Cambridge
Learner's
Dictionary

FOURTH EDITION

CAMBRIDGE
UNIVERSITY PRESS

Cambridge Learner's Dictionary

Publisher
Stella O'Shea

Development Editor
Helen Waterhouse

Editorial contributors
Carol Braham
Laura Wedgeworth

CD-ROM Project Manager
Dominic Glennon

Systems Managers
Dominic Glennon
Daniel Perrett

Dictionaries Publishing Manager
Paul Heacock

Common Learner Error Notes
Diane Nicholls

Global Corpus Manager
Ann Fiddes

Proofreading
Lucy Hollingworth
Virginia Klein
Elizabeth Walter
Kate Woodford

Design
Boag Associates
Claire Parson

Series cover design
Andrew Oliver

Typesetting
Data Standards Limited

Production
Julie Sontag
Gemma Wilkins

Illustrators
Oxford Designers and Illustrators
David Shenton
Corinne Burrows
Ray Burrows
Eikon Illustrators

Cover images
Cover photographs by Shutterstock/
Brocreative (left); Shutterstock/Vasilieva
Tatiana (centre); Shutterstock/Edyta
Pawlowska (right).

**Editorial team from the
previous edition:**

Managing Editor
Kate Woodford

Senior Commissioning Editor
Elizabeth Walter

Editorial Contributors
Melissa Good
Lucy Hollingworth
Kerry Maxwell
Duncan O'Connor

Contents

Introduction

Welcome to the new, updated edition of the **Cambridge Learner's Dictionary** (4th edition). You have in your hand the ideal dictionary for students at the A2-B2 CEFR levels.

Clear definitions
All the definitions in the dictionary are written in clear, simple English that you will understand.

Examples
This dictionary contains over 28,000 examples of how words are used in natural contexts. The examples help you to know how to use the word and what other words are often used with it.

Grammar
Grammar information is presented in a way that is clear and helpful and will show you how to avoid mistakes.

Collocations (word partners)
Collocations or word partners are words that are often used together, for example, *a good buy* and *a big decision*. Knowing how to put the right words together is extremely important for producing fluent, natural-sounding English. Collocations are highlighted in examples and also in special *word partner* boxes.

Choosing the right word
Other ways of saying boxes show a variety of words and phrases that can be used to express a main idea. Not only does this help you to expand your vocabulary, but choosing exactly the right word also helps you to express your meaning more clearly and accurately.

Common Learner Errors
The Cambridge Learner Corpus is a database of over 45 million words of Cambridge English examination scripts which has been analysed to give information about mistakes that learners make most frequently. This information is presented in the *common learner error* boxes throughout the dictionary. These boxes warn you that mistakes are common with a particular word or aspect of English and help you to avoid making them. There is also a section in the centre that shows the most common learner errors that students of English at Common European Framework levels A1, A2, B1 and B2 make when they write exam papers. This section will help you in your exam preparation.

New words
English is changing all the time. You can be confident that this dictionary is really up-to-date, with new words from many areas, such as technology, the environment, business and communications.

Self-study
This dictionary has a centre section of 70 *extra help pages* that gives clear, useful information and exercises on important topics such as phrasal verbs, grammar and spelling. There are also 16 colour pages of pictures and photographs to help you increase your vocabulary.

Cambridge English Corpus

The features described above were created using the Cambridge English Corpus (CEC). The CEC is a computer database of contemporary spoken and written English, which currently stands at over one billion words. It includes British English, American English and other varieties of English. It also includes the Cambridge Learner Corpus, developed in collaboration with the University of Cambridge ESOL Examinations. Cambridge University Press has built up the CEC to provide evidence about language use that helps to produce better language teaching materials. The corpus gives us the evidence we need to be sure that what we say in the dictionary is accurate and gives the learner a head start in making sure they are learning real, authentic English.

English Profile*

In the dictionary entries you will see the numbers and letters A1, A2, B1 and B2. These are English Vocabulary Profile levels, and they show the words, or meanings of words, that learners know at different levels. A1 words are the most basic words and should be learned first, followed by A2, B1 and B2 words. These levels relate to the international standards of the Common European Framework of Reference for Languages (CEFR). You can use these levels to decide what are the important words that you need to study.

CD-ROM

The CD-ROM contains everything that is in the dictionary plus some great extra features, including spoken pronunciations in British and American accents; a feature that allows you to record yourself for pronunciation practice; and the unique SMART thesaurus which gives you alternatives to over-used words, helping you find the exact words you need and building your vocabulary.

We hope you will enjoy using this new edition of the **Cambridge Learner's Dictionary**.

Visit the world's favourite learner dictionaries at: http://dictionary.cambridge.org

* The English Vocabulary Profile is built as part of English Profile, a collaborative programme designed to enhance the learning, teaching and assessment of English worldwide. Its main funding partners are Cambridge University Press and Cambridge ESOL and its aim is to create a 'profile' for English linked to the Common European Framework of Reference for Languages (CEFR). English Profile outcomes, such as the English Vocabulary Profile, will provide detailed information about the language that learners can be expected to demonstrate at each CEFR level, offering a clear benchmark for learners' proficiency. For more information, please visit www.englishprofile.org

How to use this dictionary

Finding a word

Each entry begins with the base form of the word.

language /'læŋgwɪdʒ/ **noun 1** COMMUNI-CATION ▷ [U] **B1** communication between people, usually using words: *She has done research into how children acquire language.* **2** ENGLISH/SPANISH/JAPANESE ETC ▷ [C] **A1** a type of communication used by the people of a particular country: *How many **languages** do you **speak**?* **3** TYPE OF WORDS ▷ [U] words of a particular type, especially the words used by people in a particular job: *legal language* ∘ *the language of business* **4** COMPUTERS ▷ [C, U] a system of instructions that is used to write computer programs → See also **body language**, **modern languages**, **second language**, **sign language**

Words which are made of two separate words (compounds) are found in alphabetical order. The stress marks (') show you which part of the word to say strongly.

'language la,boratory UK (US **'language ,laboratory**) **noun** [C] a room in a college or school where you can use equipment to help you practise listening to and speaking a foreign language

When a word can be spelled another way, or when there is another word for it, this is shown.

dialogue (also US **dialog**) /'daɪəlɒg/ **noun** [C, U] **1** **B2** the talking in a book, play, or film **2** a formal discussion between countries or groups of people

When two words have the same spelling but different parts of speech (e.g. a noun and a verb), they have separate entries.

interface¹ /'ɪntəfeɪs/ **noun** [C] **1** a connection between two pieces of electronic equipment, or between a person and a computer: *a simple **user interface*** **2** a situation, method, or place where two things can come together and have an effect on each other: *the **interface** between technology and tradition*

interface² /'ɪntə,feɪs/ **verb** [I, T] to communicate with people or electronic equipment, or to make people or electronic equipment communicate: *We use email to **interface with** our customers.*

Pronunciations use the International Phonetic Alphabet (IPA). There is a list of these symbols at the back of the dictionary. The most difficult symbols are explained at the bottom of each page. There is an explanation of the pronunciation system on page xvi.

Irregular inflections of words are clearly shown. There is a list of irregular verb inflections on page 842 and an explanation of regular inflections on page 840.

speak /spiːk/ **verb** (**spoke, spoken**) **1** [I] **(A1)** to say something using your voice: *to speak loudly/quietly* ○ *There was complete silence – nobody spoke.* **2 speak to sb** (mainly US **speak with sb**) **(A1)** to talk to someone: *Could I speak to Mr Davis, please?* ○ *Have you spoken with your new neighbors yet?* **3 speak about/of sth** to talk about something: *He refused to speak about the matter in public.* **4 speak English/French/ German, etc (A1)** to be able to communicate in English/French/German, etc: *Do you speak English?* **5** [I] to make a speech to a large group of people: *She was invited to speak at a conference in Madrid.* **6 speak for/on behalf of sb** to express the feelings, opinions, etc of another person or of a group of people: *I've been chosen to speak on behalf of the whole class.*

These labels show you when a word is used in British English or American English. See the explanation of these labels on page xv.

These labels tell you how formal, informal, etc a word is. See the explanation of all these labels on page xv.

chat¹ /tʃæt/ **verb** [I] (**chatting, chatted**) **1 (A2)** to talk with someone in a friendly and informal way: *I wanted to chat to you about the party on Saturday.* **2** to have a conversation with other people on the Internet, when you write down what you want to say, and can see immediately what other people are writing

PHRASAL VERB **chat sb up** UK informal to talk to someone in a way that shows them that you are sexually attracted to them

Learning more about a word

Cross references show you where you can find related information such as opposites, pictures, study pages, and idioms.

lamp /læmp/ **noun** [C] **(A2)** a piece of equipment that produces light: *a table lamp* ○ *an oil lamp* → See colour picture **The Living Room** on page Centre 4

Some words which are formed from the main word are shown at the end of an entry. If a word is not formed with a regular pattern, or if its meaning is not easy to guess, it has its own explanation. See **Word beginnings and endings** on page 845.

fluent /'fluːənt/ **adj 1** B2 able to use a language naturally without stopping or making mistakes: *She is **fluent** in six languages.* **2** B2 produced or done in a smooth, natural style: *Hendrik speaks fluent English.* • **fluency** /'fluːənsi/ **noun** [U] • **fluently** adv

Understanding an entry

Where a word has more than one meaning, the most frequent meaning is shown first.

Words which have several meanings have GUIDEWORDS to help you find the meaning you are looking for.

Example sentences, based on the *Cambridge English Corpus*, show how words are used in typical situations.

voice¹ /vɔɪs/ **noun 1** SOUNDS ▷ [C] B1 the sounds that you make when you speak or sing: *I could hear voices in the next room.* ∘ *Jessie has a beautiful singing voice.* ∘ *Could you please **keep your voices down** (= speak more quietly)?* ∘ *He **raised his voice** (= spoke more loudly) so that everyone could hear.* **2 lose your voice** B2 to become unable to speak, often because of an illness: *She had a bad cold and was losing her voice.* **3** OPINION ▷ [C] someone's opinion about a particular subject: *The programme gives people the opportunity to make their voices heard.* **4** PERSON ▷ [no plural] someone who expresses the opinions or wishes of a group of people: *It's important that students have a voice on the committee.* → See also **passive noun**

Each word has a part of speech label (e.g. *noun, verb, adj*). For a list of the parts of speech, see inside the front cover.

Grammar labels tell you how a word is used. See grammar labels on page xiii.

The symbols A1, A2, B1 and B2 show the *English Vocabulary Profile* level of a word, phrase, or meaning. A1 is the lowest level, followed by A2, B1 and B2. You can use these levels to decide what are the important words that you need to study.

say¹ /seɪ/ **verb** [T] (**says, said**) **1** WORDS ▷ A1 to speak words: *"I'd like to go home," she said.* ∘ *I couldn't hear what they were saying.* ∘ *How do you say this word?* **2** TELL ▷ B1 to tell someone about a fact, thought, or opinion: [+ question word] *Did she say where she was going?* ∘ [+ (that)] *The jury said that he was guilty.* **3** INFORMATION ▷ B1 to give information in writing, numbers, or signs: *My watch says one o'clock.* ∘ *What do the papers say about the election?* **4 say sth to yourself** to think something but not speak: *"I hope she likes me," he said to himself.* **5** SHOW ▷ to show what you think without using words: *His smile seemed to say that I was forgiven.* **6 (let's) say...** used to introduce a suggestion or possible example of something: *Say you were offered a better job in another city – would you take it?* **7 You can say that again!** informal used to show that you completely agree with something that someone has just said: *"That was a very bad movie!" "You can say that again!"*

Words which are often used together (*collocations* or *word partners*) are shown in **bold type** in examples.

communicate /kəˈmjuːnɪkeɪt/ **verb** [I, T] **1** ⓑ to share information with others by speaking, writing, moving your body, or using other signals: *We can now **communicate** instantly **with** people on the other side of the world.* **2** ⓑ2 to talk about your thoughts and feelings, and help other people to understand them: *He can't **communicate with** his parents.*

Some words are used as part of a phrase. This is shown clearly at the start of the definition.

spell¹ /spel/ **verb** (**spelled**, also UK **spelt**) **1** [T] ⓐ2 to write down or tell someone the letters that are used to make a word: *How do you spell that?* ◦ *Her name's spelt S-I-A-N.* **2** [I] If you can spell, you know how to write the words of a language correctly: *My grammar's all right, but I can't spell.* **3 spell disaster/trouble, etc** If something spells disaster, trouble, etc, you think it will cause something bad to happen in the future: *The new regulations could spell disaster for small businesses.*

Phrasal verbs come after the entry for the verb in alphabetical order.

PHRASAL VERB **spell sth out** to explain something in a very clear way with details: *They sent me a letter, **spelling out the details** of the agreement.*

message¹ /ˈmesɪdʒ/ **noun** [C] **1** ⓐ1 a piece of written or spoken information that one person gives to another: *Did you **get** my **message**?* ◦ *I **left** her several **messages**, but she hasn't returned my call.* **2** ⓑ2 the most important idea of a film, book, etc: *The book conveys a complex message.*

Some words are used as part of an idiom. These are shown in coloured type at the end of the entry.

IDIOM **get the message** informal to understand what someone wants you to do by their actions: *Don't return any of his calls – he'll soon get the message and leave you alone.*

All our definitions use very simple words. Where we have had to use a more difficult word than usual, that word is explained in brackets.

express¹ /ɪkˈspres/ **verb** [T] ⓑ2 to show what you think or how you feel using words or actions: *I'm simply expressing my opinion.* ◦ [often reflexive] *You're not expressing yourself (= saying what you mean) very clearly.*

The information in the boxes

These word partner boxes give you information on words that are often spoken or written together, often called *collocations* or *word partners*.
There are over 1000 of these boxes in the dictionary.

⚡ Word partners for **text message**

get/send a text message • a text message **saying** sth • a text message **from/to** sb

These thesaurus boxes show you all the different words which have the same or a similar meaning.

➕ Other ways of saying **happy**

A person who seems happy may be described as **cheerful**:
  *She's always very **cheerful**.*
If someone is happy because of something, they may be described as **pleased** or **glad**, and if they are extremely happy because of something, they may be described as **delighted**:
  *He was **pleased** that she had come back.*
  *I was so **glad** to see her.*
  *They are **delighted** with their new car.*
If someone is extremely happy and excited, they may be described as **ecstatic** or **elated**:
  *The new president was greeted by an **ecstatic** crowd.*
  *We were **elated** at the news.*

Common learner error notes based on the *Cambridge Learner Corpus* give extra information about words which often cause problems for learners.

❗ Common learner error: **advice**

Remember that this word is not countable.
  I need some advice.
  ~~I need an advice.~~
To make **advice** singular, say **a piece of advice**.

More information on using the dictionary

Grammar labels

When a word must *always* be used in a particular grammatical form, that form is shown at the beginning of the entry or the beginning of the meaning. Patterns which are common and typical, but are not *always* used, are given next to example sentences showing how they are used.

Nouns

C	countable noun	*pencil, friend, house*
U	uncountable noun, does not have a plural	*water, advice, health*
C, U	noun which can be countable or uncountable	*ability, quantity, exercise* ▶ *You should take some **exercise**.* ▶ *I do my **exercises** every morning.*

→ See also Extra help page **Countable and uncountable nouns**, on page Centre 20

group	noun which refers to a group of people or things and can be used with either a singular or plural verb	*government, class, team* ▶ *The French **team are** European Champions.* ▶ *His **team is** top of the league.*
plural	plural noun, used with a plural verb	*trousers, scissors, pliers*
no plural	noun which can be used with **a** or **an**, but does not have a plural	*rush, vicious circle, wait* ▶ *Sorry, I'm in **a rush**.*
usually plural	noun usually used in the plural form	*statistics, resources, regulations*
usually singular	noun usually used in the singular form	*mess, range, world*

Verbs

I	intransitive verb, does not have an object	*sleep, glance, fall* ▶ *Anna's **sleeping**.*
T	transitive verb, must have an object	*cure, hit, catch* ▶ *Fiona **hit** her **sister**.*
I,T	verb that can be intransitive or transitive	*sing, explain, drive* ▶ *I always **sing** in the bath.* ▶ *He **sang** a love **song**.*
+ two objects	ditransitive verb, that has two objects	*give, send, lend* ▶ *She **gave me** the **keys**.*

often passive	verb often used in the passive	*allow* ▶ *Smoking **is** not **allowed** in the restaurant.*
often reflexive	verb often used with a reflexive pronoun (**myself, yourself, herself**, etc)	*defend* ▶ *He can **defend** himself.*

If a verb or a meaning of a verb is *always* passive (e.g. **inundate, demote, affiliate**) or *always* reflexive (e.g. **brace, ingratiate, steel**) the whole grammar pattern is shown at the beginning of the entry.

Some verbs or meanings of verbs are **always followed by an adverb or preposition** (e.g. **creep, flick, trickle**). When this happens, common examples of adverbs and prepositions used are shown at the beginning of the entry or the meaning.

→ See also Extra help page **Verb patterns**, on page Centre 27

Adjectives

always before noun	attributive adjective, always comes before the noun	*major, basic, staunch* ▶ *a **staunch** supporter*
never before noun	predicative adjective, used with verbs such as **be, seem, feel**	*afraid, ready, done* ▶ *She's **afraid** of water.*
always after noun	adjective always used directly after the noun	*galore, proper, incarnate* ▶ *the devil **incarnate***

Other grammar patterns
The following patterns can refer to nouns, adjectives, and verbs:

+ that	the word is followed by a **that clause**, and the word **that** must be included	*boast, assertion, evident* ▶ *It was **evident** from her voice **that** she was upset.*
+ (that)	the word is followed by a **that clause** but the word **that** does not have to be included	*hope, amazed, doubt* ▶ *I **hope that** the bus won't be late.* ▶ *I **hope** the bus won't be late.*
+ doing sth	the word is followed by a verb in the **–ing** form	*enjoy, busy, difficulty* ▶ *I **enjoy going** to the beach.*
+ to do sth	the word is followed by a verb in the infinitive	*confidence, careful, decide* ▶ *I didn't have the **confidence to speak up**.*
+ for/of, etc + doing sth	the word is followed by a preposition (e.g. **for/of**) and then a verb in the **–ing** form	*apologize, idea, guilty* ▶ *She **apologized for** being late.*
+ question word	the word is followed by a question word (e.g. **who, what, how**)	*ask, certain, clue* ▶ *I'm not **certain who** to ask.*
used in questions and negatives	the word is used in questions and negative sentences	*mind, much, yet* ▶ *Do you **mind** if I come in?* ▶ *I haven't seen him **yet**.*

Usage labels

informal	used when you are speaking, or communicating with people you know but not normally in serious writing	*brainy, freebie, goalie*
formal	used in serious writing or for communicating with people about things like law or business	*examination, moreover, purchase*
very informal	used when you are talking to people you know well, and not usually in writing. Some of these words may offend people, and this is explained in the entry.	*prat, barf, crap*
spoken	a way of writing a word which is used in conversation	*yeah, hey, eh*
humorous	used in order to be funny or to make a joke	*couch potato, snail mail*
literary	used in books and poems, not in ordinary conversation	*beloved, slumber, weep*
old-fashioned	not used in modern English – you might find these words in books, used by older people, or used in order to be funny	*gramophone, spectacles, farewell*
trademark	the name of a product that is made by one company. Sometimes a trademark is used as a general word.	*Coke, Hoover, Sellotape*

UK/US labels

The spelling used in definitions and examples in this dictionary is British English. However, American English is also explained clearly, and where there is a difference between British and American English, this is shown.

UK	only used in British English	*pavement, petrol station*
US	only used in American English	*sidewalk, gas station*
mainly UK	mainly used in British English, but sometimes in American English	*lecturer, rubbish, nightdress*
mainly US	mainly used in American English, but sometimes in British English	*movie, apartment, semester*
also UK	another word that can also be used in British English	*truck* (also UK *lorry*) ■ *truck* is used in the UK and the US *lorry* is also used in the UK
also US	another word that can also be used in American English	*railway* (also US *railroad*) ■ *railway* is used in the UK and the US *railroad* is also used in the US

→ see also Extra help page **UK and US English**, on page Centre 38.

Pronunciation

All pronunciations use the International Phonetic Alphabet. There is a complete list of phonetic symbols at the back of the book.

Many phonetic symbols, e.g. /p/, /s/, /k/, sound exactly like the most common pronunciation of the letter they look like. Those that do not are explained at the bottom of every page of the dictionary.

Where more than one pronunciation is shown, the more common one is first, but both are often used.

British and American pronunciation

Most words are given only one pronunciation, which is acceptable in British and American English. There are some regular differences between British and American English which are not shown for every word.

The main ones are:

1 In American English, the **r** in words such as **hard** or **teacher** is pronounced, and in British English it is silent.

2 In American English, **t** and **tt** in words such as **later** and **butter**, are pronounced in a soft way, almost like a /d/ sound.

Where there is a big difference between British and American pronunciation, both forms are shown. The symbol ⓤⓢ is shown before an American pronunciation, e.g. **schedule** /ˈʃedjuːl/ ⓤⓢ /ˈskedʒuːl/

Stress patterns

Stress patterns show you which parts of the word you should emphasize when you say them.

/ˈ/ shows the main emphasis on a word. For example, in the word **picture** /ˈpɪktʃər/, you should emphasize the first part, and in the word **deny** /dɪˈnaɪ/ you should emphasize the second part.

/ˌ/ shows the second most important emphasis on the word. For example, in the word **submarine** /ˌsʌbməˈriːn/, the main emphasis is on the last part of the word, but you should also emphasize the first part of the word slightly.

Compound words (words made of two or more separate words) have their stress patterns shown on them. For example in the word **deˌsigner ˈbaby**, the main emphasis is on the first part of the second word, but you should also emphasize the middle part of the first word slightly.

Strong forms and weak forms

Some common words (e.g. **and, them, of**) have strong forms and weak forms. The weak forms are more common.

For example, in the sentence *I saw them leave*, the weak form /ðəm/ would be used.

The strong form is used when you want to emphasize the word. For instance, in the sentence *They said they saw me, but I didn't see them*, the strong form /ðem/ would be used.

Regular inflections

All inflections (e.g. plurals, past tenses) that are not regular (= are not formed in the usual way) are shown at the entry for the word. The regular way of forming inflections is shown below.

Nouns

Most nouns form their plurals by adding **–s**:
▶ *chair, chairs* ▶ *plate, plates*

Nouns which end in **–s, –ss, –ch, –x,** and **–z**, make their plurals by adding **–es**:
▶ *mass, masses* ▶ *match, matches*

Nouns which end in a consonant (e.g. **m, t, p**) + **–y**, form their plurals by taking away the **–y** and adding **–ies**:
▶ *baby, babies* ▶ *university, universities*

Adjectives

The comparative form of adjectives is used to show that someone or something has more of a particular quality than someone or something else. To make the regular comparative form, you either add **–er** to the end of the adjective, or use the word **more** before it.

The superlative form of adjectives is used to show that someone or something has more of a particular quality than anyone or anything else. To make the regular superlative form, you either add **–est** to the end of the adjective, or use the word **most** before it.

One-syllable adjectives usually form their comparative and superlative with **–er** and **–est**:
▶ *small, smaller, smallest*

Two-syllable adjectives can all form their comparative and superlative with **more** and **most**:
▶ *complex, more complex, most complex*

Some two-syllable adjectives can use **–er** and **–est** too. The most common of these are:
■ adjectives ending in **–y** and **–ow**:
  ▶ *happy, noisy, shallow*
■ adjectives ending in **–le**:
  ▶ *able, noble, simple*
■ some other common two-syllable adjectives:
  ▶ *common, cruel, handsome, pleasant, polite, quiet, solid, wicked*

Three-syllable adjectives usually form their comparative and superlative with **more** and **most**:
▶ *beautiful, more beautiful, most beautiful*

When you are using the **–er, –est** forms, if the adjective ends in **–e**, take away the **–e** before adding the ending:
▶ *pale, paler, palest*

If the adjective ends in **–y**, change this to **–i** before adding the ending:
▶ *happy, happier, happiest*

Verbs

Regular verbs add the following endings:

for the **3rd person singular** add **–s**, or **–es** to verbs that end in **–s, –ss, –ch, –x,** and **–z**

for the **present participle** add **–ing**

for the **past tense** and the **past participle** add **–ed**
▶ *pack, packs, packing, packed*

For verbs ending in **–e**, take away the **–e** before adding the present participle, past tense, and past participle endings:
▶ *hate, hates, hating, hated*

For verbs ending in **–y**, for the third person singular take away the **–y** and add **–ies**, and for the past tense and past participle take away the **–y** and add **–ied**:
▶ *cry, cries, crying, cried*

A

A, a /eɪ/ the first letter of the alphabet

a (also **an**) strong /eɪ/ weak /ə/ **determiner**
1 BEFORE NOUN ▷ **A1** used before a noun to refer to a single thing or person but not a particular thing or person or not one that you have referred to before: *I need a new car.* ∘ *I saw a woman speaking to him.* **2 ONE** ▷ **A1** one: *a hundred dollars* ∘ *a dozen eggs* **3 EVERY/EACH** ▷ **A1** every or each: *A child needs love.* ∘ *Take one tablet three times a* (= each) *day.* **4 TYPE** ▷ **A1** used to say what type of thing or person something or someone is: *It's a guinea pig.* ∘ *She's a doctor.* **5 AN ACTION** ▷ **A2** used before some action nouns when referring to one example of the action: *Take a look at this.* ∘ UK *I'm just going to have a wash.* **6 TWO NOUNS** ▷ **A2** used before the first of two nouns that are often used together: *a cup and saucer* **7 AMOUNTS** ▷ **A2** used before some phrases saying how much of something there is: *a few days* ∘ *a bit of sugar* **8 NAME** ▷ used before a person's name when referring to someone you do not know: *There's a Ms Leeming to see you.*

> ❗ Common learner error: **a** or **an**?
>
> Remember to use **an** in front of words that begin with a vowel sound. These are words that start with the letters a, e, i, o, or u, or with a sound like those letters.
>
> *a car, an orange, an hour*

a- /eɪ/ **prefix** not, without: *atypical* ∘ *amoral*

aback /əˈbæk/ **adv be taken aback** to be very surprised or shocked: *I was rather taken aback by her honesty.*

abacus /ˈæbəkəs/ **noun** [C] a square object with small balls on wires, used for counting

abandon /əˈbændən/ **verb** [T] **1** **B2** to leave someone or something somewhere, sometimes not returning to get them: *They were forced to abandon the car.* **2** to stop doing something before it is finished, or to stop following a plan, idea, etc: *The match was abandoned because of rain.* • **abandoned** adj • **abandonment** noun [U]

> 🗎 Word partners for **abandon**
>
> be **forced to** abandon sth • abandon an **attempt/effort/idea/plan/search**

abate /əˈbeɪt/ **verb** [I] formal to become less strong: *By the weekend, the storms had abated.*

abattoir /ˈæbətwɑːʳ/ **noun** [C] mainly UK (mainly US **slaughterhouse**) a place where animals are killed for meat

abbey /ˈæbi/ **noun** [C] a group of buildings that is a home for monks or nuns (= religious men or women who live separately from other people)

abbreviate /əˈbriːvieɪt/ **verb** [T] to make a word or phrase shorter: *The word 'street' is often abbreviated to 'St'.*

abbreviation /əˌbriːviˈeɪʃᵊn/ **noun** [C] a shorter form of a word or phrase, especially used in writing: *A doctor is often called a 'GP', an abbreviation for 'general practitioner'.*

abdicate /ˈæbdɪkeɪt/ **verb** **1** [I] If a king or queen abdicates, they choose to stop being king or queen. **2 abdicate responsibility** formal to decide not to be responsible for something any more • **abdication** /ˌæbdɪˈkeɪʃᵊn/ **noun** [C, U]

abdomen /ˈæbdəmən/ **noun** [C] formal the lower part of a person or animal's body, containing the stomach and other organs • **abdominal** /æbˈdɒmɪnᵊl/ **adj** to do with the abdomen: *abdominal pains*

abduct /əbˈdʌkt/ **verb** [T] to take someone away illegally: *He was abducted by a terrorist group.* • **abduction** /əbˈdʌkʃᵊn/ **noun** [C, U]

aberration /ˌæbəˈreɪʃᵊn/ **noun** [C] formal a temporary change from what usually happens

abet /əˈbet/ **verb** (**abetting, abetted**) see **aid²** and **abet (sb)**

abhor /əbˈhɔːʳ/ **verb** [T] (**abhorring, abhorred**) formal to hate something or someone very much • **abhorrence** /əbˈhɒrᵊns/ **noun** [U] formal

abhorrent /əbˈhɒrənt/ **adj** formal morally very bad: *an abhorrent crime*

abide /əˈbaɪd/ **verb can't abide sb/sth** to strongly dislike someone or something: *I can't abide rudeness.*

PHRASAL VERB **abide by sth** to obey a rule: *Staff who refused to abide by the rules were fired.*

abiding /əˈbaɪdɪŋ/ **adj** [always before noun] An abiding feeling or memory is one that you have for a long time: *My abiding memory is of him watering his plants in the garden.* → See also **law-abiding**

ability /əˈbɪləti/ **noun** [C, U] **B1** the physical or mental skill or qualities that you need to do something: *athletic/academic ability* ∘ [+ to do sth] *He had the ability to explain things clearly.* ∘ *The report questions the technical ability of the staff.* → Opposite **inability** → Compare **disability**

> 🗎 Word partners for **ability**
>
> **have/lack/possess** ability • **innate/remarkable/uncanny** ability

abject /ˈæbdʒekt/ **adj** **1 abject misery/terror/poverty etc** extreme sadness, fear etc **2** showing that you are very ashamed of what you have done: *an abject apology*

ablaze /əˈbleɪz/ **adj** [never before noun] burning strongly

able /ˈeɪbl/ **adj 1 be able to do sth** **A2** to have the ability to do something or the possibility of doing something: *He'll be able to help you.* → Opposite **be unable to do sth 2** clever or good at doing something: *She's a very able student.* • **ably adv** *Ably assisted by her mother, she learnt how to make jam.*

A

able-bodied /ˌeɪbl̩ˈbɒdɪd/ **adj** having all the physical abilities that most people have

abnormal /æbˈnɔːml̩/ **adj** different from what is normal or usual, in a way that is strange or dangerous: *abnormal behaviour/weather* ∘ *They found **abnormal levels** of lead in the water.* • **abnormally** adv *abnormally high temperatures*

abnormality /ˌæbnɔːˈmæləti/ **noun** [C, U] something abnormal, usually in the body: *a **genetic abnormality***

aboard /əˈbɔːd/ **adv, preposition** on or onto a plane, ship, bus, or train: *Welcome aboard flight BA109 to Paris.*

abode /əˈbəʊd/ **noun** [C] formal a home

abolish /əˈbɒlɪʃ/ **verb** [T] **B2** to officially end something, especially a law or system: *The slave trade was abolished in the US in 1808.* • **abolition** /ˌæbəˈlɪʃⁿn/ **noun** [U] *the abolition of slavery*

abominable /əˈbɒmɪnəbl̩/ **adj** extremely bad: *abominable behaviour* • **abominably** adv

Aboriginal /ˌæbəˈrɪdʒⁿl̩/ **adj** relating or belonging to the original race of people who lived in Australia

Aborigine /ˌæbəˈrɪdʒⁿni/ **noun** [C] an Aboriginal person

abort /əˈbɔːt/ **verb 1 STOP** ▷ [T] to stop a process before it has finished: *The take-off was aborted due to bad weather.* **2 PREGNANCY** ▷ [T] to end a pregnancy that is not wanted using a medical operation **3 COMPUTER** ▷ [I, T] to stop a computer process before it is complete: *abort a program*

abortion /əˈbɔːʃⁿn/ **noun** [C, U] a medical operation to end a pregnancy when the baby is still too small to live: *She **had an abortion**.*

abortive /əˈbɔːtɪv/ **adj** [always before noun] An abortive attempt or plan fails before it is complete.

abound /əˈbaʊnd/ **verb** [I] formal to exist in large numbers: ***Rumours abound** about a possible change of leadership.*

about¹ /əˈbaʊt/ **preposition 1** **A1** relating to a particular subject or person: *a book about the Spanish Civil War* ∘ *What was she talking about?* **2** (also US **around**) **B2** to or in different parts of a place, often without purpose or order: *We heard someone moving about outside.* **3 what/how about …? a** used to make a suggestion: *How about France for a holiday?* **b** **B1** used to ask for someone's opinion on a particular subject: *What about Ann – is she nice?*

about² /əˈbaʊt/ **adv 1 APPROXIMATELY** ▷ **A1** used before a number or amount to mean approximately: *It happened about two months ago.* **2 DIRECTION** ▷ (also US **around**) **B2** to or in different parts of a place, often without purpose or order: *She's always leaving her clothes lying about.* **3 NEAR** ▷ informal (also US **around**) If someone or something is about, they are near to the place where you are now: *Is Kate about?* **4 be about to do sth** **B2** to be going to do something very soon: *I stopped her just as she was about to leave.*

above¹ /əˈbʌv/ **adv, preposition 1 HIGHER POSITION** ▷ **A1** in or to a higher position than

something else: *There's a mirror above the washbasin.* ∘ *I could hear music coming from the room above.* **2 MORE** ▷ **A2** more than an amount or level: *It says on the box it's for children aged three and above.* ∘ *Rates of pay are above average.* **3 RANK** ▷ in a more important or advanced position than someone else: *Sally's a grade above me.* **4 TOO IMPORTANT** ▷ too good or important for something: *No one is above suspicion in this matter.* **5 above all** **B1** most importantly: *Above all, I'd like to thank everyone.*

above² /əˈbʌv/ **adj, adv** **B1** higher on the same page: *the above diagram* ∘ *the address shown above*

a,bove 'board **adj** [never before noun] honest and legal: *We hired a lawyer to make sure the agreement was all above board.*

abrasive /əˈbreɪsɪv/ **adj 1** An abrasive substance is rough and can be used for rubbing surfaces, to make them clean or smooth. **2** speaking or behaving in a rude and unpleasant way: *an abrasive manner*

abreast /əˈbrest/ **adv 1 keep (sb) abreast of sth** to make sure you or someone else knows about the most recent changes in a subject or situation: *I'll keep you abreast of any developments.* **2 two/three/four, etc abreast** If people who are moving are two/three/four, etc abreast, that number of people are next to each other, side by side: *They were cycling four abreast, completely blocking the road.*

abridged /əˈbrɪdʒd/ **adj** An abridged book or other piece of writing has been made shorter. → Opposite **unabridged** • **abridge** /əˈbrɪdʒ/ **verb** [T]

abroad /əˈbrɔːd/ **adv** **B1** in or to a foreign country: *He **goes abroad** a lot with his job.*

abrupt /əˈbrʌpt/ **adj 1** sudden and not expected: *Our conversation came to an **abrupt end**.* **2** dealing with people in a quick way that is unfriendly or rude: *She has a rather **abrupt manner**.* • **abruptly** adv

abscess /ˈæbses/ **noun** [C] a painful, swollen area on the body that contains a yellow liquid

abscond /əbˈskɒnd/ **verb** [I] formal to leave somewhere suddenly without permission because you want to escape, or because you have stolen something

absence /ˈæbsⁿns/ **noun 1** [C, U] **B2** a time when you are not in a particular place: *Lisa will be acting as manager **in** Phil's **absence** (= while Phil is not here).* ∘ *A large number of **absences from** work are caused by back problems.* **2** [U] **B2** the fact of not existing: *In the absence of any proof, it is impossible to accuse her.*

absent /ˈæbsⁿnt/ **adj** **B1** not in the place where

you are expected to be, especially at school or work: *He has been **absent from** school all week.*

absentee /ˌæbsənˈtiː/ noun [C] someone who is not in a place where they should be • **absenteeism** noun [U] a situation in which someone is often absent from work or school

absently /ˈæbsəntli/ adv without thinking about what you are doing: *He stared absently at the television screen.*

absent-minded /ˌæbsəntˈmaɪndɪd/ adj often forgetting things • **absent-mindedly** adv • **absent-mindedness** noun [U]

absolute /ˈæbsəluːt/ adj [always before noun] **1** 🅱️2 complete: *absolute power/control* ∘ *The party was an absolute disaster.* **2** definite: *There was no **absolute proof** of fraud.*

absolutely /ˌæbsəˈluːtli/ adv **1** 🅱️1 completely: *The food was absolutely delicious.* ∘ *There's absolutely nothing (= nothing at all) left.* **2 Absolutely.** used to strongly agree with someone: *"Do you think it helped his career?" "Absolutely."* **3 Absolutely not.** used to strongly disagree with someone or to agree with something negative: *"Are you suggesting that we should just ignore the problem?" "No, absolutely not."*

absolve /əbˈzɒlv/ verb [T] formal to formally say that someone is not guilty of something, or to forgive someone

absorb /əbˈzɔːb/ verb [T] **1 LIQUID** ▷ 🅱️2 If a substance absorbs a liquid, it takes it in through its surface and holds it: *The fabric absorbs all the moisture, keeping your skin dry.* **2 be absorbed in sth** 🅱️2 to give all your attention to something that you are doing: *Simon was so absorbed in his computer game, he didn't notice me come in.* **3 REMEMBER** ▷ to understand and remember facts that you read or hear: *It's hard to absorb so much **information**.* **4 BECOME PART OF** ▷ 🅱️2 If something is absorbed into something else, it becomes part of it: *The drug is quickly **absorbed into** the bloodstream.*

absorbent /əbˈzɔːbənt/ adj An absorbent substance can take liquids in through its surface and hold them.

absorbing /əbˈzɔːbɪŋ/ adj very interesting: *an absorbing book/game*

abstain /əbˈsteɪn/ verb [I] **1** formal to not do something that you enjoy because it is bad or unhealthy: *The doctor suggested that he **abstain from** alcohol.* **2** to choose not to vote for or against something: *63 members voted in favour, 39 opposed and 5 abstained.* • **abstention** /əbˈstenʃən/ noun [C, U]

abstinence /ˈæbstɪnəns/ noun [U] formal not doing something that you enjoy because it is bad or unhealthy

abstract /ˈæbstrækt/ adj **1** 🅱️2 relating to ideas and not real things: *an abstract concept* **2** 🅱️2 Abstract art involves shapes and colours and not images of real things or people.

absurd /əbˈzɜːd/ adj 🅱️2 very silly: *an absurd situation/suggestion* • **absurdity** noun [C, U] • **absurdly** adv

abundance /əˈbʌndəns/ noun [U, no plural] formal a lot of something: *an **abundance of**

flowers* ∘ *There was food **in abundance** (= a lot of food).*

abundant /əˈbʌndənt/ adj existing in large quantities: *an **abundant supply** of food* • **abundantly** adv

abuse¹ /əˈbjuːs/ noun **1 WRONG USE** ▷ [C, U] 🅱️2 the use of something for the wrong purpose in a way that is harmful or morally wrong: *drug/alcohol abuse* ∘ *abuse of public money* **2 VIOLENCE** ▷ [U] 🅱️2 violent, cruel treatment of someone: *child abuse* ∘ *sexual abuse* **3 LANGUAGE** ▷ [U] rude and offensive words said to another person: *Rival fans shouted abuse at each other.*

abuse² /əˈbjuːz/ verb [T] **1 VIOLENCE** ▷ to treat someone cruelly and violently: *He was **physically abused** by his alcoholic father.* **2 WRONG USE** ▷ to use something for the wrong purpose in a way that is harmful or morally wrong: *to abuse alcohol* **3 LANGUAGE** ▷ to say rude and offensive words to someone: *The crowd started abusing him.* • **abuser** noun [C]

abusive /əˈbjuːsɪv/ adj saying rude and offensive words to someone: *an abusive phone call*

abysmal /əˈbɪzməl/ adj very bad, especially of bad quality: *the team's **abysmal performance** last season* • **abysmally** adv

abyss /əˈbɪs/ noun [C] **1** a very bad situation that will not improve: [usually singular] *The country is sinking into an **abyss of** violence and bloodshed.* **2** literary a very deep hole

.ac /dɒtˈæk/ internet abbreviation for academic institution: used in some internet addresses for organizations such as universities

academia /ˌækəˈdiːmiə/ noun [U] the people and organizations, especially universities, involved in studying

academic¹ /ˌækəˈdemɪk/ adj **1 EDUCATION** ▷ 🅱️2 related to education, schools, universities, etc: *academic ability/standards* ∘ *It's the start of the academic year.* **2 SUBJECTS** ▷ related to subjects that involve thinking and studying and not technical or practical skills: *academic subjects* **3 CLEVER** ▷ clever and good at studying **4 NOT REAL** ▷ If what someone says is academic, it has no purpose because it relates to a situation that does not exist: *The whole discussion is academic since management won't even listen to us.* • **academically** adv

academic² /ˌækəˈdemɪk/ noun [C] someone who teaches at a university or college, or is paid to study there

academy /əˈkædəmi/ noun [C] **1** a college that teaches people the skills needed for a particular job: *a military academy* **2** an organization whose purpose is to encourage and develop an art, science, language, etc: *the Royal Academy of Music*

accelerate /əkˈseləreɪt/ verb **1** [I] to start to drive faster **2** [I, T] to start to happen more quickly, or to make something start to happen more quickly: *Inflation is likely to accelerate this year.* • **acceleration** /əkˌseləˈreɪʃən/ noun [U]

accelerator /əkˈseləreɪtər/ noun [C] (also US **gas pedal**) the part of a car that you push with your foot to make it go faster → See colour picture **Car** on page Centre 7

accent /'æksənt/ noun [C] **1 PRONUNCIATION** ▷ ⑥① the way in which someone pronounces words, influenced by the country or area they come from, or their social class: *an American accent* ◦ *a French accent* **2 WRITTEN MARK** ▷ ⑥② a mark above a letter to show you how to pronounce it, for example (â) and (é) **3 WORD EMPHASIS** ▷ the word or part of a word that you emphasize when you are speaking: *In the word 'impossible' the accent is on the second syllable.* **4 the accent on sth** particular importance or attention that you give to something: *a wonderful menu with the accent on fresh fish*

> ☑ Word partners for **accent**
>
> have/speak with a [local/northern/strong, etc] accent • lose your accent • a heavy/strong/thick accent

accentuate /ək'sentʃueɪt/ verb [T] to emphasize something so that people notice it: *make-up to accentuate the eyes*

accept /ək'sept/ verb **1 AGREE** ▷ [I, T] ⑥① to agree to take something that is offered to you: *to accept an invitation/offer* ◦ *He won't accept advice from anyone.* **2 ADMIT** ▷ [T] ⑥② to admit that something is true, often something unpleasant: [+ (that)] *He refuses to accept that he's made a mistake.* **3 ALLOW TO JOIN** ▷ [T] ⑥② to allow someone to join an organization or become part of a group: *She's been accepted by two universities.* **4 accept responsibility/blame** ⑥② to admit that you caused something bad that happened: *The company has now accepted responsibility for the accident.* **5 UNDERSTAND** ▷ [T] to understand that you cannot change a very sad or unpleasant situation: *The hardest part is accepting the fact that you'll never see that person again.*

> ❗ Common learner error: **accept** or **agree**?
>
> When you accept an invitation, job, or offer, you say yes to something that is offered.
> **Accept** is never followed by another verb.
> *They offered me the job and I've accepted it.*
> ~~They offered me the job and I've accepted to take it.~~
> When you **agree** to do something, you say that you will do something that someone asks you to do.
> *They offered me the job and I agreed to take it.*

acceptable /ək'septəbl/ adj **1** ⑥① good enough: *work of an acceptable standard* ◦ *We still hope to find a solution which is acceptable to both sides.* **2** allowed or approved of: *Smoking is less and less socially acceptable.* → Opposite **unacceptable** • acceptability /ək,septə'bɪləti/ noun [U]

acceptance /ək'septəns/ noun [C, U] the act of accepting something: *his acceptance of the award* ◦ *There is a growing public acceptance of alternative medicine.*

> ☑ Word partners for **acceptance**
>
> sb/sth gains/wins acceptance • general/growing/grudging/public acceptance • acceptance of sth

accepted /ək'septɪd/ adj agreed or approved by most people: *an accepted spelling*

access¹ /'ækses/ noun [U] **1** ⑥① the right or opportunity to use or see something: *I don't have access to that kind of information.* ◦ *Do you have Internet access?* **2** ⑥① the way in which you can enter a place or get to a place: *The only access to the village is by boat.*

access² /'ækses/ verb [T] ⑥② to find or see information, especially using a computer: *You can access the files over the Internet.*

accessible /ək'sesəbl/ adj **1** ⑥② easy to find or reach: *Information such as this is freely accessible to the public.* ◦ *The hotel is in a quiet but easily accessible part of the resort.* → Opposite **inaccessible 2** easy to understand: *They are attempting to make opera accessible to a wider audience.* • accessibility /ək,sesə'bɪləti/ noun [U]

accessory /ək'sesəri/ noun [C] **1** something extra that is not necessary but is attractive or useful: [usually plural] *bathroom accessories* ◦ *computer accessories* **2** formal someone who helps a criminal to commit a crime: *an accessory to murder*

'access pro,vider noun [C] a company that makes you able to use the Internet, so that you can use email and see or show documents

accident /'æksɪdənt/ noun [C] **1** ⑥② something bad that happens that is not intended and that causes injury or damage: *a car/traffic accident* ◦ *She had an accident in the kitchen.* ◦ *I didn't mean to spill his drink. It was an accident.* **2 by accident** ⑥① without being intended: *I deleted the wrong file by accident.*

> ☑ Word partners for **accident**
>
> have/be involved in an accident • an accident happens/occurs • a fatal/serious/tragic accident • [killed, paralyzed, etc] in an accident • a car/traffic accident

accidental /,æksɪ'dentəl/ adj ⑥② not intended: *accidental damage* • accidentally adv ⑥② *She accidentally knocked over a glass of red wine.*

accident-prone /'æksɪdənt,prəʊn/ adj Someone who is accident-prone often has accidents.

acclaim /ə'kleɪm/ noun [U] praise from a lot of people: *international/critical acclaim*

acclaimed /ə'kleɪmd/ adj praised by a lot of people: *the acclaimed singer and songwriter Norah Jones*

acclimatize (also UK **-ise**) /ə'klaɪmətaɪz/ verb [I, T] to start to feel happy with the weather, the way of life, etc in a new place, or to make someone do this • acclimatization /ə,klaɪmətaɪ'zeɪʃən/ noun [U]

accolade /'ækəleɪd/ noun [C] formal a prize or praise given to someone because they are very good at something

accommodate /ə'kɒmədeɪt/ verb [T] **1 HAVE SPACE FOR** ▷ to have enough space somewhere for a number of things or people: *We need more roads to accommodate the increase in traffic.* **2 HELP** ▷ to do what someone wants, often by providing them with something: *He requires special equipment and, where possible, we've accommodated those needs.* **3 GIVE A HOME** ▷ to provide someone with a place to live or stay: *The athletes will be accommodated in a special Olympic village.*

accommodating /ə'kɒmədeɪtɪŋ/ adj willing to change your plans in order to help people

accommodation /ə,kɒmə'deɪʃᵊn/ noun [U] 🔵 (also US **accommodations** [plural]) a place where you live or stay: *rented accommodation* ○ *The price includes travel and accommodation.*

accompaniment /ə'kʌmpᵊnɪmənt/ noun **1** [C] formal something that is nice to eat or drink with a particular food or drink: *salmon with an accompaniment of green salad* **2** [C, U] music that is played with the main instrument or with a singing voice: *a song with piano accompaniment*

accompany /ə'kʌmpəni/ verb [T] **1 GO WITH** ▷ formal 🔵 to go somewhere with someone: *We accompanied her back to their hotel.* **2 HAPPEN TOGETHER** ▷ 🔵 to happen or exist at the same time as something else: *The teachers' book is accompanied by a CD.* **3 MUSIC** ▷ to play a musical instrument with someone else who is playing or singing

accomplice /ə'kʌmplɪs/ noun [C] someone who helps a criminal to commit a crime

accomplish /ə'kʌmplɪʃ/ verb [T] to succeed in doing something good: *I feel as if I've accomplished nothing all day.*

accomplished /ə'kʌmplɪʃt/ adj having a lot of skill in art, music, writing, etc: *an accomplished musician/painter*

accomplishment /ə'kʌmplɪʃmənt/ noun **1** [U] success in doing something good: *Finishing the course gave me a great sense of accomplishment.* **2** [C] formal a skill in art, music, writing, etc

accord¹ /ə'kɔːd/ noun **1 of your own accord** If you do something of your own accord, you choose to do it and no one else forces you: *Luckily, she left of her own accord.* **2** [C] an official agreement, especially between countries: *a peace/trade accord*

accord² /ə'kɔːd/ verb [T] formal to treat someone specially, usually by showing respect: *the respect accorded to doctors*

accordance /ə'kɔːdᵊns/ noun formal **in accordance with sth** agreeing with a rule, law, or wish: *Both companies have insisted that they were acting in accordance with the law.*

accordingly /ə'kɔːdɪŋli/ adv in a way that is suitable: *We'll wait until we hear the decision and act accordingly.*

according to /ə'kɔːdɪŋtuː/ preposition **1** 🔵 as said by someone or shown by something: *According to our records, she was absent last Friday.* **2** 🔵 based on a particular system or plan: *Children are allocated to schools according to the area in which they live.*

accordion /ə'kɔːdiən/ noun [C] a musical instrument with a folding centre part and keyboards at both ends, which you play by pushing the two ends together

accost /ə'kɒst/ verb [T] If someone you do not know accosts you, they move towards you and start talking to you in an unfriendly way.

account¹ /ə'kaʊnt/ noun [C] **1 REPORT** ▷ 🔵 a written or spoken description of something that has happened: *They gave conflicting accounts of the events.* **2 BANK** ▷ (also **bank account**) 🔵 an arrangement with a bank to keep your money there and to let you take it out when you need to: *I paid the money into my account.* **3 SHOP** ▷ an agreement with a shop or company that allows you to buy things and pay for them later **4 take sth into account; take account of sth** 🔵 to consider something when judging a situation: *You have to take into account the fact that he is less experienced when judging his performance.* **5 on account of sth** formal 🔵 because of something: *He doesn't drink alcohol on account of his health.* **6 by all accounts** as said by a lot of people: *The party was, by all accounts, a great success.* **7 on my account** just for or because of me: *Please don't change your plans on my account.* **8 on no account; not on any account** UK not for any reason or in any situation: *On no account must these records be changed.* → See also **checking account, current account, deposit account**

> **🗨 Word partners for account**
>
> 1 **give** an account of sth • a **brief/detailed/full** account • an **eye-witness/first-hand** account • an account **of** sth
> 2 **close/open** an account • **have** an account **with** [name of bank] • a **joint/personal/savings** account • an account **holder/number**

account² /ə'kaʊnt/ verb

PHRASAL VERB **account for sth 1** to be part of a total number of something: *Oil accounts for 40% of Norway's exports.* **2** to be the reason for something, or to explain the reason for something: *She was asked to account for the missing money.*

accountable /ə'kaʊntəbl/ adj [never before noun] having you to be responsible for what you do and able to explain your actions: *Hospitals must be held accountable for their mistakes.* ○ *Politicians should be accountable to the public that elects them.* → Opposite **unaccountable** • **accountability** /ə,kaʊntə'bɪləti/ noun [U]

accountancy /ə'kaʊntənsi/ noun [U] UK (US **accounting**) the job of being an accountant

accountant /ə'kaʊntənt/ noun [C] 🔵 someone whose job is to keep or examine the financial records of a company or organization

accounting /ə'kaʊntɪŋ/ noun [U] (UK **accountancy**) the job of being an accountant

accounts /ə'kaʊnts/ noun [plural] an official record of all the money a company or organization has received or paid

accreditation /ə,kredɪ'teɪʃᵊn/ noun [U] official approval of an organization • **accredited** /ə'kredɪtɪd/ adj officially approved

A

accumulate /ə'kju:mjəleɪt/ **verb** [I, T] to increase in amount over a period of time, or to make something increase over a period of time: *The chemicals accumulate in your body.* • **accumulation** /ə,kju:mjə'leɪʃᵊn/ **noun** [U]

accuracy /'ækjərəsi/ **noun** [U] ⑫ how correct or exact something is: *The new system should help to improve the accuracy of weather forecasts.*

accurate /'ækjərət/ **adj** ⑥ correct or exact: ***accurate information/measurements*** ∘ *She was able to give police a fairly **accurate description** of the man.* → Opposite **inaccurate** • **accurately adv**

accusation /,ækju'zeɪʃᵊn/ **noun** [C] a statement in which you say that someone has done something bad: *He **made** a number of **accusations against** his former colleagues.*

> ✏️ **Word partners for accusation**
>
> **make** an accusation • **deny/dismiss/face/ reject** an accusation • a **false/wild** accusation • accusations **of** sth • an accusation **against** sb • an accusation **by/from** sb

accuse /ə'kju:z/ **verb** [T] ⑫ to say that someone has done something bad: *He was falsely **accused of** murder.* ∘ [+ of + doing sth] *She accused Andrew of lying to her.* • **accuser noun** [C]

the accused /ə'kju:zd/ **noun** formal the person or people who are accused of a crime in a court of law

accusing /ə'kju:zɪŋ/ **adj** showing that you think someone is responsible for something bad: *Why are you giving me that **accusing look**?* • **accusingly adv** *She looked at me accusingly.*

accustom /ə'kʌstəm/ **verb**

> PHRASAL VERB **accustom yourself to sth/doing sth** to experience something often enough for it to seem normal to you

accustomed /ə'kʌstəmd/ **adj accustomed to sth/doing sth** If you are accustomed to something, you have experienced it often enough for it to seem normal to you: *I've worked nights for years now so I've **grown accustomed to it**.*

ace¹ /eɪs/ **noun** [C] **1** a playing card with one symbol on it, that has the highest or lowest value in many games **2** a first shot by a tennis player that is too good for the other player to hit back

ace² /eɪs/ **adj** informal very good

ache¹ /eɪk/ **noun** [C] ⑥ a feeling of pain over an area of your body that continues for a long time: *There's a **dull ache** in my right shoulder.* → See also **stomach ache**

ache² /eɪk/ **verb** [I] ⑫ If a part of your body aches, it is painful: *My legs ache after all that exercise.*

achieve /ə'tʃi:v/ **verb** [T] ⑥ to succeed in doing something good, usually by working hard: *I've achieved my ambition* ∘ *I've been working all day but I feel I've achieved nothing.* • **achievable adj** possible to achieve: ***achievable goals*** • **achiever noun** [C] *He's from a family of **high achievers** (= very successful people).*

achievement /ə'tʃi:vmənt/ **noun 1** [C] ⑥ something good that you achieve: *This film is his **greatest achievement** to date.* **2** [U] success in doing something good, usually by working hard: *You get such **a sense of achievement** when you finish the course.*

> ✏️ **Word partners for achievement**
>
> a **great/notable/outstanding/remarkable** achievement • sb's **crowning** achievement • a **sense of** achievement

acid¹ /'æsɪd/ **noun** [C, U] ⑫ one of several liquid substances with a pH of less than 7 that react with other substances, often burning or dissolving them: *hydrochloric acid*

acid² /'æsɪd/ **adj 1** (also **acidic** /ə'sɪdɪk/) containing acid, or having similar qualities to an acid: *acid soil* ∘ *an acid smell/taste* **2 acid remark/ comment, etc** an unkind remark that criticizes someone

acid 'rain noun [U] rain that contains chemicals from pollution and damages plants, etc

acknowledge /ək'nɒlɪdʒ/ **verb** [T] **1** ACCEPT ▷ to accept that something is true or exists: [+ (that)] *He acknowledged that there was a problem.* **2** LETTER ▷ to tell someone, usually in a letter, that you have received something they sent you: *Send a letter acknowledging receipt of his application.* **3** SAY HELLO ▷ to let someone know that you have seen them, usually by saying hello: *She didn't even acknowledge my presence.*

> ✏️ **Word partners for acknowledge**
>
> be **generally/widely/universally** acknowledged • acknowledge sb/sth **as/to be** sth

acknowledgement (also **acknowledgment**) /ək'nɒlɪdʒmənt/ **noun 1** ACCEPT ▷ [C, U] the act of accepting that something is true or exists: *There was no acknowledgement of the extent of the problem.* **2** LETTER ▷ [C] a letter telling you that someone has received something that you sent them **3** BOOK ▷ [C] something written at the front of a book by the author to thank people who have helped them: [usually plural] *His name appears in the acknowledgements.*

acne /'ækni/ **noun** [U] a skin problem that young people often have that causes spots on the face

acorn /'eɪkɔ:n/ **noun**[C] an oval nut that grows on oak trees

acoustic /ə'ku:stɪk/ **adj 1** [always before noun] An acoustic musical instrument does not use electricity: *an acoustic guitar* **2** relating to sound and hearing

acorn

acoustics /ə'ku:stɪks/ **noun** [plural] the way in which the shape of a room affects the quality of sound: *The acoustics of the hall were terrible.*

acquaintance /ə'kweɪntᵊns/ **noun** [C] someone who you know but do not know well: *He's just a **business acquaintance**.*

acquainted /ə'kweɪntɪd/ **adj** [never before noun] formal **1** If you are acquainted with someone, you have met them but do not know them well: *We're already acquainted – we met at Elaine's party.*

2 be acquainted with sth to know about something: *I'm afraid I'm not yet acquainted with the system.*

acquiesce /ˌækwi'es/ **verb** [I] formal to agree to something, often when you do not want to • **acquiescence noun** [U] formal

acquire /ə'kwaɪə^r/ **verb** [T] **1** B2 to get something: *I managed to acquire a copy of the report.* **2** B2 to learn something: *to acquire knowledge/skills*

acquisition /ˌækwɪ'zɪʃ^ən/ **noun 1** [U] the process of learning or getting something: *children's acquisition of language* **2** [C] something that you get, usually by buying it: *And the hat – is that a recent acquisition?*

acquit /ə'kwɪt/ **verb** [T] (**acquitting, acquitted**) If someone is acquitted of a crime, a court of law decides that they are not guilty: [often passive] *Both men were acquitted of murder.*

acquittal /ə'kwɪt^əl/ **noun** [C, U] a decision by a court of law that someone is not guilty of a crime

acre /'eɪkə^r/ **noun** [C] a unit for measuring area, equal to 4047 square metres

acrid /'ækrɪd/ **adj** An acrid smell is unpleasant and causes a burning feeling in your throat.

acrimonious /ˌækrɪ'məʊniəs/ **adj** involving a lot of anger, disagreement, and bad feelings: *an acrimonious divorce* • **acrimony** /'ækrɪməni/ **noun** [U] angry, bad feelings between people

acrobat /'ækrəbæt/ **noun** [C] someone who entertains people by performing difficult physical acts, such as walking on a wire high above the ground • **acrobatic** /ˌækrə'bætɪk/ **adj** • **acrobatics** /ˌækrə'bætɪks/ **noun** [plural] the actions of an acrobat

acronym /'ækrəʊnɪm/ **noun** [C] a word made from the first letters of other words: *AIDS is the acronym for 'acquired immune deficiency syndrome'.*

across /ə'krɒs/ **adv, preposition 1** SIDES ▷ A2 from one side of something to the other: *I was walking across the road.* ○ *They've built a new bridge across the river.* **2** OPPOSITE ▷ A2 on the opposite side of: *There's a library just across the street.* **3** MEASURE ▷ used after a measurement to show how wide something is: *The window measures two metres across.*

acrylic /ə'krɪlɪk/ **noun 1** [U] a type of cloth or plastic produced by chemical processes **2** [C, U] a type of paint • **acrylic adj** *acrylic paints*

act¹ /ækt/ **verb 1** BEHAVE ▷ [I] B1 to behave in a particular way: *to act responsibly* ○ *Jeff's been acting strangely recently.* ○ *Stop acting like a child!* **2** DO SOMETHING ▷ [I] B2 to do something, especially in order to solve a problem: *We have to act now to stop the spread of this disease.* **3** PERFORM ▷ [I, T] B1 to perform in a play or film: *He's acted in a number of successful Hollywood films.*

PHRASAL VERBS **act as sth 1** B2 to do a particular job, especially one you do not normally do: *He was asked to act as an adviser on the project.* **2** to have a particular effect: *Caffeine acts as a stimulant.* • **act sth out** to perform the actions and words of a situation or story: *The children acted out a verse from their favourite poem.* • **act up** If someone, especially a child, acts up, they behave badly.

act² /ækt/ **noun 1** DO ▷ [C] B2 something that someone does: *an act of terrorism/kindness* **2** LAW ▷ [C] a law made by a government: *an act of Congress/Parliament* **3** THEATRE ▷ [C] B1 one of the parts a play is divided into: *Her character doesn't appear until Act 2.* **4** PERFORMERS ▷ [C] one or several performers who perform for a short while in a show: *a comedy double act* **5** FALSE BEHAVIOUR ▷ [no plural] behaviour that hides your real feelings or intentions: *Was she really upset or was that just an act?* **6 in the act (of doing sth)** doing something wrong: *I caught him in the act of opening one of my letters.*

IDIOMS **get your act together** informal to organize your activities so that you can make progress • **get in on the act** informal to become involved in something successful that someone else has started

---

☑ Word partners for **act**

an act **of** sth • **commit** an act • a **barbaric/cowardly** act • a **criminal/terrorist** act

---

acting¹ /'æktɪŋ/ **adj acting chairman/director,** etc someone who does a job for a short time while the person who usually does it is not there

acting² /'æktɪŋ/ **noun** [U] the job of performing in plays and films: *He's trying to get into acting.*

action /'ækʃ^ən/ **noun 1** DO ▷ [C, U] B2 something that you do: *She has to accept the consequences of her actions.* ○ *We must take action (= do something) before the problem gets worse.* ○ *So what do you think is the best course of action (= way of dealing with the situation)?* ○ *It was the first time I'd seen firemen in action (= doing a particular activity).* **2** ACTIVITY ▷ [U] B1 things that are happening, especially exciting or important things: *He likes films with a lot of action.* → Opposite **inaction 3 out of action** damaged or hurt and not able to operate or play sports: *They've got three players out of action.* **4 legal action** a legal process in a court: *They are planning to take legal action against the company.* **5** FIGHTING ▷ [U] fighting in a war: *He was killed in action (= while fighting).* **6** PROCESS ▷ [no plural] a movement or natural process: *The rocks are smoothed by the action of water.* → See also **industrial action, be all talk²** (and no action)

action movie noun [C] (also UK **action film**) a movie that has a lot of exciting action

action-packed /'ækʃ^ən,pækt/ **adj** An action-packed film or story has a lot of exciting events.

action replay noun [C] UK (US **instant replay**) a recording of a small part of a sports event that is shown immediately after it happens, often more slowly

activate /'æktɪveɪt/ **verb** [T] to make something start working: *The alarm can be activated by a laser beam.*

active /'æktɪv/ **adj 1** INVOLVED ▷ ⓑ₂ very involved in an organization or planned activity: *He played an active role in the campaign.* **2** BUSY ▷ ⓑ₁ doing a lot of things, or moving around a lot: *Even at the age of 80 she's still very active.* **3** GRAMMAR ▷ ⓑ₁ An active verb or sentence is one in which the subject of the verb is the person or thing doing the action. For example 'Andy drove the car.' is an active sentence. → Compare **passive** **4** VOLCANO ▷ An active volcano could throw out rocks, fire, etc at any time.

actively /'æktɪvli/ **adv** ⓑ₂ in a way that causes something to happen: *He actively encourages me to spend money.*

activist /'æktɪvɪst/ **noun** [C] someone who tries to cause social or political change: *a political activist* • **activism noun** [U]

activity /æk'tɪvəti/ **noun 1** EVENT ▷ [C] ⓐ₂ something that you do for enjoyment, especially an organized event: *The centre offers a range of activities, such as cycling, swimming, and tennis.* **2** WORK ▷ [C, U] ⓑ₂ the work of a group or organization to achieve an aim: *criminal/terrorist activities* **3** MOVEMENT ▷ [U] ⓑ₂ a situation in which a lot of things are happening or people are moving around: *There was a sudden flurry of activity* (= short period of activity) *at the back of the hall.* → Opposite **inactivity (inactive)**

> **Word partners for activity**
>
> do/perform an activity • frantic/strenuous activity • outdoor/leisure activity • a flurry of activity

actor /'æktər/ **noun** [C] ⓐ₂ someone, especially a man, whose job is to perform in plays and films

actress /'æktrəs/ **noun** [C] a woman whose job is to perform in plays and films

actual /'æktʃuəl/ **adj 1** ⓑ₂ real, not guessed or imagined: *We were expecting about fifty people, though the actual number was a lot higher.* **2 in actual fact** UK ⓑ₂ really: *It was due to start at ten, but in actual fact, it didn't begin until nearly eleven.*

> ❗ Common learner error: **actual** or **current**?
>
> **Actual** means 'real'. It does not mean 'happening now'.
> *His friends call him Jo-Jo, but his actual name is John.*
>
> Use **current** to talk about things that are happening or that exist now.
> *She started her current job two years ago.*

actually /'æktʃuəli/ **adv 1** TRUTH ▷ ⓐ₂ used when you are saying what is the truth of a situation: *He didn't actually say anything important.* **2** SURPRISE ▷ ⓑ₁ used when you are saying something surprising: *She sounds English but she's actually Spanish.* ○ *Did you actually meet the president?* **3** MISTAKE ▷ mainly UK ⓑ₂ used when you are disagreeing with someone or saying no to a request: *"You didn't tell me." "Actually, I did."* ○ *"Do you mind if I smoke?" "Actually, I'd rather you didn't."*

acumen /'ækjʊmən/ **noun** [U] the ability to make good judgments and decisions: *business/political acumen*

acupuncture /'ækjʊpʌŋktʃər/ **noun** [U] a way of treating pain or illness by putting thin needle into different parts of the body

acute /ə'kjuːt/ **adj 1** EXTREME ▷ An acut problem or negative feeling is extreme: *There* an *acute shortage of medical staff.* ○ *acute pai* ○ *acute anxiety* **2** ANGLE ▷ An acute angle is les than 90 degrees. **3** QUICK TO NOTICE ▷ quick to notice or understand things: *an acute min* ○ *Dogs rely on their acute sense of smell.*

acutely /ə'kjuːtli/ **adv** very strongly: *I wa acutely aware of how Alex felt about th situation.*

ad /æd/ **noun** [C] ⓑ₁ an advertisement → See als classified ad

AD /ˌeɪ'diː/ abbreviation for Anno Domini: used t show that a particular year came after the birth of Christ: *1066 AD*

adamant /'ædəmənt/ **adj** very sure of what you think and not willing to change your opinion [+ (that)] *They are adamant that they have no broken any rules.* • **adamantly adv**

Adam's apple /ˌædəmz'æpl/ **noun** [C] the lump in a man's throat that you can see moving up and down when he speaks or swallows

adapt /ə'dæpt/ **verb 1** CHANGE BEHAVIOUR ▷ [I ⓑ₂ to change your behaviour so that it i suitable for a new situation: *It takes time to adapt to a new working environment.* **2** CHANGE SOMETHING ▷ [T] ⓑ₂ to change something so that it is suitable for a different use or situation *Courses have to be adapted for different markets* **3** BOOK ▷ [T] to change a book or play so that it can be made into a film or television pro gramme: *Both novels have been adapted fo television.*

adaptable /ə'dæptəbl/ **adj** able to change t suit different situations or uses • **adaptability** /əˌdæptə'bɪləti/ **noun** [U]

adaptation /ˌædæp'teɪʃən/ **noun 1** [C] a film television programme, or play that has been made from a book **2** [C, U] the process or act o changing to suit a new situation: *Evolution occurs as a result of adaptation to new environ ments.*

adapter (also **adaptor**) /ə'dæptər/ **noun** [C something that is used for connecting two o more pieces of electrical equipment to a electrical supply

add /æd/ **verb 1** PUT WITH ▷ [T] ⓐ₂ to pu something with something else: *Add the eggs t the cream.* **2** INCREASE ▷ [I, T] to increase a amount or level: *Then there's the service charg which adds another ten percent to the bill.* **3** SA MORE ▷ [T] ⓑ₁ to say another thing: [+ that] *Sh said she liked him but added that he was difficu to work with.* **4** CALCULATE ▷ [T] ⓐ₂ to put two o more numbers or amounts together to get total → See also add **insult²** to injury

PHRASAL VERBS **add (sth) up** ⓑ₁ to put number together in order to reach a total: *When you ad up everything we've spent, it's cost well over £20(*

• **not add up** informal If something does not add up, you cannot believe it is true: *She gave me an explanation but somehow it doesn't add up.*

adder /'ædər/ **noun** [C] a small, poisonous snake

addict /'ædɪkt/ **noun** [C] **1** ⓑ someone who cannot stop taking a drug: *a heroin/drug addict* **2** informal someone who likes something very much and does it or has it very often: *a TV/computer game addict*

addicted /ə'dɪktɪd/ **adj 1** not able to stop taking a drug: *He later became **addicted to** heroin.* **2** informal liking something very much and doing or having it too often: *He's **addicted to** chocolate/football.*

addiction /ə'dɪkʃən/ **noun** [C, U] ⓑ the problem of not being able to stop doing or taking something because you are addicted to it

> **🖉 Word partners for addiction**
>
> fight/have/suffer from an addiction
> • alcohol/drug/gambling addiction
> • addiction to sth

addictive /ə'dɪktɪv/ **adj** If something is addictive, it makes you want more of it so that you become addicted: *Tobacco is **highly addictive**.*

addition /ə'dɪʃən/ **noun 1 in addition (to sth)** ⓑ added to what already exists or happens, or more than you already do or have: *In addition to teaching, she works as a nurse in the holidays.* **2** [U] ⓑ the process of adding numbers or amounts together in order to get a total **3** [C] ⓑ a new or extra thing that is added to something: *Baby Sam is the latest **addition to** their family.*

additional /ə'dɪʃənəl/ **adj** ⓑ extra to what already exists: *We plan to take on an additional ten employees over the next year.* • **additionally adv**

additive /'ædɪtɪv/ **noun** [C] a chemical that is added to food in order to make it taste or look better or to keep it fresh

add-on /'ædɒn/ **noun** [C] a piece of equipment that can be connected to a computer to give it an extra use

address¹ /ə'dres/ ⓤ /'ædres/ **noun** [C] **1 BUILDING DETAILS** ▷ ⓐ the details of where a building is, including the building number, road name, town, etc **2 ELECTRONIC** ▷ ⓐ a series of letters, signs, or numbers used to send email to someone or to reach a page of information on the Internet: *an email/web address* **3 SPEECH** ▷ a formal speech to a group of people → See also **forwarding address, public address system**

> **🖉 Word partners for address**
>
> give sb your address • your business/home/work address • a change of address

address² /ə'dres/ **verb** [T] **1 BUILDING DETAILS** ▷ to write a name or address on an envelope or parcel: *A parcel arrived **addressed to** Emma.* **2 DEAL WITH** ▷ to deal with a problem: *We have to **address** the **issue/problem** before it gets worse.* **3 SPEAK** ▷ formal to speak to someone, or to give a speech to an audience: *Today she will be addressing a major conference in London.*

4 address sb as sth formal to give someone a particular name or title when you speak or write to them: *Do you think I should address him as 'Mr Benson' or 'Albert'?*

a'ddress ˌbook noun [C] (also US **'address ˌbook**) **1** a computer document that keeps a list of names and email addresses **2** a book in which you keep a list of names and addresses

adept /æ'dept/ **adj** good at doing something difficult: *She's very **adept at** dealing with the media.*

adequate /'ædɪkwət/ **adj 1** ⓑ enough: *I didn't have **adequate time** to prepare.* **2** ⓑ good enough, but not very good: *The sound quality isn't exceptional but it's **adequate for** everyday use.* → Opposite **inadequate** • **adequately adv** ⓑ *Make sure you are adequately equipped for the journey.*

adhere /əd'hɪər/ **verb** [I] formal to stick to a surface

PHRASAL VERB **adhere to sth** to obey a rule or principle: *We always adhere strictly to the guidelines.*

adherence /əd'hɪərəns/ **noun** [U] formal the act of obeying a set of rules or principles • **adherent noun** [C] formal someone who obeys a particular set of rules, principles, etc

adhesive /əd'hiːsɪv/ **noun** [C] a substance used for sticking things together • **adhesive adj**

ad hoc /ˌæd'hɒk/ **adj** not regular or planned, but happening only when necessary: *We meet **on an ad hoc basis**.*

adjacent /ə'dʒeɪsənt/ **adj** formal If two things are adjacent, they are next to each other: *The fire started in an adjacent building.* ∘ *They live in a house **adjacent to** the railway.*

adjective /'ædʒɪktɪv/ **noun** [C] ⓐ a word that describes a noun or pronoun. The words 'big', 'boring', 'purple', and 'obvious' are all adjectives. • **adjectival** /ˌædʒɪk'taɪvəl/ **adj** containing or used like an adjective: *an adjectival phrase*

adjoining /ə'dʒɔɪnɪŋ/ **adj** next to and joined to something: *an adjoining room*

adjourn /ə'dʒɜːn/ **verb** [I, T] formal to stop a meeting, especially a legal process, for a period of time or until a later date: *The judge adjourned the case until March 31.* • **adjournment noun** [C]

adjudicate /ə'dʒuːdɪkeɪt/ **verb** [I, T] formal to make an official judgment or decision about a competition or disagreement: *Occasionally, he has to **adjudicate on** a pensions matter.* • **adjudication** /əˌdʒuːdɪ'keɪʃən/ **noun** [U] • **adjudicator noun** [C]

adjust /ə'dʒʌst/ **verb 1** [T] ⓑ to change something slightly so that it works better, fits better, or is more suitable: *You can adjust the heat using this switch here.* ∘ *The figures need to be adjusted for inflation.* **2** [I] ⓑ to change the way you behave or think in order to suit a new situation: *They found it hard **adjusting to** life in a new country.*

adjustable /ə'dʒʌstəbl/ **adj** able to be changed slightly in order to suit different people or situations: *an adjustable seat*

A

adjustment /əˈdʒʌstmənt/ **noun** [C, U] **B2** a slight change that you make to something so that it works better, fits better, or is more suitable: We've **made** a few **adjustments to** the schedule.

ad lib /ˌædˈlɪb/ **verb** [I, T] to speak in public without having planned what to say: I had no script so I had to ad lib.

admin /ˈædmɪn/ **noun** [U] UK short for administration

administer /ədˈmɪnɪstər/ **verb** [T] **1** to organize or arrange something: The fund is administered by the Economic Development Agency. **2** formal to give medicine or medical help to someone: to administer first aid

administration /ədˌmɪnɪˈstreɪʃən/ **noun 1** [U] the work of organizing and arranging the operation of something, such as a company: The job involves a lot of administration. **2** [C] mainly US the President and politicians who govern a country at a particular time, or a period of government: the Obama administration

administrative /ədˈmɪnɪstrətɪv/ **adj** relating to the organization and management of something: The work is largely administrative.

administrative asˈsistant **noun** [C] someone whose job is to do tasks such as arranging meetings and typing letters for someone

administrator /ədˈmɪnɪstreɪtər/ **noun** [C] someone who helps to manage an organization

admirable /ˈædmərəbl/ **adj** If something is admirable, you respect or approve of it: He has many **admirable qualities**. • **admirably adv**

admiral /ˈædmərəl/ **noun** [C] an officer of very high rank in the navy

admiration /ˌædməˈreɪʃən/ **noun** [U] **B2** the feeling that you admire someone or something: My **admiration for** him grows daily.

> ☑ Word partners for **admiration**
>
> express/feel/have admiration • enormous/great/grudging/profound admiration • admiration for sb

admire /ədˈmaɪər/ **verb** [T] **1** **B2** to respect or approve of someone or something: You have to **admire** him **for** being so determined. **2** **B1** to look at something or someone, thinking how attractive they are: We stood for a few minutes, admiring the view. • **admirer noun** [C]

admissible /ədˈmɪsəbl/ **adj** formal allowed or acceptable, especially in a court of law: admissible evidence

admission /ədˈmɪʃən/ **noun 1** MONEY ▷ [U] **B1** the money that you pay to enter a place: Art exhibition – admission free. **2** TRUTH ▷ [C] the act of agreeing that you did something bad, or that something bad is true: She is, **by her own admission**, lazy. ∘ His departure was seen by many as an **admission of** guilt. **3** PERMISSION ▷ [C, U] **B2** permission to enter somewhere or to become a member of a club, university, etc: She's applied for **admission to** law school.

admissions /ədˈmɪʃənz/ **noun** [plural] the people who have been accepted as students or as members of an organization, or the proces of accepting them: the college admissions office

admit /ədˈmɪt/ **verb** (**admitting**, **admitted** **1** [I, T] **B1** to agree that you did something bad or that something bad is true: Both men admitted taking illegal drugs. ∘ [+ to + doing sth] She **admitted to** stealing the keys. ∘ I wa wrong – I admit it. ∘ [+ (that)] He finally admitted that he couldn't cope. **2** [T] to allow someone to enter somewhere, especially to take someone who is sick into hospital: UK to be **admitted to** hospital/US to be **admitted to** the hospital ∘ I says on the ticket 'admits 2'.

> ➕ Other ways of saying **admit**
>
> If a person admits that something bad is true, the verbs **accept** and **acknowledge** may be used:
>
> I **accept** that things should have been done differently.
>
> He refuses to **acknowledge** the problem.
>
> If a person admits that they have done something bad, the verb **confess** is often used:
>
> Rawlinson finally **confessed** to the murder.
>
> The phrasal verbs **own up** and (informal) **fess up**, and the idiom **come clean** can also be used when a person admits that they have done something bad:
>
> I decided to **come clean** about the broken vase.
>
> Come on, **own up** – who's eaten the last sandwich?

admittance /ədˈmɪtəns/ **noun** [U] permission t enter a place

admittedly /ədˈmɪtɪdli/ **adv** **B2** used when yo are agreeing that something is true althoug you do not want to: Admittedly I was partly t blame but it wasn't all my fault.

admonish /ədˈmɒnɪʃ/ **verb** [T] formal to gentl tell someone that they have done something wrong

ado /əˈduː/ **noun without further/more ad** without waiting any more

adolescence /ˌædəˈlesəns/ **noun** [U] the perio of time in someone's life between being a chil and an adult

adolescent /ˌædəˈlesənt/ **noun** [C] a youn person who is between being a child and an adult • **adolescent adj**

adopt /əˈdɒpt/ **verb 1** [I, T] **B2** to legally become the parents of someone else's child **2** [T] **B2** t accept or start using something new: We'v **adopted** a new **approach**. • **adopted** **B** an adopted son • **adoption** /əˈdɒpʃən/ **noun** [C, U

adorable /əˈdɔːrəbl/ **adj** very attractive, ofte because of being small: an adorable little boy

adore /əˈdɔːr/ **verb** [T] **1** to love someone an have a very good opinion of them: Sarah adore her father. **2** to like something very much: I adore travelling. • **adoration** /ˌædəˈreɪʃən/ **noun** [U]

adorn /əˈdɔːn/ **verb** [T] formal to decorate some thing: The room was **adorned with** flowers • **adornment noun** [C, U]

adrenalin (also **adrenaline**) /əˈdrenəlɪn/ **noun**

[U] a substance that your body produces when you are angry, excited, or frightened that makes your heart beat faster

adrift /əˈdrɪft/ *adj* **1** [never before noun] If a boat is adrift, it floats around in the water and is not tied to anything. **2 come adrift** to become loose and not joined to anything: *A few bricks in the garden wall had come adrift.*

adulation /ˌædjʊˈleɪʃᵊn/ *noun* [U] great praise and admiration for someone, often which they do not deserve

adult¹ /ˈædʌlt, əˈdʌlt/ *noun* [C] **A1** a person or animal that has finished growing and is not now a child

adult² /ˈædʌlt, əˈdʌlt/ *adj* **1** NOT A CHILD ▷ having finished growing: *an adult male rat* **2** RELATING TO ADULTS ▷ [always before noun] **A2** for or relating to adults: *adult education* ∘ *adult life* **3** SEXUAL ▷ Adult books, films, etc show naked people or sexual acts and are not for children.

adultery /əˈdʌltᵊri/ *noun* [U] sex between a married person and someone who is not their husband or wife • **adulterous** *adj*

adulthood /ˈædʌlthʊd/ ⓤ /əˈdʌlthʊd/ *noun* [U] the part of your life when you are an adult

advance¹ /ədˈvɑːns/ *noun* **1 in advance** **B1** before a particular time: *You need to book your ticket at least 14 days in advance.* **2** PROGRESS ▷ [C, U] **B2** new discoveries and inventions: *technological/scientific advances* **3** MONEY ▷ [C] a payment given to someone before work has been completed, or before the usual time **4** FORWARD ▷ [C] a movement forward, especially by an army

> ✏ Word partners for **advance**
>
> **medical/scientific/technological** advances • a **major** advance • advances **in** sth

advance² /ədˈvɑːns/ *verb* **1** PROGRESS ▷ [I, T] to develop or progress, or to make something develop or progress: *He moved to New York with hopes of advancing his career.* **2** FORWARD ▷ [I] to move forward to a new position, especially while fighting: *Rebel soldiers advanced on the capital.*

advance³ /ədˈvɑːns/ *adj* [always before noun] happening or ready before an event: *advance planning/warning* ∘ *an advance booking*

advanced /ədˈvɑːnst/ *adj* **1** **B1** having developed or progressed to a late stage: *advanced technology* ∘ *The disease was at an advanced stage.* **2** **A2** at a higher, more difficult level: *an advanced English course*

advancement /ədˈvɑːnsmənt/ *noun* [C, U] progress: *career advancement* ∘ *technological advancements*

advances /ədˈvɑːnsɪz/ *noun* **sb's advances** things that someone says and does to try to start a sexual relationship with someone

advantage /ədˈvɑːntɪdʒ/ *noun* [C, U] **1** **B1** something good about a situation that helps you: *One of the advantages of living in town is having the shops so near.* **2** **B2** something that will help you to succeed: *These new routes will give the airline a*

considerable **advantage over** its competitors. ∘ *If we could start early it would be to our advantage* (= help us to succeed). → Opposite **disadvantage** **3 take advantage of sth** **B1** to use the good things in a situation: *I thought I'd take advantage of the sports facilities while I'm here.* **4 take advantage of sb/sth** **B2** to treat someone badly in order to get what you want

> ✏ Word partners for **advantage**
>
> a **big/enormous/main/major** advantage
> • an **unfair** advantage • take advantage **of** sth • the advantage **of** sth

advantageous /ˌædvənˈteɪdʒəs/ *adj* helping to make you more successful

advent /ˈædvent/ *noun* **1 the advent of sth** the start or arrival of something new: *the advent of the Internet* **2 Advent** the religious period before Christmas (= a Christian holiday) in the Christian year

adventure /ədˈventʃər/ *noun* [C, U] **A2** an exciting and sometimes dangerous experience: *It's a film about the adventures of two friends travelling across Africa.* • **adventurer** *noun* [C]

> ✏ Word partners for **adventure**
>
> **have** an adventure • **be looking** for adventure • a **big/exciting** adventure • an adventure **holiday/playground**

adventurous /ədˈventʃᵊrəs/ *adj* **1** **B2** willing to try new and often difficult things: *I'm trying to be more adventurous with my cooking.* **2** exciting and often dangerous: *He led an adventurous life.*

adverb /ˈædvɜːb/ *noun* [C] **A2** a word that describes or gives more information about a verb, adjective, phrase, or other adverb. In the sentences 'He ate quickly.' and 'It was extremely good.', 'quickly' and 'extremely' are both adverbs.

adversary /ˈædvəsᵊri/ *noun* [C] formal someone who you are fighting or competing against

adverse /ˈædvɜːs/ *adj* formal **1 adverse conditions/effects/impact** things that cause problems or danger: *adverse weather conditions* ∘ *Pollution levels like these will certainly have an adverse effect on health.* **2 adverse comment/publicity/reaction, etc** something negative that is said or written about someone or something • **adversely** *adv*

adversity /ədˈvɜːsəti/ *noun* [C, U] formal an extremely difficult situation: *She showed a great deal of courage in adversity.*

advert /ˈædvɜːt/ *noun* [C] UK **B1** an advertisement

advertise /ˈædvətaɪz/ *verb* **1** [I, T] **B1** to tell people about a product or service, for example in newspapers or on television, in order to persuade them to buy it: *Companies are not allowed to advertise cigarettes on television any more.* **2** [I] **B1** to put information in a newspaper or on the Internet, asking for someone or something that you need: *The university is advertising for administrative staff.* • **advertiser** *noun* [C] a company that advertises things

advertisement /ədˈvɜːtɪsmənt/ ⓤ /ˌædvərˈtaɪz-

---

yes | k cat | ŋ ring | ʃ she | θ thin | ð this | ʒ decision | dʒ jar | tʃ chip | æ cat | e bed | ə ago | ɪ sit | i cosy | ɒ hot | ʌ run | ʊ put |

A

mənt/ **noun** [C] ⓐ a picture, short film, song, etc that tries to persuade people to buy a product or service: *a newspaper/television advertisement*

advertising /'ædvətaɪzɪŋ/ **noun** [U] ⓑ the business of trying to persuade people to buy products or services: *an **advertising** agency*

advice /əd'vaɪs/ **noun** [U] ⓐ suggestions about what you think someone should do or how they should do something: *She **asked** me **for advice** about writing a book.* ∘ *There's a booklet **giving advice on** how to set up your own club.* ∘ *I **took** your **advice** (= did what you suggested) and went home early.* ∘ *Can I give you a **piece of advice**?*

> ⚠ Common learner error: **advice**
> Remember that this word is not countable.
> *I need some advice.*
> ~~I need an advice.~~
> To make **advice** singular, say **a piece of advice**.

> ⚠ Common learner error: **advice** or **advise**?
> Be careful not to confuse the noun **advice** with the verb **advise**.
> *I advise you to see a lawyer.*
> ~~I advice you to see a lawyer.~~

> 🗒 Word partners for **advice**
> ask for/give/offer/provide/seek advice • take sb's advice • bad/conflicting/expert/good advice • advice on/about sth • a piece of advice

advisable /əd'vaɪzəbl/ **adj** [never before noun] If something is advisable, it will avoid problems if you do it: *It is advisable to book seats at least a week in advance.*

advise /əd'vaɪz/ **verb 1** [I, T] ⓑ to make a suggestion about what you think someone should do or how they should do something: [+ to do sth] *His doctor **advised** him to take time off work.* ∘ *They **advise** the government on environmental matters.* ∘ *The government is **advising against** travelling in the area.* ∘ [+ that] *They're advising that children be kept out of the sun altogether.* **2** [T] formal to give someone official information about something: *They were **advised of** their rights.*

adviser (also **advisor**) /əd'vaɪzər/ **noun** [C] someone whose job is to give advice about a subject: *a **financial adviser***

advisory¹ /əd'vaɪzəri/ **adj** **advisory committee/panel/board, etc** a group of people whose purpose is to give advice

advisory² /əd'vaɪzəri/ **noun** [C] US an official announcement that contains advice, information, or a warning: [usually plural] ***weather/travel advisories***

advocate¹ /'ædvəkeɪt/ **verb** [T] to express support for a particular idea or way of doing things: *I certainly wouldn't advocate the use of violence.* • **advocacy** /'ædvəkəsi/ **noun** [U] the act of advocating something

advocate² /'ædvəkət/ **noun** [C] **1** someone who supports a particular idea or way of doing

things: *He has always been **an advocate of** stricter gun controls.* **2** UK a lawyer who defends someone in court

A&E /ˌeɪənd'iː/ **noun** [C, U] UK (US **emergency room**) abbreviation for Accident and Emergency: the part of a hospital where people go when they are injured or sick and need treatment quickly

aerial¹ /'eəriəl/ **noun** [C] UK (US **antenna**) a piece of metal that is used for receiving television or radio signals → See colour picture **Car** on page Centre 7

aerial² /'eəriəl/ **adj** [always before noun] in or from the air, especially from an aircraft: *an aerial photograph/view*

aerobic /eə'rəʊbɪk/ **adj 1** Aerobic exercise is intended to make your heart stronger. **2** needing or using oxygen

aerobics /eə'rəʊbɪks/ **noun** [U] physical exercises that you do to music, especially in a class: *She goes to aerobics (= to aerobics classes).*

aerodynamic /ˌeərəʊdaɪ'næmɪk/ **adj** having a shape that moves quickly through the air • **aerodynamics noun** [U] the study of how objects move through the air

aeroplane *UK*, **airplane** *US*

aeroplane /'eərəpleɪn/ **noun** [C] UK (US **airplane**) ⓐ a vehicle that flies and has an engine and wings

aerosol /'eərəsɒl/ **noun** [C] a metal container that forces a liquid out in small drops when you press a button

aerosol

aerospace /'eərəʊspeɪs/ **noun** [U] the design and production of aircraft

aesthetic (also US **esthetic**) /es'θetɪk/ **adj** relating to beauty and the way something looks: *the **aesthetic** appeal of cats* • **aesthetically adv**

aesthetics (also US **esthetics**) /es'θetɪks/ **noun** [U] the study of beauty, especially in art

AFAIK internet abbreviation for as far as I know: used when you believe that something is true but you are not completely certain

afar /ə'fɑːr/ **adv** literary **from afar** from a long distance: *He had admired her from afar.*

affable /'æfəbl/ **adj** pleasant and friendly

affair /ə'feər/ **noun 1** [C] ⓑ a situation or set of related events, especially bad ones: *The government's handling of the affair has been widely criticized.* **2** [C] ⓑ a sexual relationship between two people when one or both of them is married to someone else: *He's been **having an affair** with a woman at work.* **3 be sb's affair** If something is your affair, it is private and you do not want anyone else to be involved or know about it. → See also **love affair**

affairs /ə'feəz/ **noun** [plural] situations or subjects that involve you: *He refused to discuss his financial affairs.* → See also **current affairs, state of affairs**

affect /ə'fekt/ **verb** [T] **1** ⑫ to influence someone or something, or cause them to change: *It's a disease which affects many older people.* **2** ⑫ to cause a strong emotion, especially sadness: [often passive] *I was deeply affected by the film.* → See Note at **effect¹**

> ❗ Common learner error: **affect** someone or something
>
> Remember that you do not need a preposition after the verb **affect**.
> *The problem affects everyone.*
> ~~The problem affects to everyone.~~

affectation /ˌæfek'teɪʃᵊn/ **noun** [C, U] a way of speaking or behaving that is not natural

affected /ə'fektɪd/ **adj** behaving or speaking in a way that is not natural or sincere

affection /ə'fekʃᵊn/ **noun** [C, U] ⑫ a feeling of liking or loving someone: *Ann's **affection for** her grandfather was obvious.*

> ◪ Word partners for **affection**
>
> show affection • affection for sb • a display/show of affection

affectionate /ə'fekʃᵊnət/ **adj** showing that you like or love someone: *an affectionate little girl* ∘ *He's very affectionate.* • **affectionately adv**

affiliate /ə'fɪlieɪt/ **verb be affiliated to/with sth** to be officially connected to, or a member of, a larger organization: *a college affiliated to Delhi University* • **affiliation** /əˌfɪli'eɪʃᵊn/ **noun** [C, U]

affinity /ə'fɪnəti/ **noun 1** [no plural] a feeling that you like and understand someone or something: *She seems to have a natural **affinity for/with** water.* **2** [C, U] a similarity: *There are close **affinities between** the two paintings.*

affirm /ə'fɜːm/ **verb** [T] formal to say that something is true: *He gave a speech affirming the government's commitment to education.* • **affirmation** /ˌæfə'meɪʃᵊn/ **noun** [C, U]

affirmative /ə'fɜːmətɪv/ **adj** formal In language, an affirmative word or phrase expresses the meaning 'yes': *an affirmative answer*

affirmative action noun [U] If a government or an organization takes affirmative action, it gives preference to women, black people, or other groups which are often treated unfairly, when it is choosing people for a job.

affix /'æfɪks/ **noun** [C] a group of letters that you add to the beginning or the end of a word to make another word. In the word 'non-alcoholic', 'non-' is an affix. → Compare **prefix, suffix**

afflict /ə'flɪkt/ **verb** [T] formal If an illness or problem afflicts you, it makes you suffer: [often passive] *a country afflicted by civil war* • **affliction**

/ə'flɪkʃᵊn/ **noun** [C, U] something that makes you suffer

affluent /'æfluənt/ **adj** having a lot of money: *affluent families/neighbourhoods* • **affluence** /'æfluəns/ **noun** [U]

afford /ə'fɔːd/ **verb** [T] **1 can afford** ⑪ to have enough money to buy something or enough time to do something: *I can't afford a new computer.* ∘ [+ to do sth] *Can we afford to go away?* ∘ *I'd love to come out but I can't afford the time.* **2 can afford to do sth** If you can afford to do something, it is possible for you to do it without causing problems: *We can't afford to take that risk.*

> ❗ Common learner error: **afford to do** something
>
> When **afford** is followed by a verb, it is always in the **to + infinitive** form.
> *We can't afford to go on holiday this year.*
> ~~We can't afford going on holiday this year.~~

affordable /ə'fɔːdəbl/ **adj** cheap enough for most people: *affordable housing/prices*

affront /ə'frʌnt/ **noun** [C] something that is offensive or insulting to someone: *He regarded the comments as an **affront to** his dignity.*

afield /ə'fiːld/ **adv** mainly UK **far/further afield** away from the place where you are: *We hired a car so we could travel further afield.*

afloat /ə'fləʊt/ **adj 1** floating on water **2 stay afloat** to have enough money to continue a business: *Many small business are struggling to stay afloat.*

afoot /ə'fʊt/ **adj** [never before noun] being planned, or happening now: *There are **plans afoot** to launch a new radio station.*

> ➕ Other ways of saying **afraid**
>
> Other ways of saying 'afraid' are **frightened** and **scared**:
> *He's **frightened** that the other children will laugh at him.*
> *Gerry has always been **scared** of heights.*
> If someone is extremely afraid, then you can use adjectives such as **petrified**, **terrified**, **panic-stricken** or the informal phrase **scared to death**:
> *I'm **terrified** of flying.*
> *She was **panic-stricken** when her little boy disappeared.*
> *He's **scared to death** of having the operation.*
> If someone is afraid because they are worrying about something, then you can use adjectives such as **anxious**, **concerned**, **nervous**, or **worried**:
> *I'm **worried** that something will go wrong.*
> *All this waiting is making me feel **anxious**.*
> If someone is afraid of something that might happen in the future, you can use the adjectives **apprehensive** or **uneasy**:
> *He's a bit **apprehensive** about living away from home.*

afraid /əˈfreɪd/ adj [never before noun] **1 I'm afraid** ⓐ2 used to politely tell someone bad news or to politely disagree with someone: *There are no tickets left, I'm afraid.* ∘ *[+ (that)] I'm afraid that I've broken your vase.* **2 FRIGHTENED** ▷ ⓐ2 frightened: *She's afraid of water.* ∘ *He was/felt suddenly afraid.* **3 WORRIED** ▷ ⓑ1 worried that something bad might happen: *[+ (that)] Many people are afraid that they might lose their jobs.* ∘ *[+ of + doing sth] He was afraid of upsetting Clare.*

afresh /əˈfreʃ/ adv If you do something afresh, you do it again in a different way: *Juan tore up the letter he was writing and started afresh.*

African /ˈæfrɪkən/ adj relating or belonging to Africa: *African art/music* • **African noun** [C] someone from Africa

African-American /ˌæfrɪkənəˈmerɪkən/ adj (also **Afro-American** /ˌæfrəʊəˈmerɪkən/) relating or belonging to American people whose families came from Africa in the past: *the African-American community* • **African-American** (also **Afro-American**) noun [C]

Afro-Caribbean /ˌæfrəʊkærɪˈbiːən/ adj UK relating to people from the Caribbean whose families originally came from Africa: *Afro-Caribbean art/music*

after¹ /ˈɑːftər/ preposition **1 TIME/EVENT** ▷ ⓐ1 when a time or event has happened: *We went swimming after lunch.* ∘ *Let's finish the meeting. After that, we can have coffee.* **2 LIST** ▷ ⓐ2 following in order: *H comes after G in the alphabet.* **3 TIME** ▷ US (UK/US **past**) used to say how many minutes past the hour it is: *It's five after three.* **4 BECAUSE OF** ▷ ⓑ2 because of something that happened: *I'll never trust her again after what she did to me.* **5 DESPITE** ▷ ⓑ2 despite: *I can't believe he was so unpleasant after you gave him so much help.* **6 FOLLOW** ▷ ⓑ1 following someone or something: *We ran after him, but he escaped.* **7 after 5 minutes/2 weeks, etc** when five minutes, two weeks, etc have passed **8 day after day/year after year, etc** ⓑ1 continuing for a long time, or happening many times: *I'm bored with going to school day after day.* **9 NAMED FOR** ▷ used when giving someone or something the same name as another person or thing: *It was called the Biko building, after the famous South African.* **10 after all a** used to say that something happened or was true although you did not expect it to happen or be true: *Helen couldn't come to the party after all.* **b** ⓑ1 used to add information that shows that what you have just said is true: *You can't expect to be perfect – after all, it was only your first lesson.* **11 be after sth** informal to be trying to get something: *What type of job are you after?* ∘ *I'm after a tie to go with this shirt.* **12 be after sb** informal to be looking for someone: *The police are after him.*

after² /ˈɑːftər/ conjunction ⓑ1 at a later time than something else happens: *We arrived after the game had started.* ∘ *After further discussion, we decided to call the police.*

after³ /ˈɑːftər/ adv ⓐ2 later than someone or something else: *He had the operation on Monday and I saw him the day after.*

aftermath /ˈɑːftəmɑːθ/ noun [no plural] a situation that is the result of an accident, crime, or other violent event: *There are calls for tighter airport security in the aftermath of last week's bombing.*

> 🖉 Word partners for **aftermath**
>
> in the aftermath of sth • the immediate aftermath

afternoon /ˌɑːftəˈnuːn/ noun **1** ⓐ1 [C, U] the time between the middle of the day, and the evening: *I played tennis on Saturday afternoon.* ∘ *The train arrives at 3 o'clock in the afternoon.* ∘ *What are you doing this afternoon* (= today in the afternoon)*?* **2 (Good) afternoon.** ⓐ1 used to say hello to someone in the afternoon

> ❗ Common learner error: **afternoon**
>
> If you talk about what happens during the afternoon, use the preposition **in**.
> *In the afternoon I phoned my girlfriend.*
> ~~At the afternoon I phoned my girlfriend.~~
> If you say a day of the week before **afternoon**, use the preposition **on**.
> *I'm going to the dentist on Tuesday afternoon.*

aftershave /ˈɑːftəʃeɪv/ noun [C, U] a liquid with a pleasant smell that men put on their faces after shaving (= removing hair)

aftertaste /ˈɑːftəteɪst/ noun [C] the taste that a food or drink leaves in your mouth when you have swallowed it: *[usually singular] a bitter/sweet aftertaste*

afterthought /ˈɑːftəθɔːt/ noun [C] something that you say or do just later: *[usually singular] She only asked me to the party as an afterthought.*

afterwards /ˈɑːftəwədz/ adv (also US **afterward**) ⓐ2 at a later time, after something else has happened: *I did my homework and went swimming afterwards.*

again /əˈɡen/ adv **1 REPEAT** ▷ ⓐ1 once more: *I'll ask her again.* ∘ *I'll see you again next week.* **2 AS BEFORE** ▷ ⓐ2 as before: *Get some rest and you'll soon be well again.* **3 again and again** ⓑ1 many times: *He played the same song again and again* **4 all over again** ⓑ2 repeated from the beginning: *We had to start all over again.* **5 then/there again** used when adding a fact to something you have just said: *I failed my history test – but then again, I didn't do much studying for it.*

against /əˈɡenst/ preposition **1 NOT AGREE** ▷ ⓑ2 disagreeing with a plan or activity: *Andrew wants to change offices but I'm against it.* ∘ *There were 70 votes for the new proposal and 30 against.* **2 COMPETE** ▷ ⓐ2 competing with or opposing someone or something: *Liverpool is playing against AC Milan.* ∘ *the fight against racism* **3 TOUCH** ▷ touching something: *Push the bed against the wall.* **4 PROTECT** ▷ protecting you from something bad: *Fresh fruit in the diet may protect against cancer.* **5 OPPOSITE DIRECTION** ▷ ⓑ1 in the opposite direction to the way something is moving: *I was cycling against the wind.* **6 against the law/the rules** ⓑ forbidden by a law or by rules: *It's against the law to leave young children alone in the house.* **7 against sb's advice/wishes, etc** If you do something against someone's advice, wishes, etc, you do it although they have said you should not or must not: *He flew there against his doctor's advice.* **8 have sth against sb/sth** to have a reason not to like someone or something: *I have nothing against him personally, I just don't think he's the right man for the job.*

age¹ /eɪdʒ/ noun **1** HOW OLD ▷ [C, U] ⓐ the number of years that someone has lived, or that something has existed: *The show appeals to people of all ages.* ∘ *She left India at the age of 12.* ∘ *Children under 10 years of age must be accompanied by an adult.* → See Note at **year** **2** HISTORY ▷ [C] ⓑ a period of history: *the Ice Age* ∘ *We're living in the age of electronic communication.* **3** OLD ▷ [U] the quality of being old: *Some wines improve with age.* **4 under age** too young to do something legally → See also **the Middle Ages, old age**

> ◪ Word partners for **age**
>
> reach the age of [18/60/75, etc] • at/from the age of [8/12/60, etc] • [8/25/70, etc] years of age • at sb's age • an age limit

age² /eɪdʒ/ verb [I, T] (mainly UK **ageing**, US **aging**, **aged**) to become older or to make someone seem older: *Dad has aged a lot recently.*

aged¹ /eɪdʒd/ adj ⓐ having a particular age: *They have one daughter, aged three.* → See also **middle-aged**

aged² /ˈeɪdʒɪd/ adj old: *an aged dog* ∘ *improved health care for the aged*

age group noun [C] people of a particular age: *job training for people in the 16-24 age group*

ageing¹ mainly UK (UK/US **aging**) /ˈeɪdʒɪŋ/ adj becoming older: *an ageing population*

ageing² mainly UK (UK/US **aging**) /ˈeɪdʒɪŋ/ noun [U] the process of becoming older: *the ageing process*

age limit noun [C] the age at which a person is allowed or not allowed to do something: *Eighteen is the legal age limit for buying alcohol.*

agency /ˈeɪdʒənsi/ noun [C] **1** ⓑ a business that provides a service: *an advertising agency* **2** an international organization or government department: *an international development agency* → See also **travel agency**

agenda /əˈdʒendə/ noun [C] **1** a list of subjects that people will discuss at a meeting: *There are several items on the agenda.* **2** important subjects that have to be dealt with: *The issue of rail safety is back on the political agenda.*

> ◪ Word partners for **agenda**
>
> set (= decide) the agenda • be off/on the agenda • be at the top of/high on the agenda • the agenda for sth

agent /ˈeɪdʒənt/ noun [C] **1** ⓑ someone whose job is to deal with business for someone else: *a literary agent* **2** (also **secret agent**) ⓑ someone

who tries to find out secret information, especially about another country → See also **estate agent, real estate agent, travel agent**

ages /ˈeɪdʒɪz/ noun [plural] informal ⓑ a very long time: *I've been waiting here for ages.* ∘ *It takes ages to cook.*

aggravate /ˈægrəveɪt/ verb [T] **1** to make a situation or condition worse: *His comments only aggravated the problem.* **2** to annoy someone: *She's starting to really aggravate me.* • **aggravating** adj • **aggravation** /ˌægrəˈveɪʃ°n/ noun [C, U]

aggregate /ˈægrɪgət/ noun [C, U] a total: UK *Liverpool won 2-0 on aggregate* (= in total).

aggression /əˈgreʃ°n/ noun [U] angry or violent behaviour towards someone: *an act of aggression*

aggressive /əˈgresɪv/ adj **1** ⓑ behaving in an angry and violent way towards another person: *aggressive behaviour* **2** using forceful methods and determined to succeed: *an aggressive marketing campaign* • **aggressively** adv

aggressor /əˈgresər/ noun [C] someone who starts a fight or war with someone else

aggrieved /əˈgriːvd/ adj upset or angry because someone has treated you unfairly

aghast /əˈgɑːst/ adj [never before noun] very shocked: *She looked at him aghast.*

agile /ˈædʒaɪl/ ⓤ /ˈædʒ°l/ adj **1** able to move your whole body easily and quickly **2** able to think quickly in an intelligent way: *an agile mind* • **agility** /əˈdʒɪləti/ noun [U]

aging /ˈeɪdʒɪŋ/ noun, adj another spelling of ageing

agitate /ˈædʒɪteɪt/ verb [I] to argue strongly about something in order to achieve social or political changes: *They continued to agitate for changes to the legal system.* • **agitator** noun [C]

agitated /ˈædʒɪteɪtɪd/ adj very anxious or upset: *He seemed agitated, as if something was worrying him.* • **agitation** /ˌædʒɪˈteɪʃ°n/ noun [U]

AGM /ˌeɪdʒiːˈem/ noun [C] UK (US **annual meeting**) abbreviation for Annual General Meeting: a meeting that happens once every year in which an organization discusses the past year's activities and chooses the people who will be in charge of the organization

agnostic /ægˈnɒstɪk/ noun [C] someone who believes that we cannot know if God exists or not • **agnostic** adj

ago /əˈgəʊ/ adv ten minutes/six years/a long time ago ⓐ used to refer to a time in the past: *They moved to New York ten years ago.*

agonize (also UK -**ise**) /ˈægənaɪz/ verb [I] to spend a lot of time worrying about a decision: *Lee agonized over what to buy his girlfriend.*

agonizing (also UK -**ising**) /ˈægənaɪzɪŋ/ adj causing you a lot of pain or worry: *an agonizing choice*

agony /ˈægəni/ noun [C, U] extreme suffering, either physical or mental: *She lay on the bed in agony.*

agony aunt noun [C] UK someone who gives advice on personal problems, in a newspaper or magazine

agree /əˈgriː/ verb (**agreeing**, **agreed**) **1** SAME OPINION ▷ [I, T] ⓐ to have the same opinion as someone: *I **agree with** you.* ◦ *"She's definitely the right person for the job." "I agree."* ◦ [+ (that)] *We all agreed that mistakes had been made.* ◦ *We **agree about** most things.* **2 SAY YES** ▷ [I] 🄑 to say you will do something that someone asks you to do: [+ to do sth] *She agreed to help him.* → See Note at **accept 3 DECIDE** ▷ [I, T] 🄐 to decide something with someone: *We couldn't **agree on** what to buy.* ◦ [+ to do sth] *They agreed to meet on Sunday.* ◦ [+ (that)] *We agreed that they would deliver the sofa in the morning.* **4 DESCRIPTION** ▷ [I] If two descriptions agree, they are the same. → Opposite **disagree**

PHRASAL VERB **agree with sth** 🄑 to think that something is morally acceptable: *I don't agree with hunting.*

agreeable /ə'griːəbl/ **adj** formal **1** pleasant or nice: *an agreeable young man* → Opposite **disagreeable 2 be agreeable to sth** to be willing to do or accept something: *If Harvey is agreeable to the proposal, we'll go ahead.* • **agreeably adv**

agreement /ə'griːmənt/ **noun 1** [C] 🄑 a promise or decision made between two or more people: *an international agreement* ◦ *It was difficult to **reach an agreement**.* **2** [U] 🄑 a situation in which people have the same opinion as each other: *Not everyone was **in agreement**.* → Opposite **disagreement**

🗹 Word partners for **agreement**

reach/sign an agreement • a **draft/written** agreement • an agreement **between** sb

---

agriculture /'ægrɪkʌltʃər/ **noun** [U] 🄑 the work and methods of growing crops and looking after animals that are then used for food • **agricultural** /ˌægrɪ'kʌltʃərl/ **adj**

agritourism /ˌægrɪ'tʊərɪzm/ **noun** [U] the business of providing holidays for people on farms or in the countryside

aground /ə'graʊnd/ **adv run aground** If a ship runs aground, it cannot move because the water is not deep enough.

ah /ɑː/ **exclamation 1** used to show sympathy or to show pleasure at seeing a baby or attractive animal: *Ah, you poor thing!* ◦ *Ah, look at that little kitten!* **2** used to show that you have just understood something: *Ah, now I see what you're saying!*

aha /ə'hɑː/ **exclamation** used when you suddenly understand or find something: *Aha! That's where I left my keys!*

ahead /ə'hed/ **adj, adv 1 IN FRONT** ▷ 🄐 in front: *The road ahead is very busy.* ◦ *Rick walked **ahead of** us.* **2 FUTURE** ▷ 🄐 in the future: *She has a difficult time **ahead of** her.* **3 MORE POINTS** ▷ 🄑 having more points than someone else in a competition: *Barcelona was ahead after ten minutes.* **4 MORE PROGRESS** ▷ making more progress than someone or something else: *Sue is **ahead of** everyone else in French.* **5 go ahead** informal 🄑 used to allow someone to do something: *"Can I use your phone?" "Sure, go ahead."* **6 ahead of time/schedule** before the time that was planned: *We finished the project ahead of*

schedule. → See also **be one step¹ ahead (of sb)**, **be streets (street) ahead (of sb/sth)**, **be ahead of your time¹**

-aholic /-ə'hɒlɪk/ **suffix** unable to stop doing or taking something: *chocaholic* (= *someone who cannot stop eating chocolate*)

aid¹ /eɪd/ **noun 1** [U] money, food, or equipment that is given to help a country or group of people: *Emergency aid was sent to the flood victims.* ◦ *aid workers* **2 in aid of sb/sth** UK in order to collect money for a group of people who need it: *a concert in aid of famine relief* **3 with the aid of sth** using something to help you: *She can walk with the aid of a stick.* **4 come/go to sb's aid** to go to someone and help them: *Luckily a policeman came to my aid.* **5** [C] a piece of equipment that helps you to do something: *teaching aids such as books and videos* → See also **Band-Aid, first aid, visual aid**

aid² /eɪd/ **verb** formal **1** [T] to help someone **2 aid and abet (sb)** in law, to help someone do something that is illegal

aide /eɪd/ **noun** [C] someone whose job is to help someone important, especially in the government: *a former aide to the President*

AIDS /eɪdz/ **noun** [U] (also UK **Aids**) abbreviation for acquired immune deficiency syndrome: a serious disease that destroys the body's ability to fight infection → Compare **HIV**

ailing /'eɪlɪŋ/ **adj** weak or sick: *an ailing company/economy*

ailment /'eɪlmənt/ **noun** [C] an illness: *Treat minor ailments yourself.*

aim¹ /eɪm/ **noun 1** 🄐 [C] the purpose of doing something, and what you hope to achieve: *The aim of the film was to make people laugh.* ◦ [+ of + doing sth] *He went to Paris with the aim of improving his French.* **2 sb's aim** someone's ability to hit an object by throwing something or shooting at something **3 take aim** to point a weapon towards someone or something

---

🗹 Word partners for **aim**

achieve your aim • sb's/sth's **main/ultimate** aim • the aim **of** sth • **with** the aim **of** doing sth

---

aim² /eɪm/ **verb 1 aim for/at sth; aim to do sth** 🄐 to intend to achieve something: *I aim to arrive at three o'clock.* ◦ *We're aiming for a 10% increase in sales.* **2 be aimed at sb** 🄑 to be intended to influence or affect a particular person or group: *advertising aimed at students* **3 be aimed at doing sth** to be intended to achieve a particular thing: *a plan aimed at reducing traffic* **4** [I, T] to point a weapon towards someone or something: *He **aimed the** gun **at** the lion.*

aimless /'eɪmləs/ **adj** with no purpose • **aimlessly adv**

ain't /eɪnt/ informal short for am not, is not, are not, have not, or has not. This word is not considered correct by most people.

air¹ /eər/ **noun 1 GAS** ▷ [U] 🄐 the mixture of gases around the Earth that we breathe: *air pollution* ◦ *He went outside to get some **fresh air**.*

(= *clean, cool air*). **2 the air** ⑫ the space above and around things: *He fired his gun into the air.* **3 TRAVEL** ▷ [U] ⑫ travel in an aircraft: *I like travelling by air.* ○ *air safety* **4 QUALITY** ▷ [no plural] a particular appearance or quality: *He has an air of authority.* **5 be on air** to be broadcasting on television or radio

IDIOMS **clear the air** If an argument or discussion clears the air, people feel less angry or upset after it. • **disappear/vanish into thin air** to suddenly disappear in a mysterious way • **be up in the air** If something is up in the air, no decision has been made: *Our plans for the summer are still up in the air.*

→ See also a **breath** of fresh air, **mid-air**

air² /eə^r/ **verb 1 BROADCAST** ▷ [T] to broadcast something on radio or television **2 air your opinions/views, etc** to say what your opinions are: *The meeting will give everyone a chance to air their views.* **3 ROOM** ▷ [T] to make a room smell better by opening a door or window **4 CLOTHES** ▷ [I, T] If clothes air, or if you air them, you hang them up with a lot of air around them.

airbag /'eəbæg/ **noun** [C] a bag in the front of a car that protects people in an accident by filling with air: *passenger/twin airbags*

airbase /'eəbeɪs/ **noun** [C] a military airport

airborne /'eəbɔːn/ **adj** moving in, or carried by the air: *airborne troops* ○ *an airborne virus*

air con noun [U] UK abbreviation for air conditioning

air conditioner noun [C] a machine that keeps the air cool in a building or a car

air conditioning noun [U] ⑧ a system that keeps the air cool in a building or car • **air-conditioned** /'eəkən,dɪʃənd/ **adj** having air conditioning: *an air-conditioned office*

aircraft /'eəkrɑːft/ **noun** [C] (plural **aircraft**) ⑫ a vehicle that can fly

aircraft carrier noun [C] a ship on which aircraft can take off and land

airfare /'eəfeə^r/ **noun** [C] the cost of a ticket to fly somewhere

airfield /'eəfiːld/ **noun** [C] a place where small or military aircraft can take off and land

air force noun [C] ⑧ the part of a country's military organization that uses aircraft to fight wars

air hostess noun [C] UK (UK/US **flight attendant**) someone whose job is to serve passengers on an aircraft and to make sure that safety rules are obeyed

airing cupboard noun [C] UK a warm cupboard where you keep sheets, clean clothes, etc

airless /'eələs/ **adj** An airless room does not have enough fresh air.

airlift /'eəlɪft/ **noun** [C] a flight by an aircraft to move people or things when it is too difficult or too slow to travel by road: *an airlift of medical supplies* • **airlift verb** [T] [often passive] *Three small children were airlifted to safety.*

airline /'eəlaɪn/ **noun** [C] ⑧ a company that provides regular flights to places

airliner /'eəlaɪnə^r/ **noun** [C] a large plane for carrying people

airmail /'eəmeɪl/ **noun** [U] the sending of letters or parcels by plane: *an airmail letter*

airman /'eəmən/ **noun** [C] (plural **airmen**) a man who flies an aircraft in a country's air force

airplane /'eəpleɪn/ **noun** [C] US (UK **aeroplane**) a vehicle that flies and has an engine and wings → See picture at **aeroplane**

airport /'eəpɔːt/ **noun** [C] ⑫ a place where planes take off and land, with buildings for passengers to wait in

air raid noun [C] an attack by military planes

airspace /'eəspeɪs/ **noun** [U] the sky above a country that belongs to that country

airstrike /'eəstraɪk/ **noun** [C] an attack by military planes

airtight /'eətaɪt/ **adj** An airtight container does not allow air in or out.

air traffic controller noun [C] the person in an airport who tells pilots when to take off and land their aircraft

airy /'eəri/ **adj** An airy room or building is pleasant because it has a lot of space and air.

aisle

aisle /aɪl/ **noun** [C] a passage between the lines of seats or goods in a plane, church, supermarket, etc

ajar /ə'dʒɑː^r/ **adj** [never before noun] If a door is ajar, it is slightly open.

aka /,eɪkeɪ'eɪ/ **adv** abbreviation for also known as: used when giving the name that a person is generally known by, after giving their real name: *Peter Parker, aka Spiderman*

akin /ə'kɪn/ **adj** formal **be akin to sth** to be similar to something

à la carte /,ælɑː'kɑːt/ **adj, adv** choosing food as separate items from a menu (= list of food), not as a meal with a fixed price

alacrity /ə'lækrəti/ **noun** [U] formal If you do something with alacrity, you do it in a very quick and willing way.

alarm¹ /ə'lɑːm/ **noun 1 WARNING** ▷ [C] ⑧ a loud noise that warns you of danger: *a fire alarm* ○ *to set off an alarm* **2 CLOCK** ▷ [C] (also **alarm clock**) ⑧ a clock that makes a noise to wake you **3 WORRY** ▷ [U] a sudden feeling of fear or worry that something bad might happen: *There's no need for alarm – it is completely safe.*

IDIOM **raise the alarm** to warn someone of a dangerous situation: *Her parents raised the alarm when she failed to return home.*

→ See also **burglar alarm, false alarm**

> ⧉ Word partners for **alarm**
>
> an alarm **goes off/sounds** • **set off/trigger** an alarm • a **burglar/fire/smoke** alarm • a **car** alarm • an alarm **system**

alarm² /ə'lɑːm/ **verb** [T] to make someone worried or frightened: *I don't want to alarm you but he really should be here by now.*

a'larm ,clock noun [C] Ⓐ⒉ a clock that makes a noise to wake you: *I've set the alarm clock for six.*

alarm clock

alarmed /ə'lɑːmd/ **adj** worried or frightened by something: *I was a bit alarmed at the number of people in the audience.*

alarming /ə'lɑːmɪŋ/ **adj** making you feel worried or frightened: *alarming news*

alas /ə'læs/ **exclamation** literary used to show sadness

albeit /ɔːl'biːɪt/ **conjunction** formal although: *He tried, albeit without success.*

albino /æl'biːnəʊ/ ⑤ /æl'baɪnəʊ/ **noun** [C] a person or animal with white skin, white hair or fur, and pink eyes

album /'ælbəm/ **noun** [C] **1** Ⓐ⒉ several songs or pieces of music on a CD, a record, etc **2** Ⓐ⒉ a book in which you keep photographs, stamps, etc

alcohol /'ælkəhɒl/ **noun** [U] **1** Ⓐ⒉ drinks such as wine and beer that can make you drunk **2** a liquid that has no colour and is in drinks that make you drunk

alcoholic¹ /,ælkə'hɒlɪk/ **noun** [C] someone who regularly drinks too much alcohol and cannot stop the habit

alcoholic² /,ælkə'hɒlɪk/ **adj 1** Ⓑ⒈ containing alcohol: *alcoholic drinks* **2** [always before noun] regularly drinking too much alcohol and unable to stop the habit: *She lived with her alcoholic father.*

alcoholism /'ælkəhɒlɪzᵊm/ **noun** [U] the condition of being an alcoholic

alcove /'ælkəʊv/ **noun** [C] a part of a wall in a room that is further back than the rest of the wall

ale /eɪl/ **noun** [C, U] a type of beer

alert¹ /ə'lɜːt/ **adj** quick to notice and react to things around you: *A young dog should be alert and playful.* ○ *Teachers need to be alert to sudden changes in students' behaviour.* • **alertness noun** [U]

alert² /ə'lɜːt/ **verb** [T] to warn someone of a possibly dangerous situation: *Six hours later she still wasn't home so they alerted the police.*

alert³ /ə'lɜːt/ **noun 1** [C] a warning about a

possibly dangerous situation: *a bomb alert* **2 be on full/red alert** to be expecting problems and ready to deal with them: *Police in the region were on full alert against further attacks.*

'A ,level noun [C] in England and Wales, an exam taken at the age of eighteen, or the qualification itself

algae /'ældʒiː/ **noun** [U, group] a plant with no stem or leaves that grows in or near water

algebra /'ældʒɪbrə/ **noun** [U] a type of mathematics in which numbers and amounts are shown by letters and symbols

alias¹ /'eɪliəs/ **noun** [C] a false name, especially one used by a criminal

alias² /'eɪliəs/ **preposition** used when giving the name that a person is generally known by, after giving their real name: *Grace Kelly, alias Princess Grace of Monaco*

alibi /'ælɪbaɪ/ **noun** [C] proof that someone was not in the place where a crime happened and so cannot be guilty

alien¹ /'eɪliən/ **adj 1** strange and not familiar *The custom was totally alien to her.* **2** [always before noun] relating to creatures from another planet: *an alien spacecraft*

alien² /'eɪliən/ **noun** [C] **1** a creature from another planet **2** formal someone who does not legally belong to the country where they live or work

alienate /'eɪliəneɪt/ **verb** [T] **1** to make someone stop supporting and liking you: *The government's comments have alienated many teachers.* **2** to make someone feel that they are different and do not belong to a group: *Disagreements can alienate teenagers from their families.* • **alienation** /,eɪliə'neɪʃᵊn/ **noun** [U]

alight¹ /ə'laɪt/ **adj** [never before noun] mainly UK burning: *Vandals set the car alight* (= made it burn).

alight² /ə'laɪt/ **verb** [I] formal to get out of a bus, train, etc: *He alighted from the taxi.*

align /ə'laɪn/ **verb 1** [T] to put things in an exact line or make them parallel **2 align yourself with sb; be aligned with sb** to support the opinions of a political group, country, etc: *Many voters are not aligned with any party.* • **alignment noun** [C, U]

alike¹ /ə'laɪk/ **adj** [never before noun] Ⓑ⒈ similar *The children look so alike.*

alike² /ə'laɪk/ **adv 1** Ⓑ⒉ in a similar way: *We think alike.* **2** Ⓑ⒉ used to say that two people or groups are included: *It is a disease which affects men and women alike.*

alimony /'ælɪməni/ **noun** [U] money that someone must pay regularly to their wife or husband after the marriage has ended

alive /ə'laɪv/ **adj** [never before noun] **1 NOT DEAD** Ⓑ⒈ living, not dead: *Are your grandparents still alive?* **2 PLACE** ▷ full of activity and excitement: *The bar was alive with the sound of laughter.* ○ *The city comes alive at night*

3 CONTINUING ▷ continuing to exist: *Local people are fighting to keep the language alive.*

IDIOM **be alive and kicking/well** to continue to be popular or successful: *Despite rumours to the contrary, feminism is alive and kicking.*

all¹ /ɔːl/ **pronoun, determiner 1 EVERY ONE** ▷ **⚐** every person or thing in a group: *We were all dancing.* ∘ *I've watched all of the programmes in the series.* **2 WHOLE AMOUNT** ▷ **⚐** the whole amount of something: *Who's eaten all the cake?* ∘ *He spends all of his money on clothes.* **3 WHOLE TIME** ▷ **⚐** the whole of a period of time: *all week/month/year* ∘ *He's been studying all day.* **4 ONLY THING** ▷ **⚐** the only thing: *All I remember is waking up in hospital.* **5 at all** in any way: *He hasn't changed at all.* ∘ UK *Can I help at all?* **6 in all** **⚐** in total: *There were twenty people at the meeting in all.*

> ❗ Common learner error: **all** + period of time
>
> You do not say 'the' when you use **all** + a period of time.
>
> *all day/morning/week/year/summer*
> ~~all the day/morning/week/year/summer~~

all² /ɔːl/ **adv 1 ⚐** completely or very: *You're all wet!* ∘ *I'm all excited now.* **2 all over a ⚐** in every place: *Lee has travelled all over the world.* **b** finished: *It was all over very quickly.* **3 2/5/8, etc all ⚐** used to say that two players or teams have the same number of points in a game: *It was 3 all at half time.* **4 all along ⚐** from the beginning of a period of time: *I said all along that it was a mistake.* **5 all but** almost: *The film was all but over by the time we arrived.* **6 all the better/easier/more exciting, etc** much better, easier, etc: *The journey was all the more dangerous because of the bad weather.* **7 all in all ⚐** considering everything: *All in all, I think she did well.*

Allah /ˈælə/ **noun** the name of God for Muslims

allay /əˈleɪ/ **verb** formal **allay sb's concerns/ fears/suspicions, etc** to make someone feel less worried or frightened, etc: *I tried to allay his fears about the interview.*

allegation /ˌælɪˈɡeɪʃᵉn/ **noun** [C] a statement that someone has done something wrong or illegal, made without proof that this is true: *allegations of corruption* ∘ [+ that] *He denied allegations that he had cheated.*

> 🗹 Word partners for **allegation**
>
> **make/deny/face/investigate** an allegation • a **serious** allegation • an allegation **of** sth • an allegation **against** sb

allege /əˈledʒ/ **verb** [T] to say that someone has done something wrong or illegal, but not prove it: [often passive] *The teacher is alleged to have hit a student.* ∘ [+ (that)] *He alleges that Bates attacked him.*

alleged /əˈledʒd/ **adj** [always before noun] believed to be true, but not proved: *an alleged attack* • **allegedly** /əˈledʒɪdli/ **adv** *He was arrested for allegedly stealing a car.*

allegiance /əˈliːdʒᵉns/ **noun** [U] loyalty and support: *To become a citizen, you have to pledge/swear allegiance to* (= say you will be loyal to) *the United States.*

allegory /ˈælɪɡəri/ **noun** [C, U] a story, poem, or painting that has a hidden meaning, especially a moral one • **allegorical** /ˌælɪˈɡɒrɪkəl/ **adj**

allergic /əˈlɜːdʒɪk/ **adj 1** [never before noun] having an allergy: *I'm allergic to eggs.* **2** [always before noun] caused by an allergy: *an allergic reaction*

allergy /ˈælədʒi/ **noun** [C] a medical condition in which your body reacts badly to something that you eat, breathe, or touch: *an allergy to dogs*

alleviate /əˈliːvieɪt/ **verb** [T] to make problems or suffering less extreme: *She's been given some tablets to alleviate the pain.* • **alleviation** /əˌliːviˈeɪʃᵉn/ **noun** [U]

alley /ˈæli/ **noun** [C] (also **alleyway** /ˈæliweɪ/) a narrow road between buildings

IDIOM **be right up sb's alley** US informal (UK **be right up sb's street**) to be exactly the type of thing that someone knows about or likes to do

alliance /əˈlaɪəns/ **noun** [C] an agreement between countries or political parties to work together to achieve something: *an alliance between France and Britain*

> 🗹 Word partners for **alliance**
>
> **form** an alliance • an alliance **between** sb and sb • an alliance **with** sb • **in** alliance **with** sb

allied /ˈælaɪd/ **adj 1** [always before noun] joined by a formal agreement: *the allied powers* **2 be allied to/with sth** to be related to something: *a group closely allied with the Green Party*

alligator /ˈælɪɡeɪtər/ **noun** [C] a big reptile with a long mouth and sharp teeth, that lives in lakes and rivers

alligator

all-night /ˈɔːlnaɪt/ **adj** lasting all night: *Tom was tired after his all-night party.*

allocate /ˈæləkeɪt/ **verb** [T] to give some time, money, space, etc to be used for a particular purpose: *The government has promised to allocate extra money for health care.* ∘ *More police time should be allocated to crime prevention.*

allocation /ˌæləˈkeɪʃᵉn/ **noun 1** [C] an amount of money, time, space, etc that is allocated **2** [U] the process of allocating money, time, space, etc: *the allocation of money*

allot /əˈlɒt/ **verb** [T] (**allotting, allotted**) to give someone a particular amount of something: [often passive] *They were allotted seats on the front row.*

allotment /əˈlɒtmənt/ **noun 1** [C] in Britain, a

small area of land that people rent and grow vegetables and flowers on **2** [C, U] the process of sharing something, or the amount that you get

all-out /ˈɔːlˌaʊt/ **adj** [always before noun] complete and with as much effort as possible: *an all-out battle/effort*

! Common learner error: **allow** or **let**?

Allow and **let** have similar meanings. **Allow** is used in more formal or official situations, especially when talking about rules and laws. Verb patterns – **allow someone to do something / allow something to happen**.

The new legislation allows companies to charge for this service.
We can't allow this situation to continue.

Let is used in more informal and spoken situations. Verb patterns – **let someone do something / let something happen**.

Dad never lets anyone else drive his car.
She let her hair grow longer.

---

allow /əˈlaʊ/ **verb** [T] **1 GIVE PERMISSION** ▷ **B1** to give someone permission for something: [often passive] *Smoking is not allowed in the restaurant.* ○ [+ to do sth] *You are not allowed to use calculators* UK *in the exam/US on the exam.* ○ [+ two objects] *Patients are not allowed visitors after nine o'clock.* **2 NOT PREVENT** ▷ to not prevent something from happening: [+ to do sth] *They have allowed the problem to get worse.* **3 MAKE POSSIBLE** ▷ to make it possible for someone to do something: [+ to do sth] *The extra money will allow me to upgrade my computer.* **4 TIME/MONEY** ▷ to plan to use a particular amount of money, time, etc for something: *Allow three hours for the whole journey.*

PHRASAL VERB **allow for sth** to consider or include something when you are making plans: *The journey should take two hours, allowing for delays.*

allowance /əˈlaʊəns/ **noun** [C] **1** money that you are given regularly, especially to pay for a particular thing: *a clothing allowance* **2** an amount of something that you are allowed: *The luggage allowance is 25 kilos.* **3 make allowances for sb/sth** to remember that someone has a disadvantage that is not their fault when you are judging their behaviour or work: *They made allowances for the fact that he was sick.*

alloy /ˈælɔɪ/ **noun** [C] a metal that is a mixture of two or more metals

ˌall ˈright¹ (also **alright**) **adj** [never before noun], **adv 1 B1** good enough, although not very good: *The hotel wasn't great but it was all right.* ○ *It's a cheap wine but it tastes all right.* **2 A2** safe or well: *I'm all right thanks. How are you?* ○ *Did you get home all right last night?* **3 that's all right a** used as an answer when someone thanks you: *"Thanks for cleaning the kitchen." "That's all right."* **b A2** something you say when someone says sorry to show that you are not angry: *"I'm sorry – I forgot all about it." "That's all right."*

ˌall ˈright² (also **alright**) **exclamation A1** used to

agree to a suggestion or request: *"How about going out for dinner?" "All right."*

all-time /ˈɔːlˈtaɪm/ **adj** [always before noun] If something is at an all-time best/high/low, etc, it is the best/highest/lowest, etc it has ever been.

allude /əˈluːd/ **verb**

PHRASAL VERB **allude to sb/sth** formal to refer to someone or something but not directly

allure /əˈljʊəʳ/ **noun** [U] an attractive or exciting quality: *the allure of the city* • **alluring adj** attractive or exciting: *an alluring image*

allusion /əˈluːʒən/ **noun** [C, U] formal a statement in which you refer to someone or something, but not directly: *a play full of allusions to Shakespeare*

ally¹ /ˈælaɪ/ **noun** [C] **1** someone who supports you, especially when other people are against you **2** a country that has agreed to help another country, especially in a war

ally² /əˈlaɪ/ **verb**

PHRASAL VERB **ally yourself to/with sb** to join someone and support them

almighty /ɔːlˈmaɪti/ **adj 1** [always before noun] very strong or forceful: *All of a sudden I heard an almighty bang in the kitchen.* **2** having the power to do everything, like a god: *Almighty God*

almond /ˈɑːmənd/ **noun** [C, U] a flat, oval nut, often used in cooking

almost /ˈɔːlməʊst/ **adv 1 A2** If something almost happens, it does not happen but it is very close to happening: *I almost missed the bus.* **2 almost always/everyone/half, etc** not always/everyone/half, etc but very close to it: *He's almost always late.*

alone /əˈləʊn/ **adj, adv 1** [never before noun] **A2** without other people: *She lives alone.* **2** [always after noun] used to emphasize that only one person or thing is involved: *Last year alone the company made a million dollars.* **3 leave sb alone B2** to stop talking to someone or annoying them: *Leave him alone, he's tired.* **4 leave sth alone** to stop touching something: *Leave your hair alone!* → See also **let alone**

! Common learner error: **alone** or **lonely**?

Alone means without other people. If you feel sad because you are alone, you are **lonely**.

Sometimes I like to be alone to think.
She has been very lonely since her husband died.

---

along¹ /əˈlɒŋ/ **preposition 1 DIRECTION** ▷ **A2** from one part of a road, river, etc to another: *a romantic walk along the beach* **2 NEXT TO** ▷ **B1** in a line next to something long: *a row of new houses along the river* **3 PARTICULAR PLACE** ▷ at a particular place on a road, river, etc: *Somewhere along this road there's a garage.*

along² /əˈlɒŋ/ **adv 1 B1** forward: *We were just walking along, chatting.* **2 be/come along to** arrive somewhere: *You wait ages for a bus and then three come along at once.* **3 bring/take sb along B1** to take someone with you to a place

She brought some friends along to the party. **4 along with sb/sth** ⬤ in addition to someone or something else: *California along with Florida is the most popular American holiday destination.*

alongside /əˌlɒŋˈsaɪd/ **adv, preposition 1** next to someone or something: *A car pulled up alongside ours.* **2** together with someone: *She enjoyed working alongside such famous actors.*

aloof /əˈluːf/ **adj 1** not friendly, especially because you think you are better than other people: *He seems arrogant and aloof.* **2** not involved in something: *He tried to remain aloof from family arguments.*

aloud /əˈlaʊd/ **adv** ⬤ in a way that other people can hear: *to laugh aloud* ○ *The author read aloud from his new book.*

alphabet /ˈælfəbet/ **noun** [C] ⬤ a set of letters used for writing a language: *The English alphabet starts at A and ends at Z.*

alphabetical /ˌælfəˈbetɪkəl/ **adj** ⬤ arranged in the same order as the letters of the alphabet: *Put the names in alphabetical order.* • **alphabetically adv**

alpine /ˈælpaɪn/ **adj** [always before noun] existing in, or relating to high mountains: *an alpine village*

already /ɔːlˈredi/ **adv 1** ⬤ before now, or before a particular time in the past: *I've already told him.* ○ *By the time we arrived, he'd already left.* **2** ⬤ used to say that something has happened earlier than you expected: *I'm already full and I've only eaten one course.*

alright /ɔːlˈraɪt/ **adj, adv, exclamation** another spelling of all right

also /ˈɔːlsəʊ/ **adv** ⬤ in addition: *She speaks French and also a little Spanish.* ○ *The book also has a chapter on grammar.*

altar /ˈɔːltər/ **noun** [C] a table used for religious ceremonies, especially in a Christian church

alter /ˈɔːltər/ **verb** [I, T] ⬤ to change, or to make someone or something change: *We've had to alter our plans.*

alteration /ˌɔːltərˈeɪʃən/ **noun** [C, U] a change, or the process of changing something: *We've made a few alterations to the kitchen.*

> ⬛ **Word partners for alteration**
>
> **make alterations (to) sth** • a **major/minor/ slight** alteration • an alteration **in/to** sth

alternate¹ /ɔːlˈtɜːnət/ **adj 1 alternate days/ weeks/years, etc** one out of every two days, weeks, years, etc: *I work alternate Saturdays.* **2** with first one thing, then another thing, and then the first thing again, etc: *a dessert with alternate layers of chocolate and cream* **3** [always before noun] US An alternate plan, method, etc is one that you can use if you do not want to use another one. • **alternately adv**

alternate² /ˈɔːltəneɪt/ **verb 1** [I] If two things alternate, one thing happens, then the other thing happens, then the first thing happens again, etc.: *She alternates between cheerfulness and deep despair.* **2 alternate sth with sth** to use or do one thing then another thing and then the first thing again, etc: *They alternate classical*

pieces with more modern works. • **alternating adj** *alternating moods of anger and sadness*

alternative¹ /ɔːlˈtɜːnətɪv/ **noun** [C] ⬤ one of two or more things that you can choose between: *It's a low-fat alternative to butter.* ○ *After the public protests the government had no alternative but to change its policy.*

alternative² /ɔːlˈtɜːnətɪv/ **adj** [always before noun] **1** (also US **alternate**) ⬤ An alternative plan, method, etc is one that you can use if you do not want to use another one: *We can make alternative arrangements if necessary.* **2** ⬤ different to what is usual or traditional: *alternative comedy* ○ *an alternative lifestyle*

alternatively /ɔːlˈtɜːnətɪvli/ **adv** ⬤ used to give a second possibility: *We could go there by train or, alternatively, I could drive us.*

alternative ˈmedicine noun [U] any way of trying to make an illness better that uses medicines or methods that are not normally used in Western medicine

although /ɔːlˈðəʊ/ **conjunction 1** ⬤ despite the fact that: *She walked home by herself, although she knew it was dangerous.* **2** ⬤ but: *He's coming this evening, although I don't know exactly when.*

altitude /ˈæltɪtjuːd/ **noun** [C, U] the height of something above sea level: *flying at an altitude of 8000 metres.*

alto /ˈæltəʊ/ **noun** [C] a woman or boy with a low singing voice

altogether /ˌɔːltəˈɡeðər/ **adv 1 COMPLETELY** ▷ ⬤ completely: *The train slowed down and then stopped altogether.* ○ *I'm not altogether sure about the idea.* **2 TOTAL** ▷ ⬤ in total: *There were twenty people there altogether.* **3 GENERALLY** ▷ ⬤ used to make a statement about several things that you have mentioned: *Altogether, I'd say the party was a great success.*

aluminium /ˌæljəˈmɪniəm/ **noun** [U] UK (US **aluminum** /əˈluːmɪnəm/) ⬤ a light, silver-coloured metal used for making containers, cooking equipment, and aircraft parts: *aluminium cans/foil*

alumni /əˈlʌmnaɪ/ **noun** [plural] mainly US men and women who have left a school, college or university after finishing their studies there

> ➕ Other ways of saying **always**
>
> If you are using **always** to mean 'again and again', then you could also use **constantly**, **continually**, **forever**, or the fixed expressions **time after time** or **all the time**:
>
> *He's constantly/forever losing his keys.*
> *I'm fed up with you making excuses all the time.*
>
> The word **invariably** is sometimes used as a more formal way of saying **always**, especially when talking about something bad which happens:
>
> *The train is invariably late.*
>
> The fixed expression **without fail** can be used to show that someone always does something, even when it is difficult:
>
> *He visited her every Sunday without fail.*

A

always /ˈɔːlweɪz/ **adv 1 EVERY TIME** ▷ **A1** every time, or at all times: *I always walk to work.* **2 UNTIL NOW** ▷ **A2** at all times in the past: *We've always lived here.* **3 FOREVER** ▷ **A2** forever: *I will always remember you.* **4 MANY TIMES** ▷ **B2** again and again, usually in an annoying way: [+ doing sth] *He's always losing his keys.* **5 can/could always do sth B1** used to suggest something: *You can always stay with us if you miss your train.*

Alzheimer's (disease) /ˈæltshaɪməzdɪˌziːz/ **noun** [U] a brain disease mainly of old people that makes a person forget things and stops them from thinking clearly

am strong /æm/ weak /əm, m/ present simple I of be

a.m. (also **am**) /ˌeɪˈem/ **A1** used to refer to a time between 12 o'clock in the night and 12 o'clock in the day: *We're open from 9 a.m. to 5 p.m. daily.*

amalgamate /əˈmælɡəmeɪt/ **verb** [I, T] If two or more organizations amalgamate, they join to become one, and if you amalgamate them, you make them do this: *a decision to **amalgamate with** another school* • **amalgamation** /əˌmælɡəˈmeɪʃᵊn/ **noun** [C, U]

amass /əˈmæs/ **verb** [T] formal to get a lot of money or information over a period of time: *He amassed a fortune in the diamond trade.*

amateur¹ /ˈæmətər/ **adj** doing something as a hobby and not as your job: *an amateur photographer*

amateur² /ˈæmətər/ **noun** [C] **1** someone who does something as a hobby and not as their job **2** someone who is not good at what they do: *I won't be giving them any more work – they're a bunch of amateurs.*

amateurish /ˈæmətᵊrɪʃ/ ⑤ /ˌæməˈtɜːrɪʃ/ **adj** done without skill or attention

amaze /əˈmeɪz/ **verb** [T] to make someone very surprised: *It amazes me how much energy that woman has.*

amazed /əˈmeɪzd/ **adj B1** extremely surprised: *I was **amazed at** the price.* ◦ [+ (that)] *I was amazed that Paul recognized me.*

amazement /əˈmeɪzmənt/ **noun** [U] **B2** extreme surprise: *Jana looked at him **in amazement.*** ◦ **To his amazement** *they offered him the job.*

amazing /əˈmeɪzɪŋ/ **adj B1** very surprising: [+ question word] *It's amazing how many people can't read.* • **amazingly adv** *Amazingly enough, no one else applied for the job.*

ambassador /æmˈbæsədər/ **noun** [C] **B2** the main official sent by the government of a country to represent it in another country: *the French ambassador to Britain*

amber /ˈæmbər/ **noun** [U] **1** a colour between yellow and orange **2** a hard, clear, yellowish-brown substance, used for making jewellery: *an amber necklace* • **amber adj** *an amber traffic light*

ambience (also **ambiance**) /ˈæmbiəns/ **noun** [U, no plural] the qualities of a place and the way it makes you feel: *Lighting adds a lot to the ambience of a room.*

ambiguity /ˌæmbɪˈɡjuːəti/ **noun** [C, U] the state of having more than one possible meaning: *Legal documents must be free of ambiguity.*

ambiguous /æmˈbɪɡjuəs/ **adj** having more than one possible meaning: *an ambiguous statement* • **ambiguously adv**

ambition /æmˈbɪʃᵊn/ **noun 1** [C] **B1** something you want to achieve in your life: *My ambition is to retire at forty.* **2** [U] **B2** a strong feeling that you want to be successful or powerful: *My sister always had more ambition than me.*

> **🔲 Word partners for ambition**
>
> **have an ambition • achieve/fulfil/realize an ambition • a burning/lifelong ambition**

ambitious /æmˈbɪʃəs/ **adj 1 B2** wanting to be successful or powerful: *an ambitious young lawyer* **2 B2** An ambitious plan will need a lot of work and will be difficult to achieve: *This is our most ambitious project so far.*

ambivalent /æmˈbɪvələnt/ **adj** having two different feelings about something: *He was **ambivalent about** moving to London.* • **ambivalence** /æmˈbɪvᵊləns/ **noun** [U]

amble /ˈæmbl/ **verb amble along/around/through, etc** to walk somewhere in a slow and relaxed way: *We ambled home across the fields.*

ambulance /ˈæmbjələns/ **noun** [C] **A2** a vehicle that takes people to hospital when they are sick or hurt

ambush

ambush /ˈæmbʊʃ/ **verb** [T] to attack a person or vehicle after hiding somewhere and waiting for them to arrive: [often passive] *The bus was ambushed by a gang of youths.* • **ambush noun** [C] *Two policemen were killed in a terrorist ambush.*

ameliorate /əˈmiːliᵊreɪt/ **verb** [T] formal to make a problem or bad situation better

amen /ˌɑːˈmen/ **exclamation** something that Christians say at the end of a prayer

amenable /əˈmiːnəbl/ **adj** willing to do or accept something: *She may be more **amenable to** the idea now.*

amend /əˈmend/ **verb** [T] to slightly change the words of a document: [often passive] *The contract has now been amended.*

amendment /əˈmendmənt/ **noun** [C, U] a change in the words of a document, or the process of doing this: *to **make an amendment to** the human rights law*

amends /əˈmendz/ **noun make amends** to do something nice for someone to show that you are sorry for something that you have done

I want to **make amends for** *the worry I've caused you.*

amenity /əˈmiːnəti/ ⓤ /əˈmenəti/ **noun** [C] a building, piece of equipment, or service that is provided for people's comfort or enjoyment: [usually plural] *The campsite's amenities include a pool and three restaurants.*

American /əˈmerɪkən/ **adj 1** relating to the United States of America: *an American accent* **2 North/South American** relating to one or more of the countries of North/South America • **American noun** [C] someone who comes from the United States of America → See also **Native American**

American football noun [U] UK (US **football**) a game for two teams of eleven players in which each team tries to kick, run with, or throw an oval ball across the opposing team's goal line → See colour picture **Sports 2** on page Centre 15

American Indian adj relating or belonging to the original race of people who lived in North America • **American Indian noun** [C]

amiable /ˈeɪmiəbl/ **adj** pleasant and friendly: *an amiable young man* • **amiably adv**

amicable /ˈæmɪkəbl/ **adj** formal done in a friendly way, without arguments: *an amicable agreement/divorce* • **amicably adv**

amid /əˈmɪd/ **preposition** (also **amidst** /əˈmɪdst/) **1** while something else is happening: *Security was increased amid fears of further terrorist attacks.* **2** among: *a village set amid the hills*

amiss[1] /əˈmɪs/ **adj** [never before noun] If something is amiss, there is something wrong: *I knew something was amiss when he didn't answer the door.*

amiss[2] /əˈmɪs/ **adv 1 would not go amiss** UK If something would not go amiss, it would be useful or nice in a particular situation: *A cup of coffee wouldn't go amiss.* **2 take it amiss** UK to feel upset by what someone says or does: *I think she might take it amiss if I left early.*

ammonia /əˈməʊniə/ **noun** [U] a liquid or gas with a strong smell, used in substances for cleaning things

ammunition /ˌæmjəˈnɪʃⁿn/ **noun** [U] **1** a supply of bullets and bombs to be fired from guns **2** facts that you can use to criticize someone

amnesia /æmˈniːʒə/ **noun** [U] a medical condition that makes you forget things

amnesty /ˈæmnəsti/ **noun 1** [C, U] a time when a government allows political prisoners to go free **2** [C] a time when people can give weapons or drugs to the police, or admit that they have done something illegal, without being punished

among /əˈmʌŋ/ **preposition** (also **amongst** /əˈmʌŋst/) **1 IN THE MIDDLE** ▷ ⓐ2 in the middle of something: *He disappeared among the crowd.* **2 IN A GROUP** ▷ ⓐ2 in a particular group: *The decision will not be popular among students.* ◦ *I'm going to give you a minute to talk amongst yourselves* (= talk to each other). **3 ONE OF A GROUP** ▷ to be one of a small group: *He is among the top five tennis players in the country.* **4 DIVIDE** ▷ to each one in a group: *She divided the cake among the children.*

amoral /ˌeɪˈmɒrəl/ **adj** not caring if what you are doing is morally wrong: *an amoral person/act*

amorous /ˈæmⁿrəs/ **adj** full of love and sexual excitement: *amorous adventures*

amount[1] /əˈmaʊnt/ **noun** [C] ⓑ1 how much there is of something: *The project will take a huge amount of time and money.*

> **❗ Common learner error: amount of or number of?**
>
> **Amount of** is used with uncountable nouns.
> *I should reduce the amount of coffee I drink.*
> *Did you use the right amount of flour?*
> **Number of** is used with countable nouns.
> *We don't know the number of people involved yet.*
> *They received a large number of complaints.*

amount[2] /əˈmaʊnt/ **verb**

PHRASAL VERB **amount to sth 1** to be the same as something, or to have the same effect as something: *He gave what amounted to an apology on behalf of the company.* **2** to have a particular total: *goods amounting to $800*

amp /æmp/ **noun** [C] (also **ampere** /ˈæmpeər/) a unit for measuring the strength of an electric current

ample /ˈæmpl/ **adj 1** enough, or more than enough: *She's had ample time to get the work done.* **2** large: *her ample bosom* • **amply adv**

amplifier /ˈæmplɪfaɪər/ **noun** [C] a piece of electronic equipment that makes sounds louder

amplify /ˈæmplɪfaɪ/ **verb** [T] **1** to make a sound louder using electronic equipment **2** formal to make a feeling or opinion stronger or clearer • **amplification** /ˌæmplɪfɪˈkeɪʃⁿn/ **noun** [U]

amputate /ˈæmpjəteɪt/ **verb** [I, T] to cut off someone's leg, arm, finger, etc in a medical operation: *His leg was amputated at the knee.* • **amputation** /ˌæmpjəˈteɪʃⁿn/ **noun** [C, U]

amuse /əˈmjuːz/ **verb** [T] ⓑ1 to make someone smile or laugh: *I took him an article that I thought might amuse him.* **2** ⓑ2 to keep someone interested and help them to have an enjoyable time: [often reflexive] *I bought a magazine to amuse myself while I was on the train.*

amused /əˈmjuːzd/ **adj 1** ⓑ2 showing that you think something is funny: *an amused smile* ◦ *She was very amused by/at your comments.* **2 keep sb amused** ⓑ2 to keep someone interested and help them to have an enjoyable time: *How do you keep an eight-year-old boy amused?*

amusement /əˈmjuːzmənt/ **noun 1** [U] ⓑ2 the feeling that you have when something makes you smile or laugh: *I watched the performance with great amusement.* ◦ *To our amusement the tent collapsed on top of them.* **2** [C, U] ⓑ2 an enjoyable way of spending your time: *I play the piano but just for my own amusement.*

amusement park noun [C] a large park where you can ride on exciting machines

amusing /əˈmjuːzɪŋ/ **adj** ⓑ1 making you laugh or smile: *an amusing letter*

an strong /æn/ weak /ⁿn/ **determiner** ⓐ1 used

A

instead of 'a' when the next word starts with a vowel sound: *an apple* ○ *an hour* → See Note at **a**

anaemia UK (US **anemia**) /əˈniːmiə/ **noun** [U] a medical condition in which your blood does not contain enough red cells • **anaemic** UK (US **anemic**) /əˈniːmɪk/ **adj**

anaesthetic UK (US **anesthetic**) /ˌænəsˈθetɪk/ **noun** [C, U] a drug that makes you unable to feel pain during an operation: *The operation is done under anaesthetic* (= using anaesthetic). → See also **general anaesthetic, local anaesthetic**

anaesthetist UK (US **anesthetist**) /əˈniːsθətɪst/ US /əˈnesθətɪst/ **noun** [C] a doctor in a hospital who gives anaesthetics to people

anaesthetize /əˈniːsθətaɪz/ **verb** [T] UK (US **anesthetize** /əˈnesθətaɪz/) to give someone drugs that make them unable to feel pain

anagram /ˈænəɡræm/ **noun** [C] a word or phrase made by putting the letters of another word or phrase in a different order: *'Team' is an anagram of 'meat'.*

anal /ˈeɪnəl/ **adj** relating to the anus (= hole where solid waste comes out of the body)

analogous /əˈnæləɡəs/ **adj** formal similar in some ways: *It's often said that life is analogous to a journey.*

analogue (also US **analog**) /ˈænəlɒɡ/ **adj 1** using a system in which information, such as sound or images, is stored or sent in a continuously changing form, such as electrical signals, radio waves, or film: *analogue data* ○ *analogue TV/radio/phone* **2** **analogue clock/watch** a clock/watch that has hands (= narrow parts that point) that show what time it is

analogy /əˈnælədʒi/ **noun** [C, U] a comparison that shows how two things are similar: *She draws an analogy between life's events and a game of chance.*

analyse UK (US **analyze**) /ˈænəlaɪz/ **verb** [T] 🔵 to examine the details of something carefully, in order to understand or explain it: *to analyse information* ○ *Blood samples were analysed in the laboratory.*

analysis /əˈnæləsɪs/ **noun** [C, U] (plural **analyses** /əˈnæləsiːz/) 🔵 the process of analysing something: *a detailed analysis* ○ *A sample of soil was sent for analysis.*

> **🖉 Word partners for analysis**
>
> do an analysis • a **detailed** analysis • an analysis of sth • **send** sth **for** analysis

analyst /ˈænəlɪst/ **noun** [C] 🔵 someone whose job is to examine the details of a situation carefully, and give their opinion about it: *a financial/political analyst*

analytical /ˌænəˈlɪtɪkəl/ **adj** (also **analytic**) examining the details of something carefully, in order to understand or explain it: *analytical skills* ○ *an analytical mind*

analyze /ˈænəlaɪz/ **verb** [T] US spelling of analyse

anarchist /ˈænəkɪst/ **noun** [C] someone who thinks that society should not be controlled by a government and laws

anarchy /ˈænəki/ **noun** [U] a situation in which

there is no law or government, or when people ignore them • **anarchic** /ænˈɑːkɪk/ **adj**

anatomy /əˈnætəmi/ **noun 1** [U] the scientific study of the body and how its parts are arranged **2** [C] the body of a person or living thing: [usually singular] *the female anatomy* • **anatomical** /ˌænəˈtɒmɪkəl/ **adj**

ancestor /ˈænsestər/ **noun** [C] 🔵 a relative who lived a long time ago: *My ancestors came from Ireland.* • **ancestral** /ænˈsestrəl/ **adj**

ancestry /ˈænsestri/ **noun** [C, U] your relatives who lived a long time ago, or the origin of your family: *Americans of Japanese ancestry*

anchor¹ /ˈæŋkər/ **noun** [C] **1** a heavy, metal object that is dropped into water to stop a boat from moving **2** US someone who reads the news and announcements on a television or radio programme

anchor

anchor² /ˈæŋkər/ **verb** **1** **BOAT** ▷ [I, T] to stop a boat from moving by dropping a heavy metal object into the water **2** **FASTEN** ▷ [T] to make something or someone stay in one position by fastening them firmly: *We anchored ourselves to the rocks with a rope.* **3** **PROGRAMME** ▷ [T] US to read the news or announcements on television or radio as your job

ancient /ˈeɪnʃənt/ **adj 1** [always before noun] 🔵 from a long time ago: *ancient Greece/Rome* ○ *an ancient building* **2** humorous very old: *This computer is ancient.*

and strong /ænd/ weak /ənd, ən/ **conjunction 1** **JOIN** ▷ 🔵 used to join two words or two parts of a sentence: *tea and coffee* ○ *We were tired and hungry.* **2** **AFTER** ▷ 🔵 used to say that one thing happens after another thing: *I got dressed and had my breakfast.* **3** **SO** ▷ so: *The car wouldn't start and I had to get a taxi.* **4** **AFTER VERB** ▷ mainly UK 🔵 used instead of 'to' after some verbs, such as 'try' and 'go': *Try and eat something.* **5** **NUMBERS** ▷ 🔵 used when saying or adding numbers: *It cost a hundred and twenty pounds.* ○ *Two and three equals five.* **6** **EMPHASIZE** ▷ 🔵 used between two words that are the same to make their meaning stronger: *The sound grew louder and louder.*

anecdote /ˈænɪkdəʊt/ **noun** [C] a short story that you tell someone about something that happened to you or someone else: *a speech full of anecdotes* • **anecdotal** /ˌænɪkˈdəʊtəl/ **adj** consisting of things that people have said, and not facts: *anecdotal evidence*

anemia /əˈniːmiə/ **noun** [U] US spelling of anaemia (= a medical condition in which your blood does not contain enough red cells)

anemic /əˈniːmɪk/ **adj** US spelling of anaemic (= having anemia)

anesthetic /ˌænəsˈθetɪk/ **noun** [C, U] US spelling

of anaesthetic (= a drug that makes you unable to feel pain during an operation)

anesthetist /əˈnesθətɪst/ **noun** [C] US spelling of anaesthetist (= a doctor who gives anaesthetics to people)

anew /əˈnjuː/ **adv** literary If you do something anew, you do it again in a different way: *Moving to another city gave me the chance to start anew.*

angel /ˈeɪndʒəl/ **noun**
[C] **1** 🔵 a spiritual creature like a human with wings, who some people believe lives with God in heaven
2 a very good, kind person: *Be an angel and get me a drink.*
• **angelic** /ænˈdʒelɪk/
adj very beautiful or good: *an angelic child*

angel

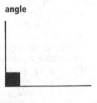

anger¹ /ˈæŋɡəʳ/ **noun** [U] 🔵 a strong feeling against someone who has behaved badly, making you want to shout at them or hurt them: *public anger at the terrorist killings* ∘ **anger at/over** sth ∘ *He never once raised his voice in anger.*

Word partners for **anger**
express/show anger • be trembling with anger • in anger • public anger • mounting/growing anger • anger at/over sth

anger² /ˈæŋɡəʳ/ **verb** [T] to make someone angry: [often passive] *Students were angered by the college's decision.*

angle¹ /ˈæŋɡl/ **noun** [C]
1 SPACE ▷ a space
between two lines or
surfaces that meet at
one point, which you
measure in degrees: *an
angle of 90 degrees* **2 at
an angle** not horizontal or vertical, but
sloping: *He wore his hat
at an angle.* **3** WAY OF
THINKING ▷ the way
you think about a
situation: *Try looking at
the problem from my
angle.* **4** DIRECTION ▷
the direction from which you look at something:
*This is the same building photographed from
different angles.* → See also **right angle**

angle

angle² /ˈæŋɡl/ **verb** [T] to aim or turn something in a direction that is not horizontal or vertical: *She angled a shot into the corner of the court.*

PHRASAL VERB **be angling for sth** to try to get something without asking for it in a direct way: *Is he angling for an invitation?*

angler /ˈæŋɡləʳ/ **noun** [C] someone who catches fish as a hobby or sport

Anglican /ˈæŋɡlɪkən/ **adj** belonging or relating to the Church of England (= the official church in England) • **Anglican noun** [C]

angling /ˈæŋɡlɪŋ/ **noun** [U] the sport or hobby of catching fish

Anglo- /ˈæŋɡləʊ-/ **prefix** of or connected with Britain or England: *Anglo-Indian, Anglo-Saxon*

angry /ˈæŋɡri/ **adj** 🔵 having a strong feeling against someone who has behaved badly, making you want to shout at them or hurt them: *He's really angry at/with me for upsetting Sophie.* ∘ *I don't understand what he's angry about.* • **angrily adv**

➕ Other ways of saying **angry**
If someone is angry about something that has happened, you can say that they are **annoyed** or **irritated**:
He was a bit annoyed with her for being late.
I was irritated that he didn't thank me.
If someone is extremely angry, you can use adjectives such as **furious**, **irate**, or **livid**:
My boss was furious with me.
Hundreds of irate passengers have complained to the airline.
If you are angry with a child, you might describe yourself as **cross**:
I'm cross with you for not telling me where you were going.
The expression **up in arms** is sometimes used when people are angry about something they think is unfair:
Local people are up in arms over plans to close the local swimming pool.
If someone suddenly becomes very angry, you can use the informal expressions **go crazy/mad**:
Dad went crazy/mad when he found out we'd broken the window.

angst /æŋst/ **noun** [U] a strong feeling of worry and unhappiness: *teenage angst*

anguish /ˈæŋɡwɪʃ/ **noun** [U] extreme suffering, especially mental suffering: *It's the anguish of knowing that I can do nothing to help.* • **anguished adj** [always before noun] *anguished parents*

angular /ˈæŋɡjʊləʳ/ **adj** An angular shape or object has a lot of straight lines and sharp points: *an angular face*

animal¹ /ˈænɪməl/ **noun** [C] **1** NOT A HUMAN ▷ 🔵 something that lives and moves but is not a person, bird, fish, or insect: *a wild animal* ∘ *She's a real animal lover.* **2** NOT A PLANT ▷ 🔵 anything that lives and moves, including people, birds, etc: *Are humans the only animals to use language?* **3** CRUEL PERSON ▷ informal a very cruel and violent person

animal² /ˈænɪməl/ **adj** [always before noun] Animal qualities and feelings relate to your basic physical needs: *animal passion*

animate /ˈænɪmət/ **adj** formal alive → Opposite **inanimate**

animated /ˈænɪmeɪtɪd/ **adj 1** showing a lot of interest and excitement: *an animated conversation* **2** An animated film is one in which drawings and models seem to move.

animation /ˌænɪˈmeɪʃᵊn/ **noun 1** [U] interest and excitement: *She spoke with great animation.*

A

2 [C, U] an animated film, or the process of making animated films: *computer animation*

animosity /ˌænɪˈmɒsəti/ **noun** [C, U] a feeling of hatred or anger towards someone: *There is no animosity between the two teams.*

ankle /ˈæŋkl/ **noun** [C] ⑤ the part of your leg that is just above your foot → See colour picture **The Body** on page Centre 13

annex¹ /æˈneks/ **verb** [T] to start to rule or control an area or country next to your own • **annexation** /ˌænekˈseɪʃᵊn/ **noun** [C, U]

annex² (also UK **annexe**) /ˈænɪks/ **noun** [C] a building that is joined to a larger one

annihilate /əˈnaɪleɪt/ **verb** [T] **1** to destroy something completely: *a city annihilated by an atomic bomb* **2** informal to defeat someone very easily • **annihilation** /əˌnaɪˈleɪʃᵊn/ **noun** [U]

anniversary /ˌænɪˈvɜːsᵊri/ **noun** [C] ⑤ a date on which you remember or celebrate something that happened on that date one or more years ago: *a wedding anniversary* ∘ *the 50th anniversary of Kennedy's death* → See also **silver wedding anniversary**

☑ Word partners for **anniversary**

the [10th/50th/500th, etc] anniversary of sth • **commemorate/mark** an anniversary • sb's **wedding** anniversary • anniversary **celebrations**

announce /əˈnaʊns/ **verb** [T] ⑤ to tell people about something officially or with force or confidence: *The company has announced plans to open six new stores.* ∘ [+ (that)] *Halfway through dinner, he announced that he was going out.*

❗ Common learner error: **announce** or **advertise**?

Announce means to tell people about something. If you want to talk about telling people about a product or service so that they will buy it, for example in newspapers or on the television, you should use **advertise**.

announcement /əˈnaʊnsmənt/ **noun 1** [C] ⑤ something that someone says officially, giving information about something: *The Prime Minister made an unexpected announcement this morning.* **2** [no plural] the act of announcing something

☑ Word partners for **announcement**

make an announcement • a **formal/official/public** announcement • an announcement **about/on** sth • an announcement **by/from** sb

announcer /əˈnaʊnsər/ **noun** [C] someone who introduces programmes on the radio or television

annoy /əˈnɔɪ/ **verb** [T] ⑤ to make someone slightly angry: *He's always late and it's starting to annoy me.*

annoyance /əˈnɔɪəns/ **noun** [U] the feeling of being annoyed: *He kept losing his keys, much to the annoyance of* (= which annoyed) *his wife.*

annoyed /əˈnɔɪd/ **adj** ⑤ slightly angry: *I was a bit annoyed with/at Kathy for not coming.*

annoying /əˈnɔɪɪŋ/ **adj** ⑤ making you feel annoyed: *an annoying habit/cough*

annual¹ /ˈænjuəl/ **adj 1** ⑤ happening or produced once a year: *an annual meeting/report* **2** measured over a period of one year: *annual rainfall* • **annually adv**

annual² /ˈænjuəl/ **noun** [C] **1** a plant that grows, produces seed, and dies within one year **2** a book produced every year containing new information about the same subject

annulment /əˈnʌlmənt/ **noun** [C, U] formal a decision by a court that a marriage or agreement does not now exist because it was never legal

anomaly /əˈnɒməli/ **noun** [C] formal something that is unusual or that does not seem right: *There are some anomalies in the data.*

anonymity /ˌænəˈnɪməti/ **noun** [U] a situation in which someone's name is not given or known: *She agreed to speak to a journalist but requested anonymity.*

anonymous /əˈnɒnɪməs/ **adj** not giving a name: *an anonymous phone call* ∘ *The winner has asked to remain anonymous.* • **anonymously adv**

anorak /ˈænəræk/ **noun** [C] UK **1** a jacket with a hood (= part that covers your head) that protects you from rain and cold **2** humorous a boring person who is too interested in the details of a hobby and who is not good in social situations

anorexia /ˌænəˈreksiə/ **noun** [U] (also **anorexia nervosa** /ænərˌeksiənsːˈvəʊsə/) a mental illness in which someone refuses to eat and becomes very thin

anorexic /ˌænəˈreksɪk/ **adj** having the illness anorexia • **anorexic noun** [C]

another /əˈnʌðər/ **pronoun, determiner 1** ⑤ one more person or thing, or an additional amount: *Would you like another piece of cake.* ∘ *We can fit another person in my car.* **2** ⑤ different person or thing: *I'm going to look for another job.* ∘ *This one's slightly damaged – I'll get you another.*

❗ Common learner error: **another** or **other**?

Another means 'one other' and is used with a singular noun. It is written as one word.

Would you like another cup of coffee?

~~Would you like other cup of coffee?~~

Other is used with a plural noun and means different things or people than the ones you are talking about.

She had other ambitions.

~~She had another ambitions.~~

answer¹ /ˈɑːnsər/ **verb 1** WORDS ▷ [I, T] ⑤ to speak or write back to someone who has asked you a question or spoken to you: *I asked where she was leaving but she didn't answer.* ∘ *I must answer his letter.* **2** DOOR ▷ [I, T] to open the door when someone has knocked on it or rung a bell: *I knocked several times but no one answered.* **3** TELEPHONE ▷ [I, T] ⑤ to pick up the telephone receiver (= part that you hold to your ear) when it rings: *Could someone **answer the phone**?* **4 TEST** ▷ [T] 🔵 to write or say something as a reply to a question in a test or competition

PHRASAL VERBS **answer (sb) back** If a child answers back, they reply rudely to an adult. • **answer for sth 1** to be responsible for something, or punished for something: *Do you think parents should have to answer for their children's behaviour?* **2 have a lot to answer for** to be the main cause of something bad that has happened: *"Why is violent crime on the increase?" "Well, I think television has a lot to answer for."*

answer² /ˈɑːnsəʳ/ **noun** [C] **1 WORDS** ▷ 🔵 what you say or write back to someone who has asked you a question or spoken to you: *I asked him if he was going but I didn't hear his answer.* ∘ *Please **give** me your **answer** by next week.* **2 DOOR/ TELEPHONE** ▷ 🔵 the act of answering the telephone or the door: [usually singular] *I rang the bell but there was no answer.* **3 SOLUTION** ▷ 🔵 a way of solving a problem: *It's a difficult situation and I don't know what the answer is.* **4 TEST** ▷ 🔵 the correct number or information given as a reply to a question in a test or competition: *Did you get the **answer to** Question 6?*

🔲 Word partners for **answer**
get/give/know/provide an answer • a correct/simple/wrong answer • the answer to sth

answerphone /ˈɑːnsəfəʊn/ **noun** [C] UK (UK/US **answering machine**) a machine that records your message if you telephone someone and they do not answer: *I left a message on her answerphone.*

ant /ænt/ **noun** [C] 🔵 a small, black or red insect that lives in groups on the ground → See picture at **insect**

antagonism /ænˈtæɡ³nɪz³m/ **noun** [U] feelings of strong disagreement or hate: *There's a history of **antagonism between** the two teams.*

antagonistic /ænˌtæɡ³nˈɪstɪk/ **adj** strongly disagreeing with someone or something: *He's **antagonistic towards** critics.*

antagonize (also UK **-ise**) /ænˈtæɡ³naɪz/ **verb** [T] to make someone angry or unfriendly towards you: *He's antagonized colleagues by making changes without discussing them.*

the Antarctic /ænˈtɑːktɪk/ **noun** the very cold area around the South Pole • **Antarctic adj** [always before noun] *Antarctic wildlife*

antelope /ˈæntɪləʊp/ **noun** [C] an animal like a large deer with long horns

antenatal /ˌæntiˈneɪt³l/ **adj** [always before noun] UK (US **prenatal**) relating to pregnant women before their babies are born: *an antenatal class*

antenna /ænˈtenə/ **noun** [C] **1** (plural **antennae**) one of two long, thin parts on the head of an insect or sea creature, used for feeling things **2** (plural **antennae, antennas**) US (UK **aerial**) a piece of metal that is used for receiving television or radio signals → See colour picture **Car** on page Centre 7

anthem /ˈænθəm/ **noun** [C] a song chosen by a country or organization to be sung on special occasions → See also **national anthem**

anthology /ænˈθɒlədʒi/ **noun** [C] a book that includes stories or poems written by different people

anthropology /ˌænθrəˈpɒlədʒi/ **noun** [U] the scientific study of human development and society or different societies • **anthropologist** /ˌænθrəˈpɒlədʒɪst/ **noun** [C] • **anthropological** /ˌænθrəpəˈlɒdʒɪk³l/ **adj**

anti- /ˈænti-/ 🔵 /ˈæntaɪ/ **prefix 1** opposed to or against: *anti-terrorist laws, anti-American protesters* **2** opposite of or preventing: *anti-clockwise movement, anti-lock brakes, anti-depressant drugs* → Compare **pro-**

antibiotic /ˌæntibaɪˈɒtɪk/ 🔵 /ˌæntaɪ-/ **noun** [C] a medicine that cures infections by destroying harmful bacteria: [usually plural] *He is **on antibiotics** for an ear infection.*

antibody /ˈæntiˌbɒdi/ **noun** [C] a substance produced in your blood to fight disease

anticipate /ænˈtɪsɪpeɪt/ **verb** [T] to expect something, or to prepare for something before it happens: *to **anticipate a problem*** ∘ [+ that] *We anticipate that prices will fall next year.*

anticipation /ænˌtɪsɪˈpeɪʃ³n/ **noun** [U] **1** the excited feeling of waiting for something to happen: *The children were breathless **with anticipation**.* **2 in anticipation (of)** in preparation for something happening: *She's even decorated the spare room in anticipation of your visit.*

anticlimax /ˌæntiˈklaɪmæks/ 🔵 /ˌæntaɪ-/ **noun** [C, U] a disappointing experience, often one that you thought would be exciting before it happened or one that comes after a more exciting experience: *After so much preparation, the party was a bit of an anticlimax.*

anti-clockwise /ˌæntiˈklɒkwaɪz/ **adj, adv** UK (US **counterclockwise**) in the opposite direction to the way the hands (= parts that point to the numbers) of a clock move: *Turn the knob anti-clockwise.* → See picture at **clockwise**

antics /ˈæntɪks/ **noun** [plural] unusual or bad behaviour that entertains or annoys people: *He's well known for his antics on and off the tennis court.*

anti-depressant /ˌæntidɪˈpres³nt/ 🔵 /ˌæntaɪ-/ **noun** [C] a medicine for people who are depressed (= severely unhappy)

antidote /ˈæntidəʊt/ **noun** [C] **1 antidote to sth** an activity that stops something bad from harming you: *Exercise is the **best antidote** to stress.* **2** a substance that stops another substance from damaging your body: *a deadly poison with no antidote*

anti-oxidant /ˌæntiˈɒksɪdənt/ 🔵 /ˌæntaɪ-/ **noun** [C] **1** a substance that slows down the rate at which something decays because of oxidization (= combining with oxygen) **2** a substance, for example a vitamin in food, that protects your body from damage

antipathy /ænˈtɪpəθi/ **noun** [U] formal a strong

A

feeling of dislike for someone: *He is a private man with a deep **antipathy to/towards** the press.*

antiperspirant /ˌænti'pɜːspºrənt/ ⓤⓢ /ˌæntaɪ-/ **noun** [C, U] a substance that prevents you from becoming wet under your arms when you are hot

antiquated /'æntɪkweɪtɪd/ **adj** very old and not modern enough: *an antiquated system*

antique /æn'tiːk/ **noun** [C] 🅱1 an object that is old, and often rare or beautiful: *His home is full of **valuable antiques**. ◦ an **antique shop*** • **antique adj** 🅱1 *antique furniture/china*

antiquity /æn'tɪkwəti/ **noun 1** [U] formal the ancient past: *the writers of antiquity* **2** [C] an ancient object: [usually plural] *priceless Egyptian antiquities*

anti-Semitism /ˌænti'semɪtɪzºm/ ⓤⓢ /ˌæntaɪ-/ **noun** [U] a feeling of hatred towards Jewish people, or cruel or unfair treatment of them • **anti-Semitic** /ˌæntɪsɪ'mɪtɪk/ **adj**

antiseptic /ˌænti'septɪk/ **noun** [C, U] a substance that you put on an injury to prevent infection • **antiseptic adj** *antiseptic cream*

anti-social /ˌænti'səʊ[ºl/ ⓤⓢ /ˌæntaɪ-/ **adj 1** Anti-social behaviour harms or upsets the people around you: *Increasingly, smoking is regarded as an anti-social habit.* **2** An anti-social person does not like being with other people.

anti-spam /ˌænti'spæm/ ⓤⓢ /ˌæntaɪ-/ **adj** [always before noun] used to stop people sending or receiving emails that are not wanted, especially advertisements: *anti-spam legislation*

anti-terrorist /ˌænti'terºrɪst/ ⓤⓢ /ˌæntaɪ-/ **adj** intended to prevent or reduce terrorism (= the use of violence for political purposes): *anti-terrorist laws/legislation*

antithesis /æn'tɪθəsɪs/ **noun** [C] (plural **antitheses** /æn'tɪθəsiːz/) formal the exact opposite: [usually singular] *She is slim and shy – the **antithesis of** her sister.*

anti-virus /ˌænti'vaɪªrəs/ ⓤⓢ /ˌæntaɪ-/ **adj** [always before noun] produced and used to protect the main memory of a computer against infection by a virus: *anti-virus software/programs*

antler /'æntlªr/ **noun** [C] a horn that looks like branches on the head of a male deer

anus /'eɪnəs/ **noun** [C] a hole where solid waste comes out of the body

anxiety /æŋ'zaɪəti/ **noun** [C, U] 🅱2 the feeling of being very worried: *That explains his **anxiety about** her health.*

🗒 **Word partners for anxiety**

a **cause/source** of anxiety • **feelings/levels** of anxiety • anxiety **about/over** sth

---

anxious /'æŋk[əs/ **adj 1** 🅱1 worried and nervous: *She's very **anxious about** her exams.* **2** 🅱2 wanting to do something or wanting something to happen: [+ to do sth] *He's anxious to get home.* ◦ [+ that] *I was anxious that no one else should know.* • **anxiously adv** 🅱2 *We **waited anxiously** by the phone.*

any¹ strong /'eni/ weak /ºni/ **pronoun, determiner 1** 🅰1 used in questions and negatives to mean 'some': *Is there any of that lemon cake left?*

◦ *I haven't seen any of his films.* ◦ *I aske Andrew for some change but he hasn't got any* → See Note at **some¹ 2** 🅰1 one of or each of particular kind of person or thing when it is no important which: *Any advice that you can giv me would be greatly appreciated.* ◦ *Any of thos shirts would be fine.*

any² strong /'eni/ weak /ºni/ **adv** 🅱1 used i questions and negatives to emphasize a com parative adjective or adverb: *Do you feel an better?* ◦ *I can't walk any faster.* ◦ *She couldn wait **any longer**.*

anybody /'eni.bɒdi/ **pronoun** another word fc anyone

anyhow /'enihaʊ/ **adv** (also **anyway**) **1** MOR IMPORTANTLY ▷ 🅱2 used to give a mor important reason for something that you ar saying: *I don't need a car and I can't afford on anyhow.* **2** DESPITE ▷ 🅱2 despite that: *He hate carrots but he ate them anyhow.* **3** I CONVERSATION ▷ 🅱2 used when you ar returning to an earlier subject: *Anyhow, as said, I'll be away next week.* **4** CHANGIN STATEMENT ▷ used when you want to slightl change something that you have just said: *Boy aren't horrible – not all of them anyhow!*

any 'more (also **anymore**) **adv** 🅰2 If you do no do something or something does not happe any more, you have stopped doing it or it doe not now happen: *This coat doesn't fit me an more.*

anyone /'eniwʌn/ **pronoun** (also **anybody**) **1** 🅰 used in questions and negatives to mean ' person or people': *I didn't know anyone at th party.* ◦ *Does **anyone else** (= another person/othe people) want to come?* **2** 🅱1 any person or an people: *Anyone can go – you don't have to b invited.*

anyplace /'enipleɪs/ **adv** US anywhere

anything /'eniθɪŋ/ **pronoun 1** 🅰1 used i questions and negatives to mean 'something' *I don't have anything to wear.* ◦ *Was ther **anything else** (= another thing) you wanted t say?* **2** 🅰1 any object, event, or situation: *We ca do anything you like.* ◦ *Tom will eat anything* **3 anything like** 🅱2 used in questions an negatives to mean 'at all similar to': *Does h look anything like his brother?*

anytime /'enitaɪm/ **adv** (also UK **any time**) at time that is not decided or agreed: *Come to m house anytime tomorrow.*

anyway /'eniweɪ/ **adv** (also **anyhow**, also U spoken **anyways**) **1** MORE IMPORTANTLY ▷ 🅱 used to give a more important reason for something that you are saying: *We can driv you to the station – we go that way anyway* **2** DESPITE ▷ 🅰2 despite that: *He hates carrots bu he ate them anyway.* **3** IN CONVERSATION ▷ 🅰 used when you are returning to an earlie subject: *Anyway, as I said, I'll be away nex week.* **4** CHANGING STATEMENT ▷ used whe you want to slightly change something that yo have just said: *Boys aren't horrible – not all yo them anyway!*

anywhere /'eniweəʳ/ **adv** (also US **anyplace** **1** 🅰2 in or to any place: *Just sit anywhere.*

---

couldn't find a post office anywhere. **2** Ⓐ used in questions and negatives to mean 'a place': *He doesn't have anywhere to stay.* ∘ *Is there **anywhere else** you'd like to visit while you're here?* **3 anywhere near sth** used in questions and negatives to mean 'close to being or doing something': *The house isn't anywhere near ready.*

IDIOM **not get anywhere** informal Ⓑ to not make any progress: *I tried discussing the problem with her but I didn't get anywhere.*

part /əˈpɑːt/ **adv 1** Ⓑ separated by a space or period of time: *Stand with your feet wide apart.* ∘ *Our kids were born just eighteen months apart.* **2** Ⓑ into separate, smaller pieces: *My jacket is coming/falling apart.* **3 apart from a** Ⓑ except for: *Apart from Jodie, who hurt her leg, all the children were fine.* **b** Ⓑ in addition to: *He works a ten-hour day and that's apart from the work he does* UK *at the weekend/US on the weekend.*

partheid /əˈpɑːtaɪt/ **noun** [U] in the past in South Africa, a political system in which white people had power over black people and made them live separately

partment /əˈpɑːtmənt/ **noun** [C] mainly US (also UK **flat**) Ⓐ a set of rooms for someone to live in on one level of a building or house

partment building noun [C] US a building that is divided into apartments

pathetic /ˌæpəˈθetɪk/ **adj** not interested in anything or willing to change things: *Young people today are so apathetic about politics.*

pathy /ˈæpəθi/ **noun** [U] a situation in which someone has no interest in anything or is not willing to change things

pe /eɪp/ **noun** [C] a hairy animal like a monkey but with no tail and long arms

ape

peritif /əˌperəˈtiːf/ **noun** [C] a small alcoholic drink before a meal

perture /ˈæpətʃər/ **noun** [C] a small hole, especially one that allows light into a camera

pex /ˈeɪpeks/ **noun** [C] the highest part of a shape: *the apex of a pyramid*

piece /əˈpiːs/ **adv** each: *Dolls from this period sell for £300 apiece.*

he apocalypse /əˈpɒkəlɪps/ **noun** in some religions, the final destruction of the world

pocalyptic /əˌpɒkəˈlɪptɪk/ **adj** showing or describing the destruction of the world: *an apocalyptic vision of the future*

pologetic /əˌpɒləˈdʒetɪk/ **adj** showing or saying that you are sorry about something: *an apologetic smile* ∘ *She was very **apologetic about** missing the meeting.*

pologize (also UK **-ise**) /əˈpɒlədʒaɪz/ **verb** [I] Ⓑ to tell someone that you are sorry about something you have done: *The bank **apologized** for the error.* ∘ *The pilot **apologized to** passengers for the delay.*

apology /əˈpɒlədʒi/ **noun** [C, U] Ⓑ something you say or write to say that you are sorry about something you have done: *I have an apology to **make** to you – I opened your letter by mistake.* ∘ *a letter of apology*

> **Ⓩ Word partners for apology**
>
> demand/make/owe sb/receive an apology • accept sb's apology • make no apology for (doing) sth • a formal/full/public apology • an apology for sth • an apology to sb

apostle /əˈpɒsl/ **noun** [C] one of the twelve men chosen by Jesus Christ to teach people about Christianity

apostrophe /əˈpɒstrəfi/ **noun** [C] **1** Ⓑ a mark (') used to show that letters or numbers are absent: *I'm (= I am) hungry.* ∘ *I graduated in '09 (= 2009).* **2** Ⓑ a punctuation mark (') used before the letter 's' to show that something belongs to someone or something: *I drove my brother's car.* → See Study Page **Punctuation** on page Centre 33

app /æp/ **noun** [C] abbreviation for application or application program: a small computer program that you can put onto a mobile phone or other electronic device: *There are apps for everything, from learning French to booking cinema tickets.*

appal (**appalling, appalled**) UK (US **appall**) /əˈpɔːl/ **verb** [T] to make someone extremely shocked or upset: *The amount of violence on television appals me.* ∘ *We were **appalled at/by** her behaviour.* • **appalled adj**

appalling /əˈpɔːlɪŋ/ **adj 1** shocking and very unpleasant: *Many live in appalling conditions.* ∘ *appalling injuries* **2** very bad: *appalling behaviour/weather* • **appallingly adv**

apparatus /ˌæpəˈreɪtəs/ ⓤ /ˌæpəˈrætəs/ **noun** [C, U] (plural **apparatus, apparatuses**) a set of equipment or tools used for a particular purpose: *The diver wore breathing apparatus.*

apparel /əˈpærəl/ **noun** [U] mainly US clothes: *children's/women's apparel*

apparent /əˈpærənt/ **adj 1** Ⓑ obvious or easy to notice: *[+ that] It soon became apparent that she had lost interest in the project.* ∘ *Suddenly, **for no apparent reason** (= without a reason) he started screaming and shouting.* **2** [always before noun] seeming to exist or be true: *I was a little surprised by her apparent lack of interest.*

apparently /əˈpærəntli/ **adv 1** Ⓑ used to say that you have read or been told something although you are not certain it is true: *Apparently it's going to rain today.* **2** Ⓑ used to say that something seems to be true, although it is not certain: *There were two apparently unrelated deaths.*

apparition /ˌæpərˈɪʃən/ **noun** [C] literary a ghost

appeal¹ /əˈpiːl/ **noun 1 REQUEST** ▷ [C] a request to the public for money, information, or help: *The appeal raised over £2 million for AIDS research.* **2 QUALITY** ▷ [U] Ⓑ the quality in someone or something that makes them attractive or enjoyable: *I've never understood the appeal of skiing.* **3 LAW** ▷ [C] a request to a court of law to change a previous legal decision: *He won his **appeal against** his jail sentence.*

A

🗹 Word partners for **appeal**

issue/launch/make an appeal • an appeal for sth

appeal² /əˈpiːl/ **verb** [I] **1 REQUEST** ▷ to strongly request something, often publicly: *The police have **appealed for** more information.* ∘ *They **appealed to** the commission to keep the hospital open.* **2 ATTRACT** ▷ **B2** to attract or interest someone: *Cycling has never **appealed to** me.* **3 FORMALLY ASK** ▷ to formally ask someone to change an official or legal decision: *He is **appealing against** a ten-year prison sentence.*

appealing /əˈpiːlɪŋ/ **adj** attractive or interesting: *The idea of living in Paris is very appealing.* • **appealingly adv**

appear /əˈpɪər/ **verb** [I] **1 SEEM** ▷ **B1** to seem to be a particular thing or have a particular quality: *He appeared calm and relaxed.* ∘ *She **appeared to be** crying.* ∘ [+ (that)] *It **appears** that we were wrong about him.* **2 BE SEEN** ▷ **B1** to start to be seen: *He suddenly **appeared** in the doorway.* ∘ *Then a bright light appeared in the sky.* → Opposite **disappear 3 BECOME AVAILABLE** ▷ **B2** to start to exist or become available: *Laptop computers first appeared in the 1990s.* ∘ *The story appeared in all the major newspapers.* **4 appear in/at/on, etc B1** to perform in a film, play, etc, or be seen in public: *She appears briefly in the new Bond movie.*

appearance /əˈpɪərəns/ **noun 1 IN PUBLIC** ▷ [C] **B2** an occasion when someone appears in public: *a television/**public appearance*** ∘ *He **made** two **appearances** during his brief visit.* **2 WAY YOU LOOK** ▷ [no plural] **B1** the way a person or thing looks: *She's very concerned with her appearance.* **3 ARRIVAL** ▷ [no plural] an occasion when you arrive somewhere or can be seen somewhere: *Her appearance at the party was a surprise.* → Opposite **disappearance 4 BECOMING AVAILABLE** ▷ [no plural] **B2** the time when something starts to exist or becomes available: *The appearance of new products on the market has increased competition.*

appease /əˈpiːz/ **verb** [T] to avoid more arguments by doing what someone wants • **appeasement noun** [U]

appendicitis /əˌpendɪˈsaɪtɪs/ **noun** [U] an illness in which your appendix becomes larger than usual and painful

appendix /əˈpendɪks/ **noun** [C] **1** (plural **appendixes**) a small tube-shaped part inside the body below the stomach, attached to the large intestine **2** (plural **appendices**) a separate part at the end of a book, article, etc that contains extra information

🗹 Word partners for **appetite**

give sb/have an appetite • lose your appetite • a good/healthy/huge appetite • loss of appetite

appetite /ˈæpɪtaɪt/ **noun** [C, U] **1** the feeling that makes you want to eat: *All that walking has **given** me an **appetite**.* **2 an appetite for sth** the feeling of wanting something very much: *his*

appetite for adventure **3 whet sb's appetite** t⟨ make someone want more of something

appetizer /ˈæpɪtaɪzər/ **noun** [C] US (mainly U⟨ **starter**) something that you eat as the first par of a meal

appetizing (also UK **-ising**) /ˈæpɪtaɪzɪŋ/ **adj** ⟨ food is appetizing, it looks or smells as if it wi⟨ taste good.

applaud /əˈplɔːd/ **verb 1** [I, T] to clap your hand to show that you have enjoyed a performance talk, etc: *The audience applauded loudly.* **2** [⟨ formal to approve of or admire something: *Mos⟨ people will surely applaud the decision.*

applause /əˈplɔːz/ **noun** [U] the sound of peopl⟨ clapping their hands to show they have enjoye⟨ or approve of something: *There was lou⟨ applause at the end of her speech.*

apple /ˈæpl/ **noun** [C] **A1** a hard, round fruit with a green or red skin → See colour picture **Fruits and Vegetables** on page Centre 10 → See also **Adam's apple**

apple

applet /ˈæplət/ **noun** [C] a small compute⟨ program that is automatically copied on to ⟨ computer when you look at a document tha⟨ needs this program to make it work

appliance /əˈplaɪəns/ **noun** [C] a piece c⟨ electrical equipment with a particular purpos⟨ in the home: *fridges, radios, and other electrica⟨ appliances*

applicable /əˈplɪkəbl/ **adj** affecting or relatin⟨ to a person or situation: *This law is onl⟨ **applicable to** people living in Europe.*

applicant /ˈæplɪkənt/ **noun** [C] someone wh⟨ asks for something officially, often by writin⟨ *There were over fifty **applicants for** the job.*

application /ˌæplɪˈkeɪʃən/ **noun 1 REQUEST** [[C] **B1** an official request for something, usuall⟨ in writing: *an **application for** a bank loa⟨* **2 USE** ▷ [C, U] a way in which something ca⟨ be used for a particular purpose: *This technolog⟨ has many practical applications.* **3 COMPUTE⟨ PROGRAM** ▷ [C] **B2** a computer progra⟨ designed for a particular purpose: *interne⟨ web/Windows™ application*

application form noun [C] a form that yo⟨ use to officially ask for something, for exampl⟨ job

applied /əˈplaɪd/ **adj applied mathematic⟨ science, etc** mathematics, science, or anothe⟨ subject that is studied for a practical use

apply /əˈplaɪ/ **verb 1 ASK** ▷ [I] **B1** to ask official⟨ for something, often by writing: *I've **applied fc⟨** a job.* ∘ *He has **applied to** several companie⟨* **2 AFFECT** ▷ [I] **B2** to affect or relate to ⟨ particular person or situation: *This law onl⟨ **applies to** married people.* **3 USE** ▷ [T] to us⟨ something in a particular situation: *The sam⟨ method can be **applied to** other situations.* **4 O⟨ SURFACE** ▷ [T] to spread a substance on ⟨ surface: *Apply the cream daily until the symptom⟨*

---

disappear. **5 apply yourself** to work hard: _If he doesn't apply himself, he'll never pass his exams._

appoint /əˈpɔɪnt/ **verb** [T] to officially choose someone for a job: _He was **appointed** as company director last year._

appointed /əˈpɔɪntɪd/ **adj appointed date/ time/place, etc** the date, time, place, etc that has been chosen for something to happen

appointment /əˈpɔɪntmənt/ **noun 1** [C] ⓐ a time you have arranged to meet someone or go somewhere: _a doctor's/dental appointment_ ∘ _I made an appointment with my hairdresser for next Monday._ **2** [C, U] an occasion when you officially choose someone for an important job, or the job itself: _the appointment of three new teachers_

> ☑ Word partners for **appointment**
>
> **have/make** an appointment • **cancel/keep/ miss** an appointment • an appointment **with sb**

apportion /əˈpɔːʃən/ **verb** [T] formal **1** to choose how much of something a person or each person should have **2 apportion blame/responsibility** to say who was responsible for something bad that happened

appraisal /əˈpreɪzəl/ **noun** [C, U] **1** an examination of someone or something in order to judge how good or successful they are: _a critical appraisal_ **2** a meeting where the manager of an employee talks to them about the quality of their work: _an appraisal scheme_

appraise /əˈpreɪz/ **verb** [T] to examine something and judge it: _We need to stop and appraise the situation._

appreciable /əˈpriːʃəbl/ **adj** formal large or important enough to be noticed: _There's an **appreciable difference** in temperatures between the two regions._

appreciate /əˈpriːʃieɪt/ **verb 1 VALUE** ▷ [T] ⓑ to understand how good something or someone is and be able to enjoy them: _There's no point buying him expensive wines – he doesn't appreciate them._ **2 GRATEFUL** ▷ [T] ⓑ to feel grateful for something: _I'd really appreciate your help._ **3 UNDERSTAND** ▷ [T] to understand something about a situation, especially that it is complicated or difficult: [+ (that)] _I appreciate that it is a difficult decision for you to make._ **4 INCREASE** ▷ [I] formal to increase in value: _Houses and antiques generally appreciate with time._

appreciation /ə,priːʃiˈeɪʃən/ **noun** [U] **1 VALUE** ▷ ⓑ an understanding of how good something or someone is so that you are able to enjoy them: _His appreciation of art increased as he grew older._ **2 FEEL GRATEFUL** ▷ a feeling of being grateful for something: _To show our appreciation, we've bought you a little gift._ **3 UNDERSTANDING** ▷ an understanding of a situation, especially that it is complicated or difficult: _He has no appreciation of the size of the problem._ **4 INCREASE** ▷ formal an increase in value

appreciative /əˈpriːʃiətɪv/ **adj** showing that you understand how good something is, or are

grateful for something: _an appreciative audience_ • **appreciatively adv**

apprehend /ˌæprɪˈhend/ **verb** [T] formal If the police apprehend someone, they catch them and take them away to ask them about a crime that they might have committed.

apprehension /ˌæprɪˈhenʃən/ **noun** [U] an anxious feeling about something that you are going to do: _It's normal to feel a little apprehension before starting a new job._

apprehensive /ˌæprɪˈhensɪv/ **adj** feeling anxious about something that you are going to do: _He's a bit **apprehensive about** living away from home._

apprentice /əˈprentɪs/ **noun** [C] a person who is learning a job by working for someone who already has skills and experience

apprenticeship /əˈprentɪʃɪp/ **noun** [C, U] a period of time when someone learns the skills needed to do a job by working for someone who already has skills and experience

approach¹ /əˈprəʊtʃ/ **noun 1 METHOD** ▷ [C] ⓑ a way of doing something: _Liam has a different approach to the problem._ ∘ _We've decided to adopt/take a new approach._ **2 ASKING** ▷ [C] an occasion when you speak or write to someone, often asking to buy something or offering them work **3 COMING CLOSER** ▷ [U] ⓑ a movement towards something, in distance or time: _the approach of winter_ **4 PATH** ▷ [C] a path or route that leads to a place

approach² /əˈprəʊtʃ/ **verb 1 COME CLOSE** ▷ [I, T] ⓑ to come close in distance or time: _The train now approaching platform 2 is the 5.35 to London, Kings Cross._ ∘ _Christmas is fast approaching._ **2 DEAL WITH** ▷ [T] ⓑ to deal with something: _I'm not sure how to approach the problem._ **3 SPEAK TO SOMEONE** ▷ [T] to speak or write to someone, often asking to buy something or offering them work: _She's been approached by a modelling agency._

> ❗ Common learner error: **approach**
>
> The verb **approach** is not normally followed by a preposition.
> _He approached the door._
> ~~He approached to the door.~~

approachable /əˈprəʊtʃəbl/ **adj** friendly and easy to talk to

appropriate¹ /əˈprəʊpriət/ **adj** ⓑ suitable or right for a particular situation or person: _Is this film **appropriate for** young children?_ → Opposite **inappropriate** • **appropriately adv** ⓑ _appropriately dressed_

appropriate² /əˈprəʊprieɪt/ **verb** [T] formal to take or steal something • **appropriation** /ə,prəʊpriˈeɪʃən/ **noun** [U]

approval /əˈpruːvəl/ **noun** [U] **1** ⓑ an opinion that something or someone is good or right: _I don't need his approval._ → Opposite **disapproval** **2** ⓑ official permission: _The project has now received approval from the government._

A

■ Word partners for **approval**

gain/get/win/receive/seek approval • **formal/ full** approval • approval **for sth**

approve /əˈpruːv/ verb **1** [T] **B1** to allow or officially agree to something: *The council has* **approved plans** *for a new shopping centre.* **2** [I] **B2** to think that something is good or right: *I don't* **approve of** *smoking.* → Opposite **disapprove**

approving /əˈpruːvɪŋ/ adj showing that you think something is good or right: *an approving smile* → Opposite **disapproving (disapprove)** • **approvingly** adv

approx written abbreviation for approximately

approximate¹ /əˈprɒksɪmət/ adj **B2** not completely accurate but close: *Do you have an approximate idea of when he's arriving?*

approximate² /əˈprɒksɪmeɪt/ verb [T] (also **approximate to**) to be almost the same as something • **approximation** /əˌprɒksɪˈmeɪʃən/ noun [C, U]

approximately /əˈprɒksɪmətli/ adv **B1** close to a particular number or time although not exactly that number or time: *The college has approximately 700 students.*

Apr written abbreviation for April

apricot /ˈeɪprɪkɒt/ noun [C] a small, soft, orange fruit

April /ˈeɪprəl/ noun [C, U] (written abbreviation **Apr**) **A1** the fourth month of the year

April 'Fool's Day noun 1 April, a day when people play tricks on people, then say 'April fool!'

apron /ˈeɪprən/ noun [C] a piece of clothing you wear when cooking to keep your clothes clean

apron

apt /æpt/ adj **1** suitable for a particular situation: *an* **apt description** **2** **be apt to do sth** to often do something: *He's apt to forget his keys.* • **aptly** adv

aptitude /ˈæptɪtjuːd/ noun [C, U] a natural skill or an ability to do something well: *He has an* **aptitude for** *learning languages.* ∘ *an* **aptitude test**

■ Word partners for **aptitude**

have/show an aptitude for (doing) sth • a **natural** aptitude • an aptitude **test**

aquarium /əˈkweəriəm/ noun [C] **1** a building where fish and other water animals are kept for people to visit **2** a glass container filled with water that fish are kept in

Aquarius /əˈkweəriəs/ noun [C, U] the sign of the zodiac that relates to the period of 21 January – 19 February, or a person born during this period → See picture at **the zodiac**

aquatic /əˈkwætɪk/ adj living or growing in water, or related to water: *aquatic animals*

Arab /ˈærəb/ adj relating or belonging to the people of the Middle East or North Africa whose families came from Arabia in the past: *Arab countries* • **Arab noun** [C] an Arab person

Arabic /ˈærəbɪk/ noun [U] the language used by Arab peoples • **Arabic adj**

arable /ˈærəbl/ adj suitable for or used for growing crops: *arable land/farming*

arbiter /ˈɑːbɪtər/ noun [C] **1** someone who judges what is right or helps to solve an argument **2 arbiter of fashion/style/taste, etc** someone who decides what is beautiful or stylish

arbitrary /ˈɑːbɪtrəri/ adj not based on a system or principles and often seeming unfair: *an* **arbitrary decision** • **arbitrarily** /ˌɑːbɪˈtreərəli/ adv

arbitrate /ˈɑːbɪtreɪt/ verb [I, T] to officially help to solve an argument between two people or groups • **arbitrator** noun [C]

arbitration /ˌɑːbɪˈtreɪʃən/ noun [U] the process of solving an argument between people by helping them to agree to an acceptable solution

arc /ɑːk/ noun [C] a curved line that looks like part of a circle

arcade /ɑːˈkeɪd/ noun [C] **1** a place where you can pay to play games on machines: *an amusement arcade* **2** a passage, especially between shops, that is covered by a roof: *a shopping arcade*

arch¹ /ɑːtʃ/ noun [C] **1** a curved structure that usually supports something, for example a bridge or wall **2** the curved, middle part of your foot that does not touch the ground

arch

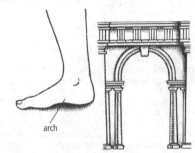

arch

arch² /ɑːtʃ/ verb [I, T] to be a curved shape or make something become a curved shape: *The bridge arched over the river.*

archaeologist (also US **archeologist**) /ˌɑːkiˈɒlədʒɪst/ noun [C] someone who studies archaeology

archaeology (also US **archeology**) /ˌɑːkiˈɒlədʒi/ noun [U] the study of ancient cultures by looking at and examining their buildings, tools, and other objects • **archaeological** (also US **archeological**) /ˌɑːkiəˈlɒdʒɪkəl/ adj

archaic /ɑːˈkeɪɪk/ adj very old and often not suitable for today: *an archaic law*

archbishop /ˌɑːtʃˈbɪʃəp/ noun [C] a priest of the highest rank in some Christian churches, responsible for a very large area: *Archbishop Desmond Tutu*

archeologist /ˌɑːkiˈɒlədʒɪst/ **noun** [C] another US spelling of archaeologist

archeology /ˌɑːkiˈɒlədʒi/ **noun** [U] another US spelling of archaeology

archery /ˈɑːtʃəri/ **noun** [U] a sport in which you shoot arrows

architect /ˈɑːkɪtekt/ **noun** [C] ⬛ someone who designs buildings

architecture /ˈɑːkɪtektʃər/ **noun** [U] **1** ⬛ the design and style of buildings: *modern architecture* **2** ⬛ the skill of designing buildings • **architectural** /ˌɑːkɪˈtektʃərəl/ **adj**

archive¹ /ˈɑːkaɪv/ **noun** [C] **1** a collection of historical documents that provides information about the past, or a place where they are kept: *the national archives* **2** a place on a computer used to store information or documents that you do not need to use often

archive² /ˈɑːkaɪv/ **verb** [T] to store paper or electronic documents in an archive

the Arctic /ˈɑːktɪk/ **noun** the very cold area around the North Pole • **Arctic adj** *Arctic temperatures*

ardent /ˈɑːdənt/ **adj** [always before noun] enthusiastic or showing strong feelings: *an ardent supporter of Real Madrid* • **ardently adv**

☑ Word partners for **ardent**

an ardent **admirer/fan/supporter**

arduous /ˈɑːdjuəs/ **adj** needing a lot of effort to do: *an arduous journey/task*

are strong /ɑːʳ/ weak /əʳ/ present simple you/we/they of be

area /ˈeəriə/ **noun 1 REGION** ▷ [C] ⬛ a region of a country or city: *an industrial area* ∘ *a mountainous area* ∘ *the London area* **2 PART** ▷ [C] ⬛ a part of a building or piece of land used for a particular purpose: *a play/picnic area* **3 SUBJECT** ▷ [C] ⬛ a part of a subject or activity: *Software is not really my area of expertise.* **4 SIZE** ▷ [C, U] the size of a flat surface calculated by multiplying its width by its length → See also **catchment area, no-go area**

area ˌcode noun [C] a set of numbers used at the beginning of all the telephone numbers in a particular area

arena /əˈriːnə/ **noun** [C] **1** a flat area with seats around where you can watch sports and other entertainments: *an Olympic/sports arena* **2 in the political/public, etc arena** involved in politics/the government, etc

aren't /ɑːnt/ **1** short for are not: *We aren't going to the party.* **2 aren't I?** short for am I not?: *I am invited, aren't I?*

arguable /ˈɑːgjuəbl/ **adj 1 It is arguable that** it is possibly true that: *It is arguable that the government has failed in this respect.* **2** If something is arguable, it is not certain if it is true: *It is arguable whether this method would even have succeeded.*

arguably /ˈɑːgjuəbli/ **adv** possibly: *He's arguably the greatest footballer in the world.*

argue /ˈɑːgjuː/ **verb** (**arguing, argued**) **1** [I] ⬛ to speak angrily to someone, telling them that you

disagree with them: *My parents are always **arguing about** money.* ∘ *Kids, will you stop **arguing with** each other?* **2** [I, T] ⬛ to give reasons to support or oppose an idea, action, etc: [+ that] *He argued that cuts in military spending were necessary.* ∘ *She **argued for/against** tax cuts.*

argument /ˈɑːgjəmənt/ **noun** [C] **1** ⬛ an angry discussion with someone in which you both disagree: *They **had** an **argument** about who should do the cleaning.* **2** ⬛ a reason or reasons why you support or oppose an idea, action, etc: *There are many **arguments for/against** nuclear energy.*

☑ Word partners for **argument**

have an argument • an argument **about/over** sth • a **heated/violent** argument

argumentative /ˌɑːgjəˈmentətɪv/ **adj** often arguing or wanting to argue

aria /ˈɑːriə/ **noun** [C] a song that one person sings in an opera

arid /ˈærɪd/ **adj** very dry and without enough rain for plants: *an arid region/climate*

Aries /ˈeəriːz/ **noun** [C, U] the sign of the zodiac that relates to the period of 21 March – 20 April, or a person born during this period → See picture at **the zodiac**

arise /əˈraɪz/ **verb** [I] (**arose, arisen**) **1** If a problem arises, it starts to happen: *The whole problem **arose from** a lack of communication.* **2** literary to get up, usually from a bed

aristocracy /ˌærɪˈstɒkrəsi/ **noun** [group] the highest social class, usually in countries that have or had a royal family

aristocrat /ˈærɪstəkræt/ **noun** [C] a member of the highest social class • **aristocratic** /ˌærɪstəˈkrætɪk/ **adj** *an aristocratic family*

arithmetic /əˈrɪθmətɪk/ **noun** [U] the act of calculating numbers, for example by multiplying or adding

arm¹ /ɑːm/ **noun** [C] **1 BODY PART** ▷ ⬛ the long part at each side of the human body, ending in a hand: *He put his arms around her.* ∘ *She was standing with her arms folded* (= *with one arm crossed over the other*). → See colour picture **The Body** on page Centre 13 **2 arm in arm** with your arm gently supporting or being supported by someone else's arm **3 CLOTHES** ▷ the part of a piece of clothing that you put your arm in **4 CHAIR** ▷ the part of a chair where your arm rests

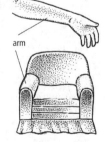
arm

arm

IDIOM **twist sb's arm** informal to persuade someone to do something

→ See also **arms**

arm² /ɑːm/ **verb** [T] to give weapons to someone: *The terrorists had **armed** themselves **with** automatic rifles.* → Opposite **disarm**

armaments /ˈɑːməmənts/ **noun** [plural] military weapons and equipment: *nuclear armaments*

armband /ˈɑːmbænd/ **noun 1** [C] a strip of material worn around your upper arm: *a black/reflective armband* **2 armbands** UK two plastic tubes that you fill with air and wear round the top of your arms when you are learning to swim

armchair /ˈɑːmˌtʃeər/ **noun** [C] 🅐🅐 a comfortable chair with sides that support your arms → See colour picture **The Living Room** on page Centre 4

armed /ɑːmd/ **adj 1** 🅑🅑 carrying or using weapons: ***armed guards/police*** ∘ *an **armed robbery*** (= robbery where guns are used) → Opposite **unarmed 2 armed with sth** carrying or knowing something that will be useful: *I like to go to a meeting armed with the relevant facts.*

the ˌarmed ˈforces noun [plural] (also **the ˌarmed ˈservices**) a country's military forces, for example the army and the navy

armful /ˈɑːmfʊl/ **noun** [C] the amount that you can carry in your arms: *an armful of books*

armistice /ˈɑːmɪstɪs/ **noun** [C] an agreement to stop fighting that is made between two countries

armour UK (US **armor**) /ˈɑːmər/ **noun** [U] metal clothing that soldiers wore in the past to protect them when fighting: *a suit of armour*

armoured UK (US **armored**) /ˈɑːməd/ **adj** covered with a protective layer of metal: *an armoured vehicle*

armpit /ˈɑːmpɪt/ **noun** [C] the part of your body under your arm, where your arm meets your shoulder → See colour picture **The Body** on page Centre 13

arms /ɑːmz/ **noun** [plural] weapons: *the sale of arms*

IDIOM **be up in arms** to be very upset and angry about something: *Local residents are up in arms over plans to close the swimming pool.*

army /ˈɑːmi/ **noun** [C] **1** 🅑🅑 a military force that fights wars on the ground: *the British Army* **2** a group of people that is organized to do the same job: *an army of cleaners/helpers*

> **✐ Word partners for army**
>
> **join** the army • **be in** the army

aroma /əˈrəʊmə/ **noun** [C] a nice smell that usually comes from food or drink: *the aroma of freshly baked bread* •**aromatic** /ˌærəʊˈmætɪk/ **adj** having a nice smell: *aromatic herbs*

aromatherapy /əˌrəʊməˈθerəpi/ **noun** [U] a way of making a person who is sick better by rubbing pleasant-smelling oils into the skin or allowing them to smell the oils

arose /əˈrəʊz/ past tense of arise

around /əˈraʊnd/ **adv, preposition 1 IN A CIRCLE** ▷ (also UK **round**) 🅐🅐 on all sides of something: *They sat around the table.* **2 DIRECTION** ▷ (also UK **round**) 🅑🅑 to the opposite direction: *He turned around and looked at her.* **3 CIRCULAR MOVEMENT** ▷ (also UK **round**)

🅐🅐 in a circular movement: *This lever turns th wheels around.* **4 ALONG OUTSIDE** ▷ (also U **round**) along the outside of something, no through it: *You have to walk around the house t get to the garden.* **5 TO A PLACE** ▷ (also UK **round** 🅐🅐 to or in different parts of a place: *I spent ∙ year travelling around Australia.* **6 SEVERAᴸ PLACES** ▷ (also UK **round**) 🅑🅑 from one plac or person to another: *She passed a plate o sandwiches around.* **7 HERE** ▷ 🅑🅑 here, or nea this place: *Is Roger around?* **8 EXISTING** ▷ present or available: *Mobile phones have bee. around for years now.* **9 APPROXIMATELY** ▷ 🅐 used before a number or amount to mea ʼapproximatelyʼ: *around four oʼclock* ∘ *aroun twenty thousand pounds* → See also **throw you weight around**

arousal /əˈraʊzᵊl/ **noun** [U] the state of bein sexually excited

arouse /əˈraʊz/ **verb** [T] **1** to make someone hav a particular feeling or reaction: *Itʼs a subjec which has **aroused** a lot of **interest**.* **2** to mak someone sexually excited

arrange /əˈreɪndʒ/ **verb** [T] **1** 🅑🅑 to make th necessary plans and preparations for somethin to happen: *to arrange a meeting* ∘ *Iʼll arrang **for** a car to come and pick you up.* ∘ *[+ to do sth We've arranged to visit the house on Saturda afternoon.* **2** 🅑🅑 to put objects in a particula order or position: *The books are arrange alphabetically by author.*

arrangement /əˈreɪndʒmənt/ **noun 1 PLANS** ▷ [C] 🅑🅑 plans for how something will happen [usually plural] *We're meeting tomorrow to discus **arrangements for** the competition.* ∘ *[+ to do sth Iʼve **made arrangements** to go home thi weekend.* **2 AGREEMENT** ▷ [C, U] 🅑🅑 an agree ment between two people or groups: *We have a arrangement whereby we share the childcar* ∘ *Viewing is by prior arrangemen* **3 POSITION** ▷ [C] 🅑🅑 a group of objects in particular order or position: *a flower arrange ment*

> **✐ Word partners for arrangement**
>
> **have/make** an arrangement • arrangements **for sth** • **alternative/necessary** arrangements

array /əˈreɪ/ **noun** [C] a large number of differen things: [usually singular] *There is **a** vast **array o** books on the subject.*

arrears /əˈrɪəz/ **noun** [plural] money that is owe and should have been paid before: *mortgage/ren arrears* ∘ *He **is** already **in arrears** with the rent.*

arrest¹ /əˈrest/ **verb** [T] 🅑🅑 If the police arres someone, they take them away to ask them about a crime that they might have committed: *He was **arrested for** possession of illegal drugs.*

arrest

arrest² /əˈrest/ **noun** [C, U] 🅑🅑 an occasion when the police take someone away to ask them about a crime that they might have committed: *Police* **made 20 arrests** *at yesterday's demonstration.* ∘ *He's* **under arrest** (= *has been arrested*). → See also **house arrest**

> **☑ Word partners for arrest**
>
> **make** an arrest • **resist** arrest • be **under** arrest • the arrest **of** sb • an arrest **for** [murder/drugs offences, etc]

arrival /əˈraɪvəl/ *noun* **1** ARRIVING ▷ [U] 🔵 an occasion when someone or something arrives somewhere: *He first met Panos soon after his arrival in Greece.* ∘ *There was a car waiting for him* **on arrival**. **2** BECOME AVAILABLE ▷ [U] the time when something new is discovered or created or becomes available: *The town grew rapidly with* **the arrival of** *the railway.* **3** NEW PERSON/THING ▷ [C] a new thing or person that has arrived: *Two teachers were there to greet the* **new arrivals**.

arrive /əˈraɪv/ *verb* [I] **1** 🔵 to get to a place: *When he first* **arrived in** *New York, he didn't speak a word of English.* ∘ *We were the last to* **arrive at** *the station.* ∘ *A letter arrived for you this morning.* **2 arrive at an answer/decision/conclusion, etc** to find an answer to a problem or make a decision after a lot of discussion: *We didn't arrive at any firm conclusions.* **3** to happen or start to exist: *Summer had finally arrived.*

> **❗ Common learner error: arrive** somewhere
>
> Be careful to choose the correct preposition after **arrive**. You **arrive at** a place such as a building.
> *We arrived at the hotel just after ten o'clock.*
> You **arrive in** a town, city, or country.
> *They arrived in Tokyo on Wednesday.*
> *When did David arrive in Australia?*
> You **arrive** home, here, or there. You do not use a preposition when **arrive** is used before these words.
> *We arrived home yesterday.*
> *I had a lot of problems when I first arrived here.*

arrogant /ˈærəgənt/ *adj* 🔵 believing that you are better or more important than other people: *I found him arrogant and rude.* • **arrogance** /ˈærəgəns/ *noun* [U] • **arrogantly** *adv*

arrow /ˈærəʊ/ *noun* [C] **1** 🔵 a symbol used on signs to show a direction **2** 🔵 a long, thin stick with a sharp point at one end which is fired from a bow (= curved piece of wood with a tight string fixed at both ends)

arrow key *noun* [C] one of the four keys on a computer keyboard that you can use to

arrow

arrow

move the cursor (= symbol on a computer screen that shows the place where you are working) up, down, left, or right on the screen: *Use the arrow keys to scroll through the page.*

arse /ɑːs/ *noun* [C] UK very informal (US **ass**) a person's bottom

arsenal /ˈɑːsənəl/ *noun* [C] a large collection of weapons

arsenic /ˈɑːsənɪk/ *noun* [U] a chemical element that is a very strong poison

arson /ˈɑːsən/ *noun* [U] the crime of intentionally burning something, such as a building • **arsonist** *noun* [C] someone who commits arson

art /ɑːt/ *noun* **1** [U] 🔵 the making or study of paintings, drawings, etc or the objects created: *fine/modern art* ∘ *an* **art exhibition/gallery** **2** [C, U] a skill in a particular activity: *the art of conversation* → See also **martial art**, **work of art**

artefact mainly UK (US **artifact**) /ˈɑːtɪfækt/ *noun* [C] an object, especially something very old of historical interest

artery /ˈɑːtəri/ *noun* [C] **1** one of the tubes in your body that carries blood from your heart **2** an important route for traffic

artful /ˈɑːtfəl/ *adj* [always before noun] showing skill: *an artful use of colour* • **artfully** *adv*

arthritis /ɑːˈθraɪtɪs/ *noun* [U] an illness that causes the parts of the body where bones meet to become painful and often big • **arthritic** /ɑːˈθrɪtɪk/ *adj* *an arthritic hip/knee*

artichoke /ˈɑːtɪtʃəʊk/ *noun* [C, U] a round, green vegetable with thick, pointed leaves covering the outside

article /ˈɑːtɪkl/ *noun* [C] **1** WRITING ▷ 🔵 a piece of writing in a magazine, newspaper, etc **2** OBJECT ▷ an object, especially one of many: *an* **article of** *clothing/furniture* **3** GRAMMAR ▷ 🔵 in grammar, used to mean the words 'the', 'a', or 'an' → See also **definite article**, **indefinite article**

articulate¹ /ɑːˈtɪkjələt/ *adj* able to express ideas and feelings clearly in words: *She's an intelligent and highly articulate young woman.* → Opposite **inarticulate**

articulate² /ɑːˈtɪkjəleɪt/ *verb* [T] formal to express ideas or feelings in words: *He articulates the views and concerns of the local community.* • **articulation** /ɑːˌtɪkjəˈleɪʃən/ *noun* [U]

articulated /ɑːˈtɪkjəleɪtɪd/ *adj* [always before noun] mainly UK An articulated vehicle is long and has two parts that are joined together to help it turn corners: *an* **articulated lorry**

artifact /ˈɑːtɪfækt/ *noun* [C] US spelling of artefact

artificial /ˌɑːtɪˈfɪʃəl/ *adj* **1** 🔵 not natural, but made by people: *an artificial flower/lake* ∘ *an artificial heart* **2** not sincere • **artificially** *adv*

artificial inˈtelligence UK (US **artiˌficial inˈtelligence**) *noun* [U] the study and development of computer systems that do jobs that previously needed human intelligence

artillery /ɑːˈtɪləri/ *noun* [U] large guns, especially those fixed on wheels used by an army

artisan /ˌɑːtɪˈzæn/ US /ˈɑːrtəzən/ *noun* [C] old-fashioned someone who does skilled work with their hands

artist /'ɑːtɪst/ **noun** [C] ⓐ someone who creates art, especially paintings and drawings

artistic /ɑːˈtɪstɪk/ **adj 1** ⓑ showing skill and imagination in creating things, especially in painting, drawing, etc: *artistic talent* **2** [always before noun] ⓑ relating to art: *the artistic director of the theatre* • **artistically adv**

artistry /'ɑːtɪstri/ **noun** [U] great skill in creating or performing something, such as in writing, music, sport, etc

arts /ɑːts/ **noun 1** [plural] (also US **liberal arts**) subjects of study that are not science, such as history, languages, etc: *an arts subject/degree* **2 the arts** ⓑ activities such as painting, music, film, dance, and literature: *public interest in the arts* → See also **the performing arts**

artwork /'ɑːtwɜːk/ **noun** [U] the pictures or patterns in a book, magazine, CD cover, etc

arty /'ɑːti/ **adj** (also US **artsy** /'ɑːtsi/) knowing a lot about art, or wanting to appear as if you do

as strong /æz/ weak /əz/ **preposition, conjunction 1 as .... as** ⓐ used to compare two things, people, amounts, etc: *He's not as tall as his brother.* ◦ *She earns three times as much as I do.* **2 WHILE** ▷ ⓑ used to describe two things happening at the same time or something happening at a particular time: *He was shot in the back as he tried to escape.* ◦ *I think your opinions change as you get older.* **3 FOR THIS PURPOSE** ▷ ⓐ used to describe the purpose, job, or appearance of something or someone: *She **works as** a waitress.* ◦ *It could be **used as** evidence against him.* **4 LIKE** ▷ ⓑ in the same way: *This year, as in previous years, tickets sold very quickly.* **5 IN THIS WAY** ▷ used to describe the way in which people see or think of something or someone: *Most people think of nursing as a female occupation.* **6 BECAUSE** ▷ ⓐ because: *You can go first as you're the oldest.* **7 as if/as though** ⓑ used to describe how a situation seems to be: *It looks as if it might rain.* **8 as for** ⓑ used to talk about how another person or thing is affected by something: *I was pleased. As for Emily, well, who cares what she thinks.* **9 as from/as of** formal starting from a particular time, date, etc: *The new conditions are effective as of Monday.* **10 as to** formal about: *There's no decision as to when the work might start.*

asap /ˌeɪeseɪˈpiː/ abbreviation for as soon as possible

asbestos /æsˈbestɒs/ **noun** [U] a soft grey-white material that does not burn easily, once used in building

Asbo (also **ASBO**) /'æzbəʊ/ abbreviation for anti-social behaviour order: an official order that a person must stop doing something bad or they might go to prison, used in the past in the UK

ascend /əˈsend/ **verb** [I, T] formal to move up or to a higher position

ascendancy (also **ascendency**) /əˈsendənsi/ **noun** [U] formal a position of power, strength, or success: *in the ascendancy*

ascending /əˈsendɪŋ/ **adj** [always before noun]

starting with the lowest or smallest and becoming greater or higher: *They announced the results in ascending order.*

ascent /əˈsent/ **noun 1 CLIMB** ▷ [C] a movement or climb up something: *his first ascent of the mountain* **2 BECOMING SUCCESSFUL** ▷ [no plural] a time when someone starts to become successful: *The book describes his rapid ascent from truck driver to film star.* **3 PATH UP** ▷ [C] a path or road that goes up a hill or mountain: *a steep ascent*

ascertain /ˌæsəˈteɪn/ **verb** [T] formal to discover something: [+ question word] *We are still trying to ascertain whether the fire was started deliberately*

ascribe /əˈskraɪb/ **verb**

PHRASAL VERB **ascribe sth to sth** formal to say that something is caused by something else: *She ascribes her success to hard work.*

ash /æʃ/ **noun 1** [U] the soft, grey powder that remains when something has burnt: *cigarette ash* **2** [C] a forest tree

ashamed /əˈʃeɪmd/ **adj 1** ⓑ feeling guilty or embarrassed about something you have done: *You've got nothing to be **ashamed of**.* ◦ [+ to do sth] *He was ashamed to admit his mistake.* **2 be ashamed of sb** ⓑ to be angry and disappointed with a family member or friend because they have behaved badly: *He was so rude to Phil – I was ashamed of him.*

ashes /'æʃɪz/ **noun sb's ashes** the powder that remains when a dead person's body has been burnt: *scatter her ashes*

ashore /əˈʃɔːʳ/ **adv** onto land from the sea, a river, a lake, etc: *We swam ashore.*

ashtray /'æʃˌtreɪ/ **noun** [C] a small, open container used to put cigarette ash and finished cigarettes in

Asian /'eɪʒən/ **adj** relating or belonging to Asia: *Asian culture* • **Asian noun** [C] someone from Asia

aside¹ /əˈsaɪd/ **adv 1** ⓑ in a direction to one side: *I gave her a plate of food but she pushed it aside.* **2** ⓑ If you put or set something aside, you do not use it now, but keep it to use later: *We've put some money aside to pay for the children's education.* **3 aside from** ⓑ except for

aside² /əˈsaɪd/ **noun** [C] something that you say quietly so that not everyone can hear it, often something funny

ask /ɑːsk/ **verb 1 QUESTION** ▷ [I, T] ⓐ to say something to someone as a question that you want them to answer: [+ two objects] *Can I ask you a few questions?* ◦ *I asked him about his hobbies.* ◦ [+ question word] *I asked why the plane was so late.* → See Note at **question** **2 WANT SOMETHING** ▷ [I, T] ⓑ to say something to someone because you want them to give you something: *He's asked for a bike for his birthday* **3 REQUEST** ▷ [I, T] ⓑ to say something to someone because you want them to do something: [+ to do sth] *They've asked me to look after their dog while they're away.* **4 INVITE** ▷ [T] ⓐ to invite someone to do something: *She asked him out to lunch the next day.* **5 WANT PERMISSION** ▷ [I, T] ⓑ to say something to someone because you want to know if you can do something

Bruce asked if he could stay with us for a few days. ○ [+ to do sth] *She asked to leave early.* **6 PRICE** ▷ [T] to want a particular amount of money for something that you sell: *How much are you asking for it?* **7 ask yourself sth** to think about something carefully: *You've got to ask yourself whether it's what you really want.* **8 ask for it/ trouble** informal to behave in a way that is likely to make something unpleasant happen to you or to cause you problems: *Drinking and driving is asking for trouble.* **9 don't ask me** informal ⑫ used to tell someone that you do not know the answer to a question and that you are surprised they have asked you: *Don't ask me why you left your last job!* **10 you may well ask** said to someone who has asked you a question that would be difficult or interesting to answer

> ❗ Common learner error: **ask for**
>
> When you use **ask** with the meaning of saying you want someone to give you something, remember to use the preposition **for** before the thing that is wanted.
>
> *I'm writing to ask for information about your products.*
>
> ~~I'm writing to ask information about your products.~~

askew /əˈskjuː/ **adj** [never before noun] not straight: *The picture was slightly askew.*

asleep /əˈsliːp/ **adj 1 be asleep** ⑤ to be sleeping: *The children are asleep.* ○ *I was fast/sound asleep* (= sleeping deeply). **2 fall asleep** ⑤ to start sleeping: *He fell asleep in front of the TV.*

> ➕ Other ways of saying **asleep**
>
> If someone starts to sleep, you can say that they **fall asleep**:
>
> *I fell asleep in front of the TV.*
>
> If someone is completely asleep, you can say they are **fast asleep**:
>
> *You were fast asleep by the time I came to bed.*
>
> The verbs **doze** and **snooze**, and the expression **have/take a nap** all mean 'to sleep, especially for a short time or during the day':
>
> *She's always dozing in front of the TV.*
>
> *Granddad was snoozing in his chair.*
>
> *Oliver is really tired so he's just taking a nap.*
>
> The phrasal verbs **doze off** and (*informal*) **nod off** mean to start to sleep, especially during the day:
>
> *I must have nodded off after lunch.*
>
> *She dozed off during the lecture.*

asparagus /əˈspærəgəs/ **noun** [U] a vegetable consisting of a long, green stem with a pointed end

aspect /ˈæspekt/ **noun 1** [C] ⑫ one part of a situation, problem, subject, etc: *His illness affects almost every aspect of his life.* **2** [U, C] the form of a verb that shows how the meaning of a verb is considered in relation to time

asphalt /ˈæsfælt/ **noun** [U] a hard, black substance used to make roads and paths

asphyxiate /əsˈfɪksieɪt/ **verb be asphyxiated** to die because you cannot breathe • **asphyxiation** /əsˌfɪksiˈeɪʃᵊn/ **noun** [U]

aspiration /ˌæspᵊrˈeɪʃᵊn/ **noun** [C, U] something you hope to achieve: *The story is about the lives and aspirations of the Irish working classes.*

> ☑ Word partners for **aspiration**
>
> **have aspirations** to do sth/of doing sth • **high aspirations** • **dreams/hopes and aspirations** • **aspirations for sth**

aspire /əˈspaɪəʳ/ **verb aspire to sth; aspire to do sth** to hope to achieve something: *He has never aspired to a position of power.*

aspirin /ˈæspᵊrɪn/ **noun** [C, U] (plural **aspirin**, **aspirins**) ⑤ a common drug used to reduce pain and fever

aspiring /əˈspaɪərɪŋ/ **adj an aspiring actor/ politician/writer, etc** someone who is trying to become a successful actor/politician/writer, etc

ass /æs/ **noun** [C] **1 BOTTOM** ▷ US very informal (UK **arse**) a person's bottom **2 PERSON** ▷ informal a stupid person **3 ANIMAL** ▷ old-fashioned a donkey (= animal like a small horse)

assailant /əˈseɪlənt/ **noun** [C] formal a person who attacks someone

assassin /əˈsæsɪn/ **noun** [C] a person who kills someone important or famous, often for money

assassinate /əˈsæsɪneɪt/ **verb** [T] to kill someone important or famous • **assassination** /əˌsæsɪˈneɪʃᵊn/ **noun** [C, U]

assault /əˈsɔːlt/ **noun** [C, U] an attack: *an assault on a police officer* ○ *sexual assault* • **assault verb** [T]

assemble /əˈsembl/ **verb 1** [I, T] to join other people somewhere to make a group, or to bring people together into a group: *They assembled in the meeting room after lunch.* **2** [T] to build something by joining parts together

assembly /əˈsembli/ **noun 1 SCHOOL** ▷ [C, U] UK a regular meeting of all the students and teachers at a school: *morning assembly* **2 GROUP** ▷ [C] a group of people, such as a government, who meet to make decisions, laws, etc: *the national assembly* **3 BUILD** ▷ [U] the act of building something by joining parts together

assemblyman /əˈsemblimən/ **noun** [C] (plural **assemblymen**) US a man who belongs to a part of the official law-making group in many US states

assemblywoman /əˈsembliˌwʊmən/ **noun** [C] (plural **assemblywomen**) US a woman who belongs to a part of the official law-making group in many US states

assent /əˈsent/ **noun** [U] formal agreement or approval: *Has she given her assent?* • **assent verb** [I] formal to agree to something

assert /əˈsɜːt/ **verb 1 assert yourself** to behave or speak in a strong, confident way: *She has to learn to assert herself.* **2 assert your authority/ control/independence, etc** to do something to show other people that you have power **3** [T] formal to say that something is certainly true: [+ that] *He asserts that she stole money from him.*

assertion /əˈsɜːʃᵊn/ **noun** [C, U] formal a state-

A

ment that something is true: [+ that] *I don't agree with his assertion that men are safer drivers than women.*

assertive /əˈsɜːtɪv/ **adj** behaving or speaking in a strong, confident way: *You need to be much more assertive.* • **assertively adv** • **assertiveness noun** [U]

assess /əˈses/ **verb** [T] ⬤ to make a judgment about the quality, size, value, etc of something: *The tests are designed to assess a child's reading skills.* • **assessment noun** [C, U]

asset /ˈæset/ **noun** [C] **1** a person, skill, or quality that is useful or helps you to succeed: *He'll be a great asset to the team.* **2** something that a person or company owns that has a value: [usually plural] *The company has $70 billion in assets.*

assiduous /əˈsɪdjuəs/ **adj** formal showing a lot of effort and determination • **assiduously adv**

assign /əˈsaɪn/ **verb** [T] to give someone a particular job or responsibility: [+ two objects] *UN troops were assigned the task of rebuilding the hospital.* ○ [often passive] *The case has been assigned to our most senior officer.*

PHRASAL VERB **assign sb to sth** to give someone a particular job or place to work: [often passive] *Which police officer has been assigned to this case?*

assignment /əˈsaɪnmənt/ **noun** [C, U] a piece of work or job that you are given to do: *a written assignment* ○ *He's on assignment in Brazil.*

assimilate /əˈsɪmɪleɪt/ **verb** formal **1** [T] to understand and remember new information **2** [I, T] to become part of a group, society, etc, or to make someone or something become part of a group, society, etc: *The refugees have now assimilated into the local community.* • **assimilation** /əˌsɪmɪˈleɪʃən/ **noun** [U]

assist /əˈsɪst/ **verb** [I, T] ⬤ to help: *The army arrived to assist in the search.* ○ *He's assisting the police with their investigation.*

assistance /əˈsɪstəns/ **noun** [U] formal ⬤ help: *financial/medical assistance* ○ *Can I be of any assistance?* (= Can I help you?)

assistant /əˈsɪstənt/ **noun** [C] **1** ⬤ someone whose job is to help a person who has a more important job: *an administrative assistant* ○ *assistant manager* **2** a **sales/shop assistant** mainly UK ⬤ someone who helps customers in a shop

associate[1] /əˈsəʊsieɪt/ **verb** [T] to relate two things, people, etc in your mind: *Most people associate this brand with good quality.*

PHRASAL VERBS **associate with sb** formal to spend time with someone • **be associated with sth** ⬤ to be related to something or caused by something: *There are many risks associated with smoking.*

associate[2] /əˈsəʊsiət/ **noun** [C] someone who you know because of work or business: *She's a business associate of mine.*

associate[3] /əˈsəʊsiət/ **adj associate director/editor/producer, etc** someone in a slightly less important position than the main person

associate's degree /əˌsəʊsiəts dɪˈɡriː/ **noun** [C]

US a college degree that is given after a course of study that typically takes two years

association /əˌsəʊsiˈeɪʃən/ **noun 1** [C] ⬤ an organization of people with the same interests or with a particular purpose: *the Football Association* **2** [C, U] a connection or relationship between two things or people **3 in association with** working together with: *The event was organized in association with the Sports Council.* → See also **savings and loan association**

assorted /əˈsɔːtɪd/ **adj** of different types: *a box of assorted chocolates*

assortment /əˈsɔːtmənt/ **noun** [C] a group of different types of something: *an assortment of vegetables*

assuage /əˈsweɪdʒ/ **verb** [T] formal to make unpleasant feelings less strong: *The government tried to assuage the public's fears.*

assume /əˈsjuːm/ **verb** [T] **1** ⬤ to think that something is likely to be true, although you have no proof: [+ (that)] *Everything was quiet when I got home so I assumed that you had gone out.* **2 assume control/power/responsibility etc** to take a position of control/power/responsibility, etc: *He has assumed the role of spokesman for the group.* **3 assume an air/expression, etc** formal to pretend to have a feeling that you do not have **4 assume a false identity/name, etc** to pretend to be someone else: *an assumed name*

assumption /əˈsʌmpʃən/ **noun** [C] **1** something that you think is true without having any proof: *People tend to make assumptions about you when you have a disability.* ○ *These calculations are based on the assumption that prices will continue to rise.* **2 the assumption of power, responsibility, etc** the act of taking a position of power/responsibility, etc

---

🗒 **Word partners for assumption**

make an assumption • be based on an assumption • a basic/common/false/underlying assumption • do sth under the assumption that • an assumption about sth

---

assurance /əˈʃʊərəns/ **noun 1** [C] a promise [+ that] *He gave us an assurance that it would not happen again.* **2** [U] confidence: *She spoke with calm assurance.*

assure /əˈʃɔːr/ **verb** [T] **1** ⬤ to tell someone that something is definitely true, especially so that they do not worry: [+ (that)] *She assured them that she would be all right.* **2** to make something certain to happen: *This loan should assure the company's future.*

assured /əˈʃʊəd/ **adj 1** showing skill and confidence: *an assured performance* **2 be assured of sth** to be certain to get or achieve something in the future: *They are now assured of a place in the final.* → See also **self-assured**

asterisk /ˈæstərɪsk/ **noun** [C] a written symbol in the shape of a star (*), often used to mark a particular word, phrase, etc

asthma /ˈæsmə/ **noun** [U] an illness that makes it difficult to breathe: *She had an asthma attack* • **asthmatic** /æsˈmætɪk/ **adj** *an asthmatic child*

astonish /əˈstɒnɪʃ/ **verb** [T] to make someone

very surprised: *Her quick recovery has astonished doctors.*

astonished /əˈstɒnɪʃt/ **adj** ⑫ very surprised: *He was astonished at her behaviour.*

astonishing /əˈstɒnɪʃɪŋ/ **adj** ⑫ very surprising: *It's astonishing that so many people believed his story.* • **astonishingly adv**

astonishment /əˈstɒnɪʃmənt/ **noun** [U] ⑫ extreme surprise: *The others stared at him **in astonishment.*** ° ***To my astonishment**, he started laughing.*

astound /əˈstaʊnd/ **verb** [T] to make someone very surprised: *The speed of her recovery has astounded doctors.*

astounded /əˈstaʊndɪd/ **adj** very surprised: *I'm **astounded at/by** these prices.*

astounding /əˈstaʊndɪŋ/ **adj** very surprising: *an astounding success* • **astoundingly adv**

astray /əˈstreɪ/ **adv 1 go astray** to get lost or go in the wrong direction: *One of my bags went astray at the airport.* **2 lead sb astray** to encourage someone to do bad things that they should not do: *He was led astray by his friends.*

astride /əˈstraɪd/ **adv** If you sit or stand astride something, you have one foot on each side of it.

astro- /æstrəʊ-/ **prefix** relating to stars or outer space: *astronomer* ° *astrophysics*

astrology /əˈstrɒlədʒi/ **noun** [U] the study of the positions and movements of stars and planets to say how they might influence people's lives • **astrologer** **noun** [C] someone who studies astrology • **astrological** /ˌæstrəˈlɒdʒɪkəl/ **adj**

astronaut /ˈæstrənɔːt/ **noun** [C] someone who travels into space

astronaut

astronomical /ˌæstrə-ˈnɒmɪkəl/ **adj 1** An astronomical amount is extremely large: *astronomical prices* **2** relating to astronomy • **astronomically adv**

astronomy /əˈstrɒnəmi/ **noun** [U] the scientific study of stars and planets • **astronomer noun** [C] a scientist who studies astronomy

astute /əˈstjuːt/ **adj** good at judging situations and making decisions that give you an advantage: *an astute businesswoman* ° *politically astute* • **astutely adv**

asylum /əˈsaɪləm/ **noun 1** [U] permission to stay in a country because you are escaping danger in your own country **2** [C] old-fashioned a hospital for people with a mental illness → See also **political asylum**

asylum seeker **noun** [C] someone who leaves their country to escape from danger, and tries to get permission to live in another country

asymmetrical /ˌeɪsɪˈmetrɪkəl/ **adj** not being exactly the same shape and size on both sides • **asymmetry** /eɪˈsɪmɪtri/ **noun** [U]

at strong /æt/ weak /ət/ **preposition 1** PLACE ▷ ⓐ used to show the place or position of something or someone: *We met at the station.* ° *She's at the library.* **2** TIME ▷ ⓐ used to show the time

something happens: *The meeting starts at three.* **3** DIRECTION ▷ ⓐ towards or in the direction of: *She threw the ball at him.* ° *He's always shouting at the children.* **4** ABILITY ▷ ⓑ used after an adjective to show a person's ability to do something: *He's good at making friends.* **5** CAUSE ▷ ⓐ used to show the cause of something, especially a feeling: *We were surprised at the news.* **6** AMOUNT ▷ ⓑ used to show the price, speed, level, etc of something: *He denied driving at 120 miles per hour.* **7** ACTIVITY ▷ used to show a state or activity: *a country at war* **8** INTERNET ▷ ⓐ the @ symbol, used in email addresses to separate the name of a person, department, etc from the name of the organization or company

ate /eɪt, et/ past tense of eat

atheist /ˈeɪθiɪst/ **noun** [C] someone who believes that there is no god • **atheism noun** [U]

athlete /ˈæθliːt/ **noun** [C] ⓑ someone who is very good at a sport and who competes with others in organized events

athletic /æθˈletɪk/ **adj 1** ⓑ strong, healthy, and good at sports **2** [always before noun] relating to athletes or to the sport of athletics

athletics /æθˈletɪks/ **noun** [U] UK (US **track and field**) ⓑ the sports that include running, jumping, and throwing → See colour picture **Sports 1** on page Centre 14

-athon /-əθɒn/ **suffix** an event or activity that lasts a long time, usually to collect money for charity: *a walkathon* (= *a long walk*)

atlas /ˈætləs/ **noun** [C] a book of maps: *a road atlas* ° *a world atlas*

ATM /ˌeɪtiːˈem/ **noun** [C] mainly US abbreviation for automated teller machine or automatic teller machine: a machine that you get money from using a plastic card

atmosphere /ˈætməsfɪər/ **noun 1** FEELING ▷ [no plural] ⓑ the feeling that exists in a place or situation: *a relaxed atmosphere* **2 the atmosphere** ⓑ the layer of gases around the Earth **3** AIR ▷ [no plural] ⓑ the air inside a room or other place: *a smoky atmosphere*

> ✏ Word partners for **atmosphere**
>
> **create** an atmosphere • an atmosphere of [fear/trust, etc] • a family/friendly/relaxed atmosphere

atmospheric /ˌætməsˈferɪk/ **adj 1** [always before noun] relating to the air or to the atmosphere: *atmospheric conditions* **2** creating a special feeling, such as mystery or romance: *atmospheric music/lighting*

atom /ˈætəm/ **noun** [C] ⓑ the smallest unit that an element can be divided into

atomic /əˈtɒmɪk/ **adj 1** [always before noun] relating to atoms: *an atomic particle* **2** ⓑ using the energy created when an atom is divided: *atomic power/weapons*

atomic bomb **noun** [C] (also **atom bomb**) a very powerful bomb that uses the energy created when an atom is divided

atomic energy **noun** [U] energy that is produced by dividing atoms

A

atop /ə'tɒp/ **preposition** mainly US on the top of

atrium /'eɪtriəm/ **noun** [C] (plural **atriums** or **atria**) a large, central room with a glass roof in an office building, restaurant, etc

atrocious /ə'trəʊʃəs/ **adj 1** extremely bad: *atrocious weather* **2** violent and shocking: *an atrocious crime*

atrocity /ə'trɒsəti/ **noun** [C, U] an extremely violent and shocking act: *Soldiers have been committing atrocities against civilians.*

attach /ə'tætʃ/ **verb** [T] **1 JOIN** ▷ 🔵 to join or fix one thing to another: *She attached a photograph to her letter.* **2 attach importance/value, etc to sb/sth** to think that someone or something has importance/value, etc: *You attach too much importance to money.* **3 INCLUDE** ▷ to include something as part of something else: *There were too many conditions attached to the deal.* → See also **no strings (string¹) (attached) 4 COMPUTER** ▷ 🔵 to add an attachment (= computer file) to an email message

attached /ə'tætʃt/ **adj be attached to sb/sth** to like someone or something very much: *I've become rather attached to my old car.*

attachment /ə'tætʃmənt/ **noun 1 FEELING** ▷ [C, U] a feeling of love or strong connection to someone or something: *I wasn't aware of any romantic attachments.* **2 EMAIL** ▷ [C] 🔵 a computer file that is sent together with an email message: *I wasn't able to open that attachment.* **3 EQUIPMENT** ▷ [C] 🔵 an extra part that can be added to a piece of equipment: *There's a special attachment for cleaning in the corners.*

attack¹ /ə'tæk/ **noun 1 VIOLENCE** ▷ [C, U] 🔵 a violent act intended to hurt or damage someone or something: *a terrorist attack on the capital* **2 CRITICISM** ▷ [C, U] a strong criticism of someone or something: *a scathing attack on the president* **3 ILLNESS** ▷ [C] a sudden, short illness: *a nasty attack of flu* **4 SPORT** ▷ [C, U] in games such as football, an attempt by the players in a team try to score points, goals, etc → See also **counter-attack**

> ☑ Word partners for **attack**
>
> 1 launch/mount an attack • be **under** attack • a **bomb/terrorist** attack • an attack **on** sb/sth
>
> 2 launch/mount an attack • be/come **under** attack • a **personal/scathing** attack • an attack **on** sb/sth

attack² /ə'tæk/ **verb 1 VIOLENCE** ▷ [I, T] 🔵 to use violence to hurt or damage someone or something: *He was attacked and seriously injured by a gang of youths.* **2 CRITICIZE** ▷ [T] to strongly criticize someone or something: *She attacked the government's new education policy.* **3 DISEASE** ▷ [T] If a disease, chemical, etc attacks someone or something, it damages them: *The virus attacks the central nervous system.* **4 SPORT** ▷ [I, T] If players in a team attack, they move forward to try to score points, goals, etc.

attacker /ə'tækər/ **noun** [C] a person who uses violence to hurt someone: *The police think she must have known her attackers.*

attain /ə'teɪn/ **verb** [T] to achieve something, especially after a lot of work: *She's attained a high level of fitness.* • **attainable adj** possible to achieve • **attainment noun** [C, U] the act of achieving something

attempt¹ /ə'tempt/ **noun** [C] **1** 🔵 If you make an attempt to do something, you try to do it: *This is his second attempt at the exam.* ○ [+ to do sth] *They closed the road in an attempt to reduce traffic in the city.* ○ *She made no attempt (= did not try) to be sociable.* **2 an attempt on sb's life** an attempt to kill someone

> ☑ Word partners for **attempt**
>
> make an attempt • a **successful/unsuccessful** attempt • an attempt **at** sth/doing sth • **in** an attempt to do sth

attempt² /ə'tempt/ **verb** [T] 🔵 to try to do something, especially something difficult: [+ to do sth] *He attempted to escape through a window.*

attempted /ə'temptɪd/ **adj attempted murder/robbery, etc** used to describe a crime that someone tries to commit but does not succeed

attend /ə'tend/ **verb** [I, T] formal **1** 🔵 to go to an event: *to attend a concert/meeting* **2 attend a church/school, etc** 🔵 to go regularly to a particular church/school, etc

> ➕ Other ways of saying **attend**
>
> Instead of the verb 'attend', people usually say **come/go to:**
>
> *How many people **came to** the meeting?*
> *He **goes to** church regularly.*
>
> The verb **make** is sometimes used when someone is talking about whether or not they are able to attend an event:
>
> *I'm afraid I can't **make** the meeting this afternoon (= I will not be able to attend).*
>
> The expression **make it** is also used, meaning 'to get to a place, even when there are problems':
>
> *The traffic was so bad we only just **made it** in time for the start of the film.*

PHRASAL VERB **attend to sb/sth** formal to deal with something or help someone

attendance /ə'tendəns/ **noun** [C, U] **1** the number of people who go to an event, meeting, etc: *falling attendance* **2** the act of going somewhere such as a church, school, etc regularly: *His attendance at school is very poor.* **3 in attendance** formal present at an event: *They have doctors in attendance at every match.*

attendant /ə'tendənt/ **noun** [C] someone whose job is to help the public in a particular place: *a parking attendant* → See also **flight attendant**

attention /ə'tenʃən/ **noun** [U] **1** 🔵 the state of watching, listening to, or thinking about something carefully or with interest: *Ladies and gentlemen, could I **have your attention**, please* **2 pay attention (to sth)** 🔵 to watch, listen to or think about something carefully or with interest: *You weren't paying attention to what was saying.* **3 bring/draw (sb's) attention to sth/sb** 🔵 to make someone notice something or someone: *If I could just draw your attention to the second paragraph.* **4 attract/get (sb's) attention** ⑫ to make someone notice you: *I waved at him to get his attention.* **5** treatment to deal with a problem: *medical attention* ∘ *This old engine needs a lot of attention.*

> ❗ Common learner error: **attention**
>
> **Attention** is usually followed by the preposition **to**.
> *You should pay attention to what she tells you.*
> *We want to draw people's attention to the risks involved.*

> ✓ Word partners for **attention**
>
> **pay** attention (to sth/sb) • **give** sth attention • **have/hold/keep** sb's attention • **careful/ full/special/undivided** attention

attentive /əˈtentɪv/ **adj** listening or watching carefully and showing that you are interested: *an attentive student* • **attentively adv**

attest /əˈtest/ **verb** [I, T] formal to show or prove that something is true

attic /ˈætɪk/ **noun** [C] a room at the top of a house under the roof

attire /əˈtaɪər/ **noun** [U] old-fashioned the clothes that you wear • **attired adj** dressed in a particular way: *suitably attired*

attitude /ˈætɪtjuːd/ **noun** [C, U] ⑤ how you think or feel about something and how this makes you behave: *a positive attitude* ∘ *He has a very bad attitude to/towards work.*

> ✓ Word partners for **attitude**
>
> **have/take** a [positive/responsible, etc] attitude • a **casual/hostile/negative/positive** attitude • (sb's) attitude **to/towards** sth/sb

attorney /əˈtɜːni/ **noun** [C] US a lawyer: *a defense attorney* → See Note at **lawyer** → See also **district attorney**

attract /əˈtrækt/ **verb** [T] **1** ⑤ to make people come to a place or do a particular thing by being interesting, enjoyable, etc: *The castle attracts more than 300,000 visitors a year.* ∘ *We need to attract more science graduates to teaching.* **2** attract attention/interest, etc ⑤ to cause people to pay attention/be interested, etc **3 be attracted to sb** ⑫ to like someone, especially sexually, because of the way they look or behave: *I was attracted to him straight away.* **4** If something attracts a substance or object, it causes it to move towards it: *Magnets attract metal.*

> ✓ Word partners for **attraction**
>
> an **added/**a **big/**the **main/**a **major/**the **star** attraction • a **tourist** attraction • the attraction **of** sth • an attraction **for** sb

attraction /əˈtrækʃən/ **noun 1** [C] ⑤ something that makes people come to a place or want to do a particular thing: *a tourist attraction* ∘ *The opportunity to travel is one of the main attractions of this job.* **2** [U] the feeling of liking

someone, especially sexually, because of the way they look or behave: *physical attraction*

attractive /əˈtræktɪv/ **adj 1** ⑫ beautiful or pleasant to look at: *an attractive woman* ∘ *I find him very attractive.* **2** ⑫ interesting or useful: *We want to make the club attractive to a wider range of people.* → Opposite **unattractive** • **attractively adv** • **attractiveness noun** [U]

> ➕ Other ways of saying **attractive**
>
> The adjectives **beautiful** and **lovely** are often used instead of 'attractive', and are used to describe both people and things:
> *His wife is very beautiful.*
> *We drove through some really beautiful/ lovely countryside.*
> *You look lovely!*
> If a person is attractive, we can say that they are **good-looking**. The adjective **handsome** is also sometimes used for men, and **pretty** for women:
> *He's certainly very good-looking.*
> *Your daughter is very pretty.*
> If someone is extremely attractive, you can say that they are **gorgeous** or **stunning**:
> *You look gorgeous in that dress!*
> *Her daughter is absolutely stunning.*
> If something is extremely attractive, you can say that it is **breathtaking**, **exquisite**, **stunning**, or **gorgeous**:
> *The views from the window were breathtaking.*
> *These hand-made decorations are exquisite.*
> If a person or thing is attractive because of being small, you can say that they are **cute** or **sweet**:
> *He's got a really cute baby brother.*
> *Look at that kitten – isn't she sweet?*
> Adjectives such as **stylish** and **chic** can be used to describe something that has been made to look attractive and fashionable:
> *He took me to a very chic restaurant.*
> *Their house is very stylish.*

attributable /əˈtrɪbjətəbl/ **adj attributable to sth** caused by something: *A lot of crime is attributable to the use of drugs.*

attribute¹ /əˈtrɪbjuːt/ **verb**

PHRASAL VERBS **attribute sth to sth** to say that something is caused by something else: *He attributes his success to hard work.* • **attribute sth to sb** to say that someone wrote, said, or made something: *This drawing has been attributed to Picasso.*

attribute² /ˈætrɪbjuːt/ **noun** [C] a quality or characteristic that someone or something has: *Her hair is her best attribute.*

attributive /əˈtrɪbjətɪv/ **adj** An attributive adjective comes before the noun it describes. → Compare **predicative**

aubergine /ˈəʊbəʒiːn/ **noun** [C, U] UK (US **eggplant**) ⑫ an oval, purple vegetable that is white inside → See colour picture **Fruits and Vegetables** on page Centre 10

A

auburn /ˈɔːbən/ **adj** Auburn hair is red-brown.

auction /ˈɔːkʃən/ **noun** [C, U] a sale in which things are sold to the person who offers the most money • **auction** (also **auction off**) **verb** [T] to sell something at an auction

auctioneer /ˌɔːkʃənˈɪər/ **noun** [C] the person who is in charge of an auction

audacity /ɔːˈdæsəti/ **noun** [U] showing too much confidence in your behaviour in a way that other people find shocking or rude: *And then he had the audacity to blame me for his mistake!* • **audacious** /ɔːˈdeɪʃəs/ **adj**

audible /ˈɔːdəbl/ **adj** If something is audible, you can hear it: *His voice was barely audible.* → Opposite **inaudible** • **audibly adv**

audience /ˈɔːdiəns/ **noun 1 GROUP** ▷ [group] 🔵 the people who sit and watch a performance at a theatre, cinema, etc: *There were a lot of children in the audience.* **2 TYPE** ▷ [group] 🔵 the type of people who watch a particular TV show, read a particular book, etc: *This magazine is aimed at a teenage audience.* **3 MEETING** ▷ [C] formal a formal meeting with an important person: *an audience with the Queen*

> ⚡ **Word partners for audience**
>
> 1 be **in** the audience • a **member** of the audience
> 2 **reach** an audience • sth's **target** audience
> • a **wide** audience

audio /ˈɔːdiəʊ/ **adj** relating to the recording or playing of sound: *audio equipment*

audio- /ɔːdiəʊ-/ **prefix** relating to hearing or sound: *audiotape*

audiovisual /ˌɔːdiəʊˈvɪʒuəl/ **adj** [always before noun] using sounds and pictures: *audiovisual equipment*

audit /ˈɔːdɪt/ **noun** [C] an examination of all the financial records of a company by an independent person in order to produce a report • **audit verb** [T] • **auditor noun** [C]

audition /ɔːˈdɪʃən/ **noun** [C] a short performance to try to get a job as an actor, singer, etc • **audition verb** [I]

auditorium /ˌɔːdɪˈtɔːriəm/ **noun** [C] the part of a theatre, hall, etc where people sit to watch a performance

Aug written abbreviation for August

augment /ɔːgˈment/ **verb** [T] formal to increase the size or value of something by adding something to it

August /ˈɔːgəst/ **noun** [C, U] (written abbreviation **Aug**) 🔵 the eighth month of the year

aunt /ɑːnt/ **noun** [C] (also **auntie, aunty** /ˈɑːnti/) 🔵 the sister of your mother or father, or the wife of your uncle → See also **agony aunt**

au pair /ˌəʊˈpeər/ **noun** [C] a young person who goes to live with a family in another country and looks after their children, does work in their house, etc

aura /ˈɔːrə/ **noun** [C] a feeling that a person or place seems to have: *an aura of mystery*

aural /ˈɔːrəl/ **adj** relating to hearing

auspices /ˈɔːspɪsɪz/ **noun under the auspices of sb/sth** formal with the help or support of a person or organization: *The conference was held under the auspices of the Red Cross.*

auspicious /ɔːˈspɪʃəs/ **adj** If an event or time is auspicious, it makes you believe that something will be successful in the future: *an auspicious start*

austere /ɒsˈtɪər/ **adj 1** plain, simple, and without unnecessary decorations or luxuries: *an austere room* **2** strict or severe: *an austere woman* • **austerity** /ɒsˈterəti/ **noun** [U]

authentic /ɔːˈθentɪk/ **adj** If something is authentic, it is real, true, or what people say it is: *authentic Italian food* • **authentically adv** • **authenticity** /ˌɔːθenˈtɪsəti/ **noun** [U]

author /ˈɔːθər/ **noun** [C] 🔵 someone who writes a book, article, etc: *a popular author of children's fiction*

authoritarian /ˌɔːθɒrɪˈteəriən/ **adj** very strict and not allowing people freedom to do what they want: *an authoritarian leader/regime*

authoritative /ɔːˈθɒrɪtətɪv/ **adj 1** An authoritative book, report, etc is respected and considered to be accurate: *an authoritative guide* **2** confident and seeming to be in control of a situation: *an authoritative manner/voice*

authority /ɔːˈθɒrəti/ **noun 1 POWER** ▷ [U] 🔵 the official power to make decisions or to control other people: *a position of authority* ○ [+ to do sth] *The investigators have the authority to examine all the company's records.* ○ *We need the support of someone in authority.* **2 OFFICIAL GROUP** ▷ [C] an official group or government department with power to control particular public services: *the local housing authority* **3 QUALITY** ▷ [U] the quality of being confident and being able to control people: *She has an air of authority.* **4 an authority on sth** someone who has a lot of knowledge about a particular subject: *She is an authority on seventeenth century English literature.* → See also **local authority**

authorize (also UK **-ise**) /ˈɔːθəraɪz/ **verb** [T] **1** to give official permission for something **2 be authorized to do sth** to be officially allowed to do something: *Only managers are authorized to sign expense forms.* • **authorization** /ˌɔːθəraɪˈzeɪʃən/ **noun** [U]

autistic /ɔːˈtɪstɪk/ **adj** Autistic people have mental condition that makes them have problems with communicating and forming relationships. • **autism** /ˈɔːtɪzəm/ **noun** [U]

auto /ˈɔːtəʊ/ **adj** mainly US relating to cars: *the auto industry*

auto- /ɔːtəʊ-/ **prefix 1** operating without being controlled by humans: *autopilot* (= *a computer that directs an aircraft*) **2** self: *an autobiograph* (= *a book that someone writes about their own life*)

autobiography /ˌɔːtəʊbaɪˈɒɡrəfi/ **noun** [C] book written by someone about their own life • **autobiographical** /ˌɔːtəʊbaɪəʊˈɡræfɪkəl/ **adj**

autograph /ˈɔːtəɡrɑːf/ **noun** [C] a famous person's name, written by that person • **autograph verb** [T] *an autographed photo*

automate /ˈɔːtəmeɪt/ **verb** [T] to control some

thing using machines and not people • **automated** adj *a fully automated system* • **automation** /ˌɔːtəˈmeɪʃən/ noun [U]

automatic¹ /ˌɔːtəˈmætɪk/ adj **1** MACHINE ▷ ⬛ An automatic machine works by itself or with little human control: *automatic doors* **2** CERTAIN ▷ certain to happen as part of the normal process or system: *You get an automatic promotion after two years.* **3** REACTION ▷ done as a natural reaction without thinking: *My automatic response was to pull my hand away.* • **automatically** adv

automatic² /ˌɔːtəˈmætɪk/ noun [C] a car in which you do not have to change the gears (= parts that control how fast the wheels turn)

automobile /ˈɔːtəməʊbiːl/ noun [C] US a car: *the automobile industry*

automotive /ˌɔːtəˈməʊtɪv/ adj [always before noun] relating to cars and car production: *the automotive industry*

autonomous /ɔːˈtɒnəməs/ adj independent and having the power to make your own decisions: *an autonomous region/state*

autonomy /ɔːˈtɒnəmi/ noun [U] the right of a country or group of people to govern itself: *Local councils need more autonomy.*

autopsy /ˈɔːtɒpsi/ noun [C] a medical examination of a dead body to discover the exact cause of death

auto-reply /ˌɔːtəʊrɪˈplaɪ/ noun [C] an email or message that is automatically sent each time you receive a message: *You can create an "out of office" auto-reply message for when you are away from your desk.*

autumn /ˈɔːtəm/ noun [C, U] (also US **fall**) ⬛ the season of the year between summer and winter, when leaves fall from the trees: *I'm starting a new job* **in the autumn.** ○ *autumn leaves* • **autumnal** /ɔːˈtʌmnəl/ adj typical of autumn

auxiliary /ɔːɡˈzɪliəri/ adj providing extra help or support: *an auxiliary nurse*

auxiliary 'verb noun [C] a verb that is used with another verb to form tenses, negatives, and questions. In English the auxiliary verbs are 'be', 'have', and 'do'.

avail /əˈveɪl/ noun **to no avail** without success, especially after a lot of effort: *She sent more than 50 letters, but to no avail.*

available /əˈveɪləbl/ adj **1** ⬛ If something is available, you can use it or get it: *This information is available free on the Internet.* ○ *The new drug is not yet* **available to** *the public.* **2** ⬛ If someone is available, they are not busy and so are able to do something: *No one from the company was available to comment on the accident.* → Opposite **unavailable** • **availability** /əˌveɪləˈbɪləti/ noun [U]

⬛ Word partners for **available**

be/become available • **make** sth available • **easily/freely/readily/widely** available • be available **to** sb

avalanche /ˈævəlɑːnʃ/ noun [C] **1** a large amount of snow that falls down the side of

a mountain **2 an avalanche of sth** a sudden, large amount of something, usually more than you can deal with: *an avalanche of mail*

avant-garde /ˌævɒŋˈɡɑːd/ adj If art, music, etc, is avant-garde, it is new and unusual in style.

avalanche

avarice /ˈævərɪs/ noun [U] formal a strong feeling that you want a lot of money and possessions

avatar /ˈævətɑːr/ noun [C] an electronic image that you create to represent yourself in a computer game, on the internet, etc.

Ave written abbreviation for avenue: *132, Gainsborough Ave*

avenge /əˈvendʒ/ verb [T] literary to punish someone for doing something bad to you, your family, etc: *He swore he would avenge his brother's death.*

avenue /ˈævənjuː/ noun [C] **1** (written abbreviation **Ave**) a wide road in a town or city, often with trees along it **2** a possible way of doing or achieving something: *We have exhausted all other avenues of treatment.*

average¹ /ˈævərɪdʒ/ adj **1** USUAL ▷ ⬛ usual and like the most common type: *an average person* ○ *an average day* **2** AMOUNT ▷ [always before noun] An average amount is calculated by adding some amounts together and then dividing by the number of amounts: *an average age/ temperature* **3** NOT EXCELLENT ▷ not excellent, although not bad: *The food was pretty average.*

average² /ˈævərɪdʒ/ noun **1** [C] ⬛ an amount calculated by adding some amounts together and then dividing by the number of amounts: *They work an average of 30.5 hours per week.* **2** [C, U] ⬛ the usual or typical amount: *well above/ below average* **3 on average** ⬛ usually, or based on an average: *Female workers earn, on average, a third less than men.*

average³ /ˈævərɪdʒ/ verb [T] to reach a particular amount as an average: *He averages about 20 points a game.*

averse /əˈvɜːs/ adj **1 not be averse to sth** UK humorous to be happy or willing to do or have something: *She's not averse to the occasional glass of champagne.* **2 be averse to sth** formal to strongly dislike something

aversion /əˈvɜːʃən/ noun **an aversion to sth** a strong dislike of something

avert /əˈvɜːt/ verb **1 avert a crisis/disaster/war, etc** to prevent something bad from happening **2 avert your eyes/face/gaze** to turn your head away so that you do not see something

avian flu /ˌeɪviənˈfluː/ noun [U] bird flu: an illness that kills birds and can sometimes pass from birds to people

aviary /ˈeɪviəri/ noun [C] a large cage for birds

aviation /ˌeɪviˈeɪʃən/ noun [U] flying aircraft or producing aircraft: *the aviation industry*

avid /ˈævɪd/ adj very interested and enthusiastic: *an avid reader* • **avidly** adv

A

avocado /ˌævəˈkɑːdəʊ/ **noun** [C, U] a dark green, oval fruit that is pale green inside and is not sweet

avoid /əˈvɔɪd/ **verb** [T] **1 ⓑ1** to stay away from a person, place, situation, etc: *Try to avoid the city centre.* **2 ⓑ2** to prevent something from happening: *Book early to avoid disappointment.* **3 avoid doing sth ⓑ2** to intentionally not do something: *She managed to avoid answering my question.* • **avoidable adj** possible to avoid → Opposite **unavoidable** • **avoidance noun** [U] the act of avoiding something

> **❗ Common learner error: avoid doing something**
>
> When **avoid** is followed by a verb, the verb is always in the **-ing** form.
>
> *I avoided seeing him for several days.*
> ~~I avoided to see him for several days.~~

await /əˈweɪt/ **verb** [T] formal **1** to wait for something: *We are awaiting the results of the tests.* **2** If something awaits you, you will experience it in the future: *A surprise awaits her when she gets home.*

awake¹ /əˈweɪk/ **adj 1 be/lie/stay, etc awake ⓑ1** to not be sleeping: *Is Tom awake yet?* ∘ *The noise from the party **kept** me **awake** all night.* **2 be wide awake** to be completely awake

awake² /əˈweɪk/ **verb** [I, T] (**awoke, awoken**) literary to wake up, or make someone wake up

awaken /əˈweɪkən/ **verb 1** [T] formal to cause an emotion, feeling, etc: *The song awakened painful memories.* **2** [I, T] literary to wake up, or make someone wake up

awakening /əˈweɪkənɪŋ/ **noun** [no plural] a time when you start to be aware of something or feel something

IDIOM **a rude awakening** If you have a rude awakening, you have a shock when you discover the truth about a situation.

award¹ /əˈwɔːd/ **noun** [C] **1 ⓑ2** a prize given to someone for something they have achieved: *the award for best actress* ∘ *to receive/win an award* **2** money given to someone because of a legal decision

> **🗹 Word partners for award**
>
> present/receive/win an award • an award for sth • an awards ceremony • an award winner

award² /əˈwɔːd/ **verb** [T] **ⓑ2** to officially give someone something such as a prize or an amount of money: [+ two objects, often passive] *He was awarded the Nobel Prize for Physics.*

aware /əˈweər/ **adj 1 be aware of/that ⓑ2** to know about something: *Are you aware of the risks involved?* ∘ *She was **well aware** that he was married.* → Opposite **unaware 2** interested in and knowing a lot about a particular subject: *politically/socially aware*

awareness /əˈweənəs/ **noun** [U] the mental state of knowing about something: *Environmental awareness is increasing all the time.*

> **🗹 Word partners for awareness**
>
> create/increase/raise awareness • a greater/growing/heightened/increased awareness • public awareness • an awareness about/of sth • an awareness among [parents/students, etc]

awash /əˈwɒʃ/ **adj be awash with sth** UK (US **be awash in sth**) to have a lot of something, often too much: *The sport is awash with money.*

away¹ /əˈweɪ/ **adv 1 DIRECTION** ▷ **ⓐ2** to or in a different place or situation: *Go away and leave me alone.* ∘ *We'd like to move **away from** the town centre.* **2 DISTANCE FROM** ▷ **ⓐ2** at a particular distance from a place: *The nearest town was ten miles away.* ∘ *How far away is the station?* **3 NOT THERE** ▷ **ⓐ2** not at the place where someone usually lives or works: *Shirley's feeding the cat while we're away.* **4 SAFE PLACE** ▷ **ⓑ1** into a usual or safe place: *Can you put everything away when you've finished?* **5 two weeks/five hours, etc away ⓑ1** at a particular time in the future: *My exam's only a week away now.* **6 CONTINUOUS ACTION** ▷ used after a verb to mean 'continuously or repeatedly': *I was still writing away when the exam finished* **7 GRADUALLY** ▷ **ⓑ2** gradually disappearing until almost or completely gone: *The snow has melted away.* **8 SPORT** ▷ If a sports team is playing away, the game is at the place where the other team usually plays. → See also **take your breath away, give the game¹ away**

away² /əˈweɪ/ **adj** In sports, an away game is played at the place where the other team usually plays.

awe /ɔː/ **noun** [U] **1** a feeling of great respect and sometimes fear: *I was filled with awe at the sheer size of the building.* **2 be in awe of sb** to feel great respect for someone: *As children we were rather in awe of our grandfather.*

awe-inspiring /ˈɔːɪnˌspaɪərɪŋ/ **adj** causing people to feel great respect or admiration

awesome /ˈɔːsəm/ **adj** very great, large, or special and making you feel respect and sometimes fear: *an awesome challenge/responsibility* ∘ *The scenery was awesome.*

awful /ˈɔːfəl/ **adj 1 ⓑ1** very bad, of low quality, or unpleasant: *an awful place* ∘ *The film was absolutely awful.* **2 an awful lot (of sth)** informal **ⓑ2** a large amount: *It cost an awful lot of money.*

awfully /ˈɔːfəli/ **adv** very: *awfully difficult/good*

awhile /əˈwaɪl/ **adv** US for a short time: *Let's wait awhile and see what happens.*

awkward /ˈɔːkwəd/ **adj 1 DIFFICULT** ▷ **ⓑ** difficult or causing problems: *an awkward customer* ∘ *an awkward question* **2 EMBARRASSING** ▷ **ⓑ2** embarrassing and not relaxed: *an awkward pause/silence* ∘ *I'm in an awkward situation.* **3 NOT ATTRACTIVE** ▷ moving in a way that is not attractive: *His movements were slow and awkward.* • **awkwardly adv** • **awkwardness noun** [U]

awoke /əˈwəʊk/ past tense of awake

awoken /əˈwəʊkən/ past participle of awake

awry /əˈraɪ/ **adv go awry** to not happen in the

correct way: *Suddenly everything started to go awry.*

axe[1] (also US **ax**) /æks/ **noun** [C] a tool consisting of a wooden handle with a sharp piece of metal at one end, used for cutting trees or wood

axe[2] (also US **ax**) /æks/ **verb** [T] to get rid of something or someone suddenly: *The company has announced plans to axe 500 jobs.*

axes /'æksiːz/ plural of axis

axis /'æksɪs/ **noun** [C] (plural **axes** /'æksiːz/) **1** an imaginary, central line around which an object turns **2** a line at the side or bottom of a graph (= picture showing measurements)

axle /'æksl/ **noun** [C] a long metal bar that connects two wheels on a vehicle

aye /aɪ/ **exclamation** informal yes, used especially in Scotland and the North of England

B

B

B, b /biː/ the second letter of the alphabet

BA /ˌbiːˈeɪ/ **noun** [C] abbreviation for Bachelor of Arts: a university or college qualification in an arts (= not science) subject that usually takes 3 or 4 years of study

baa /bɑː/ **noun** [C] the sound that a sheep makes

babble /ˈbæbl/ **verb** [I] to talk quickly in a way that is confused, silly, or has no meaning • **babble noun** [U] *the babble of voices*

babe /beɪb/ **noun** [C] **1** very informal a young, attractive woman **2** literary a baby

baby /ˈbeɪbi/ **noun** [C] **1 🅐** a very young child: *a baby girl/boy* ∘ *baby clothes* ∘ *Liz has **had a baby**.* ∘ *Maria's **expecting a baby** (= she is pregnant).* **2 🅐** a very young animal: *a baby bird*

🔲 Word partners for **baby**

have/be expecting/give birth to a baby • a baby is **born** • a new/newborn baby
---

ˈbaby ˌboom **noun** [C] a time when a lot of babies are born in a particular area: *the postwar baby boom*

ˈbaby ˌcarriage **noun** [C] US a small vehicle with four wheels for carrying a baby

babyish /ˈbeɪbiɪʃ/ **adj** Babyish behaviour is silly, like the behaviour of a young child.

babysit /ˈbeɪbisɪt/ **verb** [I, T] (**babysitting, babysat**) 🅑 to look after children while their parents are not at home • **babysitter noun** [C] 🅑 *We'd like to come, but we can't get a babysitter.* • **babysitting noun** [U]

bachelor /ˈbætʃələr/ **noun** [C] **1** a man who is not married **2 Bachelor of Arts/Science/Education, etc** a university or college qualification that usually takes 3 or 4 years of study, or a person who has this qualification

bachelor's degree /ˈbætʃələz dɪˌɡriː/ **noun** [C] (also US **bachelor's**) a university degree that is given after a course of study that usually takes three or four years

back¹ /bæk/ **adv** **1 RETURNING** ▷ 🅐 where someone or something was before: *When do you go back to college?* ∘ *I put it back in the cupboard.* **2 BEHIND** ▷ 🅑 in a direction behind you: *Anna stepped back.* ∘ *Flint leaned back in his chair.* **3 REPLY** ▷ 🅑 as a reply or reaction to something: *UK to ring back/US to call back* ∘ *I signalled to her and she waved back.* **4 STATE** ▷ 🅑 to the state something or someone was in before: *Hopefully things will **get back to normal** again now.* ∘ *I'm sure we can **put** it **back together** again (= repair it).* ∘ *Try to go back to sleep.* **5 EARLIER** ▷ 🅑 at or to an earlier time: *We first met **back in** 1973.* ∘ *Looking back, I think we did the right thing.* **6 AWAY FROM** ▷ 🅑 in a direction away from something: *He pulled back the curtain.* **7 back and forth** (also **backwards and forwards**) in one direction, then the opposite way, then in the original direction

---

again many times: *He has to travel back and forth between London and Paris every week.*

❗ Common learner error: **back to**

Remember to use the preposition **to** when you are talking about returning to a place.
I haven't seen her since she went back to Korea.
~~I haven't seen her since she went back Korea.~~
---

back² /bæk/ **noun** [C] **1 NOT FRONT** ▷ 🅐 the part of something that is furthest from the front or in the opposite direction to the front: *He wrote his number down on the back of an envelope.* ∘ *always keep a blanket in the back of the car* **2 BODY** ▷ 🅐 the part of your body from your shoulders to your bottom: *back injuries/pain* ∘ *He was lying on his back.* → See colour picture **The Body** on page Centre 13 **3 SEAT** ▷ the part of a seat that you lean against when you are sitting: *the back of a chair* **4 back to front** (also US **front to back**) with the back part of something where the front should be: *You've got your trousers on back to front.* **5 in back of** US behind: *They sat in back of us on the plane.*

IDIOMS **at/in the back of your mind** If you have a thought or idea at the back of your mind, you are always thinking about it. • **behind sb's back** If you do something behind someone's back, you do it without them knowing, often in an unfair way: *Have they been saying things about me behind my back?* • **be glad/happy, etc to see the back of sb/sth** UK to be pleased when someone leaves or something ends because you did not like them • **be on sb's back** to remind someone again and again to do something, or to criticize someone in an annoying way • **turn your back on sb/sth** to decide to stop having contact with someone or something, or to refuse to help someone: *She turned her back on Hollywood and went to live in Florida.*

→ See also **a pat² on the back, be (like) water off a duck's back**

back³ /bæk/ **verb** **1** [T] to give support or help to a person, plan, or idea: *He backed Mr Clark in the recent election.* **2** [T] to risk money by saying that you think a horse, team, etc will win a race, game, or competition in order to win more money if they do: *Many people are backing Holyfield to win the fight.* **3 back (sth) away/into/out, etc** to move backwards or drive backwards: *She saw he had a gun and backed away.*

PHRASAL VERBS **back away** to show that you do not support a plan or idea any more and do not want to be involved with it: *The government has backed away from plans to increase taxes.* • **back down** to admit that you were wrong, or agree not to do something: *The government **backed down over** tax rises.* • **back off 1** 🅑 to move away from someone, usually because you are afraid: *I saw the knife and backed off.* **2** mainly US

---

to stop supporting a plan: *The president has backed off from a threat to expel UN soldiers.* • **back out** 🄑 to decide not to do something you had planned or agreed to do: *Nigel backed out at the last minute, so we had a spare ticket.* • **back sb up 1** 🄑 to support or help someone: *My family backed me up in my fight for compensation.* **2** to say that someone is telling the truth: *Honestly, that's exactly what happened – Claire'll back me up.* • **back sth up 1** to prove that something is true: [often passive] *His claims are backed up by recent research.* **2** 🄑 to make an extra copy of computer information • **back (sth) up** to drive backwards

back⁴ /bæk/ *adj* **1** 🄐 [always before noun] at or near the back of something: *back door/page* ◦ *I put it in the back pocket of my jeans.* **2 back road/ street** a very small road or street that goes behind or between buildings → See also **put sth on the back burner**

backache /'bækeɪk/ *noun* [C, U] 🄑 a pain in your back

backbench /ˌbæk'bentʃ/ *adj* UK **a backbench MP/politician, etc** a member of the government who does not have an important position • **backbencher** *noun* [C] a backbench politician

the backbenches /ˌbæk'bentʃɪz/ *noun* [plural] UK the place where backbench politicians sit: *He prefers to remain on the backbenches.*

backboard /'bækbɔːd/ *noun* [C] in basketball, a board behind the metal ring that you have to throw the ball through to score → See colour picture **Sports 2** on page Centre 15

backbone /'bækbəʊn/ *noun* [C] **1** the main or strongest part of something: *The car industry remains the backbone of the area's economy.* **2** the line of bones down the centre of your back

backdrop /'bækdrɒp/ *noun* [C] **1** the situation that an event happens in: [usually singular] *The attack took place against a backdrop of rising tensions between the two communities.* **2** the painted cloth at the back of a stage in a theatre

backer /'bækər/ *noun* [C] someone who supports a person or plan, especially by giving them money

backfire /ˌbæk'faɪər/ *verb* [I] If something that you do backfires, it has the opposite result of what you wanted.

background /'bækgraʊnd/ *noun* **1 SOUND** ▷ [no plural] 🄑 Sounds in the background are not the main sounds you can hear: *background music/noise* ◦ *I could hear a baby crying in the background.* **2 PERSON** ▷ [C] 🄐 a person's education, family, and experience of life: *She came from a middle-class background.* **3 PICTURE** ▷ [C, U] 🄑 the parts at the back of a picture, view, etc that are not the main things you look at: *gold stars on a black background* **4 SITUATION** ▷ [C] 🄑 the situation that an event happens in, or things that have happened in the past that affect it: [usually singular] *The talks are taking place against a background of economic uncertainty.* **5 in the background** If a person stays in the background, they try not to be noticed.

✷ Word partners for background
come from a [poor/different, etc] background
• sb's **family** background

backhand /'bækhænd/ *noun* [C] a way of hitting the ball in sports such as tennis, made with your arm across your body

backing /'bækɪŋ/ *noun* [U] support, especially money, for a person or plan: *financial backing* ◦ *The proposal has the full backing of the government.*

backlash /'bæklæʃ/ *noun* [C] a reaction against an idea that was previously popular: [usually singular] *a backlash against the war*

backlog /'bæklɒg/ *noun* [C] work that should have been done earlier

backpack /'bækpæk/ *noun* [C] 🄒 a bag that you carry on your back → See picture at **luggage** • **backpacking** *noun* [U] 🄒 *to go backpacking* • **backpacker** *noun* [C]

backside /ˌbæk'saɪd/ 🅤🅢 /'bækˌsaɪd/ *noun* [C] informal the part of your body that you sit on

backslash /'bækslæʃ/ *noun* [C] the symbol '\', used in computer programs → Compare **forward slash**

backspace /'bækspeɪs/ *noun* [C, usually singular] the key that you press on a computer keyboard to move the cursor (= symbol showing your place on the screen) backwards and delete (= get rid of) the character before it • **backspace** *verb* [I] to use the backspace key

backstage /ˌbæk'steɪdʒ/ *adv* in the area behind the stage in a theatre where performers get ready

backstroke /'bækstrəʊk/ *noun* [U] a style of swimming on your back

back-to-back /ˌbæktə'bæk/ *adj, adv* **1** If two people or things are back-to-back, their backs are touching or facing each other: *They stood back-to-back.* **2** If two things happen back-to-back, one happens after the other without a pause: *back-to-back interviews*

backtrack /'bæktræk/ *verb* [I] to say that you did not mean something you said earlier: *The government has backtracked on its promises.*

backup /'bækʌp/ *noun* **1** [C, U] 🄒 extra help, support, or equipment that is available if you need it: *Medical staff are on call to provide backup in case of an emergency.* **2** [C] 🄑 an extra copy of computer information: *to make a backup*

backward /'bækwəd/ *adj* **1** [always before noun] in the direction behind you: *a backward glance* **2** less developed or slower to develop than normal: *a backward country*

backwards /'bækwədz/ *adv* (also **backward**) **1 DIRECTION** ▷ 🄒 towards the direction behind you: *She took a couple of steps backwards.* **2 EARLIER** ▷ towards an earlier time or an earlier stage of development: *Let's start with your most recent job and work backwards.* **3 OPPOSITE ORDER** ▷ in the opposite order to what is usual: *"Erehwon" is "nowhere" spelled backwards.* **4 WRONG WAY** ▷ (also **back to front**, also US **front to back**) with the part that is usually at the

front at the back: *Your T-shirt's on backwards.*
5 **backwards and forwards** (also **back and forth**) in one direction then the opposite way and back again many times: *I have to drive backwards and forwards between here and Ipswich every day.*

IDIOM **bend over backwards** to try extremely hard to help or to please someone: [+ to do sth] *She bent over backwards to help him.*

backyard /ˌbækˈjɑːd/ **noun** [C] US the area behind a house

bacon /ˈbeɪkən/ **noun** [U] **B1** meat from a pig cut into long thin slices

bacteria /bækˈtɪəriə/ **noun** [plural] very small living things that sometimes cause disease • **bacterial** **adj** made from or caused by bacteria: *bacterial infections*

bad /bæd/ **adj** (**worse, worst**) **1 NOT PLEASANT** ▷ **A1** not pleasant: *bad weather* ∘ *bad news* ∘ *My phone bill was even worse than I'd expected.* ∘ *He's in a bad mood today.* **2 LOW QUALITY** ▷ **A2** of low quality: *bad behaviour* ∘ *The service was really bad.* ∘ *He's always been **bad at** UK maths/US math.* **3 SEVERE** ▷ **B1** very serious or severe: *a bad injury* ∘ *the worst flooding for years* **4 NOT LUCKY** ▷ **B1** not lucky, not convenient, or not happening how you would like: *It was just bad luck that she heard us.* ∘ *Is this a bad time to ask?* **5 not bad** **A2** satisfactory: *"There are about 10 people in a group." "Oh well, that's not bad."* ∘ *That's **not bad for** such a small company.* **6 be bad for sb/sth** **A2** to be harmful for someone or something: *Looking at a computer screen for too long can be bad for your eyes.* **7 feel bad about sth/doing sth** **B1** to feel guilty or sorry about something that has happened: *I felt bad about letting her down.* **8 too bad a** **B1** mainly US informal used to say that you are sorry about a situation: *"He didn't get the job." "Oh, that's too bad."* **b** used to say that nothing can be done to change a situation: *I know you don't want to go but it's too bad, we have to.* **9 EVIL** ▷ **B1** evil: *She's a really bad person.* **10 NOT FRESH** ▷ **B2** Bad food is not fresh and cannot be eaten. **11 PAINFUL** ▷ [always before noun] If you have a bad arm, leg, heart, etc, there is something wrong with it and it is painful. → See also **bad blood**, **be in sb's good/bad books** (**book¹**)

baddie /ˈbædi/ **noun** [C] mainly UK informal a bad person in a film, book, etc

bade /bæd/ past tense of **bid³**

badge /bædʒ/ **noun** [C] **1** **B2** a piece of plastic, metal, etc that you wear on your clothes showing your name or the organization you work for **2** UK (US **button**) **B2** a piece of plastic, metal, etc with words or pictures on it that you wear on your clothes for decoration

badger /ˈbædʒər/ **noun** [C] a wild animal with thick black and white fur that lives under the ground and comes out at night

badly /ˈbædli/ **adv** (**worse, worst**) **1** **A2** very seriously: *badly damaged/injured* **2** **B2** in a way that is of low quality or in an unpleasant way: *to behave badly* ∘ *They played badly in the first half.*

badminton /ˈbædmɪntən/ **noun** [U] **A2** a sport

for two or four people in which you hit a shuttlecock (= a light object with feathers) over a net

bad-tempered /ˌbædˈtempəd/ **adj** **B2** a bad-tempered person gets angry or annoyed easily: *Sam's been bad-tempered recently, is something worrying him?*

baffle /ˈbæfl/ **verb** [T] If something baffles you, you cannot understand it at all: [often passive] *The police were baffled by his disappearance.*

bag

handbag

rucksack *UK*,
backpack *US*

carrier bag *UK*,
grocery bag *US*

briefcase

bag¹ /bæg/ **noun** [C] **1 CONTAINER** ▷ **A1** a container made of paper, plastic, etc, used for carrying things: *a paper/plastic bag* ∘ *He packed his **bags** and left.* **2 FOR WOMAN** ▷ (also **handbag**) mainly UK a bag with handles in which a woman carries her money, keys, etc **3 AMOUNT** ▷ the amount a bag contains: *It doesn't weigh more than a couple of bags of sugar.* **4 bags of sth** mainly UK informal a large amount of something: *There's bags of room.* **5 bags** Bags under your eyes are areas of loose or dark skin. → See also **carrier bag**, **let the cat out of the bag**, **shoulder bag**, **sleeping bag**, **tote bag**

bag² /bæg/ **verb** [T] (**bagging, bagged**) informal to get something, especially before other people have a chance to take it: *Bag us some decent seats.*

bagel /ˈbeɪɡəl/ **noun** [C] a type of bread made in the shape of a ring → See picture at **bread**

baggage /ˈbæɡɪdʒ/ **noun** [U] **1** **B1** all the cases and bags that you take with you when you travel: *We collected our suitcases from baggage reclaim.* **2** feelings and experiences from the past that influence how you think and behave now: *emotional baggage*

baggy /ˈbæɡi/ **adj** Baggy clothes are big and loose.

bagpipes /ˈbæɡpaɪps/ **noun** [plural] a Scottish musical instrument that is played by blowing air into a bag and forcing it through pipes

baguette /bæɡˈet/ **noun** [C] a French-style loaf of bread that is long and thin and white: *a ham and cheese baguette*

bail¹ /beɪl/ **noun** [U] an arrangement in which money is paid to a court so that someone can be released from prison until their trial: *He was released on bail.* ∘ *She was granted bail.*

bail² /beɪl/ **verb be bailed** If someone is bailed

B

until a particular time, they can leave prison until then if they pay money to the court.

PHRASAL VERB **bail sb out 1** to help a person or organization by giving them money: *Companies can't expect the government to keep bailing them out.* **2** to pay money to a court so that someone can be released from prison until their trial

bailiff /'beɪlɪf/ **noun** [C] **1** UK someone whose job is to take away things people own when they owe money **2** US someone whose job is to guard prisoners in a court

bailout /'beɪlaʊt/ **noun** [C] a situation in which a company is given money to solve its financial problems

bait¹ /beɪt/ **noun** [U, no plural] **1** food that is used to try to attract fish or animals so that you can catch them **2** something that you use to persuade someone to do something

bait² /beɪt/ **verb** [T] **1** to put food in or on something to try to catch fish or animals: *a mouse trap baited with cheese* **2** to try to make someone angry by laughing at them or criticizing them

bake /beɪk/ **verb** [I, T] 🅐🅐 to cook something such as bread or a cake with dry heat in an oven: *a baked apple* → See picture at **cook**

baked beans **noun** [plural] beans cooked in a tomato sauce and sold in cans

baked potato **noun** [C] a potato baked and served with the skin (= outer layer) still on

baker /'beɪkər/ **noun** [C] 🅑🅐 someone who makes and sells bread, cakes, etc: *Can you call at the baker's and get a loaf of bread?*

bakery /'beɪkəri/ **noun** [C] 🅑🅐 a shop where you can buy bread, cakes, etc

baking /'beɪkɪŋ/ **adj** informal Baking weather is very hot.

🔲 **Word partners for balance**

1 keep/lose your balance • knock/throw sb off balance • sb's sense of balance

2 find/maintain/strike a balance • redress the balance • a delicate balance • a balance between sth and sth

---

balance¹ /'bæləns/ **noun** **1** WEIGHT ▷ [U] 🅑🅐 the state of having your weight spread in such a way that you do not fall over: *I lost my balance and fell off the bike.* ∘ *The force of the explosion threw him off balance* (= it was difficult for him to stay standing). **2** EQUAL ▷ [U, no plural] 🅑🅐 a situation in which the correct amount of importance is given to each thing so that a situation is successful: *We hope to strike a balance between police powers and the protection of citizens.* → Opposite **imbalance 3** FAIR ▷ [U] the quality something has when it considers all the facts in a fair way: *I felt his report lacked balance.* **4** on balance 🅑🅐 used to give your opinion after you have considered all the facts about something: *On balance, I'd prefer a woman dentist to a man.* **5** MONEY ▷ [C] 🅑🅐 the amount of money that you still have to pay, or that you

have left to use: [usually singular] *I always pay off the balance on my credit card each month.*

IDIOM **be/hang in the balance** If something hangs in the balance, nobody knows if it will continue to exist in the future or what will happen to it: *After a bad year, Judd's career hung in the balance.*

balance² /'bæləns/ **verb 1** [I, T] 🅑🅑 to be in a position where you will not fall to either side, or to put something in this position: *She was trying to balance a book on her head.* **2** [T] 🅑🅑 to give the correct amount of importance to each thing so that a situation is successful: *I struggle to balance work and family commitments.* **3** balance the books/budget to make sure that you do not spend more money than you get

PHRASAL VERB **balance sth against sth** to compare the advantages and disadvantages of something: *The ecological effects of the factory need to be balanced against the employment it provides.*

balanced /'bælənst/ **adj 1** 🅑🅑 considering all the facts in a fair way: *a balanced discussion of his work* **2** **a balanced diet/meal** 🅑🅑 a healthy mixture of different kinds of food → See also **well-balanced**

balance of payments **noun** [no plural] mainly UK the difference between how much a country pays to other countries and how much it gets paid by other countries

balance of power **noun** [no plural] the way in which power is divided between different people or groups: *maintaining the balance of power in the European Union*

balance sheet **noun** [C] a document that shows what a company has earned and what it has spent

balcony /'bælkəni/ **noun** [C] **1** 🅑🅑 a small area joined to the wall outside a room on a high level where you can stand or sit **2** the seats in an upper area of a theatre

bald /bɔːld/ **adj 1** 🅑🅑 with little or no hair: *John started to go bald at an early age.* ∘ *I've got a bald patch/spot.* **2** [always before noun] Bald facts or ways of saying things are very clear and are not intended to comfort you. • **baldness noun** [U]

bald

balding /'bɔːldɪŋ/ **adj** becoming bald

baldly /'bɔːldli/ **adv** If you say something baldly, you say it in a very clear way that may upset the person you are speaking to: *"I don't love you any more," he said baldly.*

bale /beɪl/ **noun** [C] a large amount of something such as paper, cloth, or hay (= dried grass), that is tied together so that it can be stored or moved

baleful /'beɪlfəl/ **adj** formal evil or angry: *a baleful look*

balk (also UK **baulk**) /bɔːlk/ 🅤🅢 /bɔːk/ **verb** [I] to not want to do something that is unpleasant or difficult: *Most people balk at paying these kind of prices for clothes.*

B

ball /bɔːl/ **noun** [C] **1** ⓐ a round object that you throw, kick, or hit in a game, or something with this shape: *a tennis ball* ∘ *a ball of string* **2** a large formal occasion where people dance **3 have a ball** informal to enjoy yourself very much

IDIOMS **be on the ball** informal to be quick to understand and react to things • **set/start the ball rolling** to begin an activity that involves a group of people: *I've started the ball rolling by setting up a series of meetings.*

→ See also **ball game, crystal ball**

ballad /ˈbæləd/ **noun** [C] a song that tells a story, especially about love

ballerina /ˌbælərˈiːnə/ **noun** [C] a female ballet dancer

ballet /ˈbæleɪ/ ⓊⓈ /bælˈeɪ/ **noun 1 DANCING** ▷ [U] ⓑ a type of dancing that is done in a theatre and tells a story, usually with music **2 PERFORMANCE** ▷ [C] a particular story or performance of ballet dancing **3 DANCERS** ▷ [C] a group of ballet dancers who work together: *the Royal Ballet*

'ball ˌgame noun [C] US a game of baseball, basketball, or American football

IDIOM **a whole new ball game** (also **a different ball game**) informal a completely different situation from how things were before: *We'd been climbing in Scotland, but the Himalayas were a whole new ball game.*

ballistic /bəˈlɪstɪk/ **adj**

IDIOM **go ballistic** informal to suddenly become very angry

balloon

hot-air balloon

balloon¹ /bəˈluːn/ **noun** [C] ⓐ a small coloured rubber bag that you fill with air to play with or to use as a decoration: *Could you help me to **blow up** some **balloons**?* → See also **hot-air balloon**

balloon² /bəˈluːn/ **verb** [I] to suddenly become much larger: *I ballooned to 14 stone when I had my second baby.*

ballot¹ /ˈbælət/ **noun** [C, U] a secret written vote: *to **hold a ballot** ∘ She was the only candidate **on the ballot** (= available to vote for).* ∘ UK **ballot papers** ∘ *a **ballot box** (= box where votes are collected)*

ballot² /ˈbælət/ **verb** [T] mainly UK to ask people to vote in a ballot so that you can find out their opinion about something: *In July he will **ballot** his members **on** how they want to proceed.*

ballpark /ˈbɔːlpɑːk/ **noun 1** [C] US a place where baseball (= game where teams hit a ball and run round four fixed points) is played and watche **2 ballpark estimate/figure** a number o amount that is not exact but should be nea the correct number or amount: *$3 million woul be a ballpark figure for sales next year.*

ballpoint pen /ˌbɔːlpɔɪntˈpen/ **noun** [C] a pe with a very small ball in the end that rolls in onto the paper

ballroom /ˈbɔːlruːm/ **noun** [C] a large roon where dances are held

bamboo /bæmˈbuː/ **noun** [C, U] a tall plant with hard hollow stems, often used for making furniture

bamboo

ban¹ /bæn/ **verb** [T] (**banning, banned**) ⓑ to officially say that someone must not do something: *A lot of people think boxing should be banned.* ∘ [+ from + doing sth] *Ian's bee banned from driving for 2 years.*

ban² /bæn/ **noun** [C] ⓑ an official rule tha people must not do or use something: *There is ban on developing land around the city.*

🗹 Word partners for **ban**

impose/introduce/lift a ban • a **blanket/ complete/outright/total** ban • a ban **on** (doing) sth

banal /bəˈnɑːl/ **adj** ordinary and not exciting *banal pop songs*

banana /bəˈnɑːnə/ **noun** [C, U] ⓐ a long, curve fruit with a yellow skin → See colour picture **Fruit and Vegetables** on page Centre 10

band¹ /bænd/ **noun** [C] **1 MUSIC** ▷ ⓐ a group o musicians who play modern music together: *jazz band* **2 LINE** ▷ a line of a different colour o design: *The rugby team's shirts are white with red band around the middle.* **3 CIRCLE** ▷ a piece o material put around something: *an **elastic ban 4 PEOPLE** ▷ a group of people who do some thing together: *the Cathedral's band of regula worshippers* **5 PART** ▷ UK one of the groups tha something is divided into: *the 20-25 age ban* → See also **elastic band, rubber band**

band² /bænd/ **verb**

PHRASAL VERB **band together** to work with other people in order to achieve something: *Companies banded together to keep prices high.* → Opposite **disband**

bandage

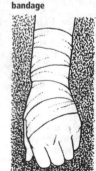

bandage¹ /ˈbændɪdʒ/ **noun** [C] ⓑ a long piece of soft cloth that you tie around an injured part of the body

bandage² /ˈbændɪdʒ/ **verb** [T] to put a

bandage around a wound or injury

Band-Aid /ˈbændeɪd/ **noun** [C] US trademark (UK **plaster**) a small piece of cloth or plastic that sticks to your skin to cover and protect a small wound

B and B /ˌbiːənˈbiː/ **noun** [C] abbreviation for bed and breakfast

bandit /ˈbændɪt/ **noun** [C] a thief who attacks people who are travelling in a wild place

bandwagon /ˈbændˌwæɡən/ **noun**

IDIOM **get/jump on the bandwagon** to become involved in an activity that is successful so that you can get the advantages of it yourself: *Publishers were rushing to get on the CD-ROM bandwagon.*

bandwidth /ˈbændwɪtθ/ **noun** [usually singular] the amount of information per second that can move between computers connected by a telephone wire

bang¹ /bæŋ/ **noun** [C] **1** ⓑ a sudden loud noise: *The door slammed with a deafening bang.* **2** an injury in which you suddenly hit part of your body on something hard: *a nasty bang on the head*

IDIOMS **go out with a bang** informal If someone or something goes out with a bang, they stop existing or doing something in an exciting way. • **more bang for your buck(s)** US informal the best result for the smallest effort

bang² /bæŋ/ **verb** [I, T] **1** ⓑ to make a loud noise, especially by hitting something against something hard: *We heard the door bang.* ◦ *Ben banged his fist on the desk.* **2** to hit part of your body against something hard: *Ted fell and banged his head.* → See also **be banging your head¹ against a brick wall**

bang³ /bæŋ/ **adv** UK informal exactly: *The books were piled up **slap bang** in the middle of the kitchen table.* ◦ *The curtain rose **bang on time.***

banger /ˈbæŋəʳ/ **noun** [C] UK informal **1** an old car that is in a bad condition **2** a sausage (= tube of meat and spices)

bangle /ˈbæŋɡl/ **noun** [C] a circle of stiff plastic, metal, etc that people wear around the arm as jewellery

bangs /bæŋz/ **noun** [plural] US (UK **fringe**) hair that is cut short and straight at the top of someone's face

banish /ˈbænɪʃ/ **verb** [T] **1** to send someone away from a place, often as a punishment: [often passive] *He was **banished to** a remote Alaskan island.* **2** to make yourself stop thinking about something or feeling a particular way: *Banish winter blues with a holiday in the sun!*

banister /ˈbænɪstəʳ/ **noun** [C] a long piece of wood that you can hold as you go up or down stairs

banjo /ˈbændʒəʊ/ **noun** [C] a musical instrument like a guitar with a round body

bank¹ /bæŋk/ **noun** [C] **1** MONEY ▷ ⓐ an organization or place where you can borrow money, save money, etc: *Most banks are reluctant to lend money to new businesses.* **2** RIVER ▷ ⓑ the land along the side of a river: *We found a*

shady spot on the river bank. **3** STORE ▷ a place where a supply of something can be kept until it is needed: *a blood bank* **4** PILE ▷ a large pile of snow, sand, or soil → See also **bottle bank, merchant bank, piggy bank**

bank² /bæŋk/ **verb 1** [I, T] to put or keep money in a bank: *to bank a cheque* ◦ *Who do you **bank with**?* ◦ *I **bank at** the First National Bank.* **2** [I] When a plane banks, it flies with one wing higher than the other when turning.

PHRASAL VERB **bank on sb/sth** to depend on someone doing something or something happening: *Chrissie might arrive on time, but I wouldn't bank on it.*

bank account **noun** [C] ⓑ an arrangement with a bank to keep your money there and take it out when you need to

banker /ˈbæŋkəʳ/ **noun** [C] ⓑ someone who has an important job in a bank

bank holiday **noun** [C] UK an official holiday when all banks and most shops and offices are closed

banking /ˈbæŋkɪŋ/ **noun** [U] ⓑ the business of operating a bank

banknote /ˈbæŋknəʊt/ **noun** [C] mainly UK (US **bill**) a piece of paper money

bankrupt¹ /ˈbæŋkrʌpt/ **adj** unable to continue in business because you cannot pay your debts: *He **went bankrupt** after only a year in business.*

bankrupt² /ˈbæŋkrʌpt/ **verb** [T] to make someone bankrupt

bankruptcy /ˈbæŋkrəptsi/ **noun** [C, U] a situation in which someone is bankrupt: *Factories that continue to make losses could soon face bankruptcy.*

bank statement **noun** [C] a piece of paper that shows how much money you have put into your bank account and how much you have taken out

banner /ˈbænəʳ/ **noun** [C] a long piece of cloth, often stretched between poles, with words or a sign written on it

banner ad **noun** [C] an advertisement that appears across the top of a page on the Internet

banquet /ˈbæŋkwɪt/ **noun** [C] a large formal dinner for a lot of people

banter /ˈbæntəʳ/ **noun** [U] conversation that is funny and not serious

baptism /ˈbæptɪzᵊm/ **noun** [C, U] a Christian ceremony in which water is put on someone to show that they are a member of the Church

Baptist /ˈbæptɪst/ **adj** belonging or relating to a Christian group that only believes in baptism for people who are old enough to understand what it means: *the Baptist Church* • **Baptist noun** [C]

baptize (also UK **-ise**) /bæpˈtaɪz/ ⓤ /ˈbæptaɪz/ **verb** [T] to perform a baptism ceremony for someone

bar¹ /bɑːʳ/ **noun** [C] **1** DRINKING ▷ ⓐ a place where alcoholic drinks are sold and drunk, or the area behind the person serving the drinks: *I met him in a bar in Soho.* **2** BLOCK ▷ ⓑ a small block of something solid: *a chocolate bar* ◦ *gold bars* → See colour picture **Pieces and Quantities**

on page Centre 1 **3 LONG PIECE** ▷ ⑫ a long, thin piece of metal or wood: *There were bars on the downstairs windows.* **4 PREVENTING SUCCESS** ▷ something that prevents you doing something or having something: *Lack of money should not be **a bar to** a good education.* **5 MUSIC** ▷ one of the short, equal groups of notes that a piece of music is divided into: *The band played the first few bars.* **6 the bar** lawyers thought of as a group: *Haughey was **called to the bar** (= became a lawyer) in 1949.*

IDIOM **behind bars** in prison

bar² /bɑːr/ **verb** [T] (**barring, barred**) **1 PREVENT** ▷ to officially prevent someone from doing something or going somewhere, or to prevent something from happening: [+ from + doing sth] *The court barred him from contacting his former wife.* **2 KEEP OUT** ▷ to stop someone going into a place: *A line of policemen barred the entrance to the camp.* **3 CLOSE** ▷ to close and lock a door or gate

bar³ /bɑːr/ **preposition 1** except: *I've read all her books, **bar one**.* **2 bar none** used to emphasize that someone or something is the best: *the best suspense writer going, bar none*

barbarian /bɑːˈbeəriən/ **noun** [C] someone who behaves in a way that shows they are not well educated and do not care about the feelings of others

barbaric /bɑːˈbærɪk/ **adj** violent and cruel: *a barbaric act of violence* • **barbarically adv**

barbecue¹ /ˈbɑːbɪkjuː/ **noun** [C] **1** ⓐ⓶ a party at which you cook food over a fire outdoors **2** ⓐ⓶ a metal frame for cooking food over a fire outdoors

barbecue

barbecue² /ˈbɑːbɪkjuː/ **verb** [I, T] (**barbecuing, barbecued**) ⓑ⓵ to cook food on a barbecue: *barbecued chicken wings*

barbed wire /ˌbɑːbdˈwaɪər/ **noun** [U] strong wire with short, sharp points on it to keep people out of a place: *a barbed wire fence*

barbed wire

barber /ˈbɑːbər/ **noun** [C] someone whose job is to cut men's hair

barber's /ˈbɑːbəz/ **noun** [C] (plural **barbers**) (also US **barbershop**) a place where men and boys get their hair cut: *Dad goes to **the barber's** once a month.*

'bar ˌcode noun [C] a row of black lines on something you buy, that a computer reads to find the price

bar-coded /ˈbɑːˌkəʊdɪd/ **adj** having a bar code (= a row of black lines on something you buy) printed on it

bare¹ /beər/ **adj 1 NO CLOTHES** ▷ ⑫ not covered by clothes: *a bare chest* ∘ *She ran out into the road **in her bare feet**.* **2 NOT COVERED** ▷ ⑫ not covered by anything: *bare floorboards* **3 EMPTY** ▷

empty: *a bare room* ∘ *The cupboard was bare.* **4 BASIC** ▷ including only the smallest amount that you need of something: *The report just gave us the barest facts about the accident.* ∘ *Tony's salary only covers **the bare essentials** for the family.* → See also **with your bare hands** (**hand¹**)

bare² /beər/ **verb** [T] to take away the thing that is covering something so that it can be seen: *He bared his chest.* ∘ *The dog bared its teeth.*

barefoot /ˈbeəfʊt/ **adj, adv** not wearing any shoes or socks: *They ran barefoot along the wet beach.*

barely /ˈbeəli/ **adv** ⑫ only just: *He was barely alive when they found him.*

barf /bɑːf/ **verb** [I] US very informal to vomit • **barf noun** [U]

bargain¹ /ˈbɑːɡɪn/ **noun** [C] **1** ⑫ something that is sold for less than its usual price or its real value: *At $8.95, it's a bargain.* **2** an agreement between two people or groups in which each promises to do something in exchange for something else: *They were prepared to **strike a bargain** to avoid more fighting.* **3 into the bargain** mainly UK as well as everything else: *Caffeine has no good effects on health and is mildly addictive into the bargain.*

> ✐ Word partners for **bargain**
>
> get/pick up/snap up a bargain • a bargain price • bargain hunting

bargain² /ˈbɑːɡɪn/ **verb** [I] to try to make someone agree to something better for you: *Do not hesitate to **bargain over** the price.*

PHRASAL VERB **bargain for/on sth** to expect or be prepared for something: *We hadn't bargained on such a long wait.* ∘ *The stormy weather proved to be **more than** anybody **bargained for**.*

barge¹ /bɑːdʒ/ **noun** [C] a long, narrow boat with a flat bottom that is used to carry goods

barge² /bɑːdʒ/ **verb** informal **barge past, through/ahead, etc** to walk somewhere quickly, pushing people or things out of the way: *Fred barged through the crowd.*

PHRASAL VERB **barge in/barge into sth** to walk into a room quickly and without being invited

baritone /ˈbærɪtəʊn/ **noun** [C] a man who sings in a voice that is quite low

bark¹ /bɑːk/ **noun 1** [U] the hard substance that covers the surface of a tree **2** [C] the sound that a dog makes

bark² /bɑːk/ **verb 1** [I] ⑫ If a dog barks, it makes loud, short sounds. **2** [I, T] to say something loudly and quickly: *I'm sorry, I had no right to bark at you like that.*

barley /ˈbɑːli/ **noun** [U] a type of grain used for making food and alcoholic drinks

barmaid /ˈbɑːmeɪd/ **noun** [C] UK (US **bartender**) a woman who serves drinks in a bar

barman /ˈbɑːmən/ **noun** [C] (plural **barmen**) UK (US **bartender**) ⑪ a man who serves drinks in a bar

bar mitzvah /ˌbɑːˈmɪtsvə/ **noun** [usually singular]

a religious ceremony for a Jewish boy when he reaches the age of 13

barmy /ˈbɑːmi/ **adj** UK informal crazy or silly: *What a barmy idea!*

barn /bɑːn/ **noun** [C] a large building on a farm where crops or animals can be kept

barometer /bəˈrɒmɪtəʳ/ **noun** [C] **1** a way of showing what people think or what the quality of something is: *Car sales are viewed as a barometer of consumer confidence.* **2** a piece of equipment that measures air pressure (= the force of the air) and shows when the weather will change

baron /ˈbærᵊn/ **noun** [C] **1** a man of high social rank in the UK and other parts of Europe **2** a man who owns or controls a lot of a particular industry: *a wealthy media baron*

baroness /ˈbærᵊnes/ **noun** [C] a woman of the same rank as a baron or married to a baron, or a title given to a woman in the UK who has earned official respect: *Baroness Thatcher*

baroque /bəˈrɒk/ **adj** relating to the style of art, building, and music that was popular in Europe in the 17th and early 18th century, and that had a lot of decoration

barracks /ˈbærəks/ **noun** [C] (plural **barracks**) a group of buildings where soldiers live

barrage /ˈbærɑːdʒ/ ⓤ /bəˈrɑːdʒ/ **noun 1** a **barrage of sth** a lot of questions, complaints, or criticisms: *He faced a barrage of questions about his decision to leave the show.* **2** [C] a continuous attack with several big guns

barrel /ˈbærᵊl/ **noun** [C] **1** a large, round container for storing liquids such as oil or wine **2** the tube in a gun that the bullet shoots out of

barrel

barren /ˈbærᵊn/ **adj 1** Land that is barren does not produce crops. **2** old-fashioned A woman who is barren cannot have children.
• **barrenness** noun [U]

barricade¹ /ˌbærɪˈkeɪd/ **noun** [C] something that is quickly put across a road or entrance to prevent people from going past

barricade² /ˌbærɪˈkeɪd/ **verb** [T] to build a barricade somewhere: [often reflexive] *They barricaded themselves in the building (= built a barricade so that nobody could get to them).*

barrier /ˈbæriəʳ/ **noun** [C] **1** a type of fence that prevents people from going into an area: *Police erected barriers to hold back the crowd.* **2** something that prevents people from doing what they want to do: *Shyness is a big barrier to making friends.* → See also **crash barrier**

> 🗹 **Word partners for barrier**
>
> act as/be/create/serve as a barrier to sth
> • break through/overcome/remove a barrier
> • the biggest/the main/a major barrier
> • [age/size, etc] is no barrier to sth

barring /ˈbɑːrɪŋ/ **preposition** if something does not happen: *We should arrive at about five o'clock, barring accidents.*

barrister /ˈbærɪstəʳ/ **noun** [C] in the UK, a lawyer who can work in the highest courts → See Note at **lawyer**

barrow /ˈbærəʊ/ UK (UK/US **wheelbarrow**) a big, open container with a wheel at the front and handles that is used to move things, especially around in a garden

bartender /ˈbɑːˌtendəʳ/ **noun** [C] US (UK **barman/barmaid**) someone who serves drinks in a bar

barter /ˈbɑːtəʳ/ **verb** [I, T] to exchange goods or services for other goods or services, without using money

base¹ /beɪs/ **noun** [C] **1 BOTTOM** ▷ ⓑ the bottom part of something, or the part something rests on: *I felt a sharp pain at the base of my thumb.* **2 MAIN PART** ▷ the most important part of something, from which other things can develop: *a solid economic base* **3 PLACE** ▷ ⓑ the main place where a person lives or works, or from where they do things: *The hotel is a good base for a holiday.* **4 ARMY** ▷ ⓑ a place where people in the army or navy live and work: *an American Air Force base* **5 ORGANIZATION** ▷ the place where the main work of an organization is done: *The company's European base is in Frankfurt.* **6 SUBSTANCE** ▷ the main substance in a mixture: *paints with an oil base* **7 BASEBALL** ▷ one of the four places in baseball that a player must run to in order to win a point **8 CHEMISTRY** ▷ a chemical substance with a pH (= measure of how acid something is) of more than 7 **9 MATHS** ▷ a number that is used as the most important unit in a system of counting: *The binary system of counting uses base 2.*

IDIOMS **be off base** US informal to be wrong: *In 1893, many of the forecasts about 1993 were way off base.* • **touch/cover all the bases** mainly US to deal with every part of a situation or activity

base² /beɪs/ **verb be based at/in, etc** ⓑ If you are based at/in, etc a particular place, that is the main place where you live or work: *The company is based in Geneva.*

PHRASAL VERB **base something on/upon sth** ⓑ If you base something on facts or ideas, you use those facts or ideas to develop it: *Her latest TV serial is based on a true story.*

baseball /ˈbeɪsbɔːl/ **noun 1** [U] ⓐ a game in which two teams try to win points by hitting a ball and running around four fixed points **2** [C] ⓐ the ball used in this game → See colour picture **Sports 2** on page Centre 15

baseball cap **noun** [C] a type of hat with a long flat piece at the front to protect the eyes from the sun → See colour picture **Clothes** on page Centre 9

base camp **noun** [C] the place from which people go to climb mountains

basement /ˈbeɪsmənt/ **noun** [C] ⓑ a room or set of rooms that is below ground level in a building

bases /ˈbeɪsiːz/ plural of basis

bash¹ /bæʃ/ **verb** [T] informal **1** to hit someone or

B

something hard: *I bashed my arm on the car door as I got out.* **2 immigrant-bashing/lawyer-bashing/union-bashing, etc** strong and unfair criticism of particular groups

bash² /bæʃ/ **noun** [C] *informal* **1** a party **2** a hard hit on something: *a bash on the nose* **3 have a bash (at sth)** UK *informal* to try to do something: *I've never been water-skiing but I'd love to have a bash at it.*

bashful /'bæʃfºl/ **adj** shy and easily embarrassed
• **bashfully** adv

basic /'beɪsɪk/ **adj 1 MAIN** ▷ [always before noun] **B1** being the main or most important part of something: *basic ideas/principles* **2 NECESSARY** ▷ **B1** including or providing only the things that are most necessary: *basic training/services/skills* **3 SIMPLE** ▷ **B1** very simple, with nothing special added: *My software is pretty basic.*

basically /'beɪsɪkºli/ **adv 1 B2** in the most important ways: *Frazier's films are basically documentaries.* ∘ *The two PCs are basically the same.* **2** used to introduce a short explanation about something: *Basically, what he's saying is that we need more time.*

the basics /'beɪsɪks/ **noun B2** the most important facts, skills, or needs: *the basics of computer technology*

basil /'bæzºl/ US /'beɪzºl/ **noun** [U] a herb with a sweet smell

basin /'beɪsºn/ **noun** [C] **1 BOWL** ▷ *mainly UK* a bowl for liquids or food: *a basin of water* **2 BATHROOM** ▷ *mainly UK* (UK/US **sink**) **B1** the bowl that is fixed to the wall in a bathroom, where you can wash your hands and face **3 LAND** ▷ a low area of land from which water flows into a river

basis /'beɪsɪs/ **noun** [C] (plural **bases** /'beɪsiːz/) **1 on a daily/monthly/regular, etc basis B2** how often something happens or is done: *Meetings are held on a weekly basis.* **2 on a commercial/full-time/percentage, etc basis B2** the way something happens or is organized: *We will consider claims for asylum on a case by case basis.* **3** the reason for something: *Marks are awarded **on the basis of** progress and performance.* ∘ *There is no legal basis for his claim.* **4** a situation, fact, or idea from which something can develop: *Dani's essay can serve as **a basis for** our discussion.*

bask /bɑːsk/ **verb** [I] to sit or lie in a place that is warm: *Seals basked on the rocks.*

PHRASAL VERB **bask in sth** to enjoy the way other people admire you: *They basked in the glory victory had brought them.*

basket /'bɑːskɪt/ **noun** [C] **1 B1** a container with a handle made of thin pieces of wood, wire, plastic, etc: *a shopping basket* **2** points scored when a player throws the ball through the net in basketball → See also **wastepaper basket**

basketball /'bɑːskɪtbɔːl/ **noun 1** [U] **A2** a game in which two teams try to win points by throwing a ball through a high net **2** [C] **A2** the large ball used in the game of basketball → See colour picture **Sports 2** on page Centre 15

bass /beɪs/ **noun 1 VOICE** ▷ [C] a man who sings

with a very low voice **2 MUSIC** ▷ [U] the lower half of the set of musical notes **3 INSTRUMENT** ▷ [C, U] (also **double bass**) a large, wooden musical instrument with four strings that you play while standing up or sitting on a high chair **4 GUITAR** ▷ [C, U] (also **bass gui'tar**) an electric guitar that makes a low sound

bassoon /bə'suːn/ **noun** [C] a long, wooden musical instrument that you blow through to make a low sound

bastard /'bɑːstəd/ **noun** [C] **1** an offensive word for a man you do not like **2** old-fashioned an offensive word for a child whose parents are not married

bastion /'bæstiən/ **noun** [C] a place, organization, etc where particular ideas or ways of doing things are protected: *The Internet has been described as a bastion of free speech.*

bat¹ /bæt/ **noun** [C] **1 A2** a piece of wood used to hit the ball in some sports **2 B1** a small animal like a mouse with wings that flies at night

bat² /bæt/ **verb** [I] (**batting, batted**) to try to hit a ball with a bat: *Rimmer batted well for Oxford.* → See also **not bat an eyelid**

batch /bætʃ/ **noun** [C] a group of things or people that are dealt with at the same time or are similar in type: *the university's first **batch of** students* ∘ *Fry the aubergines in batches.*

bated /'beɪtɪd/ **adj** → See **with bated breath**

bath¹ /bɑːθ/ **noun** [C] **1** UK (US **bathtub**) **A1** the container that you sit or lie in to wash your body → See colour picture **The Bathroom** on page Centre 3 **2 A1** the act of washing your body in a bath, or the water in the bath: [usually singular] UK *I'll just **have a** quick bath.* ∘ UK *She ran herself a bath* (= filled a bath with water).

bath

bath² /bɑːθ/ **verb** [I, T] UK (US **bathe**) to wash yourself or someone else in a bath: *Emma usually baths the kids about seven o'clock.*

bathe /beɪð/ **verb 1 WASH YOURSELF** ▷ [I, T] *mainly US* (UK **bath**) to wash yourself or someone else in a bath: *I bathe every day.* **2 PART OF BODY** ▷ [T] to wash part of someone's body, often because it is hurt: *Bathe your eye with cool salty water.* **3 SWIM** ▷ [I] old-fashioned to swim **4 be bathed in light** to look attractive in a beautiful light: *The mountain was bathed in red-gold light from the setting sun.*

'bathing suit noun [C] a piece of clothing that you wear to swim in

bathrobe /'bɑːθrəʊb/ **noun** [C] a soft coat that you wear before or after a bath

bathroom /'bɑːθruːm/ **noun** [C] **1 A1** a room with a bath, sink, and often a toilet → See colour picture **The Bathroom** on page Centre 3 **2 go to the bathroom** US to use the toilet → See Note at **toilet**

bathtub /'bɑːθtʌb/ **noun** [C] US (UK **bath**) the

container that you sit or lie in to wash your body → See colour picture **The Bathroom** on page Centre 3

bat mitzvah /ˌbætˈmitsvə/ **noun** [usually singular] a religious ceremony for a Jewish girl when she reaches the age of 12 or 13

baton /ˈbætⁿn/ ⑤ /bəˈtɑːn/ **noun** [C] **1 STICK** ▷ a thin stick used to control the rhythm of a group of musicians **2 POLICE** ▷ a thick stick that a police officer uses as a weapon **3 RACE** ▷ a stick that a runner passes to the next person in a race

batsman /ˈbætsmən/ **noun** [C] (plural **batsmen**) UK the person who is trying to hit the ball in cricket → See colour picture **Sports 2** on page Centre 15

battalion /bəˈtæliən/ **noun** [C] a large group of soldiers made from several smaller groups

batter¹ /ˈbætər/ **noun** **1** [U] a mixture of flour, milk, and often eggs used to make cakes and pancakes (= thin fried cakes), and to cover fish, etc before it is fried **2** [C] the person who is trying to hit the ball in baseball → See colour picture **Sports 2** on page Centre 15

batter² /ˈbætər/ **verb** [I, T] to hit someone or something repeatedly very hard: *If you don't open up we'll **batter** the door **down**. ∘ Waves **battered against** the rocks.*

battered /ˈbætəd/ **adj** old and not in very good condition: *a battered copy of her favourite novel*

battering /ˈbætərɪŋ/ **noun** [C] If someone or something takes a battering, they are repeatedly hit, criticized, or damaged: [usually singular] *The prime minister has **taken** quite **a battering** this week.*

battery /ˈbætəri/ **noun** **1** [C] ⓐ₂ an object that provides electricity for things such as radios, toys, or cars: UK *My car has **a flat battery** (= one that has no electricity left).* **2** [U] formal the crime of hitting someone: *assault and battery*

battery

battle¹ /ˈbætl/ **noun** **1 WAR** ▷ [C, U] ⓑ₁ a fight between two armies in a war: *the Battle of Waterloo ∘ Her grandfather was killed **in battle** (= while fighting).* **2 POWER** ▷ [C] a situation in which two people or groups compete against each other or have an argument about something: *a **battle for** control in the boardroom* **3 PROBLEMS/ILLNESS** ▷ [C] ⓑ₂ a fight against something that is hurting or destroying you: *a long battle against cancer*

IDIOM **fight a losing battle** to try hard to do something when there is no chance that you will succeed: *I try to control what my children watch on TV, but I think I'm fighting a losing battle.*

> ◪ Word partners for **battle**
>
> face/fight/lose/win a battle • a bitter/long-running/uphill battle • a legal battle • a battle for sth • a battle with sb/between sb and sb

battle² /ˈbætl/ **verb** [I] to try very hard to do something that is difficult: *Twelve teams **are**

battling for *a place in the final. ∘ Throughout the campaign Johnson was **battling against** severe health problems.*

baulk /bɔːk, bɔːlk/ **verb** [I] UK (UK/US **balk**) to not want to do something that is unpleasant or difficult: *Most people would **baulk at** paying these kinds of prices for clothes.*

bawl /bɔːl/ **verb** [I, T] informal to shout or cry loudly: *That baby's been bawling for hours.*

bay /beɪ/ **noun** **1** [C] ⓑ₁ an area of coast where the land curves in: *a sandy bay* **2** [C] a small area in a building or place that is used for a particular purpose, for example storing something: *a parking bay* **3 keep/hold sth at bay** to prevent something unpleasant from coming near you or from happening: *Gunmen kept police at bay for almost four hours.*

bayonet /ˈbeɪənət/ **noun** [C] a knife that is fastened onto the end of a long gun

bazaar /bəˈzɑːr/ **noun** [C] **1** a market in Eastern countries **2** a sale where goods are sold to raise money for a school, church, etc

B&B /ˌbiːənˈbiː/ **noun** [C] abbreviation for bed and breakfast (= a small hotel or private house where you pay for a room to sleep in for the night and a meal in the morning)

BBC /ˌbiːbiːˈsiː/ **noun** abbreviation for British Broadcasting Corporation: one of the main television and radio companies in the United Kingdom: *a cookery programme on BBC2*

BC /biːˈsiː/ abbreviation for Before Christ: used to show that a particular year came before the birth of Christ: *331 BC*

bcc abbreviation for blind carbon copy: used when you are sending a copy of a letter or an email to someone without the knowledge of the other people that it is sent to

be¹ strong /biː/ weak /bi, bɪ/ **verb** (**being, was, been**) **1** ⓐ₁ used to describe or give information about someone or something: *I'm sixteen. ∘ I'm Andy. ∘ Her mother is a teacher. ∘ He's German. ∘ They were very upset. ∘ He was very ill last year. ∘ I'm sorry I'm late. ∘ They've been unlucky. ∘ Be quiet!* **2 there is/there are/there was, etc** ⓐ₁ used to show that someone or something exists: *There were about fifty people at the party. ∘ Is there a bank near here?* **3** ⓐ₁ used to show the position of someone or something: *It's been in the cupboard for months. ∘ She's in the kitchen.* **4 it is/it was, etc** used to give a fact or your opinion about something: *It's not surprising that she left him. ∘ It's a good idea to keep a spare key somewhere safe.*

be² strong /biː/ weak /bi, bɪ/ **auxiliary verb** **1** ⓐ₂ used with the present participle of other verbs to describe actions that are or were still continuing: *Where are you going? ∘ How long have you been sitting there? ∘ He was standing by the window. ∘ He's working at the moment.* **2** ⓐ₂ used with the present participle of other verbs, and sometimes after a modal verb, to describe actions that will happen in the future: *I'm going to France next week. ∘ I'll be coming back on Tuesday.* **3** ⓐ₂ used with the past participle of other verbs to form the passive: *He was injured in a car crash. ∘ The results will be announced next* *week.* **4** used in conditional sentences to say what might happen: *If he were to offer me the job, I'd take it.* **5** used to say that someone must or should do something: *You are not to see him again.* **6** formal used to show that something has been organized: *They are to stay with us when they arrive.*

beach /biːtʃ/ **noun** [C] ⓐⓘ an area of sand or rocks next to the sea

> 🗹 Word partners for **beach**
>
> on the beach • a **sandy** beach • a beach house

beacon /ˈbiːkən/ **noun** [C] a light on a hill or in a tower that warns people of something or is a signal or guide

bead /biːd/ **noun** [C] **1** a small, round ball of glass, plastic, or wood that is used for making jewellery: *a necklace of coloured glass beads* **2** a small drop of liquid on a surface: *beads of sweat*

beak /biːk/ **noun** [C] the hard part of a bird's mouth

beak

beaker /ˈbiːkər/ **noun** [C] UK a tall cup without a handle, usually made of plastic

beam¹ /biːm/ **noun** [C] **1** ⓑ② a line of light shining from something: *a laser beam* → See picture at **light 2** a long, thick piece of wood, metal, or concrete that is used to support weight in a building or other structure

beam² /biːm/ **verb 1** SMILE ▷ [I] to smile very happily: *The baby beamed at me.* **2** SEND ▷ [T] to send a television or radio signal: [often passive] *The match was beamed live by satellite around the world.* **3** SHINE ▷ [I] If the sun or the moon beams, it shines brightly.

beamer /ˈbiːmər/ **noun** [C] a data projector: a machine that allows you to show words or images on a screen or wall

bean /biːn/ **noun** [C] **1** SEED ▷ ⓐ② a seed of some climbing plants, that is used as food: *soya beans* **2** VEGETABLE ▷ ⓐ② a part of some climbing plants that contains the seeds and is eaten as a vegetable: *green beans* **3** COFFEE/CHOCOLATE ▷ a plant seed used to make coffee and chocolate: *coffee beans* → See also **baked beans, runner bean**

bean curd /ˈbiːnkɜːd/ **noun** [U] tofu (= a soft, pale food made from the soya bean plant)

bear¹ /beər/ **verb** [T] (**bore, borne**) **1** ACCEPT ▷ ⓑ② to accept someone or something unpleasant: *She couldn't bear the thought of him suffering.* ∘ *I like her, but I can't bear her friends.* ∘ *[+ to do sth] How can you bear to watch?* ∘ *The pain was too much to bear.* **2 bear a resemblance/relation, etc to sb/sth** to be similar to someone or something: *He bears a striking resemblance to his father.* **3** CARRY ▷ formal to carry something: *He came in, bearing a tray of drinks.* **4** WEIGHT ▷ to support the weight of something: *I don't think that chair will bear his weight.* **5 bear the responsibility/cost, etc** to

accept that you are responsible for something, you should pay for something, etc: *He must bear some responsibility for the appalling conditions in the prison.* **6** FEELING ▷ to continue to have a bad feeling towards someone: *They were rude to her in the past, but she's not the kind of woman who bears grudges* (= continues to be angry). **7** HAVE CHILD ▷ formal to give birth to a child: *She has been told that she will never bear children.* **8** NAME ▷ to have or show a particular name, picture, or symbol: *The shop bore his family name.* **9 bear left/right** to turn left or right: *Bear right at the next set of traffic lights.* → See also **bear fruit, grin and bear it**

PHRASAL VERBS **bear sb/sth out** to prove that someone is right or that something is true: *The facts do not bear out his claims.* • **bear with sb** to be patient and wait while someone does something: *If you'll bear with me a moment, I'll just find your details.*

bear² /beər/ **noun** [C] ⓐ② a large, strong, wild animal with thick fur → See also **polar bear, teddy bear**

bear

bearable /ˈbeərəbl/ **adj** If an unpleasant situation is bearable, you can accept or deal with it: *Having her there made life at home more bearable for me.* → Opposite **unbearable**

beard /bɪəd/ **noun** [C] ⓐⓘ the hair that grows on a man's chin (= the bottom of his face) • **bearded adj** with a beard

bearer /ˈbeərər/ **noun** [C] a person who brings or carries something: *I am sorry to be the bearer of bad news.*

bearing /ˈbeərɪŋ/ **noun have a bearing on sth** to have an influence on something or a relationship to something: *What you decide now could have a considerable bearing on your future.*

bearings /ˈbeərɪŋz/ **noun 1 get/find your bearings a** to find out where you are: *She looked at the sun to find her bearings.* **b** to become confident in a new situation: *When you start a new job, it can take some time to get your bearings.* **2 lose your bearings** to become confused about where you are

beast /biːst/ **noun** [C] **1** an animal, especially a large or wild one: *lions, tigers and other wild beasts* **2** old-fashioned an annoying or cruel person: *Her ex-husband was an absolute beast.*

beastly /ˈbiːstli/ **adj** old-fashioned unkind or unpleasant

beat¹ /biːt/ **verb** (**beat, beaten**, also US **beat**) **1** DEFEAT ▷ ⓑⓘ to defeat someone in a competition: *Our team beat Germany 3-1.* → See Note at **win¹ 2** HIT ▷ [I, T] ⓑ② to hit a person or animal hard many times: *She beat the dog with a stick.* ∘ *She was beaten to death.* **3** SOUND ▷ [I, T] to hit against something hard, making a continuous or regular sound: *Rain beat against* the windows. ◦ The soldiers started beating their drums **4 GET RID OF** ▷ [T] to get rid of something bad: *I'm determined to beat this illness.* **5 HEART** ▷ [I] [B1] When your heart beats, it makes regular movements and sounds: *By the time the doctor arrived, his heart had stopped beating.* **6 BE BETTER** ▷ [T] informal to be better than something: [+ doing sth] *Being at the youth club beats sitting at home.* **7 you can't beat sth** used to emphasize that something is best: *You can't beat Pedro's for a great pizza.* **8 take a lot of/some, etc beating** mainly UK to be so good or enjoyable that it is hard to find anything better: *For romantic movies, The Notebook takes some beating.* **9 FOOD** ▷ [T] to mix food using hard, quick movements: *Beat the egg whites until they are stiff.* → See also **beat about the bush**, **beat/knock the (living) daylights out of sb**, **off the beaten track**[1]

IDIOM **It beats me** informal something that you say when you do not understand a situation or someone's behaviour: *It beats me why she goes out with him.*

PHRASAL VERBS **beat down** If the sun beats down, it is very hot and bright. • **beat sb down** UK to persuade someone to charge you less for something • **beat sb/sth off** to manage to defeat someone who is attacking you • **beat sb to sth** to do something before someone else does it: *I was going to ask her to the party, but you beat me to it.* • **beat sb up** [B2] to attack someone by hitting or kicking them many times: *He beat up one of the other prisoners.*

eat² /biːt/ **noun** [C] **1 REGULAR SOUND** ▷ [B2] a regular sound that is made by your heart or by something hitting a surface: *a heart beat* ◦ *the beat of a drum* **2 RHYTHM** ▷ [B2] the main rhythm of a piece of music: *loud music with a repetitive beat* **3 AREA** ▷ the area of a town or city that a police officer walks around regularly: *Having more police officers **on the beat** (= walking around their beat) should help to reduce crime.*

eating /ˈbiːtɪŋ/ **noun 1** [C] a physical attack on someone **2 take a beating** to be defeated, criticized, or damaged: *Our team took a severe beating in the tournament.*

eautician /bjuːˈtɪʃᵊn/ **noun** [C] someone whose job is to improve people's appearance by treatments to their hair, skin, etc

eautiful /ˈbjuːtɪfᵊl/ **adj 1** [A1] very attractive: *a beautiful woman* ◦ *beautiful scenery* **2** [A1] very pleasant: *beautiful music* ◦ *It's a beautiful day (= the sun is shining).* • **beautifully adv** [B1] *a beautifully illustrated book* ◦ *She sings beautifully.*

eauty /ˈbjuːti/ **noun 1 QUALITY** ▷ [U] [B1] the quality of being beautiful: *The whole area is famous for its **natural beauty**.* ◦ *a beauty contest (= competition to find the most beautiful woman)* **2 the beauty of sth** the quality that makes something especially good or attractive: *The beauty of the plan is that it won't cost anything.* **3 a beauty product/treatment** a product or treatment to make you more beautiful **4 EXCELLENT THING** ▷ [C] informal something that is an excellent example of its type: *That last goal was a beauty.* **5 WOMAN** ▷ [C] old-fashioned a beautiful woman

> [+] Other ways of saying **beautiful**
>
> If a person (man or woman), is beautiful, we can say that they are **attractive** or **good-looking**. The adjective **handsome** is also sometimes used for men, and **pretty** for women:
>
> *Her husband is really **good-looking**.*
> *Your daughter is very **pretty**.*
>
> If someone, especially a woman, is extremely beautiful, you can say that they are **gorgeous** or **stunning**:
>
> *You look **gorgeous** in that dress!*
> *I think she's **stunning**.*
>
> The adjectives **breathtaking**, **lovely** and **gorgeous** are often used to describe scenery that is very beautiful.
>
> *The views from the window were **breathtaking**.*
> *We drove through some **gorgeous** countryside.*
>
> The adjective **exquisite** is sometimes used to describe objects which are very beautiful and often delicate:
>
> *They do the most **exquisite** hand-made decorations.*

> [✎] Word partners for **beauty**
>
> **great/sheer/stunning** beauty • **natural** beauty • beauty **products**

ˈbeauty ˌsalon noun [C] (also US **ˈbeauty ˌparlor**) a place where you can have beauty treatments

ˈbeauty ˌspot noun [C] **1** UK a place in the countryside that is very beautiful **2** a small dark mark on someone's face

beaver /ˈbiːvəʳ/ **noun** [C] an animal with brown fur, a long, flat tail, and sharp teeth, which builds dams (= walls made of pieces of wood) across rivers

became /bɪˈkeɪm/ past tense of become

because /bɪˈkɒz, bɪˈkəz/ **conjunction** [A1] used to give a reason for something: *I phoned because I needed to talk to you.* ◦ *I can't come out tonight because I've got too much homework.*

because of /bɪˈkɒzəv, bɪˈkəzəv/ **preposition** [B1] as a result of someone or something: *We got into all this trouble because of you.*

beck /bek/ **noun**

IDIOM **be at sb's beck and call** to be always ready and willing to do what someone wants

beckon /ˈbekᵊn/ **verb 1 WAVE** ▷ [I, T] to move your hand, head, etc to show someone that you would like them to come nearer: *She **beckoned to** the waiter.* **2 BE LIKELY** ▷ [I] to seem very likely to happen: *A career as a lead guitarist beckoned.* **3 BE ATTRACTIVE** ▷ [I] If a place beckons, it is very attractive to you, and you want to go there: *The bright lights of London beckoned.*

become /bɪˈkʌm/ **verb** (**became**, **become**) **1 become available/rich/a writer, etc** [A2] to begin to be something: *They became great friends.* ◦ *She wants to become a teacher when she leaves school.* ◦ *This style of skirt is becoming fashionable.* **2 what/whatever became of sb/sth** something you say when you want to know what has happened to someone: *Whatever became of your friend Harry?*

bed /bed/ **noun 1 FURNITURE** ▷ [C, U] **A1** a piece of furniture that you sleep on: *a **single/double bed*** ◦ *What time did you **go to bed** last night?* ◦ *She was lying **in bed** when I arrived.* ◦ *He had only just **got out of bed**.* ◦ *Have you **made the bed** (= tidied the bed after you have slept in it)?* **2 GROUND** ▷ [C] a piece of ground that is used for growing plants, especially flowers: *a flower bed* **3 BOTTOM** ▷ [C] the ground at the bottom of the sea, a river, etc: *the sea bed* → See also **bunk beds**

🗹 **Word partners for bed**

go to bed • be in/lie in/be tucked up in bed • get into/get out of bed • make the bed • be on the bed • share a bed • a double/single bed

---

bed and breakfast noun [C] (also **B & B**) a small hotel or private house where you pay for a room to sleep in for the night and a meal in the morning

bedclothes /'bedkləʊðz/ **noun** [plural] the sheets and other pieces of cloth that cover you and keep you warm in bed

bedding /'bedɪŋ/ **noun** [U] **1** the sheets and other pieces of cloth that cover you and keep you warm in bed **2** material such as hay (= dried grass) that animals sleep on

bedraggled /bɪˈdrægld/ **adj** untidy, and often wet and dirty

bedrock /'bedrɒk/ **noun** [U] formal a situation, idea, or principle that provides a strong base for something: *Family life is **the bedrock of** a stable society.*

bedroom /'bedruːm/ **noun** [C] **A2** a room used for sleeping in

bedside /'bedsaɪd/ **noun** [no plural] **1** the area at the side of a bed: *He was at her **bedside** in the hospital.* ◦ *a **bedside table/lamp*** **2 bedside manner** a doctor's ability to make the people they are treating feel comfortable: *My surgeon has a wonderful bedside manner.*

bedsit /'bedsɪt/ **noun** [C] UK a rented room where you live, sleep, and cook your meals

bedspread /'bedspred/ **noun** [C] a cloth cover that is put over a bed

bedtime /'bedtaɪm/ **noun** [C, U] the time that you usually go to bed

bee /biː/ **noun** [C] **B1** a flying insect that has a yellow and black body and makes honey (= sweet, sticky food): *the queen bee*

beech /biːtʃ/ **noun** [C, U] a large tree with a smooth grey trunk (= main, vertical part) that produces small nuts

beef[1] /biːf/ **noun** [U] **B1** the meat of a cow: *roast beef* → See also **ground beef**

beef[2] /biːf/ **verb**

PHRASAL VERB beef sth up to make something stronger or more important: *The company wants to beef up its sales force by employing new graduates.*

beefburger /'biːfˌbɜːgər/ **noun** [C] mainly UK (UK/US **hamburger**) a flat round food made from very small pieces of meat pressed together that is cooked, and eaten between bread

beehive /'biːhaɪv/ **noun** [C] (also **hive**) a container where people keep bees

been /biːn, bɪn/ **verb have been to** to have gone to a place and come back: *Have you ever been to Thailand?* → See also **be verb**

beep /biːp/ **verb 1** [I] If a machine beeps, it makes a short, high noise. **2** [I, T] If a car horn (= part you press to make a warning sound) beeps or if you beep it, it makes a loud noise: *Beep the horn to let me know that you're here.*
• **beep noun** [C]

beeper /'biːpər/ **noun** [C] (also UK **bleeper**) a small piece of electronic equipment that you carry which makes a short high sound when someone wants to talk to you

beer /bɪər/ **noun** [C, U] **A2** an alcoholic drink made from grain, or a glass or container of this drink: *a pint of beer*

beet /biːt/ **noun** [C, U] US (UK **beetroot**) a round, dark red vegetable that grows in the ground and is usually cooked and eaten cold

beetle /'biːtl/ **noun** [C] an insect with a hard, usually black, shiny body

beetroot /'biːtruːt/ **noun** [C, U] UK (US **beet**) a round, dark red vegetable that grows in the ground and is usually cooked and eaten cold

befall /bɪˈfɔːl/ **verb** [T] (**befell**, **befallen**) formal If something bad befalls you, it happens to you: *A dreadful misfortune has befallen the family.*

befit /bɪˈfɪt/ **verb** [T] (**befitting**, **befitted**) formal to be suitable or right for someone or something: *He was given a huge welcome, **as befits** such a hero.*

before[1] /bɪˈfɔːr/ **preposition 1 EARLIER** ▷ **A1** earlier than something or someone: *a week before Christmas* ◦ *She arrived before me.* ◦ *[+ doing sth] Think hard before accepting the offer.* **2 IN FRONT OF** ▷ **B1** in a position in front of someone or something: *I've never performed this before an audience.* ◦ *He stood before her, shaking.* **3 PLACE** ▷ **A2** at a place that you arrive at first when travelling towards another place: *The hospital is just before the bridge.* **4 IN ORDER** ▷ **B1** in front of someone or something in an order or a list: *P comes before Q in the alphabet.* **5 IMPORTANCE** ▷ treated as more important than someone or something: *They always **put** the children's needs **before** their own.* **6 EXAMINATION** ▷ being formally examined or considered by a group: *He appeared before the court dressed in jeans.*

before[2] /bɪˈfɔːr/ **conjunction 1 EARLIER** ▷ **A2** earlier than the time when something happens: *He was a teacher before he became famous.* ◦ *Before I could warn him, he had fallen.* **2 TO AVOID STH** ▷ **B1** in order to avoid something

bad happening: *Put that stick down before you hurt someone.* **3 UNTIL** ▷ **B1** until: *It took a few moments before I realized that he was lying.*

before³ /bɪˈfɔːr/ *adv* **A2** at an earlier time, or on a previous occasion: *I've never seen her before.* ○ *We had spoken on the phone a few days before.*

beforehand /bɪˈfɔːhænd/ *adv* before a particular time or event: *Did you know beforehand what they had planned to do?*

befriend /bɪˈfrend/ *verb* [T] formal to be friendly to someone, especially someone who needs support or help

beg /beg/ *verb* (**begging, begged**) **1** [I] **B2** to ask someone for food or money, because you do not have any: *Young children were begging on the streets.* **2** [I, T] **B2** to make a very strong and urgent request: *She begged him for help.* ○ [+ to do sth] *I begged her not to go.* → See also **I beg your pardon.**

began /bɪˈgæn/ *past tense of begin*

beggar /ˈbegər/ *noun* [C] a poor person who lives by asking other people for money and food

begin /bɪˈgɪn/ *verb* (**beginning, began, begun**) **1** [I, T] **A2** to start to do something: [+ to do sth] *The children began to cry.* ○ [+ doing sth] *Have they begun building the wall yet?* ○ *She began her career as a journalist on a local newspaper.* **2** [I] **A1** to start to happen: *What time does the film begin?* **3 begin with sth** **B1** to have something at the start: *Local phone numbers begin with 1223.* **4 to begin with a** **B1** at the start of a situation: *To begin with, the two girls got on well.* **b** **B2** used to give the first important reason for something: *To begin with, we can't leave the children alone.*

beginner /bɪˈgɪnər/ *noun* [C] **A2** someone who is starting to do or learn something for the first time: *I'm a complete beginner at yoga.*

beginning /bɪˈgɪnɪŋ/ *noun* [C] **A2** the first part of something or the start of something: [usually singular] *We met at the beginning of 1998.* ○ *Things went well in the beginning.*

begrudge /bɪˈgrʌdʒ/ *verb* [T] **1** to feel upset because someone has something that you would like: [+ two objects] *I don't begrudge him his success.* **2** to feel upset because you have to spend money on something or spend time doing something: *They begrudge every penny that they have to spend on him.*

beguile /bɪˈgaɪl/ *verb* [T] formal to attract someone very much, sometimes in order to deceive them: [often passive] *I can see how people are beguiled by his charm.* ○ *a beguiling smile*

begun /bɪˈgʌn/ *past participle of begin*

behalf /bɪˈhɑːf/ *noun* **on sb's behalf** **B2** If you do something on someone's behalf, you do it for them or instead of them: *We are campaigning on behalf of thousands of refugees.* ○ *Will you accept the prize on my behalf?*

behave /bɪˈheɪv/ *verb* [I] **1** **B1** to do or say things in a particular way: *to behave badly/stupidly* ○ *They are behaving like children.* **2** (also **behave yourself**) **B1** to be polite and not make a situation difficult: *Try to behave.* ○ *The children can only come if they promise to behave themselves.* → Opposite **misbehave**

-behaved /bɪˈheɪvd/ *suffix* used after a word describing how someone behaves: *a badly-behaved child* → See also **well-behaved**

behaviour UK (US **behavior**) /bɪˈheɪvjər/ *noun* [U] **B1** the way that you behave: *good/bad behaviour* ○ *Did you notice anything odd about his behaviour?*

> ☑ Word partners for **behaviour**
> anti-social/bad/disruptive/good/normal behaviour

behavioural UK (US **behavioral**) /bɪˈheɪvjərəl/ *adj* relating to behaviour: *behavioural changes/problems*

behead /bɪˈhed/ *verb* [T] to cut someone's head off

beheld /bɪˈheld/ *past of behold*

behind¹ /bɪˈhaɪnd/ *preposition* **1 BACK** ▷ **A1** at or to the back of someone or something: *Close the door behind you.* ○ *The warehouse is behind the store.* **2 LESS SUCCESSFUL** ▷ **B1** slower or less successful than someone or something: *Our team is 3 points behind the winners.* ○ *The building work is already behind schedule* (= late). **3 CAUSING** ▷ causing something, or responsible for something: *What was the reason behind her decision to leave?* **4 SUPPORTING** ▷ **B1** giving your help or support to someone: *The group is 100 percent behind her.* **5 NOT AFFECTING** ▷ If a bad experience or your own bad behaviour is behind you, it does not exist or affect your life now: *He's put his criminal past behind him.*

behind² /bɪˈhaɪnd/ *adv* **1 BACK** ▷ **A2** at or to the back of someone or something: *Somebody grabbed me from behind.* **2 SLOWER** ▷ slower or later than someone else, or than you should be: *She's behind with the rent* (= is late to pay it). **3 PLACE** ▷ **A2** in the place where someone or something was before: *You go on ahead. I'll stay behind and tidy up.* ○ *When we got to the restaurant, I realized that I had left my purse behind.*

behind³ /bɪˈhaɪnd/ *noun* [C] informal the part of your body that you sit on

behold /bɪˈhəʊld/ *verb* [T] (**beheld**) literary to see something

beige /beɪʒ/ *noun* [U] a pale brown colour
• **beige** *adj* → See colour picture **Colours** on page Centre 12

being¹ /ˈbiːɪŋ/ *noun* **1** [C] a living person or imaginary creature: *human beings* **2 come into being** to start to exist: *The new law comes into being next month.* → See also **well-being**

being² /ˈbiːɪŋ/ *present participle of be*

belated /bɪˈleɪtɪd/ *adj* coming late, or later than expected: *a belated attempt to win votes* • **belatedly** *adv I belatedly realized I'd forgotten to cancel my order.*

belch¹ /beltʃ/ *verb* **1** [I] to make a sudden noise as air from your stomach comes out through your mouth **2** [T] (also **belch out**) to produce a lot of smoke, fire, gas, etc: *tall chimneys belching smoke*

belch² /beltʃ/ **noun** [C] the noise you make when you belch

beleaguered /bɪˈliːɡəd/ **adj** formal having a lot of problems: *the beleaguered farming industry*

belfry /ˈbelfri/ **noun** [C] the tower of a church where the bells are hung

belie /bɪˈlaɪ/ **verb** [T] (**belying**, **belied**) formal to give a wrong idea about something: *His shy manner belied his very sharp mind.*

belief /bɪˈliːf/ **noun 1 TRUE** ▷ [U, no plural] ⑱ something that you believe is true or real: *It is a **widely-held belief** that smoking helps you lose weight.* ◦ *She married him **in the belief that** he would change.* → Opposite **disbelief 2 IDEA** ▷ [C, U] ⑱ an idea that you are certain is true: *religious/political beliefs* **3 EFFECTIVE** ▷ [U, no plural] the feeling that someone or something is effective or right: *a **belief in** social justice* **4 beyond belief** ⑱ too bad, good, difficult, etc to be real: *The evil of this man is beyond belief.*

> 🗹 Word partners for **belief**
>
> a firm/mistaken/sincere/strong/widespread/ widely-held belief • have/hold a belief • a belief in sth • in the belief that

believable /bɪˈliːvəbl/ **adj** If something is believable, you can believe that it could be true or real. → Opposite **unbelievable**

believe /bɪˈliːv/ **verb 1 TRUE** ▷ [T] ⑫ to think that something is true, or that what someone says is true: [+ (that)] *They believe that their health has suffered because of the chemicals.* ◦ *Do you believe him?* → Opposite **disbelieve 2 THINK** ▷ [T] ⑫ to think something, without being completely sure: *The murderer is believed to be in his thirties.* **3 RELIGION** ▷ [I] to have religious beliefs **4 not believe your eyes/ears** ⑪ to be very surprised when you see someone or something, or when you hear what someone says: *I couldn't believe my ears when Dan said they were getting married.* **5 believe it or not** ⑪ used to say that something is true although it seems surprising: *He even remembered my birthday, believe it or not.*

PHRASAL VERBS **believe in sth** ⑪ to be certain that something exists: *I believe in life after death.* • **believe in sth/doing sth** ⑫ to be confident that something is effective or right: *He believes in saying what he thinks.*

believer /bɪˈliːvər/ **noun** [C] **1** a person who has a religious belief **2 a firm/great/strong, etc believer in sth/doing sth** someone who has confidence in a particular idea or way of doing things: *She's a firm believer in freedom of speech.*

belittle /bɪˈlɪtl/ **verb** [T] formal to say that someone or something is not very important or not very good

bell /bel/ **noun** [C] **1** ⑱ a hollow, metal object, shaped like a cup, with a metal part inside that hits the side of the cup and makes a ringing sound: *the sound of church bells ringing* **2** ⑪ an electrical object that makes a ringing sound

bell

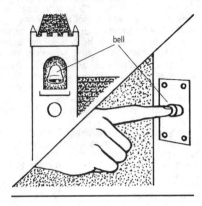

bell

when you press a switch: *Please **ring the bell** for attention.*

IDIOMS **give sb a bell** UK informal to telephone someone • **ring a bell** If a word, especially a name, rings a bell, you think you have heard it before.

belligerent /bəˈlɪdʒ³rənt/ **adj** wanting to fight or argue

bellow /ˈbeləʊ/ **verb** [I, T] to shout something in a loud voice • **bellow noun** [C]

belly /ˈbeli/ **noun** [C] informal your stomach (= organ where food is digested), or the front part of your body between your chest and your legs

'belly ,button noun [C] informal the small, round, and usually hollow place on your stomach, where you were connected to your mother before birth

belong /bɪˈlɒŋ/ **verb 1 belong in/on/there, etc** ⑱ to be in the right place: *That chair belongs in the dining room.* **2** ⑱ [I] to feel happy and comfortable in a place or with a group of people: *I never felt that I belonged there.*

PHRASAL VERBS **belong to sb** ⑫ If something belongs to you, you own it: *This necklace belonged to my grandmother.* • **belong to sth** ⑪ to be a member of a group or organization: *We belong to the same youth club.*

belongings /bɪˈlɒŋɪŋz/ **noun** [plural] ⑱ the things that you own: *I took a few **personal belongings** with me.*

beloved /bɪˈlʌvɪd/ **adj** literary very much loved: *in memory of our beloved son*

below /bɪˈləʊ/ **adv, preposition 1 POSITION** ▷ ⑪ in a lower position than someone or something else: *Send your answers to the address below (= lower on the page or on a later page).* **2 LESS** ▷ ⑪ less than an amount or level: *The temperature there rarely drops below 22°C.* ◦ *His work is **below average**.* **3 RANK** ▷ lower in rank: *Monica is a grade below me.*

belt¹ /belt/ **noun** [C] **1 WAIST** ▷ ⑫ a long, thin piece of leather, cloth, or plastic that you wear around your waist → See colour picture **Clothes** on

page Centre 9 **2 AREA** ▷ **belt**

an area of a particular type of land, or an area where a particular group of people live: *the commuter belt* ○ *a narrow belt of trees*
3 MACHINE ▷ part of a machine that moves in a circle to carry objects or to make a machine work: *The car needs a new fan belt.*

IDIOMS **have sth under your belt** to have already achieved, learnt, or done something important: *At 18, she already has several victories under her belt.* • **tighten your belt** to try to spend less money

→ See also **conveyor belt, green belt, safety belt, seat belt**

belt² /belt/ verb informal **1 belt along/down/ through, etc** UK to move very fast: *He came belting down the street.* **2** [T] to hit someone or something very hard

PHRASAL VERBS **belt sth out** to sing something very loudly • **belt up** UK informal used to tell someone to stop talking or making a noise: *Just belt up, would you? I'm trying to concentrate.*

belying /bɪˈlaɪɪŋ/ present participle of belie

bemused /bɪˈmjuːzd/ adj slightly confused: *He seemed bemused by all the attention.*

bench /benʃ/ noun [C] **1** a long seat for two or more people, usually made of wood or metal: *a park bench* **2 the bench a** in some sports, a place where players sit when they are not playing **b** a judge in court, or judges as a group: *Please address your comments to the bench.*

benchmark /ˈbenʃmɑːk/ noun [C] a level of quality with which other things of the same type can be compared: *Her performance set a new benchmark for ballet dancing.*

bend¹ /bend/ verb [I, T] (**bent**) **1** to move your body or part of your body so that it is not straight: *He was bending over to tie his shoelaces.* ○ *Bend your knees when lifting heavy objects.* **2** to become curved, or to make something become curved: *The trees were bending in the wind.* ○ *The road bent sharply to the left.* → See also **bend over backwards, bend/stretch the rules (rule¹)**

bend² /bend/ noun [C] a curved part of something: *a bend in the road/river*

IDIOM **drive/send sb round the bend** informal to make someone very angry, especially by continuing to do something annoying

→ See also **hairpin bend**

▨ Word partners for **bend**
a sharp/tight bend • a bend in sth

beneath /bɪˈniːθ/ adv, preposition **1** under something, or in a lower position than something: *He hid the letter beneath a pile of papers.* ○ *She looked out of the window at the children playing beneath.* **2** If someone or something is beneath you, you think they are not good

enough for you: *He thinks housework is beneath him.*

benefactor /ˈbenɪfæktər/ noun [C] someone who gives money to help an organization or person

beneficial /ˌbenɪˈfɪʃəl/ adj helpful or useful: *Exercise is beneficial to almost everyone.*

beneficiary /ˌbenɪˈfɪʃəri/ noun [C] formal someone who receives money, help, etc from something or someone else: *They were the beneficiaries of free education.*

benefit¹ /ˈbenɪfɪt/ noun [C, U] **1** something that helps you or gives you an advantage: *I've had the benefit of a happy childhood.* **2** UK money that the government gives to people who are sick, poor, not working, etc: *unemployment benefit* **3 for sb's benefit** in order to help someone: *We bought the piano for the children's benefit.*

IDIOM **give sb the benefit of the doubt** to choose to believe what someone tells you even though it may be wrong or a lie

→ See also **child benefit, fringe benefit**

▨ Word partners for **benefit**
enjoy/have/offer/reap benefits • [the drawbacks/risks, etc] outweigh the benefits • great/long-term/maximum/potential/tangible benefit • of benefit to sb

benefit² /ˈbenɪfɪt/ verb (**benefiting, benefited**) **1** [I] to be helped by something: *The film benefited from the excellent acting by its stars.* **2** [T] to help someone: *The charity supports activities that directly benefit children.*

benevolent /bɪˈnevələnt/ adj formal kind, generous, and helpful • **benevolence** /bɪˈnevələns/ noun [U]

benign /bɪˈnaɪn/ adj **1** not likely to kill you: *a benign tumour* **2** kind, or not intending to harm anyone: *a benign ruler*

bent¹ /bent/ adj **1** curved and not now straight or flat: *The metal bars were bent and twisted.* **2 bent on sth/doing sth** determined to do something or get something: *Both parties are bent on destroying each other's chances of winning.* **3** UK informal not honest: *a bent policeman*

bent² /bent/ past of bend

bequeath /bɪˈkwiːð/ verb [+ two objects] formal to formally arrange to give someone something after you die: *He bequeathed his art collection to the city of Glasgow.*

bequest /bɪˈkwest/ noun [C] formal money or property that you have arranged for someone to get after you die

berate /bɪˈreɪt/ verb [T] formal to speak angrily to someone: *She berated him for being late.*

bereaved /bɪˈriːvd/ adj If you have been bereaved, someone you loved has died: *bereaved parents* ○ *The minister spoke quietly with the bereaved.* • **bereavement** noun [C, U] formal

bereft /bɪˈreft/ adj formal **1 bereft of sth** completely without something: *They were bereft of new ideas.* **2** [never before noun] alone and extremely sad: *She was left bereft by his death.*

beret /'bereɪ/ ⑤ /bəˈreɪ/ **noun** [C] a round, flat hat made of soft material

berry /'beri/ **noun** [C] ⑫ a small, round fruit on some plants and trees

berserk /bəˈzɜːk/ **adj go berserk** informal to become extremely angry or violent

berth /bɜːθ/ **noun** [C] **1** a bed on a boat or train **2** a place for a boat to stay in a port

beset /bɪˈset/ **verb** [T] formal If problems beset you, they cause you continuing difficulties: [often passive] *The project has been **beset by problems** from the start.*

beside /bɪˈsaɪd/ **preposition 1** ⓐ next to someone or something, or very near them: *She knelt beside his bed.* **2 be beside yourself (with sth)** to experience a powerful emotion: *He was beside himself with rage.*

besides¹ /bɪˈsaɪdz/ **preposition** ⓑ in addition to something or someone: *Do you play any other sports besides football?*

besides² /bɪˈsaɪdz/ **adv 1** ⓑ used to give another reason for something: *She won't mind if you're late – besides, it's not your fault.* **2** ⓑ in addition to: *Besides looking after the children, she also runs a successful business.*

besiege /bɪˈsiːdʒ/ **verb 1 be besieged by/with sb** to have lots of people asking you questions or making demands: *The president was besieged by reporters.* **2 be besieged by/with sth** to receive many demands or criticisms: *The radio station was besieged with calls from angry listeners.* **3** [T] to surround a place with an army in order to attack it

best¹ /best/ **adj** ⓐ superlative of **good** adj: better than any other: *She's one of our best students.* ◦ *Give her my **best wishes**.* ◦ *Susie's my **best friend** (= the friend I like more than any other).* ◦ *What's the best way to get to the airport from here?* → See also **second best, the best/greatest thing since sliced bread**

best² /best/ **adv 1** ⓐ superlative of **well** adv: most, or more than any other: *Which of the songs did you like best?* **2** ⓑ in the most suitable or satisfactory way: *I sleep best with the windows open.*

best³ /best/ **noun 1 the best** ⓑ someone or something that is better than any other: *He's the best of the new players.* **2 at best** used to show that the most positive way of considering something is still not good: *At best, only 50 per cent of babies born at 24 weeks will survive.* **3 at his/its, etc best** ⓑ at the highest level of achievement or quality: *The article is an example of journalism at its best.* **4 do/try your best** ⓑ to make the greatest effort possible: *I did my best to persuade him.* **5 bring out the best in sb** to cause someone's best qualities to show **6 make the best of sth** ⓑ to try to be positive about a situation that you do not like but cannot change: *Our hotel room is rather small, but we'll just have to make the best of it.* **7 for the best** If something is for the best, it seems unpleasant now, but will improve a situation in the future: *Divorce is always painful, but it really*

was for the best. **8 at the best of times** used to show that something is not good when it is the best it can be: *He's not exactly patient at the best of times.*

IDIOM **have the best of both worlds** to have the advantages of two different situations: *Living in the country and working in the city you have the best of both worlds.*

best ˈman noun [no plural] a man who stands next to the man who is getting married at the marriage ceremony and helps him

bestow /bɪˈstəʊ/ **verb** [T] formal to give someone an important gift or a public reward for their achievements: *He won the Nobel Peace Prize, an honour also **bestowed on** his colleague.*

bestseller /ˌbestˈselər/ **noun** [C] ⑫ a very popular book that many people have bought ● **best-selling adj** [always before noun] best-selling authors

bet¹ /bet/ **verb** [I, T] (**betting, bet**) **1** to risk money on the result of a game, competition, etc: *He lost all his money **betting on** horses.* ◦ [+ two objects + (that)] *I bet him a dollar that I was right.* **2 I bet** informal ⓑ something that you say to show that you believe that something is true or will happen: [+ (that)] *I bet that he's forgotten my birthday again.* **3 You bet!** mainly US informal used to say that you will do something with enthusiasm: *"Are you going to Pam's party?" "You bet!"*

bet² /bet/ **noun** [C] **1** an attempt to win money on the result of a game, competition, etc: *She **won** her **bet**.* ◦ *He **put** a **bet on** Barcelona winning on Saturday.* **2 a good bet** something that would be useful, clever, or enjoyable to do: *Putting your savings in a high-interest account would be a good bet.* **3 your best bet** the best decision or choice: *Your best bet in terms of value would be the Regent Hotel.*

IDIOMS **hedge your bets** to avoid choosing one particular thing or action when it is not certain which is the right choice: *Journalists are hedging their bets on the likely outcome of the election.* ● **a safe bet** something that you are certain will happen: *Wheeler is a safe bet for a place on the team.*

🗹 **Word partners for bet**

have/place a bet (on) sth ● put a bet on sth ● lose/win a bet

---

betray /bɪˈtreɪ/ **verb** [T] **1 PERSON** ▷ ⑫ to behave in a dishonest or cruel way to someone who trusts you: *When I heard what he had said about me, I felt betrayed.* **2 SECRETS** ▷ If you betray your country or an organization, you give secret information to its enemies or to other organizations. **3 EMOTION** ▷ to show an emotion that you were trying to hide: *Her face was calm, but her hands betrayed her nervousness.*

betrayal /bɪˈtreɪəl/ **noun** [C, U] cruel or dishonest behaviour towards someone who trusts you: *a betrayal of trust*

better¹ /'betər/ **adj 1** ⓐ comparative of **good** adj: of a higher quality, more effective, or more enjoyable than something or someone else

---

Jeff's been offered a better job in the States. ◦ *The sales figures were better than expected.* ◦ *Her English has got a lot better (= improved) recently.* **2 🅐** healthy, or less sick than before: *I feel much better.* ◦ *I hope you get better soon.* **3 the bigger/brighter/hotter, etc the better** used to say that the bigger, brighter, hotter, etc something is, the more pleased you will be

better² /'betər/ **adv 1 🅐** comparative of **well** adv: to a greater degree, or in a more successful or effective way: *I'd like to get to know you better.* ◦ *Helen did much better than me in the exam.* **2 he/you, etc had better do sth 🅐** used in order to say what you think someone should do: *You'd better hurry or you'll miss the train.* **3 know better** to have enough experience not to do something stupid or something that will not achieve anything: *I thought she'd listen to me – I should have known better.*

better³ /'betər/ **noun 1 for the better** If a situation changes for the better, it improves: *Their relationship has changed for the better.* **2 get the better of sb** If a feeling gets the better of you, it becomes too strong to control: *Curiosity finally got the better of her and she opened the letter.*

better⁴ /'betər/ **verb** [T] to do something better than it has been done before: *He bettered his previous best time for a marathon.*

better 'off adj [never before noun] **1** richer: *We're a lot better off now that Jane's started work again.* **2** in a better situation: *Simon's such an idiot – you'd be better off without him.* **3 you're better off doing sth** used to give advice: *You're better off getting a taxi.*

between¹ /bɪ'twiːn/ **preposition 1 SPACE** ▷ **🅐** in the space that separates two places, people, or things: *The train lies halfway between Florence and Rome.* ◦ *A narrow path runs between the two houses.* **2 TIME** ▷ **🅐** in the period of time that separates two events or times: *The shop is closed for lunch between 12.30 and 1.30.* **3 INVOLVE** ▷ **🅐** involving two or more groups of people: *Tonight's game is between the New Orleans Saints and the Los Angeles Rams.* **4 AMOUNT** ▷ **🅐** used to show the largest and smallest amount or level of something: *Between 50 and 100 people will lose their jobs.* **5 CONNECT** ▷ **🅐** connecting two or more places or things: *There is a regular train service between the two towns.* **6 SEPARATE** ▷ **🅐** separating two or more things or people: *the gap between rich and poor* ◦ *What's the difference between these two cameras?* **7 SHARE** ▷ **🅐** shared by a particular number of people: *We drank two bottles of wine between four of us.* **8 AMOUNT** ▷ **🅐** If something is between two amounts, it is larger than the first amount but smaller than the second: *The temperature will be between 20 and 25 degrees today.* **9 CHOOSE** ▷ If you choose between two things, you choose one thing or the other.

between² /bɪ'twiːn/ **adv** (also **in between**) **1 🅐** in the space that separates two places, people, or things: *The wood is in neat piles with newspaper placed between.* **2 🅐** in the period of time that

separates two events or times: *There's a train at 6.15 and one at 10.30 but nothing in between.*

beverage /'bevərɪdʒ/ **noun** [C] formal a drink

beware /bɪ'weər/ **verb** [I] used in order to warn someone to be careful: *Beware of the dog.* ◦ [+ of + doing sth] *You should beware of spending too long in the sun.*

bewildered /bɪ'wɪldəd/ **adj** very confused and not sure what to do: *She looked bewildered.* • **bewilderment noun** [U] *He stared at me in bewilderment.*

bewildering /bɪ'wɪldərɪŋ/ **adj** making you feel confused: *There was a bewildering range of subjects to choose from.*

bewitch /bɪ'wɪtʃ/ **verb** [T] If someone or something bewitches you, you find them extremely attractive and interesting: *a bewitching smile*

beyond¹ /bi'jɒnd/ **preposition 1 DISTANCE** ▷ **🅑** on the other side of something: *Our house is just beyond the bridge.* **2 TIME** ▷ **🅑** continuing after a particular time or date: *A lot of people now live beyond the age of 80.* **3 beyond belief/repair/recognition, etc 🅑** impossible to believe/repair/recognize, etc: *Steven had changed beyond all recognition.* **4 NOT UNDERSTAND** ▷ informal If something is beyond you, you cannot understand it: *It's beyond me why anyone would want to buy that house.* **5 EXCEPT** ▷ except for: *She said very little beyond the occasional 'yes' and 'no'.* **6 INVOLVING OTHERS** ▷ involving or affecting other things or people than the ones you have talked about: *You should try to develop interests beyond the family.*

beyond² /bi'jɒnd/ **adv 1 🅑** on the other side of something: *From the top of the hill, we could see our house and the woods beyond.* **2 🅑** continuing after a particular time or date: *The strike looks set to continue into March and beyond.*

bhangra /'bæŋgrə/ **noun** [U] a type of pop music based on traditional music from North India and Pakistan

bi- /baɪ-/ **prefix** two: *bilingual (= speaking two languages)* ◦ *bimonthly (= happening twice in a month or once every two months)*

biannual /baɪ'ænjuəl/ **adj** happening twice a year → Compare **biennial**

bias /'baɪəs/ **noun** [C, U] a situation in which you support or oppose someone or something in an unfair way because you are influenced by your personal opinions: *a bias towards/against private education* ◦ *The news channel has been accused of bias in favour of the government.*

biased /'baɪəst/ **adj** showing unfair support for or opposition to someone or something because of your personal opinions: *to be biased against/towards younger workers*

bib /bɪb/ **noun** [C] a piece of cloth or plastic that is worn by young children when they are eating in order to stop their clothes getting dirty

bible /'baɪbl/ **noun 1 the Bible** the holy book of the Christian and Jewish religions **2** [C] a copy of this book **3** [C] a book or magazine that gives important information and advice about a particular subject: *'Vogue' was regarded as the fashion student's bible.*

biblical /ˈbɪblɪkəl/ **adj** relating to the Bible

bibliography /ˌbɪbliˈɒɡrəfi/ **noun** [C] a list of books and articles on a particular subject

bicentenary /ˌbaɪsenˈtiːnəri/ ⓤ /baɪˈsentəneri/ **noun** [C] UK (US **bicentennial**, ⓤ /ˌbaɪsen-ˈteniəl/) the day or year that is 200 years after an important event: *the bicentenary of Schubert's birth* ∘ *bicentennial celebrations*

biceps /ˈbaɪseps/ **noun** [C] (plural **biceps**) the large muscle at the front of your upper arm

bicker /ˈbɪkər/ **verb** [I] to argue about something that is not very important: *They were **bickering over** which channel to watch.*

bicycle /ˈbaɪsɪkl/ **noun** [C] ⓐ a vehicle with two wheels that you sit on and move by turning the two pedals (= parts you press with your feet) → See colour picture **Sports 2** on page Centre 15

bicycle

Word partners for **bicycle**
ride a bicycle • **be on** a bicycle • a bicycle **helmet**

bicycle lane **noun** [C] (also **bike lane**, UK **cycle lane**) US a part of a road or a special path that only people riding bicycles can use

bid¹ /bɪd/ **noun** [C] **1** ATTEMPT ▷ an attempt to achieve something: *a successful **bid for** re-election* ∘ [+ to do sth] *The council has banned cars from the city centre **in a bid** to reduce pollution.* **2** BUY ▷ an offer to pay a particular amount of money for something: *I made a **bid** of $150 **for** the painting.* **3** WORK ▷ an offer to do work for someone for a particular amount of money: *We put in a **bid for** the stadium contract.*

Word partners for **bid**
launch/mount a bid • **in a (desperate)** bid to do sth • a bid **for** sth

bid² /bɪd/ **verb** (**bidding, bid**) **1** [I, T] to offer to pay an amount of money for something: *They **bid** $500 million **for** the company.* **2** **bid for sth; bid to do sth** to try to do or obtain something: *Five firms have **bid for** the contract.*

bid³ /bɪd/ **verb** (**bidding, bid, bade, bid, bidden**) **bid sb farewell/goodbye/good night, etc** literary to say goodbye, good night, etc: *She **bade** her guests goodnight.*

bidder /ˈbɪdər/ **noun** [C] someone who offers to pay a particular amount of money for something: *The house will be sold to **the highest bidder** (= the person who offers to pay the most).*

bidding /ˈbɪdɪŋ/ **noun** [U] **1** the activity of offering particular amounts of money for something **2** **do sb's bidding** literary to do what someone tells you to do

bide /baɪd/ **verb** see **bide your time¹**

bidet /ˈbiːdeɪ/ ⓤ /bɪˈdeɪ/ **noun** [C] a small low bath that a person uses to wash their bottom and sex organs

biennial /baɪˈeniəl/ **adj** happening every two years → Compare **biannual**

big¹ /bɪg/ **adj** (**bigger, biggest**) **1** SIZE ▷ ⓐ large

in size or amount: *I come from a big family.* ∘ *We're looking for a bigger house* **2** IMPORTANT ▷ ⓐ important or serious *Tonight's big game is between Real Madrid and Manchester United.* ∘ *Buying that car was a big mistake.* **3** **your big brother/sister** informal ⓐ your older brother/sister **4** SUCCESSFUL ▷ informal successful or popular: *The programme's been a **big hit** (= very popular) with young children* **5** **make it big** informal to become very successful or famous

big² /bɪg/ **verb**

PHRASAL VERB **big sth/sb up** [T] informal to praise someone or something a lot, sometimes more than they deserve

big business **noun** [U] **1** an activity that makes a lot of money: *Football has become big business.* **2** large, powerful businesses

bigot /ˈbɪgət/ **noun** [C] a bigoted person

bigoted /ˈbɪgətɪd/ **adj** A bigoted person has very strong, unfair opinions and refuses to consider different opinions. • **bigotry** /ˈbɪgətri/ **noun** [U] bigoted opinions or behaviour

big-ticket /ˈbɪgˌtɪkɪt/ **adj** [always before noun] Big-ticket items are expensive things to buy such as cars or furniture.

bike /baɪk/ **noun** [C] informal **1** ⓐ short for bicycle **2** ⓑ short for motorbike/motorcycle

biker /ˈbaɪkər/ **noun** [C] someone who rides a motorcycle

bikini /bɪˈkiːni/ **noun** [C] ⓑ a piece of clothing with two parts that women wear for swimming → See colour picture **Clothes** on page Centre 9

bilateral /baɪˈlætərəl/ **adj** involving two groups or countries: *bilateral talks/agreements/trade*

bile /baɪl/ **noun** [U] a bitter liquid made and stored in the body that helps to digest fat

bilingual /baɪˈlɪŋgwəl/ **adj** using or able to speak two languages: *a bilingual dictionary* ∘ *She's bilingual.*

bill¹ /bɪl/ **noun** [C] **1** PAYMENT ▷ ⓐ a piece of paper that tells you how much you must pay for something you have bought or for a service you have used: *Have you **paid** the electricity **bill**?* **2** LAW ▷ a written plan for a law: *Parliament will vote today on whether to pass the reform bill.* **3** MONEY ▷ US (UK **note**) a piece of paper money: *a five dollar bill* **4** ENTERTAINMENT ▷ the particular entertainment being shown at a cinema or theatre **5** BEAK ▷ a bird's beak

Word partners for **bill**
pay/settle a bill • a bill **comes to** [£100/$500, etc] • a bill **for** sth • an **electricity/gas/ phone** bill

bill² /bɪl/ **verb 1** **be billed as sth** to be advertised with a particular description: *The film was billed as a romantic comedy.* **2** [T] to give or send someone a bill asking for money that they owe for a product or service: *He **billed** us **for** the materials.*

billboard /ˈbɪlbɔːd/ **noun** [C] (also UK **hoarding**) a large board used for advertising, especially by the side of a road

billfold /'bɪlfəʊld/ **noun** [C] US (UK/US **wallet**) a small, flat container for carrying paper money and credit cards (= plastic cards used for paying with)

billiards /'bɪliədz/ **noun** [U] a game in which two people try to hit coloured balls into holes around the edge of a table using long, thin sticks

billing /'bɪlɪŋ/ **noun** [U] **1** the activity of sending people letters to ask for payments **2 star/top billing** the position of being the most important performer in a show

billion /'bɪliən/ **⑫** the number 1,000,000,000

billionaire /ˌbɪljə'neə^r/ **noun** [C] a very rich person who has money and possessions to the value of at least one billion pounds or dollars

billow /'bɪləʊ/ **verb** [I] to be moved and spread out by a current of air: *Smoke **billowed** out of the building.*

bimbo /'bɪmbəʊ/ **noun** [C] very informal a young woman who is attractive but not intelligent

bin /bɪn/ **noun** [C] **1** UK (US **trash can**) **⑪** a container that is used to put waste in: *a rubbish/wastepaper bin* ∘ *I threw it in the bin.* → See colour picture **The Office** on page Centre 5 **2** a container for storing things: *a storage bin*

binary /'baɪn^əri/ **adj** The binary system expresses numbers using only 1 and 0, and is especially used for computers.

bind¹ /baɪnd/ **verb** [T] (**bound**) **1 TIE** ▷ to tie something together with string, rope, etc: *His hands were bound behind his back.* **2 KEEP PROMISE** ▷ to force someone to keep a promise: *His contract **binds** him **to** working a six-day week.* **3 UNITE** ▷ to unite people: *Culture and language **bind** people **together**.* **4 BOOK** ▷ to fasten pages together to make a book

bind² /baɪnd/ **noun** [no plural] informal **1** a difficult or unpleasant situation: *a financial bind* **2** UK a job that uses a lot of your time: *Cleaning the bathroom is a bind.*

binder /'baɪndə^r/ **noun** [C] a strong cover for holding pieces of paper together

binding /'baɪndɪŋ/ **adj** A binding agreement, promise, etc cannot be broken or changed: *It's a legally binding contract.*

binge¹ /bɪndʒ/ **noun** [C] an occasion when you eat or drink too much or spend too much money in shops

binge² /bɪndʒ/ **verb** [I] (**bingeing, binging**) to eat too much food at one time: *I've been bingeing on chocolate.*

binge drinking noun [U] the problem of drinking too much alcohol on one occasion ● **'binge drinker noun** [C]

bingo /'bɪŋgəʊ/ **noun** [U] a game in which people mark numbers on a card as they are called, and the person whose numbers are called first is the winner

binoculars /bɪ'nɒkjələz/ **noun** [plural] a piece of equipment for looking at things that are far away, made from two tubes with glass at the ends: *a pair of binoculars*

binoculars

bio- /baɪəʊ-/ **prefix** relating to living things or human life: *biodiversity* ∘ *bioethics*

biochemical /ˌbaɪəʊ'kemɪk^əl/ **adj** relating to biochemistry

biochemistry /ˌbaɪəʊ'kemɪstri/ **noun** [U] the study of the chemical processes and reactions that happen in living things such as plants, animals, or people ● **biochemist noun** [C] a scientist who studies biochemistry

biodegradable /ˌbaɪəʊdɪ'greɪdəbl/ **adj** Biodegradable substances decay naturally without damaging the environment.

biodiesel /'baɪəʊˌdiːzl/ **noun** [U] fuel used in the engines of some vehicles that is made from vegetable oil or animal fat

bioethanol /ˌbaɪəʊ'eθənɒl/ **noun** [U] fuel used in the engines of some vehicles that is partly made from ethanol (= a chemical that comes from sugar)

biofuel /'baɪəʊˌfjʊəl/ **noun** [C, U] fuel produced from plant material

biographer /baɪ'ɒgrəfə^r/ **noun** [C] someone who writes the story of a particular person's life

biography /baɪ'ɒgrəfi/ **noun** [C] **⑪** the story of a person's life written by another person ● **biographical** /ˌbaɪəʊ'græfɪk^əl/ **adj** about someone's life: *biographical information*

biohazard /'baɪəʊˌhæzəd/ **noun** [C] a risk to humans or the environment caused by something biological, such as a poisonous chemical or an infectious disease

biological /ˌbaɪə'lɒdʒɪk^əl/ **adj 1 ⑫** relating to the study of living things such as plants and animals: *biological sciences* **2** using living things or poisons made from living things: *biological weapons* ● **biologically adv**

biology /baɪ'ɒlədʒi/ **noun** [U] **⑫** the study of living things ● **biologist noun** [C] a scientist who studies biology

biopsy /'baɪɒpsi/ **noun** [C] a medical operation to remove a small number of cells from a part of the body in order to examine them to see if there is a disease

biotechnology /ˌbaɪəʊtek'nɒlədʒi/ **noun** [U] the use of living cells and bacteria in chemical processes, especially in the food and medical industries

bioterrorism /ˌbaɪəʊ'terərɪz^əm/ **noun** [U] the use of living things, such as bacteria, to hurt other people for political reasons ● **bioterrorist noun** [C]

bipartisan /baɪ'pɑːtɪzæn/ **adj** involving two political parties: *a bipartisan agreement*

birch /bɜːtʃ/ **noun** [C, U] a tree that has thin, smooth branches

bird /bɜːd/ **noun** [C] **⑪** an animal that has wings and feathers and is usually able to fly

bird flu noun [U] (also **avian flu**) an illness that kills birds and can sometimes pass from birds to people

birdie /'bɜːdi/ **noun** [C] US (mainly UK **shuttlecock**) a small object with feathers that is used like a ball in badminton (= a sport like tennis)

bird of prey noun [C] (plural **birds of prey**) a large bird that kills smaller animals for food

bird-watching /ˈbɜːdˌwɒtʃɪŋ/ **noun** [U] the hobby of looking at birds

biro /ˈbaɪərəʊ/ **noun** [C, U] UK trademark a type of pen that has a very small metal ball at its end and a thin tube of ink inside

birth /bɜːθ/ **noun 1 give birth** 🅱2 When a woman or an animal gives birth, she produces a baby from her body: *She gave birth to twins.* **2** [C, U] 🅱1 the time when a baby is born: *a difficult birth* ○ *Write your **date of birth** here.* **3** [U] literary the beginning of something: *the birth of modern science* **4 American/Italian, etc by birth** born in a particular place or having parents with a particular nationality

birth certificate noun [C] an official document that records when and where a person was born

birth control noun [U] methods of limiting the number of children you have

birthday /ˈbɜːθdeɪ/ **noun** [C] 🅰1 the day on which someone was born, or the same date each year: *She is **celebrating** her seventieth **birthday**.* ○ ***Happy Birthday!*** ○ *a birthday cake/party*

> 🗷 Word partners for **birthday**
>
> **celebrate** your birthday • **on** sb's [1st/50th/ 100th, etc] birthday • a birthday **cake/card/ party/present**

birthmark /ˈbɜːθmɑːk/ **noun** [C] a mark on someone's skin that has been there since they were born

birthplace /ˈbɜːθpleɪs/ **noun** [C] the place where someone was born

birth rate noun [C] a measurement of the number of babies born in a particular period

biscuit /ˈbɪskɪt/ **noun** [C] **1** UK (US **cookie**) 🅰3 a thin, flat cake that is dry and usually sweet → See colour picture **Food** on page Centre 11 **2** US a small, soft, round type of bread

bisexual /baɪˈsekʃuəl/ **adj** sexually attracted to both men and women

bishop /ˈbɪʃəp/ **noun** [C] a priest of high rank in some Christian churches: *the Bishop of Oxford*

bison /ˈbaɪsən/ **noun** [C] (plural **bison**) a large, wild animal similar to a cow with long hair

bistro /ˈbiːstrəʊ/ **noun** [C] an informal place to eat or drink, in a French style

bit¹ /bɪt/ **noun** [C] **1 SMALL AMOUNT** ▷ 🅰2 mainly UK a small amount or piece of something: *I wrote it down on a bit of paper.* ○ *There's a little bit more pasta left.* ○ *My favourite bit of the film is right at the end.* ○ *The books are falling **to bits** (= into separate parts).* **2 a bit** 🅰2 mainly UK slightly: *It's a bit cold in here.* ○ *It was a bit too expensive.* **b** 🅱2 mainly UK informal a short time: *I'll see you **in a bit**.* ○ *She lived in Italy **for a bit**.* **3 a bit of a change/fool/problem, etc** mainly UK a change, fool (= stupid person), problem, etc, but not an important or serious one: *I am a bit of a romantic.* ○ *It was a bit of a shock.* **4 quite a bit** informal 🅱1 a lot: *He does quite a bit of travelling.* ○ *She is quite a bit older than him.* **5 a bit much** mainly UK informal more than is fair, or more than you can deal with: *It's a bit much to expect me to tidy up their mess.* **6 bit by bit** gradually: *She*

saved up the money, bit by bit. **7 every bit as** used to emphasize that one thing is equally good, important, etc as something else: *The gardens are every bit as impressive as the castle itself.* **8 bits and pieces** small things or jobs that are not connected or not very important: *We've packed most of it up now, there are just a few bits and pieces left.* **9 COMPUTER** ▷ a unit of information in a computer: *Can I run 32-bit programs on a 64-bit computer?* **10 HORSE** ▷ a piece of metal which goes in the mouth of a horse to control it

bit² /bɪt/ past tense of bite

bitch¹ /bɪtʃ/ **noun** [C] **1** very informal an offensive name for an unpleasant woman **2** a female dog

bitch² /bɪtʃ/ **verb** [I] very informal to talk in an unkind way about people: *She's always **bitching** about her boss.*

bitchy /ˈbɪtʃi/ **adj** unkind about other people: *a bitchy comment*

bite¹ /baɪt/ **verb** (**bit**, **bitten**) **1** [I, T] 🅱1 to cut something using your teeth: *She **bit into** an apple.* ○ *He bites his fingernails.* ○ *He was bitten by a dog.* **2** [I] to begin to have a bad effect: *Government cuts are beginning to bite.* → See also **bite the bullet**, **bite the dust¹**

IDIOM **come back to bite you** If a problem will come back to bite you, it will cause more trouble for you in the future if you do not solve it now.

bite² /baɪt/ **noun 1** [C] 🅱2 a piece taken from food when you bite it: *She **took a bite** from her pizza.* **2** [C] 🅱2 an injury caused when an animal or insect bites you: *mosquito bites* **3 a bite** a small meal: *I just want to grab a bite to eat.*

biting /ˈbaɪtɪŋ/ **adj** A biting wind or biting cold is extremely cold and hurts your skin.

bitmap /ˈbɪtmæp/ **noun** [C] a computer image formed from many small points on the screen

bitten /ˈbɪtən/ past participle of bite

bitter¹ /ˈbɪtər/ **adj 1 ANGRY** ▷ 🅱2 angry and upset because of something bad that has happened that you cannot forget: *I feel very **bitter about** my childhood.* **2 HATE** ▷ 🅱2 full of hate or anger: *a bitter argument/dispute* **3 SOUR** ▷ 🅱1 having a strong, sour, usually unpleasant taste **4 COLD** ▷ 🅱2 extremely cold: *a bitter wind* **5 to/until the bitter end** until something is completely finished, usually something unpleasant: *He was determined to stay right to the bitter end.* **6 DISAPPOINTED** ▷ 🅱2 making you feel very disappointed: *Losing the championship was a bitter disappointment.* • **bitterness noun** [U]

bitter² /ˈbɪtər/ **noun** [U] UK a type of beer with a bitter taste

bitterly /ˈbɪtəli/ **adv 1** in a way that shows strong negative emotion such as anger or disappointment: *We were **bitterly disappointed** about the decision.* **2** If it is bitterly cold, the weather is extremely and unpleasantly cold.

bizarre /bɪˈzɑːr/ **adj** 🅱2 very strange and surprising: *bizarre behaviour* • **bizarrely adv**

black¹ /blæk/ **adj 1 COLOUR** ▷ 🅰1 being the colour of coal or of the sky on a very dark night: *a black jacket* → See colour picture **Colours** on

Centre 12 **2 PERSON** ▷ **A2** Someone who is black has the dark skin typical of people from Africa: *black athletes/Americans* **3 OF BLACK PEOPLE** ▷ relating to black people: *the black community* **4 DRINK** ▷ Black tea or coffee has no milk or cream added to it. **5 HUMOUR** ▷ funny about unpleasant or frightening subjects: *black comedy* **6 ANGRY** ▷ angry: *He gave her a black look.* **7 SITUATION** ▷ If your situation or future is black, it is very bad.

IDIOMS **black and blue** covered with bruises (= marks on your skin from being hit) • **black and white** very clear or simple: *The issue of nuclear weapons is not black and white.*

• **blackness** noun [U] → See also **jet-black, pitch-black**

black² /blæk/ noun **1** [C, U] **A2** the colour of coal or of the sky on a very dark night: *She always dresses in black* (= in black clothes). → See colour picture **Colours** on page Centre 12 **2** [C] a black person **3 in the black** If your bank account is in the black, it contains some money.

IDIOM **in black and white a** printed in a book, newspaper, or official document: *Look at the contract – it's all there in black and white.* **b** using or seeing no colours, but only black, white, and grey: *I saw the original film in black and white.*

→ See also **jet-black**

black³ /blæk/ verb

PHRASAL VERB **black out** informal to suddenly become unconscious

blackberry /ˈblækbəri/ noun [C] a small, soft, dark purple fruit with seeds

BlackBerry /ˈblækbəri/ noun [C] trademark a computer with no wires that fits in your hand and that you can use for documents, email, and Internet access and as a mobile phone • **BlackBerry** verb [I] to use a BlackBerry

blackbird /ˈblækbɜːd/ noun [C] a bird with black feathers and a yellow beak

blackboard /ˈblækbɔːd/ noun [C] (also US **chalkboard**) **A2** a large board with a dark surface that teachers write on with chalk (= soft, white rock) → See colour picture **The Classroom** on page Centre 6

black ˈbox noun [C] a small machine on an aircraft that people use to discover the reason for an aircraft accident

blackcurrant /ˌblækˈkʌrənt/ noun [C] UK a very small, round, sour, dark purple fruit: *blackcurrant juice/jelly*

blacken /ˈblækən/ verb **1** [I, T] to become black or to make something become black: *Storm clouds blackened the sky.* **2** [T] If you blacken someone's name, you say bad things about them.

black ˈeye noun [C] an eye that has a dark circle around it because it has been hit

black ˈhole noun [C] an area in outer space that sucks material and light into it from which they cannot escape

blacklist /ˈblæklɪst/ verb [T] to include someone on a list of people you think are bad or you will

not deal with: [often passive] *He was blacklisted by the banks and credit card companies.*

black ˈmagic noun [U] magic used for evil

blackmail /ˈblækmeɪl/ noun [U] the crime of forcing someone to do something, or to pay you money, by saying you will tell another person something that they want to keep secret • **blackmail** verb [T] [+ into + doing sth] *They used the photographs to blackmail her into spying for them.* • **blackmailer** noun [C]

black ˈmarket noun [C] illegal trading of goods that are not allowed to be bought and sold or that there are not enough of for everyone who wants them: *the black market in heroin*

blackout /ˈblækaʊt/ noun [C] **1 UNCONSCIOUS** ▷ the state of being unconscious for a short time **2 NO INFORMATION** ▷ a situation in which people are not allowed to be told about something: [usually singular] *a media/news blackout* **3 NO ELECTRICITY** ▷ a failure in the supply of electricity **4 NO LIGHTS** ▷ a period during a war when no lights must show at night

blacksmith /ˈblæksmɪθ/ noun [C] someone whose job is to make things from metal, especially shoes for horses

bladder /ˈblædər/ noun [C] the organ where waste liquid is stored before it leaves your body → See also **gall bladder**

blade /bleɪd/ noun [C] **1 B2** the flat, sharp, metal part of a knife, tool, or weapon **2** a long, narrow leaf of grass or a similar plant: *a blade of grass* → See also **razor blade, shoulder blade**

blame¹ /bleɪm/ verb [T] **1 B1** to say or think that someone or something is responsible for something bad that has happened: *Many people blame him for Tony's death.* ∘ *Poor housing is to blame for many of their health problems.* ∘ *They apologized for the delay and blamed it on technical problems.* **2 I don't blame him/them/you, etc** used to say that you understand and accept the reason for what someone is doing: *"I think I'll go home early." "I don't blame you – you look really tired."*

blame² /bleɪm/ noun [U] **B2** responsibility for something bad: *The manager should take the blame for the team's defeat.* ∘ *They put the blame on faulty equipment.*

> **🗓 Word partners for blame**
>
> apportion blame • get/shoulder/take the blame for sth • lay/put the blame on sth

blameless /ˈbleɪmləs/ adj not responsible for anything bad: *They concluded that Lucy was entirely blameless.*

bland /blænd/ adj **1** not interesting or exciting: *bland statements* **2** If food is bland, it does not have much taste.

blank¹ /blæŋk/ adj **1 B1** with no writing, pictures, or sound: *a blank page* ∘ *a blank tape* ∘ *The space for the date was left blank.* **2 go blank** If your mind goes blank, you suddenly cannot remember or think of something. **3** showing no feeling or understanding: *a blank expression* → See also **point-blank**

blank² /blæŋk/ noun [C] an empty space on a

piece of paper or form where information can be given: *Just fill in the blanks.*

IDIOM **draw a blank** to be unable to get information, think of something, or achieve something: *All their investigations have drawn a blank so far.*

blank ˈcheque UK (mainly US ˌblank ˈcheck) **noun** [C] If you give someone a blank cheque, you allow them as much money as they want or need to do something.

blanket¹ /ˈblæŋkɪt/ **noun** [C] **1** ⓐ a thick, warm cover that you sleep under **2** a thick layer of something: *a blanket of cloud/snow*

blanket² /ˈblæŋkɪt/ **adj** [always before noun] including or affecting everything: *a blanket ban*

blanket³ /ˈblæŋkɪt/ **verb** [T] to completely cover something: *The ground was blanketed with snow.*

blankly /ˈblæŋkli/ **adv** without showing any emotion or understanding: *She just stared at me blankly.*

blare /bleə^r/ **verb** [I] (also **blare out**) to make a very loud noise: *There was music blaring from his room.*

blasphemy /ˈblæsfəmi/ **noun** [U] something that you say or do that shows you do not respect God or a religion • **blasphemous** /ˈblæs-fəməs/ **adj** expressing blasphemy

blast¹ /blɑːst/ **noun 1** EXPLOSION ▷ [C] an explosion: *a bomb blast* **2** AIR ▷ [C] a sudden strong movement of air: *a blast of cold air/heat* **3** full blast If something is happening or working full blast, it is at its loudest, strongest, or fastest level: *The heating was on full blast.* **4** NOISE ▷ [C] a sudden loud noise: *a blast on the trumpet* **5** ENJOYMENT ▷ [no plural] US very informal an exciting and enjoyable experience: *Eric's party was a blast.*

blast² /blɑːst/ **verb 1** NOISE ▷ [I, T] (also **blast out**) to make a very loud noise: *Rock music blasted from the speakers.* **2** MOVE ▷ [I, T] to move through something or to hit something with force: *Dixon blasted the ball past the goalkeeper.* **3** EXPLODE ▷ [T] to break through rock using explosives: *They blasted a hole in the rock face.* **4** GUNS ▷ [T] to destroy a person or place with guns or bombs

PHRASAL VERB **blast off** When a spacecraft blasts off, it leaves the ground to go into space.

blast³ /blɑːst/ **exclamation** UK informal (US **blast it**) used when you are annoyed at something: *Blast! I forgot the keys.*

blast-off /ˈblɑːstɒf/ **noun** [U] the time when a spacecraft leaves the ground

blatant /ˈbleɪtᵊnt/ **adj** very obvious, with no attempt to be honest or behave well: *blatant lies/racism* • **blatantly adv**

> ☑ Word partners for **blatant**
>
> a blatant **attempt** to do sth • a blatant **dis-regard** for sth • a blatant **lie**

blaze¹ /bleɪz/ **verb** [I] to burn or shine very brightly or strongly: *The sun blazed down on the dry countryside.*

blaze² /bleɪz/ **noun** [C] **1** a large, strong fire: *The blaze started in the hall.* **2** a blaze of colour/lights etc very bright colour, lights, etc: *The tulips provided a blaze of colour outside her window.* **3** a blaze of glory/publicity a lot of public attention for a short time

blazer /ˈbleɪzə^r/ **noun** [C] a type of jacket, often worn as part of a school uniform

blazing /ˈbleɪzɪŋ/ **adj** [always before noun] **1** very hot: *a blazing log fire* **2** UK very angry: *a blazing row*

bleach¹ /bliːtʃ/ **noun** [U] a strong chemical used for cleaning things or removing colour from things

bleach² /bliːtʃ/ **verb** [T] to remove the colour from something or make it lighter using chemicals: *She's bleached her hair.*

bleachers /ˈbliːtʃəz/ **noun** [plural] an area of seats at a sports ground that are not covered and are therefore not expensive to sit in

bleak /bliːk/ **adj 1** If a situation is bleak, there is little or no hope for the future: *The future is looking bleak for small businesses struggling with debts.* **2** If a place is bleak, it is cold, empty, and not attractive: *a bleak landscape* • **bleakness noun** [U]

bleary /ˈblɪəri/ **adj** If you have bleary eyes, you cannot see clearly because you are tired or have just woken up.

bleat /bliːt/ **verb** [I] **1** to make the noise of a sheep or goat **2** to speak or complain in a weak and annoying way: *She keeps bleating about her lack of money.* • **bleat noun** [C]

bled /bled/ past of bleed

bleed /bliːd/ **verb** [I] (**bled**) ⓑ to have blood coming from a place in your body • **bleeding noun** [U] *Try to stop the bleeding.*

bleep /bliːp/ **noun** [C] a short, high electronic noise • **bleep verb** [I]

bleeper /ˈbliːpə^r/ **noun** [C] UK (UK/US **beeper**) a small piece of electronic equipment that you carry that makes a sound when someone wants to speak to you

blemish /ˈblemɪʃ/ **noun** [C] a mark that spoils the appearance of someone or something

blend¹ /blend/ **verb 1** [T] to mix two or more things together completely: *Blend the ingredients into a smooth paste.* **2** [I, T] to combine two or more things: *The team blends new, young players with more mature, experienced ones.*

PHRASAL VERB **blend in** If something or someone blends in, they look or seem the same as the people or things around them and so are not easily noticed.

blend² /blend/ **noun** [C] a combination of two or more things: *Their music is a blend of jazz and African rhythms.*

blender /ˈblendə^r/ **noun** [C] an electric machine for making soft foods into a smooth liquid ➔ See colour picture **The Kitchen** on page Centre 2

bless /bles/ **verb** [T] **1** to ask God to help or protect someone or something, or to make it holy: *The priest blessed their marriage.* **2** be blessed with sth to be lucky enough to have something good: *He's blessed with a wonderful singing voice.* **3 Bless you!** something you say when someone sneezes **4 bless her/him/them, etc** informal used to show your affection for the person you are talking about: *Peter, bless him, slept all the way through it.*

blessed /'blesɪd/ *adj* [always before noun] **1** pleasant and wanted very much: *The rain was a blessed relief.* **2** holy: *the Blessed Virgin Mary*

blessing /'blesɪŋ/ *noun* **1 LUCK** ▷ [C] something that is lucky or makes you happy: *It is a blessing that no one was hurt.* **2 APPROVAL** ▷ [U] approval that someone gives to a plan or action: *Mr Newton has given his blessing for the plan.* **3 RELIGION** ▷ [C, U] protection or help from God, or a prayer to ask for this

IDIOMS **a blessing in disguise** something that has a good effect, although at first it seemed that it would be bad • **a mixed blessing** something that has both good and bad effects

blew /bluː/ past tense of blow

blight /blaɪt/ *noun* [no plural] something that has a very bad effect on something, often for a long time: *the blight of poverty/unemployment* ∘ *He became a blight on their lives.* • **blight** *verb* [T] to cause damage to or have a bad effect on something: *Injury has blighted his career.*

blind¹ /blaɪnd/ *adj* **1** 🔵 not able to see: *She went blind after an accident.* ∘ *This project provides guide dogs for the blind.* **2 be blind to sth** to not notice something, or not want to notice something: *Drivers who speed are often blind to the risks they cause.* **3 blind panic/rage/trust, etc** an extremely strong feeling that makes you do things without thinking **4 a blind corner/bend** a bend or corner on a road that is dangerous because you cannot see cars coming around it • **blindness** *noun* [U] → See also **colour blind, turn a blind eye¹ (to sth)**

blind² /blaɪnd/ *verb* **1** [T] to make someone blind, either permanently or for a short time: [often passive] *I was blinded by the car headlights.* **2 blind sb to sth** to make someone unable to understand the truth about someone or something: *Love blinded her to all his faults.*

blind³ /blaɪnd/ *noun* [C] a cover that you pull down over a window → See also **venetian blind**

blind date *noun* [C] a romantic meeting between a man and a woman who have not met before

blindfold /'blaɪndfəʊld/ *noun* [C] a piece of cloth that you put over someone's eyes so they cannot see • **blindfold** *verb* [T] to put a blindfold on someone

blinding /'blaɪndɪŋ/ *adj* **1** A blinding light is extremely bright. **2** A blinding headache (= pain in the head) is extremely painful.

blindly /'blaɪndli/ *adv* **1** not able to see or not noticing what is around you: *Carly reached blindly for the light switch.* **2** not thinking about what you are doing: *They just blindly followed orders.*

blind spot *noun* [C] **1** a difficulty in accepting or understanding a particular thing: *She has a complete blind spot where relations with the press*

are concerned. **2** the part of the road just behind you, that you cannot see when you are driving

blink /blɪŋk/ *verb* **1** [I, T] 🔵 to open and close both of your eyes quickly **2** [I] If a light blinks, it goes on and off quickly. • **blink** *noun* [C]

blinkered /'blɪŋkəd/ *adj* not willing to consider new or different ideas: *a blinkered attitude*

blip /blɪp/ *noun* [C] **1** a small, temporary, and usually negative change from what usually happens: *The rise in unemployment may just be a blip.* **2** a small spot of light on an electronic screen, sometimes with a short, high sound

bliss /blɪs/ *noun* [U] complete happiness: *My idea of bliss is lying on a sunny beach.* • **blissful** *adj* making you feel very happy: *a blissful childhood* • **blissfully** *adv* *She seemed blissfully unaware of the chaos she had caused.*

blister¹ /'blɪstər/ *noun* [C] a painful, raised area of skin with liquid inside, that you get if your skin has been rubbed or burned, or a similar area on a painted surface

blister² /'blɪstər/ *verb* [I, T] to get or cause blisters

blistering /'blɪstərɪŋ/ *adj* **1 CRITICISM** ▷ using very strong criticism: *a blistering attack* **2 HEAT** ▷ extremely hot: *blistering sunshine* **3 SPEED** ▷ extremely fast: *The economy has grown at a blistering pace.*

blithely /'blaɪðli/ *adv* without thinking about what might happen: *People were blithely ignoring warnings not to swim in the river.*

blitz¹ /blɪts/ *noun* [C] **1** a lot of activity to achieve something in a short time: *We had a cleaning blitz before my parents came home.* **2 the Blitz** bomb attacks on British cities during the Second World War

blitz² /blɪts/ *verb* [T] **1** to defeat someone or something completely **2** to drop bombs on something

blizzard /'blɪzəd/ *noun* [C] a storm with strong winds and snow

bloated /'bləʊtɪd/ *adj* **1** swollen because of air or liquid inside **2** feeling uncomfortable because you have eaten too much

blob /blɒb/ *noun* [C] a small amount of a thick liquid: *a blob of cream/glue* → See colour picture **Pieces and Quantities** on page Centre 1

bloc /blɒk/ *noun* [C] a group of countries with similar political ideas, who work together: *the communist bloc*

block¹ /blɒk/ *noun* [C] **1 PIECE** ▷ 🔵 a solid piece of something, usually in the shape of a square or rectangle: *a block of ice/stone/wood* **2 DISTANCE** ▷ US 🔵 the distance along a street from where one road crosses it to the place where the next road crosses it: *They only live two blocks away from the school.* **3 BUILDING** ▷ mainly UK 🔵 a large building containing many apartments or offices: UK *a block of flats* **4 GROUP OF BUILDINGS** ▷ a square group of buildings or houses with roads on each side: *Omar took the dog for a walk round the block.* **5 CANNOT THINK** ▷ If you have a block about something, you cannot understand it or remember it: *I had a complete mental block*

block

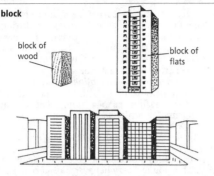

block of
wood

block of
flats

about his name. **6 STOP PROGRESS** ▷ something that makes it difficult to move or make progress **7 AMOUNT** ▷ an amount or group of something that is considered together: *This block of seats is reserved.* → See also **be a chip¹ off the old block, stumbling block, tower block**

block² /blɒk/ **verb** [T] **1 CANNOT PASS** ▷ (also **block up**) ⓑ to prevent anyone or anything from passing through a place: *A fallen tree blocked the road.* ◦ *The sink is blocked up.* ◦ *a blocked drain* **2 STOP PROGRESS** ▷ to stop something from happening or making progress: *The government has blocked plans for a new wind farm.* **3 CANNOT SEE** ▷ to be between someone and the thing they are looking at, so that they cannot see: *A pillar was blocking my view.*

PHRASAL VERBS **block sth off** to close a road, path, or entrance so that people cannot use it: *Police blocked off the road where the body was found.* • **block sth out 1** to try to stop yourself thinking about something unpleasant: *I've blocked out memories of the accident.* **2** to stop light or noise passing through something: *Most sunscreens block out UVB radiation.*

blockade /blɒk'eɪd/ **noun** [C] a situation in which a government or soldiers stop goods or people from entering or leaving a place: *The government **imposed a blockade on** oil trading.* • **blockade verb** [T]

blockage /'blɒkɪdʒ/ **noun** [C] something that stops something else passing through: *His death was caused by a blockage in his arteries.*

blockbuster /'blɒk,bʌstə^r/ **noun** [C] informal a book, film, etc that is very popular and successful: *a new blockbuster movie*

block capitals noun [plural] letters in the form A, B, C, not a, b, c

blog /blɒg/ **noun** [C] (also **weblog**) ⓑ a record of your thoughts that you put on the Internet for other people to read → See Study Page **The Web and the Internet** on page Centre 36 • **blog verb** [I] • **blogger** /'blɒgə^r/ **noun** [C] ⓑ a person who writes or reads a blog

blogging /'blɒgɪŋ/ **noun** [U] the activity of writing blogs

blogosphere /'blɒgə,sfɪə^r/ **noun** [usually singular] informal all the opinions, articles, etc. that are published by people on internet blogs: *the political blogosphere*

bloke /bləʊk/ **noun** [C] UK informal a man: *Jake's (nice bloke.*

blonde¹ (also **blond**) /blɒnd/ **adj 1** ⓐⓑ Blonde hair is pale yellow. **2** ⓐⓑ Someone who is blonde has pale yellow hair.

blonde² (also **blond**) /blɒnd/ **noun** [C] someone especially a woman, who has pale yellow hair

blood /blʌd/ **noun** [U] **1** ⓐⓑ the red liquid tha flows around your body: *a **blood test**/sample* **2** the family or place that you come from: *There' Spanish blood in me.* **3 be in your blood** I something is in your blood, you and othe people in your family are interested in it or goo(at it: *Sailing is in my blood.*

IDIOMS **bad blood** feelings of hate betwee(people because of things that have happene(in the past • **in cold blood** in a cruel way without showing any emotion: *He shot thre(policemen in cold blood.* • **new blood** new peopl(in an organization who will provide new idea and energy

→ See also **your own flesh and blood**

> **☑ Word partners for blood**
>
> **donate/give** blood (= allow blood to be taken from your body for someone else's body) • **drop/pool/trickle** of blood • a blood **test**

bloodbath /'blʌdbɑːθ/ **noun** [no plural] an extremely violent event in which many peopl(are killed

blood-curdling /'blʌd,kɜːdlɪŋ/ **adj** extremel} frightening: *a blood-curdling scream*

blood donor noun [C] someone who give(some of their blood for sick people who need i

blood group noun [C] mainly UK (UK/US **bloo(type**) one of the groups that human blood i(divided into

bloodless /'blʌdləs/ **adj** achieved without killin(or violence: *a bloodless coup*

blood pressure noun [U] the force wit} which blood flows around your body: *high/lo(blood pressure*

bloodshed /'blʌdʃed/ **noun** [U] fighting in which people are killed or injured: *Peace talk have failed to end the bloodshed in the region.*

bloodshot /'blʌdʃɒt/ **adj** Bloodshot eyes are re(in the part that should be white.

blood sport noun [C] a sport in which animal(are killed

bloodstained /'blʌdsteɪnd/ **adj** Something tha is bloodstained has blood on it.

bloodstream /'blʌdstriːm/ **noun** [no plural] th(flow of blood around your body

bloodthirsty /'blʌd,θɜːsti/ **adj** enjoying usin(or watching violence

blood transfusion noun [C] a medical treat ment in which blood is put into someone's bod}

blood type noun [C] (also UK **blood group**) on(of the groups that human blood is divided int(

blood vessel noun [C] one of the small tube that blood flows through in your body

bloody¹ /'blʌdi/ **adj 1** ⓑ covered in bloo(

bloody hands **2** violent and involving a lot of blood and injuries: *a bloody war*

bloody² /'blʌdi/ *adj, adv* UK very informal used to show anger or to emphasize what you are saying in a slightly rude way: *I can't find my bloody keys.* ∘ *We were bloody lucky to win.*

bloom¹ /bluːm/ *noun* **1** [C] a flower: *beautiful, pink blooms* **2 in bloom** with flowers that are open: *In June the roses are in bloom.*

bloom² /bluːm/ *verb* [I] **1** If a plant blooms, its flowers open. **2** to develop and become successful, happy, or healthy: *Their romance bloomed while they were in Paris.*

blossom¹ /'blɒsəm/ *noun* [C, U] a small flower, or the small flowers on a tree or plant: *cherry blossom*

blossom² /'blɒsəm/ *verb* [I] **1** If a tree blossoms, it produces flowers. **2** to develop and become successful or beautiful: *She has **blossomed into** a beautiful young woman.*

blot¹ /blɒt/ *verb* [T] (**blotting, blotted**) to dry wet marks using soft paper or a cloth

PHRASAL VERB **blot sth out 1** to stop yourself from thinking about something unpleasant: *I've tried to blot out memories of my relationship with Dieter.* **2** If smoke or cloud blots out the sun, it prevents it from being seen.

blot² /blɒt/ *noun* **1** [C] a mark on something, made by ink or paint falling on it **2 a blot on sth** something that spoils something else: *The financial scandal was a blot on his reputation.*

blotch /blɒtʃ/ *noun* [C] a mark on something, especially your skin • **blotchy** (also **blotched**) *adj* having unattractive blotches

blotting ˌpaper *noun* [U] thick paper used for drying wet ink

blouse /blaʊz/ ⓤⓈ /blaʊs/ *noun* [C] a piece of clothing like a shirt that women wear

blow¹ /bləʊ/ *verb* (**blew, blown**) **1** WIND ▷ [I] 🔓 If the wind blows, it moves and makes currents of air: *A cool sea breeze was blowing.* **2** PERSON ▷ [I] 🔓 to force air out through your mouth: *She blew on her coffee before taking a sip.* **3 blow sth down/across/off, etc** 🔓 If the wind blows something somewhere, it makes it move in that direction: *The storm blew trees across the road.* **4** MOVE ▷ [I] to move in the wind: *The branches were blowing in the breeze.* **5** INSTRUMENT ▷ [I, T] 🔓 to make a sound by forcing air out of your mouth and through an instrument: *Ann blew a few notes on the trumpet.* **6** MAKE ▷ [T] to make shapes out of something by blowing it: *to blow bubbles* **7** SPEND ▷ [T] informal to spend a lot of money quickly and without considering it seriously: *Lou blew all her prize money **on** a diamond necklace.* **8 blow it/your chance(s)** informal If you blow it or blow your chance, you lose an opportunity to do something by doing or saying the wrong thing: *Tom blew his chances of getting the job by arriving late for the interview.* **9 blow your nose** 🔓 to clear your nose by forcing air through it into a handkerchief (= piece of cloth or soft paper) **10** ELECTRICITY ▷ [I, T] If a piece of electrical equipment blows, it suddenly stops working

because the electric current is too strong. → See also **blow your mind¹**, **blow/get sth out of proportion**

PHRASAL VERBS **blow sb away** mainly US informal to surprise or please someone very much: *This movie will blow you away.* • **blow (sth) out** 🔓 If a flame blows out, or if you blow it out, it stops burning because you or the wind have blown it. • **blow over** If a storm or an argument blows over, it ends. • **blow (sb/sth) up** 🔓 to destroy something or kill someone with a bomb, or to be destroyed by a bomb: *Terrorists blew up an office building in the city.* • **blow sth up** 🔓 to fill something with air: *He blew up a balloon.* • **blow up 1** If a storm or an argument blows up, it starts suddenly. **2** informal to suddenly become very angry

blow² /bləʊ/ *noun* [C] **1** DISAPPOINTMENT ▷ a shock or disappointment: *Losing his job was a terrible **blow to** him.* **2** HIT ▷ a hard hit with a hand or heavy object: *He suffered serious **blows to** the head during the attack.* **3** INSTRUMENT ▷ the act of blowing something or blowing into an instrument or other object: *a blow on the whistle*

IDIOM **come to blows** to fight or argue

blow-by-blow /ˌbləʊbaɪ'bləʊ/ *adj* a **blow-by-blow account/description** a description of an event that gives all the details in the exact order that they happened

blow-dry /'bləʊdraɪ/ *verb* [T] to dry your hair in a particular style using a hairdryer (= electrical equipment for drying hair) • **blow-dry** *noun* [no plural] *I had a cut and blow-dry.*

blown /bləʊn/ past participle of blow

blowout /'bləʊaʊt/ *noun* [C] **1** TYRE ▷ an occasion when a tyre suddenly explodes while a vehicle is still moving **2** MEAL/PARTY ▷ informal an expensive meal or a big party **3** SPORT ▷ US informal an easy defeat of a team or player

bludgeon /'blʌdʒ³n/ *verb* [T] to hit someone several times with a heavy object: [often passive] *She was bludgeoned to death with a hammer.*

blue¹ /bluː/ *adj* **1** COLOUR ▷ 🔓 being the same colour as the sky when there are no clouds: *a dark blue jacket* → See colour picture **Colours** on page Centre 12 **2** SAD ▷ informal sad **3** SEX ▷ about sex: *a blue joke/movie* → See also **black¹** and **blue, once in a blue moon**

blue² /bluː/ *noun* [C, U] 🔓 the colour of the sky when there are no clouds → See colour picture **Colours** on page Centre 12

IDIOM **out of the blue** If something happens out of the blue, you did not expect it: *One day, completely out of the blue, I received a letter from her.*

bluebell /'bluːbel/ *noun* [C] a plant with small, blue flowers shaped like bells

blueberry /'bluːb³ri/ *noun* [C] a small, sweet, dark blue fruit that grows on bushes

blue-chip /ˌbluː'tʃɪp/ *adj* [always before noun] A blue-chip company or investment is considered certain to make a profit.

blue-collar /ˌbluːˈkɒləʳ/ **adj** [always before noun] A blue-collar worker does physical work, especially in a factory.

blueprint /ˈbluːprɪnt/ **noun** [C] a plan that shows how someone will design, build, or achieve something: *a blueprint for political reform*

blues /bluːz/ **noun** [plural] **1** a type of slow, sad music that was developed by African-Americans: *jazz and blues* **2 have/get the blues** informal to feel or become sad

Bluetooth /ˈbluːtuːθ/ **noun** [U] trademark a technology that allows equipment such as computers and mobile phones to connect with no wires or cables: *a Bluetooth headset*

bluff¹ /blʌf/ **verb** [I, T] to pretend you will do something or that you have knowledge, in order to force someone to do something: *He won't really leave her – he's only bluffing.*

bluff² /blʌf/ **noun** [C] an attempt to bluff

IDIOM **call sb's bluff** to tell someone to do the thing they say they will do, because you do not think they will do it

blunder¹ /ˈblʌndəʳ/ **noun** [C] a serious and often stupid mistake: *a series of financial blunders*

blunder² /ˈblʌndəʳ/ **verb 1** [I] to make a serious mistake **2 blunder around/into, etc** to move somewhere in a heavy way, as if you cannot see well: *He blundered around, looking for the light switch.*

blunt¹ /blʌnt/ **adj 1** not sharp: *a blunt knife* **2** saying exactly what you think without caring about people's feelings: *a blunt letter* • **bluntness noun** [U]

blunt² /blʌnt/ **verb** [T] **1** to make a feeling less strong: *Mario's comments blunted everyone's enthusiasm.* **2** to make something less sharp

bluntly /ˈblʌntli/ **adv** saying exactly what you think without caring about people's feelings

blur¹ /blɜːʳ/ **verb** [I, T] (**blurring, blurred**) **1** to make the difference between two things less clear, or to make it difficult to see the exact truth about something: *This book blurs the distinction between reality and fiction* **2** to become difficult to see clearly, or to make something become difficult to see clearly: *The soft sunlight blurred the edges of the mountains.*

blur² /blɜːʳ/ **noun** [no plural] something that you cannot see or remember clearly: *The accident happened so quickly that it's all a blur.*

blurred

blurb /blɜːb/ **noun** [C] a short description to advertise a product, especially a book

blurred /blɜːd/ **adj 1** (also **blurry** /ˈblɜːri/) not clear: *a blurred photograph* ○ *blurred memories* **2** If your sight is blurred, you cannot see clearly: *blurred vision*

blurt /blɜːt/ **verb** [T] (also **blurt out**) to say something suddenly and without thinking, especially because you are excited or nervous: *"Will you marry me?" he blurted.*

blush /blʌʃ/ **verb** [I] ⬛ If you blush, your face becomes red, especially because you are embarrassed: *He blushed with shame.* • **blush noun** [C]

blusher /ˈblʌʃəʳ/ **noun** [U] mainly UK (US **blush**) red powder or cream that women put on their faces in order to make them more attractive → See picture at **make-up**

bluster /ˈblʌstəʳ/ **verb** [I, T] to speak in a loud and angry way, often with little effect • **bluster noun** [U]

blustery /ˈblʌstəri/ **adj** very windy: *a cold, blustery day*

boar /bɔːʳ/ **noun** [C] **1** a male pig **2** (also **wild boar**) a wild pig

board

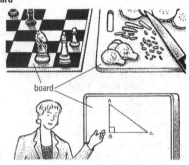

board

board¹ /bɔːd/ **noun 1** WOOD ▷ [C] a long, thin flat piece of wood: *He nailed some boards across the broken window.* **2** SURFACE ▷ [C] ⬛ a flat piece of wood, plastic, etc used for a particular purpose: *an ironing board* ○ *a chopping board* **3** INFORMATION ▷ [C] ⬛ a piece of wood, plastic, etc on a wall, where information can be put: *Have you seen the poster on the board?* **4** SCHOOL ROOM ▷ [C] ⬛ a surface on the wall of a school room that the teacher writes on: *Copy down the sentences from the board.* **5** GAMES ▷ [C] ⬛ a piece of wood, cardboard etc for playing games on: *a chess board* **6** ORGANIZATION ▷ [group] a group of people who officially control a company or organization, or a particular type of business activity: *The board approved the sales plan.* **7 on board** ⬛ on a boat, train, aircraft, etc **8** MEALS ▷ [U] ⬛ meals that are provided when you stay in a hotel: *bed and board* ○ *How much is a single room with full board (= all meals)?*

IDIOM **across the board** affecting everyone or every part of something: *Jobs are likely to be lost across the board.*

→ See also **bulletin board, diving board, drawing board, full board, half board, ironing board**

board² /bɔːd/ **verb 1** [I, T] ⬛ to get on a bus, boat, aircraft, etc: *He boarded the train to London.*

2 [I] If an aircraft, train, etc is boarding, passengers are getting onto it.

PHRASAL VERB **board sth up** to cover a door or window with wooden boards

boarder /'bɔːdər/ **noun** [C] **1 STUDENT** ▷ mainly UK a student who lives at school **2 PERSON** ▷ US (UK **lodger**) someone who pays for a place to sleep and meals in someone else's house **3 SPORT** ▷ someone who goes snowboarding (= sport where you stand on a board to move over snow)

board game noun [C] Ⓐ② a game such as chess that is played on a board

boarding house noun [C] a house where you pay for a room and meals

boarding pass noun [C] (also **boarding card**) a piece of paper you must show to get on an aircraft

boarding school noun [C] a school where students live and study

boardroom /'bɔːdruːm/ **noun** [C] a room where the people who control a company or organization have meetings

boast[1] /bəʊst/ **verb 1** [I, T] Ⓑ② to talk with too much pride about what you have done or what you own: *I wish she would stop **boasting about** her exam results.* ∘ [+ that] *Liam boasted that he owned two sports cars.* **2** [T] If a place boasts something good, it has it: *New York boasts some of the best museums in the world.*

boast[2] /bəʊst/ **noun** [C] something you are proud of and like to tell people about

boastful /'bəʊstf^əl/ **adj** talking with too much pride: *boastful remarks*

boat /bəʊt/ **noun** [C] Ⓐ① a vehicle for travelling on water: *a fishing boat*

IDIOMS **be in the same boat** to be in the same unpleasant situation as other people: *She complains that she doesn't have enough money, but we're all in the same boat.* • **miss the boat** to be too late to get what you want: *I'm afraid you've missed the boat. All the tickets have been sold.* • **push the boat out** UK to spend a lot of money, especially when you are celebrating • **rock the boat** to do or say something that changes a situation in a way that causes problems

→ See also **rowing boat**

bob /bɒb/ **verb** [I] (**bobbing**, **bobbed**) to move up and down quickly and gently: *Boats were bobbing in the harbour.*

bobby /'bɒbi/ **noun** [C] UK informal old-fashioned a police officer

bobby pin noun [C] US (UK **hairgrip**) a small, thin piece of metal, used to fasten a woman's hair in position

bode /bəʊd/ **verb** literary **bode ill/well** to be a bad or good sign for the future: *These religious differences do not bode well for their marriage.*

bodily[1] /'bɒdɪli/ **adj** [always before noun] relating to a person's body: *bodily strength*

bodily[2] /'bɒdɪli/ **adv** If you move someone bodily, you lift or push them: *He carried her bodily out of the room.*

body /'bɒdi/ **noun 1 PERSON** ▷ [C] Ⓐ① the whole physical structure of a person or animal: *the human body* → See colour picture **The Body** on page Centre 13 **2 DEAD** ▷ [C] Ⓐ② a dead person: *Police found the body in a field.* **3 NOT ARMS/ LEGS** ▷ [C] Ⓑ① the main part of a person or animal's body, not the head, arms, or legs: *a dog with a thin body and short legs* **4 GROUP** ▷ [group] an official group of people who work together: *the sport's regulatory body* **5 MAIN PART** ▷ [no plural] the main part of something: *The body of the book is about his childhood.* **6 AMOUNT** ▷ [no plural] a large amount of information: *a body of research into AIDS* **7 VEHICLE** ▷ [C] the main part of a vehicle: *The body of the ship was not damaged.*

bodybuilding /'bɒdibɪldɪŋ/ **noun** [U] exercise with heavy weights to make your muscles big • **bodybuilder noun** [C]

bodyguard /'bɒdigɑːd/ **noun** [C] someone whose job is to protect someone

body language noun [U] the way you move your body, that shows people what you are feeling

bog[1] /bɒg/ **noun** [C, U] an area of soft, wet ground

bog[2] /bɒg/ **verb** (**bogging**, **bogged**)

PHRASAL VERB **be bogged down** to become so involved in something that you cannot do anything else: *Try not to get too bogged down in details.*

boggle /'bɒgl/ **verb the mind boggles** (also US **it boggles the mind**) something you say if something is difficult for you to accept, imagine, or understand: *The mind boggles at the stupidity of some people.* → See also **mind-boggling**

BOGOF /'bɒgɒf/ **abbreviation** for buy one get one free: used in shops to tell customers that they can buy two products of a similar type but only pay for one

bogus /'bəʊgəs/ **adj** pretending to be real: *a bogus doctor* ∘ *bogus documents*

bohemian /bəʊ'hiːmiən/ **adj** typical of artists, musicians, etc, who live in a more informal way than most people

boil[1] /bɔɪl/ **verb** [I, T] **1 LIQUID** ▷ Ⓐ② If a liquid boils, or if you boil it, it reaches the temperature where bubbles rise up in it and it produces steam: *boiling water* **2 CONTAINER** ▷ Ⓑ① If a container of liquid boils, or if you boil it, the liquid inside it reaches the temperature where bubbles rise up in it and it produces steam: *I've boiled the kettle.* **3 COOK** ▷ Ⓑ① to cook food in water that is boiling: *Boil the pasta for 10 minutes.* ∘ *boiled potatoes* → See picture at **cook**

PHRASAL VERBS **boil down to sth** If a situation or problem boils down to something, that is the main reason for it: *The problem boils down to one thing – lack of money.* • **boil over 1** If a liquid that is being heated boils over, it flows over the side of the pan. **2** If a difficult situation or bad emotion boils over, it cannot be controlled any more and people start to argue or fight.

boil[2] /bɔɪl/ **noun 1 bring sth to the boil** to heat

B

B

something until it starts to produce bubbles and steam: *Bring the water to the boil, then add the rice.* **2** [C] a red swollen area on the skin that is infected

boiler /ˈbɔɪləʳ/ *noun* [C] a piece of equipment that provides hot water for a house

boiling /ˈbɔɪlɪŋ/ *adj* (also ˌboiling ˈhot) ⑫ very hot: *It's boiling in here!*

ˈboiling ˌpoint *noun* [C] the temperature that a liquid boils at

boisterous /ˈbɔɪstᵊrəs/ *adj* noisy and full of energy: *a boisterous child* • **boisterously** *adv*

bold¹ /bəʊld/ *adj* **1** NOT FRIGHTENED ▷ ⑫ not frightened of taking risks: *It was a bold decision to go and live abroad.* **2** COLOUR/SHAPE ▷ ⑪ strong in colour or shape: *bold colours* ∘ *a bold design* **3** LETTERS ▷ words that are printed in bold letters are darker and thicker than normal words • **boldly** *adv* • **boldness** *noun* [U]

🗒 Word partners for **bold**

a bold **decision/move/plan/step**

---

bold² /bəʊld/ *noun* [U] a style of printing in which the letters are darker and thicker than usual

bollard /ˈbɒlɑːd/ *noun* [C] UK a short thick post in a road, used to stop cars driving somewhere

bolster /ˈbəʊlstəʳ/ *verb* [T] to make something stronger by supporting or encouraging it: *Strong sales are bolstering the economy.*

bolt¹ /bəʊlt/ *noun* [C] **1** a metal bar that you push across a door or window to lock it **2** a small piece of metal that is used with a nut (= metal piece with a hole in the middle) to fasten pieces of wood or metal together → See picture at **tool** → See also **the nuts and bolts**

bolt² /bəʊlt/ *verb* [T] **1** FASTEN ▷ to fasten two things together with a bolt: *The seats in the cinema were bolted to the floor.* **2** LOCK ▷ to lock a door or window with a bolt **3** bolt down/out/ through, etc to move suddenly and quickly: *The cat bolted out of the door when it saw the dog.* **4** EAT ▷ (also **bolt down**) to eat something very quickly

ˌbolt ˈupright *adv* sitting or standing with your back very straight

bomb¹ /bɒm/ *noun* [C] ⑪ a weapon that explodes and causes damage: *The bomb destroyed several office buildings in the city.* → See also **atomic bomb**

🗒 Word partners for **bomb**

plant a bomb • a bomb **explodes/goes off** • a bomb **attack/blast** • a bomb **scare/ threat/warning**

---

bomb² /bɒm/ *verb* **1** ⑪ [T] to attack a place using bombs: *The factories were bombed during the war.* **2** bomb along/down/through, etc UK informal to move very quickly: *A car came bombing down the road.*

bombard /bɒmˈbɑːd/ *verb* [T] to continuously attack a place using guns and bombs

• **bombardment** *noun* [C, U] *an **aerial bom bardment***

PHRASAL VERB **bombard sb with sth** to give someone too much information, ask them too many questions, etc

bomber /ˈbɒməʳ/ *noun* [C] **1** an aircraft that drops bombs **2** ⑫ someone who puts a bomb somewhere

bombshell /ˈbɒmʃel/ *noun* [C] informal a piece of usually bad news that surprises you very much: *He **dropped a bombshell** by announcing that he was quitting the sport.*

bona fide /ˌbəʊnəˈfaɪdi/ *adj* real and honest: *Make sure you are dealing with a bona fide company.*

bonanza /bəˈnænzə/ *noun* [C] a situation in which many people are successful and get a lot of money: *The Internet is a bonanza for the computer industry.*

bond¹ /bɒnd/ *noun* [C] **1** ⑫ an interest, experience, or feeling that makes two people feel connected: *A love of opera **created** a bond **between** them.* **2** an official document from a government or company to show that you have given them money that they will pay back with a certain amount of extra money

---
🗒 Word partners for **bond**

create/forge/form/strengthen a bond • a **close** bond • a bond **with** sb/**between** sb and sb

---

bond² /bɒnd/ *verb* **1** [I, T] If two things bond, they stick together, or if you bond them, you make them stick together: *This glue bonds wood and metal in seconds.* **2** [I] to develop a strong relationship with someone: *Physical contact helps a mother **bond with** her baby.*

bondage /ˈbɒndɪdʒ/ *noun* [U] a situation in which someone is completely controlled by something or is a slave (= owned by the person they work for)

bone¹ /bəʊn/ *noun* [C, U] ⑪ one of the hard pieces that make the structure inside a person or animal: *He broke a bone in his hand.*

bone

IDIOMS **a bone of conten- tion** something that people argue about • **have a bone to pick with sb** informal to want to talk to someone because you are annoyed about something they have done • **make no bones about sth/doing sth** to say what you think or feel, without being embarrassed: *She made no bones about her reluctance to work with me.*

bone² /bəʊn/ *verb* [T] to remove the bones from meat or fish

ˈbone ˌmarrow *noun* [U] the soft substance inside bones

bonfire /ˈbɒnfaɪəʳ/ *noun* [C] a large fire outside often used for burning waste

---

bonkers /ˈbɒŋkəz/ **adj** informal crazy

bonnet /ˈbɒnɪt/ **noun** [C] **1** UK (US **hood**) the metal cover of a car's engine → See colour picture **Car** on page Centre 7 **2** a hat that you tie under your face

bonus /ˈbəʊnəs/ **noun** [C] **1** ⓑ② an extra amount of money that you are given, especially because you have worked hard: *All employees received a bonus of £500.* **2** ⓑ② another pleasant thing in addition to something you were expecting: *The sunny weather was an **added bonus**.*

bony /ˈbəʊni/ **adj** very thin, so that you can see or feel bones: *bony elbows*

boo /buː/ **verb** [I, T] (**booing, booed**) to shout the word "boo" to show that you do not like a speech, performance, etc • **boo noun** [C]

boob /buːb/ **noun** [C] informal **1** a woman's breast **2** a silly mistake

booby prize /ˈbuːbiˌpraɪz/ **noun** [C] a prize that you get if you finish last in a competition

booby trap /ˈbuːbiˌtræp/ **noun** [C] something dangerous, especially a bomb, that is hidden somewhere that looks safe • **booby-trap verb** [T] [often passive] *His car was booby-trapped.*

book¹ /bʊk/ **noun 1** [C] ⓐ① a set of pages fastened together in a cover for people to read: *a book about animals* **2 a book of stamps/ tickets, etc** a set of stamps, tickets, etc that are fastened together inside a cover **3** [C] a set of pages fastened together in a cover and used for writing on: *an **address book***

IDIOMS **do sth by the book** to do something exactly as the rules tell you • **be in sb's good/ bad books** UK informal If you are in someone's good books, they are pleased with you, and if you are in their bad books, they are angry with you.

→ See also **cookery book, take a leaf¹ out of sb's book, phone book, reference book**

book² /bʊk/ **verb 1 ARRANGE** ▷ [I, T] ⓐ② to arrange to use or do something at a particular time in the future: *to book a ticket/hotel room* ○ *We've booked a trip to Spain for next month.* ○ *Sorry, the hotel is **fully booked** (= has no more rooms).* **2 CRIME** ▷ [T] to officially accuse someone of a crime: *Detectives booked him for resisting arrest.* **3 SPORT** ▷ [T] UK If a sports official books you, they write an official record of something you have done wrong: *The referee booked two players for fighting during the game.*

PHRASAL VERBS **book in/book into sth** UK to say that you have arrived when you get to a hotel • **book sb in/book sb into sth** mainly UK ⓑ① to arrange for someone to stay at a hotel

bookcase /ˈbʊkkeɪs/ **noun** [C] ⓐ② a piece of furniture with shelves for putting books on → See colour picture **The Living Room** on page Centre 4

book ˌclub noun [C] a group of people who meet regularly to talk about books they have read

bookie /ˈbʊki/ **noun** [C] informal someone whose job is to take and pay out money that people

risk trying to guess the result of horse races, sports events, etc

booking /ˈbʊkɪŋ/ **noun** [C, U] mainly UK ⓑ① an arrangement you make to have a hotel room, tickets, etc at a particular time in the future: *advance booking*

> 🗇 Word partners for **booking**
>
> **accept/cancel/make/take** a booking • an **advance** booking • a booking **for** sth • a booking **fee/form**

bookkeeping /ˈbʊkˌkiːpɪŋ/ **noun** [U] the job of recording the money that an organization or business spends and receives • **bookkeeper noun** [C]

booklet /ˈbʊklət/ **noun** [C] ⓑ② a small, thin book that contains information: *The tourist office has booklets about the area.*

bookmaker /ˈbʊkˌmeɪkər/ **noun** [C] a bookie

bookmark¹ /ˈbʊkmɑːk/ **noun** [C] **1** something you put in a book so you can find the page you want **2** ⓑ② an address on the Internet that you record so that you can quickly find something again: *Add this website to your bookmarks.*

bookmark² /ˈbʊkmɑːk/ **verb** [T] ⓑ② to make a record of the address of an Internet document in your computer so that you can find it again easily

books /bʊks/ **noun** [plural] the written financial records of a business or organization

bookseller /ˈbʊkˌselər/ **noun** [C] a person or company that sells books

bookshelf /ˈbʊkʃelf/ **noun** [C] (plural **book-shelves**) ⓐ② a shelf for holding books

bookshop /ˈbʊkʃɒp/ **noun** [C] mainly UK (US **bookstore** /ˈbʊkstɔːr/) ⓐ② a shop that sells books

bookworm /ˈbʊkwɜːm/ **noun** [C] informal someone who enjoys reading very much

boom¹ /buːm/ **noun** [C] **1** a period when there is a big increase in sales or profits: *an **economic boom*** ○ *The 1990's saw a **boom in** computer sales.* **2** a loud, deep sound → See also **baby boom**

boom² /buːm/ **verb** [I] **1** If something is booming, it is increasing or becoming more successful or popular very quickly: *House prices are booming.* **2** to make a loud, deep sound, or to speak in a loud, deep voice

boomerang /ˈbuːməræŋ/ **noun** [C] a curved piece of wood that comes back to you when you throw it

boon /buːn/ **noun** [C] something helpful that improves your life: [usually singular] *Microwaves are a boon for busy people.*

> 🗇 Word partners for **boost**
>
> **give** sb/sth a boost • **receive** a boost • a **huge/major/massive/much-needed** boost • a **confidence/morale** boost • a boost **to** sth • a boost **for** sb

boost¹ /buːst/ **noun** [C] ⓑ② something that makes you feel more confident and happy, or that helps something increase or improve:

*Increased tourism was a major **boost to** the local economy.*

boost² /buːst/ **verb** [T] 🔵 to increase or improve something: *Getting the job has **boosted** my confidence.*

booster /ˈbuːstər/ **noun 1 a confidence/morale, etc booster** something that makes you feel happier or more confident **2** [C] an engine on a spacecraft that gives extra power for the first part of a flight

boot¹ /buːt/ **noun** [C] **1** 🅰️2 a strong shoe that covers your foot and part of your leg: *a **pair of boots** →* See colour picture **Clothes** on page Centre 9 **2** UK (US **trunk**) 🔵 a closed space at the back of a car for storing things in → See colour picture **Car** on page Centre 7 **3 get/be given the boot** informal to be told that you must leave your job

IDIOM **too big for your boots** UK (US **too big for your britches**) behaving as if you are more important or more clever than you really are

→ See also **car boot sale**

boot² /buːt/ **verb** informal **1** [T] to kick someone or something **2** [I, T] (also **boot up**) when a computer boots or is booted, it starts working and becomes ready for use

PHRASAL VERB **boot sb out** informal to make someone leave a place or job

bootcut /ˈbuːtkʌt/ **adj** bootleg

booth /buːð/ **noun** [C] a small area that is separated from a larger public area, especially used for doing something privately: *a telephone booth*

bootleg /ˈbuːtleg/ **adj** (also **bootcut**) bootleg trousers are wider at the bottom than at the knee • **bootlegs noun** [plural]

booty /ˈbuːti/ **noun** [U] valuable things stolen by thieves or by an army in a war

booze¹ /buːz/ **noun** [U] informal alcoholic drinks

booze² /buːz/ **verb** [I] informal to drink alcohol

border¹ /ˈbɔːdər/ **noun** [C] **1** 🔵 the line that separates two countries or states: *the **border between** France and Spain* ∘ *We **crossed the border** from Canada into the US.* **2** a strip around the edge of something for decoration: *white plates with a blue border*

📝 **Word partners for border**

cross the border • **across/on/over** the border • the border **between** [France and Spain/ Switzerland and Italy, etc] • [Germany's/ Syria's, etc] border **with** [France/Lebanon, etc] • the [French/Mexican, etc] **side** of the border • border **controls/guards**

---

border² /ˈbɔːdər/ **verb** [T] **1** to form a line around the edge of something: [often passive] *The fields are bordered by tall trees.* **2** to have a border with another country: [often passive] *Spain is bordered by France and Portugal.*

PHRASAL VERB **border on sth** to almost be a more extreme thing: *Her anger bordered on aggression.*

borderline¹ /ˈbɔːdəlaɪm/ **adj** If something or someone is borderline, it is not clear if they are

good enough or if they will succeed: *Borderline cases should take the exam again.*

borderline² /ˈbɔːdəlaɪm/ **noun** [no plural] the point where one feeling, quality, level, etc ends and another one begins: *My work was **on the borderline between** two grades.*

bore¹ /bɔːr/ **verb 1** [T] to make someone feel bored: *His war stories really bore me.* **2** [I, T] to make a hole in something hard with a tool

bore² /bɔːr/ **noun 1** [C] someone who talks too much about things that are not interesting **2** [no plural] a situation or job that annoys you because it causes difficulties or is not interesting: *It's a real bore not having a car.*

bore³ /bɔːr/ past tense of bear

bored /bɔːd/ **adj** 🅰️1 feeling tired and unhappy because something is not interesting or because you have nothing to do: *I'm **bored with** doing homework.* ∘ *We were **bored stiff** (= extremely bored) in her lessons.* • **boredom** /ˈbɔːdəm/ **noun** [U] the feeling of being bored: *I nearly died of boredom.*

boring /ˈbɔːrɪŋ/ **adj** 🅰️1 not interesting or exciting: *a boring job* ∘ *The film was so boring, I fell asleep.*

❗ Common learner error: **bored** or **boring**?

Bored is used to describe how someone feels.

He didn't enjoy the lesson because he was bored.

He didn't enjoy the lesson because he was boring.

If something or someone is **boring**, they make you feel bored.

The book was long and boring.

➕ Other ways of saying **boring**

We often use **bland** when describing food: *This sauce is really **bland**, it doesn't taste of anything.*

If a film, play, book, etc. or a person is boring, you can say that they are **dull**: *I find her writing a bit **dull**.*

Monotonous is often used about something that you listen to: *The teacher had a really **monotonous** voice and I almost fell asleep.*

When describing an activity, **tedious** is sometimes used: *You have to fill in various forms, which is a bit **tedious**.*

If speech or writing is boring because it is too long, we can describe it as **long-winded**: *He gave this really **long-winded** explanation about why he'd changed his mind.*

---

born¹ /bɔːn/ **verb be born a** 🅰️2 When a person or animal is born, they come out of their mother's body and start to exist: *She was born in London in 1973.* ∘ *an American-born writer* (= born in America) **b** If an idea is born, it starts to exist.

born² /bɔːn/ **adj a born actor/leader/teacher,**

etc someone who has a natural ability to act, lead, teach, etc

born-again /ˌbɔːnəˈgen/ **adj** a born-again **Christian** someone who has become a very enthusiastic member of the Christian religion

borne /bɔːn/ past participle of bear

borough /ˈbʌrə/ ⑤ /ˈbɜːrəʊ/ **noun** [C] a town or part of a city

borrow /ˈbɒrəʊ/ **verb 1 USE** ▷ [T] ⓐ2 to use something that belongs to someone else and give it back later: *Can I borrow a pen please?* ∘ *I borrowed the book from my sister.* **2 MONEY** ▷ [I, T] to take money from a bank or financial organization and pay it back over a period of time **3 IDEA** ▷ [T] to take and use a word or idea: *The English word 'rucksack' is borrowed from German.*

borrower /ˈbɒrəʊəʳ/ **noun** [C] someone who borrows money

bosom /ˈbʊzᵊm/ **noun 1** [C] a woman's breasts **2 a bosom buddy/pal, etc** a very good friend

boss¹ /bɒs/ **noun** [C] ⓐ2 someone who is responsible for employees and tells them what to do: *I'll ask my boss if I can leave work early tomorrow.*

boss² /bɒs/ **verb** [T] (also **boss about/around**) to tell someone what they should do all the time: *My older brother is always bossing me about.*

bossy /ˈbɒsi/ **adj** ⓑ2 always telling other people what to do • **bossiness noun** [U]

botanist /ˈbɒtᵊnɪst/ **noun** [C] someone who studies plants

botany /ˈbɒtᵊni/ **noun** [U] the scientific study of plants • **botanical** /bəˈtænɪkəl/ **adj** (also **botanic** /bəˈtænɪk/) relating to botany

botch /bɒtʃ/ **verb** [T] (also **botch up**) to spoil something by doing it badly: *a botched robbery*

both /bəʊθ/ **pronoun, determiner, quantifier 1** ⓐ1 used to talk about two people or things: *The children both have red hair.* ∘ *Both of my sisters are teachers.* ∘ *Would you like cream, ice cream, or both?* **2 both...and...** used to emphasize that you are talking about two people or things: *Both Jack and his wife are keen chess players.* → See also **have the best³ of both worlds**

bother¹ /ˈbɒðəʳ/ **verb 1 ANNOY** ▷ [T] ⓐ2 to annoy someone by trying to get their attention when they do not want to see you or talk to you: *Sorry to bother you, but could you spare any change?* **2 WORRY** ▷ [T] ⓑ2 to make someone feel worried or upset: *Living on my own doesn't bother me at all.* **3 DO** ▷ [I, T] ⓑ2 to make the effort to do something: [+ doing sth] *Don't bother making the bed – I'll do it later.* ∘ [+ to do sth] *He didn't even bother to call.* **4 can't be bothered** informal If you can't be bothered to do something, you are too lazy or tired to do it: [+ to do sth] *I can't be bothered to iron my clothes.* **5 not bothered** UK informal If you are not bothered about something, it is not important to you and does not worry you: *"Do you want tea or coffee?" "Either, I'm not bothered."*

bother² /ˈbɒðəʳ/ **noun** [U] trouble or problems: *"Are you sure you don't mind taking me?" "No, it's no bother, really!"*

bothered /ˈbɒðəd/ **adj** [never before noun] ⓑ2 If you are bothered about something, it is important to you and you are worried about it: *He's very bothered about what other people think.*

Botox /ˈbəʊtɒks/ **noun** [U] trademark Botulinum Toxin: a drug used in a person's face to make it look smooth and young • **Botox verb** [T]

bottle¹ /ˈbɒtl/ **noun** [C] ⓐ2 a container for liquids, usually made of glass or plastic, with a narrow top: *an empty bottle* ∘ *a bottle of wine* → See also **hot-water bottle**

bottle² /ˈbɒtl/ **verb** [T] to put liquid into a bottle: [often passive] *This wine was bottled in France.* ∘ *bottled beer/water*

PHRASAL VERB **bottle sth up** to not allow yourself to show or talk about your feelings

bottle ˌbank noun [C] UK a large container outside, where you can put empty bottles so that the glass can be used again

bottleneck /ˈbɒtlnek/ **noun** [C] **1** something that causes a process to happen more slowly than it should **2** a narrow part of a road where traffic moves slowly

bottom¹ /ˈbɒtəm/ **noun 1 LOWEST PART** ▷ [C] ⓐ1 the lowest part of something: [usually singular] *Click on the icon at the bottom of the page.* **2 FLAT SURFACE** ▷ [C] ⓐ2 the flat surface on the lowest side of something: [usually singular] *There was a price tag on the bottom of the box.* **3 LOWEST POSITION** ▷ [no plural] ⓐ2 the lowest position in a group, organization, etc: *He did badly in the exam and is at the bottom of the class.* **4 SEA/RIVER ETC** ▷ [no plural] ⓑ1 the ground under a river, lake, or sea: *Divers found the wreck on the bottom of the ocean.* **5 FURTHEST PART** ▷ [no plural] ⓑ1 the part of a road or area of land that is furthest from where you are: *Go to the bottom of the road and turn left.* **6 PART OF THE BODY** ▷ [C] ⓑ1 the part of your body that you sit on **7 be at the bottom of sth** to be the cause of a problem or situation **8 get to the bottom of sth** to discover the truth about a situation → See also **rock bottom, from top¹ to bottom**

bottom² /ˈbɒtəm/ **adj** [always before noun] in the lowest position: *the bottom drawer*

bottomless /ˈbɒtəmləs/ **adj** a **bottomless pit** a supply, especially of money, that has no limit

the ˌbottom ˈline noun the most important fact in a situation: *The bottom line is that if you don't work, you'll fail the test.*

bough /baʊ/ **noun** [C] literary a large branch on a tree

bought /bɔːt/ past of buy

boulder /ˈbəʊldəʳ/ **noun** [C] a very large rock

boulevard /ˈbuːləvɑːd/ **noun** [C] a wide road in a city, usually with trees along it

bounce¹ /baʊns/ **verb 1 BALL** ▷ [I, T] ⓑ2 to hit a surface and then move quickly away, or to make something do this: *The ball bounced high into the air.* **2 JUMP** ▷ [I] to jump up and down several times on a soft surface: *The children loved bouncing on the bed.* **3 bounce along/around/into, etc** to move somewhere in a happy and energetic way: *Sarah bounced into the room with*

---

yes | k cat | ŋ ring | ʃ she | θ thin | ð this | ʒ decision | dʒ jar | tʃ chip | æ cat | e bed | ə ago | ɪ sit | i cosy | ɒ hot | ʌ run | ʊ put |

a big smile on her face. **4 NOT PAY** ▷ [I, T] If a cheque (= piece of printed paper you write on to pay for things) bounces, or a bank bounces it, the bank will not pay it because there is not enough money in the account.

PHRASAL VERB **bounce back 1** to be successful or happy again after a failure, disappointment, etc: *After a terrible start the team bounced back and won the game.* **2** If an email bounces back, it is returned to you because the address is not correct or there is a computer problem.

bounce² /baʊns/ **noun** [C, U] an act of bouncing, or the quality that makes something able to bounce

bouncer /ˈbaʊnsər/ **noun** [C] someone whose job is to stand at the door of a bar, party, etc and keep out people who are not wanted

bouncy /ˈbaʊnsi/ **adj 1** happy and full of energy: *She's very bouncy and confident.* **2** able to bounce: *bouncy balls*

bound¹ /baʊnd/ **adj 1 bound to do sth** ❷ certain to do something, or certain to happen: *You're bound to feel nervous before your driving test.* **2 bound up with sth** closely connected with something: *A country's culture is bound up with its language and history.* **3** [never before noun] having a moral or legal duty to do something: *The witness was bound by an oath to tell the truth.* **4** [never before noun] travelling towards a particular place: *He was on a train bound for Berlin.*

bound² /baʊnd/ **verb bound across/down/into, etc** to move quickly with large steps or jumps: *Guy bounded across the room to answer the phone.*

bound³ /baʊnd/ **noun** [C] a big jump → See also **by/in leaps (leap¹) and bounds**

bound⁴ /baʊnd/ past of bind

boundary /ˈbaʊndəri/ **noun** [C] **1** a line that divides two areas or forms an edge around an area: *The mountains mark the boundary between the two countries.* **2** a limit: *Such violence is beyond the boundaries of civilized conduct.*

boundless /ˈbaʊndləs/ **adj** having no limit: *He has boundless energy/enthusiasm.*

bounds /baʊndz/ **noun 1** [plural] legal or social limits: *They have overstepped the bounds of good taste.* **2 out of bounds** If a place is out of bounds, you are not allowed to go there: *The staff room is out of bounds to students.*

bounty /ˈbaʊnti/ **noun 1** [C, U] a large or generous amount of something **2** [C] an amount of money paid as a reward

bouquet /buˈkeɪ/ **noun** [C] flowers that are tied together in an attractive way

bourbon /ˈbɜːbən/ **noun** [C, U] a type of American whisky

bourgeois /ˈbɔːʒwɑː/ **adj** typical of middle class people who are too interested in money and correct social behaviour: *bourgeois values* ● **the bourgeoisie** /ˌbɔːʒwɑːˈziː/ **noun** [group] the middle class, that owns most of society's money

bout /baʊt/ **noun** [C] **1** a short period of activity or illness: *a bout of depression* **2** a fight in boxing

boutique /buːˈtiːk/ **noun** [C] a small shop tha sells fashionable clothes

bovine /ˈbəʊvaɪn/ **adj** relating to cows

bow¹ /baʊ/ **verb** [I, T] to bend your head or body forward in order to show respect or to thank an audience: *The actors all bowed after the perfor mance.* ◦ *We **bowed** our **heads** in prayer.*

PHRASAL VERBS **bow out** to leave a job or stop doing an activity, usually after a long time: *H bowed out of politics at the age of 70.* ● **bow t sth/sb** to do what someone else wants you to do *The government are refusing to **bow to** publi pressure.*

bow² /baʊ/ **noun** [C] **1** an act of bowing: *Th actors came back on stage and **took a bow**.* **2** th front part of a ship

bow³ /bəʊ/ **noun** [C] **1 KNOT** ▷ ❷ a knot wit two curved parts and two loose ends, that i used to tie shoes or as decoration **2 MUSIC** ▷ long, thin piece of wood with hair stretche between the ends, used to play some musica instruments **3 WEAPON** ▷ ❷ a piece of curve wood with string fixed to both ends, used fo shooting arrows

bowel /ˈbaʊəl/ **noun** [C] the long tube tha carries solid waste from your stomach out o your body: [usually plural]

bowl¹ /bəʊl/ **noun** [C] ❷ a round, deep dis used for holding soup and other food: *a bowl c rice/soup*

bowl² /bəʊl/ **verb** [I, T] **1** to roll a ball along surface as part of a game **2** in cricket, to throw ball to the person who has to hit it

bowler /ˈbəʊlər/ **noun** [C] in cricket, the playe who throws the ball so someone can hit it → Se colour picture **Sports 2** on page Centre 15

bowler ˈhat noun [C] mainly UK (US **derby**) round, hard, black hat worn by men, especiall in the past

bowling /ˈbəʊlɪŋ/ **noun** [U] a game in which yo roll a large ball along a wooden track in order t knock down bottle-shaped objects

bowls /bəʊlz/ **noun** [U] UK a game in which yo roll large balls as close as possible to a smalle ball

bow ˈtie noun [C] a piece of cloth around th neck in the shape of a bow that men sometime wear, especially at formal events

box¹ /bɒks/ **noun 1 CONTAINER** ▷ [C] ❶ a squar or rectangular container: *a cardboard box* ◦ *a bo of chocolates/matches* → See picture at **containe 2 SQUARE SPACE** ▷ [C] ❷ a small square on page that gives you information or where yo write information: *Write 'Y' in the box if yo would like more details.* **3 SMALL PLACE** ▷ [C] small area of a theatre, court, etc that is separat from where other people are sitting **4 the bo** informal the television: *What's **on the box** tonight* → See also **phone box, post box, witness bo**

box² /bɒks/ **verb 1** [I, T] to do the sport of boxin **2** [T] (also **box up**) to put something in a box: *W boxed up the old books.*

PHRASAL VERB **box sb/sth in** to move so close t someone or something that they cannot mov [often passive] *When I returned I found that my car had been boxed in.*

boxer /'bɒksər/ noun [C] someone who does the sport of boxing

boxers /'bɒksəz/ noun [plural] (also **boxer shorts**) loose underwear worn by men → See colour picture **Clothes** on page Centre 9

boxing /'bɒksɪŋ/ noun
[U] ⓐ a sport in which two people hit each other while wearing big, leather gloves (= pieces of clothing for your hands) → See colour picture **Sports 1** on page Centre 14

boxing

Boxing Day noun [C, U] 26 December, a public holiday in Britain and Canada

box office noun [C] the place in a theatre, cinema, etc where you buy tickets

boy¹ /bɔɪ/ noun **1** ⓐ [C] a male child or young man: *We have three children – a boy and two girls.* **2 the boys** informal a group of male friends: *Steve's gone out with the boys.*

boy² /bɔɪ/ exclamation (also **oh boy**) used when you are excited or pleased: *Boy, that was good!*

boy band noun [C] a pop music group made up of young men who sing and dance

boycott /'bɔɪkɒt/ noun [C] a situation in which people refuse to buy, use, or do something because they do not approve of it: *Environmental groups have called for a boycott of the company's products.* • **boycott** verb [T] *Several countries boycotted the international peace talks.*

boyfriend /'bɔɪfrend/ noun [C] ⓐ a man or boy who someone is having a romantic relationship with

boyhood /'bɔɪhʊd/ noun [U] the part of a male's life when they are a boy

boyish /'bɔɪʃ/ adj like a boy: *boyish charm*

Boy Scout UK (US **Boy Scout**) noun [C] a boy who belongs to an organization that teaches boys practical skills

bra /brɑː/ noun [C] ⓑ a piece of woman's underwear that supports the breasts → See colour picture **Clothes** on page Centre 9

brace¹ /breɪs/ verb **brace yourself** to prepare for something difficult or unpleasant: *I braced myself for bad news.*

brace² /breɪs/ noun [C] **1** something that supports or holds something in the correct position: *He wore a neck brace for months after the accident.* **2** UK (US **braces**) a wire object that some children wear to make their teeth straight

bracelet /'breɪslət/ noun [C] ⓑ a piece of jewellery that you wear around your wrist → See picture at **jewellery**

braces /'breɪsɪz/ noun [plural] UK (US **suspenders**) **1** two straps fixed to a pair of trousers that go over your shoulders and stop the trousers from falling down **2** US (UK **brace**) a set of wires that some children wear to make their teeth straight

bracing /'breɪsɪŋ/ adj Bracing weather or a bracing activity makes you feel cold but healthy and full of energy: *bracing sea air* ○ *a bracing walk*

bracket¹ /'brækɪt/ noun [C] **1** a group of people whose ages, taxes, etc are between two limits: *Most heart attack victims are in the 45-65 age bracket.* **2** a piece of metal, wood, etc, that is fixed to a wall to support something, especially a shelf

bracket² /'brækɪt/ verb [T] **1** to put curved lines ( ) around words, phrases, numbers, etc to make them separate **2** to consider two or more people or things to be similar: [often passive] *Canadian accents are often bracketed with American accents.*

brackets /'brækɪts/ noun [plural] (also **parentheses**) UK ⓑ two lines ( ) or [] used around extra information or information that should be considered as separate from the main part

brag /bræg/ verb [I] (**bragging, bragged**) to talk with too much pride about what you have done or what you own: *He's always bragging about how much money he earns.*

braid¹ /breɪd/ noun **1** [C] US (mainly UK **plait**) a single piece of hair made by twisting three thinner pieces over and under each other **2** [U] a thin piece of cloth or twisted threads used for decorating clothes

braid² /breɪd/ verb [T] US (mainly UK **plait**) to twist three pieces of hair over and under each other

braille /breɪl/ noun [U] a system of printing for blind people, using raised patterns that they read by touching

brain /breɪn/ noun
1 [C] ⓐ the organ inside your head that controls your thoughts, feelings, and movements: *brain damage* **2** [C] informal an extremely intelligent person: [usually plural] *This university attracts some of the best brains in the country.* **3 brains** intelligence: *He has brains and good looks.* **4 have sth on the brain** informal to think or talk about something all the time: *You have football on the brain!* **5 the brains behind sth** informal the person who has planned and organized something successful: *Anthony is the brains behind the project.*

brain

brainchild /'breɪntʃaɪld/ noun **the brainchild of sb** someone's new and clever idea or invention: *The project is the brainchild of a Japanese designer.*

brainstorm /'breɪnstɔːm/ noun [C] US (UK **brainwave**) a sudden, clever idea

brainstorming /'breɪnˌstɔːmɪŋ/ noun [U] the activity of getting together with other people to think of new ideas: *a brainstorming session*

brainwash /'breɪnwɒʃ/ verb [T] to make someone believe something by telling them that it is true many times: [+ into + doing sth] *Advertising often brainwashes people into buying things they do not really need.* • **brainwashing** noun [U]

B

brainwave /'breɪnweɪv/ **noun** [C] UK (US **brainstorm**) a sudden, clever idea

brainy /'breɪni/ **adj** informal clever

brake¹ /breɪk/ **noun** [C] **1** ⓐ the part of a vehicle that makes it stop or go more slowly **2** something that stops or slows the progress of something: *High inflation has put the brakes on economic growth.*

> **Word partners for brake**
>
> apply/hit/slam on the brakes • the brakes fail

brake² /breɪk/ **verb** [I] ⓐ to make a vehicle stop or move more slowly, using its brake

brake pedal noun [C] the part of a car that you push with your foot to make it go more slowly → See colour picture **Car** on page Centre 7

branch¹ /brɑːnʃ/ **noun** [C] **1** TREE ▷ ⓐ one of the many parts of a tree that grows out from its trunk (= main, vertical part) → See picture at **tree** **2** BUSINESS ▷ ⓐ one of several shops, offices, etc that are part of a company or organization: *a bank with branches all over the country* **3** SUBJECT ▷ ⓐ a part of a subject: *Neurology is a branch of medicine.*

branch² /brɑːnʃ/ **verb** [I] (also **branch off**) If a road, path, etc branches, it separates into two or more roads, paths, etc.

PHRASAL VERB **branch out** to start to do something different from what you usually do, especially in your job: *After working in publishing, she branched out into journalism.*

brand¹ /brænd/ **noun** [C] **1** ⓐ a product that is made by a particular company: *Which brand of toothpaste do you use?* **2** a particular type of something: *The team plays a distinctive brand of football.*

brand² /brænd/ **verb** [T] **1** to describe someone or something in a way that makes them seem bad: *The media branded him a liar.* **2** to burn a mark on an animal to show who owns it

brandish /'brændɪʃ/ **verb** [T] to wave something in the air, especially a weapon: *He came running into the room, brandishing a gun.*

brand name noun [C] the special name that a company gives to a product

brand new adj ⓐ completely new

brandy /'brændi/ **noun** [C, U] a strong alcoholic drink made from wine

brash /bræʃ/ **adj** too confident: *a brash young businessman*

brass /brɑːs/ **noun** [U] **1** a shiny yellow metal: *a door with a brass handle* **2** the group of musical instruments made from brass: *a brass band*

brat /bræt/ **noun** [C] a child who behaves badly: *a spoilt brat*

bravado /brə'vɑːdəʊ/ **noun** [U] behaviour that is intended to make people admire you for your bravery and confidence

brave¹ /breɪv/ **adj** ⓐ showing no fear of dangerous or difficult situations: *He died after a brave fight against cancer.* • **bravely adv**

brave² /breɪv/ **verb** [T] to deal with a dangerous or unpleasant situation in a brave way: *Crowds braved the cold weather to watch the game.*

bravery /'breɪvᵊri/ **noun** [U] ⓐ brave behaviour

bravo /brɑː'vəʊ/ **exclamation** something you shout to show that you approve of something, for example a performance

brawl /brɔːl/ **noun** [C] a noisy fight, usually in public: *a drunken brawl in a bar* • **brawl verb** [I]

brazen /'breɪzᵊn/ **adj** not feeling at all ashamed about your bad behaviour: *a brazen cheat* • **brazenly adv**

BRB internet abbreviation for be right back: used when you stop taking part in a discussion on the Internet

breach¹ /briːtʃ/ **noun 1** [C, U] an action that breaks a rule, agreement, or law: *a policy that is in breach of international law* ∘ *He was sued for breach of contract.* **2** [C] formal a serious disagreement between two groups, countries, etc

> **Word partners for breach**
>
> (a) breach of sth • be in breach of sth • a flagrant breach of sth

breach² /briːtʃ/ **verb** [T] to break a rule, law, or agreement

bread

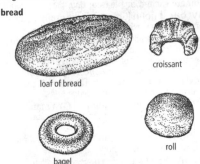

croissant

loaf of bread

bagel

roll

bread /bred/ **noun** [U] ⓐ a basic food made by mixing and baking flour, water, and sometimes yeast (= substance that makes it rise): *a slice of bread* ∘ *a loaf of white bread* → See also **the best/greatest thing since sliced bread**

bread bin noun [C] UK (US **breadbox**) container for keeping bread fresh

breadcrumbs /'bredkrʌmz/ **noun** [plural] very small pieces of dry bread, used in cooking

breadth /bretθ/ **noun** [U, no plural] **1** the distance from one side of something to the other side: *The swimming pool has a breadth of 10 metres and a length of 50 metres.* **2** sb's **breadth of experience/knowledge/interest, etc** the great number of different things that someone has done, knows, is interested in, etc → See also **the length and breadth of sth**

breadwinner /'bred,wɪnər/ **noun** [C] the person who earns the money in a family

break¹ /breɪk/ **verb** (**broke, broken**) **1** SEPARATE ▷ [I, T] ⓐ to separate into two or more pieces, or to make something separate into two or more pieces: *The vase fell on the floor*

break

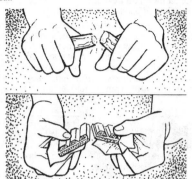

and broke. ∘ *They had to break a window to get in.*
2 break your arm/leg, etc Ⓐ② to damage a bone in your arm/leg, etc: *Carolyn broke her leg in a skiing accident.* **3 NOT WORK** ▷ [I, T] Ⓐ② If you break a machine, object, etc, or if it breaks, it stops working because it is damaged: *Who broke the video?* **4 break an agreement/promise/rule, etc** Ⓑ② to not do what you should do according to an agreement/promise/rule, etc: *Police stopped him for breaking the speed limit.* **5 break the law** Ⓑ② to do something illegal **6 break the news to sb** to tell someone about something unpleasant that has happened **7 break the silence** Ⓑ② to make a noise, speak, etc and end a period of silence: *The silence was broken by a sudden knock at the door.* **8 break a habit/routine, etc** to stop doing something that you usually do **9 break a record** Ⓑ② to do something faster, better, etc than anyone else: *He broke the world record for the 200m.* **10 REST** ▷ [I, T] Ⓑ① to stop the activity you are doing to have a short rest: *Let's break for five minutes and have a drink.* **11 BECOME KNOWN** ▷ [I, T] If news or a story breaks, or if someone breaks it, it becomes known by the public for the first time. **12 WEATHER** ▷ [I] UK If the weather breaks, it changes suddenly, and usually becomes worse. **13 VOICE** ▷ [I] When a boy's voice breaks, it becomes deeper and sounds like a man's voice. **14 WAVE** ▷ [I] When a wave breaks, it reaches its highest point as it moves towards the land, and then becomes flat and white. **15 STORM** ▷ [I] If a storm breaks, it starts suddenly. **16 break free/loose** to suddenly escape or become separate from something **17 dawn/day breaks** When dawn (= early morning)/day breaks, the sky becomes lighter because the sun is rising. → See also **break new ground¹**, **break sb's heart**, **break the ice¹**, **break the mould¹**, **break ranks (rank¹)**

PHRASAL VERBS **break away 1 ESCAPE** ▷ to suddenly leave or escape from someone who is holding you **2 LEAVE GROUP** ▷ to stop being part of a group because you disagree with them: *Some members broke away to form a new political party.* • **break down 1 MACHINE** ▷ Ⓑ① If a machine or vehicle breaks down, it stops working: *My car broke down on the way to*

work. **2 COMMUNICATION** ▷ If a system, relationship, or discussion breaks down, it fails because there is a problem or disagreement: *Their marriage broke down after only two years.* **3 CRY** ▷ to become very upset and start crying • **break sth down** to divide something into smaller, simpler parts • **break in** Ⓑ① to get into a building or car using force, usually to steal something • **break sth in** to wear something new, usually shoes, for short periods of time to make them more comfortable • **break into sth 1** Ⓑ① to get into a building or car using force, usually to steal something **2** to suddenly start doing something: *The crowd broke into a cheer when he came on stage.* • **break (sth) off** to separate a part from a larger piece, or to become separate from something: *He broke off a piece of chocolate.* • **break off** Ⓑ② to suddenly stop speaking or doing something: *She broke off in the middle of a sentence.* • **break sth off** Ⓑ② to end a relationship: *She broke off the engagement just two weeks before the wedding.* • **break out 1** Ⓑ② If a fire, disease, etc breaks out, it starts suddenly: *A fight broke out among the crowd.* **2** to escape from prison: *to break out of jail* **3 break out in a rash/sweat, etc** to suddenly have spots or sweat (= salty liquid) appear on your skin • **break through sth** Ⓑ② to force your way through something that is holding you back: *Protesters broke through the barriers.* • **break (sth) up** to divide into many pieces, or to divide something into many pieces: *The company has been broken up and sold.* • **break up 1** Ⓑ① If people break up, they stop having a relationship or stop working together: *He's just broken up with his girlfriend.* **2** UK Ⓑ① When schools or colleges break up, the classes end and the holidays begin.

break² /breɪk/ *noun* [C] **1 STOP** ▷ Ⓐ② a pause in an activity, usually to rest or to eat: *a coffee/tea break* ∘ *Take a break and come back after lunch.* **2 HOLIDAY** ▷ Ⓑ① a holiday or period of time away from work, school, etc: *the spring break* ∘ *a weekend break to Paris* **3 OPPORTUNITY** ▷ a lucky opportunity: *His big break came when he was offered a part in a TV series.* ∘ *Meeting Tom was my lucky break.* **4 DAMAGE** ▷ Ⓑ① a place where something has separated in an accident: *a break in the bone* **5 a break with sth** the end of a relationship, connection, or way of doing something: *a break with tradition*

breakable /ˈbreɪkəbl/ *adj* Ⓑ② able to break easily: *a breakable vase*

breakage /ˈbreɪkɪdʒ/ *noun* [C, U] the act of breaking something or something that is broken: *The delivery company must pay for any breakages.*

breakaway /ˈbreɪkəweɪ/ *adj* a **breakaway group/republic/region, etc** a group/republic, etc that has separated from a larger group or region because of a disagreement

breakdown /ˈbreɪkdaʊn/ *noun* [C] **1 ILLNESS** ▷ (also **nervous breakdown**) Ⓑ② a short period of mental illness when people are too ill to continue with their normal lives: *to have a breakdown* **2 FAILURE** ▷ the failure or end of

B

something such as communication or a relationship: *a breakdown in the peace talks* **3 EXPLANATION** ▷ a short explanation of the details of something: *I need a breakdown of the costs involved.* **4 NOT WORKING** ▷ **B2** an occasion when a vehicle or machine stops working for a period of time

breakfast /'brekfəst/ noun [C] **A1** the food you eat in the morning after you wake up: *She had breakfast in bed this morning.* • **breakfast** verb [I] → See also **bed and breakfast, continental breakfast, English breakfast**

break-in /'breɪkɪn/ noun [C] an occasion when someone forces their way into a building or car, usually to steal something: *There has been another break-in at the office.*

breaking point noun [U] the point at which a situation becomes so bad that it cannot continue: *Things had become so bad at work they'd almost reached breaking point.*

breakneck /'breɪknek/ adj **breakneck speed/ growth, etc** dangerously fast speed/growth, etc

breakout /'breɪkaʊt/ noun [C] an escape, usually from prison

breakthrough /'breɪkθruː/ noun [C] **B2** an important discovery or development that helps solve a problem: *a major breakthrough in the fight against cancer*

> ✏ Word partners for **breakthrough**
>
> **make/provide** a breakthrough • a breakthrough **comes** • a **big/crucial/major/real** breakthrough • a **medical/scientific** breakthrough • a breakthrough **in** sth

break-up /'breɪkʌp/ noun [C] **1** the end of a close relationship: *He moved away after the break-up of his marriage.* **2** the separation of a country, group, etc into several smaller parts

breast /brest/ noun **1** [C] **B1** one of the two soft, round parts on a woman's chest **2** [C, U] the front part of a bird's body, or the meat from this area: *chicken breast*

breast-feed /'brestfiːd/ verb [I, T] (**breast-fed**) If a woman breast-feeds, she gives a baby milk from her breast. • **breast-feeding** noun [U]

breaststroke /'breststrəʊk/ noun [U] a way of swimming in which you push your arms forward and then to the side, while you kick your legs backwards

breath /breθ/ noun **1** [U] **B1** the air that comes out of your lungs: *His breath smells of garlic.* **2** [C] **B2** the act of breathing air into or out of your lungs: *She took a deep breath before she started.* **3 be out of breath B2** to be breathing quickly because you have been running, walking fast, etc **4 catch your breath; get your breath back** to rest for a short time until you can breathe regularly again **5 under your breath** If you say something under your breath, you say it very quietly so that other people cannot hear it. **6 hold your breath B2** to keep air in your lungs and not let it out: *How long can you hold your breath under water?* **7 don't hold your breath** humorous something that you say in order to tell

someone that an event is not likely to happen: *He said he'd phone, but don't hold your breath.*

IDIOMS **a breath of fresh air** someone or something that is new, different, and exciting • **take your breath away B2** If something takes your breath away, you feel surprise and admiration because it is so beautiful or exciting: *The view from the window took my breath away.* • **with bated breath** in an excited or anxious way: *I waited with bated breath as the results were read out.*

> ❗ Common learner error: **breath** or **breathe**?
>
> Be careful not to confuse the noun **breath** with the verb **breathe**.
> *I was so excited, I could hardly breathe.*

breathalyser /'breθəlaɪzər/ noun [C] a piece of equipment that tests your breath to measure how much alcohol you have had • **breathalyse** verb [T] UK to measure the alcohol in someone's body using a breathalyser

breathe /briːð/ verb [I, T] **B1** to take air into and out of your lungs: *breathe in/out* ○ *breathe deeply* → See also **be breathing down sb's neck, not breathe a word¹**

breather /'briːðər/ noun [C] informal a short rest: *If you start to feel tired, take a breather.*

breathing /'briːðɪŋ/ noun [U] the process of taking air into and out of your lungs: *The doctor listened to my breathing.*

breathing space noun [U] an opportunity to stop, relax, or think about things

breathless /'breθləs/ adj not able to breathe enough • **breathlessly** adv

breathtaking /'breθˌteɪkɪŋ/ adj **B2** very beautiful or surprising: *breathtaking views* • **breathtakingly** adv

bred /bred/ past of breed

breed¹ /briːd/ noun [C] **1 B2** a type of dog, sheep, pig, etc: *a rare breed of cattle* **2** a type of person or thing: *a new breed of bank*

breed² /briːd/ verb (**bred** /bred/) **1** [I] If animals breed, they produce young animals. **2 breed chickens/horses/rabbits, etc B2** to keep animals in order to produce young animals **3 breed contempt/ignorance, etc** to cause something to develop, especially something bad

breeder /'briːdər/ noun [C] someone who keeps animals in order to produce young animals: *a dog/horse breeder*

breeding /'briːdɪŋ/ noun [U] **1** the process by which animals produce young animals: *the breeding season* **2** the activity of keeping animals in order to produce young animals: *horse breeding*

breeding ground noun [C] **1** a place where something develops quickly, especially something bad: *This estate is a breeding ground for crime.* **2** a place where animals breed

breeze¹ /briːz/ noun [C] **B1** a gentle wind: *a cool breeze*

breeze² /briːz/ verb informal **breeze along/into/**

through, etc to move somewhere quickly in a confident way and without worrying

breezy /'bri:zi/ **adj 1** with a slight wind: *a cool, breezy day* **2** happy, confident, and enthusiastic: *a cheerful, breezy style* • **breezily** adv

brethren /'breðrən/ **noun** [plural] members of an organized group, especially a religious group of men

brevity /'brevəti/ **noun** [U] formal **1** a quality that speech or writing has when it is short and contains few words **2** the quality of lasting for a short time

brew¹ /bru:/ **verb 1** [T] to make beer **2** [I, T] If you brew tea or coffee, you make it by adding hot water, and if it brews, it gradually develops flavour in hot water. **3 be brewing** If something bad is brewing, it is beginning to develop: *There is a row brewing over the plans.*

brew² /bru:/ **noun** [C] informal a drink made by brewing, such as beer or tea

brewer /'bru:ər/ **noun** [C] a person or organization that makes beer

brewery /'bru:əri/ **noun** [C] a company that makes beer or a factory where beer is made

bribe /braib/ **noun** [C] money or a gift given to someone so that they will do something for you, usually something dishonest: *The politician was accused of **accepting bribes** from businessmen.* • **bribe** verb [T] [+ to do sth] *He was bribed to give false evidence at the trial.*

⚡ **Word partners for bribe**

accept/take a bribe • **offer** sb/**pay** a bribe • a **cash** bribe

---

bribery /'braibəri/ **noun** [U] attempts to make someone do something, usually something dishonest, by offering them money or gifts: *bribery and corruption*

bric-a-brac /'brikə,bræk/ **noun** [U] a collection of small, decorative objects that have little value

brick /brik/ **noun** [C] ⓑ⓶ a small, hard, rectangular block used for building walls, houses, etc: *a brick wall* → See also **be banging your head¹ against a brick wall**

brick

bricklayer /'brik,leiər/ **noun** [C] someone whose job is to build houses, walls, etc with bricks

bridal /'braidəl/ **adj** [always before noun] relating to a woman who is getting married, or relating to a wedding: *a bridal gown*

bride /braid/ **noun** [C] ⓑ⓵ a woman who is getting married: *the **bride and groom***

bridegroom /'braidgru:m/ **noun** [C] (also **groom**) a man who is getting married

bridesmaid /'braidzmeid/ **noun** [C] a woman or girl who helps the bride on her wedding day

bridge¹ /brid3/ **noun 1 STRUCTURE** ▷ [C] ⓐ⓶ a structure that is built over a river, road, etc so that people or vehicles can go across it: *to go across/over a bridge* ◦ *Brooklyn Bridge* **2 CONNECTION** ▷ [C] something that connects two groups, organizations, etc and improves the

bridge

relationship between them: *After the war they tried to **build bridges** with neighbouring countries.* **3 the bridge of your nose** the hard part of your nose between your eyes **4 the bridge** the raised area of a ship where the controls are **5 GAME** ▷ [U] a card game for four players

IDIOM **I'll/We'll cross that bridge when I/we come to it.** something you say when you do not intend to worry about a possible problem now, but will deal with it if or when it happens

bridge² /brid3/ **verb bridge the gap/gulf, etc** to make the difference between two things smaller: *This course is designed to **bridge the gap between** school and work.*

bridle /'braidəl/ **noun** [C] a set of straps that you put on a horse's head to control it

brief¹ /bri:f/ **adj 1** ⓑ⓵ lasting only for a short time: *a brief visit* **2** ⓑ⓵ using only a few words: *a brief description/statement* **3 in brief** ⓑ⓶ using only a few words: *world news in brief* • **briefly** adv ⓑ⓵ *They discussed the matter briefly.*

brief² /bri:f/ **verb** [T] to give someone instructions or information: [often passive] *At the meeting reporters were **briefed on** the plans.*

brief³ /bri:f/ **noun** [C] a set of instructions or information: [+ to do sth] *My brief was to improve the image of the city.*

briefcase /'bri:fkeis/ **noun** [C] a flat, rectangular case with a handle for carrying documents, books, etc → See picture at **bag**

briefing /'bri:fiŋ/ **noun** [C, U] a meeting when people are given instructions or information: *a press briefing*

briefs /bri:fs/ **noun** [plural] underwear that you wear on your bottom: *a pair of briefs* → See colour picture **Clothes** on page Centre 9

brigade /bri'geid/ **noun** [C] **1** a large group of soldiers **2** UK humorous a group of people with a particular characteristic or interest: *the anti-smoking brigade* → See also **fire brigade**

brigadier /,brigə'diər/ **noun** [C] a British army officer of high rank

bright /brait/ **adj 1 COLOUR** ▷ ⓐ⓶ having a strong, light colour: *bright yellow/blue* **2 LIGHT** ▷ ⓑ⓵ full of light or shining strongly: *bright sunshine* **3 INTELLIGENT** ▷ ⓑ⓶ intelligent: *He's a bright boy.* **4 HAPPY** ▷ ⓑ⓶ happy or full of hope: *She's always so bright and cheerful.* • **brightly** adv ⓑ⓶ *brightly coloured flowers* • **brightness noun** [U]

---

brighten /'braɪtᵊn/ verb [I, T] (also **brighten up**)
1 to become lighter or more colourful, or to make something become lighter or more colourful: *A picture or two would brighten up the room.*
2 to become happier, or to make someone become happier: *She brightened up when she saw him.*

brilliant /'brɪliənt/ adj **1 GOOD** ▷ UK **A2** very good: *We saw a brilliant film.* **2 CLEVER** ▷ **B1** extremely clever: *a brilliant scholar* **3 LIGHT** ▷ **B1** full of light or colour: *The sky was a brilliant blue.*
• **brilliantly** adv • **brilliance** /'brɪliəns/ noun [U]

brim¹ /brɪm/ verb (**brimming**, **brimmed**) **be brimming with sth** to be full of something: *Her eyes were brimming with tears.*

brim² /brɪm/ noun [C] **1** the flat part around the bottom of a hat **2** the top edge of a container: *He filled my glass to the brim.*

brine /braɪn/ noun [U] salty water, often used for keeping food from decaying: *olives in brine*

bring /brɪŋ/ verb [T] (**brought**) **1** **A2** to take someone or something with you when you go somewhere: *Did you bring an umbrella with you?* ○ [+ two objects] *He brought me some flowers.*
2 **bring happiness/peace/shame, etc** **B1** to cause happiness/peace/shame, etc: *Money does not always bring happiness.* **3** **can not bring yourself to do sth** to not be willing to do something because it is so unpleasant: *He couldn't bring himself to talk to her.* → See also **bring sb/sth to their knees (knee)**, **bring sth to light¹**

> **⚠ Common learner error: bring or take?**
>
> Use **bring** to talk about moving something or someone towards the speaker or towards the place where you are now.
>
> *Did you bring any money?*
> *I've brought you a present.*
>
> Use **take** to talk about moving something or someone away from the speaker or away from the place where you are now.
>
> *I can take you to the station.*
> *Don't forget to take your umbrella.*

PHRASAL VERBS **bring sth about** to make something happen: *The Internet has brought about big changes in the way we work.* • **bring sth back 1** **A2** to return from somewhere with something: [+ two objects] *Can you bring me back some milk from the shop, please?* **2** to make someone think about something from the past: *The photos brought back memories.* • **bring sb down** to cause someone in a position of power to lose their job: *This scandal could bring down the government.* • **bring sth down** to reduce the level of something: *to bring down prices* • **bring sth forward** to change the date or time of an event so that it happens earlier than planned: *I've brought forward the meeting to this week.* • **bring sth in 1** to introduce something new, usually a product or a law: *New safety regulations were brought in last year.* **2** to earn or make money: *The film has brought in millions of dollars.* • **bring sb in** to ask someone to do a particular job: *We need to bring in an expert to*

sort out this problem. • **bring sth off** to succeed in doing something difficult: *How did he manage to bring that off?* • **bring sth on** to make something happen, usually something bad: [often passive] *Headaches are often brought on by stress.* • **bring sth out 1** **B2** to produce something to sell to the public: *They have just brought out a new, smaller phone.* **2** to make a particular quality or detail noticeable: *Salt can help to bring out the flavour of food.* • **bring sb together** to cause people to be friendly with each other: *The disaster brought the community closer together.* • **bring sb up** **B1** to look after a child and teach them until they are old enough to look after themselves: *She was brought up by her grandparents.* • **bring sth up 1** **B2** to start to talk about a particular subject: *There are several points I'd like to bring up at tomorrow's meeting.* **2** UK to vomit something

brink /brɪŋk/ noun **be on the brink of sth** to be in a situation where something bad is going to happen very soon: *The two countries are on the brink of war.*

brisk /brɪsk/ adj quick and energetic: *a brisk walk* • **briskly** adv

bristle¹ /'brɪsl/ verb [I] to show that you are annoyed about something: *She bristled at the suggestion that it was her fault.*

bristle² /'brɪsl/ noun [C, U] a short, stiff hair • **bristly** adj

Brit /brɪt/ noun [C] informal someone who comes from Great Britain

British¹ /'brɪtɪʃ/ adj relating to Great Britain or the United Kingdom

British² /'brɪtɪʃ/ noun **the British** [plural] the people of Great Britain or the United Kingdom

Briton /'brɪtᵊn/ noun [C] someone who comes from Great Britain

brittle /'brɪtl/ adj hard but easily broken: *brittle bones*

broach /brəʊtʃ/ verb **broach an idea/subject/topic, etc** to begin to talk about something, usually something difficult or embarrassing: *I don't know how to broach the subject of money with him.*

broad /brɔːd/ adj **1** **B1** wide: *broad shoulders* ○ *a broad smile* **2** **a broad range/variety, etc** **B1** a group that includes many different things or people: *a broad range of subjects* **3** **a broad outline/picture, etc** a general description, without detail: *This is just a broad outline of the proposal.* **4** A broad accent (= way of speaking from a region) is very noticeable. **5** **in broad daylight** during the day when it is light and people can see: *He was attacked in broad daylight.*

broadband /'brɔːdbænd/ noun [U] **B2** a system that allows large amounts of information to be sent very quickly between computers or other electronic equipment

broadcast¹ /'brɔːdkɑːst/ noun [C] a television or radio programme: *a news broadcast* • **broadcast** adj [always before noun] relating to television or radio: *broadcast news*

broadcast² /'brɔːdkɑːst/ verb [I, T] (**broadcast,**

also US **broadcasted**) ⓑ₂ to send out a programme on television or radio: [often passive]
*The concert will be **broadcast** live next week.*
• **broadcaster** noun [C] someone who speaks on
radio or television as a job • **broadcasting** noun
[U]

broaden /'brɔːdən/ verb [I, T] **1** to increase or
make something increase and include more
things or people: *We need to broaden the range of
services that we offer.* ○ *Travel **broadens your
mind**.* **2** to become wider or make something
become wider: *Her smile broadened and she
began to laugh.*

broadly /'brɔːdli/ adv in a general way and not
including everything or everyone: *The plans
have been broadly accepted.*

🗷 Word partners for **broadly**

broadly **in line with/similar** • broadly
welcome sth

---

broadsheet /'brɔːdʃiːt/ noun [C] UK a large
newspaper, usually considered to be more
serious than smaller newspapers

broccoli /'brɒkəli/ noun [U] ⓑ₁ a green vegetable with a thick stem

brochure /'brəʊʃər/ ⓤˢ /brəʊˈʃʊr/ noun [C] ⓑ₁
a thin book with pictures and information,
usually advertising something: *a **holiday/
travel brochure***

broil /brɔɪl/ verb [T] US (UK **grill**) to cook food
with strong heat coming from directly above or
below it

broiler /'brɔɪlər/ noun [C] US (UK **grill**) a piece of
equipment used for cooking food under strong
direct heat

broke[1] /brəʊk/ adj informal **1 be broke** to not
have any money **2 go broke** to lose all your
money and have to end your business

broke[2] /brəʊk/ past tense of break

➕ Other ways of saying **broken**

If a piece of equipment is broken (not
working properly), you can use adjectives
such as **dead**, **defunct**, or, informally, **bust**
(UK):

*You won't be able to watch the match, the
telly's **bust**.*

*The phone's **dead**, there must be a problem
with the line.*

If a piece of equipment or machinery in a
public place is broken, you can say that it is
out of order:

*The coffee machine was **out of order**.*

If a piece of equipment has broken, in informal situations you can use expressions like
have had it and **give up the ghost**:

*The kettle's **had it**, you'll have to boil a pan
of water.*

*I can't give you a lift – my car's **given up the
ghost**.*

---

broken[1] /'brəʊkən/ adj **1** ⓐ₂ damaged and
separated into pieces: *broken glass* → Opposite
unbroken 2 a broken arm/leg, etc ⓐ₂ an arm/
leg, etc with a damaged bone **3** ⓐ₂ If a machine

or piece of equipment is broken, it is not
working: *The DVD player's broken.* **4 a broken
heart** ⓑ₂ great sadness because someone you
love has ended a relationship with you **5 a
broken home** a family in which the parents do
not now live together **6 a broken promise** a
promise that has not been kept **7 broken
English/Spanish, etc** English/Spanish, etc that
is spoken slowly and has a lot of mistakes in it

broken[2] /'brəʊkən/ past participle of break

broken-down /ˌbrəʊkənˈdaʊn/ adj not working
or in bad condition: *a broken-down vehicle*

broken-hearted /ˌbrəʊkənˈhɑːtɪd/ adj very sad
because someone you love has ended a relationship with you

broker[1] /'brəʊkər/ noun [C] **1** (also **stockbroker**)
someone whose job is to buy and sell shares
2 an insurance/mortgage, etc broker someone
who makes other people's financial arrangements for them

broker[2] /'brəʊkər/ verb [T] to arrange an agreement: *The peace deal was brokered by the US.*

bronchitis /brɒŋˈkaɪtɪs/ noun [U] an illness in
your lungs that makes you cough and have
problems breathing

bronze[1] /brɒnz/ noun **1 METAL** ▷ [U] a shiny
orange-brown metal **2 COLOUR** ▷ [U] an orange-
brown colour **3 PRIZE** ▷ [C] a bronze medal : *He
won a bronze in the 200m.*

bronze[2] /brɒnz/ adj **1** made of bronze: *a bronze
statue* **2** being the colour of bronze

bronze ˈmedal noun [C] a small, round disc
given to someone for finishing third in a race or
competition

brooch /brəʊtʃ/ noun [C] a piece of jewellery for
women that is fastened onto clothes with a pin:
a diamond brooch

brood[1] /bruːd/ noun [C] a family of young birds
or animals, all born at the same time

brood[2] /bruːd/ verb [I] to think for a long time
about things that make you sad or angry: *I wish
he'd stop **brooding about** the past.*

brook /brʊk/ noun [C] a small stream

broom /bruːm/ noun [C] a brush with a long
handle used for cleaning the floor → See picture
at **brush**

broth /brɒθ/ noun [U] soup, usually made with
meat: *chicken broth*

brothel /'brɒθəl/ noun [C] a building where
prostitutes (= people who have sex for money)
work

brother /'brʌðər/ noun [C] **1 RELATIVE** ▷ ⓐ₁ a
boy or man who has the same parents as you:
an older/younger brother ○ *my big/little brother*
2 MEMBER ▷ a man who is a member of the
same race, religious group, organization, etc
3 RELIGION ▷ (also **Brother**) a monk (= man who
lives in a male religious group): *Brother Paul*

brotherhood /'brʌðəhʊd/ noun **1** [C] a group of
men who have the same purpose or religious
beliefs **2** [U] friendship and loyalty, like the
relationship between brothers

brother-in-law /'brʌðərɪnlɔː/ noun [C] (plural
brothers-in-law) ⓑ₂ the man married to your
sister, or the brother of your husband or wife

---

brotherly /ˈbrʌðəli/ **adj** [always before noun] relating to or typical of brothers: *brotherly love*

brought /brɔːt/ past of bring

brow /braʊ/ **noun** [C] **1** the front part of your head between your eyes and your hair: *He wiped the sweat from his brow.* **2 brow of a hill/slope** UK the top part of a hill or slope

brown /braʊn/ **adj 1** ⓐ being the same colour as chocolate or soil: *a brown leather bag* ∘ *dark brown hair/eyes* → See colour picture **Colours** on page Centre 12 **2** having darker skin because you have been in the sun • **brown noun** [C, U] ⓐ the colour brown

brownfield /ˈbraʊnfiːld/ **adj** UK describes land that was used for industry and where new buildings can be built: *a brownfield site* → Compare **greenfield**

brownie /ˈbraʊni/ **noun** [C] a small, square cake made with chocolate and nuts

browse /braʊz/ **verb 1 INTERNET** ▷ [I, T] ⓑ to look at information on the Internet: *to browse the Internet/Web* **2 READ** ▷ [I] ⓑ to read a book, magazine, etc in a relaxed way and not in detail: *She browsed through some travel brochures looking for ideas.* **3 SHOP** ▷ [I] to walk around a shop and look at things without buying anything: *I love browsing around bookshops.*

browser /ˈbraʊzər/ **noun** [C] **1** ⓑ a computer program that allows you to look at pages on the Internet **2** someone who browses

bruise /bruːz/ **noun** [C] ⓑ a dark area on your skin where you have been hurt: *He suffered cuts and bruises after falling off his bike.* • **bruise verb** [T] to cause someone or something to have a bruise: [often passive] *He was badly bruised in the accident.* • **bruising noun** [U]

brunette /bruːˈnet/ **noun** [C] a white woman with dark brown hair

brunt /brʌnt/ **noun bear/feel/take the brunt of sth** to experience the worst part of something: *He took the brunt of the criticism.*

brush¹ /brʌʃ/ **noun 1** [C] ⓐ an object made of short, thin pieces of plastic, wire, etc fixed to a handle and used to tidy hair, to clean, to paint, etc: *a stiff wire brush* **2** [no plural] the action of using a brush: *I need to give my hair a quick brush.* **3 the brush of sth** the feeling of something touching you lightly: *She felt the brush of his lips against her cheek.* **4 a brush with sth** an experience in which something unpleasant happens or almost happens: *a brush with death*

brush² /brʌʃ/ **verb** [T] **1** ⓐ to use a brush to clean or tidy something: *to brush your hair/teeth* **2 brush sth away/off, etc** ⓑ to move something somewhere using a brush or your hand: *He brushed the snow off his coat.* **3 brush against/past sb/sth** ⓑ to lightly touch someone or something as you move past: *He brushed past me as he went up the stairs.*

PHRASAL VERBS **brush sth aside/off** to refuse to think about something seriously: *He brushed aside her suggestion.* • **brush up (on) sth** to improve your skills in something: *I'm trying to brush up on my French before I go to Paris.*

brush

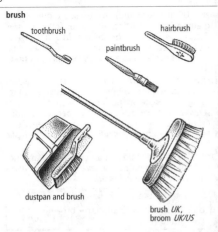

toothbrush
hairbrush
paintbrush
dustpan and brush
brush *UK*, broom *UK/US*

brush-off /ˈbrʌʃɒf/ **noun** informal **give sb the brush-off** to be unfriendly to someone by not talking to them

brusque /bruːsk/ ⓤⓢ /brʌsk/ **adj** dealing with people in a quick way that is unfriendly or rude: *a brusque manner* • **brusquely adv**

brussel sprout /ˌbrʌsˈəlˈspraʊt/ ⓤⓢ /ˈbrʌs-əlˌspraʊt/ **noun** [C] a small, green vegetable that is round and made of leaves

brutal /ˈbruːtəl/ **adj** very violent or cruel: *a brutal murder* • **brutally adv** *brutally murdered* ∘ *brutally honest* • **brutality** /bruːˈtæləti/ **noun** [C, U]

brute¹ /bruːt/ **noun** [C] someone who behaves in a very violent and cruel way • **brutish** /ˈbruːtɪʃ/ **adj** like a brute

brute² /bruːt/ **adj brute force/strength** great force or strength

BSc /ˌbiːesˈsiː/ **noun** [C] UK (US **BS** /biːˈes/) abbreviation for Bachelor of Science: a university or college qualification in a science subject that usually takes 3 or 4 years of study: *He has a BSc in computer science.*

BSE /ˌbiːesˈiː/ **noun** [U] abbreviation for bovine spongiform encephalopathy: a disease that kills cows by destroying their brains

BTW internet abbreviation for by the way: used when you write some extra information that may or may not be related to what is being discussed

bubble¹ /ˈbʌbl/ **noun** [C] a ball of air or gas with liquid around it: *an air bubble*

bubble² /ˈbʌbl/ **verb** [I] **1** If a liquid bubbles, balls of air or gas rise to its surface: *The soup was bubbling on the stove.* **2 bubble (over) with confidence/enthusiasm, etc** to be full of a positive emotion or quality

bubble gum noun [U] a sweet that you chew and blow into a bubble

bubbly /ˈbʌbli/ **adj 1** happy and enthusiastic: *a bubbly personality* **2** full of bubbles

buck¹ /bʌk/ **noun** [C] **1** US informal a dollar: *It cost me twenty bucks to get a new bike lock.* **2** a male rabbit or deer

IDIOM **pass the buck** to blame someone or to make them responsible for a problem that you should deal with yourself

buck² /bʌk/ **verb** [I] If a horse bucks, it kicks its back legs into the air.

bucket /'bʌkɪt/ **noun** [C] 🅱 a round, open container with a handle used for carrying liquids: *a bucket of water*

bucket

buckle¹ /'bʌkl/ **noun** [C] a metal object used to fasten the ends of a belt or strap: *a silver buckle*

buckle² /'bʌkl/ **verb** **1 FASTEN** ▷ [I, T] to fasten a belt or strap with a buckle **2 BEND** ▷ [I, T] to bend, or to make something bend because of too much weight, heat, etc: *His **legs buckled** as he reached the finishing line.* **3 SUFFER** ▷ [I] to suffer and stop working effectively because of too many problems or too much work

PHRASAL VERB **buckle down** to start working hard: *I must **buckle down to** some work this afternoon.*

bud /bʌd/ **noun** [C] a part of a plant that develops into a leaf or a flower: *In spring the trees are covered in buds.*

IDIOM **nip sth in the bud** to stop a small problem from getting worse by stopping it soon after it starts

→ See also **taste buds**

Buddha /'bʊdə/ ⓤⓢ /'buːdə/ **noun** the Indian holy man on whose life and teachings Buddhism is based

Buddhism /'bʊdɪz³m/ ⓤⓢ /'buːdɪz³m/ **noun** [U] a religion based on the teachings of Buddha

Buddhist /'bʊdɪst/ ⓤⓢ /'buːdɪst/ **noun** [C] someone who believes in Buddhism • **Buddhist adj** *a Buddhist temple*

budding /'bʌdɪŋ/ **adj** [always before noun] starting to develop well: *a **budding romance***

buddy /'bʌdi/ **noun** [C] informal a friend: *my best buddy*

budge /bʌdʒ/ **verb** [I, T] **1** If something will not budge, or you cannot budge it, it will not move: *I've tried to open the window, but it won't budge.* **2** If someone will not budge, or you cannot budge them, they will not change their opinion.

budgerigar /'bʌdʒ³rɪgɑːʳ/ **noun** [C] UK a budgie

budget¹ /'bʌdʒɪt/ **noun** [C] **1** a plan that shows how much money you have and how much you will spend it **2** 🅱 the amount of money you have for something: *an **annual budget** of 30 million euros* **3 the Budget** in the UK, an occasion when the government officially tells the public about its plans for taxes and spending • **budgetary adj** [always before noun] relating to a budget

budget² /'bʌdʒɪt/ **verb** [I, T] to plan how much money you will spend on something: *An extra £20 million has been **budgeted for** schools this year.*

budget³ /'bʌdʒɪt/ **adj** a budget hotel/price, etc 🅱 a very cheap hotel, price, etc

budgie /'bʌdʒi/ **noun** [C] UK a small, brightly coloured bird often kept as a pet

buff¹ /bʌf/ **noun** [C] a computer/film/wine, etc buff someone who knows a lot about computers/films/wine, etc

buff² /bʌf/ **adj** informal If someone's body is buff, it looks strong and attractive, as if they have had a lot of exercise

buffalo /'bʌf³ləʊ/ **noun** [C] (plural **buffaloes**, **buffalo**) a large, wild animal, like a cow with horns: *a herd of wild buffalo*

buffer /'bʌfəʳ/ **noun** [C] something that helps protect someone or something from harm: *I have some money saved to act as a **buffer** against unexpected bills.*

'buffer ˌzone noun [C] an area created to separate two countries that are fighting

buffet¹ /'bʊfeɪ/ ⓤⓢ /bə'feɪ/ **noun** [C] a meal in which dishes of food are arranged on a table and you serve yourself: *a cold buffet* ∘ *a buffet lunch*

buffet² /'bʌfɪt/ **verb** [T] If something is buffeted by the weather, sea, etc, it is hit repeatedly and with force: [often passive] *The little boat was buffeted by the waves.*

'buffet ˌcar noun [C] UK the part of a train where you can buy something to eat or drink

buffoon /bə'fuːn/ **noun** [C] old-fashioned someone who does silly things

bug¹ /bʌg/ **noun** [C] **1 ILLNESS** ▷ 🅱 a bacteria or virus, or the illness that it causes: *a flu / stomach bug* **2 COMPUTER** ▷ a mistake in a computer program: *This program is full of bugs.* **3 INSECT** ▷ 🅱 a small insect **4 EQUIPMENT** ▷ a small, electronic piece of equipment used to secretly listen to people talking **5 be bitten by the bug/ get the bug** informal to develop a strong interest or enthusiasm for a particular activity: *He's been bitten by the tennis bug.*

bug² /bʌg/ **verb** [T] (**bugging, bugged**) **1** to hide a piece of equipment somewhere in order to secretly listen to people talking: [often passive] *Their hotel room had been bugged.* **2** informal to annoy someone: *He's been bugging me all morning.*

buggy /'bʌgi/ **noun** [C] **1** UK (US **stroller**) a chair on wheels that is used to move small children **2** a vehicle with two wheels that is pulled by a horse, especially in the past

bugle /'bjuːgl/ **noun** [C] a small, metal musical instrument that you play by blowing into it

build¹ /bɪld/ **verb** (**built**) **1** [I, T] 🅰 to make something by putting materials and parts together: *build a house/wall* ∘ *The bridge is built of steel and aluminium.* **2** [T] to create and develop something over a long time: *They have built a solid friendship over the years.*

PHRASAL VERBS **build sth into sth** to make something a part of something else: *There are video screens built into the back of the seats.* • **build on sth** to use a success or achievement as a base from which to achieve more success • **build (sth) up** to increase or develop, or to make something increase or develop: *Traffic usually builds up in the late afternoon.*

build² /bɪld/ **noun** [C, U] the size and shape of a person's body: *He's of medium build with short brown hair.*

builder /'bɪldər/ **noun** [C] 🇬🇧 someone who makes or repairs buildings as a job

building /'bɪldɪŋ/ **noun 1** [C] 🅰️2 a structure with walls and a roof, such as a house, school, etc: *an office building* **2** [U] the activity of putting together materials and parts to make structures: *building materials* → See also **apartment building**

building so,ciety noun [C] UK an organization similar to a bank that lends you money to buy a house

build-up /'bɪldʌp/ **noun** [singular] **1** a slow increase in something: *the build-up of traffic* **2** **the build-up to sth** UK the period of preparation before something happens: *There was a lot of excitement in the build-up to the Olympics.*

built /bɪlt/ past of build

built-in /ˌbɪlt'ɪn/ **adj** [always before noun] included as part of the main structure of something: *a computer with a built-in modem*

built-up /ˌbɪlt'ʌp/ **adj** a built-up area has a lot of buildings

bulb /bʌlb/ **noun** [C] **1** (also **light bulb**) 🇧1 a glass object containing a wire which produces light from electricity: *an electric light bulb* **2** a round root that some plants grow from: *daffodil bulbs*

bulbous /'bʌlbəs/ **adj** large and round in an unattractive way: *a bulbous nose*

bulge¹ /bʌldʒ/ **verb** [I] to look larger and rounder or fuller than normal: *Her bags were bulging with shopping.*

bulge² /bʌldʒ/ **noun** [C] a round, raised area on a surface

bulimia /bʊ'lɪmiə/ **noun** [U] a mental illness in which someone eats too much and then forces themselves to vomit • **bulimic noun** [C], adj

bulk /bʌlk/ **noun 1 in bulk** in large amounts: *to buy in bulk* **2 the bulk of sth** the largest part or most of something: *He spends the bulk of his money on rent.* **3** [no plural] the large size of something or someone

bulky /'bʌlki/ **adj** too big and taking up too much space

bull /bʊl/ **noun** [C] 🇧1 a male cow → See also **be like a red rag to a bull**

bulldog /'bʊldɒg/ **noun** [C] a short, strong dog with a large head and neck

bulldozer /'bʊlˌdəʊzər/ **noun** [C] a heavy vehicle used to destroy buildings and make the ground flat • **bulldoze verb** [T]

bullet /'bʊlɪt/ **noun** [C] 🇧2 a small, metal object that is fired from a gun: *a bullet wound*

IDIOM **bite the bullet** to make yourself do something or accept something difficult or unpleasant

☑ Word partners for **bullet**
fire a bullet • a bullet flies/lodges swh • a hail of bullets • a bullet hole/wound

bullet ,(point) noun [C] a small black circle used in writing to show separate items on a list

bulletin /'bʊlətɪn/ **noun** [C] **1** a short news programme on television or radio: *the evening news bulletin* **2** a regular newspaper or report containing news about an organization

bulletin ,board noun [C] **1** US (UK **notice board**) a board on a wall where you put advertisements and announcements → See colour picture **The Classroom** on page Centre 6 **2** (also **message board**) a place on a website where you can leave messages for other people to read

bulletproof /'bʊlɪtpruːf/ **adj** made of material that a bullet cannot go through: *bulletproof vests*

bullion /'bʊliən/ **noun** [U] blocks of gold or silver

bullock /'bʊlək/ **noun** [C] a young bull (= male cow)

bully¹ /'bʊli/ **verb** [T] to intentionally frighten someone who is smaller or weaker than you: *He was bullied at school by some older boys.* ○ [+ into + doing sth] *She was bullied into leaving* • **bullying noun** [U] *Bullying is a problem in many schools.*

bully² /'bʊli/ **noun** [C] someone who intentionally frightens a person who is smaller or weaker than them

bum¹ /bʌm/ **noun** [C] informal **1** UK your bottom **2** US someone who has no home and no money

bum² /bʌm/ **verb** [T] (**bumming, bummed**) very informal to ask someone for something, such as money or cigarettes, without intending to pay for them: *Hey, could I bum a cigarette?*

PHRASAL VERBS **bum around** informal to spend time being lazy and doing very little • **bum around sth** informal to travel to different places and not do any work

bumbag /'bʌmbæg/ **noun** [C] UK (US **fanny pack**) a small bag fixed to a belt that you wear around your waist

bumblebee /'bʌmblbiː/ **noun** [C] a large, hairy bee

bumbling /'bʌmblɪŋ/ **adj** [always before noun] confused and showing no skill: *a bumbling idiot*

bummer /'bʌmər/ **noun a bummer** informal something unpleasant or annoying: *That last exam was a real bummer.*

bump¹ /bʌmp/ **verb 1** 🇧2 [T] to hurt part of your body by hitting it against something hard: *I bumped my head on the door.* **2 bump into/against sth** 🇧2 to hit your body, your car, etc against something by accident: *He kept falling* *over and bumping into things.* **3 bump along/ over sth** to move in a vehicle over a surface that is not smooth: *The bus bumped along the country road.*

PHRASAL VERBS **bump into sb** informal to meet someone you know when you have not planned to meet them: *I bumped into an old school friend in town today.* • **bump sb off** informal to murder someone

bump² /bʌmp/ noun [C] **1 SURFACE** ▷ a round, raised area on a surface: *My bike hit a bump in the road.* **2 BODY** ▷ a raised area on your body where it has been hurt by hitting something hard: *a nasty bump on the head* **3 SOUND** ▷ the sound of something hitting another thing hard: *I heard a bump upstairs.*

bumper¹ /ˈbʌmpəʳ/ noun [C] 🅱 a bar fixed along the front or back of a vehicle to protect it in an accident: *a front/rear bumper*

bumper² /ˈbʌmpəʳ/ adj [always before noun] bigger or better than usual: *a bumper year*

bumper ˌsticker noun [C] a sign that you stick on a car, often with a funny message on it

bumpy /ˈbʌmpi/ adj **1 SURFACE** ▷ A bumpy road or surface is not smooth but has raised areas on it. **2 JOURNEY** ▷ A bumpy journey is uncomfortable because the vehicle moves around a lot. **3 SITUATION** ▷ full of problems or sudden changes: *We had a bumpy start.*

bun /bʌn/ noun [C] **1 CAKE** ▷ UK 🅱 a small, round cake: *an iced bun* **2 BREAD** ▷ 🅱 a small, round piece of bread: *a hamburger/hot cross bun* **3 HAIR** ▷ a hairstyle in which the hair is arranged in a small, round shape on the back of the head

bunch¹ /bʌnʃ/ noun **1** [C] 🅱 a number of things of the same type that are joined or held together: *He handed me a **bunch of flowers.*** → See colour picture **Pieces and Quantities** on page Centre 1 **2** [C] informal 🅱 a group of people: [usually singular] *His friends are a nice bunch.* **3 a bunch of sth** US informal a large amount or number of something: *There's a whole bunch of places I'd like to visit.*

🗒 Word partners for **bunch**

a bunch of **bananas/flowers/grapes/keys**
---

bunch² /bʌnʃ/ verb

PHRASAL VERBS **bunch (sb/sth) together/up** to move close together so that you make a tight group, or to make someone or something do this: [often passive] *We were all bunched up at the back of the room.* • **bunch (sth) up** If material bunches up, or if someone bunches it up, it moves into tight folds: [often passive] *My shirt's all bunched up at the back.*

bunches /ˈbʌntʃɪz/ noun [plural] UK a hairstyle in which the hair is tied together in two parts, one on each side of the head

bundle¹ /ˈbʌndl/ noun **1** [C] a number of things that are tied together: *a bundle of letters/clothes* **2 a bundle of energy/nerves** informal a very energetic or nervous person

bundle² /ˈbʌndl/ verb **1 bundle sb into/out of/**

through sth to push or carry someone somewhere quickly and roughly: *He was bundled into the back of a car and driven away.* **2** to include an extra computer program or other product with something you sell

PHRASAL VERBS **bundle sth up** to tie a number of things together • **bundle (sb) up** to put warm clothes on yourself or someone else

bung /bʌŋ/ verb **bung sth in/on, etc** UK informal to put something somewhere in a quick, careless way: *Shall I bung a chicken in the oven for dinner?*

PHRASAL VERB **bung sth up** UK informal to cause something to be blocked so that it does not work in the way it should: [often passive] *The toilet was bunged up with paper.*

bungalow /ˈbʌŋɡələʊ/ noun [C] a house that has all its rooms on the ground floor

bungee jumping /ˈbʌndʒiˌdʒʌmpɪŋ/ noun [U] (also **bungy jumping**) the sport of jumping from a very high place while tied to a long elastic rope, so that the rope pulls you back before you hit the ground

bungle /ˈbʌŋɡl/ verb [T] to do something wrong in a very careless or stupid way: *a bungled robbery* • **bungling** noun [U]

bunk /bʌŋk/ noun [C] a narrow bed in a ship, train, etc

bunk ˌbeds noun [plural] two beds fixed together with one on top of the other

bunker /ˈbʌŋkəʳ/ noun [C] **1** an underground room where people go to be protected, especially from bombs **2** in golf, a hollow area filled with sand

bunny /ˈbʌni/ noun [C] (also **bunny ˌrabbit**) a child's word for 'rabbit'

buoy¹ /bɔɪ/ noun [C] a floating object used in water to mark dangerous areas for boats

buoy² /bɔɪ/ verb **be buoyed (up) by sth** to feel happy or confident because of something: *The team was buoyed up by their win last week.*

buoyant /ˈbɔɪənt/ adj **1 CONFIDENT** ▷ happy and confident: *in a **buoyant mood*** **2 BUSINESS** ▷ successful or making a profit: *a buoyant economy* **3 FLOATING** ▷ floating or able to float • **buoyancy** /ˈbɔɪənsi/ noun [U]

burden /ˈbɜːdən/ noun [C] something difficult or unpleasant that you have to deal with or worry about: *the **burden** of responsibility* ∘ *I'd hate to be a **burden** to you when I'm older.* • **burden** verb [T] to give someone something difficult or unpleasant to deal with or worry about: *Sorry to burden you with my problems.*

🗒 Word partners for **burden**

be/become a burden **on/to** sb • **carry** the burden of sth • **ease/lighten/share** the burden • a **heavy** burden • the burden **of (doing) sth**
---

bureau /ˈbjʊərəʊ/ noun [C] (plural **bureaux**, US **bureaus**) **1 OFFICE** ▷ a department or office **2 WRITING** ▷ UK a piece of furniture with drawers and a sloping top used for writing **3 CLOTHES** ▷ US (UK/US **chest of drawers**) a

B

piece of furniture with drawers for keeping clothes in

bureaucracy /bjʊəˈrɒkrəsi/ noun **1** [U] complicated rules and processes used by an organization, especially when they do not seem necessary: *government bureaucracy* **2** [C, U] a government or organization in which there are a lot of officials in a lot of departments • **bureaucrat** /ˈbjʊərəʊkræt/ noun [C] someone working in a bureaucracy • **bureaucratic** /ˌbjʊərəʊˈkrætɪk/ adj

burgeoning /ˈbɜːdʒənɪŋ/ adj growing very quickly: *a burgeoning population*

burger /ˈbɜːgər/ noun [C] 🅰️ a flat, round piece of food, usually made of meat, that is fried and served between pieces of bread: *burger and fries* ∘ *a veggie burger*

burglar /ˈbɜːglər/ noun [C] 🅱️ someone who gets into buildings illegally and steals things

burglar aˌlarm noun [C] something that makes a noise if someone tries to get into a building illegally

burglarize /ˈbɜːgləraɪz/ verb US burgle

burglary /ˈbɜːgləri/ noun [C, U] 🅱️ the crime of getting into a building illegally and stealing things

burgle /ˈbɜːgl/ verb [T] UK (US **burglarize**) to get into a building illegally and steal things: [often passive] *They've been burgled twice recently.*

burial /ˈberiəl/ noun [C, U] an occasion when a dead body is put into the ground

burly /ˈbɜːli/ adj A burly man is large and strong.

burn¹ /bɜːn/ verb (burnt, burned) **1 DESTROY** ▷ [I, T] 🅱️ to destroy something with fire, or to be destroyed by fire: *I burnt all his letters.* ∘ *The factory burned to the ground.* ∘ *He dropped his cigarette and burnt a hole in his jacket.* **2 FLAMES** ▷ [I] 🅱️ to produce flames: *The fire's burning well.* **3 COOK TOO LONG** ▷ [I, T] If you burn something that you are cooking, you cook it too much and if something you are cooking burns, it cooks too much: *Check the pizza – I think it's burning!* **4 burn yourself/your fingers, etc** 🅱️ to be hurt by fire or heat: *He burned his hand on the kettle.* **5 ENERGY** ▷ [T] (also **burn up**) to use fuel to produce heat or energy: *to burn calories/fuel* **6 COPY** ▷ [T] to copy music, information or images onto a CD: *He's burnt all his favourite records onto a CD.* **7 SKIN** ▷ [I] to be very hot or sore: *Her cheeks were burning.* **8 burn with anger/hatred, etc** to feel an emotion very strongly

PHRASAL VERBS **burn (sth) down** 🅱️ to destroy something, especially a building, by fire, or to be destroyed by fire: *Their house burnt down while they were at work.* • **burn out** If a fire burns out, it stops producing flames because nothing remains that can burn. • **burn out** 🅱️ to become sick or very tired from working too hard: *If Olivia keeps working late every night, she will burn out.* • **burn (sth) up** to destroy something completely, or to be destroyed completely by fire or heat: *The satellite will burn up when it enters the atmosphere.*

burn² /bɜːn/ noun [C] a place where fire or heat

has damaged or hurt something: *She has a nasty burn on her arm.*

burner /ˈbɜːnər/ noun [C] a piece of equipment used to burn or heat something

IDIOM **put sth on the back burner** to not deal with something now, but intend to deal with it at a later time

burning /ˈbɜːnɪŋ/ adj **1** very hot: *the burning heat of the midday sun* **2 burning ambition, desire, etc** a very strong need to do something **3 a burning issue/question** a subject or question that must be dealt with or answered quickly

burnout /ˈbɜːnaʊt/ noun [U] extreme tiredness, usually caused by working too much

burnt¹ /bɜːnt/ adj destroyed or made black by fire or heat: *burnt toast*

burnt² /bɜːnt/ past of burn

burnt-out /ˌbɜːntˈaʊt/ adj (also **burned-out** /bɜːndˈaʊt/) **1** A burnt-out car or building has been almost completely destroyed by fire. **2** informal tired and without enthusiasm because you have worked too hard: *a burnt-out teacher*

burp /bɜːp/ verb [I] to let air from your stomach come out of your mouth in a noisy way • **burp** noun [C]

burrow¹ /ˈbʌrəʊ/ verb [I] When an animal burrows, it digs a hole or passage in the ground to live in: *There are rabbits burrowing under the building.*

burrow² /ˈbʌrəʊ/ noun [C] a hole or passage in the ground dug by an animal to live in

burst¹ /bɜːst/ verb (burst) **1** 🅱️ [I, T] If a container bursts, or if you burst it, it breaks suddenly, so that what is inside it comes out: *A water pipe burst and flooded the cellar.* **2 burst in/out/through, etc** 🅱️ to move somewhere suddenly and forcefully: *Three masked men burst into the bank.* **3 burst into flames** to suddenly start burning **4 burst into laughter/tears, etc** 🅱️ to suddenly start laughing/crying, etc: *She burst into tears and ran away.* **5 burst open** to open suddenly and with force **6 be bursting with confidence/joy, etc** to be full of an emotion or quality: *She was bursting with pride.* **7 be bursting to do sth** informal to want to do something very much: *I was bursting to tell him about the party.*

PHRASAL VERB **burst out 1** 🅱️ to suddenly say something loudly: *'Don't go!' he burst out.* **2 burst out laughing/crying** 🅱️ to suddenly start laughing/crying: *I walked in and everyone burst out laughing.*

burst² /bɜːst/ noun **1 a burst of sth** a sudden large amount of noise, activity, etc: *a burst of applause/laughter* **2** [C] an occasion when something breaks open and what is inside it comes out

bury /ˈberi/ verb [T] **1** 🅱️ to put a dead body into the ground: [often passive] *He was buried next to his wife.* **2** 🅱️ to hide something in the ground or under something: *buried treasure* ∘ [often passive] *Two climbers were buried in the snow.* **3 bury your face/head in sth** to move your face, head somewhere where it is hidden: *She buried her face in her hands.* **4 bury yourself in sth** to give all your attention to something: *He buried himself in his work.* → See also **bury the hatchet**

bus /bʌs/ noun [C] (plural **buses**) ⒶⓁ a large vehicle that carries passengers by road, usually along a fixed route: *a school bus* ◦ *I'll go home by bus.* • **bus** verb [T] (mainly UK **bussing, bussed,** US **busing, bused**) to take a group of people somewhere in a bus → See picture at **vehicle**

> ☑ Word partners for **bus**
>
> catch a bus • miss the bus • on a bus • by bus • a bus **route**

bush

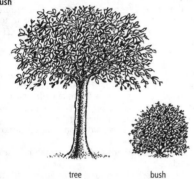

tree   bush

bush /bʊʃ/ noun **1** Ⓑ② [C] a short, thick plant with a lot of branches: *a rose bush* ◦ *There was someone hiding in the bushes.* **2 the bush** wild parts of Australia or Africa where very few people live

IDIOM **beat about the bush** to avoid talking about something difficult or embarrassing

bushy /ˈbʊʃi/ adj If hair or a plant is bushy, it has grown very thick: *bushy eyebrows*

busily /ˈbɪzɪli/ adv in a busy, active way: *He was busily writing notes.*

business /ˈbɪznɪs/ noun **1** TRADE ▷ [U] ⒶⒹ the buying and selling of goods or services: *The shop closed last year, but now they're back in business.* ◦ *We do a lot of business with China.* ◦ *His company has gone out of business* (= failed). **2** ORGANIZATION ▷ [C] ⒶⒶ an organization that sells goods or services: *My uncle runs a small decorating business.* **3** WORK ▷ [U] ⒷⒶ work that you do to earn money: *She's in Vienna on business* (= working). **4 a nasty/strange, etc business** an unpleasant/strange, etc situation **5 be sb's (own) business** to be something private that other people do not need to know **6 be none of sb's business** Ⓑ② If something is none of someone's business, they do not need to know about it, although they want to, because it does not affect them. **7 mind your own business** used to tell someone in a rude way that you do not want them to ask about something private → See also **big business, show business**

> ☑ Word partners for **business**
>
> be in business • do business with sb • go into business • go out of business

business class noun [U] a more expensive way of travelling by aircraft in which you sit in a separate part of the aircraft and are given better service • **business class** adj, adv

businesslike /ˈbɪznɪslaɪk/ adj working in a serious and effective way: *a businesslike manner*

businessman, businesswoman /ˈbɪznɪsmən, ˈbɪznɪsˌwʊmən/ noun [C] (plural **businessmen, businesswomen**) Ⓐ② someone who works in business, usually in a high position in a company

busk /bʌsk/ verb [I] UK to perform music in a public place to get money from people walking past • **busker** noun [C]

bus station noun [C] (also UK **coach station**) ⒶⓋ a building where a bus starts or ends its journey

bus stop noun [C] ⒶⓉ a place where buses stop to let passengers get on or off: *I saw her waiting at the bus stop.* → See Note at **station¹**

bust¹ /bʌst/ verb [T] (**bust,** US **busted**) informal **1** to break or damage something: *The cops had to bust the door down to get in.* **2** If the police bust someone, they catch them and accuse them of a crime: [often passive] *He was busted for selling drugs.*

bust² /bʌst/ noun [C] **1** a woman's breasts, or their size in relation to clothing: *a 36-inch bust* **2** a model of someone's head and shoulders: *a bronze bust of Mozart* **3 a drug bust** an occasion when the police catch people selling or using illegal drugs

bust³ /bʌst/ adj **1 go bust** If a business goes bust, it stops trading because it does not have enough money: *His company went bust, leaving huge debts.* **2** UK informal (US **busted,** ⓊⓈ /ˈbʌstɪd/) broken: *My phone's bust – can I use yours?*

bustle¹ /ˈbʌsl/ verb **1 bustle about/around/in, etc** to move around and do things in a quick, busy way: *There were lots of shoppers bustling about.* **2 bustle with sth** to be full of people or activity: *The street was bustling with people.*

bustle² /ˈbʌsl/ noun [U] activity and noise: *We left the bustle of the city behind us.*

bustling /ˈbʌslɪŋ/ adj full of people and activity: *a bustling city/street*

bust-up /ˈbʌstʌp/ noun [C] UK informal a serious disagreement: *He left home after a big bust-up with his dad.*

busy¹ /ˈbɪzi/ adj **1** PERSON ▷ Ⓐ② If you are busy, you are working hard, or giving your attention to a particular activity: *Mum was busy in the kitchen.* ◦ [+ doing sth] *I was busy mowing the lawn.* ◦ *There'll be plenty of jobs to keep you busy.* ◦ *He was too busy talking to notice us come in.* **2** PLACE ▷ Ⓐ② A busy place is full of activity or people: *a busy restaurant/road* **3** TIME ▷ Ⓐ② In a busy period you have a lot of things to do: *I've had a very busy week.* **4** TELEPHONE ▷ US (UK **engaged**) If a telephone line is busy, someone is using it.

busy² /ˈbɪzi/ verb **busy yourself** to spend time

working or doing something: *We busied ourselves in the kitchen preparing dinner.*

'busy ˌsignal noun [C, usually singular] mainly US a sound that means that the telephone you are calling is being used

but¹ strong /bʌt/ weak /bət/ **conjunction 1 OPPOSITE INFORMATION** ▷ **A1** used to introduce something new that you say, especially something that is different or the opposite from what you have just said: *I'd drive you there, but I don't have my car.* ∘ *The tickets were expensive, but the kids really enjoyed it.* **2 EXPLAINING WHY** ▷ used before you say why something did not happen or is not true: *I was going to go to his party, but I was sick.* **3 SHOWING SURPRISE** ▷ used to show that you are surprised about what someone has just said: *'Tim is leaving.' 'But why?'* **4 CONNECTING PHRASES** ▷ used to connect 'excuse me' or 'I'm sorry' with what you say next: *Excuse me, but would you mind shutting the door?*

but² strong /bʌt/ weak /bət/ **preposition** **B1** except: *Everyone but Andrew knows.* ∘ *Can you buy me a sandwich? Anything but ham.* ∘ *This is the **last** programme **but one** (= the programme before the last).*

but³ strong /bʌt/ weak /bət/ **adv** formal only: *We can but try.*

butcher¹ /'bʊtʃər/ **noun** [C] **B1** someone who prepares and sells meat

butcher² /'bʊtʃər/ **verb** [T] **1** to kill someone in a very violent way **2** to cut an animal into pieces of meat

butcher's /'bʊtʃəz/ **noun** [C] UK (US **butcher**, US **'butcher ˌshop**) a shop that prepares and sells meat: *I went to the butcher's to buy some sausages.*

butler /'bʌtlər/ **noun** [C] a man who opens the door, serves dinner, etc in a large house as a job

butt¹ /bʌt/ **noun 1 BOTTOM** ▷ [C] US informal your bottom: *He just sits on his butt all day long.* **2 CIGARETTE** ▷ [C] the end of a cigarette that is left after it is smoked: *There were **cigarette butts** all over the floor.* **3 GUN** ▷ [C] the end of the handle of a gun: *the butt of a rifle* **4 a head butt** the act of hitting someone with the top, front part of your head

IDIOM **kick butt** US informal to punish someone or defeat someone with a lot of force

butt² /bʌt/ **verb** [T] to hit something with the top, front part of your head: *He butted me in the stomach.*

PHRASAL VERB **butt in** to interrupt or join in a conversation or activity when the other people do not want you to: *The interviewer kept butting in and wouldn't let me answer the question.*

butter¹ /'bʌtər/ **noun** [U] **A2** a soft, pale yellow food made from cream that you put on bread and use in cooking → See colour picture **Food** on page Centre 11

IDIOM **butter wouldn't melt in sb's mouth** used to say that someone looks as if they would never do anything wrong

→ See also **peanut butter**

butter² /'bʌtər/ **verb** [T] to put a layer of butter on something: *hot buttered toast*

PHRASAL VERB **butter sb up** informal to be very nice to someone so that they will do what you want them to do

buttercup /'bʌtəkʌp/ **noun** [C] a small, bright yellow flower

butterfly /'bʌtəflaɪ/ **noun** [C] **B1** an insect with large, patterned wings → See picture at **insect**

IDIOM **have butterflies (in your stomach)** to feel very nervous about something that you are going to do

buttock /'bʌtək/ **noun** [C] one of the two sides of your bottom

button¹ /'bʌtᵊn/ **noun** [C] **1** **B1** a small, round object that you push through a hole to fasten clothing: *to **do up/undo** your **buttons*** **2** **B1** a switch that you press to control a piece of equipment: *Press the play button to listen to your recording.* → See also **belly button**

button² /'bʌtᵊn/ **verb** [T] (also **button up**) to fasten a piece of clothing with buttons: *Jack buttoned up his jacket.* → Opposite **unbutton**

buttonhole /'bʌtᵊnhəʊl/ **noun** [C] **1** a hole that you push a button through a piece of clothing **2** UK a flower worn on a jacket or coat for a special occasion

buxom /'bʌksəm/ **adj** A buxom woman has large breasts.

buy¹ /baɪ/ **verb** [T] (**bought**) **A1** to get something by paying money for it: *I went out to buy some milk.* ∘ *They **bought** their house **for** $1,000,000.* ∘ [+ two objects] *He bought me a camera for my birthday.*

PHRASAL VERBS **buy into sth** to believe in something: *I don't buy into all that dieting nonsense.* • **buy sb/sth out** to buy part of a company or building from someone else so that you own all of it • **buy sth up** to quickly buy a lot of something, often all that is available

buy² /baɪ/ **noun a good buy** something good that you buy for a cheap price: *This coat was a really good buy.*

buyer /'baɪər/ **noun** [C] **B1** someone who buys something

buyout /'baɪaʊt/ **noun** [C] an arrangement in which a group of people buy the company that they work for

buzz¹ /bʌz/ **noun 1** [no plural] informal a feeling of excitement, energy, or pleasure: *He **gets a** real **buzz from** going to the gym.* **2** [C] a continuous sound like a bee makes

buzz² /bʌz/ **verb** [I] **1** to make a continuous sound like a bee: *I can hear something buzzing.* **2** to be full of activity or excitement: *The crowd was **buzzing with** excitement.* **3 buzz about/around, etc** to move around in a quick and busy way

buzzer /'bʌzər/ **noun** [C] a piece of electronic equipment that makes a long sound as a signal: *to **press** the **buzzer***

buzzword /'bʌzwɜːd/ **noun** [C] a word or expression that has become fashionable usually in a particular subject or group of people: *a new political buzzword*

by[1] strong /baɪ/ weak /bɪ, bə/ **preposition 1 DO** ▷ **A2** used to show the person or thing that does something: *She was examined by a doctor.* ○ *a painting by Van Gogh* **2 HOW** ▷ **A2** through doing or using something: *Can I pay by cheque?* ○ *We'll get there by car.* ○ [+ doing sth] *Open the file by clicking on the icon.* **3 HOLDING** ▷ **B2** holding a particular part of someone or something: *She grabbed me by the arm.* **4 NEAR** ▷ **B1** near or next to something or someone: *I'll meet you by the post office.* ○ *A small child stood by her side.* **5 NOT LATER** ▷ **A2** not later than a particular time or date: *Applications have to be in by the 31st.* **6 ACCORDING TO** ▷ according to: *By law you must be eighteen to purchase alcohol.* **7 PAST** ▷ past: *He sped by me on a motorcycle.* **8 AMOUNT** ▷ used to show measurements or amounts: *twelve by ten metres of floor space* ○ *Interest rates have been increased by 0.25%.* ○ *I'm paid by the hour.* **9 by accident/chance/ mistake, etc** **B1** as a result of an accident/ chance/mistake, etc: *I went to the wrong room by mistake.* **10 by day/night** during the day/night **11 day by day/little by little/one by one, etc** used in particular phrases to mean 'gradually' or 'in units of': *Day by day he grew stronger.*

by[2] /baɪ/ **adv** past: *A motorcycle sped by.*

bye /baɪ/ **exclamation** (also **bye-bye**) **A1** goodbye: *Bye, see you tomorrow.*

by-election /ˈbaɪɪˌlekʃən/ **noun** [C] an election in the UK to choose a new member of parliament for an area because the old one has left or died

bygone /ˈbaɪɡɒn/ **adj** literary **bygone age/days/ era, etc** a time in the past

bygones /ˈbaɪɡɒnz/ **noun let bygones be bygones** something that you say to tell someone to forget about the unpleasant things in the past

bypass[1] /ˈbaɪpɑːs/ **noun** [C] **1** a road that goes around a town and not through it **2** a medical operation to make blood flow along a different route and avoid a damaged part of the heart: *a coronary/heart bypass*

bypass[2] /ˈbaɪpɑːs/ **verb** [T] **1** to go around a place or thing and not through it: *I was hoping to bypass the city centre.* **2** to avoid dealing with someone or something by dealing directly with someone or something else: *They bypassed him and went straight to his manager.*

by-product /ˈbaɪˌprɒdʌkt/ **noun** [C] something that is produced when you are making or doing something else: *Carbon monoxide is a by-product of burning.*

bystander /ˈbaɪˌstændər/ **noun** [C] someone who is near the place where an event happens, but not directly involved in it: *The gunman began firing at innocent bystanders.*

byte /baɪt/ **noun** [C] a unit for measuring the amount of information a computer can store, equal to 8 bits (= smallest unit of computer information)

B

C

C, c /siː/ the third letter of the alphabet

c. written abbreviation for circa (= used before a number or date to show that it is not exact): *c. 1900*

C written abbreviation for Celsius or centigrade: measurements of temperature: *30°C*

cab /kæb/ noun [C] **1** informal **B1** a taxi (= car that you pay to travel in): *We **took a cab** to the theatre.* ∘ *a cab driver* **2** the front part of a truck where the driver sits

cabaret /ˈkæbəreɪ/ noun [C, U] entertainment consisting of songs, jokes, etc in a bar or restaurant: *He's appearing **in cabaret** at the Cafe Royal.*

cabbage /ˈkæbɪdʒ/ noun [C, U] **B1** a large, round vegetable that consists of a lot of thick leaves

cabbie /ˈkæbi/ noun [C] informal someone who drives a taxi (= car that you pay to travel in)

cabin /ˈkæbɪn/ noun [C] **1** HOUSE ▷ a small, simple house made of wood: *a log cabin* **2** SHIP ▷ a small room to sleep in on a ship **3** AIRCRAFT ▷ **B1** the area where passengers sit on an aircraft

cabin crew noun [C] the people on an aircraft who take care of the passengers as their job

cabinet /ˈkæbɪnət/ noun **1 the Cabinet** a group of people in a government who are chosen by and who advise the highest leader: *a **Cabinet minister/member*** **2** **B2** [C] a cupboard with shelves or drawers to store or show things in: *a bathroom/medicine cabinet* → See also **filing cabinet**

cable /ˈkeɪbl/ noun **1** WIRE ▷ [C, U] **B2** a wire covered by plastic that carries electricity, telephone signals, etc: *overhead power cables* **2** ROPE ▷ [C, U] thick wire twisted into a rope **3** SYSTEM ▷ [U] **B1** the system of sending television programmes or telephone signals along wires under the ground: *cable TV* ∘ *This channel is only available **on cable**.*

cable (T͏V) noun [U] (also **cable television**) a system of sending television pictures and sound along wires buried under the ground

cable car noun [C] a vehicle that hangs from thick cables and carries people up hills and mountains

cache /kæʃ/ noun [C] **1** a secret supply of something: *a **cache of weapons*** **2** an area or type of computer memory in which information that is often in use can be stored temporarily, so that you can get to it quickly

cachet /ˈkæʃeɪ/ ⓤⓢ /kæʃˈeɪ/ noun [U] a quality that something or someone has that makes people admire or respect them

cacophony /kəˈkɒfəni/ noun [no plural] a loud, unpleasant mixture of sounds

cactus /ˈkæktəs/ noun [C] (plural **cacti** /ˈkæktaɪ/, **cactuses**) a plant with thick leaves for storing water and often sharp points that grows in deserts

CAD /kæd/ noun [U] computer-aided design: the use of computers to design objects

cactus

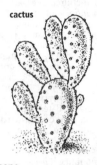

caddie /ˈkædi/ noun [C] someone who carries the equipment for someone playing golf → See colour picture **Sports 2** on page Centre 15
• **caddie** verb [I] (**caddying, caddied**) to be a caddie for someone

cadet /kəˈdet/ noun [C] a young person who is training to be in a military organization, the police, etc: *an army cadet*

caesarean (also US **cesarean**) /sɪˈzeəriən/ noun [C] an operation in which a baby is taken out of a woman through a cut in the front of her body

café (also **cafe**) /ˈkæfeɪ/ ⓤⓢ /kæˈfeɪ/ noun [C] **A1** a small restaurant where you can buy drinks and small meals

cafeteria /ˌkæfəˈtɪəriə/ noun [C] a restaurant where you collect and pay for your food and drink before you eat it: *a school cafeteria*

caffeine /ˈkæfiːn/ noun [U] a chemical in coffee, tea, etc that makes you feel more awake

cage /keɪdʒ/ noun [C] **B1** a container made of wire or metal bars used for keeping birds or animals in: *a bird cage* → See also **rib cage**

cage

cagey /ˈkeɪdʒi/ adj If someone is cagey, they are not very willing to give information, and you may think they are not honest: *He's very **cagey** about his past.*

cajole /kəˈdʒəʊl/ verb [I, T] to persuade someone to do something by being friendly or by promising them something: [+ into + doing sth] *She cajoled me into helping with the dinner.*

cake /keɪk/ noun [C, U] **A1** a sweet food made from flour, butter, sugar, and eggs mixed together and baked: *a chocolate/fruit cake* ∘ *a piece/slice of cake* ∘ *to bake/make a cake* → See colour picture **Food** on page Centre 11

IDIOM **have your cake and eat it** to have or do two things that it is usually impossible to have or do at the same time

→ See also **the icing on the cake**, **be a piece¹ of cake**

caked /keɪkt/ adj **be caked in/with sth** to be covered with a thick, dry layer of something: *His boots were caked in mud.*

calamity /kəˈlæməti/ noun [C] a sudden, bad

event that causes a lot of damage or unhappiness

calcium /'kælsiəm/ **noun** [U] a chemical element in teeth, bones, and chalk (= a soft, white rock)

calculate /'kælkjəleɪt/ **verb 1** ⓑ [T] to discover an amount or number using mathematics: *to calculate a cost/percentage* **2 be calculated to do sth** to be intended to have a particular effect: *His comments were calculated to embarrass the prime minister.*

calculated /'kælkjəleɪtɪd/ **adj** based on careful thought or planning, not on emotion: *a calculated risk/decision*

calculating /'kælkjəleɪtɪŋ/ **adj** Calculating people try to get what they want by thinking carefully and without emotion, and not caring about other people: *a cold, calculating criminal*

calculation /ˌkælkjə'leɪʃᵊn/ **noun 1** [C, U] ⓑ the use of mathematics to discover a number or amount: *I did some quick calculations to see if I could afford to buy it.* **2** [U] careful thought about something without any emotion

> 🗂 Word partners for **calculation**
>
> **do/perform** a calculation • a **complex/precise/quick/rough** calculation

calculator /'kælkjəleɪtər/ **noun** [C] ⓑ a piece of electronic equipment that you use to do mathematical calculations: *a pocket calculator*

calendar /'kæləndər/ **noun 1** ⓐ [C] something that shows all the days, weeks, and months of the year **2 the Christian/Jewish/Western, etc calendar** the system used to measure and arrange the days, weeks, months and special events of the year according to Christian/Jewish/Western, etc tradition **3 the political/school/sporting, etc calendar** the events that are arranged during the year for a particular activity or organization

calf /kɑːf/ **noun** [C] (plural **calves** /kɑːvz/) **1** ⓑ a young cow **2** the back of your leg below your knee → See colour picture **The Body** on page Centre 13

calibre UK (US **caliber**) /'kælɪbər/ **noun** [U] **1** the quality or level of ability of someone or something: *The calibre of applicants was very high.* **2** the measurement across the inside of a gun, or across a bullet

> 🗂 Word partners for **call**
>
> **make/get/take** a call • **give** sb a call • a call **from/to** sb

call¹ /kɔːl/ **verb 1 be called sth** ⓐ to have a particular name: *a man called John* ∘ *What's your dog called?* ∘ *Their latest record is called "Ecstasy".* **2 GIVE NAME** ▷ [+ two objects] ⓑ to give someone or something a particular name: *I want to call the baby Alex.* **3 DESCRIBE** ▷ [+ two objects] ⓑ to describe someone or something in a particular way: *She called him a liar.* **4 ASK TO COME** ▷ [T] ⓑ to ask someone to come somewhere: *She called me into her office.* **5 SHOUT** ▷ [I, T] (also **call out**) ⓑ to shout or say something in a loud voice: *I thought I heard someone calling my name.* **6 TELEPHONE** ▷ [I, T] ⓐ to telephone

someone: *He called me every night while he was away.* ∘ *Has anyone called the police?* → See Note at **phone²** **7 VISIT** ▷ [I] mainly UK (UK **call by/in/round**) to visit someone for a short time: *John called round earlier.* **8 call an election/meeting, etc** to arrange for an election/meeting, etc to happen: *The chairman has called an emergency meeting.* → See also **call sb's bluff²**, **call it a day**

PHRASAL VERBS **call back** mainly UK ⓑ to go back to a place in order to see someone or collect something: *I'll call back later to pick up the books.* • **call (sb) back** ⓐ to telephone someone again, or to telephone someone who telephoned you earlier: *I can't talk now – I'll call you back in ten minutes.* • **call for sth 1** to demand that something happens: *They are calling for a ban on guns.* **2** to need or deserve a particular action or quality: *You passed your test? This calls for a celebration!* • **call for sb** ⓑ to go to a place in order to collect someone: *I'll call for you at eight.* • **call sth off 1** ⓑ to decide that a planned event or activity will not happen because it is not possible, useful, or wanted now: *The game has been called off because of the weather.* **2** to decide to stop an activity: *Police have called off the search.* • **call on sb to do sth** to ask someone in a formal way to do something: *He called on the rebels to stop fighting.* • **call (sb) up** mainly US to telephone someone: *My dad called me up to tell me the good news.* • **call sth up** ⓑ to find and show information on a computer screen: *I'll just call up your account details.* • **be called up** to be ordered to join a military organization or to be asked to join an official team: *He was called up soon after the war started.*

call² /kɔːl/ **noun** [C] **1 TELEPHONE** ▷ (also **phone call**) ⓐ an occasion when you telephone someone: *Give me a call tomorrow.* ∘ *I got a call from Sue this morning.* **2 a call for sth** a demand for something to happen: *a call for action/peace* **3 VISIT** ▷ a short visit: *I thought I'd pay Gary a call.* **4 SHOUT** ▷ ⓑ a shout to someone **5 BIRD** ▷ a sound made by a bird or other animal **6 sb's call** informal someone's decision about what to do: *I don't mind what we do – it's your call.* **7 call for sth** need or demand for a particular thing: *There's not much call for interior designers round here.* **8 be on call** to be ready to go to work if you are needed, as part of your job

IDIOM **a close call** an occasion when something you do not want to happen nearly happens

→ See also **be at sb's beck and call**, **wake-up call**

CALL /kɔːl/ **abbreviation** for computer aided language learning: a way of learning languages using computers

call centre noun [C] UK a place where people use telephones to provide information to customers, or to sell goods or services

caller /'kɔːlər/ **noun** [C] **1** someone who makes a telephone call: *an anonymous caller* **2** mainly UK someone who visits for a short time

caller I'D noun [U] a telephone service that shows you the telephone number of the person who is telephoning you: *Get caller ID and then you don't have to answer the phone when he calls.*

call-in /'kɔːlɪn/ **noun** [C] US (UK **phone-in**) a television or radio programme in which the public can ask questions or give opinions over the telephone

calling /'kɔːlɪŋ/ **noun** [C] a strong feeling that you should do a particular type of work: *She found her true calling in teaching.*

callous /'kæləs/ **adj** cruel and not caring about other people: *a callous remark* • **callously adv**

calm¹ /kɑːm/ **adj 1 PERSON** ▷ **B1** relaxed and not worried, frightened, or excited: *a calm voice/manner* ° *Try to **stay calm** – the doctor will be here soon.* **2 SEA** ▷ **B1** If the sea is calm, it is still and has no large waves. **3 WEATHER** ▷ **B1** If the weather is calm, there are no storms or wind. • **calmness noun** [U]

calm² /kɑːm/ **noun** [U] calm conditions or behaviour

calm³ /kɑːm/ **verb** [T] to make someone stop feeling upset, angry, or excited: *The police tried to calm the crowd.* ° *a calming effect*

PHRASAL VERB **calm (sb) down** **B2** to stop feeling upset, angry, or excited, or to make someone stop feeling this way: *Calm down and tell me what's wrong.*

calmly /'kɑːmli/ **adv** **B2** in a relaxed way: *He spoke slowly and calmly.*

calorie /'kælᵊri/ **noun** [C] a unit for measuring the amount of energy food provides: *I try to eat about 2000 calories a day.*

calves /kɑːvz/ plural of calf

camaraderie /ˌkæmə'rɑːdᵊri/ **noun** [U] special friendship felt by people who work together or experience something together

camcorder /'kæmˌkɔːdər/ **noun** [C] a camera that you can hold in your hand and that takes moving pictures

came /keɪm/ past tense of come

camel /'kæmᵊl/ **noun** [C] **B1** a large animal that lives in the desert and has one or two humps (= raised parts on its back)

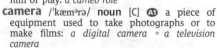
camel

cameo /'kæmiəʊ/ **noun** [C] a short appearance by someone famous in a film or play: *a cameo role*

camera /'kæmᵊrə/ **noun** [C] **A1** a piece of equipment used to take photographs or to make films: *a digital camera* ° *a television camera*

cameraman /'kæmᵊrəmæn/ **noun** [C] (plural **cameramen**) someone who operates a television camera or film camera as their job

camisole /'kæmɪsəʊl/ **noun** [C] a piece of women's underwear for the top half of the body, with thin straps that go over the shoulders: *a lace camisole* → See colour picture **Clothes** on page Centre 9

camouflage /'kæməflɑːʒ/ **noun** [U] a way of

making something difficult to see by having colour or pattern that is similar to the area around it: *a camouflage jacket* • **camouflage verb** [T]

camp¹ /kæmp/ **noun 1** **B1** [C] an area where people stay in tents for a short time, usually for a holiday **2 an army/prison/refugee, etc camp** **B2** an area containing temporary buildings or tents used for soldiers/prisoners/refugees (= people forced to leave their home), etc → See also **base camp**, **concentration camp**

camp² /kæmp/ **verb** [I] (also **camp out**) **A2** to stay in a tent or temporary shelter: *We camped on the beach for two nights.*

campaign¹ /kæm'peɪn/ **noun** [C] **1** a series of organized activities or events intended to achieve a result: *an advertising/election campaign* **2** a series of military attacks: *a bombing campaign*

> **Word partners for campaign**
>
> **launch/mount/run** a campaign • a campaign **against/for** sth • an **advertising/election** campaign

campaign² /kæm'peɪn/ **verb** [I] to organize a series of activities to try to achieve something: *to campaign against/for something* • **campaigner noun** [C] *an animal rights campaigner*

camper /'kæmpər/ **noun** [C] **1** someone who stays in a tent on holiday **2** (also **'camper ˌvan**) vehicle containing a bed, kitchen equipment, etc that you can live in

campfire /'kæmpˌfaɪər/ **noun** [C] a fire that is made and used outside, especially by people who are staying in tents

campground /'kæmpˌgraʊnd/ **noun** [C] US an area of land that has space for many people to put up tents and stay while they are travelling or on vacation

camping /'kæmpɪŋ/ **noun** [U] **A2** the activity of staying in a tent for a holiday: *We're going camping in France this summer.* ° *a camping trip*

> ⚠ Common learner error: **camping** or **campsite**?
>
> Be careful not to use **camping**, the activity of staying in a tent, when you mean **campsite**, the area of ground where you do this.

campsite /'kæmpsaɪt/ **noun** [C] (also US **campground**) **B1** an area where people can stay in tents for a holiday

campus /'kæmpəs/ **noun** [C, U] **B2** the land and buildings belonging to a college or university: *lived on campus in my first year.*

can¹ strong /kæn/ weak /kən, kn/ **modal verb** **(could) 1 ABILITY** ▷ **A1** to be able to do something: *We can't pay the rent.* ° *Can you drive?* **2 PERMISSION** ▷ **A1** to be allowed to do something: *You can't park here.* ° *Can I go now.* **3 ASK** ▷ **A1** used to ask someone to do or provide something: *Can you tell her to meet me outside?* ° *Can I have a drink of water?* **4 OFFER** ▷ **A1** used to politely offer to do something: *Can I carry those bags for you?* **5 POSSIBLE** ▷ **A2** used to talk about what is possible: *You can buy* stamps from the shop on the corner. ◦ Smoking can cause cancer. **6 TYPICAL** ▷ **B2** used to talk about how someone often behaves or what something is often like: She can be really rude at times. **7 SURPRISE** ▷ **B1** used to show surprise: You can't possibly be hungry already! ◦ Can you believe it? → See Study Page **Modal verbs** on page Centre 22

can² /kæn/ noun [C] **A2** a closed, metal container for food or liquids: a can of soup/beans ◦ a can of paint → See picture at **container**

IDIOM **a can of worms** a situation that causes a lot of trouble for you when you start to deal with it

→ See also **trash can, watering can**

can³ /kæn/ verb [T] (**canning, canned**) to put food or drink into metal containers in a factory: canned tomatoes

Canadian /kəˈneɪdiən/ adj relating to Canada • **Canadian** noun [C] someone who comes from Canada

canal /kəˈnæl/ noun [C] **B1** an artificial river built for boats to travel along or to take water where it is needed

canary /kəˈneəri/ noun [C] a small, yellow bird that sings

cancel /ˈkænsəl/ verb [T] (mainly UK **cancelling, cancelled**, US **canceling, canceled**) **1** **B1** to say that an organized event will not now happen: [often passive] The meeting has been cancelled. **2** to stop an order for goods or services that you do not now want

PHRASAL VERB **cancel sth out** If something cancels out another thing, it stops it from having any effect.

cancellation /ˌkænsəlˈeɪʃən/ noun [C, U] the act of stopping something that was going to happen or stopping an order for something: a last-minute cancellation

cancer /ˈkænsər/ noun [C, U] **B1** a serious disease that is caused when cells in the body grow in a way that is uncontrolled and not normal: breast/lung cancer ◦ His wife died of cancer. • **cancerous** adj a cancerous growth

> **☑ Word partners for cancer**
>
> get/have cancer • breast/lung/prostate/skin cancer • cancer of the [liver/stomach, etc] • cancer patients/sufferers • cancer research/treatment

Cancer /ˈkænsər/ noun [C, U] the sign of the zodiac that relates to the period of 22 June – 22 July, or a person born during this period → See picture at **the zodiac**

candid /ˈkændɪd/ adj honest, especially about something that is unpleasant or embarrassing: She was very candid about her personal life in the interview. • **candidly** adv

candidacy /ˈkændɪdəsi/ noun [U] the fact of being a candidate in an election

candidate /ˈkændɪdət/ noun [C] **1** **B2** one of the people taking part in an election or trying to get a job: a presidential candidate **2** UK **B1** someone who is taking an exam

candle /ˈkændl/ noun [C] **B1** a stick of wax with string going through it that you burn to produce light → See colour picture **The Living Room** on page Centre 4

candle

candlelight /ˈkændllaɪt/ noun [U] light produced by a candle

candlestick /ˈkændlstɪk/ noun [C] an object that holds a candle

can-do /ˈkænˌduː/ adj informal determined to deal with problems and achieve results: I really admire her **can-do attitude**.

candour UK (US **candor**) /ˈkændər/ noun [U] honest talk especially about something that is unpleasant or embarrassing

candy /ˈkændi/ noun [C, U] US a small piece of sweet food made from sugar, chocolate, etc: a box of candy ◦ a candy bar

cane¹ /keɪn/ noun **1 STEM** ▷ [C, U] the long, hard, hollow stem of some plants, sometimes used to make furniture **2 WALK** ▷ [C] a long stick used by people to help them walk **3 PUNISH** ▷ [C] UK a long stick used in the past to hit children at school

cane² /keɪn/ verb [T] UK to hit someone, especially a school student, with a stick as a punishment

canine /ˈkeɪnaɪn/ adj relating to dogs

canister /ˈkænɪstər/ noun [C] a metal container for gases or dry things: a gas canister

cannabis /ˈkænəbɪs/ noun [U] (also **marijuana**) a drug that some people smoke for pleasure and that is illegal in many countries

canned /kænd/ adj (also UK **tinned**) **B2** Canned food is sold in metal containers.

cannibal /ˈkænɪbəl/ noun [C] someone who eats human flesh • **cannibalism** noun [U]

cannon /ˈkænən/ noun [C] a very large gun, in the past one that was on wheels

cannot /ˈkænɒt/ modal verb **A1** the negative form of 'can': I cannot predict what will happen.

canny /ˈkæni/ adj clever and able to think quickly, especially about money or business: a canny businessman

canoe /kəˈnuː/ noun [C] a small, narrow boat with pointed ends that you move using a paddle (= stick with a wide, flat part) • **canoeing** noun [U] the activity of travelling in a canoe

canoe

canon /ˈkænən/ noun [C] a Christian priest who works in a cathedral (= large, important church): the Canon of Westminster

can opener noun [C] (also UK **tin opener**) a piece of kitchen equipment for opening metal food containers → See colour picture **The Kitchen** on page Centre 2

canopy /ˈkænəpi/ noun [C] a cover or type of roof for protection or decoration

can't /kɑːnt/ modal verb **1** short for cannot: I can't find my keys. **2** used to suggest that someone should do something: *Can't you ask Jonathan to help?*

canteen /kæn'tiːn/ **noun** [C] ⓑ a restaurant in an office, factory, or school

canter /'kæntər/ **verb** [I] If a horse canters, it runs quite fast. • **canter noun** [no plural]

canvas /'kænvəs/ **noun 1** [U] strong cloth used for making sails, tents, etc **2** [C] a piece of canvas used for a painting

canvass /'kænvəs/ **verb 1** [I, T] to try to persuade people to vote for someone in an election: *He's canvassing for the Labour party.* **2** [T] to ask people their opinion about something: *The study canvassed the views of over 9000 people.*

canyon /'kænjən/ **noun** [C] a deep valley with very steep sides

cap¹ /kæp/ **noun** [C] **1** ⓐ a hat with a flat, curved part at the front: *a baseball cap* → See colour picture **Clothes** on page Centre 9 **2** a small lid that covers the top or end of something → See also **skull cap**

cap² /kæp/ **verb** [T] (**capping, capped**) **1** END ▷ to be the last and the best or worst event in a series of events: *The party capped a wonderful week.* **2** LIMIT ▷ to put a limit on an amount of money that can be borrowed, charged, etc: [often passive] *The interest rate has been capped at 5%.* **3** COVER ▷ to cover the top of something: [often passive] *The mountains were capped with snow.*

capability /ˌkeɪpə'bɪləti/ **noun** [C, U] the ability or power to do something: [+ to do sth] *Both players have the capability to win this game.*

capable /'keɪpəbl/ **adj 1** ⓑ able to do things effectively and achieve results: *She's a very capable young woman.* **2 capable of sth/doing sth** ⓑ having the ability or qualities to be able to do something: *She was capable of great cruelty.* → Opposite **incapable**

capacity /kə'pæsəti/ **noun 1** CONTAIN ▷ [C, U] ⓑ the largest amount or number that a container, building, etc can hold: *The restaurant has a capacity of about 200.* ○ *The stadium was filled to capacity* (= completely full). **2** PRODUCE ▷ [U] the amount that a factory or machine can produce: *The factory is operating at full capacity* (= producing as much as possible). **3** ABILITY ▷ [C] ⓑ the ability to do, experience, or understand something: *She has a great capacity for love.* **4** JOB ▷ [C] a position or job: *He attended over 100 events last year in his capacity as mayor.*

cape /keɪp/ **noun** [C] **1** a loose coat without any sleeves that is fastened at the neck **2** a large area of land that goes out into the sea

caper /'keɪpər/ **noun** [C] something that is done as a joke, or intended to entertain people: *His new movie is a comic caper.*

capillary /kə'pɪləri/ ⓤⓢ /'kæpəleri/ **noun** [C] a very thin tube that carries blood around the body, connecting arteries to veins

capital¹ /'kæpɪtəl/ **noun 1** CITY ▷ [C] ⓐ the most important city in a country or state, where the government is based: *Paris is the capital of France.* **2** MONEY ▷ [U] an amount of money

that you can use to start a business or to make more money **3** LETTER ▷ [C] (also **capital 'letter**) ⓐ a large letter of the alphabet used at the beginning of sentences and names → See Study Page **Punctuation** on page Centre 33 → See also **block capitals**

capital² /'kæpɪtəl/ **adj a capital crime/offence** a crime that can be punished by death

capitalism /'kæpɪtəlɪzəm/ **noun** [U] a political and economic system in which industry is owned privately for profit and not by the state

capitalist /'kæpɪtəlɪst/ **noun** [C] someone who supports capitalism • **capitalist adj** *a capitalist society*

capitalize (also UK **-ise**) /'kæpɪtəlaɪz/ **verb** [T] to write something using capital letters, or starting with a capital letter

PHRASAL VERB **capitalize on sth** to use a situation to achieve something good for yourself: *He failed to capitalize on his earlier success.*

capital 'punishment noun [U] death as a punishment by the state for a serious crime

capitulate /kə'pɪtjuleɪt/ **verb** [I] to stop disagreeing or fighting with someone and agree to what they want • **capitulation** /kəˌpɪtju'leɪʃən/ **noun** [C, U]

cappuccino /ˌkæpu'tʃiːnəʊ/ **noun** [C, U] coffee made with milk that has been heated with steam to produce a lot of small bubbles

capricious /kə'prɪʃəs/ **adj** likely to suddenly change your ideas or behaviour

Capricorn /'kæprɪkɔːn/ **noun** [C, U] the sign of the zodiac that relates to the period of 2? December – 20 January, or a person born during this period → See picture at **the zodiac**

capsize /kæp'saɪz/ **verb** [I, T] If a boat capsizes, or if it is capsized, it turns over in the water.

capsule /'kæpsjuːl/ **noun** [C] **1** a small container with medicine inside that you swallow **2** the part of a spacecraft that people live in

captain¹ /'kæptɪn/ **noun** [C] **1** SHIP ▷ ⓑ the person in control of a ship or aircraft **2** ARMY ▷ an officer of middle rank in the army, navy, or air force **3** SPORT ▷ ⓑ the leader of a team

captain² /'kæptɪn/ **verb** [T] to be the captain of a team, ship, or aircraft: *He has captained the England cricket team three times.*

captaincy /'kæptɪnsi/ **noun** [U] the position of being the captain of a team

caption /'kæpʃən/ **noun** [C] words written under a picture to explain it

captivate /'kæptɪveɪt/ **verb** [T] to interest or attract someone very much: *She captivated their audiences with her beauty and charm.* • **captivating adj** *a captivating performance*

captive¹ /'kæptɪv/ **adj 1** A captive person or animal is being kept somewhere and is not allowed to leave. **2 a captive audience/market** a group of people who have to watch something or have to buy something because they do not have a choice **3 hold/take sb captive** to keep someone as a prisoner, or make someone a prisoner

aptive² /ˈkæptɪv/ **noun** [C] someone who is kept as a prisoner

aptivity /kæpˈtɪvəti/ **noun** [U] a situation in which an animal is kept in a zoo or a person is kept as a prisoner, rather than being free: *lion cubs born in captivity*

apture¹ /ˈkæptʃər/ **verb** [T] **1 PRISONER** ▷ **B2** to catch someone and make them your prisoner: *Two soldiers were captured by the enemy.* **2 CONTROL** ▷ **B2** to get control of a place with force: *Rebel troops have captured the city.* **3 GET** ▷ to succeed in getting something when you are competing against other people: *The Green Party has captured 12% of the vote.* **4 DESCRIBE** ▷ **B2** to show or describe something successfully using words or pictures: *His book really captures the spirit of the place.* **5 capture sb/sth on camera/film, etc B2** to record someone or something on camera/film, etc **6 capture sb's attention/imagination** to make someone very interested or excited: *The campaign has really captured the public's imagination.* **7 capture sb's heart** to make someone love you: *She captured the hearts of the nation.*

apture² /ˈkæptʃər/ **noun** [U] **1** the act of catching someone and making them a prisoner: *He shot himself to avoid capture.* **2** the act of getting control of a place with force: *the capture of the city by foreign troops*

ar /kɑːr/ **noun** [C] **1 A1** a vehicle with an engine, four wheels, and seats for a small number of passengers: *She goes to work by car.* ∘ *Where did you park your car?* → See colour picture **Car** on page Centre 7 **2** US a part of a train in which passengers sit, eat, sleep, etc: *the dining car* → See also **buffet car, cable car, estate car, sports car**

> 🗹 Word partners for **car**
>
> drive/park/start a car • a car breaks down • by car • a car accident/crash • a car driver

aramel /ˈkærəməl/ **noun** [C, U] sugar that has been heated until it turns brown and that is used to add colour and flavour to food, or a sweet made from sugar, milk, and butter

arat /ˈkærət/ **noun** [C] **a** a unit for measuring how much jewels (= valuable stones) weigh **b** mainly UK (US **karat**) a unit for measuring how pure gold is: *22 carat gold*

aravan /ˈkærəvæn/ **noun** [C] **1** UK a vehicle that people can live in on holiday and which is pulled by a car: *a caravan site* **2** a group of people with animals or vehicles who travel together across a desert

arbohydrate /ˌkɑːbəʊˈhaɪdreɪt/ **noun** [C, U] (also informal **carb**) a substance in food such as sugar, potatoes, etc that gives your body energy

arbon /ˈkɑːbən/ **noun** [U] **B2** a chemical element present in all animals and plants and in coal and oil

arbonated /ˈkɑːbəneɪtɪd/ **adj** Carbonated drinks contain a lot of small bubbles.

arbon 'copy noun [C] **1** a copy of a written document that is made using carbon paper (= thin paper covered in carbon) **2** an exact copy of something: *He's a **carbon copy of** his father.*

carbon dioxide /ˌkɑːbəndaɪˈɒksaɪd/ **noun** [U] **B2** a gas that is produced when people and animals breathe out, or when carbon is burned

carbon e₁missions noun [plural] carbon dioxide and carbon monoxide made by things such as factories or cars that burn carbon and cause pollution

carbon e'missions trading noun [U] a system, used by companies and countries, for buying and selling the right to release carbon dioxide (= a gas) into the environment

carbon 'footprint noun [C] a measurement of the amount of carbon dioxide produced by the activities of a person, company, organization, etc: *The company says it will **reduce the carbon footprint** of its delivery trucks.*

carbon monoxide /ˌkɑːbənməˈnɒksaɪd/ **noun** [U] **B2** a poisonous gas that is produced by burning some types of fuel, especially petrol (= fuel for cars)

carbon 'neutral adj not producing carbon emissions: *a carbon-neutral fuel/home/lifestyle*

carbon off'setting noun [U] the process of trying to stop the damage caused by activities that produce carbon dioxide by doing other things to reduce it, such as planting trees

carbon ₁paper noun [U] thin paper that is covered on one side with carbon (= a black substance) and is used for making copies of written documents

car 'boot sale noun [C] UK an event where people sell things they no longer want from the backs of their cars

carburettor UK (US **carburetor**) /ˌkɑːbəˈretər/ **US** /ˈkɑːbəreɪtər/ **noun** [C] the part of an engine that mixes fuel and air that are then burned to provide power

carcass /ˈkɑːkəs/ **noun** [C] the body of a dead animal

carcinogen /kɑːˈsɪnədʒən/ **noun** [C] a substance that can cause cancer (= a disease when cells in your body grow in an uncontrolled way) • **carcinogenic** /ˌkɑːsɪnəʊˈdʒenɪk/ **adj** *carcinogenic chemicals*

card /kɑːd/ **noun 1 MESSAGE** ▷ [C] **A2** a folded piece of stiff paper with a picture on the front and a message inside that you send to someone on a special occasion: *a **birthday card*** **2 INFORMATION** ▷ [C] **B1** a piece of stiff paper or plastic that has information printed on it: *a library card* **3 GAME** ▷ [C] (also **playing card**) **A2** one of a set of 52 pieces of stiff paper with numbers and pictures used for playing games: UK/US *a pack of cards*/US *a deck of cards* ∘ *We spent the evening **playing cards** (= playing games using cards).* **4 PAPER** ▷ [U] UK thick, stiff paper **5 WITHOUT ENVELOPE** ▷ [C] a postcard (= card with a picture on one side that you send without an envelope) **6 COMPUTER** ▷ [C] **B1** a part inside a computer that controls how the computer operates: *a graphics/sound card*

C

IDIOMS **be on the cards** UK (US **be in the cards**) to be likely to happen: *Do you think marriage is on the cards?* • **put/lay your cards on the table** to tell someone honestly what you think or plan to do

→ See also **cash card, charge card, Christmas card, credit card, debit card, phone card, smart card, swipe card, trump card, wild card**

cardboard /'kɑːdbɔːd/ *noun* [U] ⓑ thick, stiff paper that is used for making boxes

cardiac /'kɑːdiæk/ *adj* [always before noun] relating to the heart: *cardiac surgery* ∘ *cardiac arrest* (= *when the heart stops beating*)

cardigan /'kɑːdɪɡən/ *noun* [C] ⓑ a piece of clothing, often made of wool, that covers the top part of your body and fastens at the front → See colour picture **Clothes** on page Centre 8

cardinal¹ /'kɑːdɪnəl/ *noun* [C] a priest with a high rank in the Catholic Church: *Cardinal Richelieu*

cardinal² /'kɑːdɪnəl/ *adj* [always before noun] formal extremely important or serious: *One of the cardinal rules of business is know what your customer wants.*

cardinal number *noun* [C] (also **cardinal**) a number such as 1, 2, 3, etc that shows the quantity of something

care¹ /keəʳ/ *verb* **1** [I, T] ⓑ to think that something is important and to feel interested in it or worried about it: *He cares deeply about the environment.* ∘ [+ question word] *I don't care how long it takes – just get the job done.* **2** [I] ⓑ to love someone: *Your parents are only doing this because they care about you.* ∘ *I knew that Amy still cared for me.* **3** I/he, etc **couldn't care less** informal used to emphasize that someone is not interested in or worried about something or someone: [+ question word] *I couldn't care less what people think.* **4** Who cares? informal ⓑ used to emphasize that you do not think something is important: *"Manchester United will be in the final if they win this match." "Who cares?"* **5** Would you care for sth/to do sth? formal used to ask someone if they want something or want to do something: *Would you care for a drink?* ∘ *Would you care to join us for dinner?*

PHRASAL VERBS **care for sb/sth** ⓑ to look after someone or something, especially someone who is young, old, or sick: *The children are being cared for by a relative.* • **not care for sth/sb** formal to not like something or someone: *I don't care for shellfish.*

care² /keəʳ/ *noun* **1** PROTECTION ▷ [U] ⓑ the activity of looking after something or someone, especially someone who is young, old, or sick: *skin/hair care* ∘ *A small baby requires constant care.* **2** ATTENTION ▷ [U] ⓑ If you do something with care, you give a lot of attention to it so that you do not make a mistake or damage anything: *She planned the trip with great care.* ∘ *Fragile – please handle with care.* **3** take care to give a lot of attention to what you are doing so that you do not have an accident or make a mistake: *The roads are very icy so take care when you drive*

home. **4** Take care! informal ⓐ used when saying goodbye to someone: *See you soon, Bob – take care!* **5** WORRY ▷ [C] a feeling of worry: *He wa[s] sixteen years old and didn't have a care in the world* (= had no worries). **6** in care UK Childre[n] who are in care are looked after by governmen[t] organizations because their parents cannot look after them: *She was put/taken into care at th[e] age of twelve.* **7** take care of sb/sth ⓑ to look after someone or something: *My parents are going to take care of the house while we're away.* **8** take care of sth/doing sth to be responsibl[e] for dealing with something: *I sorted out the drink[s] for the party while Guy took care of the food.* → Se[e] also **intensive care**

▨ Word partners for **care**

take care of sb • need/provide/receive care • constant/long-term care • in/under sb's care

career¹ /kə'rɪəʳ/ *noun* [C] **1** ⓑ a job that you d[o] for a long period of your life and that gives yo[u] the chance to move to a higher position an[d] earn more money: *a successful career in market[ing]* **2** the time that you spend doing a particula[r] job: *She began her acting career in TV commer[cials].* → See Note at **work²**

▨ Word partners for **career**

begin/embark on/launch a career • follow/ pursue a career • a career in sth • a career change • career opportunities/prospects

career² /kə'rɪəʳ/ *verb* **career down/into/off, et[c]** UK to move quickly and in an uncontrolled way[:] *The train careered off a bridge and plunged int[o]* the river.

carefree /'keəfriː/ *adj* without any worries o[r] problems: *a carefree childhood*

careful /'keəfəl/ *adj* ⓐ giving a lot of attentio[n] to what you are doing so that you do n[o]t have an accident, make a mistake, or damag[e] something: *careful planning/consideratio[n]* ∘ *Be careful, Michael – that knife's very sharp* ∘ [+ to do sth] *We were careful to avoid the midda[y] sun.* • **carefully** *adv* ⓐ *a carefully prepare[d] speech*

➕ Other ways of saying **careful**

If someone is careful to avoid risks or danger, you can describe them as **cautious**: *She's a very cautious driver.*
The expression **play (it) safe** also means 'to be careful to avoid risks':
I think I'll play it safe and get the earlier train.
If someone does something in a very careful way, paying great attention to detail, you can use adjectives such as **meticulous, method-ical**, and **painstaking**:.
This book is the result of years of meticulous/ painstaking research.

caregiver /'keə,ɡɪvəʳ/ *noun* [C] US (UK **carer**) someone who looks after a person who is young, old, or sick

careless /'keələs/ adj ③ not giving enough attention to what you are doing: *It was very* **careless** *of you to forget your passport.* ∘ *He was fined £250 for* **careless driving.** • **carelessly** adv • **carelessness** noun [U]

carer /'keərə'/ noun [C] UK (US **caregiver**) someone who looks after a person who is young, old, or sick

caress /kə'res/ verb [T] to touch someone in a gentle way that shows that you love them • **caress** noun [C]

caretaker /'keə,teɪkə'/ noun [C] **1** someone whose job is to look after a large building, such as a school **2** US someone who looks after a person who is young, old, or sick

cargo /'kɑːgəʊ/ noun [C, U] (plural **cargoes**) goods that are carried in a vehicle: *a cargo of oil* ∘ *a cargo ship/plane*

caricature /'kærɪkətʃʊə'/ noun [C] a funny drawing or description of someone, especially someone famous, which makes part of their appearance or character more noticeable than it really is • **caricature** verb [T]

caring /'keərɪŋ/ adj ③ kind and supporting other people: *She's a very caring person.*

carjacking /'kɑː,dʒækɪŋ/ noun [C, U] the crime of attacking someone who is driving and stealing their car • **carjacker** noun [C] someone who commits the crime of carjacking

carnage /'kɑːnɪdʒ/ noun [U] formal a situation in which a lot of people are violently killed or injured

carnation /kɑː'neɪʃ°n/ noun [C] a small flower with a sweet smell that is usually white, pink, or red

carnival /'kɑːnɪv°l/ noun [C] **1** ③ a public celebration where people wear special clothes and dance and play music in the roads **2** US a place of outside entertainment where there are machines you can ride on and games that can be played for prizes

carnivore /'kɑːnɪvɔː'/ noun [C] an animal that eats meat • **carnivorous** /kɑː'nɪv°rəs/ adj eating meat

carol /'kær°l/ noun [C] (also **Christmas carol**) a song that people sing at Christmas

carousel /,kærə'sel/ noun [C] **1** a moving strip where passengers collect their bags at an airport **2** mainly US a machine that goes round and round and has toy animals or cars for children to ride on

carp¹ /kɑːp/ noun [C, U] (plural **carp**) a large fish that lives in lakes and rivers, or the meat of this fish

carp² /kɑːp/ verb [I] to complain continually about things that are not important: *He's always* **carping about** *how badly organized the office is.*

car ˌpark noun [C] UK (US **parking lot**) ③ a place where vehicles can be parked

carpenter /'kɑːp°ntə'/ noun [C] a person whose job is making and repairing wooden objects

carpentry /'kɑːp°ntri/ noun [U] the activity of making and repairing wooden objects

carpet /'kɑːpɪt/ noun **1** ③ [C, U] thick material for covering floors, often made of wool: *a new*

living room carpet ∘ UK *fitted carpets* (= carpets that cover floors from wall to wall) **2 a carpet of sth** a thick layer of something that covers the ground: *a carpet of snow* • **carpet** verb [T] to put carpet on the floor of a room: *The stairs were carpeted.* → See also **the red carpet**

carriage /'kærɪdʒ/ noun **1 TRAIN** ▷ [C] UK one of the separate parts of a train where the passengers sit: *The front carriage of the train is for first-class passengers only.* **2 WITH HORSE** ▷ [C] a vehicle with wheels that is pulled by a horse **3 GOODS** ▷ [U] UK the cost of transporting goods → See also **baby carriage**

carriageway /'kærɪdʒweɪ/ noun [C] UK one of the two sides of a motorway or main road: *the southbound carriageway* → See also **dual carriageway**

carrier /'kæriə'/ noun [C] **1 TRANSPORT** ▷ a person, vehicle, or machine that transports things from one place to another **2 DISEASE** ▷ a person who has a disease that they can give to other people without suffering from it themselves **3 COMPANY** ▷ a company that operates aircraft → See also **aircraft carrier, letter carrier**

'carrier ˌbag noun [C] UK a large paper or plastic bag with handles that you are given in a shop to carry the things you have bought → See picture at **bag**

carrot /'kærət/ noun **1** [C, U] ② an orange-coloured vegetable that is long and thin and grows in the ground → See colour picture **Fruits and Vegetables** on page Centre 10 **2** [C] informal something that is offered to someone in order to encourage them to do something

IDIOM **carrot and stick** If you use a carrot-and-stick method, you offer someone rewards if they do something and say you will punish them if they do not.

carry /'kæri/ verb **1 HOLD** ▷ [T] ④ to hold something or someone with your hands, arms, or on your back and take them from one place to another: *He was carrying my bags.* **2 TRANSPORT** ▷ [T] ② to move someone or something from one place to another: *The plane was carrying 30 passengers.* ∘ *Strong currents carried them out to sea.* **3 HAVE WITH YOU** ▷ [T] ③ to have something with you in a pocket, bag, etc: *She still carries his photo in her purse.* **4 DISEASE** ▷ [T] ② to have a disease that you might give to someone else: *Mosquitoes carry malaria and other infectious diseases.* **5 PART** ▷ [T] to have something as a part or a result of something: *All cigarette advertising must carry a government health warning.* ∘ *Murder still carries the death penalty there.* **6 SOUND** ▷ [I] If a sound or someone's voice carries, it can be heard a long way away. **7 SUPPORT** ▷ [T] ② to support the weight of something: *Is the ice thick enough to* **carry my weight?** **8 MATHS** ▷ [T] to put a number into another column when adding numbers **9 DEVELOP** ▷ [T] to develop something in a particular way: *She carried her diet to extremes.* **10 be carried** to be formally accepted by people voting at a meeting: *The **motion was***

carried by 210 votes to 160. → See also **carry weight**

PHRASAL VERBS **be carried away** ⓑ to be so excited about something that you do not control what you say or do: *There's far too much food – I'm afraid I got a bit carried away.* • **carry sth off** to succeed in doing or achieving something difficult: *It's not an easy part to act but he carried it off brilliantly.* • **carry on** ⓑ to continue doing something: [+ doing sth] *The doctors have warned him but he just carries on drinking.* ◦ *Carry on with your work while I'm gone.* • **carry out sth** ⓑ to do or complete something, especially something that you have said you would do or that you have been told to do: *I was only carrying out orders.*

carryall /ˈkæriɔːl/ *noun* [C] US (UK **holdall**) a large bag for carrying clothes → See picture at **luggage**

carry-on /ˈkæriɒn/ *adj* [always before noun] mainly US small enough to bring onto a plane with you when you travel: *carry-on luggage*

cart¹ /kɑːt/ *noun* [C] **1** a vehicle with two or four wheels that is pulled by an animal and used for carrying goods **2** US (UK **trolley**) a metal structure on wheels that is used for carrying things → See picture at **trolley** → See also **go-cart**

cart² /kɑːt/ *verb* informal **cart sb/sth around/away/off, etc** to take someone or something somewhere

carte blanche /ˌkɑːtˈblɑːnʃ/ *noun* [U] complete freedom to do what you want: [+ to do sth] *She was given carte blanche to make whatever changes she wanted.*

cartel /kɑːˈtel/ *noun* [C] a group of companies who join together to control prices and limit competition

cartilage /ˈkɑːtɪlɪdʒ/ *noun* [C, U] a strong elastic substance found where two bones connect in the human body

carton /ˈkɑːtᵊn/ *noun* [C] a container for food and drink that is made from strong, stiff paper or plastic: *a carton of milk/fruit juice* → See picture at **container**

cartoon

cartoon /kɑːˈtuːn/ *noun* [C] **1** ⓐ a film made using characters that are drawn and not real: *Mickey Mouse and other famous cartoon char-*

acters **2** ⓐ a funny drawing, especially in a newspaper or magazine • **cartoonist** *noun* [C] someone whose job is to draw cartoons

cartridge /ˈkɑːtrɪdʒ/ *noun* [C] **1** a small container that is used in a larger piece of equipment and can be easily replaced: *an ink cartridge* **2** a tube containing an explosive substance and a bullet for use in a gun

carve /kɑːv/ *verb* [I, T] **1** to make an object, a shape, or a pattern by cutting wood, stone, etc: *The statue was carved out of stone.* ◦ *They had carved their initials into the tree.* **2** to cut a large piece of cooked meat into smaller pieces **3** **carve (out) a niche/career/role, etc for yourself** to be successful in a particular job or activity

PHRASAL VERB **carve sth up** to divide something into smaller parts, in a way that people do not approve of: *The countryside has been carved up and sold to property developers.*

carving /ˈkɑːvɪŋ/ *noun* **1** [C] an object or a pattern that has been carved **2** [U] the activity of carving an object or pattern: *wood carving*

cascade /kæsˈkeɪd/ *verb* [I] to fall quickly and in large amounts: *Water cascaded from the rocks above.* • **cascade** *noun* [C] literary a large amount of something, especially something falling or hanging: *a cascade of golden hair*

case /keɪs/ *noun* **1** SITUATION ▷ [C] ⓑ a particular situation or example of something: *People were imprisoned, and, in some cases, killed for their beliefs.* ◦ *We usually ask for references, but in your case it will not be necessary.* ◦ *The whole film is based on a case of mistaken identity.* **2** COURT OF LAW ▷ [C] ⓑ something that is decided in a court of law: *a libel/criminal/ divorce case* ◦ *He lost his case.* **3** CRIME ▷ [C] ⓑ a crime that police are trying to solve: *a murder case* ◦ *Police in the town have investigated 50 cases of burglary in the past month.* **4** ILLNESS ▷ [C] an illness, or someone with an illness: *4,000 new cases of the disease are diagnosed every year.* **5** **be the case** ⓑ to be true: *Bad diet can cause tiredness, but I don't think that's the case here.* **6** REASONS ▷ [C] facts or reasons that prove a particular opinion: [usually singular] *There is a strong case for/against bringing in the new legislation.* ◦ mainly UK *He put the case for more funding very convincingly.* **7** CONTAINER ▷ [C] ⓐ a container for storing or protecting something: *a pencil case* ◦ *a cigarette case* **8** BAG ▷ [C] UK ⓐ another word for suitcase (= a rectangular bag or container with a handle which you use for carrying clothes in when you are travelling) **9** **(just) in case** ⓑ because something might happen, or might have happened: *I don't think that it's going to rain, but I'll bring a raincoat just in case.* **10** **in any case** ⓑ used to give another reason for something that you are saying, or that you have done: *I don't want to go skiing and, in any case, I can't afford it.* **11** **in that case/in which case** ⓑ because that is the situation/if that is the situation: *"Peter's coming tonight." "Oh, in that case, I'll stay in."* **12** **be a case of doing sth** to be necessary to do something: *We know that we're right. It's just a case of proving it.* **13** **in case of**

sth formal ⓑ when something happens, or in preparation for when something happens: *We keep a bucket of water backstage, in case of fire.*
14 LANGUAGE ▷ [C] any of the various types to which a noun can belong, depending on what it is doing in the sentence, usually shown by a particular ending

IDIOMS **a case in point** a good example of something: *Supermarkets often charge too much for goods. Bananas are a case in point.* • **be/get on sb's case** informal to criticize someone in an annoying way because of something that they have done: *She's always on my case about something.* • **be on the case** informal to be doing what needs to be done

→ See also **lower case, upper case**

ase ˈhistory noun [C] a record of what happens to a particular person: *The study used case histories from 500 teenage boys.*

ase ˌstudy noun [C] a report about a particular person or thing, to show an example of a general principle

ash¹ /kæʃ/ noun [U] **1** ⓐ money in the form of coins or notes (= paper money): *I'm taking 100 euros in cash.* ∘ *Are you paying by cheque or cash?* **2** informal ⓑ money in any form: *She's short of cash at the moment.* ∘ *a cash prize* → See also **e-cash, hard cash**

> ☑ Word partners for **cash**
>
> **pay (in) cash** • **[£50/$100, etc] in cash** • **a cash machine** • **cash payments**

ash² /kæʃ/ verb **cash a cheque** to exchange a cheque (= piece of paper printed by a bank and used to pay for things) for coins or paper money

PHRASAL VERB **cash in on sth** to get money or another advantage from an event or a situation, often in an unfair way: *Her family have been accused of cashing in on her death.*

ashback /ˈkæʃbæk/ noun [U] UK money that you can take from your bank account when you pay in a shop with a bank card: *£50 cashback*

ash ˌcard noun [C] UK a plastic card that you use to get money from a machine

ash ˌcrop noun [C] a crop that is grown to be sold

ash ˌdesk noun [C] UK the place in a shop where you pay for the things that you buy

ashew /ˈkæʃuː/, /kəˈʃuː/ noun [C] (also **ˈcashew ˌnut**) a curved nut that you can eat

ashflow /ˈkæʃfləʊ/ noun [U] the movement of money in and out of a business or bank account

ashier /kæʃˈɪər/ noun [C] someone whose job is to receive and pay out money in a shop, bank, etc

ash maˌchine noun [C] (also UK **cashpoint**) a machine, usually in a wall outside a bank, that you can get money from using a plastic card

ashmere /ˈkæʃmɪər/ ⓤ /ˈkæʒmɪr/ noun [U] a type of very soft, expensive wool

ashpoint /ˈkæʃpɔɪnt/ noun [C] UK (UK/US **cash machine**) ⓑ a machine, usually in a wall

outside a bank, that you can get money from using a plastic card

ˈcash ˌregister noun [C] a machine that is used in shops for keeping money in, and for recording everything that is sold

casino /kəˈsiːnəʊ/ noun [C] a place where card games and other games of risk are played for money

cask /kɑːsk/ noun [C] a strong, round, wooden container that is used for storing alcoholic drinks

casket /ˈkɑːskɪt/ noun [C] **1** UK a small, decorated box that is used for keeping valuable objects **2** US (UK/US **coffin**) a box in which a dead body is buried

casserole /ˈkæsərəʊl/ noun **1** [C, U] a mixture of meat or beans with liquid and vegetables cooked for a long time in the oven **2** [C] (also **ˈcasserole ˌdish**) a large, heavy container with a lid, that is used for cooking casseroles

cassette /kəˈset/ noun [C] a flat, plastic case containing a long piece of magnetic material that is used to record and play sound or pictures: *a video cassette*

caˈssette ˌplayer noun [C] a machine that plays cassettes of music or sound

caˈssette reˌcorder noun [C] a machine that is used for playing cassettes of music or sound and for recording music or sound onto cassettes

cast¹ /kɑːst/ verb [T] (**cast**) **1 ACTOR** ▷ ⓑ to choose an actor for a particular part in a film or play: [often passive] *Why am I always cast as the villain?* **2 THROW** ▷ literary to throw something **3 LIGHT** ▷ literary to send light or shadow (= dark shapes) in a particular direction: *The moon cast a white light into the room.* **4 cast doubt/suspicion on sb/sth** to make people feel less sure about or have less trust in someone or something: *A leading scientist has cast doubts on government claims that the drug is safe.* **5 cast a/your vote** to vote **6 cast a spell on sb a** to seem to use magic to attract someone: *The city had cast a spell on me and I never wanted to leave.* **b** to use magic to make something happen to someone **7 METAL** ▷ to make an object by pouring hot metal into a container of a particular shape → See also **cast/run your/an eye¹ over sth, cast/shed light¹ on sth, cast a pall² over sth, cast a shadow¹ over sth**

PHRASAL VERB **cast off** If a boat casts off, it leaves.

cast² /kɑːst/ noun **1** [group] ⓑ all the actors in a film or play: *The cast are in rehearsal at the moment.* **2** [C] a hard cover used to keep a broken bone in the correct position until it gets better

> ☑ Word partners for **cast**
>
> **[a play/film, etc] features a cast** • **the cast includes sb** • **the cast of sth** • **a member of the cast**

castaway /ˈkɑːstəweɪ/ noun [C] someone who is left on an island, or in a place where there are few or no other people, after their ship has sunk

caste /kɑːst/ noun [C, U] a system of dividing

Hindu society into social groups, or one of these groups: *the caste system*

castigate /'kæstɪɡeɪt/ **verb** [T] formal to criticize someone severely

cast-iron /'kɑːstˌaɪən/ **adj 1** [always before noun] able to be trusted completely, or impossible to doubt: *I need a cast-iron guarantee that the work will be finished on time.* **2** made of cast iron

cast 'iron noun [U] a type of very hard iron

castle /'kɑːsl/ **noun** [C]

castle

A2 a large, strong building with towers and high walls, that was built in the past to protect the people inside from being attacked

cast-off /'kɑːstɒf/ **noun** [C] a piece of clothing or other item that you give to someone because you do not want it any more: [usually plural] *This dress is another of my sister's cast-offs.*

castrate /kæs'treɪt/ US /'kæstreɪt/ **verb** [T] to remove a man's or male animal's testicles (= organs that produce sperm) • **castration** /kæs'treɪʃən/ **noun** [U]

casual /'kæʒuəl/ **adj 1 NOT PLANNED** ▷ [always before noun] B2 not planned, or without particular meaning or importance: *a casual remark/acquaintance/meeting* **2 RELAXED** ▷ relaxed and not seeming very interested in someone or something: *a casual manner/approach* ∘ *She's much too casual about her work.* **3 CLOTHING** ▷ B1 Casual clothing is comfortable and not suitable for formal occasions. **4 WORK** ▷ [always before noun] mainly UK Casual work is not regular or fixed: *casual labour/workers*

casually /'kæʒuəli/ **adv 1** B2 in a relaxed way, or not seeming to be interested in someone or something: *I asked as casually as I could if she was going to be at the party.* **2** B2 If you dress casually, you do not dress in a formal way.

casualty /'kæʒuəlti/ **noun 1 INJURED** ▷ [C] someone who is injured or killed in an accident or war: *Both sides in the conflict have promised to try to avoid civilian casualties.* **2 BADLY AFFECTED** ▷ [C] someone or something that is badly affected by something that happens: *The health service has been the biggest casualty of government cuts.* **3 HOSPITAL** ▷ [U] UK (US **emergency room**) the part of a hospital where people go when they have been injured or have illnesses so that they can be treated immediately

cat /kæt/ **noun** [C] **1** A1 a small animal with fur, four legs, and a tail that is kept as a pet **2** a large, wild animal that is related to the cat, such as the lion

IDIOM **let the cat out of the bag** to tell people secret information, often without intending to

cataclysmic /ˌkætə'klɪzmɪk/ **adj** sudden, shocking, and violent: *cataclysmic changes/events*

catalogue¹ (also US **catalog**) /'kætəlɒɡ/ **noun** [C] **1** B2 a book with a list of all the goods that you can buy from a shop, or of all the books, paintings, etc that you can find in a place: *clothing catalogue* **2 a catalogue of disasters/errors/failures, etc** a series of bad events

catalogue² (**cataloguing**, **catalogued**) (also US **catalog**) /'kætəlɒɡ/ **verb** [T] to make a list of things, especially in order to put it in a catalogue

catalyst /'kætəlɪst/ **noun** [C] **1** someone or something that causes change: *Recent riots and suicides have acted as a catalyst for change in the prison system.* **2** a substance that makes chemical reaction happen more quickly

catapult¹ /'kætəpʌlt/ **verb 1 catapult sb/sth into/out/through, etc** to make someone or something move through the air very quickly and with great force: [often passive] *When the two cars collided, he was catapulted out of his seat.* **2 catapult sb to stardom/into the lead, etc** to make someone suddenly very famous/successful, etc

catapult² /'kætəpʌlt/ **noun** [C] UK (US **slingshot**) a Y-shaped object with a piece of elastic used by children to shoot small stones

cataract /'kætərækt/ **noun** [C] an area of someone's eye with a disease that gradually prevents them from seeing correctly

catarrh /kə'tɑːʳ/ **noun** [U] UK the thick substance that is produced in your nose and throat when you have a cold

catastrophe /kə'tæstrəfi/ **noun** [C, U] an extremely bad event that causes a lot of suffering or destruction: *After the drought, the country is facing environmental catastrophe.*

catastrophic /ˌkætə'strɒfɪk/ **adj** causing a lot of suffering or destruction

catch¹ /kætʃ/ **verb** (**caught**) **1 GET HOLD** ▷ [T] A2 to stop someone or something that is moving through the air by taking hold of it: *Try to catch the ball.* ∘ *She fell backwards but he caught her in his arms.* **2 STOP ESCAPING** ▷ [T] B1 to find and stop a person or animal who is trying to escape: *He ran after his attacker but couldn't catch him.* ∘ *Did you catch many fish today?* **3 CRIMINAL** ▷ [T] If the police catch a criminal, they find them and take them away: *These terrorists must be caught.* **4 ILLNESS** ▷ [T] A2 to get an illness or disease: *I think I've caught a cold.* **5 TRANSPORT** ▷ [T] A1 to get on a bus, train, etc in order to travel somewhere: *You can catch the bus from the top of the hill.* **6 DISCOVER** ▷ [T] B2 to discover someone who is doing something wrong or something secret: [+ doing sth] *I caught her listening outside the door.* ∘ informal *You won't catch me wearing* (= I never wear) *a tie.* **7 STICK** ▷ [I, T] to stick somewhere, or to make something stick somewhere: *My dress caught on the door handle as I was leaving.* **8 COLLECT** ▷ [T] to collect something that is falling: *I used a bucket to catch the drips.* **9 BE IN TIME** ▷ [T] to manage to be in time to see or do something: *I only caught the end of the programme.* **10 HEAR** ▷ [T] to hear or understand something correctly: *I'm sorry. I didn't catch your name.*

11 catch fire ⓑ to start burning **12 be/get caught** to be unable to avoid something unpleasant: *I got caught in the rain.* **13 catch the sun** UK to burn your skin in the sun: *You've caught the sun on your shoulders.* **14 catch sight of sth** to see something suddenly, often only for a short time: *He caught sight of himself in the mirror.* **15 HIT** ▷ [T] to hit something or someone: *The ball flew across the garden, and caught me on the chin.* → See also **catch sb's eye¹**, **catch sb off guard¹**

PHRASAL VERBS **catch on 1** to become popular: *I wonder if the game will **catch on with** young people?* **2** informal to understand something, especially after a long time: *It took him a while to **catch on to** what she meant.* • **catch sb out** UK to trick someone so that they make a mistake • **catch (sb/sth) up 1** ⓑ to reach someone or something that is in front of you, by going faster than them: *We soon **caught up** with the car in front.* **2** ⓑ to reach the same level or quality as someone or something else: *She's doing extra work to **catch up with** the rest of the class.* • **catch up** ⓑ to learn or discuss the most recent news: *Let's meet for a chat – I need to **catch up on** all the gossip.* • **catch up on/with sth** ⓑ to do something that you did not have time to do earlier: *After the exams, I need to catch up on some sleep.* • **catch up with sb** If something bad that you have done or that has been happening to you catches up with you, it begins to cause problems for you: *I can feel the stress of the last few weeks beginning to catch up with me.* • **be/get caught up in sth** to become involved in a situation, often without wanting to: *How did the paper get caught up in a legal dispute?*

catch² /kætʃ/ **noun** [C] **1 WITH HANDS** ▷ the act of catching something that is moving through the air: *a brilliant catch* **2 FISH** ▷ the amount of fish that someone has caught **3 PROBLEM** ▷ a hidden problem or difficulty with something: *He's offering us a free flight? There must be a catch.* **4 LOCK** ▷ a part on something that fastens it and keeps it closed: *a safety catch*

Catch-22 /ˌkætʃtwentiˈtuː/ **noun** [C] an impossible situation: you do one thing until you have done another thing, but you cannot do the other thing until you have done the first thing: *a Catch-22 situation*

catching /ˈkætʃɪŋ/ **adj** [never before noun] If an illness or a mood is catching, other people can get it from you.

catchment area /ˈkætʃmənt ˌeəriə/ **noun** [C] UK the area around a school or a hospital, where most of the students or patients come from

catchphrase /ˈkætʃfreɪz/ **noun** [C] a phrase that is often repeated by a particular organization or person, and becomes connected with them

catchy /ˈkætʃi/ **adj** A catchy song, tune, or phrase is easy to remember.

categorical /ˌkætəˈɡɒrɪkəl/ **adj** If someone is categorical about what they say, they say it with force and are completely certain about it: *a categorical assurance/denial* • **categorically**

adv *They have **denied categorically** that they were involved in the conspiracy.*

categorize (also UK **-ise**) /ˈkætəɡəraɪz/ **verb** [T] to divide people or things into groups of similar types: *The books are categorized according to subject.*

category /ˈkætəɡəri/ **noun** [C] ⓑ a group of people or things of a similar type: *Our customers **fall into** two main **categories**: retired people and housewives.*

cater /ˈkeɪtər/ **verb** [I, T] to provide and often serve food and drinks for a particular event: *How many are we **catering for** at the wedding reception?*

PHRASAL VERBS **cater for sb/sth** mainly UK to provide what is wanted or needed by a particular group of people: *The club caters for children between the ages of 4 and 12.* • **cater to sb/sth** to give people exactly what they want, usually something that people think is wrong: *This legislation simply caters to unacceptable racist opinions.*

caterer /ˈkeɪtərər/ **noun** [C] a person or company that provides food and drinks for particular events, or for an organization

catering /ˈkeɪtərɪŋ/ **noun** [U] ⓑ the job of providing food and drinks for people: *Who did the catering for the party?*

caterpillar /ˈkætəpɪlər/ **caterpillar** **noun** [C] a small, long animal with many legs that eats leaves

cathartic /kəˈθɑːtɪk/ **adj** A cathartic experience or event helps you to express and get rid of strong emotions.

cathedral /kəˈθiːdrəl/ **noun** [C] ⓐ the largest and most important church in a particular area

Catholic /ˈkæθəlɪk/ **adj** (also **Roman Catholic**) belonging or relating to the part of the Christian religion that has the Pope as its leader: *a Catholic priest/school* • **Catholic noun** [C] *I think he's a Catholic.*

the ˌCatholic ˈChurch noun the Catholic religion and all the people who believe in it

Catholicism /kəˈθɒlɪsɪzəm/ **noun** [U] (also **ˌRoman Caˈtholicism**) the beliefs of the Catholic religion

catsup /ˈkætsəp/ **noun** [U] another US spelling of ketchup (= a thick, red sauce that is eaten cold with food)

cattle /ˈkætl/ **noun** [plural] ⓑ male and female cows, kept on a farm for their milk and meat

catty /ˈkæti/ **adj** informal intending to hurt someone by saying unkind things: *catty remarks*

catwalk /ˈkætwɔːk/ **noun** [C] the narrow, raised path that people walk along in a fashion show

Caucasian /kɔːˈkeɪʒən/ **adj** belonging to a race

C

of people with white or pale skin • **Caucasian** **noun** [C] a Caucasian person

caught /kɔːt/ past of catch

cauldron /ˈkɔːldrᵊn/ **noun** [C] literary a large, round metal pot that is used for cooking over a fire

cauliflower /ˈkɒlɪˌflaʊəʳ/ **noun** [C, U] a large, round, white vegetable with thick, green leaves around the outside → See colour picture **Fruits and Vegetables** on page Centre 10

cause¹ /kɔːz/ **noun** **1** MAKES HAPPEN ▷ [C] [B2] someone or something that makes something happen: *The police are still trying to* ***establish the cause of*** *the fire.* ◦ *She died of* ***natural causes.*** **2** REASON ▷ [U] a reason to feel something or to behave in a particular way: *He's never given me any* ***cause for*** *concern.* **3** PRINCIPLE ▷ [C] a principle or aim that a group of people support or fight for: *The money will all go to a* ***good cause.***

> **Word partners for cause**
>
> a **common/leading/probable/root** cause • **discover/establish/identify** the cause **of** sth • the **main** cause

cause² /kɔːz/ **verb** [T] [B2] to make something happen: *The hurricane caused widespread damage.* ◦ *Most heart attacks are* ***caused by*** *blood clots.* ◦ [+ two objects] *I hope the children haven't caused you too much trouble.* ◦ [+ to do sth] *What caused the washing machine to blow up?*

causeway /ˈkɔːzweɪ/ **noun** [C] a raised path or road over a wet area

caustic /ˈkɔːstɪk/ **adj** **1** A caustic remark is extremely unkind and intended to upset or criticize someone. **2** Caustic chemicals can burn things.

caution¹ /ˈkɔːʃᵊn/ **noun** **1** [U] great care and attention not to take risks or get into danger: *Travellers have been advised to* ***exercise*** *great* ***caution*** *when passing through the region.* ◦ *I would* ***treat*** *anything he says* ***with*** *extreme* ***caution*** *(= not be too quick to believe it).* **2** [C] UK a warning by a police officer or other person in authority telling you that you will be punished if you do something bad again

IDIOM **throw caution to the wind** to take a risk

→ See also **err on the side¹ of caution**

> **Word partners for caution**
>
> **advise/exercise/urge** caution • **extreme/great** caution • do sth **with** caution • caution **in** doing sth

caution² /ˈkɔːʃᵊn/ **verb** **1** [I, T] formal to warn someone of something: [often passive] *They were* ***cautioned against*** *buying shares in the company.* **2** [T] UK If a police officer cautions someone, they give that person a warning that they will be punished next time.

cautionary /ˈkɔːʃᵊnᵊri/ **adj** intended to warn or advise someone: *a* ***cautionary tale***

cautious /ˈkɔːʃəs/ **adj** [B2] taking care to avoid risks or danger: *She is cautious about lending money to anyone.* • **cautiously** **adv**

cavalier /ˌkævᵊlˈɪəʳ/ **adj** without caring about other people or about a dangerous or serious situation: *a* ***cavalier attitude***

the cavalry /ˈkævᵊlri/ **noun** [U, group] soldiers who fight on horses

cave¹ /keɪv/ **noun** [C] [B1] a large hole in the side of a cliff (= straight, high rock next to the sea), mountain, or under the ground

cave² /keɪv/ **verb**

PHRASAL VERB **cave in** **1** If a ceiling, roof, or other structure caves in, it breaks and falls into the space below. **2** to agree to something that you were against before, after someone has persuaded you or made you afraid: *The company has finally* ***caved in to*** *the demands of the unions.*

caveat /ˈkæviæt/ **noun** [C] something you say that warns that there is a limit on a general announcement made earlier

cavern /ˈkævᵊn/ **noun** [C] a large cave

caviar (also **caviare**) /ˈkæviɑːʳ/ **noun** [U] the eggs of a large fish, eaten as a food and usually very expensive

cavity /ˈkævəti/ **noun** [C] **1** a hole or a space inside something solid or between two surfaces **2** a hole in a tooth

cavort /kəˈvɔːt/ **verb** [I] to jump, dance, or move about in an excited way

cc /ˌsiːˈsiː/ **1** abbreviation for carbon copy: used on a letter or email to show that you are sending a copy to other people **2** abbreviation for cubic centimetre: a unit for measuring the amount of space inside an object: *a 750cc motorcycle*

CCTV /ˌsiːsiːtiːˈviː/ **noun** [U] abbreviation for closed circuit television: a system of television cameras filming in shops and public places so that people can watch and protect those places: *CCTV cameras*

CD /ˌsiːˈdiː/ **noun** [C] [A1] abbreviation for compact disc: a small disc on which music or information is recorded → See colour picture **The Office** on page Centre 5

ˌCˈD ˌburner **noun** [C] a machine that can record information onto a CD

ˌCˈD ˌplayer **noun** [C] [A1] a machine that is used for playing music CDs

CD-R /ˌsiːdiːˈɑːʳ/ **noun** [C] abbreviation for compact disc recordable: an empty compact disc for recording information only once using special computer equipment

CD-ROM /ˌsiːdiːˈrɒm/ **noun** [C] [B1] abbreviation for compact disc read-only memory: a CD that holds large amounts of information that can be read by a computer

CD-RW /ˌsiːdiːɑːˈdʌblju:/ **noun** [C] abbreviation for compact disc rewritable: an empty compact disc for recording and changing information using special computer equipment

ˌCˈD ˌwriter **noun** [C] a CD burner

cease /siːs/ **verb** [I, T] formal [B2] to stop: [+ doing sth] *He ordered his men to cease firing.* ◦ [+ to do sth] *Her behaviour never ceases to amaze me.*

ceasefire /ˈsiːsfaɪəʳ/ **noun** [C] an agreement between two armies or groups to stop fighting

ceaseless /ˈsiːsləs/ adj formal continuous: *the ceaseless movement of the sea* • **ceaselessly** adv

cedar /ˈsiːdər/ noun [C, U] a tall, evergreen (= with leaves that do not fall off in winter) tree, or the red wood of this tree

cede /siːd/ verb [T] formal to give something such as land or power to another country or person, especially because you are forced to

ceiling /ˈsiːlɪŋ/ noun [C] **1** 🅐🅑 the surface of a room that you can see when you look above you **2** a limit on the amount that can be paid for something: *They have set a ceiling on pay rises.*

celeb /sɪˈleb/ noun [C] informal a celebrity (= famous person)

celebrate /ˈseləbreɪt/ verb [I, T] 🅑🅐 to do something enjoyable because it is a special day, or because something good has happened: *Do you celebrate Christmas in your country?*

celebrated /ˈseləbreɪtɪd/ adj famous for a special ability or quality: *She is celebrated for her wit.*

celebration /ˌseləˈbreɪʃən/ noun [C, U] 🅑🅐 an occasion when you celebrate a special day or event, or the act of celebrating: *Let's buy some champagne in celebration of her safe arrival.* ◦ *You've passed? This calls for a celebration.*

> 🔲 **Word partners for celebration**
>
> anniversary/birthday/New Year celebrations • be a cause for celebration • sth calls for a celebration • a celebration to mark/of sth • in celebration of sth

celebratory /ˌseləˈbreɪtəri/ ⓤ /ˈseləbrətɔːri/ adj done to celebrate something or wanting to celebrate something: *a celebratory dinner* ◦ *in a celebratory mood*

celebrity /səˈlebrəti/ noun [C] 🅑🅐 a famous person

celery /ˈseləri/ noun [U] a vegetable with long, pale green stems, often eaten in salads → See colour picture **Fruits and Vegetables** on page Centre 10

celestial /səˈlestiəl/ adj literary relating to heaven or the sky

celibate /ˈseləbət/ adj Someone who is celibate does not have sex, especially because they have decided to never have sex. • **celibacy** /ˈseləbəsi/ noun [U] a way of life in which you do not have sex, especially because you have decided not to have sex

cell /sel/ noun [C] **1** 🅑🅐 the smallest living part of an animal or a plant: *brain/cancer cells* **2** 🅑🅐 a small room in a prison or police station where a prisoner is kept

cellar /ˈselər/ noun [C] 🅑🅐 a room under the floor of a building → See also **salt cellar**

cellist /ˈtʃelɪst/ noun [C] someone who plays the cello

cello /ˈtʃeləʊ/ noun [C] 🅑🅐 a large, wooden musical instrument with four strings that you hold between your knees to play

Cellophane /ˈseləfeɪn/ noun [U] trademark thin, transparent material that is used for wrapping goods, especially flowers and food

cell phone /ˈselfəʊn/ noun [C] (also **cellular phone, cellphone**) US a mobile phone

cellular /ˈseljələr/ adj **1** relating to animal or plant cells: *cellular damage* **2** [always before noun] relating to cellular phones: *cellular companies/communications*

cellulite /ˈseljəlaɪt/ noun [U] fat that looks like small lumps below the skin, especially on the upper legs: *I can't seem to get rid of my cellulite.*

cellulose /ˈseljələʊs/ noun [U] a substance in plants that is used to make some paper and plastics

Celsius /ˈselsiəs/ noun [U] (written abbreviation **C**) a measurement of temperature in which water freezes at 0° and boils at 100°

Celtic /ˈkeltɪk/ adj relating to the people of Ireland, Scotland, and Wales: *Celtic art/music*

cement¹ /sɪˈment/ noun [U] a grey powder used in building which is mixed with water and sand or stones to make a hard substance

cement² /sɪˈment/ verb [T] **1** to make something such as a relationship, a belief, or a position stronger: *It was that day that really cemented our friendship.* **2** (also **cement over**) to cover something with cement

cemetery /ˈsemətri/ noun [C] 🅑🅐 a place where dead people are buried

censor /ˈsensər/ verb [T] to examine books, documents, or films and remove parts of them that are offensive or not allowed by rules: [often passive] *The book was heavily censored before publication.* • **censor** noun [C]

censorship /ˈsensəʃɪp/ noun [U] the act of censoring a book, film, newspaper, or other information: *political/state censorship*

censure /ˈsensjər/ verb [T] formal to criticize someone formally for something that they have done • **censure** noun [U] formal

census /ˈsensəs/ noun [C] an occasion when people in a country are officially counted and information is taken about them

cent /sent/ noun [C] 🅐🅑 a coin or unit of money with a value of 1/100 of a dollar or euro; ¢: *The newspaper costs sixty-five cents.*

centenary /senˈtiːnəri/ ⓤ /ˈsentəneri/ noun [C] UK (US **centennial** /senˈteniəl/) the day or year that is 100 years after an important event: *This year, there will be many concerts to mark the centenary of the composer's death.*

center /ˈsentər/ noun, verb US spelling of centre

centerpiece /ˈsentəpiːs/ noun [C] US spelling of centrepiece

centi-, cent- /senti-, sent-/ prefix hundred: *a centimetre* ◦ *a century*

centigrade /ˈsentɪɡreɪd/ noun [U] (written abbreviation **C**) a measurement of temperature in which water freezes at 0° and boils at 100°

centilitre /ˈsentɪˌliːtər/ noun [C] UK (US **centiliter**, written abbreviation **cl**) a unit for measuring liquid, equal to 0.01 litres

centimetre UK (US **centimeter**, written abbreviation **cm**) /ˈsentɪˌmiːtər/ noun [C] 🅐🅑 a unit for measuring length, equal to 0.01 metres

central /ˈsentrəl/ adj **1 POSITION** ▷ 🅑🅐 in or near

C

the centre of a place or object: *central Africa/ America* ∘ *The roof is supported by a central column.* **2 ORGANIZATION** ▷ [always before noun] controlled or organized in one main place: *central authorities/government* ∘ *the US central bank* **3 IMPORTANT** ▷ main or most important: *a central character/figure* ∘ *Her role is **central to** the film.* **4 CITY** ▷ in the main part of a town or city • **centrally** adv

ˌcentral ˈheating noun [U] 🅑1 a system of heating a building by warming air or water in one place and carrying it to different rooms in pipes

centralize (also UK -**ise**) /ˈsentrəlaɪz/ verb [T] If a country or organization is centralized, it is controlled from one place: [often passive] *centralized control/government* • **centralization** /ˌsentrəlaɪˈzeɪʃən/ noun [U]

centre[1] UK (US **center**) /ˈsentər/ noun **1 MIDDLE** ▷ [C] 🅐2 the middle point or part of something: *She stood **in the centre** of the room.* ∘ *Cars are not allowed in the **town centre**.* **2 PLACE** ▷ [C] 🅐2 a place or a building used for a particular activity: *a health/advice centre* ∘ *a centre for the homeless* **3 BUSINESS** ▷ [C] a place where a lot of a particular activity or business takes place: *an industrial centre* **4 POLITICAL** ▷ [no plural] (also **the centre**) a political position with opinions that are not extreme: *His political views are left of centre.* **5 be the centre of attention** to receive more attention than anyone or anything else → See also **community centre, garden centre, shopping centre**

centre[2] UK (US **center**) /ˈsentər/ verb [T] to put something in the middle of an area

PHRASAL VERB **centre around/on sb/sth** to have someone or something as the main part of a discussion or activity: *The dispute centres on racial issues.*

ˌcentre of ˈgravity noun [C] (plural **centres of gravity**) the point in an object where its weight is balanced

centrepiece UK (US **centerpiece**) /ˈsentəpiːs/ noun [C] **1** the most important or attractive part of something: *The employment programme is **the centrepiece of** the government's economic strategy.* **2** a decoration that is put in the middle of a dinner table

century /ˈsenʃəri/ noun [C] 🅐2 a period of 100 years, especially used in giving dates: *the twentieth century*

🖉 Word partners for **century**

in the [17th/21st, etc] century • the **early/ mid/late** [15th/19th, etc] century • the **turn of** the century (= the time around the end of one century and the beginning of the next)

CEO /ˌsiːiːˈəʊ/ noun [C] abbreviation for chief executive officer: the person with the most important job in a company

ceramics /səˈræmɪks/ noun [plural] objects that are made by shaping and heating clay • **ceramic** adj made by shaping and heating clay: *a ceramic pot*

cereal /ˈsɪəriəl/ noun [C, U] **1** a plant that is

grown to produce grain for food: *cereal crops* **2** 🅐2 a food that is made from grain and eaten with milk, especially in the morning: *breakfast cereals* → See colour picture **Food** on page Centre 11

cerebral /ˈserəbrəl/ adj formal **1** Cerebral films, books, etc need a lot of thought to understand them, and cerebral people think a lot. **2** [always before noun] relating to the brain: *cerebral arteries*

ceremonial /ˌserɪˈməʊniəl/ adj relating to a ceremony • **ceremonially** adv

ceremony /ˈserɪməni/ noun **1** [C] 🅑1 a formal event that is performed on important social or religious occasions: *a wedding/marriage ceremony* ∘ *an award ceremony* **2** [U] formal behaviour, words, and actions that are part of a ceremony

---

🖉 Word partners for **ceremony**

attend/hold a ceremony • **at** a ceremony • an **award/marriage/wedding** ceremony

---

certain /ˈsɜːtən/ adj **1 NO DOUBT** ▷ [never before noun] 🅑1 completely sure of something, or knowing without doubt that something is true: [+ (that)] *I feel absolutely certain that you're doing the right thing.* ∘ [+ question word] *Nobody was certain how the accident had happened.* ∘ *He was quite **certain about/of** the thief's identity.* → Opposite **uncertain 2 know/say for certain** to know something without doubt: *We don't know for certain whether she's coming.* **3 SURE TO HAPPEN** ▷ 🅑1 sure to happen, to do something, or to be true: [+ (that)] *It now looks certain that she will resign.* ∘ [+ to do sth] *She is certain to do well in the exams.* **4 PARTICULAR** ▷ [always before noun] 🅑1 used to refer to a particular person or thing without naming or describing them exactly: *The museum is only open at certain times of the day.* **5 a certain** 🅑2 used before a noun to mean existing, but difficult to describe the exact quality or amount: *He's got a certain charm.* **6 certain of** formal used to refer to some of a group of people or things: *Certain of you already know the news.*

certainly /ˈsɜːtənli/ adv **1** 🅐2 used to emphasize something and show that there is no doubt about it: *Their team certainly deserved to win.* ∘ *"Are your parents paying for dinner?" "I certainly hope so."* ∘ *"Do you regret what you said?" "Certainly not!"* **2** 🅐2 used to agree to a request: *"Could you pass the salt, please?" "Certainly."*

certainty /ˈsɜːtənti/ noun **1** [U] 🅑2 the feeling of being completely sure about something: *I can't say with any certainty what time she left.* **2** [C] something that is very likely to happen or cannot be doubted: *There are no absolute certainties in life.*

certificate /səˈtɪfɪkət/ noun [C] 🅑1 an official document that gives details to show that something is true: *a death/marriage certificate* ∘ *an exam certificate* → See also **birth certificate**

certify /ˈsɜːtɪfaɪ/ verb [T] **1 TRUTH** ▷ formal to say in a formal or official way that something is true or correct: [+ (that)] *I certify that the information I*

ɑː **arm** | ɜː **her** | iː **see** | ɔː **saw** | uː **too** | aɪ **my** | aʊ **how** | eə **hair** | eɪ **day** | əʊ **no** | ɪə **near** | ɔɪ **boy** | ʊə **pure** | aɪə **fire** | aʊə **sour** |

have given is true. ∘ She was **certified dead** on arrival at the hospital. **2 CERTIFICATE** ▷ to give someone a certificate to say that they have completed a course of study: *a certified accountant* **3 HEALTH** ▷ to say officially that someone has a mental illness

certitude /ˈsɜːtɪtjuːd/ **noun** [U] formal a feeling of being certain about something

cervix /ˈsɜːvɪks/ **noun** [C] the narrow entrance to a woman's womb • **cervical** /səˈvaɪkəl, ˈsɜːvɪkəl/ **adj** *cervical cancer*

cesarean /sɪˈzeəriən/ **noun** [C] US spelling of caesarean

cessation /sesˈeɪʃən/ **noun** [C, U] formal the end of something that has been happening, especially violence: *the cessation of hostilities*

cf used in writing when you want the reader to make a comparison between the subject being discussed and something else

CFC /ˌsiːefˈsiː/ **noun** [C] abbreviation for chlorofluorocarbon: a type of gas used in some fridges (= containers for keeping food cold) and aerosols (= containers for making liquids come out in small drops), which damages the layer of gases around the Earth

chafe /tʃeɪf/ **verb 1** [I] to feel angry because of rules and limits: *He chafed against/at the narrow academic approach of his school.* **2** [I, T] to make part of the body painful by rubbing, or to become painful because of being rubbed

chagrin /ˈʃæɡrɪn/ ⓤ /ʃəˈɡrɪn/ **noun** [U] anger or disappointment caused by something that does not happen the way you wanted it: *To his parents' chagrin, he had no intention of becoming a lawyer.*

chain

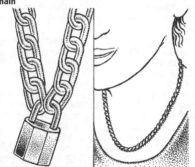

chain¹ /tʃeɪn/ **noun 1 METAL RINGS** ▷ [C, U] ⓐ a line of metal rings connected together: *a bicycle chain* ∘ *She wore a gold chain around her neck.* ∘ *The hostages were kept in chains.* **2 BUSINESS** ▷ [C] ⓑ a number of similar shops, restaurants, etc owned by the same company: *a chain of hotels/supermarkets* **3 EVENTS** ▷ [C] ⓒ a series of things that happen one after the other: *His arrival set off a surprising chain of events.*

chain² /tʃeɪn/ **verb** [T] (also **chain up**) to fasten someone or something to someone or something else using a chain: *I chained my bike to a*

lamppost. ∘ *You shouldn't keep a dog chained up like that.*

chain reˈaction **noun** [C] a series of events where each one causes the next one to happen

chain-smoke /ˈtʃeɪnsməʊk/ **verb** [I, T] to smoke cigarettes one after another • **chain smoker** **noun** [C]

chain ˌstore **noun** [C] one of a group of similar shops owned by the same company

chair¹ /tʃeər/ **noun** [C] **1 FURNITURE** ▷ ⓐ a seat for one person, with a back, usually four legs, and sometimes two arms → See colour picture **The Office** on page Centre 5 **2 MEETING** ▷ someone who controls a meeting or organization: [usually singular] *All questions should be addressed to the chair.* **3 UNIVERSITY** ▷ a very important position in a university department, or the person who has this position → See also **the electric chair**

chair² /tʃeər/ **verb** [T] to control a meeting or organization: *I've been asked to chair the committee.*

chairman, chairwoman /ˈtʃeəmən, ˈtʃeəˌwʊmən/ **noun** [C] (plural **chairmen, chairwomen**) a man/woman who controls a meeting, company, or other organization

chairperson /ˈtʃeəˌpɜːsən/ **noun** [C] someone who controls a meeting, company, or other organization

chalet /ˈʃæleɪ/ ⓤ /ʃælˈeɪ/ **noun** [C] a small wooden house, often in a mountain area, or for people who are on holiday

chalk¹ /tʃɔːk/ **noun 1** [U] a type of soft, white rock **2** [C, U] a small stick of chalk that is used for writing and drawing: *a piece of chalk* → See colour picture **The Classroom** on page Centre 6

IDIOM **be like chalk and cheese** UK If two people are like chalk and cheese, they are completely different from each other.

chalk² /tʃɔːk/ **verb** [T] UK to write something with a piece of chalk

PHRASAL VERB **chalk sth up** to achieve something: *She's chalked up five goals this season.*

chalkboard /ˈtʃɔːkbɔːd/ **noun** [C] US (UK/US **blackboard**) a large board with a dark surface that teachers write on with chalk

chalky /ˈtʃɔːki/ **adj** made of chalk, or similar to chalk

challenge¹ /ˈtʃælɪndʒ/ **noun 1 DIFFICULT** ▷ [C, U] ⓑ something that is difficult and that tests someone's ability or determination: *Finding a decision that pleases everyone is the challenge which now faces the committee.* **2 INVITATION** ▷ [C] an invitation to compete in a game or a fight: *I'm sure Paul will race you. He never refuses a challenge.* **3 DISAGREEMENT** ▷ [C] an expression of disagreement with ideas, rules, or someone's authority: *a challenge to the authority of the President*

▨ Word partners for **challenge**

face/pose/present/relish a challenge • a big/formidable/serious/tough challenge

challenge² /ˈtʃælɪndʒ/ **verb** [T] **1** ⓑ to express

---

challenger — 110

disagreement with ideas, rules, or someone's authority: *The election results are being challenged.* **2** to invite someone to compete in a game or fight: *He **challenged** Smith **to** a fight.*

challenger /'tʃæləndʒəʳ/ *noun* [C] someone who competes in a game, competition, or election, often to win a position that someone else has: *There are five **challengers for** the title.*

challenging /'tʃæləndʒɪŋ/ *adj* ⑧ difficult to do in a way that tests your ability or determination: *This has been a challenging time for us all.*

chamber /'tʃeɪmbəʳ/ *noun* [C] **1 ROOM** ▷ a room used for an official or special purpose: *a debating chamber* ∘ *a burial chamber* **2 PARLIAMENT** ▷ one of the groups that a parliament is divided into: *the **upper/lower** chamber* **3 MACHINE/BODY** ▷ a closed space in a machine or in your body: *the left chamber of the heart* → See also **gas chamber**

chambermaid /'tʃeɪmbəmeɪd/ *noun* [C] a woman whose job is to clean and tidy hotel bedrooms

chamber music *noun* [U] music that is written for a small group of musicians

chamber of commerce *noun* [C] (plural **chambers of commerce**) an organization of business people who work together to improve business in their local area

champ /tʃæmp/ *noun* [C] informal short for champion

champagne /ʃæm'peɪn/ *noun* [U] ⑫ French white wine with lots of bubbles in it that people often drink to celebrate something

champion¹ /'tʃæmpiən/ *noun* [C] **1** ⑧ a person, animal, or team that wins a competition: *a boxing champion* ∘ *the **world champions*** **2** someone who supports, defends, or fights for a person, belief, or principle: *a **champion of** human rights* → See also **reigning champion**

champion² /'tʃæmpiən/ *verb* [T] to support, defend, or fight for a person, belief, or principle: *She **championed the cause** of free speech.*

championship /'tʃæmpiənʃɪp/ *noun* [C] **1** ⑧ a competition to find the best team or player in a particular game or sport: *The **world championship** will be held in this country next year.* **2** the position of being a champion: *She is current holder of our tennis championship.*

chance¹ /tʃɑːns/ *noun* **1 POSSIBILITY** ▷ [C, U] ⑧ the possibility that something will happen: [+ (that)] *There's a chance that she'll still be there.* ∘ *She has little **chance of** passing the exam.* ∘ *Is there **any chance of** a drink?* **2 OPPORTUNITY** ▷ [C] ⑧ the opportunity to do something: [+ to do sth] *I didn't **get a chance** to speak to you at the party.* ∘ *I hope you've **had the chance** to look around the exhibition.* ∘ ***Give** me **a chance** to prove that I can do the work.* ∘ *Going on a world cruise is **the chance of a lifetime** (= an opportunity which only comes once in your life).* **3 LUCK** ▷ [U] ⑧ the way something

happens because of luck, or without being planned: *I saw her **by chance** in the shop.* **4 RISK** ▷ [C] ⑫ a risk: *I'm delivering my work by hand. I'm not **taking** any **chances**.* **5 by any chance** used to ask in a polite way whether something is possible or true: *You're not Spanish by any chance, are you?* **6 stand a chance** to have a chance of success or of achieving something: *He stands a good chance of winning the election.* **7 chances are** it is likely: [+ (that)] *Chances are that he'll refuse.* **8 No chance!/ Not a chance!** used to emphasize that there is no possibility of something happening: *"Do you think she'd go out with me?" "No chance!"*

IDIOM fat chance informal used to say that you do not think that something is likely to happen: *"Do you think we'll win?" "Fat chance."*

→ See also **off-chance, outside chance**

> **Word partners for chance**
>
> a chance **of** sth • a **fifty-fifty** chance • a **fair/ good/slim** chance

chance² /tʃɑːns/ *verb* [T] informal to take a risk by doing something

chance³ /tʃɑːns/ *adj* [always before noun] A chance event is not planned or expected: *a chance meeting*

chancellor /'tʃɑːnsələʳ/ *noun* [C] **1 GOVERNMENT** ▷ the leader of the government in some countries: *the German chancellor* **2 UNIVERSITY** ▷ the person with the highest position in some universities **3 MONEY** ▷ (also **Chancellor of the Exchequer**) UK the person in the British government who makes decisions about taxes and government spending

chandelier /ˌʃændə'lɪəʳ/ *noun* [C] a large light that hangs from the ceiling that is made of many small lights or candles and small pieces of glass

change¹ /tʃeɪndʒ/ *verb* **1 DIFFERENT** ▷ [I, T] ⑫ to become different, or to make someone or something become different: *I hadn't seen her for twenty years, but she hadn't changed a bit.* ∘ *Meeting you has changed my life.* ∘ *She's **changed from** being a happy, healthy child **to** being ill all the time.* **2 FROM ONE THING TO ANOTHER** ▷ [I, T] ⑪ to stop having or using one thing, and start having or using another: *The doctor has recommended changing my diet.* ∘ *I'll have to ask them if they can change the time of my interview.* **3 CLOTHES** ▷ [I, T] ⑫ to take off your clothes and put on different ones: *He **changed out of** his school uniform **into** jeans and a T-shirt.* ∘ *Is there somewhere I can **get changed**?* **4 JOURNEY** ▷ [I, T] ⑫ to get off a bus, plane, etc and catch another, in order to continue a journey: *I have to change trains in Paris.* **5 IN SHOP** ▷ [T] UK ⑧ to take something you have bought back to a shop and exchange it for something else: *If the dress doesn't fit, can I change it for a smaller one?* **6 MONEY** ▷ [T] ⑫ to get or give someone money in exchange for money of a different type: *Where can I change my dollars?* ∘ *Can you **change** a 20 euro note **for** two tens?* **7 BED** ▷ [T] to take dirty sheets off a bed

aː arm | ɜː her | iː see | ɔː saw | uː too | aɪ my | aʊ how | eə hair | eɪ day | əʊ no | ɪə near | ɔɪ boy | ʊə pure | aɪə fire | aʊə sour |

and put on clean ones: *to change the bed/sheets*
8 BABY ▷ [T] to put a clean nappy (= thick cloth
worn on a baby's bottom) on a baby → See also
chop and change, **change hands** (**hand**[1]),
change your tune[1]

> ### ➕ Other ways of saying change
>
> The verb **alter** is a common alternative to
> 'change':
>　　*We've had to **alter** our plans.*
> If you often change something that you do,
> you can use the verb **vary**:
>　　*Try to **vary** the children's diet a little.*
> If someone changes the purpose or appear-
> ance of something, you can use the verb
> **convert**, or the phrasal verb **turn into**:
>　　*We're going to **convert** the spare bedroom*
>　　*into an office.*
>　　*There are plans to **turn** his latest book **into** a*
>　　*film.*
> If someone changes from doing or using one
> thing to doing or using another, the verb
> **switch** is sometimes used:
>　　*We've **switched** over to low fat milk.*
>　　*Jack has just **switched** jobs.*

PHRASAL VERBS **change sth around/round** to
move objects such as furniture into different
positions • **change over** UK to stop using or
having one thing and start using or having
something else: *We've just **changed over** from
gas central heating **to** electric.*

> ### ✍ Word partners for change
>
> bring about/implement/make/undergo
> change • change occurs/takes place • a big/
> dramatic/fundamental/major/radical/sweep-
> ing change • change in/to sth

change[2] /tʃeɪndʒ/ **noun 1 DIFFERENCE** ▷ [C, U]
A2 a situation in which something becomes
different, or the result of something becoming
different: *We need to **make** a few **changes** to the
design.* ∘ *There is no **change in** the patient's
condition* (= the illness has not got better or worse).
∘ *How can we **bring about** social **change**?*
2 FROM ONE THING TO ANOTHER ▷ [C, U] **A2** a
situation in which you stop having or using one
thing and start having or using another: *This
country needs a **change of** government.* ∘ *I've
notified the school of our **change of address**.*
3 NEW EXPERIENCE ▷ [C] **B1** something that you
enjoy because it is a new experience: [usually
singular] *Going abroad for our anniversary would
make a lovely **change**.* ∘ *It's nice to eat together
as a family **for a change**.* **4 MONEY** ▷ [U] **A2** the
money that you get back when you pay more for
something than it costs: *There's your receipt and
£3 change.* **5 COINS** ▷ [U] **A2** coins, not paper
money: *Do you have any **change** for the parking
meter?* ∘ *Have you got change for £5* (= can you
give me £5 in coins in return for paper money)?
6 a change of clothes **A2** a set of clean clothes
that you can put on if you need to take off the
ones you are wearing

IDIOM **a change of heart** If you have a change of
heart, you change your opinion or feelings
about something.

→ See also **small change**

changeable /ˈtʃeɪndʒəbl/ **adj** often changing,
or likely to change

changeover /ˈtʃeɪndʒˌəʊvəʳ/ **noun** [C] a change
from one system or situation to another: [usually
singular] *the **changeover from** the old computer
system to the new one*

ˈchanging ˌroom noun [C] UK a room in a shop
where you can try clothes, or a room where you
change into clothes to do sport

channel[1] /ˈtʃænˀl/ **noun** [C] **1 TELEVISION** ▷ **A2** a
television or radio station (= broadcasting
company) **2 PASSAGE** ▷ a long, narrow
passage for water or other liquids to flow
along: *an irrigation channel* **3 COMMUNI-
CATION** ▷ a way of communicating with people
or getting something done: *a **channel of
communication*** **4 the Channel** (also **the
ˌEnglish ˈChannel**) the narrow area of water
between England and France **5 RIVER** ▷ a part
of a river or sea that is deep and wide enough
for ships to travel along: *a navigable channel*

channel[2] /ˈtʃænˀl/ **verb** [T] (mainly UK **channel-
ling**, **channelled**, US **channeling**, **channeled**)
1 to direct water along a particular route: *The
waste water is channelled through this pipe.* **2** to
use money or energy for a particular purpose:
*We've **channelled** all our resources **into** this
project.*

the ˌChannel ˈTunnel noun the three long
passages under the English Channel between
England and France

chant[1] /tʃɑːnt/ **verb** [I, T] **1** to repeat or sing a
word or phrase many times, often shouting: *The
demonstrators **chanted** anti-racist **slogans**.* **2** to
sing a religious song or phrase using a very
simple tune

chant[2] /tʃɑːnt/ **noun** [C] **1** a word or phrase that
is repeated many times **2** a religious song or
prayer that is sung using a very simple tune

Chanukah /ˈhɑːnəkə/ **noun** [C, U] Hanukkah

chaos /ˈkeɪɒs/ **noun** [U] **B2** a situation where
there is no order at all and everyone is confused:
*The country's at war and everything is **in chaos**.*

> ### ✍ Word partners for chaos
>
> cause chaos • descend into/be thrown into
> chaos • be in chaos • total/utter chaos

chaotic /keɪˈɒtɪk/ **adj** in a state of chaos: *a
chaotic situation*

chap /tʃæp/ **noun** [C] UK informal a man

chapel /ˈtʃæpˀl/ **noun** [C] a small church, or a
room used as a church in a building

chaperone[1] (also **chaperon**) /ˈʃæp^ərəʊn/ **noun**
[C] an older person who goes somewhere with a
younger person in order to make sure they
behave well, especially a woman in the past who
went with a younger woman who was not
married

chaperone[2] (also **chaperon**) /ˈʃæp^ərəʊn/ **verb**
[T] to go somewhere with someone as their
chaperone

chaplain /'tʃæplɪn/ **noun** [C] a priest in the army, a school, a hospital, or a prison

chapter /'tʃæptər/ **noun** [C] **1 🔵** one of the parts that a book is divided into **2** a period of time when something happens in history or in someone's life: *an interesting **chapter** in Spanish history*

character /'kærəktər/ **noun 1 QUALITIES** ▷ [C, U] **🔵** the combination of qualities and personality that makes one person or thing different from others: *It's **not in her character** to be jealous* (= *she would not usually be jealous*). ∘ *It would be very **out of character** (= not typical) of her to lie.* ∘ *The character of the village has changed since the road was built.* **2 STORY** ▷ [C] **🔵** a person in a book, film, etc: *a cartoon character* **3 GOOD QUALITIES** ▷ [U] **🔵** qualities that are interesting or unusual: *a hotel of character* **4 PERSON** ▷ [C] informal a particular kind of person: *an unpleasant character* **5 INTERESTING PERSON** ▷ [C] an interesting or funny person whose behaviour is different from most people's: *Your granny's a **real character**.* **6 WRITING** ▷ [C] a letter, sign, or number that you use when you are writing or printing: *Chinese characters*

> 🖉 Word partners for **character**
>
> a colourful/lovable/shady/strong/unsavoury character ∘ a real character

characteristic¹ /ˌkærəktə'rɪstɪk/ **noun** [C] **🔵** a typical or obvious quality that makes one person or thing different from others: *a national characteristic* ∘ *Does he have any distinguishing physical characteristics?*

characteristic² /ˌkærəktə'rɪstɪk/ **adj** typical of someone or something: *Grey stone is **characteristic of** buildings in that area.* → Opposite **uncharacteristic** • **characteristically** adv

characterization (also UK **-isation**) /ˌkærəktəraɪ-'zeɪʃᵊn/ **noun** [U] the way that people are described in a play, book, etc

characterize (also UK **-ise**) /'kærəktəraɪz/ **verb** [T] **1** to be typical of someone or something: [often passive] *Her behaviour in class has been characterized by rudeness and laziness.* **2** to describe or show someone or something in a particular way: *Historians have **characterized** the age **as** a period of great change.*

charade /ʃə'rɑːd/ ⓤ /ʃə'reɪd/ **noun** [C] a situation that is clearly false, but where people behave as if it is true or serious: *The interview was just a charade.*

charcoal /'tʃɑːkəʊl/ **noun** [U] a hard, black substance that is produced by burning wood without much air, and that is used as fuel or for drawing

charge¹ /tʃɑːdʒ/ **noun 1 MONEY** ▷ [C, U] **🔵** the amount of money that you have to pay for something, especially for an activity or a service: *bank charges* ∘ *There's no **charge for** children under 14.* ∘ *He repaired the computer **free of charge** (= it did not cost anything).* **2 be in charge** **🔵** to be the person who has control of or is responsible for someone or something: *She's **in charge of** a team of 20 people.* ∘ *Who's in*

charge of organizing the music for the party **3 take charge** **🔵** to take control of or make yourself responsible for something: *I was happ* to let her take charge of paying all the bills **4 CRIME** ▷ [C] **🔵** a formal police statemen saying that someone is accused of a crime: *t* **bring/press charges** ∘ *She was **arrested o** **charges of** theft and forgery.* **5 ACCUSE** ▷ [C] statement that accuses someone of something *This is a **serious charge** to make against you colleagues.* **6 ELECTRICITY** ▷ [C, U] the amount o electricity that an electrical device has in it o that a substance has in it **7 ATTACK** ▷ [C] a attack in which people or animals run forwar suddenly **8 reverse the charges** UK (US **ca** **collect**) to make a telephone call that is paid fo by the person who receives it → See also **service charge**

> 🖉 Word partners for **charge**
>
> make a charge • at no extra/free of/without charge • a charge for sth • a charge of [£10/ $12, etc] • a small charge

charge² /tʃɑːdʒ/ **verb 1 ASK TO PAY** ▷ [I, T] **🔵** t ask someone to pay an amount of money fo something, especially for an activity or a service [+ two objects] *They are going to charge motorist a tax to drive into the city centre.* ∘ *How muc do you **charge for** delivery?* **2 ACCUSE** ▷ [T] **🔵** If the police charge someone, they accus them officially of a crime: [often passive] *H was **charged with** assault.* **3 ATTACK** ▷ [I, T **🔵** to attack someone or something b moving forward quickly: *The bull looked as i it was about to charge.* **4 charge around/into through, etc** to run from one place to anothe *The children charged around the house* **5 ELECTRICITY** ▷ [I, T] **🔵** to put electricity int something

charge card **noun** [C] a small plastic card tha allows you to buy something and pay for it at particular date in the future

charged /tʃɑːdʒd/ **adj** A situation or a subjec that is charged causes strong feelings or argu ments: *a **highly charged** debate*

charger /'tʃɑːdʒər/ **noun** a piece of equipmen used for putting electricity in a battery: *a phon charger*

chariot /'tʃæriət/ **noun** [C] a vehicle with tw wheels that was used in races and fights i ancient times and was pulled by a horse

charisma /kə'rɪzmə/ **noun** [U] a natural powe that some people have to influence or attrac people • **charismatic** /ˌkærɪz'mætɪk/ **adj**

charitable /'tʃærɪtəbl/ **adj 1** [always before noun A charitable event, activity, or organization gives money, food, or help to people who nee it. **2** kind, and not judging other people in severe way • **charitably** adv

charity /'tʃærɪti/ **noun 1 ORGANIZATION** ▷ [C, U **🔵** an official organization that gives money food, or help to people who need it: *The raff will raise money **for charity**.* ∘ *A percentage o the company's profits **go to charity**.* **2 MONEY HELP** ▷ [U] **🔵** money, food, or other help that i given to people: *I won't **accept charity***

3 KINDNESS ▷ [U] kindness towards other people: *an act of charity*

> 🗹 **Word partners for charity**
>
> **donate/give** sth **to** charity • [money, etc] **goes to** charity • **do** sth **for** charity • a charity **for** [homeless people/sick children, etc] • a charity **event** (= an event to raise money for a charity)

charity shop noun [C] UK (US **thrift shop**) a shop that sells goods given by the public, especially clothes, to make money for a particular charity

charlatan /ˈʃɑːlətən/ noun [C] someone who pretends to have skills or knowledge that they do not have

charm¹ /tʃɑːm/ noun **1** [C, U] 🅱2 a quality that makes you like someone or something: *The building had a certain charm.* **2** [C] an object that you keep or wear because you believe that it is lucky: *a lucky charm*

charm² /tʃɑːm/ verb [T] to attract someone or persuade someone to do something because of your charm: [often passive] *We were charmed by his boyish manner.*

charmed /tʃɑːmd/ adj very lucky, or managing to avoid danger: *The young boy had led a charmed life.*

charmer /ˈtʃɑːmər/ noun [C] informal someone who knows how to be charming in order to attract people or persuade them to do things

charming /ˈtʃɑːmɪŋ/ adj 🅱1 pleasant or attractive: *a charming smile/place* • **charmingly** adv

charred /tʃɑːd/ adj black from having been burned: *charred wreckage*

chart¹ /tʃɑːt/ noun **1** [C] 🅱2 a drawing that shows information in a simple way, often using lines and curves to show amounts: *a sales chart* **2 the charts** 🅱2 an official list of the most popular songs each week **3** [C] a map of the sea or the sky

chart² /tʃɑːt/ verb [T] **1** to watch and record information about something over a period of time: *The documentary charted the progress of the war.* **2** to make a map of an area of land, sea, or sky

charter¹ /ˈtʃɑːtər/ noun [C] a formal, written description of the principles, activities, and purpose of an organization

charter² /ˈtʃɑːtər/ verb [T] to rent a vehicle, especially an aircraft: *The travel company chartered a plane to fly us all home.*

charter³ /ˈtʃɑːtər/ adj a **charter flight/company/plane, etc** using aircraft paid for by travel companies for their customers

chartered /ˈtʃɑːtəd/ adj [always before noun] UK having the necessary qualifications to work in a particular profession: *a chartered accountant/surveyor*

chase¹ /tʃeɪs/ verb **1** [I, T] 🅱2 to run after someone or something in order to catch them: *The dog was chasing a rabbit.* **2 chase sb/sth away/off/out, etc** to run after a person or animal to make them leave a place: *I chased the cat away.* **3** [T] UK to try very hard to get

chase

something: *There are hundreds of graduates chasing very few jobs.*

chase² /tʃeɪs/ noun **1** [C] an occasion when you go after someone or something quickly in order to catch them: *a high speed car chase* **2 give chase** to go after someone or something quickly in order to catch them

chasm /ˈkæzəm/ noun [C] **1** a long, deep, narrow hole in rock or ice **2** a very large difference between two opinions or two groups of people

chassis /ˈʃæsi/ noun [C] (plural **chassis** /ˈʃæsiz/) the structure of a vehicle that the outer metal is fixed on to

chaste /tʃeɪst/ adj not having had sex, or without sexual thoughts or intentions: *a chaste relationship*

chasten /ˈtʃeɪsən/ verb [T] formal to make someone feel ashamed by making them understand that they have failed or done something wrong: [often passive] *The team were chastened by their defeat.* • **chastening** adj

chastise /tʃæsˈtaɪz/ verb [T] formal to criticize or punish someone

chastity /ˈtʃæstəti/ noun [U] the quality of not having sex

chat¹ /tʃæt/ verb [I] (**chatting**, **chatted**) **1** 🅰2 to talk with someone in a friendly and informal way: *I wanted to chat to you about the party on Saturday.* **2** to have a conversation with other people on the Internet, when you write down what you want to say, and can see immediately what other people are writing

PHRASAL VERB **chat sb up** UK informal to talk to someone in a way that shows them that you are sexually attracted to them

chat² /tʃæt/ noun [C, U] 🅰2 a friendly, informal conversation

> 🗹 **Word partners for chat**
>
> **have** a chat • a chat **about** sth • a **good/little/long/quick** chat • a chat **with** sb

chateau /ˈʃætəʊ/ ⑤ /ʃæˈtəʊ/ noun [C] (plural **chateaux**) a large house or castle in France

chat room noun [C] a place on the Internet where you can have discussions with other people

chat show noun [C] UK (US **talk show**) 🅱1 a

television or radio programme where people are asked questions about themselves

chatter /ˈtʃætər/ **verb** [I] **1** to talk for a long time about things that are not important **2** If your teeth chatter, they knock together because you are cold or frightened. • **chatter noun** [U]

chatty /ˈtʃæti/ **adj 1** liking to talk **2** A piece of writing that is chatty has a friendly and informal style: *a chatty letter/style*

chauffeur /ˈʃəʊfər/ ⓤⓢ /ʃəʊˈfɜːr/ **noun** [C] someone whose job is to drive a car for someone else • **chauffeur verb** [T]

chauvinist /ˈʃəʊvənɪst/ **noun** [C] **1** (also **male chauvinist**) a man who believes that men are better or more important than women **2 COUNTRY/RACE** ▷ someone who believes that their country or race is better or more important than other countries or races • **chauvinism noun** [U] the beliefs and behaviour of chauvinists

chav /tʃæv/ **noun** [C] UK informal a young person who dresses in cheap clothes and jewellery that are intended to look expensive, and who does not look clever

cheap¹ /tʃiːp/ **adj 1 NOT EXPENSIVE** ▷ ⓐ1 not expensive, or costing less than usual: *I got a cheap flight to Spain at the last minute.* ∘ *It will be a lot cheaper to go by bus.* **2 PAY LESS** ▷ ⓐ1 where you have to pay less than usual or less than you expect: *Are there any cheap restaurants around here?* **3 LOW QUALITY** ▷ low in price and quality: *cheap perfume* **4 PERSON** ▷ US not willing to spend money

---

➕ Other ways of saying **cheap**

If something is cheap enough for most people to be able to buy, you can say that it is **affordable**, **inexpensive**, or **reasonable**:

*There's very little **affordable** housing around here.*

*They sell **inexpensive** children's clothes.*

*I thought the food was very **reasonable**.*

The adjective **cut-price** is sometimes used to describe something that is cheaper than usual:

*We managed to get **cut-price** tickets the day before the show.*

A piece of equipment that is cheap to use is often described as **economical**:

*I need a car that's reliable and **economical**.*

---

cheap² /tʃiːp/ **adv** informal **1** for a low price: *You'll get the table cheap if you buy the chairs too.* **2 be going cheap** UK to be offered for sale for less money than is usual **3 not come cheap** to be expensive: *Good carpets don't come cheap.*

cheaply /ˈtʃiːpli/ **adv** for a low price: *You can buy some goods more cheaply in America.*

cheat¹ /tʃiːt/ **verb** [I, T] ⓑ2 to behave in a way that is not honest or fair in order to win something or to get something: *She was caught* UK *cheating in* her French exam/US *cheating on* her French exam. ∘ *He cheats at cards.*

PHRASAL VERBS cheat on sb ⓑ2 to have a secret sexual relationship with someone who is not

your usual sexual partner • **cheat sb out of sth** to get something that belongs to someone else by deceiving them

cheat² /tʃiːt/ **noun** [C] **1** someone who cheats **2** special instructions or information that someone can use to help them play a computer game more effectively

check¹ /tʃek/ **verb 1 EXAMINE** ▷ [I, T] ⓐ2 to examine something in order to make sure that it is correct or the way it should be: [+ (that)] *I went to check that I'd locked the door.* ∘ *Have you checked your facts?* ∘ *I knelt down beside the body and checked for a pulse.* **2 FIND OUT** ▷ [I, T] ⓑ1 to find out about something: [+ question word] *I'll check whether Peter knows about the party.* **3 ASK** ▷ [I] ⓑ2 to ask someone for permission to do something: *I'd like to stay overnight, but I need to check with my parents.* **4 STOP** ▷ [T] to stop something bad from increasing or continuing: *The government needs to find a way to check rising inflation.* **5 MARK** ▷ [T] US (UK **tick**) to put a mark by an answer to show that it is correct, or by an item on a list to show that you have dealt with it **6 LEAVE** ▷ [T] US to leave your coat, bags, or other possessions temporarily in someone's care → See also **double-check**

PHRASAL VERBS check in 1 ⓑ1 to go to the desk at an airport in order to say that you have arrived and to get the number of your seat: *We have to check in three hours before the flight leaves.* **2** ⓑ1 to go to the desk at a hotel in order to say that you have arrived, and to get the key to your room • **check sth off** US (UK **tick sth off**) to put a mark next to a name or an item on a list to show that it is correct, or that it has been dealt with • **check (up) on sb/sth** to try to discover how something is progressing or whether someone is doing what they should be doing: *My boss is always checking up on me.* • **check out** ⓑ1 to leave a hotel after paying your bill • **check sth out 1 INFORMATION** ▷ informal to examine something or get more information about it in order to be certain that it is true, safe, or suitable: *We'll need to check out his story.* **2 GO TO SEE** ▷ informal to go to a place in order to see what it is like: *Let's check out that new dance club.* **3 BOOKS** ▷ mainly US to borrow books from a library

check² /tʃek/ **noun 1 EXAMINATION** ▷ [C] ⓑ1 an examination of something in order to make sure that it is correct or the way it should be: *We do safety checks on all our equipment.* **2 BANK** ▷ [C] US spelling of cheque (= a piece of paper printed by a bank that you use to pay for things) **3 RESTAURANT** ▷ [C] US (UK **bill**) a list that you are given in a restaurant showing how much your meal costs **4 MARK** ▷ [C] US (UK **tick**) a mark (✓) that shows that an answer is correct, or that you have dealt with something on a list **5 PATTERN** ▷ [C, U] a pattern of squares of different colours **6 hold/keep sth in check** to control something that could increase too quickly or become too large or powerful: *We need to keep our spending in check.* → See also **rain check**

---

checkbook /'tʃekbʊk/ **noun** [C] US spelling of
chequebook (= a book of papers printed by a
bank that you use to pay for things)

checked /tʃekt/ **adj** with a pattern of squares of
different colours: *a checked shirt/tablecloth*

checkers /'tʃekəz/ **noun** [U] US (UK **draughts**) a
game that two people play by moving flat,
round objects around on a board of black and
white squares

check in

check-in /'tʃekɪn/ **noun** [C] ⑤ the place at an
airport where you go to say that you have
arrived for your flight, or the act of going to the
check-in to say that you have arrived for your
flight: *a check-in counter/desk*

checking account **noun** [C] US (UK **current
account**) a bank account that you can take
money out of at any time

checklist /'tʃeklɪst/ **noun** [C] a list of things that
you should think about, or that you must do

checkmate /'tʃekmeɪt/ **noun** [U] the final position in the game of chess when your king
cannot escape and you have lost the game

checkout /'tʃekaʊt/ **noun** [C] **1** ⑥ (also US
'checkout ˌcounter) the place in a large shop,
especially a food shop, where you pay for your
goods: *a supermarket checkout* **2** ⑥ the place on
an Internet website where you order and pay for
things

checkpoint /'tʃekpɔɪnt/ **noun** [C] a place where
people and vehicles are stopped and examined:
a military/police checkpoint

check-up /'tʃekʌp/ **noun** [C] a general medical
examination to see if you are healthy: *I'm going
to the doctor for a check-up.*

cheddar /'tʃedər/ **noun** [U] a type of hard, yellow
cheese

cheek /tʃiːk/ **noun 1** [C] ⑥ the soft part of your
face below your eye: *Tears ran down his cheeks.* →
See colour picture **The Body** on page Centre 13 **2** [U,
no plural] mainly UK rude behaviour that shows

that you do not respect someone: [+ to do sth]
She had the cheek to ask me to pay for her!

cheekbone /'tʃiːkbəʊn/ **noun** [C] one of the two
bones below your eyes

cheeky /'tʃiːki/ **adj** UK ⑥ slightly rude or
behaving without respect, but often in a funny
way: *a cheeky grin* • **cheekily adv**

cheer¹ /tʃɪər/ **verb** ⑥ [I, T] to shout loudly in
order to show your approval or to encourage
someone: *The crowd stood up and cheered at the
end of the concert.* **2 be cheered by sth** to feel
happier or encouraged because of something

PHRASAL VERBS **cheer sb on** to shout loudly in
order to encourage someone in a competition
• **cheer (sb) up** ⑥ to stop feeling sad, or to
make someone feel happier: *Cheer up. It's not the
end of the world.* • **cheer sth up** to make a place
look brighter or more attractive

cheer² /tʃɪər/ **noun** [C] a shout of approval or
encouragement

cheerful /'tʃɪəfəl/ **adj 1** ⑥ happy: *I'm not feeling
very cheerful today.* **2** ⑥ bright and pleasant to
look at: *a bright and cheerful room* • **cheerfully
adv** • **cheerfulness noun** [U]

cheering¹ /'tʃɪərɪŋ/ **noun** [U] shouts of encouragement and approval

cheering² /'tʃɪərɪŋ/ **adj** Something cheering
encourages you and makes you feel happier:
We received some cheering news.

cheerleader /'tʃɪəˌliːdər/ **noun** [C] a girl, especially in the United States, who leads the crowd
in shouting encouragement to a team who are
playing a sport

cheers /tʃɪəz/ **exclamation 1 DRINK** ▷ ⑥ something friendly that you say before you start to
drink alcohol with someone **2 THANK YOU** ▷ UK
informal ⑥ thank you

cheery /'tʃɪəri/ **adj** bright and happy: *a cheery
wave/smile* • **cheerily adv**

cheese /tʃiːz/ **noun** [C, U] ⑥ a food that is made
from milk, is usually white or yellow, and can be
either hard or soft: *a cheese sandwich* → See
colour picture **Food** on page Centre 11

IDIOM **Say cheese!** something that you say to
make someone smile when you are taking their
photograph

→ See also be like **chalk¹** and cheese, **cottage
cheese**, **cream cheese**

cheeseburger /'tʃiːzˌbɜːgər/ **noun** [C] a hamburger (= meat cooked in a round, flat shape)
eaten between round pieces of bread with a slice
of cheese

cheesecake /'tʃiːzkeɪk/ **noun** [C, U] a sweet cake
made with soft, white cheese on a biscuit base

cheesy /'tʃiːzi/ **adj** informal **1** not fashionable and
of low quality: *cheesy music* **2 a cheesy grin** a
wide smile that is not always sincere

cheetah /'tʃiːtə/ **noun** [C] a large, wild cat that
has black spots and can run very fast

chef /ʃef/ **noun** [C] ⑥ someone who is the main
cook (= person who cooks) in a hotel or a
restaurant

chemical¹ /'kemɪkəl/ **adj** ⑥ relating to chemistry or chemicals: *a chemical reaction* ∘ *chemical weapons* • **chemically** adv

chemical² /ˈkemɪkᵊl/ noun [C] **B2** a basic substance that is used in chemistry or produced by chemistry

chemist /ˈkemɪst/ noun [C] **1** UK (US **pharmacist**) **A2** someone whose job is to prepare and sell drugs in a shop **2** **B1** a scientist who does work involving chemistry

chemistry /ˈkemɪstri/ noun [U] **A2** the scientific study of substances and how they change when they combine

chemist's /ˈkemɪsts/ noun [C] UK (US **drugstore**) **A2** a shop where you can buy drugs, soap, beauty products, etc

chemotherapy /ˌkiːməʊˈθerəpi/ noun [U] (also **chemo**) the treatment of a disease using chemicals: *Chemotherapy is often used to treat cancer.*

cheque UK (US **check**) /tʃek/ noun [C] **A2** a piece of paper printed by a bank that you use to pay for things: *a cheque for £1500* ∘ *Are you paying by cheque?* → See also **blank cheque, traveller's cheque**

┌─────────────────────────────────────┐
│ 🔲 Word partners for **cheque** │
│ │
│ pay by cheque • a cheque **bounces** • **write** a │
│ cheque • a cheque **for** [£50/£200, etc] │
└─────────────────────────────────────┘

chequebook UK (US **checkbook**) /ˈtʃekbʊk/ noun [C] a book of cheques

cheque card noun [C] a small plastic card from your bank that you show when you write a cheque

cherish /ˈtʃerɪʃ/ verb [T] **1** to love someone or something very much and take care of them **2** If you cherish an idea, hope, memory, etc, it is very important to you.

cherry /ˈtʃeri/ noun [C] **B2** a small, round red or black fruit with a large seed inside

cherub /ˈtʃerəb/ noun [C] a small child with a beautiful, round face and wings who appears in religious paintings

chess /tʃes/ noun [U] **A2** a game that two people play by moving differently shaped pieces around a board of black and white squares: *a chess set*

chest /tʃest/ noun [C] **1** **B2** the front of your body between your neck and your waist: *a hairy chest* ∘ *chest pains* → See colour picture **The Body** on page Centre 13 **2** a strong, usually wooden, container with a lid, used for keeping things in: *a treasure chest*

IDIOM **get sth off your chest** informal to tell someone about something that you have been worried or angry about for a long time

chestnut /ˈtʃesnʌt/ noun **1** [C] a nut that has a shiny, red-brown surface and is white inside, or the tree that produces these nuts: *roasted chestnuts* **2** [C, U] a dark red-brown colour → See also **horse chestnut**

chest of drawers noun [C] (also US **bureau**) **B1** a piece of furniture with drawers for keeping clothes in

chew /tʃuː/ verb [I, T] **1** **B2** to crush food between your teeth before you swallow it **2** **B2** to repeatedly bite something without swallowing it: *to chew gum*

PHRASAL VERB **chew sth over** to think carefully about something, or to discuss it

chewing gum noun [U] **B1** a sweet substance that you chew but do not swallow

chewy /ˈtʃuːi/ adj Chewy food needs to be chewed a lot before you can swallow it.

chic /ʃiːk/ adj fashionable and attractive: *a chic restaurant*

chick /tʃɪk/ noun [C] a baby bird, especially a baby chicken

chicken¹ /ˈtʃɪkɪn/ noun **1** [C] **A2** a bird kept on a farm for its meat and eggs **2** [U] **A2** the meat of a chicken: *a chicken sandwich*

chicken² /ˈtʃɪkɪn/ verb

PHRASAL VERB **chicken out** informal to decide not to do something because you are too nervous

chicken pox noun [U] a children's disease that causes a fever and red spots on the skin

chick flick noun [C] humorous a film about romantic relationships or other subjects that interest women

chick lit noun [U] humorous books about romantic relationships or other subjects that interest women

chief¹ /tʃiːf/ adj [always before noun] **1** **B2** most important: *The wonderful weather was our chief reason for coming here.* **2** **B2** highest in rank: *chief economic adviser to the government*

chief² /tʃiːf/ noun [C] **1** **B2** the leader of a group of people: *tribal chiefs* **2** **B2** a person who controls other people in an organization: *police chiefs*

chief executive noun [C] (also **chief executive officer**) the person with the most important job in a company

chiefly /ˈtʃiːfli/ adv mainly: *magazines intended chiefly for teenagers*

chieftain /ˈtʃiːftᵊn/ noun [C] the leader of a tribe (= group of people with the same language and customs)

chiffon /ˈʃɪfɒn/ US /ʃɪˈfɑːn/ noun [U] a soft, thin cloth used for making women's clothes

child /tʃaɪld/ noun [C] (plural **children**) **1** **A1** a young person who is not yet an adult: *an eight-year-old child* ∘ *How many children are there in your class?* **2** **A1** someone's son or daughter, also when they are adults: *Both our children have grown up and moved away.* → See also **only child**

child abuse noun [U] cruel or violent treatment of children by adults

child benefit noun [U] money that the British government pays every week to families with children

childbirth /ˈtʃaɪldbɜːθ/ noun [U] the process during which a baby is born: *His mother died in childbirth.*

childcare /ˈtʃaɪldkeər/ noun [U] the work of looking after children while their parents are working

childhood /ˈtʃaɪldhʊd/ **noun** [C, U] 🅱❶ the part of your life when you are a child

> ### 🔲 Word partners for **childhood**
>
> **spend** your childhood swh/doing sth • **early** childhood • **in** (sb's) childhood • a **happy/lonely/unhappy** childhood • a childhood **friend/sb's** childhood **sweetheart** • childhood **memories**

childish /ˈtʃaɪldɪʃ/ **adj 1** 🅱 Childish behaviour is silly, like that of a small child: *Don't be so childish!* **2** 🅱 typical of a child: *childish handwriting* • **childishly** adv • **childishness** noun [U]

childless /ˈtʃaɪldləs/ **adj** A childless person has no children.

childlike /ˈtʃaɪldlaɪk/ **adj** Childlike people are like children in some ways, such as trusting people or behaving in a natural way.

childminder /ˈtʃaɪldˌmaɪndər/ **noun** [C] UK someone whose job is to look after children while their parents are working

children /ˈtʃɪldrən/ plural of child

child support noun [U] money that someone gives the mother or father of their children when they do not live with them

chili /ˈtʃɪli/ **noun** US spelling of chilli

chill¹ /tʃɪl/ **verb** [I, T] to become cold, or to make someone or something become cold: *Chill the wine before serving.*

PHRASAL VERB **chill out** informal to relax completely, or not allow things to upset you: *Chill out, Dad – if we miss this train there's always another one.*

chill² /tʃɪl/ **noun 1 COLD** ▷ [no plural] a cold feeling: *There is a definite chill in the air.* **2 FEAR** ▷ [C] a sudden frightened feeling: *The scream **sent a chill down my spine**.* **3 ILLNESS** ▷ [C] UK a cold (= common illness that makes you sneeze) that is not very bad

chilli (plural **chillies**) UK (US **chili**) /ˈtʃɪli/ **noun 1** [C, U] 🅰 a small, thin, red or green vegetable that tastes very hot: *chilli powder* **2** [U] a spicy dish of beans, meat, and chillies

chilling /ˈtʃɪlɪŋ/ **adj** very frightening: *a chilling tale*

chilly /ˈtʃɪli/ **adj 1** unpleasantly cold: *a chilly evening* **2** unfriendly: *He gave me a chilly look.*

chime /tʃaɪm/ **verb** [I, T] If a bell or clock chimes, it rings. • **chime noun** [C]

PHRASAL VERB **chime in** to suddenly say something in order to add your opinion to a conversation: *"Quite right too!" Tony chimed in.*

chimney /ˈtʃɪmni/ **noun** [C] 🅱 a wide pipe that allows smoke from a fire to go out through the roof

chimney sweep noun [C] someone whose job is to clean

chimney

inside a chimney, using long brushes

chimpanzee /ˌtʃɪmpənˈziː/ **noun** [C] (informal **chimp** /tʃɪmp/) an African animal like a large monkey

chin /tʃɪn/ **noun** [C] 🅱 the bottom part of your face, below your mouth → See colour picture **The Body** on page Centre 13

china /ˈtʃaɪnə/ **noun** [U] **1** the hard substance that plates, cups, bowls, etc are made from: *a china teapot* **2** cups, plates, bowls, etc that are made from china

chink /tʃɪŋk/ **noun** [C] **1** a small, narrow opening in something **2** a short ringing sound that is made when glass or metal objects touch each other

chip¹ /tʃɪp/ **noun** [C] **1 POTATO** ▷ UK (US **French fry**) 🅰 a long, thin piece of potato that is cooked in oil: [usually plural] *fish and chips* → See colour picture **Food** on page Centre 11 **2 IN BAG** ▷ US (UK **crisp**) a very thin, dry, fried slice of potato: [usually plural] *barbecue-flavoured potato chips* → See colour picture **Food** on page Centre 11 **3 COMPUTER** ▷ 🅱 a microchip (= very small part of a computer that stores information) **4 SMALL PIECE** ▷ a small piece that has broken off something: *wood chips* **5 HOLE** ▷ a place where a small piece has broken off something: *This cup has a chip in it.*

IDIOMS **be a chip off the old block** informal to be very similar to your mother or father • **have a chip on your shoulder** informal to blame other people for something bad that has happened to you and continue to feel angry about it: *She's always had a real chip on her shoulder because she didn't go to university.*

chip² /tʃɪp/ **verb** [T] (**chipping, chipped**) to break a small piece off something: *He may have chipped a bone in his wrist.* ○ *a chipped plate*

PHRASAL VERBS **chip in** informal to interrupt a conversation in order to say something: *I'll start and you can all **chip in with** your comments.* • **chip in (sth)** If several people chip in, they each give money to buy something together: *We all chipped in to buy our teacher a present.*

chip and ˈPIN noun [U] a way to pay for goods and services using a bank card (= a small plastic card that allows you to buy things) and a secret number

chipmunk /ˈtʃɪpmʌŋk/ **noun** [C] a small North American animal with fur and dark strips along its back

chiropodist /kɪˈrɒpədɪst/ **noun** [C] UK (US **podiatrist**) someone whose job is to treat problems with people's feet

chirp /tʃɜːp/ **verb** [I] If birds or insects chirp, they make short, high sounds. • **chirp noun** [C]

chirpy /ˈtʃɜːpi/ **adj** UK informal happy and active: *Why's Ben so chirpy this morning?*

chisel /ˈtʃɪzəl/ **noun** [C] a tool with a sharp end that you use for cutting and shaping wood or stone → See picture at **tool**

chivalrous /ˈʃɪvəlrəs/ **adj** A chivalrous man behaves very politely towards women. • **chivalry noun** [U] polite behaviour towards women

C

chives /tʃaɪvz/ **noun** [plural] a plant with long, thin leaves used in cooking to give a flavour similar to onions

chlorine /ˈklɔːriːn/ **noun** [U] a gas with a strong smell, used to make water safe to drink and swim in

chocolate /ˈtʃɒkələt/ **noun 1 SUBSTANCE** ▷ [U] ④ a sweet, brown food that is usually sold in a block: *a bar of chocolate* ∘ *milk chocolate* ∘ *a chocolate cake* **2 SWEET** ▷ [C] ④ a small piece of sweet food covered in chocolate: *a box of chocolates* **3 DRINK** ▷ [C, U] ④ a sweet drink made with chocolate and hot milk

---
2 Word partners for **choice**

have/make a choice • give/offer sb a choice • a good/informed/obvious/popular/stark/wide/wrong choice • a choice between sth • by choice • have (no) choice
---

choice¹ /tʃɔɪs/ **noun 1 RIGHT** ▷ [U, no plural] ④ a situation in which you can choose between two or more things: *If I had a choice, I'd give up work.* ∘ *He had no choice but to accept their offer.* ∘ *I'm single by choice* (= because I want to be). **2 DECISION** ▷ [C] ④ the decision to choose one thing or person and not someone or something else: *In the past women had to make a choice between a career or marriage.* **3 THINGS TO CHOOSE FROM** ▷ [U, no plural] ④ the things or people you can choose from: *The dress is available in a choice of colours.* ∘ *The evening menu offers a wide choice of dishes.* **4 CHOSEN ONE** ▷ [C] ④ the person or thing that someone has chosen: [usually singular] *Harvard was not his first choice.* ∘ *The winner got 1000 euros to give to the charity of her choice.* → See also **multiple choice**

choice² /tʃɔɪs/ **adj** [always before noun] of very good quality: *the choicest cuts of meat*

choir /kwaɪəʳ/ **noun** [group] ④ a group of people who sing together: *a school/church choir*

choke¹ /tʃəʊk/ **verb 1** [I, T] If you choke, or if something chokes you, you stop breathing because something is blocking your throat: *Children can choke on peanuts.* **2** [T] (also **choke up**) to fill something such as a road or pipe so that nothing can pass through: [often passive] *The roads were choked with traffic.*

PHRASAL VERBS **choke sth back** to try not to show how angry or upset you are: *She ran to the door, choking back the tears.* • **choke (sb) up** to become unable to speak because you are starting to cry: *I can't watch that movie without choking up.*

choke² /tʃəʊk/ **noun** [C] a piece of equipment that controls the amount of air going into a car engine

cholera /ˈkɒlərə/ **noun** [U] a serious disease that affects the stomach and bowels, usually caused by dirty water or food

cholesterol /kəˈlestərɒl/ **noun** [U] a type of fat in your body that can cause heart disease if you have too much

choose /tʃuːz/ **verb** (**chose, chosen**) **1** ④ [I, T] to decide which thing you want: *I helped my sister*

choose a name for her baby. ∘ *They have to **choose between** earning a living or getting an education.* ∘ *There were lots of books to **choose from**.* ∘ [+ question word] *How did you choose which school to go to?* ∘ *Adam was **chosen as** team captain.* **2 choose to do sth** ④ to decide to do something: *Manuela chose to take a job in Paris.*

➕ Other ways of saying **choose**

The verbs **pick** and **select** are often used when someone chooses someone or something after thinking carefully:
*He's been **picked** for the school football team.*
*We've **selected** three candidates.*
In more informal situations, the phrasal verbs **go for**, **opt for**, or **decide on** are sometimes used:
*I've **decided on** blue walls for the bathroom.*
*I think I'll **go for** the chocolate cake.*
*Mike's **opted for** early retirement.*
The verbs **opt** and **decide** can also be used when someone chooses to do something:
*Most people **opt** to have the operation.*
*I've **decided** to take the job.*
---

choosy /ˈtʃuːzi/ **adj** difficult to please because of being very exact about what you like: *a choosy customer*

chop

chop¹ /tʃɒp/ **verb** [T] (**chopping, chopped**) (also **chop up**) ④ to cut something into small pieces: *Chop an onion finely.*

IDIOM **chop and change** UK informal to keep changing your opinions, activities, or job

PHRASAL VERBS **chop sth down** to cut through something to make it fall down • **chop sth off** to cut off part of something with a sharp tool

chop² /tʃɒp/ **noun** [C] **1** a flat piece of meat with a bone in it: *a lamb chop* **2** a quick, hard hit with a sharp tool or with the side of your hand

chopper /ˈtʃɒpəʳ/ **noun** [C] **1** informal a helicopter (= aircraft with turning parts on top) **2** a heavy

---

tool with a sharp edge for cutting wood, meat, etc

hoppy /ˈtʃɒpi/ **adj** Choppy water has a lot of small waves.

hopsticks /ˈtʃɒpstɪks/ **noun** [plural] thin sticks used for eating food in East Asia

horal /ˈkɔːrəl/ **adj** Choral music is written for a choir (= group of people who sing).

hord /kɔːd/ **noun** [C] two or more musical notes that are played at the same time

IDIOM **strike a chord (with sb)** If something strikes a chord with you, you like it or are interested in it because it is connected with your own life or opinions.

→ See also **vocal cords**

hore /tʃɔːʳ/ **noun** [C] a boring job that you must do: *I find cooking a real chore.*

horeograph /ˈkɒriəɡrɑːf/ **verb** [T] **1** to arrange an event or series of events carefully: *a carefully choreographed publicity stunt* **2** to design the dances for a performance • **choreographer** /ˌkɒriˈɒɡrəfəʳ/ **noun** [C]

horeography /ˌkɒriˈɒɡrəfi/ **noun** [U] the process of designing dances for a performance

horus¹ /ˈkɔːrəs/ **noun 1 SONG** ▷ [C] the part of a song that is repeated several times **2 SINGING GROUP** ▷ [group] a large group of people who sing together **3 IN A SHOW** ▷ [group] a group of dancers and singers in a show who do not have the main parts **4 a chorus of approval/demands/protest, etc** something that a lot of people say at the same time

horus² /ˈkɔːrəs/ **verb** [T] UK If two or more people chorus something, they say it at the same time.

hose /tʃəʊz/ past tense of choose

hosen /ˈtʃəʊzən/ past participle of choose

Christ /kraɪst/ **noun** (also **Jesus Christ**) the Jewish holy man believed by Christians to be the Son of God, and on whose life and teachings Christianity is based

hristen /ˈkrɪsən/ **verb** [T] to give a baby a name at a Christian ceremony and make them a member of the Christian Church: [often passive] *She's being christened in June.*

hristening /ˈkrɪsənɪŋ/ **noun** [C] a ceremony where someone is christened

Christian /ˈkrɪstʃən/ **noun** [C] someone who believes in Christianity • **Christian adj**

hristianity /ˌkrɪstiˈænəti/ **noun** [U] a religion based on belief in God and the life and teachings of Jesus Christ, and on the Bible

Christian name **noun** [C] your first name, not your family name

hristmas /ˈkrɪsməs/ **noun** [C, U] the Christian period of celebration around 25 December, when Christians celebrate the birth of Jesus Christ and people give each other presents, or the day itself: *We're going to my mother's for Christmas.* ∘ **Merry Christmas!** ∘ *Christmas dinner* → See also **Father Christmas**

Christmas card **noun** [C] a decorated card that you send to someone at Christmas

Christmas carol UK (US **Christmas carol**) **noun** [C] a song that people sing at Christmas

Christmas cracker **noun** [C] a coloured paper tube with a small toy inside, that people in the UK pull open at Christmas

Christmas Day **noun** [C, U] 25 December, the day on which Christians celebrate the birth of Jesus Christ

Christmas Eve **noun** [C, U] the day before Christmas Day

Christmas tree **noun** [C] a real or artificial tree that people decorate inside their home for Christmas

chrome /krəʊm/ **noun** [U] a hard, shiny metal that is used to cover objects: *chrome bath taps*

chromosome /ˈkrəʊməsəʊm/ **noun** [C] the part of a cell found in the nucleus, that controls what an animal or plant is like

chronic /ˈkrɒnɪk/ **adj** A chronic illness or problem continues for a long time: *a chronic shortage of nurses* ∘ *chronic back pain* • **chronically adv**

chronicle¹ /ˈkrɒnɪkl/ **noun** [C] a written record of things that happened in the past

chronicle² /ˈkrɒnɪkl/ **verb** [T] to make a record of something, or give details of something: *The book chronicles his life as an actor.*

chronological /ˌkrɒnəˈlɒdʒɪkəl/ **adj** arranged in the order in which events happened • **chronologically adv**

chubby /ˈtʃʌbi/ **adj** pleasantly fat: *the baby's chubby legs*

chuck /tʃʌk/ **verb** [T] informal to throw something: *Don't just chuck your coat on the floor!*

PHRASAL VERBS **chuck sth away/out** informal to throw something away: *I chucked out all my old clothes.* • **chuck sth in** UK informal to stop doing something because it is boring • **chuck sb out** informal to force someone to leave a place: *Pierre was chucked out of school for starting a fight.*

chuckle /ˈtʃʌkl/ **verb** [I] to laugh quietly • **chuckle noun** [C]

chug /tʃʌɡ/ **verb** (**chugging, chugged**) **chug across/along/up, etc** If a vehicle chugs somewhere, it moves slowly, making a low, regular noise with its engine: *A boat was chugging across the lake.*

chum /tʃʌm/ **noun** [C] informal a friend • **chummy adj** friendly

chunk /tʃʌŋk/ **noun** [C] **1** a large piece of something: *a chunk of cheese* → See colour picture **Pieces and Quantities** on page Centre 1 **2** a large part of something: *I spend a big chunk of my money on clothes.*

chunky /ˈtʃʌŋki/ **adj 1** A chunky person is short and heavy. **2** big, and heavy: *chunky shoes*

church /tʃɜːtʃ/ **noun 1** [C, U] ⓐ a building where Christians go to worship God: *We used to go to church every Sunday morning.* **2** [C] (also **Church**) one of the different groups that make up the Christian religion: *the Anglican Church* → See also **the Catholic Church**

C

churchgoer /'tʃɜːtʃˌgəʊəʳ/ noun [C] someone who goes to church regularly

churchyard /'tʃɜːtʃjɑːd/ noun [C] the land around a church, often where people are buried

churn[1] /tʃɜːn/ verb **1** SURFACE ▷ [T] (also **churn up**) to mix something, especially liquids, with great force: *The sea was churned up by heavy winds.* **2** STOMACH ▷ [I] If your stomach is churning, you have a slight feeling that you are going to vomit, usually because you are nervous. **3** BUTTER ▷ [T] to mix milk until it becomes butter

PHRASAL VERB **churn sth out** informal to produce large quantities of something very quickly

churn[2] /tʃɜːn/ noun [C] **1** a container in which milk is mixed to make butter **2** UK a tall, metal container for storing and transporting milk

chute /ʃuːt/ noun [C] **1** a long thin structure that people or things can slide down: *a water chute* **2** informal short for parachute

chutney /'tʃʌtni/ noun [U] a mixture of fruit, vegetables, sugar, and vinegar that you eat with meat or cheese

the CIA /ˌsiːaɪ'eɪ/ noun abbreviation for Central Intelligence Agency: the department of the US government that collects secret information about people and organizations

the CID /ˌsiːaɪ'diː/ noun abbreviation for Criminal Investigation Department: the part of the British police force that deals with serious crimes

cider /'saɪdəʳ/ noun [C, U] **1** mainly UK (US **hard cider**) a drink made from apples that contains alcohol **2** US a drink made from apples that contains no alcohol

cigar /sɪ'gɑːʳ/ noun [C] a thick tube made from rolled tobacco leaves, that people smoke

cigarette /ˌsɪgər'et/ noun [C] Ⓐ a thin tube of paper filled with tobacco, that people smoke

cilantro /sɪ'læntrəʊ/ noun [U] US (mainly UK **coriander**) the leaves of the coriander plant that are used to add flavour to food

cinder /'sɪndəʳ/ noun [C] a small piece of coal, wood, etc that has been burned

cinema /'sɪnəmə/ noun **1** [C] UK (US **movie theater**) ⒶⒷ a building where you go to watch movies **2** [U] the art or business of making movies: *an article about French cinema*

cinnamon /'sɪnəmən/ noun [U] a brown spice that is used in cooking

circa /'sɜːkə/ preposition (written abbreviation **c.**) formal used before a date to show that something happened at about that time: *Gainsborough's painting 'The Cottage Door' (circa 1780)*

circle[1] /'sɜːkl/ noun **1** [C] ⒶⒷ a round, flat shape like the letter O, or a group of people or things arranged in this shape: *We all sat on the floor in a circle.* → See picture at **shape** **2** [C] ⒷⒷ a group of people with family, work, or social connections: *a close circle of friends* ○ *It's a technical term used in medical circles.* **3** **the circle** UK the seats in the

upper area of a theatre → See also **inner circle**, **traffic circle**, **vicious circle**

circle[2] /'sɜːkl/ verb **1** [I, T] to move in a circle, often around something: *Birds circled above the trees.* **2** [T] to draw a circle around something: *Circle the answer you think is correct.*

circuit /'sɜːkɪt/ noun [C] **1** TRACK ▷ a path, route or sports track that is shaped like a circle **2** ELECTRIC ▷ a complete circle that an electric current travels around **3** EVENTS ▷ a regular series of places or events that people involved in a particular activity go to: [usually singular] *the tennis circuit* → See also **short-circuit**

circular[1] /'sɜːkjələʳ/ adj **1** ⒷⒷ shaped like a circle: *a circular rug* **2** A circular journey takes you around in a circle, back to the place where you started: *a circular walk*

circular[2] /'sɜːkjələʳ/ noun [C] a letter or advertisement that is sent to a lot of people at the same time

circulate /'sɜːkjəleɪt/ verb **1** INFORMATION ▷ If information circulates, a lot of people hear about it: *Rumours are circulating that the mayor is going to resign.* **2** SEND INFORMATION ▷ [T] to give or send information to a group of people: *A copy of the report was circulated to each director.* **3** MOVE ▷ [I, T] to move around or through something, or to make something move around or through something: *Hot water circulates through the pipes.*

circulation /ˌsɜːkjə'leɪʃən/ noun **1** BLOOD ▷ [U] the movement of blood around your body: *Exercise improves your circulation.* **2** INFORMATION ▷ [U] the movement of information, money, or goods between people: *There are a lot of fake banknotes in circulation.* **3** NEWSPAPERS ▷ [no plural] the number of copies of a newspaper or magazine that are sold each day, week, etc

circumcise (also UK **-ise**) /'sɜːkəmsaɪz/ verb [T] to cut off the skin at the end of a boy's or man's penis, or cut off part of a girl's sex organ. • **circumcision** /ˌsɜːkəm'sɪʒən/ noun [C, U] an operation or ceremony in which a boy or man is circumcised

circumference /sə'kʌmfərəns/ noun [C, U] the distance around the edge of a circle or round object: *The lake is 250km in circumference.*

circumspect /'sɜːkəmspekt/ adj formal careful about things you do or say

circumstances /'sɜːkəmstænsɪz/ noun [plural] **1** ⒷⒷ facts or events that make a situation the way it is: *I think they coped very well under the circumstances.* ○ *We oppose capital punishment in/under any circumstances.* **2** **under no circumstances** used to say that something must never happen: *Under no circumstances should you approach the man.*

C

ircumstantial /ˌsɜːkəmˈstænʃᵊl/ adj **circumstantial evidence** information about a crime that makes you believe that something is true, but does not prove it

ircumvent /ˌsɜːkəmˈvent/ verb [T] formal to find a way of avoiding something, especially a law or rule

ircus /ˈsɜːkəs/ noun [C] ⑪ a show in which a group of people and animals perform in a large tent

istern /ˈsɪstən/ noun [C] a large container to store water, especially one that supplies water to a toilet → See colour picture **The Bathroom** on page Centre 3

itadel /ˈsɪtədᵊl/ noun [C] a strong castle that was used in the past to protect people when their city was attacked

ite /saɪt/ verb [T] formal **1** to mention something as an example or proof of something else: *The doctor cited the case of a woman who had died after taking the drug.* **2** US to order someone to go to court because they have done something wrong: [often passive] *A local farmer was **cited for** breaking environmental standards.*

itizen /ˈsɪtɪzᵊn/ noun [C] **1** ⑫ someone who lives in a particular town or city: *the **citizens of** Berlin* **2** ⑫ someone who has a legal right to live in a particular country: *My husband became a British citizen in 1984.* → See also **senior citizen**

⧉ Word partners for **citizen**

a citizen **of** [Paris/Tokyo, etc] • your **fellow** citizens • **decent/law-abiding** citizens

---

itizenship /ˈsɪtɪzᵊnʃɪp/ noun [U] the legal right to be a citizen of a particular country: *British/ French citizenship*

itrus fruit /ˈsɪtrəsˌfruːt/ noun [C, U] an orange, lemon, or similar fruit

ity /ˈsɪti/ noun **1** ⑪ [C] a large town: *the city of Boston* ◦ *the **city centre*** **2 the City** UK the part of London where the large financial organizations have their offices → See also **inner city**

ivic /ˈsɪvɪk/ adj [always before noun] relating to a city or town and the people who live there: ***civic leaders*** ◦ *The opera house was a source of great **civic pride** (= people in the city were proud of it).*

ivil /ˈsɪvᵊl/ adj **1 PEOPLE** ▷ [always before noun] relating to the ordinary people or things in a country and not to military or religious organizations: *They married in a **civil ceremony**.* **2 LAW** ▷ [always before noun] relating to private arguments between people and not criminal cases: *a **civil court*** **3 POLITE** ▷ polite in a formal way: *He and his ex-wife can't even have a civil conversation.*

ivil engiˈneering noun [U] the planning and building of roads, bridges, and public buildings

ivilian /sɪˈvɪliən/ noun [C] someone who is not a member of a military organization or the police

ivility /sɪˈvɪləti/ noun [U] polite behaviour

ivilization (also UK -isation) /ˌsɪvᵊlaɪˈzeɪʃᵊn/ noun **1** [C, U] ⑫ human society with its developed social organizations, or the culture and way of life of a society at a particular period

of time: *ancient civilizations* ◦ *Nuclear war could mean the end of civilization.* **2** [U] an advanced and comfortable way of life: *modern civilization*

civilize (also UK **-ise**) /ˈsɪvᵊlaɪz/ verb [T] to educate a society so that it becomes more advanced and organized

civilized (also UK **-ised**) /ˈsɪvᵊlaɪzd/ adj **1** A civilized society is advanced and has well-developed laws and customs: *A fair justice system is an important part of **civilized society**.* **2** polite and calm: *Let's discuss this in a civilized manner.*

civil ˈliberties noun [plural] the freedom people have to do, think, and say what they want

civil ˈpartnership noun [C, U] in Britain, a legal relationship between two people of the same sex, which gives them the same rights as people who are married

civil ˈrights noun [plural] the rights that everyone in a country has

civil ˈservant noun [C] someone who works in the Civil Service

the ˌCivil ˈService noun the government departments and the people who work in them

civil ˈwar noun [C, U] a war between groups of people who live in the same country

cl written abbreviation for centilitre (= a unit for measuring liquid): *a 75 cl bottle of wine*

clad /klæd/ adj literary covered or dressed in something: *He came to the door clad only in a towel.*

claim¹ /kleɪm/ verb **1 SAY** ▷ [T] ⑫ a statement that something is true, although you have not proved it: [+ (that)] *She claimed that the dog attacked her.* ◦ [+ to do sth] *He claims to have seen a ghost.* **2 claim credit/responsibility/success, etc** to say that you have done or achieved something: *No one has claimed responsibility for yesterday's bomb attack.* → Opposite **disclaim** **3 DEMAND** ▷ [I, T] ⑫ to ask for something because it belongs to you or you have the right to have it: *She claimed $2,500 in travel expenses.* ◦ *If no one claims the watch, then you can keep it.* **4 KILL** ▷ [T] If an accident, war, etc claims lives, people are killed because of it: *The floods claimed over 200 lives.*

claim² /kleɪm/ noun [C] **1 ANNOUNCEMENT** ▷ ⑫ an announcement that something is true, although it has not been proved: [+ (that)] *She rejected claims that she had lied.* **2 DEMAND** ▷ ⑫ an official demand for something you think you have a right to: *a **claim for** compensation* **3 RIGHT** ▷ a right to have something: *You don't have any **claim to** the land.* **4 lay claim to sth** formal to say that something is yours or that you have done something

IDIOM **sb's/sth's claim to fame** a reason why someone or something is known: *My main claim to fame is that I once cooked for the president.*

⧉ Word partners for **claim**

make a claim • **deny/dismiss/reject** a claim • a **false** claim • a claim **by** sb

---

C

clam¹ /klæm/ **noun** [C] a small sea creature you can eat that has a shell in two parts

clam² /klæm/ **verb** (**clamming**, **clammed**)

PHRASAL VERB **clam up** informal to suddenly stop talking, usually because you are embarrassed or nervous

clamber /'klæmbər/ **verb clamber into/over/up, etc** to climb somewhere with difficulty, especially using your hands and feet: *The children clambered into the boat.*

clammy /'klæmi/ **adj** unpleasantly wet and sticky: *clammy hands*

clamour¹ UK (US **clamor**) /'klæmər/ **verb clamour for sth; clamour to do sth** to ask for something continuously in a loud or angry way: *Fans were clamouring for their autographs.*

clamour² UK (US **clamor**) /'klæmər/ **noun** [no plural] **1** a demand for something, or a complaint about something that is made by a lot of people: *the public's clamour for organic food* **2** a loud, continuous noise made by people talking or shouting: *We heard the clamour of voices in the street outside.*

clamp¹ /klæmp/ **noun** [C] **1** a piece of equipment that is used for holding things together tightly **2** UK a metal cover that is put on the wheel of a car so you cannot move it if you have parked in an illegal place

clamp² /klæmp/ **verb 1 clamp sth around/over/ to, etc** to put something in a particular position and hold it there tightly: *He clamped his hand over her mouth.* **2 clamp sth onto/to/together, etc** to fasten two things together using a clamp **3** [T] UK to fasten a metal cover on the wheel of a car to stop it moving because it has been parked in an illegal place

PHRASAL VERB **clamp down** to do something strict to try to stop or limit an activity: *Local police have clamped down on teenage drinking.*

clampdown /'klæmpdaun/ **noun** [C] a strict attempt to stop or limit an activity: [usually singular] *a clampdown on inner city pollution*

clan /klæn/ **noun** [C] a large group of families who are all related to each other, especially in Scotland

clandestine /klæn'destɪn/ **adj** formal secret and often illegal: *a clandestine meeting*

clang /klæŋ/ **verb** [I, T] If something metal clangs, it makes a loud ringing sound, or if you clang it, you make it do this: *The gate clanged shut behind me.* • **clang noun** [C]

clank /klæŋk/ **verb** [I] If metal objects clank, they make a low noise when they hit each other: *The bracelets on her arm clanked as she moved.* • **clank noun** [C]

clap¹ /klæp/ **verb** (**clapping**, **clapped**) **1** [I, T] 🔵 to hit your hands together, often repeatedly, especially in order to show that you enjoyed a performance: *The crowd clapped and cheered for more.* **2 clap sb on the back/shoulder** to hit someone on the back or shoulder in a friendly way **3** [T] to put something somewhere suddenly: *She clapped her hands over her ears and refused to listen.*

clap

clap² /klæp/ **noun 1** [no plural] the action of hitting your hands together, often repeatedly: *Let's give the winner a big clap.* **2 a clap of thunder** a sudden, loud sound that is made by thunder

claret /'klærət/ **noun** [U] UK red wine from the area of France around Bordeaux

clarify /'klærɪfaɪ/ **verb** [T] to make something easier to understand by explaining it: *The law aims to clarify building regulations.* • **clarification** /ˌklærɪfɪ'keɪʃən/ **noun** [C, U]

clarinet /ˌklærɪ'net/ **noun** [C] a musical instrument like a long, black tube, that you play by blowing into it and pressing metal keys

clarity /'klærəti/ **noun** [U] the quality of being clear and easy to understand

clash¹ /klæʃ/ **verb 1 FIGHT** ▷ [I] to fight or argue: *Government troops clashed with rebel soldiers* ○ *Many young people clash with their parents over what time they must be home at night* **2 COLOUR** ▷ [I] If colours or styles clash, they do not look good together: *You can't wear pink lipstick – it clashes with your dress.* **3 EVENT** ▷ [I] UK If two events clash, they happen at the same time so that you cannot go to them both: *Emma's party clashes with my brother's wedding.* **4 NOISE** ▷ [I, T] to make a loud noise by hitting metal objects together

clash² /klæʃ/ **noun** [C] **1 FIGHT** ▷ a fight or argument: *There were violent clashes between the police and demonstrators.* **2 DIFFERENCE** ▷ a big difference between ideas or qualities that causes problems: *a clash of personalities* **3 SOUND** ▷ a loud sound that is made when metal objects hit each other: *the clash of pans in the sink*

> 🔲 **Word partners for clash**
>
> be **involved in** a clash • fierce/violent clashes • clashes **between** sb and sb • a clash **with** sb • a clash **over** sth

clasp¹ /klɑːsp/ **verb** [T] to hold something or someone tightly: *He clasped his daughter in his arms.*

clasp² /klɑːsp/ **noun 1** [C] a small metal object that is used to fasten a bag, belt, or piece of jewellery **2** [no plural] a tight hold

class¹ /klɑːs/ **noun 1 STUDENTS** ▷ [C] 🔵 a group

of students who have lessons together: *Katie and Sarah are in the same class at school.* **2 LESSON** ▷ [C, U] ⓐ a period of time in which students are taught something: *My first class starts at 8.30.* ∘ *He was punished for talking in class* (= during the lesson). **3 SOCIAL GROUP** ▷ [C, U] ⓑ one of the groups of people in a society with the same social and economic position, or the system of dividing people into these groups: *She's from a working-class background.* **4 QUALITY** ▷ [C] ⓐ a group into which people or things are put according to their quality: *When it comes to mathematics, he's in a different class to his peers.* ∘ *second-class mail* **5 SIMILARITY** ▷ [C] a group of similar or related things, especially plants and animals **6 STYLE** ▷ [U] informal the quality of being stylish or fashionable: *a player with real class* → See also **middle class, upper class, working class**

> ❗ Common learner error: **class** or **classroom**?
>
> A **class** is a group of students who have lessons together.
> *The whole class arrived late.*
> A **classroom** is a room where lessons happen.
> *There is a TV and video in every classroom.*

class² /klɑːs/ *verb* **class sb/sth as sth** to put someone or something in a particular group according to their qualities: *The tower is classed as a historic monument.*

classic¹ /ˈklæsɪk/ *adj* **1 POPULAR** ▷ ⓑ A classic book, film, etc is one that has been popular for a long time and is considered to be of a high quality: *the classic film 'Gone with the Wind'* **2 TRADITIONAL** ▷ having a traditional style that is always fashionable: *a classic black jacket* **3 TYPICAL** ▷ typical

classic² /ˈklæsɪk/ *noun* [C] ⓑ a classic book, film, etc

classical /ˈklæsɪkᵊl/ *adj* **1 classical music** ⓐ serious music by people like Mozart and Stravinsky: *Do you prefer classical music or pop music?* **2** traditional in style: *classical and modern dance* **3** relating to ancient Greece and Rome: *classical literature*

classically /ˈklæsɪkᵊli/ *adv* **1** in a traditional style: *a classically trained actor* **2** in a typical style: *a classically English tea room*

classics /ˈklæsɪks/ *noun* [U] the study of ancient Greece and Rome, especially the language, literature, and history

classification /ˌklæsɪfɪˈkeɪʃᵊn/ *noun* [C, U] the process of putting people or things into groups by their type, size, etc, or one of these groups: *the classification of plants*

classified /ˈklæsɪfaɪd/ *adj* Classified information is officially kept secret by a government: *classified documents/information*

classified 'ad *noun* [C] a small advertisement that you put in a newspaper if you want to buy or sell something

classify /ˈklæsɪfaɪ/ *verb* [T] to put people or things into groups by their type, size, etc:

[often passive] *A third of the population has been classified as poor.* ∘ *The books are classified by subject.*

classmate /ˈklɑːsmeɪt/ *noun* [C] ⓐ someone who is in your class at school or college

classroom /ˈklɑːsruːm/ *noun* [C] ⓐ a room in a school where students have lessons → See colour picture **The Classroom** on page Centre 6

classy /ˈklɑːsi/ *adj* informal stylish and fashionable

clatter /ˈklætər/ *verb* **1** [I] If something clatters, it makes a lot of noise when it hits something hard. **2 clatter about/around/down, etc** to move somewhere in a very noisy way: *I could hear Sue clattering about upstairs.* • **clatter** *noun* [no plural] *He dropped his spoon with a clatter.*

clause /klɔːz/ *noun* [C] **1** a part of a legal document: *a clause in a contract* **2** ⓑ a group of words containing a subject and a verb, that is usually only part of a sentence → See also **relative clause, subordinate clause**

claustrophobia /ˌklɒstrəˈfəʊbiə/ *noun* [U] fear of being in a small or crowded place

claustrophobic /ˌklɒstrəˈfəʊbɪk/ *adj* **1** feeling very anxious when you are in a small or crowded place **2** A claustrophobic place makes you feel anxious because it is very small or crowded: *a claustrophobic room*

claw

claw¹ /klɔː/ *noun* [C] one of the sharp, curved nails on the feet of some animals and birds

claw² /klɔː/ *verb* [I, T] If a person or animal claws something, they try to get hold of it or damage it with their nails or claws: *He clawed at the rope, trying to free himself.*

> PHRASAL VERB **claw sth back** mainly UK to try to get back something that you had before: *The party is desperately trying to claw back support.*

clay /kleɪ/ *noun* [U] a type of heavy soil that becomes hard when dry, used for making things such as bricks and containers: *a clay pot*

clean¹ /kliːn/ *adj* **1 NOT DIRTY** ▷ ⓐ not dirty: *clean hands* ∘ *clean clothes* **2 NO SEX** ▷ not about sex: *a clean joke* **3 NO CRIME** ▷ showing that you have not done anything illegal: *a clean driving licence* **4 FAIR** ▷ fair and honest: *a clean election/fight*

> IDIOM **come clean** informal to tell the truth about something that you have been keeping secret

C

clean² /kliːn/ **verb** [I, T] 🅐🅵 to remove the dirt from something: *I spent the morning cleaning the house.* → See also **dry clean, spring clean**

PHRASAL VERBS **clean sth out 1** to take everything out of a room, car, container, etc and clean the inside of it **2** informal to steal everything from a place • **clean (sb/sth) up** to make a person or place clean and tidy: *We have to clean up before we leave.*

clean³ /kliːn/ **adv** informal used to emphasize that something is done completely: *The bullet went clean through his helmet.*

clean-cut /ˌkliːnˈkʌt/ **adj** Someone who is clean-cut has a tidy appearance.

cleaner /ˈkliːnər/ **noun 1** [C] 🅐🅶 someone whose job is to clean houses, offices, public places, etc **2** [C, U] a substance used for cleaning things: *carpet/oven cleaner* **3 the cleaner's** a shop where clothes are cleaned with chemicals → See also **vacuum cleaner**

cleanliness /ˈklenlɪnəs/ **noun** [U] the state of being clean, or the practice of keeping things clean

cleanly /ˈkliːnli/ **adv** in a quick and tidy way: *The branch broke cleanly away from the tree.*

cleanse /klenz/ **verb** [T] to clean your face or an injured part of your body

cleanser /ˈklenzər/ **noun** [C, U] a substance for cleaning, especially your face

clear¹ /klɪər/ **adj 1** UNDERSTAND ▷ 🅐🅶 easy to understand: *clear instructions* **2** HEAR/SEE ▷ 🅐🅶 easy to hear, read, or see: *These photos are very clear.* ○ *Can we make the sound any clearer?* **3** NO DOUBT ▷ not possible to doubt: *The evidence against him was clear.* ○ [+ (that)] *It was clear that Leif was angry.* ○ *Ella made it clear that she didn't like James.* **4** CERTAIN ▷ [never before noun] 🅱🅵 certain about something: *Are you clear about how to get there?* ○ [+ question word] *I'm not very clear why she phoned.* **5** NOT BLOCKED ▷ not covered or blocked by anything: *a clear road* ○ *a clear desk* **6** WITHOUT CLOUDS ▷ A clear sky does not have any clouds. **7** TRANSPARENT ▷ 🅐🅶 easy to see through: *clear water* ○ *clear glass* → See also **the coast¹ is clear, crystal clear**

clear² /klɪər/ **verb 1** EMPTY ▷ [T] 🅱🅵 to remove all the objects or people from a place: *to clear a room/shelf* ○ *Police cleared the building because of a bomb threat.* **2** WEATHER ▷ [I] If the sky or weather clears, the clouds and rain disappear. **3** NOT GUILTY ▷ [T] to prove that someone is not guilty of something that they were accused of: *The jury cleared him of murder.* **4** MONEY ▷ [I] If a cheque (= printed paper used to pay for things) clears, the money goes from one person's bank account to another person's bank account. **5** GO OVER ▷ [T] to jump over something without touching it: *The horse easily cleared the fence.* **6** GIVE PERMISSION ▷ [T] to give or get permission to do something: *You have to clear it with the headteacher if you want a day off school.* → See also **clear the air¹**

PHRASAL VERBS **clear sth away** to make a place tidy by removing things from it, or putting them where they should be: *The children are not very*

good at clearing away their toys. • **clear off** U[ ] informal used to tell someone to go away immediately • **clear sth out** to tidy a place b[ ] getting rid of things that you do not wan[ ] • **clear (sth) up 1** mainly UK 🅱🅶 to make a place[ ] tidy by removing things from it or putting them[ ] where they should be: *Dad was clearing up in the[ ] kitchen.* **2** to make an illness better: *Antibiotic[ ] will clear up the infection.* • **clear sth up** 🅱🅶 t[ ] give an explanation for something, or to dea[ ] with a problem or argument: *Before we sign th[ ] contract, there are a few points we should clear up[ ]* • **clear up** informal 🅱🅶 If the weather clears up[ ] the cloud and rain disappears.

clear³ /klɪər/ **adv** away from something so tha[ ] you are not touching it: *Stand **clear of** the doors[ ] please.*

IDIOM **steer clear of sb/sth** to avoid someone o[ ] something because they are unpleasant o[ ] dangerous

clear⁴ /klɪər/ **noun in the clear a** not responsibl[ ] for a mistake or crime **b** UK not in a difficul[ ] situation or having problems any more

clearance /ˈklɪərəns/ **noun** [C, U[ ]] **1** PERMISSION ▷ permission from someone i[ ] authority: *The company needs to get governmen[ ] clearance for the deal.* **2** DISTANCE ▷ the distanc[ ] that is needed for one thing to avoid touchin[ ] another thing **3** REMOVING THINGS ▷ th[ ] activity of removing waste or things you d[ ] not want from a place

clear-cut /ˌklɪəˈkʌt/ **adj** very certain or obviou[ ] *The issue is not very clear-cut.*

clearing /ˈklɪərɪŋ/ **noun** [C] a small area in th[ ] middle of a forest, where there are no trees

clearly /ˈklɪəli/ **adv 1** EASY ▷ 🅐🅶 in a way that i[ ] easy to see, hear, read, or understand: *He spok[ ] very clearly.* **2** CERTAIN ▷ 🅱🅵 used to show tha[ ] you think something is obvious or certain[ ] *Clearly he's very talented.* **3** NOT CONFUSED ▷ 🅐🅶 If you think clearly, you are not confused.

cleavage /ˈkliːvɪdʒ/ **noun** [C, U] the are[ ] between a woman's breasts

cleaver /ˈkliːvər/ **noun** [C] a heavy knife with [ ] large, square blade: *a meat cleaver*

clef /klef/ **noun** [C] a sign written at th[ ] beginning of a line of music, that shows how[ ] high or low the notes are

clemency /ˈklemənsi/ **noun** [U] formal a decisio[ ] by a judge, king, etc not to punish someon[ ] severely although they have committed a crim[ ]

clench /klenʃ/ **verb** [T] to close your hands o[ ] teeth very tightly, or to hold something tightl[ ] *Dan clenched his fists.*

clergy /ˈklɜːdʒi/ **noun** [plural] priests or religiou[ ] leaders: *a member of the clergy*

clergyman /ˈklɜːdʒɪmən/ **noun** [C] (plural **clergy[ ] men**) a man who is a member of the clergy

cleric /ˈklerɪk/ **noun** [C] a member of the clerg[ ]

clerical /ˈklerɪkəl/ **adj 1** relating to work done i[ ] an office: *a clerical assistant* **2** relating to priest[ ] or religious leaders

clerk /klɑːk/ /ⓤ/ /klɜːrk/ **noun** [C] **1** someone wh[ ] works in an office or bank, keeping records an[ ] doing general office work: *a bank clerk* **2** US someone who sells things in a shop: *a store/sales clerk*

lever /'klevər/ **adj 1** Ⓐ able to learn and understand things quickly and easily: *a clever student* **2** Ⓑ designed in an effective and intelligent way: *a clever idea* ◦ *a clever tool* ● **cleverly** adv *a cleverly designed toy* ● **cleverness** noun [U]

➕ Other ways of saying **clever**

The adjectives **intelligent** and **smart** are common alternatives to 'clever':
She's a highly intelligent woman.
He's one of the smartest kids in the class.
Young people who are clever are sometimes described as **bright**:
Jacob was a very bright boy.
The adjective **brainy** is used in informal contexts, especially by young people when describing other young people:
Ask Louisa to help you – she's really brainy.
Someone who is extremely clever is sometimes described as **brilliant** or **gifted**:
William was a brilliant/gifted scholar.

liché /'kli:ʃeɪ/ Ⓤ /kli:'ʃeɪ/ **noun** [C] something that people have said or done so much that it has become boring or has no real meaning

lick¹ /klɪk/ **verb 1 SOUND** ▷ [I, T] to make a short, sharp sound, or to use something to make this sound: *The door clicked shut behind him.* **2 COMPUTER** ▷ [I, T] Ⓐ to press on part of a computer mouse (= small computer control) to make the computer do something: *To start the program, click on its icon.* **3 PEOPLE** ▷ [I] informal If two people click, they like each other immediately. **4 IDEA** ▷ [I] informal to suddenly understand something: *Suddenly everything clicked and I realized where I'd met him.* → See also **double-click**, snap your fingers (**finger¹**)

lick² /klɪk/ **noun** [C] **1** Ⓐ a short, sharp sound: *the click of a switch* **2** the action of pressing a button on a computer mouse (= small computer control) to make the computer do something

lient /klaɪənt/ **noun** [C] Ⓑ someone who pays someone else for services or advice

lientele /ˌkli:ɒn'tel/ **noun** [group, no plural] the regular customers of a business: *The new bar aims to attract a younger clientele.*

liff /klɪf/ **noun** [C] Ⓑ an area of high, steep rocks beside the sea

cliff

limactic /klaɪ'mæktɪk/ **adj** [always before noun] literary A climactic event or time is one in which important or exciting things happen.

limate /'klaɪmət/ **noun 1** [C, U] Ⓑ the weather conditions that an area usually has: *a hot, dry climate* **2** [C] the situation, feelings, and

opinions that exist at a particular time: [usually singular] *the political/social climate* ◦ *Terrorism creates a climate of fear.*

▢ Word partners for **climate**

create a climate of [fear/trust, etc] ● **in a** climate ● **in the current/in the present** climate ● **the political/social** climate

'climate change noun [C, U] Ⓑ the way the Earth's weather is changing

climate-friendly /'klaɪmətˌfrendli/ **adj** Something that is climate-friendly does not cause any damage which will change the Earth's weather patterns: *climate-friendly technology*

climatic /klaɪ'mætɪk/ **adj** formal relating to the weather conditions that an area usually has: *climatic change*

climax¹ /'klaɪmæks/ **noun** [C] the most exciting or important part of something: [usually singular] *The climax of her career was winning a gold medal.* → Opposite **anticlimax**

▢ Word partners for **climax**

build up to/come to/reach a climax ● a **dramatic/exciting/fitting/thrilling** climax ● **the climax of** sth

climax² /'klaɪmæks/ **verb** [I, T] to reach the most important or exciting part: *The festival climaxed with/in a huge fireworks display.*

climb

He climbed a tree.   They went climbing.

climb /klaɪm/ **verb 1 PERSON** ▷ [I, T] (also **climb up**) Ⓐ to go up something, or onto the top of something: *to climb a ladder/tree/mountain* ◦ *He climbed up on a chair to change the light bulb.* **2 climb into/out of/through, etc** Ⓑ to move somewhere using your hands and legs: *The child climbed into the back of the car.* **3 NUMBER** ▷ [I] If a price, number, or amount climbs, it increases: *Profits climbed 11% last quarter.* **4 MOVE HIGHER** ▷ [I] Ⓑ to move to a higher position: *The road climbs quite steeply.* ● **climb** noun [C] *a long/steep/uphill climb*

PHRASAL VERB **climb down** UK informal to change your opinion or admit that you are wrong: *The* *government has been forced to **climb down over** the issue of increased taxes.*

climbdown /ˈklaɪmdaʊn/ **noun** [C] UK an occasion when someone admits that they were wrong about something or have changed their opinion: *an embarrassing climbdown by the government*

climber /ˈklaɪmər/ **noun** [C] someone who climbs mountains, hills, or rocks as a sport

climbing /ˈklaɪmɪŋ/ **noun** [U] ⓐ the sport of climbing mountains, hills, or rocks: *rock/mountain climbing* ∘ *climbing boots*

clinch /klɪnʃ/ **verb** [T] informal **1** to finally get or win something: *to clinch a deal* **2 clinch it** informal to make someone finally decide what to do: *When he said the job was in Paris, that clinched it for me.*

cling /klɪŋ/ **verb** [I] (**clung**) **1** to hold someone or something tightly, especially because you are frightened: *She was found clinging to the ledge.* ∘ *I clung on to his hand in the dark.* **2** to stick to something: *His damp hair clung to his forehead.*

PHRASAL VERBS **cling (on) to sth** to try very hard to keep something: *He clung on to power for ten more years.* ∘ **cling to sth** to refuse to stop believing or hoping for something: *He clung to the belief that his family were alive.*

clingfilm /ˈklɪŋfɪlm/ **noun** [U] UK trademark (US **plastic wrap**) thin, transparent plastic used for wrapping or covering food

clingy /ˈklɪŋi/ **adj** mainly UK always wanting to be with someone and not wanting to do things alone: *a clingy child*

clinic /ˈklɪnɪk/ **noun** [C] ⓑ a place where people go for medical treatment or advice: *an eye/skin clinic*

clinical /ˈklɪnɪkəl/ **adj 1** [always before noun] relating to medical treatment and tests: *clinical trials/research* **2** only considering facts and not influenced by feelings or emotions: *a clinical approach/attitude* • **clinically adv**

clinician /klɪˈnɪʃən/ **noun** [C] a doctor who treats sick people and does not just study diseases

clink /klɪŋk/ **verb** [I, T] If pieces of glass or metal clink, they make a short ringing sound when they touch, and if you clink them, you make them do this. • **clink noun** [C]

clip¹ /klɪp/ **noun** [C] **1** a small metal or plastic object used for holding things together **2** a short part of a film or television programme that is shown on its own: *They showed clips from Spielberg's new movie.* **3 a clip round the ear/earhole** UK informal a quick hit on the side of someone's head → See also **paper clip**

clip² /klɪp/ **verb** (**clipping, clipped**) **1** FASTEN ▷ [I, T] to fasten things together with a clip, or to be fastened in this way: *Clip the microphone to the collar of your jacket.* **2** CUT ▷ [T] to cut small pieces from something: *Jamie was outside clipping the hedge.* **3** HIT ▷ [T] to hit something quickly and lightly: *The plane clipped a telephone line and crashed.*

clipart /ˈklɪpɑːt/ **noun** [U] small pictures that are stored on a computer and can be easily added to a document

clipboard /ˈklɪpbɔːd/ **noun** [C] **1** a board with a clip at the top that holds paper in position for writing on **2** an area for storing information in a computer when you are moving it from one document to another

clipped /klɪpt/ **adj** If someone speaks in a clipped voice, their words sound quick, short and not friendly.

clippers /ˈklɪpəz/ **noun** [plural] a tool used to cut small pieces off something: *hedge clippers*

clipping /ˈklɪpɪŋ/ **noun** [C] **1** (also UK **cutting**) an article or picture that has been cut out of a newspaper or magazine: *a collection of newspaper clippings* about the princess **2** a small piece that has been cut off something: [usually plural] *grass clippings*

clique /kliːk/ **noun** [C] a small group of people who spend a lot of time together and are unfriendly to people who are not in the group

cloak /kləʊk/ **noun 1** [C] a loose coat without sleeves that hangs down from your shoulders **2 a cloak of sth** literary something that is intended to cover or hide the truth of something else: *a cloak of secrecy/mystery*

cloakroom /ˈkləʊkruːm/ **noun** [C] **1** a room where you leave your coat at a theatre, school etc **2** UK old-fashioned a toilet in a public building

clobber /ˈklɒbər/ **verb** [T] informal **1** to hit someone **2** to affect someone very badly: *This policy has clobbered people on low incomes.*

clock¹ /klɒk/ **noun** [C] **1** ⓐ a piece of equipment that shows you what time it is, usually in a house or on a building: *She could hear the hall clock ticking.* → See colour picture **The Living Room** on page Centre 4 **2** UK a piece of equipment in a vehicle for measuring how far it has travelled: *The car has 63,000 kilometres on the clock* **3** **around/round the clock** all day and all night: *Rescue teams are working round the clock to search for survivors of the earthquake* **4 race/work against the clock** to do something as fast as you can in order to finish before a particular time

IDIOM **turn/put the clock back** UK to make a situation the same as it was at an earlier time

→ See also **alarm clock, grandfather clock**

clock² /klɒk/ **verb**

PHRASAL VERB **clock sth up** to achieve a particular number or amount of something: *Yuri has clocked up 5,500 flying hours.*

clockwise

clockwise   anti-clockwise *UK*, counterclockwise *US*

clockwise /'klɒkwaɪz/ **adj**, **adv** in the same direction as the hands (= parts that point to the numbers) on a clock move → Opposite **anticlockwise**, UK **counterclockwise**, US

clockwork /'klɒkwɜːk/ **noun 1** [U] a system of machinery that starts when you turn a handle or key: *a clockwork toy* **2 (as) regular as clockwork** extremely regularly: *The bell rang at 8 a.m., regular as clockwork.* **3 run/go like clockwork** to happen exactly as planned, with no problems

clog /klɒg/ **verb** [I, T] **(clogging, clogged)** (also **clog up**) to fill something so that nothing can pass through it, or to be filled in this way: [often passive] *The plughole was clogged with hair.*

clogs /klɒgz/ **noun** [plural] shoes made from wood, or shoes with a wooden sole (= bottom part)

cloister /'klɔɪstər/ **noun** [C] a covered stone passage around the edges of a garden in a church or religious building

clone¹ /kləʊn/ **noun** [C] **1** an exact copy of a plant or animal that scientists make by removing one of its cells **2** informal someone or something that is very similar to someone or something else

clone² /kləʊn/ **verb** [T] to create a clone of a plant or animal: *Scientists have already cloned a sheep.* • **cloning noun** [U] *animal/human cloning*

close¹ /kləʊz/ **verb** [I, T] **1 DOOR/WINDOW ETC** ▷ ⓐ If something closes, it moves so that it is not open, and if you close something, you make it move so that it is not open: *Jane closed the window.* ○ *Lie down and close your eyes.* ○ *Suddenly the door closed.* **2 PUBLIC PLACE** ▷ ⓐ If a shop, restaurant, public place, etc closes, people cannot go in it: *The store closes at 8 p.m.* **3 ORGANIZATION** ▷ (also **close down**) ⓐ If a business or organization closes, or if someone or something closes it, it stops operating: *Many factories have closed in the last ten years.* **4 END** ▷ ⓑ to end, or to end something: *She closed the meeting with a short speech.* → See Note at **open¹** **5 COMPUTER** ▷ If a computer program or a window on a computer screen closes, or if you close it, it stops operating because you tell it to: *This file won't close.*

PHRASAL VERBS **close (sth) down** ⓑ If a business or organization closes down, or if someone or something closes it down, it stops operating. • **close in** If people close in, they gradually get nearer to someone, usually in order to attack them or stop them escaping: *Police closed in on the demonstrators.* • **close sth off** to put something across the entrance to a place in order to stop people entering it: *Police quickly closed off the area.*

close² /kləʊs/ **adj 1 DISTANCE** ▷ ⓐ near in distance: *His house is close to the airport.* **2 TIME** ▷ ⓐ near in time: *It was close to lunchtime when we arrived.* **3 FRIENDLY** ▷ ⓑ If people are close, they know each other very well and like each other a lot: *close friends* ○ *I'm very close to my brother.* **4 RELATIVE** ▷ [always before noun] ⓑ A close relative is someone who is directly related to you, for example your mother,

father, or brother. **5 RELATIONSHIP** ▷ seeing or talking with someone a lot: *Our school has close links with a school in China.* ○ *I'm still in close contact with my school friends.* **6 be/come close to doing sth** to almost achieve or do something: *We are close to reaching an agreement.* **7 be close to sth** If someone or something is close to a particular state, they are almost in that state: *She was close to tears.* **8 COMPETITION** ▷ ⓑ A close game, competition, etc is one in which people's scores are nearly the same. **9 CAREFUL** ▷ [always before noun] looking at or listening to someone or something very carefully: *On close inspection, you could see that the painting was a fake.* ○ *Keep a close watch on the children* (= watch them carefully). **10 WEATHER** ▷ Close weather is too warm and there is not enough fresh air. • **closeness noun** [U] → See also **a close call²**, **a close shave²**

close³ /kləʊs/ **adv 1** ⓑ near in distance: *He stayed close to his mother.* ○ *Come a bit closer.* ○ *We walked close behind them.* ○ *There's a great beach close by* (= near). **2** near in time: *The time for change is coming closer.*

close⁴ /kləʊz/ **noun** [no plural] the end of something: *They finally reached an agreement at the close of a week of negotiations.* ○ *The year was drawing to a close.*

close⁵ /kləʊs/ **noun** [C] (also **Close**) UK used in the name of a road that cars can only enter from one end: *They live at 7 Kings Close.*

closed /kləʊzd/ **adj 1 BUSINESS/SHOP** ▷ ⓐ not open for business: *We went to the library but it was closed.* **2 NOT OPEN** ▷ ⓐ not open: *The door was closed.* ○ *Her eyes were closed.* **3 NOT ACCEPTING IDEAS** ▷ not wanting to accept new ideas, people, customs, etc: *a closed mind* → See Note at **open¹**

closed-circuit television noun [C, U] a system of hidden cameras that take pictures of people in public places, used to help prevent crime

close-knit /ˌkləʊs'nɪt/ **adj** A close-knit group of people is one in which everyone helps and supports each other: *a close-knit community*

closely /'kləʊsli/ **adv 1 CAREFULLY** ▷ If you look at or listen to something closely, you look at it or listen to it very carefully. **2 CONNECTED** ▷ ⓑ If two things are closely connected, related, etc, they are very similar to each other or there is a relationship between them: *The two languages are closely related.* ○ *Which Amercian city most closely resembles Paris?* **3 VERY NEAR** ▷ in a way that is very near in distance or time: *Elke came into the room, closely followed by her children.* **4 WORK** ▷ ⓑ If you work closely with someone, you work together a lot: *Nurses work closely with other medical staff.*

closet¹ /'klɒzɪt/ **noun** [C] US (UK/US **wardrobe**) a large cupboard for keeping clothes in → See also **have a skeleton in the cupboard**

closet² /'klɒzɪt/ **adj a closet intellectual/liberal/socialist, etc** someone who hides their true opinions or way of life

close-up /'kləʊsʌp/ **noun** [C] a photograph of

someone or something that is taken by standing very close to them

closing /ˈkləʊzɪŋ/ **adj** [always before noun] The closing part of an event or period of time is the final part of it: *Messi scored a goal in the closing minutes of the game.*

closure /ˈkləʊʒəʳ/ **noun 1** [C, U] the time when a business, organization, etc stops operating for ever: *factory closures* ∘ *The company announced the **closure of** its Paris office.* **2** [U] the feeling that a sad or unpleasant experience has now finished so that you can think about and do other things

> 🗖 Word partners for **closure**
>
> face/be threatened with closure • save sth from closure • the closure of sth

clot¹ /klɒt/ **noun** [C] **1** a lump that forms when a liquid, especially blood, becomes almost solid **2** UK informal a stupid person

clot² /klɒt/ **verb** [I, T] (**clotting, clotted**) to form clots, or to make clots form

> ❗ Common learner error: **cloth, clothes,** or **clothing**?
>
> The most usual word for the things you wear is **clothes**. **Clothing** is slightly more formal, and often used for particular types of clothes. **Cloth** is the material that clothes are made from. Do not try to make a plural 'cloths' – it is an uncountable noun.
> *I put my clothes on.*
> ~~I put my cloth on.~~
> *They gave us money for food and clothing.*
> ~~They gave us money for food and cloths.~~

cloth /klɒθ/ **noun 1** [U] 🔁 material made from cotton, wool, etc, and used, for example, to make clothes or curtains: *a piece of cloth* **2** [C] 🔁 a piece of cloth used for cleaning or drying things

clothe /kləʊð/ **verb** [T] to supply clothes for someone

clothed /kləʊðd/ **adj** wearing clothes: *fully clothed*

clothes /kləʊðz/ **noun** [plural] 🔁 items such as shirts and trousers that you wear on your body: *She was **wearing** her sister's **clothes**.* ∘ *to **put on/take off** your **clothes** →* See colour picture **Clothes** on pages Centre 8, 9

> 🗖 Word partners for **clothes**
>
> put on/take off/wear clothes • **change** your clothes

clothesline /ˈkləʊðzlaɪn/ **noun** [C] a rope for hanging wet clothes on until they dry

'clothes ,peg noun [C] UK (US **clothespin** /ˈkləʊðzpɪn/) a short piece of wood or plastic that is used to hold clothes on a rope while they dry

clothing /ˈkləʊðɪŋ/ **noun** [U] 🔁 clothes, especially of a particular type: *outdoor/protective clothing*

cloud¹ /klaʊd/ **noun 1** [C, U] 🔁 a white or grey mass that floats in the sky, made of small water drops: *rain/storm clouds* **2** [C] 🔁 a mass of gas or

very small pieces of something floating in the air: *a cloud of dust/smoke*

cloud

> IDIOM **be under a cloud** If someone is under a cloud, they are not trusted or not popular because people think they have done something bad.

• **cloudless adj** without clouds

cloud² /klaʊd/ **verb 1** [T] to make someone confused, or make something harder to understand: *to **cloud** someone's **judgment/vision 2** [I, T] If something transparent clouds, it becomes hard to see through, and if something clouds it, it makes it hard to see through.

PHRASAL VERB **cloud over** to become covered with clouds

cloud com'puting noun [U] the use of technology, services, and software on the Internet rather than on your own computer

cloudy /ˈklaʊdi/ **adj 1** 🔁 When it is cloudy, there are clouds in the sky. **2** A cloudy liquid is not transparent: *cloudy water*

clout /klaʊt/ **noun 1** [U] power and influence over other people: *As mayor, he **has** political **clout**.* **2** [C] UK informal a heavy blow made with the hand

clove /kləʊv/ **noun** [C] **1** a small, dark-brown dried flower that is used as a spice **2** one separate part in a root of garlic (= plant with a strong taste used in cooking)

clover /ˈkləʊvəʳ/ **noun** [U] a small plant that has three round leaves and round flowers

clown¹ /klaʊn/ **noun** [C] **1** 🔁 a performer who wears brightly coloured clothes and has a painted face and makes people laugh **2** a silly person

clown

clown² /klaʊn/ **verb** [I] (also **clown around**) to behave in a silly way in order to make people laugh

club¹ /klʌb/ **noun** [C] **1** ORGANIZATION ▷ 🔁 an organization for people who want to take part in a sport or social activity together, or the building they use for this: *a fitness/football club* **2** GOLF ▷ (also **golf club**) a long, thin stick used to hit the ball in golf → See colour picture **Sports** on page Centre 15 **3** WEAPON ▷ a heavy stick used as a weapon **4** DANCE ▷ a place open late at night where people can dance **5** clubs playing cards with black shapes like three leaves on them: *the ten of clubs →* See also **fan club**

> 🗖 Word partners for **club**
>
> belong to/join a club • a member of a club

club² /klʌb/ **verb** (**clubbing, clubbed**) **1** [T] to hit a person or animal with a heavy stick **2** go

clubbing mainly UK to go to clubs where there is music and dancing

PHRASAL VERB **club together** UK If a group of people club together to buy something, they share the cost of it.

clubhouse /ˈklʌbhaʊs/ noun [C] a building that the members of a club use for social activities or for changing their clothes

cluck /klʌk/ verb [I] to make the sound that a chicken makes • **cluck** noun [C]

clue /kluː/ noun [C] **1** ⓑ a sign or a piece of information that helps you to solve a problem or answer a question: *Police are searching the area for clues to the murder.* ∘ *I can't remember who wrote it. Give me a clue.* **2 not have a clue** informal ⓑ to be completely unable to guess, understand, or deal with something: [+ question word] *I haven't a clue what you're talking about.*

clued up adj UK knowing all the most important information about something: *He's very clued up on the law.*

clueless /ˈkluːləs/ adj informal A clueless person does not know anything about a particular subject.

clump /klʌmp/ noun [C] a group of plants growing closely together: *a clump of grass*

clumsy /ˈklʌmzi/ adj **1** PERSON ▷ ⓑ Clumsy people move in a way that is not controlled or careful enough, and often knock or damage things. **2** BEHAVIOUR ▷ If you behave in a clumsy way, you upset people because you are not careful about their feelings: *a clumsy attempt to be friendly* **3** OBJECT ▷ Clumsy objects are large, not attractive, and often difficult to use. • **clumsily** adv • **clumsiness** noun [U]

clung /klʌŋ/ past of cling

cluster¹ /ˈklʌstər/ noun a group of similar things that are close together: *a cluster of galaxies*

cluster² /ˈklʌstər/ verb **cluster around/round/together, etc** to form a close group: *Photographers clustered round the film star.*

clutch¹ /klʌtʃ/ verb [T] to hold something tightly: *She clutched a coin.*

PHRASAL VERB **clutch at sth** to try very hard to hold something: *She clutched wildly at the branch.*

clutch² /klʌtʃ/ noun **1** [C] the part of a car or truck that you press with your foot when you change gear (= part that controls how fast the wheels turn) → See colour picture **Car** on page Centre 7 **2** [C, U] the action of holding something tightly or of trying to hold something tightly **3 sb's clutches** If you are in someone's clutches, they control you, often in an evil way.

clutter¹ /ˈklʌtər/ verb [T] (also **clutter up**) to cover a surface, or to fill a place with things that are not tidy or well organized: [often passive] *Every shelf is cluttered with ornaments.*

clutter² /ˈklʌtər/ noun [U] a lot of objects that are not tidy or well organized: *There's too much clutter on my desk.*

cm written abbreviation for centimetre (= a unit for measuring length)

co- /kəʊ-/ prefix with or together: *a co-author* ∘ *to coexist*

c/o written abbreviation for care of: used when you send a letter to someone who will give it to the person you are writing to

Co 1 written abbreviation for Company (= name of a business): *Williams & Co* **2** written abbreviation for County (= area with its own local government): *Co. Wexford*

coach¹ /kəʊtʃ/ noun [C] **1** BUS ▷ UK ⓐ a comfortable bus used to take groups of people on long journeys: *a coach trip* **2** PERSON ▷ ⓑ someone whose job is to teach people to improve at a sport, skill, or school subject: *a football/tennis coach* **3** OLD VEHICLE ▷ a vehicle with wheels that is pulled by horses

coach² /kəʊtʃ/ verb [T] ⓑ to teach someone so they improve at a sport, skill, or in a school subject • **coaching** noun [U]

coach station noun [C] UK (UK/US **bus station**) a building where a bus starts or ends its journey

coal /kəʊl/ noun **1** [U] a hard, black substance that is dug from under the ground and burnt as fuel: *a lump of coal* **2 coals** pieces of coal, usually burning

coalition /ˌkəʊəˈlɪʃən/ noun [C] two or more political parties that have joined together, usually to govern a country: *to form a coalition* ∘ *a coalition government*

coal mine noun [C] (also UK **colliery**) a place where people work under the ground digging coal

coarse /kɔːs/ adj **1** rough and thick, or not in very small pieces: *coarse cloth* ∘ *coarse breadcrumbs* **2** not polite: *coarse language* • **coarsely** adv

coast¹ /kəʊst/ noun [C, U] **1** ⓑ the land beside the sea: *The island lies off the North African coast* (= in the sea near North Africa). ∘ *They live on the east coast of Scotland.* **2 coast to coast** from one side of a country to the other

IDIOM **the coast is clear** If the coast is clear, you can do something or go somewhere because there is nobody who might see you.

coast² /kəʊst/ verb [I] **1** to progress or succeed without any effort or difficulty: *Pakistan coasted to a four-wicket victory over Australia.* **2** to move forward in a vehicle without using the engine, usually down a hill

coastal /ˈkəʊstəl/ adj ⓑ situated on or relating to the coast: *a coastal town/resort*

coaster /ˈkəʊstər/ noun [C] a small piece of wood, plastic or other material that you put a glass or cup on to protect a surface from heat or liquid

coastguard /ˈkəʊstɡɑːd/ noun [C] a person or the organization responsible for preventing accidents and illegal activities in the sea near a coast

coastline /ˈkəʊstlaɪn/ noun [C, U] the part of the land along the edge of the sea: *a rocky coastline*

coat¹ /kəʊt/ noun [C] **1** CLOTHES ▷ ⓐ a piece of clothing with sleeves that you wear over your other clothes, especially when you go outside: *a*

C

fur/winter coat **2 FUR** ▷ the fur that covers an animal's body **3 LAYER** ▷ a layer of a substance such as paint: *a coat of paint/varnish*

coat² /kəʊt/ **verb** [T] to cover something with a thin layer of something: *Stir the rice until it is coated with butter.*

coat hanger noun [C] a wire, wooden, or plastic object for hanging clothes on

coating /'kəʊtɪŋ/ **noun** [C] a thin layer that covers the surface of something: *a protective/non-stick coating*

coax /kəʊks/ **verb** [T] to persuade someone in a gentle way: [+ into + doing sth] *She coaxed me into joining the group.*

cobble¹ /'kɒbl/ **verb**

PHRASAL VERB **cobble sth together** to make something quickly and not very carefully

cobble² /'kɒbl/ **noun** [C] a rounded stone used on the surface of an old-fashioned road • **cobbled adj** made with cobbles: *cobbled streets*

cobbler /'kɒblər/ **noun** [C] mainly UK old-fashioned someone whose job is to make or repair shoes

cobblestone /'kɒblstəʊn/ **noun** [C] a rounded stone that is used on the surface of an old-fashioned road

cobra /'kəʊbrə/ **noun** [C] a poisonous snake that makes the skin of its neck wide and flat when it is going to attack

cobweb /'kɒbweb/ **noun** [C] a structure of fine threads made by a spider (= insect with eight legs) to catch insects

cobweb

Coca-Cola /,kəʊkə'kəʊlə/ **noun** [U] trademark a sweet, dark-brown drink with lots of bubbles

cocaine /kəʊ'keɪn/ **noun** [U] an illegal drug, often used in the form of white powder

cock¹ /kɒk/ **noun** [C] an adult male chicken

cock² /kɒk/ **verb** [T] to move part of the body up or to the side: *to cock an ear/eyebrow*

PHRASAL VERB **cock sth up** UK informal to do something wrong or badly: *I really cocked up my exams.*

cockerel /'kɒkərəl/ **noun** [C] UK a young male chicken

cockney /'kɒkni/ **noun 1** [U] a type of English spoken in East London **2** [C] someone who speaks Cockney

cockpit /'kɒkpɪt/ **noun** [C] the part of an aircraft or racing car that contains the controls

cockroach /'kɒkrəʊtʃ/ **noun** [C] a large, brown or black insect that can live in houses and places where food is prepared

cocktail /'kɒkteɪl/ **noun 1 MIXTURE** ▷ [C] a mixture of powerful substances: *a cocktail of drugs/chemicals* **2 DRINK** ▷ [C] an alcoholic drink made from two or more kinds of drink mixed together: *a cocktail bar/party* **3 DISH** ▷ [C, U] a cold dish containing small pieces of food mixed together: *a prawn cocktail* ∘ *fruit cocktail*

cocktail party noun [C] a formal party with alcoholic drinks, usually in the early evening

cock-up /'kɒkʌp/ **noun** [C] UK informal a stupid mistake or failure

cocky /'kɒki/ **adj** confident in an annoying way

cocoa /'kəʊkəʊ/ **noun** [U] **1** a dark-brown powder produced from a type of bean, used to make chocolate **2** a drink made by mixing cocoa powder with hot milk

coconut /'kəʊkənʌt/ **noun** [C] ⬤ a very large nut with a hard, hairy shell, a white part that you eat, and liquid in the centre

cocoon /kə'kuːn/ **noun** [C] a cover that protects some insects as they develop into adults

cod /kɒd/ **noun** [C, U] (plural **cod**) ⬤ a large sea fish that can be eaten as food

code /kəʊd/ **noun 1 SECRET MESSAGE** ▷ [C, U] ⬤ a set of letters, numbers, or signs that are used instead of ordinary words to keep a message secret: *The message was written in code.* ∘ *The were trying to break (= understand) the enemy code.* **2 TELEPHONE** ▷ [C] UK (UK/US **area code**) set of numbers used at the beginning of all th telephone numbers in a particular are **3 RULES** ▷ [C] a set of rules on how to behav or how to do things: *a code of conduct/practic* ∘ *The club has a strict dress code (= rules abou what you wear).* → See also **bar code, zip cod**

coded /'kəʊdɪd/ **adj** written or sent in code: *coded message/warning*

codeine /'kəʊdiːn/ **noun** [U] a medicine used t reduce pain

co-ed /,kəʊ'ed/ ⓤⓢ /'kəʊ,ed/ **adj** with both mal and female students

coerce /kəʊ'ɜːs/ **verb** [T] formal to make someon do something that they do not want to do: [+ int + doing sth] *Employees said they were coerced int signing the agreement.* • **coercion** /kəʊ'ɜːʃən **noun** [U]

coexist /,kəʊɪg'zɪst/ **verb** [I] If two things o groups coexist, they exist at the same time o together, although they may be very different *Can science and religion coexist?* • **coexistenc noun** [U]

coffee /'kɒfi/ **noun 1** [C, U] ⬤ a hot drink mad from dark beans that are made into a powder, o a cup of this drink **2** [U] ⬤ the beans from whic coffee is made, or the powder made from thes beans: *instant coffee*

coffee break noun [C] a short rest from wor in the morning or afternoon

coffee shop noun [C] (also UK **coffee bar**) small informal restaurant where drinks an small meals are served, sometimes in a large shop or building

coffee table noun [C] a low table in a roon where people sit → See colour picture **The Livin Room** on page Centre 4

coffers /'kɒfəz/ **noun** [plural] a supply of mone that a group or organization has and can spend *government/party coffers*

coffin /'kɒfɪn/ **noun** [C] (also US **casket**) a box i which a dead body is buried → See also **the fina nail¹ in the coffin**

cog /kɒg/ **noun** [C] a part shaped like a tooth o

the edge of a wheel in a machine, that makes another wheel turn

cogent /ˈkəʊdʒ^ənt/ **adj** A cogent argument, reason, or explanation is one that people will believe because it is clear and careful.

cognac /ˈkɒnjæk/ **noun** [U] good quality French brandy (= strong alcoholic drink)

cognitive /ˈkɒgnətɪv/ **adj** [always before noun] formal relating to how people think, understand, and learn

cohabit /kəʊˈhæbɪt/ **verb** [I] formal If two people cohabit, they live together and are sexual partners but are not married. • **cohabitation** /kəʊˌhæbɪˈteɪʃ^ən/ **noun** [U]

coherent /kəʊˈhɪər^ənt/ **adj 1** A coherent argument, plan, etc is clear, and each part of it has been carefully considered. **2** If someone is coherent, you can understand what they say. → Opposite **incoherent** • **coherence** /kəʊˈhɪər-^əns/ **noun** [U] • **coherently adv**

cohesion /kəʊˈhiːʒ^ən/ **noun** [U] a situation in which the members of a group or society are united: *The country needs greater social cohesion.* • **cohesive** /kəʊˈhiːsɪv/ **adj** united and working together effectively: *a cohesive unit/group*

cohort /ˈkəʊhɔːt/ **noun** [C] someone who supports someone else, especially a political leader: *the prime minister's cohorts*

coil¹ /kɔɪl/ **noun** [C] a long piece of wire, rope, etc curled into several circles: *a coil of rope*

coil² /kɔɪl/ **verb** [I, T] (also **coil up**) to twist something into circles, or to become twisted into circles: *Her hair was coiled in a bun on top of her head.*

coin¹ /kɔɪn/ **noun 1** ⓘ [C] a flat, usually round, piece of metal used as money: *a pound coin* **2 toss a coin** to throw a coin into the air so that it turns over several times, and see which side it lands on, often in order to make a decision

coin² /kɔɪn/ **verb** [T] **1** to be the first person who uses a new word or phrase **2 to coin a phrase** something you say before using a common expression: *Still, to coin a phrase, there is light at the end of the tunnel.*

coincide /ˌkəʊɪnˈsaɪd/ **verb** [I] **1** to happen at the same time as something else: *The band's American tour coincided with the release of their second album.* **2** When people's opinions or ideas coincide, they are the same.

coincidence /kəʊˈɪnsɪd^əns/ **noun** [C, U] ⓘ a situation in which two very similar things happen at the same time but there is no reason for it: *an amazing/strange coincidence* ◦ *It was pure coincidence that we both married dentists.* • **coincidental** /kəʊˌɪnsɪˈdent^əl/ **adj** happening by coincidence: *The similarities are coincidental.* • **coincidentally** /kəʊˌɪnsɪˈdent^əli/ **adv**

🔲 Word partners for **coincidence**

by coincidence • an **amazing/happy/ remarkable/strange/unfortunate** coincidence • **mere/pure** coincidence • it's no co- incidence **that**

Coke /kəʊk/ **noun** [C, U] trademark short for Coca-Cola (= a sweet, dark-brown drink with lots of bubbles)

Col written abbreviation for Colonel (= an officer of high rank in the army or air force)

cola /ˈkəʊlə/ **noun** [U] ⓐ a sweet, dark-brown drink with lots of bubbles → See also **Coca-Cola**

colander /ˈkɒləndə^r/ **noun** [C] a bowl with small holes in it used for washing food or separating water from food after cooking → See colour picture **The Kitchen** on page Centre 2

cold¹ /kəʊld/ **adj 1** TEMPERATURE ▷ ⓐ having a low temperature: *cold water/weather* ◦ *This soup has gone cold.* ◦ *My hands are getting cold.* **2** UNFRIENDLY ▷ ⓑ unfriendly or showing no emotion: *a cold stare/voice* ◦ *She became quite cold and distant with me.* **3** FOOD ▷ served cold: *cold roast beef* • **coldness noun** [U] → See also in **cold blood, get cold feet (foot**¹**)**

➕ Other ways of saying **cold**

If the weather outside or the temperature inside is very cold, you can use the adjectives **bitter** or **freezing**:

*Wrap up warmly – it's **bitter** outside!*
*It's absolutely **freezing** in here!*

If the weather, especially the wind, is so cold that it is unpleasant to be in, the adjectives **biting** and **icy** are sometimes used:

*A **biting/icy** wind blew in her face as she opened the door.*

The adjective **chilly** is often used to describe weather or temperatures that feel slightly cold and unpleasant:

*It's a bit **chilly** in here – can you turn the heater on?*

If the temperature feels cold but pleasant, you can say that it is **cool**:

*That's a nice **cool** breeze.*

Cold weather in autumn or winter that is dry and pleasant is sometimes described as **crisp**:

*We walked through the forest on a **crisp** autumn day.*

---

cold² /kəʊld/ **noun 1** ⓐ [C] a common illness that makes you sneeze and makes your nose produce liquid: *I've got a cold.* ◦ *He caught a bad cold at school.* **2 the cold** ⓑ cold weather or temperatures **3 leave sb out in the cold** to not allow someone to be part of a group or activity

---

🔲 Word partners for **cold**

catch/have a cold • a bad/heavy/stinking (= very bad) cold

---

cold³ /kəʊld/ **adv 1 be out cold** informal to be unconscious: *I hit my head and was out cold for two minutes.* **2** completely and immediately: *I offered to go with him but he turned me down cold.*

cold-blooded /ˌkəʊldˈblʌdɪd/ **adj** showing no emotion or sympathy: *a cold-blooded killer*

cold cuts noun [plural] mainly US thin, flat slices of cold cooked meat

cold-hearted /ˌkəʊldˈhɑːtɪd/ **adj** feeling no kindness or sympathy towards other people

---

coldly /ˈkəʊldli/ adv in a way that is not friendly or emotional: *He looked at me coldly.*

coleslaw /ˈkəʊl.slɔː/ noun [U] cold uncooked cabbage, carrot and onion, cut into long thin strips and covered in a thick creamy cold sauce

colic /ˈkɒlɪk/ noun [U] When a baby has colic, it has a bad pain in the stomach.

collaborate /kəˈlæbəreɪt/ verb [I] **1** When two or more people collaborate, they work together to create or achieve the same thing: *Didn't you collaborate with him on one of your books?* **2** to help people who are an enemy of your country or government: *He was accused of collaborating with the enemy.* • **collaborator** noun [C]

collaboration /kəˌlæbəˈreɪʃən/ noun **1** [C, U] the activity of working together to create or achieve the same thing, or a product of this: *The show was a result of collaboration between several museums.* **2** [U] help that someone gives to an enemy country or government

collage /ˈkɒlɑːʒ/ noun [C, U] a picture made by sticking small pieces of paper or other materials onto a surface, or the process of making pictures like this

collapse[1] /kəˈlæps/ verb **1** FALL ▷ [I] 🔵 When someone collapses, they fall down, usually because they are sick or weak. **2** OBJECT ▷ [I, T] 🔵 to fall down or towards the inside, or to make a structure or object fall down or towards its inside: *The roof collapsed under the weight of snow.* **3** FAIL ▷ [I] to fail to work or succeed: *The peace talks have collapsed.*

collapse[2] /kəˈlæps/ noun [C, U] **1** 🔵 the sudden failure of a system, organization, business, etc **2** an occasion when a person or structure becomes too weak to stand and suddenly falls

collapsible /kəˈlæpsɪbl/ adj able to be folded or made flat in order to be stored or carried: *a collapsible table/boat*

collar[1] /ˈkɒlər/ noun [C] **1** 🔵 the part of a shirt, coat, etc that is usually folded over and goes round your neck: *a shirt collar* → See picture at **jacket 2** 🔵 a narrow piece of leather or plastic that you fasten round the neck of an animal

collar[2] /ˈkɒlər/ verb [T] informal to find someone and stop them going somewhere, often so that you can talk to them about something

collarbone /ˈkɒləbəʊn/ noun [C] a bone between the base of your neck and your shoulder

collateral /kəˈlætərəl/ noun [U] things that you agree to give someone if you are not able to pay back money you have borrowed from them: *I used my car as collateral for a loan.*

colleague /ˈkɒliːg/ noun [C] 🔵 someone that you work with

collect[1] /kəˈlekt/ verb **1** BRING TOGETHER ▷ [T] 🔵 to get things from different places and bring them together: *The police are continuing to collect information.* ∘ *Would you collect up the books please, Joanne?* **2** KEEP ▷ [T] 🔵 to get and keep things of one type such as stamps or coins as a hobby: *She collects dolls.* **3** GO TO GET ▷ [T] UK 🔵 to go to a place and bring someone or something away from it: *She collects Anna from*

school at three o'clock. **4** MONEY ▷ [I, T] 🔵 to ask people to give you money for something, for example a charity (= organization that help people): *I'm collecting on behalf of the Red Cross.* **5** RECEIVE ▷ [T] to receive money that you are owed: *You can begin to collect a pension at age 62.* **6** COME TOGETHER ▷ [I] to come together in a single place: *Journalists collected outside the palace.* **7** collect yourself/your thoughts to get control over your feelings and thoughts

collect[2] /kəˈlekt/ adj, adv US If you telephone collect or make a collect telephone call, the person you telephone pays for the call.

collected /kəˈlektɪd/ adj **1** [always before noun] brought together in one book or series of books: *His collected poems were published in 1928.* **2** showing control over your feelings: *Jane wa very calm and collected.*

collection /kəˈlekʃən/ noun **1** OBJECTS ▷ [C] 🔵 a group of objects of the same type that have been collected by one person or in one place: *a private art collection* **2** TAKING AWAY ▷ [U] 🔵 the activity of taking something away from a place: *The photos will be ready for collection on Tuesday afternoon.* **3** MONEY ▷ [C] an amount o money collected from several people: *We had a collection for Emily's gift.* **4** GROUP ▷ [C] a group of things or people: *There's quite a collection of toothbrushes in the bathroom.*

> **Word partners for collection**
>
> **amass/display/have** a collection
> • an **extensive/large/priceless/private** collection

collective[1] /kəˈlektɪv/ adj involving, felt by, o owned by everyone in a group: *collective responsibility*

collective[2] /kəˈlektɪv/ noun [C] a business that i owned and controlled by the people who work in it

collectively /kəˈlektɪvli/ adv as a group: *She ha a staff of four who collectively earn almost $200,000.*

collector /kəˈlektər/ noun [C] **1** someone whose job is to collect tickets or money from people: *a tax collector* **2** 🔵 someone who collects object because they are interesting or beautiful: *a collector of modern art*

> **Word partners for college**
>
> **go to** college • **be at** college • a college **course/lecturer/student**

college /ˈkɒlɪdʒ/ noun **1** EDUCATION ▷ [C, U] 🔵 a place where students are educated when they are between 16 and 18 years old, or afte they have finished school: *a sixth-form colleg* ∘ *a teacher-training college* **2** UNIVERSITY ▷ [C, U] US a place where students, between 1 and 22 years old, are educated and receive bachelor's degree (= type of qualification **3** PART OF UNIVERSITY ▷ [C] a part of university that has its own teachers and stu dents: *Cambridge/Oxford colleges* → See als **community college, junior college 4**

place that gives degrees (= type of qualification) in a particular subject: *Royal Agricultural College*

collegiate /kə'liːdʒiət/ **adj** relating to or belonging to a college or its students: *collegiate sports*

collide /kə'laɪd/ **verb** [I] When two objects collide, they hit each other with force, usually while moving: *The car **collided with** a van.*

colliery /'kɒljəri/ **noun** [C] UK (UK/US **coal mine**) a place where people work digging coal from under the ground

collision /kə'lɪʒᵊn/ **noun** [C] an accident that happens when two vehicles hit each other with force

IDIOM **be on a collision course** If two people or groups are on a collision course, they are doing or saying things that are certain to cause a serious disagreement or fight between them.

☑ Word partners for **collision**

avoid/be involved in a collision • [a car/ train, etc] is **in** a collision **with** sth • a **head-on** collision • a collision **between** sth and sth

---

collocation /ˌkɒlə'keɪʃᵊn/ **noun** [C] **1** 🄱 a word or phrase that sounds natural and correct when it is used with another word or phrase: *In the phrase 'a hard frost', 'hard' is a collocation of 'frost', and 'strong' would not sound natural.* **2** the combination of words formed when two or more words are frequently used together in a way that sounds natural: *The phrase 'a hard frost' is a collocation.*

colloquial /kə'ləʊkwiəl/ **adj** Colloquial words or expressions are informal: *colloquial speech* • **colloquially adv**

collude /kə'luːd/ **verb** [I] formal to do something secretly with another person or group, in order to deceive or cheat others: *The company **colluded with** competitors to fix prices.* • **collusion** /kə'luːʒᵊn/ **noun** [U] *He was accused of being **in collusion with** the terrorists.*

colon /'kəʊlɒn/ **noun** [C] **1** 🄱 a mark (:) used before a list, an example, an explanation, etc → See Study Page **Punctuation** on page Centre 33 **2** the large intestine (= lower part of a person's bowels)

colonel /'kɜːnᵊl/ **noun** [C] an officer of high rank in the army or air force

colonial /kə'ləʊniəl/ **adj** [always before noun] relating to colonialism or a colony (= country controlled by another country): *colonial rule/ government*

colonialism /kə'ləʊniəlɪzᵊm/ **noun** [U] the system in which powerful countries control other countries

colonize (also UK **-ise**) /'kɒlənaɪz/ **verb** [T] **1** to send people to live in and govern another country: [often passive] *Burundi was first colonized by the Germans.* **2** to start growing or living in large numbers in a place: *Weeds quickly colonize areas of cleared ground.* • **colonist** /'kɒlənɪst/ **noun** [C] someone who goes to colonize a country • **colonization** /ˌkɒlənaɪ'zeɪʃᵊn/ **noun** [U]

colony /'kɒləni/ **noun** [C] **1 COUNTRY** ▷ a

country or area controlled in an official, political way by a more powerful country: *a French/British colony* **2 GROUP** ▷ a group of the same type of animals, insects, or plants living together in a particular place: *a colony of ants* **3 PEOPLE** ▷ a group of people with the same interests or job who live together: *an artists' colony*

color /'kʌlər/ **noun, verb** US spelling of colour

colored /'kʌləd/ **adj** US spelling of coloured

colorful /'kʌləfəl/ **adj** US spelling of colourful

coloring /'kʌlərɪŋ/ **noun** [U] US spelling of colouring

colorless /'kʌlələs/ **adj** US spelling of colourless

colossal /kə'lɒsᵊl/ **adj** extremely large: *colossal amounts of money*

colour¹ UK (US **color**) /'kʌlər/ **noun 1 RED/BLUE ETC** ▷ [C, U] 🄰 red, blue, green, yellow, etc: *Green is my favourite colour.* ∘ *What colour shall I paint the kitchen?* → See colour picture **Colours** on page Centre 12 **2 FILM/TV ETC** ▷ [U] all the colours, not only black and white: *Why didn't he shoot the film in colour?* **3 SKIN** ▷ [U] the colour of a person's skin, which shows their race **4 FACE** ▷ [U] healthy pink skin on someone's face: *The colour drained from her cheeks.* **5 INTEREST** ▷ [U] interesting or exciting qualities or parts: *We added your story for a bit of local colour.*

IDIOM **with flying colours** with a very high score or with great success: *He passed the entrance exam with flying colours.*

→ See also **primary colour**

colour² UK (US **color**) /'kʌlər/ **verb 1** [I, T] 🄰 to become a particular colour, or to make something a particular colour: *He drew a heart and coloured it red.* ∘ *Fry the onions until they start to colour.* **2** [T] to affect what someone does, says, or feels: [often passive] *Her views are coloured by her own bad experiences.*

PHRASAL VERB **colour sth in** to fill an area with colour using paint, pens, etc

colour-blind UK (US **color-blind**) /'kʌləblaɪnd/ **adj** unable to see the difference between particular colours

coloured UK (US **colored**) /'kʌləd/ **adj 1** having or producing a colour or colours: *coloured lights/ cloth* **2** an old-fashioned way of describing someone from a race with dark skin that is now considered offensive

colourful UK (US **colorful**) /'kʌləfəl/ **adj 1** 🄱 having bright colours: *a colourful painting* **2** 🄱 interesting and unusual: *a **colourful character***

colouring UK (US **coloring**) /'kʌlərɪŋ/ **noun** [U] **1** the colour of something, especially an animal or person's skin, hair, and eyes: *The boys have their father's colouring.* **2** a substance that is used to colour something: *food/artificial colouring*

colourless UK (US **colorless**) /'kʌlələs/ **adj 1** without any colour: *a colourless liquid* **2** without the qualities that make someone or something interesting and unusual

colt /kəʊlt/ **noun** [C] a young male horse

column /'kɒləm/ **noun** [C] **1 TALL POST** ▷ 🄱 a tall, solid, usually stone post which is used to

---

column

support a roof or as decoration in a building: *a stone/marble column* **2 NEWSPAPER** ▷ a regular article in a newspaper or magazine on a particular subject or by the same writer **3 PRINT** ▷ 🔢 one of the blocks of print into which a page of a newspaper, magazine, or dictionary is divided **4 NUMBERS ETC** ▷ any block of numbers or words written one under the other **5 a column of sth** something with a tall, narrow shape: *A column of smoke rose from the chimney.* **6 PEOPLE MOVING** ▷ a long line of moving people or vehicles: *a column of refugees* → See also **gossip column**

columnist /ˈkɒləmnɪst/ **noun** [C] someone who writes a regular article for a newspaper or magazine: *a sports/gossip columnist*

.com /dɒtˈkɒm/ internet abbreviation for company: used in some Internet addresses that belong to companies or businesses: *www.google.com*

coma /ˈkəʊmə/ **noun** [C] the state of being unconscious for a long time: [usually singular] *She has been in a coma for over a week.*

comb¹ /kəʊm/ **noun** [C] a flat piece of metal or plastic with a row of long, narrow parts along one side, that you use to tidy your hair

comb

comb² /kəʊm/ **verb** [T]
1 🔢 to tidy your hair using a comb **2** to search a place very carefully: *Investigators combed through the wreckage.*

combat¹ /ˈkɒmbæt/ **noun** [C, U] a fight, especially during a war: *The aircraft was shot down in combat.*

combat² /ˈkɒmbæt/ **verb** [T] (**combatting, combatted, combating, combated**) to try to stop something unpleasant or harmful from happening or increasing: *New measures have been introduced to combat the rise in crime.*

┌─────────────────────────────────────┐
│ 🔲 Word partners for **combat**   │
│   │
│ combat **crime/global warming/racism/** │
│ **terrorism** • combat the **effects** of sth │
│ • combat a **problem** • combat the **threat** of │
│ sth • combat the **rise** in [crime, etc] │
└─────────────────────────────────────┘

combatant /ˈkɒmbətənt/ **noun** [C] formal someone who fights in a war

combative /ˈkɒmbətɪv/ **adj** formal eager to fight or argue

combination /ˌkɒmbɪˈneɪʃən/ **noun 1** [C, U] 🔢 mixture of different people or things: *Strawberries and cream – a perfect combination! ◦ We won through a combination of luck and skill. ◦ This drug can be safely used in combination with other medicines.* **2** [C] a set of numbers or letters in a particular order that is needed to open some types of locks: *a combination lock*

combine /kəmˈbaɪn/ **verb 1** [I, T] 🔢 to become mixed or joined, or to mix or join things together: *My wages combined with your savings should just pay for it. ◦ The band combines jazz rhythms and romantic lyrics.* **2** [T] to do two or more activities at the same time: *don't know how she combines working with studying.*

combined /kəmˈbaɪnd/ **adj** [always before noun] joined together: *the combined effects of poverty and disease*

combine harvester /ˌkɒmbaɪnˈhɑːvɪstər/ **noun** [C] (also **combine**) a large farm machine that cuts a crop and separates the grain from the stem

combustion /kəmˈbʌstʃən/ **noun** [U] the process of burning

come /kʌm/ **verb** (**came, come**) **1 MOVE TOWARDS** ▷ [I] 🔢 to move or travel towards a person who is speaking or towards the place that they are speaking about: *Come and see what I've done. ◦ Can you come to my party? ◦ The rain came down heavily. ◦ Here comes Adam (= Adam is coming).* **2 ARRIVE** ▷ [I] 🔢 to arrive somewhere or go to a place: *I'll come and see you later. ◦ [+ to do sth] I've come to see Mr Curtis. ◦ Dad will come for you at six. ◦ We came to a crossroads.* **3 GO WITH SOMEONE** ▷ [I] 🔢 to go somewhere with the person who is speaking: *Come for a walk with us. ◦ We're going to the cinema. Do you want to come?* **4 come after/first/last, etc** 🔢 to have or achieve a particular position in a race, competition, list, etc: *Our team came third. ◦ Sunday comes after Saturday.* **5 come past/to/up to, etc** to reach a particular length, height, or depth: *The water came up to my waist.* **6 come apart/off, etc** to become separated or removed from something: *The book came apart in my hands. ◦ The handle came off. ◦ My shoelaces have come undone. ◦ The door came open.* **7 come easily/easy/naturally** to be very easy for someone: *Singing came naturally to Louise.* **8 HAPPEN** ▷ [I] 🔢 to happen: *Spring has come early. ◦ The worst problems are still to come.* **9 how come** informal used to ask why or how something has happened: *How come you didn't go to the party?* **10 come and go** to exist or happen somewhere for a short time and then go away: *The feeling of nausea comes and goes.* **11 BE AVAILABLE** ▷ [I] 🔢 to be available in a particular size, colour, etc: *The table comes in three different sizes. ◦ Furniture like this doesn't come cheap.* **12 come to do sth** to start to do something: *I have come to rely on acupuncture. ◦ This place has come to be known as 'Pheasant Corner'.* **13 when it comes to sth/doing sth** used to introduce a new idea that you want to say something about: *When it comes to baking* _cakes, she's an expert._ **14 come to think of it** used to say that you have just thought of something: _Come to think of it, there are two batteries that you can have upstairs._ → See also **come to blows (blow²)**, **I'll/We'll cross that bridge¹** when I/we come to it., **come clean¹**, **if/when it comes to the crunch¹**, **come (back) down to earth**, **come under fire¹**, **deliver/come up with the goods**, **come to grief**, **come/get to grips (grip¹) with sth**, **come to light¹**, **come into your/its own¹**, **not be/come up to scratch²**, **come to your senses (sense¹)**, **come/turn up trumps**

PHRASAL VERBS **come about** to happen, or start to happen: _How did the idea for an arts festival come about?_ • **come across sb/sth** 🅱② to meet someone or discover something by chance: _I came across a lovely little restaurant in the village._ • **come across 1** to seem to be a particular type of person: _He **came across as** shy._ **2** If an idea or emotion comes across, it is expressed clearly and people understand it: _His bitterness comes across in his poetry._ • **come along 1 ARRIVE** ▷ to arrive or appear at a place: _A taxi never comes along when you need one._ **2 GO WITH SOMEONE** ▷ 🅱① to go somewhere with someone: _We're going to the cinema. Do you want to come along?_ **3 EXIST** ▷ to start to exist: _I gave up climbing when my first child came along._ **4 be coming along** to be developing or making progress • **come around 1 VISIT** ▷ 🅰② to visit someone at their house **2 AGREE** ▷ to change your opinion about something, or agree to an idea or a plan that you were against: _I'm sure she'll **come around to** our view eventually._ **3 EVENT** ▷ If an event that happens regularly comes around, it happens, or is going to happen soon: _Thanksgiving has come around again._ **4 BECOME CONSCIOUS** ▷ to become conscious again after an accident or medical operation • **come back 1** 🅰② to return to a place: _I've just **come back from** the dentist's._ **2** If a style or a fashion comes back, it becomes popular again: _Miniskirts are coming back into fashion._ • **come back to sb** If something comes back to you, you remember it: _Suddenly, the horror of the accident came back to me._ • **come between sb** to harm the relationship between two or more people: _I won't anything come between me and my children._ • **come by sth** to get something, especially something that is unusual or difficult to find: _Cheap organic food is still **difficult to come by.**_ • **come down 1** 🅱② to break and fall to the ground: _A lot of trees came down in the storm._ **2** 🅱② If a price or a level comes down, it becomes lower: _Prices always come down after Christmas._ **3** to decide that you support a particular person or side in an argument, etc: _The government has **come down on the side of** military action._ • **come down on sb** to punish or criticize someone: _The police are **coming down hard on** people for not paying parking fines._ • **come down to sth/doing sth** If a situation, problem, decision, etc comes down to something, then that is the thing that will influence it most. • **come down with sth** informal 🅱② to get an illness: _I came down with the flu at Christmas._

• **come forward** to offer to help someone or to give information: _We need witnesses to **come forward with** information about the attack._ • **come from sth** 🅰① to be born, obtained from, or made somewhere: _She comes from Poland._ ○ _Milk comes from cows._ • **come from sth/doing sth** to be caused by something: _"I feel awful." "That comes from eating too many sweets."_ • **come in 1 ENTER** ▷ 🅰② to enter a room or building: _Do you want to come in for a cup of tea?_ **2 FASHION** ▷ If a fashion or a product comes in, it becomes available or becomes popular: _Flared trousers came in during the seventies._ **3 BE RECEIVED** ▷ If news, information, a report, etc comes in, it is received: _News is just coming in about the explosion._ **4 come in first/second, etc** to finish a race or a competition in first/second, etc position **5 SEA** ▷ If the tide (= regular change in the level of the sea) comes in, the sea moves towards the beach or coast. **6 BE INVOLVED** ▷ informal used to describe how someone is involved in a situation, story, or plan: _We need people to help clean up, and that's where you come in._ • **come in for sth** If someone comes in for criticism, praise, etc, they are criticized, praised, etc. • **come into sth 1** to get money from someone who has died: _Just after I left university, I came into a bit of money._ **2 come into it** UK informal to influence a situation: _Money doesn't come into it._ • **come of sth/doing sth** to happen as a result of something: _Did anything come of all those job applications?_ • **come off 1** to happen successfully: _His attempt to impress us all didn't quite come off._ **2 come off badly/best/well, etc** to be in a bad or good position at the end of a fight, argument, etc: _She usually comes off best in an argument._ **3 Come off it!** informal used to tell someone that you do not agree with them or do not believe them: _Oh, come off it! I saw you take it!_ • **come on 1 START** ▷ to start to happen or work: _The heating comes on at six in the morning._ ○ _I think I have a cold coming on._ **2 MAKE PROGRESS** ▷ to make progress: _How's your new novel coming on?_ **3 Come on!** informal 🅱① used to encourage someone to do something, to hurry, to try harder, etc: _Come on! We're going to be late._ **4 DISAGREEMENT** ▷ used to tell someone that you do not agree with them, do not believe them, etc: _Come on Bob! You made the same excuse last week._ • **come out 1 BECOME AVAILABLE** ▷ 🅱① If a book, record, film, etc comes out, it becomes available for people to buy or see: _When does their new album come out?_ **2 SUN** ▷ 🅱① If the sun, the moon, or a star comes out, it appears in the sky. **3 BECOME KNOWN** ▷ to become known: _The truth about him will come out in the end._ **4 SOCIAL EVENT** ▷ UK to go somewhere with someone for a social event: _Would you like to come out for a drink?_ **5 RESULT** ▷ If you describe how something comes out at the end of a process or activity, you say what it is like: _How did your chocolate cake come out?_ **6 INFORMATION** ▷ If results or information come out, they are given to people: _The exam results come out in August._ **7 BE REMOVED** ▷ If dirt or a mark comes out of something, it disappears when you clean it: _Will_ this red wine stain come out? **8 PHOTOGRAPH** ▷ If a photograph comes out, the picture can be seen clearly: *The photos didn't come out very well.* **9 BE SAID** ▷ If something that you say comes out in a particular way, you say it in that way: *I wanted to tell her that I loved her, but it came out all wrong.* **10 TELL** ▷ to tell people that you are homosexual (= sexually attracted to people of the same sex) **11 come out against/in favour of sth** to say publicly that you oppose or support something • **come out in sth** If you come out in a skin disease, it appears on your skin. • **come out of sth** If something comes out of a process or event, it is one of the results: *I hope something good can come out of this mess.* • **come out with sth** to say something suddenly that is not expected • **come over 1** to come to a place, move from one place to another, or move towards someone: *Are your family coming over from Greece for the wedding?* **2** to seem to be a particular type of person: *Henry came over as a real enthusiast.* • **come over sb** If a feeling comes over you, you suddenly experience it: *I don't usually get so angry. I don't know what came over me.* • **come round** UK **1 VISIT** ▷ 🆎 to visit someone at their house: *You must come round to the flat for dinner some time.* **2 AGREE** ▷ to change your opinion about something, or agree to an idea or a plan that you were against **3 EVENT** ▷ If an event that happens regularly comes round, it happens, or is going to happen soon: *I can't believe that winter has come round already.* **4 BECOME CONSCIOUS** ▷ to become conscious again after an accident or medical operation • **come through 1** If information or a result comes through, you receive it: *Have the results of the tests come through yet?* **2** If an emotion comes through, other people can notice it: *His nervousness came through when he spoke.* • **come through (sth)** to manage to get to the end of a difficult or dangerous situation: *We've had some hard times, but we've come through them.* • **come to** to become conscious again after an accident or medical operation • **come to sb** If a thought or idea comes to you, you suddenly remember it or start to think about it. • **come to sth 1** to be a particular total when numbers or amounts are added together: *That comes to 50 euros, please.* **2 come to a decision/conclusion/arrangement, etc** to make a decision or decide what to think about something **3** to reach a particular state or situation, especially a bad one: *You won't come to any harm.* • **come under sth 1 come under attack/criticism/scrutiny, etc** to be attacked, criticized, examined, etc **2** to be controlled or dealt with by a particular authority: *When did Hawaii come under US control?* **3** to be in a particular part of a book, list, etc: *Hairdressers come under 'beauty salons' in the Yellow Pages.* • **come up 1 MOVE TOWARDS** ▷ 🅱️ to move towards someone: *After the concert, he came up to me to ask for my autograph.* **2 BE DISCUSSED** ▷ 🅱️ to be discussed or suggested: *The issue of security came up at the meeting yesterday.* **3 OPPORTUNITY** ▷ If a job or opportunity comes up, it becomes available. **4 PROBLEM** ▷ If a problem or difficult situation

comes up, it happens. **5 be coming up** to b happening soon: *My exams are coming up ne month.* **6 SUN OR MOON** ▷ 🅱️ When the sun c the moon comes up, it rises. **7 COMPUTER** ▷ information comes up on a computer screen, appears there. • **come up against sb/sth** to hav to deal with a problem or difficulty: *She came u against a lot of sexism in her first engineering jo* • **come up to sth** to reach the usual c necessary standard: *This work doesn't come u to your usual standards.* • **come up with sth** 🅱️ to think of a plan, an idea, or a solution to problem: *We need to come up with a better way making money.*

comeback /ˈkʌmbæk/ *noun* [C] a successfu attempt to become powerful, important, c famous again: *She's made a comeback wit her first new album for twenty years.*

comedian /kəˈmiːdiən/ *noun* [C] 🅱️ someon who entertains people by telling jokes

comedown /ˈkʌmdaʊn/ *noun* [C] informal situation that is not as good as one you wer in before: [usually singular] *Cleaning windows is bit of a comedown after his last job.*

comedy /ˈkɒmədi/ *noun* [C, U] 🅱️ entertainmen such as a film, play, etc that is funny: *The film is romantic comedy.*

comet /ˈkɒmɪt/ *noun* [C] an object in space tha leaves a bright line behind it in the sky

comfort[1] /ˈkʌmfət/ *noun* **1 NO PAIN** ▷ [U] 🅱️ pleasant feeling of being relaxed and having n pain: *Now you can watch the latest films in th comfort of your sitting room.* **2 FOR SADNESS** [U] a feeling of being less worried or sad abou something: *What she said brought me gre comfort.* **3 ENOUGH MONEY** ▷ [U] a pleasant lif with enough money for everything that yo need: *He can afford to retire and live in comfo for the rest of his life.* **4 a comfort to sb** someon or something that helps you when you a anxious or sad: *The children have been a grea comfort to me since his death.* **5 PLEASAN THING** ▷ [C] something that makes your li easy and pleasant: [usually plural] *Good chocola is one of life's little comforts.* → Opposite **di comfort**

comfort[2] /ˈkʌmfət/ *verb* [T] to make someor feel better when they are anxious or sad • **com forting** *adj He said a few comforting words.*

comfortable /ˈkʌmftəbl/ *adj* **1 NOT CAUSIN PAIN** ▷ 🆎 Comfortable furniture, clothe rooms, etc make you feel relaxed and do n cause any pain: *comfortable shoes* ∘ *We had comfortable journey.* **2 PERSON** ▷ 🅱️ If you a comfortable, you are relaxed and have no pai *Make yourself comfortable while I fetch you drink.* → Opposite **uncomfortable 3 WITHOU WORRIES** ▷ 🅱️ If you are comfortable in situation, you do not have any worries about *I don't feel comfortable about leaving th children here alone.* **4 MONEY** ▷ having enoug money for everything that you need: *a con fortable retirement* **5 WIN** ▷ If you win a gam or competition by a comfortable amoun you win easily: *a comfortable lead/victor* • **comfortably** *adv*

comforter /ˈkʌmfətəʳ/ **noun** [C] US (UK/US **duvet**) a cover filled with feathers or warm material, that you sleep under

comfort ˌzone noun [C] a situation that you know well and in which you are relaxed and confident: *Owen thought about deep-sea diving but decided it was beyond his comfort zone.*

comfy /ˈkʌmfi/ **adj** informal comfortable

comic¹ /ˈkɒmɪk/ **adj** ⓑ₁ funny: *a comic actor*

comic² /ˈkɒmɪk/ **noun** [C] **1** (also ˈcomic ˌbook) ⓐ₂ a magazine with stories told in pictures **2** someone who entertains people by telling jokes

comical /ˈkɒmɪkəl/ **adj** funny in a strange or silly way: *He looked so comical in that hat.* • **comically adv**

comic ˌstrip noun [C] a set of pictures telling a story, usually in a newspaper

coming¹ /ˈkʌmɪŋ/ **noun 1 the coming of sth** the arrival of something: *the coming of spring* **2 comings and goings** people's movements to and from a particular place over a period of time

coming² /ˈkʌmɪŋ/ **adj** [always before noun] a coming time or event will come or happen soon: *the coming elections* → See also **up-and-coming**

comma /ˈkɒmə/ **noun** [C] ⓑ₁ a mark (,) used to separate parts of a sentence, or to separate the items in a list → See Study Page **Punctuation** on page Centre 33 → See also **inverted commas**

command¹ /kəˈmɑːnd/ **noun 1 CONTROL** ▷ [U] control over someone or something and responsibility for them: *The soldiers were **under the command of** a tough sergeant-major.* ○ *Jones was **in command** (= the leader).* **2 ORDER** ▷ [C] ⓑ₂ an order to do something **3 KNOWLEDGE** ▷ [no plural] ⓑ₂ knowledge of a subject, especially a language: *She **had** a good **command** of French.* **4 be at sb's command** to be ready to obey someone's orders **5 COMPUTER** ▷ [C] an instruction to a computer

command² /kəˈmɑːnd/ **verb** formal **1** [T] to control someone or something and tell them what to do: *He commanded the armed forces.* **2** [I, T] to order someone to do something: [+ to do sth] *The officer commanded his men to shoot.* **3 command attention/loyalty/respect, etc** to deserve and get attention, loyalty, respect, etc from other people

commandeer /ˌkɒmənˈdɪəʳ/ **verb** [T] formal to take something, especially for military use: *The ships were commandeered as naval vessels.*

commander /kəˈmɑːndəʳ/ **noun** [C] an officer who is in charge of a military operation, or an officer of middle rank in the navy

commanding /kəˈmɑːndɪŋ/ **adj** [always before noun] in a very successful position and likely to win or succeed: *He has a **commanding lead** in the championships.*

commandment /kəˈmɑːndmənt/ **noun** [C] one of the ten important rules of behaviour given by God in the Bible

commando /kəˈmɑːndəʊ/ **noun** [C] a soldier who is part of a small group who make surprise attacks

commemorate /kəˈmeməreɪt/ **verb** [T] to do something to show you remember an important person or event in the past with respect: *A ceremony will be held to commemorate the battle.* • **commemoration** /kəˌmeməˈreɪʃən/ **noun** [U] *a march **in commemoration of** the war of independence*

commemorative /kəˈmemərətɪv/ **adj** intended to commemorate a person or event: *a commemorative coin*

commence /kəˈmens/ **verb** [I, T] formal to begin something • **commencement noun** [C, U] formal the beginning of something

commend /kəˈmend/ **verb** [T] formal to praise someone or something: [often passive] *His courage was commended by the report.* • **commendation** /ˌkɒmenˈdeɪʃən/ **noun** [C, U]

commendable /kəˈmendəbl/ **adj** deserving praise: *She showed commendable modesty.*

comment¹ /ˈkɒment/ **noun** [C, U] **1** ⓑ₂ something that you say or write that shows what you think about something: *He **made** negative **comments** to the press.* **2 No comment.** used to say that you do not want to answer someone's question

> ☑ **Word partners for comment**
> **make** a comment • **make no** comment • **do** sth **without** comment • a comment **about/on** sth

comment² /ˈkɒment/ **verb** [I, T] ⓑ₂ to make a comment: *My mum always **comments on** what I'm wearing.* ○ [+ that] *He commented that the two pieces of work were very similar.*

commentary /ˈkɒmənt²ri/ **noun 1** [C, U] a spoken description of an event on the radio or television while the event is happening: *the football commentary* **2** [U, no plural] a discussion or explanation of something: *a **commentary on** American culture*

commentator /ˈkɒmənteɪtəʳ/ **noun** [C] someone who describes an event on the radio or television while it is happening: *a **sports commentator***

commerce /ˈkɒmɜːs/ **noun** [U] ⓑ₂ the activities involved in buying and selling things → See also **chamber of commerce, e-commerce**

commercial¹ /kəˈmɜːʃəl/ **adj 1** ⓑ₂ relating to buying and selling things **2** intended to make a profit: *commercial television* • **commercially adv**

commercial² /kəˈmɜːʃəl/ **noun** [C] ⓑ₂ an advertisement on the radio or television

commercialism /kəˈmɜːʃəlɪz²m/ **noun** [U] the idea that making money is the most important aim of an activity

commercialized (also UK **-ised**) /kəˈmɜːʃəlaɪzd/ **adj** organized to make profits: *Christmas has become so commercialized.* • **commercialization** /kəˌmɜːʃəlaɪˈzeɪʃən/ **noun** [U]

commiserate /kəˈmɪz²reɪt/ **verb** [I] to express sympathy to someone who is sad or has had bad luck

commission¹ /kəˈmɪʃən/ **noun 1 GROUP OF PEOPLE** ▷ [group] an official group of people who have been chosen to find out about

C

something and say what they think should be done about it **2 PIECE OF WORK** ▷ [C, U] a piece of work such as painting, writing, or making something that is done especially for a particular person **3 MONEY** ▷ [C, U] a payment given to someone when they sell something, which is directly related to the amount they sell: *The staff receive 5% commission on everything that they sell.* ∘ *Many salesmen work on commission.*

commission² /kəˈmɪʃ³n/ **verb** [T] to arrange for someone to do a piece of work: [+ to do sth] *I've been commissioned to write a song for their wedding.*

commissioner /kəˈmɪʃənəʳ/ **noun** [C] a member of a commission or someone with an important government job in a particular area

commit /kəˈmɪt/ **verb** [T] (**committing, committed**) **1 CRIME** ▷ **B2** to do something that is considered wrong, or that is illegal: *He was sent to prison for a crime that he didn't commit.* ∘ *to commit suicide/adultery* **2 DECISION** ▷ to make a firm decision that you will do something: *He committed himself to helping others.* **3 not commit yourself** to refuse to express an opinion about a particular subject **4 MONEY/TIME** ▷ If you commit money, time, energy, etc to something, you use it to try to achieve something: *The government has committed thousands of pounds to the research.*

commitment /kəˈmɪtmənt/ **noun 1 PROMISE** ▷ [C] **B2** a promise or firm decision to do something: *Players must make a commitment to daily training.* **2 LOYALTY** ▷ [U] **B2** a willingness to give your time and energy to something that you believe in: *We are looking for someone with talent, enthusiasm, and commitment.* **3 ACTIVITY** ▷ [C] **B2** something that you must do that takes your time: *I've got too many commitments at the moment.*

> **☑ Word partners for commitment**
>
> **make** a commitment • **fulfil/honour/meet** a commitment • a commitment **to** sth

committed /kəˈmɪtɪd/ **adj** loyal and willing to give your time and energy to something that you believe in: *a committed Christian* ∘ *She's committed to the job.*

committee /kəˈmɪti/ **noun** [group] **B2** a group of people who have been chosen to represent a larger organization and make decisions for it

commodity /kəˈmɒdəti/ **noun** [C] a product that you can buy or sell

common¹ /ˈkɒmən/ **adj 1 USUAL** ▷ **B1** happening often or existing in large numbers: *Injuries are common in sports such as hockey.* → Opposite **uncommon 2 SHARED** ▷ **B1** belonging to or shared by two or more people or things: *a common goal/interest* ∘ *English has some features common to many languages.* **3 common knowledge** **B2** something that a lot of people know: [+ that] *It's common knowledge that he spent time in jail.* **4 ORDINARY** ▷ [always before noun] not special in any way: *The herbs all have common names and Latin names.* **5 LOW CLASS** ▷ UK typical of a low social class:

My mum thinks dyed blonde hair is really common.

common² /ˈkɒmən/ **noun 1 have sth in common** **B1** to share interests, experiences, or other characteristics with someone or something: *Sue and I don't have much in common.* **2 in common with sb/sth** in the same way as someone or something: *In common with many working mothers, she feels guilty towards her children.* **3** [C] a large area of grass in a town or village that everyone is allowed to use

common 'ground noun [U] shared interests, beliefs, or ideas: *It's difficult for me to find any common ground with my dad.*

common-law /ˌkɒmənˈlɔː/ **adj** [always before noun] A common-law wife or husband is someone who is not married, but has lived with their partner for a long time as if they were married.

commonly /ˈkɒmənli/ **adv** often or usually: *These caterpillars are commonly found on nettles*

commonplace /ˈkɒmənpleɪs/ **adj** [never before noun] happening often or existing in large numbers, and so not considered special or unusual

the Commons /ˈkɒmənz/ **noun** (also **the House of Commons**) one of the two parts of the British parliament, with elected members who make laws

common 'sense noun [U] **B1** the natural ability to be practical and to make good decisions: *The children shouldn't be in any danger as long as they use their common sense.*

the Commonwealth /ˈkɒmənwelθ/ **noun** Britain and the group of countries that used to be in the British Empire (= ruled by Britain)

commotion /kəˈməʊʃ³n/ **noun** [U, no plural] a sudden period of noise and confused or excited movement: *He looked up to see what all the commotion was about.*

communal /ˈkɒmjʊn³l/ ⓤ /kəˈmjuːnəl/ **adj** belonging to or used by a group of people: *a communal changing room*

commune /ˈkɒmjuːn/ **noun** [C] a group of people who live together, sharing the work and the things they own

communicate /kəˈmjuːnɪkeɪt/ **verb** [I, T] **1 B1** to share information with others by speaking, writing, moving your body, or using other signals: *We can now communicate instantly with people on the other side of the world.* **2 B2** to talk about your thoughts and feelings, and help other people to understand them: *He can't communicate with his parents.*

> **☑ Word partners for communication**
>
> communication **between** sb and sb • **in** communication **with** sb • **a means of** communication • **a breakdown in** communication • communication **skills**

communication /kəˌmjuːnɪˈkeɪʃ³n/ **noun 1 COMMUNICATING** ▷ [U] **B1** the act of communicating with other people: *The school is improving communication between teachers and parents.* ∘ *We are in direct communication* *with* Moscow. **2 MESSAGE** ▷ [C] formal a message sent to someone by letter, email, telephone, etc

ommunications /kə͵mjuːnɪˈkeɪʃᵊnz/ **noun** [plural] the different ways of sending information between people and places, such as post, telephones, computers, and radio: *the communications industry*

ommunicative /kəˈmjuːnɪkətɪv/ **adj** ⑫ willing to talk to people and give them information

ommunion /kəˈmjuːniən/ **noun** [U] (also **Communion**) the Christian ceremony in which people eat bread and drink wine, as symbols of Christ's body and blood

ommuniqué /kəˈmjuːnɪkeɪ/ ⑤ /kə͵mjuːnɪˈkeɪ/ **noun** [C] an official announcement

ommunism, Communism /ˈkɒmjənɪzᵊm/ **noun** [U] a political system in which the government controls the production of all goods, and where everyone is treated equally

ommunist, Communist /ˈkɒmjənɪst/ **noun** [C] someone who supports communism • **communist adj** *a communist country/leader*

ommunity /kəˈmjuːnəti/ **noun 1** [C] ⑫ the people living in a particular area: *a rural/small community* **2** [group] ⑫ a group of people with the same interests, nationality, job, etc: *the business/Chinese community*

om͵munity ͵centre noun [C] UK (US **community center**) a place where people who live in an area can meet together to play sport, go to classes, etc

om͵munity ˈcollege noun [C, U] US a two-year college where students can go after high school

om͵munity ˈservice noun [U] work that someone who has committed a crime does to help other people instead of going to prison

ommute /kəˈmjuːt/ **verb** [I] to regularly travel between work and home • **commuter noun** [C]

ompact¹ /kəmˈpækt/ **adj** small and including many things in a small space

ompact² /kəmˈpækt/ **verb** [T] to press something together so that it becomes tight or solid

ompact ˈdisc noun [C] a CD

ompanion /kəmˈpænjən/ **noun** [C] ⑫ someone who you spend a lot of time with or go somewhere with: *a travelling companion*

ompanionship /kəmˈpænjənʃɪp/ **noun** [U] the feeling of having friends around you

ompany /ˈkʌmpəni/ **noun 1 BUSINESS** ▷ [C] ⑫ an organization that sells goods or services: *a software/telephone company* **2 PEOPLE** ▷ [U] ⑫ a situation in which you have a person or people with you: *I enjoy his company.* ○ *I didn't realize that you had company.* **3 keep sb company** ⑫ to stay with someone so that they are not alone **4 be good company** to be a pleasant or interesting person to spend time with **5 PERFORMERS** ▷ [C] a group of performers such as actors or dancers: *the Royal Shakespeare Company* → See also **limited company**

> ☑ **Word partners for company**
> establish/found/set up/start up a company

comparable /ˈkɒmpᵊrəbl/ **adj** similar in size, amount, or quality to something else: *Our prices are comparable to those in other stores.*

comparative¹ /kəmˈpærətɪv/ **adj 1 comparative comfort/freedom/silence, etc** a situation that is comfortable/free/silent, etc when compared to another situation or to what is usual: *I enjoyed the comparative calm of home after the busy office.* **2** comparing similar things: *a comparative study of two poems*

comparative² /kəmˈpærətɪv/ **noun** [C] ⑫ the form of an adjective or adverb that is used to show that someone or something has more of a particular quality than someone or something else. For example 'better' is the comparative of 'good' and 'smaller' is the comparative of 'small'. → Compare **superlative**

comparatively /kəmˈpærətɪvli/ **adv comparatively cheap/easy/little, etc** cheap/easy/little, etc when compared to something else or to what is usual

compare /kəmˈpeə/ **verb 1** [T] ⑬ to examine the ways in which two people or things are different or similar: *The teachers are always comparing me with/to my sister.* **2** [I] to be as good as something else: *This product compares well with more expensive brands.* **3 compared to/with sb/sth** ⑫ used when saying how one person or thing is different from another: *This room is very tidy compared to mine.* → See also **compare notes (note¹)**

PHRASAL VERB **compare sb/sth to sb/sth** to say that someone or something is similar to someone or something else

comparison /kəmˈpærɪsᵊn/ **noun** [C, U] **1** ⑫ something that compares two or more people or things, or the act of comparing them: *They published a comparison of schools in the area.* ○ *She's so tall that he looks tiny by/in comparison.* **2 There's no comparison.** used to say that someone or something is much better than someone or something else

> ☑ **Word partners for comparison**
> draw/make a comparison • a comparison **between** sth and sth • a comparison **of** sth (**with** sth) • by/in comparison (**with** sth)

compartment /kəmˈpɑːtmənt/ **noun** [C] **1** one of the separate areas inside a vehicle, especially a train: *The first class compartment is at the front of the train.* **2** a separate part of a container, bag, etc: *The refrigerator has a small freezer compartment.*

compass /ˈkʌmpəs/ **noun** [C] a piece of equipment that shows you which direction you are going in

compasses /ˈkʌmpəsɪz/ **noun** [plural, C] UK (US **compass**) a piece of equipment that is used for drawing circles

compassion /kəmˈpæʃᵊn/ **noun** [U] a

compass

feeling of sympathy for people who are suffering

compassionate /kəmˈpæʃənət/ **adj** showing compassion

compatible /kəmˈpætɪbl/ **adj 1 EQUIPMENT** ▷ compatible equipment can be used together: *This keyboard is **compatible with** all of our computers.* **2 PEOPLE** ▷ If people are compatible, they like each other and are happy to spend time together. **3 IDEAS** ▷ formal compatible ideas or situations can exist together: *Such policies are not **compatible with** democratic government.* • **compatibility** /kəmˌpætəˈbɪləti/ **noun** [U]

compatriot /kəmˈpætriət/ **noun** [C] formal someone who comes from the same country

compel /kəmˈpel/ **verb** (**compelling**, **compelled**) formal **compel sb to do sth** to force someone to do something: [often passive] *He felt compelled to resign from his job.*

compelling /kəmˈpelɪŋ/ **adj 1** very exciting or interesting and making you want to watch, listen, etc: *a compelling story* **2** If a reason, argument, etc is compelling, it makes you believe it or accept it because it is so strong: ***compelling evidence***

compensate /ˈkɒmpənseɪt/ **verb 1** [T] to pay someone money because you are responsible for injuring them or damaging something: *Victims of the crash will be **compensated for** their injuries.* **2** [I, T] to reduce the bad effect of something, or make something bad become something good: *Nothing will ever **compensate for** his lost childhood.*

compensation /ˌkɒmpənˈseɪʃən/ **noun 1** [U] money that you pay to someone because you are responsible for injuring them or damaging something: *Most of the workers have **won compensation for** losing their jobs.* **2** [C, U] something you get to make you feel better when you have suffered something bad: *Free food was no **compensation for** a very boring evening.*

compère /ˈkɒmpeəʳ/ **noun** [C] UK someone whose job is to introduce performers on television, radio, or in a theatre

compete /kəmˈpiːt/ **verb** [I] **1** [B1] to take part in a race or competition: *She's **competing for** a place in next year's Olympics.* **2** [B2] to try to be more successful than someone or something else: *It's difficult for small shops to **compete with/against** the big supermarkets.*

competent /ˈkɒmpɪtənt/ **adj** able to do something well: *a competent swimmer/teacher* • **competence** /ˈkɒmpɪtəns/ **noun** [U] the ability to do something well • **competently adv**

competition /ˌkɒmpəˈtɪʃən/ **noun 1** [C] [A2] an organized event in which people try to win a prize by being the best, fastest, etc: *to **enter** a **competition*** **2** [U] [B2] a situation in which someone is trying to win something or be more successful than someone else: *There's a lot of **competition between** computer companies.* ◦ *Applicants face stiff **competition for** university places this year.* **3 the competition** people you are competing against, especially in business

> **Word partners for competition**
>
> 1 **enter/go in for/take part in** a competition • **hold** a competition • **win** a competition
> 2 **fierce/intense/stiff** competition • competition **between** sb and sb • competition **for** sth

competitive /kəmˈpetɪtɪv/ **adj 1 SITUATION** ▷ [B2] involving competition: *competitive sports* ◦ *highly competitive industry* **2 PERSON** ▷ [B wanting to win or to be more successful tha other people: *She's very competitive.* **3 PRICE SERVICES** ▷ [B2] Competitive prices, services, e are as good as or better than other price services, etc. • **competitively adv** • **compet tiveness noun** [U]

competitor /kəmˈpetɪtəʳ/ **noun** [C] [B1] a perso team, or company that is competing with other

compilation /ˌkɒmpɪˈleɪʃən/ **noun** [C] a recor ing, book, or film containing a collection o things from many different recordings, book or films

compile /kəmˈpaɪl/ **verb** [T] to collect inform tion and arrange it in a book, report, or list

complacent /kəmˈpleɪsənt/ **adj** feeling so sati fied with your own abilities or situation th you do not feel that you need to try any harde *We must not become too complacent about o work.* • **complacency noun** [U] complace behaviour • **complacently adv**

complain /kəmˈpleɪn/ **verb** [I] [B1] to say th something is wrong or that you are annoye about something: *Lots of people have **com plained about** the noise.* ◦ [+ that] *He's alwa complaining that nobody listens to him.*

> **! Common learner error: complain about something**
>
> Be careful to choose the correct preposition after **complain**.
> *I am writing to **complain about** the trip.*
> ~~*I am writing to complain for the trip.*~~
> ~~*I am writing to complain on the trip.*~~

> **Other ways of saying complain**
>
> The verbs **grumble**, **moan** and (*UK, informal*) **whinge** are sometimes used when someone is complaining about things which are not important:
> *She's always **grumbling** about something.*
> *He's forever **moaning** about his work.*
> *I hope you don't think I'm just **whingeing**.*
> If someone, especially a child, complains in an annoying way, the verb **whine** is often used:
> *Stop **whining**, Tom – it's not that bad!*
> The expression **kick up a fuss** is sometimes used in informal contexts, especially when someone is complaining that something has not happened in the way they wanted:
> *If the food doesn't come soon, I'm going to **kick up a fuss**.*

PHRASAL VERB **complain of sth** ⑪ to tell other people that something is making you feel ill: *She's been complaining of a headache all day.*

complaint /kəm'pleɪnt/ **noun 1** NOT SATISFACTORY ▷ [C, U] ⑪ a statement that something is wrong or not satisfactory: *a letter of complaint* ∘ *I wish to* **make a complaint.** **2** ANNOYING THING ▷ [C] something that makes you complain: *My only complaint was the lack of refreshments.* **3** ILLNESS ▷ [C] an illness: *a stomach complaint*

🗹 Word partners for **complaint**

make/investigate/receive a complaint • a complaint about sb/sth • a complaint against sb • a formal/official/written complaint • a letter of complaint • have cause for/grounds for complaint

---

complement¹ /'kɒmplɪmənt/ **noun** [C] **1** MAKE GOOD ▷ something that makes something else seem good, attractive, or complete: *This wine is the perfect* **complement to** *the meal.* **2** TOTAL NUMBER ▷ the total amount or number of something that is needed to complete a group: *Do we have* **a full complement of** *players for Saturday's game?* **3** GRAMMAR ▷ a word or phrase that comes after the verb and gives more information about the subject of the verb

complement² /'kɒmplɪment/ **verb** [T] to make something seem good or attractive: *The music complements her voice perfectly.*

complementary /ˌkɒmplɪ'mentᵊri/ **adj 1** Things that are complementary are good or attractive together: *complementary colours/flavours* **2 complementary medicine/treatment, etc** ways of treating medical problems that people use instead of or in addition to ordinary medicine: *The clinic offers complementary therapies such as homeopathy.*

complete¹ /kəm'pliːt/ **adj 1** WHOLE ▷ ⑪ with all parts: *the* **complete works** *of Oscar Wilde* ∘ *The report comes* **complete with** (= including) *diagrams and colour photographs.* **2** TOTAL ▷ [always before noun] ⑪ used to emphasize what you are saying: *a complete waste of time* **3** FINISHED ▷ finished: *Our report is almost complete.*

complete² /kəm'pliːt/ **verb** [T] **1** FINISH ▷ ⑫ to finish doing or making something: *The palace took 15 years to complete.* **2** MAKE STH WHOLE ▷ ⑫ to provide the last part needed to make something whole: *Complete the sentence with one of the adjectives provided.* **3** WRITE ▷ ⑫ to write all the details asked for on a form or other document

completely /kəm'pliːtli/ **adv** ⑪ in every way or as much as possible: *I completely forgot that you were coming.*

completion /kəm'pliːʃᵊn/ **noun** [U] the time when something that you are doing or making is finished: *The stadium is due for completion in 2014.* ∘ *They will be paid* **on completion of** *the job.*

complex¹ /'kɒmpleks, kəm'pleks/ **adj** ⑫ involving a lot of different but connected parts in a way that is difficult to understand: *complex*

details/issues ∘ *The situation is very complex.* • **complexity** /kəm'pleksəti/ **noun** [C, U] the quality of being complex: *the complexities of life*

complex² /'kɒmpleks/ **noun** [C] **1** a group of buildings or rooms that are used for a particular purpose: *a sports/housing complex* **2** a mental problem that makes someone anxious or frightened about something: *an inferiority complex*

complexion /kəm'plekʃᵊn/ **noun** [C] **1** the colour and appearance of the skin on someone's face: *a clear complexion* **2** the way something seems to be: *This new information* **puts a** *completely different* **complexion on** *the situation.*

compliance /kəm'plaɪəns/ **noun** [U] formal behaviour which obeys an order, rule, or request: *The work was done* **in compliance with** *planning regulations.*

compliant /kəm'plaɪənt/ **adj** Compliant people are willing to do what other people want them to.

complicate /'kɒmplɪkeɪt/ **verb** [T] to make something more difficult to deal with or understand: *These new regulations just complicate matters further.*

complicated /'kɒmplɪkeɪtɪd/ **adj** ⑪ involving a lot of different parts, in a way that is difficult to understand: *a complicated problem/process* ∘ *The instructions were too complicated for me.*

complication /ˌkɒmplɪ'keɪʃᵊn/ **noun** [C] **1** something that makes a situation more difficult **2** a new medical problem that develops when you are already sick: *Eye problems can be a complication of diabetes.*

complicity /kəm'plɪsəti/ **noun** [U] formal the fact of being involved in doing something wrong

compliment¹ /'kɒmplɪmənt/ **noun 1** [C] something that you say or do to show praise or admiration for someone: *She was always* **paying** *him* **compliments.** **2 with the compliments of sb** formal used by someone to express good wishes when they give you something free, for example in a restaurant: *Please accept this champagne with the compliments of the manager.*

compliment² /'kɒmplɪment/ **verb** [T] to praise or express admiration for someone: *He* **complimented** *me* **on** *my writing.*

complimentary /ˌkɒmplɪ'mentᵊri/ **adj 1** praising or expressing admiration for someone: *a complimentary report* **2** given free, especially by a business: *a complimentary glass of wine*

comply /kəm'plaɪ/ **verb** [I] to obey an order, rule, or request: *The pilot* **complied with** *instructions to descend.*

component /kəm'pəʊnənt/ **noun** [C] one of the parts of something, especially a machine

compose /kəm'pəʊz/ **verb 1** PARTS ▷ [T] ⑫ to be the parts that something consists of: [often passive] *The committee* **was composed of** *elected leaders and citizens.* **2** MUSIC ▷ [I, T] ⑫ to write a piece of music **3 compose yourself** to make yourself calm again after being angry or upset **4** WRITING ▷ [T] to write a speech, letter, etc, thinking carefully about the words to use: *Laura was composing a letter of sympathy.*

---
yes | k cat | ŋ ring | ʃ she | θ thin | ð this | ʒ decision | dʒ jar | tʃ chip | æ cat | e bed | ə ago | ɪ sit | i cosy | ɒ hot | ʌ run | ʊ put |

composed /kəm'pəʊzd/ **adj** calm and in control of your emotions

composer /kəm'pəʊzə^r/ **noun** [C] ⑫ someone who writes music

composite /'kɒmpəzɪt/ **adj** consisting of several different parts: *a composite image of the killer*

composition /ˌkɒmpə'zɪʃ^ən/ **noun** **1** PARTS ▷ [U] the parts, substances, etc that something consists of: *the composition of the atmosphere* **2** MUSIC ▷ [C] ⑫ a piece of music that someone has written **3** WRITING MUSIC ▷ [U] the process or skill of writing music: *He taught composition at Yale.* **4** WRITING ▷ [C, U] ⑪ a short piece of writing about a particular subject, done by a student **5** ARRANGEMENT ▷ [U] the way that people or things are arranged in a painting or photograph

compost /'kɒmpɒst/ **noun** [U] a mixture of decayed leaves and plants that is added to the soil to improve its quality: *a compost heap*

composure /kəm'pəʊʒə^r/ **noun** [U] a feeling or look of calm and confidence: *to keep/lose your composure*

compound¹ /'kɒmpaʊnd/ **noun** [C] **1** MIXTURE ▷ a substance that is a combination of two or more elements: *a compound of hydrogen and oxygen.* **2** AREA ▷ an area of land with a group of buildings surrounded by a fence or wall: *a prison compound* **3** GRAMMAR ▷ (also **compound noun/verb/adjective**) a noun, verb, or adjective that is made by two or more words used together. For example, 'golf club' is a compound.

compound² /kəm'paʊnd/ **verb** [T] to make a problem or difficult situation worse: *Severe drought has compounded food shortages in the region.*

comprehend /ˌkɒmprɪ'hend/ **verb** [I, T] formal to understand: *I was too young to comprehend what was happening.*

comprehensible /ˌkɒmprɪ'hensəbl/ **adj** easy to understand: *Computer manuals should be easily comprehensible.*

comprehension /ˌkɒmprɪ'henʃ^ən/ **noun** **1** [U] the ability to understand something: *How anyone could be so cruel is beyond my comprehension* (= *I can't understand it*). **2** [C, U] UK a test to see how well students understand written or spoken language: *a reading comprehension*

comprehensive¹ /ˌkɒmprɪ'hensɪv/ **adj** including everything: *a comprehensive study of the subject* • **comprehensively adv** completely: *We were comprehensively beaten in the finals.*

comprehensive² /ˌkɒmprɪ'hensɪv/ **noun** [C] (also **compre'hensive ˌschool**) a school in Britain for students aged 11 to 18 of all levels of ability

compress /kəm'pres/ **verb** [T] **1** to make something smaller, especially by pressing it, so that it uses less space or time: *compressed air* ∘ *The course compresses two years' training into six months.* **2** to use a special program to make information on a computer use less space • **compression** /kəm'preʃ^ən/ **noun** [U]

comprise /kəm'praɪz/ **verb** [T] formal **1** to consist of particular parts or members: *The orchestra was comprised of amateur and professional musicians.* **2** to form part of something, especially a larger group: *Women comprise 15% of the police force.*

compromise¹ /'kɒmprəmaɪz/ **noun** [C, U] ⑫ an agreement to accept something which is not exactly what you want: *We need to reach a compromise over this issue.* ∘ *Decorating is usually a compromise between taste and cost.*

> **⚈ Word partners for compromise**
>
> accept/come to/find/reach a compromise • a compromise **between** sth and sth • a compromise **on** sth • a compromise **agreement/deal/solution**

compromise² /'kɒmprəmaɪz/ **verb** **1** AGREE ▷ [I] ⑫ to agree to something that is not exactly what you want: *The president may be willing to compromise in order to pass the bill.* ∘ *I never compromise on fresh ingredients.* **2** compromise yourself to do something dishonest or embarrassing that makes people stop admiring you **3** BELIEFS ▷ [T] to do something that does not agree with what you believe in: *I refuse to compromise my principles.* **4** HARM ▷ [T] formal to have a harmful effect on something: *The trial has been seriously compromised by sensational media coverage.*

compromising /'kɒmprəmaɪzɪŋ/ **adj** A compromising situation, photograph, etc make people think you have done something wrong: *The press printed compromising photographs of the princess and her bodyguard.*

compulsion /kəm'pʌlʃ^ən/ **noun** **1** [C] a strong wish to do something, often something that you should not do **2** [U] a situation in which you are forced to do something: *We were under no compulsion to attend.*

compulsive /kəm'pʌlsɪv/ **adj** **1** A compulsive habit is something that you do a lot because you want to so much that you cannot control yourself: *a compulsive eating disorder* **2** a compulsive eater/gambler/liar, etc someone who is unable to stop eating/lying, etc, despite knowing that they should stop **3** so interesting or exciting that you cannot stop reading, playing, or watching it: *This documentary about life in prison makes compulsive viewing.* • **compulsively adv**

compulsory /kəm'pʌls^əri/ **adj** ⑫ If something is compulsory, you must do it because of a rule or law.

computer /kəm'pju:tə^r/ **noun** [C] ⓐ⓵ an electronic machine that can store and arrange large amounts of information: *We've put all our records on computer.* ∘ *computer software* → See colour picture **The Office** on page Centre 5

com'puter aided de'sign noun [C] CAD

com'puter ˌgame noun [C] a game that is played on a computer, in which the pictures on the screen are controlled by pressing keys

computer-generated /kəmˌpju:tə^r'dʒen^əreɪtɪd/ **adj** designed or produced using a computer program: *a computer-generated image*

ɑ: arm | ɜ: her | i: see | ɔ: saw | u: too | aɪ my | aʊ how | eə hair | eɪ day | əʊ no | ɪə near | ɔɪ boy | ʊə pure | aɪə fire | aʊə sour

computer **graphics** noun [plural] images or designs that are created using a computer

computerize (also UK **-ise**) /kəm'pjuːtᵊraɪz/ verb [T] to use a computer to do something that was done by people or other machines before: *a computerized accounts system* • **computerization** /kəm,pjuːtᵊraɪ'zeɪʃᵊn/ noun [U]

computer **literacy** noun [U] the ability to use computers effectively

com,puter **literate** adj able to understand and use computer systems

computer **program** noun [C] (also **program**) a set of instructions that makes a computer do a particular thing

computer **programmer** noun [C] (also **programmer**) someone who writes computer programs as a job

computer **programming** noun [U] (also **programming**) the activity or job of writing programs for computers

com,puter **science** noun [U] the study of computers and how they can be used

computing /kəm'pjuːtɪŋ/ noun [U] the study or use of computers: *a degree in computing*

comrade /'kɒmreɪd/ ⓤ /'kɑːmræd/ noun [C] **1** literary a friend, especially someone who fights with you in a war **2** a word used by some members of trade unions (= organizations which represent people who do a particular job) or other Socialist organizations to talk to or about each other

comradeship /'kɒmreɪdʃɪp/ noun [U] the feeling of friendship between people who live or work together, especially in a difficult situation

con¹ /kɒn/ verb [T] (**conning, conned**) informal to trick someone, especially in order to take money from them: *Thieves **conned him out of** his life savings.* ∘ *She felt she had been **conned into** buying the car.*

con² /kɒn/ noun [C] informal a trick to get someone's money, or make them do what you want

con **artist** noun [C] someone who tricks people into giving them money or valuable things

concave /'kɒnkeɪv/ adj A concave surface curves inwards: *a concave lens*

conceal /kən'siːl/ verb [T] to hide something: *The listening device was concealed in a pen.* ∘ *She could barely conceal her irritation.* • **concealment** noun [U] the act of hiding something

concede /kən'siːd/ verb **1** [T] to admit that something is true, even though you do not want to: [+ (that)] *Even the company chairman concedes that the results are disappointing.* **2** [I, T] to allow someone to have something, even though you do not want to: *The government will not **concede to** rebel demands.* **3** **concede defeat** to admit that you have lost a fight, argument, game, etc

conceit /kən'siːt/ noun [U] too much pride in yourself and your actions

conceited /kən'siːtɪd/ adj too proud of yourself and your actions • **conceitedly** adv

conceivable /kən'siːvəbl/ adj possible to imagine or to believe: *every conceivable kind of*

fruit ∘ [+ (that)] *It is just conceivable that the hospital made a mistake.* • **conceivably** adv

conceive /kən'siːv/ verb **1** BABY ▷ [I, T] to become pregnant **2** IMAGINE ▷ [I, T] to be able to imagine something: *I cannot **conceive of** anything more horrible.* **3** IDEA ▷ [T] to think of an idea or plan: *The original idea for the novel was conceived in Rome.*

concentrate /'kɒnsᵊntreɪt/ verb **1** ⓐ [I] to think very carefully about something you are doing and nothing else: *Be quiet – I'm trying to concentrate.* ∘ *I can't **concentrate on** my work. It's too noisy here.* **2** **be concentrated around/in/on, etc** to be present in large numbers or amounts in a particular area: *Most of the fighting was concentrated in the mountains.*

PHRASAL VERB **concentrate on sth** to use most of your time and effort to do something: *She gave up her job to concentrate on writing a novel.*

concentrated /'kɒnsᵊntreɪtɪd/ adj **1** [always before noun] using a lot of effort to succeed at one particular thing: *a **concentrated effort** to finish the work* **2** A concentrated liquid has had most of the water removed: *concentrated tomato puree*

concentration /,kɒnsᵊn'treɪʃᵊn/ noun **1** [U] ⓑ the ability to think carefully about something you are doing and nothing else **2** [C, U] a large number or amount of something in the same place: *high **concentrations** of minerals*

> ☑ Word partners for **concentration**
>
> sth **demands/needs/requires** concentration • **lose** concentration • a **lapse in/of** concentration • your **powers of** concentration

concen'tration **camp** noun [C] a prison where large numbers of people are kept in very bad conditions, especially for political reasons

concentric /kən'sentrɪk/ adj Concentric circles have the same centre but are different sizes.

concept /'kɒnsept/ noun [C] ⓑ an idea or principle: *the concept of free speech*

conception /kən'sepʃᵊn/ noun **1** [C, U] an idea about what something is like or a way of understanding something **2** [U] the moment when a woman or animal becomes pregnant

conceptual /kən'septʃuəl/ adj formal based on ideas: *a conceptual model*

concern¹ /kən'sɜːn/ verb [T] **1** INVOLVE ▷ ⓑ to involve someone or be important to them: *Environmental issues concern us all.* **2** WORRY ▷ to worry or upset someone: *What really concerns me is her lack of experience.* **3** BE ABOUT ▷ ⓑ If a story, film, etc concerns a particular subject, it is about that subject. **4** **concern yourself** to become involved with doing something: *You needn't concern yourself with the travel arrangements.*

concern² /kən'sɜːn/ noun **1** WORRY ▷ [C, U] ⓑ a feeling of worry about something, or the thing that is worrying you: *I have **concerns about** his health.* **2** IMPORTANT THING ▷ [C, U] ⓑ something that involves or affects you or is important

C

to you: *Our primary concern is safety.*
3 BUSINESS ▷ [C] a company or business: *The perfume factory was a family concern.*

> 🗹 Word partners for **concern**
>
> **cause** concern • **express/raise/voice** concern • **grave/serious** concern • concerns **about/over** sth • a **matter of** concern • a **cause for** concern

concerned /kən'sɜ:nd/ **adj 1** 🔢 worried: [+ that] *I am very concerned that class sizes seem to be growing.* ∘ *People are becoming more **concerned about** what they eat.* → Opposite **unconcerned 2** [never before noun] involved in something or affected by it: *A letter will be sent out to everyone concerned.* **3 as far as sb is concerned** 🔢 used to show what someone thinks about something: *As far as our customers are concerned, price is the main consideration.* **4 as far as sth is concerned** 🔢 used to tell someone what you are talking about: *As far as college is concerned, everything is fine.*

concerning /kən'sɜ:nɪŋ/ **preposition** 🔢 about something: *I've had a letter concerning my tax payments.*

concert /'kɒnsət/ **noun** [C] 🔢 a performance of music and singing: *a pop concert*

concerted /kən'sɜ:rtɪd/ **adj** [always before noun] done with a lot of effort, often by a group of people working together: *Iceland has made **a concerted effort** to boost tourism.*

concerto /kən'tʃeətəʊ/ **noun** [C] a piece of music for one main instrument and an orchestra (= large group of musicians): *a piano concerto*

concession /kən'seʃ°n/ **noun 1 AGREEMENT** ▷ [C, U] something that you agree to do or give to someone in order to end an argument: *Both sides will have to **make concessions**.* **2 BUSINESS** ▷ [C] a special right to use buildings or land or to sell a product in a particular area, or the place where that business takes place: *The company was given a concession to develop oil fields in the north.* **3 LOW PRICE** ▷ [C] UK a reduction in the price of a ticket for a particular group of people such as students, people without a job, or old people

conciliation /kən,sɪli'eɪʃ°n/ **noun** [U] formal the process of trying to end an argument

conciliatory /kən'sɪliət°ri/ **adj** formal If people behave in a conciliatory manner, they try to make people stop being angry with them: *a conciliatory approach*

concise /kən'saɪs/ **adj 1** giving a lot of information clearly in a few words **2** A concise book is small: *a concise history of France* • **concisely** adv • **conciseness** noun [U]

conclude /kən'klu:d/ **verb 1 END** ▷ [I, T] formal to end something such as a meeting, speech, or piece of writing by doing or saying one last thing: *The concert **concluded with** a firework display.* ∘ *I would like to **conclude by** thanking you all for attending.* **2 DECIDE** ▷ [T] to decide something after studying all the information about it very carefully: [+ that] *The report concluded that the drug was safe.*

3 COMPLETE ▷ [T] to complete something especially an agreement or a business arrange ment: *Talks aimed at concluding the peace treat will begin tomorrow.*

concluding /kən'klu:dɪŋ/ **adj** [always befor noun] last in a series of things: *Don't mis tonight's concluding episode.*

conclusion /kən'klu:ʒ°n/ **noun 1 OPINION** ▷ [C 🔢 the opinion you have after considering a the information about something: *I've **come t the conclusion that** we'll have to sell the ca* **2 END** ▷ [C] the final part of something: *th dramatic conclusion of the film* ∘ *The case shoul finally **be brought to a conclusion** (= end) week.* **3 in conclusion** 🔢 used to introduce th last part of a speech or piece of writing: *I conclusion, I would like to thank our guest speake* **4 ARRANGEMENT** ▷ [U] the process of arrangin or agreeing something formally: *the conclusio of peace talks*

IDIOM **jump to conclusions** to guess the fact about a situation without having enough infor mation

→ See also **foregone conclusion**

> 🗹 Word partners for **conclusion**
>
> **draw/reach** a conclusion • **come to** the con clusion **that** • sth **leads** you to the conclu sion **that**

conclusive /kən'klu:sɪv/ **adj** proving that som thing is true: *conclusive evidence/proof* • **cor clusively** adv *Tests have **proved conclusivel** that the drugs are effective.*

concoct /kən'kɒkt/ **verb** [T] **1** to invent a story o explanation in order to deceive someone: *H had concocted a web of lies.* **2** to make somethin unusual, especially food, by mixing thing together • **concoction** /kən'kɒkʃ°n/ **noun** [C] concoction of meringue, ice cream, and fres strawberries*

concourse /'kɒŋkɔ:s/ **noun** [C] a large room o open area inside a building such as an airport o station

concrete¹ /'kɒŋkri:t/ **noun** [U] 🔢 a har substance that is used in building and is mad by mixing sand, water, small stones, and cemer (= grey powder that is mixed with water an becomes hard when it dries): *concrete blocks*

concrete² /'kɒŋkri:t/ **adj 1** certain or based o facts: *concrete evidence/proof* **2** existing in real form that can be seen or felt: *concret achievements/actions* ∘ *concrete objects*

concrete³ /'kɒŋkri:t/ **verb** [T] UK to cover som thing with concrete

concur /kən'kɜ:r/ **verb** [I] (**concurring, co curred**) formal to agree: *The new report concur with previous findings.*

concurrent /kən'kʌr°nt/ **adj** happening existing at the same time: *three concurre prison sentences* • **concurrently** adv

concussed /kən'kʌst/ **adj** [never before noun] someone is concussed, they are suffering fro concussion.

concussion /kən'kʌʃ°n/ **noun** [C, U] a sligh

injury to the brain that is caused by being hit on the head and that makes you unconscious or feel tired or ill

condemn /kən'dem/ **verb** [T] **1** to say very strongly that you think something is wrong or very bad: *The Prime Minister was quick to condemn the terrorists.* **2** to say that a building must be destroyed because it is not safe enough for people to use

PHRASAL VERB **condemn sb to sth 1** to say what the punishment of someone who is guilty of a serious crime will be: *He was condemned to death.* **2** to make someone suffer in a particular way: *Poor education condemns many young people to low-paid jobs.*

condemnation /,kɒndem'neɪʃᵊn/ **noun** [C, U] strong criticism of something that you think is wrong or very bad: *widespread condemnation of the war*

condensation /,kɒnden'seɪʃᵊn/ **noun** [U] small drops of water that form when warm air touches a cold surface

condense /kən'dens/ **verb 1** AIR ▷ [I, T] If hot air or a gas condenses, it changes into a liquid as it becomes colder. **2** WORDS ▷ [T] to make something such as a speech or piece of writing shorter: *You need to **condense** your conclusion **into** a single paragraph.* **3** LIQUID ▷ [T] to make a liquid thicker by taking some of the water out of it: *condensed milk*

condescend /,kɒndɪ'send/ **verb condescend to do sth** humorous to agree to do something even though you think you are too important to do it

PHRASAL VERB **condescend to sb** to treat someone as though you are better or more important than them

condescending /,kɒndɪ'sendɪŋ/ **adj** showing that you think that you are better or more important than someone else: *a condescending smile* • **condescendingly adv**

condescension /,kɒndɪ'senʃᵊn/ **noun** [U] behaviour that shows you think you are better or more important than someone

condition¹ /kən'dɪʃᵊn/ **noun 1** STATE ▷ [U, no plural] 🅱 the state that something or someone is in: *My bike's a few years old but it's **in** really **good condition**.* ◦ *He's **in no condition** (= not well enough) to travel.* **2** AGREEMENT ▷ [C] something that must happen or be agreed before something else can happen: *One of the conditions of the contract is that we can't keep pets.* **3 on condition that** 🅱 only if: *Visitors are allowed in the gardens on condition that they don't touch the plants.* **4** ILLNESS ▷ [C] 🅱 an illness: *a serious heart condition* **5 conditions** 🅱 the physical situation that people are in: ***working/living conditions*** ◦ *severe **weather conditions***

condition² /kən'dɪʃᵊn/ **verb** [T] **1** to make a person or animal behave in a particular way by influencing the way they think: [often passive, + to do sth] *The boys were conditioned to be aggressive.* **2** to put a special liquid on your hair to make it soft and healthy

conditional /kən'dɪʃᵊnᵊl/ **adj 1** If an offer or agreement is conditional, it will only happen if something else is done first: *Their fee is **conditional on** the work being completed by January.* → Opposite **unconditional 2** A conditional sentence usually begins with 'if' and says that something must be true or happen before something else can be true or happen.

conditioner /kən'dɪʃᵊnər/ **noun** [C, U] a liquid that you use when you wash your hair to make it soft

conditioning /kən'dɪʃᵊnɪŋ/ **noun** [U] ways of making a person or animal behave in a particular way, especially by influencing the way they think: *social/physical conditioning* → See also **air conditioning**

condo /'kɒndəʊ/ **noun** [C] US informal short for condominium

condolence /kən'dəʊləns/ **noun** [C, U] formal sympathy for the family or friends of a person who has recently died: *Please **offer my condolences** to your father.*

condom /'kɒndɒm/ Ⓤ /'kɑːndəm/ **noun** [C] a thin rubber covering that a man wears on his penis during sex to stop a woman becoming pregnant, or to protect against diseases

condominium /,kɒndə'mɪniəm/ **noun** [C] US a building containing apartments that are owned by the people living in them, or one of these apartments

condone /kən'dəʊn/ **verb** [T] to accept or allow behaviour that is wrong: *His comments appeared to condone drug abuse.*

conducive /kən'djuːsɪv/ **adj** making something possible or likely to happen: *Such a noisy environment was not **conducive to** a good night's sleep.*

conduct¹ /'kɒndʌkt/ **noun 1** [U] the way someone behaves: *a code of conduct (= rules about how to behave)* **2 conduct of sth** the way someone organizes or does something: *He was criticized for his conduct of the inquiry.*

conduct² /kən'dʌkt/ **verb 1** DO ▷ [T] 🅱 to organize or do something: *They're **conducting** a survey.* **2** MUSIC ▷ [I, T] 🅱 to stand in front of a group of musicians and control their performance **3** HEAT ▷ [T] If a substance conducts electricity or heat, it allows electricity or heat to go through it. **4 conduct yourself** to behave in a particular way: *She conducted herself with great dignity.* **5** LEAD ▷ [T] formal to lead someone to a place: *I was conducted to a side room.*

┌─────────────────────────────────────┐
│ 🗹 Word partners for **conduct**   │
│   │
│ conduct an **experiment/an interview/an** │
│ **inquiry/an investigation/research/** a survey │
└─────────────────────────────────────┘

conductor /kən'dʌktər/ **noun** [C] **1** MUSIC ▷ 🅱 someone who stands in front of a group of musicians or singers and controls their performance **2** BUS ▷ someone whose job is to sell or check tickets on a bus, train, etc **3** TRAIN ▷ US (UK **guard**) someone whose job is to be responsible for a train and the people who work on it **4** HEAT ▷ a substance that allows electricity or heat to go through it

cone /kəʊn/ **noun** [C] **1** a solid shape with a

C

round or oval base that narrows to a point, or an object that has this shape: *a row of traffic cones* **2** a container for ice cream (= sweet, frozen food) that you can eat

confectionery /kən'fekʃⁿⁿri/ **noun** [U] mainly UK sweet food like sweets and chocolate

confederacy /kən'fedⁿrəsi/ **noun** [C] (also **con-federation** /kənˌfedə'reɪʃⁿn/) an organization of smaller groups who have joined together for business or political purposes

confer /kən'fɜːr/ **verb** (**conferring, conferred**) **1** [I] to discuss something with other people before making a decision: *I'll need to confer with my lawyers.* **2** [T] formal to give someone something, especially an official title, an honour, or an advantage

conference /'kɒnfⁿrⁿns/ **noun** [C] **1** 🔵 a large, formal meeting, often lasting a few days, where people discuss their work, politics, subjects they are studying, etc: *the annual sales conference* **2** a small, private meeting for discussion of a particular subject → See also **press conference**

> **Word partners for conference**
>
> attend/hold a conference • a conference on sth • at a conference • a conference centre • a sales conference

'**conference ˌcall noun** [C] a telephone call between three or more people in different places

confess /kən'fes/ **verb** [I, T] **1** 🔵 to admit that you have done something wrong or something that you feel guilty about: [+ to + doing sth] *The man has confessed to stealing the painting.* ∘ *Rawlinson finally confessed to the murder.* **2** to tell a priest or God about all the wrong things that you have done

confession /kən'feʃⁿn/ **noun** [C, U] **1** 🔵 a statement in which you admit that you have done something wrong or illegal: *He has made a full confession to the police.* **2** an occasion when someone tells a priest all the wrong things they have done: *to go to confession*

confetti /kən'feti/ **noun** [U] small pieces of coloured paper that you throw when celebrating something such as a marriage

confidant, confidante /'kɒnfɪdænt/ **noun** [C] a person you can talk to about your feelings and secrets

confide /kən'faɪd/ **verb** [I, T] to tell a secret to someone who you trust not to tell anyone else: [+ that] *Holly confided to me that she was ill.*

PHRASAL VERB **confide in sb** to tell someone who you trust about things that are secret or personal

confidence /'kɒnfɪdⁿns/ **noun 1** ABILITY ▷ [U] 🔵 a feeling of being certain of your ability to do things well: *He's a good student, but he lacks confidence.* ∘ [+ to do sth] *His training has given him the confidence to deal with any problem that arises.* **2** TRUST ▷ [U] trust in someone's ability or a belief that something will produce good results: *Kate's new to the job, but I have every confidence in her.* **3** SECRET ▷ [C] something

secret that you tell someone: *to exchange confidences* **4 in confidence** If you tell something to someone in confidence, you do not want them to tell anyone else.

> **Word partners for confidence**
>
> 1 grow in/lack/lose confidence • sth gives you confidence • do sth with confidence • a lack of confidence
> 2 express/lose/restore confidence (in sth) • have (complete/every/little/no) confidence in sb/sth • consumer/public confidence • confidence in sth

confident /'kɒnfɪdⁿnt/ **adj 1** 🔵 certain about your ability to do things well: *a confident grin* ∘ *He feels confident of winning.* **2** 🔵 being certain that something will happen: [+ (that)] *Doctors are confident that she'll recover.* • **confidently adv** → See also **self-confident**

confidential /ˌkɒnfɪ'denʃⁿl/ **adj** secret, especially in an official situation: *These documents are strictly confidential.* • **confidentially adv** • **confidentiality** /ˌkɒnfɪdenʃi'æləti/ **noun** [U]

confine /kən'faɪn/ **verb** [T] to prevent someone from leaving a place or to prevent something from spreading: [often passive] *He was confined to a prison cell for several days.*

PHRASAL VERBS **be confined to sth/sb** to only exist in a particular area or group of people: *The flooding was confined to the basement.* • **confine sb/sth to sth** to limit an activity: *Please confine your discussion to the topic.*

confined /kən'faɪnd/ **adj** [always before noun] A confined space is very small.

confinement /kən'faɪnmənt/ **noun** [U] a situation in which someone is kept in a room or area usually by force → See also **solitary confinement**

confines /'kɒnfaɪnz/ **noun** [plural] the outer limits or edges of something

confirm /kən'fɜːm/ **verb** [T] **1** 🔵 to say or show that something is true: [+ (that)] *His wife confirmed that he'd left the house at 8.* **2** 🔵 to make an arrangement certain: *Flights should be confirmed 48 hours before departure.* **3 be confirmed** to become a member of the Christian Church at a special ceremony

confirmation /ˌkɒnfə'meɪʃⁿn/ **noun** [C, U] **1** 🔵 an announcement or proof that something is true or certain: *You'll receive written confirmation of your reservation within five days.* **2** a special ceremony in which someone becomes a full member of the Christian Church

confirmed /kən'fɜːmd/ **adj a confirmed atheist/bachelor/pessimist, etc** someone who has behaved in a particular way for a long time and is not likely to change

confiscate /'kɒnfɪskeɪt/ **verb** [T] to take some thing away from someone, especially as a punishment • **confiscation** /ˌkɒnfɪ'skeɪʃⁿn/ **noun** [C, U]

conflict¹ /'kɒnflɪkt/ **noun** [C, U] **1** DISAGREE MENT ▷ 🔵 serious disagreement: *The Govern ment was in conflict with the unions over pay*

○ *The peasants often came into conflict with the landowners.* **2 FIGHTING** ▷ 🅱️2 fighting between groups or countries: *armed conflict* **3 DIFFERENCE** ▷ a situation in which two or more different things cannot easily exist together: *the conflict between science and religion* **4 a conflict of interest** a situation where someone cannot make fair decisions because they are influenced by something

---

📝 **Word partners for conflict**

resolve a conflict • be in/come into conflict with sb • a conflict between sb and sb • a conflict over sth • an area of/source of conflict

---

conflict² /kənˈflɪkt/ **verb** [I] If things such as beliefs, needs, or facts conflict, they are very different and cannot easily exist together or both be true: *Her views on raising children conflict with mine.* ○ *There were conflicting accounts of how the fight started.*

conflicted /kənˈflɪktɪd/ **adj** [never before noun] confused because you have two feelings or opinions about something that are opposite

conform /kənˈfɔːm/ **verb** [I] to behave in the way that most other people behave

PHRASAL VERB conform to/with sth to obey a rule or to do things in a traditional way: *All our toys conform with safety standards.*

conformity /kənˈfɔːməti/ **noun** [U] **1** behaviour that is the same as the way that most other people behave **2 conformity to/with sth** formal following rules or traditional ways of doing things

confound /kənˈfaʊnd/ **verb** [T] If something confounds someone, it makes them surprised and confused, because they cannot explain it: *The growth in the economy continues to confound the experts.*

confront /kənˈfrʌnt/ **verb** [T] **1 ACCUSE** ▷ to tell someone something, or show them something to try to make them admit they have done something wrong: *Confronted with the evidence, she broke down and confessed.* **2 be confronted by/with sth** to be in a difficult situation, or to be shown something which may cause difficulties: *We are confronted by the possibility of war.* **3 FRIGHTEN** ▷ to stand in front of someone in a frightening way: *He was confronted by two masked men.* **4 DEAL WITH** ▷ to see that a problem exists and try to deal with it: *First, they must confront their addiction.*

confrontation /ˌkɒnfrʌnˈteɪʃən/ **noun** [C, U] a fight or argument

confrontational /ˌkɒnfrʌnˈteɪʃənəl/ **adj** intentionally causing fighting or an argument: *a confrontational style of management*

confuse /kənˈfjuːz/ **verb** [T] **1** 🅱️2 to make someone unable to think clearly or understand something: *These advertisements simply confused the public.* **2** 🅱️2 to think that one person or thing is another person or thing: *I don't see how anyone could confuse me with my mother!*

confused /kənˈfjuːzd/ **adj 1** 🅱️1 unable to think clearly or to understand something: *Sorry, I'm*

completely confused. ○ *The politicians themselves are confused about what to do.* **2** not clear: *The witnesses gave confused accounts of what happened.*

confusing /kənˈfjuːzɪŋ/ **adj** 🅱️1 difficult to understand: *I found the instructions very confusing.*

confusion /kənˈfjuːʒən/ **noun 1 NOT UNDERSTAND** ▷ [C, U] 🅱️2 a state in which people do not understand what is happening or what they should do: *There was a lot of confusion about what was actually going on.* **2 THOUGHT** ▷ [U] a feeling of not being able to think clearly: *He could see the confusion on Marion's face.* **3 BETWEEN SIMILAR THINGS** ▷ [U] the belief that one person or thing is another **4 SITUATION** ▷ [U] 🅱️2 a situation that is confusing because there is a lot of noise and activity: *In the confusion, several prisoners tried to escape.*

📝 **Word partners for confusion**

sth causes/creates/leads to confusion • confusion surrounds sth • do sth in confusion • widespread confusion • confusion about/over sth

---

congeal /kənˈdʒiːl/ **verb** [I] If a liquid congeals, it becomes thick and almost solid: *congealed fat*

congenial /kənˈdʒiːniəl/ **adj** formal pleasant and friendly: *congenial company*

congenital /kənˈdʒenɪtəl/ **adj** Congenital diseases or problems are ones that people have from when they are born: *congenital heart defects*

congested /kənˈdʒestɪd/ **adj** full or blocked, especially with traffic: *The roads are very congested.*

congestion /kənˈdʒestʃən/ **noun** [U] the state of being full or blocked, especially with traffic: *traffic congestion*

conglomerate /kənˈɡlɒmərət/ **noun** [C] a large company that is made up of several smaller companies

congratulate /kənˈɡrætʃuleɪt/ **verb** [T] 🅱️2 to tell someone that you are happy because they have done something good or something good has happened to them: *Did you congratulate Cathy on her engagement?*

congratulations /kənˌɡrætʃuˈleɪʃənz/ **exclamation** 🅰️2 something that you say when you want to congratulate someone: *Congratulations on doing an outstanding job.* ○ *I hear you're getting married. Congratulations!*

congregate /ˈkɒŋɡrɪɡeɪt/ **verb** [I] to come together in a group: *Young people congregated on street corners.*

congregation /ˌkɒŋɡrɪˈɡeɪʃən/ **noun** [group] a group of people meeting to worship in church

congress /ˈkɒŋɡres/ **noun 1** [C] a large meeting of the members of one or more organizations: *an international congress on art history* **2 Congress** the group of people who make laws in the United States. Congress consists of the Senate and the House of Representatives.

congressional /kənˈɡreʃənəl/ **adj** [always before noun] relating to the United States Congress: *a congressional committee*

---

congressman, congresswoman /ˈkɒŋgres-mən/, /ˈkɒŋgresˌwʊmən/ **noun** [C] (plural **congressmen**, **congresswomen**) a man or woman who is a member of the United States Congress

conical /ˈkɒnɪkəl/ **adj** Conical objects have a wide, round base, sloping sides and a pointed top.

conifer /ˈkɒnɪfəʳ/ **noun** [C] a tree with thin green leaves that stay green all winter and cones (= hard, brown, oval objects)

conjecture /kənˈdʒektʃəʳ/ **noun** [C, U] formal guesses about something without real evidence: *Exactly what happened that night is still a matter for conjecture.* • **conjecture verb** [I, T] formal [+ (that)] *Some people conjectured that it was an attempt to save money.*

conjugal /ˈkɒndʒʊgəl/ **adj** formal relating to marriage

conjugate /ˈkɒndʒʊgeɪt/ **verb** [T] to add different endings to a verb in order to produce all its different forms • **conjugation** /ˌkɒndʒʊˈgeɪʃən/ **noun** [C, U]

conjunction /kənˈdʒʌŋkʃən/ **noun 1** ⭲ [C] A word that is used to connect phrases or parts of a sentence. For example the words 'and', 'because', and 'although' are conjunctions. **2 in conjunction with sth/sb** working, used, or happening with something or someone else

conjure /ˈkʌndʒəʳ/ **verb**

PHRASAL VERB **conjure sth up 1** to make a picture or idea appear in someone's mind: *Familiar tunes can help us conjure up memories of the past.* **2** to make something in a quick and clever way, especially food

conjurer /ˈkʌndʒərəʳ/ **noun** [C] another spelling of conjuror

conjuring /ˈkʌndʒərɪŋ/ **noun** [U] magic tricks used to entertain people: *a conjuring trick*

conjuror /ˈkʌndʒərəʳ/ **noun** [C] a person who performs magic to entertain people

conman /ˈkɒnmæn/ **noun** [C] a man who tricks people into giving him money or valuable things

connect /kəˈnekt/ **verb 1** JOIN ▷ [I, T] ⭲ to join two things or places together: *Ferries connect the mainland · with the islands.* ∘ *Connect up the printer to your computer.* **2** INVOLVE ▷ [T] to see or show that two or more people or things are involved with each other: *There is no evidence to connect him with the crime.* **3** TRAVEL ▷ [I] If buses, trains, aircraft, etc connect, they arrive at a particular time so that passengers can get off one and onto another: *Can you get me a connecting flight?* **4** TELEPHONE ▷ [T] to make it possible for two people to talk to each other on the telephone · → Opposite **disconnect 5** COMPUTER SYSTEM ▷ [I, T] to use a computer, phone, etc. in order to use the Internet or other computer system: *You must have anti-virus software if your computer is connected to the Internet.*

connected /kəˈnektɪd/ **adj 1** If people or things are connected, there is a relationship between them: *The hospital is connected to the University of Rochester.* ∘ *He remained closely connected*

with the museum until his death. → Opposit **unconnected 2** If two things are connected they are joined together: *The Red Sea* **connected to** the Mediterranean by the Sue Canal. → Opposite **disconnected** → See als **well-connected**

connection /kəˈnekʃən/ **noun 1** RELATION SHIP ▷ [C, U] ⭲ a relationship between peopl or things: *The connection between smoking an heart disease is well known.* ∘ *He denied havin any connection with the terrorists.* **2** JOINING THINGS ▷ [C, U] ⭲ something that joins thing together: *Many companies now offer free connec tion to the Internet.* **3** TRAVEL ▷ [C] ⭲ a trair bus, or aircraft that leaves a short time afte another arrives, so that people can continu their journey: *The train was half an hour late an I missed my connection.* **4 in connection witl** ⭲ used to say what something is about: *A ma has been arrested in connection with the murder.*

🔲 Word partners for **connection**

have a/no connection with sb/sth • a **close/ direct** connection • a connection **between** sth and sth • a connection **with** sth

connections /kəˈnekʃənz/ **noun** [plural] impor tant or powerful people who you know and wh will help you: *He has connections in Washington*

connive /kəˈnaɪv/ **verb** [I] to work secretly to d something wrong or illegal, or to allow some thing wrong or illegal to happen: *They accuse the government of conniving in drug smuggling*

connoisseur /ˌkɒnəˈsɜːʳ/ **noun** [C] someone wh knows a lot about and enjoys good food, wine art, etc

connotation /ˌkɒnəˈteɪʃən/ **noun** [C, U] the feelings or ideas that words give in addition t their meanings: *The word 'second-hand' ha connotations of poor quality.*

conquer /ˈkɒŋkəʳ/ **verb 1** [I, T] to take control c a country or to defeat people by war: *Peru wa conquered by the Spanish in 1532.* **2** [T] to succee in stopping or dealing with a bad feeling or difficult problem: *He has finally conquered h fear of spiders.*

conqueror /ˈkɒŋkərəʳ/ **noun** [C] someone wh has conquered a country or its people

conquest /ˈkɒŋkwest/ **noun** [C, U] an occasio when someone takes control of a country, are or situation: *the Roman conquest of Britain*

conscience /ˈkɒnʃəns/ **noun 1** [C, U] the part c you that makes you feel guilty when you hav behaved badly: *a guilty conscience* ∘ *My con science is clear* (= I do not feel guilty) *becaus I've done nothing wrong.* **2 be on your con science** If something is on your conscience, it making you feel guilty.

conscientious /ˌkɒnʃiˈenʃəs/ **adj** always doin your work with a lot of care: *a conscientiou student* • **conscientiously adv**

conscientious objector /ˌkɒnʃiˌenʃəsəbˈdʒektə təʳ/ **noun** [C] someone who refuses to work i the armed forces because they think war wrong

conscious /ˈkɒnʃəs/ **adj 1** be conscious of/tha

C

⬛ to know that something is present or that something is happening: *I'm very conscious that a lot of people disagree with me.* **2 a conscious decision/choice/effort, etc** a decision/choice/ effort, etc that you make intentionally: *Did you make a conscious decision to lose weight?* → Opposite **subconscious adj 3** awake and able to think and notice things: *He's still conscious but he's very badly injured.* → Opposite **unconscious adj** • **consciously adv** → See also **self-conscious**

conscious /'kɒnʃəs/ **suffix** used at the end of words to mean 'thinking that something is important': *a safety-conscious mother* ◦ *fashion-conscious teenagers*

consciousness /'kɒnʃəsnəs/ **noun 1** [U] **⬛** the state of being awake and being able to think and notice things: *He lost consciousness* (= stopped being conscious) *for several minutes.* ◦ *I want to be here when she regains consciousness* (= becomes conscious again). **2** [no plural] knowledge of something: *There's a growing consciousness about environmental issues among young people.*

conscript¹ /'kɒnskrɪpt/ **noun** [C] someone who has been made to join the army

conscript² /kən'skrɪpt/ **verb** [T] to make someone join the army: [often passive] *During World War I, he was conscripted into the Russian army.*

conscription /kən'skrɪpʃ°n/ **noun** [U] a system in which people are made to join the army

consecrate /'kɒnsɪkreɪt/ **verb** [T] to make a place or object holy in a religious ceremony • **consecration** /ˌkɒnsɪ'kreɪʃ°n/ **noun** [U] *a consecration ceremony*

consecutive /kən'sekjʊtɪv/ **adj** Consecutive events, numbers, or periods of time come one after the other: *the third consecutive day of rain* • **consecutively adv**

consensus /kən'sensəs/ **noun** [U, no plural] a situation in which all the people in a group agree about something: *to reach a consensus* ◦ *The general consensus is that we should wait and see what happens.*

consent¹ /kən'sent/ **noun** [U] **1** permission for someone to do something: *You can't come without your parents' consent.* **2 by common consent** UK used to say that everyone agrees about something: *He is, by common consent, the most talented actor in Hollywood.*

consent² /kən'sent/ **verb** [I] to agree to do something, or to allow someone to do something: [+ to do sth] *They eventually consented to let us enter.*

🗹 Word partners for **consequence**

face/live with/suffer the consequences • as a consequence (of sth) • a **direct** consequence • devastating/dire/disastrous/serious consequences • the consequences of sth

---

consequence /'kɒnsɪkwəns/ **noun 1 ⬛** [C] the result of an action or situation, especially a bad result: *The ship capsized, with disastrous consequences.* ◦ *If you make him angry, you'll have*

to **suffer the consequences.** **2 of little/no consequence** formal not important: *The money was of little consequence to Tony.*

consequent /'kɒnsɪkwənt/ **adj** [always before noun] formal happening as a result of something: *the closure of the factory and the consequent loss of 400 jobs*

consequently /'kɒnsɪkwəntli/ **adv ⬛** as a result: *She was the child of two models and, consequently, she was very tall.*

conservation /ˌkɒnsə'veɪʃ°n/ **noun** [U] **1 ⬛** the protection of nature: *wildlife conservation* ◦ *conservation groups* **2** the careful use of energy, water, etc so that they are not wasted

conservationist /ˌkɒnsə'veɪʃ°nɪst/ **noun** [C] someone who believes that people should protect nature

conservatism /kən'sɜːvətɪz°m/ **noun** [U] conservative actions and beliefs

conservative /kən'sɜːvətɪv/ **adj 1** not trusting sudden changes or new ideas: *Older people tend to be very conservative.* **2 a conservative estimate/guess** a guess about a number or amount that is probably lower than the true number or amount

Conservative /kən'sɜːvətɪv/ **noun** [C] someone who supports the Conservative Party in the UK: *the Conservative candidate/MP*

the Con'servative ˌParty noun [group] one of the three main political parties in the UK

conservatory /kən'sɜːvət°ri/ **noun** [C] a room attached to a house that has windows all around it and a glass roof

conserve /kən'sɜːv/ **verb** [T] **1** to use something in a way that does not waste it: *Insulating the walls will help to conserve heat.* **2** to prevent harm or damage to animals or places

consider /kən'sɪdər/ **verb 1** [T] **⬛** to think carefully about a decision or something you might do: *Have you considered surgery?* ◦ [+ doing sth] *We're considering buying a new car.* **2** [T] to think about particular facts when you are making a decision about something: *If you buy an old house, you have to consider the cost of repairs.* **3 consider sb/sth (to be) sth; consider that ⬛** to have a particular opinion about someone or something: [often reflexive] *I don't consider myself to be a great athlete.*

considerable /kən'sɪd°rəbl/ **adj ⬛** large or important enough to have an effect: *a considerable amount of money* ◦ *The damage has been considerable.* • **considerably adv ⬛** *Rates of pay vary considerably.*

considerate /kən'sɪd°rət/ **adj** kind and helpful: *a polite and considerate child* → Opposite **inconsiderate**

consideration /kənˌsɪd°r'eɪʃ°n/ **noun 1 IMPORTANT FACT ▷** [C] **⬛** something that you have to think about when you make decisions or plans: *Safety is our main consideration.* **2 CAREFUL THOUGHT ▷** [U] **⬛** careful thought about something: *After careful consideration, we have decided to offer you the job.* ◦ *Several options are under consideration* (= being considered). **3 KINDNESS ▷** [U] kind behaviour towards someone in which you think about their feelings: *They always treated me with consideration.* **4 take sth into consideration** to think about something when you make a decision or plan

> **☑ Word partners for consideration**
>
> 1 an **important/the main/a major** consideration • **environmental/financial/political** considerations
> 2 **careful/serious** consideration • be **under** consideration • be **worthy of** consideration

considered /kən'sıdəd/ *adj* **1** [always before noun] A considered opinion or decision is based on careful thought: *It is our considered opinion that he should resign.* **2 all things considered** used when you are giving your opinion about something after thinking carefully about all the facts: *All things considered, I think we made the right choice.*

considering /kən'sıdərıŋ/ *preposition*, **conjunction** ⑫ used for saying that you have a particular opinion about something, because of a particular fact about it: *She's fairly fit considering her age.* ∘ *Considering she'd only been there once before, she did well to find the way.*

consign /kən'saın/ *verb*

PHRASAL VERB **consign sb/sth to sth** formal to get rid of someone or something or to put them in an unpleasant place or situation: *They were consigned to a life of poverty.*

consignment /kən'saınmənt/ *noun* [C] an amount of goods that is being sent somewhere: *a ship carrying a small consignment of rice*

consist /kən'sıst/ *verb*

PHRASAL VERB **consist of sth** ⑪ to be formed or made from two or more things: *a dessert consisting of fruit and cream*

consistency /kən'sıstənsi/ *noun* **1** [+ (that)] behaviour or performance that is always the same or similar: *The team has won a few games but lacks consistency.* **2** [C, U] how thick or smooth a liquid is: *Beat the mixture to a smooth consistency.*

consistent /kən'sıstənt/ *adj* **1** always behaving or happening in a similar, usually positive, way: *consistent effort/improvement* **2 consistent with sth** formal having the same principles as something else, or agreeing with other facts: *His account of events is entirely consistent with the video evidence.* • **consistently** *adv The President has consistently denied the rumours.*

consolation /ˌkɒnsə'leıʃən/ *noun* [C, U] something that makes you feel better about a bad situation: *If it's any consolation, I failed my driving test too.*

console¹ /kən'səʊl/ *verb* [T] to make someone who is sad feel better: *I tried to console her but she just kept crying.*

console² /'kɒnsəʊl/ *noun* [C] an object that contains the controls for a piece of equipment: *a video game console*

consolidate /kən'sɒlıdeıt/ *verb* **1** [I, T] to make sure that you become more powerful, or that success and achievements continue strongly: *It will take him some time to consolidate his position in the banking world.* **2** [T] to combine several things, especially businesses, so that they become more effective, or to be combined in this way: *He consolidated his businesses into one large company.* • **consolidation** /kənˌsɒlı'deıʃən/ *noun* [U]

consonant /'kɒnsənənt/ *noun* [C] ⑪ a letter of the alphabet that is not a vowel

consort /kən'sɔːt/ *verb*

PHRASAL VERB **consort with sb** to spend time with a bad person: *They claimed he had been consorting with drug dealers.*

consortium /kən'sɔːtiəm/ *noun* [C] (plural **consortiums**, **consortia**) an organization consisting of several businesses or banks: *an international consortium of airlines*

conspicuous /kən'spıkjuəs/ *adj* very easy to notice: *His army uniform made him very conspicuous.* • **conspicuously** *adv His wife was conspicuously absent.*

conspiracy /kən'spırəsi/ *noun* [C, U] secret plans by group of people to do something bad or illegal: [+ to do sth] *a conspiracy to overthrow the government*

conspirator /kən'spırətər/ *noun* [C] someone who secretly plans with other people to do something bad or illegal

conspire /kən'spaıər/ *verb* **1** [I] to join with other people to secretly plan to do something bad or illegal: [+ to do sth] *He was convicted of conspiring to sell and supply drugs.* ∘ *The king accused his advisers of conspiring against him.* **2 conspire against sb; conspire to do sth** If events or a situation conspire against you, they cause problems for you: *Circumstances had conspired to ruin her plans.*

constable /'kʌnstəbl/ *noun* [C] a British police officer of the lowest rank

constant /'kɒnstənt/ *adj* **1** ⑫ happening a lot or all the time: *These machines are in constant use* **2** staying at the same level: *The temperature remained constant.* • **constantly** *adv* ⑫ *He's constantly changing his mind.*

constellation /ˌkɒnstə'leıʃən/ *noun* [C] a group of stars

consternation /ˌkɒnstə'neıʃən/ *noun* [U] a feeling of shock or worry

constipated /'kɒnstıpeıtıd/ *adj* unable to empty your bowels as often as you should

constipation /ˌkɒnstı'peıʃən/ *noun* [U] the state of being constipated

constituency /kən'stıtjuənsi/ *noun* [C] an area of a country that elects someone to represent it in the government, or the people who live there

constituent /kən'stıtjuənt/ *noun* [C] **1** one of the parts or substances that something is made of: *Methane is the main **constituent of** natural gas.* **2** someone who lives in a particular constituency

constitute /'kɒnstıtjuːt/ *verb* [T] to be or form something: *This defeat constitutes a real setback for their championship hopes.*

constitution /ˌkɒnstɪˈtjuːʃᵊn/ noun [C] **1** the set of laws and principles that a country's government must obey: *the US Constitution* **2** the state of someone's health: *a strong/weak constitution*

constitutional /ˌkɒnstɪˈtjuːʃᵊnᵊl/ adj relating to the constitution of a country: *a constitutional crisis*

constrain /kənˈstreɪn/ verb [T] to control something by limiting it: *regulations that constrain industry* ∘ [often passive] *I'm constrained by decisions made in the past.*

constraint /kənˈstreɪnt/ noun [C] something that limits what you can do: *budget constraints* ∘ *There are constraints on the medicines doctors can prescribe.*

constrict /kənˈstrɪkt/ verb **1** [T] to limit someone's freedom to do what they want to or be the way they want to: *His creativity was constricted by the political regime he lived under.* **2** [I, T] to become narrower or tighter, or to make something narrower or tighter: *The blood vessels constricted.* • **constriction** /kənˈstrɪkʃᵊn/ noun [U]

construct /kənˈstrʌkt/ verb [T] 🔲 to build something from several parts: *The building was constructed in 1930.*

construction /kənˈstrʌkʃᵊn/ noun **1 BUILDING WORK** ▷ [U] 🔲 the work of building houses, offices, bridges, etc: *railway construction* ∘ *construction work* **2 LARGE BUILDING** ▷ [C] 🔲 something large that is built: *a large steel construction* **3 WORDS** ▷ [C] 🔲 The construction of a sentence or phrase is the way the words are arranged.

constructive /kənˈstrʌktɪv/ adj helpful or useful: *constructive advice/criticism* • **constructively** adv

construe /kənˈstruː/ verb [T] (**construing, construed**) to understand something in a particular way: *Her comments could be construed as patronizing.*

consul /ˈkɒnsᵊl/ noun [C] someone whose job is to work in a foreign country taking care of the people from their own country who go or live there

consular /ˈkɒnsjʊlər/ adj [always before noun] relating to a consul or a consulate: *consular officials*

consulate /ˈkɒnsjʊlət/ noun [C] the offices where a consul works: *the Cuban consulate in Mexico City*

consult /kənˈsʌlt/ verb [T] **1** to go to a particular person or book to get information or advice: *For more information, consult your travel agent.* **2** to discuss something with someone before you make a decision: *Why didn't you consult me about this?*

consultancy /kənˈsʌltᵊnsi/ noun **1** [C] a company that gives advice on subjects it knows a lot about: *a management/recruitment consultancy* **2** [U] the activity of giving advice on a particular subject

consultant /kənˈsʌltᵊnt/ noun [C] **1** 🔲 someone who advises people about a particular subject: *a*

tax consultant **2** UK a hospital doctor who is an expert in a particular area of medicine

consultation /ˌkɒnsᵊlˈteɪʃᵊn/ noun **1** [C] a meeting to discuss something or to get advice: *a medical consultation* **2** [U] discussion with someone in order to get their advice or opinion about it: *After consultation with his lawyers, he decided to abandon the case.*

consultative /kənˈsʌltətɪv/ adj A consultative group or document gives advice about something.

consume /kənˈsjuːm/ verb [T] **1 USE** ▷ 🔲 to use something such as a product, energy, or fuel: *These lights don't consume much electricity.* **2 EAT OR DRINK** ▷ formal 🔲 to eat or drink something **3** be consumed with/by sth to have so much of a feeling that it affects everything you do: *She was a dancer consumed by ambition.* **4 FIRE** ▷ If fire consumes something, it completely destroys it.

consumer /kənˈsjuːmər/ noun [C] 🔲 someone who buys or uses goods or services: *These price cuts are good news for consumers.*

> ☑ **Word partners for consumer**
>
> consumer **choice/confidence/demand/protection/spending**

consumerism /kənˈsjuːmərɪzᵊm/ noun [U] buying and selling things, especially when this is an important part of a society's activities

consummate¹ /ˈkɒnsəmeɪt/ verb [T] to make a marriage or relationship complete by having sex • **consummation** /ˌkɒnsəˈmeɪʃᵊn/ noun [U]

consummate² /kənˈsʌmət, ˈkɒnsəmət/ adj [always before noun] formal having great skill: *a consummate professional* ∘ *consummate ease/skill*

consumption /kənˈsʌmpʃᵊn/ noun [U] **1** the amount of something that someone uses, eats, or drinks: *China's total energy consumption* **2** the act of using, eating, or drinking something: *products sold for personal consumption*

contact¹ /ˈkɒntækt/ noun **1 COMMUNICATION** ▷ [U] 🔲 communication with someone, especially by speaking to them: *We keep in close contact with our grandparents.* ∘ *Jo and I are determined not to lose contact.* **2 TOUCH** ▷ [U] a situation in which two people or things are touching each other: *She dislikes any kind of physical contact.* ∘ *Wash your hands if they come into contact with chemicals.* **3 PERSON** ▷ [C] 🔲 someone you know who may be able to help you because of their job or position: *business contacts* **4 EYE** ▷ [C] (also **contact lens**) a small piece of plastic that you put on your eye to make you see more clearly → See also **eye contact**

> ☑ **Word partners for contact**
>
> **be in/get in/keep in/stay in** contact (**with sb**)
> • **lose/make** contact (**with sb**) • **have no** contact **with sb** • **close/regular** contact

contact² /ˈkɒntækt/ verb [T] 🔲 to telephone, email or write to someone: *I've been trying to contact you for days.*

contact ˌlens UK (US ˌcontact ˈlens) noun [C] a

small piece of plastic that you put on your eye to make you see more clearly

contagious /kən'teɪdʒəs/ **adj 1** A contagious disease is one that you can get if you touch someone who has it. **2** A contagious feeling spreads quickly amongst people: *Her excitement was contagious.*

contain /kən'teɪn/ **verb** [T] **1 INSIDE** ▷ **B1** If one thing contains another, it has it inside it: *He gave her a box containing a diamond ring.* **2 PART** ▷ **B2** to have something as a part: *Does this drink contain alcohol?* **3 CONTROL** ▷ to control something by stopping it from spreading: *The police were unable to contain the fighting.* **4 EMOTION** ▷ to control your emotions: *He could barely contain his anger.*

> **!** Common learner error: **contain** or **include**?
>
> Use **contain** to talk about objects that have something else inside them.
> *This folder contains important letters.*
> *This soup contains garlic and onions.*
> Use **include** to say that something or someone is a part of something else.
> *The team includes two new players.*
> *The price of the ticket includes insurance and tax.*

container

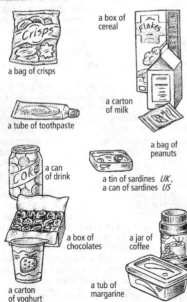

a bag of crisps

a box of cereal

a tube of toothpaste

a carton of milk

a can of drink

a bag of peanuts

a tin of sardines *UK*, a can of sardines *US*

a box of chocolates

a jar of coffee

a carton of yoghurt

a tub of margarine

container /kən'teɪnəʳ/ **noun** [C] **B2** an object such as a box or a bottle that is used for holding something

contaminate /kən'tæmɪneɪt/ **verb** [T] to make something dirty or poisonous: *contaminated drinking water* • **contamination** /kən,tæmɪ'neɪʃən/ **noun** [U]

contemplate /'kɒntəmpleɪt/ **verb** [T] to think about something for a long time or in a serious way: [+ doing sth] *I'm contemplating changing my name.* ∘ *He even contemplated suicide.* • **contemplation** /,kɒntəm'pleɪʃən/ **noun** [U]

contemporary¹ /kən'tempərəri, kən'tempəri/ **adj 1** **B2** of the present time: *contemporary music* **2** [always before noun] existing or happening at the same time as something: *Most contemporary accounts of the event have been destroyed.*

contemporary² /kən'tempərəri, kən'tempəri/ **noun** [C] Someone's contemporaries are the people who live at the same time as them: *Shakespeare and his contemporaries*

contempt /kən'tempt/ **noun 1** [U] a strong feeling that you do not respect someone or something: *He has utter contempt for anyone with power.* **2 contempt of court** behaviour that is illegal because it does not obey the rules of a law court

> **✓** Word partners for **contempt**
>
> treat sb/sth with contempt • deep/open/ utter contempt • have nothing but contempt for sb/sth • sb's contempt for sb/sth

contemptible /kən'temptəbl/ **adj** extremely bad, because of being dishonest or cruel

contemptuous /kən'temptʃuəs/ **adj** showing contempt • **contemptuously** **adv**

contend /kən'tend/ **verb 1** [T] formal to say that something is true: [+ (that)] *His lawyers contend that he is telling the truth.* **2** [I] to compete with someone to try to win something: *one of the groups contending for power*

PHRASAL VERB **contend with sth** to have to deal with a difficult or unpleasant situation: *I have enough problems of my own to contend with.*

contender /kən'tendəʳ/ **noun** [C] someone who competes with other people to try to win something: *a leading contender for an Oscar*

content¹ /'kɒntent/ **noun** [no plural] **1** **B2** the information or ideas that are talked about in a book, speech, film, etc: *The content of the article was controversial.* **2** the amount of a particular substance that something contains: *Most soft drinks have a high sugar content.*

content² /kən'tent/ **adj** **B2** happy or satisfied: *Not content with second place, Jeff played only to win.* ∘ [+ to do sth] *I was content to stay home and read.*

content³ /kən'tent/ **verb**

PHRASAL VERB **content yourself with sth** to do something or have something although it is not exactly what you want: *Since it rained we had to content ourselves with playing cards.*

contented /kən'tentɪd/ **adj** satisfied, or making you feel satisfied → Opposite **discontented** • **contentedly** **adv**

contention /kən'tenʃən/ **noun 1 OPINION** ▷ [C] formal a belief or opinion: *There's a general contention that too much violence is shown on TV.* **2 COMPETITION** ▷ [U] a situation in which people or groups compete for something and have a good chance of winning: *Johnson is back in contention for the championships.* **3 DISAGREEMENT** ▷ [U] arguments and disagreements → See also **a bone¹ of contention**

contentious /kən'tenʃəs/ *adj* likely to make people argue: *a contentious issue*

contentment /kən'tentmənt/ *noun* [U] the feeling of being happy or satisfied

contents /'kɒntents/ *noun* [plural] **1 THINGS INSIDE** ▷ **B1** all of the things that are contained inside something: *Please empty out the contents of your pockets.* **2 INFORMATION** ▷ **B1** the information or ideas that are written in a book, letter, document, etc: *the contents of his will* **3 BOOK** ▷ **B2** a list in a book that tells you what different parts the book contains: *a table of contents*

contest¹ /'kɒntest/ *noun* [C] **B1** a competition or election

---

🗹 **Word partners for contest**

enter/be in a contest • win a contest • a **close** contest • a contest **between** sb and sb • a contest **for** sth

---

contest² /kən'test/ *verb* [T] **1** to say formally that something is wrong or unfair and try to have it changed: *Mr Hughes went back to court to contest the verdict.* **2** to compete for something

contestant /kən'testənt/ *noun* [C] someone who competes in a contest

context /'kɒntekst/ *noun* [C, U] **1 B2** all the facts, opinions, situations, etc relating to a particular thing or event: *This small battle is important in the context of Scottish history.* **2** other words that were said or written at the same time as the word or words you are talking about: *Taken out of context, her remark sounded like an insult.*

continent /'kɒntɪnənt/ *noun* [C] **B1** one of the seven main areas of land on the Earth, such as Asia, Africa, or Europe

the Continent /'kɒntɪnənt/ *noun* UK the main part of land in Europe, not including Britain

continental /ˌkɒntɪ'nentəl/ *adj* relating to a continent: *the continental US*

Continental /ˌkɒntɪ'nentəl/ *adj* mainly UK relating to Europe, but not Britain

continental 'breakfast *noun* [C] a breakfast (= morning meal) consisting of fruit juice, coffee, and bread

contingency /kən'tɪndʒənsi/ *noun* [C] **1** an event or situation that might happen in the future, especially one that could cause problems: *a contingency fund/plan* (= *money or a plan that can be used if there are problems*) **2 a contingency fee** money that lawyers charge, which is a share of what the person they represent has won

contingent¹ /kən'tɪndʒənt/ *noun* [group] **1** a group of people from the same country, organization, etc who are part of a much larger group **2** a group of soldiers who are part of a larger military group

contingent² /kən'tɪndʒənt/ *adj* **contingent on sth** depending on something else in order to

happen: *Buying the new house was contingent on selling the old one.*

continual /kən'tɪnjuəl/ *adj* happening again and again over a long period of time: *I can't work with these continual interruptions.* • **continually** *adv Dad continually complains about money.*

continuation /kənˌtɪnju'eɪʃən/ *noun* **1** [C] something that comes after an event, situation, or thing to make it continue or go further: *Today's meeting will be a continuation of yesterday's talks.* **2** [U, no plural] the fact of continuing to exist, happen, or be used: *the continuation of their partnership*

continue /kən'tɪnjuː/ *verb* (**continuing, continued**) **1** [I, T] **B1** to keep happening, existing, or doing something: [+ to do sth] *It continued to snow heavily for three days.* ○ [+ doing sth] *Ann continued working part-time until June.* **2** [T] **B1** to start doing or saying something again, after stopping for a short period: *We'll have to continue this discussion tomorrow.* **3 continue along/down/up, etc** to go further in a particular direction

continued /kən'tɪnjuːd/ *adj* [always before noun] still happening, existing, or done: *his continued success*

continuity /ˌkɒntɪ'njuːəti/ *noun* [U] the state of continuing for a long period of time without being changed or stopped

continuous¹ /kən'tɪnjuəs/ *adj* **1 B2** happening or existing without stopping: *continuous pain* ○ *ten years of continuous service in the army* **2 B2** The continuous form of a verb is used to show that an action is continuing to happen. The sentence 'He was eating lunch.' is in the continuous form. • **continuously** *adv* **B2** *Their baby cried continuously all afternoon.*

continuous² /kən'tɪnjuəs/ *noun* **the continuous** the continuous form of the verb

contort /kən'tɔːt/ *verb* [I, T] If your face or body contorts, or you contort it, you twist it into a different shape, often because you are experiencing a strong emotion: *His face was contorted with pain.*

contour /'kɒntʊər/ *noun* [C] **1** the shape of the outer edge of something: *the contours of her body* **2** (also **'contour ˌline**) a line on a map joining places that are at the same height

contra- /kɒntrə-/ *prefix* against or opposite: *to contradict* (= *say the opposite*) ○ *contraception* (= *something that is used to prevent pregnancy*)

contraband /'kɒntrəbænd/ *noun* [U] goods that are brought into or taken out of a country illegally

contraception /ˌkɒntrə'sepʃən/ *noun* [U] methods that prevent a woman from becoming pregnant

contraceptive /ˌkɒntrə'septɪv/ *noun* [C] a drug or object that prevents a woman from becoming pregnant

contract¹ /'kɒntrækt/ *noun* [C] **B1** a legal agreement between two people or organizations, especially one that involves doing work for a particular amount of money

---

☑ Word partners for **contract**

enter into/negotiate/sign a contract
• breach/break/end/terminate a contract
• in a contract • the terms of a contract
• a contract between sb and sb/with sb

contract² /kən'trækt/ **verb 1 REDUCE** ▷ [I, T] to become smaller or shorter, or to make something do this: *The wood contracts in dry weather.* **2 DISEASE** ▷ [T] formal to get a serious disease: *She contracted malaria while living abroad.* **3 AGREEMENT** ▷ [I, T] to make a legal agreement with someone to do work or to have work done for you: [+ to do sth] *He's been contracted to perform in five shows.*

PHRASAL VERB **contract out sth** to make a formal arrangement for other people to do work that you are responsible for: *They've* **contracted out** *the cleaning* **to** *a private firm.*

contraction /kən'trækʃən/ **noun 1 MUSCLE** ▷ [C] a strong, painful movement of the muscles that a woman has when she is having a baby: *She was* **having contractions** *every ten minutes.* **2 WORD** ▷ [C] a short form of a word or group of words: *'Won't' is a contraction of 'will not'.* **3 REDUCTION** ▷ [U] an action in which something becomes smaller or shorter

contractor /kən'træktər/ **noun** [C] a person or company that supplies goods or does work for other people

contractual /kən'træktʃuəl/ **adj** relating to or stated in a contract (= legal agreement): *a contractual dispute*

contradict /ˌkɒntrə'dɪkt/ **verb 1** [T] If two things that are said or written about something contradict each other, they are so different that they cannot both be true: *His account of the accident contradicts the official government report.* **2** [I, T] to say that what someone else has just said is wrong

contradiction /ˌkɒntrə'dɪkʃən/ **noun 1** [C] a big difference between two things that are said or written about the same subject, or between what someone says and what they do: *There is a clear* **contradiction between** *what she says and what she does.* **2** [U] an act of saying that what someone has just said is wrong

IDIOM **a contradiction in terms** a phrase that is confusing because it contains words that seem to have opposite meanings: *An honest politician – isn't that a contradiction in terms?*

contradictory /ˌkɒntrə'dɪktəri/ **adj** If two statements about the same subject or two actions by the same person are contradictory, they are very different.

contraption /kən'træpʃən/ **noun** [C] a machine or object that looks strange or complicated

contrary¹ /'kɒntrəri/ **noun 1 to the contrary** saying or showing the opposite: *She claimed she hadn't been involved, despite evidence to the contrary.* **2 on the contrary** used to show that the opposite of what has just been said is true: *"You're a vegetarian, aren't you?" "On the contrary, I love meat."*

contrary² /'kɒntrəri/ **adj 1** opposite or very different: *a contrary opinion/view* **2 contrary to sth a** opposite to what someone said or thought: *Contrary to popular belief, bottled water is not always better than tap water.* **b** If something is contrary to a rule, it does not obey that rule.

contrast¹ /'kɒntrɑːst/ **noun** [C, U] **1** B2 an obvious difference between two people or things: *The* **contrast between** *their lifestyles couldn't be greater.* ○ *The busy north coast of the island is* **in** *sharp* **contrast** *to the peaceful south.* **2 by/in contrast** B2 used to show that someone or something is completely different from someone or something else: *She's quite petite, in contrast with her tall sister.*

☑ Word partners for **contrast**

1 a complete/sharp/striking contrast • the contrast between sth and sth
2 in direct/marked/sharp/stark contrast (to sth)

contrast² /kən'trɑːst/ **verb 1** [T] to compare two people or things in order to show the differences between them: *If you* **contrast** *his early novels* **with** *his later work, you can see how his writing has developed.* **2** [I] If one thing contrasts with another, it is very different from it: *The sharpness of the lemons* **contrasts with** *the sweetness of the honey.*

contrasting /kən'trɑːstɪŋ/ **adj** very different: *contrasting colours/styles*

contravene /ˌkɒntrə'viːn/ **verb** [T] formal to do something that is forbidden by a law or rule • **contravention** /ˌkɒntrə'venʃən/ **noun** [C, U] *By accepting the money, she was* **in contravention** *of company rules.*

contribute /kən'trɪbjuːt/, /'kɒntrɪbjuːt/ **verb** [I, T] **1** B2 to give something, especially money, in order to provide or achieve something together with other people: *I* **contributed** *$20* **towards** *Andrea's present.* **2** to write articles for a newspaper, magazine, or book: *She* **contributes to** *several magazines.*

PHRASAL VERB **contribute to sth** to be one of the causes of an event or a situation: *Smoking contributed to his early death.*

contribution /ˌkɒntrɪ'bjuːʃən/ **noun** [C] **1** B2 something that you do to help produce or develop something, or to help make something successful: *She has* **made** *a major contribution* **to** *our work.* **2** B2 an amount of money that is given to help pay for something: *a generous contribution to charity*

contributor /kən'trɪbjutər/ **noun** [C] **1 ARTICLE** ▷ someone who writes articles for a newspaper, magazine, or book **2 MONEY** ▷ someone who gives something, especially money, together with other people **3 CAUSE** ▷ one of the causes of something: *Speeding is a major contributor to road accidents.*

contributory /kən'trɪbjutəri/ **adj** helping to cause something

contrive /kən'traɪv/ **verb** [T] formal to manage to do something difficult, or to make something happen, by using your intelligence or by tricking people: [+ to do sth] *They contrived to meet in secret.*

contrived /kən'traɪvd/ **adj** Something that is contrived seems false and not natural.

control¹ /kən'trəʊl/ **noun 1 POWER** ▷ [U] ⓑ② the power to make a person, organization, or object do what you want: *The new teacher has no* **control** *over the class.* ° *The police are* **in control of** *the situation.* ° *He* **lost control** *of the vehicle.* **2 RULE** ▷ [U] ⓑ② the power to rule or govern an area: *Soldiers* **took control of** *the airport.* **3 under control** ⓑ② being dealt with successfully: *Don't worry – everything's* **under control.** ° *I couldn't* **keep** *my drinking* **under control.** **4 out of control** ⓑ② If something or someone is out of control, you cannot influence, limit, or direct them. **5 RULE** ▷ [C, U] ⓑ② a rule or law that limits something: *The government has introduced tighter immigration controls.* **6 CALM** ▷ [U] the ability to be calm: *It took a lot of control to stop myself from hitting him.* **7 EQUIPMENT** ▷ [C] ⓑ② a switch or piece of equipment that you use to operate a machine or vehicle: *Where's the volume control on your stereo?* **8 OFFICIAL PLACE** ▷ [C, U] ⓑ② a place where something official, usually a document, is checked: *passport/immigration control* **9 IN EXPERIMENT** ▷ [C] a person or thing that is used to compare with someone or something that is having an experiment done on them → See also **birth control, remote control, self-control**

control² /kən'trəʊl/ **verb** [T] (**controlling, controlled**) **1 MAKE SB DO STH** ▷ ⓑ① to make a person, organization, or object do what you want: *This switch controls the temperature.* ° *Can't you control your dogs?* **2 LIMIT** ▷ ⓑ② to limit the number, amount, or increase of something: *Fire crews struggled to control the blaze.* **3 RULE** ▷ ⓑ② to rule or govern an area: *The whole area is controlled by rebel forces.* **4 EMOTION** ▷ ⓑ① to stop yourself expressing strong emotions or behaving in a silly way: *He can't control his temper.*

con'trol ,freak noun [C] informal someone who wants to control everything about a situation and does not want other people to be involved

con'trol ,key noun [C, usually singular] the key on a computer keyboard that is usually marked 'Ctrl' and is used together with other keys to make the computer do a particular thing

controller /kən'trəʊlər/ **noun** [C] someone who directs the work of other people: *a marketing controller*

controversial /ˌkɒntrə'vɜːʃəl/ **adj** ⓑ② causing a lot of disagreement or argument: *a controversial decision/issue*

📋 **Word partners for controversy**

sth **attracts/causes/provokes/sparks** controversy • the controversy **surrounding** sth • **bitter/continuing/furious** controversy • controversy **about/over** sth • **be at the centre of** a controversy

---

controversy /'kɒntrəvɜːsi/ **noun** [C, U] a lot of disagreement and argument about something:

There is a lot of **controversy over** *mobile phone towers.*

conundrum /kə'nʌndrəm/ **noun** [C] a problem or question that is difficult to solve

convalescence /ˌkɒnvə'lesəns/ **noun** [U] the period of time when you rest and get better after a serious illness • **convalesce verb** [I]

convene /kən'viːn/ **verb** [I, T] formal to arrange a meeting, or to meet for a meeting: *The committee convenes three times a year.*

convenience /kən'viːniəns/ **noun 1** [U] ⓑ② the fact of being easy to use and suitable for what you want to do: *the convenience of credit cards* **2** [C] something that makes life easier: *Fortunately, the house has every* **modern convenience.**

con'venience ,food noun [C] food that can be prepared quickly and easily

con'venience ,store noun [C] mainly US a shop that sells food, drinks, etc, and is usually open late

convenient /kən'viːniənt/ **adj 1** ⓑ① easy to use or suiting your plans well: *When would be a convenient time to meet?* **2** ⓑ① near or easy to get to: *The new supermarket is very convenient for me.* • **conveniently adv**

convent /'kɒnvənt/ **noun** [C] a building where nuns (= religious women) live and pray together

convention /kən'venʃən/ **noun 1 MEETING** ▷ [C] a large formal meeting of people with the same interest or work: *the Democratic Party convention* **2 CUSTOM** ▷ [C, U] a usual and accepted way of behaving or doing something: *In many countries it is the convention to wear black at funerals.* **3 AGREEMENT** ▷ [C] a formal agreement between countries: *an international convention on human rights*

conventional /kən'venʃənəl/ **adj 1** ⓑ② Conventional people are traditional and not willing to try new ideas. **2** ⓑ② Conventional objects or ways of doing things are the usual ones that have been used for a long time: *conventional farming/medicine* **3 conventional arms/forces/warfare, etc** not involving the use of nuclear weapons **4 conventional wisdom** what most people believe → Opposite **unconventional**

conventionally /kən'venʃənəli/ **adv** in a traditional way: *He dressed conventionally in a suit and tie.*

converge /kən'vɜːdʒ/ **verb** [I] **1 COME TOGETHER** ▷ If lines, roads, or rivers converge, they meet at a particular point. **2 FORM GROUP** ▷ to move towards a particular point and form a group there: *The protesters* **converged on** *the town square.* **3 BECOME SIMILAR** ▷ If ideas, interests, or systems converge, they become more similar to one another. • **convergence noun** [U]

conversation /ˌkɒnvə'seɪʃən/ **noun** [C, U] ⓐ① a talk between two or more people, usually an informal one: *a telephone conversation* ° *We* **had a conversation about** *football.* • **conversational adj** relating to or like a conversation: *a conversational style*

C

converse /kən'vɜːs/ **verb** [I] formal to talk with someone

conversely /'kɒnvɜːsli/ **adv** used to introduce something that is different to something you have just said: *Dark lipsticks make your mouth look smaller. Conversely, light shades make it larger.*

conversion /kən'vɜːʒⁿn/ **noun** [C, U] **1 CHANGE FORM** ▷ a situation in which the appearance, form, or purpose of something is changed: *the country's conversion to democracy* **2 CHANGE RELIGION** ▷ a process in which someone changes to a new religion or belief: *her conversion to Christianity* **3 CHANGE DATA** ▷ the process of changing computer data so that it can be read by a different software program: *file conversion*

convert¹ /kən'vɜːt/ **verb** [I, T] **1 CHANGE FORM** ▷ 🔵 to change the appearance, form, or purpose of something: *The old warehouse was converted into offices.* ○ *How do you convert miles into kilometres?* **2 CHANGE RELIGION** ▷ to change to a new religion, belief, etc, or to make someone do this: *When did he convert to Islam?* **3 CHANGE DATA** ▷ to change computer data so that it can be read by a different software program: *Images can be converted and saved to a specific folder.*

convert² /'kɒnvɜːt/ **noun** [C] someone who has been persuaded to change to a different religion or belief: *a Catholic convert*

convertible¹ /kən'vɜːtəbl/ **adj** able to be converted

convertible² /kən'vɜːtəbl/ **noun** [C] a car with a folding roof

convex /kɒn'veks/ **adj** A convex surface curves out: *a convex mirror/lens*

convey /kən'veɪ/ **verb** [T] **1** to communicate information, feelings, or images to someone: *She always conveys a sense of enthusiasm for her work.* **2** to transport something or someone to a particular place

conveyor belt /kən'veɪə‚belt/ **noun** [C] a continuous moving piece of rubber or metal used to transport objects from one place to another

convict¹ /kən'vɪkt/ **verb** [T] to decide officially in a court of law that someone is guilty of a particular crime: [often passive] *He was convicted of murder.* ○ *a convicted criminal*

convict² /'kɒnvɪkt/ **noun** [C] someone who is in prison because they are guilty of a particular crime

conviction /kən'vɪkʃⁿn/ **noun 1** [C] an occasion when someone is officially found to be guilty of a particular crime: *He already had two convictions for burglary.* **2** [C, U] a strong opinion or belief: *religious/moral convictions*

convince /kən'vɪns/ **verb** [T] **1** 🔵 to make someone believe that something is true: [+ that]

He tried to convince me that I needed a new car ○ *She convinced the jury of her innocence.* **2** 🔵 to persuade someone to do something: [+ to do sth] *I convinced her to go to the doctor's.*

convinced /kən'vɪnst/ **adj** 🔵 completely certain about something: [+ (that)] *I'm convinced tha. he's made a mistake.*

convincing /kən'vɪnsɪŋ/ **adj 1** able to make you believe that something is true or right: *c convincing argument* **2 a convincing win, victory** a win or victory where the person or team that wins is much better than the people they are competing against • **convincingly adv**

convoluted /'kɒnvəluːtɪd/ **adj** formal extremely complicated and difficult to understand: *c convoluted argument/story*

convoy /'kɒnvɔɪ/ **noun** [C] a group of vehicles or ships that travel together

convulsion /kən'vʌlʃⁿn/ **noun** [C] a sudder uncontrollable movement of muscles in your body, caused by illness or drugs

coo /kuː/ **verb** [I] (**cooing, cooed**) **1** to make a soft, low sound, like a pigeon (= large, grey bird) **2** to speak in a soft, low voice

cook

bake

fry

boil

grill   roast

cook¹ /kʊk/ **verb 1** [I, T] 🔵 to prepare food and usually heat it: *Who's cooking this evening?* ○ *She cooked the meat in oil and spices.* **2** [I] If food cooks, it is heated until it is ready to eat: *The rice is cooking.* • **cooked adj** not raw

PHRASAL VERB **cook sth up** informal to invent a story, plan, etc, usually dishonestly

cook² /kʊk/ **noun** [C] 🔵 someone who prepares and cooks food

cookbook /'kʊkbʊk/ **noun** [C] (also UK **cookery book**) a book containing instructions for preparing food

cooker /'kʊkər/ **noun** [C] UK (UK/US **stove**) 🔵 a piece of equipment used to cook food: *an electric cooker* → See also **pressure cooker**

cookery /'kʊkəri/ **noun** [U] UK the activity of preparing or cooking food

cookery book noun [C] UK (UK/US **cookbook**) a book containing instructions for preparing food

cookie /'kʊki/ **noun** [C] **1** US (also UK **biscuit**) a thin, flat cake that is dry and usually sweet → See colour picture **Food** on page Centre 11 **2** a piece of information stored on your computer that contains information about Internet documents you have looked at

cooking /'kʊkɪŋ/ noun [U] **1** 🄰🄾 the activity of preparing or cooking food: *I do most of the cooking.* **2** 🄰🄾 a style of preparing food: *vegetarian/French cooking* • **cooking adj** [always before noun] suitable to cook with: *cooking oil/apples*

cool¹ /kuːl/ adj **1** COLD ▷ 🄱🄸 slightly cold, but not too cold: *a cool breeze/day* ∘ *cool water* **2** GOOD ▷ informal 🄰🄾 good, stylish, or fashionable: *He looks really cool in those sunglasses.* **3** CALM ▷ calm and not emotional: *She seemed cool and confident.* **4** UNFRIENDLY ▷ unfriendly

IDIOM **be cool with sth** informal to be happy to accept a situation or suggestion: *Yeah, we could leave later – I'm cool with that.*

• **coolness** noun [U]

cool² /kuːl/ verb [I, T] **1** 🄱🄾 to become less hot, or to make something become less hot: *Allow the bread to cool before slicing it.* **2** If emotions or relationships cool, or if something cools them, they become less strong.

PHRASAL VERB **cool (sb/sth) down/off 1** 🄱🄾 to become less hot, or to make someone or something become less hot: *We went for a swim to cool off.* **2** 🄱🄾 to become calmer, or to make someone become calmer

cool³ /kuːl/ noun **the cool** a cool temperature: *the cool of the early morning*

IDIOMS **keep your cool** to remain calm • **lose your cool** to suddenly become very angry

cool⁴ /kuːl/ exclamation informal 🄰🄾 used when you like something or agree to something

coolly /'kuːlli/ adv without showing emotion or interest: *Her colleagues reacted coolly to the idea.*

coop¹ /kuːp/ noun [C] a cage for birds such as chickens

coop² /kuːp/ verb

PHRASAL VERB **coop sb up** to keep a person or animal in a small area: [often passive] *Kids shouldn't be cooped up inside all day.*

co-op /'kəʊɒp/ noun [C] informal short for **co-operative noun**

cooperate (also UK **co-operate**) /kəʊ'ɒpəreɪt/ verb [I] **1** 🄱🄾 to work together with someone in order to achieve the same aim: *Witnesses are cooperating with detectives.* ∘ *Several countries are cooperating in the relief effort.* **2** 🄱🄾 to help someone or do what they ask: *We can get there early as long as the children will cooperate.*

cooperation (also UK **co-operation**) /kəʊ,ɒpə'reɪʃ³n/ noun [U] 🄱🄾 a situation in which you work together with someone or do what they ask you: *international cooperation* ∘ *The school works in close cooperation with parents.*

cooperative¹ (also UK **co-operative**) /kəʊ'ɒp³rətɪv/ adj **1** 🄱🄾 willing to help or do what people ask: *a cooperative and polite employee* **2** involving people working together

to achieve the same aim: *a cooperative relationship* • **cooperatively adv**

cooperative² (also UK **co-operative**) /kəʊ'ɒp³rətɪv/ noun [C] a business or organization owned and managed by the people who work in it

coordinate (also UK **co-ordinate**) /kəʊ'ɔːdɪneɪt/ verb [T] to make different people or things work together effectively, or to organize all the different parts of an activity: *My manager is coordinating the new project.*

coordination (also UK **co-ordination**) /kəʊ,ɔːdɪ'neɪʃ³n/ noun [U] **1** a way of organizing the different parts of an activity or making people or things work together effectively: *The President called for closer coordination between business and government.* **2** the ability to make different parts of your body move together in a controlled way: *Dancing helps develop balance and coordination.*

coordinator (also UK **co-ordinator**) /kəʊ'ɔːdɪneɪtə'/ noun [C] someone who organizes the different parts of an activity or makes people or things work together effectively

cop /kɒp/ noun [C] mainly US informal a police officer

cope /kəʊp/ verb [I] 🄱🄾 to deal quite successfully with a difficult situation: *How do you cope with stress?*

copier /'kɒpiə'/ noun [C] mainly US (UK/US **photocopier**) a machine that produces copies of documents by photographing them

copious /'kəʊpiəs/ adj [always before noun] in large amounts: *They drank copious amounts of wine.* • **copiously adv**

copper /'kɒpə'/ noun **1** METAL ▷ [U] 🄱🄾 a soft, red-brown metal, used in electrical equipment and to make coins, etc: *copper wire* **2** MONEY ▷ [C] UK a brown coin with a low value **3** POLICE ▷ [C] UK informal a police officer

copy¹ /'kɒpi/ noun [C] **1** 🄱🄸 something that is made to look exactly like something else: *Always make copies of important documents.* **2** 🄱🄾 a single book, newspaper, etc of which many have been produced: *Four million copies of the book were sold in the first year.* → See also **carbon copy**

copy² /'kɒpi/ verb **1** PRODUCE ▷ [T] 🄰🄾 to produce something that is similar or exactly the same as something else: *Copy the file onto disk.* ∘ *The design was copied from the American model.* **2** BEHAVE ▷ [T] 🄱🄾 to behave like someone else: *He likes to copy his older brother.* **3** CHEAT ▷ [I, T] 🄱🄾 to cheat by looking at and using someone else's work: *She copied his answers.*

PHRASAL VERBS **copy sth out** UK to write a piece of writing out again on a piece of paper • **copy sb in on sth** to give someone a copy of something, usually an email, that you have written for somebody else: *Please copy me in on your email to Dr White.*

copyright /'kɒpiraɪt/ noun [C, U] the legal right to control the use of an original piece of work such as a book, play, or song: *The book is protected by copyright.*

coral /'kɒrəl/ **noun** [U] a hard, usually pink or white substance produced by a type of very small sea animal: *a coral reef*

cord /kɔːd/ **noun** [C, U] **1** thick string, or a piece of this **2** (also UK **flex**) a piece of wire covered in plastic, used to connect electrical equipment to a power supply: *an electrical cord* ∘ *a telephone cord* → See also **umbilical cord**

cordial /'kɔːdiəl/ **adj** polite and friendly: *a cordial invitation* • **cordially adv**

cordless /'kɔːdləs/ **adj** able to operate without an electrical cord: *a cordless phone*

cordon¹ /'kɔːdən/ **noun** [C] a line of police, soldiers, vehicles, etc around an area, protecting it or keeping people out

cordon² /'kɔːdən/ **verb**

PHRASAL VERB **cordon sth off** If the police, army, etc cordon off an area, they stop people from entering it.

cords /kɔːdz/ **noun** [plural] informal trousers made from corduroy

corduroy /'kɔːdərɔɪ/ **noun** [U] thick, cotton cloth with raised parallel lines on the outside: *a corduroy jacket*

core /kɔːr/ **noun** **1 IMPORTANT PART** ▷ [no plural] the most important part of a system or principle: *core values* ∘ *Better health care was at the core of the senator's campaign.* **2 FRUIT** ▷ [C] the hard, central part of certain fruits, such as apples, which contains the seeds **3 PLANET** ▷ [no plural] the centre of a planet: *the Earth's core* → See also **hard core**

coriander /ˌkɒriˈændər/ **noun** [U] a plant whose leaves or seeds are added to food to give a special flavour

cork /kɔːk/ **noun** **1** [U] a light material obtained from the outer layer of a particular type of tree **2** [C] a small cylindrical piece of this material put in the top of a bottle, especially a wine bottle, to close it

corkscrew /'kɔːkskruː/ **noun** [C] a piece of equipment used for pulling corks out of wine bottles

corn /kɔːn/ **noun** [U] **1** mainly UK **🄑1** a crop of grain, or the seed from this crop used to make flour or feed animals: *fields of corn* **2** US (UK **sweetcorn**) a tall plant with yellow seeds that are cooked and eaten as a vegetable → See colour picture **Fruits and Vegetables** on page Centre 10

corner¹ /'kɔːnər/ **noun** [C] **1 POINT** ▷ **🄐2** the point or area where two lines, walls, or roads meet: *There was a television in the corner of the room.* ∘ *The restaurant is on/at the corner of Ross Street and Mill Road.* **2 PLACE** ▷ a part of a larger area, often somewhere quiet or far away: *He lives in a beautiful corner of northern California.* **3 FOOTBALL** ▷ a kick or hit taken from the corner of the field in some games, especially football **4 from/out of the corner of your eye** If

you see something out of the corner of your eye, you just see it, but do not look at it directly.

IDIOMS **around/round the corner** going to happen soon • **cut corners** to do something in the quickest or cheapest way, often harming the quality of your work

corner² /'kɔːnər/ **verb 1** [T] to force a person or animal into a situation or place from which it is hard to escape: *His attackers cornered him in a dark alley.* **2 corner the market** to become so successful at selling or making a particular product that almost no one else sells or makes it

cornerstone /'kɔːnəstəʊn/ **noun** [C] something very important that something else depends on: *Freedom of speech is the cornerstone of democracy.*

cornflakes /'kɔːnfleɪks/ **noun** [plural] a food made from corn (= grain) and eaten with milk for breakfast (= morning meal)

cornmeal /'kɔːnmiːl/ **noun** [U] rough yellow or white flour made from corn (= grain)

corn ˌsyrup noun [U] a sweet, thick liquid made from corn (= grain), used in making food

corny /'kɔːni/ **adj** informal repeated too often to be interesting or funny: *a corny joke*

coronary¹ /'kɒrənəri/ **adj** relating to the heart: *coronary heart disease*

coronary² /'kɒrənəri/ **noun** [C] a heart attack (= when the heart stops working normally)

coronation /ˌkɒrəˈneɪʃən/ **noun** [C] a ceremony at which someone is officially made king or queen

coroner /'kɒrənər/ **noun** [C] an official who examines the causes of someone's death, usually if it was violent or sudden

Corp noun [C] written abbreviation for corporation (= used after the name of a large company in the United States)

corporal /'kɔːpərəl/ **noun** [C] a soldier of low rank in the army or air force

corporal ˈpunishment noun [U] physical punishment, especially of children, usually by hitting with the hand or a stick

corporate /'kɔːpərət/ **adj** [always before noun] relating to a large company or group: *corporate finance*

corporation /ˌkɔːpərˈeɪʃən/ **noun** [C] **🄑2** a large company or group of companies

corps /kɔːr/ **noun** [C] (plural **corps**) **1** a group of people involved in the same job: *the press/diplomatic corps* **2** a special part of a military force: *the Air Corps*

corpse /kɔːps/ **noun** [C] a dead person's body

corpus /'kɔːpəs/ **noun** [C] (plural **corpora** /'kɔːpərə/) an electronic collection of many millions of words that can be studied to show how language works

correct¹ /kəˈrekt/ **adj** **1 🄐2** accurate, or having no mistakes: *Check that you have the correct information.* ∘ *Was that the correct answer?* **2 🄑1** suitable for a particular situation: *correct behaviour* ∘ *Have you got the correct number of players for the match?* • **correctly adv** • **correctness noun** [U] → See also **politically correct**

orrect² /kə'rekt/ **verb** [T] **1 MAKE RIGHT** ▷ to make a mistake or problem right or better: *The new software finds and corrects any errors on the hard disk.* **2 IMPROVE** ▷ to improve the quality of something: *These contact lenses will help to correct your vision.* **3 SHOW MISTAKE** ▷ to show someone the mistakes in something they have said or written: *Our teacher normally corrects our pronunciation.*

orrection /kə'rekʃən/ **noun** [C, U] **B1** a change to make something right or better, or the act of making such a change: *She made some corrections before handing in the essay.*

> **⚠ Word partners for correction**
>
> **make** a correction • a **minor/small** correction • a correction **to** sth

orrective /kə'rektɪv/ **adj** formal intended to improve or correct something: *corrective surgery/lenses*

orrelate /'kɒrəleɪt/ **verb** [I, T] If facts or pieces of information correlate, they are connected to each other and influence each other, and if you correlate them, you show their connections.

orrelation /ˌkɒrə'leɪʃən/ **noun** [C] a connection between two or more things, usually where one causes or influences the other: *The research showed a close correlation between smoking and lung cancer.*

> **⚠ Word partners for correlation**
>
> a **clear/close/direct/high/strong** correlation • a correlation **between** sth and sth

orrespond /ˌkɒrɪ'spɒnd/ **verb** [I] **1 B2** to be the same or very similar: *The newspaper story does not correspond with/to what really happened.* **2 B2** to communicate with someone by writing letters

orrespondence /ˌkɒrɪ'spɒndəns/ **noun 1** [U] letters or emails from one person to another, or the activity of writing and receiving letters or emails: *business correspondence* **2** [C, U] a connection or similarity between two or more things

orrespondent /ˌkɒrɪ'spɒndənt/ **noun** [C] **1** someone who reports news for newspapers, television, or radio, usually from another country **2** someone who writes letters, usually regularly

orresponding /ˌkɒrɪ'spɒndɪŋ/ **adj** [always before noun] similar or related: *Draw a line between the words with corresponding meanings.*

orridor /'kɒrɪdɔːʳ/ **noun** [C] **B2** a passage in a building or train with rooms on one or both sides

orroborate /kə'rɒbəreɪt/ **verb** [T] formal to say something or provide information that supports what someone says: *A witness corroborated his account of the accident.* • **corroboration** /kəˌrɒbə'reɪʃən/ **noun** [U]

orrode /kə'rəʊd/ **verb 1** [I, T] If metal corrodes, or rain or chemicals corrode it, it is slowly damaged by them: *Rain corroded the metal pipes.* **2** [T] to slowly damage someone or something: *He was corroded by guilt.* • **corrosion** /kə'rəʊʒən/

noun [U] • **corrosive** /kə'rəʊsɪv/ **adj** *Acid rain is highly corrosive.*

corrugated /'kɒrəgeɪtɪd/ **adj** [always before noun] Corrugated metal or cardboard has parallel rows of folds that look like waves: *a corrugated iron roof*

corrupt¹ /kə'rʌpt/ **adj 1** dishonest or illegal: *a corrupt government* **2** If information on a computer is corrupt, it has been damaged or spoiled: *corrupt files*

corrupt² /kə'rʌpt/ **verb** [T] **1** to make someone or something become dishonest or immoral: [often passive] *He became corrupted by power and money.* **2** to damage information on a computer

corruption /kə'rʌpʃən/ **noun** [U] **1 BAD BEHAVIOUR** ▷ dishonest or immoral behaviour, usually by people in positions of power: *He was arrested for corruption and bribery.* **2 MAKE DISHONEST** ▷ the act of making someone or something become dishonest or immoral: *the corruption of innocent young children* **3 COMPUTER** ▷ the fact of information on a computer being damaged in some way and not able to be used: *data corruption*

corset /'kɔːsət/ **noun** [C] a tight piece of underwear worn by women to make themselves look thinner, especially in the past

cosmetic /kɒz'metɪk/ **adj 1** intended to improve your appearance **2** involving only small changes or improvements that will not solve a problem: *Critics claimed that the changes were only cosmetic.*

cosmetics /kɒz'metɪks/ **noun** [plural] substances that you put on your face or body to improve your appearance

cos,metic 'surgery noun [U] a medical operation to make someone more attractive

cosmic /'kɒzmɪk/ **adj** relating to the whole universe: *cosmic rays*

cosmopolitan /ˌkɒzmə'pɒlɪtən/ **adj 1** consisting of people and things from many different countries: *London is a very cosmopolitan city.* **2** having experience of many different countries or cultures: *a dynamic, cosmopolitan businesswoman*

the cosmos /'kɒzmɒs/ **noun** the whole universe

> **⚠ Word partners for cost**
>
> the **cost of** sth • **at a cost of** [£500/$1000, etc] • the **high/low** cost of sth • **cover** the cost of (doing) sth • **cut/reduce** costs • **at no extra cost** • the **cost of living**

cost¹ /kɒst/ **noun 1** [C, U] **A2** the amount of money that you need to buy or do something: *The cruise ship was built at a cost of $400 million.* ○ *Software is included at no extra cost.* ○ *The cost of living* (= the cost of food, clothes, etc) *has increased.* **2** [no plural] **B2** something that you give or lose, in order to gain or achieve something else: *He rescued four people at the cost of his own life.* **3 at all costs B2** If something must be done at all costs, it is very important that it is done: *We have to succeed at all costs.* **4 to your cost** UK because of a bad experience you have had: *An ankle injury can last a long time, as I know to my cost.*

cost² /kɒst/ *verb* (**cost**) **1** [T] ⓐ If something costs a particular amount of money, you have to pay that in order to buy or do it: *How much do these shoes cost?* ∘ [+ to do sth] *It costs $5 to send the package by airmail.* ∘ [+ two objects] *It's going to cost me a lot of money to buy a new car.* **2** [+ two objects] ⓑ to make someone lose something: *His lazy attitude cost him his job.*

cost³ /kɒst/ *verb* [T] to calculate the amount of money needed to do or make something: *The building work has been costed at 30,000 euros.*

co-star¹ /ˈkəʊstɑːr/ *noun* [C] one of two famous actors who both have important parts in a particular film

co-star² /kəʊˈstɑːr/ ⓤ /ˈkəʊstɑːr/ *verb* (**co-starring, co-starred**) **1** [T] If a film, play, etc co-stars two or more famous actors, they are in it. **2** [I] to be in a film, play, etc with another famous actor: *Hugh Grant co-stars with Julia Roberts in 'Notting Hill'.*

cost-cutting /ˈkɒstˌkʌtɪŋ/ *noun* [U] actions that reduce the amount of money spent on something: *cost-cutting measures/strategies*

cost-effective /ˌkɒstɪˈfektɪv/ *adj* If something is cost-effective, it achieves good results for little money.

costly /ˈkɒstli/ *adj* **1** expensive: [+ to do sth] *It would be too costly to build a swimming pool.* **2** causing a lot of problems, or making you lose something important: *a costly mistake*

costume /ˈkɒstjuːm/ *noun* **1** [C, U] ⓑ a set of clothes that someone wears to make them look like someone or something else, for example in a play: *actors in costume* ∘ *He arrived at the party dressed in a gorilla costume.* **2** [U] ⓑ a set of clothes that are typical of a particular country or time in history: *Japanese national costume* → See also **swimming costume**

cosy UK (US **cozy**) /ˈkəʊzi/ *adj* ⓑ comfortable and warm

cot /kɒt/ *noun* [C] UK **1** (US **crib**) a bed with high sides for a baby **2** (UK **camp bed**) a narrow bed that can be folded and easily carried

cot ˌdeath *noun* [C, U] UK (US **SIDS**) the sudden death of a sleeping baby for no obvious reason

cottage /ˈkɒtɪdʒ/ *noun* [C] ⓑ a small house, usually in the countryside

cottage ˈcheese *noun* [U] a soft, white cheese with small lumps in it

cotton /ˈkɒtən/ *noun* [U] **1** CLOTH ▷ ⓑ cloth or thread that is produced from the cotton plant: *a cotton shirt/dress* **2** PLANT ▷ a plant that produces a soft, white substance used for making thread and cloth **3** FOR CLEANING ▷ US (UK **cotton wool**) a soft mass of cotton, usually used for cleaning your skin → See colour picture **The Bathroom** on page Centre 3

cotton ˈwool *noun* [U] UK (US **cotton**) a soft mass of cotton, usually used for cleaning your skin → See colour picture **The Bathroom** on page Centre 3

couch¹ /kaʊtʃ/ *noun* [C] a long, comfortable piece of furniture that two or more people ca sit on

couch² /kaʊtʃ/ *verb* **be couched in/as sth** to b expressed in a particular way: *His explanatic was* **couched in** *technical language.*

couch poˌtato *noun* [C] UK humorous a perso who is not active and spends a lot of tim watching television

cough¹ /kɒf/ *verb* [I] ⓑ to make air come out your throat with a short sound

PHRASAL VERBS **cough sth up** to make somethin come out of your lungs or throat by coughin *Doctors were worried when she started* **coughin up blood.** • **cough (sth) up** informal to giv money to someone although you do not want t

cough² /kɒf/ *noun* [C] **1** ⓑ the act of coughin or the sound this makes **2** ⓑ an illness th makes you cough a lot: *Uwe has a nasty cougl* → See also **whooping cough**

could strong /kʊd/ weak /kəd/ *modal ver* **1** CAN ▷ ⓐ used as the past form of 'can' t talk about what someone or something was abl or allowed to do: *I couldn't see what he was doin* ∘ *You said we could watch television when we finished our homework.* **2** POSSIBLE ▷ ⓑ used t talk about what is possible or might happen: *Tl baby could arrive any day now.* ∘ *This kind crime could easily be prevented.* ∘ *She could hai been seriously injured.* **3** ASK ▷ ⓐ used to as someone politely to do or provide somethin *Could you lend me £5?* ∘ *Could I have anothe drink?* **4** ASK PERMISSION ▷ ⓑ used to as politely for permission to do something: *Could speak to Mr Davis, please?* **5** SUGGEST ▷ ⓑ use to make a suggestion: *You could try painting it different colour.* **6 I could (have)** used when yo feel so happy, sad, angry, etc that you would lik to do something: *I was so grateful I could hai kissed her!* → See Study Page **Modal verbs** on pag Centre 22

couldn't /ˈkʊdənt/ short for could not: *I couldn understand what he was saying.*

could've /ˈkʊdəv/ short for could have: *It could'l been much worse.*

council, Council /ˈkaʊnsəl/ *noun* [C] **1** ⓑ group of people who are elected to control town, city, or area: *Edinburgh City Council* ∘ *council meeting* **2** a group of people who ar elected or chosen to give advice or mak decisions: *the Medical Research Council* **3** **council house/flat** in the UK a house or fla that is owned by a city or town council an rented to people

council eˌstate *noun* [C] UK (US **housin project**) a part of a city with homes owned b a council and rented to people

councillor UK (US **councilor, councilma councilwoman**) /ˈkaʊnsələr/ *noun* [C] member of a town, city, or area council

councilman /ˈkaʊnsəlmən/ *noun* [C] (plur **councilmen**) US (UK **councillor**) a man who chosen to be a member of a town, city, or are council

councilwoman /ˈkaʊnsəlˌwʊmən/ *noun* [C (plural **councilwomen**) US (UK **councillor**) woman who is chosen to be a member of a town, city, or area council

counsel¹ /ˈkaʊnsəl/ noun **1** [C] a lawyer who speaks for someone in court **2** [U] literary advice

counsel² /ˈkaʊnsəl/ verb [T] (mainly UK **counselling, counselled**, US **counseling, counseled**) **1** formal to advise someone to do something: [+ to do sth] *Lawyers had counselled him not to say anything.* **2** to give advice to someone who has problems

counselling mainly UK (US **counseling**) /ˈkaʊnsəlɪŋ/ noun [U] the job or process of listening to someone and giving them advice about their problems: *a counselling service*

counsellor mainly UK (US **counselor**) /ˈkaʊnsələr/ noun [C] someone whose job is to listen to people and give them advice about their problems

count¹ /kaʊnt/ verb **1** CALCULATE ▷ [T] ⑤ to see how many people or things there are: *I counted the money on the table.* **2** SAY NUMBERS ▷ [I] ⑤ to say numbers in their correct order: *Can you count to twenty in French?* **3** CONSIDER ▷ [T] to think of someone or something in a particular way: *She counted Tim as her closest friend.* ∘ *You should count yourself lucky you weren't hurt.* **4** IMPORTANT ▷ [I] ⑥ to be important: *I believe that health and happiness count more than money.* ∘ *Doesn't my opinion count for anything?* **5** INCLUDE ▷ [T] to include something or someone in a calculation: *There are 1500 people at my school, counting teachers.* **6** BE ACCEPTED ▷ [I] to be accepted or allowed as part of something: *I've been to sixteen different countries, but I only spent half an hour in Luxembourg, so that doesn't really count.*

PHRASAL VERBS **count against sb/sth** to make someone or something more likely to fail: *She has the qualifications for the job, but her lack of experience will count against her.* • **count sb in** to include someone in an activity: *If you're going for a pizza, you can count me in.* • **count on sb** ⑥ to be confident that you can depend on someone: *I can always count on my parents to help me.* • **count on sth** ⑥ to expect something to happen and make plans based on it: *I didn't count on so many people coming to the party.* • **count sth out** to count coins or pieces of paper money one by one as you put them down: *She counted out five crisp $20 bills.* • **count sb out** to not include someone in an activity • **count towards sth** to be part of what is needed to complete something or achieve something: *This essay counts towards my exam result.* • **count up sb/sth** to add together all the people or things in a group

count² /kaʊnt/ noun **1** NUMBER ▷ [C] an occasion when you count something, or the total number you get after counting: [usually singular] *At the last count there were 410 club members.* **2** lose count to forget how many of something there is: *I've lost count of the number of times she's arrived late.* **3** on all/both/several, etc counts in all, both, several, etc parts of a situation, argument, etc: *I had been wrong on both counts.* **4** RANK ▷ [C] (also **Count**) a man of high social rank in some European countries **5** CRIME ▷ [C] one of the times that someone has been accused of a particular crime: *He was charged with two counts of assault.* → See also **pollen count**

countable noun /ˌkaʊntəbəlˈnaʊn/ noun [C] (also **count noun**) ⑥ a noun that has both plural and singular forms → See Study Page **Countable and uncountable nouns** on page Centre 20

countdown /ˈkaʊntdaʊn/ noun [C] the time just before an important event when people are counting the time until it happens: [usually singular] *The countdown to the Olympics has begun.*

countenance¹ /ˈkaʊntənəns/ noun [C] literary the appearance or expression of someone's face

countenance² /ˈkaʊntənəns/ verb [T] formal to accept that something should happen: *They will not countenance building a new airport.*

counter¹ /ˈkaʊntər/ noun [C] **1** IN A SHOP ▷ ⑥ the place in a shop, bank, etc, where people are served: *The woman behind the counter took his money.* **2** SURFACE ▷ US a flat surface in a kitchen on which food can be prepared **3** DISC ▷ a small disc used in some games that are played on a board

counter² /ˈkaʊntər/ verb [T] **1** to prevent something or reduce the bad effect that it has: *This skin cream claims to counter the effects of sun damage.* **2** to say something to show that what someone has just said is not true: *"Of course I love him," Clare countered.*

counter³ /ˈkaʊntər/ adv **be/run counter to sth** to have the opposite effect to something : *The new road plans run counter to the government's aim of reducing pollution.*

counter- /kaʊntər-/ prefix opposing or as a reaction to: *a counter-attack (= an attack on someone who has attacked you)*

counteract /ˌkaʊntərˈækt/ verb [T] to reduce the bad effect that something else has: *There are drugs that counteract the side effects of sea sickness.*

counter-attack /ˈkaʊntərəˌtæk/ noun [C] an attack that you make against someone who has attacked you in a sport, war, or argument • **counter-attack** verb [I, T]

counterclockwise /ˌkaʊntəˈklɒkwaɪz/ adj, adv US (UK **anti-clockwise**) in the opposite direction to the way the hands (= parts that point to the numbers) of a clock move → See picture at **clockwise**

counterfeit /ˈkaʊntəfɪt/ adj made to look like the real thing, in order to trick people: *counterfeit money/jewellery*

counterpart /ˈkaʊntəpɑːt/ noun [C] someone or something that has the same job or position as someone or something in a different place or organization

counterproductive /ˌkaʊntəprəˈdʌktɪv/ adj having the opposite effect from the one you want

countess /ˈkaʊntɪs/ noun [C] a woman who has a high social rank in some European countries, especially the wife of an earl or count (= man of high social rank): *the Countess of Wessex*

countless /'kaʊntləs/ *adj* [always before noun] very many: *The song has been played* ***countless times*** *on the radio.*

country¹ /'kʌntri/ *noun* **1** Ⓐ [C] an area of land that has its own government, army, etc: *European countries* **2 the country a** Ⓐ the areas that are away from towns and cities **b** the people who live in a country: *The country was shocked by the President's decision.*

! Common learner error: **country, land, nation,** or **state**?

Country is the most general word that means 'an area of land'. It usually means an area of land with its own government and people.

China, Japan, and other countries in Asia

Nation is used to talk about a country, especially when you mean the people or the culture of that country.

The nation celebrated the 100th anniversary of independence.

State is used to talk about a country as a political or official area. Some countries are divided into political units that are also called **states**.

Belgium became an independent state in 1830.

America is divided into 50 states.

the State of Florida

Land means an area of ground, not an area with its own government.

We bought some land to build a house on.

---

country² /'kʌntri/ *adj* [always before noun] in or relating to the areas that are away from towns and cities: *country roads/hotels*

countryman /'kʌntrɪmən/ *noun* [C] (plural **countrymen**) someone from the same country as you

country 'music *noun* [U] (also ˌcountry and 'western) a style of popular music from the southern and western US

countryside /'kʌntrɪsaɪd/ *noun* [U] Ⓐ land that is not in towns or cities and has farms, fields, forests, etc → See Note at **nature**

county /'kaʊnti/ *noun* [C] Ⓑ an area of Britain, Ireland, or the US that has its own local government

coup /kuː/ *noun* [C] **1** (also **coup d'état** /ˌkuːdeɪ-'tɑː/) an occasion when a group of people suddenly takes control of a country using force: *a military coup* **2** an important achievement, often one that was not expected: *The award is a* ***major coup*** *for the university.*

couple¹ /'kʌpl/ *noun* **1** [no plural] Ⓑ two or a few: *I went to New York with* ***a couple of*** *friends.* ∘ *The weather has improved over the last* ***couple of*** *weeks.* **2** [C] Ⓑ two people who are married or having a romantic relationship: *a* ***married couple***

couple² /'kʌpl/ *verb* **coupled with sth** combined with something: *Concern about farming*

methods, coupled with health awareness, have led to a fall in meat consumption.

coupon /'kuːpɒn/ *noun* [C] **1** a piece of printed paper that you can use to buy something at a cheaper price or to get something free: *Collect 10 coupons to get a free meal.* **2** a printed form in a magazine or newspaper, that you use to send for information, enter a competition, etc

courage /'kʌrɪdʒ/ *noun* [U] Ⓑ the ability to deal with dangerous or difficult situations without being frightened: [+ to do sth] *She didn't* ***have the courage*** *to tell him the truth.*

IDIOM **pluck up the courage (to do sth)** to decide to do something that you were too frightened to do before

---

✎ Word partners for **courage**

have the courage to do sth • **show** courage • sth **takes** courage • **great/immense/ personal** courage

---

courageous /kə'reɪdʒəs/ *adj* brave • **courage-ously** *adv*

courgette /kɔː'ʒet/ *noun* [C, U] UK (US **zucchini**) Ⓑ a long, green vegetable which is white inside

courier /'kʊriər/ *noun* [C] **1** someone whose job is to take and deliver documents and parcels **2** UK someone whose job is to look after people who are on holiday

course /kɔːs/ *noun* **1 of course a** Ⓐ used to say 'yes' and emphasize your answer: *"Can you help me?" "Of course!"* **b** Ⓑ used to show that what you are saying is obvious or already known: *Of course, the Olympics are not just about money* **2 of course not** Ⓐ used to say 'no' and emphasize your answer: *"Do you mind if I borrow your pen?" "Of course not."* **3** LESSONS ▷ [C] Ⓐ a series of lessons about a particular subject: *She did a ten-week course in computing.* **4** PART OF MEAL ▷ [C] Ⓐ a part of a meal: *a three-course dinner* **5** SPORT ▷ [C] Ⓑ an area used for horse races or playing golf: *a golf course* **6** MEDICINE ▷ [C] mainly UK a fixed number of regular medical treatments: *a course of anti-biotics* **7** ROUTE ▷ [C, U] the direction in which a ship, aircraft, etc is moving: *During the storm, the boat was blown* ***off course*** *(= in the wrong direction).* **8** ACTION ▷ [C] (also ˌcourse of 'action) something that you can do in a particular situation: *I think the best course of action would be to write to him.* **9 during/in/over the course of sth** during a particular time or activity: *In the course of the interview she mentioned her previous experience.* **10 in due course** Ⓑ at a suitable time in the future: *The results will be sent to you in due course* **11** DEVELOPMENT ▷ [no plural] the way something develops, usually over a long time: *Nuclear weapons have changed* ***the course of*** *modern history.* **12 in the course of time** UK gradually, or over a period of time **13 be on course for sth/to do sth** UK to be very likely to succeed at something **14 run its course** If something runs its course, it continues naturally until it has finished. → See also **be on a collision course**, **crash course**, **be par for the course**

---

coursebook /ˈkɔːsbʊk/ **noun** [C] UK a book used by students when they do a particular course of study

coursework /ˈkɔːswɜːk/ **noun** [U] UK work done by students as part of their course of study

court¹ /kɔːt/ **noun** [C, U] **1 LAW** ▷ **B2** the place where a judge decides whether someone is guilty of a crime: *The suspect appeared in court charged with robbery.* ∘ *If they don't pay you can take them to court* (= make them be judged in court). **2 the court** the judge and group of people at a trial who decide whether someone is guilty of a crime **3 SPORT** ▷ **B1** an area for playing particular sports: *a tennis/basketball court* **4 ROYAL HOUSE** ▷ the official home of a king or queen and the people who live with them → See also **High Court, the supreme court**

court² /kɔːt/ **verb 1 PLEASE** ▷ [T] to try to please someone because you want them to support you or join you: *Adams was being courted by several football clubs.* **2 TRY TO GET** ▷ [T] to try to get or achieve something: *to court investment/publicity* **3 RELATIONSHIP** ▷ [I, T] old-fashioned to have a romantic relationship with someone that you hope to marry **4 court controversy/danger/disaster, etc** to behave in a way that risks bad results

courteous /ˈkɜːtiəs/ **adj** polite and showing respect • **courteously adv**

courtesy /ˈkɜːtəsi/ **noun 1** **B2** [U] behaviour that is polite and shows respect, or a polite action or remark: *The hotel treats all guests with courtesy.* ∘ [+ to do sth] *He didn't even have the courtesy to thank me.* **2 (by) courtesy of sb/sth** If you have something courtesy of someone, they have allowed you to have it: *The photograph is courtesy of the Natural History Museum.*

courthouse /ˈkɔːthaʊs/ **noun** [C] (plural **courthouses** /ˈkɔːthaʊzɪz/) mainly US a building with law courts inside it

courtier /ˈkɔːtiər/ **noun** [C] someone who spent a lot of time in the home of a king or queen in the past

court-martial¹ /ˌkɔːtˈmɑːʃəl/ **noun** [C] a military court, or a trial in a military court

court-martial² /ˌkɔːtˈmɑːʃəl/ **verb** [T] to judge someone in a military court

court ˌorder noun [C] an instruction from a law court that someone must do or not do something

courtroom /ˈkɔːtrʊm/ **noun** [C] the room where a judge and other people decide whether someone is guilty of a crime

courtship /ˈkɔːtʃɪp/ **noun** [C, U] formal the time when people have a romantic relationship with the intention of getting married

courtyard /ˈkɔːtjɑːd/ **noun** [C] an open area by a building with walls or buildings around it

cousin /ˈkʌzən/ **noun** [C] **A2** the child of your aunt or uncle

couture /kuːˈtjʊər/ **noun** [U] the design, making, and selling of expensive and fashionable clothes

cove /kəʊv/ **noun** [C] a place on the coast where the land curves in

covenant /ˈkʌvənənt/ **noun** [C] a formal written agreement

cover¹ /ˈkʌvər/ **verb** [T] **1 PUT** ▷ **A2** to put something over something else, in order to protect or hide it: *They covered him with a blanket.* ∘ *He covered his face with his hands.* → Opposite **uncover 2 LAYER** ▷ **B1** to form a layer on the surface of something: *Snow covered the trees.* ∘ *My legs were covered in/with mud.* **3 DISTANCE** ▷ **B2** to travel a particular distance: *We covered 700 kilometres in four days.* **4 AREA** ▷ **B2** to be a particular size or area: *The town covers an area of 10 square miles.* **5 INCLUDE** ▷ **B1** to include or deal with a subject or piece of information: *The book covers European history from 1789-1914.* **6 REPORT** ▷ **B2** to report on an event for a newspaper, television programme, etc: *Dave was asked to cover the Olympics.* **7 MONEY** ▷ to be enough money to pay for something: *100 euros should cover the cost of the repairs.* **8 FINANCIAL PROTECTION** ▷ to provide financial protection if something bad happens: *You need travel insurance that covers accident and injury.* → See also **touch/cover all the bases (base¹)**

PHRASAL VERBS **cover sth up** to put something over something else, in order to protect or hide it • **cover (sth) up** to stop people from discovering the truth about something bad: *She tried to cover up her mistakes.*

cover² /ˈkʌvər/ **noun 1 BOOK** ▷ [C] **B1** the outer part of a book, magazine, etc, that protects the pages: *Her picture was on the cover of 'Vogue' magazine.* **2 PROTECTION** ▷ [C] **B1** something you put over something else, usually to protect it: *an ironing board cover* ∘ *a lens cover* **3 FINANCIAL** ▷ [U] financial protection so that you get money if something bad happens: *The policy provides £50,000 accidental damage cover.* **4 FROM WEATHER/ATTACK** ▷ [U] protection from bad weather or an attack: *They took cover under some trees until the rain stopped.* **5 FOR ILLEGAL ACTIVITY** ▷ [C] something used to hide a secret or illegal activity: *The club is used as a cover for a gang of car thieves.*

coverage /ˈkʌvərɪdʒ/ **noun** [U] **1** the way a newspaper, television programme, etc reports an event or subject: *There is live coverage of the game on cable TV.* **2** mainly US financial protection so that you get money if something bad happens

coveralls /ˈkʌvərɔːlz/ **noun** [plural] US (UK **overalls**) a piece of clothing that you wear over your clothes to keep them clean while you are working

covering /ˈkʌvərɪŋ/ **noun** [C] a layer that covers something: *a thick covering of snow*

ˌcovering ˈletter noun [C] UK (US **ˈcover ˌletter**) a letter that you send with something to explain what it is or to give more information about it

covers /ˈkʌvəz/ **noun** [plural] the sheets and other layers of cloth on your bed that keep you warm

covert /ˈkəʊvɜːt/ **adj** done in a secret way: *covert police operations* • **covertly adv**

cover-up /'kʌvərʌp/ **noun** [C] an attempt to prevent people finding out the truth about a crime or a mistake: *Police denied accusations of a cover-up.*

'**cover** '**version noun** [C] a recording of a song already recorded by someone else: *a cover version of 'Let It Be'*

covet /'kʌvɪt/ **verb** [T] formal to want something very much, especially something that someone else has

cow /kaʊ/ **noun** [C] **1** Ⓐ a large farm animal kept for milk or meat **2** UK informal an offensive word for a woman

coward /kaʊəd/ **noun** [C] Ⓑ someone who is not brave and tries to avoid dangerous or difficult situations

cowardice /'kaʊədɪs/ **noun** [U] behaviour that shows that someone is not brave

cowardly /'kaʊədli/ **adj** Ⓑ behaving in a way that shows you are not brave

cowboy /'kaʊbɔɪ/ **noun** [C] **1** a man whose job is to look after cows in the US, and who usually rides a horse **2** UK informal someone who does their job badly or who is dishonest in business: *cowboy builders*

'**cowboy** ,**boots noun** [C] a type of boots with pointed toes, first worn by cowboys → See colour picture **Clothes** on page Centre 9

'**cowboy** ,**hat noun** [C] a type of hat with a high top and a wide lower edge, first worn by cowboys

cower /kaʊər/ **verb** [I] to bend down or move back because you are frightened

co-worker /,kəʊ'wɜːkər/ **noun** [C] (also US **co-worker**) someone that you work with

coy /kɔɪ/ **adj 1** not wanting to give people information about something: *Nigel's very coy about how much he earns.* **2** pretending to be shy: *a coy look* • **coyly adv**

coyote /kaɪ'əʊti/ **noun** [C] a wild animal similar to a dog, that lives in North America

cozy /'kəʊzi/ **adj** US spelling of cosy

crab /kræb/ **noun** [C, U] Ⓑ a sea creature with ten legs and a round, flat body covered by a shell, or the meat from this animal

crack¹ /kræk/ **verb 1** BREAK ▷ [I, T] Ⓑ to break something so that it does not separate, but very thin lines appear on its surface, or to become broken in this way: *The concrete had started to crack.* ○ *cracked dishes* **2** EGG/NUT ▷ [T] to open an egg or nut by breaking its shell **3** HIT ▷ [T] to hit a part of your body against something hard, by accident: *He cracked his head on the shelf.* **4** SOLVE ▷ [T] informal to solve a difficult problem: *It took three months to crack the enemy's code.* **5** get cracking informal to start doing something quickly **6** LOSE CONTROL ▷ [I] to lose control of your emotions and be unable to deal with a situation: *He finally cracked after years of stress.* **7** NOISE ▷ [I, T] to make a sudden, short noise, or to make something make this noise **8** crack a joke to tell a joke

IDIOM **not all it's cracked up to be** (also **not as good as it's cracked up to be**) not as good as people think or say: *Being an actor isn't all it cracked up to be.*

PHRASAL VERBS **crack down** to start dealing with bad or illegal behaviour in a more severe way: *Police are cracking down on crime in the area* • **crack up** informal to become mentally il • **crack (sb) up** informal to suddenly laugh a lot, or to make someone suddenly laugh a lot

crack² /kræk/ **noun 1** LINE ▷ [C] a line on the surface of something that is damaged: *Severa cups had cracks in them.* **2** NARROW SPACE ▷ [C a narrow space between two parts of something or between two things: *I could see sunligh through a crack in the curtains.* **3** DRUG ▷ [U] a illegal drug that is very harmful **4** NOISE ▷ [C] sudden, short noise: *a crack of thunde* **5** JOKE ▷ [C] informal an unkind joke or remark *He was always making cracks about my weigh* **6** have/take a crack at sth informal to try to d something: *I've never put up shelves before, bu I'll have a crack at it.*

IDIOM **the crack of dawn** very early in th morning: *He gets up at the crack of dawn.*

crack³ /kræk/ **adj** [always before noun] of th highest quality: *a crack regiment*

crackdown /'krækdaʊn/ **noun** [C] a perio when bad or illegal behaviour is dealt with in very severe way, in order to stop it happening *The police are having a crackdown on speeding*

cracker /'krækər/ **noun 1** FOOD ▷ [C] a dr biscuit that you eat with cheese **2** CHRISTMAS [C] (also **Christmas cracker**) a coloured pape tube with a small toy inside, that people pul open at Christmas in the UK **3** GOOD ▷ [no plura UK informal someone or something that is ver good

crackle /'krækl/ **verb** [I] to make a lot of shor dry noises: *A fire crackled in the hearth.* • **crackl noun** [no plural]

cradle¹ /'kreɪdl/ **noun 1** BED ▷ [C] a baby's bec especially one that swings from side to sid **2** TELEPHONE ▷ the part of a telephone tha holds the receiver (= the part of a telephone tha you hold in your hand and use to listen an speak) **3** MOBILE PHONE ▷ a small stand tha holds a mobile phone **4** the cradle of sth th place where something started: *Massachusetts the cradle of the American Revolution*

cradle² /'kreɪdl/ **verb** [T] to hold someone o something in a careful, gentle way: *He cradle her in his arms.*

craft¹ /krɑːft/ **noun 1** [C, U] Ⓑ an activity i which you make something using a lot of skil especially with your hands: *traditional crafts suc as weaving* **2** [C] (plural **craft**) a boat

craft² /krɑːft/ **verb** [T] to make something usin a lot of skill: [often passive] *These bowls have bee beautifully crafted from wood.*

craftsman /ˈkrɑːftsmən/ noun [C] (plural **craftsmen**) someone who uses special skill to make things, especially with their hands • **craftsmanship** noun [U] skill at making things

crafty /ˈkrɑːfti/ adj clever at getting what you want, especially by deceiving people • **craftily** adv

crag /kræg/ noun [C] a high, rough mass of rock that sticks up from the land around it

cram /kræm/ verb (**cramming, crammed**) **1 cram sth between/in/into, etc** to force things into a small space: *The refugees were crammed into the truck.* **2** [I] to study a lot before an exam

crammed /kræmd/ adj completely full of people or things: *crammed commuter trains* ○ *The room was crammed with boxes.*

cramp¹ /kræmp/ noun [C, U] a sudden, strong pain in a muscle that makes it difficult to move: *I've got cramp in my legs.*

cramp² /kræmp/ verb

cramped /kræmpt/ adj A cramped room, building, etc is unpleasant because it is not big enough.

cranberry /ˈkrænbəri/ noun [C] a small, red berry (= small round fruit) with a sour taste

crane¹ /kreɪn/ noun [C] **1** a large machine used for lifting and moving heavy things **2** a bird with long legs and a long neck

crane² /kreɪn/ verb [I, T] to stretch your neck, in order to see or hear something

crank /kræŋk/ noun [C] **1** informal someone with strange ideas or behaviour **2** a handle that you turn to make a machine work

cranny /ˈkræni/ noun see **every nook and cranny**

crap¹ /kræp/ noun [U] very informal a very impolite word for something that you think is wrong or bad: *He was talking a lot of crap!*

crap² /kræp/ adj (**crapper, crappest**) UK very informal (UK/US **crappy** /ˈkræpi/) a very impolite word for describing things that are very bad in quality: *a crap car/job*

crash¹ /kræʃ/ noun [C] **1** VEHICLE ▷ ⬛ an accident in which a vehicle hits something: *a car/plane crash* **2** NOISE ▷ ⬛ a sudden, loud noise made when something falls or breaks: *I heard a crash and hurried into the kitchen.* **3** COMPUTER ▷ an occasion when a computer or computer system suddenly stops working **4** BUSINESS ▷ an occasion when the value of a country's businesses suddenly falls by a large amount: *He lost a lot of money in the stock market crash of 1929.*

🔲 Word partners for **crash**

have/be involved in a crash • be injured in/killed in a crash • the cause of a crash • a crash victim • a car/plane/train crash

---

crash² /kræʃ/ verb **1** VEHICLE ▷ [I, T] ⬛ If a vehicle crashes, it hits something by accident, and if you crash a vehicle, you make it hit something by accident: *The van skidded and crashed into a tree.* ○ *Rick crashed his dad's car.* **2** COMPUTER ▷ [I] ⬛ If a computer or computer

system crashes, it suddenly stops working. **3 crash against/on/through, etc** to hit something and make a loud noise: *The waves crashed against the rocks.* **4** LOUD NOISE ▷ [I] ⬛ to make a sudden, loud noise: *Thunder crashed overhead.* **5** MONEY ▷ [I] If a financial market crashes, prices suddenly fall by a large amount.

crash barrier noun [C] UK a fence along the middle or edge of a road for preventing accidents

crash course noun [C] a course that teaches you a lot of basic facts in a very short time

crash helmet noun [C] a hard hat that protects your head when you ride a motorcycle

crass /kræs/ adj showing that you do not understand or care about other people's feelings: *a crass remark*

crate /kreɪt/ noun [C] a large box used for carrying or storing things

crater /ˈkreɪtər/ noun [C] **1** the round, open part at the top of a volcano **2** a big hole in the ground: *The explosion left a crater in the road.*

crave /kreɪv/ verb [T] to want something very much: *Lucy is a child who craves affection.* • **craving** noun [C] a strong feeling that you want or need a particular thing: *She had a craving for chocolate.*

crawl¹ /krɔːl/ verb
1 PERSON ▷ [I] ⬛ to move on your hands and knees: *I crawled under the desk to plug the lamp in.*
2 ANIMAL ▷ [I] If an insect crawls, it uses its legs to move: *There's an ant crawling up your leg.* **3** TRAFFIC ▷ [I] If traffic crawls, it moves extremely slowly: *We were crawling along at 10 miles per hour.* **4** TRY TO PLEASE ▷ [I] UK informal to try to please someone because you want them to like you or help you: *My brother is always crawling to Mum.* **5 be crawling with sb/sth** to be full of insects or people in a way that is unpleasant: *The kitchen's crawling with ants.*

crawl

crawl² /krɔːl/ noun **1** [no plural] a very slow speed: *Traffic slowed to a crawl.* **2** [U] a style of swimming in which you move your arms over your head and kick with straight legs

crayon /ˈkreɪɒn/ noun [C] a stick of coloured wax used for drawing

craze /kreɪz/ noun [C] something that is very popular for a short time

crazed /kreɪzd/ adj behaving in a dangerous and uncontrolled way: *a crazed gunman*

crazy /ˈkreɪzi/ adj **1** ⬛ stupid or strange: *a crazy idea* ○ *I was crazy not to take that job.* **2** ⬛ annoyed or angry: *The children are driving me crazy* (= making me annoyed). ○ *Dad went crazy when I told him what had happened.* **3 be crazy about sb/sth** ⬛ to love someone very much, or to be very interested in something: *Mia's crazy about baseball.* **4 go crazy** to become very excited about something: *When he came on stage the audience went crazy.* **5 like crazy** informal If

---

you do something like crazy, you do a lot of it, or do it very quickly: *We worked like crazy to get everything finished.* • **crazily** adv • **craziness** noun [U]

creak /kriːk/ verb [I] If something such as a door or a piece of wood creaks, it makes a long noise when it moves: *creaking floorboards* • **creak** noun [C] • **creaky** adj A creaky door, stair, etc creaks.

cream¹ /kriːm/ noun **1** FOOD ▷ [U] ⓐ a thick, yellowish-white liquid that is taken from milk: *raspberries and cream* **2** FOR SKIN ▷ [C, U] ⓑ a soft substance that you rub into your skin to make it softer or less painful: *face/hand cream* **3** COLOUR ▷ [U] ⓐ a yellowish-white colour **4 the cream of sth** the best people or things in a particular group: *the cream of Milan's designers* → See also **ice cream**

cream² /kriːm/ adj ⓐ being a yellowish-white colour

cream³ /kriːm/ verb

PHRASAL VERB **cream sth/sb off** UK to take away the best part of something, or the best people in a group, and use them for your own advantage

cream 'cheese noun [U] smooth, soft, white cheese

creamy /ˈkriːmi/ adj like cream or containing cream: *creamy sauce/soup*

crease¹ /kriːs/ noun [C] a line on cloth or paper where it has been folded or crushed

crease² /kriːs/ verb [I, T] If cloth, paper, etc creases, or if you crease it, it gets a line in it where it has been folded or crushed: *Cotton creases very easily.*

create /kriˈeɪt/ verb [T] ⓑ to make something happen or exist: *The project will create more than 500 jobs.* ◦ *The snow created further problems.*

creation /kriˈeɪʃᵊn/ noun **1** PROCESS ▷ [U] ⓑ a process in which someone makes something happen or exist: *the creation of a new political party* **2** PRODUCT ▷ [C] ⓑ something that someone has made: *The museum contains some of his best creations.* **3** UNIVERSE ▷ [U] (also **Creation**) in many religions, the process in which God made the universe and everything in it

creative /kriˈeɪtɪv/ adj ⓑ good at thinking of new ideas or using imagination to create new and unusual things: *Her book is full of creative ways to decorate your home.* • **creatively** adv • **creativity** /ˌkriːeɪˈtɪvəti/ noun [U] ⓑ the ability to produce new ideas or things using skill and imagination

creator /kriˈeɪtəʳ/ noun **1** [C] someone who invents or makes something **2 the Creator** God

creature /ˈkriːtʃəʳ/ noun [C] ⓑ anything that lives but is not a plant: *Dolphins are intelligent creatures.*

creche /kreʃ/ noun [C] UK a place where babies and young children are looked after while their parents do something

credence /ˈkriːdᵊns/ noun **add/give/lend credence to sth** to make a story, theory, etc

seem more likely to be true: *The letters lend credence to the idea that he had an unhappy life.*

credentials /krɪˈdenʃᵊlz/ noun [plural] **1** skills and experience that show you are suitable for a particular job or activity: *academic credentials* **2** documents that prove who you are

credibility /ˌkredəˈbɪləti/ noun [U] a quality that means someone can be believed and trusted: *This decision has **damaged** the President's credibility.*

☑ Word partners for **credibility**

gain/lose credibility • sth **damages/destroys/ restores/undermines** sb's credibility • sb **lacks** credibility

credible /ˈkredəbl/ adj able to be trusted or believed: *credible evidence*

credit¹ /ˈkredɪt/ noun **1** PAYMENT ▷ [U] ⓑ a way of buying something in which you arrange to pay for it at a later time: *We offer **interest-free** credit on all new cars.* ◦ *He bought most of the furniture **on credit**.* **2** PRAISE ▷ [U] ⓑ praise that is given to someone for something they have done: *I did most of the work but Dan **got all the credit!*** ◦ *We should **give** her **credit for** her honesty.* ◦ *I can't **take** full **credit for** this meal – Sam helped.* **3 be a credit to sb/sth** to do something that makes a person or organization proud of you: *Giorgio is a credit to his family.* **4 to sb's credit** If something is to someone's credit, they deserve praise for it: *To his credit, Bill never blamed her for the incident.* **5 have sth to your credit** to have achieved something: *By the age of 25, she had five novels to her credit.* **6 in credit** having money in your bank account **7** MONEY ▷ [C] ⓑ an amount of money that you put into your bank account → Opposite **debit** **8** COURSE ▷ [C] ⓑ a unit that shows you have completed part of a college course

credit² /ˈkredɪt/ verb [T] **1** to add money to someone's bank account **2** to believe that something is true: *Dean's getting married! Who would have credited it?*

PHRASAL VERBS **credit sth to sb** to say that someone is responsible for something good: *The idea was credited to Isaac Newton.* • **credit sb with sth** to believe that someone has a particular quality: *Credit me with some intelligence!* • **credit sb with sth/doing sth** to say that someone is responsible for something good: *She is credited with making the business a success.*

creditable /ˈkredɪtəbl/ adj Something that is creditable deserves praise: *a creditable performance*

'credit ˌcard noun [C] ⓐ a small plastic card that allows you to buy something and pay for it later: *He paid **by credit card**.*

'credit ˌcrunch noun (also **'credit ˌcrisis, 'credit ˌsqueeze**) **1** [C] economic conditions that make financial organizations less willing to lend money, often causing serious economic problems **2 the Credit Crunch** [usually singular] the economic situation during 2007-2009, during which there were serious economic problems all over the world when financial organizations were not willing to lend money

credit limit noun [C] the largest amount of money that a person can borrow with a credit card : *a $500 credit limit*

creditor /'kredɪtəʳ/ noun [C] a person or organization that someone owes money to

the credits /'kredɪts/ noun [plural] a list of people who made a film or television programme

creed /kriːd/ noun [C] a set of beliefs, especially religious beliefs that influence your life

creek /kriːk/ noun [C] **1** UK a narrow area of water that flows into the land from a sea or river **2** mainly US a stream or narrow river

creep¹ /kriːp/ verb (crept) **1 creep along/in/out, etc** to move very quietly and carefully: *I crept out of the room.* **2 creep across/in/into, etc** to gradually start to exist or appear: *Problems were beginning to creep into their relationship.* **3 creep along/down/through, etc** to move somewhere very slowly: *The convoy crept along in the darkness.*

PHRASAL VERB **creep up on sb 1** to surprise someone by moving closer to them from behind: *Don't creep up on me like that!* **2** If a feeling or state creeps up on you, it happens gradually so that you do not notice it: *Old age just creeps up on you.*

creep² /kriːp/ noun [C] **1** UK someone who you do not like because they are nice to people in a way that is not sincere **2** someone who you think is unpleasant

creeps /kriːps/ noun **give sb the creeps** informal to make someone feel frightened or nervous: *These old buildings give me the creeps.*

creepy /'kriːpi/ adj informal strange and frightening: *a creepy story/person*

cremate /krɪ'meɪt/ verb [T] to burn a dead body • **cremation** /krɪ'meɪʃⁿn/ noun [C, U] the ceremony where someone is cremated

crematorium /ˌkremə'tɔːriəm/ noun [C] (also US **crematory** /'kriːmətɔːri/) a place where people are cremated

crept /krept/ past of creep

crescendo /krɪ'ʃendəʊ/ noun [C] a gradual increase in volume of a piece of music

crescent /'kresⁿnt/ noun **1** [C] a curved shape that is narrow at each end and wider in the middle: *the pale crescent of the moon* **2 Crescent** used in the names of streets that have a curved shape: *57 Park Crescent*

crest /krest/ noun [C] **1 TOP** ▷ the highest part of a hill or wave **2 FEATHERS** ▷ the feathers that point upwards on a bird's head **3 DESIGN** ▷ a design used as the symbol of a school, important family, etc

crestfallen /'krestˌfɔːlⁿn/ adj disappointed or sad

crevasse /krɪ'væs/ noun [C] a deep, wide crack, especially in ice

crevice /'krevɪs/ noun [C] a small, narrow crack, especially in a rock

crew /kruː/ noun [group] **1** ⬛ the people who

work together on a ship, aircraft, or train: *a crew member* **2** ⬛ a team of people with special skills who work together: *Fire and ambulance crews were at the scene.*

crewman /'kruːmæn/ noun [C] (plural **crewmen**) a member of the crew of a ship or aircraft

crib /krɪb/ noun [C] US (UK **cot**) a bed with high sides for a baby

cricket /'krɪkɪt/ noun **1** [U] ⬛ a game in which two teams of eleven people try to score points by hitting a ball and running between two wickets (= sets of three wooden sticks): *a cricket ball/bat* → See colour picture **Sports 2** on page Centre 15 **2** [C] an insect that jumps and makes a noise by rubbing its wings together

cricketer /'krɪkɪtəʳ/ noun [C] someone who plays cricket, especially as their job

crime /kraɪm/ noun **1** [U] ⬛ illegal activities: *violent crime* ○ *Tough new measures have been introduced to* **fight** *crime.* **2** [C] ⬛ something someone does that is illegal: *He* **committed** *a serious crime.* → See also **war crime**

> ⬛ Word partners for **crime**
>
> **commit** a crime • **combat/fight/reduce** crime • a **minor/petty/terrible/violent** crime

criminal¹ /'krɪmɪnⁿl/ adj **1** [always before noun] ⬛ relating to crime: *criminal activity* ○ *He has a* **criminal record** (= the police have an official record of his crimes). **2** informal very bad or morally wrong: *It's criminal that people are having to wait so long for hospital treatment.* • **criminally** adv

criminal² /'krɪmɪnⁿl/ noun [C] ⬛ someone who has committed a crime: *a* **dangerous/violent** *criminal*

criminologist /ˌkrɪmɪ'nɒlədʒɪst/ noun [C] someone who studies crime and criminals

crimson /'krɪmzⁿn/ noun [U] a dark red colour • **crimson** adj

cringe /krɪndʒ/ verb [I] **1** to feel very embarrassed about something: *Jan* **cringed at** *the sight of her father dancing.* **2** to move away from something because you are frightened

crinkle /'krɪŋkl/ verb [I, T] to become covered in small lines or folds, or to make something become covered in small lines or folds • **crinkly** adj Something that is crinkly has crinkles in it.

cripple¹ /'krɪpl/ verb [T] **1** to injure someone so that they cannot use their arms or legs: [often passive] *His son was crippled by a riding accident.* **2** to damage something very badly and make it weak or not effective: [often passive] *It was a country crippled by war.*

cripple² /'krɪpl/ noun [C] old-fashioned an offensive word for someone who cannot use their legs or arms in a normal way

crippling /'krɪplɪŋ/ adj **1** [always before noun] A crippling illness makes someone unable to use their arms or legs in a normal way. **2** causing great damage

crisis /'kraɪsɪs/ noun [C, U] (plural **crises** /'kraɪsiːz/) ⬛ a situation or time that is extremely dangerous or difficult: *an economic/*

C

financial crisis ∘ *The country's leadership is in crisis.* → See also **mid-life crisis**

crisp¹ /krɪsp/ **adj 1 FOOD** ▷ Crisp food is pleasantly hard: *a crisp apple* ∘ *crisp pastry* **2 MATERIAL** ▷ Crisp cloth or paper money is clean and looks new, with no folds: *a crisp linen shirt* **3 WEATHER** ▷ Crisp weather is pleasantly cold and dry: *a crisp autumn day* **4 QUICK** ▷ A crisp way of talking or behaving is quick and confident. **5 IMAGE** ▷ A crisp image is very clear.

crisp² /krɪsp/ **noun** [C] UK (US **chip**) ⓐ₂ a very thin slice of potato that has been cooked in oil and is eaten cold: [usually plural] *a packet of crisps* → See colour picture **Food** on page Centre 11

crispy /ˈkrɪspi/ **adj** Crispy food is pleasantly hard and easy to bite through: *crispy bacon*

criss-cross /ˈkrɪskrɒs/ **verb** [I, T] If something criss-crosses an area, it crosses it several times in different directions: [often passive] *The forest is criss-crossed with paths and tracks.*

criterion /kraɪˈtɪəriən/ **noun** [C] (plural **criteria**) a fact or level of quality that you use when making a choice or decision: [+ for + doing sth] *We have strict criteria for deciding which students will receive a grant.*

critic /ˈkrɪtɪk/ **noun** [C] **1** someone who says that they do not approve of someone or something: *an **outspoken critic** of the government* **2** ⓑ₂ someone whose job is to give their opinion of a book, play, film, etc: *a **theatre/film critic***

critical /ˈkrɪtɪkᵊl/ **adj 1 NOT PLEASED** ▷ ⓑ₂ saying that someone or something is bad or wrong: *a critical report* ∘ *He is very **critical of** the way I work.* **2 IMPORTANT** ▷ ⓑ₂ very important for the way things will happen in the future: *a critical decision* **3 SERIOUS** ▷ ⓑ₂ extremely serious or dangerous: *The doctors said her condition was critical and she might not survive.* **4 OPINIONS** ▷ giving judgments and opinions on books, plays, films, etc: *a critical study of Tennyson's work* • **critically adv**

criticism /ˈkrɪtɪsɪzᵊm/ **noun 1** [C, U] ⓑ₂ remarks saying that something or someone is bad: *Plans to close the hospital **attracted** strong public criticism.* **2** [U] the activity of giving judgments and opinions on books, plays, movies, etc: *literary criticism*

🗎 Word partners for criticism

sb/sth **attracts/draws/faces/sparks** criticism • **deflect/dismiss** criticism • **fierce/stinging/strong** criticism • criticism **of** sb/sth • criticism **from** sb

---

criticize (also UK **-ise**) /ˈkrɪtɪsaɪz/ **verb** [I, T] ⓑ₂ to say that something or someone is bad: [often passive, + for + doing sth] *The film was criticized for being too violent.*

critique /krɪˈtiːk/ **noun** [C] a report that says what is good and bad about something

croak /krəʊk/ **verb 1** [I, T] to talk or say something in a low, rough voice: *"I don't feel well," he croaked.* **2** [I] If a bird or frog (= green jumping animal) croaks, it makes a deep, low sound.

crochet /ˈkrəʊʃeɪ/ ⓊⓈ /krəʊˈʃeɪ/ **verb** [I, T] to make clothes and other items using wool and special needle with a hook at one end

crockery /ˈkrɒkᵊri/ **noun** [U] plates, cups, and other dishes, especially those made from clay

crocodile /ˈkrɒkədaɪl/ **noun** [C] ⓑ₂ a big reptil with a long mouth and sharp teeth, that lives in lakes and rivers

crocus /ˈkrəʊkəs/ **noun** [C] a small yellow, purple, or white spring flower

croissant /ˈkwæsɒŋ/ ⓊⓈ /kwɑːˈsɒŋ/ **noun** [C] soft, curved piece of bread, eaten for breakfast

crony /ˈkrəʊni/ **noun** [C] informal one of a group of friends who help each other, especially in a way that is not fair: [usually plural] *He gave h cronies all the best jobs.*

crook /krʊk/ **noun 1** [C] informal a criminal o someone who cheats people **2 the crook o your arm** the inside part of your arm where i bends

crooked /ˈkrʊkɪd/ **adj 1** not straight: *crooke teeth* **2** informal not honest: *a crooked politician*

croon /kruːn/ **verb** [I, T] to sing in a soft, low romantic voice

crop¹ /krɒp/ **noun 1** [C] ⓑ₁ a plant such as grain, fruit, or vegetable that is grown in larg amounts by farmers **2** [C] ⓑ₁ the amount o plants of a particular type that are produced a one time: *We had a record crop of grapes this yea* **3 a crop of sth** a group of the same type o things or people that exist at the same time *He's one of the current crop of young Italian artists* → See also **cash crop**

crop² /krɒp/ **verb** (**cropping, cropped**) **1 CUT** ▷ [T] to cut something so that it is shor **2 COMPUTER** ▷ [T] to cut pieces from the side of a computer image so that it is the size yo want **3 GROW** ▷ [I] UK If a plant crops, produces fruit, flowers, etc.

PHRASAL VERB crop up to happen or appea suddenly: *The same old problems **kept croppin up.***

cropper /ˈkrɒpər/ **noun come a cropper a** t fall over: *The horse came a cropper at the firs fence.* **b** to fail in an embarrassing way, or t make an embarrassing mistake

croquet /ˈkrəʊkeɪ/ ⓊⓈ /krəʊˈkeɪ/ **noun** [U] a gam played on grass, in which you hit a ball with wooden object through curved wires pushe into the ground

cross¹ /krɒs/ **verb 1 FROM ONE SIDE TO ANOTHER** ▷ [I, T] ⓐ₂ to go from one side o something to the other side: *It's not a good plac to **cross** the road.* **2 LINE/BORDER** ▷ [I, T] ⓐ₂ t travel over a border or line into a different are country, etc: *They **crossed** from Albania int Greece.* **3 MEET AND GO ACROSS** ▷ [I, T] If tw lines, roads, etc cross, they go over or acros each other. **4 cross your arms/fingers/legs** t put one of your arms, fingers, or legs over th top of the other **5 cross yourself** to touch you head, chest, and both shoulders as a sign to Go **6 ANIMAL/PLANT** ▷ [T] to mix two breeds o animal or plant to produce a new breed **7 MAK SOMEONE ANGRY** ▷ [T] to make someone angry by refusing to do what they want you to do → Se also **I'll/We'll** cross that **bridge¹** when I/we come to it., **criss-cross, double-cross,** keep your fingers (**finger¹**) crossed, cross your **mind¹**

PHRASAL VERBS **cross sth off (sth)** to remove a word from a list by drawing a line through it: *Did you cross her name off the guest list?* • **cross sth out** to draw a line through something that you have written, usually because it is wrong: *Cross out that last sentence.*

cross² /krɒs/ noun **1** WOOD ▷ [C] 🔒 two pieces of wood that cross each other, on which people were left to die as a punishment in the past **2** SYMBOL ▷ [C] 🔒 an object in the shape of a cross, used as a symbol of the Christian religion **3** MARK ▷ [C] 🔒 a written mark (x), used for showing where something is, or that something that has been written is wrong **4 a cross between sth and sth** a mixture of two different things or people: *The dog is a cross between a terrier and a rottweiler.* **5** SPORT ▷ [C] a kick or hit of the ball across the field in sport, especially football

cross³ /krɒs/ adj annoyed or angry: *Don't be cross with me!*

cross- /krɒs-/ prefix **1** across: *cross-border* **2** including different groups or subjects: *a cross-party committee* (= one formed from many political parties) ∘ *cross-cultural*

crossbar /ˈkrɒsbɑːʳ/ noun [C] **1** the post at the top of a goal in games such as football **2** the metal tube that joins the front and back of a bicycle

cross-border /ˈkrɒsˌbɔːdəʳ/ adj [always before noun] between different countries, or involving people from different countries: *cross-border trade*

cross-Channel /ˌkrɒsˈtʃænᵊl/ adj [always before noun] connecting or happening between England and France: *a cross-Channel ferry/route*

cross-country /ˌkrɒsˈkʌntri/ adj [always before noun], adv **1** across fields and countryside: *cross-country running/skiing* **2** from one side of a country to the other side

cross-examine /ˌkrɒsɪɡˈzæmɪn/ verb [T] to ask someone a lot of questions about something they have said, in order to discover if it is true, especially in a court of law • **cross-examination** /ˌkrɒsɪɡˌzæmɪˈneɪʃᵊn/ noun [U]

cross-eyed /krɒsˈaɪd/ adj A cross-eyed person has both eyes looking towards their nose.

crossfire /ˈkrɒsfaɪəʳ/ noun **1** [U] bullets fired towards you from different directions: *Civilians died when a bus was caught in crossfire between government and rebel troops.* **2 be caught in the crossfire** to be involved in a situation where people around you are arguing

crossing /ˈkrɒsɪŋ/ noun [C] **1** WHERE PEOPLE CROSS ▷ 🔒 a place where people can go across a road, river, etc **2** SEA JOURNEY ▷ a journey across water **3** WHERE LINES CROSS ▷ a place where roads, railways, etc cross each other → See also **grade crossing, level crossing, zebra crossing**

cross-legged /ˌkrɒsˈleɡɪd/ adv sit **cross-legged**

to sit on the floor with your knees wide apart and one foot over the other foot

cross ˈpurposes noun **at cross purposes** If two people are at cross purposes, they do not understand each other because they are talking about different things but do not know this.

cross ˈreference noun [C] a note in a book that tells you to look somewhere else in the book for more information about something

crossroads /ˈkrɒsrəʊdz/ noun [C] (plural **crossroads**) **1** 🔒 a place where two roads cross each other **2** a time when you have to make an important decision that will affect your future life: *I felt I was at a crossroads in my life.*

cross-section /ˈkrɒsˌsekʃᵊn/ noun [C] **1** a small group of people or things that represents all the different types in a larger group: *a cross-section of society* **2** something that has been cut in half so that you can see the inside, or a picture of this: *a cross-section of a human heart*

crosswalk /ˈkrɒswɔːk/ noun [C] US (mainly UK **pedestrian crossing**) a special place on a road where traffic must stop if people want to cross

crossword /ˈkrɒswɜːd/ noun [C] (also ˈcrossword ˌpuzzle) a game in which you write words which are the answers to questions in a pattern of black and white squares

crotch /krɒtʃ/ noun [C] (also UK **crutch**) the part of your body between the tops of your legs, or the part of a piece of clothing that covers this area

crouch /kraʊtʃ/ verb [I] (also **crouch down**) to move your body close to the ground by bending your knees: *I crouched behind the chair to avoid being seen.*

crow¹ /krəʊ/ noun [C] a large black bird that makes a loud noise

IDIOM **as the crow flies** describes a distance when measured in a straight line: *It's about 50 miles from London to Cambridge as the crow flies.*

crow² /krəʊ/ verb [I] **1** to talk in a proud and annoying way about something you have done: *Donald wouldn't stop crowing about his exam results.* **2** If a cock (= male chicken) crows, it makes a loud noise, usually in the early morning.

crowd¹ /kraʊd/ noun **1** [C] 🔒 a large group of people who are together in one place: *A large crowd had gathered to wait for the princess.* ∘ *Shop early and avoid the crowds.* **2** [no plural] informal a group of friends or people with similar interests: *the art/theatre crowd*

> **Word partners for crowd**
>
> a crowd **gathers** • a crowd **of** [people/tourists, etc] • **in** a crowd

crowd² /kraʊd/ verb [T] **1** to stand together in large numbers: *Protesters crowded the streets.* **2** to stand too close to someone: *Don't crowd me!*

PHRASAL VERBS **crowd around/round (sb/sth)** If a group of people crowd around or crowd around someone or something, they stand very close all around them: *Everyone crowded around my desk.* • **crowd in/crowd (sb) into sth** If a large group of people crowd into somewhere, they all go there and fill the place. • **crowd sb out** to prevent someone or something from succeeding or existing by being much more successful than them or by being present in much larger numbers: *Large national companies often crowd out smaller local businesses.*

crowded /ˈkraʊdɪd/ **adj** Ⓐ② very full of people: *a crowded room/train*

crowdsourcing /ˈkraʊdˌsɔːsɪŋ/ **noun** [U] the act of giving pieces of work to a large group of people or to the general public, for example, by asking for help on the Internet, rather than having the work done within a company by employees

crown¹ /kraʊn/ **noun 1 KING/ QUEEN** ▷ [C] a round object made of gold and jewels (= valuable stones) that a king or queen wears on their head **2 TOP** ▷ [C] the top of a hat, head, or hill **3 the Crown** used to refer to the power or government of a king or queen: *All this land belongs to the Crown.* **4 TOOTH** ▷ [C] an artificial top that is put on a damaged tooth

crown² /kraʊn/ **verb** [T] **1 MAKE KING/QUEEN** ▷ to put a crown on someone's head in an official ceremony that makes them a king or queen: [often passive] *Queen Elizabeth II of England was crowned in 1952.* **2 ON TOP** ▷ literary to be on top of something : *A large domed ceiling crowns the main hall.* **3 BEST PART** ▷ to be the best or most successful part of something: *The book crowned his successful writing career.*

crowning /ˈkraʊnɪŋ/ **adj** [always before noun] more important, beautiful, etc than anything else: *It was the **crowning achievement** of his political career.*

crucial /ˈkruːʃ³l/ **adj** Ⓑ② extremely important or necessary: *a crucial decision/question* ◦ *Her work has been **crucial to** the project's success.* • **crucially adv**

crucifix /ˈkruːsɪfɪks/ **noun** [C] a model of a cross with Jesus Christ on it

crucifixion /ˌkruːsəˈfɪkʃ³n/ **noun** [C, U] in the past, the punishment of fastening someone to a cross and leaving them to die: *the crucifixion of Christ*

crucify /ˈkruːsɪfaɪ/ **verb** [T] **1** in the past, to fasten someone to a cross and leave them to die **2** informal to criticize someone or something in a cruel and damaging way: [often passive] *The film has been crucified by the media.*

crude /kruːd/ **adj 1** made or done in a simple way and without much skill: *a crude device/ weapon* **2** rude and offensive: *a crude comment/ remark* • **crudely adv**

crude 'oil noun [U] (also **crude**) oil in its natural state before it has been treated

cruel /ˈkruːəl/ **adj** (**crueller, cruellest, crueler, cruelest**) Ⓑ① extremely unkind, or causing people or animals to suffer: *a cruel joke* ◦ *Many people think hunting is **cruel to** animals.* • **cruelly adv**

cruelty /ˈkruːəlti/ **noun** [C, U] Ⓑ② cruel behaviour or a cruel action: *laws against **cruelty to** animals*

cruise¹ /kruːz/ **noun** [C] Ⓑ① a holiday on a ship sailing from place to place

cruise² /kruːz/ **verb 1** [I] to move in a vehicle at a speed that does not change: *The plane is cruising at 500 miles per hour.* **2** [I] Ⓑ② to go on a cruise **3 cruise to success/victory, etc** informal to win competition easily

cruise 'missile UK (US **'cruise ˌmissile**) **noun** [C a weapon that flies through the air, and that often carries nuclear weapons

cruiser /ˈkruːzər/ **noun** [C] **1** a large military ship used in wars **2** (also **'cabin ˌcruiser**) a motor boat with a room for people to sleep in

'cruise ˌship noun [C] (also **'cruise ˌliner**) a large ship like a hotel, which people travel on for pleasure

crumb /krʌm/ **noun 1** [C] a very small piece of bread, cake, etc **2 a crumb of sth** a very small amount of something

crumble /ˈkrʌmbl/ **verb 1** [I, T] to break into small pieces, or to make something break into small pieces: *Buildings crumbled as the earthquake struck.* **2** [I] If a relationship, system, or feeling crumbles, it fails or ends: *His first marriage crumbled after only a year.*

crummy /ˈkrʌmi/ **adj** informal unpleasant, or of bad quality: *a crummy job* ◦ *a crummy hotel*

crumple /ˈkrʌmpl/ **verb 1** [I, T] If something such as paper or cloth crumples, it becomes crushed, and if you crumple it, you crush it until it is full of folds: *a crumpled shirt* **2** [I] I someone's face crumples, they suddenly look very sad or disappointed.

PHRASAL VERB **crumple sth up** to crush a piece o paper until it is full of folds

crunch¹ /krʌnʃ/ **noun** [C] the sound of something being crushed: [usually singular] *the crunch of dried leaves under our feet*

IDIOM **if/when it comes to the crunch** if/when a situation becomes serious or you have to make an important decision

crunch² /krʌnʃ/ **verb 1** [I, T] to make a noise by chewing hard food: *She was **crunching on** an apple.* **2** [I] to make a sound as if something is being crushed: *The small stones crunched under our feet.*

crunchy /ˈkrʌnʃi/ **adj** Crunchy food is hard and makes a noise when you eat it.

crusade /kruːˈseɪd/ **noun** [C] a determined attempt to change or achieve something that you believe in strongly • **crusader noun** [C someone who is involved in a crusade

---

⚡ **Word partners for crusade**

launch/mount a crusade • be on a crusade • a moral/personal crusade • a crusade against/for sth

---

crush¹ /krʌʃ/ **verb** [T] **1** to press something so hard that it is made flat or broken into pieces *Her car was crushed by a falling tree.* **2** to defeat someone or something completely: *Government* attempts to crush the protests failed. ∘ *a crushing defeat*

crush² /krʌʃ/ noun **1** [no plural] a crowd of people forced to stand close together because there is not enough room: *Many people fell over in the crush.* **2** [C] informal a strong temporary feeling of love for someone: *Tim has a crush on Jennifer.*

crust /krʌst/ noun [C, U] **1** the hard outer surface of bread or other baked foods **2** a hard, dry layer on the surface of something

crusty /'krʌsti/ adj **1** sense-body>unfriendly and becoming annoyed very easily **2** Something that is crusty has a hard outer layer: *crusty bread*

crutch /krʌtʃ/ noun [C] **1** a stick that you put under your arm to help you walk if you have injured your leg or foot: [usually plural] *Charles was on crutches for six weeks.* **2** UK (UK/US **crotch**) the part of your body between the tops of your legs, or the part of a piece of clothing that covers this area

crux /krʌks/ noun **the crux (of sth)** the main or most important part of a problem, argument, etc

cry¹ /kraɪ/ verb **1** [I] 🄐 to produce tears from your eyes, usually because you are sad, angry, or hurt: *My baby brother cries all the time.* **2** [I, T] 🄑 to speak or say something loudly: *"Look at this!" cried Raj.*
→ See also **cry your eyes (eye¹) out, a shoulder¹ to cry on**

cry

PHRASAL VERBS **be crying out for sth** informal to need something very much: *The school is crying out for more money.* • **cry out (sth)** to shout or make a loud noise because you are frightened, hurt, etc: *She cried out in terror.*

cry² /kraɪ/ noun **1** [C] 🄑 a shout, especially one that shows that someone is frightened, hurt, etc: *a cry of horror/joy/pain* ∘ *I could hear the cries of children playing in the street.* **2** [C] a sound that a particular animal or bird makes: *an eagle's cry* **3** **have a cry** to produce tears from your eyes, usually because you are sad, angry, or hurt

IDIOM **be a far cry from sth** to be very different from something: *Her luxury mansion is a far cry from the house she grew up in.*

crying /'kraɪɪŋ/ adj **1 a crying need for sth** mainly UK a need that is very urgent: *There's a crying need for more nurses.* **2 it's a crying shame** used to say that you think a situation is very wrong

crypt /krɪpt/ noun [C] a room under a church, especially one where people are buried

cryptic /'krɪptɪk/ adj mysterious and difficult to understand: *a cryptic comment/message* • **cryptically** adv

crystal /'krɪstəl/ noun **1 ROCK** ▷ [C, U] a type of transparent rock **2 GLASS** ▷ [U] a type of high quality glass: *a crystal vase* **3 SHAPE** ▷ [C] a piece

of a substance that has become solid, with a regular shape: *ice crystals*

crystal 'ball noun [C] a large, glass ball that some people believe you can look into to see what will happen in the future

crystal 'clear adj very obvious and easy to understand: *She made her feelings crystal clear to me.*

CU internet abbreviation for see you: used when saying goodbye at the end of an email or text message

cub /kʌb/ noun [C] a young bear, fox, lion, etc

cube¹ /kjuːb/ noun **1** [C] a solid object with six square sides of the same size: *Cut the cheese into small cubes.* → See picture at **shape 2 the cube of sth** the number you get when you multiply a particular number by itself twice: *The cube of 3 is 27.* → See also **ice cube**

cube² /kjuːb/ verb [T] **1** to multiply a particular number by itself twice: *5 cubed is 125.* **2** to cut something into cubes

cubic /'kjuːbɪk/ adj **cubic centimetre/inch/ metre, etc** a unit of measurement that shows something's volume (= length multiplied by width multiplied by height): *The reservoir holds 22 million cubic metres of water.*

cubicle /'kjuːbɪkl/ noun [C] a small space with walls around it, that is separate from the rest of a room: *a shower cubicle*

cuckoo /'kʊkuː/ noun [C] a bird that makes a sound like its name and puts its eggs into other birds' nests

cucumber /'kjuːkʌmbər/ noun [C, U] 🄑 a long, green vegetable that you eat raw in salads → See colour picture **Fruits and Vegetables** on page Centre 10

cuddle /'kʌdl/ verb [I, T] to put your arms around someone to show them that you love them: *Her mother cuddled her until she stopped crying.* • **cuddle** noun [C]

PHRASAL VERB **cuddle up** to sit or lie very close to someone: *The children cuddled up to me to keep warm.*

cuddly /'kʌdli/ adj soft and pleasant to hold close to you

cue /kjuː/ noun **1 ACTION/EVENT** ▷ [C] an action or event that is a sign that something should happen: *The final goal was the cue for celebration.* **2 SIGNAL** ▷ [C] a signal that tells someone to start speaking or doing something when acting in a play, film, etc **3 on cue** If something happens on cue, it happens at exactly the right time: *Then, right on cue, Andrew appeared at the door.* **4 take your cue from sb/sth** to copy what someone else does: *I took my cue from the others and left.* **5 STICK** ▷ [C] a long, straight stick used to hit the balls in games like snooker (= a game played with small coloured balls on a table)

cuff /kʌf/ noun [C] the bottom part of a sleeve that goes around your wrist → See picture at **jacket**

IDIOM **off the cuff** If you speak off the cuff, you do it without having planned what you will say.

cuisine /kwɪˈziːn/ noun [U] a style of cooking: *French/international cuisine*

cul-de-sac /ˈkʌldəsæk/ noun [C] a short road with houses that is blocked at one end

culinary /ˈkʌlɪnəri/ adj [always before noun] formal relating to food and cooking: *culinary equipment*

cull /kʌl/ verb [T] to kill some of the animals in a group, especially the weakest ones, to limit their numbers • **cull** noun [C]

PHRASAL VERB **cull sth from sth** to collect ideas or information from several different places: [often passive] *The book is culled from over 800 pages of his diaries.*

culminate /ˈkʌlmɪneɪt/ verb formal **1 culminate in/with sth** to finish with a particular event, or reach a final result after gradual development and often a lot of effort: *His career culminated with the post of ambassador to NATO.* **2** [T] US to be the final thing in a series of events: *The discovery of a body culminated two days of desperate searching.* • **culmination** /ˌkʌlmɪˈneɪʃ°n/ noun [no plural] *This discovery is **the culmination of** years of research.*

culpable /ˈkʌlpəbl/ adj formal deserving to be blamed for something bad • **culpability** /ˌkʌlpəˈbɪləti/ noun [U]

culprit /ˈkʌlprɪt/ noun [C] **1** someone who has done something wrong **2** something that is responsible for a bad situation: *In many of these illnesses, stress is the main culprit.*

cult /kʌlt/ noun [C] **1** someone or something that has become very popular with a particular group of people: *a cult figure/movie* **2** a religious group whose ideas are considered strange by many people

cultivate /ˈkʌltɪveɪt/ verb [T] **1** to prepare land and grow crops on it: *This shrub is cultivated in Europe as a herb used in cooking.* **2** to try to develop or improve something: *She has cultivated an image as a tough negotiator.* • **cultivation** /ˌkʌltɪˈveɪʃ°n/ noun [U]

cultivated /ˈkʌltɪveɪtɪd/ adj A cultivated person has had a good education and knows a lot about art, books, music, etc.

cultural /ˈkʌltʃ°r°l/ adj **1** relating to the habits, traditions, and beliefs of a society: *cultural diversity/identity* **2** relating to music, art, theatre, literature, etc: *cultural events* • **culturally** adv

culture /ˈkʌltʃəʳ/ noun **1** SOCIETY [C, U] the habits, traditions, and beliefs of a country, society, or group of people: *American/Japanese culture* ○ *It's a good opportunity for children to learn about other cultures.* **2** ARTS [U] music, art, theatre, literature, etc: *popular culture* **3** BIOLOGY [C, U] the process of growing things, especially bacteria, for scientific purposes, or the bacteria produced by this process

cultured /ˈkʌltʃəd/ adj A cultured person knows a lot about music, art, theatre, etc.

'culture ˌshock noun [U] the feeling of confusion someone has when they go to a new and very different place

-cum- /kʌm/ used between two nouns to describe something that combines the two things: *a*

kitchen-cum-dining room (= room which is used as a kitchen and a dining room)

cumbersome /ˈkʌmbəsəm/ adj **1** large and difficult to move or use: *cumbersome safety equipment* **2** slow and not effective: *cumbersome bureaucracy*

cumulative /ˈkjuːmjələtɪv/ adj reached by gradually adding one thing after another: *a cumulative score*

cunning /ˈkʌnɪŋ/ adj clever at getting what you want, especially by tricking people: *a cunning plan/ploy* • **cunning** noun [U] • **cunningly** adv

cup

saucer

cup¹ /kʌp/ noun [C] **1** CONTAINER ▷ a small round container with a handle on the side, used to drink from: *a cup of tea/coffee* ▷ **2** SPORT ▷ a prize given to the winner of a competition, or the name of the competition: *the World Cup* **3** COOKING ▷ mainly US a measurement of amounts of food used in cooking → See also **egg cup**

cup² /kʌp/ verb [T] (**cupping, cupped**) to make your hands into the shape of a cup, or to hold something with your hands in this shape

cupboard /ˈkʌbəd/ noun [C] a piece of furniture with a door on the front and shelves inside, used for storing things → See colour picture **The Kitchen** on page Centre 2 → See also **have a skeleton in the cupboard**

cupcake /ˈkʌpˌkeɪk/ noun [C] a small, round cake, usually for one person

curate /ˈkjʊərət/ noun [C] a person who works for the Church of England and whose job is to help the vicar (= priest)

curator /kjʊəˈreɪtəʳ/ noun [C] a person who is in charge of a museum

curb¹ /kɜːb/ verb [T] to limit or control something: *to curb crime/inflation*

curb² /kɜːb/ noun [C] **1** something that limits or controls something: *They are proposing a curb on tobacco advertising.* **2** US spelling of kerb (= the edge of the raised path at the side of the road)

curdle /ˈkɜːdl/ verb [I, T] If a liquid curdles, or if you curdle it, it gets thicker and develops lumps: *Heat the sauce slowly or it will curdle.*

cure¹ /kjʊəʳ/ noun [C] **1** something that makes someone with an illness healthy again

They are trying to find a cure for cancer. **2** a solution to a problem

> ✏️ **Word partners for cure**
>
> **find/look for** a cure • a cure **for** sth • **the search for** a cure

cure² /kjʊər/ **verb** [T] **1** ⬅ to make someone with an illness healthy again: *Getting a better chair completely cured my back problems.* **2** to solve a problem: *the fight to cure social inequality*

curfew /'kɜːfjuː/ **noun** [C] a time, especially at night, when people are not allowed to leave their homes

curiosity /ˌkjʊəri'ɒsəti/ **noun 1** [U] ⬅ the feeling of wanting to know or learn about something: *My curiosity got the better of me and I opened the envelope.* ∘ *Just out of curiosity, how did you get my address?* **2** [C] something strange or unusual

> ✏️ **Word partners for curiosity**
>
> **arouse/satisfy** sb's curiosity • (do sth) **out of** curiosity • **mild/natural** curiosity • curiosity **about** sth

curious /'kjʊəriəs/ **adj 1** ⬅ wanting to know or learn about something: *I was curious about his life in India.* ∘ *I was curious to know what would happen next.* **2** strange or unusual: *The house was decorated in a curious style.* • **curiously** adv ⬅ *She looked at him curiously.*

curl¹ /kɜːl/ **noun** [C] something with a small, curved shape, especially a piece of hair: *a child with blonde curls*

curl² /kɜːl/ **verb** [I, T] to make something into the shape of a curl, or to be this shape: *The cat curled its tail around its body.*

PHRASAL VERB **curl up 1** to sit or lie in a position with your arms and legs close to your body: *She curled up and went to sleep.* **2** If something flat, such as a piece of paper, curls up, the edges start to curve up.

curly /'kɜːli/ **adj** ⬅ shaped like a curl, or with many curls: *curly hair*

currant /'kʌrənt/ **noun** [C] a small, black dried fruit used in cooking, especially in cakes

currency /'kʌrənsi/ **noun 1** [C, U] ⬅ the units of money used in a particular country: *foreign currency* **2** [U] a situation in which an idea is believed or accepted by many people: *This view is gaining currency within the government.* → See also **hard currency**

current¹ /'kʌrənt/ **adj** ⬅ happening or existing now: *What is your current address?* → See Note at **actual** • **currently** adv ⬅ *The factory currently employs 750 people.*

current² /'kʌrənt/ **noun 1** [C] the natural flow of air or water in one direction: *a current of air* ∘ *dangerous/strong currents* **2** [C, U] the flow of electricity through a wire: *an electrical current*

current ac'count noun [C] UK (US **checking account**) a bank account that you can take money out of at any time

current af'fairs noun [plural] UK (US ˌ**current**

e'vents) important political or social events that are happening in the world at the present time

curriculum /kə'rɪkjələm/ **noun** [C] (plural **curricula**, **curriculums**) ⬅ all the subjects taught in a school, college, etc or on an educational course: *the school curriculum*

curry /'kʌri/ **noun** [C, U] ⬅ a type of food from India, made of vegetables or meat cooked in hot spices

curse¹ /kɜːs/ **noun** [C] **1** MAGIC ▷ magic words that are intended to bring bad luck to someone: *to put a curse on someone* **2** RUDE WORDS ▷ a rude or offensive word or phrase **3** PROBLEM ▷ something that causes harm or unhappiness, often over a long period of time: *Traffic is one of the curses of modern living.*

curse² /kɜːs/ **verb 1** [I] to use rude or offensive words: *He cursed angrily under his breath.* **2** [T] to express anger towards someone or something: *He cursed himself for not telling David about it earlier.* **3 be cursed by/with sth** to have something that causes problems over a long period of time

cursor /'kɜːsər/ **noun** [C] ⬅ a symbol on a computer screen that shows the place where you are working

cursory /'kɜːsəri/ **adj** [always before noun] formal done quickly and without much care: *a cursory glance*

curt /kɜːt/ **adj** If something you say or write is curt, it is short and not very polite. • **curtly** adv

curtail /kɜː'teɪl/ **verb** [T] formal to reduce, limit, or stop something: *to curtail spending* • **curtailment noun** [U]

curtain /'kɜːtən/ **noun** [C] ⬅ a piece of material that hangs down to cover a window, stage, etc: *to draw the curtains* (= open or close them) ∘ *The curtain goes up* (= the performance starts) *at 8 o'clock.* → See colour picture **The Living Room** on page Centre 4

curtsey (also **curtsy**) /'kɜːtsi/ **noun** [C] a movement where a girl or woman puts one foot behind the other and bends her knees, especially to show respect to a king or queen • **curtsey verb** [I]

curve¹ /kɜːv/ **noun** [C] ⬅ a line that bends round like part of a circle: *a road with gentle curves*

curve² /kɜːv/ **verb** [I, T] to move in a curve, form a curve, or make something into the shape of a curve: *The road curves to the left.* ∘ *a chair with a curved back* → See picture at **flat**

cushion¹ /'kʊʃən/ **noun** [C] **1** ⬅ a cloth bag filled with something soft that you sit on or lean against to make you comfortable → See colour picture **The Living Room** on page Centre 4 **2** something that protects you from possible problems: *Overseas savings provide a cushion against tax rises at home.*

cushion² /'kʊʃən/ **verb** [T] **1** to reduce the bad effects of something: *Various attempts were made to cushion the impact of unemployment.* **2** to protect something, especially part of the body, with something soft: *Soft grass cushioned his fall.*

cushy /'kʊʃi/ **adj** informal very easy: *a cushy job*

custard /'kʌstəd/ **noun 1** [U] a sweet, yellow sauce made from milk and eggs, usually eaten hot with sweet food: *apple pie and custard* **2** [C, U] a soft baked mixture made from milk, eggs, and sugar: *a custard pie/tart*

custodial /kʌs'təʊdiəl/ **adj** If someone is given a custodial sentence (= punishment), they are sent to prison.

custodian /kʌs'təʊdiən/ **noun** [C] **1** VALUABLE THING ▷ formal a person who takes care of something valuable or important: *He's the grandson of Oscar Wilde and custodian of his private papers.* **2** BUILDING ▷ US someone whose job is to look after a building, especially a school

custody /'kʌstədi/ **noun** [U] **1** CHILD ▷ the legal right to look after a child, especially when parents separate: *When they divorced, it was Nicola who **won custody of** their two children.* **2** PRISON ▷ the state of being kept in prison, usually while you are waiting for a trial in court: *He is being **held in custody** in Los Angeles charged with assault.* ∘ *He was **taken into custody** by Mexican authorities.*

> 🖉 Word partners for **custody**
>
> be **awarded/given** custody (of sb) • **have/win** custody (of sb)

custom /'kʌstəm/ **noun 1** [C, U] 🄱1 a habit or tradition **2** [U] people who buy things from shops or businesses: *Free gifts are a good way of **attracting custom**.*

> 🖉 Word partners for **custom**
>
> an **ancient/local/traditional** custom • the custom **of** doing sth

custom- /'kʌstəm/ **prefix** used before another word to mean 'specially designed for a particular person or purpose': *custom-built* ∘ *custom-designed*

customary /'kʌstəmᵊri/ **adj** normal or expected for a particular person, situation, or society: [+ to do sth] *It is **customary for** the chairman to make the opening speech.* • **customarily** /ˌkʌstə'merᵊli/ **adv**

customer /'kʌstəmər/ **noun** [C] 🄰2 a person or organization that buys goods or services from a shop or business: *a **satisfied customer*** ∘ *Mrs Wilson is one of our **regular customers**.*

customise UK (US **customize**) /'kʌstəmaɪz/ **verb** [T] to change something to make it suitable for a particular person or purpose: *Our language courses are customised to each student.*

customs /'kʌstəmz/ **noun** [U] 🄱1 the place where your bags are examined when you are going into a country, to make sure you are not carrying anything illegal: *customs officials* ∘ *to **go through customs***

cut¹ /kʌt/ **verb** (**cutting, cut**) **1** KNIFE ▷ [I, T] 🄰2 to use a knife or other sharp tool to divide something, remove part of something, or make a hole in something: *Cut the meat into small pieces.* ∘ *He **cut** the piece of wood **in half**.* ∘ *I had my hair cut last week.* ∘ *She **cut off** all the diseased buds.* **2** REDUCE ▷ [T] 🄱2 to reduce the size or amount of something: *Prices have been*

cut

cut by 25%. ∘ *The company is cutting 50 jobs* **3** INJURE ▷ [T] 🄱1 to injure yourself on a sharp object that makes you bleed: *She cut her finger on a broken glass.* **4** REMOVE ▷ [T] 🄱2 to remove part of a film or piece of writing: *The film was too long so they cut some scenes.* → See also **cut corners** (**corner¹**), **cut it/things fine²**, have your **work²** cut out

PHRASAL VERBS **cut across sth 1** 🄱2 to go from one side of an area to the other instead of going round it: *If we cut across this field, it will save time.* **2** If a problem or subject cuts across different groups of people, all of those groups are affected by it or interested in it. • **cut back (sth)** to reduce the amount of money being spent on something: *We have had to **cut back on** training this year.* • **cut sth down** 🄱2 to make a tree or other plant fall to the ground by cutting it near the bottom • **cut down (sth)** 🄱2 to eat or drink less of something, or to reduce the amount or number of something: *My doctor says I should **cut down on** cigarettes.* • **cut sb off** to stop someone speaking by interrupting them or putting the telephone down: *She cut me off in the middle of our conversation.* • **cut sb/sth off 1** 🄱2 to prevent people from reaching or leaving a place, or to separate them from other people [often passive] *The whole village was cut off by flooding.* ∘ *She lives abroad and feels very **cut off from** her family.* **2** 🄱2 to stop providing something such as electricity or food supplies: [often passive] *If we don't pay the gas bill, we'll be cut off.* • **cut sth out 1** to remove something or form a shape by cutting, usually something made of paper or cloth: *She cut out his picture from the magazine.* **2** to stop eating or drinking something, usually to improve your health: *I've cut out red meat from my diet.* **3 Cut it out!** informal something you say to tell someone to stop doing something annoying **4 not be cut out to be sth/not be cut out for sth** to not have the right qualities for something: *I'm not really cut out to be a nurse.* • **cut out** If an engine, machine, or piece of equipment cuts out, it suddenly stops working. • **cut sth/sb out** to not let someone share something or be included in something • **cut sth up 1** ⓑ to cut something into pieces **2 be cut up** UK informal to be very upset about something: *He was very cut up when his brother died.*

ut² /kʌt/ noun [C] **1 INJURY** ▷ ⓑ an injury made when the skin is cut with something sharp: *He suffered cuts and bruises in the accident.* **2 OPENING** ▷ an opening made with a sharp tool: *She made a cut in the material.* **3 REDUCTION** ▷ ⓑ a reduction in the number or amount of something: *tax/job cuts* ○ *The workers were angry about the cut in pay.* **4 MEAT** ▷ a piece of meat from a particular part of an animal: *an expensive cut of beef* **5 SHARE** ▷ a share of something, usually money: *My family owns the company, so we get a cut of the profits.* **6 an electricity/power, etc cut** ⓑ an occasion when the supply of something is stopped **7 HAIR** ▷ (also **haircut**) the style in which your hair has been cut → See also **shortcut**

ut and ˈpaste verb [I, T] (**cutting and pasting, cut and pasted**) to move words or pictures from one place to another in a computer document

utback /ˈkʌtbæk/ noun [C] a reduction of something, usually to save money: *The company has made cutbacks and closed one of its factories.*

☑ Word partners for **cutback**

make cutbacks • drastic/severe/sharp cutbacks • cutbacks **in** sth

ute /kjuːt/ adj **1** attractive: *a cute baby* **2** US informal clever in a way that is annoying or rude: *He thinks it's cute to tell dirty jokes.*

utlery /ˈkʌtlᵊri/ noun [U] **1** UK (US **silverware**) knives, forks, and spoons **2** US knives and scissors

utlet /ˈkʌtlət/ noun [C] a small piece of meat still joined to the bone: *a lamb cutlet*

ut-price /ˈkʌtˌpraɪs/ adj [always before noun] mainly UK (US **cut-rate**) cheaper than usual: *cut-price tickets*

utters /ˈkʌtəz/ noun [plural] a tool for cutting something: *wire cutters*

ut-throat mainly UK (US **cutthroat**) /ˈkʌtθrəʊt/ adj a cut-throat business or other situation is where people will do anything to succeed and do not care if they hurt others: *the cut-throat world of journalism*

utting¹ /ˈkʌtɪŋ/ noun [C] **1** a piece cut from a plant and used to grow a new plant **2** UK (UK/US **clipping**) an article or picture that has been cut out of a newspaper or magazine

utting² /ˈkʌtɪŋ/ adj If something you say or write is cutting, it is unkind: *a cutting remark*

utting-edge /ˌkʌtɪŋˈedʒ/ adj very modern and with all the newest developments: *cutting-edge design/technology*

V /ˌsiːˈviː/ noun [C] mainly UK (US **résumé**) ⓑ a document that describes your qualifications and the jobs you have done, which you send to an employer that you want to work for

cwt written abbreviation for hundredweight (= a unit for measuring weight, equal to 50.8 kilograms in the UK and 45.36 kilograms in the US)

cyanide /ˈsaɪənaɪd/ noun [U] a very strong poison

cyber- /saɪbər/ prefix relating to electronic communications, especially the Internet: *cyberspace*

cybercafe /ˈsaɪbəˌkæfeɪ/ noun [C] a place where customers can buy food and drink and use computers to search for information on the Internet

cybercrime /ˈsaɪbəˌkraɪm/ noun [U] crime or illegal activity that is done using the Internet • **cybercriminal** noun [C] *hackers and other cybercriminals*

cyberslacking /ˈsaɪbəˌslækɪŋ/ noun [U] the act of spending time using the Internet at work for reasons that are not related to your job: *Cyberslacking is becoming a problem for many employers.* • **cyberslacker** noun [C]

cyberspace /ˈsaɪbəˌspeɪs/ noun [U] the Internet, considered as an imaginary area where you can communicate with people and find information

ˈcyber ˌwarfare noun [U] the activity of using the Internet to attack a country's computers in order to damage things such as communication and transport systems or water and electricity supplies

cycle¹ /ˈsaɪkl/ noun [C] **1** ⓑ a series of events that happen in a particular order and are often repeated: *the life cycle of a moth* **2** ⓑ a bicycle → See also **life cycle**

cycle² /ˈsaɪkl/ verb [I] ⓑ to ride a bicycle • **cycling** noun [U] → See colour picture **Sports 2** on page Centre 15 • **cyclist** noun [C] ⓑ someone who rides a bicycle

ˈcycle ˌhelmet noun [C] a hard hat that protects your head when you ride a bicycle → See colour picture **Clothes** on page Centre 9

ˈcycle ˌlane noun [C] UK (US **bicycle lane, bike lane**) a part of a road or a special path that only people riding bicycles can use

cyclical /ˈsɪklɪkᵊl/ adj happening in a regular and repeated pattern: *the cyclical nature of the country's history*

cyclone /ˈsaɪkləʊn/ noun [C] a violent storm with very strong winds that move in a circle

cylinder /ˈsɪlɪndər/ noun [C] **1** a shape with circular ends and long, straight sides, or a container or object shaped like this: *an oxygen cylinder* → See picture at **shape 2** a part in a car or machine's engine that is shaped like a tube, and where another part moves up and down

cylindrical /səˈlɪndrɪkᵊl/ adj having the shape of a cylinder

cymbal /ˈsɪmbᵊl/ noun [C] a musical instrument like a metal plate that is played by being hit with a stick or another cymbal

cynic /ˈsɪnɪk/ noun [C] a cynical person

cynical /ˈsɪnɪkᵊl/ adj believing that people are only interested in themselves and are not sincere: *Many people have become cynical about politicians.* • **cynically** adv • **cynicism** /'sɪnɪsɪzᵊm/ noun [U] cynical beliefs

cyst /sɪst/ noun [C] a small lump containing liquid that can grow under your skin

cystic fibrosis /ˌsɪstɪkfaɪˈbrəʊsis/ noun [U] a serious disease that causes the lungs and othe organs to become blocked

czar (also UK **tsar**) /zɑːʳ/ noun [C] **1** a mal Russian ruler before 1917 **2** informal a powerfu official who makes important decisions for the government about a particular activity: *a drug czar*

D

D, d /diː/ the fourth letter of the alphabet

dab /dæb/ **verb** [I, T] (**dabbing, dabbed**) to touch something with quick, light touches, or to put a substance on something with quick, light touches: *She dabbed at her eyes with a tissue.* • **dab noun** [C] a small amount of something: *a dab of lipstick*

DAB /ˌdiːeɪˈbiː/ **noun** [U] abbreviation for digital audio broadcasting: an electronic system for sending radio or television information using signals in the form of numbers

dabble /ˈdæbl/ **verb** [I] to try something or take part in an activity in a way that is not serious: *I only dabble in politics.* ◦ *He dabbled with drugs at university.*

dad /dæd/ **noun** [C] informal **Ⓐ** father: *Can I go to the park, Dad?*

daddy /ˈdædi/ **noun** [C] a word for 'father', used especially by children

daffodil /ˈdæfədɪl/
noun [C] a yellow flower that usually grows in spring

daffodil

daft /dɑːft/ **adj** UK informal silly: *That's a daft idea.*

dagger /ˈdægər/ **noun** [C] a short knife, used as a weapon

daily¹ /ˈdeɪli/ **adj** [always before noun], **adv 1 Ⓐ** happening or produced every day or once a day: *a daily newspaper* ◦ *The store is open daily from 8 a.m. to 6 p.m.* **2** relating to one single day: *They are paid on a daily basis.* **3 daily life Ⓑ** the usual things that happen to you every day: *Shootings are part of daily life in the region.*

daily² /ˈdeɪli/ **noun** [C] a newspaper that is published every day except Sunday

dainty /ˈdeɪnti/ **adj** small, attractive, and delicate: *dainty feet* • **daintily adv**

dairy¹ /ˈdeəri/ **noun** [C] **1** a place where milk is stored and cream and cheese are made **2** a company that sells milk and products made of milk

dairy² /ˈdeəri/ **adj** [always before noun] **Ⓑ** relating to milk or products made using milk: *dairy products* ◦ *dairy cattle*

daisy /ˈdeɪzi/ **noun** [C] a small flower with white petals and a yellow centre that often grows in grass

dam /dæm/ **noun** [C] a strong wall built across a river to stop the water and make a lake • **dam verb** [T] (**damming, dammed**) to build a dam across a river

damage¹ /ˈdæmɪdʒ/ **noun** [U] **Ⓑ** harm or injury: *He suffered brain damage in the car crash.* ◦ *The strong wind caused serious damage to the roof.*

damage² /ˈdæmɪdʒ/ **verb** [T] **Ⓑ** to harm or break something: *Many buildings were damaged*

in the storm. ◦ *Smoking can seriously damage your health.* • **damaging adj** harmful: *the damaging effects of pollution*

> **☑ Word partners for damage**
>
> cause/inflict/repair/suffer damage • extensive/permanent/serious/slight damage • damage to sth

damages /ˈdæmɪdʒɪz/ **noun** [plural] money that a person or organization pays to someone because they have harmed them or something that belongs to them: *She was awarded £400 in damages.*

> **☑ Word partners for damages**
>
> award/claim/pay/seek/win damages • substantial damages • [£400, $10,000, etc] in damages

dame /deɪm/ **noun** [C] **1** a title used in the UK before the name of a woman who has been officially respected: *Dame Agatha Christie* **2** US informal old-fashioned a woman

damn¹ /dæm/ **adj** [always before noun] (also **damned** /dæmd/) used to express anger: *He didn't listen to a damn thing I said.*

damn² /dæm/ **exclamation** (also **damn it**) **Ⓑ** used to express anger or disappointment: *Damn! I've forgotten the tickets.*

damn³ /dæm/ **adv** (also **damned** /dæmd/) very: *He worked damn hard to pass that exam.*

damn⁴ /dæm/ **noun not give a damn** informal to not be interested in or worried about someone or something: *I don't give a damn what people think.*

damn⁵ /dæm/ **verb 1 damn him/it/you, etc** used to express anger about someone or something: *Stop complaining, damn you!* **2** [T] to strongly criticize someone or something: *He was damned by the media.*

damning /ˈdæmɪŋ/ **adj** criticizing someone or something very strongly, or showing clearly that someone is guilty: *damning evidence* ◦ *a damning report on education standards*

damp /dæmp/ **adj** **Ⓑ** slightly wet, usually in an unpleasant way: *damp clothes/grass* ◦ *It was cold and damp outside.* • **damp** (also **dampness**) **noun** [U] conditions that are slightly wet

dampen /ˈdæmpən/ **verb** [T] (also **damp**) **1** to make something less strong: *Nothing you can say will dampen her enthusiasm.* **2** to make something slightly wet

damper /ˈdæmpər/ **noun**

IDIOM **put a damper on sth** to stop an occasion from being enjoyable: *The accident put a damper on their holiday.*

dance¹ /dɑːns/ **verb** [I, T] **Ⓐ** to move your feet and body to the rhythm of music: *She's dancing with Steven.* ◦ *Can you dance the tango?* • **dancer noun** [C] • **dancing noun** [U]

D

dance² /dɑ:ns/ **noun 1 MOVING** ▷ [C] **A1** the activity of moving your feet and body to music: *I had a dance with my dad.* **2 STEPS** ▷ [C] **B1** a particular set of steps or movements to music: *My favourite dance is the tango.* **3 EVENT** ▷ [C] a social event where people dance to music **4 ACTIVITY** ▷ [U] **A2** the activity or skill of dancing: *a dance school*

dandelion /'dændɪlaɪən/ **noun** [C] a yellow wild flower

dandruff /'dændrʌf/ **noun** [U] small pieces of dead skin from someone's head, in their hair or on their clothes

danger /'deɪndʒər/ **noun 1** [C, U] **A2** the possibility that someone or something will be harmed or killed, or that something bad will happen: *the dangers of rock climbing* ○ *The soldiers were in serious danger.* ○ *We were in danger of missing our flight.* **2** [C] **B1** something or someone that may harm you: *Icy roads are a danger to drivers.*

> ☑ Word partners for **danger**
>
> face danger • pose a danger • great/serious danger • be in danger • be in danger of sth

dangerous /'deɪndʒərəs/ **adj A2** If someone or something is dangerous, they could harm you: *a dangerous chemical* • **dangerously adv B1** *dangerously close to the edge*

> ➕ Other ways of saying **dangerous**
>
> If something is extremely dangerous, you can use the adjectives **hazardous**, **perilous** or **treacherous**:
>
> *Ice had made the roads **treacherous**.*
>
> *Heavy rain is causing **hazardous** driving conditions.*
>
> *A **perilous** journey through the mountains was their only escape route.*
>
> Substances which are dangerous are often described as **harmful** or **hazardous**:
>
> *Please be aware that these chemicals are **harmful**/**hazardous** to human health.*
>
> If something is dangerous because something bad might happen, you can say that it is **risky**:
>
> *Surgery at his age would be too **risky**.*

dangle /'dæŋgl/ **verb 1** [I, T] to hang loosely, or to hold something so that it hangs loosely: *Electrical wires were **dangling from** the ceiling.* **2** [T] to offer someone something they want in order to persuade them to do something: *They dangled the possibility of a job in Paris in front of him.*

dank /dæŋk/ **adj** wet, cold, and unpleasant: *a dark, dank basement*

dapper /'dæpər/ **adj** A dapper man looks stylish and tidy.

dare¹ /deər/ **verb 1 dare (to) do sth B2** to be brave enough to do something: *I didn't dare tell Dad that I'd scratched his car.* **2 dare sb to do sth** to try to make someone do something dangerous: *She dared her friend to climb onto the roof.* **3 Don't you dare** informal used to tell someone angrily not to do something: *Don't you dare hi your sister!* **4 How dare she/you, etc** used to express anger about something someone has done: *How dare you talk to me like that!* **5 I dare say** (also **I daresay**) used when you think tha something is probably true or will probably happen: *I dare say she'll change her mind.*

dare² /deər/ **noun** [C] something that you do to prove that you are not afraid: [usually singular] *She climbed down the cliff for a dare.*

daredevil /'deə,devəl/ **noun** [C] someone who enjoys doing dangerous things

daren't /deənt/ UK short for dare not: *I daren't tel my wife how much it cost.*

daring /'deərɪŋ/ **adj** brave and taking risks: *daring escape* • **daring noun** [U]

dark¹ /dɑːk/ **adj 1 NO LIGHT** ▷ **A2** with no ligh or not much light: *It's a bit dark in here.* ○ *I doesn't **get dark** until 9 o'clock in the evening* **2 NOT PALE** ▷ **A1** nearer to black than white in colour: *dark blue/green* ○ *dark clouds* ○ *He ha dark hair and blue eyes.* **3 PERSON** ▷ havin black or brown hair or brown skin: *a short, dark woman with glasses* **4 BAD** ▷ frightening or unpleasant: *a dark period in human history*

dark² /dɑːk/ **noun 1 the dark B1** somewhere where there is no light: *He's scared of the dark.* **2 before/after dark B1** before/after it become: night: *She doesn't let her children out after dark.*

IDIOM **be in the dark** to not know abou something that other people know about: *I'n completely in the dark about all this.*

→ See also **a shot¹ in the dark**

darken /'dɑːkən/ **verb** [I, T] **1** to become dark or make something dark: *the darkening sky* ○ *a darkened room* **2** If someone's mood darkens, or if something darkens it, they suddenly feel less happy.

darkly /'dɑːkli/ **adv** in a frightening or myster ious way: *"He might not be what he seems," she said darkly.*

darkness /'dɑːknəs/ **noun** [U] **B2** a state in which there is little or no light: *He stumbled around in the darkness looking for the light switch.* ○ *There was a power cut and the house was **in darkness***

darling¹ /'dɑːlɪŋ/ **noun** [C] **B2** used when you speak to someone you love: *Would you like a drink, darling?*

darling² /'dɑːlɪŋ/ **adj** [always before noun] loved very much: *my darling daughter*

darn¹ /dɑːn/ **adj** [always before noun], **adv** (also **darned** /dɑːnd/) US informal used to emphasize what you are saying, or to show that you are annoyed: *I'm too darn tired to care.*

darn² /dɑːn/ **verb** [I, T] to repair a piece of clothing by sewing across a hole with thread: *to darn socks*

dart¹ /dɑːt/ **noun** [C] a small arrow used in the game of darts or as a weapon: *a tranquilizer dart*

dart² /dɑːt/ **verb dart between/in/out, etc** to run or move somewhere quickly and suddenly *A cat darted across the street.*

darts /dɑːts/ **noun** [U] a game played by throwing small arrows at a round board

darts

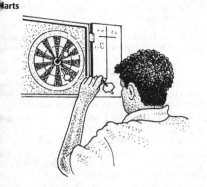

dash¹ /dæʃ/ **verb 1** 🔵 [I] to go somewhere quickly: *She dashed downstairs when she heard the phone.* ∘ *I must dash. I've got to be home by 7 p.m.* **2 dash sb's hopes** to destroy someone's hopes: *Saturday's 2-0 defeat dashed their hopes of reaching the final.* **3 dash (sth) against/on, etc** literary to hit or throw something with great force, usually causing damage: *Waves dashed against the cliffs.*

PHRASAL VERB **dash sth off** UK to write something very quickly: *She dashed off a letter to the phone company.*

dash² /dæʃ/ **noun 1** RUN ▷ [no plural] 🔵 If you make a dash somewhere, you run there very quickly: *As the rain started, we made a dash for shelter.* **2** AMOUNT ▷ [C] a small amount of something, often food: *Add a dash of milk to the sauce.* **3** MARK ▷ [C] 🔵 a mark (—) used to separate parts of sentences → See Study Page **Punctuation** on page Centre 33

dashboard /'dæʃbɔːd/ **noun** [C] the part facing the driver at the front of a car with controls and equipment to show things such as speed and temperature → See colour picture **Car** on page Centre 7

dashing /'dæʃɪŋ/ **adj** A dashing man is attractive in a confident and exciting way.

data /'deɪtə/ **noun** [U] **1** 🔵 information or facts about something: *financial data* **2** 🔵 information in the form of text, numbers, or symbols that can be used by or stored in a computer

📄 **Word partners for data**

analyse/collect data • data on sth

database /'deɪtəbeɪs/ **noun** [C] 🔵 information stored in a computer in an organized structure so that it can be searched in different ways: *a national database of missing people*

data projector **noun** [C] a machine that allows you to show words or images on a screen or wall

date¹ /deɪt/ **noun** [C] **1** PARTICULAR DAY ▷ 🔵 a particular day of the month or year: *"What's the date today?" "It's the fifth."* ∘ *Please give your name, address and date of birth.* **2** ARRANGED TIME ▷ 🔵 a time when something has been arranged to happen: *Let's make a date to have*

lunch. ∘ *We agreed to finish the report at a later date.* **3 to date** formal 🔵 up to the present time: *This novel is his best work to date.* **4** GOING OUT ▷ 🔵 a romantic meeting when two people go out somewhere, such as to a restaurant or to see a film: *He's asked her out on a date.* **5** PERSON ▷ someone who you are having a romantic meeting with: *Who's your date for the prom?* **6** FRUIT ▷ a sticky brown fruit with a long seed inside → See also **blind date, sell-by date**

📄 **Word partners for date**

make/fix/set a date • at a future/at a later date • the date of sth • sb's date of birth

date² /deɪt/ **verb 1** MEET ▷ [I, T] to regularly spend time with someone you have a romantic relationship with: *We've been dating for six months.* **2** WRITE ▷ [T] 🔵 to write the day's date on something: *a letter dated March 13th* **3** TIME ▷ [T] to say how long something has existed or when it was made: *Scientists have dated the bones to 10,000 BC.* **4** NOT MODERN ▷ [I, T] to stop seeming modern, or to make something not seem modern: *Clothes like these date really quickly.*

PHRASAL VERBS **date back** 🔵 to have existed a particular length of time or since a particular time: *This house dates back to 1650.* • **date from sth** 🔵 to have existed since a particular time: *The castle dates from the 11th century.*

dated /'deɪtɪd/ **adj** not modern: *This film seems a bit dated today.*

date rape **noun** [C] the crime of forcing someone you know or someone who you have arranged to meet to have sex with you when they do not want to

daub /dɔːb/ **verb** [T] to put a lot of a substance like paint on a surface in a careless way, often to write words or draw pictures: *The walls have been daubed with graffiti.*

daughter /'dɔːtər/ **noun** [C] 🔵 your female child

daughter-in-law /'dɔːtərɪnlɔː/ **noun** [C] (plural **daughters-in-law**) 🔵 your son's wife

daunt /dɔːnt/ **verb** [T] If someone is daunted by something, they are worried because it is difficult or frightening: [often passive] *I was a bit daunted by the idea of cooking for so many people.*

daunting /'dɔːntɪŋ/ **adj** If something is daunting, it makes you worried because it is difficult or frightening: *a daunting challenge/task*

dawdle /'dɔːdl/ **verb** [I] to walk very slowly, or do something very slowly in a way that wastes time: *Stop dawdling! You'll be late for school!*

dawn¹ /dɔːn/ **noun** [U] **1** 🔵 the early morning when light first appears in the sky: *We woke at dawn.* **2 the dawn of sth** literary the time when something began: *the dawn of civilization* → See also **the crack² of dawn**

dawn² /dɔːn/ **verb** [I] If a day or a period of time dawns, it begins: *The day of her party dawned at last.*

PHRASAL VERB **dawn on sb** If a fact dawns on you, you become aware of it after a period of not

D

being aware of it: [+ that] *It suddenly dawned on them that Mary had been lying.*

day /deɪ/ **noun 1 24 HOURS** ▷ [C] 🅐🅐 a period of 24 hours: *the days of the week* ∘ *January has 31 days.* ∘ *I saw her the day before yesterday.* **2 LIGHT HOURS** ▷ [C, U] 🅐🅑 the period during the day when there is light from the sun: *a bright, sunny day* ∘ *We've been travelling all day.* **3 WORK HOURS** ▷ [C] 🅐🅑 the time that you usually spend at work or school: *She's had a very busy day at the office.* **4 the other day** 🅑🅑 a few days ago: *I saw Terry the other day.* **5 day after day** every day for a long period of time: *Day after day they marched through the mountains.* **6 one day** 🅐🅑 used to talk about something that happened in the past: *One day, I came home to find my windows smashed.* **7 one day/some day/ one of these days** 🅑🅑 used to talk about something you think will happen in the future: *One of these days I'll tell her what really happened.* **8 days a** used to talk about a particular period of time when something happened or existed: *in my younger days* **b** 🅑🅑 a long time: *I haven't seen Jack for days.* **9 these days** 🅐🅑 used to talk about the present time: *I don't go out much these days.* **10 in those days** 🅑🅑 used to talk about a period in the past: *In those days, no-one had a TV set.* **11 the old days** a period in the past

IDIOMS **call it a day** informal to stop doing something, especially working: *It's almost midnight – let's call it a day.* • **it's early days** UK something that you say when it is too early to know what will happen: *Both teams are at the bottom of the league, but it's early days yet.* • **make sb's day** to make someone very happy: *Go on, ask him to dance – it'll make his day!* • **save the day** to do something that solves a serious problem

→ See also **April Fool's Day, Boxing Day, Christmas Day, at the end¹ of the day, field day, Independence Day, Mother's Day, New Year's Day, open day, polling day, Valentine's Day**

daybreak /'deɪbreɪk/ **noun** [U] the time in the morning when light first appears in the sky

daycare /'deɪkeəʳ/ **noun** [U] care provided during the day for people who cannot look after themselves, especially young children or old people: *a daycare centre*

day care centre noun [C] UK (US **daycare center**) a place where parents pay to leave their children while the parents work

daydream /'deɪdriːm/ **verb** [I] to have pleasant thoughts about something you would like to happen • **daydream noun** [C]

daylight /'deɪlaɪt/ **noun 1** 🅑🅑 [U] the natural light from the sun **2 in broad daylight** used to emphasize that something happens when it is light and people can see: *He was attacked in broad daylight.*

daylights /'deɪlaɪts/ **noun**

IDIOMS **beat/knock the (living) daylights out of sb** informal to hit someone very many times

• **scare/frighten the (living) daylights out of sb** informal to frighten someone very much

day re'turn noun [C] UK a ticket for a bus or train when you go somewhere and come back on the same day: *a day return to Norwich*

daytime /'deɪtaɪm/ **noun** [U] 🅑🅑 the period of the day when there is light from the sun, or the period when most people are at work: *daytime television* ∘ *a daytime telephone number*

day-to-day /ˌdeɪtə'deɪ/ **adj** [always before noun] happening every day as a regular part of your job or your life: *day-to-day activities/problems*

day trip noun [C] a visit to a place in which you go there and come back on the same day: *We're going on a day trip to London.*

daze /deɪz/ **noun in a daze** the feeling of not being able to think clearly because you are shocked or have hit your head: *The survivors were walking around in a daze.*

dazed /deɪzd/ **adj** not able to think clearly because you are shocked or have hit your head: *a dazed expression*

dazzle /'dæzl/ **verb** [T] **1** If you are dazzled by someone or something, you think they are extremely good and exciting: [often passive] *was dazzled by his intelligence and good looks.* **2** If light dazzles someone, it makes them unable to see for a short time.

dazzling /'dæzlɪŋ/ **adj 1** extremely good and exciting: *a dazzling display/performance* **2** A dazzling light is so bright that you cannot see for a short time after looking at it: *a dazzling white light*

de- /di-/ **prefix** to take something away: *deforestation* (= *when the trees in an area are cut down*)

deacon /'diːkən/ **noun** [C] an official in some Christian churches

dead¹ /ded/ **adj 1 NOT ALIVE** ▷ 🅐🅑 not now alive: *She's been dead for 20 years now.* ∘ *He was shot dead by a masked intruder.* ∘ *There were three children among the dead.* → See Note at **die** **2 EQUIPMENT** ▷ 🅑🅑 If a piece of equipment is dead, it is not working: *a dead battery* ∘ *The phone suddenly went dead.* **3 QUIET** ▷ informal If a place is dead, it is too quiet and nothing interesting is happening there. **4 COMPLETE** ▷ [always before noun] complete: *We waited in dead silence as the votes were counted.* **5 BODY** ▷ mainly UK If part of your body is dead, you cannot feel it: *My arm's gone dead.* **6 wouldn't be caught/ seen dead** informal If someone wouldn't be caught dead in a place or doing something, they would never go there or do it, usually because it would be too embarrassing: [+ doing sth] *I wouldn't be caught dead wearing a bikini.* **7 drop dead** informal to die very suddenly

dead² /ded/ **adv 1** informal extremely or completely: UK *The exam was dead easy.* ∘ US *His advice was dead wrong.* **2 be dead set against sth/doing sth** to oppose something strongly: *My parents were dead set against us getting married.* **3 stop dead** to suddenly stop moving or doing something

dead³ /ded/ **noun**

IDIOM **the dead of night/winter** the middle of the night/winter

deadbeat /'dedbiːt/ **noun** [C] US informal someone who does not pay their debts: *a deadbeat dad*

deaden /'dedᵊn/ **verb** [T] to make something less painful or less strong: *She gave me an injection to deaden the pain.*

dead 'end noun [C] **1** a road that is closed at one end **2** a situation in which it is impossible to make progress: *The peace talks have reached a dead end.* • dead-end /ˌded'end/ **adj** *a dead-end job/relationship* ◦ *a dead-end street*

dead 'heat noun [C] the result of a race in which the first two people finish at exactly the same time

deadline /'dedlaɪn/ **noun** [C] 🅱️ a time by which something must be done: *to meet/miss a deadline* ◦ *The deadline for entering the competition is tomorrow.*

> 🗹 Word partners for **deadline**
>
> set a deadline • meet/miss a deadline • a tight deadline • the deadline for (doing) sth

deadlock /'dedlɒk/ **noun** [U] a situation in which it is impossible to make progress or to reach a decision: *The talks have reached deadlock.* ◦ *There have been several attempts to break the deadlock.* • deadlocked **adj**

deadly¹ /'dedli/ **adj** 🅱️ likely to cause death: *a deadly virus* ◦ *a deadly weapon*

deadly² /'dedli/ **adv deadly dull/serious, etc** extremely dull/serious, etc

deadpan /'dedpæn/ **adj** looking or sounding serious when you are telling a joke: *a deadpan expression*

deaf /def/ **adj 1** 🅱️ unable to hear: *Many deaf people learn to lip read.* ◦ *He goes to a school for the deaf.* **2** be deaf to sth to refuse to listen to something • deafness **noun** [U] → See also **fall on deaf ears**, **tone-deaf**

deafening /'defᵊnɪŋ/ **adj** extremely loud: *a deafening noise*

deal¹ /diːl/ **noun 1** [C] 🅱️ an arrangement or an agreement, especially in business: *a business deal* ◦ *The police refused to do/make/strike a deal with the terrorists.* **2** [C] the price you pay for something, and what you get for your money: *I got a really good deal on my new car.* **3** a good/great deal 🅱️ a lot: *A great deal of time and effort went into arranging this party.*

> 🗹 Word partners for **deal**
>
> agree/do/make/strike a deal • negotiate/sign a deal • a deal between [two people/companies, etc] • a deal with sb

deal² /diːl/ **verb** [I, T] (**dealt**) to give cards to players in a game: *Whose turn is it to deal?*

PHRASAL VERBS **deal in sth** to buy and sell particular goods as a business: *He owns a shop that deals in rare books.* • **deal with sth 1** 🅱️ to take action in order to achieve something or to

solve a problem: *Can you deal with this gentleman's complaint?* **2** to be about a particular subject: *The programme dealt with teenage pregnancy.* • **deal with sb/sth** to do business with a person or organization: *I usually deal with the accounts department.* • **deal with sb** 🅱️ to meet or talk to someone, especially as part of your job: *She's used to dealing with foreign customers.*

dealer /'diːlər/ **noun** [C] **1** 🅱️ a person or company that buys and sells things for profit: *a car dealer* ◦ *a drug dealer* **2** a person who gives out cards to players in a game

dealership /'diːləʃɪp/ **noun** [C] a business that sells cars, usually cars made by a particular company: *a Ford/Toyota dealership*

dealings /'diːlɪŋz/ **noun** [plural] activities involving other people, especially in business: *Have you had any dealings with their London office?*

dealt /delt/ past of deal

dean /diːn/ **noun** [C] **1** an official in a college or university **2** an official in charge of a large church or group of churches

dear¹ /dɪər/ **adj 1** IN LETTERS ▷ 🅰️ used at the beginning of a letter, before the name of the person you are writing to: *Dear Amy* ◦ *Dear Mrs Simpson* ◦ *Dear Sir/Madam* **2** LIKED ▷ [always before noun] 🅱️ A dear person is someone who you know and like very much: *my dear Peter* ◦ *He's one of my dearest friends.* **3** EXPENSIVE ▷ UK expensive **4** dear to sb/sb's heart If something is dear to someone or dear to their heart, it is very important to them: *The charity was very dear to his heart.*

dear² /dɪər/ **exclamation oh dear** 🅰️ used to express surprise and disappointment: *Oh dear! I forgot my keys!*

dear³ /dɪər/ **noun** [C] used to address someone in a friendly way, especially a child or someone you love: *Don't cry, my dear.* ◦ *Yes, dear?*

dearly /'dɪəli/ **adv** very much: *I would dearly love to visit Rome again.*

dearth /dɜːθ/ **noun** formal **a dearth of sth** a situation in which there are not many or not enough of something available: *a dearth of new homes*

death /deθ/ **noun 1** 🅱️ [C, U] the end of life: *Do you believe in life after death?* ◦ *We need to reduce the number of deaths from heart attacks.* ◦ *a death threat* **2** to death until you die: *He was beaten to death by a gang of youths.* **3** put sb to death to kill someone as a punishment: [often passive] *She was put to death for her beliefs.* **4** frightened/bored, etc to death informal 🅱️ extremely frightened/bored, etc: *She's scared to death of dogs.*

> 🗹 Word partners for **death**
>
> bleed/choke/freeze/starve to death • be beaten/crushed/stabbed/trampled to death • sb's premature/sudden/tragic/untimely death • death from sth

deathbed /'deθbed/ **noun on your deathbed** very sick and going to die soon

deathly /'deθli/ **adj, adv** extreme in a way that is

D

unpleasant: *a **deathly** silence* ∘ *Her face turned **deathly** pale.*

death ,penalty noun [C] the legal punishment of death for a crime

death ,row noun **on death row** in prison and waiting to be killed as a punishment for a crime

death ,sentence noun [C] a legal punishment of death for a crime

death ,toll noun [C] the number of people who die because of an event such as a war or an accident: *The death toll from the earthquake has risen to 1500.*

death ,trap noun [C] something that is very dangerous and could cause death: *That old factory across the road is a real death trap.*

debase /dɪ'beɪs/ verb [T] formal to reduce the value or quality of something: *They argue that money has debased football.*

debatable /dɪ'beɪtəbl/ adj If something is debatable, it is not certain if it is true or not: *It's **debatable whether** a university degree will help you in this job.*

debate¹ /dɪ'beɪt/ noun [C, U] 🔵 discussion or argument about a subject: *a political debate* ∘ *There has been a lot of public **debate on** the safety of food.*

debate² /dɪ'beɪt/ verb **1** [I, T] to discuss a subject in a formal way: *These issues need to be debated openly.* **2** [T] to try to make a decision about something: [+ question word] *I'm still debating whether to go out tonight or not.*

debilitating /dɪ'bɪlɪteɪtɪŋ/ adj formal A debilitating illness or problem makes you weak and unable to do what you want to do: *the debilitating effects of flu*

debit¹ /'debɪt/ noun [C] 🔵 money taken out of a bank account, or a record of this → Opposite **credit** → See also **direct debit**

debit² /'debɪt/ verb [T] 🔵 to take money out of a bank account as a payment for something: *Twenty euros has been debited from my account.*

debit ,card noun [C] 🔵 a plastic card used to pay for things directly from your bank account

debris /'debri:/ 🇺🇸 /də'bri:/ noun [U] broken pieces of something: *Debris from the aircraft was scattered over a wide area.*

debt /det/ noun **1** [C] 🔵 an amount of money that you owe someone: *She's working in a bar to try to **pay off** her **debts**.* **2** [U] a situation in which you owe money to someone: *We don't want to **get into debt**.* ∘ *He's heavily **in debt**.* **3 be in sb's debt** to feel grateful to someone who has helped you or given you something

> ✏ **Word partners for debt**
> be in/fall into/get into/run into debt • get out of debt • clear/pay off/repay/settle a debt

debtor /'detər/ noun [C] someone who owes money

debt re,lief noun [U] a situation in which a bank tells a person, a company, or a government that they do not have to pay back the money they owe the bank

debug /ˌdi:'bʌg/ verb [T] (**debugging, debugged**) to remove mistakes or problems from a computer program

debut /'deɪbju:/ 🇺🇸 /deɪ'bju:/ noun [C] the first time someone performs or presents something to the public: *She **made her debut** as a pianist in 1975.* ∘ *This is the band's **debut album**.*

Dec written abbreviation for December

decade /'dekeɪd/ noun [C] 🔵 a period of ten years

decadence /'dekədəns/ noun [U] behaviour that is considered immoral because you do or have things only for your own pleasure • **decadent** adj *a decadent lifestyle*

decaf /'di:kæf/ noun [C, U] informal short for decaffeinated coffee

decaffeinated /di'kæfɪneɪtɪd/ adj Decaffeinated tea or coffee is made by removing the caffeine (= chemical that makes you feel more awake).

decay /dɪ'keɪ/ verb [I] 🔵 to gradually become bad or weak or be destroyed, often because of natural causes like bacteria or age: *decaying leaves* ∘ *Sugar makes your teeth decay.* • **decay** noun [U] the process of decaying: *tooth decay* ∘ *Many of the buildings had **fallen into decay**.*

deceased /dɪ'si:st/ adj formal **1** dead: *the deceased man's belongings* **2 the deceased** someone who has died: *The police have not yet informed the family of the deceased.*

deceit /dɪ'si:t/ noun [U] attempts to make someone believe something that is not true • **deceitful** adj *deceitful behaviour*

deceive /dɪ'si:v/ verb [T] 🔵 to make someone believe something that is not true: *The company deceived customers by selling old computers as new ones.*

December /dɪ'sembər/ noun [C, U] (written abbreviation **Dec**) 🔵 the twelfth month of the year

decency /'di:sənsi/ noun [U] behaviour that is good, moral, and acceptable in society: *a sense of decency* ∘ *She didn't even **have the decency to** tell me she wasn't coming.*

decent /'di:sənt/ adj **1** SATISFACTORY ▷ 🔵 of a satisfactory quality or level: *He earns a decent salary.* ∘ *I haven't had a decent cup of coffee since I've been here.* **2** HONEST ▷ 🔵 honest and morally good: *Decent people have had their lives ruined by his behaviour.* ∘ *She should **do the decent thing** and apologize.* **3** CLOTHES ▷ [never before noun] wearing clothes: *Can I come in? Are you decent?* • **decently** adv

decentralize (also UK **-ise**) /di:'sentrəlaɪz/ verb [T] to move the control of an organization or a government from a single place to several smaller places • **decentralization** /di:ˌsentrəlaɪ'zeɪʃən/ noun [U]

deception /dɪ'sepʃən/ noun [C, U] the act of deceiving someone by making them believe something that is not true: *He was found guilty of obtaining money by deception.*

deceptive /dɪ'septɪv/ adj If something is deceptive, it makes you believe something that is not true: *Appearances can be deceptive.* • **deceptively** adv

decibel /ˈdesɪbel/ **noun** [C] a unit for measuring how loud a sound is

decide /dɪˈsaɪd/ **verb 1** [I, T] ⓐ to choose something after thinking about several possibilities: [+ question word] *I haven't decided whether or not to tell him.* ◦ [+ to do sth] *She's decided to take the job.* ◦ [+ (that)] *The teachers decided that the school would take part in the competition.* **2** [T] to be the reason or situation that makes a particular result happen: *This match will decide the tournament.* **3 deciding factor** the thing that helps to make the final decision

> ➕ Other ways of saying **decide**
>
> If someone is deciding a time or an amount, especially an exact date or price, the verbs **fix** and **set** are often used:
> *The price has been **set/fixed** at $10.*
> *Have you **set/fixed** a date for the wedding?*
> If someone makes a final and certain decision about a plan, date, etc., the verb **finalize** is sometimes used:
> *We've chosen a venue, but we haven't **finalized** the details yet.*
> The verb **settle** and the phrasal verb **settle on/upon** are also often used when someone is making a final decision:
> *Have you **settled on** a place to live yet?*
> *Right then, we're going to Spain. That's **settled**.*
> The fixed expression **make up your mind** is often used to mean 'to decide':
> *I like them both – I just can't **make up my mind** which one to pick.*
> *Have you **made up your mind** whether you're going?*
> If someone is unable to decide between two choices, in informal situations you can use the expression **be torn between** something **and** something else:
> *I'm **torn between** the fish pie **and** the beef.*

PHRASAL VERB **decide on sth/sb** to choose someone or someone after thinking carefully: *I've decided on blue walls for the bathroom.*

decided /dɪˈsaɪdɪd/ **adj** [always before noun] certain, obvious, or easy to notice: *She had a decided advantage over her opponent.* ● **decidedly adv** *That exam was decidedly more difficult than the last one.*

deciduous /dɪˈsɪdjuəs/ **adj** A deciduous tree has leaves that drop off every autumn.

decimal¹ /ˈdesɪməl/ **adj** involving counting in units of 10: *a decimal system*

decimal² /ˈdesɪməl/ **noun** [C] a number less than one that is written as one or more numbers after a point: *The decimal 0.5 is the same as the fraction 1/2.* → See Study Page **Numbers** on page Centre 30

decimal place UK (US **decimal place**) **noun** [C] the position of a number after a decimal point: *The number is accurate to three decimal places.*

decimal point UK (US **decimal point**) **noun** [C] the point (.) that is used to separate a whole number and a decimal

decimate /ˈdesɪmeɪt/ **verb** [T] formal to destroy large numbers of people or things: *Populations of endangered animals have been decimated.*

decipher /dɪˈsaɪfər/ **verb** [T] to discover what something says or means: *It's sometimes difficult to **decipher** his **handwriting**.*

decision /dɪˈsɪʒən/ **noun** [C] ⓑ a choice that you make about something after thinking about several possibilities: *She has had to **make** some very difficult **decisions**.* ◦ [+ to do sth] *It was his decision to leave.* ◦ *The committee should **come to/reach a** final **decision** by next week.*

> 🗒 Word partners for **decision**
>
> **come to/make/reach** a decision
> ● a **big/difficult/final/important/unanimous/wise** decision ● a decision **about/on** sth

decisive /dɪˈsaɪsɪv/ **adj 1** strongly affecting how a situation will progress or end: *a **decisive goal/victory*** **2** ⓑ making decisions quickly and easily: *You need to be more decisive.* → Opposite **indecisive** ● **decisively adv** ● **decisiveness noun** [U]

deck¹ /dek/ **noun** [C] **1 SHIP/BUS/PLANE** ▷ ⓑ one of the floors of a ship, bus, or aircraft: *The children like to sit on the top deck of the bus.* **2 on deck** on the top floor of a ship that is not covered **3 CARDS** ▷ US (UK/US **pack**) a collection of cards that you use to play a game **4 MACHINE** ▷ a machine that you use to play records or tapes (= plastic cases containing magnetic material used to record sounds): *a tape deck*

deck² /dek/ **verb**

PHRASAL VERB **be decked out** to be decorated with something, or dressed in something special: *The bar was decked out with red and yellow flags.*

deckchair /ˈdektʃeər/ **noun** [C] a folding chair that you use outside

declaration /ˌdekləˈreɪʃən/ **noun** [C] an announcement, often one that is written and official: *a declaration of independence*

declare /dɪˈkleər/ **verb** [T] **1** ⓑ to announce something publicly or officially: *to declare war* ◦ [+ that] *Scientists have declared that this meat is safe to eat.* **2** ⓑ to officially tell someone the value of goods you have bought, or the amount of money you have earned because you might have to pay tax: *Do you have anything to declare?*

decline¹ /dɪˈklaɪn/ **noun** [C, U] ⓑ a situation in which something becomes less in amount, importance, quality, or strength: *a steady **decline** in sales/standards*

> 🗒 Word partners for **decline**
>
> be **in** decline ● a **sharp/steady/steep** decline ● a decline **in** sth

decline² /dɪˈklaɪn/ **verb 1** [I, T] formal ⓑ If you decline something, you refuse it politely: *She **declined** his **offer** of a lift.* ◦ [+ to do sth] *He **declined to comment**.* **2** [I] ⓑ to become less in amount, importance, quality, or strength: *Sales of records have declined steadily.*

decode /ˌdiːˈkəʊd/ **verb** [T] to discover the meaning of a message that is in code (= secret system of communication)

decoder /diːˈkəʊdər/ **noun** [C] a piece of equipment that allows you to receive particular television signals

decompose /ˌdiːkəmˈpəʊz/ **verb** [I] If a dead person, animal, or plant decomposes, it decays and is gradually destroyed: *a decomposing body*

decor /ˈdeɪkɔːr/ ⓤⓢ /deɪˈkɔːr/ **noun** [U, no plural] the style of decoration and furniture in a room or building

decorate

decorate /ˈdekəreɪt/ **verb 1** [T] ⓑ❶ to make something look more attractive by putting things on it or around it: *They decorated the room with balloons for her party.* **2** [I, T] ⓑ❶ UK to put paint or paper on the walls or other surfaces of a room or building: *The whole house needs decorating.* **3 be decorated** to be given a medal (= small, metal disc) as official respect for military action: *He was decorated for bravery.*

➕ Other ways of saying **decorate**

The verbs **refurbish**, **renovate** and **revamp** are common alternatives to 'decorate' when you are talking about improving the appearance of a room or building:
*The University library is currently being **refurbished**.*
*They were in the process of **renovating** an old barn.*
*The restaurant has recently been **revamped**.*
Another alternative used in more informal situations is the phrasal verb **do up**:
*He's bought an old cottage and is gradually **doing** it **up**.*

decoration /ˌdekəˈreɪʃən/ **noun 1 ATTRACTIVE THING** ▷ [C, U] ⓑ❷ things put on or around something to make it look more attractive, or the use of these things: *Christmas decorations* ◦ *She hung some pictures around the room for decoration.* **2 PAINT** ▷ [U] ⓑ❷ the use of paint or

paper to cover the walls or other surfaces of rooms or buildings : *This place is badly in need of decoration.* **3 OFFICIAL RESPECT** ▷ [C] an official sign of respect such as a medal (= small, metal disc)

decorative /ˈdekərətɪv/ **adj** ⓑ❷ making something or someone look more attractive: *decorative objects*

decorator /ˈdekəreɪtər/ **noun** [C] **1** UK someone whose job is to put paint or paper on the walls and other surfaces of rooms or buildings **2** US someone whose job is to design the appearance of rooms in houses and buildings

decorum /dɪˈkɔːrəm/ **noun** [U] formal behaviour that is considered to be polite and correct

decoy /ˈdiːkɔɪ/ **noun** [C] someone or something used to lead a person or animal to a place so that they can be caught

➕ Other ways of saying **decrease**

The verbs **lessen**, **lower**, and **reduce**, and the phrasal verb **bring down** are often used when someone decreases an amount or level:
*They've just **lowered** the age at which you can join.*
*Exercise **reduces** the chance of heart disease.*
*They are **bringing down** their prices.*
The verbs **drop** and **fall**, and the phrasal verbs **go down** and **come down** are often used when a level or amount decreases:
*Unemployment has **dropped/fallen** from 8% to 6% in the last year.*
*Prices always **come/go down** after Christmas.*
If a level or amount decreases very quickly, the verbs **plummet** and **plunge** are sometimes used:
*Temperatures last night **plummeted/plunged** below zero.*
If the size of something decreases, the verb **shrink** is sometimes used. The verb **contract** is used in technical contexts:
*Forests have **shrunk** to almost half the size they were 20 years ago.*
*As the metal cools, it **contracts**.*

🔲 Word partners for **decrease**

a marked/significant/slight decrease ● a decrease in sth ● a decrease of [5%/1000, etc]

decrease /dɪˈkriːs/ **verb** [I, T] ⓑ❶ to become less or to make something become less: *During the summer months, rainfall decreases.* ● **decrease** /ˈdiːkriːs/ **noun** [C, U] ⓑ❶ *There has been a decrease in the number of violent crime.* → Opposite **increase**

decree /dɪˈkriː/ **noun** [C] an official order or decision from a government or leader: *presidential/royal decree* ● **decree verb** [T] (**decreeing, decreed**)

decrepit /dɪˈkrepɪt/ **adj** old and in very bad condition: *a decrepit building*

decrypt /dɪˈkrɪpt/ **verb** [T] to change electronic information from a secret system of letters numbers, or symbols back into a form that people can understand

dedicate /'dedɪkeɪt/ **verb 1 dedicate your life/ yourself to sth** to give most of your energy and time to something: *She has dedicated her life to helping others.* **2 dedicate sth to sb** to say that something you have made or done is to show your love or respect for someone: [often passive] *This book is dedicated to my daughter.*

dedicated /'dedɪkeɪtɪd/ **adj 1** believing that something is very important and giving a lot of time and energy to it: *a dedicated teacher* **2** designed to be used for a particular purpose: *a dedicated word processor*

dedication /ˌdedɪ'keɪʃən/ **noun 1** [U] a willingness to give a lot of time and energy to something because you believe it is very important: *She thanked the staff for their dedication and enthusiasm.* **2** [C] a statement that says something has been made or done to show love and respect for someone: *a dedication to the poet's mother*

deduce /dɪ'djuːs/ **verb** [T] to decide that something is true using the available information: [+ (that)] *From the contents of his shopping basket, I deduced that he was single.*

deduct /dɪ'dʌkt/ **verb** [T] to take an amount or a part of the amount away from a total: *The company will **deduct** tax **from** your earnings.* ◦ *Marks are deducted for spelling mistakes.*

deduction /dɪ'dʌkʃən/ **noun** [C, U] **1** the act of taking an amount away from a total, or the amount that is taken: *tax deductions* **2** the process of deciding that something is true using the available information

deed /diːd/ **noun** [C] **1** formal something that you do: *good deeds* ◦ *I judge a person by their deeds, not their words.* **2** a legal document recording an agreement, especially saying who owns something: [usually plural] *Where do you keep the deeds to the house?*

deem /diːm/ **verb** [T] formal to judge or consider something in a particular way: *The book was deemed to be unsuitable for children.*

deep

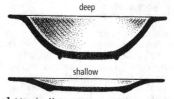

deep

shallow

deep¹ /diːp/ **adj 1 TOP TO BOTTOM** ▷ **A2** having a long distance from the top to the bottom: *The water is a lot deeper than it seems.* **2 FRONT TO BACK** ▷ having a long distance from the front to the back: *How deep are the shelves?* **3 one metre/6 ft, etc deep** **B2** one metre/6 ft, etc from the top to the bottom, or from the front to the back: *This end of the pool is two metres deep.* **4 FEELING** ▷ **B2** A deep feeling is very strong: *deep affection/regret* **5 SOUND** ▷ **B2** A deep sound is low: *a deep voice* **6 SERIOUS** ▷ serious

and difficult for most people to understand: *a deep and meaningful conversation* **7 a deep sleep** **B2** sleep that it is difficult to wake someone from **8 COLOUR** ▷ **B1** A deep colour is strong and dark: *deep brown eyes* **9 take a deep breath** **B2** to fill your lungs with air: *Take a deep breath and relax.* **10 deep in thought/ conversation** giving all of your attention to what you are thinking or talking about, and not noticing anything else → See also **throw sb in at the deep end¹**, **be in deep water¹**

deep² /diːp/ **adv 1** **B1** a long way into something from the top or outside: *They travelled deep into the forest.* **2 deep down** **B2** If you know or feel something deep down, you are certain that it is true, or you feel it strongly although you do not admit it or show it: *Deep down, I knew that I was right.* **3 go/run deep** If a feeling or a problem goes deep, it is very strong or serious and has existed for a long time.

deepen /'diːpən/ **verb** [I, T] **1** to become deeper, or to make something become deeper: *The sky deepened to a rich, dark blue.* **2** to become worse, or to make something become worse: *a **deepening crisis***

deep 'freeze **noun** [C] (US 'deep ˌfreeze) another word for freezer (= a large container in which food can be frozen and stored)

deep-fried /ˌdiːp'fraɪd/ **adj** fried in a lot of oil

deeply /'diːpli/ **adv 1** **B2** very much: *I have fallen deeply in love with her.* **2 breathe deeply** to fill your lungs with air

deep-seated /ˌdiːp'siːtɪd/ **adj** (also ˌdeep-'rooted) strongly felt or believed and difficult to change: ***deep-seated fears/problems***

deer

deer /dɪər/ **noun** [C] (plural **deer**) **B2** a large, wild animal that is sometimes hunted for food and that has antlers (= long horns) if it is male

deface /dɪ'feɪs/ **verb** [T] to spoil the appearance of something, especially by writing or painting on it: *Several posters have been defaced with political slogans.*

default¹ /dɪ'fɔːlt/ **noun 1** [no plural] what exists or happens usually if no changes are made **2 by default** If something happens by default, it happens only because something else does not happen: *No one else stood in the election, so he won by default.* • **default adj** [always before noun] *The default font size is 10.*

default² /dɪ'fɔːlt/ **verb** [I] to not do what you

have made an agreement to do, especially paying back money you have borrowed: *They have defaulted on their debt repayments.*

defeat¹ /dɪˈfiːt/ **verb** [T] **1** 🅱1 to win against someone in a fight or competition: *She was defeated by an Australian player in the first round of the tournament.* **2** 🅱2 to make someone or something fail: *The bill was narrowly defeated in parliament.*

defeat² /dɪˈfiːt/ **noun 1** [C, U] 🅱1 an occasion when someone loses against someone else in a fight or competition: *The Chicago Cubs have suffered their worst defeat of the season.* **2** [no plural] 🅱2 an occasion when someone or something is made to fail: *the defeat of apartheid*

> 🗹 Word partners for **defeat**
>
> admit/face/suffer defeat • a comprehensive/crushing/humiliating/narrow defeat

defeatism /dɪˈfiːtɪzəm/ **noun** [U] behaviour or thoughts that show that you do not expect to be successful

defeatist /dɪˈfiːtɪst/ **adj** behaving in a way that shows that you do not expect to be successful: *a defeatist attitude* • defeatist noun [C]

defect¹ /ˈdiːfekt/ **noun** [C] a fault or problem with someone or something: *a birth defect* ○ *A mechanical defect caused the plane to crash.* • defective /dɪˈfektɪv/ **adj** having a fault or problem: *defective goods*

defect² /dɪˈfekt/ **verb** [I] to leave your country or organization and go to join an enemy country or competing organization: *He defected to the West.* • defection /dɪˈfekʃən/ **noun** [C, U] the act of defecting • defector noun [C]

defence UK (US **defense**) /dɪˈfens/ **noun 1** MILITARY ▷ [U] the weapons and military forces that a country uses to protect itself against attack: *Government spending on defence is increasing.* ○ *the defence minister/industry* **2** PROTECTION ▷ [C, U] 🅱2 protection, or something that provides protection against attack or criticism: *the body's defences against infection* ○ *She argued strongly in defence of her actions.* **3 come to sb's defence** to support someone when they are being criticized **4 the defence** [group] the lawyers in a court who work in support of the person who is accused of a crime: *He was cross-examined by the defence.* ○ *a defence lawyer* **5** SPORT ▷ ⒰S /ˈdiːfens/ [C, U] 🅱1 the part of a sports team that tries to prevent the other team from scoring points → See also **self-defence**

> 🗹 Word partners for **defence**
>
> mount/put up a defence • an effective/spirited/strong/vigorous defence • defence against sth • [argue, etc] in defence of sth

defenceless UK (US **defenseless**) /dɪˈfensləs/ **adj** weak and unable to protect yourself from attack: *a small, defenceless child*

defend /dɪˈfend/ **verb 1** PROTECT ▷ [T] 🅱1 to protect someone or something from being attacked, especially by fighting: *The army was sent in to defend the country against enemy*

attack. ○ [often reflexive] *She tried to defend herself with a knife.* **2** SUPPORT ▷ [T] 🅱2 to support someone or something that is being criticized: *The newspaper's editor defended his decision to publish the photos.* **3** LAW ▷ [T] to try to show in a court that someone is not guilty of a crime: *He has hired two lawyers to defend him in court.* **4** SPORT ▷ [I, T] to try to stop the other sports team from scoring points **5 defend a championship/title, etc** to try to win a game or competition that you have won before • defender noun [C]

defendant /dɪˈfendənt/ **noun** [C] the person in a court who is accused of a crime

defense /dɪˈfens/ **noun** US spelling of defence

defenseless /dɪˈfensləs/ **adj** US spelling of defenceless

defensive¹ /dɪˈfensɪv/ **adj 1** CRITICISM ▷ quick to protect yourself from being criticized: *He's very defensive about his weight.* **2** SPORT ▷ mainly US A defensive player in a sports team tries to stop the other team scoring points **3** ATTACK ▷ done or used to protect someone or something from attack • defensively adv

defensive² /dɪˈfensɪv/ **noun on the defensive** ready to protect yourself because you are expecting to be criticized or attacked

defer /dɪˈfɜːr/ **verb** [T] (**deferring, deferred**) to arrange for something to happen at a later time *The payments can be deferred for three months.*

deference /ˈdefərəns/ **noun** [U] polite behaviour that shows that you respect someone or something • deferential /ˌdefəˈrenʃəl/ adj

defiance /dɪˈfaɪəns/ **noun** [U] refusing to obey someone or something: *an act of defiance*

defiant /dɪˈfaɪənt/ **adj** refusing to obey someone or something: *a defiant child* • defiantly adv

deficiency /dɪˈfɪʃənsi/ **noun** [C, U] **1** a situation in which you do not have enough of something: *a vitamin deficiency* **2** a mistake or fault in something so that it is not good enough: *Parents are complaining of serious deficiencies in the education system.*

> 🗹 Word partners for **deficiency**
>
> a glaring/major/serious/severe deficiency • a deficiency in sth

deficient /dɪˈfɪʃənt/ **adj 1** not having enough of something: *If you have poor night vision you may be deficient in vitamin A.* **2** not good enough: *His theory is deficient in several respects.*

deficit /ˈdefɪsɪt/ **noun** [C] the amount by which the money that you spend is more than the money that you receive: *a budget deficit*

defile /dɪˈfaɪl/ **verb** [T] formal to spoil someone or something that is pure, holy, or beautiful

define /dɪˈfaɪn/ **verb** [T] **1** 🅱2 to say exactly what something means, or what someone or something is like: *Your duties are clearly defined in the contract.* **2** to show the outer edges or shape of something: *It has sharply defined edges.*

definite /ˈdefɪnət/ **adj 1** 🅱2 certain, fixed, and not likely to change: *We need a definite answer by tomorrow.* **2** clear and obvious: *There has been a definite improvement in her behaviour.*

definite **'article** noun [C] ⓑ in grammar, the word 'the' → Compare **indefinite article**

definitely /'defɪnətli/ adv ⓑ without any doubt: *This book is definitely worth reading.* ◦ *"Do you want to come?" "Yes, definitely."*

definition /ˌdefɪ'nɪʃᵊn/ noun **1** [C] ⓑ an explanation of the meaning of a word or phrase: *a dictionary definition* **2** [U] how clear an image of something is in a photograph or on a screen

definitive /dɪ'fɪnətɪv/ adj **1** certain, clear, and not likely to change: *a definitive answer* **2** A definitive book or piece of work is the best of its type: *the definitive guide to London* • **definitively** adv

deflate /dɪ'fleɪt/ verb **1** [I, T] to let all the air or gas out of something, or to become emptied of air or gas: *to deflate a balloon/tyre* **2** [T] to make someone lose confidence or feel less important: [often passive] *They were totally deflated by losing the match.*

deflation /dɪ'fleɪʃᵊn/ noun [U] a reduction of the supply of money in an economy, and because of this a reduction of economic activity, which is often part of an intentional government plan to reduce prices → Compare **inflation**

deflect /dɪ'flekt/ verb **1** [I, T] to make something change direction by hitting or touching it, or to change direction after hitting something: *The ball was deflected into the corner of the net.* **2** **deflect attention/blame/criticism, etc** to cause attention/blame/criticism, etc to be directed away from you • **deflection** /dɪ'flekʃᵊn/ noun [C, U]

deforestation /diːˌfɒrɪ'steɪʃᵊn/ noun [U] a process in which all the trees in a large area are cut down

deformed /dɪ'fɔːmd/ adj with a shape that has not developed normally: *deformed hands* • **deform** /dɪ'fɔːm/ verb [T]

deformity /dɪ'fɔːməti/ noun [C, U] a problem in which a part of the body has not developed in the normal way, or with the normal shape

defraud /dɪ'frɔːd/ verb [T] to obtain money from someone illegally by being dishonest

defrost /ˌdiː'frɒst/ verb [I, T] **1** If food defrosts, it becomes warmer after being frozen, and if you defrost it, you make it become warmer after being frozen: *You need to defrost the fish before you can cook it.* **2** If you defrost a fridge or freezer (= machines that keep food cold), you make them warmer and remove the ice, and if they defrost, they become warmer and the ice melts.

deft /deft/ adj quick and showing great skill: *a deft movement/touch* • **deftly** adv formal

defunct /dɪ'fʌŋkt/ adj not working or existing now

defuse /ˌdiː'fjuːz/ verb [T] **1** to make a difficult or dangerous situation calmer: *He made a joke to defuse the tension.* **2** to prevent a bomb from exploding by removing the fuse (= part that starts the explosion)

defy /dɪ'faɪ/ verb **1** [T] to refuse to obey someone or something: *Some of these children openly defy their teachers.* **2** **defy belief/description/**

explanation, etc to be impossible to believe/describe/explain, etc: *His attitude defies belief.* **3** **defy sb to do sth** to tell someone to do something that you think will be impossible: *I defy you to prove that I'm wrong.*

degenerate¹ /dɪ'dʒenᵊreɪt/ verb [I] to become worse: *The protest soon degenerated into violence.* • **degeneration** /dɪˌdʒenə'reɪʃᵊn/ noun [U]

degenerate² /dɪ'dʒenᵊrət/ adj having low moral principles

degrade /dɪ'greɪd/ verb [T] **1** to treat someone without respect and as if they have no value: *They think the advert degrades women.* **2** to damage the quality or condition of something • **degradation** /ˌdegrə'deɪʃᵊn/ noun [U]

degrading /dɪ'greɪdɪŋ/ adj treating people without respect and as if they have no value: *degrading work*

degree /dɪ'griː/ noun **1** **TEMPERATURE** ▷ [C] ⓐ a unit for measuring temperature, shown by the symbol ° written after a number **2** **ANGLE** ▷ [C] a unit for measuring angles, shown by the symbol ° written after a number **3** **QUALIFICATION** ▷ [C] ⓑ a qualification given for completing a university course: *She has a degree in physics.* **4** **AMOUNT** ▷ [C, U] ⓑ an amount or level of something: *I agree with you to a degree (= in some ways but not completely).* → See also **Master's (degree)**

dehydrated /ˌdiːhaɪ'dreɪtɪd/ adj not having enough water in your body

dehydration /ˌdiːhaɪ'dreɪʃᵊn/ noun [U] the problem of not having enough water in your body

deign /deɪn/ verb **deign to do sth** to do something that you think you are too important to do

deity /'deɪti/ ⓤⓢ /'diːəti/ noun [C] formal a god or goddess (= female god)

deja vu /ˌdeɪʒɑː'vuː/ noun [U] a feeling that you have already experienced exactly what is happening now: *She suddenly had a strong sense of deja vu.*

dejected /dɪ'dʒektɪd/ adj unhappy and disappointed: *He looked tired and dejected.* • **dejection** /dɪ'dʒekʃᵊn/ noun [U]

delay¹ /dɪ'leɪ/ verb **1** [I, T] ⓐ to make something happen at a later time than originally planned or expected: *Can you delay your departure until next week?* **2** [T] ⓑ to cause someone or something to be slow or late: [often passive] *I was delayed by traffic.*

delay² /dɪ'leɪ/ noun [C, U] ⓐ a period when you have to wait longer than expected for something to happen: *An accident caused long delays on the UK motorway/ US freeway.*

> **☑ Word partners for delay**
>
> a brief/short/slight delay • a considerable/lengthy/long delay • cause delays • experience/face/suffer delays

delectable /dɪ'lektəbl/ adj formal extremely nice, especially to eat

delegate¹ /'delɪgət/ noun [C] someone who is

D

sent somewhere to represent a group of people, especially at a meeting

delegate² /ˈdelɪgeɪt/ **verb** [I, T] to give someone else part of your work or some of your responsibilities

delegation /ˌdelɪˈgeɪʃ³n/ **noun 1** [C] a group of people who have been chosen to represent a much larger group of people: *a delegation of Chinese officials* **2** [U] the act of giving someone part of your work or some of your responsibilities

delete /dɪˈliːt/ **verb** [T] 🜲 to remove something, especially from a computer's memory: *All names have been deleted from the report.* • **deletion** /dɪˈliːʃ³n/ **noun** [C, U]

deli /ˈdeli/ **noun** [C] short for delicatessen

deliberate¹ /dɪˈlɪb³rət/ **adj 1** 🜲 done intentionally, or planned: *This was a deliberate attempt by them to deceive us.* **2** careful and without hurry: *Her movements were calm and deliberate.*

deliberate² /dɪˈlɪb³reɪt/ **verb** [I, T] to consider something carefully before making a decision: *They deliberated for ten hours before reaching a decision.*

deliberately /dɪˈlɪb³rətli/ **adv** 🜲 intentionally, having planned to do something: *He deliberately lied to the police.*

deliberation /dɪˌlɪbəˈreɪʃ³n/ **noun** [C, U] careful thought or talk about a subject before a decision is made: *The jury began deliberations on Thursday.*

delicacy /ˈdelɪkəsi/ **noun 1** FOOD ▷ [C] a special food, usually something rare or expensive **2** GENTLE QUALITY ▷ [U] the quality of being soft, light, or gentle **3** EASY TO DAMAGE ▷ [U] the quality of being easy to damage or break **4** NEEDING CARE ▷ [U] the quality of needing to be treated very carefully: *You need to be very tactful because of the delicacy of the situation.* **5** ATTRACTIVE ▷ [U] the quality of having a thin, attractive shape

delicate /ˈdelɪkət/ **adj 1** GENTLE ▷ 🜲 soft, light, or gentle: *a delicate flavour* ∘ *a delicate shade of pink* **2** EASY TO DAMAGE ▷ 🜲 easy to damage or break: *a delicate china cup* **3** NEEDING CARE ▷ needing to be dealt with very carefully: *I need to discuss a very delicate matter with you.* **4** ATTRACTIVE ▷ having a thin, attractive shape: *delicate hands* • **delicately adv**

delicatessen /ˌdelɪkəˈtes³n/ **noun** [C] a shop, or a part of a shop that sells cheeses, cooked meats, salads, etc

delicious /dɪˈlɪʃəs/ **adj** 🜲 If food or drink is delicious, it smells or tastes extremely good: *This soup is absolutely delicious.* • **deliciously adv**

delight¹ /dɪˈlaɪt/ **noun 1** [U] 🜲 happiness and excited pleasure: *The children screamed with delight.* **2** [C] 🜲 someone or something that gives you pleasure: *She is a delight to have around.*

delight² /dɪˈlaɪt/ **verb** [T] to make someone feel very pleased and happy: *The new discovery has delighted scientists everywhere.*

PHRASAL VERB **delight in sth/doing sth** to get a lot of pleasure from something, especially some-

thing unpleasant: *She seems to delight in makin[g] him look stupid.*

delighted /dɪˈlaɪtɪd/ **adj** 🜲 very pleased: [+ to d[o] sth] *I'd be delighted to accept your invitatio[n]* ∘ *They are delighted with their new car.*

delightful /dɪˈlaɪtf³l/ **adj** 🜲 very pleasan[t,] attractive, or enjoyable: *We had a delightf[ul] evening.* • **delightfully adv**

delinquency /dɪˈlɪŋkwənsi/ **noun** [U] crimin[al] or bad behaviour, especially by young people

delinquent /dɪˈlɪŋkwənt/ **noun** [C] a youn[g] person who behaves badly, usually by commi[t]ting crimes • **delinquent adj** *delinquent beha[v]iour*

delirious /dɪˈlɪriəs/ **adj 1** speaking or thinking i[n] a confused way, often because of a fever o[r] drugs **2** extremely happy: *delirious fans* • **deliriously adv**

deliver /dɪˈlɪvər/ **verb 1** [I, T] 🜲 to take thing[s] such as letters, parcels, or goods to a person o[r] place: *They can deliver the sofa on Wednesda[y].* **2** [I, T] to achieve or do something that you ha[ve] promised to do, or that people expect you to d[o:] *The company failed to deliver the high quali[ty] service that we expect.* **3 deliver a speech/tal[k]** etc 🜲 to speak formally to a group of peopl[e:] *She delivered the speech on national TV.* **4 delive[r] a baby** to help take a baby out of its mothe[r] when it is being born → See also **deliver/com[e]** up with the goods

delivery /dɪˈlɪv³ri/ **noun** [C, U] **1** 🜲 the job o[f] taking things such as letters, parcels, or goods t[o] a person or place: *Is there a charge for delivery[?]* **2** the time when a baby is born and comes out o[f] its mother: *Her husband was present at th[e] delivery.*

delta /ˈdeltə/ **noun** [C] a low, flat area of lan[d] where a river divides into smaller rivers an[d] goes into the sea: *the Nile delta*

delude /dɪˈluːd/ **verb** [T] to make someon[e] believe something that is not real or true [often reflexive, + into + doing sth] *She delude[d] herself into thinking she could win.* • **deluded a[t]** believing things that are not real or true

deluge¹ /ˈdeljuːdʒ/ **noun** [C] **1** a very larg[e] amount of something that suddenly arrive[s:] *They have received a deluge of complaints.* **2** [a] sudden, large amount of rain, or a flood

deluge² /ˈdeljuːdʒ/ **verb be deluged with/b[y]** **sth** to receive very large amounts of som[e]thing suddenly: *Our switchboard was deluge[d] with calls last night.*

delusion /dɪˈluːʒ³n/ **noun** [C, U] the mental stat[e] of believing something that is not true: [+ (that[)] *She is under the delusion that her debts will ju[st]* go away.*

deluxe /dəˈlʌks/ **adj** luxurious and of very hig[h] quality: *a deluxe hotel*

delve /delv/ **verb delve in/into/inside, etc** t[o] search in a container to try to find somethin[g:] *He delved in his pocket and pulled out a pen.*

PHRASAL VERB **delve into sth** to examine som[e]thing carefully in order to discover mor[e] information about someone or something: *I don't like to delve too deeply into his past.*

demand[1] /dɪˈmɑːnd/ **noun 1** [U, no plural] ⓑ② a need for something to be sold or supplied: *There's an increasing **demand for** cheap housing.* **2** [C] ⓑ① a strong request: *They received a final **demand for** payment.* **3 in demand** wanted or needed in large numbers: *Good teachers are always in demand.*

> ☑ Word partners for **demand**
>
> **increase/meet/satisfy** demand • **great/growing/high/steady** demand • **be in** demand • demand **for** sth

demand[2] /dɪˈmɑːnd/ **verb** [T] **1** ⓑ① to ask for something in a way that shows that you do not expect to be refused: *I demanded an explanation.* ∘ [+ that] *The survivors are demanding that the airline pays them compensation.* → See Note at **ask 2** ⓑ② to need something such as time or effort: *This job demands a high level of concentration.*

demanding /dɪˈmɑːndɪŋ/ **adj** ⓑ② needing a lot of your time, attention, or effort: *a very demanding job*

demands /dɪˈmɑːndz/ **noun** [plural] the difficult things that you have to do: *the demands of modern life* ∘ *His new job **makes** a lot of **demands on** him* (= he has to work very hard).

demeaning /dɪˈmiːnɪŋ/ **adj** If something is demeaning, it makes you feel that you are not respected: *Some people consider beauty competitions **demeaning to** women.*

demeanour UK (US **demeanor**) /dɪˈmiːnər/ **noun** [C] the way that someone looks, seems, and behaves: *a quiet, serious demeanour*

demented /dɪˈmentɪd/ **adj** mentally ill, or behaving in a very strange way without any control

dementia /dɪˈmenʃə/ **noun** [U] a mental illness suffered especially by old people

demi- /demi-/ **prefix** half, partly: *demitasse* (= a small coffee cup) ∘ *demigod* (= a creature that is part god and part human)

demise /dɪˈmaɪz/ **noun 1** [no plural] the end of something, usually because it has stopped being popular or successful: *the demise of apartheid* **2 sb's demise** someone's death

demo[1] /ˈdeməʊ/ **noun** [C] **1** an example of a product, given or shown to someone to try to make them buy it: *a software demo* **2** UK short for **demonstration** (= political march): *a student demo*

demo[2] /ˈdeməʊ/ **verb** [T] to show something and explain how it works: *We need someone to demo a new piece of software.*

democracy /dɪˈmɒkrəsi/ **noun** [C, U] ⓑ② a system of government in which people elect their leaders, or a country with this system

> ☑ Word partners for **democracy**
>
> an **emerging/new** democracy • **in** a democracy

democrat /ˈdeməkræt/ **noun** [C] **1** someone who supports democracy **2 Democrat** someone who

supports the Democratic Party in the US: *the Democrat candidate* → See also **Liberal Democrat**

democratic /ˌdeməˈkrætɪk/ **adj 1** ⓑ② following or supporting the political system of democracy: *a democratic society/government* **2** where everyone has equal rights and can help to make decisions: *a democratic discussion/debate* • **democratically adv** *a democratically elected government*

the Demoˈcratic ˌParty noun [group] one of the two main political parties in the US

demolish /dɪˈmɒlɪʃ/ **verb** [T] **1** ⓑ② to destroy something such as a building: *The factory is dangerous, and will have to be demolished.* **2** to show that an idea or argument is wrong: *He completely demolished my argument.*

demolition /ˌdeməˈlɪʃən/ **noun** [C, U] the activity of destroying things such as buildings: *the demolition of dangerous buildings*

demon /ˈdiːmən/ **noun** [C] an evil spirit

demonic /dɪˈmɒnɪk/ **adj** evil

demonstrable /dɪˈmɒnstrəbl/ **adj** Something that is demonstrable can be shown to exist or be true: *a demonstrable fact* • **demonstrably adv**

demonstrate /ˈdemənstreɪt/ **verb 1 PROVE** ▷ [T] ⓑ② to show or prove that something exists or is true: [+ that] *The survey clearly demonstrates that tourism can have positive benefits.* **2 SHOW HOW** ▷ [T] to show someone how to do something, or how something works: *She demonstrated how to use the new software.* **3 EXPRESS** ▷ [T] to express or show that you have a feeling, quality, or ability: *He has demonstrated a genuine interest in the project.* **4 MARCH** ▷ [I] ⓑ② to march or stand with a group of people to show that you disagree with or support someone or something: *Thousands of people gathered to **demonstrate against** the new proposals.*

demonstration /ˌdemənˈstreɪʃən/ **noun 1 MARCH** ▷ [C] ⓑ② an occasion when a group of people march or stand together to show that they disagree with or support someone or something: *They're taking part in a **demonstration against** the causes of climate change.* **2 SHOWING HOW** ▷ [C, U] an occasion when someone shows how to do something, or how something works: *We asked the sales assistant to **give** us a **demonstration**.* **3 PROOF** ▷ [C, U] proof that something exists or is true: *This disaster is a clear demonstration of the need for tighter controls.*

> ☑ Word partners for **demonstration**
>
> **hold/organize/stage** a demonstration • **go on/take part in** a demonstration • a **mass** demonstration • a demonstration **against** sth

demonstrative /dɪˈmɒnstrətɪv/ **adj** willing to show your feelings, especially your affection

demonstrator /ˈdemənstreɪtər/ **noun** [C] a person who marches or stands with a group of people to show that they disagree with or support someone or something

demoralized (also UK **-ised**) /dɪˈmɒrəlaɪzd/ **adj** having lost your confidence, enthusiasm, and

D

hope: *After the game, the players were tired and demoralized.* • **demoralizing** adj making you lose your confidence, enthusiasm, and hope: *a demoralizing defeat* • **demoralize** /dɪ'mɒrəlaɪz/ verb [T]

demote /dɪ'məʊt/ verb **be demoted** to be moved to a less important job or position, especially as a punishment • **demotion** /dɪ'məʊʃən/ noun [C, U]

demotivated /ˌdiː'məʊtɪveɪtɪd/ adj not having any enthusiasm for your work

demure /dɪ'mjʊər/ adj If a young woman is demure, she is quiet and shy. • **demurely** adv

den /den/ noun [C] **1 ANIMAL'S HOME** ▷ the home of some wild animals: *a lions' den* **2 ILLEGAL ACTIVITY** ▷ a place where secret and illegal activity happens: *a gambling den* **3 ROOM** ▷ mainly US a room in your home where you relax, read, watch television, etc

denial /dɪ'naɪəl/ noun **1** [C, U] a statement in which you say that something is not true, or the act of making a statement like this: *a denial of his guilt* **2** [U] not allowing someone to have or do something: *the denial of medical treatment*

☑ Word partners for **denial**

issue a denial • a categorical/emphatic/strenuous/vehement denial • denial of sth

---

denigrate /'denɪɡreɪt/ verb [T] to criticize and not show much respect for someone or something

denim /'denɪm/ noun [U] ⑫ thick, strong, cotton cloth, usually blue, which is used to make clothes: *a denim jacket*

denomination /dɪˌnɒmɪ'neɪʃən/ noun [C] **1** a religious group that has slightly different beliefs from other groups that share the same religion **2** the value of a particular coin, piece of paper money, or stamp

denote /dɪ'nəʊt/ verb [T] to be a sign of something: *The colour red is used to denote passion or danger.*

denounce /dɪ'naʊns/ verb [T] to publicly criticize someone or something, or to publicly accuse someone of something: *They've been denounced as terrorists.*

dense /dens/ adj **1** with a lot of people or things close together: *dense forest* **2** ⑫ If cloud, smoke, etc is dense, it is thick and difficult to see through: *dense fog* • **densely** adv ⑫ *a densely populated area*

density /'densɪti/ noun [C, U] **1** the number of people or things in a place when compared with the size of the place: *The area has a high population density.* **2** the relationship between the weight of a substance and its size: *bone density*

dent[1] /dent/ noun [C] **1** a hollow area in a hard surface where it has been hit: *The car door had a dent in it.* **2** a reduction in something: *The cost of repairs made a serious dent in my savings.*

dent[2] /dent/ verb [T] **1** to create a hollow area in the hard surface of something by hitting it: *The side of the car was dented in the accident.* **2** to reduce someone's confidence or positive feel-

ings about something: *The defeat did little to dent her enthusiasm.*

dental /'dentəl/ adj ⑫ relating to teeth: *dental treatment*

dental floss /'dentəlˌflɒs/ noun [U] a thin thread that is used for cleaning between the teeth

dentist /'dentɪst/ noun [C] ⑫ someone who examines and repairs teeth: *I have a dentist's appointment tomorrow.* • **dentistry** noun [U] the subject or job of examining and repairing teeth

dentist

dentures /'dentʃəz/ noun [plural] false teeth

denunciation /dɪˌnʌnsi'eɪʃən/ noun [C, U] public criticism of someone or something, or publicly accusing someone of something

deny /dɪ'naɪ/ verb [T] **1** ⑫ to say that something is not true, especially something that you are accused of: [+ (that)] *He never denied that he said those things.* ○ [+ doing sth] *He denies murdering his father.* **2** ⑫ to not allow someone to have or do something: [often passive] *These children are being denied access to education.*

deodorant /di'əʊdərənt/ noun [C, U] a substance that you put on your body to prevent or hide unpleasant smells

depart /dɪ'pɑːt/ verb [I] formal ⑬ to leave a place, especially to start a journey to another place: *The train to Lincoln will depart from platform 9.* ○ *He departed for Paris on Tuesday.*

department /dɪ'pɑːtmənt/ noun [C] ⑫ a part of an organization such as a school, business, or government that deals with a particular area of work: *the sales department* ○ *head of the English department* → See also **police department**

departmental /ˌdiːpɑː'mentəl/ adj relating to a department: *the departmental budget*

de'partment store noun [C] ⑫ a large shop divided into several different parts that sell different types of things

departure /dɪ'pɑːtʃər/ noun [C, U] **1** ⑬ the act of leaving a place, especially to start a journey to another place: *the departure of flight BA11.* ○ *This fare is valid for weekday departures from Manchester.* **2** a change from what is expected, or from what has happened before: *This film is a major departure from his previous work.*

depend /dɪ'pend/ verb **it/that depends** ⑬ used to say that you are not certain about something because other things affect you answer: [+ question word] *"Are you coming out tonight?" "It depends where you're going."*

PHRASAL VERB **depend on/upon sb/sth 1 NEED** ⑫ to need the help of someone or something in order to exist or continue as before: *She depends on her son for everything.* ○ *The city's economy depends largely on the car industry.* **2 BE INFLUENCED BY** ▷ ⑬ If something depends on someone or something, it is influenced by them or changes because of them: [+ question word]

The choice depends on what you're willing to spend. **3 TRUST** ▷ ⓑ to be able to trust someone or something to help, or to do what you expect: [+ to do sth] *You can always depend on Andy to keep his promises.*

> ⚠ Common learner error: **depend on** something
>
> Be careful to choose the correct preposition after **depend**.
> *I might go on Friday – it depends on the weather.*
> ~~I might go on Friday – it depends of the weather.~~
> ~~I might go on Friday – it depends from the weather.~~

dependable /dɪˈpendəbl/ **adj** able to be trusted and very likely to do what you expect: *the team's most dependable player*

dependant UK (US **dependent**) /dɪˈpendənt/ **noun** [C] someone, usually a child, who depends on you for financial support

dependence /dɪˈpendəns/ **noun** [U] (also **dependency** /dɪˈpendəntsi/) a situation in which you need someone or something all the time in order to exist or continue as before: *Our society needs to reduce its **dependence on** the car.*

dependent¹ /dɪˈpendənt/ **adj 1** ⓑ needing the help of someone or something in order to exist or continue as before: *She's completely **dependent on** her parents for money.* **2 dependent on/upon sth** influenced by or decided by something: *The amount of tax you pay is dependent on how much you earn.*

dependent² /dɪˈpendənt/ **noun** [C] US spelling of dependant

depict /dɪˈpɪkt/ **verb** [T] to represent someone or something in a picture or story: *The cartoon **depicts** the president as a vampire.* • **depiction** /dɪˈpɪkʃən/ **noun** [C, U]

deplete /dɪˈpliːt/ **verb** [T] to reduce the amount of something, especially a natural supply: *Alcohol depletes the body of B vitamins.* • **depletion** /dɪˈpliːʃən/ **noun** [U]

deplorable /dɪˈplɔːrəbl/ **adj** very bad or morally wrong

deplore /dɪˈplɔːr/ **verb** [T] formal to feel or express strong disapproval of something: *We deeply deplore the loss of life.*

deploy /dɪˈplɔɪ/ **verb** [T] to move soldiers or equipment to a place where they can be used when they are needed • **deployment noun** [U] *the deployment of nuclear weapons*

deport /dɪˈpɔːt/ **verb** [T] to force a foreign person to leave a country: *Thousands of illegal immigrants are **deported from** the US every year.* • **deportation** /ˌdiːpɔːˈteɪʃən/ **noun** [C, U] *He now faces deportation back to his native country.*

depose /dɪˈpəʊz/ **verb** [T] to remove a ruler or leader from their position of power • **deposed adj** *the deposed president*

deposit¹ /dɪˈpɒzɪt/ **noun** [C] **1 BUYING** ▷ ⓑ a payment that you make immediately when you decide to buy something, as proof that you will

really buy it: *They've **put down** a **deposit on** a house.* **2 BANK** ▷ an amount of money that you pay into a bank: *to **make** a **deposit*** **3 SUBSTANCE** ▷ a layer of a substance that has developed from a natural or chemical process: *deposits of iron ore* **4 RENT** ▷ an amount of money that you pay when you rent something, and that is given back to you when you return it without any damage

> ☑ Word partners for **deposit**
>
> pay/put down a deposit • a deposit of [£500/$300, etc] • a deposit on sth

deposit² /dɪˈpɒzɪt/ **verb** [T] **1 PUT DOWN** ▷ to put something down somewhere: *He deposited his books on the table.* **2 MONEY** ▷ to put money into a bank or valuable things into a safe place: *She deposited $150,000 in a Swiss bank account.* **3 SUBSTANCE** ▷ to leave something lying on a surface, as a result of a natural or chemical process

deˈposit acˌcount noun [C] UK a bank account that pays interest on the money you put into it and that you use for saving

depot /ˈdepəʊ/ **noun** [C] **1 VEHICLES** ▷ a place where trains, trucks, or buses are kept **2 GOODS** ▷ a building where supplies of goods are stored **3 STATION** ▷ US a small bus or train station

depraved /dɪˈpreɪvd/ **adj** morally bad • **depravity** /dɪˈprævəti/ **noun** [U]

depreciate /dɪˈpriːʃieɪt/ **verb** [I] to lose value over a period of time: *New computers depreciate in value very quickly.* • **depreciation** /dɪˌpriːʃiˈeɪʃən/ **noun** [U]

depress /dɪˈpres/ **verb** [T] **1** to make someone feel very unhappy, especially about the future: *This place really depresses me.* **2** to reduce the value or level of something, especially in business: *Competition between stores has depressed prices.*

depressed /dɪˈprest/ **adj 1** ⓐ very unhappy, often for a long time: *She has been feeling very depressed since her marriage broke up.* **2** A depressed country, area, or economy does not have enough jobs or business activity: *an economically depressed area*

depressing /dɪˈpresɪŋ/ **adj** ⓑ making you feel unhappy and without any hope for the future: *The news is very depressing.*

depression /dɪˈpreʃən/ **noun** [C, U] **1** ⓑ the feeling of being very unhappy for a period of time, or a mental illness that makes you feel very unhappy: *Nearly three million people **suffer from depression** every year.* **2** a time when there is not much business activity: *The stock market crash marked the start of a severe depression.*

deprive /dɪˈpraɪv/ **verb**

PHRASAL VERB **deprive sb/sth of sth** ⓑ to take something important or necessary away from someone or something: *They were **deprived of** food for long periods.* • **deprivation** /ˌdeprɪˈveɪʃən/ **noun** [C, U] *sleep **deprivation***

D

D

deprived /dɪˈpraɪvd/ **adj** not having enough food, money, and the things that you need to have a normal life: *children from* **deprived** *backgrounds*

dept written abbreviation for department (= a part of an organization or government)

depth /depθ/ **noun 1** TOP TO BOTTOM ▷ [C, U] 🔒 the distance from the top of something to the bottom: *The lake reaches a maximum* **depth of** *292 metres.* ∘ *Dig a hole 10 cm* **in depth.** → See picture at **length 2** FRONT TO BACK ▷ [C, U] the distance from the front to the back of something **3** AMOUNT ▷ [U] how much someone knows or feels about something: *She was amazed at the depth of his knowledge.* **4 in depth** 🔒 giving all the details: *With access to the Internet, students can do their homework in greater depth.*

IDIOM **be out of your depth** to not have the knowledge, experience, or skills to deal with a particular subject or situation

---

🔲 Word partners for **depth**

a depth **of** [6 metres/8 inches, etc]
• [5cm/7 inches, etc] **in** depth
• **at/to** a depth of [5 metres/6 inches, etc]

---

depths /depθs/ **noun** [plural] **1** a position far below the surface or far into something: *the* **depths of** *the forest* **2** the worst period of something: *the* **depths of** *despair*

deputy /ˈdepjəti/ **noun** [C] someone who has the second most important job in an organization: *the deputy Prime Minister*

derail /dɪˈreɪl/ **verb 1** [I, T] If a train derails, or is derailed, it comes off the railway tracks. **2** [T] If you derail plans, you prevent them from happening. • **derailment noun** [C, U]

deranged /dɪˈreɪndʒd/ **adj** behaving in a way that is not normal, especially when suffering from a mental illness

derby /ˈdɑːbi/ 🇺🇸 /ˈdɜːrbi/ **noun** [C] **1** a type of sports competition: *a fishing/motorcycle derby* **2 Derby** a type of horse race **3** US (mainly UK **bowler hat**) a round, hard, black hat worn by men, especially in the past

deregulate /ˌdiːˈregjəleɪt/ **verb** [T] to remove national or local government controls from a business: *The government plans to deregulate the banking industry.* • **deregulation** /ˌdiːregjəˈleɪʃən/ **noun** [U]

derelict /ˈderəlɪkt/ **adj** A derelict building or piece of land is not used any more and is in a bad condition: *a derelict house*

deride /dɪˈraɪd/ **verb** [T] formal to talk about someone or something as if they are ridiculous and do not deserve any respect: *Her novel, once derided by critics, is now a classic.*

derision /dɪˈrɪʒən/ **noun** [U] the opinion that someone or something is ridiculous and does not deserve respect: *The novel was* **greeted with** **derision.**

derisive /dɪˈraɪsɪv/ **adj** showing derision towards someone or something

derisory /dɪˈraɪsəri/ **adj 1** so small that it seems ridiculous: *a* **derisory** *sum of money* **2** cruel an making someone feel stupid: *derisory remarks*

derivation /ˌderɪˈveɪʃən/ **noun** [C, U] the origi of something, such as a word, from whic another form has developed, or the new form itself

derivative /dɪˈrɪvətɪv/ **noun** [C] a form of som thing, such as a word, that has developed from another form

derive /dɪˈraɪv/ **verb**

PHRASAL VERB **derive (sth) from sth 1** to com from or be developed from something: *The nam derives from Latin.* **2 derive comfort/pleasur etc from sth** to get a positive feeling c advantage from someone or something: *derive great pleasure from gardening.*

dermatitis /ˌdɜːməˈtaɪtɪs/ **noun** [U] a conditic that makes your skin red and painful

derogatory /dɪˈrɒgətəri/ **adj** showing stron disapproval and not showing any respect fc someone: *derogatory comments/remarks*

descend /dɪˈsend/ **verb** [I, T] formal 🔒 to move c go down: *We descended four flights of stairs.*

PHRASAL VERB **be descended from sb/sth** to b related to a person or creature that lived a lor time ago

descendant /dɪˈsendənt/ **noun** [C] someon who is related to someone who lived a lor time ago: *She is a* **descendant of** *Queen Victori*

descent /dɪˈsent/ **noun** [C, U] **1** a movemen down: *The plane* **began** *its* **descent** *into Heathrou* **2 of Irish/French, etc descent** being related t people who lived in the past in Ireland/Franc etc

describe /dɪˈskraɪb/ **verb** [T] 🔒 to say wh someone or something is like: *Neighbou* **described** *her* **as** *a shy, quiet girl.* ∘ [+ questic word] *I tried to describe what I had seen.*

description /dɪˈskrɪpʃən/ **noun 1** 🔒 [C, something that tells you what someone c something is like: *I* **gave** *the police a* **descriptic** *of the stolen jewellery.* **2 of any/every/som description** of any/every/some type: *They se plants of every description.*

🔲 Word partners for **description**

give a description • an **accurate/detailed/ short** description • a description **of** sth/sb

---

descriptive /dɪˈskrɪptɪv/ **adj** describing som thing, especially in a detailed, interesting way

desert¹ /ˈdezət/ **noun** [C, U] 🔒 a large, hot, d area of land with very few plants: *the Saha Desert*

desert² /dɪˈzɜːt/ **verb 1** PERSON ▷ [T] to leav someone and never come back: *He deserted h family.* **2** PLACE ▷ [T] to leave a place, so that it empty: *People are deserting the countryside work in towns.* **3** ARMY ▷ [I, T] to leave the arm without permission • **desertion** /dɪˈzɜːʃər **noun** [U]

deserted /dɪˈzɜːtɪd/ **adj** If a place is deserted, has no people in it: *a deserted street*

---

deserter /dɪˈzɜːtəʳ/ **noun** [C] someone who leaves the army without permission

desert ˈisland noun [C] a tropical island where no one lives, far from any other places

deserve /dɪˈzɜːv/ **verb** [T] **㊛** If you deserve something good or bad, it should happen to you because of the way you have behaved: *The school deserves praise for the way it has raised standards.* ○ [+ to do sth] *He deserves to be locked up for life.* • **deservedly adv**

deserving /dɪˈzɜːvɪŋ/ **adj** If something or someone is deserving, people should help or support them: *The children's charity is a **deserving cause**.*

design¹ /dɪˈzaɪn/ **noun 1** PLANNING ▷ [U] **㊛** the way in which something is planned and made: *There was a fault in the design of the aircraft.* **2** DRAWING ▷ [C] a drawing that shows how an object, machine, or building will be made: *Engineers are working on the new designs.* **3** DECORATION ▷ [C] **㊛** a pattern or decoration **4** PROCESS ▷ [U] **㊛** the process of making drawings to show how something will be made: *a course in art and design* → See also **interior design**

design² /dɪˈzaɪn/ **verb** [T] **1** **㊛** to draw or plan something before making it: *She designs furniture.* **2 be designed to do sth** **㊛** to have been planned or done for a particular purpose: *The new law is designed to protect children.*

designate /ˈdezɪgneɪt/ **verb** [T] formal to choose someone or something for a particular purpose or duty: *The area has been **designated as** a nature reserve.* • **designation** /ˌdezɪgˈneɪʃᵊn/ **noun** [C, U]

designer¹ /dɪˈzaɪnəʳ/ **noun** [C] **㊛** someone who draws and plans how something will be made: *a fashion designer*

designer² /dɪˈzaɪnəʳ/ **adj designer jeans/sunglasses, etc** **㊛** clothes or objects made by a fashionable designer

deˌsigner ˈbaby noun [C] a baby with some characteristics chosen by its parents and doctors using gene therapy (= the science of changing genes in order to stop or prevent a disease)

desirable /dɪˈzaɪᵊrəbl/ **adj** **㊛** If something is desirable, it is very good or attractive and most people would want it: *A good education is highly desirable.* → Opposite **undesirable**

desire¹ /dɪˈzaɪəʳ/ **noun 1** [C, U] **㊛** a strong feeling that you want something: [+ to do sth] *I have no desire to have children.* ○ *There is a strong desire for peace among the people.* **2** [U] a strong feeling of being sexually attracted to someone

> ☑ Word partners for **desire**
>
> **express/have** a desire to do sth
> • a **burning/strong** desire • a desire **for** sth

desire² /dɪˈzaɪəʳ/ **verb** [T] formal to want something: *You can have whatever you desire.*

desired /dɪˈzaɪəd/ **adj the desired effect/result/shape, etc** the effect/result/shape, etc that is wanted: *Her medicine seems to have had the desired effect.*

desk /desk/ **noun** [C] **㊐** a table that you sit at to write or work, often with drawers → See also **cash**

desk → See colour picture **The Office** on page Centre 5

desk

desktop /ˈdesktɒp/ **noun** [C] **1** COMPUTER SCREEN ▷ **㊑** a computer screen that contains icons (= symbols that represent programs, information, or equipment) and that is usually used as a place to start and finish computer work **2** COMPUTER ▷ (also **desktop computer**) **㊑** a computer that is small enough to fit on a desk **3** SURFACE ▷ the top of a desk

ˌdesktop ˈpublishing noun [U] the production of finished designs for pages of books or documents using a small computer and printer (= machine for printing)

desolate /ˈdesᵊlət/ **adj 1** A desolate place is empty and makes you feel sad: *a desolate landscape* **2** lonely and unhappy: *She felt desolate when he left.* • **desolation** /ˌdesᵊlˈeɪʃᵊn/ **noun** [U]

despair¹ /dɪˈspeəʳ/ **noun** [U] **㊑** a feeling of having no hope: *She shook her head **in despair**.*

> ☑ Word partners for **despair**
>
> **abject/complete/utter** despair • **in** despair

despair² /dɪˈspeəʳ/ **verb** [I] to feel that you have no hope: *Don't despair – things will improve.* ○ [+ of + doing sth] *He had begun to despair of ever finding a job.* • **despairing adj**

despatch¹ UK formal (UK/US **dispatch**) /dɪˈspætʃ/ **verb** [T] to send someone or something somewhere: *They despatched a police car to arrest him.*

despatch² UK (UK/US **dispatch**) /dɪˈspætʃ/ **noun 1** [U] the act of sending someone or something somewhere: *the despatch of troops* **2** [C] an official report that someone in a foreign country sends to their organization

desperate /ˈdespᵊrət/ **adj 1** WITHOUT HOPE ▷ **㊑** feeling that you have no hope and are ready to do anything to change the situation you are in: *He was absolutely desperate and would have tried anything to get her back.* **2** NEEDING SOMETHING ▷ **㊑** needing or wanting something very much: *By two o'clock I was desperate for something to eat.* **3** BAD ▷ A desperate situation is very bad or serious: *The economy is in a really desperate situation.* • **desperately adv** • **desperation** /ˌdespᵊˈreɪʃᵊn/ **noun** [U]

despicable /dɪˈspɪkəbl/ **adj** very unpleasant or cruel: *a despicable act/crime*

despise /dɪˈspaɪz/ **verb** [T] to hate someone or something and have no respect for them: *The two groups despise each other.*

despite /dɪˈspaɪt/ **preposition 1** **㊑** used to say that something happened or is true, although something else makes this seem not probable: *I'm still pleased with the house despite all the problems we've had.* ○ [+ doing sth] *He managed to eat lunch despite having had an enormous breakfast.* **2 despite yourself** If you do something despite yourself, you do it although you did not intend to.

despondent /dɪˈspɒndənt/ **adj** unhappy and having no enthusiasm • **despondency** **noun** [U]

despot /ˈdespɒt/ **noun** [C] a very powerful person, especially someone who treats people cruelly

dessert

dessert /dɪˈzɜːt/ **noun** [C, U] **A2** sweet food that is eaten after the main part of a meal: *We had ice cream for dessert.*

dessertspoon /dɪˈzɜːtspuːn/ **noun** [C] UK a medium-sized spoon used for eating or measuring food, or the amount this spoon can hold

destabilize (also UK **-ise**) /ˌdiːˈsteɪbəlaɪz/ **verb** [T] to cause change in a country or government so that it loses its power or control: *a plot to destabilize the government*

destination /ˌdestɪˈneɪʃən/ **noun** [C] **B1** the place where someone or something is going: *Spain is a very popular **holiday destination**.*

destined /ˈdestɪnd/ **adj** be destined for sth; be destined to do sth to be certain to be something or do something in the future: *She was destined for a brilliant future.*

destiny /ˈdestɪni/ **noun** **1** [C] the things that will happen to someone in the future: *At last she feels in control of her own destiny.* **2** [U] a power that some people believe controls what will happen in the future: *Nick said it was destiny that we met.*

destitute /ˈdestɪtjuːt/ **adj** so poor that you do not have the basic things you need to live, such as food, clothes, or money • **destitution** /ˌdestɪˈtjuːʃən/ **noun** [U]

destroy /dɪˈstrɔɪ/ **verb** [T] **B1** to damage something so badly that it does not exist or cannot be used: *Many works of art were destroyed in the fire.*

destroyer /dɪˈstrɔɪər/ **noun** [C] a small, fast ship that is used in a war

destruction /dɪˈstrʌkʃən/ **noun** [U] **B2** the process of destroying something: *We are all responsible for the **destruction of** the forest.* • **destructive** /dɪˈstrʌktɪv/ **adj** causing a lot of damage: *the destructive power of nuclear weapons* → See also **self-destructive**

detach /dɪˈtætʃ/ **verb** [T] to take a part of something off so that it is separate: *Please complete and detach the form below and return it to the school.* • **detachable adj**

detached /dɪˈtætʃt/ **adj 1** UK A detached building is not joined to another building. **2** If someone is detached, they do not feel involved with someone or emotional about something → See also **semi-detached**

detachment /dɪˈtætʃmənt/ **noun 1** [U] a feeling of not being involved in a situation: *He spok with cool detachment.* **2** [C] a small group o soldiers with a particular job to do

detail¹ /ˈdiːteɪl/ ⓤ /dɪˈteɪl/ **noun** [C, U] **1** **B1** a fac or piece of information about something: *Pleas send me **details of** your training courses.* ◦ *Sh didn't include very much detail in her report.* **2** i **detail** **B1** including every part of something: *H explained it all in great detail.* **3** go into detail **B2** to include all the facts about something

> ☑ Word partners for **detail**
>
> disclose/discuss/divulge/reveal details
> • exact/full/precise/relevant details
> • details about/of/on sth

detail² /ˈdiːteɪl/ ⓤ /dɪˈteɪl/ **verb** [T] to describ something completely, giving all the facts

detailed /ˈdiːteɪld/ **adj** **B2** giving a lot o information: *a **detailed account/description***

detain /dɪˈteɪn/ **verb** [T] to keep someone some where and not allow them to leave, especially i order to ask them about a crime: *Three men wer detained by police for questioning.*

detect /dɪˈtekt/ **verb** [T] to discover or notic something, especially something that is difficul to see, hear, smell, etc: *This special camera ca detect bodies by their heat.*

detection /dɪˈtekʃən/ **noun** [U] **1** the process o discovering or noticing something: *the earl detection of cancer* **2** the discovery, by the police of information about a crime

detective /dɪˈtektɪv/ **noun** [C] **B1** someone especially a police officer, whose job is t discover information about a crime

detector /dɪˈtektər/ **noun** [C] a piece of equip ment used to discover something, especiall something that is difficult to see, hear, smel etc: *a **smoke detector***

detente /ˌdeɪˈtɒnt/ **noun** [U] formal a friendl relationship between countries that were no previously friendly

detention /dɪˈtenʃən/ **noun 1** [U] a situation i which someone is officially kept somewhere an not allowed to leave **2** [C, U] a school punish ment in which a student is kept in school afte the other students leave

deter /dɪˈtɜːr/ **verb** [T] (**deterring, deterred**) t make someone less likely to do something, or t make something less likely to happen: *We hav introduced new security measures to deter shop lifters.* ◦ *[+ from + doing sth] Higher fuel cos could deter people from driving their cars.*

detergent /dɪˈtɜːdʒənt/ **noun** [C, U] a liquid o powder that is used to clean things

deteriorate /dɪˈtɪəriəreɪt/ **verb** [I] to becom worse: *Her condition deteriorated rapidly* • **deterioration** /dɪˌtɪəriəˈreɪʃən/ **noun** [U]

determination /dɪˌtɜːmɪˈneɪʃən/ **noun** [U] **B2** quality that makes someone continue trying t do something, although it is very difficult: *And*

Murray will need great determination and skill to win this match.

determine /dɪˈtɜːmɪn/ **verb** [T] **1** to discover the facts or truth about something: [+ question word] *The doctors are still unable to determine what is wrong.* **2** to decide what will happen: [+ question word] *Her exam results will determine which university she goes to.*

determined /dɪˈtɜːmɪnd/ **adj** 🔒 wanting to do something very much, and not letting anyone stop you: [+ to do sth] *He's determined to win this match.*

determiner /dɪˈtɜːmɪnər/ **noun** [C] 🔒 a word that is used before a noun or adjective to show which person or thing you are referring to. For example 'my' in 'my old car' and 'that' in 'that man' are determiners.

deterrent /dɪˈterənt/ **noun** [C] something that stops people doing something because they are afraid of what will happen if they do: *They've installed a security camera as a **deterrent to** thieves.* • **deterrent adj** *a deterrent effect*

detest /dɪˈtest/ **verb** [T] to hate someone or something very much

detonate /ˈdetəneɪt/ **verb** [I, T] to explode or make something explode: *The **bomb** was **detonated** safely by army officers and no one was hurt.* • **detonation** /ˌdetəˈneɪʃən/ **noun** [C, U]

detonator /ˈdetəneɪtər/ **noun** [C] a piece of equipment that makes a bomb explode

detour /ˈdiːtʊər/ **noun** [C] a different, longer route to a place that is used to avoid something or to visit something: *Several roads were closed, so we had to **take a detour**.*

detox /ˈdiːtɒks/ **noun** [U] informal treatment to clean out your blood, stomach, etc and get rid of bad substances such as drugs

detract /dɪˈtrækt/ **verb**

PHRASAL VERB **detract from sth** to make something seem less good than it really is, or than it was thought to be

detriment /ˈdetrɪmənt/ **noun to the detriment of sth** causing damage to something: *He was working very long hours, to the detriment of his health.* • **detrimental** /ˌdetrɪˈmentəl/ **adj** *a detrimental effect*

devaluation /ˌdiːvæljuˈeɪʃən/ **noun** [C, U] a situation in which the value of something is reduced: *the devaluation of the dollar*

devalue /ˌdiːˈvæljuː/ **verb** [T] (**devaluing, devalued**) **1** to make something less valuable, especially a country's money: *to devalue the pound* **2** to make someone or something seem less important than they really are

devastate /ˈdevəsteɪt/ **verb** [T] to destroy or damage something very badly: *A recent hurricane devastated the city.* • **devastation** /ˌdevəˈsteɪʃən/ **noun** [U]

devastated /ˈdevəsteɪtɪd/ **adj 1** very shocked and upset: *She was devastated when her husband died.* **2** completely destroyed

devastating /ˈdevəsteɪtɪŋ/ **adj 1** making someone very shocked and upset: *Despite the devastating news, no one is giving up hope.* **2** causing a lot of damage or destruction: *The fire has had a devastating effect on the local wildlife.*

devastatingly /ˈdevəsteɪtɪŋli/ **adv** extremely: *devastatingly funny/handsome*

develop /dɪˈveləp/ **verb 1** CHANGE ▷ [I, T] 🔒 to grow or change and become more advanced, or to make someone or something do this: *The baby develops inside the mother for nine months.* ○ *He's **developing into** a very good tennis player.* **2** MAKE ▷ [T] 🔒 to make something such as a product: *Scientists are developing new drugs all the time.* **3** ILLNESS ▷ [T] 🔒 to start to have something, such as an illness, problem, or feeling: *Shortly after take-off the plane developed engine trouble.* **4** HAPPEN ▷ [I] to start to happen or exist: *Further problems may develop if you do not deal with this now.* **5** FILM ▷ [T] to use special chemicals on a piece of film to make photographs appear: *I need to get my holiday photos developed.* **6** BUILD ▷ [T] to build houses, factories, shops, etc on a piece of land

developed /dɪˈveləpt/ **adj a developed country/nation, etc** 🔒 a country with an advanced level of technology, industry, etc → Opposite **undeveloped**

developer /dɪˈveləpər/ **noun** [C] **1** a person or company that buys land and builds houses, factories, shops, etc **2** a person or company that creates new products, especially software, or services: *a software developer*

developing /dɪˈveləpɪŋ/ **adj** [always before noun] describes a country or region of the world that is poor and has few industries but that has the ability to become more advanced: *the developing countries*

development /dɪˈveləpmənt/ **noun 1** CHANGE ▷ [C, U] 🔒 the process of growing, changing, or becoming more advanced: *The nurse will do some tests to check on your child's development.* ○ *There have been some **major developments** in technology recently.* **2** MAKE ▷ [C, U] 🔒 the process of making something new: *the development of new drugs* **3** START ▷ [U] a situation in which something starts to happen or exist: *Smoking encourages the development of cancer.* **4** BUILD ▷ [U] the process of building new houses, factories, shops, etc, on an area of land: *land suitable for development* **5** BUILDINGS ▷ [C] an area of land with new houses, factories, shops, etc on it: *a new housing development* **6** EVENT ▷ [C] 🔒 something new that happens and changes a situation: *Have there been any more developments since I left?*

7 PHOTOGRAPH ▷ [U] the process of making photographs from a film

deviant /ˈdiːviənt/ **adj** different to what most people think is normal or acceptable, usually relating to sexual behaviour • **deviant noun** [C]

deviate /ˈdiːvieɪt/ **verb** [I] to do something in a different way from what is usual or expected: *The aircraft* ***deviated from*** *its original flight plan.*

D

deviation /ˌdiːviˈeɪʃən/ **noun** [C, U] a difference to what is usual, expected, or accepted by most people: ***sexual deviation***

device /dɪˈvaɪs/ **noun** [C] B2 a piece of equipment that is used for a particular purpose: *A pager is a small, electronic device for sending messages.*

IDIOM **leave someone to their own devices** to leave someone to do what they want to do: *With both parents out at work, the kids were often left to their own devices.*

devil /ˈdevəl/ **noun 1 the Devil** B2 the most powerful evil spirit, according to the Christian and Jewish religions **2** [C] B2 an evil spirit **3** [C] informal someone who behaves badly **4 lucky/poor, etc devil** informal used to describe a person who is lucky/unlucky, etc

IDIOM **speak/talk of the devil** informal something that you say when someone you have been talking about suddenly appears

devilish /ˈdevəlɪʃ/ **adj** evil or bad: *a devilish smile* • **devilishly adv** very: ***devilishly difficult***

devious /ˈdiːviəs/ **adj** clever in a way that is bad and not honest: *a devious mind*

devise /dɪˈvaɪz/ **verb** [T] to design or invent something such as a system, plan, or piece of equipment

devoid /dɪˈvɔɪd/ **adj devoid of sth** formal completely without a quality: *His voice was devoid of emotion.*

devolution /ˌdiːvəˈluːʃən/ **noun** [U] the process of moving power from a central government to local governments

devolve /dɪˈvɒlv/ **verb**

PHRASAL VERB **devolve sth to sb/sth** formal to give power or responsibility to a person or organization at a lower or more local level

devote /dɪˈvəʊt/ **verb**

PHRASAL VERB **devote sth to sb/sth 1** B2 to use time, energy, etc for a particular purpose: *She devotes most of her free time to charity work.* **2** B2 to use a space or area for a particular purpose: [often passive] *Most of the magazine was devoted to coverage of the royal wedding.*

devoted /dɪˈvəʊtɪd/ **adj** B2 loving or caring very much about someone or something: *She's absolutely* ***devoted to*** *her grandchildren.* • **devotedly adv**

devotee /ˌdevəʊˈtiː/ **noun** [C] someone who likes something or someone very much: *a* ***devotee of*** *classical music*

devotion /dɪˈvəʊʃən/ **noun** [U] **1** great love or loyalty for someone or something: *She will always be remembered for her* ***devotion to*** *her family.* **2** strong religious belief or behaviour

devour /dɪˈvaʊəʳ/ **verb** [T] **1** to eat something quickly because you are very hungry **2** to read something quickly and enthusiastically

devout /dɪˈvaʊt/ **adj** extremely religious: *devout Catholic/Muslim* • **devoutly adv**

dew /djuː/ **noun** [U] drops of water that form on surfaces outside during the night

dexterity /dekˈsterəti/ **noun** [U] skill at doing something, especially using your hands: ***manual dexterity***

diabetes /ˌdaɪəˈbiːtiːz/ **noun** [U] a serious medical condition in which your body cannot control the level of sugar in your blood • **diabetic** /ˌdaɪəˈbetɪk/ **adj** • **diabetic** /ˌdaɪəˈbetɪk/ **noun** [C] someone who has diabetes

diabolical /ˌdaɪəˈbɒlɪkəl/ **adj** extremely bad

diagnose /ˈdaɪəgnəʊz/ **verb** [T] to say what is wrong with someone who is sick: [often passive] *She was* ***diagnosed with/as having*** *cancer last year.*

diagnosis /ˌdaɪəgˈnəʊsɪs/ **noun** [C, U] (plural **diagnoses**) a doctor's opinion of what is wrong with someone who is sick

> Word partners for **diagnosis**
>
> **make** a diagnosis • a diagnosis **of** [cancer, heart disease, etc]

diagnostic /ˌdaɪəgˈnɒstɪk/ **adj diagnostic methods/tests, etc** methods/tests, etc that help you discover what is wrong with someone or something

diagonal /daɪˈægənəl/ **adj 1** A diagonal line is straight and sloping and not horizontal or vertical: *a tie with diagonal stripes* **2** going from the top corner of a square to the bottom corner on the other side • **diagonally adv**

diagram /ˈdaɪəgræm/ **noun** [C] B1 a simple picture showing what something looks like or explaining how something works

> Word partners for **diagram**
>
> **draw** a diagram • a diagram **of** sth • **in/on** a diagram

dial[1] /daɪəl/ **noun** [C] **1 TIME/MEASUREMENT** ▷ the round part of a clock, watch, or machine that shows you the time or other measurement **2 BUTTON** ▷ a round part on a piece of equipment such as a television or radio that you turn to operate it, make it louder, etc **3 TELEPHONE** ▷ the ring of holes with numbers that you turn on the front of an old telephone

dial[2] /daɪəl/ **verb** [I, T] (mainly UK **dialling**, **dialled**, US **dialing**, **dialed**) B1 to make a telephone call to a particular number: *Dial 0 for the operator.*

dialect /ˈdaɪəlekt/ **noun** [C, U] a form of a language that people speak in a particular part of a country

ˈdialog ˌbox noun [C] (also UK **dialogue box**) a small box that appears on a computer screen and asks the person using the computer fo information: *When the dialog box appears, click 'OK' to continue.*

dialogue (also US **dialog**) /'daɪəlɒg/ **noun** [C, U] **1** ⓑ the talking in a book, play, or film **2** a formal discussion between countries or groups of people

dial-up /'daɪəlʌp/ **adj** [always before noun] Dial-up computer systems and equipment and Internet services use a telephone connection to reach them. → Compare **broadband**

diameter /daɪ'æmɪtər/ **noun** [C, U] a straight line that goes from one side of a circle to the other side and through the centre, or the length of this line: *The cake was about 30 centimetres in diameter.*

diamond /'daɪəmənd/ **noun 1 STONE** ▷ [C, U] ⓑ a very hard, transparent stone that is extremely valuable and is often used in jewellery: *a diamond ring* **2 SHAPE** ▷ [C] ⓑ a shape with four straight sides of equal length that join to form two large angles and two small angles **3 BASEBALL** ▷ [C] the field where baseball is played **4 diamonds** playing cards with red, diamond shapes on them: *the queen of diamonds*

diamond

diaper /'daɪəpər/ **noun** [C] US (UK **nappy**) a thick piece of paper or cloth worn by a baby on its bottom

diaphragm /'daɪəfræm/ **noun** [C] the large muscle between your lungs and your stomach that moves up and down to move air in and out of the lungs

diarrhoea UK (US **diarrhea**) /ˌdaɪə'rɪə/ **noun** [U] an illness in which your solid waste is more liquid than usual, and comes out of your body more often

diary /'daɪəri/ **noun** [C] **1** ⓐ a book containing spaces for all the days and months of the year, in which you write meetings and other things that you must remember **2** ⓐ a book in which you write each day about your personal thoughts and experiences: *She kept a diary of her trip to Egypt.*

dice¹ /daɪs/ **noun** [C] (plural **dice**) a small object with six equal square sides, each with between one and six spots on it, used in games: *Roll the dice to see who starts the game.*

dice

dice² /daɪs/ **verb** [T] to cut food into small, square pieces: *diced onions*

dicey /'daɪsi/ **adj** informal possibly dangerous or involving a risk

dichotomy /daɪ'kɒtəmi/ **noun** [C] formal the difference between two completely opposite

ideas or things: *the dichotomy between good and evil*

dictate /dɪk'teɪt/ **verb 1** [I, T] to say or read something for someone to write down: *Tony was busy dictating letters to his secretary.* **2** [T] to decide or control what happens: [+ question word] *The weather will dictate where we hold the party.*

PHRASAL VERB **dictate to sb** to tell someone what to do, often in a way that annoys them: *I'm 15 years old – you can't dictate to me any more.*

dictation /dɪk'teɪʃən/ **noun 1** [U] the activity of saying or reading something for someone to write down **2** [C, U] the activity of saying or reading something for students to write down as a test

dictator /dɪk'teɪtər/ **noun** [C] a leader who has complete power in a country and has not been elected by the people • **dictatorial** /ˌdɪktə'tɔːriəl/ **adj**

dictatorship /dɪk'teɪtəʃɪp/ **noun** [C, U] a country or system of government with a dictator as leader

dictionary /'dɪkʃənəri/ **noun** [C] ⓐ a book that contains a list of words in alphabetical order with their meanings explained or written in another language

did /dɪd/ past tense of do

didn't /'dɪdənt/ short for did not

die /daɪ/ **verb** (**dying, died**) **1** ⓐ [I] to stop living: *Many of the refugees died of hunger.* ∘ *She died from brain injuries after a road accident.* **2 be dying for sth; be dying to do sth** informal ⓑ to very much want to have, eat, drink, or do something: *I'm dying for a drink.* **3 to die for** informal If something is to die for, it is extremely good. → See also **die hard²**

❗ Common learner error: **died** or **dead**?

Be careful not to confuse the verb and adjective forms of these words. **Died** is the past of the verb 'to die', which means 'to stop living'. *My cat died last week.*
Dead is an adjective and is used to talk about people or things that are not alive. *My cat is dead.*

PHRASAL VERBS **die away** If something, especially a sound, dies away, it gradually becomes less strong and then stops. • **die down** If something, especially noise or excitement, dies down, it gradually becomes less loud or strong until it stops. • **die off** If a group of plants, animals, or people dies off, all of that group dies over a period of time. • **die out** ⓑ to become more and more rare and then disappear completely: *Dinosaurs died out about 65 million years ago.*

diehard /'daɪhɑːd/ **adj** [always before noun] supporting something in a very determined way and refusing to change: *a diehard fan*

diesel /'diːzəl/ **noun 1** [U] fuel used in the engines of some vehicles, especially buses and trucks **2** [C] a vehicle that uses diesel in its engine

diet¹ /daɪət/ **noun 1** [C, U] ⓑ the type of food

that someone usually eats **2** [C] 🔵 a period when someone eats less food, or only particular types of food, because they want to become thinner, or because they are sick: *No cake for me, thanks – I'm **on a diet**.*

🔲 **Word partners for diet**

be on/go on a diet • follow/stick to a diet • a special/strict diet

---

diet² /ˈdaɪət/ **verb** [I] 🔵 to eat less food so that you become thinner

differ /ˈdɪfər/ **verb** [I] **1** 🔵 to be different: *How does the book **differ from** the film?* ○ *These computers **differ** quite a lot **in** price.* **2** to have a different opinion: *Economists **differ on** the cause of inflation.*

❗ **Common learner error: difference**

When you want to talk about how something or someone has changed, use the preposition **in**.

What is the difference in sales this year?

~~What is the difference of sales this year?~~

🔲 **Word partners for difference**

know/tell the difference • a big/fundamental/important/obvious difference • a difference **between** [sth and sth]

---

difference /ˈdɪfərəns/ **noun 1 WAY** ▷ [C, U] 🔵 the way in which two people or things are not the same: *What's the **difference between** an ape and a monkey?* **2 QUALITY** ▷ [U] the quality of not being the same **3 AMOUNT** ▷ [C, U] 🔵 the amount by which one thing or person is different from another: *There's a big **difference in** age between them.* **4 DISAGREEMENT** ▷ [C] a disagreement or different opinion: *They must try to resolve their differences peacefully.* **5 make a/any difference** 🔵 to have an effect on a situation: *Painting the walls white has made a big difference to this room.*

➕ **Other ways of saying different**

If something is different from what people normally expect, you can say that it is **unusual**:

*Carina – that's quite an **unusual** name.*

The adjective **alternative** is often used to describe something which is different to something else but can be used instead of it:

*The hotel's being renovated, so we're looking for an **alternative** venue.*

If something is very different and separate from other things, you can describe it as **distinct** or **distinctive**:

*She's got really **distinctive** handwriting.*

*The word has three **distinct** meanings.*

The preposition **unlike** is often used to compare people or things that are very different from each other:

*Dan's actually quite nice, **unlike** his father.*

*The furniture was **unlike** anything she had ever seen.*

---

different /ˈdɪfərənt/ **adj 1** 🔵 not the same as someone or something: *Jo's very **different from** her sister, isn't she?* ○ UK *The house is **different to** how I expected it to be.* **2** [always before noun] 🔵 used to talk about separate things or people of the same type: *I had to go to three different shops to find the book she wanted.* • **differently adv** → See also **a whole new ball game**

❗ **Common learner error: different**

Different is usually followed by the preposition **from**. In British English people also use **to**.

Anne is very different to her younger sister.

In American English people also use **than**, but teachers prefer students to use **from**.

---

differential /ˌdɪfəˈrenʃəl/ **noun** [C] a difference between amounts of things: *differentials in pay/wealth*

differentiate /ˌdɪfəˈrenʃieɪt/ **verb 1** [I, T] to understand or notice how two things or people are different from each other: *He can't **differentiate between** blue and green.* **2** [T] to make someone or something different: *We need to **differentiate** ourselves **from** the competition.* • **differentiation** /ˌdɪfərenʃiˈeɪʃən/ **noun** [U]

difficult /ˈdɪfɪkəlt/ **adj 1** 🔵 not easy and needing skill or effort to do or understand: *Japanese is a difficult language for Europeans to learn.* ○ *This game is too **difficult for** me.* ○ [+ to do sth] *It's difficult to think with all that noise.* **2** 🔵 not friendly or easy to deal with: *a difficult teenager* ○ *Please, children, don't be so difficult!*

difficulty /ˈdɪfɪkəlti/ **noun 1** [U] 🔵 problems in doing or understanding something: [+ in + doing sth] *He was **having difficulty** in breathing because of the smoke.* ○ [+ doing sth] *I had **difficulty** finding somewhere to park.* ○ *She had twisted her ankle and was walking **with difficulty**.* **2** [C] 🔵 something that is not easy to deal with: *The company is having some financial **difficulties** at the moment.*

❗ **Common learner error: have difficulty doing something**

You can say you **have difficulty doing** something or **have difficulty in doing** something.

She has difficulty walking.

She has difficulty in walking.

~~I have difficulty to walk.~~

🔲 **Word partners for difficulty**

create/experience/have difficulty • great/serious difficulty • with/without difficulty

---

diffident /ˈdɪfɪdənt/ **adj** shy and without any confidence: *a diffident young man* • **diffidence** /ˈdɪfɪdəns/ **noun** [U]

diffuse /dɪˈfjuːz/ **verb** [I, T] to spread, or to make something spread over a large area, or to a large number of people

dig¹ /dɪg/ **verb** (**digging, dug**) **1** 🔵 [I, T] to break or move the ground with a tool, machine, etc: *Digging the garden is good exercise.* **2 dig a hole,**

➕ Other ways of saying **difficult**

Hard is very often used instead of **difficult** and means exactly the same:
*The exam was really **hard**.*
*It must be **hard** to study with all this noise.*
If something is difficult to understand or do because it has a lot of different parts or stages, you can say that it is **complicated**:
*The instructions were so **complicated** I just couldn't follow them.*
Tricky describes something difficult that needs skill or needs you to be very careful:
*It's quite **tricky** getting the bits to fit together.*
*It's a **tricky** situation – I don't want to upset anyone.*
Fiddly (*UK*) describes something that you do with your hands which is difficult because the parts involved are so small:
*Repairing a watch is very **fiddly**.*
Awkward describes something or someone that is difficult to deal with and could cause problems:
*Dealing with **awkward** customers is just part of the job.*
*Luckily, she didn't ask any **awkward** questions.*
Demanding means 'needing a lot of your time, attention, or effort':
*She has a very **demanding** job.*
*Like most young children, he's very **demanding**.*
A situation or piece of work that is **challenging** is difficult and needs all your skills and determination:
*This has been a **challenging** time for us all.*
*I found the course very **challenging**.*
You say **easier said than done** about something that is impossible or very difficult to do:
*I suppose I should stop smoking but it's **easier said than done**.*

tunnel, etc ⬛ to make a hole in the ground by moving some of the ground or soil away: *They've dug a huge hole in the road.* → See also **dig the/up dirt¹ on sb**

dig

PHRASAL VERBS **dig in/ dig into sth** informal to start eating food: *Dig in, there's plenty for everyone.* • **dig (sth) into sb/sth** to press or push hard into someone or something, or to press something hard into someone or something: *A stone was digging into my heel.* • **dig sb/sth out** to get someone or something out of somewhere by digging • **dig sth out** to find something that you have not

seen or used for a long time: *Mum dug out some old family photographs to show me.* • **dig sth up**
1 TAKE OUT ▷ to take something out of the ground by digging: *Could you dig up a few potatoes for dinner?* **2 BREAK GROUND** ▷ to break the ground or make a hole in the ground with a tool, machine, etc: *They're digging up the road outside my house.* **3 INFORMATION** ▷ to discover information that is secret or forgotten by searching very carefully: *See if you can dig up anything interesting about his past.*

dig² /dɪg/ noun **1 REMARK** ▷ [C] something that you say to annoy or criticize someone: *He was having a dig at me.* **2 PLACE** ▷ [C] a place where people are digging in the ground looking for ancient things to study: *an archaeological dig* **3 PUSH** ▷ [no plural] informal a quick, hard push: *a dig in the ribs*

digerati /ˌdɪdʒəˈrɑːti/ noun [plural] informal people who understand computer technology and the Internet and are able to use them confidently

digest /daɪˈdʒest/ verb [T] **1** to change food in your stomach into substances that your body can use **2** to read and understand new information: *You need to give me time to digest this report.* • **digestible** adj easy to digest

digestion /daɪˈdʒestʃən/ noun [U] the process in which your body changes food in your stomach into substances that it can use

digestive /daɪˈdʒestɪv/ adj [always before noun] relating to digestion: *the **digestive** system*

digger /ˈdɪgər/ noun [C] a large machine that is used to lift and move soil, or a person who digs

Digibox /ˈdɪdʒɪbɒks/ noun [C] trademark a piece of electronic equipment that allows you to watch digital broadcasts (= television sounds and pictures sent as signals in the form of numbers) on an ordinary television

digit /ˈdɪdʒɪt/ noun [C] any of the numbers from 0 to 9, especially when they form part of a longer number: *a seven digit telephone number*

digital /ˈdɪdʒɪtəl/ adj **1 SYSTEM** ▷ 🅰2 using an electronic system that changes sounds or images into signals in the form of numbers before it stores them or sends them: *digital television* **2 CLOCK** ▷ 🅱1 A digital clock or watch shows the time in the form of numbers. **3 COMPUTER** ▷ relating to computer technology, especially the Internet: *the digital world*

digital ˈcamera noun [C] 🅰2 a type of camera that records images that you can use and store on a computer

digitize (also UK **-ise**) /ˈdɪdʒɪtaɪz/ verb [T] to put information into the form of a series of the numbers 0 and 1, usually so that it can be used by a computer • **digitizer** /ˈdɪdʒɪtaɪzər/ noun [C] a piece of software that digitizes information

dignified /ˈdɪgnɪfaɪd/ adj calm, serious, and behaving in a way that makes people respect you: *a quiet, dignified woman*

dignitary /ˈdɪgnɪtəri/ noun [C] someone with an important, official position: *a group of **visiting** dignitaries*

dignity /ˈdɪgnəti/ noun [U] calm and serious

D

behaviour that makes people respect you: *He behaved with great dignity and courage.*

digress /daɪˈgres/ **verb** [I] to start talking about something that is not related to what you were talking about before • **digression** /daɪˈgreʃᵊn/ **noun** [C, U]

digs /dɪgz/ **noun** [plural] UK informal a room in someone's house that you pay rent to live in

dike (also **dyke**) /daɪk/ **noun 1** a wall built to stop water from a sea or river going onto the land **2** UK a passage that has been dug to take water away from fields

dilapidated /dɪˈlæpɪdeɪtɪd/ **adj** A dilapidated building or vehicle is old and in bad condition. • **dilapidation** /dɪˌlæpɪˈdeɪʃᵊn/ **noun** [U]

dilate /daɪˈleɪt/ **verb** [I, T] If a part of your body dilates, or if you dilate it, it becomes wider or more open: *The drug causes your pupils to dilate.* • **dilation** /daɪˈleɪʃᵊn/ **noun** [U]

dilemma /dɪˈlemə/ **noun** [C] 🅱️2 a difficult choice you have to make between two things you could do: *She's still in a dilemma about whether she should go or not.*

> 🖉 Word partners for **dilemma**
>
> face/have/be in a dilemma • sth poses/presents a dilemma • a **moral** dilemma • a dilemma **for** sb • a dilemma **about/over** sth

diligence /ˈdɪlɪdʒᵊns/ **noun** [U] the quality of working hard with care and effort

diligent /ˈdɪlɪdʒᵊnt/ **adj** working hard with care and effort: *a diligent student* • **diligently** adv

dilute /daɪˈluːt/ **verb** [T] to make a liquid thinner or weaker by adding water or another liquid to it • **dilute** adj *dilute solution*

dim¹ /dɪm/ **adj** (**dimmer, dimmest**) **1** not bright or clear: *He could hardly see her in the dim light.* **2** a dim memory/recollection, etc something you remember slightly, but not very well **3** UK informal stupid: *He's nice, but a bit dim.* • **dimly** adv *a dimly lit room*

dim² /dɪm/ **verb** [I, T] (**dimming, dimmed**) to become less bright, or to make something become less bright: *He dimmed the lights and turned up the music.*

dime /daɪm/ **noun** [C] a US or Canadian coin with a value of 10 cents

> IDIOM **a dime a dozen** mainly US informal easy to find and very ordinary: *Millionaires are now a dime a dozen.*

dimension /ˌdaɪˈmenʃᵊn/ **noun** [C] **1** 🅱️2 a particular part of a situation, especially something that affects how you think or feel: *Music has added a new dimension to my life.* **2** 🅱️2 a measurement of the length, width, or height of something

> 🖉 Word partners for **dimension**
>
> add/give a [new/extra, etc] dimension (**to** sth) • an added/extra/new dimension

diminish /dɪˈmɪnɪʃ/ **verb** [I, T] to become less, or to make something become less: *Your pain should diminish gradually after taking these tablets.*

diminutive /dɪˈmɪnjətɪv/ **adj** formal extremely small: *a diminutive figure*

dimple /ˈdɪmpl/ **noun** [C] a small hollow place on your skin, often one that appears on your face when you smile • **dimpled** adj

din /dɪn/ **noun** [no plural] a lot of loud unpleasant noise

dine /daɪn/ **verb** [I] formal to eat dinner: *O Saturday we dined with friends.*

PHRASAL VERB **dine out** formal to eat your evenin meal in a restaurant

diner /ˈdaɪnəʳ/ **noun** [C] **1** someone who is eatin in a restaurant **2** mainly US a small, informa restaurant

dinghy /ˈdɪŋi/ **noun** [C] a small boat: *a inflatable dinghy*

dingy /ˈdɪndʒi/ **adj** dirty and not bright: *a ding basement*

dining hall **noun** [C, usually singular] a larg room in a school or other building, where man people can eat at the same time

dining room **noun** [C] 🅐1 a room where yo eat your meals in a house or hotel

dinner /ˈdɪnəʳ/ **noun** [C, U] 🅐1 the main meal c the day that people usually eat in the evenin *What's for dinner tonight?*

> 🖉 Word partners for **dinner**
>
> eat/have dinner • have sth **for** dinner

dinner jacket **noun** [C] a black or white jacket that a man wears on a very formal occasion

dinner jacket *UK*, tuxedo *US*

dinosaur /ˈdaɪnəsɔːʳ/ **noun** [C] 🅐2 a very large animal that used to live millions of years ago

dinosaur

diocese /ˈdaɪəsɪs/ **noun** [C] the area controlled by a bishop (= an important Christian official)

dip¹ /dɪp/ **noun 1** FOOD ▷ [C, U] a thick sauce tha you can put pieces of food into before you e them: *a blue cheese dip* **2** SURFACE ▷ [C] a lowe area on a surface: *a sudden dip in the roa* **3** AMOUNT ▷ [C] a sudden fall in the level c amount of something: *a dip in profits* **4** SWIM ▷ [C] informal a short swim: *Let's have a quick dip i the pool before breakfast.*

dip² /dɪp/ **verb** (**dipping, dipped**) **1** [T] 🅱️2 to p something into a liquid for a short time: *She dipped the brush into the paint.* **2** [I] ⑫ to become lower in level or amount: *The number of students taking sciences has dipped sharply.*

PHRASAL VERB **dip into sth 1** UK to read small parts of a book or magazine: *It's the sort of book you can dip into now and then.* **2** to spend part of a supply of money that you have been keeping: *I had to dip into my savings to pay for the repairs.*

diphtheria /dɪpˈθɪəriə/ **noun** [U] a very serious disease of the throat

diphthong /ˈdɪfθɒŋ/ **noun** [C] a sound made by two vowels that are said together

diploma /dɪˈpləʊmə/ **noun** [C] ⑫ a qualification from a school, college, or university, or an official document showing that someone has completed a course of study: *a diploma in art and design*

diplomacy /dɪˈpləʊməsi/ **noun** [U] **1** the job of dealing with the relationships between governments: *international diplomacy* **2** skill in dealing with people well and not upsetting them: *She showed great tact and diplomacy in the meeting.*

diplomat /ˈdɪpləmæt/ **noun** [C] ⑫ someone whose job is to live in another country and to keep a good relationship between their government and that country's government

diplomatic /ˌdɪpləˈmætɪk/ **adj 1** [always before noun] relating to diplomacy or diplomats: *diplomatic relations* **2** good at dealing with people without upsetting them: *That's a very diplomatic answer.* • **diplomatically** adv

dire /daɪər/ **adj** very serious or bad: *He's in dire need of help.*

direct¹ /dɪˈrekt/, /daɪˈrekt/ **adj 1 STRAIGHT** ▷ ⑪ going straight from one place to another without turning or stopping: *We went by the most direct route.* **2 NOTHING BETWEEN** ▷ ⑫ with no other person or thing involved or between: *There is a direct link between smoking and cancer.* **3 CLEAR** ▷ saying clearly and honestly what you think: *a direct answer* → Opposite **indirect**

direct² /dɪˈrekt/, /daɪˈrekt/ **adv** going straight from one place to another without turning or stopping: *Several airlines now fly direct to Vancouver.*

direct³ /dɪˈrekt/, /daɪˈrekt/ **verb 1 FILM/PLAY** ▷ [T] ⑪ to tell the actors in a film or play what to do: *a film directed by Alfred Hitchcock* **2 direct sth against/at/towards, etc sb/sth** to aim something at someone or something: *The demonstrators' anger was directed at the police.* **3 ROUTE** ▷ [T] ⑪ to show or tell someone how to get to a place: *Can you direct me to the manager's office please?* **4 ORGANIZE** ▷ [T] to organize and control the way something is done: *He directed the building of the new art gallery.* **5 direct sb to do sth** formal to officially order someone to do something: *They directed us not to discuss the matter.*

direct 'debit noun [C, U] an arrangement that allows an organization to take money from your

bank account at regular times to pay for goods or services: *I pay my council tax by direct debit.*

direction /dɪˈrekʃən/ **noun 1 WAY** ▷ [C] ⑪ the way that someone or something is going or facing: *The car sped away in the direction of the airport.* ○ *I think we're going in the wrong direction.* **2 in sb's direction** ⑫ towards someone: *She keeps looking in my direction.* **3 DEVELOPMENT** ▷ [C] the way that someone or something changes or develops: *Our careers have gone in very different directions.* **4 CONTROL** ▷ [U] control or instructions: *Under his direction the company has doubled its profits.* **5 PURPOSE** ▷ [U] the ability to know what you want to do: *According to his teachers, he lacks direction.*

> ✏️ Word partners for **direction**
>
> change direction • in the opposite/other direction • in the right/wrong direction • in the direction of sth • from all/in all directions

directions /dɪˈrekʃənz/ **noun** [plural] ⑫ instructions that tell you how to get to a place, or how to do something: *We stopped to ask for directions.* ○ *Just follow the directions on the label.*

directive /dɪˈrektɪv/ **noun** [C] formal an official instruction: *The government has issued new directives on food hygiene.*

directly /dɪˈrektli/ **adv 1** ⑪ with no other person or thing involved or between: *Why don't you speak to him directly?* **2 directly after/ behind/opposite, etc** exactly or immediately after/behind/opposite, etc: *She was sitting directly opposite me.* **3** ⑫ clearly and honestly: *Let me answer that question directly.*

directness /dɪˈrektnəs/ **noun** [U] the quality of being clear and honest in your speech or behaviour: *He liked her directness and simplicity.*

direct 'object noun [C] the direct object of a transitive verb is the person or thing that is affected by the action of the verb. In the sentence 'I bought a new car yesterday.', 'a new car' is the direct object. → Compare **indirect object**

director /dɪˈrektər/ **noun** [C] **1** ⑪ an important manager in an organization or company: *Meet the new sales director.* **2** ⑪ someone who tells the actors in a film or play what to do: *the famous film director, Alfred Hitchcock* → See also **funeral director, managing director**

directorate /dɪˈrektərət/ **noun** [C] a part of a government or other organization with responsibility for a particular activity

directory /dɪˈrektəri/ **noun** [C] **1** a book or list of names, numbers, or other facts → See also **telephone directory 2 (file directory)** a place on a computer for putting files and folders together

dirt¹ /dɜːt/ **noun** [U] **1** ⑪ an unpleasant substance that makes something not clean: *There's dirt all over the floor.* **2** soil or rough ground: *a dirt road/track*

D

IDIOM **dig the/up dirt on sb** informal to try to discover bad things about someone to stop other people admiring them

dirt² /dɜːt/ **adv dirt cheap/poor** extremely cheap/poor

dirty¹ /ˈdɜːti/ **adj 1 NOT CLEAN** ▷ 🅐 not clean: *dirty clothes* ∘ *dirty dishes* **2 OFFENSIVE** ▷ talking about sex in a way that some people find offensive: *dirty books/jokes* **3 DISHONEST** ▷ dishonest or unfair: *a dirty business* → See also **do sb's dirty work²** **4 HARMFUL** ▷ containing dangerous substances that may be harmful to the environment: *dirty air*

➕ Other ways of saying **dirty**

If something is extremely dirty, you can say it is **filthy**:
*Wash your hands – they're **filthy**!*

If someone or something looks dirty and untidy, you can say that they are **scruffy** or **messy**:
*He's the typical **scruffy** student.*
*Ben's bedroom is always really **messy**.*

If something is covered in dirt and needs washing, the adjectives **grimy** and **grubby** are often used:
*Don't wipe your **grimy** hands on that clean towel!*
*He was wearing an old pair of jeans and a **grubby** T-shirt.*

The adjective **soiled** is sometimes used to describe material that is dirty:
Soiled tablecloths should be soaked in detergent.

If a place is extremely dirty and unpleasant, the adjective **squalid** is sometimes used:
*The prisoners lived in **squalid** conditions.*
---

dirty² /ˈdɜːti/ **verb** [T] to make something dirty

dis- /dɪs-/ **prefix** not or the opposite of: *dishonest* ∘ *disbelief* ∘ *to disagree*

disability /ˌdɪsəˈbɪləti/ **noun** [C, U] 🅑 an illness, injury, or condition that makes it difficult for someone to do the things that other people do

disable /dɪˈseɪbl/ **verb** [T] **1** If someone is disabled by an illness or injury, it makes it difficult for them to live in the way that most other people do: [often passive] *Some children were permanently disabled by the bomb.* **2** to stop a piece of equipment from working: *The thieves must have disabled the alarm system.*

disabled /dɪˈseɪbld/ **adj** 🅑 having an illness, injury, or condition that makes it difficult to do the things that other people do: *They are demanding equal rights for **the disabled**.*

🖉 Word partners for **disadvantage**

have/face a disadvantage • a **big/the main/a major/a serious** disadvantage • a disadvantage **of/to** (doing) sth • a disadvantage **for** sb • the **advantages** and disadvantages (of sth)
---

disadvantage /ˌdɪsədˈvɑːntɪdʒ/ **noun 1** 🅑 [C] something that makes a situation more difficult, or makes you less likely to succeed: *One*

disadvantage of living in the country is th lack of public transport. **2 at a disadvantag** having problems that other people do not hav *Being shy puts him at a disadvantage.*

disadvantaged /ˌdɪsədˈvɑːntɪdʒd/ **adj** Disa● vantaged people are poor and do not hav many opportunities: *disadvantaged children*

disaffected /ˌdɪsəˈfektɪd/ **adj** disappointed wi● someone or something and not supportin● them as you did before: *disaffected vote●* • **disaffection** /ˌdɪsəˈfekʃən/ **noun** [U]

disagree /ˌdɪsəˈɡriː/ **verb** [I] (**disagreeing, di● agreed**) 🅑 to have a different opinion fro● someone else about something: *I **disagree** wit● most of what he said.* ∘ *Experts **disagree** abou● on the causes of the disease.*

disagreeable /ˌdɪsəˈɡriːəbl/ **adj** formal unplea● ant: *a disagreeable old man*

disagreement /ˌdɪsəˈɡriːmənt/ **noun** [C, U] 🅑 situation in which people have a differen● opinion about something or have an argumen● *They **had** a **disagreement** about/over mone● ∘ There is a lot of **disagreement among** docto● on this matter.*

disallow /ˌdɪsəˈlaʊ/ **verb** [T] to officially refuse t● accept something because the rules have bee● broken: *The goal was disallowed by the referee.*

disappear /ˌdɪsəˈpɪər/ **verb** [I] **1 NOT SEE** ▷ 🅑 ● become impossible to see: *She watched hi● disappear into the crowd.* **2 GO** ▷ 🅑 to sudden● go somewhere and become impossible to fin● *Her husband disappeared in 1991.* **3 STO● EXISTING** ▷ 🅑 to stop existing: *These flower● are disappearing from our countryside.* • **disa● pearance** /ˌdɪsəˈpɪərəns/ **noun** [C, U] 🅑 *Police a● investigating the girl's disappearance.* → See als● **disappear/vanish into thin air¹**

disappoint /ˌdɪsəˈpɔɪnt/ **verb** [T] 🅑 to mak● someone feel unhappy because someone ● something was not as good as they ha● expected: *We don't want to disappoint the fans.*

➕ Other ways of saying **disappointed**

If someone feels very disappointed about something that has happened, you can use the adjectives **disheartened** or, in informal situations, (UK) **gutted**:
*He was very **disheartened** by the results*
*Nick's absolutely **gutted** that he's been dropped from the team.*

If a person disappoints someone by not doing what they agreed to do, then the phrasal verb **let down** is sometimes used:
*John had promised to go but he **let** me **down** at the last minute.*

A situation which makes someone feel disappointed is often described as a **letdown**:
After all that planning the party was a bit of a letdown.

An **anticlimax** is a disappointing experience, often one that you thought would be exciting before it happened or one that comes after a more exciting experience:
*After so much preparation, the party itself was a bit of an **anticlimax**.*
---

disappointed /ˌdɪsəˈpɔɪntɪd/ **adj** ⬛ unhappy because someone or something was not as good as you hoped or expected, or because something did not happen: [+ (that)] *I was very disappointed that he didn't come.* ∘ *I'm really disappointed in you.*

disappointing /ˌdɪsəˈpɔɪntɪŋ/ **adj** ⬛ making you feel disappointed: *a disappointing performance/result* • **disappointingly adv** *a disappointingly small audience*

disappointment /ˌdɪsəˈpɔɪntmənt/ **noun 1** [U] ⬛ the feeling of being disappointed: *She couldn't hide her disappointment when she lost.* **2** [C] ⬛ someone or something that disappoints you: *I'm sorry I'm such a disappointment to you.*

disapproval /ˌdɪsəˈpruːvəl/ **noun** [U] the opinion that someone or something is bad or wrong *She could sense their disapproval of her suggestion.*

disapprove /ˌdɪsəˈpruːv/ **verb** [I] ⬛ to think that someone or something is bad or wrong: *Her family disapproved of the marriage.* • **disapproving adj** showing that you think someone or something is bad or wrong: *a disapproving look*

disarm /dɪˈsɑːm/ **verb 1** [I, T] to give up your weapons, or to take away someone else's weapons: *Both sides have agreed to disarm.* **2** [T] to make someone feel less angry: *His smile disarmed her.*

disarmament /dɪˈsɑːməmənt/ **noun** [U] a process in which a country or group gets rid of some or all of its weapons: *nuclear disarmament*

disarming /dɪˈsɑːmɪŋ/ **adj** behaving in a way that stops people feeling angry with you or criticizing you: *a disarming smile*

disarray /ˌdɪsərˈeɪ/ **noun** [U] a situation in which something is untidy and not organized: *The house was in complete disarray.*

disaster /dɪˈzɑːstər/ **noun 1** DAMAGE ▷ [C] ⬛ something that causes a lot of harm or damage: *floods and other natural disasters* **2** FAILURE ▷ [C] ⬛ a failure or something that has a very bad result: *His idea was a total disaster.* **3** BAD SITUATION ▷ [U] an extremely bad situation: *The holiday ended in disaster.*

> 🗹 Word partners for **disaster**
>
> bring/cause/prevent disaster • disaster happens/strikes • a complete/major/terrible/unmitigated disaster • a natural disaster

disastrous /dɪˈzɑːstrəs/ **adj** extremely bad: *disastrous consequences* ∘ *a disastrous week*

disband /dɪsˈbænd/ **verb** [I, T] formal to stop working together as a group, or to stop a group from working together

disbelief /ˌdɪsbɪˈliːf/ **noun** [U] the feeling of not being able to believe that something is true or real: *She shook her head in disbelief.*

disbelieve /ˌdɪsbɪˈliːv/ **verb** [T] to not believe someone or something

disc (also US **disk**) /dɪsk/ **noun** [C] **1** SHAPE ▷ ⬛ a flat, round shape or object **2** RECORDING ▷ ⬛ a CD or DVD **3** BACK ▷ a piece of cartilage (= strong material in the body) between the bones in your back → See also **compact disc**

discard /dɪˈskɑːd/ **verb** [T] to throw something away: *discarded food wrappers*

discern /dɪˈsɜːn/ **verb** [T] formal to see or recognize something • **discernible adj** *There was no discernible difference between them.*

discerning /dɪˈsɜːnɪŋ/ **adj** having or showing good judgment, especially about style and quality: *a discerning customer/reader*

discharge¹ /dɪsˈtʃɑːdʒ/ **verb** [T] **1** to allow someone to leave a hospital or prison, or to order or allow someone to leave an organization such as the army: [often passive] *She was discharged from the army yesterday.* **2** If a liquid or gas is discharged from something, it comes out of it.

discharge² /ˈdɪstʃɑːdʒ/ **noun** [C, U] **1** LEAVE ▷ the time when someone is officially allowed or ordered to leave somewhere such as a prison, hospital, or the army **2** COME OUT ▷ a situation in which a liquid or gas comes out of something: *the discharge of carbon dioxide* **3** SUBSTANCE ▷ a liquid or gas that comes out of something

disciple /dɪˈsaɪpl/ **noun** [C] someone who follows the ideas and teaching of someone, especially of a religious leader

disciplinarian /ˌdɪsəplɪˈneəriən/ **noun** [C] someone who is very strict and gives punishments when people break rules

disciplinary /ˌdɪsəˈplɪnəri/ ⑤ /ˈdɪsəplɪneri/ **adj** [always before noun] relating to punishment for someone who has broken rules: *disciplinary action*

discipline¹ /ˈdɪsəplɪn/ **noun 1** CONTROL ▷ [U] ⬛ the control of people's behaviour using rules and punishments: *There should be better discipline in schools.* **2** SELF CONTROL ▷ [U] the ability to control your own behaviour carefully: *I don't have enough discipline to save money.* **3** KNOWLEDGE ▷ [C] formal a particular subject of study: *the scientific disciplines* → See also **self-discipline**

> 🗹 Word partners for **discipline**
>
> enforce/establish/restore discipline • firm/harsh/rigorous discipline • lax/poor discipline

discipline² /ˈdɪsəplɪn/ **verb** [T] **1** to punish someone: [often passive] *He was disciplined for missing a training session.* **2** to teach someone to behave in a controlled way: [often reflexive] *You have to learn to discipline yourself.*

disciplined /ˈdɪsəplɪnd/ **adj** behaving in a very controlled way: *the most disciplined army in the world*

disc jockey noun [C] (also **DJ**) ⬛ someone who plays music on the radio or at discos

disclaim /dɪsˈkleɪm/ **verb** [T] formal to say that you know nothing about something, or are not responsible for something: *The terrorists disclaimed responsibility for the bomb.*

disclaimer /dɪsˈkleɪmər/ **noun** [C] a statement in which someone officially says that they are not responsible for something

disclose /dɪsˈkləʊz/ **verb** [T] formal to give new or secret information to someone: *He refused to disclose details of the report.*

disclosure /dɪsˈkləʊʒər/ **noun** [C, U] the act of giving people new or secret information

disco /ˈdɪskəʊ/ **noun** [C] 🅐🅩 a place or event where people dance to pop music

discoloured UK (US **discolored**) /dɪsˈkʌləd/ **adj** If something is discoloured, it has become a less attractive colour than it was originally: *discoloured teeth*

discomfort /dɪsˈkʌmfət/ **noun 1 PAIN** ▷ [U] 🅑🅩 slight pain: *You may feel some discomfort for a few days.* **2 MENTAL FEELING** ▷ [U] the feeling of being slightly embarrassed or anxious **3 SITUATION** ▷ [C, U] a physically uncomfortable situation

disconcert /ˌdɪskənˈsɜːt/ **verb** [T] to make someone feel confused or anxious: [often passive] *She was disconcerted by his questions.*

disconcerting /ˌdɪskənˈsɜːtɪŋ/ **adj** making you feel confused or anxious: *a disconcerting silence* • **disconcertingly adv**

disconnect /ˌdɪskəˈnekt/ **verb** [T] **1** to separate two things that are joined or connected, especially a piece of equipment and a power supply: *Switch off the machine before disconnecting it from the power supply.* **2** to stop being connected to the Internet

disconnected /ˌdɪskəˈnektɪd/ **adj** not joined in any way: *disconnected thoughts*

discontent /ˌdɪskənˈtent/ **noun** [U] unhappiness about a situation: *There is growing discontent with this government.* • **discontented adj**

discontinue /ˌdɪskənˈtɪnjuː/ **verb** [T] (**discontinuing, discontinued**) to stop producing or providing something such as a product or service: [often passive] *I'm afraid this model has been discontinued.*

discord /ˈdɪskɔːd/ **noun** [U] disagreement between people

discount¹ /ˈdɪskaʊnt/ **noun** [C, U] 🅐🅩 a reduction in price: *They offer a 10 percent discount on rail travel for students.*

discount² /dɪˈskaʊnt/ **verb** [T] **1** to ignore something because you do not believe that it is true or that it will happen: *You shouldn't discount the possibility of him coming back.* **2** to reduce the price of something: *discounted goods/rates*

discount store noun [C] a shop which sells products at cheap prices

discourage /dɪˈskʌrɪdʒ/ **verb 1 discourage sb from doing sth** 🅑🅩 to try to persuade someone not to do something: *a campaign to discourage people from smoking* **2** [T] to try to prevent something from happening: *a campaign to discourage smoking* **3** [T] 🅑🅩 to make someone less confident or enthusiastic about something: *I didn't mean to discourage her.* • **discouragement noun** [U] → Opposite **encourage**

discouraged /dɪˈskʌrɪdʒd/ **adj** having lost your confidence or enthusiasm for something

discouraging /dɪˈskʌrɪdʒɪŋ/ **adj** making you feel less enthusiastic or confident about something: *discouraging results*

discover /dɪˈskʌvər/ **verb** [T] **1 FIND** ▷ 🅑🅐 to find something: *The body was discovered in a ditch.* **2 FIRST** ▷ 🅑🅐 to be the first person to find something important: *Who discovered America?* **3 GET INFORMATION** ▷ 🅑🅐 to get information about something for the first time: [+ (that)] *Sh discovered that he had been married three time before.* ◦ [+ question word] *Have they discovere what was causing your headaches?*

discoverer /dɪˈskʌvərər/ **noun** [C] someone wh is the first person to find something important

discovery /dɪˈskʌvəri/ **noun 1** [C, U] 🅑🅩 a occasion when someone discovers something *the discovery of bones in the garden* ◦ *Scientist have made some important discoveries abou genetics recently.* **2** [C] something or someon that is discovered

> 🗹 **Word partners for discovery**
> make a discovery • a chance/new discovery
> • the discovery of sth

discredit /dɪˈskredɪt/ **verb** [T] to make someon or something appear bad and lose the respect o other people: *They're always looking for ways t discredit her.*

discreet /dɪˈskriːt/ **adj** careful not to caus embarrassment or attract too much attention especially by keeping something secret: *Can trust you to be discreet?* → Opposite **indiscree** • **discreetly adv**

discrepancy /dɪˈskrepənsi/ **noun** [C, U] a differ ence between two things that should be th same: *There is a slight discrepancy between th two statements.*

discrete /dɪˈskriːt/ **adj** separate and different: *word that has two discrete meanings*

discretion /dɪˈskreʃən/ **noun** [U] **1** care not t cause embarrassment or attract too muc attention, especially by keeping somethin secret: *You can rely on my discretion.* → Opposit **indiscretion (indiscreet) 2** the right to decid something: *Students can be expelled at th discretion of* the head teacher (= *if the hea teacher decides it*).

discretionary /dɪˈskreʃənəri/ **adj** decided b officials and not fixed by rules: *Judges hav great discretionary powers.*

discriminate /dɪˈskrɪmɪneɪt/ **verb** [I] **1** to trea someone unfairly because of their sex, race religion, etc: *The company was accused o discriminating against people on the basis c age.* **2** to notice a difference between two things *Police dogs are very good at discriminatin between different smells.*

discriminating /dɪˈskrɪmɪneɪtɪŋ/ **adj** good a judging what is good quality: *a discriminatin shopper*

discrimination /dɪˌskrɪmɪˈneɪʃən/ **noun** [U unfair treatment of someone because of thei sex, race, religion, etc: *racial/sex discriminatio* ◦ *discrimination against older workers*

> 🗹 **Word partners for discrimination**
> face/suffer discrimination • age/racial/sex
> discrimination • discrimination against sb

discus /'dɪskəs/ **noun** [C] a round, flat, heavy object that people throw as a sport

discuss /dɪ'skʌs/ **verb** [T] **A2** to talk about something with someone and tell each other your ideas or opinions: *Have you discussed this matter with anyone else?*

> **! Common learner error: discuss**
>
> **Discuss** is not followed by a preposition.
> *We discussed the plans for the wedding.*
> ~~We discussed about the plans for the wedding.~~
> You can **discuss something with someone**.
> *Can I discuss this report with you?*

discussion /dɪ'skʌʃ°n/ **noun** [C, U] **B1** a conversation in which people talk about something and tell each other their ideas or opinions: *They were **having** a **discussion about** football.* ∘ *Several ideas are still **under discussion** (= being discussed).*

> **✓ Word partners for discussion**
>
> have/hold a discussion • a heated/lengthy discussion • a discussion about sth • be under discussion

disdain /dɪs'deɪn/ **noun** [U] a feeling of dislike towards someone or something and the opinion that they do not deserve any respect: *His **disdain for** politicians is obvious.* • **disdainful adj** *disdainful remarks* • **disdainfully adv**

disease /dɪ'ziːz/ **noun** [C, U] **B1** an illness caused by an infection or by a failure of health and not by an accident: *heart disease* ∘ *an infectious disease* • **diseased adj** affected by a disease: *a diseased lung*

> **✓ Word partners for disease**
>
> be affected by/have/suffer from a disease • contract/develop a disease • cure/detect/diagnose/treat a disease • a chronic/deadly/hereditary/infectious disease

disembark /ˌdɪsɪm'bɑːk/ **verb** [I] formal to leave a ship, boat, or aircraft: *All passengers must disembark in Vancouver.* • **disembarkation** /ˌdɪsɪmbɑː'keɪʃ°n/ **noun** [U]

disembodied /ˌdɪsɪm'bɒdid/ **adj** seeming not to have a body or not to be connected to a body: *a disembodied voice*

disenchanted /ˌdɪsɪn'tʃɑːntɪd/ **adj** disappointed with something that you thought was good in the past: *He became **disenchanted with** politics.* • **disenchantment noun** [U]

disengage /ˌdɪsɪn'geɪdʒ/ **verb** [I, T] to become separated from something, or to make two things become separate from each other: *He gently disengaged his hand from hers.*

disentangle /ˌdɪsɪn'tæŋgl/ **verb** [T] **1** to separate someone or something that is connected to something else in a complicated way: *He disentangled himself from her arms.* **2** to separate things such as pieces of string, hair, or wire that have become twisted together

disfigure /dɪs'fɪgər/ **verb** [T] to spoil someone's or something's appearance: [often passive] *Her face was disfigured by a huge scar.*

disgrace¹ /dɪs'greɪs/ **verb** [T] to make people stop respecting you or your family, team, etc by doing something very bad

disgrace² /dɪs'greɪs/ **noun** [U] **1** **B2** a situation in which someone does something very bad that makes people stop respecting them or their family, team, etc: *They were sent home **in disgrace**.* **2 be a disgrace** **B2** to be very bad: [+ that] *It's a disgrace that money is being wasted like this.* **3 be a disgrace to sb/sth** to be so bad or unacceptable that you make people stop respecting a particular group, activity, etc: *You are a disgrace to your profession.*

disgraced /dɪs'greɪst/ **adj** A disgraced person has lost people's respect because they have done something very bad: *a disgraced politician*

disgraceful /dɪs'greɪsf°l/ **adj** very bad: *disgraceful behaviour* • **disgracefully adv**

disgruntled /dɪs'grʌntld/ **adj** angry and upset: *Disgruntled workers have decided to go on strike.*

disguise¹ /dɪs'gaɪz/ **noun** [C, U] **B2** clothes and other things that you wear to change the way you look so that people cannot recognize you: *She usually goes out **in disguise** to avoid being bothered by the public.* → See also a **blessing** in disguise

disguise² /dɪs'gaɪz/ **verb** **1 disguise yourself/your voice, etc** **B2** to change your appearance/voice, etc so that people cannot recognize you: *He managed to escape by **disguising** himself **as** a woman.* **2 be disguised as sb/sth** **B2** to be wearing clothes and other things that make you look like someone or something else **3** [T] to hide something such as a feeling or opinion: *She couldn't disguise her disappointment.*

disgust¹ /dɪs'gʌst/ **noun** [U] a very strong feeling of dislike or disapproval: *She walked out **in disgust**.*

disgust² /dɪs'gʌst/ **verb** [T] If something disgusts you, it makes you feel extreme dislike or disapproval: *These pictures disgust me.*

disgusted /dɪs'gʌstɪd/ **adj** feeling extreme dislike or disapproval of something: *I'm totally **disgusted with** your behaviour.*

disgusting /dɪs'gʌstɪŋ/ **adj** **B1** extremely unpleasant: *What's that disgusting smell?*

dish¹ /dɪʃ/ **noun** [C] **1** **A2** a curved container for eating or serving food from: *a baking/serving dish* **2** **A2** food that is prepared in a particular way as part of a meal: *a chicken/vegetarian dish* **3 the dishes** **A2** dirty plates, bowls, and other objects for cooking or eating food: *Who's going to **wash the dishes**?*

dish² /dɪʃ/ **verb**

> PHRASAL VERB **dish sth out** informal to give or say things to people without thinking about them carefully

dishcloth /'dɪʃklɒθ/ **noun** [C] a cloth used for washing dirty dishes

disheartened /dɪsˈhɑːtᵊnd/ **adj** disappointed or without hope: *She was very disheartened by the results of the test.*

disheartening /dɪsˈhɑːtᵊnɪŋ/ **adj** making you feel disappointed or without hope: *a disheartening experience*

dishevelled mainly UK (US **disheveled**) /dɪˈʃevᵊld/ **adj** very untidy: *dishevelled hair*

dishonest /dɪˈsɒnɪst/ **adj** ⑫ not honest and likely to lie or do something illegal • **dishonestly adv** • **dishonesty noun** [U] ⑫ behaviour that is not honest

dishonour¹ UK (US **dishonor**) /dɪˈsɒnər/ **noun** [U] If you bring dishonour on yourself, your family. etc, people stop respecting you because you have done something bad. • **dishonourable adj** bad or not deserving respect: *dishonourable conduct*

dishonour² UK (US **dishonor**) /dɪˈsɒnər/ **verb** [T] **1** to show no respect for someone or something by behaving badly: *He felt that he had dishonoured his country.* **2** to refuse to accept or pay a cheque or a bill (= amount charged)

dish soap **noun** [U] US (UK **washing-up liquid**) a thick liquid soap used to wash pans, plates, knives, and forks etc.

dishtowel /ˈdɪʃtaʊəl/ **noun** [C] US (UK **tea towel**) a cloth that is used for drying plates, dishes, etc

dishwasher /ˈdɪʃˌwɒʃər/ **noun** [C] ⑪ a machine that washes plates, glasses and other kitchen equipment: *I'll load the dishwasher.* → See colour picture **The Kitchen** on page Centre 2

disillusion /ˌdɪsɪˈluːʒᵊn/ **verb** [T] to cause someone to discover that something they believed is not true

disillusioned /ˌdɪsɪˈluːʒᵊnd/ **adj** feeling disappointed because something is not as good as you thought it was: *She says she's disillusioned with the music business.*

disillusionment /ˌdɪsɪˈluːʒᵊnmənt/ **noun** [U] (also **disillusion**) the disappointment someone feels when they discover something is not as good as they thought it was: *There's growing disillusionment with the government.*

disinfect /ˌdɪsɪnˈfekt/ **verb** [T] to clean something with a chemical that destroys bacteria

disinfectant /ˌdɪsɪnˈfektənt/ **noun** [C, U] a chemical substance that destroys bacteria

disintegrate /dɪˈsɪntɪɡreɪt/ **verb** [I] **1** to break into a lot of small pieces **2** to become much worse: *The situation is disintegrating into total chaos.* • **disintegration** /dɪˌsɪntɪˈɡreɪʃᵊn/ **noun** [U]

disinterested /dɪˈsɪntrəstɪd/ **adj** not involved in a situation and so able to judge it without supporting a particular side: *a disinterested observer*

disjointed /dɪsˈdʒɔɪntɪd/ **adj** having words or ideas that are not in a clear order: *a disjointed conversation*

disk /dɪsk/ **noun** [C] **1** another US spelling of disc **2** ⑪ a piece of computer equipment that records and stores information electronically: *How much disk space is there?* → See colour picture **The Office** on page Centre 5 → See also **floppy disk, hard disk**

☑ Word partners for **disk**

save/write sth to disk • on a disk • disk space

disk drive **noun** [C] the part of a computer that allows the person using the computer to store and read information from a disk

diskette /dɪˈsket/ **noun** [C] a small, flat, plastic object that you put in your computer to record and store information electronically

dislike¹ /dɪˈslaɪk/ **verb** [T] ⑪ to not like someone or something: *Why do you dislike her so much?* ◦ [+ doing sth] *I dislike ironing intensely.*

dislike² /dɪˈslaɪk/ **noun** [C, U] ⑫ the feeling of not liking someone or something: *a dislike of cold weather* ◦ *I took an instant dislike to her* (= disliked her immediately).

dislocate /ˈdɪsləʊkeɪt/ **verb** [T] If you dislocate a part of your body, the bones move away from their correct position: *I think you've dislocated your shoulder.* ◦ *a dislocated hip* • **dislocation** /ˌdɪsləʊˈkeɪʃᵊn/ **noun** [U]

dislodge /dɪˈslɒdʒ/ **verb** [T] to move something away from a fixed position

disloyal /dɪˈslɔɪəl/ **adj** not loyal or not supporting someone who you should support: *I don't want to be disloyal to my friend.* • **disloyalty noun** [U] *They accused her of disloyalty.*

dismal /ˈdɪzməl/ **adj** very bad or unpleasant and making you feel unhappy: *What dismal weather.* ◦ *That was a dismal performance* • **dismally adv** *I tried to cheer her up, but failed dismally* (= completely failed).

dismantle /dɪˈsmæntl/ **verb** [T] **1** to take something apart so that it is in several pieces: *He's specially trained to dismantle bombs.* **2** to get rid of a system or organization

dismay /dɪˈsmeɪ/ **noun** [U] a feeling of unhappiness and disappointment: *To our dismay, it started raining.*

dismayed /dɪˈsmeɪd/ **adj** unhappy and disappointed: [+ to do sth] *I was dismayed to discover that he'd lied to me.*

dismember /dɪˈsmembər/ **verb** [T] to cut the arms and legs off the body of a person or animal: *a dismembered body*

dismiss /dɪˈsmɪs/ **verb** [T] **1 NOT CONSIDER** ▷ to refuse to consider an idea or opinion: *The committee dismissed the idea as rubbish.* **2 MAKE LEAVE** ▷ to officially make someone leave their job: [often passive] *Anyone who breaks company rules will be dismissed.* **3 ALLOW TO LEAVE** ▷ to give someone official permission to leave: *The bell rang and the teacher dismissed the class.*

dismissal /dɪˈsmɪsᵊl/ **noun 1** [U] the act of refusing to consider an idea or opinion **2** [C, U] an occasion when an employer officially makes someone leave their job

dismissive /dɪˈsmɪsɪv/ **adj** treating something as if it is not important: *He's so dismissive of all my suggestions.* • **dismissively adv**

dismount /dɪˈsmaʊnt/ **verb** [I] formal to get off a horse or bicycle

disobedience /ˌdɪsəʊˈbiːdiəns/ **noun** [U] beha

viour in which someone refuses to do what someone in authority tells them to do

isobedient /ˌdɪsəʊˈbiːdiənt/ **adj** refusing to do what someone in authority tells you to do: *a disobedient child*

isobey /ˌdɪsəʊˈbeɪ/ **verb** [T] to not do what you are told to do by someone in authority: *How dare you disobey me!*

isorder /dɪˈsɔːdər/ **noun 1** ILLNESS ▷ [C] a disease or mental problem: *a blood disorder* **2** BAD BEHAVIOUR ▷ [U] uncontrolled, bad behaviour, especially by large groups of people: *crime and disorder* **3** NOT ORGANIZED ▷ [U] a situation in which things are untidy or confused and not organized: *His financial affairs are in complete disorder.* → See also **eating disorder**

isordered /dɪˈsɔːdəd/ **adj** confused and not organized: *a disordered mind*

isorderly /dɪˈsɔːdəli/ **adj 1** behaving badly by being noisy or violent: *He was charged with being drunk and disorderly.* **2** untidy

isorganized (also UK -ised) /dɪˈsɔːgənaɪzd/ **adj 1** not planned or organized well: *The competition was completely disorganized.* **2** not good at planning or organizing things

isorient /dɪˈsɔːriənt/ **verb** [T] (also UK **disorientate** /dɪˈsɔːriənteɪt/) to make someone not know where to go or what to do

isoriented /dɪˈsɔːriəntɪd/ **adj** (also UK **disorientated** /dɪˈsɔːriənteɪtɪd/) confused and not knowing where to go or what to do: *Whales become disoriented in shallow water.*

isown /dɪˈsəʊn/ **verb** [T] to say that you do not want to have any involvement or connection with someone: *Even his parents have disowned him.*

isparage /dɪˈspærɪdʒ/ **verb** [T] to say that you think someone or something is not very good: [often passive] *He is often disparaged by the critics.*

isparaging /dɪˈspærɪdʒɪŋ/ **adj** criticizing someone or something: *disparaging remarks*

isparate /ˈdɪspərət/ **adj** formal completely different: *people from disparate cultures*

isparity /dɪˈspærəti/ **noun** [C, U] formal difference, usually relating to the money people earn or their position

ispatch¹ formal (also UK **despatch**) /dɪˈspætʃ/ **verb** [T] to send someone or something somewhere: *They dispatched a police car to arrest him.*

ispatch² (also UK **despatch**) /dɪˈspætʃ/ **noun 1** [U] the act of sending someone or something somewhere: *the dispatch of troops* **2** [C] an official report that someone in a foreign country sends to their organization

ispel /dɪˈspel/ **verb** [T] (**dispelling, dispelled**) to get rid of a feeling, thought, or belief: *He appeared on TV to dispel rumours that he was dying.*

ispensary /dɪˈspensəri/ **noun** [C] a place where medicines are given out

ispensation /ˌdɪspenˈseɪʃən/ **noun** [C, U] special permission to do something: [+ to do sth] *The court would not grant him a dispensation to visit his children.*

dispense /dɪˈspens/ **verb** [T] to give something out: *These machines dispense drinks and snacks.*

PHRASAL VERB **dispense with sth/sb** to stop using something or someone, or to get rid of something or someone, usually because you do not need them

dispenser /dɪˈspensər/ **noun** [C] a machine that you can get something from: *a cash/drink/soap dispenser*

disperse /dɪˈspɜːs/ **verb** [I, T] to separate and go in different directions, or to make something do this: *We waited until the crowds had dispersed.* • **dispersal noun** [U]

dispirited /dɪˈspɪrɪtɪd/ **adj** unhappy and without hope

displace /dɪˈspleɪs/ **verb** [T] **1** to take the place of someone or something: *Many of these workers will be displaced by modern technology.* **2** to make someone or something leave their usual place or position: *The earthquake displaced thousands of people.* • **displacement noun** [U]

display¹ /dɪˈspleɪ/ **noun 1** ARRANGEMENT ▷ [C] ⓑ a collection of objects or pictures arranged for people to look at: *a display of children's paintings* **2** on display ⓑ If something is on display, it is there for people to look at: *Many old aircraft are on display at the museum.* **3** SHOW ▷ [C] ⓑ a performance or show for people to watch: *a firework display* **4** ON SCREEN ▷ [C, U] ⓑ electronic information that is shown on a computer screen: *The display problems might be due to a shortage of disk space.* **5** a display of affection/anger, etc behaviour that shows someone has a particular feeling

display² /dɪˈspleɪ/ **verb 1** ARRANGE ▷ [T] ⓑ to arrange something somewhere so that people can see it: *There were some family photographs displayed on his desk.* **2** ON SCREEN ▷ [I, T] ⓑ to show something electronically such as on a computer screen: *The text can be displayed and edited on screen.* **3** FEELING ▷ [T] to show how you feel by your expression or behaviour: *He never displayed any interest in girls.*

displease /dɪˈspliːz/ **verb** [T] formal to make someone annoyed or unhappy • **displeased adj**

displeasure /dɪˈspleʒər/ **noun** [U] formal a feeling of being annoyed or unhappy about something: *She expressed great displeasure at his behaviour.*

disposable /dɪˈspəʊzəbl/ **adj** intended to be used only once and then thrown away: *a disposable camera/razor*

dis,posable 'income noun [C, U] the amount of money that you have available to spend after tax, rent and other basic things that you must pay for

disposal /dɪˈspəʊzəl/ **noun** [U] **1** ⓑ the job or activity of getting rid of something, especially by throwing it away: *waste disposal* ○ *the disposal of hazardous substances* **2** at sb's disposal ⓑ available for someone to use: *We will have a car at our disposal for the whole trip.*

dispose /dɪˈspəʊz/ **verb**

PHRASAL VERB **dispose of sth** to get rid of something, especially by throwing it away

disposed /dɪˈspəʊzd/ **adj** formal **1 be disposed to do sth** to be willing or likely to do something: *I tried to tell her but she didn't seem disposed to listen.* **2 be favourably/well, etc disposed towards sth** to like or approve of something: *She seems well disposed towards the idea.*

disposition /ˌdɪspəˈzɪʃ³n/ **noun** [C] the type of character someone has: *a **cheerful/nervous disposition***

disproportionate /ˌdɪsprəˈpɔːʃ³nət/ **adj** too large or small in comparison to something: *There are a **disproportionate number** of girls in the class.* • **disproportionately** adv

disprove /dɪˈspruːv/ **verb** [T] to prove that something is not true

dispute¹ /ˈdɪspjuːt/ **noun** [C, U] a disagreement, especially one that lasts a long time: *A man stabbed his neighbour in a **dispute over** noise.*

> ☑ Word partners for **dispute**
>
> have/be involved in a dispute • resolve/settle a dispute • a bitter/long-running dispute • a dispute about/over sth

dispute² /dɪˈspjuːt/ **verb** [T] to disagree with something someone says: [+ (that)] *I'm not disputing that the drug has benefits.*

disqualify /dɪˈskwɒlɪfaɪ/ **verb** [T] to stop someone from being in a competition or doing some other activity because they have done something wrong: [often passive] *She was **disqualified from** the race after a drugs test.* • **disqualification** /dɪˌskwɒlɪfɪˈkeɪʃ³n/ **noun** [U, C]

disquiet /dɪˈskwaɪət/ **noun** [U] formal a situation in which people are anxious or worried about something: *His health has been causing disquiet.*

disregard¹ /ˌdɪsrɪˈɡɑːd/ **noun** [U, no plural] behaviour that shows you do not care about or have any interest in someone or something: *His behaviour shows a total **disregard for** other people.*

> ☑ Word partners for **disregard**
>
> blatant/callous/flagrant/total disregard • disregard for/of sb/sth

disregard² /ˌdɪsrɪˈɡɑːd/ **verb** [T] to ignore something: *She chose to disregard my advice.*

disrepair /ˌdɪsrɪˈpeər/ **noun** [U] the bad condition of a building that has not been taken care of: *The house has **fallen into disrepair**.*

disreputable /dɪsˈrepjətəbl/ **adj** not respected or trusted by people: *a disreputable company*

disrepute /ˌdɪsrɪˈpjuːt/ **noun bring sb/sth into disrepute** formal to make people not respect or trust someone or something: *Corrupt policemen are bringing the law into disrepute.*

disrespect /ˌdɪsrɪˈspekt/ **noun** [U] impolite behaviour that shows no respect towards someone or something: *a **disrespect for** authority*

disrespectful /ˌdɪsrɪˈspektf³l/ **adj** being rude and not showing any respect: *Don't be **disrespectful to** your mother.* • **disrespectfully** adv

disrupt /dɪsˈrʌpt/ **verb** [T] ⓷ to interrupt som thing and stop it continuing as it should: *I disturbs other children and disrupts the class.* • **di ruption** /dɪsˈrʌpʃ³n/ **noun** [C, U] *the disruption services* • **disruptive** adj *disruptive behaviour*

dissatisfaction /dɪsˌsætɪsˈfækʃ³n/ **noun** [U] ⓷ feeling of not being pleased or happy wit something: *He expressed his **dissatisfaction wit** the legal system.*

dissatisfied /dɪsˈsætɪsfaɪd/ **adj** ⓷ not please or happy with something: *a dissatisfied custom* ○ *Are you **dissatisfied with** our service?*

dissect /daɪˈsekt/ **verb** [T] to cut something in pieces for scientific study: *We had to dissect a r in biology.* • **dissection** /daɪˈsekʃ³n/ **noun** [U]

disseminate /dɪˈsemɪneɪt/ **verb** [T] to sprea information or ideas: *They are using their websi to disseminate political propaganda.* • **dissemi ation** /dɪˌsemɪˈneɪʃ³n/ **noun** [U]

dissent /dɪˈsent/ **noun** [U] a situation in whic someone does not agree with something: *The is a lot of dissent within the Church about g priests.* • **dissent verb** [I] to not agree with oth people about something • **dissenter noun** [C]

dissertation /ˌdɪsəˈteɪʃ³n/ **noun** [C] a very lon piece of writing done as part of a course (study: *She's writing a **dissertation on** America poetry.*

disservice /ˌdɪsˈsɜːvɪs/ **noun** [no plural] a situ tion in which something causes harm t someone or something: *Bad teaching **does** great **disservice to** children.*

dissident /ˈdɪsɪd³nt/ **noun** [C] someone wh criticizes their government in a public wa *political dissidents*

dissimilar /dɪˈsɪmɪlər/ **adj** different: *Her hair not **dissimilar to** yours (= is similar to yours).*

dissipate /ˈdɪsɪpeɪt/ **verb** [I, T] to disappear, or t make something disappear: *The heat gradual dissipates into the atmosphere.*

dissociate /dɪˈsəʊʃieɪt/ **verb dissociate yourse from sb/sth** to say that you do not have an connection or involvement with someone (something: *He's trying to dissociate himself fro his former friends.*

dissolution /ˌdɪsəˈluːʃ³n/ **noun** [U] the ending (an organization or an official arrangement

dissolve /dɪˈzɒlv/ **verb 1** [I, T] If a solid dissolve it becomes part of a liquid, and if you dissolve you make it become part of a liquid: *Thes tablets dissolve in water.* **2** [T] to end a organization or official arrangement: [ofte passive] *Their marriage was dissolved in 201* **3 dissolve into laughter/tears, etc** to sudden start to laugh/cry, etc

dissuade /dɪˈsweɪd/ **verb** [T] to persuad someone not to do something: [+ from + doir sth] *We tried to dissuade him from leaving.*

distance¹ /ˈdɪst³ns/ **noun 1** [C, U] ⓷ the lengt of the space between two places or things: *We'r only a short **distance from** my house.* ○ *H calculated the **distance between** the Earth an the Sun.* ○ *Are the shops **within walkin distance**?* **2** [no plural] ⓷ somewhere that is f away, but close enough for you to see or hea the things that are there: *I could see Mary in the distance.* ∘ *From a distance, it sounded like a bell ringing.*

---

distance² /ˈdɪst³ns/ **verb distance yourself from sb/sth** to say or show that you are not connected or involved with someone or something: *She has tried to distance herself from the book.*

distant /ˈdɪst³nt/ **adj 1 FAR AWAY** ▷ 🅱️ far away in space or time: *distant galaxies* ∘ *the distant sound of traffic* ∘ *We hope to see you in the not too distant future.* **2 RELATIVE** ▷ A distant relative is not very closely related to you: *a distant cousin* **3 NOT FRIENDLY** ▷ [never before noun] not friendly: *She seemed cold and distant.* • **distantly adv distantly related**

distaste /dɪsˈteɪst/ **noun** [U] a feeling of dislike towards something you think is unpleasant: *I have developed a distaste for meat.*

distasteful /dɪsˈteɪstf³l/ **adj** unpleasant or offensive: *I find this advertisement extremely distasteful.* • **distastefully adv**

distil (distilling, distilled) UK (US **distill**) /dɪˈstɪl/ **verb** [T] to make a liquid stronger or more pure by heating it until it changes into a gas and then changing it into a liquid again: *distilled water* • **distillation** /ˌdɪstɪˈleɪʃ³n/ **noun** [U] • **distillery** /dɪˈstɪl³ri/ **noun** [C] a place where strong alcoholic drinks are produced

distinct /dɪˈstɪŋkt/ **adj 1 DIFFERENT** ▷ different and separate: *This word has three distinct meanings.* **2 HEAR/SEE** ▷ easy to hear, see, or smell: *The voices gradually became louder and more distinct.* → Opposite **indistinct 3 CLEAR** ▷ [always before noun] clear and certain: *There's been a distinct improvement in your work.* • **distinctly adv**

distinction /dɪˈstɪŋkʃ³n/ **noun** [C, U] **1** 🅱️ a difference between two similar things: *the distinction between spoken and written language* **2** a quality or fact that makes someone or something special or different: *wines of distinction* ∘ *He has the distinction of being the youngest player in the World Cup finals.*

---

distinctive /dɪˈstɪŋktɪv/ **adj** Something that is distinctive is easy to recognize because it is different from other things: *a distinctive style of writing* • **distinctively adv**

distinguish /dɪˈstɪŋgwɪʃ/ **verb 1 RECOGNIZE DIFFERENCES** ▷ [I, T] 🅱️ to recognize the differences between two people, ideas, or things: *Children must learn to distinguish between right and wrong.* ∘ *People have difficulty distinguishing Tracy from her twin sister Mary.* **2 SHOW DIFFERENCES** ▷ [T] 🅱️ to make one person or thing seem different from

another: *His great skill distinguishes him from the rest of the team.* **3 SEE/HEAR** ▷ [T] 🅱️ to be able to see, hear, or understand something **4 distinguish yourself** to do something so well that people notice and admire you • **distinguishable adj**

distinguished /dɪˈstɪŋgwɪʃt/ **adj** 🅱️ famous, praised, or admired: *a distinguished writer*

distort /dɪˈstɔːt/ **verb** [T] **1** to change the shape, sound, or appearance of something so that it seems strange: *It's a bad recording – the microphone distorted our voices.* **2** to change information so that it is not true or realistic: *Newspapers distorted the truth about their marriage.* • **distorted adj** • **distortion** /dɪˈstɔːʃ³n/ **noun** [C, U] *a gross distortion of the facts*

distract /dɪˈstrækt/ **verb** [T] 🅱️ to make someone stop giving their attention to something: *Stop distracting me – I'm trying to finish my essay.*

distracted /dɪˈstræktɪd/ **adj** anxious and unable to think carefully

distraction /dɪˈstrækʃ³n/ **noun 1** [C, U] something that makes you stop giving your attention to something else: *The phone calls were a constant distraction.* **2 drive sb to distraction** UK to make someone very annoyed

distraught /dɪˈstrɔːt/ **adj** extremely upset and unhappy

distress¹ /dɪˈstres/ **noun** [U] **1** the feeling of being extremely upset or worried: *The newspaper reports caused her a great deal of distress.* **2** a situation in which someone is in danger and needs help: *an aircraft in distress*

---

distress² /dɪˈstres/ **verb** [T] to make someone feel very upset or worried • **distressing adj** 🅱️ *a distressing experience*

distribute /dɪˈstrɪbjuːt/ **verb** [T] **1** 🅱️ to give something out to people or places: *The books will be distributed free to local schools.* **2** to supply goods to shops and companies: *The company manufactures and distributes computer equipment worldwide.*

distribution /ˌdɪstrɪˈbjuːʃ³n/ **noun 1** [U] the activity or work of supplying something or giving something out to people: *the sale and distribution of DVDs* **2** [U, no plural] the way something is divided and shared in a group or area: *The distribution of wealth was very unequal.*

distributor /dɪˈstrɪbjətə²/ **noun** [C] a person or organization that supplies goods to shops and companies

district /ˈdɪstrɪkt/ **noun** [C] 🅱️ a part of a city or country, either an official area or one that is known for having a particular characteristic or business: *the fashion district of New York*

district attorney noun [C] (abbreviation **DA**) US a lawyer who works for the government of a particular district

distrust /dɪˈstrʌst/ **noun** [U] a feeling of not trusting someone or something • **distrust verb** [T]

disturb /dɪˈstɜːb/ **verb** [T] **1 INTERRUPT** ▷ to

---

interrupt what someone is doing by making noise or annoying them: *Don't disturb him, he needs to sleep.* **2 UPSET** ▷ to make someone feel anxious or upset: *Some scenes are violent and may disturb younger viewers.* **3 CHANGE** ▷ to change something by touching it or moving it from its original position

disturbance /dɪˈstɜːbəns/ **noun 1** [C, U] something that interrupts what you are doing, especially something loud or annoying **2** [C] loud or violent behaviour

disturbed /dɪˈstɜːbd/ **adj** not thinking or behaving normally because of mental or emotional problems

disturbing /dɪˈstɜːbɪŋ/ **adj** unpleasant in a way that makes people feel anxious or upset: *disturbing images* • **disturbingly adv**

disused /dɪˈsjuːzd/ **adj** not used now: *a disused warehouse* • **disuse** /dɪˈsjuːs/ **noun** [U] the state of not being used: *to fall into disuse*

ditch¹ /dɪtʃ/ **noun** [C] a long, narrow hole in the ground next to a road or field, which water can flow through

ditch² /dɪtʃ/ **verb** [T] informal to get rid of someone or something that you do not need or want now: *He ditched his girlfriend when she got pregnant.*

dither /ˈdɪðər/ **verb** [I] to spend too much time trying to make a decision: *Stop dithering and tell me which one you want!*

ditto¹ /ˈdɪtəʊ/ **adv** used to agree with something that has been said, or to avoid repeating something that has been said

ditto² /ˈdɪtəʊ/ **noun** [C] a mark (") used instead of words to show that you are repeating what is written above it

ditty /ˈdɪti/ **noun** [C] a short, simple song

diva /ˈdiːvə/ **noun** [C] a successful and famous female singer

Divali /dɪˈvɑːli/ **noun** [U] Diwali (= a Hindu festival)

dive

dive¹ /daɪv/ **verb** [I] (**dived**, also US **dove**, **dived**) **1 JUMP IN** ▷ 🔒 to jump into water with your head and arms going in first: *He dived off the side*

of the boat into the sea. **2 SWIM** ▷ 🔒 to swim under water, usually with breathing equipment **3 dive into/over/under, etc** to move somewhere quickly: *He heard footsteps and dived under the table.* **4 FLY** ▷ to fly down through the air very quickly: *Suddenly the plane dived to the ground.* **5 VALUE** ▷ If a value or price dives, it suddenly becomes less.

dive² /daɪv/ **noun** [C] **1 JUMP** ▷ 🔒 a jump into water with your arms and head going in first **2 MOVEMENT** ▷ a quick movement somewhere **3 VALUE** ▷ a sudden reduction in the value or price of something: *Share prices took a dive today.* **4 PLACE** ▷ informal a place such as a bar that is considered to be dirty or of low quality

diver /ˈdaɪvər/ **noun** [C] 🔒 someone who swims under water, usually with breathing equipment

diverge /daɪˈvɜːdʒ/ **verb** [I] **1** to be different, or to develop in a different way: *Over the years our interests have diverged.* **2** to go in different directions: *At that point, the paths diverged* • **divergence noun** [C, U]

diverse /daɪˈvɜːs/ **adj** 🔒 including many different types: *a diverse collection of music*

diversify /daɪˈvɜːsɪfaɪ/ **verb** [I, T] If a business diversifies, it starts making new products or offering new services: *Many designers are diversifying into casual wear.* • **diversification** /daɪˌvɜːsɪfɪˈkeɪʃən/ **noun** [U]

diversion /daɪˈvɜːʃən/ **noun 1 CHANGE** ▷ [C, U] change to where something is being sent, so it goes to a different place to that originally intended: *the diversion of money to other projects* **2 ROUTE** ▷ [C] UK (US **detour**) a different route that is used because a road is closed **3 ATTENTION** ▷ [C] something that takes your attention away from something else: *John created a diversion while the rest of us escaped.* **4 ENTERTAINMENT** ▷ [C] an activity you do for entertainment or pleasure: *Reading is a pleasant diversion.*

diversity /daɪˈvɜːsəti/ **noun** [U] a situation in which many different types of things or people are included in something: *ethnic diversity*

divert /daɪˈvɜːt/ **verb 1** [T] to send someone or something somewhere different from where they were expecting to go: *The plane was diverted to Newark because of engine trouble.* **2 divert sb's attention/thoughts, etc** to take someone's attention away from something

divide /dɪˈvaɪd/ **verb 1 SEPARATE** ▷ [I, T] 🔒 to separate into parts or groups, or to make something separate into parts or groups: *We divided up into teams of six.* ∘ *Each school year is divided into two semesters.* **2 divide sth (up) among/between sb** to separate something into parts and give a part to each person in a group: *The prize money will be divided equally among the winners.* **3 PLACE** ▷ [T] 🔒 to separate a place into two areas: *An ancient wall divides the city.* **4 NUMBERS** ▷ [I, T] to calculate how many times a number can go into another number: *6 divided by 6 equals 2.* **5 DISAGREE** ▷ [T] to make people disagree about something: [often passive] *Council members were divided over plans to build a new stadium.*

ividend /ˈdɪvɪdend/ **noun** [C] an amount of money paid regularly to someone who owns shares in a company from the company's profits

ivine /dɪˈvaɪn/ **adj** relating to or coming from God or a god

iving /ˈdaɪvɪŋ/ **noun** [U] **1** 🅑1 the activity or sport of swimming under water, usually using special breathing equipment **2** the activity or sport of jumping into water with your arms and head going in first → See also **scuba diving**

iving ˌboard noun [C] a raised board next to a swimming pool that you jump from into the water

ivisible /dɪˈvɪzəbl/ **adj divisible by 2/7/50, etc** able to be divided by 2/7/50, etc

ivision /dɪˈvɪʒən/ **noun 1** SEPARATED ▷ [U] 🅑2 the separation of something into parts or groups, or the way that it is separated: *the equal division of labour among workers* **2** ORGANIZATION ▷ [C] 🅑2 one of the groups in a business or organization: *the sales division* **3** DISAGREEMENT ▷ [C, U] disagreement between people about something: *a division over the issue of free medical care* **4** CALCULATION ▷ [U] calculations of how many times one number goes into another number

ivisive /dɪˈvaɪsɪv/ **adj** causing disagreements between people: *a divisive issue*

ivorce /dɪˈvɔːs/ **noun** [C, U] 🅑1 the official ending of a marriage: *My parents are getting a divorce.* • **divorce verb** [I, T] 🅑2 *She's divorcing her husband.*

┌───┐
│ 🗹 Word partners for **divorce**   │
│   │
│ **get** a divorce • a divorce **from** sb • divorce │
│ **proceedings/rate/settlement**   │
└───┘

ivorced /dɪˈvɔːst/ **adj 1** 🅑1 married before but not married now **2 get divorced** to officially stop being married: *My parents got divorced when I was seven.* → See Note at **married**

ivorcée /dɪˌvɔːˈsiː/ ⒰ /-seɪ/ **noun** [C] a person, usually a woman, who is divorced

ivulge /daɪˈvʌldʒ/ **verb** [T] to give secret or private information to someone: *He would not divulge how much the house cost.*

Diwali /dɪˈwɑːli/ **noun** [C, U] (also **Divali**) a Hindu holiday in October/November that celebrates light and the new year

DIY /ˌdiːaɪˈwaɪ/ **noun** [U] UK abbreviation for do it yourself: the activity of doing building, decorating, or repairs in your own home

izzy /ˈdɪzi/ **adj** 🅑2 feeling like everything is turning round, so that you feel sick or as if you might fall

DJ /ˈdiːˌdʒeɪ/ **noun** [C] (also **disc jockey**) 🅑1 someone who plays music on the radio or at discos

DNA /ˌdiːenˈeɪ/ **noun** [U] abbreviation for deoxyribonucleic acid; a chemical in the cells of living things that contains genetic information

do¹ strong /duː/ weak /də/ **auxiliary verb 1** QUESTIONS/NEGATIVES ▷ 🅐1 used with another verb to form questions and negative phrases: *Do you need any help?* ∘ *When does the*

next bus leave? ∘ *I don't know.* **2** MAKE QUESTION ▷ 🅐2 used in a phrase at the end of a sentence to make it into a question: *Sarah lives near here, doesn't she?* ∘ *That doesn't make any sense, does it?* **3** AVOID REPEATING ▷ 🅑1 used to avoid repeating a verb that has just been used: *"I hate that song." "So do I."* ∘ *My sister reads a lot more than I do.* **4** EMPHASIZE ▷ 🅑2 used to emphasize the main verb: *He does like you, he's just shy.* ∘ *Do come and visit us soon.*

do² /duː/ **verb** (**did**, **done**) **1** ACTION/JOB ▷ [T] 🅐1 to perform an action or job: *Go upstairs and do your homework.* ∘ *What are you doing this weekend?* ∘ *What does she do?* (= What is her job?) **2** MAKE ▷ [T] 🅐2 to make or prepare something: *Our printer only does black and white copies.* ∘ *Max's Cafe does great sandwiches.* **3 do badly/well, etc** 🅑1 to be unsuccessful/successful: *Sam did very well UK in her exams/ US on her exams.* **4 do biology/French/history, etc** UK 🅐1 to study biology/French/history, etc **5 do your hair/make-up, etc** 🅑1 to make your hair/make-up, etc look nice **6 do sb good** 🅑2 to have a good effect on someone: *A holiday would do you good.* **7 do damage/harm, etc** 🅑2 to cause damage/harm, etc: *Luckily the fire didn't do much damage.* **8 will do** will be satisfactory: *You don't have to pay now, next week will do.* **9** SPEED ▷ [T] to travel at a particular speed: *For most of the journey we were doing 70 miles an hour.*

┌───┐
│ ❗ Common learner error: **do** or **make**? │
│   │
│ **Do** generally means to perform an activity │
│ or job.   │
│ *I should do more exercise.*   │
│ ~~I should make more exercise.~~   │
│ **Make** generally means to create or produce │
│ something.   │
│ *Did you make the dress yourself?*   │
│ ~~Did you do the dress yourself?~~   │
└───┘

PHRASAL VERBS **do away with sth** to get rid of something, or to stop using something: *We may do away with the school uniform soon.* • **do away with sb** informal to kill someone • **do sb in** informal **1** to make someone extremely tired: *All that exercise has done me in.* **2** to attack or kill someone • **do sth over** US to do something again because you did not do it well the first time • **do sth up 1** mainly UK to fasten something: *Do your coat up. It's cold outside.* **2** 🅑2 to repair or decorate a building so that it looks attractive • **do with sth** used to ask where someone put something: *What did you do with my keys?* • **do with sb/sth 1 could do with sb/sth** to need or want someone or something: *I could do with a few days off work.* **2 be/have to do with sb/sth** 🅑2 to be about or connected with someone or something: *My question has to do with yesterday's homework.* • **do without (sb/sth)** 🅑2 to manage without having someone or something: *Jack's the kind of player we can't do without.*

do³ /duː/ **noun** [C] UK informal a party: *Are you going to the Christmas do?*

docile /'dəʊsaɪl/ ⓤⓢ /'dɑːsəl/ **adj** A docile person or animal is quiet and easily controlled.

dock¹ /dɒk/ **noun** **1** [C] the place where ships stop and goods are taken off or put on **2 the dock** (also **the stand**) the place in a law court where the person who is accused of a crime sits

dock² /dɒk/ **verb** **1** [I, T] If a ship docks, it arrives at a dock. **2 dock sb's pay/wages** to take away part of the money you pay someone, usually as a punishment

doctor¹ /'dɒktər/ **noun** **1** ⓐ [C] a person whose job is to treat people who have an illness or injury: *I have to go to the doctor's for a check-up.* **2 Doctor of Philosophy/Divinity, etc** someone who has the most advanced type of qualification from a university → See also **spin doctor**

> ☑ Word partners for **doctor**
>
> consult/see a doctor • go to the doctor's • a doctor's **appointment**

doctor² /'dɒktər/ **verb** [T] to change something, usually in a dishonest way: *The photo in his passport had been doctored.*

doctorate /'dɒktərət/ **noun** [C] the most advanced type of qualification from a university: *He has a doctorate in physics from Cambridge.*

doctrine /'dɒktrɪn/ **noun** [C, U] a belief or set of beliefs taught by a religious or political group: *Christian doctrine*

document /'dɒkjəmənt/ **noun** [C] **1** ⓐ a piece of paper with official information on it: *Please sign and return the insurance documents enclosed.* **2** ⓑ a piece of text produced electronically on a computer: *How do I create a new document?*

> ☑ Word partners for **document**
>
> draw up/produce a document • in a document • a document **about/concerning/on** sth

documentary /ˌdɒkjə'mentəri/ **noun** [C] ⓑ a film or television programme that gives facts about a real situation or real people: *a TV documentary about the Russian Revolution*

documentation /ˌdɒkjəmen'teɪʃən/ **noun** [U] **1** pieces of paper containing official information **2** the instructions written for a piece of computer software or equipment

docusoap /'dɒkjuːsəʊp/ **noun** [C] UK an entertaining television programme about the lives of real people who live in the same place or who do the same thing

doddle /'dɒdl/ **noun** UK **be a doddle** informal to be very easy: *This computer's a doddle to use.*

dodge¹ /dɒdʒ/ **verb** **1** [I, T] to move quickly to avoid someone or something: *He managed to dodge past the security guard.* **2** [T] to avoid talking about something or doing something you should do: *The minister dodged questions about his relationship with the actress.*

dodge² /dɒdʒ/ **noun** [C] a way of avoiding something, usually a dishonest one: *a tax dodge*

dodgy /'dɒdʒi/ **adj** UK informal bad, or not able to be trusted: *His friend's a bit dodgy.*

doe /dəʊ/ **noun** [C] a female deer

does strong /dʌz/ weak /dəz/ present simple he/she/ of do

doesn't /'dʌzənt/ short for does not: *Keith doesn't like mushrooms or garlic.*

dog¹ /dɒg/ **noun** [C] ⓐ an animal with fur, fou legs, and a tail that is kept as a pet, or trained t guard buildings and guide blind people: *Let take the dog for a walk.* → See also **guide dog hot dog**

dog² /dɒg/ **verb** [T] (**dogging, dogged**) to caus someone or something trouble for a long tim [often passive] *His football career has been dogge by injury.*

dog-eared /'dɒgɪəd/ **adj** If a piece of paper or book is dog-eared, its corners are folded an torn from being touched a lot.

dogged /'dɒgɪd/ **adj** [always before noun] co tinuing to do or believe in something, althoug it is difficult: *dogged determination* • **do gedly adv**

doghouse /'dɒghaʊs/ **noun** **1** [C] US (mainly U **kennel**) a small building for a dog to sleep **2 be in the doghouse** If you are in th doghouse, you have done something to mak people angry or annoyed with you.

dogma /'dɒgmə/ **noun** [C, U] a belief or set o beliefs that people are expected to accept as th truth, without ever doubting them: *politic dogma*

dogmatic /dɒg'mætɪk/ **adj** not willing to accep other ideas or opinions because you think you are right

dogsbody /'dɒgzbɒdi/ **noun** [C] UK someon who has to do boring jobs for someone else

doing /'duːɪŋ/ **noun** **1 be sb's doing** to hav been done or caused by someone: *The problem not all his doing.* **2 take some/a lot of doin** informal to be difficult to do: *It took some doin to convince him to come.*

doldrums /'dɒldrəmz/ **noun in the doldrum a** If a business or job is in the doldrums, it is nc very successful and nothing new is happenin in it. **b** UK sad and with no energy or enthusias

dole¹ /dəʊl/ **verb**

PHRASAL VERB **dole sth out** to give somethin especially money, to several people or in larg amounts

dole² /dəʊl/ **noun** UK **the dole** money that th government gives someone when they ar unemployed: *He's been on the dole for years.*

doleful /'dəʊlfəl/ **adj** very sad: *doleful eyes*

doll /dɒl/ **noun** [C] ⓐ a child's toy that looks lik a small person

dollar /'dɒlər/ **noun** [C] ⓐ the unit of mone used in the US, Canada, and some othe countries; $: *a hundred dollars/$100* ◦ *a dolla bill*

dollop /'dɒləp/ **noun** [C] a lump or mass of a so substance, usually food: *a dollop of cream*

dolphin /'dɒlfɪn/ **noun** [C] ⓑ an intelligen animal that lives in the sea, breathes air, an looks like a large, smooth, grey fish

domain /dəʊ'meɪn/ **noun** [C] a particular are activity, or subject that someone controls o deals with: *The garden is his domain.* ∘ *This information should be* **in the public domain** (= *known by the public*).

do'main ˌname noun [C] the part of an email or website address that shows the name of the organization that the address belongs to

dome /dəʊm/ noun [C] a curved, round roof of a building • **domed** adj *a domed roof*

domestic /dəˈmestɪk/ adj **1 HOME** ▷ **B2** relating to the home and family relationships: *domestic violence* ∘ *What are his* **domestic arrangements?** **2 COUNTRY** ▷ **B2** inside one country and not international: *a domestic flight* **3 ANIMAL** ▷ A domestic animal is kept as a pet.

domesticated /dəˈmestɪkeɪtɪd/ adj **1** A domesticated animal is kept as a pet or lives on a farm. **2** A domesticated person is able or willing to do cleaning, cooking, and other jobs in the home.

domesticity /ˌdɒmesˈtɪsəti/ noun [U] life at home looking after a house and family

dominance /ˈdɒmɪnəns/ noun [U] power, influence, and control: *the company's dominance in the software industry*

dominant /ˈdɒmɪnənt/ adj **1** main or most important: *Her mother was the dominant influence in her life.* **2** strongest and wanting to take control: *a dominant older brother*

dominate /ˈdɒmɪneɪt/ verb [I, T] **B2** to control or have power over someone or something: *The US continues to dominate the world politically.* **2** to be the largest, most important, or most noticeable part of something: *The cathedral dominates the skyline.*

domination /ˌdɒmɪˈneɪʃᵊn/ noun [U] great power and control over someone or something else: *world domination*

🗹 Word partners for **domination**

global/world domination • domination **of** sth • domination **over** sb/sth

---

domineering /ˌdɒmɪˈnɪərɪŋ/ adj trying to control people too much: *a domineering mother*

dominion /dəˈmɪnjən/ noun [U] formal the power and right to control someone or something

domino /ˈdɒmɪnəʊ/ noun [C] (plural **dominoes**) a small, rectangular object that has spots on it, used in a game • **dominoes** noun [U] a game played using dominoes

don /dɒn/ verb [T] (**donning, donned**) formal to put on a piece of clothing such as a coat or hat

donate /dəʊˈneɪt/ verb [T] **1 B2** to give money or goods to a person or organization that needs help: *Four hundred new computers were* **donated to** *the college.* **2** to allow some of your blood or part of your body to be used for medical purposes

---
🗹 Word partners for **donation**

make a donation • a donation **of** [$50/food/ clothing, etc] • a donation **to** sb/sth

---

donation /dəʊˈneɪʃᵊn/ noun [C, U] **B2** money or goods that are given to help a person or organization, or the act of giving them: *Would you like to* **make a donation?**

done¹ /dʌn/ adj **1** finished or completed: *Did you get your essay* **done** *in time?* **2** cooked enough: *The potatoes aren't quite done yet.* → See also **easier said than done** (**easy¹**), **well-done**

done² /dʌn/ exclamation something that you say to show that you accept someone's offer: *"I'll give you 50 euros for the whole lot." "Done!"*

done³ /dʌn/ past participle of do

dongle /ˈdɒŋgl/ noun [C] a piece of equipment that is connected to a computer in order to allow the computer to use a particular piece of software

donkey /ˈdɒŋki/ noun [C] **B1** an animal that looks like a small horse with long ears

donkey

IDIOM **for donkey's years** UK informal for a long time

---

donkey ˌwork noun [U] UK informal the most boring or difficult parts of a job

donor /ˈdəʊnəʳ/ noun [C] **1** someone who gives some of their blood or part of their body to be used for medical purposes **2** someone who gives money or goods to a person or organization that needs help: *Ten thousand dollars was given by an* **anonymous donor.** → See also **blood donor**

don't /dəʊnt/ short for do not: *Please don't talk during the exam.*

donut /ˈdəʊnʌt/ noun [C] another US spelling of doughnut (= a small, round, fried cake)

doodle /ˈduːdl/ verb [I, T] to draw little pictures or patterns on something without thinking about it • **doodle** noun [C]

doodle

doom /duːm/ noun [U] **1** death, destruction, and other unpleasant events that cannot be avoided: *a horrible* **sense of doom** **2 doom and gloom** unhappiness and feeling no hope for the future: *Life's* **not all doom and gloom,** *you know.*

doomed /duːmd/ adj certain to fail, die, or have problems: *Their marriage was doomed from the start.*

door /dɔːʳ/ noun [C] **1 A1** the part of a building, room, vehicle, or piece of furniture that you open or close to get inside it or out of it: *Please* **shut the door** *behind you.* ∘ *I can't* **open the door.** ∘ *There's someone* **at the door.** **2** the space in a wall where you enter a building or room: *He led us through the door to the rear of the building.* **3 behind closed doors** privately and not in public: *Most of the deals were done behind closed doors.* **4 two/three, etc doors away** in a place that is two/three, etc houses away: *We live just a*

D

few doors away from the Smiths. → See also **trap door**

> ☑ Word partners for **door**
>
> **close/open/shut/slam** a door • **knock on** a door • **be at the** door

doorbell /'dɔːbel/ **noun** [C] a button that you press next to a door that makes a noise to let someone know that you are there

doorknob /'dɔːnɒb/ **noun** [C] a round object on a door that you hold and turn to open or close it

doorman /'dɔːmən/ **noun** [C] (plural **doormen**) a man who stands near the doors of a large building such as a hotel to watch and help the visitors

doormat /'dɔːmæt/ **noun** [C] **1** a piece of thick material on the floor by a door used to clean your shoes before entering a building **2** informal someone who allows other people to treat them very badly

doorstep /'dɔːstep/ **noun** [C] **1** a step in front of the door of a building **2 on your doorstep** very near to where you live: *They have the Rocky Mountains on their doorstep.*

door-to-door /ˌdɔːtə'dɔːʳ/ **adj** [always before noun], **adv 1** going from one house or building to another: *The hotel offers a **door-to-door service** to the airport.* **2** going to every house in an area: *a **door-to-door salesman***

doorway /'dɔːweɪ/ **noun** [C] an entrance to a building or room through a door: *She waited **in the doorway** while I ran back inside.*

dope[1] /dəʊp/ **noun** informal **1** [U] an illegal drug taken for pleasure, especially cannabis (= drug that you smoke) **2** [C] informal a stupid or silly person

dope[2] /dəʊp/ **verb 1** [T] to give a drug to a person or animal, usually so that they become sleepy **2 be doped up** to have a lot of a drug in your body affecting your behaviour

dork /dɔːk/ **noun** [C] mainly US informal a stupid or silly person

dormant /'dɔːmənt/ **adj** not active or developing now, but possibly active in the future: *a dormant volcano*

dormitory /'dɔːmɪtᵊri/ **noun** [C] (informal **dorm**) **1** a large bedroom with a lot of beds, especially in a school **2** US (UK **hall of residence**) a large building at a college or university where students live

dosage /'dəʊsɪdʒ/ **noun** [C] how much medicine you should take and how often you should take it: *the recommended daily dosage*

dose /dəʊs/ **noun** [C] **1** ⑱ a measured amount of medicine that is taken at one time or during a period of time: *What is the recommended dose?* ○ *a **lethal dose*** **2 a dose of sth** ⑲ an amount of something, often something unpleasant: *a dose of bad news* • **dose verb** [T] to give someone a drug or medicine

> ☑ Word partners for **dose**
>
> a **high/low** dose • a **fatal/lethal** dose • a dose **of** sth

dosh /dɒʃ/ **noun** [U] UK informal money

doss /dɒs/ **verb** [I] (also **doss down**) UK informal to sleep somewhere temporarily, such as on the floor: *Can I doss at your house tonight?*
PHRASAL VERB **doss about/around** UK informal to spend your time doing very little

dossier /'dɒsieɪ/ **noun** a set of documents that contain information about a particular person or subject: *The officers **compiled** a **dossier** on the case.*

dot[1] /dɒt/ **noun 1** [C] ⑱ a small, round mark or spot: *a pattern of blue and green dots* **2** [U] spoken ⑳ the spoken form of '.' in an internet address: *dot co dot uk* (= .co.uk) **3 on the dot** at that exact time: *We have to leave at 7.30 on the dot.*

dot[2] /dɒt/ **verb** [T] (**dotting, dotted**) **1** to put a dot or dots on something **2** (also **dot around**) to be spread across an area: *The company has 4. hotels dotted around the UK.*

dot.com /ˌdɒt'kɒm/ **noun** [C] (also **dotcom**) a company that does most of its business on the Internet: *a dot.com company/millionaire*

dote /dəʊt/ **verb**
PHRASAL VERB **dote on sb** to love someone completely and believe that they are perfect: *She absolutely dotes on that little boy.*

doting /dəʊtɪŋ/ **adj** [always before noun] extremely loving and caring: *doting parents*

dotted 'line noun 1 [C] a line of printed dots on a piece of paper **2 sign on the dotted line** to make an agreement official by writing your name on it

dotty /'dɒti/ **adj** UK slightly crazy: *a dotty old woman*

double[1] /'dʌbl/ **adj 1 TWO PARTS** ▷ having two parts of the same type or size: *double doors* ○ *My number is four, two, six, double two, five* (= 426225). **2 TWICE THE SIZE** ▷ ⑫ twice the amount, number, or size of something: *a double vodka* ○ *a double hamburger* **3 FOR TWO** ▷ made to be used by two people: *a **double bed**/room*

double[2] /'dʌbl/ **verb** [I, T] ⑫ to increase and become twice the original size or amount, or to make something do this: *Our house has almost doubled in value.*
PHRASAL VERBS **double (up) as sth** If something doubles up as something else, it also has the purpose of that thing: *The school's gymnasium doubles up as a dining room.* • **double back** to turn and go back in the direction that you have come from • **double (sb) over/up** to suddenly bend your body forward, usually because of pain or laughter, or to make someone do this

double[3] /'dʌbl/ **noun 1** [C, U] something that is twice the usual amount, number, or size **2 sb's double** someone who looks exactly the same as someone else

double[4] /'dʌbl/ **determiner** ⑪ twice as much or as many: *Our new house is double the size of our old one.*

double-barrelled mainly UK (US **double-barreled**) /ˌdʌbl'bærᵊld/ **adj 1** A double-barrelled gun has two of the cylindrical parts that bullets come out of. **2** UK A double-barrelled name is two names joined together.

double ˈbass noun [C] a wooden musical instrument with four strings, like a very large violin (= instrument you hold against your neck), that you play while standing up or sitting on a high chair

double ˈbed noun [C] a bed big enough for two people to sleep in

double-breasted /ˌdʌbl'brestɪd/ **adj** A double-breasted jacket or coat has two sets of buttons to fasten at the front.

double-check /ˌdʌbl'tʃek/ **verb** [I, T] to examine something again so that you are certain it is safe or correct

double-click /ˌdʌbl'klɪk/ **verb** [I, T] to quickly press a button twice on a mouse (= small computer control) to make something happen on a computer screen: *Double-click on the icon to start the program.*

double-cross /ˌdʌbl'krɒs/ **verb** [T] to deceive someone who you should be helping

double-decker /ˌdʌbl'dekər/ **noun** [C] UK a tall bus with two levels: *a double-decker bus*

double-glazing /ˌdʌbl'gleɪzɪŋ/ **noun** [U] UK windows that have two layers of glass to keep a building warm or quiet

doubles /'dʌblz/ **noun** [U] a game, especially tennis, in which two people play together against two other people

double ˈstandard noun [C] a situation in which people are given different treatment in an unfair way: [usually plural] *Critics accused the government of double standards in its policies.*

double ˈtake noun [C] a second look at someone or something because you cannot believe you have seen something or heard something: [usually singular] *He did a double take when he saw her.*

doubly /'dʌbli/ **adv** twice as much, or very much more: *It is doubly important to drink plenty of water when it's hot.*

doubt¹ /daʊt/ **noun 1** ⑤ [C, U] the feeling of not being certain about something, or not trusting someone or something: *I have some doubts about his ability to do the job.* **2 have no doubt** ⑤ to be certain: [+ (that)] *I have no doubt that I made the right decision.* **3 there's no doubt** ⑤ it is certain: [+ (that)] *There is no doubt that he's a good player.* **4 be in doubt** ⑥ to not be certain: *The future of the project is in doubt.* **5 cast doubt on sth** to make something seem uncertain: *Witnesses have cast doubt on the suspect's innocence.* **6 without (a) doubt** ⑥ certainly: *She is without doubt a great musician.* **7 no doubt** used to say that something is very likely: *No doubt she'll spend the money on new clothes.* → See also **give sb the benefit¹ of the doubt, beyond/without a shadow¹ of a doubt**

> ☑ Word partners for **doubt**
>
> express/have/raise doubts • a nagging/serious doubt • doubts about sth

doubt² /daʊt/ **verb** [T] **1** ⑥ to feel uncertain about something or think that something is not

probable: [+ (that)] *I doubt that I'll get the job.* ○ *I doubt if/whether he'll win.* **2** to not believe someone or something: *Do you have any reason to doubt her?*

doubtful /'daʊtf°l/ **adj 1** ⑥ not probable: *It's doubtful if/whether he'll be able to come.* ○ [+ (that)] *It's doubtful that anyone survived the fire.* **2** ⑥ not feeling certain about something • **doubtfully adv**

doubtless /'daʊtləs/ **adv** probably: *He will doubtless be criticized by journalists.*

dough /dəʊ/ **noun** [U] a thick mixture of flour and liquid used to make foods such as bread or pastry

doughnut (also US donut) /'dəʊnʌt/ **noun** [C] a small, round, fried cake, sometimes with a hole in the middle

dour /dʊər, daʊər/ **adj** unfriendly and serious: *a dour expression*

doughnut

douse /daʊs/ **verb** [T] **1** to pour a lot of liquid over someone or something: *The dessert was doused with brandy and set alight.* **2** to stop a fire burning by putting a lot of water on it: *to douse the flames/fire*

dove¹ /dʌv/ **noun** [C] a white bird, sometimes used as a symbol of peace

dove² /dəʊv/ US past tense of dive

dowdy /'daʊdi/ **adj** plain and not fashionable

down¹ /daʊn/ **adv, preposition 1 LOWER PLACE** ▷ ⓐ towards or in a lower place: *The kids ran down the hill to the gate.* ○ *I bent down to have a look.* **2 LEVEL/AMOUNT** ▷ towards or at a lower level or amount: *Can you turn the music down?* ○ *Slow down so they can see us.* **3 SURFACE** ▷ ⓐ moving from above and onto a surface: *I sat down and turned on the TV.* ○ *Put that box down on the floor.* **4 DIRECTION** ▷ in or towards a particular direction, usually south: *Pete's moved down to London.* **5 down the road/river, etc** ⓐ along or further along the road/river, etc: *There's another pub further down the street.* **6 note/write, etc sth down** ⑤ to write something on a piece of paper: *Can I just take down your phone number?* **7 STOMACH** ▷ inside your stomach: *He's had food poisoning and can't keep anything down.* **8 be down to sb** UK to be someone's responsibility or decision: *I've done all I can now, the rest is down to you.* **9 come/go down with sth** to become sick: *The whole family came down with food poisoning.*

IDIOM **down under** informal Australia, or in Australia

down² /daʊn/ **adj** [never before noun] **1** ⑥ sad: *What's the matter? You look a bit down today.* **2** If a computer or machine is down, it is temporarily not working: *The network was down all morning.*

down³ /daʊn/ **noun** [U] soft feathers, often used as a warm filling for bed covers → See also **ups and downs**

D

down⁴ /daʊn/ **verb** [T] informal to drink something quickly

down-and-out /ˌdaʊnənˈaʊt/ **adj** If someone is down-and-out, they have no money, possessions, or opportunities. • **down-and-out noun** [C]

downcast /ˈdaʊnkɑːst/ **adj 1** sad or disappointed **2** If someone's eyes are downcast, they are looking down.

downgrade /ˌdaʊnˈɡreɪd/ **verb** [T] to move someone or something to a less important position

downhearted /ˌdaʊnˈhɑːtɪd/ **adj** sad or disappointed

downhill¹ /ˌdaʊnˈhɪl/ **adv 1** towards the bottom of a hill or slope: *It's so much easier cycling downhill.* **2 go downhill** to gradually become worse: *After his wife died, his health started to go downhill.*

downhill² /ˌdaʊnˈhɪl/ **adj 1** leading down towards the bottom of a hill or slope: *downhill skiing* **2 be all downhill; be downhill all the way** to be much easier: *From now on it will be all downhill.*

download¹ /ˌdaʊnˈləʊd/ (US) /ˈdaʊnˌləʊd/ **verb** [T] ⓐ to copy computer programs, music or other information electronically using the Internet: *You can **download** this software free **from** their website.* → See Study Page **The Web and the Internet** on page Centre 36 • **downloadable adj** able to be downloaded: ***downloadable** files/images*

download² /ˈdaʊnləʊd/ **noun** [C] ⓑ a computer program, music, or other information that has been or can be downloaded

downmarket /ˌdaʊnˈmɑːkɪt/ **adj** UK cheap and low quality

down 'payment noun [C] the first amount of money that you pay when you buy something expensive and pay over a period of time: *a **down payment** on a house*

downplay /daʊnˈpleɪ/ **verb** [T] to make something seem less important or bad than it really is: *The report downplays the risks of nuclear power.*

downpour /ˈdaʊnpɔːʳ/ **noun** [C] a period when it suddenly rains a lot

downright /ˈdaʊnraɪt/ **adv downright dangerous/rude/ugly, etc** extremely dangerous/rude/ugly, etc

downside /ˈdaʊnsaɪd/ **noun** [no plural] the disadvantage of a situation: *The **downside of** living in a city is all the pollution.*

downsize /ˈdaʊnˌsaɪz/ **verb** [I, T] to make a company or organization smaller by reducing the number of people who work there • **downsizing noun** [U]

Down's syndrome /ˈdaʊnzˌsɪndrəʊm/ **noun** [U] a condition that some babies are born with that affects their mental and physical development

downstairs /ˌdaʊnˈsteəz/ **adv** ⓐ on or to a lower level of a building: *She **went downstairs** to see who was at the door.* • **downstairs adj** ⓑ *a downstairs bathroom*

downstream /ˌdaʊnˈstriːm/ **adv** in the direction that the water in a river is moving in

downtime /ˈdaʊntaɪm/ **noun** [U] **1 MACHINE** the time during which a machine, especially a computer, is not working or is not able to ▶ used: *Website downtime can damage your bu..ness.* **2 BUSINESS** ▷ time when a business do◄ not operate, for example when machines brea or there is no work to do **3 PERSON** ▷ time whe you relax and do not do very much, especial time when you are not at work: *He wanted to ▶ able to spend his downtime on the beach.*

down-to-earth /ˌdaʊntuˈɜːθ/ **adj** practical an realistic

downtown /ˌdaʊnˈtaʊn/ **adj** [always before noun **adv** US in or to the central part or main busine: area of a city: *downtown Chicago*

downtrodden /ˈdaʊnˌtrɒdᵊn/ **adj** treated bad and without respect from other people: *dow..trodden workers*

downturn /ˈdaʊntɜːn/ **noun** [C] a period when business or economy becomes less successfu *There has been a sharp **downturn in** sales.*

downwards /ˈdaʊnwədz/ (also US **downwar◄ adv** towards a lower place or level: *The roc slopes downwards to the river.* • **downward a◄** → See also **a downward spiral**

downwind /ˌdaʊnˈwɪnd/ **adj, adv** in the dire▶ tion that the wind is blowing

dowry /ˈdaʊri/ **noun** [C] money that a woman family gives to the man she is marrying in som cultures

doze /dəʊz/ **verb** [I] to sleep lightly: *Grandma w◄ dozing in front of the TV.*

PHRASAL VERB **doze off** to gradually start sleepin usually during the day: *He dozed off during t▶ film.*

dozen /ˈdʌzᵊn/ **noun, determiner 1** ⓑ twelv or a group of twelve: *There were about a doze people at the party.* **2 dozens** informal a lot: *She got **dozens of** friends.* → See also **a dime a doze**

Dr ⓐ written abbreviation for doctor: *Dr Pa◄ Thomas*

drab /dræb/ **adj** without colour and boring ▶ look at: *drab, grey buildings*

draconian /drəˈkəʊniən/ **adj** very severe: *drac▶ nian laws*

draft¹ /drɑːft/ **noun 1** [C] ⓑ a piece of writing ◄ a plan that is not yet in its finished form: *F◄ made several changes to the **first draft**.* **2 th draft** US an arrangement in which people a◄ told that they must join the armed forces **3** [◄ US spelling of draught (= a current of cold air in room)

draft² /drɑːft/ **verb** [T] **1** to produce a piece ◄ writing or a plan that you intend to chang◄ later: *to **draft** a letter* **2** to order someone ▶ join the armed forces

---

☑ Word partners for **draft**

draft a constitution/legislation/a letter/a proposal

PHRASAL VERB **draft sb in/draft sb into sth** main UK to bring someone somewhere to do particular job: *Extra police were drafted in to stop the demonstration.*

raftsman (plural **draftsmen**) US (UK **draughts-man**) /'drɑːftsmən/ **noun** [C] someone who draws detailed drawings as plans for something

rafty /'drɑːfti/ **adj** US spelling of draughty

rag¹ /dræg/ **verb** (**dragging, dragged**) **1 drag sth/sb across/along/over, etc** 🔵 to pull something or someone along the ground somewhere, usually with difficulty: *The table was too heavy to lift, so we had to drag it across the room.* **2 drag sb along/out/to, etc** to make someone go somewhere they do not want to go: *I have to drag myself out of bed every morning.* **3** [T] 🔵 to move something somewhere on a computer screen using a mouse (= small computer control) **4** [I] (also **drag on**) to continue for too much time in a boring way → See also **drag your feet (foot¹)**

PHRASAL VERBS **drag sb down** UK If an unpleasant situation drags someone down, it makes them feel unhappy or sick. • **drag sb into sth** to force someone to become involved in an unpleasant or difficult situation: *I don't want to be dragged into this argument.* • **drag sth out** to make something continue for more time than is necessary

rag² /dræg/ **noun 1 in drag** informal If a man is in drag, he is wearing women's clothes. **2 be a drag** informal to be boring and unpleasant: *Cleaning the house is such a drag.* **3** [C] the action of breathing in smoke from a cigarette: *He took a drag on his cigarette.*

rag and 'drop verb [I, T] 🔵 to move something on a computer screen using a mouse

ragon /'drægən/ **noun** [C] a big, imaginary creature that breathes out fire

dragon

ragonfly /'drægənflaɪ/ **noun** [C] an insect with long wings and a thin, colourful body, often seen flying near water → See picture at **insect**

rain¹ /dreɪn/ **verb 1 REMOVE LIQUID** ▷ [T] to remove the liquid from something, usually by pouring it away: *Drain the pasta and add the tomatoes.* **2 FLOW AWAY** ▷ [I] If something drains, liquid flows away or out of it. **3 MAKE TIRED** ▷ [T] to make someone very tired: *The long journey drained him.* **4 DRINK** ▷ [T] If you drain a glass or cup, you drink all the liquid in it.

rain² /dreɪn/ **noun 1** [C] a pipe or hole that takes away waste liquids or water: *She poured the dirty water down the drain.* **2 a drain on sth** something that uses or wastes a lot of money or energy

IDIOM **down the drain** informal If money or work goes down the drain, it is wasted.

rainage /'dreɪnɪdʒ/ **noun** [U] the system of water or waste liquids flowing away from somewhere into the ground or down pipes

drained /dreɪnd/ **adj** If someone is drained, they are extremely tired.

drainpipe /'dreɪnpaɪp/ **noun** [C] a pipe that carries waste water away from a building

drama /'drɑːmə/ **noun 1 PLAY** ▷ [C] 🔵 a play in a theatre or on television or radio: *a historical drama* **2 PLAYS/ACTING** ▷ [U] 🔵 plays and acting generally: *modern drama* **3 EXCITEMENT** ▷ [C, U] 🔵 exciting things that happen: *There was a lot of drama in the courtroom.*

> ✏️ **Word partners for drama**
>
> a drama **unfolds** • **high** drama • **human** drama

'drama ,queen noun [C] informal someone who gets far too upset or angry over small problems

dramatic /drə'mætɪk/ **adj 1 SUDDEN** ▷ 🔵 very sudden or noticeable: *a dramatic change/improvement* **2 EXCITING** ▷ 🔵 full of action and excitement: *a dramatic rescue* **3 THEATRE** ▷ [always before noun] relating to plays and acting **4 BEHAVIOUR** ▷ showing your emotions in a very obvious way because you want other people to notice you: *Stop being so dramatic!* • **dramatically adv**

dramatist /'dræmətɪst/ **noun** [C] someone who writes plays

dramatize (also UK **-ise**) /'dræmətaɪz/ **verb** [T] **1** to make an event or situation seem more exciting than it really is: *The media tends to dramatize things.* **2** to change a story so that it can be performed as a play • **dramatization** /ˌdræmətaɪ'zeɪʃ°n/ **noun** [C, U]

drank /dræŋk/ past tense of drink

drape /dreɪp/ **verb 1 drape sth across/on/over, etc** to put something such as cloth or a piece of clothing loosely over something: *He draped his jacket over the chair and sat down to eat.* **2 be draped in/with sth** to be loosely covered with a cloth: *The coffin was draped in a flag.*

drapes /dreɪps/ **noun** [plural] mainly US long, heavy curtains

drastic /'dræstɪk/ **adj** Drastic action or change is sudden and extreme: *drastic reductions in price* • **drastically adv**

draught¹ UK (US **draft**) /drɑːft/ **noun** [C] a current of cold air in a room

draught² UK (US **draft**) /drɑːft/ **adj draught beer/lager, etc** a drink that comes from a large container and not from a can or bottle

draughts /drɑːfts/ **noun** [U] UK (US **checkers**) a game that two people play by moving flat, round objects around on a board of black and white squares

draughtsman (plural **draughtsmen**) UK (US **draftsman**) /'drɑːftsmən/ **noun** [C] someone who draws detailed drawings as plans for something

draughty UK (US **drafty**) /'drɑːfti/ **adj** having currents of cold air blowing through: *a draughty old building*

draw¹ /drɔː/ **verb** (**drew, drawn**) **1 PICTURE** ▷ [I, T] 🔵 to produce a picture by making lines or marks, usually with a pen or pencil: *She drew a picture of a tree.* **2 draw sth/sb across/back/**

D

D

over, etc to pull something or someone gently in a particular direction: *He took her hand and drew her towards him.* **3 draw into/out/away, etc** Ⓑ to move somewhere, usually in a vehicle: *The train drew into the station.* **4 draw the curtains** to pull curtains open or closed **5 draw (sb's) attention to sth/sb** Ⓑ to make someone notice someone or something: *I don't want to draw too much attention to myself.* **6 ATTRACT** ▷ [T] Ⓑ to attract someone to a place or person: *Thousands of tourists are drawn to the city every year.* **7 SPORT** ▷ [I, T] UK to finish a game or competition with each team or player having the same score: *England drew 2-2 against Italy.* **8 TAKE OUT** ▷ [T] to take something out of a container or from your pocket, especially a weapon: *He drew a knife and started threatening me.* **9 draw near/close** Ⓑ to become nearer in space or time: *Her birthday's drawing nearer every day.* **10 draw (a) breath** to breathe in air: *She drew a deep breath and started her speech.* **11 MONEY** ▷ [T] (also **draw out**) to take money from your bank account **12 draw to a close/end** to be almost finished **13 draw conclusions** Ⓑ to make judgments after considering a subject or situation **14 draw a comparison/distinction** to say that there is a similarity or difference between two things ▷ See also **draw a blank²**, **draw the line¹ at sth**, **draw a veil over sth**

PHRASAL VERBS **draw back** to move away from someone or something, usually because you are surprised or frightened • **draw sb/sth into sth** to make someone or something become involved in a difficult or unpleasant situation: *I'm not going to be drawn into this argument.* • **draw on sth** to use information or your knowledge or experience of something to help you do something: *His novels draw heavily on his childhood.* • **draw sth up** to prepare something, usually a plan, list, or an official agreement, by writing it

draw² /drɔː/ **noun** [C] **1** the result of a game or competition in which each player or team has the same score: *The match ended in a draw.* **2** mainly UK (US **drawing**) a competition that is decided by choosing a particular ticket or number: *the National Lottery draw* → See also **the luck of the draw**

drawback /'drɔːbæk/ **noun** [C] a problem or disadvantage: *The only **drawback with** this camera is the price.*

> 🖉 Word partners for **drawback**
>
> have drawbacks • a big/major drawback • the main/only drawback • a drawback of/to/with sth

drawer /drɔːʳ/ **noun** [C] Ⓐ a container like a box without a lid that is part of a piece of furniture and that slides in and out: *She opened the **drawer** and took out a knife.* → See also **chest of drawers**

drawing /'drɔːɪŋ/ **noun 1 PICTURE** ▷ [C] Ⓐ a picture made with a pencil or pen: *There were some children's drawings pinned up on the wall.* **2 ACTIVITY** ▷ [U] Ⓐ the skill or activity of

making pictures using a pencil or pen: *Do yo[u] want to do some drawing?* **3 NUMBER/TICKET** [[[C] US (mainly UK **draw**) a competition that [decided by choosing a particular ticket o[r] number

drawing board **noun**

IDIOM **back to the drawing board** If you go bac[k] to the drawing board, you have to start plannin[g] a piece of work again because the first pla[n] failed.

drawing pin **noun** [C] UK (US **thumbtack**) [a] pin with a wide, flat top, used for fastenin[g] pieces of paper to a wall

drawing room **noun** [C] old-fashioned a roo[m] in a large house used for sitting in and talkin[g] with guests

drawl /drɔːl/ **noun** [no plural] a lazy way o[f] speaking that uses long vowel sounds • **draw[l]** **verb** [I]

drawn¹ /drɔːn/ **adj** looking very tired or sic[k]: *She looked pale and drawn after the operatio[n]* → See also **horse-drawn**

drawn² /drɔːn/ past participle of draw

drawn-out /ˌdrɔːnˈaʊt/ **adj** continuing f[or] longer than you think is necessary: *lon[g]* *drawn-out negotiations*

dread¹ /dred/ **verb 1** [T] to feel worried [or] frightened about something that has not ha[p]pened yet: *I'm dreading the first day at my ne[w]* *school.* ○ [+ doing sth] *I dread seeing him agai[n]* **2 I dread to think** UK used to say that you d[o] not want to think about something because it [is] too worrying: *I dread to think what could ha[ve]* *happened if we hadn't been wearing seat belts.*

dread² /dred/ **noun** [U, no plural] a strong feelin[g] of fear or worry: [+ of + doing sth] *a dread of bein[g]* *lonely*

dreadful /'dredf°l/ **adj** Ⓑ extremely bad [or] unpleasant: *a dreadful mistake* ○ *a dreadful m[a...]*

dreadfully /'dredfəli/ **adv 1** mainly UK form[al] very: *I'm dreadfully sorry.* **2** very badly: *Th[e]* *children behaved dreadfully.*

dreadlocks /'dredlɒks/ **noun** [plural] a hairsty[le] in which the hair is twisted together in length[s] and is never brushed

dream¹ /driːm/ **noun 1** [C] Ⓐ a series of even[ts] and images that happen in your mind while yo[u] are sleeping: *a bad dream* ○ *I had a ve[ry]* *strange dream last night.* **2** [C] Ⓑ something th[at] you want to happen although it is not ve[ry] likely: *It was his dream to become an actor.* **3 be i[n]** **a dream** UK Ⓑ to not notice things that a[re] around you because you are thinking abo[ut] something else

IDIOMS **beyond your wildest dreams** bigger [or] better than anything you could imagine or hop[e] for • **like a dream** If something or someon[e] does something like a dream, they do it ve[ry] well.

> 🖉 Word partners for **dream**
>
> have a dream • in sb's dream • a bad dream • a recurring dream

ream² /driːm/ verb (**dreamed, dreamt**) **1** [I, T] **A2** to experience events and images in your mind while you are sleeping: [+ (that)] *Last night I dreamed that I was flying.* **2** [I, T] **B1** to imagine something that you would like to happen: [+ of + doing sth] *I dream of living on a desert island.* ○ [+ (that)] *He never dreamed that one day he would become President.* **3 wouldn't dream of doing sth** used to say that you would not do something because you think it is wrong or silly

PHRASAL VERB **dream sth up** to think of an idea or plan, usually using a lot of imagination: *Who dreams up these new designs?*

ream³ /driːm/ adj **dream house/job/car, etc** the perfect house/job/car, etc

reamer /ˈdriːmər/ noun [C] someone who is not practical and thinks about things that are not likely to happen

reamy /ˈdriːmi/ adj **1** seeming to be in a dream and thinking about pleasant things instead of what is happening around you: *She had a dreamy look in her eyes.* **2** very pleasant: *a dreamy dessert* ● **dreamily** adv

reary /ˈdrɪəri/ adj boring and making you feel unhappy: *a rainy, dreary day* ○ *a dreary job*

redge /dredʒ/ verb [T] to clean the bottom of a lake or river by removing dirt, plants, or rubbish

PHRASAL VERB **dredge sth up** to talk about something bad or unpleasant that happened in the past

regs /dregz/ noun **1** [plural] the part of a drink at the bottom of a glass or other container that usually contains small solid bits **2 the dregs of society/humanity** people who you think are extremely bad or unimportant

rench /drenʃ/ verb [T] to make something or someone completely wet: [often passive] *He was completely drenched by the time he got home.*

ress¹ /dres/ verb **1** [I, T] **A2** to put clothes on yourself or someone else: *I usually get dressed before having breakfast.* → Opposite **undress 2** [I] **B1** to wear a particular type, style, or colour of clothes: *Ali always dresses smartly for work.* ○ [often passive] *She was dressed in black.* **3 dress a burn/cut/wound, etc** to clean an injury and put a covering over it to protect it

PHRASAL VERB **dress up 1** to put on formal clothes for a special occasion **2** to wear special clothes in order to change your appearance, usually for a game or party: *He dressed up as Superman for the party.*

> ⚠ Common learner error: **be/get dressed**
>
> Be careful to use the correct preposition. You do not always need one.
>
> *I got dressed and went to school.*
> *Are you dressed yet?*
> *He was dressed in a black suit.*
> ~~He was dressed with a black suit.~~

ress² /dres/ noun **1** [C] **A1** a piece of clothing for women or girls that covers the top of the body and hangs down over the legs: *She was wearing a short, black dress.* → See colour picture

Clothes on page Centre 8 **2** [U] **B2** a particular style of clothes: *casual/formal dress* → See also **fancy dress**

dresser /ˈdresər/ noun [C] **1** mainly US a piece of bedroom furniture with a mirror and drawers for keeping clothes in **2** UK a piece of furniture consisting of a cupboard with shelves above for keeping plates, cups, and other kitchen equipment

dressing /ˈdresɪŋ/ noun **1** [C, U] a sauce, especially a mixture of oil and vinegar for salad **2** [C] a covering that protects an injury

dressing gown noun [C] mainly UK (US **robe**) a piece of clothing, like a long coat, that you wear at home when you are not dressed

dressing room noun [C] a room where actors or sports teams get dressed before a performance or game

dressing table noun [C] mainly UK a piece of bedroom furniture like a table with a mirror and drawers

dressy /ˈdresi/ adj Dressy clothes are suitable for a formal occasion.

drew /druː/ past tense of draw

dribble /ˈdrɪbl/ verb **1** MOUTH ▷ [I] If someone dribbles, a small amount of liquid comes out of their mouth and goes down their face: *Babies dribble a lot.* **2** LIQUID ▷ [I, T] If a liquid dribbles, it falls slowly in small amounts, and if you dribble a liquid, you pour it so it falls slowly in small amounts: *Dribble some oil over the vegetables.* **3** SPORT ▷ [I, T] to move a ball along by using your hand to hit it against the ground or kicking it several times ● **dribble** noun [C, U]

dried /draɪd/ past of dry

drier /ˈdraɪər/ noun [C] another spelling of dryer (= a machine for drying wet things)

drift¹ /drɪft/ verb **1 drift across/down/towards, etc** to be moved slowly somewhere by currents of wind or water: *Smoke drifted across the rooftops.* **2 drift in/out/into, etc** to move somewhere slowly: *Guests were drifting out onto the terrace.* **3** [I] to get into a situation or job without having any particular plan: *He drifted into acting after university.* **4** [I] If snow or leaves drift, they are blown into piles by the wind.

PHRASAL VERBS **drift apart** If two people drift apart, they gradually become less friendly and the relationship ends. ● **drift off** to gradually start to sleep: *I drifted off during the lecture.*

drift² /drɪft/ noun **1** [C] slow, gradual movement from one place to another: *the drift of people into Western Europe* **2 catch/get sb's drift** to understand the general meaning of what someone is saying **3** [C] a pile of snow or leaves that has been blown somewhere

drill¹ /drɪl/ noun **1** TOOL ▷ [C] a tool or machine for making holes in a hard substance: *an electric drill* → See picture at **tool 2** FOR LEARNING ▷ [C, U] a teaching method in which students repeat something several times to help them learn it: *We do lots of drills to practise pronunciation.* **3 an emergency/fire, etc drill** an occasion when you practise what to do in an emergency/

fire, etc **4 SOLDIERS** ▷ [C, U] an occasion when soldiers do training for marching

drill² /drɪl/ **verb 1** [I, T] to make a hole in a hard substance using a special tool: *Billy drilled a hole in the wall.* ∘ *The engineers were **drilling for** oil.* **2** [T] to make someone repeat something several times so that they learn it

drily /'draɪli/ **adv** another spelling of dryly (= in a serious voice but trying to be funny)

drink¹ /drɪŋk/ **verb (drank, drunk) 1** [I, T] ⓐ to put liquid into your mouth and swallow it: *Would you like something to drink?* ∘ *He was drinking a glass of milk.* **2** [I] ⓐ to drink alcohol, usually regularly: *She doesn't smoke or drink.*

PHRASAL VERBS **drink to sb/sth** to hold your glass up before drinking from it, in order to wish someone or something good luck or success • **drink (sth) up** to finish your drink completely: *Drink up! We've got to leave soon.*

drink² /drɪŋk/ **noun 1** [C] ⓐ a liquid or an amount of liquid that you drink: *a hot/cold drink* ∘ *Can I **have a drink** of water please?* **2** [C, U] ⓐ alcohol, or an alcoholic drink: *Do you fancy a drink tonight to celebrate?* → See also **soft drink**

> 🖉 Word partners for **drink**
>
> **have** a drink • a drink **of** [water/milk, etc] • a **hot/cold** drink

drink-driving /ˌdrɪŋk'draɪvɪŋ/ **noun** [U] UK (US **drunk driving**) driving a vehicle after drinking too much alcohol: *He was convicted of drink-driving.*

drinker /'drɪŋkər/ **noun 1** [C] someone who regularly drinks alcohol: *He's a **heavy drinker** (= he drinks a lot of alcohol).* **2** a **coffee/tea/wine, etc drinker** someone who regularly drinks a particular drink

drinking /'drɪŋkɪŋ/ **noun** [U] the activity of drinking alcohol

drinking water **noun** [U] water that is safe for people to drink

drip¹ /drɪp/ **verb (dripping, dripped) 1** [I, T] If a liquid drips, it falls in drops or you make it fall in drops: *There was water **dripping from** the ceiling.* **2** [I] to produce drops of liquid: *The candle's dripping.*

drip² /drɪp/ **noun 1 DROP** ▷ [C] a drop of liquid that falls from something **2 SOUND** ▷ [no plural] the sound or action of a liquid falling in drops **3 MEDICAL** ▷ [C] (also US **IV**) a piece of medical equipment used for putting liquids into your body: *The doctor's put him **on a drip**.*

drive¹ /draɪv/ **verb (drove, driven) 1 CONTROL VEHICLE** ▷ [I, T] to make a car, bus, or train move, and control what it does: *She's learning to drive.* ∘ *He drives a red sports car.* **2 TRAVEL** ▷ [I, T] ⓐ to travel somewhere in a car, or to take someone somewhere in a car: *My friend drove me home last night.* **3 drive sb out/away/from, etc** to force someone to leave a place: *The supermarket has driven many small shops out of the area.* **4 drive sb crazy/mad/wild, etc** ⓑ to make someone feel crazy, annoyed, or excited: *That noise is driving me mad.* **5 drive sb to sth; drive sb to do**

sth to make someone have a bad feeling or ⬦ something bad: *The arguments and violen⬦ drove her to leave home.* **6 drive sth int⬦ through/towards, etc** to push something som⬦ where by hitting it hard: *He drove the nail in⬦ the wall with a hammer.* **7 MAKE WORK** ▷ [T] provide the power or energy that mak⬦ someone or something work: [often passive] *S⬦ was driven by greed and ambition.* → See a⬦ **drive/send sb round the bend²**, **drive sb ⬦ the wall**

> ❗ Common learner error: **drive** or **ride**?
>
> You **drive** a car, truck, or bus.
> *She drives an expensive sports car.*
> You **ride** a bicycle, motorcycle, or horse.
> *My brother is learning to ride a bicycle.*
> ~~My brother is learning to drive a bicycle.~~

PHRASAL VERBS **be driving at sth** used to ask wh⬦ someone really means: *Just what are you drivi⬦ at?* • **drive off** to leave in a car

drive² /draɪv/ **noun 1 JOURNEY** ▷ [C] ⬦ journey in a car: *The drive from Boston to Ne⬦ York took 4 hours.* **2 GROUND** ▷ [C] the area ⬦ ground that you drive on to get from your hou⬦ to the road: *You can park on the dri⬦* **3 COMPUTER** ▷ [C] ⬦ a part of a comput⬦ that can read or store information: *a DVD dri⬦* ∘ *Save your work **on the** C: **drive**.* **4 EFFORT** ▷ ⬦ a great effort to achieve something: [+ to do s⬦ *The government started a drive to impro⬦ standards in schools.* **5 ENERGY** ▷ [U] ener⬦ and determination to achieve things: *She h⬦ drive and ambition.*

> 🖉 Word partners for **drive**
>
> **go for** a drive

drive-by /'draɪvbaɪ/ **adj** describes somethi⬦ that someone does when they are inside ⬦ vehicle that is moving: *a drive-by shooting*

drive-in /'draɪvɪn/ **noun** [C] mainly US a cinem⬦ or restaurant that you can visit without getti⬦ out of your car

drivel /'drɪvəl/ **noun** [U] nonsense: *He was talki⬦ complete drivel.*

driven /'drɪvən/ past participle of drive

driver /'draɪvər/ **noun** [C] **1** ⓐ someone wh⬦ drives a vehicle: *a bus/train driver* → See a⬦ **engine driver 2** a computer program th⬦ makes it possible for a computer to use oth⬦ pieces of equipment such as a printer: *printer driver*

> 🖉 Word partners for **driver**
>
> a **bus/taxi/train/truck** driver • the driver **of** sth

driver's license **noun** [C] US (UK **drivi⬦ licence**) an official document that allows yc⬦ to drive a car

drive-through /'draɪvθruː/ **noun** [C] a pla⬦ where you can get a type of service by drivi⬦ through, without needing to get out of your ca⬦ *a drive-through restaurant*

---

driveway /ˈdraɪvweɪ/ **noun** [C] the area of ground that you drive on to get from your house to the road

driving¹ /ˈdraɪvɪŋ/ **noun** [U] the activity of driving a vehicle, or the way someone drives

driving² /ˈdraɪvɪŋ/ **adj 1 driving rain/snow** rain or snow that is falling very fast and being blown by the wind **2 the driving force** a person or thing that has a very strong effect and makes something happen: She was **the driving force** *behind* the project.

driving licence noun [C] UK (US **driver's license**) Ⓐ an official document that allows you to drive a car

drizzle /ˈdrɪzl/ **noun** [U] light rain • **drizzle verb** [I]

drone /drəʊn/ **verb** [I] to make a continuous, low sound, like an engine: I could hear traffic droning in the distance.

PHRASAL VERB **drone on** to talk for a long time in a very boring way: I wish he'd stop **droning on** *about* school.

drool /druːl/ **verb** [I] If a person or animal drools, liquid comes out of the side of their mouth.

PHRASAL VERB **drool over sb/sth** to look at someone or something in a way that shows you think they are very attractive

droop /druːp/ **verb** [I] to hang down, often because of being weak, tired, or unhappy: He was tired and his eyelids were starting to droop.

drop¹ /drɒp/ **verb** (**dropping, dropped**)
1 LET FALL ▷ [T] to let something you are carrying fall to the ground: She tripped and dropped the vase.
2 FALL ▷ [I] Ⓑ to fall: The ball dropped to the ground. **3 BECOME LESS** ▷ [I] Ⓑ If a level or amount drops, it becomes less: Unemployment has **dropped** *from* 8% *to* 6% in the last year. **4 TAKE** ▷ [T] (also **drop off**) to take someone or something to a place, usually by car as you travel somewhere else: I can drop you at the station on my way to work. **5 STOP ACTIVITY** ▷ [T] Ⓑ If you drop a plan, activity, or idea, you stop doing or planning it: Plans for a new supermarket have been dropped. ∘ When we heard the news, we **dropped everything** (= stopped what we were doing) and rushed to the hospital. **6 STOP INCLUDING** ▷ [T] to decide to stop including someone in a group or team: The coach **dropped** me *from* the team. **7 drop it/the subject** to stop talking about something, especially because it is annoying or upsetting someone **8 VOICE** ▷ [I, T] If your voice drops, or if you drop your voice, you talk more quietly. → See also **be dropping like flies (fly²)** **9 COMPUTING** ▷ [T] to put text, a file, a picture, etc. in a particular place on a computer screen using your mouse: Just **drag and drop** the images into your presentation.

drop

PHRASAL VERBS **drop by/in** to visit someone for a short time, usually without arranging it before: I **dropped in** *on* George on my way home from school. • **drop sb/sth off** to take someone or something to a place, usually by car as you travel somewhere else • **drop off 1** informal to start to sleep: She dropped off in front of the TV. **2** If the amount, number, or quality of something drops off, it becomes less: The demand for mobile phones shows no signs of dropping off. • **drop out** to stop doing something before you have completely finished: He **dropped out of** school at 14.

drop² /drɒp/ **noun 1 LIQUID** ▷ [C] Ⓑ a small, round-shaped amount of liquid: I felt a few drops of rain. → See colour picture **Pieces and Quantities** on page Centre 1 **2 REDUCTION** ▷ [no plural] Ⓑ a reduction in the level or amount of something: There has been a **drop** *in* crime recently. **3 SMALL AMOUNT** ▷ [no plural] a small amount of a liquid you can drink: Would you like a **drop** *more* milk? **4 DISTANCE** ▷ [no plural] a vertical distance down from somewhere to the ground: It's a drop of about 50 metres from the top of the cliff.

🗹 Word partners for **drop**

a **big/dramatic/sharp/steep** drop • a drop **in** sth

---

drop-down menu noun [C] a pop-up menu: a list of choices on a computer screen that is hidden until you choose to look at it

droplet /ˈdrɒplət/ **noun** [C] a very small, round amount of liquid

dropout /ˈdrɒpaʊt/ **noun** [C] **1** a student who leaves school or university before they have completely finished: a high-school dropout **2** someone who does not want to have a job, possessions, etc because they do not want to be like everyone else

droppings /ˈdrɒpɪŋz/ **noun** [plural] solid waste from birds and some small animals: rabbit droppings

drought /draʊt/ **noun** [C, U] a long period when there is no rain and people do not have enough water: A severe drought ruined the crops.

drove /drəʊv/ past tense of drive

droves /drəʊvz/ **noun in droves** If people do something in droves, they do it in large numbers.

drown /draʊn/ **verb 1** [I, T] to die because you are under water and cannot breathe, or to kill someone in this way: Two people drowned in a boating accident yesterday. **2** [T] (also **drown out**) If a loud noise drowns the sound of something else, it prevents that sound from being heard: His voice was drowned out by the traffic.

drowning /ˈdraʊnɪŋ/ **noun** [C, U] a death caused by someone being under water and not being able to breathe

drowsy /ˈdraʊzi/ **adj** feeling tired and wanting to sleep: The sun was making me drowsy. • **drowsily adv** • **drowsiness noun** [U]

drudgery /ˈdrʌdʒəri/ **noun** [U] work that is very boring

drug¹ /drʌg/ **noun** [C] **1** ⓑ² an illegal substance that people take to make them feel happy: [usually plural] *He started taking/using drugs such as heroin and cocaine.* ∘ *Greg is on drugs* (= he uses drugs regularly). ∘ *a drug dealer* **2** ⓑ² a chemical substance used as a medicine: *Scientists are developing a new drug to treat cancer.* → See also **hard drugs**

> ☑ Word partners for **drug**
>
> be on/take/use drugs • drug abuse/addiction
> • a drug addict/dealer/user

drug² /drʌg/ **verb** [T] (**drugging, drugged**) to give someone a chemical substance that makes them sleep or stop feeling pain: *He drugged his victims before robbing them.*

drug addict noun [C] someone who cannot stop taking drugs

drugstore /'drʌgstɔːʳ/ **noun** [C] US (UK **chemist's**) a shop that sells medicines and also things such as soap and beauty products

drum¹ /drʌm/ **noun** [C] **1** ⓐ² a round, hollow, musical instrument that you hit with your hands or with sticks: *Anna plays the drums.* **2** a large, round container for holding substances such as oil or chemicals

drum

drum² /drʌm/ **verb** [I, T] (**drumming, drummed**) to hit something several times and make a sound like a drum, or to make something do this: *I listened to the rain drumming on the roof.* ∘ *She drummed her fingers nervously on the desk.*

PHRASAL VERBS **drum sth into sb** to make someone remember or believe an idea or fact by repeating it to them many times: [often passive] *The importance of good manners was drummed into me by my father.* • **drum up sth** to increase interest in something or support for something: *He was trying to drum up some enthusiasm for his idea.*

drummer /'drʌməʳ/ **noun** [C] someone who plays a drum

drunk¹ /drʌŋk/ **adj** ⓑ² unable to behave or speak normally because you have drunk too much alcohol: *He usually gets drunk at parties.*

drunk² /drʌŋk/ past participle of drink

drunken /'drʌŋkən/ **adj** [always before noun] drunk, or involving people who are drunk: *a drunken man* ∘ *drunken behaviour* • **drunkenly** adv • **drunkenness noun** [U]

dry¹ /draɪ/ **adj** (**drier, driest, dryer, dryest**) **1 NOT WET** ▷ ⓐ² Something that is dry does not have water or liquid in it or on its surface: *dry paint* ∘ *Is your hair dry yet?* **2 NO RAIN** ▷ ⓐ² with no or not much rain: *a dry summer* **3 HAIR/ SKIN** ▷ Dry skin or hair does not feel soft or smooth: *My lips feel really dry.* **4 WINE** ▷ Dry wine is not sweet. **5 BORING** ▷ If a book, talk, or subject is dry, it is not interesting. **6 FUNNY** ▷ saying something in a serious way but trying to be funny: *a dry sense of humour* • **dryness** /'draɪnəs/ **noun** [U]

dry² /draɪ/ **verb** [I, T] ⓐ² to become dry, or to make something become dry: *He dried his hand on a towel.* → See also **blow-dry**

PHRASAL VERBS **dry (sb/sth) off** to make someone or something dry, or to become dry, especially on the surface: [often reflexive] *I dried myself off with a towel and got dressed.* • **dry (sth) out** to become dry, or to make something become dry • **dry (sth) up** mainly UK to make plates, cups, etc dry with a cloth after they have been washed • **dry up 1** If a supply of something dries up, it ends: *The work dried up and he went out of business.* **2** If a river or lake dries up, the water in it disappears.

dry clean verb [T] to clean clothes using a special chemical and not with water • **dry cleaner's noun** [C] a shop where you can have your clothes cleaned this way • **dry cleaning noun** [U]

dryer (also **drier**) /'draɪəʳ/ **noun** [C] a machine for drying wet things, usually clothes or hair → See also **tumble dryer**

dryly (also **drily**) /'draɪli/ **adv** If you say something dryly, you say it in a serious way but you are trying to be funny.

dual /'djuːəl/ **adj** [always before noun] having two parts, or having two of something: *dual nationality*

dual carriageway noun [C] UK a road that consists of two parallel roads, so that traffic travelling in opposite directions is separated by a central strip of land

dub /dʌb/ **verb** [T] (**dubbing, dubbed**) **1** to give someone or something an unofficial or funny name: [often passive] *He was dubbed 'Big Ears' by the media.* **2** to change the language in a film or television programme into a different language: [often passive] *The film was dubbed into English.*

dubious /'djuːbiəs/ **adj 1** thought not to be completely true, honest, or legal: *dubious evidence* ∘ *a man with a dubious reputation* **2** not certain that something is good or true: *He dubious about the benefits of acupuncture* • **dubiously adv**

duchess /'dʌtʃɪs/ **noun** [C] a woman of very high social rank in some European countries: *the Duchess of Windsor*

duck

duck¹ /dʌk/ **noun** [C, U] ⓐ² a bird with short legs that lives in or near water, or the meat from this bird → See also **be (like) water¹ off a duck's back**

uck² /dʌk/ **verb 1** [I, T] to move your head or body down quickly to avoid being hit or seen: *Billy ducked behind a car when he saw his teacher.* **2** [T] informal to avoid something that is difficult or unpleasant: *He managed to **duck** the **issue**.*

PHRASAL VERB **duck out of sth** to avoid doing something that other people are expecting you to do: [+ doing sth] *She was trying to duck out of doing her homework.*

uckling /ˈdʌklɪŋ/ **noun** [C] a young duck

uct /dʌkt/ **noun** [C] **1** a tube in the body that a liquid substance can flow through: *a **tear duct*** **2** a tube or passage for air or wires that is part of the structure of a building: *a heating duct*

ud /dʌd/ **noun** [C] something that does not work correctly ● **dud adj**

ude /duːd/ **noun** [C] mainly US very informal a man: *a cool dude*

ue¹ /djuː/ **adj 1** EVENT ▷ [never before noun] ⓺ expected or planned: [+ to do sth] *He was due to fly back this morning.* ○ *Her book is **due out** (= expected to be published) next week.* ○ *When is the baby due (= expected to be born)?* **2 due to sth** ⓺ because of something: *The train was late due to snow.* **3** MONEY ▷ [never before noun] Money that is due is owed to someone and must be paid: *The rent is due today.* **4** DESERVE ▷ Something that is due to you is something that is owed to you or something you deserve: *He didn't get the praise and recognition that was **due to** him.* **5** BEHAVIOUR ▷ [always before noun] formal correct and suitable: *He was fined for driving without due care and attention.* → Opposite **undue 6 be due for sth** If you are due for something, it should happen very soon: *I'm due for a check-up at the dentist's.*

ue² /djuː/ **noun give sb their due** something that you say when you want to describe someone's good qualities after they have done something wrong or after you have criticized them: *Joe's a bit slow but, to give him his due, he does work hard.*

ue³ /djuː/ **adv due east/north/south/west, etc** directly east/north/south/west, etc: *sail/fly due south*

uel /ˈdjuːəl/ **noun** [C] **1** a type of fight in the past between two people with weapons, used as a way of deciding an argument: *He challenged him to a duel.* **2** an argument or competition between two people or groups

ues /djuːz/ **noun** [plural] money that you must pay to be a member of an organization: *annual dues*

uet /djuˈet/ **noun** [C] a piece of music for two people to perform together

uffel ˌbag noun [C] (also **duffle bag**) a strong bag with thick string at the top that is used to close it and carry it

ug /dʌg/ past of dig

uke /djuːk/ **noun** [C] a man of very high social rank in some European countries: *the Duke of Beaufort*

dull¹ /dʌl/ **adj 1** BORING ▷ ⓺ not interesting: *a dull place* ○ *a dull person* **2** NOT BRIGHT ▷ not bright: *dull colours* ○ *dull weather* **3** SOUND ▷ A dull sound is not loud or clear: *a dull thud* **4** PAIN ▷ [always before noun] A dull pain is not strong: *a dull ache* ● **dullness noun** [U] ● **dully adv**

dull² /dʌl/ **verb** [T] to make a feeling or quality become less strong: *He's on morphine to dull the pain.*

duly /ˈdjuːli/ **adv** formal at the correct time, in the correct way, or as you would expect: *I ordered it over the Internet and within a few days, it duly arrived.* ○ *I was duly impressed.*

dumb /dʌm/ **adj 1** mainly US informal stupid: *a dumb idea/question* ○ *He's too dumb to understand.* **2** physically unable to talk

IDIOM **be struck dumb** to be unable to speak because you are so shocked or angry

● **dumbly adv**

dumbfounded /ˌdʌmˈfaʊndɪd/ **adj** extremely surprised

dummy¹ /ˈdʌmi/ **noun** [C] **1** BABY EQUIPMENT ▷ UK (US **pacifier**) a small, rubber object that a baby sucks to stop it crying **2** STUPID PERSON ▷ mainly US informal a stupid person: *She's no dummy.* **3** MODEL ▷ a model of a person

dummy² /ˈdʌmi/ **adj** [always before noun] not real but made to look real: *dummy weapons*

dump¹ /dʌmp/ **verb 1** [T] to put something somewhere to get rid of it, especially in a place where you should not put it: *The company was fined for illegally dumping toxic chemicals.* **2 dump sth on/in/down, etc** to put something somewhere quickly and carelessly: *Henri dumped his bag on the table and went upstairs.*

dump² /dʌmp/ **noun** [C] (also UK **tip**) **1** a place where people take things that they do not want: *We took our old mattress to the dump.* **2** informal a place that is dirty and untidy: *His room is a dump.*

dumping /ˈdʌmpɪŋ/ **noun** [U] **1** SELL CHEAPLY ▷ the activity of selling goods in another country so cheaply that companies in that country cannot compete fairly **2** SELL LARGE AMOUNTS ▷ the act of selling large amounts of something that you do not want to keep **3** GET RID OF ▷ the act of throwing something away in a place that is not suitable or allowed by law: *chemical dumping*

dumpling /ˈdʌmplɪŋ/ **noun** [C] a round mixture of fat and flour that has been cooked in boiling liquid: *stew and dumplings*

dumps /dʌmps/ **noun**

IDIOM **be down in the dumps** informal to be unhappy: *He looks a bit down in the dumps.*

Dumpster /ˈdʌmpstəʳ/ **noun** [C] US trademark (UK **skip**) a very large, metal container for big pieces of rubbish

dumpy /ˈdʌmpi/ **adj** informal short and fat

dune /djuːn/ **noun** [C] (also **sand dune**) a hill of sand in the desert or on the coast

dung /dʌŋ/ **noun** [U] solid waste from a large animal

dungarees /ˌdʌŋgəˈriːz/ **noun** [plural] UK (US **overalls**) trousers with a part that covers your chest and straps that go over your shoulders

dungeon /ˈdʌndʒən/ **noun** [C] a dark, underground prison, used in the past

dunk /dʌŋk/ **verb** [T] to quickly put something into liquid and take it out again: *He dunked the roll in his soup.*

dunno /dəˈnəʊ/ informal **I dunno** I do not know.

duo /ˈdjuːəʊ/ **noun** [C] two people who perform together: *a comedy/pop duo*

dupe /djuːp/ **verb** [T] to trick someone: [often passive, + into + doing sth] *He was duped into paying $4000 for a fake painting.*

duplicate¹ /ˈdjuːplɪkeɪt/ **verb** [T] **1** to make an exact copy of something: *The document has been duplicated.* **2** to do something that has already been done, in exactly the same way: *Ajax hope to duplicate last year's success.* • **duplication** /ˌdjuː-plɪˈkeɪʃən/ **noun** [U]

duplicate² /ˈdjuːplɪkət/ **noun 1** [C] something that is an exact copy of something else: *I lost my passport and had to get a duplicate.* **2 in duplicate** If a document is in duplicate, there are two copies of it. • **duplicate adj** *a duplicate key*

duplicity /djuːˈplɪsəti/ **noun** [U] attempts to trick people by dishonestly telling different people different things

durable /ˈdjʊərəbl/ **adj** remaining in good condition for a long time: *durable goods* ∘ *a fabric that is comfortable and durable* • **durability** /ˌdjʊərəˈbɪləti/ **noun** [U]

duration /djʊəˈreɪʃən/ **noun** [U] formal the amount of time that something lasts: *The singer remained in the hotel for the duration of his stay in the UK.*

duress /djʊˈres/ **noun** formal **under duress** If you do something under duress, you do it because someone is forcing you to: *The confession was made under duress.*

during /ˈdjʊərɪŋ/ **preposition 1** ⓐ₂ for the whole of a period of time: *Emma's usually at home during the day.* **2** ⓐ₂ at a particular moment in a period of time: *We'll arrange a meeting some time during the week.*

> **⚠ Common learner error: during or for?**
>
> Use **during** to talk about a period of time when something happens.
> *I'm at work during the day, so it's better to phone in the evening.*
> *Please don't take photos during the performance.*
> Use **for** to say how long something happens or continues, for example 'for two hours', 'for three days'.
> *I've been in Cambridge for six months now.*
> *We waited for an hour and then left.*
> ~~We waited during an hour and then left.~~

dusk /dʌsk/ **noun** [U] the time in the evening when it starts to become dark: *As dusk fell, u, headed back to the hotel.*

dust¹ /dʌst/ **noun** [U] ⓑ₁ a powder of dirt or sc that you see on a surface or in the air: *He drou off in a cloud of dust.*

IDIOMS **bite the dust** informal to die, fail, or sto existing • **the dust settles** If the dust settle after an argument or big change, the situatio becomes calmer: *Let the dust settle a bit befo. you make any decisions about the future.*

dust² /dʌst/ **verb** [I, T] to remove dust fro something: *I tidied and dusted the shelves.*

dustbin /ˈdʌstbɪn/ **noun** [C] UK (US **garbage ca** ⓑ₁ a large container for rubbish kept outsid your house

duster /ˈdʌstər/ **noun** [C] UK a cloth used fo removing dust (= powder of dirt) from furnitur and other objects

dustman /ˈdʌstmən/ **noun** [C] (plural U **dustmen**) UK (US **garbage man**) someor whose job is to remove rubbish from containe outside people's houses

dustpan /ˈdʌstpæn/ **noun** [C] a flat containe with a handle, used with a brush for removin dirt from a floor: *Get the dustpan and brush ar I'll sweep this up.* → See picture at **brush**

dusty /ˈdʌsti/ **adj** ⓑ₁ covered with dust (= powde of dirt): *a dusty old chair* ∘ *dusty streets*

dutiful /ˈdjuːtɪfəl/ **adj** doing everything that yo should in your position or job: *a dutiful sc* • **dutifully adv**

duty /ˈdjuːti/ **noun** [C, U] **1** RIGHT THING TO DO [ⓑ₁ something you must do because it is moral or legally right: *a moral duty* ∘ [+ to do sth] *Ro companies have a duty to provide safe transpor* **2** JOB ▷ ⓑ₂ something you do as part of your jc or because of your position: *professional/offici duties* **3 on/off duty** ⓑ₂ If a doctor, police office etc is on duty, they are working, and if they ar off duty, they are not working. **4** TAX ▷ tax tha you pay on something you buy

> **✎ Word partners for duty**
>
> have/neglect/perform a duty • a duty to/ towards sb

duty-free /ˌdjuːtiˈfriː/ **adj** ⓑ₁ Duty-free goods ar things that you can buy and bring into country without paying tax.

duvet /duːˈveɪ/ **noun** [C] (also US **comforter**) ⓑ₁ cover filled with feathers or warm material tha you sleep under

DVD /ˌdiːviːˈdiː/ **noun** [C] ⓐ₁ abbreviation fo digital versatile disc: a small disc for storin music, films and information: *a DVD playe drive* ∘ *Is this film available on DVD?*

dwarf¹ /dwɔːf/ **noun** [C] **1** an imaginary creatur like a little man, in children's stories: *Snow Whi and the Seven Dwarves* **2** an offensive word fo someone who is very short • **dwarf adj** A dwa animal or plant is much smaller than th normal size.

dwarf² /dwɔːf/ **verb** [T] If something dwarf other things, it is very big and makes them seer small: [often passive] *The hotel is dwarfed by skyscrapers.*

dwell /dwel/ **verb** (**dwelt, dwelled**) **dwell in/ among/with**, etc literary to live somewhere

PHRASAL VERB **dwell on/upon sth** to keep thinking or talking about something, especially something bad or unpleasant: *I don't want to **dwell on the past**.*

dweller /'dwelə^r/ **noun an apartment/city/ country**, etc **dweller** someone who lives in an apartment/city/the country, etc

dwelling /'dwelɪŋ/ **noun** [C] formal a house or place to live in

dwindle /'dwɪndl/ **verb** [I] to become smaller or less: *The number of students in the school has **dwindled to** 200.* ∘ *Our savings slowly **dwindled away**.* ∘ *dwindling supplies of oil*

dye¹ /daɪ/ **noun** [C, U] a substance that is used to change the colour of something

dye² /daɪ/ **verb** [T] (**dyeing, dyed**) to change the colour of something by using a dye: *He dyed his hair pink last week.*

dying /'daɪɪŋ/ present participle of die

dyke (also **dike**) /daɪk/ **noun** [C] **1** a wall built to stop water from a sea or river going onto the land **2** UK a passage that has been dug to take water away from fields

dynamic /daɪ'næmɪk/ **adj 1** ACTIVE ▷ ⓑ full of ideas, energy, and enthusiasm: *a dynamic, young*

teacher ∘ *dynamic leadership* **2** CHANGING ▷ continuously changing or moving: *a dynamic economy* **3** PRODUCING MOVEMENT ▷ A dynamic force makes something move. • **dynamically** adv

dynamics /daɪ'næmɪks/ **noun 1** [plural] the way that parts of a situation, group, or system affect each other: *political dynamics* ∘ *The **dynamics of family life** have changed greatly.* **2** [U] the scientific study of the movement of objects

dynamism /'daɪnəmɪz^əm/ **noun** [U] the quality of being dynamic

dynamite /'daɪnəmaɪt/ **noun** [U] **1** a type of explosive: *a stick of dynamite* **2** informal someone or something that is very exciting, powerful, or dangerous: *The issue is political dynamite.*

dynasty /'dɪnəsti/ ⓤⓢ /'daɪnəsti/ **noun** [C] a series of rulers who are all from the same family: *the Ming dynasty*

dysentery /'dɪs^ənt^əri/ **noun** [U] an infectious disease that causes severe problems with the bowels, making solid waste become liquid

dysfunctional /dɪs'fʌŋkʃ^ən^əl/ **adj** formal not behaving, working, or happening in the way that most people think is normal: *a **dysfunctional family/childhood***

dyslexia /dɪ'sleksiə/ **noun** [U] a condition affecting the brain that makes it difficult for someone to read and write • **dyslexic** /dɪ'sleksɪk/ **adj** having dyslexia

D

E

E, e /iː/ the fifth letter of the alphabet

e- /iː-/ **prefix** electronic, usually relating to the Internet: *an e-ticket* ∘ *e-commerce*

each /iːtʃ/ **pronoun, determiner** ⓐ every one in a group of two or more things or people when they are considered separately: *A player from **each of** the teams volunteered to be captain.* ∘ *The bill is $36 between the four of us, that's $9 each.*

each ˈother pronoun ⓐ used to show that each person in a group of two or more people does something to the others: *The kids are always arguing with each other.*

eager /ˈiːgər/ **adj** ⓑ wanting to do or have something very much: [+ to do sth] *Sam was eager to go home and play on his computer.* • **eagerly adv** ⓑ *an **eagerly awaited** announcement* • **eagerness noun** [U]

eagle

eagle /ˈiːgl/ **noun** [C] ⓑ a large, wild bird with a big, curved beak, that hunts smaller animals

ear /ɪər/ **noun 1** [C] ⓐ one of the two organs on your head that you hear with: *The child whispered something in her mother's ear.* → See colour picture **The Body** on page Centre 13 **2** [C] the top part of some crop plants, which produces grain: *an ear of wheat/corn* **3 have an ear for sth** to be good at hearing, repeating, or understanding a particular type of sound: *He has no ear for music.*

IDIOMS **fall on deaf ears** If advice or a request falls on deaf ears, people ignore it. • **play it by ear** to decide how to deal with a situation as it develops • **play sth by ear** to play a piece of music by remembering the notes

earache /ˈɪəreɪk/ **noun** [C, U] ⓑ pain in your ear: *I've got UK earache/US an earache.*

eardrum /ˈɪədrʌm/ **noun** [C] a part inside your ear made of thin, tight skin that allows you to hear sounds

earl /ɜːl/ **noun** [C] a man of high social rank in the UK: *the Earl of Northumberland*

earlobe /ˈɪələʊb/ **noun** [C] the soft part at the bottom of your ear

early /ˈɜːli/ **adj, adv** (**earlier, earliest**) **1** ⓐ near the beginning of a period of time, process, etc:

the early 1980s ∘ *It is too early to say whether h will recover completely.* **2** ⓑ before the usu time or the time that was arranged: *earl retirement* ∘ *The plane arrived ten minutes earl* **3 at the earliest** used after a time or date t show that something will not happen befor then: *Building will not begin until July at th earliest.* **4 early on** in the first stage or part o something: *I lost interest quite early on in th book.* → See also **it's early days (day)**

earmark /ˈɪəmɑːk/ **verb** [T] to decide th something, especially money, will be used for particular purpose: [often passive] *More than $ million has been **earmarked for** schools in th area.* ∘ *The land is earmarked for development.*

earn /ɜːn/ **verb 1 GET MONEY** ▷ [I, T] ⓐ to g money for doing work: *She earns more tha £40,000 a year.* **2 earn a/your living** to work get money for the things you need **3 DESERVE [T] to get something that you deserve because your work, qualities, etc: *As a teacher you have t earn the respect of your students.* **4 PROFIT** ▷ [to make a profit: *I want an account that earns high rate of interest.*

earner /ˈɜːnər/ **noun** [C] **1** someone who ear money: *a **high earner*** **2** UK informal a product service that earns you money: *She has a nic little earner making curtains.*

> ☑ Word partners for **earner**
> high/low/top earners • wage earners

earnest /ˈɜːnɪst/ **adj 1** very serious and sincer *an earnest young man* ∘ *an earnest effort* **2 i earnest** If something begins to happen i earnest, it really starts to happen in a seriou way: *The research will begin in earnest early ne: year.* **3 be in earnest** to be very serious abou something and mean what you are sayin • **earnestly adv** • **earnestness noun** [U]

earnings /ˈɜːnɪŋz/ **noun** [plural] ⓑ money tha you get from working

earphones /ˈɪəfəʊnz/ **noun** [plural] a piece of electronic equipment that you put on your ears so that you can listen privately to radio, recorded music, etc

earring

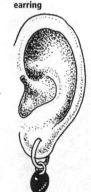

earring /ˈɪərɪŋ/ **noun** [C] ⓐ a piece of jewellery that you wear on or through your ear: [usually plural] *diamond earrings*

earshot /ˈɪəʃɒt/ **noun be out of/within earshot** If you are out of earshot, you are too far away to hear something, and if you are within earshot, you are close enough to hear something.

arth /ɜːθ/ noun **1** PLANET ▷ [no plural] (also **the Earth**) 🔒 the planet that we live on **2** SUBSTANCE ▷ [U] 🔒 soil or ground: *a mound of earth* **3** ELECTRICAL WIRE ▷ [C] UK (US **ground**) a wire that makes electrical equipment safer **4** cost/charge, etc the earth UK informal to cost/charge, etc an extremely large amount of money

IDIOMS **come (back) down to earth** to start dealing with life and problems again after you have had a very exciting time • **how/what/why, etc on earth?** informal used when you are extremely surprised, confused, or angry about something: *Why on earth didn't you tell me before?*

arthly /ˈɜːθli/ adj **1** no earthly doubt/reason/use, etc used to emphasize that there is not any doubt/reason/use, etc: *There's no earthly reason why you should feel guilty.* **2** literary relating to this world and not any spiritual life: *earthly powers*

arthquake /ˈɜːθkweɪk/ noun [C] 🔒 a sudden movement of the Earth's surface, often causing severe damage: *A powerful **earthquake struck** eastern Turkey last night.*

🖉 **Word partners for earthquake**

an earthquake **hits/strikes** [a place] • a **devastating/major/massive/powerful** earthquake

---

arthy /ˈɜːθi/ adj **1** referring to sex and the human body in a direct way: *earthy jokes* **2** similar to soil in colour, smell, or taste

arwig /ˈɪəwɪɡ/ noun [C] a small dark-brown insect with two curved parts on its tail

arworm /ˈɪəwɜːm/ noun [C] a song or part of a song that you keep hearing in your head

ase¹ /iːz/ noun **1** 🔒 [U] If you do something with ease, it is very easy for you to do it: *Gary passed his exams **with ease**.* ∘ *I'm amazed at **the ease with which** he learnt the language.* **2** at ease 🔒 feeling relaxed and comfortable: *I felt completely at ease with him.*

IDIOM **ill at ease** feeling anxious

ase² /iːz/ verb **1** [I, T] to become less severe, or to make something become less severe: *The new road should ease traffic problems in the village.* **2** ease sb/sth back/out/up, etc to move someone or something gradually and gently to another position: [often reflexive] *Tom eased himself back in his chair.*

PHRASAL VERB **ease off/up 1** STOP ▷ to gradually stop or become less: *The storm is easing off.* **2** WORK LESS ▷ to start to work less or do things with less energy: *As he got older, he started to ease up a little.* **3** TREAT LESS SEVERELY ▷ to start to treat someone less severely: *I wish his supervisor would **ease up on** him a bit.*

asel /ˈiːzəl/ noun [C] something used to support a painting while you paint it

asily /ˈiːzɪli/ adv **1** EASY ▷ 🔒 with no difficulty: *She makes friends easily.* **2** LIKELY ▷ used to

emphasize that something is likely: *A comment like that could easily be misunderstood.* **3** easily the best/worst/biggest, etc certainly the best/worst/biggest, etc

easel

east, East /iːst/ noun **1** 🔒 [U] the direction that you face to see the sun rise: *Which way's east?* **2** the east 🔒 the part of an area that is further towards the east than the rest **3** the East 🔒 the countries of Asia, especially Japan and China • **east** adj 🔒 *New York is **east of** Chicago.* • **east** adv 🔒 towards the east: *They sailed east.* → See also the **Middle East**

Easter /ˈiːstər/ noun [C, U] the Christian period of celebration around Easter Sunday (= the special Sunday in March or April on which Christians celebrate Jesus Christ's return to life): *the Easter holidays*

Easter egg noun [C] a chocolate egg that people give and receive at Easter

easterly /ˈiːstəli/ adj **1** towards or in the east: *The river flows in an easterly direction.* **2** An easterly wind comes from the east: *a strong, easterly breeze*

eastern, Eastern /ˈiːstən/ adj [always before noun] **1** 🔒 in or from the east part of an area: *eastern Europe* **2** 🔒 in or from the countries of Asia: *Eastern philosophy* ∘ *an Eastern religion*

easterner, Easterner /ˈiːstənər/ noun [C] mainly US someone from the east part of a country or area

Easter Sunday noun [C, U] (also **Easter Day**) the special Sunday in March or April on which Christians celebrate Jesus Christ's return to life

eastward, eastwards /ˈiːstwəd, ˈiːstwədz/ adv towards the east • **eastward** adj *an eastward direction*

easy¹ /ˈiːzi/ adj **1** 🔒 not difficult: *an easy choice* ∘ *He thought the exam was very easy.* ∘ [+ to do sth] *It's easy to see why he's so popular.* **2** relaxed and comfortable: *She has a very easy manner.* **3** I'm easy informal used to say that you do not mind which choice is made: *"Would you like pizza or curry?" "I'm easy. You choose."*

⚠️ **Common learner error: easy or easily?**

Remember, **easy** is an adjective and usually describes a noun.

an easy question
The exam was easy.

Easily is an adverb and usually describes a verb.

You should pass the exam easily.
~~You should pass the exam easy.~~

---

easy² /ˈiːzi/ adv **1** take it/things easy 🔒 to relax and not use too much energy: *After his heart attack, he had to take things easy for a while.* **2** go easy on sb informal to treat someone in a gentle way and not be too strict : *Go easy on the boy – he's only young.* **3** go easy on sth informal to not eat or use too much of something: *Go easy on the chips, there aren't many left.*

IDIOM **easier said than done** used to say that something seems like a good idea but it would be difficult to do

---

➕ Other ways of saying **easy**

If something is easy to do or understand, we often use the adjectives **simple** or **straightforward**:
> *The recipe is so simple, you just mix all the ingredients together.*
> *It seems like a fairly straightforward task.*

If a machine or system is easy to use, we often describe it as **user-friendly**:
> *This latest version of the software is much more user-friendly.*

In informal situations there are also some fixed expressions you can use to say that something is very easy to do, for example:
> (UK) *This machine's a doddle to use.*
> *My last exam was a piece of cake.*
> *Once we reached the main road the journey was plain sailing.*

---

easy-going /ˌiːziˈɡəʊɪŋ/ **adj** 🔵 relaxed and not easily upset or worried

---

➕ Other ways of saying **eat**

A more formal alternative is the verb **consume**:
> *He consumes vast quantities of bread with every meal.*

If someone eats something quickly because they are very hungry, the verb **devour** is sometimes used:
> *The children devoured a whole packet of biscuits.*

The phrasal verbs **bolt down**, **gobble up**, and **wolf down** are also used to describe the action of eating something very quickly:
> *He gobbled up his food before anyone else had started.*
> *She wolfed down a plate of pasta.*

The verb **scoff** (**scarf** US) can be used in informal situations when someone eats a lot of something very quickly:
> *Who scoffed/scarfed all the cake?*

The verb **snack** means 'to eat a little food between main meals':
> *I've been snacking on biscuits and chocolate all afternoon.*

To **eat out** is to eat in a restaurant:
> *I thought we could eat out tonight.*

The phrasal verb **pick at** is sometimes used when someone eats only a little of something:
> *He didn't feel hungry, and sat at the table picking at his food.*

The phrasal verb **tuck into** means 'to start to eat something with enthusiasm':
> *I was just about to tuck into a huge bowl of ice cream.*

---

eat /iːt/ **verb** (**ate**, **eaten**) **1** [I, T] 🔵 to put foo into your mouth and then swallow it: *Who ate a the cake?* ∘ *I haven't eaten since breakfast.* ∘ *Let have something to eat* (= some food). **2** [I] 🔵 t eat a meal: *We usually eat in the kitchen.* → Se also **have your cake and eat it**

PHRASAL VERBS **eat away at sb** If a memory or ba feeling eats away at someone, it makes them fe more and more unhappy. • **eat away at sth** t gradually damage or destroy something • **ea into sth** to use or take away a large part c something valuable, such as money or tim • **eat out** 🔵 to eat at a restaurant → See colo picture **Phrasal Verbs** on page Centre 16 • **ea (sth) up** 🔵 to eat all the food you have bee given: *Be a good boy and eat up your spinac* • **eat up sth** to use or take away a large part c something valuable, such as money or tim *Cities are eating up more and more farmland.*

eater /ˈiːtər/ **noun a big/fussy/meat, etc eate** someone who eats in a particular way or eats particular food

eatery /ˈiːtəri/ **noun** [C] informal a restaurant

'eating diˌsorder noun [C] a mental illness i which someone cannot eat normal amounts food

eaves /iːvz/ **noun** [plural] the edges of a roc where it is wider than the walls

eavesdrop /ˈiːvzdrɒp/ **verb** [I] (**eavesdroppin eavesdropped**) to secretly listen to a convers tion: *He stood outside the door eavesdropping o their conversation.* • **eavesdropper noun** [C]

e-bank[1] (also **ebank**) /ˈiːbæŋk/ **noun** [C] a ban that operates over the Internet

e-bank[2] (also **ebank**) /ˈiːbæŋk/ **verb** [I] to manag your bank accounts and pay money in and ou using the Internet

eBay /ˈiːbeɪ/ **noun** [U] trademark a website tha allows users to buy and sell things online

ebb[1] /eb/ **noun the ebb (tide)** the movement c the sea when it flows away from the land

IDIOMS **be at a low ebb** If someone's enthusiasn confidence, etc is at a low ebb, it is much les than before: *Staff morale is at a low ebb.* • **eb and flow** the way in which the level of som thing regularly becomes higher or lower in situation: *the ebb and flow of the economy*

ebb[2] /eb/ **verb** [I] **1** (also **ebb away**) to graduall disappear: *She watched her father's life slowl ebbing away.* **2** When the tide ebbs, the sea flow away from the land.

ebony /ˈebəni/ **noun** [U] hard, black wood

ebook (also **e-book**, **electronic book**) /ˈiːbʊk **noun** [C] a book that is published in electroni form, for example on the Internet or on a dis and not printed on paper

ebullient /ɪˈbʊliənt/ **adj** energetic, enthusiasti and excited: *an ebullient personality*

e-business /ˈiːbɪznɪs/ **noun** [C, U] the business c buying and selling goods and services on th Internet, or a company that does this

---

e-cash /ˈiːkæʃ/ **noun** [U] money in an electronic form, used for buying goods and services on the Internet

eccentric¹ /ɪkˈsentrɪk/ **adj** behaving in a strange and unusual way: *an eccentric professor* ∘ *eccentric behaviour* • **eccentrically** adv • **eccentricity** /ˌeksenˈtrɪsəti/ **noun** [U] eccentric behaviour

eccentric² /ɪkˈsentrɪk/ **noun** [C] someone who is eccentric: *a harmless eccentric*

ecclesiastical /ɪˌkliːziˈæstɪkəl/ **adj** relating to the Christian Church: *ecclesiastical law/history*

echelon /ˈeʃəlɒn/ **noun** formal **the lower/upper echelons** the people at the lower/upper level of a large organization or society: *the upper echelons of government/management*

echinacea /ˌekɪˈneɪʃə/ **noun** [U] a plant that is used as a medicine, especially to help your body fight illness

echo¹ /ˈekəʊ/ **verb** (**echoing, echoed**) **1** [I] If a sound echoes, or a place echoes with a sound, you hear the sound again because you are in a large, empty space: *Their voices echoed around the room.* **2** [T] to repeat something that someone else has said because you agree with it: *This report echoes some of the earlier research I've read.*

echo² /ˈekəʊ/ **noun** [C] (plural **echoes**) **1** a sound that you hear more than once because you are in a big, empty space **2** something that is very much like something else and makes you think of it: [usually plural] *There are echoes of Shakespeare's work in the play.*

eclectic /ekˈlektɪk/ **adj** including many different styles and types: *an eclectic mix*

eclipse¹ /ɪˈklɪps/ **noun** [C] a situation in which the sun is covered by the moon, or the moon is covered by the Earth's shadow (= dark area): *a solar/lunar eclipse*

eclipse² /ɪˈklɪps/ **verb** [T] **1** to make another person or thing seem much less important, good, or famous: [often passive] *Braque was somewhat eclipsed by Picasso.* **2** to make an eclipse of the moon or sun

eco- /iːkəʊ-/ **prefix** relating to the environment: *eco-friendly cleaning products*

eco-friendly /ˌiːkəʊˈfrendli/ **adj** describes a product that is designed so that it does not damage the environment: *eco-friendly washing powder*

ecological /ˌiːkəˈlɒdʒɪkəl/ **adj** ⏱ relating to ecology or to the environment: *an ecological disaster* • **ecologically** adv

ecological footprint **noun** [C] the amount of the earth's energy that someone or something uses: *You can reduce your ecological footprint by cycling more and driving less.*

ecology /iˈkɒlədʒi/ **noun** [U, no plural] the relationship between living things and the environment, or the scientific study of this • **ecologist** **noun** [C] someone who studies ecology

e-commerce /ˈiːˌkɒmɜːs/ **noun** [U] the buying and selling of goods and services on the Internet

economic /ˌiːkəˈnɒmɪk, ˌekəˈnɒmɪk/ **adj 1** [always before noun] ⏱ relating to trade, industry, and money: *economic growth* ∘ *economic policies* **2** making a profit, or likely to make a profit: *It's not economic to produce goods in small quantities.* → Opposite **uneconomic** • **economically** adv *The country would benefit economically.*

economical /ˌiːkəˈnɒmɪkəl, ˌekəˈnɒmɪkəl/ **adj** ⏱ not using a lot of money, fuel, etc: *I need a car that's economical and reliable.* • **economically** adv

economic migrant **noun** [C] a person who leaves their home country to live in another country with better work or living conditions

economics /ˌiːkəˈnɒmɪks/ **noun** [U] ⏱ the study of the way in which trade, industry, and money are organized • **economist** /ɪˈkɒnəmɪst/ **noun** [C] ⏱ someone who studies economics → See also **home economics**

economize (also UK **-ise**) /ɪˈkɒnəmaɪz/ **verb** [I] to use less of something that you want to save money

economy /ɪˈkɒnəmi/ **noun 1** [C] ⏱ the system by which a country produces and uses goods and money: *the German/US economy* ∘ *a global economy* **2** [C, U] a situation in which someone or something does not use much money, fuel, etc: *The car's design combines comfort with economy.* ∘ UK *We'll need to make some economies when I stop work.*

> **🗹 Word partners for economy**
>
> a **booming/stable/strong/weak** economy
> • the **global/local/national** economy • the economy **grows/improves/recovers/slows**

economy class **noun** [U] the cheapest and least comfortable seats on an aircraft • **economy class** adj, adv

ecosystem /ˈiːkəʊˌsɪstəm/ **noun** [C] all the living things in an area and the way they affect each other and the environment: *Tourism is damaging the fragile ecosystem of the reef.*

ecotourism /ˈiːkəʊˌtʊərɪzəm/ **noun** [U] the business of providing holidays for people so that they can help local people and not damage the environment

eco town **noun** [C] a town consisting of houses that are built in a way that is designed to cause less damage than usual to the environment, for example, by not using much electricity

eco-warrior /ˈiːkəʊˌwɒriər/ **noun** [C] someone who tries to stop activities that damage the environment

ecstasy /ˈekstəsi/ **noun 1** [U] a feeling of extreme happiness: *She danced about in ecstasy.* **2 Ecstasy** an illegal drug that makes you feel happier and more active

ecstatic /ɪkˈstætɪk/ **adj** extremely happy • **ecstatically** adv

ecumenical /ˌekjʊˈmenɪkəl/ **adj** encouraging different types of Christian churches to unite: *an ecumenical service*

eczema /ˈeksmə/ **noun** [U] a medical condition that makes areas of skin become red and dry

edge¹ /edʒ/ **noun** [C] **1** ⓑ the part around something that is furthest from the centre: *Rick was sitting **on the edge of** the bed.* ∘ *She ran down to the water's edge.* **2** ⓑ the part of a blade of a knife or tool that cuts: *a sharp/cutting edge*

IDIOMS **have the edge on/over sb/sth** to be slightly better than someone or something else • **be on edge** to be nervous or worried: *Sorry for shouting – I'm a bit on edge today.* • **take the edge off sth** to make something unpleasant have less of an effect on someone: *Have an apple. It'll **take the edge off** your **hunger.***

edge² /edʒ/ **verb 1** **edge (sth) up/down/past, etc** to move somewhere gradually, or to make something move somewhere gradually: *She edged her way through the crowd of reporters.* **2** [T] to put something around the edge of something else as a decoration: *The cloth was edged with gold.*

edgeways /'edʒweɪz/ **adv** mainly UK (US **edgewise**, ⓤⓢ /'edʒwaɪz/) with the narrowest part going first: *We should be able to get the sofa through edgeways.* → See also **not get a word¹ in edgeways**

edgy /'edʒi/ **adj** nervous: *David was starting to feel a bit edgy.*

edible /'edɪbl/ **adj** safe to eat and not harmful: *edible berries* → Compare **inedible**

edict /'iːdɪkt/ **noun** [C] formal an official order from someone in authority

edifice /'edɪfɪs/ **noun** [C] formal a very large building

edit /'edɪt/ **verb** [T] ⓑ to prepare text, film, etc by deciding what to include and making mistakes correct

edition /ɪ'dɪʃᵊn/ **noun** [C] **1** ⓑ a book, newspaper, etc that is one of several that are the same and were produced at the same time: *a new edition* ∘ *The paperback edition costs £7.95.* **2** a radio or television programme that is one of a series

editor /'edɪtər/ **noun** [C] **1** ⓑ someone whose job is to prepare text, film, etc by deciding what to include and making mistakes correct **2** ⓑ someone who is in charge of a newspaper or magazine

editorial¹ /ˌedɪ'tɔːriəl/ **adj** [always before noun] **1** relating to editors or editing: *editorial skills* **2** written by or expressing the opinions of a newspaper editor: *editorial pages*

editorial² /ˌedɪ'tɔːriəl/ **noun** [C] an article in a newspaper expressing the editor's opinion

educate /'edʒukeɪt/ **verb** [T] **1** ⓑ to teach someone at a school or college: [often passive] *She was educated at a private school.* **2** ⓑ to give people information about something so that they understand it better: *This is part of a campaign to **educate** people **about** the dangers of smoking.*

educated /'edʒukeɪtɪd/ **adj 1** ⓑ Someone who is educated has learned a lot at school or university and has a good level of knowledge. **2** an **educated guess** a guess that is probably correct

because you have enough knowledge about something → See also **well-educated**

education /ˌedʒu'keɪʃᵊn/ **noun** [U, no plural] ⓑ the process of teaching and learning in a school or college, or the knowledge that you get from this: *We expect a good standard of education for our children.* • **educational adj** ⓑ providing education, or relating to education: *the educational system* • **educationally adv** → See also **further education, higher education**

☑ Word partners for **education**

continue/have/provide/receive education • compulsory/good education

⚠ Common learner error: **education** or **upbringing**?

If you want to talk about the way your parents treated you when you were growing up, you should use **upbringing**, not 'education'.

My parents were old-fashioned, and my upbringing was rather strict.

eel /iːl/ **noun** [C] a long fish that looks like a snake

eerie /'ɪəri/ **adj** unusual and slightly frightening: *an eerie silence* • **eerily adv** • **eeriness noun** [U]

effect¹ /ɪ'fekt/ **noun 1** ⓑ [C, U] a change, reaction, or result that is caused by something: *The accident **had a** huge **effect on** her life.* ∘ *We don't know the long-term **effects of** this drug.* **2 in effect** used to say what the real situation is: *This means, in effect, that the plan has been scrapped.* **3 come/go into effect** to start being used: *New food safety rules come into effect on Monday.* **4 take effect** ⓑ to start to produce results or changes: *The anaesthetic takes effect in about ten minutes.* **5 to that effect** used to say that you are giving the general meaning of something but not the exact words: *He said he was bored with school or something to that effect.* **6 a sound/special/visual, etc effect** ⓑ a sound, image, etc that is created artificially → See also **side effect**

⚠ Common learner error: **affect** or **effect**?

Be careful not to confuse these two words.

Affect is a verb that means to cause a change.

Pollution seriously affects the environment.

Use the noun **effect** to talk about the change, reaction, or result caused by something.

Global warming is one of the effects of pollution.

☑ Word partners for **effect**

have/produce an effect • an adverse/beneficial/devastating/harmful/profound effect • an effect on sb/sth • the effects of sth

effect² /ɪ'fekt/ **verb** [T] formal to make something happen: *The civil rights movement **effected** a huge **change** in America.*

effective /ɪ'fektɪv/ **adj 1** ⓑ successful or

achieving the result that you want: *effective management* ∘ *What is the most effective way of teaching grammar?* **2 become/be effective** If changes, laws, etc become effective, they officially start. **3** [always before noun] used to say what the real situation is although officially it is different: *She has effective control of the company.* → Opposite **ineffective** • **effectiveness** noun [U]

effectively /ɪˈfektɪvli/ adv **1** 🅑 in a way that is successful and achieves what you want: *Teachers need to be able to communicate ideas effectively.* **2** used when you describe what the real result of a situation is: *His illness effectively ended his career.*

effects /ɪˈfekts/ noun [plural] formal possessions: *my personal effects.*

effeminate /ɪˈfemɪnət/ adj An effeminate man behaves or looks like a woman.

efficiency /ɪˈfɪʃ⁰nsi/ noun [U] 🅑 a good use of time and energy, without wasting any: *fuel efficiency* ∘ *We must improve the efficiency of the industry.*

efficient /ɪˈfɪʃ⁰nt/ adj 🅐 working well and not wasting time or energy: *an efficient person/organization* ∘ *Email is a quick and efficient way of contacting people.* → Opposite **inefficient** • **efficiently** adv

effigy /ˈefɪdʒi/ noun [C] a model of a person: *Protesters burned effigies of the president.*

effort /ˈefət/ noun **1** [C, U] 🅐 an attempt to do something: [+ to do sth] *We huddled together in an effort to keep warm.* ∘ *He was making an effort to be sociable.* **2** [U] 🅐 the energy that you need to do something: *I put a lot of effort into organizing the party.* ∘ [+ to do sth] *It would take too much effort to tidy my bedroom.* **3** [U] the force that is used to make something move **4 be an effort** to be difficult or painful: *After his accident, walking was an effort.*

> ### Word partners for **effort**
> make an effort • require/take effort • a big/brave/concerted/frantic/valiant effort • in an effort to do sth

effortless /ˈefətləs/ adj achieved without any special or obvious effort: *effortless grace/style* • **effortlessly** adv

effusive /ɪˈfjuːsɪv/ adj showing a lot of enthusiasm or approval for someone or something, often too much

EFL /ˌiːefˈel/ noun [U] abbreviation for English as a Foreign Language: the teaching of English to students whose first language is not English

e.g. (also **eg**) /ˌiːˈdʒiː/ used to give an example of what you mean: *crime writers, e.g. Agatha Christie and Ruth Rendell*

egalitarian /ɪˌɡælɪˈteəriən/ adj formal believing that everyone should have the same freedom and opportunities

egg¹ /eɡ/ noun **1 FOOD** ▷ [C, U] 🅐 an oval object produced by a female chicken, that you eat as food: *a boiled/fried egg* → See colour picture **Food** on page Centre 11 **2 BABY** ▷ [C] 🅑 an oval object with a hard shell that contains a baby bird, insect, or other creature: *The bird lays* (= *produces*) *its eggs in a nest.* **3 FEMALE CELL** ▷ [C] a cell inside a female person or animal that can develop into a baby

IDIOM **have egg on your face** to seem stupid because of something you have done

→ See also **Easter egg**, **scrambled eggs**

egg² /eɡ/ verb

PHRASAL VERB **egg sb on** to encourage someone to do something, usually something that is wrong, stupid, or dangerous: *Two girls were fighting outside the club, egged on by a group of friends.*

'egg ˌcup noun [C] a small container for holding a boiled egg while you eat it

eggplant /ˈeɡplɑːnt/ noun [C, U] US (UK **aubergine**) an oval, purple vegetable that is white inside → See colour picture **Fruits and Vegetables** on page Centre 10

eggshell /ˈeɡˌʃel/ noun [C] the hard outer covering of an egg

ego /ˈiːɡəʊ/, /ˈeɡəʊ/ noun [C] your opinion of yourself: *He has a huge ego.*

egocentric /ˌiːɡəʊˈsentrɪk/ adj interested only in yourself

egotism /ˈiːɡəʊtɪz⁰m/ noun [U] (also **egoism** /ˈiːɡəʊɪz⁰m/) the opinion that you are very important so you are not interested in other people • **egotist** noun [C] • **egotistic** /ˌiːɡəʊˈtɪstɪk/ adj (also **egotistical** /ˌiːɡəʊˈtɪstɪk⁰l/)

egregious /ɪˈɡriːdʒəs/ adj formal extremely bad or shocking in an obvious way: *an egregious example of racism*

eh? /eɪ/ exclamation UK informal spoken **1** used to ask someone to repeat something because you did not hear or understand it: *"You're looking tired." "Eh?" "I said, you're looking tired."* **2** used to show interest or surprise at something: *Sue's had a baby girl, eh?*

Eid /iːd/ noun the name of two Muslim festivals. The more important one celebrates the end of Ramadan.

eight /eɪt/ 🅐 the number 8

eighteen /ˌeɪˈtiːn/ 🅐 the number 18 • **eighteenth** 18th written as a word

eighth¹ /eɪtθ/ 🅐 8th written as a word

eighth² /eɪtθ/ noun [C] one of eight equal parts of something; ⅛

eighty /ˈeɪti/ **1** 🅐 the number 80 **2 the eighties** the years from 1980-1989 **3 be in your eighties** to be aged between 80 and 89 • **eightieth** 80th written as a word

either¹ /ˈaɪðər/, /ˈiːðər/ conjunction **either... or** 🅐 used when you are giving a choice of two or more things: *Either call me tonight or I'll speak to you tomorrow.*

either² /ˈaɪðər, ˈiːðər/ pronoun, determiner **1** 🅐 one of two people or things when it is not important which: *"Would you like red or white wine?" – "Oh, either."* ∘ *Ask Dom or Andrew, either of them will help you.* **2** 🅑 both: *People were smoking on either side* (= *at both sides*) *of me.* ∘ *You can use the train or the bus, either way it'll take an hour.*

either³ /ˈaɪðər/, /ˈiːðər/ adv 🅐 used in negative

sentences to mean that something else is also true: *The menu is boring and it's not cheap either.* → See Note at **not**

eject /ɪ'dʒekt/ verb **1 LEAVE PLACE** ▷ [T] formal to make someone leave a place, usually using force: [often passive] *He was ejected from the courtroom for shouting.* **2 LEAVE MACHINE** ▷ [I, T] to come out of a machine when a button is pressed, or to make something do this: *How do you eject the disc?* **3 LEAVE AIRCRAFT** ▷ [I] to leave an aircraft in an emergency by being pushed out while still in your seat

eke /iːk/ verb

PHRASAL VERB **eke sth out 1** to use something slowly or carefully because you only have a small amount of it **2 eke out a living/existence** to earn only just enough money to pay for things you need: *He ekes out a living by cleaning windows.*

elaborate¹ /ɪ'læbᵊrət/ adj complicated, detailed, or made carefully from many parts: *an elaborate system/scheme* ∘ *an elaborate design* • **elaborately** adv

elaborate² /ɪ'læbᵊreɪt/ verb [I, T] to explain something and give more details: *He wouldn't elaborate on the details.* • **elaboration** /ɪ,læbə-'reɪʃᵊn/ noun [U]

elapse /ɪ'læps/ verb [I] formal If time elapses, it passes: *Two years have elapsed since the attack.*

elastic¹ /ɪ'læstɪk/ adj Something that is elastic can stretch and return to its original size: *Your skin is more elastic when you are young.* • **elasticity** /,ɪlæs'tɪsəti/ noun [U] the quality of being elastic

elastic² /ɪ'læstɪk/ noun [U] a type of rubber that returns to its original size and shape after you stretch it

e,lastic 'band noun [C] UK (UK/US **rubber band**) a thin circle of rubber used to hold things together

elated /ɪ'leɪtɪd/ adj extremely happy and excited: *We were elated by/at the news.* • **elation** /ɪ'leɪʃᵊn/ noun [U]

elbow¹ /'elbəʊ/ noun [C] ⑤ the part in the middle of your arm where it bends → See colour picture **The Body** on page Centre 13

elbow² /'elbəʊ/ verb [T] to push someone with your elbow, especially so you can move past them: *He elbowed his way through the crowds of shoppers.*

'elbow ,room noun [U] space to move easily

elder¹ /'eldər/ adj **elder brother/daughter/ sister, etc** ⑤ the older of two brothers/daughters/sisters, etc → See Note at **old**

elder² /'eldər/ noun **1 the elder** ⑫ the oldest of two people: *He's the elder of two sons.* **2 your elders** people older than you: *I was taught to respect my elders.* **3** [C] an important, respected, older member of a group

elderly /'eldᵊli/ adj ⑤ a more polite word for 'old', used to describe people: *an elderly man* ∘ *Children should show respect for the elderly.*

eldest /'eldɪst/ adj **eldest child/daughter/ brother, etc** ⑥ the oldest child/daughter/

brother, etc: *My eldest brother is a doctor.* ∘ *Susan is the eldest of three sisters.*

e-learning /'iːlɜːnɪŋ/ noun [U] electronic learning: the business of providing courses online for students so that they can study and learn from home

elect /ɪ'lekt/ verb **1** ⑫ [T] to choose someone for a particular job or position by voting: [often passive] *She was elected to the US Senate in 2000.* ∘ *He was elected president in 2008.* **2 elect to do sth** formal to choose to do something: *The child elected to stay with his mother.* → See also **re-elect**

election /ɪ'lekʃᵊn/ noun [C, U] ⑪ a time when people vote in order to choose someone for a political or official job: *a presidential election* ∘ *Who do you think will win the election?* ∘ *Will you stand/run for election again this year?* → See also **by-election, general election, re-election**

┌─────────────────────────────────────┐
│ 🗹 Word partners for **election** │
│ │
│ hold an election • run for/stand for election │
│ • lose/win an election • an election cam- │
│ paign │
└─────────────────────────────────────┘

e'lection ,day noun [C] US (UK **polling day**) the day when people vote in an election

electoral /ɪ'lektᵊrᵊl/ adj [always before noun] relating to elections: *the electoral system* ∘ *electoral reform*

electorate /ɪ'lektᵊrət/ noun [group] the people who are allowed to vote in an election: *the British electorate*

electric /ɪ'lektrɪk/ adj **1 EQUIPMENT** ▷ ⓐ Electric lights, tools, etc work using electricity: *an electric light/heater* **2 SUPPLY** ▷ ⑥ supplying electricity: *an electric socket* ∘ *electric current* **3 EXCITING** ▷ full of excitement and emotion: *The atmosphere backstage was electric.*

electrical /ɪ'lektrɪkᵊl/ adj **1** ⑥ Electrical goods or equipment work using electricity: *electrical appliances/goods* **2** relating to the production and supply of electricity: *an electrical engineer*

the e,lectric 'chair noun a chair used in parts of the US to kill a criminal using electricity

electrician /ɪ,lek'trɪʃᵊn/ noun [C] ⑫ someone whose job is to put in, check, or repair electric wires and equipment

electricity /ɪ,lek'trɪsəti/ noun [U] ⑫ a type of energy that can produce light and heat, or make machines work: *The electricity has been turned off.* ∘ *an electricity bill*

┌─────────────────────────────────────┐
│ 🗹 Word partners for **electricity** │
│ │
│ generate/produce electricity • be operated │
│ by/be powered by electricity • an electricity │
│ supply │
└─────────────────────────────────────┘

e,lectric 'shock noun [C] a sudden, painful feeling that you get when electricity flows through your body

electrify /ɪ'lektrɪfaɪ/ verb [T] **1** to make people who are watching something feel very excited: *She electrified the crowd with her fantastic performance.* **2** to supply something with electricity: *an electrified railway*

---

ectrocute /ɪˈlektrəkjuːt/ **verb** [T] to kill someone by causing electricity to flow through their body: [often passive] *He was electrocuted while playing on a railway line.* • **electrocution** /ɪˌlektrəˈkjuːʃ°n/ **noun** [U]

ectrode /ɪˈlektrəʊd/ **noun** [C] the point where an electric current enters or leaves something such as a battery (= object which provides electricity)

ectron /ɪˈlektrɒn/ **noun** [C] an extremely small piece of an atom with a negative electrical charge

ectronic /ɪˌlekˈtrɒnɪk/ **adj 1 EQUIPMENT** ▷ **B1** Electronic equipment consists of things such as computers, televisions, and radios. **2 MUSIC/ GAMES** ▷ **B1** Electronic music, games, etc use electronic equipment. **3 COMPUTING** ▷ using the Internet or another electronic communication system in order to operate: *electronic publishing* • **electronically adv**

ectronic ˈbook noun [C] (also **ebook, digital book**) a book that is published in electronic form, for example on the Internet or on a disk, and not printed on paper

ectronics /ˌɪlekˈtrɒnɪks/ **noun** [U] **B2** the science of making electronic equipment: *the electronics industry*

egance /ˈelɪɡ°ns/ **noun** [U] the quality of being stylish or attractive in appearance or behaviour

egant /ˈelɪɡ°nt/ **adj B2** stylish or attractive in appearance or behaviour: *an elegant dining room* ◦ *She's a very elegant woman.* • **elegantly adv**

ement /ˈelɪmənt/ **noun 1 PART** ▷ [C] **B2** a part of something: *This book has all the elements of a good detective story.* **2 an element of sth** a small amount of an emotion or quality: *There's an element of truth in what she says.* **3 PEOPLE** ▷ [C] a group of people of a particular type: *The disruptive element on the committee voted against the proposal.* **4 SIMPLE SUBSTANCE** ▷ [C] **B2** a simple substance which cannot be reduced to smaller chemical parts: *Iron is one of the elements of the Earth's crust.* **5 HEAT** ▷ [C] the part of a piece of electrical equipment that produces heat

IDIOM **be in your element** to be happy because you are doing what you like doing and what you are good at: *I'm in my element at a children's party.*

ementary /ˌelɪˈment°ri/ **adj 1 B1** basic: *I only have an elementary knowledge of physics.* ◦ *an elementary mistake* **2 B1** relating to the early stages of studying a subject: *students at elementary level*

eˈmentary ˌschool noun [C] US (mainly UK **primary school**) a school for children from the ages of five to about eleven

ements /ˈelɪmənts/ **noun the elements** the weather, especially bad weather: *Shall we **brave the elements** and go out for a walk?*

ephant /ˈelɪfənt/ **noun** [C] **A2** a very large, grey animal with big ears and a very long nose

evate /ˈelɪveɪt/ **verb** formal **1 be elevated to sth** to be given a more important position: *She has been elevated to deputy manager.* ◦ *an elevated position* **2** [T] to move something to a

higher level or height: *High stress levels elevate blood pressure.* ◦ *Try to keep your leg elevated.*

elevation /ˌelɪˈveɪʃ°n/ **noun 1** [C] the height of a place above the level of the sea: *The hotel is situated at an elevation of 1000m.* **2** [U] formal a situation in which someone or something is given a more important position: *his sudden **elevation to** stardom*

elevator /ˈelɪveɪtə‌r/ **noun** [C] US (UK **lift**) a machine that carries people up and down in tall buildings

eleven /ɪˈlev°n/ **A1** the number 11 • **eleventh** 11th written as a word

elf /elf/ **noun** [C] (plural **elves**) a small person with pointed ears who has magic powers in children's stories

elicit /ɪˈlɪsɪt/ **verb** [T] formal to get information or a reaction from someone: *You have to ask the right questions to **elicit** the **information** you want.*

eligible /ˈelɪdʒəbl/ **adj 1** If you are eligible to do something, you can do it because you are in the right situation: [+ to do sth] *Only people over 18 are eligible to vote.* ◦ *You might be **eligible for** a grant for your studies.* → Opposite **ineligible 2** If someone who is not married is eligible, they would be a good husband or wife because they are rich, attractive, etc.: *an eligible young bachelor* • **eligibility** /ˌelɪdʒəˈbɪləti/ **noun** [U]

eliminate /ɪˈlɪmɪneɪt/ **verb** [T] **1** to remove something from something, or get rid of something: *The doctor advised me to **eliminate** salt **from** my diet.* **2** to defeat someone so that they cannot go any further in a competition: [often passive] *She was eliminated after the first round of the tournament.*

elimination /ɪˌlɪmɪˈneɪʃ°n/ **noun 1** [U] the act of eliminating someone or something **2 a process of elimination** a method that involves removing all possible answers to something until only one remains

elite /ɪˈliːt/ **noun** [group] the richest, most powerful, or best educated group in a society: *a member of the elite* ◦ *an elite group*

elitism /ɪˈliːtɪz°m/ **noun** [U] a way of organizing a society so that only a small group of rich, powerful, or educated people are given an advantage in a situation • **elitist adj** *elitist attitudes*

elm /elm/ **noun** [C, U] a large tree that loses its leaves in winter

elocution /ˌeləˈkjuːʃən/ **noun** [U] the skill of speaking in a careful, clear way

elongated /ˈiːlɒŋgeɪtɪd/ ⑤ /iːˈlɒŋgeɪtɪd/ **adj** longer and thinner than usual

elope /ɪˈləʊp/ **verb** [I] to leave home secretly with someone in order to get married

eloquent /ˈeləkwənt/ **adj** expressing ideas clearly and in a way that influences people: *the most eloquent speaker at the conference* • **eloquence** /ˈeləkwəns/ **noun** [U] an eloquent way of expressing ideas • **eloquently adv**

else /els/ **adv 1 IN ADDITION** ▷ ⓐ in addition to someone or something: *Would you like* **anything else** *to eat?* ○ **What else** *did he say?* **2 DIFFERENT** ▷ ⓐ different from someone or something: *I don't like it here. Let's go* **somewhere else**. ○ *I didn't say that. It must have been* **someone else**. **3 OTHER** ▷ ⓐ other things or people: *I forgot my toothbrush, but I remembered* **everything else**. **4 or else a** used to compare two different things or situations: *He talks to her all the time, or else he completely ignores her.* **b** ⓑ used to say what will happen if another thing does not happen: *We must be there by six, or else we'll miss the beginning.* **5 if all else fails** if no other plan is successful: *If all else fails, you're welcome to stay at our house.*

elsewhere /ˌelsˈweər/ **adv** ⓑ in or to another place: *The report studies economic growth in Europe and elsewhere.* ○ *If we can't find it here, we'll have to* **go elsewhere**.

ELT /ˌiːelˈtiː/ **noun** [U] abbreviation for English Language Teaching: the teaching of English to students whose first language is not English

elucidate /ɪˈluːsɪdeɪt/ **verb** [T] formal to explain something, or make it clear

elude /ɪˈluːd/ **verb** [T] formal **1 NOT ACHIEVE** ▷ If something that you want eludes you, you do not succeed in achieving it: *The gold medal continues to elude her.* **2 NOT BE CAUGHT** ▷ to not be caught by someone: *He eluded the police for years before he was arrested.* **3 NOT REMEMBER** ▷ If a piece of information eludes you, you cannot remember it.

elusive /ɪˈluːsɪv/ **adj** difficult to describe, find, achieve, or remember: *The answers to these questions remain as elusive as ever.*

elves /elvz/ plural of elf

'em /əm/ informal spoken short for them

emaciated /ɪˈmeɪsieɪtɪd/ **adj** very thin and weak because of being sick or not eating enough food

email (also **e-mail**) /ˈiːmeɪl/ **noun 1** [U] ⓐ a system for sending messages electronically, especially from one computer to another using the Internet: *You can contact me* **by email**. ○ *What's your* **email address**? **2** [C, U] ⓐ a message sent electronically: *I got an email from Danielle yesterday.* • **email verb** [T] ⓐ to send a message using email

> 🔲 Word partners for **email**
>
> **get/send** an email • **by** email • **in** an email • an email **address/attachment**

emanate /ˈemaneɪt/ **verb** formal

> PHRASAL VERB **emanate from sth** to come from something: *Strange noises emanated from th[e] room next door.*

emancipate /ɪˈmænsɪpeɪt/ **verb** [T] formal to giv[e] people more freedom or rights by removin[g] social, legal, or political controls that lim[it] them: *emancipated women* • **emancipatio[n]** /ɪˌmænsɪˈpeɪʃən/ **noun** [U]

embalm /ɪmˈbɑːm/ **verb** [T] to use oils an[d] chemicals to prevent a dead body from decayin[g]

embankment /ɪmˈbæŋkmənt/ **noun** [C] a artificial slope built from soil or stones to sto[p] floods, or to support a road or railway: *a railwa[y]* **embankment**

embargo /ɪmˈbɑːgəʊ/ **noun** [C] (plural **emba[rgoes]**) an order by a government to stop trad[e] with another country: *an* **arms/oil embarg[o]** ○ *We will not* **lift** (= stop) *the trade* **embarg[o]** *until they end this war.*

embark /ɪmˈbɑːk/ **verb** [I] to get on a ship, boa[t] or aircraft to begin a journey → Oppos[ite] **disembark**

> PHRASAL VERB **embark on/upon sth** to sta[rt] something new or important: *You're never to[o]* old to embark on a new career.

embarrass /ɪmˈbærəs/ **verb** [T] to mak[e] someone feel ashamed or shy: *My dad's alway[s] embarrassing me in front of my friends.*

embarrassed /ɪmˈbærəst/ **adj** ⓑ feelin[g] ashamed or shy: *She felt* **embarrassed** *abou[t] undressing in front of the doctor.* ○ [+ to do sth] *was too embarrassed to admit that I was scared.*

embarrassing /ɪmˈbærəsɪŋ/ **adj** ⓑ making yo[u] feel embarrassed: *an embarrassing defeat* ○ *Wh[at] has been your most embarrassing momen[t]* • **embarrassingly adv** *The play was embarras[s]ingly bad.*

embarrassment /ɪmˈbærəsmənt/ **noun 1** [U] ⓑ the feeling of being embarrassed: *He blushe[d] with embarrassment.* ○ *Her behaviour has cause[d] great embarrassment to her family.* **2** [C] ⓔ something or someone that makes you fee[l] embarrassed: *He is becoming an* **embarrassmen[t] to** *the government.*

> 🔲 Word partners for **embarrassment**
>
> **acute/great/huge** embarrassment • **a source of** embarrassment • the embarrassment of doing sth

embassy /ˈembəsi/ **noun** [C] ⓑ the offici[al] group of people who live in a foreign countr[y] and represent their government there, or th[e] building where they work

embedded /ɪmˈbedɪd/ **adj 1** fixed into th[e] surface of something: *A small piece of glass wa[s]* **embedded in** *his finger.* **2** If an emotion, attitud[e] etc is embedded in someone or something, it [is] a very strong and important part of them: *sense of guilt was deeply* **embedded in** *m[y] conscience.*

embellish /ɪmˈbelɪʃ/ **verb** [T] to make somethin[g] more beautiful or interesting by adding som[e] thing to it: *He embellished the story with lots of dramatic detail.* • **embellishment noun** [C, U]

mbers /'embəz/ **noun** [plural] pieces of wood or coal that continue to burn after a fire has no more flames

mbezzle /ɪm'bezl/ **verb** [T] to steal money that belongs to the company or organization that you work for • **embezzlement noun** [U]

mbittered /ɪm'bɪtəd/ **adj** very angry about unfair things that have happened to you

mblazoned /ɪm'bleɪzᵊnd/ **adj** decorated in a very obvious way with something such as a name or a design: *Her T-shirt was **emblazoned** **with** the company logo.*

mblem /'embləm/ **noun** [C] a picture, object, or symbol that is used to represent a person, group, or idea: *The rose is the national emblem of England.*

mbodiment /ɪm'bɒdɪmənt/ **noun the embodiment of sth** If someone or something is the embodiment of a particular idea or quality, they express or represent it exactly: *The mother in the story is the embodiment of evil.*

mbody /ɪm'bɒdi/ **verb** [T] to represent an idea or quality exactly: *He embodies the values of hard work and fair play.*

mbrace¹ /ɪm'breɪs/ **verb 1 HOLD** ▷ [I, T] If you embrace someone, you put your arms around them, and if two people embrace, they put their arms around each other. **2 ACCEPT** ▷ [T] to accept new ideas, beliefs, methods, etc in an enthusiastic way: *We are always eager to embrace the latest technology.* **3 INCLUDE** ▷ [T] formal to include a number of things: *The report embraces a wide range of opinions.*

mbrace² /ɪm'breɪs/ **noun** [C] the action of putting your arms around someone: *a passionate embrace*

mbroider /ɪm'brɔɪdəʳ/ **verb 1** [I, T] to decorate cloth by sewing small patterns or pictures onto it **2** [T] to add imaginary details to a story to make it more interesting: *They accused him of embroidering the facts.*

mbroidery /ɪm'brɔɪdᵊri/ **noun** [U] **1** the activity of sewing small patterns or pictures onto things **2** decoration on cloth made by sewing small patterns or pictures onto it

mbroil /ɪm'brɔɪl/ **verb** formal **be embroiled in sth** to be involved in an argument or difficult situation: *We don't want to become embroiled in a dispute over ownership.*

mbryo /'embriəʊ/ **noun** [C] a human or an animal that is starting to develop in its mother's uterus

mbryonic /ˌembri'ɒnɪk/ **adj** starting to develop: *The project is still at an embryonic stage.*

merald /'emᵊrᵊld/ **noun 1** [C] a bright green stone used in jewellery **2** [U] (also **emerald green**) a bright green colour • **emerald adj**

merge /ɪ'mɜːdʒ/ **verb** [I] **1 COME OUT** ▷ ⑫ to appear from somewhere or come out of somewhere: *A figure emerged from the shadows.* **2 BECOME KNOWN** ▷ to become known: *It emerged that she had lied to her employers.* **3 DIFFICULT SITUATION** ▷ to reach the end of a

difficult situation: *They emerged victorious from the fight.* • **emergence noun** [U]

emergency /ɪ'mɜːdʒᵊnsi/ **noun** [C] ⑬ a serious or dangerous situation that needs immediate action: *You should only call this number in an emergency.* ○ *an emergency exit*

> 🗂 Word partners for **emergency**
>
> cope with/respond to an emergency • a major/real emergency • in an emergency

e**'mergency** **brake** **noun** [C] US (UK/US **handbrake**, also US **parking brake**) a stick inside a car that you can pull up to stop the car from moving → See colour picture **Car** on page Centre 7

e**'mergency** **room** **noun** [C] US (UK **casualty**) the part of a hospital where people go when they have been injured or have urgent illnesses so that they can be treated immediately

e**ˌmergency** **'services** **noun** [plural] the organizations who deal with accidents and urgent problems such as fire, illness, or crime

emerging /ɪ'mɜːdʒɪŋ/ **adj** [always before noun] starting to exist or develop: *emerging economies/markets*

emigrant /'emɪgrənt/ **noun** [C] someone who leaves their own country to go and live in another one

emigrate /'emɪgreɪt/ **verb** [I] to leave your own country to go and live in another one: *We're thinking of emigrating to New Zealand.* • **emigration** /ˌemɪ'greɪʃᵊn/ **noun** [U]

eminent /'emɪnənt/ **adj** famous, respected, or important: *an eminent historian* • **eminence** /'emɪnəns/ **noun** [U] → See also **preeminent**

eminently /'emɪnəntli/ **adv** formal very: *He is eminently qualified for the job.*

emission /ɪ'mɪʃᵊn/ **noun** [C, U] the act of sending gas, heat, light, etc. out into the air, or an amount of gas, heat, light, etc that is sent out: *Carbon dioxide emissions will be reduced by 20%.*

emit /ɪ'mɪt/ **verb** [T] (**emitting, emitted**) to send out gas, heat, light, etc into the air: *The machine emits a high-pitched sound when you press the button.*

emoticon /ɪ'məʊtɪkɒn/ **noun** [C] an image that looks like a face, used in emails and texts to show emotions → See Study Page **Emailing and texting** on page Centre 37

emotion /ɪ'məʊʃᵊn/ **noun** [C, U] ⑫ a strong feeling such as love or anger, or strong feelings in general: *He finds it hard to express his emotions.* ○ *She was overcome with emotion and burst into tears.*

> 🗂 Word partners for **emotion**
>
> display/experience/feel/show emotion • deep/powerful/strong emotion

emotional /ɪ'məʊʃᵊnᵊl/ **adj 1 EMOTIONS** ▷ ⑫ relating to emotions: *a child's emotional development* **2 STRONG FEELINGS** ▷ ⑫ showing strong feelings, or making people have strong feelings: *an emotional speech* ○ *After the argument, I was feeling confused and emotional.*

3 PERSON ▷ An emotional person shows their emotions very easily or very often. • **emotionally** adv

emotive /ɪˈməʊtɪv/ adj making people feel strong emotions: *Animal experimentation is a very emotive issue.*

empathy /ˈempəθi/ noun [U] the ability to imagine what it must be like to be in someone's situation • **empathize** (also UK **-ise**) /ˈempəθaɪz/ verb [I] to feel empathy with someone: *I think people find it easy to empathize with the main character.*

emperor /ˈempᵊrər/ noun [C] the male ruler of an empire (= group of countries ruled by one person or government): *Emperor Charlemagne*

emphasis /ˈemfəsɪs/ noun [C, U] (plural **emphases** /ˈemfəsiːz/) **1** ☉ particular importance or attention that you give to something: *Schools are starting to place/put greater emphasis on passing exams.* **2** the extra force that you give to a word or part of a word when you are saying it: *The emphasis is on the final syllable.*

emphasize (also UK **-ise**) /ˈemfəsaɪz/ verb [T] ☉ to show that something is especially important or needs special attention: *The government is emphasizing the importance of voting in the election.* ○ [+ that] *He emphasized that the driver was not to blame for the accident.*

emphatic /ɪmˈfætɪk/ adj done or said in a strong way and without any doubt: *an emphatic victory* • **emphatically** adv

empire /ˈempaɪər/ noun [C] **1** a group of countries that is ruled by one person or government **2** a large group of businesses that is controlled by one person or company: *a publishing empire*

empirical /ɪmˈpɪrɪkᵊl/ adj formal based on experience or scientific experiments and not only on ideas: *empirical evidence* • **empirically** adv

employ /ɪmˈplɔɪ/ verb [T] **1** ☉ If a person or company employs someone, they pay that person to work for them: *The company employs 2500 staff.* ○ [+ to do sth] *They employ her to look after their children.* **2** formal to use something: *Companies employ clever tactics to persuade us to buy their products.*

employee /ɪmˈplɔɪiː/ noun [C] ☉ someone who is paid to work for a person or company

employer /ɪmˈplɔɪər/ noun [C] ☉ a person or company that pays people to work for them

employment /ɪmˈplɔɪmənt/ noun [U] **1** ☉ paid work that someone does for a person or company: *full-time/part-time employment* ○ *It is not easy to find employment in the countryside.* ○ *employment opportunities/rights* → Compare **unemployment 2** formal the use of something

☐ Word partners for **employment**

find/offer/provide/seek employment • gainful/paid/full-time/part-time/temporary employment • be in employment

empower /ɪmˈpaʊər/ verb **1** [T] to give someone

the confidence, skills, freedom, etc to do something: [+ to do sth] *Education empowers people t* take control of their lives. **2 be empowered to d sth** to have the legal or official right to c something

empress /ˈemprəs/ noun [C] the female ruler, c the wife of a male ruler, of an empire (= group c countries ruled by one person or government *Empress Josephine*

empty¹ /ˈempti/ adj **1** ☉ If something is empty it does not contain any things or people: *a empty house/street* ○ *empty bottles/glasses* ○ *Th train was completely empty when it reache London.* → See picture at **full 2** having n meaning or value: *an empty promise/threa* • **emptiness** noun [U]

empty² /ˈempti/ verb **1** [T] (also **empty out**) you empty a container, or if you empty th things inside it, you remove everything from i *He emptied the dirty water into the sink.* **2** [I] t become empty: *The room emptied rapidly whe the fire started.*

empty-handed /ˌemptiˈhændɪd/ adj withou bringing or taking anything: *We can't go to th party empty-handed.*

emulate /ˈemjəleɪt/ verb [T] formal to try to b like someone or something that you admire c that is successful: *They hope to emulate th success of other software companies.*

emulsion /ɪˈmʌlʃᵊn/ noun [C, U] (**emulsio paint**) a water-based paint that is not shin when dry

enable /ɪˈneɪbl/ verb [T] ☉ to make someon able to do something, or to make somethin possible: [+ to do sth] *This money has enabled m to buy a new computer.*

-enabled /ɪˈneɪbᵊld/ suffix **1** having the nece sary equipment or system to use somethin *Bluetooth-enabled mobile phones* **2** used or mad possible by using a particular thing: *voic enabled software*

enact /ɪˈnækt/ verb [T] **1** to make something int a law: [often passive] *When was this legislatic enacted?* **2** formal to perform a story or pla • **enactment** noun [U]

enamel /ɪˈnæmᵊl/ noun [U] **1** a hard, shin substance that is used to decorate or prote metal or clay **2** the hard, white substance th covers your teeth

enamoured UK (US **enamored**) /ɪˈnæməd/ a **be enamoured of/with sb/sth** formal to lik someone or something very much

enc (also **encl**) written abbreviation for enclose used at the end of a business letter to show th there is something else in the envelope

encapsulate /ɪnˈkæpsjəleɪt/ verb [T] to expre or show the most important facts about som thing: *The film encapsulates the essence of th period.*

encase /ɪnˈkeɪs/ verb **be encased in sth** formal t be completely covered in something: *The outsi walls are encased in concrete.*

enchanted /ɪnˈtʃɑːntɪd/ adj **1** If you a enchanted by something, you like it ver much: *She was enchanted by the Scottish landscape.* **2** affected by magic: *an enchanted forest*

enchanting /ɪn'tʃɑːntɪŋ/ **adj** very nice: *What an enchanting child!*

encircle /ɪn'sɜːkl/ **verb** [T] formal to form a circle around something: [often passive] *The house is encircled by a high fence.*

enclave /'enkleɪv/ **noun** [C] a place that is different from the area that is around it because its people have a different language or culture: *an Italian enclave in Switzerland*

enclose /ɪn'kləʊz/ **verb** [T] **1** ⑫ to send something in the same envelope or parcel as something else: *I enclose a map of the area.* **2** to be all around something and separate it from other things or places • **enclosed adj** *He doesn't like enclosed spaces.*

enclosure /ɪn'kləʊʒər/ **noun** [C] a small area of land that has a wall or fence around it

encompass /ɪn'kʌmpəs/ **verb** [T] to include a lot of things, ideas, places, etc: *Their albums encompass a wide range of music.*

encore /'ɒŋkɔːr/ **noun** [C] an extra song or piece of music that is performed at the end of a show because the audience shout for it

encounter¹ /ɪn'kaʊntər/ **verb** [T] **1** ⑫ to experience something unpleasant: *We encountered quite a few problems at the beginning.* **2** literary to meet someone, especially when you do not expect it

encounter² /ɪn'kaʊntər/ **noun** [C] a meeting, especially one that happens by chance

> ☑ **Word partners for encounter**
>
> **have** an encounter • a **chance** encounter
> • an encounter **with** sb

encourage /ɪn'kʌrɪdʒ/ **verb** [T] **1** ⑥ to make someone more likely to do something, or make something more likely to happen: [+ to do sth] *My parents encouraged me to try new things.* ◦ *Cutting back plants will encourage growth.* **2** ⑥ to give someone confidence or hope: *My parents encouraged me when things weren't going well at school.* → Opposite **discourage** • **encouragement noun** [C, U] ⑫ *Children need lots of encouragement from their parents.*

encouraged /ɪn'kʌrɪdʒd/ **adj** having more confidence or hope about something: *We were very encouraged by his exam results.*

encouraging /ɪn'kʌrɪdʒɪŋ/ **adj** ⑫ making you feel more hope and confidence: *The team's performance was very encouraging.* → Opposite **discouraging** • **encouragingly adv**

encroach /ɪn'krəʊtʃ/ **verb**

PHRASAL VERB **encroach on/upon sth** to gradually take away someone's rights, power, etc, or get control of something, often without being noticed: *My job is starting to encroach on my family life.*

encrusted /ɪn'krʌstɪd/ **adj** covered with something hard, for example dirt or stones: *My trousers were encrusted with mud.*

encrypt /ɪn'krɪpt/ **verb** [T] to change electronic information into a secret system of letters,

numbers, or symbols: *The email is encrypted, so you need to enter a password to read it.* • **encryption noun** [U]

encyclopedia (also UK **encyclopaedia**) /ɪnˌsaɪklə'piːdiə/ **noun** [C] a book or a set of books containing facts about a lot of subjects

end¹ /end/ **noun 1** FINAL PART ▷ [no plural] ⓐ the final part of something such as a period of time, activity, or story: *I'll pay you at the end of next month.* ◦ *I didn't meet him until the end of the course.* ◦ *a film with a twist at the end* **2** FURTHEST PART ▷ [C] ⓐ the furthest part or final part of a place or thing: *They live at the other end of the street.* ◦ *They were standing at opposite ends of the room.* **3** STOP ▷ [C] ⑫ the time when something stops happening: [usually singular] *They are calling for an end to the violence.* **4** in the end ⑧ finally, after something has been thought about or discussed a lot **5** come to an end to finish **6** put an end to sth ⑫ to make something stop happening or existing: *He's determined to put an end to these rumours.* **7** bring sth to an end to make something finish: *The stories in the newspaper brought her career to a sudden end.* **8** no end informal a lot: *I've had no end of trouble finding a hotel room.* **9** for hours/days, etc on end for hours/days, etc without stopping: *He waited by the telephone for hours on end.* **10** INTENTION ▷ [C] an intention or purpose: *She only has one end in mind.*

IDIOMS **be at a loose end** UK (US **be at loose ends**) to have nothing to do: *Come and visit us if you're at a loose end over the weekend.* • **at the end of the day** something that you say before you give the most important fact of a situation: *At the end of the day, what matters is that you're safe.* • **at the end of your tether** mainly UK (US **at the end of your rope**) so tired, annoyed, or worried by something that you do not feel that you can deal with it • **get (hold of) the wrong end of the stick** to not understand a situation correctly: *My mum got the wrong end of the stick and thought that Jim was my boyfriend.* • **make ends meet** to have just enough money to pay for the things that you need: *I've taken a second job in the evenings just to make ends meet.* • **not be the end of the world** If something is not the end of the world, it will not cause very serious problems: *It won't be the end of the world if I don't get the job.* • **be on/at the receiving end of sth** If you are on the receiving end of something, you suffer something unpleasant when you have done nothing to deserve it: *They are often on the receiving end of verbal abuse from angry customers.* • **throw sb in at the deep end** to make someone start a new and difficult job or activity without helping them or preparing them for it

→ See also **dead end**, **light¹** at the end of the tunnel, **odds and ends**, the **tail¹** end of sth, the **West End**, be at your **wits' end**

> ☑ **Word partners for end**
>
> **at the** end (of sth) • **by the** end (of sth)
> • the **very** end

end² /end/ **verb** [I, T] ⓐ to finish or stop, or to make something finish or stop: *What time does the concert end?* ○ *These talks do not look likely to end the war.*

PHRASAL VERBS **end in/with sth** to finish in a particular way: *The evening ended in a big argument.* • **end up** ⓑ to finally be in a particular place or situation: *I never thought he'd end up in prison.* ○ [+ doing sth] *He always ends up doing what Alan wants to do.* ○ *She'll end up unemployed.*

endanger /ɪnˈdeɪndʒər/ **verb** [T] to put someone or something in a situation where they might be harmed or seriously damaged: *He would never do anything to endanger the children's lives.*

endangered /ɪnˈdeɪndʒəd/ **adj endangered birds/plants/species, etc** ⓑ animals or plants that may soon not exist because there are very few now alive

endear /ɪnˈdɪər/ **verb**

PHRASAL VERB **endear sb to sb** If a quality in someone's character, or their behaviour endears them to you, it makes you like them.

endearing /ɪnˈdɪərɪŋ/ **adj** An endearing quality is one that makes people like you.

endeavour UK (US **endeavor**) /ɪnˈdevər/ **verb endeavour to do sth** formal to try very hard to do something: *I endeavoured to help her, but she wouldn't let me.* • **endeavour** UK (US **endeavor**) **noun** [C, U] *human/artistic endeavour*

endemic /enˈdemɪk/ **adj** formal If something unpleasant is endemic in a place or among a group of people, there is a lot of it there: *Corruption is endemic in some parts of the police force.*

ending /ˈendɪŋ/ **noun** [C] **1** ⓑ the last part of a story: *I hope this film has a **happy ending**.* **2** ⓑ a part added to the end of a word: *To make the plural of 'dog', you add the plural ending '-s'.*

endive /ˈendaɪv/ **noun** [C, U] a plant with bitter green leaves that are eaten in salads

endless /ˈendləs/ **adj** ⓑ continuing for a long time and never finishing, or never seeming to finish: *He seems to think that I have an **endless supply** of money.* • **endlessly adv**

endorse /ɪnˈdɔːs/ **verb** [T] formal to say publicly that you support a person or action: [often passive] *The idea was endorsed by a majority of members.* • **endorsement noun** [C, U]

endow /ɪnˈdaʊ/ **verb 1 be endowed with sth** to have a particular quality or characteristic: *The country is richly endowed with natural resources.* **2** [T] to give a large amount of money to a college, hospital, etc

end-product /ˈendˌprɒdʌkt/ **noun** [C] the thing that you get at the end of a process or activity

endurance /ɪnˈdjʊərəns/ **noun** [U] the ability to keep doing something difficult, unpleasant, or painful for a long time: *The race will test athletes' endurance.*

endure /ɪnˈdjʊər/ **verb** [T] formal ⓑ to suffer something difficult, unpleasant, or painful: *She's already had to endure three painful operations on her leg.*

enduring /ɪnˈdjʊərɪŋ/ **adj** existing for a long time: *the enduring popularity of cartoons*

enemy /ˈenəmi/ **noun 1** [C] ⓑ a person who you dislike or oppose: *I try not to **make** any **enemies**.* **2** [group] ⓑ a country or army that your country or army is fighting against in a war: *enemy forces/territory*

☑ Word partners for **enemy**

have/make enemies • arch/bitter/deadly enemies

energetic /ˌenəˈdʒetɪk/ **adj** ⓑ having or involving a lot of energy: *an energetic young woman* ○ *Aerobics is too energetic for me.* • **energetically adv**

energy /ˈenədʒi/ **noun** [C, U] **1** ⓑ the power and ability to be very active without becoming tired: *Looking after children takes up a lot of time and energy.* ○ [+ to do sth] *I didn't even have the energy to get out of bed.* **2** ⓑ the power that comes from electricity, gas, etc: *nuclear energy* ○ *energy conservation* → See also **atomic energy**

☑ Word partners for **energy**

expend/have/save/waste energy • boundless/ high/restless/surplus energy

energy efficient adj (also **energy-efficient**) used to describe things that use only as much energy as is needed without wasting any: *energy efficient lighting*

energy-saving /ˈenədʒiˌseɪvɪŋ/ **adj** [always before noun] relating to products and systems that use as little electricity, gas, etc as possible: *an energy-saving light*

enforce /ɪnˈfɔːs/ **verb** [T] **1** to make people obey a rule or law: *It is the duty of the police to enforce the law.* **2** to make a particular situation happen or to make people accept it: *The new teacher failed to enforce discipline.* • **enforcement noun** [U] *law enforcement*

engage /ɪnˈgeɪdʒ/ **verb** [T] formal **1** to interest someone in something and keep them thinking about it: *The debate about food safety has engaged the whole nation.* **2** formal to employ someone: [+ to do sth] *I have engaged a secretary to deal with all my paperwork.*

PHRASAL VERBS **engage in sth** to take part in something • **engage sb in sth** If you engage someone in conversation, you start a conversation with them.

engaged /ɪnˈgeɪdʒd/ **adj 1** ⓑ If two people are engaged, they have formally agreed to marry each other: *When did they **get engaged**?* **2** UK If a telephone line or a toilet is engaged, it is already being used.

engagement /ɪnˈgeɪdʒmənt/ **noun** [C] **1** an agreement to get married to someone: *an engagement ring* **2** an arrangement to meet someone or do something at a particular time

☑ Word partners for **engagement**

announce/break off your engagement • your engagement to sb • an engagement party/ ring

engaging /ɪnˈɡeɪdʒɪŋ/ **adj** pleasant, interesting, or attractive: *She has a very engaging personality.*

engender /ɪnˈdʒendər/ **verb** [T] formal to make people have a particular feeling or make a situation start to exist: *We want to engender loyalty to our products.*

engine /ˈendʒɪn/ **noun** [C] **1 ⚫** the part of a vehicle that uses energy from oil, electricity, or steam to make it move: *a diesel engine* **2** the part of a train that pulls it along → See also **fire engine**, **search engine**

> 🔲 Word partners for **engine**
>
> start/switch on/switch off/turn off the engine

engine driver **noun** [C] UK (US **engineer**) someone whose job is to drive a train

engineer¹ /ˌendʒɪˈnɪər/ **noun** [C] **1 ⚫** someone whose job is to design, build, or repair machines, engines, roads, bridges, etc: *a mechanical/structural engineer* ◦ *a software engineer* **2** US someone whose job is to drive a train

engineer² /ˌendʒɪˈnɪər/ **verb** [T] to arrange for something to happen, especially in a clever and secret way: [often passive] *She was convinced that the accident had been engineered by his enemies.*

engineering /ˌendʒɪˈnɪərɪŋ/ **noun** [U] **⚫** the work of an engineer, or the study of this work: *mechanical engineering* → See also **civil engineering**, **genetic engineering**

English¹ /ˈɪŋɡlɪʃ/ **noun 1** [U] the language that is spoken in the UK, the US, and in many other countries: *American/British English* ◦ *Do you speak English?* **2 the English** [plural] the people of England

English² /ˈɪŋɡlɪʃ/ **adj 1** relating to the English language: *an English teacher* **2** relating to England: *English law*

English breakfast **noun** [C] UK a dish including cooked meat and eggs, eaten as the first meal of the day

English muffin **noun** [C] US (UK **muffin**) a small, round, flat type of bread that is often eaten hot with butter → See picture at **muffin**

engrave /ɪnˈɡreɪv/ **verb** [T] to cut words or pictures into the surface of metal, stone, etc: *He gave her a silver pen engraved with her name.* • **engraver** **noun** [C]

engraving /ɪnˈɡreɪvɪŋ/ **noun** [C] a picture printed from an engraved piece of metal or wood

engrossed /ɪnˈɡrəʊst/ **adj** giving all your attention to something: *He was so engrossed in what he was doing that he didn't hear the bell.*

engrossing /ɪnˈɡrəʊsɪŋ/ **adj** very interesting, and needing all your attention: *an engrossing book*

engulf /ɪnˈɡʌlf/ **verb** [T] **1** to surround or cover someone or something completely: [often passive] *The house was quickly engulfed in flames.* **2** to affect a place or a group of people quickly and strongly: *Panic is threatening to engulf the country.*

enhance /ɪnˈhɑːns/ **verb** [T] formal to improve something: *Winning that award greatly enhanced her reputation.* • **enhancement** **noun** [C, U] improvement

enigma /ɪˈnɪɡmə/ **noun** [C] someone or something that is mysterious and difficult to understand: *She is a complete enigma to me.*

enigmatic /ˌenɪɡˈmætɪk/ **adj** mysterious and impossible to understand completely

enjoy /ɪnˈdʒɔɪ/ **verb** [T] **1 ⚫** If you enjoy something, it gives you pleasure: *I hope you enjoy your meal.* ◦ [+ doing sth] *I really enjoyed being with him.* **2 enjoy yourself ⚫** to get pleasure from something that you are doing: *Everyone eventually relaxed and began to enjoy themselves.* **3** formal to have or experience something good such as success: *His play enjoyed great success on Broadway.*

> ➕ Other ways of saying **enjoy**
>
> A more formal way of saying 'enjoy' is **relish**:
>
> *Jonathan always relishes a challenge.*
>
> When someone enjoys a situation or activity very much, you can use the phrasal verbs **lap up** or **revel in**:
>
> *He lapped up all the attention they gave him.*
>
> *She revelled in her role as team manager.*
>
> If someone enjoys doing something that other people think is unpleasant, the phrasal verb **delight in** is sometimes used:
>
> *She seems to delight in making other people look stupid.*
>
> The verb **savour** (UK) (**savor** US) is sometimes used when someone enjoys something slowly so that they can appreciate it as much as possible:
>
> *It was the first chocolate he'd had for over a year, so he savoured every mouthful.*
>
> When someone enjoys themselves very much, in informal situations you can use the expression **have a ball**:
>
> *We had a ball in Miami.*

> ❗ Common learner error: **enjoy doing something**
>
> When **enjoy** is followed by a verb, the verb must be in the **-ing** form.
>
> *My parents enjoy walking in the mountains.*
>
> ~~My parents enjoy to walk in the mountains.~~

enjoyable /ɪnˈdʒɔɪəbl/ **adj** **⚫** An enjoyable event or experience gives you pleasure: *We had a very enjoyable evening.*

enjoyment /ɪnˈdʒɔɪmənt/ **noun** [U] **⚫** the feeling of enjoying something: *She gets a lot of enjoyment from music.*

enlarge /ɪnˈlɑːdʒ/ **verb** [I, T] to become bigger or to make something become bigger: [often passive] *I want to get this photo enlarged.* ◦ *an enlarged view*

PHRASAL VERB enlarge on/upon sth formal to give more details about something that you have said or written

E

E

enlargement /ɪnˈlɑːdʒmənt/ **noun** [C, U] the process of enlarging something, or something that has been enlarged: *I'm going to get an enlargement of this wedding photo.*

enlighten /ɪnˈlaɪtᵊn/ **verb** [T] formal to give someone information about something, so that they understand a situation: *He believes he has a duty to enlighten the public on these matters.*

enlightened /ɪnˈlaɪtᵊnd/ **adj** having practical, modern ideas and ways of dealing with things: *an enlightened attitude*

enlightening /ɪnˈlaɪtᵊnɪŋ/ **adj** giving you more information and understanding about something: *an enlightening book*

enlist /ɪnˈlɪst/ **verb 1 enlist the help/support of sb** to ask for and get help or support from someone: *They are hoping to enlist the support of local politicians.* **2** [I] to join the army, navy, etc

enliven /ɪnˈlaɪvᵊn/ **verb** [T] to make something more interesting: *The children's arrival enlivened a boring evening.*

en masse /ɒnˈmæs/ **adv** If a group of people do something en masse, they do it together as a group: *They surrendered en masse.*

enmity /ˈenməti/ **noun** [U] formal a strong feeling of hate

enormity /ɪˈnɔːməti/ **noun the enormity of sth** how big or important something is: *He hadn't realized the enormity of the problem.*

enormous /ɪˈnɔːməs/ **adj** ⑤ extremely large: *This living room is enormous.*

enormously /ɪˈnɔːməsli/ **adv** extremely: *an enormously popular show*

enough¹ /ɪˈnʌf/ **pronoun, quantifier 1** ⓐ as much as is necessary: *They had enough fuel for one week.* ○ [+ to do sth] *Have you had enough to eat?* **2** ⑤ as much or more than you want: *I've got enough work at the moment, without being given any more.* **3 have had enough** to want something to stop because it is annoying you: *I've had enough of your excuses.* **4 that's enough** used to tell someone to stop behaving badly

enough² /ɪˈnʌf/ **adv 1** ⓐ as much as is necessary: [+ to do sth] *Are you old enough to vote?* ○ *You're not going fast enough.* **2** slightly, but not very: *He's nice enough, but I don't really want to go out with him.* **3 funnily/oddly/strangely enough** ⑤ although it may seem strange: *I was dreading the party, but I really enjoyed it, funnily enough.*

enquire UK (UK/US **inquire**) /ɪnˈkwaɪər/ **verb** [I, T] ⑤ to ask someone for information about something: *"Are you staying long?" she enquired.* ○ *I'm enquiring about dentists in the area.* ● **enquirer** UK (UK/US **inquirer**) **noun** [C]

PHRASAL VERBS **enquire after sb** UK formal to ask someone for information about someone else's health and what they are doing, in order to be polite ● **enquire into sth** formal to try to discover the facts about something

enquiring UK (UK/US **inquiring**) /ɪnˈkwaɪərɪŋ/ **adj** [always before noun] **1** always wanting to learn new things: *an enquiring mind* **2** An enquiring

expression on your face shows that you want to know something.

enquiry UK (UK/US **inquiry**) /ɪnˈkwaɪəri/ **nou 1 QUESTION** ▷ [C] formal ⑤ a question that y ask when you want more information: *We recei a lot of enquiries about tax issues.* **2 OFFICIAL PROCESS** ▷ [C] an official process to discover th facts about something bad that has happene *The hospital is holding an enquiry into t accident.* **3 ASKING QUESTIONS** ▷ [U] formal th process of asking questions in order to g information

☑ Word partners for **enquiry**

make/receive an enquiry ● an enquiry **about** sth

enrage /ɪnˈreɪdʒ/ **verb** [T] to make someone ve angry: [often passive] *Farmers are enraged by t government's refusal to help.*

enrich /ɪnˈrɪtʃ/ **verb** [T] to improve the quality something by adding something to it: [oft passive] *Our culture has been enriched by the ma immigrants who live here.* ● **enrichment noun**

enrol (**enrolling, enrolled**) UK (US **enroll**) /ɪ ˈrəʊl/ **verb** [I, T] to become or make someo become an official member of a course, colleg or group: *I've* UK **enrolled on**/US **enrolled** *a creative writing course.* ● **enrolment** (US **enrollment**) **noun** [C, U]

en route /ˌɒnˈruːt/ **adv** on the way to or fro somewhere: *We stopped in Monaco en route Switzerland.*

ensemble /ɒnˈsɒmbᵊl/ **noun** [C] a small group musicians or actors who regularly play perform together

enshrined /ɪnˈʃraɪnd/ **verb** formal **be enshrine in sth** If a political or social right is enshrined something, it is protected by being included it: *These fundamental human rights are enshrin in the constitution.*

enslave /ɪnˈsleɪv/ **verb** [T] formal to contr someone and keep them in a bad situatio [often passive] *These workers are enslaved poverty.*

ensue /ɪnˈsjuː/ **verb** [I] (**ensuing, ensued**) form to happen after something, often as a result of ● **ensuing adj** [always before noun] *the ensui hours/months*

en suite /ˌɒnˈswiːt/ **adj** UK An en suite bathroo is directly connected to a bedroom.

ensure /ɪnˈʃɔːr/ **verb** [T] formal ⑤ to make certa that something is done or happens: [+ (tha *Please ensure that all examination papers ha your name at the top.*

entail /ɪnˈteɪl/ **verb** [T] to involve somethin *What exactly does the job entail?*

entangled /ɪnˈtæŋgld/ **adj 1** involved wi someone or something so that it is difficult escape: *I don't know how I ever got entangled this relationship.* **2** caught in something such as net or ropes: *The dolphin had become entangl in the fishing net.*

enter /ˈentər/ **verb 1 PLACE** ▷ [I, T] ⓐ to come go into a place: *The police entered by the ba door.* ○ *She is accused of entering the count* *illegally.* **2 INFORMATION** ▷ [T] **⑥** to put information into a computer, book, or document: *You have to enter a password to access this information.* **3 COMPETITION** ▷ [I, T] **⑥** to take part in a competition, race, or exam, or to arrange for someone else to do this: *Are you going to enter the photography competition?* **4 ORGANIZATION** ▷ [T] to become a member of a particular organization, or start working in a particular type of job: *She didn't enter the legal profession until she was 40.* **5 PERIOD OF TIME** ▷ [T] to begin a period of time: *The violence is now entering its third week.*

> **!** Common learner error: **enter** a place
>
> You do not need to use a preposition after **enter.**
>
> *I entered the classroom.*
> ~~I entered in the classroom.~~
>
> Be careful not to use **enter** with vehicles.
> *The children got on the bus.*
> ~~The children entered the bus.~~

PHRASAL VERB **enter into sth** to start to become involved in something, especially a discussion or agreement

nterprise /'entəpraɪz/ *noun* **1 BUSINESS** ▷ [C] a business or organization: *a state-owned enterprise* **2 PLAN** ▷ [C] a difficult and important plan: *Putting on the concert will be a joint enterprise between the two schools.* **3 QUALITY** ▷ [U] the quality of being enthusiastic and willing to do new and clever things, although there are risks involved: *The venture shows imagination and enterprise.* → See also **free enterprise**

nterprising /'entəpraɪzɪŋ/ *adj* enthusiastic and willing to do new, clever, and difficult things: *The film was made by an enterprising group of students.*

ntertain /ˌentə'teɪn/ *verb* **1 INTEREST** ▷ [T] **⑥** to keep someone interested and help them to have an enjoyable time: *We hired a clown to entertain the children.* **2 GUEST** ▷ [I, T] to invite someone to be your guest and give them food, drink, etc: *We don't entertain as much as we used to.* **3 THINK ABOUT** ▷ [T] formal to consider or be willing to accept an idea or suggestion: *He had never even entertained the idea of her returning.*

ntertainer /ˌentə'teɪnər/ *noun* [C] **⑥** someone whose job is to entertain people by singing, telling jokes, etc

ntertaining /ˌentə'teɪnɪŋ/ *adj* **⑥** interesting and helping someone to have an enjoyable time: *an entertaining and informative book*

ntertainment /ˌentə'teɪnmənt/ *noun* [C, U] **⑥** shows, films, television, or other performances or activities that entertain people: *popular entertainment* ○ *There is live entertainment in the bar every night.*

nthral (**enthralling**, **enthralled**) UK (US **enthrall**) /ɪn'θrɔːl/ *verb* [T] to keep someone's interest and attention completely: [often passive] *The children were enthralled by the circus.* ● **enthralling** *adj* keeping someone's interest and attention completely

enthuse /ɪn'θjuːz/ *verb* [I] to express excitement about something or great interest in it: *She couldn't stop enthusing about the film.*

enthusiasm /ɪn'θjuːziæzᵊm/ *noun* [U] **⑫** the feeling of being very interested in something and wanting very much to be involved in it: *She has always had a lot of enthusiasm for her work.*

enthusiast /ɪn'θjuːziæst/ *noun* [C] someone who is very interested in and involved with a particular activity or subject: *a sports enthusiast*

enthusiastic /ɪnˌθjuːzi'æstɪk/ *adj* **⑫** showing enthusiasm: *The teacher was very enthusiastic about my project.* ● **enthusiastically** *adv*

entice /ɪn'taɪs/ *verb* [T] to persuade someone to do something by offering them something pleasant: [+ to do sth] *Supermarkets use all sorts of tricks to entice you to buy things.* ● **enticing** *adj* attracting you by offering you something pleasant

entire /ɪn'taɪər/ *adj* [always before noun] **⑫** whole or complete: *She spent her entire life caring for other people.*

entirely /ɪn'taɪəli/ *adv* **⑫** completely: *I'm not entirely convinced that it will work.*

entirety /ɪn'taɪərəti/ *noun* **in its entirety** with all parts included: *This is the first time that the book has been published in its entirety.*

entitle /ɪn'taɪtl/ *verb* **1 entitle sb to (do) sth** **⑫** to give someone the right to do or have something: [often passive] *I'm entitled to apply for citizenship.* **2** [T] to give something a particular title: *a lecture entitled "Language, Learning and Literacy"*

entitlement /ɪn'taɪtlmənt/ *noun* [C, U] the right to do or have something

entity /'entɪti/ *noun* [C] something that exists apart from other things: *They want the area recognized as a separate political entity.*

entourage /'ɒntʊrɑːʒ/ *(US)* /ɒntʊ'rɑːʒ/ *noun* [group] the group of people who travel with an important or famous person: *She arrived with her usual entourage of dancers and musicians.*

entrance /'entrəns/ *noun* **1 DOOR** ▷ [C] **⑫** a door or other opening that you use to enter a building or place: *They must have used the back entrance to the building.* ○ *I'll meet you at the main entrance.* **2 COMING IN** ▷ [C] the time when someone comes into or goes into a place, especially in a way that makes people notice them: *The whole room went quiet when he made his entrance.* **3 RIGHT** ▷ [U] **⑥** the right to enter a place or to join an organization, college, etc: *Entrance is free, but you have to pay for your drinks.*

> **✓** Word partners for **entrance**
>
> the **back/front/main** entrance ● **at** the entrance ● the entrance **to** sth

entranced /ɪn'trɑːnst/ *adj* If you are entranced by someone or something, you cannot stop watching them because they are very interesting or very beautiful: *The children were entranced by the puppet show.*

entrant /'entrənt/ *noun* [C] someone who enters a competition, organization, or examination

entreat /ɪnˈtriːt/ **verb** [T] formal to try very hard to persuade someone to do something

entrenched /ɪnˈtrentʃt/ **adj** Entrenched ideas are so fixed or have existed for so long that they cannot be changed: *These **attitudes** are firmly **entrenched** in our culture.*

entrepreneur /ˌɒntrəprəˈnɜːr/ **noun** [C] someone who starts their own business, especially when this involves risks • **entrepreneurial** **adj** *an **entrepreneurial** spirit*

entrust /ɪnˈtrʌst/ **verb** [T] to make someone responsible for doing something or looking after something: [often passive] *I was **entrusted** with the task of organizing the party.*

entry /ˈentri/ **noun 1** COMING IN ▷ [U] ❷ the act of coming into or going into a place: *She was **refused** entry to the US.* ∘ *Police **gained** entry by breaking a window.* **2** JOINING/TAKING PART ▷ [U] ❷ the act of joining an organization or taking part in a competition: *Are there lots of exams for **entry** into the legal profession?* ∘ *an entry form* **3** COMPETITION WORK ▷ [C] ❶ a piece of work that you do to try to win a competition: *The first ten correct entries will receive a prize.* **4** PIECE OF INFORMATION ▷ [C] ❷ one of the pieces of information or writing that is recorded in a book such as a dictionary, or in a computer system: *a diary entry* **5** ADDING INFORMATION ▷ [U] the act of putting information into something such as a computer system: *data entry*

> 🗹 **Word partners for entry**
>
> **allow/gain/refuse** entry • entry **into/to** [a place]

entwined /ɪnˈtwaɪnd/ **adj 1** twisted together or twisted around something: *Their arms were entwined.* **2** unable to be separated: *My fate is entwined with his.*

enumerate /ɪˈnjuːməreɪt/ **verb** [T] formal to name each thing on a list

envelop /ɪnˈveləp/ **verb** [T] to completely cover something: [often passive] *The farm was enveloped in fog.*

envelope /ˈenvələʊp/ **noun** [C] ❷ a flat paper container for a letter → See colour picture **The Office** on page Centre 5

enviable /ˈenviəbl/ **adj** If someone is in an enviable situation, you wish that you were also in that situation: *She's in the **enviable position** of being able to choose who she works for.*

envious /ˈenviəs/ **adj** wishing that you had what someone else has: *She was **envious of** his successful career.* • **enviously** adv

environment /ɪnˈvaɪərənmənt/ **noun 1** the **environment** ❷ the air, land, and water where people, animals, and plants live: *The new road may cause damage to the environment.* → See Note at **nature 2** ❷ [C] the situation that you live or work in, and how it influences how you feel: *We are working in a very competitive environment.*

> 🗹 **Word partners for environment**
>
> **damage/harm/pollute/protect** the environment

environmental /ɪnˌvaɪərənˈmentəl/ **adj** ❸ relating to the environment: *environmental damage* ∘ *an environmental disaster* • **environmentally** adv ❷ *environmentally damaging chemicals*

environmentalism /ɪnˌvaɪərənˈmentəlɪzəm/ (US) /-ˌvaɪrənˈmentəl-/ **noun** [U] the study of the environment and the belief that it must be protected from damage by human activities

environmentalist /ɪnˌvaɪərənˈmentəlɪst/ **noun** [C] someone who tries to protect the natural environment from being damaged

environmentally friendly **adj** ❷ not damaging the environment: *environmentally friendly washing powder*

envisage /ɪnˈvɪzɪdʒ/ **verb** [T] mainly UK (mainly US **envision** /ɪnˈvɪʒən/) to imagine something happening, or think that something is likely to happen: *The police don't envisage any trouble at the festival.*

envoy /ˈenvɔɪ/ **noun** [C] someone who is sent to represent their government in another country

envy¹ /ˈenvi/ **noun 1** ❷ [U] the feeling that you wish you had something that someone else has: *I watched with envy as he climbed into his brand new sports car.* **2 be the envy of sb** to be liked and wanted by someone: *Her new office was the envy of the whole company.*

envy² /ˈenvi/ **verb** [T] ❷ to wish that you had something that someone else has: *I envy her good looks.* ∘ [+ two objects] *I don't envy him the job.*

enzyme /ˈenzaɪm/ **noun** [C] a chemical substance produced by living cells that make particular chemical reactions happen in animals and plants

ephemeral /ɪˈfemərəl/ **adj** formal lasting for only a short time

epic /ˈepɪk/ **noun** [C] a story or film that is very long and contains a lot of action • **epic adj** *an epic journey*

epidemic /ˌepɪˈdemɪk/ **noun** [C] a situation in which a large number of people get the same disease over the same period of time: *the AIDS epidemic*

epilepsy /ˈepɪlepsi/ **noun** [U] a condition of the brain that causes a person to become unconscious and have fits (= periods when you shake in an uncontrolled way)

epileptic /ˌepɪˈleptɪk/ **noun** [C] someone who suffers from epilepsy • **epileptic adj**

epilogue /ˈepɪlɒg/ **noun** [C] a speech or piece of writing that is added to the end of a play or book

epiphany /ɪˈpɪfəni/ **noun** [U] literary a moment when you suddenly understand or become aware of something

episode /ˈepɪsəʊd/ **noun** [C] **1** ❷ one programme of a series shown on television: *Did you see last week's episode of The X-Factor?* **2** ❷ single event or period of time: *an important episode in British history*

epitaph /ˈepɪtɑːf/ **noun** [C] words that are written to remember a dead person, usually on the stone where they are buried

epitome /ɪˈpɪtəmi/ **noun be the epitome of st**

to be a perfect example of a quality or type of thing: *The hotel was the epitome of luxury.*

pitomize (also UK **-ise**) /ɪˈpɪtəmaɪz/ **verb** [T] to be a perfect example of a quality or type of thing: *She epitomizes elegance and good taste.*

poch /ˈiːpɒk/ ⓤⓢ /ˈepək/ **noun** [C] (plural **epochs**) a long period of time in history

ponymous /ɪˈpɒnɪməs/ **adj** [always before noun] literary An eponymous character in a play, book, etc, has the same name as the title.

-publishing /ˈiːˌpʌblɪʃɪŋ/ **noun** [U] the production of books, magazines, newspapers, etc that can be read using a computer, for example on the Internet or on a CD

qual¹ /ˈiːkwəl/ **adj 1** ⑤ⓘ the same in amount, number, or size: *The sides are of equal length.* ∘ *One metre is **equal to** 39.37 inches.* **2 equal opportunities/rights, etc** ⑥② opportunities/ rights, etc that are the same for everyone without anyone having an unfair advantage → Opposite **unequal**

qual² /ˈiːkwəl/ **verb** [T] (mainly UK **equalling, equalled**, US **equaling, equaled**) **1** to have the same value, size, etc as something else, often shown using a symbol (=): *Two plus two equals four.* **2** to be as good as someone or something else: *She equalled her own world record in the race.*

qual³ /ˈiːkwəl/ **noun** [C] ⑥② someone who has the same ability, opportunities, or rights as someone else: *The teacher treats us all as equals.*

quality /ɪˈkwɒləti/ **noun** [U] ⑥② the situation when everyone is equal and has the same opportunities, rights, etc: *racial/sexual equality* ∘ *equality between* men and women → Opposite **inequality**

qualize (also UK **-ise**) /ˈiːkwəlaɪz/ **verb 1** [I] UK to get the point in a game or competition that makes your score the same as the other team or player **2** [T] to make things or people equal

qually /ˈiːkwəli/ **adv 1 SAME DEGREE** ▷ to the same degree or level: *an equally important question* ∘ *She did **equally well** in the competition last year.* **2 SAME AMOUNTS** ▷ into amounts or parts that are the same size: *She shared the money equally between the four children.* **3 SAME WAY** ▷ ⑥② If you treat people equally, you treat everyone in the same way so that no one has an unfair advantage.

qual ˌsign noun [C] (also **ˈequals ˌsign**) the symbol =, used to show that two things are the same in value, size, meaning, etc

quanimity /ˌekwəˈnɪməti/ **noun** [U] formal the ability to react calmly, especially in difficult situations

quate /ɪˈkweɪt/ **verb** [T] to consider one thing to be the same as or equal to another thing: *Many people **equate** wealth **with** happiness.*

quation /ɪˈkweɪʒᵊn/ **noun** [C] a mathematical statement that shows two amounts are equal using mathematical symbols

equator /ɪˈkweɪtᵊr/ **noun** [U] the imaginary line around the Earth that divides it into equal north and south parts • **equatorial** /ˌekwəˈtɔːriəl/ **adj** relating to the equator

equestrian /ɪˈkwestriən/ **adj** relating to riding horses

equi- /ekwɪ-/ **prefix** equal, equally: *equidistant* (= *the same distance from two or more places*)

equip /ɪˈkwɪp/ **verb** (**equipping, equipped**) **1 be equipped with sth** ⑥② to include the things that are needed for a particular purpose: *The new trains are equipped with all the latest technology.* **2** [T] to give someone the skills they need to do a particular thing: [+ to do sth] *The course didn't really equip me to be a journalist.*

equipment /ɪˈkwɪpmənt/ **noun 1** ⑤ⓘ [U] the things that are used for a particular activity or purpose: *kitchen/office equipment* ∘ *electrical equipment* (= *equipment that uses electricity*) **2 a piece of equipment** ⑤ⓘ a tool or object used for a particular activity or purpose

> **❗** Common learner error: **equipment**
>
> Remember you cannot make **equipment** plural. Do not say 'equipments'.
>
> *The computer room has all the equipment you need.*

equitable /ˈekwɪtəbl/ **adj** formal treating everyone in an equal way: *a fair and equitable voting system* • **equitably adv**

equity /ˈekwɪti/ **noun** [U] formal the situation when everyone is treated fairly and equally: *pay equity* → Compare **inequity**

equivalent¹ /ɪˈkwɪvᵊlənt/ **adj** equal in amount, value, importance, or meaning: *The UK's Bafta Awards are roughly **equivalent to** the Oscars.*

equivalent² /ɪˈkwɪvᵊlənt/ **noun** [C] something that has the same value, importance, size, or meaning as something else: *She won **the equivalent of** $5 million.*

er /ɜːr/ **exclamation** mainly UK spoken (US **uh**) something that you say while you are thinking what to say next: *Well, er, I'm not too sure about that.*

ER /ˌiːˈɑːr/ **noun** [C] US abbreviation for emergency room: the part of a hospital where people go when they have been injured or have urgent illnesses so that they can be treated immediately

era /ˈɪərə/ **noun** [C] ⑥② a period of time in history that is special for a particular reason: *the Victorian era* ∘ *a new era of peace*

eradicate /ɪˈrædɪkeɪt/ **verb** [T] formal to destroy or completely get rid of something such as a social problem or a disease • **eradication** /ɪˌrædɪˈkeɪʃᵊn/ **noun** [U]

erase /ɪˈreɪz/ ⓤⓢ /ɪˈreɪs/ **verb** [T] to completely remove words, music, pictures, etc that are written or stored on a computer or other piece of equipment: *How do I erase the disc?*

E

E

eraser /ɪ'reɪzəʳ/ ⑤ /ɪ'reɪsər/ **noun** [C] US (UK **rubber**) **1** a small object that is used to remove pencil marks from paper **2** an object that is used to remove marks from a board that teachers write on → See colour picture **The Classroom** on page Centre 6

erect¹ /ɪ'rekt/ **adj** straight and standing up: *She stood very erect, with her hands behind her back.*

erect² /ɪ'rekt/ **verb** [T] formal to build or put up a structure: *When was this building erected?*

erection /ɪ'rekʃ³n/ **noun 1** [C] If a man has an erection, his penis is harder and bigger than usual. **2** [C, U] formal the activity of building or putting up a building, or the building itself

erode /ɪ'rəʊd/ **verb 1** [I, T] If soil, stone, etc erodes or is eroded, it is gradually damaged and removed by the sea, rain, or wind: [often passive] *The coastline is slowly being eroded by the sea.* **2** [T] formal to gradually destroy a good quality or situation: *Reports of corruption have eroded people's confidence in the police.* • **erosion** /ɪ'rəʊʒ³n/ **noun** [U] *soil erosion*

erotic /ɪ'rɒtɪk/ **adj** making you feel strong sexual feelings, or involving sexual love: *an erotic film* • **erotically adv**

err /ɜːʳ/ **verb** [I] formal to make a mistake or do something that is wrong → See also **err on the side¹ of caution**

errand /'erənd/ **noun** [C] a short journey in order to buy or do something for someone: *I've got to **run** a few **errands** this morning before we go.*

errant /'erənt/ **adj** [always before noun] An errant person has behaved badly: *an errant husband*

erratic /ɪ'rætɪk/ **adj** often changing suddenly and not regular: *His behaviour is becoming more and more erratic.* • **erratically adv**

erroneous /ɪ'rəʊniəs/ **adj** formal not correct: *an erroneous answer*

error /'erəʳ/ **noun** [C, U] ⑫ a mistake, especially one that can cause problems: *a computer error/* **human error** ∘ *to **make** an **error*** ∘ *The documents were destroyed **in error** (= by mistake) by the police.*

☑ **Word partners for error**

make/correct an error • a **fundamental/ glaring** error • do sth **in** error • **human** error
---

erupt /ɪ'rʌpt/ **verb** [I] **1** VOLCANO ▷ If a volcano erupts, it suddenly throws out smoke, fire, and melted rocks. **2** HAPPEN ▷ to happen suddenly or violently: *Violence erupted in the city on Friday night.* **3** PERSON ▷ to suddenly become very excited or angry, or start to shout: *The whole stadium erupted when he scored the second goal.* • **eruption** /ɪ'rʌpʃ³n/ **noun** [C, U] *a volcanic eruption*

escalate /'eskəleɪt/ **verb 1** [I, T] If a violent or bad situation escalates or is escalated, it quickly becomes worse or more serious: *The fight quickly **escalated into** a riot.* **2** [I] to rise or increase quickly: *Airline **prices escalate** during the holiday season.* • **escalation** /ˌeskə'leɪʃ³n/ **noun** [C, U] *an **escalation in** violence*

escalator /'eskəleɪtəʳ/ **noun** [C] ⑫ moving stairs

that take people from one level of a building t another: *We **took** the **escalator** down to th basement.*

escapade /ˌeskə'peɪd/ **noun** [C] an exciting an sometimes dangerous experience

escape¹ /ɪ'skeɪp/ **verb 1** GET AWAY ▷ [I] ⑧ t succeed in getting away from a place where yo do not want to be: *The two killers **escaped fro** prison last night.* **2** AVOID ▷ [I, T] ⑫ to avoid dangerous or unpleasant situation: *to **escap** capture/injury* **3** FORGET ▷ [T] If somethin such as a name escapes you, you canne remember it: *The **name** of her book **escapes** n at the moment.* **4** NOT NOTICE ▷ [T] If somethin escapes your notice or attention, you do ne notice or see it: *Nothing that goes on in this offi **escapes** her **attention**.* **5** GAS/LIQUID ▷ [I] If gas or liquid escapes from a pipe or containe it comes out, especially when it should no • **escaped adj** *an escaped prisoner*

escape² /ɪ'skeɪp/ **noun 1** [C, U] ⑫ an occasio when someone succeeds in getting out of place or a dangerous or bad situation **2 narrow escape** an occasion when someon almost dies or almost has a very bad experienc **3** [U, no plural] something that helps you t forget about your usual life or problems: *I lo old movies, they're such an **escape from** the re world.* → See also **fire escape**

☑ **Word partners for escape**

attempt/make/plan an escape • a **lucky/ remarkable** escape • an escape **from** sth/sb
---

es'cape (key) noun [C] (written abbreviation Es the key on a computer keyboard that allows yo to leave a particular screen or program: *If yo press the escape key, you will return to the ma menu.*

escapism /ɪ'skeɪpɪz³m/ **noun** [U] entertainme or imagination that helps you to forget abo your work and your problems • **escapist adj**

escort¹ /'eskɔːt/ **noun 1** [C, U] a person or vehic that goes somewhere with someone to protect guard them: *She was driven to court **under** poli **escort**.* **2** [C] a person who goes with someone a social event, sometimes for payment

escort² /ɪ'skɔːt/ **verb** [T] to go somewhere wit someone, often to protect or guard them: *H offered to escort me home.*

Eskimo /'eskɪməʊ/ **noun** [C, U] (plural **Eskimo Eskimo**) old-fashioned another word for Inuit (= group of people who live in the cold, norther areas of North America, Russia, and Greenlan or a member of this group): *an Eskimo village*

ESL /ˌiːes'el/ **noun** [U] abbreviation for English as Second Language: the teaching of English t students whose first language is not English, b who live in a country where it is the ma language

especially /ɪ'speʃ³li/ **adv 1** ⑫ more than othe things or people, or much more than usual: *He always making comments about her appearanc especially her weight.* ∘ *She's especially intereste in American poetry.* **2** for one particular perso

---

purpose, or reason: *I cooked this meal **especially for you**.* → See Note at **specially**

espionage /ˈespiənɑːʒ/ **noun** [U] the activity of discovering secret information about a country or company that is fighting or competing against you: *industrial espionage*

espouse /ɪˈspaʊz/ **verb** [T] formal to support a belief or way of life

espresso /esˈpresəʊ/ **noun** [C, U] strong, black coffee

essay /ˈeseɪ/ **noun** [C] 🔵 a short piece of writing about a particular subject, especially one written by a student: *He wrote an **essay on** modern Japanese literature.*

> 🗹 **Word partners for essay**
>
> **do/write** an essay • **in** an essay • an essay **on** sth

essence /ˈesᵊns/ **noun 1** [U, no plural] the basic or most important idea or quality of something: *The essence of his argument is that we should not eat meat.* **2** [C, U] a strong liquid, usually made from a plant or flower, that is used to add a flavour or smell to something: *vanilla essence*

essential /ɪˈsenʃᵊl/ **adj 1** 🔵 very important and necessary: *Computers are an **essential part** of our lives.* ○ *Fibre is **essential for** a healthy digestive system.* ○ [+ to do sth] *It is essential to arrive early for the show.* ○ [+ (that)] *It is absolutely essential that she gets this message.* **2** the most basic and important: *There's one essential point I think you've forgotten.*

essentially /ɪˈsenʃᵊli/ **adv** 🔵 used when you are emphasizing the basic facts about something: *What he is saying is essentially true.*

essential 'oil noun [C, U] a strong oil made from a plant that contains its smell or other special qualities

essentials /ɪˈsenʃᵊlz/ **noun** [plural] the most important or necessary things

establish /ɪˈstæblɪʃ/ **verb 1 START** ▷ [T] 🔵 to start a company or organization that will continue for a long time: [often passive] *The brewery was established in 1822.* **2 establish sb/sth as sth** to put someone or something into a successful and lasting position: [often reflexive] *He quickly established himself as a talented actor.* **3 establish communication/relations, etc** to start having a relationship or communicating with another company, country, or organization: *The two countries have only recently established diplomatic relations.* **4 DECIDE** ▷ [T] to decide something: *Our first step must be to establish priorities for the weeks ahead.* **5 DISCOVER** ▷ [T] to find out information or prove something: [+ question word] *The police are trying to establish how he died.* • **established adj**

establishment /ɪˈstæblɪʃmənt/ **noun 1** [C] an organization or business **2** [U] the process of starting an organization, school, business, etc: *the establishment of a new national bank* **3 the Establishment** the people and organizations that have most power and influence in a country **4 the legal/medical, etc establishment** the

group of people with most influence in a particular area of work or activity

estate /ɪˈsteɪt/ **noun** [C] **1 LAND** ▷ 🔵 a large area of land in the countryside that is owned by one person or organization: *a country estate* **2 BUILDINGS** ▷ UK 🔵 an area with a lot of buildings of the same type: *an industrial estate* **3 POSSESSIONS** ▷ the possessions and money that someone owns when they die → See also **housing estate, real estate**

es'tate ˌagent noun [C] UK (US **real estate agent**) someone who sells buildings and land as their job

es'tate ˌcar noun [C] UK (US **station wagon**) a big car with a large space for bags behind the back seat

esteem /ɪˈstiːm/ **noun** [U] formal respect and admiration for someone: *My father was **held in high esteem** by everyone who knew him.* → See also **self-esteem**

esteemed /ɪˈstiːmd/ **adj** formal respected and admired: *a **highly esteemed** professor*

esthetic /esˈθetɪk/ **adj** another US spelling of aesthetic (= relating to beauty and the way something looks) • **esthetically adv**

esthetics /esˈθetɪks/ **noun** [U] another US spelling of aesthetics (= the study of beauty)

estimate¹ /ˈestɪmət/ **noun** [C] **1** 🔵 a guess of what a size, value, amount, etc might be: *a rough estimate* **2** a written document saying how much it will probably cost to do a job: *Can you **give** me an **estimate** for the work?*

> 🗹 **Word partners for estimate**
>
> an **accurate/rough** estimate • an estimate **of** sth • **give** sb an estimate

estimate² /ˈestɪmeɪt/ **verb** [T] 🔵 to guess the cost, size, value, etc of something: [+ that] *They estimate that a hundred people were killed in the accident.* ○ *The number of dead **is estimated at** a hundred.* • **estimated adj** 🔵 *an estimated cost*

estimation /ˌestɪˈmeɪʃᵊn/ **noun** [U] your opinion of someone or something: *He is a total genius, **in my estimation**.*

estranged /ɪˈstreɪndʒd/ **adj** formal **1** not now communicating with a friend or a member of your family, because you have argued **2** not now living with your husband or wife: *his estranged wife* • **estrangement noun** [C, U]

estrogen /ˈiːstrədʒᵊn/ ⑮ /ˈestrədʒᵊn/ **noun** [U] US spelling of oestrogen (= a chemical substance in a woman's body)

estuary /ˈestjʊəri/ **noun** [C] the wide part of a river where it goes into the sea

etc /etˈsetᵊrə/ **abbreviation** for et cetera: used at the end of a list to show that other things or people could also be added to it

etch /etʃ/ **verb** [I, T] to cut lines on a hard surface to make a picture or words

eternal /ɪˈtɜːnᵊl/ **adj** continuing forever, or seeming to continue forever: *eternal youth* • **eternally adv** *I will be **eternally grateful** to you.*

eternity /ɪˈtɜːnəti/ **noun 1** [U] time that continues forever, especially after death **2 an**

eternity informal a very long time: *It seemed like an eternity until she came back.*

ethereal /ɪˈθɪəriəl/ adj very delicate and light and almost seeming not to be from this world • **ethereally** adv

ethic /ˈeθɪk/ noun [no plural] a belief or idea that influences the way you think or behave

ethical /ˈeθɪkᵊl/ adj **1** relating to what is right or wrong: *The book raises some serious ethical questions.* **2** morally correct and good: *He dealt with this case in a completely professional and ethical manner.* → Opposite **unethical** • **ethically** adv

ethics /ˈeθɪks/ noun [plural] ideas and beliefs about what type of behaviour is morally right and wrong: *a code of ethics* ○ *the ethics of genetic engineering*

ethnic /ˈeθnɪk/ adj relating to a particular race of people: *ethnic minorities*

ethnic cleansing /ˌeθnɪkˈklenzɪŋ/ noun [U] the use of violence to remove everyone of a particular race or religion from a country or area

ethos /ˈiːθɒs/ noun [no plural] the ideas and beliefs of a particular person or group

e-ticket /ˈiːˌtɪkɪt/ noun [C] a ticket, usually for someone to travel on an aircraft, that is held on a computer and is not printed on paper

etiquette /ˈetɪket/ noun [U] rules about what is polite and correct behaviour

etymology /ˌetɪˈmɒlədʒi/ noun [U] the study of the history and origin of words and their meanings • **etymological** /ˌetɪməˈlɒdʒɪkᵊl/ adj • **etymologically** adv

.eu /ˌdɒtˈiːjuː/ abbreviation for Europe: used by some European companies in their internet address instead of .com

the EU /ˌiːˈjuː/ noun abbreviation for the European Union: a European political and economic organization that encourages business and good relationships between the countries that are members

euphemism /ˈjuːfəmɪzᵊm/ noun [C, U] a polite word or phrase that is used to avoid saying something embarrassing or offensive: *'Passed away' is a euphemism for 'died'.* • **euphemistic** /ˌjuːfəˈmɪstɪk/ adj • **euphemistically** adv

euphoria /juːˈfɔːriə/ noun [U] a feeling of extreme happiness and excitement • **euphoric** /juːˈfɒrɪk/ adj

euro /ˈjʊərəʊ/ noun [C] **⚫** a unit of money used in European countries that belong to the European Union; €

Euro- /jʊərəʊ-/ prefix relating to Europe: *Europop (= pop music from Europe)*

European /ˌjʊərəˈpiːən/ adj relating or belonging to Europe: *European countries/languages* ○ *the European Parliament* • **European** noun [C] *Many Europeans speak English.*

the European Union noun (also **the EU**) a European political and economic organization that encourages business and good relationships between the countries that are members

euthanasia /ˌjuːθəˈneɪziə/ noun [U] the ending of someone's life so that they do not suffer any more: *voluntary euthanasia*

evacuate /ɪˈvækjueɪt/ verb [T] to move people from a dangerous place to somewhere safer: *The police quickly evacuated the area after the bomb threat.* • **evacuation** /ɪˌvækjuˈeɪʃᵊn/ noun [C, U] *the evacuation of civilians from the war zone*

evacuee /ɪˌvækjuˈiː/ noun [C] someone who is evacuated from a place to somewhere safer

evade /ɪˈveɪd/ verb **1** [T] to avoid something or someone, especially in a dishonest way: *to evade capture* ○ *to evade paying tax* **2** **evade the issue/question**, etc to intentionally not talk about something or not answer something

evaluate /ɪˈvæljueɪt/ verb [T] formal to consider or study something carefully and decide how good or bad it is • **evaluation** /ɪˌvæljuˈeɪʃᵊn/ noun [C, U]

evangelical /ˌiːvænˈdʒelɪkᵊl/ adj Evangelical Christians believe that faith in Jesus Christ and studying the Bible are more important than religious ceremonies.

evaporate /ɪˈvæpᵊreɪt/ verb **1** [I, T] If a liquid evaporates or is evaporated, it changes into gas or vapour (= very small drops of water). **2** [I] If feelings evaporate, they disappear. • **evaporation** /ɪˌvæpəˈreɪʃᵊn/ noun [U]

evasion /ɪˈveɪʒᵊn/ noun [C, U] activities aimed at avoiding something, especially in a dishonest way: *tax evasion*

evasive /ɪˈveɪsɪv/ adj **1** trying to avoid talking about something: *He was very evasive about his past.* ○ *an evasive answer* **2** **take evasive action** to do something to avoid an accident or bad situation • **evasively** adv • **evasiveness** noun [U]

eve /iːv/ noun **1 Christmas Eve/New Year's Eve** the day or night before Christmas Day/New Year's Day **2** **the eve of sth** the time just before something important happens: *They were married in Washington on the eve of the Second World War.*

even¹ /ˈiːvᵊn/ adj **1 FLAT** ▷ flat, level, or smooth: *Find an even surface to work on.* → Opposite **uneven 2 NOT CHANGING** ▷ An even temperature or rate is regular and does not change very much. **3 NUMBER** ▷ An even number is a number that can be exactly divided by two, for example four, six, or eight. → Opposite **odd 4 MONEY** ▷ informal not now owing someone money: *If you pay for my cinema ticket, we'll be even.* **5 COMPETITION** ▷ An even race or competition is one that both players, teams, or people involved have an equal chance of winning. **6 get even (with sb)** informal If you get even with someone who has done something bad to you, you do something bad to them.

even² /ˈiːvᵊn/ adv **1 ⚫** used to emphasize something that is surprising: *Everyone danced even Mick.* **2 even better/faster/smaller, etc ⚫** used when comparing things, to emphasize the difference: *I think Alex is going to be even taller than his father.* **3 even if ⚫** used to emphasize that a particular situation would not change what you have just said: *I would never eat meat, even if I was really hungry.* **4 even though ⚫**

although: *He still smokes, even though he's got asthma.* **5 even so** used to emphasize that something surprising is true despite what you have just said: *Car prices have gone down a lot, but even so, we couldn't afford to buy one.*

even³ /ˈiːvən/ **verb**

PHRASAL VERB **even (sth) out** to become equal, or to make something equal: *Sometimes I pay and sometimes Tom does – it usually evens out in the end.*

evening /ˈiːvnɪŋ/ **noun 1** ⓐ [C, U] the part of the day between the afternoon and the night: *Are you doing anything this evening?* ∘ *I go to band practice on Monday evenings.* ∘ *We usually eat our main meal in the evening.* **2 (Good) evening.** something that you say when you meet someone in the evening

> 🔲 **Word partners for evening**
>
> this/tomorrow/yesterday evening • in the evening

evening class noun [C] a class for adult students that happens in the evening: *I've been going to evening classes to improve my German.*

evenly /ˈiːvənli/ **adv 1** into equal amounts, or in a regular way: *They decided to divide the prize money evenly between them.* **2 evenly matched** Two people or teams who are evenly matched are equally good, or have an equal chance of winning.

event /ɪˈvent/ **noun** [C] **1** ⓑ something that happens, especially something important or unusual: *Local people have been shocked by recent events in the town.* **2** ⓑ a race, party, competition, etc that has been organized for a particular time: *a social/sporting event* **3 in the event** UK used to emphasize what did happen when it was not what you had expected: *In the event, we didn't need the extra money.* **4 in the event of sth** formal if something happens: *An airbag could save your life in the event of an accident.* **5 in any event** whatever happens: *I'm not sure if I'm coming on Friday, but in any event, I'll see you next week.* → See also **non-event**

> 🔲 **Word partners for event**
>
> an event **happens/occurs/takes place**
> • **witness** an event • a **dramatic/major/rare/
> tragic** event • **recent** events

eventful /ɪˈventf³l/ **adj** full of interesting or important events: *a very eventful day/journey*

eventual /ɪˈventʃuəl/ **adj** [always before noun] happening or existing at the end of a process or period of time: *the eventual winner of the competition*

eventually /ɪˈventʃuəli/ **adv** ⓑ in the end, especially after a long time: *We all hope that an agreement can be reached eventually.*

ever /ˈevər/ **adv 1** ⓐ at any time: *Have you ever been skiing?* ∘ *No one ever calls me anymore.* **2 better/faster/happier, etc than ever** better/faster/happier, etc than at any time before **3 hardly ever** ⓑ almost never: *We hardly ever go out these days.* **4 ever since** ⓑ always since

that time: *We met at school and have been friends ever since.* **5 ever so/ever such a** mainly UK ⓑ very/a very: *She's ever so pretty.* **6 for ever** UK (UK/US **forever**) ⓑ always in the future: *I'm not going to live here for ever.* **7 ever-changing/ growing/increasing, etc** always changing/ growing/increasing, etc

evergreen /ˈevəgriːn/ **adj** An evergreen plant has green leaves that do not fall off in winter. • **evergreen noun** [C] a plant with leaves that do not fall off in winter

everlasting /ˌevəˈlɑːstɪŋ/ **adj** continuing for a long time or always: *everlasting love*

evermore /ˌevəˈmɔːr/ **adv** literary always in the future

every /ˈevri/ **determiner 1** EACH ▷ ⓐ each one of a group of people or things: *He knows the name of every child in the school.* ∘ *Every one of the paintings was a fake.* **2** HOW OFTEN ▷ ⓐ used to show that something is repeated regularly: *He goes to Spain every summer.* **3** POSSIBLE ▷ ⓑ as much as is possible: *I'd like to wish you every success in your new job.* ∘ *Every effort is being made to solve the problem.* **4 every now and then/every so often** sometimes, but not often: *We still meet up every now and then.* **5 one in every five/ten, etc** used to show how many people or things in a group are affected by or involved in something

> ❗ Common learner error: **every**
>
> When **every** is followed by **body, one, thing,** or **where,** you write the words together.
> *Everybody needs to bring something to eat.*
> *Can everyone see that?*
> *Have you got everything you need?*
> *I've looked everywhere for it.*
> In other situations you use **every** as a separate word.
> *You have to take your membership card every time you go.*
> *Do you go jogging every morning?*

everybody /ˈevriˌbɒdi/ **pronoun** ⓐ another word for everyone

everyday /ˈevrideɪ/ **adj** [always before noun] normal, usual, or happening every day: *Computers are now part of everyday life.*

everyone /ˈevriwʌn/ **pronoun** (also **everybody**) **1** ⓐ every person: *Everyone agreed with the decision.* **2 everyone else** every other person: *Everyone else was wearing jeans.*

everyplace /ˈevripleɪs/ **adv** US another word for everywhere

everything /ˈevriθɪŋ/ **pronoun 1** ⓐ all things or each thing: *They lost everything in the fire.* ∘ *What's the matter Nick, is everything all right?* **2 everything else** all the other things: *The meat tasted strange, but everything else was okay.* **3 be/mean everything** to be the most important part of someone's life: *His children mean everything to him.* ∘ *Money isn't everything.*

everywhere /ˈevriweər/ **adv** ⓐ in or to every place: *I've looked everywhere, but I still can't find that letter.*

E

evict /ɪ'vɪkt/ **verb** [T] to legally force someone to leave the house they are living in: *They were evicted after complaints from their neighbours.* • **eviction** /ɪ'vɪkʃən/ **noun** [C, U]

evidence /'evɪdəns/ **noun** [U] **1** 🅱️2 something that makes you believe that something is true or exists: *evidence of global warming* ○ [+ that] *There is no scientific evidence that the drug is addictive.* **2** information that is given or objects that are shown in a court of law to help to prove if someone has committed a crime: *He was arrested despite the lack of evidence against him.* **3** **give evidence** UK to give information and answer questions in a court of law: *She was called to give evidence at his trial.* **4** **be in evidence** formal to be noticeable

⊘ Word partners for **evidence**

compelling/conclusive/hard/scientific/strong evidence • evidence of sth

evident /'evɪdənt/ **adj** formal 🅱️2 obvious to everyone and easy to see or understand: [+ that] *It was evident from his voice that he was upset.* → See also **self-evident**

evidently /'evɪdəntli/ **adv 1** 🅱️2 used to say that something can easily be noticed: *He evidently likes her.* **2** used to say that something seems probable from the information you have: *The intruder evidently got in through an open window.*

evil¹ /'iːvəl/ **adj** 🅱️2 very cruel, bad, or harmful: *an evil monster*

evil² /'iːvəl/ **noun** [C, U] 🅱️2 something that is very bad and harmful: *The theme of the play is the battle between good and evil.* → See also **the lesser of two evils**

evocative /ɪ'vɒkətɪv/ **adj** making you remember or imagine something that is pleasant: *evocative music* ○ *The sound is evocative of the sea.*

evoke /ɪ'vəʊk/ **verb** [T] to make someone remember something or feel an emotion: *The story evoked memories of my childhood.*

evolution /ˌiːvə'luːʃən/ **noun** [U] **1** 🅱️2 the way in which living things gradually change and develop over millions of years: *Darwin's theory of evolution* **2** 🅱️2 a gradual process of change and development: *the evolution of language* • **evolutionary adj**

evolve /ɪ'vɒlv/ **verb 1** [I] to develop from other forms of life over millions of years **2** [I, T] to develop or make something develop, usually gradually: *rapidly evolving technology*

e-waste /'iːweɪst/ **noun** [U] computers, phones, and other electronic products that are thrown away because they are old, broken, etc

ewe /juː/ **noun** [C] a female sheep

ex /eks/ **noun** [C] informal someone who used to be your husband, wife, or partner: *My ex and his new wife live abroad.*

ex- /eks-/ **prefix** from before: *an ex-boyfriend* ○ *an ex-boss*

exacerbate /ɪg'zæsəbeɪt/ **verb** [T] to make something worse: *Sunny weather exacerbates the effects of pollution.*

exact¹ /ɪg'zækt/ **adj** 🅱️1 completely correct in every detail: *I'm afraid I can't give you the exact*

details of the show yet. ○ *They've lived here a lor time – 25 years to be exact.* • **exactness noun** [

exact² /ɪg'zækt/ **verb** [T] formal to demand ar get something from someone

exacting /ɪg'zæktɪŋ/ **adj** needing a lot of effo and attention: *an exacting training schedule*

exactly /ɪg'zæktli/ **adv 1** COMPLETEL CORRECT ▷ 🅰️2 used when you are giving ↓ asking for information that is complete correct: *What exactly seems to be the problen* ○ *The train got in at exactly ten o'cloc* **2** EMPHASIS ▷ 🅱️1 used to emphasize what yc are saying: *I found a dress that's exactly the san colour as my shoes.* **3** AGREEMENT ▷ 🅱️2 som thing you say when you agree completely wit someone: *"Surely they should have told us abo this problem sooner?" "Exactly."* **4** **not exactly** 🅲 used to say that something is not complete true: *"Do you live here?" "Not exactly, I'm stayir with friends."* **5** **not exactly easy/new/clear, et** informal used to say that a description i completely untrue: *Let's face it, we're n exactly rich, are we?*

exaggerate /ɪg'zædʒəreɪt/ **verb** [I, T] to mal something seem larger, better, worse, etc than really is: *Don't exaggerate – it didn't cost th much!*

exaggeration /ɪgˌzædʒə'reɪʃən/ **noun** [C, U] t use of descriptions that say something is large better, worse, etc than it really is: *a gro exaggeration of the facts*

⊘ Word partners for **exaggeration**

a **gross/slight** exaggeration • an exagger- ation **of** sth

exalted /ɪg'zɔːltɪd/ **adj** formal very high respected, or with a very high position

exam /ɪg'zæm/ **noun** [C] **1** 🅰️2 an official test ↓ how much you know about something, or ho well you can do something: *a geography exa* ○ *to fail/pass an exam* ○ UK *to sit/*UK/US *to tak (= do) an exam* **2** US a series of medical tests: *c eye exam*

❗ Common learner error: **take/sit an exam**

To **take an exam** means to do an official test. 'Sit' is slightly more formal than 'take' in this phrase and is only used in the UK. *We have to take an exam at the end of the course.* ~~We have to write an exam at the end of the course.~~

If you **pass an exam**, you are successful because you get a good mark. If you **fail an exam**, you are not successful because you get a bad mark.

⊘ Word partners for **exam**

do UK/sit/take an exam • fail/pass an exam • exam **results**

examination /ɪgˌzæmɪ'neɪʃən/ **noun 1** [C, U] 🅱️ an occasion when someone looks at somethin very carefully: *a medical examination* ○ *a clos*

examination *of the facts* **2** [C] formal Ⓐ2 an exam: *a written examination*

examine /ɪgˈzæmɪn/ **verb** [T] **1** LOOK AT ▷ Ⓑ2 to look at someone or something very carefully, especially to try to discover something: *She picked up the knife and examined it closely.* ∘ *He was examined by a doctor as soon as he arrived.* **2** TEST ▷ formal to test someone to see how much they know or how well they can do something: *You'll be examined in three main areas: speaking, listening, and reading comprehension.* **3** CONSIDER ▷ to consider a plan or an idea carefully: *They have called a special meeting to examine the proposal.* → See also **cross-examine**

examiner /ɪgˈzæmɪnər/ **noun** [C] Ⓑ1 someone who tests how much you know about something, or how well you can do something

example /ɪgˈzɑːmpl/ **noun** **1** [C] Ⓐ1 something that is typical of the group of things that you are talking about: *This is a good example of medieval Chinese architecture.* **2 for example** Ⓐ1 used to give an example of what you are talking about: *Some people, students for example, can get cheaper tickets.* **3** [C] someone or something that is very good and should be copied: *He is a very good example to the rest of the class.* **4 set an example** Ⓑ2 to behave in a way that other people should copy

> ☑ Word partners for **example**
>
> a **classic/good/prime** example • an example **of** sth

exasperate /ɪgˈzæspəreɪt/ **verb** [T] to annoy someone a lot

exasperated /ɪgˈzæspəreɪtɪd/ **adj** extremely annoyed: *He's become increasingly exasperated with the situation.*

exasperating /ɪgˈzæspəreɪtɪŋ/ **adj** extremely annoying

exasperation /ɪgˌzæspəˈreɪʃən/ **noun** [U] the feeling of being extremely annoyed with someone or something

excavate /ˈekskəveɪt/ **verb** [I, T] to dig in the ground, especially with a machine, or to look for objects from the past: *These Roman coins were excavated from a site in Cambridge.* • **excavation** /ˌekskəˈveɪʃən/ **noun** [C, U]

exceed /ɪkˈsiːd/ **verb** **1** [T] to be more than a particular number or amount: *Sales have exceeded $1 million so far this year.* **2 exceed the speed limit** to drive faster than you are allowed to according to the law

exceedingly /ɪkˈsiːdɪŋli/ **adv** formal very: *He was clever, attractive, and exceedingly rich.*

excel /ɪkˈsel/ **verb** (**excelling, excelled**) formal **1** [I] to be very good at something: *Paula always excelled in languages at school.* **2 excel yourself** to do something better than you usually do

excellent /ˈeksələnt/ **adj** Ⓐ2 very good, or of a very high quality: *That was an excellent meal.* • **excellently adv** • **excellence** /ˈeksələns/ **noun** [U]

except /ɪkˈsept/ **preposition, conjunction** Ⓐ2 not including a particular fact, thing, or person: *The boat sails from Oban every day except Sunday.*

∘ *Everyone passed the exam **except for** Rory.* ∘ [+ (that)] *So nothing changed, except that Anna saw her son less and less.*

excepted /ɪkˈseptɪd/ **adj** [always after noun] formal not included: *Everybody who was asked, myself excepted, said no.*

excepting /ɪkˈseptɪŋ/ **preposition** not including

exception /ɪkˈsepʃən/ **noun** **1** Ⓑ2 [C, U] someone or something that is not included in a rule, group, or list: *There are **exceptions to** every rule.* ∘ *I like all kinds of movies, **with the exception of** horror films.* ∘ *All our pupils, **without exception**, have access to the Internet.* ∘ *Her films are always popular and this one **is no exception**.* **2 make an exception** to not treat someone or something according to the usual rules: *They don't usually give refunds, but they said they'd make an exception in my case.* **3 take exception to sth** formal to be annoyed or insulted by something

exceptional /ɪkˈsepʃənəl/ **adj** **1** Ⓑ2 extremely good: *an exceptional student* **2** Ⓑ2 very unusual and not likely to happen very often: *Visitors are only allowed in exceptional circumstances.* • **exceptionally adv** *an exceptionally gifted pianist*

excerpt /ˈeksɜːpt/ **noun** [C] a short piece from a book, film, piece of music, etc

excess¹ /ɪkˈses/ **noun** **1** [U, no plural] more of something than is usual or needed: *An excess of oil on the markets has caused prices to fall sharply.* **2 in excess of sth** more than a particular amount or level: *He earns in excess of £60,000 a year.* **3 do sth to excess** to do something too much: *He occasionally has a beer, but he never drinks to excess.*

excess² /ɪkˈses/ **adj** [always before noun] more than is usual or allowed: *We had to pay $100 for excess baggage.*

excesses /ɪkˈsesɪz/ **noun** [plural] extreme, harmful, or immoral actions or behaviour

excessive /ɪkˈsesɪv/ **adj** more than is necessary or wanted: *They accused the police of using excessive force.* • **excessively adv**

exchange¹ /ɪksˈtʃeɪndʒ/ **noun** **1** GIVING ▷ [C, U] Ⓑ1 an occasion when you give something to someone and they give you something else: *an exchange of ideas/information* ∘ *They were given food and shelter in exchange for work.* **2** STUDENTS ▷ [C] Ⓑ1 an arrangement by which students and teachers from one country go to stay with students and teachers in another **3** CONVERSATION ▷ [C] a short conversation or argument: *There were angry exchanges between the police and demonstrators.* → See also **the stock exchange**

exchange² /ɪksˈtʃeɪndʒ/ **verb** **1** [T] Ⓑ1 to give something to someone and receive something similar from them: *It's traditional for the two teams to exchange shirts after the game.* **2** [T] Ⓑ2 to take something back to the shop where you bought it and change it for something else: *Could I exchange this shirt for a larger size?* **3 exchange looks/smiles/words, etc** Ⓑ2 If two people exchange looks, smiles, words, etc, they look at each other/smile at each other/talk to each other, etc.

exˈchange ˌrate noun [C] Ⓑ1 the amount of

another country's money that you can buy with a particular amount of your own country's money

excise /ˈeksaɪz/ **noun** [U] government taxes that must be paid on some things that are made or sold in a particular country

excitable /ɪkˈsaɪtəbl/ **adj** easily becoming excited: *a very excitable child/puppy*

excite /ɪkˈsaɪt/ **verb** [T] **1** to make someone feel very happy and enthusiastic: *Try not to excite the children too much.* **2** formal to cause a particular reaction in someone: *This product has excited a great deal of interest.*

excited /ɪkˈsaɪtɪd/ **adj** ⓐ feeling very happy and enthusiastic: *happy, excited faces* ∘ *The children are getting really excited about the party.* • **excitedly adv**

> ⚠ Common learner error: **excited** or **exciting**?
>
> **Excited** is used to describe how someone feels.
>
> *She was very excited about the visit.*
> ~~She was very exciting about the visit.~~
>
> **Exciting** is used to describe the thing that makes you excited.
>
> *I've had some exciting news!*

excitement /ɪkˈsaɪtmənt/ **noun** [U] ⓑ a feeling of being very happy and enthusiastic: *The competition is causing a lot of excitement.*

> 🗎 Word partners for **excitement**
>
> cause/feel excitement • excitement mounts • great/wild excitement • excitement about/at/over sth

exciting /ɪkˈsaɪtɪŋ/ **adj** ⓐ making you feel very happy and enthusiastic: *an exciting football match* ∘ *You're going to Africa? How exciting!*

> ➕ Other ways of saying **exciting**
>
> If something is so exciting that it holds your attention completely, you can say that it is **gripping** or **riveting**:
>
> *The book was gripping – I couldn't put it down.*
> *I found the film absolutely riveting.*
>
> Sports and outdoor activities which are exciting are often described as **exhilarating**:
>
> *I find skiing absolutely exhilarating.*
>
> The adjective **action-packed** is often used to describe a story or period of time which is full of exciting events:
>
> *We had an action-packed weekend in Berlin.*
> *The film is described as 'an action-packed thriller'.*
>
> An exciting atmosphere is sometimes described as **electric**:
>
> *The atmosphere backstage was electric.*
>
> **Vibrant** is often used to describe places which are exciting:
>
> *This is one of Europe's most vibrant cities.*

exclaim /ɪksˈkleɪm/ **verb** [I, T] to say something suddenly and loudly because you are surprised, annoyed, excited, etc: *"How terrible!" sh* exclaimed.

exclamation /ˌekskləˈmeɪʃən/ **noun** [C] some thing that you say loudly and suddenly becaus you are surprised, angry, excited, etc: *a exclamation of delight*

excla'mation ˌmark noun [C] (also US **excla** 'mation ˌpoint) ⓑ a mark (!) used at the end o a sentence that expresses surprise, excitement or shock, or that is a greeting or an order → Se Study Page **Punctuation** on page Centre 33

exclude /ɪksˈkluːd/ **verb** [T] **1 KEEP OUT** ▷ to no allow someone or something to take part in a activity or enter a place: [often passive] *Women ar still excluded from the club.* **2 NOT INCLUDE** ▷ t intentionally not include something: *The insu ance cover excludes particular medical conditions* **3 POSSIBILITY** ▷ to decide that something certainly not true or possible: *We can't exclud the possibility that he is dead.*

excluding /ɪksˈkluːdɪŋ/ **preposition** not includ ing: *That's $600 per person for seven days excluding travel costs.*

exclusion /ɪksˈkluːʒən/ **noun 1** [C, U] a situatio in which someone or something is not allowe to take part in an activity or to enter a place *the exclusion of disruptive pupils* → Opposit **inclusion 2 to the exclusion of sth** If yo do something to the exclusion of somethin else, you do it so much that you have no tim to do anything else.

exclusive¹ /ɪksˈkluːsɪv/ **adj 1** ⓑ expensive an only for people who are rich or of a high socia class: *an exclusive private club* **2 exclusive of st** not including something: *The price of the meal exclusive of drinks.* → Opposite **inclusive 3** n shared with another person, organization, news paper, etc: *an exclusive interview*

exclusive² /ɪksˈkluːsɪv/ **noun** [C] a news stor that appears in only one newspaper or on on television programme

exclusively /ɪksˈkluːsɪvli/ **adv** only: *an exclu sively female audience*

excrement /ˈekskrəmənt/ **noun** [U] formal soli waste that comes out of the bottom of a perso or animal

excrete /ɪkˈskriːt/ **verb** [I, T] to get rid of waste sub stances from the body • **excretion** /ɪkˈskriːʃən noun [C, U]

excruciating /ɪkˈskruːʃieɪtɪŋ/ **adj** very bad o painful: *Her illness causes her excruciating pain* • **excruciatingly adv** *an excruciatingly embar rassing situation*

excursion /ɪkˈskɜːʒən/ **noun** [C] a short journe made by a group of people for pleasure: *We'v booked to go on an excursion to Pompeii.*

excusable /ɪkˈskjuːzəbl/ **adj** easy to forgive → Op posite **inexcusable**

excuse¹ /ɪkˈskjuːz/ **verb** [T] **1 FORGIVE** ▷ ⓑ t forgive someone for something that is not ver serious: *Please excuse my appearance, I've bee painting.* ∘ [+ for + doing sth] *She asked him t excuse her for being so rude.* **2 NOT DO** ▷ to sa that someone does not have to do somethin that they usually have to do: *Could I be excuse* *from football training today?* **3 EXPLAIN** ▷ **B2** to be given as a reason for someone's bad behaviour, so that it does not seem so bad: *Nothing can excuse what he did.* **4 excuse me a A1** used to politely get someone's attention: *Excuse me, does this bus go to Oxford Street?* **b A2** used to say sorry for something that you do without intending to: *Oh, excuse me, did I take your seat?* • **excusable** adj

xcuse² /ɪkˈskjuːs/ **noun** [C] **1 B1** a reason that you give to explain why you did something wrong: [+ for + doing sth] *I hope he's got a good excuse for being so late.* **2 B1** a false reason that you give to explain why you do something: *Nick was just looking for an excuse to call her.*

> ☑ Word partners for **excuse**
>
> have/make/offer/think up an excuse • a feeble/good excuse

xecute /ˈeksɪkjuːt/ **verb** [T] **1** to kill someone as a legal punishment: *He was executed for murder.* **2** formal to do something, such as follow a plan or order: *to execute a deal/plan*

xecution /ˌeksɪˈkjuːʃən/ **noun 1** [C, U] the legal punishment of killing someone **2** [U] the act of doing something, such as following a plan or order: *He was killed in the execution of his duties as a soldier.*

xecutioner /ˌeksɪˈkjuːʃənər/ **noun** [C] someone whose job is to execute criminals

xecutive¹ /ɪɡˈzekjətɪv/ **adj** [always before noun] **1** relating to making decisions and managing businesses: *an executive director* **2** suitable for people who have important jobs in business: *Peter always stays in the executive suite.*

xecutive² /ɪɡˈzekjətɪv/ **noun 1** [C] someone who has an important job in a business: *a company executive* **2 the executive** mainly UK the people who have the power to make decisions in an organization

xemplary /ɪɡˈzempləri/ **adj** formal very good and suitable to be copied by people: *Sarah's behaviour is always exemplary.*

xemplify /ɪɡˈzemplɪfaɪ/ **verb** [T] formal to be or give a typical example of something

xempt¹ /ɪɡˈzempt/ **adj** [never before noun] with special permission not to have to do something or pay something: *The first £6,000 that you earn is exempt from tax.*

xempt² /ɪɡˈzempt/ **verb** [T] formal to officially say that someone does not have to do something or pay for something: [often passive] *Students are exempted from payment.* • **exemption** /ɪɡˈzempʃən/ **noun** [C, U]

xercise¹ /ˈeksəsaɪz/ **noun 1 PHYSICAL ACTIVITY** ▷ [C, U] **A2** physical activity that you do to make your body strong and healthy: *Swimming is my favourite form of exercise.* ∘ *Let's do some stretching exercises to start with.* **2 TEST** ▷ [C] **A2** a piece of written work that helps you learn something: *For your homework, please do exercise 3 on page 24.* **3 ACTIVITY WITH PURPOSE** ▷ [C] **A2** an activity that is intended to achieve a particular thing: *The whole point of the exercise was to get people to*

exercise

share their ideas. ∘ *a team-building exercise.* **4 MILITARY** ▷ [C] a set of actions that a group of soldiers do to practise their skills: *The cadets are out on military exercises.* **5 USE** ▷ [U] formal the use of something such as a power or right

> ☑ Word partners for **exercise**
>
> do/get/take exercise • daily/gentle/regular/strenuous exercise • a form of exercise

exercise² /ˈeksəsaɪz/ **verb 1** [I, T] **A2** to do physical activities to make your body strong and healthy: *I try to exercise every day.* **2** [T] formal to use a power, right, or ability: *You should always exercise your right to vote.*

exert /ɪɡˈzɜːt/ **verb** [T] **1** to use something such as authority, power, influence, etc in order to make something happen: *My parents exerted a lot of pressure on me to do well at school.* **2 exert yourself** to use a lot of physical or mental energy to do something: *She was too sick to exert herself much.*

exertion /ɪɡˈzɜːʃən/ **noun** [C, U] the use of a lot of physical or mental energy to do something: *I get out of breath with any kind of physical exertion.*

exhale /eksˈheɪl/ **verb** [I, T] formal to send air out of your lungs → Opposite **inhale**

exhaust¹ /ɪɡˈzɔːst/ **verb** [T] **1 SUPPLY** ▷ to finish all of the supply of something: *How long will it be before the world's fuel supplies are exhausted?* **2 TIRED** ▷ to make someone very tired **3 SUBJECT** ▷ to say everything possible about a subject: *We seem to have exhausted that topic of conversation.*

exhaust² /ɪɡˈzɔːst/ **noun 1** [U] the waste gas from a vehicle's engine: *exhaust fumes* **2** [C] (also **exhaust pipe**) mainly UK the pipe that waste gas from a vehicle's engine flows through → See colour picture **Car** on page Centre 7

exhausted /ɪɡˈzɔːstɪd/ **adj B1** very tired

exhausting /ɪɡˈzɔːstɪŋ/ **adj B2** making you feel very tired: *What an exhausting day!*

exhaustion /ɪɡˈzɔːstʃən/ **noun** [U] **B2** the state of being extremely tired: *The tennis star was suffering from exhaustion.*

exhaustive /ɪɡˈzɔːstɪv/ **adj** complete and including everything: *an exhaustive account of the incident*

ex'haust ,pipe noun [C] mainly UK (US **tailpipe**) the pipe that waste gas from a vehicle's engine flows through

exhibit¹ /ɪɡ'zɪbɪt/ verb **1** [I, T] to show objects such as paintings to the public: *She's exhibiting her roses at the local flower show.* **2** [T] formal to show a feeling, quality, or ability: *The crew exhibited great courage when the plane crashed.*

exhibit² /ɪɡ'zɪbɪt/ noun [C] an object such as a painting that is shown to the public: *a museum exhibit* • **exhibitor** noun [C] someone who shows something that they own or have made to the public

exhibition /ˌeksɪ'bɪʃᵊn/ noun **1** [C, U] ⓔ1 an occasion when objects such as paintings are shown to the public: *There's a new exhibition of sculpture on at the city gallery.* ○ *an exhibition centre* **2** [C] an occasion when someone shows a particular skill or quality that they have to the public

exhibitionist /ˌeksɪ'bɪʃᵊnɪst/ noun [C] someone who tries to attract attention to themselves with their behaviour • **exhibitionism** /ˌeksɪ'bɪʃᵊnɪzᵊm/ noun [U] behaviour that tries to attract attention

exhilarated /ɪɡ'zɪləreɪtɪd/ adj very excited and happy

exhilarating /ɪɡ'zɪləreɪtɪŋ/ adj making you feel very excited and happy: *There's nothing more exhilarating than water-skiing.*

exhilaration /ɪɡˌzɪlᵊr'eɪʃᵊn/ noun [U] a very excited and happy feeling

exhort /ɪɡ'zɔːt/ verb [T] formal to strongly encourage someone to do something • **exhortation** /ˌeɡzɔː'teɪʃᵊn/ noun [C, U]

exile /'eksaɪl/, /'eɡzaɪl/ noun **1** [U] a situation in which someone has to leave their home and live in another country, often for political reasons: *He spent the war years in exile in New York.* ○ *The King was forced into exile.* **2** [C] someone who is forced to live in another country: *She lived the rest of her life as an exile in the UK.* • **exile** verb [T] to force someone to leave their home and live in another country, often for political reasons • **exiled** adj

exist /ɪɡ'zɪst/ verb [I] **1** ⓔ1 to be real or present: *Poverty still exists in this country.* **2** to live in difficult conditions: *You can't exist without water for more than a week.*

existence /ɪɡ'zɪstᵊns/ noun **1** [U] ⓔ2 the state of existing: *She never doubted the existence of God.* ○ *The theatre company that we started is still in existence today.* ○ *When did the Football League come into existence (= begin to exist)?* **2** [C] a particular way of life: *We could have a much more peaceful existence in the countryside.*

☑ Word partners for **existence**

come into/go out of existence • **be in** existence • **the existence of** sth

existing /ɪɡ'zɪstɪŋ/ adj [always before noun] ⓔ2 which exist or are used at the present time: *Existing schools will have to be expanded to*

accommodate the extra students. → See also **pre** existing

exit¹ /'eksɪt/ noun [C] **1** DOOR ▷ ⓐ2 the door ○ gate that you use to leave a public building ○ place: *a fire exit* ○ *an emergency ex* **2** LEAVING ▷ the act of leaving a place: *Su made a quick exit when she saw Mick come i.* **3** ROAD ▷ ⓐ2 a road that you use to leave motorway (= wide, fast road) or roundabou (= place where three or more main roads meet *Take the third exit at the next roundabout.*

exit² /'eksɪt/ verb [I, T] **1** ⓑ1 to stop using program on a computer: *Press escape to exit th game.* **2** formal to leave a place or a competitio

exit ,strategy noun [C] a plan that you use t get out of a difficult situation: *A good politicia will plan his exit strategy before announcing h retirement from office.*

exodus /'eksədəs/ noun [no plural] a situation i which a large number of people all leave a plac together: *There has been a mass exodus ○ workers from the villages to the towns.*

exonerate /ɪɡ'zɒnᵊreɪt/ verb [T] formal to sa that someone is not guilty of doing somethin that they have been blamed for: [often passive] *H was exonerated of all blame by the investigatio* • **exoneration** /ɪɡˌzɒnᵊ'reɪʃᵊn/ noun [U]

exorbitant /ɪɡ'zɔːbɪtᵊnt/ adj Exorbitant price or costs are much too high.

exorcism /'eksɔːsɪzᵊm/ noun [C, U] the activit of exorcising an evil spirit

exorcise (also UK **-ise**) /'eksɔːsaɪz/ verb [T] **1** t make evil spirits leave a person or place b saying special prayers and having a specia ceremony **2** to get rid of something such as bad memory: *She moved to Paris to try to exorciz the past.*

exotic /ɪɡ'zɒtɪk/ adj ⓑ2 unusual, interesting, an often foreign: *exotic fruits*

expand /ɪk'spænd/ verb [I, T] ⓑ2 to increase i size or amount, or to make something increase *We are hoping to expand our range of products.*

PHRASAL VERB **expand on sth** to give more detai about something that you have said or writter *She mentioned a few ideas, but she didn't expan on them.*

expanse /ɪk'spæns/ noun [C] a large, open are of land, sea, or sky: *a vast expanse of water*

expansion /ɪk'spænʃᵊn/ noun [U] ⓑ2 an increas in the size or amount of something: *the rapi expansion of the software industry*

expansive /ɪk'spænsɪv/ adj formal very happy t talk to people in a friendly way: *He was in a expansive mood on the night of the party.*

expatriate /ɪk'spætriət/ noun [C] (also U informal **expat** /ˌek'spat/) someone who doe not live in their own country • **expatriate** adj

expect /ɪk'spekt/ verb **1** [T] ⓑ1 to think tha something will happen: [+ to do sth] *He didn expect to see me.* ○ [+ (that)] *I expect that she'll b very angry about this.* **2** be expecting sb/sth ⓑ to be waiting for someone or something t arrive: *I'm expecting a letter from my sister.* **3** ⓑ2 to think that someone should behave in particular way or do a particular thing: [+ to do sth] *You will be expected to work some weekends.* **4 I expect** mainly UK informal ⓑ② used to show that you think that something is likely to be true: *I expect Isabel's told you about me?* ∘ *"Will you be coming to the party?" "I expect so."* **5 be expecting** ⓑ② to be going to have a baby: *I'm expecting my first baby in May.* → See Note at **wait¹**

expectancy /ɪk'spekt³nsi/ **noun** [U] the feeling that something pleasant or exciting is going to happen: *An air of expectancy filled the room.* → See also **life expectancy**

expectant /ɪk'spekt³nt/ **adj 1** thinking that something pleasant or exciting is going to happen: *the children's expectant faces* **2 an expectant mother/father, etc** someone who is going to have a baby soon • **expectantly** adv

expectation /ˌekspek'teɪʃ³n/ **noun 1** [C] ⓑ② the feeling that good things are going to happen in the future: [usually plural] *The holiday **lived up to** all our **expectations** (= was as good as we expected).* ∘ *My parents **had high expectations** for me (= expected me to be successful).* **2** [C, U] the feeling of expecting something to happen: *He had gone away and there was no **expectation of** his return.*

> **Word partners for expectation**
>
> have high/have low expectations • live up to/meet (sb's) expectations • expectations of sth

expedient¹ /ɪk'spiːdiənt/ **adj** formal An expedient action achieves a useful purpose, although it may not be moral: *It might be expedient not to pay him until the work is finished.* • **expediency** /ɪk'spiːdiənsi/ **noun** [U] the quality of being expedient: *an issue of political expediency*

expedient² /ɪk'spiːdiənt/ **noun** [C] formal a useful or clever action

expedite /'ekspɪdaɪt/ **verb** [T] formal to make an action or process happen more quickly

expedition /ˌekspɪ'dɪʃ³n/ **noun** [C] ⓑ① an organized journey, especially a long one for a particular purpose: *Peary **led** the first **expedition** to the North Pole.* ∘ *a **shopping expedition***

expel /ɪk'spel/ **verb** [T] (**expelling, expelled**) **1** to make someone leave a school, organization, or country because of their behaviour: [often passive] *He was **expelled from** school **for** hitting another student.* **2** formal to force air, gas, or liquid out of something

expend /ɪk'spend/ **verb** [T] formal to use effort, time, or money to do something: [+ doing sth] *You **expend** far too much **energy** doing things for other people.* ∘ *Governments **expend** a lot of resources **on** war.*

expendable /ɪk'spendəbl/ **adj** If someone or something is expendable, people can do something or deal with a situation without them: *He considers his staff as temporary and expendable.*

expenditure /ɪk'spendɪtʃə⁰/ **noun** [U] formal **1** the total amount of money that a government or person spends: *The government's annual*

expenditure on *arms has been reduced.* **2** the use of energy, time, or money

expense /ɪk'spens/ **noun 1** ⓑ② [C, U] the money that you spend on something: *You have to **pay** your own medical **expenses**.* ∘ *He eventually found her the car she wanted, **at great expense** (= it cost him a lot of money).* **2 at the expense of sth** If you do one thing at the expense of another, doing the first thing harms the second thing: *He spent a lot of time at work, at the expense of his marriage.* **3 at sb's expense a** If you do something at someone's expense, they pay for it: *We went on holiday at my father's expense.* **b** in order to make someone look stupid: *Stop making jokes at my expense.*

expenses /ɪk'spensɪz/ **noun** [plural] money that you spend when you are doing your job, that your employer will pay back to you: *travel expenses* ∘ *They pay us two hundred euros a week, plus expenses.*

expensive /ɪk'spensɪv/ **adj** ⓐ① costing a lot of money: *expensive jewellery* ∘ [+ to do sth] *It's too expensive to go out every night.* → Opposite **inexpensive** • **expensively** adv *expensively dressed*

experience¹ /ɪk'spɪəriəns/ **noun 1** [U] ⓑ① knowledge that you get from doing a job, or from doing, seeing, or feeling something: *Do you have any **experience of** working with children?* ∘ *He knows **from experience** not to play with fire.* ∘ *In my experience, people smile back if you smile at them.* **2** [C] ⓑ① something that happens to you that affects how you feel: *My trip to Australia was an experience I'll never forget.*

> **Word partners for experience**
>
> gain/have/lack experience • good/previous/ useful/wide experience • experience in/of sth • from experience • in my experience

experience² /ɪk'spɪəriəns/ **verb** [T] ⓑ① If you experience something, it happens to you, or you feel it: *It was the worst pain I had ever experienced.* ∘ *We experienced a lot of difficulty in selling our house.*

experienced /ɪk'spɪəriənst/ **adj** ⓑ① having skill and knowledge because you have done something many times: *Karsten's a very experienced ski instructor.* → Opposite **inexperienced**

experiment¹ /ɪk'sperɪmənt/ **noun** [C] ⓑ① a test, especially a scientific one, that you do in order to learn something or discover if something is true: *to **conduct/do/perform** an **experiment*** ∘ *They're conducting **experiments on** hamster cells to test the effects of the drug.*

> **Word partners for experiment**
>
> conduct/do/perform an experiment • an experiment on sth

experiment² /ɪk'sperɪment/ **verb** [I] **1** ⓑ② to try something in order to discover what it is like: *Did he ever **experiment with** drugs?* **2** to do an experiment: *Experimenting on mice can give us an idea of the effect of the disease in humans.* • **experimentation** /ɪkˌsperɪmen'teɪʃ³n/ **noun** [U]

experimental /ɪkˌsperɪ'ment³l/ **adj** relating to

E

expert¹ /'eksp3:t/ **noun** [C] 🄑 someone who has a lot of skill in something or a lot of knowledge about something: *He's **an expert on** Japanese literature.*

expert² /'eksp3:t/ **adj** [always before noun] 🄒 having a lot of skill in something or knowing a lot about something: *I need some **expert advice** on investments.* ◦ *What's your **expert opinion**?* • **expertly** adv *He carved the roast expertly.*

expertise /ˌeksp3:'ti:z/ **noun** [U] skill: *the technical expertise of the engineers*

expire /ɪk'spaɪəʳ/ **verb** [I] If a legal document or agreement expires, you can no longer use it: *Your contract expired six months ago.*

expiry /ɪk'spaɪəri/ **noun** [U] UK the end of a period when something can be used: *What's **the expiry date** on your passport?*

explain /ɪk'spleɪn/ **verb** [I, T] 🄐 to make something clear or easy to understand by giving reasons for it or details about it: [+ question word] *Can you explain why you did this?* ◦ *Can you **explain to** me how this machine works?* ◦ [+ (that)] *He explained that he was going to stay with his sister.* • **explaining** noun [U] things you say to explain or give a good reason for your actions: *You'll **have** a lot of **explaining to do** when dad finds out what happened.*

> ⚠ Common learner error: **explain** something
>
> **Explain** is followed by the thing you are explaining.
> *I'll explain the situation.*
> Remember to use the preposition **to** before a person.
> *I'll explain the situation to my parents.*
> ~~I'll explain my parents the situation.~~

> ➕ Other ways of saying **explain**
>
> If someone is explaining something in order to make it easier for someone else to understand, you can use the verb **clarify**:
> *Let me just **clarify** what I mean here.*
> The verb **define** is sometimes used when explaining exactly what something means:
> *Your responsibilities are clearly **defined** in the contract.*
> If something is being explained clearly in writing, the phrasal verb **set out** is sometimes used:
> *Your contract will **set out** the terms of your employment.*
> If something is being explained in great detail, the phrasal verb **spell out** is often used:
> *They sent me a letter, **spelling out** the details of the agreement.*

explanation /ˌeksplə'neɪʃən/ **noun** [C, U] 🄑 the details or reasons that someone gives to make something clear or easy to understand: *What's your **explanation for** the team's poor perfor-*

mance? ◦ *Could you give me a quick **explanatior of** how it works?*

> 🄑 Word partners for **explanation**
>
> **demand/give/have/offer** an explanation • a **clear/possible/satisfactory/simple** explanation • an explanation **for** sth

explanatory /ɪk'splænətəri/ **adj** giving an ex planation about something: *There are **explana tory notes** with the diagram.* → See also **self explanatory**

expletive /ɪk'spli:tɪv/ 🄤 /'eksplətɪv/ **noun** [C formal a swear word (= word which people thinl is rude or offensive)

explicable /ɪk'splɪkəbl/ **adj** formal Something that is explicable can be explained. → Opposite **inexplicable**

explicit /ɪk'splɪsɪt/ **adj 1** clear and exact: *She wa very **explicit about** her plans.* ◦ *He made nc **explicit references** to Tess.* **2** showing or talking about sex or violence in a very detailed way: *c **sexually explicit** film* • **explicitly** adv *She **explicitly stated** that she did not want her nam to be revealed.*

explode /ɪk'spləʊd/ **verb 1** [I, T] 🄑 If something such as a bomb explodes, it bursts (= break: suddenly from inside) with noise and force, anc if you explode it, you make it burst with noise and force: *One of the bombs did not explode.* **2** [to suddenly start shouting because you are ver) angry

exploit¹ /ɪk'splɔɪt/ **verb** [T] **1** 🄒 to not pay o: reward someone enough for something: [ofte passive] *I felt as though I was being exploited.* **2** 🄒 to use or develop something for your advantage *We are not fully exploiting all the resources that w have.* • **exploitation** /ˌeksplɔɪ'teɪʃən/ **noun** [U] *th exploitation of child workers*

exploit² /'eksplɔɪt/ **noun** [C] something unusual brave, or interesting that someone has done [usually plural] *Have you heard about her amazin exploits travelling in Africa?*

exploratory /ɪk'splɒrətəri/ **adj** done in order tc discover or learn about something: *an explora tory expedition* ◦ *an exploratory operation*

explore /ɪk'splɔ:ʳ/ **verb 1** [I, T] 🄑 to go around a place where you have never been in order tc find out what is there: *The children love explor ing.* ◦ *The best way to explore the countryside i: on foot.* **2** [T] 🄒 to think about something ver) carefully before you make a decision about it *We're **exploring** the **possibility** of buying c holiday home.* • **exploration** /ˌeksplə'reɪʃən noun [C, U] *She's always loved travel anc exploration.*

explorer /ɪk'splɔ:rəʳ/ **noun** [C] someone whc travels to places where no one has ever been ir order to find out what is there

explosion /ɪk'spləʊʒən/ **noun** [C] **1** 🄒 the actior of something such as a bomb exploding: *Forty people were killed in the explosion.* **2** a sudder large increase in the amount of something: *th recent **population explosion***

explosive¹ /ɪk'spləʊsɪv/ **adj 1** An explosive substance or piece of equipment can cause explosions: *The **explosive device** was hidden in a suitcase.* **2** An explosive situation or subject causes strong feelings, and may make people angry or violent: *a highly explosive political issue*

explosive² /ɪkˈspləʊsɪv/ **noun** [C] a substance or piece of equipment that can cause explosions

exponent /ɪkˈspəʊnənt/ **noun** [C] someone who supports a particular idea or belief, or performs a particular activity: *The early **exponents of** votes for women suffered greatly.*

export¹ /ˈekspɔːt/ **noun 1** [C] ⬛ a product that you sell in another country: *Scottish beef exports to Japan* **2** [U] ⬛ the business of sending goods to another country in order to sell them there: *the export of industrial goods* → Opposite **import**

export² /ɪkˈspɔːt/ **verb** [I, T] **1** ⬛ to send goods to another country in order to sell them there: *Singapore exports large quantities of rubber.* → Opposite **import 2** If you export information from a computer, you copy it to another place. • **exporter noun** [C] *Brazil is the world's largest exporter of coffee.*

expose /ɪkˈspəʊz/ **verb** [T] **1 HIDDEN THING** ▷ to remove what is covering something so that it can be seen: *Our bodies need to be exposed to sunlight in order to make vitamin D.* **2 BAD THING** ▷ ⬛ to make public something bad or something that is not honest: *The review exposed widespread corruption in the police force.* **3 be exposed to sth** ⬛ to experience something or be affected by something because you are in a particular situation or place: *It was the first time I'd been exposed to violence.* **4 PHOTOGRAPHY** ▷ to allow light to reach a piece of camera film in order to produce a photograph

exposed /ɪkˈspəʊzd/ **adj** having no protection from bad weather: *an exposed cliff*

exposure /ɪkˈspəʊʒər/ **noun 1 EXPERIENCING** ▷ [U] a situation in which someone experiences something or is affected by it because they are in a particular situation or place: *There is a risk of **exposure** to radiation.* ○ *Many young children now have exposure to computers in the home.* **2 MAKING PUBLIC** ▷ [C, U] a situation in which something bad that you have done is made public: *She was threatened with exposure by a journalist.* **3 MEDICAL** ▷ [U] a serious medical condition that is caused by being outside in very cold weather **4 PHOTOGRAPH** ▷ [C] a single photograph on a piece of film: *This film has 24 exposures.*

expound /ɪkˈspaʊnd/ **verb** [I, T] formal to give a detailed explanation of something: *He's always **expounding on** what's wrong with the world.* ○ *She uses her newspaper column to **expound** her **views** on environmental issues.*

express¹ /ɪkˈspres/ **verb** [T] ⬛ to show what you think or how you feel using words or actions: *I'm simply expressing my opinion.* ○ [often reflexive] *You're not expressing yourself (= saying what you mean) very clearly.*

express² /ɪkˈspres/ **adj 1 an express service/ train, etc** a service/train, etc that is much faster than usual **2 an express aim/intention/ purpose, etc** a clear and certain aim/intention/

purpose, etc: *You came here with the express purpose of causing trouble.*

express³ /ɪkˈspres/ **noun** [C] (also **ex¦press ˌtrain**) a fast train: *I took the express to London.*

expression /ɪkˈspreʃən/ **noun 1 LOOK** ▷ [C] ⬛ the look on someone's face showing what they feel or think: *your **facial expression*** ○ *He had a sad expression on his face.* **2 PHRASE** ▷ [C] ⬛ a phrase that has a special meaning: *'A can of worms' is an expression meaning a difficult situation.* **3 SHOWING THOUGHTS** ▷ [C, U] ⬛ ways of saying what you think or showing how you feel using words or actions: *As **an expression of** our disapproval, we will no longer use his shop.*

> ✎ Word partners for **expression**
>
> have a [pained, puzzled, etc] expression **on your face** • an expression **changes** • an **angry/dazed/pained/puzzled** expression • **facial** expression

expressive /ɪkˈspresɪv/ **adj** showing your feelings: *a very expressive face*

expressly /ɪkˈspresli/ **adv** formal **1** If you say something expressly, you say it in a clear way, so that your meaning cannot be doubted: *I **expressly stated** that I did not want any visitors.* **2** If something is expressly for a particular reason or person, it is for that reason or person only: *The picture was painted expressly for me.*

expressway /ɪkˈspreswei/ **noun** [C] US (UK **motorway**) a long, wide road, usually used by traffic travelling fast over long distances

expulsion /ɪkˈspʌlʃən/ **noun** [C, U] the punishment of making someone leave their school, organization, or country because of their behaviour: *They threatened him with **expulsion from** school.*

exquisite /ɪkˈskwɪzɪt/ **adj** very beautiful or perfect: *a garden of exquisite flowers* • **exquisitely adv** *an exquisitely dressed woman*

extend /ɪkˈstend/ **verb 1 MAKE BIGGER** ▷ [T] ⬛ to make something bigger or longer: *We're going to extend our kitchen.* **2 MAKE LAST** ▷ [T] to make an activity, agreement, etc last for a longer time: *They have extended the deadline by one week.* **3 extend from/into/over, etc** to continue or stretch over a particular area of land or period of time: *Will the building work extend into next week?* **4 STRETCH OUT** ▷ [T] to stretch out a part of your body: *She smiled and extended her hand.* **5 extend an invitation/thanks, etc to sb** formal to give someone an invitation/thanks, etc: *I'd like to extend a warm welcome to our guests.*

extension /ɪkˈstenʃən/ **noun** [C] **1 PART OF A BUILDING** ▷ a new room or rooms that are added to a building: *You could build an extension onto the back of the house.* **2 EXTRA TIME** ▷ ⬛ extra time that you are given to do or use something: *You might be able to get an extension on your visa.* **3 TELEPHONE** ▷ ⬛ a telephone that is connected to the main telephone in an office or other large building: *Call me on extension 213.*

extensive /ɪkˈstensɪv/ **adj** ⬛ large in amount or

E

size: *an **extensive** art **collection*** ∘ *The hurricane caused **extensive** damage.* • **extensively** adv *I have **travelled** extensively in Europe.*

extent /ɪkˈstent/ noun **1**ⓑ⓶ [no plural] the size or importance of something: *They are just beginning to realize the **full** extent of the damage.* ∘ *Her face was injured **to such an** extent (= so much) that he didn't recognize her.* **2 to some extent/to a certain extent** ⓑ⓶ in some ways: *I was, **to some** extent, responsible for the accident.*

> 🗹 Word partners for **extent**
>
> the **full/true** extent of sth • **to such** an extent • the extent **of** sth

exterior /ɪkˈstɪəriər/ noun [C] the outside part of something or someone: [usually singular] *The exterior of the house was painted white.* • **exterior** adj [always before noun] *an exterior wall* → Opposite **interior**

exterminate /ɪkˈstɜːmɪneɪt/ verb [T] to kill a large group of people or animals • **extermination** /ɪkˌstɜːmɪˈneɪʃən/ noun [C, U]

external /ɪkˈstɜːnəl/ adj **1** ⓑ⓶ relating to the outside part of something: *the **external walls** of the house* ∘ *The ointment is **for external use** only (= it must not be put inside the body).* **2**ⓑ⓶ coming from or relating to another country, group, or organization: *All exams are marked by an **external examiner**.* → Opposite **internal** • **externally** adv

extinct /ɪkˈstɪŋkt/ adj If a type of animal is extinct, it does not now exist.

extinction /ɪkˈstɪŋkʃən/ noun [U] a situation in which a type of animal no longer exists: *Many species of animal are **threatened with extinction**.*

extinguish /ɪkˈstɪŋgwɪʃ/ verb [T] formal to stop something burning or giving out light: *The fire took two hours to extinguish.*

extinguisher /ɪkˈstɪŋgwɪʃər/ noun [C] (also **fire extinguisher**) a piece of equipment shaped like a tube, which is used to spread a substance onto a fire to stop it burning

extol /ɪkˈstəʊl/ verb [T] (**extolling, extolled**) to say that you think that something is very good: *He always **extols the virtues of** (= praises) French cooking.*

extort /ɪkˈstɔːt/ verb [T] to get money from someone by saying that you will harm them • **extortion** /ɪkˈstɔːʃən/ noun [U]

extortionate /ɪkˈstɔːʃənət/ adj Extortionate prices or costs are very high.

extra¹ /ˈekstrə/ adj ⓐ⓶ more, or more than usual: *Can I invite a few extra people?* ∘ *She's been babysitting to earn some extra cash.*

extra² /ˈekstrə/ noun [C] **1**ⓑ⓵ something that costs more when you buy goods or pay for a service: *The hi-fi comes with **optional extras** such as headphones and remote control.* **2** an actor in a film who does not have a main part and usually plays someone in a crowd

> 🗹 Word partners for **extra**
>
> an added/hidden/optional extra

extra³ /ˈekstrə/ adv ⓑ⓵ more than usual: *Do yo get paid extra for working late?*

extra- /ekstrə-/ prefix outside of or in additio to: *extracurricular activities (= activities that are addition to the usual school work)*

extract¹ /ɪkˈstrækt/ verb [T] formal **1**ⓑ⓶ to tal something out, especially using force: *Th dentist may decide to extract the tooth.* **2** to g the money, information, etc that you want fro someone who does not want to give it to yo *They were not able to extract a confession from he*

extract² /ˈekstrækt/ noun [C] **1**ⓑ⓶ a particula part of a book, poem, etc that is chosen so that can be used in a discussion, article, etc: *Th teacher read out **an extract from** 'Brave Ne World'.* **2** a substance taken from a plant, flowe etc and used especially in food or medicine: *pu vanilla extract*

extraction /ɪkˈstrækʃən/ noun **1** [C, U] the act taking something out, especially using forc **2 of Chinese/Italian, etc extraction** having family whose origin is Chinese, Italian, etc

extracurricular /ˌekstrəkəˈrɪkjʊlər/ a describes an activity or subject that is not pa of the usual school or college course: *Popul extracurricular activities include pottery, ches and choir.*

extradite /ˈekstrədaɪt/ verb [T] to send someon back to the country where they are accused a crime, so that a court there can decide if the are guilty: [often passive] *The suspects were extr dited to the UK.* • **extradition** /ˌekstrəˈdɪʃə noun [C, U]

extraneous /ɪkˈstreɪniəs/ adj not directly co nected to something: *extraneous informatio noise*

extraordinary /ɪkˈstrɔːdənəri/ adj ⓑ⓵ ve special, unusual, or strange: *an extraordinar tale of courage* ∘ *She was an extraordinary youn woman.* • **extraordinarily** adv ⓑ⓶ *Their la album was extraordinarily successful.*

extravagant /ɪkˈstrævəgənt/ adj **1** costing to much or spending a lot more money tha you need to: *the **extravagant lifestyle** of movie star* **2** too unusual and extreme to b believed or controlled: *the extravagant claim made by cosmetics companies* • **extravaganc** /ɪkˈstrævəgəns/ noun [C, U] extravagant beh viour • **extravagantly** adv

extravaganza /ɪkˌstrævəˈgænzə/ noun [C] large, exciting, and expensive event or ente tainment: *a three-hour extravaganza of countr music*

extreme¹ /ɪkˈstriːm/ adj **1 SERIOUS** ▷ ⓑ⓶ th most unusual or most serious possible: *extrem weather conditions* ∘ *In **extreme cases**, th disease can lead to blindness.* **2 VERY LARGE** ▷ ⓑ⓶ very large in amount or degree: *extreme pa* ∘ *extreme wealth* **3 OPINIONS** ▷ having suc strong opinions or beliefs that most peopl cannot agree with you: *extreme views* ∘ *th extreme right* **4 FURTHEST** ▷ [always before noun at the furthest point of something: *in the extrem south of the island*

extreme² /ɪkˈstriːm/ noun [C] the largest po sible amount or degree of something: *Anna* moods went **from one extreme to another** (= first she was very happy, then she was very unhappy). ○ Coach Wilson **took** our training **to extremes** (= made us train extremely hard).

extremely /ık'striːmli/ adv ⓐ very, or much more than usual: *extremely beautiful*

extreme 'sports noun [C, U] ⓐ dangerous games or activities: *extreme sports such as bungee jumping and snowboarding*

extremist /ık'striːmıst/ noun [C] someone who has such strong opinions or beliefs that most people cannot agree with them • **extremism** /ık'striːmızᵊm/ noun [U] • **extremist** adj

extremities /ık'stremətiz/ noun [plural] the end parts of your body such as your hands and feet

extremity /ık'streməti/ noun formal **1** [C] the part of something that is furthest from the centre: *at the north-west extremity of Europe* **2** [U] a situation in which a feeling is very strong or a bad situation that is very serious

extricate /'ekstrıkeıt/ verb **extricate yourself from sth** to get yourself out of a difficult situation or unpleasant place: *I didn't know how to extricate myself from such an embarrassing situation.*

extrovert /'ekstrəvɜːt/ noun [C] someone who is very confident and likes being with other people → Opposite **introvert** • **extrovert** adj *an extrovert personality* → Opposite **introverted**

exuberant /ıg'zjuːbᵊrᵊnt/ adj full of happiness, excitement, and energy: *a warm and exuberant personality* • **exuberance** /ıg'zjuːbᵊrᵊns/ noun [U]

exude /ıg'zjuːd/ verb [T] If you exude love, confidence, pain, etc, you show that you have a lot of that feeling.

exult /ıg'zʌlt/ verb [I] to show great pleasure, especially at someone else's defeat or failure: *She seems to **exult in** her power.* • **exultation** /ˌegzʌl'teıʃᵊn/ noun [U]

eye¹ /aı/ noun **1** [C] ⓐ   eye
one of the two organs in your face, which you use to see with: *Sara has black hair and brown eyes.* ○ *She **closed** her **eyes** and drifted off to sleep.*

2 [C] the small hole at the end of a needle, which you put the thread through **3 have an eye for sth** to be good at noticing a particular type of thing: *Your son has a very good eye for detail.* **4 keep your/an eye on sb/sth** ⓑ to watch or look after someone or something: *Could you keep an eye on this pan of soup for a moment?* **5 have your eye on sth** *informal* to want something and intend to get it: *Jane's got her eye on that new advertising job.* **6 can't keep/ take your eyes off sb/sth** to be unable to stop looking at someone or something because they are so attractive or interesting: *He couldn't take his eyes off her all night.* **7 lay/set eyes on sb/sth** to see someone or something for the first time: *They fell in love the moment they laid eyes on each other.* **8 look sb in the eye/eyes** to look at someone in a direct way, without showing fear

or shame: *Look me in the eye and say that you didn't steal it.* **9 in sb's eyes** ⓑ in someone's opinion: *In my parents' eyes, I'll always be a child.*

IDIOMS **cast/run your/an eye over sth** to look at something quickly, often in order to give your opinion about it: *Would you cast an eye over our work so far?* • **catch sb's eye a** to get someone's attention by looking at them: *I tried to catch her eye, but she had already turned away.* **b** to be attractive or different enough to be noticed by people: *It was the colour of his jacket that caught my eye.* • **cry your eyes out** to cry a lot about a problem or situation • **keep your eyes open/ peeled (for sb/sth)** to watch carefully for someone or something: *Keep your eyes peeled, he should be here any minute.* • **keep an eye out for sb/sth** to watch carefully for someone or something to appear: *Keep an eye out for the delivery van.* • **see eye to eye (with sb)** If two people see eye to eye, they agree with each other. • **turn a blind eye (to sth)** to choose to ignore something that you know is wrong or illegal • **with your eyes open** knowing about all of the problems that could happen if you do something: *I went into this marriage with my eyes open.*

→ See also **black eye**

eye² /aı/ verb [T] (**eyeing**, also US **eying**, **eyed**) to look at someone or something with interest: *The two women eyed each other suspiciously.*

eyeball /'aıbɔːl/ noun [C] the whole of the eye, that has the shape of a small ball

eyebrow /'aıbraʊ/ noun [C] ⓑ the thin line of hair that is above each eye → See colour picture **The Body** on page Centre 13

eye-catching /'aıˌkætʃıŋ/ adj attractive, interesting, or different enough to be noticed: *an eye-catching poster*

'eye ˌcontact noun [U] UK If two people make eye contact, they look at each other at the same time.

-eyed /aıd/ suffix used at the end of a word describing a person's eyes: *Both sisters are brown-eyed.* → See also **cross-eyed, wide-eyed**

eyeglasses /'aıˌglɑːsız/ noun [plural] US (UK/US **glasses**) a piece of equipment with two transparent parts that you wear in front of your eyes to help you see better

eyelash /'aılæʃ/ noun [C] (also **lash**) ⓑ one of the short hairs that grow from the edge of your eyelids: [usually plural] *false eyelashes*

eyelid /'aılıd/ noun [C] ⓑ the piece of skin that covers your eye when you close it

IDIOM **not bat an eyelid** to not react to something unusual

eyeliner /'aıˌlaınər/ noun [C, U] a coloured substance, usually contained in a pencil, which you put in a line above or below your eyes in order to make them more attractive → See picture at **make-up**

eye-opener /'aıˌəʊpᵊnər/ noun [C] something that surprises you and teaches you new facts about life, people, etc: *Living in another country can be a real eye-opener.*

eyeshadow /'aɪʃædəʊ/ **noun** [C, U] a coloured cream or powder that you put above or around your eyes in order to make them more attractive

eyesight /'aɪsaɪt/ **noun** [U] ⑤ the ability to see: *My eyesight is getting worse.*

eyesore /'aɪsɔːʳ/ **noun** [C] a building, area, etc that looks ugly compared to the things that are around it

eyewitness /ˌaɪ'wɪtnɪs/ **noun** [C] (also **witness**) someone who saw something such as a crime or an accident happen: *Eyewitnesses saw two men running away from the bank.*

E

F

F, f /ef/ the sixth letter of the alphabet

F written abbreviation for Fahrenheit (= a measurement of temperature): *a body temperature of 98.6 °F*

FA /ˌefˈeɪ/ **noun** abbreviation for Football Association: the national organization for football in England: *the FA Cup*

fable /ˈfeɪbl/ **noun** [C] a short, traditional story, usually involving animals, which is intended to show people how to behave: *Aesop's fables*

fabric /ˈfæbrɪk/ **noun 1** [C, U] cloth: *a light/ woollen fabric* **2 the fabric of sth a** the basic way in which a society or other social group is organized: *The family is part of **the fabric of society*. **b** UK the walls, floor, and roof of a building

fabricate /ˈfæbrɪkeɪt/ **verb** [T] to invent facts, a story, etc in order to deceive someone: *He claims that the police **fabricated evidence** against him.*
• **fabrication** /ˌfæbrɪˈkeɪʃᵊn/ **noun** [C, U]

fabulous /ˈfæbjələs/ **adj** extremely good: *They've got a fabulous house.* ○ *We had an absolutely fabulous holiday.* • **fabulously adv** extremely: *Her family is **fabulously wealthy**.*

facade (also **façade**) /fəˈsɑːd/ **noun** [C] **1** a false appearance: ***Behind** that amiable **facade**, he's a deeply unpleasant man.* **2** the front of a large building: *the gallery's elegant 18th century facade*

face¹ /feɪs/ **noun 1** [C] **④** the front part of the head where the eyes, nose, and mouth are, or the expression on this part: *She's got a long, thin face.* ○ *I can't wait to see her face when she opens the present.* **2 make a face** (also UK **pull a face**) **③** to show with your face that you do not like someone or something: *The baby made a face every time I offered her some food.* **3 make faces** to make silly expressions with your face in order to try and make people laugh **4 sb's face falls/ lights up** someone starts to look disappointed/ happy: *His face fell when I said that she wasn't coming.* **5 to sb's face ③** If you say something unpleasant to someone's face, you say it to them directly, when you are with them: *If you've got something to say, say it to my face.* **6** the front or surface of something: *the north face of the cliff* ○ *a clock face* **7 in the face of sth** while having to deal with a difficult situation or problem: *She refused to leave him, in the face of increasing pressure from friends and family.* **8 on the face of it** used when you are describing how a situation seems, when this is different to what it is really like: *On the face of it, it seems like a bargain, but I bet there are hidden costs.*

IDIOMS **keep a straight face** to manage to stop yourself from smiling or laughing: *I can never play jokes on people because I can't keep a straight face.* • **lose/save face** to do something so that people stop respecting you/still respect you: *He seemed more interested in saving face than telling the truth.*

→ See also **have egg¹** on your face, **a slap²** in the face

face² /feɪs/ **verb** [T] **1 DIRECTION** ▷ **④** to be or turn in a particular direction: *The room faces south.* ○ *She turned to face him.* **2 PROBLEM** ▷ **④** If you face a problem, or a problem faces you, you have to deal with it: [often passive] *This is one of the many problems faced by working mothers.* **3 can't face sth/doing sth ④** to not want to do something or deal with something because it is so unpleasant: *I had intended to go for a run, but now I just can't face it.* **4 ACCEPT** ▷ **④** to accept that something unpleasant is true and start to deal with the situation: *She's going to have to **face the fact that** he's not coming back to her.* **5 let's face it** something that you say before you say something that is unpleasant but true: *Let's face it, none of us are getting any younger.* **6 PUNISHMENT** ▷ If you face something unpleasant, especially a punishment, then it might happen to you: *If found guilty, the pair face fines of up to $40,000.* **7 DEAL WITH** ▷ to deal with someone when the situation between you is difficult: *How can I face him now that he knows what I've done?* **8 COMPETITION** ▷ to play against another player or team in a competition, sport, etc: *We face Spain in the semifinal.* → See also **face the music**

PHRASAL VERB **face up to sth ④** to accept that a difficult situation exists

Facebook¹ /ˈfeɪsbʊk/ **noun** [U] trademark a website where you can show information about yourself, and communicate with friends

Facebook² /ˈfeɪsbʊk/ **verb** [T] trademark to communicate with someone using Facebook™

facelift /ˈfeɪslɪft/ **noun** [C] **1** medical treatment that makes the skin of your face tighter so that you look younger: *She looks like she's **had** a **facelift**.* **2** If a place is given a facelift, it is improved and made to look more attractive: *The council is planning a £6 million facelift for the old harbour area.*

facet /ˈfæsɪt/ **noun** [C] one part of a subject, situation, etc that has many parts: *She has many **facets to** her personality.*

facetious /fəˈsiːʃəs/ **adj** trying to make a joke or a clever remark in a way that annoys people

face-to-face /ˌfeɪstəˈfeɪs/ **adj, adv ④** directly, meeting someone in the same place: *We need to talk face-to-face.* ○ *She **came face-to-face with** the gunman as he strode into the playground.*

face value **noun take sth at face value** to accept the way that something first appears without thinking about what it really means: *You can't just take everything you read in the papers at face value.*

facial /ˈfeɪʃᵊl/ **adj** of or on the face: *facial expressions/hair*

facile /ˈfæsaɪl/ ⑤ /ˈfæsᵊl/ **adj** formal A facile

remark is too simple and has not been thought about enough.

facilitate /fə'sɪlɪteɪt/ **verb** [T] formal to make something possible or easier: *I will do everything in my power to facilitate the process.*

facilities /fə'sɪlətiz/ **noun** [plural] **B1** buildings, equipment, or services that are provided for a particular purpose: *sports/washing facilities* ◦ *childcare facilities*

> **Word partners for facilities**
>
> offer/provide facilities • facilities for sb/ (doing) sth • **sports** facilities

facility /fə'sɪləti/ **noun** [C] **1 B2** a part of a system or machine that makes it possible to do something: *This phone has a memory facility.* **2** a place where a particular activity happens: *a new medical facility*

fact /fækt/ **noun 1 TRUE THING** ▷ [C] **A2** something that you know is true, exists, or has happened: *I'm not angry that you drove my car, it's just the fact that you didn't ask me first.* ◦ *No decision will be made until we know all the facts.* ◦ *He knew for a fact* (= was certain) *that Natalie was lying.* **2 REAL THINGS** ▷ [U] **B1** real events and experiences, not things that are imagined: *It's hard to separate fact from fiction in what she says.* **3 in fact/in actual fact/as a matter of fact a B1** used to emphasize what is really true: *I was told there were some tickets left, but in actual fact they were sold out.* **b B2** used when giving more information about something: *"Is Isabel coming?" "Yes. As a matter of fact, she should be here soon."* **4 the fact (of the matter) is B2** used to tell someone that something is the truth: *I wouldn't usually ask for your help, but the fact is I'm desperate.*

IDIOM **the facts of life** details about sexual activity and the way that babies are born

> **Word partners for fact**
>
> accept/face up to/establish/explain/ignore a fact • the fact remains • an important/interesting/simple/undeniable fact • the facts about sth • know for a fact

faction /'fækʃən/ **noun** [C] a small group of people who are part of a larger group, and oppose the ideas of everyone else

factor /'fæktər/ **noun** [C] **1 B2** one of the things that has an effect on a particular situation, decision, event, etc: *Money was an important factor in their decision to move.* **2** a number that another larger number can be divided by exactly: *5 is a factor of 10.*

factory /'fæktəri/ **noun** [C] **A2** a building or group of buildings where large amounts of products are made or put together: *a textile factory*

factual /'fæktʃuəl/ **adj** using or consisting of facts • **factually adv** *factually correct/incorrect*

faculty /'fækəlti/ **noun 1** [C] a natural ability to hear, see, think, move, etc **2 the English/law/ science, etc faculty** a particular department at a college or university, or the teachers in that

department **3 the faculty** US all of the teachers at a school or college

fad /fæd/ **noun** [C] something that is fashionable to do, wear, say, etc for a short period of time: *the latest health fad*

fade /feɪd/ **verb 1** [I, T] **B2** If a colour or a sound fades, or if something fades it, it becomes less bright or strong: *The music began to fade.* ◦ *The walls had been faded by the sun.* **2** [I] (also **fade away**) **B2** to slowly disappear, lose importance or become weaker: *With time, memories of the painful summer would fade away.*

faeces /'fiːsiːz/ UK formal (US **feces**) **noun** [plural] solid waste that comes out of the bottom of a person or animal

fag /fæg/ **noun** [C] UK informal a cigarette

Fahrenheit /'færənhaɪt/ **noun** [U] (written abbreviation **F**) a measurement of temperature in which water freezes at 32° and boils at 212°

fail¹ /feɪl/ **verb 1 NOT SUCCEED** ▷ [I] **B2** to not be successful: *Dad's business failed after just three years.* ◦ *She keeps failing in her attempt to lose weight.* **2 fail to do sth B2** to not do what is necessary or expected: *John failed to turn up for football practice yesterday.* **3 EXAM** ▷ [I, T] **A2** to not pass a test or an exam, or to decide that someone has not passed: *I'm worried about failing my driving test.* **4 STOP WORKING** ▷ **B2** to stop working normally, or to become weaker: *Two of the plane's engines had failed.* **5 NOT HELPING** ▷ [T] to stop being helpful or useful to someone when they need you: *The government is failing the poor and unemployed.* **6 I fail to see/understand** used to show that you do not accept something: [+ question word] *I fail to see why you cannot work on a Sunday.*

fail² /feɪl/ **noun without fail** If you do something without fail, you always do it, even when it is difficult: *I go to the gym every Monday and Thursday without fail.*

failing¹ /'feɪlɪŋ/ **noun** [C] a bad quality or fault that someone or something has: *Despite one or two failings, he's basically a nice guy.*

failing² /'feɪlɪŋ/ **preposition failing that** something is not possible or does not happen: *Our goal is to move out by January, or failing that, by March.*

failure /'feɪljər/ **noun 1 NO SUCCESS** ▷ [U] **B2** a situation in which someone or something does not succeed: *Their attempt to climb Everest ended in failure.* **2 PERSON/ACTION** ▷ [C] **B2** someone or something that does not succeed: *All my life I've felt like a failure.* **3 failure to do sth B2** a situation in which you do not do something that you must do or are expected to do: *Failure to pay within 14 days will result in prosecution.* **4 NOT WORKING** ▷ [C, U] **B2** a situation in which something does not work, or stops working as well as it should: *heart failure* ◦ *All trains were delayed due to a power failure.*

> **Word partners for failure**
>
> admit/end in failure • be doomed to failure • an abject/complete/humiliating/total failure

aint[1] /feɪnt/ **adj 1** 🅱️2 slight and not easy to notice, smell, hear, etc: *a faint smell of smoke* ◦ *Faint laughter was coming from next door.* **2 feel faint** to feel very weak and as if you might fall down: *Seeing all the blood made me feel faint.* **3 faint hope/praise/chance, etc** very little hope, praise, chance, etc: *a faint hope of winning the gold medal* **4 not have the faintest idea** used to emphasize that you do not know something: [+ question word] *I haven't the faintest idea what you're talking about.*

aint[2] /feɪnt/ **verb** [I] 🅱️2 to suddenly become unconscious for a short time, usually falling down onto the floor: *She fainted with exhaustion.*

aintly /'feɪntli/ **adv** slightly: *faintly embarrassed*

air[1] /feəʳ/ **adj 1** EQUAL ▷ 🅱️1 treating everyone in the same way, so that no one has an advantage: *a fair trial* ◦ *That's not fair. You always go first!* **2** RIGHT ▷ 🅱️1 acceptable or right: *a fair deal* ◦ *We'd like to move abroad, but it's just not fair on the children.* → Opposite **unfair 3** HAIR/SKIN ▷ 🅰️2 having pale skin or a light colour of hair: *a boy with fair hair and blue eyes* → Opposite **dark 4 a fair amount/distance/size, etc** quite a large amount, distance, size, etc: *There's still a fair bit of work to be done on the house.* **5** WEATHER ▷ sunny and not raining: *Tomorrow will be fair, with some early morning frost.* **6** AVERAGE ▷ not very good but not very bad: *He has a fair chance of winning.* **7 fair enough** informal 🅱️2 used to say that you agree, or think that something is acceptable: *"He'll only work on Sunday if he gets paid extra." "Fair enough."* → See also **fair play**[2], **have your (fair) share**[2] **of sth**

air

air[2] /feəʳ/ **noun** [C] **1** 🅱️1 an event outside where you can ride large machines for pleasure and play games to win prizes **2** an event where people show and sell goods or services relating to a particular business or hobby: *a trade fair*

air[3] /feəʳ/ **adv play fair** to do something in a fair and honest way

IDIOM **fair and square** in an honest way and without any doubt: *We won the game fair and square.*

airground /'feəgraʊnd/ **noun** [C] an outside area that is used for fairs

air-haired /ˌfeə'heəd/ **adj** having a light colour of hair: *a fair-haired child*

airly /'feəli/ **adv 1** 🅱️1 more than average, but less than very: *a fairly big family* ◦ *fairly quickly* **2** 🅱️2 done in a fair way: *treating people fairly*

fairness /'feənəs/ **noun** [U] treatment of everyone in the same way, so that no one has an advantage

fair 'trade noun [U] a way of buying and selling products that makes certain that the original producer receives a fair price: *fair trade coffee/ chocolate* → Compare **free trade** • **fairly traded adv**

fairy /'feəri/ **noun** [C] a small, imaginary creature that looks like a person with wings, and has magic powers

fairy

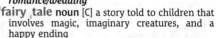

fairytale /'feəriteɪl/ **adj** [always before noun] happy and beautiful, like something in a fairy tale: *a fairytale romance/wedding*

fairy ˌtale noun [C] a story told to children that involves magic, imaginary creatures, and a happy ending

faith /feɪθ/ **noun 1** TRUST ▷ [U] 🅱️2 the belief that someone or something is good, right, and able to be trusted: *Have faith in me. I won't let you down.* **2** STRONG BELIEF ▷ [U] 🅱️2 strong belief in a god or gods: *Throughout her illness, she never lost her faith in God.* **3** RELIGION ▷ [C] 🅱️2 a religion: *the Jewish and Christian faiths* **4 in good faith** If you act in good faith, you believe that what you are doing is good, honest, or legal.

> 🗎 Word partners for **faith**
> have/lose faith • sb's faith in sb/sth

faithful /'feɪθfl/ **adj 1** RELATIONSHIP ▷ If your husband, wife, or partner is faithful, they do not have a sexual relationship with anyone else: *a faithful husband* ◦ *They remained faithful to each other throughout their long marriage.* **2** LOYAL ▷ 🅱️2 always loyal: *his trusted and faithful servant* **3** NOT CHANGED ▷ not changing any of the original details, facts, style, etc: *Does the film adaptation stay faithful to the novel?* → Opposite **unfaithful** • **faithfulness noun** [U]

faithfully /'feɪθfli/ **adv 1** in a faithful way **2 Yours faithfully** 🅱️2 used to end a formal letter to someone whose name you do not know

fake[1] /feɪk/ **adj** not real, but made to look or seem real: *fake fur* ◦ *a fake passport*

fake[2] /feɪk/ **noun** [C] **1** a copy of something that is intended to look real or valuable and deceive people: *Experts say that the painting is a fake.* **2** someone who pretends to have particular skills or qualities so that they can deceive people or get their admiration

fake[3] /feɪk/ **verb** [T] **1** to copy something in order to deceive people: *faked documents* **2** to pretend that you have a particular feeling or emotion: *He said he was feeling sick, but he was just faking it.*

falcon /'fɔːlkən/ **noun** [C] a large bird that eats small animals and is often taught to hunt by people

fall[1] /fɔːl/ **verb** [I] (**fell, fallen**) **1** MOVE DOWN ▷ 🅰️2 to move down towards the ground: *Huge drops of rain were falling from the sky.* ◦ *By* winter, all the leaves had **fallen off** the trees. **2 STOP STANDING** ▷ **A2** to suddenly go down and hit the ground without intending to: *She fell off her bike and broke her arm.* **3 BECOME LESS** ▷ **B1** to become less in number or amount: *Housing prices have fallen by 15% since last year.* ○ *Temperatures are expected to fall from 15° C to 9°C.* **4 BECOME WORSE** ▷ to become worse, or start to be in a bad situation or condition: *Education standards are continuing to fall.* ○ *Empty for 30 years, the building had fallen into ruin* (= become very damaged). **5 fall asleep/ill/still, etc B1** to start to sleep/become sick/become quiet, etc: *I fell asleep on the sofa watching TV.* **6 darkness/night falls** literary used to say that it is becoming dark **7 LOSE POWER** ▷ to lose power and start to be controlled by a different leader: *In 1453 the city fell to the Turks.* **8 HANG DOWN** ▷ to hang down: *Her long blonde hair fell softly over her shoulders.* → See also **fall on deaf ears (ear)**, **fall flat³**, **fall foul¹ of sb/sth**, **go/fall to pieces (piece¹)**, **fall into place¹**, **fall prey¹ to sth**, **fall by the wayside**

> **!** Common learner error: **fall** and **feel**
>
> Be careful not to confuse the past forms of the verbs **fall** and **feel**. The past tense of **fall** is **fell**.
> *Chris fell off the ladder and broke his arm.*
> The past tense of **feel** is **felt**.
> *I felt really happy and relaxed.*

PHRASAL VERBS **fall apart 1 BREAK** ▷ **B2** to break into pieces: *My poor old boots are falling apart.* **2 HAVE PROBLEMS** ▷ **B2** to start having problems that you cannot deal with: *Their relationship fell apart after they moved to Detroit.* • **fall back on sb/sth** to use someone or something when other things have failed, or when there are no other choices: *We've been saving up the past few years, to have something to fall back on.* • **fall behind** to not do something fast enough, or not do something by a particular time: *Lucy's been falling behind in her homework again.* • **fall for sb B2** to suddenly have strong, romantic feelings about someone • **fall for sth** to be tricked into believing something that is not true: *He told me he owned a mansion in Spain and I fell for it.* • **fall in** If a roof or ceiling falls in, it drops to the ground because it is damaged. • **fall off** If the amount, rate, or quality of something falls off, it becomes smaller or lower: *Demand for new cars is falling off.* • **fall on sth** to happen on a particular day or date: *New Year's Day falls on a Tuesday this year.* • **fall out** UK **B2** to argue with someone and stop being friendly with them: *Have you and Sam fallen out with each other again?* • **fall over B1** If someone or something falls over, they fall to the ground or onto their side: *The fence fell over in the wind.* → See colour picture **Phrasal Verbs** on page Centre 16 • **fall through B2** If a plan or agreement falls through, it does not happen.

fall² /fɔːl/ *noun* **1 AMOUNT** ▷ [C] **B1** a reduction in the number or amount of something: *There's*

been a sharp **fall in** prices. **2 MOVEMENT** ▷ [C] **B** a movement of someone or something down t the ground: *a heavy fall of snow* **3 SEASON** ▷ [C U] US (UK/US **autumn**) the season of the yea between summer and winter, when leaves fa from the trees: *He started a new job in the fal* **4 DEFEAT** ▷ [no plural] an occasion when a city government, leader, etc loses power or contro *the fall of communism*

> **✷** Word partners for **fall**
>
> a dramatic/sharp/steep fall • a fall in sth

fallacy /ˈfæləsi/ *noun* [C, U] a belief that is nc true or correct: *It's a fallacy that problems wi disappear if you ignore them.*

fallen /ˈfɔːlən/ past participle of fall

fallible /ˈfæləbl/ *adj* able to make mistakes: *W place our trust in doctors, but even they ar fallible.* → Opposite **infallible** • **fallibility** /ˌfælə-ˈbɪləti/ *noun* [U]

fallout /ˈfɔːlaʊt/ *noun* [U] the radiation (= powe ful and dangerous energy) from a nuclea explosion

fallow /ˈfæləʊ/ *adj* If land is left fallow, it is nc planted with crops, in order to improve th quality of the soil.

false /fɔːls/ *adj* **1 NOT TRUE** ▷ **B1** not true c correct: *a false name* ○ *Many rumours about he life were later proved to be false.* **2 NOT REAL** ▷ **B** not real, but made to look or seem real: *fals teeth* ○ *false documents* **3 NOT SINCERE** ▷ nc sincere or expressing real emotions: *false pr mises* • **falsely** *adv*

false aˈlarm *noun* [C] an occasion when peopl believe that something dangerous is happening but it is not: *Fire engines rushed to the scene, bu it was a false alarm.*

falsehood /ˈfɔːlshʊd/ *noun* [C] formal a lie

false ˈstart *noun* [C] an occasion when you tr to start an activity, event, or process, but fa and have to stop: *After several false start the company has finally opened for business.*

false ˈteeth *noun* [plural] a set of artificial teetl worn by someone who does not have their ow teeth

falsify /ˈfɔːlsɪfaɪ/ *verb* [T] to change importan information, especially in documents, in orde to deceive people

falter /ˈfɔːltər/ *verb* [I] **1** to stop being confiden powerful, or successful: *In the late 1980s hi career began to falter.* **2** to pause, make mistake or seem weak when you are talking or movinç *Her voice didn't falter once during the ceremony* ○ *a few faltering steps*

fame /feɪm/ *noun* [U] **B2** the quality of bein known by many people because of your achieve ments, skills, etc: *fame and fortune* ○ *She firs rose to fame as a pop star at the age of 16* → See also **sb's/sth's claim² to fame**

famed /feɪmd/ *adj* famous, especially for havinç particular qualities: *It is a city famed for its sk slopes and casinos.*

familiar /fəˈmɪliər/ *adj* **1 B1** easy to recogniz because of being seen, met, heard, etc before It's nice to see a few **familiar faces** (= people tha

I recognize) around here. ◦ *This street doesn't look **familiar to** me.* **2 be familiar with sth** B2 to know about something or have experienced it many times before: *Anyone who's familiar with his poetry will find the course easy.* → Opposite **unfamiliar** **3** friendly and very informal: *He doesn't like to be too familiar with his staff.*

amiliarity /fəˌmɪliˈærəti/ **noun** [U] **1** a good knowledge of something, or experience of doing or using it: *Her **familiarity with** computers is very impressive.* **2** friendly and informal behaviour

amiliarize (also UK **-ise**) /fəˈmɪliəraɪz/ **verb familiarize sb/yourself with sth** to teach someone more about something new, or try to understand more about it yourself: *We spent a few minutes familiarizing ourselves with the day's schedule.*

amily /ˈfæməli/ **noun** **1** RELATED PEOPLE ▷ [group] A1 a group of people who are related to each other, such as a mother, a father, and their children: *Her* UK *family are*/US *family is originally from Ireland.* ◦ *a family business* **2** CHILDREN ▷ [C] B1 the children in a family: [usually singular] *Single parents have to **raise a family** on their own.* ◦ *Paul and Alison are hoping to **start a family** soon.* **3** PLANTS/ANIMALS ▷ [C] a group of similar types of plants or animals that are related to each other

> Word partners for **family**
>
> **have/raise/start/support** a family • a **big/close/happy** family • your **close/extended/immediate** family

amily ˌname **noun** [C] the name that is used by all the members of a family

amily ˈplanning **noun** [U] controlling how many children you have by using contraceptives (= pills or objects that prevent a woman from becoming pregnant)

amily ˌroom **noun** [C] US a room in a family's home that is used for relaxing, especially for watching television

amily ˈtree **noun** [C] a drawing that shows the relationships between the different members of a family, especially over a long period of time

amine /ˈfæmɪn/ **noun** [C, U] a long period when people living in a particular area do not have enough food, and many of them suffer and die

amous /ˈfeɪməs/ **adj** A1 known or recognized by many people: *a famous actress* ◦ *New York is a city **famous for** its shopping and nightlife.* → See also **world-famous**

amously /ˈfeɪməsli/ **adv** **1 get on famously (with sb)** to have a very friendly relationship with someone **2** in a way that is famous

an¹ /fæn/ **noun** [C] **1** A2 someone who admires and supports a famous person, sport, type of music, etc: *More than 15,000 Liverpool fans attended Saturday's game.* ◦ *He's a big **fan of** country music.* **2** B1 something that is used to move the air around so that it feels cooler, such as a machine or an object that you wave with your hand: *an electric fan*

fan

> Word partners for **fan**
>
> a **big/huge** fan • a fan **of** sb/sth • **football/soccer** fans

fan² /fæn/ **verb** [T] (**fanning**, **fanned**) to move the air around with a fan or something used like a fan, to make it feel cooler: [often reflexive] *The spectators sat in the bright sun, fanning themselves with newspapers.*

PHRASAL VERB **fan out** If a group of people fan out, they move out in different directions from a single point.

fanatic /fəˈnætɪk/ **noun** [C] someone whose interest in something or enthusiasm for something is extreme • **fanatical adj** extremely enthusiastic about something: *She's fanatical about football.* • **fanaticism** /fəˈnætɪsɪzəm/ **noun** [U]

fanciable /ˈfænsiəbl/ **adj** UK informal sexually attractive

fanciful /ˈfænsɪfəl/ **adj** Something that is fanciful comes from someone's imagination and so is probably not true or real: *a fanciful story*

ˈfan ˌclub **noun** [C] an organization for the people who support and admire a particular singer, actor, sports team, etc

fancy¹ /ˈfænsi/ **verb** [T] **1** WANT ▷ UK B1 to want to have or do something: *Do you fancy a drink?* ◦ [+ doing sth] *We fancy going to the Caribbean for our holiday.* **2** PERSON ▷ UK informal to feel sexually attracted to someone: *I fancied him the first time I saw him.* **3 fancy (that)!** UK informal used to show that you are surprised or shocked by something: [+ doing sth] *Fancy seeing you here!* **4** THINK ▷ old-fashioned to think that something is true: [+ (that)] *I fancy that he was smiling, but I can't be sure.*

fancy² /ˈfænsi/ **adj** **1** Fancy things and places are expensive and fashionable: *a fancy restaurant* **2** with lots of decoration, or very complicated: *fancy cakes*

fancy³ /ˈfænsi/ **noun** **1 take a fancy to sb/sth** to start to like someone or something a lot: *Marina had taken a fancy to her.* **2 take sb's fancy** If something or someone takes your fancy, you find them interesting or attractive: *We can go anywhere that takes your fancy.*

ˌfancy ˈdress **noun** [U] UK special clothes that people wear for a party, which make them look like a different person: *a **fancy dress party***

fanfare /ˈfænfeər/ **noun** [C] a short, loud tune played on a trumpet (= metal musical instrument) to announce an important person or event

fang

fang

fang /fæŋ/ **noun** [C] a long, sharp tooth of an animal such as a dog or a snake

'fanny ,pack noun [C] US (UK **bumbag**) a small bag fixed to a belt that you wear around your waist

fantasize (also UK **-ise**) /'fæntəsaɪz/ **verb** [I, T] to imagine something that you would like to happen, but is not likely to happen: *We used to **fantasize about** becoming famous actresses.*

fantastic /fæn'tæstɪk/ **adj 1 GOOD** ▷ informal ⓐ2 very good: *I've had a fantastic time.* **2 LARGE** ▷ informal A fantastic amount or number of something is very large: *They're making fantastic amounts of money.* **3 STRANGE** ▷ very strange and probably not true: *fantastic stories about monsters and witches*

fantastically /fæn'tæstɪkᵊli/ **adv** ⓑ2 extremely: *fantastically rich*

fantasy /'fæntəsi/ **noun** [C, U] ⓑ2 a situation or event that you imagine, which is not real or true

> 🔲 **Word partners for fantasy**
>
> have fantasies **about/of** (doing) sth • a fantasy **world**

FAQ /ˌefeɪˈkjuː/ **noun** [C] abbreviation for frequently asked question: something that many people ask when they use the Internet or a computer program, or a file (= collection) of these questions with their answers

far¹ /fɑːʳ/ **adv** (**farther, farthest or further, furthest**) **1 DISTANCE** ▷ ⓐ2 used to talk about how distant something is: *It's the first time I've been so **far away** from home.* ∘ ***How far** is it to the supermarket?* ∘ *Versailles is **not far from** Paris.* ∘ *In the summer the herds move farther north.* **2 TIME** ▷ ⓐ2 a long time: *How far back can you remember?* ∘ *We need to plan further ahead.* **3 far better/cheaper/more, etc** ⓑ2 much better/cheaper/more, etc: *Young people are far more independent these days.* **4 far too difficult/expensive/late, etc** ⓑ2 much too difficult/expensive/late, etc: *She was wearing a coat that was far too big for her.* **5 as far as I know** informal ⓑ2 used to say what you think is true, although you do

not know all the facts: *As far as I know, they haven't reached a decision yet.* **6 as far as sb concerned** ⓑ2 used to say what someone opinion is: *It's all over as far as I'm concerne* **7 as far as sth is concerned** ⓑ2 used to say wh you are talking about: *As far as sport's concerne I like tennis and football.* **8 by far** ⓑ2 used emphasize that something is the biggest, th best, etc: *This is his best film by far.* **9 far fro sth** certainly not something: *The situation is fᵣ from clear.* **10 far from doing sth** certainly nᵣ doing something: *Far from being pleased, he wᵣ embarrassed by the praise.* **11 far from it** inforᵣ used to tell someone that something is certainᵣ not true: *He's not handsome – far from it.* **12 ᵣ far as possible** as much as is possible: *We try buy organic food as far as possible.* **13 go so far ᵣ to do sth** to take the extreme action of doiᵣ something: *He even went so far as to stop her froᵣ using the telephone.* **14 go too far** to behave in ᵣ way that upsets or annoys other people **15 hoᵣ far** used to talk about how true something ᵣ *How far do politicians represent the views ᵣ ordinary people?* **16 so far** ⓑ1 until now: *So fᵣ we haven't made much progress.* **17 so far ᵣ good** informal used to say that something hᵣ gone well until now **18 not go (very) far ᵣ something such as money does not go far, yᵣ cannot do very much with it: £100 doesn't ᵣ very far these days.*

far² /fɑːʳ/ **adj** (**farther, farthest or furtheᵣ furthest**) **1** ⓑ2 [always before noun] describes thᵣ part of something that is most distant from yᵣ or from the centre: *His office is at the far end ᵣ the corridor.* ∘ *They live in the far south of tᵣ country.* **2 the far left/right** used to describᵣ political groups whose opinions are veᵣ extreme → See also **be a far cry² from sth**

faraway /ˌfɑːrəˈweɪ/ **adj 1** [always before nouᵣ literary a long distance away: *faraway places* **2ᵣ faraway look/expression** an expression oᵣ someone's face that shows that they are nᵣ thinking about what is happening around theᵣ *He had a faraway look in his eyes.*

farce /fɑːs/ **noun 1 SITUATION** ▷ [no plural] ᵣ serious event or situation that becomes ridiᵣ lous because it is so badly organized: *Tᵣ meeting was a complete farce.* **2 PLAY** ▷ [C] ᵣ funny play in which a lot of silly things happeᵣ • **farcical** /'fɑːsɪkᵊl/ **adj** like a farce

fare¹ /feəʳ/ **noun** [C] ⓑ1 the price that you pay ᵣ travel on an aircraft, train, bus, etc: *air/traiᵣ fares*

> 🔲 **Word partners for fare**
>
> a **return/single** fare • the fare **to** [Seattle/ Moscow, etc]

fare² /feəʳ/ **verb** formal **fare well/badly/betteᵣ etc** used to say how well or badly someone ᵣ something does in a particular situation: *All tᵣ children fared well in the exams.*

farewell /ˌfeəˈwel/ **exclamation** old-fashioneᵣ goodbye • **farewell noun** [C] an occasion wheᵣ someone says goodbye: *a sad farewell* ∘ ᵣ *farewell party*

far-fetched /ˌfɑːˈfetʃt/ **adj** difficult to believ

and not likely to be true: *The idea is not as far-fetched as it might sound.*

arm

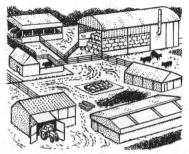

arm¹ /fɑːm/ **noun** [C] Ⓐ① an area of land with fields and buildings that is used for growing crops and keeping animals as a business: *a dairy farm* ○ *farm animals/buildings*

> ☑ Word partners for **farm**
>
> on a farm • farm **workers** • farm **animals**

arm² /fɑːm/ **verb** [I, T] to grow crops or keep animals as a business: *Only 2% of the country's farmland is farmed organically.*

armer /'fɑːmər/ **noun** [C] Ⓐ② someone who owns or looks after a farm

armhouse /'fɑːmhaʊs/ **noun** [C] (plural **farmhouses** /'fɑːmhaʊzɪz/) the house on a farm where the farmer lives

arming /'fɑːmɪŋ/ **noun** [U] Ⓑ① the job of working on a farm or organizing the work there

armland /'fɑːmlænd/ **noun** [U] land that is used for or suitable for farming

armyard /'fɑːmjɑːd/ **noun** [C] an area of ground with farm buildings around it

ar-off /ˌfɑːr'ɒf/ **adj** literary a long distance away or a long time in the past or future: *far-off lands*

ar-reaching /ˌfɑːˈriːtʃɪŋ/ **adj** Far-reaching acts, events, or ideas have very big effects: *far-reaching changes in the education system*

arsighted /'fɑːˌsaɪtɪd/ **adj** US (UK **long-sighted**) able to see objects that are far away, but not things that are near to you

art /fɑːt/ **verb** [I] very informal to release gas from the bowels through the bottom • **fart noun** [C]

arther /'fɑːðər/ **adj, adv** comparative of **far adv**: more distant: *I couldn't walk any farther.*

arthest /'fɑːðɪst/ **adj, adv** superlative of **far adv**: most distant: *They walked to the farthest edge of the garden.*

ascinate /'fæsɪneɪt/ **verb** [T] to interest someone a lot: *Science has always fascinated me.*

ascinated /'fæsɪneɪtɪd/ **adj** Ⓑ② extremely interested: *They were absolutely fascinated by the game.*

ascinating /'fæsɪneɪtɪŋ/ **adj** Ⓑ② extremely interesting: *I found the movie fascinating.*

ascination /ˌfæsɪ'neɪʃən/ **noun** [U, no plural] a very great interest in something: *Her fascination with fashion started at an early age.*

fascism, Fascism /'fæʃɪzəm/ **noun** [U] a political system in which the government is extremely powerful and controls people's lives

fascist /'fæʃɪst/ **noun** [C] **1** (also **Fascist**) someone who supports fascism **2** someone who you do not like because they try to control other people's behaviour • **fascist adj** *a fascist dictator/regime*

fashion¹ /'fæʃən/ **noun** **1** STYLE ▷ [C, U] Ⓐ② the most popular style of clothes, appearance, or behaviour at a particular time: *Long hair is back in fashion for men.* ○ *Fur coats have gone out of fashion.* **2** BUSINESS ▷ [U] Ⓑ① the business of making and selling clothes: *the fashion industry* **3** WAY ▷ [no plural] formal the way in which someone does something: *He told the story in a very amusing fashion.*

> ☑ Word partners for **fashion**
>
> be in fashion • come into/go out of fashion • a fashion for sth

fashion² /'fæʃən/ **verb** [T] formal to make something: *Their jewellery is fashioned from recycled metal.*

fashionable /'fæʃənəbl/ **adj** Ⓑ① popular at a particular time: *fashionable clothes* ○ *It's no longer fashionable to smoke.* → Opposite **unfashionable** • **fashionably adv** *fashionably dressed*

> ➕ Other ways of saying **fast**
>
> If you want to use fast as an adjective, a very common alternative is **quick**:
>
> > *I tried to catch him, but he was too **quick** for me.*
>
> If something is done fast, without waiting, you can use the adjectives **prompt** or **speedy**:
>
> > *A **prompt** reply would be very much appreciated.*
> > *He made a **speedy** recovery.*
>
> If something is done too fast, without thinking carefully, the adjectives **hasty** and **hurried** are often used:
>
> > *I don't want to make a **hasty** decision.*
> > *We left early after a **hurried** breakfast.*
>
> A fast walk is often described as **brisk**:
>
> > *We took a **brisk** walk through the park.*
>
> The adjective **rapid** is often used to describe fast growth or change:
>
> > *The 1990's were a period of **rapid** change/growth.*
>
> If you want to use fast as an adverb, a very common alternative is **quickly**:
>
> > *The problem needs to be sorted out as **quickly** as possible.*
>
> If someone does something very fast, in informal situations you can use the expressions **in a flash** and **like a shot**:
>
> > *I'll be back **in a flash**.*
> > *There was an almighty crash and he got up **like a shot**.*

fast¹ /fɑːst/ **adj** **1** Ⓐ① moving, happening, or doing something quickly: *fast cars* ○ *a fast*

F

swimmer ∘ *Computers are getting faster all the time.* **2** [never before noun] If a clock or watch is fast, it shows a time that is later than the correct time. → See also **a fast track¹ (to sth)**

fast² /fɑːst/ **adv 1** ⓐ moving or happening quickly: *We ran as fast as we could.* ∘ *You'll have to act fast.* **2 fast asleep** completely asleep (= sleeping) **3** in a firm or tight way: *He tried to get away, but she* **held** *him* **fast.** → See also **thick¹ and fast**

> **❗ Common learner error: fast**
>
> Remember that there is no adverb 'fastly'.
> Use the adverbs **fast** or **quickly** instead.
> *The situation is changing fast.*
> *Alice got dressed very quickly.*

fast³ /fɑːst/ **verb** [I] to eat nothing, or much less than you usually eat for a period of time • **fast noun** [C]

fasten /ˈfɑːsən/ **verb 1** ⓑ [I, T] to close or fix something together, or to become closed or fixed together: *Fasten your seat belts.* ∘ *This dress fastens at the side.* **2 fasten sth on/to/together, etc** ⓑ to fix one thing to another: *He fastened the rope to a tree.* → Opposite **unfasten**

fastener /ˈfɑːsənər/ **noun** [C] something that is used to close or fix things together

fast food **noun** [U] ⓐ hot food that can be served very quickly in a restaurant because it is already prepared: *fast food restaurants*

fast-forward /ˌfɑːstˈfɔːwəd/ **verb** [I, T] If you fast-forward a recording, or if it fast-forwards, you make it play at very high speed so that you get to the end more quickly. • **fast-forward noun** [U]

fastidious /fæsˈtɪdiəs/ **adj** Someone who is fastidious wants every detail of something to be correct and perfect.

fat¹ /fæt/ **adj (fatter, fattest) 1** ⓐ Someone who is fat weighs too much: *She eats all the time but never* **gets fat.** **2** thick or large: *a fat book* → See also **fat chance¹**

fat² /fæt/ **noun 1** [U] the substance under the skin of people and animals that keeps them warm: *body fat* **2** [C, U] ⓑ a solid or liquid substance like oil that is taken from plants or animals and used in cooking: *animal/vegetable fat* → See also **saturated fat**

fatal /ˈfeɪtəl/ **adj 1** ⓑ A fatal accident or illness causes death: *a fatal car crash* **2** ⓑ Fatal actions have very bad effects: *a* **fatal error** • **fatally adv** *fatally injured*

fatalism /ˈfeɪtəlɪzəm/ **noun** [U] the belief that people cannot change events, and that bad events cannot be avoided • **fatalistic** /ˌfeɪtəlˈɪstɪk/ **adj**

fatality /fəˈtæləti/ **noun** [C] formal the death of a person caused by violence or an accident

fat cat **noun** [C] someone who has a lot of money, especially someone in charge of a company

fate /feɪt/ **noun 1** [C] ⓑ what happens to someone, especially when it is something bad: *His fate is now in the hands of the jury.* **2** [U] ⓑ a power that some people believe decides what

will happen: *I believe it was fate that caused us t meet again.* → See also **quirk of fate**

> **❷ Word partners for fate**
>
> **suffer** a fate • **decide/seal** sb's fate • [suffer] the **same/a similar** fate

fated /ˈfeɪtɪd/ **adj** [never before noun] If somethin that happens or someone's actions are fated they are decided by a power that contro events, and cannot be avoided: [+ to do sth] *seem fated to meet him wherever I go.* → See als **ill-fated**

fateful /ˈfeɪtfəl/ **adj** A fateful event has a important and usually bad effect on th future: *a fateful decision*

fat-free /ˌfætˈfriː/ **adj** describes food that co tains no fat

father¹ /ˈfɑːðər/ **noun 1** ⓐ [C] your male paren **2 Father** the title of some Christian priest *Father O'Brian* **3 the father of sth** the man wh invented or started something: *Descartes known as the father of modern philosophy.*

father² /ˈfɑːðər/ **verb** [T] formal to become a mal parent: *He fathered three children.*

Father Christmas **noun** [no plural] UK a kin fat, old man in red clothes who people sa brings presents to children at Christmas

father figure **noun** [C] an older man who give you advice and support like a father

fatherhood /ˈfɑːðəhʊd/ **noun** [U] the state c being a father

father-in-law /ˈfɑːðərɪnlɔː/ **noun** [C] (plur. **fathers-in-law**) ⓑ the father of your husban or wife

fathom¹ /ˈfæðəm/ **verb** [T] (also UK **fathom ou** to be able to understand something afte thinking about it a lot: [+ question word] *No on could fathom why she had left so early.*

fathom² /ˈfæðəm/ **noun** [C] a unit for measurin the depth of water, equal to 1.8 metres

fatigue /fəˈtiːɡ/ **noun** [U] the feeling of bein tired • **fatigued adj**

fatigues /fəˈtiːɡz/ **noun** [plural] special clothe that soldiers wear when they are fighting c working

fat tax **noun** [C] a tax on food that is bad fo your body and will make you fat: *The prim minister said a fat tax could help stop health cos rising.*

fatten /ˈfætən/ **verb** [T] to make animals fatter s that they can be eaten

PHRASAL VERB **fatten sb/sth up** to give a thi person or animal lots of food so that the become fatter

fattening /ˈfætənɪŋ/ **adj** Fattening food ca make you fat: *I don't eat chips, they're to fattening.*

fatty /ˈfæti/ **adj** Fatty foods contain a lot of fat

fatuous /ˈfætjuəs/ **adj** very stupid and nc deserving your attention or respect: *a fatuou comment/remark*

aucet /ˈfɔːsɪt/ **noun** [C] US (mainly UK **tap**) an object at the end of a pipe that you turn to control the flow of water → See picture at **tap** → See colour picture **The Kitchen** on page Centre 2

ault¹ /fɔːlt/ **noun 1** sb's fault 🅱1 If something bad that has happened is someone's fault, they are responsible for it: *She believes it was the doctor's fault that Peter died.* **2 at fault** 🅱2 responsible for something bad that has happened: *I was at fault and I would like to apologize.* **3** 🅱2 [C] something that is wrong with something or with someone's character: *The car has a serious design fault.* **4 find fault with sb/sth** to criticize someone or something, especially without good reasons

> ❗ Common learner error: **fault** or **mistake**?
>
> Use **fault** for explaining who is responsible when something bad happens.
>
> *It's my fault that the car was stolen. I left the window open.*
>
> ~~It's my mistake the car was stolen. I left the window open.~~
>
> Use **mistake** for talking about something that you did or thought that was wrong.
>
> *I still make lots of mistakes in my essays.*
>
> ~~I still make lots of faults in my essays.~~

> 🗹 Word partners for **fault**
>
> all/entirely sb's fault • it's sb's **own** fault • be **at** fault

ault² /fɔːlt/ **verb** [T] to find a reason to criticize someone or something: *I can't fault the way that they dealt with the complaint.*

aultless /ˈfɔːltləs/ **adj** perfect, or without any mistakes: *a faultless performance*

aulty /ˈfɔːlti/ **adj** 🅱2 not working correctly: *faulty brakes/wiring*

auna /ˈfɔːnə/ **noun** [group] all the animals that live in a particular area: *the flora and fauna of the area*

avour¹ UK (US **favor**) /ˈfeɪvər/ **noun 1 HELP** ▷ [C] 🅱1 something that you do to help someone: *Could you do me a favour please?* ∘ *I wanted to ask you a favour.* **2 be in favour of sth** 🅱2 to agree with or approve of a plan or idea: *Most people are in favour of reducing traffic in cities.* **3 in favour of sb/sth** If you refuse or get rid of someone or something in favour of someone or something else, you choose them instead: *They dropped him from the team in favour of a much younger player.* **4 in sb's favour a** If something is in your favour, it helps you to win or succeed: *Both sides have strong arguments in their favour.* **b** If a game, vote, or judgment is in someone's favour, they win: *The final score was 16-10 in England's favour.* **5 LIKE** ▷ [U] formal approval of something or someone: *Her work never found favour among the critics.* **6 be in favour/out of favour** to be popular/unpopular: *He has fallen out of favour recently.*

avour² UK (US **favor**) /ˈfeɪvər/ **verb** [T] **1** to choose or prefer one possibility: [often passive] *These are the running shoes favoured by marathon runners.* **2** to act unfairly by treating one person

better than another: *She always felt that her parents favoured her brother.*

favourable UK (US **favorable**) /ˈfeɪvərəbl/ **adj 1** 🅱2 showing that you like or approve of someone or something, or making you like or approve of them: *She made a very favourable impression on us.* **2** making something more likely to be successful: *favourable weather conditions* → Opposite **unfavourable** • **favourably** UK (US **favorably**) adv

favourite¹ UK (US **favorite**) /ˈfeɪvərət/ **adj** [always before noun] 🅰1 Your favourite person or thing is the one that you like best: *What's your favourite band?*

favourite² UK (US **favorite**) /ˈfeɪvərət/ **noun** [C] **1** 🅱1 a person or thing that you like more than all others: *These chocolates are my favourites.* **2** the person or animal that is most likely to win a competition: *The Dallas Cowboys are now favourites to win.*

favouritism UK (US **favoritism**) /ˈfeɪvərətɪzəm/ **noun** [U] unfair treatment of one person or group in a better way than another

fawn¹ /fɔːn/ **noun 1** [C] a young deer **2** [U] a light brown colour

fawn² /fɔːn/ **verb**

> **PHRASAL VERB fawn on/over sb** to praise someone or be nice to someone in a way that is false in order to get something or to make them like you

fax¹ /fæks/ **noun 1 DOCUMENT** ▷ [C] a document that is sent or received using a special machine and a telephone line: *I got a fax from them this morning.* **2 SYSTEM** ▷ [U] the system of sending or receiving documents using a special machine and a telephone line: *Some products can be ordered by fax.* **3 MACHINE** ▷ [C] (also ˈfax ˌmachine) a machine that is used to send and receive faxes → See colour picture **The Office** on page Centre 5

fax² /fæks/ **verb** [T] 🅱1 to send documents using a fax machine: [+ two objects] *Can you fax me a price list?*

the FBI /ˌefbiːˈaɪ/ **noun** abbreviation for the Federal Bureau of Investigation: one of the national police forces in the US that is controlled by the central government: *He is wanted by the FBI for fraud.*

fear¹ /fɪər/ **noun 1** 🅱1 [C, U] a strong, unpleasant feeling that you get when you think that something bad, dangerous, or frightening might happen: *She was trembling with fear.* ∘ *Unlike the rest of us, Dave had no fear of snakes.* ∘ [+ (that)] *There are fears that the disease will spread to other countries.* **2 for fear of sth/ doing sth** because you are worried about something/doing something: *I didn't want to move for fear of waking her up.*

> 🗹 Word partners for **fear**
>
> allay/calm/cause/heighten fear • hold no fear for sb • great/morbid/widespread fear • fear **of** sth

fear² /fɪər/ **verb** [T] **1** 🅱2 to be worried or frightened that something bad might happen or might have happened: [+ (that)] *Police fear that the couple may have drowned.* **2** ⓑ to be frightened of something or someone unpleasant: *Most older employees fear unemployment.* **3 fear the worst** ⓑ If you fear the worst, you are frightened that an unpleasant situation will become much worse: *When there was no sign of the children, rescuers feared the worst.*

PHRASAL VERB **fear for sth/sb** to be worried about something, or to be worried that someone is in danger: *Her parents **fear for** her **safety** (= worry that she may not be safe).*

fearful /ˈfɪəfəl/ **adj** formal **1** frightened or worried: [+ of + doing sth] *Many women are fearful of travelling alone.* **2** [always before noun] UK very bad: *Nigel has a fearful temper.* • **fearfully adv**

fearless /ˈfɪələs/ **adj** not frightened of anything: *a fearless fighter* • **fearlessly adv**

fearsome /ˈfɪəsəm/ **adj** very frightening: *a fearsome opponent*

feasible /ˈfiːzəbl/ **adj** possible to do: *a feasible plan* ◦ [+ to do sth] *It may be feasible to clone human beings, but is it ethical?* • **feasibility** /ˌfiːzəˈbɪləti/ **noun** [U]

feast[1] /fiːst/ **noun** [C] a large meal, especially to celebrate something special: *a wedding feast*

feast[2] /fiːst/ **verb**

PHRASAL VERB **feast on sth** to eat a lot of food and enjoy it very much: *We feasted on fried chicken, ice cream, and chocolate cake.*

feat /fiːt/ **noun 1** [C] an act or achievement that shows great skill or strength: *The Eiffel Tower is a remarkable **feat of** engineering.* **2 be no mean feat** used when you want to emphasize that an act or achievement is very difficult: *Learning to ski at 60 is no mean feat!*

feather /ˈfeðər/ **noun** [C] ⓑ one of the soft, light things that grow from and cover a bird's skin • **feathery adj** like feathers: *feathery leaves*

feature[1] /ˈfiːtʃər/ **noun** [C] **1 PART** ▷ ⓑ a typical quality, or important part of something: *This phone has several **new features**.* **2 FACE** ▷ ⓑ Someone's features are the parts of their face that you notice when you look at them: *His eyes are his **best feature**.* **3 NEWSPAPER** ▷ a special article in a newspaper or magazine, or a special television programme: *a double-page **feature on** global warming*

┌─────────────────────────────────────┐
│ 🗹 Word partners for **feature**   │
│   │
│ a **distinguishing/important/notable** feature • │
│ a **redeeming** feature • a feature **of** sth • a │
│ **new** feature   │
└─────────────────────────────────────┘

feature[2] /ˈfiːtʃər/ **verb** [T] ⓑ to include someone or something as an important part: *a new movie featuring Will Smith*

PHRASAL VERB **feature in sth** to be an important part of something

feature film noun [C] a film that is usually 90 or more minutes long

February /ˈfebruəri/ **noun** [C, U] (written abbreviation **Feb**) ⓐ the second month of the year

feces /ˈfiːsiːz/ **noun** [plural] US spelling of faeces

feckless /ˈfekləs/ **adj** A feckless person is no willing to work or take responsibility for thei actions.

fed /fed/ past of feed

federal /ˈfedərəl/ **adj** [always before noun] **1** rela ing to the central government, and not to th government of a region, of some countries suc as the United States: *the **federal governmen*** ◦ *a federal agency/employee* **2** A federal syster of government consists of a group of region that is controlled by a central government.

federal holiday noun [C] US (UK/US **nationa holiday**) a day when most people in a countr do not have to work

federalism /ˈfedərəlɪzəm/ **noun** [U] a politica system in which separate states are organize under a central government • **federalist nou** [C] someone who supports federalism

federation /ˌfedərˈeɪʃən/ **noun** [C] a group c organizations, countries, regions, etc that hav joined together to form a larger organization c government: *the International Tennis Federatior*

fed up adj [never before noun] informal ⓑ annoyed or bored by something that you hav experienced for too long: *I'm **fed up with** m job.*

fee /fiː/ **noun** [C] ⓑ an amount of money tha you pay to do something, to use something, c to get a service: *an entrance fee* ◦ *university fee*

feeble /ˈfiːbl/ **adj 1** extremely weak: *She becam too feeble to get out of bed.* **2** not very good c effective: *a **feeble argument/excuse*** • **feebl adv**

feed[1] /fiːd/ **verb** (**fed**) **1 GIVE FOOD** ▷ [T] ⓑ t give food to a person, group, or animal: *I fe Simone's cat while she was away.* **2 EAT FOOD** [I] If an animal or a baby feeds, it eats: *Th caterpillars **feed on** cabbage leaves.* **3 SUPPLY** [T] to supply something such as information to person or a machine, especially in a regular o continuous way: *We feed them false informatio about our plans.* → See also **breast-feed**

feed[2] /fiːd/ **noun 1** [U] food for animals that ar not kept as pets: *cattle/chicken feed* **2** [C] UK (U **feeding**) a meal for a baby or an animal: *He ha three feeds during the night.*

feedback /ˈfiːdbæk/ **noun** [U] ⓑ an opinio from someone about something that you hav done or made: *positive/negative **feedbac*** ◦ *We've had lots of **feedback on** these ne products **from** our customers.*

┌─────────────────────────────────────┐
│ 🗹 Word partners for **feedback**   │
│   │
│ **get/give/provide** feedback • **negative/posi** │
│ **tive** feedback • feedback **on** sth • feedback │
│ **from** sb   │
└─────────────────────────────────────┘

feel[1] /fiːl/ **verb** (**felt**) **1 EXPERIENCE** ▷ [I, T] ⓐ t experience an emotion or a physical feeling: *Yo shouldn't feel embarrassed about making mistake.* ◦ *I felt a sharp pain in my side when stood up.* ◦ *"Are you feeling better?" "Yes, thanks feel fine now."* **2 feel better/different/strange etc; feel like/as if** ⓑ If you describe the way place, situation, or object feels, you say how i seems to you, or what your experience of it is like: *It felt strange to see him again after so long.* ○ *The house feels empty without the children.* ○ *This shirt feels tight under my arms.* ○ *I feel as if I've known you for ages.* **3 feel like sb/sth** ⑤ to seem to be similar to a type of person, thing, or situation: *My feet feel like blocks of ice.* ○ *I felt like a fool when I saw what everyone else was wearing.* **4 OPINION** ▷ [I, T] ⑤ to think something or have an opinion: [+ (that)] *I feel that he's the best person for the job.* ○ *How do you feel strongly (= have strong opinions) about it?* **5 TOUCH** ▷ [I, T] ⑤ to touch something, especially with your hands, in order to examine it: *He felt her ankle to see if it was broken.* **6 feel like sth/doing sth** ⑤ to want something, or want to do something: *I feel like some chocolate.* ○ *Jane felt like crying.* **7 BE AWARE** ▷ [T] ⑤ to be aware of something: *You could feel the tension in the room.* ○ *I could feel them watching me.* → See Note at **fall¹** → See also **feel free¹, feel the pinch², be/feel under the weather¹**

PHRASAL VERB **feel for sb** to feel sorry for someone because they are very unhappy, or in a difficult situation

feel² /fiːl/ **noun 1** [no plural] the way that something seems, or feels when you touch it: *I love the feel of silk against my skin.* ○ *His art has a very modern feel to it.* **2 a feel for sth** informal the ability to do something or use something well: *Once you get a feel for it, using the mouse is easy.* ○ *Claire has a real feel for this kind of work.*

feel-good /'fiːlɡʊd/ **adj** causing happy feelings about life: *a feel-good story*

feeling /'fiːlɪŋ/ **noun 1 EMOTION** ▷ [C, U] ⑤ emotion: *guilty feelings* ○ *a feeling of joy/sadness* ○ *Her performance was completely lacking in feeling.* **2 PHYSICAL** ▷ [C, U] ⑤ the way something feels physically: *I had a tingling feeling in my fingers.* ○ *Pablo lost all feeling (= could not feel anything) in his feet.* **3 OPINION** ▷ [C] ⑤ an opinion or belief: *My feeling is that we should wait until they come back.* **4 have/get a feeling (that)...** ⑤ to think that something is likely: *I had a feeling he'd be there.* ○ *I get the feeling that he doesn't like me.* **5 bad/ill feeling** a situation in which people are upset or angry with each other

➕ Other ways of saying **feeling**

A very common alternative to the noun 'feeling' is **emotion**:
*He finds it hard to express his **emotions**.*
The nouns **pang** or **stab** are sometimes used to describe a sudden, strong, bad feeling:
*Amelia felt a sharp **pang** of jealousy when she saw her.*
*He felt a **stab** of regret as he looked at his son.*
A small amount of a sad feeling is often described as a **tinge**:
*It was with a **tinge** of sadness that she finally said goodbye.*

feelings /'fiːlɪŋz/ **noun 1** ⑤ [plural] Your feelings are your beliefs and emotions: *You can't hide*

your feelings from me. **2 hurt sb's feelings** ⑤ to make someone feel unhappy

🗒 Word partners for **feelings**

express/hide/show your feelings ● hurt sb's feelings ● mixed/strong feelings

feet /fiːt/ plural of foot

feign /feɪn/ **verb** [T] formal If you feign an emotion, illness, etc, you pretend to have it: *He feigned illness to avoid having to work.*

feisty /'faɪsti/ **adj** active, confident, and determined: *a feisty young woman*

feline /'fiːlaɪn/ **adj** relating to cats, or like a cat

fell¹ /fel/ **verb** [T] **1** to cut down a tree **2** to knock someone down: *He was felled with a single punch.*

fell² /fel/ past tense of fall

fella (also **feller**) /'felə/ **noun** [C] informal a man

fellow¹ /'feləʊ/ **noun** [C] **1 MAN** ▷ old-fashioned a man: *a big fellow with broad shoulders* **2 COLLEGE** ▷ someone whose job is to teach or study a particular subject at some colleges or universities: *She's a research fellow at St Peter's college.* **3 MEMBER** ▷ a member of an official organization for a particular subject or job

fellow² /'feləʊ/ **adj fellow countrymen/students, etc** ⑤ used to describe people who share your interests or situation: *She's earned enormous respect from her fellow artists.*

fellowship /'feləʊʃɪp/ **noun 1 JOB** ▷ [C] a job teaching or studying a particular subject at some colleges or universities: *a research fellowship at Harvard* **2 FEELING** ▷ [U] a friendly feeling among people **3 GROUP** ▷ [C] a group of people who share the same interests or beliefs

felon /'felən/ **noun** [C] someone who is guilty of a serious crime in the US: *a convicted felon*

felony /'feləni/ **noun** [C, U] a serious crime in the US: *to commit a felony*

felt¹ /felt/ **noun** [U] a soft, thick cloth that is made from wool, hair, or fur that has been pressed together

felt² /felt/ past of feel

felt-tip 'pen noun [C] a pen with a point made of soft material, usually with brightly coloured ink for colouring pictures

female¹ /'fiːmeɪl/ **adj** ⑤ belonging to or relating to women, or to the sex that can produce eggs or have babies: *a female athlete/employee* ○ *a female butterfly/elephant* ○ *Is it male or female?*

female² /'fiːmeɪl/ **noun** [C] ⑤ a person or animal that belongs to the sex that can produce eggs or have babies: *Our dog's just had puppies – three males and two females.*

feminine /'femɪnɪn/ **adj 1** showing qualities that people generally think are typical of women: *a feminine voice* ○ *feminine beauty* **2** in some languages, belonging to a group of nouns or adjectives that have the same grammatical behaviour. The other groups are 'masculine' and 'neuter'.

femininity /ˌfemɪ'nɪnəti/ **noun** [U] qualities that people generally think are typical of women

feminism /'femɪnɪzᵊm/ **noun** [U] the belief that women should have the same economic, social, and political rights as men • **feminist noun** [C] someone who supports feminism: *a radical feminist* • **feminist adj** *feminist literature*

fence¹ /fens/ **noun** [C] 🔵 a wood, wire, or metal structure that divides or goes around an area: *a garden/electric fence*

IDIOM **sit on the fence** to wait before you choose between two possibilities

→ See also **picket fence**

fence² /fens/ **verb** [I] to take part in the sport of fencing

PHRASAL VERBS **fence sth in** to build a fence around an area • **fence sth off** to separate one area from another by building a fence

fencing /'fensɪŋ/ **noun** [U] **1** the sport of fighting with thin swords (= weapons like long knives) **2** fences, or the material that is used to make them

fend /fend/ **verb**

PHRASAL VERBS **fend for yourself** to take care of yourself without help • **fend sb/sth off** to defend yourself against someone or something that is attacking or annoying you: *They managed to fend off their attackers with rocks and sticks.*

fender /'fendəʳ/ **noun** [C] **1** CAR ▷ US (UK **wing**) one of the parts at each corner of a car above the wheels **2** BICYCLE ▷ US (UK **mudguard**) a curved piece of metal or plastic fixed above a wheel of a bicycle or motorcycle to prevent water or dirt from hitting the legs of the person who is riding it **3** FIREPLACE ▷ UK a low, metal structure around an open fireplace that stops the coal or wood from falling out

feng shui /fʌŋ'ʃweɪ/ **noun** [U] an ancient Chinese belief that the way your house is built and the way that you arrange objects affects your success, health, and happiness

fennel /'fenᵊl/ **noun** [U] a plant whose base can be eaten, and whose leaves and seeds are used as a spice in cooking

ferment¹ /fə'ment/ **verb** [I, T] If food or drink ferments, or if you ferment it, the sugar in it changes into alcohol because of a chemical process: *The wine ferments in barrels.* • **fermentation** /ˌfɜːmen'teɪʃᵊn/ **noun** [U]

ferment² /'fɜːment/ **noun** [U] formal excitement or disagreement caused by change or a difficult situation

fern /fɜːn/ **noun** [C] a green plant with long stems, narrow leaves like feathers, and no flowers

ferocious /fə'rəʊʃəs/ **adj** extremely angry,

fern

violent, or forceful: *a ferocious dog* ∘ *a ferociou* *attack* • **ferociously adv**

ferocity /fə'rɒsəti/ **noun** [U] extreme violence or force: *a storm of incredible ferocity*

ferret¹ /'ferɪt/ **noun** [C] a small animal with long, thin body that is sometimes used to hur rabbits

ferret² /'ferɪt/ **verb**

PHRASAL VERB **ferret sth out** to find somethin after searching carefully for it

Ferris wheel /'ferɪsˌwiːl/ **noun** [C] an entertai ment consisting of a large wheel that turn slowly with seats for people to sit in

ferry¹ /'feri/ **noun** [C] 🔵 a boat that regularl carries passengers and vehicles across an area c water: *a car/passenger ferry*

ferry² /'feri/ **verb** [T] to regularly carry passer gers or goods from one place to another in vehicle

fertile /'fɜːtaɪl/ US /'fɜːrtᵊl/ **adj 1** Fertile land c soil produces a lot of healthy plants. **2** If peopl or animals are fertile, they are able to hav babies. **3 fertile ground (for sth)** a situation c place where an idea, activity, etc is likely t succeed **4 a fertile imagination** If someone ha a fertile imagination, they have lots of interes ing and unusual ideas. • **fertility** /fə'tɪləti/ **nou** [U]

fertilize (also UK **-ise**) /'fɜːtɪlaɪz/ **verb** [T] **1** t cause an egg to start to develop into a youn animal or baby by combining it with a male cel *Once an egg is fertilized it becomes an embryo* **2** to put a natural or chemical substance on lan in order to make plants grow well • **fertilizatio** /ˌfɜːtɪlaɪ'zeɪʃᵊn/ **noun** [U]

fertilizer (also UK **-iser**) /'fɜːtɪlaɪzəʳ/ **noun** [C, U natural or chemical substance that you put o land in order to make plants grow well

fervent /'fɜːvᵊnt/ **adj** showing sincere an enthusiastic beliefs or feelings: *a fervent sup porter of animal rights* • **fervently adv**

fervour UK (US **fervor**) /'fɜːrvəʳ/ **noun** [l extremely strong beliefs or feelings: *religiou patriotic fervour*

fess /fes/ **verb**

PHRASAL VERB **fess up** informal to admit that yo have done something bad: *He eventually fesse up to having spilt coffee on it.*

fest /fest/ **noun a beer/film/jazz, etc fest** special event where people can enjoy a par cular activity or thing

fester /'festəʳ/ **verb** [I] **1** If a bad feeling c situation festers, it becomes worse over a perio of time: *Hatred between the two groups h festered for years.* **2** If an injury festers, becomes infected: *a festering wound*

festival /'festɪvᵊl/ **noun** [C] **1** 🔵 a series o special events, performances, etc that ofte takes place over several days: *a dance/musi festival* ∘ *the Berlin Film Festival* **2** 🔵 a speci day or period when people celebrate somethin especially a religious event: *the Jewish festival c Hanukkah*

festive /'festɪv/ **adj** happy and enjoyable because people are celebrating: *a festive mood/occasion* ○ *What are you doing for the festive season* (= Christmas)? • **festivity** /fes'tɪvəti/ **noun** [U] a period when people are happy and celebrating

festivities /fes'tɪvətiz/ **noun** [plural] events that people organize in order to celebrate something

festoon /fes'tuːn/ **verb** [T] to cover something with objects, especially decorations: [often passive] *The balcony was festooned with flags and ribbons.*

fetch /fetʃ/ **verb** [T] **1** ⑤ to go to a place to get something or someone and bring them back: *Can you fetch my glasses from the bedroom?* **2** If something fetches a particular amount of money, it is sold for that amount: *The painting is expected to fetch $50,000 in the auction.*

fetching /'fetʃɪŋ/ **adj** attractive: *That scarf looks rather fetching on you.*

fête /feɪt/ **noun** [C] **1** UK an event that is held outside and includes competitions, games, and things for sale: *a village fête* **2** US a special event to celebrate someone or something • **fête** **verb** [T] to publicly celebrate someone, often by having a special party: [often passive] *She was fêted by audiences all over the world.*

fetish /'fetɪʃ/ **noun** [C] **1** a strong sexual interest in something unusual: *a rubber fetish* **2** something that someone spends too much time thinking about or doing: *a fetish for cleanliness*

fetus /'fiːtəs/ **noun** [C] US spelling of foetus (= a young human or animal that is still developing inside its mother) • **fetal** /'fiːt³l/ **adj** US spelling of foetal

feud /fjuːd/ **noun** [C] a serious and sometimes violent argument between two people or groups that continues for a long period • **feud** **verb** [I] *The families have been feuding for years.*

🗹 Word partners for **feud**

a **bitter/long-running** feud • a **family** feud • a feud **with** sb/**between** sb and sb

---

feudal /'fjuːd³l/ **adj** relating to a social system in the past in which people worked and fought for a lord (= a man of high rank) in exchange for land and protection • **feudalism** **noun** [U]

fever /'fiːvə r/ **noun** [C, U] ⑤ a high body temperature because you are sick: *a high/slight fever* **2** [U] a situation in which people are very excited about something: *Election fever has gripped the nation.* → See also **glandular fever**, **hay fever**

🗹 Word partners for **fever**

develop/have/run a fever • a **high** fever

---

feverish /'fiːv³rɪʃ/ **adj 1** having a fever: *I feel a bit feverish.* **2** Feverish activity is done quickly, often because of excitement or fear: *The rescuers worked at a feverish pace.* • **feverishly** **adv** *They worked feverishly to put out the fire.*

fever ˌpitch **noun** reach fever pitch If emotions reach fever pitch, they become so strong that they are difficult to control.

few /fjuː/ **quantifier 1** a few ⓐ some, or a small number of: *It'll be here in a few minutes.* ○ *I met a few of the other employees at my interview.* **2** quite a few/a good few ⓐ quite a large number of: *Quite a few people have had the same problem.* **3** ⓑ not many, or only a small number of: *We get few complaints.* • *Few of the children can read or write yet.* ○ *Very few people can afford to pay those prices.* → See Note at **less** **4** few and far between not happening or existing very often: *Opportunities like this are few and far between.*

fiancé /fi'ɑːnseɪ/ **noun** [C] A woman's fiancé is the man that she has promised to marry.

fiancée /fi'ɑːnseɪ/ **noun** [C] A man's fiancée is the woman that he has promised to marry.

fiasco /fi'æskəʊ/ **noun** [C] a complete failure, especially one that embarrasses people: *My last dinner party was a complete fiasco.*

fib /fɪb/ **noun** [C] informal a small lie that is not very important: *Don't tell fibs.* • **fib** **verb** [I] (**fibbing, fibbed**) to say something that is not true

fibre UK (US **fiber**) /'faɪbə r/ **noun 1** CLOTH ▷ [C, U] cloth made from thin threads twisted together: *Man-made fibres like nylon are easy to wash.* **2** THIN THREAD ▷ [C] one of the thin threads that forms a substance such as cloth: *The fibres are woven into fabric.* **3** FOOD ▷ [U] the substance in plants that cannot be digested and helps food pass through your body: *Broccoli is a good source of fibre.* **4** BODY ▷ [C] a structure like a thread in your body: *muscle/nerve fibres*

fibreglass UK (US **fiberglass**) /'faɪbəglɑːs/ **noun** [U] a strong, light material made by twisting together glass or plastic threads

fickle /'fɪkl/ **adj** Someone who is fickle often changes their opinion about things.

fiction /'fɪkʃ³n/ **noun 1** [U] ⑤ literature and stories about imaginary people or events: *What's the best-selling children's fiction title?* → Opposite **nonfiction 2** [U, no plural] something that is not true or real → See also **science fiction**

fictional /'fɪkʃ³n³l/ **adj** existing only in fiction: *a fictional character*

fictitious /fɪk'tɪʃəs/ **adj** invented and not real or true: *a fictitious name*

fiddle¹ /'fɪdl/ **verb** [T] UK informal to change something dishonestly in order to get money: *She was fired for fiddling her travel expenses.*

PHRASAL VERB **fiddle (about/around) with sth** **1** to touch or move things with your fingers because you are nervous or bored: *Stop fiddling with your hair!* **2** to make small changes to something to try to make it work: *He fiddled with the wires to get the radio working again.*

fiddle² /'fɪdl/ **noun** [C] **1** informal a violin (= a wooden musical instrument with strings) **2** UK a dishonest way to get money: *a tax fiddle*

fiddler /'fɪdlə r/ **noun** [C] someone who plays the violin (= a wooden musical instrument with strings)

fiddly /'fɪdli/ **adj** UK difficult to do because the parts involved are small: *Repairing a watch is very fiddly.*

F

fidelity /fɪˈdeləti/ **noun** [U] loyalty, especially to a sexual partner → Opposite **infidelity**

fidget /ˈfɪdʒɪt/ **verb** [I] to keep making small movements with your hands or feet because you are nervous or bored: *She fidgeted all the way through the job interview.* • **fidgety** adj

field¹ /ˈfiːld/ **noun 1 LAND** ▷ [C] **A2** an area of land used for growing crops or keeping animals: *a wheat field* ∘ *a field of cows* **2 SPORT** ▷ [C] **B1** an area of grass where you can play a sport: *a football field* **3 AREA OF STUDY** ▷ [C] **B2** an area of study or activity: *He's an expert in the field of biochemistry.* **4 IN RACE/BUSINESS** ▷ [no plural] the people who are competing in a race, activity, or business: *We lead the field in genetic research.* **5 a gas/oil field** an area of land containing gas or oil **6 a gravitational/magnetic field** an area affected by a particular physical force → See also **paddy field, playing field**

field² /ˈfiːld/ **verb 1** [I, T] to try to catch or stop a ball after it has been hit in a game such as cricket or baseball: *Are we fielding or batting?* **2** [T] to send out a team or player to play in a game: *Brazil fielded a strong team in the World Cup.* **3 field questions/telephone calls** to answer or deal with questions/telephone calls

field day noun have a field day to have the opportunity to do a lot of something you want to do, especially to criticize someone: *The press had a field day when they found out about the scandal.*

fielder /ˈfiːldər/ **noun** [C] a player who tries to catch or stop the ball in games such as cricket or baseball

field hockey noun [U] US (UK/US **hockey**) a team game played on grass where you hit a small ball with a long, curved stick

field marshal UK (US **field marshal**) **noun** [C] an officer of the highest rank in the British army

fiend /fiːnd/ **noun** [C] **1** an evil or cruel person **2** someone who is very interested in a particular thing

fiendish /ˈfiːndɪʃ/ **adj 1** evil or cruel: *a fiendish attack* **2** very difficult or complicated: *a fiendish crossword* • **fiendishly** adv mainly UK extremely: *fiendishly clever/difficult*

fierce /fɪəs/ **adj 1** **B2** violent or angry: *a fierce attack* ∘ *a fierce dog* **2** **B2** very strong or powerful: *fierce winds/storms* ∘ *There is fierce competition between car manufacturers.* • **fiercely** adv

fiery /ˈfaɪəri/ **adj 1** showing strong emotion, especially anger: *a fiery temper* **2** bright or burning like a fire: *a fiery sunset*

fifteen /fɪfˈtiːn/ **A1** the number 15 • **fifteenth** 15th written as a word

fifth¹ /fɪfθ/ **A2** 5th written as a word

fifth² /fɪfθ/ **noun** [C] **B1** one of five equal parts of something; ⅕

fifty /ˈfɪfti/ **1** **A2** the number 50 **2 the fifties** the years from 1950 to 1959 **3 be in your fifties** to be aged between 50 and 59 • **fiftieth** 50th written as a word

fifty-fifty /ˌfɪftiˈfɪfti/ **adj, adv** informal **1** shared equally between two people: *Let's divide the bill*

fifty-fifty. **2 a fifty-fifty chance** If something has a fifty-fifty chance, it is equally likely to happen or not to happen: *We have a fifty-fifty chance of winning the game.*

fig /fɪg/ **noun** [C] a dark, sweet fruit with lots of seeds, that is often eaten dried

fig. written abbreviation for figure (= a picture or drawing in a book or document, usually with a number) : *See fig. 1.*

fight¹ /faɪt/ **verb (fought) 1 USE FORCE** ▷ [I, T] **B1** When people fight, they use physical force to try to defeat each other: *Two men were arrested for fighting outside a bar.* ∘ *Sam's always fighting with his little brother.* **2 JOIN WAR** ▷ [I, T] **B2** take part in a war: *Millions of young men fought in World War I.* **3 ARGUE** ▷ [I] **B2** to argue: *We've got to stop fighting in front of the children.* **4 TRY TO STOP** ▷ [I, T] **B2** to try hard to stop something bad happening: *He fought against racism.* ∘ *New measures have been introduced to fight crime.* **5 TRY TO ACHIEVE** ▷ [I] **B2** to try hard to achieve something you want or think is right: *They are fighting for their freedom.* ∘ [+ to do sth] *He had to fight very hard to keep his job.* **6 be fighting for your life** to be trying very hard to stay alive when you are very sick or badly injured → See also **fight a losing battle¹**

PHRASAL VERB **fight back** to defend yourself when someone or something attacks you or causes problems for you

fight² /faɪt/ **noun** [C] **1 PHYSICAL FORCE** ▷ **B1** an occasion when people use physical force to hurt or attack others: *He's always getting into fights.* **2 EFFORT** ▷ **B2** a determined effort to achieve or stop something: *She was very active in the fight against drugs.* ∘ *Join us in our fight for freedom.* ∘ [+ to do sth] *the fight to save the whale.* **3 ARGUMENT** ▷ **B2** an argument: *I don't want to have a fight over this.* **4 SPORT** ▷ a boxing competition

📓 Word partners for **fight**

a fight with sb • have/get into/pick/start a fight • lose/win a fight

fighter /ˈfaɪtər/ **noun** [C] **1** (also **fighter plane**) a fast military aircraft that can attack other aircraft: *a fighter pilot* **2** someone who fights in a war or as a sport

fighting /ˈfaɪtɪŋ/ **noun** [U] **B2** the activity of fighting, usually in a war: *Thousands of civilians were killed in the fighting.*

figment /ˈfɪgmənt/ **noun a figment of sb's imagination** something that someone believes is real but that only exists in their imagination

figurative /ˈfɪgjərətɪv/ **adj 1** A figurative meaning of a word or phrase is a more imaginative meaning developed from the usual meaning. **2** Figurative art shows people, places, or things in a similar way to how they look in real life. • **figuratively** adv

figure¹ /ˈfɪgər/ **noun** [C] **1 SYMBOL** ▷ **B1** a symbol for a number: *Write down the amount in words and figures.* ∘ *He's now being paid a six-figure salary.* **2 single/double, etc figure** numbers from 0 to 9/numbers from 10 to 99 etc **3 AMOUNT** ▷ **B1** a number that expresses an amount, especially in official documents: *Government figures show a rise in unemployment.* **4 TYPE OF PERSON** ▷ **B2** a particular type of person, often someone important or famous: *a mysterious figure ∘ Lincoln was a major figure in American politics.* **5 PERSON** ▷ **B2** a person that you cannot see clearly: *I could see two figures in the distance.* **6 BODY SHAPE** ▷ **B1** the shape of someone's body, usually an attractive shape: *She's got a good figure for her age.* **7 PICTURE** ▷ (written abbreviation **fig.**) a picture or drawing in a book or document, usually with a number: *Look at the graph shown in Figure 2.* → See also **father figure**

> ☑ Word partners for **figure**
>
> a key/leading/major/prominent figure • a public figure

figure² /ˈfɪɡəʳ/ verb **1** [I] to be a part of something, or to appear in something: *Love figures in most pop songs.* **2** [T] to decide something after thinking about it: [+ (that)] *I figured that it was time to tell her the truth.* **3 that/it figures** informal something you say when you expected something to happen: *"I've run out of money, Mum." "That figures."*

PHRASAL VERB **figure sth/sb out** **B2** to finally understand something or someone after a lot of thought: [+ question word] *I never could figure out what she saw in him.*

figurehead /ˈfɪɡəhed/ **noun** [C] a leader who has no real power

figure of speech **noun** [C] (plural **figures of speech**) words that are used together in an imaginative way to mean something different from their usual meaning

file¹ /faɪl/ **noun 1 COMPUTER** ▷ [C] **A2** a piece of text, a picture, or a computer program stored on a computer: *Do you want to **download** all these files?* **2 INFORMATION** ▷ [C] **A2** a collection of information and documents about someone or something: *The school **keeps files on** all its pupils.* **3 CONTAINER** ▷ [C] a box or folded piece of thick paper used to put documents in: *He keeps all his bank statements in a file.* → See colour picture **The Office** on page Centre 5 → See colour picture **The Classroom** on page Centre 6 **4 on file** If information is on file, it is recorded and stored somewhere. **5 TOOL** ▷ [C] a small tool with a rough edge that is used to make a surface smooth: *a nail file* **6 in single file** in a line with one person following the other → See also **the rank¹ and file**

> ☑ Word partners for **file**
>
> 1 close/create/download/open/save a file
> 2 hold/keep a file on sb/sth

file² /faɪl/ **verb 1 PAPER** ▷ [T] (also **file away**) to put documents into an ordered system of boxes or files where you can easily find them again: *She filed all her tax returns under T.* **2 LAW** ▷ [I, T] to officially state that you are going to take someone to court: *The police **filed charges** against the suspect. ∘ His wife's **filing for**

divorce. **3 RUB** ▷ [T] to rub something with a rough tool in order to make it smooth **4 file along/into/through, etc** to walk somewhere in a line, one behind the other: *The audience slowly filed back to their seats.*

file ex,tension **noun** [C] a dot followed by three letters, such as .doc or .jpg, that forms the end of the name of a computer document and shows what sort of document it is

filename /ˈfaɪlneɪm/ **noun** [C] a name given to a computer file

file ,sharing **noun** [U] the activity of putting a file onto a special place on your computer so that many other people can copy it, look at it, or use it by using the Internet → See Study Page **The Web and the Internet** on page Centre 36

filet /fɪˈleɪ/ **noun** [C] another US spelling of fillet (= a piece of meat or fish with the bones taken out)

filing ,cabinet **noun** [C] (also US **file ,cabinet**) a piece of office furniture with deep drawers for storing documents → See colour picture **The Office** on page Centre 5

fill¹ /fɪl/ **verb 1 MAKE FULL** ▷ [I, T] (also **fill up**) **A2** to make a container or space full, or to become full: *He filled the bucket with water. ∘ I made a drink while the bath was filling.* **2 TAKE SPACE** ▷ [T] **B1** If people or things fill a place, there are a lot of them in it: *The streets were **filled with** tourists. ∘ Dark clouds filled the sky.* **3 BE NOTICEABLE** ▷ [T] **B1** If light, sound, or a smell fills a place, you can easily notice it: *The smell of smoke filled the room.* **4 fill sb with anger/joy/pride, etc** **B2** to make someone feel very angry/happy/proud, etc: *The thought of losing him filled her with fear.* **5 fill a post/position/vacancy** **B2** to give someone a new job: *They still haven't filled the vacancy.* **6 fill a need/gap/demand** to provide something that people need or want

PHRASAL VERBS **fill sth in/out** **A2** to write the necessary information on an official document: *to **fill in** a form/questionnaire* • **fill (sth) up** **B1** to become full, or to make something become full: *The restaurant soon filled up with people.*

fill² /fɪl/ **noun your fill** as much of something as you want or need: *I've **had my fill of** living in the city.*

fillet (also US **filet**) /ˈfɪlɪt/ ⓤⓢ /fɪˈleɪ/ **noun** [C] a piece of meat or fish with the bones taken out

filling

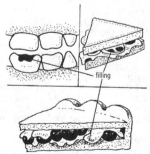

filling

filling¹ /ˈfɪlɪŋ/ **noun 1** [C, U] food that is put

inside things such as cakes, pastry, pieces of bread, etc: *What sort of filling do you want in your sandwich?* **2** [C] a hard substance that fills a hole in a tooth

filling² /'fɪlɪŋ/ **adj** Food that is filling makes your stomach feel full: *This soup is very filling.*

filling ˌstation **noun** [C] a petrol station (= place where you can buy fuel for your car)

film¹ /fɪlm/ **noun 1 PICTURES** ▷ [C] (also **movie**) 🅐1 a story shown in moving pictures, shown at the cinema or on television: *'Titanic' was one of the most popular Hollywood **films** ever **made**.* **2 MATERIAL** ▷ [C, U] special thin plastic used for making photographs or moving pictures, or a length of this: *I need to buy another **roll of film**.* **3 LAYER** ▷ [no plural] a thin layer of something on a surface: *A thick film of dust covered the furniture.*

> ✓ Word partners for **film**
>
> make a film • a film about sb/sth • in a film • a horror film • a classic film • the film industry

film² /fɪlm/ **verb** [I, T] 🅑1 to record moving pictures with a camera, usually to make a film for the cinema or television: *Most of the scenes were filmed in a studio.* • **filming noun** [U]

film-maker UK (US **filmmaker**) /'fɪlmmeɪkər/ **noun** [C] 🅑1 someone who makes films for the cinema or television

ˈfilm ˌstar **noun** [C] a famous cinema actor or actress

filter¹ /'fɪltər/ **verb 1** [T] to pass a liquid or gas through a piece of equipment in order to remove solid pieces or other substances: *The water was filtered to remove any impurities.* **2 filter down/in/through, etc** to gradually appear or become known: *News is filtering in of an earthquake in Mexico.*

PHRASAL VERB filter sth out to remove a particular substance from a liquid or gas. *They use special equipment to filter out the dust.*

filter² /'fɪltər/ **noun** [C] a piece of equipment that you pass a liquid or gas through in order to remove particular substances: *a coffee filter*

filth /fɪlθ/ **noun** [U] **1** thick and unpleasant dirt: *His clothes were covered in filth and mud.* **2** offensive language or pictures, usually relating to sex

filthy /'fɪlθi/ **adj 1** extremely dirty: *Wash your hands, they're filthy!* **2** rude or offensive: *filthy language/jokes* ○ *Smoking is a **filthy habit**.*

fin /fɪn/ **noun** [C] a thin, triangular part on a fish, which helps it to swim

final¹ /'faɪnəl/ **adj 1** [always before noun] 🅐2 last in a series or coming at the end of something: *the final paragraph* ○ *They scored a goal in the final minute.* **2** If a decision, agreement, or answer is final, it will not be changed or discussed any more: *The committee's decision is final.* → See also **the final nail¹ in the coffin, the final/last straw**

final² /'faɪnəl/ **noun 1** 🅑1 [C] the last part of a competition to decide which person or team will be the winner: *the European Cup Final* ○ *The*

finals will be shown on TV. **2 finals** exams taken at the end of a university course

finale /fɪ'nɑːli/ **noun** [C] the last part of a show, event, or piece of music

finalist /'faɪnəlɪst/ **noun** [C] a person or team in the last part of a competition

finalize (also UK **-ise**) /'faɪnəlaɪz/ **verb** [T] to make a final and certain decision about a plan, date, etc: *to **finalize arrangements/details***

finally /'faɪnəli/ **adv 1 AFTER A LONG TIME** ▷ 🅐 after a long time or some difficulty: *After months of looking, he finally found a job.* **2 LAST POINT** ▷ 🅑1 used to introduce the last point or idea: *Finally, I'd like to thank everyone for coming this evening.* **3 CERTAINLY** ▷ in a way that will not be changed: *The date of the wedding hasn't been finally decided yet.*

finance¹ /'faɪnæns/ **noun 1** [U] 🅑2 the control of how large amounts of money should be spent **2** [U] the money that is needed to support a business: *Who **put up** the **finance** for the project?* **3 sb's finances** 🅑2 the money that a person, company, or country has: *You must learn how to manage your own finances.*

finance² /'faɪnæns/ **verb** [T] 🅑2 to provide the money needed to do something: *Who's financing the project?*

financial /faɪ'nænʃəl/ **adj** 🅑1 relating to money or how money is managed: *a **financial adviser*** ○ *She's having some financial difficulties at the moment.* • **financially adv** 🅑2 *Many students are still financially dependent on their parents.*

finch /fɪntʃ/ **noun** [C] a small singing bird with a short beak

> ➕ Other ways of saying **find**
>
> A very common alternative to 'find' is the verb **discover**:
>
> *The victim's wallet was **discovered** in a ditch.*
>
> *I finally **discovered** the letters in a drawer.*
>
> If someone finds the exact position of someone or something, in formal situations the verb **locate** is sometimes used:
>
> *Police are still trying to **locate** the suspect.*
>
> If someone finds something that has been secret or hidden, then the verbs **uncover** or **unearth** are sometimes used:
>
> *Reporters **uncovered/unearthed** evidence of corruption.*
>
> The phrasal verbs **come across** and **stumble across/on** are used when someone finds something by chance:
>
> *I **stumbled on** these photographs when I was cleaning out my desk.*
>
> *We **came across** a lovely little restaurant in the village.*
>
> If someone finds something or someone after looking carefully in different places, you can use the verb **trace** or the phrasal verb **track down**:
>
> *Police have so far failed to **trace/track down** the missing woman.*

find¹ /faɪnd/ **verb** [T] (**found**) **1 DISCOVER WHEN SEARCHING** ▷ 🅐1 to discover something or someone that you have been searching for: *I can't find my glasses and I've looked everywhere.* ∘ *Police found the missing girl at a London railway station.* ∘ [+ two objects] *Has he found himself a place to live yet?* **2 DISCOVER BY CHANCE** ▷ **A2** to discover something or someone by chance: *The body was found by a man walking his dog.* **3 BECOME AWARE** ▷ **B1** to become aware that something exists, or has happened: *I came home to find that my cat had had kittens.* **4 find the energy/money/time, etc** to have or get enough energy/money/time, etc to do something: *Where do you find the energy to do all these things?* **5 find sb/sth easy/boring/funny, etc** **B1** to think or feel a particular way about someone or something: *I still find exams very stressful.* **6 find yourself somewhere/doing sth** **B2** to become aware that you have gone somewhere or done something without intending to: *I suddenly found myself making everyone's lunch.* **7 be found** **B2** to exist or be present somewhere: *Vitamin C is found in oranges and other citrus fruit.* **8 find sb guilty/not guilty** to judge that someone is guilty or not guilty in a law court: [often passive] *She was **found guilty of** murder.*

PHRASAL VERB **find (sth) out** **A2** to get information about something, or to learn a fact for the first time: *I must find out the train times.* ∘ [+ question word] *Peter was shocked when he found out what we had done.* → See Note at **know¹**

find² /faɪnd/ **noun** [C] something or someone valuable, interesting, or useful that you discover: [usually singular] *This hotel was a real find.*

finding /ˈfaɪndɪŋ/ **noun** [C] a piece of information that has been discovered as a result of an official study: [usually plural] *The findings of this research will be published next year.*

fine¹ /faɪn/ **adj 1 WELL** ▷ **A1** well, healthy, or happy: *"How are you?" "I'm **fine thanks**. And you?"* ∘ *I had a cold last week, but I'm fine now.* **2 GOOD** ▷ **A2** good or good enough: *"Is the soup hot enough?" "Yes, it's fine."* **3 EXCELLENT** ▷ **B2** excellent, or of very good quality: *fine wines* ∘ *He's a fine musician.* **4 (that's) fine** **A1** used to agree with a suggestion, plan, decision, etc: *"Shall we meet at 8 o'clock?" "Yes, that's **fine by me**."* **5 THIN** ▷ thin or made of very small pieces: *fine, brown hair* ∘ *fine sand* **6 SUNNY** ▷ mainly UK **B1** sunny and not raining: *If it's fine, we could have a picnic.* **7 the finer details/points, etc of sth** the more detailed or more difficult parts of an argument, idea, etc

fine² /faɪn/ **adv** informal **B2** very well or without any problems: *"How did your exam go?" "It went fine thanks."*

IDIOM **cut it/things fine** to leave yourself only just enough time to do something: *Twenty minutes to get to the station? That's cutting it a bit fine!*

fine³ /faɪn/ **verb** [T] **B2** to make someone pay an amount of money as a punishment for breaking a law or rule: [often passive] *The company was **fined** £60,000 **for** air pollution.*

fine⁴ /faɪn/ **noun** [C] **B1** an amount of money that you must pay for breaking a law or rule: *a **parking fine*** ∘ *The court gave her two weeks to **pay** the **fine**.*

> **☑ Word partners for fine**
>
> face/get/receive a fine • pay a fine • a heavy/hefty/stiff fine • a parking fine

finely /ˈfaɪnli/ **adv 1** **B2** into small pieces: *Finely chop the garlic.* **2** very exactly: *a finely tuned machine*

finger¹ /ˈfɪŋɡər/ **noun** [C] **A2** one of the five, long, separate parts at the end of your hand, including your thumb → See colour picture **The Body** on page Centre 13

IDIOMS **have green fingers** UK (US **have a green thumb**) to be good at gardening and making plants grow well • **keep your fingers crossed** informal to hope that things will happen in the way that you want them to: *Let's keep our fingers crossed that it doesn't rain.* • **not lift a finger** informal to not help someone do something, usually because you are too lazy: *He never lifts a finger to help with the housework.* • **put your finger on sth** to understand exactly why a situation is the way it is: *Something was wrong, but I couldn't put my finger on it.* • **snap your fingers** (also UK **click your fingers**) to press your thumb and middle finger together until the finger hits your hand and makes a short sound

→ See also **index finger**

finger² /ˈfɪŋɡər/ **verb** [T] to touch or feel something with your fingers

fingernail /ˈfɪŋɡəneɪl/ **noun** [C] **B2** the hard, thin part on the top of the end of your finger

fingerprint /ˈfɪŋɡəprɪnt/ **noun** [C] the mark made on something by the pattern of curved lines on the end of someone's finger: *The police found fingerprints all over the murder weapon.*

fingertip /ˈfɪŋɡətɪp/ **noun** [C] the end of your finger

IDIOM **at your fingertips** If you have something at your fingertips, you can get it and use it very easily: *He had all the information he needed at his fingertips.*

finish¹ /ˈfɪnɪʃ/ **verb 1 COMPLETE** ▷ [I, T] **A1** to complete something, or come to the end of an activity: *When I finish my homework, can I watch TV?* ∘ [+ doing sth] *Have you finished reading that book yet?* **2 END** ▷ [I] **A1** to end: *The meeting should finish at five o'clock.* **3 USE COMPLETELY** ▷ [T] (also **finish off**) **B1** to eat, drink, or use something completely: *They finished their drinks and left the bar.* **4 finish first/second, etc** to be in the first/second, etc winning position at the end of a race or competition

PHRASAL VERBS **finish sth off 1** **B2** to complete the last part of something that you are doing: *I have to finish off this report by Friday.* **2** to eat, drink, or use the last part of something: *Would you like to finish off the pizza?* • **finish up** mainly UK to finally be in a particular place, state, or situation, usually without having planned it: *I only went for two days, but finished up staying for a* week. • **finish with sth** to stop using or needing something: *Have you finished with the newspaper?* • **finish with sb** UK ⓔⓔ to stop having a romantic relationship with someone

---

➕ Other ways of saying **finish**

The verb **end** is a common alternative to 'finish' when it means 'stop':
What time does the concert end?

When someone finishes doing or making something, the verb **complete** is sometimes used:
Have you completed all the questions?
The project took 5 years to complete.

If someone finishes something quickly and easily, especially food or a piece of work, in informal situations you can use the phrasal verb **polish off**:
He's just polished off two huge bowls of pasta.

The phrasal verb **wind up** is sometimes used when an activity is gradually finishing:
It's time to wind up the game now.

---

finish² /ˈfɪnɪʃ/ **noun** [C] **1** ⓔⓔ the end of a race, or the last part of something: *a close/exciting finish* ∘ *I enjoyed the film from start to finish.* **2** the way the surface of something feels or looks: *The table has a smooth, shiny finish.*

finished /ˈfɪnɪʃt/ **adj 1** completed: *How much does the finished product cost?* → Opposite **unfinished 2 be finished** If you are finished, you have completed something: *I hope I'll be finished before 5 p.m.*

fir /fɜːr/ **noun** [C] (also **ˈfir ˌtree**) a tree with thin, straight leaves shaped like needles that do not fall in winter

fire

fire¹ /faɪər/ **noun 1** FLAME ▷ [U] ⓐⓐ heat, light, and flames that are produced when something burns **2 catch fire** ⓑⓑ to start burning: *The car crashed and caught fire.* **3 on fire** burning: *That house is on fire.* **4 set fire to sth; set sth on fire** to make something start burning, usually to cause damage: *Enemy troops set fire to the village.* **5** EVENT ▷ [C] an event when something burns in a way that causes damage and cannot be controlled: *Three people were killed in the fire.* ∘ *It took the firefighters two hours to put the fire out* (= stop it burning). **6** NATURAL HEAT ▷ [C] ⓑⓑ a pile of wood, coal, etc that is burning to produce heat: *We sat by the fire.* ∘ *They put up the tents and lit a fire.* **7 an electric/gas fire** UK a piece of equipment that uses electricity/gas to heat a room **8** SHOOTING ▷ [U] the shooting of

guns and other weapons: *The soldiers opened fire* (= started shooting).

IDIOM **come under fire** to be criticized: *The government has come under fire for closing the hospital.*

🔲 Word partners for **fire**

put out/start a fire • a fire **breaks out/burns/rages** • **be on** fire • **catch** fire

---

fire² /faɪər/ **verb 1** [I, T] ⓔⓔ to shoot a bullet from gun: *She fired three shots at him.* **2** [T] informal ⓑ to tell someone they must leave their job: [often passive] *I was fired for being late.* **3 fire sb's imagination** to make someone very excited or interested in something **4 fire questions at sb** to ask someone questions quickly one after the other

PHRASAL VERB **fire sb up** to make someone excited or angry

ˈfire aˌlarm noun [C] a piece of equipment such as a bell that warns the people in a building that the building is on fire: *If you hear the fire alarm, you must leave the building immediately.*

firearm /ˈfaɪərɑːm/ **noun** [C] a gun that you can carry easily

ˈfire briˌgade noun [C] UK (US **ˈfire deˌpartment**) ⓑⓑ an organization of people whose job is to stop fires burning

ˈfire deˌpartment noun [C] US (UK **fire brigade**) an organization of people whose job is to stop fires burning

ˈfire ˌdrill noun [C] an occasion when people practise what they must do to leave a burning building safely

ˈfire ˌengine noun [C] (also US **fire truck**) vehicle for carrying firefighters and equipment for stopping large fires

ˈfire esˌcape noun [C] a set of metal stairs on the outside of a building that allows people to leave if there is an emergency

ˈfire exˌtinguisher noun [C] a piece of equipment kept inside buildings which is used to stop small fires

firefighter /ˈfaɪəfaɪtər/ **noun** [C] ⓑⓑ someone whose job is to stop fires burning

firefighting /ˈfaɪəˌfaɪtɪŋ/ **noun** [U] the time and effort that someone uses to deal with problems at work that need to be dealt with quickly instead of dealing with their ordinary business: *seem to be so busy firefighting that I never have time to do routine jobs.*

ˈfire ˌhouse noun [C] (plural **fire houses** /ˈfaɪə ˌhaʊzɪz/) US (UK/US **fire station**) the building where fire engines are kept, and firefighters wait for emergencies

ˈfire ˌhydrant noun [C] a large pipe in the street that firefighters can get water from to use to stop fires burning

fireman /ˈfaɪəmən/ **noun** [C] (plural **firemen**) man whose job is to stop fires burning

fireplace /ˈfaɪəpleɪs/ **noun** [C] a space in the wall of a room where you can have a fire, or the

---

structure around this space → See colour picture **The Living Room** on page Centre 4

fireside /ˈfaɪəsaɪd/ **noun** [U] the area next to a fireplace

fire station noun [C] (also US **fire house**) the building where fire engines are kept, and firefighters wait for emergencies

fire truck noun [C] (UK/US **fire engine**) a vehicle for carrying firefighters and equipment for stopping large fires

firewall /ˈfaɪəwɔːl/ **noun** [C] a system that controls what information can be sent from your computer using the Internet

firewood /ˈfaɪəwʊd/ **noun** [U] wood that is used for burning on a fire

fireworks

firework /ˈfaɪəwɜːk/ **noun** [C] ⓐ a small object that explodes to produce a loud noise and bright colours and is often used to celebrate special events: *a firework display*

> 🗹 Word partners for **firework**
>
> let off/set off a firework • a firework(s) display

firing squad noun [C] a group of soldiers who are ordered to shoot and kill a prisoner

firm¹ /fɜːm/ **adj 1 NOT SOFT** ▷ ⓑ not soft, but not completely hard: *A firm bed is better for your back.* **2 FIXED** ▷ [always before noun] ⓑ certain or fixed and not likely to change: *We don't have any firm plans for the weekend yet.* ∘ *I'm a firm believer in equal rights.* **3 STRONG** ▷ strong and tight: *a firm handshake/grip* **4 STRICT** ▷ strict and making certain that people do what you want: *You've got to be firm with children.* • **firmly adv** • **firmness noun** [U]

firm² /fɜːm/ **noun** [C] ⓑ a company that sells goods or services: *a law firm*

> 🗹 Word partners for **firm**
>
> run/set up a firm • a firm of [solicitors, accountants, etc]

first¹ /fɜːst/ **adj 1 BEFORE** ▷ ⓐ coming before all others: *Who was the first person to arrive at the party?* ∘ *He was nervous on his first day at school.* ∘ *They went abroad last year for the first time*

since having children. **2 NUMBER** ▷ 1st written as a word **3 IMPORTANT** ▷ ⓐ most important: *Sheila won first prize in the photo competition.* → See also **in the first place¹**

first² /fɜːst/ **adv 1 BEFORE** ▷ ⓐ before everything or everyone else: *I can go to the cinema, but I've got to do my homework first.* ∘ *Jason came first in the 400 metres (= he won).* **2 FIRST TIME** ▷ ⓑ for the first time: *I first heard the song on the radio.* ∘ *He first started playing the piano at school.* **3 at first** ⓑ at the beginning of a situation or period of time: *At first I thought she was unfriendly, but actually she is just shy.* **4 first; first of all a** ⓑ used to introduce the first idea, reason, etc in a series: *First, I think we have to change our marketing strategy.* **b** ⓐ before doing anything else: *First of all check you have all the correct ingredients.* **5 come first** to be the most important person or thing: *Her career always comes first.* **6 put sb/sth first** to consider someone or something to be the most important thing: *Most couples put their children first when sorting out their problems.* **7 First come, first served.** something you say when there is not enough of something for everyone and only the first people who ask for it will get it

first³ /fɜːst/ **noun, pronoun 1 the first** ⓑ the first person, people, thing, or things: *Hillary and Norgay were the first to climb Everest.* **2 be a first** to be something that has never happened before: *Man walking on the moon was a first in space history.* **3** [C] the highest exam result that you can achieve at the end of a university course in the UK

first aid noun [U] basic medical treatment that you give someone who is sick or injured in an emergency: *The policeman gave him first aid before the ambulance arrived.*

first-class /ˌfɜːstˈklɑːs/ **adj 1** relating to the best and most expensive available service, especially when travelling or sending something somewhere: *a first-class ticket* ∘ *a first-class stamp* **2** of very good quality: *It was a first-class restaurant.* • **first class adv** *How much is it to send this letter first class?*

first floor noun [no plural] **1** UK ⓑ the level of a building directly above the ground level **2** US (UK **ground floor**) the level of a building on the same level as the ground

firsthand /ˌfɜːstˈhænd/ **adj, adv** experienced, seen, or learnt directly: *Police heard firsthand accounts of the accident from witnesses.* ∘ *firsthand experience*

first language noun [C] ⓑ the language that someone learns to speak first: *Madeleine's first language is French, but she also knows English and German.*

firstly /ˈfɜːstli/ **adv** ⓑ used to introduce the first idea, reason, etc in a series: *The aim of this activity is firstly to have fun, and secondly to keep fit.*

first name noun [C] ⓐ the name that people who know you call you and that comes before your family name

the first person noun ⓑ the form of a verb or pronoun that is used when people are speaking or writing about themselves. For example, 'I' and 'we' are first person pronouns.

first-rate /ˌfɜːstˈreɪt/ **adj** extremely good: *a first-rate team/writer*

fiscal /ˈfɪskəl/ **adj** relating to government money, especially taxes

fish¹ /fɪʃ/ **noun** (plural **fish**, **fishes**) **1** [C] Ⓐ an animal that lives only in water and swims using its tail and fins (= thin, triangular parts): *Are there any fish in the pond?* **2** [U] Ⓐ fish eaten as food: *fish and chips* → See colour picture **Food** on page Centre 11

> ❗ **Common learner error: fish or fishes?**
>
> **Fish** is the usual plural of **fish**.
> *I caught six fish in the river.*
> ~~I caught six fishes in the river.~~
> **Fishes** is sometimes used to talk about different types of fish.

fish² /fɪʃ/ **verb** [I] Ⓑ to try to catch fish: *They're fishing for tuna.*

PHRASAL VERB **fish sth out** informal to pull or take something out of a bag or pocket, especially after searching

fisherman /ˈfɪʃəmən/ **noun** [C] (plural **fishermen**) someone who catches fish as a job or as a hobby

fishing /ˈfɪʃɪŋ/ **noun** [U] Ⓐ the sport or job of catching fish: *Dad loves to go fishing.*

fish slice noun [C] UK a kitchen tool with a wide, flat end used for lifting and serving food → See colour picture **The Kitchen** on page Centre 2

fishy /ˈfɪʃi/ **adj 1** smelling or tasting like fish **2** making you feel that someone is lying or something dishonest is happening: *His story sounds a bit fishy to me.*

fist /fɪst/ **noun** [C] a hand closed into a ball with the fingers and thumb curled tightly together: *He banged his fist down angrily on the table.*

fist

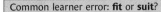

fit¹ /fɪt/ **verb** (**fitting**, **fitted**) **1 RIGHT SHAPE** ▷ [I, T] Ⓑ to be the right shape or size for someone or something: *This skirt doesn't fit any more.* ∘ *I can't find a lid to fit this jar.* **2 fit (sth) in/through/ under, etc** Ⓑ If people or things fit somewhere, or if you can fit them somewhere, that place is big enough for them: *How many people can you fit in your car?* ∘ *This radio is small enough to fit into my pocket.* **3 PUT** ▷ [T] mainly UK Ⓑ to put or fix something somewhere: *You ought to fit a smoke alarm in the kitchen.* **4 SAME** ▷ [I, T] to be the same as or like something: *She seems to fit the police description.* **5 SUITABLE** ▷ [T] to be suitable for something: *The punishment should fit the crime.*

> **Common learner error: fit or suit?**
>
> Remember that the verb **fit** means to be the right shape or size.
> *This jacket doesn't fit me. It's too tight.*
> Use the verb **suit** when you want to say that something is right for someone or makes them look more attractive.
> *That dress looks lovely. Red really suits you.*
> *Life in the big city didn't suit him.*
> ~~Life in the big city didn't fit him.~~

PHRASAL VERBS **fit in** to feel that you belong to a particular group and are accepted by them: *He doesn't fit in with the other pupils in his class.* • **fit sb/sth in** to find the time to see someone or do something: *The dentist can fit you in on Tuesday morning.* • **fit in with sth** Ⓑ If one activity or event fits in with another, they exist or happen together in a way that is convenient: *The party is in early June. How does that fit in with your plans?*

fit² /fɪt/ **adj** (**fitter**, **fittest**) **1** of a good enough quality or suitable type for a particular purpose [+ to do sth] *Is this water fit to drink?* ∘ *She's not in a fit state to drive.* **2** Ⓐ healthy, especially because you exercise regularly: *He's very fit for his age.* → Opposite **unfit 3 do sth as you see/think fit** to do something that you feel is the right thing to do, although other people might disapprove: *You must spend the money as you see fit.*

fit³ /fɪt/ **noun 1** a good/loose/tight, etc fit used to say how something fits someone or somewhere: *These shoes are a perfect fit.* **2** [C] a sudden, uncontrolled period of doing something or feeling something: *a coughing fit* ∘ *I hit him in a fit of anger.* **3** [C] a short period of illness when someone cannot control their movements and becomes unconscious: *to have an epileptic fit* **4 have a fit** informal to become extremely angry

fitful /ˈfɪtfəl/ **adj** stopping and starting and not happening in a regular or continuous way: *fitful sleep* • **fitfully adv**

fitness /ˈfɪtnəs/ **noun** [U] **1** Ⓑ the condition of being physically strong and healthy: *physical fitness* **2** the quality of being suitable for particular purpose, job, course of study, etc: *The purpose of the exercise is to judge a soldier's fitness for combat.*

> ✎ **Word partners for fitness**
>
> **improve** your fitness • sb's fitness **level(s)** • a fitness **programme/regime/test** • **physical** fitness

fitness centre noun [C] UK (US **fitness center**) a building or a place in a building with equipment that people can use for exercising

fitted /ˈfɪtɪd/ **adj 1** UK made or cut to fill a particular space exactly: *fitted carpets/kitchens* **2** Fitted clothes fit tightly to your body: *a fitted jacket*

fitting /ˈfɪtɪŋ/ **adj** suitable or right for particular situation: *The promotion was a fitting reward for all his hard work.*

fitting room noun [C] a room in a shop where you can put on clothes to check that they fit before you buy them

fittings /ˈfɪtɪŋz/ noun [plural] mainly UK **1** parts that are fixed to a piece of furniture or equipment: *a circular bath with gold fittings* **2** things that are fixed to the walls, floors, and ceilings inside a house but that can be moved

five /faɪv/ ⓐ the number 5

fiver /ˈfaɪvər/ noun [C] UK informal a piece of paper money worth £5: *You owe me a fiver.*

five-star /faɪvˈstɑːr/ adj describes a hotel or resort of very high quality

fix¹ /fɪks/ verb [T] **1 REPAIR** ▷ ⓑ to repair something: *My watch is broken – can you fix it?* **2 DECIDE** ▷ ⓑ to decide a certain and exact date, price, plan, etc: *Let's fix a day to have lunch together.* ○ *The price has been fixed at $10.* **3 fix sth onto/to/under, etc** ⓑ to fasten something in a particular place: *They fixed the bookcase to the wall.* **4 PREPARE** ▷ ⓑ to prepare a drink or meal: [+ two objects] *I'll fix you a sandwich.* **5 CHEAT** ▷ to do something dishonest to make certain that a competition, race, or election is won by a particular person: [often passive] *People are saying that the elections were fixed.*

PHRASAL VERBS **fix sth up 1** UK to arrange a meeting, date, event, etc: *Can we fix up a date for the next meeting?* **2** to repair or change something in order to improve it: *Nick loves fixing up old cars.* • **fix sb up** to provide someone with something that they need: *My uncle has **fixed me up with** a summer job.*

fix² /fɪks/ noun **1 a quick fix** a way of solving a problem easily: *There is no quick fix for unemployment.* **2 be in a fix** informal to be in a difficult situation: *I'm in a fix and need your help.* **3** [C] informal an amount of an illegal drug or something that you want very much: *Cath needs her **fix of** chocolate every day.*

fixation /fɪkˈseɪʃən/ noun [C] a very strong interest in a particular person or thing: *She's got an unhealthy **fixation with** her weight.*

fixed /fɪkst/ adj **1** ⓑ decided already and not able to be changed: *a **fixed price*** ○ *Is the date of the wedding fixed yet?* **2** fastened somewhere and not able to be moved

fixture /ˈfɪkstʃər/ noun [C] **1** a piece of furniture or equipment that is fixed inside a house or building and is usually sold with it: [usually plural] *It comes with the usual **fixtures and fittings**.* **2** UK a sports event that is arranged for a particular day

fizz /fɪz/ noun [U] bubbles of gas in a liquid or the sound that they make • **fizz** verb [I]

fizzle /ˈfɪzl/ verb

PHRASAL VERB **fizzle out** to gradually end in a disappointing way: *Their relationship soon fizzled out when they got back from holiday.*

fizzy /ˈfɪzi/ adj A fizzy drink has lots of bubbles of gas in it.

flabbergasted /ˈflæbəgɑːstɪd/ adj informal extremely surprised

flabby /ˈflæbi/ adj having too much loose fat on your body: *flabby arms/ thighs*

flag¹ /flæg/ noun [C] ⓑ a piece of cloth with a special design and colours, that is fixed to a pole as the symbol of a country or group: *the French flag* ○ *There was a flag flying above the castle.*

flag² /flæg/ verb [I] (**flagging, flagged**) to become tired or less interested in something: *The players started to flag towards the end of the game.*

PHRASAL VERB **flag sth down** to make a vehicle stop by waving at the driver

flagrant /ˈfleɪɡrənt/ adj shocking because of being so obviously wrong or bad: *a flagrant disregard for the law* • **flagrantly** adv

flagship /ˈflæɡʃɪp/ noun [C] a product or service that is the best and most admired that a company has

flail /fleɪl/ verb [I, T] (also **flail about/around**) to wave or move your arms and legs about energetically and in an uncontrolled way: *The wasp came towards us and Howard started flailing his arms around.*

flair /fleər/ noun **1** [no plural] a natural ability to do something well: *She has a **flair for** languages.* **2** [U] the ability to do something in an exciting and interesting way: *He played with great imagination and flair.*

flak /flæk/ noun [U] informal criticism: *The government **took** a lot of **flak for** breaking its election promises.*

flake¹ /fleɪk/ noun [C] a small, flat, thin piece of something: *flakes of paint/snow*

flake off

flake² /fleɪk/ verb [I] to come off in small, flat, thin pieces: *The paint was flaking off the walls.* • **flaky** adj coming off easily in small, flat, thin pieces: *dry, flaky skin*

flamboyant /flæmˈbɔɪənt/ adj **1** A flamboyant person is loud, stylish, and confident: *a flamboyant pop star* **2** Flamboyant clothes or colours are very bright and noticeable. • **flamboyance** /flæmˈbɔɪəns/ noun [U]

flame¹ /fleɪm/ noun **1** [C, U] ⓑ hot, bright, burning gas produced by something on fire: *Smoke and flames were pouring out of the burning factory.* ○ *The whole building was soon **in flames** (= burning).* ○ *The car crashed and **burst into flames** (= suddenly started burning).* **2** [C] an angry email or message in a chat room, etc.

fizzy

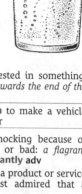

F

flame

flame² /fleɪm/ **verb** [I, T] to send an angry email to someone

flaming /'fleɪmɪŋ/ **adj** [always before noun] **1 BURNING** ▷ burning with a bright light: *a flaming building* **2 BRIGHT** ▷ very bright in colour or light: *flaming red hair* **3 ANNOYED** ▷ UK informal used to emphasize something when you are annoyed: *What a flaming idiot!*

flamingo /flə'mɪŋgəʊ/ **noun** [C] a large bird with long, thin legs and pink feathers that lives near water in some hot countries

flammable /'flæməbl/ **adj** (also **inflammable**) Flammable liquids, gases, or materials burn very easily.

flan /flæn/ **noun** [C, U] a round, open pastry base filled with something such as fruit, or cheese and vegetables: *cheese and onion flan*

flank¹ /flæŋk/ **verb be flanked by sb/sth** to have someone or something at the side or at each side: *The President was flanked by police officers.*

flank² /flæŋk/ **noun** [C] **1** the side of the body of an animal or person from the chest to the hips **2** the side of an army when it is ready to fight

flannel /'flænəl/ **noun 1** [U] soft, warm cloth for making clothes: *flannel pyjamas* **2** [C] UK (US **washcloth**) a small cloth that you use to wash your face and body → See colour picture **The Bathroom** on page Centre 3

flap¹ /flæp/ **noun 1** [C] a piece of cloth or material fixed along one edge to cover or close an opening **2** [C, U] informal the feeling of being worried or excited, or a situation that causes someone to feel this way: *The President's remarks caused a huge flap.*

IDIOM **be/get in a flap** mainly UK informal to be or become worried or excited

flap² /flæp/ **verb** (**flapping, flapped**) **1 WINGS** ▷ [T] If a bird flaps its wings, it moves them up and down. **2 MOVE** ▷ [I] If something such as cloth or paper flaps, the side that is not fixed to something moves around, especially in the wind: *The curtains were flapping around in the breeze.* **3 WORRY** ▷ [I] informal to become worried or excited about something: *Don't flap! We've got plenty of time to get to the airport.*

flare¹ /fleə^r/ **verb** [I] (also **flare up**) **1** If something bad such as anger or pain flares or flares up, it suddenly starts or gets worse: *Violence flared up between football fans yesterday.* **2** to suddenly burn brightly, usually for a short time: *The rocket flared in the sky and disappeared into space.*

flare² /fleə^r/ **noun** [C] **1** a piece of safety equipment that produces a bright signal when you are lost or injured **2** a sudden, bright light

flared /fleəd/ **adj** wide at the bottom: *flared trousers*

flash¹ /flæʃ/ **verb 1** [I, T] ⏾ to shine brightly and suddenly, or to make something shine in this way: *The doctor flashed a light into my eye.* ○ *Lightning flashed across the sky.* **2** [I, T] (also

flash up) to appear for a short time, or to make something appear for a short time: *An icon flashed up on the screen.* **3 flash by/past/through, etc** to move somewhere fast: *The motorcycle flashed past us and around the corner.* **4 flash (sb) a look/smile, etc** to look/smile, etc at someone quickly: *She flashed him a smile as he came in.*

PHRASAL VERB **flash back** If your mind or thoughts flash back to something that happened in the past, you suddenly remember it.

flash² /flæʃ/ **noun 1 BRIGHT LIGHT** ▷ [C] ⏾ a sudden bright light: *The bomb exploded in a flash of yellow light.* **2 CAMERA** ▷ [C, U] ⏾ a piece of camera equipment that produces a bright light when you take a photograph in a dark place **3 SUDDEN EXPERIENCE** ▷ [C] a sudden experience of something such as a feeling or idea: *a flash of anger* ○ *I had a flash of inspiration.* **4 in a flash** immediately, or very quickly: *I'll be back in a flash.*

IDIOM **a flash in the pan** a sudden success that does not continue

flashback /'flæʃbæk/ **noun** [C] **1** a sudden memory of something that happened in the past, usually something bad **2** part of a film or book that goes back in time to something that happened before the main story began

flash drive **noun** [C] (also **flash memory drive** also **flash memory pen drive**) a small object for storing electronic information that can be connected to a computer and that can be carried about easily

flashlight /'flæʃlaɪt/ **noun** [C] US (UK **torch**) an electric light that you can hold in your hand

flashy /'flæʃi/ **adj** looking too bright, big, and expensive, in a way that is intended to get attention: *flashy gold jewellery*

flask

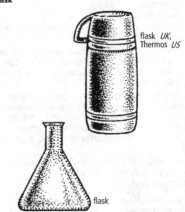

flask *UK*, Thermos *US*

flask

flask /flɑːsk/ **noun** [C] **1 HOT DRINKS** ▷ UK (UK/US **Thermos**) a special container that keeps drinks hot or cold: *a flask of coffee* **2 ALCOHOL** ▷ a flat bottle that is used to carry alcohol in your pocket **3 SCIENCE** ▷ a glass container with a wide base and a narrow opening used in science

flat¹ /flæt/ **noun** [C] UK (mainly US **apartment**) ⓐ a set of rooms to live in, with all the rooms on one level of a building: *a large **block of flats***

> ☑ Word partners for **flat**
>
> in a flat • a block of flats • a one-bedroom/ two-bedroom flat • a basement flat

flat

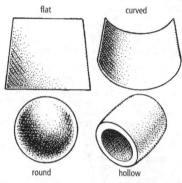

flat   curved

round   hollow

flat² /flæt/ **adj** (**flatter**, **flattest**) **1** SMOOTH ▷ ⓑ smooth and level, with no curved, high, or hollow parts: *a flat surface* ∘ *The countryside around here is very flat.* **2** WITHOUT EMOTION ▷ without any energy, interest, or emotion: *Her voice sounded very flat.* **3** WITHOUT AIR ▷ If a tyre is flat, it does not contain enough air. **4** WITHOUT GAS ▷ If a drink is flat, it does not contain enough bubbles of gas. **5** WITHOUT POWER ▷ UK If a battery (= object which provides electricity) is flat, it does not contain any more electrical power. **6 a flat price/rate, etc** a price/rate, etc that is the same for everyone and does not change: *He charges a flat rate of 15 euros an hour.* **7 B flat/E flat, etc** the musical note that is between the note B/E, etc and the note below it **8** TOO LOW ▷ A flat musical note sounds unpleasant because it is slightly lower than it should be. **9** LOW ▷ Flat shoes do not raise your feet far from the ground.

flat³ /flæt/ **adv** (**flatter**, **flattest**) **1** ⓒ in a horizontal or level position on a surface: *She spread the cloth flat across the kitchen table.* **2 flat out** using all your energy or effort: *We've all been working flat out to finish the project on time.* **3 in 5 minutes/30 seconds, etc flat** in exactly and only 5 minutes, 30 seconds, etc: *He showered and got dressed in 10 minutes flat.*

IDIOM **fall flat** If an event or joke falls flat, it fails to have the effect that you wanted, such as making people laugh.

flatly /'flætli/ **adv 1 flatly deny/refuse, etc** to say something in a direct and certain way: *He flatly refused to answer our questions.* **2** without showing any emotion or interest: *"He's gone,"* she said flatly.

flatmate /'flætmeɪt/ **noun** [C] UK (US **roommate**) someone who you share a flat with

flatpack /'flætpæk/ **adj** used to describe furni-

ture that is sold in pieces inside a flat box, ready to be put together: *a flatpack table*

flat-screen /'flæt,skriːn/ **adj** [always before noun] (also **flat-panel**) having a screen that is thin and flat: *a flat-screen TV*

flat-screen TV noun [C] a type of television with a screen that is very thin and shows a very clear picture

flatten /'flætªn/ **verb** [I, T] to become flat or to make something become flat: *Roll out the dough into balls and flatten them slightly.*

flatter /'flætəʳ/ **verb 1** [T] to say nice things to someone in order to make them feel attractive or important, sometimes in a way that is not sincere: *The interviewer flattered him about his recent work.* **2 be flattered** to feel very pleased and proud: *She was flattered by his attention.* **3** [T] to make someone look more attractive than usual: *That new hairstyle really flatters you.* **4 flatter yourself** to believe something good about yourself, although it might not be true: *He flatters himself that he's a good driver.*

flattering /'flætərɪŋ/ **adj** making you look more attractive than usual: *a flattering picture*

flattery /'flætəri/ **noun** [U] nice things that you say to someone, often because you want something from that person

flatware /'flæt,weəʳ/ **noun** [U] US objects used for eating and serving food

flaunt /flɔːnt/ **verb** [T] to make your success, money, beauty, etc very obvious so that people notice it and admire you: *Although he's a millionaire, he doesn't flaunt his wealth.*

flavour¹ UK (US **flavor**) /'fleɪvəʳ/ **noun 1** [C, U] ⓐ the taste of a particular type of food or drink: *We sell 50 different flavours of ice cream.* ∘ *Add some salt to give the soup more flavour.* **2** [no plural] a particular quality or style that something has: *London has a very international flavour.*

> ☑ Word partners for **flavour**
>
> have a [mild/spicy/strong, etc] flavour • a delicate/delicious flavour

flavour² UK (US **flavor**) /'fleɪvəʳ/ **verb 1** [T] to give a particular taste to food or drink: [often passive] *This sauce is flavoured with garlic and herbs.* **2 cheese/chocolate, etc -flavoured** tasting of cheese/chocolate, etc: *lemon-flavoured sweets*

flavouring UK (US **flavoring**) /'fleɪvərɪŋ/ **noun** [C, U] something that is added to food or drink to give it a particular taste

flaw /flɔː/ **noun** [C] a mistake or bad character-istic that stops someone or something from being perfect: *There's a flaw in your reasoning.* • **flawed adj** *a flawed argument*

flawless /'flɔːləs/ **adj** with no mistakes or bad characteristics: *a flawless complexion* • **flaw-lessly adv**

flea /fliː/ **noun** [C] a small, jumping insect that lives on animals or people and drinks their blood

flea market noun [C] a market where you can buy old or used things cheaply

fleck /flek/ **noun** [C] a mark, or a very small piece

of something: *His shirt was covered in **flecks of paint.***

fledgling /ˈfledʒlɪŋ/ **adj** [always before noun] A fledgling company, country, or organization is new and not yet developed: *a fledgling democracy*

flee /fliː/ **verb** [I, T] (**fleeing, fled**) to leave a place quickly because you are in danger or are afraid: *Police think the suspect has now fled the country.*

fleece /fliːs/ **noun** [C, U] **1** a warm, soft, light jacket, or the material used to make it **2** the thick covering of wool on a sheep

fleet /fliːt/ **noun** [C] **1** a group of ships, or all of the ships in a country's navy **2** a group of vehicles that are owned and controlled by one person or organization: *a **fleet** of aircraft/cars*

flesh /fleʃ/ **noun** [U] **1** the soft part of a person's or animal's body between the skin and bones **2 in the flesh** in real life and not on television or in a film: *She looks much taller in the flesh.* **3** the soft part of a fruit or vegetable that you can eat

IDIOM **your own flesh and blood** a member of your family

• **fleshy adj** fat or thick, or with a lot of flesh

flew /fluː/ past tense of fly

flex[1] /fleks/ **verb** [T] to bend a part of your body so that the muscle becomes tight

flex[2] /fleks/ **noun** [C, U] UK (UK/US **cord**) a piece of wire covered in plastic, that is used to connect electrical equipment to a power supply

flexible /ˈfleksɪbl/ **adj 1** able to change or be changed easily according to the situation: *I'd like a job with more flexible working hours.* **2** A flexible substance can bend easily without breaking. • **flexibility** /ˌfleksɪˈbɪləti/ **noun** [U]

flick[1] /flɪk/ **verb 1 flick sth into/off/over, etc** to move something somewhere suddenly and quickly through the air, usually with your fingers: *He quickly flicked the crumbs off the table.* **2 flick down/out/towards, etc** to make a sudden, quick movement somewhere: *His eyes flicked between her and the door.* **3 flick a switch** to move a switch in order to make electrical equipment start or stop working

PHRASAL VERBS **flick sth on/off** to move a switch in order to make electrical equipment start/stop working • **flick through sth** to look quickly at the pages of a magazine, book, etc

flick[2] /flɪk/ **noun** [C] a sudden, quick movement: *With a **flick** of her wrist, she threw the pebble into the water.*

flicker[1] /ˈflɪkər/ **verb** [I] **1** to shine with a light that is sometimes bright and sometimes weak: *A candle flickered in the window.* **2** to appear for a short time or make a sudden movement somewhere: *A smile **flickered across** her face.*

flicker[2] /ˈflɪkər/ **noun** [no plural] **1** a light that is sometimes bright and sometimes weak: *the soft flicker of candlelight* **2** a slight, brief feeling or expression of an emotion: *a **flicker** of hope*

flier (also **flyer**) /ˈflaɪər/ **noun** [C] **1** a small piece of paper advertising a business, show, event, etc **2** someone who flies, especially a passenger on an aircraft

flies /flaɪz/ **noun** [plural] UK (UK/US **fly**) the par where trousers open and close at the front

flight /flaɪt/ **noun 1** JOURNEY ▷ [C] ⓐ a journey in an aircraft: *The **flight** to Chicago took · hours.* **2** AIRCRAFT ▷ [C] an aircraft that carrie passengers from one place to another: *Flight 10. is ready for boarding at Gate 3.* **3** MOVEMENT ▷ [U] the movement of flying or moving through the air: *an eagle in flight* **4 a flight of stairs** steps a set of stairs

---
🗌 **Word partners for flight**

on a flight • a flight **from/to** [Paris/Tokyo, etc] • a **long-haul/short-haul** flight

---

flight atˌtendant noun [C] someone whose job is to look after passengers on an aircraft

flimsy /ˈflɪmzi/ **adj 1** thin and not solid o strong: *a flimsy cardboard box* **2** A flimsy argument, excuse, etc is weak and difficult t believe: *I'm sick of his **flimsy excuses** for bein late.*

flinch /flɪnʃ/ **verb** [I] **1** to make a sudde movement backwards because you are afrai or in pain: *She didn't flinch when the nurs cleaned the wound.* **2** to avoid doing somethin that is unpleasant: *Nick never **flinches fron** difficult decisions.*

fling[1] /flɪŋ/ **verb** (**flung**) **fling sth around across/down, etc** to throw or move somethin suddenly and with a lot of force: *She flung he arms around his neck.*

fling[2] /flɪŋ/ **noun** [C] **1** a sexual relationship tha is short and not serious: *She had a **fling** wit someone last summer.* **2** a short period of tim when you have a lot of enjoyment or pleasure *This is my last fling before the exams.*

flint /flɪnt/ **noun** [C, U] a very hard, grey ston that can be used to produce a flame

flip /flɪp/ **verb** (**flipping, flipped**) **1** [I, T] to turn o make something turn onto a different side, or s that it is the wrong way up: *to flip a coin/pancak* ◦ *The boat **flipped** right **over**.* **2** [I] informal t become uncontrollably angry, crazy, or excited *Dad completely flipped when he saw the car.*

PHRASAL VERB **flip through sth** to look quickly a the pages of a magazine, book, etc

flip ˌchart noun [C] large pieces of pape attached to a board on legs, which you write o draw on when you are talking to a group o people

flip-flop /ˈflɪpflɒp/ **noun** [usually plural] (also U **thong**) a type of shoe, often made of rubbe with a V-shaped strap in between the big toe an the toe next to it → See colour picture **Clothes** o page Centre 9

flippant /ˈflɪpənt/ **adj** without respect or n serious: *a flippant remark* • **flippantly ad** • **flippancy** /ˈflɪpənsi/ **noun** [U]

flipper /ˈflɪpər/ **noun** [C] **1** a part like a wide, fla arm without fingers that some sea animals us for swimming **2** a long, flat, rubber shoe tha you use when swimming under water

flipping /ˈflɪpɪŋ/ **adj** [always before noun] U

---

informal used to emphasize something, or to show slight anger: *Where are my flipping keys?*

the **'flip ˌside** noun the opposite, less good, or less popular side of something

flirt¹ /flɜːt/ **verb** [I] to behave as if you are sexually attracted to someone, usually not in a very serious way: *She was flirting with a guy at the bar.*

PHRASAL VERB **flirt with sth 1** to be interested in an idea, activity, etc but not seriously, or for only a short time: *He flirted with the idea of becoming a priest.* **2 flirt with danger/disaster, etc** to risk experiencing something bad • **flirtation** /flɜːˈteɪʃᵊn/ noun [C, U]

flirt² /flɜːt/ **noun** [C] someone who often flirts with people

flirtatious /flɜːˈteɪʃəs/ **adj** behaving as if you are sexually attracted to someone, usually not in a very serious way

flit /flɪt/ **verb** (**flitting, flitted**) **flit about/around/ in and out, etc** to fly or move quickly from one place to another: *Birds were flitting from tree to tree.*

float

float   sink

float¹ /fləʊt/ **verb 1** LIQUID ▷ [I, T] to stay on the surface of a liquid instead of sinking, or to make something do this: *I like floating on my back in the pool.* **2** AIR ▷ [I] to stay in the air, or move gently through the air: *A balloon floated across the sky.* **3** BUSINESS ▷ [I, T] to start selling a company's shares to the public

IDIOM **float sb's boat** informal to interest someone: *Georgia likes William, but he just doesn't float my boat.*

float² /fləʊt/ **noun** [C] **1** VEHICLE ▷ a large, decorated vehicle that is used in public celebrations **2** WATER ▷ an object that floats on water, used in fishing or when learning to swim **3** BUSINESS ▷ an occasion when someone floats a business

flock¹ /flɒk/ **noun** [group] **1** a group of birds or sheep: *a flock of geese* **2** a group of people led by one person: *a flock of children/visitors*

flock² /flɒk/ **verb** [I] to move or come together in large numbers: *Tourists are flocking to the*

beaches. ◦ [+ to do sth] *People flocked to hear him speak.*

flog /flɒg/ **verb** [T] (**flogging, flogged**) **1** to hit someone repeatedly as a punishment with something such as a stick **2** UK informal to sell something quickly or cheaply: *I had to flog the car to pay my bills.* • **flogging** noun [C, U]

flood¹ /flʌd/ **verb** [I, T] **1** If a place floods or is flooded, it becomes covered in water: [often passive] *The town was flooded when the river burst its banks.* ◦ *I left the taps running and flooded the bathroom.* **2** to fill or enter a place in large numbers or amounts: *Light flooded the room.* ◦ *Shoppers flooded into the store.* • **flooding** noun [U] *There is widespread flooding in the South.*

PHRASAL VERB **be flooded with sth** to receive so many letters, telephone calls, etc that you cannot deal with them

flood

flood² /flʌd/ **noun** [C] **1** a situation in which a lot of water covers an area that is usually dry, especially when a river becomes too full **2** a large number or amount of things or people that arrive at the same time: *a flood of letters/ calls*

IDIOM **in floods of tears** UK crying a lot

> 🗌 **Word partners for flood**
>
> **catastrophic/devastating** floods • **flood damage/victims/warnings**

floodgates /ˈflʌdgeɪts/ **noun**

IDIOM **open the floodgates** to make it possible for a lot of people to do something

floodlights /ˈflʌdlaɪts/ **noun** [plural] powerful lights used to light up sports fields or the outside of buildings at night • **floodlit** /ˈflʌdlɪt/ **adj** lit up by floodlights

floor /flɔːʳ/ **noun 1** SURFACE ▷ [C] a surface that you walk on inside a building: *a wooden/ tiled floor* ◦ *I must sweep the kitchen floor.* **2** BUILDING ▷ [C] a particular level of a building: *the second/third floor* **3** BOTTOM ▷ [no plural] the ground or surface at the bottom of something: *the forest/sea floor* **4** AREA ▷ [C] an area where a particular activity happens: *a dance floor* → See also **first floor, ground floor, shop floor**

floorboard /'flɔːbɔːd/ **noun** [C] a long, narrow, flat board that forms part of a wooden floor in a building

flooring /'flɔːrɪŋ/ **noun** [U] the material used to make or cover a floor: *vinyl flooring*

flop¹ /flɒp/ **verb** [I] (**flopping, flopped**) **1 flop down/into/onto, etc** to fall or sit somewhere suddenly in a heavy or relaxed way: *He flopped down on the sofa.* **2** to hang loosely: *Her hair kept flopping in her eyes.* **3** informal If a film, product, plan, etc flops, it is not successful.

flop² /flɒp/ **noun** [C] informal **1** something that is not a success: *The party was a bit of a flop.* **2** a movement towards the ground, or the noise someone or something makes as they fall down: *She fell onto the bed with a flop.*

floppy /'flɒpi/ **adj** soft and loose or hanging down loosely: *floppy hair* ◦ *a floppy hat*

floppy disk noun [C] (also **floppy**) a small disk inside a flat, square piece of plastic used in the past for storing information from a computer

flora /'flɔːrə/ **noun** [group] the plants that grow naturally in a particular area: *Scotland's flora and fauna*

floral /'flɔːrᵊl/ **adj** [always before noun] made from flowers or relating to flowers: *a floral arrangement/pattern*

florist /'flɒrɪst/ **noun** [C] **1** someone who sells and arranges flowers in a shop **2** (also **florist's**) a shop that sells flowers

flotation /fləʊ'teɪʃᵊn/ **noun 1** [C, U] a sale of a company's shares to the public for the first time **2** [U] the act of floating on or in liquid

flounder /'flaʊndər/ **verb** [I] **1 MOVEMENT** ▷ to make wild movements with your arms or body, especially because you are trying not to sink **2 NOT KNOW** ▷ to not know what to do or say: *When he resigned, the team was left floundering.* **3 FAIL** ▷ If a relationship, organization, or plan flounders, it fails or begins to experience problems: *By 1993 his marriage was floundering.*

flour /flaʊər/ **noun** [U] ⑤ a powder made from grain that is used to make bread, cakes, and other food

flourish¹ /'flʌrɪʃ/ **verb 1** [I] to grow or develop well: *a flourishing tourist industry* **2** [T] to wave something around in the air

flourish² /'flʌrɪʃ/ **noun** [no plural] a special and noticeable action or way of doing something: *The waiter handed me the menu with a flourish.*

flout /flaʊt/ **verb** [T] to intentionally not obey or accept something: *to flout the law/rules*

flow¹ /fləʊ/ **verb** [I] **1** ⑤ If something such as a liquid flows, it moves somewhere in a smooth, continuous way: *The river flows from the Andes to the ocean.* **2** If words, ideas, or conversations flow, they continue in an easy and relaxed way without stopping: *At dinner, the conversation flowed freely.*

flow² /fləʊ/ **noun** [no plural] ⑥ a smooth continuous movement of something such as a liquid: *the flow of blood* ◦ *the flow of information*

IDIOM **go with the flow** informal to do or accept what other people are doing because it is the easiest thing to do: *Just relax and go with the flow!*

→ See also **ebb¹** and **flow**

flower¹ /flaʊər/ **noun 1** [C] ⓐ the attractive coloured part of a plant where the seeds grow: *bunch of flowers* **2** [C] a type of plant that produces flowers: *spring/wild flowers* **3 be in flower** When plants are in flower, they have flowers on them. **4 the flower of sth** literary the best part of something: *the flower of our nation's youth*

> ☑ Word partners for **flower**
>
> a **bouquet of**/**bunch of** flowers • **wild** flowers • **cut**/**fresh** flowers • **dried** flowers

flower² /flaʊər/ **verb** [I] to produce flowers: *These pansies flower all summer.*

flower bed noun [C] an area of soil in a garden that you grow flowers in

flowerpot /'flaʊəpɒt/ **noun** [C] a container usually made of clay or plastic in which a plant is grown

flowery /'flaʊəri/ **adj 1** (also **flowered** /flaʊəd/) decorated with a pattern of flowers: *a flowery dress* **2** Flowery language contains unnecessarily complicated and unusual words.

flowing /'fləʊɪŋ/ **adj 1** hanging down in a long, loose way: *flowing robes/hair* **2** produced in a smooth, continuous, or relaxed style: *flowing lines*

flown /fləʊn/ past participle of fly

fl oz written abbreviation for fluid ounce (= a unit for measuring liquid)

flu /fluː/ **noun** [U] ⑤ an illness like a very bad cold, that makes you feel hot and weak: *I had the flu last week.*

fluctuate /'flʌktʃueɪt/ **verb** [I] to keep changing, especially in level or amount: *Oil prices have fluctuated wildly in recent weeks.* • **fluctuation** /ˌflʌktʃu'eɪʃᵊn/ **noun** [C, U] *fluctuations in house prices*

fluent /'fluːənt/ **adj 1** ⑫ able to use a language naturally without stopping or making mistakes: *She is fluent in six languages.* **2** ⑫ produced or done in a smooth, natural style: *Hendrik speaks fluent English.* • **fluency** /'fluːənsi/ **noun** [U] • **fluently adv**

fluff¹ /flʌf/ **noun** [U] small, loose bits of wool or other soft material: *There's a piece of fluff on your jacket.*

fluff² /flʌf/ **verb** [T] informal to fail to do something successfully: *I had a great chance to score but I fluffed it.*

PHRASAL VERB **fluff sth out/up** to make something appear bigger or fuller by hitting or shaking so that it contains more air: *I'll fluff up your pillows for you.*

fluffy /'flʌfi/ **adj** made or covered with soft fur or cloth: *a fluffy toy*

fluid¹ /'fluːɪd/ **noun** [C, U] a liquid: *cleaning fluid* ◦ *Drink plenty of fluids.*

fluid² /'fluːɪd/ **adj 1 LIQUID** ▷ able to flow easily like liquid **2 CHANGING** ▷ likely or able change: *a fluid situation* **3 SMOOTH** ▷ smooth and continuous: *fluid movements*

uid 'ounce noun [C] (written abbreviation **fl oz**) a unit for measuring liquid, equal to 0.0284 litres in the UK and 0.0296 litres in the US

uke /fluːk/ noun [C, U] something good that happens only because of luck or chance: *That first goal was just a fluke.*

ume /fluːm/ noun [C] a large tube for people to slide down at a swimming pool

ung /flʌŋ/ past of fling

uorescent /flɔːˈresᵊnt/ adj **1** Fluorescent lights are very bright, tube-shaped, electric lights, often used in offices. **2** Fluorescent colours, clothes, etc are very bright and can be seen in the dark: *fluorescent pink* ∘ *a fluorescent jacket*

uoride /ˈflɔːraɪd/ noun [U] a chemical that helps to prevent tooth decay: *fluoride toothpaste*

urry /ˈflʌri/ noun [C] **1** a sudden, short period of activity, interest, or excitement: *a flurry of phone calls* **2** a sudden, short period of snow and wind

ush¹ /flʌʃ/ verb **1** [I, T] If you flush a toilet, or if it flushes, its contents empty and it fills with water again. **2 flush sth away/down/out, etc** to get rid of something by pushing it somewhere with lots of water, such as down a toilet **3** [I] If you flush, your face becomes red and hot, usually because you are embarrassed or angry.

PHRASAL VERB **flush sb/sth out** to force a person or animal to come out from where they are hiding

ush² /flʌʃ/ noun [C] **1** a hot red face that you get suddenly: *a hot flush* **2 a flush of excitement/pleasure, etc** a sudden feeling of excitement/pleasure, etc

ush³ /flʌʃ/ adj [never before noun] **1** at the same level as another surface: *I want the door flush with the wall.* **2** informal rich: *flush with cash*

ustered /ˈflʌstəd/ adj upset and confused: *She arrived very late, looking flustered.*

ute /fluːt/ noun [C] **B1** a musical instrument in the shape of a tube that is held out to the side and played by blowing across a hole near one end

utter¹ /ˈflʌtəʳ/ verb **1** [I, T] to move quickly and gently up and down or from side to side in the air, or to make something move in this way: *The flag was fluttering in the breeze.* **2 flutter about/around/down, etc** to move somewhere quickly and gently, usually without any particular purpose: *There were several moths fluttering around the light.*

utter² /ˈflʌtəʳ/ noun [C] **1 MOVEMENT** ▷ a quick, gentle movement: *the flutter of wings* **2 EMOTION** ▷ a state of excitement or worry: *a flutter of excitement* **3 RISK MONEY** ▷ UK informal an occasion when you risk money on the result of a game, competition, etc

ux /flʌks/ noun [U] continuous change: *The housing market is still in a state of flux.*

y¹ /flaɪ/ verb (**flew, flown**) **1 MOVE THROUGH AIR** ▷ [I] **A2** When a bird, insect, aircraft, etc flies, it moves through the air: *The robin flew up into a tree.* ∘ *The plane was flying at 5000 feet.*

2 TRAVEL ▷ [I] **A1** to travel through the air in an aircraft: *I'm flying to Delhi tomorrow.* **3 CONTROL AIRCRAFT** ▷ [I, T] **B2** to control an aircraft: *She learned to fly at the age of 18.* **4 TAKE/SEND** ▷ [T] to take or send people or goods somewhere by aircraft: [often passive] *She was flown to the hospital by helicopter.* **5 fly along/down/past, etc** to move somewhere very quickly: *He grabbed some clothes and flew down the stairs.* **6 send sb/sth flying** to cause someone or something to move through the air suddenly, usually in an accident **7 LEAVE** ▷ [I] UK to leave suddenly: *I must fly – I'm late for work.* **8 let fly (at sb/sth)** mainly UK informal to start shouting angrily or attacking someone **9 TIME** ▷ [I] If time flies, it passes very quickly. **10 FLAG** ▷ [I, T] If you fly a flag, or a flag is flying, it is fixed to a rope or pole and raised in the air. • **flying** noun [U] *Ben's afraid of flying.* → See also **as the crow¹ flies, fly off the handle²**

PHRASAL VERBS **fly about/around** If ideas or remarks are flying about, they are being passed quickly from one person to another and causing excitement: *All kinds of rumours are flying around about the school closing.* • **fly into a rage/temper** to suddenly become very angry

fly² /flaɪ/ noun [C] **1 B1** a small insect with two wings: *There was a fly buzzing around in the kitchen.* → See picture at **insect 2** (also UK **flies** [plural]) the part where trousers open and close at the front: *a button/zip fly*

IDIOMS **fly on the wall** If you say that you would like to be a fly on the wall in a certain situation, you mean that you would like to be there secretly to see and hear what happens. • **a fly-on-the-wall documentary/film** a television programme or film in which people do not act but are recorded in real situations, sometimes without knowing • **be dropping like flies** to be dying or becoming sick in large numbers • **wouldn't hurt a fly** If you say that someone wouldn't hurt a fly, you mean that they are very gentle and would never do anything to injure or upset anyone.

flyer (also **flier**) /ˈflaɪəʳ/ noun [C] **1** a small piece of paper advertising a business, show, event, etc: *She's handing out flyers outside the store.* **2** someone who flies, especially a passenger on an aircraft: *a frequent flyer* → See also **high-flyer**

flying /ˈflaɪɪŋ/ adj [always before noun] **1** A flying creature or object moves or is able to move through the air: *flying ants* **2 a flying visit** UK a very brief visit → See also **with flying colours (colour¹)**

flyover /ˈflaɪˌəʊvəʳ/ noun [C] UK (US **overpass**) a bridge that carries a road over another road

FM /ˌefˈem/ noun [U] abbreviation for frequency modulation; a system of radio signals used for broadcasting programmes

foal /fəʊl/ noun [C] a young horse

foam /fəʊm/ noun [U] **1 BUBBLES** ▷ a mass of small, white bubbles on the surface of a liquid **2 PRODUCT** ▷ a thick substance of small, white bubbles used as a cleaning or beauty product:

F

shaving foam **3** FILLING ▷ a soft substance used to fill furniture and other objects

focal point /'fəʊkᵊl,pɔɪnt/ noun [no plural] the thing that attracts most of your attention or interest in a place, picture, etc: *The fireplace is the focal point of the room.*

focus¹ /'fəʊkəs/ verb (**focusing, focused**) **1** [T] If you focus a camera or something else than you look through, you make small changes to it until you can see something clearly. **2** [I, T] If you focus your eyes, or your eyes focus, they change so that you can see clearly: *Give your eyes time to focus in the darkness.*

PHRASAL VERB **focus (sth) on sth** ⓑ to give a lot of attention to one particular subject or thing: *The research focused on men under thirty.*

focus² /'fəʊkəs/ noun **1** the focus of sth ⓑ the person or thing that is getting most attention in a situation or activity: *the focus of our attention* ◦ *He is the focus of a police investigation.* **2** [U] the special attention you give to something: *Their main focus must be on reducing crime.* **3** in focus If an image is in focus, you are able to see it clearly. **4** out of focus If an image is out of focus, you are not able to see it clearly.

> ☑ Word partners for **focus**
>
> be the focus of sth • the focus is on (doing) sth

'focus ,group noun [group] a group of people who are brought together to discuss what they think about something such as a new product

fodder /'fɒdər/ noun [U] food such as dried grass for animals that are kept on farms: *cattle fodder*

foe /fəʊ/ noun [C] literary an enemy

foetus UK (US **fetus**) /'fiːtəs/ noun [C] a young human or animal that is still developing inside its mother • **foetal** UK (US **fetal**) /'fiːtᵊl/ adj *foetal development*

fog /fɒg/ noun [U] ⓐ thick cloud just above the ground or sea that makes it difficult to see

> ☑ Word partners for **fog**
>
> fog descends • fog clears/lifts • dense/heavy/thick fog

foggy /'fɒgi/ adj ⓐ with fog: *a foggy day*

IDIOM **not have the foggiest (idea)** informal to not know anything about something: [+ question word] *I haven't the foggiest idea what you're talking about.*

foible /'fɔɪbl/ noun [C] a slightly unusual or annoying habit: [usually plural] *Married couples must learn to accept each other's **little foibles.***

foil¹ /fɔɪl/ noun **1** [U] metal made into very thin sheets like paper and used mainly for covering food: UK *aluminium foil*/US *aluminum foil* **2** a foil for sb/sth a person or thing that shows or emphasizes how different someone or something else is

foil² /fɔɪl/ verb [T] to stop a crime, plan, etc from succeeding, or to stop someone doing what they want to do: [often passive] *The plot was foiled by undercover police officers.*

fold¹ /fəʊld/ verb **1** MATERIAL ▷ [T] ⓑ If you fold paper, cloth, etc, you bend it so that one part of it lies flat on top of another part: *He folded the letter in half.* **2** FURNITURE ▷ [I, T] (also **fold up**) to make something such as a chair or table smaller or flatter by closing it or bending it together: *a folding chair* → Opposite **unfold** **3** BUSINESS ▷ [I] informal If a business folds, it fails and is unable to continue: *The magazine folded last year.* **4** fold your arms to bend your arms across your chest, with one crossing over the other: *He sat with his arms folded.*

fold² /fəʊld/ noun [C] **1** a line or mark where paper, cloth, etc was or is folded: *Make a fold across the centre of the card.* **2** a thick part where something folds or hangs over itself: [usually plural] *folds of skin/fabric*

folder /'fəʊldər/ noun [C] **1** ⓐ a piece of plastic or thick paper folded down the middle and used to store loose papers → See colour picture **The Office** on page Centre 5 **2** ⓑ a place on a computer where particular files (= documents, pictures, etc) are kept

foliage /'fəʊliɪdʒ/ noun [U] the leaves on a plant

folk¹ /fəʊk/ noun **1** [plural] UK informal (US **folks**) people: *country folk* ◦ *old folk* **2** sb's folk informal someone's parents: *We always spend Christmas with my folks.* **3** [U] ⓑ folk music

folk² /fəʊk/ adj folk art/dancing, etc ⓑ the traditional style of art, dancing, etc among a particular group of people

'folk ,music noun [U] music written and played in a traditional style

'folk ,song noun [C] a traditional song of a particular region or group of people

follow /'fɒləʊ/ verb **1** GO ▷ [I, T] ⓐ to move behind someone or something and go where they go, sometimes secretly: *She followed me into the kitchen.* **2** HAPPEN ▷ [I, T] ⓑ to happen or come after something: *There was a bang followed by a cloud of smoke.* **3** follow a path/road, etc ⓑ to travel along a path/road, etc: *Follow the main road down to the traffic lights.* **4** follow instructions/orders/rules, etc ⓑ to do what the instructions/orders/rules, etc say you should do: *I followed your advice and stayed at home.* **5** follow sb's example/lead to copy someone's behaviour or idea **6** UNDERSTAND ▷ [I, T] ⓑ to understand something: *Could you say that again? I didn't quite follow.* **7** BE INTERESTED ▷ [T] to be interested in an event or activity: *I followed the trial closely.* **8** as follows ⓑ used to introduce a list or description **9** it follows that used to say that if one thing is true, another thing will also be true: *He's big, but it doesn't follow that he's strong.* → See also **follow in sb's footsteps, follow suit¹**

PHRASAL VERBS **follow on** mainly UK to happen or exist as the next part of something: *This report follows on from my earlier study.* • **follow sth through** to do something as the next part of an activity or period of development, usually to make certain that it is completed or successful • **follow sth up** ⓑ to discover more about situation or take further action in connection with it

ollower /'fɒləʊəʳ/ noun [C] someone who believes in a particular person or set of ideas: a **follower of** Jesus

ollowing¹ /'fɒləʊɪŋ/ adj **1 the following day/morning, etc** ⓑ the next day/morning, etc **2 the following** ⓑ what comes next, often used to introduce a list, report, etc: The following is an extract from her diary: Today I stayed in bed all day.

ollowing² /'fɒləʊɪŋ/ noun [no plural] a group of people who support a leader, sport, etc, or admire a particular performer: He has a large and loyal following.

ollowing³ /'fɒləʊɪŋ/ preposition ⓑ after or as a result of: He died on October 23rd, following several years of illness.

ollow-up /'fɒləʊʌp/ noun [C] something that is done to continue or complete something that was done before: a follow-up meeting

ond /fɒnd/ adj **1 be fond of sb/sth** ⓑ to like someone or something: to be fond of animals/music ∘ [+ doing sth] He's not very fond of dancing. **2** ⓑ [always before noun] expressing or causing happy feelings: fond memories **3 a fond hope/belief, etc** something that you wish were true, but probably is not • **fondly** adv • **fondness** noun [C, U] We both have a fondness for cricket.

ondle /'fɒndl/ verb [T] to touch and rub part of someone's body, in a loving or sexual way

ont /fɒnt/ noun [C] **1** a set of letters and symbols that are printed in a particular design and size: What size font are you using? **2** a container in a church that holds the water for a baptism (= Christian ceremony)

ood /fuːd/ noun [C, U] ⓐ something that people and animals eat, or plants absorb, to keep them alive: **baby/dog food** ∘ His favourite food is pizza. → See colour picture **Food** on page Centre 11 → See also **fast food, junk food**

> ☑ Word partners for **food**
>
> cold/hot/savoury/sweet food • baby/cat/dog food • canned/frozen/organic/processed food

oodie /'fuːdi/ noun [C] informal someone who loves food and knows a lot about it

ood ˌmile noun [C] a unit for measuring how far food travels from where it is made or grown to where it is eaten: People are becoming more concerned about how many food miles their produce has travelled.

ood ˌpoisoning noun [U] an illness caused by eating food containing harmful bacteria

ood ˌprocessor noun [C] a piece of electrical equipment with a sharp blade, for cutting and mixing food → See colour picture **The Kitchen** on page Centre 2

oodstuff /'fuːdstʌf/ noun [C] formal a substance used as food or to make food: [usually plural] They need **basic foodstuffs** like rice and corn.

ool¹ /fuːl/ noun **1** ⓑ [C] a stupid person: I was a fool to trust him. **2 make a fool (out) of sb** ⓑ to

try to make someone look stupid intentionally: She was always trying to make a fool out of me in front of my friends. **3 make a fool of yourself** ⓑ to behave in a silly or embarrassing way: I got drunk and started singing and making a fool of myself. **4 act/play the fool** to behave in a silly way, usually in order to make people laugh: Joe is always playing the fool in class.

fool² /fuːl/ verb **1** ⓑ [T] to trick someone: Don't be fooled by his appearance. ∘ [+ into + doing sth] He fooled the old man into giving him the money. **2 you could have fooled me** informal something that you say when you do not believe what someone says about something that you saw or experienced yourself: "I wasn't cross." "Really? You could have fooled me."

PHRASAL VERBS **fool around/about** to behave in a silly way or have a good time: Stop fooling around – this is serious! • **fool with sb/sth** mainly US to deal with someone or something that could be dangerous in a stupid or careless way

foolhardy /'fuːlˌhɑːdi/ adj taking or involving silly and unnecessary risks: a **foolhardy decision**

foolish /'fuːlɪʃ/ adj ⓑ silly and not wise: [+ to do sth] It would be foolish to ignore his advice. • **foolishly** adv • **foolishness** noun [U]

foolproof /'fuːlpruːf/ adj A foolproof method, plan, or system is certain to succeed and not fail.

foot¹ /fʊt/ noun **1** [C] (plural **feet**) ⓐ one of the two flat parts on the ends of your legs that you stand on: bare feet ∘ He stepped on my foot. → See colour picture **The Body** on page Centre 13 **2** [C] (plural **foot, feet**) (written abbreviation **ft**) ⓑ a unit for measuring length, equal to 0.3048 metres or 12 inches: Alex is about 6 feet tall. → See Study Page **Measurements** on page Centre 31 **3 the foot of sth** the bottom of something such as stairs, a hill, a bed, or a page: Put the notes at the foot of the page. **4 on foot** ⓑ If you go somewhere on foot, you walk there. → See Note at **walk**² **5 be on your feet** to be standing and not sitting: I'm exhausted, I've been on my feet all day. **6 put your feet up** to relax, especially by sitting with your feet supported above the ground **7 set foot in/on sth** to go into a place or onto a piece of land: He told me never to set foot in his house again. **8 get/rise to your feet** to stand up after you have been sitting: The audience rose to their feet.

IDIOMS **drag your feet** to deal with something slowly because you do not really want to do it • **get cold feet** to suddenly become too frightened to do what you had planned to do, especially something important • **get/start off on the wrong foot** to start a relationship or activity badly: He got off on the wrong foot with my parents by arriving late. • **not put a foot wrong** UK to not make any mistakes • **put your foot down** to tell someone in a strong way that they must do something or must stop doing something • **put your foot in it** UK (US **put your foot in your mouth**) to say something silly or embarrassing, without intending to • **stand on your own two feet** to do things for yourself

F

without wanting or needing anyone else to help you

foot² /fʊt/ **verb foot the bill** to pay for something: *Why should taxpayers have to foot the bill?*

footage /'fʊtɪdʒ/ **noun** [U] film of an event: *news/TV footage*

football /'fʊtbɔːl/ **noun 1 UK GAME** ▷ [U] UK (UK/ US **soccer**) ⓐ a game in which two teams of players kick a round ball and try to score goals: *a game of football* ○ *a football match/team* → See colour picture **Sports 2** on page Centre 15 **2 US GAME** ▷ [U] US (UK **American football**) a game in which two teams of players try to kick, run with, or throw an oval ball across each other's goal line → See colour picture **Sports 2** on page Centre 15 **3 BALL** ▷ [C] ⓐ a large ball for kicking, especially in football ● **footballer noun** [C] UK someone who plays football, especially as their job ● **footballing adj** [always before noun] relating to or playing football: *his footballing career*

> ☑ Word partners for **football**
>
> play football ● a football club/match/player/ team ● a game of football

foothills /'fʊthɪlz/ **noun** [plural] the lower hills next to a mountain or line of mountains

foothold /'fʊthəʊld/ **noun** [C] **1** a place where it is safe to put your foot when you are climbing **2** a safe position from which you can make more progress, for example in business: *We are still trying to gain a foothold in the Japanese market.*

footing /'fʊtɪŋ/ **noun 1** [no plural] If you have a footing on a surface, you are standing on it firmly: *I lost my footing and fell.* **2 be on an equal/firm, etc footing** to be in an equal/safe, etc position or situation

footnote /'fʊtnəʊt/ **noun** [C] extra information that is printed at the bottom of a page

footpath /'fʊtpɑːθ/ **noun** [C] mainly UK a path or track for people to walk along, especially in the countryside: *a public footpath*

footprint /'fʊtprɪnt/ **noun** [C] **1** a mark made by a foot or shoe: [usually plural] *The police found some footprints in the mud.* **2** the amount of space on a surface that something needs, especially a computer → Compare **ecological footprint**

footstep /'fʊtstep/ **noun** [C] the sound of a foot hitting the ground when someone walks: [usually plural] *I heard footsteps behind me and quickly turned round.*

IDIOM **follow in sb's footsteps** to do the same job or the same things in your life as someone else, especially a member of your family: *He followed in his father's footsteps and became an actor.*

footwear /'fʊtweə^r/ **noun** [U] shoes, boots, and other things that you wear on your feet

for strong /fɔː^r/ weak /fə^r/ **preposition 1 GIVEN/ USED** ▷ ⓐ intended to be given to or used by someone or something: *I've bought a few clothes for the new baby.* ○ *parking for residents only* **2 PURPOSE** ▷ ⓐ having a particular purpose: *a cream for dry skin* ○ *What are those large scissors*

for? **3 BECAUSE OF** ▷ ⓐ because of or as a resul of something: [+ doing sth] *I got fined fc travelling without a ticket.* ○ *Scotland is famou for its spectacular countryside.* **4 TIMI DISTANCE** ▷ ⓐ used to show an amount c time or distance: *We drove for miles before w found a phone box.* ○ *I've been living with m parents for a few months.* → See Note at **durin 5 GET** ▷ ⓐ in order to get or achieve something *I've sent off for an application form.* ○ *We had t wait for a taxi.* **6 HELP** ▷ ⓑ in order to hel someone: *I'll carry those bags for yo* **7 OCCASION** ▷ ⓐ on the occasion of: *We'r having a party for Jim's 60th birthday.* **8 AT TIME** ▷ ⓐ at a particular time: *I've booked table for 9 o'clock.* **9 IN EXCHANGE** ▷ ⓐ i exchange for something, especially an amoun of money: *How much did you pay for you computer?* ○ *I'd like to change it for a smaller one* **10 SUPPORT** ▷ ⓑ supporting or agreeing wit someone or something: *Who did you vote for* ○ *There were 16 people for the motion and 1 against.* **11 REPRESENT** ▷ ⓑ representing c working with a country, organization, etc: *H plays football for Manchester United.* ○ *She work for a charity.* **12 TOWARDS** ▷ ⓐ towards or i the direction of: *Just follow the signs for th airport.* **13 COMPARE** ▷ when compared to particular fact: *She's quite tall for her age* **14 MEANING** ▷ ⓐ meaning or representin something: *What's the German word for 'cucun ber'?* **15 RESPONSIBILITY** ▷ used to say whos responsibility something is: *I can't tell yo whether you should go or not – that's for you t decide.* **16 for all** despite: *For all her qualifio tions, she's useless at the job.* **17 for all I care know** used to say that a fact is not important t you: *He could be married by now, for all I care* **18 for now** used to say that something shoul happen or be done now but can be change later: *Just put everything on the table for nou* **19 be for it** UK informal (UK/US **be in for it**) t be in trouble: *If Hilary finds out I'll be for it!*

forage /'fɒrɪdʒ/ **verb** [I] to move about searchin for things you need, especially food: *Chimpai zees spend most of the day foraging for frui leaves, and insects.*

foray /'fɒreɪ/ **noun** [C] an occasion when you tr to do something that is not familiar to you, o go somewhere different, for a short time: *I 2004, she made her first foray into politics.*

forbid /fə'bɪd/ **verb** [T] (**forbidding, forbade forbidden**) **1** ⓑ to order someone not to d something, or to say that something must no happen: [+ to do sth] *I forbid you to see that bo again.* ○ [often passive, + from + doing sth] *He forbidden from leaving the country.* **2 God Heaven forbid!** something you say when yo hope that something will not happen: [+ (that) *God forbid that he should die during the operatio* ● **forbidden adj** ⓑ not allowed by an officia rule: *Smoking is strictly forbidden in this area.*

forbidding /fə'bɪdɪŋ/ **adj** looking unpleasant unfriendly, or frightening: *a cold and forbiddin landscape*

force¹ /fɔːs/ **noun 1 POWER** ▷ [U] ⓑ physica

power or strength: *The force of the explosion shattered every window in the street.* ◦ *The army has seized power by force.* **2 ORGANIZED GROUP** ▷ [C] 🔵 a group of people organized to work together for a particular purpose, for example in military service: *the Royal Air Force* ◦ *a skilled work force* **3 INFLUENCE** ▷ [C, U] power and influence, or a person or thing that has it: *the forces of good/evil* **4 in/into force** If a law, rule, etc is in force, it is being used, and if it comes into force, it starts to be used: *The new law came into force in April.* **5 be out in force** to be somewhere in large numbers: *Photographers were out in force at the palace today.*

IDIOMS **a force to be reckoned with** a very powerful person or organization ● **join forces** When two people or groups join forces, they act or work together: [+ to do sth] *She joined forces with her sister-in-law to set up a restaurant.*

→ See also **air force, the armed forces, market forces, police force, task force**

📋 Word partners for **force**

exert/use force ● **brute/sheer** force ● **do sth by** force ● **the force of** sth

force² /fɔːs/ verb [T] **1** 🔵 to make someone do something that they do not want to do: [+ to do sth] *The hijacker forced the pilot to fly to New York.* ◦ [often passive] *She was forced out of the race by a knee injury.* **2** 🔵 to make an object move or open by physical strength or effort: *They had to force the lock.* ◦ *She forced the window open.*

forceful /ˈfɔːsfəl/ adj expressing opinions strongly and demanding attention or action: *a forceful manner/personality* ● **forcefully adv** *to argue forcefully*

forcible /ˈfɔːsəbl/ adj A forcible action is done using force: *forcible entry/arrest* ● **forcibly adv** *Thousands of people were forcibly removed from their homes.*

fore /fɔːʳ/ noun to the fore in or to an important or popular position: *The band first came to the fore in 2009.*

forearm /ˈfɔːrɑːm/ noun [C] the lower part of your arm between your hand and your elbow (= the place where it bends)

foreboding /fɔːˈbəʊdɪŋ/ noun [U, no plural] a feeling that something very bad is going to happen: *a sense of foreboding*

forecast¹ /ˈfɔːkɑːst/ noun [C] 🔵 a report saying what is likely to happen in the future: *economic forecasts* → See also **weather forecast**

📋 Word partners for **forecast**

a forecast **of** sth ● **an economic** forecast ● **a gloomy** forecast

forecast² /ˈfɔːkɑːst/ verb [T] (**forecast, forecasted**) to say what you expect to happen in the future: *In 2001 a serious earthquake was forecast for the area.* ● **forecaster noun** [C] *a weather forecaster*

forecourt /ˈfɔːkɔːt/ noun [C] UK a large area with a hard surface at the front of a building: *a garage forecourt*

forefather /ˈfɔːˌfɑːðəʳ/ noun formal **sb's forefathers** someone's relatives who lived a long time ago

forefinger /ˈfɔːˌfɪŋɡəʳ/ noun [C] the finger next to your thumb

forefront /ˈfɔːfrʌnt/ noun be at/in the forefront of sth to have an important position or job in an area of activity: *The company is at the forefront of developing new technology.*

forego /fɔːˈɡəʊ/ verb [T] (**foregoing, forewent, foregone**) another spelling of forgo (= to decide not to have or do something you want)

foregone conˈclusion noun [no plural] a result that is obvious before it happens: [+ (that)] *It was a foregone conclusion that he'd go into politics.*

the foreground /ˈfɔːɡraʊnd/ noun 1 the area of a view or picture that seems closest to you: *There's a seated figure in the foreground of the painting.* **2** the subject or person that people give most attention to: *Environmental issues have recently moved to the foreground.*

forehand /ˈfɔːhænd/ noun [C] a way of hitting the ball in sports such as tennis, with your arm held out on the side that you hold the racket (= object to hit balls with): *a forehand volley*

forehead /ˈfɔːhed, ˈfɒrɪd/ noun [C] 🔵 the part of your face between your eyes and your hair → See colour picture **The Body** on page Centre 13

foreign /ˈfɒrɪn/ adj 1 🔵 belonging to or coming from another country, not your own: *a foreign language/student* ◦ *foreign cars/films* **2** [always before noun] 🔵 relating to or dealing with countries that are not your own: *foreign policy* ◦ *the Foreign Minister* **3 be foreign to sb** to be something you know nothing about or do not understand: *The concept of loyalty is completely foreign to him.*

foreigner /ˈfɒrɪnəʳ/ noun [C] 🔵 someone from another country

foreman /ˈfɔːmən/ noun [C] (plural **foremen**) someone who leads a group of workers: *a factory foreman*

foremost /ˈfɔːməʊst/ adj, adv formal most important: *He's one of the country's foremost experts on military law.*

forename /ˈfɔːneɪm/ noun [C] UK formal your first name, which comes before your family name

forensic /fəˈrensɪk/ adj [always before noun] relating to scientific methods of solving crimes: *forensic evidence/medicine* ◦ *a forensic scientist*

forerunner /ˈfɔːˌrʌnəʳ/ noun [C] an earlier, less developed example: *the forerunner of the modern car*

foresee /fɔːˈsiː/ verb [T] (**foreseeing, foresaw, foreseen**) to expect a future situation or event: *I don't foresee any problems in the future.*

foreseeable /fɔːˈsiːəbl/ adj for/in the foreseeable future as far in the future as you can imagine: *Prices will remain high for the foreseeable future.*

foreshadow /fɔːˈʃædəʊ/ verb [T] formal to show or warn that something bigger, worse, or more important is coming

foresight /ˈfɔːsaɪt/ **noun** [U] the ability to know or judge what will happen or what you will need in the future: *She had the foresight to book her flight early.*

foreskin /ˈfɔːskɪn/ **noun** [C, U] the loose skin that covers the end of a penis

forest /ˈfɒrɪst/ **noun** [C, U] **A2** a large area of trees growing closely together: *pine forest* • **forested** adj covered by forest: *heavily forested areas*

forest

forestall /fɔːˈstɔːl/ **verb** [T] to prevent something from happening by taking action before it does: *to forestall an attack/crisis*

forestry /ˈfɒrɪstri/ **noun** [U] the work of looking after or making forests

foretell /fɔːˈtel/ **verb** [T] (**foretold**) formal to say what is going to happen in the future

forever /fəˈrevəʳ/ **adv 1 IN FUTURE** ▷ **B1** for all time in the future: *I'll love you forever.* **2 A LONG TIME** ▷ informal **B2** used to emphasize that something takes a long time: *The journey home took forever.* **3 OFTEN** ▷ used to emphasize that something happens often: *She is forever helping people.*

foreword /ˈfɔːwɜːd/ **noun** [C] a short piece of writing at the front of a book that introduces the book or its writer

forfeit /ˈfɔːfɪt/ **verb** [T] to lose the right to do something or have something because you have done something wrong: *They have **forfeited** the **right** to live in society.*

forgave /fəˈɡeɪv/ past tense of forgive

forge¹ /fɔːdʒ/ **verb** [T] **1** to make an illegal copy of something in order to deceive people: *a **forged passport*** **2** to develop a good relationship with someone or something: *The group **forged friendships** that have lasted more than twenty years.*

PHRASAL VERB **forge ahead** to suddenly make a lot of progress with something: *The organizers are **forging ahead with** a programme of public events.*

forge² /fɔːdʒ/ **noun** [C] a place where metal objects are made by heating and shaping metal

forgery /ˈfɔːdʒəʳri/ **noun 1** [C] an illegal copy of a document, painting, etc **2** [U] the crime of making an illegal copy of something

forget /fəˈɡet/ **verb** (**forgetting, forgot, forgotten**) **1 NOT REMEMBER** ▷ [I, T] **B1** to be unable to remember a fact, something that happened, or how to do something: *I've forgotten his name.* ○ [+ (that)] *Don't forget that Lucy and John are coming this weekend.* ○ *He'd completely **forgotten about** their quarrel.* ○ [+ question word] *You never forget how to ride a bike.* **2 NOT DO** ▷ [I, T] **A2** to not remember to do something: [+ to do sth] *Dad's always forgetting to take his pills.* **3 NOT**

BRING ▷ [T] **A2** to not bring something with you because you did not remember it: *Oh no, I've forgotten my passport.* **4 STOP THINKING** ▷ [T (also **forget about**) **B1** to stop thinking about someone or something: *I'll never forget him for as long as I live.* **5 forget it** used to tell someone not to worry about something as it is not important **6 I forget** used instead of 'I have forgotten': *I forget when we last saw him* **7 forget yourself** to do or say something that is not acceptable in a particular situation: *She completely forgot herself and started screaming at him.*

➕ Other ways of saying **forget**

The expression **slip someone's mind** is often used informally when someone forgets to do something:

*I meant to tell you that he'd phoned, but I completely **slipped my mind**.*

If a word is **on the tip of your tongue**, you have forgotten it but think that you will very soon remember it:

*Oh, what was that film called? – it's **on the tip of my tongue**.*

If something such as a name **escapes** you, you cannot remember it:

*The name of her book **escapes** me at the moment.*

forgetful /fəˈɡetfəl/ **adj** often forgetting things *James is 84 now and getting a bit forgetful* • **forgetfulness** noun [U]

forgive /fəˈɡɪv/ **verb** (**forgave, forgiven**) **1** **B1** [I T] to decide not to be angry with someone or not to punish them for something they have done *I've apologized, but I don't think she'll ever forgive me.* ○ [often reflexive] *Mike would never forgive himself if anything happened to the children.* ○ [+ for + doing sth] *Jane never forgave her mother for lying to her.* **2 forgive me** **B2** used before you ask or say something that might seem rude: *Forgive me for asking, but how much did you pay for your bag?* **3 sb could be forgiven for doing sth** used to say that you can understand if someone might think, believe, or do something

forgiveness /fəˈɡɪvnəs/ **noun** [U] the kindness of forgiving someone for something they have done

🔲 Word partners for **forgiveness**

ask (for)/beg (for) forgiveness • forgiveness **for sth**

forgiving /fəˈɡɪvɪŋ/ **adj** ready to forgive someone for something they have done

forgo /fɔːˈɡəʊ/ **verb** [T] (**forgoing, forwent, forgone**) formal to decide not to have or do something, although you want to have it or do it: *She had to forgo her early ambition to be a writer.*

forgot /fəˈɡɒt/ past tense of forget

forgotten /fəˈɡɒtən/ past participle of forget

fork¹ /fɔːk/ **noun** [C] **1 FOOD** ▷ **A2** a small object with three or four points and a handle, that you use to pick up food and eat with: *a knife and fork* **2 DIGGING** ▷ a tool with a long handle three or four points, used for digging and breaking soil into pieces: *a garden fork* **3 ROAD** ▷ a place where a road or river divides into two parts: *Turn right when you reach a **fork in the road**.*

ork² /fɔːk/ **verb** [I] If a road or river forks, it divides into two parts.

PHRASAL VERB **fork sth out** mainly UK (US **fork sth over**) to pay or give money for something, especially when you do not want to

orlorn /fəˈlɔːn/ **adj** lonely and unhappy: *The captured soldiers looked forlorn and helpless.*
• **forlornly adv**

orm¹ /fɔːm/ **noun 1 TYPE** ▷ [C] 🔵 a type of something or way of doing something: *Swimming is the best **form of** exercise.* **2 PAPER** ▷ [C] 🔵 a printed document with spaces for you to write information: *Please **fill in/out the form** using black ink.* **3** the form of sth the particular way in which something exists: *The novel is written **in the form of** a series of letters.* **4 SPORT** ▷ [U] In sport, someone's form is how well or badly they are performing: *The team seems to have **lost its form** lately.* **5 be in/on/off form** UK If someone is in form or on form, they are feeling or performing well, and if they are off form they are not feeling or performing well: *Harry was **on good form** last night.* **6 SCHOOL GROUP** ▷ [C] UK (US **grade**) 🔵 a school class or group of classes for students of the same age or ability: *He's **in the** third **form**.* **7 SHAPE** ▷ [C] the body or shape of someone or something **8 GRAMMAR** ▷ [C] 🔵 a way of writing or saying a word that shows if it is singular or plural, past or present, etc: *The plural form of 'sheep' is 'sheep'.* → See also **application form, sixth form**

orm² /fɔːm/ **verb 1 BEGIN** ▷ [I, T] 🔵 to begin to exist, or to make something begin to exist: [often passive] *We are learning more about how stars are formed.* **2 SHAPE** ▷ [I, T] to take or to make something take a particular shape: ***Form*** *the dough **into** little balls.* **3 COMBINE** ▷ [T] 🔵 to make something by combining different parts: *In English you form the present participle by adding -ing to the verb.* **4 START** ▷ [T] 🔵 to start an organization or business: *Brown formed her own company eleven years ago.* **5 BE** ▷ [T] to be the thing talked about or be part of it: *The Alps form a natural barrier between Italy and Switzerland.* **6 form an opinion/impression, etc** to begin to have a particular opinion or idea about something because of the information you have

ormal /ˈfɔːməl/ **adj 1 SERIOUS** ▷ 🔵 used about clothes, language, and behaviour that are serious and not friendly or relaxed: *a formal dinner party* **2 OFFICIAL** ▷ [always before noun] public or official: *a formal announcement/apology* **3 IN SCHOOL** ▷ [always before noun] Formal education, training, etc happens in a school or college: *Tom had little **formal schooling**.*

ormality /fɔːˈmæləti/ **noun 1** [C] something that the law or an official process says must be done: *There are certain **legal formalities** to be*
completed. **2** [U] formal and polite behaviour: *the formality of a royal funeral*

formally /ˈfɔːməli/ **adv 1** officially: *The deal will be **formally announced** on Tuesday.* **2** in a polite way: *They shook hands formally.*

format¹ /ˈfɔːmæt/ **noun** [C] the way something is designed, arranged, or produced: *This year's event will have a **new format**.*

format² /ˈfɔːmæt/ **verb** [T] (**formatting, formatted**) **1** to prepare a computer disk so that information can be stored on it **2** to organize and design the words on a page or document

formation /fɔːˈmeɪʃən/ **noun 1** [U] the development of something into a particular thing or shape: *the formation of a crystal* **2** [C, U] the particular shape of something or the way things are arranged: *rock/cloud formations* ○ *The planes flew overhead **in formation** (= in a pattern).*

formative /ˈfɔːmətɪv/ **adj** relating to the time when your character and opinions are developing: *She spent **her formative years** in New York.*

former¹ /ˈfɔːmər/ **adj** [always before noun] 🔵 happening, existing, or true in the past but not now: *the former Soviet Union* ○ *former President Bill Clinton*

former² /ˈfɔːmər/ **noun the former** 🔵 the first of two people or things that have just been talked about

formerly /ˈfɔːməli/ **adv** 🔵 in the past: *The European Union was formerly called the European Community.*

formidable /ˈfɔːmɪdəbl/ **adj 1** Someone who is formidable is strong and slightly frightening: *a formidable woman* **2** difficult and needing a lot of effort or thought: *a formidable task*

formula /ˈfɔːmjələ/ **noun** [C] (plural **formulas, formulae**) **1 METHOD** ▷ a plan or method that is used to achieve something: *There's no magic **formula for** success.* **2 RULE** ▷ a set of letters, numbers, or symbols that are used to express a mathematical or scientific rule **3 LIST** ▷ a list of the substances that something is made of

formulate /ˈfɔːmjəleɪt/ **verb** [T] **1** to develop all the details of a plan for doing something: *They **formulated** a **plan** to save the company.* **2** to say what you think or feel after thinking carefully: *to **formulate** an **answer/reply*** • **formulation** /ˌfɔːmjəˈleɪʃən/ **noun** [C, U]

forsake /fəˈseɪk/ **verb** [T] (**forsook, forsaken**) formal **1** to leave someone, especially when they need you: *He felt he couldn't forsake her when she was so ill.* **2** to stop doing or having something: *He decided to forsake politics for journalism.*

fort /fɔːt/ **noun** [C] a strong building that soldiers use to defend a place

forth /fɔːθ/ **adv** literary out of a place or away from it: *The knights rode forth into battle.*

forthcoming /ˌfɔːθˈkʌmɪŋ/ **adj 1 SOON** ▷ [always before noun] formal 🔵 going to happen soon: *the forthcoming election/visit* **2 OFFERED** ▷ [never before noun] If money or help is forthcoming, it is offered or given: *He insisted that no more money would be forthcoming.* **3 WILLING** ▷ [never before noun] willing to give information: *Elaine wasn't very forthcoming about her love life.*

forthright /ˈfɔːθraɪt/ **adj** saying what you think honestly and clearly: *They dealt with all our questions in a very forthright manner.*

forthwith /ˌfɔːθˈwɪθ/ **adv** formal immediately: *to cease forthwith*

fortifications /ˌfɔːtɪfɪˈkeɪʃᵊnz/ **noun** [plural] strong walls, towers, etc that are built to protect a place

fortify /ˈfɔːtɪfaɪ/ **verb** [T] **1** to build strong walls, towers, etc around a place to protect it: *a fortified city/town* **2** to make someone feel stronger physically or mentally: *She had a sandwich to fortify herself before going on.*

fortitude /ˈfɔːtɪtjuːd/ **noun** [U] formal brave behaviour, and not complaining about pain or problems

fortnight /ˈfɔːtnaɪt/ **noun** [C] UK 🔵 two weeks: [usually singular] *a fortnight's holiday* ∘ *We usually get together about once a fortnight.* • **fortnightly adv** UK happening every two weeks: *a fortnightly meeting*

fortress /ˈfɔːtrəs/ **noun** [C] a castle or other strong building built to defend a place

fortunate /ˈfɔːtʃᵊnət/ **adj** 🔵 lucky: [+ to do sth] *I'm very fortunate to be alive.* ∘ [+ (that)] *It was fortunate that someone was available to take over.* → Opposite **unfortunate**

fortunately /ˈfɔːtʃᵊnətli/ **adv** 🔵 happening because of good luck: *Fortunately, no one was hurt in the accident.* → Opposite **unfortunately**

fortune /ˈfɔːtʃuːn/ **noun 1** [C] 🔵 a lot of money: *She made a fortune selling her story to the newspapers.* **2** [C, U] 🔵 the good or bad things that happen to you: [usually plural] *The family's fortunes changed almost overnight.*

IDIOM **tell sb's fortune** to say what is going to happen to someone in the future

> ⊘ Word partners for **fortune**
>
> cost/earn/make/spend a fortune • a personal fortune • the family fortune

fortune-teller /ˈfɔːtʃuːnˌtelər/ **noun** [C] someone who tells you what will happen to you in the future

forty /ˈfɔːti/ **1** 🔵 the number 40 **2 the forties** the years from 1940 to 1949 **3 be in your forties** to be aged between 40 and 49 • **fortieth** 40th written as a word

forum /ˈfɔːrəm/ **noun** [C] **1** a situation or meeting in which people can exchange ideas and discuss things: *a forum for debate/discussion* **2** an area of a website where people go to discuss things

forward¹ /ˈfɔːwəd/ **adv** (also **forwards**) **1 DIRECTION** ▷ 🔵 towards the direction that is in front of you: *She leaned forward to make sure I could hear her.* **2 FUTURE** ▷ 🔵 towards the future: *I always look forward, not back.* **3 PROGRESS** ▷ used to say that something is making good progress: *This is a big step forward for democracy.*

forward² /ˈfɔːwəd/ **adj 1 forward motion/movement, etc** movement towards the direction that is in front of you **2 forward planning/**

thinking, etc the activity of planning or thinking about something for the future **3** to confident or too friendly with people you d not know

forward³ /ˈfɔːwəd/ **verb** [T] to send a lette email, etc that you have received to someon else: *Could you forward my mail to me while I'r away?* → See also **fast-forward**

forward⁴ /ˈfɔːwəd/ **noun** [C] a player in a spor such as football who plays near the front an tries to score goals

forwarding a'ddress noun [C] a new addres that letters and parcels should be sent to

forward-looking /ˈfɔːwədlʊkɪŋ/ **adj** plannin for the future and using new ideas or techno ogy: *a forward-looking plan/policy*

forwards /ˈfɔːwədz/ **adv** another word for forwar

forward ˌslash noun [C] (also **slash**) the symbc '/', used in Internet addresses and used to sho where on a computer files are kept → Compar **backslash**

forwent /fɔːˈwent/ past tense of forgo

fossil /ˈfɒsᵊl/ **noun** [C] part of an animal or plan from thousands of years ago, preserved in roc

fossil ˌfuel noun [C, U] a fuel such as coal or o that is obtained from under the ground

foster¹ /ˈfɒstər/ **verb** [T] **1** to encourage particular feeling, situation, or idea to develop *The growth of the Internet could foster economi development worldwide.* **2** to look after a child a part of your family for a time, without becomin their legal parent

foster² /ˈfɒstər/ **adj 1 foster home/mothe parent, etc** the home where a child who i fostered lives, or the person or people wh foster a child **2 foster child/daughter/son, etc** child who is fostered

fought /fɔːt/ past of fight

foul¹ /faʊl/ **adj 1** very dirty, or with a unpleasant smell: *the foul smell of rotting fis* **2** very bad or unpleasant: *foul weather* ∘ *She's i a foul mood.* **3 foul language/words** very rud and offensive words

IDIOM **fall foul of sb/sth** UK to do something tha causes you to be in trouble

foul² /faʊl/ **verb 1** [T] to make something ver dirty: *The beaches had been fouled by dogs.* **2** [I,] to do something that is against the rules in sport: *He was fouled as he was about to shoot* goal.

PHRASAL VERB **foul sth up** informal to spoil some thing completely: *The travel company completel fouled up our holiday.*

foul³ /faʊl/ **noun** [C] something that someon does in a sport that is not allowed by the rule

> ⊘ Word partners for **foul**
>
> commit a foul • a foul against/on sb

foul ˈplay noun [U] a situation in which som one's death is caused by a violent crime: *Polic do not suspect foul play at present.*

found¹ /faʊnd/ **verb** [T] **1** 🔵 to start a organization, especially by providing money

The company was founded in 1861. **2** to base something on a set of ideas or beliefs: [often passive] *a society founded on principles of equality*

found² /faʊnd/ past of find

foundation /faʊnˈdeɪʃən/ noun **1 IDEA** ▷ [C] the idea or principle that something is based on: *Jefferson's document formed the foundation of a new nation.* **2 STARTING** ▷ [U] the process of establishing an organization, state, or country: *the foundation of a new state* **3 ORGANIZATION** ▷ [C] an organization that gives money for a particular purpose: *the Mental Health Foundation* **4 foundations** [plural] mainly UK (US **foundation** [C]) the part of a building, road, bridge, etc that is under the ground and supports it: *concrete foundations* **5 MAKE-UP** ▷ [U] make-up that is worn all over the face to give it a smooth appearance **6 be without foundation; have no foundation** If something is without foundation, there is no proof that it is true: *The allegations are completely without foundation.*

IDIOM **lay the foundation(s) for/of sth** to provide the conditions that make it possible for something to happen: *His reforms laid the foundation of future greatness.*

foun'dation ˌcourse noun [C] UK (US **introductory course**) a college or university course on a subject that students take to prepare them for a more advanced course on that subject

founder /ˈfaʊndər/ noun [C] someone who establishes an organization

foundry /ˈfaʊndri/ noun [C] a place where metal or glass is melted and made into objects

fountain /ˈfaʊntɪn/ noun [C] 🄰 a structure that forces water up into the air as a decoration

fountain

fountain ˌpen noun [C] a pen that you fill with ink

four /fɔːr/ 🄐 the number 4

four-by-four /ˌfɔːbaɪˈfɔːr/ a four-wheel drive

fours /fɔːz/ noun

IDIOM **on all fours** with your hands and knees on the ground

foursome /ˈfɔːsəm/ noun [C] a group of four people: *We could go out as a foursome.*

fourteen /ˌfɔːˈtiːn/ 🄐 the number 14 • **fourteenth** 14th written as a word

fourth¹ /fɔːθ/ 🄑 4th written as a word

fourth² /fɔːθ/ noun [C] US (UK/US **quarter**) one of four equal parts of something; ¼

fourth-generation /ˌfɔːθˌdʒenərˈeɪʃən/ adj (also **4G**) relating to technology that gives mobile phone and computer users more advanced features: *4G phones/technology/networks* ○ *Fourth-generation technology allows networks to handle larger amounts of data at faster speeds.*

Fourth of Juˈly noun [U] (also **Independence**

Day) 4 July, a national holiday in the US to celebrate the country's freedom from Great Britain in 1776

four-wheel ˈdrive noun [C] (written abbreviation **4WD**) a vehicle with an engine that supplies power to all four wheels so that it can drive easily over rough ground • **four-wheel ˈdrive** adj *a four-wheel drive car*

fowl /faʊl/ noun [C] (plural **fowl**, **fowls**) a bird that is kept for its eggs and meat, especially a chicken

fox /fɒks/ noun [C] 🄑 a wild animal like a dog with red-brown fur, a pointed nose, and a long, thick tail

foyer /ˈfɔɪeɪ/ ⓤ /ˈfɔɪər/ noun [C] a room at the entrance of a hotel, theatre, cinema, etc

fracas /ˈfrækɑː/ ⓤ /ˈfreɪkəs/ noun [no plural] a noisy fight or argument

fraction /ˈfrækʃən/ noun [C] **1** a number less than 1, such as ½ or ¾ → See Study Page **Numbers** on page Centre 30 **2** a very small number or amount: *a fraction of a second* • **fractionally** adv by a very small amount: *Harry is fractionally taller than Ben.*

📝 Word partners for **fraction**

a minute/small/tiny fraction of sth • a fraction of sth

---

fracture /ˈfræktʃər/ verb [T] to break something hard such as a bone, or a piece of rock: *She's fractured her ankle.* • **fracture** noun [C]

fragile /ˈfrædʒaɪl/ ⓤ /ˈfrædʒəl/ adj **1** easily broken, damaged, or destroyed: *a fragile china cup* ○ *a fragile economy* **2** physically or emotionally weak: *a fragile little girl* • **fragility** /frəˈdʒɪləti/ noun [U]

fragment¹ /ˈfrægmənt/ noun [C] a small piece of something: *fragments of pottery*

fragment² /frægˈment/ verb [I, T] to break something into small parts, or to be broken in this way: *The opposition has fragmented into a number of small groups.* • **fragmented** adj *a fragmented society*

fragrance /ˈfreɪɡrəns/ noun [C, U] **1** a pleasant smell: *the delicate fragrance of roses* **2** a substance that people put on their bodies to make themselves smell nice: *a new fragrance for men*

fragrant /ˈfreɪɡrənt/ adj with a pleasant smell: *fragrant flowers*

frail /freɪl/ adj not strong or healthy: *a frail old lady*

frailty /ˈfreɪlti/ noun [C, U] the quality of being physically or morally weak

frame¹ /freɪm/ noun [C] **1 PICTURE** ▷ 🄑 a structure that goes around the edge of something such as a door, picture, window, or mirror: *a picture frame* ○ *a window frame* **2 STRUCTURE** ▷ 🄑 the basic structure of a building, vehicle, or piece of furniture that other parts are added onto: *a bicycle frame* **3 BODY** ▷

frame

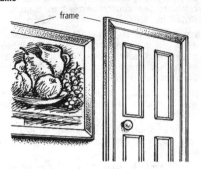

frame

the shape of someone's body: *his large/small frame*

IDIOM **frame of mind** the way someone feels at a particular time: *She was in a much more positive frame of mind today.*

frame² /freɪm/ **verb** [T] **1 PICTURE** ▷ to put something such as a picture into a frame: *I'm going to frame this and put it on the wall.* **2 EDGE** ▷ to form an edge to something in an attractive way: *Dark hair framed her face.* **3 CRIME** ▷ to intentionally make it seem as if someone is guilty of a crime: [often passive] *He claimed he had been framed by the police.* **4 EXPRESS** ▷ formal to express something choosing your words carefully: *I tried to frame a suitable reply.*

frames /freɪmz/ **noun** [plural] the plastic or metal structure that holds together a pair of glasses

framework /ˈfreɪmwɜːk/ **noun** [C] **1** a system of rules, ideas, or beliefs that is used to plan or decide something: *a legal framework for resolving disputes* **2** the basic structure that supports something such as a vehicle or building and gives it its shape

> 🔲 Word partners for **framework**
> create/develop/establish/provide a framework • a framework **for (doing) sth**

franchise /ˈfræntʃaɪz/ **noun 1** [C] the right to sell a company's products or services in a particular area using the company's name: *a fast food franchise* **2** [U] the legal right to vote in elections

frank /fræŋk/ **adj** speaking honestly and saying what you really think: *a full and frank discussion* ∘ **To be frank**, *I don't really want to see him.* • **frankness noun** [U]

frankfurter /ˈfræŋkfɜːtər/ **noun** [C] a long, thin sausage (= tube of meat and spices), often eaten with bread

frankly /ˈfræŋkli/ **adv** ⓑ in an honest and direct way: *Quite frankly, I think you're making a big mistake.*

frantic /ˈfræntɪk/ **adj 1** done in a fast and excited way and not calm or organized: *a frantic search* **2** very worried or frightened: *frantic calls for help* ∘ *I got home to find Joe frantic with worry.* • **frantically adv** *Laura was searching frantically for her keys.*

fraternal /frəˈtɜːnəl/ **adj** like or relating to a brother

fraternity /frəˈtɜːnəti/ **noun 1** [U] a feeling of friendship between people **2** [C] in the US, a social organization of male college students

fraud /frɔːd/ **noun 1** [U, C] the crime of doing something illegal in order to get money: *credit card fraud* **2** [C] someone who deceives people by pretending to be someone or something that they are not

> 🔲 Word partners for **fraud**
> commit fraud • a fraud **case/charge/investigation**

fraudulent /ˈfrɔːdjələnt/ **adj** formal dishonest and illegal: *fraudulent insurance claims* • **fraudulently adv**

fraught /frɔːt/ **adj 1 fraught with danger/difficulties, etc** full of danger/difficulties, etc: *The present situation is fraught with danger.* **2** mainly UK causing worry, or feeling worried: *fraught silence*

fray¹ /freɪ/ **verb 1** [I, T] If material or clothing frays, or if it is frayed, the threads at the edge break and become loose. **2** [I] If your temper (= mood) frays or your nerves fray, you gradually become annoyed or upset: *After hours of waiting, **tempers** were beginning to **fray**.*

fray² /freɪ/ **noun enter/join, etc the fray** to start taking part in an argument or fight: *The time had come for the US to enter the fray.*

freak¹ /friːk/ **noun** [C] **1** informal someone who is very interested in a particular subject or activity: *My brother's a bit of a computer freak.* **2** someone who looks strange or behaves in a strange way: *They made me feel like a freak.*

freak² /friːk/ **adj a freak accident/storm, etc** A freak event is one that is very unusual.

freak³ /friːk/ **verb** [I, T] (also **freak out**) to suddenly become very angry, frightened, or surprised, or to make someone do this: *I hated that film, it totally freaked me out.*

freckle /ˈfrekl/ **noun** [C] a very small, brown spot on your skin from the sun • **freckled adj**

free¹ /friː/ **adj 1 NOT CONTROLLED** ▷ ⓐ able to live, happen, or exist without being controlled by anyone or anything: *free trade* ∘ *a free society* ∘ [+ to do sth] *People should be free to say what they think.* **2 NO COST** ▷ ⓐ not costing any money: *a free sample of perfume* ∘ *Entry is free for children under 12.* ∘ *Children get into the museum free of charge.* **3 NOT A PRISONER** ▷ ⓑ not in prison or in a cage: *He opened the cage and set the birds free.* **4 NOT BUSY** ▷ ⓐ not busy doing anything: *Are you free this evening?* ∘ *I don't have much free time.* **5 NOT USED** ▷ no being used by anyone: *Is this seat free?* **6 free from/of sth** not containing or having anything harmful or unpleasant: *a life free from pain*

IDIOM **feel free** something that you say in order to tell someone that they are allowed to do something: [+ to do sth] *Please feel free to ask questions.*

→ See also **duty-free**, a free **hand¹**, free **rein**, **tax-free**, **toll-free**

free² /friː/ adv **1** without cost or payment: *Children under five travel free.* ∘ *He offered to do it for free.* **2** in a way that is not tied, limited, or controlled: *She broke free from his grasp and ran away.*

free³ /friː/ verb [T] (**freeing**, **freed**) **1 ALLOW TO LEAVE** ▷ to allow someone to leave a prison or place where they have been kept: *The last hostages were finally freed yesterday.* **2 GET OUT** ▷ to get someone out of a situation or place that they cannot escape from: *Firefighters worked for two hours to free the driver from the wreckage.* **3 TAKE AWAY** ▷ to help someone by taking something unpleasant away from them: *The book's success freed her from her financial worries.* **4 MAKE AVAILABLE** ▷ (also **free up**) to make something available for someone to use: *I need to free up some space for these files.*

-free /friː/ suffix used at the end of words to mean 'without' or 'not containing': *sugarfree gum* ∘ *an interest-free loan*

freebie /ˈfriːbi/ noun [C] informal something that you are given, usually by a company, and do not have to pay for

freecycle /ˈfriːsaɪkl/ verb [I, T] trademark to use a local Freecycle email group to give away things that you do not want now • **freecycler** noun [C]

freedom /ˈfriːdəm/ noun **1** [C, U] the right to live in the way you want, say what you think, and make your own decisions without being controlled by anyone else: *religious freedom* ∘ *freedom of choice/speech* ∘ [+ to do sth] *You have the freedom to do what you want to do.* **2 freedom from sth** a situation in which you are not suffering because of something unpleasant or harmful: *freedom from fear/poverty* **3** [U] a situation in which someone is no longer a prisoner

☑ **Word partners for freedom**

be given/have the freedom to do sth • freedom **of choice/of expression/of movement/of speech**

free enterprise noun [U] trade and business that is allowed to operate without much control from the government

freegan /ˈfriːgən/ noun [C] someone who tries not to spend money by eating food and using things that have been thrown away or that are found in nature: *Freegans rarely go hungry thanks to the huge amount of food thrown away every day.*

free kick noun [C] a kick that a player in a game of football is allowed to take after a player from the other team has broken the rules

freelance /ˈfriːlɑːns/ adj, adv working for

several different organizations, and paid according to the hours you work: *a freelance photographer* ∘ *Most of our producers work freelance.* • **freelance** verb [I] • **freelancer** noun [C]

freely /ˈfriːli/ adv **1** without being controlled or limited: *For the first time in months she could move freely.* ∘ *Exotic foods are freely available in supermarkets.* **2** If you freely admit something, you are very willing to agree that it is true: *I freely admit that I was wrong about him.*

free market noun [no plural] a situation in which the government does not control prices and trade: *a free-market economy*

freephone /ˈfriːfəʊn/ adj [always before noun] UK (US **toll-free**) A freephone number is a telephone number that you can connect to without paying.

free-range /ˌfriːˈreɪndʒ/ adj relating to or produced by farm animals that are allowed to move around outside and are not kept in cages: *free-range eggs*

freesheet /ˈfriːʃiːt/ noun [C] a free newspaper

free speech noun [U] the right to express your opinions in public

free trade noun [C] a way to buy and sell products between countries, without limits on the amount of goods that can be bought and sold, and without special taxes on the goods → Compare **fair trade**

freeware /ˈfriːweər/ noun [U] computer software that you do not have to pay for, for example from the Internet

freeway /ˈfriːweɪ/ noun [C] US (UK **motorway**) a long, wide road, usually used by traffic travelling fast over long distances

free will noun **1** [U] a situation in which people choose and decide what they want to do in their own lives **2 do sth of your own free will** to do something because you want to, not because someone forces you to: *She had gone there of her own free will.*

freeze¹ /friːz/ verb (**froze**, **frozen**) **1 ICE** ▷ [I, T] If something freezes or is frozen, it becomes hard and solid because it is very cold: *The river had frozen overnight.* ∘ *Water freezes at 0° Celsius.* **2 FOOD** ▷ [I, T] to make food last a long time by making it very cold and hard: *You can freeze any cakes that you have left over.* **3 PERSON** ▷ [I] to feel very cold: *One of the climbers froze to death on the mountain.* **4 NOT MOVE** ▷ [I] to suddenly stop moving, especially because you are frightened: *She saw someone outside the window and froze.* **5 LEVEL** ▷ [T] to fix the level of something such as a price or rate so that it does not increase **6 COMPUTER** ▷ [I] if a computer freezes, it suddenly stops working and the screen will not change even when you use the keyboard or mouse (= small computer control)

freeze² /friːz/ noun **1 LEVEL** ▷ [C] a situation in which the level of something such as a price or rate is fixed so that it does not increase: *a pay freeze* **2 PROCESS** ▷ [C] a situation in which a process is stopped for a period of time: *There was an immediate freeze on all new building in the city.* **3 COLD** ▷ [no plural] informal a period of extremely cold weather

freezer /ˈfriːzər/ **noun** [C] **B1** a large container operated by electricity in which food can be frozen and stored → See colour picture **The Kitchen** on page Centre 2

freezing¹ /ˈfriːzɪŋ/ **adj** informal **B1** very cold: *It's absolutely freezing in here.*

freezing² /ˈfriːzɪŋ/ **noun** [U] the temperature at which water freezes: *It was five degrees below/above freezing.*

freezing point noun [C, U] the temperature at which a liquid freezes

freight /freɪt/ **noun** [U] goods that are carried by trains, trucks, ships, or aircraft

freighter /ˈfreɪtər/ **noun** [C] a large ship or aircraft that carries goods

French fries noun [plural] US (UK **chips**) long, thin pieces of potato that have been cooked in hot oil → See colour picture **Food** on page Centre 11

French knickers noun [plural] women's loose underwear that covers all the bottom → See colour picture **Clothes** on page Centre 9

French windows noun [plural] (also **French doors**) a pair of glass doors that usually open into a garden

frenetic /frəˈnetɪk/ **adj** fast and exciting in an uncontrolled way: *a frenetic pace* ◦ *frenetic activity*

frenzied /ˈfrenzɪd/ **adj** wild and uncontrolled: *a frenzied dance*

frenzy /ˈfrenzi/ **noun** [U, no plural] the state of being so excited, nervous, or anxious that you cannot control what you are doing: *She hit him in a frenzy of rage.*

frequency /ˈfriːkwənsi/ **noun** [C, U] **1** the number of times something happens in a particular period, or the fact that something happens often or a large number of times: *The frequency of attacks seems to have increased recently.* **2** the rate at which a sound wave or radio wave is repeated: *the very high frequencies of a television signal*

frequent¹ /ˈfriːkwənt/ **adj** **B1** happening often: *He is a frequent visitor to the US.*

frequent² /frɪˈkwent/ **US** /ˈfriːkwent/ **verb** [T] to go to a place often: *a bar frequented by criminals*

frequently /ˈfriːkwəntli/ **adv** formal **B1** often: *a frequently asked question*

fresh /freʃ/ **adj** **1 DIFFERENT** ▷ **B1** new or different from what was there before: *We're looking for fresh ideas.* ◦ *They decided to move abroad and make a fresh start.* **2 NOT OLD** ▷ **A2** Fresh food has been produced or collected recently and has not been frozen, dried, etc.: *fresh fruit/vegetables* ◦ *fresh bread* **3 CLEAN/COOL** ▷ **B1** smelling clean or feeling pleasantly cool: *a fresh breeze* ◦ *a fresh smell* **4 fresh air B1** air outside buildings that is clean and cool: *Let's go outside and get some fresh air.* **5 fresh water** water from lakes, rivers, etc that has no salt in it **6 NOT TIRED** ▷ having a lot of energy and not feeling tired: *We got up the next day feeling fresh and relaxed.* **7 SKIN** ▷ Fresh skin looks healthy: *a fresh complexion* **8 RECENT** ▷ **B2** recently made or done and not yet changed by time: *The memory of the accident is still very fresh in my* mind. **9 fresh from/out of sth** having just left place: *The new French teacher's fresh out of college.* ● **freshness noun** [U] → See also breath of fresh air

freshen /ˈfreʃ°n/ **verb**

PHRASAL VERBS **freshen up** to quickly wash yourself so that you feel clean: *Would you lik to freshen up before dinner?* ● **freshen sth up** t make something look cleaner and more attrac tive: *A coat of paint would help to freshen th place up.*

fresher /ˈfreʃər/ **noun** [C] UK informal a student i the first year of university

freshly /ˈfreʃli/ **adv** recently: *freshly bake bread*

freshman /ˈfreʃmən/ **noun** [C] (plural **freshmer** US a student in their first year of study at a American college or high school (= school fc students aged 15 to 18)

freshwater /ˈfreʃˌwɔːtər/ **adj** relating to wate that is not salty: *freshwater fish*

fret /fret/ **verb** [I] (**fretting, fretted**) to b anxious or worried: *There's no point in frettin about what you cannot change.* ● **fretful** ac anxious and unhappy

Fri written abbreviation for Friday

friar /fraɪər/ **noun** [C] a member of a religiou group of men

friction /ˈfrɪkʃ°n/ **noun** [U] **1** the action rubbing against something, often making mov ment more difficult **2** argument or disagre ment about something, often over a long perio of time: *There's a lot of friction between my wif and my mother.*

Friday /ˈfraɪdeɪ/ **noun** [C, U] (written abbreviatio **Fri**) **A1** the day of the week after Thursday an before Saturday → See also **Good Friday**

fridge /frɪdʒ/ **noun** [C] **A2** a large container tha uses electricity to keep food cold → See colo picture **The Kitchen** on page Centre 2

fridge-freezer /ˌfrɪdʒˈfriːzər/ **noun** [C] a piece c equipment for storing food that has two parts: fridge (= a container that keeps food cold) and freezer (= a container that keeps food frozen)

fried /fraɪd/ **adj** **A2** cooked in hot oil or fat: *fried egg* → See also **deep-fried**

friend /frend/ **noun** [C] **1 A1** someone who yo know well and like: *Sarah's my best friend (= th friend I like most).* ◦ *Gordon is a friend of min* **2 an old friend A2** someone who you hav known and liked for a long time **3 be friend (with sb) B1** to know and like someone: *I hav been friends with Jo for years.* **4 make friend (with sb) B1** to begin to know and like someon *He's shy and finds it difficult to make friends.*

🗹 Word partners for friend

sb's best friend ● a close/good friend ● a family friend ● an old friend ● a friend of mine

---

friendly¹ /ˈfrendli/ **adj** **1 A2** behaving in pleasant, kind way towards someone: *a friendl face/smile* ◦ *The other students have been ver friendly to us.* → Opposite **unfriendly 2 b**

➕ Other ways of saying **friend**

The words **chum, mate** (*UK*), and **pal** are all informal words for 'friend':
*Pete was there with a couple of his **mates**.*
An **old friend** is someone you have known and liked for many years:
*Rachel is one of my **oldest friends**.*
An **acquaintance** is someone you know, but do not know well:
*He had a few business **acquaintances**.*
A **confidant** is a friend whom you can talk to about your feelings and secrets:
*Sarah was my **confidant** throughout this period and I told her everything.*
A group of friends with similar interests are sometimes described informally as a **crowd**:
*"Who was there?" "Oh, you know, Dave, Fiona, and all that **crowd**."*
The informal word **crony** is sometimes used disapprovingly to describe one of a group of friends who help each other in an unfair way:
*He always gives his **cronies** all the best jobs.*

friendly with sb to know and like someone • **friendliness** noun [U]

riendly² /ˈfrendli/ **noun** [C] UK a sports match that is not part of an official competition

friendly /ˈfrendli/ **suffix 1** used at the end of words to mean 'not harmful': *environmentally-friendly detergent* **2** used at the end of words to mean 'suitable for particular people to use': *family-friendly restaurant* → See also **user-friendly**

riendship /ˈfrendʃɪp/ **noun** [C, U] 🔵 the relationship between people who are friends: *a close friendship*

🔲 Word partners for **friendship**

strike up a friendship • a **close** friendship • sb's friendship **with** sb • a friendship **between** sb and sb

ries /fraɪz/ **noun** [plural] mainly US (UK **chips**) long, thin pieces of potato that have been cooked in hot oil

rieze /friːz/ **noun** [C] an area of decoration along a wall

rigate /ˈfrɪɡət/ **noun** [C] a small, fast military ship

right /fraɪt/ **noun** [U, no plural] a sudden feeling of shock and fear: *That dog **gave me a** terrible **fright**.* ∘ *She screamed **in fright** when she saw him.*

righten /ˈfraɪtⁿn/ **verb** [T] 🔵 to make someone afraid or nervous: *It frightens me when he drives so fast.* → See also **scare/frighten the (living) daylights** out of sb, **scare/frighten sb out of their wits**

PHRASAL VERB **frighten sb away/off** to make a person or animal afraid or nervous so that they go away

rightened /ˈfraɪtⁿnd/ **adj** 🔵 afraid or nervous:

*I've always been **frightened of** going to the dentist.* ∘ *[+ (that)] Gerry was frightened that people would laugh at him.*

➕ Other ways of saying **frightened**

The adjectives **afraid** and **scared** are common alternatives to 'frightened':
*She's very **afraid** of dogs.*
*Gerry has always been **scared** of heights.*
If someone is extremely frightened, then you can use adjectives like **petrified, terrified, panic-stricken**, or the informal phrase **scared to death**:
*I'm **terrified** of flying.*
*She was **panic-stricken** when her little boy disappeared.*
*He's **scared to death** of having the operation.*
If someone is frightened because they are worrying about something, then you can use the adjectives **afraid** and **worried**:
*I'm **afraid/worried** that something will go wrong.*
If someone is frightened about something that might happen in the future, you can use the adjectives **apprehensive** or **uneasy**:
*He's a bit **apprehensive** about living away from home.*

frightening /ˈfraɪtⁿnɪŋ/ **adj** 🔵 making you feel afraid or nervous: *a very frightening film* • **frighteningly adv**

frightful /ˈfraɪtfⁿl/ **adj** UK old-fashioned very bad: *The house was in a frightful mess.*

frightfully /ˈfraɪtfⁿli/ **adv** UK old-fashioned very: *They're frightfully rich, you know.*

frigid /ˈfrɪdʒɪd/ **adj 1** not enjoying sexual activity, usually said about a woman **2** literary not friendly or emotional

frill /frɪl/ **noun 1** [C] a strip of material with a lot of folds that is used to decorate the edge of cloth **2 frills** extra things that are added to something to make it nicer or more attractive, but that are not really necessary: *a cheap, **no frills** airline service*

frilly /ˈfrɪli/ **adj** with a lot of frills: *a frilly dress*

fringe¹ /frɪndʒ/ **noun** [C] **1** HAIR ▷ UK (US **bangs** [plural]) hair that is cut short and straight at the top of someone's face **2** DECORATION ▷ loose threads that hang along the edge of cloth as a decoration **3** EDGE ▷ the outside edge of an area, group, or subject and not the main part

fringe² /frɪndʒ/ **verb** **be fringed with sth** If a place or object is fringed with something, that thing forms a border along the edge: *The river is fringed with wild flowers.*

fringe³ /frɪndʒ/ **adj** [always before noun] not belonging to the main part of a group, activity, or subject: *fringe politics/theatre*

fringe ˈbenefit noun [C] something extra that you get from your employer in addition to money: [usually plural] *fringe benefits such as private health care*

frisk /frɪsk/ **verb 1** [T] to move your hands over someone's body to discover if they are hiding something such as a weapon: *There were guards frisking people as they went into the building.* **2** [I] to run and jump happily like a young animal

frisky /ˈfrɪski/ **adj** energetic and wanting to be active or play: *a frisky puppy*

fritter /ˈfrɪtər/ **verb**

PHRASAL VERB **fritter sth away** to waste money or time on something that is not important

frivolity /frɪˈvɒləti/ **noun** [C, U] behaviour that is silly and not serious

frivolous /ˈfrɪvələs/ **adj** silly and not serious • **frivolously adv**

frizzy /ˈfrɪzi/ **adj** Frizzy hair has a lot of very small, tight curls.

fro /frəʊ/ **adv** see **to³** and **fro**

frog /frɒg/ **noun** [C] **B1** a small, green animal with long back legs for jumping that lives in or near water

frogman /ˈfrɒgmən/ **noun** [C] (plural **frogmen**) someone whose job is to swim under water wearing a rubber suit and using special breathing equipment: *Police frogmen are searching the lake.*

from strong /frɒm/ weak /frəm/ **preposition** **1** STARTING PLACE ▷ **A1** used to show the place, time, or level that someone or something started at: *Did you walk all the way from Bond Street?* ◦ *The museum is open from 9.30 to 6.00, Tuesday to Sunday.* ◦ *Prices start from $5,595.* **2** HOME ▷ **A1** used to say where someone was born, or where someone lives or works: *His mother's originally from Poland.* ◦ *Our speaker tonight is from the BBC.* **3** DISTANCE ▷ **A1** used to say how far away something is: *The hotel is about 15 kilometres from the coast.* **4** GIVING ▷ **A1** used to say who gave or sent something to someone: *Have you received a Christmas card from Faye yet?* **5** REMOVING ▷ If you take something from a person, place, or amount, you take it away: *Two from ten leaves eight.* ◦ *We had to borrow some money from my father to pay the bill.* **6** PRODUCED ▷ **A1** used to say where something was produced or grown: *These vegetables are fresh from the garden.* **7** MATERIAL ▷ **A2** used to say what something is made of: *juice made from oranges* **8** AVOID ▷ **B2** used to show something that you want to avoid or prevent: *There's a bar across the front to prevent you from falling out.* **9** POSITION ▷ **B2** used to show where you are when you look at something or how you see something: *The view from the top was absolutely breathtaking.* **10** REASON ▷ used to say why you think or believe something: *I guessed from her accent that she must be French.* ◦ *From what I've heard, the new exam is going to be a lot more difficult.* **11** CAUSE ▷ **B2** used to say what causes something: *Deaths from heart disease continue to rise every year.* ◦ *He was rushed to hospital suffering from severe burns.* **12** COMPARE ▷ **B1** used when you are saying how similar or different two things, people, or places are: *College is very different from school.* **13 a week/ six months/ten years, etc from now** a week/six months/ten years, etc after the time when you are speaking: *Who knows what we'll all be doing*

five years from now? **14 from now/then, etc on** starting now/then, etc and continuing into the future: *They were good friends from that day on.*

front¹ /frʌnt/ **noun 1 the front a** **A2** the side of something that is most important or most often seen because it faces forward: *You need to write the address clearly* **on the front of** *the envelope.* ◦ *There was blood on the front of his shirt.* **b** **A2** the part of something that is furthest forward: *We asked to sit* **in the front of** *the plane.* ◦ *He was standing right* **at the front.** **2 in front a** **B1** further forward than someone or something else: *She started a conversation with the man sitting* **in front of** *her.* **b** winning in a game or competition: *By half time the Italians were well in front.* **3 in front of a** **A2** close to the front part of something: *He parked the car in front of the house.* **b** **A2** where someone can see or hear you: *Please don't swear in front of the children.* **4** BEHAVIOUR ▷ [C] a way of behaving that hides how someone really feels: [usually singular] *Many parents decide to stay together,* **putting up a front** *for the children's sake.* **5** ILLEGAL ACTIVITY ▷ [C] an organization or activity that is used to hide a different, illegal activity: [usually singular] *Police discovered the restaurant was just a front for a drugs operation.* **6 the front** an area of land where soldiers fight during a war: *Thousands of young men were sent to the front to fight.* **7 on the business/jobs/politics, etc front** in a particular area of activity: *How are things on the work front at the moment?* **8** WEATHER ▷ [C] a line where warm air meets cold air affecting the weather: *A cold front is moving across the Atlantic.*

front² /frʌnt/ **adj** [always before noun] **B1** in or at the front of something: *the front door/UK garden/ US yard* ◦ *the front page of the newspaper*

frontal /ˈfrʌntəl/ **adj 1** relating to the front of something **2 a frontal attack/assault** a very strong and direct way of criticizing or attacking someone

frontier /frʌnˈtɪər/ **noun 1** [C] a line or border between two countries **2 the frontiers of sth** the limits of what is known or what has been done before in an area of knowledge or activity: *the frontiers of science and technology*

front ˈline noun the front line a the place where soldiers fight in a war **b** a position of direct and important influence: *doctors working* **in the front line** *of medicine* • **front-line** /ˈfrʌntlaɪn/ **adj** [always before noun] *front-line troops*

front-page /ˈfrʌntˌpeɪdʒ/ **adj front-page news/ story, etc** news that is very important and suitable for the front page of a newspaper

front-runner /ˌfrʌntˈrʌnər/ US /ˈfrʌntˌrʌnər/ **noun** [C] the person or organization that will most probably win something

frost¹ /frɒst/ **noun 1** [U] **B2** a thin, white layer of ice that forms on surfaces, especially at night when it is very cold **2** [C] **B2** weather that is cold and in which water freezes, especially at night: *We're expecting a* **hard frost** *tonight.*

frost² /frɒst/ **verb** [T] US (UK/US **ice**) to cover a cake with frosting (= sweet mixture)

frostbite /ˈfrɒstbaɪt/ **noun** [U] a painful

condition in which extreme cold injures your fingers and toes

rosted /'frɒstɪd/ **adj** Frosted glass has a special surface so that you cannot see through it.

rosting /'frɒstɪŋ/ **noun** [U] US (UK/US **icing**) a sweet mixture used to cover or fill cakes, made from sugar and water or sugar and butter

rosty /'frɒsti/ **adj 1** very cold, with a thin layer of white ice covering everything: *a frosty morning* **2** not friendly: *She gave me a very frosty look.*

roth /frɒθ/ **noun** [U] small, white bubbles such as on the surface of a liquid • **froth verb** [I] • **frothy adj** *frothy coffee*

rown[1] /fraʊn/ **verb** [I] to make your face show that you are annoyed or worried by moving your eyebrows (= lines of hair above your eyes) : *She frowned when I mentioned his name.*

PHRASAL VERB **frown on/upon sth** to think that something is wrong and that you should not do it: [often passive] *Smoking is frowned upon in many public places.*

rown[2] /fraʊn/ **noun** [C] the expression on your face when you frown: *He looked at me with a puzzled frown.*

roze /frəʊz/ past tense of freeze

rozen[1] /'frəʊzᵊn/ **adj 1** FOOD ▷ **B1** Frozen food has been made so that it will last a long time by freezing: *frozen peas* **2** WATER ▷ **B1** turned into ice: *The pond was frozen and people were skating on it.* **3** PERSON ▷ informal **B1** extremely cold: *Is there any heating in here? I'm frozen!*

rozen[2] /'frəʊzᵊn/ past participle of freeze

rugal /'fruːɡᵊl/ **adj** careful not to spend very much money

ruit /fruːt/ **noun 1** **A1** [C, U] something such as an apple or orange that grows on a tree or a bush, contains seeds, and can be eaten as food: *dried/fresh fruit* ∘ *fruit juice* → See colour picture **Fruits and Vegetables** on page Centre 10 **2 the fruit(s) of sth** the good result of someone's work or actions: *This book is the fruit of 15 years' research.*

IDIOM **bear fruit** If something that someone does bears fruit, it produces successful results: *Our decision is just beginning to bear fruit.*

→ See also **citrus fruit**

☑ Word partners for **fruit**

dried/fresh fruit • a piece of fruit • fruit juice • citrus/tropical fruit

ruitful /'fruːtfᵊl/ **adj** producing good or useful results: *We had a very fruitful discussion.*

ruition /fruˈɪʃᵊn/ **noun** [U] formal the time when a plan or an idea really begins to happen, exist, or be successful: *The plan never really came to fruition.*

ruitless /'fruːtləs/ **adj** not successful or achieving good results: *a long and fruitless search*

ruit 'salad noun [C, U] a mixture of pieces of different types of fruit, which is usually served at the end of a meal

fruity /'fruːti/ **adj** smelling or tasting of fruit: *a fruity wine/taste*

frustrate /frʌsˈtreɪt/ ⑤ /ˈfrʌstreɪt/ **verb** [T] **1** to make someone feel annoyed because things are not happening in the way that they want, or in the way that they should: *It really frustrates me when she arrives late for meetings.* **2** to prevent someone from achieving something, or to prevent something from happening: *They have frustrated all our attempts to find a solution to this problem.*

frustrated /frʌsˈtreɪtɪd/ ⑤ /ˈfrʌstreɪtɪd/ **adj** annoyed because things are not happening in the way that you want, or in the way that they should: *I'm very frustrated at/with my lack of progress.*

frustrating /frʌsˈtreɪtɪŋ/ ⑤ /ˈfrʌstreɪtɪŋ/ **adj** making you feel frustrated: *a frustrating situation*

frustration /frʌsˈtreɪʃᵊn/ **noun** [C, U] **B2** the feeling of being annoyed because things are not happening in the way that you want, or in the way that they should: *I could sense his frustration at not being able to help.*

☑ Word partners for **frustration**

sheer frustration • in frustration • frustration at (doing) sth

fry /fraɪ/ **verb** [I, T] **B1** to cook something in hot oil or fat or to be cooked in hot oil or fat: *Fry the onions in a little butter.* → See picture at **cook**

'frying ,pan noun [C] **B1** a flat, metal pan with a long handle that is used for frying food → See colour picture **The Kitchen** on page Centre 2

ft written abbreviation for foot (= a unit for measuring length)

fudge[1] /fʌdʒ/ **noun** [U] a soft, sweet food made from butter, sugar, and milk

fudge[2] /fʌdʒ/ **verb** informal **1** [T] UK to avoid making a decision or giving a clear answer about something: *The government continues to fudge the issue.* **2** [I, T] US to slightly cheat, often by not telling the exact truth: *He fudged on his income tax return.*

fuel[1] /ˈfjuːəl/ **noun** [C, U] **B1** a substance that is burned to provide heat or power: *The plane ran out of fuel and had to land at sea.*

☑ Word partners for **fuel**

fuel bills/consumption/prices/supplies • fuel efficiency

fuel[2] /ˈfjuːəl/ **verb** [T] (mainly UK **fuelling, fuelled**, US **fueling, fueled**) to make people's ideas or feelings stronger, or to make a situation worse: *Newspaper reports are fuelling fears about GM foods.*

fugitive /ˈfjuːdʒətɪv/ **noun** [C] someone who is escaping or hiding from the police or from a dangerous situation

fulfil UK (US **fulfill**) /fʊlˈfɪl/ **verb** (**fulfilling, fulfilled**) **1 fulfil a duty/promise/responsibility, etc** to do something that you have promised to do or that you are expected to do: *He has failed to fulfil his duties as a father.* **2 fulfil an ambition/dream/goal, etc** to do something that you really wanted to do **3 fulfil a function/need/role, etc**

to do something that is necessary or useful: *You seem to fulfil a very useful role in the organization.* **4 fulfil criteria/requirements/qualifications, etc** to have all the qualities that are wanted or needed for something: *You have to fulfil certain requirements to qualify for the competition.*

fulfilled /fʊlˈfɪld/ **adj** feeling happy that you are receiving everything that you want from your life → Opposite **unfulfilled**

fulfilling /fʊlˈfɪlɪŋ/ **adj** If something is fulfilling, it satisfies you and makes you happy: *a fulfilling job*

fulfilment UK (US **fulfillment**) /fʊlˈfɪlmənt/ **noun** [U] **1** a feeling of pleasure because you are receiving or achieving what you want: *I hope that you'll find happiness and fulfilment in your life together.* **2** the act of doing something necessary or something that you have wanted or promised to do: *Being here is the **fulfilment of** a lifelong ambition.*

full¹ /fʊl/ **adj 1 NO MORE POSSIBLE** ▷ **A2** If a container or a space is full, it contains as many things or people as possible or as much of something as possible: *We couldn't get in, the cinema was full.* ∘ *The shelves were **full of** books.* **2 A LOT** ▷ **A2** containing a lot of things or people or a lot of something: *The room was **full of** people.* ∘ *His face was full of anger.* **3 COMPLETE** ▷ [always before noun] **A2** complete and including every part: *Please give your full name and address.* **4 full speed/strength/volume, etc** **B1** the greatest speed/strength/volume, etc possible: *We were driving at full speed.* ∘ UK *She got full marks in the test.* **5 be full of yourself** to think that you are very important **6 be full of sth** to be talking or thinking a lot about a particular thing: *He's full of stories about his trip.* **7 FOOD** ▷ informal (also UK **full up**) **B2** having eaten enough food: *No more for me, thanks, I'm full.* **8 a full face/figure** a face or body shape that is large and round → See also **have your hands (hand¹) full**, **be in full swing²**

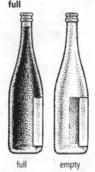

full   empty

full² /fʊl/ **noun 1 in full** **B1** completely and with nothing missing: *The speech will be published in full in tomorrow's newspaper.* **2 to the full** mainly UK as much or as well as possible: *She certainly lived life to the full.*

full-blown /ˈfʊlˌbləʊn/ **adj** completely developed: *a full-blown crisis* ∘ *a full-blown disease*

full board **noun** [U] UK an arrangement in which all your meals are provided in a hotel

full-fledged /fʊlˈfledʒd/ **adj** [always before noun] US (UK **fully-fledged**) having finished developing, studying, or establishing yourself

full-grown /fʊlˈgrəʊn/ **adj** A full-grown person, animal, or plant has developed completely, and is not expected to grow more: *a full-grown man*

full house **noun** [C] a theatre or cinema in which all the seats are full

full-length /fʊlˈleŋθ/ **adj 1** a full-length book, film, etc a book/film, etc that is the usual length and not shorter: *a full-length feature film* **2** a full-length mirror/photograph, etc a mirror/image, etc that shows a person's whole body from the head to the feet **3** a full-length coat/dress/skirt, etc a long piece of clothing that reaches to your feet

full moon **noun** [no plural] the moon when it appears as a complete circle

full-on /fʊlˈɒn/ **adj 1** very great or to the greatest degree: *full-on luxury* **2** very serious and enthusiastic, often in a way that annoys other people

full-page /fʊlˈpeɪdʒ/ **adj** [always before noun] filling a complete page in a newspaper or magazine: *a **full-page ad***

full-scale /fʊlˈskeɪl/ **adj** [always before noun] **1** very large or serious and involving everything that is possible or expected: *The violence had developed into a full-scale war.* **2** A full-scale model is the same size as the original thing that it is representing.

full stop **noun** [C] UK (US **period**) **B1** a mark (.) used at the end of a sentence, or to show that the letters before it are an abbreviation → See Study Page **Punctuation** on page Centre 33

full-time /fʊlˈtaɪm/ **adj** **B1** happening or working for the whole of the working week and not only part of it: *a **full-time job/course*** ∘ **full-time adv** *She **works full-time** for the council.*

fully /ˈfʊli/ **adv** **B1** completely: *The restaurant was **fully booked**.* ∘ *He is **fully aware** of the danger involved.*

fully-fledged /ˌfʊliˈfledʒd/ **adj** [always before noun] UK (US **full-fledged**) having finished developing, studying, or establishing yourself: *I won't be a fully-fledged doctor until after the exams.*

fumble /ˈfʌmbl/ **verb** [I] to use your hands with difficulty to try to get hold of something or find something: *She fumbled in her bag for her glasses.*

fume /fjuːm/ **verb** [I] to be extremely angry, especially in a quiet way: *A week later, she was still fuming about his behaviour.*

fumes /fjuːmz/ **noun** [plural] strong, unpleasant, and often dangerous gas or smoke: *car exhaust fumes*

fun¹ /fʌn/ **noun** [U] **1** **A1** enjoyment or pleasure or something that gives you enjoyment or pleasure: *She's **great fun** to be with.* ∘ *Have fun!* (= enjoy yourself) ∘ *It's **no fun** having to work late every night.* **2 for fun/for the fun of it** **B1** for pleasure and not for any other reason **3 make fun of sb/sth** **B2** to make a joke about someone or something in an unkind way: *The other children at school used to make fun of his hair.*

> ☑ Word partners for **fun**
>
> have fun • good/great fun • be no fun • for fun

fun² /fʌn/ **adj** **A2** enjoyable or entertaining: *There are lots of fun things to do here.*

function¹ /ˈfʌŋkʃən/ **noun** [C] **1** **B2** the purpos of something or someone: *Each button has a different function.* **2** a large, formal party or ceremony: *a charity function*

> ☑ Word partners for **function**
>
> a basic/important/primary/vital function • carry out/fulfil/provide/serve a function

function² /'fʌŋkʃən/ **verb** [I] to work or operate: *The operation should help his lungs to function properly again.*

PHRASAL VERB **function as sth** to have a particular purpose: *The spare bedroom also functions as a study.*

functional /'fʌŋkʃənəl/ **adj 1** 🔵 designed to be practical or useful and not only attractive: *functional clothing* **2** operating or working correctly: *The system is not yet fully functional.*

function key noun [C] (written abbreviation **F**) one of the keys on a computer keyboard that has the letter F and a number on it and that makes the computer do particular jobs: *Press F4 to print.*

fund /fʌnd/ **noun 1** [C] an amount of money collected, saved, or provided for a purpose: *a pension fund* **2 funds** [plural] money needed or available to spend on something: *The charity closed down due to **lack of funds**.* • **fund verb** [T] to provide money for an event, activity, or organization: *Who is the project funded by?*

fundamental /ˌfʌndə'mentəl/ **adj** relating to the most important or main part of something: *a fundamental change/difference* ∘ *Training is **fundamental to** success.* • **fundamentally adv** *The world has changed fundamentally over the last century.*

fundamentalism /ˌfʌndə'mentəlɪzəm/ **noun** [U] the belief that the traditions and rules of a religion should be followed exactly

fundamentalist /ˌfʌndə'mentəlɪst/ **noun** [C] someone who believes that the rules of their religion should be followed exactly • **fundamentalist adj**

fundamentals /ˌfʌndə'mentəlz/ **noun** [plural] the main principles, or most important parts of something

funding /'fʌndɪŋ/ **noun** [U] money given by a government or organization for an event or activity: *The company received state funding for the project.*

fundraiser /'fʌndˌreɪzər/ **noun** [C] a person or an event that collects money for a particular purpose

fundraising /'fʌndˌreɪzɪŋ/ **noun** [U] the activity of collecting money for a particular purpose: *a fundraising event*

funeral /'fjuːnərəl/ **noun** [C] 🔵 a ceremony for burying or burning the body of a dead person

funeral diˌrector noun [C] someone whose job is to organize funerals and prepare dead bodies to be buried or burned

funfair /'fʌnfeər/ **noun** [C] UK (also **fair**, US **carnival**) an event outside where you can ride large machines for pleasure and play games to win prizes

fungus /'fʌŋgəs/ **noun** [C, U] (plural **fungi**, **funguses**) a type of plant without leaves and without green colouring that gets its food from other living or decaying things

funk /fʌŋk/ **noun** [U] a style of popular music with a strong rhythm that is influenced by African and jazz music

funky /'fʌŋki/ **adj** informal **1** fashionable in an unusual and noticeable way: *She's got some very funky clothes.* **2** Funky music has a strong rhythm, and is good to dance to.

funnel /'fʌnəl/ **noun** [C] **1** a tube with a wide part at the top that you use to pour liquid or powder into something that has a small opening **2** a metal pipe on the top of a ship or train that smoke comes out of

funnel

funnily /'fʌnɪli/ **adv** UK **funnily enough** although it seems strange and surprising: *Funnily enough, I was just thinking about you when you called.*

funny /'fʌni/ **adj 1** 🔵 making you smile or laugh: *a funny story* ∘ *It's not funny. Don't laugh!* **2** 🔵 strange or unusual and not what you expect: *This chicken tastes a bit funny.*

> ❗ Common learner error: **fun** or **funny**?
>
> Use **fun** to talk about something that you enjoy doing.
> *Going to the cinema is fun.*
> Use **funny** to describe something that makes you laugh.
> *The film was really funny.*

> ➕ Other ways of saying **funny**
>
> The adjective **amusing** is a more formal alternative to 'funny':
> *I gave her an article that I thought she would find amusing.*
> If something is extremely funny, you can use the adjectives **hilarious** or (*informal*) **hysterical**:
> *I've just read his autobiography – it's absolutely hilarious/hysterical.*
> If someone talks in a way that is clever and funny, you can use the adjective **witty**:
> *He was a very witty man.*
> The adjective **comical** is sometimes used if someone or something looks funny:
> *She looked so comical in that hat!*
> If you want to describe a person as very funny, in informal situations you can use the expressions **be a good laugh** (*UK*) and **be a scream**.
> *You'd like Amanda – she's a scream/good laugh.*

fur /fɜːr/ **noun 1** [U] 🔵 the thick hair that covers

the bodies of some animals like cats and rabbits **2** [C, U] the skin of an animal covered in thick hair and used for making clothes, or a piece of clothing made from this

furious /'fjʊəriəs/ adj **1** 🄱🄿 extremely angry: *He's furious at the way he's been treated.* ∘ *My boss was furious with me.* **2** very energetic or fast: *a furious attack* • **furiously** adv

furlong /'fɜːlɒŋ/ noun [C] a unit of length used in horse races equal to 201 metres

furnace /'fɜːnɪs/ noun [C] a container that is heated to a very high temperature and used to heat buildings, melt metal, or burn things

furnish /'fɜːnɪʃ/ verb [T] to put furniture into a room or building: *They have furnished the room very simply.*

PHRASAL VERB **furnish sb with sth** formal to provide someone with something: *Can you furnish me with any further information?*

furnished /'fɜːnɪʃt/ adj If a room or building is furnished, there is furniture in it.

furnishings /'fɜːnɪʃɪŋz/ noun [plural] the furniture, curtains and other decorations in a room or building

furniture /'fɜːnɪtʃər/ noun [U] 🄰🄲 objects such as chairs, tables, and beds that you put into a room or building: *antique furniture*

> **!** Common learner error: **furniture**
>
> Remember you cannot make **furniture** plural. Do not say 'furnitures'.
> *I want to buy some new furniture for my bedroom.*

> **✓** Word partners for **furniture**
>
> a **piece of** furniture • **garden/office** furniture • **antique** furniture

furore /fjʊə'rɔːri/ noun [no plural] UK (US **furor**, Ⓤ /'fjʊrɔːr/) a sudden, excited, or angry reaction to something by a lot of people: *The book caused a furore when it was published.*

furrow¹ /'fʌrəʊ/ noun [C] **1** a deep line cut into a field that seeds are planted in **2** a deep line on someone's face, especially above their eyes

furrow² /'fʌrəʊ/ verb **furrow your brow** to make deep lines appear on your face above your eyes: *He furrowed his brow as he struggled to think of a solution.*

furry /'fɜːri/ adj covered with fur or with something that feels like fur

further¹ /'fɜːðər/ adv **1** 🄱🄿 more: *He refused to discuss the matter further.* ∘ *Have you got any further* (= achieved any more) *with your research?* **2** 🄱🄹 comparative of **far**: at or to a place or time that is a longer distance away: *Let's walk a bit further down the road.*

further² /'fɜːðər/ adj [always before noun] 🄰🄲 more or extra: *For further details about the offer, call this number.* ∘ *We will let you know if there are any further developments.*

further³ /'fɜːðər/ verb [T] to make something develop or become more successful: *He'll do anything to further his career.*

> **!** Common learner error: **further** or **farther**?
>
> **Further** means the same as **farther** when you are talking about distance.
> *We walked further down the street.*
> *We walked farther down the street.*
> In all other situations you should use **further**.
> *Petrol prices have increased further.*
> *For further information contact our office.*

further edu'cation noun [U] UK education at a college for people who have left school but are not at a university

furthermore /ˌfɜːðə'mɔːr/ Ⓤ /'fɜːðərmɔːr/ adv 🄱🄿 in addition to what has just been said

furthest /'fɜːðɪst/ adj, adv 🄱🄹 superlative of **far** adv: most distant

furtive /'fɜːtɪv/ adj doing something secretly, or done secretly, so that people do not notice: *He gave her a furtive glance as soon as his wife le_ the room.* • **furtively** adv

fury /'fjʊəri/ noun [U, no plural] extreme anger: *H_ could hardly control his fury.*

fuse¹ /fjuːz/ noun [C] **1** a small object that stop_ electrical equipment working if there is to_ much electricity going through it: *The fuse ha_ blown. You'll have to change it.* ∘ *a fuse bo_* **2** the part of a bomb or other explosive objec_ that starts the explosion: *Light the fuse, and the_ stand back.*

fuse² /fjuːz/ verb [I, T] **1** UK If a piece of electrica_ equipment fuses, or if you fuse it, it stop_ working because there is too much electricit_ going through it: *You've fused the lights.* **2** t_ join or become combined: *The bones of the sku_ are not properly fused at birth.*

fuselage /'fjuːzəlɑːʒ/ noun [C] the main body c_ an aircraft

fusion /'fjuːʒən/ noun [C, U] the process in whic_ two or more things join or become combined, c_ the result of this process: *nuclear fusion* ∘ *Sh_ describes her music as a fusion of folk and rock.*

fuss¹ /fʌs/ noun **1** 🄱🄿 [U, no plural] a situation i_ which people become excited, annoyed, c_ anxious about something, especially abou_ something unimportant: *What's all the fus_ about?* ∘ *They were making a big fuss ove_ nothing.* **2 kick up/make a fuss** to complai_ about something: *If they don't bring our foo_ soon, I'll have to kick up a fuss.* **3 make a fuss o_ over sb** to give someone a lot of attention an_ treat them well: *My uncle always makes a b_ fuss of the children.*

fuss² /fʌs/ verb [I] to worry too much or get to_ excited, especially about unimportant thing_ *Please don't fuss, Mum. Everything's under contro_*

PHRASAL VERB **fuss over sb/sth** to give someone c_ something too much attention because yo_ want to show that you like them

fussy /'fʌsi/ adj **1 NOT LIKING** ▷ only likin_ particular things and very difficult to pleas_ *She's a very fussy eater.* **2 CAREFUL** ▷ to_

F

careful about unimportant details **3 TOO COMPLICATED** ▷ If something is fussy, it is too complicated in design and has too many details.

futile /ˈfjuːtaɪl/ ⑤ /ˈfjuːtəl/ **adj** certain not to have a successful effect or result: *a futile attempt to escape* • **futility** /fjuːˈtɪləti/ **noun** [U] the state of being futile

futon /ˈfuːtɒn/ **noun** [C] a flat bed filled with soft material that can be used on the floor or on a wooden base, or folded into a seat

future¹ /ˈfjuːtʃər/ **noun 1 the future a** ⓑ1 the time that is to come: *He likes to **plan for the future**.* ∘ *They hope to get married **in the near future*** (= soon). **b** ⓐ2 In grammar, the future is the form of the verb used to talk about something that will happen. **2 in future** UK (mainly US **in the future**) ⓑ1 beginning from now: *In future, I'll be more careful about who I lend my bike to.* **3 WHAT WILL HAPPEN** ▷ [C] ⓑ2 what will happen to someone or something in the time that is to come: *We need to discuss the future of the company.* **4 SUCCESS** ▷ [U, no plural] ⓑ1 the chance of continuing to exist or succeed: *She's got a very promising future ahead of her.*

> 🗹 Word partners for **future**
>
> the **distant/foreseeable/near** future • **plan for/predict** the future • **in the** future

future² /ˈfjuːtʃər/ **adj** [always before noun] **1** ⓑ1 happening or existing in the time that is to come: *future plans* ∘ *in future years* ∘ *What will we leave for future generations?* **2 future tense** the form of the verb that is used to talk about something that will happen

the ˌfuture ˈperfect noun the form of the verb that is used to show that an action will have been completed before a particular time in the future. The sentence 'I'll probably have left by then.' is in the future perfect.

future-proof /ˈfjuːtʃəpruːf/ **verb** [T] to design software, a computer, etc. so that it can still be used in the future, even when technology changes: *Here are some tips for future-proofing your computer network.*

futuristic /ˌfjuːtʃəˈrɪstɪk/ **adj** very modern and strange and seeming to come from some imagined time in the future: *a futuristic steel building*

fuzzy /ˈfʌzi/ **adj 1** confused and not clear: *We could only get a fuzzy picture on the television.* **2** covered in soft, short hairs, or material like this: *a fuzzy kitten* ∘ *fuzzy slippers*

FYI internet abbreviation for for your information: used when you send someone a document or tell them something you think they should know about

F

G

G, g /dʒiː/ the seventh letter of the alphabet

g written abbreviation for gram (= a unit for measuring weight)

gabble /ˈɡæbl/ **verb** [I, T] UK informal to talk quickly or in a way that people cannot understand: *He gabbled something in Italian.*

gable /ˈɡeɪbl/ **noun** [C] the top end of a wall of a building where two sloping parts of a roof meet at a point

gadget /ˈɡædʒɪt/ **noun** [C] a small piece of equipment that does a particular job, especially a new type: *a kitchen gadget*

Gaelic /ˈɡeɪlɪk/, /ˈɡælɪk/ **noun** [U] a language spoken in parts of Scotland and Ireland • **Gaelic adj** relating to Gaelic or to the Gaelic culture of Scotland and Ireland

gaffe /ɡæf/ **noun** [C] something embarrassing that someone says or does without intending to: *The minister has made a series of embarrassing gaffes.*

gag¹ /ɡæg/ **verb** (**gagging, gagged**) **1 COVER MOUTH** ▷ [T] to fasten something over someone's mouth so that they cannot speak: *The owners of the house were found **bound and gagged** in the cellar.* **2 STOP INFORMATION** ▷ [T] to prevent someone from giving their opinion or giving information about something: *The government is trying to gag the press over the issue.* **3 ALMOST VOMIT** ▷ [I] to feel that you are going to vomit: *The sight of the body made him gag.*

IDIOM **be gagging for sth** UK informal to want something or want to do something very much: *I'm gagging for a coffee.*

gag² /ɡæg/ **noun** [C] **1** informal a joke or funny story **2** something that is fastened over someone's mouth to stop them speaking

gaggle /ˈɡægl/ **noun** [C] a group of people, especially when they are noisy: *a gaggle of newspaper reporters*

gaiety /ˈɡeɪəti/ **noun** [U] old-fashioned happiness or excitement

gaily /ˈɡeɪli/ **adv** old-fashioned in a happy way

gain¹ /ɡeɪn/ **verb 1 GET** ▷ [T] 🔟 to get something useful or positive: *The country gained independence in 1948.* ∘ *You'll gain a lot of experience working there.* **2 gain by/from sth** to get an advantage or something valuable from something: *Who stands to gain from the will?* **3 INCREASE** ▷ [T] 🔢 to increase in something such as size, weight, or amount: *He's gained a lot of weight in the last few months.* **4 CLOCK** ▷ [I, T] If a clock or a watch gains, it works too quickly and shows a time that is later than the real time. → See also **gain/lose ground¹**, **get/gain the upper hand¹**

PHRASAL VERB **gain on sb/sth** to get nearer to someone or something that you are chasing: *Quick! They're gaining on us.*

gain² /ɡeɪn/ **noun** [C, U] **1** something useful or positive that you get: *financial gain* **2** a increase in something such as size, weight, o amount

gait /ɡeɪt/ **noun** [C] someone's particular way walking: *I recognized his gait from a distance.*

gal. written abbreviation for gallon (= a unit fo measuring liquid)

gala /ˈɡɑːlə/ ⓤⓢ /ˈɡeɪlə/ **noun** [C] a special soci event, performance, or sports competition: *gala concert*

galaxy /ˈɡæləksi/ **noun** [C] a very large group o stars held together in the universe

gale /ɡeɪl/ **noun** [C] a very strong wind

gall¹ /ɡɔːl/ **noun have the gall to do sth** to b rude enough to do something that is no considered acceptable: *I can't believe he had th gall to complain.*

gall² /ɡɔːl/ **verb** [T] to annoy someone: *What gal me is that he escaped without punishmen* • **galling adj** annoying: *It's particularly gallin for me that she gets paid more than I do.*

gallant /ˈɡælənt/ **adj** literary **1** brave: *a gallar attempt to rescue a drowning man* **2** polite an kind, especially to women • **gallantly ad** • **gallantry noun** [U] gallant behaviour

'gall ˌbladder noun [C] an organ in the bod that contains a substance that helps you t digest food

gallery /ˈɡælⁿri/ **noun** [C] **1** 🔟 a room o building that is used for showing painting and other art to the public: *a museum and ar gallery* **2** a floor at a higher level that look over a lower floor inside a large room o building: *The courtroom has a **public gallery**.*

galley /ˈɡæli/ **noun** [C] a kitchen in a ship o aircraft

gallon /ˈɡælən/ **noun** [C] (written abbreviation **gal** a unit for measuring liquid, equal to 4.546 litre in the UK and 3.785 litres in the US → See Stud Page **Measurements** on page Centre 31

gallop /ˈɡæləp/ **verb** [I] If a horse gallops, it run very fast. • **gallop noun** [no plural]

gallows /ˈɡæləʊz/ **noun** [C] (plural **gallows**) wooden structure used in the past to han criminals from to kill them

galore /ɡəˈlɔːr/ **adj** [always after noun] in larg amounts or numbers: *There are bargains galor at the new supermarket.*

galvanize (also UK **-ise**) /ˈɡælvənaɪz/ **verb** [T] t make someone suddenly decide to do some thing: *His words galvanized the team into actio* • **galvanization** (also UK **-isation**) **noun** [U]

gamble¹ /ˈɡæmbl/ **verb** [I, T] to risk money o the result of a game, race, or competition: *H gambled away all of our savings.* • **gambler nou** [C] • **gambling noun** [U]

PHRASAL VERB **gamble on sth** to take a risk tha something will happen

---

gamble² /ˈgæmbl/ **noun** [C] a risk that you take that something will succeed: *Buying this place was a big **gamble**, but it seems to have **paid off**.*

> ☑ Word partners for **gamble**
>
> take a gamble • a gamble backfires/pays off • a gamble on sth

game¹ /geɪm/ **noun 1 ACTIVITY** ▷ [C] **A1** an entertaining activity or sport that people play, usually needing some skill and played according to rules: *a **computer game*** ∘ *Do you want to **play** a different **game**? **2 OCCASION** ▷ [C] **A2** a particular occasion when people play a game: *Would you like a **game** of chess?* ∘ *Who won yesterday's **game**? **3 games** UK organized sports that children do at school: *I always hated games at school.* ∘ *a games teacher* **4 the European/ Commonwealth, etc Games** a special event where there are lots of competitions for different sports **5 SECRET PLAN** ▷ [C] UK informal a secret plan: *What's your game?* **6 ANIMALS** ▷ [U] wild animals and birds that are hunted for food or sport

IDIOMS **give the game away** UK to spoil a surprise or joke by letting someone know something that should have been kept secret • **play games** to not deal with a situation seriously or honestly: *Someone's life is in danger here – we're not playing games.*

→ See also **ball game, board game, the Olympic Games, video game**

> ☑ Word partners for **game**
>
> play a game • lose/win a game • a game of [chess/football, etc] • a computer game

game² /geɪm/ **adj** willing to do new things, or things that involve a risk: *She's **game for** anything.*

Gameboy /ˈgeɪmbɔɪ/ **noun** [C] trademark a small machine that you play computer games on and that you can carry with you

gamekeeper /ˈgeɪmˌkiːpər/ **noun** [C] someone whose job is to look after wild animals and birds that are going to be hunted

gamepad /ˈgeɪmpæd/ **noun** [C] a small piece of equipment that you hold in your hands and use to control a computer game or video game (= a game in which you make pictures move on a screen)

gamer /ˈgeɪmər/ **noun** [C] someone who plays games, especially computer games

game show noun [C] a programme on television in which people play games to try to win prizes

gammon /ˈgæmən/ **noun** [U] UK a type of meat from a pig, usually cut in thick slices

gamut /ˈgæmət/ **noun** [no plural] the whole group of things that can be included in something: *The film explores **the whole gamut** of emotions from despair to joy.*

gang¹ /gæŋ/ **noun** [C] **1 YOUNG PEOPLE** ▷ **B2** a group of young people who spend time together, usually fighting with other groups and behaving badly: *a **member** of a **gang***

∘ *gang violence* **2 CRIMINALS** ▷ **B2** a group of criminals who work together: *a **gang of** armed robbers* **3 FRIENDS** ▷ informal a group of young friends

> ☑ Word partners for **gang**
>
> in a gang • a gang of sth • a gang leader/ member

gang² /gæŋ/ **verb**

PHRASAL VERB **gang up against/on sb** to form a group to attack or criticize someone, usually unfairly: *Some older girls have been ganging up on her at school.*

gangly /ˈgæŋgli/ **adj** (also **gangling**) tall and thin: *a gangly youth*

gangrene /ˈgæŋgriːn/ **noun** [U] the death and decay of a part of the body because blood is not flowing through it

gangster /ˈgæŋstər/ **noun** [C] a member of a group of violent criminals

gangway /ˈgæŋweɪ/ **noun** [C] **1** UK a space that people can walk down between two rows of seats in a vehicle or public place **2** a board or stairs for people to get on and off a ship

gaol /dʒeɪl/ **noun** [C, U] another UK spelling of jail (= prison)

gap

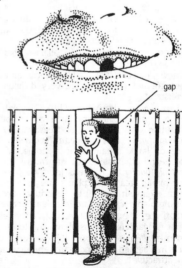

gap

gap /gæp/ **noun** [C] **1 SPACE** ▷ **B1** an empty space or hole in the middle of something, or between two things: *There's quite a big **gap between** the door and the floor.* ∘ *The sun was shining through a **gap in** the curtains.* **2 DIFFERENCE** ▷ **B2** a difference between two groups of people, two situations, etc: *an age gap* ∘ *This course **bridges the gap** between school and university.* **3 ABSENT THING** ▷ **B2** something that is absent and stops something from being complete: *There are huge gaps in my memory.* **4 a gap in the market** an opportunity for a product or service that does not already exist **5 TIME** ▷ **B2** a period of time when nothing happens, or when you are doing something different than usual: *I decided to go back to teaching after a gap of 10 years.* → See also **the generation gap**

> **2** Word partners for **gap**
>
> bridge/close/narrow the gap • the gap between sth and sth

gape /geɪp/ **verb** [I] **1** to look at someone or something with your mouth open because you are so surprised: *We stood there gaping in wonder at the beautiful landscape.* **2** to be wide open

gaping /'geɪpɪŋ/ **adj** a gaping hole/wound, etc a hole/wound, etc that is open very wide

gap year noun [C] UK a year between leaving school and starting university that you usually spend travelling or working

garage /'gæraːʒ/ ⓤ /gə'rɑːʒ/ **noun** [C] **1** **A2** a small building, often built next to a house, that you can put a car in **2** **B1** a business that repairs or sells cars, and sometimes also sells fuel

garbage /'gɑːbɪdʒ/ **noun** [U] US (UK **rubbish**) **1** things that you throw away because you do not want them **2** something that you think is nonsense, wrong, or very bad quality: *How can you listen to that garbage on the radio!*

garbage can noun [C] US (UK **dustbin**) a large container for waste kept outside your house

garbage collector noun [C] US (UK **dustman**) someone whose job is to remove the waste from containers left outside houses

garbage man noun [C] US another word for garbage collector

garbled /'gɑːbəld/ **adj** Garbled words or messages are not clear and are very difficult to understand.

garden /'gɑːdən/ **noun 1** **A1** [C] UK (US **yard**) an area of ground belonging to a house, often containing grass, flowers, or trees: *the front/back garden* ○ *Dad's outside in the garden.* **2** a piece of land, usually near a home, where flowers and other plants are grown: *We have a vegetable garden.* **3** gardens [plural] a park or large public area where plants and flowers are grown • **garden verb** [I] to work in a garden, growing plants and making it look attractive

garden centre noun [C] UK a place that sells things for gardens such as plants and tools

gardener /'gɑːdənər/ **noun** [C] someone who works in a garden, growing plants and making it look attractive

gardening /'gɑːdənɪŋ/ **noun** [U] the job or activity of growing a garden and keeping it attractive

gargle /'gɑːgl/ **verb** [I] to move liquid or medicine around in your throat without swallowing, especially to clean it or stop it feeling painful

garish /'geərɪʃ/ **adj** unpleasantly bright in colour, or decorated too much: *a garish red jacket*

garlic /'gɑːlɪk/ **noun** [U] **A2** a vegetable like a small onion with a very strong taste and smell:

a clove of garlic → See colour picture **Fruits and Vegetables** on page Centre 10

garment /'gɑːmənt/ **noun** [C] formal a piece of clothing

garnish /'gɑːnɪʃ/ **verb** [T] to decorate food with something such as herbs or pieces of fruit: *salmon garnished with herbs and lemon* • **garnish noun** [C]

garrison /'gærɪsən/ **noun** [C] a group of soldiers living in a particular area or building to defend it

garter /'gɑːtər/ **noun** [C] a piece of elastic that holds up a woman's stockings (= very thin pieces of clothing that cover a woman's foot and leg)

gas¹ /gæs/ **noun 1 SUBSTANCE** ▷ [C, U] **B2** a substance in a form like air and not solid or liquid: *poisonous gases* **2 FUEL** ▷ [U] **A2** a substance in a form like air used as a fuel for heating and cooking: UK *a gas cooker*/US *a gas stove* **3 CAR FUEL** ▷ [U] US (UK **petrol**) a liquid fuel used in cars: *half a tank of gas* **4 STOMACH** ▷ [U] US (UK **wind**) air in your stomach that makes you feel uncomfortable and sometimes makes noises **5 the gas** US informal the part of a car that you push with your foot to make it go faster: *We'd better step on the gas* (= drive faster). → See also **natural gas, tear gas**

gas² /gæs/ **verb** [T] (**gassing, gassed**) to poison or kill someone with gas

gas chamber noun [C] a room that is filled with poisonous gas to kill people

gash /gæʃ/ **noun** [C] a long, deep wound or cut • **gash verb** [T]

gas mask noun [C] a cover you wear over your face to protect you from breathing poisonous gas

gasoline /'gæsəliːn/ **noun** [U] US (UK **petrol**) another word for gas (= a liquid fuel used in cars)

gasp /gɑːsp/ **verb** [I] **1** to make a noise by suddenly breathing in because you are shocked or surprised: *She gasped in horror as the car spun out of control.* **2** to breathe loudly and with difficulty trying to get more air: *He clutched his heart, gasping for breath.* • **gasp noun** [C] *gasp of surprise*

gas pedal noun [C] US (UK/US **accelerator**) the part of a car that you push with your foot to make it go faster

gas station noun [C] US (UK **petrol station**) a place where you can buy fuel for cars

gastric /'gæstrɪk/ **adj** relating to the stomach

gastronomic /ˌgæstrə'nɒmɪk/ **adj** relating to good food and cooking

gate /geɪt/ **noun** [C] **1** **A2** the part of a fence or outside wall that opens and closes like a door: *Please shut the gate.* **2** **B1** the part of an airport where passengers get on or off an aircraft: *The flight to Dublin is now boarding at gate 8.*

gateau /'gætəʊ/ ⓤ /gæ'təʊ/ **noun** [C, U] (plural **gateaux**) UK a large cake, usually filled and decorated with cream

gatecrash /'geɪtkræʃ/ **verb** [I, T] to go to a party or private event without an invitation • **gate crasher noun** [C] someone who gatecrashes

gateway /'geɪtweɪ/ **noun 1** [C] an opening in

fence or outside wall that is closed with a gate **2 the gateway to sth** the way to get into something or somewhere: *the gateway to the North*

gather /ˈɡæðər/ verb **1 MAKE A GROUP** ▷ [I, T] ⑫ to join other people somewhere to make a group, or to bring people together into a group: *Crowds of fans gathered at the stadium for the big match.* **2 COLLECT** ▷ [T] ⑫ to collect several things together, often from different places or people: *They interviewed 1000 people to gather data on TV viewing habits.* ∘ *She gathered her things together and left.* **3 THINK** ▷ [T] to think something is true because you have heard or seen information about it: *From what I can gather, they haven't sold their house yet.* **4 gather speed/strength/support, etc** to increase in speed/strength/support, etc

gathering /ˈɡæðərɪŋ/ noun [C] a party or a meeting when many people get together as a group: *a family gathering*

> **Word partners for gathering**
>
> at a gathering • a gathering of [teachers/ world leaders, etc] • a family gathering

gaudy /ˈɡɔːdi/ adj unpleasantly bright in colour or decoration: *a gaudy pink sweatshirt with gold embroidery*

gauge¹ /ɡeɪdʒ/ verb [T] **1** to make a judgment about a situation or about what someone thinks or feels: [+ question word] *It's impossible to gauge what her reaction will be.* **2** to measure a distance, size, or amount

gauge² /ɡeɪdʒ/ noun [C] **1** a way of judging something such as a situation or what someone thinks or feels: *Street interviews aren't an accurate gauge of public opinion.* **2** a method or piece of equipment that you use to measure something: *a fuel gauge*

gaunt /ɡɔːnt/ adj very thin, especially because of being sick or old: *a pale, gaunt face*

gauntlet /ˈɡɔːntlət/ noun [C] a long, thick glove (= piece of clothing for your hand)

IDIOMS **run the gauntlet** to have to deal with a lot of people who are criticizing or attacking you • **throw down the gauntlet** to invite someone to argue, fight, or compete with you

gauze /ɡɔːz/ noun [U] thin, transparent cloth, especially used to cover injuries

gave /ɡeɪv/ past tense of give

gawp /ɡɔːp/ verb [I] UK (US **gawk**, ⑤ /ɡɔːk/) to look at someone or something with your mouth open because you are shocked or surprised: *He just stood there gawping at me.*

gay¹ /ɡeɪ/ adj **1** ⑪ homosexual: *Have you told your parents you're gay yet?* ∘ *a gay bar/club* **2** old-fashioned very happy and enjoying yourself

gay² /ɡeɪ/ noun [C] someone who is homosexual, especially a man: *equal rights for gays and lesbians*

gaze /ɡeɪz/ verb gaze at/into, etc ⑫ to look for a long time at someone or something or in a particular direction: *They gazed into each other's eyes.* • **gaze** noun [no plural]

GB written abbreviation for gigabyte (= a unit for measuring the amount of information a computer can store): *a 200 GB hard drive*

GCSE /ˌdʒiːsiːesˈiː/ noun [C] abbreviation for General Certificate of Secondary Education: in the UK, an exam taken by students at the age of sixteen, or the qualification itself: *Mary's got nine GCSEs.*

GDP /ˌdʒiːdiːˈpiː/ noun [U] abbreviation for Gross Domestic Product: the total value of goods and services that a country produces in a year → Compare **GNP**

gear¹ /ɡɪər/ noun **1** [C] ⑫ a set of parts in a motor vehicle or bicycle that control how fast the wheels turn: [usually plural] *a mountain bike with 21 gears* ∘ *to change gear* **2 first/second/third, etc gear** ⑫ a particular position of the gears in a motor vehicle or bicycle that controls how fast the wheels turn: *The lights turned green, but I couldn't get into first gear.* **3** [U] ⑫ the clothes and equipment used for a particular purpose: *sports/swimming gear*

gear² /ɡɪər/ verb

PHRASAL VERBS **gear sth to/towards sb/sth** to design or organize something so that it is suitable for a particular purpose, situation, or group of people: [often passive] *These advertisements are geared towards a younger audience.* • **gear (sb/sth) up** to prepare for something that you have to do, or to prepare someone else for something: [often reflexive] *I'm trying to gear myself up for the exams.*

gearbox /ˈɡɪəbɒks/ noun [C] the set of gears in a motor vehicle and the metal box that contains them

gear lever noun [C] UK (US **gearshift**, ⑤ /ˈɡɪəʃɪft/) a stick with a handle that you move to change gear in a vehicle → See colour picture **Car** on page Centre 7

gearstick /ˈɡɪəstɪk/ noun [C] UK another word for gear lever → See colour picture **Car** on page Centre 7

GED /ˌdʒiːiːˈdiː/ noun [C] abbreviation for General Equivalency Diploma: an official document in the US that is given to someone who did not complete high school (= school for students aged 15 to 18) but who has passed a government exam instead

geek /ɡiːk/ noun [C] informal **1** a man who is boring and not fashionable **2** someone who knows a lot about science or technology, especially computers: *a brilliant computer geek* • **geeky** adj informal *a geeky guy with a beard and glasses*

geese /ɡiːs/ plural of goose

geezer /ˈɡiːzər/ noun [C] UK very informal a man

gel /dʒel/ noun [C, U] a thick, clear, liquid substance, especially a product used to style hair: *hair gel* ∘ *shower gel*

gelatine mainly UK /ˈdʒelətiːn/ (US **gelatin** /ˈdʒelətɪn/) noun [U] a clear substance made from animal bones, often used to make food thicker

gem /dʒem/ noun [C] **1** a valuable stone, especially one that has been cut to be used in jewellery **2** informal someone or something that you like very much and think is very special

Gemini /'dʒemɪnaɪ/ noun [C, U] the sign of the zodiac that relates to the period of 23 May – 21 June, or a person born during this period → See picture at **the zodiac**

gender /'dʒendər/ noun [C, U] **1** 🔒 the state of being male or female **2** 🔒 the division of nouns, pronouns, and adjectives into masculine, feminine, and neuter types

gene /dʒiːn/ noun [C] a part of a cell that is passed on from a parent to a child and that controls particular characteristics

> ☑ Word partners for **gene**
>
> carry/have a gene • a gene (responsible) for sth • gene therapy

general¹ /'dʒenᵊrᵊl/ adj **1** NOT DETAILED ▷ 🔒 not detailed, but including the most basic or necessary information: *These leaflets contain some general information about the school.* ∘ *I've got a general idea of how it works.* **2** MOST PEOPLE ▷ [always before noun] 🔒 relating to or involving all or most people, things, or places: *There seems to be general agreement on this matter.* **3** NOT LIMITED ▷ [always before noun] 🔒 including a lot of things or subjects and not limited to only one or a few: *general knowledge* **4** **in general a** 🔒 considering the whole of someone or something, and not just a particular part of them: *I still have a sore throat, but I feel much better in general.* **b** 🔒 usually, or in most situations: *In general, the weather here stays sunny.*

general² /'dʒenᵊrᵊl/ noun [C] an officer of very high rank in the army or air force

general anaes'thetic UK (US **general anesthetic**) noun [C, U] a substance that is used to stop someone being conscious when they have an operation so that they do not feel any pain

general e'lection noun [C] an election in which the people living in a country vote to decide who will represent them in the government

generalization (also UK **-isation**) /,dʒenᵊrᵊlaɪ'zeɪʃᵊn/ noun [C, U] something very basic that someone says is true, when it is sometimes but not always true

> ☑ Word partners for **generalization**
>
> make a generalization • a broad/gross/sweeping generalization

generalize (also UK **-ise**) /'dʒenᵊrᵊlaɪz/ verb [I] to say something very basic that is often true but not always true

general 'knowledge noun [U] knowledge of many different subjects

generally /'dʒenᵊrᵊli/ adv **1** USUALLY ▷ 🔒 usually, or in most situations: *I generally wake up early.* **2** AS A WHOLE ▷ 🔒 considering the whole of someone or something, and not just a particular part of them: *The police said that the crowd was generally well-behaved.* **3** BY MOST PEOPLE ▷ 🔒 by most people, or to most people: *He is generally believed to be their best player.*

general prac'titioner noun [C] (also **GP**) a doctor who sees people in the local area and treats illnesses that do not need a hospital visit

generate /'dʒenᵊreɪt/ verb [T] **1** 🔒 to cause something to exist: *to generate income/profit* ∘ *This film has generated a lot of interest.* **2** 🔒 to produce energy: *Many countries use nuclear fuels to generate electricity.*

generation /,dʒenᵊ'reɪʃᵊn/ noun **1** PEOPLE ▷ [C] 🔒 all the people in a society or family who are approximately the same age: *the older/younger generation* ∘ *This is the story of three generations of women.* **2** TIME ▷ [C] 🔒 a period of about 25 to 30 years, the time it takes for a child to become an adult and take the place of their parents in society: *Our family has lived in this village for generations.* **3** PRODUCT ▷ [C] 🔒 a product when it is at a particular stage of development: *a new generation of computers* **4** ENERGY ▷ [U] 🔒 the production of energy: *the generation of electricity*

the gener'ation ,gap noun the difference between young people and old people who do not understand each other because of their age difference

generator /'dʒenᵊreɪtər/ noun [C] a machine that produces electricity

generic /dʒə'nerɪk/ adj **1** relating to a whole group of things or type of thing **2** A generic product such as a drug is not sold with the name of the company that produced it.

generosity /,dʒenᵊ'rɒsəti/ noun [U] 🔒 the quality of being generous

generous /'dʒenᵊrəs/ adj **1** 🔒 giving people a lot of money, presents, or time in a kind way: *very generous man* **2** larger than usual or than expected: *a generous discount for students* ∘ *a generous portion* • **generously** adv

gene ,therapy noun [U] the science of changing genes (= parts of cells which control particular characteristics) in order to stop or prevent a disease

genetic /dʒə'netɪk/ adj relating to genes (= parts of cells which control particular characteristics): *a rare genetic disorder* ∘ *genetic research* • **genetically** adv

ge,netically 'modified adj Genetically modified plants or animals have had some of their genes (= parts of cells which control particular characteristics) changed.

ge,netic engi'neering noun [U] the activity of changing the genes (= parts of cells which control particular characteristics) in the cells of plants or animals

genetics /dʒə'netɪks/ noun [U] 🔒 the scientific study of genes (= parts of cells which control particular characteristics)

genial /'dʒiːniəl/ adj kind and friendly

genitals /'dʒenɪtᵊlz/ noun [plural] the sexual organs

genius /'dʒiːniəs/ noun **1** [C] someone who is extremely intelligent or extremely good at doing something: *Einstein was a genius.* **2** [U] the quality of being extremely intelligent or extremely good at doing something: *Einstein's genius*

enocide /'dʒenəsaɪd/ **noun** [U] the intentional killing of a large group of people who belong to a particular race or country

enre /'ʒɒnrə/ **noun** [C] a type of art or writing with a particular style: *a literary/musical genre*

ent /dʒent/ **noun** [C] informal short for gentleman

enteel /dʒen'tiːl/ **adj** very polite, especially in a way that is typical of someone from a high social class

entle /'dʒentl/ **adj 1 KIND** ▷ **③** kind and careful not to hurt or upset anyone or anything: *My mother was such a gentle, loving person.* **2 NOT STRONG** ▷ **③** not strong or severe: *Use a mild soap that is gentle on your skin.* ∘ *a gentle breeze* **3 SLOPE** ▷ A gentle slope or climb is not steep. • **gently** adv • **gentleness** noun [U]

entleman /'dʒentlmən/ **noun** [C] (plural **gentlemen**) **1** a man who behaves politely and treats people with respect: *He was a **perfect gentleman**.* **2** **③** a polite word for 'man', used especially when talking to or about a man you do not know: *There's a gentleman here to see you.*

he gents /dʒents/ **noun** [group] UK informal a toilet in a public place for men → See Note at **toilet**

enuine /'dʒenjuɪn/ **adj 1** If a person or their feelings are genuine, they are sincere and honest: *He shows a genuine concern for the welfare of his students.* **2** **③** If something is genuine, it is really what it seems to be: *a genuine gold necklace* • **genuinely** adv

enus /'dʒiːnəs/, /'dʒenəs/ **noun** [C] (plural **genera**) a group of animals or plants that have the same characteristics

eo- /dʒiːəʊ-/ **prefix** relating to the earth: *geothermal (= of or connected with the heat inside the Earth)*

eo-engineering /ˌdʒiːəʊendʒɪ'nɪərɪŋ/ **noun** [U] the use of scientific methods to artificially control the environment, particularly the world's temperature, in order to deal with the problem of climate change (= way the Earth's weather is changing)

eography /dʒi'ɒgrəfi/ **noun** [U] **②** the study of all the countries of the world, and of the surface of the Earth such as the mountains and seas • **geographer** noun [C] someone who studies geography • **geographical** /ˌdʒiːəʊ'græfɪkəl/ **adj** (also **geographic** /dʒiːəʊ'græfɪk/) • **geographically** adv

eology /dʒi'ɒlədʒi/ **noun** [U] the study of rocks and soil and the physical structure of the Earth • **geological** /ˌdʒiːəʊ'lɒdʒɪkəl/ **adj** • **geologist** noun [C] someone who studies geology

eometric /ˌdʒiːəʊ'metrɪk/ **adj** (also **geometrical**) **1** having a regular shape such as a circle or triangle, or having a pattern made of regular shapes **2** relating to geometry

eometry /dʒi'ɒmɪtri/ **noun** [U] a type of mathematics that deals with points, lines, angles and shapes

eriatric /ˌdʒeri'ætrɪk/ **adj** relating to very old people: *geriatric patients* ∘ *a geriatric hospital* • **geriatrics** noun [U] care and medical treatment for very old people

germ /dʒɜːm/ **noun 1** [C] a very small living thing that causes disease: *Wash your hands before cooking so that you don't spread germs.* **2 the germ of sth** the beginning of something: *the germ of a brilliant idea*

German measles **noun** [U] (also **rubella**) a disease which causes red spots on your skin

germinate /'dʒɜːmɪneɪt/ **verb** [I, T] If a seed germinates or is germinated, it begins to grow. • **germination** /ˌdʒɜːmɪ'neɪʃən/ **noun** [U]

gerund /'dʒerənd/ **noun** [C] a noun made from the form of a verb that ends with -ing, for example 'fishing' in 'John loves fishing.'

gesticulate /dʒes'tɪkjəleɪt/ **verb** [I] to move your hands and arms around to emphasize what you are saying or to express something

gesture¹ /'dʒestʃər/ **noun** [C] **1** a movement you make with your hand, arm, or head to express what you are thinking or feeling: *He **made a** rude **gesture** at the crowd.* **2** something you do to show people how you feel about a person or situation: *It would be a **nice gesture** to invite her to dinner.*

> **☑ Word partners for gesture**
>
> a **grand/token** gesture • a gesture **of** [friendship/goodwill, etc] • a **nice** gesture

gesture² /'dʒestʃər/ **verb** [I] to point at something or express something using your hand, arm, or head: *He **gestured towards** the window.*

get /get/ **verb** (**getting, got, got,** US **gotten**) **1 OBTAIN** ▷ [T] **④** to obtain or buy something: *I need to get some bread on the way home.* ∘ [+ two objects] *I'll try to get you a ticket.* **2 BRING** ▷ [T] **④** to go somewhere and bring back someone or something: *Wait here while I get the car.* **3 RECEIVE** ▷ [T] **④** to receive something or be given something: *Did you get anything nice for your birthday?* ∘ *Guy still hasn't got my email yet.* **4 UNDERSTAND** ▷ [T] **③** to understand something: *He never gets any of my jokes.* **5 get into/off/through, etc** **④** to move somewhere: *Get over here right now!* **6 get sth into/down/out, etc** to move something somewhere: *Could you get that bowl down from the shelf for me?* **7 get here/there/to the bank, etc** **④** to arrive somewhere: *What time do you normally get home from work?* **8 get sb/sth to do sth** **④** to make someone or something do something: *Sorry, I couldn't get the window to shut properly.* **9 get to do sth** **④** to have an opportunity to do something: *I never get to sit in the front seat.* **10 get sick/rich/wet, etc** **④** to become sick/rich/ wet, etc: *We should go. It's getting late.* **11 get caught/killed/married, etc** **④** to have something done to you **12 get sth painted/repaired, etc** **④** to arrange for someone to do something for you, usually for money: *I need to get my hair cut.* **13 get cancer/flu/malaria, etc** **④** to become sick or develop an illness: *I feel like I'm getting a cold.* **14 get a bus/train, etc** **④** to travel somewhere on a bus/train, etc: *Maybe we should get a taxi home.* **15 get the phone/door** informal **④** to answer someone calling on the telephone or waiting at the door: *Can you get the phone?*

> **Common learner error: got** or **gotten**?
>
> The past participle of the verb 'get' is **got** in British English and **gotten** in American English.
>
> *Have you got my email yet?* UK
> *Have you gotten my email yet?* US

PHRASAL VERBS **get about** mainly UK (US **get around**) **1** TRAVEL ▷ to travel to a lot of places **2** MOVE ▷ to be able to go to different places without difficulty, especially if you are old or sick **3** INFORMATION ▷ If news or information gets about, a lot of people hear about it. • **get sth across** ⓑ to successfully communicate information to other people: *This is the message that we want to **get across to** the public.* • **get ahead** to be successful in the work that you do: *It's tough for any woman who wants to **get ahead in** politics.* • **get along** mainly US (mainly UK **get on**) **1** If two or more people get along, they like each other and are friendly to each other: *I don't really **get along with** my sister's husband.* **2** to deal with a situation, especially successfully: *I wonder how Michael's getting along in his new job?* • **get around sth** (also UK **get round sth**) to find a way of dealing with or avoiding a problem: *Our lawyer found a way of getting around the adoption laws.* • **get around to sth** (also UK **get round to sth**) ⓑ to do something that you have intended to do for a long time: *I finally **got around to** calling her yesterday.* • **get at sb** UK informal to criticize someone in an unkind way • **be getting at sth** informal If you ask someone what they are getting at, you are asking them what they really mean. • **get at sth** ⓑ to be able to reach or get something • **get away 1** ⓑ to leave or escape from a place or person, often when it is difficult to do this: *We walked to the next beach to **get away from** the crowds.* **2** ⓑ to go somewhere to have a holiday, especially because you need to rest: *We decided to go up to Scotland to **get away from it all** (= have a relaxing holiday).* • **get away with sth** ⓑ to succeed in doing something bad or wrong without being punished or criticized: *He shouldn't treat you like that. Don't let him get away with it.* • **get back** ⓐ to return to a place after you have been somewhere else: *By the time we got back to the hotel, Lydia had already left.* • **get sth back** If you get something back, something that you had before is given to you again: *I wouldn't lend him anything, you'll never get it back.* • **get sb back** informal to do something unpleasant to someone because they have done something unpleasant to you • **get back to sb** to talk to someone, usually on the telephone, to give them some information they have asked for or because you were not able to speak to them before • **get back to sth** to start doing or talking about something again: *Anyway, I'd better get back to work.* • **get behind** If you get behind with work or payments, you have not done as much work or paid as much money as you should by a particular time. • **get by** to be able to live or deal with a situation with

difficulty, usually by having just enough ◆ something you need, such as money: *I don⸿ know how he **gets by** on so little money.* • **get s⸿ down** ⓑ to make someone feel unhappy: *A⸿ this uncertainty is really getting me down.* • **g⸿ sth down** to write something, especially som⸿ thing that someone has said • **get down to st⸿** ⓑ to start doing something seriously and with ⸿ lot of attention and effort: *Before we get down ⸿ business, I'd like to thank you all for coming toda⸿* • **get in 1** ENTER ▷ ⓑ to succeed in entering ⸿ place, especially a building: *They must have g⸿ in through the bathroom window.* **2** PERSO⸿ ARRIVING ▷ ⓑ to arrive at your home or th⸿ place where you work: *What time did you get ⸿ last night?* **3** VEHICLE ARRIVING ▷ ⓑ If a train ⸿ other vehicle gets in at a particular time, that ⸿ when it arrives: *Our flight's getting in later th⸿ expected.* **4** BE CHOSEN ▷ ⓑ to succeed in bein⸿ chosen or elected for a position in a school ⸿ other organization: *He wanted to go to Oxfo⸿ University but he didn't get in.* • **get into sth 1** ⓑ to succeed in being chosen or elected for ⸿ position in a school or other organization **2** t⸿ become interested in an activity or subject, ⸿ start being involved in an activity: *How did yo⸿ get into journalism?* • **get into sb** If you do n⸿ know what has got into someone, you do n⸿ understand why they are behaving strangel⸿ • **get off (sth) 1** ⓐ to leave a bus, train, aircraf⸿ or boat: *We should get off at the next stop.* → Se⸿ colour picture **Phrasal Verbs** on page Centre 16 **2** t⸿ leave the place where you work, usually at th⸿ end of the day: *What time do you get off work⸿* • **Get off!** UK informal something that you say i⸿ order to tell someone to stop touching someon⸿ or something • **get (sb) off (sth)** to avoid bein⸿ punished for something you have done wron⸿ or to help someone avoid getting punished f⸿ something they have done wrong: *He got o⸿ with a 20 euro fine.* • **get off on sth** informal If yo⸿ get off on something, it makes you feel ver⸿ excited, especially in a sexual way. • **get off wit⸿ sb** UK informal to begin a sexual relationship wit⸿ someone • **get on (sth)** ⓐ to go onto a bu⸿ train, aircraft, or boat: *I think we got on th⸿ wrong bus.* → See colour picture **Phrasal Verbs** ⸿ page Centre 16 • **be getting on** informal **1** t⸿ old **2** mainly UK If time is getting on, it ⸿ becoming late. • **get on** mainly UK (mainly US **g⸿ along**) **1** ⓑ If two or more people get on, the⸿ like each other and are friendly to each other: *⸿ never knew that Karen didn't **get on with** Su⸿* **2** ⓑ to deal with a situation, especially succes⸿ fully: *How's Frank getting on in his new job?* • **g⸿ on with sth** to continue doing somethin⸿ especially work: *Get on with your homewor⸿* • **get onto sth** to start talking about a subjec⸿ after discussing something else: *How did we ge⸿ onto this subject?* • **get out 1** MOVE OUT ▷ ⓑ t⸿ move out of something, especially a vehicle: *⸿ get out when you stop at the traffic light⸿* **2** DIFFERENT PLACES ▷ to go out to differen⸿ places and meet people in order to enjo⸿ yourself: *She doesn't get out so much now tha⸿ she's got the baby.* **3** NEWS ▷ If news ⸿ information gets out, people hear about

---

although someone is trying to keep it secret. • **get (sb) out** to escape from or leave a place, or to help someone do this: *I left the door open and the cat got out.* • **get out of sth** ⓑ to avoid doing something that you should do, often by giving an excuse: *You're just trying to get out of doing the housework!* • **get sth out of sb** to persuade or force someone to tell or give you something: *He was determined to get the truth out of her.* • **get sth out of sth** to enjoy something or think that something is useful: *It was an interesting course but I'm not sure I got much out of it.* • **get over sth 1** ⓑ to begin to feel better after being unhappy or sick: *It took her months to get over the shock of Richard leaving.* **2 can't/couldn't get over sth** informal to be very shocked or surprised about something: *I can't get over how different you look with short hair.* • **get sth over with** to do and complete something difficult or unpleasant that must be done: *I'll be glad to get these exams over with.* • **get round** UK (US **get around**) If news or information gets round, a lot of people hear about it. • **get round sth** UK (US **get around sth**) to find a way of dealing with or avoiding a problem • **get round sb** UK (US **get around sb**) to persuade someone to do what you want by being kind to them • **get through** to manage to talk to someone on the telephone: *I called you earlier, but I couldn't get through.* • **get through to sb** to succeed in making someone understand or believe something: *I just don't seem to be able to get through to him these days.* • **get through sth 1** ⓑ to deal with a difficult or unpleasant experience successfully, or to help someone do this: *If I can just get through my exams I'll be so happy.* **2** mainly UK to finish doing or using something: *We got through a whole jar of coffee last week.* • **get to sb** informal to make someone feel upset or angry: *I know he's annoying, but you shouldn't let him get to you.* • **get together 1** ⓑ to meet in order to do something or spend time together: *Jan and I are getting together next week for lunch.* **2** to begin a romantic relationship: *She got together with Phil two years ago.* • **get (sb) up** ⓐ to wake up and get out of bed, or to make someone do this: *I had to get up at five o'clock this morning.* → See colour picture **Phrasal Verbs** on page Centre 16 • **get up** to stand up: *The whole audience got up and started clapping.* • **get up to sth** UK to do something, especially something that other people think is wrong: *She's been getting up to all sorts of mischief lately.*

getaway /ˈɡetəweɪ/ noun [C] an occasion when someone leaves a place quickly, especially after committing a crime: *They had a car waiting outside so they could **make** a quick **getaway**.*

get-together /ˈɡettəɡeðə/ noun [C] an informal meeting or party: *We have a big family get-together every year.*

ghastly /ˈɡɑːstli/ adj very bad or unpleasant: *a ghastly mistake* ◦ *a ghastly man*

ghetto /ˈɡetəʊ/ noun [C] (plural **ghettos, ghettoes**) an area of a city where people of a particular race or religion live, especially a poor area

ghost /ɡəʊst/ noun [C] ⓑ the spirit of a dead person that appears to people who are alive: *Do you believe in ghosts?* ◦ *a ghost story*

ghost

IDIOM **give up the ghost** UK humorous If a machine gives up the ghost, it stops working completely.

• **ghostly** adj *a ghostly figure*

ghost town noun [C] a town where few or no people now live

ghoul /ɡuːl/ noun [C] an evil spirit

GI /ˌdʒiːˈaɪ/ noun [C] a soldier in the US army

giant¹ /ˈdʒaɪənt/ adj [always before noun] ⓑ extremely big, or much bigger than other similar things: *a giant spider*

giant² /ˈdʒaɪənt/ noun [C] **1** an imaginary man who is much bigger and stronger than ordinary men **2** a very large and important company or organization: *a media/software giant*

gibberish /ˈdʒɪbərɪʃ/ noun [U] something that someone says that has no meaning or that cannot be understood

gibe /dʒaɪb/ noun [C] another spelling of jibe (= an insulting remark)

giddy /ˈɡɪdi/ adj feeling as if you cannot balance and are going to fall

gift /ɡɪft/ noun [C] **1** ⓐ something that you give to someone, usually for a particular occasion: *a birthday/wedding gift* **2** a natural ability or skill: *She **has a gift for** design.*

gifted /ˈɡɪftɪd/ adj A gifted person has a natural ability or is extremely intelligent: *a gifted athlete* ◦ *a school for gifted children*

gift shop noun [C] a shop which sells goods which are suitable for giving as presents

gift token/voucher noun [C] UK (US **gift certificate, gift card**) a card with an amount of money printed on it that you exchange in a shop for goods that cost that amount of money: *a £20 gift voucher*

gig /ɡɪɡ/ noun [C] informal a performance of pop or rock music

gigabyte /ˈɡɪɡəbaɪt/ noun [C] (written abbreviation **GB**) a unit for measuring the amount of information a computer can store, equal to 1,000,000,000 bytes

gigantic /dʒaɪˈɡæntɪk/ adj extremely big: *a gigantic teddy bear*

giggle /ˈɡɪɡl/ verb [I] to laugh in a nervous or silly way: *She started giggling and couldn't stop.* • **giggle** noun [C]

gilded /ˈɡɪldɪd/ adj covered with a thin layer of gold or gold paint: *a gilded frame/mirror*

gill /ɡɪl/ noun [C] an organ on each side of a fish or other water creature which it uses to breathe

gilt /ɡɪlt/ noun [U] a thin covering of gold or gold paint • **gilt** adj

gimmick /ˈɡɪmɪk/ noun [C] something that is used only to get people's attention, especially to make them buy something: *a **marketing/pub-licity gimmick*** • **gimmicky** adj

gin /dʒɪn/ **noun** [C, U] a strong alcoholic drink that has no colour

ginger[1] /ˈdʒɪndʒər/ **noun** [U] a pale brown root with a strong taste used as a spice in cooking: *ginger cake*

ginger[2] /ˈdʒɪndʒər/ **adj** UK Ginger hair is an orange-brown colour: *She's got ginger hair and freckles.*

ginger[3] /ˈɡɪŋər/ **noun** [C] UK informal an offensive word for a person with red hair

gingerly /ˈdʒɪndʒəli/ **adv** slowly and carefully: *He lowered himself gingerly into the water.*

gipsy /ˈdʒɪpsi/ **noun** [C] another UK spelling of gypsy (= a member of a race of people who travel from place to place, especially in Europe)

giraffe /dʒɪˈrɑːf/ **noun** [C] ⓐ a large African animal with a very long neck and long, thin legs

giraffe

girder /ˈɡɜːdər/ **noun** [C] a long, thick piece of metal that is used to support bridges or large buildings

girl /ɡɜːl/ **noun 1** ⓐ [C] a female child or young woman: *We have three children – a boy and two girls.* **2 the girls** a group of female friends: *I'm going out with the girls tonight.*

girlfriend /ˈɡɜːlfrend/ **noun** [C] **1** ⓐ a woman or girl who someone is having a romantic relationship with: *Have you met Steve's new girlfriend?* **2** a female friend, especially of a woman

girth /ɡɜːθ/ **noun** [C, U] the measurement around something round, such as someone's waist

gist /dʒɪst/ **noun the gist of sth** the main point or meaning of something without the details

give[1] /ɡɪv/ **verb** (**gave, given**) **1 PROVIDE** ▷ [+ two objects] ⓐ to provide someone with something: *Her parents gave her a car for her birthday.* ∘ *Do you **give** money **to** charity?* ∘ *Could you give me a lift to the station, please?* **2 PUT NEAR** ▷ [+ two objects] ⓐ to put something near someone or in their hand so that they can use it or look at it: *Can you give me that pen?* ∘ *He poured a cup of coffee and **gave** it **to** Isabel.* **3 ALLOW** ▷ [+ two objects] ⓑ to allow someone to have a right or an opportunity: *We didn't really give him a chance to explain.* **4 TELL** ▷ [T] ⓐ to tell someone something: *The woman refused to give her name.* ∘ [+ two objects] *Can you give Jo a message?* **5 CAUSE** ▷ [+ two objects] ⓑ to make someone have or feel something: *I hope he hasn't given you any trouble.* ∘ *This news will **give** hope **to** thousands of sufferers.* **6 ALLOW TIME** ▷ [+ two objects] ⓑ to allow someone or something a particular amount of time: *I'm nearly ready – just give me a few minutes.* **7 PAY MONEY** ▷ [+ two objects] ⓑ to pay someone for

Other ways of saying give

Very common alternatives to 'give' are verbs such as **offer**, **provide**, and **supply**:
*This booklet **provides** useful information about local services.*
*Your doctor should be able to **offer** advice.*
*The lake **supplies** the whole town **with** water.*

The verb **donate** is often used when someone gives money or goods to an organisation that needs help:
*Four hundred pounds has been **donated** to the school book fund.*

If one of many people gives something, especially money, in order to provide or achieve something, the verb **contribute** is used:
*I **contributed** twenty dollars towards Jamie's present.*

If you put something from your hand into someone else's hand, you can use verbs such as **pass** and **hand**:
*Could you **hand** me that book, please?*
*He **passed** a note to her during the meeting.*

The phrasal verb **hand in** is sometimes used when you give something to someone in a position of authority:
*Have you **handed in** your history essay yet?*

The phrasal verb **pass on** is often used when you ask someone to give something to someone else:
*Could you **pass** this **on** to Laura when you've finished reading it?*

If something like a prize or an amount of money is given in an official way, you can use verbs like **award** or **present**:
*She was **presented** with a bouquet of flowers and a cheque for £500.*
*He was **awarded** the Nobel Prize for Physics.*

particular amount of money for something: *gave him $40 for his old camera.* **8 DO** ▷ [T] ⓑ t perform an action: *to give a cry/shout* ∘ [+ tw objects] *He gave her a kiss on the cheek.* **9 give s a call** ⓐ (also UK **give sb a ring**) to telephon someone: *Why don't you just give him a cal.* **10 give a performance/speech, etc** ⓑ t perform or speak in public: *Tony gave a gre speech.* **11 give a party** ⓐ to have a party Claire's giving a birthday party for Eri **12 MOVE** ▷ [I] to bend, stretch, or brea because of too much weight **13 give way U** (US **yield**) to stop in order to allow other vehicle to go past before you drive onto a bigger road

PHRASAL VERBS **give sth away 1** ⓑ to giv something to someone without asking for an money: *They're giving away a CD with th magazine.* **2** ⓑ to let someone know a secre often without intending to: *The party was mean to be a surprise, but Caroline gave it away.* • **giv sth back** ⓐ to return something to the perso who gave it to you: *Has she given you those book back yet?* • **give in 1** ⓑ to finally agree to wha someone wants after a period when you refus to agree: *We will never **give in to** terrorist* demands. **2** ⓑ to accept that you have been beaten and agree to stop competing or fighting • **give sth in** mainly UK ⓑ to give a piece of written work or a document to someone for them to read, judge, or deal with: *I have to give my essay in on Monday.* • **give off sth** to produce heat, light, a smell, or a gas: *The fire was giving off a lot of smoke.* • **give sth out** ⓑ to give something to a large number of people: *He gave out copies of the report at the end of the meeting.* • **give out** If a machine or part of your body gives out, it stops working correctly: *She read until her eyes gave out.* • **give up (sth) 1** ⓑ If you give up a habit such as smoking, or give up something unhealthy such as alcohol, you stop doing it or having it: *I gave up smoking two years ago.* **2** ⓑ to stop doing something before you have completed it, usually because it is too difficult: [+ doing sth] *I've given up trying to help her.* • **give up sth** ⓑ to stop doing a regular activity or job: *Are you going to give up work when you have your baby?* • **give up** to stop trying to think of the answer to a joke or question: *Do you give up?* • **give it up for sb** used to ask people to clap their hands to show that they like a performance: *Ladies and gentlemen, give it up for the star of our show, Amy Jones!* • **give yourself up** to allow the police or an enemy to catch you • **give up on sb** to stop hoping that someone will do what you want them to do: *The doctors have given up on him.* • **give up on sth** to stop hoping that something will achieve what you want it to achieve

give² /gɪv/ **noun** [U] something's ability to bend or move from its normal shape to take extra weight or size

IDIOM **give and take** a way in which people reach agreement by letting each person have part of what they want

giveaway /ˈgɪvəweɪ/ **noun 1** [C] something that is given to people free **2** [no plural] something that makes it easy for people to guess something

given¹ /ˈgɪvᵊn/ **adj 1** [always before noun] already arranged or agreed: *They can only stay for a given amount of time.* **2 any given day/time/week, etc** any day/time/week, etc: *About 4 million women are pregnant in the US at any given time.*

given² /ˈgɪvᵊn/ **preposition** considering a particular thing: *Given the force of the explosion, it's a miracle they survived.*

given³ /ˈgɪvᵊn/ past participle of give

glacial /ˈgleɪsiəl/ ⓤ /ˈgleɪʃᵊl/ **adj** [always before noun] relating to glaciers or ice: *glacial lakes*

glacier /ˈglæsiəʳ/ ⓤ /ˈgleɪʃər/ **noun** [C] a large mass of ice that moves very slowly, usually down a slope or valley

glad /glæd/ **adj** [never before noun] **1** ⓐ happy about something: [+ (that)] *She's very glad that she left.* ∘ [+ to do sth] *I'm so glad to see you.* **2** very willing to do something: [+ to do sth] *She's always glad to help.* **3 be glad of sth** formal to be grateful for something: *I was glad of a few days off before going back to work.*

gladly /ˈglædli/ **adv** willingly or happily: *I would gladly pay extra for better service.*

glamorize (also UK **-ise**) /ˈglæmᵊraɪz/ **verb** [T] to make something seem glamorous

glamorous /ˈglæmᵊrəs/ **adj** attractive in an exciting and special way: *a glamorous woman* ∘ *a glamorous lifestyle*

glamour (also US **glamor**) /ˈglæməʳ/ **noun** [U] the quality of being attractive, exciting and special: *the glamour of Hollywood*

glance¹ /glɑːns/ **verb 1 glance at/around/ towards, etc** ⓑ to look somewhere for a short time: *He glanced at his watch.* **2 glance at/over/ through, etc** ⓑ to read something quickly: *She glanced through the newspaper.*

glance² /glɑːns/ **noun 1** ⓑ [C] a quick look: *She had a quick glance around the restaurant.* **2 at a glance** If you see something at a glance, you see it very quickly or immediately.

> ⓩ **Word partners for glance**
>
> cast/give/have a glance [at/around, etc] sb/ sth • **exchange** glances • a **cursory/quick** glance

gland /glænd/ **noun** [C] an organ in the body that produces a particular chemical substance or liquid

glandular fever /ˌglændjʊləˈfiːvəʳ/ **noun** [U] UK (US **mononucleosis**) an infectious disease that makes your glands swell and makes you feel tired

glare¹ /gleəʳ/ **noun 1** [U] strong, bright light that hurts your eyes: *I get a lot of glare from my computer screen.* **2** [C] a long, angry look **3 the glare of publicity/the media, etc** too much attention that someone gets from newspapers and television

glare² /gleəʳ/ **verb** [I] to look at someone in an angry way

glaring /ˈgleərɪŋ/ **adj 1 a glaring error/mistake/ omission, etc** a very noticeable mistake or problem **2 glaring light/sun, etc** light that is too strong and bright

glass

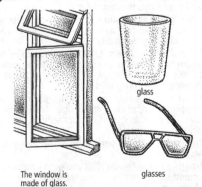

The window is made of glass.

glasses

glass /glɑːs/ **noun 1** [U] ⓐ a hard, transparent substance that objects such as windows and bottles are made of: ***broken glass*** ∘ *glass jars*

2 [C] ⚠ a container made of glass that is used for drinking: *Would you like* **a glass of** *water?*
→ See also **magnifying glass, stained glass**

glasses /ˈglɑːsɪz/ **noun** [plural] ⚠ a piece of equipment with two transparent parts that you wear in front of your eyes to help you see better: *a pair of glasses* ∘ *She was wearing glasses.*

glassy /ˈglɑːsi/ **adj 1** A glassy surface is smooth and shiny like glass. **2** Glassy eyes show no expression and seem not to see anything.

glaze¹ /gleɪz/ **verb 1 EYES** ▷ [I] (also **glaze over**) If someone's eyes glaze or glaze over, they stop showing any interest or expression because they are bored or tired. **2 CLAY** ▷ [T] to cover the surface of objects made of clay with a liquid that makes them hard and shiny when they are baked **3 FOOD** ▷ [T] to put a liquid on food to make it shiny and more attractive **4 GLASS** ▷ [T] to put glass in a window or door

glaze² /gleɪz/ **noun** [C, U] **1** a liquid that is put on objects made of clay to make them hard and shiny when they are baked **2** a liquid that is put on food to make it shiny and attractive

gleam¹ /gliːm/ **verb** [I] to shine in a pleasant, soft way: *a gleaming new car*

gleam² /gliːm/ **noun** [no plural] **1** a pleasant, soft light from something that shines: *the gleam of sunlight on the frozen lake* **2** an expression in someone's eyes: *She had a strange gleam in her eye.*

glean /gliːn/ **verb** [T] to discover information slowly or with difficulty: [often passive] *Some useful information can be gleaned from this study.*

glee /gliː/ **noun** [U] a feeling of great happiness, usually because of your good luck or someone else's bad luck: *Rosa began laughing with glee.* • **gleeful** adj • **gleefully** adv

glee club noun [C] US a group organized to sing together, often at a school or university

glib /glɪb/ **adj** using words in a way that is clever and confident, but not sincere

glide /glaɪd/ **verb glide along/into/over, etc** to move somewhere smoothly and quietly: *The train slowly glided out of the station.*

glider /ˈglaɪdər/ **noun** [C] an aircraft that has no engine and flies on air currents • **gliding noun** [U] the activity of flying in a glider → See also **hang glider, hang gliding**

glimmer¹ /ˈglɪmər/ **noun 1 a glimmer of happiness/hope, etc** a small sign of something good **2** [C] the light from something that is shining in a weak way

glimmer² /ˈglɪmər/ **verb** [I] to shine in a weak way

glimpse /glɪmps/ **noun** [C] If you get a glimpse of something or someone, you see them for a very short time: *He caught/got a glimpse of her as she got into the car.* • **glimpse verb** [T] to see something or someone for a very short time: *She glimpsed him out of the corner of her eye.*

glint /glɪnt/ **noun** [no plural] **1** If you have a glint in your eye, your eyes shine with excitement or because you are going to do something bad: *Sh had a wicked glint in her eye.* **2** a quick flash of light that shines from something or is reflected from it • **glint verb** [I]

glisten /ˈglɪsən/ **verb** [I] If something glistens, i shines, often because it is wet: *Their faces were glistening with sweat.*

glitch /glɪtʃ/ **noun** [C] informal a mistake or problem that stops something from working correctly: *technical glitches*

glitter¹ /ˈglɪtər/ **verb** [I] to shine with small flashes of light: *Snow glittered on the mountains*

glitter² /ˈglɪtər/ **noun** [U] **1** very small, shin pieces of metal used for decoration **2** the quality of being exciting and attractive

glittering /ˈglɪtərɪŋ/ **adj 1** shining with small flashes of light: *glittering jewels* **2** successful an exciting: *a glittering party/career*

glitz /glɪts/ **noun** [U] the quality of being attractive, exciting and showing money in a obvious way • **glitzy adj** *a glitzy nightclub*

gloat /gləʊt/ **verb** [I] to show pleasure at you success or at someone else's failure: *His enemie were gloating over his defeat.*

global /ˈgləʊbəl/ **adj** ⚠ relating to the whol world: *the global problem of nuclear wast* • **globally adv**

globalization /ˌgləʊbəlaɪˈzeɪʃən/ **noun** [U] **1** th increase of business around the world, espe cially by big companies operating in man countries **2** the process in which things a over the world become more similar: *th globalization of fashion*

global warming noun [U] ⚠ an increase i the temperature of the air around the worl because of pollution

globe /gləʊb/ **noun** **1 the globe** the world: *This event is being watched by 200 million people around the globe.* **2** [C] a model of the world shaped like a ball with a map of all the countries on it

globe

globule /ˈglɒbjuːl/ **noun** [C] a small, round mass or lump of a liquid substance: *a globule of oil*

gloom /gluːm/ **noun** [U] **1** a feeling of unhappiness and of not havin any hope: *an atmosphere of gloom* **2** darknes but not complete darkness

gloomy /ˈgluːmi/ **adj 1 NEGATIVE** ▷ ver negative about a situation: *a gloomy repor* **2 DARK** ▷ dark in an unpleasant way: *a smal gloomy room* **3 UNHAPPY** ▷ unhappy and without hope: *a gloomy face* • **gloomily adv**

glorify /ˈglɔːrɪfaɪ/ **verb** [T] **1** to describe or represent something in a way that makes it seem better or more important than it really is: *I don't like films that glorify violence.* **2** to praise someone, especially God

glorious /ˈglɔːriəs/ **adj 1** beautiful or wonderful: *We had four days of glorious sunshine.* ◦ *glorious colours* **2** deserving praise and respect: *a glorious career* • **gloriously adv**

glory¹ /ˈglɔːri/ **noun** [U] **1** praise and respect you get from people for achieving something important **2** great beauty: *The castle has been restored to its former glory.*

glory² /ˈglɔːri/ **verb**

PHRASAL VERB **glory in sth** to enjoy something and be very proud of it

gloss¹ /glɒs/ **noun 1** PAINT ▷ [U] paint that creates a shiny surface **2** SHINE ▷ [U] shine on a surface **3** EXPLANATION ▷ [C] a short explanation of a word or phrase in a text

gloss² /glɒs/ **verb** [T] to give a short explanation of a word or phrase

PHRASAL VERB **gloss over sth** to avoid discussing something, or to discuss something without any details in order to make it seem unimportant

glossary /ˈglɒsəri/ **noun** [C] a list of difficult words with their meanings like a small dictionary, especially at the end of a book

glossy /ˈglɒsi/ **adj 1** smooth and shiny: *glossy hair* **2** Glossy magazines and pictures are printed on shiny paper: *a glossy brochure*

glove /glʌv/ **noun** [C] ⚫ a piece of clothing that covers your fingers and hand: *a pair of gloves* → See colour picture **Clothes** on page Centre 9

glove compartment noun [C] (also **glove box**) a small cupboard in the front of a car, used to hold small things

glow¹ /gləʊ/ **noun** [no plural] **1** a soft, warm light: *the warm glow of the moon* **2** the warm and healthy appearance of someone's face: *Sam's face had lost its rosy glow.* **3 a glow of happiness/pride, etc** a strong feeling of being happy/proud, etc

glow² /gləʊ/ **verb** [I] **1** to produce a soft, warm light: *These toys glow in the dark.* **2** to have a warm and healthy appearance: *Her eyes were bright and her cheeks were glowing.* **3 glow with happiness/pride, etc** to feel very happy/proud, etc: *Glowing with pride, she showed me her painting.*

glower /ˈglaʊər/ **verb** [I] to look at someone in a very angry way: *The woman glowered at her husband.*

glowing /ˈgləʊɪŋ/ **adj** praising someone a lot: *She got a glowing report from her teacher.*

☑ Word partners for **glowing**

a glowing reference/report/tribute • in glowing terms

glucose /ˈgluːkəʊs/ **noun** [U] a type of sugar

glue¹ /gluː/ **noun** [U] a substance used to stick things together: *Put a bit of glue on both edges*

and hold them together. → See colour picture **The Classroom** on page Centre 6

glue² /gluː/ **verb** [T] (**glueing, gluing, glued**) to stick something to something else with glue: *Do you think you can glue this vase back together?*

PHRASAL VERB **be glued to sth** to be watching something, especially television, with all your attention: *The kids were glued to the TV all morning.*

glum /glʌm/ **adj** unhappy: *Why are you looking so glum today?* • **glumly adv**

glut /glʌt/ **noun** [C] more of something than is needed: [usually singular] *There is a glut of houses for sale in this area.*

glutton /ˈglʌtən/ **noun** [C] someone who eats too much

IDIOM **be a glutton for punishment** to enjoy doing things that are unpleasant or difficult

gluttony /ˈglʌtəni/ **noun** [U] the quality of eating too much

gm written abbreviation for gram (= a unit for measuring weight)

GM /ˌdʒiːˈem/ **adj** abbreviation for genetically modified: genetically modified plants or animals have had some of their genes (= parts of cells which control particular characteristics) changed: *GM foods*

GMO /ˌdʒiːemˈəʊ/ **noun** [U] abbreviation for genetically modified organism: a plant or animal in which scientists have changed the genes (= parts of cells which control particular characteristics)

GMT /ˌdʒiːemˈtiː/ **noun** [U] abbreviation for Greenwich Mean Time: the time at Greenwich in London, which is used as an international measurement for time

gnarled /nɑːld/ **adj** rough and twisted, usually because of being old: *a gnarled tree trunk*

gnat /næt/ **noun** [C] a small flying insect that can bite you

gnaw /nɔː/ **verb** [I, T] to bite something with a lot of small bites: *He was gnawing on a bone.*

PHRASAL VERB **gnaw at sb** to make someone feel more and more anxious or annoyed: *Doubt kept gnawing at him.*

gnome /nəʊm/ **noun** [C] an imaginary little man with a pointed hat: *a garden gnome*

GNP /ˌdʒiːenˈpiː/ **noun** [U] abbreviation for gross national product: the total value of goods and services produced in a country in a year, including the profits made in foreign countries → Compare **GDP**

go¹ /gəʊ/ **verb** [I] (**going, went, gone**) **1** MOVE ▷ ⚫ to move or travel somewhere: *I'd love to go to America.* ◦ *We went into the house.* ◦ *Are you going by train?* **2** DO SOMETHING ▷ ⚫ to move or travel somewhere in order to do something: *Let's go for a walk.* ◦ [+ doing sth] *We're going camping tomorrow.* **3** DISAPPEAR ▷ ⚫ to disappear or no longer exist: *When I turned round the man had gone.* **4 go badly/well, etc** ⚫ to develop in a particular way: *My exams went really badly.* **5** CONTINUE ▷ to continue to be in a particular state: *We won't let anyone go hungry.* **6 WORKING** ▷ **B2** to work correctly: *Did you manage to get the car going?* **7 STOP WORKING** ▷ **B2** to stop working correctly: *Her hearing is going, so speak loudly.* **8 MATCH** ▷ **B1** If two things go, they match each other: *Any colour* **goes with** *jeans.* **9 TIME** ▷ **B2** If time goes, it passes: *The day went very quickly.* **10 SONG** ▷ **B2** to have a particular tune or words: *I can't remember how it goes.* **11 SOUND/MOVEMENT** ▷ **B2** to make a particular sound or movement: *My dog goes like this when he wants some food.*

❗ Common learner error: go, gone, and been

Gone is the usual past participle of the verb **go**. Sometimes you use the past participle **been** when you want to say that you have gone somewhere and come back, or to say that you have visited somewhere.

Paul has gone to the hospital this morning (= he is still there).

Paul has been to the hospital this morning (= he went and has come back).

He has gone to New York (= he is still there).

Have you ever been to New York? (= Have you ever visited New York?)

IDIOM **not go there** to not think or talk about a subject that makes you feel bad: *"Then there's the guilt I feel about leaving my child with another woman." "Don't even go there!"*

PHRASAL VERBS **go about sth** to start to do something or deal with something: *What's the best way to go about this?* • **go after sb** to chase or follow someone in order to catch them: *He ran away, but the police went after him.* • **go against sth** If something goes against a rule or something you believe in, it does not obey it or agree with it: *It goes against my principles to lie.* • **go against sb** If a decision or vote goes against someone, they do not get the result that they needed: *The judge's decision went against us.* • **go ahead 1** **B2** to start to do something: *We have permission to go ahead with the project.* **2** **B2** something that you say to someone to give them permission to do something: *"Can I borrow your book?" "Yes, go ahead."* • **go-ahead** noun *get/give the go-ahead* • **go along 1** UK to go to a place or event, usually without much planning: *I might go along to the party after work.* **2** to continue doing something: *I'll tell you the rules as we go along.* • **go along with sth/sb** to support an idea, or to agree with someone's opinion: *She'll never go along with this idea.* • **go around** (also mainly UK **go round**) **1** to be enough for everyone in a group: *There aren't enough chairs to go around.* **2** **go around doing sth** to spend your time behaving badly or doing something that is unpleasant for other people: *She's been going around telling people I'm stupid.* • **go at sth** informal to start doing something with a lot of energy and enthusiasm: *There were a lot of dishes to wash so we went at it straight away.* • **go away 1** LEAVE ▷ **B1** to leave a place: *Go away – I'm busy.* **2** HOLIDAY ▷ **B1** to leave

your home in order to spend time in a differen[t] place, usually for a holiday: *They're going awa[y] for a few weeks in the summer.* **3 DISAPPEAR** ▷ t[o] disappear: *That smell seems to have gone away.* • **go back** **B1** to return to a place where you wer[e] or where you have been before: *When are yo[u] going back to London?* • **go back on sth** to not d[o] something that you promised you would do: *never go back on my word* (= not do what I said [I] would do). • **go back to sb** to start a relationshi[p] again with a person who you had a romanti[c] relationship with in the past: *Jim's gone back t[o] his ex-wife.* • **go back to sth** to start doin[g] something again that you were doing before: *It[']s time to go back to work now.* • **go by 1** **B2** If tim[e] goes by, it passes: *The days went by really slowl[y].* **2** to move past: *A green sports car went by.* • **g[o] by sth** to use information about something t[o] help you make a decision about the best thin[g] to do: *You can't go by anything she says.* • **g[o] down 1** BECOME LESS ▷ **B1** to become lower i[n] level: *Interest rates are going down at the momen[t].* **2 SUN** ▷ **B1** When the sun goes down, it move[s] down in the sky until it cannot be seen an[y] more. **3 COMPUTER** ▷ If a computer goes dow[n] it stops working. **4 REMEMBER** ▷ to b[e] considered or remembered in a particular wa[y]: *This will go down as one of the most excitin[g] soccer games ever played.* ○ *I don't think my pla[n] will go down well at all.* • **go down with sth** U[K] informal **B2** to become sick, usually with a[n] illness that is not very serious: *Our whole clas[s] went down with the flu.* • **go for sth 1** CHOOSE [▷] **B1** to choose something: *What sort of printer ar[e] you going to go for?* **2** HAVE ▷ informal **B2** to try t[o] have or achieve something: *He'll be going for h[is] third straight Olympic gold medal.* ○ *If you wan[t] it, go for it* (= do what you need to do in order t[o] have or achieve it). **3** GET ▷ **B2** to try to ge[t] something: *He tripped as he was going for th[e] ball.* **4 MONEY** ▷ If something goes for [a] particular amount of money, it is sold for tha[t] amount. • **go for sb** to attack someone: *H[e] suddenly went for me with a knife.* • **go in** **A2** t[o] enter a place: *I looked through the window, but [I] didn't actually go in.* • **go in for sth** to like [a] particular activity: *I don't really go in for sports.* • **go into sth 1** START ▷ to start to do a particula[r] type of work: *What made you decide to go int[o] politics?* **2** DESCRIBE ▷ to describe, discuss, o[r] examine something in a detailed way: *She didn['t] go into any detail about the job.* **3** BE USED ▷ If a[n] amount of time, money, or effort goes into [a] product or activity, it is used or spent creatin[g] that product or doing that activity: *A lot of effo[rt] has gone into producing this play.* • **go of[f]** **1** LEAVE ▷ **B1** to leave a place and go somewher[e] else: *She's gone off to a bar with Tony.* **2 FOOD** [▷] UK informal **B2** If food goes off, it is not good t[o] eat any more because it is too old. **3 STOP** ▷ **B[2]** If a light or machine goes off, it stops workin[g]: *The heating goes off at 10 o'clock.* **4 EXPLODE** [▷] **B2** If a bomb or gun goes off, it explodes or fire[s]. **5 MAKE NOISE** ▷ **B2** If something that make[s] noise goes off, it suddenly starts making a nois[e]: *His car alarm goes off every time it rains.* **6 go o[ff] on one** informal to react angrily to somethin[g]

• **go off sb/sth** UK ⓑ to stop liking someone or something: *I've gone off fish recently.* • **go on** ❶ **LAST** ▷ ⓑ to last for a particular period of time: *The film seemed to go on forever.* ❷ **CONTINUE** ▷ ⓑ to continue doing something: [+ doing sth] *We can't go on living like this.* ❸ **go on to do sth** to do something else in the future: *He went on to win the final.* ❹ **HAPPEN** ▷ ⓑ to happen: *What's going on?* ❺ **TALK** ▷ to talk in an annoying way about something for a long time: *I wish she'd stop going on about her boyfriend.* ❻ **TALK AGAIN** ▷ to start talking again after stopping for a short time: *He paused and then went on with his story.* ❼ **Go on** informal something that you say to encourage someone to do something: *Go on, what happened next?* • **go on sth** to use a piece of information to help you discover or understand something: *Her first name was all we had to go on.* • **go out** ❶ **LEAVE** ▷ ⓐ to leave a place in order to go somewhere else: *Are you going out tonight?* ❷ **LIGHT/FIRE** ▷ ⓑ If a light or something that is burning goes out, it stops producing light or heat: *It took ages for the fire to go out.* ❸ **RELATIONSHIP** ▷ ⓑ If two people go out together, they have a romantic relationship with each other: *I've been going out with him for a year.* • **go over** US to be thought of in a particular way: *I wonder how my speech will go over this afternoon.* • **go over sth** ⓑ to talk or think about something in order to explain it or make certain that it is correct: *Let's go over the plan one more time.* • **go round** mainly UK (UK/US **go around**) ❶ to be enough for everyone in a group: *There aren't enough chairs to go round.* ❷ **go round doing sth** to spend your time behaving badly or doing something that is unpleasant for other people: *She's been going round telling people I'm stupid.* • **go through sth** ❶ **EXPERIENCE** ▷ ⓑ to experience a difficult or unpleasant situation: *She's going through a difficult time with her job.* ❷ **EXAMINE** ▷ to carefully examine the contents of something or a collection of things in order to find something: *A customs officer went through my suitcase.* ❸ **USE** ▷ to use a lot of something: *I've gone through two boxes of tissues this week.* • **go through** If a law, plan, or deal goes through, it is officially accepted or approved. • **go through with sth** to do something unpleasant or difficult that you have planned or promised to do: *He was too scared to go through with the operation.* • **go under** If a company or business goes under, it fails financially. • **go up** ❶ **INCREASE** ▷ ⓑ to become higher in level: *House prices keep going up.* ❷ **BE FIXED** ▷ If a building or sign goes up, it is fixed into position. ❸ **EXPLODE** ▷ to suddenly explode: *There was a loud bang, and then the building went up in flames.* • **go without (sth)** to not have something that you usually have: *They went without food for four days.*

go² /gəʊ/ **noun** [C] (plural **goes**) ❶ ⓑ an attempt to do something: *I had a go at catching a fish.* ◦ *If you think you might like skiing, why don't you give it a go* (= try to do it)? ❷ UK ⓑ someone's turn to do something: *Throw the dice*

Jane, it's your go. ❸ **have a go at sb** UK to criticize someone angrily: *My mother's always having a go at me about my hair.* ❹ **make a go of sth** to try to make something succeed, usually by working hard

goad /gəʊd/ **verb** [T] to make someone angry or annoyed so that they react in the way that you want: [+ into + doing sth] *They tried to goad us into attacking the police.*

goal /gəʊl/ **noun** [C] ❶ **POINT** ▷ ⓐ a point scored in sports such as football when a player sends a ball or other object into a particular area, such as between two posts: *He scored two goals in the second half.* ❷ **AREA** ▷ ⓐ in some sports, the area between two posts where players try to send the ball → See colour picture **Sports 2** on page Centre 15 ❸ **AIM** ▷ ⓑ something you want to do successfully in the future: *Andy's goal is to run in the New York Marathon.*

> ✏ Word partners for **goal**
>
> **score** a goal • the **winning** goal
> **set yourself** a goal • **achieve** a goal

goalie /'gəʊli/ **noun** [C] informal short for goalkeeper

goalkeeper
/'gəʊlˌkiːpər/ **noun** [C]
(also US **goaltender**
/'gəʊlˌtendər/) ⓑ the
player in a sport such
as football who tries
to stop the ball going
into the goal → See
colour picture **Sports 2**
on page Centre 15

goalkeeper

goalpost /'gəʊlpəʊst/ **noun** [C] either of the two posts that are each side of the area where goals are scored in sports such as football → See colour picture **Sports 2** on page Centre 15

goat /gəʊt/ **noun** [C] ⓑ an animal with horns that is kept for the milk it produces

gobble /'gɒbl/ **verb** [T] (also **gobble up/down**) to eat food very quickly

gobbledygook (also **gobbledegook**) /'gɒbldiˌguːk/ **noun** [U] informal nonsense or very complicated language that you cannot understand

go-between /'gəʊbɪˌtwiːn/ **noun** [C] someone who talks and gives messages to people who will not or cannot talk to each other

goblin /'gɒblɪn/ **noun** [C] a short, ugly, imaginary creature who behaves badly

go-cart (also UK **go-kart**) /'gəʊkɑːt/ **noun** [C] a small, low racing car with no roof or windows

god /gɒd/ **noun** ❶ **God** ⓐ in Jewish, Christian, or Muslim belief, the spirit who created the universe and everything in it, and who rules over it ❷ ⓑ [C] a spirit, especially a male one, that people pray to and who has control over parts of the world or nature: *the ancient Greek gods and goddesses* ❸ **(Oh) (my) God!** informal ⓑ used to emphasize how surprised, angry, shocked, etc you are: *Oh my God! The car has been stolen.* ❹ **thank God** informal ⓑ something you say when you are happy because something

G

bad did not happen: *Thank God nobody was hurt in the accident.*

godchild /ˈgɒdtʃaɪld/ noun [C] (plural **godchildren**) a child who has godparents (= people who take responsibility for the child's moral and religious development)

goddess /ˈgɒdes/ noun [C] a female spirit that people pray to and who has control over parts of the world or nature

godfather /ˈgɒdfɑːðər/ noun [C] a man who is responsible for the moral and religious development of another person's child

godforsaken /ˈgɒdfəˌseɪkən/ adj [always before noun] informal A godforsaken place is very unpleasant and usually far from other places.

godlike /ˈgɒdlaɪk/ adj having qualities that make someone admired and respected as if they were a god or God

godmother /ˈgɒdˌmʌðər/ noun [C] a woman who is responsible for the moral and religious development of another person's child

godparent /ˈgɒdˌpeərənt/ noun [C] a person who is responsible for the moral and religious development of another person's child

godsend /ˈgɒdsend/ noun [no plural] something good that happens unexpectedly, usually when you really need it: *The lottery win was a godsend for her.*

goes /ɡəʊz/ present simple he/she/it of go

goggles /ˈgɒglz/ noun [plural] special glasses that fit close to your face to protect your eyes: *a pair of goggles* → See colour picture **Sports 1** on page Centre 14

going¹ /ˈɡəʊɪŋ/ noun **1 DIFFICULTY** ▷ [U] how easy or difficult something is: *I found the exam quite hard going.* **2 GROUND** ▷ [U] the condition of the ground for walking, riding, etc **3 LEAVING** ▷ [no plural] the fact that someone leaves somewhere: *His going came as a big surprise.*

☑ Word partners for **going**
hard/heavy/slow/tough going

going² /ˈɡəʊɪŋ/ adj **the going price/rate, etc** the usual amount of money you would expect to pay for something: *What's the going rate for babysitting these days?* → See also **easy-going**

going³ /ˈɡəʊɪŋ/ present participle of go

goings-on /ˌɡəʊɪŋzˈɒn/ noun [plural] informal unusual events or activities: *strange goings-on*

go-kart /ˈɡəʊkɑːt/ noun [C] another UK spelling of go-cart (= a small, low racing car with no roof or windows)

gold¹ /ɡəʊld/ noun **1** [U] ⓐ² a valuable, shiny, yellow metal used to make coins and jewellery **2** [C, U] a gold medal (= a small, round disc given to someone for winning a race or competition)

gold² /ɡəʊld/ adj **1** ⓐ² made of gold: *gold coins* **2** ⓐ² being the colour of gold: *gold paint*

golden /ˈɡəʊldən/ adj **1** ⓐ² being a bright yellow colour: *bright golden hair* **2** literary ⓐ² made of gold or like gold: *a golden ring* **3 a golden opportunity** ⓑ² a very exciting and good opportunity

golden wedding noun [C] the day when two people have been married for 50 years

goldfish /ˈɡəʊldfɪʃ/ noun [C] (plural **goldfish**, **goldfishes**) a small, orange fish that is often kept as a pet

gold medal noun [C] a small, round disc given to someone for winning a race or competition: *to win an Olympic gold medal*

gold mine noun [C] **1** a place where gold is taken from the ground **2** something that provides you with a lot of money

golf /ɡɒlf/ noun [U] ⓐ² a game on grass where players try to hit a small ball into a series of holes using a long, thin stick • **golfer** noun [C] → See colour picture **Sports 2** on page Centre 15

golf

golf ball noun [C] a small, hard, white ball used for playing golf

golf club noun [C] **1** a place where people can play golf **2** a long, thin stick used to play golf → See colour picture **Sports 2** on page Centre 15

golf course noun [C] an area of land used for playing golf

gone /ɡɒn/ past participle of go

gong /ɡɒŋ/ noun [C] a metal disc that makes a loud sound when you hit it with a stick

gonna /ˈɡənə/ informal short for going to

goo /ɡuː/ noun [U] a thick, sticky substance

good¹ /ɡʊd/ adj (**better**, **best**) **1 PLEASANT** ▷ enjoyable, pleasant, or interesting: *a good book* ◦ *Did you have a good time at the party?* **2 HIGH QUALITY** ▷ ⓐ¹ of a high quality or level: *She speaks good French.* ◦ *The food at this restaurant is very good.* **3 SUCCESSFUL** ▷ ⓐ¹ successful, able to do something well: *Anne's a good cook* ◦ *She's very good at geography.* **4 KIND** ▷ kind or helpful: *a good friend* ◦ *My granddaughter is very good to me.* **5 HEALTHY** ▷ something that you say when a person asks how you are: *'Hi, how are you?' 'I'm good, thanks.'* **6 POSITIVE** ▷ ⓐ¹ having a positive or useful effect: *Exercise is good for you.* **7 SUITABLE** ▷ suitable or satisfactory: *When would be a good time to call?* **8 BEHAVIOUR** ▷ ⓐ² A good child or animal behaves well. **9 MORALLY RIGHT** ▷ morally right: *a good person* ◦ *He sets a good example to the rest of the class.* **10 COMPLETE** complete and detailed: *She got a good look at the robbers.* **11 LARGE** ▷ ⓑ² used to emphasize the number, amount, quality, etc of something: *There's a good chance he'll pass the exam.* **12 SATISFACTION** ▷ ⓐ¹ something you say when you are satisfied or pleased about something: *good, he's arrived at last.* **13 Good God/good heavens!, etc** used to express surprise or shock: *Good heavens! It's already 11 p.m.* **14 a good minutes/30 miles, etc** not less than 20 minutes/30 miles, etc and probably a bit more → See also **be in sb's good/bad books (book¹)**, *it's a good* job, for good **measure²**, stand sb in good stead

IDIOM **good to go** informal be ready to go: *I'll get my coat and then I'm good to go.*

> ❗ Common learner error: **good** or **well**?
> **Good** is an adjective and is used to describe nouns.
> *She's a good cook.*
> *Her children had a good education.*
> **Well** is an adverb and is used to describe verbs.
> *She cooks well.*
> *Her children were well educated.*

good² /gʊd/ noun **1** [U] ⑫ something that is an advantage or help to a person or situation: *It's hard work, but it's for your own good.* **2 be no good/not any good** ⑫ to not be useful, helpful, or valuable **3 do sb good** ⑫ to be useful or helpful to someone: *A holiday will do you good.* **4** [U] what people think is morally right: *Children don't always understand the difference between good and bad.* **5 for good** forever: *When he was 20, he left home for good.* → See also **do sb a/the world¹ of good**

good after'noon exclamation Ⓐ something you say to greet someone when you meet them in the afternoon

goodbye /gʊd'baɪ/ exclamation Ⓐ something you say when you leave someone or when they leave you: *Goodbye Vicki! See you next week.*

> 🗒 Word partners for **goodbye**
> kiss/say/wave goodbye • a final goodbye

good 'evening exclamation Ⓐ something you say to greet someone in the evening

Good 'Friday noun [C, U] the Friday before Easter (= a Christian holiday), a day when Christians remember the death of Jesus Christ

good-humoured UK (US **good-humored**) /ˌgʊd'hjuːməd/ adj pleasant and friendly

goodies /'gʊdiz/ noun [plural] informal special or nice things that you will enjoy: *She gave the children some sweets and other goodies.*

good-looking /ˌgʊd'lʊkɪŋ/ adj ⑫ If someone is good-looking, they have an attractive face: *a good-looking woman*

good 'looks noun [plural] an attractive face

good 'morning exclamation Ⓐ something you say to greet someone when you meet them in the morning

good-natured /ˌgʊd'neɪtʃəd/ adj pleasant and friendly: *a good-natured smile/crowd*

goodness /'gʊdnəs/ noun **1** [U] the quality of being good: *She believes in the goodness of human nature.* **2 my goodness** informal something you say when you are surprised: *My goodness, he's a big baby, isn't he?* **3 thank goodness** informal something you say when you are happy because something bad did not happen: *Thank goodness that dog didn't bite you.* **4 for goodness sake** used when you are annoyed or when you want something to

happen quickly: *For goodness sake, come in out of the rain.*

good 'night exclamation Ⓐ something you say when you leave someone or when they leave you in the evening or when someone is going to bed

goods /gʊdz/ noun [plural] ⑪ items that are made to be sold: *televisions, washing machines, and other electrical goods*

IDIOM **deliver/come up with the goods** If you deliver the goods, you do what people hope you will do.

goodwill /gʊd'wɪl/ noun [U] kind, friendly, or helpful feelings towards other people: *He gave them a full refund as a gesture of goodwill.*

goody-goody /'gʊdiˌgʊdi/ noun [C] informal someone who tries too hard to be good, usually to parents or teachers

gooey /'guːi/ adj soft and sticky: *a sweet, gooey sauce*

goof /guːf/ verb [I] (also **goof up**) US informal to make a silly mistake

PHRASAL VERBS **goof around** US to spend your time doing silly or unimportant things • **goof off** US to avoid doing any work

goofy /'guːfi/ adj mainly US silly: *a goofy sense of humour*

Google¹ /'guːgl/ noun trademark a popular Internet search engine (= a computer program which finds things on the Internet by looking for words which you have typed in)

Google² /'guːgl/ verb [T] ⑫ to use the Google® search engine

goose /guːs/ noun [C, U] (plural **geese**) a large water bird similar to a duck, or the meat from this bird

gooseberry /'gʊzbəri/ ⓊⓈ /'guːsberi/ noun [C] a small, sour, green fruit with a hairy skin

goose ˌpimples noun [plural] (also **goose ˌbumps**) small, raised lumps that appear on your skin when you are cold or frightened

gore¹ /gɔːʳ/ noun [U] blood, usually from a violent injury

gore² /gɔːʳ/ verb [T] If an animal gores someone, it injures them with its horn.

gorge¹ /gɔːdʒ/ noun [C] a narrow and usually steep valley

gorge² /gɔːdʒ/ verb **gorge (yourself) on sth** to eat food until you cannot eat any more: *She gorged herself on chocolate biscuits.*

gorgeous /'gɔːdʒəs/ adj ⑪ very beautiful or pleasant: *You look gorgeous in that dress.*

gorilla /gə'rɪlə/ noun [C] a big, black, hairy animal, like a large monkey

gorse /gɔːs/ noun [U] a bush with yellow flowers and sharp, pointed leaves

gory /'gɔːri/ adj involving violence and blood: *a gory murder*

gosh /gɒʃ/ exclamation used to express surprise or shock: *Gosh! I didn't realize it was that late.*

gosling /'gɒzlɪŋ/ noun [C] a young goose (= large water bird)

gospel /'gɒspəl/ noun **1** TEACHING ▷ [no plural]

G

the teachings of Jesus Christ: *to preach the gospel* **2 BOOK** ▷ [C] one of the four books in the Bible that tells the life of Jesus Christ **3 the gospel truth** something that is completely true **4 MUSIC** ▷ [U] a style of Christian music, originally sung by black Americans

gossip¹ /'gɒsɪp/ noun **1** [U] 🄲 conversation or reports about other people's private lives that might or might not be true: *an interesting **piece of gossip*** **2** [C] someone who likes to talk about other people's private lives

> ☑ Word partners for **gossip**
>
> a bit of/piece of gossip • juicy gossip

gossip² /'gɒsɪp/ verb [I] 🄲 to talk about other people's private lives: *They were **gossiping** about her boss.*

gossip ˌcolumn noun [C] an article appearing regularly in a newspaper giving information about famous people's private lives

got /gɒt/ past of get

gotta /'gɒtə/ informal short for got to

gotten /'gɒtᵊn/ US past participle of get

gouge /gaʊdʒ/ verb [T] to make a hole or long cut in something

PHRASAL VERB **gouge sth out** to remove something by digging or cutting it out of a surface, often violently

gourmet¹ /'gʊəmeɪ/ noun [C] someone who enjoys good food and drink and knows a lot about it

gourmet² /'gʊəmeɪ/ adj [always before noun] relating to good food and drink: *a gourmet meal*

govern /'gʌvᵊn/ verb **1** [I, T] 🄲 to officially control a country: *The country is now governed by a coalition government.* ◦ *a **governing body*** **2** [T] to influence or control the way something happens or is done: *There are rules that govern how teachers treat children.*

governess /'gʌvᵊnəs/ noun [C] a woman employed to teach the children in a family at home

government /'gʌvᵊnmənt/ noun **1** [group] 🄱 the group of people who officially control a country: *The Government has cut taxes.* **2** [U] 🄲 the method or process of governing a country: *a new style of government* • **governmental** /ˌgʌvᵊn-'mentᵊl/ adj relating to government

> ☑ Word partners for **government**
>
> bring down/elect/form/overthrow a government • a democratic/elected government • be in government

governor /'gʌvᵊnəʳ/ noun [C] someone who is officially responsible for controlling a region, city, or organization: *a prison/school governor* ◦ *the Governor of Texas*

gown /gaʊn/ noun [C] **1** a woman's dress, usually worn on formal occasions: *a silk gown* **2** a loose piece of clothing like a coat worn for a particular purpose: *a hospital gown* → See also **dressing gown**

GP /ˌdʒiː'piː/ noun [C] abbreviation for general practitioner: a doctor who sees people in a

local area and treats illnesses that do not nee(a hospital visit

GPA /ˌdʒiːpiː'eɪ/ noun [C] US abbreviation for grad(point average: a number which is the averag(mark received for all the courses a student take(and shows how well the student is doing

GPS /ˌdʒiːpiː'es/ noun [U] abbreviation for Globa Positioning System: a system of computers and satellites (= equipment that is sent into spac(around the Earth to receive and send signals that work together to tell a user where they ar(

grab¹ /græb/ verb [T] (**grabbing, grabbed** **1 TAKE SUDDENLY** ▷ 🄱 to take hold of some thing or someone suddenly: *He grabbed my arₘ and pulled me away.* **2 DO QUICKLY** ▷ informal t(eat, do, or get something quickly because yo(do not have much time: *I grabbed a sandwich oₙ the way to the station.* **3 grab sb's attentioₙ** informal to attract someone's attention **4 TAK(OPPORTUNITY** ▷ 🄲 If someone grabs a chanc(or opportunity, they take it quickly and witₕ enthusiasm.

PHRASAL VERB **grab at sb/sth** to try to get hold o(someone or something quickly, with your hanₔ

grab² /græb/ noun **make a grab for sth/sb** to trː to take hold of something or someone suddenlː *He made a grab for the gun.*

IDIOM **up for grabs** informal If something is up fo grabs, it is available to anyone who wants to trː to get it: *Ten free concert tickets are up for grabs*

grace¹ /greɪs/ noun [U] **1 MOVEMENT** ▷ thᵉ quality of moving in a smooth, relaxed, anₔ attractive way: *She moved **with** grace anₔ elegance.* **2 POLITENESS** ▷ the quality of beinₔ pleasantly polite: *He **had the grace to** apologizᵉ for his mistake the next day.* **3 with good gracᵉ** in a willing and happy way: *He accepted thᵉ failure with good grace.* **4 a month's/week's, etᵉ grace** an extra month/week, etc you are giveₙ before something must be paid or donᵉ **5 PRAYER** ▷ a prayer of thanks said before o(after a meal: *to say grace*

grace² /greɪs/ verb [T] When a person or objecᵗ graces a place or thing, they make it morᵉ attractive: *Her face has graced the covers o₁ magazines across the world.*

graceful /'greɪsfᵊl/ adj **1** moving in a smoothˏ relaxed, and attractive way, or having a smootₕ attractive shape: *graceful movements* ◦ *a gracefu₁ neck* **2** behaving in a polite and pleasant waʸ • **gracefully** adv

gracious /'greɪʃəs/ adj **1** behaving in a pleasanᵗ polite, calm way: *He was gracious enough to thanₖ me.* **2** comfortable and with a good appearancᵉ and quality: *gracious homes/living* **3 Good/Good ness gracious!** used to express polite surprisᵉ • **graciously** adv

grade¹ /greɪd/ noun [C] **1 SCORE** ▷ 🄱 a numbe₁ or letter that shows how good someone's worₖ or performance is: *Steve never studies, but hᵉ always **gets** good **grades**.* ◦ UK *Carla got a gradᵉ A in German.* **2 LEVEL** ▷ 🄲 a level of quality, sizᵉ importance, etc: *I applied for a position a gradᵉ higher than my current job.* **3 SCHOOL GROUP** ▷

G

US a school class or group of classes for students of the same age or ability: *My son is in fifth grade.*

IDIOM **make the grade** to perform well enough to succeed: *He wanted to get into the team but he didn't make the grade.*

grade² /greɪd/ verb [T] **1** to separate people or things into different levels of quality, size, importance, etc: *The fruit is washed and then graded by size.* **2** US (UK **mark**) to give a score to a student's piece of work: *to grade work/papers*

grade ˌcrossing noun [C] US (UK **level crossing**) a place where a railway crosses a road

grade ˌschool noun [C, U] US a school for the first six to eight years of a child's education

gradient /ˈgreɪdiənt/ noun [C] how steep a slope is: *a steep/gentle gradient*

gradual /ˈgrædʒuəl/ adj **B2** happening slowly over a period of time: *a gradual change/improvement*

gradually /ˈgrædʒuəli/ adv **B2** slowly over a period of time: *Gradually he began to get better.*

graduate¹ /ˈgrædʒuət/ noun [C] **1** UK **B2** someone who has studied for and received a degree from a university: *a science graduate* **2** US a person who has finished their school, college or university education: *a high-school graduate*

graduate² /ˈgrædjueɪt/ verb **1** **B2** [I] to complete your education successfully at a university, college, or, in the US, at school: *He graduated from Cambridge University in 2006.* **2 graduate to sth** to move up to something more advanced or important

graduated /ˈgrædjueɪtɪd/ adj divided into levels or stages: *a graduated scale*

graduation /ˌgrædʒuˈeɪʃᵊn/ noun [C, U] an occasion when you receive your degree for completing your education or a course of study: *a graduation ceremony*

graffiti

graffiti /grəˈfiːti/ noun [U] writing or pictures painted on walls and public places, usually illegally

graft¹ /grɑːft/ noun **1** SKIN/BONE ▷ [C] a piece of skin or bone taken from one part of a body and joined to another part: *a skin/bone graft* **2** PLANT ▷ [C] a piece cut from one plant and joined onto another plant **3** WORK ▷ [U] UK informal work: *hard graft*

graft² /grɑːft/ verb **1** SKIN/BONE ▷ [T] to join a

piece of skin or bone taken from one part of the body to another part **2** PLANT ▷ [T] to join a piece cut from one plant onto another plant **3** WORK ▷ [I] UK informal to work hard

grain /greɪn/ noun **1** SEED ▷ [C, U] a seed or seeds from types of grass that are eaten as food: *grains of wheat/rice* **2** PIECE ▷ [C] a very small piece of something: *a grain of sand/sugar* **3** QUALITY ▷ [no plural] a very small amount of a quality: *There isn't a grain of truth in her story.* **4 the grain** the natural direction and pattern of lines which you can see in wood or material: *to cut something along/against the grain*

IDIOM **go against the grain** If something goes against the grain, you would not normally do it because it would be unusual or morally wrong.

→ See also **take sth with a pinch of salt¹**

gram (also UK **gramme**) (written abbreviation **g, gm**) /græm/ noun [C] **A2** a unit for measuring weight, equal to 0.001 kilograms

grammar /ˈgræmər/ noun **1** [U] **A2** the way you combine words and change their form and position in a sentence, or the rules or study of this **2** [C] mainly UK a book of grammar rules

ˈgrammar ˌschool noun [C, U] **1** in the UK, a school that clever children over 11 years old can go to if they pass a special exam **2** US old-fashioned another word for elementary school (= a school for children from the ages of five to eleven in the US)

grammatical /grəˈmætɪkᵊl/ adj relating to grammar, or obeying the rules of grammar: *grammatical rules* ◦ *a grammatical sentence* • **grammatically** adv

gramme /græm/ noun [C] another UK spelling of gram

gramophone /ˈgræməfəʊn/ noun [C] old-fashioned a machine for playing music

gran /græn/ noun [C] UK informal short for grandmother

grand¹ /grænd/ adj **1** LARGE ▷ very large and special: *a grand hotel* ◦ *the Grand Canal* **2** IMPORTANT ▷ rich and important, or behaving as if you are: *a grand old lady* **3** GOOD ▷ informal very good or enjoyable

grand² /grænd/ noun [C] (plural **grand**) informal one thousand dollars or pounds: *The holiday cost me two grand.*

grandad /ˈgrændæd/ noun [C] another UK spelling of granddad

grandchild /ˈgrændtʃaɪld/ noun [C] (plural **grandchildren**) **A2** the child of your son or daughter

granddad /ˈgrændæd/ noun [C] mainly UK informal **A2** grandfather

granddaughter /ˈgrændˌdɔːtər/ noun [C] **A2** the daughter of your son or daughter

grandeur /ˈgrændjər/ noun [U] the quality of being very large and special or beautiful: *the grandeur of the hills*

grandfather /ˈgrændˌfɑːðər/ noun [C] **A2** the father of your mother or father

ˌgrandfather ˈclock noun [C] a clock in a very tall, wooden case

grandiose /ˈɡrændiəʊs/ **adj** large or detailed and made to appear important, often in an unnecessary and annoying way: *grandiose plans*

grandly /ˈɡrændli/ **adv** in a very important way, or as if you are very important

grandma /ˈɡrændmɑː/ **noun** [C] informal ⒶⒶ another word for grandmother

grandmother /ˈɡrændˌmʌðər/ **noun** [C] Ⓐ the mother of your mother or father

grandpa /ˈɡrændpɑː/ **noun** [C] informal Ⓐ another word for grandfather

grandparent /ˈɡrændˌpeərənt/ **noun** [C] Ⓐ the parent of your mother or father

grand piˈano noun [C] a very large piano, usually used in public performances

grand prix /ˌɡrɒnˈpriː/ **noun** [C] (plural **grands prix**) one of a series of important international races for very fast cars: *the Italian Grand Prix*

grand ˈslam noun [C] all the important competitions that are held in one year for a particular sport when they are won by the same person

grandson /ˈɡrændsʌn/ **noun** [C] Ⓐ the son of your son or daughter

grandstand /ˈɡrændstænd/ **noun** [C] a large, open structure containing rows of seats, used for watching sporting events

granite /ˈɡrænɪt/ **noun** [U] a type of very hard, grey rock

granny /ˈɡræni/ **noun** [C] informal Ⓐ another word for grandmother

grant¹ /ɡrɑːnt/ **verb** [T] formal **1** Ⓑ to give or allow someone something, usually in an official way: [+ two objects] *to grant someone a licence/visa* **2** to admit or agree that something is true: *She's a good-looking woman, I grant you.*

IDIOMS **take sb/sth for granted** Ⓑ to not show that you are grateful for someone or something, and forget that you are lucky to have them: *Most of us take our freedom for granted.* • **take it for granted** Ⓑ to believe that something is true without checking or thinking about it: [+ (that)] *I took it for granted that we'd be invited.*

grant² /ɡrɑːnt/ **noun** [C] Ⓑ an amount of money provided by a government or organization for a special purpose: *They received a research grant for the project.*

> ✐ Word partners for **grant**
>
> apply for/get/receive a grant • a grant for/ towards sth • a research grant

granule /ˈɡrænjuːl/ **noun** [C] a small, hard piece of a substance: *coffee granules* • **granulated** /ˈɡrænjəleɪtɪd/ **adj** *granulated sugar*

grape /ɡreɪp/ **noun** [C] Ⓐ a small, round, green, purple or red fruit that grows in large, close groups and is often used to make wine: *a bunch of grapes* → See colour picture **Fruits and Vegetables** on page Centre 10

grapefruit /ˈɡreɪpfruːt/ **noun** [C, U] (plural **grapefruit**, **grapefruits**) a large, round, yellow fruit with a sour taste

grapevine /ˈɡreɪpvaɪn/ **noun**

IDIOM **hear sth on/through the grapevine** to hear news from someone who heard the news from someone else

graph /ɡrɑːf/ **noun** [C] Ⓑ a picture with measurements marked on it as lines or curves, used to compare different things or show the development of something

graph

> ✐ Word partners for **graph**
>
> draw a graph • a graph **indicates/shows** sth • a graph **of** sth

graphic /ˈɡræfɪk/ **adj** A graphic description or image is extremely clear and detailed: *The film contains graphic violence.* • **graphically adv**

graphical user ˈinterface noun [C] a way of arranging information on a computer screen that is easy to understand because it uses pictures and symbols as well as words

graphic deˈsign noun [U] the art of designing pictures and text for books, magazines, advertisements, etc

graphics /ˈɡræfɪks/ **noun** [plural] Ⓑ images shown on a computer screen

graphite /ˈɡræfaɪt/ **noun** [U] a soft, grey-black form of carbon used in pencils

grapple /ˈɡræpl/ **verb**

PHRASAL VERBS **grapple with sth** to try to deal with or understand something difficult • **grapple with sb** to hold onto someone and fight with them

grasp¹ /ɡrɑːsp/ **verb** [T] **1** to take hold of something or someone firmly: *He grasped my hand enthusiastically.* **2** to understand something: *I find these mathematical problems difficult to grasp.*

PHRASAL VERB **grasp at sth** to quickly try to get hold of something

grasp² /ɡrɑːsp/ **noun** [no plural] **1** UNDERSTAND ▷ an understanding of something: *He has an excellent grasp of of English* **2** HOLD ▷ your hold on someone or something: *I tried to pull him out but he slipped from my grasp.* **3** ABILITY ▷ the ability to obtain or achieve something: *Victory is within our grasp.*

> ✐ Word partners for **grasp**
>
> have a [good/poor, etc] grasp of sth

grasping /ˈɡrɑːspɪŋ/ **adj** wanting much more of something than you need, especially money: *a grasping, greedy man*

grass /ɡrɑːs/ **noun 1** [U] Ⓐ a common plant with narrow green leaves that grows close to the ground in gardens and fields: *to mow/cut the grass* ○ *We lay on the grass in the sunshine.* **2** [C] a particular type of grass: *ornamental grasses*

grasshopper /ˈɡrɑːsˌhɒpər/ **noun** [C] a green insect that jumps about using its long back legs

grass ˈroots noun [plural] ordinary people in a

society or political organization and not the leaders

grassy /ˈɡrɑːsi/ adj covered with grass: *a grassy slope/meadow*

grasshopper

grate¹ /ɡreɪt/ verb **1** [T] to break food such as cheese into small, thin pieces by rubbing it against a grater (= kitchen tool with holes): *grated cheese/carrot* **2** [I] to make an unpleasant noise when rubbing against something: *The chair grated against the floor.*

PHRASAL VERB **grate on sb** If someone's voice or behaviour grates on you, it annoys you.

grate² /ɡreɪt/ noun [C] a metal structure for holding the wood or coal in a fireplace

grateful /ˈɡreɪtfᵊl/ adj ⓒ feeling or showing thanks: *I'm really grateful to you for all your help.* → Opposite **ungrateful** • **gratefully** adv *All donations gratefully received.*

> **Other ways of saying grateful**
>
> The adjective **appreciative** is sometimes used to show that someone is grateful, or you can use the verb **appreciate** to express the same idea:
> *I'm really appreciative of all the help you've given me.*
> *I really appreciate all the help you've given me.*
> The expression **be glad of** is another alternative:
> *We were very glad of some extra help.*
> The expression **be indebted to** is a more formal way of saying that someone is very grateful for something:
> *I'm indebted to my parents for all their love and support.*
> The adjectives **thankful** or **relieved** are often used when a person is grateful that something bad did not happen:
> *I'm just thankful/relieved that she's safe and well.*
> If a person is grateful that someone has done something kind, the adjective **touched** is sometimes used:
> *She was really touched that he remembered her birthday.*

grater /ˈɡreɪtər/ noun [C] a kitchen tool with a surface full of holes with sharp edges, used to grate (= break into small pieces) foods such as cheese → See colour picture **The Kitchen** on page Centre 2

gratify /ˈɡrætɪfaɪ/ verb [T] formal to please someone or satisfy their wishes or needs: *I was gratified by their decision.* ◦ *a gratifying result* • **gratification** /ˌɡrætɪfɪˈkeɪʃᵊn/ noun [U]

grating /ˈɡreɪtɪŋ/ noun [C] a flat structure made of long, thin pieces of metal crossing each other over a hole in the ground or a window

gratitude /ˈɡrætɪtjuːd/ noun [U] the feeling or quality of being grateful: *I would like to express my deep gratitude to all the hospital staff.*

gratuitous /ɡrəˈtjuːɪtəs/ adj unnecessary and done without a good reason: *gratuitous violence*

gratuity /ɡrəˈtjuːəti/ noun [C] formal an extra amount of money given to someone to thank them for providing a service

grave¹ /ɡreɪv/ noun [C] ⓒ a place in the ground where a dead body is buried

grave² /ɡreɪv/ adj very serious: *grave doubts* ◦ *a grave mistake* • **gravely** adv

gravel /ˈɡrævᵊl/ noun [U] small pieces of stone used to make paths and road surfaces

gravestone /ˈɡreɪvstəʊn/ noun [C] a stone that shows the name of a dead person who is buried under it

graveyard /ˈɡreɪvjɑːd/ noun [C] an area of land where dead bodies are buried, usually next to a church

gravitate /ˈɡrævɪteɪt/ verb

PHRASAL VERB **gravitate to/towards sth/sb** to be attracted to something or someone, or to move in the direction of something or someone

gravitational /ˌɡrævɪˈteɪʃᵊnᵊl/ adj relating to gravity: *gravitational force*

gravity /ˈɡrævəti/ noun [U] **1** the force that makes objects fall to the ground or that pulls objects towards a planet or other body: *the laws of gravity* **2** formal the quality of being very serious: *You don't seem to realize the gravity of the situation.* → See also **centre of gravity**

gravy /ˈɡreɪvi/ noun [U] a warm, brown sauce made from the fat and liquid that comes from meat when it is being cooked

gray /ɡreɪ/ noun [C, U], adj US spelling of grey

graying /ˈɡreɪɪŋ/ adj US spelling of greying (= having hair that is becoming grey or white)

graze¹ /ɡreɪz/ verb **1** EAT ▷ [I] When cows or other animals graze, they eat grass: *Cattle grazed in the meadow.* **2** INJURE ▷ [T] mainly UK (UK/US **skin**) to injure your skin by rubbing it against something rough: *I fell and grazed my knee.* **3** TOUCH ▷ [T] to touch or move lightly along the surface or edge of something: *A bullet grazed his cheek.*

graze² /ɡreɪz/ noun [C] mainly UK an injury on the surface of your skin caused by rubbing against something: *She has a nasty graze on her elbow.*

grease¹ /ɡriːs/ noun [U] **1** a substance such as oil or fat **2** a substance like thick oil that is put on parts in an engine or machine to make them move more smoothly

grease² /ɡriːs/ verb [T] to put fat or oil on or in something

greasy /ˈɡriːsi/ adj containing or covered with fat or oil: *greasy food/fingers*

great /ɡreɪt/ adj **1** EXCELLENT ▷ ⓐ very good: *We had a great time.* ◦ *I've had a great idea!* **2** IMPORTANT ▷ ⓑ important or famous: *a great statesman/novelist* **3** LARGE ▷ ⓒ large in amount, size, or degree: *a great crowd of people* **4** EXTREME ▷ ⓓ extreme: *great success/difficulty* **5** great big/long, etc ⓑ very big/long, etc: *I gave her a great big hug.* **6** a great many a large

G

number • **greatness** noun [U] → See also **go to great lengths** (**length**) **to do sth**, **set great store** by sth, **the best/greatest thing since sliced bread**

great- /greɪt/ prefix **1** **great-grandfather/-grandmother** the father/mother of your grandfather or grandmother **2** **great-aunt/-uncle** the aunt/uncle of your mother or father **3** **great-grandchild/-granddaughter, etc** the child/daughter, etc of your grandson or granddaughter **4** **great-niece/-nephew** the daughter/son of your niece or nephew

greatly /'greɪtli/ adv ⓑ very much: *I greatly admire your paintings.* ∘ *We will miss her greatly.*

greed /griːd/ noun [U] the wish to have a lot more food, money, etc, than you need

greedy /'griːdi/ adj ⓑ wanting a lot more food, money, etc, than you need: *greedy, selfish people* ∘ *They were greedy for money.* • **greedily** adv • **greediness** noun [U]

Greek /griːk/ adj relating to the culture, language, or people of Greece or ancient Greece

green¹ /griːn/ adj **1** COLOUR ▷ ⓐ being the same colour as grass: *The traffic lights turned green.* → See colour picture **Colours** on page Centre 12 **2** ENVIRONMENT ▷ [always before noun] ⓑ relating to nature and protecting the environment: *a green activist/campaigner* **3** GRASS ▷ ⓑ covered with grass or other plants: *green spaces* **4** NOT EXPERIENCED ▷ informal having little experience or understanding: *I was very green when I joined the company.*

IDIOM **be green with envy** to wish very much that you had something that another person has

→ See also **have green fingers** (**finger¹**) , **green light**

green² /griːn/ noun **1** COLOUR ▷ [C, U] ⓐ the colour of grass → See colour picture **Colours** on page Centre 12 **2** GOLF ▷ [C] a special area of very short, smooth grass on a golf course: *the 18th green* **3** VILLAGE ▷ [C] an area of grass in the middle of a village

green belt noun [C] an area of land around a city or town where no new building is allowed

green card noun [C] an official document allowing a foreigner to live and work in the US permanently

green consumer noun [C] a customer who wants to buy things that have been produced in a way that protects the natural environment

green consumerism noun [U] the situation in which consumers want to buy things that have been produced in a way that protects the natural environment

greenery /'griːnəri/ noun [U] green leaves, plants, or branches

greenfield /'griːnfiːld/ adj UK describes land where there were no buildings before, or buildings on land that have never had buildings: *a greenfield site* → Compare **brownfield**

greengrocer /'griːnˌɡrəʊsəʳ/ noun [C] UK **1** **greengrocer's** a shop where you buy fruit and vegetables **2** someone who sells fruit and vegetables

greenhouse /'ɡriːnhaʊs/ noun [C] (plural **greenhouses** /'griːnhaʊzɪz/) a building made of glass for growing plants in

the greenhouse effect noun the gradual warming of the Earth's surface caused by an increase in pollution and gases in the air

greenhouse gas noun [C] a gas that causes the greenhouse effect, especially carbon dioxide (= a gas produced when carbon is burned)

green job noun [C] (also **green-collar job**) a job that is related to the protection of the environment

green light noun [no plural] permission to do something: [+ to do sth] *They've been given the green light to build two new supermarkets.*

the Green Party noun [group] a political party whose main aim is to protect the environment

greens /griːnz/ noun [plural] green leaves that are cooked and eaten as a vegetable

greenwash /'ɡriːnwɒʃ/ verb [T] to make people believe that your company is doing more to protect the environment than it really is

greet /griːt/ verb [T] **1** ⓑ to welcome someone: *He greeted me at the door.* **2** to react to something in a particular way: [often passive] *His story was greeted with shrieks of laughter.*

greeting /'ɡriːtɪŋ/ noun [C] formal ⓑ something friendly or polite that you say or do when you meet or welcome someone

greetings card noun [C] UK (US **greeting card**) a card with a picture on the outside and a message inside that you give to someone to celebrate an event such as a birthday

gregarious /ɡrɪ'ɡeəriəs/ adj If you are gregarious, you enjoy being with other people.

grenade /ɡrə'neɪd/ noun [C] a small bomb that is thrown or fired from a weapon

grew /ɡruː/ past tense of **grow**

grey¹ UK (US **gray**) /ɡreɪ/ adj **1** COLOUR ▷ ⓐ being a colour that is a mixture of black and white: *grey clouds* → See colour picture **Colours** on page Centre 12 **2** HAIR ▷ having hair that has become grey or white: *She went grey in her thirties.* **3** WEATHER ▷ cloudy and not bright: *a cold, grey morning* **4** BORING ▷ not interesting or attractive: *Life was grey and tedious.* **5** grey area something that people are not certain about, usually because there are no clear rules for it

grey² UK (US **gray**) /ɡreɪ/ noun [C, U] ⓐ a colour that is a mixture of black and white → See colour picture **Colours** on page Centre 12

greyhound /'ɡreɪhaʊnd/ noun [C] a thin dog with short hair that runs very fast, sometimes in races

greying UK (US **graying**) /'ɡreɪɪŋ/ adj having hair that is becoming grey or white

grey water (US **gray water**) noun [U] water that has been used before, for example for washing, that can be stored and used again: *If more homes had a grey water system we would save up to 30% of our fresh water.*

grid /ɡrɪd/ noun **1** PATTERN ▷ [C] a pattern or structure made from horizontal and vertical

G

lines crossing each other to form squares **2 POWER** ▷ [no plural] a system of connected wires used to supply electrical power to a large area: *the National Grid* **3 MAP** ▷ [C] a pattern of squares with numbers or letters used to find places on a map

gridlock /ˈɡrɪdlɒk/ **noun** [U] a situation in which the traffic cannot move in any direction because all of the roads are blocked with cars

grief /griːf/ **noun 1** ⑫ [U] great sadness, especially caused by someone's death **2 Good grief!** informal something that you say when you are surprised or annoyed

IDIOMS **come to grief** informal to suddenly fail or have an accident • **cause/give sb grief** informal to annoy someone or cause trouble or problems for them

grievance /ˈɡriːvəns/ **noun** [C] formal a complaint, especially about unfair behaviour

grieve /griːv/ **verb 1** [I] to feel or express great sadness, especially when someone dies: *He is still grieving for his wife.* **2** [T] formal to make someone feel very sad

grievous /ˈɡriːvəs/ **adj** formal very serious: *grievous injuries* • **grievously adv**

grill¹ /ɡrɪl/ **noun** [C] **1** UK (US **broiler**) ⑥ a piece of equipment used for cooking food under strong direct heat → See colour picture **The Kitchen** on page Centre 2 **2** a flat, metal structure used to cook food over a fire

grill² /ɡrɪl/ **verb** [T] **1 COOK** ▷ ⑥ to cook food on a flat, metal structure over a fire: *Grill the fish for 2 to 3 minutes on each side.* → See picture at **cook 2 COOK** ▷ UK (US **broil**) to cook food with strong heat coming from directly above or below it **3 QUESTION** ▷ to ask someone questions continuously and for a long time: *I was grilled by the police for two days.*

grille /ɡrɪl/ **noun** [C] a metal structure of bars built across something to protect it

grim /ɡrɪm/ **adj** (**grimmer, grimmest**) **1 BAD** ▷ worrying and bad: *grim news* ∘ *The future looks grim.* **2 SERIOUS** ▷ sad and serious: *a grim expression* **3 UNPLEASANT** ▷ A grim place is ugly and unpleasant. • **grimly adv**

grimace /ˈɡrɪməs/ **verb** [I] to make your face show an expression of pain or unhappiness: *He grimaced at the bitter taste.* • **grimace noun** [C]

grime /ɡraɪm/ **noun** [U] dirt that covers a surface: *The walls were covered in grime.* • **grimy adj** covered in dirt: *grimy hands*

grin /ɡrɪn/ **verb** [I] (**grinning, grinned**) to smile a big smile: *He grinned at me from the doorway.*

IDIOM **grin and bear it** to accept an unpleasant or difficult situation because there is nothing you can do to improve it

• **grin noun** [C] *She had a big grin on her face.*

grind¹ /ɡraɪnd/ **verb** [T] (**ground**) **1** to keep rubbing something between two rough, hard surfaces until it becomes a powder: *to grind coffee* **2** to rub a blade against a hard surface to

make it sharp **3 grind your teeth** to rub your teeth together, making an unpleasant sound

PHRASAL VERB **grind sb down** to gradually make someone lose hope, energy, or confidence

grind² /ɡraɪnd/ **noun** [no plural] informal work or effort that is boring and unpleasant and makes you tired because it does not change: *the daily grind*

grinder /ˈɡraɪndər/ **noun** [C] a machine used to rub or press something until it becomes a powder: *a coffee grinder*

grip¹ /ɡrɪp/ **noun** [no plural] **1** ⑫ a tight hold on something: *She tightened her grip on my arm.* **2** control over something or someone: *He has a firm grip on the economy.*

IDIOMS **come/get to grips with sth** to understand and deal with a problem or situation: *It's a difficult subject to get to grips with.* • **get a grip (on yourself)** to make an effort to control your emotions and behave more calmly

> ☑ **Word partners for grip**
>
> loosen/release/tighten your grip • sb's grip on sth

grip² /ɡrɪp/ **verb** [T] (**gripping, gripped**) **1 HOLD** ▷ ⑫ to hold something tightly: *She gripped his arm.* **2 INTEREST** ▷ to keep someone's attention completely: *This trial has gripped the whole nation.* **3 EMOTION** ▷ When an emotion grips you, you feel it very strongly: [often passive] *He was gripped by fear.*

gripe /ɡraɪp/ **verb** [I] informal to complain, often in an annoying way • **gripe noun** [C]

gripping /ˈɡrɪpɪŋ/ **adj** If something is gripping, it is so interesting that it holds your attention completely: *a gripping story*

grisly /ˈɡrɪzli/ **adj** very unpleasant, especially because death or blood is involved: *a grisly murder*

grit¹ /ɡrɪt/ **noun** [U] **1** very small pieces of stone or sand: *I've got a bit of grit in my eye.* **2** the quality of being brave and determined

grit² /ɡrɪt/ **verb** [T] (**gritting, gritted**) to put grit onto a road surface when the road has ice on it → See also **grit your teeth** (**tooth**)

gritty /ˈɡrɪti/ **adj 1** showing unpleasant details about a situation in a way that seems very real: *a gritty drama* ∘ *gritty realism* **2** brave and determined: *gritty determination*

groan /ɡrəʊn/ **verb** [I] to make a long, low sound such as when expressing pain, unhappiness, etc: *He collapsed, groaning with pain.* • **groan noun** [C]

grocer /ˈɡrəʊsər/ **noun 1 grocer's** UK a shop that sells food and other products used in the home **2** [C] someone who owns or works in a grocer's

groceries /ˈɡrəʊsəriz/ **noun** [plural] goods bought to be used in the home such as food and cleaning products

grocery /ˈɡrəʊsəri/ **noun** [C] (also US **'grocery store**) a shop that sells food and products used in the home

groggy /ˈɡrɒɡi/ **adj** informal unable to think or

act quickly because you have just woken up, are sick, etc: *I felt a bit groggy after the operation.*

groin /grɔɪn/ noun [C] the area where the legs join the rest of the body near the sexual organs: *He pulled a muscle in his groin.*

groom¹ /gruːm/ verb [T] **1** to prepare someone carefully for a special position or job: *He's being **groomed for** stardom.* **2** to clean and brush an animal's fur

groom² /gruːm/ noun [C] **1** (also **bridegroom**) ⓑ a man who is getting married **2** someone who cleans and looks after horses

groove /gruːv/ noun [C] a long, narrow line that has been cut into a surface

grope /grəʊp/ verb **1** [I, T] to try to get hold of something with your hand, usually when you cannot see it: *I **groped** in my bag **for** my keys.* **2 grope your way along/through, etc** to move somewhere with difficulty, feeling with your hands because you cannot see clearly: *We groped our way through the smoke to the exit.*

PHRASAL VERB **grope for sth** to try to think of the right words or the right way to express something: *He groped for the words to tell her.*

gross¹ /grəʊs/ adj **1** TOTAL ▷ A gross amount of money has not had taxes or other costs taken from it: *gross earnings/profit* **2** SERIOUS ▷ [always before noun] formal very serious or unacceptable: *This was **gross misconduct**.* **3** UNPLEASANT ▷ informal very unpleasant: *Oh, yuck. That's really gross.*

gross² /grəʊs/ verb [T] to earn a particular amount of money as a total before tax or other costs are taken from it: *The movie grossed $250 million.*

grossly /ˈgrəʊsli/ adv extremely: *grossly unfair/exaggerated*

grotesque /grəʊˈtesk/ adj very strange and unpleasant, especially in a ridiculous or slightly frightening way: *a grotesque image* • **grotesquely** adv

grotto /ˈgrɒtəʊ/ noun [C] a small cave

ground¹ /graʊnd/ noun **1 the ground** ⓑ the surface of the Earth: *I sat down on the ground.* **2** SOIL ▷ [U] ⓑ the soil in an area: *soft/stony ground* **3** AREA ▷ [C] ⓑ an area of land used for a particular purpose or activity: *a football ground* **4** KNOWLEDGE ▷ [U] an area of knowledge, information, interest, or experience: *He had to go over the same ground several times before I understood it.*

IDIOMS **break new ground** to do something that is different to anything that has been done before • **gain/lose ground** to become more/less popular and accepted: *The idea is gradually gaining ground.* • **get (sth) off the ground** If a plan or activity gets off the ground, or if you get it off the ground, it starts or succeeds: *He worked hard at getting the project off the ground.* • **stand your ground** to refuse to change your opinion or move your position despite attempts to make you • **suit sb down to the ground** UK to be exactly right or suitable for someone: *That job would suit you down to the ground.* • **be thin on**

the ground UK to exist only in small numbers or amounts

→ See also **breeding ground**, **common ground**

ground² /graʊnd/ verb **1 be grounded** If a vehicle that travels on water or in the air is grounded, it cannot or may not leave the ground: *The aircraft was **grounded by** fog.* **2 be grounded in sth** formal to be based firmly on something: *Fiction should be grounded in reality.*

ground³ /graʊnd/ past of grind

ground ˈbeef noun [U] US (UK **mince**) beef (= meat from a cow) that has been cut into very small pieces by a machine

groundbreaking /ˈgraʊndˌbreɪkɪŋ/ adj based on or containing completely new ideas: *groundbreaking research*

ground ˈfloor noun [C] (US **first floor**) ⓑ the level of a building that is on the ground

grounding /ˈgraʊndɪŋ/ noun [no plural] knowledge of the basic facts and principles of a subject: *The course gave me a good **grounding in** bookkeeping.*

groundless /ˈgraʊndləs/ adj Groundless fears, worries, etc have no reason or facts to support them.

ground ˈrules noun [plural] the basic rules or principles for doing something

grounds /graʊndz/ noun [plural] **1** ⓑ the reason for doing or believing something: *He resigned on medical **grounds**.* ○ *I refused **on the grounds that** (= because) it was too risky.* **2** the land around and belonging to a particular building or organization: *We strolled around the hospital grounds.*

groundwork /ˈgraʊndwɜːk/ noun [U] work or events that prepare for something that will be done or produced in the future: *The project is **laying the groundwork for** a new approach to research.*

ground ˈzero noun [U] **1** the exact place where a nuclear bomb explodes **2 Ground Zero** the place in New York City where the World Trade Center stood before it was destroyed in an attack on September 11, 2001

group¹ /gruːp/ noun [C] **1** ⓐ a number of people or things that are together in one place or are connected: *She went camping with a small **group of** friends.* **2** ⓐ a few musicians or singers who perform together, usually playing popular music: *a pop group*

🗒 Word partners for group

form/join a group • divide/split sth into groups • a large/small group • a group of sth

---

group² /gruːp/ verb [I, T] to form a group or put people or things into a group or groups: *The children are grouped according to their ability.*

grouping /ˈgruːpɪŋ/ noun [C] a group of people or things that have the same aims or qualities: *regional groupings*

grouse¹ /graʊs/ noun [C] **1** (plural **grouse**) a fat

---

brown bird that some people hunt for food **2** a small complaint about something

rouse² /graʊs/ **verb** [I] to complain about something

rove /grəʊv/ **noun** [C] a small group of trees: *an olive grove*

rovel /'grɒvəl/ **verb** [I] (mainly UK **grovelling, grovelled**, US **groveling, groveled**) **1** to try very hard to be nice to someone important so that they will be nice to you or forgive you: *She grovelled to the producer to get that part.* **2** to move around on your hands and knees: *He was grovelling around on the floor.*

row /grəʊ/ **verb** (**grew, grown**) **1** DEVELOP ▷ [I] ⓐ to develop and become bigger or taller as time passes: *Children grow very quickly.* **2** PLANT ▷ [I, T] ⓐ If a plant grows, or you grow it, it develops from a seed to a full plant: *These shrubs grow well in sandy soil.* **3** INCREASE ▷ [I] ⓑ to increase: *The number of people living alone grows each year.* **4** **grow tired/old/calm, etc** ⓒ to gradually become tired/old/calm, etc: *The music grew louder and louder.* **5** HAIR ▷ [I, T] ⓑ If your hair or nails grow, or if you grow them, they get longer.

PHRASAL VERBS **grow into sb/sth** to develop into a particular type of person or thing • **grow into sth** If a child grows into clothes, they gradually become big enough to wear them. • **grow on sb** If someone or something grows on you, you start to like them: *I didn't like her at first but she's grown on me over the years.* • **grow out of sth 1** If children grow out of clothes, they gradually become too big to wear them: *Adam's grown out of his shoes.* **2** to stop doing something as you get older: *He still bites his nails, but hopefully he'll grow out of it.* • **grow up 1** ⓐ to become older or an adult: *She grew up in New York.* **2** to develop or become bigger or stronger: *A close friendship had grown up between them.*

rower /'grəʊəʳ/ **noun** [C] someone who grows fruit or vegetables to sell to people

rowing /'grəʊɪŋ/ **adj** ⓑ increasing: *A growing number of people are choosing to live alone.*

rowl /graʊl/ **verb** [I] If a dog or similar animal growls, it makes a deep, angry noise in its throat. • **growl noun** [C]

rown¹ /grəʊn/ **adj a grown man/woman** an adult, used especially when they are not behaving like an adult

rown² /grəʊn/ past participle of grow

rown-up¹ /'grəʊnʌp/ **noun** [C] ⓑ an adult, used especially when talking to children: *Ask a grown-up to cut the shape out for you.*

rown-up² /ˌgrəʊn'ʌp/ **adj** ⓑ with the physical and mental development of an adult: *Jenny has a grown-up son of 24.*

> 🖉 Word partners for **growth**
>
> encourage/slow/stimulate/stunt growth •
> healthy/long-term/low/rapid/slow/steady
> growth • a growth in sth

rowth /grəʊθ/ **noun 1** [U, no plural] ⓑ the process of growing, increasing, or developing:

population growth ∘ *A balanced diet is essential for healthy growth.* **2** [C] something that grows on your skin or inside your body, that should not be there

grub /grʌb/ **noun 1** [U] informal food **2** [C] a young, developing insect that has a fat, white tube shape

grubby /'grʌbi/ **adj** quite dirty: *a grubby little boy*

grudge¹ /grʌdʒ/ **noun** [C] a feeling of dislike or anger towards someone because of something they have done in the past: *He is not the type of person to **bear a grudge against** anyone.*

grudge² /grʌdʒ/ **verb** [T] to not want to spend time or money or to give something to someone: *He grudged the time he spent in meetings.*

grudging /'grʌdʒɪŋ/ **adj** done against your will, in a way that shows you do not want to do it: *He treated her with **grudging respect**.* • **grudgingly adv**

gruelling mainly UK (US **grueling**) /'gruːəlɪŋ/ **adj** Gruelling activities are very difficult and make you very tired: *a gruelling bicycle race*

gruesome /'gruːsəm/ **adj** very unpleasant or violent, usually involving injury or death: *a gruesome murder*

gruff /grʌf/ **adj** sounding unfriendly: *a gruff voice* • **gruffly adv**

grumble /'grʌmbl/ **verb** [I] to complain about something in a quiet but angry way: *She's always **grumbling about** something.* • **grumble noun** [C]

grumpy /'grʌmpi/ **adj** easily annoyed and often complaining: *a **grumpy old man*** • **grumpily adv** • **grumpiness noun** [U]

grunt /grʌnt/ **verb 1** [I, T] to make a short, low sound instead of speaking, usually when you are angry or in pain **2** [I] If a pig grunts, it makes short, low sounds. • **grunt noun** [C]

guarantee¹ /ˌgærən'tiː/ **verb** [T] (**guaranteeing, guaranteed**) **1** ⓑ to promise that something is true or will happen: *Every child is guaranteed a place at a local school.* ∘ [+ (that)] *We can't guarantee that it will arrive in time.* **2** If a company guarantees its products, it makes a written promise to repair them or give you a new one if they have a fault.

guarantee² /ˌgærən'tiː/ **noun** [C, U] **1** ⓑ a written promise made by a company to repair one of its products or give you a new one if it has a fault: *a three-year guarantee* ∘ *I'm afraid this camera is no longer **under guarantee**.* **2** a promise that something will be done or will happen: [+ (that)] *There's no guarantee that it actually works.*

guard¹ /gɑːd/ **noun 1** PROTECT ▷ [C] ⓑ someone whose job is to make certain someone does not escape or to protect a place or another person: *a security guard* ∘ *prison guards* **2** SOLDIERS ▷ [no plural] a group of soldiers or police officers who are protecting a person or place **3** TRAIN ▷ [C] (also **conductor**) someone who is in charge of a train **4** THING ▷ [C] something that covers or protects someone

G

or something: *a fire guard* **5 be on guard; stand guard** to be responsible for protecting a place or a person: *Armed police stood guard outside the house.* **6 be under guard** to be kept in a place by a group of people who have weapons: *The suspect is now under guard in the local hospital.*

IDIOMS **catch sb off guard** to surprise someone by doing something when they are not ready to deal with it • **be on (your) guard** to be ready to deal with something difficult that might happen: *Companies were warned to be **on their guard** for suspicious packages.*

guard² /gɑːd/ **verb** [T] **1 ☻** to protect someone or something from being attacked or stolen: *Soldiers guarded the main doors of the embassy.* **2 ☻** to watch someone and make certain that they do not escape from a place: *Five prison officers guarded the prisoners.*

PHRASAL VERB **guard against sth** to try to make certain that something does not happen by being very careful: *Regular exercise helps guard against heart disease.*

guarded /ˈɡɑːdɪd/ **adj** careful not to give too much information or show how you really feel: *a guarded response* • **guardedly adv**

guardian /ˈɡɑːdiən/ **noun** [C] **1** someone who is legally responsible for someone else's child: *The consent form must be signed by the child's parent or guardian.* **2** a person or organization that protects laws, principles, etc • **guardianship noun** [U]

guerrilla /ɡəˈrɪlə/ **noun** [C] a member of an unofficial group of soldiers fighting to achieve their political beliefs: *guerrilla warfare*

guess¹ /ɡes/ **verb 1** [I, T] **☻** to give an answer or opinion about something without having all the facts: *Can you guess how old he is?* **2** [I, T] **☻** to give a correct answer without having all the facts: *"You've got a promotion!" "Yes, how did you guess?"* ○ [+ (that)] *I'd never have guessed that you two were related.* **3 I guess ☻** used when you think that something is probably true or likely: *I've known her for about 12 years, I guess.* **4 I guess so/not ☻** used when you agree/disagree but are not completely certain about something **5 Guess what? ☻** something you say when you have some surprising news for someone: *Guess what? I'm pregnant.*

guess² /ɡes/ **noun** [C] **1 ☻** an attempt to give the right answer when you are not certain what it is: *How old do you think John is? Go on, mainly UK have a guess/US take a guess.* ○ *At a guess, I'd say there were about 70 people there.* **2** an opinion that you have formed by guessing: *My guess is they'll announce their engagement soon.* **3 be anybody's guess** informal to be something that no one can be certain about: *What happens after the election is anybody's guess.*

> ### 🖉 Word partners for **guess**
>
> **have/hazard/make/take** a guess • a **rough** guess • **at** a guess • a guess **as to/at** sth

guesswork /ˈɡeswɜːk/ **noun** [U] a way of trying to find an answer that involves guessing

guest /ɡest/ **noun** [C] **1 VISITOR** ▷ **☻** someone who comes to visit you in your home, at a party etc: *We've got some guests coming this weekend.* **2 HOTEL** ▷ **☻** someone who is staying in a hotel: *The hotel has accommodation for 200 guests.* **3 TV** ▷ **☻** a famous person who takes part in a television programme or other entertainment: *Our special guest tonight is Sandra Bullock.*

IDIOM **Be my guest.** something you say when you give someone permission to use something or do something

> ### 🖉 Word partners for **guest**
>
> **entertain/invite/welcome** guests • a **frequent/honoured/special/uninvited** guest

guesthouse /ˈɡesthaʊs/ **noun** [C] a small cheap hotel

GUI /ˈɡuːi/ **noun** [C] graphical user interface: a way of arranging information on a computer screen that is easy to understand because it uses pictures and symbols as well as words

guidance /ˈɡaɪdəns/ **noun** [U] **☻** help or advice: *Students make choices about their future, with the guidance of their teachers.*

guide¹ /ɡaɪd/ **noun** [C] **1 PERSON** ▷ **☻** someone whose job is to show interesting places to visitors, or to help people get somewhere: *tour guide* **2 BOOK** ▷ **☻** a book that gives information about something or tells you how to do something: *a hotel/restaurant guide* ○ *user's guide* **3 PLAN** ▷ something that helps you plan or decide what to do: [usually singular] *Parents use this report as a guide when choosing schools for their children.* **4 Guide** (also **Girl Guide**) a girl who belongs to an organization in the UK that teaches practical things like living outside, and how to work as part of a team **5 the Guides** an organization in the UK that teaches girls practical skills and how to work as part of a team

guide² /ɡaɪd/ **verb** [T] **1 ☻** to help someone or something go somewhere: *He gently guided her back to her seat.* **2** to tell someone what they should do: *She had no one to guide her as a teenager.*

guidebook /ˈɡaɪdbʊk/ **noun** [C] **☻** a book that gives visitors information about a particular place

guide dog noun [C] (also US **seeing eye dog**) a dog that is trained to help blind people

guided tour noun [C] a visit to a place such as a museum with a guide who explains facts about the place

guidelines /ˈɡaɪdlaɪnz/ **noun** [plural] advice about how to do something: *government guidelines on tobacco advertising*

> ### 🖉 Word partners for **guidelines**
>
> **draw up/issue/lay down/produce** guidelines • guidelines **on** sth

guild /ɡɪld/ **noun** [C] an organization of people

who have the same job or interests: *the Designers' Guild*

guile /gaɪl/ **noun** [U] formal clever but sometimes dishonest behaviour that you use to deceive someone

guillotine /ˈgɪlətiːn/ **noun** [C] a piece of equipment used to cut off criminals' heads in the past • **guillotine verb** [T]

guilt /gɪlt/ **noun** [U] **1 FEELING** ▷ ⑩ the strong feeling of shame that you feel when you have done something wrong: *He was overcome with guilt over what he had done.* **2 ILLEGAL** ▷ ⑫ the fact that someone has done something illegal: *The prosecution must convince the jury of his guilt.* **3 WRONG** ▷ the responsibility for doing something bad

guilt-ridden /ˈgɪltrɪdᵊn/ **adj** feeling very guilty

guilty /ˈgɪlti/ **adj 1** ⑪ ashamed because you have done something wrong: [+ about + doing sth] *I feel so guilty about not going to see them.* **2** ⑫ having broken a law: *The jury found her guilty* (= decided that she was guilty of a crime). ○ *They found him guilty of rape.* • **guiltily adv** • **guiltiness noun** [U]

guinea pig /ˈgɪniˌpɪg/ **noun** [C] **1** a small animal with fur and no tail that people sometimes keep as a pet **2** informal someone who is used in a test for something such as a new medicine or product

guise /gaɪz/ **noun** [C] formal what something seems to be, although it is not: *Banks are facing new competition in the guise of supermarkets.*

guitar /gɪˈtɑːʳ/ **noun** [C] ⑪ a musical instrument with strings that you play by pulling the strings with your fingers or a piece of plastic: *an electric guitar*

guitar

guitarist /gɪˈtɑːrɪst/ **noun** [C] ⑪ someone who plays the guitar, especially as their job

gulf /gʌlf/ **noun** [C] **1** a large area of sea that has land almost all the way around it: *the Arabian Gulf* **2** an important difference between the opinions or situations of two groups of people: *There is a growing gulf between the rich and the poor.*

gull /gʌl/ **noun** [C] (also **seagull**) a white or grey bird that lives near the sea and has a loud cry

gullible /ˈgʌlɪbl/ **adj** Someone who is gullible is easily tricked because they trust people too much: *How could you be so gullible?*

gully /ˈgʌli/ **noun** [C] a narrow valley that is usually dry except after a lot of rain

gulp /gʌlp/ **verb 1 DRINK/EAT** ▷ [T] (also **gulp down**) to drink or eat something quickly: *I just had time to gulp down a cup of coffee before I left.* **2 BREATHE** ▷ [I, T] to breathe in large amounts of air **3 SWALLOW** ▷ [I] to swallow suddenly, sometimes making a noise, because you are

nervous or surprised • **gulp noun** [C] *He took a large gulp of tea.*

gum¹ /gʌm/ **noun 1 MOUTH** ▷ [C] ⑫ the hard, pink part inside your mouth that your teeth grow out of: [usually plural] *Protect your teeth and gums by visiting your dentist regularly.* ○ *gum disease* **2 SWEET** ▷ [U] (also **chewing gum**) a sweet substance that you chew (= bite repeatedly) but do not swallow: *a stick of gum* **3 STICKY** ▷ [U] a sticky substance like glue, used for sticking papers together → See also **bubble gum**

gum² /gʌm/ **verb** [T] (**gumming, gummed**) UK to stick things together using glue

gun¹ /gʌn/ **noun** [C] ⑪ a weapon that you fire bullets out of

IDIOMS **jump the gun** to do something too soon, before you have thought about it carefully • **stick to your guns** informal to refuse to change your ideas although other people try to make you

→ See also **machine gun**

> ☑ Word partners for **gun**
>
> **point** a gun at sb/sth • **fire** a gun

gun² /gʌn/ **verb** (**gunning, gunned**)

PHRASAL VERB **gun sb down** to shoot someone and kill them or injure them badly

gunboat /ˈgʌnbəʊt/ **noun** [C] a small ship used during a war

gunfire /ˈgʌnfaɪəʳ/ **noun** [U] the sound of guns being fired

gunman /ˈgʌnmən/ **noun** [C] (plural **gunmen**) a criminal with a gun

gunner /ˈgʌnəʳ/ **noun** [C] a soldier or sailor whose job is to fire a large gun

gunpoint /ˈgʌnpɔɪnt/ **noun at gunpoint** with someone aiming a gun towards you: *The hostages are being held at gunpoint.*

gunpowder /ˈgʌnˌpaʊdəʳ/ **noun** [U] an explosive powder

gunshot /ˈgʌnʃɒt/ **noun** [C] the sound or action of a gun being fired: *I heard a gunshot and rushed into the street.* ○ *gunshot wounds to the chest*

gurgle /ˈgɜːgl/ **verb** [I] to make a sound like bubbling liquid: *The baby was gurgling happily.* • **gurgle noun** [C]

guru /ˈguːruː/ **noun** [C] **1** someone whose opinion you respect because they know a lot about a particular thing **2** a teacher or leader in the Hindu religion

gush¹ /gʌʃ/ **verb** [I, T] **1** If liquid gushes from an opening, it comes out quickly and in large amounts: *He ran down the street, blood gushing from a wound in his neck.* **2** to praise someone so much that they do not believe you are sincere: *"Darling! I'm so excited!" she gushed.*

gush² /gʌʃ/ **noun** [C] **1** a large amount of liquid or gas that flows quickly **2** a sudden feeling of a particular emotion

gust /gʌst/ **verb** [I] If winds gust, they blow strongly: *Winds gusting to 50 mph brought down* *power cables.* • **gust** noun [C] *a gust of air* • **gusty** adj

gusto /ˈɡʌstəʊ/ **noun with gusto** with a lot of energy and enthusiasm: *Everyone joined in the singing with great gusto.*

gut¹ /ɡʌt/ **noun** [C] the tube in your body that takes food from your stomach to be passed out as waste

gut² /ɡʌt/ **adj gut reaction/feeling/instinct** a reaction/feeling, etc that you feel certain is right, although you have no reason to think so: *I had a gut feeling that he was going to come back.*

gut³ /ɡʌt/ **verb** [T] (**gutting, gutted**) **1** to remove the organs from inside a fish or other animal **2** to completely destroy or remove the inside of a building: *A fire gutted the bookshop last week.*

guts /ɡʌts/ **noun** [plural] informal **1** ⓑ the bravery and determination that is needed to do something difficult or unpleasant: *It **took guts** to stand up and tell the boss how she felt.* **2** the organs inside a person's or animal's body

IDIOM **hate sb's guts** informal to dislike someone very much

gutsy /ˈɡʌtsi/ **adj** brave and determined: *a gutsy performance*

gutted /ˈɡʌtɪd/ **adj** UK informal very disappointed and upset: [+ (that)] *Neil's absolutely gutted that he's been dropped from the team.*

gutter /ˈɡʌtər/ **noun** [C] **1** a long, open pipe that is fixed to the edge of a roof to carry water away **2** the edge of a road where water flows away

guy /ɡaɪ/ **noun** informal **1** ⓐ [C] a man: *What a nice guy!* **2 guys** used when you are talking to or about two or more people: *Come on, you guys, let's go home.*

guzzle /ˈɡʌzl/ **verb** [I, T] informal to eat or drink lot of something quickly: *Who's guzzled all th beer?*

gym /dʒɪm/ **noun 1** [C] ⓑ a building with equipment for doing exercises: *Nick goes to th gym three times a week.* **2** [U] ⓑ exercises don inside, especially as a school subject

gymnasium /dʒɪmˈneɪziəm/ **noun** [C] a gym

gymnast /ˈdʒɪmnæst/ **noun** [C] someone who does gymnastics: *an Olympic gymnast*

gymnastics /dʒɪmˈnæstɪks/ **noun** [U] ⓑ a sport in which you do physical exercises on the floor and on different pieces of equipment, often in competitions

gymnastics

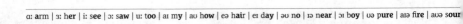

gynaecologist UK (US **gynecologist**) /ɡaɪnə-ˈkɒlədʒɪst/ **noun** [C] a doctor who treats medical conditions that only affect women

gynaecology UK (US **gynecology**) /ɡaɪnəˈkɒlədʒi/ **noun** [U] the study and treatment of diseases an medical conditions that only affect wome • **gynaecological** /ˌɡaɪnəkəˈlɒdʒɪkəl/ **adj** UK

gypsy (also UK **gipsy**) /ˈdʒɪpsi/ **noun** [C] member of a race of people who travel from place to place, especially in Europe: *a gyps caravan*

H

H, h /eɪtʃ/ the eighth letter of the alphabet

ha /hɑː/ **exclamation** something you say when you are surprised or pleased

habit /ˈhæbɪt/ **noun 1 REGULAR ACTIVITY** ▷ [C, U] ⓑ something that you do regularly, almost without thinking about it: *He's just eating out of habit – he's not really hungry.* **2 be in/get into the habit of doing sth** to be used/get used to doing something regularly: *We don't want the children to get into the habit of watching a lot of TV.* **3 BAD ACTIVITY** ▷ [C, U] ⓑ something that you often do that is bad for your health or is annoying: *He has some really nasty habits.* ◦ *We offer help to alcoholics who want to **kick the habit.*** **4 CLOTHING** ▷ [C] a long, loose piece of clothing worn by some religious groups: *a monk's habit*

> **⧉ Word partners for habit**
>
> **get into/get out of** the habit of doing sth • **have/kick** a habit • an **annoying/bad/good** habit • do sth **from/out of/through** habit

habitable /ˈhæbɪtəbl/ **adj** A habitable building is in good enough condition to live in.

habitat /ˈhæbɪtæt/ **noun** [C] the natural environment of an animal or plant

habitation /ˌhæbɪˈteɪʃᵊn/ **noun** [U] the fact of living in a place: *This place is not fit for **human habitation.***

habitual /həˈbɪtʃuəl/ **adj 1** usual or typical: *an habitual expression/gesture* **2** doing something often because it is a habit: *a habitual drug user* • **habitually adv**

hack¹ /hæk/ **verb** [I, T] **1 CUT** ▷ to cut something roughly into pieces: *The victim had been **hacked to death.*** **2 COMPUTER** ▷ to use a computer to illegally get into someone else's computer system and read the information that is kept there: *Two British youths were caught **hacking into** government computers.* **3 TELEPHONE** ▷ [often passive] to illegally and secretly listen to someone else's telephone conversations or to the messages left on someone else's telephone: *The actor believes that his phone was hacked by the newspaper.*

hack² /hæk/ **noun** [C] informal someone who produces low quality writing for books, newspapers, etc

hacker /ˈhækər/ **noun** [C] **1** someone who illegally gets into someone else's computer system: *The hacker obtained names and e-mail accounts of the company's one million customers.* **2** someone who illegally and secretly listens to someone else's telephone conversations and telephone messages: *The **mobile phone** hackers face five years in jail.*

hacking /ˈhækɪŋ/ **noun** [U] the activity of using a computer illegally to get into another computer system to read the information kept there, or to spread a computer virus: *He was convicted of*
hacking into numerous corporate computer networks.

hacktivist /ˈhæktɪvɪst/ **noun** [C] someone who uses computers to try to achieve political change, for example by attacking websites or illegally entering another computer system: *A hacktivist invaded part of the bank's website last week.*

had strong /hæd/ weak /həd/, /əd/, /d/ **verb 1** past of have **2 be had** informal to be tricked or made to look silly: *I think I've been had – this camera doesn't work.*

haddock /ˈhædək/ **noun** [C, U] (plural **haddock**) a fish that lives in northern seas and is eaten as food

hadn't /ˈhædᵊnt/ short for had not: *I hadn't seen Megan since college.*

haemophilia UK (US **hemophilia**) /ˌhiːməˈfɪliə/ **noun** [U] a serious disease in which the flow of blood from someone's body cannot be stopped when they are hurt • **haemophiliac** UK (US **hemophiliac**) **noun** [C] someone who has haemophilia

haemorrhage UK (US **hemorrhage**) /ˈhemᵊrɪdʒ/ **noun** [C, U] the medical problem of suddenly losing a lot of blood from a part of your body: *a brain haemorrhage*

haemorrhoids UK (US **hemorrhoids**) /ˈhemərɔɪdz/ **noun** [plural] painful swollen tissue around the opening of a person's bottom

haggard /ˈhægəd/ **adj** Someone who is haggard has a thin face with dark marks around their eyes because they are sick or tired.

haggle /ˈhægl/ **verb** [I] to argue, especially about the price of something: *I spent 20 minutes **haggling over** the price of a leather bag.*

ha ha exclamation used in writing to represent the sound someone makes when they laugh

hail¹ /heɪl/ **noun 1** [U] small, hard pieces of frozen rain that fall from the sky **2 a hail of bullets/stones/bottles, etc** a lot of bullets/ stones/bottles, etc that are fired or thrown at the same time

hail² /heɪl/ **verb 1** [T] to call or wave to someone to get their attention: *She stepped into the road and **hailed a taxi.*** **2 it hails** If it hails, small, hard pieces of frozen rain fall from the sky.

PHRASAL VERBS **hail sb/sth as sth** to say publicly and enthusiastically that someone or something is something very good • **hail from** to come from a particular place

hailstone /ˈheɪlstəʊn/ **noun** [C] a small, hard ball of ice that falls from the sky like rain

hair /heər/ **noun 1** [U] ⓐ the thin, thread-like parts that grow on your head: *a girl with long, fair hair* **2** [C] ⓑ one of the thin thread-like parts that grow on a person's or animal's skin: *My black skirt was covered in cat hairs.*

IDIOMS **let your hair down** informal to relax and enjoy yourself • **pull/tear your hair out** to be very anxious about something: *When they still weren't home by midnight, I was pulling my hair out.* • **split hairs** to argue about small details that are not important

→ See also **pubic hair**

hairbrush /ˈheəbrʌʃ/ *noun* [C] a brush that you use to make your hair look tidy → See picture at **brush**

haircut /ˈheəkʌt/ *noun* [C] **1** ⑤ If you have a haircut, someone cuts your hair: *I really need a haircut.* **2** ⑥ the style in which your hair has been cut

hairdo /ˈheəduː/ *noun* [C] informal the style in which someone arranges their hair

hairdresser /ˈheəˌdresər/ *noun* **1** ⑤ [C] someone whose job is to wash, cut, colour, etc people's hair **2 hairdresser's** ⑥ the place where you go to have your hair washed, cut, coloured, etc

hairdryer /ˈheəˌdraɪər/ *noun* [C] ⑤ a piece of electrical equipment for drying your hair with hot air

-haired /-ˈheəd/ *suffix* used after a word describing someone's hair: *a red-haired woman* ∘ *a short-haired cat* → See also **fair-haired**

hairgrip /ˈheəɡrɪp/ *noun* [C] UK (US **bobby pin**) a small, thin piece of metal, used to fasten a woman's hair in position

hairline /ˈheəlaɪn/ *noun* **1** [C] the place at the top of your face where your hair starts growing **2 a hairline crack/fracture** a very thin line where something hard such as a bone or cup is broken

hairpin /ˈheəpɪn/ *noun* [C] a piece of metal shaped like a U, used to fasten a woman's hair in position

hairpin ˈbend *noun* [C] UK (US ˌhairpin ˈturn, ˌhairpin ˈcurve) a bend shaped like a U on a steep road

hair-raising /ˈheəˌreɪzɪŋ/ *adj* frightening but in an enjoyable way: *It was a rather **hair-raising** journey down the mountain road.*

hairstyle /ˈheəstaɪl/ *noun* [C] the style in which someone arranges their hair: *Do you like my new hairstyle?*

hairy /ˈheəri/ *adj* **1** covered in hair: *a **hairy** chest* ∘ *hairy legs* **2** informal frightening or dangerous: *There were some rather **hairy** moments during the race.* • **hairiness** *noun* [U]

hajj (*plural* **hajjes**) (also **haj** *plural* **hajes**) /hædʒ/ *noun* [C] the religious journey to Mecca that all Muslims try to make at least once in their life

halal /hælˈæl/ *adj* Halal meat is prepared according to Islamic law.

hale /heɪl/ *adj* **hale and hearty** healthy and full of life

half¹ /hɑːf/ *noun, determiner* (*plural* **halves**) **1** ⑫ [C, U] one of two equal parts of something; ½: *Rice is eaten by **half** of the world's population.* ∘ *Cut the lemons into halves.* ∘ *It'll take **half an hour** to get there.* ∘ *Jenny lived in Beijing for a year and a half.* **2 break/cut/split sth in half** ⑥

to divide something into two equal parts: *Divide the dough in half and roll it out into two circles* **3 decrease/increase, etc sth by half** to make something smaller/larger, etc by half its size: *The drug reduces the risk of stroke by half.* **4 half past one/two/three, etc** mainly UK ⑬ 30 minutes past one o'clock/two o'clock/three o'clock, etc: *We go back to our hotel at half past seven.* **5 half one, two/three, etc** UK informal ⑬ 30 minutes past one o'clock/two o'clock/three o'clock, etc: *"What time does it start?" "About half six."*

IDIOMS **go halves with sb** informal to divide the cost of something with someone: *Shall we go halves on a present for Laura?* • **half the fun, time/pleasure, etc** informal ⑫ a large part of the enjoyment/time, etc: *Kids today – parents don't know where they are half the time.* • **not half as good/bad/exciting, etc** informal ⑫ to be much less good/bad/exciting, etc than something else: *Her new book's not half as good as the last one.*

half² /hɑːf/ *adv* ⑬ partly, but not completely: *half empty/full* ∘ *Sophia is half Greek and half Spanish (= she has one Greek parent and one Spanish parent).* ∘ *She was only half aware of what was happening.*

ˌhalf ˈboard *noun* [U] mainly UK the price for a room in a hotel, which includes breakfast and dinner

half-brother /ˈhɑːfˌbrʌðər/ *noun* [C] a brother who is the son of only one of your parents

half-hearted /ˌhɑːfˈhɑːtɪd/ *adj* without much effort or interest: *a **half-hearted** attempt* • **half-heartedly** *adv*

half-price /ˌhɑːfˈpraɪs/ *adj, adv* ⑫ costing half the usual price: *I got some **half-price** pizzas at the supermarket.* ∘ *Children under the age of 16 can travel half-price on most trains.*

half-sister /ˈhɑːfˌsɪstər/ *noun* [C] a sister who is the daughter of only one of your parents

half-term /ˌhɑːfˈtɜːm/ *noun* [C, U] UK a short holiday in the middle of a school term (= one of the periods the school year is divided into)

half-time /ˌhɑːfˈtaɪm/ *noun* [U] a short period of rest between the two halves of a game

halfway /ˌhɑːfˈweɪ/ *adj, adv* at an equal distance between two places, or in the middle of a period of time: *the **halfway** point* ∘ *He was released **halfway through** his prison sentence.*

hall /hɔːl/ *noun* [C] **1** (also **hallway** /ˈhɔːlweɪ/) ⑬ a room or passage in a building, which leads to other rooms **2** ⑫ a large room or building where meetings, concerts, etc are held: *the Albert Hall* ∘ *The disco will be held in the school hall.* → See also **town hall**

hallmark /ˈhɔːlmɑːk/ *noun* [C] **1** an official mark that is put on something made of silver or gold to prove that it is real **2** a quality or method that is typical of a particular type of person or thing: *Simplicity is a **hallmark of** his design.*

hallo UK (UK/US **hello**) /həˈləʊ/ *exclamation* **1** used to greet someone: *Hallo, Chris, how are things?* **2** used to start a conversation on the telephone: *Hallo, this is Alex.*

ˌhall of ˈresidence *noun* [C] (*plural* **halls of residence**) UK (US **dormitory, residence hall**) building where university or college students live

hallowed /ˈhæləʊd/ **adj 1** respected and considered important: *a **hallowed tradition*** **2** made holy by a priest: *the **hallowed ground** of the churchyard*

Halloween /ˌhæləʊˈiːn/ **noun** [U] the night of 31 October when children dress in special clothes and people try to frighten each other

hallucinate /həˈluːsɪneɪt/ **verb** [I] to see things that are not really there, because you are sick or have taken an illegal drug

hallucination /həˌluːsɪˈneɪʃᵊn/ **noun** [C, U] things you see that are not really there because you are sick or have taken an illegal drug

halo /ˈheɪləʊ/ **noun** [C] a gold circle of light that is shown around the head of a holy person in a painting

halt¹ /hɒlt/ **noun 1** [no plural] the act of stopping moving or happening: *The car **came to a halt** just inches from the edge of the cliff.* ∘ *News of the accident **brought** the party **to a halt**.* **2 call a halt to sth** to officially order something to stop: *The government has called a halt to all new building in the area.*

> ✎ Word partners for **halt**
>
> **bring sth to/come to** a halt • an **abrupt/ grinding/sudden** halt

halt² /hɒlt/ **verb** [I, T] formal to stop or make something stop: *The council ordered that work on the project should be halted immediately.*

halting /ˈhɒltɪŋ/ **adj** stopping often while you are saying or doing something, especially because you are nervous: *He spoke quietly, in halting English.*

halve /hɑːv/ **verb 1** [T] to divide something into two equal parts: *Peel and halve the potatoes.* **2** [I, T] If you halve something, or if it halves, it is reduced to half the size it was before: *They have almost halved the price of flights to New York.*

ham /hæm/ **noun** [C, U] 🅰🄿 meat from a pig's back or upper leg: *a ham sandwich*

hamburger /ˈhæmˌbɜːɡər/ **noun 1** [C] a round, flat shape of meat that is cooked in hot oil and eaten between round pieces of bread: *a hamburger and fries* **2** [U] US (UK **mince**) beef (= meat from a cow) that is cut into very small pieces

hamlet /ˈhæmlət/ **noun** [C] a very small village

hammer¹ /ˈhæmər/ **noun** [C] 🄱🄲 a tool with a heavy, metal part at the top that you use to hit nails into something → See picture at **tool**

hammer

hammer² /ˈhæmər/ **verb** [I, T] to hit something with a hammer

PHRASAL VERBS **hammer sth into sb** to repeat something to someone a lot of times until they remember it • **hammer on sth** to hit something many times, making a lot of noise: *They were woken up by someone **hammering on** the door.*

• **hammer sth out** to finally agree on a plan, business agreement, etc after arguing about the details for a long time

hammering /ˈhæmᵊrɪŋ/ **noun 1** [U] the noise made by hitting something with a hammer or hitting something hard with your hands **2** [no plural] UK informal a very bad defeat

hammock /ˈhæmək/ **noun** [C] a large piece of cloth or strong net that you hang between two trees or poles to sleep on

hamper¹ /ˈhæmpər/ **verb** [T] to make it difficult for someone to do something: *The police investigation was hampered by a lack of help from the community.*

hamper² /ˈhæmpər/ **noun** [C] a large basket (= container made of thin pieces of wood) with a lid: *a **picnic hamper***

hamster /ˈhæmstər/ **noun** [C] a small animal with soft fur and no tail that is often kept as a pet

hamstring¹ /ˈhæmstrɪŋ/ **noun** [C] a tendon (= part that connects a muscle to a bone) at the back of the upper part of your leg: *a hamstring injury*

hamstring² /ˈhæmstrɪŋ/ **verb** [T] (**hamstrung**) to make it difficult for a person, team, or organization to do something

hand¹ /hænd/ **noun 1 ARM** ▷ [C] 🅰🄰 the part of your body on the end of your arm that has fingers and a thumb: *Take your hands out of your pockets.* → See colour picture **The Body** on page Centre 13 **2 take sb by the hand** to get hold of someone's hand: *Bill took her by the hand and led her into the garden.* **3 hand in hand** holding each other's hand: *The young couple walked hand in hand by the lake.* **4 hold hands** to hold each other's hand **5 at hand** near in time or space: *Teachers are always close at hand to give help to any child who needs it.* **6 by hand** 🄱🄹 done or made by a person instead of a machine: *This sweater has to be washed by hand.* **7 in hand** being worked on or dealt with now: *Despite the pressures we are determined to get on with the job in hand.* **8 be in sb's hands** to be in someone's control or care: *The matter is now in the hands of my lawyer.* **9 on hand** (also UK **to hand**) near to someone or something, and ready to help or be used when necessary: *Extra supplies will be on hand, should they be needed.* **10 at the hands of sb** If you suffer at the hands of someone, they hurt you or treat you badly. **11 CLOCK** ▷ [C] one of the long, thin pieces that point to the numbers on a clock or watch **12 CARDS** ▷ [C] the set of playing cards that one player has been given in a game **13 a hand** 🄱🄹 some help, especially to do something practical: *Could you **give me a hand with** these suitcases?* ∘ *I think Matthew might **need a hand with** his homework.* **14 on the one hand ... on the other hand** 🄱🄲 used when you are comparing two different ideas or opinions: *On the one hand, computer games develop many skills, but on the other, they mean kids don't get enough exercise.* **15 hands off**

H

informal used to tell someone not to touch something: *Hands off – that's mine!*

IDIOMS **change hands** to be sold by someone and bought by someone else: *The hotel has changed hands twice since 2009.* • **a free hand** permission to make your own decisions about how you want to do something • **get out of hand** to become difficult to control: *It was the end of term and the children were getting a little out of hand.* • **go hand in hand** If two things go hand in hand, they exist together and are connected with each other. • **have your hands full** to be very busy: *Shelley has her hands full with three kids under 5.* • **get/lay your hands on sth** to find something • **get/gain the upper hand** to get into a stronger position than someone else so that you are controlling a situation: *Government troops are gradually gaining the upper hand over the rebels.* • **with your bare hands** without using a weapon or tool • **wring your hands** to press your hands together because you are upset or worried about something

hand² /hænd/ **verb** [+ two objects] ⓑ to give something to someone: *Could you hand me that book, please?*

IDIOM **you have to hand it to sb** informal used when you want to show that you admire someone: *You have to hand it to Mick, he's done a good job on that kitchen.*

PHRASAL VERBS **hand sth back** to return something to the person who gave it to you • **hand sth down 1** to give toys, clothes, books, etc to children who are younger than you in your family **2** to pass traditions from older people to younger ones: *This custom has been handed down through the generations.* • **hand sth in** ⓑ to give something to someone in a position of authority: *Have you handed your history essay in yet?* • **hand sth out** ⓑ to give something to all the people in a group: *A girl was handing out leaflets at the station.* • **hand sb/sth over** ⓑ to give someone or something to someone else: *The hijacker was handed over to the French police.*

handbag /'hændbæg/ **noun** [C] mainly UK (mainly US **purse**) ⓐ a bag carried by a woman with her money, keys, etc inside → See picture at **bag**

handbook /'hændbʊk/ **noun** [C] a book that contains information and advice about a particular subject: *a teacher's handbook*

handbrake /'hændbreɪk/ **noun** [C] (also US **emergency brake**, **parking brake**) a stick inside a car that you can pull up to stop the car from moving → See colour picture **Car** on page Centre 7

handcuffs /'hændkʌfs/ **noun** [plural] two metal rings that are joined by a chain and are put on a prisoner's wrists (= lower arms)

handful /'hændfʊl/ **noun 1** [C] the amount of something that you can hold in one hand **2 a handful of sth** ⓑ a small number of people or things: *Only a handful of people came to the meeting.* **3 a handful** informal someone who is difficult to control, especially a child

handgun /'hændgʌn/ **noun** [C] a small gun that you can hold in one hand

handheld¹ (also **hand-held**) /'hændheld/ **adj** ⓑ small enough to be held in your hand: *a handheld computer*

handheld² /'hændheld/ **noun** [C] a piece of electronic equipment that is small enough to be used while holding it in your hand

handicap /'hændɪkæp/ **noun** [C] old-fashioned **1** something that is wrong with your mind or body permanently: *a mental/physical handicap* **2** something that makes it more difficult for you to do something: *I found not having a car quite a handicap in the countryside.*

handicapped /'hændɪkæpt/ **adj** old-fashioned not able to use part of your body or your mind because it has been damaged in some way: *mentally/physically handicapped*

handicraft /'hændɪkrɑːft/ **noun 1** [C] an activity that involves making things with your hand and that needs skill and artistic ability **2 handicrafts** things that people make with their hands: *a sale of handicrafts*

handiwork /'hændɪwɜːk/ **noun** [U] something that someone makes or does: *She put down the brush and stood back to admire her handiwork.*

handkerchief /'hæŋkətʃiːf/ **noun** [C] ⓑ a small piece of cloth or soft paper that you use to dry your eyes or nose

handle¹ /'hændl/ **verb** [T] **1** DEAL WITH ▷ ⓑ to deal with something: *He handled the situation very well.* ◦ *This office handles thousands of enquiries every day.* **2** TOUCH ▷ to touch, hold or pick up something: *You must wash your hands before handling food.* **3** BUY ▷ to buy and sell goods: *He's been charged with handling stolen goods.*

handle

handle

handle² /'hændl/ **noun** [C] ⓑ the part of something that you use to hold it or open it: *door handle* ◦ *the handle on a suitcase*

IDIOM **fly off the handle** informal to suddenly become very angry

handlebars /'hændlbɑːz/ **noun** [plural] the meta

bars at the front of a bicycle or motorcycle that you hold onto to control direction

handler /'hændlə^r/ *noun* [C] someone whose job is to deal with or control a particular type of thing: *a police dog handler*

hand ,luggage *noun* [U] small bags that you can carry onto an aircraft with you when you travel

handmade /ˌhænd'meɪd/ *adj* made by hand instead of by machine

handout /'hændaʊt/ *noun* [C] **1** money or food that is given to people who are poor: *Increasing numbers of people are dependent on government handouts.* **2** ⓑ² a copy of a document that is given to all the people in a class or meeting

handpicked /ˌhænd'pɪkt/ *adj* carefully chosen for a particular purpose or job: *a handpicked audience*

handset /'hændset/ *noun* [C] **1** the outer part of a mobile phone **2** the part of a telephone that you hold in front of your mouth and against your ear

hands ˈfree *adj* describes a piece of equipment, especially a telephone, that you can use without needing to hold it in your hand

handshake /'hændʃeɪk/ *noun* [C] the action of taking someone's right hand and shaking it when you meet or leave each other

handsome /'hændsəm/ *adj* **1** ⓑ¹ A handsome man is attractive: *tall, dark and handsome* **2 a handsome profit/sum, etc** a large amount of money

hands-on /ˌhændz'ɒn/ *adj* physically doing something and not only studying it or watching someone else do it: *hands-on experience*

handwriting /'hændˌraɪtɪŋ/ *noun* [U] ⓑ¹ the way that someone forms the letters when they write with a pen or pencil

handwritten /ˌhænd'rɪtˀn/ *adj* written with a pen or pencil: *a handwritten letter*

handy /'hændi/ *adj* **1** useful or easy to use: *a handy container/tool* **2 come in handy** informal to be useful at some time in the future: *Don't throw those jars away – they might come in handy.* **3** UK informal near to a place: *It's a nice house and it's handy for the station.* **4 be handy with sth** to be good at using something, usually a tool: *He's very handy with a paintbrush.*

handyman /'hændimæn/ *noun* [C] (plural **handymen**) someone who is good at making things or repairing them

hang¹ /hæŋ/ *verb* (**hung**) **1 FASTEN** ▷ [I, T] ⓑ¹ to fasten something so that the top part is fixed but the lower part is free to move, or to be fastened in this way: *He **hung** his coat **on** the hook behind the door.* **2 KILL** ▷ [I, T] (past also **hanged**) ⓑ² to kill someone by putting a rope around their neck and making them drop, or to die in this way **3 IN AIR** ▷ [I] to stay in the air for a long time: *Thick fog hung over the town.* → See also **be/hang in the balance¹**, **hang your head¹ (in shame)**

PHRASAL VERBS **hang around** informal (also UK **hang about**) **1** ⓑ¹ to spend time somewhere, usually without doing very much: *There's*

nowhere for teenagers to go, so they just **hang around on street corners.** **2 hang around with sb** to spend time with someone • **hang on 1** informal ⓑ¹ to wait for a short time: *Hang on – I'm almost finished.* **2** to hold something tightly: *Hang on, we're going over a big bump here.* • **hang onto sth** informal to keep something: *You should hang onto that – it might be worth something.* • **hang out** informal ⓑ¹ to spend a lot of time in a particular place or with a particular group of people • **hang up** ⓑ¹ to finish a conversation on the telephone by putting the phone down • **hang sth up** ⓑ¹ to put something such as a coat somewhere where it can hang: *You can hang up your jacket over there.*

hang² /hæŋ/ *noun* **get the hang of sth** informal to gradually learn how to do or use something

hangar /'hæŋə^r/ *noun* [C] a large building where aircraft are kept

hanger /'hæŋə^r/ *noun* [C] (also **coat hanger**) a wire, wooden, or plastic object for hanging clothes on

ˈhang ˌglider *noun* [C] a structure covered in cloth that you hold onto and float through the air

ˈhang ˌgliding *noun* [U] the sport of flying using a structure covered in cloth that you hang from

hangover /'hæŋəʊvə^r/ *noun* [C] If you have a hangover, you feel ill because you drank too much alcohol the day before.

hanker /'hæŋkə^r/ *verb*

PHRASAL VERB **hanker after/for sth** to want something very much, especially over a long period of time

hankie (also **hanky**) /'hæŋki/ *noun* [C] informal short for handkerchief

Hanukkah (also **Chanukah**) /'hɑːnəkə/ *noun* [C, U] a Jewish religious holiday lasting for eight days in December

haphazard /ˌhæp'hæzəd/ *adj* not planned, organized, controlled, or done regularly: *The whole examination process seemed completely haphazard.* • **haphazardly** *adv*

hapless /'hæpləs/ *adj* literary having bad luck

happen /'hæpˀn/ *verb* [I] **1** ⓐ² If an event or situation happens, it exists or starts to be done, usually by chance: *Were you anywhere nearby when the accident happened?* ◦ *We can't let a mistake like this happen again.* **2** ⓐ² to be the result of an action, situation, or event that someone or something experiences: *Did you hear what **happened to** Jamie last night?* ◦ *What happens if we can't get enough tickets?* **3 happen to do sth** to do something by chance: *If you happen to see Peter, say "hi" for me.* ◦ *You don't happen to know her phone number, do you?* **4 as it happens; it so happens** something that you say in order to introduce a surprising fact: *As it happens, her birthday is the day after mine.*

PHRASAL VERB **happen on/upon sth/sb** to find something or meet someone without planning to

happening /ˈhæpⁿnɪŋ/ **noun** [C] something that happens, often a strange event that is difficult to explain

happily /ˈhæpɪli/ **adv 1 HAPPY** ▷ **B1** in a happy way: *happily married* **2 WILLING** ▷ **B2** in a way that is very willing: *I'd happily drive you to the airport.* **3 LUCKY** ▷ having a good or lucky result: *Happily, the operation was a complete success.*

happiness /ˈhæpɪnəs/ **noun** [U] **B1** the feeling of being happy

> 🗌 Word partners for **happiness**
>
> find happiness

happy /ˈhæpi/ **adj 1 PLEASED** ▷ **A1** pleased and in a good mood, especially because something good has happened: *I'm glad you've finally found someone who **makes** you **happy**.* ∘ *Jean seems much happier now that she's moved out.* **2 happy to do sth** **A2** to be willing to do something: *I'd be very happy to help, if you need me to.* **3 SHOWING HAPPINESS** ▷ **A1** making you feel happy, or expressing happiness: *Did the book have a **happy ending**?* **4 SATISFIED** ▷ **A2** satisfied and not worried: *Are you **happy with** your exam results?* ∘ *I'm not very **happy about** you travelling alone at night.* **5 Happy Birthday/New Year, etc A1** something friendly that you say to someone on a special day or holiday: *Happy Anniversary!* → Opposite **unhappy**

> ➕ Other ways of saying **happy**
>
> A person who seems happy may be described as **cheerful**:
>
> > *She's always very **cheerful**.*
>
> If someone is happy because of something, they may be described as **pleased** or **glad**, and if they are extremely happy because of something, they may be described as **delighted**:
>
> > *He was **pleased** that she had come back.*
> > *I was so **glad** to see her.*
> > *They are **delighted** with their new car.*
>
> If someone is extremely happy and excited, they may be described as **ecstatic** or **elated**:
>
> > *The new president was greeted by an **ecstatic** crowd.*
> > *We were **elated** at the news.*

happy-go-lucky /ˌhæpɪɡəʊˈlʌki/ **adj** not worried and not having any responsibilities

happy hour noun [usually singular] a period of time, usually in the early evening, when a bar sells drinks more cheaply than usual

happy slapping noun [U] an attack on someone by a group of young people who photograph their attack with mobile phones

harass /ˈhærəs/, /həˈræs/ **verb** [T] to continue to annoy or upset someone over a period of time

harassed /ˈhærəst/ **adj** tired and feeling anxious: *harassed passengers*

> 🗌 Word partners for **harassment**
>
> be subjected to/suffer harassment • racial/sexual harassment • harassment of sb

harassment /ˈhærəsmənt/ **noun** [U] behaviour that annoys or upsets someone: *sexual harassment*

harbour

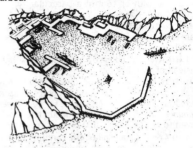

harbour¹ UK (US **harbor**) /ˈhɑːbər/ **noun** [C] **B2** an area of water near the coast where ships are kept and are safe from the sea

harbour² UK (US **harbor**) /ˈhɑːbər/ **verb** [T] **1 I** you harbour doubts, hopes, thoughts, etc, you feel or think about them for a long time: *H harboured dreams of one day becoming a profes sional footballer.* **2** to hide someone or some thing bad: *to **harbour** a **criminal***

hard¹ /hɑːd/ **adj 1 FIRM** ▷ **A2** firm and stiff, an not easy to press or bend: *a hard surface* ∘ *Th seats in the waiting room were hard and uncom fortable.* **2 DIFFICULT** ▷ **A1** difficult to do o understand: [+ to do sth] *It must be hard to stud with all this noise.* ∘ *Quitting my job was th hardest decision I ever had to make.* **3 WITH EFFORT** ▷ **B1** using or done with a lot of effort *the long, **hard** struggle* ∘ *With a bit of **har work** and determination we might still finish o time.* **4 UNPLEASANT** ▷ full of problems an difficult to deal with: *My grandparents had a ver **hard** life.* **5 NOT KIND** ▷ not gentle or kind: *Sh had a cold, hard look in her eyes.* **6 be hard on s a** **B2** to criticize someone too much or trea them unfairly: *You shouldn't be so hard o yourself.* **b** to make someone unhappy b causing them problems: *Our divorce has bee particularly hard on the children.* **7 be hard o sth** to damage something or make it hav problems: *Stress can be hard on any relationshi* **8 do/learn sth the hard way** to do or lear something by experiencing a lot of problems o difficulty **9 give sb a hard time** informal t criticize someone or to treat them unfairly: *H gave me a hard time about losing his keys.*

hard² /hɑːd/ **adv 1 A1** with a lot of effort: *Sh tried very hard but she wasn't quite fast enough* ∘ *You'll have to **work harder**, if you want to pas this exam.* **2 B1** with a lot of force: *It's bee raining hard all day.* ∘ *She kicked the ball as har as she could.*

IDIOMS **die hard** If a belief, custom, or habit die hard, it is very difficult to change: *I'm afraid tha **old habits die hard**.* • **hit sb hard** UK If situation or experience hits you hard, it make you so upset that you have difficulty dealin with it.

ardback /'hɑ:dbæk/ **noun** [C] a book that has a thick, stiff cover

ard-boiled /,hɑ:d'bɔɪld/ **adj** A hard-boiled egg has been boiled with its shell on, until the inside is solid.

ard 'cash noun [U] coins and paper money

ard 'copy noun [C, U] information from a computer that has been printed on paper

ardcore (also **hard-core**) /'hɑ:dkɔ:/ **adj 1** extremely loyal to someone or something, and not willing to change: a **hard-core following 2** Hardcore magazines, films, etc show very active or offensive sexual acts: **hardcore pornography**

ard 'core noun [no plural] a small group of people in society or an organization who are very active and determined not to change: a hard core of activists

ard 'currency noun [U] money that is valuable and can be exchanged easily because it comes from a powerful country

ard 'disk noun [C] a hard drive

ard 'drive noun [C] (also **hard disk**) ⑫ the part inside a computer that is not removed and stores very large amounts of information

ard 'drugs noun [plural] very strong, illegal drugs

arden /'hɑ:dən/ **verb** [I, T] **1** to become hard and stiff, or to make something become hard and stiff: This island is formed from volcanic lava that has hardened into rock. **2** to stop feeling emotions about someone or something, so that you seem less kind, gentle, or weak: **hardened criminals**

ard-headed /,hɑ:d'hedɪd/ **adj** very determined, and not willing to be influenced by your emotions: a hard-headed manager

ard-hearted /,hɑ:d'hɑ:tɪd/ **adj** not caring how other people feel

ard-hitting /,hɑ:d'hɪtɪŋ/ **adj** A hard-hitting speech, report, article, etc is very severe or criticizes someone or something a lot.

ard 'line noun [no plural] a very strict and severe way of dealing with someone or something: Judge Tucker has a reputation for **taking a hard line on** criminals. • **hardline** /,hɑ:d'laɪn/ adj a **hardline policy** on illegal immigrants

ardly /'hɑ:dli/ **adv 1** ⑪ almost not, or only a very small amount: I was so tired that I could hardly walk. ○ We've **hardly ever** spoken to each other. ○ There's **hardly any** food left in the fridge. **2** ⑫ used to emphasize that you think something is not likely, true, possible, etc: I hardly think she'll want to talk to me now that I have a new girlfriend.

⚠ Common learner error: **hardly** or **hard**?

When you mean 'with a lot of effort or force', you should use the adverb **hard**, not 'hardly'.
We worked very hard.
~~We worked very hardly.~~

---

ard-nosed /,hɑ:d'nəʊzd/ **adj** very determined, and not willing to be influenced by your emotions: a hard-nosed lawyer

ard-pressed /,hɑ:d'prest/ **adj 1** be hard-

pressed to do sth to not be able to do something, or have difficulty doing something: You'd be hard-pressed to find a better worker than Jeff. **2** having problems because you are poor: hard-pressed farmers

hardship /'hɑ:dʃɪp/ **noun** [C, U] a problem or situation that makes you suffer a lot, especially because you are very poor: They have suffered years of **financial hardship**.

🗎 Word partners for **hardship**

suffer hardship • **economic/financial/physical** hardship

---

hard 'shoulder noun [C] UK (US **shoulder**) the area on the edge of a main road where a car can stop in an emergency

hard 'up adj informal not having enough money

hardware /'hɑ:dweər/ **noun** [U] ⑪ **1** the machines or equipment that your computer system is made from, not the programs **2** tools and strong equipment, such as those used in the home or garden

hard-working /,hɑ:d'wɜ:kɪŋ/ **adj** doing a job seriously and with a lot of effort

hardy /'hɑ:di/ **adj** strong enough to deal with bad conditions or difficult situations: Goats are very **hardy animals**.

hare /heər/ **noun** [C] an animal like a large rabbit that can run very fast and has long ears

harem /'hɑ:ri:m/ ⑤ /'herəm/ **noun** [C] a group of women who live with or are married to one man in some Muslim societies, or the place where these women live

harm¹ /hɑ:m/ **noun 1** ⑫ [U] hurt or damage: Smoking can **cause** serious **harm to** the lungs. ○ Alan would never **do** anyone any **harm**. **2** not **come to any harm** to not be hurt or damaged **3** not do any harm to not be a bad thing to do and possibly be a good thing: [+ to do sth] It wouldn't **do** any **harm** to have another look. **4** there's no harm in doing sth used to say that something is not a bad thing to do and could possibly have a good effect: I suppose there's no harm in trying. **5** not mean any harm to not intend to hurt someone or damage something: I never meant him any harm, I just wanted him to leave me alone. **6** out of harm's way safe from a dangerous place or situation

---

🗎 Word partners for **harm**

cause/do (sb/sth) harm • not **come to** any harm • **great/serious/untold** harm • harm **to** sb

---

harm² /hɑ:m/ **verb** [T] ⑫ to hurt someone or damage something: Thankfully no one was harmed in the accident.

harmful /'hɑ:mfəl/ **adj** ⑫ causing or likely to cause harm: Doctors believe that smoking is **harmful to** your health.

harmless /'hɑ:mləs/ **adj 1** ⑫ not able or not likely to cause any hurt or damage: Taken in small doses, this drug is completely harmless. **2** not likely to shock or upset people: Their jokes seemed harmless enough. • **harmlessly adv**

harmonica /hɑ:'mɒnɪkə/ **noun** [C] a small

musical instrument that you blow into as you move it across your mouth

harmonious /hɑːˈməʊniəs/ adj **1** friendly and peaceful: *a harmonious business relationship* **2** having or making a pleasant sound

harmonize (also UK **-ise**) /ˈhɑːmənaɪz/ verb [I, T] **1** to be suitable together, or to make different people, plans, situations, etc suitable for each other: *The gardens had been designed to harmonize with the natural landscape.* **2** to sing or play music in harmony

harmony /ˈhɑːməni/ noun **1** [U] ② a situation in which people are peaceful and agree with each other, or when different things seem right or suitable together: *living together in peace and harmony* **2** [C, U] a pleasant sound in music, made by playing or singing a group of different notes together

harness[1] /ˈhɑːnɪs/ noun [C] **1** a set of straps fastened around a horse's body and connecting it to a vehicle that it will pull **2** a set of strong, flat ropes that fasten equipment to your body or fasten you to a vehicle to prevent you from moving too much: *All climbers must wear safety harnesses and helmets.*

harness[2] /ˈhɑːnɪs/ verb [T] **1** to put a harness on a horse, or to connect a horse to a vehicle using a harness **2** to control something so that you can use its power or qualities for a particular purpose

harp[1] /hɑːp/ noun [C] a large wooden musical instrument with many strings that you play with your fingers

harp[2] /hɑːp/ verb

PHRASAL VERB **harp on (about sb/sth)** to talk about someone or something too much

harpoon /hɑːˈpuːn/ noun [C] a weapon with a sharp point, used especially for hunting whales (= large sea animals)

harrowing /ˈhærəʊɪŋ/ adj making you feel extremely frightened or upset: *a harrowing experience*

harsh /hɑːʃ/ adj **1** CRUEL ▷ cruel, unkind, or unpleasant in a way that seems unfair: *harsh criticism/punishment* ∘ *Taking him out of the game was a bit harsh.* **2** DIFFICULT ▷ very cold, dangerous, or unpleasant and difficult to live in: *harsh conditions* **3** STRONG ▷ too strong, bright, loud, etc: *harsh chemicals* ∘ *harsh lighting* • **harshly** adv • **harshness** noun [U]

harvest[1] /ˈhɑːvɪst/ noun **1** [C, U] ② the time when crops are cut and collected from fields **2** [C] the quality or amount of crops that are collected

harvest[2] /ˈhɑːvɪst/ verb [I, T] to cut and collect crops when they are ready

has strong /hæz/ weak /həz/, /əz/, /z/ present simple he/she/it of have

has-been /ˈhæzbiːn/ noun [C] informal someone who was famous or important in the past but is now ignored

hash /hæʃ/ noun UK **1 make a hash of sth** informal to do something very badly **2** [U] (also **the hash key**) a key on a computer keyboard or

a phone with the symbol #: *Please press the hash key to continue.*

hashish /ˈhæʃiːʃ/ noun [U] (also **hash**) an illegal drug that is usually smoked for pleasure

hasn't /ˈhæzᵊnt/ short for has not: *It hasn't rained for three weeks.*

hassle[1] /ˈhæsl/ noun [C, U] **1** something that is annoying because it is difficult or unpleasant to do: *I don't want to drive – it's such a hassle finding a place to park.* **2** an argument or fight: *They aren't giving you any hassle, are they?*

hassle[2] /ˈhæsl/ verb [T] to annoy someone especially by asking them something again and again: *He's always hassling me about money*

haste /heɪst/ noun [U] a situation in which you are in a hurry and do something more quickly than you should: *In their haste to escape, they left behind all their belongings.*

> ☑ Word partners for **haste**
>
> indecent/undue haste • in sb's haste • do sth in haste

hasten /ˈheɪsᵊn/ verb **1** [T] to make something happen faster than usual **2 hasten to do sth** to hurry to do or say something: *I was not, I hasten to add, the only male there.*

hasty /ˈheɪsti/ adj done very quickly, usually too quickly and without thinking enough: *a hasty decision/remark* • **hastily** adv

hat /hæt/ noun [C] ② something you wear to cover your head, for fashion or protection: *cowboy hat* → See also **bowler hat, top hat**

hatch[1] /hætʃ/ verb **1** [I, T] If an egg hatches or is hatched, it is broken open by a baby creature such as a bird, fish, or snake being born. **2 hatch a plan/plot, etc** to plan something secretly especially something bad: *He hatched a plot to kill his wife.*

hatch[2] /hætʃ/ noun [C] a small door or opening especially in a ship, aircraft, or spacecraft: *escape hatch*

hatchback /ˈhætʃbæk/ noun [C] a car that has a large door at the back, which you lift up to open

hatchet /ˈhætʃɪt/ noun [C] a small axe (= tool for cutting wood)

IDIOM **bury the hatchet** to forget about your arguments and become friends with someone again

hate[1] /heɪt/ verb [T] **1** ② to dislike someone or something very much: *They've hated each other since they were kids.* ∘ [+ doing sth] *He hates going to the dentist's.* ∘ [+ to do sth] *I hate to see you look so upset.* **2** used to emphasize that you are sorry you have to do something: *I hate to interrupt, John, but we need to leave.* → See also **hate sb's guts**

hate[2] /heɪt/ noun [U] a very strong dislike of someone or something → See also **pet hate**

hateful /ˈheɪtfᵊl/ adj extremely unpleasant or unkind: *She called me the most hateful names.*

hatred /ˈheɪtrɪd/ noun [U] a very strong dislike of someone or something: *He developed a intense hatred of all women.*

☑ Word partners for **hatred**

deep/intense hatred • racial hatred • hatred of sb/sth

---

at ˌtrick noun [C] three successes by a player or team, one after the other, especially three goals in a game

aughty /'hɔːti/ adj showing that you think you are much better or more important than other people: *a haughty young actress* • **haughtily** adv

aul¹ /hɔːl/ verb [T] to pull something somewhere slowly and with difficulty: *They hauled the piano into the living room.*

aul² /hɔːl/ noun **1** [C] an amount of something that has been stolen or that is owned illegally: *a haul of arms/drugs* **2** **be a long haul** to be difficult and take a long time

aulage /'hɔːlɪdʒ/ noun [U] UK the business of moving things by road or railway: *a road haulage firm*

aunt¹ /hɔːnt/ verb [T] **1** ⬤ If a ghost haunts a place, it appears there often: *a haunted house* **2** ⬤ If an unpleasant memory or feeling haunts you, you think about or feel it often: [often passive] *He was haunted by memories of the war.*

aunt² /hɔːnt/ noun [C] a place that someone visits often: *Regents Park is one of my favourite haunts in London.*

aunting /'hɔːntɪŋ/ adj beautiful, but in a sad way: *the haunting beauty of Africa*

ave¹ strong /hæv/ weak /həv, əv, v/ **auxiliary verb** (**had**, singular **has**) ⬤ used with the past participle of another verb to form the present and past perfect tenses: *Have you seen Roz?* ◦ *I've passed my test.* ◦ *He hasn't visited London before.* ◦ *It would have been better to tell the truth.* ◦ *He's been working in France for two years now.* ◦ *I had met his wife before.*

ave² /hæv/ **modal verb 1 have to do sth; have got to do sth** ⬤ to need to do something or be forced to do something: *I have to go to Berlin tomorrow.* ◦ *Do we have to finish this today?* ◦ *They've had to change their plans.* **2** ⬤ used when you are telling someone how to do something: *You've got to type in your name, then your password.* **3** used to say that you feel certain that something is true or will happen: *Interest rates have to come down at some point.* ◦ *There's (= there has) got to be a better way of doing this.* → See Study Page **Modal verbs** on page Centre 22

ave³ strong /hæv/ weak /həv, əv, v/ **verb** (**had**, singular **has**) **1** OWN ▷ [T] (also mainly UK **have got**) ⬤ to own something: *I have two horses.* ◦ *Laura has got beautiful blue eyes.* **2** HOLD ▷ [T] ⬤ used to say that someone is holding something, or that someone or something is with them: *He had a pen in his hand.* ◦ *She had a small child with her.* **3** BE SICK ▷ [T] (also mainly UK **have got**) ⬤ If you have a particular illness, you are suffering from it: *Have you ever had the measles?* **4** EAT/DRINK ▷ [T] ⬤ to eat or drink something: *We are having dinner at 7 o'clock.* ◦ *Can I have a drink of water?* **5 have a bath/sleep/walk, etc** ⬤ used with nouns to say that someone does some-

thing: *Can I have a quick shower?* ◦ *Let Mark have a try.* **6 have difficulty/fun/problems, etc** ⬤ used with nouns to say that someone experiences something: *We had a great time in Barcelona.* **7 have a baby** ⬤ to give birth to a baby **8 have sth done** ⬤ If you have something done, someone does it for you: *I'm having my hair cut tomorrow.* ◦ *We had the carpets cleaned.*

IDIOMS **have had it** to be broken or not working well: *I think the car engine's had it.* • **have it in for sb** to dislike someone and want to cause problems for them: *She really has it in for me – I don't know what I've done to offend her.* • **have it out (with sb)** to talk to someone about something they have done that made you angry, in order to try to solve the problem

PHRASAL VERBS **have (got) sth on** ⬤ to be wearing something: *The only had a bikini on.* • **have sb on** UK to make someone think that something is true, as a joke: *He's not really angry – he's just having you on.* • **have sth out** to have something removed from your body: *I'm having two teeth out next week.*

haven /'heɪvᵊn/ noun [C] a safe place: *a haven for wildlife*

haven't /'hævᵊnt/ short for have not: *I haven't finished eating.*

havoc /'hævək/ noun [U] a very confused and possibly dangerous situation: *The snow has caused havoc on Scotland's roads today.*

☑ Word partners for **havoc**

cause/create/wreak havoc • play havoc with sth

---

hawk /hɔːk/ noun [C] a large hunting bird

hay /heɪ/ noun [U] dried grass for animals to eat

ˈhay ˌfever noun [U] an illness caused by a bad reaction to plants that some people get in the summer, especially affecting the nose and eyes

haystack /'heɪstæk/ noun [C] a large pile of hay

hazard¹ /'hæzəd/ noun **1** [C] something that is dangerous: *a fire hazard* ◦ *a health hazard* **2 an occupational hazard** something unpleasant that sometimes happens to people who do a particular job

hazard² /'hæzəd/ verb **hazard a guess** to risk guessing something: *I don't know where he is, but I'd be willing to hazard a guess.*

hazardous /'hæzədəs/ adj dangerous: *hazardous chemicals*

haze /heɪz/ noun [U] the air when it is not very clear because of something such as heat or smoke, making it difficult to see well

hazel /'heɪzᵊl/ adj green-brown in colour: *hazel eyes*

hazy /'heɪzi/ adj **1** If the air is hazy, it is not very clear because of something such as heat or smoke, making it difficult to see well: *a hazy day* **2** not remembering things clearly: *He has only a hazy recollection of what happened.*

HD adj abbreviation for high definition: used to describe a system for showing very clear

H

---

pictures on a television or computer screen or for producing very clear sound: **HD DVD/radio**

he strong /hiː/ weak /hi/ **pronoun** 🅐 used as the subject of the verb when referring to someone male who has already been talked about: *"When is Paul coming?" "He'll be here in a minute."*

head¹ /hed/ **noun** [C] **1 BODY** ▷ 🅐 the part of your body above your neck that contains your brain, eyes, ears, mouth, nose, etc and on which your hair grows: *He fell and hit his head on the table.* → See colour picture **The Body** on page Centre 13 **2 MIND** ▷ 🅑 your mind: *All the time these thoughts were going round in my head.* **3 ORGANIZATION** ▷ 🅑 the person who is in charge of an organization: *Her father is the head of an oil company.* **4 SCHOOL** ▷ (also ˌhead ˈteacher) UK 🅐 the person in charge of a school: *You'll have to ask the head if you can have a day off school.* **5 FRONT/TOP** ▷ the front or top part of something: *Who is that at the head of the table?* **6 £10/$6, etc a head** costing £10/$6, etc for each person: *The meal costs 20 euros a head.* **7 heads** the side of a coin that has a picture of someone's head on it: *Heads or tails?*

IDIOMS **be banging your head against a brick wall** to do, say, or ask for something repeatedly but to be unable to change a situation • **come to a head** If a problem or disagreement comes to a head, it becomes so bad that you have to start dealing with it. • **go over sb's head** to be too difficult for someone to understand: *All this talk about philosophy went right over my head.* • **go to your head** If something that you have achieved goes to your head, it makes you too proud: *Fame and fortune had gone to his head.* • **hang your head (in shame)** to look ashamed or embarrassed • **keep your head** to stay calm in a difficult situation • **lose your head** to stop being calm in a difficult situation • **raise/rear its ugly head** If a problem or something unpleasant raises its ugly head, it becomes a problem that people have to deal with. • **laugh/shout/scream, etc your head off** to laugh/shout/scream, etc very much and very loudly

→ See also **hit the nail¹ on the head**, **a roof over your head**, **off the top¹ of your head**

head² /hed/ **verb 1 head back/down/towards, etc** 🅑 to move in a particular direction: *They headed back to the shore.* **2 LEAD** ▷ [T] 🅑 to lead an organization or group: [often passive] *The company is headed by a young entrepreneur.* **3 FRONT/TOP** ▷ [T] to be at the front or top of something: *Jo headed a very short list of candidates.* **4 HIT** ▷ [T] to hit a ball with your head: *Owen headed the ball straight into the back of the net.*

PHRASAL VERBS **be heading for sth** 🅑 to be likely to get or experience something soon: *Those children are heading for trouble.* • **head off** to start a journey or leave a place

headache /ˈhedeɪk/ **noun** [C] 🅐 pain inside your head: *I've got a bad headache.* → See also **splitting headache**

headhunt /ˈhedhʌnt/ **verb** [T] to persuade someone to leave their job for a job with a

different company: *She was headhunted by rival firm.* • **headhunter noun** [C]

heading /ˈhedɪŋ/ **noun** [C] words at the top of a piece of writing that tell you what it is about

headlight /ˈhedlaɪt/ **noun** [C] one of the two large lights on the front of a car → See picture **light**

headline /ˈhedlaɪn/ **noun 1** 🅑 [C] the title of a newspaper story that is printed in large letters above it: *a front-page headline* **2 the headline** 🅑 the main stories in newspapers, on television, etc: *The story hit the headlines the very next day.*

headlong /ˈhedlɒŋ/ **adv** quickly and directly: *The plane plunged headlong into the sea.*

headmaster /ˌhedˈmɑːstər/ **noun** [C] UK (U **principal**) a man who is in charge of a school

headmistress /ˌhedˈmɪstrəs/ **noun** [C] UK (U **principal**) a woman who is in charge of a school

ˌhead ˈoffice **noun** [usually singular] the most important office of a company, or the people who work there: *Head office handles all complaints made against the company.*

ˌhead ˈon **adv 1** If two vehicles hit each other head on, the front parts hit each other as they are moving forward. **2** If you deal with something head on, you deal with it directly, although it is difficult. • **head-on** /ˌhedˈɒn/ **adj** *a head-on collision*

headphones

headphones

earphones

headphones /ˈhedfəʊnz/ **noun** [plural] a piece of equipment that you wear over your ears so that you can listen to music without anyone else hearing it: *a pair of headphones*

headquarters /ˈhedˌkwɔːtəz/ **noun** [group] (plural **headquarters**) 🅑 the place from where an organization is controlled: *police headquarters*

headset /ˈhedset/ **noun** [C] a piece of equipment that you wear over your ears so that you can hear things, especially one with a microphone (= a piece of equipment that you speak into) attached to it: *a mobile phone headset*

head start noun [C] an advantage that someone has over other people: *Caroline's language skills should give her a head start over/on other people applying for the job.*

headstone /ˈhedstəʊn/ noun [C] a stone that shows the name of a dead person who is buried under it

headstrong /ˈhedstrɒŋ/ adj extremely determined: *a headstrong young girl*

heads-up /ˈhedzʌp/ noun [usually singular] informal a warning that something is going to happen, usually so that you can prepare for it

headteacher /ˌhedˈtiːtʃər/ noun [C] UK (US **principal**) ⓐ the person in charge of a school

headway /ˈhedweɪ/ noun **make headway** to make progress in what you are doing: *The builders aren't making much headway with our new house.*

heady /ˈhedi/ adj having a powerful effect on the way you feel, for example by making you feel excited: *a heady experience*

heal /hiːl/ verb [I, T] (also **heal up**) ⓑ If a wound or broken bone heals, it becomes healthy again, and if something heals it, it makes it healthy again: *The wound on his head had begun to heal.* • **healer** noun [C] someone who makes sick people well again using something such as prayer or magic

health /helθ/ noun [U] **1** ⓐ the condition of your body: *to be in good/poor health* ◦ *Regular exercise is good for your health.* **2** how successful and strong something is: *the financial health of the business* → See also **the National Health Service**

☑ Word partners for **health**
damage/improve sb's health • **excellent/good/ill/poor** health • **be in** [good/bad, etc] health

health and safety noun [U] a set of rules intended to protect people from illness or injury caused by their work: *health and safety regulations*

health-care /ˈhelθˌkeər/ noun [U] the set of services provided by a country or an organization for treating people who are sick

health club noun [C] a private club where people can go to do exercise to keep fit

health food noun [C, U] food that is believed to be good for you because it does not contain artificial chemicals or much sugar or fat

health service noun [C] UK the National Health Service: *the system providing free medical service in the UK*

healthy /ˈhelθi/ adj **1** PHYSICALLY STRONG ▷ ⓐ physically strong and well: *Sue is a normal healthy child.* **2** GOOD ▷ ⓐ good for your health: *a healthy diet* **3** SUCCESSFUL ▷ successful and strong: *a healthy economy* → Opposite **unhealthy**

Common learner error: **healthy** or **health**?
Remember not to use 'healthy' as a noun. If you need a noun, use **health**.
She has some health problems.
~~She has some healthy problems.~~

heap¹ /hiːp/ noun **1** [C] an untidy pile of things: *a heap of rubbish* **2 heaps of sth** informal a lot of something: *He's got heaps of money.*

☑ Word partners for **heap**
a heap **of** sth • **in** a heap

heap² /hiːp/ verb informal **1** [T] to put things into an untidy pile: *He heaped more food onto his plate.* **2 heap criticism/insults/praise, etc on sb** to criticize/insult/praise, etc someone a lot

hear /hɪər/ verb (**heard**) **1** SOUND ▷ [I, T] ⓐ to be aware of a sound through your ears: *I could hear his voice in the distance.* ◦ *I can't hear – can you turn the sound up?* **2** INFORMATION ▷ [I, T] ⓑ to be told some information: *When did you first hear about this?* ◦ *Have you heard the news? Jane's back.* ◦ *[+ (that)] I hear that you're leaving.* **3** LAW ▷ [T] If a judge hears a case, they listen to it in a law court, to decide if someone is guilty or not. **4 will not hear of sth** If someone will not hear of something, they will not allow it: *I wanted to pay for her meal but she wouldn't hear of it.*

PHRASAL VERBS **hear from sb** ⓑ to receive a letter, telephone call, or other message from someone: *Have you heard from Sue recently?* • **have heard of sb/sth** ⓑ to know that someone or something exists: *I've never heard of her.*

hearing /ˈhɪərɪŋ/ noun **1** [U] the ability to hear sounds: *He lost his hearing when he was a child.* **2** [C] a meeting in a law court when a judge hears the facts of a case: *The preliminary hearing will take place next week.* **3 a fair hearing** If you get a fair hearing, someone listens to your opinion.

hearing aid noun [C] a small piece of equipment worn inside or next to the ear by people who cannot hear well in order to help them to hear better

hearing-impaired /ˈhɪərɪŋɪmˌpeəd/ adj A person who is hearing-impaired cannot hear or cannot hear well. → Compare **deaf**

hearsay /ˈhɪəseɪ/ noun [U] things that people have told you and that may or may not be true: *Everything we heard was based on hearsay and rumour.*

hearse /hɜːs/ noun [C] a large car that is used to take a dead body to a funeral

heart /hɑːt/ noun **1** ORGAN ▷ [C] ⓐ the organ inside your chest that sends blood around your body: *Isabel's heart was beating fast.* ◦ *heart disease/failure* **2** CENTRE ▷ [no plural] the centre of something: *Her office is in the heart of Tokyo.* **3 the heart of sth** ⓑ the most important part of something: *We need to get to the heart of the matter.* **4** FEELINGS ▷ [C, U] ⓑ someone's deepest feelings and true character: *She has a kind heart.* **5** SHAPE ▷ [C] a shape that is used to

heart

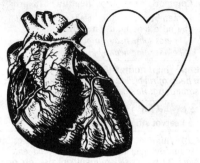

H

mean love **6 hearts** playing cards with red, heart shapes on them **7 at heart** used to say what someone is really like: *I'm just a kid at heart.* **8 in your heart** used to say what you really think: *In his heart he felt they were wrong.* **9 with all your heart** used to say that you feel something very strongly: *I thank you with all my heart.* **10 not have the heart to do sth** to decide not to do something that would make someone unhappy **11 learn/know, etc sth by heart** ⓑ to be able to remember all of something

IDIOMS **break sb's heart** ⓑ to make someone very unhappy • **heart and soul** used to say that you give all your attention and enthusiasm to something: *She threw herself into teaching heart and soul.*

→ See also **a change² of heart**

> 🗹 Word partners for **heart**
>
> your heart **beats** • heart **disease/failure** • a heart **condition/problem**

heartache /ˈhɑːteɪk/ noun [C, U] extreme sadness

ˈheart atˌtack noun [C] ⓑ a medical problem in which someone's heart suddenly stops working correctly, sometimes causing death: *I think he's had a heart attack.*

heartbeat /ˈhɑːtbiːt/ noun [C, U] the regular movement of the heart as it moves blood around the body

heartbreaking /ˈhɑːtˌbreɪkɪŋ/ adj causing extreme sadness: *heartbreaking news*

heartbroken /ˈhɑːtˌbrəʊkən/ adj If you are heartbroken, you feel extremely sad about something that has happened.

heartened /ˈhɑːtənd/ adj feeling happier because of something: *We all felt heartened by the news.* → Opposite **disheartened**

heartening /ˈhɑːtənɪŋ/ adj making you feel happier: *heartening news* → Opposite **disheartening**

ˈheart ˌfailure noun [U] a serious medical problem in which someone's heart stops working, often causing death

heartfelt /ˈhɑːtfelt/ adj Heartfelt feelings and words are strong and sincere: *heartfelt thanks/gratitude*

hearth /hɑːθ/ noun [C] the floor around a fireplace

heartily /ˈhɑːtɪli/ adv **1** with a lot of enthusiasm: *We all laughed heartily at the joke.* **2** completely or very much: *I am heartily sick of the situation.*

heartland /ˈhɑːtlænd/ noun [C] the place where an activity or belief is strongest: *the traditional heartland of the motor industry*

heartless /ˈhɑːtləs/ adj cruel and not caring about other people

heart-to-heart /ˌhɑːttəˈhɑːt/ noun [C] a serious conversation between two people in which they talk honestly about their feelings

hearty /ˈhɑːti/ adj **1** friendly and full of energy: *hearty laugh/welcome* **2** Hearty meals are large and satisfy you.

heat¹ /hiːt/ noun **1** HOT ▷ [U] ⓑ the quality of being hot or warm: *the heat of summer* **2** the heat hot weather: *I don't really like the heat.* **3** TEMPERATURE ▷ [U, no plural] ⓑ the temperature of something: *Cook on a low heat.* **4** the heat US (UK the heating) the system that keeps a building warm: *Could you turn the heat up a little?* **5** RACE ▷ [C] a competition, especially a race, which decides who will be in the final event

IDIOM **in the heat of the moment** If you do or say something in the heat of the moment, you do or say it without thinking because you are angry or excited.

→ See also **dead heat**

> 🗹 Word partners for **heat**
>
> **generate/give out** heat • **intense/searing** heat

heat² /hiːt/ verb [I, T] (also **heat up**) ⓑ to make something become hot or warm, or to become hot or warm: *I'll just heat up some soup.*

heated /ˈhiːtɪd/ adj **1** made warm or hot **2** a **heated argument/debate, etc** an angry or excited argument

heater /ˈhiːtər/ noun [C] ⓑ a machine that heats air or water

heath /hiːθ/ noun [C] an open area of land covered with wild plants and rough grass

heather /ˈheðər/ noun [C, U] a small plant with purple or white flowers that grows on hills

heating /ˈhiːtɪŋ/ noun [U] UK (US **heat**) ⓐ the system that keeps a building warm → See also **central heating**

heatwave /ˈhiːtweɪv/ noun [C] a period of time, usually a few days or weeks, when the weather is much hotter than usual

heave /hiːv/ verb **1** [I, T] to move something heavy using a lot of effort: *He heaved the bag on to his shoulder.* **2** [I] to move up and down: *He chest heaved as she started to cry.* **3 heave a sigh of relief** to breathe out loudly because you are pleased that something bad has not happened • **heave** noun [C]

heaven /ˈhevən/ noun [U] **1** ⓑ according to some religions, the place where good people go when they die **2** informal ⓑ something very nice that gives you great pleasure: *This cake is absolute heaven.*

heavenly /ˈhevᵊnli/ **adj 1** [always before noun] relating to heaven: *the heavenly kingdom* **2** informal very nice: *a heavenly day*

heavens /ˈhevᵊnz/ **noun 1 the heavens** literary the sky **2 (Good) Heavens!** used when you are surprised or annoyed: *Heavens, what's the matter?*

heavily /ˈhevɪli/ **adv 1** 🔒 a lot or to a great degree: *She's heavily involved in politics.* **2 drink/smoke heavily** to drink/smoke a lot **3 rain/snow heavily** to rain/snow a lot **4** using a lot of force: *to breathe heavily*

heavy /ˈhevi/ **adj 1 WEIGHING A LOT** ▷ 🔒 Heavy objects weigh a lot: *heavy bags* ∘ *heavy machinery/equipment* **2 HOW MUCH** ▷ 🔒 used to say how much someone or something weighs: *How heavy are you?* ∘ *Oxygen is sixteen times heavier than hydrogen.* **3 A LOT** ▷ 🔒 large in amount or degree: *heavy traffic* ∘ *heavy costs* **4 a heavy drinker/smoker** someone who drinks/smokes a lot **5 heavy snow/rain** an occasion when a lot of snow/rain falls **6 FORCE** ▷ using a lot of force: *a heavy blow* ∘ *heavy breathing* **7 SERIOUS** ▷ informal serious: *The discussion got a bit too heavy.* **8 heavy going** mainly UK too serious or difficult: *I found the book very heavy going.*

heavy-handed /ˌheviˈhændɪd/ **adj** using too much force in dealing with people

heavy ˈmetal noun [U] a type of very loud, modern music

heavyweight /ˈheviweɪt/ **noun** [C] **1** a fighter such as a boxer who is in the heaviest weight group: *the heavyweight champion of the world* **2** someone who is powerful and important: *a political heavyweight*

Hebrew /ˈhiːbruː/ **noun** [U] the language used in the Jewish religion and in Israel • **Hebrew adj**

hectare /ˈhekteər/ **noun** [C] a unit for measuring area, equal to 10,000 square metres

hectic /ˈhektɪk/ **adj** extremely busy and full of activity: *a hectic day/week*

he'd /hiːd/ **1** short for he had: *We knew he'd taken the money.* **2** short for he would: *No one thought he'd get the job.*

hedge¹ /hedʒ/ **noun** [C] 🔒 a row of bushes growing close together, often used to divide land into separate areas

hedge² /hedʒ/ **verb** [I, T] to avoid giving a direct answer → See also **hedge your bets (bet²)**

hedge

hedgehog /ˈhedʒhɒg/ **noun** [C] a small animal whose body is covered with sharp points

hedgerow /ˈhedʒrəʊ/ **noun** [C] UK a row of bushes and small trees along the edge of a field or road

heed¹ /hiːd/ **verb** [T] formal to pay attention to some advice or a warning: *Officials failed to heed his warning.*

heed² /hiːd/ **noun** formal **take heed of sth** to pay

attention to something, especially some advice or a warning

heel /hiːl/ **noun** [C] **1** 🔒 the back part of your foot → See colour picture **The Body** on page Centre 13 **2** 🔒 the part of a shoe that is under your heel: *high heels*

hefty /ˈhefti/ **adj** informal very large: *a hefty bill/fine* ∘ *a hefty woman with dyed hair*

height /haɪt/ **noun 1 HOW TALL** ▷ [C, U] 🔒 how tall or high something or someone is: *a man of average height* ∘ *The tower measures 27.28 metres in height.* **2 HOW FAR UP** ▷ [C, U] 🔒 how far above the ground something is: *The aircraft was flying at a height of about 6000 metres.* **3 TALL** ▷ [U] being tall: *People always make comments about his height.* **4 the height of sth** the strongest or most important part of something: *I met him when he was at the height of his fame.*

> 🗒 Word partners for **height**
>
> **grow to/reach** a height of sth • be [3 metres, etc] **in** height

heighten /ˈhaɪtᵊn/ **verb** [I, T] to increase or make something increase: *heightened awareness* ∘ [often passive] *The book's success was heightened by the scandal.*

heights /haɪts/ **noun** [plural] high places: *I've always been afraid of heights.*

IDIOM **new heights** more success or improvement than ever before: *Our athletes have reached new heights of sporting glory.*

heinous /ˈheɪnəs/ **adj** formal very bad and shocking: *heinous crimes*

heir /eər/ **noun** [C] a person who will have the legal right to someone's money and possessions when they die: *He is the heir to a huge fortune.*

heiress /ˈeəres/ **noun** [C] a woman who will have the legal right to someone's money and possessions when they die

held /held/ past of hold

helicopter

helicopter /ˈhelɪkɒptər/ **noun** [C] 🔒 an aircraft that flies using long, thin parts on top of it that turn round and round very fast

helium /ˈhiːliəm/ **noun** [U] a gas that is lighter than air and that will not burn: *a helium balloon*

hell /hel/ **noun 1** [U] 🔒 according to some religions, the place where bad people go when they die **2** [U] informal 🔒 an experience that is

H

very unpleasant: *It's been hell working with him.*
3 the hell informal ⓑ② used to emphasize something in a rude or angry way: *What the hell are you doing here?* **4 a/one hell of a** informal used to say that someone or something is very good, big, etc: *a hell of a noise* ○ *He's one hell of a tennis player.* **5 from hell** informal used to say that someone or something is extremely bad: *We had the holiday from hell.* **6 like hell** informal very much: *It's raining like hell out there.*

he'll /hiːl/ short for he will: *He'll be home soon.*

hellish /'helɪʃ/ **adj** informal extremely bad or unpleasant: *a hellish place/journey*

hello (also UK **hallo**) /hel'əʊ/ **exclamation 1** ⓐ① used to greet someone: *Hello, Chris, how are things?* **2** ⓐ① used to start a conversation on the telephone: *Hello, this is Alex.*

helm /helm/ **noun 1** [C] the part that you use to direct a boat or ship **2 at the helm** controlling a group or organization: *With Lewis at the helm we are certain of success.*

helmet

helmet /'helmət/ **noun** [C] ⓑ② a hard hat that protects your head: *a cycling helmet* → See also **crash helmet** → See colour picture **Sports 2** on page Centre 15

> ➕ **Other ways of saying help**
>
> The verbs **aid** and **assist** are more formal alternatives to 'help':
> *The army arrived to **assist** in the search.*
> *The project is designed to **aid** poorer countries.*
>
> If two or more people help each other in order to achieve the same thing, verbs such as **collaborate** or **cooperate** are sometimes used:
> *Several countries are **collaborating/cooperating** in the relief effort.*
>
> The verb **benefit** is sometimes used when someone is helped by something:
> *The children have **benefited** greatly from the new facilities.*
>
> If someone is asking for help, in informal situations the expression **give** someone **a hand** is sometimes used:
> *Do you think you could **give** me **a hand** with these heavy boxes?*

help¹ /help/ **verb 1** [I, T] ⓐ① to make it easier for someone to do something: *Thank you for helping.* ○ [+ (to) do sth] *Shall I help you to set the table?* ○ *Dad always helps me with my homework.* **2** [I, T] ⓑ② to make something easier or better: [+ to do sth] *When you're nervous or frightened, it helps to breathe slowly and deeply.* **3 can't/couldn't help sth** ⓑ① to be unable to stop yourself doing something or to stop something happening: [+ doing sth] *I couldn't help thinking about what had happened.* ○ *He couldn't help it, he slipped.* **4 help yourself (to sth)** ⓑ① to take

something, especially food or drink, without asking: *Please help yourself to some coffee.*

PHRASAL VERB **help (sb) out** ⓑ② to help someone, especially by giving them money or working for them: *Carol's been helping out in the shop this week.*

help² /help/ **noun 1** [U] ⓐ② the things someone does to help another person: *I was too embarrassed to **ask for help**.* ○ *Do you want any help?* **2** [no plural] ⓑ② something or someone that helps: *Dave has been a great help to me.* **3 with the help of sth** ⓑ① using something: *We assembled the computer with the help of the manual.*

> 🔲 **Word partners for help**
>
> ask for/need/offer/provide/refuse help ● a big/great help ● extra/professional help

help³ /help/ **exclamation** ⓐ② something that you shout when you are in danger

help desk **noun** [C] a service that provides help to the people who use a computer network (= group of computers that share information and programs)

helper /'helpər/ **noun** [C] ⓑ② someone who helps another person to do something

helpful /'helpfᵊl/ **adj 1** ⓑ① useful: *helpful advice/comments* **2** ⓑ① willing to help: *The staff here are very helpful.* → Opposite **unhelpful** ● **helpfully** **adv** ● **helpfulness** **noun** [U]

helping /'helpɪŋ/ **noun** [C] an amount of food given to one person at one time: *She gave me a very large helping of pasta.*

helpless /'helpləs/ **adj** not able to defend yourself or do things without help: *a helpless animal/child* ● **helplessly** **adv**

helpline /'helplaɪn/ **noun** [C] UK a telephone number that you can ring for help or information: *If you have any questions about any of our products, just **call** our **helpline**.*

hem /hem/ **noun** [C] the edge of a piece of clothing or cloth that has been folded under and sewn ● **hem** **verb** [T] (**hemming, hemmed**) to sew a hem on a piece of clothing or cloth

hemisphere /'hemɪsfɪər/ **noun** [C] one half of the Earth: *birds of the northern hemisphere*

hemophilia /ˌhiːməˈfɪliə/ **noun** [U] US spelling of haemophilia (= a serious disease in which the flow of blood from someone's body cannot be stopped when they are hurt)

hemophiliac /ˌhiːməˈfɪliæk/ **noun** [C] US spelling of haemophiliac (= someone who has haemophilia)

hemorrhage /'hemᵊrɪdʒ/ **noun** [C, U] US spelling of haemorrhage (= a medical problem in which someone suddenly loses a lot of blood from part of their body)

hemorrhoids /'hemᵊrɔɪdz/ **noun** [plural] US spelling of haemorrhoids (= painful swollen tissue around the opening of a person's bottom)

hemp /hemp/ **noun** [U] a plant that is used for making rope, cloth, and the drug cannabis

en /hen/ **noun** [C] a female bird, especially a chicken

ence /hens/ **adv 1** for this reason: *He's got an interview today, hence the suit.* **2 three weeks/ two months, etc hence** formal three weeks/two months, etc from this time

enceforth /ˌhens'fɔːθ/ **adv** formal from this time: *Henceforth only English may be spoken in this classroom.*

enchman /'henʃmən/ **noun** [C] (plural **henchmen**) someone who does unpleasant jobs for a powerful person

en ˌnight noun [C] (also ˈhen ˌparty) a party for women only, usually one held for a woman before she gets married → Compare **stag night**

epatitis /ˌhepə'taɪtɪs/ **noun** [U] a serious disease that affects your liver (= the organ that cleans your blood)

er¹ strong /hɜːʳ/ weak /hǝʳ/, /ǝʳ/ **pronoun 1** ⓐ used after a verb or preposition to refer to someone female who has already been talked about: *Where's Kath – have you seen her?* **2** used to refer to a country or ship: *God bless HMS Victoria and all who sail in her.*

er² strong /hɜːʳ/ weak /hǝʳ/ **determiner** ⓐ belonging to or relating to someone female who has already been talked about: *That's her house on the corner.* ◦ *It's not her fault.*

erald¹ /'herǝld/ **verb** [T] to be a sign that a particular event will happen soon: *Thick black clouds heralded rain.*

erald² /'herǝld/ **noun** [C] a sign that a particular event will happen soon: *A fall in unemployment was the **herald of** economic recovery.*

erb /hɜːb/ ⓤ /ɜːrb/ **noun** [C] ⓑ a plant that is used in cooking to add flavour to food or used in medicines • **herbal** /'hɜːbᵊl/ **adj** *herbal medicine*

erd¹ /hɜːd/ **noun** [C] a large group of animals such as cows that live and eat together: *a herd of cattle/deer*

erd² /hɜːd/ **verb** [T] If people or animals are herded somewhere, they are moved there in a group: [often passive] *The passengers were quickly herded onto a bus.*

ere /hɪǝʳ/ **adv 1 IN THIS PLACE** ▷ ⓐ in the place where you are: *Does Jane live near here?* ◦ *Come here!* **2 GETTING ATTENTION** ▷ used to bring someone's attention to someone or something: *Look, here's our bus.* ◦ *Here, put this on.* **3 here you are/ here he is, etc** ⓐ used when you see someone or something you have been looking for or waiting for: *Here she is at last.* ◦ *Here we are, this is the place.* **4 GIVING** ▷ ⓐ used when you are giving someone something: *Here's a present for you.* **5 Here you are.** ⓐ used when you are giving someone something: *"Have you got the paper?" "Here you are."* **6 AT THIS POINT** ▷ ⓑ at this point in a discussion: *I don't have time here to go into all the arguments.* **7 ON THE TELEPHONE** ▷ ⓐ used when saying who you are on the telephone: *Hello, it's Tim here.* **8 here and there** ⓑ in several different places but without any pattern: *Tall trees were growing here and there.*

hereafter /ˌhɪǝr'ɑːftǝʳ/ **adv** formal from now or after this time

hereby /ˌhɪǝ'baɪ/ **adv** formal with these words or this action: *I hereby declare you the winner.*

hereditary /hɪ'redɪtᵊri/ **adj 1** passed to a child from its parents before birth: *Depression is often hereditary.* **2** passed from parent to child as a right: *a **hereditary title***

heredity /hɪ'redǝti/ **noun** [U] the way in which mental or physical qualities pass from parent to child

heresy /'herǝsi/ **noun** [C, U] a belief that is against what a group or society generally believes to be right or good

heretic /'herǝtɪk/ **noun** [C] someone with a belief that is against what a group or society generally believes to be right or good • **heretical** /hǝ'retɪkᵊl/ **adj**

heritage /'herɪtɪdʒ/ **noun** [U] the buildings, paintings, customs, etc that are important in a culture or society because they have existed for a long time: *our architectural/cultural heritage*

hermit /'hɜːmɪt/ **noun** [C] someone who chooses to live alone and away from other people

hernia /'hɜːnɪǝ/ **noun** [C] a medical condition in which an organ pushes through the muscle which is around it

hero /'hɪǝrǝʊ/ **noun** [C] (plural **heroes**) **1** ⓑ someone who does something brave or good that people respect or admire them for: *He became a **national hero** for his part in the revolution.* **2** ⓑ the main male character in a book or film who is usually good: *the hero of her new novel*

✔ Word partners for **hero**
a **local/national** hero • an **unsung** hero

heroic /hɪ'rǝʊɪk/ **adj 1** very brave: *a **heroic figure*** ◦ *a heroic act/deed* **2** If someone makes a heroic effort to do something, they work very hard to try to do it: *In spite of England's **heroic efforts**, they lost the match.* • **heroically adv**

heroics /hɪ'rǝʊɪks/ **noun** [plural] actions that seem brave but are stupid because they are dangerous

heroin /'herǝʊɪn/ **noun** [U] a very strong drug that some people use illegally for pleasure: *a **heroin** addict*

heroine /'herǝʊɪn/ **noun** [C] **1** the main female character in a book or film, who is usually good: *the heroine of the film 'Alien'* **2** a woman who does something brave or good that people respect or admire her for

heroism /'herǝʊɪzᵊm/ **noun** [U] very brave behaviour: *an act of heroism*

herring /'herɪŋ/ **noun** [C, U] a small, silver-coloured fish that lives in the sea and is eaten as food → See also **red herring**

hers /hɜːz/ **pronoun** ⓐ the things that belong to or relate to someone female who has already been talked about: *That's Ann's coat over there – at least I think it's hers.* ◦ *I borrowed it from a friend of hers.*

herself /hǝ'self/ **pronoun 1** ⓐ the reflexive form

of the pronoun 'she': *She kept telling herself that nothing was wrong.* **2** ⓐ used to emphasize the pronoun 'she' or the particular female person you are referring to: *She decorated the cake herself.* **3 (all) by herself** ⓐ alone or without anyone else's help: *She managed to put her shoes on all by herself.* **4 (all) to herself** for her use only: *My sister's got the house to herself this weekend.*

hertz /hɜːts/ **noun** [C] (plural **hertz**) (written abbreviation **Hz**) a unit for measuring the frequency (= how often the wave is repeated) of a sound wave

he's /hiːz/ **1** short for he is: *He's my best friend.* **2** short for he has: *Sam must be tired – he's been dancing all night!*

hesitant /ˈhezɪtᵊnt/ **adj** If you are hesitant, you do not do something immediately or quickly because you are nervous or not certain: *She was hesitant about returning to her home town.* • **hesitantly adv** • **hesitancy noun** [U]

hesitate /ˈhezɪteɪt/ **verb 1** ⓑ [I] to pause before doing something, especially because you are nervous or not certain: *Richard hesitated before answering.* **2 not hesitate to do sth** ⓑ to be very willing to do something because you are certain it is right: *They would not hesitate to call the police at the first sign of trouble.*

hesitation /ˌhezɪˈteɪʃᵊn/ **noun 1** [C, U] a pause before doing something, especially because you are nervous or not certain: *After a **moment's** hesitation, he unlocked the door.* **2 have no hesitation in doing sth** used to show you are very willing to do something because you know it is the right thing to do: *He had no hesitation in signing for the team.*

> 🖉 Word partners for **hesitation**
>
> **without** hesitation • a **brief/momentary/ moment's/slight** hesitation

heterogeneous /ˌhetᵊrəʊˈdʒiːniəs/ **adj** formal consisting of parts or things of different types: *a heterogeneous sample of people*

heterosexual /ˌhetᵊrəʊˈsekʃuᵊl/ **adj** sexually attracted to people of the opposite sex • **heterosexual noun** [C]

het up /hetˈʌp/ **adj** [never before noun] UK informal worried and upset: *Why are you **getting** so **het up** about this?*

hexagon /ˈheksəɡən/ **noun** [C] a flat shape with six sides of the same length • **hexagonal** /hekˈsæɡᵊnᵊl/ **adj** shaped like a hexagon

hey /heɪ/ **exclamation** spoken ⓐ used to get someone's attention or to show that you are interested, excited, angry, etc: *Hey, Helen, look at this!* ◦ *Hey, wait a minute!*

heyday /ˈheɪdeɪ/ **noun** [no plural] the time when something or someone was most successful or popular: *In its **heyday**, the company employed over a thousand workers.*

hi /haɪ/ **exclamation** ⓐ hello: *Hi! How's it going?*

hiatus /haɪˈeɪtəs/ **noun** [no plural] formal a short pause in which nothing happens or is said

hibernate /ˈhaɪbəneɪt/ **verb** [I] If an animal hibernates, it goes to sleep for the winter.

• **hibernation** /ˌhaɪbəˈneɪʃᵊn/ **noun** [U] *Bea go into hibernation in the autumn.*

hiccup (also **hiccough**) /ˈhɪkʌp/ **noun** [C] **1** quick noise you make in your throat when muscle in your chest moves suddenly: [usual plural] *I got hiccups from drinking too quickly.* **2** small, temporary problem: *I'm afraid there's bee a slight hiccup.*

hide

hide¹ /haɪd/ **verb** (**hid**, **hidden**) **1 THING** ▷ [T] ⓑ to put something in a place where it cannot b seen or found: *I hid the money in a vase.* ◦ [ofte passive] *She kept the diary hidden in a drawe* **2 PERSON** ▷ [I] (also **hide yourself**) ⓑ to go to place where you cannot be seen or found: *Sh ran off and hid behind a tree.* **3 FEELINC INFORMATION** ▷ [T] ⓑ to keep a feeling c information secret: *He couldn't hide his emba rassment.* ◦ *There's something about her past th she's trying to **hide from** me.*

hide² /haɪd/ **noun** [C, U] the skin of an anim that is used for making leather

hide-and-seek /ˌhaɪdᵊnˈsiːk/ **noun** [U] a chi dren's game in which one child hides and th others try to find them

hideaway /ˈhaɪdəweɪ/ **noun** [C] a place wher you go to hide or to be alone

hideous /ˈhɪdiəs/ **adj** very ugly: *a hideou monster* • **hideously adv**

hideout /ˈhaɪdaʊt/ **noun** [C] a place where yo go to hide, especially from the police or if yo are in danger

hiding /'haɪdɪŋ/ **noun be in hiding; go into hiding** to hide in a place, especially from the police or if you are in danger

hierarchy /'haɪərɑːki/ **noun** [C] a system or organization in which people or things are arranged according to their importance • **hierarchical** /ˌhaɪə'rɑːkɪkəl/ **adj** *a hierarchical structure*

☑ Word partners for **hierarchy**

in a hierarchy • a hierarchy of sth

hieroglyphics /ˌhaɪərəʊ'glɪfɪks/ **noun** [plural] a system of writing that uses pictures instead of words, especially used in ancient Egypt

hi-fi /'haɪfaɪ/ **noun** [C] a set of electronic equipment for playing music, consisting of a CD player, radio, etc

high¹ /haɪ/ **adj 1 TALL** ▷ **A2** having a large distance from the bottom to the top: *a high building/mountain* **2 ABOVE GROUND** ▷ **B1** a large distance above the ground or the level of the sea: *a high shelf/window* ○ *The village was high up in the mountains.* **3 MEASUREMENT** ▷ used to say how big the distance is from the top of something to the bottom, or how far above the ground something is: *How high is it?* ○ *It's ten metres high.* **4 AMOUNT** ▷ **B1** great in amount, size, or level: *a high temperature* ○ *high prices/costs* ○ *The car sped away at high speed.* **5 VERY GOOD** ▷ **B1** very good: *high standards/quality* **6 IMPORTANT** ▷ **B2** important, powerful, or at the top level of something: *a high rank* ○ *Safety is our highest priority.* **7 DRUGS** ▷ If someone is high, they are behaving in an unusual way because they have taken an illegal drug. **8 SOUND** ▷ A high sound or note is near the top of the set of sounds that people can hear. **9 high in sth** If a food is high in something, it contains a lot of it: *Avoid foods that are high in salt.*

high² /haɪ/ **adv 1 B1** at or to a large distance above the ground: *We flew high above the city.* ○ *He threw the ball high into the air.* **2 B1** at or to a large amount or level: *Temperatures rose as high as 40 degrees.*

high³ /haɪ/ **noun** [C] **1** the top amount or level that something reaches: *Computer ownership has reached an all-time high* (= more people own computers than ever before). **2** a feeling of excitement or happiness: [usually singular] *The players are still on a high from their last match.*

☑ Word partners for **high**

hit/reach a high • an all-time/new/record high

highbrow /'haɪbraʊ/ **adj** A highbrow book, film, etc is serious and intended for very intelligent or well-educated people.

high-class /ˌhaɪ'klɑːs/ **adj** of very good quality: *a high-class hotel*

High Court noun [C] the most important law court in some countries: *a High Court judge*

higher education noun [U] education at a college or university

high-flyer (also **high-flier**) /ˌhaɪ'flaɪər/ **noun** [C] someone who is very successful or who is likely to be very successful, especially in business • **high-flying adj**

high heels noun [plural] (also **heels**) women's shoes with heels raised high off the ground • **high-heeled adj**

the high jump noun a sports event in which people try to jump over a bar that gets higher and higher during the competition → See colour picture **Sports 1** on page Centre 14

highlands /'haɪləndz/ **noun** [plural] an area with a lot of mountains: *the Scottish highlands* • **highland** /'haɪlənd/ **adj** in or relating to the highlands: *a highland village*

high-level /ˌhaɪ'levəl/ **adj** involving important or powerful people: *high-level meetings/talks*

highlight¹ /'haɪlaɪt/ **verb** [T] **1 B2** to emphasize something or make people notice something: *to highlight a problem/danger* ○ *The report highlights the need for stricter regulations.* **2 B2** to make something a different colour so that it is more easily noticed, especially written words

☑ Word partners for **highlight**

highlight a **danger/need/issue/problem** • highlight **the need for** something

highlight² /'haɪlaɪt/ **noun** [C] **B2** the best or most important part of something: *The boat trip was one of the highlights of the holiday.*

highlighter /'haɪlaɪtər/ **noun** [C] a pen with bright, transparent ink that is used to emphasize words in a book, article, etc → See colour picture **The Office** on page Centre 5

highly /'haɪli/ **adv 1 B2** very or to a large degree: *a highly effective treatment* ○ *It is highly unlikely that they will succeed.* **2 B2** at a high level: *a highly paid worker* **3 to speak/think highly of sb/sth** to have or express a very good opinion of someone or something

Highness /'haɪnəs/ **noun Her/His/Your Highness** used when you are speaking to or about a royal person: *Thank you, Your Highness.*

high-pitched /ˌhaɪ'pɪtʃt/ **adj 1** A voice that is high-pitched is higher than usual. **2** describes a noise that is high and sometimes also loud or unpleasant: *a high-pitched whine*

high-powered /ˌhaɪ'paʊəd/ **adj** very important or responsible: *a high-powered executive/job*

high-profile /ˌhaɪ'prəʊfaɪl/ **adj** A high-profile person or event is known about by a lot of people and receives a lot of attention from television, newspapers, etc.: *a high-profile campaign/case*

high-resolution /ˌhaɪrezə'luːʃən/ **adj** (also informal **hi-res**, also **high-res**) used to describe a television or computer screen that can show things extremely clearly

high-rise /'haɪraɪz/ **adj** A high-rise building is very tall and has a lot of floors.

high school noun [C, U] a school in the US that children go to between the ages of 14 and 18: *I played violin when I was in high school.* ○ *a high-school student/teacher*

high street noun [C] UK (US **main street**) the

H

main road in the centre of a town where there are a lot of shops

high-tech (also UK **hi-tech**) /ˌhaɪˈtek/ adj ⑫ using or involved with the most recent and advanced electronic machines, computers, etc: *high-tech companies/industry* → Compare **low-tech**

highway /ˈhaɪweɪ/ noun [C] mainly US a main road, especially between two towns or cities

hijack /ˈhaɪdʒæk/ verb [T] to take control of an aircraft during a journey, especially using violence: [often passive] *The plane was hijacked by terrorists.* • **hijacker** noun [C] • **hijacking** noun [C, U]

hike¹ /haɪk/ noun [C] a long walk, usually in the countryside

hike² /haɪk/ verb [I] to go for a long walk in the countryside • **hiker** noun [C] • **hiking** noun [U] *to go hiking in the mountains*

hilarious /hɪˈleəriəs/ adj extremely funny: *They all thought the film was hilarious.* • **hilariously** adv *hilariously funny*

hilarity /hɪˈlærəti/ noun [U] a lot of loud laughter because people think something is very funny

hill /hɪl/ noun [C] ⑫ a raised area of land, smaller than a mountain: *They climbed up the hill to get a better view.*

hillside /ˈhɪlsaɪd/ noun [C] the sloping side of a hill

hilly /ˈhɪli/ adj having a lot of hills: *hilly countryside*

hilt /hɪlt/ noun

IDIOM **to the hilt** very much or as much as is possible: *Mark borrowed to the hilt to pay for his new car.*

him strong /hɪm/ weak /ɪm/ pronoun ⑪ used after a verb or preposition to refer to someone male who has already been talked about: *Where's Serge – have you seen him?*

himself /hɪmˈself/ pronoun **1** ⑫ the reflexive form of the pronoun 'he': *John always cuts himself when he's shaving.* **2** ⑫ used to emphasize the pronoun 'he' or the particular male person you are referring to: *Do you want to speak to Dr Randall himself or his secretary?* ◦ *He made the bookcase himself.* **3 (all) by himself** ⑫ alone or without anyone else's help: *Joe made that snowman all by himself.* **4 (all) to himself** for his use only: *Tim wants a desk all to himself.*

hind /haɪnd/ adj **a hind foot/leg** a foot/leg at the back of an animal

hinder /ˈhɪndər/ verb [T] to make it difficult to do something or for something to develop: [often passive] *His performance at the Olympics was hindered by a knee injury.*

hindrance /ˈhɪndrəns/ noun [C] something or someone that makes it difficult for you to do something: *Large class sizes are a **hindrance to** teachers.*

hindsight /ˈhaɪndsaɪt/ noun [U] the ability to understand an event or situation only after it has happened: **With hindsight**, *I should have taken the job.*

Hindu /ˈhɪnduː/ noun [C] someone who believe in Hinduism • **Hindu** adj *a Hindu temple*

Hinduism /ˈhɪnduːɪzªm/ noun [U] the mai religion of India, based on belief in many god and the belief that when someone dies thei spirit returns to life in another body

hinge¹ /ˈhɪndʒ/ noun [C] a metal fastening tha joins the edge of a door, window, or lid t something else and allows you to open or clos it

hinge² /ˈhɪndʒ/ verb

PHRASAL VERB **hinge on sth** to depend completel on something: *Her career hinges on the success o this project.*

hint¹ /hɪnt/ noun **1** [C] ⑫ something you sa that suggests what you think or want, but not i a direct way: *He **dropped** (= made) several hint that he wanted an MP3 player for his birthda* **2** [C] ⑫ a small piece of advice: *The magazin gives lots of **useful hints** on how to save money* **3 a hint of sth** a small amount of something *There was a hint of anger in her voice.*

> ☑ **Word partners for hint**
>
> drop a hint • a broad/heavy/subtle hint

hint² /hɪnt/ verb [I, T] to suggest something, bu not in a direct way: [+ (that)] *He hinted that h wants to retire next year.* ◦ *She **hinted at** th possibility of moving to America.*

hip¹ /hɪp/ noun [C] ⑫ one of the two parts o your body above your leg and below your wais → See colour picture **The Body** on page Centre 13

hip² /hɪp/ adj informal fashionable

hip-hop /ˈhɪphɒp/ noun [U] ⑫ a type of po music with songs about problems in society an words that are spoken and not sung

hippie /ˈhɪpi/ noun [C] (also UK **hippy**) someon who believes in peace and love and has lon hair, especially someone who was young in th 1960s

hippo /ˈhɪpəʊ/ noun [C] short for hippopotamus

hippopotamus /ˌhɪpəˈpɒtəməs/ noun [C] (plura **hippopotamuses**, **hippopotami**) a very larg animal with a thick skin that lives near water i parts of Africa

hire¹ /haɪər/ verb [T] **1** UK (US **rent**) ⑪ to pa money in order to use something for a shor time: *They hired a car for a few weeks.* → See Not at **rent¹ 2** ⑫ to begin to employ someone: *W hired a new secretary last week.*

PHRASAL VERB **hire sth out** to allow someone t borrow something from you in exchange fo money: *The shop hires out electrical equipment.*

hire² /haɪər/ noun [U] UK an arrangement to pa to use something for a short time: *The pric includes flights and **car hire**.* ◦ *Do you have bike **for hire**?*

his¹ strong /hɪz/ weak /ɪz/ determiner ⑪ belong ing to or relating to someone male who ha already been talked about: *Alex is sitting ove there with his daughter.* ◦ *It's not his fault.*

his² /hɪz/ pronoun ⑫ the things that belong o relate to someone male who has already bee

H

talked about: *That's Frank's coat over there – at least I think it's his.* ∘ *I borrowed them from a friend of his.*

ispanic /hɪˈspænɪk/ **adj** relating or belonging to people whose families came from Spain or Latin America in the past • **Hispanic noun** [C] a Hispanic person

iss /hɪs/ **verb 1** [I] to make a long noise like the letter 's': *The gas hissed through the pipes.* **2** [T] to speak in an angry or urgent way: *"Will you be quiet," she hissed.* • **hiss noun** [C] a sound like the letter 's'

issy (fit) /ˈhɪsiˌfɪt/ **noun** [C] informal a sudden strong feeling of anger that someone cannot control: *David, of course, **threw a hissy fit** when he found out.*

istorian /hɪˈstɔːriən/ **noun** [C] someone who studies or writes about history

istoric /hɪˈstɒrɪk/ **adj** ⑤ important in history or likely to be important in history: *historic buildings* ∘ *a historic day/moment*

istorical /hɪˈstɒrɪkəl/ **adj** ⑤ relating to events or people in the past, or the study of history: *a historical novel* ∘ *historical documents* • **historically adv**

istory /ˈhɪstəri/ **noun 1 PAST** ▷ [U] ⓐ the whole series of events in the past that relate to the development of a country, subject, or person: *The Civil War was a terrible time in American history.* **2 SUBJECT** ▷ [U] ⓐ the study of events in the past: *He's very interested in modern European history.* ∘ *a history book* **3 a history of sth** If you have a history of a particular problem or illness, you have already suffered from it: *a man with a history of drug addiction* **4 DESCRIPTION** ▷ [C] a description or record of events in the past relating to someone or something: *The doctor read through his **medical history**.* → See also **case history, natural history**

> ⓘ Common learner error: **history** or **story**?
>
> **History** is events that happened in the past.
> *He's studying history at university.*
> A **story** is a description of real or imaginary events, often told to entertain people.
> *The story is about two friends travelling across India.*

> ❷ Word partners for **history**
>
> in sth's history • recent history

it¹ /hɪt/ **verb (hitting, hit) 1 HAND** ▷ [T] ⓐ to touch something quickly and with force using your hand or an object in your hand: *She hit him on the head with her tennis racket.* **2 TOUCH** ▷ [T] ⑥ to touch someone or something quickly and with force, usually causing injury or damage: *The car skidded and hit a wall.* ∘ *As she fell, she hit her head on the pavement.* **3 AFFECT** ▷ [I, T] ⑥ to affect something badly: [often passive] *The economy has been hit by high unemployment.* **4 REACH** ▷ [T] to reach a place, position, or state: *Our profits have already hit $1 million.* **5 THINK** ▷ [T] informal If an idea or thought hits you, you suddenly think of it: *The idea for the book hit me in the middle of the night.* → See also **hit sb hard²**,

hit

hit the jackpot, hit the nail¹ on the head, hit the roof

IDIOM **hit it off** informal ⑥ If people hit it off, they like each other and become friendly immediately.

PHRASAL VERBS **hit back** to criticize or attack someone who has criticized or attacked you: *The President **hit back at** journalists who said he was a liar.* • **hit on/upon sth** to have a good idea, especially one that solves a problem: *We **hit upon the idea** of writing to the mayor to ask for his help.*

> ❷ Word partners for **hit**
>
> a big/massive/smash hit • a hit single

hit² /hɪt/ **noun** [C] **1 SONG/FILM** ▷ ⑥ a very successful song, film, book, etc: *The film 'Avatar' was a **big hit**.* **2 PERSON/THING** ▷ ⑥ a popular person or thing: *The chocolate cake was a **big hit** with the children.* **3 TOUCH** ▷ the action when you touch something or when something touches you quickly and with force **4 INTERNET** ▷ ⑥ a request to see a document on the Internet that is then counted to calculate the number of people looking at the page

hit-and-miss /ˌhɪtənˈmɪs/ **adj** (also **hit or miss**) not planned, but happening by chance

hit-and-run /ˌhɪtənˈrʌn/ **adj** A hit-and-run accident is when the driver of a vehicle hits and injures someone, but then drives away without helping.

hitch¹ /hɪtʃ/ **noun** [C] a small problem: *The ceremony **went without a hitch**.*

hitch² /hɪtʃ/ **verb 1 hitch a ride** (also UK **hitch a lift**) to get a free ride in someone's vehicle, by standing next to the road and waiting for someone to pick you up **2** [T] (also US **hitch up**) to fasten something to an object or vehicle: *They hitched the caravan to the car.*

PHRASAL VERB **hitch sth up** to pull up a piece of clothing

hitchhike /ˈhɪtʃhaɪk/ **verb** [I] ⑥ to get free rides in people's vehicles by standing next to the road and waiting for someone to pick you up • **hitchhiker noun** [C]

hi-tech (also **high-tech**) /ˌhaɪˈtek/ **adj** ⑫ using or involved with the most recent and advanced electronic machines, computers, etc

hitherto /ˌhɪðəˈtuː/ **adv** formal until now, or until a particular point in time

'hit ˌrate noun [C] the total number of visits to a website in a particular period

HIV /ˌeɪtʃaɪˈviː/ **noun** [U] abbreviation for human immunodeficiency virus: a virus that causes AIDS (= a serious disease that destroys the body's ability to fight infection)

hive /haɪv/ **noun 1** [C] (also **beehive**) a special container where people keep bees **2 a hive of activity** a place where people are busy and working hard

HIV-positive /ˌeɪtʃaɪviːˈpɒzətɪv/ **adj** If a person is HIV-positive, they are infected with HIV although they might not have AIDS.

hiya /ˈhaɪjə/ **exclamation** informal a way to say hello to someone you know well: *Hiya, Mike, how are you doing?*

hm (also **hmm**) /həm/ spoken something you say when you pause while talking or when you are uncertain: *"Which one do you like best?" "Hmm. I'm not sure."*

hoard /hɔːd/ **verb** [T] to collect and store a large supply of something, often secretly: *He hoarded antique books in the attic.* • **hoard noun** [C] a large, secret supply or collection of something: *Police found a hoard of stolen jewellery in the car.*

hoarding /ˈhɔːdɪŋ/ **noun** [C] UK (UK/US **billboard**) a large board used for advertising, especially by the side of a road

hoarse /hɔːs/ **adj** If you are hoarse, your voice sounds rough when you speak, often because you are sick: *The teacher was hoarse from shouting.* • **hoarsely adv**

hoax /həʊks/ **noun** [C] a trick in which someone tries to make people believe something that is not true: *The police said the bomb threat was a hoax.*

hob /hɒb/ **noun** [C] UK the flat part on top of an oven where you heat food in pans → See colour picture **The Kitchen** on page Centre 2

hobble /ˈhɒbl/ **verb** [I] to walk with small, uncomfortable steps, especially because your feet hurt

hobby /ˈhɒbi/ **noun** [C] ⑫ an activity that you enjoy and do regularly when you are not working: *Do you have any hobbies?*

hockey /ˈhɒki/ **noun** [U] **1** (also US **field hockey**) ⑫ a team game played on grass where you hit a small ball with a long, curved stick **2** US (UK/US **ice hockey**) a team game played on ice where you hit a small, hard object with a long, curved stick → See colour picture **Sports 1** on page Centre 14

hoe /həʊ/ **noun** [C] a garden tool with a long handle used for removing weeds (= plants you do not want)

hog¹ /hɒg/ **noun** [C] mainly US a large pig

hog² /hɒg/ **verb** [T] (**hogging, hogged**) inform to use or keep all of something for yourself: *Sto hogging the newspaper! I want to read it too.*

hoist /hɔɪst/ **verb** [T] to raise something, som times using a rope or machine: *They slow hoisted the flag.*

hold¹ /həʊld/ **verb** (**held**) **1 IN HAND** ▷ [T] ⑫ have something in your hand or arms: *He w holding a glass of wine.* ○ *They were holdin hands and kissing.* **2 KEEP IN POSITION** ▷ [T] ⑥ to keep something in a particular position: *Ca you hold the door open please?* ○ *Hold your har up if you know the answer.* ○ *The frame was he together with screws.* **3 ORGANIZE** ▷ [T] ⑥ t organize an event: *to hold talks/an electi* **4 CONTAIN** ▷ [T] ⑥ to contain something to be able to contain a particular amount something: *The bucket holds about 10 litres.* **5 JO OR QUALIFICATION** ▷ [T] to have a particular jo position, or qualification: *She held the post treasurer.* **6 COMPETITION** ▷ [T] to have particular position in a competition: *to hold th world record* ○ *to hold the lead* **7 STORE** ▷ [T] t store documents, information, etc in a partic lar place: *The documents are held in the loc library.* **8 PRISONER** ▷ [T] ⑫ to keep someone a prisoner: *Police held the suspect overnigh* ○ *The hijackers are holding them hostage/pri oner.* **9 ARMY** ▷ [T] If soldiers hold a place, the control it: *Rebel troops held the village.* **10 hol an opinion/belief/view** to believe somethin They held the view that it was wrong to smac children. **11 hold a conversation** to have conversation **12 hold sb's attention/interest t keep someone interested in something: The fil held my attention from beginning to en **13 TELEPHONE** ▷ [I, T] to wait on the telephon until someone can speak to you: *Her line's bus Would you like to hold?* ○ **Hold the line,** pleas **14 NOT BREAK** ▷ [I] to not break: *The rope hel* **15 Hold it!** informal used to tell someone to wa or stop doing something: *Hold it! I've forgott my coat.* **16 hold shares** to own shares (= sma equal parts of the value of a company) **17 hol your breath a** ⑫ to intentionally stop breat ing for a time **b** to wait for something t happen, often feeling anxious **18 hold you nose** to close your nose with your fingers t avoid smelling something unpleasant → See als **hold your own¹**

PHRASAL VERBS hold sth against sb to lik someone less because they have done som thing wrong or behaved badly: *It was h mistake, but I won't hold it against him.* • **hol sb/sth back 1** to prevent someone or somethin from moving forward: *The police held back th protesters.* **2** to prevent someone or somethin from making progress: *She felt that havin children would hold her back.* • **hold sth bac 1** to stop yourself showing an emotion: *Sh couldn't hold back the tears.* **2** to not giv information to someone • **hold sth/sb dow 1** to stop someone moving or escaping: *It too three officers to hold down the suspect.* **2** to kee the cost of something at a low level: *to hold dou prices/wages* **3 hold down a job** to keep a jo

H

It's difficult for mothers to hold down a full-time job. • **hold off (sth/doing sth)** to wait before doing something: *They are holding off making a decision until next week.* • **hold on** informal **1** 🔵 to wait: *Hold on! I'll just check my diary.* **2** to hold something or someone firmly with your hands or arms: *Hold on tight!* • **hold onto sth/sb** to hold something or someone firmly with your hands or arms: *Hold onto the rope and don't let go.* • **hold onto/on to sth** to keep something you have: *It was a tough election, but they held onto their majority.* • **hold sth out** to move your hand or an object in your hand towards someone: *She held out her glass for some more wine.* • **hold out 1** If a supply of food or money holds out, you have enough for a particular period of time. **2** to continue to defend yourself against an attack: *The city is still **holding out** against rebel troops.* • **hold out for sth** to wait until you get what you want: *I decided to hold out for a better offer.* • **hold sth up** to prevent something from falling down: *The tent was held up by ropes.* • **hold sth/sb up** 🔵 to make someone or something slow or late: *Sorry I'm late. I got held up in traffic.* • **hold sb up** to try to steal money from a bank, shop, or vehicle using force

hold² /həʊld/ noun **1 WITH HANDS** ▷ [C] 🔵 the action of holding something or someone, or the way you do this: *Keep a tight **hold on** your tickets.* **2 catch/grab/take, etc hold of sth/sb** 🔵 to start holding something or someone: *He tried to escape, but I grabbed hold of his jacket.* **3 get hold of sth/sb** 🔵 to obtain something, or to manage to speak to someone: *I got hold of a copy at the local library.* ∘ *I rang three times, but couldn't get hold of her.* **4 on hold a** If a plan or activity is on hold, it will not be done until a later time: *The project is on hold until we get more money.* **b** waiting to speak to someone on the telephone: *His secretary put me on hold.* **5 keep hold of sth** to keep something: *Keep hold of this. You might need it later.* **6 hold on/over sth/sb** power or control over something or someone: *Their company has a strong hold on the computer market.* **7 SPACE** ▷ [C] an area on a ship or aircraft for storing things: *a cargo hold* → See also **get (hold of) the wrong end¹ of the stick**

holdall /'həʊldɔːl/ noun [C] UK (US **carryall**) a large bag for carrying clothes → See picture at **luggage**

holder /'həʊldər/ noun [C] someone who officially owns something: *the world record holder* ∘ *passport holders* → See also **title-holder**

holding /'həʊldɪŋ/ noun [C] part of a company that someone owns

hold-up mainly UK (US **holdup**) /'həʊldʌp/ noun [C] **1** something that slows you down or makes you late: *There were several hold-ups on the motorway.* **2** an occasion when someone steals money from a bank, shop, or vehicle using force

hole¹ /həʊl/ noun **1** [C] 🔵 a hollow space in something, or an opening in a surface: *a bullet hole* ∘ *There's a **hole in** the roof.* ∘ *We dug a hole to plant the tree.* **2 a rabbit/mouse, etc hole** a hollow space where a rabbit/mouse, etc lives **3** a small, hollow space in the ground that you try to hit a ball into in a game of golf

hole² /həʊl/ verb

PHRASAL VERB **hole up** (also **be holed up**) informal to stay or hide somewhere

holiday¹ /'hɒlədeɪ/ noun **1 NO WORK** ▷ [C, U] UK (US **vacation**) 🔵 a time when you do not have to go to work or school: *My aunt looks after us during the **school holidays**.* **2 VISIT** ▷ [C, U] UK (US **vacation**) 🔵 a long visit to a place away from where you live, for pleasure: *a skiing/walking holiday* ∘ *Are you **going on holiday** this year?* **3 DAY** ▷ [C] 🔵 an official day when you do not have to go to school or work: *a **public holiday*** → See also **bank holiday, federal holiday, national holiday, package holiday, summer holiday**

holiday² /'hɒlədeɪ/ verb [I] UK (US **vacation**) to have your holiday somewhere: *We usually holiday in Spain.*

holidaymaker /'hɒlədeɪˌmeɪkər/ noun [C] UK someone who is away from home on holiday

holiness /'həʊlɪnəs/ noun [U] the quality of being holy

holistic /həʊˈlɪstɪk/ adj dealing with or treating the whole of something or someone and not just some parts

holler /'hɒlər/ verb [I] US informal to shout or call loudly • **holler** noun [C]

hollow¹ /'hɒləʊ/ adj   **hollow**
1 having a hole or empty space inside: *a hollow shell/tube* → See picture at **flat**
2 without meaning or real feeling: *a hollow victory* ∘ *a hollow laugh* **3 hollow cheeks/eyes** If someone has hollow cheeks/eyes, their face seems to curve in around these areas.

hollow² /'hɒləʊ/ noun [C] a hole or empty space in something, or a low area in a surface

hollow³ /'hɒləʊ/ verb

PHRASAL VERB **hollow sth out** to make an empty space inside something

holly /'hɒli/ noun [U] a green bush with sharp, pointed leaves and small, red fruit

Hollywood /'hɒliwʊd/ noun the centre of the US film industry

holocaust /'hɒləkɔːst/ noun [C] a situation in which a very large number of people are killed

H

and things destroyed, such as in a war or fire: *a nuclear holocaust*

hologram /ˈhɒləɡræm/ **noun** [C] a photograph or image that appears to be solid and have depth when light shines on it in a particular way

holster /ˈhəʊlstər/ **noun** [C] a leather container for carrying a gun on your body

holy /ˈhəʊli/ **adj 1** relating to a religion or a god: *the holy city of Jerusalem* **2** very religious or pure: *a holy man*

homage /ˈhɒmɪdʒ/ **noun pay homage to sb** to show your respect for someone, especially by praising them in public: *Fans paid homage to the actress who died yesterday.*

home¹ /həʊm/ **noun 1** [C, U] ⓐ the place where you live or feel you belong: *I tried to call him, but he wasn't at home.* ∘ *He left home* (= stopped living with his family) *when he was eighteen.* **2** [C] a place where people who need special care live: *a children's home* ∘ *My grandmother lives in a home now.* **3 feel at home** ⓑ to feel happy and confident in a place or situation: *After a month she felt at home in her new job.* **4 make yourself at home** to behave in a relaxed way in a place, as if it was your own home: *Take off your coat and make yourself at home.* **5 the home of sth/sb** the place where you usually find something or someone, or where they come from: *France, the home of good food* → See also **nursing home, stately home**

> **!** Common learner error: **home**
>
> When you use verbs of movement with **home**, for example 'go' or 'come', you do not use a preposition.
> *What time did you go home?*
> *I'll call you as soon as I get home.*
> When you use the verbs **be** or **stay** with **home**, you can use the preposition **at**.
> *I was at home all afternoon.*
> *I'll stay at home to look after the children.*
> *Let's stay home instead and watch a movie.* mainly US

> **2** Word partners for **home**
> go home • be at home

home² /həʊm/ **adv 1** ⓐ to the place where you live: *He didn't come home until midnight.* ∘ *I went home to visit my parents.* **2** at or in the place someone lives: *Will you be home tomorrow evening?*

home³ /həʊm/ **adj 1 sb's home address/phone number, etc** an address/telephone number, etc for the place where someone lives **2 FOR/FROM HOME** ▷ made or used in the place where someone lives: *home cooking* ∘ *a home computer* **3 SPORT** ▷ relating to the place where a sporting event happens: *The home team won 2-0.* **4 COUNTRY** ▷ relating to things in your own country: *home affairs*

home⁴ /həʊm/ **verb**

PHRASAL VERB **home in on sth/sb** to give a lot of attention to something or someone: *The report only homes in on the negative points.*

homeboy /ˈhəʊmbɔɪ/ **noun** [C] (also **homey**) mainly US informal a boy or man who is a clos[e] friend or who is from your own town

homecoming /ˈhəʊmˌkʌmɪŋ/ **noun** [C, U] a[n] occasion when someone returns home, usuall[y] after being away for a long time

home ecoˈnomics noun [U] a school subje[ct] in which you learn how to cook and sew

home-grown /ˌhəʊmˈɡrəʊn/ **adj 1** from you[r] own garden: *home-grown vegetables* **2** [if] someone or something is home-grown, the[y] belong to or were developed in your ow[n] country: *Our football team has many hom[e]-grown players.*

homeland /ˈhəʊmlænd/ **noun** [C] the countr[y] where you were born

homeless /ˈhəʊmləs/ **adj** without a place to liv[e] *10,000 people were made homeless by the flood[s]* ∘ *They're opening a new shelter for the homeles[s]* • **homelessness noun** [U]

homely /ˈhəʊmli/ **adj 1** UK A homely place [is] simple, but comfortable and pleasant: *It's [a] small restaurant with a homely atmosphere.* **2** U[S] Someone who is homely is not very attractive.

homemade (also UK **home-made**) /ˌhəʊmˈmeɪd/ **adj** made at home and not bought from a sho[p] *homemade bread/cookies*

homeopathy /ˌhəʊmiˈɒpəθi/ **noun** [U] a way [of] treating illnesses using very small amounts [of] natural substances • **homeopathic** /ˌhəʊmiəʊ[ˈ]æθɪk/ adj *a homeopathic remedy*

homeowner /ˈhəʊmˌəʊnər/ **noun** [C] someon[e] who owns the house that they live in

home ˈpage noun [C] the first page that you se[e] when you look at a website on the Internet → Se[e] Study Page **The Web and the Internet** on pa[ge] Centre 36

home ˈrun noun [C] (also informal **homer**) US [a] point scored in baseball by hitting the ball so f[ar] that you have time to run all the way round th[e] four corners of the playing field before it returned

home ˈshopping noun [U] shopping from [a] magazine, a television programme, or a websi[te]

homesick /ˈhəʊmsɪk/ **adj** feeling sad becaus[e] you are away from your home • **homesicknes[s] noun** [U]

homestead /ˈhəʊmsted/ **noun** [C] mainly US [a] house and area of land usually used as a far[m]

hometown (also **home ˈtown**) /ˌhəʊmˈtaʊ[n]/ **noun** [C] the town or city that you come fro[m]

homeward /ˈhəʊmwəd/ **adj, adv** towar[d] home: *the homeward journey*

homework /ˈhəʊmwɜːk/ **noun** [U] **1** ⓐ wo[rk] that teachers give students to do at home: *Ha[ve] you done your homework yet?* **2 do you[r] homework** to prepare carefully for a situatio[n] *It was clear that she had done her homewo[rk] before the meeting.*

homey¹ /ˈhəʊmi/ **adj** US (UK **homely**) A hom[ey] place is simple, but comfortable and pleasant

homey² /ˈhəʊmi/ **noun** [C] (also **homeboy**) main[ly] US informal a boy or man who is a close friend [or] who is from your own town

homicide /ˈhɒmɪsaɪd/ **noun** [C, U] US the crim[e]

of killing someone: *There were over 400 homicides in Chicago last year.* • **homicidal** /ˌhɒmɪˈsaɪdəl/ **adj** likely to murder someone: *a homicidal maniac*

homogeneous /ˌhɒməˈdʒiːniəs/, /ˌhəʊməˈdʒiːniəs/ **adj** formal consisting of parts or members that are all the same: *The village was a fairly homogeneous community.*

homophobia /ˌhəʊməˈfəʊbiə/ **noun** [U] hate of homosexual people • **homophobic adj** hating homosexual people

homosexual /ˌhəʊməˈsekʃuəl/ **adj** sexually attracted to people of the same sex • **homosexual noun** [C] someone who is homosexual • **homosexuality** /ˌhəʊməʊˌsekʃuˈæləti/ **noun** [U] the fact of being homosexual

hone /həʊn/ **verb** [T] to improve something and make it perfect: *This is an opportunity for you to hone your skills.*

honest /ˈɒnɪst/ **adj 1** 🔵 sincere and telling the truth: *If you want my honest opinion, I think your hair looks awful.* **2** 🔵 not likely to lie, cheat, or steal: *an honest man* → Opposite **dishonest 3 to be honest** informal 🔵 used to express your real opinion: *To be honest, I didn't really enjoy the party.*

honestly /ˈɒnɪstli/ **adv 1 EMPHASIZE** ▷ 🔵 used to emphasize that you are telling the truth: *Thanks, but I honestly couldn't eat another piece of cake.* **2 HONEST** ▷ 🔵 in an honest way **3 ANNOYED** ▷ used to show that you are annoyed or do not approve of something: *Honestly! He should have been here hours ago.*

honesty /ˈɒnɪsti/ **noun 1** 🔵 [U] the quality of being honest **2 in all honesty** used when you are saying what you really think or feel about something: *In all honesty, I'd rather not go.* → Opposite **dishonesty**

honey /ˈhʌni/ **noun 1** [U] 🔵 a sweet, sticky food that is made by bees → See colour picture **Food** on page Centre 11 **2** [C] mainly US a name that you call someone you love or like very much

honeymoon /ˈhʌnimuːn/ **noun** [C] 🔵 a holiday taken by two people who have just got married: *We went to Paris on our honeymoon.* • **honeymooner noun** [C]

🔲 Word partners for **honeymoon**

be **on** (your) honeymoon • a honeymoon **couple**

---

honk /hɒŋk/ **verb** [I, T] to make a short sound with your car's horn (= part you press to make a warning noise): *The truck driver honked his horn at me.*

honor /ˈɒnər/ **noun, verb** US spelling of honour

honorable /ˈɒnərəbl/ **adj** US spelling of honourable

honorary /ˈɒnərəri/ **adj 1** given as a reward to show respect: *He was given an honorary degree from Cambridge University.* **2** If you have an honorary job, you are not paid for it: *the honorary chairman*

honour¹ UK (US **honor**) /ˈɒnər/ **noun 1 RESPECT** ▷ [U] 🔵 respect that people have for you because you have done what you believe

is honest and right, or the quality of doing this: *a man of honour* ○ *The soldiers fought for the honour of their country.* → Opposite **dishonour 2 in honour of sb/sth** 🔵 in order to celebrate or show great respect for someone or something: *A banquet was held in honour of the President.* **3 PRIDE** ▷ [no plural] 🔵 something that makes you feel proud and pleased: [+ to do sth] *It's an honour to be team captain.* ○ [+ of + doing sth] *I had the great honour of meeting the King.* **4 REWARD** ▷ [C] something that you give to someone in public to show respect for them and their achievements: *She was granted the Order of Merit – one of the nation's highest honours.* **5 Her/His/Your Honour** used when you are speaking to or about a judge **6 honours** A qualification or university course with honours is of a very high level: *an honours degree*

honour² UK (US **honor**) /ˈɒnər/ **verb 1** [T] to show great respect for someone or something, usually in public: [often passive] *He was honoured for his bravery.* ○ *She was honoured with an Oscar.* **2 honour an agreement/contract/promise, etc** to do what you agreed or promised to do → Opposite **dishonour**

honourable /ˈɒnərəbl/ **adj** UK **1** (US **honorable**) honest and fair, or deserving praise and respect: *a decent, honourable man* → Opposite **dishonourable 2 the Honourable a** a title used before the name of some important government officials **b** a title used in the UK before the name of certain people of high social rank • **honourably adv**

hood /hʊd/ **noun** [C] **1** 🔵 a part of a coat or jacket that covers your head and neck: *a waterproof jacket with a hood* → See colour picture **Clothes** on page Centre 8 **2** US (UK **bonnet**) the metal part that covers a car engine → See colour picture **Car** on page Centre 7

hooded /ˈhʊdɪd/ **adj** having or wearing a hood: *a hooded sweatshirt* ○ *hooded figures*

hoodie (also **hoody**) /ˈhʊdi/ **noun** [C] a sweatshirt (= a piece of clothing made of soft cotton which covers the top of your body) with a hood (= part which covers your head) → See colour picture **Clothes** on page Centre 8

hoof /huːf/ **noun** [C] (plural **hooves**, **hoofs**) the hard part on the foot of a horse and some other large animals

hook¹ /hʊk/ **noun 1** 🔵 [C] a curved piece of metal or plastic used for hanging something on, or a similar object used for catching fish: *His coat was hanging from a hook on the door.* **2 off the hook** If a telephone is off the hook, the part you speak into is not in its correct position, so the telephone will not ring. **3 a left/right hook** a hard hit with your left/right hand

IDIOM **get/let sb off the hook** informal to allow someone to escape from a difficult situation or to avoid doing something that they do not want to do

---

hook² /hʊk/ **verb 1** [T] to fasten something with a hook, hang something on a hook, or catch something with a hook **2 be/get hooked on sth a** 🔵 to like or start to like doing something very

---

much and want to do it all the time: *He's completely hooked on computer games.* **b** If you are hooked on a drug, you cannot stop taking it. • **hooked** adj shaped like a hook: *a hooked nose*

PHRASAL VERB **hook sth/sb up** to connect a machine to a power supply or to another machine, or to connect someone to a piece of medical equipment

hooligan /'hu:lɪgᵊn/ noun [C] someone who behaves badly or violently and causes damage in a public place • **hooliganism** noun [U]

hoop /hu:p/ noun [C] a ring made of metal, plastic, or wood

hooray (also **hurrah**) /hʊ'reɪ/ **exclamation** something that you shout when you are happy, excited, etc or when you approve of someone or something: *Hip, hip, hooray!*

hoot¹ /hu:t/ noun **1** [C] a short sound made by an owl (= bird that hunts animals at night) or by a car horn (= warning equipment) **2 a hoot of laughter** a loud laugh **3** [no plural] informal something or someone that is very funny: *The film was an absolute hoot.*

hoot² /hu:t/ verb **1** [I, T] mainly UK to make a short sound with your car's horn (= part you press to make a warning noise): *The van driver hooted his horn impatiently.* **2** [I] If an owl (= bird that hunts animals at night) hoots, it makes a low 'oo' sound. **3 hoot with laughter** to laugh a lot very loudly

Hoover /'hu:vᵊr/ noun [C] UK trademark (UK/US **vacuum cleaner**) an electric machine that cleans floors by sucking up dirt • **hoover** verb [I, T]

hooves /hu:vz/ plural of hoof

hop¹ /hɒp/ verb [I] (**hopping, hopped**) **1 ONE FOOT** ▷ to jump on one foot or to move about in this way **2 ANIMAL** ▷ If a small animal, bird, or insect hops, it moves by jumping on all of its feet at the same time: *Rabbits were hopping across the field.* **3 MOVE QUICKLY** ▷ informal to go somewhere quickly or get into or out of a vehicle quickly: *to hop on a plane/train*

hop² /hɒp/ noun **1** [C] a short jump, especially on one leg **2 a short hop** informal a short journey or distance: *London to Paris is only a short hop by plane.*

hope¹ /həʊp/ verb **1** ⓐ [I, T] to want something to happen or be true: [+ (that)] *I hope that the bus won't be late.* ◦ *We had hoped for better weather than this.* ◦ *"Do you think it's going to rain?" "I hope not!"* ◦ *"Is he coming?" "I hope so."* **2 hope to do sth** ⓑ to intend to do something: *Dad hopes to retire next year.*

hope² /həʊp/ noun **1** ⓑ [C, U] a positive feeling about the future, or something that you want to happen: *a message full of hope* ◦ *What are your hopes and dreams for the future?* ◦ [+ of + doing sth] *Young people are growing up in our cities without any hope of getting a job.* **2 sb's best/last/only hope** the best/last/only person or thing that can help you and make you succeed: *Doctors say his only hope is a transplant.* **3 in the hope of/that** because you want something

good to happen: [+ doing sth] *She went to Paris ⟨in⟩ the hope of improving her French.*

IDIOM **pin your hopes on sb/sth** to hope tha⟨t⟩ someone or something will help you achiev⟨e⟩ what you want

🗒 Word partners for **hope**
bring/give/give up/hold out/lose/offer hope • fresh/great/renewed/vain hope • hope of sth/ doing sth

hopeful /'həʊpfᵊl/ adj **1** ⓑ feeling positiv⟨e⟩ about a future event or situation: *Many teen⟨-⟩ agers do not feel hopeful about the future.* ◦ [⟨+⟩ (that)] *Police are still hopeful that they will find th⟨e⟩ missing family.* **2** If something is hopeful, i⟨t⟩ makes you feel that what you want to happe⟨n⟩ will happen: *There are hopeful signs that she wi⟨ll⟩ make a full recovery.* • **hopefulness** noun [⟨U⟩] • **hopeful** noun [C] someone who hopes t⟨o⟩ succeed, especially in the entertainment bus⟨i-⟩ ness: *a young hopeful*

hopefully /'həʊpfᵊli/ adv **1** ⓑ used, often at th⟨e⟩ start of a sentence, to express what you woul⟨d⟩ like to happen: *Hopefully it won't rain.* **2** ⓑ in ⟨a⟩ hopeful way: *"Are there any tickets left?" she aske⟨d⟩ hopefully.*

hopeless /'həʊpləs/ adj **1 VERY BAD** ▷ ⓑ ver⟨y⟩ bad and not likely to succeed or improve: *⟨a⟩ hopeless situation* ◦ *They searched for survivor⟨s⟩ but it was hopeless.* **2 NOT ABLE** ▷ ⓑ very bad ⟨at⟩ a particular activity: *Dad's a hopeless cook.* ◦ *I'⟨m⟩ hopeless at sports.* **3 NOT POSITIVE** ▷ ⓑ feelin⟨g⟩ no hope: *She was depressed and felt totall⟨y⟩ hopeless about the future.* • **hopelessness** nou⟨n⟩ [U]

hopelessly /'həʊpləsli/ adv extremely, or in ⟨a⟩ way that makes you lose hope: *hopelessly lo⟨st⟩* ◦ *They met at university and fell hopelessly i⟨n⟩ love.*

hops /hɒps/ noun [plural] the flowers of a plan⟨t⟩ that are used to make beer

horde /hɔ:d/ noun [C] a large group of peopl⟨e⟩ *There was a horde of tourists outside Buckingha⟨m⟩ Palace.*

horizon /hə'raɪzᵊn/ noun **1** [C] the line in th⟨e⟩ distance where the sky seems to touch the lan⟨d⟩ or sea **2 broaden/expand/widen your horizon⟨s⟩** to increase the number of things that you kno⟨w⟩ about, have experienced, or can do: *Travellin⟨g⟩ certainly broadens your horizons.*

IDIOM **on the horizon** likely to happen soo⟨n⟩ *Economic recovery is on the horizon.*

horizontal /ˌhɒrɪ'zɒntᵊl/ adj level and flat, ⟨or⟩ parallel to the ground or to the bottom of ⟨a⟩ page: *a horizontal line/stripe* • **horizontally** ad⟨v⟩

hormone /'hɔ:məʊn/ noun [C] one of severa⟨l⟩ chemicals produced in your body that influenc⟨e⟩ its growth and development • **hormonal** /hɔ:⟨-⟩ 'məʊnᵊl/ adj *a hormonal imbalance*

horn /hɔ:n/ noun [C] **1 ANIMAL** ▷ one of the tw⟨o⟩ hard, pointed growths on the heads of cow⟨s,⟩ goats, and some other animals **2 EQUIPMENT** ⟨▷⟩ ⓑ a piece of equipment used to make a lou⟨d⟩ sound as a warning or signal: *a car horn* ◦ *Th⟨e⟩*

orizontal/vertical

horizontal stripes

vertical stripes

taxi driver **hooted** *his* **horn.** **3** MUSIC ▷ a curved musical instrument that you blow into to make a sound: *the French horn*

oroscope /'hɒrəskəʊp/ **noun** [C] a description of what someone is like and what might happen to them in the future, based on the position of the stars and planets when they were born

orrendous /hər'endəs/ **adj** extremely unpleasant or bad: *She suffered horrendous injuries in the accident.* • **horrendously** **adv** extremely or extremely badly: *horrendously expensive*

orrible /'hɒrəbl/ **adj** ⓐ very unpleasant or bad: *What's that horrible smell?* ∘ *That was a horrible thing to say to your sister.* • **horribly** **adv** extremely, or in a very bad way: *His plan went horribly wrong.*

orrid /'hɒrɪd/ **adj** very unpleasant or unkind

orrific /hɒr'ɪfɪk/ **adj** very bad and shocking: *a horrific accident/crime* ∘ *horrific injuries* • **horrifically** **adv**

orrify /'hɒrɪfaɪ/ **verb** [T] to make someone feel very shocked: [often passive] *I was horrified to hear about your accident.* • **horrifying** **adj**

orror /'hɒrər/ **noun 1** ⓑ [C, U] a strong feeling of shock or fear, or something that makes you feel shocked or afraid: *She watched* **in horror** *as the car skidded across the road.* **2 a horror film/ movie/story** ⓑ a film or story that entertains people by shocking or frightening them

orse /hɔːs/ **noun** [C] ⓐ a large animal with four legs, which people ride or use to pull heavy things

orseback /'hɔːsbæk/ **noun 1 on horseback** riding a horse: *police on horseback* **2 horseback riding** US (UK **horse riding**) the sport or activity of riding a horse → See colour picture **Sports 1** on page Centre 14

orse 'chestnut noun [C] a tree that produces shiny, brown nuts in thick, green shells with sharp points, or one of these nuts

orse-drawn /'hɔːsdrɔːn/ **adj** [always before noun] A horse-drawn vehicle is pulled by a horse.

orseman, horsewoman /'hɔːsmən/, /'hɔːs-ˌwʊmən/ **noun** [C] (plural **horsemen, horse-women**) a man/woman who rides horses well

orsepower /'hɔːsˌpaʊər/ **noun** [U] (written abbreviation **hp**) a unit for measuring the power of an engine

'horse ˌracing noun [U] the sport where people race on horses, usually to win money

'horse ˌriding noun [U] UK (US **'horseback ˌriding**) the sport or activity of riding a horse → See colour picture **Sports 1** on page Centre 14

horseshoe /'hɔːsʃuː/ **noun** [C] a U-shaped piece of metal that is nailed to a horse's foot

horticulture /'hɔːtɪkʌltʃər/ **noun** [U] the study or activity of growing plants • **horticultural** /ˌhɔːtɪ'kʌltʃərəl/ **adj** relating to gardening

hose /həʊz/ **noun 1** [C] (also UK **hosepipe** /'həʊz-paɪp/) a long pipe made of rubber or plastic and used for directing water somewhere, usually onto a garden or fire **2** [plural] (also **pantyhose**) US a piece of women's clothing made of very thin material that covers the legs and bottom

hospice /'hɒspɪs/ **noun** [C] a place where people who are dying live and are cared for

hospitable /hɒs'pɪtəbl/ **adj** A hospitable person or place is friendly, pleasant, and welcomes visitors.

hospital /'hɒspɪtəl/ **noun** [C, U] ⓐ a place where sick or injured people go to be treated by doctors and nurses: *He was* UK **in hospital**/US **in the hospital** *for two weeks.*

> ✏ Word partners for **hospital**
>
> be **admitted to/discharged from** hospital • be **in** UK/**in the** US hospital

hospitalize (also UK **-ise**) /'hɒspɪtəlaɪz/ **verb** [T] to take someone to hospital and keep them there for treatment: [often passive] *My wife was often hospitalized for depression.*

host¹ /həʊst/ **noun 1** PARTY ▷ [C] ⓑ someone who organizes a party and invites the guests **2** TELEVISION ▷ [C] someone who introduces the guests on a radio or television programme: *a talk show host* **3** PLACE ▷ [C] a country or city that provides the place and equipment for an organized event: *China* **played host to** *the Olympics in 2008.* **4** COMPUTERS ▷ a company that hosts websites on the Internet **5 a host of sth** a large number of people or things: *I've got a whole host of questions to ask you.*

host² /həʊst/ **verb** [T] **1** to be the host of an event: *to host a party/dinner* **2** to provide the computer equipment and programs that allow a website to operate on the Internet

hostage /'hɒstɪdʒ/ **noun 1** [C] someone who is kept as a prisoner and may be hurt or killed in order to force other people to do something **2 take/hold sb hostage** to catch or keep someone as a prisoner: *Two tourists were held hostage by terrorists.*

hostel /'hɒstəl/ **noun** [C] ⓑ a place like a cheap hotel, where you can live when you are away from home or have no home: *a hostel for the homeless* ∘ *a student hostel* → See also **youth hostel**

hostess /'həʊstɪs/ **noun** [C] **1** a woman who organizes a party and invites the guests **2** a woman who introduces the guests on a televi-sion programme → See also **air hostess**

hostile /'hɒstaɪl/ **adj 1** unfriendly and not liking or agreeing with something: *Some politicians*

H

were very **hostile to** the idea. **2** unpleasant or not suitable for living or growing: *a hostile climate*

hostility /hɒsˈtɪləti/ noun **1** [U] unfriendly, angry behaviour that shows that you dislike someone: *hostility towards outsiders* **2** [U] strong disagreement with something or someone: *There is still open hostility to the idea.* **3 hostilities** [plural] formal fighting in a war

> ☑ Word partners for **hostility**
>
> arouse/provoke hostility • open hostility • hostility **to/towards** sb

hot¹ /hɒt/ adj (**hotter, hottest**) **1** VERY WARM ▷ ⓐ having a high temperature: *a hot summer's day* ◦ *a hot drink/meal* ◦ *I'm too hot in this jacket.* **2** SPICY ▷ ⓑ Hot food contains strong spices that cause a burning feeling in your mouth: *Be careful. The chilli sauce is very hot.* **3** EXCITING ▷ informal exciting or interesting: *Hollywood's hottest new actress* **4 a hot issue/topic** a subject that people discuss and have strong feelings about: *The legalization of drugs is a hot topic.* → See also **piping hot, red-hot**

hot² /hɒt/ verb (**hotting, hotted**)

PHRASAL VERB **hot up** UK informal If a situation or event hots up, it becomes more exciting and more things start to happen.

hot-'air bal,loon noun [C] a very large balloon filled with hot air, that has a container below it where people can travel → See picture at **balloon**

hotbed /ˈhɒtbed/ noun [C] a place where there is a lot of a particular activity, usually something bad: *The government was a hotbed of corruption.*

'**hot 'chocolate** noun [C, U] a hot, sweet drink with a chocolate flavour

'**hot ,dog** noun [C] a cooked sausage (= tube of meat and spices) that you usually eat inside bread

hotel /həʊˈtel/ noun [C] ⓐ a place where you pay to stay when you are away from home: *We spent our honeymoon in a luxury hotel.* ◦ *a hotel room*

> ☑ Word partners for **hotel**
>
> at/in a hotel • a hotel **guest/room** • a **luxury** hotel

hotelier /həʊˈteliei/ ⓤ /həʊˈteljər/ noun [C] someone who owns or is in charge of a hotel

hotline /ˈhɒtlaɪn/ noun [C] a telephone number that you can ring for help or information: *Ring our 24-hour hotline for advice.*

hotly /ˈhɒtli/ adv **1** in an angry or excited way: *He hotly denied the rumours.* **2 hotly contested** If a race, election, or other competition is hotly contested, everyone is trying very hard to win it.

'**hot ,spot** (also **hotspot**) noun [C] a public place where people can use computers, mobile phones, etc. to connect to the Internet without using wires: *There are wi-fi hotspots in all our cafés.*

,**hot-'water bottle** noun [C] a flat, rubber container that you fill with hot water to keep you warm

hound¹ /haʊnd/ noun [C] a dog that is used when people hunt animals

hound² /haʊnd/ verb [T] to follow someone an annoy them by asking questions or takin photographs: [often passive] *She is always bein hounded by photographers.*

> ❗ Common learner error: **hour** or **time**?
>
> An **hour** is a period of 60 minutes.
> *The journey takes about three hours.*
> *We went for a two-hour walk.*
> **Time** is measured in hours and minutes. We use **time** to refer to a particular point during the day or night, or to say when something happens.
> *What time do you get up in the morning?*
> *There's only one bus at that time of night.*
> Remember to use **time**, not 'hour', when you are talking about what time it is.
> *"What time is it?" "Two o'clock."*
> ~~"What hour is it?" "Two o'clock."~~

hour /aʊər/ noun **1** [C] ⓐ a period of time equa to 60 minutes: *half an hour* ◦ *It's a six-hour fligh* ◦ *The job pays $5 an hour.* **2** [C] the period c time when a particular activity happens or whe a shop or public building is open: [usually plura **working hours** ◦ *Our opening hours are from to 6.* ◦ *I've got to go to the bank* UK *in my lunch hour/*US *on my lunch hour.* **3 hours** informal ⓑ long time: *I spent hours doing my homework* **4 the hour** the point when a new hour begins *The train leaves at two minutes past the hour.* ◦ *M watch beeps on the hour.* **5 all hours** very late a night, until early morning, or almost all th time: *Our neighbours are up till all hours ever night, playing loud music.* **6 the early/smal hours** the hours between midnight and th time that the sun rises → See also **rush hour**

hourly /ˈaʊəli/ adj, adv **1** ⓑ happening ever hour: *There is an hourly bus service.* **2** ⓑ for eac hour: *an hourly rate/wage*

house¹ /haʊs/ noun (plural **houses** /ˈhaʊzɪz/) **1** BUILDING ▷ [C] ⓐ a building where peopl live, usually one family or group: *a three bedroomed house* ◦ *We went to my aunt's hous for dinner.* **2** PEOPLE ▷ [no plural] the people wh live in a house: *The baby's screaming woke th whole house up.* **3** PLACE FOR ACTIVITY ▷ [C] th place where a particular business or activit happens: *an opera house* ◦ *a publishing hous* **4 the House** a group of people that makes country's laws, or the place where they meet: *th House of Commons/Representatives* ◦ *The Hous voted on the proposals.* **5** THEATRE ▷ [C] th people watching a performance or the are where they sit: [usually singular] *The actors playe to a full house.*

IDIOM **on the house** If food or drink is on th house in a bar or restaurant, it is free.

→ See also **boarding house, full house, rov house, terraced house, the White House**

> ☑ Word partners for **house**
>
> build/buy/rent/sell a house • a **detached/ semi-detached/terraced** house

house² /haʊz/ verb [T] **1** to give a person c

animal a place to live: *This development will house over 100 families.* **2** to provide space for something: *The museum houses a huge collection of paintings.*

ouse ar'rest noun **under house arrest** kept as a prisoner in your own home

ouseboat /'haʊsbəʊt/ noun [C] a boat that people can live on

ousebound /'haʊsbaʊnd/ adj unable to leave your home because you are too sick or old

ousehold[1] /'haʊshəʊld/ noun [C] B2 a family or group of people who live together in a house: *Many households own more than one television.*

ousehold[2] /'haʊshəʊld/ adj **1** [always before noun] connected with or belonging to a home: **household bills/expenses** ∘ **household products/goods 2 a household name** someone or something that everyone knows: *Her TV roles made her a household name.*

ouseholder /'haʊshəʊldəʳ/ noun [C] UK someone who owns or rents a house

ouse ˌhusband noun [C] a man who takes care of the house and children while his wife or partner earns money for the family

ousekeeper /'haʊsˌkiːpəʳ/ noun [C] someone who is paid to clean and cook in someone else's house

ousekeeping /'haʊsˌkiːpɪŋ/ noun [U] the cleaning and cooking that you do in your home

ousemate /'haʊsmeɪt/ noun [C] someone you live with in a house but are not related to

ouse ˌ(music) noun [U] a type of electronic pop music with a strong beat for dancing

ouse of ˈCommons noun [no plural] one of the two parts of the British parliament, with elected members who make laws

ouse of ˈLords noun [no plural] one of the two parts of the British parliament, with members who are chosen by the government

ouse of Repreˈsentatives noun [no plural] a group of politicians elected by people in the US to make laws

ouses of ˈParliament noun [plural] the House of Commons and the House of Lords, or the building in London where they meet

ouse ˌwarming noun [C] a party to celebrate moving into a new house

ousewife /'haʊswaɪf/ noun [C] (plural **housewives** /'haʊswaɪvz/) A2 a woman who stays at home to cook, clean, and take care of her family

ousework /'haʊswɜːk/ noun [U] B1 the work that you do to keep your house clean: *I hate doing housework.*

ousing /'haʊzɪŋ/ noun [U] buildings for people to live in: *a shortage of local housing*

ousing eˌstate noun [C] UK (US **ˈhousing deˌvelopment**) an area with a large number of houses that were built at the same time

ousing ˌproject noun [C] US (UK **council estate**) a group of houses or apartments, usually provided by the government for families who have low incomes

over /'hɒvəʳ/ verb [I] **1** to stay up in the air but without moving anywhere: *A helicopter hovered*

overhead. **2** If you hover, you stand and wait near someone or something: *A waiter hovered at the table ready to take our order.*

hovercraft /'hɒvəkrɑːft/ noun [C] a boat that moves across the surface of water or land supported by a large cushion (= soft container) of air

how[1] /haʊ/ adv **1 WAY** ▷ A2 used to ask about the way something happens or is done: *How did he die?* ∘ *How does she manage to keep the house so tidy?* **2 QUANTITY** ▷ A1 used to ask about quantity, size, or age: *How big is the house?* ∘ *How old are they?* ∘ *How much (= what price) was that dress?* **3 EMPHASIZE** ▷ B1 used before an adjective or adverb to emphasize it: *I was amazed at how quickly she finished.* **4 HEALTH** ▷ A2 used to ask about someone's health: *How are you feeling today?* **5 SITUATION** ▷ B1 used to ask about the success or progress of a situation: *How's everything going?* ∘ *How was the exam?* **6 How are you?** A1 used to ask someone if they are well and happy: *"How are you Jane?"* – *"Oh, not so bad thanks."* **7 How about..?** A2 used to make a suggestion: *How about a drink?* ∘ [+ doing sth] *How about going to the cinema?* **8 How come?** informal used to ask about the reason for something, especially when you feel surprised about it: *"Kate's gone to the party on her own." "How come?"*

IDIOM **How strange/stupid/weird, etc. is that?** said to mean that something is strange/stupid, etc.

→ See also **know-how**

> ❗ Common learner error: **how** or **what**?
>
> In these expressions we use **what**. Be careful not to use 'how'.
> **what something is called**
> *I don't know what it's called in English.*
> ~~I don't know how it's called in English.~~
> **what something/someone looks like**
> *I'd like to see what it looks like before I buy it.*
> *What does your brother look like?*

how[2] /haʊ/ conjunction used to talk about the way that something happens or is done: [+ to do sth] *I don't know how to copy a file onto a CD-ROM.*

however[1] /haʊˈevəʳ/ adv **1 however cold/difficult/slowly, etc** B2 used to say that it does not make any difference how cold/difficult/slowly, etc something is or happens: *We're not going to get there in time, however fast we drive.* **2** A2 used when you are about to say something that is surprising compared with what you have just said: *He had always been a successful businessman. Recently, however, things have not been going well for him.* **3** UK used to ask about how something happened when the person asking feels surprised: *However did you manage to persuade her?*

however[2] /haʊˈevəʳ/ conjunction in any way: *However you look at it, it's still a mess.* ∘ *You can do it however you like.*

howl /haʊl/ verb [I] **1 ANIMAL** ▷ If a dog or wolf

(= wild animal like a dog) howls, it makes a long, sad sound. **2 MAKE SOUND** ▷ to make a loud sound, usually to express pain, sadness, or another strong emotion: *He **howled in** pain.* ○ *The audience was **howling with** laughter.* **3 WIND** ▷ If the wind howls, it blows hard and makes a lot of noise. • **howl** noun [C]

hp written abbreviation for horsepower (= a unit for measuring the power of an engine)

HQ /ˌeɪtʃˈkjuː/ noun [C, U] abbreviation for headquarters (= the place from where an organization is controlled)

hr written abbreviation for hour

HRH /ˌeɪtʃɑːrˈeɪtʃ/ abbreviation for His/Her Royal Highness: used when speaking to or about a royal person

HTH internet abbreviation for hope this helps: used when you send someone information you think is useful, especially when you answer a question

HTML /ˌeɪtʃtiːemˈel/ abbreviation for hypertext markup language: a way of marking text so that it can be seen on the Internet

http /ˌeɪtʃtiːtiːˈpiː/ abbreviation for hypertext transfer protocol: a set of instructions made by a computer program that allows your computer to connect to an Internet document

hub /hʌb/ noun [C] **1** a place that is the centre of a particular activity: [usually singular] *Silicon Valley has become the **hub of** the electronics industry.* **2** the round part in the centre of a wheel

huddle¹ /ˈhʌdl/ verb [I] (also **huddle together/ up**) to move closer to other people, or to hold your arms and legs close to your body, usually because you are cold or frightened: *They huddled around the fire to keep warm.*

huddle² /ˈhʌdl/ noun [C] a group of people or things that are standing close together

hue /hjuː/ noun [C] literary a colour

huff¹ /hʌf/ verb **huff and puff** informal to breathe loudly, especially because you have been exercising

huff² /hʌf/ noun **in a huff** informal angry with someone: *Mum's in a huff because I didn't call yesterday.*

hug¹ /hʌɡ/ verb (**hugging, hugged**) **1** [I, T] 🔒 to put your arms around someone and hold them tightly, usually because you love them: *They hugged and kissed each other.* **2** [T] to stay very close to the edge of something: *The road hugs the coast for several miles.*

hug² /hʌɡ/ noun [C] 🔒 the action of putting your arms around someone and holding them tightly: *She **gave** me a big **hug** before she left.*

huge /hjuːdʒ/ adj 🔒 extremely large: *a huge house*

hugely /ˈhjuːdʒli/ adv extremely: *hugely popular/successful*

huh /hʌ/ exclamation informal used to ask a question, or to express surprise, anger, etc: *So you're leaving, huh?*

hull /hʌl/ noun [C] the main part of a ship that i mostly under water

hullo UK (UK/US **hello**) /həˈləʊ/ exclamation **1** used to greet someone: *Hullo, Chris, how ar things?* **2** used to start a conversation on th telephone: *Hullo, this is Alex.*

hum /hʌm/ verb (**humming, hummed**) **1** [I, T] t sing without opening your mouth: *She humme to herself as she walked to school.* **2** [I] to make continuous, low sound: *The computers wer humming in the background.* **3 be humming** a place is humming, it is busy and full of activity • **hum** noun [C] a low, continuous sound: *th hum of traffic*

human¹ /ˈhjuːmən/ adj **1** 🔒 relating to peopl or their characteristics: *the human body* ○ *huma behaviour* ○ *The accident was caused by huma error* (= a person's mistake). **2 be only human** t not be perfect: *Of course Tom makes mistakes he's only human.*

human² /ˈhjuːmən/ noun [C] (also ˌhuma **ˈbeing**) 🔒 a man, woman, or child: *The diseas affects both humans and animals.*

humane /hjuːˈmeɪn/ adj kind, especially toward people or animals that are suffering: *They fough for more humane treatment of prisoners of wa* → Opposite **inhumane** • **humanely** adv

humanism /ˈhjuːmənɪzəm/ noun [U] a belie system based on human needs and values an not on a god or religion • **humanist** noun [C • **humanistic** /ˌhjuːməˈnɪstɪk/ adj

humanitarian /hjuːˌmænɪˈteəriən/ adj con nected with improving people's lives and redu cing suffering: *The UN is sending **humanitaria** **aid** to the refugees.*

humanities /hjuːˈmænətiz/ noun [plural] su jects that you study that are not connected wit science, such as literature and history

humanity /hjuːˈmænəti/ noun [U] **1 AL PEOPLE** ▷ all people: *The massacre was a crim against humanity.* **2 KINDNESS** ▷ kindness an sympathy towards others → Opposite **inhuma ity 3 BEING HUMAN** ▷ the condition of bein human

humankind /ˌhjuːmənˈkaɪnd/ noun [U] all th people in the world

humanly /ˈhjuːmənli/ adv **humanly possibl** able to be done by people: *Doctors did everythin humanly possible to save her life.*

ˌhuman ˈnature noun [U] feelings, qualitie and behaviour that are typical of most peopl *It's human nature to want to be loved.*

the ˌhuman ˈrace noun [no plural] all th people in the world

ˌhuman reˈsources UK (US **ˌhuman ˈresources** noun [U] the department of an organizatic that deals with finding new people to wor there, keeping records about all the organiza tion's employees, and helping them with an problems

ˌhuman ˈrights noun [plural] 🔒 the basic right that every person should have, such as justic and the freedom to say what you thin international laws protecting human rights ∘ the human rights group Amnesty International

humble¹ /ˈhʌmbl/ **adj 1** not proud or not believing that you are important: *He's very humble about his success.* **2** poor or of a low social rank: *She rose from **humble beginnings** to become Prime Minister.* • **humbly** adv

humble² /ˈhʌmbl/ **verb** [T] to make someone understand that they are not as important or special as they think they are: *She was humbled by the unexpected defeat.* • **humbling** adj *a humbling experience*

humdrum /ˈhʌmdrʌm/ **adj** boring and ordinary: *a humdrum existence*

humid /ˈhjuːmɪd/ **adj** Humid air or weather is hot and slightly wet: *a hot and humid climate*

humidity /hjuːˈmɪdəti/ **noun** [U] a measurement of how much water there is in the air

humiliate /hjuːˈmɪlieɪt/ **verb** [T] to make someone feel stupid or ashamed: *How could you humiliate me in front of all my friends!* • **humiliated** adj *Sue felt completely humiliated.* • **humiliation** /hjuːˌmɪliˈeɪʃən/ **noun** [C, U]

humiliating /hjuːˈmɪlieɪtɪŋ/ **adj** making you feel stupid or ashamed: *a humiliating defeat*

humility /hjuːˈmɪləti/ **noun** [U] the quality of not being proud or not thinking that you are better than other people

humor /ˈhjuːmər/ **noun, verb** US spelling of humour

humorless /ˈhjuːmələs/ **adj** US spelling of humourless

humorous /ˈhjuːmərəs/ **adj** funny, or making you laugh: *a humorous book* • **humorously** adv

humour¹ UK (US **humor**) /ˈhjuːmər/ **noun** [U] **1 ABILITY** ▷ **B1** the ability to laugh and recognize that something is funny: *He's got a great **sense of humour.*** **2 FUNNY QUALITY** ▷ **B2** the quality of being funny, or things that are funny: *His speech was full of humour.* **3 MOOD** ▷ formal the way you are feeling, or your mood: *good humour*

☑ Word partners for **humour**
a sense of humour • a dry/wry humour

humour² UK (US **humor**) /ˈhjuːmər/ **verb** [T] to do what someone wants so that they do not become annoyed or upset: *Carol applied for the job just to humour me.*

humourless UK (US **humorless**) /ˈhjuːmələs/ **adj** unable to laugh and recognize when something is funny, or being without funny qualities

hump /hʌmp/ **noun** [C] **1** a round, raised area on a road or other surface **2** a round, hard part on an animal's or person's back: *a camel's hump*

hunch¹ /hʌnʃ/ **noun** [C] a feeling or guess that something might be true, when there is no proof: *I **had a hunch** that he would get the job.*

hunch² /hʌnʃ/ **verb** [I] to stand or sit with your shoulders and back curved forward: *Sitting **hunched over** a computer all day can cause back problems.*

hunchback /ˈhʌnʃbæk/ **noun** [C] someone with

a large lump on their back, which makes them lean forward

hundred /ˈhʌndrəd/ **1** **A2** the number 100 **2 hundreds** informal a lot: *Hundreds of people wrote in to complain.*

hundredth¹ /ˈhʌndrədθ/ ¹⁄₁₀₀ written as a word

hundredth² /ˈhʌndrədθ/ **noun** [C] one of a hundred equal parts of something; ¹⁄₁₀₀, .01: *a hundredth of a second*

hundredweight /ˈhʌndrədweɪt/ **noun** [C] (plural **hundredweight**) (written abbreviation **cwt**) a unit for measuring weight, equal to 50.8 kilograms in the UK and 45.36 kilograms in the US

hung /hʌŋ/ past of hang

hunger /ˈhʌŋgər/ **noun 1 FEELING** ▷ [U] **B1** the feeling you have when you need to eat: *The children were almost crying with hunger by the time we got home.* **2 NOT ENOUGH FOOD** ▷ [U] **B2** the state of not having enough food: *Many of the refugees **died of hunger.*** **3 WISH** ▷ [no plural] a strong wish for something: *a **hunger for** success/knowledge*

'hunger ˌstrike noun [C, U] a situation in which someone, especially a prisoner, refuses to eat in order to show that they strongly disagree with something: *The prisoners **went on hunger strike**.*

hungover /ˌhʌŋˈəʊvər/ **adj** feeling ill after drinking too much alcohol the day before

hungry /ˈhʌŋgri/ **adj 1** **A1** wanting or needing food: *I'm hungry. What's for supper?* **2 go hungry** to not have enough food to eat: *In an ideal world, nobody should go hungry.* **3 be hungry for sth** to have a strong wish for something: *The journalists were **hungry for** more details of the accident.* • **hungrily** adv

hunk /hʌŋk/ **noun** [C] **1** informal an attractive man who is often young and has a strong body **2** a piece of something, usually large and not flat or smooth: *a **hunk of** bread* → See colour picture **Pieces and Quantities** on page Centre 1

hunt¹ /hʌnt/ **verb** [I, T] **1** **B1** to chase and kill wild animals: *to hunt deer/rabbits* **2** **B2** to search for something: *The children **hunted for** sea shells on the beach.* • **hunter noun** [C] a person who hunts wild animals

PHRASAL VERB **hunt sb/sth down** to search everywhere for someone or something until you find them

hunt² /hʌnt/ **noun** [C] **1** a search for something or someone: *a job hunt* ∘ *The detective leading the **hunt for** the killer spoke at the news conference.* **2** an occasion when people chase and kill wild animals: *a fox/deer hunt* → See also **witch-hunt**

☑ Word partners for **hunt**
launch a hunt • a hunt for sb/sth

hunting /ˈhʌntɪŋ/ **noun** [U] **B2** the sport of chasing and killing animals: *fox-hunting*

hurdle¹ /ˈhɜːdl/ **noun** [C] **1** a bar or fence that people or horses jump over in a race **2** a problem or difficulty that you have to deal with in order to be able to make progress: *Getting a work permit was the **first hurdle** to overcome.*

hurdle² /'hɜ:dl/ verb [I, T] to jump over something, such as a bar or a fence, when you are running • **hurdler** noun [C]

hurl /hɜ:l/ verb **1** [T] to throw something with a lot of force, usually in an angry or violent way: *The demonstrators **hurled** stones **at** police.* **2 hurl abuse/insults, etc at sb** to shout something at someone in a rude or angry way

hurrah (also **hooray**) /hə'rɑ:/ exclamation something that you shout when you are happy, excited, etc, or when you approve of someone or something: *Hurrah! Ian's won!*

hurricane /'hʌrɪkən/ noun [C] a violent storm with very strong winds

hurried /'hʌrid/ adj done more quickly than normal: *a hurried explanation/meeting/meal* • **hurriedly** adv

hurry¹ /'hʌri/ verb [I, T] **(A2)** to move or do things more quickly than normal or to make someone do this: *to hurry away/home* ∘ *Please hurry, the train is about to leave.* ∘ [+ to do sth] *We had to hurry to get there on time.*

PHRASAL VERB **hurry up** **(B1)** to start moving or doing something more quickly: *Hurry up! We're going to be late.*

hurry² /'hʌri/ noun **1 be in a hurry** **(B1)** If you are in a hurry, you want or need to do something quickly: *If you're in a hurry, it's better to take a taxi.* **2 be in no hurry; not be in any hurry** If you are in no hurry to do something, either you do not need to do it soon or you do not really want to do it : [+ to do sth] *They are in no hurry to sign a contract.*

hurt¹ /hɜ:t/ verb (**hurt**) **1 CAUSE PAIN** ▷ [T] **(A2)** to cause someone pain or to injure them: *Simon hurt his knee playing football.* ∘ [often reflexive] *She hurt herself when she slipped on an icy step.* **2 BE PAINFUL** ▷ [I] **(A2)** If a part of your body hurts, it is painful: *My eyes really hurt.* ∘ [+ to do sth] *It hurts to walk on it.* **3 UPSET** ▷ [I, T] **(B1)** to cause emotional pain to someone: *Her comments about my work really hurt.* **4 AFFECT** ▷ [T] to have a harmful effect on something: *His chances of re-election were hurt by allegations of corruption.* **5 it won't/wouldn't hurt (sb) to do sth** informal used to say that someone should do something: *It wouldn't hurt to get there a bit earlier than usual.* → See also **wouldn't hurt a fly²**

hurt² /hɜ:t/ adj [never before noun] **1 (B1)** injured or in pain: *Several people were **seriously hurt** in the accident.* ∘ *Put that knife away before someone **gets hurt**.* **2 (B1)** upset or unhappy: *She was deeply hurt by what he said.*

hurt³ /hɜ:t/ noun [U] emotional pain: *She has **caused** a lot of **hurt**.*

hurtful /'hɜ:tfəl/ adj Hurtful behaviour or remarks make someone feel upset: *hurtful comments/remarks*

hurtle /'hɜ:tl/ verb [I] to move very quickly in a way that is not controlled and may be dangerous: *The explosion sent pieces of glass and metal hurtling through the air.*

husband /'hʌzbənd/ noun [C] **(A1)** the man you are married to: *Janet's husband is in the Navy.*

hush¹ /hʌʃ/ exclamation used to tell someone to be quiet, especially if they are crying: *It's okay. Hush now and wipe your eyes.*

hush² /hʌʃ/ noun [no plural] a period of silence: *A **hush fell** over the room.* • **hushed** adj *a hushed atmosphere/crowd*

> ☑ **Word partners for hush**
>
> a hush **descends/falls** • a **deathly** hush

hush³ /hʌʃ/ verb [T] to make someone be quiet

PHRASAL VERB **hush sth up** to keep something secret, especially from the public, because it could cause embarrassment or trouble: *The whole affair was hushed up by the management.*

hush-hush /ˌhʌʃ'hʌʃ/ adj informal If something is hush-hush, it is kept secret: *The project's **all very** hush-hush.*

husky¹ /'hʌski/ adj **1** A husky voice is low and rough but usually sounds attractive. **2** US A husky man or boy is big and strong.

husky² /'hʌski/ noun [C] a large, strong dog that is used to pull heavy things across snow

hustle¹ /'hʌsl/ verb **1** [T] to make someone move somewhere, especially by pushing them quickly: *The security men hustled him out of the back door.* **2** [I, T] informal to try to persuade someone, especially to buy something, often illegally: *to hustle for business/customers*

hustle² /'hʌsl/ noun **hustle and bustle** busy movement and noise, especially where there are a lot of people: *He wanted to escape the hustle and bustle of city life.*

hustler /'hʌslə/ noun [C] someone who tries to persuade people to give them what they want, especially in order to make money illegally

hut /hʌt/ noun [C] **(B1)** a small, simple building, often made of wood: *a mountain hut*

hybrid /'haɪbrɪd/ noun [C] **1 PLANT/ANIMAL** ▷ plant or animal that is produced from two different types of plant or animal **2 THING** ▷ something, for example a machine, which is made using ideas or parts from two different things **3 CAR** ▷ (also **hybrid car**) a vehicle with an engine that uses both petrol (= a liquid fuel made from oil) and another type of energy, usually electricity • **hybrid** adj

hydrant /'haɪdrənt/ noun [C] a pipe, especially at the side of the road, which is connected to the water system and is used to get water to stop fires: *a fire hydrant*

hydraulic /haɪ'drɔ:lɪk/ adj operated using the force of water or another liquid

hydro- /haɪdrəʊ-/ prefix relating to water: *hydroponics (= a method of growing plants in water)*

hydroelectric /ˌhaɪdrəʊɪ'lektrɪk/ adj using the force of water to create electricity: *hydroelectric power*

hydrogen /'haɪdrədʒən/ noun [U] a gas that combines with oxygen to form water

hydrogenated /haɪ'drɒdʒɪneɪtɪd/ adj Hydrogenated substances, for example fats, have had hydrogen added to them. • **hydrogenation** /haɪˌdrɒdʒɪˈneɪʃʲn/ **noun** [U]

hygiene /ˈhaɪdʒiːn/ **noun** [U] the process of keeping things clean, especially to prevent disease: *health and hygiene regulations* ∘ *dental/personal hygiene* • **hygienic** /haɪˈdʒiːnɪk/ **adj** very clean, so that bacteria cannot spread

☑ Word partners for **hygiene**

standards of hygiene • dental/personal hygiene

hymn /hɪm/ **noun** [C] a song sung by Christians in church to praise God

hype¹ /haɪp/ **noun** [U] a lot of attention that something gets, especially in newspapers, on television, etc, making it seem more important or exciting than it really is: *media hype* ∘ *There's been a lot of hype about/surrounding his latest film.*

hype² /haɪp/ **verb** [T] (also **hype up**) to make something seem more important or exciting than it really is by talking about it a lot, especially in newspapers, on television, etc: *It's being hyped as the musical event of the year.* • **hyped adj**

hyper /ˈhaɪpər/ **adj** informal Someone who is hyper has more energy than is normal and is very excited.

hyper- /haɪpər/ **prefix** having a lot of or too much of a quality: *hyperactive* ∘ *hypersensitive* (= *more than normally sensitive*)

hyperactive /ˌhaɪpərˈæktɪv/ **adj** Someone who is hyperactive has more energy than is normal, gets excited easily, and cannot stay still or think about their work: *hyperactive children* • **hyperactivity** /ˌhaɪpəˈræktɪvəti/ **noun** [U]

hyperbole /haɪˈpɜːbəli/ **noun** [U] formal the use of descriptions that say something is much better, more important, etc than it really is

hyperlink /ˈhaɪpəlɪŋk/ **noun** [C] text that you can click on that lets you move easily between two computer documents or two pages on the Internet

hypermarket /ˈhaɪpəˌmɑːkɪt/ **noun** [C] a very large shop, usually outside the centre of town

hypertext /ˈhaɪpətekst/ **noun** [U] a way of joining a word or image to another page, document, etc on the Internet or in another computer program so that you can move from one to the other easily

hyphen /ˈhaɪfʲn/ **noun** [C] 🅱 a mark (-) used to join two words together, or to show that a word has been divided and continues on the next line → See Study Page **Punctuation** on page Centre 33 • **hyphenated adj** written with a hyphen

ypnosis /hɪpˈnəʊsɪs/ **noun** [U] a mental state

like sleep, in which a person's thoughts can be easily influenced by someone else: *Police placed witnesses under hypnosis in an effort to gain additional information.*

hypnotic /hɪpˈnɒtɪk/ **adj 1** making you feel like sleeping, especially because of being repeated in a regular way: *The chugging of the machinery had a hypnotic effect on me.* **2** relating to hypnosis: *a hypnotic trance*

hypnotize (also UK **-ise**) /ˈhɪpnətaɪz/ **verb** [T] to place someone in a mental state like sleep, in which their thoughts can be easily influenced • **hypnotist noun** [C] someone who hypnotizes people • **hypnotism** /ˈhɪpnətɪzʲm/ **noun** [U] the activity of hypnotizing people

hypochondriac /ˌhaɪpəˈkɒndriæk/ **noun** [C] someone who worries about their health more than is normal, although they are not really sick • **hypochondria** /ˌhaɪpəʊˈkɒndriə/ **noun** [U]

hypocrisy /hɪˈpɒkrəsi/ **noun** [C, U] behaviour which shows that someone does not really believe something that they say they believe or that is the opposite of what they do or say at another time

hypocrite /ˈhɪpəkrɪt/ **noun** [C] someone who pretends to believe something that they do not really believe or that is the opposite of what they do or say at another time • **hypocritical** /ˌhɪpəʊˈkrɪtɪkʲl/ **adj** • **hypocritically adv**

hypothermia /ˌhaɪpəʊˈθɜːmiə/ **noun** [U] a serious illness caused by someone's body becoming too cold

hypothesis /haɪˈpɒθəsɪs/ **noun** [C] (plural **hypotheses** /haɪˈpɒθəsiːz/) a suggested explanation for something that has not yet been proved to be true

hypothetical /ˌhaɪpəˈθetɪkʲl/ **adj** A hypothetical situation or idea has been suggested but does not yet really exist or has not been proved to be true.

hysteria /hɪˈstɪəriə/ **noun** [U] extreme fear, excitement, anger, etc which cannot be controlled: *mass hysteria*

hysterical /hɪˈsterɪkʲl/ **adj 1** If someone is hysterical, they cannot control their feelings or behaviour because they are extremely frightened, angry, excited, etc.: *hysterical laughter* ∘ *As soon as Wendy saw the blood, she became hysterical.* **2** informal extremely funny • **hysterically adv** *They all thought it was hysterically funny.*

hysterics /hɪˈsterɪks/ **noun 1** [plural] uncontrolled behaviour **2 in hysterics** informal laughing so much that you cannot stop

Hz written abbreviation for hertz (= a unit of measurement used in electronics)

H

I, i /aɪ/ the ninth letter of the alphabet

I /aɪ/ pronoun ⓐ used when the person speaking or writing is the subject of the verb: *I had lunch with Glen yesterday.* ◦ *Chris and I have been married for twelve years.* → See Note at **me**

ice¹ /aɪs/ noun [U] ⓐ water that has frozen and become solid: *Gerry slipped on the ice and broke his arm.* ◦ *I've put a couple of bottles of champagne **on ice** (= in a bucket of ice to get cold).*

IDIOM **break the ice** ⓐ to make people who have not met before feel relaxed with each other, often by starting a conversation

ice² /aɪs/ verb [T] (also US **frost**) to cover a cake with icing (= sweet mixture): *an iced bun*

iceberg /ˈaɪsbɜːɡ/ noun [C] a very large piece of ice that floats in the sea → See also **be the tip¹ of the iceberg**

ice ˈcream UK (US **ice ˌcream**) noun [C, U] ⓐ a sweet food made from frozen milk or cream and sugar: *chocolate/vanilla ice cream*

ice ˌcube noun [C] a small block of ice that you put into drinks to make them cold

ice ˌhockey noun [U] (also US **hockey**) ⓑ a game played on ice in which two teams try to hit a small hard object into a goal using long curved sticks → See colour picture **Sports 1** on page Centre 14

ice ˌlolly noun [C] UK (US trademark **Popsicle**) a sweet, fruit-flavoured piece of ice on a small stick

ice ˌrink noun [C] an area of ice, usually inside a building, which is prepared for people to ice skate on

ice ˌskate noun [C] a boot with a metal part on the bottom, used for moving across ice • **ice skate** verb [I] to move across ice using ice skates • **ice skating** noun [U] ⓑ the activity or sport of moving across ice using ice skates → See colour picture **Sports 1** on page Centre 14

icicle /ˈaɪsɪkl/ noun [C] a long, thin piece of ice that hangs down from something

icicles

icing /ˈaɪsɪŋ/ noun [U] (also US **frosting**) a sweet mixture used to cover or fill cakes, made from sugar and water or sugar and butter: *chocolate butter icing*

IDIOM **the icing on the cake** something that makes a good situation better: *He was delighted to get the article published and the payment was the icing on the cake.*

icon /ˈaɪkɒn/ noun [C] **1** ⓑ a small picture on a computer screen that you choose in order to make the computer do something: *Click on the print icon.* **2** ⓑ a person or thing that is famous because it represents a particular idea or way of life: *a cultural/fashion/national icon*

ICT /ˌaɪsiːˈtiː/ noun [U] abbreviation for information and communication technology: the use of computers and other electronic equipment to store and send information

icy /ˈaɪsi/ adj **1** WITH ICE ▷ ⓑ covered in ice: *icy conditions/roads* **2** COLD ▷ ⓑ extremely cold: *an icy wind* ◦ *icy water* **3** WITHOUT EMOTION ▷ ⓑ without showing any emotion: *an icy look/stare* • **icily** adv

I'd /aɪd/ **1** short for I had: *Everyone thought I'd gone.* **2** short for I would: *I'd like to buy some stamps, please.*

ID /ˌaɪˈdiː/ noun [C, U] ⓐ abbreviation for identification: an official document that shows or proves who you are: *You'll need to show some form of ID, such as a passport or driving licence.*

I'D ˌcard noun [C] ⓐ an identity card

idea /aɪˈdɪə/ noun **1** SUGGESTION ▷ [C] ⓐ a suggestion or plan: *"Why don't we ask George?" "That's a good idea."* ◦ [+ for + doing sth] *Steven explained his ideas for improving production.* ◦ [+ to do sth] *It was Kate's idea to hire a car.* **2** THOUGHT ▷ [U, no plural] ⓑ an understanding, thought, or picture in your mind: [+ of + doing sth] *Clive soon got used to the idea of having children around the house again.* ◦ [+ (that)] *I don't want them to get the idea that we're not interested.* **3** have no idea ⓑ to not know: *Bett had no idea where he'd gone.* **4** OPINION ▷ [C] ⓑ an opinion or belief: *My husband and I have very different ideas about school discipline.* **5** AIM ▷ [no plural] the aim or purpose of something: *The idea is to give local people a chance to voice their opinions.* → See also **not have the foggiest (idea) (foggy)**

🔲 **Word partners for idea**

come up with/have an idea • a bad/bright/brilliant/good/stupid idea

---

➕ **Other ways of saying idea**

An idea about how to do something is often described as a **plan**, **thought** or **suggestion**:
*The **plan** is to hire a car when we get there.*
*Have you got any **suggestions** for improvements?*
*Have you had any **thoughts** on presents for your mother?*

A sudden, clever idea is sometimes described as a **brainwave** in the UK and a **brainstorm** in the US:
*I wasn't sure what to do and then I had a **brainwave** – I could ask Anna for help.*

The noun **theory** is sometimes used to describe a set of ideas intended to explain something:
*He was giving a lecture on Darwin's **theory** of evolution.*

---

ideal¹ /aɪˈdɪəl/ adj ⓑ perfect, or the be

possible: *an ideal candidate/solution* ◦ *The book is* **ideal for** *children aged 4 to 6.* ◦ **In an ideal world,** *you wouldn't need to use a keyboard at all.*

ideal² /aɪˈdɪəl/ *noun* **1** [C] a belief about the way you think something should be: *democratic ideals* ◦ *They are committed to the ideal of equality.* **2** [no plural] a perfect thing or situation: *The ideal would be to have a house in the country and an apartment in the city too.*

idealism /aɪˈdɪəlɪzᵊm/ *noun* [U] the belief that your ideals can be achieved, often when this does not seem likely to others • **idealist** *noun* [C] a person who believes that it is possible to achieve your ideals • **idealistic** /aɪˌdɪəˈlɪstɪk/ *adj*

ideally /aɪˈdɪəli/ *adv* **1** 🄑 used to describe how something would be in a perfect situation: *Ideally, I'd like to work at home.* **2** 🄑 in a perfect way: *She seemed* **ideally suited** *for the job.*

identical /aɪˈdentɪkᵊl/ *adj* 🄑 exactly the same: *The two rooms were almost/virtually identical.* ◦ *She found a dress* **identical to** *the one in the picture.* • **identically** *adv*

identical ˈtwin *noun* [C] one of two babies who are born at the same time from the same egg, and look exactly the same

identifiable /aɪˌdentɪˈfaɪəbl/ *adj* If someone or something is identifiable, you can recognize them and say or prove who or what they are: *clearly/readily identifiable*

identification /aɪˌdentɪfɪˈkeɪʃᵊn/ *noun* [U] **1** 🄑 the act of recognizing and naming someone or something: *Most of the bodies were badly burned, making identification almost impossible.* **2** 🄐 an official document that shows or proves who you are: *an identification card/number*

> 🄩 Word partners for **identification**
>
> a form/a means/proof of identification

identify /aɪˈdentɪfaɪ/ *verb* [T] **1 RECOGNIZE** ▷ 🄑 to recognize someone or something and say or prove who or what they are: *Some of the children in the photographs have still not been identified.* **2 NAME** ▷ to tell people who someone is: *My informant asked not to be identified.* **3 DISCOVER** ▷ 🄑 to find a particular thing or all the things of a particular group: *You need to identify your priorities.*

PHRASAL VERBS **identify sb/sth with sb/sth** to connect one person or thing with another: *As a politician he was identified with liberal causes.* • **identify with sb/sth** 🄑 to feel that you are similar to someone, and can understand them or their situation because of this

identity /aɪˈdentəti/ *noun* [C, U] **1** 🄑 who someone is: *Police are trying to* **establish the identity** *of a woman seen walking away from the accident.* **2** 🄑 the things that make one person or group of people different from others: *cultural/national identity*

> 🄩 Word partners for **identity**
>
> cultural/national/personal identity • a sense of identity

iˈdentity ˌcard *noun* [C] 🄑 a piece of paper or a card that shows your name, photograph, and information to prove who you are

ideological /ˌaɪdɪəˈlɒdʒɪkᵊl/ *adj* based on or relating to a particular set of ideas or beliefs: *ideological conflicts/disagreements* • **ideologically** *adv*

ideology /ˌaɪdiˈɒlədʒi/ *noun* [C, U] a set of ideas or beliefs, especially about politics: *socialist ideology*

idiom /ˈɪdiəm/ *noun* [C] 🄑 a group of words used together with a meaning that you cannot guess from the meanings of the separate words → See Study Page **Idioms** on page Centre 26 • **idiomatic** /ˌɪdiəˈmætɪk/ *adj idiomatic language*

idiosyncratic /ˌɪdiəʊsɪŋˈkrætɪk/ *adj* An idiosyncratic quality or way of behaving is typical of only one person and is often strange or unusual. • **idiosyncrasy** /ˌɪdiəʊˈsɪŋkrəsi/ *noun* [C] an idiosyncratic habit or way of behaving

idiot /ˈɪdiət/ *noun* [C] 🄑 a stupid person or someone who is behaving in a stupid way: *Like an idiot, I believed him.* • **idiocy** /ˈɪdiəsi/ *noun* [C, U] stupid behaviour • **idiotic** /ˌɪdiˈɒtɪk/ *adj* stupid: *an idiotic grin/idea* • **idiotically** *adv*

idle¹ /ˈaɪdl/ *adj* **1 NOT WORKING** ▷ not working or being used: *The factory has* **stood idle** *for over a year.* **2 NOT SERIOUS** ▷ [always before noun] not serious or having no real purpose: *idle gossip* ◦ *This is no* **idle threat**. **3 LAZY** ▷ lazy and not willing to work: *He knows what has to be done, he's just* **bone idle** (= *extremely lazy*). • **idleness** *noun* [U] • **idly** *adv* *We cannot* **stand idly by** (= *not do anything*) *and let this plan go ahead.*

idle² /ˈaɪdl/ *verb* **1 ENGINE** ▷ [I] If an engine or machine idles, it runs slowly but does not move or do any work. **2 STOP WORKING** ▷ [T] US to stop someone or something working or being used, often because there is not enough work to do: *The closure of the factory idled about 300 workers.* **3 TIME** ▷ [I] to spend time doing nothing: *We saw her idling in the school grounds.*

PHRASAL VERB **idle sth away** to waste time doing nothing: *I idled away a few hours watching TV.*

idol /ˈaɪdᵊl/ *noun* [C] **1** someone that you admire and respect very much: *a pop/sporting idol* **2** a picture or object that people pray to as part of their religion • **idolize** (also UK **-ise**) *verb* [T] to admire and respect someone very much

idyllic /ɪˈdɪlɪk/ *adj* An idyllic place or experience is extremely pleasant, beautiful, or peaceful: *an* **idyllic childhood** ◦ *an* **idyllic existence**

i.e. (also **ie**) /ˌaɪˈiː/ used to explain exactly what you are referring to or what you mean: *The price must be more realistic, i.e. lower.*

if¹ /ɪf/ *conjunction* **1 DEPEND** ▷ 🄐 used to say that something will happen only after something else happens or is true: *We'll have the party in the garden if the weather's good.* ◦ *If you eat up all your dinner you can have some chocolate.* **2 MIGHT** ▷ 🄑 used to talk about something that might happen or be true: *What will we do if this doesn't work?* **3 WHETHER** ▷ 🄑 whether: *I wonder if he'll get the job.* **4 ALWAYS** ▷ 🄑 used to mean always or every time: *If you mention his mother, he always cries.*

if² /ɪf/ **noun** [C] informal something that is not certain or not yet decided: *There are still a lot of ifs.* ∘ *There are **no ifs and buts** (= no doubts or excuses) about it – we'll have to start again.*

iffy /ˈɪfi/ **adj** informal **1** not completely good, honest, or suitable: *The milk smells a bit iffy.* **2** not certain or decided: *Simon's still kind of iffy about going to Colombia.*

igloo /ˈɪglu:/ **noun** [C] a house made of blocks of hard snow

igloo

ignite /ɪgˈnaɪt/ **verb** formal **1** [I, T] to start to burn or make something start to burn: *A spark ignited the fumes.* **2** [T] to start an argument or fight

ignition /ɪgˈnɪʃ°n/ **noun 1** [no plural] the part of a car that starts the engine: *He turned the key in the ignition.* → See colour picture **Car** on page Centre 7 **2** [U] formal the process of making something start to burn or of starting to burn

ignominious /ˌɪgnəʊˈmɪniəs/ **adj** formal making you feel embarrassed or ashamed: *an ignominious defeat* • **ignominiously adv**

ignorance /ˈɪgn°r°ns/ **noun** [U] not enough knowledge, understanding, or information about something: *There is still widespread ignorance about the disease.* ∘ *I was shocked by her total ignorance of world history.*

ignorant /ˈɪgn°r°nt/ **adj 1** not having enough knowledge, understanding, or information about something: *He was a newcomer to Formula One and ignorant of many of the circuits.* **2** UK not polite or showing respect: *an ignorant lout*

ignore /ɪgˈnɔ:ʳ/ **verb** [T] to pay no attention to something or someone: *They just ignored him and carried on with the game.* ∘ *We cannot afford to ignore the fact that the world's population is increasing rapidly.*

IIRC internet abbreviation for if I remember correctly

il- /ɪl-/ **prefix** not: *illegal* ∘ *illegible*

ill¹ /ɪl/ **adj 1** not feeling well, or suffering from a disease: *critically/seriously ill* ∘ *Mark had been feeling ill for a couple of days.* → See Note at **sick¹** **2** [always before noun] formal bad: *ill health* ∘ *He suffered no ill effects from his fall.* → See also **ill at ease**

ill² /ɪl/ **noun** [C] formal a problem: [usually plural] *social and economic ills*

ill³ /ɪl/ **adv** formal **1** badly: *Many of the nurses were ill prepared to deal with such badly burned patients.* **2 can ill afford (to do) sth** If you can ill afford to do something, it is likely to make things difficult for you if you do it: *This is a match United can ill afford to lose.* **3 speak ill of sb** formal to say bad things about someone

I'll /aɪl/ short for I shall/I will: *I'll be there at 6:0C*

ill- /ɪl-/ **prefix** in a way that is bad or not suitabl *ill-prepared* ∘ *an ill-judged remark*

ill-advised /ˌɪləd'vaɪzd/ **adj** not wise, and like to cause problems in the future

ill-conceived /ˌɪlkən'si:vd/ **adj** badly planned (not wise

illegal /ɪˈli:g°l/ **adj** not allowed by law: *illeg drugs/weapons* ∘ *[+ to do sth] It is illegal to se cigarettes to anyone under 16.* • **illegally adv** *an illegally parked car*

illegal immigrant **noun** [C] (also US **il,leg, 'alien**) someone who goes to live or work another country when they do not have th legal right to

illegible /ɪˈledʒəbl/ **adj** Illegible writing difficult or impossible to read.

illegitimate /ˌɪlɪ'dʒɪtəmət/ **adj 1** An illegitima child is born to parents who are not married each other. **2** not legal, honest, or fair: *illegitimate use of council funds* • **illegitimac** /ˌɪlɪ'dʒɪtəməsi/ **noun** [U]

ill-equipped /ˌɪlɪ'kwɪpt/ **adj 1** not having th necessary equipment **2** not having the nece sary ability or qualities to do something: *[+ to sth] These teachers were ill-equipped to deal wi rowdy students.*

ill-fated /ˌɪl'feɪtɪd/ **adj** unlucky and often unsu cessful: *an ill-fated expedition to the South Pole*

ill-fitting /ˌɪl'fɪtɪŋ/ **adj** Ill-fitting clothes do not f well.

ill-gotten /ˌɪl'gɒt°n/ **adj** literary obtained in dishonest or illegal way: *He deposited his il gotten gains in foreign bank accounts.*

illicit /ɪ'lɪsɪt/ **adj** not legal or not approved of b society: *an illicit love affair*

ill-informed /ˌɪlɪn'fɔ:md/ **adj** without enoug knowledge or information: *an ill-informed dec sion*

illiterate /ɪ'lɪt°rət/ **adj** not able to read or wri

illness /ˈɪlnəs/ **noun 1** [C] a disease of th body or mind: *a serious/terminal illness* ∘ *H died at the age of 83 after a long illness.* **2** [U] the state of being ill

🗹 Word partners for **illness**

cause/develop/have/recover from/treat an illness • a critical/minor/rare/serious/terminal illness

logical /ɪˈlɒdʒɪkəl/ **adj** not based on careful thought: *It would be illogical for them to stop at this stage.*

illuminate /ɪˈluːmɪneɪt/ **verb** [T] **1** to shine lights on something: *The paintings and sculptures are illuminated by spotlights.* **2** to explain something clearly or make it easier to understand • **illumination** /ɪˌluːmɪˈneɪʃən/ **noun** [C, U] formal

illuminating /ɪˈluːmɪneɪtɪŋ/ **adj** giving you new information about something or making it easier to understand: *a most illuminating discussion*

illusion /ɪˈluːʒən/ **noun** **1** [C, U] an idea or belief that is not true: *He had no illusions about his talents as a singer.* ○ *We are not under any illusion – we know the world is dangerous.* **2** [C] something that is not really what it seems to be: *There is a large mirror at one end to create the illusion of more space.* → See also **optical illusion**

illustrate /ˈɪləstreɪt/ **verb** [T] **1** to give more information or examples to explain or prove something: *to illustrate a point/problem* ○ [+ question word] *This new discovery illustrates how little we know about early human history.* **2** 🅱️ to draw pictures for a book, magazine, etc: *an illustrated children's book*

illustration /ˌɪləˈstreɪʃən/ **noun** **1** [C] 🅱️ a picture in a book, magazine, etc: *a full-page colour illustration* **2** [C, U] an example that explains or proves something: *This is another illustration of the power of the media.*

illustrator /ˈɪləstreɪtər/ **noun** [C] a person whose job is to draw or paint pictures for books

illustrious /ɪˈlʌstriəs/ **adj** formal famous and well respected: *an illustrious career*

ill will noun [U] bad feelings between people because of things that happened in the past

im- /ɪm-/ **prefix** not: *impossible* ○ *immortal*

I'm /aɪm/ short for I am

image /ˈɪmɪdʒ/ **noun 1 PUBLIC** ▷ [C, U] 🅱️ the way that people think someone or something is: *The aim is to improve the public image of the police.* **2 PICTURE** ▷ [C] 🅱️ a picture, especially on film or television or in a mirror: *television images of starving children* **3 IDEA** ▷ [C] a picture in your mind or an idea of how someone or something is: *I have an image in my mind of the way I want the garden to look.*

🗹 Word partners for **image**

create/project an image • sb's/sth's public image • an image of sth

imagery /ˈɪmɪdʒəri/ **noun** [U] the use of words or pictures in books, films, paintings, etc to describe ideas or situations

imaginable /ɪˈmædʒɪnəbl/ **adj** possible to think of: *ice cream of every imaginable flavour* → Opposite **unimaginable**

imaginary /ɪˈmædʒɪnəri/ **adj** not real but imagined in your mind: *The story takes place in an imaginary world.*

imagination /ɪˌmædʒɪˈneɪʃən/ **noun 1** [C] 🅱️ the part of your mind that creates ideas or pictures of things that are not real or that you have not seen: [usually singular] *There's nothing out here – it's just your imagination.* **2** [U] 🅱️ the ability to create ideas or pictures in your mind: *The job needs someone with creativity and imagination.* → See also **not by any stretch² of the imagination**

🗹 Word partners for **imagination**

have/lack/show imagination • use your imagination • capture sb's imagination • a fertile/vivid imagination

imaginative /ɪˈmædʒɪnətɪv/ **adj 1** Something that is imaginative is new or clever and often unusual: *an imaginative use of colour* **2** Someone who is imaginative is able to create new and interesting ideas or things: *a highly imaginative poet* • **imaginatively adv**

imagine /ɪˈmædʒɪn/ **verb** [T] **1 CREATE** ▷ 🅱️ to create an idea or picture of something in your mind: [+ doing sth] *Imagine being able to travel in space.* ○ [+ question word] *You can imagine how pleased I was when the letter arrived.* **2 BELIEVE** ▷ 🅱️ to believe that something is probably true: *I imagine he must be under a lot of pressure at the moment.* **3 NOT REAL** ▷ 🅱️ to think that you hear or see something that does not really exist: *I can't hear anything – you must be imagining it.*

imaging /ˈɪmɪdʒɪŋ/ **noun** [U] the process of producing an exact picture of something, especially on a computer screen: *computer/digital imaging*

imbalance /ˌɪmˈbæləns/ **noun** [C] a difference between two things that should be equal or are normally equal: *There is a huge economic imbalance between the two countries.*

imbue /ɪmˈbjuː/ **verb** (imbuing, imbued)

PHRASAL VERB **imbue sb/sth with sth** formal to fill someone or something with a particular feeling, quality, or idea: *His poetry is imbued with deep religious feeling.*

IMHO internet abbreviation for in my humble opinion: used when you tell someone your opinion

imitate /ˈɪmɪteɪt/ **verb** [T] to copy the way someone or something looks, sounds, or behaves: *She tried to imitate the way the models walked.* • **imitator noun** [C]

imitation /ˌɪmɪˈteɪʃən/ **noun 1** [C] a copy of something that is made to look like the real thing: *It wasn't a genuine Gucci handbag, just a cheap imitation.* ○ *imitation leather/fur* **2** [C, U] a copy of another person's way of speaking or behaving: *He does a very good imitation of the Prime Minister.*

🗹 Word partners for **imitation**

a cheap/convincing/good/pale imitation • an imitation of sb/sth

immaculate /ɪˈmækjələt/ **adj 1** perfectly clean

and tidy or in perfect condition: *an immaculate garden/room* **2** perfect and without any mistakes: *an immaculate performance* • **immaculately** **adv**

immaterial /ˌɪməˈtɪəriəl/ **adj** If something is immaterial, it is not important because it does not affect a situation.

immature /ˌɪ.məˈtjʊər/ **adj 1** not behaving in a way that is as wise and calm as people expect from someone your age: *Some of the boys are quite immature for their age.* **2** not completely developed: *immature cells* • **immaturity** **noun** [U]

immeasurable /ɪˈmeʒ³rəbl/ **adj** very large or extreme and so impossible to measure: *the immeasurable pain of losing a child* • **immeasurably** **adv** *His confidence has grown immeasurably since he got the job.*

immediate /ɪˈmiːdiət/ **adj 1** WITHOUT WAITING ▷ ❷ happening or done without waiting or very soon after something else: *The government has promised to take immediate action.* ○ *The drugs will have an immediate effect.* **2** IMPORTANT NOW ▷ ❷ important now and needing attention: *Our immediate concern is getting food and water to the refugees.* **3** CLOSEST ▷ [always before noun] closest to something or someone: *Police cleared people from the immediate area following the bomb warning.* **4 the immediate future** the period of time that is coming next **5 sb's immediate family** someone's closest relatives, such as their parents, children, husband, or wife

immediately¹ /ɪˈmiːdiətli/ **adv 1** ❷ now or without waiting or thinking about something: *The cause of the problem wasn't immediately obvious.* **2** next to something, or close to something in time: *There are fields immediately behind the house.* ○ *Cole scored again immediately after half-time.*

immediately² /ɪˈmiːdiətli/ **conjunction** UK as soon as: *Immediately I saw her I knew something terrible had happened.*

immense /ɪˈmens/ **adj** extremely big: *immense pressure/value* ○ *Health care costs the country an immense amount of money.*

immensely /ɪˈmensli/ **adv** extremely: *immensely powerful/popular*

immerse /ɪˈmɜːs/ **verb 1 be immersed in sth; immerse yourself in sth** to be or become completely involved in something, so that you do not notice anything else **2** [T] to put something in a liquid so that it is completely covered • **immersion** /ɪˈmɜːʃ³n/ **noun** [U]

immigrant /ˈɪmɪgrənt/ **noun** [C] ❷ someone who comes to live in a different country → See also **illegal immigrant**

immigration /ˌɪmɪˈgreɪʃ³n/ **noun** [U] **1** ❷ the process in which people come to live in a different country: *immigration policy* **2** ❸ the place where people's official documents are checked when they enter a country at an airport, port, border, etc: *immigration control* • **immigrate** /ˈɪmɪgreɪt/ **verb** [I] to come to live in a different country

imminent /ˈɪmɪnənt/ **adj** coming or happening very soon: *imminent danger*

immobile /ɪˈməʊbaɪl/ ⑤ /ɪˈməʊb³l/ **adj** not moving or not able to move • **immobili** /ˌɪməʊˈbɪləti/ **noun** [U]

immoral /ɪˈmɒr³l/ **adj** ❷ morally wron *immoral behaviour* • **immorality** /ˌɪməˈrælə **noun** [U]

immortal /ɪˈmɔːt³l/ **adj 1** living or lastin forever: *an immortal soul/God* **2** famous remembered for a very long time: *Then uttered the immortal line – "My name is Bon* • **immortality** /ˌɪmɔːˈtæləti/ **noun** [U]

immortalize (also UK **-ise**) /ɪˈmɔːt³laɪz/ **verb** to make someone or something famous for long time

immune /ɪˈmjuːn/ **adj 1** PROTECTED ▷ [nev before noun] If you are immune to a disease, yo will not get it: *Once you've had the virus, you a immune to it.* **2** BODY SYSTEM ▷ [always befo noun] relating to the way your body figh disease: *an immune deficiency/respon* **3** NOT AFFECTED ▷ [never before noun] n affected by a particular type of behaviour emotion: *He is immune to flattery.* **4** NO PUNISHED ▷ [never before noun] not able to ¹ punished or damaged by something: *His dip. matic passport makes him immune from prosec tion.*

imˈmune ˌsystem **noun** [C] the cells ar tissues in your body that fight against infectio [usually singular] *Vitamins help boost (= ma stronger) your immune system.*

immunity /ɪˈmjuːnəti/ **noun** [U] the state being immune, especially to disease or fro legal action: *diplomatic immunity* ○ *T vaccine gives you lifelong immunity to the viru*

immunize (also UK **-ise**) /ˈɪmjənaɪz/ **verb** [T] make a person or animal immune by givin them special medicine: *He was immuniz against measles as a child.* • **immunizatio** /ˌɪmjənaɪˈzeɪʃ³n/ **noun** [C, U] *a programme mass immunization*

IMO internet abbreviation for in my opinion: us when you want to give an opinion

impact¹ /ˈɪmpækt/ **noun 1** [no plural] ❷ t effect that a person, event, or situation has someone or something: *Latino singers have h a major impact on pop music this year.* **2** [U] the force or action of one object hitting anothe *The missile explodes on impact (= when it h another object).*

> ✏ Word partners for **impact**
>
> have/make an impact • a major/negative/ significant impact • an impact on sth

impact² /ɪmˈpækt/ **verb** [T] (also **impact o upon**) to affect something or someone: *Risi interest rates are sure to impact on the housi market.*

impair /ɪmˈpeər/ **verb** [T] formal to harm som thing and make it less good: [often passive] *Wh you're tired your judgment is impaire* • **impairment** **noun** [C, U] the state of bei impaired: *mental/physical impairment*

impaired /ɪmˈpeəd/ **adj** **visually/hearing impaired** unable to see or hear as well as most people

impale /ɪmˈpeɪl/ **verb** [T] to push a sharp object through someone or something

impart /ɪmˈpɑːt/ **verb** [T] formal **1** to communicate information or knowledge to someone: *I have disappointing news to impart.* **2** to give something a particular feeling, quality, or taste: *Preservatives can impart colour and flavour to a product.*

impartial /ɪmˈpɑːʃ³l/ **adj** not supporting or preferring any person, group, plan, etc more than others: *impartial advice* ∘ *A trial must be fair and impartial.* • **impartiality** /ɪmˌpɑːʃiˈæləti/ **noun** [U] the quality of being impartial

impassable /ɪmˈpɑːsəbl/ **adj** If roads or paths are impassable, vehicles cannot move along them.

impasse /ˈæmpæs/ ⑤ /ˈɪmpæs/ **noun** [U] a situation in which it is impossible to make any progress: *He is determined to break (= end) the impasse in the peace process.*

Word partners for impasse

break/reach an impasse • an impasse **in** sth

---

impassioned /ɪmˈpæʃ³nd/ **adj** showing and expressing strong emotion: *an impassioned plea/speech*

impassive /ɪmˈpæsɪv/ **adj** An impassive person or face shows no emotion. • **impassively** adv

impatience /ɪmˈpeɪʃ³ns/ **noun** [U] impatient behaviour

impatient /ɪmˈpeɪʃ³nt/ **adj 1** ⑫ easily annoyed by someone's mistakes or because you have to wait: *I get impatient with the children when they won't do their homework.* **2** [never before noun] ⑫ wanting something to happen as soon as possible: *People are increasingly impatient for change in this country.* • **impatiently** adv ⑫ *We waited impatiently for the show to begin.*

impeccable /ɪmˈpekəbl/ **adj** perfect and with no mistakes: *She speaks impeccable English.* • **impeccably** adv *impeccably dressed*

impede /ɪmˈpiːd/ **verb** [T] formal to make it difficult or impossible for someone or something to move or make progress: *A broken-down car is impeding the flow of traffic.*

impediment /ɪmˈpedɪmənt/ **noun** [C] **1** formal something that makes it difficult or impossible for someone or something to move or make progress: *Cramped classrooms are an impediment to learning.* **2** a problem that makes speaking, hearing, or moving difficult: *a speech impediment*

impel /ɪmˈpel/ **verb** [T] (**impelling, impelled**) formal to make you feel that you must do something: [+ to do sth] *Harry felt impelled to tell the truth.*

impending /ɪmˈpendɪŋ/ **adj** [always before noun] An impending event will happen soon and is usually bad or unpleasant: *impending disaster/doom* ∘ *I've just heard about the impending departure of our chairman.*

impenetrable /ɪmˈpenɪtrəbl/ **adj 1** impossible to understand: *impenetrable jargon* **2** impossible to see through or go through: *impenetrable fog*

imperative¹ /ɪmˈperətɪv/ **adj 1** formal When an action or process is imperative, it is extremely important that it happens or is done: [+ (that)] *It is imperative that I speak with him at once.* **2** An imperative form of a verb is used to express an order. In the sentence 'Stop the machine!', the verb 'stop' is an imperative verb.

imperative² /ɪmˈperətɪv/ **noun** [C] **1** something that must happen, exist, or be done: *a moral/political imperative* **2** ⑫ the imperative form of a verb

imperceptible /ˌɪmpəˈseptəbl/ **adj** not able to be noticed or felt: *She heard a faint, almost imperceptible cry.* • **imperceptibly** adv

imperfect¹ /ɪmˈpɜːfɪkt/ **adj** not perfect and with some mistakes: *an imperfect solution* • **imperfectly** adv

the imperfect² /ɪmˈpɜːfɪkt/ **noun** (also **the imperfect 'tense**) **the imperfect** The form of the verb that is used to show an action in the past that has not been completed. In the sentence 'We were crossing the road', 'were crossing' is in the imperfect.

imperfection /ˌɪmpəˈfekʃ³n/ **noun** [C, U] a part of something or someone that is not perfect: *Make-up can hide small skin imperfections.*

imperial /ɪmˈpɪəriəl/ **adj 1** [always before noun] relating or belonging to an empire (= group of countries ruled by one person or government) or the person who rules it: *imperial rule* ∘ *the imperial family* **2** The imperial system of measurement uses units based on measurements such as inches, pints, and ounces.

imperialism /ɪmˈpɪəriəlɪz³m/ **noun** [U] **1** a system in which one government or person rules a group of other countries: *the age of imperialism* **2** a situation in which one country has a lot of power or influence over others: *cultural/economic imperialism* • **imperialist** adj relating to imperialism

imperil /ɪmˈper³l/ **verb** [T] (mainly UK **imperilling, imperilled**, US **imperiling, imperiled**) formal to put someone or something in a dangerous situation

imperious /ɪmˈpɪəriəs/ **adj** formal showing that you think that you are important and expect others to obey you: *an imperious manner*

impersonal /ɪmˈpɜːs³n³l/ **adj** not being friendly towards people or showing any interest in them: *a cold and impersonal letter*

impersonate /ɪmˈpɜːs³neɪt/ **verb** [T] to copy the way someone looks and behaves in order to pretend to be them or to make people laugh: *Impersonating a police officer is a serious offence.* • **impersonation** /ɪmˌpɜːs³nˈeɪʃ³n/ **noun** [C, U] *He did an impersonation of Barack Obama.* • **impersonator** **noun** [C] *an Elvis impersonator*

impertinent /ɪmˈpɜːtɪnənt/ **adj** formal rude or not showing respect: *an impertinent remark*

impervious /ɪmˈpɜːviəs/ **adj 1** not affected by something: *She was impervious to the pain.* **2** formal Impervious material does not let liquid into or through it: *impervious rock*

impetuous /ɪmˈpetʃuəs/ **adj** done or acting quickly and without thinking carefully: *an impetuous outburst*

impetus /ˈɪmpɪtəs/ **noun** [U] **1** something that makes an activity or process happen or continue with more speed and energy: *His visit gave new impetus to the peace process.* **2** a physical force that makes an object start or continue to move

> ☑ Word partners for **impetus**
>
> give/provide [new, fresh, added, etc] impetus to sth • the impetus **behind/for** sth

impinge /ɪmˈpɪndʒ/ **verb** formal

PHRASAL VERB **impinge on/upon** sb/sth to affect or limit someone or something: *How does your religious commitment impinge upon your professional life?*

implacable /ɪmˈplækəbl/ **adj** formal determined not to change the strong feelings you have against someone or something: *implacable opposition/hostility*

implant¹ /ˈɪmplɑːnt/ **noun** [C] an object placed inside part of your body in an operation, to improve your appearance or treat a medical condition: *breast implants*

implant² /ɪmˈplɑːnt/ **verb** [T] to place something into someone's body in a medical operation: *Two embryos were implanted in her womb.*

implausible /ɪmˈplɔːzəbl/ **adj** difficult to believe or imagine: *an implausible explanation*

implement¹ /ˈɪmplɪment/ **verb** [T] formal ⑫ to make a law, system, plan, etc start to happen or operate: *Our new computerized system will soon be fully implemented.* • **implementation** /ˌɪmplɪmenˈteɪʃⁿn/ **noun** [U]

implement² /ˈɪmplɪmənt/ **noun** [C] a tool: *a garden/farm implement*

implicate /ˈɪmplɪkeɪt/ **verb** [T] to show that someone or something is involved in something bad, especially a crime: [often passive] *Two senior officers are implicated in the latest drugs scandal.*

implication /ˌɪmplɪˈkeɪʃⁿn/ **noun 1** EFFECT ▷ [C] a result or effect that seems likely in the future: [usually plural] *financial/health implications* ○ *This scheme has serious implications for the local economy.* **2** SUGGESTION ▷ [C, U] the act of suggesting something without saying it directly: *The implication was that the school had to do much better or it would be closed.* **3** INVOLVEMENT ▷ [U] the act of implicating something or someone in something bad

> ☑ Word partners for **implication**
>
> have implications for sth • far-reaching/profound/serious implications • the implications of sth

implicit /ɪmˈplɪsɪt/ **adj 1** suggested but not stated directly: *an implicit threat* ○ *We interpreted his silence as implicit agreement.* **2** complete: *implicit faith/trust* • **implicitly** adv *I trust him implicitly.*

implore /ɪmˈplɔːʳ/ **verb** [T] literary to ask for something in a serious and emotional way: [+ to do sth] *I implored him to let the child go.*

imply /ɪmˈplaɪ/ **verb** [T] to suggest or sho⟨w⟩ something, without saying it directly: [+ (tha⟨t⟩] *Are you implying that I'm fat?* ○ *an implie⟨d⟩ criticism*

impolite /ˌɪmpəˈlaɪt/ **adj** formal ⑫ not polite

import¹ /ɪmˈpɔːt/ **verb** [T] **1** ⑫ to bring som⟨e⟩thing into your country from another count⟨ry⟩ for people to buy: *We import about 20 percent ⟨of⟩ our food.* **2** to copy information from o⟨ne⟩ computer or computer program to another: ⟨to⟩ **import data** ○ *imported files* → Opposite **expo⟨rt⟩** • **importation** /ˌɪmpɔːˈteɪʃⁿn/ **noun** [U] • **impo⟨r⟩ter noun** [C]

import² /ˈɪmpɔːt/ **noun 1** [C] a product that ⟨is⟩ imported from another country: [usually plura⟨l⟩] *Japanese/American imports* **2** [U] the process ⟨of⟩ importing goods: *a ban on the import of be⟨ef⟩* → Opposite **export**

importance /ɪmˈpɔːtⁿns/ **noun** [U] ⑥ ho⟨w⟩ important someone or something is: *He emph⟨a⟩sized the importance of following safety proc⟨e⟩dures.* ○ *She attaches a lot of importance ⟨to⟩ personal possessions (= she thinks they a⟨re⟩ important).*

> ☑ Word partners for **importance**
>
> central/great/major/paramount/the utmost/vital importance • emphasize/stress the importance of sth • attach (great) importance to sth • the importance of sth

important /ɪmˈpɔːtⁿnt/ **adj 1** ④ valuabl⟨e⟩ useful, or necessary: *My family is very importan⟨t⟩ to me.* ○ [+ to do sth] *Listen, Donna has somethin⟨g⟩ important to say.* **2** ⑥ having a lot of powe⟨r⟩ influence, or effect: *an important person/decisio⟨n⟩* → Opposite **unimportant** • **importantly** adv ⑥ *They provided hot showers and, more importantl⟨y⟩ clean clothes.*

> ⊞ Other ways of saying **important**
>
> Adjectives such as **big**, **major** and **significant** are often used to mean 'important' in this sense:
>
> *This is a **big** game tonight – if Manchester lose, they're out of the championship.*
>
> *This is a **major** decision so we'd better get it right.*
>
> *Did he make any **significant** changes to my suggestions?*
>
> Someone or something **of note** is important or famous:
>
> *Did she say anything **of note** at the meeting?*
>
> A person who is important and famous is sometimes described as **eminent**, **prominent**, or **great**:
>
> *Her father was an **eminent** historian.*

impose /ɪmˈpəʊz/ **verb** [T] **1** to officially orde⟨r⟩ that a rule, tax, punishment, etc will happen: ⟨to⟩ **impose a ban/tax** ○ *The judge imposed the dea⟨th⟩ penalty on both men.* **2** to force someone ⟨to⟩ accept a belief or way of living: *I don't want the⟨m⟩ to impose their religious beliefs on my children.*

PHRASAL VERB **impose on** sb to ask or expe⟨ct⟩ someone to do something that may give the⟨m⟩

extra work or trouble: *I hate to impose on you, but could I stay the night?*

imposing /ɪmˈpəʊzɪŋ/ **adj** looking big and important in a way that people admire: *He was an imposing figure – tall and broad-chested.*

imposition /ˌɪmpəˈzɪʃᵊn/ **noun 1** [U] the act of imposing something: *the imposition of a fine* **2** [C] the cause of extra work or trouble for someone else: *It's a bit of an imposition, but could you take me to the airport?*

impossible¹ /ɪmˈpɒsəbl/ **adj 1** 🚫 If an action or event is impossible, it cannot happen or be done: *an impossible task* ∘ *He finds walking almost impossible.* ∘ [+ to do sth] *It was impossible to sleep because of the noise.* **2** very difficult to deal with: *You're putting me in an impossible position.* • **impossibility** /ɪmˌpɒsəˈbɪləti/ **noun** [C, U] something that is impossible: [usually singular] *I can't do it – it's a physical impossibility.*

impossible² /ɪmˈpɒsəbl/ **noun the impossible** something that it is not possible to have or achieve

impossibly /ɪmˈpɒsəbli/ **adv** extremely, in a way that is very difficult to achieve or deal with: *a picture of an impossibly pretty woman*

impostor (also **imposter**) /ɪmˈpɒstər/ **noun** [C] someone who pretends to be someone else in order to deceive people

impotent /ˈɪmpətᵊnt/ **adj 1** An impotent man is unable to have sex because his penis does not become or stay hard. **2** not having the power or strength to do anything to change a situation: *When your child is ill, you feel so impotent.* • **impotence** /ˈɪmpətᵊns/ **noun** [U]

impound /ɪmˈpaʊnd/ **verb** [T] If the police or someone in authority impounds something that belongs to you, for example your car, they take it away because you have broken the law.

impoverished /ɪmˈpɒvᵊrɪʃt/ **adj** formal **1** poor or made poor: *an impoverished country/family* **2** made worse or weaker: *culturally impoverished*

impractical /ɪmˈpræktɪkᵊl/ **adj 1** METHOD/ IDEA ▷ Impractical ideas, methods, etc cannot be used or done easily. **2** PERSON ▷ Impractical people are not good at making, repairing, or planning things. **3** MATERIAL/CLOTHING ▷ not suitable for using in normal situations: *I love high heels but they're rather impractical.*

imprecise /ˌɪmprɪˈsaɪs/ **adj** not accurate or exact: *an imprecise description*

impress /ɪmˈpres/ **verb** [T] 🚫 to make someone admire or respect you: *I was impressed by her professionalism.* ∘ *Sarah was hoping to impress him with her cooking.*

PHRASAL VERB **impress sth on sb** to make someone understand the importance of something: *He tried to impress the importance of hygiene on them.*

impression /ɪmˈpreʃᵊn/ **noun 1** OPINION ▷ [no plural] 🚫 an idea, feeling, or opinion about something or someone: [+ (that)] *I got/had the impression that he was bored.* ∘ *Monica gives the impression of being shy.* ∘ *Remember that it makes a bad impression if you're late.* ∘ *I think*

Mick was under the impression that (= thought that) *we were married.* **2** COPY ▷ [C, U] a copy of the way someone speaks or behaves, often to make people laugh: *He does a brilliant impression of the president.* **3** MARK ▷ [C] a mark left when an object is pressed into something soft

---

🔲 **Word partners for impression**

convey/create/give/make an impression •
get an impression • be under an impression
• a distinct/false/favourable/indelible/lasting/
misleading impression

---

impressionable /ɪmˈpreʃᵊnəbl/ **adj** easy to influence: *impressionable young people*

impressive /ɪmˈpresɪv/ **adj** 🚫 Someone or something that is impressive makes you admire and respect them: *an impressive performance/view* • **impressively adv**

imprint /ˈɪmprɪnt/ **noun 1** [C] a mark left when an object is pressed into something soft: *The steps showed the imprint of his boots in the snow.* **2** [no plural] the effect that something leaves behind: *Much of the house still bears the imprint of her personality.*

imprison /ɪmˈprɪzᵊn/ **verb** [T] to put someone in prison or keep them as a prisoner: [often passive] *He was imprisoned for burglary two years ago.* • **imprisonment noun** [U]

improbable /ɪmˈprɒbəbl/ **adj 1** not likely to be true or to happen **2** surprising: *She was an improbable choice for a supermodel.* • **improbably adv**

impromptu /ɪmˈprɒmptjuː/ **adj, adv** not planned or prepared: *an impromptu party*

improper /ɪmˈprɒpər/ **adj** formal not correct, suitable, honest, or acceptable: *improper conduct* • **improperly adv** *The court ruled that he had acted improperly.*

impropriety /ˌɪmprəˈpraɪəti/ **noun** [U] formal behaviour that is not correct, suitable, or honest: *The enquiry found no evidence of financial impropriety.*

➕ **Other ways of saying improve**

If something improves after a period of doing badly, you can use the verbs **rally** and **recover**:

The team played badly in the first half but rallied in the second.

We are still waiting for the economy to recover.

The phrasal verbs **look up** and **pick up** can be used informally to say that a situation is improving:

Our financial situation is looking up.

Business is really beginning to pick up.

The phrasal verb **work on** means 'to try to improve something':

You need to work on your technique.

The verb **refine** can be used when someone improves something by making small changes:

A team of experts spent several months refining the software.

---

improve /ɪmˈpruːv/ **verb** [I, T] **A2** to get better or to make something better: *Scott's behaviour has improved a lot lately.* ◦ *Every year thousands of students come to London to improve their English.* ◦ *improved earnings/productivity*

PHRASAL VERB **improve on sth** to do something in a better way or with better results than before: *I hope our team can improve on last Saturday's performance.*

> ☑ Word partners for **improvement**
>
> a continuous/dramatic/gradual/significant/ slight improvement • bring about/notice/ produce an improvement • an improvement in/to sth

improvement /ɪmˈpruːvmənt/ **noun** [C, U] **B1** If there is an improvement in something, it gets better: *home improvements* ◦ *There's been a noticeable improvement in her work this year.* ◦ *He's a definite improvement on her last boyfriend.* ◦ *Sadly, her health has shown no improvement.*

improvise /ˈɪmprəvaɪz/ **verb** [I, T] **1** to make or do something without any preparation, using only the things that are available: *For a football, we improvised with some rolled-up socks.* **2** to play music or say words that you are inventing, not reading or remembering • **improvisation** /ˌɪmprəvaɪˈzeɪʃən/ **noun** [C, U]

impulse /ˈɪmpʌls/ **noun 1** [C] a sudden feeling that you must do something, without thinking about the results: [usually singular] *Her first impulse was to run away.* **2 on impulse** suddenly and without thinking first: *I tend to act on impulse.* **3** [C] a short signal that carries information through a system, for example an electrical system or the nerves in your body

> ☑ Word partners for **impulse**
>
> resist an impulse • sb's first impulse

impulsive /ɪmˈpʌlsɪv/ **adj** Impulsive people do things suddenly, without planning or thinking carefully, but because they want to. • **impulsively adv** *He often acted rather impulsively.*

impunity /ɪmˈpjuːnəti/ **noun** formal **with impunity** without being punished: *Criminal gangs are terrorizing the city with apparent impunity.*

impure /ɪmˈpjʊər/ **adj** not pure, but mixed with other substances • **impurity noun** [C, U] the quality of being impure or a substance that is impure

in¹ /ɪn/ **preposition 1** POSITION ▷ **A1** inside or towards the inside of a container, place, or area: *There's milk in the fridge.* ◦ *a shop in Cambridge* ◦ *He put his hand in his pocket.* **2** DURING ▷ **A1** during part or all of a period of time: *We're going to Italy in April.* ◦ *I started working here in 2003.* **3** USING TIME ▷ **A2** needing or using no more than a particular amount of time: *I'll be ready in a few minutes.* **4** PART OF ▷ **A2** part of something: *Who's the woman in the painting?* ◦ *There are a few spelling mistakes in your essay.* **5** JOB ▷ **B1** involved in a particular kind of job:

a career in publishing/politics **6** SUBJECT ▷ **B** connected with a particular subject: *a degree i philosophy* ◦ *advances in medical scienc* **7** WEARING ▷ **B1** wearing: *Do you know tha man in the grey suit?* **8** EXPRESSED ▷ **B1** expressed or written in a particular way Complete the form in black ink. ◦ *She spoke t him in Russian.* **9** ARRANGED ▷ **B1** arranged in particular way: *We sat down in a circle.* ◦ *Is thi list in alphabetical order?* **10** EXPERIENCE ▷ **B1** experiencing an emotion or condition: *She's i a bad mood this morning.* ◦ *The kitchen's in terrible state.* **11 in all** **B2** used to show the tota amount of something: *Some of the childre came, so there were 15 of us in all.*

in² /ɪn/ **adv 1** INTO A SPACE ▷ **A2** into an area o space from the outside of it: *He rushed i halfway through the meeting.* ◦ *Annie opene the car door and threw her luggage in.* **2** AT *A* PLACE ▷ **B1** at the place where a person usuall lives or works: *I called her, but she wasn't ir* ◦ *Could you ask him to phone me when he get in?* **3** TRAIN/PLANE ▷ **B1** If a train, plane, etc i in, it has arrived at the place where was going to: *M train gets in at 17.54.* **4** SENT ▷ **B2** given or sen to someone official in order to be read: *Applic tions must be in by 28th February.* **5** TOWARD LAND ▷ used when the sea or a ship moves clos to land: *Let's go – the tide is coming in.* **6 be i for sth** informal If someone is in for a surprise treat, shock, etc, it will happen to them soon: *A he thinks looking after a baby is easy, he's in for shock.* **7 be in on sth** informal If you are in o something, you know about it or are involved i it: *Were you in on the surprise?* ◦ *Please let me i on (= tell me) the secret.* **8** SPORT ▷ UK In cricke and similar sports, if a person or team is in, the are taking a turn to play. **9 be in for it** inform (also UK **be for it**) to be in trouble

in³ /ɪn/ **adj** informal fashionable or popular: *Pink i in this season.*

in⁴ /ɪn/ **noun**

IDIOM **the ins and outs of sth** the details of particular subject: *the ins and outs of the leg system*

in⁵ (also **in.**) **B1** written abbreviation for inch (= unit for measuring length)

in- /ɪn-/ **prefix** not: *inaccurate* ◦ *insensitive*

inability /ˌɪnəˈbɪləti/ **noun** [no plural] the fact not being able to do something

inaccessible /ˌɪnækˈsesəbl/ **adj** impossible o extremely difficult to get to: *The plane crashed i a mountain area that was totally inaccessible t vehicles.*

inaccurate /ɪnˈækjərət/ **adj** **B2** not correct c exact: *inaccurate information/figures* • **inaccurac** /ɪnˈækjərəsi/ **noun** [C, U] the quality of not bein correct or exact: *His book contains historica inaccuracies.*

inaction /ɪnˈækʃən/ **noun** [U] a failure to tak any action, especially about a problem: *Th announcement follows months of inaction an delay.*

inactive /ɪnˈæktɪv/ **adj** not active or workin

Beetle grubs stay inactive underground until spring. • **inactivity** /ˌmækˈtɪvəti/ **noun** [U] the fact of not being active or working: *a **period of inactivity***

inadequacy /ɪˈnædɪkwəsi/ **noun 1** [C, U] the quality of not being good enough or not being of a high enough quality: *feelings of inadequacy* ◦ *He pointed out several **inadequacies in** the present system.* **2** [U] the quality of not being enough: *The basic problem is the inadequacy of our school budget.*

inadequate /ɪˈnædɪkwət/ **adj 1** not good enough or too low in quality: *inadequate facilities/training* ◦ *Our equipment is totally **inadequate for** a job like this.* **2** not enough: *We were given inadequate funds for the expedition.* • **inadequately** adv

inadvertent /ˌmədˈvɜːtᵊnt/ **adj** not done intentionally: *an inadvertent error* • **inadvertently** adv *I had inadvertently picked up the wrong keys.*

inadvisable /ˌmədˈvaɪzəbl/ **adj** likely to cause problems: *It is inadvisable for women to travel alone in this region.*

inane /ɪˈneɪn/ **adj** very silly and annoying: *an inane question*

inanimate /ɪˈnænɪmət/ **adj** not alive: *an inanimate object*

inappropriate /ˌməˈprəʊpriət/ **adj** not suitable: *inappropriate behaviour* ◦ *It would **be inappropriate for** me to comment, without knowing the facts.* • **inappropriately** adv

inarticulate /ˌmɑːˈtɪkjələt/ **adj** unable to express clearly what you feel or mean in words

inasmuch as /ɪnəzˈmʌtʃˌəz/ **conjunction** formal used to introduce a phrase that explains the degree to which something you have just said is true: *They were strict about our appearance inasmuch as we weren't allowed to wear jewellery or make-up.*

inaudible /ɪˈnɔːdəbl/ **adj** impossible to hear: *His voice was almost inaudible.*

inaugural /ɪˈnɔːgjᵊrᵊl/ **adj** [always before noun] An inaugural speech, meeting, etc is the first one of a new organization or leader: *the President's inaugural address*

inaugurate /ɪˈnɔːgjəreɪt/ **verb** [T] **1** to have a ceremony to celebrate an important person starting a new job, a new building opening, etc: *Barack Obama was inaugurated in 2009.* **2** formal to start a new system or organization: *He inaugurated a programme to fight tuberculosis.* • **inauguration** /ɪˌnɔːgjəˈreɪʃᵊn/ **noun** [C, U] *the inauguration of the Lord Mayor*

in-box (also **inbox**) /ˈɪnbɒks/ **noun** [C] **1** the place on a computer where email messages arrive **2** US (UK **in-tray**) a container where you keep letters and documents that need to be dealt with

Inc. written abbreviation for incorporated (= used after the name of some companies): *Macmillan Inc.*

incalculable /ɪnˈkælkjələbl/ **adj** too big to measure: *The cost in human terms is incalculable.*

incapable /ɪnˈkeɪpəbl/ **adj incapable of sth/ doing sth** not able to do something or to feel a

particular emotion: *He's incapable of controlling his temper.*

incapacitate /ˌmkəˈpæsɪteɪt/ **verb** [T] formal to make someone too sick or weak to work or do things normally: [often passive] *He was incapacitated by illness.* • **incapacity** /ˌmkəˈpæsəti/ **noun** [U] the fact of being unable to do something because you do not have the ability or you are too weak

incarcerate /ɪnˈkɑːsᵊreɪt/ **verb** [T] formal to put and keep someone in prison: [often passive] *Marks was incarcerated for robbery.* • **incarceration** /ɪnˌkɑːsᵊrˈeɪʃᵊn/ **noun** [U]

incarnate /ɪnˈkɑːnət/ **adj** [always after noun] in human form: *He was acting like **the devil incarnate.***

incarnation /ˌmkɑːˈneɪʃᵊn/ **noun 1** [C] a particular form of something or someone that is changing or developing: *In their new incarnation, the band have acquired a female singer.* **2 the incarnation of sth** the physical form of a god or quality: *the incarnation of evil/freedom* **3** [C] a particular life, in religions that believe we have many lives

incendiary /ɪnˈsendiᵊri/ **adj** [always before noun] designed to cause a fire: *an **incendiary bomb/ device***

incense /ˈɪnsens/ **noun** [U] a substance that burns with a strong, sweet smell, often used in religious ceremonies

incensed /ɪnˈsenst/ **adj** extremely angry

incentive /ɪnˈsentɪv/ **noun** [C, U] something that encourages you to act in a particular way: [+ to do sth] *People had little incentive to save.* ◦ *The government should **provide incentives for** young people to stay in school.*

> **🗹 Word partners for incentive**
>
> have/provide an incentive • an **added/ powerful/strong** incentive • an incentive **for** sb

inception /ɪnˈsepʃᵊn/ **noun** [no plural] formal the time when an organization or official activity began: *He has directed the project since its inception.*

incessant /ɪnˈsesᵊnt/ **adj** continuous, especially in a way that is annoying or unpleasant: *incessant rain/noise* • **incessantly** adv *The phone rang incessantly.*

incest /ˈɪnsest/ **noun** [U] sex that is illegal because it is between closely related people, for example a father and daughter

incestuous /ɪnˈsestjuəs/ **adj 1** involving sex between people who are closely related **2** involving a group of people who are not interested in people or things outside the group: *Universities can be very incestuous places.*

inch¹ /ɪntʃ/ **noun** [C] **1** 🔊 (written abbreviation **in.**) a unit for measuring length, equal to 2.54 centimetres → See Study Page **Measurements** on page Centre 31. **2 not budge/give an inch** informal to refuse to change your opinions **3 to be every inch sth** to be a particular kind of person in every way: *He is every inch a gentleman.*

inch² /ɪntʃ/ **verb** **inch closer/forward/up, etc** to move somewhere slowly or by very small amounts

incidence /'ɪnsɪdᵊns/ noun [C] how often something happens, especially something bad: [usually singular] *There's a high incidence of crime in the area.*

> ☑ **Word partners for incidence**
>
> a **high/increased/low** incidence • the incidence **of** sth

incident /'ɪnsɪdᵊnt/ noun [C] formal ⑬ an event, especially one that is bad or unusual: *Police are investigating the incident.*

> ☑ **Word partners for incident**
>
> an incident **happens/occurs** • an **isolated** incident

incidental /ˌɪnsɪ'dentᵊl/ adj less important than the thing something is connected with or part of: *The lyrics here are incidental to the music.*

incidentally /ˌɪnsɪ'dentᵊli/ adv used when you say something that is not as important as the main subject of conversation but is connected to it: *Incidentally, talking of Stephen, have you met his girlfriend?*

incinerator /ɪn'sɪnᵊreɪtᵊr/ noun [C] a machine that is used to burn waste, especially harmful materials

incipient /ɪn'sɪpiənt/ adj [always before noun] formal just beginning: *incipient wrinkles*

incision /ɪn'sɪʒᵊn/ noun [C] formal an opening that is made in something with a sharp tool, especially in someone's body during an operation

incisive /ɪn'saɪsɪv/ adj showing an ability to think quickly and clearly and deal with situations effectively: *incisive questions*

incite /ɪn'saɪt/ verb [T] to do or say something that encourages people to behave violently or illegally: *They denied inciting the crowd to violence.* • **incitement** noun [C, U] something someone does or says that incites people

incl written abbreviation for including or inclusive

inclination /ˌɪnklɪ'neɪʃᵊn/ noun [C, U] a feeling that you want to do something: [+ to do sth] *She showed little inclination to leave.*

incline¹ /ɪn'klaɪn/ verb [T] formal If you incline your head, you bend your neck so that your face bends down.

PHRASAL VERB **incline to/towards sth** formal to think that a belief or opinion is probably correct: *I incline to the view that peace can be achieved.*

incline² /'ɪnklaɪn/ noun [C] formal a slope: *a steep/gentle incline*

inclined /ɪn'klaɪnd/ adj [never before noun] **1 be inclined to think/believe/agree, etc** to have an opinion, but not a strong opinion: *I'm inclined to agree with you.* **2 inclined to do sth a** often behaving in a particular way: *Tom is inclined to be forgetful.* **b** wanting to do something: *No one seemed inclined to help.* **3 artistically/technically, etc inclined** having natural artistic/technical, etc ability: *She's very bright, but not academically inclined.*

include /ɪn'kluːd/ verb [T] **1** ⓐ to have something or someone as part of something larger or more general, such as a group, price, or process: *His books include the best-selling novel 'The Foundling'.* ○ *The price includes flights and three nights' accommodation.* → See Note at **contain 2** to allow someone to take part in an activity: [often passive] *Local residents were included in the initial planning discussions.* → Opposite **exclude**

including /ɪn'kluːdɪŋ/ preposition ⓐ used to show that someone or something is part of a larger group, amount, or process: *Fourteen people, including a prison warden, were killed.* ○ *It's $24.99, including shipping and handling.*

inclusion /ɪn'kluːʒᵊn/ noun [C, U] the fact of including someone or something, especially in a group, amount, or event: *Her self-portrait was chosen for inclusion in the exhibition.* → Opposite **exclusion**

inclusive /ɪn'kluːsɪv/ adj **1 COST** ▷ An inclusive price or amount includes everything: *Prices are inclusive of flights and accommodation.* **2 NUMBERS** ▷ [always after noun] including the first and last date or number stated: *The course will run from October 19 to November 13, inclusive.* **3 PEOPLE** ▷ Inclusive groups try to include many different types of people: *Our aim is to create a fairer, more inclusive society.* → Opposite **exclusive**

incoherent /ˌɪnkəʊ'hɪərᵊnt/ adj not using clear words or ideas, and difficult to understand: *His statement to the police was rambling and incoherent.* • **incoherence** /ˌɪnkəʊ'hɪərᵊns/ noun [U]

income /'ɪŋkʌm/ noun [C, U] ⑫ money that you earn by working, investing, or producing goods: *families on low incomes* ○ *Tourism accounts for 25% of the country's national income.* → See Note at **pay²**

> ☑ **Word partners for income**
>
> an **average/good/high/low/steady** income • **earn/have/provide** an income • be **on a** (high/low, etc) income

'income sup,port noun [U] in the UK, money that is paid by the government to people who have very little or no income

'income ,tax noun [C, U] tax that you have to pay on your income

incoming /'ɪn,kʌmɪŋ/ adj [always before noun] **1** coming into a place or starting a job: *the incoming government* **2** If a telephone call or message is incoming, it is being received rather than sent. *an incoming email* ○ *incoming phone calls/mail*

incomparable /ɪn'kɒmpᵊrəbl/ adj too good to be compared with anything or anyone else: *incomparable beauty*

incompatible /ˌɪnkəm'pætəbl/ adj **1** too different to exist or live together: *He regarded being a soldier as incompatible with his Christian faith.* **2** If equipment or software is incompatible with other equipment or software, it will not work with it. • **incompatibility** /ˌɪnkəmˌpætə'bɪləti/ noun [U] the fact of being incompatible

incompetent /ɪn'kɒmpɪtᵊnt/ adj not able to do

your job, or things that you are expected to do, successfully: *incompetent managers* • **incompetence** /ɪnˈkɒmpɪtᵊns/ **noun** [U]

incomplete /ˌɪnkəmˈpliːt/ **adj** not finished, or having one or more parts missing: *Decisions were made on the basis of incomplete information.* • **incompleteness noun** [U]

incomprehensible /ɪnˌkɒmprɪˈhensəbl/ **adj** impossible to understand: *The instructions are almost incomprehensible.* ◦ *His behaviour is quite incomprehensible to me.*

incomprehension /ɪnˌkɒmprɪˈhenʃᵊn/ **noun** [U] formal the state of not being able to understand something: *She looked at him in total incomprehension.*

inconceivable /ˌɪnkənˈsiːvəbl/ **adj** impossible to imagine: [+ that] *I find it inconceivable that she could be a killer.*

inconclusive /ˌɪnkənˈkluːsɪv/ **adj** not leading to a definite decision or result: *inconclusive evidence/results* ◦ *The battle was inconclusive.*

incongruous /ɪnˈkɒŋgruəs/ **adj** formal strange or not suitable for a particular situation: *Bill was an incongruous sight, standing on the beach in his suit.*

inconsequential /ɪnˌkɒnsɪˈkwenʃᵊl/ **adj** formal not important: *inconsequential remarks*

inconsiderate /ˌɪnkənˈsɪdᵊrət/ **adj** not caring about other people's situations or the way they feel: *It was very inconsiderate of you to keep us all waiting.*

inconsistency /ˌɪnkənˈsɪstᵊnsi/ **noun** [C, U] something that is inconsistent or the quality of being inconsistent : *The report was full of errors and inconsistencies.*

> **✏ Word partners for inconsistency**
>
> (an) **apparent/glaring** inconsistency • (an) inconsistency **in** sth

inconsistent /ˌɪnkənˈsɪstənt/ **adj 1** not staying the same in quality or behaviour: *His homework is very inconsistent.* **2** not having the same principles as something else, or not agreeing with other facts: *The story Robert told his mother is totally inconsistent with what he told me.*

inconspicuous /ˌɪnkənˈspɪkjuəs/ **adj** not noticeable or attracting attention: *Emma tried to make herself as inconspicuous as possible.*

incontinent /ɪnˈkɒntɪnənt/ **adj** not able to control when urine or faeces come out of your body

incontrovertible /ˌɪnˌkɒntrəˈvɜːtəbl/ **adj** formal certainly true: *incontrovertible evidence/proof*

inconvenience /ˌɪnkənˈviːniəns/ **noun** [C, U] the quality of being inconvenient, or something that is inconvenient: *The Director apologized for any inconvenience caused.* ◦ [usually singular] *Having to wait for ten minutes was a minor inconvenience.* • **inconvenience verb** [T] *There were complaints from travellers inconvenienced by delays and cancellations.*

inconvenient /ˌɪnkənˈviːniənt/ **adj** ⑬ involving or causing difficulty, such as unexpected changes or effort: *I'm sorry, I seem to have called at an inconvenient time.*

incorporate /ɪnˈkɔːpᵊreɪt/ **verb** [T] to include something as part of another thing: *He began to incorporate dance and mime into his plays.* • **incorporation** /ɪnˌkɔːpᵊrˈeɪʃᵊn/ **noun** [U]

Incorporated /ɪnˈkɔːpᵊreɪtɪd/ **adj** (written abbreviation **Inc.**) used after the name of companies that have been organized in a particular legal way: *They formed their own company, Broadcast Music Incorporated.*

incorrect /ˌɪnkərˈekt/ **adj** ⑬ not correct: *His answers were incorrect.* • **incorrectly adv** *My name is spelled incorrectly on your list.*

incorrigible /ɪnˈkɒrɪdʒəbl/ **adj** having particular faults and impossible to change

increase¹ /ɪnˈkriːs/ **verb** [I, T] ⑬ to get bigger or to make something bigger in size or amount: *Eating fatty food increases the risk of heart disease.* ◦ *Exports of computers have increased by 15% since January.* ◦ *increased demand/ competition* → Opposite **decrease**

> **➕ Other ways of saying increase**
>
> The verbs **grow** and **rise** are common alternatives to 'increase':
> *The number of people living alone grows each year.*
> *Prices rose by ten percent.*
> The phrasal verb **go up** is often used when prices increase:
> *House prices keep going up.*
> *The price of fuel has gone up by 5p a litre.*
> If something suddenly increases by a large amount, you can use verbs such as **escalate, rocket**, or **soar**:
> *Crime in the city has escalated in recent weeks.*
> *Building costs have rocketed by seventy percent.*
> *House prices have soared this year.*
> If someone makes something increase in size or amount, you can use verbs like **expand** or **extend**:
> *We're hoping to expand/extend our range of products.*
> The verb **maximize** is sometimes used when someone tries to increase something as much as possible:
> *We need to maximize profits.*

increase² /ˈɪnkriːs/ **noun 1** ⑫ [C, U] a rise in the number, size, or amount of something: *a price/ tax increase* ◦ *We are seeing an increase in standards of living.* **2 on the increase** If something is on the increase, it is happening more often: *Violent crime is on the increase.* → Opposite **decrease**

> **❗ Common learner error: increase in or increase of?**
>
> Use **increase in** before the thing that is increasing.
> *an increase in profits/sales*
> Use **increase of** before the size of the increase.
> *an increase of 30%*

🗂 Word partners for **increase**

a dramatic/sharp/significant/slight/substantial increase • an increase in sth

---

increasingly /ɪn'kriːsɪŋli/ adv Ⓑ more and more: *increasingly important* ○ *Increasingly, education is seen as a right, not a privilege.*

incredible /ɪn'kredɪbl/ adj **1** informal Ⓑ very good, exciting, or large: *We had an incredible time that summer.* ○ *an incredible noise* **2** Ⓑ too strange to be believed: *an incredible story*

incredibly /ɪn'kredɪbli/ adv **1** informal Ⓑ extremely: *The team played incredibly well.* **2** in a way that is difficult to believe: *Incredibly, no one was hurt.*

incredulous /ɪn'kredjələs/ adj not able to believe something: *He looked incredulous when I told him the results.* • **incredulity** /ˌɪnkrə'djuːləti/ noun [U] • **incredulously** adv

increment /'ɪnkrəmənt/ noun [C] formal one of a series of increases: *pay increments*

incremental /ˌɪnkrə'mentəl/ adj formal increasing by small amounts: *incremental changes*

incriminate /ɪn'krɪmɪneɪt/ verb [T] to make someone seem guilty of a crime or to show that they are guilty: [often reflexive] *He refused to answer questions on the grounds that he might incriminate himself.*

incriminating /ɪn'krɪmɪneɪtɪŋ/ adj Something that is incriminating makes someone seem guilty of a crime: *incriminating evidence/remarks*

incubator /'ɪŋkjubeɪtər/ noun [C] a heated container that provides the right conditions for a baby born too early, or for very young birds, animals, or eggs

incumbent¹ /ɪn'kʌmbənt/ noun [C] formal someone who has an official job, especially a political one: *the previous incumbent*

incumbent² /ɪn'kʌmbənt/ adj **1 be incumbent on/upon sb to do sth** formal to be someone's duty or responsibility to do something **2** [always before noun] holding an official job, especially a political one: *the incumbent president*

incur /ɪn'kɜːr/ verb [T] (**incurring, incurred**) formal to experience something unpleasant as a result of something you have done: *to incur debts* ○ *I am sorry to have incurred his anger.*

incurable /ɪn'kjʊərəbl/ adj impossible to cure: *an incurable disease*

incursion /ɪn'kɜːʃən/ noun [C] formal a sudden attack or entry into an area that belongs to other people: *incursions into enemy territory*

indebted /ɪn'detɪd/ adj **1 be indebted to sb** to be very grateful to someone: *I'm indebted to my parents for all their support.* **2** having a debt to pay: *indebted countries* • **indebtedness** noun [U]

indecent /ɪn'diːsᵊnt/ adj showing or consisting of sexual behaviour, language, etc that is unacceptable to most people: *indecent photographs* • **indecency** /ɪn'diːsᵊnsi/ noun [U] indecent behaviour, or the fact of being indecent • **indecently** adv

indecision /ˌɪndɪ'sɪʒᵊn/ noun [U] the feeling c not being able to make a decision: *a moment c indecision*

indecisive /ˌɪndɪ'saɪsɪv/ adj not good at makin decisions, or not producing a decision: *She wa weak and indecisive.*

indeed /ɪn'diːd/ adv **1 EMPHASIS** ▷ Ⓑ used t add emphasis after 'very' followed by a adjective or adverb: *For a four-year-old, he vocabulary is very good indeed.* ○ *Thank yo very much indeed.* **2 REACTION** ▷ used whe someone has said something that surprise interests, or annoys you: *"She asked if you wer married." "Did she, indeed?"* **3 TRUE** ▷ Ⓑ used t emphasize that something is true or that yo agree with it: *"He sounds a very interesting man "He is indeed."* **4 MORE** ▷ formal used when yo say more to support or develop what has alread been said: *For such creatures speed is no important, indeed it is counterproductive.*

indefatigable /ˌɪndɪ'fætɪgəbl/ adj formal neve becoming tired: *She was indefatigable i promoting her cause.*

indefensible /ˌɪndɪ'fensəbl/ adj completel wrong, and so impossible to defend c support: *Racism is **morally indefensible**.*

indefinable /ˌɪndɪ'faɪnəbl/ adj difficult t describe or explain: *an indefinable atmospher of tension*

indefinite /ɪn'defɪnət/ adj with no fixed time size, end, or limit: *an **indefinite period***

in,definite 'article noun [C] Ⓑ in gramma a phrase used to mean the words 'a' or 'ar → Compare **definite article**

indefinitely /ɪn'defɪnətli/ adv for a period c time for which no end has been fixed: *His vis has been **postponed indefinitely**.*

indelible /ɪn'deləbl/ adj **1** impossible to forge *an indelible impression/image* **2** impossible t wash away or remove: *indelible ink*

indemnity /ɪn'demnəti/ noun formal **1** [U] pr tection against possible damage or punishmer **2** [C, U] money paid or promised to you something valuable to you is lost or damage *indemnity insurance*

indentation /ˌɪnden'teɪʃᵊn/ noun [C] a marl cut, or hole in the surface of something

independence /ˌɪndɪ'pendəns/ noun [U] **1** Ⓑ the quality of being able to look after yourse and not need money, help, or permission fro other people: *My parents gave me a lot c independence.* ○ *Many old people are afraid c **losing** their **independence**.* **2** Ⓑ a situation i which a country has its own government and i not ruled by another country: *Mexico **gained i independence** from Spain in 1821.*

🗂 Word partners for **independence**

achieve/gain independence • independence from sth

Inde'pendence Day noun (also **Fourth c July**) 4 July, a national holiday in the US t celebrate the country's freedom from Grea Britain in 1776

---

independent¹ /ˌɪndɪˈpendənt/ **adj 1 RULE** ▷ **B2** not controlled or ruled by anyone else: *an independent state/company* ∘ *The group is independent of any political party.* **2 NEED** ▷ **B1** not wanting or needing anyone else to help you or do things for you: *She's a proud, independent woman.* **3 INFLUENCE** ▷ **B2** not influenced by anyone or anything else: *an independent expert/study* • **independently adv B2** *to operate independently*

independent² /ˌɪndɪˈpendənt/ **noun** [C] a politician who does not belong to a political party

in-depth /ˈɪnˌdepθ/ **adj** [always before noun] involving or considering all the details of something: *in-depth knowledge*

indescribable /ˌɪndɪˈskraɪbəbl/ **adj** so good, bad, large, etc that it is impossible to describe: *an indescribable feeling* ∘ *indescribable agony*

indestructible /ˌɪndɪˈstrʌktəbl/ **adj** impossible to destroy or break

indeterminate /ˌɪndɪˈtɜːmɪnət/ **adj** impossible to know: *a large woman of indeterminate age*

index¹ /ˈɪndeks/ **noun** [C] **1 LIST** ▷ (plural **indexes**) an alphabetical list of subjects or names at the end of a book, showing on what page they are found in the text: *Look up 'heart disease' in the index.* **2 INFORMATION** ▷ (plural **indexes**) a collection of information stored on a computer or on cards in alphabetical order **3 SYSTEM** ▷ (plural **indices, indexes**) a system for comparing different values and recording changes, especially in financial markets: *the retail price index*

index² /ˈɪndeks/ **verb** [T] to make an index for text or information, or arrange it in an index

index ˌfinger noun [C] the finger next to your thumb

Indian /ˈɪndiən/ **noun** [C] **1** someone from India **2** an American Indian (= one of the original race of people who lived in North America) → See also **West Indian**

indicate /ˈɪndɪkeɪt/ **verb 1 SHOW** ▷ [T] to show that something exists or is likely to be true: [+ (that)] *Recent evidence indicates that the skeleton is about 3 million years old.* **2 SAY** ▷ [T] **B2** to say something or give a signal to show what you mean or what you intend to do: *He has indicated his intention to resign.* **3 POINT** ▷ [T] to point to someone or something: *He indicated a man in a dark coat.* **4 SIGNAL** ▷ [I, T] UK to show that you intend to turn left or right when you are driving: *The driver turned right without indicating.*

indication /ˌɪndɪˈkeɪʃⁿn/ **noun** [C, U] **1** a sign showing that something exists or is likely to be true: [+ (that)] *There are strong indications that the case will be referred to the Court of Appeal.* **2** a sign showing what someone means or what they intend to do: *Helen's face gave no indication of what she was thinking.*

🔲 **Word partners for indication**

a **clear/good/strong** indication • an indication **of** sth

indicative¹ /ɪnˈdɪkətɪv/ **adj** formal **1** be **indicative of sth** to be a sign that something exists, is

true, or is likely to happen: *These statistics are indicative of a widespread problem.* **2** An indicative form of a verb is used to express a fact or action.

indicative² /ɪnˈdɪkətɪv/ **noun** [no plural] the indicative form of a verb

indicator /ˈɪndɪkeɪtər/ **noun** [C] **1** a fact, measurement, or condition that shows what something is like or how it is changing: *With some goods, cost is the most reliable indicator of quality.* **2** UK (US **turn signal**) a light that flashes on a vehicle to show that the driver intends to turn right or left → See colour picture **Car** on page Centre 7

🔲 **Word partners for indicator**

a **good/reliable/useful** indicator • an indicator **of** sth

indict /ɪnˈdaɪt/ **verb** [T] formal to accuse someone officially of a crime: [often passive] *Pound was indicted for treason.*

indictment /ɪnˈdaɪtmənt/ **noun 1** [C] something that shows the bad things that a person or system is responsible for: *The novel is a scathing indictment of the slave trade.* **2** [C, U] the process of legally indicting someone, or the official document for doing this

indie /ˈɪndi/ **noun** [C, U] informal a small independent music company or film producer: *indie music/bands*

indifference /ɪnˈdɪfⁿrⁿns/ **noun** [U] the feeling of not caring about something or having any particular opinions about it: *an air of indifference*

🔲 **Word partners for indifference**

callous/casual/cold indifference • indifference **to/towards** sth

indifferent /ɪnˈdɪfⁿrⁿnt/ **adj 1** not caring about or interested in someone or something: *They are indifferent to the plight of the unemployed.* **2** neither good nor bad: *an indifferent performance*

indigenous /ɪnˈdɪdʒɪnəs/ **adj** having always lived or existed in a place: *indigenous peoples* ∘ *The kangaroo is indigenous to Australia.*

indigestion /ˌɪndɪˈdʒestʃⁿn/ **noun** [U] pain that you feel when your stomach is unable to digest food correctly

indignant /ɪnˈdɪɡnənt/ **adj** angry because you have been treated badly or unfairly: *Consumers are indignant at/about the high prices charged by car dealers.* • **indignantly adv**

indignation /ˌɪndɪɡˈneɪʃⁿn/ **noun** [U] the feeling of being indignant: *His voice was trembling with indignation.*

indignity /ɪnˈdɪɡnəti/ **noun** [C, U] a situation that makes you lose respect or look silly, or the feeling of shame and embarrassment it gives you: [+ of + doing sth] *They suffered the indignity of being searched like common criminals.*

indigo /ˈɪndɪɡəʊ/ **noun** [U] a blue-purple colour • **indigo adj**

indirect /ˌɪndɪˈrekt/ **adj 1 NOT CONNECTED** ▷ not directly caused by or connected with something: *Indirect effects of the fighting include disease and food shortages.* **2 NOT OBVIOUS** ▷ hidden, or not taken or given in a way that is obvious: *indirect taxes/costs* ○ *an indirect criticism* **3 NOT STRAIGHT** ▷ not going straight from one place or person to another: *an indirect route* • **indirectly** adv

ˌindirect ˈobject **noun** [C] The indirect object of a verb with two objects is the person or thing that is affected by the result of the action of the verb. In the sentence 'Give Val some cake.', 'Val' is the indirect object. → Compare **direct object**

indiscreet /ˌɪndɪˈskriːt/ **adj** saying or doing things that let people know things that should be secret: *indiscreet remarks* • **indiscretion** /ˌɪndɪˈskreʃən/ **noun** [C, U]

indiscriminate /ˌɪndɪˈskrɪmɪnət/ **adj** not planned or controlled in a responsible or careful way: *the indiscriminate use of pesticides* • **indiscriminately** adv *The gunman fired indiscriminately into the crowd.*

indispensable /ˌɪndɪˈspensəbl/ **adj** completely necessary: *an indispensable tool/guide* ○ *She quickly became indispensable to him.*

indisputable /ˌɪndɪˈspjuːtəbl/ **adj** obviously and certainly true: *an indisputable fact*

indistinct /ˌɪndɪˈstɪŋkt/ **adj** not clear: *His words became indistinct.*

indistinguishable /ˌɪndɪˈstɪŋgwɪʃəbl/ **adj** impossible to see or hear as different or separate: *Many toy pistols are indistinguishable from real guns.*

individual¹ /ˌɪndɪˈvɪdʒuəl/ **adj 1** [always before noun] **🔒** considered separately from other things in a group: *Read out the individual letters of each word.* **2 🔒** given to or relating to one particular person or thing: *We deal with each case on an individual basis.*

individual² /ˌɪndɪˈvɪdʒuəl/ **noun** [C] **1 🔒** a person, especially when considered separately and not as part of a group: *We try to treat our students as individuals.* **2** informal a person with a special characteristic, usually one you dislike: *a ruthless individual*

individualism /ˌɪndɪˈvɪdʒuəlɪzəm/ **noun** [U] the quality of being different from other people

individualist /ˌɪndɪˈvɪdʒuəlɪst/ **noun** [C] someone who likes to behave or do things differently from other people • **individualistic** /ˌɪndɪˌvɪdʒuəˈlɪstɪk/ **adj** behaving or doing things differently from other people

individuality /ˌɪndɪˌvɪdʒuˈæləti/ **noun** [U] the quality of being different from others: *The houses had no character and no individuality.*

individually /ˌɪndɪˈvɪdʒuəli/ **adv** separately and not as a group: *He apologized to each person individually.*

indoctrinate /ɪnˈdɒktrɪneɪt/ **verb** [T] to make someone accept your ideas and beliefs by repeating them so often that they do not consider any others: *They try to indoctrinate young people with their religious beliefs.*

• **indoctrination** /ɪnˌdɒktrɪˈneɪʃən/ **noun** [U *political indoctrination*

indoor /ˌɪnˈdɔːʳ/ **adj** [always before noun] **🅐** happening, used, or existing in a building: *an indoor swimming pool*

indoors /ˌɪnˈdɔːz/ **adv 🔒** into or inside building: *If you're feeling cold, we can go indoor*

induce /ɪnˈdjuːs/ **verb** [T] **1 PERSUADE** ▷ formal t persuade someone do something: [+ to do st *Nothing would induce me to marry that mar* **2 CAUSE** ▷ formal to cause a particular conditio *High doses of the drug may induce depressio* **3 BABY** ▷ to give a woman a drug to make he have a baby earlier than she would naturally

inducement /ɪnˈdjuːsmənt/ **noun** [C, U] form something that someone offers you to try persuade you to do something: *They offered m more money as an inducement to stay.*

induct /ɪnˈdʌkt/ **verb** [T] formal to accep someone officially as a member of an organiz tion: *He was inducted into the army in 1943.*

induction /ɪnˈdʌkʃən/ **noun** [C, U] the process ↄ officially accepting someone into a new job ○ an organization: *a two-week induction course*

indulge /ɪnˈdʌldʒ/ **verb 1** [I, T] to let yourself d or have something that you enjoy but that ma be bad for you: *They indulged in a bit of gossi* ○ [often reflexive] *Go on, indulge yourself! Hav another chocolate.* **2** [T] to let someone do have anything they want: *Their children a dreadfully indulged.*

indulgence /ɪnˈdʌldʒəns/ **noun 1** [U] behaviou in which you eat or drink too much or d anything you want **2** [C] something that you d or have because you want to, not because yo need it: *Silk sheets are one of my indulgences.*

indulgent /ɪnˈdʌldʒənt/ **adj** If you are indulge to someone, you give them anything they wa and do not mind if they behave badly: *c indulgent father* • **indulgently** adv *She smile indulgently at her son.* → See also **self-indu gent**

industrial /ɪnˈdʌstriəl/ **adj 1 🔒** connected wi industry: *the industrial revolution* **2 🔒** with lot of factories: *an industrial city such as Sheffie*

inˌdustrial ˈaction **noun** [U] UK a situation i which workers stop working or do less wor because they want better pay or conditions

inˌdustrial esˈtate **noun** [C] UK (US **industri park**) an area where there are a lot of factori and businesses

industrialist /ɪnˈdʌstriəlɪst/ **noun** [C] someor who owns or has an important position in large industrial company

industrialization /ɪnˌdʌstriəlaɪˈzeɪʃən/ **nou** [U] the process of developing industries in country: *Japan's rapid industrialization*

industrialized (also UK **-ised**) /ɪnˈdʌstriəlaɪzͻ **adj** Industrialized countries have a lot industry: *the industrialized nations*

inˈdustrial ˌpark **noun** [C] US (UK **industri estate**) an area where there are a lot of factori and businesses

inˌdustrial triˈbunal **noun** [C] in the UK,

type of law court that decides on disagreements between companies and their workers

ndustrious /ɪnˈdʌstriəs/ adj formal Industrious people work hard. • **industriously** adv

ndustry /ˈɪndəstri/ noun **1** [U] 🔢 the production of goods in factories: *heavy industry* **2** [C] 🔢 all the companies involved in a particular type of business: *the entertainment industry*

> 🔲 **Word partners for industry**
>
> an **important/major/thriving** industry • an industry **booms/grows**

nedible /ɪˈnedɪbl/ adj not suitable for eating: *The meat was inedible.*

neffective /ˌɪnɪˈfektɪv/ adj If something is ineffective, it does not work well. • **ineffectively** adv • **ineffectiveness** noun [U]

neffectual /ˌɪnɪˈfektʃuəl/ adj Ineffectual people or actions do not achieve much: *a weak and ineffectual president* • **ineffectually** adv

nefficient /ˌɪnɪˈfɪʃənt/ adj Inefficient people or things waste time, money, or effort, and do not achieve as much as they should: *an inefficient heating system* • **inefficiently** adv • **inefficiency** /ˌɪnɪˈfɪʃənsi/ noun [C, U]

neligible /ɪˈnelɪdʒəbl/ adj not allowed to do something or have something: [+ to do sth] *Foreign residents are ineligible to vote.* ◦ *Non-graduates are ineligible for this position.* • **ineligibility** /ˌɪnelɪdʒəˈbɪləti/ noun [U]

nept /ɪˈnept/ adj unable to do something well: *socially inept* ◦ *She was totally inept at telling jokes.* • **ineptly** adv • **ineptitude** /ɪˈneptɪtjuːd/ noun [U]

nequality /ˌɪnɪˈkwɒləti/ noun [C, U] a situation in which some groups in a society have more advantages than others: *inequality between the sexes*

> 🔲 **Word partners for inequality**
>
> **gender/racial/social** inequality • inequality **between** sb and sb

nequity /ɪˈnekwəti/ noun [C, U] the state of being unfair, or something that is unfair: *inequities in the health care system*

nert /ɪˈnɜːt/ adj formal **1** Inert substances do not produce a chemical reaction when another substance is added: *inert gases* **2** not moving: *Vanessa lay inert on the sofa.* • **inertly** adv

nertia /ɪˈnɜːʃə/ noun [U] **1** NO CHANGE ▷ If there is inertia, a situation remains the same or changes very slowly: *the inertia of larger organizations* **2** LAZY ▷ a failure to do anything, especially because you are too lazy: *International inertia could lead to a major disaster in the war zone.* **3** FORCE ▷ the physical force that keeps something in the same position or moving in the same direction

nescapable /ˌɪnɪˈskeɪpəbl/ adj An inescapable fact cannot be ignored: *Racial discrimination is an inescapable fact of life for some people.* • **inescapably** adv

nevitable /ɪˈnevɪtəbl/ adj **1** If something is inevitable, you cannot avoid or prevent it: [+

(that)] *It was inevitable that his crime would be discovered.* **2** **the inevitable** something that cannot be prevented: *Eventually the inevitable happened and he had a heart attack.* • **inevitably** adv *Inevitably, there was a certain amount of fighting between the groups.* • **inevitability** /ɪˌnevɪtəˈbɪləti/ noun [U]

inexcusable /ˌɪnɪkˈskjuːzəbl/ adj Inexcusable behaviour is too bad to be forgiven: *His rudeness was inexcusable.* • **inexcusably** adv

inexhaustible /ˌɪnɪɡˈzɔːstəbl/ adj existing in very large amounts that will never be finished: *The Internet is an inexhaustible source of information.*

inexorable /ɪˈneksərəbl/ adj formal continuing without any possibility of being stopped: *the inexorable progress of civilization* • **inexorably** adv *These events led inexorably to war.*

inexpensive /ˌɪnɪkˈspensɪv/ adj 🔢 cheap but of good quality: *inexpensive children's clothes*

inexperience /ˌɪnɪkˈspɪəriəns/ noun [U] the quality of not knowing how to do something because you have not done it or experienced it much before: *The accident was probably caused by the driver's inexperience.*

inexperienced /ˌɪnɪkˈspɪəriənst/ adj 🔢 without much experience or knowledge of something: *Kennedy was young and inexperienced.*

inexplicable /ˌɪnɪkˈsplɪkəbl/ adj so strange or unusual that you cannot understand or explain it: *To me his behaviour was quite inexplicable.* • **inexplicably** adv

inextricably /ˌɪnɪkˈstrɪkəbli/ adv If things are inextricably connected, they are so closely connected that you cannot separate them: *His story is inextricably linked with that of his brother.*

infallible /ɪnˈfæləbl/ adj always right, true, or correct: *infallible evidence of guilt* ◦ *They're experts, but they're not infallible.* • **infallibility** /ɪnˌfæləˈbɪləti/ noun [U]

infamous /ˈɪnfəməs/ adj famous for being bad: *The area became infamous for its slums.*

infancy /ˈɪnfənsi/ noun **1** [U] the period during which you are a baby or a very young child: *Their fourth child died in infancy.* **2** **in its infancy** Something that is in its infancy has only just begun to develop: *In the 1950s, space travel was in its infancy.*

infant /ˈɪnfənt/ noun [C] formal a baby or very young child

infantile /ˈɪnfəntaɪl/ adj behaving like a young child in a way that seems silly: *Don't be so infantile.*

infantry /ˈɪnfəntri/ noun [U, group] soldiers who fight on foot

infatuated /ɪnˈfætjueɪtɪd/ adj If you are infatuated with someone, you feel extremely strongly attracted to them: *As the weeks passed he became totally infatuated with her.* • **infatuation** /ɪnˌfætjuˈeɪʃən/ noun [C, U]

infect /ɪnˈfekt/ verb [T] **1** DISEASE ▷ to give someone a disease: [often passive] *Thousands of people were infected with the virus.* **2** PLACE/ SUBSTANCE ▷ If a place, wound, or substance is

infected, it contains bacteria or other things that can cause disease: [often passive] *The wound became infected.* ◦ *infected water/meat* →
Compare **disinfect 3 FEELING** ▷ to make other people feel the same way as you do: [often passive] *They became infected by the general excitement.*

infection /ɪnˈfekʃⁿn/ **noun** [C, U] **B2** a disease in a part of your body that is caused by bacteria or a virus: *an ear/throat infection*

infectious /ɪnˈfekʃəs/ **adj 1** An infectious disease can be passed from one person to another. **2** Infectious laughter or feelings quickly spread from one person to another: *infectious enthusiasm*

infer /ɪnˈfɜːʳ/ **verb** [T] (**inferring, inferred**) formal to guess that something is true because of the information that you have: [+ (that)] *I inferred from the number of cups that he was expecting visitors.*

inference /ˈɪnfⁿrⁿns/ **noun** [C] formal a fact that you decide is true because of the information that you have: *What inferences can we draw from this?*

inferior¹ /ɪnˈfɪəriəʳ/ **adj** not good, or not as good as someone or something else: *I've never felt inferior to anyone.* ◦ *They're selling inferior products at inflated prices.* • **inferiority** /ɪnˌfɪəriˈɒrəti/ **noun** [U] the fact of not being as good as another thing, or the feeling that you are not as good as other people

inferior² /ɪnˈfɪəriəʳ/ **noun** [C] someone who is considered to be less important than other people

inferno /ɪnˈfɜːnəʊ/ **noun** [C] literary a very large hot fire

infertile /ɪnˈfɜːtaɪl/ ⓤⓢ /ɪnˈfɜːrtⁿl/ **adj 1** An infertile person or animal cannot have babies. **2** Infertile land is not good enough for plants to grow well there. • **infertility** /ˌɪnfəˈtɪləti/ **noun** [U] the problem of being infertile

infest /ɪnˈfest/ **verb** [T] If insects, animals, weeds (= plants you do not want), etc infest a place, they cause problems by being there in large numbers: [often passive] *The hotel was infested with cockroaches.*

infidelity /ˌɪnfɪˈdeləti/ **noun** [C, U] behaviour in which someone who is married or in a relationship has sex with someone who is not their wife, husband, or regular partner

infighting /ˈɪnˌfaɪtɪŋ/ **noun** [U] arguments between the members of a group: *political infighting*

infiltrate /ˈɪnfɪltreɪt/ **verb** [T] to secretly join a group or organization so that you can learn more about them: *A journalist managed to infiltrate the gang of drug dealers.* • **infiltration** /ˌɪnfɪlˈtreɪʃⁿn/ **noun** [C, U] • **infiltrator** **noun** [C]

infinite /ˈɪnfɪnət/ **adj 1** extremely large or great: *She took infinite care with the painting.* **2** without limits or without an end: *God's power is infinite.*

infinitely /ˈɪnfɪnətli/ **adv** very or very much: *Travel is infinitely more comfortable now than it used to be.*

infinitive /ɪnˈfɪnətɪv/ **noun** [C] **C1** the basic form

of a verb that usually follows 'to'. In th sentence 'She decided to leave.', 'to leave' is a infinitive.

infinity /ɪnˈfɪnəti/ **noun** [U] **1** time or space th has no end **2** a number that is larger than a other numbers

infirm /ɪnˈfɜːm/ **adj** formal weak or sick, esp cially because of being old

infirmary /ɪnˈfɜːmⁿri/ **noun** [C] **1** UK formal use in the name of some hospitals: *Leicester Roy Infirmary* **2** mainly US a room in a school, priso etc where people go when they are sick

infirmity /ɪnˈfɜːməti/ **noun** [C, U] formal the sta of being weak and unhealthy, or an illness

inflame /ɪnˈfleɪm/ **verb** [T] to cause or increa strong emotions: *These brutal attacks ha inflamed passions in a peaceful country.*

inflamed /ɪnˈfleɪmd/ **adj** If part of your body inflamed, it is red and often painful and swolle

inflammable /ɪnˈflæməbl/ **adj** Inflammab liquids, gases, or materials burn very easily.

inflammation /ˌɪnfləˈmeɪʃⁿn/ **noun** [C, U] a re painful, and often swollen area in or ɑ a part of your body

inflammatory /ɪnˈflæmətⁿri/ **adj** intended ɑ likely to cause anger or hate: *inflammator statements/speeches*

inflatable /ɪnˈfleɪtəbl/ **adj** An inflatable obje has to be filled with air before you can use it: ɑ *inflatable boat*

inflate /ɪnˈfleɪt/ **verb 1** [I, T] to fill something wiɪ air or gas, or to become filled with air or gas **2** [to make something such as a number, price, e larger

inflated /ɪnˈfleɪtɪd/ **adj** Inflated prices, cost numbers, etc are higher than they should be.

inflation /ɪnˈfleɪʃⁿn/ **noun** [U] **B2** the rate which prices increase, or a continuing increaɪ in prices: *low/rising inflation*

inflationary /ɪnˈfleɪʃⁿⁿri/ **adj** likely to maɪ prices rise

inflection /ɪnˈflekʃⁿn/ **noun** [C, U] **1** the way th end of a word changes to show tense, plurɪ forms, etc **2** the way that your voice goes up ar down when you speak, for example to show th you are asking a question

inflexible /ɪnˈfleksəbl/ **adj 1** Inflexible ruleɪ opinions, beliefs, etc do not change easily: *a co and inflexible man* **2** Inflexible materials do n bend easily. • **inflexibility** /ɪnˌfleksəˈbɪləɪ **noun** [U]

inflict /ɪnˈflɪkt/ **verb** [T] to make someone sufɪ by doing something unpleasant to them: *would never have inflicted such suffering on yo*

in-flight /ˈɪnˌflaɪt/ **adj** [always before noun] haɪ pening or available during a flight: *in-fligɪ entertainment*

influence¹ /ˈɪnfluəns/ **noun 1** [C, U] **B2** th power to affect how someone thinks or behavɪ or how something develops: *The drug compani have a lot of influence on doctors.* **2** [C] ɑ someone or something that has an effect ɑ another person or thing: *His grandfather was strong influence on him.*

☑ **Word partners for influence**

exert/have/wield influence • bad/consider-able/disruptive/good/powerful influence • influence on/over sb/sth • be under the influence of sb/sth

influence² /ˈɪnfluəns/ **verb** [T] ⓑ to affect or change how someone or something develops, behaves, or thinks: *Many factors influence a film's success.* ○ [often passive] *Were you influenced by anybody when you were starting your career?*

influential /ˌɪnfluˈenʃəl/ **adj** having a lot of influence: *an **influential figure** in modern jazz*

influenza /ˌɪnfluˈenzə/ **noun** [U] formal flu (= an illness like a very bad cold, that makes you feel hot and weak)

influx /ˈɪnflʌks/ **noun** [C] the arrival of a lot of people or things at the same time: [usually singular] *The 1990s saw an **influx of** foreign players into British football.*

info /ˈɪnfəʊ/ **noun** [U] informal short for information

inform /ɪnˈfɔːm/ **verb** [T] **1** ⓑ to tell someone about something: *If he calls me again, I shall inform the police.* ○ [+ (that)] *He informed us that we would have to leave.* **2** ⓑ to give someone information about something: [often passive] *Patients should be **informed about** the risks.* ○ *He keeps his parents **informed of** his whereabouts.*

PHRASAL VERB **inform against/on sb** to tell the police about something illegal that someone has done

informal /ɪnˈfɔːməl/ **adj 1** ⓑ relaxed and friendly: *an **informal discussion/meeting* **2** ⓑ suitable for normal situations: *informal clothes* ○ *informal language* • **informality** /ˌɪnfɔːˈmæləti/ **noun** [U] • **informally adv**

informant /ɪnˈfɔːmənt/ **noun** [C] someone who gives information to another person: *Our survey is based on over 200 informants.*

information /ˌɪnfəˈmeɪʃən/ **noun** [U] ⓐ facts about a situation, person, event, etc: *a vital **piece of information*** ○ *Police are urging anyone with **information about** the crime to contact them.*

❗ Common learner error: **information**

Remember you cannot make **information** plural. Do not say 'informations'.

*Could you send me some **information** about your courses?*

*For more **information** contact our office.*

*That's the only piece of **information** we've been able to find out.*

☑ **Word partners for information**

accurate/confidential/detailed/further/useful information • access/exchange/gather/give/need/provide information • information about/on sth

➕ **Other ways of saying information**

The plural noun **details** is often used to describe facts or pieces of information grouped together:

*Please send me **details** of your training courses.*

The plural nouns **directions** and **instructions** are often used to talk about information which describes how to do something:

*Just follow the **directions/instructions** on the label.*

The plural noun **directions** is also used to mean 'information about how to get to a place':

*We had to stop and ask for **directions**.*

The noun **data** is sometimes used to describe information in the form of facts and numbers:

*Our consultants have been collecting financial **data**.*

Written information about a subject is sometimes described as **literature**:

*Some **literature** on our current policy is enclosed.*

information technology noun [U] (abbreviation **IT**) the use of computers and other electronic equipment to store and send information

informative /ɪnˈfɔːmətɪv/ **adj** containing a lot of useful facts: *a very informative lecture*

informed /ɪnˈfɔːmd/ **adj** having a lot of information or knowledge about something: *an **informed choice/decision*** → See also **well-informed**

informer /ɪnˈfɔːmər/ **noun** [C] someone who secretly gives information to the police about a crime

infraction /ɪnˈfrækʃən/ **noun** [C, U] formal an occasion when someone breaks a rule or the law

infrared /ˌɪnfrəˈred/ **adj** Infrared light feels warm but cannot be seen.

infrastructure /ˈɪnfrəˌstrʌktʃər/ **noun** [C] the basic systems, such as transport and communication, that a country or organization uses in order to work effectively: [usually singular] *The country's infrastructure is in ruins.*

infrequent /ɪnˈfriːkwənt/ **adj** not happening very often • **infrequently adv**

infringe /ɪnˈfrɪndʒ/ **verb** [T] **1** formal to break a law or rule: *They infringed building regulations.* **2** (also **infringe on**) to limit someone's rights or freedom: *This law infringes on a citizen's right to bear arms.* • **infringement noun** [C, U] *an infringement of copyright*

infuriate /ɪnˈfjʊərieɪt/ **verb** [T] to make someone very angry: *What really infuriated me was the fact that he'd lied.* • **infuriating adj** extremely annoying

infuse /ɪnˈfjuːz/ **verb 1** [T] formal to fill someone or something with a lot of a particular emotion or quality: [often passive] *His work is **infused with** a love for tradition.* **2** [I, T] to put something into a liquid so that its taste goes into the liquid

infusion /ɪnˈfjuːʒᵊn/ noun [C, U] formal the addition of one thing to another thing to make it stronger or better: *an infusion of cash*

ingenious /ɪnˈdʒiːniəs/ adj very clever and involving new ideas, equipment, or methods: *It was an ingenious idea/scheme/solution.* • ingeniously adv

ingenuity /ˌɪndʒɪˈnjuːəti/ noun [U] skill at inventing things or finding new ways to solve problems

ingest /ɪnˈdʒest/ verb [T] formal to eat or drink something • ingestion noun [U]

ingrained /ɪnˈɡreɪnd/ adj 1 Ingrained beliefs, behaviour, problems, etc have existed for a long time and are difficult to change: *For most of us, watching television is a deeply ingrained habit.* 2 Ingrained dirt has got under the surface of something and is difficult to remove.

ingratiate /ɪnˈɡreɪʃieɪt/ verb ingratiate yourself (with sb) to try to make people like you by doing things to please them • ingratiating adj Ingratiating behaviour is done to try to make people like you: *an ingratiating smile/manner*

ingratitude /ɪnˈɡrætɪtjuːd/ noun [U] the feeling of not being grateful for something

ingredient /ɪnˈɡriːdiənt/ noun [C] 1 🅱 one of the different foods that a particular type of food is made from 2 🅱 one of the parts of something successful: *Trust is an essential ingredient in a successful marriage.*

> ☑ Word partners for **ingredient**
> a basic/essential/vital ingredient • an ingredient in/of sth

inhabit /ɪnˈhæbɪt/ verb [T] formal to live in a place: [often passive] *The area is inhabited by artists and writers.*

inhabitant /ɪnˈhæbɪtᵊnt/ noun [C] 🅱 someone who lives in a particular place: *a city with 10 million inhabitants*

inhabited /ɪnˈhæbɪtɪd/ adj An inhabited place or building has people living in it: *Is the island inhabited?*

inhale /ɪnˈheɪl/ verb [I, T] formal 1 to breathe air, smoke, or gas into your lungs 2 US informal to eat something very quickly: *Slow down, you're inhaling that pizza!*

inherent /ɪnˈherᵊnt/ adj existing as a natural and basic part of something: *The desire for freedom is inherent in all people.* • inherently adv *There's nothing inherently wrong with his ideas.*

inherit /ɪnˈherɪt/ verb [T] 1 FROM DEAD PERSON ▷ to receive possessions or money from someone who has died: *In 1842 he inherited a small estate near Liverpool.* 2 QUALITY ▷ to have the same physical or mental characteristics as one of your parents or grandparents: *Miranda has inherited her father's red hair.* 3 PROBLEM ▷ If you inherit a problem, situation, or belief, it is passed on to you by someone who had it before: *The mayor will inherit a city hopelessly in debt.*

inheritance /ɪnˈherɪtᵊns/ noun [C, U] money or possessions that someone gives you when they die: *Nick has sold off much of his inheritance.*

inhibit /ɪnˈhɪbɪt/ verb [T] 1 to make the progress or growth of something slower: *This product inhibits the growth of harmful bacteria.* 2 to make it more difficult for someone to do something: *Their threats inhibited witnesses from giving evidence.*

inhibited /ɪnˈhɪbɪtɪd/ adj not confident enough to say or do what you want

inhibition /ˌɪnhɪˈbɪʃᵊn/ noun [C, U] a feeling of embarrassment or worry that prevents you from saying or doing what you want: *The whole point about dancing is to lose all your inhibitions.*

> ☑ Word partners for **inhibition**
> have no inhibitions about doing sth • lose your inhibitions

inhospitable /ˌɪnhɒsˈpɪtəbl/ adj 1 An inhospitable place is not pleasant or easy to live in because it is too hot, cold, etc.: *the world's most inhospitable deserts* 2 not friendly toward people who are visiting you

in-house /ˌɪnˈhaʊs/ adj, adv done in the office of a company or organization by employees of that company: *in-house training of staff*

inhuman /ɪnˈhjuːmən/ adj extremely cruel: *the inhuman treatment of prisoners*

inhumane /ˌɪnhjuːˈmeɪn/ adj treating people or animals in a cruel way: *inhumane experiments on monkeys* • inhumanely adv

inhumanity /ˌɪnhjuːˈmænəti/ noun [U] extremely cruel behaviour: *the inhumanity of war*

initial¹ /ɪˈnɪʃᵊl/ adj [always before noun] 🅱 first, or happening at the beginning: *My initial reaction was one of anger.*

initial² /ɪˈnɪʃᵊl/ noun [C] 🅱 the first letter of a name: [usually plural] *His initials are S.G.M.*

initial³ /ɪˈnɪʃᵊl/ verb [T] (mainly UK initialling, initialled, US initialing, initialed) to write your initials on something

initialize /ɪˈnɪʃᵊlaɪz/ verb [T] to make a computer program ready to use

initially /ɪˈnɪʃᵊli/ adv 🅱 at the beginning: *The situation was worse than they initially thought.*

initiate /ɪˈnɪʃieɪt/ verb [T] 1 to make something begin: [often passive] *The program was initiated by the state government.* 2 to make someone a member of a group or organization in a special ceremony, or to show someone how to do an activity: *At the age of 50, he was initiated into the priesthood.* • initiation /ɪˌnɪʃiˈeɪʃᵊn/ noun [C, U]

initiative /ɪˈnɪʃətɪv/ noun 1 [C] a plan or activity that is done to solve a problem or improve a situation: *a new government initiative to reduce crime* 2 [U] the ability to make decisions and do things without needing to be told what to do: *We need someone who can work on their own initiative* (= without anyone telling them what to do). 3 take the initiative to be the first person to do something that solves a problem or improves a situation: *Jackson had taken the initiative and prepared a report.*

inject /ɪnˈdʒekt/ verb [T] 1 DRUG ▷ to put a drug into someone's body using a needle: *Phil is diabetic and has to inject himself with insulin every day.* 2 IMPROVE ▷ to add a good quality to something: *The new teacher has **injected** a bit of enthusiasm **into** the school.* **3** MONEY ▷ to provide a large amount of money for a plan, service, organization, etc: *The government plans to **inject** £100 million **into** schools.*

injection

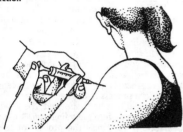

injection /ɪnˈdʒekʃən/ **noun 1** [C, U] If you have an injection, someone puts a drug into your body using a needle: *an injection of insulin* **2** [C] a large amount of money that is provided for a plan, service, organization, etc: *The university has welcomed the $5 million **cash injection**.*

injunction /ɪnˈdʒʌŋkʃən/ **noun** [C] an official order from a court that prevents someone from doing something: *The courts have **issued an injunction** to prevent the book from being published.*

injure /ˈɪndʒər/ **verb** [T] ⑤ to hurt a person, animal, or part of your body: *She injured her ankle when she fell.*

injured /ˈɪndʒəd/ **adj** ⑥ hurt: *Fortunately, no one was **seriously injured** in the accident.*

injury /ˈɪndʒəri/ **noun** [C, U] ⑥ damage to someone's body in an accident or attack: *head injuries* ∘ *The passenger in the car escaped with **minor injuries**.* → See also **add insult² to injury**

> 🗌 Word partners for **injury**
>
> a **fatal/major/minor/serious** injury • **cause/ prevent/receive/recover from/suffer** an injury • an injury **to** sth

injustice /ɪnˈdʒʌstɪs/ **noun** [C, U] a situation or action in which people are treated unfairly: *the fight against racial injustice*

ink /ɪŋk/ **noun** [C, U] ⑥ a coloured liquid that you use for writing, printing, or drawing

ink cartridge noun [C] a small container of ink for use in a printer (= machine which is connected to a computer and which produces writing or pictures)

inkjet printer noun [C] (also **inkjet**) an electronic printer (= machine which is connected to a computer and which produces writing or pictures) that blows small amounts of ink onto paper

inkling /ˈɪŋklɪŋ/ **noun have an inkling** to think that something might be true or might happen: *She **had** absolutely no **inkling** that we were planning the party.*

inland¹ /ˈɪnlənd/ **adj** [always before noun] Inland areas, lakes, towns, etc are a long way from the coast.

inland² /ˈɪnlænd/ **adv** towards the middle of a country and away from the coast

in-laws /ˈɪnlɔːz/ **noun** [plural] informal the parents of your husband or wife, or other people in their family

inlet /ˈɪnlet/ **noun** [C] a narrow part of a sea, river, or lake where it flows into a curve in the land

in-line skate noun [C] (also **rollerblade**) a boot with a single line of wheels on the bottom, used for moving across the ground → See colour picture **Sports 1** on page Centre 14

inmate /ˈɪnmeɪt/ **noun** [C] someone who lives in a prison or in a hospital for people with mental illnesses

inn /ɪn/ **noun** [C] a small hotel in the countryside

innate /ɪˈneɪt/ **adj** An innate quality or ability is one that you were born with, not one you have learned: *He has an innate desire to win.*
• **innately adv**

inner /ˈɪnər/ **adj** [always before noun] **1** ⑥ on the inside, or near the middle of something: *The monastery is built around an inner courtyard.* → Opposite **outer 2** ⑥ Inner feelings, thoughts, etc are ones that you do not show or tell other people: *a profound sense of inner peace*

inner circle noun [C] the small group of people who control an organization, political party, etc: *The statement was made by a member of the President's inner circle.*

inner city noun [C] the part of a city that is closest to the centre, often where buildings are in a bad condition and there are social problems: *a plan to tackle rising crime in inner cities* • **inner-city** /ˌɪnəˈsɪti/ **adj** [always before noun] *inner-city schools*

innermost /ˈɪnəməʊst/ **adj** [always before noun] **1** Your innermost feelings, thoughts, etc are the most private ones that you do not want other people to know about. **2** formal closest to the middle of something

inning /ˈɪnɪŋ/ **noun** [C] one of the nine playing periods in a baseball game

innings /ˈɪnɪŋz/ **noun** [C] (plural **innings**) the period of time in a game of cricket when one player or one team hits the ball

innit /ˈɪnɪt/ **exclamation** UK very informal used to change a statement into a question: *It's wrong, innit?*

innocence /ˈɪnəsəns/ **noun** [U] **1** the fact of not being guilty of a crime: *She fought to **prove** her son's **innocence**.* **2** the quality of not having much experience of life and not knowing about the bad things that happen: *the innocence of childhood*

> 🗌 Word partners for **innocence**
>
> **proclaim/protest/prove** sb's innocence

innocent /ˈɪnəsənt/ **adj 1** NOT GUILTY ▷ ⑥ not guilty of committing a crime: *He claims to be **innocent** of the crime.* **2** NO EXPERIENCE ▷ ⑥ not having much experience of life and not knowing about the bad things that happen: *an innocent young woman* **3** NOT DESERVED ▷ ⑥ used to emphasize that someone who was hurt had done nothing wrong: *Several innocent civilians were killed in the bombing.* **4 NOT INTENDED TO HARM** ▷ not intended to harm or upset anyone: *It was an innocent mistake.* • **innocently adv**

innocuous /ɪˈnɒkjuəs/ **adj** not likely to upset or harm anyone: *The parcel looked innocuous enough.* • **innocuously adv**

innovation /ˌɪnəʊˈveɪʃᵊn/ **noun** [C, U] a new idea or method that is being tried for the first time, or the use of such ideas or methods: *the latest innovations in education*

innovative /ˈɪnəvətɪv/ ⑩ /ˈɪnəveɪtɪv/ **adj** using new methods or ideas: *an innovative approach to programme making*

innovator /ˈɪnəveɪtər/ **noun** [C] someone who uses or designs new methods or products

innuendo /ˌɪnjuˈendəʊ/ **noun** [C, U] (plural **innuendoes**, **innuendos**) a remark that intentionally suggests something about sex, or something unpleasant about someone, without saying it directly: *The advertisement was criticized for its sexual innuendo.*

innumerable /ɪˈnjuːmᵊrəbl/ **adj** very many, or too many to count: *innumerable problems*

inoffensive /ˌɪnəˈfensɪv/ **adj** not likely to upset anyone or make them angry: *an inoffensive colour*

inordinate /ɪˈnɔːdɪnət/ **adj** formal much more than is usual or suitable: *James seems to spend an inordinate amount of time on his computer.* • **inordinately adv**

inorganic /ˌɪnɔːˈɡænɪk/ **adj** not being or consisting of living things: *inorganic waste*

in-patient /ˈɪnˌpeɪʃᵊnt/ **noun** [C] someone who stays in hospital for one or more nights while they are receiving treatment

input¹ /ˈɪnpʊt/ **noun 1 IDEAS** ▷ [C, U] ⑫ ideas, money, effort, etc that you put into an activity or process in order to help it succeed: *Input from students is used to develop new and exciting courses.* **2 ELECTRICAL** ▷ [C, U] electrical energy that is put into a machine to make it work **3 COMPUTER** ▷ [U] ⑫ information that is put into a computer

input² /ˈɪnpʊt/ **verb** [T] (**inputting**, **inputted**, **input**) to put information into a computer

inquest /ˈɪŋkwest/ **noun** [C] a legal process to discover the cause of an unexpected death: *There will be an inquest into the deaths of the three men.*

> **Word partners for inquest**
> hold an inquest • an inquest into sth

inquire formal (also UK **enquire**) /ɪnˈkwaɪər/ **verb** [I, T] ⑫ to ask someone for information about something: *If you like languages, why don't you inquire about French classes in your area?* ○ [+ question word] *Vronsky inquired whether the picture was for sale.* • **inquirer** (also UK **enquirer**) **noun** [C]

PHRASAL VERBS **inquire after sb** UK formal to ask someone for information about someone else's health and what they are doing, in order to be polite: *Jane inquired after your mother.* • **inquire into sth** formal to try to discover the facts about something: *a report inquiring into the causes ⸰ the region's housing problem*

inquiring (also UK **enquiring**) /ɪnˈkwaɪərɪŋ/ **ad** [always before noun] **1** always wanting to lear. new things: *an inquiring mind* **2** An inquirin. expression on your face shows that you want t know something. • **inquiringly adv**

inquiry (also UK **enquiry**) /ɪnˈkwaɪəri/ **nou 1 QUESTION** ▷ [C] formal ⑪ a question that yo ask when you want more information: *Th company has received a lot of inquiries abou its new Internet service.* **2 OFFICIAL PROCESS** [C] an official process to discover the facts abou something bad that has happened: *There will b an official inquiry into the train crash.* **3 ASKIN QUESTIONS** ▷ [U] formal the process of askin questions in order to get information

> **Word partners for inquiry**
> make/receive an inquiry • an inquiry about sth

inquisitive /ɪnˈkwɪzətɪv/ **adj** wanting to di cover as much as you can about things: *a inquisitive child* • **inquisitively adv** • **inquis tiveness noun** [U]

inroads /ˈɪnrəʊdz/ **noun make inroads (into/o sth)** to start to become successful by gettin sales, power, votes, etc that someone else ha before: *Women have made great inroads into th male-dominated legal profession.*

the ins and outs **noun** all the details an facts about something: *Tolya is someone wh knows the ins and outs of the music industry.*

insane /ɪnˈseɪn/ **adj 1** seriously mentally ill: *hospital for the criminally insane* **2** very silly c stupid: *an insane decision* • **insanely adv**

insanity /ɪnˈsænəti/ **noun** [U] **1** serious menta illness **2** a very stupid thing to do: *It would b insanity to expand the business at the moment.*

insatiable /ɪnˈseɪʃəbl/ **adj** always wanting mor of something: *There is an insatiable demand f energy fuels.* • **insatiably adv**

inscribe /ɪnˈskraɪb/ **verb** [T] formal to write word in a book or cut them on an object: [often passiv. *The child's bracelet was inscribed with the nam 'Amy'.*

inscription /ɪnˈskrɪpʃᵊn/ **noun** [C, U] words tha are written or cut in something: *The inscriptio on the gravestone was almost illegible.*

insect /ˈɪnsekt/ **noun** [C] ⑫ a small creature wit six legs, for example a bee or a fly

insecticide /ɪnˈsektɪsaɪd/ **noun** [C, U] a chemic. that is used for killing insects

insecure /ˌɪnsɪˈkjʊər/ **adj 1** having no confidenc in yourself and what you can do: *a shy, insecu. teenager* **2** not safe or protected: *Many of ou staff are worried because their jobs are insecur* • **insecurely adv** • **insecurity** /ˌɪnsɪˈkjʊərət noun** [U, C]

insensitive /ɪnˈsensətɪv/ **adj 1** not noticing c not caring about other people's feelings: *a insensitive remark* ○ *He was completely insen*

---

nsect

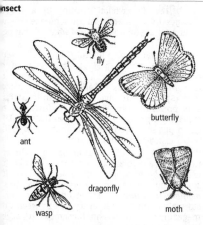

fly

butterfly

ant

dragonfly

moth

wasp

sitive to Maria's feelings. **2** not able to feel something, or not affected by it: *She was insensitive to the pain.* • **insensitively** adv • **insensitivity** /ɪnˌsensəˈtɪvəti/ noun [U]

nseparable /ɪnˈsepərəbl/ adj **1** formal Two things that are inseparable are so closely connected that you cannot consider them separately: *Rossetti's work was inseparable from his life.* **2** People who are inseparable are always together because they are such good friends. • **inseparably** adv

nsert¹ /ɪnˈsɜːt/ verb [T] formal **1** to put something into something else: *Insert the coin in the slot.* **2** to add something to the middle of a document or piece of writing: *He inserted a new paragraph.* • **insertion** /ɪnˈsɜːʃən/ noun [C, U]

nsert² /ˈɪnsɜːt/ noun [C] something that is made to go inside or into something else: *The leaflet is designed as an insert for a magazine.*

nshore /ɪnˈʃɔːr/ adj, adv near or towards the coast: *inshore waters*

nside¹ /ɪnˈsaɪd/ noun **1 the inside** ⏴ the part of something that is under its surface: *I cleaned the inside of the oven.* **2 inside out** ⏴ If a piece of clothing is inside out, the part that is usually outside is on the inside: *Harry, you've got your sweater on inside out again.*

IDIOM **know sth inside out** to know everything about something

nside² /ɪnˈsaɪd/ adj **1** ⏴ [always before noun] in or on the part of something under its surface: *Put your wallet in the inside pocket of your jacket.* **2 inside information/knowledge, etc** information that is only known by people who are part of an organization, group, etc

nside³ /ɪnˈsaɪd/ preposition **1 CONTAINER** ▷ ⏴ in or into a room, building, container, etc: *There were some keys inside the box.* ∘ *Luckily, no one was inside the house when the fire started.* **2 TIME** ▷ in less than a particular length of time: *The doctor's promised to be here inside an hour.* **3 ORGANIZATION** ▷ in an organization, group, etc and not known or happening outside it: *rumours of disputes inside the company*

inside⁴ /ˌɪnˈsaɪd/ adv **1 CONTAINER** ▷ ⏴ in or into a room, building, container, etc: *I'm freezing, let's go back inside.* **2 FEELING** ▷ ⏴ If you have a feeling inside, people do not know about it if you do not tell them: *She looked calm but was feeling nervous inside.* **3 PRISON** ▷ informal in prison

insider /ɪnˈsaɪdər/ noun [C] someone who knows about a business or organization because they are part of it: *Industry insiders say they are surprised by the company's success.* → Compare **outsider**

insides /ˌɪnˈsaɪdz/ noun [plural] informal your stomach

insidious /ɪnˈsɪdiəs/ adj having harmful effects that happen gradually so you do not notice them for a long time: *the insidious effects of pollution* • **insidiously** adv • **insidiousness** noun [U]

insight /ˈɪnsaɪt/ noun [C, U] the ability to understand what something is really like, or an example of this: *The book provides a fascinating insight into the world of art.*

> **Word partners for insight**
> gain/give/provide an insight into sth • a fascinating/rare/unique/valuable insight

insignia /ɪnˈsɪgniə/ noun [C] (plural **insignia**) a piece of cloth or a symbol that shows someone's military rank or official position

insignificant /ˌɪnsɪgˈnɪfɪkənt/ adj not important or large enough to consider or worry about: *insignificant differences* • **insignificance** /ˌɪnsɪgˈnɪfɪkəns/ noun [U] • **insignificantly** adv

insincere /ˌɪnsɪnˈsɪər/ adj pretending to feel something that you do not really feel, or not meaning what you say: *an insincere apology* • **insincerely** adv • **insincerity** /ˌɪnsɪnˈserəti/ noun [U]

insinuate /ɪnˈsɪnjueɪt/ verb [T] to suggest that something bad is true without saying it directly: [+ that] *She insinuated that Perez had lied.* • **insinuation** /ɪnˌsɪnjuˈeɪʃən/ noun [C, U]

insipid /ɪnˈsɪpɪd/ adj not interesting, exciting, or colourful: *a dull, insipid man* ∘ *The soup was rather insipid.* • **insipidly** adv

insist /ɪnˈsɪst/ verb [I, T] **1** ⏴ to say firmly that something is true, especially when other people do not believe you: [+ (that)] *Mia insisted that she and Carlo were just friends.* **2** ⏴ to demand that something must be done or that you must have a particular thing: *The school insists on good behaviour from its students.* ∘ [+ on + doing sth] *Frank insisted on doing all the work himself.* ∘ [+ (that)] *Gerlinde insisted that I stay for dinner.*

insistence /ɪnˈsɪstəns/ noun [U] **1** a demand that something must be done or that you must have a particular thing: [+ that] *his insistence that his children should have a good education* ∘ *Clare's insistence on a vegetarian diet caused arguments with her mother.* **2** the act of saying firmly that something is true, especially when other people do not believe you: [+ that] *Jane was in trouble despite her insistence that she had done nothing wrong.*

insistent /ɪnˈsɪstənt/ **adj** firmly saying that something is true or must be done: [+ that] *Pedro is absolutely insistent that Sinda should be invited too.* • **insistently adv**

insofar as /ˌɪnsəʊˈfɑːrˌəz/ **conjunction** formal to the degree that: *The story is based insofar as possible on notes made by Scott himself.*

insolent /ˈɪnsələnt/ **adj** formal rude and not showing respect: *an insolent reply* • **insolence** /ˈɪnsələns/ **noun** [U] • **insolently adv**

insoluble /ɪnˈsɒljəbl/ **adj 1** An insoluble problem, mystery, etc is impossible to solve. **2** An insoluble substance does not dissolve when you put it in liquid.

insomnia /ɪnˈsɒmniə/ **noun** [U] the problem of not being able to sleep • **insomniac** /ɪnˈsɒmniæk/ **noun** [C] someone who often finds it difficult to sleep

inspect /ɪnˈspekt/ **verb** [T] **1** to officially visit a building or organization, in order to check that everything is correct and legal: *Schools will be inspected regularly to maintain standards.* **2** to look at something very carefully: *Clara inspected her make-up in the mirror.*

inspection /ɪnˈspekʃən/ **noun** [C, U] **1** an official visit to a building or organization to check that everything is correct and legal: *Fire officers carried out an inspection of the building.* **2** careful examination of something by looking at it: *On closer inspection (= when looked at more carefully), the painting was discovered to be a fake.*

> **Word partners for inspection**
> carry out an inspection • an inspection of sth

inspector /ɪnˈspektər/ **noun** [C] **1** someone whose job is to check that things are being done correctly: *a factory inspector* **2** a police officer of middle rank

inspiration /ˌɪnspərˈeɪʃən/ **noun 1** [C, U] someone or something that gives you ideas for doing something: *Africa has long been a source of inspiration for his painting.* **2** [C] a sudden good idea about what you should do **3 be an inspiration to sb** to be so good that someone else admires you and is encouraged by your behaviour: *The way she has dealt with her illness is an inspiration to us all.*

inspire /ɪnˈspaɪər/ **verb** [T] **1 ENCOURAGE** ▷ to make someone feel that they want to do something and can do it: [+ to do sth] *A drama teacher at school had inspired Sam to become an actor.* **2 FEELING** ▷ to make someone have a particular feeling or reaction: *Robson's first task will be to inspire his team with some confidence.* ∘ *He inspires great loyalty in his staff.* **3 PROVIDE IDEA** ▷ to give someone an idea for a book, play, painting, etc: [often passive] *The television drama was inspired by a true story.* • **inspiring adj** giving you new ideas and making you feel you want to do something: *an inspiring teacher* ∘ *an inspiring book*

inspired /ɪnˈspaɪəd/ **adj** showing a lot of skill and good ideas: *an inspired performance*

instability /ˌɪnstəˈbɪləti/ **noun** [U] a lot of changes in a situation or in someone's behaviour so that you do not know what will happen next

install (also UK **instal**) /ɪnˈstɔːl/ **ver 1 EQUIPMENT** ▷ [T] to put a piece of equipment somewhere and make it ready to use: *The school has installed a burglar alarm.* **2 PERSON** ▷ [T] to give someone an important and powerful job: *She will be installed as Managing Director in May.* **3 COMPUTER** ▷ [I, to put software onto a computer • **installation** /ˌɪnstəˈleɪʃən/ **noun** [C, U]

instalment UK (US **installment**) /ɪnˈstɔːlmənt/ **noun** [C] **1** a regular payment that you make, for example each month, in order to pay for something: *You can pay for your computer in six monthly instalments.* **2** one of the parts of a story that you can see every day or week in a magazine or on television: *Don't miss next week's exciting instalment.*

instance /ˈɪnstəns/ **noun 1 for instance** for example: *Many teenagers earn money, for instance by babysitting or cleaning cars.* **2** [C] an example of a particular type of event, situation or behaviour: *There have been several instances of violence in the school.*

instant¹ /ˈɪnstənt/ **adj 1** happening immediately: *The book was an instant success in the US.* **2** Instant food or drink is dried, usually in the form of a powder, and can be made quickly by adding hot water: *instant coffee* → See also **instant replay**

instant² /ˈɪnstənt/ **noun** [C] a moment: *Take a seat, I'll be with you in an instant.*

instantaneous /ˌɪnstənˈteɪniəs/ **adj** happening immediately: *The Internet offers almost instantaneous access to vast amounts of information.* • **instantaneously adv**

instantly /ˈɪnstəntli/ **adv** immediately: *A car hit them, killing them both instantly.*

instant message¹ **noun** [C] (abbreviation **IM**) a written message that can be sent over the Internet to someone who is using the Internet at the same time

instant message² **verb** [I or T] (abbreviation **IM**) to use the Internet to exchange written messages very quickly with someone who is using the Internet at the same time: *I need to be able to instant message my friends.*

instant messaging /ˌɪnstənt ˈmesɪdʒɪŋ/ **noun** [U] a system on the Internet that makes it possible to send messages quickly between two people using the system

instant replay **noun** [C] US (UK **action replay**) a recording of part of a sporting event that is shown again immediately after it happens, often more slowly

instead /ɪnˈsted/ **adv** in the place of someone or something else: *If you don't want pizza, you can have pasta instead.* ∘ *I'm going swimming on Monday instead of Friday now.* ∘ [+ of + doing sth] *Why don't you help instead of just complaining?*

instigate /ˈɪnstɪɡeɪt/ **verb** [T] formal to make

something start to happen: *My mother had instigated divorce proceedings.* • **instigation** /ˌɪnstɪˈɡeɪʃᵊn/ **noun** [U] • **instigator noun** [C]

nstil (**instilling, instilled**) UK (US **instill**) /ɪnˈstɪl/ **verb** [T] to make someone have a particular feeling or idea: *He's a coach with great skill at instilling confidence in/into his players.*

nstinct /ˈɪnstɪŋkt/ **noun** [C, U] the way someone naturally reacts or behaves, without having to think or learn about it: [+ to do sth] *a mother's instinct to protect her children*

> ☑ Word partners for **instinct**
> **follow/trust** your instincts • instinct **tells** sb sth • sb's **first/gut** instinct

nstinctive /ɪnˈstɪŋktɪv/ **adj** behaving or reacting naturally and without thinking: *Her instinctive response was to fight back.* • **instinctively adv**

nstitute¹ /ˈɪnstɪtjuːt/ **noun** [C] ⓑ an organization where people do a particular kind of scientific, educational, or social work: *the Massachusetts Institute of Technology*

nstitute² /ˈɪnstɪtjuːt/ **verb** [T] formal to start a plan, law, system, etc: *Major reforms were instituted in the company's finance department.*

nstitution /ˌɪnstɪˈtjuːʃᵊn/ **noun** [C] **1 ORGANIZATION** ▷ ⓑ a large and important organization, such as a university or bank: *one of the country's top medical institutions* **2 PLACE** ▷ ⓑ a building where people are sent so they can be looked after, for example a prison or hospital **3 TRADITION** ▷ a custom that has existed for a long time: *the institution of marriage* • **institutional adj** relating to an institution

nstruct /ɪnˈstrʌkt/ **verb** [T] **1** to officially tell someone to do something: [+ to do sth] *Staff are instructed not to use the telephones for personal calls.* **2** formal to teach someone about something: *She is there to instruct people in the safe use of the gym equipment.*

nstruction /ɪnˈstrʌkʃᵊn/ **noun 1** [C] something that you have been told to do: [+ to do sth] *I had strict instructions to call him as soon as I arrived home.* **2** [U] formal the activity of teaching or training someone, or the information you are being taught: *religious instruction*

nstructions /ɪnˈstrʌkʃᵊnz/ **noun** [plural] ⓐ information that explains how to do or use something: *Are there any instructions on how to load the software?* ◦ *I just followed the instructions.*

> ☑ Word partners for **instructions**
> **follow** the instructions • **give** instructions • **detailed/full** instructions • instructions **on** sth

nstructive /ɪnˈstrʌktɪv/ **adj** providing useful information: *an instructive discussion/talk* • **instructively adv**

nstructor /ɪnˈstrʌktər/ **noun** [C] someone who teaches a particular sport or activity: *a driving instructor*

nstrument /ˈɪnstrəmənt/ **noun** [C] **1 TOOL** ▷ a tool that is used for doing something: *scientific*

instruments **2 MUSIC** ▷ ⓐ an object that is used for playing music, for example a piano or drum **3 EQUIPMENT** ▷ a piece of equipment that is used for measuring speed, light, fuel level, etc **4 FOR ACHIEVING SOMETHING** ▷ someone or something that is used for achieving something: *The Internet is a very powerful instrument of communication.* → See also **wind instrument**

instrumental /ˌɪnstrəˈmentᵊl/ **adj 1 be instrumental in sth/doing sth** to be one of the main people or things that make something happen: *Mikan was instrumental in establishing professional basketball in the US.* **2** involving only musical instruments, and no singing

insubordinate /ˌɪnsəˈbɔːdᵊnət/ **adj** not willing to obey rules or people in authority • **insubordination** /ˌɪnsəˌbɔːdɪˈneɪʃᵊn/ **noun** [U]

insubstantial /ˌɪnsəbˈstænʃᵊl/ **adj** not very large, strong, or good: *The meal was rather insubstantial.*

insufferable /ɪnˈsʌfᵊrəbl/ **adj** extremely annoying or unpleasant: *insufferable arrogance* • **insufferably adv**

insufficient /ˌɪnsəˈfɪʃᵊnt/ **adj** not enough: *insufficient information* ◦ [+ to do sth] *Her income is insufficient to support a family.* • **insufficiently adv**

insular /ˈɪnsjələr/ **adj** only interested in your own country, life, etc and not willing to accept new ideas or people • **insularity** /ˌɪnsjəˈlærəti/ **noun** [U]

insulate /ˈɪnsjəleɪt/ **verb** [T] **1** to cover something with a special material so that heat, electricity, or sound cannot escape through it **2** to protect someone from unpleasant experiences or bad influences: *Some parents want to insulate their children from real life.*

insulation /ˌɪnsjəˈleɪʃᵊn/ **noun** [U] **1** a special material used for insulating something such as a wall, roof, or building **2** the process of insulating something, or being insulated

insulin /ˈɪnsjəlɪn/ **noun** [U] a substance produced by the body that controls the amount of sugar in your blood

insult¹ /ɪnˈsʌlt/ **verb** [T] ⓑ to say or do something to someone that is rude and offensive: *How dare you insult me in front of my friends!* • **insulting adj** rude and offensive: *an insulting remark*

insult² /ˈɪnsʌlt/ **noun** [C] ⓑ a rude and offensive remark or action: *They were shouting insults at each other.* ◦ *His comments are an insult to the victims of the war.*

IDIOM add insult to injury to make someone's bad situation worse by doing something else to upset them

> ☑ Word partners for **insurance**
> **take out** insurance • insurance **against** [sickness/fire, etc] • an insurance **company/policy/premium** • **car/travel** insurance

insurance /ɪnˈʃʊərᵊns/ **noun** [U] ⓑ an agreement in which you pay a company money and they pay your costs if you have an accident,

insure /ɪnˈʃʊər/ verb [T] to buy insurance from a company, or to provide insurance for someone: *I need to get my car insured.* ∘ *The policy insures you against damage and theft.*

injury, etc: *car/travel insurance* ∘ *an insurance policy*

insurmountable /ˌɪnsəˈmaʊntəbl/ adj formal impossible to deal with: *an insurmountable problem/task*

insurrection /ˌɪnsərˈekʃən/ noun [C, U] the use of force by a group of people to try to get control of a government

intact /ɪnˈtækt/ adj not damaged or destroyed: *Many of the old buildings are still intact.*

intake /ˈɪnteɪk/ noun [C] **1** the amount of food or drink that you take into your body: [usually singular] *Reducing your salt intake can help to lower blood pressure.* **2** UK the group of people who start working or studying somewhere at the same time: *a new intake of students*

intangible /ɪnˈtændʒəbl/ adj An intangible feeling or quality exists but you cannot describe or prove it.

integral /ˈɪntɪgrəl/ adj necessary and important as part of something: *The Internet has become an integral part of modern life.*

integrate /ˈɪntɪgreɪt/ verb **1** [I, T] to become part of a group or society, or to help someone do this: *After a few weeks of training he was fully integrated into the team.* **2** [T] to combine two or more things to make something more effective: *There are plans to integrate the two schools.* • **integration** /ˌɪntɪˈgreɪʃən/ noun [U]

integrity /ɪnˈtegrəti/ noun [U] honesty and the ability to do or know what is morally right: *a woman of great integrity*

intellect /ˈɪntəlekt/ noun [C, U] the ability to learn and understand something, and to form ideas, judgments, and opinions about what you have learned: *His energy and intellect are respected by many people.*

intellectual¹ /ˌɪntəˈlektjuəl/ adj **1** using or relating to your ability to think and understand things: *intellectual work* ∘ *intellectual and physical development* **2** interested in learning and in thinking about complicated ideas: *She's very intellectual.* • **intellectually** adv

intellectual² /ˌɪntəˈlektjuəl/ noun [C] someone who enjoys studying and thinking about complicated ideas

intelligence /ɪnˈtelɪdʒəns/ noun [U] **1** the ability to learn, understand, and think about things: *a child of low intelligence* **2** secret information about the governments of other countries, or the group of people who get this information: *military intelligence* → See also **artificial intelligence**

Word partners for **intelligence**
average/great/high/low intelligence • have/show/use intelligence

intelligent /ɪnˈtelɪdʒənt/ adj able to learn and understand things easily: *a highly intelligent young woman* • **intelligently** adv

intelligible /ɪnˈtelɪdʒəbl/ adj able to be understood → Opposite **unintelligible**

intend /ɪnˈtend/ verb **1** [T] to want and plan to do something: [+ to do sth] *How long are you intending to stay in Paris?* ∘ [+ doing sth] *I don't intend seeing him again.* **2** be intended for sb/be intended as sth to be made, designed, or provided for a particular person or purpose: *The book is intended for anyone who wants to learn more about the Internet.*

intense /ɪnˈtens/ adj **1** extreme or very strong: *intense heat/pain* **2** Intense people are very serious, and usually have strong emotions or opinions. • **intensely** adv *Clare disliked him intensely.* • **intensity** noun [U]

intensify /ɪnˈtensɪfaɪ/ verb [I, T] to become greater, more serious, or more extreme, or to make something do this: *The fighting has intensified in the past week.*

intensive /ɪnˈtensɪv/ adj involving a lot of work in a short period of time: *ten weeks of intensive training* • **intensively** adv

inˌtensive ˈcare noun [U] the part of a hospital used for treating people who are very sick or very badly injured

intent¹ /ɪnˈtent/ noun [U, no plural] formal what someone wants and plans to do: [+ to do sth] *It had not been his intent to hurt anyone.*
IDIOM **to/for all intents (and purposes)** in all the most important ways: *To all intents and purposes, the project was a disaster.*

intent² /ɪnˈtent/ adj **1** be intent on sth/doing sth to be determined to do or achieve something: *She seems intent on winning this year's tennis tournament.* **2** giving a lot of attention to something: *She had an intent look on her face.* • **intently** adv

intention /ɪnˈtenʃən/ noun [C, U] something that you want and plan to do: [+ to do sth] *She announced her intention to resign.* ∘ [+ of + doing sth] *I have no intention of seeing him again.*

Word partners for **intention**
announce/declare/signal your intention • have no intention of doing sth

intentional /ɪnˈtenʃənəl/ adj planned or intended: *I'm sorry if I said something that offended you, Isabel. It really wasn't intentional.* • **intentionally** adv

inter- /ɪntər-/ prefix between or among: *international* ∘ *an interdepartmental meeting*

interact /ˌɪntərˈækt/ verb [I] **1** to talk and do things with other people: *At school, teachers said he interacted well with students.* **2** If things interact, they have an effect on each other: *We are looking at how these chemicals interact.*

interaction /ˌɪntərˈækʃən/ noun [C, U] **1** the activity of talking and doing things with other people, or the way you do this: *Our work involves a lot of interaction with the customers.* **2** the way that two or more things combine and have an effect on each other

interactive /ˌɪntərˈæktɪv/ adj **1** Interactive

computer programs, games, etc involve the person using them by reacting to the way they use them. **2** involving communication between people

ntercept /ˌɪntəˈsept/ **verb** [T] to stop someone or something before they are able to reach a particular place: *Johnson intercepted the pass and went on to score the third goal.* • **interception** /ˌɪntəˈsepʃən/ **noun** [C, U]

nterchangeable /ˌɪntəˈtʃeɪndʒəbl/ **adj** If things are interchangeable, you can exchange them because they can be used in the same way: *interchangeable words* • **interchangeably** adv

ntercom /ˈɪntəkɒm/ **noun** [C] an electronic system used for communicating with people in different parts of a building, aircraft, ship, etc: *A stewardess asked **over the intercom** if there was a doctor on board.*

ntercontinental /ˌɪntəˌkɒntɪˈnentəl/ **adj** in or between two continents: *an intercontinental flight*

ntercourse /ˈɪntəkɔːs/ **noun** [U] (also **sexual intercourse**) the activity of having sex

nterest[1] /ˈɪntrəst/ **noun 1** FEELING ▷ [U, no plural] **B1** the feeling of wanting to give attention to something or discover more about it: *Mark **had an interest in** the media and wanted to become a journalist.* ◦ *After a while he simply **lost interest in** (= stopped being interested) his studies.* ◦ *Bindi felt that her father didn't **take** much of **an interest in** her (= he was not very interested).* **2** ACTIVITY/SUBJECT ▷ [C] **B1** something you enjoy doing, studying, or experiencing: *We **share** a lot of the same **interests**, particularly music and football.* **3** MONEY YOU PAY ▷ [U] **B2** the extra money that you must pay to a bank, company, etc which has lent you money: *low interest rates* **4** MONEY YOU EARN ▷ [U] **B2** the money you earn from keeping your money in a bank account **5** QUALITY ▷ [U] **B1** a quality that makes you think something is interesting: *Would this book **be** of any **interest to** you?* **6** ADVANTAGE ▷ [C, U] something that gives someone or something an advantage: *A union looks after the interests of its members.* **7 be in sb's interest(s)** to help someone and give them an advantage: *It may not be in your interests to change jobs so soon.* **8 in the interest(s) of sth** in order to achieve a particular situation or quality: *In the interest of safety, passengers are advised to wear their seat belts at all times.* **9** LEGAL RIGHT ▷ [C] formal the legal right to own or receive part of a building, company, profits, etc → See also **self-interest, vested interest**

Word partners for interest

develop/generate/have/show/take an interest • a genuine/keen/passionate/strong interest • an interest in sth • be of interest

---

nterest[2] /ˈɪntrəst/ **verb** [T] **B1** If someone or something interests you, you want to give them your attention and discover more about them: *History doesn't really interest me.*

nterested /ˈɪntrəstɪd/ **adj 1** [never before noun] **A2** wanting to give your attention to something and discover more about it: *Sarah's only inter-ested in boys, music, and clothes.* ◦ [+ to do sth] *I'd be interested to find out more about the course.* → Opposite **uninterested** **2** [never before noun] wanting to do, get, or achieve something: [+ in + doing sth] *Mark said he's interested in buying his bike.* **3 interested parties/groups** people who will be affected by a situation → Opposite **disinterested**

interesting /ˈɪntrəstɪŋ/ **adj** **A1** Someone or something that is interesting keeps your attention because they are unusual, exciting, or have lots of ideas: *an interesting person* ◦ *The museum was really interesting.* ◦ [+ to do sth] *It'll be interesting to see what John's sister thinks of his new girlfriend.*

⚠ Common learner error: **interesting** or **interested**?

Interested is used to describe how someone feels about a person or thing.
I'm interested in theatre.
~~I'm interesting in theatre.~~
If a person or thing is **interesting**, they make you feel interested.
It was an interesting film.

⚠ Common learner error: **interesting**

Interesting does not mean 'useful'. Use a word like **useful, beneficial** or **valuable** instead.
This course could be very useful for my colleagues.
~~This course could be very interesting for my colleagues.~~

➕ Other ways of saying **interesting**

You can use **absorbing** or **gripping** to describe a game, book, film, etc. which is so interesting that it keeps your attention completely:
*I found the book absolutely **gripping** – I couldn't put it down.*
*It was a very **absorbing** film.*
A game, book, TV programme, etc. which is so interesting that you cannot stop playing, reading, or watching it, may be described as **compulsive**:
*I found the whole series **compulsive** viewing.*
Fascinating is often used to describe someone or something you have seen or heard that you have found extremely interesting:
*The history of the place was absolutely **fascinating**.*
*He's **fascinating** on the subject.*
If something or someone is interesting because they seem mysterious and make you want to know more about them, you can say that they are **intriguing**:
*It's a very **intriguing** situation.*

---

interestingly /ˈɪntrəstɪŋli/ **adv** used to show that the speaker finds something interesting: *Interestingly, he never actually said he was innocent.*

interest ˌrate noun [C] the percentage of an amount of money that is charged or paid by a bank or other financial company

interface¹ /'ɪntəfeɪs/ noun [C] **1** a connection between two pieces of electronic equipment, or between a person and a computer: *a simple **user interface*** **2** a situation, method, or place where two things can come together and have an effect on each other: *the **interface between** technology and tradition*

interface² /'ɪntəfeɪs/ verb [I, T] to communicate with people or electronic equipment, or to make people or electronic equipment communicate: *We use email to **interface with** our customers.*

interfere /ˌɪntə'fɪər/ verb [I] ⑫ to try to control or become involved in a situation, in a way that is annoying: *I know he's worried about us, but I wish he wouldn't interfere.* ∘ *You shouldn't **interfere in** other people's business.*

PHRASAL VERB **interfere with sth 1** to prevent something from working effectively or from developing successfully: *I try not to let my dancing classes interfere with my schoolwork.* **2** If something interferes with radio or television signals, it stops you from getting good pictures or sound.

interference /ˌɪntə'fɪərəns/ noun [U] **1** attempts to interfere in a situation: *There have been claims of too much political **interference in** education.* **2** noise or other electronic signals that stop you from getting good pictures or sound on a television or radio

> 🗹 Word partners for **interference**
>
> interference **in** sth • interference **from** sb

interim¹ /'ɪntərɪm/ adj [always before noun] temporary and intended to be used or accepted until something permanent exists: *an interim solution* ∘ *an **interim government***

interim² /'ɪntərɪm/ noun **in the interim** in the time between two particular periods or events

interior /ɪn'tɪəriər/ noun [C] ⑫ the inside part of something: *the grand interior of the hotel* → Opposite **exterior**

inˌterior deˈsign noun [U] the job of choosing colours, designs, etc for the inside of a house or room • **interior designer** noun [C] someone whose job is to do interior design

interjection /ˌɪntə'dʒekʃən/ noun [C] an exclamation or sudden expression of your feelings. For example 'Hey' in 'Hey you!' is an interjection.

interlude /'ɪntəluːd/ noun [C] a period of time between two events, activities, etc: *a **brief interlude** of peace*

intermediary /ˌɪntə'miːdiəri/ noun [C] someone who works with two people or groups to help them agree on something important

intermediate /ˌɪntə'miːdiət/ adj **1** ⑪ between the highest and lowest levels of knowledge or skill: *intermediate students* **2** between two different stages in a process: ***intermediate steps** towards achieving our goal*

interminable /ɪn'tɜːmɪnəbl/ adj lasting a very

long time, in a way that is boring: *an interminable train journey* • **interminably** adv

intermission /ˌɪntə'mɪʃən/ noun [C] a short period between the parts of a play performance, etc

intermittent /ˌɪntə'mɪtənt/ adj stopping and starting again for short periods of time: *intermittent rain* • **intermittently** adv

intern¹ /'ɪntɜːn/ noun [C] **1** US a young doctor who works in a hospital to finish their medical education **2** a student who learns about a particular job by doing it for a short period of time • **internship** noun [C] the time when someone is an intern

intern² /ɪn'tɜːn/ verb [T] to put someone in prison for political reasons, especially during a war • **internment** noun [U] the punishment of interning someone

internal /ɪn'tɜːnəl/ adj **1** INSIDE A PLACE ▷ ⑫ happening or coming from inside a particular country, group, or organization: *an internal report* ∘ *internal disputes* **2** BODY ▷ ⑫ inside your body: *internal injuries* **3** PLACE ▷ ⑫ inside a country, building, area, etc: *an internal flight* ∘ *internal walls* → Opposite **external** • **internally** adv

international¹ /ˌɪntə'næʃənəl/ adj ⑫ relating to or involving two or more countries: *international politics* ∘ *an international team of scientist* • **internationally** adv

international² /ˌɪntə'næʃənəl/ noun [C] UK a game of sport involving two or more countries or a player in one of these games: *a one-day international in South Africa*

the interˌnational comˈmunity noun countries of the world considered or acting together as a group: *The international community expressed shock at the terrorist attacks.*

> 🗹 Word partners for **the Internet**
>
> browse/surf the Internet • on the Internet • download sth from the Internet • Internet access • an Internet provider/service provi- der

the Internet /'ɪntənet/ noun (also **the Net**) ⑫ the system that connects computers all over the world and allows people who use computers to look at websites (= electronic documents): *She found a lot of information **on the Internet.*** ∘ *company that provides cheap **Internet access*** → See Study Page **The Web and the Internet** on page Centre 36

Internet ˌaccess noun [U] the ability to connect to the Internet: *The hotel offers free **wireless internet access** to all guests.*

Internet ˌbank noun [C] a bank that operates over the Internet

Internet ˌbanking noun [U] the process of activity of managing bank accounts or operating as a bank over the Internet

Internet ˌcafe noun [C] a place where custo- mers can buy food and drink and use computers to search for information on the Internet

Internet ˌdating noun [U] a way to meet people for possible romantic relationships, w which you look at descriptions of people on a website and arrange to meet them if you like them

nternet piracy noun [U] (also **internet pirating**) the illegal activity of using the Internet to illegally copy software and sell it to other people

nternet service provider noun [C] (also **Internet provider**) a company that provides customers with an Internet connection

nterplay /ˈɪntəpleɪ/ noun [U] the effect that two or more things have on each other: *I'm interested in the **interplay between** Latin and English.*

nterpret /ɪnˈtɜːprɪt/ verb **1** [T] to explain or decide what you think a particular phrase, performance, action, etc means: *His comments were **interpreted as** an attack on the government.* **2** [I, T] ⓑ to change what someone has said into another language: *We had to ask the guide to interpret for us.*

nterpretation /ɪnˌtɜːprɪˈteɪʃən/ noun **1** [C, U] an explanation or opinion of what something means: *traditional interpretations of the Bible* **2** [C] the way someone performs a particular play, piece of music, etc: *a beautiful interpretation of Swan Lake*

nterpreter /ɪnˈtɜːprɪtər/ noun [C] someone whose job is to change what someone else is saying into another language

nterrogate /ɪnˈterəgeɪt/ verb [T] to ask someone a lot of questions, often with great force: *Police have arrested and interrogated the two suspects.* • **interrogation** /ɪnˌterəˈgeɪʃən/ noun [C, U] *twelve hours of brutal interrogation* • **interrogator** noun [C]

nterrogative /ˌɪntəˈrɒgətɪv/ noun [C] a word or sentence used when asking a question. For example 'Who' and 'Why' are interrogatives. • **interrogative** adj

nterrupt /ˌɪntəˈrʌpt/ verb **1** [I, T] ⓑ to stop someone while they are talking or doing something, by saying or doing something yourself: *I was trying to work but the children were interrupting me.* **2** [T] ⓑ to stop an action or activity, usually for a short period of time: *A leg injury interrupted his sporting career.*

nterruption /ˌɪntəˈrʌpʃən/ noun [C, U] ⓑ an occasion when an action or activity is interrupted, or something that interrupts someone or something

ntersect /ˌɪntəˈsekt/ verb [I, T] If two things such as lines or roads intersect, they go across each other at a particular point.

ntersection /ˌɪntəˈsekʃən/ noun [C] US (UK/US **junction**) the place where two roads meet or cross each other

nterspersed /ˌɪntəˈspɜːst/ adj **interspersed with sth** having something in several places among something else: *farmland interspersed with forests and lakes*

nterstate¹ /ˌɪntəˈsteɪt/ adj [always before noun]

relating to, or involving two or more US states: *interstate commerce/travel* ∘ *an interstate highway*

interstate² /ˈɪntəˌsteɪt/ noun [C] a fast wide road which goes between states and connects important cities in the United States

interval /ˈɪntəvəl/ noun **1** [C] a period of time between two actions, activities, or events: *After an interval of three days the peace talks resumed.* **2 at intervals** repeated after a particular period of time or particular distance: *Patients were injected with the drug at four-hour intervals* (= *every four hours*). **3** [C] UK (UK/US **intermission**) ⓑ a short period of time between the parts of a play, performance, etc

intervene /ˌɪntəˈviːn/ verb [I] **1** BECOME INVOLVED ▷ to become involved in a situation in order to try to stop a fight, argument, problem, etc: *Government officials refused to **intervene in** the recent disputes.* ∘ *[+ to do sth] The forces intervened to stop the attack.* **2** INTERRUPT ▷ to interrupt someone who is talking: *"Mr Lawrence," the judge intervened, "please be silent."* **3** PREVENT ▷ If something intervenes, it stops something or prevents it from happening: *She was going to marry Barratt but tragedy intervened.*

intervening /ˌɪntəˈviːnɪŋ/ adj **the intervening months/period/years, etc** the time between two events: *In the intervening years, his illness had become a lot worse.*

intervention /ˌɪntəˈvenʃən/ noun [C, U] the act of intervening, especially to prevent something from happening: *Without **medical intervention**, the child would have died.*

interview¹ /ˈɪntəvjuː/ noun [C] **1** JOB/COURSE ▷ ⓑ a meeting in which someone asks you questions to see if you are suitable for a job or course: *I **had an interview** last week for a job in London.* **2** NEWS ▷ ⓑ a meeting in which someone is asked questions for a newspaper article, television show, etc: *an **exclusive interview** with Madonna* **3** POLICE ▷ a meeting in which the police ask someone questions to see if they have committed a crime

interview² /ˈɪntəvjuː/ verb [T] ⓑ to ask someone questions in an interview: *Police are interviewing a 43-year-old man in connection with the murder.* ∘ *So far we've **interviewed** five applicants **for** the Managing Director's job.* • **interviewer** noun [C]

interviewee /ˌɪntəvjuːˈiː/ noun [C] someone who is being interviewed

intestine /ɪnˈtestɪn/ noun [C] a long tube that carries food from your stomach • **intestinal** /ˌɪntesˈtaɪnəl, ɪnˈtestɪnəl/ adj relating to your intestine

intimacy /ˈɪntɪməsi/ noun [U] a very special friendship or sexual relationship with someone

intimate¹ /ˈɪntɪmət/ adj **1** PRIVATE ▷ private

and personal: *intimate details* of her family life ∘ *intimate conversations* **2 RELATIONSHIP** ▷ having a special relationship with someone who you like or love very much: *an intimate friend* **3 SMALL** ▷ If a place or event is intimate, it is small in a way that feels comfortable or private: *an intimate hotel* **4 an intimate knowledge/understanding of sth** a very good knowledge/understanding of something, so you know all of the facts about it or about how it works • **intimately** adv

intimate² /'ɪntɪmeɪt/ verb [T] formal to suggest that something is true without saying it directly

intimidate /ɪn'tɪmɪdeɪt/ verb [T] to intentionally frighten someone, especially so that they will do what you want • **intimidation** /ɪnˌtɪmɪ'deɪʃᵊn/ noun [U]

intimidated /ɪn'tɪmɪdeɪtɪd/ adj frightened or nervous because you are not confident in a situation: *Older people can feel very intimidated by computers.* • **intimidating** adj making you feel intimidated: *I find speaking in front of a crowd very intimidating.*

into /'ɪntə/, /'ɪntu/ preposition **1 IN** ▷ ⓐ towards the inside or middle of something: *Stop running around and get into bed!* ∘ *He's gone into a shop across the road.* **2 CHANGE** ▷ ⓐ used to show when a person or thing changes from one form or condition to another: *We're planning to turn the smallest bedroom into an office.* ∘ *Her last novel was translated into nineteen languages.* **3 ABOUT** ▷ involving or about something: *an investigation into the cause of the fire* **4 TOWARDS** ▷ ⓑ in the direction of something or someone: *She was looking straight into his eyes.* **5 HIT** ▷ ⓑ moving towards something or someone and hitting them: *I backed the car into the garden wall.* **6 be into sth** informal ⓑ to be very interested in something: *Kate's really into classical music.* **7 DIVIDE** ▷ used when dividing one number by another: *What's 5 into 125?*

intolerable /ɪn'tɒlᵊrəbl/ adj too bad or unpleasant to deal with or accept: *an intolerable situation* • **intolerably** adv

intolerance /ɪn'tɒlᵊrᵊns/ noun [U] intolerant behaviour: *religious intolerance*

intolerant /ɪn'tɒlᵊrᵊnt/ adj refusing to accept any opinions, beliefs, customs, etc that are different from your own

intonation /ˌɪntəʊ'neɪʃᵊn/ noun [C, U] the way your voice goes up and down when you speak

intoxicated /ɪn'tɒksɪkeɪtɪd/ adj **1** formal drunk **2** literary very excited or enthusiastic about someone or something • **intoxicating** adj making you intoxicated • **intoxication** /ɪnˌtɒksɪ'keɪʃᵊn/ noun [U]

intra- /ɪntrə-/ prefix within: *an intranet*

intranet /'ɪntrənet/ noun [C] a system that connects the computers in a company or organization so that people can share information and send messages

intransitive /ɪn'trænsətɪv/ adj ⓐ An intransitive verb does not have an object. In the sentence 'John arrived first.', 'arrived' is an intransitive verb. → See Study Page **Verb patterns** on page Centre 27. → Compare **transitive**

intravenous /ˌɪntrə'viːnəs/ adj Intravenou medicines or drugs are put directly int your veins (= tubes that carry your blood • **intravenously** adv

in-tray /'ɪntreɪ/ noun [C] UK (US **in-box**) container where you keep letters and doc ments that need to be dealt with → See colo picture **The Office** on page Centre 5

intrepid /ɪn'trepɪd/ adj brave and willing to d dangerous things: *intrepid travellers*

intricacy /'ɪntrɪkəsi/ noun **1 the intricacies** sth the complicated details of something: *Th booklet explains the intricacies of the game's rule* **2** [U] the quality of being intricate: *the intricac of the stone carvings*

intricate /'ɪntrɪkət/ adj having many small complicated parts and details: *an intricat pattern* • **intricately** adv

intrigue¹ /ɪn'triːg/ verb [T] (**intriguing, intr gued**) If someone or something intrigues yo they interest you very much: *Ancient Egyptia art has always intrigued me.*

intrigue² /'ɪntriːg/ noun [C, U] a secret, cleve plan to deceive someone or do something ba *a tale of romance, intrigue, and betrayal*

intriguing /ɪn'triːgɪŋ/ adj very interesting: *intriguing story*

intrinsic /ɪn'trɪnsɪk/ adj [always before noun] A intrinsic quality or thing forms part of the bas character of something or someone: *Dram is an intrinsic part of the school's curriculum* • **intrinsically** adv

introduce /ˌɪntrə'djuːs/ verb [T] **1 SOMETHIN NEW** ▷ ⓑ to make something exist, happen, be used for the first time: *CD players were fir introduced in 1983.* ∘ *We have introduced a ne training schedule for employees.* **2 MEETIN PEOPLE** ▷ ⓑ to tell someone another person name the first time that they meet: *He took m round the room and introduced me to everyon* ∘ [often reflexive] *Emma introduced herself an they shook hands.* **3 TO AN AUDIENCE** ▷ to tell a audience who is going to speak to them perform for them: *I'd like to introduce Rache Elliott who is our speaker this evening.*

PHRASAL VERB **introduce sb to sth** to hel someone experience something for the fir time: *His father introduced him to the pleasure of good food.*

introduction /ˌɪntrə'dʌkʃᵊn/ noun **1 SOM THING NEW** ▷ [U] ⓑ the process of makin something exist, happen, or be used for the fir time: *the introduction of a minimum wag* **2 BOOK** ▷ [C] ⓑ the first part of a book speech **3 BASIC KNOWLEDGE** ▷ [C] ⓑ a book course that provides basic knowledge about subject: *an introduction to psychology* **4 FIRS EXPERIENCE** ▷ [no plural] the first time someon experiences something: *It was our first introdu tion to great poetry.* **5 FIRST MEETING** ▷ [C] ⓑ a occasion when you tell someone anothe person's name the first time that they mee [usually plural] *Can you do the introductions?* **6 T AN AUDIENCE** ▷ [C, U] something you say to te an audience who is going to speak to them o perform for them: *My next guest needs no introduction.*

introductory /ˌɪntrəˈdʌktᵊri/ **adj 1 an introductory chapter/essay/message, etc** a part that comes at the beginning of a piece of writing or a speech and explains what will come later **2 an introductory book/course/lesson, etc** something that provides basic information about a subject: *an introductory course in economics* **3 an introductory discount/fare/offer, etc** something that you get when you start buying something or using a service

introspective /ˌɪntrəʊˈspektɪv/ **adj** thinking a lot about your own thoughts and feelings, in a way that is not always good for you • **introspection** /ˌɪntrəʊˈspekʃᵊn/ **noun** [U]

introvert /ˈɪntrəʊvɜːt/ **noun** [C] someone who is quiet and shy and prefers to be alone • **introverted** **adj** *an introverted child* → Opposite **extrovert**

intrude /ɪnˈtruːd/ **verb** [I] to become involved in a situation that people want to be private: *They should not have **intruded on** the family's grief.*

intruder /ɪnˈtruːdər/ **noun** [C] someone who enters a place where they are not allowed to be, often to commit a crime

intrusion /ɪnˈtruːʒᵊn/ **noun** [C, U] involvement in a situation that people want to be private: *She could not bear the **intrusion into** her private life.*

🗹 Word partners for **intrusion**

an **unwarranted/unwelcome** intrusion • an intrusion **into/on** sth

---

intrusive /ɪnˈtruːsɪv/ **adj** If something or someone is intrusive, they become involved in things that should be private: *The magazine published intrusive pictures of the princess's family.*

intuition /ˌɪntjuˈɪʃᵊn/ **noun** [C, U] the feeling that you know something without being able to explain why: *Her approach to childcare is based on intuition.*

intuitive /ɪnˈtjuːɪtɪv/ **adj** using intuition: *He has an intuitive understanding of animals.* • **intuitively adv**

Inuit /ˈɪnuɪt/ **noun** [C, U] (plural **Inuit**, **Inuits**) a group of people who live in the cold, northern areas of North America, Russia, and Greenland, or a member of this group

inundate /ˈɪnʌndeɪt/ **verb be inundated with/by sth** to receive so much of something that you cannot deal with it: *Laura was inundated with flowers, cards, and other gifts.*

invade /ɪnˈveɪd/ **verb 1** [I, T] ⬛ to enter a country by force in order to take control of it: *Portugal was invaded by the French in 1807.* **2** [T] to enter a place in large numbers: *Every summer the town is invaded by tourists.* **3 invade sb's privacy** to become involved in someone's private life when they do not want you to

invader /ɪnˈveɪdər/ **noun** [C] someone who enters a country by force in order to take control of it

invalid¹ /ˈɪnvəlɪd/ **noun** [C] someone who is so sick that they have to be looked after by other people

invalid² /ɪnˈvælɪd/ **adj 1** An invalid document, ticket, law, etc is not legally or officially acceptable. **2** An invalid argument is not correct.

invaluable /ɪnˈvæljuəbl/ **adj** extremely useful: *Her contacts in government **proved invaluable** to the company.*

invariably /ɪnˈveəriəbli/ **adv** always: *The train is invariably packed.*

invasion /ɪnˈveɪʒᵊn/ **noun 1** ⬛ [C, U] an occasion when an army enters a country by force in order to take control of it **2 an invasion of privacy** becoming involved in someone's private life when they do not want you to

invent /ɪnˈvent/ **verb** [T] **1** ⬛ to design or create something that has never existed before: *We've invented a new game.* **2** ⬛ to think of a story or explanation in order to deceive someone: *She invented an excuse to leave.*

invention /ɪnˈvenʃᵊn/ **noun 1** [C] ⬛ something that has been designed or created for the first time **2** [U] ⬛ the process of designing or creating something new: *the invention of printing*

inventive /ɪnˈventɪv/ **adj** full of clever and interesting ideas: *inventive designs* • **inventively adv** • **inventiveness noun** [U]

inventor /ɪnˈventər/ **noun** [C] ⬛ someone who designs and makes new things

inventory /ˈɪnvᵊntri/, /ɪnˈventᵊri/ **noun** [C] a list of all the things that are in a place

invert /ɪnˈvɜːt/ **verb** [T] formal to turn something upside-down, or put something in the opposite order from how it usually is

inverted commas /ɪnˌvɜːtɪdˈkɒməz/ **noun** [plural] UK ⬛ a pair of marks (" ") or (' ') used before and after a group of words to show that they are spoken or that someone else originally wrote them → See Study Page **Punctuation** on page Centre 33

invest /ɪnˈvest/ **verb 1** [I, T] ⬛ to give money to a bank, business, etc, or buy something, because you hope to get a profit: *He's **invested** over a million euros **in** the city's waterfront restoration project.* **2** [T] ⬛ to use a lot of time, effort, or emotions because you want to succeed: *I think she **invests** too much time and energy **in** her career.*

PHRASAL VERB **invest in sth** to buy something because you think it will be useful: *Dad's decided to invest in a computer.*

---

investigate /ɪnˈvestɪgeɪt/ **verb** [I, T] ⬛ to try to discover all the facts about something, especially a crime or accident: *He has been questioned by detectives investigating Jenkins' murder.*

🗹 Word partners for **investigation**

carry out/conduct/launch an investigation • a **detailed/full/thorough** investigation • an investigation **into** sth • be **under** investigation

---

investigation /ɪnˌvestɪˈgeɪʃᵊn/ **noun** [C, U] ⬛ a process in which officials try to discover all the facts about something, especially a crime or an accident: *Police have begun an* **investigation into** *his death.* ∘ *The cause of the fire is still* **under investigation** (= *being investigated*).

investigative /ɪn'vestɪɡətɪv/ ⑤ /ɪn'vestɪɡeɪtɪv/ **adj** trying to discover all the facts about something: *investigative journalists*

investigator /ɪn'vestɪɡeɪtər/ **noun** [C] ⑧² someone who tries to discover all the facts about something, especially as their job

investment /ɪn'vestmənt/ **noun 1** [C, U] ⑧² the money that you put in a bank, business, etc in order to make a profit, or the act of doing this: *Businesses need to increase their* **investment** in *new technology.* **2** [C] ⑧² something that you do or have, in order to have more in the future: *Going to college is an* **investment in** *the future.*

investor /ɪn'vestər/ **noun** [C] ⑧² someone who puts money in a bank, business, etc in order to make a profit

inveterate /ɪn'vetərət/ **adj an inveterate liar/ gambler/reader, etc** someone who does something very often

invigorating /ɪn'vɪɡəreɪtɪŋ/ **adj** making you feel very healthy and energetic: *a long, invigorating walk* • **invigorate verb** [T] to make you feel very healthy and energetic

invincible /ɪn'vɪnsəbl/ **adj** If someone or something is invincible, it is impossible to defeat or destroy them: *The French army seemed invincible.*

invisible /ɪn'vɪzəbl/ **adj** ⑧² Someone or something that is invisible cannot be seen: *invisible particles called electrons* ∘ *The house was invisible from the road.* • **invisibility** /ɪn,vɪzə'bɪləti/ **noun** [U]

invitation /,ɪnvɪ'teɪʃᵊn/ **noun 1 INVITING SOMEONE** ▷ [C, U] ⑧² an offer from someone to do something or go somewhere: *an* **invitation to** *dinner* ∘ [+ to do sth] *He has* **accepted** *their* **invitation** *to visit China.* **2 PIECE OF PAPER** ▷ [C] a piece of paper or card that invites someone to an event **3 CAUSE RESULT** ▷ [no plural] something that is likely to cause a particular result, especially a bad one: *It is* **an invitation to** *violence.*

☑ Word partners for **invitation**

accept/decline/turn down an invitation • an invitation **to** sth

---

❗ Common learner error: **invite** someone **to** something

If you are talking about a social event, use the preposition **to**.

She invited me to the party.
~~She invited me for the party.~~
~~She invited me at the party.~~

If you are talking about a meal, you can use **to** or **for**.

He invited me for dinner/to dinner.

If you are talking about a particular type of food, or inviting someone for a particular activity, use **for**.

I was invited for an interview.
They invited her for a pizza.

---

invite¹ /ɪn'vaɪt/ **verb** [T] **1 SOCIAL EVENT** ▷ ⑬ to ask someone to come to a social event: *They've* **invited** *us to the wedding.* **2 ASK OFFICIALLY** ▷ to officially ask someone to do something: [+ to do sth] *I was invited to appear on television* **3 REACTION** ▷ to do something that is likely to cause a particular reaction or result, especially a bad one: *Unconventional ideas often invite attack*

PHRASAL VERBS **invite sb in** to ask someone to come into your house: *The neighbours invited u. in for coffee.* • **invite sb over** (also UK **invite sb round**) to invite someone to come to your house

invite² /'ɪnvaɪt/ **noun** [C] informal an invitation

inviting /ɪn'vaɪtɪŋ/ **adj** pleasant and attractive *an inviting smile* ∘ *The room looked cosy and inviting.* • **invitingly adv**

invoice¹ /'ɪnvɔɪs/ **noun** [C] a list that shows you how much you owe someone for work they have done or for goods they have supplied

invoice² /'ɪnvɔɪs/ **verb** [T] to send someone an invoice

invoke /ɪn'vəuk/ **verb** [T] formal to use a law, rule, etc to support what you are saying o doing: *The President may* **invoke** *federal law to stop the strike.*

involuntary /ɪn'vɒlᵊntᵊri/ **adj** An involuntary movement or action is something you do but cannot control: *an involuntary shudder* • **involuntarily adv**

involve /ɪn'vɒlv/ **verb** [T] **1 NECESSARY PART** ▷ ⑬ If a situation or activity involves something, that thing is a necessary part of it: *The trips often involve a lot of walking.* ∘ *There are a lot of risk involved.* **2 AFFECT/INCLUDE** ▷ ⑬ to affect o include someone or something in an activity: *a event involving hundreds of people* **3 TAKE PART** ▷ ⑧² to make someone be part of a activity or process: *I prefer teaching methods tha* **actively involve** *students* **in** *learning.*

involved /ɪn'vɒlvd/ **adj 1 be/get involved (in with sth)** ⑧² to do things and be part of a activity or event: *How did you get involved i acting?* **2 be/get involved with sb** to have sexual or romantic relationship with someone *She got* **involved with** *a boy from college* **3** complicated: *a long and involved story*

involvement /ɪn'vɒlvmənt/ **noun** [U] ⑧² th state of being involved in an activity or event *He denies any* **involvement in** *the attack.*

☑ Word partners for **involvement**

close/direct/personal involvement • involvement **in** sth

---

inward¹ /'ɪnwəd/ **adj 1** [always before noun] towards the centre or the inside of somethin **2 inward investment** UK money from foreig companies that is put into businesses in you own country **3** [always before noun] inside you mind and not shown to other people: *inwar feelings* → Opposite **outward adj**

inward² /'ɪnwəd/ **adv** (also UK **inwards**) toward the inside or the centre: *The door slowly opene inward.*

inwardly /'ɪnwədli/ **adv** in your mind withou

anyone else seeing or knowing: *She smiled inwardly.* → Opposite **outwardly**

in-your-face (also **in-yer-face**) /ˌɪnjəˈfeɪs/ **adj** informal describes something that is done in a forceful way that intends to shock people: *in-your-face television advertising*

iodine /ˈaɪədiːn/ **noun** [U] a chemical element found in sea water, and used in some medicines

IOU /ˌaɪəʊˈjuː/ **noun** [C] abbreviation for I owe you: a piece of paper saying that you will pay back money you owe

IOW internet abbreviation for in other words: used when you want to express something in a different way in order to explain it clearly

IPA /ˌaɪpiːˈeɪ/ **noun** [U] abbreviation for International Phonetic Alphabet: a system of symbols for showing how words are spoken

iPad /ˈaɪpæd/ **noun** [C] trademark a tablet (= small computer) made by Apple, that is controlled by touch rather than having a keyboard

iPod /ˈaɪpɒd/ **noun** [C] trademark a small piece of electronic equipment for storing and playing music

IQ /ˌaɪˈkjuː/ **noun** [C, U] abbreviation for intelligence quotient: a person's intelligence when measured by a special test: *a high/low IQ*

ir- /ɪr-/ **prefix** not: *irregular*

irate /aɪˈreɪt/ **adj** extremely angry: *Hundreds of irate passengers have complained to the airline.*

iris /ˈaɪərɪs/ **noun** [C] **1** a tall plant with purple, yellow, or white flowers **2** the coloured part of your eye

Irish¹ /ˈaɪərɪʃ/ **adj** relating to Ireland: *Irish music/ culture* ○ *Irish whiskey*

Irish² /ˈaɪərɪʃ/ **noun 1** [U] the language that is spoken in some parts of Ireland **2 the Irish** [plural] the people of Ireland

iron¹ /aɪən/ **noun 1** [U] 🔵 a dark grey metal used to make steel (= very strong metal) and found in small amounts in blood and food (formula Fe): *an iron bar/gate* **2** [C] 🔵 a piece of electrical equipment that you use for making clothes flat and smooth → See also **cast iron**, **wrought iron**

iron² /aɪən/ **verb** [I, T] 🔵 to make clothes flat and smooth using an iron: *I need to iron a shirt to wear tomorrow.*

PHRASAL VERB **iron sth out** to solve a problem or difficulty: *We're still trying to **iron out** a few **problems** with the computer system.*

iron³ /aɪən/ **adj** [always before noun] extremely strong and determined: *a man of **iron will*** → See also **cast-iron**

ironic /aɪəˈrɒnɪk/ **adj 1** saying something that you do not mean, as a joke: *ironic comments* **2** An ironic situation is strange because it is the opposite of what you expected: [+ that] *It's ironic that she was hurt by the very person she's trying to help.* ● **ironically adv**

ironing /ˈaɪənɪŋ/ **noun** [U] **1** 🔵 the activity of making clothes flat and smooth using an iron (= a piece of electrical equipment): *John was doing the ironing.* **2** the clothes that are waiting to be ironed, or those that have just been ironed: *a basket full of ironing*

ironing board **noun** [C] a narrow table that you use for ironing

irony /ˈaɪərəni/ **noun 1** [C, U] a situation that is strange because it is the opposite of what you expected: *The irony is that now he's retired, he's busier than ever.* **2** [U] a type of humour in which people say something they do not mean

irrational /ɪˈræʃ(ə)nəl/ **adj** Irrational feelings and actions are based on your emotions and not on good reasons: *irrational behaviour* ○ *an **irrational fear** of flying* ● **irrationality** /ɪˌræʃənˈæləti/ **noun** [U] ● **irrationally adv**

irreconcilable /ˌɪrekənˈsaɪləbl/ **adj** formal Irreconcilable beliefs, opinions, etc are so different that no agreement is possible: ***Irreconcilable differences*** led to their divorce.

irregular /ɪˈregjələr/ **adj 1** TIME ▷ 🔵 Irregular actions or events happen with a different amount of time between each one: *an irregular heartbeat* ○ *They met at irregular intervals.* **2** SHAPE ▷ 🔵 not smooth or straight, or having parts that are different sizes: *an irregular coastline* **3** GRAMMAR ▷ 🔵 not following the general rules in grammar: *irregular verbs/plurals* **4** BEHAVIOUR ▷ UK formal slightly illegal, or not done in the usual and acceptable way: *He led a very irregular life.* ● **irregularity** /ɪˌregjəˈlærəti/ **noun** [C, U] ● **irregularly adv**

irrelevant /ɪˈreləvənt/ **adj** not important in a particular situation: *The car had faults but these were **irrelevant to** the crash.* ● **irrelevance** /ɪˈreləvəns/ **noun** [C, U] something that is irrelevant, or the quality of being irrelevant ● **irrelevantly adv**

irreparable /ɪˈrepərəbl/ **adj** Irreparable damage, harm, injury, etc is so bad that it can never be repaired. ● **irreparably adv**

irreplaceable /ˌɪrɪˈpleɪsəbl/ **adj** Someone or something that is irreplaceable is so valuable or special that you could not get another one like them.

irrepressible /ˌɪrɪˈpresəbl/ **adj 1** always happy and energetic **2** An irrepressible feeling is impossible to control: *an irrepressible urge to travel* ● **irrepressibly adv**

irresistible /ˌɪrɪˈzɪstəbl/ **adj 1** extremely attractive and impossible not to like or want: *an irresistible smile* **2** too powerful to control or ignore: *irresistible pressure* ○ *an irresistible desire to run away* ● **irresistibly adv**

irrespective /ˌɪrɪˈspektɪv/ **adv irrespective of sth** used to say that something does not affect a situation: *Everyone should be treated equally, irrespective of skin colour.*

irresponsible /ˌɪrɪˈspɒnsəbl/ **adj** 🔵 not thinking about the possible bad results of what you are doing: *an irresponsible attitude* ● **irresponsibility** /ˌɪrɪˌspɒnsəˈbɪləti/ **noun** [U] ● **irresponsibly adv**

irreverent /ɪˈrevərənt/ **adj** not showing any respect for people or traditions that are usually respected: *irreverent humour* ● **irreverence** /ɪˈrevərəns/ **noun** [U] irreverent behaviour ● **irreverently adv**

irreversible /ˌɪrɪˈvɜːsəbl/ **adj** Something that is

irreversible cannot be changed back to how it was before: *Smoking has caused **irreversible** damage to his lungs.* • **irreversibly** adv

irrevocable /ɪˈrevəkəbl/ adj formal impossible to change or stop: ***irrevocable decisions*** • **irrevocably** adv

irrigate /ˈɪrɪgeɪt/ verb [T] to provide water for an area of land so that crops can be grown • **irrigation** /ˌɪrɪˈgeɪʃən/ noun [U]

irritable /ˈɪrɪtəbl/ adj becoming annoyed very easily: *Jack's been irritable all day.* • **irritability** /ˌɪrɪtəˈbɪləti/ noun [U] • **irritably** adv

irritant /ˈɪrɪtənt/ noun [C] **1** someone or something that makes you feel annoyed **2** a substance that makes part of your body hurt

irritate /ˈɪrɪteɪt/ verb [T] **1** to annoy someone: *His comments really irritated me.* **2** to make a part of your body hurt: *The smoke irritated her eyes.* • **irritation** /ˌɪrɪˈteɪʃən/ noun [C, U]

irritated /ˈɪrɪteɪtɪd/ adj ⓔ annoyed: *Ben began to get increasingly **irritated by/at** her questions.* ◦ *[+ that] I was irritated that he didn't thank me.*

irritating /ˈɪrɪteɪtɪŋ/ adj ⓑ making you feel annoyed: *an irritating habit* • **irritatingly** adv

is strong /ɪz/ weak /z/ present simple he/she/it of be

Islam /ˈɪzlɑːm/ noun [U] a religion based on belief in Allah, on the Koran, and on the teachings of Mohammed: *The followers of Islam are called Muslims.*

Islamic /ɪzˈlæmɪk/ adj related to Islam: *Islamic art* ◦ *an Islamic country*

island /ˈaɪlənd/ noun [C] ⓐⓩ an area of land that has water around it: *the Caribbean island of Grenada* ◦ *the Hawaiian Islands* • **islander** noun [C] someone who lives on an island → See also **desert island**

isle /aɪl/ noun [C] an island, often used in the name of a particular island: *the British Isles*

isn't /ˈɪzənt/ short for is not: *Mike isn't coming with us.*

isolate /ˈaɪsəleɪt/ verb [T] to separate someone or something from other people or things: *Scientists have been able to isolate the gene responsible for causing the illness.* ◦ *He had been **isolated from** other prisoners.*

isolated /ˈaɪsəleɪtɪd/ adj **1** a long way from other places: *an isolated village in the mountains* **2** alone and not having help or support from other people: *Kazuo felt very isolated at his new school.* **3 an isolated case/example/incident, etc** an event/action, etc that happens only once

isolation /ˌaɪsəˈleɪʃən/ noun **1** [U] the state of being separate from other people, places, or things: *the country's economic isolation from the rest of the world* **2 in isolation** alone, or separately from other people, places, or things: *These poems cannot be considered in isolation.* **3** [U] a feeling of being lonely: *I had this awful sense of isolation.*

ISP /ˌaɪesˈpiː/ noun [C] abbreviation for Internet service provider: a company that connects your computer to the Internet, and lets you use email and other services

issue¹ /ˈɪʃuː/ noun **1** [C] ⓑ an important subject or problem that people are discussing: *the issues*

of race and social class ◦ *political issues* ◦ *Ch[...] has **raised** a very important **issue**.* **2** [C] ⓔⓩ t[...] newspaper, magazine, etc that is produced on[...] particular day: *Have you seen the latest issue [...] Computer World?* **3 at issue** most important [...] what is being discussed: *The point at issue is wh[...] is best for the child.* **4 take issue (with sb/sth)** [...] disagree with what someone says or writes: [...] *would take issue with you on that.*

IDIOM **have issues with sth** to often be sa[...] anxious, or angry because of something: *A ve[...] high proportion of women diet frequently a[...] have issues with their bodies.*

🗎 Word partners for **issue** noun

a **contentious/important/key/major/thorny** issue • **address/discuss/raise/resolve** an issue • **the issue of** sth

---

issue² /ˈɪʃuː/ verb [T] (**issuing, issued**) **1** to s[...] something officially: *The Prime Minister w[...]* ***issue** a **statement** tomorrow.* ◦ *Police **issued** [...] **warning** about the dangers of playing near wat[...]* **2** to officially give something to someone: *[...]* ***issue** a passport/ticket/invitation* ◦ *All me[...] bers will be **issued with** a membership card.*

🗎 Word partners for **issue** verb

issue an **order/statement/warning** • issue **guidelines/instructions**

---

it /ɪt/ pronoun **1 THING** ▷ ⓐⓩ used to refer to th[...] thing, situation, or idea that has already bee[...] talked about: *"Have you seen my bag?" "It's in t[...] hall."* **2 DESCRIPTION** ▷ ⓐⓞ used before certa[...] adjectives, nouns, or verbs to introduce a[...] opinion or description of a situation: *It's unlike[...] that she'll arrive on time.* **3 SUBJECT/OBJECT** ▷ ⓐ[...] used with certain verbs that need a subject [...] object but do not refer to a particular noun: [...] *costs less if you travel UK at the weekend/US on t[...] weekend.* ◦ *I liked it in Scotland.* **4 TIM[...] WEATHER** ▷ ⓐⓩ used with the verb 'be' [...] sentences giving the time, date, weather, [...] distances: *It rained all day.* ◦ *What time is [...]* **5 SEEM** ▷ used as the subject of verbs such [...] 'seem', 'appear' and 'look': *It seemed unfair [...] leave her at home.* **6 EMPHASIZE** ▷ used [...] emphasize one part of a sentence: *It's th[...] children I'm concerned about, not me.* **7 it's s[...] sth** used to say the name of a person or thin[...] when the person you are speaking to does n[...] know: *It's your Dad on the phone.*

IT /ˌaɪˈtiː/ noun [U] ⓐⓩ abbreviation for informatic[...] technology: the use of computers and oth[...] electronic equipment to store and ser[...] information

italics /ɪˈtælɪks/ noun [plural] a style of writing [...] printing in which the letters slope to the rig[...] • **italic** adj written in italics

itch¹ /ɪtʃ/ verb **1** [I] If a part of your body itches, [...] feels uncomfortable and you want to rub it wi[...] your nails: *Woollen sweaters make my arms itc[...]* **2 be itching to do sth** informal to want to d[...] something very much: *You could tell that the[...] were itching to leave.*

itch² /ɪtʃ/ noun [C] an uncomfortable feeling [...]

---

your skin that makes you want to rub it with your nails: *I've **got an itch** in the middle of my back.*

tching /ˈɪtʃɪŋ/ **noun** [U] the feeling when a part of your body itches: *a lotion to stop itching*

tchy /ˈɪtʃi/ **adj** If a part of your body is itchy, it feels uncomfortable and you want to rub it with your nails: *an itchy nose* • **itchiness noun** [U]

t'd /ˈɪtəd/ **1** short for it would: *It'd be great if we could meet next week.* **2** short for it had: *It'd taken us an hour to find Bruce's house.*

tem /ˈaɪtəm/ **noun** [C] **1 🔵** a single thing in a set or on a list: *the last item on the list* ∘ *Various stolen items were found.* **2 🔵** a piece of news on television or radio, or in a newspaper: *a small item on the back page of the local newspaper*

temize (also UK **-ise**) /ˈaɪtəmaɪz/ **verb** [T] to list things separately, often including details about each thing: *an itemized phone bill*

tinerant /aɪˈtɪnᵊrᵊnt/ **adj** [always before noun] formal travelling from one place to another: *an itinerant preacher*

tinerary /aɪˈtɪnᵊrᵊri/ **noun** [C] a list of places that you plan to visit on a journey: *The President's itinerary includes visits to Boston and New York.*

t'll /ˈɪtᵊl/ short for it will: *It'll take about twenty minutes to get there.*

ts /ɪts/ **determiner 🔵** belonging to or relating to the thing that has already been talked about: *The house has its own swimming pool.*

t's /ɪts/ **1** short for it is: *"What time is it?" "It's one o'clock."* **2** short for it has: *It's been a long day and I'm tired.*

tself /ɪtˈself/ **pronoun 1 🔵** the reflexive form of the pronoun 'it': *The cat licked itself clean.* **2 🔵** used to emphasize the particular thing you are referring to: *The garden is enormous but the house itself is very small.* **3 (all) by itself a 🔵** alone: *The dog was in the house by itself for several days.* **b** automatically: *The UK heating/ US heat comes on by itself.* **4 in itself** as the only thing being talked about and nothing else: *You've managed to complete the course – that in itself is an achievement.*

ITV /ˌaɪtiːˈviː/ **noun** abbreviation for Independent Television: one of the main television companies in the United Kingdom

IV /ˌaɪˈviː/ **noun** [C] US (UK/US **drip**) a piece of medical equipment used for putting liquids into your body

I've /aɪv/ short for I have: *I've decided not to go.*

IVF /ˌaɪviːˈef/ **noun** [U] abbreviation for in vitro fertilization: a treatment where a woman's egg is fertilized outside her body and put back in her body for the baby to grow

ivy

ivory /ˈaɪvᵊri/ **noun** [U] a hard, white substance from the tusks (= long teeth) of some animals, such as elephants (= large, grey animals)

ivy /ˈaɪvi/ **noun** [U] a dark green plant that often grows up walls

I

J

J, j /dʒeɪ/ the tenth letter of the alphabet

jab¹ /dʒæb/ **verb** [I, T] (**jabbing, jabbed**) to push something quickly and hard into or towards another thing: *He jabbed a finger into her back.*

jab² /dʒæb/ **noun** [C] **1** a quick, hard push into or towards something **2** UK informal an injection (= when a drug is put in your body with a needle): *a flu jab*

jack¹ /dʒæk/ **noun** [C] **1** a piece of equipment for lifting a heavy object such as a car **2** a playing card that comes between a ten and a queen: *the jack of diamonds*

jack² /dʒæk/ **verb**

PHRASAL VERBS **jack sth in** UK informal to stop doing something, especially a job: *She's jacked in her job.* • **jack sth up** informal to increase a price or rate suddenly and by a large amount

jackal /ˈdʒækəl/ **noun** [C] a wild dog that hunts in groups

jacket

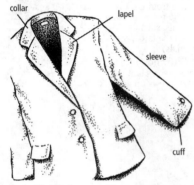

collar
lapel
sleeve
cuff

jacket /ˈdʒækɪt/ **noun** [C] **A2** a short coat: *a leather jacket* → See colour picture **Clothes** on page Centre 8 → See also **dinner jacket, life jacket, strait-jacket**

jacket po'tato **noun** [C] (plural **jacket potatoes**) UK a potato that has been baked in the oven with its skin on

jack-knife¹ /ˈdʒækˌnaɪf/ **noun** [C] (plural **jack-knives**) a knife with a blade that can be folded away into the handle

jack-knife² /ˈdʒækˌnaɪf/ **verb** [I] If a large truck jack-knifes, the front part turns round to face the back in a way that is not controlled.

jackpot /ˈdʒækpɒt/ **noun** [C] an amount of money that is the largest prize anyone can win in a competition

IDIOM **hit the jackpot** to be very successful, especially by winning or earning a lot of money

Jacuzzi /dʒəˈkuːzi/ **noun** [C] trademark a bath or pool that produces bubbles in the water

jade /dʒeɪd/ **noun** [U] a green stone used in making jewellery

jaded /ˈdʒeɪdɪd/ **adj** tired or bored with something, especially because you have done it too much

jagged /ˈdʒægɪd/ **adj** very rough and sharp: *jagged rocks*

jaguar /ˈdʒægjuər/ **noun** [C] a large, wild cat that lives in Central and South America

jail¹ (also UK **gaol**) /dʒeɪl/ **noun** [C, U] **B1** a place where criminals are kept as a punishment: *He ended up in jail.*

> 🗂 Word partners for **jail**
>
> be released from/be sent to jail • in jail • a jail **sentence**

jail² /dʒeɪl/ **verb** [T] to put someone in a jail: [often passive] *He was jailed for two years.*

jailer /ˈdʒeɪlər/ **noun** [C] someone who guards prisoners in a jail

jam¹ /dʒæm/ **noun 1** [C, U] (also US **jelly**) **A2** a sweet food made from fruit that you spread on bread: *a jar of strawberry jam* → See colour picture **Food** on page Centre 11 **2** [C] (also **traffic jam**) **B2** a line of cars, trucks, etc that are moving slowly or not moving: *We were stuck in a jam for hours.*

jam² /dʒæm/ **verb** (**jamming, jammed**) **1** **jam sth in/into/on, etc** to push something somewhere firmly and tightly: *She jammed her hands into her pockets.* **2 STUCK** ▷ [I, T] to get stuck or make something get stuck: *The machine keeps jamming.* **3 FILL** ▷ [T] to fill a place completely. [often passive] *The streets were jammed with cars* **4 STOP RADIO** ▷ [T] to send a signal that stops a radio being able to broadcast

jamboree /ˌdʒæmbəˈriː/ **noun** [C] a big celebration or party

Jan written abbreviation for January

jangle /ˈdʒæŋgl/ **verb** [I, T] If small metal objects jangle, they hit together making a ringing noise and if you jangle them, you make them make this noise: *He was jangling his keys.* • **jangle** **noun** [C]

janitor /ˈdʒænɪtər/ **noun** [C] US someone whose job is to look after a building: *the school janitor*

January /ˈdʒænjuəri/ **noun** [C, U] (written abbreviation **Jan**) **A1** the first month of the year

jar¹ /dʒɑːr/ **noun** [C] **B1** a glass container used for storing food: *a jar of jam* → See picture a **container**

jar² /dʒɑːr/ **verb** [I, T] (**jarring, jarred**) to move suddenly, hitting something and causing pain or damage: *The movement jarred his injured leg.*

PHRASAL VERB **jar on sb** UK to annoy someone: *Her voice jars on me.*

jargon /ˈdʒɑːgən/ **noun** [U] words and phrases used by particular groups of people that are difficult for other people to understand: *legal jargon*

jaundice /'dʒɔːndɪs/ **noun** [U] a disease that makes your eyes and skin yellow

jaundiced /'dʒɔːndɪst/ **adj** having a negative opinion of something because of bad things that have happened to you: *a jaundiced view of marriage*

jaunt /dʒɔːnt/ **noun** [C] a short, enjoyable journey

jaunty /'dʒɔːnti/ **adj** happy and confident: *a jaunty walk*

javelin /'dʒævəlɪn/ **noun 1** [C] a long, pointed stick that you throw as a sport **2 the javelin** a sport in which you throw a javelin as far as you can → See colour picture **Sports 1** on page Centre 14

jaw /dʒɔː/ **noun** [C] **1** ⓬ either of the two bones in your mouth that contain your teeth → See colour picture **The Body** on page Centre 13 **2 sb's jaw drops** If someone's jaw drops, their mouth opens because they are very surprised.

jazz /dʒæz/ **noun** [U] ⓪ music with a strong beat that is often played without written music: *a jazz band*

jealous /'dʒeləs/ **adj 1** ⓫ unhappy and angry because you want something that someone else has: *His new bike was **making** his friends **jealous**.* ◦ *Steve has always been **jealous of** his brother's good looks.* **2** ⓫ upset and angry because someone you love seems too interested in another person: *a jealous husband* ● **jealously adv**

> **Word partners for jealous**
>
> **make sb jealous** ● **insanely/madly jealous** ● **jealous of sb/sth**

jealousy /'dʒeləsi/ **noun** [U] jealous feelings

jeans /dʒiːnz/ **noun** [plural] ⓐ trousers made from denim (= a strong, usually blue, material): *a pair of jeans* → See colour picture **Clothes** on page Centre 8

jeep /dʒiːp/ **noun** [C] trademark a strongly built vehicle with big wheels that is used for driving over rough ground

jeer /dʒɪəʳ/ **verb** [I, T] to laugh and shout insults at someone: *The crowd outside his house jeered as he left.* ● **jeer noun** [C]

Jell-O /'dʒeləʊ/ **noun** [U] US trademark jelly

jelly /'dʒeli/ **noun** [C, U] **1** UK (US **Jell-O**) a soft but solid sweet food that shakes when you move it: *jelly and ice cream* **2** US (UK/US **jam**) a sweet food made from fruit that you spread on bread

jellyfish /'dʒelifɪʃ/ **noun** [C] (plural **jellyfish**) a sea creature with a clear body that may sting you (= put poison into your skin)

jeopardize (also UK **-ise**) /'dʒepədaɪz/ **verb** [T] to put something in a situation where there is a risk of failing or being harmed: *Bad weather could jeopardize all our plans.*

jeopardy /'dʒepədi/ **noun in jeopardy** in danger of failing or being harmed: *If the factory closes, local jobs will be in jeopardy.*

jerk¹ /dʒɜːk/ **verb** [I, T] to move very quickly and suddenly, or to make something move like this: *The truck jerked forward.*

jerk² /dʒɜːk/ **noun** [C] **1** a quick, sudden move-

ment: *a sudden jerk of the head* **2** informal a stupid or annoying person

jerky /'dʒɜːki/ **adj** Jerky movements are quick and sudden. ● **jerkily adv**

jersey /'dʒɜːzi/ **noun 1** [C] a piece of clothing that covers the top of your body and is pulled on over your head **2** [U] soft wool or cotton cloth used for making clothes

jest /dʒest/ **noun in jest** said as a joke

Jesus Christ /ˌdʒiːzəsˈkraɪst/ **noun** the Jewish holy man believed by Christians to be the Son of God, and on whose life and teachings Christianity is based

jet¹ /dʒet/ **noun** [C] **1** ⓑ an aircraft that flies very fast → See also **jumbo jet 2** liquid or gas that is forced out of something in a thin, strong line

jet² /dʒet/ **verb** [I] (**jetting, jetted**) **jet in/off, etc** to fly somewhere in an aircraft: *She jetted off to Athens for a week.*

jet-black /ˌdʒetˈblæk/ **noun** [U] a very dark black colour ● **jet-black adj** *jet-black hair*

jet engine noun [C] an engine that makes an aircraft fly very fast

jet lag noun [U] the tired feeling you get when you have just travelled a long distance on an aircraft

jettison /'dʒetɪsən/ **verb** [T] **1** to get rid of something you do not want or need: *The station has jettisoned educational broadcasts.* **2** If an aircraft or a ship jettisons something, it throws it off to make itself lighter.

jetty /'dʒeti/ **noun** [C] a wooden structure at the edge of the sea or a lake where people can get on and off boats

Jew /dʒuː/ **noun** [C] someone whose religion is Judaism, or who is related to the ancient people of Israel

jewel /'dʒuːəl/ **noun** [C] ⓬ a valuable stone that is used to make jewellery

jeweller UK (US **jeweler**) /'dʒuːələʳ/ **noun** [C] someone whose job is to sell or make jewellery

jewellery *UK*, **jewelry** *US*

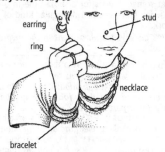

earring   stud   ring   necklace   bracelet

jewellery UK (US **jewelry**) /'dʒuːəlri/ **noun** [U] ⓐ objects made from gold, silver, and valuable stones that you wear for decoration

Jewish /'dʒuːɪʃ/ **adj** relating or belonging to the Jews: *Jewish history/law*

jibe (also **gibe**) /dʒaɪb/ **noun** [C] an insulting remark: *He kept making **jibes at** me about my weight.*

---

jig /dʒɪg/ **noun** [C] a traditional, quick dance, or the music it is danced to

jiggle /'dʒɪgl/ **verb** [I, T] to make quick, short movements from side to side or to make something else move like this

jigsaw /'dʒɪgsɔː/ **noun** [C] (also '**jigsaw ˌpuzzle**) a picture in many small pieces that you put together as a game

jingle¹ /'dʒɪŋgl/ **noun** [C] **1** a short song that is used to advertise a product on the radio or television **2** a sound made when small metal objects hit against each other

jingle² /'dʒɪŋgl/ **verb** [I, T] to make the sound of small metal objects hitting against each other: *a pocket full of jingling coins*

jinx /dʒɪŋks/ **noun** [C] someone or something that brings bad luck: *There seems to be **a jinx on** the school.* • **jinx verb** [T]

jitters /'dʒɪtəz/ **noun** [plural] a nervous feeling: *Hospitals give me **the jitters**.*

jittery /'dʒɪtᵊri/ **adj** nervous: *She gets quite **jittery about** exams.*

Jnr UK (UK/US **Jr**) written abbreviation for junior (= the younger of two men in a family with the same name)

➕ Other ways of saying **job**

A more formal alternative is the noun **occupation**:

*Please fill in your name, age, and **occupation**.*

The nouns **post** and **position** are often used to talk about a particular job within an organisation:

*She's applied for a part-time teaching **post/position**.*

The noun **career** is sometimes used to describe a job that a person does for a long period in their life:

*She's had a very successful **career** in marketing.*

A **placement** (*UK*) (**internship** *US*) is a job that someone does for a short time in order to learn more about a particular kind of work:

*He's got a year's **placement** in the medical labs.*

---

job /dʒɒb/ **noun** [C] **1 PAID EMPLOYMENT** ▷ **A1** the regular work that you do in order to earn money: *She **got a job** in publishing.* ∘ *Hundreds of workers could **lose** their **jobs**.* ∘ *Why don't you **apply for** a part-time **job**?* → See Note at **work²** **2 PIECE OF WORK** ▷ **A2** a piece of work that you have to do: *cooking, cleaning and other household jobs* **3 RESPONSIBILITY** ▷ **B2** something that is your responsibility: *It's my job to water the plants.* **4 make a bad/good, etc job of sth** UK to do sth badly/well, etc **5 do a good/excellent, etc job** **B2** to do something well/very well, etc: *She did a great job of organizing the event.* **6 out of a job** without a job: *How long have you been out of a job?*

IDIOMS **do the job** If something does the job, it is suitable for a particular purpose: *Here, this knife should do the job.* • **it's a good job** UK informal I it is a good job that something happened, it is lucky that it happened: [+ (that)] *It's a good job that Jo was there to help you.* • **just the job** UK If something is just the job, it is exactly what you want or need.

☑ Word partners for **job**

a **dead-end/full-time/good/part-time/temporary** job • **apply for/create/do/find/get/lose** a job • a job **as** sth

---

'**job deˌscription noun** [C] a list of the things you must do in your work

jobless /'dʒɒbləs/ **adj** without a job: *young jobless people*

jobshare /'dʒɒbʃeəʳ/ **verb** [I] UK If two people jobshare, they do one job between them, working at different times. • **jobshare noun** [C] UK

jockey /'dʒɒki/ **noun** [C] someone who rides horses in races → See also **disc jockey**

jog /dʒɒg/ **verb** (**jogging, jogged**) **1** [I] **B1** to run slowly for exercise: *I jog through the park every morning.* **2** [T] to hit something gently by mistake: *He jogged her arm.* **3 jog sb's memory** to make someone remember something: *They hoped the photographs would jog his memory.* • **jog noun** [no plural] *Let's go for a jog.* • **jogging noun** [U]

jogger /'dʒɒgəʳ/ **noun** [C] someone who runs for exercise

join¹ /dʒɔɪn/ **verb 1 BECOME MEMBER** ▷ [T] **A2** to become a member of a group or organization: *He joined the army when he was eighteen.* **2 DO WITH OTHERS** ▷ [T] **A2** to do something or go somewhere with someone: *Would you like to join us for dinner?* **3 FASTEN** ▷ [T] **B1** to fasten or connect things together: *Join the ends together with strong glue.* **4 MEET** ▷ [I, T] **B1** to meet at a particular point: *The Mississippi River and the Missouri join near St Louis.* **5 join a line** (also UK **join a queue**) to go and stand at the end of a row of people waiting for something → See also **join forces** (**force¹**)

❗ Common learner error: **join**

Join is not followed by a preposition when it is used in expressions such as 'join a company'.

He joined the team in 1998.

~~He joined to the team in 1998.~~

PHRASAL VERBS **join in** (**sth**) **B1** to become involved in an activity with other people: *We're playing cards. Would you like to join in?* • **join up** to become a member of the army or other military group

join² /dʒɔɪn/ **noun** [C] UK the place where two or more things are fastened together

joined-up /ˌdʒɔɪn'dʌp/ **adj** UK **1 joined-up writing** a style of writing where each letter in a word is connected to the next one **2 joined-up thinking** thinking about a complicated problem in an intelligent and original way, and considering everything that is connected with it

oint¹ /dʒɔɪnt/ **adj** [always before noun] ⓐ belonging to or done by two or more people: *a joint statement* ○ *The project was a joint effort by all the children in the class.* • **jointly** adv

oint² /dʒɔɪnt/ **noun** [C] **1 BODY PART** ▷ a place in your body where two bones meet: *the knee joint* **2 MEAT** ▷ UK a large piece of meat, usually cooked in the oven: *a joint of beef* **3 CONNECTION** ▷ a place where parts of a structure or machine are connected **4 PLACE** ▷ informal a place where something is sold, especially a restaurant or bar: *a pizza joint*

joint

oint 'venture noun [C] a business activity that is done by two separate companies working together

oke¹ /dʒəʊk/ **noun 1** ⓐ [C] something that someone says to make people laugh, usually a short story with a funny ending: *to tell/make a joke* **2 be a joke** informal to not be serious or not deserve respect: *The investigation was a joke.* **3 be no joke** to be serious or difficult: *It's no joke driving on icy roads.* **4 take a joke** to understand and accept a trick without becoming angry or upset → See also **practical joke**

🗌 Word partners for **joke**

crack/make/tell a joke • a **dirty/sick** joke • a joke **about** sth

oke² /dʒəʊk/ **verb 1** ⓐ [I] to say funny things, or not be serious: *She always jokes about her husband's cooking.* **2 You must be joking!/ You're joking!** informal ⓐ something you say to show that you are surprised by what someone has said, or do not believe it is true • **jokingly** adv

oker /'dʒəʊkəʳ/ **noun** [C] **1** someone who likes saying or doing funny things **2** one of a set of playing cards that can be used instead of another card in some games

olly¹ /'dʒɒli/ **adj** happy or enjoyable: *We had a jolly evening.*

olly² /'dʒɒli/ **adv** old-fashioned very: *a jolly good idea*

olt¹ /dʒəʊlt/ **noun** [C] **1** a sudden, violent movement: *With a sudden jolt the train started moving again.* **2** an unpleasant shock or surprise: *The reminder that he was dead gave her a jolt.*

olt² /dʒəʊlt/ **verb** [I, T] to move suddenly and forcefully, or to make someone or something do this: *The bus stopped suddenly and the passengers were jolted forward.*

ostle /'dʒɒsl/ **verb** [I, T] to push other people in order to get somewhere in a crowd

PHRASAL VERB **jostle for sth** to try hard to get something: *Thousands of companies are jostling for business on the Internet.*

jot /dʒɒt/ **verb** [T] (**jotting, jotted**) to write something quickly: *She jotted a note to Sue.*

PHRASAL VERB **jot sth down** to write something quickly on a piece of paper so that you remember it: *I jotted down some notes during his speech.*

journal /'dʒɜːnəl/ **noun** [C] **1** a magazine containing articles about a particular subject: *a medical journal* **2** a book in which you regularly write about what has happened to you

journalism /'dʒɜːnəlɪzəm/ **noun** [U] ⓐ the work of writing articles for newspapers, magazines, television, or radio

journalist /'dʒɜːnəlɪst/ **noun** [C] ⓐ someone whose job is journalism

journalistic /ˌdʒɜːnəlˈɪstɪk/ **adj** relating to journalism or typical of journalism

journey /'dʒɜːni/ **noun** [C] ⓐ If you go on a journey, you travel from one place to another: *a car/train journey* ○ *We take games for the children when we go on long journeys.* → See Note at **travel²**

🗌 Word partners for **journey**

an **arduous/long/perilous/short** journey • **begin/complete/embark on/go on/make** a journey

jovial /'dʒəʊviəl/ **adj** happy and friendly: *a jovial man*

joy /dʒɔɪ/ **noun 1 HAPPINESS** ▷ [U] ⓐ a feeling of great happiness: *the joy of winning* **2 PLEASURE** ▷ [C] ⓐ something or someone that makes you feel very happy: *She's a joy to work with.* **3 SUCCESS** ▷ [U] UK informal success: *I tried ringing for a plumber, but had no joy.*

joyful /'dʒɔɪfl/ **adj** very happy, or making people feel very happy: *joyful news* • **joyfully** adv

joyous /'dʒɔɪəs/ **adj** literary extremely happy, or making people extremely happy • **joyously** adv

joypad /'dʒɔɪpæd/ **noun** [C] a gamepad (= a small piece of equipment that you hold in your hands and use to control a computer game)

joyriding /'dʒɔɪˌraɪdɪŋ/ **noun** [U] the crime of stealing cars and driving them fast and dangerously • **joyride** /'dʒɔɪraɪd/ **noun** [C] *They took the car for a joyride.* • **joyrider noun** [C]

joystick /'dʒɔɪstɪk/ **noun** [C] a vertical handle you move to control a computer game, machine, or aircraft

JP /ˌdʒeɪˈpiː/ **noun** [C] abbreviation for Justice of the Peace: a judge in a small or local court of law

JPEG /'dʒeɪpeg/ **noun 1** [U] abbreviation for joint photographics experts group: a system for making electronic pictures use less space **2** [C] a type of computer file (= collection of information) that contains pictures or photographs

Jr (also UK **Jnr**) written abbreviation for junior (= the younger of two men in a family with the same name): *John F. Kennedy, Jr.*

jubilant /'dʒuːbɪlənt/ **adj** feeling or showing great happiness, usually because of a success: *jubilant Man United supporters* • **jubilation**

/ˌdʒuːbɪˈleɪʃ^ən/ noun [U] a feeling of great happiness and success

jubilee /ˈdʒuːbɪliː/ noun [C] a celebration of an important event in the past, usually one that happened 25 or 50 years ago: *a golden jubilee* (= 50 years) ○ *a silver jubilee* (= 25 years)

Judaism /ˈdʒuːdeɪɪz^əm/ noun [U] the religion of the Jewish people, based on belief in one God and on the laws contained in the Torah

judge¹ /dʒʌdʒ/ noun [C] **1** 🔒 someone who controls a trial in court, decides how criminals should be punished, and makes decisions about legal things: *Judge Moylan* ○ *The judge ruled that they had acted correctly.* **2** 🔒 someone who decides which person or thing wins a competition: *the Olympic judges* **3 a bad/good, etc judge of sth** someone who is usually wrong/usually right, etc when they judge something: *a good judge of character*

judge² /dʒʌdʒ/ verb **1 DEVELOP OPINION** ▷ [I, T] 🔒 to have or develop an opinion about something or someone, usually after thinking carefully: [+ question word] *I can't judge whether he's telling the truth or not.* ○ *You shouldn't judge people on their appearances.* ○ *He was judged guilty/insane.* **2 judging by/from** 🔒 used to express the reasons why you have a particular opinion: *She must be popular judging by the huge number of letters that she receives.* **3 COMPETITION** ▷ [I, T] to decide the winner or results of a competition: *I've been asked to judge the art contest.* **4 BAD OPINION** ▷ [I, T] to have a bad opinion of someone's behaviour, often because you think you are better than them: *What gives you the right to judge people?* **5 GUESS** ▷ [T] to try to guess something, especially a measurement: *I find it difficult to judge distances.*

judgment (also UK **judgement**) /ˈdʒʌdʒmənt/ noun **1 OPINION** ▷ [C, U] 🔒 an opinion about someone or something that you decide on after thinking carefully: *The inspector needs to make a judgment about how the school is performing.* **2 ABILITY** ▷ [U] the ability to make good decisions or to be right in your opinions: *to have good/bad judgment* **3 LEGAL DECISION** ▷ [C, U] an official legal decision, usually made by a judge

> 🔲 **Word partners for judgment**
>
> make/pass/reserve judgment • poor/good judgment • a harsh/subjective judgment • an error/lapse of judgment

judgmental (also UK **judgemental**) /dʒʌdʒˈmentˀl/ adj quick to criticize people

judicial /dʒuːˈdɪʃ^əl/ adj relating to a court of law or the legal system: *a judicial inquiry*

the judiciary /dʒuːˈdɪʃ^əri/ noun all the judges in a country

judicious /dʒuːˈdɪʃəs/ adj done or decided carefully and with good judgment

judo /ˈdʒuːdəʊ/ noun [U] a sport from Japan in which two people try to throw each other to the ground

jug /dʒʌg/ noun [C] 🔒 **jug** a container with a handle used for pouring out liquids: *a jug of water*

juggle /ˈdʒʌgl/ verb **1** [T] to try to do several things at once, when it is difficult to have enough time: *Many women have to juggle work and family.* **2** [I, T] to keep two or more objects such as balls in the air by throwing them repeatedly, usually in order to entertain people

juggler /ˈdʒʌglə^r/ noun [C] someone who juggles objects to entertain people

juice /dʒuːs/ noun [C, U] 🔒 the liquid that comes from fruit or vegetables → See also **orange juice**

juices /ˈdʒuːsɪz/ noun [plural] the liquid that comes from cooked meat

juicy /ˈdʒuːsi/ adj **1** 🔒 full of juice: *juicy apple.* **2** interesting because of shocking or personal information: *juicy gossip*

jukebox /ˈdʒuːkbɒks/ noun [C] a machine usually in a bar, which plays a song when you put money into it

July /dʒʊˈlaɪ/ noun [C, U] 🔒 the seventh month of the year → See also **Fourth of July**

jumble¹ /ˈdʒʌmbl/ noun [no plural] a confused mixture or group of things: *Her handbag is a jumble of pens, make-up, and keys.*

jumble² /ˈdʒʌmbl/ verb [T] (also **jumble up**) to mix things together in an untidy way: [often passive] *Her clothes were all jumbled up in the suitcase.*

jumble sale noun [C] UK (US **rummage sale**) a sale of old items, especially clothes, usually to make money for an organization

jumbo /ˈdʒʌmbəʊ/ adj [always before noun] extra large: *a jumbo bag of sweets*

jumbo jet noun [C] a very large aircraft for carrying passengers

jump¹ /dʒʌmp/ verb **1 INTO AIR** ▷ [I] 🔒 to push your body up and away from the ground using your feet and legs: *The children were jumping up and down with excitement.* ○ *I jumped over the log.* ○ *They jumped into the water.* **2 jump into, up, etc** 🔒 to move somewhere suddenly and quickly: *She jumped into a taxi and rushed to the station.* **3 GO OVER** ▷ [T] 🔒 to move over something by moving up into the air: *The horse jumped the last fence.* **4 INCREASE** ▷ [I, T] to suddenly increase by a large amount: *House prices have jumped by 20%.* **5 FEAR** ▷ [I] 🔒 to make a sudden movement because you are frightened or surprised: *Her scream made me jump.* → See also get/jump on the bandwagon, jump to conclusions , jump the gun¹, jump the queue

PHRASAL VERB **jump at sth** to take an opportunity to have or do something in a very willing and excited way: *He jumped at the chance to join the band.*

jump² /dʒʌmp/ **noun** [C] **1** 🔵 the movement of pushing your body up into the air using your feet and legs: *He won with a jump of 8.5 metres.* **2** a sudden increase in the amount of something: *a **jump** in profits* → See also **the high jump**, **the long jump**

jumper /'dʒʌmpər/ **noun** [C] **1** UK (UK/US **sweater**) 🔵 a warm piece of clothing that covers the top of your body and is pulled on over your head → See colour picture **Clothes** on page Centre 5 **2** US (mainly UK **pinafore**) a loose dress with no sleeves that is worn over other clothes such as a shirt

jump rope **noun** [C] US (UK **skipping rope**) a rope that you move over your head and then jump over as you move it under your feet

jumpy /'dʒʌmpi/ **adj** nervous or anxious

junction /'dʒʌŋkʃən/ **noun** [C] the place where two roads or railway lines meet or cross each other: *The accident happened at a busy road junction.* → See also **T-junction**

juncture /'dʒʌŋktʃər/ **noun** [C] formal a particular point in an event or period of time

June /dʒuːn/ **noun** [C, U] 🔵 the sixth month of the year

jungle /'dʒʌŋgl/ **noun** [C, U] 🔵 an area of land, usually in tropical countries, where trees and plants grow close together

junior¹ /'dʒuːniər/ **adj 1** LOW RANK ▷ 🔵 low or lower in rank: *a junior minister/senator* **2** YOUNG PEOPLE ▷ 🔵 for or relating to young people: *a junior tennis tournament* **3** NAME ▷ (written abbreviation **Jr**) mainly US used at the end of a man's name to show that he is the younger of two men in the same family who have the same name: *Hello, I'd like to speak to Mr Anderson, Junior.*

junior² /'dʒuːniər/ **noun 1 be 10/20, etc years sb's junior** to be 10, 20, etc years younger than someone: *My wife is 8 years my junior.* **2** [C] US a student in their third year of study at an American college or high school (= school for students aged 15 to 18) **3** [C] UK a child who goes to a junior school

junior college **noun** [C, U] a two-year college in the US where students can learn a skill or prepare to enter a university

junior high school **noun** [C, U] (also **junior high**) a school in the US or Canada for children who are 12 to 15 years old

junior school **noun** [C, U] a school in the UK for children who are 7 to 11 years old

junk /dʒʌŋk/ **noun** [U] informal old things that have little value

junk food **noun** [U] 🔵 food that is unhealthy but is quick and easy to eat

junkie /'dʒʌŋki/ **noun** [C] informal **1** someone who cannot stop taking illegal drugs **2** someone who wants something or wants to do something very much: *a publicity junkie*

junk mail **noun** [U] letters sent by companies to advertise their goods and services

junta /'dʒʌntə/ **noun** [C] a military government that has taken power in a country by force

Jupiter /'dʒuːpɪtər/ **noun** [no plural] the planet that is fifth from the Sun, after Mars and before Saturn

jurisdiction /ˌdʒʊərɪsˈdɪkʃən/ **noun** [U] the legal power to make decisions and judgments: *The school is **under the jurisdiction of** the local council.*

juror /'dʒʊərər/ **noun** [C] a member of a jury

jury /'dʒʊəri/ **noun** [group] **1** 🔵 a group of people in a court of law who decide if someone is guilty or not **2** a group of people who decide the winner of a competition

just¹ strong /dʒʌst/ weak /dʒəst/ **adv 1** ONLY ▷ 🔵 only: *I'll just have a small piece.* ∘ *He just wants to win.* ∘ *The film is not just about love.* **2** RECENTLY ▷ 🔵 a very short time ago: *I've just been on a trip to France.* ∘ *We've only just begun.* **3** EMPHASIS ▷ 🔵 used to emphasize something you say: *I just can't bear it!* **4** ALMOST NOT ▷ UK 🔵 almost not: *This dress **only just** fits.* **5** EXACTLY ▷ 🔵 exactly: *Tim looks **just like** his father.* ∘ *This carpet would be **just right** for my bedroom.* **6** ALMOST NOW ▷ 🔵 now or very soon: *I'm **just** coming!* **7 just before/over/under, etc** 🔵 a little before/over/under, etc something else: *It costs just over $10.* ∘ *She left just before Michael.* **8 just about** 🔵 almost: *I think I've remembered just about everything.* **9 be just about to do sth** 🔵 to be going to do something very soon: *I was just about to phone you.* **10 just as bad/good/tall, etc (as sb/sth)** 🔵 equally bad/good/tall, etc: *He's just as talented as his brother.* **11 I/you/we, etc will just have to do sth** used to say that there is nothing else someone can do: *You'll just have to wait.* **12 just as** 🔵 at the same time as: *She woke up just as we got there.* **13 it's just as well** used to say that it is lucky that something happened: *It's just as well we brought an umbrella.* → See also **just the job**

just² /dʒʌst/ **adj** fair or morally right: *a just society* → Opposite **unjust** • **justly adv**

justice /'dʒʌstɪs/ **noun 1** FAIR BEHAVIOUR ▷ [U] 🔵 behaviour or treatment that is fair and morally correct: *She tried to bring about fairness and **justice for** all.* → Opposite **injustice 2** LAW ▷ [U] 🔵 the system of laws that judges or punishes people: *the **criminal justice system*** **3** JUDGE ▷ [C] US someone who judges in a court of law **4 bring sb to justice** to catch a criminal and decide if they are guilty or not **5 do sb/sth justice; do justice to sb/sth** to show the best or real qualities of something or someone: *This postcard doesn't do justice to the wonderful scenery.*

,Justice of the 'Peace **noun** [C] someone who acts as a judge in a small or local court of law

justifiable /'dʒʌstɪfaɪəbl/ **adj** having a good reason: *justifiable anger* • **justifiably adv**

justification /ˌdʒʌstɪfɪ'keɪʃən/ **noun** [C, U] a reason for something: *There's no justification for treating her so badly.*

justified /'dʒʌstɪfaɪd/ **adj** fair or having a good reason: *justified criticism* ∘ *He's perfectly justified in asking for a larger salary.* → Opposite **unjustified**

justify /'dʒʌstɪfaɪ/ **verb** [T] ⬛ to give a good enough reason to make something seem acceptable: *I don't know how they can justify those ticket prices.*

jut /dʒʌt/ **verb** (**jutting, jutted**) **jut into/out, etc**

If something juts out, it comes out further tha the edge or surface around it: *The rocks jutted o into the sea.*

juvenile¹ /'dʒuːvənaɪl/ **adj 1** [always before nou by, for, or relating to young people: *juveni crime* **2** behaving in a silly way as if you were young child

juvenile² /'dʒuːvənaɪl/ **noun** [C] especially law, a young person

,juvenile de'linquent **noun** [C] a your criminal

juxtapose /ˌdʒʌkstə'pəʊz/ **verb** [T] formal place very different things or people close each other: *The exhibition juxtaposes paintin with black and white photographs.* • **juxtapos tion** /ˌdʒʌkstəpə'zɪʃən/ **noun** [C, U]

J

K

K, k /keɪ/ the eleventh letter of the alphabet

K /keɪ/ abbreviation for kilobyte: a unit for measuring the amount of information a computer can store

kaleidoscope /kəˈlaɪdəskəʊp/ **noun 1** [C] a tube-shaped toy you look through that contains mirrors and pieces of coloured glass that make patterns **2** [no plural] a mixture of different things: *The fashion show was a kaleidoscope of colours.*

kangaroo /ˌkæŋgəˈruː/ **noun** [C] 🔵 a large Australian animal that moves by jumping on its back legs

kangaroo

karaoke /ˌkæriˈəʊki/ **noun** [U] a type of entertainment in which people sing songs with recorded music that is played by a machine: *a karaoke night*

karat /ˈkærət/ **noun** [C] US (mainly UK **carat**) a unit for measuring how pure gold is

karate /kəˈrɑːti/ **noun** [U] a sport from Japan in which people fight using fast, hard hits with the hands or feet

karma /ˈkɑːmə/ **noun** [U] in some religions, the actions of a person in this life or earlier lives, which influence their future

kayak /ˈkaɪæk/ **noun** [C] a light, narrow boat, usually for one person, which you move using a paddle (= stick with a wide, flat part) • **kayaking noun** [U] the activity of travelling in a kayak

kebab /kɪˈbæb/ **noun** [C] (also **shish kebab**) small pieces of meat or vegetables cooked on a long, thin stick

keel¹ /kiːl/ **noun** [C] a long piece of wood or metal at the bottom of a boat that helps it to balance

keel² /kiːl/ **verb**

PHRASAL VERB **keel over** to fall over suddenly

keen /kiːn/ **adj 1** INTERESTED ▷ 🔵 very interested or enthusiastic: *a keen golfer/photographer* ◦ *He's very **keen** on travelling.* **2** WANTING TO DO ▷ 🔵 wanting to do something very much: [+ to do sth] *The shop is keen to attract new customers.* **3** VERY GOOD ▷ very good or well developed: *a keen sense of smell* • **keenness noun** [U] • **keenly adv**

keep¹ /kiːp/ **verb** (**kept**) **1** HAVE ▷ [T] 🔵 to have something permanently or for the whole of a period of time: *You can keep that dress if you like it.* ◦ *He borrowed my bike and kept it all week.* **2 keep sth in/on, etc** 🔵 to regularly store something in a particular place: *I think he keeps his keys in the desk drawer.* ◦ *We'll keep your application on file.* **3 keep doing sth** 🔵 to continue to do something, or to do something repeatedly: *I keep telling her not to leave her clothes on the floor.* ◦ *He keeps hitting me.* **4 keep**

(sb/sth) awake/clean/safe, etc 🔵 to remain in a particular state or make someone or something remain in a particular state: *He goes jogging twice a week to keep fit.* ◦ *He keeps his car spotlessly clean.* **5 keep sb/sth in/inside, etc** to make someone or something stay in the same place: *They will keep her at home for a few more days.* **6 MAKE DO STH** ▷ [T] 🔵 to make someone do something that stops them doing something else: [+ doing sth] *She kept me talking for ages.* ◦ *Sorry to keep you waiting.* ◦ *Don't let me keep you from your work.* **7 keep a secret** 🔵 to not tell anyone a secret **8 keep a promise/your word, etc** 🔵 to do what you have promised to do **9 keep an appointment** to meet someone when you have arranged to meet them **10 MAKE LATE** ▷ [T] to make someone arrive later than they planned: *I was expecting you at six – what kept you?* **11 WRITE** ▷ [T] 🔵 to write down something in order to remember it: *to keep records/notes* **12 FOOD** ▷ [I] 🔵 If food or drink keeps, it remains fresh. **13 PROVIDE MONEY** ▷ [T] to provide enough money for someone to live: *I can't keep a family on that salary.* **14 ANIMALS** ▷ [T] 🔵 to have and look after animals: *Our neighbours keep pigs.* **15 keep sb going** to provide what someone needs for a short period of time: *Dinner is at eight, but I had an apple to keep me going.* → See also **keep your cool³, keep a straight face¹, keep your fingers (finger¹) crossed, put/keep sb in the picture¹, keep a low profile¹, keep a tight rein on sb/sth, keep tabs on sb/sth, keep sb on their toes (toe¹)**

PHRASAL VERBS **keep at sth** 🔵 to continue working hard at something difficult: *Learning a language is hard but you've just got to keep at it.* • **keep (sb/sth) away** 🔵 to not go somewhere or near something, or to prevent someone from going somewhere or near something: *I told them to keep away from the edge of the cliff.* • **keep (sb/sth) back** 🔵 to not go near something, or to prevent someone or something from going past a particular place: *Barriers were built to keep back the flood water.* • **keep sth back** to not tell someone everything you know about a situation or an event: *I was sure she was keeping something back.* • **keep sth down 1** 🔵 to stop the number, level, or size of something from increasing: *I have to exercise to keep my weight down.* **2** to be able to eat or drink without vomiting • **keep sb/sth from doing sth** to prevent someone or something from doing something • **keep sth from sb** to not tell someone about something: *Is there something you're keeping from me?* • **keep sb in** 🔵 to make a child stay inside as a punishment, or to make someone stay in hospital • **keep (sb/sth) off sth** 🔵 to not go onto an area, or to stop someone or something going onto an area: *Keep off the grass.* • **keep sth off (sb/sth)** 🔵 to stop something touching or

K

➕ Other ways of saying **keep**

If someone keeps something somewhere until they need it, the verb **store** is sometimes used:

*I've **stored** all Helen's books in the attic.*

The verb **stash** (*informal*) and the phrasal verb **stash away** (*informal*) are sometimes used if someone keeps a lot of something in a secret place:

*His money was **stashed** (**away**) in a cupboard.*

The verb **save** is often used when someone keeps something to use in the future:

*I have some really good chocolates that I've been **saving** for a special occasion.*

The phrasal verbs **hang onto** and **hold onto** are also often used when someone keeps something that they might need in the future:

*You should **hang/hold onto** that picture – it might be worth something.*

---

harming someone or something: *He put a cloth over the salad to keep the flies off.* • **keep on doing sth** ⓑ to continue to do something, or to do something again and again: *She kept on asking me questions the whole time.* • **keep on** UK to continue to talk in an annoying way about something: *I wish he wouldn't **keep on about** how much he earns.* • **keep (sb/sth) out** ⓑ to not go into a place, or to stop someone or something from going into a place: *He locked the room and put up a sign asking people to keep out.* • **keep to sth 1** ⓑ to stay in one particular area: *We kept to main roads all the way.* **2** ⓑ to do what you have promised or planned to do: *I think we should keep to our original plan.* • **keep sth to sth** If you keep something to a particular number or amount, you make sure it does not become larger than that: *I'm trying to keep costs to a minimum.* • **keep sth to yourself** to keep something secret and not tell anyone else about it • **keep up 1 SAME SPEED** ▷ ⓑ to move at the same speed as someone or something that is moving forward so that you stay level with them: *She was walking so fast I couldn't **keep up with** her.* **2 MAKE PROGRESS** ▷ to increase or make progress at the same speed as something or someone else so that you stay at the same level as them: *Prices have been rising very fast and wages haven't kept up.* **3 UNDERSTAND** ▷ ⓑ to be able to understand or deal with something that is happening or changing very fast: *I feel it's important to **keep up with** current events.* • **keep sth up** ⓑ to not allow something that is at a high level to fall to a lower level: *Make sure you eat properly – you've got to keep your strength up.* • **keep (sth) up to** continue without stopping or changing or to continue something without allowing it to stop or change: *People are having difficulties keeping up the repayments on their loans.*

keep² /kiːp/ noun [no plural] the money needed to pay for someone to eat and live in a place: *He **earns** his **keep** working in a garage.*

keeper /ˈkiːpər/ noun [C] **1** ⓑ someone wh‌ looks after a place and the things, people, ‌ animals there: *a park keeper* **2** *informal* ⓑ short f‌ goalkeeper (= the player in a sport such ‌ football who tries to stop the ball going into th‌ goal)

keeping /ˈkiːpɪŋ/ noun **1 for safe keeping** i‌ order to keep something safe: *She put the mone‌ into a bank for safe keeping.* **2 in keeping wit‌ sth** suitable or right for a situation, style, ‌ tradition: *The antique desk was in keeping wit‌ the rest of the furniture in the room.*

keg /keg/ noun [C] a large, round container use‌ for storing beer

kennel /ˈkenᵊl/ noun [C] **1** mainly UK a small building for a dog to sleep in **2** US (UK **kennels**) a place where dogs are cared for while their owners are away

kennel

kept /kept/ past of keep

kerb UK (US **curb**) /kɜːb/ noun [C] the edge of the raised path at the sid‌ of the road

kernel /ˈkɜːnᵊl/ noun [C] the part of a nut or see‌ inside the hard shell which you can usually ea‌

kerosene /ˈkerəsiːn/ noun [U] US (UK **paraffi‌** oil used for heating and in lamps (= equipmer‌ that produces light)

ketchup /ˈketʃʌp/ noun [U] a thick sauce mad‌ from tomatoes that is eaten cold with food

kettle /ˈketl/ noun [C] ⓑ a metal or plasti‌ container with a lid, used for boiling wate‌ *Charlotte **put the kettle on** to make some te‌* → See colour picture **The Kitchen** on page Centre

key¹ /kiː/ noun [C]
1 FOR LOCKS ▷ ⓐ a piece of metal cut into a particular shape and used for locking things such as doors, or for starting an engine: *I've lost my car keys.* **2 METHOD** ▷ ⓑ a way of explaining or achieving something: *Hard work is **the key to** success.*
3 KEYBOARD ▷ ⓑ one of the parts you press with your fingers on a keyboard or musical instrument to produce letters, numbers, or to make a sound **4 MUSIC** ▷ a set of musical notes based on one particular note: *the key of D major* **5 SYMBOLS** ▷ a list that explains the symbols on a map or picture **6 ANSWERS** ▷ ⓐ a list of answers to an exercise or game → See also **under lock²** and key

key

key

🔲 Word partners for **key**

a **bunch of/set of** keys • the key **for/to** sth • a **car** key

---

key² /kiː/ adj ⓑ very important in influencing o‌ achieving something: *a **key factor***

key³ /kiː/ *verb*

PHRASAL VERB **key sth in** ⑫ to put information into a computer or machine using a keyboard

keyboard /ˈkiːbɔːd/ *noun* [C] **1** ⑫ a set of keys on a computer, which you press to make it work, or the rows of keys on a piano → See colour picture **The Office** on page Centre 5 **2** ⑫ an electrical musical instrument similar to a piano

keyhole /ˈkiːhəʊl/ *noun* [C] a hole in a lock where you put a key

keynote /ˈkiːnəʊt/ *noun* [C] the most important part of an event, idea, or speech, or something that is emphasized strongly: *the keynote speech/ speaker*

keypad /ˈkiːpæd/ *noun* [C] a set of buttons with numbers on them used to operate a television, telephone, etc

key ˌring *noun* [C] a metal ring used for keeping keys together

kg written abbreviation for kilogram (= a unit for measuring weight)

khaki /ˈkɑːki/ *noun* [U] a pale green-brown colour, often worn by soldiers • **khaki** *adj* → See colour picture **Colours** on page Centre 12

kibbutz /kɪˈbʊts/ *noun* [C] (plural **kibbutzim**) a place in Israel where people live and work together, often a farm or a factory

kick¹ /kɪk/ *verb* **1** [I, T] ⑪ to hit or move something or someone with your foot: *The boys were kicking a ball back and forth.* ◦ *They tried to kick the door down.* **2** [I] to move your feet and legs forwards or backwards quickly and with force: *I kicked at them and screamed for help.* **3 kick yourself** informal to be very annoyed with yourself for doing something stupid or wrong: *I could have kicked myself for saying that.* → See also **be alive and kicking/well**

PHRASAL VERBS **be kicking about/around** informal If something is kicking about, it is in a particular place, but nobody is using it or paying attention to it: *We've probably got a copy of the document kicking around the office.* • **kick in** informal to start to be effective or to happen: *The new tax rate kicks in next month.* • **kick off 1** When a football match or other event kicks off, it starts. **2** informal to start to get angry or complain • **kick (sth) off** informal When you kick off a discussion or activity, you start it. • **kick sb out** informal to force someone to leave a place or organization: *His wife kicked him out.*

kick² /kɪk/ *noun* [C] **1** ⑫ the action of kicking something with your foot: *He gave her a kick in the shins.* **2** informal a special feeling of excitement and energy: *She gets a kick out of performing live.*

IDIOM **a kick in the teeth** used when someone treats you badly or unfairly, especially when you need or expect support: *This latest pay award amounts to a kick in the teeth.*

→ See also **free kick**

kickback /ˈkɪkbæk/ *noun* [C] US money given to someone, especially illegally, for providing help, a job, or a piece of business

kickboxing /ˈkɪkˌbɒksɪŋ/ *noun* [U] a sport in which two people fight by hitting each other with their hands and kicking each other with their feet

kick-off /ˈkɪkɒf/ *noun* [C, U] the time when a football match begins

kid¹ /kɪd/ *noun* [C] **1** informal ⑪ a child or young person: *school kids* **2** a young goat

kid² /kɪd/ *verb* [I, T] (**kidding, kidded**) **1** to make a joke, or to trick someone with a joke **2** to deceive or trick someone into believing something: [often reflexive] *You've got to stop kidding yourself. She's not coming back.*

kiddie /ˈkɪdi/ *noun* [C] informal a child

kidnap /ˈkɪdnæp/ *verb* [T] (**kidnapping, kidnapped**) to take someone away using force, usually to obtain money in exchange for releasing them • **kidnap** *noun* [C] *a kidnap victim/attempt* • **kidnapper** *noun* [C]

kidnapping /ˈkɪdnæpɪŋ/ *noun* [C, U] a crime in which someone is kidnapped

kidney /ˈkɪdni/ *noun* [C] one of the two organs in your body that remove waste from the blood and produce urine

kidult /ˈkɪdʌlt/ *noun* [C] informal an adult who likes doing or buying things that are intended for children

kill¹ /kɪl/ *verb* **1** DEATH ▷ [I, T] ⑫ to make someone or something die: *Sunday's bomb killed 19 people.* ◦ *Their son was killed in a road accident.* **2 sb will kill sb** ⑫ informal used to say that someone will be very angry with someone else: *Dad will kill me for being late.* **3** END ▷ [T] to stop an activity or experience completely: *His remark killed the conversation.* **4** CAUSE PAIN ▷ [T] informal to cause you a lot of pain or effort: *My feet are killing me.* ◦ *It wouldn't kill you to tidy up occasionally.* → See also **kill time¹**

PHRASAL VERB **kill sth/sb off** to stop something or someone from existing any more: *Lack of funding is killing off local theatres.*

kill² /kɪl/ *noun* **1** [no plural] an occasion when an animal is killed **2 go/move in for the kill** to prepare to defeat someone completely or to kill them

killer /ˈkɪləʳ/ *noun* [C] ⑪ someone who kills, or a disease, substance, or animal that kills: *Cancer and heart disease are the UK's biggest killers.* → See also **serial killer**

ˈkiller ˌapp *noun* [C] (also **killer application**) **1** computer software that is very popular or useful, especially software that is the reason people buy certain computer systems, mobile phones, etc.: *Mobile access to social networking sites is the next killer app.* **2** a use for a particular technology that becomes extremely popular and is the reason people want that technology: *At the time they thought that e-learning would be the killer app of the Internet.*

killing /ˈkɪlɪŋ/ *noun* **1** ⑪ [C] a murder, or when someone or something is killed: *the killing of civilians* **2 make a killing** informal to make a lot of money very quickly

K

kiln /kɪln/ **noun** [C] a large oven for baking bricks and other clay objects until they are hard

kilo /'kiːləʊ/ **noun** [C] **A2** short for kilogram

kilo- /'kɪlə-/ **prefix** a thousand: *a kilometre* ∘ *a kilogram*

kilobyte /'kɪləʊbaɪt/ **noun** [C] (written abbreviation **K**) a unit for measuring the amount of information a computer can store, equal to 1024 bytes

kilogram (also UK **kilogramme**, written abbreviation **kg**) /'kɪləʊgræm/ **noun** [C] **A2** a unit for measuring weight, equal to 1000 grams

kilometre UK (US **kilometer**, written abbreviation **km**) /kɪ'lɒmɪtər, 'kɪləˌmiːtər/ **noun** [C] **A2** a unit for measuring distance, equal to 1000 metres

kilowatt /'kɪləʊwɒt/ **noun** [C] (written abbreviation **kW**) a unit for measuring electrical power, equal to 1000 watts

kilt /kɪlt/ **noun** [C] a traditional Scottish skirt for men, made of heavy material with close vertical folds at the back

kin /kɪn/ **noun** [plural] formal the members of your family → See also **next of kin**

kind¹ /kaɪnd/ **noun 1 A1** [C] a type of thing or person: *What **kind of** music do you like?* ∘ **All kinds** *of people come to our church.* ∘ *Older kids like board games and that **kind of thing**.* ∘ *Her travel company was the first **of its kind** (= the first one like it).* **2 some kind of B1** used to talk about something when you are not sure of its exact type: *She has some kind of disability.* **3 kind of** informal **B2** used when you are trying to explain or describe something, but you cannot be exact: *It's kind of unusual.* **4 of a kind** used to describe something that exists but is not very good: *The school had a swimming pool of a kind, but it was too small for most classes to use.*

kind² /kaɪnd/ **adj** **A2** Kind people do things to help others and show that they care about them: *Your mother was very **kind** to us.* ∘ *It was very **kind of** you to come and see me.* → Opposite **unkind**

➕ Other ways of saying **kind**

The adjectives **nice** and **sweet** are common alternatives to 'kind':
> *It was really **nice** of you to come.*
> *Wasn't it **sweet** of Heidi to call?*

If someone is **good to** you, they do things to help you:
> *Jay's mother has been very **good to** us.*

If someone is very willing to help, you can describe them as **helpful**:
> *The staff here are very **helpful**.*

Someone who is **caring** is kind to other people and tries to make them happy and well:
> *I've always thought of Mary as a very **caring** person.*

The expression **mean well** is sometimes used to describe a person who tries to be kind and help but who does not improve a situation:
> *I know my parents **mean well**, but I do wish they wouldn't interfere.*

---

kinda /'kaɪndə/ mainly US informal short for kind o *I'm kinda busy right now.*

kindergarten /'kɪndəˌgɑːtən/ **noun** [C, U] **1** i the UK, a school for children under five **2** in th US, a class in school for children aged five

kind-hearted /ˌkaɪnd'hɑːtɪd/ **adj** having a kin character: *a kind-hearted family man*

kindly¹ /'kaɪndli/ **adv 1 B1** in a kind or generou way: *She **kindly offered** to cook me lunch* **2** formal used in instructions to mean 'please usually when you are annoyed: *Would you kindl get out of my car?* **3 not take kindly to sth** to n like something that someone says or does: *H doesn't take kindly to criticism.*

kindly² /'kaɪndli/ **adj** old-fashioned kind: *a kindl old gentleman*

kindness /'kaɪndnəs/ **noun** [C, U] **B2** kin behaviour: *Thanks for all your kindness th morning.*

king /kɪŋ/ **noun** [C] **1 RULER** ▷ **A2** a male ruler i some countries: *King Richard II* ∘ *the kings an queens of England* **2 BEST PERSON** ▷ the best o most important person in a particular activity *He's the new king of pop music.* **3 PLAYIN CARD** ▷ a playing card with a picture of a kin on it: *the king of spades*

kingdom /'kɪŋdəm/ **noun 1 B2** [C] a countr with a king or queen: *the Kingdom of Belgiu* **2 the animal/plant kingdom** all animals o plants considered together

kingfisher /'kɪŋˌfɪʃər/ **noun** [C] a small, brightl coloured bird that catches fish from rivers an lakes

king-size (also **king-sized**) /'kɪŋsaɪz/ **adj** ver big: *a king-size bed*

kink /kɪŋk/ **noun** [C] a bend in something lon and thin: *There was a kink in the hosepipe.*

kinky /'kɪŋki/ **adj** informal involving strange o unusual sexual behaviour

kiosk /'kiːɒsk/ **noun** [C] a small building with window where things like tickets or newspaper are sold

kip /kɪp/ **noun** [C, U] UK informal a short period o sleep • **kip verb** [I] (**kipping, kipped**)

kipper /'kɪpər/ **noun** [C] UK a type of fish that ha been cut open and dried over smoke

kiss¹ /kɪs/ **verb** [I, T] **A2** to press your lips against another person's lips or skin to show love or affection: *He kissed her cheek.* ∘ *Len kissed Samantha goodbye at the front gate.*

kiss

kiss² /kɪs/ **noun** [C] **A2** an act of kissing someone: *She ran up and **gave** me **a big kiss**.*

IDIOM **give sb the kiss of life** UK to help to kee someone who has stopped breathing alive b blowing into their mouth

---

☑ Word partners for **kiss**

give sb a kiss • plant a kiss on sb's [lips/ cheek, etc] • a lingering/passionate kiss

kit /kɪt/ **noun 1** COLLECTION ▷ [C] ⑤ a collection of things kept in a container ready for a particular use: *a first-aid/tool kit* **2** CLOTHES ▷ [C, U] UK ⑫ a set of clothes worn for sport or military service: *a football kit* **3** PARTS ▷ [C] a set of parts that you put together to make something: *He's making a model car from a kit.*

kitchen /'kɪtʃɪn/ **noun** [C] ⑪ a room used to prepare and cook food in → See colour picture **The Kitchen** on page Centre 2

kite /kaɪt/ **noun** [C] ⑫ a toy made of paper or cloth that flies in the air on the end of a long string

kitsch /kɪtʃ/ **noun** [U] decorative objects or pieces of art that are ugly, silly, or have little value

kitten /'kɪtᵊn/ **noun** [C] ⑤ a young cat

kitty /'kɪti/ **noun** [C] an amount of money consisting of a share from everyone in a group, used for a special purpose: [usually singular] *We all put money into a kitty to pay for drinks.*

kiwi /'kiːwiː/ **noun** [C] (also **'kiwi ,fruit**) a small, green fruit with black seeds and brown, hairy skin

km written abbreviation for kilometre (= a unit for measuring distance)

knack /næk/ **noun** [no plural] a special skill, or the ability to use or do something easily: *a knack for remembering faces* ◦ *She has the knack of making people feel comfortable.*

☑ Word partners for **knack**

have/lose the knack of doing sth • an uncanny knack • a knack for doing sth

knackered /'nækəd/ **adj** UK informal extremely tired

knead /niːd/ **verb** [T] to press and shape the mixture for making bread firmly and repeatedly with your hands

knee /niː/ **noun** [C] **1** ⑤ the middle part of your leg where it bends: *a knee injury* → See colour picture **The Body** on page Centre 13 **2** the part of a pair of trousers that covers the knee

IDIOM **bring sb/sth to their knees** to destroy or defeat someone or something: *The war brought the country to its knees.*

kneecap /'niːkæp/ **noun** [C] the round bone at the front of your knee

knee-deep /ˌniːˈdiːp/ **adj 1** reaching as high as someone's knees: *knee-deep in cold water* **2 be knee-deep in sth** to have a lot of something to deal with: *I'm knee-deep in paperwork.*

knee-jerk /'niːdʒɜːk/ **adj** a **knee-jerk reaction/ response, etc** an immediate reaction that does not allow you time to consider something carefully

kneel /niːl/ **verb** [I] (**knelt** or **kneeled**) ⑫ to go down into or stay in a position where one or

both of your knees are on the ground: *She knelt down beside the child.*

knew /njuː/ past tense of know

knickers /'nɪkəz/ **noun** [plural] UK (US **panties**) ⑤ women's underwear that covers the bottom → See Note at **underwear** → See colour picture **Clothes** on page Centre 9

knife¹ /naɪf/ **noun** [C] (plural **knives**) ⑪ a sharp tool or weapon for cutting, usually with a metal blade and a handle: *a knife and fork*

knife² /naɪf/ **verb** [T] to attack someone using a knife → See also **jack-knife²**

knight¹ /naɪt/ **noun** [C] **1** a man of high social rank who fought as a soldier on a horse in the past **2** a man who has been given the title 'Sir' by the King or Queen in the UK

knight² /naɪt/ **verb be knighted** to be given a knighthood

knighthood /'naɪthʊd/ **noun** [C] the title of 'Sir' given to someone by the King or Queen in the UK

knit /nɪt/ **verb** [I, T] (**knitting, knitted, knit**) ⑤ to make clothes using wool and two long needles to join the wool into rows: *She was knitting him a jumper.*

knit

knitting /'nɪtɪŋ/ **noun** [U] the activity of knitting things, or the thing that is being knitted: *She put down her knitting.*

knitwear /'nɪtweəʳ/ **noun** [U] knitted clothes

knob /nɒb/ **noun 1** [C] a round handle, or a round button on a machine: *a door knob* ◦ *Turn the black knob to switch on the radio.* **2 a knob of butter** UK a small lump of butter

knock¹ /nɒk/ **verb 1** MAKE NOISE ▷ [I] ⑤ to make a noise by hitting something, especially a door, with your closed hand in order to attract someone's attention: *There's someone knocking at/on the door.* ◦ *Please knock before entering.* **2** HIT ▷ [T] ⑤ to hit something or someone and make them move or fall down: *He accidentally knocked the vase off the table.* ◦ *I knocked over the mug.* **3** CRITICIZE ▷ [T] informal to criticize someone or something, often unfairly: *She knocks every suggestion I make.* → See also **beat/ knock the (living) daylights out of sb**

K

IDIOM **Knock it off!** informal something you say when you want someone to stop doing something that is annoying you

> ⚠ **Common learner error: knock**
>
> Be careful to use the correct prepositions. You do not always need one.
>
> The policeman **knocked on/knocked at** the door.
>
> ~~Listen! There is someone knocking to the door.~~
>
> **Knock** before you come in.

PHRASAL VERBS **knock sth back** informal to drink alcohol very quickly • **knock sb down** UK ⑥ to hit someone with a vehicle and injure or kill them: [often passive] She was knocked down by a bus. • **knock sb/sth down** US to make someone or something fall to the ground by hitting them • **knock sth down** ⑫ to destroy a building or part of a building • **knock off** informal to stop working, usually at the end of a day: I don't knock off until six. • **knock sth off (sth)** to take a particular amount away from something, usually a price: The manager knocked $5 off because it was damaged. • **knock sb out 1**⑫ to make someone become unconscious, usually by hitting them on the head: He was knocked out halfway through the fight. **2**⑫ to defeat a person or team in a competition so they cannot take part any more: [often passive] The French team were knocked out in the semifinal.

knock² /nɒk/ **noun** [C] **1** a sudden short noise made when something or someone hits a surface: a **knock at/on** the door **2** a hit, sometimes causing damage or injury: a knock on the head

> 🔲 **Word partners for knock**
>
> a **sharp** knock • a knock **at/on** [the door/ window, etc.]

knocker /ˈnɒkər/ **noun** [C] a metal object fixed to the outside of a door that visitors use to knock

knock-on /ˌnɒkˈɒn/ **adj** UK a **knock-on effect** When an event or situation has a knock-on effect, it causes another event or situation: Cutting schools' budgets will have a knock-on effect on teachers' jobs.

knockout /ˈnɒkaʊt/ **noun** [C] in boxing, a hard hit that makes a player unconscious

knot¹ /nɒt/ **noun** [C] **1** a place where pieces of string, rope, etc have been tied together **2** a unit for measuring the speed of the wind, ships, or aircraft

IDIOM **tie the knot** informal to get married

> 🔲 **Word partners for knot**
>
> tie a knot (in sth) • undo/untie a knot

knot² /nɒt/ **verb** [T] (**knotting, knotted**) to tie knots in pieces of string, rope, etc

know¹ /nəʊ/ **verb** (**knew, known**) **1** HAVE INFORMATION ▷ [I, T] ⑪ to have knowledge or information about something in your mind:

"How old is she?" "I don't know." ∘ Andre **knows** a lot **about** computers. ∘ [+ question wor Do you know where the station is? ∘ [+ (tha He knew that she was lying. **2** BE FAMILIA WITH ▷ [T] ⑥ to be familiar with a person, plac or thing because you have met them, bee there, used it, etc before: I've known Tim sinc primary school. ∘ I grew up in Brussels so I kno it well. ∘ Since moving to London, I've **got t know** (= become familiar with) some nice peopl **3** BE ABLE ▷ [T] ⑫ to be able to do somethin [+ question word] Do you know how to ski? ∘ I on know (= understand and speak) a little Spanis **4 let sb know**⑫ to tell someone something: L me know if you're going to the party. **5** GUES CORRECTLY ▷ [T] to guess something correctl I knew she'd arrive late. ∘ I **should have know** he wouldn't come. **6** UNDERSTAND ▷ [I, T] understand and agree with someone: I kno what you mean about Pete – I wouldn't trust hi at all. **7** be known as sth ⑥ to be calle something: California is also known as th Sunshine State. **8 have known sth** to have ha experience of something: I've never known th weather be so hot. **9 know better (than to d sth)**⑫ to have the intelligence or judgment n to do something: She should have known bett than to eat so much. No wonder she feels sick no **10 I know a** ⑫ used when you agree wit something someone has just said: "It's a love day, isn't it?" "I know – let's hope it lasts." **b** ⑥ used when you have an idea: I know – let's go Helen's house. **11 you know a** used to emphasiz that someone does know what you are referrin to: You know, he's the one with curly hair. **b** ⑥ something that you say while you are thinkin what to say next: It's, you know, supposed to be surprise. **c** ⑥ used to emphasize what you a saying: I'm not an idiot, you know. **12 as far as know** ⑫ used to say that you think somethin is true, but cannot be sure: As far as I know, he never been in prison. **13 you never know** ⑥ used to say that something could be possibl although it does not seem likely: You never kno – you might win the lottery. **14 before you kno it** very soon: We'll be there before you know → See also know sth **inside¹** out, learn/kno the ropes (**rope¹**), know your **stuff¹**

> ⚠ **Common learner error: meet, get to know, and know**
>
> When you **meet someone**, you see or speak to them for the first time. When you **get to know someone**, you learn more about them. After this you can say that you **know** them.
>
> I **met** Nick on holiday.
>
> ~~I knew Nick on holiday.~~
>
> We **got to know** each other and became good friends.
>
> ~~We knew each other and became friends.~~
>
> How long have you **known** Nick?
>
> ~~How long have you got to know Nick?~~

PHRASAL VERB **know of sth/sb** ⑫ to have heard something or someone and have a little info mation about them: *I know of a good restaurant near the station.*

now² /nəʊ/ **noun be in the know** to have knowledge about something that not everyone knows: *People in the know were sure the film would win an Oscar.*

> **⚠ Common learner error: know or find out?**
>
> To **know** something means to already have information about something.
> *Kelly knows what time the train leaves.*
> *His parents already know about the problem.*
> To **find out** something means to learn new information for the first time.
> *Can you find out what time the train leaves?*
> *His parents were angry when they found out about the problem.*

now-how /'nəʊhaʊ/ **noun** [U] practical skill and knowledge: *technical know-how*

nowing /'nəʊɪŋ/ **adj** A knowing smile, look, etc shows that you know what another person is really thinking: *He gave me a knowing wink.*

nowingly /'nəʊɪŋli/ **adv 1** If you knowingly do something, you mean to do it although it is wrong. **2** showing that you know what another person is really thinking: *He smiled knowingly.*

nowledge /'nɒlɪdʒ/ **noun 1** ⓐ [U, no plural] information and understanding that you have in your mind: *He has a detailed knowledge of naval history.* ◦ *He took the car without my knowledge* (= I did not know). **2 to (the best of) sb's knowledge** ⓑ used to say that someone thinks that something is true, but cannot be sure: *To the best of my knowledge, she's never worked abroad.*

> **✍ Word partners for knowledge**
>
> common/detailed/firsthand/poor/thorough knowledge • knowledge **about/of** sth • **have/ gain/impart** knowledge

> **⚠ Common learner error: knowledge**
>
> Remember you cannot make **knowledge** plural. Do not say 'knowledges'.
> *I have some knowledge of French and German.*

knowledgeable /'nɒlɪdʒəbl/ **adj** knowing a lot: *He's very knowledgeable about art.*

known¹ /nəʊn/ **adj** ⓑ recognized or known about by most people: *He's a member of a known terrorist organization.* → Opposite **unknown** → See also **well-known**

known² /nəʊn/ past participle of know

knuckle¹ /'nʌkl/ **noun** [C] one of the parts of your finger where it bends → See also **a rap on/across/over the knuckles**

knuckle² /'nʌkl/ **verb**

PHRASAL VERB **knuckle down** to start to work or study hard

koala /kəʊˈɑːlə/ **noun** [C] (also **ko'ala ˌbear**) an Australian animal like a small bear with grey fur that lives in trees and eats leaves

koala

the Koran /kɒrˈɑːn/ ⓤⓢ /kəˈræn/ **noun** the holy book of Islam

kosher /'kəʊʃər/ **adj** Kosher food is prepared according to Jewish law.

kph written abbreviation for kilometres per hour: a unit for measuring speed: *a car travelling at 100 kph*

kudos /'kjuːdɒs/ **noun** [U] praise and respect for what you have done

kung fu /kʌŋˈfuː/ **noun** [U] a sport from China in which people fight using their hands and feet

kW (also **kw**) written abbreviation for kilowatt (= a unit for measuring electrical power)

K

L

L, l /el/ the twelfth letter of the alphabet

l written abbreviation for litre (= a unit for measuring liquid)

lab /læb/ **noun** [C] 🔵 short for laboratory (= a room used for scientific work)

label¹ /'leɪbəl/ **noun** [C] **1** INFORMATION ▷ 🔵 a small piece of paper or other material that gives information about the thing it is fixed to: *There should be washing instructions on the label.* **2** WORD ▷ a word or phrase that is used to describe the qualities of someone or something, usually in a way that is not fair: *He seems to be stuck with the label of 'troublemaker'.* **3** MUSIC ▷ (also **record label**) 🔵 a company that records and sells music: *They've just signed a deal with a major record label.*

label² /'leɪbəl/ **verb** [T] (mainly UK **labelling, labelled**, US **labeling, labeled**) **1** to fix a small piece of paper or other material to something which gives information about it: *All food has to be labelled with 'best before' or 'use by' dates.* **2** to describe the qualities of someone or something using a word or phrase, usually in a way that is not fair: [often passive] *They've been unfairly labelled as criminals.*

labor /'leɪbər/ **noun, verb** US spelling of labour

laboratory /ləˈbɒrətʰri/ ⓤⓢ /ˈlæbrətɔːri/ **noun** [C] 🔵 a room used for scientific work: *research laboratories ∘ a computer laboratory* → See also **language laboratory**

laborer /'leɪbərər/ **noun** [C] US spelling of labourer

laborious /ləˈbɔːriəs/ **adj** Laborious work is very difficult and needs a lot of effort: *a laborious task*

labors /'leɪbəz/ **noun** [plural] US spelling of labours

labor union **noun** [C] US (UK **trade union**) an organization that represents people who do a particular job

labour¹ UK (US **labor**) /'leɪbər/ **noun 1** WORK ▷ [U] work, especially the type of work that needs a lot of physical effort: **manual labour** **2** WORKERS ▷ [U] people who work: **cheap/ skilled labour** **3** BIRTH ▷ [C, U] the stage of pregnancy when a woman has pain in the lower part of her body because the baby is coming out: *to be **in labour**/go into labour ∘ labour pains* **4** **Labour** [group] short for the Labour Party: *I voted Labour (= for the Labour party) at the last election. ∘ a Labour MP*

IDIOM **a labour of love** work that you do because you like it, not because you are paid for it

labour² UK formal (US **labor**) /'leɪbər/ **verb** [I] to work hard: *He laboured night and day to get the house finished on time.*

labourer UK (US **laborer**) /'leɪbərər/ **noun** [C] a worker who uses a lot of physical effort in their job: *a farm labourer*

the 'Labour ˌParty noun [group] one of the three main political parties in the UK

labours (US **labors**) /'leɪbəz/ **noun** [plural] **sb** **labours** work done with a lot of effort: *He earne a mere $15 for his labours.*

lace¹ /leɪs/ **noun 1** [U] a delicate cloth wi patterns of holes: *a lace curtain* **2** [C] a stri used to tie shoes: *to tie/untie your laces*

lace² /leɪs/ **verb**

PHRASAL VERBS **lace sth up** to fasten somethin with laces: *He laced up his boots.* • **be laced wit sth** If food or drink is laced with alcohol or drug, a small amount has been added to *coffee laced with brandy*

lacerate /'læsʰreɪt/ **verb** [T] formal to make dee cuts in someone's skin: *a badly lacerated ar* • **laceration** /ˌlæsʰrˈeɪʃʰn/ **noun** [C] formal a cu

lack¹ /læk/ **noun** lack of sth 🔵 not havin something, or not having enough of somethin *a lack of food/money*

> 🗹 **Word partners for lack**
>
> a **complete/distinct/marked/total** lack of sth
> • an **apparent** lack of sth

---

lack² /læk/ **verb 1** 🔵 [T] to not have somethin or not have enough of something: *She real lacks confidence.* **2** **be lacking** If something th you need is lacking, you do not have enough it: *Enthusiasm has been sadly lacking these pc few months at work.* **3** **be lacking in sth** to n have a quality: *He's totally lacking in charm any sort.*

lacklustre UK (US **lackluster**) /'lækˌlʌstər/ **a** without energy or excitement: *a lacklustr performance*

laconic /ləˈkɒnɪk/ **adj** formal using very fe words to express yourself: *laconic humour/wit*

lacquer /'lækər/ **noun** [U] a clear, hard substanc that is painted on wood or metal to protect i

lad /læd/ **noun** [C] UK a boy or young man: *a ni young lad* ∘ informal *He's having a night out wi **the lads** (= his male friends).*

ladder /'lædər/ **noun** [C] 🔵 a piece of equipment that is used to reach high places, consisting of short steps fixed between two long sides → See also **the first/highest/next, etc rung¹** of the ladder

ladder

laddish /'lædɪʃ/ **adj** UK rude, noisy and typical of the way that young men behave in groups

laden /'leɪdʰn/ **adj** be **laden with sth** to be holding a lot of something: *She staggered*

---

home, laden with shopping.

he ladies /'leɪdiz/ **noun** [group] UK a toilet in a public place for women: *Where's the ladies?* → See Note at **toilet**

adies' room noun [C] mainly US (also US **women's room**) a room in a public place where there are women's toilets → See Note at **toilet**

adle /'leɪdl/ **noun** [C] a large, deep spoon, used to serve soup → See colour picture **The Kitchen** on page Centre 2

ady /'leɪdi/ **noun 1** ⑪ [C] a polite way of saying 'woman': *There's a young lady here to see you.* ○ *Ladies and gentlemen, can I have your attention please?* **2 Lady** a title used before the name of some women of high social rank in the UK: *Lady Alison Weir*

adybird /'leɪdibɜːd/ **noun** [C] UK (US **ladybug**, ⓤⓢ /'leɪdibʌg/) a small flying insect that is usually red with black spots

ag¹ /læg/ **noun** [C] (also **time lag**) a period of time between two things happening: *You have to allow for a time lag between order and delivery.* → See also **jet lag**

ag² /læg/ **verb** (**lagging, lagged**)

PHRASAL VERB **lag behind (sb/sth) 1** to move more slowly than someone or something else so that you are behind them **2** to achieve less than someone or something else: *Britain is lagging far behind the rest of Europe on this issue.*

ager /'lɑːgəʳ/ **noun** [C, U] a pale yellow beer: *A pint of lager, please.*

agoon /ləˈguːn/ **noun** [C] a lake that contains sea water

aid /leɪd/ past of lay

aid-back /ˌleɪdˈbæk/ **adj** informal very relaxed and not seeming worried about anything: *a laid-back style of teaching* ○ *He's very laid-back.*

ain /leɪn/ past participle of lie¹

aissez-faire /ˌleɪseɪˈfeəʳ/ **adj** allowing things to happen and not trying to control them: *a laissez-faire attitude*

ake /leɪk/ **noun** [C] ⑫ a large area of water that has land all around it: *Lake Garda*

amb /læm/ **noun 1** [C] ⑪ a young sheep: *a newborn lamb* **2** [U] ⑪ meat from a young sheep: *grilled lamb chops* ○ *roast leg of lamb* → See also **mutton dressed as lamb**

ame /leɪm/ **adj 1** A lame excuse or explanation is one that you cannot believe: *He said he didn't go because it was raining, which is a pretty lame excuse if you ask me.* **2** A lame animal or person cannot walk because they have an injured foot or leg: *a lame horse*

ament /ləˈment/ **verb** [I, T] formal to say that you are disappointed about a situation: *He was lamenting the fact that so few people read fiction nowadays.*

amentable /'læməntəbl/ **adj** formal extremely bad: *a lamentable performance*

amp /læmp/ **noun** [C] ⑫ a piece of equipment that produces light: *a table lamp* ○ *an oil lamp* → See colour picture **The Living Room** on page Centre 4

lamppost /'læmppəʊst/ **noun** [C] a tall post with a light at the top, which you see on roads where there are houses

lampshade /'læmpʃeɪd/ **noun** [C] a decorative cover for an electric light → See colour picture **The Living Room** on page Centre 4

LAN /læn/, /ˌeləˈen/ **noun** [C] abbreviation for local area network: a system that connects the computers of people who work in the same building → Compare **wan**

land¹ /lænd/ **noun 1** AREA ▷ [U] ⑪ an area of ground: *agricultural land* ○ *undeveloped land* → See Note at **country¹ 2** NOT SEA ▷ [U] ⑫ the surface of the Earth that is not sea: *to travel over land and sea* **3** COUNTRY ▷ [C] literary a country: *a land of ice and snow* → See also **no-man's land**

> ❗ Common learner error: **land** or **country**?
>
> **Land** is only used to mean 'country' in literary writing or poems. In ordinary speech or writing, it is better to use **country**.
> *I enjoyed visiting their country.*
> ~~I enjoyed visiting their land.~~

land² /lænd/ **verb 1** [I, T] ⑪ If an aircraft lands, it arrives on the ground after a journey, or if you land it, you make it arrive on the ground: *We should land in Madrid at 7 a.m.* ○ *He managed to land the helicopter on the cliff.* **2 land in/on, etc** If an object or person lands somewhere, they fall to the ground there: *She landed flat on her back.* **3** [T] to get something, usually something good: *He's just landed a new job at an agency in London.*

PHRASAL VERBS **land sb in sth** to put someone in a difficult situation: *His remarks have landed him in a lot of trouble.* • **land sb with sth** If something lands you with problems, it causes problems for you: *The project's failure has landed him with debts of over £50,000.*

landfill /'lændfɪl/ **noun** [C] a place where waste is buried in the ground: *a landfill site*

landing /'lændɪŋ/ **noun** [C] **1** ⑫ an arrival on the ground, usually of an aircraft or boat: *They had to make an emergency landing in Chicago.* **2** the area of floor at the top of a set of stairs

landlady /'lændˌleɪdi/ **noun** [C] ⑫ a woman who you rent a room or house from

landline /'lændlaɪn/ **noun** [C] a telephone that is not a mobile phone

landlord /'lændlɔːd/ **noun** [C] ⑫ a man who you rent a room or house from

landmark /'lændmɑːk/ **noun** [C] **1** a building that you can easily recognize, especially one that helps you to know where you are: *a historic landmark* **2** an event that is famous or important in the history of something: *His speech was a landmark in the history of civil rights.*

landmine /'lændmaɪn/ **noun** [C] a bomb that is hidden in the ground

landowner /'lændəʊnəʳ/ **noun** [C] someone who owns a lot of land: *a wealthy landowner*

landscape /'lændskeɪp/ **noun** [C] ⑪ the appearance of an area of land, especially in the countryside: *The cathedral dominates the landscape for miles around.*

L

landslide /'lændslaɪd/ **noun** [C] **1** a movement of rocks and soil down a mountain or hill **2** an easy victory in an election: *a* **landslide defeat/victory**

lane /leɪn/ **noun** [C] **1** PART ▷ ⑫ part of a road or track that is separated from the other parts, usually by a painted line: *the inside/middle/outside lane* ∘ *the* **fast/slow lane** **2** ROAD ▷ ⑫ a narrow road, usually in the countryside: *We drove down a winding country lane.* **3** BOATS/AIRCRAFT ▷ a route that is regularly used by boats or aircraft: *It's one of the world's busiest shipping lanes.*

> 🗹 Word partners for **lane**
>
> in the [inside/fast, etc] lane • the fast/slow lane

language /'læŋgwɪdʒ/ **noun 1** COMMUNICATION ▷ [U] ㉛ communication between people, usually using words: *She has done research into how children acquire language.* **2** ENGLISH/SPANISH/JAPANESE ETC ▷ [C] ㉑ a type of communication used by the people of a particular country: *How many* **languages** *do you* **speak**? **3** TYPE OF WORDS ▷ [U] words of a particular type, especially the words used by people in a particular job: *legal language* ∘ *the language of business* **4** COMPUTERS ▷ [C, U] a system of instructions that is used to write computer programs → See also **body language, modern languages, second language, sign language**

> 🗹 Word partners for **language**
>
> learn/speak a language • foreign languages • foul/native/official/strong language

language laboratory UK (US **language laboratory**) **noun** [C] a room in a college or school where you can use equipment to help you practise listening to and speaking a foreign language

languid /'læŋgwɪd/ **adj** literary moving or speaking slowly and with little energy, often in an attractive way: *a languid manner/voice*

languish /'læŋgwɪʃ/ **verb** [I] formal **languish at/in, etc sth** to stay in an unpleasant or difficult situation for a long time: *to languish in jail*

lanky /'læŋki/ **adj** informal A lanky person is very tall and thin.

lantern /'læntən/ **noun** [C] a light that can be carried, usually with a candle inside it: *a paper lantern*

lap¹ /læp/ **noun** [C] **1** ⑫ Your lap is the top part of your legs when you are sitting down: *Sit on my lap and I'll read you a story.* **2** ⑫ one journey around a circular race track: *He's two laps behind the leaders.*

lap² /læp/ **verb** (**lapping, lapped**) **lap against/on, etc sth** If water laps against something, it touches it gently in waves.

PHRASAL VERB **lap sth up** informal to enjoy something very much: *He loved all the attention – he was lapping it up!*

lapel /lə'pel/ **noun** [C] the part of a collar that is folded against the front of a shirt or jacket: *wic lapels* → See picture at **jacket**

lapse¹ /læps/ **noun** [C] **1** a period of time whe something does not happen as it should: *memory lapse* ∘ *It is thought that the accident w caused by a* **lapse of** *concentration.* **2** a period time passing between two things happening: *time lapse/a* **lapse of time** ∘ *He turned up aga after a lapse of two years.*

> 🗹 Word partners for **lapse**
>
> a momentary lapse • a lapse in/of sth

lapse² /læps/ **verb** [I] If an arrangement lapses, stops existing because of the amount of tim that has passed: *I've allowed my membership lapse.*

PHRASAL VERB **lapse into sth** If you lapse int something, you change to a different, an usually bad, condition: *to lapse into silence*

laptop /'læptɒp/ **noun** [C] ⑫ a computer that is small enough to be carried around and used where you are sitting

laptop

large /lɑːdʒ/ **adj 1** ⑫ big in size or amount: *a large number of people* ∘ *a large amount of money* ∘ *She come from quite a large family.* ∘ *The shirt was a bit to large.* → Opposite **small 2 be at large** If someor dangerous is at large, they are not in priso **3 sb/sth at large** people or things in genera *This group is not representative of the populatic at large.*

IDIOM **by and large** in most situations: *By ar large, people have welcomed the changes.*

largely /'lɑːdʒli/ **adv** ⑫ mainly: *Their complain have been largely ignored.*

large-scale /ˌlɑːdʒ'skeɪl/ **adj** involving a lot c people or happening in big numbers: *a larg scale development* ∘ *large-scale redundancies*

lark /lɑːk/ **noun** [C] a small brown bird that known for its beautiful singing

larva /'lɑːvə/ **noun** [C] (plural **larvae** /'lɑːviː/) th form of some creatures, for example insect before they develop into a different form: *inse larvae*

lasagne mainly UK (US **lasagna**) /lə'zænjə/ /lə'zɑːnjə/ **noun** [U] a type of Italian foo consisting of flat pieces of pasta with layers c meat and sauce in between

laser /'leɪzər/ **noun** [C] ⑫ a strong beam of ligh that has medical and technical uses: *a lase beam* ∘ *laser surgery*

laser printer noun [C] a printer (= machin which is connected to a computer and whic produces writing or pictures) that uses a lase (= a strong beam of light) to produce very clea writing or pictures

lash¹ /læʃ/ **verb 1** [I, T] If wind or rain lashe against something, the wind or rain is ver strong and hits or blows hard against it: *Rai lashed against the window.* **2 lash sth dow**

together, etc to tie something firmly to something else

PHRASAL VERB **lash out 1** to suddenly hit someone: *He lashed out and caught her on the side of the face.* **2** to criticize someone angrily: *He **lashed out at** the government for refusing to take action.*

ash² /læʃ/ **noun** [C] a hit with a whip (= long, thin piece of leather): *He was given forty lashes.*

ashes /'læʃɪz/ **noun** [plural] the small hairs on the edges of your eye

ass /læs/ **noun** [C] UK informal a girl or a young woman: *a young lass*

ast¹ /lɑːst/ **adj, determiner 1** MOST RECENT ▷ [always before noun] 🄰🄰 the most recent: *What was the last film you saw?* ∘ *It's rained for the last three days.* 🄰🄰 **2** ONE BEFORE PRESENT ▷ [always before noun] 🄰🄰 The last book, house, job, etc is the one before the present one: *I liked his last book but I'm not so keen on this latest one.* **3** FINAL ▷ 🄰🄰 happening or coming at the end: *It's the last room on the left.* ∘ *That's the last programme of the series.* ∘ *I was the last one to arrive.* ∘ *"How did she get on in her race?" "She was last."* **4** REMAINING ▷ [always before noun] 🄱🄱 only remaining: *Who wants the last piece of cake?* **5 the last person/thing, etc** 🄱🄱 the least expected or wanted person or thing: *Three extra people to feed – that's the last thing I need!* ∘ *He's the last person you'd expect to see at an aerobics class.* → Opposite **first** → See also **be on its last legs (leg), the final/last straw, have the last word¹**

ast² /lɑːst/ **adv 1** 🄱🄱 after everything or everyone else: *I wasn't expecting to win the race but I didn't think I'd come last!* ∘ *We've still got to check the figures but we'll do that last.* **2** 🄱🄱 used to talk about the most recent time you did something: *When did you last see her?*

IDIOM **last but not least** 🄱🄱 something that you say to introduce the last person or thing on a list: *This is Jeremy, this is Cath and, last but not least, this is Eva.*

→ Opposite **first**

ast³ /lɑːst/ **noun, pronoun 1 the last** 🄱🄱 a person or thing that comes after all the others: [+ to do sth] *We were the last to get there.* **2 the last of sth** the only part of something that remains: *We've just finished the last of the wine.* **3 the day/week/year before last** 🄱🄱 the day, week, or year before the one that has just finished **4 at (long) last** 🄱🄱 finally: *At last, I've found a pair of jeans that actually fit.* **5 the last I heard** used before saying a piece of information about someone that you previously heard: *The last I heard, they were selling their house.*

ast⁴ /lɑːst/ **verb** [I, T] **1** 🄱🄱 to continue to happen, exist, or be useful: *How long will the meeting last?* ∘ *We don't get much sun – enjoy it while it lasts!* ∘ *The batteries only last about five hours.* **2** to be enough for a period of time: *I've only got £30 to last me till the end of the month.* ∘ *We've got enough food to last another week.*

ast-ditch /ˌlɑːst'dɪtʃ/ **adj a last-ditch attempt/effort** a final attempt to solve a problem that

you have failed to solve several times before: *a last-ditch effort to prevent war*

lasting /'lɑːstɪŋ/ **adj** continuing to exist for a long time: **lasting damage** ∘ *a lasting friendship*

lastly /'lɑːstli/ **adv** finally: *And lastly, I'd like to thank everyone who took part in the event.*

last-minute /ˌlɑːst'mɪnɪt/ **adj** 🄱🄱 done at the last possible time: *I was just doing some **last-minute** preparations.*

last name noun [C] the name that you and other members of your family all have

latch¹ /lætʃ/ **noun** [C] **1** a small piece of metal on a door that you move down so that the door will stay closed **2** a type of lock for a door that you need a key to open from the outside

latch² /lætʃ/ **verb**

PHRASAL VERB **latch on** informal to begin to understand something: *It took me ages to **latch on to** what she was saying.*

late /leɪt/ **adj, adv 1** AFTER THE USUAL TIME ▷ 🄰🄰 after the usual time or the time that was arranged: *I was late for work this morning.* ∘ *We got there too late and all the tickets had been sold.* ∘ *We had a late lunch.* **2** NEAR END OF PERIOD ▷ 🄰🄰 near the end of a period of time: *It was built in the late nineteenth century.* ∘ *It was late at night.* ∘ *Marsha is in her late twenties.* **3 it's late** something that you say when it is near the end of a day: *It's late – I really should be going.* ∘ *It's getting late and I'm a bit tired.* **4** DEAD ▷ [always before noun] not now alive: *the late Mrs Walker* **5 of late** formal recently: *We've scarcely seen him of late.*

lately /'leɪtli/ **adv** 🄱🄱 recently: *I haven't been feeling so well lately.* ∘ *Lately, I've been walking to work.*

latent /'leɪtᵊnt/ **adj** A feeling or quality that is latent exists now but is hidden or not yet developed: *latent hostility/racism*

later /'leɪtᵊr/ **adj 1** 🄱🄱 after some time: *I might arrange for a later date.* **2** more recent: *I'm not so familiar with his later work.*

later (on) /'leɪtᵊr/ **adv** 🄰🄰 after some time: *I'm off now – see you later.* ∘ *If you're busy now we could do it later on.*

latest¹ /'leɪtɪst/ **adj** [always before noun] 🄰🄰 most recent: *the latest fashions/news/technology*

latest² /'leɪtɪst/ **noun 1 the latest in sth** the most recent of its type: *This is the latest in a series of terrorist attacks in the region.* **2 at the latest** If you tell someone to do something by a particular time at the latest, you mean they must do it before that time: *She said to be there by 8 o'clock at the latest.*

lather /'lɑːðᵊr/ **noun 1** [U] small white bubbles that are produced when soap is used with water **2 get into a lather** informal to become anxious or upset about something

Latin /'lætɪn/ **noun** [U] the language used by ancient Romans • **Latin adj**

Latin American adj relating or belonging to the countries of South and Central America, and Mexico • **Latin American noun** [C] a Latin American person

L

Latino /ləˈtiːnəʊ/ **noun** [C] US someone who lives in the US whose family came from Latin America

latitude /ˈlætɪtjuːd/ **noun 1** [C, U] the distance of a place north or south of the Equator (= imaginary line around the Earth's middle), measured in degrees: *The latitude of Helsinki is approximately 60 degrees north.* **2** [U] formal freedom to do what you want: *She should be allowed the latitude to choose the people she wants.*

latte /ˈlæteɪ/ ⑤ /ˈlɑːteɪ/ **noun** [C, U] a drink of coffee made from espresso (= strong coffee) and milk

latter /ˈlætər/ **adj** [always before noun] formal ⑧ near the end of a period: *the **latter half** of the twentieth century* ∘ *She had moved to California in the **latter part** of the year.* ∘ *She is now in the **latter stages** of the disease.*

the latter /ˈlætər/ **noun** the second of two people or things that have just been talked about: *She offered me more money or a car, and I chose the latter.*

latterly /ˈlætəli/ **adv** UK formal recently: *She started her career in radio, but latterly she has been working in television.*

laudable /ˈlɔːdəbl/ **adj** formal A laudable idea or action deserves admiration, even if it is not successful: *a **laudable aim/ambition/goal***

laugh¹ /lɑːf/ **verb** [I] ⑫ to smile while making sounds with your voice that show you are happy or think something is funny: *You never **laugh at** my jokes.* ∘ *She really **makes** me **laugh**.* ∘ *It's very rare that a book is so good you **laugh out loud**.* ∘ *It was so funny, we **burst out laughing** (= laughed suddenly and loudly).* → See also **be no laughing matter**¹

PHRASAL VERBS **laugh at sb/sth** ⑪ to show that you think someone or something is stupid: *I can't go into work looking like this – everyone will laugh at me.* • **laugh sth off** to laugh about something unpleasant so that it seems less important: *He was upset by the criticism though he tried to laugh it off at the time.*

laugh² /lɑːf/ **noun** [C] **1** ⑪ the act or sound of laughing: *a loud/nervous laugh* ∘ *At the time, I was embarrassed, but I **had a good laugh** (= laughed a lot) about it later.* **2 be a (good) laugh** UK informal to be funny: *You'd like David – he's a good laugh.* **3 for a laugh** informal If you do something for a laugh, you do it because you think it will be funny: *Just for a laugh, I pretended that I'd forgotten it was his birthday.*

laughable /ˈlɑːfəbl/ **adj** If something is laughable, it is stupid and you cannot believe it or respect it: *Most people thought his suggestions were laughable.*

laughing stock **noun** [no plural] someone who does something very stupid that makes other people laugh at them: *If I wear this hat, I'll be the laughing stock of the party!*

laughter /ˈlɑːftər/ **noun** [U] ⑫ the sound or act of laughing: *I heard the sound of laughter in the room next door.* ∘ *The crowd **roared with laughter** (= laughed very loudly).*

☑ **Word partners for laughter**

burst into laughter • **roar with** laughter • **be in fits of** laughter

---

launch¹ /lɔːnʃ/ **verb** [T] **1** SEND ▷ to send spacecraft or bomb into the sky, or a ship int the water: *to **launch** a **rocket/satellite*** ∘ *to **launch** a **boat/fleet*** **2** BEGIN ▷ ⑧ to begin a important activity: *to **launch** an **attack/inquir** investigation* **3** NEW PRODUCT ▷ ⑧ If company launches a product or service, makes it available for the first time: *The boo was launched last February.* ∘ *The airline w launch its new transatlantic service next month.*

PHRASAL VERB **launch into sth** to start saying c criticizing something with a lot of anger c energy: *Then he launched into a verbal attack o her management of the situation.*

launch² /lɔːnʃ/ **noun** [C] **1** SENDING ▷ a occasion when a spacecraft, ship, or weapon launched: *Poor weather delayed the space shu tle's launch.* **2** BEGINNING ▷ the beginning of a activity: *The campaign's launch was a we publicized event.* **3** NEW PRODUCT ▷ the tim when a new product or service becomes avai able: *The film's launch attracted a lot of Hollywoo stars.* **4** BOAT ▷ a large boat with a motor: *police launch*

launder /ˈlɔːndər/ **verb** [T] to hide the fact th an amount of money has been made illegally b putting the money into legal bank accounts c businesses: *to **launder** drug money* • **launder ing noun** [U] *money laundering*

launderette /ˌlɔːndərˈet/ **noun** [C] mainly UK (US trademark **laundromat** /ˈlɔːndrəmæt/) a plac where you pay to use machines that wash an dry your clothes

laundry /ˈlɔːndri/ **noun** [U] ⑧ clothes, sheet etc that need to be washed: *to **do the laundr*** ∘ *a **laundry basket***

laundry detergent **noun** [C, U] US washin powder (= soap in the form of a powder, used fc washing clothes)

laurels /ˈlɒrəlz/ **noun** [plural]

IDIOM **rest on your laurels** to be so satisfied wit what you have achieved that you make no effo to improve: *Just because you've passed you exams, that's no reason to rest on your laurels.*

lava /ˈlɑːvə/ **noun** [U] hot melted rock that come out of a volcano

lavatory /ˈlævətəri/ **noun** [C] formal mainly U a toilet: *to go to the lavatory* ∘ *public lavatorie* → See Note at **toilet**

lavender /ˈlævəndər/ **noun** [U] a plant wit purple flowers and a strong, pleasant smel *lavender oil*

lavish¹ /ˈlævɪʃ/ **adj** showing that a lot of mone has been spent: *a lavish meal/party* • **lavishl adv** *a lavishly illustrated book*

lavish² /ˈlævɪʃ/ **verb**

PHRASAL VERB **lavish sth on sb/sth** to give a larg amount of money, gifts, attention, etc t someone or something: *They have lavished more than £6 million on the new stadium.*

law /lɔː/ noun **1 the law** 🔵 the system of official rules in a country: *You're **breaking the law**.* ∘ *It's **against the law** (= illegal) not to wear seat belts.* ∘ *It's their job to **enforce the law**.* **2 by law** 🔵 If you have to do something by law, it is illegal not to do it: *They have to provide a contract by law.* **3** RULE ▷ [C] 🔵 an official rule in a country: *There are **laws against** drinking in the street.* ∘ *They led the fight to impose **laws on** smoking.* **4 law and order** the obeying of laws in society: *a breakdown in law and order* **5** SUBJECT ▷ [U] 🔵 the subject or job of understanding and dealing with the official laws of a country: *to study/practise law* ∘ *a law school/firm* ∘ *a specialist in civil/criminal law* **6** ALWAYS TRUE ▷ [C] something that is always true in science, mathematics, etc.: *the laws of nature/physics* ∘ *the law of averages/gravity*

IDIOM **lay down the law** to repeatedly tell people what they should do, without caring about how they feel: *People are fed up with him laying down the law the whole time.*

→ See also **brother-in-law, common-law, daughter-in-law, father-in-law, in-laws, martial law, mother-in-law, sister-in-law, son-in-law**

> 🗹 Word partners for **law**
>
> break/enforce/obey/pass a law • the law forbids/prohibits/requires sth • a law against sth • be against the law

law-abiding /ˈlɔːəˌbaɪdɪŋ/ adj A law-abiding person always obeys the law: *a **law-abiding citizen***

lawful /ˈlɔːfᵊl/ adj allowed by the law: *He was going about his lawful business as a press photographer.*

lawmaker /ˈlɔːˌmeɪkəʳ/ noun [C] US someone who makes laws: *state lawmakers*

lawn /lɔːn/ noun [C] an area of grass that is cut: *to mow the lawn*

lawn ˌmower noun [C] a machine that you use to cut grass

lawsuit /ˈlɔːsuːt/ noun [C] a legal complaint against someone that does not usually involve the police: *The tenants have **filed a lawsuit against** their landlord.*

lawyer /ˈlɔɪəʳ/ noun [C] 🔵 someone whose job is to understand the law and deal with legal situations: *I want to see my lawyer before I say anything else.*

> ❗ Common learner error: **lawyer, solicitor, barrister, attorney**
>
> In Britain, **lawyers** are divided into two types, **solicitors** and **barristers**. Solicitors give advice on legal subjects and work in the lower courts of law. **Barristers** can represent people in the higher courts of law. In America, there is only one type of lawyer, who is sometimes called an **attorney**.

lax /læks/ adj not careful enough or not well controlled: *They seem to have a very lax attitude towards security.*

lay¹ /leɪ/ verb (**laid**) **1 lay sth down/in/on, etc** to put something down somewhere carefully: *She laid the baby on the bed.* ∘ *He laid the tray down on the table.* **2** [T] to put something into its correct position: *to lay a carpet* ∘ *to lay bricks* **3 lay eggs** 🔵 If an animal lays eggs, it produces them out of its body. **4 lay the blame on sb** to blame someone, usually when this is not fair: *You always lay the blame on me!* **5 lay the table** UK 🔵 to put plates, knives, forks, etc on the table to prepare for a meal → See also put/lay your cards on the table, lay the foundation(s) for/of sth, get/lay your hands (hand¹) on sth, lay down the law

> ❗ Common learner error: **lay** and **lie**
>
> Be careful not to confuse these verbs. **Lay** means 'put down carefully' or 'put down flat'. This verb is always followed by an object. **Laying** is the present participle. **Laid** is the past simple and the past participle.
> *She laid the papers on the desk.*
> **Lie** means 'be in a horizontal position' or 'be in a particular place'. This verb is irregular and is never followed by an object. **Lying** is the present participle. **Lay** is the past simple and **lain** is the past participle.
> *The papers were lying on the desk.*
> ~~The papers were laying on the desk.~~
> *I lay down and went to sleep.*
> ~~I laid down and went to sleep.~~
> The regular verb **lie** means 'not say the truth'.
> *He lied to me about his age.*

PHRASAL VERBS **lay sth down 1** to officially make new rules, or to officially say how something must be done: *The committee has **laid down** guidelines for future cases.* **2** If someone lays down their weapons, they stop fighting: *It is hoped the two sides will lay down their arms and return to peace.* • **lay into sb** informal to attack or criticize someone: *They started laying into me for no reason.* • **lay sb off** to stop employing someone, usually because there is no more work for them: [often passive] *Thirty more people were laid off last week.* • **lay sth on** to provide something for a group of people: *They're laying on free buses to and from the concert.* • **lay sth out 1** to arrange something on a surface: *He'd laid his tools out all over the kitchen floor.* **2** to explain something clearly, usually in writing: *I've just laid out some proposals.*

lay² /leɪ/ adj [always before noun] **1** involved in religious activities, but not trained as a priest: *a **lay preacher*** **2** not having special or detailed knowledge of a subject: *a lay person/audience*

lay³ /leɪ/ past tense of lie¹

lay-by /ˈleɪbaɪ/ noun [C] UK a small area where cars can stop at the side of a road

> 🗹 Word partners for **layer**
>
> a layer of sth • an outer/top layer • a thick layer of sth

layer /leɪər/ **noun** [C]
B2 an amount of a
substance covering a
surface, or one of
several amounts of
substance, each on
top of the other: *the
outer/top layer*
○ *Place alternate
layers of pasta and
meat sauce in a
shallow dish.* ○ *The
shelf was covered in a
thick **layer of** dust.*
• **layer verb** [T] [often
passive] *The potatoes
are **layered with**
onion.* → See also **the
ozone layer**

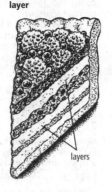

layer

layers

layman /'leɪmən/ **noun** [C] (plural **laymen**) (also
layperson) someone who does not have special
knowledge of a subject: *Could you please explain
that **in layman's terms** (= in a simple way)?*

layoff /'leɪɒf/ **noun** [C] the ending of someone's
job by an employer, usually because there is no
more work: [usually plural] *Several hundred more
layoffs are planned next month.*

layout /'leɪaʊt/ **noun** [C] the way that something
is arranged: *Do you like the **layout of** the kitchen?*

lazy /'leɪzi/ **adj 1** A2 Someone who is lazy does
not like working or using any effort: *You lazy
thing!* ○ *He's too lazy to make his bed in the
morning.* **2** slow and relaxed: *a lazy morning/
weekend* • **lazily adv** • **laziness noun** [U]

lb written abbreviation for pound (= a unit for
measuring weight)

LCD /ˌelsiː'diː/ **noun** [C] abbreviation for liquid
crystal display: a screen for showing words or
pictures which uses a liquid and an electric
current: *LCD TV*

lead¹ /liːd/ **verb** (**led** /led/) **1** TAKE SOMEONE ▷ [I,
T] B1 to show someone where to go, usually by
taking them to a place or by going in front of
them: *She led them down the hall.* ○ *We followed
a path that led us up the mountain.* ○ *You lead and
we'll follow.* ○ *I'll **lead the way** (= go first to show
the route).* **2** lead **into/to/towards, etc** B2 If a
path or road leads somewhere, it goes there:
That path leads to the beach. **3** BE WINNING ▷ [I,
T] B2 to be winning a game: *They were **leading
by** 11 points at half-time.* ○ *The Lions lead the
Hawks 28-9.* **4** BE THE BEST ▷ [T] to be better
than anyone else: *I still believe that we lead the
world in acting talent.* **5** CONTROL ▷ [T] to be in
control of a group, country, or situation: *to lead
a discussion* ○ *Is this man really capable of
leading the country?* ○ *Casillas **led** his team **to**
victory.* **6 lead sb to do sth** to make someone do
or think something: *What led you to think that?*
○ *I was **led to believe** that breakfast was
included.* **7 lead a busy/normal/quiet, etc life**
B2 to live in a particular way: *He was able to lead
a normal life despite his illness.* **8 lead sb to a
conclusion** to make you think that something is

probably true: *So you thought I was leaving, di
you? What led you to that conclusion?*

PHRASAL VERBS **lead to sth** B2 to make somethin
happen or exist: *A poor diet can lead to healt
problems in later life.* • **lead up to sth** to happe
before an event: *The shops are always busy in th
weeks leading up to Christmas.*

lead² /liːd/ **noun 1** WINNING ▷ [no plural] B2 a
winning position during a race or other situa
tion where people are competing: *She's **in th
lead** (= winning).* ○ *France has just **taken th
lead** (= started to win).* ○ *a three-goal lead* **2** FILM
PLAY ▷ [C] the main person in a film or play: *Sh
plays the **lead** in both movies.* **3** DOG ▷ [C] UK (US
leash) a chain or piece of leather fixed to a dog'
collar so that it can be controlled: *Dogs must b
kept **on a lead** at all times.* **4** ELECTRICITY ▷ [C
UK (US **cord**) the wire that connects a piece o
electrical equipment to the electricity suppl
5 INFORMATION ▷ [C] information about
crime that police are trying to solve: *Police ar
chasing up a new lead.*

> ☑ **Word partners for lead noun**
>
> **take the lead** • **increase/stretch your lead** •
> **be in the lead**

lead³ /liːd/ **adj** [always before noun] The lea
performer or lead part in a performance is th
main performer or part: *the **lead singer*** ○ *Wh
played the **lead role**?*

lead⁴ /led/ **noun 1** [U] a soft, heavy, grey
poisonous metal used for roofs, pipes, etc:
lead pipe ○ *lead-free petrol/gasoline* **2** [C, U] the
black part inside a pencil

leader /'liːdər/ **noun** [C] **1** B1 a person in contro
of a group, country, or situation: *a religiou
leader* ○ *Who's the **leader of** the Democratic Part
in the Senate?* **2** someone or something that i
winning during a race or other situation wher
people are competing: *He's fallen two laps behin
the leaders.* ○ *Microsoft is a world leader i
software design.*

leadership /'liːdəʃɪp/ **noun 1** [U] the job o
being in control of a group, country, o
situation: *the **leadership of** the Conservativ
party* ○ **leadership skills/qualities** ○ *a leader
ship contest* **2** [group] the people in control of
group, country, or situation: *There is growin
discontent with the leadership.*

> ☑ **Word partners for leadership**
>
> **leadership of** sth • **under** sb's **leadership** •
> **leadership skills/qualities** • a **leadership
> contest**

leading /'liːdɪŋ/ **adj** [always before noun] B2 ver
important or most important:
*He's a leading Hollywood
producer.*

leaf

leaf¹ /liːf/ **noun** [C] plural **leaves**
/liːvz/) B1 a flat, green part of a
plant that grows from a stem
or branch: *an oak leaf* ○ *a
lettuce leaf* ○ *the falling leaves*

IDIOMS **take a leaf out of sb's book** mainly UK to copy something good that someone else does • **turn over a new leaf** to start to behave in a better way

leaf² /li:f/ **verb**

PHRASAL VERB **leaf through sth** to turn the pages of a book or magazine and look at them quickly: *She lay on the sofa, leafing through glossy magazines.*

leaflet /ˈli:flət/ **noun** [C] a piece of folded paper or a small book that contains information: *I picked up a useful **leaflet on** how to fill in tax forms.*

leafy /ˈli:fi/ **adj** [always before noun] A leafy place is pleasant and quiet with a lot of trees: *a **leafy lane/suburb***

league /li:g/ **noun 1** [B1] [C] a group of teams that compete against each other in a sport: *top/bottom of the league* ◦ ***major/minor league baseball*** ◦ *Who won the league championship this year?* **2 be in league with sb** to be secretly working or planning something with someone, usually to do something bad **3 not be in the same league as sb/sth** informal to not be as good as someone or something: *It's a nice enough restaurant but it's not in the same league as Rossi's.*

leak¹ /li:k/ **verb 1** [I, T] [B2] If a liquid or gas leaks, it comes out of a hole by accident, and if a container leaks, it allows liquid or gas to come out when it should not: *Water had leaked all over the floor.* ◦ *The bottle must have leaked because the bag's all wet.* **2** [T] If someone leaks secret information, they intentionally tell people about it: *Details of the report had been **leaked to** the press.*

PHRASAL VERB **leak out** If secret information leaks out, people find out about it.

leak² /li:k/ **noun** [C] **1** [B2] a hole in something that a liquid or gas comes out of, or the liquid or gas that comes out: *I think we may have a leak in the roof.* ◦ *a **gas leak*** **2** the act of intentionally telling people a secret

leakage /ˈli:kɪdʒ/ **noun** [U] the problem of a liquid or gas coming out of something when it should not

leaky /ˈli:ki/ **adj** informal Something that is leaky has a hole in it and liquid or gas can get through: *a leaky boat/roof*

lean¹ /li:n/ **verb** (**leaned**, also UK **leant** /lent/) **lean (sth) back/forward/out, etc** [B2] to move the top part of your body in a particular direction: *She leaned forward and whispered in my ear.* ◦ *Lean your head back a bit.*

PHRASAL VERBS **lean (sth) against/on sth** [B2] to sit or stand with part of your body touching something as a support: *He leaned against the wall.* ◦ *She leaned her head on his shoulder.* • **lean sth against/on sth** [B2] to put something against a wall or other surface so that it is supported: *Lean the ladder against the wall.* • **lean on sb/sth** to use someone or something to help you, especially in a difficult situation: *Her mother had always leaned on her for support.*

lean² /li:n/ **adj 1** thin and healthy: *lean and fit* **2** Lean meat has very little fat on it.

leaning /ˈli:nɪŋ/ **noun** [C] a belief or idea: [usually plural] *I don't know what his **political leanings** are.*

leap¹ /li:p/ **verb** (**leapt** /lept/, **leaped**) **1 leap into/out of/up, etc** to suddenly move somewhere: *He leapt out of his car and ran towards the house.* ◦ *I leapt up to answer the phone.* **2 leap off/over/into, etc** to jump somewhere: *She leapt over the wall and disappeared down the alley.*

PHRASAL VERB **leap at sth** to accept the chance to have or do something with enthusiasm: *I'd **leap at** the **opportunity** to work in Japan.*

leap² /li:p/ **noun** [C] **1** a sudden improvement or increase: *There was a big **leap in** profits last year.* ◦ *This represents a great **leap forward** in technology.* **2** a big jump: *He finished third in the long jump with a leap of 26 feet.*

IDIOM **by/in leaps and bounds** If progress or growth happens in leaps and bounds, it happens very quickly.

→ See also **quantum leap**

> Word partners for **leap noun**
>
> a leap **in** sth • a leap **of** [75%/5 million, etc] • a leap **forward**

ˈleap ˌyear **noun** [C] a year that happens every four years, in which February has 29 days instead of 28

> **!** Common learner error: **learn**, **teach**, or **study**?
>
> To **learn** is to get new knowledge or skills.
>
> *I want to learn how to drive.*
>
> When you **teach** someone, you give them new knowledge or skills.
>
> *My dad taught me how to drive.*
>
> ~~*My dad learnt me how to drive.*~~
>
> When you study, you go to classes, read books, etc. to try to understand new ideas and facts.
>
> *He is studying biology at university.*

learn /lɜ:n/ **verb** (**learned**, also UK **learnt** /lɜ:nt/) **1 GET SKILL** ▷ [I, T] [A1] to get knowledge or skill in a new subject or activity: *I learned Russian at school.* ◦ *"Can you drive?" "I'm learning."* ◦ *She's **learned** a lot **about** computers in the last three months.* ◦ [+ to do sth] *I'm learning to play the piano.* **2 REMEMBER** ▷ [T] [B1] to make yourself remember a piece of writing by reading or repeating it many times: *I don't know how actors learn all those lines.* **3 UNDERSTAND** ▷ [I, T] [B2] to start to understand that you must change the way you behave: [+ (that)] *She'll have to learn that she can't have everything she wants.* ◦ *The good thing is, he's not afraid to **learn from his mistakes**.* → See also **learn your lesson**, **learn/know the ropes (rope¹)**

PHRASAL VERB **learn about/of sth** to hear facts or information that you did not know: *We only learned about the accident later.*

learned /'lɜːnɪd/ **adj** formal Someone who is learned has a lot of knowledge from reading and studying: *He was a very learned man.*

learner /'lɜːnəʳ/ **noun** [C] ⑫ someone who is getting knowledge or a new skill: *learners of English*

learning /'lɜːnɪŋ/ **noun** [U] ⑫ the process of getting knowledge or a new skill: *language learning*

learning curve **noun** [C] how quickly or slowly someone learns a new skill: *I've been on a steep learning curve since I started my new job.*

lease¹ /liːs/ **noun** [C] a legal agreement in which you pay money in order to use a building or a piece of land for a period of time: *We signed a three-year lease when we moved into the house.*

IDIOM **give sb/sth a new lease of life** UK (US **give sb/sth a new lease on life**) **a** to make someone feel happy or healthy after a period of illness or sadness: *The operation has given her a new lease of life.* **b** to improve something that was old so that it works much better

☑ Word partners for **lease**
renew/sign/take a lease • a lease of/on sth

lease² /liːs/ **verb** [T] to use a building or piece of land, or to allow someone to use a building or piece of land, in exchange for money: *We want to lease some office space in the centre of town.* ∘ *They leased the land to a local company.*

leash /liːʃ/ **noun** [C] (also UK **lead**) a chain or piece of leather fixed to a dog's collar so that it can be controlled

least¹ /liːst/ **adv 1** ⑬ less than anyone or anything else: *Which car costs least?* ∘ *I chose the least expensive dish on the menu.* ∘ *No one, least of all (= especially not) James, is going to be angry with you.* **2 at least a** ⑫ as much as, or more than, a number or amount: *You'll have to wait at least an hour.* **b** ⑬ something that you say when you are telling someone about an advantage in a bad situation: *It's a small house but at least there's a garden.* **c** used to say that someone should give a small amount of help although they do not intend to give a lot: *Even if you didn't want to send a present, you could at least have sent a card.* **d** something that you say in order to correct something you said that was wrong: *I've seen that film. At least, I saw the beginning then I fell asleep.* **3 not least** formal especially: *The whole trip was fascinating, not least because of the people I met.* **4 not in the least** not at all: *I don't mind staying at home, not in the least.* → See also **last² but not least**

least² /liːst/ **quantifier 1** ⑫ the smallest amount: *She earns the least money of all of us.* ∘ *Jake had more experience than anyone else and I probably had the least.* **2 to say the least** used to emphasize that you could have said something in a much stronger way: *We were surprised, to say the least.*

leather /'leðəʳ/ **noun** [U] ⑫ the skin of animals that is used to make things such as shoes and bags: *a leather jacket*

leave¹ /liːv/ **verb** (**left** /left/) **1 GO AWAY** ▷ [I, T] ⓐ to go away from a place or a situation, either permanently or for a temporary period: *I'm leaving work early this afternoon.* ∘ *What time does the bus leave?* ∘ *They left for Paris last night.* ∘ "*Does Trevor still work there?*" "*No, he left* (= he does not work there now).* ∘ *She left school at 16.* **2 END RELATIONSHIP** ▷ [I, T] ⓑ to end a relationship with a husband, wife, or partner and stop living with them: *I'll never leave you.* ∘ *She left him for a younger man.* **3 NOT TAKE** ▷ [T] ⓐ to not take something with you when you go away from a place, either intentionally or by accident: *Why don't you leave your jacket in the car?* ∘ *She'd left a note for him in the kitchen.* ∘ *That's the second umbrella I've left on the train.* **4 NOT USE ALL** ▷ [T] ⓐ to not use all of something: *They'd drunk all the wine but they'd left some food.* ∘ *Are there any biscuits left?* **5 REMAIN** ▷ [T] to make a permanent mark: *The operation may leave a scar.* **6 leave sth open/on/off, etc** ⑫ to make something stay in a particular condition: *Who left the window open?* **7 DO LATER** ▷ [T] to do something later that you could do immediately: *Don't leave your packing till the night before you go.* **8 GIVE** ▷ [T] to arrange for someone to receive something after you die: *His aunt left him a lot of money.* ∘ *He left the house to Julia.* **9 leave sb alone** to stop speaking to or annoying someone: *Leave me alone! I'm trying to work.* **10 leave sth alone** to stop touching something: *Leave your hair alone!*
→ See also **leave someone to their own devices**, **leave/make your mark¹**

PHRASAL VERBS **leave sb/sth behind** ⓐ to leave a place without taking something or someone with you: *We were in a hurry and I think I must have left my keys behind.* • **leave behind sth, leave sth behind (sb)** to make a situation exist after you have left a place: *The army left a trail of destruction behind them.* • **leave sth for/to sb** to give someone the responsibility for dealing with something: *I've left the paperwork for you.* • **leave sb/sth out** ⑫ to not include someone or something: *I've made a list of names – I hope I haven't left anyone out.* • **be left out** If someone feels left out, they are unhappy because they have not been included in an activity: *The older children had gone upstairs to play and she felt left out.* • **be left over** If an amount of money or food is left over, it remains when the rest has been used or eaten: *There was a lot of food left over from the party.*

leave² /liːv/ **noun** [U] a period of time when you do not go to work: *She's on maternity/sick leave.*

☑ Word partners for **leave**
annual/maternity/paternity/sick leave • on leave • leave from [work/your job, etc]

leaves /liːvz/ plural of leaf

lecherous /'letʃərəs/ **adj** A lecherous man shows too much interest in sex, in a way that is unpleasant.

lecture¹ /'lektʃəʳ/ **noun** [C] **1** ⑬ a formal talk given to a group of people in order to teach them about a subject: *We went to a lecture on*

α: arm | ɜː her | iː see | ɔː saw | uː too | aɪ my | aʊ how | eə hair | eɪ day | əʊ no | ɪə near | ɔɪ boy | ʊə pure | aɪə fire | aʊə sour

Italian art. ∘ *Do you know who's giving the lecture this afternoon?* **2** an angry or serious talk given to someone in order to criticize their behaviour: *My dad gave me a lecture on smoking last night.*

:cture² /'lektʃər/ **verb 1** [I] to give a formal talk to a group of people, often at a university: *She travelled widely throughout North America lecturing on women's rights.* ∘ *For ten years she lectured in law.* **2** [T] to talk angrily to someone in order to criticize their behaviour: *Stop lecturing me!* ∘ *His parents used to lecture him on his table manners.*

:cturer /'lektʃərər/ **noun** [C] mainly UK **⑫** someone who teaches at a university or college: *a lecturer in psychology* ∘ *a senior lecturer*

> **⚠** Common learner error: **lecturer** or **teacher**?
>
> In American English, **lecturer** is formal, and **teacher** or **professor** is usually used instead.

:d /led/ past of lead

:dge /ledʒ/ **noun** [C] a long, flat surface that comes out under a window or from the side of a mountain: *The birds landed on a ledge about halfway up the cliff.*

:ek /liːk/ **noun** [C, U] **⑫** a long, white and green vegetable that smells and tastes similar to an onion

:er /lɪər/ **verb** [I] to look at someone in an unpleasant and sexually interested way: *He was always leering at female members of staff.* • **leer** **noun** [C]

:ery /'lɪəri/ **adj** US worried and not able to trust someone: *I've gotten more leery of the media.*

:eway /'liːweɪ/ **noun** [U] freedom to do what you want: *My current boss gives me much more leeway.*

:ft¹ /left/ **adj** [always before noun], **adv ⑫** on or towards the side of your body that is to the west when you are facing north: *Step forward on your left leg.* ∘ *She had a diamond earring in her left ear.* ∘ *Turn left at the end of the hallway.* → Opposite **right**

:ft² /left/ **noun 1 ⑫** [no plural] the left side: *Ned's the man sitting on my left in that photo.* ∘ *Jean's house is last on the left.* **2 the Left/left** political groups that believe that power and money should be shared more equally among people: *The proposals were sharply criticized by the Left.* → Opposite **right**

> **🗹** Word partners for **left noun**
> **on the left** • **the left of sth** • **be to sb's left**

:ft³ /left/ past of leave

:ft 'click verb [I] to press the button on the left of a computer mouse (= a small piece of equipment that you move with your hand to control what the computer does)

:ft 'field noun US informal **1 (come) out of/from left field** strange and not expected: *His question came out of left field, and I didn't know what to say.* **2 (be) out in left field** strange and different

from other people or things: *She's kind of out in left field but she's fun.*

left-hand /ˌleft'hænd/ **adj** [always before noun] **⑫** on the left: *a left-hand drive car* (= *car which you drive sitting on the left-hand side*) ∘ *The swimming pool is on the left-hand side of the road.*

left-handed /ˌleft'hændɪd/ **adj** Someone who is left-handed uses their left hand to do most things.

leftist /'leftɪst/ **adj** supporting the ideas of parties on the political left: *leftist politics/ideas*

leftover /'leftˌəʊvər/ **adj** [always before noun] Leftover food remains after a meal: *If there's any leftover food we can take it home with us.* • **leftovers** **noun** [plural] food that remains after a meal: *We've been eating up the leftovers from the party all week.*

left-wing /ˌleft'wɪŋ/ **adj** supporting the ideas of parties on the political left: *a left-wing newspaper* • **left-winger** **noun** [C]

leg

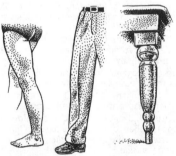

leg /leg/ **noun** [C] **1 PART OF BODY** ▷ **⑪** one of the parts of the body of a human or animal that is used for standing and walking: *He broke his leg in the accident.* ∘ *There were cuts on her arms and legs.* ∘ *She had bare legs and wore only a light summer dress.* → See colour picture **The Body** on page Centre 13 **2 FOOD** ▷ the meat of an animal's leg eaten as food: *a chicken leg* **3 FURNITURE** ▷ one of the vertical parts of a chair, table, etc that is on the floor: *a chair/table leg* **4 CLOTHES** ▷ the part of a pair of trousers that covers one of your legs: *He rolled up his trouser legs and waded into the water.* **5 PART OF JOURNEY** ▷ one part of a journey or competition: *the first/second/third leg of the journey*

IDIOMS **not have a leg to stand on** informal to have no chance of proving that something is true: *If you don't have a witness, you don't have a leg to stand on.* • **be on its last legs** informal If a machine is on its last legs, it will stop working soon because it is so old: *We've had the same oven for twenty years now and it really is on its last legs.* • **stretch your legs** informal to go for a walk

legacy /'legəsi/ **noun** [C] **1** a situation that was caused by something from an earlier time: *The war has left a legacy of hatred.* **2** money or buildings, etc that you receive after someone dies

legal /'li:gəl/ **adj 1** B2 relating to the law: *legal action/advice* ∘ *the legal profession/system* **2** B2 allowed by law: *Is it legal to carry a handgun?* → Opposite **illegal** • **legally** adv B2 *Children under sixteen are not legally allowed to buy cigarettes.*

legal 'aid **noun** [U] a system that provides free advice about the law to people who are too poor to pay for it

legality /li:'gæləti/ **noun** [U] the legal quality of a situation or action: *Some board members have questioned the legality of the proposal.*

legalize /'li:gəlaɪz/ **verb** [T] to make something legal: *How many Americans want to legalize drugs?* • **legalization** /ˌli:gəlaɪ'zeɪʃən/ **noun** [U] *the legalization of abortion*

legend /'ledʒənd/ **noun 1** [C, U] B2 an old story or set of stories from ancient times: *the legends of King Arthur* ∘ *She's writing a book on Greek legend.* **2** [C] a famous person: *a living legend* ∘ *Jazz legend, Ella Fitzgerald, once sang in this bar.*

legendary /'ledʒəndəri/ **adj 1** from a legend (= old story): *a legendary Greek hero* **2** very famous: *He became editor of the legendary Irish journal, 'The Bell'.*

leggings /'legɪŋz/ **noun** [plural] tight trousers made of soft material that stretches and are worn mainly by women: *a pair of leggings*

legible /'ledʒəbl/ **adj** If writing is legible, you can read it easily. → Opposite **illegible**

legion /'li:dʒən/ **noun** [C] a large group of soldiers that forms part of an army

legions /'li:dʒənz/ **noun** [plural] **legions of sb** large numbers of people: *He failed to turn up for the concert, disappointing the legions of fans waiting outside.*

legislate /'ledʒɪsleɪt/ **verb** [I] If a government legislates, it makes a new law: *We believe it is possible to legislate against racism.* ∘ *It's hard to legislate for* (= make a law that will protect) *the ownership of an idea.*

legislation /ˌledʒɪ'sleɪʃən/ **noun** [U] a law or a set of laws: *Most people want tougher environmental legislation but large corporations continue to oppose it.*

📝 Word partners for **legislation**

introduce/pass legislation • a piece of legislation • legislation on sth

---

legislature /'ledʒɪslətʃʊər/ **noun** [C] formal the group of people in a country or part of a country who have the power to make and change laws

legit /lə'dʒɪt/ **adj** informal short for legitimate

legitimate /lɪ'dʒɪtəmət/ **adj 1** allowed by law: *Sales of illegal CDs now exceed those of legitimate recordings.* → Opposite **illegitimate 2** A legitimate complaint or fear can be understood or believed: *People have expressed legitimate fears about the spread of the disease.* • **legitimately** adv

leisure /'leʒər/ US /'li:ʒər/ **noun** [U] **1** B1 the time when you are not working: *leisure activities* ∘ *Try to spend your leisure time doing activities you really enjoy.* **2** at your leisure If you do

something at your leisure, you do it when you have the time: *Take it home and read it at your leisure.*

'leisure ˌcentre **noun** [C] UK a building with a swimming pool and places where you can play sports

leisurely /'leʒəli/ US /'li:ʒərli/ **adj** in a relaxed way without hurrying: *a leisurely stroll*

lemon /'lemən/ **noun** [C, U] A2 an oval, yellow fruit that has sour juice: *a slice of lemon* ∘ *lemon juice* → See colour picture **Fruit and Vegetables** on page Centre 10

lemon

lemonade /ˌlemə'neɪd/ **noun** [C, U] **1** UK A2 cold drink with a lemon flavour that is sweet and has bubbles **2** mainly US a cold drink that is made from lemon juice, water, and sugar

lend /lend/ **verb** (lent /lent/) **1** [+ two objects] to give something to someone for a period of time, expecting that they will then give it back to you: *She lent me her car for the weekend.* ∘ *I don't have a bike but I've lent it to Sara.* **2** [I, T] B2 If a bank lends money, it gives money to someone who then pays the money back in small amounts over a period: *The bank refused to lend us any more money.*

PHRASAL VERBS **lend itself to sth** formal to be suitable for a particular purpose: *The old system doesn't lend itself to mass production.* • **lend sth to sb/sth** formal to add a quality to something or someone: *We will continue to lend support to our allies.*

lender /'lendər/ **noun** [C] a person or organization that lends money to people: *mortgage lenders*

length /leŋθ/ **noun** **1** DISTANCE ▷ [C, U] B1 the measurement or distance of something from one end to the other: *The carpet is over three metres in length.* ∘ *The length of the bay is roughly 200 miles.* → See Study Page **Measurements** on page Centre 31 **2** TIME ▷ [C, U] B1 the amount of time something takes: *the length of a film/play/speech* ∘ *Sitting still for any length of time is quite hard for most children.* **3** WRITING ▷ [C, U] the amount of writing in a book or document: *He's written books of various lengths on the subject.* **4** at length If you talk about something at length, you talk for a long time: *We discussed both topics at length.* **5** PIECE ▷ [C] a long piece of something: *length of cloth/cord/rope*

length

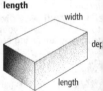

IDIOMS **go to great lengths to do sth** to try very hard to achieve something: *He'll go to great lengths to get what he wants.* • **the length and breadth of sth** in every part of a place: *They travelled the length and breadth of Scotland together.*

engthen /ˈleŋθən/ **verb** [I, T] to become longer or to make something longer: *lengthening waiting lists*

engthy /ˈleŋθi/ **adj** continuing for a long time: *a lengthy discussion/process*

enient /ˈliːniənt/ **adj** A lenient punishment is not severe: *He asked the judge to pass a lenient sentence.*

ens /lenz/ **noun** [C] a curved piece of glass in cameras, glasses, and scientific equipment used for looking at things → See also **contact lens, zoom lens**

lens

lens

ent /lent/ past of lend

ent /lent/ **noun** [U] the religious period before Easter (= a Christian holiday), in which some Christians do not allow themselves something that they usually enjoy: *She's given up chocolate for Lent.*

entil /ˈlentᵊl/ **noun** [C] a very small, dried bean which is cooked and eaten: *lentil soup*

eo /ˈliːəʊ/ **noun** [C, U] the sign of the zodiac that relates to the period of 23 July – 22 August, or a person born during this period → See picture at **the zodiac**

eopard

eopard /ˈlepəd/ **noun** [C] ⓑ a large, wild animal of the cat family, with yellow fur and dark spots

eper /ˈlepəʳ/ **noun** [C] a person who has leprosy

eprosy /ˈleprəsi/ **noun** [U] a serious skin disease that can destroy parts of the body

esbian /ˈlezbiən/ **noun** [C] a woman who is sexually attracted to other women: *a lesbian affair*

ess¹ /les/ **quantifier** ⓐ a smaller amount: *She gets about $50 a week or less.* ∘ *I was driving at less than 20 miles per hour.* ∘ *Tuberculosis is less of a threat these days.* ∘ *I prefer my coffee with a little less sugar.*

🔲 Common learner error: **less** or **fewer**?

Less is used before uncountable nouns.
I should eat less fat.

Fewer is used before countable nouns.
I should smoke fewer cigarettes.

ess² /les/ **adv 1** ⓐ not as much: *I'm trying to exercise more and eat less.* ∘ *Plastic bottles are less*

expensive to produce. **2** less and less If something happens less and less, it gradually becomes smaller in amount or not so frequent: *I find I'm eating less and less red meat.*

-less /-ləs/ **suffix** changes a noun into an adjective meaning 'without': *homeless people* ∘ *a meaningless statement* ∘ *a hopeless situation*

lessen /ˈlesᵊn/ **verb** [I, T] to become less or to make something less: *Exercise and a healthy diet lessen the chance of heart disease.*

lesser /ˈlesəʳ/ **adj** not as large, important, or of such good quality: *The price increase was due to labour shortages and, to a lesser extent, the recent earthquake.* ∘ *He faces the lesser charge of assault.*

IDIOM **the lesser of two evils** the less bad of two bad things: *I suppose I regard the Democratic candidate as the lesser of two evils.*

lesser-known /ˌlesəˈnəʊn/ **adj** not as popular or famous as something else: *We stayed on one of the lesser-known Greek islands.*

lesson /ˈlesᵊn/ **noun** [C] **1** ⓐ a period of time when a teacher teaches people: *The best way to improve your game is to **take lessons**.* ∘ *She gives French **lessons**.* ∘ *Lessons start at 9 a.m.* **2** ⓑ an experience that teaches you how to behave better in a similar situation in the future: *My parents made me pay back all the money, and it was a lesson I never forgot.*

IDIOMS **learn your lesson** to decide not to do something again because it has caused you problems in the past: *I'm not going out without my umbrella again – I've learnt my lesson!* • **teach sb a lesson** to punish someone so that they will not behave badly again: *The next time she's late, go without her. That should teach her a lesson.*

let /let/ **verb** [T] (**letting, let**) **1** ⓑ to allow someone to do something, or to allow something to happen: *Let them play outside.* ∘ *Don't let the camera get wet.* ∘ *We let a whole year go by before we tried again.* → See Note at **allow 2 let sb/sth in/past/through, etc** ⓑ to allow someone or something to move to or past a particular place: *They won't let us past the gate.* ∘ *I won't let him near my children.* ∘ *The roof lets in a lot of rain.* **3 let's** ⓐ something that you say when you are making a suggestion: *Let's eat out tonight.* **4 let me/us** something that you say when you are offering to help someone: *Let me carry your cases.* **5** If you let a building or part of a building, you allow someone to live there and they pay you money: *I let the top floor of my house to a student.* **6 Let's see/Let me see** something that you say when you are trying to remember something or calculate something: *Let's see – there are five people and only three beds.* ∘ *It must have been – let me see – three years ago.* **7 Let's say** something that you say when you are suggesting a possible situation or action: *Let's say we'll meet back here in an hour.* **8 let sb know (sth)** ⓐ to tell someone something: [+ question

L

word] *I'll let you know when we've fixed a date for the meeting.* **9 let (sth) go** to stop holding something: *I let go of the rope.* **10 let yourself go a** to allow yourself to become less attractive or healthy **b** to relax completely and enjoy yourself: *It's a party – let yourself go!* **11 let's face it** something that you say when the truth is unpleasant but must be accepted: *Let's face it, we're not getting any younger.* → See also **let the cat out of the bag, let your hair down, get/let sb off the hook¹, let off steam¹**

IDIOM **let alone** used to emphasize that something is more impossible than another thing: *You couldn't trust her to look after your dog, let alone your child.*

PHRASAL VERBS **let sb down** ⑫ to disappoint someone by not doing what you agreed to do: *I promised to go to the party with Jane and I can't let her down.* • **let sb in** to allow someone to enter a room or building, often by opening the door: *Could you go down and let Darren in?* • **let yourself in for sth** to become involved in an unpleasant situation without intending to: *Do you realize how much work you're letting yourself in for?* • **let sb off** ⑫ to not punish someone who has done something wrong, or to not punish them severely: *I'll let you off this time, but don't ever lie to me again.* ◦ *The judge let her off with* (= only punished her with) *a fine.* • **let on** to tell someone about something secret: *She let on to* a friend that she'd lied in court. • **let sb/sth out** ⑫ to allow a person or animal to leave somewhere, especially by opening a locked or closed door • **let up** If bad weather or an unpleasant situation lets up, it stops or improves: *I hope the rain lets up for the weekend.*

letdown /ˈletdaʊn/ **noun** [no plural] informal a disappointment: *After all I'd heard about the film it was a bit of a letdown when I finally saw it.*

lethal /ˈliːθəl/ **adj** able to cause death

lethargic /ləˈθɑːdʒɪk/ **adj** having no energy and not wanting to do anything • **lethargy** /ˈleθədʒi/ **noun** [U] the feeling of being tired and having no energy

letter /ˈletər/ **noun** [C] **1** ④ a written message that you send to someone, usually by post: *I got a letter from Paul this morning.* **2** ④ a symbol that is used in written language and that represents a sound in that language: *the letter K* → See also **covering letter**

⚡ Word partners for **letter**

get/receive/send/write a letter • in a letter • a letter from/to sb

letterbox /ˈletəbɒks/ **noun** [C] UK **1** a small hole in a door that letters are put through **2** (US **mailbox**) a large, metal container in a public place where you can post letters

letter carrier noun [C] US (UK **postman**) someone who takes and brings letters and parcels as a job

lettuce /ˈletɪs/ **noun** [C] ⑤ a plant with green leaves, which is eaten in salads → See colour picture **Fruit and Vegetables** on page Centre 10

leukaemia UK (US **leukemia**) /luːˈkiːmiə/ **noun** [U] a serious disease in which a person's body produces too many white blood cells

levee /ˈlevi/ **noun** [C] a wall made of earth or other materials that is built next to a river to stop the river from flooding (= covering everywhere in water)

level¹ /ˈlevəl/ **noun** [C] **1** HEIGHT ▷ ⑫ the height of something: *the water level* **2** AMOUNT ▷ ⑥ the amount or number of something: *Che requires a high level of concentration.* **3** ABILITY ⑫ someone's ability compared to other people: *Students at this level need a lot of help* **4** FLOOR ▷ a floor in a building: *The store ha three levels.* → See also **A level, a level playing field, sea level**

⚡ Word partners for **level**

the level of sth • at a (high/low, etc) level

level² /ˈlevəl/ **adj 1** [never before noun] at the same height: *I got down till my face was level with h* **2** ⑫ flat or horizontal: *Make sure the camera level before you take the picture.*

level³ /ˈlevəl/ **verb** [T] (mainly UK **levelling, levelled**, US **leveling, leveled**) **1** to make som thing flat: *He levelled the wet cement before it se* **2** to completely destroy a building: *Artillery fi levelled the town.*

PHRASAL VERBS **level sth against/at sb** to say th someone has done something wrong: [oft passive] *Charges of corruption have been levell against him.* • **level sth at sb** to aim a gun someone or something: *He levelled the gun at h head.* • **level off/out** to stop rising or falling ar stay at the same level: *Road deaths have levell off since the speed limit was lowered.*

level crossing noun [C] UK (US **grade cros ing**) a place where a railway crosses a road

lever /ˈliːvər/ ⑤ /ˈlevər/ **noun** [C] **1** a handle th you push or pull to make a machine work **2** long bar that you use to lift or move somethir by pressing one end

leverage /ˈliːvərɪdʒ/ ⑤ /ˈlevərɪdʒ/ **noun** [U] th power to influence people in order to get wh you want

levy /ˈlevi/ **verb** **levy a charge/fine/tax, etc** t officially demand money: [often passive] *A ne tax was levied on consumers of luxury goods.*

lewd /luːd/ **adj** sexual in a way that is unple sant: *lewd comments/gestures*

liability /ˌlaɪəˈbɪləti/ **noun 1** [U] legal respon bility for something: *They have admitted liab lity for the damage caused.* **2** [no plural] someo or something that is likely to cause you a lot trouble: *Wherever we go she upsets someone she's a real liability.*

liable /ˈlaɪəbl/ **adj 1** **be liable to do sth** to likely to do something: *He's liable to make a fu if you wake him.* **2** legally responsible: *Corpora officials are liable for the safety of their emplo ees.*

liaise /liˈeɪz/ **verb** [I] to speak to other people work in order to exchange information wit them: *Our head office will* **liaise with** *the suppliers to ensure delivery.*

liaison /li'eɪzᵊn/ *noun* **1 COMMUNICATION** ▷ [U] communication between people or groups that work with each other **2 PERSON** ▷ [C] US someone who helps groups to communicate effectively with each another: *She served as an informal liaison between employees and management.* **3 RELATIONSHIP** ▷ [C] a short, secret sexual relationship between people who are not married

liar /'laɪər/ *noun* [C] 🅱️2 someone who tells lies

Lib Dem /lɪb'dem/ *noun* [C] short for Liberal Democrat

libel /'laɪbᵊl/ *noun* [U] writing that contains bad information about someone which is not true: *Tabloid magazines are often sued for libel.*

liberal /'lɪbᵊrᵊl/ *adj* **1** accepting beliefs and behaviour that are new or different from your own: *a liberal attitude* **2** Liberal political ideas emphasize the need to make new laws as society changes and the need for government to provide social services. • **liberal** *noun* [C] someone who is liberal

liberal '**arts** *noun* [plural] US (UK/US **arts**) subjects of study that are not science, such as history, languages, etc

Liberal '**Democrat** *noun* [C] **1 the Liberal Democrats** one of the three main political parties in the UK: *He's the leader of the Liberal Democrats.* **2** someone who supports the Liberal Democrats

liberally /'lɪbᵊrᵊli/ *adv* in large amounts: *fruit liberally sprinkled with sugar*

liberate /'lɪbᵊreɪt/ *verb* [T] to help someone or something to be free: *Troops liberated the city.* • **liberation** /ˌlɪbᵊr'eɪʃᵊn/ *noun* [U] *the invasion and liberation of France*

liberated /'lɪbᵊreɪtɪd/ *adj* not following traditional ways of behaving or old ideas: *a liberated woman*

liberating /'lɪbᵊreɪtɪŋ/ *adj* making you feel that you can behave in exactly the way that you want to: *Taking all your clothes off can be a very liberating experience.*

liberty /'lɪbᵊti/ *noun* [C, U] **1** 🅱️2 the freedom to live, work, and travel as you want to: *Many would willingly fight to preserve their liberty.* **2 be at liberty to do sth** formal to be allowed to do something: *I'm not at liberty to discuss the matter at present.* **3 take the liberty of doing sth** formal to do something that will have an effect on someone else, without asking their permission: *I took the liberty of booking theatre seats for us.* → See also **civil liberties**

Libra /'liːbrə/ *noun* [C, U] the sign of the zodiac that relates to the period of 23 September – 22 October, or a person born during this period

librarian /laɪ'breəriən/ *noun* [C] someone who works in a library

library /'laɪbrᵊri/ *noun* [C] 🅰️2 a room or building that contains a collection of books and other written material that you can read and borrow

lice /laɪs/ plural of louse

licence UK (US **license**) /'laɪsᵊns/ *noun* [C] 🅰️2 an official document that allows you to do or have something: *a hunting licence* ◦ *a marriage licence* → See also **driving licence, off-licence**

🗹 Word partners for **licence**

apply for/hold/issue a licence • a licence **for** sth

---

license /'laɪsᵊns/ *verb* [T] to give someone official permission to do or have something: [often passive, + to do sth] *Undercover agents are licensed to carry guns.*

licensed /'laɪsᵊnst/ *adj* **1** mainly US officially approved: *a licensed physician* **2** A licensed bar or restaurant is officially allowed to serve alcoholic drinks.

'license ˌplate *noun* [C] US (UK **number plate**) an official metal sign with numbers and letters on the front and back of a car → See colour picture **Car** on page Centre 7

lick¹ /lɪk/ *verb* [T] 🅱️2 to move your tongue across the surface of something: *to lick your lips* ◦ *We licked the chocolate off our fingers.*

lick

lick² /lɪk/ *noun* **1** [C] the act of licking something: [usually singular] *Here, have a lick of my ice cream.* **2 a lick of paint** UK informal If you give a wall or other surface a lick of paint, you paint it.

lid /lɪd/ *noun* [C] 🅱️2 the top part of a container that can be removed in order to put something in or take something out

lie¹ /laɪ/ *verb* [I] (**lying, lay, lain**) **1 lie in/on, etc** 🅰️2 to be in a horizontal or flat position on a surface: *to lie in bed* ◦ *to lie on a beach* ◦ *to lie on your side* ◦ *The pen lay on the desk.* ◦ *She had lain where she fell until morning.* **2 lie below/in/on/to, etc** 🅱️1 to be in a particular place: *The river lies 30 km to the south of the city.* → See Note at **lay¹**

PHRASAL VERBS **lie around 1** informal to spend time lying down and doing very little: *We spent a week by the sea, lying around on the beach.* **2** If things are lying around, they are left in an untidy way in places where they should not be: *He's always leaving money lying around.* • **lie back** to lower the top half of your body from a sitting position to a lying position: *Lie back and relax.* • **lie down** 🅰️2 to move into a position in which your body is flat, usually in order to sleep or rest: *I'm not feeling well – I'm going to lie down.* → See colour picture **Phrasal Verbs** on page Centre 16 • **lie in** UK to stay in bed in the morning later than usual: *I lay in till eleven o'clock this morning.* • **lie in sth** to exist or be found in something: *Her strength lies in her faith.* • **lie with sb** If the responsibility or blame for something lies with someone, it is their responsibility: *The final decision lies with me.*

lie² /laɪ/ *verb* [I] (**lying, lied**) 🅱️1 to say or write something that is not true in order to deceive someone: *Are you **lying** to me?* ∘ *He **lied** about his qualifications for the job.*

lie³ /laɪ/ *noun* [C] 🔵 something that you say or write which you know is not true: *I **told a lie** when I said I liked her haircut.* → See also **white lie**

lie-in /'laɪˌɪn/ *noun* [no plural] UK If you have a lie-in, you stay in bed in the morning longer than usual: *I **had a long lie-in** this morning.*

lieu /luː/ *noun* **in lieu of sth** formal instead of something: *She took the money in lieu of the prize.*

lieutenant /lef'tenənt/ 🇺🇸 /luː'tenənt/ *noun* [C] an officer of middle rank in the army, navy, or air force: *first/second lieutenant*

life /laɪf/ *noun* (plural **lives** /laɪvz/) **1 ANIMALS/PLANTS** ▷ [U] 🔵 living things and their activities: *human/marine life* ∘ *Is there life in outer space?* **2 PERSON'S EXISTENCE** ▷ [C] 🔵 the existence of a person: *How many lives will be lost to AIDS?* **3 TIME** ▷ [C, U] 🔵 the time between a person's birth and their death: *I'm not sure I want to **spend** the rest of my **life** with him.* ∘ ***Life's too short** to worry about stuff like that.* ∘ *Unfortunately, accidents are **part of life.*** ∘ *He had a happy **life.*** **4 WAY OF LIVING** ▷ [C, U] 🔵 a way of living: *You **lead** an exciting **life.*** **5 family/private/sex, etc life** 🔵 one part of someone's existence: *My private life is nobody's business but mine.* **6 ACTIVITY** ▷ [U] 🔵 energy and activity: *She was always bubbly and **full of life.*** ∘ *I looked through the window but couldn't see any **signs of life** (= people moving).* **7 ACTIVE PERIOD** ▷ [no plural] The amount of time that a machine, system, etc exists or can be used: *Careful use will prolong the life of your machine.*

IDIOMS **bring sth to life/come to life** to make something more real or exciting, or to become more real or exciting ∘ **That's life.** something you say which means bad things happen and you cannot prevent them: *You don't get everything you want but that's life, isn't it?* ∘ **Get a life.** informal something you say to a boring person when you want them to do more exciting things: *Surely you're not cleaning the house on Saturday night? Get a life!*

→ See Note at **live³** → See also **the facts of life**, **give sb the kiss² of life**, **give sb/sth a new lease¹ of life**, **shelf life**, **walk² of life**

> ✏ Word partners for **life**
>
> have/lead/live a [charmed/normal, etc] life ∘ spend your life (doing sth) ∘ an aspect/part of sb's life

lifeboat /'laɪfbəʊt/ *noun* [C] a small boat that is used to help people who are in danger at sea

life ˌcoach *noun* [C] someone whose job is to teach people how to solve problems and make decisions in their daily life

life ˌcycle *noun* [C] the changes that happen in the life of an animal or plant

life exˌpectancy *noun* [C, U] the number of years that someone is likely to live

lifeguard /'laɪfɡɑːd/ *noun* [C] someone at a swimming pool or beach whose job is to help people who are in danger in the water

life inˌsurance *noun* [U] (also UK **life aˌssurance**) a system of payments to an insurance company that will pay money to your family when you die

life ˌjacket *noun* [C] a piece of equipment that you wear on the upper part of your body to help you float if you fall into water

life jacket

lifeless /'laɪfləs/ *adj* **1** without life: *his lifeless body* **2** without energy or feeling: *a lifeless performance*

lifelike /'laɪflaɪk/ *adj* If something is lifelike, it looks real: *a lifelike portrait/sculpture*

lifeline /'laɪflaɪn/ *noun* [C] something that helps you when you are in a difficult or dangerous situation: *For a lot of old people who live on their own, the telephone is a lifeline.*

lifelong /ˌlaɪf'lɒŋ/ *adj* [always before noun] for all of your life: *a lifelong friend/interest*

life ˌpeer *noun* [C] someone who has been officially respected in the UK by being given an important title, for example 'Lord', 'Lady', or 'Baroness'

life ˌsentence *noun* [U] (informal **life**) the punishment of spending a very long time, or the rest of your life, in prison

lifespan /'laɪfspæn/ *noun* [C] the amount of time that a person lives or a thing exists

lifestyle /'laɪfstaɪl/ *noun* [C] 🔵 the way that you live: *a healthy lifestyle*

life-threatening /'laɪfˌθretᵊnɪŋ/ *adj* likely to cause death: *life-threatening conditions/diseases*

lifetime /'laɪftaɪm/ *noun* [C] 🔵 the period of time that someone is alive: [usually singular] *We'll see such huge changes in our lifetime.*

lift¹ /lɪft/ *verb* **1 UP** ▷ [T] 🔵 to put something or someone in a higher position: *Could you help me lift this table, please?* ∘ *She **lifted** the baby **up** and put him in his chair.* **2 WEATHER** ▷ [I] If fog lifts, it disappears: *By noon the fog had lifted and the day turned hot.* **3 RULES** ▷ [T] to stop a rule: *The government had already **lifted** the **ban** on beef imports.* **4 STEAL** ▷ [T] informal to steal or copy something: *Entire paragraphs of his thesis were lifted from other sources.* → See also **not lift a finger¹**

lift² /lɪft/ *noun* [C] **1 MACHINE** ▷ UK (US **elevator**) 🔵 a machine that carries people up and down in tall buildings: *Shall we use the stairs or take the lift?* **2 RIDE** ▷ 🔵 a free ride somewhere, usually in a car: [usually singular] *Can you **give** me **a lift** to the airport?* **3 MOVE** ▷ the act of moving someone or something up to a higher position

lift-off /'lɪftɒf/ *noun* [C] the moment when a spacecraft leaves the ground

ligament /'lɪɡəmənt/ *noun* [C] a piece of strong

tissue in the body that holds bones together: *ankle/knee ligaments* ∘ *torn ligaments*

light

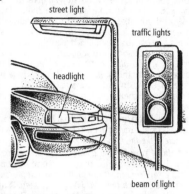

street light

traffic lights

headlight

beam of light

light¹ /laɪt/ **noun 1** [U] ⓑ the brightness that shines from the sun, from fire, or from electrical equipment, allowing you to see things: *bright/ dim light* ∘ *fluorescent/ultraviolet light* ∘ *a beam/ray of light* ∘ *Light was streaming in through the open door.* **2** [C] ⓐ a device that produces light: *car lights* ∘ *to switch/turn the light on* ∘ *They must be in bed – I can't see any lights on anywhere.* **3 a light** a flame from a match, etc used to make a cigarette start burning: *Have you got a light, please?* **4 set light to sth** mainly UK to make something start burning **5 in the light of sth** (also US **in light of sth**) If something is done or happens in the light of facts, it is done or happens because of those facts: *The drug has been withdrawn in the light of new research.*

IDIOMS **bring sth to light** If information about something bad is brought to light, it is discovered: *The trial brought to light numerous contradictions in his story.* • **cast/shed light on sth** to help people understand a situation: *We were hoping you might be able to shed some light on the matter.* • **come to light** If information about something bad comes to light, it is discovered. • **light at the end of the tunnel** something that makes you believe that an unpleasant situation will soon end

→ See also **green light, street light, tail light, traffic lights**

> 🗹 Word partners for **light**
>
> light **shines** • a **beam/ray/shaft** of light • **bright** light

light² /laɪt/ **adj 1 NOT HEAVY** ▷ ⓐ not heavy: *light clothing/machinery* ∘ *I can carry both bags – they're quite light.* **2 NOT MUCH** ▷ ⓑ small in amount: *light rain/snow* ∘ *I only had a light lunch.* **3 NOT STRONG** ▷ not strong or not forceful: *a light breeze* ∘ *a light embrace* **4 PALE** ▷ ⓐ Light colours are pale: *light brown/green* ∘ *a light blue cardigan* **5 NOT SERIOUS** ▷ easy to understand and not serious: *light entertainment* ∘ *I'm taking some light reading on holiday.* **6 make light of sth** to talk

or behave as if you do not think a problem is serious **7 it is light** ⓑ it is bright from the sun: *Let's go now while it's still light.* • **lightness noun** [U]

light³ /laɪt/ **verb** (**lit, lighted**) **1** [I, T] ⓑ to start to burn, or to make something start to burn: *to light a candle/cigarette/fire* ∘ *The wood was damp and wouldn't light.* **2** [T] ⓑ to produce light somewhere so that you can see things: [often passive] *The room was lit by a single light bulb.* ∘ *Burning buildings lit up the sky.*

PHRASAL VERBS **light up** If your face or your eyes light up, you suddenly look happy or excited: *His eyes lit up when you mentioned her name.* • **light (sth) up** to make a cigarette, etc start burning: *He made himself a coffee and lit up a cigarette.*

light bulb noun [C] a glass object containing a wire which produces light from electricity

light bulb

lighten /ˈlaɪtᵊn/ **verb 1** [I, T] If a serious situation lightens, it becomes less serious, and if something or someone lightens it, they make it less serious: *Her mood lightened a bit when I asked about her holiday.* ∘ *He tried to lighten the atmosphere by telling a joke.* **2 lighten the burden/load** to reduce the amount of work or trouble someone has to deal with **3** [I, T] to become less dark, or to make something less dark: *The sun had lightened her hair.*

PHRASAL VERB **lighten up** informal to become more relaxed and less serious: *I wish she'd lighten up a bit.*

lighter /ˈlaɪtᵊr/ **noun** [C] ⓑ a small object that produces a flame and is used to make cigarettes start burning

light-hearted /ˌlaɪtˈhɑːtɪd/ **adj** not serious: *a light-hearted remark*

lighthouse /ˈlaɪthaʊs/ **noun** [C] (plural **lighthouses** /ˈlaɪthaʊzɪz/) a tall building on the coast containing a large light which warns ships that there are rocks

lighthouse

lighting /ˈlaɪtɪŋ/ **noun** [U] ⓑ the light created by electrical equipment, candles, etc: *soft lighting*

lightly /ˈlaɪtli/ **adv 1** ⓑ gently: *He kissed her lightly on the cheek.* **2** not much: *lightly cooked vegetables* **3 not do sth lightly** to think carefully about something before you do it, knowing that it is serious: *It's not a decision that I take lightly.* **4 get off lightly** (also UK **escape lightly**) to have less trouble or punishment than you expected

lightning /ˈlaɪtnɪŋ/ **noun** [U] ⓑ a sudden flash of light in the sky during a storm: *thunder and lightning* ∘ *He was struck by lightning and killed.*

L

Word partners for lightning

be **struck by** lightning • a **bolt/flash** of lightning • **thunder and** lightning

lights /laɪts/ noun [plural] (also **'traffic ˌlights**) a set of red, green, and yellow lights that is used to stop and start traffic

lightweight /'laɪtweɪt/ adj not weighing much: *a lightweight jacket for the summer* • **lightweight** noun [C] a sportsman such as a boxer who is not in the heaviest weight group

like¹ /laɪk/ preposition **1** SIMILAR ▷ **A2** similar to or in the same way as someone or something: *They were acting like children.* ○ *He looks like his father.* ○ *It sounded like Harry.* **2 What is sb/sth like?** **A2** something you say when you want someone to describe someone or something: *I haven't met him – what's he like?* ○ *So what's your new dress like?* **3 What are you like?** UK informal used when someone has said or done something silly: *You've bought another jacket? What are you like?* **4** TYPICAL ▷ **B2** If behaviour is like someone, it is typical of the way that they behave: *It's just like Anita to miss her train.* ○ *It's not like Tim to be late.* **5** FOR EXAMPLE ▷ **B1** for example: *She looks best in bright colours, like red and pink.*

➕ Other ways of saying like

If a person likes someone or something very much, you can use the verbs **love** and **adore**:
I adore/love seafood.
Oliver loves animals.
Kate adored her grandfather.

The expressions **think the world of** someone and **have a soft spot for** someone can also be used when a person likes someone very much:
I've always had a soft spot for Rebecca ever since she was tiny.
Annabel's like a daughter to him, he thinks the world of her.

The expression **be fond of** is sometimes used to talk about someone or something that someone likes:
She's very fond of Chinese food.
I think she's very fond of you.

The phrasal verbs **grow on** and **take to/ warm to** can be used when someone starts to like someone or something:
I wasn't sure about the colour at first, but it's growing on me.
For some reason, I just didn't take/warm to him.

The expressions **take a shine to** or **take a liking to** are sometimes used when someone immediately likes a person:
I think he's taken a bit of a shine to you.

like² /laɪk/ verb [T] **1** **A1** to enjoy something or feel that someone or something is pleasant: [+ doing sth] *Most kids like playing computer games.* ○ [+ to do sth] *I like to paint in my spare time.* ○ *He really likes her.* ○ *What do you like about him?* → Opposite **dislike¹** **2 not like to do sth/**

not like doing sth to not usually do somethin because you think it is wrong: *I don't like criticize her too much.* **3 would like sth** **A1** t want something: [+ to do sth] *I'd like to thir about it.* ○ *I'd like some chips with that, pleas* **4 Would you like...?** **A1** used to offer someon something: *Would you like a drink?* ○ [+ to do sth Would you like to eat now?* **5 if you like a** used t say 'yes' when someone suggests a plan: *"Shall come?" "If you like."* **b** **A2** used when you off someone something: *If you like I could drive yo there.* **6 How do you like sb/sth?** used to as someone for their opinion: *How do you like m new shoes?*

like³ /laɪk/ conjunction informal **1** in the sam way as: *Do it exactly like I told you to.* **2** **B1** as **i** *He acted like he didn't hear me.*

like⁴ /laɪk/ noun **1** [no plural] formal someone **c** something that is similar to someone or som thing else: *Economists are predicting a depressio* **the like of which** *the world has never seen.* **2 an the like** informal and similar things: *There's gym that they use for dance and aerobics and th like.* **3 sb's likes and dislikes** **B1** the things th someone likes and does not like

-like /-laɪk/ suffix changes a noun into a adjective meaning 'typical of or similar tc *childlike trust* ○ *a cabbage-like vegetable*

likeable /'laɪkəbl/ adj If you are likeable, you a pleasant and easy to like: *a likeable character*

likelihood /'laɪklihʊd/ noun [U] the chanc that something will happen: *There's not muc* **likelihood of** *that happening.*

Word partners for likelihood

increase/reduce the likelihood of sth • a **real/strong** likelihood • the likelihood of (doing) sth

likely¹ /'laɪkli/ adj **1** **B1** expected: [+ to do sth] *D* remind me because I'm likely to forget.* ○ [+ (that It's likely that he'll say no.* **2** probably true: th most likely explanation* → Opposite **unlikely**

likely² /'laɪkli/ adv **1** probably: *She'll most like* come without him.* **2 Not likely!** UK informal use to say that you will certainly not do somethin "So are you coming running with me?" "N likely!"*

liken /'laɪkən/ verb

PHRASAL VERB **liken sth/sb to sth/sb** formal to sa that two people are similar or two things ar similar: *She's been likened to a young Elizabe Taylor.*

likeness /'laɪknəs/ noun [C, U] being similar **i** appearance: *There's a definite family likenes around the eyes.*

likewise /'laɪkwaɪz/ adv formal in the same wa Water these plants twice a week and likewise th ones in the bedroom.* ○ *Watch what she does an then do likewise.*

liking /'laɪkɪŋ/ noun **1** [no plural] a feeling tha you like someone or something: *He has a likin for young women.* **2 take a liking to sb** to lik someone immediately: *He obviously took a likin to her.* **3 be too bright/sweet, etc for you**

liking to be brighter/sweeter, etc than you like **4 be to sb's liking** formal to be the way that someone prefers something: *Is the wine to your liking, sir?*

lilac /ˈlaɪlək/ noun [C, U] a small tree that has sweet-smelling purple, pink, or white flowers

lily /ˈlɪli/ noun [C] a plant with large, bell-shaped flowers that are often white

limb /lɪm/ noun [C] **1** a leg or an arm of a person **2** a large branch of a tree

lime /laɪm/ noun **1** FRUIT ▷ [C, U] a small, green fruit that is sour like a lemon **2** TREE ▷ [C] (also **ˈlime ˌtree**) a large tree that has pale green leaves and yellow flowers **3** SUBSTANCE ▷ [U] a white substance that is found in water and soil and is used to improve the quality of soil **4** COLOUR ▷ [U] (also **ˌlime ˈgreen**) a bright colour that is a mixture of yellow and green → See colour picture **Colours** on page Centre 12 • **lime** (also **lime-green**) adj

the limelight /ˈlaɪmlaɪt/ noun attention from the public: *She's been in the limelight for most of her career.*

limit¹ /ˈlɪmɪt/ noun [C] **1** ⑤ the largest amount of something that is possible or allowed: *a time limit* ◦ *Is there a limit on the amount of money you can claim?* ◦ *There's a limit to how much time we can spend on this.* **2 be over the limit** UK to have more alcohol in your blood than is legally allowed while driving **3 within limits** avoiding behaviour that is extreme or silly: *You can wear what you want, within limits.* **4 off limits** If an area is off limits, you are not allowed to enter it. → See also **speed limit**

> 🗹 **Word partners for limit**
>
> an **age/height/speed/time** limit • a **legal/ maximum/strict/an upper** limit • **exceed/ impose** a limit • a limit **on/to** sth

limit² /ˈlɪmɪt/ verb [T] ⑤ to control something so that it is less than a particular amount or number: *We'll have to limit the number of guests.*

PHRASAL VERBS **be limited to sth** to only exist in a particular area: *Racial problems are certainly not limited to the south.* • **limit sb to sth** to only allow someone a particular amount or number of something: [often passive] *We're limited to two pieces of luggage each.* ◦ [often reflexive] *I try to limit myself to two cups of coffee a day.*

limitation /ˌlɪmɪˈteɪʃⁿn/ noun [C, U] the control of something so that it is less than a particular amount or number: *the limitation of free speech* ◦ *You can't write everything you want to because of space limitations.*

limitations /ˌlɪmɪˈteɪʃⁿnz/ noun [plural] things that someone is not good at doing: *Both films show her limitations as an actress.*

limited /ˈlɪmɪtɪd/ adj ⑤ small in amount or number: *a limited choice* ◦ *limited resources* → Opposite **unlimited**

ˌlimited ˈcompany noun [C] a company, especially one in the UK, whose owners only have to pay part of the money they owe if the company fails financially

limousine /ˌlɪməˈziːn/ noun [C] (also **limo** /ˈlɪməʊ/) a large, expensive car, usually for rich or important people: *a chauffeur-driven limousine*

limp¹ /lɪmp/ adj soft and weak: *a limp hand-shake* ◦ *a limp lettuce*

limp² /lɪmp/ verb [I] to walk with difficulty because one of your legs or feet is hurt • **limp** noun [no plural] *She walks with a limp.*

line¹ /laɪn/ noun **1** MARK ▷ [C] ⑫ a long, thin mark: *a horizontal/straight/vertical line* ◦ *Sign your name on the dotted line.* ◦ *Draw a line around your hand.* **2** ROW ▷ [C] a row of people or things: *a line of trees* ◦ *We formed two lines, men on one side and women on the other.* **3** ROPE ETC ▷ [C] a piece of rope or wire with a particular purpose: *a clothes/fishing line* **4** TELEPHONE ▷ [C] ⑫ the connection between two telephones: *I've got Neil on the line for you (= waiting to speak to you).* ◦ *I'll be with you in a moment – could you hold the line (= wait), please?* **5** WAITING ▷ [C, U] US (UK **queue**) a row of people waiting for something, one behind the other: *We were standing in line for hours to get tickets.* **6** SONG/POEM ▷ [C] ⑪ a row of words on a page, for example in a song or poem: *The same line is repeated throughout the poem.* **7 lines** the words spoken by an actor in a performance: *I don't know how actors remember all their lines.* **8** OPINION ▷ [C] the official opinion of an organization: [usually singular] *the government's line on immigration* **9 along the lines of sth** based on and similar to something: *He gave a talk along the lines of the one he gave in Oxford.* **10 sb's line of reasoning/thinking, etc** your reasons for believing that something is true or right **11** PRODUCT ▷ [C] a type of product that a company sells: *They're advertising a new line in garden furniture.* **12** DIRECTION ▷ [C] the direction that something moves in: *He can't kick the ball in a straight line.* **13 lines** the marks that older people have on their faces, when the skin is loose **14** BORDER ▷ [C] US a border between two areas: *the New York state line* **15 be on the line** If someone's job is on the line, they may lose it. **16 be in line for sth** to be likely to get something good, especially a job **17 be in line with sth** to be similar to and suitable for something: *a pay increase in line with inflation*

IDIOMS **draw the line at sth** to never do something because you think it is wrong: *I swear a lot but even I draw the line at certain words.* • **toe the (party) line** to do what someone in authority tells you to do although you may not agree with it

→ See also **the bottom line, dotted line, front line, hard line**

> 🗹 **Word partners for line**
>
> **draw** a line • a **diagonal/horizontal/straight/ vertical** line

line² /laɪn/ verb [T] **1** to form a row along the side of something: *Trees and cafes lined the street.* **2 be lined with sth** If a piece of clothing is lined with a material, its inside is covered with it: *a jacket lined with fur*

L

PHRASAL VERBS **line (sb/sth) up** to stand in a row, or to arrange people or things in a row: *Books were neatly lined up on the shelves.* • **line sb/sth up** to plan for something to happen: *What future projects have you lined up?*

line manager noun [C] mainly UK the person who manages another person in a company or business

linen /'lɪnɪn/ noun [U] **1** an expensive cloth that is like rough cotton: *a linen jacket* **2** pieces of cloth that you use to cover tables and beds: *bed linen*

liner /'laɪnə^r/ noun [C] a large ship like a hotel, which people travel on for pleasure: *a cruise/ ocean liner*

linesman /'laɪnzmən/ noun [C] (plural **linesmen**) in a sport, someone who watches to see if a ball goes into areas where it is not allowed

linger /'lɪŋɡə^r/ verb [I] to stay somewhere for a long time: *The smell from the fire still lingered hours later.*

lingerie /'lɒnʒ³ri/ ⑩ /ˌlɑːnʒə'reɪ/ noun [U] women's underwear

lingering /'lɪŋɡ³rɪŋ/ adj [always before noun] lasting a long time: *lingering doubts*

linguist /'lɪŋɡwɪst/ noun [C] someone who is good at learning foreign languages, or someone who studies or teaches linguistics

linguistic /lɪŋ'ɡwɪstɪk/ adj [always before noun] relating to language or linguistics

linguistics /lɪŋ'ɡwɪstɪks/ noun [U] the scientific study of languages

lining /'laɪnɪŋ/ noun [C, U] a material or substance that covers the inside of something: *a coat/jacket lining* ◦ *the lining of the stomach*

link¹ /lɪŋk/ noun [C] **1** CONNECTION ▷ 🔵 a connection between two people, things, or ideas: *There's a direct link between diet and heart disease.* ◦ *Their links with Britain are still strong.* **2** CHAIN ▷ one ring of a chain **3** INTERNET ▷ (also **hyperlink**) 🔵 a connection between documents or areas on the Internet: *Click on this link to visit our online bookstore.* → See Study Page **The Web and the Internet** on page Centre 36

> 🗹 Word partners for **link**
>
> **discover/establish/find** a link • a **close/ direct/strong** link • a link **between** sth and sth • a link **with** sth

link² /lɪŋk/ verb [T] 🔵 to make a connection between two or more people, things, or ideas: [often passive] *Both men have been **linked with** the robberies.* ◦ *The drug has been **linked to** the deaths of several athletes.*

PHRASAL VERB **link (sb/sth) up** If two or more things or people link up, or if you link them up, they form a connection so that they can operate or work together: *Each house will be linked up with the new communications network.*

lion /'laɪən/ noun [C] 🔵 a large, wild animal of the cat family, with light brown fur → See also **sea lion**

lion

lip /lɪp/ noun [C] **1** 🔵 one of the two soft, r... edges of the mouth: *He licked his lips.* → S... colour picture **The Body** on page Centre 13 **2** t... edge of a container that liquid is poured from...

lip-read /'lɪpriːd/ verb [I, T] (**lip-read**) to und... stand what someone is saying by looking at t... way their mouth moves • **lip-reading** noun [...

lip-service /'lɪpsɜːvɪs/ noun [no plural] **give/p**... **lip-service to sth** informal to say that y... support an idea or plan, but not do anythi... to help it succeed

lipstick /'lɪpstɪk/ noun [C, U] a coloured substance that women put on their lips → See picture at **make-up**

lipstick

liqueur /li'kjʊə^r/ noun [C] a strong, sweet alcoholic drink that people usually drink a little of at the end of a meal

liquid /'lɪkwɪd/ noun [C, U] 🔵 a substance, for example water, that is not so... and that can be poured easily • **liquid** adj ... *liquid fuel/nitrogen*

liquidate /'lɪkwɪdeɪt/ verb [T] to close a busine... because it has no money left • **liquidati**... /ˌlɪkwɪ'deɪʃ³n/ noun [C, U] *The store went in... liquidation.*

liquid-crystal display /ˌlɪkwɪdˌkrɪst³ldɪ'spl**... noun [C] LCD

liquor /'lɪkə^r/ noun [U] US an alcoholic drin... especially a strong alcoholic drink

liquor store noun [C] US (UK **off-licence**) ... shop that sells alcoholic drink

lisp /lɪsp/ noun [C] a way of speaking where ... and 'z' sound like 'th' • **lisp** verb [I]

list¹ /lɪst/ noun [C] 🔵 a series of nam... numbers, or items that are written one belo... the other: *a shopping list* ◦ *Is your name on t... list?* ◦ *Make a list of everything you need.* → S... also **mailing list**, **waiting list**

> 🗹 Word partners for **list**
>
> **compile/draw up/make/write** a list • a list of... sth • **on** a list • a **shopping** list

list² /lɪst/ verb [T] 🔵 to make a list, or to inclu... something in a list: *All participants' names a... listed alphabetically.*

listen /'lɪs³n/ verb [I] **1** 🔵 to give attention ... someone or something in order to hear the... *What kind of music do you **listen to**?* ◦ *She do... all the talking – I just sit and listen.* ◦ *You have... listened to a word I've said.* ◦ *Listen, if you ne... money, I'm happy to lend you some.* **2** 🔵

---

accept someone's advice: *I told you she wouldn't like it but you wouldn't listen to me!*

> ⚠ Common learner error: **listen, listen to, or hear?**
>
> Use **hear** when you want to say that sounds, music, etc. come to your ears. You can **hear** something without wanting to.
> *I could hear his music through the wall.*
> Use **listen** to say that you pay attention to sounds or try to hear something.
> *The audience listened carefully.*
> *Ssh! I'm listening!*
> Use **listen to** when you want to say what it is that you are trying to hear.
> *The audience listened to the speaker.*
> *Ssh! I'm listening to the radio!*

PHRASAL VERBS **listen (out) for sth** to try to hear something: *Could you listen out for the phone while I'm upstairs?* • **listen in** to secretly listen to a conversation, especially a telephone conversation • **Listen up!** mainly US something you say to tell people to listen to you: *Okay, everyone, listen up! I have an announcement to make.*

stener /'lɪsənər/ **noun** [C] someone who listens: *The new radio station already has twelve million listeners.* ○ *She's a **good listener** (= she gives you all her attention when you speak).*

t /lɪt/ past of light

ter /'liːtər/ **noun** [C] US spelling of litre

teracy /'lɪtərəsi/ **noun** [U] the ability to read and write

teral /'lɪtərəl/ **adj** The literal meaning of a word or phrase is its real or original meaning: *the literal meaning/sense*

terally /'lɪtərəli/ **adv 1** 🔵 having the real or original meaning of a word or phrase: *They were responsible for literally millions of deaths.* **2** informal used to emphasize what you are saying: *He missed that kick literally by miles!*

terary /'lɪtərəri/ **adj** 🔵 relating to literature, or typical of the type of language that is used in literature: *literary criticism*

terate /'lɪtərət/ **adj** able to read and write
→ Opposite **illiterate**

terature /'lɪtrətʃər/ **noun** [U] **1** 🔵 books, poems, etc that are considered to be art: *classical/modern literature* **2** written information about a subject: *There is very little literature on the disease.*

tre UK (US **liter**) (written abbreviation l) /'liːtər/ **noun** [C] 🔵 a unit for measuring liquid

tter¹ /'lɪtər/ **noun 1** [U] 🔵 pieces of paper and other waste that are left in public places **2** [C] a group of baby animals that are from the same mother and born at the same time: *a litter of kittens/puppies*

> 🔲 Word partners for **litter**
>
> drop litter • a piece of litter • a litter bin

tter² /'lɪtər/ **verb** [T] If things litter an area, they

cover parts of it in an untidy way: *Clothes littered the floor.*

PHRASAL VERB **be littered with sth** to contain a lot of something: *The whole book is littered with errors.*

little¹ /'lɪtl/ **adj 1** SMALL ▷ 🔵 small in size or amount: *a little bag/box/town* ○ *She's so little.* ○ *It costs **as little as** one dollar.* ○ *I might have a **little bit of** cake.* **2** SHORT ▷ [always before noun] 🔵 short in time or distance: *Sit down **for a little while**.* ○ *Let's have a little break.* **3** NOT IMPORTANT ▷ [always before noun] 🔵 not important: *It's only a little problem.* ○ *I'm having a little trouble with my back.* **4** YOUNG ▷ [always before noun] 🔵 young and small: *She was my little sister and I looked after her.* → See Note at **small¹**

little² /'lɪtl/ **quantifier 1** 🔵 not much or not enough: *He has little chance of winning.* ○ *There's so little choice.* **2 a little sth** 🔵 a small amount of something: *It just needs a little effort.*

> ⚠ Common learner error: **little**
>
> When **little** is used as a quantifier, it can only be used with uncountable nouns.

little³ /'lɪtl/ **pronoun 1** 🔵 not much, or not enough: *We did very little on Sunday.* **2 a little** 🔵 a small amount: *I only know a little about my grandparents.* ○ *"More dessert?" "Just a little, please."*

little⁴ /'lɪtl/ **adv** 🔵 not much or not enough: *It matters little.* ○ *a little-known fact*

live¹ /lɪv/ **verb 1** [I] 🔵 to be alive: *She only lived a few days after the accident.* ○ *I hope I live to see my grandchildren.* **2 live at/in/near, etc** 🔵 to have your home somewhere: *They live in New York.* ○ *We live near each other.* ○ *Where do you live?* **3** [I, T] 🔵 to spend your life in a particular way: *Many people are living in poverty.* **4 I'll never live it down!** humorous something you say about an embarrassing experience that other people will not forget

PHRASAL VERBS **live for sth/sb** 🔵 to have something or someone as the most important thing in your life: *I love dancing – I just live for it.* • **live on** to continue to live: *She lived on well into her nineties.* • **live on sth 1** 🔵 Money that you live on is the money you use to buy the things that you need: *We lived on very little when we were students.* **2** 🔵 to only eat a particular type of food: *All summer we live on hamburgers and hot dogs.* • **live together** 🔵 If two people live together, they live in the same home and have a sexual relationship, but are not married. • **live up to sth** 🔵 to be as good as someone hopes: *Did the trip **live up to** your **expectations**?* • **live with sb** 🔵 to live in the same home as someone and have a sexual relationship with them although you are not married • **live with sth** to accept a difficult or unpleasant situation: *It's a problem she's going to have to live with.*

live² /laɪv/ **adj 1** LIFE ▷ having life: *Millions of live animals are shipped around the world each year.* **2** ELECTRICITY ▷ A live wire has electricity in it.

---

yes | k cat | ŋ ring | ʃ she | θ thin | ð this | ʒ decision | dʒ jar | tʃ chip | æ cat | e bed | ə ago | ɪ sit | i cosy | ɒ hot | ʌ run | ʊ put |

3 BROADCAST ▷ **B1** A live radio or television programme is seen or heard as it happens: *live coverage* ∘ *a live broadcast* **4 AUDIENCE** ▷ A live performance or recording of a performance is done with an audience: *a live concert* **5 BOMB** ▷ A live bomb has not yet exploded.

live³ /laɪv/ **adv** broadcast at the same time that something happens: *We'll be bringing the match to you live on Wednesday.*

> ❗ Common learner error: **live** or **life**?
>
> **Live** cannot be used as a noun. The correct noun to use is **life**.
>
> *It was the best day of my life.*

livelihood /ˈlaɪvlihʊd/ **noun** [C, U] the way that you earn the money you need for living: *The farm is his livelihood.*

lively /ˈlaɪvli/ **adj** **B1** full of energy and interest: *a lively conversation/debate* ∘ *a lively child* • **liveliness noun** [U]

liver /ˈlɪvər/ **noun 1** [C] **B2** a large organ in your body that cleans your blood **2** [U] the liver of an animal that is eaten by people

lives /laɪvz/ plural of life

livestock /ˈlaɪvstɒk/ **noun** [U] animals that are kept on a farm

livid /ˈlɪvɪd/ **adj** very angry

living¹ /ˈlɪvɪŋ/ **noun 1** **B2** [C] the money that you earn from your job: [usually singular] *to earn/make a living* ∘ *What does he do for a living* (= how does he earn money)? **2 country/healthy, etc living** the way in which you live your life → See also **standard of living**

living² /ˈlɪvɪŋ/ **adj** [always before noun] **1** **B2** alive now: *He's probably the best known living photographer.* **2** **B2** alive: *living organisms* ∘ *living things* → See also **beat/knock the (living) daylights** out of sb, **scare/frighten the (living) daylights** out of sb

living room noun [C] (also UK **sitting room**) **A2** the room in a house where people sit to relax and, for example, watch television → See colour picture **The Living Room** on page Centre 4

lizard /ˈlɪzəd/ **noun** [C] a small animal with thick skin, a long tail, and four short legs

load¹ /ləʊd/ **noun 1** **B2** [C] something that is carried, often by a vehicle: *We were behind a truck carrying a load of coal.* **2 a load/loads** informal **B1** a lot of something: *There were loads of people there.* ∘ *Have some more food – there's loads.* **3 a load of rubbish/nonsense, etc** UK informal nonsense

load² /ləʊd/ **verb 1** [I, T] (also **load up**) **B2** to put a lot of things into a vehicle or machine: *Bring the car up to the door and I'll start loading up.* ∘ *to load the dishwasher/washing machine* → Opposite **unload 2** [T] to put film in a camera or bullets in a gun

PHRASAL VERBS **be loaded down with sth** to have too much to carry, or too much work to do: *I was loaded down with shopping.* • **be loaded with sth** to contain a lot of something: *Most fast foods are loaded with fat.*

-load /ləʊd/ **suffix** used at the end of a word to describe an amount of something that is being carried: *a truckload of soldiers*

loaded /ˈləʊdɪd/ **adj 1** A loaded gun, or similar weapon, has a bullet in it. **2** [never before noun] informal very rich

loaded question noun [C] a question that makes you answer in a particular way

loaf /ləʊf/ **noun** [C] (plural **loaves** /ləʊvz/) **B** bread that has been baked in one large piece so that it can be cut into smaller pieces: *a loaf of bread* → See picture at **bread**

loan¹ /ləʊn/ **noun 1** **B1** [C] money that someone has borrowed: *a bank loan* ∘ *He repaid the loan within two years.* **2 be on loan** If something is on loan, someone is borrowing it: *Both paintings are on loan from the city museum.*

> ✍ Word partners for **loan**
>
> **apply for/repay/take out** a loan • a **bank loan**

loan² /ləʊn/ **verb** [+ two objects] to lend something to someone: *I was glad to loan my old books to her.* ∘ *My dad loaned me the money.*

loath /ləʊθ/ **adj be loath to do sth** formal to not want to do something because it will cause problems: *I'm loath to spend it all.*

loathe /ləʊð/ **verb** [T] to hate someone or something • **loathing noun** [U] a feeling of hating someone or something

loaves /ləʊvz/ plural of loaf

lobby¹ /ˈlɒbi/ **noun** [C] **1** **B2** a room at the main entrance of a building, often with doors and stairs that lead to other parts of the building: *hotel lobby* **2** a group of people who try to persuade the government to do something: *the anti-smoking lobby*

lobby² /ˈlɒbi/ **verb** [I, T] to try to persuade the government to do something: *They're lobbying for changes to the law.*

lobster /ˈlɒbstər/ **noun** [C, U] a sea creature that has two claws (= sharp, curved parts) and eight legs, or the meat of this animal

local¹ /ˈləʊkəl/ **adj** **B1** relating to an area near you: *the local school/newspaper/radio station* • **locally adv** *locally grown vegetables*

local² /ˈləʊkəl/ **noun** [C] **1** someone who lives in the area you are talking about **2 sb's local** UK informal a bar that is near someone's home

local anaesthetic UK (US **local anesthetic**) **noun** [C, U] a substance that is put into a part of your body so that you do not feel pain there: *The procedure is carried out under local anaesthetic*

local authority noun [group] the group of people who govern a small area of a country: *Local authorities are looking for new ways to promote investment.*

local time noun [U] the official time in an area or country: *We will shortly be landing in London where the local time is 3.15.*

locate /ləʊˈkeɪt/ **verb** [T] formal **1** **B2** to find the exact position of someone or something: *Police are still trying to locate the suspect.* **2 be located in/near/on, etc** **B1** to be in a particular place: *Both schools are located in the town.*

ocation /ləʊˈkeɪʃᵊn/ **noun 1** ⑪ [C] a place or position: *They haven't yet decided on the location of the new store.* **2 on location** If a film or television programme is made on location, it is made at a place suitable to the story.

🗷 Word partners for **location**
at/in a [remote/secret, etc] location ● the location **of** sth

och /lɒk/, /lɒx/ **noun** [C] a lake in Scotland: *Loch Lomond*

ock¹ /lɒk/ **verb 1** [I, T] ⑪ to fasten something with a key, or to be fastened with a key: *Did you lock the door?* ○ *If you shut the door it will lock automatically.* → Opposite **unlock 2 lock sth/sb away/in, etc** ⑫ to put something or someone in a place or container that is fastened with a key: *She locked herself in her bedroom.* ○ *Most of my jewellery is locked away in a safe.* **3** [I] to become fixed in one position: *I tried to move forward but the wheels had locked.*

PHRASAL VERBS **lock sb in/out** ⑫ to prevent someone from entering/leaving a room or building by locking the door ● **lock (sth) up** to lock all the doors and windows of a building when you leave it ● **lock sb up** to put someone in prison or a hospital for people who are mentally ill

ock² /lɒk/ **noun** [C] **1** ⑪ the thing that is used to close a door, window, etc, and that needs a key to open it: *I heard someone turn a key in the lock.* ○ *safety locks* **2** a place on a river with gates to allow boats to move to a different water level

IDIOM **under lock and key** kept safely in a room or container that is locked: *I tend to keep medicines under lock and key because of the kids.*

🗷 Word partners for **lock** (noun)
fit a lock ● a lock **on** sth ● a **safety** lock

ocker /ˈlɒkəʳ/ **noun** [C] a small cupboard in a public area where your personal possessions can be kept: *a gym/luggage/school locker*

ocker room **noun** [C] a room where you change your clothes and leave those and other personal possessions in a locker

ocomotive /ˌləʊkəˈməʊtɪv/ **noun** [C] the part of a train that makes it move: *a steam locomotive*

odge¹ /lɒdʒ/ **noun** [C] a small house in the country that is used especially by people on holiday: *a hunting/mountain/ski lodge*

odge² /lɒdʒ/ **verb 1 lodge in/on, etc** to become stuck somewhere: *The bullet had lodged near his heart.* → Compare **dislodge 2 lodge at/with, etc** to live in someone's home and give them money for it **3 lodge a claim/complaint/protest, etc** to officially complain about something: *He lodged an official complaint against the officers responsible.*

odger /ˈlɒdʒəʳ/ **noun** [C] UK (US **boarder**) someone who pays for a place to sleep and meals in someone else's house

odgings /ˈlɒdʒɪŋz/ **noun** [plural] mainly UK a room in someone's home that you pay money to live in: *temporary lodgings*

loft /lɒft/ **noun** [C] **1** the space under the roof of a house or other building **2** US the space where someone lives or works in a building that used to be a factory

log¹ /lɒg/ **noun** [C] **1** a thick piece of wood that has been cut from a tree **2** a written record of events, often on a ship or aircraft

log² /lɒg/ **verb** [T] (**logging, logged**) to make a written record of events, often on a ship or aircraft

PHRASAL VERBS **log in/on** ⑫ to connect a computer to a system of computers by typing your name and often a password, usually so that you can start working ● **log off/out** ⑫ to stop a computer being connected to a computer system, usually when you want to stop working

loggerheads /ˈlɒgəhedz/ **noun**

IDIOM **be at loggerheads (with sb)** If two people or groups are at loggerheads, they disagree strongly about something: *He is at loggerheads with the Prime Minister over public spending.*

logging /ˈlɒgɪŋ/ **noun** [U] the activity of cutting down trees in order to get wood that can be sold: *a logging company*

logic /ˈlɒdʒɪk/ **noun** [U] the use of reason, or the science of using reason: *It was difficult to understand the **logic behind** his argument.*

🗷 Word partners for **logic**
the logic **behind/in/of** sth

logical /ˈlɒdʒɪkᵊl/ **adj** ⑫ using reason: *a logical choice/conclusion* → Opposite **illogical** ● **logically adv**

login /ˈlɒgɪn/ **noun** [C, U] a box that appears on your computer screen when you start to use a computer into which you put your name and password (= secret word)

logistics /ləˈdʒɪstɪks/ **noun the logistics of sth/ doing sth** the practical arrangements for something: *We could all use the one car but I'm not sure about the logistics of it.*

logo /ˈləʊgəʊ/ **noun** [C] ⑪ a design or symbol used by a company to advertise its products: *a corporate logo*

loiter /ˈlɔɪtəʳ/ **verb** [I] to stand in a place or walk slowly around without any purpose: *A gang of youths were loitering outside the cinema.*

LOL internet abbreviation for laughing out loud: used when you think something is very funny

lollipop /ˈlɒlipɒp/ **noun** [C] (also UK **lolly** /ˈlɒli/) a large, hard sweet on a stick

lollipop

lone /ləʊn/ **adj** [always before noun] alone: *lone parents* ○ *the lone survivor*

lonely /ˈləʊnli/ **adj 1** ⑪ unhappy because you are not with other people: *She gets lonely now that the kids have all left home.* → See Note at **alone 2** ⑫ A lonely place is a long way from where people live. ● **loneliness noun** [U]

loner /'ləʊnəʳ/ noun [C] someone who likes to be alone: *He was always a bit of a loner at school.*

lonesome /'ləʊnsəm/ adj US lonely

long¹ /lɒŋ/ adj **1** DISTANCE ▷ Ⓐ1 having a large distance from one end to the other: *long, brown hair* ∘ *a long dress* ∘ *It's a long way to travel to work.* **2** TIME ▷ Ⓐ1 continuing for a large amount of time: *a long film/meeting* ∘ *Have you been waiting a long time?* **3** HOW LONG ▷ used when asking for or giving information about the distance or time of something: *It's about three metres long.* ∘ *Most of the concerts are over three hours long.* ∘ *Do you know how long the film is?* **4** BOOK ▷ Ⓐ2 A long book or other piece of writing has a lot of pages or words: *a long article/letter* → See also **in the long/short run²**

long² /lɒŋ/ adv **1** Ⓐ2 for a long time: *We didn't have to* ***wait long*** *for the train.* ∘ *The band played long into the night.* **2** ***as long as*** Ⓑ1 used when you are talking about something that must happen before something else can happen: *You can play football as long as you do your homework first.* **3** ***before long*** Ⓑ2 soon: *He'll be home before long.* **4** ***long ago*** If something happened long ago, it happened a great amount of time ago. **5** ***no longer/not any longer*** Ⓑ1 not now: *He no longer works here.*

long³ /lɒŋ/ noun [U] a large amount of time: *She won't be away for long.*

long⁴ /lɒŋ/ verb formal ***long for sth; long to do sth*** to want something very much: *She longed to see him again.*

long-distance /ˌlɒŋ'dɪstəns/ adj Ⓑ2 travelling or communicating between two places that are a long way apart: *a long-distance race* ∘ *a long-distance phone call*

long-haul /'lɒŋhɔːl/ adj [always before noun] travelling a long distance: *a long-haul flight*

longing /'lɒŋɪŋ/ noun [U, no plural] a feeling of wanting something or someone very much: *He gazed at her, his eyes full of longing.* ∘ *a longing for his homeland* • **longingly** adv *She looked longingly at the silk dresses.*

longitude /'lɒndʒɪtjuːd/ noun [U] the distance of a place east or west of an imaginary line from the top to the bottom of the Earth, measured in degrees

the ***long jump*** noun a sports event where people try to jump as far as possible

long-life /ˌlɒŋ'laɪf/ adj UK Long-life drink or food has been treated so that it will last a long time: *long-life milk*

long-lost /'lɒŋˌlɒst/ adj **long-lost friend/cousin, etc** a friend or relative that you have not seen for a long time

long-range /ˌlɒŋ'reɪndʒ/ adj [always before noun] **1** relating to a time in the future: *a long-range weather* ***forecast*** **2** able to be sent long distances: *a long-range bomber/missile*

long shot noun [C] informal something that is not likely to succeed: *It's a long shot, but you could try phoning him at home.*

long-sighted /ˌlɒŋ'saɪtɪd/ adj UK (US **far-**sighted) able to see objects that are far away but not things which are near to you

long-standing /ˌlɒŋ'stændɪŋ/ adj having existed for a long time: *a long-standing relationship*

long-suffering /ˌlɒŋ'sʌfərɪŋ/ adj A long-suffering person has been very patient for a long time about all the trouble that someone has caused them: *Bill and his long-suffering wife*

long-term /ˌlɒŋ'tɜːm/ adj Ⓑ2 continuing a long time into the future: *long-term unemployment*

long-winded /ˌlɒŋ'wɪndɪd/ adj If what someone says or writes is long-winded, it is boring because it is too long: *a long-winded explanation*

loo /luː/ noun [C] UK informal toilet: *I'll just go to the loo.* → See Note **toilet**

look¹ /lʊk/ verb **1** SEE ▷ [I] Ⓐ1 to turn your eye in the direction of something or someone so that you can see them: ***Look at*** *the picture on page two.* ∘ *He was looking out of the window.* ∘ *I looked around and there she was.* **2** SEARCH ▷ [I] Ⓐ1 to try to find someone or something: *I'm* ***looking for*** *my keys.* ∘ *I've looked everywhere but I can't find my bag.* **3** ***look nice/strange, etc*** **look like/as if** Ⓐ2 used to describe the appearance of a person or thing: *That food looks nice.* ∘ *You look tired, my love.* ∘ *Do I look silly in this hat?* ∘ *He looked like a drug addict.* **4** ***it looks like; it looks as if*** Ⓑ1 used to say that something is likely to happen: *It looks like there'll be three of us.* ∘ *It looks as if he isn't coming.* **5** ***be looking to do sth*** to plan to do something: *I'm looking to start my own business.* **6** ***Look!*** something you say when you are annoyed and you want people to know that what you are saying is important: *Look, I've had enough of your complaints.* → See also **look the part¹**

❗ Common learner error: look, see, or watch?

See means to notice people and things with your eyes.

She saw a big spider and screamed.

Did you see anyone you knew at the party?

Look (at) is used when you are trying to see something or someone. **Look** cannot be followed by an object.

I've looked everywhere, but I can't find my keys.

He looked at the map to find the road.

~~He looked the photographs.~~

Watch means to look at something for a period of time, usually something that moves or changes.

He watched television all evening.

I watched them playing football.

PHRASAL VERBS **look after sb/sth** Ⓐ2 to take care of someone or something by keeping them healthy or in a good condition: *Could you look after the children while I'm out?* • **look ahead** to think about something that will happen in the future and plan for it • **look at sth 1** THINK ▷ Ⓑ to think about a subject carefully so that you ca make a decision about it: *Management is looking at ways of cutting costs.* **2 READ** ▷ ⑳ to read something: *Can you look at my essay sometime?* **3 EXPERT** ▷ ⑳ If an expert looks at something, they examine it: *Did you get the doctor to look at your knee?* **4 OPINION** ▷ to consider something in a particular way: *If I'd been a mother I might have looked at things differently.* • **look back** ⑳ to remember something in the past: *He looked back on his childhood with affection.* • **look down on sb** ⑳ to think that someone is less important than you • **look forward to sth/doing sth** ㉛ to feel happy and excited about something that is going to happen: *I'm really looking forward to seeing him.*

> ⚠ Common learner error: **look forward to**
>
> Remember always to use the preposition **to** when you use this verb.
> *We are looking forward to your visit.*
> ~~We are looking forward your visit.~~

• **look into sth** ⑳ to examine the facts about a situation: *They are looking into the causes of the accident.* • **look on** to watch something happen but not become involved in it • **look on sb/sth** to think about someone or something in a particular way: *We look on him almost as our own son.* • **Look out!** ㉛ something you say when someone is in danger: *Look out – there's a car coming!* • **look out for sb/sth** ⑳ to try to notice someone or something: *Look out for Anna while you're there.* • **look over sth** to examine something quickly: *I'm just looking over what you've written.* • **look through sth** ⑳ to read something quickly: *I've looked through a few catalogues.* • **look up** to become better: *Our financial situation is looking up.* • **look sth up** ㉛ to look at a book or computer in order to find information: *I looked it up in the dictionary.* • **look up to sb** ⑳ to respect and admire someone

ook² /lʊk/ **noun 1 SEE** ▷ [C] ㉛ an act of looking at someone or something: [usually singular] *Take a look at these pictures.* ○ *You've got your photos back – can I **have a look**?* **2 have/take a look** ㉛ to try to find something: *I've had a look in the drawer but I can't find my passport.* **3 FACE** ▷ [C] ⑳ an expression on someone's face: *She had a worried look about her.* ○ *She gave me a questioning look.* **4 FASHION** ▷ [no plural] a style or fashion: *the new look for the summer* **5 the look of sb/sth** ⑳ the appearance of someone or something: *I like the look of that new music programme they're advertising.* **6 sb's looks** a person's appearance, especially how attractive they are → See also **good looks**

> 🗹 Word partners for **look** noun
>
> have/take a look • a close/good look • a look at sb/sth

ookalike /ˈlʊkəlaɪk/ **noun** [C] informal someone who looks very similar to a famous person: *an Elvis lookalike*

ook-in /ˈlʊkɪn/ **noun** UK informal **not get a look-in** to get no chance to achieve what you want

or to succeed in something: *He played so well, nobody else got a look-in.*

lookout /ˈlʊkaʊt/ **noun 1** [C] a person who watches for danger and warns other people **2 be on the lookout** to be continuing to search for something or someone: *I'm always on the lookout for interesting new recipes.*

loom¹ /luːm/ **verb** [I] **1** to appear as a large, sometimes frightening shape: *Dark storm clouds loomed on the horizon.* **2** If an unpleasant event looms, it is likely to happen soon: *The threat of closure looms over the workforce.*

loom² /luːm/ **noun** [C] a machine for making cloth by weaving together (= crossing over) threads

loony /ˈluːni/ **noun** [C] informal someone who behaves in a crazy way: *The man's a complete loony.* • **loony adj** informal crazy: *loony ideas*

loop¹ /luːp/ **noun** [C] a circle of something long and thin, such as a piece of string or wire

loop² /luːp/ **verb loop sth around/over, etc sth** to make something into the shape of a loop: *Loop the rope around your waist.*

loophole /ˈluːphəʊl/ **noun** [C] a mistake in an agreement or law which gives someone the chance to avoid having to do something

> 🗹 Word partners for **loophole**
>
> a loophole in sth • a legal loophole

loose /luːs/ **adj 1 NOT FIXED** ▷ ⑳ not firmly fixed: *There were some loose wires hanging out of the wall.* ○ *One of my buttons is loose.* **2 CLOTHES** ▷ ㉛ large and not fitting tightly: *a loose dress/sweater* **3 FREE** ▷ An animal that is loose is free to move around: *Two lions escaped and are still loose.* **4 NOT EXACT** ▷ not exact: *It's only a loose translation of the poem.* • **loosely adv** *The film is based very loosely (= not exactly) on the novel.* → See also **be at a loose end¹**

> ⚠ Common learner error: **loose** or **lose**?
>
> Be careful! These two words look and sound similar but have completely different meanings. **Loose** is an adjective, meaning 'not fixed or not tight'.
> *These trousers are a bit loose.*
> Be careful not to use **loose** when you really mean the verb **lose**.
> *I hope he doesn't lose his job.*
> ~~I hope he doesn't loose his job.~~

loosen /ˈluːsən/ **verb** [I, T] to become loose or make something loose: *He loosened his tie.*

PHRASAL VERB **loosen up** to become more relaxed with other people: *After a while he loosened up.*

loot¹ /luːt/ **verb** [I, T] to steal from shops and houses during a war or period of fighting: *Rioters looted the capital.*

loot² /luːt/ **noun** [U] goods that have been stolen

lop /lɒp/ **verb** (**lopping, lopped**)

PHRASAL VERB **lop sth off** to cut off something in one quick movement: *I lopped off the biggest branches.*

L

lopsided /ˌlɒpˈsaɪdɪd/ ⓤⓈ /ˈlɒpsaɪdɪd/ **adj** with one side lower than the other: *a lopsided grin*

loquacious /ləʊˈkweɪʃəs/ **adj** formal talking a lot

lord /lɔːd/ **noun 1** [C, U] (also **Lord**) a man of high social rank, or a title given to a man who has earned official respect, in the UK: *Lord Lichfield* **2 the Lord** God or Christ **3 Good Lord!** informal something you say when you are surprised or angry: *Good Lord! Is that the time?* → See also **House of Lords**

the Lords /lɔːdz/ **noun** [group] (also **House of Lords**) one of the two parts of the British parliament, with members who are chosen by the government

lorry /ˈlɒri/ **noun** [C] UK (UK/US **truck**) ⓑ1 a large road vehicle for carrying goods from place to place → See picture at **vehicle**

lose /luːz/ **verb** (**lost**) **1 NOT FIND** ▷ [T] ⓐ2 to not be able to find someone or something: *I've lost my passport.* ○ *She's always losing her car keys.* **2 NOT HAVE** ▷ [T] ⓑ1 to stop having someone or something that you had before: *She lost a leg in a car accident.* ○ *I hope he doesn't lose his job.* ○ *He lost his mother (= his mother died) last year.* **3 HAVE LESS** ▷ [T] ⓑ1 to have less of something than you had before: *She's lost a lot of weight.* ○ *He's losing his hair.* ○ *to lose your memory* **4 NOT WIN** ▷ [I, T] ⓑ1 If you lose a game, competition, or election, the team or person that you are competing with wins: *Chelsea lost by a goal.* ○ *They're losing 3-1.* ○ *They hadn't lost an election in 15 years.* **5 lose faith/interest/ patience, etc** ⓑ2 to stop feeling something good: *I'm rapidly losing interest in the whole subject.* ○ *He kept on crying and I lost my patience.* **6 TIME** ▷ [T] ⓑ2 If you lose a number of hours or days, you cannot work during this time: *Four million hours were lost last year through stress-related illnesses.* **7 CLOCK** ▷ [T] If a clock loses time, it goes slower than it should. **8 CONFUSE** ▷ [T] informal to confuse someone so that they do not understand something: *No, you've lost me there – can you explain that again?* **9 GET RID OF** ▷ informal to take something away, usually because it looks bad: *Lose the belt, Andrea, it looks ridiculous with that dress.* **10 lose your balance** to fall because you are leaning too much to one side **11 lose count of sth** to forget the exact number: *I've lost count of how many times I've called her.* **12 lose your life** ⓑ2 to die: *Millions of young men lost their lives in the war.*

IDIOMS **be losing it** informal to start to become crazy: *I can't even remember my own telephone number – I think I must be losing it.* • **lose it** informal to stop being able to control your emotions and suddenly start to laugh, shout or cry: *I was trying so hard to stay calm but in the end I just lost it.*

→ See Note at **loose** → See also **fight a losing battle**¹, **lose your cool**³, **lose/save face**¹, **gain/lose ground**¹, **lose sight**¹ **of** sth, **lose sleep**² **over** sth

PHRASAL VERB **lose out** to not have an advantage that someone else has

---

❗ **Common learner error: lose or miss?**

Usually you **miss** something that happens, such as an event, a train leaving, or an opportunity.

I do not want to miss my class.

~~I do not want to lose my class.~~

Usually you **lose** a thing.

I've lost my umbrella.

---

loser /ˈluːzəʳ/ **noun** [C] **1** someone who does n̶ win a game or competition: *The losers of bo̶ games will play each other for third plac̶* **2** informal someone who is not successful ̶ anything they do

loss /lɒs/ **noun 1 NOT HAVING** ▷ [C, U] ⓑ2 the fa̶ of not having someone or something that yc̶ had before, or of having less of something tha̶ before: *loss of income/memory* ○ *blood/ha̶ weight loss* ○ *job losses* **2 MONEY** ▷ [C, U] ̶ situation in which a company spends mo̶ money than it earns: *Both companies suffer̶ losses this year.* **3 DISADVANTAGE** ▷ [no plural] ̶ disadvantage caused by someone leaving a̶ organization: *It would be a great loss to t̶ department if you left.* **4 be at a loss** to not kno̶ what to do or say: [+ to do sth] *I'm at a loss ̶ explain his disappearance.* **5 a sense of lo̶** sadness because someone has died or le̶ **6 DEATH** ▷ [C, U] ⓑ2 the death of a perso̶ *They never got over the loss of their son.*

☑ **Word partners for loss**

make/suffer a loss • a loss **of** [$50,000/£3̶ million, etc]

---

lost¹ /lɒst/ **adj 1 PERSON** ▷ ⓐ2 not knowing whe̶ you are or where you should go: *I got lost on t̶ way.* **2 OBJECT** ▷ ⓑ1 If something is lost, no o̶ knows where it is: *Things tend to get lost whe̶ you move house.* ○ *Lost: black cat with white pau̶* **3 NEW SITUATION** ▷ not knowing what to do in̶ new situation: *It was his first day in the office a̶ he seemed a bit lost.* **4 be lost without sb/s̶** informal to be unable to live or work witho̶ someone or something: *She's lost without h̶ computer.* **5 be lost on sb** If a joke or remark ̶ lost on someone, they do not understand ̶ **6 Get lost!** informal an impolite way of tellin̶ someone to go away → See also **long-lost**

lost² /lɒst/ past of lose

lost property noun [U] UK things that peop̶ have left in public places which are kept som̶ where until the owners can collect them

lot /lɒt/ **noun 1 a lot; lots** ⓐ1 a large number ̶ amount of people or things: *There were a lot ̶ people outside the building.* ○ *He earns lots ̶ money.* ○ *I've got a lot to do this morning.* ○ S̶ Note at **many 2 a lot better/older/quicker, e̶** ⓐ1 much better/older/quicker, etc: *It's a lot bett̶ than the old system.* ○ *It's a lot quicker by trai̶* **3 the lot** UK informal all of an amount or numbe̶ *I made enough curry for three people and he a̶ the lot.* **4 GROUP** ▷ [C] UK a group of people ̶ things that you deal with together: *I've alread̶ done one lot of washing.* **5 AREA** ▷ [C] US an are̶ of land: *a parking lot* ○ *an empty lot* **6 SALE** ▷ [̶

---

something being sold at an auction (= sale where things are sold to the people who pay the most): *Lot 3: a Victorian chest.* **7 sb's lot** the quality of someone's life and the type of experiences they have: *They've done much to improve the lot of working people.*

> ⚠ Common learner error: **a lot of** sth
>
> Remember to use the preposition **of** before the thing that there is a large number of.
>
> *A lot of people enjoy travelling to other countries.*
>
> ~~A lot people enjoy travelling to other countries.~~

otion /'ləʊʃ³n/ *noun* [C, U] a liquid that you put on your skin to make it soft or healthy: *suntan lotion* ∘ *body lotion*

ottery /'lɒt³ri/ *noun* [C] 🄱1 a way of making money by selling numbered tickets to people who then have a chance of winning a prize if their number is chosen: *the national lottery*

oud¹ /laʊd/ *adj* **1** 🄐2 making a lot of noise: *a loud noise* ∘ *a loud voice* ∘ *a loud explosion* **2** Loud clothes are too bright or have too many colours. • **loudly** *adv* 🄱1 *She was speaking very loudly.*

oud² /laʊd/ *adv* **1** 🄱1 loudly: *Can you speak a bit louder?* **2 out loud** 🄱1 If you say or read something out loud, you say or read it so that other people can hear you.

oudspeaker /ˌlaʊd'spiːkə³/ 🅤⒮ /'laʊdˌspiːkə³/ *noun* [C] a piece of equipment used for making voices or sounds louder

ounge¹ /laʊndʒ/ *noun* [C] **1** UK the room in a home where you sit and relax **2** a room in a hotel, theatre, airport, etc where people can relax or wait

ounge² /laʊndʒ/ *verb*
PHRASAL VERB **lounge about/around (sth)** to spend your time in a relaxed way, doing very little: *Most days were spent lounging around the pool.*

ouse /laʊs/ *noun* [C] (plural **lice** /laɪs/) a very small insect that lives on the bodies or in the hair of people or animals

ousy /'laʊzi/ *adj informal* very bad: *lousy food/service* ∘ *I felt lousy when I woke up this morning.*

out /laʊt/ *noun* [C] a man who behaves in a rude or violent way

ovable (also **loveable**) /'lʌvəbl/ *adj* A person or animal that is lovable has qualities that make them easy to love.

ove¹ /lʌv/ *verb* [T] **1** ROMANCE/SEX ▷ 🄐1 to like someone very much and have romantic or sexual feelings for them: *Last night he told me he loved me.* ∘ *I've only ever loved one woman.* **2** FRIENDS/FAMILY ▷ 🄐1 to like a friend or a person in your family very much: *I'm sure he loves his kids.* **3** ENJOY ▷ 🄐1 to enjoy something very much or have a strong interest in something: *He loves his music.* ∘ *She loves animals.* ∘ [+ doing sth] *I love eating out.* **4 I'd love to** 🄐2 used to say that you would very much like to do something that someone is offering: *"I won-*

dered if you'd like to meet up sometime?" "I'd love to."

love² /lʌv/ *noun* **1** ROMANCE/SEX ▷ [U] 🄱1 the feeling of liking someone very much and having romantic or sexual feelings for them: *He's madly in love with* (= he loves) *her.* ∘ *I was 20 when I first fell in love* (= started to love someone). ∘ *a love song/story* **2 make love** to have sex **3** PERSON ▷ [C] 🄱1 someone who you like very much and have a romantic or sexual relationship with: *He was my first love.* **4** FRIENDS/FAMILY ▷ [U] 🄱1 the feeling of liking a friend or person in your family very much: *Nothing is as strong as the love you have for your kids.* **5** INTEREST ▷ [C, U] 🄱2 something that interests you a lot: *his love of books* **6 Love from; All my love** 🄐2 something you write at the end of a letter to a friend or someone in your family: *Love from* UK *Mum/* US *Mom.* ∘ *All my love, Louise.* **7** SPEAKING TO SOMEONE ▷ mainly UK You call someone 'love' to show affection or to be friendly: *"Margot?" "Yes, love."* ∘ *Two portions of chips please, love.* **8** SPORTS ▷ [U] in games such as tennis, a score of zero: *She's leading by two sets to love.* → See also **a labour¹ of love**

> 🔲 Word partners for **love**
>
> **in love with** sb • **fall in love** • **madly in love** • **brotherly/unconditional love**

'love af,fair *noun* [C] a romantic or sexual relationship

loveless /'lʌvləs/ *adj* without love: *She was trapped in a loveless marriage.*

'love ,life *noun* [C] the romantic relationships in a person's life: *How's your love life these days?*

lovely /'lʌvli/ *adj* **1** 🄐2 pleasant or enjoyable: *We had a lovely day together.* ∘ *What lovely weather.* **2** 🄐2 very attractive: *a lovely dress/house/village* ∘ *You look lovely!*

lover /'lʌvə³/ *noun* **1** 🄱1 [C] If two people are lovers, they have a sexual relationship but they are not married: *She had a string of lovers before her marriage finally broke up.* **2 a book/cat/dog, etc lover** 🄱1 someone who is very interested in books/cats/dogs, etc: *She's a real cat lover.*

loving /'lʌvɪŋ/ *adj* showing a lot of affection and kindness towards someone: *a loving relationship* ∘ *a loving father* • **lovingly** *adv*

low¹ /ləʊ/ *adj* **1** NOT HIGH ▷ 🄱1 near the ground, not high: *low aircraft* ∘ *a low fence* **2** LEVEL ▷ 🄐2 below the usual level: *a low income* ∘ *low temperatures/prices* ∘ *a low number* ∘ *Fish is very low in* (= has little) *fat.* **3** SOUND ▷ deep or quiet: *a low voice* ∘ *a low note* **4** LIGHTS ▷ If lights are low, they are not bright: *We have very low lighting in the main room.* **5** UNHAPPY ▷ unhappy and without energy: *Illness of any sort can leave you feeling low.* → See also **be at a low ebb¹**, **keep a low profile¹**

low² /ləʊ/ *adv* **1** 🄱1 in or to a low position or level: *low-paid workers* ∘ *Turn the oven on low.* **2** with deep notes: *You can sing lower than me.*

low³ /ləʊ/ *noun* **a new/record/all-time, etc low** the lowest level: *Temperatures in the region hit a record low yesterday.*

L

low-alcohol /ˌləʊˈælkəhɒl/ *adj* A low-alcohol drink has less alcohol in it than the normal type: *low-alcohol beer*

low-calorie /ˌləʊˈkælᵊri/ *adj* (abbreviation **low-cal, lo-cal**) A low-calorie food or drink will not make you fat because it has fewer calories (= units for measuring the amount of energy a food provides) than normal food or drink.

low-cut /ˌləʊˈkʌt/ *adj* describes a piece of clothing that does not cover the top part of a woman's chest: *a low-cut dress*

the lowdown /ˈləʊdaʊn/ *noun* informal the most important information about something: *Jenny will give you the lowdown on what happened at yesterday's meeting.*

lower[1] /ˈləʊəʳ/ *adj* being the bottom part of something: *I've got a pain in my lower back.* ◦ *She bit her lower lip.*

lower[2] /ˈləʊəʳ/ *verb* [T] **1**🔵 to move something to a low position: *They lowered the coffin into the grave.* **2**🔵 to reduce the amount of something: *I'll join if they lower the entrance fee.*

lower case *noun* [U] letters of the alphabet that are not written as capital letters, for example a, b, c

low-fat /ˌləʊˈfæt/ *adj* Low-fat foods do not contain much fat: *low-fat cheese* ◦ *a low-fat diet*

low-key /ˌləʊˈkiː/ *adj* not attracting attention: *The reception itself was surprisingly low-key.*

lowly /ˈləʊli/ *adj* not important or respected: *He took a lowly job in an insurance firm.*

low-rise /ˈləʊˌraɪz/ *adj* describes trousers in which the top part of the trousers ends below the person's waist

low-tech /ˌləʊˈtek/ *adj* Something that is low-tech does not use the most recent technology. → Compare **high-tech**

loyal /lɔɪəl/ *adj*🔵 always liking and supporting someone or something, sometimes when other people do not: *a loyal supporter* ◦ *She's very loyal to her friends.* → Opposite **disloyal** • **loyally** *adv*

loyalties /ˈlɔɪəltiz/ *noun* [plural] a feeling of support for someone: *My loyalties to my family come before work.*

loyalty /ˈlɔɪəlti/ *noun* [U]🔵 the quality of being loyal: *Your loyalty to the company is impressive.* → Opposite **disloyalty**

lozenge /ˈlɒzɪndʒ/ *noun* [C] a sweet that you suck to make your throat feel better

LP /ˌelˈpiː/ *noun* [C] a record that has about 25 minutes of music on each side

LPG /ˌelpiːˈdʒiː/ *noun* [U] abbreviation for liquid petroleum gas: a type of fuel used for heating, cooking, and in some vehicles

L-plate /ˈelpleɪt/ *noun* [C] UK a red and white 'L' symbol on the car of someone learning to drive

Ltd written abbreviation for limited company (= used after the name of some companies): *Pinewood Supplies Ltd*

lubricant /ˈluːbrɪkənt/ *noun* [C, U] a liquid, such as oil, which is used to make the parts of an engine move smoothly together

lubricate /ˈluːbrɪkeɪt/ *verb* [T] to put a lubricant on something •**lubrication** /ˌluːbrɪˈkeɪʃᵊn/ *noun* [U]

lucid /ˈluːsɪd/ *adj* **1** clear and easy to understand:

a lucid account **2** able to think and speak clearly: *In a lucid moment, she spoke about her son.* • **lucidly** *adv*

luck /lʌk/ *noun* [U] **1**🔵 good and bad things caused by chance and not by your own actions: *It was just luck that I asked for a job at the right time.* ◦ *Then I met this gorgeous woman and couldn't believe my luck.* ◦ *He seems to have had a lot of bad luck in his life.* **2**🔵 success: *Have you had any luck finding your bag?* ◦ *He been trying to find work but with no luck so far.* **3 be in luck** informal to be able to have or do what you want: *"Do you have any tuna sandwiches?" "You're in luck – there's one left."* **4 Good luck** something you say to someone when you hope that they will be successful: *Good luck with your exam!* **5 Bad/Hard luck!** used to show sympathy when someone is unsuccessful or unlucky: *"They've run out of tickets." "Oh, bad luck!"*

IDIOM **the luck of the draw** If something is the luck of the draw, it is the result of chance and you have no control over it.

→ See also **a stroke**[1] **of luck**

> 🗪 Word partners for **luck**
>
> bad/beginner's/good/rotten luck • bring/wish sb luck • curse your luck • a stroke of luck

lucky /ˈlʌki/ *adj* **1**🔵 having good things happen to you: *"I'm going on holiday." "Lucky you!"* ◦ *The lucky winner will be able to choose from three different holidays.* ◦ *[+ to do sth] You're lucky to have such a nice office to work in.* **2** If an object is lucky, some people believe that it gives you luck: *I chose six – it's my lucky number.* → Opposite **unlucky** • **luckily** *adv*🔵 *Luckily I had some money with me.* → See also **happy-go-lucky**

lucrative /ˈluːkrətɪv/ *adj* If something is lucrative, it makes a lot of money: *a lucrative contract/job/offer*

ludicrous /ˈluːdɪkrəs/ *adj* stupid: *a ludicrous idea/suggestion* • **ludicrously** *adv*

lug /lʌg/ *verb* [T] (**lugging, lugged**) informal to carry or pull a heavy object: *You don't want to lug your suitcase across London.*

luggage

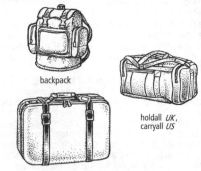

backpack

holdall *UK*, carryall *US*

suitcase

luggage /ˈlʌgɪdʒ/ *noun* [U]🔵 bags and cases

that you carry with you when you are travelling → See also **hand luggage**

lukewarm /ˌluːkˈwɔːm/ adj **1** A liquid that is lukewarm is only slightly warm: *Dissolve yeast and one tablespoon of sugar in lukewarm water.* **2** showing little interest or enthusiasm: *She seemed rather lukewarm about the idea.*

lull[1] /lʌl/ verb [T] to make someone feel calm and make them want to sleep: *Soft music lulled him to sleep.*

PHRASAL VERB **lull sb into sth/doing sth** to make someone feel safe so that you can then trick them

lull[2] /lʌl/ noun [C] a short period of calm in which little happens: *a lull in the conversation/traffic*

lullaby /ˈlʌləbaɪ/ noun [C] a song that you sing to children to make them sleep

lumber[1] /ˈlʌmbər/ verb **lumber along/around/off, etc** to move slowly with heavy steps: *The bear lumbered off into the forest.*

PHRASAL VERB **be lumbered with sth/sb** mainly UK to have to deal with something or someone that you do not want to: *I've been lumbered with my neighbours' cat while they're away.*

lumber[2] /ˈlʌmbər/ noun [U] US (UK **timber**) wood that is used for building

lumberjack /ˈlʌmbədʒæk/ noun [C] a person whose job is to cut down trees in a forest

luminary /ˈluːmɪnəri/ noun [C] formal a famous person who is respected for their skills or knowledge

luminous /ˈluːmɪnəs/ adj Something that is luminous shines in the dark.

lump[1] /lʌmp/ noun [C] **1** a piece of a solid substance with no particular shape: *a lump of coal* ○ *You don't want lumps in the sauce.* → See colour picture **Pieces and Quantities** on page Centre 1 **2** a hard piece of tissue under the skin caused by injury or illness: *She found a lump in her breast.*

lump[2] /lʌmp/ verb

PHRASAL VERB **lump sth/sb together** to put different groups together and think about them or deal with them in the same way: *American and Canadian authors tend to be lumped together.*

lump sum noun [C] a large amount of money given as a single payment: *She received a tax-free lump sum on leaving the company.*

lumpy /ˈlʌmpi/ adj covered with or containing lumps (= bits of solid substance): *a lumpy sauce*

lunacy /ˈluːnəsi/ noun [U] stupid behaviour that will have bad results: *It was lunacy spending all that money.*

lunar /ˈluːnər/ adj [always before noun] relating to the moon

lunatic /ˈluːnətɪk/ noun [C] someone who behaves in a crazy way: *He drives like a lunatic.*

lunch[1] /lʌnʃ/ noun [C, U] **A2** a meal that you eat in the middle of the day → See also **packed lunch**

🔲 Word partners for **lunch**
eat/have lunch • have sth for lunch • a light lunch

lunch[2] /lʌnʃ/ verb [I] to eat lunch

luncheon /ˈlʌnʃən/ noun [C] formal lunch

lunchtime /ˈlʌnʃtaɪm/ noun [C, U] **A2** the time when lunch is eaten

lung /lʌŋ/ noun [C] **B2** one of the two organs inside your chest that are used for breathing: *lung cancer*

lurch /lɜːtʃ/ verb **lurch forward/towards, etc** to suddenly move in a way that is not controlled: *The car lurched forward before hitting the tree.*

lure[1] /lʊər/ verb [T] to persuade someone to go somewhere or do something by offering them something exciting: *It seems that he was lured into a trap.* ○ *They had been lured to the big city by the promise of high wages.*

lure[2] /lʊər/ noun [U] the power to attract people: *the lure of fame/power/money*

lurid /ˈlʊərɪd/ adj **1** shocking in a way that involves sex or violence: *lurid details/stories* **2** too brightly coloured: *a lurid green miniskirt*

lurk /lɜːk/ verb [I] **1** to wait somewhere secretly, especially before doing something bad: *Someone was lurking in the shadows.* **2** to enter a place on the Internet and read what other people have written without them knowing you are there • **lurker** noun [C]

lush /lʌʃ/ adj A lush area has a lot of healthy grass, plants, or trees.

lust[1] /lʌst/ noun [U] **1** a strong feeling of sexual attraction to someone **2** a very strong wish to have something: *a lust for power*

lust[2] /lʌst/ verb

PHRASAL VERBS **lust after sb** to feel strong sexual attraction for someone • **lust after sth** to want something very much: *to lust after fame/power*

Lutheran /ˈluːθərən/ adj belonging or relating to a Christian group based on the teachings of Martin Luther • **Lutheran** noun [C]

luxurious /lʌɡˈʒʊəriəs/ adj very comfortable and expensive: *a luxurious hotel* ○ *luxurious fabrics*

luxury /ˈlʌkʃəri/ noun **1** COMFORT/PLEASURE ▷ [U] **B1** great comfort or pleasure from expensive or beautiful things: *to live in luxury* ○ *a luxury apartment/car* **2** NOT NECESSARY ▷ [C] something expensive that you enjoy but do not need: *It's nice to buy people the little luxuries that they wouldn't buy themselves.* **3** RARE PLEASURE ▷ [U, no plural] **B2** something that gives you a lot of pleasure but which you cannot often do: *A day off work is such a luxury.*

lying /ˈlaɪɪŋ/ present participle of lie[1,2]

lyrical /ˈlɪrɪkəl/ adj Lyrical writing expresses the writer's emotions in a beautiful way: *lyrical poetry/verse*

lyrics /ˈlɪrɪks/ noun [plural] **B2** the words of a song

M

M, m /em/ the thirteenth letter of the alphabet

m written abbreviation for metre (= a unit of length)

MA /,em'eɪ/ **noun** [C] abbreviation for Master of Arts: a higher university qualification in an arts (= not science) subject

ma'am /mæm/, /maːm/ US short for madam: *Can I help you, Ma'am?*

mac /mæk/ **noun** [C] UK a coat that you wear in the rain → See colour picture **Clothes** on page Centre 8

macabre /mə'kɑːbrə/ **adj** strange and frightening, and often connected with death: *a macabre story*

macaroni /,mækər'əʊni/ **noun** [U] pasta that is shaped like small tubes

machete /mə'ʃeti/ **noun** [C] a large knife with a wide blade

machinations /,mæʃɪ'neɪʃᵊnz/ **noun** [plural] complicated and secret plans and activities: *political machinations*

machine /mə'ʃiːn/ **noun** [C] **1 EQUIPMENT** ▷ **A2** a piece of equipment with moving parts that uses power to do a particular job: *a fax machine* ∘ *a coffee machine* ∘ *Clothes are generally sewn by machine these days.* **2 GROUP** ▷ a group of people all working together to achieve the same result: *a political/war machine* **3 COMPUTER** ▷ a computer → See also **answerphone, cash machine, sewing machine, slot machine, vending machine, washing machine**

> ☑ Word partners for **machine**
>
> operate/use a machine • turn off/turn on a machine • do sth by machine • a machine for doing sth

ma'chine ,gun noun [C] a gun that fires a lot of bullets very quickly

machine-readable /mə,ʃiːn'riːdəbl/ **adj** able to be understood by a computer: *a machine-readable dictionary*

machinery /mə'ʃiːnᵊri/ **noun** [U] **1** machines, often large machines: *industrial/farm machinery* **2** the system that a group of people uses to achieve something: *the machinery of government*

macho /'mætʃəʊ/ ⓤ /'mɑːtʃəʊ/ **adj** informal Men who are macho emphasize their traditional male qualities, such as physical strength, and do not show emotion.

mackerel /'mækrᵊl/ **noun** [C, U] (plural **mackerel, mackerels**) a type of sea fish, or the meat from this fish

mackintosh /'mækɪntɒʃ/ **noun** [C] old-fashioned a mac

macro- /'mækrəʊ-/ **prefix** large or on a large scale: *macroeconomics* (= *the study of financial systems at a national level*)

mad /mæd/ **adj 1 CRAZY** ▷ mainly UK informal **B1** stupid or crazy: [+ to do sth] *You're mad to walk home alone at night.* **2 ANGRY** ▷ **A2** mainly US angry: *Were your parents **mad at** you when yo* came home late? **3 go mad a** UK to become ver angry: *Dad'll go mad when he finds out you too the car.* **b** to suddenly become very excited: *Whe the band arrived on stage, the crowd went ma* **4 be mad about sb/sth** informal **B1** to lov someone or something: *Jo's mad about skiin* **5 SICK** ▷ mainly UK **B1** mentally ill **6 NO CONTROLLED** ▷ not controlled: *We made a ma dash for the exit.* **7 like mad a** **B2** If you ru work, etc like mad, you do it very quickly an with a lot of energy. **b** **B2** If something hurts li mad, it hurts a lot.

> ❗ Common learner error: **mad** or **mentally ill**?
>
> If someone has mental health problems, it is not polite to say that they are **mad**, use **mentally ill** instead.

madam /'mædəm/ **noun** formal **1** **B1** (als **Madam**) You call a woman 'madam' when yo are speaking to her politely: *This way, madan* **2 Madam** **B2** You write 'Madam' at th beginning of a formal letter to a woma when you do not know her name: *Dear Madan I am writing to...*

made /meɪd/ past of make

-made /meɪd/ **suffix** used after nouns adjectives to make a word that describes ho something is produced → See **man-made, se made, tailor-made**

madhouse /'mædhaʊs/ **noun** [C] informal a plac where there is a lot of uncontrolled noise an activity

madly /'mædli/ **adv 1** with a lot of energy an enthusiasm: *We cheered madly as the team cam out onto the field.* **2 be madly in love** to lov someone very much

madman, madwoman /'mædmən/, /'mæ ,wʊmən/ **noun** [C] (plural **madmen, ma women**) a crazy person: *He was runnir around **like a madman**.*

madness /'mædnəs/ **noun** [U] **1** stupid dangerous behaviour: *It would be madness give up your job when you've just bought a hous* **2** mental illness

maestro /'maɪstrəʊ/ **noun** [C] someone who very good at something, especially playir music

the mafia /'mæfiə/ ⓤ /'mɑːfiə/ **noun** a larg group of organized criminals: *Drug-smuggling activities have been linked to the Mafia.*

magazine

magazine /,mægə'ziːn/ **noun** [C] **A2** a thin book published every week or month, that has shiny, colourful pages with articles and pictures: *a fashion/news magazine*

maggot /'mægət/ **noun** [C] a small insect with a soft body and no legs that often lives in decaying food

magic¹ /'mædʒɪk/ **noun** [U] **1** SPECIAL POWERS ▷ **A2** special powers that can make things happen that seem impossible: *Do you believe in magic?* **2** ENTERTAINMENT ▷ **A2** clever actions intended to entertain people, often making objects appear and disappear **3** SPECIAL QUALITY ▷ **B2** a quality that makes something or someone seem special or exciting: *No one could fail to be charmed by **the magic of** this beautiful city.* **4 as if by magic** in a way that is surprising and impossible to explain: *Food would appear on the table every day, as if by magic.* → See also **black magic**

magic² /'mædʒɪk/ **adj 1** **B1** with special powers: *a magic spell/wand* **2** **A2** relating to magic: *a magic trick* **3 magic moments** special and exciting experiences

magical /'mædʒɪkəl/ **adj 1** with special powers: *Diamonds were once thought to have **magical** powers.* **2** **B2** special or exciting: *It was a magical night.* • **magically** adv *I knew my problems would not just magically disappear.*

magician /mə'dʒɪʃən/ **noun** [C] **1** someone who entertains people by performing magic tricks **2** a character in old stories who has magic powers

magistrate /'mædʒɪstreɪt/ **noun** [C] a type of judge (= person who decides what punishments should be given) who deals with less serious crimes

magnate /'mægneɪt/ **noun** [C] someone who is rich and successful in business: *a media magnate*

magnesium /mæg'niːziəm/ **noun** [U] a metallic element that burns very brightly, used to make fireworks (= explosives used to entertain people)

magnet

magnet /'mægnət/ **noun 1** [C] an iron object that makes pieces of iron or steel (= metal made with iron) move towards it **2 be a magnet for sb** If a place or event is a magnet for people, a lot of people go there: *Airports are a magnet for thieves.*

magnetic /mæg'netɪk/ **adj 1** with the power of a magnet: *a magnetic field* **2 magnetic tape/disk/storage, etc** equipment used in the past for storing information from a computer **3** having a character that attracts people to you

magnificent /mæg'nɪfɪsənt/ **adj** **B1** very good or very beautiful: *a magnificent view* • **magnificently** adv

magnify /'mægnɪfaɪ/ **verb** [T] **1** to make an object look larger than it is by looking through special equipment: *The cells are first magnified under a microscope.* **2** to make a bad situation worse: *All your problems are magnified when you're ill.*

magnifying glass noun [C] a piece of curved glass that makes objects look larger than they are

magnitude /'mægnɪtjuːd/ **noun** [U] formal the large size or importance of something: *People were still unaware of **the magnitude of** the problem.*

mahogany /mə'hɒgəni/ **noun** [U] a dark, red-brown wood used to make furniture

maid /meɪd/ **noun** [C] a woman who works as a servant in a hotel or in someone's home

maiden¹ /'meɪdən/ **noun** [C] literary old-fashioned a young woman who is not married

maiden² /'meɪdən/ **adj a maiden flight/voyage** the first journey of a new aircraft or ship

maiden name noun [C] the family name that a woman has before she gets married

mail¹ /meɪl/ **noun** [U] **1** **A2** (also UK **post**) letters and parcels that are brought by post **2** (also UK **post**) **A2** the system by which letters and parcels are taken and brought: *Send it **by mail**.* ∘ *The letter is **in the mail**.* → See also **email, junk mail, snail mail, surface mail, voice mail**

mail² /meɪl/ **verb** [T] (also UK **post**) to send a letter or parcel or email something: *Could you **mail** it **to** me?*

mail bomb noun [C] (also **email bomb**) an occasion when many email messages are sent to a single address at the same time, for example as a way of complaining or showing anger about something

mailbox /'meɪlbɒks/ **noun** [C] US **1** AT HOME ▷ a small box outside your home where letters are delivered **2** IN PUBLIC PLACE ▷ (UK **letterbox, post box**) a large, metal container in a public place where you can post letters **3** ON COMPUTER ▷ the part of a computer program that shows on a computer screen where electronic messages are stored

mail carrier noun [C] US (UK **postman**) someone who takes and brings letters and packages as a job

mailing list noun [C] a list of names and addresses that an organization uses in order to send information to people

mailman /'meɪlmæn/ **noun** [C] (plural **mailmen**) US (UK **postman**) a man who takes and brings letters and parcels as a job

mail order noun [U] a way of buying goods by ordering them from a catalogue (= book) and receiving them by post

maim /meɪm/ **verb** [T] to injure someone permanently: *Thousands of innocent people have been killed or maimed by landmines.*

main¹ /meɪn/ **adj** [always before noun] **1** **B1** most important or largest: *the main problem/reason* ∘ *The main airport is 15 miles from the capital.* **2 the main thing** **B2** the most important fact in a situation: *You're happy and that's the main thing.*

M

main² /meɪn/ **noun** [C] **1 gas/water main** a pipe that carries gas or water to a building **2 in the main** generally or mostly: *Her friends are teachers in the main.*

main ˌcourse noun [C] ⓐ the largest or most important part of a meal

mainframe /'meɪnfreɪm/ **noun** [C] a large, powerful computer that many people can use at the same time

mainland /'meɪnlənd/ **noun the mainland** the main part of a country, not including the islands around it: *A daily ferry links the islands to the mainland.* • **mainland adj** [always before noun] *mainland Britain*

mainly /'meɪnli/ **adv** ⓑ mostly or to a large degree: *The waitresses are mainly French.*

ˌmain ˈroad noun [C] a large road that leads from one town to another: *Stay on the main road for about three miles and you'll be there.*

the mains /meɪnz/ **noun** [group] UK **1** the system of pipes or wires that carries gas, water, or electricity to a building: *The house isn't connected to the mains yet.* **2** the place inside a building where you can connect a machine to a supply of electricity: *Is the cooker turned off at the mains?*

mainstay /'meɪnsteɪ/ **noun a/the mainstay of sth** the most important thing or activity: *Cattle farming is the mainstay of the country's economy.*

mainstream /'meɪnstriːm/ **noun the mainstream** the beliefs or way of living accepted by most people: *The party is now in the mainstream of politics.* • **mainstream adj** [always before noun] *mainstream culture/politics*

ˈmain ˌstreet noun [C] US (UK **high street**) the main road in the centre of a town where there are shops

maintain /meɪn'teɪn/ **verb** [T] **1 NOT CHANGE** ▷ ⓑ to make a situation or activity continue in the same way: *The army has been brought in to maintain order in the region.* **2 CONDITION** ▷ ⓑ to keep a building or area in good condition: *A large house is very expensive to maintain.* **3 SPEAK TRUTH** ▷ formal to say that you are certain something is true: [+ (that)] *He has always maintained that he is innocent.*

maintenance /'meɪntⁿnəns/ **noun** [U] **1** ⓑ the work that is done to keep something in good condition: *car maintenance* ◦ *I want a garden that's very low maintenance* (= easy to look after). **2** UK regular amounts of money that someone must pay after they have left their family so that the family still has money to live on: *child maintenance*

☑ Word partners for **maintenance**

carry out maintenance • **high/low** maintenance • maintenance of sth

maize /meɪz/ **noun** [U] UK (US **corn**) a tall plant with yellow seeds that are eaten as food

majestic /mə'dʒestɪk/ **adj** very beautiful or powerful in a way that people admire: *majestic scenery*

majesty /'mædʒəsti/ **noun 1** [U] the quality of being majestic: *the majesty of the pyramids* **2 His/Her/Your Majesty** used when you are

speaking to or about a king or queen: *H. Majesty King Edward VII*

major¹ /'meɪdʒər/ **adj 1** [always before noun] ⓑ more important or more serious than othe things or people of a similar type: *a majo problem/issue* ◦ *a major city* ◦ *America ha played a major role in the peace process.* **2** i music, belonging to a key (= set of musica notes) that often produces a happy soun → Opposite **minor**

major² /'meɪdʒər/ **noun** [C] **1** US the mos important subject that a college or universit student studies, or the student who is studying What's your major? ◦ *Diane's an English majo* **2** an officer of middle rank in the army or ai force

major³ /'meɪdʒər/ **verb**

PHRASAL VERB **major in sth** If you major in subject, it is the most important part of you course at a college or university.

majority /mə'dʒɒrəti/ **noun 1** [no plural] ⓑ more than half of a group of people or things *The majority of people in this country own the houses.* ◦ *The vast majority of smokers clain they would like to give up.* **2 be in a/the majority** to be larger than other similar groups: *Wome are in the majority in the publishing world.* **3** [C] i an election, the difference between the numbe of votes for the winner, and the votes for th party that came second: *Labour has a strong majority.* → Opposite **minority**

☑ Word partners for **majority**

a **narrow/outright/overwhelming/tiny/vast** majority • the majority **of** sth • **in** the majority

make¹ /meɪk/ **verb** [T] (**made**) **1 CREATE** ▷ ⓐ t produce or create something: *Shall I make som coffee?* ◦ *They've made a film about her life.* → Se Note at **do²** **2 make a promise/remark/mistake etc** to promise something, to say something, t do something wrong, etc: *We have to make decision today.* ◦ *You're making a big mistake* ◦ *She made some useful suggestions.* **3 make s do sth** ⓑ to force someone to do something *You can't make me go.* **4 make sb/sth happy/sac difficult, etc** ⓑ to cause someone or something to become happy, sad, difficult, etc: *You've mad me very happy.* ◦ *This is the song that made her star.* **5 GO TO** ▷ ⓑ to be able to go to an even *I'm afraid I can't make the meeting this afternoor* **6 EARN MONEY** ▷ ⓑ If you make an amount money, you earn it: *He makes $80,000 a yea* **7 NUMBERS** ▷ If two or more numbers make particular amount, that is the amount whe they are added together: *That makes $4 altogether.* **8 PERSONAL QUALITIES** ▷ [T] t have the right qualities to become a father c mother or to do a particular job: *Andy woul make a good teacher.* **9 GIVE A JOB** ▷ [+ tw objects] to give someone a particular job: *The made her a director of the company.* **10 make a appointment** to arrange to do something at particular time: *I've made an appointment wit the doctor.* **11 make the bed** to make the sheet and covers on a bed tidy **12 make time** to leave enough time to do something although you are busy: [+ to do sth] *You must make time to do your homework.* **13 make do (with)** to accept that something is less good than you would like: *If we can't get a bigger room we'll have to make do with this.* **14 make it a** to manage to arrive at a place: *Will we make it in time for the film?* **b** to be successful: *Very few actors actually make it.*

PHRASAL VERBS **make for sth** to move towards a place: *He got up and made for the exit.* • **make sth into sth** ® to change something into something else: *We're going to make the spare room into an office.* • **make of sb/sth** If you ask someone what they make of someone or something, you want to know their opinion about that person or thing: *What do you make of this letter?* • **make off with sth** informal to steal something • **make sth/sb out** ® to be able to see, hear, or understand something or someone: *We could just make out a building through the trees.* • **make out sth** to say something that is not true: [+ (that)] *He made out that he'd been living in Boston all year.* • **make out** US informal **1** to deal with a situation, usually in a successful way: *How is Jake **making out in** his new school?* **2** to kiss and touch someone in a sexual way • **make it up to sb** to do something good for someone because you have done something bad to them in the past: *I'm sorry I missed your birthday. I'll make it up to you, I promise.* • **make sth up** ® to say or write something that is not true: *I made up some story about having to go and see my sick mother.* • **make up sth** to form the whole of an amount: *Women make up nearly 50% of medical school entrants.* • **make up** to become friendly with someone again after you have argued with them: *Have you **made up with** Daryl yet?* • **make up for sth** ® to reduce the bad effect of something, or make something bad become something good: *I hope this money will make up for the inconvenience.*

make² /meɪk/ *noun* [C] the name of a company that makes a particular product: *I like your bike. What make is it?*

make-believe /ˈmeɪkbɪˌliːv/ *noun* [U] the activity of pretending that something is real: *Disneyland creates a world of make-believe.*

makeover /ˈmeɪkˌəʊvəʳ/ *noun* [C] the process of suddenly improving your appearance by wearing better clothes, cutting your hair, etc: *to **have** a **makeover***

maker /ˈmeɪkəʳ/ *noun* [C] ® 'the person or company that makes a product: *makers of top quality electrical products*

makeshift /ˈmeɪkʃɪft/ *adj* [always before noun] temporary and low quality: *makeshift shelters*

make-up, makeup /ˈmeɪkʌp/ *noun* [U] ® coloured substances that a woman puts on her face in order to make herself more attractive: *to **put on/take off** make-up* ○ *She doesn't **wear** much **make-up**.*

making /ˈmeɪkɪŋ/ *noun* [U] **1** the process of making or producing something: *There's an article on **the making of** a television series.*

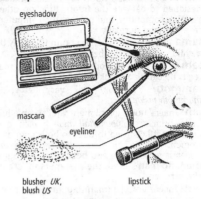

make-up

eyeshadow

mascara

eyeliner

blusher *UK*,
blush *US*

lipstick

○ *the art of film making* **2 be a sth/sb in the making** to be likely to develop into a particular thing or type of person: *What we're seeing is a disaster in the making.* **3 have the makings of sth** to seem likely to develop into something: *She has the makings of a great violinist.*

malaria /məˈleəriə/ *noun* [U] a serious disease that you can get in hot countries if a mosquito (= small insect) bites you

male¹ /meɪl/ *adj* ® belonging to or relating to the sex that cannot have babies: *a male colleague* → Opposite **female**

male² /meɪl/ *noun* [C] ® a male person or animal: *In 1987, 27 percent of adult males smoked.*

male chauvinist *noun* [C] a man who believes that men are better or more important than women

malice /ˈmælɪs/ *noun* [U] the feeling of wanting to harm or upset someone: *There was no malice in her comments.*

malicious /məˈlɪʃəs/ *adj* **1** intended to harm or upset someone: *malicious gossip* **2** Malicious software or computer programs are designed to damage other people's computers and prevent them from working normally. *malicious programs*

malignant /məˈlɪgnənt/ *adj* A malignant tumour (= group of diseased cells) is one that could cause death.

mall /mɔːl/ *noun* [C] (also **shopping mall**) ® a large, covered shopping area

malleable /ˈmæliəbl/ *adj* **1** easy to bend or make into a different shape **2** formal easily influenced and controlled

mallet /ˈmælɪt/ *noun* [C] a tool like a hammer with a large, flat end made of wood or rubber → See picture at **tool**

malnutrition /ˌmælnjuˈtrɪʃən/ *noun* [U] a serious illness caused by having too little food

malpractice /ˌmælˈpræktɪs/ *noun* [U] failure to act correctly or legally when doing your job, often causing injury or loss: *medical malpractice*

malt /mɔːlt/ *noun* [U] a substance made from grain that is used to make drinks, for example beer and whisky (= strong alcoholic drink)

M

malware /'mælweə^r/ **noun** [U] software that is designed to damage the information on other people's computers, and prevent the computers from working normally

mama /mə'mɑː/ ⓤⓢ /'mɑː.mə/ **noun** [C] mainly US a child's word for 'mother'

mammal /'mæm^əl/ **noun** [C] an animal that feeds its babies on milk from its body

mammoth /'mæməθ/ **adj** very large: *a mammoth task/project*

man[1] /mæn/ **noun** (plural **men**) **1** [C] ⓐⓘ an adult male human: *a young/tall man* ∘ *men and women* **2** [U] ⓑ② used to refer to both men and women: *Man is still more intelligent than the cleverest robot.* → See also **best man, garbage man, no-man's land, the man/person, etc in the street**

man[2] /mæn/ **verb** [T] (**manning, manned**) to be present somewhere, especially in order to operate a machine: *The emergency room is manned 24 hours a day.*

manage /'mænɪdʒ/ **verb 1** DO SUCCESSFULLY ▷ [I, T] ⓑⓘ to do something or deal with something successfully: *Will you be able to manage on your own?* ∘ [+ to do sth] *Anyway, we managed to get there on time.* **2** CONTROL ▷ [T] ⓑⓘ to be in control of an office, shop, team, etc: *He used to manage the bookshop on King Street.* **3** USE TIME/MONEY ▷ [T] to use or organize your time or money: *He's no good at managing his money.* **4** HAVE ENOUGH MONEY ▷ [I] to have enough money to live: *How can anyone manage on such a low income?*

manageable /'mænɪdʒəbl/ **adj** easy to control: *Are they going to reduce classes to a more manageable size?*

management /'mænɪdʒmənt/ **noun 1** [U] ⓑ② being in control of an office, shop, team, etc: *management skills/training* **2** [group] the people who are in control of an office, shop, team, etc: *middle/senior management*

> ✅ **Word partners for management**
>
> management **of** sth • management **skills** • **middle/senior** management

manager /'mænɪdʒə^r/ **noun** [C] ⓐ② someone in control of an office, shop, team, etc: *a sales manager* ∘ *She's the manager of the local sports club.*

managerial /ˌmænə'dʒɪəriəl/ **adj** relating to a manager or management: *managerial skills*

managing di'rector noun [C] mainly UK the main person in control of a company

mandate /'mændeɪt/ **noun** [C] formal support for action given to someone by the people voting for them: *The electorate have given them a clear mandate for social reform.*

mandatory /'mændət^əri/ **adj** formal If something is mandatory, it must be done.

mane /meɪn/ **noun** [C] the long, thick hair that grows on the necks of animals such as horses or lions

maneuver[1] US (UK **manoeuvre**) /mə'nuːvə^r/ **noun** [C] **1** a movement that needs care or skill

2 a clever action, usually done to trick someone: *a political/tactical maneuver*

maneuver[2] US (UK **manoeuvre**) /mə'nuːvə^r/ **verb** [I, T] to move with care or skill: *I find big cars difficult to maneuver.*

mangled /'mæŋgld/ **adj** badly crushed and damaged: *a mangled body*

mango /'mæŋgəʊ/ **noun** [C] (plural **mangoes, mangos**) ⓐ② a tropical fruit that has a green skin and is orange inside

manhood /'mænhʊd/ **noun** [U] the qualities related to being a man and not a boy

mania /'meɪniə/ **noun** [U] extreme enthusiasm or interest: *football mania*

maniac /'meɪniæk/ **noun** [C] informal someone who behaves in an extreme or uncontrolled way: *a sex maniac* ∘ *He drives like a maniac.*

manic /'mænɪk/ **adj** behaving in an excited and uncontrolled way

manicure /'mænɪkjʊə^r/ **noun** [C, U] a treatment for the hands to make them more attractive by cleaning and cutting the nails, etc

manifest[1] /'mænɪfest/ **verb** [T] formal to show a quality or condition: [often reflexive] *Grief manifests itself in a number of different ways.*

manifest[2] /'mænɪfest/ **adj** [always before noun] formal obvious: *her manifest lack of interest*

manifestation /ˌmænɪfes'teɪʃ^ən/ **noun** [C, U] formal something which shows that a quality or condition exists: *one of the manifestations of the disease*

manifesto /ˌmænɪ'festəʊ/ **noun** [C] a written statement that says publicly what a political group intends to do

manipulate /mə'nɪpjəleɪt/ **verb** [T] to control someone or something in a clever way so that they do what you want them to do: *She knows how to manipulate the press.* • **manipulation** /məˌnɪpjə'leɪʃ^ən/ **noun** [U]

manipulative /mə'nɪpjələtɪv/ **adj** A manipulative person controls people in a clever and unpleasant way: *a devious, manipulative little boy*

mankind /mæn'kaɪnd/ **noun** [U] ⓑ② all people considered as a group: *the history of mankind*

manly /'mænli/ **adj** having the qualities and appearance that people think a man should have: *a deep, manly voice*

man-made /ˌmæn'meɪd/ **adj** not natural, but made by people: *man-made fibres* ∘ *a man-made lake*

manned /mænd/ **adj** A place or vehicle that is manned has people working in it: *a manned space flight*

manner /'mænə^r/ **noun** [no plural] **1** ⓑ② the way in which a person talks and behaves with other people: *an aggressive/friendly manner* **2** ⓑ② the way something happens or something is done: *They dealt with the problem in a very efficient manner.*

> ✅ **Word partners for manner**
>
> in a [similar/traditional/professional, etc] manner • the manner of sth

mannerism /'mæn^ərɪz^əm/ **noun** [C] somethin

M

strange that someone often does with their face, hands, or voice, and that is part of their personality

manners /ˈmænəz/ noun [plural] ⑫ polite ways of behaving with other people: *bad/good manners* ∘ *table manners*

manoeuvre¹ UK (US **maneuver**) /məˈnuːvər/ noun [C] **1** a movement that needs care or skill **2** a clever action, usually done to trick someone: *a political/tactical manoeuvre*

> ☑ Word partners for **manoeuvre** noun
> carry out/perform a manoeuvre

manoeuvre² UK (US **maneuver**) /məˈnuːvər/ verb [I, T] to move with care or skill: *I find big cars difficult to manoeuvre.*

manpower /ˈmænˌpaʊər/ noun [U] the people needed or available to do a job: *a manpower shortage*

mansion /ˈmænʃən/ noun [C] a very large house

manslaughter /ˈmænˌslɔːtər/ noun [U] the crime of killing someone without intending to kill them

mantelpiece /ˈmæntəlpiːs/ noun [C] (also US **mantel**) the shelf above a fireplace (= place in a room where wood, etc is burned): *There was an old family photo on the mantelpiece.* → See colour picture **The Living Room** on page Centre 4

mantra /ˈmæntrə/ noun [C] an idea or belief that people often say but do not think about: *the mantra of 'democratic reform'*

manual¹ /ˈmænjuəl/ adj ⑫ using your hands: *manual labour/work* ∘ *a manual control/gearbox* • **manually** adv

manual² /ˈmænjuəl/ noun [C] ⑫ a book that tells you how to use something or do something

manufacture /ˌmænjəˈfæktʃər/ verb [T] ⑫ to produce something, usually in large numbers in a factory: *Local industries manufacture plastic products, boats, and clothing.* • **manufacture** noun [U] *the manufacture of computers/margarine*

manufacturer /ˌmænjəˈfæktʃərər/ noun [C] ⑫ a company that manufactures something: *a shoe manufacturer*

manufacturing /ˌmænjəˈfæktʃərɪŋ/ noun [U] ⑫ the production of something, usually in large quantities in a factory: *car/food manufacturing*

manure /məˈnjʊər/ noun [U] solid waste from animals that is used to make plants grow well: *cow/horse manure*

manuscript /ˈmænjəskrɪpt/ noun [C] a piece of writing or music that has been written, but not yet published

many /ˈmeni/ pronoun, quantifier **1** ⓐ used mainly in negative sentences and questions to mean 'a large number of': *I don't have many clothes.* ∘ *Were there many cars on the road?* ∘ *I've got so many things to do this morning.* ∘ *You've given me too many potatoes (= more than I want).* ∘ *There aren't as many people here as last year.* **2 how many** ⓐ used in questions to ask about the number of something: *How many hours a week do you work?* ∘ *How many do you want?* **3 as many as** used before a number or amount to show that the number or amount is large: *As*

> ⓘ Common learner error: **many, much,** or **a lot of**?
>
> **Many** is used with countable nouns in negative sentences and questions. **Much** is used with uncountable nouns in negative sentences and questions.
> *Do you have many friends?*
> *I don't earn much money.*
> **A lot of** can be used to mean **much** or **many**. In positive sentences it sounds formal to use **much** or **many**. You can use **a lot of** instead.
> ~~There was much enthusiasm for the project.~~
> *There was a lot of enthusiasm for the project.*

many as 6000 people may have been infected with the disease.

Maori /ˈmaʊəri/ adj relating or belonging to the original group of people who lived in New Zealand: *Maori culture* • **Maori** noun [C] a Maori person

map /mæp/ noun [C] ⓐ a picture that shows where countries, towns, roads, rivers, etc are: *a road map* ∘ *a large-scale map of Europe*

map

> ☑ Word partners for **map**
> read a map • a **detailed** map • a map of sth • be **(marked)** on a map • a **road** map

maple /ˈmeɪpl/ noun [C, U] a tree that has colourful leaves in the autumn and that produces a substance like sugar: *a **maple leaf*** ∘ **maple syrup**

mar /maːr/ verb [T] (**marring, marred**) formal to spoil something: [often passive] *The evening was marred by Meg's appalling behaviour.*

Mar written abbreviation for March

marathon /ˈmærəθən/ noun [C] **1** ⑫ a race in which people run for about 26 miles/42 km: *the London marathon* ∘ *a marathon runner* **2** a very long event: *a dance marathon*

marble /ˈmaːbl/ noun [U] hard, smooth stone that is often used for decoration: *green/pink marble* ∘ *a marble statue*

march¹ /maːtʃ/ noun [C] **1** an organized walk by a group to show that they disagree with something: *to go on a march* **2** the special type of walking that soldiers do

march² /maːtʃ/ verb [I] **1** to walk somewhere as a group to show that you disagree with something: *They marched to London to protest against government spending cuts.* **2** When soldiers march, they walk together with regular steps. **3 march off/up/down, etc** to walk somewhere fast, often because you are angry

March /maːtʃ/ noun [C, U] (written abbreviation **Mar**) ⓐ the third month of the year

mare /meər/ noun [C] a female horse

margarine /ˌmaːdʒəˈriːn/ ⓤ /ˈmaːrdʒərɪn/ noun [U] a yellow substance made from vegetable oil that you put on bread and use in cooking

margin /'mɑ:dʒɪn/ noun [C] **1** the difference between two amounts of time, money, etc, usually between people in a competition: *to win by a **narrow/wide margin*** ∘ *He took third place **by a margin of** seven minutes.* **2** an empty space down the side of a page of writing: *You can make notes **in the margin**.* **3 a margin of error** the amount by which a calculation can be wrong but still produce a good result: *a margin of error of 5 percent*

marginal /'mɑ:dʒɪnᵊl/ adj small and not important: *a marginal effect/improvement*

marginalize (also UK **-ise**) /'mɑ:dʒɪnᵊlaɪz/ verb [T] to treat someone or something as if they are not important: [often passive] *The poorest countries are increasingly marginalized from the world economy.*

marginally /'mɑ:dʒɪnᵊli/ adv by a small amount: *marginally more expensive*

marijuana /ˌmærɪ'wɑ:nə/ noun [U] (also **cannabis**) a drug that some people smoke for pleasure and that is illegal in many countries

marina /mə'ri:nə/ noun [C] an area of water where people keep their boats

marinade[1] /ˌmærɪ'neɪd/ noun [C,U] a mixture of oil, wine, herbs etc that you put food in before you cook it, to give it a pleasant flavour

marinade[2] /'mærɪneɪd/ verb [T] to marinate food

marinate /'mærɪneɪt/ verb [T] (also **marinade** /'mærɪneɪd/) to put food in a mixture of oil, wine, herbs, etc before cooking it, to give it a pleasant flavour

marine[1] /mə'ri:n/ adj [always before noun] found in the sea, or relating to the sea: *marine creatures/life* ∘ *marine biology*

marine[2] /mə'ri:n/ noun [C] a soldier who has been trained to fight at sea and on land: *the Marine Corps*

marital /'mærɪtᵊl/ adj [always before noun] relating to marriage: *marital problems*

marital status noun [U] whether or not someone is married: *The form asks for personal information such as name, date of birth, and marital status.*

maritime /'mærɪtaɪm/ adj [always before noun] relating to ships and sea travel: *a maritime museum*

mark[1] /mɑ:k/ noun **1** AREA ▷ [C] 🅱️ an area of dirt, damage, etc that is left on something: *You've got a black mark on your nose.* ∘ *He's **left dirty marks** all over the carpet.* **2** SCORE ▷ [C] 🅰️ mainly UK a number or letter that is written on a piece of work, saying how good the work is: *She always gets good marks in English.* **3** LEVEL ▷ [no plural] a particular level, degree, distance, etc: *They've just passed **the 5000m mark**.* ∘ *Interest rates are somewhere around the seven percent mark.* **4 a mark of sth** a sign or proof that something exists: *a mark of genius* ∘ *There was a*

*minute's silence everywhere **as a mark** of respect.*

IDIOMS **leave/make your mark** to do something that makes you successful or makes people notice you • **On your marks. Get set. Go** something that you say to start a running race • **be wide of the mark** to not be correct or accurate

→ See also **punctuation mark**, **quotation marks**

mark[2] /mɑ:k/ verb **1** HAPPEN ▷ [T] If an event marks the beginning, end, etc of something, it causes it, or happens at the same time as it: *H death marks the end of an era in television.* **2** CELEBRATE ▷ [T] If you mark an occasion, you do something to celebrate it: *They've declared Tuesday a national holiday to mark the 10th anniversary of Independence.* **3** SHOW A PLACE ▷ [T] 🅱️ to show where something is by drawing or putting something somewhere: *I've marked m street on the map for you.* **4** GIVE RESULTS ▷ [I, 🅱️ to check a piece of work or an exam, showing mistakes and giving a letter or number to say how good it is: *to mark essays* **5** DIRTY ▷ [T] to leave an area of dirt on something

PHRASAL VERB **mark sth out** to show the shape or position of something by drawing a line around it

marked /mɑ:kt/ adj very noticeable: *There has been a **marked improvement** since last year.* • **markedly** adv

marker /'mɑ:kər/ noun [C] **1** (also '**marker pen**) a thick pen used especially for writing on boards: *a black felt marker* → See colour picture **The Classroom** on page Centre 6 **2** a sign that shows where something is

market

market[1] /'mɑ:kɪt/ noun [C] **1** SELLING PLACE 🅰️ a place where people go to buy or sell things, often outside: *a cattle/fish/flower market* ∘ *market stall* **2** SHOP ▷ US a supermarket (= large shop that sells food) **3** BUSINESS ▷ the buying and selling of something: *the insurance/personal computer market* **4** BUYING GROUP ▷ all the people who want to buy particular product, or the area where they live: *South America is our largest market.* ◦ *Is there **a market for** (= will people buy) second-hand jewellery?* **5 on the market** available to buy: *His house has been on the market for over a year.* → See also **black market, flea market, free market, niche market, the stock exchange**

> 🗹 Word partners for **market**
>
> the market **is booming/is growing** • a market **collapses** • the market **in** sth

---

market² /ˈmɑːkɪt/ verb [T] to try to sell products using advertising or other ways of making people want to buy them: *Their products are very cleverly marketed.*

marketable /ˈmɑːkɪtəbl/ adj Marketable products or skills are easy to sell because people want them.

market 'forces noun [plural] the way that prices and wages are influenced by how many people want to buy a particular product and how much is available

marketing /ˈmɑːkɪtɪŋ/ noun [U] ⑫ the work of encouraging people to buy a product or service: *a career in marketing/**sales and marketing***

marketplace /ˈmɑːkɪtpleɪs/ noun **1 the market- place** in business, the buying and selling of products: *We have to learn to compete **in the** international **marketplace**.* **2** [C] an area in a town where there is a market

market re'search noun [U] the activity of finding out what people like about products and what new things they want to buy: *a market research company*

market ˌshare noun [C] the number of things that a company sells compared with the number of things of the same type that other companies sell

markings /ˈmɑːkɪŋz/ noun [plural] the shapes and colours on an animal or bird

mark-up /ˈmɑːkʌp/ noun [C] the amount by which the price of something is increased before it is sold again: *The usual mark-up on clothes is around 20%.*

marmalade /ˈmɑːməleɪd/ noun [U] a sweet, soft food made with oranges or lemons and often eaten on toast (= cooked bread)

maroon¹ /məˈruːn/ noun [U] a dark red-purple colour • **maroon** adj → See colour picture **Colours** on page Centre 12

maroon² /məˈruːn/ verb **be marooned** to be left somewhere where you cannot get away

marquee /mɑːˈkiː/ noun [C] **1** UK a large tent used for parties, shows, etc **2** US a large sign over a cinema or theatre that says what films or shows are playing

---

> 🗹 Word partners for **marriage**
>
> sb's marriage **breaks up/fails** • sb's marriage **to** sb • a **happy** marriage

---

marriage /ˈmærɪdʒ/ noun **1** [C, U] ⑪ the legal relationship of a man and a woman being a husband and a wife: *a **happy marriage*** **2** [C] ⑪ the ceremony where people become a husband and a wife: *a marriage ceremony/certificate*

married /ˈmærɪd/ adj **1** ⑫ A married man or woman has a wife or husband: *a **married couple*** ◦ *She's been **married to** David for nearly ten years.* ◦ *As far as I know, they're very happily married.* → Opposite **unmarried 2 get married** ⑫ to begin a legal relationship with someone as their husband or wife: *We got married last year.*

marrow /ˈmærəʊ/ noun **1** [C, U] UK a large vegetable that has dark green skin and is white on the inside **2** [U] (also **bone marrow**) the soft substance inside bones

marry /ˈmæri/ verb **1** [I, T] ⑪ to begin a legal relationship with someone as their husband or wife: ***Will you marry me?*** ◦ *He never married.* **2** [T] to officially make people become a husband and a wife in a ceremony: *We were married by our local vicar.*

Mars /mɑːz/ noun [no plural] the planet that is fourth from the Sun, after the Earth and before Jupiter

marsh /mɑːʃ/ noun [C, U] an area of soft, wet land

marshal /ˈmɑːʃəl/ noun [C] **1** someone who helps to organize or control a large public event: *race marshals* **2** an important officer in police or fire departments in the US → See also **field marshal**

marshmallow /ˌmɑːʃˈmæləʊ/ ⑩ /ˈmɑːrʃˌmæləʊ/ noun [C, U] a soft, white food made from sugar

martial art /ˌmɑːʃəlˈɑːt/ noun [C] ⑫ one of the traditional Japanese or Chinese skills of fighting, done as a sport in western countries

martial law /ˌmɑːʃəlˈlɔː/ noun [U] the control of a country by its army instead of by its usual leaders: *to declare martial law*

Martian /ˈmɑːʃən/ noun [C] in stories, someone from the planet Mars

martyr /ˈmɑːtər/ noun [C] someone who dies for their beliefs: *a Catholic martyr* • **martyrdom** noun [U] a situation in which someone dies for their beliefs

marvel¹ /ˈmɑːvəl/ noun [C] something really surprising, exciting, or good: *a marvel of modern technology*

marvel² /ˈmɑːvəl/ verb [I] (mainly UK **marvelling, marvelled**, US **marveling, marveled**) to admire something very much: *I'm just **marvelling at** your skills.*

marvellous UK (US **marvelous**) /ˈmɑːvələs/ adj ⑪ extremely good: *What a marvellous idea!* • **marvellously** UK (US **marvelously**) adv

Marxism /ˈmɑːksɪzəm/ noun [U] the political and economic ideas of Karl Marx

Marxist /ˈmɑːksɪst/ adj relating to Marxism: *Marxist ideology* • **Marxist** noun [C] someone who supports Marxism

mascara /mæsˈkɑːrə/ noun [U] a dark substance that you put on your eyelashes (= hairs that grow above and below your eyes) to make them look longer and thicker → See picture at **make-up**

mascot /ˈmæskɒt/ noun [C] a toy or a child that a person or a team takes with them to bring them luck: *He's our **lucky mascot**.*

masculine /ˈmæskjəlɪn/ adj **1** having qualities

M

---

that are typical of men: *a masculine appearance/ voice* **2** in some languages, belonging to a group of nouns or adjectives that have the same grammatical behaviour. The other groups are 'feminine' and 'neuter'.

masculinity /ˌmæskjəˈlɪnəti/ noun [U] the qualities that are typical of men

mash /mæʃ/ verb [T] to crush food until it is soft: *UK/US mashed potato/US mashed potatoes*

mask

mask¹ /mɑːsk/ noun [C] ⏚ a covering for the face that protects, hides, or decorates the person wearing it → See also **gas mask**

mask² /mɑːsk/ verb [T] to prevent something from being noticed: *I've had to put some flowers in there to mask the smell.*

masked /mɑːskt/ adj wearing a mask: *a masked gunman*

masochism /ˈmæsəkɪzᵊm/ noun [U] pleasure from being hurt • **masochist** noun [C] someone who gets pleasure from being hurt

masochistic /ˌmæsəˈkɪstɪk/ adj getting pleasure from being hurt: *masochistic behaviour*

masonry /ˈmeɪsᵊnri/ noun [U] the parts of a building that are made of bricks or stone

masquerade /ˌmæskᵊrˈeɪd/ verb

PHRASAL VERB **masquerade as sb/sth** to pretend to be someone or something: *She's just a teacher masquerading as an academic.*

Mass, mass /mæs/ noun [C, U] a religious ceremony in some Christian churches in which people eat bread and drink wine: *to go to Mass*

mass¹ /mæs/ noun **1** [C] a solid lump with no clear shape: *The sauce was now a sticky mass in the bottom of the pan.* **2 a mass of sth** ⏚ a large amount or number of something: *She had a mass of blond curls.* **3** [U] in physics, the amount of substance that something contains: *One litre of water has a mass of one kilogram.* **4 masses** informal ⏚ a large amount or number of something: *I've got masses of work to do.* **5 the masses** the ordinary people who form the largest part of society: *He failed to win the support of the masses.*

mass² /mæs/ adj [always before noun] involving a lot of people: *mass destruction/unemployment* ∘ *a mass murderer*

mass³ /mæs/ verb [I, T] formal to come together somewhere in large numbers, or make people or things do this: *Over 20,000 demonstrators massed in the town's main square.*

massacre /ˈmæsəkər/ noun [C] the killing of a lot of people: *He ordered the massacre of over*

2,000 women and children. • **massacre** verb [*Hundreds of civilians were massacred in the rai*

massage /ˈmæsɑːdʒ/ ⓤ /məˈsɑːdʒ/ noun [C, the activity of rubbing or pressing parts someone's body in order to make them rel or to stop their muscles hurting: *to ha a massage* ∘ *She gave me a foot massag* • **massage** verb [T] *Would you massag my shoulders?*

massive /ˈmæsɪv/ adj ⏚ very big: *a massi building* ∘ *massive debts*

mass-market /ˌmæsˈmɑːkɪt/ adj describ something that is made to be sold to as man people as possible • **ˈmass ˌmarket** noun [C]

the ˌmass ˈmedia noun [group] newspaper television, and radio

mast /mɑːst/ noun [C] **1** a tall pole on a boat th supports its sails **2** a tall metal pole that sen out television, radio, or mobile phone signals

master¹ /ˈmɑːstər/ noun [C] **1 IN CHARGE** ▷ ⏚ the past, a servant's master was the man th they worked for. **2 TEACHER** ▷ old-fashioned male teacher: *the Latin master* **3 SKILL** someone who does something very well: *P was a master of disguise.* **4 FOR COPYING** ▷ document or recording from which copies ca be made **5 Master of Arts/Science, etc** a high university qualification that usually takes 1 or more years of study after your first qualificatio or a person who has this qualificatio **6 Master's (degree)** ⏚ a higher universi qualification: *to study for a Master's degre* **7 Master** formal a title for a boy, used befo his family name or full name: *Master Thom Mills*

master² /ˈmɑːstər/ verb [T] to learn how to d something well: *to master a technique* ∘ *I lived for several years in Italy but never qui mastered the language.*

master³ /ˈmɑːstər/ adj [always before noun] havin the skills for a particular job: *a master che craftsman*

masterful /ˈmɑːstᵊfᵊl/ adj done with great ski *a masterful display* of golf

mastermind /ˈmɑːstəmaɪnd/ verb [T] to pla every detail of a complicated event or activi and make sure that it happens: *He allege masterminded both bomb attacks in the regio* • **mastermind** noun [C] *It is thought he was t mastermind behind* (= the person who planne last year's bombing campaign.

masterpiece /ˈmɑːstəpiːs/ noun [C] a paintin book, or film that is generally considered to of excellent quality: *'Mona Lisa' is wide regarded as Leonardo da Vinci's masterpiece.*

mastery /ˈmɑːstᵊri/ noun [U] **1 mastery of s** great skill or understanding of something: *h mastery of the Japanese language* **2 mastery over sth** control over something: *The tu countries battled for mastery over the region.*

masturbate /ˈmæstəbeɪt/ verb [I] to ma yourself feel sexually excited by rubbing yo sexual organs • **masturbation** /ˌmæstəˈbeɪʃᵊ noun [U]

mat /mæt/ noun [C] **1** a piece of thick materi

that you put on the floor, often in order to protect it: *There's a mat by the door for you to wipe your feet on.* **2** a small piece of plastic or other material that you put on a table so that hot plates and liquid will not damage it

match¹ /mætʃ/ **noun 1 GAME** ▷ [C] ⓐ a sports competition in which two people or teams compete against each other: *a football/tennis match* **2 FIRE** ▷ [C] ⓑ a thin, wooden stick that produces a flame when you rub one end of it against a rough surface: *a box of matches* **3 ATTRACTIVE** ▷ [no plural] If something is a good match for something else, it looks attractive next to it, usually because it is the right colour: *The curtains look nice – they're a perfect match for the sofa.* **4 RELATIONSHIP** ▷ [no plural] If two people who are having a relationship are a good match, they are very suitable for each other. **5 be no match for sb/sth** to not be as good as someone or something else: *Gibson ran well but was no match for the young Italian.*

> **☑ Word partners for match**
>
> play/lose/win a match • a match **against** sb • **in** a match

match² /mætʃ/ **verb 1 BE THE SAME** ▷ [I, T] ⓑ If two things match, they are the same colour or type: *I can't find anything to match my green shirt.* ∘ *Your socks don't match.* ∘ *Traces of blood found on Walker's clothing matched the victim's blood type.* **2 CHOOSE** ▷ [T] ⓑ to choose someone or something that is suitable for a particular person, activity, or purpose: *In the first exercise, you have to match the famous person to their country of origin.* **3 BE AS GOOD AS** ▷ [T] to be as good as someone or something else: *It would be difficult to match the service this airline gives to its customers.*

PHRASAL VERBS **match up** If two pieces of information match up, they are the same: *Their accounts of what happened that evening didn't match up.* • **match sb/sth up** to choose someone or something that is suitable for a particular person, activity, or purpose: *They look at your interests and try to match you up with someone suitable.* • **match up to sth** to be as good as something else: *Nothing that he wrote after this point ever matched up to his early work.*

matchbox /'mætʃbɒks/ **noun** [C] a small box containing matches

matching /'mætʃɪŋ/ **adj** [always before noun] having the same colour or pattern as something else: *She wore purple shorts and a matching T-shirt.*

mate¹ /meɪt/ **noun** [C] **1 FRIEND** ▷ UK informal ⓑ a friend: *She's my best mate.* ∘ *Pete was there with a couple of mates.* **2 TALKING TO A MAN** ▷ UK informal You call a man 'mate' when you are speaking to him informally: *Thanks, mate.* **3 ANIMAL** ▷ an animal's sexual partner

mate² /meɪt/ **verb** [I] When animals mate, they have sex in order to produce babies.

material¹ /mə'tɪəriəl/ **noun 1 SUBSTANCE** ▷ [C, U] ⓑ a solid substance from which things can be made: *building materials* ∘ *Crude oil is used as the*

raw material for making plastics. **2 CLOTH** ▷ [C, U] ⓑ cloth for making clothes, curtains, etc: *Her dress was made of a soft, silky material.* **3 INFORMATION** ▷ [U] the facts or ideas in a piece of writing: *I'm collecting material for an article that I'm writing.*

material² /mə'tɪəriəl/ **adj** relating to money and possessions and not emotions or thoughts: *the material world*

materialism /mə'tɪəriəlɪzᵊm/ **noun** [U] the belief that having money and possessions is the most important thing in life • **materialistic** /mə,tɪəriə'lɪstɪk/ **adj** believing in materialism

materialize (also UK **-ise**) /mə'tɪəriəlaɪz/ **verb** [I] If something does not materialize, it does not happen: *She was promised a promotion but it never materialized.*

materials /mə'tɪəriəlz/ **noun** [plural] the equipment that you need for a particular activity: *teaching/writing materials*

maternal /mə'tɜːnᵊl/ **adj 1** like a mother: *I've never had much of a maternal instinct* (= natural ability to be a good mother). **2** [always before noun] A maternal relation is part of your mother's family: *He's my maternal grandfather.*

maternity /mə'tɜːnəti/ **adj** [always before noun] related to pregnancy and birth: *maternity clothes*

maternity leave /mə'tɜːnəti,liːv/ **noun** [U] a period of weeks or months that a mother spends away from her usual job so that she can look after a new baby

math /mæθ/ **noun** [U] US short for mathematics

mathematical /,mæθᵊm'ætɪkᵊl/ **adj** ⓑ relating to mathematics: *a mathematical formula/ equation* • **mathematically adv**

mathematician /,mæθᵊmə'tɪʃᵊn/ **noun** [C] someone who studies mathematics

mathematics /,mæθᵊm'ætɪks/ **noun** [U] formal the study or science of numbers and shapes

maths /mæθs/ **noun** [U] UK ⓐ short for mathematics

matinée /'mætɪneɪ/ ⓤ /mætə'neɪ/ **noun** [C] an afternoon performance of a play or film

matrimony /'mætrɪməni/ **noun** [U] formal the state of being married

matron /'meɪtrᵊn/ **noun** [C] **1 NURSE** ▷ UK old-fashioned a female nurse in a school, or a female nurse who is in charge of other nurses in a hospital **2 WOMAN** ▷ US a married woman, especially one who is old or a widow (= woman whose husband has died) **3 PRISON/SCHOOL** ▷ US a woman who is a manager at some hospitals, schools, prisons, etc

matt UK (US **matte**) /mæt/ **adj** not shiny: *a matt photograph* ∘ *matt paint*

matter¹ /'mætər/ **noun 1 SUBJECT** ▷ [C] ⓑ a subject or situation that you need to think about, discuss, or deal with: *I've been thinking about this matter for a long time.* ∘ *He denied any knowledge of the matter.* ∘ *To make matters worse, our car broke down!* **2 SUBSTANCE** ▷ [U] the physical substances that exist in the universe **3 TYPE OF THING** ▷ [U] a particular type of substance or thing: *vegetable matter* ∘ *printed*

M

matter **4 what's the matter** ⓐ② used to ask or talk about the reason for a problem: *What's the matter with your leg?* **5 there's something/nothing the matter** ⓐ② used to say that there is/is not a problem: *There's something the matter with the washing machine.* **6 a matter of days/weeks/feet, etc** used in expressions describing how small a period of time or an amount is: *The aircraft missed each other by a matter of feet.* **7 a matter of confidence/luck/waiting, etc** If something is a matter of confidence/luck/waiting, etc, that is what you need for it to happen: *Learning languages is just a matter of hard work.* **8 no matter how/what/when, etc** ⓑ② used to emphasize that something cannot be changed: *I never manage to lose any weight, no matter how hard I try.* **9 as a matter of fact** ⓑ② used to emphasize that something is true, especially when it is surprising: *As a matter of fact, I used to live next door to him.* **10 a matter of course** If something happens as a matter of course, it always happens as part of the normal process or system: *Babies were tested for the disease as a matter of course.* **11 a matter of life and/or death** a serious situation where people could die: *Getting water to these people is a matter of life and death.* **12 it's only a matter of time** If you say that it is only a matter of time before something happens, you are sure it will happen but you do not know when.

IDIOM **be no laughing matter** If a subject is no laughing matter, it is serious and not something that people should joke about.

→ See also **subject matter**

> 🗹 Word partners for **matter**
>
> consider/discuss/pursue/raise/resolve a matter • on the matter (of sth)

matter² /ˈmætər/ **verb** [I] ⓐ② to be important, or to affect what happens: *It doesn't matter to me whether he comes or not.* ∘ *"I've forgotten to bring your book back." "It doesn't matter – there's no hurry."*

matter-of-fact /ˌmætərəvˈfækt/ **adj** not showing emotion when you talk about something: *a matter-of-fact tone/manner* • **matter-of-factly adv**

matting /ˈmætɪŋ/ **noun** [U] strong, rough material for covering floors

mattress /ˈmætrəs/ **noun** [C] the soft, comfortable part of a bed that you lie on

mature¹ /məˈtjʊər/ **adj 1** completely grown or developed: *sexually mature* ∘ *mature trees* **2** ⓑ② Mature people behave like adults in a way that shows they are well developed emotionally: *She seems very mature for thirteen.* → Opposite **immature**

mature² /məˈtjʊər/ **verb** [I] **1 AGE** ▷ to become completely grown or developed **2 BEHAVIOUR** ▷ to start to behave in a more mature way: *Girls mature sooner than boys.* **3 MONEY** ▷ If an investment (= money you have given to a bank or a company in order to make a profit) matures, you receive the money you have made from it.

ma,ture 'student noun [C] a college o university student who is older than the usua age

maturity /məˈtjʊərəti/ **noun** [U] **1** the quality o behaving like an adult, in a way which show that you are well developed emotionally: *Sh shows remarkable maturity for a child of 13.* **2** th time when someone or something is complete grown or developed: *Penguins reach maturit in late summer.*

maul /mɔːl/ **verb** [T] **1** If you are mauled by a animal, you are injured by its teeth or claw (= the sharp parts of its feet): [often passive] *H was mauled by a lion.* **2** to criticize someone o something very badly: [often passive] *His film wa mauled by critics.*

mausoleum /ˌmɔːsəˈliːəm/ **noun** [C] a buildin where dead people are buried

mauve /məʊv/ **noun** [U] a pale purple colou • **mauve adj**

maverick /ˈmævərɪk/ **noun** [C] someone wh thinks and behaves in an unusual way: *maverick cop/politician*

max¹ /mæks/ **adj 1** informal maximum (= th largest amount allowed or possible), often use after numbers: *The trip should take 30 minute max.* **2 to the max** informal as much as possibl *He lived life to the max.*

max² verb

PHRASAL VERB **max out** informal to use all that i available of something, especially money: *W maxed out our credit cards when we bought a that new furniture.*

maxim /ˈmæksɪm/ **noun** [C] a phrase that give advice: *Our company works on the maxim tha small is beautiful.*

maximize (also UK **-ise**) /ˈmæksɪmaɪz/ **verb** [T] t increase something as much as you can: *t maximize profits*

maximum¹ /ˈmæksɪməm/ **adj** [always befor noun] ⓑ① The maximum amount of somethin is the largest amount that is allowed or possibl *the maximum temperature/speed* → Opposit **minimum**

maximum² /ˈmæksɪməm/ **noun** [no plural] ⓒ the largest amount that is allowed or possibl *The school has a maximum of 30 students pe class.*

> 🗹 Word partners for **maximum**
>
> reach a maximum • a maximum of [10/50%, etc] • up to a maximum [of 10/50%, etc]

may /meɪ/ **modal verb 1** ⓑ① used to talk abou what is possibly true or will possibly happer *There may be other problems that we don't kno about.* ∘ *I think I may have a cold.* **2** formal ⓒ used to ask or give permission: *May I be excuse please?* ∘ *You may begin.* **3 may (well) ... bu** used to show that the first thing you say is no important when compared to another fact: *may be cheap but it's not very good.* → See Stud Page **Modal verbs** on page Centre 22

May /meɪ/ **noun** [C, U] ⓐ① the fifth month of th year

M

> **!** Common learner error: **may be** or **maybe**?
>
> **May be** is written as two separate words when **be** is used as a verb. Here **may** is being used as a modal verb.
>
> *I may be late this evening.*
>
> ~~I maybe late this evening.~~
>
> **Maybe** is an adverb, and is written as one word.
>
> *Maybe we should do it tomorrow.*
>
> ~~May be we should do it tomorrow.~~

maybe /ˈmeɪbi/ **adv 1** ⓐ possibly: *Maybe we're too early.* ◦ *It could take a month, or maybe more, to complete.* **2** ⓐ used to suggest something: *Maybe Ted would like to go.*

mayhem /ˈmeɪhem/ **noun** [U] a situation in which there is no order or control: *With five kids running around, it was complete mayhem.*

mayonnaise /ˌmeɪəˈneɪz/ **noun** [U] a thick, cold, white sauce that is made from eggs and oil

mayor /meər/ **noun** [C] ⓑ the person who is elected to be the leader of the group that governs a town or city

maze /meɪz/ **noun** [C] a complicated system of paths where you can easily become lost

MB written abbreviation for megabyte (= a unit for measuring the amount of information a computer can store): *This program needs 8 MB of hard-disk space.*

MBA /ˌembiːˈeɪ/ **noun** [C] abbreviation for Master of Business Administration: an advanced degree in business, or a person who has this degree: *a Harvard MBA*

McCoy /məˈkɔɪ/ **noun**

IDIOM **the real McCoy** informal the real thing, and not a copy or something similar: *Cheap sparkling wines cannot be labelled 'champagne' – it has to be the real McCoy.*

MD /ˌemˈdiː/ abbreviation for Doctor of Medicine

me /miː/ **pronoun** ⓐ used after a verb or preposition to refer to the person who is speaking or writing: *She gave me some money.* ◦ *She never gave it to me.* ◦ *Lydia is three years younger than me.* ◦ *It wasn't me!*

> **!** Common learner error: **me** or **I**?
>
> **Me** is used after 'than', 'as', or 'be'. It would sound very formal if you used **I**.
>
> *She's taller than me.*
>
> *David is not as tall as me.*
>
> *"Who's there?" "It's me."*
>
> ~~"Who's there?" "It's I."~~
>
> Sometimes **me** is used with another noun as the subject of a sentence, especially in informal English.
>
> *Jane and me went to the cinema yesterday.* (informal)
>
> *Jane and I went to the cinema yesterday.*

meadow /ˈmedəʊ/ **noun** [C] a field of grass, often with flowers

meagre UK (US **meager**) /ˈmiːgər/ **adj** not enough in amount: *a meagre ration/salary*

meal /miːl/ **noun** [C] ⓐ the time when you eat, or the food that you eat at that time: *a three-course meal*

IDIOM **make a meal of sth** UK to spend more time and energy doing something than is necessary: *A simple apology will do. There's no need to make a meal of it!*

→ See also a **square meal**

> **✓** Word partners for **meal**
>
> cook/eat/have/prepare a meal • a [two/three, etc.] **course meal**

mealtime /ˈmiːltaɪm/ **noun** [C] the time when you eat: *These days I only see him at mealtimes.*

mean¹ /miːn/ **verb** [T] (**mean** /ment/) **1** MEANING ▷ ⓐ to have a particular meaning: *What does 'perpendicular' mean?* ◦ *The red light means stop.* **2** EXPRESS ▷ ⓑ to intend to express a fact or opinion: *I didn't mean that as a criticism.* ◦ *What exactly do you mean by 'old-fashioned'?* **3 mean to do sth** ⓑ to intend to do something: *I didn't mean to hurt her.* **4** RESULT ▷ ⓑ to have a particular result: *These changes will mean better health care for everyone.* ◦ *[+ (that)] It doesn't mean that you can stop working.* **5** SERIOUS ▷ to be serious about something that you have said: *I'll take that sandwich away if you don't eat it properly – I mean it!* **6** IMPORTANT ▷ ⓑ to have an important emotional effect on someone: *You don't know what it means to me to get this letter.* ◦ *Their support has meant a lot to us.* **7 have been meaning to do sth** ⓑ to have been wanting and planning to do something: *I've been meaning to call you for weeks.* **8 be meant to do sth** If you are meant to do something, that is what you should do in order to behave correctly: *You're meant to shake the bottle first.* **9 mean well** to intend to behave in a kind way: *I know my parents mean well, but I wish they wouldn't interfere.* **10 I mean a** something people often say before they continue their sentence: *I mean, I don't dislike her.* **b** ⓐ something that you say in order to correct yourself: *We went there in May – I mean June.*

mean² /miːn/ **adj 1** UNKIND ▷ ⓑ unkind and unpleasant: *I thought my sister was being mean to me.* **2** NOT GENEROUS ▷ mainly UK ⓑ A mean person does not like spending money, especially on other people: *He's too mean to buy her a ring.* **3** VIOLENT ▷ mainly US A mean person or animal is strong and violent, and makes people frightened: *He's a big, mean guy.* **4** GOOD ▷ [always before noun] informal very good: *I make a mean spaghetti.* **5** AVERAGE ▷ [always before noun] In maths, a mean number is an average number: *Their mean age at death was 84.6.*

IDIOM **no mean** used to describe something very difficult: *Setting up a business in two days was no mean feat* (= was a difficult thing to do).

mean³ /miːn/ **noun** [no plural] formal the average

meander /miˈændər/ **verb** [I] **1 meander along/**

around/through, etc If a river, a road, or a line of something meanders, it has many curves: *The coast road meanders along the beach for miles.* **2 meander around/from/off, etc** to move around with no clear purpose: *We meandered around town for a couple of hours.*

meaning /ˈmiːnɪŋ/ *noun* **1** [C, U] ⓑ The meaning of words, signs, or actions is what they express or represent: *The word 'squash' has several meanings.* ◦ *The meaning of her gesture was clear.* **2** [U, no plural] ⓑ purpose or emotional importance: *She felt that her life had no meaning.*

☑ Word partners for **meaning**
different/hidden/precise/real/true meaning • convey/explain/grasp/understand the meaning of sth

meaningful /ˈmiːnɪŋfəl/ *adj* **1 USEFUL** ▷ ⓑ useful, serious, or important: *a meaningful discussion* **2 WITH MEANING** ▷ ⓑ having a clear meaning that people can understand: *a meaningful comparison/conclusion* **3 LOOK** ▷ intended to show a meaning, often secretly: *a meaningful look* • **meaningfully** *adv*

meaningless /ˈmiːnɪŋləs/ *adj* without any meaning or purpose: *He produced yet another set of meaningless statistics.*

means /miːnz/ *noun* **1** [C] (plural **means**) ⓑ a way of doing something: *We had no means of communication.* ◦ *It was a means of making money.* **2** [plural] money: *We don't have the means to buy the house.* **3 by no means; not by any means** not at all: *I'm not an expert by any means.* **4 by all means** something that you say when you are agreeing to let someone do something: *I have a copy of the report on my desk. By all means have a look at it.*

☑ Word partners for **means**
(as) a means of (doing) sth • the means by which sth happens/sb does sth

means-tested /ˈmiːnztestɪd/ *adj* mainly UK If an amount of money or an activity such as education is means-tested, it is only given to people who are poor enough: *means-tested benefits*

meant /ment/ past of mean

meantime /ˈmiːnˌtaɪm/ *noun* **in the meantime** ⓑ in the time between two things happening, or while something else is happening: *Your computer won't be arriving till Friday. In the meantime, you can use Julie's.*

meanwhile /ˈmiːnˌwaɪl/ *adv* ⓑ in the time between two things happening, or while something else is happening: *The mother is ill. The child, meanwhile, is living with foster parents.*

measles /ˈmiːzlz/ *noun* [U] an infectious disease that covers your skin in small, red spots → See also **German measles**

measurable /ˈmeʒərəbl/ *adj* If something is measurable, it is big enough to be measured: *Extra training has led to measurable improvements in performance.* → Opposite **immeasurable**

measure¹ /ˈmeʒər/ *verb* **1 JUDGE** ▷ [T] to judge the quality, effect, importance, or value of

something: *We will soon be able to measure the results of these policy changes.* ◦ *They measure the performance of three different engines.* **2 FIND SIZE** ▷ [T] ⓑ to find the size, weight, amount, or speed of something: *I've measured all the windows.* ◦ *The distances were measured in kilometres.* **3 BE SIZE** ▷ [I] ⓑ to be a certain size: *a whale measuring around 60 feet in length*

PHRASAL VERBS **measure sth out** to weigh or measure a small amount of something and remove it from a larger amount: *Use a hot spoon to measure out honey into a bowl.* • **measure up** to be good enough, or as good as something or someone else: *He did not measure up to the requirements of the job.*

measure² /ˈmeʒər/ *noun* **1** [C] ⓑ a way of achieving something or dealing with a situation: *This arrangement is only a temporary measure.* ◦ *We must take preventative measures to stop the spread of the disease.* ◦ *security measures* **2 a measure of sth** a good way of judging something: *Ticket sales are a good measure of a show's popularity.* **3 a/some measure of sth** formal an amount of something: *Bulletproof vests give some measure of protection.* **4** [U] a way of measuring something: *units of measure such as centimetres, grams and litres*

IDIOM **for good measure** as well as something you have already done or given to someone: *They stole his passport and wallet, and for good measure beat him unconscious.*

→ See also **tape measure**

measurement /ˈmeʒəmənt/ *noun* **1 PROCESS** ▷ [U] the process of measuring something **2 SIZE** ▷ [C] ⓑ the size and shape of something: *I've taken measurements of all the rooms.* **3 WAY OF MEASURING** ▷ [U] a way of measuring something: *SI units are the standard units of measurement used all over the world.*

meat /miːt/ *noun* [U] ⓐ muscles and other soft parts of animals, used as food: *I don't eat meat.* ◦ *red/white meat* → See colour picture **Food on page Centre 11**

meatball /ˈmiːtbɔːl/ *noun* [C] one of several small balls made of meat that has been cut into small pieces, which are eaten hot with a sauce

meatloaf (also **meat loaf**) /ˈmiːtləʊf/ *noun* [U] meat that has been cut into small pieces, mixed with other things, then shaped and baked in one piece

mecca /ˈmekə/ *noun* [no plural] a place where particular groups of people like to go because they feel happy there: *His Indiana bookstore became a mecca for writers and artists.*

mechanic /mɪˈkænɪk/ *noun* [C] ⓐ someone whose job is to repair machines: *a car mechanic*

mechanical /mɪˈkænɪkəl/ *adj* **1** ⓑ relating to or operated by machines: *a mechanical engineer* ◦ *a mechanical device* **2** If you do something in a mechanical way, you do it without emotion or without thinking about it: *a mechanical performance* • **mechanically** *adv*

mechanics /mɪˈkænɪks/ *noun* [U] the study of physical forces on objects and their movement

M

mechanism /ˈmekənɪzᵊm/ noun [C] **1** a part of a piece of equipment that does a particular job: *The clock's winding mechanism had broken.* **2** a system for achieving something, or the way that a system works: *We need a mechanism for resolving this sort of dispute.*

mechanized (also UK **-ised**) /ˈmekənaɪzd/ adj A mechanized organization or activity uses machines: *mechanized farming/production*

medal /ˈmedᵊl/ noun [C] ⬤ a metal disc given as a prize in a competition or given to someone who has been very brave: *a bronze medal* ○ *an Olympic medal* → See also **gold medal, silver medal**

medallist UK (US **medalist**) /ˈmedᵊlɪst/ noun [C] someone who has received a medal in a sports event: *an Olympic medallist*

meddle /ˈmedl/ verb [I] to try to influence people or change things that are not your responsibility: *He's always meddling in other people's business.*

the media /ˈmiːdiə/ noun [group] ⬤ television, newspapers, magazines, and radio considered as a group: *media coverage/attention* ○ *The issue has been much discussed in the media.* → See also **the mass media**

mediaeval /mediˈiːvᵊl/ adj another spelling of medieval (= relating to the period in Europe between about AD 500 and AD 1500)

median /ˈmiːdiən/ adj [always before noun] relating to the middle number or amount in a series: *the median age/income*

media player noun [C] a computer program that can store, copy, and play sound and picture files (= collections of information)

mediate /ˈmiːdieɪt/ verb [I, T] to try to find a solution between two or more people who disagree about something: *Negotiators were called in to mediate between the two sides.* • **mediation** /ˌmiːdiˈeɪʃᵊn/ noun [U]

mediator /ˈmiːdieɪtᵊr/ noun [C] someone who mediates between people who disagree about something

medic /ˈmedɪk/ noun [C] informal **1** UK a medical student or doctor **2** US someone who does medical work in a military organization

medical¹ /ˈmedɪkᵊl/ adj ⬤ relating to medicine and different ways of curing illness: *medical treatment* ○ *a medical student* ○ *She has a medical condition that makes it hard for her to work.* • **medically** adv

medical² /ˈmedɪkᵊl/ noun [C] UK (US **physical**) an examination of your body by a doctor to find out if you are healthy

medicated /ˈmedɪkeɪtɪd/ adj A medicated substance contains medicine: *medicated soap*

medication /ˌmedɪˈkeɪʃᵊn/ noun [C, U] medicine that is used to treat an illness: *Paolo is on medication to control his depression.*

medicinal /məˈdɪsɪnᵊl/ adj Medicinal substances are used to cure illnesses: *I keep some brandy for medicinal purposes.*

medicine /ˈmedɪsᵊn/ noun **1** [C, U] ⬤ a substance used to cure an illness or injury: *cough medicine* ○ *Have you taken your medicine*

medicine

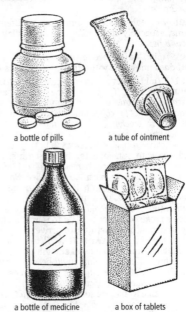

a bottle of pills   a tube of ointment

a bottle of medicine   a box of tablets

M

today? **2** [U] ⬤ the science of curing and preventing illness and injury: *to study medicine* ○ *western/Chinese medicine*

> ◪ Word partners for **medicine**
> take medicine • a medicine **for** sth

medieval (also **mediaeval**) /ˌmediˈiːvᵊl/ adj ⬤ relating to the period in Europe between about AD 500 and AD 1500: *medieval literature/art*

mediocre /ˌmiːdiˈəʊkᵊr/ adj not good in quality: *The acting was mediocre.* • **mediocrity** /ˌmiːdiˈɒkrəti/ noun [U]

meditate /ˈmedɪteɪt/ verb [I] **1** to think calm thoughts for a long period in order to relax or as a religious activity: *I meditate twice a day.* **2** formal to think seriously about something: *He meditated on the consequences of his decision.* • **meditation** /ˌmedɪˈteɪʃᵊn/ noun [U] *Let's now spend a few moments in quiet meditation.*

the Mediterranean /ˌmedɪtᵊrˈeɪniən/ noun the sea that has southern Europe, northern Africa, and the Middle East around it, or the countries around this sea • **Mediterranean** adj *a Mediterranean climate/island*

medium¹ /ˈmiːdiəm/ adj ⬤ in the middle of a group of different amounts or sizes: *people of medium weight* ○ *She bought a medium-sized car.* ○ *The shirt comes in small, medium, and large.*

medium² /ˈmiːdiəm/ noun [C] (plural **media, mediums**) a way of communicating or expressing something: *the medium of television/radio* ○ *The Internet has become yet another medium for marketing.*

medium-term /ˈmiːdiəmˌtɜːm/ adj continuing into the future for a time that is neither short nor long: *The medium-term outlook remains favourable.*

medley /ˈmedli/ **noun** [C] a mixture of different items, especially songs: *She sang **a medley of** show tunes.*

meek /miːk/ **adj** Someone who is meek is quiet and does not argue with others. • **meekly** adv

meet¹ /miːt/ **verb** (**met** /met/) **1** COME TOGETHER ▷ [I, T] **A1** to come to the same place as someone else by arrangement or by chance: *We met for coffee last Sunday.* ○ *I met my old English teacher while trekking in the Alps.* ○ *Each student **meets with** an adviser at the start of the school year.* **2** INTRODUCE ▷ [I, T] **A1** to see and speak to someone for the first time: *I've always wanted to meet a movie star.* ○ *"This is Helen." "Pleased to meet you."* → See Note at **know¹ 3** GROUP ▷ [I] **B1** If a group of people meet, they come to a place in order to do something: *The shareholders meet once a year to discuss profits.* **4** PLACE ▷ [T] **B1** to wait at a place for someone or something to arrive: *They met me at the airport.* **5** ENOUGH ▷ [T] to be a big enough amount or of a good enough quality for something: *This old building will never meet the new fire regulations.* ○ *Can your product **meet** the **needs** of a wide range of consumers?* **6** ACHIEVE ▷ [T] to be able to achieve something: *He **met** every **goal** he set for himself.* ○ *to **meet** a **deadline*** **7** JOIN ▷ [I, T] to join something: *There's a large crack where the ceiling meets the wall.* → See also **make ends (end¹) meet**

PHRASAL VERBS **meet up 1** to meet another person in order to do something together: *I **met up with** a few friends yesterday.* **2** If roads or paths meet up, they join at a particular place: *This path **meets up with** the main road.* • **meet with sth** to cause a particular reaction or result: *Both proposals have **met with** fierce opposition.* ○ *I trust the arrangements **meet with your approval** (= I hope that you like them).*

! Common learner error: **meet** or **visit**?

You **meet** a person, but not a place or thing.
I met John's parents for the first time last week.
You **visit** a person, place, or thing.
I visited my aunt today.
We visited Paris and the Eiffel Tower.

---

meet² /miːt/ **noun** [C] US a sports competition: *a swim/track meet* ○ *His final jump set a new **meet record**.*

meeting /ˈmiːtɪŋ/ **noun** [C] **1** **A2** an event where people come together for a reason, usually to discuss something: *We're **having** a **meeting** on Thursday to discuss the problem.* ○ *He's **in a meeting** – I'll ask him to call you back later.* **2** UK a sporting competition: *an international meeting*

✍ Word partners for **meeting**

arrange/attend/chair/convene/have/hold a meeting • an emergency/private/recent/urgent meeting • a meeting between sb • be **in** a meeting

---

mega- /megə-/ **prefix 1** informal extremely: *megarich* (= extremely rich) **2** one million: *4 megabytes*

megabyte /ˈmegəbaɪt/ **noun** [C] (written abbreviation **MB**) a unit for measuring the amount of information a computer can store, equal to 1,000,000 bytes

megaphone /ˈmegəfəʊn/ **noun** [C] a thing that you hold in your hand and speak into to make your voice louder

megapixel /ˈmegəˌpɪksəl/ **noun** [C] one million pixels (= small points that form part of the image on a computer screen), used to describe the amount of detail in images made by a digital camera, computer screen, etc

megawatt /ˈmegəwɒt/ **noun** [C] a unit for measuring electrical power, equal to 1,000,000 watts

melancholy /ˈmelənkɒli/ **adj** formal sad: *melancholy expression* • **melancholy noun** [U] formal a feeling of sadness

melanoma /ˌmeləˈnəʊmə/ **noun** [C] a type of skin cancer (= a serious disease) that appears as a coloured mark on the skin

melee /ˈmeleɪ/ **noun** [C] a situation where many people are behaving in a noisy, confused, and sometimes violent way: *In the melee his jaw was broken.*

mellow¹ /ˈmeləʊ/ **adj 1** pleasant and soft: *mellow voice* ○ *a mellow flavour/wine* **2** calm and relaxed: *After a few drinks, he became very mellow.*

mellow² /ˈmeləʊ/ **verb** [I, T] to become more relaxed and gentle, or to make someone become more relaxed and gentle: *Age has mellowed him.*

melodic /məˈlɒdɪk/ **adj** Melodic music has a pleasant tune, and melodic sounds are pleasant and like music.

melodrama /ˈmeləʊˌdrɑːmə/ **noun** [C, U] a story in which the characters show much stronger emotions than in real life

melodramatic /ˌmeləʊdrəˈmætɪk/ **adj** showing much stronger emotions than are necessary for a situation: *Don't be so melodramatic! It's only a scratch.*

melody /ˈmelədi/ **noun** [C] a song or tune

melon /ˈmelən/ **noun** [C, U] **A2** a large, round, sweet fruit with a thick, green or yellow skin and a lot of seeds → See colour picture **Fruit and Vegetables** on page Centre 10

melt /melt/ **verb 1** [I, T] **B2** If something melts, it changes from a solid into a liquid because of heat and if you melt something, you heat it until it becomes liquid: *The sun soon melted the ice on the pond.* ○ *The chocolate had melted in my pocket.* ○ *melted cheese* **2** [I] to start to feel love or sympathy, especially after feeling angry: *When he smiles at me, I just melt.* → See also **butter¹ wouldn't melt in sb's mouth**

PHRASAL VERBS **melt away** to disappear: *Then I saw her and all my fears just melted away.* • **melt down** If you melt something down, especially a metal object, you heat it until it changes to liquid.

---

eltdown /'meltdaʊn/ **noun** [C, U] **1** informal a situation of complete failure and no control: *economic meltdown* **2** a serious accident in which nuclear fuel melts through its container and escapes into the environment

elting ,pot noun [C] a place where people of many different races and from different countries live together

ember /'membər/ **noun** [C] ⓐ a person who belongs to a group or an organization: *family/staff members* ∘ *He was a member of the university rowing club.*

lember of 'Parliament noun [C] (plural **Members of Parliament**) a person who has been elected to represent people in their country's parliament

embership /'membəʃɪp/ **noun 1** [C, U] ⓑ the state of belonging to a group or an organization: *I've **applied for membership** of the union.* ∘ *a **membership card/fee 2** [group] the people who belong to a group or an organization: *Union membership is now over three million and rising.*

embrane /'membreɪn/ **noun** [C] a thin layer of tissue that covers some parts inside the body in order to protect, connect or separate them

emento /mɪ'mentəʊ/ **noun** [C] (plural **mementos, mementoes**) an object that you keep to remember a person, place, or event

emo /'meməʊ/ **noun** [C] a written message sent from one member of an organization to another

emoirs /'memwɑːz/ **noun** [plural] a written story of a person's own life and experiences

emorabilia /ˌmemərə'bɪliə/ **noun** [plural] objects relating to famous people or events that people collect: *an auction of pop memorabilia*

emorable /'memərəbl/ **adj** ⓑ If an occasion is memorable, you will remember it for a long time because it is so good: *a memorable performance* • **memorably** adv

emorandum /ˌmemər'ændəm/ **noun** (plural **memoranda**) formal a memo

emorial /mə'mɔːriəl/ **noun** [C] an object, often made of stone, that is built to help people remember an important person or event: *a **war memorial** ∘ *a **memorial service**

emorize (also UK **-ise**) /'memərɑɪz/ **verb** [T] to learn something so that you remember it exactly: *I've memorized all my friends' birthdays.*

emory /'memri/ **noun 1** ABILITY ▷ [C, U] ⓑ your ability to remember: *John has an amazing **memory for** historical facts.* ∘ *She had a **photographic memory** (= was able to remember every detail).* **2** THOUGHT ▷ [C] ⓑ something that you remember: [usually plural] *I have fond **memories** of my childhood.* **3** MIND ▷ [C, U] ⓑ the part of your mind that stores what you remember: *He recited the poem **from memory**.* **4 in memory of sb** If you do something in memory of a dead person, you do it to show your respect or love

for them: *They built a statue in memory of those who died in the fire.* **5** COMPUTING ▷ [C, U] ⓐ the part of a computer where information and instructions are stored, or the amount of information that can be stored there: *You need 32 megabytes of memory to run this software.*

'memory ,card noun [C] a device for storing information in computers or digital cameras

'Memory ,Stick noun [C] trademark a small electronic device designed to store information that can be put into a computer, mobile phone, etc

men /men/ plural of man

menace¹ /'menɪs/ **noun 1** [C] something that is likely to cause harm: [usually singular] *Drunk drivers are **a menace to** everyone.* **2** [U] a dangerous quality that makes you think someone is going to do something bad: *His eyes were cold and filled with menace.*

menace² /'menɪs/ **verb** [T] formal to cause harm to someone or something, or be likely to cause harm: *Hurricane Bonnie continued to menace the east coast.*

menacing /'menɪsɪŋ/ **adj** making you think that someone is going to do something bad: *a menacing gesture/voice*

mend¹ /mend/ **verb** [T] ⓑ to repair something that is broken, torn, or not working correctly: *I've mended that hole in your skirt for you.*

mend² /mend/ **noun be on the mend** informal If you are on the mend, your health is improving after an illness.

mendacious /men'deɪʃəs/ **adj** formal not telling the truth

menial /'miːniəl/ **adj** Menial work is boring, and not well paid or respected: *a **menial job/task**

meningitis /ˌmenɪn'dʒɑɪtɪs/ **noun** [U] a serious infectious disease that affects a person's brain and spinal cord (= the nerves in your back)

menopause /'menəʊpɔːz/ **noun** [U] the time, usually between the ages of 45 and 55, when a woman gradually stops having periods (= monthly blood from the uterus)

'men's ,room noun [C] US a room in a public place where there are men's toilets → See Note at **toilet**

menstrual /'menstruəl/ **adj** [always before noun] formal relating to menstruating: *a **menstrual cycle**

menstruate /'menstrueɪt/ **verb** [I] formal to have a monthly flow of blood from the uterus • **menstruation** /ˌmenstru'eɪʃən/ **noun** [U]

mental /'mentəl/ **adj** [always before noun] ⓑ relating to the mind, or involving the process of thinking: *mental health/illness* • **mentally** adv ⓑ *a mentally ill person*

mentality /men'tæləti/ **noun** [C] a person's opinions or way of thinking: *I can't understand the mentality of people who hunt animals for fun.*

M

mention¹ /'menʃən/ **verb** [T] **1** 🔵B1 to briefly speak or write about something or someone: *I'll mention your ideas to Caroline.* ○ *She didn't mention her daughter.* ○ [+ (that)] *He mentioned that he liked skydiving.* **2 not to mention** 🔵B2 used to emphasize the importance of something that you are adding to a list: *The resort has great hotels and restaurants, not to mention some of the best skiing in the region.*

> **❗ Common learner error: mention**
>
> No preposition is normally needed after the verb **mention**.
> *He didn't mention the price.*
> ~~He didn't mention about the price.~~

mention² /'menʃən/ **noun** [C] 🔵B2 a brief remark: *The report made no mention of the problem.*

> **✏ Word partners for mention noun**
>
> deserve/get/be worth a mention • make no mention of sth • a brief/passing/special mention • mention of sth

mentor /'mentɔːʳ/ **noun** [C] formal an experienced person who gives help and advice to someone with less experience

menu /'menjuː/ **noun** [C] **1** 🔵A2 a list of food and drinks that you can order in a restaurant: *a lunch/dinner menu* ○ *I ordered the most expensive thing on the menu* (= available in the restaurant). **2** 🔵A2 a list that appears on a computer screen of the choices available in a computer program: *a pop-up menu*

menu bar noun [C] a long, narrow area, usually at the top of a computer screen, that contains computer menus

menu option noun [C] one of the choices on a computer menu

meow /miːˈaʊ/ **noun** [C] US spelling of miaow (= the sound that a cat makes)

MEP /ˌemiːˈpiː/ **noun** [C] abbreviation for Member of European Parliament: a person who represents an area of a European country in the European Parliament: *the MEP for Glasgow*

mercenary¹ /'mɜːsənəri/ **noun** [C] a soldier who fights for any country or organization who pays them

mercenary² /'mɜːsənəri/ **adj** interested only in getting money or an advantage from a situation

merchandise /'mɜːtʃəndaɪz/ **noun** [U] formal goods that are traded, or sold in shops: *We stock a broad range of merchandise.*

merchandising /'mɜːtʃəndaɪzɪŋ/ **noun** [U] the selling of products relating to films, television programmes, and famous people

merchant¹ /'mɜːtʃənt/ **noun** [C] formal someone whose job is buying and selling goods, usually in large amounts: *a wine/grain merchant*

merchant² /'mɜːtʃənt/ **adj** [always before noun] relating to the trade of large amounts of goods: *a merchant ship/seaman*

merchant bank noun [C] a bank that organizes investments in companies or lends money to them • **merchant banker noun** [C]

mercifully /'mɜːsɪfəli/ **adv** used to show that you

are pleased that something unpleasant has be avoided: *Her illness was mercifully short.*

merciless /'mɜːsɪləs/ **adj** cruel, or showing kindness: *a merciless attack* ○ *She was mercil in her criticism of his work.* • **mercilessly adv**

mercury /'mɜːkjʊri/ **noun** [U] a heavy, silv coloured metal that is liquid at ordina temperatures

Mercury /'mɜːkjʊri/ **noun** [no plural] the pla that is closest to the Sun, before Venus

mercy /'mɜːsi/ **noun** [U] kindness that mak you forgive someone, usually someone that y have authority over: *The judge showed mercy.*

IDIOM **be at the mercy of sth/sb** to not be able protect yourself from something or someo that you cannot control: *Farmers are often at mercy of the weather.*

> **✏ Word partners for mercy**
>
> ask for/beg for/plead for mercy • show (no) mercy

mere /mɪəʳ/ **adj** [always before noun] **1** 🔵B2 used emphasize that something is not large important: *It costs a mere twenty dollars.* ○ *T mere thought of* (= Just thinking about) eati octopus makes me feel sick. **2 the merest** used emphasize that something is small, often wh it has an important effect: *She's upset by t merest hint of criticism.*

merely /'mɪəli/ **adv 1** 🔵B2 used to emphasize th you mean exactly what you are saying a nothing more: *I'm not arguing with you – I merely explaining the problem.* **2** used to emp size that something is not large, important, effective when compared to something else: *T medicine doesn't make you better, it merely sto the pain.*

merge /mɜːdʒ/ **verb** [I, T] If two or more thin merge, they combine or join, and if you mer two or more things, you combine or join the *The two companies merged, forming the larg brewery in Canada.* ○ *The city's smaller librar will be merged into a large, central one.*

merger /'mɜːdʒəʳ/ **noun** [C, U] an arrangeme in which two or more companies or organi tions join together

meringue /məˈræŋ/ **noun** [C, U] a light, swe food that is made by baking the white part an egg mixed with sugar

merit¹ /'merɪt/ **noun** [C, U] formal good qualiti that deserve praise: *His ideas have merit.* ○ debated **the merits of** using television in t classroom.* ○ *Every application has to be judg on its own merits* (= judged by considering t qualities of each).

merit² /'merɪt/ **verb** [T] formal to be importa enough to receive attention or punishment: *H crimes were serious enough to merit a pris sentence.*

mermaid /'mɜːmeɪd/ **noun** [C] an imagina creature that lives in the sea and has the upp body of a woman and the tail of a fish

merry /'meri/ **adj** showing enjoyment a

M

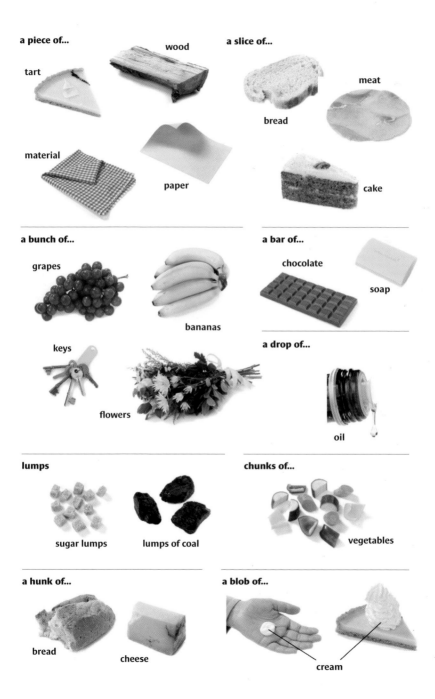

a piece of...
wood
tart
material
paper

a slice of...
meat
bread
cake

a bunch of...
grapes
bananas
keys
flowers

a bar of...
chocolate
soap

a drop of...
oil

lumps
sugar lumps
lumps of coal

chunks of...
vegetables

a hunk of...
bread
cheese

a blob of...
cream

THE KITCHEN

chopping board

toaster

bread bin *UK*,
bread box *US*

tin opener *UK*,
can opener *US*

food processor

grater

oven glove

kettle

blender

coffee maker

cupboard

tap *UK*,
faucet *US*

microwave

freezer

teapot

sink

fridge/
refrigerator

oven

sieve

dishwasher

cake tin *UK*,
cake pan *US*

rolling pin

scales *UK*,
scale *US*

utensils

saucepan

measuring
spoons

baking tray

frying pan

shower

shower curtain

bathroom cabinet *UK*,
medicine cabinet *US*

towel

cistern *UK*,
tank *US*

soap

toilet roll *UK*,
toilet paper *US*

sink

bath *UK*,
bathtub *US*

toilet

scales *UK*,
scale *US*

bath mat

toothbrush

nail brush

toothpaste

razor

cotton wool *UK*,
cotton *US*

electric razor

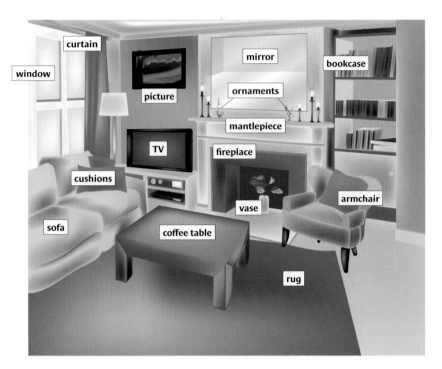

curtain

window

mirror

bookcase

picture

ornaments

mantlepiece

TV

fireplace

cushions

armchair

vase

sofa

coffee table

rug

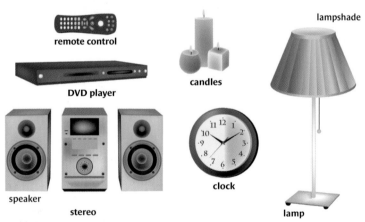

remote control

DVD player

candles

lampshade

speaker

stereo

clock

lamp

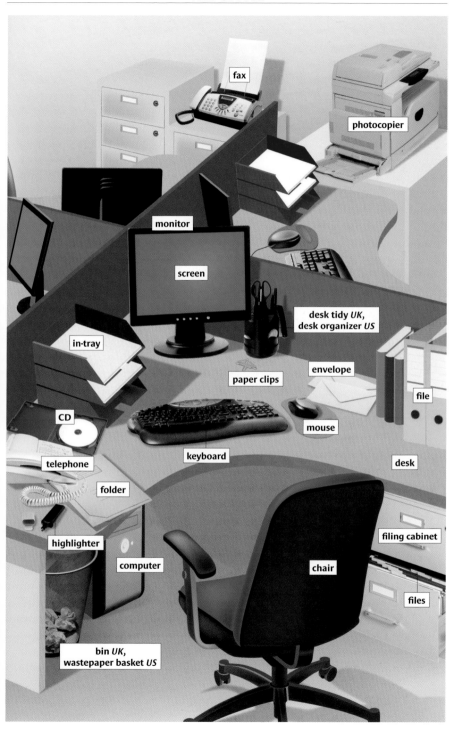

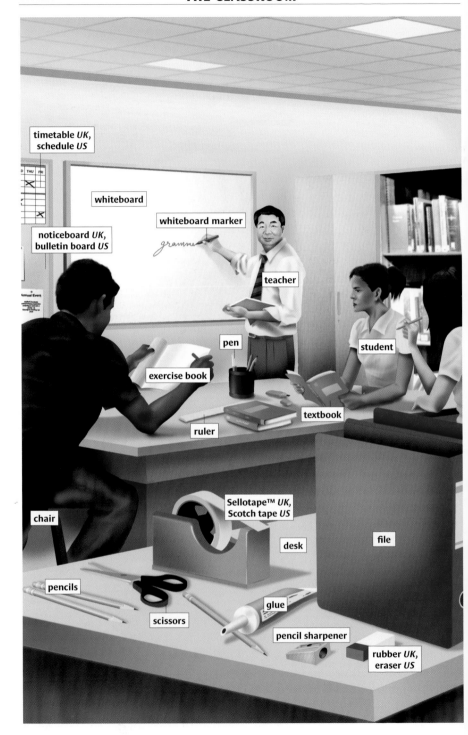

aerial *UK*, antenna *US*

rear window

number plate *UK*, license plate *US*

bonnet *UK*, hood *US*

boot *UK*, trunk *US*

indicator *UK*, turn signal *US*

tyre *UK*, tire *US*

rear light *UK*, tail light *US*

exhaust *UK*, tailpipe *US*

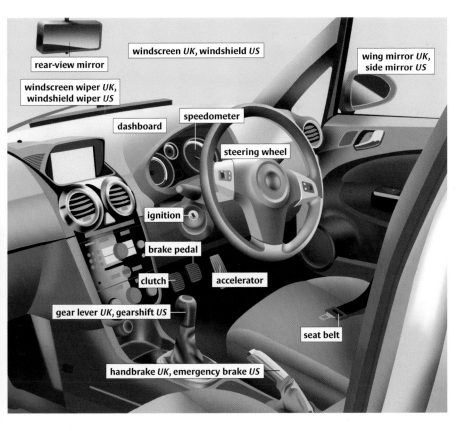

rear-view mirror

windscreen *UK*, windshield *US*

wing mirror *UK*, side mirror *US*

windscreen wiper *UK*, windshield wiper *US*

dashboard

speedometer

steering wheel

ignition

brake pedal

clutch

accelerator

gear lever *UK*, gearshift *US*

seat belt

handbrake *UK*, emergency brake *US*

CLOTHES

jacket

cardigan

sweater

halter top

trousers *UK*, pants *US*

jeans

skirt

miniskirt

suit

salwar kameez

t-shirt

shorts

dress

pyjamas

slippers

sweatshirt

fur collar

coat

hood

mac *UK*, raincoat *US*

boots

jacket

hoodie

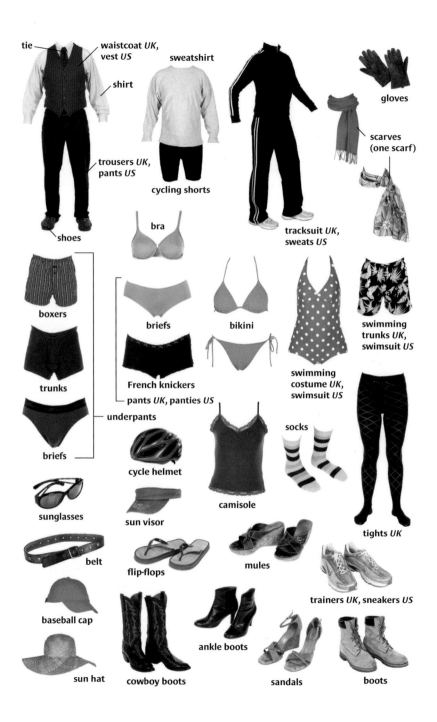

tie
waistcoat *UK*, vest *US*
sweatshirt
shirt
gloves
scarves (one scarf)
trousers *UK*, pants *US*
cycling shorts
shoes
bra
tracksuit *UK*, sweats *US*
boxers
briefs
bikini
swimming trunks *UK*, swimsuit *US*
trunks
French knickers
pants *UK*, panties *US*
swimming costume *UK*, swimsuit *US*
underpants
socks
briefs
cycle helmet
camisole
tights *UK*
sunglasses
sun visor
belt
flip-flops
mules
trainers *UK*, sneakers *US*
baseball cap
ankle boots
sun hat
cowboy boots
sandals
boots

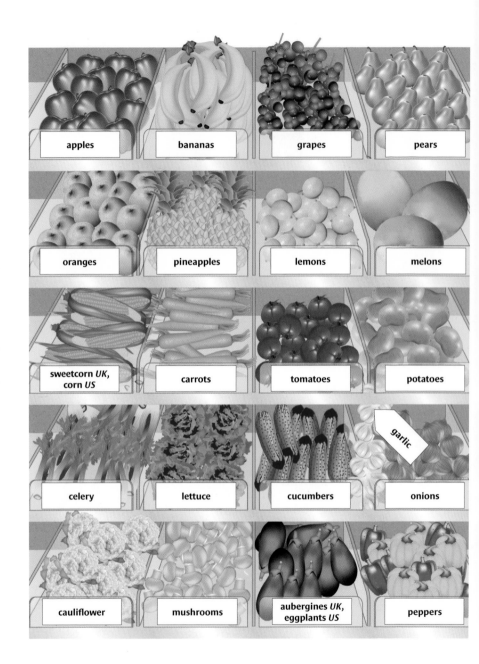

apples

bananas

grapes

pears

oranges

pineapples

lemons

melons

sweetcorn *UK*, corn *US*

carrots

tomatoes

potatoes

celery

lettuce

cucumbers

garlic

onions

cauliflower

mushrooms

aubergines *UK*, eggplants *US*

peppers

FOOD

roll *UK*,
sandwich *US*

sandwich *UK & US*

soup

biscuits *UK*,
cookies *US*

cake

salad

vegetables

pizza

rice

chips *UK*,
french fries *US*

cereal

pasta

honey

jam

crisps *UK*,
chips *US*

peanuts

eggs

butter

fish

yoghurt

cheese

meat

COLOURS

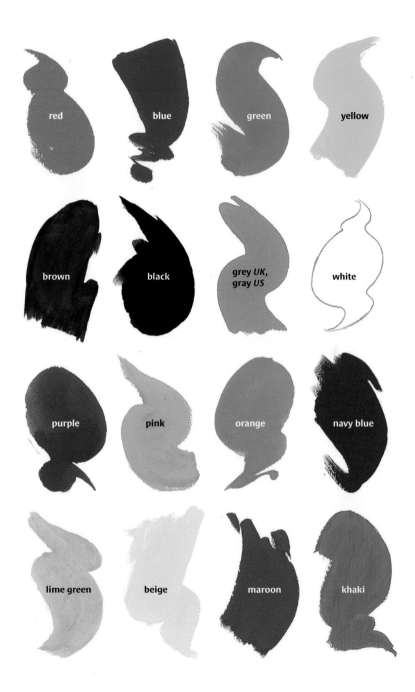

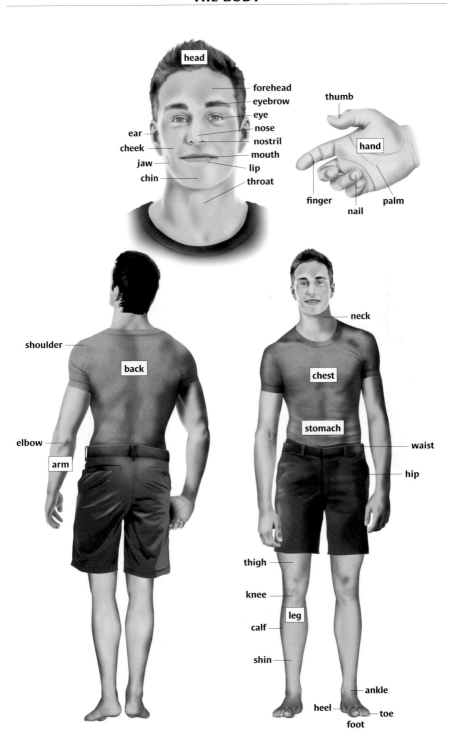

SPORTS (1)

athletics *UK*, **track and field** *US*

javelin

boxing

skiing

goggles

pole

running

skis

high jump

boxing gloves

snowboarding

ice hockey

ice skating

snowboard

puck

skateboarding

skateboard

rollerblading

rollerblades/
inline skates

skate

swimming   lane

horse riding *UK*,
horseback riding *US*

rider

reins

saddle

goggles   cap

football *UK*, **soccer** *US* — goal goalkeeper — referee

American football *UK*, **football** *US* — goal post — helmet

rugby

golf — club

cricket — batsman — bowler — stumps

basketball — backboard — basket

baseball — cap — glove/mitt — pitcher — batter

tennis — racket — net

cycling — helmet — bicycle

net — **volleyball**

PHRASAL VERBS

wake up

get up

put on

take off

lie down

sit down

stand up

put down

pick up

throw away

put away

wash up

tell off

eat out

turn on

turn off

get on

get off

fall over

work out

Extra help pages

Checking your work

There are many ways that this dictionary can help you avoid common mistakes.

Common Learner Error notes

Words that often cause difficulty for learners of English have special common learner error notes explaining how to use them correctly. These are all based on the *Cambridge Learner Corpus*.

1 Correct the following sentences by looking up the underlined word and reading the Common Learner Error notes for that word:

  1 The new rule affects to everyone.
  2 What hour is it?
  3 It's quiet hot in here.
  4 Where can I find informations about volcanoes?

Grammar

Always check the grammar of the words you want to use. There is an explanation of all the grammar labels on page xiii, and the Extra help pages on **Countable and uncountable nouns** and **Verb patterns** will help you too.

Using the right words

Look carefully at the example sentences in the dictionary entries. They will show you how words are used in typical situations. When a word is often used with another word we call it a *collocation* or *word partner*. These collocations or word partners are shown in **bold type** in the example sentences.

2 Fill in the gaps in these sentences by looking at examples at the entry for the underlined word:

  1 You must _____ your homework before you go out.
  2 Shall we _____ a taxi to the station?
  3 He has no chance _____ getting there on time.
  4 I'm _____ rather ill this morning.

  → See also Extra help pages **Punctuation** on page Centre 33, **Spelling** on page Centre 34, **What is a collocation/word partner?** on page Centre 41

3 There are seven mistakes in the paragraph below. Can you find them and correct them?

Ancient tribes moved to the area hundreds of years ago, bringing sheeps and cattle with them. They also hunted deer and catched fish, and learned grind wheat to make loafs of bread. They builded simple houses with mud walls and roofs made of sticks, and in the evenings, they sung songs and told storys around the fire.

Classroom language

Asking about words

What does 'impatient' mean?

How do you say _____ in English?

How do you spell 'castle'?

How do you pronounce this word?

What's the past tense/past participle of 'lie'?

Can you give me an example?

Could you say that again, please?

Asking about activities

I'm sorry, I don't understand what we have to do.

Can you repeat the instructions please?

Could you repeat that, please?

Could you speak more slowly, please?

Could I borrow a pen/pencil, please?

Can you lend me a pen/pencil, please?

How long do we have to do this?

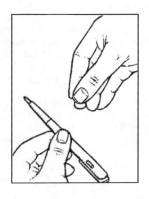

Classroom instructions

Open your books at page 28.

Turn to page 40.

Close your books.

Work in pairs/groups of three, four, etc.

Listen to the tape, then try to answer the questions.

Write the answers on a piece of paper.

Work with your partner.

Look up these words in your dictionary.

No talking, please.

Hand in your homework as you leave.

Countable and uncountable nouns

Countable nouns can have *a/an* or *the* before them and can be used both in the singular and the plural:	**Uncountable nouns** cannot have *a/an* before them and cannot be used in the plural:
▶ *There's a* **plate***, three* **spoons** *and a* **cup** *on the* **table***.*	▶ *We have* **rice** *and some* **cheese** *but we haven't any* **wine***.*

In this dictionary, countable nouns have the symbol [C], and uncountable nouns have the symbol [U].

1 Are these sentences correct? Look up the noun that is <u>underlined</u>.

1 We get a lot of English <u>homeworks</u>.
2 I've got some <u>sands</u> in my shoe.
3 They bought some new <u>equipment</u>.
4 Can I have some more <u>pasta</u>?
5 She carried my <u>luggages</u> to the taxi.

2 Some of these sentences need 'a' or 'an' in the gaps. Put them in if necessary.

1 Why are you taking _____ umbrella? It's not raining.
2 I had _____ soup and _____ bread roll for lunch.
3 It was _____ good idea to have a party.
4 She's looking for _____ work in Madrid.
5 I often go to her for _____ advice.

Top 10 uncountable noun errors

In the *Cambridge Learner Corpus* these are the ten most common uncountable nouns that intermediate students try to make plural by adding an 's'. Try to remember that these nouns cannot be used in the plural.

1	information	5	transport	8	knowledge
2	equipment	6	homework	9	countryside
3	advice	7	paper (= material used for writing on)	10	stuff
4	furniture				

Some and any

You can use **some** and **any** with plural countable nouns:	You can use **some** and **any** with uncountable nouns:
▶ *There are* **some cakes** *left.*	▶ *I'd like* **some sugar** *in my coffee.*
▶ *Are there* **any biscuits***?*	▶ *Is there* **any water** *in the jug?*

3 Fill in the gaps with a noun from the box:

chair	suitcase	fly	rice	furniture
day	weather	accidents	luggage	

1 There's a _____ in my soup.
2 I have to buy some _____ for my new house.
3 I haven't got much _____ with me. Just this bag.
4 It's a sunny _____ today.
5 There weren't any _____ on the roads yesterday.

Much, many, a lot of, a few

You can use **many** and **a few** with plural countable nouns:

▶ *Did you take **many photographs**?*

▶ *I've got **a few friends** who live in London.*

You can use **much** with uncountable nouns:

▶ *I haven't got **much news** to tell you.*

You can use **a lot of** with both plural countable nouns and with uncountable nouns:

▶ *Did you take **a lot of photographs**?*

▶ *I haven't got **a lot of news** to tell you.*

NOTE: **Many** and **much** are used especially in questions and negatives.

4 Which of the underlined parts of these sentences is right? Put a circle around the correct part.

1 Hurry up! We haven't got many/a lot of time.
2 I don't eat much/many chocolate.
3 I didn't take much/many photographs.
4 I don't listen to much/many classical music.

Nouns which can be both countable and uncountable

Some nouns can be countable or uncountable, depending on how they are used:

▶ e.g.: *a fish/fish, a glass/glass, a hair/hair, a chocolate/chocolate*

You can use them as **countable** nouns to talk about particular things:

▶ *There are **some glasses** on the table.*

▶ *I caught **a fish** at the lake.*

You can use them as **uncountable** nouns to talk about the thing in general:

▶ *Careful. There's broken **glass** on the floor.*

▶ *I'd like **fish** and chips for dinner.*

5 Look at the items below. How many of them can be used as countable and uncountable nouns?

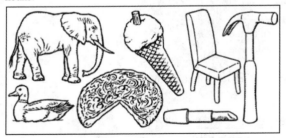

It is important to check the symbols [C], [U] and [C, U] for every meaning of a word, because the same word can be countable for some meanings and uncountable for others. For example, look at these entries for 'thread' and 'fibre'.

thread¹ /θred/ noun **1** MATERIAL ▷ [C, U] a long, thin piece of cotton, wool, etc that is used for sewing: *a needle and thread* **2** CONNECTION ▷ [C] the connection between different events or different parts of a story or discussion: *By that point I'd **lost the thread** of the conversation.* **3** INTERNET ▷ [C] a group of pieces of writing on the Internet in which people discuss one subject

fibre UK (US **fiber**) /ˈfaɪbər/ noun **1** CLOTH ▷ [C, U] cloth made from thin threads twisted together: *Man-made fibres like nylon are easy to wash.* **2** THIN THREAD ▷ [C] one of the thin threads that forms a substance such as cloth: *The fibres are woven into fabric.* **3** FOOD ▷ [U] the substance in plants that cannot be digested and helps food pass through your body: *Broccoli is a good source of fibre.* **4** BODY ▷ [C] a structure like a thread in your body: *muscle/nerve fibres*

Modal verbs

A modal verb is a verb that is used before another verb to express meanings such as ability, permission, possibility, necessity or advice. These pages will show you some of the uses of modal verbs. Look at their dictionary entries for more information.

These are the main modal verbs of English:

MODAL VERB	SHORT FORM	NEGATIVE	SHORT FORM
can		cannot	can't
could		could not	couldn't
may		may not	
might		might not	mightn't
must		must not	mustn't
ought to		ought not to	oughtn't to
shall		shall not	shan't
will	'll	will not	won't
would	'd	would not	wouldn't

We also use **need** and **have to** as modal verbs.

Saying how certain you think something is

This is an important use of some modal verbs. Look at the sentences below:

The speaker is sure that John has the car:
▶ *The car's not here – John **must** have taken it.*

The speaker thinks this is Clare's sister but is not sure:
▶ *She **might/could** be Clare's sister. She looks a lot like her.*

The speaker thinks it is not possible that the metal is real silver:
▶ *It **can't** be real silver – it's too cheap.*

The speaker is sure that Harry will be there:
▶ *If Harry promised to come, he **will** come.*

The speaker thinks it is possible that the rain will stop later:
▶ *Let's wait a bit – the rain **may** stop later.*

1 Fill in the gaps in these sentences with a word from the box:

may	will	mustn't	can't	might not

1 If we don't hurry, we _____ get there on time.
2 Don't worry. Everything _____ be fine.
3 You _____ forget to lock the door.
4 He _____ have failed his exams – he's always top of the class.
5 We_____ have to catch a later train – I'm not sure.

Expressing instructions, advice, permission, and necessity

Modal verbs are also used to:

give instructions or to say that something is necessary
▶ You **must** wear a helmet when riding a bike.
▶ You **mustn't** smoke in here.
▶ I **have to** be at the dentist at 3 o'clock.
▶ You **needn't** shut the door.

give advice or to express a strong opinion
▶ You **should/ought to** go to bed if you're tired.
▶ She **shouldn't** worry about me.

give and ask for permission
▶ She **can** borrow my dress.
▶ **Can/May/Could** I open the window?

2 Match the sentences on the left with the use on the right:

1 You can borrow my camera if you like.   a instructions
2 If you feel very ill you should go to the doctor.   b permission
3 You must lock the door.   c necessary
4 You don't need to bring food – just something to drink.   d advice
5 I need to make a phone call before I go out.   e not necessary

Same word, different use

Each modal verb has more than one use. The dictionary tells you what they are.

3 Look at the modal verb **can** in these sentences and match each use to a word on the right.
Use the dictionary to help you.

1 **Can** you hand out these books for me, please?   a possible
2 You **can** leave early today.   b offering
3 I **can't** speak Russian.   c permission
4 **Can** you get to work by train?   d asking
5 **Can** I help you with those bags?   e ability

Forming modal verbs

Modal verbs are always followed by a main verb and cannot be used as a main verb by themselves.

▶ I **must make** a phone call. / We **won't wait** for you.

They do not use **do** and **did** to form questions, negatives, and short answers.

▶ 'He **wouldn't** steal anything, would he?' 'Oh yes he **would**.'

Phrasal verbs

What are phrasal verbs?

A phrasal verb is a verb followed by one or two adverbs or prepositions, which together make a meaning that is usually impossible to guess from the meanings of the words on their own.

Look at the meanings of these common phrasal verbs:

break down	If a machine or vehicle breaks down, it stops working.
look forward to something	to feel happy and excited about something that is going to happen
pick sth up	to lift something by using your hands

Of course, verbs are often used with their normal meanings with adverbs and prepositions too, e.g.:

▶ I **went into** the classroom.

▶ He **put** the book **on** the desk.

These are not phrasal verbs. They are just the normal meaning explained at the entries for the verbs, adverbs and prepositions.

Finding phrasal verbs

In this dictionary, phrasal verbs follow the entry for the main verb, and are in alphabetical order. For instance, the phrasal verb 'lose out' comes after all the meanings of the verb 'lose'.

1 Look at the dictionary entries for the following verbs. How many phrasal verbs can you find formed with these verbs?

   1 drag   2 hand   3 pack   4 make

2 Use the dictionary to help you fill in the gaps in the sentences below to make phrasal verbs.

   1 If you carry _____ spending like that you'll have no money left.
   2 I nodded _____ after lunch.
   3 The brakes suddenly seized _____.
   4 It took him a long time to get _____ her death.

Phrasal verbs with more than one meaning

A phrasal verb can have more than one meaning. Often, the meanings are not related:

▶ Just **pick up** the phone and ring her! (pick up = lift)

▶ She **picks up** languages really easily. (pick up = learn)

3 Write two sentences for each of these phrasal verbs, using different meanings for each sentence:

   turn out   catch on   come under sth   fall apart

The grammar of phrasal verbs

Some phrasal verbs have objects, some do not, and some sometimes have objects and sometimes do not. This is shown in the way the phrasal verb is written in the dictionary. The dictionary also shows you whether the object is a person, a thing, or an action.

Phrasal verbs that do not need an object are shown like this:

hurry up   ▶ *Hurry up, or we'll be late!*

If a phrasal verb needs an object, the dictionary shows whether the object is 'something' (sth) or 'somebody' (sb). Here are some examples:

go over sth   ▶ *Let's go over the figures one more time.*

look up to sb   ▶ *He really looks up to his brother.*

make sb/sth out   ▶ *I could just make Julie out at the back of the room.*

                           ▶ *I could make out a faint mark on the wood.*

Phrasal verbs that sometimes use an object and sometimes do not use an object are shown like this:

pack (sth) up   ▶ *I packed up all my belongings and left the house.*

                           ▶ *Could you help me pack up?*

Some phrasal verbs have two objects. They are shown like this:

put sth down to sth ▶ *We put his bad temper down to tiredness.*

Prepositions following phrasal verbs

Many phrasal verbs are often followed by a particular preposition. This is shown in **bold type** in an example:

▶ *He dressed up as a ghost.*

4 Fill in the gaps in these sentences with the correct prepositions.

1 She stood in _____ her boss while he was sick.
2 Just carry on _____ your work.
3 She looked back _____ her days as a student with nostalgia.
4 He's always going on _____ his car.
5 We will have to cut back _____ our spending.

Idioms

Idioms are groups of words that together have a meaning that is different from the usual meanings of the words on their own. It is often impossible to guess what idioms mean. They are used in all types of language, but especially in informal situations. Idioms often have a stronger meaning than ordinary words. For example, 'be at loggerheads with someone' has more emphasis than 'be arguing with someone', but they mean the same thing.

Finding idioms in this dictionary

Most idioms are found at the entry for the first noun in the idiom.

1 Underline the first noun in each idiom on the left.

Then match each idiom with its meaning on the right.

1 be up to your neck in sth	a try to do something you cannot achieve
2 the final nail in the coffin	b be very busy
3 fight a losing battle	c have nothing to do
4 be at a loose end	d not laugh
5 keep a straight face	e something that causes failure

If the idiom does not contain a noun, try the first verb or adjective. But don't worry if you do not know where to look for an idiom. If you look in the wrong place, you will find an arrow telling you where to go.

> **breathe** /briːð/ verb [I, T] ⑤ to take air into and out of your lungs: *breathe in/out* ∘ *breathe deeply* → See also **be breathing down sb's neck**, **not breathe a word¹**

2 The following sentences all use idioms that contain a part of the body. Choose a body part from the box below to complete each sentence.

> head   face   arm   leg   ear

1 The accident was clearly his fault – he doesn't have a _____ to stand on.
2 Most of her lecture went over my _____ .
3 Dad might lend you his camera if you twist his _____ .
4 I've never taught this class before, so I'll have to play it by _____ .
5 When I saw his hat, I could hardly keep a straight _____

Verb patterns

Some verbs must have something (an object) after them:	Other verbs don't need anything after them:
▶ She put **the cup** on the table.	▶ He **fell**.
▶ Did you **bring** any **money**?	▶ They don't want to **stay**.
These verbs are **transitive** verbs. They are marked [T] in the dictionary.	These verbs are **intransitive** verbs. They are marked [I] in the dictionary.

Some verbs can be both transitive and intransitive:

▶ We **sold three cars** today. [T]   ▶ Her new novel is **selling** well. [I]

▶ Did you **pay the bill?** [T]   ▶ Have you **paid?** [I]

1 Look up these verbs in the dictionary to find out if they are transitive or intransitive or both.

1 like	3 drive	5 tell	7 hate	9 fall
2 hear	4 smoke	6 explain	8 play	10 hit

Sometimes a verb has to be followed by other grammar patterns, for example an infinitive verb, or a verb ending **-ing**:

[+ to do sth]   ▶ I **promise to help** you.

[+ doing sth]   ▶ Have you **finished reading** the newspaper?

[+ (that)]   ▶ He **told** me **(that)** it was safe.

These patterns are shown in the dictionary entries, at the beginning of the entry if they are *always* used, and in example sentences if they are *often* used. There is a full explanation of all the grammar codes on page xiii.

Some verbs are followed by particular prepositions. These are shown in **bold type** in the example sentences in this dictionary:

▶ I **apologized to** her.

2 Can you describe what follows these verbs? Match the underlined parts on the left with a description from the list on the right.

1 He's always **complaining** that nobody listens to him.	a **+ to do sth**
2 Did she **say** where she was going?	b **+ two objects**
3 He doesn't **like** watching TV.	c **+ that**
4 They **want** to go shopping.	d **+ doing sth**
5 He **brought** me some flowers.	e **+ question word**

3 Write a sentence using each of these verbs and the patterns that are shown in the following grammar codes.

1 forget	**+ [that]**
2 tell	**+ question word**
3 like	**+ doing sth**
4 start	**+ to do sth**
5 sell	**+ two objects**

Word formation

Prefixes

Prefixes are added to the beginning of words to change their meaning. There is a list of common prefixes at the end of this book on page 845.

Here are some common prefixes that are used to give opposite and often negative meanings. They are all used with adjectives, and **dis-** and **un-** are used with some verbs too:

dis-	*dissimilar, disappear*	**in-**	*inaccurate, inexpensive*
il-	*illegal, illogical*	**ir-**	*irregular, irresponsible*
im-	*impossible, impatient*	**un-**	*uncertain, uncover*

1 Match the prefixes on the left to the adjectives and verbs on the right to make new words.

1 un-	lock
2 dis-	responsible
3 il-	possible
4 im-	legal
5 ir-	agree

2 Now use the words you have made to fill in the gaps in the sentences below.

1 Which key do I need to _____ this door?
2 The tide is so strong it's _____ to swim against it.
3 It is _____ to drive without a licence.
4 I _____ with her views on immigration.
5 Leaving the children alone was a very _____ thing to do.

3 There are many other prefixes used in English. Match the prefix on the left with the meaning on the right. Then form new words by choosing a suitable word from the box to combine with each prefix.

1 multi-	a half
2 semi-	b in favour of
3 anti-	c former (not now)
4 pro-	d not enough
5 ex-	e many
6 post-	f against
7 over-	g after
8 under-	h too much

president	war
cooked	racial
graduate	worked
circle	democracy

Suffixes

Suffixes are added at the end of words to change their meaning. There is a list of suffixes at the end of this book on page 846. Here are some common ones:

-er **-or**	■ for people who do activities and for things that have a particular function	*worker, swimmer, golfer, driver, actor, sailor, conductor; tin opener, screwdriver, hanger, projector*
-ist	■ for people with certain beliefs ■ for people who play musical instruments ■ for some professions	*Buddhist, socialist* *violinist, pianist, guitarist* *journalist, pharmacist, artist*
-ness	■ to make nouns from adjectives	*happiness, sadness, rudeness*
-(t)ion	■ to make nouns from verbs	*education, television, pollution*
-ment	■ to make nouns from verbs	*improvement, government*

Note: Adding a suffix to a word sometimes changes its pronunciation.

Look at how the stress changes in these words:

photograph ⇒ pho**tog**rapher   **ed**ucate ⇒ edu**ca**tion

Noun, verb, adjective?

Most suffixes can tell you whether a word is a noun, verb or adjective. This table shows some common ones:

adjectives	-able, -al, -ful, -ible, -ive, -less, -ous, -y	*washable, natural, beautiful, flexible, active, helpless, adventurous, happy*
nouns	-al, -ance, -(t)ion, -ence, -hood, -ity, -ment, -ness, -ship	*performance, reduction, independence, parenthood, similarity, enjoyment, politeness, friendship, arrival*
verbs	-en, -ify, -ize	*harden, solidify, modernize*

Note: **-al** can be used to make nouns, e.g. **arrival**, and adjectives, e.g. **comical**

4 Use suffixes to change the following adjectives and verbs into nouns.

1 rude	4 ignorant
2 create	5 hilarious
3 prefer	6 develop

Numbers

Saying numbers

Don't forget to say 'and' after hundreds:

- ▶ 569   *five hundred and sixty nine*
- ▶ 7,892   *seven thousand, eight hundred and ninety two*
- ▶ 4,680,022 *four million, six hundred and eighty thousand and twenty two*

Parts of numbers: decimals and fractions

For decimals we say each number separately after the point (.):

- ▶ 2.5   *two point five*
- ▶ 3.65 *three point six five*
- ▶ 22.33 *twenty two point three three*

When you use fractions, if you are talking about a half or quarters, you say:

- ▶ $2\frac{1}{4}$ *two and a quarter*
- ▶ $4\frac{1}{2}$ *four and a half*
- ▶ $5\frac{3}{4}$ *five and three quarters*

For other fractions, use ordinal numbers for the second number:

- ▶ $\frac{3}{8}$ *three eighths*
- ▶ $\frac{1}{3}$ *a third* or *one third*
- ▶ $\frac{1}{12}$ *a twelfth* or *one twelfth*

Percentages and other symbols

Here are some other symbols used with numbers:

%	percent	45%	*forty five percent*
°	degree	22°C	*twenty two degrees Celsius*
		70°F	*seventy degrees Fahrenheit*
+	addition	6 + 2 = 8	*six plus two is/equals eight*
−	subtraction	6 − 2 = 4	*six minus two is/equals four*
×	multiplication	6 × 3 = 18	*six times three/six multiplied by three is/equals eighteen*
÷	division	24 ÷ 4 = 6	*twenty four divided by four is/equals six*

Saying 0

'0' can be said in different ways. It is usually said as 'oh' or 'zero' ('zero' is especially used in American English). Here are some ways of saying '0':

MATHS:	0.65 (UK): *nought point six five*, (US): *zero point six five*
FOOTBALL:	6 – 0 (UK): *six nil*, (US): *six to zero*
TENNIS:	15–0 *fifteen love*
TELEPHONE NUMBER:	965703 *nine six five seven oh three* (also US *seven zero three*)

Measurements

Metric and imperial measurements

The international system of metric units of measurement is not used in the US. It is used in the UK, but many people still use the older system of imperial units such as pounds, feet, and gallons.

Some units have the same name but mean different amounts in the UK and the US.

IMPERIAL	METRIC		IMPERIAL	METRIC
1 inch (in)	2.5 centimetres (cm)		1 ounce (oz)	28 grams (g)
1 foot (ft)	30 centimetres		1 pound (lb)	450 grams
	(100 cm = 1 metre (m))		1 pint	(UK) 0.6 litres (US) 0.5 litres
1 yard (yd)	90 centimetres		1 gallon	(UK) 4.5 litres (US) 3.8 litres
1 mile (m)	2.2 kilometres (km)			

Saying how tall you are

Most people in the UK and the US say their height in imperial units.

▶ I'm **six feet** tall.   ▶ I'm **five foot seven**. (often written 5' 7")

Saying how much you weigh

In the UK, people usually say their weight in stones and pounds. There are fourteen pounds in a stone.

▶ I weigh **nine stone three**. (Note that you do not have to say 'pounds'.)

▶ I weigh **seven and a half stone**.

In the US, people usually say their weight in pounds.

▶ I weigh **160 pounds**.

Talking about measurements

We normally use adjectives to talk or ask about measurements:

▶ The box is 30cm **long**.   ▶ How **tall** is David?

We can also use nouns, but they are more formal:

▶ The **length** of the box is 30cm.   ▶ What is David's **height**?

1 Look at the words in the box. Decide which are adjectives and which are nouns. Use them to complete the table below.

height	deep	length	width	depth	high	long	wide

QUESTION	ANSWER	FORMAL
1 How wide is it?	It's 5m _____.	The _____ of the x is 5m.
2 How _____ is it?	It's 50m long.	The length of the x is 50m.
3 How deep is it?	It's 10m deep.	The _____ of the x is 10m.
4 How _____ is it?	It's 70m _____.	The height of the x is 70m.

Pronunciation

Pronouncing words in English can be very difficult. Often, words are not written the way they are pronounced. The phonetic symbols after each word in the dictionary show you how to say each word. There is an explanation of all these symbols at the back of the book, and more information about the pronunciation system on page xvi.

Some of the symbols are pronounced in the same way as the letter they look like, e.g. /b/ sounds like 'b' in 'bad'. All the others are explained at the bottom of every page in the dictionary.

1 Look at these words and match them with their pronunciations.

1 cough	a /sɪnəmə/
2 throw	b /θruː/
3 through	c /sɪŋ/
4 cup	d /kɒf/
5 cinema	e /θrəʊ/
6 sing	f /kʌp/

2 All these words are names of animals. Write the name of the animal next to the phonetic symbols.

1 /məʊl/   3 /hɔːs/   5 /laɪən/
2 /dʒɪrɑːf/   4 /ʃiːp/   6 /tʃɪmp/

Silent letters

Many words in English contain letters that are not pronounced, for example the 't' in 'listen' /lɪsn/.

3 Which is the silent letter in each of these words?

1 know   3 island   5 two
2 honest   4 wrong   6 talk

Word stress

Probably the most important thing about pronunciation is to make sure that you put the stress (emphasis) on the right part of the word.

The symbol /'/ shows you where to put the main stress. Some words have another, less important stress too, and that is shown with the symbol /ˌ/.

information /ˌɪnfəˈmeɪʃən/   **important** /ɪmˈpɔːtənt/   **difficult** /ˈdɪfɪkəlt/

4 Underline the part of each word that has the main stress.

1 brother   3 photographer   5 computer
2 education   4 below   6 necessary

Punctuation

	Uses	Examples
capital letter	■ the first letter of a sentence ■ for people's names and titles ■ for countries, nationalities, languages, places, religions ■ for organizations, trademarks ■ for days, months ■ for titles of books, films, etc ■ for most abbreviations ■ for the personal pronoun 'I'	*Football is very popular in Britain.* *Joanne, John, Professor Rose* *Portugal, Africa, Russian, Islam, Dubai, Geneva* *Oxfam, Nike* *Sunday, February* *The Dark Knight* *UK, AIDS, WWF* *I opened the book.*
full stop (UK)/ period (US) [.]	■ at the end of a sentence ■ after some abbreviations ■ to separate parts of an email or website address	*I'm going for a walk.* *Marton Rd./Mrs. White* *info@cambridge.org*
question mark [?]	■ after a direct question	*What's your name?*
exclamation mark [!]	■ at the end of a sentence to express surprise, shock, etc. ■ to indicate a loud sound ■ to emphasize what you have said	*I can't believe it!* *Ouch! Yes!* *I want this mess tidied up – fast!*
comma [,]	■ between items in a list ■ to show a pause in a long sentence ■ when you add extra information ■ in direct speech	*I need some peas, butter, sugar and eggs.* *They didn't want to eat before I'd arrived, but I was an hour late.* *The woman, who I'd met last week, waved as she went past.* *'I will tell you,' he said.*
apostrophe [']	■ for missing letters ■ for possessives (showing that something belongs to someone) Note: for words ending in 's' the apostrophe goes after the 's', but there is no need to add another 's'	*don't, I'll, it's (= it is)* *Paul's bike* *James' house* *the boys' homework*
colon [:]	■ to introduce a list or a quotation in a sentence	*You need the following: paint, brushes, water, cloths.*
semi-colon [;]	■ to separate two parts of a sentence	*I spoke to Linda on Monday; she can't come to the meeting today.*
hyphen [-]	■ to join two words together ■ when you have to divide a word at the end of a line	*blue-black* *Everyone there was absolutely horri-fied by the news.*
dash [–]	■ to separate parts of sentences	*The car – the one with the broken window – was parked outside our house.*
quotation marks/ UK also inverted commas [" or ""]	■ to show that words are spoken ■ to show that someone else originally wrote the words	*'I'm tired,' she said.* *'Let's go,' he suggested.* *She had described the school as 'not attracting the best pupils'.*
brackets (UK)/ parentheses (US) [() or []]	■ to add extra information but keep it separate from the rest of the sentence ■ after numbers or letters in a list	*You will need suitable clothing (waterproof coat, strong shoes) and a picnic lunch.* *These are my favourite foods:* *1) cheese* *2) pizza* *3) tomatoes*

Spelling

Because of its history, the English language does not have simple spelling rules. Often words are not written exactly as they sound, so it is important to check the spelling of any new word and to copy it down correctly.

Top 10 learner spelling errors

In the *Cambridge Learner Corpus* these are the ten most common spelling errors made by intermediate students taking exams such as PET (the Preliminary English Test) and FCE (the First Certificate in English).

1	accommodation	double **c** and double **m**
2	restaurant	remember the two vowels (**au**) after the **t**
3	advertisement	don't forget the **e** in the middle (-is**e**ment)
4	because	remember **au** after the **c**
5	which	remember the **h** after the **w**
6	beautiful	remember the three vowels (**eau**) after the **b**
7	different	double **f** and remember the **e** after the second **f**
8	environment	remember the **n** before **–ment**
9	receive	remember the **ei** after the **c**
10	comfortable	remember the **m** before the **f**

Regular inflections

There are many rules you can learn which will help a lot with your spelling. Look at page xvii, which explains the rules for regular inflections (e.g. plurals, past tenses).

1 Write the plural of these nouns.

 1 house   2 watch   3 brick   4 minute   5 fax   6 loss

Word beginnings

Even the first letter of a word can sometimes be difficult to guess.

c   Some words beginning with **c** sound as though they begin with **s**.

  ▶ *cell*, *centre*, *circle*

ps Words beginning with **ps** sound as though they start with **s**.

  ▶ *pseudonym*, *psychiatrist*

ph Words beginning with **ph** sound as though they start with **f**.

  ▶ *philosophy*, *phone*, *physical*

Same or similar sound, different spelling

Some words in English have the same or very similar sounds, but are spelled differently.

2 Choose the correct word from the pair on the right to fill in the gaps.

1 I don't know _____ he will come.   weather/whether
2 It's _____ a long way to my brother's house.   quite/quiet
3 _____ of these pictures do you like best?   Which/Witch
4 They didn't have _____ coats with them.   their/there
5 We stayed in a cottage by the _____.   see/sea

Doubling consonants

Some adjectives have a double
consonant at the end when they make
the comparative form with **-er** and the
superlative form with **-est**. When this
happens, it is clearly shown in the
entry for those adjectives.

Some verbs have a double consonant
when they make the present participle
or the past tense and past participle.
This is also shown clearly in the entry
for those verbs.

A lot of verbs ending in **l** (e.g. **travel**,
level) have a double consonant in UK
English, and a single consonant in US
English. This is also shown in the entry
for those verbs.

> **big**[1] /bɪg/ **adj** (**bigger**, **biggest**) **1** SIZE ▷ **A1** large
> in size or amount: *I come from a big family.*
> ∘ *We're looking for a bigger house.*

> **acquit** /əˈkwɪt/ **verb** [T] (**acquitting**, **acquitted**)
> If someone is acquitted of a crime, a court of law
> decides that they are not guilty: [often passive]
> *Both men were **acquitted** of murder.*

> **travel**[1] /ˈtrævəl/ **verb** (mainly UK **travelling**,
> **travelled**, US **traveling**, **traveled**) **1** [I, T] **A1** to
> make a journey: *I spent a year travelling around
> Asia.* ∘ *He has to travel abroad a lot on business.*

3 Fill in the gaps in the sentences below with the correct inflection of the word on the right. Be
careful not to double the consonant where it is not correct to do so.

1 It's usually _____ than this in the summer.   (hot)
2 The use of mobile phones is _____ on aircraft.   (ban)
3 The concert was the _____ I've ever been to.   (loud)
4 I'm _____ to find my way around the city.   (begin)
5 I'm tired of _____ ten hours a day.   (work)

British and American children learn this rhyme to help them with their
spelling:

'**I** before **E**, except after **C**.'

▶ *friend, receive*

The Web and the Internet

The Web or the World Wide Web (www) refers to all the websites that you can look at using the Internet. The Internet or the Net is the system that connects computers all over the world and allows people to share information, visit websites, communicate using email, etc.

The Internet is a very important part of many people's lives and has generated a lot of words and phrases. Here are some important ones:

Accessing the Internet

You can access the Internet via your computer or a handheld device, such as a smartphone or PDA. Many public places such as cafes, restaurants and airports usually have a wireless LAN (local area network) or wi-fi so people can use the Internet in these locations. Most mobile devices come already loaded with apps (applications) which allow the user to listen to music, play games, write emails, etc.

Online

To be online is to be connected to the Internet or to be available on the Internet. To go online is to start to connect your computer to the Internet.

Moving around on the Web

You can use your mouse to click on links (= connections between the documents or areas on the Internet), to go to a different website, or to move from one part of a website to another.

Websites

Websites usually consist of a series of web pages. The main page on a website is called the homepage. If you know the web address or URL of a website you can type it in at the top of the screen. Otherwise you can use a search engine. A search engine is a computer program that allows you to search for information on the Internet by typing in one or more words. To surf or to surf the Internet is to spend time looking at many different websites, often without knowing where you are going next.

Blogs

A blog is a record of news, opinions, photos and videos about a particular subject that someone puts on the Internet and adds to regularly. A blogger is someone who writes or contributes to a blog. A microblog is a blog in the form of short messages for anyone to read, sent especially from a mobile phone. The word blogosphere is used to refer to all the opinions, articles, etc. that are published by people on Internet blogs.

Podcasts

A podcast is a recording from the Internet that you can listen to on your computer or MP3 player. You can also sign up to (= say that you want to receive) a podcast which is then updated (= new information is added to it) through the Internet when you plug your MP3 player into your computer.

Downloading and uploading

If you download information, a film, a game, music, etc., you copy it onto your computer from the Internet. To upload something is to copy something from your computer onto a website or other place where, through the Internet, many people can look at it and use it.

File sharing

File sharing is the activity of putting a file from your computer onto a special place on your computer so that other people can, through the Internet, copy it, look at it, or use it.

Social networking

Social networking is the activity of using a website to share information and communicate with people. To start you usually need to register, which means choosing a username, a password, and possibly an avatar to create a profile of yourself. Once you have created a profile, you can post comments and share messages, photos, music and videos with other people using the website.

Emailing and texting

Emails are usually shorter and more informal than letters and people sometimes use abbreviations in them.

Text messages are written messages sent from one mobile phone to another. They usually use abbreviations. Here are some frequently used abbreviations:

Abbreviations

AFAIK	as far as I know	MSG	message
ASAP	as soon as possible	OMG	oh my God (= used to show surprise
B	be		or excitement)
BDAY	birthday	OTOH	on the other hand
B4	before	PLS	please
BTW	by the way	R	are
C	see	SHUD	should
CU	see you!	SPK	speak
CUD	could	TBH	to be honest
EOM	end of message	THX/TNX	thanks
4	for	2	to
FWIW	for what it's worth	2DAY	today
FYA	for your amusement	2MORO	tomorrow
FYI	for your information	2NITE	tonight
GD	good	TXT	text
GR8	great	U	you
IMO	in my opinion	UR	you are/your
IMHO	in my humble opinion	W/E	weekend
IOU	I owe you	WK	week
LOL	laughing out loud/lots of love	WKEND	weekend
L8R	later	WUD	would

UK and US English

Although English in the UK and the US is very similar, there are a lot of differences in vocabulary, spelling, grammar, and pronunciation.

This dictionary shows you when there are differences. For a full explanation of the UK and US labels, see page xv.

Vocabulary

Many common words for items we see or use every day are different in UK and US English.

1 The words on the left are UK English. Match each one with a US word from the list on the right.

1 aubergine	4 windscreen	a elevator	d eggplant
2 wardrobe	5 queue	b truck	e closet
3 lift	6 lorry	c windshield	f line

In informal language there are lots of differences between UK and US English.

2 The underlined word in each sentence is used in UK English only. Replace it with a word from the list on the right which would be understood in both UK and US English.

1 I got it from a bloke at work.	a complaining
2 I'm feeling rather poorly today.	b man
3 I wish he'd stop whingeing and do some work.	c weak
4 I was gutted when I heard I hadn't got the job.	d disappointed
5 My brother's too weedy to climb that tree.	e ill

Spelling

3 Look at these pairs of words. Which is the UK spelling and which is the US spelling?

1 labour/labor
2 center/centre
3 offence/offense
4 color/colour
5 metre/meter
6 traveller/traveler

Pronunciation

In this dictionary, words which are pronounced very differently in UK and US English have both pronunciations shown at the word. The US pronunciation follows the symbol ⓤⓢ.

4 Which of these words have different pronunciations in UK and US English?

1 peach	4 ballet
2 schedule	5 zebra
3 colour	6 bicycle

albino /æl'biːnəʊ/ ⓤⓢ /æl'baɪnəʊ/ **noun** [C] a person or animal with white skin, white hair or fur, and pink eyes

Writing letters and emails

Formal letters

19 Garden St
Cambridge
CB4 3AL

20 June 2012

Ms R. Philips
Evening News
104 Wolfs Way
Newtown
NT7 0PE

Dear Ms Philips ❶

I am ❸ writing to inquire about ❷ the possibility of holiday work with your company this summer. I am very interested in gaining some experience working for a newspaper.

For the last two years I have been editor of the student magazine at my school. Next year I am planning to do a one-year course in newspaper journalism.

I have good computer skills and accurate written English.

I very much hope you have a vacancy for me. I enclose a copy of my CV and look forward to hearing from you soon. ❹

Yours sincerely ❶

Anna Thompson

❶ If you know the name of the person you are writing to, but the letter is formal, end the letter: *Yours sincerely.*

If you do not know the name of the person you are writing to, begin the letter: *Dear Sir/Madam* and end it: *Yours faithfully.*

❷ Other ways of beginning a formal letter:
- ▶ *I am writing to inform you of/that ...*
- ▶ *I am writing to complain about ...*
- ▶ *I am writing regarding your advertisement ...*
- ▶ *Please send me ...*
- ▶ *Further to my letter of June 1st ...*

❸ You should not use contractions (e.g. *I'm, I'd*) in a formal letter.

❹ Other ways of ending a formal letter:
- ▶ *Thank you in advance for your help.*
- ▶ *Wishing you all the best for the future.*

Informal emails

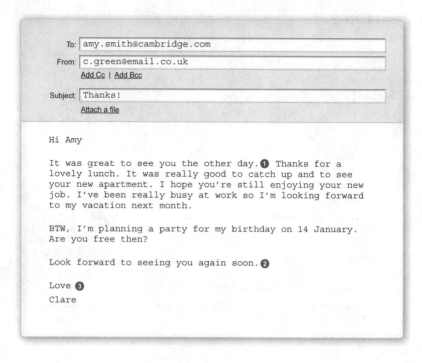

To: amy.smith@cambridge.com

From: c.green@email.co.uk

Add Cc | Add Bcc

Subject: Thanks!

Attach a file

Hi Amy

It was great to see you the other day. ❶ Thanks for a
lovely lunch. It was really good to catch up and to see
your new apartment. I hope you're still enjoying your new
job. I've been really busy at work so I'm looking forward
to my vacation next month.

BTW, I'm planning a party for my birthday on 14 January.
Are you free then?

Look forward to seeing you again soon. ❷

Love ❸
Clare

---

❶ Other ways of starting an informal
   email:

  ► *Thanks for your email.*
  ► *How are you?*
  ► *I hope you're well.*
  ► *Sorry it's been so long since I last
    wrote.*
  ► *It was lovely to hear from you.*

❷ Other ways of ending an informal email:

  ► *Drop me a line soon.*
  ► *Write soon.*
  ► *Take care.*
  ► *Keep in touch.*
  ► *Give my love to Paul.*
  ► *Hope to hear from you soon.*

❸ At the end, before your name, you write:

   to close friends:

  ► *love from*
  ► *all my love*
  ► *lots of love*

   to less close friends:

  ► *best wishes*
  ► *all the best*
  ► *yours*
  ► *kind regards*

What is a collocation/word partner?

A **collocation** is a combination of two or more words which are often used together. In the boxes in the a-z part of this dictionary we call them **word partners**. For example, a native speaker of English would say:

*He **made** a **mistake**.*

But would not say:

*He **did** a **mistake**.*

If you can use collocations or word partners correctly, your English will sound more natural and it will be easier to understand.

What types of collocation are there?

Verbs and nouns
There are verb + noun collocations. For example:

take a photo   *have* fun   *make* a decision

Or noun + verb collocations. For example:

an accident *happens*   disaster *strikes*   a problem *arises*

Adjectives and nouns
There are adjective + noun collocations. For example:

heavy traffic   a *written* agreement   a *useful* skill

Nouns and prepositions
There are noun + preposition collocations. For example:

an answer *to* sth   an argument *with* sb   a choice *between* sth and sth

Or preposition + noun collocations. For example:

by mistake   *in* pain   be *of* interest

Collocations are sometimes used with a lot of words in the same topic. For example, in the topic 'clothes' the collocation 'wear' is used with words such as 'jeans', 'skirt', 'shirt', etc.

On the pages that follow, you will find the most important collocations for these topics. These are very useful collocations to learn.

1	Age	7	Meals
2	Clothes	8	Months
3	Crimes	9	Musical instruments
4	Days of the week	10	Seasons
5	Illnesses	11	Software
6	Languages	12	Subjects for study

1 Age

• be [15/30/50, etc.] **years old**
*She's only four **years old**.*

• be **in your** [30s/40s/50s, etc.]
*Many women now have children **in their** thirties.*

• *formal* [32/57/70, etc.] **years of age**
*The prices apply to children between 2 and 15 **years of age**.*

• [a man/woman/daughter, etc.] **of** [20/30/65, etc.]
*She has a son **of** 10 and a daughter **of** 8.*

• **about** [17/40/65, etc.]
*Their son must be **about** 25 now.*

• **approaching/nearly** [50/60/70, etc.]
*I would think he's **approaching** 70. • She's **nearly** twenty and still lives with her parents.*

• **over/under** [18/35/80, etc.]
*You have to be **over** 21 to get in the club. • People **under** 18 are not allowed to drive.*

• **over the age of/under the age of**
*You must be **over the age of** 16 to buy cigarettes. • We don't sell alcohol to anyone **under the age of** 18.*

• *humorous* **be the wrong side of** [40/50/60, etc.] (= be older than 40, 50, 60, etc.)
*She's **the wrong side of** 50 but she's still attractive.*

2 Clothes

• **wear** [jeans/a skirt/a shirt, etc.]
*I **wear** a uniform for work.*

• **in** sth/be **dressed in** sth/**wearing** sth
*a woman **in** a red coat • He was **dressed in** a grey suit. • She was **wearing** a green dress.*

• **have** [a dress/skirt/T-shirt, etc.] **on**
*I only **had** a thin shirt **on**.*

• **put on/take off** [your dress/jeans/coat, etc.]
***Put** your hat **on** – it's cold. • She **took off** her coat.*

• **do up/fasten/undo/unfasten** [your skirt/belt/coat, etc.]
***Fasten** your coat. • She **undid** her jacket and took it off.*

• **loose/tight** [jeans/T-shirt, etc.]
*He was wearing a pair of **tight** black jeans. • Wear **loose** clothes in hot weather.*

3 Crimes

• be **accused of/charged with** (doing) sth
*He appeared in court, **accused of** stabbing a man. • He has been **charged with** the murder of his neighbour.*

• **face charges of** [murder/burglary, etc.]
*He arrived in the country to **face charges of** theft and kidnapping.*

• **confess to/admit** (doing) sth
*She **confessed to** the murder. • He **admitted** driving while drunk.*

• **deny** (doing) sth
*He has **denied** murdering his girlfriend.*

• be **convicted of/found guilty of** (doing) sth
*Jenkins was **convicted of** murdering his mother in 2011. • Bates was **found guilty of** assault.*

• be **arrested for/jailed for** (doing) sth
*She was **arrested for** shoplifting. • He was **jailed for** stealing cars.*

• **investigate** [a murder, assault, etc.]
*Police are **investigating** the murder of a young mother.*

• the [murder/rape, etc.] **of** sb
*The murder **of** the 85-year-old woman has shocked everyone.*

• a [crime/murder/rape, etc.] **victim**
*The organization offers help to rape **victims**.*

• a [murder/rape, etc.] **inquiry/investigation**
*Police have launched a murder **inquiry** after a woman's body was found.*

• a [murder/rape, etc.] **case**
*The police still have 110 unsolved rape **cases**.*

• a **brutal** [murder/attack/rape, etc.]
*He was jailed for the **brutal** attack on an elderly man.*

4 Days of the week

• **on** [Monday/Tuesday, etc.]
*I'm going to London **on** Friday.*

• **on** [Mondays/Tuesdays, etc.] (= every Monday/Tuesday, etc.)
*She works **on** Wednesdays and Fridays.*

• **every** [Saturday/Tuesday, etc.]
*I have a piano lesson **every** Saturday.*

• **last/next** [Wednesday/Thursday, etc.]
*The meeting was **last** Monday. • It's my birthday **next** Tuesday.*

• **the following** [Tuesday/Friday, etc.]
*She went into hospital on Friday for an operation **on the following** Monday.*

• [Monday/Friday, etc.] **afternoon/evening/morning/night**
*I have to work on Monday **morning**. • I'm going to a party on Friday **night**.*

5 Illnesses

• **have (got)/suffer from** [a cold/cancer, etc.]
*I've got a really bad cold. • He was **suffering from** flu.*

• be **diagnosed with** [AIDS/a brain tumour/cancer, etc.]
*In 2001, she **was diagnosed with** breast cancer.*

• **catch** [a cold/chickenpox/measles, etc.]
*I **caught** chickenpox from one of the children.*

• **develop** [cancer/an infection/asthma, etc.]
*People who smoke are more likely to **develop** cancer.*

• **go down with** [flu/a stomach upset, etc.]
*He **went down with** flu two days before we were due to leave.*

• **shake off** [a cold, flu, etc.]
*I've had a cold for two weeks now and I can't **shake** it **off**.*

• **Cure/treat** [a cold/infection/cancer, etc.]
*Scientists are searching for a drug to **cure** colds. • Antibiotics can be used to **treat** some throat infections.*

• [AIDS/asthma/cancer, etc.] **sufferers**
*The drug offers new hope to cancer **sufferers**.*

6 Languages

• **speak** [French/Italian/Arabic, etc.]
*She **speaks** very good Russian.*

• **learn/study** [Cantonese/Urdu/Spanish, etc.]
*I'm **learning** German at school. • She wants to **study** Icelandic at university.*

• **in** [Danish/Mandarin/Portuguese, etc.]
*All the signs were **in** French.*

• **fluent/be fluent in** [German/Japanese/Russian, etc.]
*He speaks **fluent** Italian. • Anna is **fluent in** Japanese.*

• **broken** (= not good and full of mistakes) [French/Italian/Spanish, etc.]
*I tried to make myself understood in **broken** French.*

• a [French/Latin/Russian, etc.] **teacher**
*She's a Spanish **teacher** at the local school.*

7 Meals

• **eat/have** [breakfast/lunch, etc.]
*More workers are **eating** lunch at their desks. • He was sitting in a café **having** lunch.*

• **make/prepare** [breakfast/lunch, etc.]
*He was in the kitchen **making** lunch. • She'd **prepared** a lovely meal for us.*

• **have** sth **for** [lunch/dinner, etc.]
*I **had** toast **for** breakfast. • What did you **have for** dinner?*

• **serve** [breakfast/lunch, etc.]
*Breakfast is **served** in the hotel restaurant between 7 and 9.30am.*

• **skip** [breakfast/lunch, etc.] (= not eat breakfast, lunch, etc.)
*I was late for school so I had to **skip** breakfast.*

• a **big/light** [breakfast/lunch, etc.]
*He always eats a **big** breakfast. • I usually have a **light** lunch.*

• an **early/late** [breakfast/lunch, etc.]
*We had an **early** lunch and then set off. • I got up at 11am and had a **late** breakfast.*

• a **leisurely/quick** [breakfast/lunch, etc.]
*They enjoyed a **leisurely** lunch on the hotel terrace. • We set off early after a **quick** breakfast.*

• **at/over** [lunch/dinner, etc.]
*He didn't say a word **at** breakfast. • We discussed it **over** dinner.*

8 Months

• **in** [December/March, etc.]
*My birthday's **in** July.*

• **on** [August 24th/May 12th, etc.]
*Her birthday's **on** August 24th.*

• **early/mid/late** [January/June, etc.]
*The weather is usually very nice in **early** July.* • *By **late** May, the situation had improved.*

• **the beginning of/the end of** [May/October, etc.]
*The work should be finished by **the beginning of** April.* • *He's coming at **the end of** November.*

• **last/next** [May/June, etc.]
*They got married **last** December.* • *The elections will be held **next** June.*

9 Musical instruments

• **play the/play** [guitar/piano, etc.]
*He **plays** saxophone in a band.* • *She was **playing the** violin.*

• **learn (to play) the** [flute/violin, etc.]
*John's **learning** the clarinet.*

• **on the/on** [drums/violin, etc.]
*Sam was **on the** trumpet and Jim was **on** drums.*

• a [piano/guitar, etc.] **lesson/player/teacher**
*I'm having piano **lessons**.* • *He's a great guitar **player**.*

10 Seasons

• **during the/in the/in** [spring/summer, etc.]
*We're very busy **during the** summer.* • *The park is open for longer **in** summer.* • *It often snows **in** the winter.*

• **through the/throughout the** [summer/winter, etc.]
*The plant produces flowers **throughout the** summer.*

• **early/late** [autumn/spring, etc.]
*Sow the seeds in **early** spring.* • *It was a cold night in **late** autumn.*

• **last/next** [winter/summer, etc.]
*The book was published **last** autumn.* • *They're getting married **next** summer.*

• **the depths of winter/the height of spring/summer**
*He never wears a coat, even in **the depths of winter**.* • *It was **the height of summer** and very hot.*

• **the** [spring/summer, etc.] **of** [1995/2004, etc.]
*He had a heart attack in **the** summer **of** 2002.*

• **the** [summer/winter, etc.] **months**
*In **the** winter **months**, people visit the area to ski.*

11 Software

• **download** [files/music/software, etc.]
*You can just **download** the software from the Internet.*

• **install/uninstall** [a program/software, etc.]
*Follow the on-screen instructions to **install** the program.* • ***Uninstall** the software if you want to free up more disk space.*

• **run** [a program, etc.]
*Click on the icon to **run** the program.*

• **copy/paste** [a file, etc.]
***Copy** the file onto the C-drive.*

• **develop** [software/a program, etc.]
*The software was **developed** in the US.*

12 Subjects for study

• **do/study** [physics/German, etc.]
*I'm **doing** French and German this year.* • *Amy's **studying** law at Cambridge University.*

• **have a degree in** [French/history/law, etc.]
*She **has a degree in** chemistry.*

• a [geography/history/maths, etc.] **class/course/lesson**
*He fell asleep in the geography **class**.* • *The college offers language and computer **courses**.*
• *She's having French **lessons**.*

• a [history/maths, etc.] **lecturer/student/teacher**
*Our English **teacher** is called Mrs Jackson.* • *She's a maths **lecturer** at the university.*

Speaking naturally
1: language for different situations

These pages will help you to speak English naturally. They give you the phrases (= groups of words that are often used together) that you need in lots of different situations. Try to learn these phrases.

1 Saying hello
2 Saying goodbye
3 When someone says sorry
4 Asking if you can do something
5 Asking if you can have something

6 Offering something
7 Offering to help someone
8 Inviting someone
9 What to say when someone thanks you

1 Saying hello

There are other ways to say hello to someone as well as the usual 'Hello' or, 'Hello, how are you?' Here are a few:

Hello/Hi, **how's it going?**

Hello/Hi, **how are you doing?**

Hello/Hi, **how are things?**

Answering

If you are well or happy:

Fine, thanks. How are you?

Good thanks. And you?

All right, thanks. How are you doing?

Not too bad, thanks. And you?

If you are not well or happy:

Not too good today.

Not brilliant, actually.

So-so.

2 Saying goodbye

Other ways to say 'goodbye' informally to friends and family:

Bye. **See you later!**

See you soon.

Bye. **Take care.**

See you!

3 When someone says sorry

If someone says they are sorry about something they have done, you can say one of these:

It doesn't matter.

That's all right.

Don't worry about it!

4 Asking if you can do something

Is it all right if I open a window?

Do you mind if I smoke?

May I sit here?

Saying 'yes':

Saying 'no':

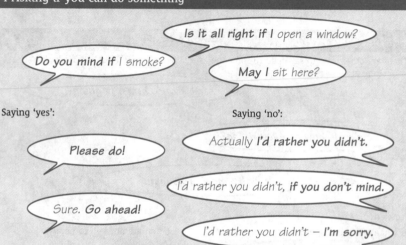

Please do!

Actually **I'd rather you didn't.**

I'd rather you didn't, **if you don't mind.**

Sure. **Go ahead!**

I'd rather you didn't – **I'm sorry.**

5 Asking if you can have something

May I take this chair?

Could I have a hand-out, please?

Saying 'yes':

Saying 'no':

Yes, of course!

I'm sorry – that's the only one I've got.

Please do!

I'm afraid I need it myself.

Be my guest!

Help yourself!

6 Offering something

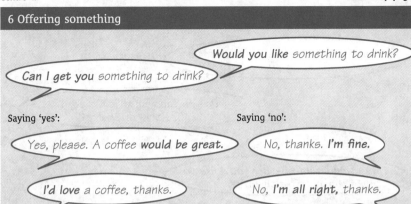

Would you like *something to drink?*

Can I get you *something to drink?*

Saying 'yes':

Yes, please. A coffee **would be great.**

I'd **love** a coffee, thanks.

Saying 'no':

No, thanks. **I'm fine.**

No, **I'm all right,** thanks.

7 Offering to help someone

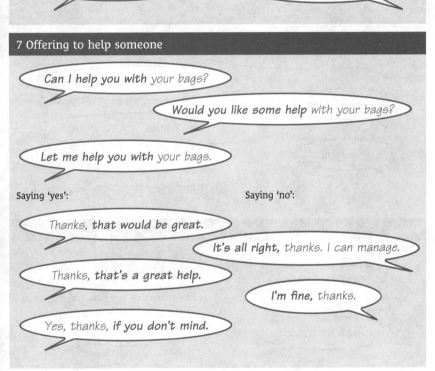

Can I help you with *your bags?*

Would you like **some help** *with your bags?*

Let me help you with *your bags.*

Saying 'yes':

Thanks, **that would be great.**

Thanks, **that's a great help.**

Yes, thanks, **if you don't mind.**

Saying 'no':

It's all right, thanks. I can manage.

I'm fine, thanks.

TALK! TALK! TALK! TALK! TALK! TALK! TALK! TALK! TALK! TALK! TALK! TALK! TALK!

8 Inviting someone

Would you like to get together for a coffee this afternoon?

Do you fancy meeting up for a coffee this afternoon?

I was wondering whether you'd like to meet for a coffee this afternoon.

Saying 'yes':   Saying 'no':

Yes, *that would be lovely.*

I'd love to but I can't this afternoon.

Yes, *great idea.*

I'm afraid I can't make it this afternoon.

Sure, why not?

I wish I could, but I'm busy.

9 What to say when someone thanks you...

... for something you have done:

That's all right.

... for something you have given them:

It was no trouble.

You're very welcome.

Not at all.

It was my pleasure.

Don't mention it.

I'm glad you like it.

Don't mention it.

Speaking naturally

2: conversation exercises

These pages contain twelve longer conversations that take place in different situations. There are gaps in the conversations. Under each conversation you will find some phrases (= groups of words which are often used together). Try to find the right phrases to fill the gaps. Then try to learn these phrases. Again, they will help your English to sound natural, like the English that native speakers of English use.

1 **Making an appointment**
2 **Making phone calls**
3 **Invitations**
4 **Apologizing (saying you are sorry)**
5 **At the restaurant**
6 **Visiting someone's house**
7 **Asking someone how their family are**
8 **Talking about where you come from**
9 **Talking about your plans (for the weekend and for your holiday)**
10 **Talking about the past weekend**
11 **Cancelling an arrangement**
12 **When someone tells you news (good and bad)**

---

1 Making an appointment

Complete the dialogue with the phrases below:

Making an appointment with a doctor
Mark: I'd like to (1) _____ Dr Parker, please.
Receptionist: Right, let me see. The first appointment available is 3.30, Wednesday.
Mark: I'm afraid Wednesday is no good. (2) _____ on Friday?
Receptionist: 4.20 on Friday?
Mark: Yes, that's fine - (3) _____
Receptionist: What's the name, please?
Mark: Mark Klein, (4) _____ K-L-E-I-N.
Receptionist: So, that's 4.20 on Friday with Dr Parker.

a. I'll take that
b. make an appointment to see
c. Do you have anything
d. that's spelled

---

2 Making phone calls

Complete the dialogues with the phrases below:

An informal call
Sue: Hello.
Anna: Hi, can I speak to Jane, please?
Sue: I'm afraid she's not here at the moment. (1) _____
Anna: Yes, please. It's Anna calling. Could you ask her to call me when she gets back?
Sue: Sure. (2) _____
Anna: I think so but I'll give it to you anyway. It's 0209 435876.
Sue: Ok, (3) _____
Anna: Thanks very much.
Sue: Bye.
Anna: Goodbye.

A business call
Receptionist: Good morning. Smith and Dawson. (4) _____
John: Hello. Could I speak to Sylvie Roberts, please?
Receptionist: Certainly. (5) _____
John: It's John Wilson.
Receptionist: OK. (6) _____

a. I'll just put you through.
b. Does she have your number?
c. I'll ask her to call you when she gets in.
d. How can I help you?
e. Could I ask who's calling, please?
f. Can I take a message?

3 Invitations

Complete the dialogues with the phrases below:

Saying 'yes' to an invitation
Sasha: I was wondering whether you'd like to come over for dinner one evening.
Nihal: Yes, thank you (1) _____
Sasha: Are you free on Thursday evening?
Nihal: Yes. (2) _____
Sasha: About 7 o'clock?
Nihal: Yes, thanks, that would be great. (3) _____
Sasha: OK, see you on Thursday, then.
Nihal: (4) _____

a. I'll put it in my diary.
b. What sort of time?
c. I'd love to.
d. I'll look forward to it.

Saying 'no' politely to an invitation
Tomas: Suki, would you like to join us for dinner this evening?
Suki: I'd love to but (1) _____ - I'm meeting a friend.
Tomas: That's a shame.
Suki: Yes, (2) _____
Tomas: Maybe another time, then?
Suki: (3) _____

a. I'd love to have come otherwise.
b. Definitely.
c. I'm afraid I can't

4 Apologizing (saying you are sorry)

Complete the dialogues with the phrases below:

Vikram: Maria, (1) _____ I said I'd call you last night, and I completely forgot.
Maria: Oh, (2) _____ It doesn't matter. I know you're really busy.
Vikram: (3) _____ - it just completely slipped my mind.
Maria: Really, Vikram, it doesn't matter. (4) _____

a. Don't give it another thought.
b. don't worry about it.
c. I owe you an apology.
d. I feel really bad about it

5 At the restaurant

Complete the dialogues with the phrases below:

Before the meal
Waiter: Good evening.
Alexandra: Good evening. (1) _____
Waiter: (2) _____
Alexandra: No, I phoned earlier and the person I spoke to said I didn't need to reserve a table.
Waiter: Okay, please take a seat near the window.
Alexandra: Thanks. (3) _____ and wine list, please?

a. Do you have a reservation?
b. Could we see the menu
c. A table for two, please.

Ordering the meal
Waiter: Are you (1) _____
Alexandra: Yes, I think so. (2) _____ salmon, please.
Waiter: And for you, madam?
Danielle: Do you have (3) _____
Waiter: Yes, we have several dishes without meat, at the bottom of the menu.
Danielle: Ah yes, I'll have the mushroom tart, please.
Waiter: Okay. (4) _____
Danielle: Yes, one mixed salad, please.
Waiter: (5) _____
Danielle: A bottle of house red and some mineral water, please.
Waiter: (6) _____
Danielle: Sparkling, please.
Waiter: (7) _____
Danielle: Yes, thank you.

a. a vegetarian option?
b. I'll have the
c. Any side dishes with that?
d. And to drink?
e. ready to order?
f. Is that everything?
g. Sparkling or still?

During the meal
Waiter: (1) _____
Alexandra: Yes, thanks. (2) _____ bread, please?
Waiter: Certainly. And (3) _____ wine?
Alexandra: No thanks, but could we have another bottle of sparkling water?

a. Could we have some more
b. Is everything all right for you?
c. can I get you any more

After the meal
Waiter: (1) _____
Danielle: Yes, thanks. It was lovely.
Waiter: Good. (2) _____ More coffee?
Danielle: No thanks. (3) _____
Waiter: Of course.

a. Would you like anything else?
b. Could we have the (UK) bill/(US) check, please?
c. Did you enjoy your meal?

6 Visiting someone's house

Complete the dialogues with the phrases below:
Ethan arrives at Linda's house to have dinner.

Welcoming someone
Linda: Hello. (1) _____
Ethan: Hello. (2) _____
Linda: Not at all. Perfect timing. (3) _____
Ethan: Thank you.
Linda: (4) _____
Ethan: No, not at all. We've brought you these flowers.
Linda: Oh, (5) _____ They're beautiful - thank you!

a. I'm sorry we're late.
b. Did you have any problems finding us?
c. Lovely to see you.
d. you shouldn't have!
e. Let me take your coats.

Saying goodbye
Ethan: It's been a lovely evening. (1) _____
Linda: Not at all. (2) _____Thank you for coming.
Ethan: We'll see you soon. (3) _____
Linda: That would be great. See you soon. (4) _____
Ethan: Thanks. Bye!
Linda: Bye!

a. You must come over to us next time.
b. Thank you very much for having us.
c. It's been a pleasure.
d. Drive carefully

7 Asking someone how their family are

Complete the dialogue with the phrases below:

Luis: Juan, hello!
Juan: Hello Luis, how are you?
Luis: (1) _____, thanks, and you?
Juan: Fine. How's the family?
Luis: (2) _____, thanks. Julia has just been promoted at work.
Juan: (3) _____
Luis: Yes, she's very pleased.
Juan: Do (4) _____
Luis: Yes, I will. By the way, (5) _____, how is your father these days?
Juan: He's much better, thank you.
Luis: That's good. (6) _____, won't you?
Juan: Yes, I will. Thanks. (7) _____
Luis: Nice to see you too.

a. They're doing well
b. tell her I was asking after her.
c. Not too bad
d. Good for her!
e. Give him my regards when you see him
f. I was meaning to ask you
g. Nice to see you.

8 Talking about where you come from

Complete the dialogue with the phrases below:

Jude: So (1) _____, Thomas?
Thomas: I'm from Germany.
Jude: (2) _____ in Germany?
Thomas: From the north – Osnabrück. Do you know it?
Jude: No, I've been to Karlsruhe but I don't know the north of Germany at all.
Thomas: (3) _____ Where are you from?
Jude: (4) _____ Edinburgh but I live in London now.
Thomas: (5) _____ London?
Jude: North London – a place called Hampstead. (6) _____
Thomas: Yes, I know the name but I've never been there.

a. Have you heard of it?
b. What about you?
c. where are you from
d. I'm originally from
e. Whereabouts
f. Which part of

9 Talking about your plans...

Complete the dialogues with the phrases below:

...for the weekend

Akbar: (1) _____ this weekend?
Carolina: (2) _____ Just having (3) _____ at home. How about you?
Akbar: We're going to visit my brother in Paris.
Carolina: Paris? That'll be nice. (4) _____
Akbar: Yes, it should be good.

a. a quiet weekend
b. What are you doing
c. Are you looking forward to it?
d. Nothing special.

...for your (UK) holiday / (US) vacation

Georgia: (1) _____ this summer?
Leo: Yes, we're going camping in France. How about you?
Georgia: (2) _____ yet but (3) _____ Switzerland for a couple of weeks.
Leo: Switzerland. We went there last year and really enjoyed it. (4) _____

a. I think you'll like it.
b. we're thinking of going to
c. Are you going away
d. We haven't booked anything

10 Talking about the past weekend

Complete the dialogue with the phrases below:

Ava: (1) _____
Owen: Yes, thanks - very good. Did you?
Ava: Yes, it was nice.
Owen: Did you (2) _____
Ava: No not really – we just (3) _____ How about you?
Owen: We went to the coast on Saturday.
Ava: (4) _____
Owen: It was really nice. The weather was perfect.
Ava: (5) _____

a. Sounds great!
b. Did you have a good weekend?
c. do anything special?
d. had a quiet one.
e. How was that?

11 Cancelling an arrangement

Complete the dialogue with the phrases below:

Marta: I'm really sorry, Michel, but (1) _____ dinner tonight. (2) _____
Michel: Oh what a shame. (3) _____
Marta: Can we arrange it for another time?
Michel: Yes, (4) _____
Marta: Next week sometime would be great. (5) _____
Michel: Don't worry about it – it's not a problem.

a. Something's come up.
b. I'm going to have to cancel
c. I'm free most evenings next week.
d. Never mind.
e. I'm really sorry about tonight.

12 When someone tells you news

Complete the dialogues with the phrases below:

Good news
James: I've just heard that I've got the job.
Erin: (1) _____
James: Thank you!
Erin: Well done! (2) _____
James: Yes, I am. It's really good news.
Erin: I'm so pleased for you, James – you deserve it.
James: Thank you – (3) _____

Bad news
Conor: I'm afraid I won't be able to make it to the party tonight. I've got to work.
Patrice: Oh no, (4) _____ You were really looking forward to it.
Conor: Yes, I'm really disappointed.
Patrice: (5) _____ Is there no way round it?

a. You must be really pleased.
b. what a shame!
c. that's very kind.
d. Congratulations!
e. I bet you are.

Common learner errors at levels A1, A2, B1 and B2

The following pages focus on the sorts of mistakes that students of English at Common European Framework of Reference (CEFR) levels A1, A2, B1 and B2 make when they write exam papers. The information in these pages will help you avoid common mistakes in your exams.

All our information on typical student mistakes comes from the *Cambridge Learner Corpus*. The *Cambridge Learner Corpus* (*CLC*) is a large collection of exam scripts written by students taking Cambridge ESOL English exams. It currently contains over 45 million words of English written by learners and is growing all the time. 28 million words of the *CLC* have been coded according to the mistakes learners make. Many of these mistakes will be well-known to teachers. Others may seem strange, yet are very much in evidence in our corpus. The *CLC* has been developed in partnership with Cambridge ESOL, whose exams are taken by students all over the world.

Top 10 spelling mistakes

The words in the columns below are, in order of frequency, the most frequently misspelled words in the *Cambridge Learner Corpus* at CEFR levels A1, A2, B1 and B2. The **bold letters** in the column below show you which parts of the words students commonly get wrong. To ensure that you spell these words correctly, pay particular attention to these letters.

Correct spelling

A1	A2	B1	B2
1. be**cause**	1. be**cause**	1. be**cause**	1. advertis**e**ment
2. wi**th**	2. b**eau**tiful	2. rec**ei**ve	2. **wh**ich
3. ver**y**	3. tomorr**o**w	3. a**ccommo**dation	3. a**ccommo**dation
4. di**ff**erent	4. comfor**t**able	4. **wh**ich	4. be**cause**
5. b**eau**tiful	5. rec**ei**ve	5. b**eau**tiful	5. rec**ei**ve
6. tea**ch**er	6. mobil**e**	6. comfor**t**able	6. **en**vironment
7. lear**n**	7. **in**teresting	7. resta**u**rant	7. re**comm**end
8. ki**tch**en	8. **H**i	8. di**ff**erent	8. be**ginn**ing
9. co**u**ntry	9. fri**e**nd	9. sin**cere**ly	9. beli**e**ve
10. to**ge**ther	10. watch**ed**	10. re**comm**end	10. comfor**t**able

Spelling words in English can be difficult for learners because sometimes a word is very similar to a word in their own language but is not spelled the same. This is why French learners of English, for example, spell **success** with only one 's', or **colleague** without an 'a' . This is not just a problem for French speakers. Another thing that makes spelling difficult is that some words in English do not sound exactly as they are spelled. When an English person says **definitely**, for example, the second 'i' sounds more like an 'a'. It is important that students of English learn these differences.

Top 10 noun plural form mistakes

The following lists, taken from the *Cambridge Learner Corpus*, show you, in order of frequency, the ten nouns with plural forms that cause the most difficulty for students of English at A1, A2, B1 and B2 CEFR levels. The left column shows the singular form of the noun and the right column shows the correct plural form. Make sure you know the plural form of these nouns.

A1

Singular	Plural
1. person	people
2. potato	potatoes
3. country	countries
4. child	children
5. wish	wishes
6. year	years
7. movie	movies
8. family	families
9. city	cities
10. church	churches

A2

Singular	Plural
1. person	people
2. wish	wishes
3. photo	photos
4. class	classes
5. church	churches
6. potato	potatoes
7. kiss	kisses
8. child	children
9. beach	beaches
10. man	men

B1

Singular	Plural
1. member of staff	staff
2. person	people
3. man	men
4. city	cities
5. child	children
6. party	parties
7. life	lives
8. company	companies
9. woman	women
10. country	countries

B2

Singular	Plural
1. member of staff	staff
2. life	lives
3. child	children
4. company	companies
5. person	people
6. country	countries
7. city	cities
8. activity	activities
9. man	men
10. family	families

Top 10 verb form mistakes

The following lists, taken from the *Cambridge Learner Corpus* show the ten verbs that cause the most difficulty for students of English at A1, A2, B1 and B2 CEFR levels. The **bold letters** in this list show you the letters that students most often get wrong.

A1

Verb	Correct inflection
1. study	present participle: study**ing**
2. write	present participle: wri**t**ing
3. travel	present participle: trave**ll**ing*
4. swim	present participle: swi**mm**ing
5. come	present participle: co**m**ing
6. live	present participle: li**v**ing
7. learn	past simple: lear**ned**/lear**nt**
8. chat	present participle: cha**tt**ing
9. watch	3rd person singular present simple: watch**es**
10. use	present participle: us**ing**

* in US English, the correct inflection is *traveling.*

A2

Verb	Correct inflection
1. cost	past simple: cost
2. pay	past smple: **pai**d
3. write	present participle: wri**t**ing
4. buy	past simple: b**ough**t
5. come	present participle: co**m**ing
6. give	past simple: **gave**
7. enjoy	past simple: enjo**yed**
8. travel	past simple: trave**lle**d*
9. choose	past simple: ch**o**se
10. study	present participle: study**ing**

* in US English, the correct inflection is *traveled.*

B1

Verb	Correct inflection
1. write	present participle: wri**t**ing; past participle: wri**tt**en
2. choose	past participle: ch**o**sen; past simple: ch**o**se
3. plan	present participle: pla**nn**ing; past simple: pla**nn**ed
4. come	present participle: co**m**ing
5. happen	past simple: happen**ed**
6. study	present participle: study**ing**
7. travel	present participle: trave**ll**ing; past simple: trave**lle**d*
8. enjoy	past simple: enjo**yed**
9. hear	past simple: hea**rd**
10. read	past simple: read

* in US English, the correct inflections is *traveling* and *traveled.*

B2

Verb	Correct inflection
1. write	present participle: wri**t**ing; past participle: wri**tt**en
2. happen	past simple: happen**ed**
3. study	present participle: study**ing**
4. choose	past participle: ch**o**sen; past simple: ch**o**se
5. travel	present participle: trave**ll**ing; past simple: trave**lle**d*
6. refer	present participle: refe**rr**ing; past simple: refe**rr**ed
7. plan	present participle: pla**nn**ing; past simple: pla**nn**ed
8. pay	past simple: **pai**d
9. hear	past simple: hea**rd**
10. come	present participle: co**m**ing

* in US English, the correct inflections are *traveling* and *traveled.*

Top 10 uncountable noun mistakes

An uncountable noun is a noun that cannot be counted. It does not have a plural form and it cannot be used with 'a' or 'one'. Examples of uncountable nouns are 'music' and 'furniture'.

The lists below, taken from the *Cambridge Learner Corpus*, show the ten most frequent uncountable nouns that A2, B1 and B2 students try to make plural by adding 's'. Remember not to make a plural form of these nouns by adding 's'. Some of these nouns can be made plural by adding phrases such as 'piece of' or 'item of' before the noun, e.g. *She gave me two very useful **pieces of** advice*. Where such phrases are used, we have provided them in the right column. The corpus does not show data for this error at A1 level.

A2			B1	
1. information	**pieces of** information		1. information	**pieces of** information
2. music	**pieces of** music		2. equipment	**pieces of** equipment
3. paper*	**pieces of** paper		3. advice	**pieces of** advice
4. love			4. homework	**pieces of** homework
5. homework	**pieces of** homework		5. furniture	**pieces of** furniture
6. seafood			6. countryside	
7. equipment	**pieces of** equipment		7. work*	**pieces of** work
8. popcorn			8. training	
9. work*	**pieces of** work		9. scenery	
10. stuff			10. transport	

B2	
1. information	**pieces of** information
2. advice	**pieces of** advice
3. equipment	**pieces of** equipment
4. transport	**modes/means of** transport
5. knowledge	
6. training	
7. spending	
8. work*	**pieces of** work
9. homework	**pieces of** homework
10. furniture	**pieces of** furniture

*This word also has a meaning that can be made plural. See the main dictionary for this.

Although a lot of languages have words which do not have a plural form, these are not usually the same words. The words for **furniture** in German, Russian and Italian, for example, all have a plural form. It is easy for learners of English to make a mistake.

Top 10 plural nouns without a singular form

The following list, taken from the *Cambridge Learner Corpus* shows you, in order of frequency, the ten plural nouns or nouns ending in 's' which do not have a singular form without 's' that cause the most difficulty for A2, B1 and B2 students of English. The corpus does not show data for this error at A1 level.

A2
1. shorts
2. jeans
3. trousers
4. clothes
5. pants
6. pyjamas
7. overalls
8. news
9. maths*
10. congratulations

* in US English, *maths* is singular, i.e. *math*.

B1
1. clothes
2. trousers
3. news
4. jeans
5. shorts
6. series
7. goods
8. headquarters
9. premises
10. sheep

B2
1. means
2. gymnastics
3. surroundings
4. news
5. headquarters
6. goods
7. thanks
8. aerobics
9. mathematics
10. trousers

Words that are often confused

The following lists show words that are, in order of frequency, commonly confused by A1, A2, B1 and B2 students of English. Look up these words in the dictionary and make sure you know the difference.

Top 10 spellings that are often confused

A1

1. to	too	
2. quite	quiet	
3. now	know	
4. hear	here	
5. thing	think	
6. than	then	
7. with	which	witch
8. now	new	
9. four	for	
10. an	and	

A2

1. to	too	
2. by	bye	buy
3. an	and	
4. than	then	
5. thing	think	
6. now	know	
7. cheep	cheap	
8. where	were	
9. some	same	
10. there	their	

B1

1. to	too	two
2. than	then	that
3. an	and	
4. by	bye	buy
5. were	where	
6. thing	think	
7. now	know	
8. quite	quiet	
9. though	thought	
10. their	there	

B2

1. to	too	
2. think	thing	
3. than	then	that
4. an	and	
5. the	they	
6. there	their	
7. now	know	
8. hole	whole	
9. quiet	quite	
10. by	buy	

Top 10 nouns that are often confused

A1

1. home	house
2. collage	college
3. think	thing
4. meet	meat
5. place	space
6. meter	metre
7. diner	dinner
8. topic	subject (in school)
9. desert	dessert
10. cost	coast

A2

1. home	house
2. cloth	clothes
3. name	title
4. play	game
5. travel	trip
6. cost	price
7. class	classroom
8. hour	time
9. basket	basketball
10. sweat	sweatshirt

B1

1. cloth	clothes
2. program	programme
3. travel	trip
4. home	house
5. hour	time
6. shopping	shopping centre
7. notice	news
8. night	evening
9. job	work
10. possibility	opportunity

B2

1. possibility	opportunity	
2. travel	trip	journey
3. place	space	
4. advertisement	advertising	
5. work	job	
6. parking	car park	
7. way	journey	
8. hour	time	moment
9. trouble	problem	
10. food	dish	

Top 10 adjectives that are often confused

A1*

1. best	favourite
2. well	good
3. boring	bored
4. poorly	poor
5. interesting	interested

* The corpus data shows only five commonly confused adjectives for A1 level.

A2

1. interesting	interested
2. funny	fun
3. classic	classical
4. well	good
5. best	favourite
6. last	latest
7. exciting	excited
8. historical	historic
9. long	far
10. comfortable	convenient

B1

1. funny	fun
2. interesting	interested
3. historical	historic
4. last	latest
5. well	good
6. exciting	excited
7. afraid	sorry
8. interested	interesting
9. suitable	convenient
10. comfortable	convenient

B2

1. interesting	interested
2. historical	historic
3. funny	fun
4. last	latest
5. grateful	great
6. exciting	excited
7. typical	traditional
8. actual	current
9. economical	economic
10. common	ordinary

Top 10 verbs that are often confused

A1*

1. learn   study   teach
2. go   come
3. spend (time)   have (time)
4. know   get to know
5. say   tell   ask

* The corpus data shows only five commonly confused verbs for A1 level.

A2

1. go   come
2. use   wear
3. have   be (+ age)
4. bring   take
5. do   have (party, meeting, fun)
6. forget   leave
7. take   get
8. see   watch
9. say   tell
10. hear   listen to

B1

1. use   wear
2. say   tell
3. come   go
4. watch   see
5. wish   hope
6. get   have
7. know   meet   get to know
8. borrow   lend
9. bring   take
10. know   find out

B2

1. come   go
2. get   have
3. wish   hope
4. say   tell
5. like   want
6. bring   take
7. know   find out/learn   get to know
8. require   request
9. join   attend
10. reach   achieve

Some verbs that are commonly confused are not included in these lists because the difference is too subtle for dictionary definitions alone to provide a clear explanation and the correct choice often depends on context or collocation. The commonly confused verbs not included are **have/do**, **make/do**, **be/have**. Look at the section on modal verbs on page Centre 22 and the common learner error note at **do** to help you with these verbs.

Top 10 following verb form mistakes

This is a list of the most frequent mistakes that students make with the form of a verb that follows another verb.

A1*

* The corpus data shows only eight common verb form mistakes at A1 level.

1 Main Verb like
✗ ~~like do sth~~
✗ ~~I like play football at college.~~
✓ like doing sth
✓ I **like playing** football at college.

2 Main Verb want
✗ ~~want do sth~~
✗ ~~I want invite you to dinner.~~
✓ want to do sth
✓ I **want to invite** you to dinner.

3 Main Verb can
✗ ~~can to do sth; can doing sth~~
✗ ~~I can skiing in winter, too; I can to meet you this afternoon.~~
✓ can do sth
✓ I **can ski** in winter, too; I **can meet** you this afternoon.

4 Main Verb love
✗ ~~love do sth~~
✗ ~~I love spend time with my friends.~~
✓ love doing sth
✓ I **love spending** time with my friends.

5 Main Verb need
✗ ~~need do sth~~
✗ ~~After the bridge, you need turn left.~~
✓ need to do sth
✓ After the bridge, you **need to turn** left.

6 Main Verb learn
✗ ~~learn do sth~~
✗ ~~At college I can learn speaking English.~~
✓ learn to do sth
✓ At college I can **learn to speak** English.

7 Main Verb will
✗ ~~will doing sth~~
✗ ~~I will coming to your house.~~
✓ will do sth
✓ I **will come** to your house.

8 Main Verb enjoy
✗ ~~enjoy do sth~~
✗ ~~I enjoy go to college.~~
✓ enjoy doing sth
✓ I **enjoy going** to college.

A2

1 Main Verb (would) like
✗ ~~would like do sth; would like doing sth; would like did sth~~
✗ ~~I would like have a pen friend in another country; I would like watching the tennis match with you.~~
✓ would like to do sth
✓ I **would like to have** a pen friend in another country; I **would like to watch** the tennis match with you.

2 Main Verb want
✗ ~~want do sth~~
✗ ~~I want invite you to my house.~~
✓ want to do sth
✓ I **want to invite** you to my house.

3 Main Verb can
✗ ~~can did sth; can doing sth~~
✗ ~~I can met you at 8 o'clock; After the film we can going to a restaurant.~~
✓ can do sth
✓ I **can meet** you at 8 o'clock; After the film **we can** go to a restaurant.

4 Main Verb need
✗ ~~need do sth~~
✗ ~~You need wear warm clothes because it's cold here.~~
✓ need to do sth
✓ You **need to wear** warm clothes because it's cold here.

5 Main Verb will
✗ ~~will doing sth; will did sth~~
✗ ~~We will going to the sports centre by car; I will arrived tomorrow at 7 p.m.~~
✓ will do sth
✓ We **will go** to the sports centre by car; I **will arrive** tomorrow at 7 p.m.

6 Main Verb hope
✗ ~~hope do sth~~
✗ ~~I hope see you very soon.~~
✓ hope to do sth
✓ I **hope to see** you very soon.

7 Main Verb must
✗ ~~must to do sth~~
✗ ~~You must to wear comfortable clothes and trainers.~~
✓ must do sth
✓ You **must wear** comfortable clothes and trainers.

8 Main Verb look forward to
✗ ~~look forward to do sth~~
✗ ~~I'm looking forward to see you next week.~~
✓ look forward to doing sth
✓ I'm **looking forward to seeing** you next week.

9 Main Verb should
✗ ~~should to do sth~~
✗ ~~You should to bring some money for the cinema.~~
✓ should do sth
✓ You **should bring** some money for the cinema.

10 Main Verb like
✗ ~~like do sth~~
✗ ~~I like play computer games.~~
✓ like doing sth / like to do sth
✓ I **like playing** computer games; I **like to play** computer games.

B1

1 Main Verb look forward to
✗ ~~look forward to do sth~~
✗ ~~I'm looking forward to meet you in April.~~
✓ look forward to doing sth
✓ I'm **looking forward to meeting** you in April.

2 Main Verb would like
✗ ~~would like do sth; would like doing sth~~
✗ ~~I would like live closer to the city centre.~~
✓ would like to do sth
✓ I **would like to live** closer to the city centre.

3 Main Verb want
✗ ~~want do sth~~
✗ ~~I want invite you to my birthday party.~~
✓ want to do sth
✓ I **want to invite** you to my birthday party.

4 Main Verb suggest
✗ ~~suggest to do sth~~
✗ ~~I suggest to ask Peter Hobbs for help.~~
✓ suggest doing sth
✓ I **suggest asking** Peter Hobbs for help.

5 Main Verb hope
✗ hope do sth
✗ I hope see you very soon.
✓ hope to do sth
✓ I **hope to see** you very soon.

6 Main Verb can
✗ can did sth; can doing sth
✗ I hope you can came to visit me soon.; You can staying with my family.
✓ can do sth
✓ I hope you **can come** to visit me soon; You **can stay** with my family.

7 Main Verb like
✗ like do sth
✗ I like go shopping with my friends.
✓ like doing sth / like to do sth
✓ I **like going** shopping with my friends; I **like to go** shopping with my friends.

8 Main Verb will
✗ will doing sth; will did sth
✗ I will meeting you in the park tomorrow; I will arrived at the airport at 10 am.
✓ will do sth
✓ I **will meet** you in the park tomorrow; I **will arrive** at the airport at 10 am.

9 Main Verb must
✗ must to do sth
✗ I must to thank you for an amazing weekend.
✓ must do sth
✓ I **must thank** you for an amazing weekend.

10 Main Verb love
✗ love do sth
✗ I love go shopping with my friends.
✓ love doing sth / love to do sth
✓ I **love going** shopping with my friends; I **love to go** shopping with my friends.

B2

1 Main Verb look forward to
✗ look forward to do sth
✗ I am looking forward to go to the festival.
✓ look forward to doing sth
✓ I'm **looking forward to going** to the festival.

2 Main Verb suggest
✗ suggest to do sth
✗ I suggest to meet at 9pm.
✓ suggest doing sth
✓ I **suggest meeting** at 9pm.

3 Main Verb like
✗ like do sth
✗ I like to live here, and I find this an attractive town.
✓ like doing sth
✓ I **like living** here and I find this an attractive town.

4 Main Verb recommend
✗ recommend to do sth
✗ I recommend to take the train.
✓ recommend doing sth / recommend sb does sth
✓ I **recommend taking** the train; I **recommend you take** the train.

5 Main Verb can
✗ can did sth; can doing sth
✗ We can discussing it later; She can worked with all kinds of people.
✓ can do sth
✓ We **can discuss** it later; She **can work** with all kinds of people.

6 Main Verb will
✗ will did sth; will doing sth
✗ I have something you will enjoyed; Tonight we will eating in a beautiful restaurant.
✓ will do sth
✓ I have something you **will enjoy**; Tonight we **will eat** in a beautiful restaurant.

7 Main Verb want
✗ want do sth
✗ I want know about the English course.
✓ want to do sth
✓ I **want to know** about the English course.

8 Main Verb would like
✗ would like do sth; would like doing sth
✗ I would like apply for the job.
✓ would like to do sth
✓ I **would like to apply** for the job.

9 Main Verb should
✗ should to do sth
✗ I think you should to apply for this job.
✓ should do sth
✓ I think you **should apply** for this job.

10 Main Verb prefer
✗ prefer to do sth
✗ I prefer to read books to watching television.
✓ prefer doing sth / prefer to do sth
✓ I **prefer reading** books to watching television; I **would prefer to work** with animals.

Answer Key

Checking your work

1 1 The new rule affects everyone.
  2 What time is it?
  3 It's quite hot in here.
  4 Where can I find information about volcanoes?
2 1 do 2 take 3 of 4 feeling
  3 Ancient tribes moved to the area hundreds of years ago, bringing *sheep* and cattle with them. They also hunted deer and *caught* fish, and *learned to* grind wheat to makes *loaves* of bread. They *built* simple houses with mud walls and roofs made of sticks, and in the evenings, they *sang* songs and told *stories* around the fire.

Countable and uncountable nouns

1 1 homework 2 sand 3 ✓ 4 ✓ 5 luggage
2 1 an 2 —, a 3 a 4 — 5 —
3 1 fly 2 furniture 3 luggage 4 day 5 accidents
4 1 a lot of 2 much 3 many 4 much
  5 duck, ice cream, lipstick, pizza

Modal verbs

1 1 might not 2 will 3 mustn't 4 can't 5 may
2 1 b 2 d 3 a 4 e 5 c
3 1 d 2 c 3 e 4 a 5 b

Phrasal verbs

1 1 drag: 3 2 hand: 5 3 pack: 3 4 make: 12
2 1 on 2 off 3 up 4 over
3 your own answers
4 1 for 2 with 3 on 4 about 5 on

Idioms

1 1 neck: b 2 nail: e 3 battle: a 4 end: c 5 face: d
2 1 leg 2 head 3 arm 4 ear 5 face

Verb patterns

1 1 T 2 I, T 3 I, T 4 I, T 5 T 6 I, T 7 T 8 I, T 9 I 10 T
2 1 c 2 e 3 d 4 a 5 b
3 your own answers

Word formation

1 1 unlock 2 disagree 3 illegal 4 impossible 5 irresponsible
2 1 unlock 2 impossible 3 illegal 4 disagree 5 irresponsible
3 1 e, multiracial 2 a, semicircle 3 f, anti-war 4 b, pro-democracy 5 c, ex-president

6 g, postgraduate 7 h, overworked 8 d, under-cooked
4 1 rudeness 2 creation 3 preference 4 ignorance 5 hilarity 6 development

Measurements

1 wide, width 2 long 3 depth 4 high, high

Pronunciation

1 1 d 2 e 3 b 4 f 5 a 6 c
2 1 mole 2 giraffe 3 horse 4 sheep 5 lion 6 chimp
3 1 k 2 h 3 s 4 w 5 w 6 l
4 1 **bro**ther 2 edu**ca**tion 3 pho**tog**rapher 4 be**low** 5 com**pu**ter 6 **ne**cessary

Spelling

1 1 houses 2 watches 3 bricks 4 minutes 5 faxes 6 losses
2 1 whether 2 quite 3 which 4 their 5 sea
3 1 hotter 2 banned 3 loudest 4 beginning 5 working

UK and US English

1 1 d 2 e 3 a 4 c 5 f 6 b
2 1 b 2 e 3 a 4 d 5 c
3 in each case, UK comes first:
  1 labour/labor 2 centre/center 3 offence/offense 4 colour/color 5 metre/meter 6 traveller/traveler
4 schedule, ballet, zebra

Speaking naturally

1 conversation exercises
  1 1 b 2 c 3 a 4 d
2 An informal call
  1 f 2 b 3 c
  A business call
  4 d 5 e 6 a
3 Saying 'yes' to an invitation
  1 c 2 b 3 a 4 d
  Saying 'no' politely to an invitation
  1 c 2 a 3 b
4 Apologizing
  1 c 2 b 3 d 4 a
5 Before the meal
  1 c 2 a 3 b
  Ordering the meal
  1 e 2 b 3 a 4 c 5 d 6 g 7 f
  During the meal
  1 b 2 a 3 c
  After the meal
  1 c 2 a 3 b
6 Welcoming someone
  1 c 2 a 3 e 4 b 5 d
  Saying goodbye
  1 b 2 c 3 a 4 d

7 Asking someone how their family are
  1 c **2** a **3** d **4** b **5** f **6** e **7** g
8 Talking about where you come from
  1 c **2** e **3** b **4** d **5** f **6** a
9 For this weekend
  1 b **2** d **3** a **4** c
  For a (UK) holiday/(US) vacation
  1 c **2** d **3** b **4** a
10 Talking about the past weekend
   1 b **2** c **3** d **4** e **5** a
11 Cancelling an arrangement
   1 b **2** a **3** d **4** c **5** e
12 Good news
   1 d **2** a **3** c
   Bad news
   4 b **5** e

happiness: *a merry laugh* ◦ ***Merry Christmas!***
• **merrily** adv

merry-go-round /ˈmerigəʊˌraʊnd/ **noun** [C]
(also UK **roundabout**, also US **carousel**) a
machine that goes round and round and has
toy animals or cars for children to ride on

mesh¹ /meʃ/ **noun** [C, U] material that is like a
net and is made of wire, plastic, or thread:
a wire mesh fence

mesh² /meʃ/ **verb** [I] If two or more things mesh,
they are suitable for each other: *Her ideas **mesh**
well **with** our plans for the future.*

mess¹ /mes/ **noun** [C] **1 UNTIDY** ▷ 🅑 Someone
or something that is a mess, or is in a mess, is
dirty or untidy: [usually singular] *My hair's such a
mess!* ◦ *The house is **in a mess**.* ◦ *Don't **make a
mess** in the kitchen!* **2 DIFFICULT** ▷ 🅒 a confused
or difficult situation: [usually singular] *She told me
that her life was a mess.* ◦ *If he hadn't lied, he
wouldn't be **in** this **mess** now.* **3 make a mess of
sth** to damage or spoil something: *He made a
mess of his first marriage.* **4 MILITARY** ▷ a place
where members of the armed forces eat:
[usually singular] *the officers' mess*

> ☑ Word partners for **mess**
>
> **make** a mess • **clean up/clear up** a mess •
> be **in** a mess

mess² /mes/ **verb**

PHRASAL VERBS **mess about/around** informal **1** to
waste time, often by doing things that are not
important: *Stop messing around and do your
homework!* **2** to spend time playing and doing
things with no particular purpose: *I can spend
hours **messing around with** my computer.* •
mess sb about/around UK informal to treat
someone badly, often by not doing something
that you have promised • **mess about/around
with sth** informal to use or treat something in a
careless or harmful way: *Who's been messing
around with my computer?* • **mess sth up 1** to
make something untidy or dirty: *I hate wearing
hats – they always mess up my hair.* **2** 🅒 to spoil
something, or to do something badly: *Don't try
to cook lunch by yourself – you'll only mess it up.*
• **mess with sb/sth** informal to become involved
with someone or something dangerous: *Anyone
who messes with drugs is stupid.*

message¹ /ˈmesɪdʒ/ **noun** [C] **1** 🅐 a piece of
written or spoken information that one person
gives to another: *Did you **get** my **message**?* ◦ *I
left her several **messages**, but she hasn't returned
my call.* **2** 🅒 the most important idea of a film,
book, etc: *The book conveys a complex message.*

IDIOM **get the message** informal to understand
what someone wants you to do by their actions:
*Don't return any of his calls – he'll soon get the
message and leave you alone.*

> ☑ Word partners for **message**
>
> **get/leave/send/take** a message • a message
> **for/from** sb

message² /ˈmesɪdʒ/ **verb** [T] to send someone

an email or text message (= a written message
sent from one mobile phone to another)

message board noun [C] 🅒 a place on a
website where you can leave messages for other
people to read

messaging /ˈmesɪdʒɪŋ/ **noun** [U] the act of
sending a message to someone using electronic
equipment: *a messaging service*

messenger /ˈmesɪndʒər/ **noun** [C] someone who
takes a message between two people

the Messiah /məˈsaɪə/ **noun 1** Jesus Christ
2 the leader that Jews believe God will send
them

Messrs /ˈmesəz/ **noun** formal a title used before
the names of two or more men: *Messrs Davis and
Dixon led the discussion on tax reform.*

messy /ˈmesi/ **adj 1** 🅑 untidy or dirty: *messy
hair* ◦ *a messy house/car* ◦ *My son's bedroom is
always messy.* **2** unpleasant and complicated:
*Ian's just gone through a **messy divorce**.*

met /met/ past of meet

metabolism /məˈtæbəlɪzəm/ **noun** [C] all the
chemical processes in your body, especially the
ones that use food

metal /ˈmetəl/ **noun** [C, U] 🅑 a usually hard,
shiny material such as iron, gold, or silver which
heat and electricity can travel through: *scrap
metal* ◦ *Metals are used for making machinery
and tools.* ◦ *a metal sheet/bar* • **metallic** /məˈtæ
lɪk/ **adj** having a quality that is similar to metal:
a metallic paint/taste → See also **heavy metal**

metamorphosis /ˌmetəˈmɔːfəsɪs/ **noun** (plural
metamorphoses /ˌmetəˈmɔːfiːz/) **1** [C] a
gradual change into something very different:
*The past year has seen a complete metamorphosis
of the country's economy.* **2** [U] in biology, the
process by which the young forms of some
animals, such as insects, develop into very
different adult forms: *Caterpillars changing into
butterflies is an example of metamorphosis.*

metaphor /ˈmetəfər/ **noun** [C, U] a way of
describing something by comparing it with
something else that has some of the same
qualities: *She used a computer metaphor to
explain how the brain works.* • **metaphorical**
/ˌmetəˈfɒrɪkəl/ **adj** using a metaphor

mete /miːt/ **verb** (**meting, meted**)

PHRASAL VERB **mete sth out** formal to punish
someone: [often passive] *Long jail sentences are
meted out to drug smugglers.*

meteor /ˈmiːtiər/ **noun** [C] a rock from outer
space that becomes very hot and burns brightly
in the sky at night as it enters Earth's
atmosphere (= air surrounding Earth)

meteoric /ˌmiːtiˈɒrɪk/ **adj** If the development of
something is meteoric, it happens very quickly
or causes great success: *a meteoric career* ◦ *The
band's rise to fame was meteoric.*

meteorite /ˈmiːtiəraɪt/ **noun** [C] a piece of rock
from outer space that has fallen on Earth's
surface

meteorological /ˌmiːtiərəˈlɒdʒɪkəl/ **adj** [always
before noun] relating to the scientific study of
weather

M

meteorologist /ˌmiːtiˀrˈɒlədʒɪst/ **noun** [C] someone who studies weather, especially to say how it will be in the near future • **meteorology noun** [U] the scientific study of weather

meter /ˈmiːtər/ **noun** [C] **1** a piece of equipment for measuring the amount of something such as electricity, time, or light: *a gas/water meter* ∘ *a parking/taxi meter* **2** US spelling of metre

methadone /ˈmeθədəʊn/ **noun** [U] a drug for treating people who want to stop using heroin (= an illegal drug)

methane /ˈmiːθeɪn/ Ⓤ /ˈmeθeɪn/ **noun** [U] a gas that has no colour or smell, used for cooking and heating

method /ˈmeθəd/ **noun** [C] Ⓑ a way of doing something, often one that involves a system or plan: *What's the best method of/for solving this problem?* ∘ *traditional teaching methods*

> 🗹 Word partners for **method**
>
> an **alternative/new/reliable/simple/traditional** method • **develop/devise/use a** method

methodical /məˈθɒdɪkˀl/ **adj** careful and well organized, using a plan or system: *a methodical researcher* • **methodically adv**

Methodist /ˈmeθədɪst/ **adj** belonging or relating to a Christian group that was started by John Wesley • **Methodist noun** [C]

methodological /ˌmeθədəˀlˈɒdʒɪkˀl/ **adj** relating to a methodology: *methodological problems*

methodology /ˌmeθəˈdɒlədʒi/ **noun** [C, U] the system of methods used for doing, teaching, or studying something

meticulous /məˈtɪkjələs/ **adj** very careful, and giving great attention to detail: *This book is the result of meticulous research.* • **meticulously adv**

me time /ˈmiːtaɪm/ **noun** [U] informal time when you can do exactly what you want

metre UK (US **meter**) /ˈmiːtər/ **noun 1** [C] (written abbreviation **m**) Ⓐ a unit for measuring length, equal to 100 centimetres: *Our bedroom is five metres wide.* ∘ *She finished third in the women's 400 metres (= running race).* **2** [C, U] a pattern of rhythm in poetry

metric /ˈmetrɪk/ **adj** The metric system of measurement uses units based on the gram, metre, and litre.

ˌmetric ˈton **noun** [C] a unit for measuring weight, equal to 1000 kilograms

metro¹ /ˈmetrəʊ/ **noun** [C] an underground railway system in a large city: *the Paris metro*

> ❗ Common learner error: **metro, subway, or underground**?
>
> All these words mean an underground railway system in a large city. **Metro** is the most general word. The usual word in British English is **underground**. In American English it is **subway**.
> *the Paris metro*
> *the London underground*
> *the New York subway*

metro² /ˈmetrəʊ/ **adj** [always before noun] Ⓤ informal relating to a large city and the towns around it: *the New York metro area*

metropolis /məˈtrɒpəlɪs/ **noun** [C] a very large city, often the capital of a country or region

metropolitan /ˌmetrəˈpɒlɪtˀn/ **adj** [always before noun] relating to a large city: *a metropolitan area, council*

metrosexual /ˌmetrəʊˈseksjuəl/ **noun** [C] a man who is sexually attracted to women but is also interested in fashion and the way he looks → Compare **retrosexual**

mg written abbreviation for milligram (= a unit for measuring weight)

miaow UK (US **meow**) /ˌmiːˈaʊ/ **noun** [C] the sound that a cat makes

mice /maɪs/ plural of mouse

mickey /ˈmɪki/ **take the mickey (out of sb)** UK informal to laugh at someone and make them seem silly

micro- /maɪkrəʊ-/ **prefix** very small: *a microchip* ∘ *microscopic (= very small)*

microbe /ˈmaɪkrəʊb/ **noun** [C] a very small organism, often a bacterium that causes disease

microblog¹ (also **micro-blog**) /ˈmaɪkrəʊˌblɒɡ/ **noun** [C] a blog (= record of thoughts put on the Internet) in the form of short messages for anyone to read, sent especially from a mobile phone: *Microblogs, for example on Twitter, can be for anything from "what I'm doing now" to coverage of serious political events.*

microblog² (**microblogging, microblogged**) (also **micro-blog**) /ˈmaɪkrəʊˌblɒɡ/ **verb** [I] to send short messages for anyone to read on the Internet, especially from a mobile phone

microblogging (also **micro-blogging**) /ˈmaɪkrəʊˌblɒɡɪŋ/ **noun** [U] the activity of sending short messages for anyone to read on the Internet, especially from a mobile phone

microchip /ˈmaɪkrəʊtʃɪp/ **noun** [C] a very small part of a computer or machine that does calculations or stores information

microcosm /ˈmaɪkrəʊˌkɒzˀm/ **noun** [C] formal a place, group of people, or situation that has the same characteristics as a larger one: *The town is a microcosm of French culture.*

microphone /ˈmaɪkrəfəʊn/ **noun** [C] Ⓑ a piece of electrical equipment for recording or broadcasting sounds, or for making sounds louder

microprocessor /ˌmaɪkrəʊˈprəʊsesər/ Ⓤ /ˈmaɪkrəʊˌprɑːsesər/ **noun** [C] the part of a computer that controls all the other parts

microscope /ˈmaɪkrəskəʊp/ **noun** [C] a piece of scientific equipment that uses lenses (= pieces of curved glass) to make very small objects look bigger

microscope

microscopic /ˌmaɪkrə'skɒpɪk/ adj extremely small and needing a microscope to be seen, or using a microscope to see something: *microscopic organisms/particles*

microsite /'maɪkrəʊˌsaɪt/ noun [C] a small website, usually one advertising a particular product or service for a company

microwave¹ /'maɪkrəʊweɪv/ noun [C] **1** (also ˌmicrowave 'oven) an electric oven that uses waves of energy to cook or heat food → See colour picture **The Kitchen** on page Centre 2 **2** a very short wave similar to a radio wave that is used for sending information and cooking

microwave² /'maɪkrəʊweɪv/ verb [T] to cook or heat food using a microwave oven

mid- /mɪd-/ prefix among or in the middle of: *mid-March* ∘ *mid-afternoon*

mid-air /ˌmɪd'eəʳ/ noun **in mid-air** in the air or sky: *She jumped up and caught the ball in mid-air.* • **mid-air** adj [always before noun] *a mid-air collision*

midday /ˌmɪd'deɪ/ noun [U] 🄰🄰 12 o'clock in the middle of the day, or the period around this time: *the heat of the midday sun*

middle¹ /'mɪdl/ noun **1 the middle** 🄱🄰 the central part, position, or point in time: *We used to live just outside Boston but now we live right (= exactly) in the middle.* ∘ *The letter should arrive by the middle of next week.* **2 be in the middle of doing sth** 🄱🄰 to be busy: *I can't talk now – I'm in the middle of cooking a meal.* **3 your middle** informal your waist, or your waist and stomach: *He wrapped the towel round his middle.*

IDIOM **in the middle of nowhere** 🄱🄰 a long way from places where people live: *His car broke down in the middle of nowhere.*

middle² /'mɪdl/ adj [always before noun] **1** 🄱🄰 in a central position: *The middle layer is made of plastic.* ∘ *Our company rents the middle warehouse.* **2** neither high nor low in importance or amount: *middle managers*

middle-aged /ˌmɪdl'eɪdʒd/ adj 🄱🄰 in the middle of your life before you are old: *a middle-aged couple/man/woman*

the ˌMiddle 'Ages noun the period in European history between the end of the Roman Empire and the start of the Renaissance

middle 'class noun [group] a social group that consists of well-educated people, such as doctors, lawyers, and teachers, who have good jobs and are neither very rich nor very poor • **middle-class** /ˌmɪdl'klɑːs/ adj belonging or relating to the middle class: *a middle-class suburb*

the ˌMiddle 'East noun a group of countries in the area where Africa, Asia, and Europe meet • **Middle Eastern** adj relating to the Middle East: *Middle Eastern cuisine*

middleman /'mɪdlmæn/ noun [C] (plural **middlemen**) someone who buys goods from one person and sells them to someone else for a higher price: *Selling direct from the factory cuts out the middleman.*

middle 'name noun [C] an extra name between someone's first and family names

middle ˌschool noun [C] a school in the US for children usually between the ages of 11 and 14

midget /'mɪdʒɪt/ noun [C] someone who is very small

the Midlands /'mɪdləndz/ noun the central area of England that includes several large industrial cities

mid-life 'crisis noun [C] (plural **mid-life crises**) a period in the middle of your life when you lose confidence in your abilities and worry about the future

midnight /'mɪdnaɪt/ noun [U] 🄰🄰 12 o'clock at night: *He died shortly after midnight.*

midriff /'mɪdrɪf/ noun [C] the front of your body between your chest and waist

midst /mɪdst/ noun **1 in the midst of sth** in the middle of something, usually an event or activity **2 in your midst** among the group of people that you belong to: *Residents are protesting about a convicted murderer living in their midst.*

midsummer /ˌmɪd'sʌməʳ/ noun [U] the longest day of the year, or the period around this

midterm /'mɪdtɜːm/ adj in the middle of a school or university term (= fixed period of time that the school or university year is divided into): *Midterm exams start next week.*

midtown /'mɪdˌtaʊn/ noun [U] US the part of a city near the centre

midway /ˌmɪd'weɪ/ adv **1 midway between sth and sth** at the middle point between two places or things: *Leeds is midway between London and Edinburgh.* **2 midway through sth** at the middle point of an activity or a period of time: *He scored the third goal midway through the second half.*

midweek /ˌmɪd'wiːk/ noun [U] the middle of the week, usually from Tuesday to Thursday • **midweek** adj, adv [always before noun] in the middle of the week: *a midweek game/match* ∘ *Flights are cheaper if you travel midweek.*

the Midwest /ˌmɪd'west/ noun the northern central area of the United States • **Midwestern** adj [always before noun] relating to the Midwest

midwife /'mɪdwaɪf/ noun [C] (plural **midwives** /'mɪdwaɪvz/) a nurse who has had special training to help women give birth

midwifery /mɪd'wɪfʳri/ noun [U] the work of a midwife

midwinter /ˌmɪd'wɪntəʳ/ noun [U] the shortest day of the year, or the period around this

might¹ /maɪt/ modal verb **1** 🄰🄰 used to talk about what will possibly happen: *It might be finished by Thursday.* ∘ *She might not come.* **2** 🄱🄰 used to talk about what is possibly true: *I think Isabel might be pregnant.* ∘ *The rain might have stopped by now.* **3 you might like/want to** UK formal used to politely suggest something: *You might want to try a different approach next time.* → See Study Page **Modal verbs** on page Centre 22

might² /maɪt/ noun [U] formal great strength or power: *economic/military might* ∘ *She pushed*

M

the door **with all her might** (= *with as much force as possible*).

mightn't /'maɪt^ənt/ mainly UK formal short for might not: *It mightn't be true.*

might've /'maɪtəv/ short for might have: *The children might've seen her in the park.*

mighty¹ /'maɪti/ adj very powerful or successful: *In their next game they're playing the mighty Redskins.*

mighty² /'maɪti/ adv mainly US informal very: *It's mighty tempting to stay in bed on a rainy morning.*

migraine /'maɪɡreɪn/ noun [C, U] a very bad pain in the head, often one that makes you vomit

migrant /'maɪɡr^ənt/ noun [C] someone who goes to live in a different place in order to find work: *migrant labour/workers*

migrate /maɪˈɡreɪt/ ⓤⓢ /'maɪɡreɪt/ verb [I] **1** When birds, fish, or animals migrate, they travel from one place to another at the same time each year: *Many birds migrate from Europe to African forests for the winter.* **2** When people migrate, they move to another place, often a different country, in order to find work and a better life: *Between 1900 and 1914, 3.1 million people migrated to the US from central Europe.* • migration /maɪˈɡreɪʃ^ən/ noun [C, U]

migratory /'maɪɡreɪt^əri/ ⓤⓢ /'maɪɡrətɔːri/ adj [always before noun] relating to birds, fish, or animals that migrate

mike /maɪk/ noun [C] informal short for microphone

mild /maɪld/ adj **1** WEATHER ▷ ⓑ① When weather is mild, it is less cold than you would expect: *a mild winter* **2** ILLNESS ▷ When an illness is mild, it is not as serious as it could be: *My doctor said I had a mild form of pneumonia.* **3** WEAK ▷ ⓑ② not having a strong effect: *a mild taste* ∘ *a mild detergent* **4** KIND ▷ calm and gentle: *He has a very mild manner.*

mildly /'maɪldli/ adv **1** slightly: *I find his films mildly amusing.* **2 to put it mildly** something you say when an opinion is not expressed as strongly as it should be: *The building is unsafe, to put it mildly.*

mile /maɪl/ noun [C] **1** ⓑ① a unit for measuring distance, equal to 1609 metres or 1760 yards: *The nearest station is two miles from here.* ∘ *It's a five-mile walk to the next village.* ∘ *The latest high-speed trains can travel at 190 **miles per hour**.* → See Study Page **Measurements** on page Centre 31 **2 miles** a very long distance: *We drove for miles along dusty roads.* ∘ *Her cottage is miles from the nearest village.*

mileage /'maɪlɪdʒ/ noun **1** DISTANCE ▷ [C, U] the number of miles that a vehicle has travelled since it was new: *low mileage* **2** FUEL ▷ [C, U] the number of miles a vehicle can travel using a particular amount of fuel **3** ADVANTAGE ▷ [U] informal an advantage got from something: *There's no **mileage in** taking your employer to court.*

milestone /'maɪlstəʊn/ noun [C] an important event in the history or development of some-

thing or someone: *Passing my driving test was an important milestone for me.*

militant¹ /'mɪlɪt^ənt/ adj expressing strong support for a political or social idea, and willing to use extreme or violent methods to achieve it: *a **militant group/organization*** • militancy /'mɪlɪt^ənsi/ noun [U] militant beliefs or behaviour

militant² /'mɪlɪt^ənt/ noun [C] a militant person

military¹ /'mɪlɪtri/ adj ⓑ② relating to the army, navy, or air force: *military action/service*

military² /'mɪlɪtri/ noun **the military** a country's army, navy, and air force

military service noun [U] army training that young people must do in some countries

militia /mɪˈlɪʃə/ noun [C] a group of people who have been trained as soldiers but are not part of a country's official army • militiaman noun [C] (plural **militiamen**) a member of a militia

milk¹ /mɪlk/ noun [U] ⓐ① a white liquid produced by women and other female animals, such as cows, for feeding their babies: *a carton of milk* ∘ *breast milk* → See also **skimmed milk**

milk² /mɪlk/ verb [T] **1** to get as much money or as many advantages as possible from a person or situation: *She **milked** her grandfather **for** all his savings.* **2** to take milk from a cow using your hands or a machine

milkman /'mɪlkmən/ noun [C] (plural **milkmen**) a man whose job is bringing milk to people's homes early in the morning

milkshake /'mɪlkʃeɪk/ noun [C, U] a sweet drink made of milk and chocolate or fruit: *a banana milkshake*

milky /'mɪlki/ adj **1** containing milk, often a lot of it: *milky coffee/tea* **2** similar to milk: *a milky liquid*

the Milky Way /ˌmɪlkiˈweɪ/ noun the group of very many stars that includes the sun

mill¹ /mɪl/ noun [C] **1** FLOUR ▷ a machine for crushing grain into flour, or a building with this machine: *a flour mill* **2** POWDER ▷ a small machine used in the kitchen for crushing things such as coffee beans into a powder: *a coffee/pepper mill* **3** MATERIAL ▷ a factory where one material or substance is made: *a cotton/woollen mill* ∘ *a paper/steel mill*

mill² /mɪl/ verb [T] to use a machine to crush something into a powder: *freshly milled black pepper*

PHRASAL VERB **mill about/around (sth)** When people mill around, they come together in a place, usually to wait for someone or something.

millennium /mɪˈleniəm/ noun [C] (plural **millennia**) **1** a period of 1000 years, often calculated from the date when Christ is thought to have been born **2 the Millennium** the change from the year 1999 to 2000 in the Western calendar: *Where did you celebrate the Millennium?*

milli- /mɪli-/ prefix a thousandth: *a millisecond*

milligram /'mɪlɪɡræm/ noun [C] (written abbreviation **mg**) a unit for measuring weight, equal to 0.001 grams

millilitre UK (US **milliliter**) (written abbreviation

ml) /ˈmɪlɪˌliːtər/ **noun** [C] a unit for measuring liquid, equal to 0.001 litres

millimetre UK (US **millimeter**) (written abbreviation **mm**) /ˈmɪlɪˌmiːtər/ **noun** [C] ⓑ a unit for measuring length, equal to 0.001 metres

million /ˈmɪljən/ **1** ⓐ the number 1,000,000 **2 millions** informal a lot: *I've seen that film millions of times.*

millionaire /ˌmɪljəˈneər/ **noun** [C] a very rich person who has money and possessions to the value of at least one million pounds or dollars

millionth¹ /ˈmɪljənθ/ 1,000,000th written as a word

millionth² /ˈmɪljənθ/ **noun** [C] one of a million equal parts of something; ¹⁄₁,₀₀₀,₀₀₀; .000001

mime /maɪm/ **verb** [I, T] to act or tell a story without speaking, using movements of your hands and body, and expressions on your face: *Pop stars often mime (= pretend to sing while their song is played) on TV.* • **mime noun** [C, U] *a mime artist*

mimic¹ /ˈmɪmɪk/ **verb** [T] (**mimicking, mimicked**) **1** to copy the way someone talks and behaves, usually to make people laugh: *He's always getting into trouble for mimicking his teachers.* **2** to have the same behaviour or qualities as something else: *The drug mimics the effects of a natural hormone.*

mimic² /ˈmɪmɪk/ **noun** [C] someone who is good at mimicking other people

mince¹ /mɪns/ **noun** [U] UK (US **ground beef**) meat, usually from a cow, which has been cut into very small pieces by a machine

mince² /mɪns/ **verb** [T] to cut food into small pieces in a machine: *minced beef/onions*

mincemeat /ˈmɪnsmiːt/ **noun** [U] a spicy, sweet mixture of apples, dried fruit, and nuts, which have been cut into small pieces

IDIOM **make mincemeat of sb** informal to defeat someone very easily

mince ˈpie noun [C] a small pastry filled with mincemeat that is eaten mainly at Christmas

mind¹ /maɪnd/ **noun** [C] **1** ⓑ someone's memory or their ability to think, feel emotions, and be aware of things: *For some reason her words stuck in my mind.* ◦ *She has a very logical mind.* **2 have sth on your mind** to think or worry about something: *Jim has a lot on his mind at the moment.* **3 bear/keep sb/sth in mind** ⓑ to remember someone or something that may be useful in the future: *I'll keep you in mind if another job comes up.* ◦ [+ (that)] *Bear in mind that there's a bank holiday next week.* **4 make your mind up** ⓑ to make a decision: [+ question word] *I haven't made up my mind whether to go yet.* **5 change your mind** ⓑ to change a decision or opinion: *We've changed our minds about selling the house.* **6 come/spring to mind** If an idea comes to mind, it is the first thing you think of: *I was thinking about who might be suitable for this job, and your name came to mind.* **7 put your mind to sth** to give your full attention to something: *You could win if you put your mind to it.* **8 be out of your mind** informal to be crazy or very stupid **9 be out of your**

mind with worry/grief, etc to be very worried or upset

IDIOMS **blow your mind** informal If something blows your mind, you are very excited or surprised by it: *There was one scene in the film that really blew my mind.* • **cross your mind** ⓑ If an idea crosses your mind, you think about it for a short time: [+ (that)] *It never crossed my mind (= I never thought) that she might be married.* • **be in two minds** UK (US **be of two minds**) to have difficulty making a decision: *I'm in two minds about accepting his offer.* • **put/set sb's mind at rest** to say something to someone to stop them worrying: *I was really worried about the tests, but talking to the doctor put my mind at rest.* • **read sb's mind** to know what someone is thinking • **slip your mind** If something slips your mind, you forget it. • **speak your mind** to say exactly what you think without worrying if it will upset anyone: *She has very strong opinions and she's not afraid to speak her mind.* • **take your mind off sth** to stop you thinking about something unpleasant: *Talking to him took my mind off the pain.*

→ See also **at/in the back² of your mind, frame¹, give sb a piece¹ of your mind, a weight off your mind**

mind² /maɪnd/ **verb 1** BE ANNOYED ▷ [I, T] ⓑ to be annoyed or worried by something: *Do you think he'd mind if I borrowed his book?* ◦ [+ doing sth] *Tim won't mind lending you his car.* ◦ *He doesn't seem to mind doing all the driving.* ◦ *I don't mind taking her (= I am willing to take her) if you're too busy.* **2** LOOK AFTER ▷ [T] to look after someone or something: *Who's minding the baby?* **3 do you mind/would you mind** ⓐ something you say when politely asking someone to do something: *Do you mind not smoking in here, please?* ◦ *Would you mind if I borrowed your phone?* **4** BE CAREFUL ▷ [T] ⓑ something you say when telling someone to be careful with something dangerous: *Mind the iron – it's still very hot!* **5 never mind a** ⓐ something that you say to tell someone that something is not important: *"I forgot to bring any money." "Never mind, you can pay me next week."* **b** something you say to emphasize that something is impossible: *I can't afford to buy a bike, never mind a car!* **6 mind you** something you say before saying the opposite of what you have just said: *We had a lovely holiday in France. Mind you, the weather was appalling.*

PHRASAL VERB **Mind out!** UK something you say to warn someone about a danger or to tell them to move: *Mind out – this plate's very hot!*

mind-boggling /ˈmaɪndˌbɒɡlɪŋ/ **adj** informal difficult to accept, imagine, or understand: *The amount of information available on the Internet is mind-boggling.*

-minded /ˈmaɪndɪd/ used after adjectives or adverbs to describe someone's character, interests or way of thinking about things → See **absent-minded, narrow-minded, open-minded, single-minded**

minder /ˈmaɪndər/ **noun** [C] UK someone who

M

physically protects a famous, important, or very rich person

mindless /ˈmaɪndləs/ **adj** stupid and done without a good reason: *mindless violence*

mine¹ /maɪn/ **pronoun** Ⓐ② the things that belong or relate to the person who is speaking or writing: *I borrowed them from a friend of mine.* ∘ *"Whose book is this?" "It's mine."* ∘ *Can I use your pen? Mine's not working.*

mine² /maɪn/ **noun** [C] **1** Ⓑ② an underground system of holes and passages where people dig out coal or other minerals **2** a bomb hidden in the ground or water that explodes when it is touched → See also **gold mine**

mine³ /maɪn/ **verb 1** [I, T] to dig out of the ground minerals such as coal, metals, and valuable stones: *Tin was mined in this area for hundreds of years.* ∘ *He made his fortune **mining** for gold and diamonds.* **2** [T] to put mines (= bombs) in the ground or water: *The southern coast was heavily mined during the war.*

minefield /ˈmaɪnfiːld/ **noun** [C] **1** a situation with many complicated problems: *a **legal** minefield* **2** an area of land or sea where bombs have been hidden

miner /ˈmaɪnər/ **noun** [C] someone who works in a mine: *a coal miner*

mineral /ˈmɪnərəl/ **noun** [C] **1** a valuable or useful substance that is dug out of the ground: *The region's rich mineral deposits include oil, gold, and aluminium.* **2** a chemical that your body needs to stay healthy

mineral water **noun** [C, U] Ⓐ② water that is taken from the ground and contains chemicals that are good for your health

mingle /ˈmɪŋgl/ **verb 1** [I, T] to mix, or be mixed: *the smell of fresh coffee **mingled with** cigarette smoke* **2** [I] to meet and talk to a lot of people at a party or similar event: *The party will be a good opportunity to **mingle with** the other students.*

mini- /mɪni-/ **prefix** small: *a miniskirt (= very short skirt)* ∘ *a minibus*

miniature¹ /ˈmɪnətʃər/ **adj** [always before noun] extremely small: *a miniature camera*

miniature² /ˈmɪnətʃər/ **noun 1** [C] a very small copy of an object: *You can buy miniatures of the statue in the museum shop.* **2 in miniature** If something is in miniature, it is a very small copy of something else.

mini-break /ˈmɪnibreɪk/ **noun** [C] a very short holiday

minibus /ˈmɪnibʌs/ **noun** [C] a small bus with seats for about ten people

minimal /ˈmɪnɪməl/ **adj** very small in amount: *Damage to the building was minimal.* • **minimally adv**

minimize (also UK **-ise**) /ˈmɪnɪmaɪz/ **verb** [T] **1** to make the amount of something that is unpleasant or not wanted as small as possible: *Airport staff are trying to minimize the inconvenience caused to passengers.* **2** to click on the corner of a computer window to reduce it to a small title and hide its contents

minimum¹ /ˈmɪnɪməm/ **adj** [always before noun] Ⓑ① The minimum amount of something is the

smallest amount that is allowed, needed, or possible: *How much is the **minimum wage**?* ∘ *There is a **minimum charge** of $5 for postage.* → Opposite **maximum**

minimum² /ˈmɪnɪməm/ **noun** [no plural] Ⓑ① the smallest amount that is allowed, needed, or possible: *The judge sentenced him to a minimum of five years in prison.* ∘ *Please **keep** noise **to an** absolute **minimum**.*

> **⬛ Word partners for minimum**
>
> a minimum **of** [5/2%, etc] • **keep** sth **to a** minimum • an **absolute/bare** minimum • **with the** minimum **of** sth

mining /ˈmaɪnɪŋ/ **noun** [U] the industrial process of digging coal or other minerals out of the ground

miniscule /ˈmɪnɪskjuːl/ **adj** a common spelling of 'minuscule' that is not correct

miniskirt /ˈmɪniskɜːt/ **noun** [C] a very short skirt → See colour picture **Clothes** on page Centre 8

minister /ˈmɪnɪstər/ **noun** [C] **1** Ⓑ② a politician who is responsible for a government department or has an important position in it: *a finance/health minister* **2** a priest in some Christian churches: *a Baptist/Methodist minister* → See also **prime minister**

ministerial /ˌmɪnɪˈstɪəriəl/ **adj** relating to a government minister: *a ministerial job/post*

ministry /ˈmɪnɪstri/ **noun 1** [C] a government department that is responsible for a particular subject: *the Ministry of Defence* ∘ *a Foreign Ministry spokesman* **2 the ministry** the job of being a priest

minivan /ˈmɪnivæn/ **noun** [C] US a people carrier (= large, high car for many people)

mink /mɪŋk/ **noun** [C, U] a small animal with valuable fur which is used to make expensive coats, or the fur from this animal: *a mink coat*

minor¹ /ˈmaɪnər/ **adj 1** Ⓑ② not important or serious: *a minor offence* ∘ *Most of the passengers suffered only minor injuries.* **2** [always before noun] in music, belonging to a key (= set of musical notes) that often produces a sad sound → Opposite **major**

minor² /ˈmaɪnər/ **noun** [C] formal someone who is too young to have the legal responsibilities of an adult

minority /maɪˈnɒrəti/ **noun 1** [no plural] Ⓑ② part of a group that is less than half of the whole group, often much less: *The violence was caused by a **small minority** of football supporters.* ∘ *I voted to accept the proposal, but I was **in the minority**.* → Opposite **majority 2** [C] a group of people whose race is different from the race of most of the people where they live: *ethnic minorities*

> **⬛ Word partners for minority**
>
> be **in** a minority • a **sizeable/small/substantial/tiny** minority • a minority **of** sth

mint¹ /mɪnt/ **noun 1 SWEET** ▷ [C] a sweet with a fresh, strong taste **2 HERB** ▷ [U] Ⓑ② a plant whose leaves are used to add flavour to food and drinks **3** FACTORY ▷ [C] a factory that produces coins for the government

mint² /mɪnt/ **verb** [T] to produce a coin for the government

minus¹ /'maɪnəs/ **preposition 1** ⓐ used when the second of two numbers should be taken away from the first: *Five minus three is two.* **2** informal without something that should be there: *She arrived at the meeting minus her briefcase.*

minus² /'maɪnəs/ **adj 1** [always before noun] A minus number is less than zero: *The temperature last night was minus ten.* **2 A minus/B minus, etc** used with scores given to written work meaning 'slightly lower than': *I got an A minus for my last essay.*

minus³ /'maɪnəs/ **noun** [C] **1** (also '**minus ,sign**) the sign which shows that the second of two numbers should be taken away from the first, or that a number is less than zero, shown by the symbol '–' **2** a problem or difficulty: *It isn't easy having a child but the pluses outweigh the minuses.*

minuscule /'mɪnəskjuːl/ **adj** extremely small: *The cost of vaccination is minuscule compared to the cost of treating the disease.*

minute¹ /'mɪnɪt/ **noun** [C] **1** ⓐ a period of time equal to 60 seconds: *She was ten minutes late for her interview.* ∘ *"Did you have a good holiday?" "Yes, thanks. I enjoyed every minute of it."* ∘ *a thirty-minute journey* **2** ⓐ a very short period of time: *It'll only **take a minute** to call him.* ∘ *I'll be with you **in a minute**.* ∘ *She died **within minutes of** (= very soon after) the attack.* **3 (at) any minute** very soon: *Her train should be arriving any minute.* **4 the last minute** ⓑ the latest time possible: *The concert was cancelled at the last minute.* **5 the minute (that)** as soon as: *I'll tell you the minute we hear any news.* **6 Wait/Just a minute; Hold on a minute. a** used when asking someone to wait for a short time: *Just a minute – I've left my coat in the restaurant.* **b** used when you disagree with something that someone has said or done: *Hold on a minute, Pete! I never said you could borrow my car.*

minute² /maɪ'njuːt/ **adj 1** extremely small: *a minute amount/quantity* **2** [always before noun] done in great detail: *He explained everything in minute detail.*

the minutes /'mɪnɪts/ **noun** [plural] an official record of what is said and decided during a meeting: *Michael has kindly agreed to **take the minutes** (= write them down).*

miracle /'mɪrəkl/ **noun** [C] **1** ⓑ something that is very surprising or difficult to believe: *an economic miracle* ∘ *[+ (that)] It's a miracle that he's still alive.* ∘ *a **miracle cure*** **2** an event that should be impossible and cannot be explained by science

miraculous /mɪ'rækjələs/ **adj** very surprising or difficult to believe: *John's made a **miraculous recovery** from his illness.* • **miraculously adv**

mirage /'mɪrɑːʒ/ ⓤⓢ /mɪ'rɑːʒ/ **noun** [C] an image of water in a desert or on a road produced by hot air

mirror¹ /'mɪrər/ **noun** [C] ⓐ a piece of glass with a shiny metallic material on one side that produces an image of anything that is in front of it: *a bathroom mirror* ∘ *He looked at his reflection **in the mirror**.* → See colour picture **The Living Room** on page Centre 4 → See also **rearview mirror, wing mirror**

mirror² /'mɪrər/ **verb** [T] to be similar to or represent something: *Our newspaper mirrors the opinions of ordinary people.*

mirth /mɜːθ/ **noun** [U] formal laughter or happiness

mis- /mɪs-/ **prefix** not or badly: *mistrust* ∘ *to misbehave*

misadventure /ˌmɪsəd'ventʃər/ **noun 1** [U] UK formal a situation in which someone is killed by accident and no one is legally responsible for the death: *The coroner recorded a verdict of **death by misadventure**.* **2** [C] an unlucky event

misanthrope /'mɪsənθrəʊp/ **noun** [C] formal someone who hates people in general and avoids being with them

misapprehension /ˌmɪsæprɪ'henʃən/ **noun** [C] formal an idea or opinion about someone or something that is wrong: *[+ that] He was **labouring under the misapprehension** (= wrongly believed) that she loved him.*

misbehave /ˌmɪsbɪ'heɪv/ **verb** [I] to behave badly • **misbehaviour** UK (US **misbehavior**) **noun** [U] bad behaviour

misc written abbreviation for miscellaneous

miscalculate /mɪs'kælkjəleɪt/ **verb** [I, T] **1** to make a mistake when calculating something: *I think I've miscalculated how much wine we'll need for the party.* **2** to make a bad decision because you do not completely understand a situation: *If she thinks Mike will support her plan, then she's seriously miscalculated.* • **miscalculation** /ˌmɪskælkjə'leɪʃən/ **noun** [C, U]

miscarriage /'mɪsˌkærɪdʒ/ **noun** [C, U] **1** If a pregnant woman has a miscarriage, her baby is born too early and dies because it has not developed enough: *She **had a miscarriage** after her car accident.* **2 miscarriage of justice** a wrong or unfair decision by a court

miscarry /mɪs'kæri/ **verb** [I, T] to give birth to a baby too early so that it dies

miscellaneous /ˌmɪsəl'eɪniəs/ **adj** [always before noun] consisting of a mixture of several different things: *The plumber tried to charge me fifty pounds for miscellaneous items.*

mischief /'mɪstʃɪf/ **noun** [U] behaviour, usually of a child, which is slightly bad but not serious

mischievous /'mɪstʃɪvəs/ **adj** behaving in a way that is slightly bad but not serious: *a mischievous grin* ∘ *a mischievous five-year-old* • **mischievously adv**

misconceived /ˌmɪskən'siːvd/ **adj** If a plan is misconceived, it is not suitable or has not been thought about carefully.

☑ **Word partners for misconception**

be **based on** a misconception • a **common/ popular** misconception • a misconception **about sth**

misconception /ˌmɪskən'sepʃən/ **noun** [C] an

understanding of something that is wrong: [+ that] *It's a **common misconception** that older workers cannot learn to use new technology.*

misconduct /mɪˈskɒndʌkt/ **noun** [U] formal behaviour by someone in a position of responsibility that is morally wrong or breaks the rules while doing their job: ***professional misconduct***

misdemeanour UK (US **misdemeanor**) /ˌmɪsdɪˈmiːnər/ **noun** [C] **1** behaviour that is bad or not moral: *political/sexual misdemeanours* **2** US a crime that is not serious

misdirect /ˌmɪsdaɪˈrekt/ **verb** [T] to use money or people's skills in a way that is not suitable: [often passive] *Large quantities of money and expertise have been misdirected.*

miserable /ˈmɪzərəbl/ **adj 1 SAD** ▷ **⑤⑨** unhappy: *I just woke up feeling miserable.* **2 NOT PLEASANT** ▷ **⑥②** very unpleasant or bad, and causing someone to feel unhappy: *Some families are living in miserable conditions.* **3 NOT ENOUGH** ▷ informal A miserable amount is too small to be acceptable: *She offered me a miserable 50 euros for my old computer.*

miserably /ˈmɪzərəbli/ **adv 1** in a way that causes disappointment or suffering: *miserably low wages* ∘ *Every job application that I've made has **failed miserably** (= has been extremely unsuccessful).* **2** in a very unhappy way: *"I feel so ill," said Rachel miserably.*

misery /ˈmɪzəri/ **noun** [C, U] **⑥②** great suffering or unhappiness: *The war brought misery to millions of people.* ∘ *Her husband's drinking is **making her life a misery**.*

IDIOM **put sb out of their misery** to stop someone worrying by telling them what they want to know

misfire /mɪsˈfaɪər/ **verb** [I] When something that you do misfires, it does not have the result that you intended: *His joke misfired badly, and he was forced to make a public apology.*

misfit /ˈmɪsfɪt/ **noun** [C] someone with strange or unusual behaviour who is not accepted by other people: *a **social misfit***

misfortune /mɪsˈfɔːtʃuːn/ **noun** [C, U] bad luck, or an unlucky event: [+ to do sth] *He **had the misfortune** to fall in love with a married woman.*

misgiving /mɪsˈɡɪvɪŋ/ **noun** [C] a feeling of doubt or worry about a future event: [usually plural] *She **has serious misgivings about** giving birth at home.*

> 🖉 **Word partners for misgiving**
>
> **express/have** misgivings • **grave/serious/ strong** misgivings • misgivings **about** sth

misguided /mɪsˈɡaɪdɪd/ **adj** not likely to succeed because of a bad judgment or understanding of a situation: *The government's policy seems to me completely misguided.*

mishandle /mɪsˈhændl/ **verb** [T] to deal with a problem or situation badly: *The murder investigation was mishandled from the beginning.*

mishap /ˈmɪshæp/ **noun** [C, U] an accident or unlucky event that usually is not serious: *They suffered a series of mishaps during the trip.*

misinform /ˌmɪsɪnˈfɔːm/ **verb** [T] to give someone false information: [often passive] *I'm afraid you've been misinformed about your exam results.*

misinterpret /ˌmɪsɪnˈtɜːprɪt/ **verb** [T] to understand something in the wrong way: [often passive] *He claims his speech was deliberately misinterpreted by journalists.*

misjudge /mɪsˈdʒʌdʒ/ **verb** [T] **1** to form a wrong opinion about a person or situation: *W believe that the government has seriously misjudged the public mood.* **2** to guess an amount o distance wrongly

misjudgment (also UK **misjudgement**) /mɪsˈdʒʌdʒmənt/ **noun** [C, U] a wrong opinion or wrong guess: *Her outspoken criticism of her bos was a serious misjudgment.*

mislay /mɪsˈleɪ/ **verb** [T] (**mislaid** /mɪsˈleɪd/ formal to lose something for a short time b forgetting where you put it: *I seem to hav mislaid my car keys.*

mislead /mɪsˈliːd/ **verb** [T] (**misled** /mɪsˈled/) t make someone believe something that is untru by giving them information that is wrong or no complete: [often passive] *She claims the public wa misled by the government.*

misleading /mɪsˈliːdɪŋ/ **adj** **⑥②** making someon believe something that is untrue: *misleadin information/statements*

mismanage /ˌmɪsˈmænɪdʒ/ **verb** [T] to contro or organize something badly: *He accused th government of mismanaging the crisis.* • **mis management noun** [U]

misnomer /mɪsˈnəʊmər/ **noun** [C] a name that i not suitable for the person or thing that it refer to: [usually singular] *It's a misnomer to call youn car thieves 'joyriders'.*

misogynist /mɪˈsɒdʒɪnɪst/ **noun** [C] a man wh dislikes women very much • **misogynistic** /m ˌsɒdʒəˈnɪstɪk/ **adj** (also **misogynist**) expressing great dislike of women: *a misogynistic attitude writer*

misogyny /mɪˈsɒdʒɪni/ **noun** [U] a great dislik of women

misplaced /mɪsˈpleɪst/ **adj** If you have misplaced feeling or belief, it is wrong becaus you have not understood the situation correctly *misplaced loyalty/trust*

misprint /ˈmɪsprɪnt/ **noun** [C] a mistake made i the printing of a newspaper or book: *The articl is full of misprints.*

mispronounce /ˌmɪsprəˈnaʊns/ **verb** [T] t pronounce a word or sound wrongly: *I alway mispronounce his name.* • **mispronunciatio** /ˌmɪsprəˌnʌnsiˈeɪʃən/ **noun** [C, U]

misread /mɪsˈriːd/ **verb** [T] (**misread** /mɪsˈred/ **1** to make a mistake when you are readin something: *He misread the cooking instruction on the packet.* **2** to not understand somethin correctly: *She completely **misread the situation***

misrepresent /ˌmɪsreprɪˈzent/ **verb** [T] to sa things that are not true about someone o something: *He claims that the article misrepre sented his views.* • **misrepresentation** /ˌmɪsrepr rɪzenˈteɪʃən/ **noun** [C, U]

miss[1] /mɪs/ **verb 1 FEEL SAD** ▷ [T] **A2** to feel sad about someone that you do not see now or something that you do not have or do now: *I'll miss you when you go.* ∘ [+ doing sth] *He misses having a room of his own.* **2 NOT GO TO** ▷ [T] **A2** to not go to something: *I missed my class this morning.* **3 NOT SEE/HEAR** ▷ [T] **B1** to not see or hear something or someone: *Sorry, I missed that, could you repeat it please?* ∘ *We missed the first five minutes of the film.* **4 NOT HIT** ▷ [I, T] **B2** to not hit or catch something as you intended: *It should have been such an easy goal and he missed.* **5 TOO LATE** ▷ [T] **A2** to arrive too late to get on a bus, train, or aircraft: *If I don't leave now, I'll miss my train.* → See Note at **lose 6 NOT NOTICE** ▷ [T] **B1** to not notice someone or something: *It's the big house on the corner – you can't miss it.* **7 miss a chance/opportunity** **B1** to not use an opportunity to do something: *You can't afford to miss a chance like this.* **8 miss the point** to not understand something correctly → See also **miss the boat**

PHRASAL VERBS **miss sb/sth out** UK to not include someone or something • **miss out** **B2** to not do or have something that you would enjoy or something that other people do or have: *I got there late and* **missed out on** *all the fun.*

> **!** Common learner error: **miss** or **lack**?
>
> Be careful not to confuse the verb **lack** with **miss**. Lack means to not have something, or to not have enough of something.
> *Our town lacks a cinema.*
> ~~Our town misses a cinema.~~

miss[2] /mɪs/ **noun** [C] a failure to hit or catch something as you intended

IDIOMS **give sth a miss** UK informal to not do an activity: *I think I'll give aerobics a miss this evening.* • **a near miss** something bad that does not happen but almost happens

Miss /mɪs/ **noun** **A1** a title for a girl or woman who is not married, used before her family name or full name: *Miss Olivia Allenby* ∘ *Tell Miss Russell I'm here.* → See Note at **Mr**

misshapen /mɪsˈʃeɪp³n/ **adj** not the correct or normal shape

missile /ˈmɪsaɪl/ ⑤ /ˈmɪsəl/ **noun** [C] **1** an explosive weapon that can travel long distances through the air: *nuclear missiles* ∘ *a missile attack* **2** an object that is thrown through the air to hit someone or something

missing /ˈmɪsɪŋ/ **adj 1** **A2** If someone or something is missing, you cannot find them because they are not in their usual place: *Have you found those missing documents?* ∘ *Her daughter went missing a week ago.* **2** **B1** not included in something: *There are a couple of things missing from the list.*

> **⚲** Word partners for **missing**
>
> go missing • report sb missing • missing from sth

mission /ˈmɪʃ³n/ **noun** [C] **1 JOB** ▷ an important job, usually travelling somewhere: *I'll be going on a fact-finding mission to Paris next week.* **2 GROUP** ▷ an official group of people who are sent somewhere, usually to discover information about something: *a trade mission* **3 JOURNEY** ▷ an important journey that a spacecraft or military aircraft goes on **4 PURPOSE** ▷ someone's duty or purpose in life: *Her mission in life was to help the poor.*

missionary /ˈmɪʃ³n³ri/ **noun** [C] someone who travels to another country to teach people about the Christian religion

missive /ˈmɪsɪv/ **noun** [C] literary a letter or message

misspell /mɪsˈspel/ **verb** [T] (**misspelled**, UK **misspelt**) to spell something wrongly

mist[1] /mɪst/ **noun** [C, U] **B2** small drops of water in the air that make it difficult to see objects which are not near: *Gradually the mist cleared and the sun began to shine.*

mist[2] /mɪst/ **verb**

PHRASAL VERB **mist over/up** If a glass surface mists over, it becomes covered with very small drops of water so that you cannot see through it easily.

> **➕** Other ways of saying **mistake**
>
> A common alternative is the noun **error**:
> *He admitted that he'd made an* **error***.*
> *The letter contained a number of typing* **errors***.*
> A stupid mistake is sometimes described as a **blunder**:
> *The company was struggling after a series of financial* **blunders***.*
> A mistake which causes confusion is often described as a **mix-up**:
> *There was a* **mix-up** *with the bags at the airport.*
> An embarrassing mistake that someone makes when they are talking is sometimes described as a **gaffe**:
> *I made a real* **gaffe** *by calling her 'Emma' which is the name of his previous girlfriend.*
> The noun **oversight** is sometimes used to describe a mistake which someone makes by forgetting to do something:
> *The payment was delayed because of an* **oversight** *in the accounts department.*

mistake[1] /mɪˈsteɪk/ **noun** [C] **1** **A2** something that you do or think that is wrong: *a spelling mistake* ∘ *He* **made** *a lot of* **mistakes** *in his written test.* ∘ [+ to do sth] *It would be a* **big mistake** *to leave school.* ∘ [+ of + doing sth] *She* **made the mistake of** *giving him her phone number.* **2 by mistake** **B1** If you do something by mistake, you do it without intending to: *I picked up someone else's book by mistake.*

> **!** Common learner error: **mistake**
>
> Remember to use the correct verb with this word.
> *I always* **make mistakes** *in my essays.*
> ~~I always do mistakes in my essays.~~

> ☑ Word partners for **mistake**
>
> correct/make/repeat a mistake • a big/costly/
> fatal/serious/terrible mistake • by mistake

mistake² /mɪˈsteɪk/ **verb** [T] (**mistook, mistaken**) to not understand something correctly: *I think you mistook my meaning.*

PHRASAL VERB **mistake sb/sth for sb/sth** to confuse someone or something with someone or something else: *People sometimes mistake him for a girl.*

mistaken /mɪˈsteɪkᵊn/ **adj** If you are mistaken, or you have a mistaken belief, you are wrong about something: *If you think you can behave like that, you are mistaken.* • **mistakenly adv** *I mistakenly* (= wrongly) *thought he had left.*

Mister /ˈmɪstər/ **noun** [U] US informal used when calling or talking to a man that you do not know: *Hey Mister, you forgot your suitcase!*

mistletoe /ˈmɪsltəʊ/ **noun** [U] a plant with white berries (= small, round fruit) which is often used as a decoration at Christmas

mistook /mɪˈstʊk/ past tense of mistake

mistreat /mɪsˈtriːt/ **verb** [T] to treat a person or animal in a bad or cruel way: *A local farmer has been accused of mistreating horses.* • **mistreatment noun** [U]

mistress /ˈmɪstrəs/ **noun** [C] a woman who has a sexual relationship with a man who is married to someone else

mistrust /mɪsˈtrʌst/ **noun** [U] a feeling of not believing or not having confidence in someone or something: *They have a deep mistrust of strangers.* • **mistrust verb** [T]

misty /ˈmɪsti/ **adj** ⬚ If the weather is misty, there is a cloud of small drops of water in the air, which makes it difficult to see objects which are not near: *a cold and misty morning*

misunderstand /ˌmɪsʌndəˈstænd/ **verb** [T] (**misunderstood**) **1** ⬚ to not understand someone or something correctly: *He misunderstood the question completely.* **2 be misunderstood** If someone is misunderstood, other people do not understand that they have good qualities.

misunderstanding /ˌmɪsʌndəˈstændɪŋ/ **noun** **1** [C, U] ⬚ If there is a misunderstanding, someone does not understand something correctly: *There must have been a misunderstanding.* **2** [C] a slight disagreement

misuse /ˌmɪsˈjuːz/ **verb** [T] to use something in the wrong way or for the wrong purpose: *He misused his position to obtain money dishonestly.* • **misuse** /ˌmɪsˈjuːs/ **noun** [C, U] *the misuse of drugs/power*

mite /maɪt/ **noun** [C] **1** an extremely small insect with eight legs: *dust mites* **2** informal a small child: *You're so cold, you poor little mite!* **3 a mite** mainly UK informal slightly: *He seemed a mite embarrassed.*

mitigate /ˈmɪtɪgeɪt/ **verb** [T] to reduce the harmful effects of something • **mitigation** /ˌmɪtɪˈgeɪʃᵊn/ **noun** [U]

mitigating /ˈmɪtɪgeɪtɪŋ/ **adj mitigating circumstances/factors** facts that make something bad that someone has done seem less bad or less serious

mitt /mɪt/ **noun** [C] a thick leather glove (= cover for the hand) used for catching a baseball → See colour picture **Sports 2** on page Centre 15

mix¹ /mɪks/ **verb 1 COMBINE SUBSTANCES** ▷ [I, T] ⬚ If two or more substances mix, they combine to make one substance, and if you mix two or more substances, you combine them to make one substance: *Mix the powder with water to form a paste.* ○ *Put the chocolate, butter, and egg in a bowl and mix them all together.* ○ *Oil and water don't mix.* **2 COMBINE QUALITIES ETC** ▷ [I, T] ⬚ to have or do two or more things, such as qualities, styles, activities, etc, at the same time: *a feeling of anger mixed with sadness* **3 MEET** ▷ [I] ⬚ to meet and talk to people: *She enjoys going to parties and mixing with people.*

PHRASAL VERBS **mix sb/sth up** ⬚ to confuse two people or things by thinking that one person or thing is the other person or thing: *People often mix them up because they look so similar.* • **mix sth up** to cause a group of things to be untidy or badly organized: *The books were all mixed up in a box.*

mix² /mɪks/ **noun 1** [C] ⬚ a combination of things or people, often in a group: [usually singular] *There's a good mix of nationalities in the class.* **2** [C, U] a powder to which you add liquid in order to make something: *cake mix*

> ☑ Word partners for **mix**
>
> a mix of sth • an ethnic/racial/social mix

mixed /mɪkst/ **adj 1** made of a combination of different people or things: *a racially mixed area* ○ *a mixed salad* **2 mixed feelings** If you have mixed feelings about something, you are pleased and not pleased at the same time → See also **a mixed blessing**

mixed-race /mɪkstˈreɪs/ **adj** describes a person whose parents are of different races (= the groups that people are divided into according to their physical characteristics, such as skin colour)

mixed up adj informal **1** confused: *I got a bit mixed up and thought we were supposed to be there at eight.* **2 be mixed up in sth** to be involved in an activity that is bad or illegal **3 be mixed up with sb** to be involved with someone who has a bad influence on you: *Her son got mixed up with the wrong people.*

mixer /ˈmɪksər/ **noun** [C] a machine that mixes things: *an electric mixer*

mixture /ˈmɪkstʃər/ **noun 1** [C, U] ⬚ a substance made of other substances that have been combined: *Add milk to the mixture and stir until smooth.* **2** [no plural] ⬚ a combination of two or more ideas, qualities, styles, etc: *Their house is decorated in a mixture of styles.*

mix-up /ˈmɪksʌp/ **noun** [C] informal a mistake because things are confused: [usually singular] *There was a mix-up with the bags at the airport.*

ml written abbreviation for millilitre (= a unit for measuring liquid)

mm written abbreviation for millimetre (= a unit for measuring length)

moan /məʊn/ **verb** [I] **1** to complain or speak in a way that shows you are unhappy: *She's always moaning about something.* **2** to make a low sound, especially because you are in pain: *He lay on the floor moaning.* ● **moan noun** [C]

mob¹ /mɒb/ **noun** [C] a large group of people that is often violent or not organized: *an angry mob*

mob² /mɒb/ **verb** [T] (**mobbing, mobbed**) If a group of people mob someone, they get close to them and surround them, often to try to see them: [often passive] *She was mobbed by photographers.*

mobile¹ /ˈməʊbaɪl/ Ⓤ /ˈməʊbəl/ **adj** able to move or be moved easily: *a mobile home* → Opposite **immobile**

mobile² /ˈməʊbaɪl/ Ⓤ /ˈməʊbiːl/ **noun** [C] **1** Ⓐ⃝ UK a mobile phone **2** a decoration made of objects on threads that hang down and move in the air

mobile appli'cation noun [C] (also **mobile app**) a software program that operates on a mobile phone: *One popular mobile application gives driving directions to any place with a street address.*

mobile 'phone noun [C] UK Ⓐ⃝ a telephone that you can carry everywhere with you

mobile phone UK, **cell phone** US

mobilize (also UK **-ise**) /ˈməʊbɪlaɪz/ **verb 1** [T] to organize a group of people so that they support or oppose something or someone: *He's trying to mobilize support* for the strike. **2** [I, T] formal to prepare for a war: *The forces were fully mobilized for action.* ● **mobilization** /ˌməʊbɪlaɪˈzeɪʃᵊn/ **noun** [U]

mock¹ /mɒk/ **verb** [I, T] to laugh at someone or something in an unkind way: *The older kids mocked him whenever he made a mistake.*

mock² /mɒk/ **adj** [always before noun] not real but appearing or pretending to be exactly like something: *a **mock exam*** ○ *mock surprise* ○ *mock leather*

mockery /ˈmɒkᵊri/ **noun** [U] **1** behaviour in which someone laughs at someone or something in an unkind way **2 make a mockery of sth** to make something seem stupid: *The latest outbreak of fighting makes a mockery of the peace process.*

modal verb /ˈməʊdᵊlˌvɜːb/ **noun** [C] (also **modal**) Ⓑ⃝ a verb, for example 'can', 'might', or 'must', that is used before another verb to show that something is possible, necessary, etc → See Study Page **Modal verbs** on page Centre 22

mode /məʊd/ **noun** [C] formal a way of doing something: *a mode of transport*

model¹ /ˈmɒdᵊl/ **noun** [C] **1 PERSON** ▷ Ⓑ⃝ someone whose job is to wear fashionable clothes, be in photographs, etc in order to advertise things: *a fashion model* **2 COPY** ▷ Ⓐ⃝ a smaller copy of a real object, often used to show how something works or what it looks like **3 EXAMPLE** ▷ someone or something that is an example for others to copy: *a model of good behaviour* **4 DESIGN** ▷ Ⓐ⃝ a design of machine or car that is made by a particular company: *I think her car is a slightly older model.* → See also **role model**

model² /ˈmɒdᵊl/ **verb** [I, T] (mainly UK **modelling, modelled,** US **modeling, modeled**) to wear clothes in fashion shows, magazines, etc as a model

PHRASAL VERBS **be modelled on sth** to be based on the design of something else: *The house is modelled on a 16th century castle.* ● **model yourself on sb** to try to make yourself very similar to someone else: *He models himself on Mohammed Ali.*

modem /ˈməʊdem/ **noun** [C] a piece of equipment that is used to send information from a computer through a telephone line, cable or other link → See Study Page **The Web and the Internet** on page Centre 36

moderate¹ /ˈmɒdᵊrət/ **adj 1** average in size or amount and not too much: *Eating a moderate amount of fat is healthy.* **2** not extreme, especially relating to political opinions: *a moderate political group* ● **moderately adv**

moderate² /ˈmɒdᵊrət/ **noun** [C] someone who does not have extreme political opinions

moderate³ /ˈmɒdᵊreɪt/ **verb** [T] to make something less extreme: *He's trying to moderate his drinking.*

moderation /ˌmɒdᵊrˈeɪʃᵊn/ **noun 1 in moderation** If you do something in moderation, you do not do it too much: *I only drink alcohol in moderation now.* **2** [U] control of your feelings or actions so they do not become extreme

modern /ˈmɒdᵊn/ **adj 1** Ⓑ⃝ relating to the present time and not to the past: *modern society* ○ *the stresses of modern life* **2** Ⓐ⃝ using the newest ideas, design, technology, etc and not traditional: *modern art/architecture* ○ *modern medicine* ● **modernity** /mɒdˈɜːnəti/ **noun** [U] formal modern ideas, design, technology, etc

modern-day /ˈmɒdᵊndeɪ/ **adj** [always before noun] relating to the present time and not to the past: *a modern-day version of Shakespeare*

modernize (also UK **-ise**) /ˈmɒdᵊnaɪz/ **verb** [I, T] to make something more modern or to become more modern: *We really need to modernize our image.* ● **modernization** /ˌmɒdᵊnaɪˈzeɪʃᵊn/ **noun** [U]

modern 'languages noun [plural] languages that are spoken now such as Spanish or German

modest /ˈmɒdɪst/ **adj 1** Ⓑ⃝ not large in size or amount, or not expensive: *a modest amount of money* ○ *Their house is quite modest in size.* **2** If you are modest, you do not talk in a proud way about your skills or successes: *He's very modest about his achievements.* ● **modestly adv**

modesty /ˈmɒdɪsti/ **noun** [U] the quality of not

talking too much or too proudly about your skills or successes

modicum /'mɒdɪkəm/ noun formal **a modicum of sth** a small amount of something: *a modicum of success*

modification /ˌmɒdɪfɪ'keɪʃᵊn/ noun [C, U] a small change to something: *We've made a few modifications to the system.*

modifier /'mɒdɪfaɪəʳ/ noun [C] in grammar, a word that describes or limits the meaning of another word

modify /'mɒdɪfaɪ/ verb [T] **1** to change something in order to improve it: [often passive] *The plans will have to be modified to reduce costs.* ○ *genetically modified food* **2** In grammar, a word that modifies another word describes or limits the meaning of that word: *Adjectives modify nouns.*

module /'mɒdjuːl/ noun [C] **1** UK a part of a university or college course **2** a part of an object that can operate alone, especially a part of a spacecraft

mogul /'məʊgᵊl/ noun [C] an important, powerful person: *media/movie moguls*

Mohammed /mə'hæmɪd/ noun the main prophet of Islam, who revealed the Koran (= the Islamic holy book)

moist /mɔɪst/ adj slightly wet: *Keep the soil moist but not wet.* ○ *It was a lovely, moist cake.* • **moisten** /'mɔɪsᵊn/ verb [I, T] to make something slightly wet, or to become slightly wet

moisture /'mɔɪstʃəʳ/ noun [U] very small drops of water in the air or on a surface

moisturizer (also UK **-iser**) /'mɔɪstʃəraɪzəʳ/ noun [C, U] a substance that you put on your skin to make it less dry • **moisturize** (also UK **-ise**) /'mɔɪstʃəraɪz/ verb [T] to put moisturizer on your skin

molasses /məʊ'læsɪz/ noun [U] (also UK **treacle**) a sweet, thick, dark liquid used in sweet dishes

mold /məʊld/ noun, verb US spelling of mould

moldy /'məʊldi/ adj US spelling of mouldy

mole /məʊl/ noun [C] **1** SKIN ▷ a small, dark mark on the skin **2** ANIMAL ▷ a small animal with black fur that digs holes in the soil and lives under the ground **3** PERSON ▷ informal someone who gives other organizations or governments secret information about the organization where they work

molecule /'mɒlɪkjuːl/ noun [C] the smallest unit of a substance, consisting of one or more atoms

molehill /'məʊlhɪl/ noun [C] see **make a mountain out of a molehill**

molest /məʊ'lest/ verb [T] to hurt or attack someone in a sexual way: *He was accused of molesting children.* • **molestation** /ˌməʊles'teɪʃən/ noun [U]

mom /mɒm/ noun [C] US (UK **mum**) mother: *My mom phoned last night.* ○ *Can we go now, Mom?*

moment /'məʊmənt/ noun **1** [C] a very short period of time: *I'll be back in a moment.* ○ *For a moment I thought it was Anna.* ○ *Could you wait a moment?* **2** [C] a point in time: *Just at that moment, the phone rang.* **3** at the moment now: *I'm afraid she's not here at the moment.* **4** for the moment If you do something for

the moment, you are doing it now but might do something different in the future. **5** the moment (that) as soon as: *I'll call you the moment I hear anything.*

IDIOM **have a senior, blond, etc moment** inform to behave, for a short time, in a way that show you are old, silly, etc: *I've just had a seni moment – I couldn't remember why I'd gone in the kitchen.*

→ See also **on the spur² of the moment**

momentarily /'məʊmənt°r°li/ adv for a ver short time: *I momentarily forgot his name.*

momentary /'məʊmənt°ri/ adj lasting for very short time: *a momentary lapse of memor*

momentous /məʊ'mentəs/ adj A momentou decision, event, etc is very important because has a big effect on the future.

momentum /məʊ'mentəm/ noun [U] **1** the wa in which something continues to move increase, or develop: *to gain/gather momentu* ○ *The players seemed to lose momentu* halfway through the game. **2** in science, th force that makes something continue to move

☑ **Word partners for momentum**

gain/gather/lose momentum • **keep up/ maintain** the momentum • **the momentum for/of** sth

momma /'mɒmə/ noun [C] US another word f mommy

mommy /'mɒmi/ noun [C] US (UK **mummy**) word for 'mother', used especially by children: *want my mommy!* ○ *Can I have some cand Mommy?*

Mon written abbreviation for Monday

monarch /'mɒnək/ noun [C] a king or queen

monarchy /'mɒnəki/ noun **1** [U, no plural] system in which a country is ruled by a king c queen **2** [C] a country that is ruled by a king c queen

monastery /'mɒnəst°ri/ noun [C] a buildin where men live as a religious group

monastic /mə'næstɪk/ adj relating to a mon (= religious man) or a monastery

Monday /'mʌndeɪ/ noun [C, U] (written abbrevi tion **Mon**) ⑪ the day of the week after Sunda and before Tuesday

monetary /'mʌnɪt°ri/ adj relating to money

money /'mʌni/ noun [U] ⑪ the coins or ban notes (= pieces of paper with values) that ar used to buy things: *How much money have yo got?* ○ *He spends all his money on clothes.* ○ *Th company's not making (= earning) any money c the moment.* → See also **pocket money**

☑ **Word partners for money**

borrow/earn/lend/pay/raise/save/spend money

money order noun [C] US (UK **postal order**) a official piece of paper bought at a post offic that you can send instead of money

mongrel /'mʌŋgr°l/ noun [C] a dog that is a mi of different breeds

monies /ˈmʌniz/ **noun** [plural] formal amounts of money

monitor¹ /ˈmɒnɪtər/ **noun** [C] **1 SCREEN** ▷ **B2** a screen that shows information or pictures, usually connected to a computer: *a colour monitor* → See colour picture **The Office** on page Centre 5 **2 MACHINE** ▷ a machine, often in a hospital, that measures something such as the rate that your heart beats: *a **heart monitor*** **3 PERSON** ▷ someone who watches something to make certain that it is done correctly or fairly: *a human rights monitor*

monitor² /ˈmɒnɪtər/ **verb** [T] to watch something carefully and record your results: *to monitor progress*

monk /mʌŋk/ **noun** [C] a member of a group of religious men living apart from other people

monkey /ˈmʌŋki/ **noun** [C] **A2** a hairy animal with a long tail that lives in hot countries and climbs trees

mono- /mɒnəʊ-/ **prefix** one or single: *monolingual* ∘ *a monologue*

monochrome /ˈmɒnəkrəʊm/ **adj** A monochrome image is only in black, white, and grey and not in colour.

monogamy /məˈnɒɡəmi/ **noun** [U] the behaviour of having a sexual relationship with only one person ● **monogamous adj** relating to monogamy: *a **monogamous relationship***

monolingual /ˌmɒnəʊˈlɪŋɡwəl/ **adj** using only one language: *monolingual dictionaries*

monolithic /ˌmɒnəʊˈlɪθɪk/ **adj** large and powerful

monologue (also US **monolog**) /ˈmɒnəlɒɡ/ **noun** [C] a long speech by one person, often in a performance

mononucleosis /ˌmɒnəʊˌnjuːkliˈəʊsɪs/ **noun** [U] US (UK **glandular fever**) an infectious disease that makes your glands (= small organs in your body) swell and makes you feel tired

monopolize (also UK **-ise**) /məˈnɒpəlaɪz/ **verb** [T] to control a situation by being the only person or organization involved in it

monopoly /məˈnɒpəli/ **noun** [C] **1** a situation in which a company or organization is the only one in an area of business or activity and has complete control of it: *They **have a monopoly on** the postal service.* **2** a company or other organization that has a monopoly in a particular industry

monosyllabic /ˌmɒnəʊsɪˈlæbɪk/ **adj** using only short words such as 'yes' or 'no', usually because you do not want to talk

monotonous /məˈnɒtənəs/ **adj** If something is monotonous, it is boring because it stays the same: *a **monotonous voice*** ∘ ***monotonous work*** ● **monotonously adv**

monsoon /mɒnˈsuːn/ **noun** [C] the season when there is heavy rain in Southern Asia

monster /ˈmɒnstər/ **noun** [C] **B1** an imaginary creature that is large, ugly, and frightening

monstrous /ˈmɒnstrəs/ **adj 1** very bad or cruel: *a **monstrous crime*** **2** like a monster

month /mʌnθ/ **noun** [C] **1 A1** one of the twelve periods of time that a year is divided into: *last/*

next month ∘ *Your birthday's this month, isn't it?* **2 A1** a period of approximately four weeks: *I saw him about three months ago.*

monthly /ˈmʌnθli/ **adj, adv B1** happening or produced once a month: *a monthly meeting* ∘ *a monthly magazine*

monument /ˈmɒnjəmənt/ **noun** [C] **1 B2** a building or other structure that is built to make people remember an event in history or a famous person: *a national monument* ∘ *They built the statue as **a monument to** all the soldiers who died.* **2 B1** an old building or place that is important in history: *an ancient monument*

monumental /ˌmɒnjəˈmentəl/ **adj** very large: *a **monumental task***

moo /muː/ **noun** [C] the sound that a cow makes ● **moo verb** [I] (**mooing**, **mooed**)

mood /muːd/ **noun 1** [C, U] **B1** the way someone feels at a particular time: *to be in a **good/bad mood*** ∘ *The public mood changed dramatically after the bombing.* **2 be in a mood** to not be friendly to other people because you are feeling angry **3 be in the mood for sth/to do sth** to want to do or have something: *I'm not really in the mood for shopping at the moment.* **4 be in no mood for sth/to do sth** to not want to do something with someone else, often because you are angry with them **5** [C] in grammar, one of the different ways a sentence is being used, for example to give an order, express a fact, etc: *the indicative/imperative mood*

> 🔲 Word partners for **mood**
>
> be **in** a [bad/confident/foul/good, etc] mood ●
> mood **changes/swings** ● a **bad/foul/good**
> mood

moody /ˈmuːdi/ **adj** If someone is moody, they are often unfriendly because they feel angry or unhappy. ● **moodily adv** ● **moodiness noun** [U]

moon /muːn/ **noun 1 the moon A2** the round object that shines in the sky at night and moves around the Earth **2 crescent/full/new moon** the shape made by the amount of the moon that you can see at a particular time **3** [C] a round object like the moon that moves around another planet

IDIOMS **once in a blue moon** rarely: *We only go out once in a blue moon.* ● **be over the moon** UK to be very pleased about something: *"I bet she was pleased with her results." "She was over the moon."*

moonlight /ˈmuːnlaɪt/ **noun** [U] **B2** light that comes from the moon: *In the moonlight she looked even more beautiful.* ● **moonlit adj** [always before noun] with light from the moon

moor /mɔːr/ **noun** [C] an open area in the countryside that is covered with rough grass and bushes: [usually plural] *the Yorkshire Moors*

moose /muːs/ **noun** [C] (plural **moose**) a large deer that comes from North America

moot point /ˌmuːtˈpɔɪnt/ **noun** [C] a subject that people cannot agree about

mop¹ /mɒp/ **noun** [C] a piece of equipment used

M

for cleaning floors that has a long handle and thick strings at one end

mop² /mɒp/ **verb** [T] (**mopping, mopped**) to use a mop: *to **mop** the floor*

PHRASAL VERB **mop sth up** to use a cloth or mop to remove liquid from a surface

moral¹ /ˈmɒrəl/ **adj 1** [always before noun] ⑰ relating to beliefs about what is right or wrong: ***moral** standards/values* ∘ *a **moral** issue* **2** behaving in a way that most people think is correct and honest: *He's a very moral person.* → Opposite **immoral** → Compare **amoral** • **morally adv** ⑰ *morally wrong*

moral² /ˈmɒrəl/ **noun** [C] something you learn from a story or event about how to behave: *The **moral of the story** is never to lie.*

morale /məˈrɑːl/ **noun** [U] the amount of confidence or hope for the future that people feel: *The pay increase should help to **improve** staff **morale**.*

> ☑ **Word partners for morale**
> boost/damage/improve/raise/undermine morale • high/low morale

morality /məˈrælɪti/ **noun** [U] ideas and beliefs about what is right or wrong

morals /ˈmɒrəlz/ **noun** [plural] principles of good behaviour: *He doesn't care what he does, he has no morals at all.*

moral suˈ**pport** **noun** [U] help and encouragement: *Roz has said she'll come with me for moral support.*

morbid /ˈmɔːbɪd/ **adj** showing too much interest in unpleasant things such as death: *a **morbid** fascination with death*

more¹ /mɔːʳ/ **quantifier 1** ⑪ something in addition to what you already have: *Would anyone like some more food?* ∘ *I need a bit more money.* **2** ⑪ a greater number or amount of people or things: *There are a lot more people here today than yesterday.* ∘ *He knows more about computers than I do.* **3 more and more** ⑰ an increasing number: *More and more people are choosing not to get married.* → See also **any more**

> ❗ **Common learner error: more**
> The opposite of **more** is **fewer** for countable nouns and **less** for uncountable nouns.
> *He takes more exercise now.*
> *He takes less exercise now.*
> *He smokes fewer cigarettes.*

more² /mɔːʳ/ **adv 1 more beautiful/difficult/ interesting, etc** ⑪ used to show that someone or something has a greater amount of a quality than someone or something else: *It's **more** expensive **than** the others.* ∘ *She's far more intelligent than her sister.* **2** ⑬ used to show that something happens a greater number of times than before: *We eat out a lot **more than** we used to.* **3 more or less** ⑬ almost: *We've more or less finished work on the house.* **4 more and more** ⑬ more as time passes: *It's becoming more and more difficult to pass the exam.* → See also **any more**

> ❗ **Common learner error: more**
> **More** is used to form the comparative of many adjectives and adverbs that have two or more syllables.
> *a more expensive hotel*
> *Could you drive more slowly please?*
> ~~an expensiver hotel~~
> The opposite of the adverb **more** is **less**.
> *a less expensive hotel*

moreover /mɔːrˈəʊvəʳ/ **adv** formal ⑬ also: *It a cheap and, moreover, effective way of dealin with the problem.*

morgue /mɔːg/ **noun** [C] a building or roor where dead bodies are prepared and kept befor a funeral

Mormon /ˈmɔːmən/ **adj** belonging or relating t a Christian group that was started in the US b Joseph Smith • **Mormon noun** [C]

morning /ˈmɔːnɪŋ/ **noun** [C, U] **1** ⑪ the first hal of the day, from the time when the sun rises c you wake up until the middle of the day: *Frida morning* ∘ ***tomorrow morning*** ∘ *I got up lat **this morning**.* **2 in the morning a** ⑪ during th early part of the day: *I listen to the radio in th morning.* **b** ⑬ tomorrow morning: *I'll pack m bags in the morning.* **3 3/4, etc o'clock in th morning** ⑬ 3/4, etc o'clock in the night: *My co alarm went off at 3 o'clock in the morning* **4 (Good) morning.** ⑪ used to say hello t someone in the morning

moron /ˈmɔːrɒn/ **noun** [C] informal a very stupi person • **moronic** /mɔːˈrɒnɪk/ **adj** informal stupi

morose /məˈrəʊs/ **adj** If someone is morose they are not friendly or happy and they tal very little.

morphine /ˈmɔːfiːn/ **noun** [U] a powerful dru that is used to reduce pain

morsel /ˈmɔːsəl/ **noun** [C] a small piece c something: *a morsel of food*

mortal¹ /ˈmɔːtəl/ **adj 1** not living foreve → Opposite **immortal 2 mortal danger/fea terror, etc** extreme danger/fear/terror, etc because you could die • **mortally adv mortall** *wounded*

mortal² /ˈmɔːtəl/ **noun** [C] literary a human bein

mortality /mɔːˈtælɪti/ **noun** [U] **1** the number c deaths at a particular time or in a particula place: *infant mortality* ∘ *the mortality rat* **2** the way that people do not live forever: *He death made him more aware of his own mortality*

mortar /ˈmɔːtəʳ/ **noun 1** [C] a heavy gun tha fires explosives high into the air: *a morta attack/bomb* **2** [U] a mixture of substances, fo example sand and water, that is used betwee bricks or stones to keep them together

mortgage /ˈmɔːgɪdʒ/ **noun** [C] money that yo borrow to buy a home: *a monthly mortgag payment*

> ☑ **Word partners for mortgage**
> get/have/pay off/take out a mortgage • a mortgage **payment**

mortified /ˈmɔːtɪfaɪd/ **adj** very embarrassed

ortify /ˈmɔːtɪfaɪ/ **verb be mortified** to feel very embarrassed or upset about something: *I told her she'd upset John and she was mortified.*

ortuary /ˈmɔːtʃuᵊri/ **noun** [C] a building or room where dead bodies are prepared and kept before a funeral

osaic

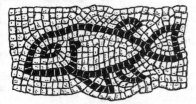

osaic /məʊˈzeɪɪk/ **noun** [C, U] a picture or pattern that is made with small pieces of coloured stone, glass, etc

Moslem /ˈmɒzləm/ **noun** [C] another spelling of Muslim (= someone who believes in Islam) • **Moslem adj**

osque /mɒsk/ **noun** [C] **A2** a building where Muslims say their prayers

osquito /mɒˈskiːtəʊ/ **noun** [C] (plural **mosquitoes**) **B1** a small flying insect that sucks your blood, sometimes causing malaria (= a serious disease): *mosquito bites*

oss /mɒs/ **noun** [C, U] a very small, green plant that grows on the surface of rocks, trees, etc

ost¹ /məʊst/ **adv 1** the **most attractive/ important/popular, etc A2** used to show that someone or something has the greatest amount of a quality: *She's the most beautiful girl I've ever seen.* ∘ *There are various reasons but this is the most important.* **2 A2** more than anyone or anything else: *Which subject do you like most?* ∘ *Sam enjoyed the swings most of all.*

> ❗ Common learner error: **most**
> The adverb **most** is used to form the superlative of many adjectives and adverbs.
> *the most beautiful actress in the world*

ost² /məʊst/ **quantifier 1 A2** almost all of a group of people or things: *Most people think he's guilty.* ∘ *Most of our students walk to school.* **2 B1** a larger amount than anyone or anything else: *This one costs the most.* ∘ *Which of you earns most?* **3 the most B1** the largest number or amount possible: *That's the most I can pay you.* **4 make the most of sth B2** to take full advantage of something because it may not last long: *We should make the most of this good weather.* **5 at (the) most** not more than a particular amount or number: *The journey will take an hour at the most.*

ostly /ˈməʊstli/ **adv B1** mainly or most of the time: *She reads mostly romantic novels.*

otel /məʊˈtel/ **noun** [C] a hotel for people who are travelling by car

oth /mɒθ/ **noun** [C] an insect with large wings that often flies at night and is attracted to light → See picture at **insect**

other /ˈmʌðəʳ/ **noun** [C] **1 A1** your female

parent: *a single mother* ∘ *My mother and father are divorced.* **2 Mother** the title of an important nun (= woman who lives in a female religious group): *Mother Teresa* → See also **surrogate mother**

motherhood /ˈmʌðəhʊd/ **noun** [U] the state of being a mother

mother-in-law /ˈmʌðᵊrɪnˌlɔː/ **noun** [C] (plural **mothers-in-law**) **B2** the mother of your husband or wife

motherly /ˈmʌðᵊli/ **adj** A motherly woman is like a mother, usually because she is kind and looks after people.

Mother's Day noun [C, U] a Sunday in the spring when people give their mothers presents to show their love

mother tongue noun [C] **B2** the first language that you learn when you are a child

motif /məʊˈtiːf/ **noun** [C] a small design used as a decoration on something: *a floral motif*

motion¹ /ˈməʊʃᵊn/ **noun 1 MOVEMENT** ▷ [U] the way something moves or the fact that it is moving: *The motion of the boat made him feel sick.* **2 ACTION** ▷ [C] a single action or movement: *She made a motion with her hand.* **3 SUGGESTION** ▷ [C] a suggestion that you make in a formal meeting or court of law: *to propose/oppose a motion* **4 set sth in motion** to make something start to happen

IDIOM **go through the motions** to do something that you have to do without enthusiasm

→ See also **slow motion**

motion² /ˈməʊʃᵊn/ **verb motion (for/to) sb to do sth** to make a movement as a sign for someone to do something: *She motioned him to sit down.*

motionless /ˈməʊʃᵊnləs/ **adj** not moving: *He stood motionless in the middle of the road.*

motivate /ˈməʊtɪveɪt/ **verb** [T] **1** to make someone enthusiastic about doing something: [+ to do sth] *Teaching is all about motivating people to learn.* **2** to make someone behave in a particular way: [often passive] *Some people are motivated by greed.* • **motivated adj B2** *a racially motivated crime* ∘ *a very motivated student (= one who works hard and wants to succeed)*

motivation /ˌməʊtɪˈveɪʃᵊn/ **noun 1** [U] **B2** enthusiasm for doing something: *There is a lack of motivation among the staff.* **2** [C] the need or reason for doing something: *What was the motivation for the attack?*

> ✅ Word partners for **motivation**
> sb's **main/primary** motivation • the motivation **behind/for** sth

motivational /ˌməʊtɪˈveɪʃᵊnᵊl/ **adj** [always before noun] giving you encouragement to do something: *a motivational speaker*

> ✅ Word partners for **motive**
> **have** a motive • an **ulterior/underlying** motive • the motive **behind/for** sth

motive /ˈməʊtɪv/ **noun** [C] **B2** a reason for doing

M

something: *The police don't yet know the **motive** for the killing.*

motor¹ /ˈməʊtər/ **noun** [C] 🅱2 the part of a machine or vehicle that changes electricity or fuel into movement and makes it work: *an electric motor*

motor² /ˈməʊtər/ **adj** [always before noun] relating to cars: *motor racing*

motorbike /ˈməʊtəbaɪk/ **noun** [C] 🅰2 a vehicle with two wheels and an engine

motorcycle /ˈməʊtəˌsaɪkl/ **noun** [C] a motorbike

motoring /ˈməʊtərɪŋ/ **adj** [always before noun] UK relating to driving: *a motoring offence*

motorist /ˈməʊtərɪst/ **noun** [C] 🅱2 someone who drives a car

motor racing **noun** [U] the sport of driving extremely fast and powerful cars around a track

motorway /ˈməʊtəweɪ/ **noun** [C] UK (US **freeway**, **expressway**) 🅰2 a long, wide road, usually used by traffic travelling fast over long distances

mottled /ˈmɒtld/ **adj** A mottled pattern has a mixture of dark and light areas: *mottled skin*

motto /ˈmɒtəʊ/ **noun** [C] a short phrase that expresses someone's purpose or beliefs: *Her motto is, "Work hard, play hard".*

mould¹ UK (US **mold**) /məʊld/ **noun 1** [U] a green or black substance that grows in wet places or on old food **2** [C] a container that is used to make something in a particular shape: *a chocolate mould*

IDIOM **break the mould** to do something differently after it has been done in the same way for a long time

mould² UK (US **mold**) /məʊld/ **verb** [T] to make a soft substance a particular shape: *moulded plastic*

mouldy UK (US **moldy**) /ˈməʊldi/ **adj** covered with mould: *mouldy cheese*

mound /maʊnd/ **noun** [C] **1** a large pile of something: *a mound of clothes waiting to be ironed* **2** a higher area of soil, like a small hill: *an ancient burial mound*

mount /maʊnt/ **verb 1** **mount a campaign/challenge/protest, etc** to arrange a series of organized activities that will achieve a particular result **2** INCREASE ▷ [I] to increase in amount or level: *Tension in the room was mounting.* **3** **mount sth on/to, etc** to fix an object onto something: *They've mounted a camera on the wall by the door.* **4** GO UP ▷ [T] to go up something: *to mount the stairs* **5** RIDE ▷ [T] to get on a horse or bicycle → Opposite **dismount**

PHRASAL VERB **mount up** to gradually become a large amount: *My homework is really mounting up this week.*

Mount /maʊnt/ **noun** [C] used in the names of mountains: *Mount Everest*

mountain /ˈmaʊntɪn/ **noun** [C] **1** 🅰2 a very high hill: *to **climb** a mountain* ∘ *a **mountain range*** **2** informal a large pile of something: *There's a*

mountain of papers on my desk.

mountain

IDIOM **make a mountain out of a molehill** to deal with a small problem as if it were a big problem

mountain bike **noun** [C] a bicycle with thick tyres, originall made for people to ride on hills and roug ground

mountainous /ˈmaʊntɪnəs/ **adj** A mountainou area has a lot of mountains.

mourn /mɔːn/ **verb** [I, T] to feel very sad becaus someone has died: *He **mourned for** his dead so every day.*

mourner /ˈmɔːnər/ **noun** [C] someone at funeral

mournful /ˈmɔːnfəl/ **adj** very sad: *a mournfu voice* • **mournfully** adv

mourning /ˈmɔːnɪŋ/ **noun** [U] a period durin which someone mourns the death of someon else: *a **period of mourning*** ∘ *She's **in mournin** for her husband.*

mouse

mouse /maʊs/ **noun** [C] (plural **mice**) **1** 🅰2 a sma piece of equipment connected to a compute that you move with your hand to control wha the computer does → See colour picture **The Offic** on page Centre 5 **2** 🅰2 a small animal with fur an a long, thin tail

mouse click (also **mouse-click**) **noun** [C] th action of pressing a button on a compute mouse (= small computer control) to make th computer do something

mouse mat **noun** [C] a flat piece of material o which you move the mouse of your computer

mousse /muːs/ **noun** [C, U] **1** a soft, cold foo that is often sweet and usually has eggs c cream in it: *chocolate mousse* **2** a substanc that you put in your hair so that it stays in a particular shape

moustache

moustache (also US **mustache**) /məˈstɑːʃ/ US /ˈmʌstæʃ/ **noun** [C] 🅱1 a line of hair that some men grow above their mouths

mousy (also **mousey**) /ˈmaʊsi/ **adj 1** Mousy

hair is light brown. **2** A mousy person is shy and not very interesting.

mouth /maʊθ/ **noun** [C] **1** 🅐 the part of the face that is used for eating and speaking → See colour picture **The Body** on page Centre 13 **2 mouth of a cave/tunnel, etc** the opening or entrance of a cave/tunnel, etc **3 mouth of a river** where a river goes into the sea → See also **butter¹ wouldn't melt in sb's mouth**

> 🗹 Word partners for **mouth**
>
> close/open your mouth • in your mouth

mouthful /ˈmaʊθfʊl/ **noun** [C] the amount of food or drink that you can put into your mouth at one time

mouthpiece /ˈmaʊθpiːs/ **noun** [C] a person, newspaper, etc that expresses the opinions of the government or a political group

mouthwash /ˈmaʊθwɒʃ/ **noun** [U] a liquid used to make your mouth clean and fresh

movable /ˈmuːvəbl/ **adj** able to be moved

move¹ /muːv/ **verb 1** CHANGE PLACE ▷ [I] 🅑 If a person or an organization moves, they go to a different place to live or work: *Eventually, he moved to Germany.* ○ *She's moving into a new apartment.* ○ *Our children have all moved away.* **2** POSITION ▷ [I, T] 🅐 to change place or position, or to make something change place or position: *We moved the chairs to another room.* ○ *Someone was moving around upstairs.* **3 move ahead/along/forward, etc** to make progress with something that you have planned to do: *The department is moving ahead with changes to its teaching programme.* **4** ACTION ▷ [I] to take action: [+ to do sth] *The company moved swiftly to find new products.* **5** TIME ▷ [T] to change the time or order of something: *We need to move the meeting back a few days.* **6** FEELING ▷ [T] 🅑 to make someone have strong feelings of sadness or sympathy: [often passive] *I was deeply moved by his speech.* ○ *Many people were moved to tears* (= were so sad they cried). → Compare **unmoved 7 move house** UK 🅑 to leave your home in order to live in a new one

> ❗ Common learner error: move or travel?
>
> **Move** means to change position or put something in a different position.
> *Could you move back a bit, please?*
> *Why don't you move the table over there?*
> **Travel** means to go from one place to another, usually in a vehicle.
> *Most people travel to work by car.*

IDIOM **get moving** informal to hurry

PHRASAL VERBS **move in** 🅑 to begin living in a new home: *She's just moved in with her boyfriend.* ○ *They want to move in together before they get married.* • **move on 1** NEW PLACE ▷ to leave the place where you are staying and go somewhere else: *After three days in Madrid we thought we'd move on.* **2** NEW ACTIVITY ▷ to start doing a new activity: *I'd done the same job for ten years and felt it was time to*

move on. **3** NEW SUBJECT ▷ to change from one subject to another when you are talking or writing: *Let's move on to the next topic.* • **move out** 🅑 to stop living in a particular home *He moved out when he was only eighteen.* • **move over** to change the place where you are sitting or standing so that there is space for someone else to sit or stand

move² /muːv/ **noun** [C] **1** something that you do in order to achieve something or to make progress in a situation: *"I've told her she's got to find somewhere else to live." "Good move!"* ○ *The latest policies are clearly a move towards democracy.* ○ *a good career move* **2** an occasion when you go to live or work in a different place: *The move will cost us a lot of money.* **3 make a move a** to change from one place or position to another: *He made a move as if to leave.* **b** UK informal to leave somewhere: *I'd better make a move or I'll be late.*

IDIOM **get a move on** informal to hurry: *Come on, get a move on!*

movement /ˈmuːvmənt/ **noun 1** GROUP ▷ [C] a group of people with the same beliefs who work together to achieve something: *the women's movement* ○ *the labour movement* **2** CHANGE ▷ [C] a change or development in the way people think or behave: *a movement towards democracy* **3** POSITION ▷ [C, U] 🅑 a change of position or place: *His movements were rather clumsy.* **4** MUSIC ▷ [C] a part of a piece of music: *The symphony opens with a slow movement.* **5 sb's movements** what someone is doing during a particular period of time: *I don't know his movements this week.*

movie /ˈmuːvi/ **noun** [C] **1** 🅐 a film **2 the movies** US (UK **the cinema**) a cinema, or group of cinemas: *What's playing at the movies?* ○ *Why don't we go to the movies tonight?*

> 🗹 Word partners for **movie**
>
> make/see/watch a movie • in a movie

movie star noun [C] a famous movie actor or actress

movie theater noun [C] US (UK **cinema**) a building where you go to watch films

moving /ˈmuːvɪŋ/ **adj 1** 🅑 causing strong feelings of sadness or sympathy: *a moving tribute* **2** [always before noun] A moving object is one that moves: *a moving target*

mow /məʊ/ **verb** [T] (**mowed**, **mown**, **mowed**) to cut grass using a machine: *to mow the lawn*

mower /ˈməʊəʳ/ **noun** [C] (also **lawn mower**) a machine that you use to cut grass

MP /ˌemˈpiː/ **noun** [C] abbreviation for Member of Parliament: someone who has been elected to the government of the United Kingdom

MP3 /ˌempiːˈθriː/ **noun** [C, U] a computer file (= collection of information) that stores good-quality sound in a small amount of space, or the technology that makes this possible

MP3 player noun [C] 🅐 a piece of electronic equipment or a computer program for playing

M

music that has been stored as MP3 files (= collections of information)

mph written abbreviation for miles per hour: a unit for measuring speed: *a 30 mph speed limit*

MPV /ˌempiːˈviː/ **noun** [C] UK (US **minivan**) abbreviation for multi-purpose vehicle: a large, high car that can carry more people than a normal car

Mr /ˈmɪstər/ **noun** ⓐ a title for a man, used before his family name or full name: *Good morning, Mr Smith.* ∘ *This package is addressed to Mr Gordon Harper.*

> **❗ Common learner error: Mr, Mrs, Ms, Miss**
>
> All these titles are used before someone's name. **Mr** is used for men. **Mrs** is used for women who are married. **Miss** is used for girls or for women who are not married. **Ms** is used for women and does not show if a woman is married. Many women prefer to use this title to **Miss** or **Mrs**. We do not use these titles on their own as a way of speaking to someone. Usually, we use no name.
> *Can I help you?*
> ~~*Can I help you, Mrs?*~~

MRI /ˌemɑːrˈaɪ/ **noun** [C] abbreviation for magnetic resonance imaging: a system that produces electronic pictures of the organs inside a person's body

Mrs /ˈmɪsɪz/ **noun** ⓐ a title for a married woman, used before her family name or full name: *Hello, Mrs. Jones.* ∘ *Please send your application to the finance director, Mrs Laura Fox.*

MRSA /ˌemɑːresˈeɪ/ **noun** abbreviation for Methicillin Resistant Staphylococcus Aureus: a type of bacteria that is often found in hospitals and can make people very sick

Ms /mɪz/ **noun** ⓐ a title for a woman, used before her family name or full name: *Ms Holly Fox*

MS /ˌemˈes/ **noun** [U] abbreviation for multiple sclerosis (= a serious disease that gradually makes it difficult for a person to see, speak, or move)

MSc UK (US **MS**) /ˌemesˈsiː/ **noun** [C] abbreviation for Master of Science: a higher university qualification in a science subject

MTV /ˌemtiːˈviː/ **noun** trademark [U] abbreviation for Music Television: an organization that broadcasts pop music around the world

much¹ /mʌtʃ/ **quantifier 1** QUESTION ▷ ⓐ In questions, 'much' is used to ask about the amount of something: *Was there much food there?* ∘ *How much money will I need for the taxi?* **2** NEGATIVE ▷ ⓐ In negative sentences, 'much' is used to say that there is not a large amount of something: *She doesn't earn much money.* ∘ *Pete didn't say much at dinner.* ∘ *"Is there any coffee left?" "Not much."* **3 too much/so much** ⓐ a large amount of something, often more than you want: *I'd love to come, but I've got too much work.* ∘ *We were having so much fun, I didn't want to go home.* **4 A LOT OF** ▷ formal a lot of: *Much work remains to be done.* ∘ *Much of his*

evidence was unreliable. **5 not much of a st** used when you want to say that a person thing is a bad example of something: *I'm n much of a cook.* **6 not be up to much** UK inform to be of bad quality: *Her latest novel isn't up much.* → See Note at **many**

much² /mʌtʃ/ **adv** (**more, most**) **1** ⓐ often or lot: *Do you go to London much?* ∘ *I don't like cur very much.* **2** ⓐ used before comparativ adjectives (= adjectives like 'better' an 'smaller', that are used to compare things) mean 'a lot': *Their old house was much bigg* ∘ *That's a much more sensible idea.* ∘ *"Is her ne car faster than her old one?" "Oh yes, much."*

muck¹ /mʌk/ **noun** [U] informal dirt: *You've g muck on your shoes.*

muck² /mʌk/ **verb**

PHRASAL VERBS **muck about/around** mainly ᵁ informal to behave stupidly and waste time: *Sto mucking around, will you!* • **muck sth up** inform to do something badly, or to spoil something *mucked up the interview.*

mucus /ˈmjuːkəs/ **noun** [U] a thick liqu produced inside the nose and other parts the body

mud /mʌd/ **noun** [U] ⓑ a thick liquid mixture soil and water, or this mixture after it has drie *He'd been playing football and was covered mud.*

muddle¹ /ˈmʌdl/ **noun** [C, U] a situation confusion or bad organization: *There was a b* **muddle over** *who was buying the tickets.* ∘ *I'm* such **a muddle** *with these bills.*

> **② Word partners for muddle**
> be/get **in** a muddle • a muddle **over/with** sth

muddle² /ˈmʌdl/ **verb get sb/sth muddled up** think that a person or thing is someone ∘ something else: *I often get Jonathan and I brother muddled up.*

PHRASAL VERBS **muddle through (sth)** to mana to do something although you do not know hc to do it well: *None of us has any formal trainir but somehow we muddle through.* • **muddle st up** to arrange things in the wrong order: *Plea don't muddle up those books – I've just sorted the out.*

muddled /ˈmʌdld/ **adj 1** A person who muddled is confused: *He became increasing muddled as he grew older.* **2** Things that a muddled are badly organized: *He left his cloth in a muddled pile in the corner.*

muddy /ˈmʌdi/ **adj** ⓑ covered by or containir mud (= mixture of soil and water): *a mudc stream* ∘ *muddy boots*

mudguard /ˈmʌdɡɑːd/ **noun** [C] UK (US **fende** a curved piece of metal or plastic fixed above wheel of a bicycle or motorcycle to preven water or dirt from hitting the person's legs

muesli /ˈmjuːzli/ **noun** [U] a mixture of grair dried fruit, and nuts that people eat with milk part of the first meal of the day

muffin /ˈmʌfɪn/ **noun** [C] **1** a small, sweet cake: *blueberry muffin* **2** UK (US **English muffin**)

muffin

muffin *UK*,
English muffin *US*

muffin

small, round, flat bread that is often eaten hot with butter: *toasted muffins*

muffle /ˈmʌfl/ **verb** [T] to make a noise quieter and less clear: *The pillow muffled her screams.* • **muffled** adj Muffled sounds cannot be heard clearly: *a muffled sound/voice* ∘ *a muffled scream/cry*

muffler /ˈmʌflər/ **noun** [C] US (UK **silencer**) a part of a vehicle that reduces noise

mug¹ /mʌg/ **noun** [C] **1** 🅐🅑 a large cup with straight sides usually used for hot drinks: *a coffee mug* ∘ *a steaming mug of tea* **2** informal someone who is stupid and easily deceived: *I was such a mug to think he'd pay me back.*

mug² /mʌg/ **verb** [T] (**mugging, mugged**) to attack and rob someone in a public place: [often passive] *He was mugged as he walked across the park.* • **mugger** noun [C] someone who mugs people

mugging /ˈmʌgɪŋ/ **noun** [C, U] an attack in a public place in which money, etc is stolen from someone

muggy /ˈmʌgi/ **adj** When the weather is muggy, it is unpleasantly warm and the air contains a lot of water: *a muggy afternoon*

Muhammad /məˈhæmɪd/ **noun** another spelling of Mohammed (= the main prophet of Islam)

mule /mjuːl/ **noun** [C] an animal whose mother is a horse and whose father is a donkey (= animal like a small horse)

mules /mjuːlz/ **noun** [plural] women's shoes that have no back → See colour picture **Clothes** on page Centre 9

null /mʌl/ **verb**

PHRASAL VERB **mull sth over** to think carefully about something for a long time, often before you make a decision

nullah /ˈmʌlə/ **noun** [C] a Muslim religious teacher or leader

multi- /mʌlti-/ **prefix** many: *a multi-millionaire* ∘ *a multi-storey car park*

multicultural /ˌmʌltiˈkʌltʃərəl/ **adj** including people of different races and religions: *a multicultural society*

multilingual /ˌmʌltiˈlɪŋgwəl/ **adj** using or speaking more than two languages

multimedia /ˌmʌltiˈmiːdiə/ **adj** [always before noun] Multimedia computers and programs use

sound, pictures, film, and text: *multimedia software/technology*

multinational¹ /ˌmʌltiˈnæʃənəl/ **adj** active in several countries, or involving people from several countries: *a multinational company/corporation*

multinational² /ˌmʌltiˈnæʃənəl/ **noun** [C] a large company that produces goods or services in several countries

multiple¹ /ˈmʌltɪpl/ **adj** with several parts: *multiple injuries*

multiple² /ˈmʌltɪpl/ **noun** [C] a number that can be divided by another number an exact number of times: *Nine is a multiple of three.*

multiple choice **adj** A multiple choice exam or question gives you different answers and you choose the correct one.

multiple sclerosis /ˌmʌltɪplskləˈrəʊsɪs/ **noun** [U] a serious disease that gradually makes it difficult for a person to see, speak, or move

multiplex /ˈmʌltipleks/ **noun** [C] a cinema that has separate screens and shows different films at the same time

multiplication /ˌmʌltɪplɪˈkeɪʃən/ **noun** [U] the process of multiplying a number with other numbers

multiply /ˈmʌltɪplaɪ/ **verb 1** [I, T] to increase by a large number, or to make something increase by a large number: *In warm weather, germs multiply rapidly.* **2** [T] to add one number to itself a particular number of times: *Three multiplied by six equals eighteen.*

multi-purpose /ˌmʌltiˈpɜːpəs/ **adj** describes something that can be used in many different ways

multiracial /ˌmʌltiˈreɪʃəl/ **adj** involving people from different races: *a multiracial society*

multi-storey /ˌmʌltiˈstɔːri/ **adj** UK (US **multistory**) describes a building with many floors: *UK: a multi-storey car park/US: a multistory office building*

multitasking /ˌmʌltiˈtɑːskɪŋ/ **noun** [U] the ability of a person to do more than one thing at a time: *Women are often very good at multitasking.*

multitude /ˈmʌltɪtjuːd/ **noun** [C] formal a large number of people or things: *a multitude of problems/questions*

mum /mʌm/ **noun** [C] UK (US **mom**) 🅐🅑 mother: *I asked my mum but she said no.* ∘ *Can we go now, Mum?*

mumble /ˈmʌmbl/ **verb** [I, T] 🅑🅑 to speak too quietly and not clearly enough for someone to understand you: *He mumbled something about it being a waste of time.*

mummy /ˈmʌmi/ **noun** [C] **1** UK informal (US **mommy**) a word for 'mother', used especially by children: *Come here, Mummy!* ∘ *My mummy and daddy came too.* **2** a dead body covered in cloth, especially from ancient Egypt

mumps /mʌmps/ **noun** [U] an illness that children get which makes the throat and neck swell: *to have mumps*

munch /mʌnʃ/ **verb** [I, T] to eat something in a

noisy way: *She was sitting on the lawn munching an apple.*

mundane /mʌnˈdeɪn/ **adj** ordinary, or not interesting: *a mundane task/life*

municipal /mjuːˈnɪsɪpᵊl/ **adj** [always before noun] relating to the government of a town or city: *a municipal council/election*

munitions /mjuːˈnɪʃᵊnz/ **noun** [plural] bombs, guns, and other military equipment: *a munitions factory*

mural /ˈmjʊərᵊl/ **noun** [C] a picture that is painted on a wall

murder¹ /ˈmɜːdər/ **noun** [C, U] **1** ⬤ the crime of intentionally killing someone: *to* ***commit murder.*** ◦ *She was charged with* ***attempted murder.*** ◦ *a murder charge/trial* **2** **be murder** informal to be unpleasant or cause difficulty: *Driving in Chicago at rush hour is murder.*

> ☑ Word partners for **murder**
>
> **commit** (a) murder • the murder of sb • a murder **charge/investigation/victim/weapon**

murder² /ˈmɜːdər/ **verb** [T] ⬤ to kill someone intentionally and illegally: [often passive] *He was murdered by a former employee.*

murderer /ˈmɜːdᵊrər/ **noun** [C] ⬤ someone who has committed murder: *a convicted murderer*

murderous /ˈmɜːdᵊrəs/ **adj** [always before noun] likely to kill someone, or wanting to kill them: *a murderous dictator/regime*

murky /ˈmɜːki/ **adj 1** secret, and involving dishonest or illegal activities: *He has a* ***murky past*** *as an arms dealer.* ◦ *the* ***murky world*** *of drug dealing* **2** dirty and dark: *murky water*

murmur¹ /ˈmɜːmər/ **verb** [I, T] to speak quietly so that you can only be heard by someone near you: *"Go to sleep now," she murmured.* ◦ *He murmured a few words of sympathy.*

murmur² /ˈmɜːmər/ **noun** [C] the sound of something being said quietly: *I could hear the low* ***murmur of voices*** *from behind the door.*

muscle¹ /ˈmʌsl/ **noun 1** [C, U] ⬤ one of many pieces of tissue in the body that are connected to bones and which produce movement by becoming longer or shorter: *aching joints and muscles* ◦ *stomach/thigh muscles* ◦ *I think I may have* ***pulled*** (= injured) *a muscle.* **2** [U] the ability to control or influence people: *political/military muscle*

muscle² /ˈmʌsl/ **verb**

PHRASAL VERB **muscle in** informal to force yourself into an activity in which other people do not want you to be involved: *How can we stop him* ***muscling in*** *on this project?*

muscular /ˈmʌskjələr/ **adj 1** having firm, strong muscles: *muscular legs/arms* **2** relating to muscles: *muscular aches/pains*

muse /mjuːz/ **verb** [I] formal to think carefully about something for a long time: *I was just* ***musing about*** *relationships.*

museum /mjuːˈziːəm/ **noun** [C] ⬤ a building where you can look at important objects connected with art, history, or science: *a museum of modern art*

mush /mʌʃ/ **noun** [U] informal food that is unpleasantly soft and wet, usually because has been cooked for too long

mushroom¹
/ˈmʌʃruːm/ **noun** [C]
⬤ a type of fungus
(= organism like a
plant) with a short
stem and a round top,
some types of which
can be eaten: *pasta
with wild mushrooms*

mushroom

mushroom²
/ˈmʌʃruːm/ **verb** [I] to
increase or develop
very quickly: *mush-
rooming costs*

music /ˈmjuːzɪk/ **noun** [U] **1** ⬤ a pattern o sounds that is made by playing instruments o singing, or a recording of this: ***pop/dance musi*** ◦ ***classical music*** ◦ *He likes* ***listening to music*** ◦ *Could you* ***put on*** *some music?* ◦ *a musi festival* ◦ *a music lesson/teacher* **2** written sign that represent sounds that can be sung o played with instruments: *I never learnt to* ***rea music*** (= understand written music)*.*

IDIOM **face the music** to accept punishment o criticism for something bad that you have don

→ See also **chamber music, country music folk music**

> ☑ Word partners for **music**
>
> **compose/listen to/play** music • a piece of music • **dance/pop/classical** music • **put on** some music

musical¹ /ˈmjuːzɪkᵊl/ **adj 1** [always before noun] ⬤ relating to music: *a musical instrument* **2** goo at playing music: *She comes from a very musica family.* • **musically adv**

musical² /ˈmjuːzɪkᵊl/ **noun** [C] ⬤ a play or filn in which singing and dancing tell part of th story: *a Broadway/Hollywood musical*

musician /mjuːˈzɪʃᵊn/ **noun** [C] ⬤ someone wh plays a musical instrument, often as a job: « *talented jazz/classical musician*

Muslim (also **Moslem**) /ˈmʊzlɪm/ ⓤ /ˈmʌzləm/ **noun** [C] someone who believes in Islam • **Muslim adj** *a Muslim family*

muslin /ˈmʌzlɪn/ **noun** [U] a very thin cotton cloth

mussel /ˈmʌsᵊl/ **noun** [C] a small sea creature that has a black shell in two parts and that ca» be eaten

must¹ strong /mʌst/ weak /məst/, /məs/ **moda verb 1** NECESSARY ▷ ⬤ used to say that it i necessary that something happens or is done *The meat must be cooked thoroughly.* ◦ *Yoʋ mustn't show this letter to anyone else.* ◦ *I mus get some sleep.* **2** LIKELY ▷ ⬤ used to show tha you think something is very likely or certain to be true: *You must be exhausted.* ◦ *She must be very wealthy.* **3** SUGGEST ▷ ⬤ used to show tha you think it is a good idea for someone to d something: *You must come and stay with us som*

M

time. → See Study Page **Modal verbs** on page Centre 22

must² /mʌst/ **noun be a must** informal If something is a must, it is very important to have or do it: *The restaurant has become so popular that reservations are a must.*

mustache /'mʌstæʃ/ **noun** [C] another US spelling of moustache (= a line of hair above the mouth)

mustard /'mʌstəd/ **noun** [U] a thick, spicy, yellow or brown sauce often eaten in small amounts with meat: *a teaspoon of mustard*

muster /'mʌstə^r/ **verb** [T] (also **muster up**) to get enough support, bravery, or energy to do something difficult: *I hope she **musters** the **courage** to invite him for dinner.*

mustn't /'mʌsᵊnt/ short for must not: *You mustn't let her know I'm coming.*

musty /'mʌsti/ **adj** smelling old and slightly wet in an unpleasant way: *a musty room* ∘ *the **musty smell** of old books*

mutant /'mju:tᵊnt/ **noun** [C] an organism or cell that is different from others of the same type because of a change in its genes: *a mutant virus*

mutation /mju:'teɪʃᵊn/ **noun** [C, U] a permanent change in the genes of an organism, or an organism with such a change: *The disease is caused by a mutation in a single gene.*

mute /mju:t/ **adj 1** expressed in thoughts but not in speech or writing: *The president has **remained mute** about whether he will resign.* ∘ *I gazed at her in **mute admiration**.* **2** unable to speak for physical or mental reasons: *a school for deaf and mute children*

muted /'mju:tɪd/ **adj 1** FEELING ▷ not strongly expressed: *a muted response/reaction* ∘ *muted criticism* **2** SOUND ▷ A muted sound is quieter than usual: *muted voices* **3** COLOUR ▷ [always before noun] A muted colour is not bright or easily noticed.

mutilate /'mju:tɪleɪt/ **verb** [T] to damage someone's body violently and severely, often by cutting off a part of it: *a **mutilated body/corpse*** • **mutilation** /ˌmju:tɪ'leɪʃᵊn/ **noun** [C, U]

mutiny /'mju:tɪni/ **noun** [C, U] a situation in which a group of people, usually soldiers or sailors, refuse to obey orders, often because they want to be in control themselves • **mutiny verb** [I] to take part in a mutiny

mutt /mʌt/ **noun** [C] informal a dog that is a mixture of different breeds (= types)

mutter /'mʌtə^r/ **verb** [I, T] to speak quietly so that your voice is difficult to hear, often when complaining about something: *She walked past me, **muttering to herself.*** ∘ *He muttered some-thing about the restaurant being too expensive.* • **mutter noun** [C]

mutton /'mʌtᵊn/ **noun** [U] meat from an adult sheep: *a leg/shoulder of mutton*

IDIOM **mutton dressed as lamb** UK informal an older woman who wears clothes that would be more suitable for a young woman

mutual /'mju:tʃuəl/ **adj 1** When two or more people have a mutual feeling, they have the same opinion about each other: *mutual admiration/respect* ∘ *He doesn't like her, and I suspect **the feeling's mutual.*** **2** When two or more people have a mutual friend or interest, they have the same one: *Andrew and Jean were introduced to each other by a **mutual friend.***

mutually /'mju:tʃuəli/ **adv** You use mutually before an adjective when the adjective describes all sides of a situation: *a **mutually dependent** relationship* ∘ *Being attractive and intelligent are not **mutually exclusive** (= someone can be both attractive and intelligent).*

muzzle¹ /'mʌzl/ **noun** [C] **1** the mouth and nose of a dog, or a covering put over these to prevent the dog biting **2** the open end of the long cylindrical part of a gun

muzzle² /'mʌzl/ **verb** [T] **1** to put a muzzle on a dog **2** to prevent someone expressing their own opinions

my /maɪ/ **determiner** ⓐ belonging to or relating to the person who is speaking or writing: *Tom's my older son.* ∘ *It's not my fault.* ∘ *My house is near the station.*

MYOB informal internet abbreviation for mind your own business: used in emails and text messages to say rudely that you do not want to talk about something

myriad /'mɪriəd/ **adj** literary very many: *myriad problems* • **myriad noun** [C] literary *Digital technology resulted in **a myriad of** (= many) new TV channels.*

myself /maɪ'self/ **pronoun 1** ⓐ the reflexive form of the pronouns 'me' or 'I': *I've bought myself a new coat.* ∘ *I looked at myself in the mirror.* **2** ⓑ used to emphasize the pronoun 'I', especially when the speaker wants to talk about their actions and not someone else's: *I'll tell her myself.* ∘ *Jack always drinks red wine but I prefer white myself.* **3 (all) by myself** ⓐ alone or without anyone else's help: *I live by myself in a small house.* ∘ *I did the whole job all by myself.* **4 (all) to myself** for my use only: *I'll have the house all to myself this weekend.*

mysterious /mɪ'stɪəriəs/ **adj 1** ⓑ strange or unknown, and not explained or understood: *a mysterious stranger* ∘ *the mysterious death of her son* **2** refusing to talk about something and behaving in a secretive way: *Nick is being very **mysterious about** where he's going on holiday.* • **mysteriously adv** *to disappear/vanish myster-iously*

mystery¹ /'mɪstᵊri/ **noun 1** [C, U] ⓑ something strange or unknown that cannot be explained or understood: *an **unsolved mystery*** ∘ *He never gave up hope that he would **solve the mystery of** his son's disappearance.* ∘ *He's out of work, so how he pays his rent is **a mystery** to me (= I cannot explain it).* **2** [C] a story, often about a crime, in which the strange events that happen are explained at the end: *a **murder mystery***

> ☑ Word partners for **mystery**
>
> **explain/solve/unravel** a mystery • the mystery **surrounding** sth • an **unexplained/ unsolved** mystery • the mystery **of** sth • be a mystery **to** sb

M

mystery² /ˈmɪstəri/ **adj** [always before noun] A mystery person or thing is one who is unknown: *I saw her with a **mystery man** in a restaurant last night.*

mystic /ˈmɪstɪk/ **noun** [C] someone who attempts to be united with God through prayer

mystical /ˈmɪstɪkəl/ **adj** (also **mystic**) **1** relating to the religious beliefs and activities of mystics **2** involving magical or spiritual powers that are not understood

mysticism /ˈmɪstɪsɪzəm/ **noun** [U] the religious beliefs and activities of mystics

mystify /ˈmɪstɪfaɪ/ **verb** [T] If something mystifies someone, they cannot understand or explain it because it is confusing or complicated: [often passive] *I was mystified by the decision.*

mystique /mɪˈstiːk/ **noun** [U] a mysterious quality that makes a person or thing seem interesting or special: *the mystique of the princess*

myth /mɪθ/ **noun** [C] **1** 🇧2 an ancient story abou gods and brave people, often one that explain an event in history or the natural world: *a Gree myth* **2** an idea that is not true but is believed b many people: *It's a myth that men are bette drivers than women.*

☑ Word partners for **myth**

debunk/dispel/explode a myth (= show that an idea is not true) • a common/popular myth • the myth of sth

---

mythical /ˈmɪθɪkəl/ **adj** (also **mythic**) **1** existin in a myth: *a mythical character* **2** imaginary o not true

mythology /mɪˈθɒlədʒi/ **noun** [U] myths, ofte those relating to a single religion or culture *classical mythology* ○ *the mythology of th ancient Greeks* • **mythological** /ˌmɪθəˈlɒdʒɪk adj

N

l, n /en/ the fourteenth letter of the alphabet

I/A (also US **NA**) written abbreviation for not applicable: used on official forms to show that you do not need to answer a question

naff /næf/ **adj** UK informal silly and not fashionable: *naff lyrics*

nag /næg/ **verb** [I, T] (**nagging, nagged**) to keep criticizing or giving advice to someone in an annoying way: *They keep nagging me about going to university.*

PHRASAL VERB **nag (away) at sb** If doubts or worries nag at you, you think about them all the time: *The same thought has been nagging away at me since last week.*

nagging /'nægɪŋ/ **adj** [always before noun] Nagging doubts or worries make you worried and you cannot forget them.

nail¹ /neɪl/ **noun** [C]

nail

nail

1 🅱2 a thin piece of metal with a sharp end, used to join pieces of wood together: *a hammer and nails* **2** 🅱2 the hard surface at the end of your fingers and toes: *fingernails/toenails* ∘ *to cut your nails* ∘ *nail clippers/scissors* ∘ *Stop biting your nails.*

IDIOMS **hit the nail on the head** to describe exactly what is causing a situation or problem • **the final nail in the coffin** an event that causes the failure of something that had already started to fail: *This latest evidence could be the final nail in the coffin for Jackson's case.*

nail² /neɪl/ **verb 1 nail sth down/on/to, etc** to fasten something with nails: *There was a 'private property' sign nailed to the tree.* **2** [T] mainly US informal to catch someone who has committed a crime: *They eventually **nailed** him **for** handling stolen goods.*

PHRASAL VERBS **nail sb down** to make someone give you exact details or a decision about something • **nail sth down** US to understand something completely, or to describe something correctly: *We haven't been able to nail down the cause of the fire yet.*

nail brush noun [C] a small brush, used for cleaning your nails → See colour picture **The Bathroom** on page Centre 3

nail file noun [C] a small strip of metal or paper with a rough surface used for for smoothing and shaping the ends of your nails

nail polish noun [U] (also UK **nail varnish**) paint that you put on your nails

naive /naɪˈiːv/ **adj** If someone is naive, they believe things too easily and do not have enough experience of the world: *I was much younger then, and very naive.* • **naively adv**

I naively believed that we would be treated as equals. • **naivety** /naɪˈiːvəti/ **noun** [U] the quality of being naive

naked /'neɪkɪd/ **adj 1** 🅱2 not wearing clothes or not covered by anything: *a naked thigh/shoulder* ∘ *He was **stark naked** (= completely naked).* **2** [always before noun] A naked feeling or quality is not hidden, although it is bad: **naked aggression 3 the naked eye** If something can be seen by the naked eye, it is big enough to be seen without special equipment.

> 🗹 Word partners for **naked**
> US **buck**/UK/US **stark** naked • **half** naked

name¹ /neɪm/ **noun 1** 🅰1 [C] the word or group of words that is used to refer to a person, thing, or place: *What's your name?* ∘ *My name's Alexis.* ∘ *I can't remember the name of the street he lives on.* ∘ *He didn't mention her **by name** (= he did not say her name).* **2 in the name of sth** If bad things are done in the name of something, they are done in order to help that thing succeed: *So much blood has been spilt in the name of religion.* **3 a bad/good name** 🅱2 If things or people have a bad/good name, people have a bad/good opinion of them: *Their behaviour gives us all a bad name.* **4 call sb names** to use impolite or unpleasant words to describe someone

IDIOMS **make a name for yourself** to become famous or respected by a lot of people • **the name of the game** the main purpose or most important part of an activity: *Popularity is the name of the game in television.*

→ See also **brand name**, **Christian name**, **family name**, **first name**, **last name**, **maiden name**, **middle name**

name² /neɪm/ **verb** [T] **1 GIVE A NAME** ▷ 🅱1 to give someone or something a name: [+ two objects] *We named our first son Mike.* ∘ *A young boy named Peter answered the phone.* **2 SAY NAME** ▷ 🅱1 to say what the name of someone or something is: [often passive] *The dead man has been **named as** John Kramer.* ∘ *She cannot be named for legal reasons.* **3 ANNOUNCE** ▷ 🅱2 to announce who has got a new job or won a prize: [+ two objects] *She has been named manager of the new Edinburgh branch.* **4 you name it** something that you say that means anything you say or choose: *I've never seen such a wide selection. You name it, they've got it.*

IDIOM **name and shame** UK to publicly say that a person or business has done something wrong

PHRASAL VERB **name sb after sb** to give someone the same name as someone else: *We named him after my wife's brother.*

nameless /'neɪmləs/ **adj** If someone or something is nameless, they have no name or their name is not known: *a nameless soldier* → Compare **unnamed**

namely /ˈneɪmli/ **adv** a word used when you are going to give more detail about something you have just said: *She learned an important lesson from failing that exam, namely that nothing is ever certain.*

namesake /ˈneɪmseɪk/ **noun** [C] **your name-sake** someone who has the same name as you

nan /næn/ **noun** [C] UK informal grandmother

nanny /ˈnæni/ **noun** [C] someone whose job is to look after a family's children

nano- /nænəʊ-/ **prefix 1** extremely small: *nano-technology* **2** one billionth (= a thousand millionth): *a nanosecond*

nap /næp/ **noun** [C] a short sleep: *He likes to have/ take a nap after lunch.* • **nap verb** [I] (**napping, napped**)

nape /neɪp/ **noun** [C] the back of your neck

napkin /ˈnæpkɪn/ **noun** [C] (also UK **serviette**) a piece of cloth or paper used when you eat to keep your clothes clean and to clean your mouth and hands: *a paper napkin*

nappy /ˈnæpi/ **noun** [C] UK (US **diaper**) a thick piece of paper or cloth worn by a baby on its bottom: *disposable nappies* ∘ *to change a nappy*

narcissism /ˈnɑːsɪsɪzᵊm/ **noun** [U] formal great interest in and pleasure at your own appearance and qualities • **narcissistic** /ˌnɑːsɪˈsɪstɪk/ **adj** If people or their actions are narcissistic, they show narcissism.

narcotic /nɑːˈkɒtɪk/ **noun** [C] a drug that stops you feeling pain or makes you sleep, and that is addictive (= difficult to stop using)

narrate /nəˈreɪt/ **verb** [T] formal to tell the story in a book, film, play, etc: *'Peter and the Wolf,' narrated by actress Glenn Close* • **narration** /nəˈreɪʃᵊn/ **noun** [U] formal

narrative /ˈnærətɪv/ **noun** [C] formal a story or description of a series of events

narrator /nəˈreɪtəʳ/ **noun** [C] the person who tells the story in a book, film, play, etc

narrow¹ /ˈnærəʊ/ **adj 1** Narrow things measure a small distance from one side to the other: *a narrow lane/street* ∘ *a narrow tie* **2** including only a small number: *He has very narrow interests.* **3 a narrow defeat/victory** If you have a narrow defeat/victory, you only just lose/win. **4 a narrow escape** If you have a narrow escape, you only just avoid danger.

narrow² /ˈnærəʊ/ **verb** [I, T] **1** to become less wide or to make something less wide: *The road has been narrowed to one lane.* **2** to become less or to make something become less: *to narrow the gap between rich and poor*

PHRASAL VERB **narrow sth down** to make something, for example a list or a choice, smaller and clearer by removing the things that are less important: *We've managed to narrow the list down to four.*

narrowly /ˈnærəʊli/ **adv** only by a small amount: *A tile fell off the roof, narrowly missing my head.*

narrow-minded /ˌnærəʊˈmaɪndɪd/ **adj** not

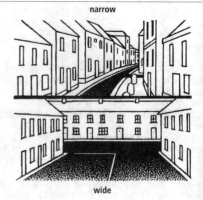

narrow

wide

willing to accept new ideas or opinion different from your own

nasal /ˈneɪzᵊl/ **adj** relating to the nose: *the nasʌ passages*

nascent /ˈnæsᵊnt/, /ˈneɪsᵊnt/ **adj** formal startin to develop: *a nascent democracy*

nasty /ˈnɑːsti/ **adj 1 BAD** very bad: *a nast shock/surprise* ∘ *a nasty smell/taste* ∘ *a nasty cu burn* **2 UNKIND** unkind: *She's always bein nasty to her little brother.* **3 ANGRY** ver angry or violent: *When I asked for the money, h turned really nasty.* • **nastiness noun** [U]

nation /ˈneɪʃᵊn/ **noun** [C] a country or th people living in a country: *Asian nation* ∘ *industrial nations* ∘ *The entire nation mourne her death.* ∘ *a nation of dog lovers.* → See Note **country¹** → See also **the United Nations**

✍ Word partners for **nation**
a **civilized/industrialized/poor/powerful** nation • **govern/lead** a nation • **across** the nation • a nation **of** sth

national¹ /ˈnæʃᵊnᵊl/ **adj 1** relating to th whole of a country: *to threaten national securit* ∘ *a sense of national identity* ∘ *a national new. paper* ∘ *national elections* ∘ *His income is wa above the national average.* ∘ *Gambling is national pastime (= many people do it) here* **2** [always before noun] connected with th traditions of a particular nation: *national dres customs* • **nationally adv**

national² /ˈnæʃᵊnᵊl/ **noun** [C] someone wh officially belongs to a particular country: *British/Chinese national*

national ˈanthem noun [C] the official son of a country, played at public events

the ˌNational ˈHealth Service noun th system providing free medical services in the U

national ˈholiday noun [C] (also US **federa holiday**) a day when most people in a countr do not have to work

National Inˈsurance noun [U] the system i the UK in which people regularly pay mone to the government in order to help people wh are old, sick or have no work

nationalism /ˈnæʃᵊnᵊlɪzᵊm/ **noun** [U] **1** a feelin

f pride in your own country **2** the belief that a
particular area should have its own government:
Welsh nationalism

ationalist /'næʃ°n°lɪst/ **noun** [C] someone who
wants a particular area to have its own
government

ationalistic /ˌnæʃ°n°l'ɪstɪk/ **adj** having a lot of
pride, often too much pride, in your own
country: nationalistic fervour

ationality /ˌnæʃ°n'æləti/ **noun** [C, U] **A1** If you
have American/British/Swiss, etc nationality, you
are legally a member of that country: What
nationality is she? ○ She has **dual nationality**
(= nationality of two countries).

ationalize /'næʃ°n°laɪz/ **verb** [T] If private
companies are nationalized, the government
takes control of them. • **nationalization**
ˌnæʃ°n°laɪ'zeɪʃ°n/ **noun** [U]

ational 'park noun [C] a large area of park for
use by the public, usually an area of special
beauty

ational 'service noun [U] the period of time
young people in some countries have to spend
in the army

ationwide /ˌneɪʃ°n'waɪd/ **adj**, **adv** **B2** including all parts of a country: a **nationwide**
campaign ○ Surveys have been carried out
nationwide.

ative¹ /'neɪtɪv/ **adj** **1** BORN IN ▷ [always before
noun] **B2** Your native town or country is the place
where you were born: It was a custom in his
native Algeria. ○ She is a **native-born** Texan.
2 LANGUAGE ▷ [always before noun] **B2** Your
native language is the first language you learn.
3 PEOPLE ▷ [always before noun] **B2** relating to
the people who lived in a country first, before
other people took control of it: the native
inhabitants/population **4** ANIMALS AND
PLANTS ▷ Native animals or plants live or
grow naturally in a place, and have not been
brought from somewhere else: a large bird
native to Europe

ative² /'neɪtɪv/ **noun** [C] **1** someone who was
born in a particular place: He's a **native of** Texas.
2 an old-fashioned and often offensive word for
a person who lived in a country, for example an
African country, before Europeans went there

ative A'merican adj relating or belonging to
the original groups of people who lived in North
America • **Native American noun** [C]

ative 'speaker noun [C] **B2** someone who
speaks a language as their first language

ATO (also UK **Nato**) /'neɪtəʊ/ **noun** abbreviation
for North Atlantic Treaty Organization: an international military organization formed in 1949
to improve the defence of Western Europe

atter /'nætə'/ **verb** [I] mainly UK informal to talk
about things that are not important • **natter
noun** [no plural] UK to **have a natter**

atural /'nætʃ°r°l/ **adj** **1** NATURE ▷ **B1** Something that is natural exists or happens because
of nature, not because it was made or done by
people: **natural gas/resources** ○ **natural
beauty** ○ to die of **natural causes** (= because
you are sick or old) ○ This product contains only

natural ingredients. **2** NORMAL ▷ **B2** normal or
expected: a **natural impulse/instinct** ○ It's
perfectly natural to feel nervous. → Opposite
unnatural 3 FROM BIRTH ▷ If you have a
natural characteristic, it is something you have
been born with: a natural talent ○ She's a natural
athlete/blonde. • **naturalness noun** [U]

natural 'gas noun [U] a gas that is found under
the ground and is used for cooking and heating

natural 'history noun [U] the study of animals
and plants

naturalist /'nætʃ°r°lɪst/ **noun** [C] someone who
studies animals and plants

naturalistic /ˌnætʃ°r°l'ɪstɪk/ **adj** Naturalistic art,
writing, or acting tries to show things as they
really are.

naturalize /'nætʃ°r°laɪz/ **verb** be **naturalized** to
officially become a member of another country:
a naturalized US citizen • **naturalization**
/ˌnætʃ°r°laɪ'zeɪʃ°n/ **noun** [U]

naturally /'nætʃ°r°li/ **adv** **1** AS EXPECTED ▷ **B2**
as you would expect: Naturally, he was very
disappointed. **2** NORMALLY ▷ **B2** in a normal
way: Relax and try to behave naturally. **3** FROM
BIRTH ▷ having been born with a characteristic:
naturally aggressive/funny/slim **4** NATURE ▷
Something that exists or happens naturally is
part of nature and not made or done by people:
Organic tomatoes are grown naturally without
chemical fertilizers.

natural re'sources noun [plural] things such
as minerals, wood, coal, etc. that exist naturally
in a place and can be used by people: The region
is rich in natural resources.

natural 'sciences noun [plural] sciences that
relate to the physical world such as biology,
chemistry, and physics

natural se'lection noun [U] the way that
plants and animals die when they are weak or
not suitable for the place where they live, while
stronger ones continue to exist

N

❗ Common learner error: **nature, the environment,** and **countryside**

Nature means all the things in the world
that exist naturally and were not created by
people.
   He's interested in wildlife and anything to do
with nature.

The environment means the land, water,
and air that animals and plants live in. It is
usually used when talking about the way
people use or damage the natural world.
   The government has introduced new policies
to protect the environment.

Countryside means land where there are no
towns or cities.
   I love walking in the countryside.

---

nature /'neɪtʃə'/ **noun** **1** PLANTS AND
ANIMALS ▷ [U] **A2** all the plants, creatures,
substances, and forces that exist in the universe,
which are not made by people: the laws of nature
○ I like to get out and enjoy nature. ○ a nature
trail **2** CHARACTER ▷ [no plural] **B2** someone's
character: I didn't think it was **in his nature** to

behave like that. **3 TYPE** ▷ [no plural] formal type: *What exactly is the nature of your business?* ∘ *I don't like hunting and things of that nature.* → See also **human nature, second nature**

> 🔲 **Word partners for nature**
>
> in sb's nature ∘ [happy/optimistic, etc.] by nature

'**nature re,serve** noun [C] a place where animals and plants live and are protected

naught /nɔːt/ noun [U, C] **1** (also **nought**) old-fashioned nothing **2** US (UK **nought**) the number 0

naughty /'nɔːti/ adj **1** 🇬🇧 If a child is naughty, they behave badly: *a naughty little boy/girl* **2** a word used humorously to describe things that are sexual: *naughty films/magazines*

nausea /'nɔːziə/ noun [U] the unpleasant feeling of wanting to vomit: *She was hit by a sudden wave of nausea.*

nauseating /'nɔːsieɪtɪŋ/ adj If something is nauseating, it makes you want to vomit: *a nauseating smell*

nauseous /'nɔːsiəs/ adj If you feel nauseous, you feel like you might vomit, and if something is nauseous, it makes you want to vomit.

nautical /'nɔːtɪkᵊl/ adj relating to boats or sailing: *a nautical mile*

naval /'neɪvᵊl/ adj [always before noun] relating to the navy: *a naval base/officer*

navel /'neɪvᵊl/ noun [C] the small, round, and usually hollow place on your stomach, where you were connected to your mother before birth

navigable /'nævɪɡəbl/ adj If an area of water is navigable, it is wide, deep, and safe enough to sail a boat on.

navigate /'nævɪɡeɪt/ verb **1 WITH MAP** ▷ [I, T] to find the right direction to travel by using maps or other equipment: *He navigated the ship back to Plymouth.* ∘ *We navigated using a map and compass.* ∘ *I drive and he navigates.* **2 BOAT** ▷ [T] to successfully sail along an area of water **3 DIFFICULT JOURNEY** ▷ [T] to find your way through a difficult place: *We had to navigate several flights of stairs.* **4 SYSTEM** ▷ [T] to successfully use a complicated system: *to navigate a website* ● **navigation** /,nævɪ'ɡeɪʃᵊn/ noun [U] ● **navigator** noun [C] a person who navigates

navy /'neɪvi/ noun **1 the Navy** 🇬🇧 ships and soldiers used for fighting wars at sea: *to be in the navy* **2** 🇬🇧 [U] (also ,navy 'blue) a very dark blue colour → See colour picture **Colours** on page Centre 12

Nazi /'nɑːtsi/ noun [C] someone who supported the ideas of Hitler in Germany in the 1930s and 1940s: *Nazi propaganda*

nb, NB /,en'biː/ used to tell the reader that a particular piece of information is very important

near¹ /nɪəʳ/ adv, preposition **1 DISTANCE** ▷ 🇦 not far away in distance: *Could you come a bit nearer, please?* ∘ *I stood near the window.* ∘ *Are you going anywhere near the post office?* **2 be/come near to doing sth** to almost achieve or do something: *This is the nearest I've ever got to*

winning anything. ∘ *He came near to punching him.* **3 STATE** ▷ If something or someone is ne a particular state, they are almost in that stat *She looked near exhaustion.* ∘ *She was near tears* (= almost crying) when I told her. **4 TIME** 🇬🇧 not far away in time: *She shouldn't be partyir so near her exams.* ∘ *We can decide nearer tl time.* **5 SIMILAR** ▷ similar: *The feelings I h were near hysteria.* ∘ *He is Russia's nearest thir to a rock legend.* **6 nowhere near** not close distance, amount, time, or quality: *It wasn't me I was nowhere near him.* ∘ *That's nowhere ne enough for six people.* ∘ *It was nowhere near difficult as I thought it would be.* **7 near enouc** almost: *The books were ordered near enouc alphabetically.*

near² /nɪəʳ/ adj **1** 🇬🇧 not far away in distance time: *The school's very near.* ∘ *The nearest gara is 10 miles away.* ∘ *The baby's due date we getting nearer.* **2 in the near future** 🇬🇧 at a tin that is not far away: *Space travel may becom very common in the near future.* → See also **a nea miss²**

near³ /nɪəʳ/ verb [T] to get close to something distance or time: *The building work is nearir completion at last.*

nearby /,nɪə'baɪ/ adj, adv 🇬🇧 not far away: *nearby town/village*

nearly /'nɪəli/ adv **1** 🇦 almost: *It's nearly thr weeks since I last saw her.* ∘ *Nearly all the foc had gone when I arrived.* ∘ *She nearly drowne when she was eight.* ∘ *I'll be with you in a minu – I've nearly finished.* **2 not nearly (as/so)** a l less: *It's not nearly as expensive as I thought.*

nearsighted /,nɪə'saɪtɪd/ adj US (UK **shor sighted**) If you are nearsighted, you cann see things very well if they are too far away.

neat /niːt/ adj **1 TIDY** ▷ 🇬🇧 tidy and clean: *t always looks very neat and tidy.* **2 GOOD** ▷ l informal good: *That's really neat.* ∘ *What a ne idea.* **3 ALCOHOL** ▷ A neat alcoholic drink drunk on its own, and not mixed with ar other liquid.

neatly /'niːtli/ adv in a tidy way: *neatly dresse* ∘ *a neatly folded pile of clothes*

necessarily /nesə'serᵊli/ adv **not necessarily** (not for certain: *That's not necessarily true.* ∘ *l know she doesn't say much, but it doesr necessarily mean she's not interested.*

necessary /'nesəsᵊri/ adj 🇬🇧 needed in order t achieve something: *[+ to do sth] Is it real. necessary to give so much detail?* ∘ *Does he hav the necessary skills and experience?* ∘ *The poli are prepared to use force, if necessary.* → Opposi **unnecessary**

necessitate /nə'sesɪteɪt/ verb [T] formal to mak something necessary

necessity /nə'sesəti/ noun **1** [U] the need fc something: *There's no financial necessity for h to work.* ∘ *Sewing is something I do out c necessity, not for pleasure.* **2** [C] something yc need: *Most people seem to consider a car necessity, not a luxury.*

➕ **Other ways of saying necessary**

The verbs **need** and **require** and the modal verb **must** are very commonly used to show that something is necessary:

*The meat **must** be cooked thoroughly.*
*Does she have the skills **needed/required** for work of that sort?*

If something is very important and necessary, you can use adjectives such as **essential**, **fundamental**, and **indispensable**:

*Some understanding of grammar is **essential/fundamental** to learning a language.*
*This book is an **indispensable** resource for teachers.*

The expression **be a must** is sometimes used in informal situations to describe things that are necessary to have or do:

*If you live in the country a car **is a must**.*

🔲 **Word partners for necessity**

out of necessity • the necessity **for/of** sth • **financial** necessity

neck /nek/ **noun** [C] **1** 🅰2 the part of the body between your head and your shoulders: *He was wearing a gold chain **around** his neck.* → See colour picture **The Body** on page Centre 13 **2** the part of a piece of clothing that goes around your neck: *a UK polo-neck/ US turtleneck ○ a V-neck sweater*

IDIOMS **be breathing down sb's neck** to watch what someone does all the time in a way that annoys them: *The last thing I want is a boss breathing down my neck.* • **neck and neck** If two people who are competing are neck and neck, they are very close and either of them could win. • **be up to your neck (in sth)** to be very busy

→ See also **polo neck**, by the **scruff** of the/your neck

necklace /ˈnekləs/ **noun** [C] 🅰2 a piece of jewellery that you wear around your neck: *a pearl necklace* → See picture at **jewellery**

neckline /ˈneklaɪn/ **noun** [C] the shape made by the edge of a dress or shirt at the front of the neck: *a low neckline*

nectar /ˈnektər/ **noun** [U] a sweet liquid produced by plants and collected by bees

nectarine /ˈnektəriːn/ **noun** [C] a soft, round fruit that is sweet and juicy and has a smooth red and yellow skin

née /neɪ/ **adj** [always before noun] a word used to introduce the family name that a woman had before she got married: *Margaret Hughes, née Johnson*

need¹ /niːd/ **verb** [T] **1** 🅰1 If you need something, you must have it, and if you need to do something, you must do it: *I need some new shoes. ○ The country still desperately needs help. ○ [+ to do sth] If there's anything else you need to know, just give me a call. ○ We need you to look after the children for us.* **2 don't need to do sth/needn't do sth** 🅰2 used in order to say that someone does not have to do something or

should not do something: *You didn't need to come all this way. ○ You don't need to be frightened. ○ She needn't have taken him to the hospital.* **3** 🅱1 If something needs something to be done to it, that thing should be done in order to improve it: *Do the clothes on this chair need washing? ○ The car needs to be serviced.* **4 There needs to be sth** used to say that something is necessary: *There needs to be more funding for education in this country.*

❗ **Common learner error: needed or necessary?**

It is not usual to use 'needed' as an adjective. We usually say **necessary** instead.

He gave us the necessary information.
~~He gave us the needed information.~~

need² /niːd/ **noun 1** 🅱2 [no plural] something that is necessary to have or do: *There's an urgent **need** for more medical supplies. ○ [+ to do sth] Is there any need to change the current system? ○ There's really **no need for** that sort of behaviour.* **2 be in need of sth** 🅱2 to need something: *My car's in desperate **need** of repair.*

🔲 **Word partners for need noun**

identify a need • meet a need (= provide what is needed) • a need **for** sth

needle /ˈniːdl/ **noun** [C]
1 MEDICAL ▷ the thin, sharp, metal part of a piece of medical equipment used to take blood out of the body, or to put medicine or drugs in **2 SEWING** ▷ 🅱2 a thin, pointed metal object with a small hole at one end for thread, used in sewing: *a needle and thread* **3 MEASURING** ▷ a thin, pointed piece of metal or plastic that moves to point to numbers on equipment used for measuring things → See also **pins and needles**

needle

needless /ˈniːdləs/ **adj** not necessary: *a **needless** expense ○ **Needless to say** (= as you would expect), it rained the whole time we were there.* • **needlessly adv**

needn't /ˈniːdənt/ short for need not: *You needn't have come.*

needs /niːdz/ **noun** [plural] 🅱2 the things you need in order to have a good life: *her emotional needs ○ The city is struggling to **meet the needs of** its homeless people.*

needy /ˈniːdi/ **adj** Needy people do not have enough money: *The mayor wants to establish permanent housing for **the needy**.*

neet /niːt/ **noun** abbreviation for not in education, employment or training: a name for people aged 16 to 24 who have finished their education and are unemployed: *The number of neets in Britain has risen to over one million.*

negate /nɪˈɡeɪt/ **verb** [T] formal to make something lose its effect or value • **negation** /nɪˈɡeɪʃən/ **noun** [U] formal

negative¹ /ˈneɡətɪv/ **adj 1 NO ENTHUSIASM** ▷

N

⑥① not having enthusiasm or positive opinions about something: ***negative feelings*** ○ *Many people have a **negative attitude** towards ageing.* **2 BAD** ▷ **⑥②** A negative effect is bad and causes damage to something: *Terrorist threats have had a very **negative impact** on tourism.* **3 MEDICINE** ▷ If the result of a test to prove if someone is pregnant or sick is negative, that person is not pregnant or sick. **4 NUMBERS** ▷ A negative number is less than zero. **5 GRAMMAR** ▷ **⑥②** In language, a negative word or phrase expresses the meaning 'no' or 'not'.

negative² /'negətɪv/ **noun** [C] **1** a piece of film from which a photograph can be produced, where dark areas look light and light areas look dark **2** a word or phrase that expresses the meaning 'no' or 'not'

negatively /'negətɪvli/ **adv 1** without enthusiasm or positive opinions: *to **react/respond negatively*** **2 ⑥②** with a bad effect: ***negatively affected***

negativity /ˌnegə'tɪvəti/ **noun** [U] a way of reacting that shows you do not feel enthusiastic or positive about things

neglect¹ /nɪ'glekt/ **verb** [T] **1** to not give enough care or attention to something or someone: *to neglect your appearance/the garden* ○ [often passive] *Some of these kids have been badly neglected in the past.* ○ *neglected animals* **2 neglect to do sth** to not do something, often intentionally: *He neglected to mention the fact that we could lose money on the deal.*

neglect² /nɪ'glekt/ **noun** [U] a failure to give enough care or attention to something or someone: *to suffer years of neglect*

negligence /'neglɪdʒəns/ **noun** [U] a failure to be careful enough in something you do, especially in a job where your actions affect other people: *Her parents plan to sue the surgeon for medical negligence.*

negligent /'neglɪdʒənt/ **adj** not giving enough care or attention to a job or activity, especially where your actions affect someone else: *The report found him negligent in his duties.*

negligible /'neglɪdʒəbl/ **adj** small and not important: *a **negligible effect/result***

negotiable /nɪ'gəʊʃiəbl/ **adj** If something is negotiable, it is not completely fixed, and can be changed after discussion: *The January deadline is not negotiable.*

negotiate /nɪ'gəʊʃieɪt/ **verb 1** [I, T] to try to make or change an agreement by discussion: *to negotiate with employers about working conditions* **2** [T] to successfully move around, through, or past something: *to negotiate your way around/through a city* ● **negotiator noun** [C] *a peace negotiator*

⊘ Word partners for negotiation

enter into/be in negotiations • negotiations break down/fail • negotiations about/on/over sth • negotiations with sb • negotiations between sb and sb

---

negotiation /nɪˌgəʊʃi'eɪʃən/ **noun** [C] the process of trying to make or change an agreement by discussion: ***Peace negotiations*** *are due to start.*

Negro /'niːgrəʊ/ **noun** [C] (plural **Negroes**) old-fashioned a word that means a black person, which some people think is offensive

neighbour UK (US **neighbor**) /'neɪbər/ **noun** [C] **1 ⑥②** someone who lives very near you, especially in the next house: *Our **next-door neighbours** are always arguing.* **2 ⑥②** someone or something that is near or next to someone or something else: *The French make more films than their European neighbours.*

neighbourhood UK (US **neighborhood**) /'neɪbəhʊd/ **noun** [C] **⑥①** an area of a town or city that people live in: *I grew up in a very poor neighbourhood.* ○ *Are there any good restaurants **in the neighbourhood** (= in this area)?*

neighbouring UK (US **neighboring**) /'neɪbərɪŋ/ **adj** [always before noun] **⑥②** near or next to somewhere: *neighbouring countries/villages*

neither¹ /'naɪðər/, /'niːðər/ **adv ⑥②** used to say that a negative fact is also true of someone or something else: *Jerry doesn't like it, and neither do I.* ○ *Her family wouldn't help her and neither would anyone else.* ○ *She's not very tall and neither is her husband.*

neither² /'naɪðər/, /'niːðər/ **pronoun, determiner ⑥②** not either of two people or things: *Luckily, neither child was hurt in the accident.* ○ ***Neither of*** *us had ever been to London before.* ○ *They gave us two keys, but neither worked.*

neither³ /'naɪðər/, /'niːðər/ **conjunction neither ... nor ⑥②** used when a negative fact is true of two people or things or when someone or something does not have either of two qualities: *Neither he nor his mother would talk to the police.* ○ *Their performance was neither entertaining nor educational.*

❗ Common learner error: Neither...nor

This expression can be used with a singular or plural verb.

Neither Jack nor Philip likes/like football.

---

neo- /niːəʊ-/ **prefix** new: *neo-facists*

neon /'niːɒn/ **noun** [U] a gas that produces bright, colourful light when electricity passes through it, often used in signs: *neon lights/signs*

nephew /'nefjuː/ **noun** [C] **⑥①** the son of your brother or sister, or the son of your husband's or wife's brother or sister

Neptune /'neptjuːn/ **noun** [no plural] the planet that is eighth from the Sun, after Uranus and before Pluto

nerd /nɜːd/ **noun** [C] informal someone, especially a man, who is not fashionable and who is interested in boring things ● **nerdy adj** informal boring and not fashionable

nerve /nɜːv/ **noun 1 PART OF THE BODY** ▷ [C] one of the threads in your body that carry messages between your brain and other parts of the body: *the optic nerve* ○ ***nerve cells/endings*** **2 BEING BRAVE** ▷ [no plural] the quality of being brave: [+ to do sth] *I **haven't got the nerve** to tell him I'm leaving.* ○ *He **lost his nerve** and couldn't* go through with it. **3 RUDENESS** ▷ [no plural] the rudeness necessary to do something you know will upset someone: *You've **got a nerve**, coming here!* ○ [+ to do sth] *I can't believe she **had the nerve** to talk to me after what happened.*

IDIOM **hit/touch a (raw) nerve** to upset someone by talking about a particular subject

nerve-racking /ˈnɜːvˌrækɪŋ/ **adj** If an experience is nerve-racking, it makes you very nervous: *a nerve-racking experience*

nerves /nɜːvz/ **noun** [plural] **1** ⬛ the state of being nervous: *I need something to **calm my nerves**.* ○ *I always **suffer from nerves** before a match.* **2 steady/strong nerves** ⬛ the ability to be calm in difficult situations: *You need a cool head and steady nerves for this job.*

IDIOM **get on sb's nerves** ⬛ to annoy someone, especially by doing something again and again: *If we spend too much time together we end up getting on each other's nerves.*

> ☑ Word partners for **nerves**
>
> **suffer from** nerves • **calm/settle/steady** your nerves

nervous /ˈnɜːvəs/ **adj 1** ⬛ worried and anxious: *a nervous cough/laugh* ○ *She's very **nervous about** her driving test.* **2** [always before noun] relating to the nerves in the body: *a nervous disorder*

> ❗ Common learner error: **nervous, agitated**, or **irritable?**
>
> **Nervous** means 'worried or frightened'. It does not mean 'angry' or 'upset'.
>
> *I get very nervous if I have to speak in public.*
>
> If you want to describe someone who cannot control their voice and movements because they are anxious and upset, use **agitated**.
>
> *He was very agitated and aggressive.*
>
> If you want to describe someone who becomes annoyed easily, use **irritable** or **bad-tempered**.
>
> *She was tired and irritable.*

nervous breakdown noun [C] a short period of mental illness when people are too sick to continue with their normal lives

nervously /ˈnɜːvəsli/ **adv** in a worried and anxious way: *to giggle/laugh nervously* • **nervousness noun** [U]

nervous system noun [C] your brain and all the nerves in your body that control your feelings and actions: *a disease of the central nervous system*

nest¹ /nest/ **noun** [C] a home built by birds for their eggs and by some other creatures to live in: *a birds'/wasps' nest*

nest² /nest/ **verb** [I] to live in a nest or build a nest

nestle /ˈnesl/ **verb 1 nestle (sth) against/in/on, etc** to rest yourself or part of your body in a comfortable, protected position: *The cat was nestling in her lap.* **2 nestle beneath/between/in, etc** If a building, town, or object nestles

somewhere, it is in a protected position, with bigger things around it: *a village nestled in the Carpathian mountains*

net

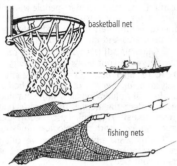

basketball net

fishing nets

net¹ /net/ **noun 1** [U] material made of crossed threads with holes between them **2** [C] ⬛ something made with a piece of net, for example for catching fish or insects, or for sports: *a fishing net* ○ *a tennis/basketball net* **3 the Net** ⬛ short for the Internet → See also **safety net**

net² (also UK **nett**) /net/ **adj** A net amount of money has had costs such as tax taken away from it: *a net income/profit of 10,000 euros*

net³ /net/ **verb** [T] (**netting, netted**) **1** to get an amount of money as profit: *One trader netted a bonus of £1 million.* **2** to hit, throw, or kick a ball into a net: *He netted a great penalty.*

.net /ˌdɒtˈnet/ part of an internet address that shows that it belongs to a business, often a network that provides internet services

netball /ˈnetbɔːl/ **noun** [U] a game usually played by teams of women, where a ball is thrown from player to player and goals are scored by throwing the ball through a high net

netbook /ˈnetbʊk/ **noun** [C] a small computer that can be carried around and that is designed especially for using the Internet and sending emails

netting /ˈnetɪŋ/ **noun** [U] material made of crossed threads or wires with holes between them: *wire netting*

nettle /ˈnetl/ **noun** [C] a wild plant whose leaves hurt you if you touch them

network¹ /ˈnetwɜːk/ **noun** [C] **1 SYSTEM** ▷ ⬛ a system or group of connected parts: *a rail/road network* ○ *a network of cables/tunnels* **2 PEOPLE** ▷ a group of people who know each other or who work together: *a large network of friends* **3 COMPANY** ▷ a large television or radio company that broadcasts programmes in many areas **4 COMPUTERS** ▷ a system of computers connected together so that they can share information

> ☑ Word partners for **network**
>
> **build/create/establish/form** a network • a network **of** sth • a **rail/road** network

network² /ˈnetwɜːk/ **verb 1** [I] to use social

N

events to meet people who might be useful for your business **2** [T] **B2** to connect computers together so that they can share information and programs

networking /'netwɜːkɪŋ/ **noun** [U] **1** the activity of using social events to meet people who might be useful for your business **2** the process of connecting computers together so that they can share programs and information

neural /'njʊərəl/ **adj** [always before noun] relating to the nerves in your body: *neural activity*

neurology /njʊə'rɒlədʒi/ **noun** [U] the study of the system of nerves in people's bodies • **neurological** /ˌnjʊərə'lɒdʒɪkəl/ **adj** Neurological illnesses affect the nerves in people's bodies. • **neurologist** /njʊə'rɒlədʒɪst/ **noun** [C] a doctor who deals with neurological illnesses

neuron /'njʊərɒn/ **noun** [C] a nerve cell that carries messages between your brain and other parts of your body

neurosis /njʊə'rəʊsɪs/ **noun** [C] (plural **neuroses** /njʊə'rəʊsiːz/) a mental illness, often causing you to worry too much about something

neurotic /njʊə'rɒtɪk/ **adj** If you are neurotic, you worry about things too much.

neuter /'njuːtər/ **adj** in some languages, belonging to a group of nouns or adjectives that have the same grammatical behaviour. The other groups are 'masculine' and 'feminine'.

neutral[1] /'njuːtrəl/ **adj 1** independent and not supporting any side in an argument, fight, or competition: *neutral ground/territory* ◦ *He decided to remain neutral on the issue.* **2** Neutral colours are not strong or bright.

neutral[2] /'njuːtrəl/ **noun** [U] In driving, neutral is the position of the gears (= parts of a vehicle that control how fast the wheels turn) when they are not connected: *to be in neutral*

neutrality /njuː'træləti/ **noun** [U] the state of being independent and not supporting any side in an argument, war, etc: *political neutrality*

neutron /'njuːtrɒn/ **noun** [C] a part of an atom that has no electrical charge (= the electricity something stores or carries)

never /'nevər/ **adv 1** **A1** not ever, not one time: *"Have you ever been to Australia?" "No, never."* ◦ *I've never even thought about that before.* ◦ *She'll never be able to have children.* ◦ *He just walked out of the door one day and never came back.* **2** used to emphasize something negative: *I never knew you lived around here.*

never-ending /ˌnevər'endɪŋ/ **adj** If something is never-ending, it continues for ever: *The housework in this place is just never-ending.*

nevertheless /ˌnevəðə'les/ **adv** **B2** despite that: *I knew a lot about the subject already, but her talk was interesting nevertheless.*

new /njuː/ **adj 1 DIFFERENT** ▷ **A1** different from before: *I need some new shoes.* ◦ *Have you met Fiona's new boyfriend?* ◦ *He's starting his new job on Monday.* ◦ *We're always looking for new ways to improve our services.* **2 RECENTLY MADE** ▷ **A1** recently made: *Their house is quite new – it's about five years old.* ◦ *The factory will provide hundreds of new jobs for the area.* **3 NOT KNOWN**

BEFORE ▷ **A1** not known before: *to discover* a *new gene/star* **4 be new to sb B1** If a situation or activity is new to you, you have not had experience of it before. **5 be new to sth B1** If you are new to a situation or activity, you have only recently started experiencing it: *I'm new to the job.* → See also **a whole new ball game**, new **blood**, **brand new**, break new **ground**[1], new **heights**, turn over a new **leaf**[1], give sb/sth a new **lease**[1] of life

newborn /ˌnjuː'bɔːn/ **adj** [always before noun] A newborn baby has just been born. • **newborn noun** [C] a newborn baby

newcomer /'njuːˌkʌmər/ **noun** [C] someone who has only recently arrived or started doing something: *He's a relative newcomer to the area.*

new-found /'njuːˌfaʊnd/ **adj** [always before noun] A new-found quality or ability has started recently: *This success is a reflection of their new-found confidence.*

newly /'njuːli/ **adv** **B2** recently: *a newly married couple* ◦ *newly built houses*

news /njuːz/ **noun** [U] **1** the news **B1** the announcement of important events on television, radio, and in newspapers: *the local/national news* ◦ *to watch the 6 o'clock news* ◦ *Did you see that report about child labour on the news last night?* ◦ *a news bulletin/report* **2** **A2** new information: *Have you had any news about your job yet?* ◦ *I've got some good news for you.* ◦ *Any news from John?* **3 be news to sb** informal to be a surprise to someone: *He's leaving? Well that's certainly news to me.*

IDIOM be bad/good news for sb to affect someone badly/well: *This weather is bad news for farmers.*

☑ Word partners for news

the latest news • hear/listen to/see/watch the news • in/on the news

---

newsagent /'njuːzˌeɪdʒənt/ **noun** [C] UK **1 newsagent's** a shop that sells newspapers, magazines, and things like sweets and cigarettes **2** someone who owns or works in a newsagent's

newscast /'njuːzkɑːst/ **noun** [C] US a television or radio broadcast of the news: *the evening newscast*

newscaster /'njuːzkɑːstər/ **noun** [C] someone who reads the news on the radio or television

newsgroup /'njuːzgruːp/ **noun** [group] a collection of messages on the Internet that people write about a particular subject: *a political newsgroup*

newsletter /'njuːzˌletər/ **noun** [C] a regular report with information for people who belong to an organization or who are interested in a particular subject: *a monthly newsletter about business and the environment*

newspaper /'njuːsˌpeɪpər/ **US** /'nuːzˌpeɪpər/ **noun 1** [C] **A1** large, folded sheets of paper that are printed with the news and sold every day or every week: *a local/national newspaper* ◦ *I read about his death in the newspaper.* ◦ *newspaper article/headline* **2** [U] **A2** paper

---

N

from newspapers: *The cups were wrapped in newspaper.*

newsprint /'njuːzprɪnt/ **noun** [U] cheap, low quality paper used to print newspapers

newsreader /'njuːzˌriːdər/ **noun** [C] UK someone who reads the news on the radio or television

newsstand /'njuːzstænd/ **noun** [C] US a small shop in a public area of a building or station, or part of a bigger shop, where newspapers and magazines are sold

newsworthy /'njuːzˌwɜːði/ **adj** interesting or important enough to be included in the news

the ˌNew ˈTestament noun the part of the Bible (= holy book) written after the birth of Jesus Christ

new ˈwave noun [usually singular] people who are doing activities in a new and different way: *the new wave of wine producers*

new ˈyear noun [C] (also **New Year**) the period in January when another year begins: *Happy New Year!* ∘ *We're going away in the new year.*

New ˌYear's ˈDay noun [C, U] 1 January, the first day of the year and a public holiday in many countries

New ˌYear's ˈEve noun [C, U] 31 December, the last day of the year

next¹ /nekst/ **adj** **1** next week/year/Monday, etc ⒶⓉ the week/year/Monday, etc that follows the present one: *I'm planning to visit California next year.* ∘ *Are you doing anything next Wednesday?* ∘ *Next time, ask my permission before you borrow the car.* **2** ⒶⓉ The next time, event, person, or thing is the one nearest to now or the one that follows the present one: *What time's the next train to London?* ∘ *We're going to be very busy for the next few months.* **3** ⒶⓉ The next place is the one nearest to the present one: *She only lives in the next village.* ∘ *Turn left at the next set of traffic lights.* **4** **the next best thing** the thing that is best, if you cannot have or do the thing you really want: *Coaching football is the next best thing to playing.* **5** **the next thing I knew** used to talk about part of a story that happens in a sudden and surprising way: *A car came speeding round the corner, and the next thing I knew I was lying on the ground.*

next² /nekst/ **adv** **1** ⒶⓉ immediately after: *You'll never guess what happened next.* ∘ *Where shall we go next?* **2** The time when you next do something is the first time you do it again: *Could you get some coffee when you next go to the supermarket?*

next³ /nekst/ **preposition** next to sth/sb ⒶⓉ very close to something or someone, with nothing in between: *Come and sit next to me.* ∘ *The factory is right next to a residential area.*

next⁴ /nekst/ **pronoun** **1** ⒷⓉ the person or thing that follows the present person or thing: *Who's next to see the nurse?* ∘ *Blue roses? Whatever next?* (= *What other strange things might happen?*) **2** **the weekend/week/Thursday, etc after next** ⒷⓉ the weekend/week/Thursday, etc that follows the next one

next ˈdoor adj, adv ⒷⓉ in the next room, house, or building: *What are your next-door neighbours*

like? ∘ *That's the old man who lives next door to Paul.*

ˌnext of ˈkin noun [C] (plural **next of kin**) formal the person you are most closely related to: *The names of the dead cannot be released until their next of kin have been notified.*

the NHS /ˌeneɪtʃˈes/ **noun** abbreviation for the National Health Service: the system providing free medical services in the UK: *Did she get it done privately or on the NHS?*

nib /nɪb/ **noun** [C] the pointed end of a pen, where the ink comes out

nibble /'nɪbl/ **verb** [I, T] to eat something by taking very small bites or to bite something gently: *He was nibbling a biscuit.* ∘ *She nibbled playfully at his ear.*

➕ Other ways of saying nice

If a person is nice because they are kind to other people, you can say that they are **kind** or **sweet**:

*She's a very **kind** person.*
*Thank you so much for the card – it was very **sweet** of you!*

If something that you do is nice, you can describe it as **fun**, **enjoyable**, or **lovely**:

*We had a really **lovely** day at the beach.*
*You'd have liked the party – it was **fun**.*

If something is nice to look at, then adjectives such as **attractive**, **beautiful**, **pleasant**, **lovely**, and **pretty** are often used:

*There's some **beautiful** countryside in Yorkshire.*
*That's a **pretty** dress you're wearing.*

If food tastes nice, then we can say that it is **delicious** or **tasty**:

*This chicken soup is absolutely **delicious**.*

---

nice /naɪs/ **adj** **1** ⒶⓉ pleasant: *They live in a nice old house on Market Street.* ∘ *We could go to the coast tomorrow, if the weather's nice.* ∘ [+ to do sth] *It was very nice to meet you.* ∘ [+ doing sth] *Nice talking to you.* **2** ⒶⓉ kind and friendly: *He seems like a really nice guy.* ∘ *She's always been very nice to me.* **3** **nice and sth** informal used to emphasize a positive quality: *nice and clean* ∘ *This chair's nice and comfy.*

nicely /'naɪsli/ **adv** **1** ⒷⓉ well: *That table would fit nicely in the bedroom.* ∘ *His business is doing very nicely.* **2** ⒷⓉ in a pleasant way: *nicely dressed*

niche /niːʃ/ ⓊⓈ /nɪtʃ/ **noun** [C] **1** a job or activity that is very suitable for someone: *After years of job dissatisfaction, he's at last found his niche in financial services.* **2** a hollow space cut into a wall

ˌniche ˈmarket noun [C] a small number of people who buy a particular product or service, especially an unusual or expensive one: *They make luxury cars for a small but significant niche market.*

nick¹ /nɪk/ **verb** [T] **1** STEAL ▷ UK informal to steal something: *She got caught nicking CDs from HMV.* **2** CATCH ▷ UK informal If the police nick someone, they catch that person because they have committed a crime: [often passive] *He got* nicked for handling stolen goods. **3 CUT** ▷ to make a small cut in something without intending to: *He nicked himself shaving.*

nick² /nɪk/ **noun 1** [C] mainly UK informal a prison or police station: *They spent the night **in the nick**.* **2** [C] a small cut: *He has a little nick on his cheek.* **3 in bad/good nick** UK informal in bad/good condition

IDIOM **in the nick of time** just before it was too late: *The ambulance arrived in the nick of time.*

nickel /ˈnɪkl/ **noun 1** [C] a US or Canadian coin with a value of 5 cents **2** [U] a silver-white metal that is often mixed with other metals

nickname /ˈnɪkneɪm/ **noun** [C] a name used informally instead of your real name: *His behaviour has earned him the nickname 'Mad Dog'.* • **nickname verb** [+ two objects] *They nicknamed her 'The Iron Lady'.*

nicotine /ˈnɪkətiːn/ **noun** [U] a poisonous chemical substance in tobacco

niece /niːs/ **noun** [C] ⓐ the daughter of your brother or sister, or the daughter of your husband's or wife's brother or sister

nifty /ˈnɪfti/ **adj** informal well-designed and effective: *a nifty piece of software*

nigger /ˈnɪɡəʳ/ **noun** [C] offensive a very offensive word for a black person

niggle /ˈnɪɡl/ **verb 1** [I, T] to worry or annoy someone slightly for a long time: *a **niggling injury*** **2 niggle about/over, etc** UK to complain about things that are not very important: *She kept niggling about the extra work.* • **niggle noun** [C]

nigh /naɪ/ **adv 1** literary near: *The end of the world is nigh.* **2 well nigh/nigh on** old-fashioned almost: *Our family has lived here well nigh two hundred years.*

night /naɪt/ **noun** [C, U] **1 DARK** ▷ ⓐ the time in every 24 hours when it is dark and people usually sleep: *I didn't get any sleep **last night**.* ∘ *It's warm during the day, but it can get quite cold **at night**.* ∘ *The phone rang in the **middle of the night**.* ∘ *We stayed up almost all night talking.* ∘ *Tim's working nights this week.* **2 EVENING** ▷ ⓐ the period from the evening to the time when you go to sleep: *Did you have a good time **last night**?* ∘ *Are you doing anything **on Friday night**?* **3 SAYING THE TIME** ▷ used to describe the hours from the evening until just after 12 midnight: *They're open from 7 in the morning until 10 o'clock at night.* **4 have an early/a late night** to go to bed early/late **5 a night out** an evening spent away from home doing something enjoyable: *a night out at the theatre* **6 Good night.** You say 'Good night' to someone who is going to bed: *Good night, sleep well.* → See also **the dead³ of night/winter**

☑ Word partners for **night**

spend the night • **at** night • **in** the night • the **middle** of the night • **last** night

nightclub /ˈnaɪtklʌb/ **noun** [C] ⓑ a place where you can dance and drink at night

nightdress /ˈnaɪtdres/ **noun** [C] mainly UK a loose dress that women wear in bed

nightfall /ˈnaɪtfɔːl/ **noun** [U] the time in the evening when it gets dark

nightgown /ˈnaɪtɡaʊn/ **noun** [C] a loose dress that women wear in bed

nightie /ˈnaɪti/ **noun** [C] a loose dress that women wear in bed

nightingale /ˈnaɪtɪŋɡeɪl/ **noun** [C] a small brown bird that sings very well

nightlife /ˈnaɪtlaɪf/ **noun** [U] ⓑ entertainment for the night such as bars, restaurants, and theatres: *What's the nightlife like around here?*

nightly /ˈnaɪtli/ **adj** [always before noun], **adv** happening every night: *the nightly news* ∘ *The show, lasting ninety minutes, will be broadcast nightly from Monday to Friday.*

nightmare /ˈnaɪtmeəʳ/ **noun** [C] **1** ⓑ a very unpleasant experience: *The traffic can be a real nightmare after 4.30.* **2** ⓑ a frightening dream

☑ Word partners for **nightmare**

an **absolute/complete/living/total** nightmare • be sb's **worst** nightmare • the nightmare **of (doing)** sth • a nightmare **for** sb

ˈnight ˌschool noun [U] classes for adults that are taught in the evening

nightstick /ˈnaɪtstɪk/ **noun** [C] US (UK **truncheon**) a short stick that police officers carry to use as a weapon

night-time /ˈnaɪttaɪm/ **noun** [U] the period of time when it is dark at night

nil /nɪl/ **noun** [U] **1** UK In sports results, nil means 'zero': *Germany beat England three nil (= 3-0)* **2** not existing: *The chances of that happening are virtually nil.*

nimble /ˈnɪmbl/ **adj** able to move quickly and easily: *nimble fingers*

nine /naɪn/ ⓐ the number 9

nineteen /ˌnaɪnˈtiːn/ ⓐ the number 19 • **nineteenth** 19th written as a word

nine-to-five /ˌnaɪntəˈfaɪv/ **adj, adv** describe work that begins at nine o'clock in the morning and ends at five o'clock, which are the hours that people work in many offices from Monday to Friday: *She's tired of **working nine-to-five**.* • **nine-to-five** /ˌnaɪntəˈfaɪv/ **noun** [C]

ninety /ˈnaɪnti/ **1** ⓐ the number 90 **2 the nineties** the years from 1990 to 1999 **3 be in your nineties** to be aged between 90 and 99 • **ninetieth** 90th written as a word

ninth¹ /naɪnθ/ ⓐ 9th written as a word

ninth² /naɪnθ/ **noun** [C] one of nine equal parts of something; ⅑

nip /nɪp/ **verb** (**nipping, nipped**) **1 nip down out/up, etc** UK informal to go somewhere quickly and for a short time: *I'm just nipping down the road to get a paper.* **2** [T] If something nips you, it gives you a small, sharp bite: *His parrot nipped him on the nose.* → See also **nip sth in the bud**

nipple /ˈnɪpl/ **noun** [C] the small, circular area of slightly darker, harder skin in the centre of each breast in women, or on each side of the chest in men

irvana /nɪəˈvɑːnə/ noun [U] a state of perfection

itrate /ˈnaɪtreɪt/ noun [C, U] a chemical containing nitrogen and oxygen that is used on crops to make them grow better

itrogen /ˈnaɪtrədʒən/ noun [U] a gas that has no colour or smell and is the main part of air

he nitty-gritty /ˌnɪtiˈɡrɪti/ noun the important details of a subject or activity: *English teachers should concentrate on **the nitty-gritty of** teaching grammar.*

o¹ /nəʊ/ exclamation **1** ⓐ something that you say in order to disagree, give a negative answer, or say that something is not true: *"Have you seen Louise?" "No, I haven't."* ○ *"Have you ever been to Ireland?" "No."* ○ *"Can I have some more cake?" "No, you'll be sick."* ○ *"He's really ugly." "No he isn't!"* **2** ⓐ something that you say to agree with something that is negative: *"He's not very bright, is he?" "No, I'm afraid not."* **3 Oh no!** ⓐ something that you say when you are shocked and upset: *Oh no! It's gone all over the carpet!*

o² /nəʊ/ determiner **1** ⓐ not any: *There were no signposts anywhere.* ○ *I had no difficulty getting work.* ○ *There was no mention of money.* **2** ⓐ a word used to say that something is forbidden: *No smoking.* ○ *There was no talking in her classes.* **3 There's no doing sth** something that you say when an action is impossible: *There's no pleasing some people* (= nothing that you do will make them happy).

o³ /nəʊ/ adv **no ... than** ⓑ not any: *The work should be done no later than Friday.* ○ *There were no more than ten people there.*

o. written abbreviation for number

obility /nəʊˈbɪləti/ noun **1 the nobility** [group] the people from the highest social group in a society **2** [U] the quality of being noble

oble¹ /ˈnəʊbl/ adj **1** honest, brave, and kind: *a noble gesture* **2** belonging to the highest social group of a society

oble² /ˈnəʊbl/ noun [C] a person of the highest social group in some countries

obleman, noblewoman /ˈnəʊblmən/, /ˈnəʊblˌwʊmən/ noun [C] (plural **noblemen**, **noblewomen**) someone belonging to the highest social group in some countries

obly /ˈnəʊbli/ adv in a brave or generous way: *She nobly offered to sell her jewellery.*

obody /ˈnəʊbədi/ pronoun ⓐ no person: *There was nobody I could talk to.* ○ *Nobody's listening.* ○ *Sally helped me, but **nobody else** bothered.*

o-brainer /ˌnəʊˈbreɪnər/ noun [C] informal something that is very simple to do or to understand, or a decision that is very easy to take

octurnal /nɒkˈtɜːnl/ adj **1** Nocturnal animals and birds are active at night. **2** happening at night: *nocturnal activities/habits*

od /nɒd/ verb [I, T] (**nodding, nodded**) ⓑ to move your head up and down as a way of agreeing, to give someone a sign, or to point to something: *They nodded enthusiastically at the*

proposal. ○ *Barbara nodded in approval.* ● **nod** noun [C] *He gave a nod of approval.*

PHRASAL VERB **nod off** informal to start sleeping

nodule /ˈnɒdjuːl/ noun [C] a small lump, especially on a plant or someone's body

no-fault /ˈnəʊfɔːlt/ adj [always before noun] US No-fault laws or systems are ones where it is not important who is responsible for what has happened: *no-fault insurance*

no-go ˈarea noun [C] mainly UK an area, usually in a city, where it is too dangerous to go because there is a lot of violent crime there

noise /nɔɪz/ noun [C, U] ⓐ a sound, often a loud, unpleasant sound: *a deafening/loud noise* ○ *Stop **making** so much **noise**!* ○ *The engine's making funny noises.* ○ *There is some **background noise** on the recording.* ○ *I had to shout above the noise of the party.*

> 🔲 Word partners for **noise**
>
> background noise ● a deafening/faint/loud/ strange noise ● hear/make a noise

noise polˈlution noun [U] noise, often from traffic, which upsets people where they live or work

noisy /ˈnɔɪzi/ adj ⓐ Noisy people or things make a lot of noise: *A crowd of noisy protesters gathered in the square.* ○ *We've had problems with noisy neighbours.* ● **noisily** adv

nomad /ˈnəʊmæd/ noun [C] a member of a group of people who move from one place to another instead of living in the same place all the time ● **nomadic** /nəʊˈmædɪk/ adj Nomadic people move from place to place.

no-man's ˈland noun [U, no plural] an area of land that no one owns or controls, especially in a war

nominal /ˈnɒmɪnl/ adj **1** existing officially, but not in reality: *a nominal leader* **2** A nominal sum of money is a small amount of money: *a nominal charge/fee*

nominally /ˈnɒmɪnəli/ adv officially but not in reality: *nominally Catholic areas*

nominate /ˈnɒmɪneɪt/ verb [T] **1** to officially suggest a person for a job or a position in an organization, or to suggest a person or their work for a prize: [often passive] *Judges are nominated by the governor.* ○ *The film was **nominated for** an Academy Award.* ○ *He was **nominated as** best actor.* **2** to choose someone for a job or to do something: *He has **nominated** his brother **as** his heir.* ○ [+ to do sth] *Two colleagues were nominated to attend the conference.*

nomination /ˌnɒmɪˈneɪʃən/ noun [C, U] **1** the act of officially suggesting a person for a job or their work for a prize: *to **seek/win** a nomination* ○ *He won the Democratic **nomination for** mayor of Chicago.* ○ *She has just **received** her fourth Oscar **nomination**.* **2** the choice of someone for a job or to do something: *They did everything they could to defeat his nomination to be surgeon general.*

📝 **Word partners for nomination**

make/receive/seek/win a nomination • a nomination as/for sth

nominee /ˌnɒmɪˈniː/ noun [C] a person or a piece of work that has been nominated

non- /nɒn-/ prefix not or the opposite of: *non-alcoholic drinks* ∘ *non-smokers*

non-alcoholic /ˌnɒnælkəˈhɒlɪk/ adj describes a drink that does not contain alcohol

nonchalant /ˈnɒnʃ°lənt/ ⑤ /ˌnɑːnʃəˈlɑːnt/ adj calm and not worried: *a nonchalant shrug* • **nonchalantly** adv

noncommittal /ˌnɒnkəˈmɪt°l/ adj not showing your opinion about something: *a noncommittal expression/response*

nondescript /ˈnɒndɪskrɪpt/ adj not interesting: *a nondescript building/man*

none /nʌn/ quantifier **1** 🅱 not any: *None of them smoke.* ∘ *In 1992, the company had 2,700 part-time workers. Today it has none.* ∘ *There were only three births here in March and none at all in April.* ∘ *He asked if there was any hope. I told him frankly that there was none.* **2 none too clean/clever/pleased, etc** not at all clean/clever/pleased, etc: *His handkerchief was none too clean.* **3 none the happier/poorer/wiser, etc** not any happier/poorer/wiser, etc than before: *She must have explained the theory three times, but I'm still none the wiser.*

nonetheless /ˌnʌnðəˈles/ adv despite what has just been said: *He was extremely rude in meetings. Nonetheless, his arguments found some support.*

non-event /ˌnɒnɪˈvent/ noun [no plural] informal an event that was not as exciting or interesting as you expected it to be: *Her party was a bit of a non-event.*

non-existent /ˌnɒnɪgˈzɪst°nt/ adj not existing: *We knew our chances of success were non-existent.*

nonfiction /ˌnɒnˈfɪkʃ°n/ noun [U] writing about things that are true: *nonfiction books/titles*

no-no /ˈnəʊnəʊ/ noun [C] informal something that is forbidden or not socially acceptable: *Cardigans are a fashion no-no this season.*

no-nonsense /ˌnəʊˈnɒns°ns/ adj [always before noun] not having or allowing others to have any silly ideas or behaviour: *a no-nonsense approach to child rearing*

nonplussed /ˌnɒnˈplʌst/ adj extremely surprised

non-profit-making /ˌnɒnˈprɒfɪtˌmeɪkɪŋ/ adj UK (US **nonprofit**) A non-profit-making organization does not make money from its activities.

non-renewable /ˌnɒnrɪˈnjuːəbl/ adj relating to materials, etc. that are not able to be replaced once they have all been used: *non-renewable fuel*

nonsense /ˈnɒns°ns/ noun [U] **1** 🅱 If something someone has said or written is nonsense, it is silly and not true: *She talks such nonsense sometimes.* ∘ *That's a load of nonsense.* ∘ *It's nonsense to suggest they could have cheated.* **2** silly behaviour: *Will you stop this childish nonsense!* **3 make a nonsense of sth** UK to spoil something or make it seem stupid: *Cuts to the text made a nonsense of the play.*

📝 **Word partners for nonsense**

talk nonsense • absolute/complete/utter nonsense • a load of nonsense

non-smoker /ˌnɒnˈsməʊkər/ noun [C] a perso who does not smoke

non-smoking /ˌnɒnˈsməʊkɪŋ/ adj 🅱 A no smoking area is one where people are n allowed to smoke.

non-starter /ˌnɒnˈstɑːtər/ noun [C] inform something that will not be successful: *Th amount of money needed makes his project non-starter.*

non-stop /ˌnɒnˈstɒp/ adj, adv without stoppin or resting: *non-stop flights from Germany to th West Indies* ∘ *We've been talking non-stop th whole way.*

non-violent /ˌnɒnˈvaɪələnt/ adj not usin violent methods: *non-violent action/protes* ∘ *non-violent crimes/offenders*

noodles /ˈnuːdlz/ noun [plural] thin pieces pasta (= food made from flour, eggs, and wate used in Chinese cooking

nook /nʊk/ noun

IDIOM **every nook and cranny** every part of place: *I know every nook and cranny of this plac*

noon /nuːn/ noun [U] 🅱 12 o'clock in th middle of the day: *He has until noon to act. The service will be held at 12 noon.*

no one pronoun 🅱 no person: *No one bothere to read the report.* ∘ *No one knows where he now.* ∘ *There was no one there.* ∘ *No one els makes cakes like my mother.*

noose /nuːs/ noun [C] a piece of rope tied in circle, used to catch animals or to hang (= ki people

nor /nɔːr/ adv, conjunction **1 neither...nor...** ⓖ used after 'neither' to introduce the secon thing in a negative sentence: *Strangely, neith James nor Emma saw what happened.* ∘ *H neither spoke nor moved.* **2 nor can I/nor d you, etc** mainly UK 🅱 used after somethin negative to say that the same thing is true fo someone or something else: *"I don't like cats* *"Nor do I."* ∘ *"I won't get to see him tomorrow* *"Nor will Tom."* ∘ *She couldn't speak a word* *Italian and nor could I.*

Nordic /ˈnɔːdɪk/ adj from or relating to th North European countries of Sweden, Denmar Norway, Finland, and Iceland

norm /nɔːm/ noun **1 the norm** the usual wa that something happens: *Short-term job contrac are the norm nowadays.* **2** [C] an accepted way behaving in a particular society: [usually plura *cultural/social norms*

normal /ˈnɔːm°l/ adj 🅰 usual, ordinary, an expected: *to lead a normal life* ∘ *It's perfect normal to feel some degree of stress at work.* ∘ *It normal for couples to argue now and then.* ∘ *It that trains are running again things are back normal.*

Word partners for normal

be back to/return to normal • perfectly normal

normality /nɔːˈmæləti/ **noun** [U] (also US **normalcy** /ˈnɔːmᵊlsi/) a situation in which everything is happening normally: *a **return to** normality*

normally /ˈnɔːməli/ **adv 1** ③ usually: *Normally, I start work around nine o'clock.* **2** ③ in the ordinary way that you would expect: *Both lungs are now functioning normally.*

north

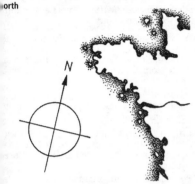

N

north, North /nɔːθ/ **noun** [U] **1** ④ the direction that is on your left when you face towards the rising sun: *The stadium is to the north of the city.* **2 the north** ④ the part of an area that is further towards the north than the rest: *She's from the north of England.* • **north** adj ④ *a north wind* • **north** adv ④ towards the north: *I live north of the river.* ∘ *We're going to visit Paul's family up north.*

northbound /ˈnɔːθbaʊnd/ **adj** going or leading towards the north

northeast, Northeast /ˌnɔːθˈiːst/ **noun** [U] **1** ⑤ the direction between north and east **2 the northeast** ⑤ the northeast part of a country • **northeast, Northeast** adj, adv

northeastern, Northeastern /ˌnɔːθˈiːstən/ **adj** in or from the northeast

northerly /ˈnɔːðᵊli/ **adj 1** towards or in the north: *Canada's most **northerly** point* **2** A northerly wind comes from the north.

northern, Northern /ˈnɔːðᵊn/ **adj** ⑤ in or from the north part of an area: *Northern England* ∘ *a northern accent*

northerner, Northerner /ˈnɔːðᵊnᵊr/ **noun** [C] someone from the north part of a country

northernmost /ˈnɔːðᵊnməʊst/ **adj** The northernmost part of an area is the part furthest to the north.

north-facing /ˈnɔːθˌfeɪsɪŋ/ **adj** [always before noun] positioned towards the north: *a north-facing slope*

the North Pole noun the point on the Earth's surface that is furthest north

northward, northwards /ˈnɔːθwəd/, /ˈnɔːθ**wədz/ **adv** towards the north • **northward adj** *a northward direction*

northwest, Northwest /ˌnɔːθˈwest/ **noun** [U] **1** ⑤ the direction between north and west **2 the northwest** ⑤ the northwest part of a country • **northwest, Northwest** adj, adv

northwestern, Northwestern /ˌnɔːθˈwestən/ **adj** in or from the northwest

nose¹ /nəʊz/ **noun** [C] ④ the part of your face through which you breathe and smell: *a big/broken nose* ∘ *She paused to **blow her nose** (= breathe out hard to empty it into a piece of cloth).* → See colour picture **The Body** on page Centre 13

IDIOMS **get up sb's nose** UK informal to annoy someone • **poke/stick your nose into sth** informal to show too much interest in a situation that does not involve you: *You shouldn't go sticking your nose into other people's business!* • **thumb your nose at sth/sb** to show that you do not respect rules, laws, or powerful people • **turn your nose up at sth** informal to not accept something because you do not think it is good enough for you: *He turned his nose up at my offer of soup, saying he wanted a proper meal.* • **under your nose** If something bad happens under your nose, it happens close to you but you do not notice it.

nose² /nəʊz/ **verb**

PHRASAL VERB **nose about/around (sth)** informal to look around a place, often in order to find something: *I caught him nosing around in my office.*

nosebleed /ˈnəʊzbliːd/ **noun** [C] **have a nosebleed** to have blood coming from your nose

nosedive /ˈnəʊzdaɪv/ **verb** [I] to fall very quickly in value: *The economy nosedived after the war.* • **nosedive noun** [C]

nosey /ˈnəʊzi/ another spelling of nosy

nostalgia /nɒsˈtældʒə/ **noun** [U] a feeling of happiness mixed with sadness when you think about things that happened in the past: *his nostalgia for his college days*

nostalgic /nɒsˈtældʒɪk/ **adj** feeling both happy and sad when you think about things that happened in the past: *Talking about those holidays has made me feel quite nostalgic.*

nostril /ˈnɒstrᵊl/ **noun** [C] one of the two holes at the end of your nose → See colour picture **The Body** on page Centre 13

nosy /ˈnəʊzi/ **adj** always trying to find out private things about other people: *nosy neighbours* ∘ *Don't be so nosy!*

not /nɒt/ **adv 1** ④ used to form a negative phrase after verbs like 'be', 'can', 'have', 'will', 'must', etc, usually used in the short form 'n't' in speech: *I won't tell her.* ∘ *I can't go.* ∘ *He hasn't eaten yet.* ∘ *Don't you like her?* ∘ *It isn't difficult (= It is easy).* ∘ *The service isn't very good (= it is bad).* ∘ *You're coming, aren't you?* ∘ *I will not tolerate laziness.* **2** ④ used to give the next word or group of words a negative meaning: *I told you not to do that.* ∘ *I like most vegetables but not cabbage.* ∘ *"Come and play football, Dad." "Not*

N

now, Jamie." ◦ "Whose are these?" "Not mine."
3 ⓐ2 used after verbs like 'be afraid', 'hope',
'suspect', etc in short, negative replies: "Do you
think it's going to rain?" "I hope not." ◦ "Have you
finished?" "I'm afraid not." **4 certainly/hopefully
not** used after an adverb in short, negative
replies: "She's not exactly poor, is she?" "Certainly
not." ◦ "We won't need much money, will we?"
"Hopefully not." **5 not at all** ⓑ2 used instead of
'no' or 'not' to emphasize what you are saying: "I
hope this won't cause you any trouble." "No, not at
all." ◦ I'm not at all happy about it. **6 Not at all.**
ⓑ1 used as a polite reply after someone has
thanked you: "Thanks for all your help." "Not at
all." **7 if not** ⓐ2 used to say what the situation
will be if something does not happen: I hope to
see you there but, if not, I'll call you. **8 or not** ⓐ2
used to express the possibility that something
might not happen: Are you coming or not? **9 not
a/one** used to emphasize that there is nothing of
what you are talking about: Not one person came
to hear him talk. ◦ "You haven't heard from Nick,
have you?" "Not a word."

> ⚠ Common learner error: **not ... either**
>
> The words **not ... either** are used to add
> another piece of negative information.
> I'd forgotten my credit card and I didn't have
> any cash either.
> ~~I'd forgotten my credit card and I didn't have
> any cash neither.~~
> Helen didn't enjoy it either.
> ~~Helen didn't enjoy it too.~~

notable /ˈnəʊtəbl/ **adj** If someone or something
is notable, they are important or interesting.
notably /ˈnəʊtəbli/ **adv** used to emphasize an
important example of something: Florida is well
known for many of its fruits, notably oranges and
avocados.
notation /nəʊˈteɪʃən/ **noun** [U] a system of
written symbols used especially in mathematics
or to represent musical notes
notch¹ /nɒtʃ/ **noun** [C] **1** a level of quality or
amount: Interest rates have moved up another
notch. **2** a cut in the shape of the letter V on the
edge or surface of something
notch² /nɒtʃ/ **verb**

PHRASAL VERB **notch up sth** to achieve something:
He has notched up a total of 34 goals this season.

note¹ /nəʊt/ **noun 1** LETTER ▷ [C] ⓐ1 a short
letter: He **left** a **note** on her desk. ◦ Did you **get**
my **note**? **2** INFORMATION ▷ [C] ⓐ2 words that
you write down to help you remember something: She studied her notes before the exam. ◦ Let
me **make a note of** (= write) your phone number.
◦ The doctor **took notes** (= wrote information)
while my wife described her symptoms.
3 EXPLANATION ▷ [C] a short explanation or
an extra piece of information that is given at the
bottom of a page or at the back of a book: See
note 3, page 37. **4** FEELING ▷ [no plural] a
particular feeling or mood: a **sad/serious/posi-
tive note** ◦ His speech had just the **right note** of
sympathy. **5** MUSIC ▷ [C] a single musical sound
or the symbol that represents it **6** MONEY ▷ [C]

UK (US **bill**) ⓑ1 a piece of paper money: a ten
pound note **7 take note (of sth)** to pay careful
attention to something: Make sure you take note
of what she says. **8 sb/sth of note** form
someone or something famous or important
A medieval church is the only monument of note
in the town.

IDIOM **compare notes** If two people compare
notes, they tell each other what they think about
something that they have both done: We
compared notes about our experiences in China.

> ☑ Word partners for **note noun**
> leave/scribble/send/write a note • a note for/
> from sb • get sb's note

note² /nəʊt/ **verb** [T] **1** ⓑ1 to notice something
She noted a distinct chill in the air. ◦ [+ (that)] We
noted that their idea had never been tried. **2** to say
or write something: In the article, she notes
several cases of medical incompetence.

PHRASAL VERB **note sth down** ⓑ2 to write something so that you do not forget it: I noted down
the telephone number for the police.

notebook /ˈnəʊtbʊk/ **noun** [C] **1** ⓐ2 a book with
empty pages that you can write in **2** a small
computer that can be carried around and used
anywhere
noted /ˈnəʊtɪd/ **adj** important or famous: a noted
artist ◦ He was **noted for** his modern approach t
architecture.
notepad (computer) noun [C] a very small
computer that you can carry easily
notepaper /ˈnəʊtˌpeɪpər/ **noun** [U] paper that
you write letters on
noteworthy /ˈnəʊtˌwɜːði/ **adj** If someone or
something is noteworthy, they are important or
interesting: a **noteworthy example**
nothing /ˈnʌθɪŋ/ **pronoun 1** ⓐ2 not anything
I've had nothing to eat since breakfast. ◦ He
claimed that he did nothing wrong. ◦ He had
nothing in his pockets. ◦ There was **nothing else**
(= no other thing) I could do to help. ◦ She did
nothing but criticize (= criticized a lot). **2** ⓑ1 no
something important or of value: He's a dange
ous person – human life means nothing to him. ◦ A
thousand pounds is nothing to a woman of her
wealth. **3 for nothing** without a successful
result: I've come all this way for nothing. **4 be
nothing to do with sb** ⓑ2 If something is or ha
nothing to do with you, you have no good
reason to know about it or be involved with it:
wish he wouldn't offer advice on my marriage – it
nothing to do with him. **5 have nothing to d
with sb/sth** ⓑ2 to have no connection o
influence with someone or something: H
made his own decision – I had nothing to d
with it. **6 to say nothing of sth** used t
emphasize other problems you have not talke
about: Most wild otters have disappeared fron
populated areas, to say nothing of wilderness
areas. **7 nothing of the sort** used to emphasiz
that something is not true: He said that he was
legitimate businessman – in fact, he was nothing o
the sort. **8 It was nothing.** a polite reply t

someone who has thanked you for doing something

IDIOMS **be nothing if not sth** used to emphasize a quality: *The senator was nothing if not honest* (= *he was very honest*). • **stop at nothing** to be willing to do anything in order to achieve something: *He will stop at nothing to get what he wants.*

nothingness /'nʌθɪŋnəs/ **noun** [U] a state where nothing exists

notice¹ /'nəʊtɪs/ **verb** [I, T] to see something and be aware of it: *If the sign's too small, no one will notice it.* ◦ [+ (that)] *I noticed that he walked with a limp.*

notice² /'nəʊtɪs/ **noun 1 SIGN** ▷ [C] a sign giving information about something: *The notice said that the pool was closed for repairs.* ◦ *Have you seen any* **notices about** *the new sports club?* **2 WARNING** ▷ [U] a warning that something will happen: *I had to give my landlord a month's notice before moving.* **3 at short notice** UK (US **on short notice**) only a short time before something happens **4 ATTENTION** ▷ [U] attention: *I didn't* **take** *any* **notice of** (= *give attention to*) *his advice.* ◦ *It has* **come to** *our* **notice** (= *we became aware*) *that you are being overcharged for your insurance.* **5 hand/give in your notice** to tell your employer that you are going to stop working for them: *I handed in my notice yesterday.*

📝 Word partners for **notice** noun

display/put up a notice • a notice **says** sth • a notice **about** sth • **on** a notice

noticeable /'nəʊtɪsəbl/ **adj** easy to see or be aware of: *There was a noticeable difference in his behaviour after the injury.* • **noticeably adv**

noticeboard /'nəʊtɪsbɔːd/ **noun** [C] UK (US **bulletin board**) **1** 🅑 a board on a wall where you put advertisements and announcements: *I saw the ad on the noticeboard.* → See colour picture **The Classroom** on page Centre 6 **2** an area on a website where messages containing information for other users can be left: *online noticeboards*

notify /'nəʊtɪfaɪ/ **verb** [T] formal to officially tell someone about something: *You should notify the police if you are involved in a road accident.* ◦ [+ (that)] *The court notified her that her trial date had been postponed.* • **notification** /ˌnəʊtɪfɪ-ˈkeɪʃən/ **noun** [C, U]

notion /'nəʊʃən/ **noun** [C] an idea or belief: *The notion of sharing is unknown to most two-year-olds.*

notoriety /ˌnəʊtərˈaɪəti/ **noun** [U] the quality of being famous for something bad: *He* **gained** **notoriety** *for his racist speeches.*

notorious /nəʊˈtɔːriəs/ **adj** famous for something bad: *a notorious criminal* ◦ *She was* **notorious for** *her bad temper.* • **notoriously adv** *Mount Everest is a notoriously difficult mountain to climb.*

notwithstanding /ˌnɒtwɪθˈstændɪŋ/ **adv, preposition** formal despite: *Injuries notwithstanding, he won the semi-final match.*

nought /nɔːt/ **noun** [C, U] **1** UK the number 0 **2** old-fashioned (mainly US **naught**) nothing

noun /naʊn/ **noun** [C] 🅐 a word that refers to a person, place, object, event, substance, idea, feeling, or quality. For example the words 'teacher', 'book', 'development', and 'beauty' are nouns. → See also **countable noun, proper noun, uncountable noun**

nourish /'nʌrɪʃ/ **verb** [T] formal to provide living things with food in order to make them grow or stay healthy: *Mammals provide milk to nourish their young.*

nourishing /'nʌrɪʃɪŋ/ **adj** Nourishing food makes you healthy.

nourishment /'nʌrɪʃmənt/ **noun** [U] formal the food that you need to stay alive and healthy

Nov written abbreviation for November

novel¹ /'nɒvəl/ **noun** [C] 🅑 a book that tells a story about imaginary people and events: *Have you* **read** *any good* **novels** *lately?* • **novelist noun** [C] 🅑 someone who writes novels

📝 Word partners for **novel**

read/write a novel • a novel **by** sb • a novel **about** sth • **in** a novel

novel² /'nɒvəl/ **adj** new or different from anything else

novelty /'nɒvəlti/ **noun 1 QUALITY** ▷ [U] the quality of being new or unusual: *The fashion industry relies on novelty, and photographers are always looking for new faces.* **2 NEW THING** ▷ [C] an object, event, or experience that is new or unusual: *Tourists are still a novelty on this remote island.* **3 CHEAP TOY** ▷ [C] a cheap toy or unusual object, often given as a gift

November /nəʊˈvembər/ **noun** [C, U] (written abbreviation **Nov**) 🅐 the eleventh month of the year

novice /'nɒvɪs/ **noun** [C] someone who is beginning to learn how to do something: *I've never used a computer before – I'm a complete novice.*

now¹ /naʊ/ **adv 1 AT PRESENT** ▷ 🅐 at the present time: *She's finished her degree and now she teaches English.* ◦ *Do you know where Eva is* **right now** (= *at this moment*)? **2 IMMEDIATELY** ▷ 🅐 immediately: *Come on, Andreas, we're going home now.* ◦ *I don't want to wait – I want it now!* **3 LENGTH OF TIME** ▷ 🅑 used to show the length of time that something has been happening, from the time it began until the present: *I've lived in Canada for two years now.* **4 IN SPEECH** ▷ used when you start to tell someone something: *Now, I have been to Glasgow many times before.* ◦ **Now then**, *would anyone else like to ask a question?* **5 just now** a very short time ago: *When I came in just now, everyone was laughing.* ◦ *Who was that woman who was speaking just now?* **6 (every) now and then/again** 🅑 If something happens now and then, it happens sometimes but not very often: *I love chocolate, but I only eat it now and then.* **7 any day/minute/time, etc now** used to say that something will happen very soon: *We're expecting our second child any day now.*

now² /naʊ/ **conjunction** (also **now that**) **B2** as a result of a new situation: *Now that I've got a car I can visit her more often.* ∘ *You should help in the house more, now you're older.*

now³ /naʊ/ **pronoun** the present time or moment: *Now isn't a good time to speak to him.* ∘ *She'd kept calm until now.* ∘ *I'll be more careful* **from now on** (= from this moment and always in the future).

nowadays /ˈnaʊədeɪz/ **adv** **B1** at the present time, especially when compared to the past: *Everything seems more expensive nowadays.*

nowhere /ˈnəʊweəʳ/ **adv** **B1** not anywhere: *The room was very crowded – there was nowhere to sit.* ∘ *We had **nowhere else** to go.* **2 out of nowhere** **B2** If someone or something appears out of nowhere, they appear suddenly or unexpectedly: *The car came out of nowhere and we had to swerve to miss it.*

IDIOMS **get/go nowhere** informal to not make any progress or achieve anything: *They're getting nowhere on this project.* • **get you nowhere** If something gets you nowhere, it does not help you to succeed: *Bad manners will get you nowhere.*

noxious /ˈnɒkʃəs/ **adj** [always before noun] formal poisonous or harmful: *noxious fumes/gases*

nozzle /ˈnɒzl/ **noun** [C] a narrow, hollow object that is fixed to a tube and which helps you to control the liquid or air that comes out

n't /ənt/ short for not: *She isn't* (= is not) *going.* ∘ *I can't* (= cannot) *hear you.* ∘ *They didn't* (= did not) *believe me.*

nuance /ˈnjuːɑːns/ **noun** [C] a very slight difference in meaning, appearance, sound, etc.: *a **subtle nuance*** ∘ *Linguists explore the nuances of language.*

nuclear /ˈnjuːkliəʳ/ **adj** [always before noun] **1** **B2** relating to the energy that is released when the nucleus (= central part) of an atom is divided: ***nuclear weapons/waste*** ∘ *a **nuclear power** plant* **2** relating to the nucleus (= central part) of an atom: *nuclear physics*

ˌnuclear reˈactor **noun** [C] a large machine that uses nuclear fuel to produce power

nucleus /ˈnjuːkliəs/ **noun** [C] (plural **nuclei** /ˈnjuːkliaɪ/) **1** the central part of an atom or cell **2** the central or most important part of a group or idea: *Senior coaches handpicked the nucleus of the team.*

nude¹ /njuːd/ **adj** not wearing any clothes: *Our children were running around the garden **in the nude*** (= not wearing any clothes).

nude² /njuːd/ **noun** [C] a painting or other piece of art that shows a nude person

nudge /nʌdʒ/ **verb** [T] to gently push someone or something: *She nudged me towards the door.* • **nudge noun** [C] *I gave him a nudge.*

nudism /ˈnjuːdɪzəm/ **noun** [U] the activity of wearing no clothes when you are outside with other people • **nudist noun** [C] someone who practices nudism

nudity /ˈnjuːdəti/ **noun** [U] the fact of wearing no clothes: *Some people are offended by nudity.*

nugget /ˈnʌgɪt/ **noun** [C] **1** a small amount of something good: ***nuggets of wisdom*** **2** a small round piece of a solid substance: *gold nuggets*

nuisance /ˈnjuːsᵊns/ **noun** [C] **1** **B2** a person, thing, or situation that annoys you or causes problems for you: *Not being able to use my computer is a real nuisance.* **2 make a nuisance of yourself** to annoy someone or cause problems for them

nullify /ˈnʌlɪfaɪ/ **verb** [T] formal **1** to make something lose its effect: *Advances in medicine have nullified the disease's effect.* **2** to say officially that something has no legal power: *The judge could nullify the entire trial.*

numb /nʌm/ **adj 1** If a part of your body is numb, you cannot feel it: *My fingers and toes were **numb with cold**.* **2** If you are numb with a bad emotion, you are so shocked that you are not able to think clearly: *I was **numb with** grief after his death.*

number¹ /ˈnʌmbəʳ/ **noun** [C] **1 SYMBOL** ▷ **A1** a symbol or word used in a counting system or used to show the position or order of something: *Think of a number smaller than 100.* ∘ *The Prime Minister lives at number 10, Downing Street.* ∘ *Look at item number three on your agenda.* **2 GROUP OF NUMBERS** ▷ **A1** a group of numbers that represents something: *What's your **phone number**?* ∘ *Each person receives a membership number when they join.* **3 AMOUNT** ▷ **B1** an amount: *a **small number** of* (= a few) ∘ *a **large number** of* (= many) ∘ *There were **a number** of* (= several) *soldiers present at the rally.* ∘ *Scientists have noticed a drop in the number of song birds in Britain.* → See Note at **amount¹** → See also **cardinal number, ordinal number, phone number, telephone number**

> **!** Common learner error: **number**
>
> We use the adjectives **large** and **small** with the word **number**, not 'big' and 'little'.
> *A large number of people attended the concert.*
> ~~A big number of people attended the concert.~~

number² /ˈnʌmbəʳ/ **verb** [T] **1** to give something a number: [often passive] *Each volume was numbered and indexed.* **2** If people or things number a particular amount, there are that many of them: *Our company's sales force numbered over 5,000.*

ˈnumber ˌplate **noun** [C] UK (US **license plate**) an official metal sign with numbers and letters on the front and back of a car → See colour picture **Car** on page Centre 7

numeral /ˈnjuːmᵊrᵊl/ **noun** [C] a symbol used to represent a number → See also **Roman numeral**

numerical /njuːˈmerɪkl/ **adj** [always before noun] relating to or expressed by numbers: *The exams were filed in numerical order.*

numerous /ˈnjuːmᵊrəs/ **adj** formal many: *He is the author of numerous articles.*

nun /nʌn/ **noun** [C] a member of a group of religious women living apart from other people

nurse¹ /nɜːs/ **noun** [C] (A2) someone whose job is to care for sick and injured people

nurse² /nɜːs/ **verb** [T] **1 CARE FOR** ▷ to care for a person or animal that is sick: *We nursed the injured bird back to health.* **2 FEED** ▷ US to feed a baby milk from its mother's breast: *She nursed her son until he was a year old.* **3 INJURY** ▷ to try to cure an illness or injury by resting: *He was nursing a broken nose.* **4 EMOTION** ▷ to think about an idea or an emotion for a long time: *She nursed a great hatred towards her older sister.*

nursery /'nɜːsəri/ **noun** [C] **1** (B2) a place where babies and young children are looked after without their parents **2** a place where plants are grown and sold

nursery ˌrhyme noun [C] a short poem or song for young children

nursery ˌschool noun [C] a school for very young children

nursing /'nɜːsɪŋ/ **noun** [U] the job of being a nurse

nursing ˌhome noun [C] a place where old people live to receive medical care

nurture /'nɜːtʃər/ **verb** [T] formal **1** to encourage or support the development of someone or something: *He was an inspiring leader who **nurtured** the **talents** of his colleagues.* **2** to look after, feed, and protect young children, animals, or plants: *The rains nurtured the newly planted crops.*

nut /nʌt/ **noun** [C] **1 FOOD** ▷ (B2) the dry fruit of some trees that grows in a hard shell, and can often be eaten: *a brazil/cashew nut* **2 METAL** ▷ a piece of metal with a hole in it through which you put a bolt (= metal pin) to hold pieces of wood or metal together → See picture at **tool** **3 KEEN** ▷ informal a person who is keen on a

particular subject or hobby: *She's a real sports nut.*

IDIOM **the nuts and bolts** the basic parts of a job or an activity: *Law school can teach you theory, but it can't teach you the nuts and bolts of the profession.*

nutrient /'njuːtriənt/ **noun** [C] formal any substance that animals need to eat and plants need from the soil in order to live and grow: *A healthy diet should provide all your **essential nutrients**.*

nutrition /nju'trɪʃən/ **noun** [U] the food that you eat and the way that it affects your health: *Good nutrition is essential for growing children.*
• **nutritional adj** relating to nutrition: *Some snacks have little **nutritional value**.*

nutritionist /nju'trɪʃənɪst/ **noun** [C] someone who gives advice on the subject of nutrition

nutritious /nju'trɪʃəs/ **adj** Nutritious food contains substances that your body needs to stay healthy: *a nutritious meal*

nuts /nʌts/ **adj** informal **1** crazy: *They thought I was nuts to go parachuting.* **2 go nuts** to become very excited, angry, or upset: *If I don't have a holiday soon, I'll go nuts.*

nutshell /'nʌtʃel/ **noun**

IDIOM **in a nutshell** something that you say when you are describing something using as few words as possible: *The answer, in a nutshell, is yes.*

nutty /'nʌti/ **adj 1** informal crazy: *nutty ideas* **2** Something nutty tastes of nuts.

nylon /'naɪlɒn/ **noun** [U] a strong, artificial material used to make clothes, ropes, etc: *nylon stockings* ∘ *a nylon shirt/bag*

nymph /nɪmf/ **noun** [C] in Greek and Roman stories, a spirit in the form of a young girl who lives in trees, rivers, mountains, etc

N

O

O, o /əʊ/ the fifteenth letter of the alphabet

oak /əʊk/ **noun** [C, U] **B2** a large tree found in northern countries, or the wood of this tree

OAP /ˌəʊeɪˈpiː/ **noun** [C] UK abbreviation for old-age pensioner: a person who regularly receives money from the state because they are too old to work

oar /ɔːʳ/ **noun** [C] a long pole with a wide, flat end that you use to move a boat through water

IDIOM **stick/put your oar in** UK informal to involve yourself in a discussion or situation when other people do not want you to

oasis /əʊˈeɪsɪs/ **noun** [C] (plural **oases** /əʊˈeɪsiːz/) **1** a place in the desert where there is water and where plants grow **2** a place that is much calmer and more pleasant than what is around it: *The cafe was an oasis in the busy, noisy city.*

oath /əʊθ/ **noun 1** [C] a formal promise: *an oath of allegiance* ◦ *They refused to* **take an oath** *of* (= *to promise*) *loyalty to the king.* **2 under oath** If someone is under oath, they have promised to tell the truth in a law court: *He denied under oath that he was involved in the crime.*

oatmeal /ˈəʊtmiːl/ **noun** [U] **1** a type of flour made from oats **2** US (UK **porridge**) a soft, white food made of oats (= type of grain) and water or milk

oats /əʊts/ **noun** [plural] grain that people eat or feed to animals

obedience /əʊˈbiːdiəns/ **noun** [U] the quality of being willing to do what you are told to do: *He demanded complete obedience from his soldiers.* → Opposite **disobedience** • **obedient** /əʊˈbiːdiənt/ **adj** willing to do what you are told to do: *an obedient child/dog* → Opposite **disobedient**

obese /əʊˈbiːs/ **adj** extremely fat • **obesity noun** [U] the state of being obese

obey /əʊˈbeɪ/ **verb** [I, T] **B2** to do what you are told to do by a person, rule, or instruction: *He gave the command, and we obeyed.* → Opposite **disobey**

obfuscate /ˈɒbfʌskeɪt/ **verb** [T] formal to make something harder to understand or less clear

obituary /əʊˈbɪtʃʊəri/ **noun** [C] a report in a newspaper that gives details about a person who has recently died

object¹ /ˈɒbdʒɪkt/ **noun 1** [C] **B1** a thing that you can see or touch but that is usually not alive: *a bright, shiny object* **2 the object of sth** the purpose of something: *The object of the game is to score more points than the opposing team.* **3 the object of sb's affection/desire, etc** the cause of someone's feelings: *He's the object of my affection.* **4** **B1** [C] in grammar, the person or thing that is affected by the action of the verb → See also **direct object, indirect object**

object² /əbˈdʒekt/ **verb** [I] **B2** to feel or say that you do not like or do not approve of something or someone: *We objected to his unreasonable*

demands. ◦ *Would anyone object if I were to leav* early? → See also **conscientious objector**

objection /əbˈdʒekʃən/ **noun** [C, U] **B2** a reason why you do not like or approve of something or someone, or the fact that you do not lik or approve of them: *Our main objection to th new factory is that it's noisy.* ◦ *I have n objections, if you want to stay an extra day.*

🗪 Word partners for **objection**
lodge/make/raise/voice an objection • **have no** objections • a **serious/strong** objection • an objection **to** sth

objectionable /əbˈdʒekʃənəbl/ **adj** formal ver unpleasant

objective¹ /əbˈdʒektɪv/ **noun** [C] **B2** somethin that you are trying to achieve: *His main objectiv was to increase profits.*

objective² /əbˈdʒektɪv/ **adj** **B2** only influence by facts and not by feelings: *I try to be objectiv when I criticize someone's work.*

obligation /ˌɒblɪˈɡeɪʃən/ **noun** [C, U] **B2** some thing that you do because it is your duty o because you feel you have to: *a moral/lega obligation* ◦ *to fulfil an obligation* ◦ *He wa under no obligation to answer any questions.* [+ to do sth] *Parents have an obligation to mak sure their children receive a proper education.*

🗪 Word partners for **obligation**
feel/have an obligation to do sth • **carry out/ fulfil/meet** an obligation • be **under** an obli- gation

obligatory /əˈblɪɡətᵊri/ **adj** If something i obligatory, you must do it because of a rule or because everyone else does it: *obligatory military service*

oblige /əˈblaɪdʒ/ **verb 1 be obliged to do sth** **B** to be forced to do something: *Sellers are no legally obliged to accept the highest offer.* **2** [I, T formal to be helpful: *The manager was only to happy to oblige.*

obliged /əˈblaɪdʒd/ **adj 1 feel obliged to do st** to think that you must do something: *The helped us when we moved so I feel obliged to d the same.* **2** formal old-fashioned grateful o pleased: *Thank you, I'm much obliged to you.*

oblique /əʊˈbliːk/ **adj** formal not expressed in direct way: *an oblique comment* • **obliquely ad** formal

obliterate /əˈblɪtᵊreɪt/ **verb** [T] to destroy some thing completely: [often passive] *The town wa obliterated by bombs.*

oblivion /əˈblɪviən/ **noun** [U] **1** a situation i which someone or something is not remem bered: *to disappear into oblivion* **2** a situation i which you are not aware of what is happening around you: *He drank himself into oblivion.*

oblivious /əˈblɪviəs/ **adj** not aware of some

thing: *She seemed completely **oblivious to** what was happening around her.*

obnoxious /əbˈnɒkʃəs/ **adj** very unpleasant or rude: *He was loud and obnoxious.*

obscene /əbˈsiːn/ **adj 1** relating to sex in a way that is unpleasant or shocking: *an **obscene** gesture* ∘ *obscene language* **2** An obscene amount of something is morally wrong because it is too large: *obscene profits*

obscenity /əbˈsenəti/ **noun 1** [U] the state of being sexually shocking: *obscenity laws/trials* **2** [C] a sexually shocking word or expression: [usually plural] *He was shouting obscenities at people walking by.*

obscure¹ /əbˈskjʊər/ **adj 1** not known by many people: *an obscure figure/writer* **2** difficult to understand: *His answers were obscure and confusing.*

obscure² /əbˈskjʊər/ **verb** [T] **1** to prevent something from being seen or heard: [often passive] *The moon was partially obscured by clouds.* **2** to make something difficult to understand: *He deliberately obscured details of his career in the army.*

obscurity /əbˈskjʊərəti/ **noun** [U] the fact of not being known by many people: *to fade into obscurity* ∘ *He rose from relative obscurity to worldwide recognition.*

obsequious /əbˈsiːkwiəs/ **adj** formal too willing to praise or obey someone

observance /əbˈzɜːvəns/ **noun** [C, U] formal the fact of obeying a law or following a religious custom: *strict observance of the law* ∘ *religious observances*

observant /əbˈzɜːvənt/ **adj** good or quick at noticing things: *He's very observant.*

observation /ˌɒbzəˈveɪʃən/ **noun 1** [U] ⑫ the act of watching someone or something carefully: *The doctor wants to keep him **under observation** for a week.* ∘ *to have good **powers of observation** (= to be good at noticing things)* **2** [C] a remark about something that you have noticed: *He **made an** interesting **observation**.*

> ☑ Word partners for **observation**
>
> careful/close observation • observation of sth • under observation • powers of observation

observatory /əbˈzɜːvətri/ **noun** [C] a building that is used by scientists to look at stars and planets

observe /əbˈzɜːv/ **verb** [T] **1** WATCH ▷ ⑫ to watch someone or something carefully: *Children learn by observing adults.* **2** NOTICE ▷ formal to notice something **3** SAY ▷ formal to make a remark about something you have noticed: *"It's still raining," he observed.* **4** OBEY ▷ to obey a law, rule, or religious custom: *to observe the law*

observer /əbˈzɜːvər/ **noun** [C] **1** someone who watches people and events as a job: *a UN observer* ∘ *a political observer* **2** someone who sees something: *a casual observer*

obsess /əbˈses/ **verb** [I, T] If something or someone obsesses you, or if you obsess about

something or someone, you think about them all the time: *She used to obsess about her weight.*

obsessed /əbˈsest/ **adj be obsessed by/with sb/sth** ⑫ to think about someone or something all the time: *to be obsessed with money/sex*

obsession /əbˈseʃən/ **noun** [C, U] ⑫ someone or something that you think about all the time: *an unhealthy obsession with death* ∘ *a lifelong/national obsession*

obsessive /əbˈsesɪv/ **adj** thinking too much about something, or doing something too much: *obsessive behaviour* ∘ *He's obsessive about his health.* • **obsessively adv**

obsolete /ˈɒbsəliːt/ **adj** not used now: *obsolete equipment* ∘ *Will books become obsolete because of computers?*

obstacle /ˈɒbstəkl/ **noun** [C] something that makes it difficult for you to go somewhere or to succeed at something: *to **overcome an obstacle*** ∘ *His refusal to talk is the main **obstacle to** peace.*

> ☑ Word partners for **obstacle**
>
> face/overcome an obstacle • the biggest/the main/a major obstacle • an obstacle to sth

obstetrician /ˌɒbstəˈtrɪʃən/ **noun** [C] a doctor who looks after pregnant women and helps in the birth of children

obstinate /ˈɒbstɪnət/ **adj** not willing to change your ideas or behaviour although you are wrong: *He's a very rude and obstinate man.*

obstruct /əbˈstrʌkt/ **verb** [T] **1** to be in a place that stops someone or something from moving or stops someone from seeing something: *to **obstruct** the **traffic*** ∘ *There was a pillar **obstructing** our view.* **2** to try to stop something from happening or developing: *to obstruct a police investigation* • **obstruction** /əbˈstrʌkʃən/ **noun** [C, U] *Your car's **causing an obstruction**.* ∘ *the obstruction of justice*

obtain /əbˈteɪn/ **verb** [T] formal ⑫ to get something: *to obtain permission* ∘ *He obtained a law degree from the University of California.* • **obtainable adj** If something is obtainable, you can get it: *This information is easily obtainable on the Internet.*

obvious /ˈɒbviəs/ **adj** ⑪ easy to understand or see: *an obvious choice/answer* ∘ [+ (that)] *It's obvious that he doesn't really care about her.*

obviously /ˈɒbviəsli/ **adv** ⑪ in a way that is easy to understand or see: *They're obviously in love.* ∘ *Obviously we want to start as soon as possible.*

occasion /əˈkeɪʒən/ **noun 1** [C] ⑫ a time when something happens: *a previous/separate occasion* ∘ *We met **on** several **occasions** to discuss the issue.* → See Note at **possibility 2** [C] ⑪ an important event or ceremony: *a **special occasion*** ∘ *She bought a new dress for the occasion.* **3 on occasion(s)** sometimes, but not often: *I only drink alcohol on occasion.*

occasional /əˈkeɪʒənəl/ **adj** not happening often: *He still plays the occasional game of football.* • **occasionally adv** ⑫ *They only meet occasionally.*

the occult /ˈɒkʌlt/ **noun** the study of magic or mysterious powers

occupant /ˈɒkjəpənt/ **noun** [C] formal someone who lives or works in a room or building: *the occupant of No. 46*

occupation /ˌɒkjəˈpeɪʃən/ **noun 1** JOB ▷ [C] formal your job: *You have to give your name, age, and occupation on the application form.* → See Note at **work²** **2** CONTROL ▷ [usually singular] a situation in which an army moves into a place and takes control of it: *a military occupation* **3** HOBBY ▷ [C] formal something that you do in your free time

occupational /ˌɒkjəˈpeɪʃənəl/ **adj** relating to your job: *an occupational hazard*

occupied /ˈɒkjəpaɪd/ **adj 1** being used by someone: *All of these seats are occupied.* → Opposite **unoccupied 2** busy doing something or thinking about something: *There was enough to keep us occupied.*

occupier /ˈɒkjəpaɪər/ **noun** [C] UK someone who lives or works in a room or building

occupy /ˈɒkjəpaɪ/ **verb** [T] **1** FILL ▷ 🅑2 to fill a place or period of time: *His book collection occupies most of the room.* ◦ *The baby seems to occupy all our time.* **2** LIVE ▷ to live or work in a room or building: *They occupy the second floor of the building.* **3** CONTROL ▷ to move into a place and take control of it: *The troops eventually occupied most of the island.*

occur /əˈkɜːr/ **verb** [I] (**occurring, occurred**) **1** 🅑2 formal to happen, often without being planned: *According to the police, the shooting occurred at about 12.30 a.m.* **2 occur in/among, etc sth/sb** to exist or be present in a particular place or group of people: *Minerals occur naturally in the Earth's crust.* ◦ *The disease mainly occurs in women over 40.*

PHRASAL VERB **occur to sb** if something occurs to you, you suddenly think of it: [+ (that)] *It had never occurred to me that he might be lying.*

occurrence /əˈkʌrəns/ **noun** [C] something that happens: *a common/everyday occurrence*

Word partners for **occurrence**
a common/everyday/rare/regular occurrence

ocean /ˈəʊʃən/ **noun 1** [no plural] 🅑1 the sea: *to swim in the ocean* **2** [C] one of the five main areas that the sea is divided into: *the Pacific Ocean*

o'clock /əˈklɒk/ **adv one/two/three, etc o'clock** 🅐1 used after the numbers one to twelve to mean exactly that hour when you tell the time: *It was ten o'clock when we got home.*

Oct written abbreviation for October

octagon /ˈɒktəgən/ **noun** [C] a flat shape with eight equal sides

octave /ˈɒktɪv/ **noun** [C] the space between two musical notes that are eight notes apart

October /ɒkˈtəʊbər/ **noun** [C, U] (written abbreviation **Oct**) 🅐1 the tenth month of the year

octopus /ˈɒktəpəs/ **noun** [C] a sea creature with eight long arms

odd /ɒd/ **adj 1** STRANGE ▷ 🅑2 strange or unusual: *I always thought there was something*

odd about her. ◦ *It's a bit odd that he didn't come.* **2** NOT OFTEN ▷ [always before noun] not happening often: *He does odd jobs here and there.* **3** SEPARATED ▷ [always before noun] being one of a pair when the other item is missing: *an odd sock* **4** APPROXIMATELY ▷ used after a number to mean approximately: *There are thirty odd kids in the class.* **5** NUMBER ▷ An odd number does not produce a whole number when it i divided by two.

octopus

oddity /ˈɒdɪti/ **noun** [C] someone or somethin that is strange or unusual

oddly /ˈɒdli/ **adv** in a strange way: *He's bee behaving very oddly lately.* ◦ *Oddly enough business was good during the bad weather month.*

odds /ɒdz/ **noun** [plural] **1** the probability tha something will happen: *What are the odds o winning the top prizes?* ◦ *I'm afraid the odds ar against us.* **2 against all (the) odds** If you do o achieve something against all the odds, yo succeed although you were not likely to: *We wo the game against all odds.* **3 be at odds with sb sth** to not agree with someone or something: *H remark was at odds with our report.*

IDIOM **odds and ends** informal a group of sma objects of different types that are not valuabl or important

Word partners for **odds**
the odds of/on sth happening • the odds are (stacked) against sb

odious /ˈəʊdiəs/ **adj** formal very unpleasant: *a odious little man*

odour UK (US **odor**) /ˈəʊdər/ **noun** [C] a smel often one that is unpleasant: *body odour*

odyssey /ˈɒdɪsi/ **noun** [C] literary a long, excitin journey

oestrogen UK (US **estrogen**) /ˈiːstrəʊdʒən/ 🅤 /ˈestrədʒən/ **noun** [U] a chemical substance i a woman's body that prepares her eggs fo fertilization (= joining with the male seed t make a baby)

of strong /ɒv/ weak /əv/ **preposition 1** BELONG ▷ 🅐1 belonging or relating to someone or some thing: *a friend of mine* ◦ *the colour of her ha* ◦ *part of the problem* **2** AMOUNT ▷ 🅐1 used afte words that show an amount: *a kilo of apple* ◦ *both of us* ◦ *a handful of raisins* **3** NUMBER ▷ 🅐1 used with numbers, ages, and dates: *a boy o six* ◦ *a decrease of 10%* ◦ *the 14th of Februar 2012* **4** CONTAIN ▷ 🅐1 containing: *a glass of mil* ◦ *sacks of rubbish* **5** MADE ▷ made or consistin of: *dresses of lace and silk* **6** ADJECTIVE/VERB ▷ used to connect particular adjectives and verb with nouns: *frightened of spiders* ◦ *smelling o garlic* **7** SHOW ▷ 🅐2 showing someone o something: *a map of the city* **8** CAUSE ▷ 🅑

showing a reason or cause: *He died of a heart attack.* **9 POSITION** ▷ ⓐ2 showing position or direction: *the front of the queue* ∘ *a small town north of Seattle* **10 ACTION/FEELING** ▷ used after nouns describing actions or feelings to mean 'done to' or 'experienced by': *the destruction of the rain forest* ∘ *the suffering of millions* **11 WRITTEN** ▷ ⓑ1 written or made by: *the collected works of William Shakespeare*

of course /əvˈkɔːs/ *adv* **1** ⓐ1 used to say 'yes' and emphasize your answer: *'Can you help me?' 'Of course!'* **2** ⓑ1 used to show that what you are saying is obvious or already known: *The rain meant, of course, that the match was cancelled.* ∘ *Of course, the Olympics are not just about money.* **3 of course not** ⓐ2 used to say 'no' and emphasize your answer: *'Do you mind if I borrow your pen?' 'Of course not.'*

off[1] /ɒf/ *adv, preposition* **1 NOT TOUCHING** ▷ ⓐ2 not touching or connected to something or not on a surface: *Keep off the grass!* ∘ *A button came off my coat.* **2 AWAY** ▷ ⓑ1 away from a place or position: *He ran off to find his friend.* ∘ *I'll be off* (= *will go*) *soon.* **3 NOT OPERATING** ▷ ⓐ2 not operating or being used: *Make sure you switch your computer off.* **4 NEAR** ▷ ⓑ2 near to a building or place: *an island off the coast of Spain* **5 PRICE** ▷ ⓑ1 If a price has a certain amount of money off, it costs that much less than the usual price: *These jeans were $10 off.* **6 DISTANCE/TIME** ▷ far in distance or time: *My holidays seem a long way off.* **7 go off sth/sb** UK ⓑ2 to stop liking something or someone: *I've gone off meat.* **8 NOT AT WORK** ▷ ⓐ2 not at work: *I had 6 months off when my son was born.* → See also **off the cuff**, **on**[2] **and off**

off[2] /ɒf/ *adj* [never before noun] **1 NOT CORRECT** ▷ not correct: *Our sales figures were off by ten percent.* **2 FOOD** ▷ ⓑ2 If food or drink is off, it is not now fresh and good to eat or drink: *This milk smells off.* **3 NOT AT WORK** ▷ ⓐ2 not at work: *He's off today – I think he's ill.* → See also **off-chance**

offal /ˈɒfl/ *noun* [U] organs from the inside of animals that are killed for food

off 'balance *adj, adv* If someone or something is off balance, they are in a position where they are likely to fall or be knocked down: *to knock/throw someone off balance*

off-chance /ˈɒftʃɑːns/ *noun* UK informal **on the off-chance** hoping that something may be possible, although it is not likely: *I went to the station on the off-chance that she'd be there.*

off 'duty *adj* When an official such as a police officer is off duty, they are not working.

offence UK (US **offense**) /əˈfens/ *noun* **1** [U] ⓑ2 the feeling of being upset or angry by something rude someone says : *to cause/give offence* ∘ *Many people take offence at swearing.* **2** [C] ⓑ2 a crime: *a criminal offence* ∘ *He committed several serious offences.*

> ⚡ Word partners for **offence**
> **cause/give/take** offence • **grave** offence

offend /əˈfend/ *verb* **1** [T] ⓑ2 to make someone upset or angry: [often passive] *I was deeply*

offended by her comments. **2** [I] formal to commit a crime: *If she offends again, she'll go to prison.*

offender /əˈfendər/ *noun* [C] ⓑ2 someone who has committed a crime: *a sex offender* ∘ *a young offender*

offense /əˈfens/ *noun* US spelling of offence

offensive[1] /əˈfensɪv/ *adj* **1** ⓑ2 likely to make people angry or upset: *an offensive remark* → Opposite **inoffensive 2** used for attacking: *an offensive weapon* • **offensively** *adv*

offensive[2] /əˈfensɪv/ *noun* [C] an attack: *It's time to launch a major offensive against terrorism.*

offer[1] /ˈɒfər/ *verb* **1 ASK** ▷ [+ two objects] ⓑ1 to ask someone if they would like something: *They offered me a job.* **2 SAY YOU WILL DO** ▷ [I, T] ⓐ2 to say that you are willing to do something: [+ to do sth] *He offered to get me a cab.* **3 AGREE TO PAY** ▷ [T] ⓑ2 to say that you will pay a particular amount of money: [+ two objects] *I offered him £500 for the car.* ∘ *Police have offered a $1,000 reward for information.* **4 PROVIDE** ▷ [T] ⓑ1 to give or provide something: *to offer advice* ∘ *The hotel offers a wide range of facilities.*

offer[2] /ˈɒfər/ *noun* [C] **1 ASK** ▷ ⓐ2 a question in which you ask someone if they would like something: *an offer of help* ∘ *a job offer* ∘ *to accept/refuse an offer* **2 PAYMENT** ▷ an amount of money that you say you will pay for something: *The highest offer anyone has made so far is a thousand euros.* **3 CHEAP** ▷ ⓑ1 a cheap price or special arrangement for something you are buying: *This special offer ends on Friday.* **4 on offer a** at a cheaper price than usual: *Are these jeans still on offer?* **b** ⓑ2 available to do or have: *We were amazed at the range of products on offer.*

> ⚡ Word partners for **offer**
> **accept/make/receive/turn down** an offer • a **generous/tempting** offer • an offer **of** sth

offering /ˈɒfərɪŋ/ *noun* [C] something that you give to someone: *a peace offering*

offhand[1] /ˌɒfˈhænd/ *adj* not friendly or polite: *He was a bit offhand with me.*

offhand[2] /ɒfˈhænd/ *adv* immediately, without thinking about something: *I don't know offhand how much it will cost.*

office /ˈɒfɪs/ *noun* **1 PLACE** ▷ [C] ⓐ2 a room or building where people work: *an office worker* ∘ *I never get to the office before nine.* → See colour picture **The Office** on page Centre 5 **2 INFORMATION** ▷ [C] ⓐ2 a room or building where you can get information, tickets, or a particular service: *a ticket office* ∘ *the tourist office* **3 JOB** ▷ [U] an important job in an organization: *Some people think he has been in office for too long.* ∘ *She held the office of mayor for eight years.* → See also **box office**, **the Oval Office**, **post office**, **register office**, **registry office**

office building *noun* [C] (also UK **office block**) a large building that contains offices

office hours *noun* [plural] the hours during the day when people who work in offices are usually at work

officer /ˈɒfɪsəʳ/ **noun** [C] **1 MILITARY** ▷ **B2** someone with an important job in a military organization: *an* ***army/naval officer*** **2 GOVERNMENT** ▷ **B1** someone who works for a government department: *a customs officer* ∘ *a prison officer* **3 POLICE** ▷ **B1** a police officer: *a uniformed officer* → See also **probation officer**

official¹ /əˈfɪʃ³l/ **adj 1 APPROVED** ▷ **B2** approved by the government or someone in authority: *the* ***official language*** *of Singapore* ∘ *an* ***official document*** **2 JOB** ▷ [always before noun] relating to the duties of someone in a position of authority: *the* ***official residence*** *of the ambassador* ∘ *an* ***official visit*** **3 KNOWN** ▷ known by the public: *It's official – they're getting married!* **4 NOT TRUE** ▷ [always before noun] An official explanation or statement is one that is given, but which may not be true: *The* ***official reason*** *for the delay is bad weather.* → Opposite **unofficial**
• **officially adv** *The new hospital was officially opened yesterday.*

official² /əˈfɪʃ³l/ **noun** [C] **B1** someone who has an important position in an organization such as the government: *a senior official* ∘ *a UN official*

offing /ˈɒfɪŋ/ **noun be in the offing** If something is in the offing, it will happen or be offered soon: *He thinks there might be a promotion in the offing.*

off-licence /ˈɒfˌlaɪs³ns/ **noun** [C] UK (US **liquor store**) a shop that sells alcoholic drink

offline /ɒfˈlaɪn/ **adj, adv** (**off-line**) A computer is offline when it is not connected to a central system, or not connected to the Internet: *to* ***work offline***

off-peak /ˌɒfˈpiːk/ **adj** not at the most popular and expensive time: *an off-peak phone call*

offset /ˌɒfˈset/ **verb** [T] (**offsetting**, **offset**) If one thing offsets another thing, it has the opposite effect and so creates a more balanced situation: [often passive] *The costs have been offset by savings in other areas.*

offshore /ˌɒfˈʃɔːʳ/ **adj** [always before noun] **1** in the sea and away from the coast: *an offshore island* **2** An offshore bank or bank account is based in another country and so less tax has to be paid: *an* ***offshore account/trust***

offside /ˌɒfˈsaɪd/ **adj** (also US **offsides**) In sports such as football, a player who is offside is in a position that is not allowed.

offspring /ˈɒfsprɪŋ/ **noun** [C] (plural **offspring**) formal the child of a person or animal: *to produce offspring*

off-the-cuff /ˌɒfðəˈkʌf/ **adj** An off-the-cuff remark is one that is not planned.

often /ˈɒf³n/, /ˈɒftˀn/ **adv 1** **A1** many times or regularly: *I often see her there.* ∘ *He said I could visit as often as I liked.* ∘ ***How often*** (= How many times) *do you go to the gym?* ∘ *I don't see her* ***very often.*** **2** **B2** If something often happens or is often true, it is normal for it to happen or it is usually true: *Headaches are often caused by stress.* ∘ *Brothers and sisters often argue.*

ogre /ˈəʊgəʳ/ **noun** [C] an unpleasant, frightening person

oh /əʊ/ **exclamation 1** **A1** used before you say something, often before replying to what someone has said: *"Ian's going." "Oh, I didn't realize."* ∘ *"I'm so sorry." "Oh, don't worry."* **2** **A** used to show an emotion or to emphasize your opinion about something: *Oh, no! I don't believe it!* ∘ *"I don't think I can come." "Oh, that's a shame."* ∘ *Oh, how sweet of you!*

oil /ɔɪl/ **noun** [U] **1** **B1** a thick liquid that comes from under the Earth's surface that is used as fuel and for making parts of machines move smoothly: *an oil company* ∘ *an oil well* **2** **A2** a thick liquid produced from plants or animals that is used in cooking: *vegetable oil* → See also **crude oil, olive oil**

oilfield /ˈɔɪlˌfiːld/ **noun** [C] an area under the ground where oil is found: *an offshore oilfield*

oil painting **noun** [C] a picture made using paint that contains oil

oil spill **noun** [C] an accident in which oil has come out of a ship and caused pollution

oily /ˈɔɪli/ **adj** containing a lot of oil or covered with oil: *oily fish* ∘ *oily hands*

oink /ɔɪŋk/ **noun** [C] the sound that a pig makes

ointment /ˈɔɪntmənt/ **noun** [C, U] a smooth thick substance that is used on painful or damaged skin

okay¹ (also **OK**) /əʊˈkeɪ/ **exclamation 1** **A1** used when agreeing to do something or when allowing someone to do something: *"Let's meet this afternoon." "Okay."* ∘ *"Can I use the car?" "Okay."* **2** **A2** used before you start speaking, especially to a group of people: *Okay, I'm going to start by showing you a few figures.*

okay² (also **OK**) /əʊˈkeɪ/ **adj, adv** informal **1 GOOD** ▷ **A2** good or good enough: *Is your food okay?* ∘ *It was okay, but it wasn't as good as his last film.* **2 SAFE** ▷ **A1** safe or healthy: *Is your grandmother okay now?* **3 ALLOWED** ▷ **A** allowed or acceptable: *Is it okay if I leave early today?* ∘ [+ to do sth] *Is it okay to smoke in here?*

> **!** Common learner error: **older, oldest, elder, eldest**
>
> **Older** and **oldest** are the comparative and superlative forms of the adjective 'old'.
> *I'm four years older than my sister.*
> *Pedro is the oldest student in the class.*
> The adjectives **elder** and **eldest** are only used before nouns. They are usually used when you are comparing members of a family.
> *My elder brother is a doctor.*
> *Mary has three sons. Her eldest boy is called Mark.*

old /əʊld/ **adj 1 LIVED LONG** ▷ **A1** having lived or existed for a long time: *an old man/woman* ∘ *an old house* ∘ *We're all* ***getting older.*** ∘ *Children should show some respect for* ***the old.*** **2 USED A LOT** ▷ **A2** having been used or owned for a long time: *You might get dirty so wear some old clothes.* **3 AGE** ▷ **A1** used to describe or ask about someone's age: ***How old*** *are you?* ∘ *She'll be* ***years old*** *this month.* → See Note at **year 4 an old friend/enemy, etc** **A2** someone who has been your friend/enemy, etc for a long time: *I met an old friend who I was at college with.* **5 BEFORE** ▷ [always before noun] used before or in the past: *I think the old system was better in many ways.*

old 'age noun [U] the period of time when you are old

old-age 'pension noun [U] UK money that people receive regularly from the government when they are old and have stopped working

old-age 'pensioner noun [C] UK someone who gets an old-age pension

olden /'əʊldən/ adj **in the olden days/in olden times** a long time ago

old-fashioned /ˌəʊld'fæʃ°nd/ adj ⑤ not modern: *old-fashioned clothes/furniture*

oldie /'əʊldi/ noun [C] informal an old song or film, or an old person: *a golden oldie*

old-style /'əʊldstaɪl/ adj [always before noun] used or done in the past: *old-style politics*

the ˌOld 'Testament noun the part of the Bible (= holy book) written before the birth of Jesus Christ

the 'Old ˌWorld noun Asia, Africa, and Europe

olive /'ɒlɪv/ noun **1** [C] ⑤ a small green or black fruit with a bitter taste that is eaten or used to produce oil **2** [U] (also ˌolive 'green) a colour that is a mixture of green and yellow • **olive** (also **olive-green**) adj

olive ˌoil noun [U] oil produced from olives, used for cooking or on salads

-ology /-ɒlədʒi/ suffix makes a noun meaning 'the study of something': *psychology* (= the study of the mind) ∘ *sociology* (= the study of society)

the Olympic Games /əˌlɪmpɪk'ɡeɪmz/ noun [plural] (also **the Olympics**) an international sports competition that happens every four years • **Olympic** adj [always before noun] relating to the Olympic Games: *She broke the Olympic record.*

ombudsman /'ɒmbʊdzmən/ noun [C] (plural **ombudsmen**) someone who deals with complaints that people make against the government or public organizations

omelette /'ɒmlət/ noun [C] (also US **omelet**) ⑤ a food made with eggs that have been mixed and fried, often with other foods added: *a cheese omelette*

omen /'əʊmən/ noun [C] a sign of what will happen in the future: *a good/bad omen*

☑ **Word partners for omen**
a **bad/good/lucky** omen • an omen **of** [death/disaster/good fortune, etc] • an omen **for** sb/sth

ominous /'ɒmɪnəs/ adj making you think that something bad is going to happen: *an ominous sign* ∘ *ominous clouds*

☑ **Word partners for omission**
a **glaring/serious/surprising** omission • sb/sth's omission **from** sth • the omission **of** sb/sth

omission /əʊ'mɪʃ°n/ noun [C, U] something that

has not been included but should have been: *There are some **serious omissions** in the book.*

omit /əʊ'mɪt/ verb (**omitting**, **omitted**) **1** [T] to not include something or someone: [often passive] *He was **omitted from** the team because of his behaviour.* **2 omit to do sth** mainly UK formal to not do something: *She omitted to mention where she was going.*

on¹ /ɒn/ preposition **1** SURFACE ▷ ④ on a surface of something: *We put all of our medicine on a high shelf.* **2** PLACE ▷ ④ in a particular place: *the diagram on page 22* ∘ *I met her on a ship.* **3** RECORDING/PERFORMANCE ▷ ④ used to show the way in which something is recorded or performed: *What's on television tonight?* **4** TOUCHING ▷ ⑤ used to show what happens as a result of touching something: *I cut myself on a knife.* **5** SUBJECT ▷ ⑤ about: *a book on pregnancy* **6** MONEY/TIME ▷ ④ used to show what money or time is used for: *I've wasted too much time on this already.* ∘ *She spends a lot of money on clothes.* **7** NEXT TO ▷ ⑤ next to or along the side of: *The post office is on Bateman Street.* **8** DATE/DAY ▷ ④ used to show the date or day when something happens: *He's due to arrive on 14 February.* ∘ *I'm working on my birthday.* **9** USING ▷ ⑤ using something: *I spoke to Mum on the phone.* **10** AFTER ▷ happening after something and often because of it: *The Prince was informed on his return to the UK.* **11** TRANSPORT ▷ ④ used to show some methods of travelling: *Did you go over on the ferry?* ∘ *Sam loves travelling on buses.* **12** FOOD/FUEL/DRUGS ▷ ⑤ used to show something that is used as food, fuel, or a drug: *This radio runs on batteries.* ∘ *I can't drink wine because I'm on antibiotics.* **13 be on a committee/panel, etc** to be a member of a group or organization: *She's on the playgroup committee.* **14 have/carry sth on you** to have something with you: *Do you have your driving licence on you?* **15 be on me/him, etc** informal used to show who is paying for something: *This meal is on me.*

on² /ɒn/ adv **1** CONTINUE ▷ used to show that an action or event continues: *The old tradition lives on.* ∘ *It was a complicated situation that dragged on for weeks.* **2** WEAR ▷ ④ If you have something on, you are wearing it: *She's got a black coat on.* ∘ *Why don't you **put** your new dress **on**?* **3** WORKING ▷ working or being used: *The heating has been on all day.* **4** TRAVEL ▷ ⑤ into a bus, train, plane, etc: *Amy got on in Stamford.* **5** HAPPENING ▷ ⑤ happening or planned: *I've got a lot on at the moment.* ∘ *Have you checked what's on at the cinema?*

IDIOM **on and off** (also **off and on**) If something happens on and off during a period of time, it happens sometimes: *They've been seeing each other on and off since Christmas.*

once¹ /wʌns/ adv **1** ④ one time: *It's only snowed once or twice this year.* ∘ *I go swimming **once a week** (= one time every week).* **2** ⑤ in the past, but not now: *This house once belonged to my grandfather.* **3 once again** ⑤ again: *Once again I'm left with all the washing up.* **4 all at once** suddenly: *All at once he stood up and walked out* *of the room.* **5 at once a** ⓑ1 immediately: *I knew at once that I would like it here.* **b** at the same time: *They all started talking at once.* **6 once in a while** ⓑ2 sometimes but not often: *He plays tennis once in a while.* **7 once and for all** If you do something once and for all, you do it now so that it does not have to be dealt with again: *Let's get to the bottom of this matter once and for all!* **8 once more** ⓑ1 one more time: *If you say that once more, I'm going to leave.* **9 for once** ⓑ2 used to mean that something is happening that does not usually happen: *For once, I think I have good news for him.* **10 once upon a time** ⓑ1 used at the beginning of a children's story to mean that something happened a long time ago → See also **once in a blue moon**

once² /wʌns/ **conjunction** ⓑ2 as soon as: *Once I've found somewhere to live, I'll send you my new address.* ∘ *We'll send your tickets once we've received your cheque.*

oncoming /ˈɒnˌkʌmɪŋ/ **adj** [always before noun] Oncoming vehicles are coming towards you.

one¹ /wʌn/ ⓐ1 the number 1 → See also **back to square¹ one**

one² /wʌn/ **pronoun 1** ⓐ2 used to refer to a particular person or thing in a group that has already been talked about: *I've just made some biscuits, do you want one?* ∘ *Throw those gloves away and get some new ones.* ∘ *Chris is the one with glasses.* **2** formal any person in general: *One ought to respect one's parents.* **3 one at a time** ⓑ2 separately: *Eat them one at a time.* **4 one by one** ⓑ2 separately, with one thing happening after another: *One by one the old buildings have been demolished.* **5 one another** ⓑ1 each other: *How can they reach an agreement if they won't talk to one another?* **6 (all) in one** combined into a single thing: *It's a vacation and art course all in one.*

one³ /wʌn/ **determiner 1** PARTICULAR PERSON/ THING ▷ ⓐ2 used to refer to a particular person or thing in a group: *One drawback is the cost of housing in the area.* ∘ *One of our daughters has just got married.* **2** FUTURE TIME ▷ ⓑ2 used to refer to a time in the future that is not yet decided: *We must have a drink together one evening.* **3** TIME IN PAST ▷ ⓑ2 at a particular time in the past: *I first met him one day in the park.* **4** ONLY ▷ ⓑ2 only: *He's the one person you can rely on in this place.* **5** WITH ADJECTIVE ▷ mainly US used to emphasize an adjective: *That's one big ice cream you've got there!* **6 one or two** ⓑ1 a few: *I'd like to make one or two suggestions.* → See also **put sth to one side¹**, **be one step¹ ahead (of sb)**

one-man /ˌwʌnˈmæn/ **adj** [always before noun] with only one person doing something: *a one-man show*

one-night ˈstand **noun** [C] an occasion when two people have sex just after they meet but do not then have a relationship

one-off /ˌwʌnˈɒf/ **adj** [always before noun] UK only happening once: *a one-off payment* • **one-off noun** [C] UK something that only happens once: *His Olympic victory was not just a one-off.*

one-on-one /ˌwʌnɒnˈwʌn/ **adj, adv** mainly U only including two people

onerous /ˈəʊnərəs/ **adj** formal difficult an⦁ needing a lot of effort: *an onerous task*

oneself /wʌnˈself/ **pronoun** formal the reflexiv⦁ form of the pronoun 'one' when it refers to th⦁ person speaking or people in general: *How els⦁ should one protect oneself and one's family?*

one-sided /ˌwʌnˈsaɪdɪd/ **adj 1** If a competition i⦁ one-sided, one team or player is much bette⦁ than the other: *a one-sided contest/game* **2** onl⦁ considering one opinion in an argument in ⦁ way that is unfair: *a one-sided view*

one-time /ˈwʌntaɪm/ **adj** [always before noun] ⦁ one-time position or job is one that you had o⦁ did in the past, but not now: *a one-time frien⦁ minister*

one-to-one /ˌwʌntəˈwʌn/ **adj, adv** mainly U⦁ only including two people: *She's having privat⦁ lessons on a one-to-one basis.*

one-trick ˈpony **noun** [C] someone or some⦁ thing that is good at doing only one thing, o⦁ that can work in only one area

one-way /ˌwʌnˈweɪ/ **adj** If a road is one-way, yo⦁ can only drive on it in one direction: *a one-wa⦁ street*

one-way ˈticket **noun** [C] (also UK **single**) ⦁ one-way ticket for a journey can only be used t⦁ travel in one direction and not for returning.

ongoing /ˈɒnˌɡəʊɪŋ/ **adj** [always before noun] stil⦁ happening: *an ongoing process/investigation*

onion /ˈʌnjən/ **noun** [C, U] ⓐ2 a round vegetabl⦁ with layers that has a strong taste and smel⦁ → See colour picture **Fruit and Vegetables** on pag⦁ Centre 10 → See also **spring onion**

online /ˌɒnˈlaɪn/ **adj, adv** ⓐ2 connected to ⦁ system of computers, especially the Internet⦁ *online services* ∘ *to go online* (= *start using th⦁ Internet*) ∘ *Most newspapers are now available⦁ online.* → See Study Page **The Web and th⦁ Internet** on page Centre 36

online ˈbank **noun** [C] a bank that operate⦁ over the Internet

online ˈbanking **noun** [U] the process o⦁ activity of managing bank accounts o⦁ operating as a bank over the Internet

onlooker /ˈɒnˌlʊkəʳ/ **noun** [C] someone wh⦁ watches something happening without becom⦁ ing involved in it: *a crowd of onlookers*

only¹ /ˈəʊnli/ **adv 1** NOT MORE ▷ ⓐ1 not mor⦁ than a particular size or amount: *It'll only take ⦁ few minutes.* ∘ *She's only fifteen.* **2** NO ONE⦁ NOTHING ELSE ▷ ⓐ2 not anyone or anything⦁ else: *The offer is available to UK residents only⦁* **3** RECENTLY ▷ ⓑ1 used to mean that something⦁ happened very recently: *She's only just finishe⦁ writing it.* **4 not only ... (but) also** ⓑ2 used t⦁ say that one thing is true and another thing i⦁ true too, especially a surprising thing: *Not onl⦁ did he turn up late, he also forgot his books.*

only² /ˈəʊnli/ **adj** [always before noun] ⓐ1 used t⦁ mean that there are not any others: *This coul⦁ be our only chance.* ∘ *You're the only perso⦁ here I know.*

only³ /ˈəʊnli/ **conjunction** used to introduce ⦁

statement that explains why something you have just said cannot happen or is not completely true: *I'd phone him myself only I know he's not there at the moment.*

only child noun [C] (plural **only children**) someone who has no brothers or sisters

onscreen¹ /ˌɒnˈskriːn/ adj appearing on a computer screen or a television screen: *Insert the disk and then follow the onscreen prompts to restore your system.* ○ *Select which programme you want to record from the onscreen TV guide.*

onscreen² /ˌɒnˈskriːn/ adv on a computer screen or on a television screen: *Most editing is now done onscreen.*

onset /ˈɒnset/ noun **the onset of sth** the beginning of something, usually something unpleasant: *the onset of cancer*

onslaught /ˈɒnslɔːt/ noun [C] an attack on someone or something or criticism of them: *Staff have to deal with a constant onslaught of complaints.*

> ✎ **Word partners for onslaught**
>
> launch/mount an onslaught • an onslaught against/on sb

onstage /ˌɒnˈsteɪdʒ/ adj, adv onto or on a stage for a performance: *The audience cheered as the band walked onstage.*

onto (also **on to**) /ˈɒntuː/ preposition **1** ⑪ used to show movement into or on a particular place: *The sheep were loaded onto trucks.* ○ *Can you get back onto the path?* **2 hold/grip, etc onto sth** to hold something: *Hold onto my hand before we cross the road.* **3** ⑫ used to show that you are starting to talk about a different subject: *Can we move onto the next item on the agenda?* **4 be onto sb** to know that someone has done something wrong or illegal: *She knows we're onto her and she's trying to get away.* ○ *Who put the police onto (= told the police about) her?* **5 be onto sth** to know or discover something useful or important: *Researchers think they may be onto something big.* ○ *Can you put me onto (= tell me about) a good dentist?*

the onus /ˈəʊnəs/ noun formal the responsibility for doing something: *The onus is on parents to make sure their children attend school.*

onward /ˈɒnwəd/ adv (also **onwards**) **1** from the 1870s/March/6.30 pm, etc **onwards** beginning at a time and continuing after it **2** If you move onwards, you continue to go forwards.

oops /uːps/ exclamation something you say when you make a mistake or have a slight accident: *Oops! I've spilled my coffee.*

ooze /uːz/ verb **1** [I, T] If a liquid oozes from something or if something oozes a liquid, the liquid comes out slowly: *Blood was oozing out of the wound.* **2** [T] informal to show a lot of a quality: *to ooze charm*

opaque /əʊˈpeɪk/ adj **1** If an object or substance is opaque, you cannot see through it. **2** formal difficult to understand

op-ed /ˌɒpˈed/ adj [always before noun] US describes a piece of writing in a newspaper in which a writer gives an opinion about a subject: *an op-ed article/page*

open

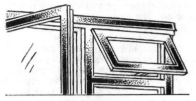

The window is open.

The book is open.

open¹ /ˈəʊpən/ adj **1 NOT CLOSED** ▷ ⓐ₂ not closed or fastened: *an* **open** *door/window* ○ *Someone had left the gate* **wide open**. ○ *Is there a bottle of wine already open?* ○ *A magazine was lying open on her lap.* **2 DOING BUSINESS** ▷ ⓐ₁ A shop or business is open during the time it is available for business or serving customers: *Most shops are open on Sundays now.* **3 COMPUTERS** ▷ If a computer document or program is open, it is ready to be read or used. **4 WITHOUT BUILDINGS** ▷ [always before noun] ⓑ₁ An open area of land has no buildings on it or near it: *large* **open** *spaces* **5 NOT COVERED** ▷ [always before noun] without a roof or cover: *an open courtyard* **6 FOR EVERYONE** ▷ If a place or event is open, everyone can go to it or become involved in it: *an* **open** *debate* ○ *Are the gardens* **open to** *the public?* **7 HONEST** ▷ An open person is honest and does not hide their feelings. **8 NOT HIDDEN** ▷ [always before noun] Open feelings, usually negative ones, are not hidden: *open hostility/rivalry* **9 NOT DECIDED** ▷ If a decision or question is open, it has not yet been decided: *We don't have to make a firm arrangement now. Let's* **leave** *it* **open**. **10 have/keep an open mind** ⓑ₂ to wait until you know all the facts before you form an opinion about something or judge someone: *The cause of the fire is still unclear and we are keeping an open mind.* **11 open to discussion/suggestions, etc** willing to consider a discussion/suggestions, etc: *This is only a proposal. I'm open to suggestions.* **12 open to abuse/criticism, etc** likely to be abused/criticized, etc: *The system is wide open to abuse.* → See also with your eyes (**eye¹**) open

open² /ˈəʊpən/ verb **1 NOT CLOSED** ▷ [I, T] ⓐ₁ If something opens, it changes to a position that is not closed, and if you open it, you make it change to a position that is not closed: *to open a door/window* ○ *The gate won't open.* ○ *Don't open your eyes yet.* **2 REMOVE COVER** ▷ [T] ⓐ₂ to remove part of a container or parcel so that you can see or use what it contains: *Karen opened the* box and looked inside. ∘ Why don't you open the envelope? ∘ I can't open this bottle. **3 PREPARE FOR USE** ▷ [I, T] If an object opens, the parts that are folded together move apart, and if you open it, you make the parts that are folded together move apart: Shall I open the umbrella? ∘ Open your books at page 22. **4 START WORK** ▷ [I] ⓐ If a shop or office opens at a particular time of day, it starts to do business at that time: What time does the bank open? **5 COMPUTERS** ▷ [T] ⓑ to make a computer document or program ready to be read or used **6 START OFFICIALLY** ▷ [I, T] ⓑ If a business or activity opens, it starts officially for the first time, and if you open it, you make it start officially for the first time: That restaurant's new – it only opened last month. ∘ Several shops have **opened up** in the last year. **7 MAKE AVAILABLE** ▷ [T] to allow people to use a road or area: They **opened up** the roads again the day after the flooding. **8 open an account** to make an arrangement to keep your money with a bank: Have you opened a bank account yet? → See also **open the floodgates**

PHRASAL VERBS **open (sth) up 1** to create a new opportunity or possibility: A teaching qualification can **open up** many more career **opportunities**. **2** to open the lock on the door of a building: The caretaker **opens up** the school every morning at seven. • **open up** to start to talk more about yourself and your feelings: I've tried to get him to **open up to** me, but with no success.

> **!** Common learner error: **open** and **close**
>
> Be careful not to confuse the adjective and verb forms of these words. The adjectives are **open** and **closed**.
> Is the supermarket open on Sunday?
> The museum is closed today.
> The verbs are **open** and **close**.
> The supermarket opens at 8 a.m.
> The museum closes at 5 p.m. today.

open³ /ˈəʊpᵊn/ noun **1 in the open** outside: We spent the night in the open. **2 bring sth out into the open** to tell people information that was secret: [often passive] It's time this issue was brought out into the open.

open-air /ˌəʊpənˈeəʳ/ adj [always before noun] An open-air place does not have a roof: an **open-air swimming pool**

ˈopen ˌday noun [C] UK (US **open house**) a day when people can visit a school or organization to see what happens there

open-ended /ˌəʊpᵊnˈendɪd/ adj An open-ended activity or situation does not have a planned ending: We are not willing to enter into **open-ended discussions**.

opener /ˈəʊpᵊnəʳ/ noun [C] **1 bottle/can/tin, etc opener** a piece of kitchen equipment used to open bottles/cans, etc **2** someone or something that begins a series of events, usually in sports → See also **eye-opener**

opening¹ /ˈəʊpᵊnɪŋ/ noun [C] **1 HOLE** ▷ a hole or space that something or someone can pass through: We found an opening in the fence and

climbed through. **2 START** ▷ ⓑ the beginning of something: The **opening** of the opera is quite dramatic. **3 CEREMONY** ▷ ⓑ a ceremony at the beginning of an event or activity: I've been invited to the **opening** of the new exhibition on Tuesday. **4 OPPORTUNITY** ▷ a job or an opportunity to do something: There's an **opening for** an editorial assistant in our department.

opening² /ˈəʊpᵊnɪŋ/ adj [always before noun] happening at the beginning of an event or activity: the **opening night** ∘ her **opening remarks**

openly /ˈəʊpᵊnli/ adv without hiding any of your thoughts or feelings: He **talks** quite openly about his feelings.

open-minded /ˌəʊpᵊnˈmaɪndɪd/ adj willing to consider ideas and opinions that are new or different to your own

openness /ˈəʊpᵊnnəs/ noun [U] honesty about your thoughts and feelings: I appreciated his openness.

open-plan /ˌəʊpᵊnˈplæn/ adj describes a room or a building without many walls: an **open-plan office**

opera /ˈɒpᵊrə/ noun [C, U] ⓐ a musical play in which most of the words are sung: to go to the opera ∘ **opera singers** ∘ an **opera house** (= building for opera) • **operatic** /ˌɒpᵊrˈætɪk/ adj relating to opera: an operatic society

operate /ˈɒpᵊreɪt/ verb **1 ORGANIZATION** ▷ [I, T] ⓑ If an organization or business operates, it is working, and if you operate it, you manage it and make it work: Our company is operating under very difficult conditions at present. **2 MACHINE** ▷ [I, T] ⓑ If a machine operates, it does what it is designed to do, and if you operate it, you make it do what it is designed to do: You have to be trained to operate the machinery. **3 TREATMENT** ▷ [I] ⓑ to treat an illness or injury by cutting someone's body and removing or repairing part of it: Did they have to **operate** on him?

ˈoperating ˌroom noun [C] US (UK **operating theatre**) a room in a hospital where doctors do operations

ˈoperating ˌsystem noun [C] (abbreviation **OS**, **O/S**) computer software that controls how different parts of a computer work together

ˈoperating ˌtheatre noun [C] UK (US **operating room**) a room in a hospital where doctors do operations

operation /ˌɒpᵊrˈeɪʃᵊn/ noun [C] **1 MEDICAL TREATMENT** ▷ ⓑ If you have an operation, a doctor cuts your body to remove or repair part of it: a heart/lung operation ∘ a **major/minor operation** ∘ My son's got to **have an operation**. **2 ORGANIZATION** ▷ an organization or business: a large commercial operation **3 ACTIVITY** ▷ an activity that is intended to achieve a particular purpose: a military/peacekeeping operation ∘ a joint operation by French and Spanish police **4 in operation** If a machine or system is in operation, it is working or being used: The new rail link is now in operation. ∘ Most of the machines are now back in operation.

operational /ˌɒpəˈreɪʃ^ən^əl/ **adj 1** If a system is operational, it is working: *The service becomes* **fully operational** *next June.* **2** [always before noun] relating to a particular activity: *operational control/responsibility*

operative¹ /ˈɒp^ərətɪv/ **adj** formal working or being used: *The agreement will not become operative until all members have signed.*

operative² /ˈɒp^ərətɪv/ **noun** [C] mainly US someone who does secret work for a government or other organization: *a former CIA operative*

operator /ˈɒpəreɪtə^r/ **noun** [C] **1** TELEPHONE ▷ someone who helps to connect people on a telephone system: *Why don't you call the operator?* **2** MACHINE ▷ ⑫ someone whose job is to use and control a machine or vehicle: *a computer operator* **3** BUSINESS ▷ ⑫ a company that does a particular type of business: *a tour operator*

opinion /əˈpɪnjən/ **noun 1** ⑪ [C] a thought or belief about something or someone: *What's your* **opinion about/on** *the matter?* ○ *He has fairly strong* **opinions** *on most subjects.* ○ **In my opinion** (= I think) *he's the best football player we have in this country.* **2** **public opinion** ⑫ the thoughts and beliefs that most people have about a subject: *Eventually, the government will have to take notice of public opinion.* **3** **have a high/low opinion of sb/sth** to think that someone or something is good/bad: *He has a low opinion of doctors.*

opinionated /əˈpɪnjəneɪtɪd/ **adj** being too certain that your strong opinions are correct

opinion poll **noun** [C] the results of questions that people are asked to discover what they think about a subject: *The latest opinion poll shows that the president's popularity has improved.*

opium /ˈəʊpiəm/ **noun** [U] a drug made from the seeds of a poppy (= a red flower)

opponent /əˈpəʊnənt/ **noun** [C] **1** ⑫ someone who you compete against in a game or competition: *He beat his opponent six games to two.* **2** ⑫ someone who disagrees with an action or belief and tries to change it: *an opponent of slavery* ○ *a political opponent*

opportune /ˈɒpətjuːn/ **adj** formal **an opportune moment/time** a good time for something to happen: *His letter arrived at an opportune moment.*

opportunist /ˌɒpəˈtjuːnɪst/ **noun** [C] someone who tries to get power or an advantage in every situation • **opportunistic** /ˌɒpətjuːˈnɪstɪk/ **adj** using a situation to get power or an advantage

opportunity /ˌɒpəˈtjuːnəti/ **noun 1** [C, U] ⑪ a situation in which it is possible for you to do something, or a possibility of doing something: *a* **unique opportunity** ○ *a* **golden** (= very good) **opportunity** ○ [+ to do sth] *Everyone will have* **an opportunity** *to comment.* ○ *There are plenty of* **opportunities for** *research.* ○ *Don't* **miss** *this* **opportunity** *to win a million pounds.* ○ *She talks about her boyfriend* **at every opportunity.** **2** [C] ⑫ the chance to get a job: [usually plural] *opportunities for young graduates* ○ **job/employment opportunities 3** **take the opportunity to do sth** ⑫ to use an occasion to do or say something: *I'd like to take this opportunity to thank all of you.* → See Note at **possibility**

oppose /əˈpəʊz/ **verb** [T] ⑫ to disagree with a plan or activity and to try to change or stop it: *The committee opposed a proposal to allow women to join the club.*

opposed /əˈpəʊzd/ **adj 1** **be opposed to sth** to disagree with a plan or activity: *We're not opposed to tax increases.* **2** **as opposed to** used to say that two things are very different: *I'm talking about English football, as opposed to European football.*

opposing /əˈpəʊzɪŋ/ **adj 1** **opposing teams/players, etc** Opposing teams/players, etc are competing against each other. **2** **opposing ideas/beliefs, etc** Opposing ideas/beliefs, etc are completely different: *The book presents two opposing views.*

opposite¹ /ˈɒpəzɪt/ **adj 1** ⑪ in a position facing something or someone but on the other side: *on the* **opposite page** ○ *in the* **opposite corner** ○ *We live on* **opposite sides** *of the city.* ○ *I noticed a gate at the* **opposite end** *of the courtyard.* **2** ⑫ completely different: *Police attempts to calm the violence had completely the* **opposite effect.**

opposite² /ˈɒpəzɪt/ **adv, preposition** ⑪ in a position facing something or someone but on the other side: *The couple sat down opposite her.* ○ UK *She lives opposite* (= on the other side of the road). ○ *Is there a bakery opposite your house?*

opposite³ /ˈɒpəzɪt/ **noun** [C] ⑪ someone or something that is completely different from another person or thing: *They're* **complete opposites.** ○ *He's* **the exact opposite of** *my father.*

the opposite sex **noun** someone who is male if you are female, or female if you are male: *It's not always easy to meet* **members of the opposite sex.**

opposition /ˌɒpəˈzɪʃ^ən/ **noun 1** [U] strong disagreement: *Is there much* **opposition to** *the proposed changes?* ○ *There has been strong* **opposition from** *local residents.* **2** **the Opposition/opposition** political parties that are not in power

oppress /əˈpres/ **verb** [T] **1** to treat a group of people in an unfair way, often by limiting their freedom: [often passive] *Women were oppressed by* *a society which considered them inferior.* **2** to make someone feel anxious

oppression /ə'preʃ⁰n/ **noun** [U] unfair treatment that limits people's freedom: *political oppression* ∘ *the oppression of women*

oppressive /ə'presɪv/ **adj 1 UNFAIR** ▷ cruel and unfair: *an oppressive government/regime* **2 HOT** ▷ If the weather or heat is oppressive, it is too hot and there is no wind: *oppressive heat* **3 NOT RELAXING** ▷ not relaxing or pleasant: *an oppressive silence*

oppressor /ə'presər/ **noun** [C] someone who treats people in an unfair way, often by limiting their freedom

opt /ɒpt/ **verb opt for sth; opt to do sth** to choose something or to decide to do something: *Mike opted for early retirement.* ∘ *Most people opt to have the operation.*

PHRASAL VERB **opt out** to choose not to be part of an activity or to stop being involved in it: *He's decided to opt out of the company's pension scheme.*

optical /'ɒptɪk⁰l/ **adj** relating to light or the ability to see: *optical equipment/instruments*

optical i'llusion noun [C] something that you think you see, but which is not really there

optician /ɒp'tɪʃ⁰n/ **noun** [C] **1** someone whose job is to make eye glasses **2** UK a shop where you can have your eyes tested and have your glasses made

optimism /'ɒptɪmɪz⁰m/ **noun** [U] the belief that good things will happen: *a mood/spirit of optimism* ∘ *There is cause/reason for optimism.* ∘ *He expressed cautious optimism about the future.* → Opposite **pessimism**

> ☑ Word partners for **optimism**
>
> express optimism • cautious/renewed optimism • cause for/grounds for/reason for optimism • optimism about sth

optimist /'ɒptɪmɪst/ **noun** [C] someone who always believes that good things will happen

optimistic /ˌɒptɪ'mɪstɪk/ **adj** always believing that good things will happen: *We're optimistic about our chances of success.* ∘ [+ (that)] *I'm not optimistic that we'll reach an agreement.* → Opposite **pessimistic**

optimum /'ɒptɪməm/ **adj** [always before noun] formal best or most suitable: *the optimum temperature*

option /'ɒpʃ⁰n/ **noun 1** ⑬ [C] a choice: *That's an option you might like to consider.* ∘ *We don't have many options.* ∘ [+ of + doing sth] *You always have the option of not attending.* **2 have no option (but to do sth)** to not have the possibility of doing something else: *We didn't want to dismiss him, but we had no option.* **3 keep/leave your options open** to wait and not make a decision or choice yet → See also **soft option**

> ☑ Word partners for **option**
>
> consider/examine the options • be given/ have the option of doing sth • an attractive/ viable option • an option for sb

optional /'ɒpʃ⁰n⁰l/ **adj** ⑬ If something i optional, it is available but you do not have t have it: *an optional extra*

opulent /'ɒpjələnt/ **adj** Opulent things ar expensive and give a feeling of luxury: *ar opulent bathroom*

or strong /ɔːr/ weak /ər/ **conjunction 1 BETWEEN POSSIBILITIES** ▷ ⑪ used between possibilities or before the last in a list of possibilities: *Woul you like toast or cereal?* ∘ *Is that a boy or a girl.* ∘ *You can have beer, wine, or mineral water.* ∘ *Th house will take two or three years to complete* **2 CHANGE** ▷ ⑫ used to change or correc something you have said: *We told the truth, o most of it.* **3 REASON** ▷ used to give a reason fo something you have said: *She must love him o she wouldn't have stayed with him all these years* **4 NOT EITHER** ▷ ⑫ used after a negative ver between a list of things to mean not any c those things or people: *Tim doesn't eat meat o fish.*

oral¹ /'ɔːr⁰l/ **adj 1** ⑫ spoken: *an oral examina tion* ∘ *an oral agreement* **2** relating to or usin the mouth: *oral medication* • **orally adv**

oral² /'ɔːr⁰l/ **noun** [C] an examination that i spoken, usually in a foreign language

orange¹ /'ɒrɪndʒ/ **adj** ⑪ being a colour that is . mixture of red and yellow: *a deep orange sunse* → See colour picture **Colours** on page Centre 12

orange² /'ɒrɪndʒ/ **noun 1 FRUIT** ▷ [C] ⑪ round, sweet fruit with a thick skin and a centr that is divided into many equal parts: *orang juice* → See colour picture **Fruit and Vegetables** o page Centre 10 **2 COLOUR** ▷ [C, U] ⑫ a colour tha is a mixture of red and yellow → See colour pictur **Colours** on page Centre 12 **3 DRINK** ▷ [U] UK . drink made with oranges: *Would you like som orange?*

orange 'juice noun [U] a drink made from th juice of oranges

orator /'ɒrətər/ **noun** [C] formal someone wh gives good speeches: *a brilliant orator*

oratory /'ɒrət⁰ri/ **noun** [U] formal the skill c making good public speeches: *political oratory*

orbit /'ɔːbɪt/ **noun** [C, U] the circular journey tha a spacecraft or planet makes around the sun the moon, or another planet: *the Earth's orbi* ∘ *Two satellites are already in orbit.* ∘ *It was th first spacecraft to go into orbit around Jupite* • **orbit verb** [I, T] *The moon orbits the Earth.*

orchard /'ɔːtʃəd/ **noun** [C] a piece of land wher fruit trees are grown: *an apple/cherry orchard*

orchestra /'ɔːkɪstrə/ **noun** [C] **1** ⑪ a large grou of musicians who play different instrument together: *a symphony orchestra* ∘ *a youth orches tra* **2** US (UK **the stalls**) the seats on the mai floor near the front of a theatre or cinem • **orchestral** /ɔː'kestr⁰l/ **adj** ⑫ [always befor noun] Orchestral music is played by or written fo an orchestra.

orchestrate /'ɔːkɪstreɪt/ **verb** [T] to intentionally organize something in order to achieve what you want: *a carefully orchestrated demonstration of support*

orchid /'ɔːkɪd/ **noun** [C] a plant with flowers that are an unusual shape and beautiful colours

orchid

ordain /ɔː'deɪn/ **verb** [T] to officially make someone a Christian priest: [often passive] *He was ordained by the Bishop of London.*

ordeal /ɔː'diːl/ **noun** [C] a very unpleasant experience: *a terrible ordeal* ∘ *They feared he would not survive the ordeal.* ∘ *She went through the ordeal of being interviewed by a panel of ten people.*

order¹ /'ɔːdər/ **noun 1 ARRANGEMENT** ▷ [C, U] **B1** the arrangement of a group of people or things in a list from first to last: *in alphabetical order* ∘ *in the right/wrong order* ∘ *We ranked the various tasks in order of importance.* **2 INSTRUCTION** ▷ [C] **B2** an instruction that someone must obey: *to obey orders* ∘ *to give orders* **3 under orders** If you are under orders, someone has told you to do something: [+ to do sth] *Team members are under orders to behave well.* ∘ *They claimed they were under orders from the president.* **4 REQUEST** ▷ [C] **A2** a request for food or goods in return for payment: *Can I take your order now?* **5 TIDINESS** ▷ [U] **B2** a situation in which everything is in its correct place: *It's nice to see some order around here for a change.* ∘ *I want to put all my things in order before I go away.* → Opposite **disorder 6 out of order a B1** If a machine or system is out of order, it is not working as it should: *The coffee machine's out of order.* **b** If someone's behaviour is out of order, it is not acceptable: *What he did was completely out of order.* **7 in order to do/for sth to do sth B1** with the purpose of achieving something: *She worked all summer in order to save enough money for a holiday.* **8 NO TROUBLE** ▷ [U] a situation in which people obey laws and there is no trouble: *The army was brought in to restore order to the troubled province.* → Opposite **disorder 9 economic/political/social order** the way that the economy, politics, or society is organized: *a threat to the established social order* **10 GROUP** ▷ [C] a religious group who live together and have the same rules: *an order of nuns* ∘ *a monastic order* → See also **mail order**, **postal order**, **standing order**

📝 Word partners for **order**

follow/give/ignore/issue/obey orders • clear/strict orders

---

order² /'ɔːdər/ **verb 1 TELL** ▷ [T] **B2** to give someone an instruction that they must obey: [+ to do sth] *He ordered them to leave.* **2 REQUEST** ▷ [I, T] **A2** to ask for food, goods, etc: *to order a drink/pizza* ∘ *to order tickets* ∘ *We've ordered new lights for the kitchen.* ∘ [+ two objects] *Can I order you a drink?* **3 ARRANGE** ▷ [T] to arrange a group of people or things in a list from first to last: *Have you ordered the pages correctly?*

PHRASAL VERB **order sb about/around** to tell someone what they should do all the time: *You can't just come in here and start ordering people around.*

orderly¹ /'ɔːdəli/ **adj** tidy or organized: *an orderly pile* ∘ *Please form an orderly queue.* → Opposite **disorderly**

orderly² /'ɔːdəli/ **noun** [C] a hospital worker who has no special skills or training

ordinal number /ˌɔːdɪnəl'nʌmbər/ **noun** [C] (also **ordinal**) a number such as 1st, 2nd, 3rd, etc that shows the order of things in a list

ordinance /'ɔːdɪnəns/ **noun** [C] mainly US a law or rule that limits or controls something: *a tax ordinance*

ordinarily /'ɔːdɪnərəli/ **adv** usually: *These are people who would not ordinarily carry guns.*

ordinary /'ɔːdənəri/ **adj 1 B1** not special, different, or unusual in any way: *ordinary life* ∘ *an ordinary day* ∘ *I had a very ordinary childhood.* **2** Ordinary people are not rich or famous and do not have special skills: *ordinary people/citizens* ∘ *an ordinary man/woman* **3 out of the ordinary** unusual or different: *Their relationship was a little out of the ordinary.* ∘ *The investigation revealed nothing out of the ordinary.*

ore /ɔːr/ **noun** [U] rock or soil from which metal can be obtained: *iron ore*

.org /dɒt'ɔːg/ abbreviation for organization: used in some Internet addresses: *You can search Cambridge dictionaries online at www. dictionary.cambridge.org*

organ /'ɔːgən/ **noun** [C] **1** a part of an animal or plant that has a special purpose: *reproductive/sexual organs* ∘ *The liver is a vital organ (= you need it to stay alive).* ∘ *an organ donor/transplant* **2** a large musical instrument that has keys like a piano and produces different notes when air is blown through pipes of different lengths: *a church organ*

organic /ɔː'gænɪk/ **adj 1 FARMING** ▷ **B2** not using artificial chemicals when keeping animals or growing plants for food: *organic farming/farmers* ∘ *organic fruit/food/vegetables* **2 CHEMISTRY** ▷ In chemistry, 'organic' describes chemicals that contain carbon: *organic compounds* **3 LIVING** ▷ from a living organism: *organic matter/material* → Opposite **inorganic** • **organically adv** *organically grown vegetables*

organism /'ɔːgənɪzəm/ **noun** [C] a living thing, often one that is extremely small: *Plants, animals, bacteria, and viruses are organisms.*

organist /'ɔːgənɪst/ **noun** [C] someone who plays the organ (= an instrument like a piano): *a church organist*

organization (also UK **-isation**) /ˌɔːgənaɪ'zeɪʃən/ **noun 1 GROUP** ▷ [C] **B1** an official group of people who work together for the same purpose: *a charitable/voluntary organization* **2 ARRANGEMENT** ▷ [U] the way that parts of something are arranged: *Better organization of the office would improve efficiency.* **3 PLAN** ▷ [U]

61 the planning of an activity or event: *Who was responsible for the organization of the conference?*
• **organizational** adj *organizational skills*

> 🗹 Word partners for **organization**
>
> a **charitable/international/voluntary** organization • **join/set up** an organization

organize (also UK **-ise**) /'ɔːgᵊnaɪz/ verb [T] **61** to plan or arrange something: *to organize a meeting/wedding*

organized (also UK **-ised**) /'ɔːgᵊnaɪzd/ adj **1** **62** An organized person plans things well and does not waste time or effort. → Opposite **disorganized** **2** [always before noun] involving a group of people who have planned to do something together: *organized crime/religion* → See also **well-organized**

organizer (also UK **-iser**) /'ɔːgᵊnaɪzər/ noun [C] **62** someone who plans an event or activity: *conference/exhibition organizers*

orgasm /'ɔːgæzᵊm/ noun [C, U] the time of greatest pleasure and excitement during sex: *to have an orgasm*

orgy /'ɔːdʒi/ noun [C] **1** a noisy party at which people have a lot of sex, alcohol, or illegal drugs **2 an orgy of sth** a period when there is too much of an often bad activity: *an orgy of destruction*

the Orient /'ɔːriənt/ noun old-fashioned the countries of east Asia

Oriental /ˌɔːri'entᵊl/ adj relating or belonging to the countries of east Asia: *Oriental art*

orientated /'ɔːriənteɪtɪd/ adj mainly UK (UK/US **oriented**) directed towards or interested in something

orientation /ˌɔːrien'teɪʃᵊn/ noun **1** [C, U] the type of beliefs that a person has: *He's very secretive about his political orientation.* **2** [U] training or preparation for a new job or activity: *an orientation session*

oriented /'ɔːrientɪd/ adj (also UK **orientated**) directed towards or interested in something: *His new TV series is oriented towards teenage viewers.* ○ *He's very family oriented.*

origin /'ɒrɪdʒɪn/ noun [C, U] **1** **62** the cause of something, or where something begins or comes from: *the origin of the universe* ○ *This dish is Greek in origin.* **2** the country, race, or social class of a person's family: *ethnic origin* ○ *She's of Irish origin.*

> 🗹 Word partners for **origin**
>
> sth **has** its origins **in** sth • the origin(s) **of** sth • be [Chinese/French, etc] **in** origin

original¹ /ə'rɪdʒᵊnᵊl/ adj **1** **61** special and interesting because of not being the same as others: *Her essay was full of original ideas.* ○ *He's a highly original thinker.* **2** [always before noun] **61** existing since the beginning, or being the earliest form of something: *His original plan was to stay for a week, but he ended up staying for a month.* ○ *Do you still have the original version of this document?*

original² /ə'rɪdʒᵊnᵊl/ noun [C] **62** something that is in the form in which it was first created

and has not been copied or changed: *If the painting were an original, it would be very valuable.*

originality /əˌrɪdʒᵊn'æləti/ noun [U] the quality of being interesting and different from everyone or everything else: *The judges were impressed by the originality of his work.*

originally /ə'rɪdʒᵊnᵊli/ adv **62** at the beginning or before any changes: *The bathroom was originally a bedroom.*

originate /ə'rɪdʒᵊneɪt/ verb [I] **originate from/in/with, etc** to come from a particular place or person, or to begin during a particular period: *Citrus fruits originated in China and Southeast Asia.*

originator /ə'rɪdʒᵊneɪtər/ noun [C] formal The originator of an idea is the person who first thought of it.

ornament /'ɔːnəmənt/ noun [C] an attractive object that is used as a decoration in a home or garden → See colour picture **The Living Room** on page Centre 4

ornamental /ˌɔːnə'mentᵊl/ adj used for decoration and having no other purpose

ornate /ɔː'neɪt/ adj decorated with a lot of complicated patterns: *ornate wooden doors*

ornithology /ˌɔːnɪ'θɒlədʒi/ noun [U] the scientific study of birds • **ornithologist** noun [C] a scientist who studies birds

orphan¹ /'ɔːfᵊn/ noun [C] a child whose parents are dead

orphan² /'ɔːfᵊn/ verb **be orphaned** When a child is orphaned, both their parents die: *She was orphaned at the age of six.*

orphanage /'ɔːfᵊnɪdʒ/ noun [C] a home for children whose parents are dead

orthodox /'ɔːθədɒks/ adj **1** keeping the traditional beliefs and customs of Judaism or some types of Christianity: *an orthodox Jewish family* ○ *the Russian/Greek Orthodox Church* **2** If ideas or methods are orthodox, most people think they are correct, usually because they have existed for a long time: *orthodox medicine* → Opposite **unorthodox**

orthodoxy /'ɔːθədɒksi/ noun [C, U] formal an idea of a society, religion, political party, or subject that most people believe is correct, or a set of such ideas

orthopaedic UK (US **orthopedic**) /ˌɔːθə'piːdɪk/ adj [always before noun] relating to the treatment or study of bones that have been injured or have not grown correctly: *an orthopaedic surgeon*

Oscar /'ɒskər/ noun [C] trademark one of several prizes given to actors and people who make films every year in Hollywood in the US: *Who won the Oscar for best actress this year?*

oscillate /'ɒsɪleɪt/ verb [I] formal to move repeatedly between two positions or opinions: *an oscillating fan* ○ *The story oscillates between comedy and tragedy.* • **oscillation** /ˌɒsɪ'leɪʃᵊn/ noun [C, U]

ostensibly /ɒs'tensɪbli/ adv If something is ostensibly the reason for something else, people say it is the reason, although you do not believe it: *He was discharged from the army, ostensibly for medical reasons.*

ostentatious /ˌɒsten'teɪʃəs/ **adj** intended to attract attention or admiration, often by showing money or power: *an ostentatious display of wealth* • **ostentatiously adv**

osteopath /'ɒstiəʊpæθ/ **noun** [C] someone who treats injuries to bones and muscles by moving and rubbing them • **osteopathy noun** [C]

osteoporosis /ˌɒstiəʊpə'rəʊsɪs/ **noun** [U] a disease that makes bones weak and makes them break easily

ostracize (also UK **-ise**) /'ɒstrəsaɪz/ **verb** [T] When a group of people ostracizes someone, they refuse to talk to or do things with that person: [often passive] *He was ostracized by the other children at school.*

ostrich /'ɒstrɪtʃ/ **noun** [C] a very large bird from Africa that cannot fly but can run very fast

ostrich

other¹ /'ʌðər/ **adj, determiner 1 MORE** ▷ **A1** used to refer to people or things that are similar to or in addition to those you have talked about: *I don't like custard – do you have any other desserts?* ∘ *I don't think he's funny, but other people do.* **2 PART OF SET** ▷ **A2** used to talk about the remaining members of a group or items in a set: *Mario and Anna sat down to watch the other dancers.* ∘ *I found one shoe – have you seen the other one?* **3 DIFFERENT** ▷ **B1** different from a thing or person that you have talked about: *Ask me some other time, when I'm not so busy.* → See Note at **another 4 the other side/end (of sth)** **B1** the opposite side/end of something: *Our house is on the other side of town.* **5 the other day/week, etc** **B1** used to mean recently, without giving a particular date: *I asked Kevin about it just the other day.* **6 every other day/week, etc** happening one day/week, etc but not the next: *Alice goes to the gym every other day.* **7 other than** except: *The form cannot be signed by anyone other than the child's parent.* ∘ [+ to do sth] *They had no choice other than to surrender.* **8 other than that** informal except for the thing you have just said: *My arm was a bit sore – other than that I was fine.*

other² /'ʌðər/ **pronoun 1** **A2** used to refer to a person or thing that belongs to a group or set that you have already talked about: *Hold the racket in one hand, and the ball in the other.* ∘ *Some of the pieces were damaged, others were missing.* **2 others** **B1** used to refer to people or things that are similar to people or things you have already talked about: *This is broken – do you have any others?* → See also **each other**

others /'ʌðəz/ **pronoun** [plural] **B1** other people: *Don't expect others to do your work for you.*

otherwise¹ /'ʌðəwaɪz/ **adv 1** **B2** except for what has just been referred to: *She hurt her arm in the accident, but otherwise she was fine.* **2** different to what has just been stated: *I'll meet you there at 6*

o'clock *unless I hear otherwise.* ∘ *I'd like to help you with any problems, financial or otherwise.*

otherwise² /'ʌðəwaɪz/ **conjunction** **B1** used when saying what will happen if someone does not obey an order or do what has been suggested: *You'd better phone home, otherwise your parents will start to worry.*

otter /'ɒtər/ **noun** [C] a small animal with short, brown fur and a long body, that swims well and eats fish

ouch /aʊtʃ/ **exclamation** something you say when you experience sudden physical pain: *Ouch! This radiator's really hot.*

ought /ɔːt/ **modal verb 1 ought to do sth** **B1** used to say or ask what is the correct or best thing to do: *You ought to see a doctor.* ∘ *He ought to have told her the truth.* ∘ *Ought I to phone her?* **2 ought to be/do sth** **B2** used to say that you expect something to be true or that you expect something to happen: *He ought to pass the exam this time.* → See Study Page **Modal verbs** on page Centre 22

oughtn't /'ɔːtənt/ formal short for ought not: *He oughtn't to have shouted at us.*

ounce /aʊns/ **noun 1** [C] (written abbreviation **oz**) a unit for measuring weight, equal to 28.35 grams → See Study Page **Measurements** on page Centre 31 → See also **fluid ounce 2 not have an ounce of sth** to not have any of a quality or emotion: *His new novel doesn't have an ounce of originality.* **3 every ounce of sth** all of a quality or emotion that is available: *He deserves every ounce of support that we can give him.*

our /aʊər/ **determiner** **A1** belonging to or relating to the person who is speaking and one or more other people: *Janice is our youngest daughter.*

ours /aʊəz/ **pronoun** **A2** the things that belong or relate to the person who is speaking and one or more other people: *Matt's a friend of ours.* ∘ *That's their problem – not ours.*

ourselves /ˌaʊə'selvz/ **pronoun 1** **A2** the reflexive form of the pronoun 'we': *We've promised ourselves a holiday abroad this year.* **2** used for emphasis with the pronoun 'we' or when referring to yourself and at least one other person: *John and I arranged the wedding reception ourselves.* **3 (all) by ourselves** **A2** alone or without anyone else's help: *It's a big garden but we manage to look after it by ourselves.* **4 (all) to ourselves** for our use only: *We arrived early and had the swimming pool all to ourselves.*

oust /aʊst/ **verb** [T] to force someone to leave a position of power or responsibility: [often passive] *He was ousted from power by a military coup.*

out¹ /aʊt/ **adj, adv 1 AWAY FROM** ▷ **B1** used to show movement away from the inside of a place or container: *He dropped the bag and all the apples fell out.* ∘ *She opened the window and stuck her head out.* **2 OUTSIDE** ▷ outside a building or room: *Would you like to wait out here?* ∘ *It's bitterly cold out today.* **3 NOT THERE** ▷ **A2** not in the place where you usually live or work, especially for a short time: *I came round to see you this morning but you were out.* **4 FIRE/LIGHT** ▷ A fire or light that is out is not

o

burning or shining: *Bring some more wood, the fire's gone out.* **5 AVAILABLE** ▷ 🔵 available to buy or see: *When's the new Spielberg film out?* **6 FASHION** ▷ no longer fashionable or popular: *Trousers like that **went out** years ago.* **7 NOT ACCURATE** ▷ not accurate: *Your figures are out by £300.* **8 GAME** ▷ no longer able to play or take part in a game or competition: *Two of the best players were out after ten minutes.* **9 APPEAR** ▷ 🔵 able to be seen: *After a few minutes the sun came out.* **10 NOT POSSIBLE** ▷ not possible or not acceptable: *Next weekend is out because we're going away.* **11 be out of sth** 🔵 to have no more of something left: *We're nearly out of petrol.* **12 be out for sth; be out to do sth** to intend to do something, especially for an unpleasant reason: *He's only out to impress the boss.* → See also **out of**

out² /aʊt/ verb [T] to report to the public the secret that someone is homosexual: [often passive] *He was outed by a tabloid newspaper.*

out- /aʊt-/ prefix more than or better than: *to outgrow something* ∘ *to outnumber* ∘ *to outdo someone* (= *show that you are better than someone*)

out-and-out /ˌaʊtᵊn'aʊt/ adj [always before noun] complete or in every way: *an out-and-out lie*

the outback /'aʊtbæk/ noun the areas of Australia where few people live, especially the central desert areas

outbid /ˌaʊt'bɪd/ verb [T] (**outbidding**, **outbid**) to offer to pay more for something than someone else: *She had to outbid two rivals to buy the business.*

out-box /'aʊtbɒks/ noun [C] (also **outbox**) **1** the place on a computer where email messages that you are going to send are kept **2** US (UK **out-tray**) a container where you keep letters and documents that you want to send to someone

outbreak /'aʊtbreɪk/ noun [C] the time when something unpleasant and difficult to control starts, such as a war or disease: *an outbreak of flu/fighting*

outburst /'aʊtbɜːst/ noun [C] a sudden, forceful expression of emotion in words or actions: *an angry outburst*

outcast /'aʊtkɑːst/ noun [C] someone who is not accepted by society because they are different to most other people: *a social outcast*

outcome /'aʊtkʌm/ noun [C] the final result of an activity or process: *the outcome of an election*

> 🗒 **Word partners for outcome**
>
> announce/await/determine the outcome • the eventual/final outcome • the outcome of sth

outcrop /'aʊtkrɒp/ noun [C] (also US **outcropping**) a rock or group of rocks that sticks out above the surface of the ground: *a rocky outcrop*

outcry /'aʊtkraɪ/ noun [C] a strong public expression of anger and disapproval about a recent event or decision: *There has been a public **outcry against** the new road.*

> 🗒 **Word partners for outcry**
>
> cause/provoke/spark an outcry • an international/national/public outcry • an outcry against/over sth

outdated /ˌaʊt'deɪtɪd/ adj not modern enough: *outdated equipment* ∘ *an outdated idea*

outdo /ˌaʊt'duː/ verb [T] (**outdid, outdone**) to do something better than someone else: *They are always trying to outdo each other with their jokes and funny stories.*

outdoor /ˌaʊt'dɔːr/ adj [always before noun] 🔵 happening, used, or in a place that is outside and not inside a building: *outdoor activities* ∘ *an outdoor concert* ∘ *an outdoor swimming pool* ∘ *outdoor clothing* → Opposite **indoor**

outdoors¹ /ˌaʊt'dɔːz/ adv 🔵 not inside a building: *If it's warm this evening, we could eat outdoors.* → Opposite **indoors**

outdoors² /ˌaʊt'dɔːz/ noun **the outdoors** the countryside: *He enjoys hunting, fishing, and the outdoors.*

outer /'aʊtər/ adj [always before noun] 🔵 on the edge or surface of something: *Remove the outer layers of the onion.* → Opposite **inner**

outer space noun [U] the universe outside the Earth and its gases where other planets and stars are

the outfield /'aʊtfiːld/ noun the outer area of the playing field in sports such as cricket and baseball • **outfielder** noun [C] a baseball player who stands in the outfield

outfit¹ /'aʊtfɪt/ noun [C] **1** a set of clothes for a particular event or activity: *a cowboy outfit* **2** informal an organization, company, or any group of people who work together

outfit² /'aʊtfɪt/ verb [T] (**outfitting, outfitted**) US to provide equipment for something: [often passive] *My hotel room was small and outfitted with cheap wooden furniture.*

outgoing /ˌaʊt'gəʊɪŋ/ 🇺🇸 /'aʊtgəʊɪŋ/ adj **1 FRIENDLY** ▷ Someone who is outgoing is friendly, talks a lot, and enjoys meeting people **2 LEAVING POWER** ▷ [always before noun] leaving a position of power or responsibility: *the outgoing president* **3 LEAVING A PLACE** ▷ [always before noun] going to another place: *outgoing calls/messages*

outgoings /'aʊtgəʊɪŋz/ noun [plural] UK money that you have to spend on rent, food, etc

outgrow /ˌaʊt'grəʊ/ verb [T] (**outgrew, outgrown**) **1** to grow too big for something: *He's already outgrown these shoes.* **2** to develop so that something is not now suitable: *She's outgrown her current job and needs a new challenge.*

outing /'aʊtɪŋ/ noun **1** [C] an occasion when a group of people go on a short journey for pleasure or education: *a **family/school outing*** ∘ *to **go on an outing*** **2** [U] a situation in which someone says publicly that someone else is homosexual

outlandish /ˌaʊt'lændɪʃ/ adj very strange and unusual: *an outlandish story/idea* ∘ *outlandish behaviour/clothes*

outlast /ˌaʊtˈlɑːst/ **verb** [T] to continue for longer than someone or something else

outlaw¹ /ˈaʊtlɔː/ **verb** [T] to make something officially illegal: *I think all handguns should be outlawed.*

outlaw² /ˈaʊtlɔː/ **noun** [C] old-fashioned a criminal: *a dangerous outlaw*

outlay /ˈaʊtleɪ/ **noun** [C] an amount of money spent by a business or government: *The project requires an **initial outlay** of $450,000.*

outlet /ˈaʊtlet/ **noun** [C] **1 SHOP** ▷ In business, an outlet is a shop that sells one type of product or the products of one company. **2 CHEAP SHOP** ▷ US a shop that sells goods for a lower price than usual **3 EXPRESS** ▷ a way for someone to express an emotion, idea, or ability: *She needs a job that will provide **an outlet for** her creative talent.* **4 WAY OUT** ▷ a place where a liquid or gas can flow out of something **5 CONNECTION** ▷ US (UK/US **socket**) a place where you can connect a wire on a piece of electrical equipment: *an electrical outlet*

outline¹ /ˈaʊtlaɪn/ **verb** [T] ⑫ to describe only the most important ideas or facts about something: *He outlined the department's plans for next year.*

outline² /ˈaʊtlaɪn/ **noun** [C] **1** ⑫ a short description of the most important ideas or facts about something: *He gave us a **brief outline** of the town's history.* **2** the shape made by the outside edge of something

outlive /ˌaʊtˈlɪv/ **verb** [T] to continue living or existing after someone or something else has died or stopped existing: *She outlived both her children.*

outlook /ˈaʊtlʊk/ **noun 1** [no plural] the likely future situation: *The **outlook for** the economy next year is bleak.* **2** [C] the way a person thinks about something: *Despite her illness, she has a very positive **outlook on** life.*

outlying /ˈaʊtˌlaɪɪŋ/ **adj** [always before noun] far from towns and cities, or far from the centre of a place: *outlying farms/villages*

outmanoeuvre UK (US **outmaneuver**) /ˌaʊtməˈnuːvəʳ/ **verb** [T] to do something clever that gives you an advantage over someone you are competing against: *She outmanoeuvred her opponents throughout the election campaign.*

outmoded /ˌaʊtˈməʊdɪd/ **adj** not modern enough: *outmoded equipment*

outnumber /ˌaʊtˈnʌmbəʳ/ **verb** [T] to be larger in number than another group: *Women now far outnumber men on language courses.*

out of /aʊt əv/ **preposition 1 AWAY FROM** ▷ ⑪ used to show movement away from the inside of a place or container: *A bunch of keys fell out of her bag.* ∘ *She stepped out of the car and walked towards me.* **2 NO LONGER IN** ▷ ⑫ no longer in a place or situation: *He's out of the country until next month.* ∘ *I've been out of work for the past year.* **3 MADE FROM** ▷ ⑪ used to show what something is made from: *The statue was carved out of a single block of stone.* **4 BECAUSE OF** ▷ ⑫ used to show the reason why someone does something: *I only gave her the job out of pity.*

5 FROM AMONG ▷ ⑪ from among an amount or number: *Nine out of ten people said they preferred it.* **6 NOT INVOLVED** ▷ no longer involved in something: *He missed the practice session and now he's out of the team.*

out-of-court /ˌaʊtəvˈkɔːt/ **adj** [always before noun] agreed without involving a law court: *an **out-of-court settlement***

out-of-date /ˌaʊtəvˈdeɪt/ **adj** ⑪ old and not useful or correct any more: *I do have a road map but I think it's out-of-date.*

out-of-town /ˌaʊtəvˈtaʊn/ **adj** [always before noun] positioned or happening in the countryside or on the edge of a town: *an out-of-town supermarket*

outpace /ˌaʊtˈpeɪs/ **verb** [T] to move or develop more quickly than someone or something else

outpatient /ˈaʊtˌpeɪʃᵊnt/ **noun** [C] someone who is treated in a hospital but does not sleep there at night

outperform /ˌaʊtpəˈfɔːm/ **verb** [T] to do something better than someone or something else: *Girls are consistently outperforming boys at school.*

outplay /ˌaʊtˈpleɪ/ **verb** [T] to play a game or sport better than another player or team

outpost /ˈaʊtpəʊst/ **noun** [C] a small place that is far from large towns or cities, often where a government or company is represented

outpouring /ˈaʊtˌpɔːrɪŋ/ **noun** [C] a situation in which an emotion is expressed a lot in public: *His death provoked a national **outpouring of** grief.*

output /ˈaʊtpʊt/ **noun** [U] **1 AMOUNT** ▷ the amount of something that is produced: *Over the past year the factory's output has fallen by 15%.* **2 INFORMATION** ▷ information produced by a computer: *You can look at the output on screen before you print it out.* **3 POWER** ▷ the power or energy produced by an electrical or electronic system

outrage¹ /ˈaʊtreɪdʒ/ **noun 1** [U] a strong feeling of anger or shock: *moral outrage* ∘ *The scandal caused **public outrage**.* **2** [C] something that causes great anger or shock: *a terrorist outrage* ∘ [+ (that)] *It's an outrage that these children don't have enough to eat.*

> 🗹 Word partners for **outrage**
>
> cause/express/provoke/spark outrage ∘
> moral/public outrage ∘ outrage at/over sth

outrage² /ˈaʊtreɪdʒ/ **verb** [T] to make someone feel very angry or shocked: [often passive] *The audience was outraged by his racist comments.* ∘ *Local people were **outraged at** the bombing.*

outrageous /aʊtˈreɪdʒəs/ **adj** ⑫ shocking or extreme: *outrageous behaviour/clothes* ∘ *The prices in that restaurant were outrageous.* • **outrageously adv** *outrageously expensive*

outran /ˌaʊtˈræn/ past tense of outrun

outreach /ˈaʊtriːtʃ/ **noun** [U] mainly US the activity of an organization that helps people with their social, medical, or educational problems: *an **outreach programme*** ∘ *an **outreach worker***

outright /ˈaʊtraɪt/ **adj** [always before noun] total, clear, and certain: *an **outright ban** on smoking*

° an **outright victory** • **outright** /ˌaʊtˈraɪt/ **adv** She needs 51% of the vote to **win outright**. ° He was **killed outright** (= immediately) when the car hit him.

outrun /ˌaʊtˈrʌn/ **verb** [T] (**outrunning, outran, outrun**) to move or develop faster or further than someone or something

outscore /ˌaʊtˈskɔːr/ **verb** [T] mainly US to score more points than another player or team

outset /ˈaʊtset/ **noun at/from the outset** at or from the beginning of something: I made my views clear at the outset.

outshine /ˌaʊtˈʃaɪn/ **verb** [T] (**outshone**) to be much better than someone else: She easily outshone the other students on the course.

outside¹ /ˌaʊtˈsaɪd/ **preposition** (also US **outside of**) **1** ⓐ2 not in a particular building or room, but near it: She waited outside his room for nearly two hours. **2** ⓐ2 not in: a town just outside Munich ° You have to phone a different number outside office hours.

outside² /ˌaʊtˈsaɪd/ **adv 1** ⓐ1 not inside a building: Go and play outside for a while. ° It's cold outside today. **2** ⓐ2 not in a particular building or room, but near it: She knocked on his bedroom door and left the tray outside.

outside³ /ˌaʊtˈsaɪd/ **adj** [always before noun] **1** ⓑ2 not in a building: an outside light ° outside activities **2** from a different organization or group of people: **outside help** ° **outside influences** → See also **the outside world**

outside⁴ /ˌaʊtˈsaɪd/ **noun the outside** ⓑ2 the outer part or surface of something: The pie was cooked on the outside but cold in the middle.

ˌoutside ˈchance **noun** [no plural] a very small chance: She has an outside chance of reaching the final.

outsider /ˌaʊtˈsaɪdər/ **noun** [C] someone who does not belong to a particular group, organization, or place: The villagers are very suspicious of outsiders. → Compare **insider**

the ˌoutside ˈworld **noun** other people in other places: When he was in prison, his radio was his only contact with the outside world.

outsize /ˌaʊtˈsaɪz/ **adj** [always before noun] (also **outsized**) larger than usual: an outsize jumper

the **outskirts** /ˈaʊtskɜːts/ **noun** ⓑ2 the outer area of a city, town, or village: We stayed in a hotel **on the outskirts of** Palma.

outspoken /ˌaʊtˈspəʊkən/ **adj** expressing an opinion forcefully and not worrying about what other people think: **outspoken comments** ° He's an **outspoken critic** of nuclear energy.

outstanding /ˌaʊtˈstændɪŋ/ **adj 1** ⓑ2 excellent and much better than most: an **outstanding achievement 2** waiting to be paid or dealt with: an outstanding debt

outstandingly /ˌaʊtˈstændɪŋli/ **adv** used to emphasize how good something is: outstandingly successful

outstay /ˌaʊtˈsteɪ/ **verb** see **outstay/overstay your welcome⁴**

outstretched /ˌaʊtˈstretʃt/ **adj** When a part of your body is outstretched, it is reaching out as

far as possible: He ran towards me with his arm outstretched.

outstrip /ˌaʊtˈstrɪp/ **verb** [T] (**outstripping, out▪ stripped**) When one amount outstrips anothe▪ amount, it is much greater than it: **Demand fo** the toys far **outstrips supply**.

outta /ˈaʊtə/ informal short for out of: Let's ge▪ outta here!

out-take /ˈaʊtteɪk/ **noun** [C] a short part of ▪ film, television programme, or music recording▪ that was removed, usually because it contain▪ mistakes: They showed a video with funny ou▪ takes from famous films.

outward¹ /ˈaʊtwəd/ **adj** [always before noun▪ **1** showing on the outside: He had a seriou▪ illness, but there was no **outward sign** of it▪ **2 outward flight/journey, etc** a flight/journey▪ etc away from a place that you will return t▪ → Opposite **inward adj**

outward² /ˈaʊtwəd/ **adv** (also UK **outwards**▪ towards the outside or away from the centre▪ This door opens outward.

outwardly /ˈaʊtwədli/ **adv** If someone is out▪ wardly calm, confident, etc, they seem to b▪ calm, confident, etc, although they may not fee▪ that way: She was very nervous, but she remaine▪ **outwardly calm**. → Opposite **inwardly**

outweigh /ˌaʊtˈweɪ/ **verb** [T] to be greater o▪ more important than something else: Th▪ benefits of this treatment far outweigh the risks.

outwit /ˌaʊtˈwɪt/ **verb** [T] (**outwitting, out▪ witted**) to get an advantage over someone b▪ doing something clever and deceiving them: Sh▪ outwitted her kidnappers and managed to escape▪

oval /ˈəʊvəl/ **adj** ⓑ2 in the shape of an egg or ▪ slightly flat circle: an oval face ° an oval tabl▪ • **oval noun** [C] an oval shape → See pictur▪ at **shape**

the ˈOval ˌOffice **noun** the office of th▪ president of the United States

ovary /ˈəʊvəri/ **noun** [C] the part of a woma▪ or female animal that produces eggs, or the par▪ of a plant that produces seeds • **ovaria** /əʊˈveəriən/ **adj** [always before noun] relatin▪ to the ovaries: ovarian cancer

ovation /əʊˈveɪʃən/ **noun** [C] a way in which ▪ group of people show their approval of ▪ performance or speech by clapping for a lon▪ time → See also **standing ovation**

oven /ˈʌvən/ **noun** [C] ⓑ1 a piece of kitche▪ equipment with a door, which is used fo▪ cooking food: an electric oven ° a microwav▪ oven → See colour picture **The Kitchen** on pag▪ Centre 2

over¹ /ˈəʊvər/ **adv, preposition 1 ABOVE** ▷ ⓐ▪ above or higher than something: The sign over the door said "Private, No Entry". ° A fighter plan▪ flew over. **2 SIDE TO SIDE** ▷ ⓑ1 If you walk, jump▪ climb, etc over an object or place, you go from one side of it to the other side: We had to clim▪ over large rocks to get to the beach. **3 AMOUNT** ▷ ⓐ2 more than a particular amount, number, o▪ age: Over 5,000 Internet users contact our websit▪ every year. ° Suitable for children aged 5 and ove▪ **4 OPPOSITE SIDE** ▷ ⓑ1 on or to the opposite side▪

of a road, bridge, path, etc: *The station is over the bridge.* **5 COVER** ▷ (A2) covering someone or something: *She placed the quilt over the bed.* **6 DOWN** ▷ down from a higher to a lower position: *The little boy fell over and started to cry.* ◦ *She tripped over the rug.* **7 PLACE** ▷ (B1) to a particular place: *Could you bring the plates over here* (= bring them to this place). ◦ *He was sent over there during the war.* **8 TIME** ▷ (B1) during a particular period of time: *I was in Seattle over the summer.* **9 ABOUT** ▷ connected with or about: *It's stupid arguing over something so trivial.* **10 NOT USED** ▷ not used: *There's some food left over from the party.* **11 USING** ▷ (B2) using the radio or telephone: *I made the booking over the phone.* **12 be/get over sth** to feel better after being sick or feeling unhappy about something: *It took him months to get over breaking up with his girlfriend.* **13 do sth over** US to do something again from the beginning because you did not do it well the first time: *You've ruined it! Now I'll have to do it over.* **14 (all) over again** (B2) again from the beginning: *It looks all messy. I'm going to have to do it all over again.* **15 over and over (again)** (B2) repeatedly: *He was whistling the same tune over and over.* **16 roll/turn, etc (sth) over** (B2) to move so that a different part is showing, or to make something go this: *She turned the page over.* **17 CONTROL** ▷ in control of someone or something: *Her husband has a lot of influence over her.*

over² /ˈəʊvəʳ/ **adj 1** (B1) [never before noun] finished: *The exams will be over next week.* ◦ *It was all over very quickly.* **2 get sth over (and done) with** to do something difficult or unpleasant as soon as you can so that you do not have to worry about it any more

over- /ˈəʊvəʳ/ **prefix** too much: *to overeat* ◦ *overpopulated*

overall /ˈəʊvəʳrɔːl/ **adj** [always before noun] (B2) considering everything or everyone: *the overall cost of the holiday* ◦ *the overall effect* ● **overall** /ˌəʊvəʳrˈɔːl/ **adv** (B2) *How would you rate the school overall?*

overalls /ˈəʊvəʳrɔːlz/ **noun** [plural] **1** UK (US **coveralls**) a piece of clothing that you wear over your clothes to keep them clean while you are working **2** US (UK **dungarees**) trousers with a part that covers your chest and straps that go over your shoulders

overbearing /ˌəʊvəˈbeərɪŋ/ **adj** trying to have too much control over other people: *an overbearing mother*

overblown /ˌəʊvəˈbləʊn/ **adj** If something is overblown, it is made to seem more important or serious than it really is.

overboard /ˈəʊvəbɔːd/ **adv** over the side of a boat and into the water: *to fall overboard*

IDIOM **go overboard** informal to do something too much, or to be too excited about something: *I think people go overboard at Christmas.*

overburdened /ˌəʊvəˈbɜːdənd/ **adj** having too much to deal with: *overburdened with work*

overcame /ˌəʊvəˈkeɪm/ past tense of overcome

overcast /ˈəʊvəkɑːst/ **adj** cloudy and dark: *an overcast sky/day*

overcharge /ˌəʊvəˈtʃɑːdʒ/ **verb** [I, T] to charge someone too much money for something: *The shop overcharged me by $5.*

overcoat /ˈəʊvəkəʊt/ **noun** [C] a long, warm coat

overcome /ˌəʊvəˈkʌm/ **verb** (**overcame, overcome**) **1** (B2) [T] to deal with and control a problem or feeling: *He's trying to overcome his drug addiction and find a job.* ◦ *Let's hope she overcomes her shyness.* **2 be overcome by excitement/fear/sadness, etc** to suddenly have too much of a feeling: *She was overcome by emotion.* **3 be overcome by smoke/fumes, etc** to become sick or weak because you have been breathing smoke or poisonous gas: *One worker died when he was overcome by chemical fumes.*

overcrowded /ˌəʊvəˈkraʊdɪd/ **adj** containing too many people or things: *an overcrowded classroom/prison* ● **overcrowding noun** [U]

overdo /ˌəʊvəˈduː/ **verb** [T] (**overdid, overdone**) to do or use too much of something: *I went to the gym yesterday, but I think I overdid it a bit.*

overdone /ˌəʊvəˈdʌn/ **adj** cooked for too long

overdose /ˈəʊvədəʊs/ **noun** [C] too much of a drug taken at one time: *Her daughter died of a drug overdose.* ● **overdose** /ˌəʊvəˈdəʊs/ **verb** [I]

overdraft /ˈəʊvədrɑːft/ **noun** [C] If you have an overdraft, you have taken more money out of your bank account than you had in it: *a £1000 overdraft*

overdrawn /ˌəʊvəˈdrɔːn/ **adj** If you are overdrawn, you have taken more money out of your bank account than you had in it: *We've gone overdrawn again!*

overdue /ˌəʊvəˈdjuː/ **adj** happening later than expected: *This decision is long overdue.*

overestimate /ˌəʊvəʳrˈestɪmeɪt/ **verb** [I, T] to guess or think that something is bigger or better than it really is: *They overestimated her ability to do the job.* → Opposite **underestimate**

over-fishing /ˌəʊvəˈfɪʃɪŋ/ **noun** [U] the problem of catching so many fish in a part of the sea that there are not many fish left there: *low fish stocks caused by over-fishing*

overflow

overflow /ˌəʊvəˈfləʊ/ **verb 1** [I] If a container or a place overflows, the thing that is inside it starts coming out because it is too full: *The bath overflowed, and there's water all over the floor!* ◦ *The bin was overflowing with rubbish.* **2** [I, T] to come out of a container or a place because it

O

is too full: *The river overflowed its banks after the heavy rainfall.* **3 overflow with confidence/happiness/love, etc** to have a lot of a quality or emotion • **overflow** /ˈəʊvəfləʊ/ **noun** [C, U]

overgrown /ˌəʊvəˈgrəʊn/ **adj** covered with plants that have become too big: *an overgrown garden*

overhang /ˌəʊvəˈhæŋ/ **verb** [T] (**overhung**) to hang over something: ***overhanging branches***

overhaul /ˌəʊvəˈhɔːl/ **verb** [T] to examine a machine or a system carefully and improve it or repair it: *to overhaul an engine* • **overhaul** /ˈəʊvəhɔːl/ **noun** [C]

overhead /ˌəʊvəˈhed/ **adj, adv** above you, usually in the sky: *overhead power cables* ◦ *A police helicopter was hovering overhead.*

overheads /ˈəʊvəhedz/ **noun** [plural] UK (US **overhead**) money that a company spends on its regular and necessary costs, for example rent and heating

overhear /ˌəʊvəˈhɪəʳ/ **verb** [T] (**overheard**) to hear what someone is saying when they are not talking to you: [+ doing sth] *I overheard him telling her he was leaving.*

overheat /ˌəʊvəˈhiːt/ **verb** [I] to become too hot: *The engine keeps overheating.*

overhung /ˌəʊvəˈhʌŋ/ past of overhang

overjoyed /ˌəʊvəˈdʒɔɪd/ **adj** very happy: [+ to do sth] *He was overjoyed to hear from his old friend.*

overkill /ˈəʊvəkɪl/ **noun** [U] a situation in which something is done too much: *Should I add an explanation or would that be overkill?*

overlap /ˌəʊvəˈlæp/ **verb** [I, T] (**overlapping, overlapped**) **1** If two subjects or activities overlap, they are the same in some way: *Although our job titles are different, our responsibilities overlap quite a lot.* **2** If two objects overlap, part of one covers part of the other. • **overlap** /ˈəʊvəlæp/ **noun** [C, U]

overload /ˌəʊvəˈləʊd/ **verb** [T] **1** to put too many people or things into or onto a vehicle: [often passive] *The coach was overloaded with passengers.* **2** to give someone more work or problems than they can deal with

overlook /ˌəʊvəˈlʊk/ **verb** [T] **1 VIEW** ▷ [B2] to have a view of something from above: *a balcony overlooking the sea* **2 NOT NOTICE** ▷ to not notice or consider something: *Two important facts have been overlooked in this case.* **3 FORGIVE** ▷ to forgive or ignore someone's bad behaviour

overly /ˈəʊvəli/ **adv** in a way that is extreme or too much: *overly optimistic* ◦ *It wasn't overly expensive.*

overnight /ˌəʊvəˈnaɪt/ **adv 1** [B1] for or during the night: *Sometimes we would **stay overnight** at my grandmother's house.* **2** very quickly or suddenly: *Change does not happen overnight.* • **overnight adj** [always before noun] *overnight rain* ◦ *an **overnight** (= sudden) **success***

overpass /ˈəʊvəpɑːs/ **noun** [C] US (UK **flyover**) a bridge that carries a road over another road

overpower /ˌəʊvəˈpaʊəʳ/ **verb** [T] **1** to defeat someone by being stronger than they are: [often passive] *The gunman was overpowered by two security guards.* **2** If a feeling, smell, etc overpowers you, it is very strong and makes you fee weak.

overpowering /ˌəʊvəˈpaʊərɪŋ/ **adj** unpleasantl strong or powerful: *an **overpowering smell***

overpriced /ˌəʊvəˈpraɪst/ **adj** too expensive

overran /ˌəʊvəˈræn/ past tense of overrun

overrated /ˌəʊvəˈreɪtɪd/ **adj** If something i overrated, it is considered to be better or mor important than it really is.

overreact /ˌəʊvəriˈækt/ **verb** [I] to react in way that is more extreme than you should: *Sh tends to **overreact to** criticism.*

override /ˌəʊvəˈraɪd/ **verb** [T] (**overrode, over ridden**) **1** If someone in authority overrides decision or order, they officially decide that it i wrong: *I don't have the power to **override** hi **decision**.* **2** to be more important than some thing else: *His desire for money seems to overrid anything else.*

overriding /ˌəʊvəˈraɪdɪŋ/ **adj** [always before nour more important than others: *an **overridin concern***

overrule /ˌəʊvəˈruːl/ **verb** [T] If someone i authority overrules a decision or order, the officially decide that it is wrong: *Does the judg have the power to overrule the jury?*

overrun /ˌəʊvəˈrʌn/ **verb** (**overrunning overran, overrun**) **1** [T] If something unpleasar overruns a place, it fills it in large number [often passive] *The house was overrun by rat* ◦ *Troops overran the city.* **2** [I] UK to continue fo a longer time than planned: *Sorry I'm late, bu the meeting overran by 20 minutes.*

overseas /ˌəʊvəˈsiːz/ **adj** [always before noun] [B in, to, or from another country: *an **oversea student*** • **overseas adv** *to live/work overseas*

oversee /ˌəʊvəˈsiː/ **verb** [T] (**overseeing oversaw, overseen**) to watch work as it is don in order to make certain that it is done correctl *A committee has been set up to oversee the projec*

overshadow /ˌəʊvəˈʃædəʊ/ **verb** [T] **1** to mak something less enjoyable: [often passive] *Th party was overshadowed by a family argumen* **2** to make someone or something less importar or successful

oversight /ˈəʊvəsaɪt/ **noun** [C, U] a mistake tha you make by not noticing something or b forgetting to do something

oversleep /əʊvəˈsliːp/ **verb** [I] (**overslept**) t sleep longer than you had intended: *Sorry I'r late, I overslept.*

overstate /ˌəʊvəˈsteɪt/ **verb** [T] to talk abou something in a way that makes it seem mo important than it really is

overstep /ˌəʊvəˈstep/ **verb** (**overstepping, ove stepped**) **overstep the mark** to behave in a wa that is not allowed or not acceptable

overt /əʊˈvɜːt/ **adj** done or shown publicly an not hidden: ***overt criticism*** • **overtly ad** *overtly racist remarks*

overtake /ˌəʊvəˈteɪk/ **verb** (**overtook, overta ken**) **1** [T] to become more successful tha someone or something else: *Tobacco has ove taken coffee to become the country's leadin* *export.* **2** [I, T] 🔵 to go past a vehicle or person that is going in the same direction

over-the-counter /ˌəʊvəðə'kaʊntər/ adj [always before noun] Over-the-counter medicines can be bought in a shop without first visiting a doctor. • **over-the-counter** adv *Most of these drugs can be bought over-the-counter.*

overthrow /ˌəʊvə'θrəʊ/ verb [T] (**overthrew**, **overthrown**) to remove someone from power by using force: *They were accused of plotting to* **overthrow** *the* **government**. • **overthrow** /'əʊvəθrəʊ/ noun [no plural]

overtime /'əʊvətaɪm/ noun [U] 🔵 extra time that you work after your usual working hours: *unpaid overtime* • **overtime** adv

overtones /'əʊvətəʊnz/ noun [plural] ideas that seem to be expressed but that are not stated directly: *His speech had political overtones.*

overtook /ˌəʊvə'tʊk/ past tense of overtake

overture /'əʊvətjʊər/ noun [C] a piece of classical music that introduces another longer piece such as an opera

overturn /ˌəʊvə'tɜːn/ verb **1** **overturn a conviction/ruling/verdict, etc** to officially change a legal decision **2** [I, T] If something overturns or if you overturn something, it turns over onto its top or onto its side: *She overturned her car in the accident.*

overview /'əʊvəvjuː/ noun [C] a short description giving the most important facts about something: *I'll just* **give** *you* **an overview** *of the job.*

> ✏ **Word partners for overview**
>
> give/provide an overview • a brief/broad/comprehensive/general overview • an overview of sth

overweight /ˌəʊvə'weɪt/ adj too heavy or too fat: *He's still a few pounds overweight.* → Opposite **underweight**

overwhelm /ˌəʊvə'welm/ verb [T] If a feeling or situation overwhelms someone, it has an effect that is too strong or extreme: [often passive] *She was overwhelmed by the excitement of it all.*

overwhelming /ˌəʊvə'welmɪŋ/ adj very strong in effect or large in amount: *an* **overwhelming feeling** *of sadness* ∘ *They won by an over-whelming majority.* • **overwhelmingly** adv

overworked /ˌəʊvə'wɜːkt/ adj Someone who is overworked has to work too much: *We're* **overworked and underpaid.**

overwrite /ˌəʊvə'raɪt/ verb [T] If you overwrite a computer file, you replace it with a different one.

ovulate /'ɒvjəleɪt/ verb [I] When a woman ovulates, her body produces eggs.

owe /əʊ/ verb [T] **1** 🔵 to have to pay money back to someone: [+ two objects] *You still owe me money.* ∘ *He* **owes** *a lot of money* **to** *the bank.* **2** **owe sb an apology/favour/drink, etc** 🔵 to have to give something to someone because they deserve it: *I think I* **owe** *you an apology.* **3** **owe your existence/success, etc to sb/sth** to have something or achieve something because of someone or something else: *The museum owes much of its success to the present generation of young British artists.*

owing to /'əʊɪŋ tuː/ preposition 🔵 because of: *The concert has been cancelled owing to lack of support.*

owl /aʊl/ noun [C] 🔵 a bird that has large eyes and hunts small animals at night

owl

own¹ /əʊn/ adj, pronoun, determiner **1** 🔵 belonging to or done by a particular person or thing: *Each student has their own dictionary.* ∘ *Petra makes all her own clothes.* ∘ *"Is that your mum's car?" "No, it's my own (= it belongs to me).* **2** **of your own** belonging to someone or something: *I'll have a home of my own (= home belonging only to me) someday.* **3** **(all) on your own a** 🔵 alone: *Jessica lives on her own.* **b** 🔵 If you do something on your own, you do it without any help from other people: *She's raised three kids on her own.*

IDIOMS **come into your/its own** to be very useful or successful: *By the 1970s, Abrams was starting to come into his own as a soloist.* • **get your own back (on sb)** UK to do something unpleasant to someone because they have done something unpleasant to you • **hold your own** to be as successful as other people or things: *She could always hold her own in political debates.*

own² /əʊn/ verb [T] 🔵 to have something that legally belongs to you: *The University owns a lot of the land around here.*

PHRASAL VERB **own up** to admit that you have done something wrong: [+ to + doing sth] *No one has owned up to breaking that window.*

owner /əʊnər/ noun [C] 🔵 someone who legally owns something: *a property owner* • **ownership** noun [U] the right of owning something

> ✏ **Word partners for owner**
>
> the current/original/previous owner • the owner of sth

ox /ɒks/ noun [C] (plural **oxen**) a large, male cow, used especially in the past to pull farm vehicles

oxygen /'ɒksɪdʒən/ noun [U] 🔵 a gas that is in the air and that animals need to live

oxymoron /ˌɒksɪ'mɔːrɒn/ noun [C] two words used together, which mean two different or opposite things, such as 'bitter-sweet' or 'smart casual'

oyster /'ɔɪstər/ noun [C] a sea creature that lives in a flat shell and is eaten as food

oz written abbreviation for ounce (= a unit for measuring weight): *an 8 oz steak*

ozone /'əʊzəʊn/ noun [U] a form of oxygen that has a powerful smell (formula O_3)

ozone-friendly /ˌəʊzəʊn'frendli/ adj used to describe a product that does not produce gases that are harmful to the ozone layer (= the layer of gases around the earth)

the 'ozone ˌlayer noun the layer of ozone high above the Earth's surface that prevents the sun from harming the Earth

P

P, p /piː/ the sixteenth letter of the alphabet

p. 1 written abbreviation for page: *See diagram on p.135.* **2** abbreviation for penny or pence (= units of British money): *a 20p coin* → See Note at **pence**

PA /piːˈeɪ/ UK abbreviation for personal assistant: a person who organizes letters, meetings, and telephone calls for someone with an important job

pace¹ /peɪs/ **noun 1** [no plural] ⓑ² the speed at which someone or something moves or does something: *We started to walk at a much faster pace.* ∘ *the* **pace** *of life* **2** [C] a step: *Every few paces I stopped to listen.* **3 keep pace with sb/sth** to move or develop at the same speed as someone or something else: *We have to keep pace with the changing times.* → See also **at a snail's pace**

> 🗌 Word partners for **pace**
>
> quicken/slow your pace • at a [blistering/ brisk/leisurely, etc] pace • the pace of sth

pace² /peɪs/ **verb 1 pace about/up and down, etc** to walk around because you are worried or excited about something: *He kept pacing up and down, glancing at his watch.* **2 pace yourself** to be careful not to do something too quickly so that you do not get too tired to finish it

pacemaker /ˈpeɪsˌmeɪkər/ **noun** [C] a small piece of medical equipment in someone's heart that makes it work at the correct speed

pacifier /ˈpæsɪfaɪər/ **noun** [C] US (UK **dummy**) a small rubber object that you give to a baby to suck in order to make it calm

pacifism /ˈpæsɪfɪzəm/ **noun** [U] the belief that war or fighting of any type is wrong • **pacifist** /ˈpæsɪfɪst/ **noun** [C] someone who believes in pacifism

pacify /ˈpæsɪfaɪ/ **verb** [T] to do something in order to make someone less angry or upset: *She smiled at Jamie to pacify him.*

pack¹ /pæk/ **verb 1** [I, T] ⓐ² to put your things into bags or boxes when you are going on holiday or leaving the place where you live: *I've got to go home and pack.* ∘ *to* **pack** *your* **bags** → Opposite **unpack 2** [T] If people pack a place, there are so many of them in it that it is very crowded: *Thousands of fans packed the club.*

PHRASAL VERBS **pack sth in 1** informal to stop doing something: *If this job doesn't get any better, I'm going to* **pack it in.** **2** to manage to do a lot of things in a short period of time: *We were only there four days but we packed so much in.* • **pack sb off** informal to send someone away: *We were* **packed off to** *our grandparents' for the summer holidays.* • **pack (sth) up** ⓑ² to collect all your things together when you have finished doing something: *I'm about to* **pack** *my* **things up** *and go home.*

pack² /pæk/ **noun** [C] **1 BOX** ▷ mainly US ⓑ² small box that contains several of the sam thing: *a pack of cigarettes* **2 BAG** ▷ mainly US bag that you carry on your back **3 ANIMALS** ▷ group of animals that live together, especiall those of the dog family: *a* **pack of wolve 4 CARDS** ▷ (also US **deck**) a set of playing card → See also **fanny pack**

package

packet *UK*, pack *US*

package

packaging

package¹ /ˈpækɪdʒ/ **noun** [C] **1 PARCEL** ▷ ⓑ² a object that is covered in paper, inside a box, et especially so that it can be sent somewher **2 GROUP OF THINGS** ▷ ⓑ² a group of object plans, or arrangements that are sold or con sidered together: *a computer package* ∘ *This s package includes hotel, transport, and four days c skiing.* **3 BOX** ▷ US a box or container in whic something is put to be sold: *a package of raisin. cookies*

package² /ˈpækɪdʒ/ **verb** [T] **1** to put somethin into a box or container so that it can be sold: *It neatly packaged in a blue and white box.* **2** t show someone or something in an attractiv way so that people will like or buy them: *What important is the way we package the programme*

package 'holiday noun [C] UK (also UK/U 'package ˌtour) a holiday that is arranged fc you by a travel company and for which you pa a fixed price before you go

packaging /ˈpækɪdʒɪŋ/ **noun** [U] the paper, bo etc that something is inside so that it can be sol or sent somewhere

packed /pækt/ **adj** (also UK **packed out**) ⓑ² ver crowded: *The hall was packed.*

packed 'lunch noun [C] UK food that you put i a bag or box and take to eat at work, school, et

packet /ˈpækɪt/ **noun** [C] UK (US **pack**) **1** ⓑ¹ small container that contains several of th same thing: *a packet of cigarettes/sweets* **2** US set of documents that give information about something: *a packet of information* **3** US (UK **sachet**) a small closed container made of paper or plastic, containing a small amount of something: *a packet of sugar*

packing /'pækɪŋ/ **noun** [U] **1** the activity of putting things into bags or boxes in order to take them somewhere: *I've got to do my packing because I'm going tomorrow.* **2** paper, material, etc that you put around an object in a box so that it does not get damaged

pact /pækt/ **noun** [C] an agreement between two people or groups: *We have a pact never to talk about each other.*

> ☑ Word partners for **pact**
>
> have/make/sign a pact • a pact between sb and sb • a pact with sb

pad[1] /pæd/ **noun** [C] **1** (also US **tablet**) sheets of paper that have been fastened together at one edge, used for writing or drawing: *There's a pad and pencil by the phone.* **2** a small piece of soft material used to protect something or to make something more comfortable: *knee/shin pads*

pad[2] /pæd/ **verb** (**padding**, **padded**) **1** pad **about/around/down, etc** to walk somewhere with small, quiet steps: *He padded downstairs and out of the front door.* **2** [T] to protect something or make something more comfortable by filling or surrounding it with soft material

PHRASAL VERB **pad sth out** to make a piece of writing or a speech longer by adding more information to it

padding /'pædɪŋ/ **noun** [U] soft material that is used to fill or cover something to protect it or make it more comfortable

paddle[1] /'pædl/ **noun 1** [C] a short pole with one flat end that you use to make a small boat move through the water **2** [no plural] UK a walk in water that is not deep: *to go for a paddle*

paddle[2] /'pædl/ **verb 1** BOAT ▷ [I, T] to move a small boat through water with a paddle **2** WALK ▷ [I] UK (US **wade**) to walk in water that is not deep **3** SWIM ▷ [I] US to swim using short, quick movements with your arms and legs

paddock /'pædək/ **noun** [C] a small field where animals are kept, especially horses

paddy field /'pædi,fiːld/ **noun** [C] UK (also UK/US **rice paddy**) a field in which rice is grown

padlock /'pædlɒk/ **noun** [C] a metal lock with a U-shaped part that is used for fastening bicycles, doors, etc • **padlock verb** [T]

paediatrician UK (US **pediatrician**) /ˌpiːdiə-'trɪʃᵊn/ **noun** [C] a children's doctor

paedophile UK (US **pedophile**) /'piːdəʊfaɪl/ **noun** [C] someone who is sexually interested in children

pagan /'peɪgᵊn/ **adj** relating to religious beliefs that do not belong to any of the main religions of the world: *a pagan festival* • **pagan noun** [C] someone who has pagan religious beliefs

page[1] /peɪdʒ/ **noun** [C] **1** PAPER ▷ ⓐ a piece of paper in a book, magazine, etc, or one side of a

piece of paper: *The article is on page 36.* ◦ *I've only read 50 pages so far.* **2** INTERNET ▷ (also **web page**) ⓐ one part of a website that you can see or print separately → See also **home page, the Yellow Pages 3** ELECTRONIC ▷ the text of an electronic document that you can see on a computer screen: *You have to scroll down the page to find the information you're looking for.*

> ☑ Word partners for **page**
>
> turn a page • the back/front page • on page [25/36, etc.]

page[2] /peɪdʒ/ **verb** [T] **1** to call someone using a sound system in a public place **2** to send a message to someone's pager (= small piece of electronic equipment)

pageant /'pædʒᵊnt/ **noun** [C] a show that happens outside in which people dress and act as if they are from a time in history

pageantry /'pædʒᵊntri/ **noun** [U] ceremonies in which there are a lot of people in special clothes

pager /'peɪdʒəʳ/ **noun** [C] a small piece of electronic equipment that you carry that makes a noise or movement when someone sends a message

pagoda /pə'gəʊdə/ **noun** [C] a tall religious building in Asia with many levels, each of which has a curved roof

paid /peɪd/ past of pay

pail /peɪl/ **noun** [C] a container with an open top and a handle used for carrying liquids

pain[1] /peɪn/ **noun 1** [C, U] ⓐ an unpleasant physical feeling caused by an illness or injury: *chest/stomach pains* ◦ *Are you in pain?* ◦ *I felt a sharp pain in my foot.* **2** [U] ⓑ sadness or mental suffering caused by an unpleasant event: *I can't describe the pain I suffered when he died.* **3 be a pain (in the neck)** informal to be annoying: *My brother can be a real pain in the neck sometimes.* **4 be at pains to do sth; take pains to do sth** to make a lot of effort to do something: *He was at great pains to explain the reasons for his decision.*

> ☑ Word partners for **pain**
>
> excruciating/severe/sharp/unbearable pain • ease/inflict/relieve/suffer pain • in pain

pain[2] /peɪn/ **verb** [T] formal If something pains you, it makes you feel sad or upset: [+ to infinitive] *It pained him to see animals being treated so cruelly.*

pained /peɪnd/ **adj** appearing to be sad or upset: *a pained expression*

painful /'peɪnfᵊl/ **adj 1** ⓑ causing physical pain: *Recovery from the operation is a slow and painful process.* **2** ⓑ making you feel sad or upset: *a painful memory*

painfully /'peɪnfᵊli/ **adv 1** in a painful way: *He landed painfully on his elbow.* **2 painfully clear/obvious, etc** If a problem is painfully clear/obvious, etc, it is embarrassing because it is so clear/obvious, etc.: *It was painfully obvious that she didn't like him.* **3** used to emphasize an unpleasant situation or quality: *She's painfully thin.*

painkiller /ˈpeɪnˌkɪlər/ **noun** [C] a drug that reduces pain

painless /ˈpeɪnləs/ **adj 1** causing no physical pain: *a painless death* **2** causing no problems or difficulties: *There is no painless way of learning a language.* • **painlessly adv**

painstaking /ˈpeɪnzˌteɪkɪŋ/ **adj** done with a lot of care: *It took months of **painstaking research** to write the book.* • **painstakingly adv**

paint¹ /peɪnt/ **noun** [C, U] 🅐 a coloured liquid that you put on a surface to decorate it: *a gallon of blue paint* ∘ *The door needs another **coat** of blue paint* (= layer) **of paint**.

paint² /peɪnt/ **verb 1** [T] 🅐 to cover a surface with paint in order to decorate it: *We've painted the kitchen yellow.* **2** [I, T] 🅐 to produce a picture of something or someone using paint: *These pictures were all painted by local artists.* → See also **paint a bleak/rosy, etc picture of sth**

paintbrush /ˈpeɪntbrʌʃ/ **noun** [C] a brush that is used for painting pictures or for painting surfaces such as walls and doors → See picture at **brush**

painter /ˈpeɪntər/ **noun** [C] **1** 🅐 someone who paints pictures **2** someone whose job is to paint surfaces, such as walls and doors: *a painter and decorator*

painting /ˈpeɪntɪŋ/ **noun 1** [C] 🅐 a picture that someone has painted **2** [U] 🅐 the activity of painting pictures or painting surfaces → See also **oil painting**

> 🖉 Word partners for **painting**
>
> **do** a painting • a painting **of** sth/sb • a painting **by** sb

pair

a pair of trousers   a pair of scissors

a pair of gloves

pair¹ /peər/ **noun** [C] **1 TWO THINGS** ▷ 🅐 two things that look the same and that are used together: *a pair of socks/shoes* **2 TWO PARTS** ▷ 🅐 something that is made of two parts that are joined together: *a pair of scissors* ∘ *a new pair of jeans/trousers* **3 TWO PEOPLE** ▷ 🅐 two people who are doing something together: *For the next exercise, you'll need to work **in pairs**.*

pair² /peər/ **verb**

PHRASAL VERBS **pair off** If two people pair off, the begin a romantic or sexual relationship. • **pair sb off with sb** to introduce one person t another because you hope they will begin romantic relationship: *Caroline tried to pair m off with her sister.* • **pair up** to join anothe person for a short time in order to do some thing: *I **paired up with** Chris for the last dance*

pajamas /pəˈdʒɑːməz/ **noun** [plural] US spelling ◂ pyjamas (= shirt and trousers that you wear i bed)

pal /pæl/ **noun** [C] informal a friend: *He's an old pc of mine.*

palace /ˈpælɪs/ **noun** [C] 🅑 a large house where king or queen lives: *Buckingham Palace*

palatable /ˈpælətəbl/ **adj** formal **1** If food c drink is palatable, it has a pleasant taste: *palatable local wine* **2** If an idea or plan i palatable, it is acceptable: *They need to make th project more palatable to local people.* → Opposit **unpalatable**

palate /ˈpælət/ **noun** [C] **1** the top part of th inside of your mouth **2** the ability to judge an enjoy good food and drink

pale /peɪl/ **adj 1 pale blue/green/red, etc** 🅐 light blue/green/red, etc: *a pale yellow dress* **2** 🅑 If your face is pale, it has less colour than usua because you are sick or frightened.

pall¹ /pɔːl/ **verb** [I] to become less interesting an enjoyable: *The pleasure of not having to wor soon began to pall.*

pall² /pɔːl/ **noun a pall of dust/smoke, etc** thick cloud of dust/smoke, etc

IDIOM **cast a pall over sth** If an unpleasan situation or piece of news casts a pall over a event, it spoils it: *The news of Nick's accident cas a pall over the celebrations.*

palm¹ /pɑːm/ **noun** [C] **1** the inside surface c your hand → See colour picture **The Body** on pag Centre 13 **2** a palm tree

palm² /pɑːm/ **verb**

PHRASAL VERBS **palm sb off** to tell someon something that is not true so that they wi stop asking questions: *He **palmed** me **off** wit an excuse about why he couldn't pay.* • **palm st off as sth** to deceive people by saying tha something has a particular quality or value tha it does not have • **palm sth off on sb** to give c sell something to someone because you want t get rid of it: *He palmed his old computer off o me.*

Palm /pɑːm/ **noun** [C] trademark a small compu ter that you can carry with you

palm tree noun [C] a tall tree with long leave at the top that grows in hot countries

palpable /ˈpælpəbl/ **adj** very obvious: *There wa a palpable sense of tension in the crowd.*

paltry /ˈpɔːltri/ **adj** A paltry amount of some thing, especially money, is very small: *a **paltr sum** of money*

pamper /ˈpæmpər/ **verb** [T] to treat someone in kind way and give them everything they wan

She pampered herself with a trip to the beauty salon.

pamphlet /'pæmflɪt/ **noun** [C] a very thin book with a paper cover that gives information about something: *The tourist office gave me a pamphlet about places to visit in the city.*

pan¹ /pæn/ **noun** [C] **1** 🔒 a metal container with a handle that is used for cooking food in → See also a **flash²** in the pan, **frying pan 2** US (UK **tin**) a metal container without a handle that is used for cooking food in the oven

pan² /pæn/ **verb** [T] (**panning**, **panned**) *informal* to criticize something severely: [often passive] *His last novel was panned by the critics.*

PHRASAL VERB **pan out** to develop in a particular way: *Not all his ideas had panned out in the way he would have liked.*

panacea /ˌpænə'siːə/ **noun** [C] something that people believe can solve all their problems

panache /pə'næʃ/ **noun** [U] a confident and attractive way of doing things: *The orchestra played with great panache.*

pancake /'pænkeɪk/ **noun** [C] 🔒 a thin, flat food made from flour, milk, and egg mixed together and cooked in a pan

panda /'pændə/ **noun**
[C] a large, black and white animal that lives in forests in China

panda

pandemonium /ˌpændə'məʊniəm/ **noun** [U] a lot of noise and confusion because people are angry or excited about something that has happened: *Pandemonium broke out in the courtroom as they took him away.*

pander /'pændər/ **verb**

PHRASAL VERB **pander to sb/sth** to do what someone wants although it is wrong: *He said he would not pander to public pressure.*

pane /peɪn/ **noun** [C] a flat piece of glass in a window or door

panel /'pænəl/ **noun** [C] **1** PIECE ▷ a flat, rectangular piece of wood, metal, etc that forms the surface of a door, wall, etc **2** PEOPLE ▷ a group of people who are chosen to discuss something or make a decision about something: *a panel of experts* **3** CONTROLS ▷ the part of a car, aircraft, etc that the controls are fixed to → See also **solar panel**

panelling *mainly UK* (US **paneling**) /'pænəlɪŋ/ **noun** [U] flat, rectangular pieces of wood that form the surface of walls, doors, etc: *carved oak panelling*

panellist *mainly UK* (US **panelist**) /'pænəlɪst/ **noun** [C] one of a group of people who are chosen to discuss something or make a decision about something

pang /pæŋ/ **noun** [C] a sudden, strong feeling of an unpleasant emotion: *Bernard felt a sharp pang of jealousy.*

panhandle /'pæn,hændl/ **verb** [I] US to ask people for money in a public place • **panhandler noun** [C] US

panic¹ /'pænɪk/ **noun** [C, U] 🔒 a sudden, strong feeling of worry or fear that makes you unable to think or behave calmly: *He was in a panic about his exams.* ∘ *She had a panic attack* (= suddenly felt extreme panic) *in the supermarket.*

> ☑ **Word partners for panic**
>
> be **in** a panic • panic **breaks out** • **absolute/ blind** panic • panic **about/over** sth • do sth in panic • a panic **attack**

panic² /'pænɪk/ **verb** [I, T] (**panicking**, **panicked**) 🔒 to suddenly feel so worried or frightened that you cannot think or behave calmly, or to make someone feel this way: *Don't panic, we've got plenty of time.*

panic-stricken /'pænɪk,strɪkən/ **adj** extremely frightened

panorama /ˌpænər'ɑːmə/ **noun** [C] a view of a wide area

panoramic /ˌpænə'ræmɪk/ **adj** A panoramic view is very wide: *a panoramic view of the city*

pansy /'pænzi/ **noun** [C] a small garden flower with round petals that can be many different colours

pant /pænt/ **verb** [I] to breathe quickly and loudly because it is hot or because you have been running, etc

panther /'pænθər/ **noun** [C] a large, black, wild cat

panties /'pæntiːz/ **noun** [plural] *mainly US* (UK **knickers**) women's underwear that covers the bottom → See Note at **underwear** → See colour picture **Clothes** on page Centre 9

pantomime /'pæntəmaɪm/ **noun** [C, U] a funny play performed in the UK around Christmas, based on traditional children's stories

pantry /'pæntri/ **noun** [C] a small room where food is kept

pants /pænts/ **noun** [plural] **1** US (UK/US **trousers**) a piece of clothing that covers the legs and has a separate part for each leg → See **Clothes** on page Centre 8 **2** UK (US **underpants**) 🔒 underwear that covers the bottom → See Note at **underwear** → See colour picture **Clothes** on page Centre 9.

pant suit **noun** [C] US (UK **trouser suit**) a woman's jacket and trousers made of the same material

pantyhose /'pæntihəʊz/ **noun** [plural] US (UK **tights**) a piece of women's clothing made of very thin material that covers the legs and bottom

papa /pə'pɑː/ **noun** [C] old-fashioned another word for father

the papacy /'peɪpəsi/ **noun** the position or authority of the Pope (= leader of the Roman Catholic Church)

papal /'peɪpəl/ **adj** relating to the Pope (= leader of the Roman Catholic Church)

paparazzi /ˌpæpə'rætsi/ **noun** [plural] photographers whose job is to follow famous people and take photographs of them for newspapers and magazines

paper¹ /'peɪpər/ **noun 1** MATERIAL ▷ [U] 🔒 thin, flat material used for writing on, covering things in, etc: *a piece/sheet of paper* **2** NEWSPAPER ▷ [C] **B1** a newspaper **3** EXAM ▷ [C] UK **A2** an examination: *Candidates must answer two questions from each paper.* **4** WRITING ▷ [C] a piece of writing about a particular subject written by someone who has been studying that subject: *She's just published a paper on language acquisition.* → See also **blotting paper, carbon paper, toilet paper, White Paper, wrapping paper**

paper² /ˈpeɪpər/ **verb** [T] to decorate the walls of a room by covering them with paper

paperback /ˈpeɪpəbæk/ **noun** [C] a book that has a soft paper cover

paper clip noun [C] a small piece of metal used to hold several pieces of paper together → See colour picture **The Office** on page Centre 5

paper clips

papers /ˈpeɪpəz/ **noun** [plural] official documents: *My papers are safely locked away.*

paperweight noun [C] a small, heavy object that you put on top of pieces of paper to stop them from moving

paperwork /ˈpeɪpəwɜːk/ **noun** [U] **B2** the part of a job that involves writing letters, organizing information, etc

par /pɑːr/ **noun 1 be on a par with sb/sth** to be the same as or equal to someone or something **2 below par** not as good as usual: *I'm feeling a bit below par today.*

IDIOM **be par for the course** If a type of behaviour, event, or situation is par for the course, it is not good but it is normal or as you would expect: *"Simon was late." "That's just par for the course, isn't it?"*

parable /ˈpærəbl/ **noun** [C] a short story, especially in the Bible, that shows you how you should behave

paracetamol /ˌpærəˈsiːtəmɒl/ **noun** [C, U] UK a common drug used to reduce pain and fever

parachute /ˈpærəʃuːt/ **noun** [C] **B2** a large piece of cloth that is fixed to your body by strings and helps you to drop safely from an aircraft • **parachute verb** [I] to jump from an aircraft using a parachute

parachute

parade¹ /pəˈreɪd/ **noun** [C] **B2** a line of people or vehicles that moves through a public place as a way of celebrating an occasion: *a victory parade*

parade² /pəˈreɪd/ **verb 1 parade down/past/through sth** to walk as a group, usually to show disagreement about something: *Thousands of workers paraded through the streets.* **2 parade around/up and down, etc** to walk somewhere so that people will see and admire you: *The kids were parading around in their new clothes.* **3** [T] to try to make someone notice something that you are proud of, especially how rich you are or how much you know

paradigm /ˈpærədaɪm/ **noun** [C] formal a typical example or model of something: *Career women are establishing a new paradigm of work and family life.*

paradise /ˈpærədaɪs/ **noun 1** [no plural] in some religions, a place where good people go after they die **2** [C, U] a perfect place or situation: *tropical paradise* ∘ *a shoppers' paradise*

paradox /ˈpærədɒks/ **noun** [C] a situation that seems very strange or impossible because of two opposite qualities or facts • **paradoxical** /ˌpærəˈdɒksɪkəl/ **adj** involving a paradox • **paradoxically adv**

paraffin /ˈpærəfɪn/ **noun** [U] UK (US **kerosene**) oil used for heating and lights

paragraph /ˈpærəɡrɑːf/ **noun** [C] **B1** a part of a text that contains at least one sentence and starts on a new line

parallel¹ /ˈpærəlel/ **adj 1** If two or more lines are parallel, the distance between them is the same along all their length: *The streets are parallel.* **2** similar and happening at the same time: *Parallel experiments are being conducted in both countries.*

parallel² /ˈpærəlel/ **noun** [C] a similarity: *There are a number of **parallels between** our two situations.* ∘ *People are **drawing parallel** (= describing similarities) between the two cases.*

> ☑ Word partners for **parallel noun**
>
> **draw** a parallel • a **clear/close/strong** parallel • a parallel **between** sth and sth • a parallel **with** sth

the Paralympic Games /ˌpærəˌlɪmpɪkˈɡeɪmz/ **noun** [plural] (also **Paralympics**) an international sports competition for people who have a disability (= a condition that makes it difficult for a person to do the things that other people do) • **Paralympic adj** • **Paralympian noun** [C

paralyse UK (US **paralyze**) /ˈpærəlaɪz/ **verb** [T] **1** to make someone unable to move all or part of their body: [often passive] *He was paralysed from the waist down by polio.* **2** to make something stop working: *Rail strikes have paralysed the city's transport system.*

paralysed UK (US **paralyzed**) /ˈpærəlaɪzd/ **adj 1** unable to move all or part of your body because of an injury or illness **2** unable to move or speak because you are so frightened: *to be paralysed with fear*

paralysis /pəˈræləsɪs/ **noun** [U] **1** being unable to move all or part of your body because of injury or illness: *muscular paralysis* **2** not being able to take action: *political paralysis*

paralyze /ˈpærəlaɪz/ **verb** [T] US spelling of paralyse

paramedic /ˌpærəˈmedɪk/ **noun** [C] someone who is trained to give medical treatment to people who are injured or very sick, but who is not a doctor or nurse

parameter /pəˈræmɪtər/ **noun** [C] a limit that

controls the way that you can do something: [usually plural] *Before we can start the research we need to* **set** *some* **parameters** (= *decide some limits*).

paramilitaries /ˌpærə'mɪlɪtᵊriz/ **noun** [plural] people who belong to paramilitary organizations

paramilitary /ˌpærə'mɪlɪtᵊri/ **adj** [always before noun] organized like an army, but not belonging to an official army: *a* **paramilitary organization/group**

paramount /'pærəmaʊnt/ **adj** formal more important than anything else: *Safety, of course, is paramount.* ◦ *Communication is* **of paramount importance**. ◦

paranoia /ˌpærə'nɔɪə/ **noun** [U] **1** the feeling that other people do not like you and are always criticizing you: *Do you think his boss really hates him or is it just paranoia?* **2** a mental illness that makes people wrongly think that other people are trying to harm them • **paranoid** /'pærᵊnɔɪd/ **adj** having paranoia: *Stop being so paranoid – no one's talking about you.*

paraphernalia /ˌpærəfə'neɪliə/ **noun** [U] all the objects used in a particular activity: *the painter's paraphernalia of brushes, paints, and pencils*

paraphrase /'pærəfreɪz/ **verb** [I, T] to express something that has been said or written in a different way, usually so that it is clearer • **paraphrase noun** [C]

parasite /'pærəsaɪt/ **noun** [C] **1** a plant or animal that lives on or inside another plant or animal in order to get food **2** a lazy person who expects other people to give them money and food

paratrooper /'pærətru:pər/ **noun** [C] a soldier who is trained to be dropped from an aircraft using a parachute (= large piece of cloth fixed to the body by strings)

parcel /'pɑːsᵊl/ **noun** [C] ⓑ something that is covered in paper so that it can be sent by post → See also **part¹** and parcel

parched /pɑːtʃt/ **adj 1 be parched** informal to be very thirsty: *I'm going to get a drink – I'm parched.* **2** very dry: *a parched desert/land*

pardon¹ /'pɑːdᵊn/ **exclamation 1** ⓐ (also US **pardon me**) a polite way of asking someone to repeat what they have just said: *"You'll need an umbrella." "Pardon?" "I said you'll need an umbrella."* **2 Pardon me.** used to say 'sorry' after you have done something rude, for example after burping (= letting air from your stomach out of your mouth)

pardon² /'pɑːdᵊn/ **noun** [C] an official decision to forgive someone who has committed a crime and allow them to be free

IDIOM **I beg your pardon.** formal spoken **a** used for saying 'sorry' when you have made a mistake or done something wrong: *I beg your pardon – I thought you were speaking to me.* **b** used to show that you strongly disagree or that you are angry about something that someone has said: *I beg your pardon, young man – I don't want to hear you speak like that again!*

pardon³ /'pɑːdᵊn/ **verb** [T] to officially forgive

someone who has committed a crime and allow them to be free

parent /'peᵊrᵊnt/ **noun** [C] ⓐ your mother or father: *Her parents live in Oxford.* • **parental** /pə'rentᵊl/ **adj** relating to a parent: *parental responsibility*

> ❗ Common learner error: **parents** or **relations/relatives?**
>
> Your **parents** are only your mother and father. The other people in your family are **relations** or **relatives.**
> *We spent the holidays visiting all our relatives.*
> ~~We spent the holidays visiting all our parents.~~

parent company noun [C] a company that controls other smaller companies

parentheses /pə'renθəsi:z/ **noun** [plural] (also UK **brackets**) two curved lines ( ) used around extra information or information that should be considered as separate from the main part: *The age of each student is listed* **in parentheses**.

parenthood /'peᵊrᵊnthʊd/ **noun** [U] being a parent: *the demands of parenthood* ◦ *single parenthood*

parenting /'peᵊrᵊntɪŋ/ **noun** [U] the things that you do during the time when you take care of your baby or child

parish /'pærɪʃ/ **noun** [C] an area that has its own church

parishioner /pə'rɪʃᵊnər/ **noun** [C] someone who lives in a parish and often goes to church

parity /'pærəti/ **noun** [U] formal equality, usually relating to the money people earn or their position: *The union has asked for wage* **parity with** *similar public-sector workers.* → Opposite **disparity**

park¹ /pɑːk/ **noun** [C] ⓐ a large area of grass, often in a town, where people can walk and enjoy themselves: *We went for a walk in the park.* → See also **amusement park, car park, industrial park, national park, theme park, trailer park**

park² /pɑːk/ **verb** [I, T] ⓐ to leave a vehicle in a particular place for a period of time: *I parked the car near the old bridge.* ◦ *You can park outside the school.*

parking /'pɑːkɪŋ/ **noun** [U] ⓑ leaving a vehicle in a particular place for a period of time: *free/ underground parking*

> ❗ Common learner error: **parking** or **car park?**
>
> Be careful not to use **parking** (leaving a vehicle) when you mean **car park**, the place where you leave it.

parking brake noun [C] US (UK/US **handbrake**, also US **emergency brake**) a stick inside a car that you can pull up to stop the car from moving

parking lot noun [C] US (UK **car park**) a place where vehicles can be parked

parking meter noun [C] a device next to a road that you put money into so that you can park your vehicle on that road

parking ticket noun [C] a piece of paper that tells you that you must pay money because you have parked your car where you should not

parkway /ˈpɑːkweɪ/ noun [C] US a wide road, usually divided, with an area of grass and trees on both sides and in the middle

parliament /ˈpɑːləmənt/ noun [C, U] ⑫ in some countries, a group of people who make the laws for the country: *the Russian parliament* • **parliamentary** /ˌpɑːləˈmentˤri/ adj [always before noun] relating to a parliament: *a parliamentary candidate/election* → See also **Houses of Parliament, Member of Parliament**

> ☑ Word partners for **parliament**
>
> **dissolve/elect** a parliament • **enter** parliament • **in** parliament

parlour UK (US **parlor**) /ˈpɑːlər/ noun [C] a shop that provides a particular type of goods or services: *a beauty/pizza parlour*

paˈrochial ˌschool noun [C] a school in the US that is controlled by a church or religious organization

parody /ˈpærədi/ noun [C, U] a film, book, etc that copies someone else's style in a way that is funny: *It's a parody of a low-budget 1950's horror movie.* • **parody** verb [T]

parole /pəˈrəʊl/ noun [U] If someone gets parole, they are allowed to leave prison early but are only allowed to remain free if they behave well: *He's hoping to get released on parole.*

parrot /ˈpærət/ noun [C] ⑬ a tropical bird with a curved beak and colourful feathers that can be taught to copy what people say

parsimonious /ˌpɑːsɪˈməʊniəs/ adj formal not willing to spend money or give something

parsley /ˈpɑːsli/ noun [U] a herb that is added to food to give it flavour

parsnip /ˈpɑːsnɪp/ noun [C] a long, cream-coloured root that is eaten as a vegetable

part¹ /pɑːt/ noun **1 NOT ALL** ▷ [C, U] ⓐ one of the things that, with other things, makes the whole of something: *Part of this form seems to be missing.* ∘ *I did French as part of my degree course.* ∘ *It's all part of growing up.* ∘ *You're part of the family.* **2 take part (in sth)** ⓑ to be involved in an activity with other people: *She doesn't usually take part in any of the class activities.* **3 FILM/PLAY** ▷ [C] ⓑ a person in a film or play: *He plays the part of the father.* **4 have/ play a part in sth** ⓑ to be one of the people or things that are involved in an event or situation: *Alcohol plays a part in 60 percent of violent crime.* **5 MACHINE** ▷ [C] ⓑ a piece of a machine or vehicle: *aircraft parts* ∘ *spare parts* **6 HAIR** ▷ [C] US (UK **parting**) the line on your head made by brushing your hair in two different directions **7 the best/better part of sth** most of a period of time: *It took the better part of the afternoon to put those shelves up.* **8 in part** formal partly: *He is in part to blame for the accident.* **9 for the most part** mostly or usually: *I enjoyed it for the most part.*

IDIOMS **look the part** to look suitable for a particular situation: *If you're going to be a* *successful businesswoman, you've got to look th* *part.* • **part and parcel** If something is part an parcel of an experience, it is a necessary part o that experience and cannot be avoided: *Stress* ▪ *part and parcel of the job.*

part² /pɑːt/ adv not completely: *She's part Iris* *and part English.*

part³ /pɑːt/ verb **1 SEPARATE** ▷ [I, T] If two side of something part, they become separated, an if you part them, you make them separate *Slowly her lips parted and she smiled.* **2 LEAVE** [I, T] formal If two people part, or if one perso parts from another, they leave each other: *Tha summer, after six years of marriage, we parte* ∘ *Even after we parted company, we remaine* *in contact.* **3 HAIR** ▷ [T] to brush your hair in tw directions so that there is a straight line showin on your head: *In my school days, I had long ha* *parted in the middle.*

PHRASAL VERB **part with sth** to give something t someone else, often when you do not want to *You know how hard it is to get Simon to part wit* *his money.*

partial /ˈpɑːʃˤl/ adj **1** ⓑ not complete: *He mad* *a partial recovery.* **2 be partial to sth** If you ar partial to something, you like it: *I'm rathe* *partial to red wine myself.*

partially /ˈpɑːʃˤli/ adv not completely: *partiall* *cooked*

participant /pɑːˈtɪsɪpˤnt/ noun [C] someon who is involved in an activity: *All participant finishing the race will receive a medal.*

> ☑ Word partners for **participant**
>
> an **active/unwilling** participant • a partici-pant **in** sth

participate /pɑːˈtɪsɪpeɪt/ verb [I] ⑫ to b involved with other people in an activity: *Sh* *rarely participates in any of the discussions* • **participation** /pɑːˌtɪsɪˈpeɪʃˤn/ noun [U] *Bot* *shows encourage audience participation.*

participle /pɑːˈtɪsɪpl/ ⓤ /ˈpɑːtɪsɪpl/ noun [C] th form of a verb that usually ends with '-ed' o '-ing' and is used in some verb tenses or as a adjective → See also **past participle, presen participle**

particle /ˈpɑːtɪkl/ noun [C] **1** a very small piec of something: *particles of dust* **2** a very small par of an atom, for example an electron or a proto

particular /pəˈtɪkjələr/ adj **1 ONE PERSON THING** ▷ [always before noun] ⑫ used to tal about one thing or person and not others: *I there any particular restaurant you'd like to go to* ∘ *"Why did you ask?" "No particular reason.* **2 SPECIAL** ▷ [always before noun] ⑫ special: *"Wa anything important said at the meeting?* *"Nothing of particular interest."* **3 NOT EASIL' SATISFIED** ▷ [never before noun] choosing thing carefully and not easily satisfied: *Teenagers ar very particular about the clothes they'll wear.* **4 in particular** ⑥ especially: *Are you looking fo anything in particular?*

particularly /pəˈtɪkjələli/ adv ⑥ especially: *Sh*

didn't seem particularly interested. ∘ *"Was the food good?" "Not particularly."*

particulars /pəˈtɪkjələz/ **noun** [plural] formal details about something or someone: *There's a form for you to note down all your particulars.*

parting¹ /ˈpɑːtɪŋ/ **noun 1** [C, U] formal separation from someone, often for a long time: *The pain of parting gradually lessened over the years.* **2** [C] UK (US **part**) the line on your head made by brushing your hair in two different directions

parting² /ˈpɑːtɪŋ/ **adj parting glance/words, etc** something that you do or say as you leave

partisan¹ /ˌpɑːtɪˈzæn/ ⓤⓢ /ˈpɑːrtɪzən/ **adj** showing support for a particular political system or leader: *partisan politics* ∘ *a partisan crowd*

partisan² /ˌpɑːtɪˈzæn/ ⓤⓢ /ˈpɑːrtɪzən/ **noun** [C] **1** someone who supports a particular political system or leader **2** a member of a group that secretly fights against soldiers who are controlling their country

partition /pɑːˈtɪʃᵊn/ **noun 1** [C] a wall that divides a room into two parts **2** [U] the division of a country into two or more countries or areas of government • **partition verb** [T]

partly /ˈpɑːtli/ **adv** ⓑ① used to show that something is true to some degree but not completely: *The house is partly owned by her father.* ∘ *He was partly responsible.*

partner¹ /ˈpɑːtnər/ **noun** [C] **1** RELATIONSHIP ▷ ⓑ① someone that you are married to or having a sexual relationship with: *sexual partners* ∘ *Are partners invited to the office dinner?* **2** SPORTS/ DANCING ▷ ⓐ② someone that you are dancing or playing a sport or game with **3** BUSINESS ▷ ⓑ② someone who owns a business with another person: *a junior/senior partner* ∘ *He's a partner in a law firm.* **4** COUNTRY ▷ a country that has an agreement with another country: *a trading partner* ∘ *Britain and its European partners*

partner² /ˈpɑːtnər/ **verb** [T] to be someone's partner in a dance, sport, or game: *He looks certain to partner him again in the finals.*

partnership /ˈpɑːtnəʃɪp/ **noun 1** [C, U] ⓑ② an arrangement in which two people or organizations work together to achieve something: *She's gone into partnership* (= started to work together) *with an ex-colleague.* **2** [C] a company that is owned by two or more people

☑ Word partners for **partnership**

enter into/go into partnership • be in partnership with sb • a partnership between sb and sb

part of ˈspeech noun [C] one of the grammatical groups into which words are divided, such as noun, verb, and adjective

part-time /ˌpɑːtˈtaɪm/ **adj, adv** ⓑ① working or studying only for part of the day or the week: *a part-time job* ∘ *He works part-time as a waiter.*

party¹ /ˈpɑːti/ **noun** [C] **1** EVENT ▷ ⓐ① an event where people enjoy themselves by talking, eating, drinking, and dancing: *a birthday party* ∘ *We're having a party to celebrate the* occasion. **2** POLITICS ▷ ⓑ① an organization that shares the same political beliefs and tries to win elections: *a political party* **3** GROUP ▷ a group of people who are working or travelling together: *a party of tourists* **4** LEGAL ▷ one of the sides in a legal agreement or disagreement: *the guilty party* ∘ *We hope to provide a solution that is acceptable to both parties.* → See also **the Conservative Party, the Democratic Party, the Green Party, the Labour Party, toe the (party) line¹, the Republican Party, search party, slumber party, third party**

☑ Word partners for **party**

go to/have/throw a party • a birthday/ Christmas party • be at a party

party² /ˈpɑːti/ **verb** [I] to enjoy yourself by talking, eating, drinking, and dancing with a group of people: *They were out partying till five o'clock in the morning.*

pass¹ /pɑːs/ **verb 1** GO PAST ▷ [I, T] (also **pass by**) ⓑ① to go past something or someone: *She passed me this morning in the corridor.* ∘ *Cars kept passing us on the motorway.* **2 pass (sth) over/ through, etc** ⓑ① to go in a particular direction, or to cause something to go in a particular direction: *Another plane passed over our heads.* ∘ *We pass through your village on the way home.* **3** GIVE ▷ [T] ⓑ① to give something to someone: *Could you pass the salt, please?* ∘ *He passed a note to her in the meeting.* **4** TIME ▷ [I] ⓑ① If a period of time passes, it happens: *Four years have passed since that day.* **5 pass (the) time** ⓑ② to spend time doing something: *She was eating only to pass the time.* **6** EXAM ▷ [I, T] ⓐ② to succeed at a test or an exam, or to decide that someone has been successful: *I passed my driving test the first time.* **7** BE MORE THAN ▷ [T] to be more than a particular level: *Donations have passed the one million mark.* **8** SPORTS ▷ [I, T] in sports, to throw or kick a ball to someone: *Edwards passes to Brinkworth.* **9 pass a law/ motion, etc** ⓑ② to officially approve of something and make it into a law or rule: *They passed a law banning the sale of alcohol.* **10** GO AWAY ▷ [I] If a feeling passes, it goes away: *I know he's angry now but it'll pass.* **11 pass judgment** to judge someone's behaviour **12 pass sentence** If a judge passes sentence, they state what the criminal's punishment will be. **13 let sth pass** to decide not to criticize someone when they say something unpleasant or they make a mistake → See also **pass the buck¹**

PHRASAL VERBS **pass sth around/round** ⓑ② to offer something to each person in a group of people: *Take a copy for yourself and pass the rest around.* • **pass as/for sb** If someone or something passes as or for someone or something else, they appear like that person or thing: *She's fifteen but could easily pass for eighteen.* • **pass away** ⓑ② to die: *She passed away peacefully in her sleep.* • **pass sth down** to teach or give something to someone who will be alive after you have died: [often passive] *Folk tales have been passed down from generation to generation.* • **pass sth/sb off as sth/sb** to pretend that something or someone is different from what they really are: *He tried to pass himself off as some sort of expert.* • **pass on** to die • **pass sth on 1** TELL ▷ ⓑ to tell someone something that someone else has told you: *Did you pass on my message to him?* **2** GIVE ▷ ⓑ to give something to someone else: *Could you pass it on to Laura when you've finished reading it?* **3** DISEASE ▷ to give a disease to another person: *The virus can be passed on through physical contact.* • **pass out** ⓑ to become unconscious: *I don't remember any more because I passed out at that point.* • **pass sth up** to not use an opportunity to do something interesting: *It's a great opportunity – you'd be a fool to pass it up.*

pass² /pɑːs/ **noun** [C] **1** TEST ▷ ⓑ a successful result in a test or a course: *A pass is above 60%.* **2** DOCUMENT ▷ ⓑ an official document that allows you to do something: *a bus/rail pass* ∘ *You need a pass to get into the building.* **3** SPORTS ▷ in sports, a throw or kick of a ball to someone else **4** PATH ▷ a narrow path between two mountains: *a mountain pass* → See also **boarding pass**

passage /ˈpæsɪdʒ/ **noun 1** SPACE ▷ [C] (also **passageway** /ˈpæsɪdzweɪ/) ⓑ a long, narrow space that connects one place to another: *There's a passage to the side of the house, leading to the garden.* **2** WRITING/MUSIC ▷ [C] ⓑ a short part of a book, speech, or piece of music: *She can quote whole passages from the novel.* **3** TUBE ▷ [C] a tube in your body that allows air, liquid, etc to pass through it: *the nasal/respiratory passages* **4** PROGRESS ▷ [U, no plural] the movement or progress from one stage or place to another: *It's a difficult passage from boyhood to manhood.* **5 the passage of time** literary the way that time passes: *Love changes with the passage of time.*

passenger /ˈpæsəndʒər/ **noun** [C] ⓐ someone who is travelling in a vehicle, but not controlling the vehicle: *a front-seat passenger*

passer-by /ˌpɑːsəˈbaɪ/ **noun** [C] (plural **passers-by**) someone who is walking past something by chance: *Police were alerted by a passer-by who saw the accident.*

passing¹ /ˈpɑːsɪŋ/ **adj** [always before noun] lasting only for a short time and not important: *a passing interest*

passing² /ˈpɑːsɪŋ/ **noun 1 the passing of time/ years** the way that time passes: *With the passing of time their love had changed.* **2 in passing** If you say something in passing, you talk about one thing briefly while talking mainly about something else: *She mentioned in passing that she'd seen Stuart.*

passion /ˈpæʃən/ **noun 1** [U] ⓑ a strong, sexual feeling for someone: *She saw the passion in his eyes.* **2** [C, U] ⓑ a strong belief in something or a strong feeling about a subject: *She spoke with passion about the injustice.* **3 a passion for sth** a very strong feeling of liking something: *a passion for football*

passionate /ˈpæʃənət/ **adj 1** ⓑ having a strong, sexual feeling for someone: *a passionate affair/ lover.* **2** ⓑ showing a strong belief in something

or a strong feeling about a subject: *a passionat[e] speaker* • **passionately adv**

passive¹ /ˈpæsɪv/ **adj 1** ⓑ letting things happe[n] to you and not taking action: *Women at that tim[e] were expected to be passive.* **2** ⓑ A passive ver[b] or sentence is one in which the subject does n[o] do or cause the action but is affected by it. Fo[r] example 'He was released from prison.' is [a] passive sentence.

passive² /ˈpæsɪv/ **noun** (also **the ˌpassive ˈvoice**[)] **the passive** ⓑ the passive form of a verb

ˌpassive ˈsmoking noun [U] breathing i[n] smoke from other people's cigarettes

Passover /ˈpɑːsˌəʊvər/ **noun** [U] the Jewis[h] period of religious celebration held in Marc[h] or April

passport /ˈpɑːspɔːt/ **noun 1** ⓐ [C] an officia[l] document, often a small book, that you need t[o] enter or leave a country: *a British passport* **2** [a] **passport to sth** something that allows you t[o] achieve something else: *Education is a passpor[t] to a better life.*

> ☑ Word partners for **passport**
>
> **apply for** a passport • **have/hold** a [British/ Japanese, etc] passport • a **valid** passport

ˈpassport conˌtrol noun [U] the place wher[e] your passport is officially checked when yo[u] enter or leave a country

password /ˈpɑːswɜːd/ **noun** [C] ⓑ a secret wor[d] that allows you to do something, such as us[e] your computer

> ☑ Word partners for **password**
>
> **enter/put in** your password • a **secret** password • **forget** a password • **change** a password

past¹ /pɑːst/ **adj 1** BEFORE NOW ▷ [always befor[e] noun] ⓑ having happened or existed befor[e] now: *past relationships* ∘ *I know this from pas[t] experience.* **2** UNTIL NOW ▷ [always before noun] ⓑ used to refer to a period of time before an[d] until the present: *It's been raining for the pas[t] three days.* **3** FINISHED ▷ [never before noun] Something that is past has now finished: *M[y] student days are past.* **4 past tense** ⓐ the form of the verb that is used to show what happene[d] in the past

past² /pɑːst/ **noun 1 the past a** ⓑ the tim[e] before the present and all the things tha[t] happened then: *In the past people would bath[e] once a month.* **b** ⓐ the form of the verb which i[s] used to show what happened in the past **2 sb'[s] past** ⓑ all of the things that someone has don[e] in their life: *I knew nothing about his past.*

past³ /pɑːst/ **adv, preposition 1** FURTHER ▷ ⓐ further than: *I live on Station Road, just past th[e] Post Office.* **2** UP TO AND FURTHER ▷ ⓐ up t[o] and further than something or someone: *Three boys went past us on mountain bikes.* ∘ *I've jus[t] seen the bus go past.* **3** AFTER HOUR ▷ ⓐ used t[o] say 'after' the hour when you are saying wha[t] time it is: *It's five past three.* **4** AFTER LIMIT ▷ ⓑ after a particular time or age limit: *This bacon i[s]*

P

past its sell-by date. **5 past it** informal too old to do something

IDIOM **I wouldn't put it past sb (to do sth)** informal used to say that you would not be surprised if someone did something, especially something bad, because it is a typical thing for them to do: *I wouldn't put it past him to sell her jewellery.*

pasta /ˈpæstə/ ⓤ /ˈpɑːstə/ **noun** [U] Ⓐ⒉ a food that is made from flour, water, and sometimes eggs and is made in many different shapes → See colour picture **Food** on page Centre 11

paste¹ /peɪst/ **noun** [C, U] **1** a soft, wet, sticky substance that is used to stick things together: *wallpaper paste* **2** a soft food that spreads easily: *tomato/almond paste*

paste² /peɪst/ **verb 1** [T] to stick a piece of paper to another piece of paper: *The cuttings had been pasted into a scrapbook.* **2** [I, T] to move a piece of text to a particular place in a computer document → See also **cut and paste**

pastel /ˈpæstəl/ ⓤ /pæsˈtel/ **adj** A pastel colour is light: *pastel colours/shades* ∘ *pastel pink* ● **pastel noun** [C] *The bedroom is decorated in pastels (= pale colours).*

pastime /ˈpɑːstaɪm/ **noun** [C] an activity that you enjoy doing when you are not working: *Shopping is one of her favourite pastimes.*

pastor /ˈpɑːstər/ **noun** [C] a priest in some Protestant churches

pastoral /ˈpɑːstərəl/ **adj 1** related to giving advice and looking after people: *the teacher's pastoral role* **2** [always before noun] literary relating to life in the country: *a pastoral song/ tradition*

past par'ticiple UK (US ˌpast ˈparticiple) **noun** [C] the form of a verb that usually ends with '-ed' and can be used in the perfect tense, the passive tense, or as an adjective. For example 'baked' is the past participle of 'bake'.

the ˌpast ˈperfect noun (also **the pluperfect**) the form of a verb that is used to show that an action had already finished when another action happened. In English, the past perfect is made with 'had' and a past participle.

pastry /ˈpeɪstri/ **noun 1** [U] a mixture of flour, fat, and water that is cooked, usually used to cover or contain other food **2** [C] a small cake that is made with pastry

pasture /ˈpɑːstʃər/ **noun** [C] an area of land with grass where animals can feed

pat¹ /pæt/ **verb** [T] (**patting, patted**) to touch a person or animal with a flat hand in a gentle, friendly way: *She stopped to pat the dog.*

pat² /pæt/ **noun** [C] the action of patting a person or animal: *He gave her an encouraging pat on the shoulder.*

IDIOM **a pat on the back** praise for something good that someone has done: *I got a pat on the back for all my hard work.*

patch¹ /pætʃ/ **noun** [C] **1** AREA ▷ a small area that is different from the area around it: *a bald patch.* ∘ *There are icy patches on the road.* **2** MATERIAL ▷ a piece of material that you use

to cover a hole in your clothes or in other material: *He had leather patches sewn on the elbows of his jacket.* **3** EYE ▷ a small piece of material used to cover an injured eye **4** LAND ▷ a small area of land used for a particular purpose: *a cabbage/vegetable patch* **5 a bad/ rough, etc patch** a difficult time: *I think their marriage is going through a bad patch.*

IDIOM **not be a patch on sb/sth** UK informal to not be as good as someone or something else: *Her cooking is okay but it's not a patch on yours.*

patch² /pætʃ/ **verb** [T] to repair a hole in a piece of clothing or other material by sewing a piece of material over it: *to patch your trousers*

PHRASAL VERB **patch sth up** to try to improve your relationship with someone after you have had an argument: *Has he managed to patch things up with her?*

patchwork /ˈpætʃwɜːk/ **noun 1** [U] a type of sewing in which a lot of small pieces of different material are sewn together: *a patchwork quilt* **2 a patchwork of sth** something that seems to be made of many different pieces: *We flew over a patchwork of fields.*

patchy /ˈpætʃi/ **adj 1** not complete or not good in every way: *a patchy knowledge of Spanish* **2** existing only in some areas: *patchy clouds/fog*

pâté /ˈpæteɪ/ ⓤ /pæˈteɪ/ **noun** [U] a soft food, usually made of meat or fish, that you spread on bread, etc: *liver pâté*

patent¹ /ˈpeɪtənt/ ⓤ /ˈpætənt/ **noun** [C] a legal right that a person or company receives to make or sell a particular product so that others cannot copy it ● **patent verb** [T] to get a patent for something

patent² /ˈpeɪtənt, ˈpætənt/ **adj** formal **patent lie/ nonsense** something that is obviously false: *The explanation he gave – that was patent nonsense.* ● **patently adv** formal *Her claims are patently (= obviously) false.*

paternal /pəˈtɜːnəl/ **adj 1** like a father: *paternal affection* **2** [always before noun] A paternal relative is part of your father's family: *He was my paternal grandfather.*

paternity /pəˈtɜːnəti/ **noun** [U] the state of being a father

pa'ternity ˌleave noun [U] a period of weeks or months that a father spends away from his usual job so that he can look after his baby or child

path /pɑːθ/ **noun** [C] **1** GROUND ▷ Ⓐ⒉ a long, narrow area of ground for people to walk along: *There's a path through the forest.* ∘ *a garden path* **2** DIRECTION ▷ the direction that a person or vehicle moves in: *a flight path* **3** CHOOSING ▷ Ⓑ⒉ a particular way of doing something over a period of time: *a career path* ∘ *Whichever path we choose, we'll have difficulties.*

pathetic /pəˈθetɪk/ **adj 1** informal showing no skill, effort, or bravery: *He made a rather pathetic attempt to apologize.* ∘ *You're too frightened to speak to her? Come on, that's pathetic!* ∘ *It was a pathetic performance.* **2** sad and weak: *Four times the pathetic little creature*

P

fell to the ground. • **pathetically** adv *a patheti-cally small amount of money*

pathological /ˌpæθəˈlɒdʒɪkᵊl/ adj **1** Pathological behaviour or feelings are extreme and cannot be controlled: *a **pathological** liar* ∘ ***pathological** hatred* **2** relating to pathology (= the study of disease)

pathologist /pəˈθɒlədʒɪst/ noun [C] a doctor who has studied pathology, especially one who tries to find out why people have died

pathology /pəˈθɒlədʒi/ noun [U] the scientific study of disease and causes of death

pathos /ˈpeɪθɒs/ noun [U] literary a quality in a situation that makes you feel sympathy and sadness

patience /ˈpeɪʃns/ noun [U] **1** ⑩ the quality of being able to stay calm and not get angry, especially when something takes a long time: *Finally, I **lost** my **patience** and shouted at her.* ∘ *Making small scale models **takes** a lot of **patience**.* → Opposite **impatience 2** UK (US **solitaire**) a card game for one person

> **☑ Word partners for patience**
>
> **have/run out of** patience • **lose** (your) patience • **test/try** sb's patience • sth **takes** patience • patience **with** sb/sth

patient¹ /ˈpeɪʃnt/ adj ⑩ having patience: *You need to be **patient with** children.* • **patiently** adv → Opposite **impatient**

patient² /ˈpeɪʃnt/ noun [C] ⑩ someone who is being treated by a doctor, nurse, etc: *a cancer patient*

patio /ˈpætiəʊ/ noun [C] an outside area with a stone floor next to a house, where people can sit to eat and relax

patriot /ˈpeɪtriət/ noun [C] someone who loves their country and is proud of it

patriotic /ˌpeɪtriˈɒtɪk/ adj showing love for your country and pride in it: *patriotic duty* ∘ *a patriotic song* • **patriotism** /ˈpeɪtriətɪzᵊm/ noun [U] love for and pride in your country

patrol¹ /pəˈtrəʊl/ noun **1** [C, U] the act of looking for trouble or danger around an area or building: *We passed a group of soldiers **on patrol**.* ∘ *a patrol boat/car* **2** [C] a group of soldiers or vehicles that patrol an area or building: *a border patrol* ∘ *an armed patrol*

patrol² /pəˈtrəʊl/ verb [I, T] (**patrolling, patrolled**) to look for trouble or danger in an area or around a building: *Police patrol the streets night and day.*

patron /ˈpeɪtrᵊn/ noun [C] **1** someone who supports and gives money to artists, writers, musicians, etc: *a generous patron* ∘ *a patron of the arts* **2** a customer at a bar, restaurant, or hotel

patronize (also UK **-ise**) /ˈpætrᵊnaɪz/ verb [T] **1** to speak or behave towards someone as if you were better than them: *Don't patronize me! I know what I'm doing.* **2** formal to go to a store, business, etc, especially if you go regularly

patron ˈ**saint** noun [C] a saint (= a special, famous Christian) who is believed to help a

particular place, person, or activity: *St. Chris-topher is the patron saint of travellers.*

pattern /ˈpætᵊn/ noun [C] **1** WAY ▷ ⑫ a particular way that something is often done o repeated: *behaviour patterns* **2** DESIGN ▷ ⑪ design of lines, shapes, colours, etc **3** SHAPE [⑫ a drawing or shape that helps you to mak something: *a dress pattern*

> **☑ Word partners for pattern**
>
> **alter/establish/fall into/follow** a pattern • a **consistent/familiar/traditional** pattern

patty /ˈpæti/ noun [C] mainly US a piece of food especially meat, made into a disc shape which i then cooked

pause /pɔːz/ verb [I] ⑪ to stop doing something for a short time: *She **paused for** a moment an looked around her.* • **pause** noun [C] ⑫ *There wa a short pause before he spoke.*

pave /peɪv/ verb [T] to cover a path or road with flat stones, bricks, concrete, etc

pavement /ˈpeɪvmənt/ noun **1** UK (US **side-walk**) ⑪ [C] a path by the side of a road that people walk on: *It's illegal to park on the pavement.* **2** US [U] the hard surface of a road

pavement

pavilion /pəˈvɪljən/ noun [C] **1** TENT ▷ a large tent that is used for outside event **2** SPORTS ▷ UK a building next to a sport field where players can change their clothe **3** BUILDING ▷ US one of a group of relate buildings, such as a hospital

paw /pɔː/ noun [C] ⑫ the foot of certai animals, such as cats and dogs • **paw** (als **paw at**) verb [T] to touch something with a paw *I could hear the dog pawing at the door.*

pawn¹ /pɔːn/ noun [C] **1** in the game of chess the smallest piece and the one that has th lowest value **2** someone who does not hav power and is used by other people

pawn² /pɔːn/ verb [T] to leave something with pawnbroker, who gives you money for it and wi sell it if you do not pay the money back: *Sh pawned her wedding ring to pay the rent.*

pawnbroker /ˈpɔːnˌbrəʊkəʳ/ noun [C] someon who lends you money in exchange for items tha they will sell if you cannot pay the money bac

pay¹ /peɪ/ verb (**paid**) **1** BUY ▷ [I, T] ⑬ to giv money to someone because you are buyin something from them, or because you owe ther money: *Helen **paid for** the tickets.* ∘ *Did you pa the telephone bill?* ∘ *You can pay by cash or credi card.* **2** WORK ▷ [I, T] ⑪ to give someone mone for the work that they do: *She **gets paid** twice month.* ∘ *People work for them because they pa well.* ∘ *[+ two objects] **We paid** them 1000 euro **for** the work.* ∘ *a paid job* **3** ADVANTAGE ▷ [I] t be a good thing to do because it gives yo money or an advantage: *Crime doesn't pay* **4** SUFFER ▷ [I, T] to suffer because of somethin bad you have done: *He's certainly **paying for** h* mistakes. **5 pay attention** ⓵ to look at or listen to someone or something carefully: *I missed what she was saying because I wasn't paying attention.* **6 pay sb a compliment** to tell someone that you admire something about them **7 pay tribute to sb/sth** to thank someone or say that you admire someone or something, especially in public: *He paid tribute to his former teacher.* **8 pay sb/sth a visit; pay a visit to sb/sth** ⓰ to visit a place or a person, usually for a short time

> ❗ Common learner error: **pay for** something
>
> Remember that when **pay** means give money to buy something, it is usually followed by the preposition **for**.
> *Rachel paid for the meal.*
> ~~Rachel paid the meal.~~

PHRASAL VERBS **pay sb/sth back** ⓰ to pay someone the money that you owe them: *Only borrow money if you're sure you can pay it back.* ○ *I lent him $10 last month and he still hasn't paid me back.* • **pay sth off** ⓰ to pay all of the money that you owe: *I'm planning to pay off my bank loan in five years.* • **pay (sth) out** to spend a lot of money on something, or to pay a lot of money to someone: *I've just paid out £700 to get the car fixed.* • **pay up** informal to give someone all of the money that you owe them, especially when you do not want to: *Come on, pay up!*

pay² /peɪ/ **noun** [U] ⓰ the money you receive from your employer for doing your job: UK *a pay rise*/US *a pay raise* ○ *good rates of pay*

> ❗ Common learner error: **pay, wage, salary,** or **income**?
>
> **Pay** is a general word that means the money that you receive for working.
> *Doctors usually get more pay than teachers.*
> A **wage** is an amount of money you receive each day or week. It is often paid in cash (= notes and coins).
> *His weekly wage is $400.*
> A **salary** is the money you receive each month. A person's **salary** is often expressed as the total amount in a year.
> *His salary is £20,000.*
> Your **income** is the total amount of money that you earn by working or investing money.
> *She has a monthly income of £1,300.*

> ✏ Word partners for **pay**
>
> a pay UK **cheque cut**/UK **raise**/US **rise** • **rates** of pay

payable /ˈpeɪəbl/ **adj 1** describes something to be paid: *Rent is payable monthly.* **2** If a cheque (= a piece of paper printed by a bank that you use to pay for things) is payable to a person, that person's name is written on the cheque and the money will be paid to them.

pay-as-you-go /ˌpeɪəzjəˈɡəʊ/ **adj** [always before noun] describes a system in which you pay for a service before you use it: *a pay-as-you-go mobile phone* • **pay-as-you-go noun** [U]

pay channel noun [C] a television channel (= a broadcasting company) that you pay money to watch: *Most of the best football matches are on the pay channels.*

pay check noun [C] US pay cheque

pay cheque noun [C] the amount of money a person earns

payday /ˈpeɪdeɪ/ **noun** [C] the day on which a worker is paid

payment /ˈpeɪmənt/ **noun 1** [U] the act of paying: *They will accept payment by credit card.* **2** [C] ⓰ the amount of money that is paid: *monthly payments* → See also **balance of payments, down payment**

> ✏ Word partners for **payment**
>
> **make/receive** payment • a **form/method** of payment • payment **for/of** sth

pay-per-view /ˌpeɪpəˈvjuː/ **noun** [U] a system in which you choose particular television programmes and then pay to watch them: *pay-per-view television/channels*

payphone noun [C] a telephone in a public place that you pay to use

PC¹ /ˌpiːˈsiː/ **noun** [C] **1** ⓐ a personal computer **2** UK abbreviation for police constable (= a police officer of the lowest rank)

PC² /ˌpiːˈsiː/ **adj** abbreviation for politically correct (= careful to speak or behave in a way which is not offensive to women, people of a particular race, or people who have physical or mental problems)

PDA /ˌpiːdiːˈeɪ/ **noun** [C] abbreviation for personal digital assistant: a small computer that you can carry with you

PDF /ˌpiːdiːˈef/ **1** [U] abbreviation for portable document format: a system for storing and moving documents between computers that usually only allows them to be looked at or printed **2** [C] a document using the PDF system

PE /ˌpiːˈiː/ **noun** [U] abbreviation for physical education: classes at school where children do exercise and play sport

pea /piː/ **noun** [C] ⓰ a small, round, green seed that people eat as a vegetable

> ✏ Word partners for **peace**
>
> **bring about/establish/restore** peace • **keep** the peace • the peace **process** • a peace **agreement/initiative/treaty**

peace /piːs/ **noun** [U] **1** ⓰ a situation in which there is no war, violence, or arguing: *peace talks* ○ *a peace agreement/treaty* ○ *There seems little hope for world peace.* ○ *The UN sent troops to the region to keep the peace.* **2** ⓰ quiet and calm: *a feeling of peace* ○ *After a busy day, all I want is peace and quiet.* ○ *I wish you'd stop complaining and leave me in peace!* **3 peace of mind** a feeling that you do not need to worry about anything: *We lock our doors and windows at night*

P

for peace of mind. → See also **Justice of the Peace**

peaceful /ˈpiːsfəl/ adj **1** 🔵 without violence: *a peaceful protest* **2** 🔵 quiet and calm: *The churchyard was empty and peaceful.* • **peacefully** adv 🔵 *He died peacefully at home.*

peacekeeping /ˈpiːsˌkiːpɪŋ/ adj [always before noun] relating to the activity of preventing war and violence: *peacekeeping forces/troops* ○ *a peacekeeping effort/operation* • **peacekeeper** /ˈpiːsˌkiːpər/ noun [C] someone, usually a soldier, who tries to prevent war and violence in countries where there is trouble: *UN peacekeepers*

peacetime /ˈpiːstaɪm/ noun [U] a time when a country is not at war

peach /piːtʃ/ noun [C] 🔵 a soft, sweet, round fruit with red and yellow skin

peacock /ˈpiːkɒk/ noun [C] a large, male bird with long tail feathers that it can lift up to show a lot of colours

peak

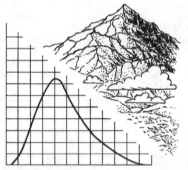

peak¹ /piːk/ noun [C] **1** 🔵 the highest level or value of something: *Here we see an athlete **at the peak of** fitness.* ○ *The price of gold **reached its peak** during the last recession.* ○ **peak travel times** **2** 🔵 the top of a mountain, or the mountain itself: *snow-covered/mountain peaks*

peak² /piːk/ verb [I] to reach the highest level or value of something: *Her singing career peaked in the 1990s.*

peanut /ˈpiːnʌt/ noun [C] 🔵 an oval-shaped nut with a soft, brown shell: *salted peanuts* ○ *peanut oil* → See colour picture **Food** on page Centre 11

peanut butter UK (US **peanut butter**) noun [U] a pale brown food made by crushing peanuts: *a peanut butter and jelly sandwich*

pear /peər/ noun [C] 🔵 an oval-shaped, pale green or yellow fruit → See colour picture **Fruit and Vegetables** on page Centre 10

pear

pearl /pɜːl/ noun [C] a hard, white, round object that is made inside the shell of an oyster (= a sea creature) and that is used to make jewellery: *a string of pearls* ○ *a pearl necklace* ○ *pearl earrings*

pear-shaped /ˈpeəʃeɪpt/ adj **go pear-shaped** UK informal If a plan goes pear-shaped, it fails.

peasant /ˈpezənt/ noun [C] a poor person who works on the land, usually in a poor country: *a peasant farmer*

peat /piːt/ noun [U] a dark brown soil made from decaying plants that you can burn as fuel or that you can put around living plants to help them grow

pebble /ˈpebl/ noun [C] a small stone

pecan /ˈpiːkæn/ 🇺🇸 /pɪˈkɑːn/ noun [C] a nut that grows on a tree, or the tree itself: *chopped pecan* ○ *pecan pie*

peck¹ /pek/ verb [T] (also **peck at**) If a bird pecks something, it lifts or hits it with its beak: *chickens pecking at corn*

peck² /pek/ noun [C] **1 give sb a peck on the cheek** to give someone a quick, gentle kiss on the face **2** the action of a bird pecking something

peckish /ˈpekɪʃ/ adj UK slightly hungry

peculiar /pɪˈkjuːliər/ adj **1** 🔵 strange, often in an unpleasant way: *The wine had a peculiar musty smell.* **2 peculiar to sb/sth** belonging to or relating to a particular person or thing: *Her accent is peculiar to the region.*

peculiarity /pɪˌkjuːliˈærəti/ noun [C] **1** something that is typical of a person, place, or thing: *Each college has its own traditions and peculiarities.* **2** a strange or unusual characteristic: *My mother always hummed – it was one of her little peculiarities.*

peculiarly /pɪˈkjuːliəli/ adv **1** in a way that is typical of someone or something: *a peculiarly American sense of humour* **2** in a strange way: *The birds were peculiarly quiet just before the earthquake.*

pedagogue /ˈpedəgɒg/ noun [C] formal a teacher, usually a very strict one

pedal /ˈpedəl/ noun [C] 🔵 a part of a machine that you press with your foot to operate or move the machine: *bicycle pedals* ○ *a gas/brake pedal*

pedant /ˈpedənt/ noun [C] someone who thinks too much about details and rules • **pedantic** /pɪˈdæntɪk/ adj thinking too much about details and rules: *I hate to be pedantic, but Freud was actually Austrian, not German.*

peddle /ˈpedl/ verb [T] to sell things, especially drugs or things of bad quality: *The shops on the pier peddled cheap souvenirs to the tourists.* ○ *He was arrested for peddling drugs.*

pedestal /ˈpedɪstəl/ noun [C] the base for a statue (= model of a person or animal)

IDIOM **put sb on a pedestal** to believe that someone is perfect

pedestrian¹ /pɪˈdestriən/ noun [C] 🔵 a person who is walking and not travelling in a vehicle: *Many streets are reserved for cyclists and pedestrians.* ○ *a pedestrian precinct/crossing*

pedestrian² /pɪˈdestriən/ adj formal ordinary or not interesting: *pedestrian ideas* ○ *a pedestrian speech*

pedestrian crossing noun [C] UK (US **cross**

walk) a special place on a road where traffic must stop if people want to cross

pediatrician /ˌpiːdiəˈtrɪʃⁿn/ **noun** [C] US spelling of paediatrician

pedicure /ˈpedɪkjʊəʳ/ **noun** [C, U] treatment to make your feet look attractive → Compare **manicure**

pedigree¹ /ˈpedɪɡriː/ **noun** [C] **1** a list of the parents and other relatives of an animal **2** someone's family history, or their education and experience

pedigree² /ˈpedɪɡriː/ **adj** [always before noun] A pedigree animal has parents and other relatives all from the same breed and is thought to be of high quality: *a pedigree dog*

pedophile /ˈpiːdəʊfaɪl/ **noun** [C] US spelling of paedophile

pee /piː/ **verb** [I] (**peeing, peed**) informal to urinate • **pee noun** [no plural] informal *Do I have time for a pee before we go?*

peek¹ /piːk/ **verb** [I] to look at something for a short time, often when you do not want other people to see you: *I peeked out the window to see who was there.*

peek² /piːk/ **noun have/take a peek** to look at something for a short time

peel¹ /piːl/ **verb 1** [T] 🔒 to remove the skin of fruit or vegetables: *Peel and chop the onions.* **2** [I, T] If you peel something from a surface, you remove it and if something peels, it comes away from a surface: *The paint is starting to peel off where the wall is damp.* → See also **keep your eyes (eye¹) open/peeled (for sb/sth)**

PHRASAL VERB **peel sth off** to take off clothes, especially wet or tight clothes: *We peeled off our muddy socks and left them outside.*

peel² /piːl/ **noun** [U] the skin of fruit or vegetables, especially after it has been removed: *Combine nuts, sugar, and orange peel in a small bowl.*

peep /piːp/ **verb** [I] **1 peep at/ through/out, etc** to look at something for a short time, often when you do not want other people to see you: *She peeped at them through the fence.* **2 peep through/over/out from, etc** to appear but not be seen completely: *The sun peeped out from behind the clouds.* • **peep noun** [no plural] *She took a peep at herself in the mirror.*

peer¹ /pɪəʳ/ **noun** [C] **1** someone who is the same age, or who has the same social position or abilities as other members of a group: *Most teenagers want to be accepted by their peers.* **2** in the UK, a person who has a title and a high social position

peer² /pɪəʳ/ **verb peer at/into/through, etc** to look carefully or with difficulty: *She peered at me over her glasses.*

peer group **noun** [C] a group of people of about the same age, social position, etc: *He was the first of his peer group to get married.*

peer pressure **noun** [U] strong influence on a member of a group to behave in the same way as other members in the group, although that

behaviour is not good: *Many teenagers take drugs because of boredom or peer pressure.*

peg¹ /peɡ/ **noun** [C] **1 ON WALL** ▷ an object on a wall or door that you hang things on **2 ON ROPE** ▷ (also **clothes peg**) UK a short piece of wood, plastic, etc that is used to hold clothes on a rope while they dry **3 STICK** ▷ a stick made of metal or wood that has a sharp end and which is used to fix something somewhere: *a tent peg*

peg² /peɡ/ **verb** [T] (**pegging, pegged**) to fix the cost of borrowing money or the value of a country's money at a particular level: [often passive] *Interest rates were pegged at 8.2%.*

pellet /ˈpelɪt/ **noun** [C] a small, hard ball of metal, grain, etc: *shotgun/feed pellets*

pelvic /ˈpelvɪk/ **adj** [always before noun] relating to the area below your waist and above your legs

pelvis /ˈpelvɪs/ **noun** [C] the group of bones that forms the area below your waist and above your legs and to which your leg bones are joined

pen¹ /pen/ **noun** [C] **1** 🅐 a long, thin object that you use to write or draw in ink → See colour picture **The Classroom** on page Centre 6 **2** a small area with a fence around it that you keep animals in: *a pig/sheep pen* → See also **ballpoint pen, felt-tip pen, fountain pen**

pen² /pen/ **verb** [T] (**penning, penned**) literary to write something: *sonnets penned by Shakespeare*

PHRASAL VERB **pen sb/sth in/up** to keep people or animals in a small area: [often passive] *The soldiers were penned up in their barracks.*

penal /ˈpiːnⁿl/ **adj** [always before noun] relating to the punishment of criminals: *a penal code/ system*

penalize (also UK **-ise**) /ˈpiːnⁿlaɪz/ **verb** [T] **1** to cause someone a disadvantage: *The present tax system penalizes poor people.* **2** to punish someone for breaking a rule: *He was penalized early in the game for dangerous play.*

penalty /ˈpenⁿlti/ **noun** [C] **1** 🔒 a punishment for doing something which is against a law or rule: *There's a £50 penalty for late cancellation of tickets.* **2** 🔒 in sports, an advantage given to a team when the opposing team has broken a rule: *They won a penalty in the first five minutes of the game.* ◦ *a penalty goal/kick* → See also **death penalty**

☑ Word partners for **penalty**

face a penalty • a heavy/severe/stiff penalty • a penalty **for** (doing) sth

penance /ˈpenəns/ **noun** [C, U] an act that shows you are sorry for something that you have done

❗ Common learner error: **pence, pennies, or p?**

Pence is the usual plural of penny (UK) and is used to talk about amounts of money. In informal UK English you can also say **p**.

Can you lend me 50 pence?
Can you lend me 50p?

The plural form **pennies** is only used to talk about the coins as objects.

He found some pennies in his pocket.

pence /pens/ **noun** ⓐ plural of British penny; p

penchant /'ɒnʃɒŋ/ ⑤ /'pentʃənt/ **noun have a penchant for sth** formal to like something very much: *Miguel has a penchant for fast cars.*

pencil /'pensəl/ **noun** [C, U] ⓐ a long, thin wooden object with a black or coloured point that you write or draw with → See colour picture **The Classroom** on page Centre 6

pencil sharpener noun [C] a tool that you use to make pencils sharp → See colour picture **The Classroom** on page Centre 6

pendant /'pendənt/ **noun** [C] a piece of jewellery on a chain that you wear around your neck

pending¹ /'pendɪŋ/ **preposition** formal used to say that one thing must wait until another thing happens: *Several employees have been suspended pending an investigation.*

pending² /'pendɪŋ/ **adj** formal not decided or finished: *Their court case is still pending.*

pendulum /'pendjələm/ **noun** [C] a heavy object on a chain or stick that moves from side to side, especially inside a large clock

penetrate /'penɪtreɪt/ **verb** [I, T] **1** If something penetrates an object, it moves into that object: *The bullet penetrated his skull.* **2** [T] If someone penetrates a place or a group, they succeed in moving into or joining it: *No one in our industry has successfully penetrated the Asian market.* • **penetration** /ˌpenɪ'treɪʃən/ **noun** [U]

penetrating /'penɪtreɪtɪŋ/ **adj 1** intelligent and full of careful thought: *a penetrating discussion/mind.* • *She wrote a penetrating analysis of Shakespeare's Hamlet.* **2 a penetrating gaze/look/stare, etc** If someone gives you a penetrating look, you feel as if they know what you are thinking. **3** If a sound is penetrating, it is very strong and unpleasant: *a penetrating voice/scream*

penfriend /'penfrend/ **noun** [C] UK (US **pen pal**) ⓐ someone that you write to regularly but have never met

penguin /'peŋgwɪn/ **noun** [C] ⑥ a large, black and white sea bird that swims and cannot fly

penicillin /ˌpenɪ'sɪlɪn/ **noun** [U] a type of medicine that kills bacteria and is used to treat illness

peninsula /pə'nɪnsjələ/ **noun** [C] a long, thin piece of land that has water around most of it: *the Korean peninsula*

penis /'piːnɪs/ **noun** [C] the part of a man's or male animal's body that is used for urinating and having sex

penitentiary /ˌpenɪ'tenʃəri/ **noun** [C] a prison in the US

pennant /'penənt/ **noun** [C] a long, pointed flag

penniless /'penɪləs/ **adj** having no money

penny /'peni/ **noun** [C] (plural **pence, p, pennies**) **1** ⑥ a coin or unit of money with a value of ¹⁄₁₀₀ of a pound (= UK unit of money); p: *There are 100 pence in a pound.* ∘ *fifty pence/50p* → See Note at **pence 2** a coin with a value of one US cent (= ¹⁄₁₀₀ of a dollar): *My dad always let us have his pennies to buy candy.* **3 every penny** all of an

amount of money: *They had spent every penny of their savings.*

pen pal noun [C] US (UK **penfriend**) someone that you write to regularly but have never met

pension¹ /'penʃən/ **noun** [C] ⑥ money that is paid regularly by the government or a private company to a person who has stopped working because they are old or sick: *a state/private pension* ∘ *a pension plan/scheme* • **pensioner noun** [C] mainly UK someone who receives pension → See also **old-age pension, old-age pensioner**

> ☑ Word partners for **pension**
>
> get/be on/receive a pension • a pension fund/plan/scheme • a state/private pension

pension² /'penʃən/ **verb**

PHRASAL VERB **pension sb off** mainly UK If an organization pensions someone off, it forces that person to leave their job but pays them a pension.

the Pentagon /'pentəgɒn/ **noun** the department of the US government that controls the army, navy, etc, or the building where it is: *The Pentagon refused to comment on potential military targets.*

penthouse /'penthaʊs/ **noun** [C] (plural **penthouses** /'penthaʊzɪz/) an expensive apartment at the top of a building

pent-up /ˌpent'ʌp/ **adj** [always before noun] Pent-up feelings are feelings that you have not expressed for a long time: *pent-up anger*

penultimate /pə'nʌltɪmət/ **adj** [always before noun] formal next to the last: *Y is the penultimate letter of the alphabet.*

people¹ /'piːpl/ **noun 1** [plural] ⓐ more than one person: *Our company employs over 400 people.* ∘ *People live much longer than they used to* **2 the people** [plural] all the ordinary people in a country: *The rebels have gained the support of the people.* **3** [C] formal all the people of a race: *Europe is made up of many different peoples.*

people² /'piːpl/ **verb**

PHRASAL VERB **be peopled by/with sb** literary to be filled with a particular kind of person: *His novels are peopled with angry young men.*

people carrier noun [C] UK (US **minivan**) a large, high car that can carry more people than a normal car

pepper¹ /'pepər/ **noun 1** [U] ⓐ a black, grey, or red powder that is made from crushed seeds, used to give food a slightly spicy flavour: *salt and pepper* **2** [C] ⑥ a hollow green, red, or yellow vegetable: *green/red pepper* → See colour picture **Fruit and Vegetables** on page Centre 10

pepper² /'pepər/ **verb**

PHRASAL VERB **pepper sth with sth** to include a lot of something: [often passive] *His speech was peppered with quotations.*

peppermint /'pepəmɪnt/ **noun 1** [U] oil from a plant that is added to food to give it a strong, fresh taste, or the taste itself: *peppermint tea*

P

2 [C] a small, hard sweet that tastes like peppermint

per strong /pɜːr/ weak /pər/ **preposition** 🅐🅑 for each: *Our hotel room costs $60 per night.* ∘ *The speed limit is 100 kilometres per hour.* ∘ *The wedding dinner will cost £30 per head* (= *for each person*).

per annum /pɜːrˈænʌm/ **adv** formal every year: *a salary of $19,000 per annum*

per capita /pɜːˈkæpɪtə/ **adj, adv** formal for each person: *This county has the lowest per capita income in the country.* ∘ *Belgians eat more chocolate per capita than any other nation in Europe.*

perceive /pəˈsiːv/ **verb** [T] formal **1** to think of something or someone in a particular way: [often passive] *The British are often perceived as being very formal.* **2** to notice something that is not easy to notice: *We perceived a faint light in the distance.*

percent (also **per cent**) /pəˈsent/ **adj, adv** 🅑 for or out of every 100, shown by the symbol %: *a 40 percent increase in prices* • **percent** (also **per cent**) noun [C] *Nearly 70 percent of all cars in the UK are less than five years old.*

percentage /pəˈsentɪdʒ/ **noun** [C] 🅑 an amount of something, expressed as a number out of 100: *The **percentage of** women who work has risen steadily.* ∘ *The **percentage of** people who are left-handed is small – only about 10%.*

perceptible /pəˈseptəbl/ **adj** formal just able to be noticed: *a perceptible difference in colour* ∘ *His pulse was barely perceptible.*

perception /pəˈsepʃən/ **noun 1** [C] what you think or believe about someone or something: *The **public perception** of him as a hero is surprising.* **2** [U] the ability to notice something: *Alcohol reduces your perception of pain.*

perceptive /pəˈseptɪv/ **adj** quick to notice or understand things: *a perceptive writer*

perch¹ /pɜːtʃ/ **verb 1 perch (sth) on/in/above, etc** to be in a high position or in a position near the edge of something, or to put something in this position: [often passive] *The village was perched on the side of a mountain.* ∘ *She wore glasses perched on the end of her nose.* **2 perch on/in, etc** to sit near the edge of something: *The children perched on the edges of their seats.*

perch² /pɜːtʃ/ **noun** [C] a place where a bird sits, especially a stick inside a cage

percussion /pəˈkʌʃən/ **noun** [U] musical instruments that make a sound when you hit them with a stick or your hand: *Drums, tambourines, and cymbals are percussion instruments.*

perennial¹ /pəˈreniəl/ **adj** happening again and again, or continuing for a long time: *the perennial problem of unemployment*

perennial² /pəˈreniəl/ **noun** [C] a plant that lives for several years

perfect¹ /ˈpɜːfɪkt/ **adj 1 WITHOUT FAULT** ▷ 🅐🅑 without fault, or as good as possible: *James is a*

perfect husband and father. ∘ *Her performance was perfect.* **2 SUITABLE** ▷ exactly right for someone or something: *You'd be **perfect for** the job.* ∘ *The weather's just perfect for a picnic.* **3 TO EMPHASIZE** ▷ [always before noun] used to emphasize a noun: *His suggestion makes perfect sense.*

perfect² /pəˈfekt/ **verb** [T] to make something as good as it can be: *I've spent hours perfecting my speech.*

the perfect /ˈpɜːfɪkt/ **noun** (also **the perfect tense**) 🅑 the form of the verb that is used to show an action that has happened in the past or before another time or event. In English, the perfect is made with 'have' and a past participle. → See also **the future perfect, the past perfect, the present perfect**

perfection /pəˈfekʃən/ **noun** [U] the quality of being perfect: *She strives for perfection in everything she does.* ∘ *chicken legs cooked to perfection*

perfectionist /pəˈfekʃənɪst/ **noun** [C] someone who wants everything to be perfect

perfectly /ˈpɜːfɪktli/ **adv 1** 🅑 used to emphasize the word that follows it: *To be perfectly honest, I don't care any more.* ∘ *I made it perfectly clear to him what I meant.* **2** 🅑 in a perfect way: *The jacket fits perfectly, the skirt not so well.*

perforated /ˈpɜːfəreɪtɪd/ **adj 1** Perforated materials such as paper have small holes in them so that they can be torn or liquid can pass through them. **2** If an organ of your body is perforated, it has a hole in it: *a perforated eardrum* • **perforate** verb [T]

perform /pəˈfɔːm/ **verb 1** [I, T] 🅑 to entertain people by acting, singing, dancing, etc: *She has performed all over the world.* ∘ *The orchestra will perform music by Mozart.* **2** [T] formal 🅑 to do a job or a piece of work: *In the future, many **tasks** will be **performed** by robots.* ∘ *Surgeons **performed** the **operation** in less than two hours.* **3 perform well/badly, etc** If something performs well, badly, etc, it works that way: *These cars perform poorly at high speeds.*

P

performance /pəˈfɔːməns/ **noun 1** [C] acting, singing, dancing, or playing music to entertain people: *a performance of Shakespeare's Hamlet* **2** [U] how successful someone or something is: *The company's performance was poor for the first two years.* ◦ *Some athletes take drugs to improve their performance.*

☑ Word partners for **performance**

give/put on a performance • a brilliant/virtuoso/wonderful performance

performer /pəˈfɔːmər/ **noun** [C] someone who entertains people

the performing arts noun [plural] types of entertainment that are performed in front of people, such as dancing, singing, and acting

perfume /ˈpɜːfjuːm/ **noun** [C, U] a liquid with a pleasant smell that women put on their skin • **perfumed** adj containing perfume

perhaps /pəˈhæps/ **adv 1** possibly: *Perhaps I'll go to the gym after work.* ◦ *Ben won't be coming but perhaps it's better that way.* **2** used when you want to suggest or ask someone something: *Perhaps you should leave now.*

peril /ˈperəl/ **noun** [C, U] formal extreme danger: *A shortage of firefighters is putting lives in peril.* ◦ *His book describes the perils of war.*

perilous /ˈperələs/ **adj** formal very dangerous: *a perilous journey* • **perilously** adv

perimeter /pəˈrɪmɪtər/ **noun** [C] the outer edge of an area: *the perimeter of the airport*

period /ˈpɪəriəd/ **noun** [C] **1** TIME ▷ a length of time: *a 24-hour period* ◦ *a period of four months* **2** SCHOOL/SPORTS ▷ one of the equal parts of time that a school day or sports game is divided into **3** WOMEN ▷ the time each month when blood comes out of a woman's uterus **4** MARK ▷ US (UK full stop) a mark (.) used at the end of a sentence, or to show that the letters before it are an abbreviation → See Study Page **Punctuation** on page Centre 33

periodic /ˌpɪəriˈɒdɪk/ **adj** happening regularly: *Our sales team makes periodic trips to Asia.* • **periodically** adv

periodical /ˌpɪəriˈɒdɪkəl/ **noun** [C] a magazine about a particular subject

peripheral¹ /pəˈrɪfərəl/ **adj** not as important as someone or something else

peripheral² /pəˈrɪfərəl/ **noun** [C] a piece of equipment, such as a printer, that can be connected to a computer

periphery /pəˈrɪfəri/ **noun** [C] the outer edge of an area: *The soldiers were camped on the periphery of the village.*

perish /ˈperɪʃ/ **verb** [I] literary to die: *Hundreds of people perished in the flood.*

perishable /ˈperɪʃəbl/ **adj** Food that is perishable goes bad very quickly.

perjury /ˈpɜːdʒəri/ **noun** [U] the crime of telling a lie in a court of law: *The witness was accused of committing perjury.*

perk¹ /pɜːk/ **noun** [C] an advantage, such as money or a car, that you are given because of your job: [usually plural] *A mobile phone is one of the perks of the job.*

perk² /pɜːk/ **verb**

PHRASAL VERB **perk (sb) up** informal to start to feel happier, or to make someone feel happier: *A cup of coffee always perks me up in the morning.*

perm /pɜːm/ **noun** [C] the use of chemicals on someone's hair to make it have curls for several months, or the hairstyle that is made in this way: *I'm thinking of having a perm.* • **perm verb** [T]

permanence /ˈpɜːmənəns/ **noun** [U] the state of continuing forever or for a long time

permanent /ˈpɜːmənənt/ **adj** continuing forever or for a long time: *permanent damage* ◦ *a permanent job* • **permanently** adv *He moved here permanently in 2008.*

permeate /ˈpɜːmieɪt/ **verb** [T] formal to move gradually into every part of something: *The pungent smell of vinegar permeated the air.* ◦ *Drug dealers have permeated every level of society.*

permissible /pəˈmɪsəbl/ **adj** formal allowed by the rules: [+ to do sth] *It is not permissible to smoke inside the building.*

permission /pəˈmɪʃən/ **noun** [U] If you give someone permission to do something, you allow them to do it: *She gave him permission without asking any questions.* ◦ [+ to do sth] *He has permission to stay in the country for one more year.* ◦ *They even have to ask for permission before they go to the toilet.* ◦ *He took the car without permission.*

☑ Word partners for **permission**

ask for/give/grant/obtain/receive/refuse/seek permission • permission for sth

permissive /pəˈmɪsɪv/ **adj** allowing people to behave in ways that other people may not approve of: *permissive attitudes*

permit¹ /pəˈmɪt/ **verb** (**permitting, permitted**) **1** [T] formal to allow something: [often passive] *Photography is not permitted inside the museum.* ◦ [+ to do sth] *He permitted them to leave.* **2** [I] to make something possible: *The match starts at 3 p.m., weather permitting.*

permit² /ˈpɜːmɪt/ **noun** [C] an official document that allows you to do something: *a work permit* ◦ *You need a permit to park your car here.*

pernicious /pəˈnɪʃəs/ **adj** formal very harmful

perpendicular /ˌpɜːpənˈdɪkjʊlər/ **adj** at an angle of 90 degrees to something

perpetrate /ˈpɜːpɪtreɪt/ **verb** [T] formal to do something very bad: [often passive] *They heard of torture perpetrated by the army.*

perpetrator /ˈpɜːpɪtreɪtər/ **noun** [C] formal someone who has done something very bad: *There is great public pressure to bring the perpetrators of these crimes to justice.*

perpetual /pəˈpetʃuəl/ **adj** never ending: *He seems to be in a perpetual state of confusion.* • **perpetually** adv

perpetuate /pəˈpetʃueɪt/ **verb** [T] formal to make something continue, especially something bad

People think of him as a cruel man, an image perpetuated by the media.

perplexed /pəˈplekst/ **adj** confused: *He seemed a little perplexed by the question.* • **perplex verb** [T]

perplexing /pəˈpleksɪŋ/ **adj** confusing: *a perplexing problem*

persecute /ˈpɜːsɪkjuːt/ **verb** [T] to treat someone unfairly or cruelly because of their race, religion, or beliefs: [often passive] *He was persecuted for his religious beliefs.* • **persecution** /ˌpɜːsɪˈkjuːʃən/ **noun** [U] *political/religious persecution*

persecutor /ˈpɜːsɪkjuːtər/ **noun** [C] someone who persecutes people

perseverance /ˌpɜːsɪˈvɪərəns/ **noun** [U] the quality of persevering when things are difficult: *Hard work and perseverance do pay off in the end.*

persevere /ˌpɜːsɪˈvɪər/ **verb** [I] to continue to try to do something although it is difficult: *Despite the difficulties, I decided to **persevere with** the project.*

persist /pəˈsɪst/ **verb** [I] **1** If an unpleasant feeling or situation persists, it continues to exist: *If symptoms persist, consult a doctor.* **2** to continue to do something although it is annoying other people: *He **persists in** calling me Jane, even though I've corrected him twice.*

persistence /pəˈsɪstəns/ **noun** [U] the state or action of persisting

persistent /pəˈsɪstənt/ **adj 1** Something unpleasant that is persistent continues for a long time or is difficult to get rid of: *a persistent cough* **2** A persistent person continues to do something although other people do not want them to: *He can be very persistent sometimes.* • **persistently adv** *He has persistently lied to us.*

person /ˈpɜːsən/ **noun** (plural **people**) **1** 🅐 [C] a human being: *You're the only person I know here.* ◦ *He is a very dangerous person.* **2 in person** 🅑 If you do something in person, you go somewhere to do it yourself: *If you can't be there in person the next best thing is watching it on TV.* → See also **the first person, the second person, the third person**

persona /pəˈsəʊnə/ **noun** [C] (plural **personae**, **personas**) the way your character seems to other people: *He's trying to improve his **public persona**.*

personal /ˈpɜːsənəl/ **adj 1** RELATING TO A PERSON ▷ [always before noun] 🅑 relating to or belonging to a particular person: *I can only speak from my own **personal experience**.* ◦ *Please ensure you take all **personal belongings** with you when you leave the train.* ◦ *This is a personal view and not that of the government.* **2** PRIVATE ▷ 🅑 relating to the private parts of someone's life, including their relationships and feelings: *He's got a few **personal problems** at the moment.* ◦ *She prefers to keep her personal and professional lives separate.* **3** FOR ONE PERSON ▷ [always before noun] 🅑 designed for or used by one person: *a personal computer/tutor* ◦ *a personal loan/pension* **4** RUDE ▷ rude about or offensive towards someone: *I know you're upset, but there's no need to **get personal** (= start making offensive remarks).* **5** BODY ▷

[always before noun] relating to your body: *personal hygiene*

personal digital aˈssistant noun [C] (abbreviation **PDA**) a small computer that you can carry with you

personality /ˌpɜːsənˈæləti/ **noun 1** CHARACTER ▷ [C] 🅑 the way you are as a person: *She's got a lovely, **bubbly personality**.* **2** FAMOUS ▷ [C] 🅑 a famous person: *a well-known TV personality* **3** INTERESTING ▷ [U] 🅑 the quality of having a very strong or interesting character: *Sales people need a lot of personality.*

☑ Word partners for **personality**

a **bubbly/forceful/outgoing/warm** personality

personalized (also UK **-ised**) /ˈpɜːsənəlaɪzd/ **adj** A personalized object has someone's name on it, or has been made for a particular person: *a personalized fitness plan* • **personalize** (also UK **-ise**) **verb** [T]

personally /ˈpɜːsənəli/ **adv 1** 🅑 done by you and not someone else: *I'd like to personally apologize for the delay.* **2** 🅑 used when you are going to give your opinion: *Personally, I'd rather stay at home and watch TV.* **3 take sth personally** to think that someone is criticizing you when they are not: *You mustn't take everything so personally.*

personal ˈorganizer noun [C] a small book or computer containing a calendar, address book, etc → See **PDA**

personal ˈpronoun noun [C] a word that is used to refer to a person in speech or in writing. For example the words 'I', 'you', and 'they' are personal pronouns.

personal ˈtrainer noun [C] a person whose job is to help you improve the shape of your body by showing you what exercises to do

personify /pəˈsɒnɪfaɪ/ **verb** [T] If someone personifies a particular quality, they are a perfect example of that quality: *She seems to personify honesty and goodness.* • **personified adj** [always after noun] *Tom has always been laziness personified.* • **personification** /pəˌsɒnɪfɪˈkeɪʃən/ **noun** [U]

personnel /ˌpɜːsənˈel/ **noun 1** [plural] the people who work for an organization: *military personnel* **2** [U] the department of an organization that deals with finding people to work there, keeping records about them, etc: *I need to speak to someone in Personnel.* ◦ *the personnel manager*

perspective /pəˈspektɪv/ **noun 1** [C] the way you think about something: *Being unemployed has made me see things **from a different perspective**.* **2** [U] a way of drawing things so that they appear to be a realistic size and in a realistic position **3 put sth in/into perspective** If something puts a problem into perspective, it makes you understand how unimportant that problem is.

☑ Word partners for **perspective**

from sb's perspective • **from** a [historical/political, etc] perspective • perspective **on** sth

perspicacious /ˌpɜːspɪˈkeɪʃəs/ **adj** formal quick in noticing, understanding, or judging things accurately

perspiration /ˌpɜːspəˈreɪʃⁱn/ **noun** [U] formal the liquid that comes out of your skin when you get hot

perspire /pəˈspaɪəʳ/ **verb** [I] formal to produce liquid through your skin because you are hot or nervous

persuade /pəˈsweɪd/ **verb** [T] ⓘ to make someone agree to do something by talking to them a lot about it: [+ to do sth] *We managed to persuade him to come with us.* ○ [+ (that)] *I persuaded her that it was the right thing to do.* → Opposite **dissuade**

persuasion /pəˈsweɪʒⁱn/ **noun 1** [U] the act of persuading someone: *I'm sure she'll agree, she just needs a little **gentle persuasion**.* **2** [C] formal a political, religious, or moral belief: *There were people of all persuasions there.*

persuasive /pəˈsweɪsɪv/ **adj** able to make people agree to do something: *It's a very **persuasive argument**.* • **persuasively adv**

pertain /pəˈteɪn/ **verb**

PHRASAL VERB **pertain to sth** formal to relate to something: *Some important evidence pertaining to the case has been overlooked.*

pertinent /ˈpɜːtɪnənt/ **adj** formal relating directly to a subject: *a pertinent question*

perturbed /pəˈtɜːbd/ **adj** worried or upset: *He seemed slightly perturbed by the news.* • **perturb verb** [T]

peruse /pəˈruːz/ **verb** [T] formal to look at or read something in order to find what interests you

pervade /pəˈveɪd/ **verb** [T] formal to move gradually through every part of something: *Cheap perfume and tobacco pervaded the room.*

pervasive /pəˈveɪsɪv/ **adj** formal moving into or through everywhere or everything: *a pervasive smell* ○ *the **pervasive influence** of television*

perverse /pəˈvɜːs/ **adj** strange and not what most people would expect or enjoy: *In a perverse way, I enjoy going to the dentist.* • **perversely adv**

perversion /pəˈvɜːʃⁱn/ **noun** [C, U] **1** getting sexual pleasure in a way that seems strange or unpleasant **2** changing something that is right into something that is wrong: *the perversion of justice*

pervert¹ /ˈpɜːvɜːt/ **noun** [C] someone who gets sexual pleasure in a strange or unpleasant way

pervert² /pəˈvɜːt/ **verb** [T] to change something that is right into something that is wrong: *They were charged with conspiracy to **pervert the course of justice.***

perverted /pəˈvɜːtɪd/ **adj** relating to getting sexual pleasure in a strange or unpleasant way

pessimism /ˈpesɪmɪzⁱm/ **noun** [U] the belief that bad things will happen → Opposite **optimism**

pessimist /ˈpesɪmɪst/ **noun** [C] someone who always believes that bad things will happen: *Don't be such a pessimist!*

pessimistic /ˌpesɪˈmɪstɪk/ **adj** ⓘ always believing that bad things will happen: *He was feelin*(g) that bad things will happen: *He was feelin* **pessimistic about** the future. → Opposite **opti****mistic**

pest /pest/ **noun** [C] **1** an animal that cause(s) damage to plants, food, etc: *Most farmers thin*(k) *foxes are pests.* **2** informal an annoying person

pester /ˈpestəʳ/ **verb** [T] to annoy someone b(y) asking them something again and again: [+ to d(o) sth] *He's been pestering me to go out with him a(ll) week.*

pesticide /ˈpestɪsaɪd/ **noun** [C, U] a chemical tha(t) is used to kill insects which damage plants

pet¹ /pet/ **noun** [C] ⓐ an animal that someon(e) keeps in their home: *my pet rabbit*

pet² /pet/ **verb** [T] (**petting, petted**) **1** to touch a(n) animal because you feel affection for it **2** t(o) touch someone in a sexual way

petal /ˈpetⁱl/ **noun** [C] one of the thin, flat(,) coloured parts on the outside of a flower: *ros*(e) *petals*

peter /ˈpiːtəʳ/ **verb**

PHRASAL VERB **peter out** to gradually stop o(r) disappear: *The track petered out after a mile or s*(o)

pet 'hate **noun** [C] UK (US **pet 'peeve**) some(-) thing that annoys you a lot: *That's one of my pe*(t) *hates – people who smoke while other people ar*(e) *eating.*

petite /pəˈtiːt/ **adj** A petite woman is small an(d) thin in an attractive way.

petition¹ /pəˈtɪʃⁱn/ **verb** [I, T] to officially as(k) someone in authority to do something: [+ to d(o) sth] *They are petitioning the government t*(o) *increase funding for the project.*

petition² /pəˈtɪʃⁱn/ **noun** [C] a document tha(t) has been signed by a lot of people officiall(y) asking someone in authority to do something: *Will you sign this **petition against** experiments o*(n) *animals?*

> ⧉ Word partners for **petition**
>
> launch/organize/sign a petition • a petition against/(calling) for sth

petrified /ˈpetrɪfaɪd/ **adj** extremely frightened(:) *I'm **petrified of** spiders.*

petrol /ˈpetrⁱl/ **noun** [U] UK (US **gas**) ⓐ a liqui(d) fuel used in cars: *unleaded petrol*

petroleum /pəˈtrəʊliəm/ **noun** [U] thick oi(l) found under the Earth's surface which is use(d) to produce petrol and other substances

'petrol ,station noun [C] UK (US **'gas ,station**) ⓐ a place where you can buy petrol

petticoat /ˈpetɪkəʊt/ **noun** [C] a thin piece o(f) women's clothing worn under a dress or skirt

petty /ˈpeti/ **adj 1** [always before noun] unim(-) portant or not serious: *petty crime* **2** [neve(r) before noun] complaining too much about unim(-) portant things: *You can be so petty sometimes!*

petulant /ˈpetʃələnt/ **adj** behaving in an angry(,) silly way like a child

pew /pjuː/ **noun** [C] a long seat in a church

pewter /ˈpjuːtəʳ/ **noun** [U] a blue-grey metal

phantom¹ /ˈfæntəm/ **noun** [C] the spirit of (a) dead person

phantom² /'fæntəm/ **adj** [always before noun] imagined, not real: *phantom pains*

pharaoh /'feərəʊ/ **noun** [C] a king of ancient Egypt

pharmaceutical /ˌfɑːmə'sjuːtɪkəl/ **adj** relating to the production of medicines: *a pharmaceutical company* ○ *the pharmaceutical industry* • **pharmaceuticals noun** [plural] medicines

pharmacist /'fɑːməsɪst/ **noun** [C] ⑫ someone who is trained to prepare or sell medicines

pharmacy /'fɑːməsi/ **noun 1** [C] ⑪ a shop or part of a shop that prepares and sells medicines **2** [U] the study of the preparation of medicines

phase¹ /feɪz/ **noun** [C] ⑫ a stage or period that is part of a longer period: *The first phase of the project is scheduled for completion next year.* ○ *My younger daughter is going through a phase of only wearing black.*

> 🗨 Word partners for **phase**
>
> **enter/go through** a phase • a **passing** phase • a phase **of** sth

phase² /feɪz/ **verb**

PHRASAL VERBS **phase sth in** to gradually start using a new system, process, or law: *The new tax will be phased in over five years.* • **phase sth out** to gradually stop using something

phat /fæt/ **adj** very informal very good: *The band had a really phat sound.*

PhD /ˌpiːeɪtʃ'diː/ **noun** [C] an advanced university qualification, or a person who has this qualification: *a PhD course/programme* ○ *Maria has a PhD in mathematics.*

pheasant /'fezənt/ **noun** [C] (plural **pheasants** or **pheasant**) a bird with a long tail that is shot for food

phenomenal /fɪ'nɒmɪnəl/ **adj** extremely successful or showing great qualities or abilities: *The film has been a phenomenal success.* • **phenomenally adv**

phenomenon /fɪ'nɒmɪnən/ **noun** [C] (plural **phenomena**) something that exists or happens, usually something unusual: *storms, lightning, and other natural phenomena* ○ *Road rage seems to be a fairly recent phenomenon.*

phew (also **whew**) /fjuː/ **exclamation** used when you are happy that something is not going to happen, or when you are tired or hot

philanthropist /fɪ'lænθrəpɪst/ **noun** [C] someone who gives money to people who need help

phile /-faɪl/ **suffix** makes a noun meaning 'enjoying or liking something': *a Francophile* (= *someone who loves France*) ○ *a bibliophile* (= *someone who loves books*)

philosopher /fɪ'lɒsəfər/ **noun** [C] ⑫ someone who studies or writes about the meaning of life

philosophical /ˌfɪlə'sɒfɪkəl/ **adj 1** relating to the study or writing of philosophy: *a philosophical problem/question* **2** accepting unpleasant situations in a calm and wise way: *She seems fairly philosophical about the failure of her marriage.* • **philosophically adv**

philosophy /fɪ'lɒsəfi/ **noun 1** [C, U] ⑫ the study or writing of ideas about the meaning of life, or a particular set of ideas about the meaning of life: *Descartes is considered by many to be the father of modern philosophy.* **2** [C] a way of thinking about what you should do in life: *My philosophy has always been to give those with ability the chance to progress.*

phisher /'fɪʃər/ **noun** [C] a person who tries to trick people into giving information over the Internet or by email so that they can take money out of their bank account: *Phishers use emails to steal your identity.*

phishing /'fɪʃɪŋ/ **noun** [U] the practice of sending emails to people to trick them into giving information that would let someone take money from their Internet bank account (= an arrangement with your bank to keep your money there and take it out when you need it)

phlegm /flem/ **noun** [U] a thick liquid produced in your lungs, throat, and nose when you have a cold (= common illness that makes you sneeze)

phlegmatic /fleg'mætɪk/ **adj** formal Someone who is phlegmatic is calm and does not get excited easily.

-phobe /-fəʊb/ **suffix** someone who hates something: *a commitment-phobe* (= *a person who hates commitment*)

phobia /'fəʊbiə/ **noun** [C] an extreme fear of something: *My mum's got a phobia about birds.*

phone¹ /fəʊn/ **noun** (also **telephone**) **1** [U] a communication system that is used to talk to someone who is in another place: *We'll contact you by phone when we get the results.* **2** [C] ⑩ a piece of equipment that is used to talk to someone who is in another place: *Would someone please answer the phone?* ○ *I could hear the phone ringing.* **3 on the phone** using the phone: *She's been on the phone all night.*

> 🗨 Word partners for **phone**
>
> **answer/pick up** the phone • **put** the phone **down** • a phone **rings** • **by/over** the phone • a phone **bill/company/conversation**

phone² /fəʊn/ **verb** [I, T] (also **phone up**) ⑪ to communicate with someone by telephone: *I tried to phone her last night, but she was out.* ○ *I'm going to phone for a taxi.* → See Note at **telephone²**

> ❗ Common learner error: **phone** or **call**?
>
> In British English the verbs **phone** or **call** are used to mean communicate with someone by telephone. You can also use the expressions 'give someone a ring/call' or 'ring (someone)'.
> *I'll phone you tomorrow.*
> *I'll give you a ring tomorrow.*
> *I'll ring you tomorrow.*
> In American English **call** is the usual verb that means telephone someone.
> *Call me later.*
> *I'll call you tomorrow.*

'**phone appli,cation noun** [C] (also informal

phone app) a small computer program that you can put onto a mobile phone

phone book noun [C] a book that contains the telephone numbers of people who live in a particular area

phone box noun [C] UK (US **phone booth**) a small structure containing a public telephone → See picture at **telephone**

phone call noun [C] If you make a phone call, you use the telephone: *Will you excuse me, I've got to **make a phone call**.*

phone card noun [C] a small piece of plastic used to pay for the use of some telephones

phone hacking noun [U] the activity of illegally listening to someone else's telephone conversations and telephone messages: *The editor of the newspaper is due to stand trial in July on charges of mobile **phone hacking**.*

phone-in /'fəʊnɪn/ noun [C] UK (US **call-in**) a television or radio programme in which the public can ask questions or give opinions over the telephone

phone number noun [C] the number of a particular telephone

phonetic /fəˈnetɪk/ adj relating to the sounds you make when you speak: *the international phonetic alphabet* • **phonetically** adv

phonetics /fəˈnetɪks/ noun [U] the study of the sounds made by the human voice in speech

phoney¹ UK informal (US **phony**) /'fəʊni/ adj not real: *He gave the police a phoney number.*

phoney² UK informal (US **phony**) /'fəʊni/ noun [C] someone who is not sincere • **phoney** UK (US **phony**) adj informal *a phoney smile*

phosphate /'fɒsfeɪt/ noun [C, U] a chemical that is used in cleaning products and to help plants grow

photo /'fəʊtəʊ/ noun [C] ⓐ a picture produced with a camera: *a black-and-white/colour photo* ○ *I **took** a photo of Jack lying on the beach.*

photocopier /'fəʊtəʊˌkɒpiə'/ noun [C] a machine that produces copies of documents by photographing them → See colour picture **The Office** on page Centre 5

photocopy /'fəʊtəʊˌkɒpi/ noun [C] ⓑ a copy of a document made with a photocopier: *I **made** a photocopy of my letter before sending it.* • **photocopy** verb [T]

photogenic /ˌfəʊtəʊˈdʒenɪk/ adj Someone who is photogenic has the type of face that looks attractive in a photograph.

photograph¹ /'fəʊtəgrɑːf/ noun [C] ⓐ a picture produced with a camera: *a black-and-white/colour photograph* ○ *He **took** a lovely photograph of the children in the garden.*

photograph² /'fəʊtəgrɑːf/ verb [T] ⓑ to take a photograph of someone or something: *They were photographed leaving a nightclub together.*

photographer /fəˈtɒɡrəfə'/ noun [C] ⓐ someone whose job is to take photographs

photographic /ˌfəʊtəˈɡræfɪk/ adj [always before noun] relating to photographs: *photographic equipment/film* ○ **photographic evidence**

photography /fəˈtɒɡrəfi/ noun [U] ⓐ the activity or job of taking photographs

phrasal verb /ˌfreɪzəlˈvɜːb/ noun [C] ⓑ a verb together with an adverb or preposition that has a different meaning to the meaning of its separate parts. For example 'look up' and 'carry on' are phrasal verbs. → See Study Page **Phrasal verbs** on page Centre 24 → See colour picture **Phrasal Verbs** on page Centre 16

phrase¹ /freɪz/ noun [C] ⓑ a group of words that are often used together and have a particular meaning

phrase² /freɪz/ verb [T] to express something by choosing to use particular words: *It might have been better if he had phrased it differently.*

physical¹ /'fɪzɪkəl/ adj **1** ⓑ relating to the body: *physical fitness/strength* ○ *People put too much emphasis on **physical appearance** (= what you look like).* **2** [always before noun] relating to real things that you can see and touch: *There was no physical evidence linking Jones to Shaw's murder.*

physical² /'fɪzɪkəl/ noun [C] US (UK **medical**) an examination of your body by a doctor to find out if you are healthy

physical education noun [U] (abbreviation **PE**) classes at school where children do exercise and play sport

physically /'fɪzɪkəli/ adv ⓑ in a way that relates to the body: *physically attractive/fit*

physical therapist noun [C] US (also UK/US **physiotherapist**) someone whose job is to give people physical therapy

physical therapy noun [U] US (also UK/US **physiotherapy**) treatment for illness or injury in which you practise moving parts of your body

physician /fɪˈzɪʃən/ noun [C] formal a doctor

physicist /'fɪzɪsɪst/ noun [C] someone who studies physics

physics /'fɪzɪks/ noun [U] ⓐ the scientific study of natural forces, such as energy, heat, light, etc

physio /'fɪziəʊ/ noun [C, U] UK informal short for physiotherapy or physiotherapist

physiological /ˌfɪziəˈlɒdʒɪkəl/ adj relating to how the bodies of living things work

physiology /ˌfɪziˈɒlədʒi/ noun [U] the scientific study of how the bodies of living things work

physiotherapist /ˌfɪziəʊˈθerəpɪst/ noun [C] (also US **physical therapist**) someone whose job is to give people physiotherapy

physiotherapy /ˌfɪziəʊˈθerəpi/ noun [U] (also US **physical therapy**) treatment for illness or injury in which you practise moving parts of your body

physique /fɪˈziːk/ noun [C] the shape and size of your body: *He has a very muscular physique.*

pianist /'piːənɪst/ noun [C] someone who plays the piano

piano /piˈænəʊ/ noun [C] ⓐ a large wooden musical instrument with strings inside and black and white bars that produce sounds when you press them

piano

→ See also **grand piano**

pick¹ /pɪk/ verb [T] **1** CHOOSE ▷ ⓐ to choose something or someone: *Do you want to help me pick some numbers for my lottery ticket?* ∘ *I was never picked for the school football team.* **2** FLOWERS/FRUIT, ETC ▷ ⓐ If you pick flowers, fruit, etc, you take them off a tree or out of the ground: *I picked some apples this morning.* **3** REMOVE ▷ to remove small pieces from something with your fingers: *You'll have to let the glue dry and then you can pick it off.* **4 pick a fight/argument** to start a fight or argument with someone **5 pick sb's pocket** to steal something from someone's pocket → See also **have a bone¹ to pick with sb**

PHRASAL VERBS **pick at sth 1** FOOD ▷ to only eat a small amount of your food because you are worried or ill: *He picked at his food but had no appetite.* **2** REMOVE ▷ to remove small pieces from something with your fingers: *If you keep picking at that scab, it'll never heal.* • **pick on sb** ⓑ to choose a person and criticize or treat them unfairly: *He just started picking on me for no reason.* • **pick sth/sb out** to choose someone or something from a group of people or things: *She picked out a red shirt for me to try on.* • **pick sth/ sb up 1** ⓐ to lift something or someone by using your hands: *He picked his coat up off the floor.* ∘ *Just pick up the phone and call him.* → See colour picture **Phrasal Verbs** on page Centre 16 **2** ⓐ to collect someone who is waiting for you, or to collect something that you have left somewhere: *Can you pick me up from the airport?* • **pick sth up 1** GET ▷ to get something: *She picked up some real bargains in the sale.* **2** LEARN ▷ ⓑ to learn a new skill or language by practising it and not by being taught it: *He hadn't done any skiing before, but he picked it up really quickly.* **3** ILLNESS ▷ to get an illness from someone or something: *She picked up a nasty stomach bug while she was on holiday.* **4** SIGNAL ▷ If a piece of equipment picks up a signal, it receives it: *Antennas around the top of the ship picked up the radar signals.* **5** NOTICE ▷ to notice something: *Police dogs picked up the scent of the two men from clothes they had left behind.* • **pick sb up 1** to start talking to someone in order to try to begin a romantic relationship with them **2** If the police pick someone up, they take that person to the police station. • **pick up 1** If a business or social situation picks up, it improves: *Business is really starting to pick up now.* **2** If the wind picks up, it becomes stronger. • **pick up sth** If a vehicle picks up speed, it starts to go faster.

pick² /pɪk/ noun **1** [C] a sharp metal stick used to break hard ground or rocks **2 the pick of sth** the best of a group of things or people **3 have/take your pick** to choose what you want: *We've got tea, coffee, or hot chocolate – take your pick.*

picket /'pɪkɪt/ noun [C] (also **'picket ˌline**) a group of people who stand outside a building in order to show their anger about something and to try to stop people going inside • **picket** verb [I, T] *Protesters picketed cinemas across the whole country.*

ˌpicket 'fence noun [C] US a low fence made from a row of flat sticks that are pointed at the top

pickle /'pɪkl/ noun **1** [C, U] UK food that has been put into vinegar or salt water for a long time and has a sour taste: *cold meat and pickles* **2** [C] US a small cucumber (= a green, cylindrical vegetable) that has been put in vinegar or in a liquid containing salt and spices • **pickled** adj *pickled onions*

pickpocket /'pɪkˌpɒkɪt/ noun [C] someone who steals things from people's pockets

pickup /'pɪkʌp/ noun [C] (also **'pickup ˌtruck**) US a small, open truck

picky /'pɪki/ adj informal Someone who is picky does not like many things: *a **picky eater***

picnic /'pɪknɪk/ noun [C] ⓐ a meal that you make and take with you somewhere to eat outside: *We're going to **have a picnic** down by the lake.* • **picnic** verb [I] (**picnicking, picnicked**)

pictorial /pɪk'tɔːriəl/ adj relating to pictures or shown using pictures

picture¹ /'pɪktʃər/ noun [C] **1** DRAWING ETC ▷ ⓐ a drawing, painting, or photograph of something or someone: *to **draw/paint** a picture* ∘ *She's got pictures of pop stars all over her bedroom wall.* ∘ *Did you **take** many pictures (= photograph many things) while you were in Sydney?* → See colour picture **The Living Room** on page Centre 4 **2** IDEA ▷ ⓑ an idea of what something is like: [usually singular] *I've got a much clearer picture of what's happening now.* **3** TV ▷ ⓑ the image on a television screen: *I'm afraid it's not a very good picture.* **4** FILM ▷ ⓑ a film: *Could this be the first animated film to win a best picture award?* **5 the pictures** old-fashioned the cinema: *I really fancy going to the pictures tonight.*

IDIOMS **get the picture** informal used to say that someone understands a situation: *Oh right, I get the picture.* • **paint a bleak/rosy, etc picture of sth** to describe something in a particular way: *She paints a rosy (= happy) picture of family life.* • **put/keep sb in the picture** informal to explain to someone what is happening: *Jim had no idea what was going on till I put him in the picture.*

☑ Word partners for **picture**

draw/paint a picture • **take** a picture • a picture **of** sb/sth • **in** a picture

---

picture² /'pɪktʃər/ verb [T] **1** to imagine something in a particular way: *The house isn't at all how I had pictured it.* **2** to show someone or something in a picture: [often passive] *They were pictured holding hands on the beach.*

'picture ˌmessaging noun [C] sending and receiving pictures on a mobile phone

picturesque /ˌpɪktʃər'esk/ adj ⓑ A picturesque place is attractive to look at: *a picturesque cottage on the edge of the Yorkshire Moors*

pie /paɪ/ noun [C, U] ⓑ a type of food made with meat, vegetables, or fruit which is covered in pastry and baked: *apple/meat pie* → See also **mince pie**

P

piece¹ /piːs/ **noun** [C]
1 AMOUNT/PART ▷ **A2**
an amount of something, or a part of something: *a **piece** of paper/wood* ◦ *She cut the flan into eight pieces.* ◦ *Some of the*

pie

pieces seem to be missing. ◦ *These shoes are **falling to pieces** (= breaking into pieces).* → See colour picture **Pieces and Quantities** on page Centre 1 **2 ONE** ▷ **A2** one of a particular type of thing: *a useful **piece** of equipment* **3 SOME** ▷ **B1** some of a particular type of thing: *a **piece** of news/information* ◦ *Can I give you a **piece** of advice?* **4 ART/WRITING, ETC** ▷ **B2** an example of artistic, musical, or written work: *There was an interesting piece on alternative medicine in the paper yesterday.* **5 ten-/twenty-, etc pence piece** a coin with a value of ten/twenty, etc pence (= British money)

IDIOMS **be a piece of cake** informal **B2** to be very easy: *The test was a piece of cake.* ● **give sb a piece of your mind** informal to speak angrily to someone because they have done something wrong ● **go/fall to pieces** If someone goes to pieces, they become so upset that they cannot control their feelings or think clearly: *He went to pieces when his mother died.*

→ See also **set-piece**

piece² /piːs/ **verb**

PHRASAL VERB **piece sth together** to try to understand something or discover the truth about something by collecting different pieces of information: *Police are trying to piece together a profile of the murderer.*

piecemeal /'piːsmiːl/ **adj, adv** happening very gradually: *The land is being sold in a **piecemeal** fashion over a number of years.*

pier

pier /pɪər/ **noun** [C] a long structure that is built from the land out over the sea and sometimes has entertainments, restaurants, etc on it

pierce /pɪəs/ **verb** [T] **1** to make a hole in something using a sharp point: *I'd like to have my **ears** pierced.* **2** literary If a light or a sound pierces something, it is suddenly seen or heard: *A few rays of sunlight pierced the bedroom shutters.*

piercing /'pɪəsɪŋ/ **adj 1** A piercing noise, light etc is very strong and unpleasant: *I heard a loud **piercing scream**.* **2** Piercing eyes seem to look at you very closely.

piety /'paɪəti/ **noun** [U] a strong belief in religious morals

pig¹ /pɪg/ **noun** [C] **1** **A1** a large pink, brown, or black farm animal that is kept for its meat **2** informal someone who is very unpleasant, or someone who eats a lot: *He's an ignorant pig.* → See also **guinea pig**

pig² /pɪg/ **verb** (**pigging, pigged**)

PHRASAL VERB **pig out** informal to eat too much: *We pigged out on the cakes and pastries.*

pigeon /'pɪdʒən/ **noun** [C] a grey bird that often lives on buildings in towns

pigeonhole¹ /'pɪdʒənhəʊl/ **noun** [C] one of a set of small open boxes in which letters or messages are left, especially in an office or hotel

pigeonhole² /'pɪdʒənhəʊl/ **verb** [T] If you pigeonhole someone, you unfairly decide what type of person they are.

piggyback /'pɪgibæk/ **noun** [C] (also **'piggyback ,ride**) a way of carrying someone on your back in which they put their arms and legs around you

piggy bank /'pɪgiˌbæŋk/ **noun** [C] a small container, often in the shape of a pig, used by children to keep money in

pigheaded /ˌpɪg'hedɪd/ **adj** refusing to change your opinion or the way you are doing something although it would be better if you did

piglet /'pɪglət/ **noun** [C] a baby pig

pigment /'pɪgmənt/ **noun** [C, U] a substance that gives something colour ● **pigmentation** /ˌpɪgmən'teɪʃən/ **noun** [U] the natural colour of a living thing

pigsty /'pɪgstaɪ/ **noun** [C] (also US **pigpen** /'pɪgpen/) a place where pigs are kept

pigtail /'pɪgteɪl/ **noun** [C] a hairstyle in which the hair is twisted together and tied: [usually plural] *A little girl in pigtails presented the flowers.*

pike /paɪk/ **noun** [C, U] (plural **pike**) a large river fish with sharp teeth, or the meat of this fish

Pilates /pɪ'lɑːtiːz/ **noun** [U] a system of physical exercise involving controlled movements, stretching and breathing

pile¹ /paɪl/ **noun 1** **B1** [C] an amount of a substance in the shape of a small hill or a number of objects on top of each other: *a **pile** of books/bricks* ◦ *a **pile** of sand/rubbish* ◦ *The clothes were arranged in piles on the floor.* **2 a pile of sth, piles of sth** informal **B2** a lot of something: *It's all right for him, he's got piles of money.*

> ☑ **Word partners for pile**
>
> a pile **of** sth ● be **in/put** sth **into** a pile

pile² /paɪl/ **verb**

PHRASAL VERBS **pile in/out** informal to enter/leave a place quickly and not in an organized way: *She opened the door and we all piled in.* ● **pile sth up** to make a lot of things into a pile by putting them on top of each other: *Just pile those books* up over there. • **pile up** ⓑ If something unpleasant piles up, you get more of it: *My work's really starting to pile up.*

ile-up /'paɪlʌp/ **noun** [C] an accident involving several cars

ilfer /'pɪlfər/ **verb** [I, T] to steal things that do not have much value

ilgrim /'pɪlgrɪm/ **noun** [C] someone who travels to a place that is important in their religion

ilgrimage /'pɪlgrɪmɪdʒ/ **noun** [C, U] a journey to a place that has religious importance: *to go on a pilgrimage to Mecca*

ill /pɪl/ **noun 1** ⓑ [C] a small, hard piece of medicine that you swallow: *a vitamin pill* ∘ *I've taken a couple of pills, but my headache still hasn't gone.* → See picture at **medicine 2 the pill** a pill that prevents a woman from becoming pregnant → See also **sleeping pill**

illar /'pɪlər/ **noun 1** [C] a tall structure made of stone, wood, etc that supports something above it: *The new bridge will be supported by 100 concrete pillars.* **2 a pillar of sth** someone or something who is very important to a place, organization, etc: *He was a pillar of the local community.*

illow /'pɪləʊ/ **noun** [C] ⓐ a soft object that you rest your head on in bed

illowcase /'pɪləʊkeɪs/ **noun** [C] a cloth cover for a pillow

ilot /'paɪlət/ **noun** [C] ⓐ someone who flies an aircraft • **pilot verb** [T]

imp /pɪmp/ **noun** [C] someone who controls the work and money of a prostitute (= person who has sex for money)

imple /'pɪmpl/ **noun** [C] a small spot on your skin • **pimply adj** → See also **goose pimple**

in¹ /pɪn/ **noun** [C] **1** ⓑ a thin piece of metal with a sharp point used to fasten pieces of cloth, etc together: *She pricked her finger on a pin.* **2** a thin piece of metal, wood, plastic, etc that holds or fastens things together: *He's had a metal pin put in his leg so that the bones heal properly.* → See also **drawing pin, pins and needles, rolling pin, safety pin**

in² /pɪn/ **verb** [T] (**pinning, pinned**) **1** ⓑ to fasten something with a pin: *We're not allowed to pin anything on these walls.* ∘ *She had a red ribbon pinned to her collar.* **2 pin sb to/against/under, etc** to force someone to stay in a position by holding them: *They pinned him to the ground.* → See also **pin your hopes (hope²) on sb/sth**

PHRASAL VERBS **pin sb down 1** to make someone give you details or a decision about something: *I've been trying to get a decision from Jim, but he's very difficult to pin down.* **2** to force someone to stay in a horizontal position by holding them: *They pinned him down on the floor.* • **pin sth down** to discover exact details about something: *Investigators are trying to pin down the cause of the fire.* • **pin sth on sb** informal to blame someone for something they did not do: *They tried to pin the murder on the dead woman's husband.* • **pin sth up** to fasten something to a wall using a pin: *The exam results have been pinned up on the noticeboard.*

PIN /pɪn/ **noun** [C] (also **'PIN ,number**) abbreviation for Personal Identification Number: the secret number that allows you to use a bank card in a machine

pinafore /'pɪnəfɔːr/ **noun** [C] mainly UK (US **jumper**) a loose dress with no sleeves that is worn over other clothes such as a shirt

pincer /'pɪnsər/ **noun** [C] one of a pair of curved hand-like parts of an animal such as a crab (= round, flat sea animal with ten legs)

pinch¹ /pɪntʃ/ **verb** [T] **1** to press someone's skin tightly between your thumb and first finger, sometimes causing pain: *One of the kids had been pinching her and she was crying.* **2** mainly UK informal to steal something that does not have much value: *Who's pinched my ruler?*

pinch² /pɪntʃ/ **noun** [C] **1** a small amount of a substance that you pick up between your thumb and your first finger: *a pinch of salt* **2** the act of pressing part of the body or an area of skin tightly between your thumb and first finger **3 at a pinch** UK (US **in a pinch**) If something can be done at a pinch, it is possible but it is difficult: *We can fit ten round the table, at a pinch.*

IDIOM **feel the pinch** to have problems because you do not have enough money

→ See also **take sth with a pinch of salt¹**

pinched /pɪntʃt/ **adj** A pinched face looks thin and sick.

pine¹ /paɪn/ **noun 1** [C, U] (also **'pine ,tree**) ⓑ a tall tree with long, thin leaves shaped like needles **2** [U] the pale coloured wood from this tree

pine² /paɪn/ **verb** [I] (also **pine away**) to be sad because you want someone or something that has gone away: *He's pining for his ex-girlfriend.*

pineapple /'paɪnæpl/ **noun** [C, U] ⓑ a large fruit with thick skin and sharp leaves sticking out of the top, which is sweet and yellow inside

pineapple

pinecone /'paɪnˌkəʊn/ **noun** [C] a hard, brown, oval object that grows on pine and fir trees (= tall trees which stay green all winter)

ping /pɪŋ/ **verb** [I] to make a short, high noise like a bell: *They could hear the microwave pinging in the kitchen.* • **ping noun** [C]

Ping-Pong /'pɪŋpɒŋ/ **noun** [U] (also **table tennis**) trademark informal a game in which two or four people hit a small ball over a low net on a large table

pink /pɪŋk/ **adj** ⓐ being a pale red colour: *pretty, pink flowers* • **pink noun** [C, U] → See colour picture **Colours** on page Centre 12

pinnacle /'pɪnəkl/ **noun** [no plural] the highest or

best part of something: *At 35, she is at the* **pinnacle of** *her career.*

pinpoint /'pɪnpɔɪnt/ **verb** [T] to say exactly what or where something is: *It is difficult to pinpoint the exact time of death.*

pins and needles noun have **pins and needles** to feel slight sharp pains in a part of your body when you move it after keeping it still for a period of time

pint /paɪnt/ **noun** [C] **1** (written abbreviation **pt**) ⓑ a unit for measuring liquid, equal to 0.568 litres in the UK and 0.473 litres in the US → See Study Page **Measurements** on page Centre 31 **2** UK informal a pint of beer

pin-up /'pɪnʌp/ **noun** [C] an attractive, famous person who is often in big photographs that people stick to their walls, or the photograph of that person

pioneer /ˌpaɪə'nɪər/ **noun** [C] someone who is one of the first people to do something: *one of the pioneers of modern science* • **pioneer verb** [T] *He pioneered the use of lasers in surgery.*

pioneering /ˌpaɪə'nɪərɪŋ/ **adj** [always before noun] starting the development of something important: **pioneering work/research** on atomic energy

pious /'paɪəs/ **adj** having strong religious beliefs, and living or behaving in a way which shows these beliefs

pip¹ /pɪp/ **noun** [C] UK a small seed inside fruit such as apples and oranges

pip² /pɪp/ **verb** [T] (**pipping**, **pipped**) UK informal to beat someone by a very small amount

pipe¹ /paɪp/ **noun** [C] **1** ⓑ a long tube that liquid or gas can move through: *A water pipe had burst, flooding the basement.* **2** a tube with a bowl-shaped part at one end, used to smoke tobacco: *to smoke a pipe* → See also **exhaust pipe**

🗹 **Word partners for pipe**

a pipe **leads/runs** [from/to, etc] sth • a pipe **bursts/leaks** • **through** a pipe

---

pipe² /paɪp/ **verb** [T] to send something through a pipe: *Water is piped from a spring to houses in the local area.*

PHRASAL VERBS **pipe down** informal to stop making noise and become quieter • **pipe up** informal to suddenly say something: *Then Lydia piped up with her view of things.*

pipeline /'paɪplaɪn/ **noun** [C] a series of pipes that carry liquid or gas over a long distance

IDIOM **be in the pipeline** If a plan is in the pipeline, it is being developed and will happen in the future: *We have several projects in the pipeline.*

piping /'paɪpɪŋ/ **noun** [U] a piece of pipe: *copper piping*

piping hot adj Piping hot food is very hot.

piquant /'piːkənt/ **adj** formal having a pleasant, spicy taste

pique¹ /piːk/ **noun** [U] formal the feeling of being annoyed

pique² /piːk/ **verb** (**piquing**, **piqued**) **pique sb's**

curiosity/interest, etc to make someone interested in something

piqued /piːkt/ **adj** annoyed

piracy /'paɪərəsi/ **noun** [U] **1** attacking and stealing from ships **2** the illegal activity of copying and selling music, films, etc: *software/video piracy*

pirate¹ /'paɪrət/ **noun** [C] **1** ⓑ someone who attacks ships and steals from them **2** someone who illegally copies and sells music, films, etc

pirate² /'paɪrət/ **verb** [T] to illegally copy and sell music, films, etc

pirate³ /'paɪrət/ **adj** [always before noun] illegally copied: *a pirate CD/DVD*

Pisces /'paɪsiːz/ **noun** [C, U] the sign of the zodiac that relates to the period of 20 February – 20 March, or a person born during this period → See picture at **the zodiac**

piss¹ /pɪs/ **verb** [I] very informal a very impolite word meaning to pass urine from the body

PHRASAL VERB **piss sb off** very informal to annoy someone

piss² /pɪs/ **noun**

IDIOM **take the piss** UK very informal an impolite phrase meaning to make jokes about someone

pissed /pɪst/ **adj** very informal **1** mainly UK an impolite way of describing someone who has drunk too much alcohol **2** US an impolite way of describing someone who is angry

pissed off adj very informal an impolite way of describing someone who is angry

pistol /'pɪstəl/ **noun** [C] a small gun

piston /'pɪstən/ **noun** [C] a part of an engine that moves up and down and makes other parts of the engine move

pit¹ /pɪt/ **noun** [C] **1** HOLE ▷ a large hole that has been dug in the ground **2** SEED ▷ US (UK **stone**) a large, hard seed that grows inside some types of fruit and vegetables **3** COAL ▷ (also US **pit mine**) a place where coal is dug out from under the ground **4** the pits UK (US the pit) the place where racing cars stop to be repaired or filled with fuel during a race **5** be the pits informal to be very bad: *Our hotel was the absolute pits.*

pit² /pɪt/ **verb** (**pitting**, **pitted**)

PHRASAL VERB **pit sb/sth against sb/sth** to make someone or something compete against someone or something else: *Teams of athletes were pitted against each other.*

pitch¹ /pɪtʃ/ **verb 1** LEVEL ▷ [T] to make something suitable for a particular level or group of people: [often passive] *His talk was pitched at slightly too high a level for the audience.* **2** PERSUADE ▷ [I, T] mainly US to try to persuade someone to do something: *They are pitching for new business at the moment.* **3** pitch (sb/sth) forward/into, etc to suddenly move in a particular direction, or to make someone or something suddenly move in a particular direction: *He braked too hard and the car pitched forward.* **4** pitch a tent to choose a place for a tent and put it there **5** BALL ▷ [I, T] in baseball to throw the ball towards the person who going to hit it: *He used to pitch for the Chicago White Sox.* **6 SOUND** ▷ [T] to make sound at a particular level: *The tune was pitched much too high for me.*

PHRASAL VERB **pitch in** informal to help a group of people to do some work that needs to be done: *If we all pitch in, we'll get this kitchen cleaned up in no time.*

pitch² /pɪtʃ/ **noun 1 SPORT** ▷ [C] UK ⓔ (US **field**) an area of ground where a sport is played: *a cricket/football pitch* **2 THROW** ▷ [C] in baseball, a throw towards the person who is going to hit the ball: *He struck out two batters with six pitches.* **3 SOUND** ▷ [U] how high or low a sound is **4 PERSUADING** ▷ [C, U] the things someone says in order to persuade you to do something: *I wasn't very impressed by his **sales pitch**.* → See also **fever pitch**

pitch-black /ˌpɪtʃˈblæk/ **adj** (also **pitch-dark**) very dark: *Outside it was pitch-black.*

pitcher /ˈpɪtʃər/ **noun** [C] **1** in baseball, someone who throws the ball at the person who is going to hit it → See colour picture **Sports 2** on page Centre 15 **2** US a container for holding and pouring out liquids: *a pitcher of water*

pitfall /ˈpɪtfɔːl/ **noun** [C] a likely mistake or problem in a situation: *the pitfalls of buying a house*

pithy /ˈpɪθi/ **adj** A pithy remark expresses something in a very clear and direct way.

pitiful /ˈpɪtɪfəl/ **adj 1** making you feel pity: *I didn't recognize him, he looked so pitiful.* **2** very bad: *a pitiful excuse* • **pitifully adv**

pittance /ˈpɪtəns/ **noun** [no plural] a very small amount of money: *She works very long hours and yet she **earns a pittance**.*

pity¹ /ˈpɪti/ **noun 1 It's a pity...** ⓐ used to say that something is disappointing: *It's a pity you're not staying longer.* **2** ⓔ [U] a feeling of sympathy for someone: *I was hoping someone would **take pity on** me* (= help me in a difficult situation) *and give me a lift home.* → See also **self-pity**

> 🟩 **Word partners for pity**
> feel pity • take pity on sb • pity for sb

pity² /ˈpɪti/ **verb** [T] to feel sorry for someone: *She doesn't want people to pity her.*

pivot /ˈpɪvət/ **noun** [C] **1** a fixed point on which something balances or turns **2** the most important part of something • **pivot verb** [I, T]

pivotal /ˈpɪvətəl/ **adj** having a very important influence on something: *He has played a **pivotal role** in the negotiations.*

pixel /ˈpɪksəl/ **noun** [C] a small point that forms part of the image on a computer screen

pixie /ˈpɪksi/ **noun** [C] a small imaginary person who can do magic things

pizza /ˈpiːtsə/ **noun** [C, U] a food made from a flat, round piece of bread covered with cheese, vegetables, etc and cooked in an oven → See colour picture **Food** on page Centre 11

placard /ˈplækɑːd/ **noun** [C] a large sign with writing that someone carries, often to show that they disagree with something

placate /pləˈkeɪt/ ⓤ /ˈpleɪkeɪt/ **verb** [T] formal to make someone less angry about something

place¹ /pleɪs/ **noun 1 SOMEWHERE** ▷ [C] ⓐ a position, building, town, area, etc: *His leg's broken in two places.* ◦ *Edinburgh would be a nice place to live.* ◦ *What a stupid place to park.* **2 take place** ⓑ to happen: *The meeting will take place next week.* **3 in place a** in the correct position: *The chairs are all in place.* **b** If a rule, system, etc is in place, it has started to exist: *There are now laws in place to prevent this from happening.* **4 out of place a** not in the correct position: *Why are my files all out of place?* **b** not right or suitable for a particular situation: *Everyone else was wearing jeans and I felt completely out of place in my office clothes.* **5 all over the place** ⓔ in or to many different places: *There was blood all over the place.* **6 in place of sth** ⓔ instead of something: *Try adding fruit to your breakfast cereal in place of sugar.* **7 HOME** ▷ [C] informal ⓐ someone's home: *They've just bought a place in Spain.* **8 OPPORTUNITY** ▷ [C] ⓑ an opportunity to take part in something: *She's got a place at Liverpool University to do Spanish.* **9 in first/second/third, etc place** ⓑ If you are in first/second, etc place in a race or competition, that is your position: *He finished in fifth place.*

IDIOMS **fall into place** When events or details that you did not understand before fall into place, they become easy to understand. • **in the first place** ⓔ used to refer to the time when something started: *How did this error happen in the first place?* • **put sb in their place** to let someone know that they are not as important as they think they are

→ See also **decimal place, have/take pride¹ of place**

place² /pleɪs/ **verb 1 place sth in/on, etc** ⓔ to put something somewhere carefully: *She placed a large dish in front of me.* **2** [T] to cause someone to be in a situation: *One stupid action has placed us all at risk.* **3 can't place sb** to not be able to remember who someone is or where you have met them: *I recognize her face, but I can't quite place her.* **4 place an advertisement/bet/order, etc** to arrange to have an advertisement/bet/order, etc **5 place emphasis/importance, etc on sth** to give something emphasis/importance, etc: *They place a lot of importance on qualifications.*

place mat noun [C] a piece of cloth, paper, or plastic put on a table under someone's plate

placement /ˈpleɪsmənt/ **noun 1** [C] UK a position that someone has with an organization for a short time in order to learn about the work that is done there: *He got a month's placement on a national newspaper.* **2** [U, no plural] the act of putting something or someone somewhere: *the placement of additional police on the streets*

placid /ˈplæsɪd/ **adj** A placid person is calm and does not often get angry or excited. • **placidly adv**

plagiarism /ˈpleɪdʒərɪzəm/ **noun** [U] copying someone else's work or ideas: *He was accused of plagiarism.*

P

plagiarize (also UK **-ise**) /ˈpleɪdʒ°raɪz/ verb [I, T] to copy someone else's work or ideas • **plagiarist** /ˈpleɪdʒ°rɪst/ noun [C] someone who plagiarizes

plague¹ /pleɪg/ noun [C] **1** a serious disease that spreads quickly and kills a lot of people **2** a **plague of sth** a large number of something unpleasant that causes a lot of damage: *a plague of rats*

plague² /pleɪg/ verb [T] (**plaguing, plagued**) to make someone suffer for a long time: [often passive] *He's been plagued by bad luck ever since he bought that house.*

plaid /plæd/ noun [C, U] US cloth with a pattern of different coloured squares and crossing lines: *a plaid dress*

plain¹ /pleɪn/ adj **1 SIMPLE** ▷ **B1** simple and not complicated: *plain food* **2 NOT MIXED** ▷ **B1** not mixed with other colours, substances, etc: *a plain blue carpet* ∘ *plain yoghurt* **3 PERSON** ▷ A plain person is not attractive to look at. **4 OBVIOUS** ▷ obvious and clear: [+ (that)] *It's quite plain that she doesn't want to talk to me about it.* → See also **be plain sailing**

plain² /pleɪn/ adv informal **plain stupid/wrong, etc** completely stupid/wrong, etc: *That's just plain stupid!*

plain³ /pleɪn/ noun [C] a large area of flat land

plainclothes /ˈpleɪnˌkləʊðz/ adj [always before noun] Plainclothes police wear normal clothes and not a uniform.

plainly /ˈpleɪnli/ adv **1** in a simple way that is not complicated: *plainly dressed* **2** in a clear and obvious way: *This is plainly wrong.*

plaintiff /ˈpleɪntɪf/ noun [C] someone who takes legal action against someone else in a court of law

plaintive /ˈpleɪntɪv/ adj sounding sad: *a plaintive cry*

plait /plæt/ verb [T] mainly UK (US **braid**) to twist three pieces of hair, rope, etc together so that they form one long piece • **plait** mainly UK (US **braid**) noun [C] *She wore her hair in plaits.*

plan¹ /plæn/ noun [C] **1** ⓐ an arrangement for what you intend to do or how you intend to do something: *the country's economic plan* ∘ *Do you have any plans for the weekend?* ∘ *The plan is that we'll buy a car once we're there.* ∘ *There's been a change of plan and we're going on Wednesday instead.* ∘ *Luckily, everything went according to plan* (= happened the way it was planned). **2** ⓑ a drawing that shows how something appears from above or will appear from above when it is built: *a street plan.* ∘ *We had a designer draw up a plan for the yard.*

> ▢ **Word partners for plan**
> announce/approve/implement/oppose/outline/unveil a plan • an ambitious/controversial/strategic plan

plan² /plæn/ verb (**planning, planned**) **1** ⓑ to think about and decide what you are going to do or how you are going to do something: *We're just planning our trip.* ∘ *As a manager, you've got to plan ahead.* ∘ *I'd planned the meeting for*

Friday. **2 plan to do sth** ⓐ to intend to do something: *He plans to go to college next yea* **3** [T] to decide how something will be built: *W* got an architect to help us plan our new kitchen.

PHRASAL VERBS **plan on doing sth** to intend to do something: *We're planning on catching the earl train.* • **plan sth out** to think about and decid what you are going to do or how you are goin to do something: *Have you planned out you journey?* ∘ *I'm just planning out my day.*

plane¹ /pleɪn/ noun [C] **1 FLYING** ▷ ⓐ a vehicl that flies and has an engine and wings: *Whc time does her plane get in* (= arrive)? ∘ *He likes t watch the planes taking off and landing.* ∘ *plane crash* **2 TOOL** ▷ a tool that you use to mak wood smooth **3 SURFACE** ▷ in mathematics, flat surface

> ▢ **Word partners for plane**
> board/catch/get on/get off a plane • a plane gets in/lands/takes off • on a plane • by plane

plane² /pleɪn/ verb [T] to make a piece of woo smooth using a tool called a plane

planet /ˈplænɪt/ noun [C] ⓑ a large, roun object in space that moves around the sun o another star: *Jupiter is the largest planet of ou solar system.* • **planetary** adj relating to planet

planetarium /ˌplænɪˈteəriəm/ noun [C] (plur **planetariums** or **planetaria**) a building that ha a machine for showing the positions and move ments of the stars and planets

plank /plæŋk/ noun [C] a long, flat piece o wood: *wooden planks*

plankton /ˈplæŋktən/ noun [U] very smal plants and animals in the sea that are eaten b fish and other sea creatures

planner /ˈplænər/ noun [C] someone whose jo is to plan things, especially which buildings ar built in towns: *urban planners*

planning /ˈplænɪŋ/ noun [U] **1** ⓑ the activity o thinking about and deciding what you are goin to do or how you are going to do something *Events like these take months of careful planning* **2** control over which buildings are built in a area: *town planning* → See also **family plannin**

plant¹ /plɑːnt/ noun [C] **1** ⓐ a living thing tha grows in the soil or water and has leaves an roots, especially one that is smaller than a tree *Have you watered the plants?* ∘ *tomato plant* **2** a large factory where an industrial proces happens: *a nuclear power plant* → See als **potted plant**

plant² /plɑːnt/ verb [T] **1 SEEDS/PLANTS** ▷ ⓑ to put seeds or plants in the ground so tha they will grow: *to plant bulbs/seeds/tree* **2 SECRETLY** ▷ to secretly put something in place that will make someone seem guilty: *Sh insisted that the drugs had been planted on he without her knowledge.* **3 plant a bomb** ⓑ to pu a bomb somewhere so that it will explode ther **4 plant sth in/next/on, etc** to put somethin firmly in a particular place: *He planted himse next to me on the sofa.* **5 IDEA/DOUBTS** ▷ to mak someone start thinking something: *I was confident till you **planted doubts** in my mind.*

plantation /plæn'teɪʃᵊn/ **noun** [C] **1** an area of land in a hot country where a crop is grown: *a banana/cotton/sugar plantation* **2** an area of land where trees are grown to produce wood

plaque /plɑːk/ **noun 1** [C] a flat piece of metal or stone with writing on it which is fixed to a wall, often in order to make people remember a dead person **2** [U] a harmful substance that forms on your teeth

plasma /'plæzmə/ **noun** [U] the clear liquid part of blood that contains the blood cells

plasma ˌscreen noun [C] a screen for showing very clear words or pictures which uses special gases pressed between two flat pieces of glass

plaster¹ /'plɑːstəʳ/ **noun 1** [U] a substance that is spread on walls in order to make them smooth **2** [C] UK (US trademark **Band-Aid**) a small piece of sticky material that you put on cuts on your body **3 be in plaster** UK (US **be in a cast**) If your arm or leg is in plaster, it is covered in a hard, white substance to protect a broken bone.

plaster² /'plɑːstəʳ/ **verb** [T] **1** to cover most of a surface with something: *My boots were **plastered with** mud.* **2** to cover a wall with a substance in order to make it smooth

plastered /'plɑːstəd/ **adj** informal very drunk

plastic /'plæstɪk/ **noun** [C, U] ⓐ a light, artificial substance that can be made into different shapes when it is soft and is used in a lot of different ways: *Most children's toys are made of plastic.* • **plastic adj** ⓐ *a plastic bag*

plasticity /plæs'tɪsəti/ **noun** [U] formal the quality of being soft enough to make into many different shapes

plastic ˈsurgery noun [U] operations on someone's face or body to make them more attractive: *to have plastic surgery*

plastic ˌwrap noun [U] US (UK **clingfilm**) thin, transparent plastic used for wrapping or covering food

plate /pleɪt/ **noun 1 FOOD** ▷ [C] ⓐ a flat, round object that is used for putting food on: *a dinner plate* ∘ *a plate of biscuits* **2 METAL/GLASS** ▷ [C] a flat piece of metal or glass: *I had a metal plate put in my knee after the accident.* **3 gold/silver plate** metal with a thin layer of gold or silver on top **4 PICTURE** ▷ [C] a picture in a book → See also **license plate**, **L-plate**, **number plate**

plateau /'plætəʊ/ ⓤ /plæ'təʊ/ **noun** [C] (plural mainly UK **plateaux**, US **plateaus**) **1** a large area of high, flat land **2** a period when the level of something stays the same: [usually singular] *Sales are still good but they've **reached a plateau**.*

platform /'plætfɔːm/ **noun** [C] **1 RAISED SURFACE** ▷ ⓑ a raised surface for people to stand on, especially when they are speaking to a lot of people: *The speakers all stood on a platform.* **2 TRAIN** ▷ ⓐ the area in a railway station where you get on and off the train: *The train for London Paddington will depart from platform 12.* **3 POLITICS** ▷ all the things that a political party promises to do if they are elected: *They campaigned on a platform of low taxation.* **4 FOR**

OPINIONS ▷ a way of telling the public about your opinions: *Basically, he uses the newspaper as a **platform for** airing his political views.*

platinum /'plætɪnəm/ ⓤ /'plætnəm/ **noun** [U] a silver-coloured metal that is very valuable

platitude /'plætɪtjuːd/ **noun** [C] something that is boring because it has been said many times before

platonic /plə'tɒnɪk/ **adj** A platonic relationship is friendly and not sexual.

platoon /plə'tuːn/ **noun** [C] a small group of soldiers

platter /'plætəʳ/ **noun** [C] a large plate used for serving food

plaudit /'plɔːdɪt/ **noun** [C] formal praise: [usually plural] *He has **earned/won** plaudits (= been praised) for his latest novel.*

plausible /'plɔːzɪbl/ **adj** If something that someone says or writes is plausible, it could be true: *a **plausible excuse/explanation** →* Opposite **implausible** • **plausibility** /ˌplɔːzɪ'bɪləti/ **noun** [U] whether or not something is plausible

play¹ /pleɪ/ **verb 1 SPORTS/GAMES** ▷ [I, T] ⓐ to take part in a sport or game: *You play tennis, don't you Sam? ∘ We often used to play cards. ∘ I used to **play** netball **for** my school. ∘ I'm playing Tony (= playing against Tony) at squash tonight. ∘ Barcelona are **playing against** Real Madrid tonight.* **2 CHILDREN** ▷ [I, T] ⓐ If children play, they enjoy themselves with toys and games: *She likes **playing with** her dolls.* **3 MUSIC** ▷ [I, T] ⓐ to make music with a musical instrument: *Tim was playing the piano.* **4 RECORD/RADIO** ▷ [I, T] ⓐ If a radio, record, etc plays, it produces sounds, or if you play a radio, record, etc you make it produce sounds: *A radio was playing in the background. ∘ He plays his records late into the night.* **5 ACTING** ▷ [T] ⓑ to be a character in a film or play: *Morgan played the father in the film version.* **6 play a joke/trick on sb** ⓑ to deceive someone as a joke: *I played a trick on her and pretended we'd eaten all the food. →* See also **play it by ear**, **play games (game¹)**, **play (it) safe¹**, **play for time¹**, **play truant**

PHRASAL VERBS play about/around to behave in a silly way: *Stop playing around and get on with your homework!* • **be playing at sth** UK If you ask what someone is playing at, you are angry because they are doing something silly: *What do you think you're playing at?* • **play sth back** to listen to sounds or watch pictures that you have just recorded: *When I played back our conversation, I realized I hadn't made myself clear.* • **play sth down** to try to make people think that something is less important or bad than it really is: *The government have tried to play down the seriousness of the incident.* • **play on sth** to use someone's fears in order to make that person do or believe what you want: *A lot of marketing strategies just **play on** your **fears** and insecurities.* • **play up** UK **1** If a child plays up, he or she behaves badly. **2** If a machine plays up, it does not work as it should. • **play (about/around) with sth 1** to think about or try different ways of doing something: *We've been playing around with ideas for a new TV show.* **2** to keep touching or moving something, often when you are bored or nervous: *Stop playing with your hair!*

play² /pleɪ/ **noun 1 THEATRE** ▷ [C] **A2** a story that is written for actors to perform, usually in a theatre: *We saw a play at the National Theatre.* ∘ *Most schools usually **put on a play** (= perform a play) at Christmas.* **2 SPORTS/GAMES** ▷ [U] the activity of taking part in a sport or a game: *The West Indies were in the lead when rain stopped play.* **3 CHILDREN** ▷ [U] **B2** the activity of enjoying yourself with toys and games: *a **play area***

IDIOMS **fair play** behaviour that is fair, honest, and does not take advantage of people • **a play on words** a joke using a word or phrase that has two meanings

→ See also **foul play, role-play**

> ✏ Word partners for **play** noun
>
> **perform/put on/write** a play • **in** a play • a play **about** sth

playboy /'pleɪbɔɪ/ **noun** [C] a rich man who spends his time enjoying himself and has relationships with a lot of beautiful women

player /'pleɪə'/ **noun** [C] **1 A1** someone who plays a sport or game: *football/tennis players* **2 A2** someone who plays a musical instrument: *a piano player* → See also **cassette player, CD player, record player**

playful /'pleɪf³l/ **adj** funny and not serious: *a playful mood/remark* • **playfulness noun** [U] • **playfully adv**

playground /'pleɪgraʊnd/ **noun** [C] **A2** an area of land where children can play, especially at school

playgroup /'pleɪgruːp/ **noun** [C] a place where small children go during the day when they are too young to go to school

'playing ,card noun [C] one of a set of 52 small pieces of stiff paper with numbers and pictures on, used for playing games

'playing ,field noun [C] an area of land used for sports such as football

IDIOM **a level playing field** a situation in which everyone has the same chance of succeeding

playlist /'pleɪlɪst/ **noun 1** a list of all the songs or pieces of music played by a particular radio or TV station: *The song was on the radio station's playlist for ten weeks.* **2** a group of songs that have been stored electronically and are organized in a particular way on a computer or on a device such as an MP3 player (= piece of electronic equipment): *Users can search for a track or album, download it then put it in a playlist.*

playoff /'pleɪɒf/ **noun** [C] a game between two teams that have equal points in order to decide which is the winner

playpen /'pleɪpen/ **noun** [C] a small structure with net or bars around the sides that young children are put into so that they can play safely

playroom /'pleɪruːm/ **noun** [C] a room in a house for children to play in

PlayStation /'pleɪˌsteɪʃ³n/ **noun** [C] trademark a machine that you use to play games on your television

plaything /'pleɪθɪŋ/ **noun** [C] someone who is treated without respect and is forced to do things for someone else's enjoyment

playtime /'pleɪtaɪm/ **noun** [C, U] UK a period of time when children at school can play outside

playwright /'pleɪraɪt/ **noun** [C] someone who writes plays

plaza /'plɑːzə/ **noun** [C] US **1** an open, public area in a city or town: *Mexico City's main plaza is called the Zocalo.* **2** a group of buildings with shops, often including an open, public area: *a shopping plaza*

plc, PLC /ˌpiːel'siː/ **noun** [C] abbreviation for Public Limited Company: used after the name of a large company in Britain whose shares (= equal parts of its total value) can be bought and sold by the public

plea /pliː/ **noun** [C] **1** a statement by someone in a court of law that they are guilty or not guilty of the crime they have been accused of: *a plea of guilty/not guilty* **2** a strong request: *an emotional plea for forgiveness*

> ✏ Word partners for **plea**
>
> **issue/make/reject** a plea • a **desperate/emotional/impassioned** plea • a plea **for** sth • a plea **from** sb

plead /pliːd/ **verb** (**pleaded**, also US **pled**) **1 LEGAL** ▷ [T] to say in a court of law if you are guilty or not guilty of the crime you have been accused of: *He **pleaded** not guilty **to** five felony charges.* **2 ASK** ▷ [I] to ask for something in a strong and emotional way: *He **pleaded with** her to come back.* ∘ *She **pleaded for** mercy.* **3 EXCUSE** ▷ [T] to say something as an excuse: *You'll just have to **plead ignorance** (= say you did not know).* **4 plead sb's case/cause** to say something to try to help someone get what they want or avoid punishment

pleasant /'plez³nt/ **adj 1 A2** enjoyable or attractive: *pleasant weather/surroundings* ∘ *We had a very pleasant evening.* **2 A2** A pleasant person has a friendly character. → Opposite **unpleasant** • **pleasantly adv B1** *I was pleasantly surprised.*

pleasantry /'plez³ntri/ **noun** [C] a polite thing that you say when you meet someone: [usually plural] *They **exchanged pleasantries** about the weather.*

please¹ /pliːz/ **exclamation 1 A1** something that you say to be polite when you are asking for something or asking someone to do something: *Could you fill in the form, please? ∘ Please may I use your telephone?* **2 Yes, please. A1** used to accept something politely: *"Would you like a lift home?" "Oh yes, please."*

please² /pliːz/ **verb 1 B1** [I, T] to make someone happy: *the desire to please ∘ I only got married to please my parents.* → Opposite **displease 2 anything/as/what/whatever, etc you please** used to say that someone can have or do anything they want: *Feel free to talk about anything you*

please. ∘ *He can come and go as he pleases.*
3 Please yourself. a slightly rude way of telling someone that you do not care what they choose to do: *"I don't want anything to eat." "Please yourself."*

pleased /pliːzd/ **adj 1** Ⓐ② happy or satisfied: *I wasn't very pleased about having to pay.* ∘ [+ to do sth] *I'm pleased to be back in England.* ∘ [+ (that)] *He was pleased that she had come back.* ∘ *I'm really pleased with the quality of his work.* **2 Pleased to meet you.** Ⓐ② a polite way of greeting someone you are meeting for the first time

> **❗ Common learner error: pleased**
>
> Be careful to use the correct preposition or verb pattern after this word.
> *I'm pleased with my new computer.*
> *He wasn't very pleased about the news.*
> *I'm pleased to be in London.*
> ~~I'm pleased for my new computer.~~
> ~~He wasn't very pleased of the news.~~
> ~~I'm pleased for being in London.~~

pleasing /ˈpliːzɪŋ/ **adj** Something that is pleasing gives pleasure: *the most pleasing aspect of her work* ∘ *These buildings are very pleasing to the eye.*

pleasurable /ˈpleʒərəbl/ **adj** enjoyable: *a pleasurable experience*

pleasure /ˈpleʒəʳ/ **noun 1 HAPPINESS** ▷ [U] Ⓑ① a feeling of happiness or enjoyment: *His visits used to give us such pleasure.* ∘ *She seemed to take pleasure in (= enjoy) humiliating people.* ∘ *It gives me great pleasure to introduce our next guest.* → Opposite **displeasure 2 ENJOYABLE EXPERIENCE** ▷ [C, U] Ⓑ① an enjoyable activity or experience: *Food is one of life's great pleasures.* ∘ *I once had the pleasure of sharing a taxi with her.* **3 NOT WORK** ▷ [U] If you do something for pleasure, you do it because you enjoy it and not because it is your job: *reading for pleasure* **4 It's a pleasure.; My pleasure.** a polite way of replying to someone who has thanked you: *"Thank you for a wonderful evening." "My pleasure."*

> **✏ Word partners for pleasure**
>
> derive/express/give pleasure • take pleasure in sth • enormous/great/perverse/pure/sheer pleasure

pleated /ˈpliːtɪd/ **adj** A pleated piece of clothing or piece of cloth has regular, vertical folds in it: *a pleated skirt*

pled /pled/ US past of plead

pledge¹ /pledʒ/ **noun** [C] a serious promise: [+ to do sth] *a pledge to create jobs* ∘ *He made a solemn pledge to the American people.*

> **✏ Word partners for pledge noun**
>
> break/fulfil/make a pledge • a pledge on sth

pledge² /pledʒ/ **verb** [T] to promise seriously to do something or give something: *Foreign donors have pledged $550 million.* ∘ *He pledged his*

support to Mandela. ∘ [+ to do sth] *He pledged to cut government salaries.*

plentiful /ˈplentɪfªl/ **adj** If something is plentiful, there is a lot of it available: *a plentiful supply of meat*

plenty /ˈplenti/ **quantifier 1** Ⓑ① easily as much or as many as you need: *Don't bring any food – we've got plenty.* ∘ *There is plenty of evidence to support her claims.* ∘ *There's plenty of room.* ∘ *Help yourself to food – there's plenty more.* **2 plenty big/large/wide, etc enough** easily as big/large/wide, etc as you need something to be: *This house is plenty big enough for two families.* **3** Ⓑ① a lot: *I know plenty of unemployed musicians.* ∘ *There's plenty for you to do.*

plethora /ˈpleθ°rə/ **noun a plethora of sth** formal a large number of something: *There is a confusing plethora of pension plans.*

pliers /ˈplaɪəz/ **noun** [plural] a tool for holding or pulling small things like nails or for cutting wire: *a pair of pliers* → See picture at **tool**

plight /plaɪt/ **noun** [no plural] formal an unpleasant or difficult situation: *the plight of the sick and the poor*

plod /plɒd/ **verb** (**plodding, plodded**) **plod along/on/through, etc** to walk with slow, heavy steps: *We plodded through the mud.*

plonk¹ /plɒŋk/ **verb** UK informal **plonk sth down/in/on, etc** to put something somewhere quickly and without care: *She plonked her bag on the floor.*

PHRASAL VERB plonk yourself down to sit down quickly and without care

plonk² /plɒŋk/ **noun** [U] UK informal cheap wine

plop¹ /plɒp/ **noun** [C] the sound made by an object when it falls into water

plop² /plɒp/ **verb** (**plopping, plopped**) US informal **plop (sth) down/onto, etc** to put something somewhere quickly and without care: *She plopped down next to me.*

plot¹ /plɒt/ **noun** [C] **1 STORY** ▷ Ⓑ② the things that happen in a story: *I don't like movies with complicated plots.* **2 PLAN** ▷ a plan to do something bad: [+ to do sth] *a plot to blow up the embassy* **3 LAND** ▷ a piece of land, often for growing food or for building on: *a building plot*

plot² /plɒt/ **verb** (**plotting, plotted**) **1** [I, T] to plan to do something bad: [+ to do sth] *They plotted to bring down the government.* ∘ *He fired all those accused of plotting against him.* **2** [T] to make marks on a map, picture, etc to show the position or development of something: *This chart plots the position of all aircraft.*

plough¹ UK (US **plow**) /plaʊ/ **noun** [C] a large tool used by farmers to turn over the soil before planting crops

plough² UK (US **plow**) /plaʊ/ **verb** [I, T] to turn over soil with a plough

PHRASAL VERBS plough sth back to spend the money that a business has earned on improving that business: *All profits are ploughed back into the company.* • **plough into sth** to hit something with great force: *My car ploughed straight into the car in front.* • **plough on** to continue doing

P

plough UK, **plow** US

something, although it is difficult or boring
• **plough through sth** to finish what you are
reading, eating, or working on, although there is
a lot of it: *I had to plough through the whole
report.*

plow /plaʊ/ **noun, verb** US spelling of plough

ploy /plɔɪ/ **noun** [C] a slightly dishonest method
used to try to achieve something: [+ to do sth]
The phone call was just a ploy to get rid of her.

☑ Word partners for **ploy**

use a ploy • a ploy backfires/works • a
clever/cunning/cynical/deliberate ploy • a
ploy by sb

PLS informal written abbeviation for please: used in
emails and text messages

pluck /plʌk/ **verb 1 pluck sth/sb from/out, etc**
to quickly pull something or someone from the
place where they are: *A helicopter plucked him
from the sea.* **2 BIRD** ▷ [T] to pull all the feathers
out of a bird before cooking it **3 MUSIC** ▷ [T] If
you pluck the strings of a musical instrument,
you pull them with your fingers to make a
sound. **4 PLANT** ▷ [T] literary to pick a flower or
part of a plant **5 pluck your eyebrows** to pull
hairs out of your eyebrows (= lines of hair above
your eyes) to make them look tidy → See also
pluck up the courage (to do sth)

plug

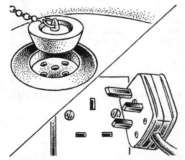

plug¹ /plʌg/ **noun** [C] **1 ELECTRICITY** ▷ 🔒 a
plastic or rubber object with metal pins, used to
connect electrical equipment to an electricity
supply: *I need to change the plug on my hairdryer.*

2 HOLE ▷ 🔒 something you put in a hole to
block it: *a bath plug* **3 ADVERTISEMENT** ▷
talking about about a new book, film, etc in
public to advertise it: *She managed to get in a
plug for her new book.*

IDIOM **pull the plug** to prevent an activity from
continuing: *They have pulled the plug on jazz
broadcasts.*

→ See also **spark plug**

plug² /plʌg/ **verb** [T] (**plugging, plugged**) **1 plug
a gap/hole** mainly UK to solve a problem by
supplying something that is needed: *The new
computer system will help to plug the gap in the
county's ability to collect taxes.* **2** to talk about a
new book, film, etc in public in order to
advertise it: *He was on TV, plugging his new
book.* **3** to block a hole

PHRASAL VERBS **plug away** informal to work hard at
something for a long time: *I'm still plugging
away at my article.* • **plug sth in** 🔒 to connect
a piece of electrical equipment to an electricity
supply: *Could you plug the iron in for me?* -
Opposite **unplug** • **plug sth into sth** to connect
one piece of electrical equipment to another:
*You need to plug the speakers into the back of the
computer.*

plughole /'plʌghəʊl/ **noun** [C] UK (US **drain**) the
hole in a bath or sink (= place in a kitchen where
dishes are washed) where the water flows away

plug-in (also **plugin**) /'plʌgɪn/ **noun** [C] a small
computer program that makes a larger one work
faster or be able to do more things

plum /plʌm/ **noun** [C] a soft, round fruit with
red, yellow, or purple skin and a stone in the
middle

plumage /'pluːmɪdʒ/ **noun** [U] a bird's feathers

plumber /'plʌmər/ **noun** [C] 🔒 someone whose
job is to repair or connect water pipes and
things like toilets and baths

plumbing /'plʌmɪŋ/ **noun** [U] the water pipes in
a building

plume /pluːm/ **noun 1 a plume of dust/smoke,
etc** a tall, thin amount of dust/smoke, etc rising
into the air. **2** [C] a large feather, often worn for
decoration

plummet /'plʌmɪt/ **verb** [I] to fall very quickly in
amount or value: *Temperatures plummeted to
minus 20.*

plump¹ /plʌmp/ **adj 1** quite fat: *a plump child*
2 pleasantly round or full: *nice plump cloves of
garlic*

plump² /plʌmp/ **verb**

PHRASAL VERB **plump for sth** UK to choose
something, especially after thinking about it
for a time: *I plumped for the salmon.*

plunder /'plʌndər/ **verb** [I, T] to steal, especially
during a war: *Many of the region's churches have
been plundered.* • **plunder noun** [U]

plunge¹ /plʌndʒ/ **verb 1 plunge down/into, etc**
to fall or move down very quickly and with
force: *The car came off the road and plunged down
the hillside.* **2** [I] to become lower in temperature

ɑː arm | ɜː her | iː see | ɔː saw | uː too | aɪ my | aʊ how | eə hair | eɪ day | əʊ no | ɪə near | ɔɪ boy | ʊə pure | aɪə fire | aʊə sour

value, etc very suddenly and quickly: *Temperatures plunged below zero.*

PHRASAL VERBS **plunge sth into sth** to push something very hard into something else: *He plunged the knife into the man's stomach.* • **plunge sb/sth into sth** to make someone or something suddenly be unhappy or in an unpleasant situation: [often passive] *The country had been plunged into chaos.* • **plunge into sth** to start doing something with a lot of energy: *Trying to forget about her, he plunged into his work.*

•lunge² /plʌndʒ/ **noun** [C] a sudden and quick decrease in the value, amount, or level of something: *Prices have **taken a plunge** (= suddenly become less).*

IDIOM **take the plunge** to do something important or difficult, especially after thinking about it for a long time: *We're finally going to take the plunge and buy a house.*

☑ Word partners for **plunge**

take a plunge • a plunge **in** sth • a stock market plunge

---

he pluperfect /ˌpluːˈpɜːfɪkt/ **noun** (also **the past perfect**) the form of the verb that is used to show that an action had already finished when another action happened. In English, the pluperfect is made with 'had' and a past participle.

•lural /ˈplʊərəl/ **noun** [C] ⓐ a word or part of a word that shows that you are talking about more than one person or thing. For example 'babies' is the plural of 'baby'. • **plural adj** *'Cattle' and 'trousers' are plural nouns.*

•luralism /ˈplʊərəlɪzəm/ **noun** [U] the existence in a society of many different types of people with many different beliefs and opinions: *political pluralism* • **pluralist adj** (also **pluralistic** /ˌplʊərəlˈɪstɪk/) relating to pluralism: *a pluralist society*

•lus¹ /plʌs/ **preposition 1** ⓐ added to: *Five plus three is eight.* **2** ⓑ and also: *You've won their latest CD plus two tickets for their concert.*

•lus² /plʌs/ **adj 40 plus, 150 plus, etc** more than the amount stated: *temperatures of 40 plus*

•lus³ /plʌs/ **conjunction** informal ⓑ and also: *Don't go there in August. It'll be too hot, plus it'll be really expensive.*

•lus⁴ /plʌs/ **noun** [C] **1** informal ⓑ an advantage: *Well, the apartment has a garden so that's a plus.* **2** (also **plus ˌsign**) the symbol +, used between two numbers to show that they are being added together

•lush /plʌʃ/ **adj** Plush furniture, buildings, rooms, etc are very expensive and comfortable: *a plush red carpet*

•luto /ˈpluːtəʊ/ **noun** [no plural] a dwarf planet (= an object in space like a small planet) that comes after Neptune in distance from the sun. Pluto was considered to be a proper planet until 2006, when it was officially decided that it was a dwarf planet.

•lutonium /pluːˈtəʊniəm/ **noun** [U] a chemical element that is used in the production of nuclear power and nuclear weapons

ply /plaɪ/ **verb 1 ply across/between, etc** old-fashioned to often make a particular journey: *Fishing boats were plying across the harbour.* **2 ply your trade** to work at your job, especially selling things

PHRASAL VERB **ply sb with sth 1** to give someone a lot of something again and again: *They plied me with food and drink.* **2** to ask someone a lot of questions: *They **plied** him **with questions** about where he had been.*

plywood /ˈplaɪwʊd/ **noun** [U] wood that is made by sticking several thin layers of wood together

p.m. (also **pm**) /ˌpiːˈem/ ⓐ used when you are referring to a time after 12 o'clock in the middle of the day, but before 12 o'clock in the middle of the night: *Opening hours: 9 a.m. – 6 p.m.*

PM /ˌpiːˈem/ **noun** [C] abbreviation for prime minister: the leader of an elected government in some countries

pneumatic /njuːˈmætɪk/ **adj** filled with air, or operated using air: *pneumatic tyres*

pneumonia /njuːˈməʊniə/ **noun** [U] a serious illness in which your lungs fill with liquid and it is difficult to breathe

poach /pəʊtʃ/ **verb 1 COOK** ▷ [T] to cook something, especially an egg without its shell, by putting it into liquid that is gently boiling **2 ANIMALS** ▷ [I, T] to illegally catch or kill animals, especially by going onto land without the permission of the person who owns it **3 PERSON** ▷ [I, T] to persuade someone to leave a company or team in order to work or play for yours: *They can poach experienced people easily because they offer higher salaries.*

poacher /ˈpəʊtʃər/ **noun** [C] someone who illegally catches or kills animals

pocket¹ /ˈpɒkɪt/ **noun** [C]   **pocket**
1 BAG ▷ ⓐ a small bag that is sewn or fixed onto or into a piece of clothing, a bag, the back of a seat, etc: *a coat/shirt/trouser pocket* ∘ *He was asked to empty his **pockets**.* ∘ *Safety instructions are in the pocket on the seat in front of you.* **2 SMALL AREA/ AMOUNT** ▷ a small area or small amount of something that is different from what is around it: *There was real poverty in some **pockets of** the country.* ∘ *small pockets of air trapped inside the glass* **3 MONEY** ▷ the amount of money that you have for spending: *I shouldn't have to pay for travel **out of my own pocket** (= with my own money).* **4 be out of pocket** to have less money than you should have because you have paid for something: *The travel company cancelled our trip and we were left hundreds of pounds out of pocket.*

pocket² /ˈpɒkɪt/ **verb** [T] **1** to take something, especially money, which does not belong to you: *His plan was to **pocket the money** from the sale of the business and leave the country.* **2** to put something in your pocket: *Juan pocketed the knife and walked away.*

pocket³ /'pɒkɪt/ **adj** [always before noun] small enough to fit in your pocket: *a pocket dictionary*

pocketbook /'pɒkɪtbʊk/ **noun** [C] US **1** a woman's bag **2** Someone's pocketbook is their ability to pay for something: *The sales tax hits consumers in the pocketbook.*

pocketful /'pɒkɪtfʊl/ **noun** [C] the amount you can fit in a pocket: *a pocketful of coins*

pocketknife /'pɒkɪtnaɪf/ **noun** [C] (plural **pocketknives**) a small knife that folds into a case

pocket money **noun** [U] 🔵 an amount of money given regularly to a child by its parents

pod /pɒd/ **noun** [C] the long, flat part of some plants that has seeds in it: *a pea pod*

podcast¹ /'pɒdkɑːst/ **noun** [C] a recording that you can listen to on your computer or MP3 player from a website. You can also sign up to (= say that you want to receive) a podcast which is then updated (= new information is added to it) through the Internet when you plug your MP3 player into a computer: *You can download the weekly Business News as a podcast.* → See Study Page **The Web and the Internet** on page Centre 36

podcast² /'pɒdkɑːst/ **verb** [I, T] (**podcast**) to record something as a podcast

podiatrist /pəʊˈdaɪətrɪst/ **noun** [C] US (UK **chiropodist**) someone whose job is to treat problems with people's feet

podium /'pəʊdiəm/ **noun** [C] a small, raised area, sometimes with a tall table on it, that someone stands on when they are performing or speaking

poem /'pəʊɪm/ **noun** [C] 🔵 a piece of writing, especially one that has short lines and uses words that sound the same: *love/war poems*

> ☑ Word partners for **poem**
>
> read/recite/write a poem • in a poem • a poem **about** sth • a poem **by** sb • a **love** poem

poet /'pəʊɪt/ **noun** [C] 🔵 someone who writes poems

poetic /pəʊˈetɪk/ **adj 1** Something that is poetic makes you feel strong emotions because it is so beautiful: *To him, life seemed poetic.* **2** relating to poetry: *poetic language*

poetry /'pəʊɪtri/ **noun** [U] 🔵 poems in general, or the writing of poetry: *I enjoy all kinds of poetry, especially love poetry.*

poignant /'pɔɪnjənt/ **adj** making you feel sad: *It's a poignant story about a poor family's struggle to survive.* • **poignancy** /'pɔɪnjənsi/ **noun** [U] the quality of being poignant • **poignantly adv**

> ❗ Common learner error: **point**
>
> A **point** (.) is used to separate a whole number from a fraction (= number less than 1).
> *Normal body temperature is 36.9° Celsius.*
> A **comma** (,) is used to divide large numbers into groups of three so that they are easier to read.
> *28,071,973*
> *1,378*

> ☑ Word partners for **point**
>
> illustrate/make/prove/raise a point • take sb's point • a point **about** sth

point¹ /pɔɪnt/ **noun 1** OPINION ▷ [C] 🔵 an opinion, idea, or fact that someone says c writes: *Could I make a point about noise levels* ∘ *I take your point* (= I agree with you) abou cycling, but I still prefer to walk. **2** IMPORTANT OPINION ▷ [no plural] 🔵 an opinion or fact tha deserves to be considered seriously, or whic other people agree is true: *"She's alway complaining that the office is cold." "Well, she got a point."* ∘ *"How are we going to get there there are no trains?" "Good point."* **3 the point** 🔵 the most important part of what has been sai or written: *I thought he was never going to get t the point.* ∘ *The point is, if you don't claim th money now you might never get it.* ∘ *To say his a is simplistic is missing the point* (= not unde standing the most important thing about it) **4** SHARP ▷ [C] 🔵 the thin, sharp end c something: *the point of a needle* **5** PLACE ▷ [C a particular place: *a stopping/fuelling poin* ∘ *the point where the pipes enter the buildin* **6** TIME ▷ [C] 🔵 a particular time in an event c process: *At this point, people started to leave.* ∘ *has got to the point where I can hardly bear t speak to him.* **7 be at/on the point of doing st** 🔵 to be going to do something very soon: *Am was on the point of crying.* **8** REASON ▷ [no plura 🔵 the reason for or purpose of somethin *What's the point of studying if you can't get a jo afterwards?* ∘ *There's no point inviting her – sh never comes to parties.* **9 beside the point** n important or not connected with what you ar talking about: *The fact that he doesn't want t come is beside the point – he should have bee invited.* **10 make a point of doing sth** to b certain that you always do a particular thing: *H made a point of learning all the names of his staf* **11 to the point** If something someone says c writes is to the point, it expresses the mo important things without extra details: *His repo was short and to the point.* **12 up to a point** 🔵 partly: *What he says is true up to a poin* **13** GAME ▷ [C] 🔵 a unit used for showing wh is winning in a game or competition: *With games still to play, Manchester United are 5 poin ahead.* **14** MEASUREMENT ▷ [C] a unit used i some systems of measuring and comparin things: *The stock exchange fell by five point* **15 boiling/freezing/melting point** the temper ture at which a substance boils, freezes, or mel **16** QUALITY ▷ [C] 🔵 a quality that someone ha *I know she's bossy, but she has lots of good poin too.* ∘ *Chemistry never was my strong point* (= *was never good at it*). **17** MATHEMATICS ▷ [C (also **decimal point**) 🔵 the mark (.) that is use to separate the two parts of a decimal: *One mi equals one point six* (= 1.6) *kilometre* **18** DIRECTION ▷ [C] 🔵 one of the marks on compass (= object used for showing direction **19** LETTERS ▷ [C] a unit of measurement of th size of letters, used in printing and on compt ters → See also **breaking point, a case in poin decimal point, focal point, moot poin**

point of view, starting-point, turning point, vantage point

▶**oint²** /pɔɪnt/ **verb 1 SHOW** ▷ [I] 🄐 to show where someone or something is by holding your finger or a thin object towards it: *She **pointed at/ to** a bird flying overhead.* **2 AIM** ▷ [T] 🄑 to hold something so that it faces towards something else: *She **pointed** her camera **at** them.* **3 FACE** ▷ [I] 🄑 to face towards a particular direction: *The solar panels were pointing away from the sun.*

PHRASAL VERBS **point sb/sth out** to make a person notice someone or something: *I didn't think about the disadvantages until you pointed them out to me.* • **point sth out** 🄒 to tell someone a fact: *If he makes a mistake I always think it's best to point it out immediately.* • **point to/towards sth** to show that something probably exists, is happening, or is true: *All the evidence points to suicide.*

▶**oint-blank** /ˌpɔɪntˈblæŋk/ **adj, adv 1** If you refuse point-blank, you refuse completely and will not change your decision. **2 at point-blank range** If someone is shot at point-blank range, they are shot from a very short distance away.

▶**ointed** /ˈpɔɪntɪd/ **adj 1** If someone says something in a pointed way, they intend to criticize someone: *He made some **pointed references** to her history of drug problems.* **2** A pointed object has a thin, sharp end: *a pointed chin/beard*

▶**ointer** /ˈpɔɪntər/ **noun** [C] **1** a piece of information that can help you understand a situation or do something better: *I asked for some pointers on applying for jobs.* **2** an object that you use to point at something

▶**ointless** /ˈpɔɪntləs/ **adj** Something that is pointless has no purpose: *pointless arguments/ conflict* ○ [+ to do sth] *It would be pointless to argue with him.* • **pointlessly** adv

▶**oint of ˈview noun** [C] (plural **points of view**) **1** 🄒 a way of thinking about a situation: ***From** a medical **point of view**, there was no need for the operation.* **2** 🄒 an opinion: *You have to be willing to see other people's points of view.*

> ❗ Common learner error: **point of view** or **opinion**?
>
> When you want to talk about your own opinion, you should say **In my opinion ...**, not 'In my point of view'.

> 🗹 Word partners for **point of view**
>
> from sb's point of view • from a [political/ financial, etc] point of view

▶**oise** /pɔɪz/ **noun** [U] **1** the ability to behave in a calm and confident way: *Recovering his poise, he congratulated his opponent.* **2** the ability to move or stand in a careful, pleasant way

▶**oised** /pɔɪzd/ **adj 1** [never before noun] ready to do something: [+ to do sth] *They have three hundred ships, all poised to attack.* **2** [never before noun] in a particular position or situation, ready to move or change: *a helicopter poised above the crowd* **3** calm and confident: *a poised performance*

poison¹ /ˈpɔɪzən/ **noun** [C, U] 🄑 a substance that can make you sick or kill you if you eat or drink it: *Someone had put poison in her drink.*

poison² /ˈpɔɪzən/ **verb** [T] **1 KILL** ▷ 🄑 to try to kill someone by giving them a dangerous substance to drink or eat: *He tried to poison his wife.* **2 MAKE DANGEROUS** ▷ 🄑 to put poison or a dangerous substance in something: *They poisoned the city's water supply.* **3 SPOIL** ▷ to make something very unpleasant: *These arguments were poisoning his life.* **4 poison sb's mind** to make someone think bad things about someone or something: *Her father had **poisoned** her mind **against** me.* • **poisoned** adj

poisoning /ˈpɔɪzənɪŋ/ **noun** [U] an illness caused by eating, drinking, or breathing a dangerous substance: ***alcohol/lead poisoning*** → See also **food poisoning**

poisonous /ˈpɔɪzənəs/ **adj 1** 🄒 containing poison: *poisonous gas* **2** 🄑 A poisonous animal uses poison in order to defend itself: *a poisonous snake*

poke

She poked her head
out of the window.

She poked him.

poke¹ /pəʊk/ **verb 1** [T] to quickly push your finger or other pointed object into someone or something: *Nell kept poking me in the arm.* ○ *He poked the fire with his stick.* **2 poke (sth) round/ out/through, etc** to appear through or from behind something, or to make something do this: *Grace poked her head round the door.* → See also **poke/stick your nose¹ into sth**

PHRASAL VERB **poke about/around** informal to look for something by moving other things: *I was poking around in the garage, looking for a paintbrush.*

poke² /pəʊk/ **noun** [C] the action of quickly pushing your finger or other pointed object into someone or something: *I gave him a poke in the back.*

poker /ˈpəʊkər/ **noun 1** [U] a game played with cards in which people try to win money from each other **2** [C] a long, metal stick used for moving the coal or wood in a fire so that it burns better

poker-faced /ˈpəʊkəˌfeɪst/ **adj** not showing on your face what you are really thinking or feeling

poky (also **pokey**) /ˈpəʊki/ adj informal **1** A room or house that is poky is unpleasant because it is too small. **2** US too slow

polar /ˈpəʊlər/ adj relating to the North or South Pole

ˌpolar ˈbear noun [C] 🅱️2 (US ˈpolar ˌbear) a large, white bear that lives in the Arctic (= most northern part of the Earth)

Polaroid /ˈpəʊlərɔɪd/ noun [C] trademark a camera that prints a photograph immediately after you have taken it, or a picture taken with this type of camera

pole /pəʊl/ noun **1** [C] a long, thin stick made of wood or metal, often used to hold something up: *tent poles* **2 the North/South Pole** the part of the Earth that is furthest north/south

IDIOM **be poles apart** to be complete opposites

polemic /pəˈlemɪk/ noun [C, U] formal writing or speech that strongly criticizes or defends an idea, a belief, etc

ˈpole ˌvault noun [no plural] a sport in which you use a very long stick to jump over a high bar

police¹ /pəˈliːs/ noun [plural] 🅰️2 the official organization that makes people obey the law and that protects people and places against crime, or the people who work for this organization: *I heard a gun shot and decided to **call the police**.* ○ *A 30-year-old taxi driver is being interviewed by police.* ○ *a police investigation*

> ☑ Word partners for **police**
>
> **call** the police • **report** sb/sth **to** the police • police **arrest/question** sb

police² /pəˈliːs/ verb [T] to make sure that people obey the law in a particular place or when they are doing a particular activity: *Clubs have to pay for the cost of policing matches.*

poˌlice ˈconstable noun [C] in the UK, a police officer of the lowest rank

poˈlice deˌpartment noun [C] in the US, the police force in an area or city

poˈlice ˌforce noun [C] the police in a country or area

policeman, policewoman /pəˈliːsmən, pəˈliːsˌwʊmən/ noun [C] (plural **policemen**, **policewomen**) 🅰️2 a man/woman who is a member of the police

poˈlice ˌofficer noun [C] 🅰️2 someone who is a member of the police

poˌlice ˈstate noun [C] (US poˈlice ˌstate) a country in which the people are not free to do what they want because the government controls them

poˈlice ˌstation noun [C] 🅰️2 the office of the police in a town or part of a city

policy /ˈpɒləsi/ noun **1** [C, U] 🅱️2 a set of ideas or a plan of what to do in particular situations that has been agreed by a government, business, etc: *foreign policy* ○ *It is **company policy** to help staff progress in their careers.* **2** [C] an agreement that you have with an insurance company (= company that pays the costs if you are injured, etc)

> ☑ Word partners for **policy**
>
> **adopt/formulate/implement/pursue** a policy • a policy **on** sth • a policy **of** (doing) sth • **company** policy • **foreign** policy

polio /ˈpəʊliəʊ/ noun [U] a serious disease that sometimes makes it impossible for you to move your muscles

polish¹ /ˈpɒlɪʃ/ noun **1** [C, U] a substance that you rub on something in order to make it clean and shiny **2** [no plural] the act of rubbing something in order to make it clean and shiny: *Just give the table a polish.* → See also **nail polish**

polish² /ˈpɒlɪʃ/ verb [T] to rub something with a cloth in order to make it clean or to make it shine: *to polish your shoes*

PHRASAL VERB **polish sth off** informal to finish something quickly: *I gave him a bowl of ice cream which he soon polished off.*

polished /ˈpɒlɪʃt/ adj **1** clean and shiny after polishing: *a polished floor* **2** done with skill and style: *He gave a highly **polished performance**.*

polite /pəˈlaɪt/ adj 🅰️2 behaving in a way that is not rude and shows that you do not only think about yourself: *She was too polite to point out my mistake.* • **politely** adv 🅱️1 *He thanked them politely.* • **politeness** noun [U]

> ➕ Other ways of saying **polite**
>
> The adjectives **courteous**, **respectful**, and **well-mannered** are sometimes used when someone is polite and shows respect for other people:
> *Although she often disagreed with me, she was always **courteous**.*
> *They were quiet, **well-mannered** children.*
> A man who is polite to a woman is sometimes described as **chivalrous**:
> *He held open the door in that **chivalrous** way of his.*
> The expression **politically correct** and its abbreviation, **PC**, are regularly used to show that someone is being polite by speaking in a way which does not offend women, people of a particular race, or people who have physical or mental problems:
> *'Fireman' has been replaced by the **politically correct** term 'firefighter'.*
> *Calling them 'ladies' – that's not very **PC** of you!*
> Conversation which is polite and calm is sometimes described as **civilized**:
> *Let's discuss this in a **civilized** manner.*

political /pəˈlɪtɪkəl/ adj 🅱️1 relating to or involved in politics: *There are two main political parties in my country.* ○ *The church has a strong political influence.* • **politically** adv

poˌlitical aˈsylum noun [U] protection given by a government to someone whose political activities have made it too dangerous for them to live in their own country

poˌlitically coˈrrect adj careful to speak or behave in a way that is not offensive to women, people of a particular race, or people who have physical or mental problems: *It's not politically correct to call women 'girls'.* • **political correctness** noun [U]

political prisoner noun [C] someone who is in prison because their political activities or opinions oppose the government

politician /ˌpɒlɪˈtɪʃᵊn/ noun [C] ⓑ someone who works in politics, especially a member of the government

politicize (also UK **-ise**) /pəˈlɪtɪsaɪz/ verb [T] to make something or someone become more involved with politics: [often passive] *The whole issue has been politicized.* ∘ *a highly **politicized** debate*

politics /ˈpɒlətɪks/ noun **1** ACTIVITIES ▷ [U] ⓑ ideas and activities relating to how a country or area is governed: *He has little interest in local politics.* **2** JOB ▷ [U] ⓑ a job in politics: *She's planning to retire from politics next year.* **3** sb's **politics** [plural] someone's opinions about how a country or area should be governed: *I don't know what his politics are, but he strongly disagreed with the decision.* **4** RELATIONSHIPS ▷ [plural] the relationships in a group that allow particular people to have power over others: *I try not to get involved in office politics.*

> ✏ Word partners for **politics**
>
> enter/go into/be involved in politics • domestic/international/local politics

polka /ˈpɒlkə/ noun [C] a type of dance, or a piece of music used for this type of dance

polka-dot /ˈpɒlkəˌdɒt/ adj [always before noun] having a regular pattern of small, round spots: *a polka-dot bikini*

poll¹ /pəʊl/ noun [C] (also **opinion poll**) the results of a set of questions people are asked to discover what they think about a subject: *A recent **poll indicated** that 77 percent of Americans supported the president.*

> ✏ Word partners for **poll**
>
> carry out/conduct a poll • a poll indicates/reveals/shows/suggests sth • a poll of sb

poll² /pəʊl/ verb [T] **1** to ask someone's opinion as part of a study on what people think about a subject: [often passive] *Most students polled said they preferred the new system.* **2** to receive a particular number of votes in an election: *Labour polled only 45 percent of the Scottish vote.*

pollen /ˈpɒlən/ noun [U] a powder produced by flowers, which is carried by insects or the wind and makes other flowers produce seeds

pollen count noun [C] the measurement of the amount of pollen in the air

polling day noun [C] UK (US **election day**) the day when people vote in an election

polling station noun [C] UK (US **polling place**) a building where people go to vote in an election

the polls /pəʊlz/ noun [plural] voting in an election: *The country will go to the polls (= vote) on 13 September.*

pollster /ˈpəʊlstər/ noun [C] someone who tries

to discover what most people think about a subject by asking questions

pollutant /pəˈluːtᵊnt/ noun [C] a substance that pollutes water, air, etc

pollute /pəˈluːt/ verb [T] ⓑ to make water, air, soil, etc dirty or harmful: *We need a fuel that won't pollute the environment.*

polluter /pəˈluːtər/ noun [C] a person or organization that puts harmful substances or waste into the water, air, soil, etc, causing damage to the environment

pollution /pəˈluːʃᵊn/ noun [U] ⓑ damage caused to water, air, etc by harmful substances or waste: *The book shows simple things you can do to reduce pollution from your car.*

polo /ˈpəʊləʊ/ noun [U] a game played between two teams who ride horses and hit a ball with long, wooden hammers

polo neck noun [C] UK (US **turtleneck**) a piece of clothing that covers the top part of the body and has a tube-like part covering the neck: *a black polo neck sweater*

polo neck

polo neck *UK*, turtleneck *US*

polo shirt noun [C] a cotton shirt with short sleeves, a collar, and buttons at the front

poly- /pɒli-/ prefix many: *polygamy* (= *having more than one husband or wife at the same time*) ∘ *a polygon* (= *a shape with many sides*)

polyester /ˌpɒliˈestər/ noun [U] a type of artificial cloth used for making clothes: *a polyester shirt/skirt*

polystyrene /ˌpɒliˈstaɪriːn/ noun [U] UK (US trademark **Styrofoam**) a light plastic material that is wrapped around delicate objects to protect them, and around hot things to keep them hot: *polystyrene packaging/polystyrene cups*

polytechnic /ˌpɒliˈteknɪk/ noun [C] a college where students study scientific and technical subjects

polythene /ˈpɒliθiːn/ noun [U] UK (US **polyethylene**, ⓤⓢ /ˌpɒliˈeθəliːn/) a thin, soft plastic, often used for making bags

pomp /pɒmp/ noun [U] formal special clothes, decorations, and music at an official ceremony

pompous /ˈpɒmpəs/ adj Someone who is pompous is too serious and thinks they are more important than they really are. • **pompously** adv • **pomposity** /pɒmˈpɒsəti/ noun [U] pompous behaviour or speech

pond /pɒnd/ noun [C] ⓑ a small area of water, especially one that has been made artificially in a park or garden

ponder /ˈpɒndər/ verb [I, T] literary to think carefully about something: [+ question word] *He*

P

ponderous 550

pondered what might have happened if he hadn't gone home.

ponderous /ˈpɒndᵊrəs/ *adj* **1** Ponderous speech or writing is boring or too serious. **2** slow because of being very heavy or large • **ponderously** *adv*

pony /ˈpəʊni/ *noun* [C] a small horse

ponytail /ˈpəʊniteɪl/ *noun* [C] hair tied at the back of your head so that it hangs down like a horse's tail

ponytail

poodle /ˈpuːdl/ *noun* [C] a type of dog with thick, curly hair

pool¹ /puːl/ *noun* **1 SWIM** ▷ [C] (also **swimming pool**) ⏎ an area of water that has been made for people to swim in: *The hotel has two outdoor pools.* **2 LIQUID** ▷ [C] ⏎ a small area of water or a small amount of liquid on a surface: *We dipped our feet in a shallow pool by the rocks.* ○ *a **pool of** blood* **3 GAME** ▷ [U] ⏎ a game in which two people use long, thin sticks to hit coloured balls into holes around the edge of a table **4 COLLECTION** ▷ [C] a collection of money, people, or equipment that is shared by a group of people: *a car pool for company business*

pool² /puːl/ *verb* [T] If a group of people pool their money, knowledge, or equipment, they collect it together so that it can be shared or used for a particular purpose: *Several villages pooled their resources to set up a building project.*

the pools /puːlz/ *noun* [plural] in Britain, a game in which people try to win a lot of money by guessing the results of football games

poor /pɔːr/ ⓤ /pʊr/ *adj* **1 NO MONEY** ▷ ⏎ having very little money or few possessions: *Most of these people are desperately poor.* ○ *Modern fertilizers are too expensive for poorer countries to afford.* ○ *housing for the poor* **2 BAD** ▷ ⏎ of very low quality: *poor health* ○ *Last year's exam results were poor.* ○ *a poor harvest* ○ *The meeting went smoothly but attendance was poor* (= not many people came). **3 NO SKILL** ▷ ⏎ not having much skill at a particular activity: *She's always been poor at spelling.* **4 SYMPATHY** ▷ [always before noun] ⏎ used to show sympathy for someone: *That cold sounds terrible, you poor thing.* **5 be poor in sth** ⏎ If something is poor in a particular substance, it has very little of the substance: *Avoid foods which are high in calories but poor in nutrients.*

poorly¹ /ˈpɔːli/ *adv* badly: *poorly educated*

poorly² /ˈpɔːli/ *adj* UK informal sick: *Rosie was feeling poorly so I put her to bed.*

pop¹ /pɒp/ *verb* (**popping, popped**) **1** [I, T] to make a short sound like a small explosion, or to make something do this by breaking it: *The music played and champagne corks popped.* **2 pop in/out/over, etc** informal ⏎ to go to a particular place: *Doug's just popped out for a few minutes.* ○ *I'll pop into the supermarket on my way home.* **3 pop sth in/into/on, etc** informal to quickly put something in a particular place: *Can you pop the pizza in the oven?* **4 pop out/up** to

move quickly and suddenly, especially out of something

PHRASAL VERB **pop up** informal to suddenly appear or happen, often unexpectedly: *A message just popped up on my screen.*

pop² /pɒp/ *noun* **1 MUSIC** ▷ [U] (also **pop music**) ⏎ modern music with a strong beat which is popular with young people **2 SOUND** ▷ [C] a short sound like a small explosion **3 DRINK** ▷ [U] informal (US usually **soda**) a sweet drink with bubbles **4 FATHER** ▷ [no plural] US informal father

popcorn /ˈpɒpkɔːn/ *noun* [U] yellow seeds of grain that break open when heated and are eaten with salt, sugar, or butter

Pope /pəʊp/ *noun* [C] the leader of the Roman Catholic Church: *Pope John Paul II* ○ *The Pope was due to visit Paraguay in May.*

poplar /ˈpɒplər/ *noun* [C, U] a tall tree with branches that grow up to form a thin, pointed shape

popper /ˈpɒpər/ *noun* [C] UK (US **snap**) a metal or plastic object used to fasten clothing, made of two parts that fit together with a short, loud sound

poppy /ˈpɒpi/ *noun* [C] a red flower with small black seeds

populace /ˈpɒpjələs/ *noun* [group] formal all the people who live in a particular country or place

popular /ˈpɒpjələr/ *adj* **1 LIKED** ▷ ⏎ liked by many people: *'Jack' was the most popular boy's name.* ○ *The North African coast is becoming increasingly popular with British tourists.* → Opposite **unpopular 2 GENERAL** ▷ [always before noun] ⏎ for or involving ordinary people and not specialists or people who are very educated: *The issue was given full coverage in the popular press.* **3 MANY PEOPLE** ▷ [always before noun] A popular belief, opinion, etc is one that many people have: *The allegations are false, contrary to popular belief.*

popularity /ˌpɒpjəˈlærəti/ *noun* [U] ⏎ the quality of being liked by many people: *the increasing popularity of organic produce* → Opposite **unpopularity**

☑ Word partners for **popularity**

gain popularity • be growing in/increasing in popularity • sb's/sth's popularity increases/soars/wanes • the popularity of sth • sb/sth's popularity with sb

popularize (also UK **-ise**) /ˈpɒpjəlaraɪz/ *verb* [T] to make something become known or liked by many people: *It was the World Cup which popularized professional soccer in the United States.* • **popularization** (also UK **-isation**) /ˌpɒpjəlaraɪˈzeɪʃᵊn/ *noun* [U]

popularly /ˈpɒpjələli/ *adv* **popularly believed/called/known, etc** believed, called, etc by most people: *Los Angeles is popularly known as 'LA'.*

populate /ˈpɒpjəleɪt/ *verb* **be populated** If an area is populated by people or animals, they live in that area: *The countryside is densely/sparsely populated* (= there are many/few people). ○ *The forest was populated by rare and colourful birds.*

α: arm | ɜː her | iː see | ɔː saw | uː too | aɪ my | aʊ how | eə hair | eɪ day | əʊ no | ɪə near | ɔɪ boy | ʊə pure | aɪə fire | aʊə sour

population /ˌpɒpjəˈleɪʃᵊn/ **noun 1** [C, U] 🔵 the number of people living in a particular area: *What's the population of Brazil?* **2** [group] 🔵 all the people living in a particular area, or all the people or animals of a particular type: *a 9% rise in the prison population*

> ☑ Word partners for **population**
>
> **have** a population of [50 million, etc] • population **growth**

populous /ˈpɒpjələs/ **adj** formal A populous area has a lot of people living in it: *It's one of the world's most populous cities.*

pop-up /ˈpɒpʌp/ **adj** [always before noun] **1** A pop-up book is a book that has pictures that stand up from the pages when the book is opened. **2** A pop-up menu is a list of choices on a computer screen that is hidden until you choose to look at it: *Select the option you want from the **pop-up menu**.*

porcelain /ˈpɔːsᵊlɪn/ **noun** [U] a hard, shiny, white substance used to make cups, plates, etc, or the cups and plates themselves: *a porcelain dish* ∘ *a fine collection of porcelain*

porch /pɔːtʃ/ **noun** [C] a covered area built onto the entrance to a house

pore¹ /pɔːʳ/ **noun** [C] a very small hole in your skin that sweat (= salty liquid) can pass through

pore² /pɔːʳ/ **verb**

PHRASAL VERB **pore over sth** to study or look carefully at something, especially a book or document: *Jeremy spent the afternoon poring over his exam notes.*

pork /pɔːk/ **noun** [U] 🔵 meat from a pig: *pork chops*

pornography /pɔːˈnɒgrəfi/ **noun** [U] (informal **porn**) magazines and films showing naked people or sexual acts that are intended to make people feel sexually excited • **pornographic** /ˌpɔːnəˈgræfɪk/ **adj** relating to pornography: *pornographic images/videos*

porous /ˈpɔːrəs/ **adj** allowing liquid or air to pass through: *porous rock*

porridge /ˈpɒrɪdʒ/ **noun** [U] a soft, white food made of oats (= type of grain) and water or milk

port /pɔːt/ **noun 1** SHIPS ▷ [C] 🔵 a town or an area of a town next to water where ships arrive and leave from: *a fishing port* ∘ *the Belgian port of Zeebrugge* **2** DRINK ▷ [U] a sweet, strong, red wine that is made in Portugal **3** LEFT ▷ [U] the left side of a ship or aircraft: *the port side*

portable /ˈpɔːtəbl/ **adj** able to be carried: *a portable computer*

portal /ˈpɔːtᵊl/ **noun** [C] a page on the Internet with links to many other pages or websites that people use to start searching the World Wide Web

porter /ˈpɔːtəʳ/ **noun** [C] someone whose job is to carry other people's bags in hotels, stations, etc

portfolio /ˌpɔːtˈfəʊliəʊ/ **noun** [C] **1** a collection of designs, pictures, documents, etc that represents a person's work, or the large, flat container that it is carried in **2** a collection of accounts,

money, etc that is owned by a person or organization: *a stock portfolio*

porthole /ˈpɔːthəʊl/ **noun** [C] a small, round window in the side of a ship or aircraft

portion /ˈpɔːʃᵊn/ **noun** [C] **1** a part of something: *A large portion of their profits go straight back into new projects.* **2** 🔵 the amount of food served to one person, especially in a restaurant

portly /ˈpɔːtli/ **adj** humorous quite fat: *a portly gentleman*

portrait /ˈpɔːtrɪt/ **noun 1** 🔵 [C] a painting, drawing, or photograph of someone: *a **portrait of** the princess* ∘ *a portrait gallery/painter* **2 a portrait of sb/sth** a film or book that describes someone or something in detail: *His latest film is a portrait of life in the 1920s.* → See also **self-portrait**

portray /pɔːˈtreɪ/ **verb** [T] **1** If a book or film portrays someone or something, it describes or shows them: *Both novels portray the lives of professional athletes.* ∘ *In the movie he's **portrayed as** a hero.* **2** to act the part of a character in a film or play • **portrayal noun** [C, U] the way someone or something is portrayed: *He won several awards for his portrayal of the dictator.*

pose¹ /pəʊz/ **verb 1 pose a danger/problem/threat**, etc to cause a problem: *A lot of these chemicals pose very real threats to our health.* **2** [I] to stay in a particular position so that someone can paint or photograph you: *The two leaders **posed for** photographs outside the White House.* **3** [I] mainly UK to try to make people notice and admire you, especially by looking fashionable: *Pascal was posing in his new sunglasses.* **4 pose a question** formal to ask a question

PHRASAL VERB **pose as sb** to pretend that you are someone else: *He got into her house by posing as an electrician.*

pose² /pəʊz/ **noun 1** [C] the position that you stay in while someone photographs or paints you: *an elegant pose* **2** [no plural] a way of pretending to be more clever or interesting than you really are: *She's not really interested in art, it's just a pose.*

posh /pɒʃ/ **adj 1** 🔵 expensive and used or owned by rich people: *a posh hotel/restaurant* **2** UK from a high social class: *a posh voice*

position¹ /pəˈzɪʃᵊn/ **noun 1** SITTING/STANDING ▷ [C, U] 🔵 the way someone is sitting, standing, or lying, or if something is pointing up or down, etc: *a kneeling position* ∘ *I go to sleep on my back but I always wake up in a different **position**.* ∘ *Make sure your chair is in the upright **position**.* **2** SITUATION ▷ [C] 🔵 the situation that someone is in: [usually singular] *She's in a very difficult **position**.* **3 be in a position to do sth** to be able to do something because of your situation: *I'm not in a position to talk about this at the moment.* **4** PLACE ▷ [C] 🔵 the place where someone or something is: *I'm trying to find our position on the map.* ∘ *You're in a good **position** next to the window.* **5 be in position** If someone or something is in position, they are in the place that they should be in. **6 in first/second/third, etc position** in first/second/

P

third, etc place in a race or other competition: *She finished the race in third position.* **7** JOB ▷ [C] formal ⓑ a job: *to apply for a position in a company* **8** OPINION ▷ [C] formal a way of thinking about a subject: *What's the company's* ***position on*** *recycling?* **9** GAME ▷ [C] ⓑ the part that someone plays in a game such as football: *What* ***position*** *does he* ***play?*** **10** IMPORTANCE ▷ [C] ⓑ your level of importance in society: *the position of women in society*

position² /pə'zɪʃən/ verb [T] to put someone or something in a place for a reason: [often reflexive] *I positioned myself as far away from her as possible.*

positive /'pɒzətɪv/ adj **1** HAPPY ▷ ⓑ feeling happy about your life and your future: *a* ***positive attitude*** ○ *I'm feeling much more positive about things now.* **2** ENCOURAGING ▷ ⓑ Something that is positive makes you feel better about a situation: *We've shown people samples of the product and had a very* ***positive response.*** **3** CERTAIN ▷ [never before noun] ⓑ certain that something is true: *"Are you sure you saw him?" "Absolutely positive."* ○ [+ (that)] *I'm positive that I switched it off.* **4** PROOF ▷ [always before noun] showing without any doubt that something is true: ***positive proof*** **5** MEDICAL TEST ▷ If a medical test is positive, it shows that the person being tested has a disease or condition: *She did a pregnancy test and it was positive.* **6** NUMBER ▷ In mathematics, a positive number is greater than zero. **7** ***positive charge*** the electrical charge that is carried by protons (= parts of atoms)

positively /'pɒzətɪvli/ adv **1** ⓑ in a good way that makes you feel happier: *Most children* ***respond positively*** *to praise and encouragement.* **2** used to emphasize something that you say, especially when it is surprising: *Our waiter was* ***positively*** *rude.*

possess /pə'zes/ verb **1** [T] formal to have or own something: *He was found guilty of possessing an illegal weapon.* **2** ***what possessed her/him/you, etc?*** something that you say when someone has done something stupid: [+ to do sth] *What possessed you to tell him?*

possessed /pə'zest/ adj controlled by evil spirits

possession /pə'zeʃən/ noun **1** [C] ⓑ a thing that you own: [usually plural] ***personal possessions*** ○ *He woke up to discover that all his possessions had been stolen.* **2** [U] formal the fact of having or owning something: *I have* ***in my possession*** *a photograph which may be of interest to you.* ○ *He was caught* ***in possession of*** *explosives.*

> 🔲 Word partners for **possession**
>
> sb's **prized/most treasured** possessions • **material/personal** possessions

possessive /pə'zesɪv/ adj **1** wanting someone to love and spend time with you and no one else **2** ⓑ In grammar, a possessive word or form of a word shows who or what something belongs to. For example the words 'mine' and 'yours' are possessive pronouns.

possibility /,pɒsə'bɪləti/ noun **1** [C, U] ⓑ a chance that something may happen or be true:

Is there any ***possibility of*** *changing this ticket?* ○ [+ (that)] *There is a* ***strong possibility*** *that she wa lying.* **2** [C] ⓑ something that you can choose to do: *Have you considered the* ***possibility of*** *flying* → Opposite **impossibility (impossible)**

> ⚠ Common learner error: **possibility, occasion**, or **opportunity**?
>
> A **possibility** is a chance that something may happen or be true. **Possibility** cannot be followed by an infinitive.
>
> *Is there a possibility of finding a cure for AIDS?*
>
> ~~Is there a possibility to find a cure for AIDS?~~
>
> An **occasion** is an event, or a time when something happens. **Occasion** does not mean 'chance' or 'opportunity'.
>
> *Birthdays are always special occasions.*
>
> An **opportunity** is a possibility of doing something, or a situation that gives you the possibility of doing something.
>
> *The trip to Paris gave me an opportunity to speak French.*
>
> *Students had the opportunity to ask questions during the lecture.*
>
> *I have more opportunity to travel than my parents did.*
>
> ~~I have more possibility to travel than my parents did.~~

> 🔲 Word partners for **possibility**
>
> **consider/discuss/raise/rule out** a possibility • a **distinct/real/strong** possibility • possibility **of doing sth**

possible /'pɒsəbl/ adj **1** ⓐ If something i possible, it can happen or be done: [+ to do sth] *I it possible to speak to the manager please?* ○ *Th operation will* ***make it possible*** *for her to wal without crutches.* ○ *I'll send it today,* ***if possible*** → Opposite **impossible 2** ⓑ If something i possible, it might or might not exist or be true *possible safety problems* ○ [+ (that)] *It's possibl that the tapes were stolen.* **3** ***as much/quickly soon, etc as possible*** ⓐ as much/quickly/soor etc as something can happen or be done: *I'll g as soon as possible.* **4** ***the best/cheapest/wors etc possible*** the best/cheapest/worst, etc tha can happen or exist: *the shortest possible time*

possibly /'pɒsəbli/ adv **1** NOT CERTAIN ▷ ⓐ used when something is not certain: *Someone possibly Tom, had left the window oper* **2** EMPHASIS ▷ ⓑ used with 'can' or 'could' fc emphasis: *We'll do everything we possibly can t help.* ○ *I couldn't possibly ask you to do tha.* **3** QUESTIONS ▷ ⓑ used in polite questions *Could I possibly borrow your bike?*

post¹ /pəust/ noun **1** SYSTEM ▷ [no plural] UK (UP US **mail**) ⓐ the system for sending letters parcels, etc: *Your letter is* ***in the post.*** ○ *I'r sending the documents* ***by post.*** **2** LETTERS ▷ [U UK (UK/US **mail**) ⓐ letters, parcels, etc that yo send or receive: *Has the* ***post arrived/come*** *yet* **3** JOB ▷ [C] formal ⓑ a job: *a part-time post* ○ *teaching post* **4** POLE ▷ [C] a long, vertical piec of wood or metal fixed into the ground at on end: *I found the dog tied to a post.* **5 PLACE** ▷ [C] a place where someone stands to guard something

post² /pəʊst/ **verb** [T] **1** Ⓐ2 UK (UK/US **mail**) to send a letter or parcel by post: *Did you post my letter?* **2** Ⓑ1 to leave a message on a website: *I posted a query about arthritis treatment.* **3 be posted to France/London/Singapore, etc** to be sent to France/London/Singapore, etc to work, usually for the government or army **4 post a notice/sign, etc** to put a notice/sign, etc somewhere: *He posted the message on the noticeboard.* **5 keep sb posted** to make certain that someone always knows what is happening: *Keep me posted on anything that happens while I'm away.*

postage /ˈpəʊstɪdʒ/ **noun** [U] money that you pay to send a letter or parcel: *first-class postage* ∘ *postage and packing*

postage and packing **noun** [U] UK (US **shipping and handling**) money that you pay so that a company will send you something through the post

postage stamp **noun** [C] formal a small, official piece of paper that you buy and stick onto a letter or parcel before you post it

postal /ˈpəʊstəl/ **adj** [always before noun] relating to the system of sending letters and parcels: *the postal service/system*

postal order **noun** [C] UK (US **money order**) an official piece of paper bought at a post office that you can send instead of money

post box **noun** [C] UK (US **mailbox**) a large, metal container in a public place where you can post letters

postcard /ˈpəʊstkɑːd/ **noun** [C] Ⓐ2 a card with a picture on one side that you send without an envelope: *Send me a postcard.*

postcode /ˈpəʊstkəʊd/ **noun** [C] a group of letters and numbers that comes at the end of someone's address in the UK → Compare **zip code**

poster /ˈpəʊstər/ **noun** [C] Ⓐ2 a large, printed picture or notice that you put on a wall, in order to decorate a place or to advertise something

posterity /pɒsˈterəti/ **noun** [U] the people who will be alive in the future: *These works of art should be preserved for posterity.*

postgraduate /ˌpəʊstˈɡrædʒuət/ **noun** [C] (informal **postgrad**) **1** UK (US **graduate student**) a student who has one degree and now studies at a university for a more advanced degree **2** US a student who has a master's degree or PhD. and now studies for a more advanced degree • **postgraduate adj** *a postgraduate degree in mathematics*

posthumous /ˈpɒstjəməs/ **adj** happening after someone's death: *the posthumous publication of her letters* • **posthumously adv**

posting /ˈpəʊstɪŋ/ **noun** [C] mainly UK a job in another country that you have been sent to by the company you work for: *a posting to Madrid*

Post-it (note) /ˈpəʊstɪtˌnəʊt/ **noun** [C] trademark a small piece of paper that you can write on and then stick to other papers or surfaces

postman /ˈpəʊstmən/ **noun** [C] (plural **postmen**)

UK (US **mailman, letter carrier, mail carrier**) Ⓑ1 someone who takes and brings letters and parcels as a job

postmark /ˈpəʊstmɑːk/ **noun** [C] an official mark on a letter or parcel, showing the place and time it was sent

post-mortem /ˌpəʊstˈmɔːtəm/ **noun** [C] a medical examination of a dead body to find out why the person died

post office **noun** [C] Ⓐ2 a place where you can buy stamps and send letters and parcels

postpone /pəʊstˈpəʊn/ **verb** [T] Ⓑ1 to arrange for something to happen at a later time: *The trip to the museum has been postponed until next week.*

postscript /ˈpəʊstskrɪpt/ **noun** [C] extra information at the end of a letter or email, usually added after writing the letters 'PS'

posture /ˈpɒstʃər/ **noun** [U] the position of your back, shoulders, etc when you are standing or sitting: *She has very good posture.*

postwar /ˌpəʊstˈwɔːr/ **adj** happening or existing in the period after a war: *postwar Europe*

pot¹ /pɒt/ **noun** [C] Ⓑ1 a round container, usually used for storing things or cooking: *a flower pot* ∘ *a pot of coffee/tea* ∘ *pots and pans*

IDIOM **go to pot** to be damaged or spoilt because no effort has been made: *My diet's gone to pot since the holidays.*

→ See also **melting pot**

pot² /pɒt/ **verb** [T] (**potting, potted**) to put a plant into a pot filled with soil

potassium /pəˈtæsiəm/ **noun** [U] a chemical element that combines easily with other elements, often used to help plants grow well

potato /pəˈteɪtəʊ/ **noun** [C, U] (plural **potatoes**) Ⓐ1 a round vegetable with a brown, yellow, or red skin that grows in the ground: *boiled/fried potatoes* ∘ *mashed potato* → See colour picture **Fruit and Vegetables** on page Centre 10 → See also **couch potato, jacket potato, sweet potato**

potato chip **noun** [C] US (UK **crisp**) a very thin, dry, fried slice of potato

potent /ˈpəʊtənt/ **adj** very powerful or very effective: *a potent drug/weapon* • **potency** /ˈpəʊtənsi/ **noun** [U] the quality of being potent

potential¹ /pəˈtenʃəl/ **adj** [always before noun] Ⓑ2 A potential problem, employer, partner, etc may become one in the future, although they are not one now: *a potential danger/threat* ∘ *a potential customer* ∘ *A number of potential buyers have expressed interest in the building.* • **potentially adv** Ⓑ2 *a potentially fatal condition*

> 🗹 Word partners for **potential**
>
> **have** [enormous/great, etc] potential • **achieve/fulfil/reach/realize** your (full) potential • **see/spot** sb's/sth's potential • sb's/sth's potential **as** sth

potential² /pəˈtenʃəl/ **noun 1** [U] Ⓑ2 qualities or abilities that may develop and allow someone or something to succeed: *to achieve your full potential* **2 potential for sth/doing sth** the possibility that something may happen: *There is the potential for some really interesting research.*

pothole /'pɒthəʊl/ **noun** [C] a hole in the surface of a road

potted /'pɒtɪd/ **adj 1** planted in a container: *potted plants/flowers* ∘ *a potted palm* **2 potted history/version, etc of sth** UK a story or report that has been changed to make it shorter and more simple: *a potted version of Shakespeare*

potted plant noun [C] (also UK **pot plant**) a plant that is grown in a container, and usually kept inside

potter¹ /'pɒtər/ **noun** [C] a person who makes plates, bowls, etc from clay

potter² /'pɒtər/ **verb**

PHRASAL VERB **potter about/around (sth)** mainly UK to spend time in a pleasant, relaxed way, often doing small jobs in your house

pottery /'pɒtəri/ **noun 1** OBJECTS ▷ [U] ⑫ plates, bowls, etc that are made from clay **2** ACTIVITY ▷ [U] ⑫ the activity of making plates, bowls, etc from clay **3** PLACE ▷ [C] a place where plates, bowls, etc made from clay are made or sold

potty¹ /'pɒti/ **noun** [C] a small toilet that young children use

potty² /'pɒti/ **adj** UK informal crazy or stupid

pouch /paʊtʃ/ **noun** [C] **1** a small, soft bag made of leather or cloth **2** a pocket of skin in which some female animals carry their babies

poultry /'pəʊltri/ **noun 1** [plural] chickens and other birds that people breed for meat and eggs **2** [U] the meat of chickens and other birds eaten as food

pounce /paʊns/ **verb** [I] to suddenly move towards a person or animal that you want to catch: *The police were waiting to pounce when he arrived at the airport.*

PHRASAL VERB **pounce on sth/sb** to immediately criticize a mistake

pound¹ /paʊnd/ **noun** [C] **1** ⑫ the unit of money used in the UK: *a hundred pounds/£100* ∘ *a pound coin* **2** (written abbreviation **lb**) ⑫ a unit for measuring weight, equal to 453.6 grams or 16 ounces: *a pound of potatoes* ∘ *The baby weighed just four pounds when she was born* → See Study Page **Measurements** on page Centre 31

pound² /paʊnd/ **verb 1** [I, T] ⑫ to hit something many times using a lot of force: *Someone was pounding on the door.* **2** [I] ⑫ If your heart pounds, it beats very quickly: *My heart was pounding as I walked out onto the stage.* **3 pound along/down/up, etc** to run somewhere with quick, loud steps: *He pounded up the stairs.*

pour /pɔːr/ **verb 1** [T] ⑪ to make a liquid flow from or into a container: *I poured the milk into a jug.* ∘ [+ two objects] *Can I pour you a drink?* **2** [I] (also UK **pour down**) ⑪ to rain, producing a lot of water: *We can't go out in this weather – it's*

pour

pouring! **3 pour into/out/from, etc a** ⑫ to flow quickly and in large amounts: *Blood we pouring from my leg.* **b** to enter or leave a plac in large numbers: *The crowd poured out into th street.*

PHRASAL VERB **pour sth out** ⑫ If you pour o your feelings or thoughts, you talk very ho estly about what is making you sad: *She listene quietly while he* **poured out** *his* **troubles**.

pout /paʊt/ **verb** [I] to push your lips forwar because you are annoyed or because you wa to look sexually attractive • **pout noun** [C]

poverty /'pɒvəti/ **noun** [U] ⑫ the state of bein very poor: *to live in poverty*

☑ Word partners for **poverty**

die in/live in poverty • alleviate/fight/tackle poverty • abject/extreme poverty

poverty-stricken /'pɒvətiˌstrɪkən/ **adj** poverty-stricken area or person is very poor.

POW /ˌpiːəʊˈdʌbljuː/ **noun** [C] abbreviation f prisoner of war: a soldier who is caught b enemy soldiers during a war

powder /'paʊdər/ **noun** [C, U] ⑪ a dry substanc made of many small, loose grains: *curry powde* ∘ *face powder* • **powdered adj** in the form o powder: *powdered milk/sugar* → See also **talcu powder**

power¹ /paʊər/ **noun 1** CONTROL ▷ [U] ⑥ control or influence over people and event *He likes to have* **power over** *people.* **2** POLITICS [U] ⑫ political control in a country: *They hav been* **in power** *too long.* ∘ *When did this gover ment* **come to power** *(= start to control th country)?* **3** ENERGY ▷ [U] ⑪ energy, usuall electricity, that is used to provide light, heat, et nuclear power ∘ *Turn off the power at the ma switch.* **4** COUNTRY ▷ [C] a country that has a l of influence over others: *a major world pow* **5** OFFICIAL RIGHT ▷ [C, U] an official or leg right to do something: [+ to do sth] *It's not in m* **power** *to stop him publishing this boo* **6** STRENGTH ▷ [U] strength or force: *economi military power* **7** ABILITY ▷ [U] a natur ability: *to lose the power of speech* **8 do ever thing in your power to do sth** to do everythin that you are able and allowed to do: *I've don everything in my power to help him.* **9 th powers that be** important people who hav authority over others → See also **balance • power**

☑ Word partners for **power**

come to/devolve/seize/take/wield power • considerable/enormous power

power² /paʊər/ **verb** [T] to supply energy to machine and make it work: [often passive] *Th clock is powered by two small batteries.*

power cut noun [C] UK (US **power outage**) there is a power cut, the supply of electrici suddenly stops.

powerful /'paʊəfəl/ **adj 1** CONTROL ▷ ⑪ powerful person is able to control and influenc people and events: *a powerful man/woma*

2 STRENGTH ▷ **B1** having a lot of strength or force: *a powerful engine/weapon* **3 EFFECT** ▷ **B2** having a strong effect on people: *a powerful effect/influence* • **powerfully** adv

powerless /ˈpaʊələs/ adj not able to control events: [+ to do sth] *The police were powerless to stop the fighting.*

power outage /ˈpaʊərˌaʊtɪdʒ/ noun [C] US (UK **power cut**) If there is a power outage, the supply of electricity suddenly stops.

power ˌstation noun [C] (also US ˈpower ˌplant) a place where electricity is produced

power ˌtool noun [C] a tool that uses electricity

pp written abbreviation for pages: *See pp 10 – 12 for more information.*

P&P /ˌpiːənˈpiː/ noun [U] UK abbreviation for postage and packing

PR /ˌpiːˈɑːr/ noun [U] abbreviation for public relations: writing and activities that are intended to make a person, company, or product more popular: *good/bad PR* ∘ *a PR campaign*

practicable /ˈpræktɪkəbl/ adj formal able to be done successfully: *It's just not practicable to travel in this weather.*

practical¹ /ˈpræktɪkəl/ adj **1 REAL** ▷ **B2** relating to real situations or actions and not to thoughts or ideas: *practical experience* ∘ *They can offer practical help.* **2 SUITABLE** ▷ suitable or useful for a situation which may involve some difficulty: *practical clothes/shoes* ∘ *Pale carpets just aren't practical if you have kids.* **3 POSSIBLE** ▷ able to be done successfully: *a practical solution* ∘ *The plan is simply not practical.* **4 GOOD AT PLANNING** ▷ Someone who is practical is good at planning things and dealing with problems: *She has a lot of interesting ideas but she's not very practical.* **5 GOOD WITH HANDS** ▷ good at repairing and making things

practical² /ˈpræktɪkəl/ noun [C] a lesson or examination in which you do or make something instead of only writing

practicalities /ˌpræktɪˈkælətiz/ noun [plural] real situations or facts: *the practicalities of running your own business*

practicality /ˌpræktɪˈkæləti/ noun [U] **1** the possibility that something can be done successfully: *I like the idea but I'm not sure about the practicality of it.* **2** how suitable or useful something is for a situation that may involve some difficulty

practical ˈjoke noun [C] a trick using actions and not words to make people laugh: *to play a practical joke on someone*

practically /ˈpræktɪkəli/ adv **1 B2** almost: *It's practically impossible to get there.* ∘ *We see her practically every day.* **2** in a suitable or useful way: *We need to think practically.*

practice /ˈpræktɪs/ noun **1 REPEATING** ▷ [U] **A2** repeatedly doing an activity to improve your ability: *We need a bit more practice before the concert.* ∘ *I've got basketball practice tonight.* **2 ACTIVITY** ▷ [C, U] what people do or how they do it: *business/working practices* ∘ [+ of + doing sth] *the illegal practice of copying CDs* ∘

[+ to do sth] *It is common practice to bury waste in landfills.* **3 WORK** ▷ [C] a business in which several doctors or lawyers work together, or the work that they do: *a legal/medical practice* **4 in practice** **B2** If something is true in practice, this is the real situation: *In practice, the new laws have had little effect.* **5 be out of practice** to not do something well because you have not done it recently **6 put something into practice** to try a plan or idea: *Next month we will have a chance to put these ideas into practice.*

> ⚠ Common learner error: **practice** or **practise**?
>
> In British English, **practice** is used for the noun, and **practise** for the verb.
> *He needs more practice before he can sail on his own.*
> In US English, **practice** is used for the noun and the verb.

practise UK (US **practice**) /ˈpræktɪs/ verb **1 REPEAT** ▷ [I, T] **A1** to repeat something regularly in order to improve your ability: *You need to practise your pronunciation.* ∘ *They're practising for tomorrow's concert.* **2 WORK** ▷ [I, T] to work as a doctor or a lawyer: *to practise medicine/law* **3 CUSTOM/RELIGION** ▷ [T] to do something regularly according to a custom, religion, or a set of rules: *to practise a religion*

IDIOM practise what you preach to behave as well as you often tell other people they should behave: *I'd have more respect for him if he practised what he preached.*

practised UK (US **practiced**) /ˈpræktɪst/ adj very good at doing something because you have done it so often: *She answered the questions with practised ease.*

practising UK (US **practicing**) /ˈpræktɪsɪŋ/ adj a **practising Catholic/Jew/Muslim, etc** someone who follows the rules of a religion

practitioner /prækˈtɪʃənər/ noun [C] formal someone who works as a doctor or a lawyer: *a medical practitioner* → See also **general practitioner**

pragmatic /prægˈmætɪk/ adj doing things in a practical and realistic way and not using only ideas: *a pragmatic approach to a problem*

pragmatism /ˈprægmətɪzəm/ noun [U] pragmatic behaviour or ways of doing things • **pragmatist** noun [C] someone who is pragmatic

prairie /ˈpreəri/ noun [C] a large, flat area of land in North America that is usually covered in grass

praise¹ /preɪz/ verb [T] **1 B2** to say that you admire someone or something, or that they are very good: *He praised the team's performance.* ∘ *Residents praised the firemen for their swift action.* **2** to give respect and thanks to a god: *Praise God, no one was hurt.*

praise² /preɪz/ noun [U] words you say to show that you admire someone or something: *They deserve praise for their achievements.* ∘ *Her first novel won a lot of praise from the critics.*

praiseworthy /ˈpreɪzˌwɜːði/ adj formal deserving praise

pram /præm/ noun [C] mainly UK a small vehicle with four wheels for carrying a baby

prance /prɑːns/ verb [I] to walk or dance in a proud way, often because you want people to look at you: She was **prancing around** in a bikini.

prank /præŋk/ noun [C] a trick that is intended to be funny

prat /præt/ noun [C] UK very informal a stupid person

prawn /prɔːn/ noun [C] 🅑 a small sea animal that you can eat, and which has a shell and ten legs

pray /preɪ/ verb [I, T] 1 🅐 to speak to a god in order to show your feelings or to ask for something: Let us **pray for** all the sick children. ◦ [+ that] She prayed that God would forgive her. 2 🅑 to hope very much that something will happen: We're just **praying for** rain.

prayer /preəʳ/ noun 1 [C] 🅑 the words you say to a god: Shall we **say a prayer for** him? 2 [U] the activity of praying: They knelt **in prayer**.

preach /priːtʃ/ verb 1 [I, T] to talk to a group of people about a religious subject, usually as a priest in a church: to preach the gospel 2 [I] to try to persuade people to believe or support something, often in an annoying way → See also **practise what you preach**

preacher /ˈpriːtʃəʳ/ noun [C] someone who speaks in public about a religious subject, especially someone whose job is to do this

preamble /ˈpriːæmbl/ noun [C] formal an introduction to a speech or piece of writing

precarious /prɪˈkeəriəs/ adj 1 A precarious situation is likely to become worse: Many illegal immigrants are in a **precarious position**. 2 not fixed and likely to fall: That shelf looks a bit precarious. • **precariously** adv Her cup was **balanced precariously** on the arm of the chair.

precaution /prɪˈkɔːʃən/ noun [C] something that you do to prevent bad things happening in the future: Driving alone at night can be dangerous, so always **take precautions**. ◦ They called the doctor **as a precaution**. ◦ [+ of + doing sth] He took the precaution of locking the door. • **precautionary** adj a precautionary measure/step something that you do in order to prevent something bad from happening

precede /priːˈsiːd/ verb [T] formal to happen or exist before something else: [often passive] The formal ceremony was **preceded by** a parade.

• **preceding** adj [always before noun] happenin⟩ or coming before: the preceding months

precedence /ˈpresɪdəns/ noun [U] If one perso⟩ or thing has precedence over another, it ⟩ considered to be more important: to giv⟩ **precedence to** something ◦ Quality should tak⟩ precedence over cost.

precedent /ˈpresɪdənt/ noun [C, U] an action ⟨ decision that is used as an example whe⟩ someone wants to do a similar thing in th⟩ future: This decision has **set an** important leg⟩ precedent for other countries.

precinct /ˈpriːsɪŋkt/ noun 1 a pedestrian/shop⟩ ping precinct UK an area in a town where ther⟩ are shops and no cars are allowed 2 [C] US a⟩ area in a city that a particular group of polic⟩ are responsible for, or the building in which the⟩ work: the 45th precinct

precincts /ˈpriːsɪŋkts/ noun [plural] the area ⟨ land around a building, especially a larg⟩ church: the cathedral precincts

precious[1] /ˈpreʃəs/ adj 1 🅑 very important t⟩ you: His books are his most precious possession⟩ 2 🅑 rare and very valuable: a precious vase ◦ precious metal/stone

precious[2] /ˈpreʃəs/ adv precious few/little ver⟩ little or very few of something: We have preciou⟩ little money at present.

precipice /ˈpresɪpɪs/ noun [C] 1 a dangerou⟩ situation that could lead to failure or harm: Th⟩ two countries stood **on the precipice** of war. 2 ⟩ steep side of a mountain or high area of land

precipitate /prɪˈsɪpɪteɪt/ verb [T] formal to mak⟩ something happen: [often passive] The war w⟩ precipitated by an invasion.

precipitation /prɪˌsɪpɪˈteɪʃən/ noun [U] ⟩ science, precipitation is rain or snow that fal⟩ to the ground.

precis /ˈpreɪsiː/ noun [C, U] formal a report givin⟩ the main ideas of a piece of writing or speech

precise /prɪˈsaɪs/ adj 1 🅑 exact and accurat⟩ precise details/instructions → Opposite **imprecis⟩** 2 **to be precise** 🅑 used to give exact detai⟩ about something: We met in 1994 – October 1st t⟩ be precise. 3 [always before noun] used ⟩ emphasize something that you are referring t⟩ At that **precise moment**, the door opened.

precisely /prɪˈsaɪsli/ adv 1 EXACTLY ▷ 🅑 exactl⟩ at 6 o'clock precisely 2 EMPHASIS ▷ 🅑 used t⟩ emphasize something: This is precisely the kin⟩ of thing I was hoping to avoid. 3 AGREEMENT ⟩ used to agree with what someone else says: "It⟩ the shape I dislike, not the colour." "Precisely!"

precision /prɪˈsɪʒən/ noun [U] the quality ⟨ being very exact and accurate: She parked the c⟩ with great precision.

preclude /prɪˈkluːd/ verb [T] formal to prever⟩ something from happening: [+ from + doing st⟩ His illness precludes him from taking part in an⟩ sports.

precocious /prɪˈkəʊʃəs/ adj Children who ar⟩ precocious have the confidence or skill of a⟩ adult: A precocious child, she went to university ⟩ the age of 15.

preconceived /ˌpriːkənˈsiːvd/ adj Preconceive⟩

ideas are decided before the facts of a situation are known: *preconceived ideas*

preconception /ˌpriːkənˈsepʃən/ noun [C] what you believe before you know the facts of a situation: *People have so many preconceptions about unmarried mothers.*

precondition /ˌpriːkənˈdɪʃən/ noun [C] formal what must happen before something else can happen: *The ceasefire is a precondition for peace talks.*

precursor /ˌpriːˈkɜːsər/ noun [C] formal something that happens or exists before something else and influences its development: *Infection with HIV is a precursor to AIDS.*

predate /ˌpriːˈdeɪt/ verb [T] to exist or happen before something else: *The drinking of alcohol predates the Greeks and Romans.*

predator /ˈpredətər/ noun [C] an animal that kills and eats other animals

predatory /ˈpredətəri/ adj **1** A predatory person tries to get things from other people in a way that is unfair. **2** A predatory animal kills and eats other animals.

predecessor /ˈpriːdɪˌsesər/ ⓤⓢ /ˈpredəsesər/ noun [C] **1** the person who was in a job or position before: *He seems a lot better than his predecessor.* **2** something that existed before another, similar thing: *The predecessors to these computers were much larger and heavier.*

predetermined /ˌpriːdɪˈtɜːmɪnd/ adj formal decided before: *They met at a predetermined time and place.*

predeterminer /ˌpriːdɪˈtɜːmɪnər/ noun [C] a word that is used before a determiner to give more information about a noun. For example 'all' in 'all these children' is a predeterminer.

predicament /prɪˈdɪkəmənt/ noun [C] a problem or a difficult situation: *I sympathize with your predicament.*

⏹ Word partners for **predicament**

face a predicament • explain your predicament • be in a predicament

predicate /ˈpredɪkət/ noun [C] the part of a sentence that gives information about the subject. In the sentence 'We went to the airport.', 'went to the airport' is the predicate.

predicative /prɪˈdɪkətɪv/ adj A predicative adjective comes after a verb. In the sentence 'She is happy.', 'happy' is a predicative adjective. → Compare **attributive**

predict /prɪˈdɪkt/ verb [T] ⓑ to say what you think will happen in the future: *Companies are predicting massive profits.* ° [+ (that)] *They predicted that the temperature would reach 80 degrees today.*

predictable /prɪˈdɪktəbl/ adj ⓑ happening or behaving in a way that you expect and not unusual or interesting: *a predictable result* ° *She's so predictable.* → Opposite **unpredictable** • **predictably** adv

prediction /prɪˈdɪkʃən/ noun [C, U] ⓑ the act of saying what you think will happen in the future: *I wouldn't like to make any predictions about the result of this match.*

⏹ Word partners for **prediction**

make a prediction • an accurate/gloomy prediction • a prediction about sth • a prediction of [disaster/an improvement, etc]

pre‚dictive ˈtexting noun [U] a way of writing text messages on your mobile phone in which words are suggested automatically when you write the first few letters

predilection /ˌpriːdɪˈlekʃən/ noun [C] formal If you have a predilection for something, you like it very much: *She has a predilection for chocolate.*

predisposed /ˌpriːdɪˈspəʊzd/ adj be predisposed to sth to be more likely than other people to have a medical problem or to behave in a particular way: *Some people are predisposed to addiction.* • **predisposition** /ˌpriːdɪspəˈzɪʃən/ noun [C] If you have a predisposition to a medical problem or type of behaviour, you are likely to have it or do it: *people with a predisposition to heart disease*

predominant /prɪˈdɒmɪnənt/ adj more important or noticeable than other things: *He has played a predominant role in these talks.* • **predominance** /prɪˈdɒmɪnəns/ noun [U] the fact of being more important or noticeable than things: *the predominance of English on the Internet*

predominantly /prɪˈdɒmɪnəntli/ adv mostly or mainly: *a predominantly Asian community*

predominate /prɪˈdɒmɪneɪt/ verb [I] to be the largest in number or the most important: *Olive trees predominate in this area.*

pre-eminent /ˌpriːˈemɪnənt/ adj more important or better than others: *a pre-eminent artist/scholar* • **pre-eminence** /ˌpriːˈemɪnəns/ noun [U] the quality of being pre-eminent

pre-empt /ˌpriːˈempt/ verb [T] to do something before something else happens in order to prevent it or reduce its effect • **pre-emptive** adj preventing something else from happening: *to take pre-emptive action*

preen /priːn/ verb [I, T] **1** If a bird preens or preens itself, it makes its feathers clean and tidy. **2** to try to look attractive: [often reflexive] *The actors preened themselves in the dressing room.*

pre-existing /ˌpriːɪgˈzɪstɪŋ/ adj existing before something else: *a pre-existing medical condition*

prefabricated /ˌpriːˈfæbrɪkeɪtɪd/ adj a prefabricated building/home/house, etc a building that has already been partly built when it is put together

preface /ˈprefɪs/ noun [C] a piece of writing at the beginning of a book that explains why it was written

prefect /ˈpriːfekt/ noun [C] in the UK, an older student in a school who has special duties and some authority

prefer /prɪˈfɜːr/ verb [T] (preferring, preferred) **1** ⓐ to like someone or something more than another person or thing: *I prefer dogs to cats.* ° [+ doing sth] *She prefers watching tennis to playing.* **2** would prefer ⓐ used to say what you want or ask someone what they want: [+ to

P

do sth] *I'd prefer to go alone.* ○ *Would you prefer red or white wine?*

> **!** Common learner error: **prefer**
>
> Remember that **prefer** is often followed by **to do sth** or **doing sth.**
> *I prefer to walk.*
> *I prefer walking.*
> ~~I prefer walk.~~

preferable /'pref°rəbl/ **adj** ⓑ better or more suitable: *Staying at home is* ***preferable to*** *going out with someone you don't like.*

preferably /'pref°rəbli/ **adv** ⓑ if possible: *Serve the pudding with ice cream, preferably vanilla.*

preference /'pref°r°ns/ **noun 1** ⓑ [C, U] the feeling of liking something or someone more than another person or thing: *personal* ***preferences*** ○ *We have white and brown bread. Do you* ***have a preference?*** ○ *I have a* ***preference for*** *dark-haired men.* **2 give preference to sb** to give special treatment to someone: *Hospitals must give preference to urgent cases.*

> **2** Word partners for **preference**
>
> **express/have** a preference • a **clear/marked** preference • a **personal** preference • a preference **for** sth

preferential /ˌpref°r'enʃ°l/ **adj** **preferential treatment** If you are given preferential treatment, you are treated in a better way than other people: *There were complaints that some guests had been given preferential treatment.*

prefix /'priːfɪks/ **noun** [C] ⓑ a group of letters that you add to the beginning of a word to make another word. In the word 'unimportant', 'un-' is a prefix. → Compare **suffix** → See Study Page **Word formation** on page Centre 28.

pregnancy /'pregnənsi/ **noun** [C, U] the state of being pregnant: *a teenage pregnancy*

pregnant /'pregnənt/ **adj 1** ⓑ A pregnant woman has a baby developing inside her uterus: *to* ***get pregnant*** ○ *She's five months pregnant.* **2 a pregnant pause/silence** a pause or silence full of meaning that is not said in words

preheat /priː'hiːt/ **verb** [T] to heat an oven to a particular temperature before putting food in it: *Preheat the oven to 180 degrees.*

prehistoric /ˌpriːhɪ'stɒrɪk/ **adj** relating to a time in the past before there were written records of events: *prehistoric remains*

prejudice¹ /'predʒədɪs/ **noun** [C, U] ⓑ the feeling of not liking a group of people or unfair treatment of them because they are a different race, sex, religion, etc: *racial prejudice* ○ ***prejudice against*** *women*

> **2** Word partners for **prejudice**
>
> **encounter/experience/face** prejudice • prejudice **against** sb

prejudice² /'predʒədɪs/ **verb** [T] **1** to influence someone in an unfair way so that they have a bad opinion of someone or something: *Her comments may have* ***prejudiced*** *the voters*

against *him.* **2** to have a harmful effect on situation: *Newspaper reports have prejudiced th trial.*

prejudiced /'predʒədɪst/ **adj** feeling dislike for group of people or treating them unfairl because they are a different race, sex, religion etc: *Are the police* ***prejudiced against*** *blac people?*

preliminary /prɪ'lɪmɪn°ri/ **adj** [always befor noun] done or happening in order to prepar for the main event or activity: *a preliminar discussion/meeting* • **preliminary noun** [C] some thing that you do at the start of an event o activity

prelude /'preljuːd/ **noun 1 a prelude to sth** something that happens before another even or activity, usually as an introduction to it: *Ther are hopes that the talks are a prelude to a agreement.* **2** [C] a short piece of music tha introduces the main piece

premature /'premətʃər/ /ˌpriːmə'tʊr/ **ad** happening too soon or before the usual time *premature ageing/death* ○ *a* ***premature bab*** ○ [+ to do sth] *It seems a bit premature to star talking about it already.* • **prematurely adv** *H died prematurely of cancer.*

premeditated /ˌpriː'medɪteɪtɪd/ **adj** If a crime **i** premeditated, it is planned: ***premeditate*** *murder* ○ *a premeditated attack*

premenstrual /ˌpriː'menstruəl/ **adj** related t the time just before a woman's perio (= monthly blood from the uterus): ***premen strual syndrome/tension***

premier¹ /'premiər/ /prɪ'mɪr/ **noun** [C] th leader of a government: *the Chinese premie* • **premiership noun** [U] the period in whic someone is premier

premier² /'premiər/ /prɪ'mɪr/ **adj** [alway before noun] best or most important: *the city premier hotel*

premiere /'premieər/ /prɪ'mɪr/ **noun** [C] th first public performance of a film, play, etc: *film premiere* ○ *the world premiere* • **premier verb** [I, T] [often passive] *The opera was premiere in Paris.*

the Premiership /'premiəʃɪp/ **noun** the grou of the best English football teams who compet against each other

premise /'premɪs/ **noun** [C] formal an idea tha you use to support another theory

premises /'premɪsɪz/ **noun** [plural] the land o buildings used by an organization: *We're movin to new premises.* ○ *Smoking is not allowed an where* ***on the premises****.*

premium¹ /'priːmiəm/ **noun 1** [C] an amount c money you pay for insurance (= payments for a accident or illness): *How much is the monthl premium?* **2** [C] an amount or rate that is highe than average: *You* ***pay a premium*** *for apartment in the city centre.* **3 be at a premium** *I* something useful is at a premium, there is nc enough of it: *Time is at a premium just before th start of exams.* **4 place/put a premium on sth** t consider a quality or achievement as ver important: *She puts a premium on honesty.*

premium² /ˈpriːmiəm/ **adj** [always before noun] A premium product is of a higher quality or value than others: *premium beer/cigars*

premonition /ˌpreməˈnɪʃᵊn/ **noun** [C] a feeling that something, especially something unpleasant, is going to happen: *to have a premonition* ∘ *a premonition of disaster*

prenatal /ˌpriːˈneɪtᵊl/ **adj** US (UK **antenatal**) relating to pregnant women before their babies are born: *prenatal care*

preoccupation /priːˌɒkjəˈpeɪʃᵊn/ **noun 1** [C, U] the state of thinking or worrying about something so much that you do not think about other things: *a preoccupation with death/food* **2** [C] something that you think or worry about a lot: *His main preoccupations are football and women.*

preoccupied /ˌpriːˈɒkjəpaɪd/ **adj** thinking or worrying about something a lot: *She's been very preoccupied recently.* ∘ *He's far too preoccupied with his own problems to notice mine.* • **preoccupy** /ˌpriːˈɒkjəpaɪ/ **verb** [T] If something preoccupies you, you think or worry about it a lot.

prepaid /priːˈpeɪd/ **adj** If something is prepaid, you pay for it before a particular time: *Susan just got prepaid tickets for the show next weekend.*

preparation /ˌprepᵊrˈeɪʃᵊn/ **noun** [U] 🔵 the things that you do or the time that you spend preparing for something: *Did you do much preparation for your interview?* ∘ *He's been painting the outside of the house in preparation for winter.* ∘ *the preparation of the document*

preparations /ˌprepərˈeɪʃᵊnz/ **noun** [plural] 🔵 things that you do to get ready for something: *wedding preparations* ∘ *We've been making preparations for the journey.* ∘ *I've been busy with last-minute preparations for our trip.*

🔲 Word partners for **preparations**

begin/finalize/make preparations • final/last-minute preparations • preparations are underway • preparations for sth

---

preparatory /prɪˈpærətᵊri/ **adj** done in order to get ready for something: *preparatory work*

pre'paratory ˌschool noun [C] formal a prep school

prepare /prɪˈpeᵊr/ **verb 1** [I, T] 🔵 to get someone or something ready for something that will happen in the future: *They're preparing for the big game.* ∘ *We're preparing the students for their end-of-year exam.* ∘ *[+ to do sth] I was busy preparing to go on a trip.* **2 prepare yourself** 🔵 to make yourself ready to deal with a difficult situation: *Prepare yourself for a shock.* **3** [T] 🔵 to make food ready to be eaten: *to prepare lunch*

prepared /prɪˈpeəd/ **adj 1** 🔵 ready to deal with a situation: *I wasn't prepared for the cold.* **2 be prepared to do sth** 🔵 to be willing to do something: *You must be prepared to work hard.*

preponderance /prɪˈpɒndᵊrᵊns/ **noun** formal a **preponderance of sth** a larger amount of one thing than of others: *There is a preponderance of older people in this area.*

preposition /ˌprepəˈzɪʃᵊn/ **noun** [C] 🔵 a word or group of words that is used before a noun or pronoun to show place, direction, time, etc. For example 'on' in 'Your keys are on the table.' is a preposition.

preposterous /prɪˈpɒstᵊrəs/ **adj** extremely stupid: *That's a preposterous idea!*

prep school /ˈprepskuːl/ **noun** [C] **1** in the UK, a private school for children aged between 8 and 13 **2** in the US, a private school that prepares students for college

prerequisite /ˌpriːˈrekwɪzɪt/ **noun** [C] formal something that is necessary in order for something else to happen or exist: *Trust is a prerequisite for any sort of relationship.*

prerogative /prɪˈrɒgətɪv/ **noun** [C] formal something that you have the right to do because of who you are: *Alex makes the decisions – that's his prerogative as company director.*

Presbyterian /ˌprezbɪˈtɪəriən/ **adj** belonging or relating to a type of Christian church with elected groups of local members involved in the official organization of local churches • **Presbyterian noun** [C]

pre-school /ˈpriːskuːl/ **adj** [always before noun] relating to children who are too young to go to school: *pre-school children/education* • **pre-school noun** [C] a school for children younger than five years old

prescribe /prɪˈskraɪb/ **verb** [T] **1** to say what medical treatment someone needs: [often passive] *Painkillers are the most common drugs prescribed by doctors.* **2** formal to say officially what people must do: *rules prescribed by law*

prescription /prɪˈskrɪpʃᵊn/ **noun 1** 🔵 [C] a piece of paper saying what medicine someone needs or the medicine itself: *a doctor's prescription* **2 on prescription** UK (US **by prescription**) If you get a medicine on prescription, you only get it if you have a written instruction from your doctor.

prescriptive /prɪˈskrɪptɪv/ **adj** formal saying exactly what must happen: *The government's homework guidelines are too prescriptive.*

presence /ˈprezᵊns/ **noun 1 IN A PLACE** ▷ [U] 🔵 the fact of being in a place: *She signed the document in the presence of two witnesses.* **2 POLICE/SOLDIERS** ▷ [no plural] a group of police or soldiers who are watching or controlling a situation: *a strong police presence* **3 QUALITY** ▷ [U] a quality that makes people notice and admire you **4 presence of mind** the ability to deal with a difficult situation quickly and effectively: *She had the presence of mind to press the alarm.* **5 make your presence felt** to have a strong effect on other people: *The new police chief has really made his presence felt.*

🔲 Word partners for **presence**

the presence of sb/sth • in the presence of sb/sth

---

present¹ /ˈprezᵊnt/ **adj 1 be present** 🔵 to be in a particular place: *The whole family was present.* **2** [always before noun] happening or existing now: *the present situation* ∘ *What is your present occupation?* **3 present tense** 🔵 the form of the verb that is used to show what happens or exists now

P

present² /ˈprezᵊnt/

present

noun 1 the present
a ⑤ the period of time that is happening now: *The play is set in the present.* **b** ㉑ the form of the verb which is used to show what happens or exists now
2 ㉒ [C] something that you give to someone, usually for a particular occasion: *a birthday/wedding present* ∘ *to give someone a present* **3 at present** ⑤ now: *At present she's working abroad.*

> 🗒 **Word partners for present**
>
> buy/get/give sb/wrap (up) a present • a present for/from sb • a birthday/wedding present

present³ /prɪˈzent/ verb [T] **1 GIVE** ▷ ㉒ to give something to someone, often at a formal ceremony: *to present a prize* ∘ *They presented her with a bouquet.* **2 INFORMATION** ▷ ㉒ to give people information in a formal way: *He presented the report to his colleagues.* **3 present a danger/threat/problem, etc** to cause a danger/threat/problem, etc: *The final exam may present some problems.* **4 TV/RADIO** ▷ UK (US **host**) ㉒ to introduce a television or radio programme: *He presents a weekly sports quiz.* **5 PLAY/FILM** ▷ to show a new play or film: *The school is presenting 'West Side Story' this term.* **6 INTRODUCE** ▷ to introduce someone formally: *May I present my daughters?* **7 OPPORTUNITY** ▷ If an opportunity presents itself, it becomes possible: *I'd be happy to go to New York, if the opportunity presented itself.*

presentable /prɪˈzentəbl/ adj looking clean and tidy enough: *He was looking quite presentable in his jacket and tie.*

presentation /ˌprezᵊnˈteɪʃᵊn/ noun **1 SHOW** ▷ [U] the way something is arranged or shown to people: *Presentation is important if you want people to buy your products.* **2 TALK** ▷ [C] ⑤ a talk giving information about something: *a sales presentation* ∘ *She gave an excellent presentation.* **3 CEREMONY** ▷ [C] ㉒ a formal ceremony at which you give someone something: *a presentation ceremony*

present-day /ˌprezᵊntˈdeɪ/ adj existing now: *present-day attitudes*

presenter /prɪˈzentər/ noun [C] **1** ㉒ UK (US **host**) someone who introduces a radio or television programme **2** US a person who gives someone a prize at a ceremony

presently /ˈprezᵊntli/ adv **1** formal now: *He's presently living with his parents.* **2** old-fashioned soon or after a short time: *I'll be back presently.*

present parˈticiple UK (US **present ˈparticiple**) noun [C] the form of a verb that ends with '-ing'

the ˌpresent ˈperfect noun the form of the verb that is used to show actions or events that have happened in a period of time up to now. The sentence 'I have never been to Australia.' is in the present perfect.

preservation /ˌprezəˈveɪʃᵊn/ noun [U] keepin something the same or preventing it from bein damaged or destroyed: *the preservation of peac* ∘ *the preservation of wildlife*

preservative /prɪˈzɜːvətɪv/ noun [C, U] a sut stance used to prevent decay in food or in woo

preserve¹ /prɪˈzɜːv/ verb [T] **1** ㉒ to kee something the same or prevent it from bein damaged or destroyed: *to preserve peace* ∘ *t preserve the environment* **2** to add substances t something so that it stays in good condition fc a long time: *to preserve food/wood*

preserve² /prɪˈzɜːv/ noun **1 FOOD** ▷ [C, U] UK (U **preserves**) a sweet food made from frui sugar, and water: *apricot/strawberry preserv* **2 ACTIVITY** ▷ [no plural] an activity that only particular group of people can do: *Sport used t be a male preserve.* ∘ *Owning racehorses is th preserve of the rich.* **3 AREA** ▷ [C] mainly US a area where wild animals and plants are pro tected

preside /prɪˈzaɪd/ verb [I] to be officially respor sible for a formal meeting or ceremony: *A elderly priest presided at the marriage ceremon*

PHRASAL VERB **preside over sth** to be in charge • a situation, especially a formal meeting or leg· trial: *The case was presided over by a senic judge.*

presidency /ˈprezɪdᵊnsi/ noun **1** ㉒ [C] th period when someone is president: *Her pres dency lasted seven years.* **2 the presidency** ㉒ the job of being president: *He won the pre sidency by a wide margin.*

president /ˈprezɪdᵊnt/ noun [C] **1** ㉖ the highes political position in some countries, usually th leader of the government: *President Obama* **2** th person in charge of a company or organizatio: → See also **vice president**

presidential /ˌprezɪˈdenʃᵊl/ adj ㉒ relating t the president of a country: *a presidentic campaign*

press¹ /pres/ verb **1 PUSH** ▷ [I, T] ㉖ to pus something firmly: *Press the button to start th machine.* ∘ *He pressed his face against th window.* **2 PERSUADE** ▷ [T] to try hard t persuade someone to do something: *[+ to c sth] The committee pressed him to reveal mor information.* ∘ *We pressed him for an answer b he refused.* **3 press charges** to complain off cially about someone in a court of law: *Th family decided not to press charges against him* **4 MAKE SMOOTH** ▷ [T] to make clothes smoot by ironing them: *I need to press these trouser.* **5 MAKE FLAT** ▷ [T] to make something flat b putting something heavy on it for a long time: *press fruit/flowers* **6 press a case/claim** to try t make people accept your demands

PHRASAL VERB **press ahead/forward/on** to cor tinue to do something in a determined way *They're determined to press ahead with their plar despite opposition.*

press² /pres/ noun **1 the press** ㉒ newspaper and magazines, or the people who write them *the local/national press* ∘ *press report*

2 good/bad press praise or criticism from newspapers, magazines, television, etc: *She's had a lot of bad press recently.* **3 BUSINESS** ▷ [C] a business that prints and sells books: *Cambridge University Press* **4 PRINT** ▷ [C] (also **printing press**) a machine used to print books, newspapers, and magazines **5 MAKE FLAT** ▷ [no plural] the use of an iron (= a piece of electrical equipment used for making clothes flat and smooth): *Can you give these trousers a press?*

press ˌconference noun [C] a meeting at which someone officially gives information to the newspapers, television, etc: *to call/hold a press conference*

pressed /prest/ **adj be pressed for time/money** to not have much time/money

pressing /'presɪŋ/ **adj** A pressing problem or situation needs to be dealt with immediately: *a pressing need for housing*

press ˌoffice noun [C] the part of an organization that is responsible for giving information to journalists (= someone who writes articles for newspapers, magazines, etc)

press ˌofficer noun [C] a person whose job is to give a person or organization advice on what to say to newspapers, or on television, etc., and who gives information about a person or organization to newspapers, etc.

press reˌlease noun [C] an official piece of information that is given to newspapers, television, etc

press-up /'presʌp/ **noun** [C] UK (US **push-up**) a physical exercise in which you lie facing the floor and use your hands to push your body up

pressure[1] /'preʃər/ **noun 1 MAKE SOMEONE DO** ▷ [U] 🅱️ attempts to make someone do something by arguing, persuading, etc: *public/political pressure* ∘ [+ to do sth] *Teachers are under increasing pressure to work longer hours.* ∘ *The government is facing pressure from environmental campaigners.* **2 PROBLEMS** ▷ [C, U] 🅱️ difficult situations that make you feel worried or unhappy: *the pressures of work* ∘ *He's been under a lot of pressure recently.* **3 LIQUID/GAS** ▷ [C, U] the force that a liquid or gas produces when it presses against an area: *water pressure* **4 PUSH** ▷ [U] 🅱️ the force that you produce when you push something **5 put pressure on sb** 🅱️ to try to force someone to do something: [+ to do sth] *They're putting pressure on me to make a decision.* → See also **blood pressure, peer pressure**

🔲 Word partners for **pressure**

face/feel pressure • be under/come under pressure • pressure on sb • pressure from sb • pressure for sth

---

pressure[2] /'preʃər/ **verb** [T] (also UK **pressurize, -ise** /'preʃəraɪz/) to try to force someone to do something: [often passive, + into + doing sth] *We will not be pressured into making a decision.*

pressure ˌcooker noun [C] a pan with a lid which you use to cook food quickly in steam

pressure ˌgroup noun [C] a group of people who try to influence what the public or the government think about something

pressurize (also UK **-ise**) /'preʃəraɪz/ **verb** [T] UK to try to force someone to do something: [often passive, + into + doing sth] *He was pressurized into signing the agreement.*

pressurized (also UK **-ised**) /'preʃəraɪzd/ **adj** containing air or gas that is kept at a controlled pressure: *a pressurized container*

prestige /pres'tiːʒ/ **noun** [U] If someone or something has prestige, people feel respect and admiration for them, often because they are successful: *His company has gained international prestige.* • **prestigious** /pres'tɪdʒəs/ **adj** respected and admired, usually because of being important: *a prestigious award* ∘ *a prestigious university*

presumably /prɪ'zjuːməbli/ **adv** 🅱️ used to say what you think is the likely situation: *Presumably he just forgot to send the letter.*

presume /prɪ'zjuːm/ **verb 1** [T] to think that something is likely to be true, although you are not certain: [+ (that)] *I presume that you've done your homework.* **2 be presumed dead/innocent, etc** If someone is presumed dead/innocent, etc, it seems very likely that they are dead/innocent, etc. **3 presume to do sth** formal to do something that you do not have the right or the skills to do: *I certainly wouldn't presume to tell you how to do your job.*

presumption /prɪ'zʌmpʃən/ **noun 1** [C] the belief that something is true without any proof: [+ (that)] *I object to the presumption that young people are only interested in pop music.* **2** [U] behaviour that is rude and does not show respect

presumptuous /prɪ'zʌmptʃuəs/ **adj** Someone who is presumptuous confidently does things that they have no right to do: *It was a bit presumptuous of her to take the car without asking.*

presuppose /ˌpriːsə'pəʊz/ **verb** [T] formal If an idea or situation presupposes something, that thing must be true for the idea or situation to work.

pre-teen /priː'tiːn/ **noun** [C] a boy or girl between the ages of 9 and 12: *a magazine for pre-teens* • **pre-teen adj** *pre-teen fashions*

pretence UK (US **pretense**) /prɪ'tens/ **noun 1** [U] behaviour that makes someone believe something that is not true: *I can't keep up the pretence (= continue pretending) any longer.* ∘ *They made absolutely no pretence of being interested.* **2 under false pretences** If you do something under false pretences, you do it when you have lied about who you are or what you are doing: *The police charged him with obtaining money under false pretences.*

pretend /prɪ'tend/ **verb** [I, T] 🅱️ to behave as if something is true when it is not: [+ (that)] *I can't pretend that I like him.* ∘ [+ to do sth] *Were you just pretending to be interested?*

pretense /prɪ'tens/ **noun** US spelling of pretence

pretension /prɪ'tenʃən/ **noun** [C, U] behaviour in which you try to seem better or more important than you really are: [usually plural] *He seems to be without pretensions of any sort.*

pretentious /prɪˈtenʃəs/ **adj** trying to seem more important or clever than you really are: *a pretentious film*

pretext /ˈpriːtekst/ **noun** [C] a false reason that you use to explain why you are doing something: *I called her **on the pretext of** needing some information.*

pretty¹ /ˈprɪti/ **adv** informal **1** ⓑ quite, but not extremely: *The traffic was pretty bad.* ◦ *I'm pretty sure they'll accept.* **2 pretty much/well** ⓑ almost: *We've pretty much finished here.*

pretty² /ˈprɪti/ **adj 1** ⓐ If a woman or girl is pretty, she is attractive: *Your daughter is very pretty.* **2** ⓑ If a place or an object is pretty, it is pleasant to look at: *a pretty little village*

pretzel /ˈpretsəl/ **noun** [C] A hard salty biscuit that is baked in the shape of a loose knot or stick

prevail /prɪˈveɪl/ **verb** [I] formal **1** to get control or influence: *We can only hope that **common sense** will **prevail**.* **2** to be common among a group of people: *The use of guns prevails among the gangs in this area.*

PHRASAL VERB **prevail on/upon sb to do sth** formal to persuade someone to do something that they do not want to do: *He was eventually prevailed upon to accept the appointment.*

prevailing /prɪˈveɪlɪŋ/ **adj** [always before noun] **1** existing a lot in a particular group, area, or at a particular time: *a prevailing attitude/mood* **2 a prevailing wind** a wind that usually blows in a particular place

prevalent /ˈprevələnt/ **adj** existing a lot in a particular group, area, or at a particular time: *These diseases are more prevalent among young children.* • **prevalence** /ˈprevələns/ **noun** [U] the large amount of something in a particular group, area, or at a particular time: *the prevalence of smoking among teenagers*

prevent /prɪˈvent/ **verb** [T] ⓑ to stop something happening or to stop someone doing something: *to prevent accidents/crime* ◦ [+ from + doing sth] *Members of the public were prevented from entering the building.* • **preventable adj** If something is preventable, it can be prevented.

❗ Common learner error: prevent

Prevent should not be followed by 'to do sth'.

We must prevent such a disaster from happening again.

~~We must prevent such a disaster to happen again.~~

❗ Common learner error: protect or prevent?

Protect means to keep someone or something safe from bad things.

You should wear sunscreen to protect your skin.

Prevent means to stop something from happening.

Wearing sunscreen can help prevent skin cancer.

---

preventative /prɪˈventətɪv/ **adj** another word for preventive

prevention /prɪˈvenʃən/ **noun** [U] ⓑ ways of stopping something happening or stopping someone doing something: *crime prevention* ◦ *the **prevention of** diseases*

preventive /prɪˈventɪv/ **adj** (also **preventative**) Preventive action is intended to stop something before it happens: *preventive measures* ◦ *preventive medicine*

preview /ˈpriːvjuː/ **noun** [C] **1** an opportunity to see a film, play, etc before it is shown to the public **2** a short film that advertises a film or television programme • **preview verb** [T]

previous /ˈpriːviəs/ **adj** ⓑ existing or happening before something or someone else: *the previous day/year* ◦ *a previous attempt* ◦ *his previous marriage* • **previously adv** ⓑ *He previously worked as a teacher.*

prey¹ /preɪ/ **noun** [U] an animal that is hunted and killed by another animal

IDIOM **fall prey to sth** to be hurt or deceived by something or someone bad

→ See also **bird of prey**

prey² /preɪ/ **verb**

PHRASAL VERBS **prey on sth** If an animal preys on another animal, it catches it and eats it: *Spiders prey on flies and other small insects.* • **prey on/upon sb** to hurt or deceive people who are weak and easy to deceive: *These young thieves prey on the elderly.*

price¹ /praɪs/ **noun 1** [C] ⓐ the amount of money that you pay to buy something: *high/low prices* ◦ *House prices are falling/rising.* ◦ *The price of fuel has gone up again.* **2** [no plural] the unpleasant results that you must accept or experience for getting or doing something: *Suspension from the club was a high/small price to pay* (= very bad/not very bad thing to experience) *for his mistake.* **3 at a price** If you can get something at a price, you have to pay a lot of money for it: *False passports are available, at a price.* **4 at any price** If you want something at any price, you will do anything to get it: *She wanted the job at any price.*

❗ Common learner error: price or prize?

These two words sound very similar but have different spellings and very different meanings – be careful not to confuse them.

Price means 'the amount of money that you pay to buy something'.

The price of oil has risen by 20%.

Prize means 'something valuable that is given to someone who wins a competition or who has done good work'.

She won first prize in the competition.

☑ Word partners for price

charge/increase/pay/put up prices • prices fall • an average/exorbitant/high/low/reasonable price

---

price² /praɪs/ **verb** [T] to say what the price of

something is: [often passive] *The book is **priced at** $40.*

priceless /'praɪsləs/ **adj 1** very valuable: *a priceless antique/painting* **2** very important or useful: *A trip round the world is a priceless opportunity.*

price tag noun [C] (also '**price ticket**) a piece of paper attached to a product that shows the amount a product costs

pricey (also **pricy**) /'praɪsi/ **adj** informal expensive: *That jacket's a bit pricey!*

prick /prɪk/ **verb** [T] to make a very small hole in something with a sharp object: *Prick the potatoes all over before baking.* ∘ *I pricked my finger on a pin.* • **prick** noun [C] *The injection won't hurt – you'll just feel a slight prick.*

prickle¹ /'prɪkl/ **noun** [C] a sharp point on the surface of some plants or the skin of some animals

prickle² /'prɪkl/ **verb** [I] If part of your body prickles, it feels as if a lot of sharp points are touching it because you are frightened or excited: *a prickling sensation*

prickly /'prɪkli/ **adj 1** covered with prickles: *a prickly bush* **2** informal A prickly person or relationship is unfriendly or difficult to deal with.

pricy /'praɪsi/ **adj** another spelling of pricey

pride¹ /praɪd/ **noun** [U] **1 SATISFACTION** ▷ ⑫ a feeling of satisfaction at your achievements or the achievements of your family or friends: *She felt **a great sense of pride** as she watched him accept the award.* ∘ *The whole community **takes pride in** (= feels proud about) the school.* **2 RESPECT** ▷ ⑫ the respect that you feel for yourself: *Defeat in the World Cup had badly damaged **national pride**.* **3 IMPORTANCE** ▷ the belief that you are better or more important than other people: *His pride prevented him from asking for help.* **4 sb's **pride and joy** something or someone that is very important to you: *He spends hours cleaning that motorcycle – it's his pride and joy.*

IDIOMS **have/take pride of place** If something takes pride of place, you put it in the best position so that it can be seen easily: *A photo of her grandchildren took pride of place on the wall.* • **swallow your pride** to decide to do something although it will embarrass you: *He swallowed his pride and asked if he could have his old job back.*

📋 **Word partners for pride**

take pride **in** sth • a **sense/source** of pride • **great** pride • sb's pride **at/in** sth

---

pride² /praɪd/ **verb**

PHRASAL VERB **pride yourself on sth/doing sth** to feel satisfaction at a quality or skill that you have: *The company prides itself on having the latest technology.*

priest /priːst/ **noun** [C] ⑧ someone who performs religious duties and ceremonies

the priesthood /'priːsthʊd/ **noun** the job of being a priest

prim /prɪm/ **adj** Someone who is prim behaves in a very formal way and is easily shocked by anything rude: *Sarah wouldn't find that funny – she's far too **prim and proper** (= shocked by anything rude).* • **primly adv**

prima donna /ˌpriːməˈdɒnə/ **noun** [C] someone who behaves badly and expects to get everything they want because they think that they are very important

primal /'praɪməl/ **adj** formal very basic, or relating to the time when human life on Earth began: *primal instincts*

primarily /praɪˈmerəli/ **adv** ⑫ mainly: *She's known primarily as a novelist but she also writes poetry.*

primary¹ /'praɪməri/ **adj** [always before noun] ⑫ most important: *Her primary responsibility is to train new employees.*

primary² /'praɪməri/ **noun** [C] a vote in which people in a political party in the US choose the person who will represent them in an election

primary colour UK (US **primary color**) **noun** [C] one of the three colours, which in paint, etc are red, blue, and yellow, that can be mixed together to make any other colour

primary school noun [C] mainly UK (US **elementary school**) ⑧ a school for children aged 5 to 11

primate /'praɪmeɪt/ **noun** [C] a member of the group of animals that includes monkeys and people, which have large brains and hands and feet developed for climbing

prime¹ /praɪm/ **adj** [always before noun] **1** main, or most important: *the prime suspect in a murder investigation* **2** of the best quality: *The hotel is in a prime location in the city centre.* **3** a **prime example** a very good example of something

prime² /praɪm/ **noun** [no plural] the period in your life when you are most active or successful: *At 35, she's **in her prime**.* ∘ *the prime of life*

prime³ /praɪm/ **verb** [T] to prepare someone for an event or situation, often by giving them the information that they need: *The president had been well primed before the debate.*

prime minister noun [C] ⑫ the leader of an elected government in some countries

prime time noun [U] the time in the evening when the largest number of people watch television: *prime-time television*

primeval /praɪˈmiːvəl/ **adj** belonging to a very early period in the history of the world: *primeval forest*

primitive /'prɪmɪtɪv/ **adj 1** relating to human society at a very early stage of development, with people living in a simple way without machines or a writing system: *primitive man* ∘ *primitive societies* **2** very basic or old-fashioned: *The conditions at the campsite were rather primitive.*

primrose /'prɪmrəʊz/ **noun** [C] a wild plant with pale yellow flowers

prince /prɪns/ **noun** [C] **1** ⑧ the son of a king or queen, or one of their close male relatives:

P

Prince Edward **2** the male ruler of a small country

princely /'prɪnsli/ adj **a princely sum** a large amount of money: *It cost the princely sum of $2 million.*

princess /prɪn'ses/ ⑤ /'prɪnsəs/ noun [C] **1** ㉛ the daughter of a king or queen, or one of their close female relatives **2** ㉛ the wife of a prince

principal¹ /'prɪnsəpᵊl/ adj [always before noun] ㉛ main, or most important: *Her principal reason for moving is to be nearer her mother.*

principal² /'prɪnsəpᵊl/ noun [C] ㉜ the person in charge of a school or college

principality /ˌprɪnsɪ'pæləti/ noun [C] a country ruled by a prince

principally /'prɪnsəpᵊli/ adv mainly: *The advertising campaign is aimed principally at women.*

principle /'prɪnsəpl/ noun **1** [C, U] a rule or belief that influences your behaviour and which is based on what you think is right: *He must be punished – it's a **matter of principle**.* **2** [C] ㉜ a basic idea or rule that explains how something happens or works: *The organization works **on the principle that** all members have the same rights.* **3 in principle** If you agree with something in principle, you agree with the idea or plan although you do not know the details or you do not know if it will be possible: *They have approved the changes in principle.* **4 on principle** If you refuse to do something on principle, you refuse to do it because you think it is morally wrong: *She doesn't wear fur on principle.*

🗌 Word partners for **principle**

stick to your principles • a **guiding** principle • be **against** sb's principles • be a **matter of** principle

---

principled /'prɪnsᵊpld/ adj showing strong beliefs about what is right and wrong

print¹ /prɪnt/ verb **1 WRITING/IMAGES** ▷ [T] ㉓ to produce writing or images on paper or other material with a machine: *The instructions are printed on the side of the box.* **2 BOOKS/ NEWSPAPERS** ▷ [T] ㉜ to produce books, newspapers, magazines, etc, usually in large quantities, using machines: *Fifty thousand booklets have been printed for the exhibition.* **3 INCLUDE** ▷ [T] ㉜ to include a piece of writing in a newspaper or magazine: *They printed his letter in Tuesday's paper.* **4 WRITE** ▷ [I, T] to write words without joining the letters together: *Please print your name and address clearly using capitals.* **5 PATTERN** ▷ [T] to produce a pattern on material or paper

PHRASAL VERB print sth out to produce a printed copy of a document that has been written on a computer: *Can you print out a copy of that letter for me?*

print² /prɪnt/ noun **1 WORDS** ▷ [U] words, letters, or numbers that are produced on paper by a machine **2 in/out of print** If a book is in print, it is possible to buy a new copy of it, and if it is out of print, it is not now possible. **3 PICTURE** ▷ [C] a copy of a picture made using photography or by pressing paper onto a design covered in ink: *a*

print of Van Gogh's 'Sunflowers' **4 PHOTO GRAPH** ▷ [C] a photograph that is produced o₁ paper **5 PATTERN** ▷ [C] a pattern that i produced on material or paper: *a floral prir* **6 HAND** ▷ [C] (also **fingerprint**) a mark that i left on a surface where someone has touched i *His prints were found all over the house and h was arrested the next day.* **7 MARK** ▷ [C] a mar that is left on a surface where someone ha walked: *The dog left prints all over the kitche floor.* → See also **small print**

printer /'prɪntər/ noun [C] **1 ㉔** a machine that i connected to a computer and that produce writing or images on paper: *a laser printer* **2** person or company that prints books, new papers, magazines, etc

printing /'prɪntɪŋ/ noun [U] the process c producing writing or images on paper or othe material using a machine

printing press noun [C] a machine that print books, newspapers, magazines, etc

printout /'prɪntaʊt/ noun [C] information or document that is printed from a computer: *H asked for a printout of the year's sales figures.*

prior /praɪər/ adj formal **1** [always before noun existing or happening before something else *The course requires no **prior knowledge** c Spanish.* **2 prior to sth** before a particular tim or event: *the weeks prior to her death*

prioritize (also UK **-ise**) /praɪ'ɒrɪtaɪz/ verb [I, T] t decide which of a group of things are the mos important so that you can deal with them first *You must learn to **prioritize** your **work**.*

priority /praɪ'ɒrəti/ noun **1 ㉜** [C] somethin that is very important and that must be deal with before other things: *My **first/top priority** i to find somewhere to live.* **2 give priority to sth** to consider that something is more importar than other things and deal with it first **3 have take priority (over sth)** to be more importar than other things and to be dealt with first: *H job seems to take priority over everything else.*

prise /praɪz/ verb UK **prise sth apart/off/open** etc to use force to move, remove, or ope₁ something: *I prised the lid off with a spoon.*

prism /'prɪzᵊm/ noun [C] an object made of clea glass which separates the light that passe through it into different colours

prison /'prɪzᵊn/ noun [C, U] ㉛ a place wher criminals are kept as a punishment: *He's sper most of his life **in prison**.* ∘ *She was **sent t prison** for two years.*

🗌 Word partners for **prison**

go to/be sent to prison • be **released from** prison • **in/out of** prison • a prison **sentence**

---

prisoner /'prɪzᵊnər/ noun **1 ㉛** [C] someone wh is being kept in prison as a punishment, o because they have been caught by an enem **2 hold/keep/take sb prisoner** to catch someon and guard them so that they cannot escap → See also **political prisoner**

prisoner of war noun [C] (plural **prisoners o war**) a soldier who is caught by enemy soldier during a war: *a prisoner of war camp*

---

pristine /'prɪstiːn/ **adj** in very good condition, as if new: *Her car is in pristine condition.*

privacy /'prɪvəsi/ ⓤ /'praɪvəsi/ **noun** [U] ⓑ② the state of being alone so that people cannot see or hear what you are doing: *I hate sharing a bedroom – I never get any privacy.*

private[1] /'praɪvɪt/ **adj 1** NOT EVERYONE ▷ ⓑ① only for one person or group and not for everyone: *Each room has a balcony and a private bathroom.* ◦ *You can't park here – this is private property.* **2** NOT GOVERNMENT ▷ ⓑ② controlled by or paid for by a person or company and not by the government: *Charles went to a private school.* **3** SECRET ▷ ⓑ① If information or an emotion is private, you do not want other people to know about it: *This is a private matter – it doesn't concern you.* **4 in private** ⓑ② If you do something in private, you do it where other people cannot see or hear you: *I need to talk to you in private.* **5 sb's private life** someone's personal relationships and activities and not their work **6** QUIET ▷ A place which is private is quiet and there are no other people there to see or hear what you are doing: *Is there somewhere private where we can talk?* • **privately adv**

private[2] /'praɪvɪt/ **noun** [C] a soldier of the lowest rank in the army

private 'school noun [C] a school that does not receive its main financial support from the government

the 'private ˌsector noun businesses and industries that are not owned or controlled by the government

privatize (also UK **-ise**) /'praɪvɪtaɪz/ **verb** [T] If an industry or organization owned by the government is privatized, it is sold to private companies. • **privatization** /ˌpraɪvɪtaɪ'zeɪʃ³n/ **noun** [U]

privilege /'prɪv³lɪdʒ/ **noun 1** [C, U] an advantage that only one person or group has, usually because of their position or because they are rich **2** [no plural] an opportunity to do something special or enjoyable: [+ of + doing sth] *I had the privilege of meeting the Queen.* • **privileged adj** having a privilege: *to be in a privileged position*

privy /'prɪvi/ **adj** formal **privy to sth** knowing information that is not known by many people

prize[1] /praɪz/ **noun** [C] ⓐ② something valuable that is given to someone who wins a competition or who has done good work: *to win a prize* ◦ *first/second prize* → See Note at **price**[1] → See also **booby prize**

> 🗎 **Word partners for prize**
>
> be awarded/win a prize • first/second/the runner's-up/the top prize • a prize for sth • a prize of [£500/a car, etc] • prize money/winner

prize[2] /praɪz/ **adj** [always before noun] A prize animal or vegetable is good enough to win a competition.

prize[3] /praɪz/ **verb** [T] to think that something is very valuable or important: *His car is his prized possession.*

prize-winning /'praɪzˌwɪnɪŋ/ **adj** [always before noun] having won a prize: *a prize-winning author*

pro /prəʊ/ **noun** [C] **1** informal someone who earns money for playing a sport: *a golf/tennis pro* **2 the pros and cons** ⓑ② the advantages and disadvantages of something: [+ of + doing sth] *We discussed the pros and cons of buying a bigger house.*

pro- /prəʊ-/ **prefix** supporting or approving of something: *pro-European* ◦ *pro-democracy demonstrations* → Compare **anti-**

proactive /ˌprəʊ'æktɪv/ **adj** taking action by causing change and not only reacting to change when it happens

probability /ˌprɒbə'bɪləti/ **noun 1** [C, U] how likely it is that something will happen: [+ of + doing sth] *What's the probability of winning?* ◦ [+ (that)] *There's a high probability that he'll get the job.* **2 in all probability** used to mean that something is very likely: *She will, in all probability, have left before we arrive.*

probable /'prɒbəbl/ **adj** ⓑ② likely to be true or to happen: *The probable cause of death was heart failure.* ◦ [+ (that)] *It's highly probable that he'll lose his job.*

probably /'prɒbəbli/ **adv** ⓐ② used to mean that something is very likely: *I'll probably be home by midnight.*

probation /prəʊ'beɪʃ³n/ **noun** [U] **1** a period of time when a criminal must behave well and not commit any more crimes in order to avoid being sent to prison: *to be on probation* **2** a period of time at the start of a new job when you are watched and tested to see if you are suitable for the job • **probationary adj** relating to probation: *a probationary period*

pro'bation ˌofficer noun [C] someone whose job is to watch and help criminals who have been put on probation

probe[1] /prəʊb/ **verb** [I, T] to ask a lot of questions in order to discover information about something or someone: *The interviewer probed deep into her private life.* ◦ *probing questions*

probe[2] /prəʊb/ **noun** [C] **1** a process in which someone tries to discover information about something by asking a lot of questions: *an FBI probe into corruption* **2** a long, thin, metal tool used by doctors to examine parts of the body

problem /'prɒbləm/ **noun 1** [C] ⓐ① a situation that causes difficulties and that needs to be dealt with: *health problems* ◦ *I'm having problems with my computer.* ◦ *Drugs have become a serious problem in the area.* → See Note at **trouble**[1] **2** [C] a question that you use mathematics to solve **3 have a problem with sth/sb** to find something or someone annoying or offensive: *Yes, she can smoke in the house – I don't have a problem with that.* **4 No problem. a** ⓐ② something that you say to mean you can or will do what someone has asked you to do: *"Can you get me to the airport by 11.30?" "No problem."* **b** ⓐ② something that you say when someone has thanked you for something: *"Thanks for taking me home." "No problem."*

P

> 🔲 Word partners for **problem**
>
> cause/face/have/tackle/pose a problem • a problem arises • a big/major/real/serious problem

> ➕ Other ways of saying **problem**
>
> The noun **difficulty** is a common alternative to 'problem':
> *The company is having some financial **difficulties** at the moment.*
> A small, temporary problem may be described informally as a **hitch** or a **hiccup**:
> *The ceremony went without a **hitch**.*
> *I'm afraid there's been a slight **hiccup** with the arrangements.*
> A **glitch** is a problem that stops something from working properly:
> *We've had a few technical **glitches**, but I'm confident we'll be ready on time.*
> A **hurdle** or **obstacle** is a problem that you need to deal with so that you can continue to make progress:
> *Getting a work permit is the first **hurdle/ obstacle**.*
> A **pitfall** is a problem that is likely to happen in a particular situation:
> *It's just one of the **pitfalls** of buying a house.*
> A **setback** is a problem that makes something happen less quickly than it should:
> *The project has suffered a series of **setbacks** this year.*

problematic /ˌprɒbləˈmætɪk/ **adj** full of problems or difficulties: *He has a very problematic relationship with his father.*

procedure /prəˈsiːdʒər/ **noun** [C, U] 🅱️ the official or usual way of doing something: *The company has new **procedures for** dealing with complaints.*

> 🔲 Word partners for **procedure**
>
> follow a procedure • correct/proper/standard procedure • a procedure for (doing) sth

proceed /prəˈsiːd/ **verb** [I] formal **1** to continue as planned: *His lawyers have decided not to **proceed with** the case.* **2 proceed to do sth** to do something after you have done something else: *She sat down and proceeded to tell me about her skiing trip.* **3 proceed along/down/to, etc** formal to move or travel in a particular direction: *Passengers for Sydney should proceed to gate 21.*

proceedings /prəˈsiːdɪŋz/ **noun** [plural] **1** legal action against someone: *The bank is threatening to start **legal proceedings** against him.* **2** a series of organized events or actions: *The chairman opened the proceedings with a short speech.*

proceeds /ˈprəʊsiːdz/ **noun** [plural] the money that is earned from an event or activity: *All proceeds from the concert will go to charity.*

process¹ /ˈprəʊses/ 🇺🇸 /ˈprɑːses/ **noun** [C] **1** 🅱️ a series of actions that you take in order to achieve a result: *Buying a house can be a long and complicated process.* **2** [C] 🅱️ a series of changes that happen naturally: *the **ageing***

process **3 in the process** If you are doing something, and you do something else in the process, the second thing happens as a result of doing the first thing: *She stood up to say hello and spilled her drink in the process.* **4 be in the process of doing sth** to have started doing something: *We're in the process of painting our apartment.*

process² /ˈprəʊses/ 🇺🇸 /ˈprɑːses/ **verb** [T] **1 CHEMICALS** ▷ to add chemicals to a substance, especially food, in order to change it or make it last longer: ***processed food*** **2 INFORMATION** ▷ 🅱️ to deal with information or documents in an official way: *Visa applications take 28 days to process.* **3 COMPUTER** ▷ When a computer processes data (= information), it does things to it so that it can be used and understood. • **processing noun** [U] *data processing*

procession /prəˈseʃən/ **noun** [C] a line of people or vehicles that moves forward slowly as part of a ceremony or public event: *a funeral procession*

processor /ˈprəʊsesər/ **noun** [C] the main part of a computer that controls all the other parts → See also **food processor, word processor**

proclaim /prəˈkleɪm/ **verb** [T] formal to announce something officially or in public • **proclamation** /ˌprɒkləˈmeɪʃən/ **noun** [C] an official announcement about something important

procrastinate /prəʊˈkræstɪneɪt/ **verb** [I] formal to wait a long time before doing something that you must do: *I know I've got to deal with the problem at some point – I'm just procrastinating.*

procure /prəˈkjʊər/ **verb** [T] formal to obtain something that is difficult to get

prod /prɒd/ **verb (prodding, prodded)** **1** [I, T] to push someone or something with your finger or with a pointed object: *He prodded me in the back and told me to hurry up.* **2** [T] to encourage someone to do something: [+ into + doing sth] *We need to prod him into making a decision.* • **prod noun** [C] usually singular] *to **give** someone a prod*

prodigious /prəˈdɪdʒəs/ **adj** formal extremely great in size or ability: *a prodigious talent* ∘ *a prodigious appetite*

prodigy /ˈprɒdɪdʒi/ **noun** [C] a young person who is very good at something: *A **child prodigy**, she entered university at the age of eleven.*

produce¹ /prəˈdjuːs/ **verb** [T] **1 MAKE** ▷ 🆎 to make or grow something: *The factory produces about 900 cars a year.* ∘ *This plant will produce small yellow flowers in the spring.* **2 CAUSE** ▷ 🅱️ to cause a particular reaction or result: *Nuts produce an allergic reaction in some people.* **3 SHOW** ▷ to take an object from somewhere so that people can see it: *One of the men suddenly produced a gun from his pocket.* **4 FILM/PLAY** ▷ to control how a film, play, programme, or musical recording is made: *He's produced some of the top Broadway shows.*

produce² /ˈprɒdjuːs/ **noun** [U] food that is grown or made in large quantities to be sold: *dairy produce*

producer /prəˈdjuːsər/ **noun** [C] **1** a company, country, or person that makes goods or grows food: *Australia is one of the world's main* *producers of wool.* **2** ⑫ someone who controls how a film, play, programme, or musical recording is made: *a film/record producer*

product /'prɒdʌkt/ *noun* [C] **1** ⑬ something that is made or grown to be sold: *They have a new range of skin-care products.* ∘ *Does she eat dairy products (= things made from milk)?* **2 product of sth** someone or something that is the result of a particular experience or process: *His lack of confidence is the product of an unhappy childhood.* → See also **by-product, end-product**

production /prə'dʌkʃ°n/ *noun* **1 MAKING** ▷ [U] ⑫ the process of making or growing something: *Sand is used in the production of glass.* ∘ *The new model goes into production (= starts being made) next year.* **2 AMOUNT** ▷ [U] ⑫ the amount of something that is made or grown: *We need to increase production by 20%.* **3 PERFORMANCE** ▷ [C] a performance or series of performances of a play or show: *a school production of 'Romeo and Juliet'* **4 ORGANIZING FILM/PLAY** ▷ [U] ⑫ the job of controlling how a film, play, programme, or musical recording is made: *She wants a career in TV production.*

> ☑ Word partners for **production**
>
> sth **goes into** production • production **of** sth

productive /prə'dʌktɪv/ *adj* **1** ⑫ producing a good or useful result: *We had a very productive meeting and sorted out a lot of problems.* **2** ⑫ producing a large amount of goods, food, work, etc: *productive land* ∘ *a productive worker*

productivity /ˌprɒdʌk'tɪvəti/ *noun* [U] the rate at which goods are produced: *We need to increase productivity by 50%.*

Prof /prɒf/ *noun* [C] short for professor: *Prof Susan Nishio*

profane /prə'feɪn/ *adj* formal showing no respect for God or for religious or moral rules: *profane language* • **profanity** /prə'fænəti/ *noun* [U] formal

profess /prə'fes/ *verb* [T] formal to express a quality or belief, often when it is not true: [+ to do sth] *She professes to hate shopping, but she's always buying new things.*

profession /prə'feʃ°n/ *noun* **1** [C] ⑬ a type of work that needs special training or education: *He's working in a restaurant, but he's a teacher by profession (= he trained to be a teacher).* → See Note at **work²** **2** [group] ⑫ the people who do a type of work considered as a group: *The medical profession has expressed concern about the new drug.*

professional¹ /prə'feʃ°n°l/ *adj* **1 JOB** ▷ [always before noun] ⑫ relating to a job that needs special training or education: *You should get some professional advice about your finances.* **2 EARNING MONEY** ▷ ⑬ Someone is professional if they earn money for a sport or activity that most people do as a hobby: *a professional athlete/musician* → Opposite **amateur 3 SKILL** ▷ ⑬ showing skill and careful attention: *a professional attitude* ∘ *He looks very professional in that suit.* → Opposite **unprofessional**

professional² /prə'feʃ°n°l/ *noun* [C] **1 TRAINED** ▷ someone who does a job that needs special training or education **2 WITH EXPERIENCE** ▷ someone who has done a job for a long time and who does it with a lot of skill: *She dealt with the problem like a true professional.* **3 SPORTS** ▷ ⑫ someone who earns money for doing a sport or activity that most other people do as a hobby: *a rugby professional* → Opposite **amateur**

professionalism /prə'feʃ°n°lɪz°m/ *noun* [U] the skill and careful attention that trained people are expected to have: *He complained about the lack of professionalism in the company.*

professionally /prə'feʃ°n°li/ *adv* **1 WORK** ▷ in a way that relates to your work: *I know him professionally, but he's not a close friend.* **2 WITH TRAINING** ▷ Work that is done professionally is done by someone who has had special training: *Their house has been professionally decorated.* **3 HIGH STANDARDS** ▷ in a way that shows high standards or skill: *He dealt with the situation very professionally.* **4 SPORT** ▷ If someone does an activity or sport professionally, they earn money for doing it: *He's good enough at football to play professionally.*

professor /prə'fesər/ *noun* [C] ⑬ the highest rank of teacher in a British university, or a teacher in an American university or college: *a professor of history at Oxford* ∘ *Professor Blackman.*

proffer /'prɒfər/ *verb* [T] formal to offer something to someone: *to proffer advice*

proficiency /prə'fɪʃ°nsi/ *noun* [U] the ability to do something very well: *The job requires proficiency in written and spoken English.*

proficient /prə'fɪʃ°nt/ *adj* very good at something: *She's proficient in two languages.* ∘ *I've become quite proficient at repairing bicycles.*

profile¹ /'prəʊfaɪl/ *noun* [C] **1 DESCRIPTION** ▷ ⑫ a short description of someone's character, work, etc **2 HEAD** ▷ a side view of someone's face or head: *The picture shows him in profile.* **3 ATTENTION** ▷ the amount of attention that something receives: *We need to increase our company's profile in Asia.* **4 high profile** important and noticeable: *a high-profile job* **5** a description of yourself and your interests on a website

profile

IDIOM **keep a low profile** to try not to be noticed

> ☑ Word partners for **profile**
>
> **build up/create** a profile • a profile **of** sb/sth

profile² /'prəʊfaɪl/ *verb* [T] to describe someone's life, character, work, etc

profit¹ /'prɒfɪt/ *noun* [C, U] ⑫ money that you get from selling goods or services for more than they cost to produce or provide: *a profit of $4.5 million* ∘ *It's very hard for a new business to **make a profit** in its first year.*

> ☑ Word partners for **profit**
>
> boost/increase profits • make a profit • profits fall/rise • an annual/big/gross/healthy/large/small profit

profit² /ˈprɒfɪt/ **verb**

PHRASAL VERB **profit from sth** to earn a profit or get an advantage from something: *Investors have profited from a rise in interest rates.*

profitable /ˈprɒfɪtəbl/ **adj 1** ⓑ making or likely to make a profit: *a profitable business* **2** ⓑ useful or likely to give you an advantage: *a profitable discussion* • **profitability** /ˌprɒfɪtəˈbɪlɪti/ **noun** [U] • **profitably** adv

profound /prəˈfaʊnd/ **adj 1** EFFECT ▷ If an effect is profound, it is extreme: *The war had a **profound impact** on people's lives.* **2** FEELING ▷ If a feeling is profound, you feel it very strongly: *a **profound sense of** sadness* **3** UNDERSTANDING ▷ If an idea or piece of work is profound, it shows intelligence or a great ability to understand: *a profound question* ∘ *His theories were simple, but profound.* • **profoundly** adv

profusely /prəˈfjuːsli/ **adv** a lot: *He apologized profusely for being late.*

profusion /prəˈfjuːʒən/ **noun** [U, no plural] formal an extremely large amount of something: *a profusion of wild flowers* ∘ *Bacteria grow **in profusion** in the warm, wet soil.*

prognosis /prɒɡˈnəʊsɪs/ **noun** [C] (plural **prognoses** /prɒɡˈnəʊsiːz/) formal **1** a judgment that a doctor makes about a sick person's chance of becoming healthy **2** an opinion about the future of someone or something: *The prognosis for economic growth is good.*

program¹ /ˈprəʊɡræm/ **noun** [C] **1** ⓐ a set of instructions that you put into a computer to make it do something: *to write a **computer program*** **2** US spelling of programme

program² /ˈprəʊɡræm/ **verb** [T] (**programming**, **programmed**) **1** If you program a computer, you give it a set of instructions to do something. **2** US spelling of programme

programme¹ UK (US **program**) /ˈprəʊɡræm/ **noun** [C] **1** TELEVISION/RADIO ▷ ⓐ a show on television or radio: *a **TV programme*** ∘ *Did you see that programme about spiders last night?* **2** PLAN ▷ ⓑ a plan of events or activities with a particular purpose: *a health education programme* **3** THIN BOOK ▷ a thin book that you buy at a theatre, sports event, etc which tells you who or what you are going to see

programme² UK (US **program**) /ˈprəʊɡræm/ **verb** [T] If you programme a machine, you give it a set of instructions to do something: [+ to do sth] *The robot can be programmed to follow instructions.*

programmer /ˈprəʊɡræmər/ **noun** [C] someone who writes computer programs as a job • **programming noun** [U] ⓑ the job or activity of writing computer programs

progress¹ /ˈprəʊɡres/ ⓤⓢ /ˈprɒɡres/ **noun** [U] **1** ⓑ development and improvement of skills, knowledge, etc: *slow/rapid progress* ∘ *technological progress* ∘ *He has **made good progress** in French this year.* **2 in progress** formal ⓑ happening or being done now: *Quiet please - Exams in progress.* **3** movement towards a place

> ☑ Word partners for **progress**
>
> halt/impede/make/monitor progress • rapid/real/significant/slow/steady progress • progress on/toward sth

progress² /prəˈɡres/ **verb** [I] **1** ⓑ to improve or develop in skills, knowledge, etc: *Technology has progressed rapidly in the last 100 years.* **2** to continue gradually: *I began to feel more relaxed as the evening progressed.*

progression /prəˈɡreʃən/ **noun** [C, U] a change to the next stage of development: *a **logical/natural progression*** ∘ *Drugs can stop the progression of the disease.*

progressive¹ /prəˈɡresɪv/ **adj 1** ⓑ thinking or behaving in a new or modern way: *progressive ideas/attitudes* **2** developing or happening gradually: *a progressive disease* • **progressively** adv gradually: *My headaches are getting progressively worse.*

progressive² /prəˈɡresɪv/ **noun the progressive** the form of the verb that is used to show that an action is continuing. In English, the progressive is made with 'be' and the present participle.

prohibit /prəˈhɪbɪt/ **verb** [T] formal ⓑ to officially forbid something: [often passive] *Smoking is prohibited on most international flights.* ∘ [+ from + doing sth] *The new law prohibits people from drinking alcohol in the street.* ∘ *a **prohibited substance*** • **prohibition** /ˌprəʊɪˈbɪʃən/ **noun** [U]

prohibitive /prəˈhɪbɪtɪv/ **adj** If the cost of something is prohibitive, it is too expensive for many people: *The cost of flying first class is prohibitive for most people.* • **prohibitively** adv *prohibitively expensive*

project¹ /ˈprɒdʒekt/ **noun** [C] **1** ⓑ a carefully planned piece of work that has a particular purpose: *a research project* ∘ *The new building project will cost $45 million.* **2** ⓐ a piece of school work that involves detailed study of a subject: *We're **doing** a class **project on** the environment.*

project² /prəˈdʒekt/ **verb 1** CALCULATE ▷ [T] to calculate an amount or make a guess about the future based on information that you have [often passive, + to do sth] *As people live longer, the demand for health care is projected to increase dramatically.* ∘ *projected growth* **2** IMAGE ▷ [T] to show a film or other image on a screen or a wall: *Laser images were **projected onto** a screen.* **3** QUALITY ▷ [T] If you project a particular quality, that quality is what most people notice about you: *She projected **an image** of strong leadership.* **4** **project from/into/out, etc** formal to stick out

projection /prəˈdʒekʃən/ **noun 1** [C] a calculation or guess about the future based on

P

information that you have: *government projections of population growth* **2** [U] the use of a projector to show a film or an image on a screen or wall

projector /prəʊˈdʒektəʳ/ **noun** [C] a machine that projects films, pictures, or words onto a screen or a wall

proliferate /prəʊˈlɪfəreɪt/ **verb** [I] formal to increase in number very quickly

proliferation /prəʊˌlɪfəˈreɪʃən/ **noun** [U] a very quick increase in the number of something: *the proliferation of new TV channels*

prolific /prəʊˈlɪfɪk/ **adj** producing a lot of something: *a **prolific writer**/composer*

prologue /ˈprəʊlɒg/ **noun** [C] an introduction to a book, film, or play

prolong /prəʊˈlɒŋ/ **verb** [T] to make something last longer: *Eating a good diet can prolong your life.*

prolonged /prəʊˈlɒŋd/ **adj** continuing for a long time: *a prolonged illness*

prom /prɒm/ **noun** [C] a formal dance party for older students held at the end of the school year: *a school prom*

promenade /ˌprɒməˈnɑːd/ **noun** [C] a wide path by the sea

prominence /ˈprɒmɪnəns/ **noun** [U] a position of being important or famous: *He first **came to prominence** as a singer in the 1980s.*

prominent /ˈprɒmɪnənt/ **adj** **1** important or famous: *a **prominent figure*** **2** very easy to see or notice: *a **prominent feature*** • **prominently** adv

promiscuous /prəˈmɪskjuəs/ **adj** Someone who is promiscuous has sex with a lot of people. • **promiscuity** /ˌprɒmɪˈskjuːəti/ **noun** [U] promiscuous behaviour

promise¹ /ˈprɒmɪs/ **verb** **1** [I, T] B1 to say that you will certainly do something or that something will certainly happen: [+ to do sth] *She promised to write to me every week.* ◦ [+ (that)] *Paul promised me that he'd cook dinner tonight.* **2** [+ two objects] B1 to say that you will certainly give something to someone: *They promised us a reward.* **3 promise to be sth** B2 If something promises to be good, exciting, etc, people expect that it will be good, exciting, etc.

> **! Common learner error: promise**
>
> When you use the expression **promise someone something**, no preposition is needed after the verb.
>
> *He promised his mum that he would clean his room.*
>
> ~~*He promised to his mum that he would clean his room.*~~

promise² /ˈprɒmɪs/ **noun** **1** B1 [C] a statement that you will certainly do something: *I'm not sure I can do it so I won't **make** any **promises**.* **2 keep/break a promise** B2 to do/not do what you said that you would do **3 show promise** If someone or something shows promise, they are likely to be successful: *As a child, he showed great promise as an athlete.*

> **Word partners for promise**
>
> **break/keep/make/renege on** a promise • a **broken/rash/solemn/vague** promise

promising /ˈprɒmɪsɪŋ/ **adj** likely to be very good or successful in the future: *a promising student* ◦ *a **promising start** to the game*

promo /ˈprəʊməʊ/ **noun** [C] informal an advertisement, especially a short film

promote /prəˈməʊt/ **verb** [T] **1 ENCOURAGE** ▷ to encourage something to happen or develop: *to **promote** good **health/peace*** **2 ADVERTISE** ▷ B2 to advertise something: *The band is promoting their new album.* **3 JOB** ▷ B1 to give someone a more important job in the same organization: [often passive] *She's just been **promoted to** manager.*

promoter /prəˈməʊtəʳ/ **noun** [C] **1** someone who organizes a large event: *a concert promoter* **2** someone who tries to encourage something to happen or develop: *a promoter of sexual equality*

promotion /prəˈməʊʃən/ **noun** **1 ADVERTISEMENT** ▷ [C, U] B2 activities to advertise something: *a **sales promotion*** ◦ *They're giving away free T-shirts as a special promotion.* **2 JOB** ▷ [C, U] B2 If you get a promotion, you get a more important job in your organization: *She was **given a promotion** in her first month with the company.* **3 ENCOURAGE** ▷ [U, no plural] ways of encouraging something to happen or develop: *the promotion of a healthy lifestyle*

> **Word partners for promotion**
>
> **gain/get/be given** a promotion • promotion **to** sth

promotional /prəˈməʊʃənəl/ **adj** Promotional items or activities are used to advertise something: *a **promotional campaign***

prompt¹ /prɒmpt/ **verb** [T] **1** to cause something: *His remarks prompted a lot of discussion.* **2 prompt sb to do sth** to cause someone to do something: *What prompted him to leave?* **3** to help someone, often an actor, remember what they were going to say or do

prompt² /prɒmpt/ **adj** B2 done or acting quickly and without waiting, or arriving at the correct time: *a **prompt reply*** ◦ ***prompt payment*** • **promptly** adv

prone /prəʊn/ **adj** **1 be prone to sth/doing sth** to often do something or suffer from something, especially something bad: *I'm prone to headaches.* **2 accident-/injury-, etc prone** often having accidents/injuries, etc → See also **accident-prone**

pronoun /ˈprəʊnaʊn/ **noun** [C] B1 a word that is used instead of a noun which has usually already been talked about. For example the words 'she', 'it', and 'mine' are pronouns. → See also **personal pronoun, relative pronoun**

pronounce /prəˈnaʊns/ **verb** [T] **1** B1 to make the sound of a letter or word: *How do you pronounce his name?* **2 pronounce sb/sth dead/a success, etc** formal to state that something is

P

true in an official or formal way: *Doctors pronounced him dead at 12.23 a.m.*

pronounced /prə'naʊnst/ **adj** very easy to notice: *She spoke with a pronounced American accent.*

pronouncement /prə'naʊnsmənt/ **noun** [C] formal an official announcement: *to **make** a **pronouncement***

pronunciation /prəˌnʌnsi'eɪʃən/ **noun** [C, U] **⑤** how words are pronounced: *There are two different pronunciations of this word.*

proof /pruːf/ **noun** [U] **1** **⑥** a fact or a piece of information that shows something exists or is true: *She showed us her passport as **proof of** her identity.* ○ [+ (that)] *My landlord has asked for proof that I'm employed.* **2** a printed copy of something which is examined and corrected before the final copies are printed

> ☑ Word partners for **proof**
>
> have/provide proof • conclusive/positive/ scientific proof • proof of sth

-proof /pruːf/ **suffix** used at the end of words to mean 'protecting against' or 'not damaged by': *a bulletproof vest* ○ *a waterproof jacket*

proofread /'pruːfriːd/ **verb** [I, T] to find and correct mistakes in proofs (= copies of printed text) before the final copies are printed

prop¹ /prɒp/ **verb** (**propping, propped**) **prop sth against/on, etc** to put something somewhere so that it is supported on or against something: *He propped the ladder against the wall.*

PHRASAL VERB **prop sth up 1** to lift and give support to something by putting something under it: *We had to prop up the bed with some bricks.* **2** to help something to continue: *For years the industry was propped up by the government.*

prop² /prɒp/ **noun** [C] an object used in a film or play: *a **stage prop***

propaganda /ˌprɒpə'gændə/ **noun** [U] information or ideas, which are often false, that an organization prints or broadcasts to make people agree with what it is saying: *political propaganda* • **propagandist noun** [C] someone who creates, prints, or broadcasts propaganda

propagate /'prɒpəgeɪt/ **verb** formal **1** [I, T] If you propagate plants, you help them to produce new plants, and if plants propagate, they produce new plants. **2** [T] to tell your ideas or opinions to a lot of people in order to make them agree with what you are saying: *to **propagate lies/rumours*** • **propagation** /ˌprɒpə'geɪʃən/ **noun** [U] formal

propel /prə'pel/ **verb** [T] (**propelling, propelled**) **1** **propel sb into/to sth** to make someone do an activity or be in a situation: *The film propelled him to international stardom.* **2** to push or move something somewhere, often with a lot of force: *a rocket propelled through space*

propeller /prə'pelər/ **noun** [C] a piece of equipment made of two or more flat metal pieces that turn around and cause a ship or aircraft to move

propensity /prə'pensəti/ **noun** [C] formal If

someone has a propensity for something or to do something, they often do it: *to have a **propensity for** violence* ○ *a propensity to talk too much*

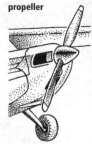

propeller

proper /'prɒpər/ **adj** **1** CORRECT ▷ [always before noun] **⑤** correct or suitable: *the **proper way** to do something* ○ *Please put those books back in the **proper place**.* **2** REAL ▷ [always before noun] mainly UK **⑥** real and satisfactory: *his first **proper job*** ○ *You should eat some proper food instead of just sweets.* **3** ACCEPTABLE ▷ socially acceptable: *It's not proper to interrupt someone when they're speaking.* **4** MAIN ▷ [always after noun] referring to the main or most important part of something: *I live outside Cambridge – I don't live in the city proper.*

properly /'prɒpəli/ **adv** **⑥** correctly, or in a satisfactory way: *She doesn't eat properly.*

proper noun noun [C] **⑥** a word or group of words that is the name of a person or place and always begins with a capital letter. For example 'Tony' and 'London' are proper nouns.

property /'prɒpəti/ **noun** **1** BUILDING ▷ [C, U] **⑥** a building or area of land: *There are several properties for sale in this area.* ○ *Private property – no parking.* ○ *a property developer.* **2** OBJECT ▷ [U] **⑥** objects that belong to someone: *The police recovered a large amount of stolen property.* **3** QUALITY ▷ [C] a quality of something: *the **medicinal properties** of wild plants* → See also **lost property**

> ☑ Word partners for **property**
>
> private property • property prices • a property developer

the property ladder noun a process in which you buy a small house and then sell it to buy a bigger house when you have more money: *When house prices are high, it is hard for buyers to move up the property ladder.*

prophecy /'prɒfəsi/ **noun** [C, U] something someone says about what will happen in the future • **prophesy** /'prɒfəsaɪ/ **verb** [I, T] to say that you believe something will happen in the future

prophet /'prɒfɪt/ **noun** [C] someone sent by God to tell people what to do, or to say what will happen in the future

prophetic /prə'fetɪk/ **adj** saying what will happen in the future: *a **prophetic dream/vision*** ○ *Her warnings proved prophetic.*

proponent /prə'pəʊnənt/ **noun** [C] formal someone who supports a particular idea or plan of action: *a proponent of nuclear energy*

proportion /prə'pɔːʃən/ **noun** **1** [C] a part of a total number or amount: *Children make up a large **proportion of** the world's population.* ○ *The class consists of both men and women in roughly*

equal proportions. **2 out of proportion** If something is out of proportion, it is much bigger or smaller than it should be, when compared to other things: *The punishment is completely out of proportion to the crime.* **3 in proportion** If something is in proportion, it is the right size or shape when compared to other things. **4 in proportion to** If something changes in proportion to another thing, it changes to the same degree as that thing: *Your tax payment increases in proportion to your salary.*

IDIOM **blow/get sth out of proportion** to behave as if something that has happened is much worse than it really is

proportional /prə'pɔ:ʃəl/ **adj** If two amounts are proportional, they change at the same rate so that the relationship between them does not change: *Weight is proportional to size.*

pro,portional ,represen'tation noun [U] a system of voting in which the number of a political party's elected representatives is related to the number of votes the party gets

proportionate /prə'pɔ:ʃənət/ **adj** If two amounts are proportionate, they change at the same rate so that the relationship between them does not change: *His success was proportionate to his efforts.* → Opposite **disproportionate** • **proportionately adv**

proportions /prə'pɔ:ʃənz/ **noun** [plural] the size, shape, or level of something: *Crime has increased to alarming proportions.*

proposal /prə'pəuzəl/ **noun** [C] **1** 💬 a suggestion for a plan: [+ to do sth] *a proposal to raise taxes* ◦ *The proposal for a new sports hall has been rejected.* **2** 💬 a request in which you ask someone to marry you

propose /prə'pəuz/ **verb 1** [T] 💬 to suggest a plan or action: [+ (that)] *I propose that we delay our decision until we have more information.* ◦ *proposed changes* **2 propose to do sth** 💬 to intend to do something: *They propose to cycle across Europe.* **3** [I] 💬 to ask someone to marry you: *He proposed to me on my birthday.*

proposition /ˌprɒpə'zɪʃən/ **noun** [C] **1 OFFER** ▷ an offer or suggestion, usually in business: *an attractive/interesting proposition* **2 IDEA** ▷ an idea or opinion: [+ that] *the proposition that all people are created equal* **3 PLAN** ▷ in the US, a formal plan that people accept or refuse by voting

proprietary /prə'praɪətəri/ **adj** [always before noun] formal owned or controlled by a company

proprietor /prə'praɪətər/ **noun** [C] formal the owner of a business such as a hotel, shop, newspaper, etc

propriety /prə'praɪəti/ **noun** [U] formal socially acceptable behaviour

propulsion /prə'pʌlʃən/ **noun** [U] a force that pushes something forward: *jet propulsion*

prosaic /prəu'zeɪk/ **adj** formal ordinary and not interesting

prose /prəuz/ **noun** [U] ordinary written language that is not poetry: *He's a wonderful writer – readers love his clear and lively prose.*

prosecute /'prɒsɪkju:t/ **verb** [I, T] to accuse

someone of a crime in a law court: *No one has been **prosecuted for** the murders.*

prosecution /ˌprɒsɪ'kju:ʃən/ **noun 1 the prosecution** [group] the lawyers who are prosecuting someone in a court of law: *The prosecution will begin presenting evidence today.* **2** [C, U] the process of prosecuting someone

prosecutor /'prɒsɪkju:tər/ **noun** [C] a lawyer who prosecutes people

prospect /'prɒspekt/ **noun 1** [C, U] 💬 the possibility that something good might happen in the future: *Is there any prospect of the weather improving?* **2** [no plural] the idea of something that will happen in the future: [+ of + doing sth] *We face the prospect of having to start all over again.* ◦ *I'm very excited at the prospect of seeing her again.* **3 sb's prospects** 💬 the possibility of being successful at work: *He's hoping the course will improve his career prospects.*

☑ **Word partners for prospect**

face the prospect of sth • **with** the prospect of sth • **at** the prospect of sth

prospective /prə'spektɪv/ **adj prospective buyers/employers/parents, etc** Prospective buyers, employers, parents, etc are not yet buyers, employers, parents, etc but are expected to be in the future.

prospectus /prə'spektəs/ **noun** [C] a book or magazine that gives information about a school, college, or business for future students or customers

prosper /'prɒspər/ **verb** [I] to be successful, usually by earning a lot of money

prosperity /prɒs'perəti/ **noun** [U] a situation in which someone is successful, usually by earning a lot of money

prosperous /'prɒspərəs/ **adj** successful, usually by earning a lot of money

prostitute /'prɒstɪtju:t/ **noun** [C] someone whose job is having sex with people • **prostitution** /ˌprɒstɪ'tju:ʃən/ **noun** [U]

prostrate /'prɒstreɪt/ **adj** lying flat on the ground with your face pointing down

protagonist /prəu'tægənɪst/ **noun** [C] formal the main character in a play, film, or story

protect /prə'tekt/ **verb** [I, T] 💬 to keep someone or something safe from something dangerous or bad: *It's important to **protect** your skin **from** the harmful effects of the sun.* ◦ *Vitamin C may help **protect against** cancer.* → See Note at **prevent** • **protection** /prə'tekʃən/ **noun** [U] 💬 *This coat doesn't provide any **protection against** the rain.*

protected /prə'tektɪd/ **adj** protected animals, plants, and land are kept safe by laws that stop people from harming or damaging them: *Tigers are a protected species.*

protective /prə'tektɪv/ **adj 1** 💬 giving protection: *protective clothing* ◦ *a protective mask* **2** wanting to protect someone from criticism, hurt, danger, etc because you like them: *She's fiercely **protective of** her children.*

protector /prə'tektər/ **noun** [C] someone or something that protects

P

protégé /ˈprɒtəʒeɪ/ **noun** [C] a young person who is helped and taught by an older and usually famous person

protein /ˈprəʊtiːn/ **noun** [U] food such as meat, cheese, fish, or eggs that is necessary for the body to grow and be strong

protest¹ /ˈprəʊtest/ **noun** [C, U] ⱬ an occasion when people show that they disagree with something by standing somewhere, shouting, carrying signs, etc: *a **protest against** the war* ∘ *a **peaceful/violent protest***

> ☑ Word partners for **protest**
>
> **hold/stage** a protest • **do** sth **as** a protest • **in** protest **at** sth • a protest **against/over** sth • a protest **by/from** sb

protest² /prəˈtest/ **verb 1 protest (about/ against/at sth)** ⱬ to show that you disagree with something by standing somewhere, shouting, carrying signs, etc: *Students were protesting about cuts to the education budget.* **2 protest sth** US ⱬ to show that you disagree with something by standing somewhere, shouting, carrying signs, etc: *Thousands gathered to protest the plan.* **3** ⱬ [I, T] to say something forcefully or complain about something: [+ that] *The girl was crying, protesting that she didn't want to leave her mother.*

Protestant /ˈprɒtɪstənt/ **adj** belonging or relating to the part of the Christian religion that separated from the Roman Catholic Church in the 1500s • **Protestant noun** [C] • **Protestantism noun** [U] the beliefs of the Protestant Churches

protestation /ˌprɒtesˈteɪʃən/ **noun** [C] formal something someone says forcefully or when complaining about something: *He was arrested despite his protestations of innocence.*

protester (also **protestor**) /prəˈtestər/ **noun** [C] someone who shows that they disagree with something by standing somewhere, shouting, carrying signs, etc

protocol /ˈprəʊtəkɒl/ **noun** [C, U] the rules about what you must do and how you must behave in official or very formal situations: *royal protocol*

proton /ˈprəʊtɒn/ **noun** [C] a part of an atom with a positive electrical charge

prototype /ˈprəʊtəʊtaɪp/ **noun** [C] the first model or example of something new that can be developed or copied in the future: *a **prototype for** a new car*

protracted /prəˈtræktɪd/ **adj** If an unpleasant situation is protracted, it lasts a long time: *a **protracted dispute/struggle***

protrude /prəˈtruːd/ **verb** [I] If something such as a part of the body protrudes, it comes out from the surface more than usual: *protruding ears/teeth*

proud /praʊd/ **adj 1** ⱬ feeling very pleased about something you have done, something you own, or someone you know: *She was so **proud of** her son.* ∘ [+ to do sth] *I'm very proud to be involved in this project.* **2 be too proud to do sth** ⱬ to not be able to do something, especially ask

for help, because you are too embarrassed: *He too proud to ask you for any money.* **3** feeling tha you are more important than you really are

> ☑ Word partners for **proud**
>
> **fiercely/immensely/rightly** proud • proud **of** sth/sb

proudly /ˈpraʊdli/ **adv** ⱬ in a way that show you are pleased about something you hav done, something you own, or someone yo know: *He proudly showed us a photo of h grandchildren.*

prove /pruːv/ **verb** [T] (**proved**, mainly US **prover 1** ⱬ to show that something is true: *They knew who had stolen the money, but they couldn't prov it.* ∘ [+ (that)] *Can you prove that you weren there?* → Opposite **disprove 2 prove (to be) st** ⱬ to show a particular quality after a period c time: *The new treatment has proved to be ver effective.* **3 prove yourself** to show that you ar good at something: *I wish he'd stop trying t prove himself all the time.*

proven /ˈpruːvən/ **adj** If something is proven, i has been shown to be true: *proven ability/skill*

proverb /ˈprɒvɜːb/ **noun** [C] a famous phrase c sentence that gives you advice: *an ancien Chinese proverb* • **proverbial** /prəˈvɜːbiəl/ **ad** relating to a proverb

provide /prəˈvaɪd/ **verb** [T] ⱬ to supply some thing to someone: *This booklet provides usefu information about local services.* ∘ *It's a new scheme to **provide** schools **with** free computers* • **provider noun** [C] someone who provide something: *an Internet service provider*

PHRASAL VERB **provide for sb** to give someone th things they need such as money, food, o clothes: *He has a wife and two young childre to provide for.*

provided (that) /prəˈvaɪdɪd/ **conjunction** (als **providing (that)**) ⱬ only if: *He's welcome t come along, provided that he behaves himself.*

provider /prəˈvaɪdər/ **noun** [C] **1** a company o organization that sells a particular type o product or service: *a **healthcare provide 2** (also **internet service provider**, also **servic provider**) a company that provides interne connections and services: *a **broadband prov der***

province /ˈprɒvɪns/ **noun 1** [C] one of the larg areas that some countries are divided int because of the type of government they have *the Canadian province of Alberta* **2 the province** the areas of a country that are not the capita city and so are not considered exciting o fashionable

provincial /prəˈvɪnʃəl/ **adj 1** relating to province **2** relating to or typical of th provinces: *a provincial town* ∘ *provincial att tudes*

provision /prəˈvɪʒən/ **noun 1** [U, no plural] th act of providing something for someone: *W need to increase the **provision of** health care fc the elderly.* **2 make provision for sth** to mak arrangements to deal with something: *He hasn* *made any provision for his retirement yet.* **3** [C] a rule that is part of a law or an agreement

provisional /prə'vɪʒ³n³l/ **adj** If a situation or arrangement is provisional, it is not certain and might change in the future: *These dates are only provisional at the moment.* • **provisionally adv**

provisions /prə'vɪʒ³nz/ **noun** [plural] supplies of food and other necessary items

proviso /prə'vaɪzəʊ/ **noun** [C] formal something that must happen as part of an agreement: *He was released from prison **with the proviso that** he doesn't leave the country.*

provocation /ˌprɒvə'keɪʃ³n/ **noun** [C, U] something you do that makes someone angry: *He'll start a fight **at the slightest provocation**.*

provocative /prə'vɒkətɪv/ **adj** **1** causing an angry reaction, usually intentionally: *a provocative question/remark* **2** Provocative clothes, images, etc are sexually exciting. • **provocatively adv** *She dresses very provocatively.*

provoke /prə'vəʊk/ **verb** [T] **1** to cause a strong and usually angry reaction: *to **provoke** an **argument*** ° *Her statement has **provoked** a public **outcry**.* **2** to intentionally make someone angry so that they react in an angry or violent way: *He claimed he was provoked by the victim.*

prowess /'praʊɪs/ **noun** [U] formal great skill at doing something: ***athletic/sporting prowess***

prowl¹ /praʊl/ **verb** [I, T] to walk around somewhere slowly as if hunting someone or something: *to prowl the streets*

prowl² /praʊl/ **noun be on the prowl** to be hunting for someone or something

proximity /prɒk'sɪməti/ **noun** [U] formal how near one thing is to another, or the fact of being near something: *What's good about this hotel is its **proximity to** the airport.*

proxy /'prɒksi/ **noun by proxy** using another person to do something instead of doing something yourself: *to vote by proxy*

Prozac /'prəʊzæk/ **noun** [U] trademark a drug that is used to make people feel happier and less worried: *She's **on Prozac** because of her depression.*

prude /pruːd/ **noun** [C] someone who does not like to hear or see things relating to sex: *Don't be such a prude.* • **prudish adj** *a prudish woman*

prudent /'pruːd³nt/ **adj** formal wise and careful: [+ to do sth] *I think it would be prudent to leave now before it starts raining.* • **prudence** /'pruːd³ns/ **noun** [U] formal • **prudently adv**

prune¹ /pruːn/ **verb** [T] If you prune a tree or bush, you cut off some of the branches or flowers to help it grow better.

prune² /pruːn/ **noun** [C] a dried plum (= type of fruit)

pry /praɪ/ **verb** **1** [I] to try to discover private things about people: *to **pry into** someone's personal life.* ° *She wanted a private holiday away from **prying eyes**.* **2 pry sth apart/loose/open, etc** to open something with difficulty: *She managed to pry open a window and escape.*

PS /ˌpiː'es/ used when you want to add extra information at the end of a letter or email: *PS Give my love to Emma.*

psalm /sɑːm/ **noun** [C] a song or poem from the Bible (= holy book)

pseudo- /sjuː'dəʊ-/ **prefix** false: *a pseudonym* (= *a false name, especially by a writer*) ° *pseudo-academic*

pseudonym /'sjuːdənɪm/ **noun** [C] a name used by a writer instead of their own name: *He writes **under a pseudonym**.*

psych /saɪk/ **verb**

PHRASAL VERB **psych yourself up** informal to try to make yourself feel confident and ready to do something difficult

psyche /'saɪki/ **noun** [C] the human mind and feelings: *the male psyche*

psychedelic /ˌsaɪkə'delɪk/ **adj** **1** Psychedelic drugs make you see things that are not really there. **2** Psychedelic colours or patterns are very strong, bright, and strange.

psychiatrist /saɪ'kaɪətrɪst/ **noun** [C] a doctor who is trained in psychiatry

psychiatry /saɪ'kaɪətri/ **noun** [U] the study and treatment of mental illness • **psychiatric** /ˌsaɪki-'ætrɪk/ **adj** relating to psychiatry: *a psychiatric disorder* ° *a psychiatric nurse*

psychic /'saɪkɪk/ **adj** having a special mental ability, for example so that you are able to know what will happen in the future or know what people are thinking: ***psychic powers***

psycho /'saɪkəʊ/ **noun** [C] informal someone who is crazy and frightening

psychoanalysis /ˌsaɪkəʊə'næləsɪs/ **noun** [U] the treatment of mental problems by studying and talking about people's dreams, fears, and experiences • **psychoanalytic** /ˌsaɪkəʊˌæn³l'ɪtɪk/ **adj** relating to psychoanalysis

psychoanalyst /ˌsaɪkəʊ'æn³lɪst/ **noun** [C] someone who treats people using psychoanalysis

psychological /ˌsaɪk³'lɒdʒɪk³l/ **adj** ⓑ relating to the human mind and feelings: *psychological problems* • **psychologically adv**

psychologist /saɪ'kɒlədʒɪst/ **noun** [C] ⓑ someone who has studied the human mind and feelings

psychology /saɪ'kɒlədʒi/ **noun** [U] **1** ⓑ the study of the human mind and feelings: *child psychology* ° *He's studying psychology and philosophy.* **2** ⓑ the way someone thinks and behaves: *the psychology of serial killers*

psychopath /'saɪkəʊpæθ/ **noun** [C] someone who is very mentally ill and usually dangerous • **psychopathic** /ˌsaɪkəʊ'pæθɪk/ **adj** *a psychopathic killer*

psychosis /saɪ'kəʊsɪs/ **noun** [C] (plural **psychoses** /saɪ'kəʊsiːz/) a mental illness that makes you believe things that are not real

psychotherapy /ˌsaɪkəʊ'θerəpi/ **noun** [U] the treatment of mental problems by talking about your feelings instead of taking medicine • **psychotherapist noun** [C] someone who gives people psychotherapy

psychotic /saɪ'kɒtɪk/ **adj** suffering from a

mental illness that makes you believe things that are not true

pt noun [C] **1** written abbreviation for point (=a unit used for showing who is winning in a game or competition): *They are leading by 4 pts.* **2** written abbreviation for pint (= a unit for measuring liquid)

PTO /ˌpiːtiːˈəʊ/ UK abbreviation for please turn over: used at the bottom of a page of writing to show that there is more information on the other side

pub /pʌb/ noun [C] ⓐ a place where you can get drinks such as beer and usually food: *We're all going to the pub after work.*

puberty /ˈpjuːbəti/ noun [U] the time when children's bodies change and become like adults' bodies: *to reach puberty*

pubic hair /ˌpjuːbɪkˈheər/ noun [U] the hair that grows around the sexual organs

public¹ /ˈpʌblɪk/ adj **1** public awareness/health/support, etc ⓑ the awareness/health/support, etc of all ordinary people: *Public opinion has turned against him.* ∘ *Is it really in the public interest* (= useful for people) *to publish this information?* **2** public parks/toilets/transport, etc ⓑ parks/toilets/transport, etc that are for everyone to use and are not private: *Smoking is banned in public places.* **3** a public announcement/appearance/statement, etc ⓑ an announcement/appearance/statement, etc that can be seen or heard or known by everyone: *The Prime Minister is due to make a public statement later today.* **4** make sth public to allow everyone to know about something: *The government does not plan to make its findings public.* **5** public funds/services/spending, etc ⓑ funds/services/spending, etc controlled by the government and not by a private company

public² /ˈpʌblɪk/ noun **1** the (general) public ⓑ [group] all ordinary people: *a member of the public* ∘ *The public has a right to know about this.* ∘ *The house is only open to the general public on Sundays.* **2** in public ⓑ where everyone can see you: *He shouldn't behave like that in public.*

public adˈdress system noun [C] (also UK **tannoy**) a system of equipment used in public places that someone speaks into in order to make their voice loud enough to hear

publication /ˌpʌblɪˈkeɪʃən/ noun **1** [U] ⓑ the act of printing and selling a book, newspaper, etc **2** [C] ⓑ a book, newspaper, or magazine: *a monthly/weekly publication*

public ˈholiday noun [C] mainly UK (US **national holiday**) a day when most people in a particular country do not have to go to work or school

publicist /ˈpʌblɪsɪst/ noun [C] someone whose job is to make people know about someone or something by advertising or giving information in the newspaper, on television, etc

publicity /pʌbˈlɪsəti/ noun [U] ⓑ advertising or information about someone or something in the newspaper, on television, etc: *a publicity campaign* ∘ *to get bad/good publicity*

☑ Word partners for **publicity**

attract/get/receive/seek publicity • adverse/bad/good/negative publicity • publicity about/for sth • publicity surrounding sth • a publicity campaign/stunt

---

publicize (also UK **-ise**) /ˈpʌblɪsaɪz/ verb [T] to make people know about something by advertising or giving information in newspapers, on television, etc: *a highly/widely publicized event*

publicly /ˈpʌblɪkli/ adv If you do something publicly, everyone can see it, hear it, or know about it.

public reˈlations noun [U] formal PR (=writing and activities that are intended to make a person, company, or product more popular)

public ˈschool (US **public ˌschool**) noun [C] **1** in the UK, a school that you pay to go to **2** (US **state school**) in the US, a school that is free to go to because the government provides the money for it

the ˌpublic ˈsector noun [usually singular] businesses and industries that are owned or controlled by the government: *public sector workers*

ˌpublic ˈtransport noun [U] ⓑ a system of vehicles such as buses and trains which operate at regular times and that the public use

ˌpublic uˈtility noun [C] an organization that supplies the public with water, gas, or electricity

publish /ˈpʌblɪʃ/ verb [T] **1** PRINT ▷ ⓑ to prepare and print a book, newspaper, magazine, article, etc so that people can buy it: [often passive] *This book is published by Cambridge University Press.* **2** WRITE ▷ to write something that is then printed in a book, newspaper, magazine, etc: *He's published several short stories in national magazines.* **3** MAKE PUBLIC ▷ ⓑ to make information available to the public

publisher /ˈpʌblɪʃər/ noun [C] ⓑ a company or person who prepares and prints books, newspapers, magazines, etc

publishing /ˈpʌblɪʃɪŋ/ noun [U] the business of preparing and printing books, newspapers, magazines, etc: *a career in publishing*

puck /pʌk/ noun [C] in ice hockey (= a sport), small, hard disc that players hit with a stick → See colour picture **Sports 1** on page Centre 14

pudding /ˈpʊdɪŋ/ noun **1** [C, U] ⓑ in the UK, sweet dish that is usually eaten as the last part of a meal: *We've got apple pie for pudding.* **2** [U] in the US, a soft, sweet food made from milk, sugar, eggs, and sometimes flour: *chocolate/vanilla pudding*

puddle /ˈpʌdl/ noun [C] a pool of liquid on the ground, usually from rain

puerile /ˈpjʊəraɪl/ ⓤⓢ /ˈpjuːərɪl/ adj formal behaving in a silly way like a child

puff¹ /pʌf/ verb **1** [I] to breathe fast and with difficulty, usually because you have been doing exercise **2** [I, T] to smoke something: *to puff on a cigarette*

PHRASAL VERBS **puff sth out** to make your chest or your face become bigger by filling them with air

• **puff up** If part of your body puffs up, it becomes larger because it is infected or injured.

puff² /pʌf/ **noun** [C] **1** a small amount of smoke, gas, powder, etc: *a puff of smoke/air* **2** the act of breathing in smoke from a cigarette: *to take a puff on a cigarette*

puffin /'pʌfɪn/ **noun** [C] a black and white sea bird with a large head and brightly coloured beak

puffy /'pʌfi/ **adj** If the skin around your eyes is puffy, it is slightly swollen: *His **eyes** were still **puffy** with sleep.*

puke /pjuːk/ **verb** [I, T] (also **puke up**) informal to vomit

pull

pull¹ /pʊl/ **verb 1** ⒶⒶ [I, T] to take hold of something and move it somewhere: *If you keep pulling his tail, he'll bite you.* ○ *No wonder it's not working, someone's **pulled** the plug **out**.* ○ *He **pulled off** his boots.* ○ *She bent down and **pulled up** her socks.* **2 pull a muscle** to injure a muscle by stretching it too much **3 pull a gun/knife, etc on sb** to suddenly take out a weapon: *He pulled a gun on us and demanded money.* → See also **pull/ tear your hair** out, **pull the plug¹**, not **pull any punches (punch²)**, **pull out all the stops (stop²)**, **pull strings**, **pull your weight**

PHRASAL VERBS **pull sth apart 1** to destroy something by tearing it into pieces **2** to say that something, usually a piece of work, is very bad: *He really pulled apart the last essay I gave him.* • **pull sb/sth apart** to separate two people or things • **pull at sth** to pull something several times, usually with quick, light movements: *Stop pulling at my sleeve.* • **pull away 1** If a vehicle pulls away, it starts moving: *I just managed to get on the bus before it pulled away.* **2** If you pull away from someone who is holding you, you suddenly move your body backwards, away from them. • **pull sth down** ⒷⒷ to destroy a building because it is not wanted any more: *They've started pulling down the old cinema.* • **pull in/ into sth** ⒷⒷ If a vehicle pulls in or pulls into somewhere, it moves in that direction and stops there: *They pulled in at the side of the road.* • **pull sth off** to succeed in doing or achieving something difficult: *He is about to pull off his biggest deal yet.* • **pull off** UK If a vehicle pulls off, it starts moving: *The car pulled off and sped up the*

road. • **pull sth on** to put on clothes quickly: *I pulled on my jeans and ran downstairs.* • **pull out** ⒷⒷ If a vehicle pulls out, it starts moving onto a road or onto a different part of the road: *That car pulled out right in front of me.* • **pull over** ⒷⒷ If a vehicle pulls over, it moves to the side of the road and stops. • **pull through** to continue to live after you have been badly injured or very sick • **pull yourself together** informal to become calm and behave normally again after being angry or upset • **pull up 1** ⒷⒷ If a vehicle pulls up, it stops, often for a short time: *A car pulled up outside the bank and two men got out.* **2 pull up a chair** to move a chair nearer to something or someone: *Why don't you pull up a chair and join us?*

pull² /pʊl/ **noun** [no plural] a strong force that causes something to move somewhere or be attracted to something

pull-down /'pʊldaʊn/ **adj** [always before noun] A pull-down menu is a list of choices on a computer screen which is hidden until you choose to look at it.

pulley /'pʊli/ **noun** [C] a wheel with a rope going round it which is used to lift things

pulley

pullover /'pʊləʊvəʳ/ **noun** [C] ⒷⒷ a warm piece of clothing that covers the top of your body and is pulled on over your head: *a black woolly pullover*

pulp /pʌlp/ **noun** [U] **1** a soft, wet substance made from wood, which is used to make paper **2** the soft part inside a fruit or vegetable

pulpit /'pʊlpɪt/ **noun** [C] the raised structure in a church where the priest stands when he or she speaks to everyone

pulsate /pʌl'seɪt/ ⓤⓈ /'pʌlseɪt/ **verb** [I] to beat or move with a strong, regular rhythm: *The whole room was pulsating with music.*

pulse /pʌls/ **noun** [C] the regular movement of blood through your body when your heart is beating: *She put her fingers on my wrist to **take my pulse** (= count the number of beats per minute).* ○ *My **pulse rate** is 70.*

pulses /pʌlsɪz/ **noun** [plural] UK seeds such as beans or peas which are cooked and eaten as food

pump¹ /pʌmp/ **noun** [C] ⒷⒷ a piece of equipment that forces liquid or gas to move somewhere: *a gas/petrol pump* ○ *a water pump*

pump² /pʌmp/ **verb** [T] to force liquid or gas to move somewhere: *Your heart pumps blood around your body.* ○ *Firemen used powerful hoses to **pump** water **into** the building.*

PHRASAL VERBS **pump sth into sth** to give a lot of money to a plan or organization: *They've pumped millions of pounds into the economy.*

P

pump

bicycle pump

petrol pump *UK*,
gas pump *US*

• **pump sth out** informal to continuously produce a lot of something: *a radio pumping out music* • **pump sth up** to fill something with air using a pump: *You should pump your tyres up.*

pumpkin /'pʌmpkɪn/ **noun** [C, U] a large, round vegetable with thick, orange skin

pun /pʌn/ **noun** [C] a joke that you make by using a word that has two meanings

punch¹ /pʌnʃ/ **verb** [T] **1** 🔂 to hit someone or something with your fist (= closed hand): *He punched me twice in the stomach.* **2 punch a hole in sth** to make a hole in something with a special piece of equipment

punch² /pʌnʃ/ **noun 1** HIT ▷ [C] 🔂 the act of hitting someone or something with your fist (= closed hand): *a punch on the nose* **2** DRINK ▷ [U] a sweet, mixed drink made from fruit juice, spices, and usually alcohol **3** HOLE ▷ [C] a piece of equipment that makes a hole in something

IDIOM **not pull any punches** to speak in an honest way without trying to be kind

🔲 Word partners for **punch**

aim a punch at sb • **deliver/land/swing/ throw** a punch

punchline /'pʌntʃlaɪn/ **noun** [C] the last part of a joke that makes it funny

punch-up /'pʌntʃʌp/ **noun** [C] UK informal a fight in which people hit each other with their fists (= closed hands)

punctual /'pʌŋktʃuəl/ **adj** arriving at the right time and not too late • **punctuality** /ˌpʌŋktʃu-'æləti/ **noun** [U] the quality of being punctual • **punctually adv**

punctuate /'pʌŋktʃueɪt/ **verb** [T] to add punctuation marks to written words so that people can see when a sentence begins and finishes, that something is a question, etc

punctuation /ˌpʌŋktʃu'eɪʃ°n/ **noun** [U] 🔂 the use of punctuation marks in writing so that people can see when a sentence begins and finishes, that something is a question, etc → See Study Page **Punctuation** on page Centre 33

punctu'ation ˌmark noun [C] a symbol such as a full stop (.) or a question mark (?) used in

writing to show where a sentence begins and finishes, etc.

puncture¹ /'pʌŋktʃər/ **noun** [C] **1** a small hole made by a sharp object **2** UK a hole in a tyre that makes the air come out: *to have a puncture*

puncture² /'pʌŋktʃər/ **verb** [T] to make a hole in something: *The knife went through his ribs and punctured his lung.*

pundit /'pʌndɪt/ **noun** [C] an expert in a subject who often gives their opinions on television, radio, etc: *a political pundit*

pungent /'pʌndʒ°nt/ **adj** A pungent smell is very strong: *the pungent smell of vinegar*

punish /'pʌnɪʃ/ **verb** [T] 🔂 to make someone suffer because they have done something bad [often passive] *They must be severely punished for these crimes.*

punishable /'pʌnɪʃəbl/ **adj** A crime that is punishable is one that you can be punished for: *Drug dealing is punishable by death in some countries.*

punishing /'pʌnɪʃɪŋ/ **adj** very difficult and making you tired: *a punishing schedule*

punishment /'pʌnɪʃmənt/ **noun** [C, U] 🔂 something that is done to punish someone: *He had to stay in his bedroom as a punishment for fighting* → See also **capital punishment, corporal punishment, be a glutton for punishment**

🔲 Word partners for **punishment**

capital/corporal punishment • **an appropriate/cruel/harsh/severe** punishment • **deserve/escape/impose/inflict/receive** punishment

punitive /'pjuːnətɪv/ **adj** formal given as a punishment or seeming like a punishment: *punitive action*

punk /pʌŋk/ **noun 1** STYLE ▷ [U] (also ˌpunk 'rock) a style of music and fashion in the 1970s which was wild, loud, and violent **2** PERSON ▷ [C] someone who wears punk clothes and likes punk music **3** BAD MAN ▷ [C] US informal a bad young man

punt¹ /pʌnt/ **noun** [C] **1** a long boat with a flat bottom that you push along the river with a long pole **2** in some sports, a powerful kick which causes the ball to go very far

punt² /pʌnt/ **verb 1** [I, T] to go or take someone along a river in a punt **2** [T] in some sports, to kick a ball after you have dropped it from your hands and before it touches the ground

punter /'pʌntər/ **noun** [C] UK informal someone who is buying something or making a bet (= risking money on a competition)

puny /'pjuːni/ **adj** very small and weak

pup /pʌp/ **noun** [C] a young dog or other particular type of baby mammal: *a seal pup*

pupil /'pjuːp°l/ **noun** [C] **1** 🔂 a student at school: *The school has 1,100 pupils aged 11 to 18.* → See colour picture **The Classroom** on page Centre 6 **2** the black, round part in the centre of your eye

puppet /'pʌpɪt/ **noun** [C] **1** a toy in the shape of a person or animal that you can move with strings or by putting your hand inside: *a glove* *puppet* **2** someone who is controlled by someone else: *a political puppet*

puppy /ˈpʌpi/ **noun** [C] 🄱 a young dog: *a litter of puppies*

purchase¹ /ˈpɜːtʃəs/ **verb** [T] formal 🄱 to buy something: *Tickets must be purchased two weeks in advance.*

purchase² /ˈpɜːtʃəs/ **noun** formal **1** [C, U] 🄱 the act of buying something: *the illegal purchase of guns* **2** [C] 🄱 something that you buy: *a major purchase*

pure /pjʊəʳ/ **adj 1 NOT MIXED** ▷ 🄱 A pure substance is not mixed with anything else: *pure gold* ∘ *pure wool* **2 EMPHASIS** ▷ [always before noun] 🄱 used to emphasize that a feeling, quality, or state is completely and only that thing: *pure delight.* ∘ *Her face had a look of pure delight.* **3 CLEAN** ▷ 🄱 clean and healthy: *pure air/water* **4 pure mathematics/physics, etc** the study of mathematics/physics, etc based only on ideas and not on practical use **5 GOOD** ▷ completely good and not having any bad qualities or bad morals

puree /ˈpjʊəreɪ/ 🅤🅢 /pjʊəˈreɪ/ **noun** [U] a thick, smooth, liquid food made by crushing and mixing fruit or vegetables: *tomato puree*

purely /pjʊəli/ **adv** only: *She married him **purely** for his money.*

purgatory /ˈpɜːgətəri/ **noun** [U] **1** in the Catholic religion, a very unpleasant place where you have to go and suffer before you go to heaven **2** a very unpleasant situation: *This diet is purgatory.*

purge /pɜːdʒ/ **verb** [T] **1** to get rid of bad feelings that you do not want: [often reflexive] *She wanted to purge herself of guilt.* **2** to get rid of people from an organization because you do not agree with them ∘ **purge noun** [C]

purify /ˈpjʊərɪfaɪ/ **verb** [T] to remove bad substances from something to make it pure: *Plants help to purify the air.* ∘ *purified water* ∘ **purification** /ˌpjʊərɪfɪˈkeɪʃⁿn/ **noun** [U]

purist /ˈpjʊərɪst/ **noun** [C] someone who believes in and follows very traditional rules or ideas in a subject

puritanical /ˌpjʊərɪˈtænɪkⁿl/ **adj** having severe religious morals and not wanting people to enjoy themselves ∘ **puritan** /ˈpjʊərɪtⁿn/ **noun** [C] a puritanical person

purity /ˈpjʊərəti/ **noun** [U] the quality of being pure: *air purity*

purple /ˈpɜːpl/ **adj** 🄐 being a colour that is a mixture of red and blue: *purple flowers* ∘ **purple noun** [C, U] → See colour picture **Colours** on page Centre 12

purport /pəˈpɔːt/ **verb**

PHRASAL VERB **purport to be/do sth** formal to pretend to be or do something: *a man purporting to be a police officer*

purpose /ˈpɜːpəs/ **noun 1** [C] 🄱 why you do something or why something exists: *The main **purpose of** the meeting is to discuss the future of the company.* ∘ *The drug may be legalized for medical purposes.* **2** [U] the feeling of knowing

what you want to do: *He seems to have lost all **sense of purpose.*** **3 on purpose** 🄱 intentionally: *I didn't do it on purpose, it was an accident.* **4 serve a purpose** to have a use: *These small village shops serve a very useful purpose.* → See also **cross purposes, to/for all intents (intent¹) (and purposes)**

> 🔲 Word partners for **purpose**
>
> defeat/have/fulfil/serve a purpose ∘ a clear/good/primary/practical/useful purpose ∘ the purpose of sth

purpose-built /ˌpɜːpəsˈbɪlt/ **adj** mainly UK A purpose-built building has been specially designed for the way it will be used.

purposeful /ˈpɜːpəsfⁿl/ **adj** showing that you know what you want to do: *He has a quiet, purposeful air.* ∘ **purposefully adv**

purposely /ˈpɜːpəsli/ **adv** intentionally: *I wasn't purposely trying to hurt you.*

purr /pɜːʳ/ **verb** [I] **1 CAT** ▷ If a cat purrs, it makes a soft sound in its throat to show pleasure. **2 PERSON** ▷ to talk in a soft, low voice **3 CAR** ▷ If a car purrs, its engine is very smooth and makes a soft sound.

purse¹ /pɜːs/ **noun** [C] **1** mainly UK 🄐 a small container for money, usually used by a woman: *a leather purse* **2** mainly US (UK/US **handbag**) a bag, usually carried by a woman: *I always carry aspirin in my purse.*

purse² /pɜːs/ **verb** **purse your lips** to press your lips tightly together, often to show that you are angry

pursue /pəˈsjuː/ 🅤🅢 /pərˈsuː/ **verb** [T] (**pursuing, pursued**) **1** If you pursue a plan, activity, or situation, you try to do it or achieve it, usually over a long period of time: *She decided to pursue a career in television.* **2** to follow someone or something, usually to try to catch them: *The car was pursued by helicopters.* **3 pursue a matter** to try to discover information about something: *We will not be pursuing this matter any further.*

pursuit /pəˈsjuːt/ 🅤🅢 /pərˈsuːt/ **noun** [U] **1** an attempt to achieve a plan, activity, or situation, usually over a long period of time: *the pursuit of pleasure* ∘ *He left his native country **in pursuit of** freedom.* **2** the act of following someone or something to try to catch them: *The police are **in pursuit of** a 25-year-old murder suspect.*

pursuits /pəˈsjuːts/ 🅤🅢 /pərˈsuːts/ **noun** [plural] formal activities or hobbies: *He enjoys climbing and other **outdoor pursuits**.*

purveyor /pəˈveɪəʳ/ **noun** [C] formal someone who sells or provides something: *a purveyor of antiques*

pus /pʌs/ **noun** [U] a yellow substance that is produced when part of your body is infected

push¹ /pʊʃ/ **verb 1 MOVE SOMETHING** ▷ [I, T] 🄐 to move someone or something by pressing them with your hands or body: *She **pushed** the books **aside** and sat down on my desk.* ∘ *We **pushed** the children **down** the slide.* ∘ *He **pushed** me violently **out** of the door.* ∘ *Someone **pushed** him **into** the river.* → See picture at **pull 2 MOVE YOURSELF** ▷ [I, T] 🄱 to move somewhere by

P

moving someone or something away from you: *He pushed me past me.* ◦ *She pushed her way to the front of the crowd.* **3 PRESS** ▷ [T] **B1** to press something: *If you push this button, your seat goes back.* **4 push (sb) for sth/to do sth** **B2** to try hard to achieve something or to make someone else do something: *Local residents are pushing for the road to be made safer.* **5 ENCOURAGE** ▷ [T] to try to make someone do something that they do not want to do: [+ into + doing sth] *My mother pushed me into having ballet lessons.* **6 push yourself** **B2** to make yourself work very hard to achieve something → See also **push the boat out**

PHRASAL VERBS **push sb about/around** to tell someone what to do in a rude way: *I'm fed up with being pushed around.* • **push ahead/forward** to continue doing something, especially when this is difficult: *They have decided to* **push ahead with** *legal action.* • **push sth/sb aside** to decide to forget about or ignore something or someone: *We can't just push these problems aside – we have to deal with them.* • **push in** UK informal to rudely join a line of people who are waiting for something by moving in front of some of the people who are already there • **push on** to continue doing something, especially when this is difficult • **push sb/sth over** to push someone or something so that they fall to the ground • **push sth through** to make a plan or suggestion be officially accepted: *We're trying to push this deal through as quickly as possible.* • **push sth up** to increase the amount, number, or value of something: *If you want to travel on Saturday, it will push the price up a bit.*

push² /pʊʃ/ *noun* **1 a push for sth/to do sth** a big effort to achieve something or make someone do something: *a push for higher standards in education* **2** [C] **B1** the act of moving someone or something by pressing them with your hands or body: [usually singular] *She* **gave** *him a little* **push** *towards the door.* **3 give sb the push** UK informal to get rid of someone from a job or relationship **4** [C] encouragement to make someone do something: [usually singular] *I'm sure he'll go, he just needs a little push that's all.* **5 at a push** UK If you can do something at a push, you can do it but it will be difficult.

IDIOM **if/when push comes to shove** informal If you say that something can be done if push comes to shove, you mean that it can be done if the situation becomes so bad that you have to do it: *If push comes to shove, we'll just have to sell the car.*

pushchair /ˈpʊʃtʃeəʳ/ *noun* [C] UK (US **stroller**) a chair on wheels that is used to move small children

pushed /pʊʃt/ *adj* UK informal **be pushed for sth** to not have much of something: *I can't stop, I'm a bit pushed for time.*

pusher /ˈpʊʃəʳ/ *noun* [C] someone who sells illegal drugs

push-up /ˈpʊʃʌp/ *noun* [C] US (UK **press-up**) a

physical exercise in which you lie facing th floor and use your hands to push your body up *I did forty push-ups yesterday.*

pushy /ˈpʊʃi/ *adj* behaving in an unpleasant wa by trying too much to get something or to mak someone do something: *a pushy salesman*

put /pʊt/ *verb* [T] (**putting, put**) **1 put sth down in/on, etc** **A1** to move something to a place o position: *Where have you put the keys?* ◦ *She pu her bag on the floor.* ◦ *You can put your coat in th car.* ◦ *He put his arm around her.* **2 put sb in mood/position, etc** **B2** to make someone o something be in a particular situation: *They' had an argument and it had put her in a ba mood.* ◦ *This puts me in a very difficult position* **3** to say something using particular words: *don't know quite* **how to put this**, *but I'm leaving* **4** **A2** to write something: *Please put your nam on the list by Monday evening.*

PHRASAL VERBS **put sth across** to explain o express something clearly so that people under stand it easily • **put sth aside** **B2** to sav something so that you can use it later: *I've bee putting a bit of money aside every month.* • **pu sth away** **B1** to put something in the plac where you usually keep it: *She folded the towe and put them away in the cupboard.* → See colou picture **Phrasal Verbs** on page Centre 16 • **put stl back** **B1** to put something where it was before i was moved: *I put the book back on the shelf.* • **pu sth down 1 STOP HOLDING** ▷ **B1** to pu something that you are holding onto the floo or onto another surface: *I'll just put my ba down for a minute, it's rather heavy.* → See colou picture **Phrasal Verbs** on page Centre 1 **2 TELEPHONE** ▷ UK **B1** If you put the phon down, you put the part of the telephone tha you speak into back to its usual position **3 ANIMAL** ▷ to kill an animal, usually becaus it is suffering • **put sb down 1** to make someon feel stupid or unimportant by criticizing them *I'm tired of him putting me down all the time.* **2 B** to write someone's name on a list or document usually in order to arrange for them to d something: *I've* **put** *you* **down for** *the trip t Rome next week.* • **put sth down to sth** UK t think that a problem or situation is caused by particular thing • **put sth forward** to state a idea or opinion, or to suggest a plan, so that i can be considered or discussed • **put sb/sth i sth** **B2** to arrange for someone or something t go somewhere: *to put someone in prison* ◦ *to pu some money in the bank* ◦ *I'd never put m mother in an old people's home.* • **put sth in** to fi something into a room or building: *I've just hac a new kitchen put in.* • **put sth into sth/doin sth** If you put time, work, or effort into some thing, you spend a lot of time or effort doing it *We've put a lot of effort into this project and w want it to succeed.* • **put sth off** **B1** to decide o arrange to do something at a later time: *I mus talk to her about this, I can't put it off any longer* • **put sb off (sth/sb)** **B2** to make someone no like someone or something, or not want to d something: *Jan was talking about her operatior and it put me off my food.* • **put sth o**

1 CLOTHES ▷ **A2** to put clothes or shoes onto your body: *You'd better put your coat on, it's cold outside.* → See colour picture **Phrasal Verbs** on page Centre 16 **2 EQUIPMENT** ▷ mainly UK **B1** to make a piece of equipment work by pressing a switch: *Can you put the light on please?* **3 BEHAVIOUR** ▷ to pretend to have a particular feeling, or to behave in a way which is not real or natural for you: *He's not really upset, he's just putting it on.* **4 MUSIC/FILM** ▷ **A2** to make music, a film, or some other recording start playing on a machine: *Why don't you put on some music?* **5 put on weight** UK **B1** to become fatter and heavier • **put sth out 1 STOP SHINING** ▷ mainly UK to make a light stop shining by pressing a switch: *Please put the lights out when you leave.* **2 STOP BURNING** ▷ **B1** to make something that is burning stop burning: *to put out a fire* **3 PUT OUTSIDE** ▷ to put something outside the house: *to put out the rubbish/trash* • **put sb out** to cause trouble or extra work for someone: *It would be great if you could help, but I don't want to put you out.* • **be put out** to be annoyed, often because of something that someone has done or said to you: *He seemed a bit put out at not having been invited.* • **put sb through sth** to make someone experience or do something unpleasant or difficult: *Why did they put themselves through this ordeal?* • **put sb through** **B1** to connect someone using a telephone to the person they want to speak to: *Can you put me through to customer services, please?* • **put sth to sb 1** to suggest an idea or plan to someone so that they can consider it or discuss it **2** to ask someone a question • **put sth together 1** **B2** to put the parts of something in the correct place and join them to each other: *You buy it in a kit and then you put it together yourself.* **2** to prepare a piece of work by collecting several ideas and suggestions and organizing them: *to put together a plan/proposal* • **put sth up 1 BUILD** ▷ **B2** to build something: *to put up a tent* ∘ *We spent the weekend putting up a fence in the backyard.* **2 FASTEN** ▷ **B1** to fasten something to a wall or ceiling: *to put up shelves* ∘ *I need to put up some curtains in the back bedroom.* **3 INCREASE** ▷ mainly UK **B1** to increase the price or value of something: *They're going to put up the price of fuel.* • **put sb up** **B2** to let someone stay in your home for a short period: *If you need somewhere to stay, we can put you up for the night.* • **put up with sb/sth** **B2** to accept unpleasant behaviour or an unpleasant situation, although you do not like it: *He's so rude, I don't know how you put up with him.*

putrid /ˈpjuːtrɪd/ **adj** decaying and smelling bad: *a putrid smell*

putt /pʌt/ **verb** [I, T] in golf, to hit the ball gently when you are near the hole • **putt noun** [C]

putty /ˈpʌti/ **noun** [U] a soft, grey substance that becomes hard when it is dry and is used to fasten glass into windows or to fill small holes in wood

puzzle¹ /ˈpʌzl/ **noun** [C] **1** **A2** a game or activity in which you have to put pieces together or answer questions using skill: *to do/solve a puzzle* ∘ *a crossword puzzle* ∘ *a jigsaw puzzle* **2** a situation that is very difficult to understand: *Scientists have been trying to solve this puzzle for years.*

> ☑ **Word partners for puzzle**
> resolve/solve a puzzle • the puzzle of sth

puzzle² /ˈpʌzl/ **verb** [T] to make someone confused because they do not understand something: [often passive] *I was puzzled by what he said.*

PHRASAL VERB **puzzle over sth** to try to solve a problem or understand a situation by thinking carefully about it

puzzled /ˈpʌzld/ **adj** **B2** confused because you do not understand something: *He had a puzzled look on his face.*

puzzling /ˈpʌzlɪŋ/ **adj** If something is puzzling, it confuses you because you do not understand it.

PVC /ˌpiːviːˈsiː/ **noun** [U] a strong material similar to thick plastic

pyjamas UK (US **pajamas**) /pɪˈdʒɑːməz/ **noun** [plural] **B2** a shirt and trousers that you wear in bed: *a pair of blue pyjamas* → See colour picture **Clothes** on page Centre 8

pyjamas

pylon /ˈpaɪlɒn/ **noun** [C] a tall structure that supports electrical wires above the ground

pyramid /ˈpɪrəmɪd/ **noun** [C] a shape with a square base and four triangular sides that meet to form a point at the top → See picture at **shape**

pyre /paɪər/ **noun** [C] a pile of wood on which a dead person is burned in some countries

python /ˈpaɪθən/ **noun** [C] a large snake that kills other animals by putting itself tightly around them

P

Q

Q, q /kjuː/ the seventeenth letter of the alphabet

QC /ˌkjuːˈsiː/ **noun** [C] abbreviation for Queen's Counsel: a lawyer of high rank in the UK: *Horace Rumpole QC*

qt written abbreviation for quart (= a unit for measuring liquid)

quack /kwæk/ **noun** [C] the sound made by a duck (= water bird) • **quack verb** [I]

quadruple /kwɒdˈruːpl/ **verb** [I, T] If an amount quadruples, it becomes multiplied by four, or if you quadruple it, you multiply it by four.

quagmire /ˈkwɒgmaɪəʳ/ **noun** [C] **1** a difficult and unpleasant situation: *a legal quagmire* **2** an area of wet ground that you can sink into

quail /kweɪl/ **noun** [C] (plural **quail, quails**) a small bird that is shot for food

quaint /kweɪnt/ **adj** attractive or unusual in an old-fashioned way: *a quaint little village*

quake¹ /kweɪk/ **noun** [C] short for earthquake (= when the Earth shakes)

quake² /kweɪk/ **verb** [I] to shake because you are frightened

qualification /ˌkwɒlɪfɪˈkeɪʃən/ **noun 1 EXAMS** ▷ [C] mainly UK ⑥ what you get when you pass an exam or a course: [usually plural] *legal/medical qualifications* ° *What qualifications do you need to be a nanny?* **2 SKILLS** ▷ [C] the skills, qualities, or experience that you need in order to do something: *The only qualification needed for this job is an eye for detail.* **3 COMPETITION** ▷ [U] success in getting into a competition: *England's qualification for the World Cup* **4 ADDITION** ▷ [C, U] an addition to something that is said that makes its meaning less certain

> **☑ Word partners for qualification**
>
> an **academic/basic/formal/recognized** qualification • **gain/get/have/need** a qualification • a qualification **in** sth

qualified /ˈkwɒlɪfaɪd/ **adj 1** ⑥ having passed exams or courses: *a newly qualified teacher* **2 qualified to do sth** ⑥ having the skills, qualities, or experience that you need in order to do something: *I think John is the best qualified to make that decision.* **3** If something someone says is qualified, they have added something to it to make it less certain: *The answer was a qualified yes.* → Opposite **unqualified**

qualifier /ˈkwɒlɪfaɪəʳ/ **noun** [C] **1** a game or competition that decides whether you can enter another competition **2** someone who has succeeded in getting into a competition

qualify /ˈkwɒlɪfaɪ/ **verb 1 BE ALLOWED** ▷ [I, T] ⑥ If you qualify for something, you are allowed to do it or have it, and if something qualifies you for something, it allows you to do it or have it: *To qualify for the competition, you must be over 18.* → Opposite **disqualify 2 PASS EXAMS** ▷ [I] mainly UK ⑥ to pass exams so that you are able to do a job: *He's recently qualified as a doctor.* **3 GET INTO COMPETITION** ▷ [I] ⑥ to succeed in getting into a competition: *Nigeria were the first team to qualify for the World Cup.* **4 ADD** ▷ [T] to add something to what you say to make it meaning less certain

qualitative /ˈkwɒlɪtətɪv/ ⑤ /ˈkwɑːlɪteɪtɪv/ **adj** formal relating to how good something is and not how much of it there is • **qualitatively adv**

quality¹ /ˈkwɒləti/ **noun 1 GOOD OR BAD** ▷ [U] ⑥ how good or bad something is: *good/high quality* ° *poor/low quality* ° *The air quality in this area is terrible.* ° *All we are asking for is a decent quality of life.* ° *The spokeswoman says a quality control system is being developed for next year.* **2 GOOD** ▷ [U] ⑥ the fact of being very good or well made: *A designer label isn't necessarily a guarantee of quality.* **3 CHARACTER** ▷ [C] ⑥ part of the character or personality of someone or something: *leadership qualities*

> **☑ Word partners for quality**
>
> **affect/enhance/improve/maintain** quality • **good/high/inferior/low/poor** quality

quality² /ˈkwɒləti/ **adj** [always before noun] ⑥ very good: *We only sell quality products in this store.*

quality time noun [U] time that you spend with someone when you can give them all of your attention: *We've been too busy to give the children much quality time this week.*

qualm /kwɑːm/ **noun** [C] a worry or doubt about something: *I would have no qualms about reporting her to the police.*

quandary /ˈkwɒndəri/ **noun** [no plural] a situation in which you are trying to make a difficult choice: *We're in a quandary over which school to send her to.*

quantifier /ˈkwɒntɪfaɪəʳ/ **noun** [C] a word or group of words that is used before a noun to show an amount of that noun. For example the words 'many', 'some', and 'a lot of' are quantifiers.

quantify /ˈkwɒntɪfaɪ/ **verb** [T] to measure or state the amount of something: *It is difficult to quantify the damage that this storm has caused.*

quantitative /ˈkwɒntɪtətɪv/ ⑤ /ˈkwɑːntɪteɪtɪv/ **adj** relating to quantity

quantity /ˈkwɒntəti/ **noun** [C, U] ⑥ the amount or number of something: *A vast quantity of information is available on the Internet.* ° *They are now developing ways to produce the vaccine in large quantities and cheaply.* → See colour picture **Pieces and Quantities** on page Centre 1

IDIOM **an unknown quantity** someone or something that you do not know and so you cannot be certain about

quantum leap /ˌkwɒntʌmˈliːp/ noun [C] a sudden, large increase or improvement in something: [usually singular] *a quantum leap in information technology*

quarantine /ˈkwɒrᵊntiːn/ noun [U] If an animal or person is put into quarantine, they are kept away from other animals or people because they have or might have a disease.

quarrel¹ /ˈkwɒrᵊl/ noun **1** ☻ [C] an argument: *She walked out after **having a quarrel with** her boss.* **2 have no quarrel with sb/sth** to not disagree with someone or something: *We have no quarrel with either of those ideas.*

quarrel² /ˈkwɒrᵊl/ verb [I] (mainly UK **quarrelling**, **quarrelled**, US **quarreling**, **quarreled**) ☻ to have an argument with someone: *She'd been **quarrelling with** her mother all morning.*

quarry /ˈkwɒri/ noun [C] a place where stone is dug out of a large hole in the ground: *a marble quarry* • **quarry** verb [T] to dig stone out of a quarry

quart /kwɔːt/ noun [C] (written abbreviation **qt**) a unit for measuring liquid, equal to 1.14 litres in the UK and 0.95 litres in the US

quarter /ˈkwɔːtər/   quarter
noun **1 EQUAL PART** ▷
[C] (also US **fourth**) ☻
one of four equal parts
of something; ¼ : *Three
quarters of the island's
residents speak English.*
∘ *My house is one and
three-quarter miles/a
mile and three-quarters

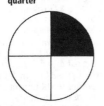

from here.* ∘ *I waited a
quarter of an hour for her.* **2 BEFORE/AFTER HOUR** ▷ [no plural] ☻ a period of 15 minutes before or after the hour: *It's (a) **quarter to** three (= 2.45).* ∘ also US *It's (a) **quarter of** three (= 2.45).* ∘ *We're leaving at (a) **quarter past** six (= 6.15).* ∘ also US *We're leaving at (a) **quarter after** six (= 6.15).* **3 BUSINESS** ▷ [C] one of four periods of time into which a year is divided for financial calculations such as profits or bills (= orders for payment): *I get an electricity bill every quarter.* **4 SCHOOL** ▷ [C] US one of four periods of time into which a year at school is divided **5 SPORT** ▷ [C] US one of four periods of time into which some sports games are divided **6 PART OF TOWN** ▷ [C] a part of a town, often where people from a particular country or religion live: *the Jewish quarter* **7 COIN** ▷ [C] a US or Canadian coin with a value of 25 cents, which is a quarter of a dollar

quarterback /ˈkwɔːtəbæk/ noun [C] a player in American football who controls the attack

quarter-final /ˌkwɔːtəˈfaɪnᵊl/ noun [C] the part of a competition when eight people or teams are left and there are four games to decide who will reach the semi-final (= when only four people or teams are left): *She was knocked out of the competition **in the quarter-finals**.*

quarterly /ˈkwɔːtᵊli/ adj, adv produced or happening every three months: *Water and electricity bills are paid quarterly.* ∘ *a quarterly magazine/report*

quarters /ˈkwɔːtəz/ noun [plural] rooms to live in or sleep in, usually for people in a military organization

quartet /kwɔːˈtet/ noun [C] four people singing or playing music in a group

quartz /kwɔːts/ noun [U] a mineral used to make watches and clocks accurate

quash /kwɒʃ/ verb [T] **1** formal to officially change a legal decision so that it stops existing: *His **conviction** was **quashed** last month.* **2** to stop something that you do not want to happen: *He appeared on television to **quash rumours** that he was seriously ill.*

quasi- /kweɪzaɪ-/ prefix partly: *quasi-religious ideas*

quay /kiː/ noun [C] a structure built next to water where ships stop and goods are taken on and off

queasy /ˈkwiːzi/ adj If you feel queasy, you feel slightly sick as if you might vomit.

queen /kwiːn/ noun [C] **1 FEMALE RULER** ▷ ☻ a female ruler in some countries: *Queen Elizabeth II* ∘ *God save the Queen!* **2 KING'S WIFE** ▷ ☻ the wife of a king when he is the main ruler in a country **3 PLAYING CARD** ▷ a playing card with a picture of a queen on it: *the queen of diamonds* **4 INSECT** ▷ a large female insect that is the most important in a group and which produces all the eggs: *queen bee*

queen-size /ˈkwiːnˌsaɪz/ adj (also **queen-sized**) US larger than the ordinary size, but not the largest size: *a **queen-size** bed*

queer /kwɪər/ adj **1** informal an offensive word meaning homosexual **2** old-fashioned strange

quell /kwel/ verb [T] formal to stop something that you do not want to happen: *to **quell** a riot* ∘ *to **quell** rumours*

quench /kwenʃ/ verb **quench your thirst** to drink liquid so that you stop being thirsty

query¹ /ˈkwɪəri/ noun [C] ☻ a question: *His job is to answer telephone **queries about** airline schedules.*

query² /ˈkwɪəri/ verb [T] to ask questions in order to check that something is true or correct: [+ question word] *A few students have queried whether exam marks were added up correctly.*

quest /kwest/ noun [C] formal an attempt to get something or do something difficult: *the **quest for** truth* ∘ [+ to do sth] *She is continuing her quest to find a husband for her daughter.*

question¹ /ˈkwestʃən/ noun **1 SENTENCE** ▷ [C] ☻ a sentence or phrase that asks you for information: *Is it OK if I **ask** you a few **questions**?* ∘ *He refused to **answer** my **question**.* ∘ *If you have any **questions** about the scheme, do ask me.* ∘ *"So where's the money coming from?" "That's a*

Q

good question" (= I do not know). **2 SITUATION** ▷ [C] **B2** a situation or problem that needs to be considered: *This documentary* **raises** *important* **questions** *about the American legal system.* ∘ *Two important* **questions arise** *from this debate.* **3 DOUBT** ▷ [U] **B2** doubt: [+ that] *There is* **no question** *that this was an accidental fire.* ∘ *His ability as a chef has never been* **in question.** ∘ *"So you agree she's the right person for the job." "Yes, absolutely,* **without question.**" ∘ *The report* **brings/calls into question** (= causes doubts about) *the safety of this drug.* **4 sb/sth in question** the person or thing that is being discussed: *He claims that he was at home with his girlfriend on the night in question.* **5 be out of the question** If something is out of the question, it is not possible or not allowed. → See also **loaded question, rhetorical question**

> ❗ Common learner error: **ask a question**
>
> Remember to use the verb **ask** with **question.**
>
> *We weren't allowed to ask any questions.*
> ~~We weren't allowed to make any questions.~~

> ✍ Word partners for **question**
>
> **ask/answer/pose/raise/reply to** a question ∙ a question **arises** ∙ an **awkward/fundamental/important/interesting/hypothetical** question ∙ a question **about** sth

question² /'kwestʃən/ **verb** [T] **1 B2** to ask someone questions: *Detectives were* **questioning** *a boy* **about** *the murder.* ∘ [often passive] *Two out of three people questioned in the survey were non-smokers.* **2 B2** to show or feel doubt about something: *I'm not for a moment questioning your decision.* ∘ [+ question word] *I'm just* **questioning whether** *we need the extra staff.*

questionable /'kwestʃənəbl/ **adj 1** possibly not true or correct: [+ question word] *It is highly* **questionable whether** *this drug has any benefits at all.* **2** not honest or not legal: *He's being investigated for questionable business practices.*

questioning /'kwestʃənɪŋ/ **noun** [U] a process in which the police ask someone questions about a crime: *She was taken in* **for questioning** *by police yesterday morning.*

'question ˌmark noun [C] **B1** a mark (?) used at the end of a question → See Study Page **Punctuation** on page Centre 33

questionnaire /ˌkwestʃə'neər/ **noun** [C] **B1** a set of questions asked of a large number of people to discover information about a subject: *Residents have been sent* **questionnaires about** *their homes and energy use.*

> ✍ Word partners for **questionnaire**
>
> **complete/fill in** a questionnaire ∙ **draw up** a questionnaire ∙ a questionnaire **asks** sth ∙ a questionnaire **about/on** sth

'question ˌtag noun [C] a short phrase such as 'isn't it?' or 'don't you?' that is added to the end of a sentence to check information or to ask if someone agrees with you. In the sentence, 'It's hot, isn't it?', 'isn't it?' is a question tag.

queue¹ /kjuː/ **noun** [C] UK (US **line**) **B1** a row of people waiting for something, one behind the other: *to* **join** *the queue* ∘ *Are you* **in the queue**?

IDIOM **jump the queue** to move in front of people who have been waiting longer for something than you

queue² /kjuː/ **verb** [I] (also UK **queue up**) (US **line up**) **B2** to stand in a row in order to wait for something: [+ to do sth] *They're queueing up to get tickets.*

> ✍ Word partners for **queue**
>
> **form/be in/join** a queue ∙ a queue **stretches** [for miles/around sth, etc] ∙ a **big/long/short/small** queue ∙ a queue **of** [cars/people, etc] ∙ a queue **for** sth

quibble /'kwɪbl/ **verb quibble about/over/with sth** to argue about something that is not important: *They spend far too much time quibbling over details.* ∙ **quibble noun** [C]

quiche /kiːʃ/ **noun** [C, U] a dish made of a pastry base filled with a mixture of egg and milk and usually cheese, vegetables, or meat

quick¹ /kwɪk/ **adj 1 A1** doing something fast or taking only a short time: *I tried to catch him but he was too quick for me.* ∘ [+ to do sth] *Publishers were quick to realize that a profit could be made.* **2 A2** lasting a short time: *Can I ask you a quick question?*

quick² /kwɪk/ **adv** informal fast: *Come here, quick!*

quicken /'kwɪkən/ **verb** [I, T] to become faster or to cause something to become faster: *His breathing quickened.*

quickly /'kwɪkli/ **adv A2** fast or in a short time: *quickly shut the door.* ∘ *These people need to be treated as quickly as possible.*

quid /kwɪd/ **noun** [C] (plural **quid**) UK informal a pound (= UK unit of money): *This bike's not bad for twenty quid.*

quiet¹ /'kwaɪət/ **adj 1 NOT NOISY** ▷ **A2** making little or no noise: *Can you* **be quiet,** *please?* ∘ *The children are very quiet.* **2 NOT BUSY** ▷ **A2** without much noise or activity: *I fancy a* **quiet night in** *tonight.* ∘ *They found a table in a quiet corner of the restaurant.* **3 NOT TALKING MUCH** ▷ **B1** If someone is quiet, they do not talk very much: *He was a shy, quiet man.* **4 keep (sth) quiet** to not talk about something that is secret: *It might be wise to keep this quiet for a while.*

> ❗ Common learner error: **quiet** or **quite**?
>
> Be careful, these two words look very similar, but they are spelled differently and have completely different meanings.
> **Quiet** means making little or no noise.
> *The house was very quiet without the children around.*
> **Quite** means a little or a lot but not completely.
> *It's quite cold today.*

quiet² /kwaɪət/ **noun** [U] 🅱️2 a situation in which there is little or no noise: *She needs a bit of **peace and quiet**.*

quieten /ˈkwaɪətᵊn/ **verb** [T] UK (US **quiet**) to make someone or something quiet

PHRASAL VERB **quieten (sb/sth) down** UK (US **quiet (sb/sth) down**) to become quieter or calmer, or to make a person or animal become quieter or calmer

quietly /ˈkwaɪətli/ **adv 1** 🅱️1 making little or no noise: *"Don't worry," she said quietly.* **2** 🅱️1 doing something without much noise or activity: *He sat quietly on the sofa, waiting for her to come home.*

quilt /kwɪlt/ **noun** [C] a cover for a bed, which is filled with feathers or other warm material

quip /kwɪp/ **verb** [I, T] (**quipping, quipped**) to say something in a funny and clever way • **quip noun** [C]

quirk /kwɜːk/ **noun** [C] a strange habit: *My aunt has a few odd quirks.*

IDIOM **quirk of fate** a strange and unexpected event: *By some **quirk of fate**, we came to live in the same town.*

• **quirky adj** strange: *a quirky sense of humour*

quit /kwɪt/ **verb** (**quitting, quit**) **1** NOT WORK ▷ [I, T] 🅱️1 to leave your job or school permanently: *She recently **quit** her **job** to spend more time with her family.* **2** NOT DO ▷ [T] 🅱️1 to stop doing something: *I **quit** smoking and put on weight.* **3** COMPUTER ▷ [I, T] to end a program on a computer

quite /kwaɪt/ **adv 1** NOT COMPLETELY ▷ UK 🅰️2 a little or a lot but not completely: *I'm quite tired, but I'm happy to walk a little further.* ◦ *He's quite attractive but not what I'd call gorgeous.* **2** VERY ▷ US very: *My sister and I are quite different.* **3** COMPLETELY ▷ 🅱️1 completely: *The two situations are quite different.* ◦ *Are you quite sure you want to go?* **4** not quite 🅱️2 almost but not completely: *I'm not quite sure that I understand this.* ◦ *He didn't get quite enough votes to*

win. **5 quite a bit/a few/a lot, etc** 🅰️2 a large amount or number: *There are quite a few letters for you here.* ◦ *He's changed quite a bit.*

quiver /ˈkwɪvər/ **verb** [I] to shake slightly • **quiver noun** [C]

quiz¹ /kwɪz/ **noun** [C] (plural **quizzes**) **1** 🅰️2 a game in which you answer questions: *a television quiz show* **2** US a short test on a subject in school

quiz² /kwɪz/ **verb** [T] (**quizzing, quizzed**) to ask someone questions about something: *A group of journalists **quizzed** them **about/on** the day's events.*

quizzical /ˈkwɪzɪkᵊl/ **adj** A quizzical expression or look seems to ask a question without words.

quota /ˈkwəʊtə/ **noun** [C] a limited amount of something that is officially allowed: *an import quota*

quotation /kwəʊˈteɪʃᵊn/ **noun** [C] **1** a sentence or phrase that is taken out of a book, poem, or play: *a **quotation from** Shakespeare/the Bible* **2** the amount that a piece of work will probably cost: *Make sure you **get** a **quotation** for all the work before they start.*

quot'ation ˌmarks noun [plural] a pair of marks (" ") or (' ') used before and after a group of words to show that they are spoken or that someone else originally wrote them → See Study Page **Punctuation** on page Centre 33

quote¹ /kwəʊt/ **verb 1** REPEAT ▷ [I, T] to repeat what someone has said or written: *I was **quoting** from Marx.* ◦ *Witnesses were **quoted as saying** there were two gunmen.* **2** GIVE EXAMPLE ▷ [T] to give a fact or example in order to support what you are saying: *The minister **quoted** recent unemployment figures.* **3** COST ▷ [T] to say how much a piece of work will cost before you do it

quote² /kwəʊt/ **noun** [C] short for quotation

quotes /kwəʊts/ **noun** [plural] short for quotation marks

the Qur'an /kɒrˈɑːn/ **noun** another spelling of the Koran (= the holy book of Islam)

Q

R

R, r /ɑːr/ the eighteenth letter of the alphabet

R informal written abbeviation for are: used in emails and text messages

rabbi /'ræbaɪ/ **noun** [C] a leader and teacher in the Jewish religion

rabbit /'ræbɪt/ **noun** [C] **A2** a small animal with fur and long ears that lives in a hole in the ground

rabble /'ræbl/ **noun** [no plural] a group of noisy, uncontrolled people

rabies /'reɪbiːz/ **noun** [U] a serious disease that people can get if they are bitten by an infected animal

raccoon /ræˈkuːn/ **noun** [C] a small North American animal with black marks on its face and a long tail with black rings on it

race¹ /reɪs/ **noun** **1 COMPETITION** ▷ [C] **A2** a competition in which people run, ride, drive, etc against each other in order to see who is the fastest: *a horse race* **2 PEOPLE** ▷ [C, U] one of the groups that people are divided into according to their physical characteristics, such as skin colour: *people of many different races* **3 FOR POWER** ▷ [C] a situation in which people compete against each other for power or control: *the race for governor* **4 the races** an event when horses race against each other

IDIOM **a race against time/the clock** a situation in which something has to be done very quickly

→ See also **the human race, the rat race**

> **!** Common learner error: **race** or **species**?
>
> **Race** is used to talk about one of the groups that people are divided into according to their physical characteristics.
>
> *the human race*
> *People of all races and religions live in America.*
>
> **Species** is used to talk about types of animals and plants.
>
> *eagles, vultures and other species of bird*

> **✓** Word partners for **race**
>
> drop out of/lose/win a race • in a race

race² /reɪs/ **verb 1** [I, T] **B1** to compete in a race: *I'll race you to the end of the road.* ∘ *I used to race against him at school.* **2 race along/down/over, etc** to move somewhere very quickly: *I raced over to see what was the matter.* **3 race sb to/back, etc** to take someone somewhere very quickly: *Ambulances raced the injured to a nearby hospital.* **4** [T] to put a horse, dog, etc in a race

racecourse /'reɪskɔːs/ **noun** [C] UK the place where horses race

racehorse /'reɪshɔːs/ **noun** [C] a horse that has been trained to run in races

race reˈlations noun [plural] the relationship between people from different races who live together in the same place

racetrack /'reɪstræk/ **noun** [C] the place where horses, cars, etc race

racial /'reɪʃəl/ **adj B2** relating to people's race: *racial minority* ∘ **racial discrimination/tension** • **racially** adv *a racially motivated crime*

racing /'reɪsɪŋ/ **noun** [U] the activity or sport in which people, animals, or vehicles race against each other: *motor racing* → See also **horse racing**

racism /'reɪsɪzəm/ **noun** [U] **B2** the belief that other races of people are not as good as your own, or the unfair treatment of people because they belong to a particular race

> **✓** Word partners for **racism**
>
> combat/encounter/face/tackle racism • a form of racism • racism against sb

racist /'reɪsɪst/ **noun** [C] someone who believes that other races of people are not as good as their own • **racist** adj *a racist attack*

rack¹ /ræk/ **noun** [C] a type of shelf that you can put things on or hang things from: *a magazine/luggage rack*

rack² /ræk/ **verb 1 be racked with pain/guilt** etc If someone is racked with pain or an emotion, they suffer a lot because of it. **2 rack your brain/brains** informal to think very hard, usually to try to remember something or solve a problem

PHRASAL VERB **rack up sth** informal to get or achieve a lot of something: *He's racked up debts of over thirty thousand pounds.*

racket /'rækɪt/ **noun**   racket
1 SPORT ▷ [C] (also **racquet**) **A2**
a piece of equipment that you
use to hit a ball in sports such
as tennis → See colour picture
Sports 2 on page Centre 15
2 ILLEGAL ▷ [C] informal an
illegal activity that is used to make money: *a drugs smuggling racket* **3 NOISE** ▷ [no plural] informal a loud noise: *The neighbours were making such a racket.*

radar /'reɪdɑːr/ **noun** [U] a system that uses radio waves to find out the position of something you cannot see

radiant /'reɪdiənt/ **adj 1** showing that you are very happy: *a radiant smile* **2** very bright • **radiance** /'reɪdiəns/ **noun** [U]

radiate /'reɪdieɪt/ **verb 1 radiate from/out, etc** to spread out in all directions from a particular point: *A number of roads radiate out from the centre.* **2** [T] to show an emotion or quality in your face or behaviour: *His face just radiates happiness.* **3** [T] to send out heat or light

radiation /ˌreɪdiˈeɪʃən/ **noun** [U] **1** a form of energy that comes from a nuclear reaction and that in large amounts can be very dangerous:

dangerously high **levels of radiation** ∘ radiation sickness **2** energy from heat or light that you cannot see: *solar/microwave radiation*

adiator /ˈreɪdieɪtə/̩/ noun [C] **1** a metal piece of equipment that is filled with hot water and is used to heat a room → See colour picture **The Living Room** on page Centre 4 **2** a part of a vehicle engine that is used to make the engine cool

adical¹ /ˈrædɪkəl/ adj **1** A radical change is very big and important: *a radical reform* **2** believing that there should be big social and political changes: *a radical group/movement* ∘ *a radical proposal* • **radically** adv *The company has changed radically in recent years.*

adical² /ˈrædɪkəl/ noun [C] someone who supports the idea that there should be big social and political changes

adio¹ /ˈreɪdiəʊ/ noun **1** BROADCASTS ▷ [C] ⒶⒷ a piece of equipment used for listening to radio broadcasts: *a car radio* **2** **the radio** ⒶⒷ the programmes that you hear when you listen to the radio: *We heard him speaking on the radio this morning.* **3** SYSTEM ▷ [U] ⒷⒶ a system of sending and receiving sound through the air: *local radio* ∘ *a radio station* **4** MESSAGES ▷ [C] a piece of equipment for sending and receiving messages by sound

adio² /ˈreɪdiəʊ/ verb [I, T] (**radioing, radioed**) to send a message to someone by radio: *They radioed for help.*

adioactive /ˌreɪdiəʊˈæktɪv/ adj containing harmful radiation (= energy from a nuclear reaction): *radioactive waste*

adioactivity /ˌreɪdiəʊækˈtɪvəti/ noun [U] the quality of being radioactive

adish /ˈrædɪʃ/ noun [C] a small, round, white or red vegetable with a slightly hot taste that you eat in salad

adius /ˈreɪdiəs/ noun [C] (plural **radii**) **1** a certain distance from a particular point in any direction: *Most facilities lie within a two-mile radius of the house.* **2** the distance from the centre of a circle to its edge

radius

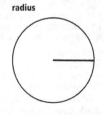

affle /ˈræfl/ noun [C] a competition in which people buy tickets with numbers on them and win a prize if any of their numbers are chosen: *raffle tickets* • **raffle** verb [T] to offer something as a prize in a raffle

aft /rɑːft/ noun **1** [C] a small, flat boat made by tying pieces of wood together **2** **a raft of sth/sb** a lot of things or people: *a raft of data*

after /ˈrɑːftə/̩/ noun [C] one of the long pieces of wood that supports a roof

ag /ræg/ noun [C] a piece of old cloth that you use to clean things

IDIOM **be like a red rag to a bull** UK If a particular subject is like a red rag to a bull, it always makes someone angry.

rage¹ /reɪdʒ/ noun [C, U] ⒷⒶ strong anger that you cannot control: *a jealous rage* ∘ *He **flew into a rage** (= suddenly became angry) over the smallest mistake.*

IDIOM **be all the rage** informal old-fashioned to be very popular

→ See also **road rage**

rage² /reɪdʒ/ verb [I] **1** to continue with great force or violence: *The battle raged well into the night.* **2** to speak or behave in a very angry way

ragged

ragged /ˈrægɪd/ adj **1** CLOTHES ▷ old and torn: *ragged jeans* **2** PERSON ▷ wearing clothes that are old and torn: *a ragged child* **3** ROUGH ▷ rough and not smooth: *a ragged edge*

rags /rægz/ noun [plural] clothes that are old and torn: *an old man dressed **in rags***

IDIOM **go from rags to riches** to start your life very poor and then later in life become very rich

raid¹ /reɪd/ noun [C] **1** SOLDIERS ▷ a sudden attack on a place by soldiers: *an air raid* ∘ *a dawn raid* **2** POLICE ▷ a sudden visit to a place by police in order to find someone or something: *a police raid to recover illegal weapons* **3** STEAL ▷ the illegal activity of entering a place by force in order to steal from it: *a bank raid* → See also **air raid**

> ☑ Word partners for **raid**
>
> **carry out** a raid • a raid **on** sth • an **air** raid • a **dawn** raid

raid² /reɪd/ verb [T] **1** SOLDIERS ▷ If soldiers raid a place, they suddenly attack it. **2** POLICE ▷ If the police raid a place, they suddenly visit it in order to find someone or something: *Police raided nine properties in search of the documents.* **3** STEAL ▷ to steal many things from somewhere: *to **raid** the **fridge***

rail

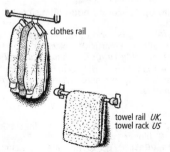

clothes rail

towel rail *UK*,
towel rack *US*

rail /reɪl/ noun **1** FOR HANGING ▷ [C] UK a

R

horizontal bar on the wall that you hang things on: *a curtain rail* **2 FOR SUPPORTING** ▷ [C] a bar around or along something which you can hold to stop you from falling: *a hand rail* **3 TRAIN SYSTEM** ▷ [U] 🅱 trains as a method of transport: *rail travel* ∘ *a rail link* ∘ *They sent the shipment by rail.* **4 TRAIN** ▷ [C] the metal tracks that trains run on → See also **towel rail**

railing /ˈreɪlɪŋ/ *noun* [C] a fence made from posts and bars: *an iron railing*

railroad tie *noun* [C] US (UK **sleeper**) a piece of wood that is used to support a railway track

railway /ˈreɪlweɪ/ *noun* **1** 🅰 [C] mainly UK (US **railroad** /ˈreɪlrəʊd/) the metal tracks that trains travel on: *Repairs are being carried out on the railway.* **2 the railway(s)** mainly UK (US **the railroad(s)**) 🅰 the organizations connected with trains: *He worked on the railways all his life.*

rain¹ /reɪn/ *noun* **1** 🅰 [U] water that falls from the sky in small drops: *heavy rain* ∘ *It looks like rain* (= *as if it will rain*). **2 the rains** [plural] in tropical countries, the time of year when there is a lot of rain: *They were waiting for the rains to come.* → See also **acid rain**

> ✒ Word partners for **rain**
>
> rain **falls** • **heavy/light/pouring/torrential** rain • be **pouring with** rain • a **drop of/spot of** rain • **in the** rain

rain² /reɪn/ *verb* **it rains** 🅰 If it rains, water falls from the sky in small drops: *It was raining all weekend.*

PHRASAL VERB **be rained off** UK (US **be rained out**) If a sport or outside activity is rained off, it cannot start or continue because it is raining.

rainbow /ˈreɪnbəʊ/ *noun* [C] 🅱 a half circle with seven colours that sometimes appears in the sky when the sun shines through rain

rain check *noun* [C] **1** US a piece of paper that allows you to buy something at a low price although that thing is now being sold at a higher price **2** US a ticket that allows you to see an event at a later time if bad weather stops that event from happening **3 take a rain check on sth** something you say when you cannot accept someone's invitation, but would like to do it at a later time

raincoat /ˈreɪnkəʊt/ *noun* [C] 🅰 a coat that you wear when it is raining → See colour picture **Clothes** on page Centre 8

raindrop /ˈreɪndrɒp/ *noun* [C] a single drop of rain

rainfall /ˈreɪnfɔːl/ *noun* [U] the amount of rain that falls in a particular place at a particular time: *monthly rainfall* ∘ *heavy rainfall*

rainforest /ˈreɪnˌfɒrɪst/ *noun* [C] 🅱 a forest with a lot of tall trees where it rains a lot: *a tropical rainforest*

rainy /ˈreɪni/ *adj* 🅱 raining a lot: *a rainy afternoon*

raise¹ /reɪz/ *verb* [T] **1 LIFT** ▷ 🅱 to lift something to a higher position: *to raise your hand* **2 INCREASE** ▷ 🅱 to increase an amount or level: *to raise prices/taxes* **3 IMPROVE** ▷ to

improve something: *to raise standard* **4 MONEY** ▷ 🅱 to collect money from othe people: *They're raising money for charity* **5 raise your voice** to speak loudly and angril to someone **6 raise hopes/fears/doubts, etc** t cause emotions or thoughts: *Her answers raise doubts in my mind.* **7 raise a question/subject etc** 🅱 to start talking about a subject that yo want other people to consider **8 CHILD** ▷ 🅱 t look after and educate a child until they hav become an adult: *Their ideas on how to rais children didn't always agree.* **9 ANIMALS CROPS** ▷ to make an animal or crop grow: *t raise chickens/sheep* → See Note at **rise¹** → See als **raise the alarm¹**

raise² /reɪz/ *noun* [C] US (UK **rise**) an increase i the amount of money that you earn: *We usuall get a raise at the start of a year.*

raisin /ˈreɪzᵊn/ *noun* [C] a dried grape (= smal round fruit)

rake¹ /reɪk/ *noun* [C] a garden tool with a lon handle that is used for moving dead leaves grass, etc

rake² /reɪk/ *verb* [I, T] to use a rake to move dea leaves, grass, etc

PHRASAL VERB **rake sth in** informal to earn a larg amount of money: *He's raking it in.*

rally¹ /ˈræli/ *noun* [C] **1** a large public meeting i support of something: *an election/campaig rally* **2** a car or motorcycle race: *a rally driver*

> ✒ Word partners for **rally**
>
> **hold/organize/stage** a rally • a **mass** rally • **at a** rally

rally² /ˈræli/ *verb* **1** [I, T] to come together o bring people together to support something *Her fans rallied behind her from the start.* **2** [I] t get stronger or better after being weak: *The stoc market rallied late in the day.*

PHRASAL VERB **rally around/round (sb)** to help o give support to someone: *If one of the family ha a crisis, we rally round them.*

ram¹ /ræm/ *verb* [T] (**ramming, rammed**) to hi something or push something into somethin with great force: *He had to stop suddenly and car rammed into him.*

ram² /ræm/ *noun* [C] a male sheep

RAM /ræm/ *noun* [U] abbreviation for randon access memory: a computer's ability to immedi ately store information

Ramadan /ˈræmədæn/ *noun* [U] the Muslin religious period in which Muslims do not eat o drink during the day

ramble¹ /ˈræmbl/ *verb* **1 ramble along through, etc** to walk for a long time, especiall in the countryside **2** [I] (also **ramble on**) to tal for a long time in a boring and often confuse way: *He rambled on for hours about his time in th army.*

ramble² /ˈræmbl/ *noun* [C] a long walk in th countryside

rambler /ˈræmblər/ *noun* [C] someone wh walks in the countryside

ambling /ˈræmblɪŋ/ **adj 1** A rambling speech, letter, etc is very long and confused. **2** A rambling building is big and without a regular shape.

amifications /ˌræmɪfɪˈkeɪʃᵊnz/ **noun** [plural] the possible results of an action

amp /ræmp/ **noun** [C] **1** a sloping surface that joins two places that are at different heights: *a wheelchair ramp* **2** US (UK **slip road**) a short road that is used to drive onto or off a large, fast road

ampage¹ /ræmˈpeɪdʒ/ **verb** [I] to run around or through an area, making a lot of noise and causing damage: *Angry citizens rampaged through the city.*

ampage² /ˈræmpeɪdʒ/ **noun** [no plural] an occasion when a group of people rampage: *Rioters went on a rampage through the city.*

ampant /ˈræmpᵊnt/ **adj** growing or spreading quickly, in a way that cannot be controlled: *rampant corruption/inflation*

amshackle /ˈræmˌʃækl/ **adj** A ramshackle building is in very bad condition.

an /ræn/ past tense of run

anch /rɑːnʃ/ **noun** [C] a large farm where animals are kept: *a cattle/sheep ranch*

ancher /ˈrɑːnʃər/ **noun** [C] someone who owns or works on a ranch

ancid /ˈrænsɪd/ **adj** Rancid fat, such as oil or butter, smells and tastes bad because it is not fresh.

andom /ˈrændəm/ **adj 1** 🄱② done or chosen without any plan or system: *random testing* ∘ *a random selection* **2 at random** chosen by chance: *Winners will be chosen at random.* • **randomly adv**

ang /ræŋ/ past tense of ring²

ange¹ /reɪndʒ/ **noun 1** OF THINGS ▷ [C] 🄱① a group of different things of the same general type: *a range of colours/patterns* ∘ *We discussed a wide range of subjects.* **2** AMOUNT ▷ [C] 🄱② the amount or number between a particular set of limits: [usually singular] *The price range is from $100 to $200.* ∘ *The product is aimed at young people in the 18-25 age range.* **3** DISTANCE ▷ [U] the distance from which things can be seen, heard, or reached: *The soldiers came within firing range.* ∘ *He was shot at close range* (= *from very near*). **4** MOUNTAINS ▷ [C] a line of hills or mountains **5** SHOOTING ▷ [C] a place where you can practise shooting a gun: *a rifle/shooting range*

> 🗹 Word partners for **range**
> a full/wide range • a range of sth

ange² /reɪndʒ/ **verb 1 range from sth to sth** 🄱② to have several different amounts or types: *Tickets range from $12 to $35.* ∘ *Choose from 13 colours, ranging from classic white to antique blue.* **2** [I] to deal with a large number of subjects: *The discussion ranged over many topics.*

anger /ˈreɪndʒər/ **noun** [C] someone whose job is to look after a forest or a park: *a forest ranger*

ank¹ /ræŋk/ **noun 1** [C, U] a position in society or in an organization, for example the army: *He holds the rank of colonel.* **2 the ranks** the

ordinary members of an organization, especially the army

IDIOMS **break ranks** to publicly show that you disagree with a group that you belong to • **the rank and file** the ordinary members of an organization and not its leaders

→ See also **taxi rank**

rank² /ræŋk/ **verb** [I, T] to have a position in a list that shows things or people in order of importance, or to give someone or something a position on such a list: *He ranked number one in the world at the start of the competition.* ∘ *The city's canals now rank among the world's dirtiest.*

ransom /ˈrænsᵊm/ **noun** [C, U] the money that is demanded for the return of someone who is being kept as a prisoner: *a ransom note/letter*

rant /rænt/ **verb** [I] to talk a lot about something in an excited or angry way: *He was ranting and raving about the injustice of the situation.*

rap¹ /ræp/ **noun 1** [U] 🄰② a type of music in which the words are spoken and there is a strong beat: *a rap artist* **2** [C] a sudden, short sound made when someone or something hits a hard surface: *There was a rap on the window.*

IDIOM **a rap on/across/over the knuckles** a punishment that is not severe

rap² /ræp/ **verb** (**rapping, rapped**) **1** [I, T] to hit a hard surface to make a sudden, short noise: *He rapped on the door.* **2** [I] to perform rap music

rape /reɪp/ **verb** [T] 🄱② to force someone to have sex when they do not want to • **rape noun** [C, U]

rapid /ˈræpɪd/ **adj** 🄱② happening or moving very quickly: *rapid change/growth* • **rapidity** /rəˈpɪdəti/ **noun** [U] • **rapidly adv**

rapids /ˈræpɪdz/ **noun** [plural] a part of a river where the water moves very fast

rapist /ˈreɪpɪst/ **noun** [C] someone who forces another person to have sex when they do not want to

rapper /ˈræpər/ **noun** [C] someone who performs rap music (= a type of music in which the words are spoken and there is a strong beat)

rapport /ræˈpɔːr/ **noun** [U, no plural] a good understanding of someone and ability to communicate with them: *She has a good rapport with her staff.*

rapture /ˈræptʃər/ **noun** [U] a feeling of extreme pleasure and excitement

rare /reər/ **adj 1** 🄱① very unusual: *a rare disease/species* ∘ [+ to do sth] *It's very rare to see these birds in England.* **2** If meat is rare, it is still red because it has only been cooked for a short time: *a rare steak*

rarely /ˈreəli/ **adv** 🄱① not often: *I rarely see her these days.*

raring /ˈreərɪŋ/ **adj be raring to do sth** informal to be very enthusiastic about starting something

rarity /ˈreərəti/ **noun 1 be a rarity** to be unusual: *Genuine enthusiasm is a rarity.* **2** [U] the fact that something is not common: *Precious stones are valued for their rarity.*

rascal /ˈrɑːskᵊl/ **noun** [C] **1** humorous a person

R

who behaves badly, but who you still like **2** old-fashioned a dishonest man

rash¹ /ræʃ/ **noun 1** [C] a group of small, red spots on the skin: *an itchy rash* ∘ *Certain foods give him a rash.* **2 a rash of sth** a group of unpleasant events of the same type, happening at the same time: *There has been a rash of burglaries in the area.*

rash² /ræʃ/ **adj** done suddenly and without thinking carefully: *a rash decision/promise*

rasher /ˈræʃər/ **noun** [C] UK a slice of bacon (= meat from a pig)

raspberry /ˈrɑːzbəri/ **noun** [C] a small, soft, red fruit that grows on bushes

rat /ræt/ **noun** [C] **1** ⓐ2   rat

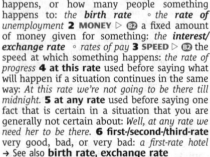

an animal that looks like a large mouse and has a long tail: *Rats carry disease.* **2** informal an unpleasant, dishonest person

rate¹ /reɪt/ **noun** [C]
1 HOW MANY ▷ ⓑ2 how often something happens, or how many people something happens to: *the **birth rate*** ∘ *the **rate of** unemployment* **2 MONEY** ▷ ⓑ2 a fixed amount of money given for something: *the **interest/exchange rate*** ∘ *rates of pay* **3 SPEED** ▷ ⓑ2 the speed at which something happens: *the rate of progress* **4 at this rate** used before saying what will happen if a situation continues in the same way: *At this rate we're not going to be there till midnight.* **5 at any rate** used before saying one fact that is certain in a situation that you are generally not certain about: *Well, at any rate we need her to be there.* **6 first-/second-/third-rate** very good, bad, or very bad: *a first-rate hotel* → See also **birth rate, exchange rate**

> **Word partners for rate**
> a **cut in/drop in/increase in/rise in** the rate ∘ **at** a rate (**of**) ∘ the rate **for/of**

rate² /reɪt/ **verb** [T] **1** to judge the quality or ability of someone or something: *How do you **rate** her **as** a singer?* **2** to deserve something: *The incident didn't even **rate a mention** (= was not written about) in the local newspaper.*

rather /ˈrɑːðər/ **adv 1** ⓑ1 slightly or to a degree: *I rather like it.* ∘ *I find her books rather dull.* **2 rather than** ⓑ1 instead of: *He saw his music as a hobby rather than a career.* **3 would rather** ⓑ1 If you would rather do something, you would prefer to do that thing: *I'd much rather go out for a meal than stay in and watch TV.* **4** ⓑ2 used to change something you have just said and make it more correct: *I tried writing some drama, or rather comedy-drama, but it wasn't very good.*

ratify /ˈrætɪfaɪ/ **verb** [T] to make an agreement official: *Sixty-five nations need to **ratify** the **treaty**.*

rating /ˈreɪtɪŋ/ **noun 1** [C] a measurement of how good or popular something or someone is: *A high percentage of Americans gave the President a positive rating.* **2 the ratings** a list of television

and radio programmes showing how popular they are

> **Word partners for rating**
> **give** sb/sth/**have** a rating ∘ sb's/sth's rating **drops/falls/improves/increases** ∘ a **high/low** rating ∘ a rating **of** [5/28%, etc]

ratio /ˈreɪʃiəʊ/ **noun** [C] the relationship between two things expressed in numbers to show how much bigger one is than the other: *The female to male ratio at the college is 2 to 1.*

ration¹ /ˈræʃən/ **noun** [C] the amount of something that you are allowed to have when there is little of it available: *a **food/petrol ration***

ration² /ˈræʃən/ **verb** [T] to give people only a small amount of something because there is little of it available: *They might have to start rationing water.*

rational /ˈræʃənəl/ **adj 1** based on facts and not affected by someone's emotions or imagination: *a rational argument/debate/explanation* **2** able to make decisions based on facts and not be influenced by your emotions or imagination: *Look, we've got to try to be rational about this.* → Opposite **irrational** ∘ **rationally adv**

rationale /ˌræʃəˈnɑːl/ **noun** [C] a group of reasons for a decision or belief: *I don't understand **the rationale behind** the policy.*

rationalize (also UK **-ise**) /ˈræʃənəlaɪz/ **verb 1** [I, T] to try to find reasons to explain your behaviour or emotions: *I can't rationalize the way I feel towards him.* **2** [T] mainly UK to improve the way a business is organized, usually by getting rid of people ∘ **rationalization** (also UK **-isation**) /ˌræʃənəlaɪˈzeɪʃən/ **noun** [C, U]

the ˈrat ˌrace noun informal the unpleasant way that people compete against each other at work in order to succeed

rattle¹ /ˈrætl/ **verb 1** [I, T] to make a noise like something knocking repeatedly, or to cause something to make this noise: *The wind blew hard, rattling the doors and windows.* **2** [T] to make someone nervous: [often passive] *He was clearly rattled by their angry reaction.*

PHRASAL VERB **rattle sth off** to quickly say a list of something that you have learned: *She can rattle off the names of all the players.*

rattle² /ˈrætl/ **noun** [C] a toy that a baby shakes to make a noise

raucous /ˈrɔːkəs/ **adj** loud and unpleasant: *raucous laughter*

ravage /ˈrævɪdʒ/ **verb** [T] to damage or destroy something: [often passive] *The whole area has been ravaged by war.*

ravages /ˈrævɪdʒɪz/ **noun** [plural] **the ravages of disease/time/war, etc** the damaging effects of disease/time/war, etc

rave¹ /reɪv/ **verb** [I] **1** to talk about something that you think is very good in an excited way: *He went there last year and he's been **raving about** it ever since.* **2** to talk in an angry, uncontrolled way

rave² /reɪv/ **noun** [C] an event where people dance to modern, electronic music

ʳaven /ˈreɪvᵊn/ **noun** [C] a large, black bird

ʳavenous /ˈrævᵊnəs/ **adj** very hungry ● **ravenously adv**

ʳavine /rəˈviːn/ **noun** [C] a narrow, deep valley with very steep sides

ravine

ʳaving /ˈreɪvɪŋ/ **adj** informal completely uncontrolled: *He was acting like a **raving** lunatic.*

ʳavings /ˈreɪvɪŋz/ **noun** [plural] the strange things that a crazy person says: *the ravings of a madman*

ʳavishing /ˈrævɪʃɪŋ/ **adj** very beautiful

ʳaw /rɔː/ **adj 1 FOOD** ▷ 🔵 not cooked: ***raw** meat/ vegetables* **2 NATURAL** ▷ 🔵 in the natural state: *raw materials ∘ raw sugar* **3 INJURY** ▷ If a part of the body is raw, the skin has come off and it is red and painful. ● **rawness noun** [U] → See also **hit/touch a raw nerve**

ʳay /reɪ/ **noun 1** 🔵 [C] a narrow beam of light, heat, or energy: *an ultraviolet ray ∘ the rays of the sun* **2 a ray of hope/comfort, etc** a small amount of hope, etc → See also **X-ray**

ʳazor /ˈreɪzəʳ/ **noun** [C]
🔵 a piece of equipment with a sharp blade used for removing hair from the face, legs, etc → See colour picture **The Bathroom** on page Centre 3

razor

ʳazor ˌblade noun [C] a very thin, sharp blade that you put in a razor

ʳd written abbreviation for road: *17, Lynton Rd*

ʳe /reɪ/ ⓤ /riː/ **preposition 1** used in the subject line of an email (= line at the top of an email that tells you the subject of the message) to show that you are replying to an email that was sent to you with the same title: *The email was titled 'Re: Our Meeting Next Week'.* **2** used in business letters to refer to a letter or something in a letter you have received and are replying to: *Re your communication of 15 February…*

ʳe- /riː-/ **prefix** again: *to remarry ∘ a reusable container*

ʳeach¹ /riːtʃ/ **verb 1 ARRIVE** ▷ [T] 🔵 to arrive somewhere: *We won't reach Miami till five or six o'clock.* **2 STRETCH** ▷ [I, T] 🔵 to stretch your arm and hand to touch or take something: *She **reached** for a cigarette. ∘ She **reached down** to stroke the dog's head. ∘ He **reached out** and grabbed her arm.* **3 can reach (sth)** 🔵 to be able to touch or take something with your hand: *Could you get that book down for me – I can't reach.* **4 BE LONG ENOUGH** ▷ [I, T] If something reaches, or reaches something, it is long enough to touch something: *The rope won't be long enough to reach the ground.* **5 LEVEL** ▷ [T] 🔵 to get to a particular level, situation, etc: *We hope to* reach our goal by May next year. ∘ *I've **reached** the point where I'm about to give up.* **6 reach a decision/agreement/conclusion, etc** 🔵 to make a decision, agreement, etc about something **7 TELEPHONE** ▷ [T] 🔵 to speak to someone on the telephone: *You can reach him at home.*

> ⚠ Common learner error: **reach**
>
> When **reach** means 'arrive somewhere' or 'get to a particular level' it is not normally followed by a preposition.
> *We finally reached the hotel just after midnight.*
> *The project has now reached the final stage.*
> ~~The project has now reached to the final stage.~~

reach² /riːtʃ/ **noun 1 out of/beyond (sb's) reach** 🔵 too far away for someone to take hold of: *I keep the medicines up here, out of the kids' reach.* **2 beyond (sb's) reach** not possible for someone to have: *With all this money we can buy things previously beyond our reach.* **3 be within reach (of sth)** 🔵 to be close enough to travel to: *You'll be within easy reach of London.* **4 be within (sb's) reach a** 🔵 to be close enough for someone to take hold of: *The gun lay within reach.* **b** possible for someone to achieve: *Winning the championship suddenly seemed within their reach.*

react /riˈækt/ **verb** [I] **1 SAY/DO** ▷ 🔵 to say, do, or feel something because of something else that has been said or done: *He **reacted** angrily **to** her comments.* **2 BAD EFFECT** ▷ to become sick because something that you have eaten or used on your body has had a bad effect on you: *My skin **reacts to** most perfumes.* **3 SUBSTANCES** ▷ In science, if a substance reacts with another substance, it changes: *Carbon **reacts with** oxygen to produce carbon dioxide.*

PHRASAL VERB **react against sth** to do the opposite of what someone wants you to do because you do not like their rules or ideas

> 🔁 Word partners for **reaction**
>
> an **adverse/angry/immediate/initial/ instinctive/negative/rapid** reaction
> ● **gauge/produce/provoke** a reaction
> ● a reaction **to/towards** sth

reaction /riˈækʃᵊn/ **noun 1 CAUSED BY SOMETHING** ▷ [C, U] 🔵 something you say, feel, or do because of something that has happened: *What was his **reaction to** the news?* **2 reactions** mainly UK the ability to move quickly when something suddenly happens: *Drivers need to have quick reactions.* **3 CHANGE** ▷ [no plural] a change in the way people behave or think because they do not agree with the way people behaved or thought in the past: *In art, there was a **reaction against** Realism.* **4 BAD EFFECT** ▷ [C] 🔵 an unpleasant feeling or illness caused by something you have eaten or used on your body: *A number of people have **had a bad reaction to** this drug.* **5 SUBSTANCES** ▷ [C] a change that happens when two substances are

R

put together: *a **chemical reaction*** → See also **chain reaction**

reactionary /riˈækʃənªri/ **adj** being against political or social progress • **reactionary noun** [C] someone who is against political or social progress

reactor /riˈæktər/ **noun** [C] (also **nuclear reactor**) a large machine that uses nuclear fuel to produce power

read¹ /riːd/ **verb** (**read** /red/) **1 WORDS** ▷ [I, T] 🅐 to look at words and understand what they mean: *What was the last **book** you **read**?* ∘ *I've been **reading about** John F Kennedy.* ∘ [+ that] *I've read that the economy is going to improve by the end of the year.* **2 SAY** ▷ [I, T] 🅐 to look at words that are written and say them aloud for other people to listen to: *Do you want me to **read** it **to** you?* ∘ [+ two objects] *I **read** him a **story** at bedtime.* **3 SIGNS** ▷ [T] to look at signs and be able to understand them: *Can you **read** music?* **4 MEASUREMENT** ▷ [T] to show the temperature, time, etc on a piece of measuring equipment: *The thermometer **read** 20 degrees this morning.* → See also **lip-read**

PHRASAL VERBS **read sth into sth** to believe that an action, remark, etc has a particular meaning when it has not: *Don't **read** too much into anything he says.* • **read sth out** 🅑 to read something and say the words aloud so that other people can hear: *He **read** out the names of all the winners.* • **read sth over/through** 🅑 to read something from the beginning to the end, especially to find mistakes: *I **read** over my essay to check for errors.*

read² /riːd/ **noun** [no plural] **1** the act of reading something: *It's not brilliant but it's worth a **read**.* **2 a good/easy, etc read** something that is enjoyable, easy, etc to read

readable /ˈriːdəbl/ **adj** enjoyable and easy to read

reader /ˈriːdər/ **noun** [C] **1** 🅑 someone who reads: *She's a slow **reader**.* **2** a piece of equipment or software that can read printed material or electronic data (= information)

readership /ˈriːdəʃɪp/ **noun** [no plural] the number and type of people who read a particular newspaper, magazine, etc: *These magazines have a very young **readership**.*

readily /ˈredɪli/ **adv 1** 🅑 quickly and easily: *Information is **readily** available on the Internet.* **2** 🅑 willingly and without stopping to think: *He **readily** admits to having problems himself.*

readiness /ˈredinəs/ **noun 1** [U, no plural] being willing to do something: [+ to do sth] *They expressed a **readiness** to accept our demands.* **2** [U] the state of being prepared for something: *It was time to repair their shelters **in readiness for** the winter.*

reading /ˈriːdɪŋ/ **noun 1 ACTIVITY** ▷ [U] 🅐 the activity or skill of reading books: *I **did** a lot of **reading** on holiday.* **2 EVENT** ▷ [C] an event at which someone reads something to an audience: *a **poetry reading*** **3 MEASUREMENT** ▷ [C] the measurement that is shown on a piece of

measuring equipment: *It's best to **take** a mete. **reading** as soon as you move in.*

readjust /ˌriːəˈdʒʌst/ **verb 1** [I] to change in order to deal with a new situation, such as a new job or home: *The children will have to **readjust** to a new school.* **2** [T] to move something slightly or make a small change to something: *He **read**. justed his tie.*

ready /ˈredi/ **adj 1** [never before noun] 🅐 prepared for doing something: *Give me a call when you're ready.* ∘ [+ to do sth] *Are you **ready** to go yet.* ∘ *We're going at eight, so you've got an hour to **get ready**.* ∘ *The army was **ready for** action* **2** [never before noun] 🅑 prepared and available to be eaten, drunk, used, etc: *Is dinner ready.* ∘ *When will the book be **ready for** publication.* **3 be ready to do sth** to be willing to do something: *We are **ready** to die for our country* → See also **rough¹** and **ready**

ready-made /ˌrediˈmeɪd/ **adj** made and ready to use: ***ready-made** meals*

ready meal **noun** [C] a meal that has already been cooked, that is bought at a shop but taken home to be heated and eaten

real¹ /rɪəl/ **adj 1 NOT IMAGINED** ▷ 🅐 existing and not imagined: *Romance is never like that in **real life**.* **2 TRUE** ▷ 🅑 true and not pretended: *What was the **real reason** she didn't come?* ∘ *I. that your **real** name?* **3 NOT ARTIFICIAL** ▷ 🅐 not artificial or false: *real fur/leather* ∘ *It's not a toy gun, it's the **real thing**.* **4 FOR EMPHASIS** ▷ [always before noun] 🅑 used to emphasize a noun: *She was a **real** help.*

IDIOM **Get real!** informal used to tell someone that they are hoping for something that will never happen, or that they believe something that is not true

→ See also **the real McCoy**

real² /rɪəl/ **adv** US informal very: *It's **real** easy to get there from here.*

real estate **noun** [U] US buildings and land

real estate agent **noun** [C] US (UK **estate agent**) someone who sells buildings and land a their job

realism /ˈrɪəlɪzªm/ **noun** [U] **1** a style in art literature, etc in which things and people are shown as they are in real life **2** behaviour in which you accept and deal with the true facts of a situation and do not hope for things that will not happen

realist /ˈrɪəlɪst/ **noun** [C] **1** someone who accept the true facts of a situation and does not hope for things that will not happen **2** an artist or writer who shows people and things in their work as they are in real life

realistic /ˌrɪəˈlɪstɪk/ **adj 1** 🅑 accepting the true facts of a situation and not basing decisions or things that will not happen: *Let's be realistic - we're not going to finish this by Friday.* **2** 🅑 showing things and people as they really are, or making them seem to be real: *realistic specia. effects in a film* → Opposite **unrealistic** • **realistically adv**

reality /riˈæləti/ **noun 1** 🅑 [U] the way things or situations really are and not the way you would like them to be: *Sooner or later you have to face up to reality.* ∘ *He may seem charming but in reality he's actually quite unpleasant.* **2 the reality/realities of sth** ⑫ the truth about an unpleasant situation: *the harsh realities of life* **3 become a reality** to start to happen or exist: *New jobs could become a reality next month.* → See also **virtual reality**

☑ Word partners for **reality**

face up to reality • **turn** [an idea/dream, etc] **into** reality • **lose touch with** reality • **in** reality

---

reality T'V noun [U] television programmes about ordinary people who are filmed in real situations

realization (also UK **-isation**) /ˌrɪələˈzeɪʃᵊn/ noun **1** [U, no plural] the process of noticing or understanding something that you did not notice or understand before: [+ that] *There is a growing realization that education has benefits at many levels.* **2** [U] the process of achieving something that you wanted: *the **realization of** an ambition*

realize (also UK **-ise**) /ˈrɪəlaɪz/ verb [T] **1 NOTICE** ▷ ⑪ to notice or understand something that you did not notice or understand before: [+ question word] *I didn't realize how unhappy she was.* ∘ *I suddenly realized I'd met him before.* ∘ [+ (that)] *Some people just don't seem to realize that the world has changed.* **2 realize an ambition/ dream/goal, etc** to achieve something that you have wanted for a long time: *He had realized all his ambitions by the age of 30.* **3 SELL** ▷ to sell things that you own: *to realize your assets* **4 MAKE MONEY** ▷ to be sold for a particular amount of money: *The shares realized £1.4 million.*

really /ˈrɪəli/ adv **1** ⑪ very or very much: *She's really nice.* ∘ *I really don't want to go.* ∘ "*Did you like it then?*" "*Er, **not really**" (= no).* **2** ⑪ used when you are saying what is the truth of a situation: *She tried to hide what she was really thinking.* **3 Really?** ⑫ used when you are surprised at what someone has just said: "*Apparently, he's leaving.*" "*Really?*"

realm /relm/ noun [C] **1** formal an area of knowledge or activity: *successes in the realm of foreign policy* **2** literary a country that has a king or queen

real-time /ˈrɪəltaɪm/ adj describes computing systems that are able to deal with and use new information immediately

realtor /ˈriːltər/ noun [C] US trademark (also **realtor**, UK **estate agent**) someone who sells buildings or land as their job

reap /riːp/ verb **1 reap the benefits/profits/ rewards** to get something good by working hard for it: *Sometimes, this approach can reap tremendous rewards.* **2** [I, T] to cut and collect a crop of grain

reappear /ˌriːəˈpɪər/ verb [I] to appear again or return after a period of time: *He reappeared later that day.* • **reappearance** /ˌriːəˈpɪərᵊns/ noun [C, U]

rear¹ /rɪər/ noun **1 the rear** the back part of something: *First class accommodation is towards the rear of the train.* **2 bring up the rear** to be at the back of a group of people who are walking or running • **rear** adj [always before noun] ⑫ *a rear window/wheel*

rear² /rɪər/ verb **1** [T] If you rear children or young animals, you care for them until they are adults: *In these waters they breed and rear their young.* **2** [I] (also **rear up**) If a horse rears, it stands on its back legs. → See also **raise/rear its ugly head¹**

rear 'light noun [C] UK (US **tail light**) either of the two red lights on the back of a vehicle → See **Car** on page Centre 7

rearrange /ˌriːəˈreɪndʒ/ verb [T] **1** ⑫ to change the order or position of things: *I've **rearranged** the furniture.* **2** to change the time of an event or meeting: *I've **rearranged** the **meeting** for Monday.*

rear-view 'mirror noun [C] a small mirror inside a car which the driver looks in to see what is happening behind the car → See colour picture **Car** on page Centre 7

reason¹ /ˈriːzᵊn/ noun **1 WHY** ▷ [C] ⑫ the facts about why something happens or why someone does something: *Is there any particular **reason why** he doesn't want to come?* ∘ *He left without giving a reason.* ∘ *That was the **reason for** telling her.* **2 RIGHT** ▷ [C, U] ⑫ something that makes it right for you to do something: [+ to do sth] *There is **every reason** to believe the project will be finished on time.* **3 ABILITY** ▷ [U] the ability to think and make good decisions: *By this time he'd lost his powers of reason.* **4 within reason** If something is within reason, it is acceptable and possible: *You can have as much as you like, within reason.*

IDIOM **it stands to reason** If it stands to reason that something happens or is true, it is what you would expect: *It stands to reason that a child who is constantly criticized will have little self-confidence.*

❗ Common learner error: **reason**

Be careful to choose the correct preposition.
*That was the main **reason for** the trip.*
~~That was the main reason of the trip.~~

☑ Word partners for **reason**

a **compelling/good/obvious/simple** reason • **have/give/understand** a reason • the reason **for** sth • the reason **why** sth happens

---

reason² /ˈriːzᵊn/ verb [T] to decide that something is true after considering the facts: [+ that] *We reasoned that it was unlikely he would be a serious threat to the public.*

PHRASAL VERB **reason with sb** to persuade someone not to do something stupid by giving them good reasons not to

reasonable /ˈriːzᵊnəbl/ adj **1 FAIR** ▷ ⑫ fair and showing good judgment: [+ to do sth] *It's not reasonable to expect people to work those hours.* → Opposite **unreasonable 2 BIG ENOUGH** ▷ ⑪ big enough or large enough in number, although not big or not many: *There were a reasonable number of people there.* **3 GOOD ENOUGH** ▷ **B1** good enough but not the best: *I'd say her work is of a reasonable standard.* **4 CHEAP** ▷ **B1** not expensive: *reasonable prices*

reasonably /ˈriːzᵊnəbli/ **adv 1 B2** in a fair way, showing good judgment: *Why can't we discuss this reasonably, like adults?* **2 reasonably good/ successful/well, etc** **B2** good/successful/well, etc enough but not very good or very well: *I did reasonably well at school but not as well as my sister.* **3 reasonably priced** **B1** not expensive

reasoning /ˈriːzᵊnɪŋ/ **noun** [U] the process of thinking about something in order to make a decision: *I don't understand the **reasoning** **behind** this decision.*

reassure /ˌriːəˈʃʊər/ **verb** [T] to say something to stop someone from worrying: [+ that] *He reassured me that I would be paid soon.* • **reassurance** /ˌriːəˈʃʊərᵊns/ **noun** [C, U] something that you say to make someone stop worrying: *Despite my repeated reassurances that she was welcome, she wouldn't come.*

reassuring /ˌriːəˈʃʊərɪŋ/ **adj** making you feel less worried: *a reassuring smile/voice* • **reassuringly adv**

rebate /ˈriːbeɪt/ **noun** [C] an amount of money that is given back to you because you have paid too much: *a tax/rent rebate*

rebel¹ /ˈrebᵊl/ **noun** [C] **1 B2** someone who fights against the government in their country, especially a soldier: *Rebels seized control of the airport.* **2** someone who does not like authority and refuses to obey rules

rebel² /rɪˈbel/ **verb** [I] (**rebelling, rebelled**) **1** to fight against the government **2 B2** to refuse to obey rules because you do not like authority: *She **rebelled against** her family.*

rebellion /rɪˈbeliən/ **noun** [C, U] a situation in which people fight against the government in their country

☑ Word partners for **rebellion**

launch/lead/quash/stage a rebellion • a rebellion **against** sb/sth • a rebellion **by** sb

rebellious /rɪˈbeliəs/ **adj** refusing to obey rules because you do not like authority: *a rebellious teenager*

rebirth /ˈriːbɜːθ/ **noun** [no plural] the second time that something becomes popular or active: *the rebirth of the women's movement*

reboot /ˌriːˈbuːt/ **verb** [T, I] When a computer reboots, it switches off and then starts again immediately, and when you reboot a computer, you make it do this.

rebound¹ /rɪˈbaʊnd/ **verb** [I] to move back through the air after hitting something: *The ball rebounded off the post.*

rebound² /ˈriːbaʊnd/ **noun be on the rebound** to be unhappy because your romantic relationship has ended: *She was on the rebound when she met her second husband.*

rebuff /rɪˈbʌf/ **verb** [T] formal to refuse someone's suggestion or offer, especially in an unfriendly

way: *The company has rebuffed several buyou offers.* • **rebuff noun** [C]

rebuild /ˌriːˈbɪld/ **verb** [T] (**rebuilt**) **1 B1** to buil something again after it has been damaged: *Th cathedral was rebuilt after being destroyed by fir* **2 B2** to make a situation succeed again afte something bad caused it to fail: *The country i still struggling to rebuild its economy.*

rebuke /rɪˈbjuːk/ **verb** [T] formal to speak angri to someone because they have done somethin wrong • **rebuke noun** [C] formal

recalcitrant /rɪˈkælsɪtrᵊnt/ **adj** formal not willin to obey or respect someone: *recalcitrant schoo children*

recall /rɪˈkɔːl/ **verb** [T] **1 B2** to remember some thing: *I don't recall arranging a time to meet.* **2** t order the return of someone or somethin [often passive] *The ambassador was recalled t London.* • **recall** /ˈriːkɔːl/ **noun** [U]

recap /ˈriːkæp/ **verb** [I] (**recapping, recapped**) t repeat the most important parts of what yo have just said • **recap** /ˈriːkæp/ **noun** [C]

recapture /ˌriːˈkæptʃər/ **verb** [T] **1** to catch person or animal that has escaped **2** to exper ence or feel something from the past agai *Some men try to recapture their youth by goin out with younger women.*

recede /rɪˈsiːd/ **verb** [I] **1 MOVE AWAY** ▷ t become further and further away: *The coastlir receded into the distance.* **2 LESS STRONG** ▷ If memory or feeling recedes, it becomes less clea or strong. **3 HAIR** ▷ If a man's hair recedes, stops growing at the front of his head: *receding hairline*

receipt /rɪˈsiːt/ **noun 1** [C] **A2** a piece of pape that proves that you have received goods c money: *Could I have a receipt?* ∘ *Remember t keep **receipts for** any work done.* **2** [U] formal th act of receiving something: *Items must b returned within fourteen days of receipt.*

receipts /rɪˈsiːts/ **noun** [plural] US (UK **taking** the amount of money that a business gets fror selling things: *box-office receipts*

receive /rɪˈsiːv/ **verb** [T] **1 GET** ▷ **A2** to ge something that someone has given or sent t you: *Occasionally, he **receives** letters **from** fan* **2 REACT** ▷ to react to a suggestion or piece c work in a particular way: [often passive] *His fir. book was not **well received** (= people did not lik it).* **3 WELCOME** ▷ to formally welcome guest → See also **be on/at the receiving end¹** of sth

receiver /rɪˈsiːvər/ **noun** [C] **1 TELEPHONE** ▷ th part of a telephone that you hold in your han and use for listening and speaking **2 RADIC TV** ▷ the part of a radio or television tha receives signals from the air **3 PERSON** ▷ someone who officially deals with a compan when it has to stop business because it canno pay the money it owes

recent /ˈriːsᵊnt/ **adj** **B1** happening or startin from a short time ago: *a recent photo* ∘ *In rece years, sales have decreased quite markedly.*

recently /ˈriːsᵊntli/ **adv** **B1** not long ago: *Hav you seen any good films recently?* ∘ *Until recentl he worked as a teacher.*

ɑː arm | ɜː her | iː see | ɔː saw | uː too | aɪ my | aʊ how | eə hair | eɪ day | əʊ no | ɪə near | ɔɪ boy | ʊə pure | aɪə fire | aʊə sou

eception /rɪ'sepʃən/ **noun 1** HOTEL/OFFICE ▷ [no plural] 🖪 the place in a hotel or office building where people go when they arrive: *Ask for me at reception.* ○ *a reception area/desk* **2** PARTY ▷ [C] 🖪 a formal party that is given to celebrate a special event or to welcome someone: *a wedding reception* **3** REACTION ▷ [no plural] the way people react to something or someone: *We were given a very warm reception.* **4** RADIO/TV ▷ [U] the quality of a radio or television signal

> 🗒 Word partners for **reception**
>
> **get/be given/receive** a [cool/good, etc] reception • a **cool/chilly/frosty/hostile** reception • a **good/great/rapturous/warm** reception • a **lukewarm/mixed** reception • reception **from** sb

eceptionist /rɪ'sepʃənɪst/ **noun** [C] 🖪 someone who works in a hotel or office building, answering the telephone and dealing with guests: *a hotel receptionist*

eceptive /rɪ'septɪv/ **adj** willing to think about and accept new ideas: *She's generally very receptive to ideas and suggestions.*

ecess /rɪ'ses/ **noun 1** NOT WORKING ▷ [C, U] a time in the day or in the year when a parliament or law court is not working: *a parliamentary/ congressional recess* ○ *The court is in recess for thirty minutes.* **2** SCHOOL ▷ [C, U] US (UK **break**) a period of free time between classes at school: *At recess the boys would fight.* **3** WALL ▷ [C] a part of a wall in a room that is further back than the rest of the wall

ecession /rɪ'seʃən/ **noun** [C, U] 🖪 a time when the economy of a country is not successful: *The latest report confirms that the economy is in recession.*

echarge /ˌriː'tʃɑːdʒ/ **verb** [T] to fill a battery (= object that provides a machine with power) with electricity so that it can work again

ecipe /'resɪpi/ **noun 1** 🖪 [C] a list of foods and a set of instructions telling you how to cook something: *a recipe for carrot cake* **2 be a recipe for disaster/trouble/success, etc** to be likely to become a disaster, a success, etc

ecipient /rɪ'sɪpiənt/ **noun** [C] someone who receives something: *a recipient of an award*

eciprocal[1] /rɪ'sɪprəkəl/ **adj** involving two people or groups that agree to help each other in a similar way: *a reciprocal arrangement*

eciprocal[2] /rɪ'sɪprəkəl/ **noun** [C] a number that when multiplied with another particular number give the answer 1: *The reciprocal of 2 is 0.5.*

eciprocate /rɪ'sɪprəkeɪt/ **verb** [I, T] to do something for someone because they have done something similar for you

ecital /rɪ'saɪtəl/ **noun** [C] a performance of music or poetry: *a piano recital*

ecite /rɪ'saɪt/ **verb** [I, T] to say something aloud from memory: *She can recite the whole poem.*

eckless /'rekləs/ **adj** doing something dangerous and not caring about what might happen: *reckless driving* • **recklessly** *adv*

reckon /'rekən/ **verb** [T] **1** 🖪 to think that something is probably true: *I reckon he likes her.* ○ [+ (that)] *He reckons that he earns more in a week than I do in a month.* **2** to guess that a particular number is correct: *His fortune is reckoned at $5 million.* → See also **a force**[1] **to be reckoned with**

PHRASAL VERBS **reckon on sth/doing sth** to think that something is going to happen and make it part of your plans • **reckon with sb/sth** to deal with someone or something difficult

reclaim /rɪ'kleɪm/ **verb** [T] **1** to get something back from someone: *You can reclaim the tax at the airport.* **2** to make land good enough to be used for growing crops

recline /rɪ'klaɪn/ **verb 1** [I] to lie back with the upper part of your body in a horizontal position: *I found him reclining on the sofa.* **2** [I, T] If a chair reclines, you can lower the back part so that you can lie in it, and if you recline a chair, you put it in this position: *a reclining chair/seat*

recluse /rɪ'kluːs/ **noun** [C] someone who lives alone and does not like being with other people • **reclusive** *adj* living alone and avoiding other people

recognition /ˌrekəg'nɪʃən/ **noun 1** ACCEPT ▷ [U, no plural] agreement that something is true or real: *There is a growing recognition of the scale of the problem.* ○ [+ that] *There is a general recognition that she's the best person for the job.* **2** HONOUR ▷ [U] a situation in which when someone is publicly thanked for something good that they have done: *Ellen gained recognition for her outstanding work.* ○ *He was given a medal in recognition of his bravery.* **3** KNOW ▷ [U] knowledge of something or someone because you have seen or experienced them before: *I waved at her, but she showed no sign of recognition.*

> 🗒 Word partners for **recognition**
>
> **achieve/deserve/gain** recognition • **in** recognition **of** sth • recognition **for** sth

recognizable (also UK **-isable**) /'rekəgnaɪzəbl/ **adj** able to be recognized (= able to be known): *Megan's voice is instantly recognizable.* • **recognizably** *adv*

recognize (also UK **-ise**) /'rekəgnaɪz/ **verb** [T] **1** KNOW ▷ 🖪 to know someone or something because you have seen or experienced them before: *I recognized her from her picture.* ○ *Doctors are trained to recognize the symptoms of disease.* **2** ACCEPT ▷ 🖪 to accept that something is true or real: [+ (that)] *She recognized that she had been partly to blame.* ○ *Smoking is recognized as a leading cause of lung cancer.* **3** SHOW RESPECT ▷ to officially show respect for someone for an achievement: *He was recognized by the governor for his work with teenagers.*

recoil /rɪ'kɔɪl/ **verb** [I] to react to something with fear or hate: *She recoiled in horror at the thought of touching a snake.*

recollect /ˌrekə'lekt/ **verb** [T] to remember something: *I didn't recollect having seen him.*

recollection /ˌrekə'lekʃən/ **noun** [C, U] the

feeling of remembering something: *He* **had** *no* **recollection** *of the incident.*

recommend /ˌrekəˈmend/ **verb** [T] **1** ⓑ⒈ to say that someone or something is good or suitable for a particular purpose: *Can you recommend a good wine to go with this dish?* ◦ *She has been* **recommended for** *promotion.* **2** ⓑ⒉ to advise someone that something should be done: *The judge is likely to recommend a long jail sentence.* ◦ [+ that] *The report recommended that tourists avoid the region.*

recommendation /ˌrekəmenˈdeɪʃən/ **noun 1** [C] ⓑ⒉ a piece of advice about what to do in a particular situation: *The marketing department* **made** *several* **recommendations** *to improve sales.* ◦ [+ that] *It's my recommendation that this factory be closed immediately.* **2** [C, U] a suggestion that someone or something is good or suitable for a particular purpose: *I bought this book* **on** *Andy's* **recommendation.**

> ✐ Word partners for **recommendation**
>
> accept/follow/implement/make a recommendation • a recommendation for/on sth

recompense /ˈrekəmpens/ **noun** [U] formal payment that you give to someone when you have caused them difficulty or an injury: *Angry soccer fans sought* **recompense for** *the cancelled match.* • **recompense verb** [T] formal *He was* **recompensed for** *loss of earnings.*

reconcile /ˈrekənsaɪl/ **verb** [T] **1** to make two different ideas, beliefs, or situations agree or able to exist together: *It is sometimes difficult to reconcile science and religion.* ◦ *How can you* **reconcile** *your love of animals* **with** *your habit of eating them?* **2** **be reconciled (with sb)** to become friendly with someone after you have argued with them

PHRASAL VERB **reconcile yourself to sth** to accept a situation although you do not like it: *Eventually he reconciled himself to living without her.*

reconciliation /ˌrekənˌsɪliˈeɪʃən/ **noun 1** [C, U] a process in which two people or groups become friendly again after they have argued: *to* **seek** *a* **reconciliation 2** [U, no plural] the process of making two opposite ideas, beliefs, or situations agree: *the reconciliation of facts with theory*

reconnaissance /rɪˈkɒnɪsəns/ **noun** [U] the process of getting information about a place or an area for military use

reconnect /ˌriːkəˈnekt/ **verb** [I, T] **1** EQUIP-MENT ▷ to connect a piece of equipment with the power supply or a telephone service again after that connection has been broken: *You need to reconnect the cables.* **2** INTERNET ▷ to use a computer, mobile phone, etc. to connect to the Internet again after the connection has been broken: *We reconnected to the Internet.* **3** TELEPHONE ▷ to connect again a person who is phoning someone to the person they want to speak to, after the connection has been broken: *One moment please, I'll try to reconnect you.*

reconsider /ˌriːkənˈsɪdər/ **verb** [I, T] to think again about a decision or opinion and decide if

you want to change it: *We've been asked to reconsider the proposal.* • **reconsideration** /ˌriː-kənˌsɪdərˈeɪʃən/ **noun** [U]

reconstruct /ˌriːkənˈstrʌkt/ **verb** [T] **1** to create a description of a past event using all the information that you have: *The police tried to reconstruct the crime using evidence found at the scene.* **2** to build something again after it has been damaged or destroyed

reconstruction /ˌriːkənˈstrʌkʃən/ **noun** [C, U] **1** the process of creating a description of a past event using all the information that you have: *A reconstruction of the crime was shown on TV.* **2** the process of building something again after it has been damaged or destroyed

record¹ /ˈrekɔːd/ **noun 1** STORED INFORMATION ▷ [C, U] ⓑ⒉ information that is written on paper or stored on computer so that it can be used in the future: *medical/dental* **records** ◦ *My teacher* **keeps** *a* **record** *of my absences.* ◦ *This has been the hottest summer* **on record** (= the hottest summer known about) **2** BEHAVIOUR ▷ [C] A person's or company's record is their behaviour or achievements [usually singular] *She has an outstanding academic record* (= has done very well in school). ◦ *Of all airlines they have the best* **safety record 3** BEST ▷ [C] ⓑ⒈ the best, biggest, longest, tallest, etc: *to* **set/break** *a* **record** ◦ *He* **holds the** *world* **record** *for 100 metres.* **4** MUSIC ▷ [C] ⓑ⒈ a flat, round, plastic disc that music is stored on used especially in the past: *to play a record* **5 off the record** If you say something off the record, you do not want the public to know about it **6 put/set the record straight** to tell people the true facts about a situation **7** COMPUTER ▷ [C] a collection of pieces of information in a computer database that is treated as one unit: *You can sort the records on any field.* → See also **track record**

> ✐ Word partners for **record**
>
> have/keep a record • records indicate/reveal/show sth • a record of sth • [the hottest/the lowest, etc] on record

record² /rɪˈkɔːd/ **verb 1** [T] ⓑ⒉ to write down information or store it on a computer so that it can be used in the future: *He* **recorded details of** *their conversation in his diary.* **2** [I, T] ⓐ⒉ to store sounds or pictures using electronic equipment, a camera, etc so that you can listen to them or see them again: *to record a new album* ◦ *a* **recorded message**

record-breaking /ˈrekɔːdˌbreɪkɪŋ/ **adj** [always before noun] better, bigger, longer, etc than anything else before: *record-breaking sales of the new movie*

recorder /rɪˈkɔːdər/ **noun** [C] **1** a machine for storing sounds or pictures: *a video recorder* **2** a long, thin, hollow instrument that you play by blowing into it → See also **cassette recorder**, **tape recorder**

recording /rɪˈkɔːdɪŋ/ **noun** [C, U] ⓑ⒈ sounds or moving pictures that have been recorded, or the process of recording: *a recording of classical music* ◦ *a new system of digital recording*

ɑː arm | ɜː her | iː see | ɔː saw | uː too | aɪ my | aʊ how | eə hair | eɪ day | əʊ no | ɪə near | ɔɪ boy | ʊə pure | aɪə fire | aʊə sour

record ˌlabel noun [C] a company that records and sells music

record ˌplayer noun [C] a machine that makes it possible to hear the music on a record (= a flat, round disc used especially in the past)

recount¹ /rɪˈkaʊnt/ verb [T] formal to tell a story or describe an event: *He was **recounting** a **story** about a woman he'd met on a train.*

recount² /ˌriːˈkaʊnt/ verb [T] to count something again

recount³ /ˈriːkaʊnt/ noun [C] a second count of votes in an election: *They **demanded** a **recount**.*

recoup /rɪˈkuːp/ verb [T] to get back money that you have lost or spent: *to recoup your **losses***

recourse /rɪˈkɔːs/ noun [U] formal someone or something that can help you in a difficult situation: *For many cancer patients, surgery is the **only recourse**. ○ They solved their problem **without recourse to** (= without using) violence.*

recover /rɪˈkʌvəʳ/ verb **1** HEALTH ▷ [I] 🔵 to become healthy or happy again after an illness, injury, or period of sadness: *It takes a long time to **recover from** surgery. ○ She never **recovered from** the death of her husband.* **2** SITUATION ▷ [I] 🔵 If a system or situation recovers, it returns to the way it was before something bad happened: *The economy was quick to recover after the election.* **3** BODY ▷ [T] to be able to use or feel again part of your body which has been damaged: *He never fully recovered the use of his legs.* **4** GET BACK ▷ [T] to get something back that has been lost or stolen: *Police recovered the stolen money.*

recovery /rɪˈkʌvəʳi/ noun **1** HEALTH ▷ [U, no plural] 🔵 the process of getting better after an illness, injury, or period of sadness: *She only had the operation last month but she's **made a** good **recovery**.* **2** SITUATION ▷ [U, no plural] a process in which a system or situation returns to the way it was before something bad happened: *economic recovery ○ The housing industry has **made a** remarkable **recovery**.* **3** GET BACK ▷ [U] the act of getting back something that was lost or stolen: *the recovery of stolen jewels*

☑ **Word partners for recovery**

make a recovery • a **full/miraculous/slow/speedy** recovery • recovery **from** sth

---

recreate /ˌriːkriˈeɪt/ verb [T] to make something exist or happen again: *They plan to recreate a typical English village in Japan.*

recreation /ˌrekriˈeɪʃᵊn/ noun [C, U] 🔵 activities that you do for enjoyment when you are not working: *Shopping seems to be her only form of recreation.* • **recreational** adj

recrimination /rɪˌkrɪmɪˈneɪʃᵊn/ noun [C, U] formal the things you say when you blame someone for something, or the act of blaming someone for something

recruit¹ /rɪˈkruːt/ verb [I, T] to try to persuade someone to work for a company or to join an organization • **recruitment** noun [U] the job or activity of recruiting people: *graduate recruitment*

recruit² /rɪˈkruːt/ noun [C] someone who has recently joined an organization: *a **new recruit***

☑ **Word partners for recruit**

a **new** recruit • a recruit **to** sth

---

rectangle /ˈrektæŋgl/ noun [C] a shape with four 90° angles and four sides, with opposite sides of equal length and two sides longer than the other two → See picture at **shape** • **rectangular** /rekˈtæŋgjələʳ/ adj 🔵 shaped like a rectangle: *a rectangular room*

rectify /ˈrektɪfaɪ/ verb [T] formal to correct something or change it so that it is acceptable: *The government has promised to **rectify the situation**.*

rector /ˈrektəʳ/ noun [C] a priest in some Christian churches

rectum /ˈrektəm/ noun [C] the last part of a tube in the body that solid waste travels through before coming out of the bottom

recuperate /rɪˈkuːpᵊreɪt/ verb [I] to become healthy again after an illness or injury: *She's still **recuperating from** her injuries.* • **recuperation** /rɪˌkjuːpᵊrˈeɪʃᵊn/ noun [U]

recur /rɪˈkɜːʳ/ verb [I] (**recurring, recurred**) to happen again or many times: *The same ideas recur throughout her books.* • **recurrence** /rɪˈkʌrᵊns/ noun [C, U] an occasion when something recurs: *a recurrence of the disease*

recurring /rɪˈkɜːrɪŋ/ adj (also **recurrent**) happening again or many times: *a recurring dream*

recycle /ˌriːˈsaɪkl/ verb [I, T] 🔵 to put used paper, glass, plastic, etc through a process so that it can be used again: *We recycle all our newspapers and bottles.* • **recyclable** /ˌriːˈsaɪkləbl/ adj able to be recycled: *Glass is recyclable.*

recycled /ˌriːˈsaɪkld/ adj 🔵 Recycled paper, glass, plastic, etc has been used before and put through a process so that it can be used again.

recycling /ˌriːˈsaɪklɪŋ/ noun [U] 🔵 the process of putting paper, glass, plastic, etc through a process so that it can be used again: *ways to encourage recycling ○ a recycling centre*

red¹ /red/ adj (**redder, reddest**) **1** COLOUR ▷ 🔵 being the same colour as blood: *a red shirt* → See **Colours** on page Centre 12 **2** HAIR ▷ 🔵 Red hair is an orange-brown colour. **3** go red UK (US turn red) 🔵 If someone goes red, their face becomes red because they are embarrassed or angry. **4** WINE ▷ 🔵 Red wine is made from black grapes (= small, round, purple fruits). → See also **be like a red rag to a bull**

red² /red/ noun **1** 🔵 [C, U] the colour of blood → See colour picture **Colours** on page Centre 12 **2 in the red** If your bank account is in the red, you have spent more money than there was in it.

IDIOM **see red** to become very angry

red ˈcard noun [C] in football, a small red card which the referee (= someone who makes sure the players follow the rules) shows to a player to make them stop playing because they have broken a rule

the ˌred ˈcarpet noun special treatment that is given to an important person when they go

R

---

somewhere: *She's given **the red carpet treatment** wherever she goes.*

redden /'redᵊn/ verb [I, T] to become red or to make something become red: *His face reddened with anger.*

redeem /rɪ'diːm/ verb [T] **1** IMPROVE ▷ to make something seem less bad: *He tried to **redeem** his **reputation** by working extra hard.* ◦ *a **redeeming feature*** **2 redeem yourself** to do something that makes people have a better opinion of you after you have done something bad: *He was two hours late, but he redeemed himself by bringing presents.* **3** GET SOMETHING ▷ to exchange something for something else **4** RELIGION ▷ to save someone from evil, especially according to the Christian religion

redemption /rɪ'demʃᵊn/ noun **1** [U] being saved from evil, especially according to the Christian religion **2 be beyond redemption** to be too bad to be improved or saved

redeploy /ˌriːdɪ'plɔɪ/ verb [T] to move employees, soldiers, equipment, etc to a different place or use them in a more effective way • **redeployment** noun [C, U] the act of redeploying someone or something

redevelop /ˌriːdɪ'veləp/ verb [T] to make a place more modern by improving old buildings or building new ones: *There are plans to redevelop the city's waterfront area.* • **redevelopment** noun [C, U] the process of redeveloping a place

red-handed /ˌred'hændɪd/ adv **catch sb red-handed** informal to discover someone doing something wrong: *He was caught red-handed trying to steal a car.*

redhead /'redhed/ noun [C] someone who has red hair

red 'herring noun [C] a fact or idea that takes your attention away from something that is important

red-hot /ˌred'hɒt/ adj extremely hot

redirect /ˌriːdɪ'rekt/ verb [T] **1** to send something in a different direction: *Traffic should be redirected away from the city centre.* **2** to use money, energy, etc for a different purpose: *Money spent on weapons could be **redirected to** hospitals and schools.*

redistribute /ˌriːdɪ'strɪbjuːt/ verb [T] to share money, land, power, etc between people in a different way from before: *to **redistribute wealth*** • **redistribution** /ˌriːdɪstrɪ'bjuːʃᵊn/ noun [U] the process of redistributing something

red 'meat noun [U] meat from animals and not birds or fish

redo /ˌriː'duː/ verb [T] to do something again: *I'm going to have to redo that report.*

redress¹ /rɪ'dres/ verb [T] formal to correct something that is wrong, unfair, or not equal: *laws aimed at redressing racial inequality*

redress² /rɪ'dres/ ⓤⓢ /'riːdres/ noun [U] formal payment for an action or situation that is wrong or unfair

red 'tape noun [U] official rules that do not seem necessary and make things happen very slowly

reduce /rɪ'djuːs/ verb [T] **1** ⓔ to make something less: *to reduce air pollution* ◦ *The number of employees was **reduced from** 500 **to** 300.* **2** to add one or more electrons to a substance or to remove oxygen from a substance

PHRASAL VERBS **reduce sb to sth/doing sth** to make someone unhappy or cause them to be in a bad situation: *She was **reduced to tears** by his comments.* • **reduce sth to sth** to destroy something, especially something that has been built: *The earthquake reduced the city to rubble.*

reduction /rɪ'dʌkʃᵊn/ noun [C, U] **1** ⓔ the act of reducing something: *She refused to accept a **reduction in** wages.* ◦ *price reductions* **2** the process of adding one or more electrons to a substance or removing oxygen from a substance

> **⧉ Word partners for reduction**
>
> a **dramatic/drastic/sharp/significant** reduction • a reduction **in** sth

redundancy /rɪ'dʌndᵊnsi/ noun **1** [C, U] UK an occasion when your employer makes you stop working because there is not enough work: *There have been a lot of redundancies in the mining industry.* **2** [U] a situation in which something is not needed or used because there are other similar or more modern things

redundant /rɪ'dʌndᵊnt/ adj **1** NOT WORKING ▷ UK ⓔ not working because your employer has told you there is not enough work: *Eight thousand people have been **made redundant** in Britain this year.* **2** NOT NEEDED ▷ UK not needed or used any more because there are other similar or more modern things: *redundant weapons* **3** TOO MUCH ▷ more than is needed, especially extra words that mean the same thing

redwood /'redwʊd/ noun [C, U] a very tall tree that grows on the west coast of the US, or the wood of this tree

reed /riːd/ noun [C] a tall, stiff plant like grass that grows near water

reef /riːf/ noun [C] a line of rocks or sand near the surface of the sea: *a **coral reef***

reek /riːk/ verb [I] to have a very unpleasant smell: *The whole room **reeked of** sweat.* • **reek** noun [no plural]

reel¹ /riːl/ verb [I] **1** to feel very shocked: *She was still **reeling from** the news of his death.* **2** to walk in a way that looks as if you are going to fall over: *He came reeling down the street like a drunk.*

PHRASAL VERB **reel sth off** to say a long list of things quickly and without stopping: *She **reeled off** a list of all the countries she'd been to.*

reel² /riːl/ noun [C] an object shaped like a wheel that you can roll film, thread, etc around

re-elect /ˌriːɪ'lekt/ verb [T] to elect someone again to a particular position

re-election /ˌriːɪ'lekʃᵊn/ noun [C, U] the election of someone again to the same position: *She's UK **standing for**/US **running for** re-election (= she wants to be re-elected).*

ref /ref/ noun [C] informal short for referee

efer /rɪˈfɜːr/ **verb** (**referring, referred**)

PHRASAL VERBS **refer to sb/sth 1** ⬤ to talk or write about someone or something, especially briefly: *She didn't once refer to her son.* ◦ *He always referred to his father as 'the old man'.* **2** If writing or information refers to someone or something, it relates to that person or thing: *The sales figures refer to UK sales only.* • **refer to sth** to read something in order to get information: *Please refer to your owner's manual for more information.* • **refer sb/sth to sb/sth** to send someone or something to a different place or person for information or help: *My doctor referred me to a specialist.*

eferee¹ /ˌrefəˈriː/ **noun** [C] ⬤ someone who makes sure that players follow the rules during a sports game → See colour picture **Sports 2** on page Centre 15

eferee² /ˌrefəˈriː/ **verb** [I, T] (**refereeing, refereed**) to be the referee in a sports game

eference /ˈrefərəns/ **noun 1** SAY ▷ [C, U] a few words that you say or write about someone or something: *In his book, he makes several references to his time in France.* **2** **with/in reference to sth** formal ⬤ relating to something: *I am writing to you with reference to the job advertised in yesterday's newspaper.* **3** LOOK AT ▷ [C, U] the act of looking at information, or the thing that you look at for information: *Please keep this handout for future reference* (= to look at in the future). **4** LETTER ▷ [C] ⬤ a letter that is written by someone who knows you, to say if you are suitable for a job or course → See also **cross reference**

eference book noun [C] a book that you look at in order to find information

eferendum /ˌrefəˈrendəm/ **noun** [C] an occasion when all the people in a country can vote in order to show their opinion about a political question

eferral /rɪˈfɜːrəl/ **noun** [C, U] the act of sending someone or something to a different place or person for information or help

efill /ˌriːˈfɪl/ **verb** [T] to fill something again: *He got up and refilled their glasses.* • **refill** /ˈriːfɪl/ **noun** [C]

efine /rɪˈfaɪn/ **verb** [T] **1** to make a substance pure by removing other substances from it **2** to improve an idea, method, system, etc by making small changes: *The engineers spent months refining the software.*

efined /rɪˈfaɪnd/ **adj 1** PURE ▷ A refined substance has been made more pure by removing other substances from it: *refined sugar* **2** POLITE ▷ very polite and showing knowledge of social rules **3** IMPROVED ▷ improved by many small changes: *a refined method*

efinement /rɪˈfaɪnmənt/ **noun 1** IMPROVEMENT ▷ [C, U] a small change that improves something: *Several refinements have been made to improve the car's performance.* **2** POLITE ▷ [U] polite behaviour and knowledge of social rules: *a woman of refinement* **3** PURE ▷ [U] the process of making a substance pure

refinery /rɪˈfaɪnəri/ **noun** [C] a factory where substances, such as sugar, oil, etc are made pure

reflect /rɪˈflekt/ **verb 1** SHOW ▷ [T] ⬤ to show or be a sign of something: *The statistics reflect a change in people's spending habits.* **2** SEND BACK ▷ [T] If a surface reflects heat, light, sound, etc, it sends the light, etc back and does not absorb it. **3** IMAGE ▷ [I, T] ⬤ If a surface such as a mirror or water reflects something, you can see the image of that thing in the mirror, water, etc.: *He saw himself reflected in the shop window.* **4** THINK ▷ [I] formal ⬤ to think in a serious and careful way: *In prison, he had plenty of time to reflect on the crimes he had committed.*

PHRASAL VERB **reflect on sb/sth** If something reflects on someone or something, it affects other people's opinion of them, especially in a bad way: *The whole affair reflects badly on the government.*

reflection

reflection /rɪˈflekʃən/ **noun 1** [C] ⬤ the image of something in a mirror, on a shiny surface, etc: *I saw my reflection in the window.* **2** [C, U] formal serious and careful thought: *He paused for reflection before answering my question.* ◦ **On reflection** (= after thinking again), *I think I was wrong.* **3 a reflection of sth** something that is a sign or result of a particular situation: *His poor job performance is a reflection of his lack of training.* **4 a reflection on sb/sth** something that makes people have a particular opinion about someone or something, especially a bad opinion: *Low test scores are a sad reflection on our school system.*

reflective /rɪˈflektɪv/ **adj 1** thinking carefully and quietly: *a reflective mood* **2** A reflective surface is one that you can see easily when a light shines on it: *a jacket made of reflective material*

reflex /ˈriːfleks/ **noun** [C] a physical reaction that you cannot control: *Shivering and blushing are reflexes.*

reflexes /ˈriːfleksɪz/ **noun** [plural] your ability to react quickly: *A boxer needs to have good reflexes.*

reflexive /rɪˈfleksɪv/ **adj** A reflexive verb or pronoun is used to show that the person who does the action is also the person who is affected by it. In the sentence 'I looked at myself in the mirror', 'myself' is a reflexive pronoun.

reflexology /ˌriːflekˈsɒlədʒi/ **noun** [U] the treatment of your feet by rubbing and pressing them in a special way in order to make the blood flow and help you relax

reform¹ /rɪˈfɔːm/ **noun** [C, U] changes made to improve a system, organization, or law: *economic/political reform*

> ☑ Word partners for **reform**
>
> **introduce/propose** a reform • a **major/ radical/sweeping** reform • reform **in/of** sth • **economic/political** reform

reform² /rɪˈfɔːm/ **verb 1** [T] to change a system, organization, or law in order to improve it: *efforts to reform the education system* **2** [I, T] to change your behaviour and stop doing bad things, or to make someone else do this: *a programme to reform criminals* ∘ *a reformed drug addict*

reformer /rɪˈfɔːmər/ **noun** [C] someone who tries to improve a system or law by changing it: *a social reformer*

refrain¹ /rɪˈfreɪn/ **verb** [I] formal to stop yourself from doing something: [+ from + doing sth] *Please refrain from talking during the performance.*

refrain² /rɪˈfreɪn/ **noun** [C] **1** formal a phrase or idea that you repeat often: *'Every vote counts' is a familiar refrain in politics.* **2** a part of a song that you repeat

refresh /rɪˈfreʃ/ **verb 1** [T] to make you feel less hot or tired: *A cool drink should refresh you.* **2** [I, T] to make the most recent information on an Internet page appear on your computer **3 refresh sb's memory** to help someone remember something

refreshing /rɪˈfreʃɪŋ/ **adj 1** different and interesting: *a refreshing change* ∘ [+ to do sth] *It's refreshing to see a film that's so original.* **2** making you feel less hot or tired: *a refreshing shower/ swim* • **refreshingly** adv

refreshments /rɪˈfreʃmənts/ **noun** [plural] ⬤ food and drinks that are available at a meeting, event, on a journey, etc: *Refreshments are available in the lobby.*

refrigerate /rɪˈfrɪdʒəreɪt/ **verb** [T] to make or keep food cold so that it stays fresh: *You should refrigerate any leftover food immediately.* • **refrigeration** /rɪˌfrɪdʒərˈeɪʃən/ **noun** [U]

refrigerated /rɪˈfrɪdʒəreɪtɪd/ **adj 1** A refrigerated container or vehicle keeps the things inside it cold. **2** Refrigerated food or drink is cold because it has been kept in a refrigerator.

refrigerator /rɪˈfrɪdʒəreɪtər/ **noun** [C] a large container that uses electricity to keep food cold → See colour picture **The Kitchen** on page Centre 2

refuel /ˌriːˈfjuːəl/ **verb** [I, T] to put more fuel into an aircraft, ship, etc so that it can continue its journey

refuge /ˈrefjuːdʒ/ **noun 1** [U] protection from danger or unpleasant conditions: *We took refuge from the storm in an old barn.* **2** [C] a place where you are protected from danger: *a refuge for homeless people*

refugee /ˌrefjʊˈdʒiː/ **noun** [C] ⬤ someone who has been forced to leave their country, especially because of a war: *a refugee camp*

refund¹ /ˈriːfʌnd/ **noun** [C] ⬤ an amount of money that is given back to you, especially because you are not happy with something you have bought: *The travel company apologized and gave us a full refund.*

> ☑ Word partners for **refund**
>
> **claim/give** sb/**get** a refund • a **full** refund • a refund **of** sth

refund² /ˌriːˈfʌnd/ **verb** [T] to give back money that someone has paid to you

refurbish /ˌriːˈfɜːbɪʃ/ **verb** [T] formal to repair or improve a building • **refurbishment noun** [C, U] the process of refurbishing a building: *The library was closed for refurbishment.*

refusal /rɪˈfjuːzəl/ **noun** [C, U] the act of refusing to do or accept something: [+ to do sth] *his refusal to admit his mistake*

refuse¹ /rɪˈfjuːz/ **verb** [I, T] ⬤ to say that you will not do or accept something: *I asked him to leave but he refused.* ∘ [+ to do sth] *Cathy refuses to admit that she was wrong.*

refuse² /ˈrefjuːs/ **noun** [U] formal waste: *a pile of refuse*

refute /rɪˈfjuːt/ **verb** [T] formal to say or prove that something is not true or correct: *attempts to refute his theory* ∘ *She angrily refuted their claims.*

regain /rɪˈɡeɪn/ **verb** [T] ⬤ to get something back again: *Armed troops have regained control of the capital.* ∘ *It was several hours before he regained consciousness.*

regal /ˈriːɡəl/ **adj** very special and suitable for a king or queen: *a regal dress*

regard¹ /rɪˈɡɑːd/ **verb** [T] **1** ⬤ to think of someone or something in a particular way: *She is generally regarded as one of the greatest singers this century.* ∘ *The plans were regarded with suspicion.* **2** formal to look carefully at someone or something

regard² /rɪˈɡɑːd/ **noun 1** [U] respect or admiration for someone or something: *I have the greatest regard for her.* → Opposite **disregard noun 2 in/with regard to sth** formal ⬤ relating to something: *I am writing in regard to your letter of 24 June.*

regarding /rɪˈɡɑːdɪŋ/ **preposition** formal ⬤ about or relating to: *I am writing to you regarding your application dated 29 April.*

regardless /rɪˈɡɑːdləs/ **adv 1 regardless of sth** despite something: *She'll make a decision regardless of what we think.* **2** without thinking about problems or difficulties: *Mr Redwood claimed he would carry on with his campaign regardless.*

regards /rɪˈɡɑːdz/ **noun** [plural] ⬤ friendly greetings: *Give/send my regards to your mother when you see her.*

regeneration /rɪˌdʒenərˈeɪʃən/ **noun** [U] the process of improving a place or system, especially to make it more active or successful: *a programme of urban regeneration* • **regenerate**

/rɪˈdʒenᵊreɪt/ **verb** [T] to improve a place or system

eggae /ˈregeɪ/ **noun** [U] a type of popular music from Jamaica with a strong beat

egime /reɪˈʒiːm/ **noun** [C] a system of government or other control, especially one that people do not approve of: *the former Communist regime*

egiment /ˈredʒɪmənt/ **noun** [group] a large group of soldiers • **regimental** /ˌredʒɪˈmentᵊl/ **adj** relating to a regiment

egimented /ˈredʒɪmentɪd/ **adj** too controlled or organized: *a regimented lifestyle*

egion /ˈriːdʒᵊn/ **noun 1** [C] ⓰ a particular area in a country or the world: *China's coastal region* **2** [C] an area of the body: *pain in the lower abdominal region* **3 in the region of sth** approximately: *It probably cost somewhere in the region of 900 euros.*

egional /ˈriːdʒᵊnᵊl/ **adj** ⓲ relating to a region (= particular area in a country): *a regional dialect/newspaper*

egister¹ /ˈredʒɪstəʳ/ **noun 1** [C] an official list of names: *a **register of** approved builders* ∘ *the **electoral register*** **2** [C, U] the style of language, grammar, and words used in particular situations: *a formal/informal register* → See also **cash register**

☑ Word partners for **register**

compile a register • **on** a register • a register **of** sth

egister² /ˈredʒɪstəʳ/ **verb 1 ON A LIST** ▷ [I, T] ⓳ to put information about someone or something, especially a name, on an official list: *Is he **registered with** the authorities to sell alcohol?* ∘ *Students need to **register for** the course by the end of April.* ∘ *a registered nurse* **2 SHOW A FEELING** ▷ [T] to show an opinion or feeling: *People gathered to **register** their **opposition** to the plans.* **3 SHOW AMOUNT** ▷ [I, T] to show an amount on an instrument that measures something: *The earthquake registered 7.3 on the Richter scale.*

egistered /ˈredʒɪstəd/ **adj registered mail/ post** a special service that records when a letter or parcel is sent and received

egister ˌoffice noun [C] in Britain, a place where births, deaths, and marriages are officially recorded and where you can get married

egistrar /ˌredʒɪˈstrɑːʳ/ **noun** [C] **1** someone whose job is to keep official records, especially of births, deaths, and marriages, or of students at a university **2** UK a type of hospital doctor

egistration /ˌredʒɪˈstreɪʃᵊn/ **noun 1** [U] ⓳ the recording of a name or information on an official list **2** [C] (also **regisˈtration ˌnumber**) mainly UK the official set of numbers and letters on the front and back of a vehicle

egistry /ˈredʒɪstri/ **noun** [C] a place where official records are kept: *the land registry*

egistry ˌoffice noun [C] in Britain, a place where births, deaths, and marriages are officially recorded and where you can get married

egress /rɪˈgres/ **verb** [I] formal to go back to an earlier, less advanced state • **regression** /rɪˈgreʃᵊn/ **noun** [U] formal the process of regressing

regret¹ /rɪˈgret/ **verb** [T] (**regretting, regretted**) **1** ⓳ to feel sorry about a situation, especially something that you wish you had not done: [+ doing sth] *I really regret leaving school so young.* ∘ [+ (that)] *He began to regret that he hadn't paid more attention in class.* **2** formal ⓲ used to say that you are sorry that you have to tell someone about a situation: [+ to do sth] *We regret to inform you that the application has been refused.*

regret² /rɪˈgret/ **noun** [C, U] ⓲ a feeling of sadness about a situation, especially something that you wish you had not done: *We married very young but we've been really happy and I've **no regrets**.* ∘ *It is **with** great regret that I announce Steve Adam's resignation.* • **regretful** adj expressing regret • **regretfully** adv

☑ Word partners for **regret**

express regret • **have (no)** regrets • sb's **biggest/only** regret • **with** regret • regret **about/at/over** sth

regrettable /rɪˈgretəbl/ **adj** If something is regrettable, you wish it had not happened and you feel sorry about it: *a deeply regrettable incident* • **regrettably** adv

regular¹ /ˈregjələʳ/ **adj 1 SAME TIME/SPACE** ▷ ⓲ repeated with the same amount of time or space between one thing and the next: *a regular pulse* ∘ *Plant the seedlings at regular intervals.* **2 OFTEN** ▷ ⓳ happening or doing something often, especially at the same time every week, year, etc: *a **regular occurrence*** ∘ *We arranged to meet **on a regular basis**.* **3 USUAL** ▷ US usual or normal: *I couldn't see my regular dentist.* **4 SIZE** ▷ informal ⓳ being a standard size: *a burger and regular fries* **5 SHAPE** ▷ Something that has a regular shape is the same on both or all sides: *She's got lovely, regular teeth.* **6 GRAMMAR** ▷ ⓳ following the usual rules or patterns in grammar: *'Talk' is a regular verb but 'go' is not.* → Opposite **irregular** • **regularity** /ˌregjəˈlærəti/ **noun** [U] the state of being regular

regular² /ˈregjələʳ/ **noun** [C] informal someone who often goes to a particular shop, restaurant, etc: *Mick was one of the regulars at the local pub.*

regularly /ˈregjələli/ **adv 1** ⓳ often: *Accidents occur regularly on this stretch of the road.* **2** ⓳ at the same time each day, week, month, etc: *They meet regularly – usually once a week.*

regulate /ˈregjəleɪt/ **verb** [T] **1** to control an activity or process, especially by using rules: *There are laws regulating advertising.* **2** to control the speed, temperature, etc of something: *Babies find it difficult to regulate their body temperature.*

☑ Word partners for **regulation**

breach/comply with/enforce/introduce regulations • regulations **governing** sth • **strict/ stringent/tough** regulations • **under** a regulation

regulation /ˌregjəˈleɪʃᵊn/ **noun 1** [C] ⓲ an official rule that controls how something is

R

done: [usually plural] *building regulations* **2** [U] the control of a process or activity: *government regulation of interest rates*

regulator /'regjəleɪtər/ **noun** [C] **1** someone whose job is to make sure that a system works in a fair way: *the water industry regulator* **2** a piece of equipment that is used to control the temperature, speed, etc of something

regulatory /'regjələtəri/ **adj** controlling an activity or process, especially by using rules

rehab /'ri:hæb/ **noun** [U] informal treatment to help someone stop drinking too much alcohol or taking drugs: *He spent six months in rehab.*

rehabilitate /ˌri:hə'bɪlɪteɪt/ **verb** [T] to help someone live a normal life again after they have had a serious illness or been in prison: *a programme to rehabilitate young offenders* • **rehabilitation** /ˌri:həˌbɪlɪ'teɪʃən/ **noun** [U]

rehearsal /rɪ'hɜ:səl/ **noun** [C, U] a time when all the people involved in a play, dance, etc practise in order to prepare for a performance

rehearse /rɪ'hɜ:s/ **verb** [I, T] to practise a play, dance, etc in order to prepare for a performance

reign[1] /reɪn/ **noun 1** [C] a period of time when a king or queen rules a country: *the reign of Henry VIII* **2** [no plural] a period of time when someone controls a sports team, an organization, etc: *Christie's reign as captain of the British athletics team*

IDIOM **reign of terror** a period of time when someone uses violence to control people

reign[2] /reɪn/ **verb** [I] **1** to be the king or queen of a country: *Queen Victoria reigned for 64 years.* **2** formal to be the main feeling or quality in a situation: *Chaos reigned as angry protesters hammered on the doors.*

reigning champion **noun** [C] the most recent winner of a competition

reimburse /ˌri:ɪm'bɜ:s/ **verb** [T] formal to pay money back to someone, especially money that they have spent because of their work: *Employees will no longer be reimbursed for taxi fares.* • **reimbursement** **noun** [U] formal the act of reimbursing someone

rein /reɪn/ **noun** [C] a long, thin piece of leather that helps you to control a horse: [usually plural] *Hold the reins in your left hand.* → See colour picture **Sports 1** on page Centre 14

IDIOMS **free rein** the freedom to do or say what you want: [+ to do sth] *The school gives teachers free rein to try out new teaching methods.* • **keep a tight rein on sb/sth** to have a lot of control over someone or something: *We've been told to keep a tight rein on spending.*

reincarnation /ˌri:ɪnkɑ:'neɪʃən/ **noun** [U] the belief that a dead person's spirit returns to life in another body

reindeer /'reɪndɪər/ **noun** [C] (plural **reindeer**) a type of deer with large horns that lives in northern parts of Europe, Asia, and America

reinforce /ˌri:ɪn'fɔ:s/ **verb** [T] **1** to make an existing opinion or idea stronger: *to reinforce a view/feeling* **2** to make something stronger: *a security door reinforced by steel bars* ∘ *reinforced*

concrete • **reinforcement** **noun** [C, U] the act o reinforcing something

reinforcements /ˌri:ɪn'fɔ:smənts/ **noun** [plura soldiers who are sent to make an army stronge

reinstate /ˌri:ɪn'steɪt/ **verb** [T] **1** to give someon the job or position that they had before **2** t cause a rule, law, etc to exist again • **reinstate ment** **noun** [C, U] the act of reinstating someon or something

reinvent /ˌri:ɪn'vent/ **verb 1** [T] to produc something new that is based on somethin that already exists: *The story of Romeo and Juli was reinvented as a Los Angeles gangster movie* **2 reinvent yourself** to change the way you loo and behave so that you seem very differen → See also **reinvent the wheel**

reiterate /ri'ɪtəreɪt/ **verb** [T] formal to say som thing again so that people take notice of it: [that] *I must reiterate that we have no intention o signing this contract.* • **reiteration** /riˌɪtər'eɪʃən noun** [C, U]

reject[1] /rɪ'dʒekt/ **verb** [T] **1 NOT ACCEPT** ▷ **B2** refuse to accept or agree with something: *Th United States government rejected the proposa* **2 JOB/COURSE** ▷ **B2** to refuse to accept someon for a job, course, etc: *I applied to Cambridg University but I was rejected.* **3 PERSON** ▷ **B2** not give someone the love or attention the were expecting: *She felt rejected by her husban*

reject[2] /'ri:dʒekt/ **noun** [C] a product that damaged or not perfect in some way

rejection /rɪ'dʒekʃən/ **noun 1 NOT ACCEPT** ▷ [C U] the act of refusing to accept or agree wit something: *Their rejection of the peace plan very disappointing for the government.* **2 JO COLLEGE** ▷ [C] a letter that says you have n been successful in getting a job, a place college, etc **3 PERSON** ▷ [U] the feeling tha someone does not give you the love or attentio you were expecting: *a feeling of rejection*

rejoice /rɪ'dʒɔɪs/ **verb** [I] literary to feel ver happy because something good has happened

rejoicing /rɪ'dʒɔɪsɪŋ/ **noun** [U] happy celebra tions by people because something good ha happened

rejoin /rɪ'dʒɔɪn/ **verb** [T] to return to a person o place: *I was feeling better, so I rejoined the part*

rejuvenate /rɪ'dʒu:vəneɪt/ **verb** [T] to mak someone look or feel young and energeti again: *You're supposed to come back from holiday feeling rejuvenated.* • **rejuvenatio** /rɪˌdʒu:və'neɪʃən/ **noun** [U]

rekindle /ˌri:'kɪndl/ **verb** [T] to make someor have a feeling that they had in the past: *The tri seemed to rekindle their love for each other.*

relapse /rɪ'læps/, /'ri:læps/ **noun** [C, U] **1** a occasion when someone becomes sick agai after a period of feeling better: *I had a relaps last year and was off work for a month.* **2** a occasion when something or someone get worse again after being better: *The company share prices have suffered a relapse this wee* • **relapse** /rɪ'læps/ **verb** [I]

relate /rɪ'leɪt/ **verb 1** [I, T] to be connected, or t

R

find or show the connection between two or more things: *How do the two proposals relate?* **2** [T] formal to tell a story or describe a series of events

PHRASAL VERBS **relate to sb/sth** to be connected to, or to be about, someone or something: *Please provide all information relating to the claim.* • **relate to sb** to understand how someone feels: *Most teenagers find it hard to relate to their parents.*

related /rɪ'leɪtɪd/ **adj 1** ⑫ connected: *There's been an increase in criminal activity related to drugs.* **2** ⑫ If two or more people are related, they belong to the same family: *Did you know that I'm related to Jackie?* → Opposite **unrelated**

relation /rɪ'leɪʃᵊn/ **noun 1** [C, U] ⑫ a connection between two or more things: *the relation between smoking and lung cancer* **2** [C] ⑪ someone who belongs to the same family as you: *He's called Ken Russell, no relation to* (= he is not from the same family as) *the film director.* → See Note at **parent 3 in relation to sth a** ⑫ when compared with something: *Salaries are low in relation to the cost of living.* **b** about or relating to something: *I'd like to ask you something in relation to what you said earlier.*

relations /rɪ'leɪʃᵊnz/ **noun** [plural] ⑫ the way two people or groups feel and behave towards each other: *It was an attempt to restore diplomatic relations between the two countries.* → See also **public relations, race relations**

relationship /rɪ'leɪʃᵊnʃɪp/ **noun 1** BEHAVIOUR ▷ [C] ⑪ the way two people or groups feel and behave towards each other: *He has a very good relationship with his older sister.* **2** ROMANTIC ▷ [C] ⑪ a sexual or romantic friendship: *I don't feel ready for a relationship at the moment.* **3** CONNECTION ▷ [C, U] ⑫ a connection between two or more things: *the relationship between sunburn and skin cancer*

> ❗ Common learner error: **have a relationship with** someone
>
> Be careful to use the correct preposition in this expression.
>
> *I have a good relationship with my parents.*
> ~~I have a good relationship to my parents.~~

> ✅ Word partners for **relationship**
>
> a **close/intimate/personal/loving/stormy** relationship • **end/forge/form/have** a relationship • a relationship **between** sb and sb

relative¹ /'relətɪv/ **noun** [C] ⑪ a member of your family: *a party for friends and relatives* → See Note at **parent**

relative² /'relətɪv/ **adj 1** [always before noun] compared to other similar things or people: *the relative prosperity of the West* **2 relative to sth** when compared to something else: *The economy has been declining relative to other countries.*

relative 'clause noun [C] a part of a sentence that is used to describe the noun that comes just before it. In the sentence, 'The woman who I saw yesterday wasn't his wife.', 'who I saw yesterday' is a relative clause.

relatively /'relətɪvli/ **adv** ⑫ quite, when compared to other things or people: *Eating out is relatively cheap.*

relative 'pronoun noun [C] a word such as 'that', 'which', or 'who' that is used to begin a relative clause

relax /rɪ'læks/ **verb 1** PERSON ▷ [I, T] ⑪ to become happy and comfortable because nothing is worrying you, or to make someone do this: *I find it difficult to relax.* ◦ *The wine had relaxed him and he began to talk.* **2** LESS STIFF ▷ [I, T] If a part of your body relaxes, it becomes less stiff, and if you relax it, you make it become less stiff: *Try these exercises to relax your neck muscles.* **3** RULES ▷ [T] to make laws or rules less severe: *The government has recently relaxed laws on bringing animals into Britain.* • **relaxation** /ˌriːlæk'seɪʃᵊn/ **noun** [U]

> ➕ Other ways of saying **relax**
>
> The verb **chill** and the phrasal verb **chill out** are very common, informal ways of saying 'relax':
>
> *We spent the whole week chilling out on the beach.*
>
> The phrasal verb **wind down** and the verb **unwind** mean 'to start to relax after working or doing something difficult':
>
> *It takes me a while to wind down when I get back from work.*
>
> *Music helps me to unwind.*
>
> If a person relaxes so that they don't use too much energy, the fixed expression **take it easy/take things easy** is often used:
>
> *You'll need to spend a few days taking it easy/taking things easy after the operation.*
>
> The fixed expression **put your feet up** is also often used to mean 'sit down and relax':
>
> *I'm going to make myself a cup of coffee and put my feet up for half an hour.*

relaxed /rɪ'lækst/ **adj 1** ⑪ feeling happy and comfortable because nothing is worrying you: *She seemed relaxed and in control of the situation.* **2** ⑫ A relaxed situation is comfortable and informal: *There was a very relaxed atmosphere at the party.*

relaxing /rɪ'læksɪŋ/ **adj** ⑪ making you feel relaxed: *a relaxing bath*

relay¹ /ˌriː'leɪ/ **verb** [T] **1** to send a message from one person to another: *Cory had an idea which he relayed to his friend immediately.* **2** to broadcast radio or television signals

relay² /'riːleɪ/ **noun** [C] (also **'relay ˌrace**) a race in which each member of a team runs or swims part of the race

release¹ /rɪ'liːs/ **verb** [T] **1** PRISONER ▷ ⑫ to allow a prisoner to be free: *Six hostages were released shortly before midday.* **2** STOP HOLDING ▷ to stop holding someone or something: *Release the handle.* **3** INFORMATION ▷ to let the public have news or information about something: *Police have not released the dead woman's name.* **4** RECORD/FILM ▷ ⑫ to make a

R

record or film available for people to buy or see: *The album is due to be released in time for Christmas.* **5 SUBSTANCE** ▷ to let a substance flow out from somewhere: *Dangerous chemicals were accidentally released into the river.*

release² /rɪˈliːs/ **noun 1 FROM PRISON** ▷ [C] the occasion when someone is allowed to leave prison: *After his release from jail, Jackson found it difficult to find work.* **2 FILM/RECORD** ▷ [C] ⓑ a new film or record that you can buy: *Have you heard the group's latest release?* **3 SUBSTANCE** ▷ [C, U] an occasion when a substance is allowed to flow out of somewhere: *a release of toxic gas from the factory* → See also **press release**

> **Word partners for release**
>
> demand/secure sb's release • release from sth

relegate /ˈrelɪɡeɪt/ **verb** [T] to put someone or something in a less important position: [often passive] *He'd been relegated to the B team.* • **relegation** /ˌrelɪˈɡeɪʃⁿn/ **noun** [U]

relent /rɪˈlent/ **verb** [I] to allow something that you refused to allow before: *The security guard relented and let them through.*

relentless /rɪˈlentləs/ **adj** never stopping or getting any less extreme: *relentless criticism* • **relentlessly adv**

relevance /ˈreləvəns/ **noun** [U] (also US **relevancy** /ˈreləvəntsi/) the degree to which something is related or useful to what is happening or being talked about: *This point has no relevance to the discussion.*

relevant /ˈreləvənt/ **adj** ⓑ related or useful to what is happening or being talked about: *relevant information* ◦ *Education should be relevant to children's needs.* → Opposite **irrelevant**

reliable /rɪˈlaɪəbl/ **adj** ⓑ able to be trusted or believed: *a reliable car* ◦ *reliable information* ◦ *Andy's very reliable – if he says he'll do something, he'll do it.* → Opposite **unreliable** • **reliability** /rɪˌlaɪəˈbɪləti/ **noun** [U] how reliable someone or something is • **reliably adv** *I am reliably informed that the concert has been cancelled.*

reliance /rɪˈlaɪəns/ **noun reliance on sb/sth** the fact of depending on someone or something : *our increasing reliance on computers*

reliant /rɪˈlaɪənt/ **adj be reliant on sb/sth** to depend on someone or something: *I don't want to be reliant on anybody.* → See also **self-reliant**

relic /ˈrelɪk/ **noun** [C] a very old thing from the past: *an Egyptian relic*

relief /rɪˈliːf/ **noun 1 EMOTION** ▷ [U, no plural] ⓑ the good feeling that you have when something unpleasant stops or does not happen: *It'll be such a relief when these exams are over.* ◦ *"James can't come tonight." "Well, that's a relief!"* **2 HELP** ▷ [U] money, food, or clothes that are given to people because they need help: *an international relief operation* **3 PHYSICAL FEELING** ▷ [U] an end to or pause in a feeling of pain: *I'd been trying to sleep to find relief from the pain.*

> **Word partners for relief**
>
> a big/great/tremendous relief • a sense of relief • to sb's relief

relieve /rɪˈliːv/ **verb** [T] **1** to make pain or a bad feeling less severe: *Breathing exercises can help t relieve stress.* **2** to allow someone to stop workin by taking their place: *The 7 a.m. team arrived t relieve the night workers.*

PHRASAL VERB **relieve sb of sth** formal to tak something away from someone: *Let me reliev you of your luggage.*

relieved /rɪˈliːvd/ **adj** ⓑ feeling happy becaus something unpleasant did not happen or yo are not worried about something any more [+ (that)] *I'm just relieved that she's safe and wel* ◦ [+ to do sth] *I heard a noise and was relieved t find that it was only a cat.*

religion /rɪˈlɪdʒⁿn/ **noun** [C, U] ⓑ the belief in god or gods, or a particular system of belief in god or gods: *the Christian religion*

> **Word partners for religion**
>
> believe in/practise a religion • a major religion • be against sb's religion

religious /rɪˈlɪdʒəs/ **adj 1** ⓑ relating to religio *religious paintings* **2** ⓑ having a strong belief i a religion: *He's a very religious man.*

religiously /rɪˈlɪdʒəsli/ **adv 1** regularly: *H visited the old woman religiously every weeken* **2** in a religious way

relinquish /rɪˈlɪŋkwɪʃ/ **verb** [T] formal to allo something to be taken away from you: *At 80 h still refuses to relinquish control of the company.*

relish¹ /ˈrelɪʃ/ **verb** [T] to enjoy something: *I don relish the thought of a twelve-hour flight.*

relish² /ˈrelɪʃ/ **noun 1** [U] enjoyment: *He ha baked a cake which the children now ate wit relish.* **2** [C] a sauce that you put on food to giv it more taste

relive /ˌriːˈlɪv/ **verb** [T] to remember somethin so clearly that you feel as if it is happening no

relocate /ˌriːləʊˈkeɪt/ ⓤⓢ /riːˈləʊˌkeɪt/ **verb** [I, T] t move to another place: *The company relocate to Tokyo.* • **relocation** /ˌriːləʊˈkeɪʃⁿn/ **noun** [U *relocation costs*

reluctant /rɪˈlʌktⁿnt/ **adj** not wanting to d something: [+ to do sth] *Many victims of crime ar reluctant to go to the police.* • **reluctance** /rɪˈlʌk tⁿns/ **noun** [U] a feeling of not wanting to d something: [+ to do sth] *a reluctance to accep changes* • **reluctantly adv**

rely /rɪˈlaɪ/ **verb**

PHRASAL VERB **rely on sb/sth 1** ⓑ to nee someone or something in order to be successfu work correctly, etc: *Families rely more on wive earnings than before.* **2** ⓑ to trust someone o something: [+ to do sth] *I know I can rely on yo to help me.*

remain /rɪˈmeɪn/ **verb 1** ⓑ [I] to continue t exist when everything or everyone else ha gone: *Only a few hundred of these animals remai today.* → See Note at **rest²** **2 remain calm/open**

etc; **remain a secret/mystery/prisoner, etc** ⑤ to continue to be in the same state: *The exact date of the wedding remains a secret.* **3 remain at/in/with, etc** formal ⑥ to stay in the same place: *She will remain at her mother's until I return.*

remainder /rɪ'meɪndəʳ/ **noun** [no plural] the things or people that are left when everything or everyone else has gone or been dealt with: *He drank **the remainder of** his coffee and got up to leave.*

remaining /rɪ'meɪnɪŋ/ **adj** [always before noun] ⑥ continuing to exist when everything or everyone else has gone or been dealt with: *Mix in half the butter and keep the remaining 50g for later.*

remains /rɪ'meɪnz/ **noun** [plural] **1** ⑥ the parts of something, especially a building, that continue to exist when the rest of it has been destroyed: *the remains of a Buddhist temple* **2** formal someone's body after they have died

remake /'riːmeɪk/ **noun** [C] a film that is the same as one that has been made before: *a remake of 'King Kong'* • **remake** /ˌriː'meɪk/ **verb** [T] (**remade**)

remand[1] /rɪ'mɑːnd/ **noun on remand** UK in prison before your trial: *He spent two weeks on remand in Bullingdon prison.*

remand[2] /rɪ'mɑːnd/ **verb be remanded in custody** UK to be kept in prison on remand: *He was charged with murder and remanded in custody.*

remark[1] /rɪ'mɑːk/ **noun** [C] ⑥ something that you say: *He **made a remark** about her clothes.*

📝 **Word partners for remark**

make a remark • a remark about/on sth

---

remark[2] /rɪ'mɑːk/ **verb** [I] ⑥ to say something: [+ that] *He remarked that she was looking thin.*

PHRASAL VERB **remark on/upon sth** ⑥ to say something about something that you have just noticed: *He remarked on how well you were looking.*

remarkable /rɪ'mɑːkəbl/ **adj** ⑥ very unusual or noticeable in a way that you admire: *a remarkable woman* ∘ *He has a remarkable memory.* → Opposite **unremarkable**

remarkably /rɪ'mɑːkəbli/ **adv** in a way that makes you feel surprised: *She has remarkably good skin for her age.*

remarry /ˌriː'mæri/ **verb** [I] to get married again: *His wife died in 1970 and he never remarried.*

remedial /rɪ'miːdiəl/ **adj** [always before noun] **1** intended to help people who are having difficulty learning something: *remedial English classes* **2** formal intended to improve something: *Remedial action is needed.*

remedy[1] /'remədi/ **noun** [C] **1** ⑥ something that makes you better when you are sick: *a flu remedy* **2** ⑥ something that solves a problem: *The **remedy for** the traffic problem is to encourage people to use public transport.*

remedy[2] /'remədi/ **verb** [T] to solve a problem,

or to improve a bad situation: *They were able to **remedy** the **problem** very easily.*

remember /rɪ'membəʳ/ **verb** [I, T] **1** ⓐ If you remember a fact or something from the past, you keep it in your mind, or bring it back into your mind: *I can't remember his name.* ∘ [+ doing sth] *I don't remember signing a contract.* ∘ [+ (that)] *Just as the door closed he remembered that his keys were inside the room.* **2** ⓐ to not forget to do something: [+ to do sth] *I must remember to send Carol a birthday card.*

❗ Common learner error: **remember** or **memory**?

Remember is a verb. Use **remember** when you think about or bring thoughts into your mind about a person, place, or event from the past.
I can remember when I was at school.
Memory is a noun. Use **memory** to talk about the person, place, or event from the past that you think about.
I have good memories of when I was at school.

➕ Other ways of saying **remember**

More formal alternatives are verbs such as **recall** and (*UK*) **recollect**:
*I don't **recall** arranging a time to meet.*
*I didn't **recollect** having seen him.*
Remind means 'to make someone remember something', or 'to make someone remember to do something':
*Every time we meet he **reminds** me about the money he lent me.*
*Will you **remind** me to buy some eggs?*
The phrasal verbs **come back to** and **come to** are often used when someone suddenly remembers something:
*I'd forgotten his name but it's just **come** (**back**) **to** me.*
To **reminisce** is to remember and talk about pleasant things that happened in the past:
*We were just **reminiscing** about our school days.*
To **bear** something **in mind** is to remember someone or something that may be useful in the future:
*When you book, **bear in mind** that Christmas is the busiest period.*

---

remembrance /rɪ'membrəns/ **noun** [U] the act of remembering and showing respect for someone who has died: *They erected a statue **in remembrance of** him.*

remind /rɪ'maɪnd/ **verb** [T] ⑤ to make someone remember something, or remember to do something: *Every time we meet he **reminds** me **about** the money he lent me.* ∘ [+ to do sth] *Will you remind me to buy some eggs?*

PHRASAL VERB **remind sb of sth/sb** ⑤ to make someone think of something or someone else: *Harry reminds me of my father.* ∘ *This song reminds me of our trip to Spain.*

Common learner error: **remind** or **remember**?

If you **remember** a fact or something from the past, you keep it in your mind, or bring it back into your mind.

I can't remember the name of the film.
Did you remember to bring your passport?

When you **remind** someone to do something, you make them remember it.

Can you remind me to phone Anna tomorrow?
Can you remember me to phone Anna tomorrow?

reminder /rɪ'maɪndər/ **noun** [C] something that makes you remember something else: *Her scars are a constant **reminder of** the attack.*

🔲 Word partners for **reminder**

need/serve as a reminder • a constant/gentle/timely reminder • a grim/poignant/sharp/stark reminder • a reminder of sth

reminisce /ˌremɪ'nɪs/ **verb** [I] to talk about pleasant things that happened in the past: *We were just **reminiscing about** our school days.*
• **reminiscence noun** [C, U] talk in which you reminisce

reminiscent /ˌremɪ'nɪs⁰nt/ **adj reminiscent of sb/sth** making you think of someone or something that is similar: *a smell reminiscent of an old church*

remission /rɪ'mɪʃ⁰n/ **noun be in remission** to be in a period of time when a serious illness is better: *He is in remission at the moment.*

remit¹ /'ri:mɪt/ **noun** [no plural] UK the things that you are responsible for in your job

remit² /rɪ'mɪt/ **verb** [T] (**remitting, remitted**) formal to send money to someone

remnant /'remnənt/ **noun** [C] a piece of something that continues to exist when the rest of that thing has gone: *the remnants of last night's meal*

remorse /rɪ'mɔ:s/ **noun** [U] the feeling that you are sorry for something bad that you have done: *He has **shown** no **remorse for** his actions.*
• **remorseful adj** feeling remorse

remorseless /rɪ'mɔ:sləs/ **adj 1** UK never stopping: *remorseless pressure to succeed* **2** cruel
• **remorselessly adv**

remote /rɪ'məʊt/ **adj 1 PLACE** ▷ 🅑2 far away: *It was a remote mountain village with no electricity supply.* **2 TIME** ▷ far in time: *in the remote past* **3 SLIGHT** ▷ slight: *There is a **remote possibility** that it could be cancer.* • **remote control**
• **remoteness noun** [U]

re,mote con'trol
noun 1 [C] (also **remote**) 🅑1 a piece of equipment that is used to control something such as a television from a distance → See colour picture **The Living Room** on page

Centre 4 **2** [U] the use of radio waves to contro[l] something such as a television from a distance

remotely /rɪ'məʊtli/ **adv not remotely inter**-**ested/surprised/possible, etc** not at all inter[est]ested, etc: *I'm not remotely intereste[d] in football.*

removal /rɪ'mu:v⁰l/ **noun 1** [U] the act o[f] removing something: *stain removal* **2** [C, U] U[K] the job or activity of removing everything from one house to take to another: *a removals firm*

remove /rɪ'mu:v/ **verb** [T] **1 TAKE AWAY** ▷ 🅑1 t[o] take something away: *An operation was needed to* **remove** the bullets **from** his chest. **2 TAKE OFF** ▷ 🅑2 to take something off: *Carefully remove th[e] lid, then stir the paint.* **3 JOB** ▷ formal to mak[e] someone stop doing their job: [often passive] *H[e] had been **removed from** his job on medica[l] grounds.* **4 be far removed from sth** to b[e] very different from something: *The princess['] world was far removed from reality.*

remuneration /rɪˌmju:n⁰r'eɪʃ⁰n/ **noun** [U] forma[l] the money someone is paid for work they hav[e] done

renaissance /rə'neɪs⁰ns/ 🅤🅢 /ˌrenə'sɑ:ns/ **noun** [no plural] a time when something become[s] popular or fashionable again: *The British film industry is **enjoying a renaissance**.*

the Renaissance /rə'neɪs⁰ns/ 🅤🅢 /ˌrenə'sɑ:ns/ **noun** the period during the 14th, 15th, and 16t[h] centuries in Europe when there was a lot o[f] interest and activity in art, literature, ideas, et[c]

rename /ˌri:'neɪm/ **verb** [T] to give something [a] new name: [+ two objects] *Siam was rename[d] Thailand in 1939.*

render /'rendər/ **verb** [T] formal **1** to mak[e] something or someone be in a particular stat[e] or condition: *She was rendered speechless upo[n] hearing the news.* **2** to give someone a decision[,] opinion, help, etc: *payment for **services ren**dered*

rendering /'rend⁰rɪŋ/ **noun** [C] the way tha[t] something is performed, written, drawn, etc: *[a] child's rendering of a house*

rendezvous /'rɒndɪvu:/ **noun** [C] (plural **rendez**-**vous**) an arrangement to meet someone, or th[e] place you have arranged to meet the[m]
• **rendezvous verb** [I]

rendition /ren'dɪʃ⁰n/ **noun** [C] the way in whic[h] a song, piece of music, etc is performed

renegade /'renɪɡeɪd/ **noun** [C] someone wh[o] changes and joins a group that is against thei[r] own group: *a group of renegade soldiers*

renege /rə'neɪɡ/ 🅤🅢 /rə'nɪɡ/ **verb**

PHRASAL VERB **renege on sth** formal to not do wha[t] you said you were going to do: *to renege on [a] promise*

renew /rɪ'nju:/ **verb** [T] **1 OFFICIAL[LY] AGREEMENT** ▷ 🅑2 to arrange to continue a[n] official agreement that was going to end soon: *I've decided not to **renew** my golf club **member**-**ship** this year.* **2 BUY** ▷ UK to get a new one o[f] something that is old: *A car isn't the sort of thing you renew every year.* **3 DO AGAIN** ▷ to start t[o] do something again: *The next morning enem[y]* *war planes renewed their bombing.* • **renewal** **noun** [C, U] the act of renewing something

renewable /rɪˈnjuːəbl/ **adj 1** A renewable form of energy can be produced as quickly as it is used: *a **renewable energy** source such as wind power* **2** A renewable official agreement is one that you can arrange to continue when the time limit is reached: *a 6-month **renewable contract***

renewables /rɪˈnjuːəblz/ **noun** [plural] types of energy such as wind power and power from the sun that can be replaced as quickly as they are used

renewed /rɪˈnjuːd/ **adj** starting again in a stronger way than before: *He sang now with renewed confidence.*

renounce /rɪˈnaʊns/ **verb** [T] to officially say that you do not have the right to something any more, or that you do not want to be involved in something any more: *They had renounced all rights to ownership of the land.*

renovate /ˈrenəveɪt/ **verb** [T] to repair and decorate a building that is old and in bad condition • **renovation** /ˌrenəˈveɪʃᵊn/ **noun** [C, U]

renowned /rɪˈnaʊnd/ **adj** famous: *The island of Crete is **renowned for** its beauty.*

rent¹ /rent/ **verb 1** HOME ▷ [I, T] 🅰2 to pay money to live in a building that someone else owns: *He'll be renting an apartment until he can find a house to buy.* **2** PAY TO USE ▷ [T] US (UK **hire**) 🅰2 to pay money to use something for a short time: *We could rent a car for the weekend.* **3** RECEIVE MONEY ▷ [T] (also **rent out**) 🅱1 to allow someone to pay you money to live in your building: *I rented out my house and went travelling for a year.*

> ⚠ Common learner error: **rent** and **hire**
>
> In British English you **rent** something for a long time.
> *I rent a two-bedroom flat.*
> In British English you **hire** something for a short time.
> *We hired a car for the weekend.*
> In American English the word **rent** is used in both situations.
> *I rent a two-bedroom apartment.*
> *We rented a car for the weekend.*

rent² /rent/ **noun** [C, U] 🅰2 the amount of money that you pay to live in a building that someone else owns: *They couldn't afford the rent.*

> ✐ Word partners for **rent**
>
> pay the rent • the rent on sth

rental /ˈrentᵊl/ **noun** [C, U] an arrangement to rent something, or the amount of money that you pay to rent something: *The price includes flights and car rental.*

rented /ˈrentɪd/ **adj** describes something that you rent: ***rented accommodation***

renter /ˈrentər/ **noun** [C] US someone who pays money to live in a house or an apartment that someone else owns

renunciation /rɪˌnʌnsiˈeɪʃᵊn/ **noun** [U, no plural] a statement in which you say that you do not

want something or believe in something any more: *a renunciation of violence*

reorganize (also UK **-ise**) /ˌriːˈɔːgənaɪz/ **verb** [I, T] to organize something again in order to improve it: *He's completely reorganized his schedule for the week.* • **reorganization** /riːˌɔːgənaɪˈzeɪʃᵊn/ **noun** [C, U]

rep /rep/ **noun** [C] informal someone whose job is to sell things for a company: *the UK **sales rep***

repaid /ˌriːˈpeɪd/ past of repay

repair¹ /rɪˈpeər/ **verb** [T] **1** 🅰2 to fix something that is broken or damaged: *I must **get** my bike **repaired**.* **2** to improve a bad situation: *It will take a long time to repair relations between the two countries.*

> ➕ Other ways of saying **repair**
>
> The verbs **fix** and **mend** are common alternatives:
> *I must get my bike **fixed**.*
> *Can you **mend** that hole in my trousers?*
> The phrasal verbs **do up** (*UK*) and **fix up** are often used when someone repairs something and improves it:
> *Nick loves **fixing up** old cars.*
> *They're planning to buy an old cottage and **do** it **up**.*
> The verb **service** (*UK*) is often used when examining and repairing cars or other machines:
> *I'm taking the car to the garage to have it **serviced** this afternoon.*

repair² /rɪˈpeər/ **noun 1** 🅱1 [C, U] something that you do to fix something that is broken or damaged: [usually plural] *The repairs cost me £150.* **2 be in good/bad repair** to be in good/bad condition

> ✐ Word partners for **repair** (noun)
>
> carry out/do repairs • be in need of repair • extensive/major/minor repairs • the repair of sth

repairman /rɪˈpeəmən/ **noun** [C] (plural **repairmen**) a person who is paid to repair things: *a TV repairman*

repatriate /riːˈpætrieɪt/ 🇺🇸 /riːˈpeɪtrieɪt/ **verb** [T] to send someone back to their own country • **repatriation** /ˌriːpætriˈeɪʃᵊn/ 🇺🇸 /rɪˌpeɪtriˈeɪʃᵊn/ **noun** [U]

repay /ˌriːˈpeɪ/ **verb** [T] (**repaid**) **1** 🅱2 to pay back money that you have borrowed: *to **repay** a **loan*** **2** 🅱2 to do something kind for someone who has done something to help you: *What can I do to repay you for your kindness?* • **repayment** /rɪˈpeɪmənt/ **noun** [C, U] the act of repaying someone or the money that you pay back

repeal /rɪˈpiːl/ **verb** [T] to officially make a law end

repeat¹ /rɪˈpiːt/ **verb** [T] **1** 🅰2 to say or do something more than once: *He repeated the number.* ○ *The test must be repeated several times.* **2** to tell someone something that someone else has told you: *I've got some news for you but you mustn't **repeat** it **to** anyone.*

R

repeat² /rɪˈpiːt/ **noun 1** [no plural] something that happens or is done more than once: *Everything is being done to avoid a repeat of the tragedy.* **2** [C] (also US **rerun**) a television or radio programme that is broadcast again

repeated /rɪˈpiːtɪd/ **adj** [always before noun] done or happening more than once: *He has refused repeated requests to be interviewed.* • **repeatedly** adv *The victim was stabbed repeatedly.*

repel /rɪˈpel/ **verb** [T] (**repelling, repelled**) **1** to make someone or something move away or stop attacking you: *a smell that repels insects* **2** If someone or something repels you, you think they are extremely unpleasant.

repellent¹ /rɪˈpelənt/ **adj** extremely unpleasant: *I find his views utterly repellent.*

repellent² /rɪˈpelənt/ **noun** [C, U] **insect/mosquito repellent** a substance that you use to keep insects away

repent /rɪˈpent/ **verb** [I, T] formal to say that you are sorry for doing something bad • **repentance** noun [U] formal the act of repenting

repentant /rɪˈpentənt/ **adj** formal feeling sorry about something bad that you have done → Opposite **unrepentant**

repercussions /ˌriːpəˈkʌʃənz/ **noun** [plural] the effects that an action or event has on something, especially bad effects: *Any decrease in tourism could have serious repercussions for the local economy.*

repertoire /ˈrepətwɑːr/ **noun** [C] all the songs, plays, etc that someone can perform

repertory /ˈrepətəri/ **noun 1** [C, U] an arrangement in which a group of actors performs several different plays during a period of time: *They have four plays in repertory this season.* ◦ *a repertory company/theatre* **2** [C] all the songs, plays, etc that someone can perform

repetition /ˌrepɪˈtɪʃən/ **noun** [C, U] the act of repeating something: *We don't want a repetition of last year's disaster.*

repetitive /rɪˈpetətɪv/ **adj** (also **repetitious** /ˌrepɪˈtɪʃəs/) doing or saying the same thing several times, especially in a way that is boring: *a repetitive job* • **repetitively** adv

reˌpetitive ˈstrain ˌinjury RSI

replace /rɪˈpleɪs/ **verb** [T] **1 USE INSTEAD** ▷ **B1** to start using another thing or person instead of the one that you are using now: *We're thinking of replacing our old TV with a fancy new one.* **2 BE USED INSTEAD** ▷ **B2** to start to be used instead of the thing or person that is being used now: *This system will replace the old one.* **3 GET SOMETHING NEW** ▷ **B1** to get something new because the one you had before has been lost or damaged: *We'll have to replace this carpet soon.* **4 PUT BACK** ▷ formal to put something back in the place where it usually is: *She picked up the books and carefully replaced them on the shelf.*

replacement /rɪˈpleɪsmənt/ **noun 1** [C] **B2** the thing or person that replaces something or someone: *It's not going to be easy to find a replacement for you.* **2** [U] the act of replacing something or someone

replay /ˈriːpleɪ/ **noun** [C] **1** an important part of a sports game or other event on television that i shown again immediately after it has happene **2** a game of sport that is played again • **repla** /ˌriːˈpleɪ/ **verb** [T] → See also **action replay instant replay**

replenish /rɪˈplenɪʃ/ **verb** [T] formal to fill some thing or make it complete again: *to replenish supplies* • **replenishment** noun [U] formal the ac of filling something or making it complete agai

replica /ˈreplɪkə/ **noun** [C] something that i made to look almost exactly the same a something else: *a replica of the White House*

replicate /ˈreplɪkeɪt/ **verb** [T] formal to make o do something again in exactly the same wa • **replication** /ˌreplɪˈkeɪʃən/ **noun** [C, U]

reply¹ /rɪˈplaɪ/ **verb** [I, T] **B1** to answer: *"I don understand," she replied.* ◦ *He didn't reply to m email.* ◦ [+ that] *Henry replied that he had no ide what I was talking about.*

reply² /rɪˈplaɪ/ **noun** [C, U] **B1** an answer: *He reply was short and unfriendly.* ◦ *Have you had reply to your letter?* ◦ *She sent me an email i reply (= as an answer).*

🗒 **Word partners for reply noun**

give/make/send a reply • get/have/receive a reply • a reply to sth • in reply

---

report¹ /rɪˈpɔːt/ **noun** [C] **1 B1** a description of a event or situation: *a police report* ◦ *an annua report on the economy* **2** UK (US **reˈport ˌcard** something teachers write about a child's pr gress at school for their parents

report² /rɪˈpɔːt/ **verb 1 DESCRIBE** ▷ [I, T] **B1** t describe a recent event or situation, especially on television, radio, or in a newspaper: *Jo Smit reports on recent developments.* ◦ [+ that] *Sh reported that the situation had changed dramati cally.* ◦ [+ doing sth] *A woman outside the sho reported seeing the gun.* **2 TELL** ▷ [T] **B1** to te someone in authority that something ha happened, especially an accident or crime: *H should have reported the accident immediately* ◦ *Have you reported the fault to a technician* **3 COMPLAIN** ▷ [T] to complain about someone behaviour to someone in authority: *I'm going t report him to the police.* ◦ *Duncan's bee reported for smoking.*

PHRASAL VERB report to sb/sth to go to someon or a place and say that you have arrived: *A visitors please report to reception.*

reportedly /rɪˈpɔːtɪdli/ **adv** If something ha reportedly happened or is reportedly a fact people say it has happened or is true: *Tw students were reportedly killed and severa wounded.*

reˌported ˈspeech noun [U] speech or writin that is used to report what someone has said but not using exactly the same words

reporter /rɪˈpɔːtər/ **noun** [C] **B1** someone whos job is to discover information about news event and describe them on television, radio, or in newspaper

repossess /ˌriːpəˈzes/ **verb** [T] to take bac someone's house, car, furniture, etc becaus they cannot finish paying for them • **repossession** /ˌriːpəˈzeʃᵊn/ **noun** [C, U] the process of repossessing something, or the thing that is repossessed

reprehensible /ˌreprɪˈhensəbl/ **adj** formal Reprehensible behaviour is extremely bad.

represent /ˌreprɪˈzent/ **verb** [T] **1** BE ▷ ⑫ to be equal to something: *In practice the figure represents a 10% pay cut.* ∘ *The cancellation of the new road project represents a victory for protesters.* **2** SPEAK FOR ▷ to officially speak or do something for someone else because they have asked you to: *The union represents over 200 employees.* **3** COMPETITION ▷ ⑫ to be the person from a country, school, etc that is in a competition **4** SIGN ▷ ⑫ to be a sign or symbol of something: *The crosses on the map represent churches.* **5** SHOW ▷ to show someone or something in a particular way

representation /ˌreprɪzenˈteɪʃᵊn/ **noun 1** [U] speaking or doing something officially for another person: *Can he afford **legal representation**?* **2** [C, U] the way someone or something is shown: *an accurate representation of country life* → See also **proportional representation**

representative¹ /ˌreprɪˈzentətɪv/ **noun** [C] ⑫ someone who speaks or does something officially for another person → See also **House of Representatives**

representative² /ˌreprɪˈzentətɪv/ **adj** the same as other people or things in a particular group: *Are his views **representative of** the rest of the department?*

repress /rɪˈpres/ **verb** [T] **1** to stop yourself from showing your true feelings: *Brigitta repressed a sudden desire to cry.* **2** to control what people do, especially by using force • **repression** /rɪˈpreʃᵊn/ **noun** [U] the act of repressing someone or something

repressed /rɪˈprest/ **adj 1** unable to show your true feelings and emotions: *a lonely, repressed man* **2** A repressed feeling or emotion is one that you do not show: *repressed anger*

repressive /rɪˈpresɪv/ **adj** cruel and not allowing people to have freedom: *a **repressive** military regime*

reprieve /rɪˈpriːv/ **noun** [C] **1** an official order that stops a prisoner from being killed as a punishment **2** something that happens to stop a bad situation • **reprieve verb** [T]

reprimand /ˈreprɪmɑːnd/ **verb** [T] to tell someone in an official way that they have done something wrong: [+ for + doing sth] *He was reprimanded for disclosing confidential information.* • **reprimand noun** [C]

reprint /riːˈprɪnt/ **verb** [T, I] to print a book again

reprisal /rɪˈpraɪzᵊl/ **noun** [C, U] something violent or unpleasant that is done to punish an enemy for something they have done: *The attack was **in reprisal** for police raids.* ∘ *He did not wish to be filmed because he **feared reprisals**.*

☑ Word partners for **reprisal**

fear reprisals • in reprisal for sth • a reprisal against/from sb

reproach¹ /rɪˈprəʊtʃ/ **noun** [C, U] criticism of someone, especially for not being successful or not doing what is expected: *There was a hint of reproach in his voice.* ∘ *The article gave the impression that the teachers were **above/beyond reproach** (= could not be criticized).* • **reproachful adj** showing criticism: *a **reproachful** look* • **reproachfully adv**

reproach² /rɪˈprəʊtʃ/ **verb** [T] to criticize someone for not being successful or not doing what is expected: [often reflexive] *You've no reason to reproach yourself.*

reproduce /ˌriːprəˈdjuːs/ **verb 1** [T] to make a copy of something: *The diagram is reproduced by permission of the original author.* **2** [I] formal If people, animals, or plants reproduce, they produce babies or young animals or plants.

reproduction /ˌriːprəˈdʌkʃᵊn/ **noun 1** [U] the process of producing babies or young animals and plants **2** [C] a copy of something, especially a painting

reproductive /ˌriːprəˈdʌktɪv/ **adj** [always before noun] relating to the process of producing babies or young animals and plants: *the **reproductive** organs*

reptile /ˈreptaɪl/ **noun** [C] an animal whose body is covered with scales (= pieces of hard skin), and whose blood changes temperature, for example a snake • **reptilian** /repˈtɪliən/ **adj** like a reptile, or relating to reptiles

republic /rɪˈpʌblɪk/ **noun** [C] a country with no king or queen but with an elected government

republican /rɪˈpʌblɪkən/ **noun** [C] **1** someone who supports the principles of a republic **2** **Republican** someone who supports the Republican Party in the US: *the Republican candidate* • **republican adj** relating to a republic

the Reˈpublican ˌParty noun [group] one of the two main political parties in the US

repudiate /rɪˈpjuːdieɪt/ **verb** [T] formal to refuse to accept or agree with something: *Cousteau **repudiated** the **criticism/claims**.* • **repudiation** /rɪˌpjuːdiˈeɪʃᵊn/ **noun** [U] formal

repugnant /rɪˈpʌɡnənt/ **adj** formal extremely unpleasant: *She thought the idea **morally repugnant**.* • **repugnance** /rɪˈpʌɡnəns/ **noun** [U] formal the state of being repugnant

repulse /rɪˈpʌls/ **verb** [T] **1** If someone or something repulses you, you think they are extremely unpleasant: *The smell of him repulsed her.* **2** to successfully stop a military attack: [often passive] *The enemy attack was quickly repulsed.*

repulsion /rɪˈpʌlʃᵊn/ **noun** [U, no plural] a strong feeling that someone or something is extremely unpleasant

repulsive /rɪˈpʌlsɪv/ **adj** extremely unpleasant, especially to look at: *a repulsive man with long, greasy hair*

reputable /ˈrepjətəbl/ **adj** known to be good and honest: *a reputable organization* → Opposite **disreputable**

reputation /ˌrepjəˈteɪʃᵊn/ **noun** [C] ⑫ the opinion that people have about someone or something based on their behaviour or char-

R

acter in the past: *Both hotels* **have a good reputation**. ∘ *He has a* **reputation for** *efficiency*.

☑ **Word partners for reputation**

have a reputation • a reputation **for** sth • a **bad/good** reputation • **acquire/establish/get** a reputation • **damage/destroy/ruin** sb's reputation

---

reputed /rɪˈpjuːtɪd/ *adj formal* believed by most people to be true: [+ to do sth] *The ghost of a young woman is reputed to haunt the building.* • **reputedly** *adv*

request¹ /rɪˈkwest/ *noun* [C, U] ⑤ a question which politely or officially asks for something: *His doctor* **made** *an urgent* **request for** *a copy of the report*. ∘ *An application form is available* **on request** (= *if you ask for it*). ∘ *A clause was added to the contract* **at his request** (= *because he asked*).

request² /rɪˈkwest/ *verb* [T] ⑤ to politely or officially ask for something: *We've requested a further two computers.* ∘ [+ that] *They requested that no photographs be taken in the church.*

requiem /ˈrekwiəm/ *noun* [C] a Christian ceremony where people pray for someone who has died, or a piece of music written for this ceremony

require /rɪˈkwaɪəʳ/ *verb* [T] **1** ⑤ to need or demand something: *Training to be a doctor requires a lot of hard work.* ∘ [+ that] *A recent law requires that all programmes are censored.* **2 require sb to do sth** ⑤ to officially demand that someone does something: [often passive] *You are required by law to produce a valid passport.*

❗ **Common learner error: require** or **request?**

The main meaning of **require** is 'need'.
Learning a language requires time and effort.
Request means 'ask for'.
I wrote a letter to request more information.
~~I wrote a letter to require more information.~~

---

requirement /rɪˈkwaɪəmənt/ *noun* [C] ⑫ something that is needed or demanded: *college* **entrance requirements** ∘ *Valid insurance is a* **legal requirement**.

requisite /ˈrekwɪzɪt/ *adj* [always before noun] *formal* needed for a particular purpose: *I felt that he lacked the* **requisite skills** *for the job.*

re-release /ˌriːrɪˈliːs/ *verb* [T] to make a record or film available for people to buy or see for a second time

rerun /ˈriːrʌn/ *noun* [C] *US* (*UK/US* **repeat**) a television or radio programme or film that is broadcast again

reschedule /ˌriːˈʃedjuːl/ ⓤ /ˌriːˈskedʒuːl/ *verb* [T] to agree a new and later date for something to happen

rescue¹ /ˈreskjuː/ *verb* [T] (**rescuing, rescued**) ⑤ to save someone from a dangerous or unpleasant situation: *Fifty passengers had to be rescued from a sinking ship.* • **rescuer** *noun* [C]

rescue² /ˈreskjuː/ *noun* **1** ⑤ [C, U] an occasion when someone is saved from a dangerous or unpleasant situation: *an unsuccessful* **rescue attempt** **2** **come to the/sb's rescue** to help someone who is in a difficult situation: *I forgot my purse but Anna came to the rescue and lent me some money.*

research¹ /rɪˈsɜːtʃ/ *noun* [U] ⑤ detailed study of a subject in order to discover new information: *research into language development* ∘ *They are* **doing research** *into the effects of passive smoking.* ∘ *a* **research project** → *See also:* **market research**

☑ **Word partners for research**

carry out/conduct/do research • research **indicates/proves/reveals/suggests** sth • research **into** sth • a research **assistant/institute/programme/project**

---

research² /rɪˈsɜːtʃ/ *verb* [I, T] ⑫ to study a subject in detail in order to discover new information about it: *He spent several years researching a rare African dialect.* • **researcher** *noun* [C]

resemblance /rɪˈzembləns/ *noun* [C, U] similarity between two people or things, especially in their appearance: *There's a striking* **resemblance between** *Diane and her mother.* ∘ *He* **bears a resemblance to** (= *looks like*) *someone I used to know.*

resemble /rɪˈzembl/ *verb* [T] to look like or be like someone or something: *She resembles her father.*

resent /rɪˈzent/ *verb* [T] to feel angry and upset about a situation or about something that someone has done: [+ doing sth] *I resent having to work late.* ∘ *He* **resents the fact** *that she gets more money than he does.*

resentful /rɪˈzentfˀl/ *adj* angry and upset about a situation that you think is unfair: *He was bitterly* **resentful of** *his brother's success.* • **resentfully** *adv* • **resentfulness** *noun* [U]

resentment /rɪˈzentmənt/ *noun* [U] a feeling of anger about a situation that you think is unfair

reservation /ˌrezəˈveɪʃˀn/ *noun* **1** [C] ⑤ an arrangement that you make to have a seat on an aircraft, a room in a hotel, etc: *I'd like to* **make** *a* **reservation** *for Friday evening.* **2** [C, U] a doubt or a feeling that you do not agree with something completely: *I still* **have reservations** *about her ability to do the job.*

reserve¹ /rɪˈzɜːv/ *verb* [T] **1** ⑤ to arrange to have a seat on an aircraft, a room in a hotel, etc: *I'd like to reserve two seats on the 9:15 to Birmingham.* **2** ⑤ to not allow people to use something because it is only for a particular person or for a particular purpose: *This seat is* **reserved for** *elderly or disabled passengers.*

reserve² /rɪˈzɜːv/ *noun* **1** SUPPLY ▷ [C] a supply of something that you keep until it is needed: *emergency cash reserves* **2 in reserve** ready to be used if you need it: *I always keep a little money in reserve.* **3** QUALITY ▷ [U] behaviour that does not show what you are thinking or feeling **4** SPORT ▷ [C] in sport, an extra player who is ready to play if one of the other players has an

---

R

injury **5** AREA ▷ [C] 🅱️ an area of land where animals and plants are protected → See also **nature reserve**

reserved /rɪˈzɜːvd/ **adj** not wanting to show what you are thinking or feeling: *a quiet, reserved woman*

reservoir /ˈrezəvwɑːʳ/ **noun** [C] an artificial lake where water is stored before it goes to people's houses

reset (button) noun [C] a button or switch on a computer that allows the user to turn the computer off and then on again when a program does not work correctly

reshuffle /ˌriːˈʃʌfl/ **noun** [C] a change in who has which job in an organization, especially a government: *a government reshuffle* • **reshuffle verb** [T]

reside /rɪˈzaɪd/ **verb** formal **reside in/with, etc** to live somewhere: *My sister currently resides in Seattle.*

residence /ˈrezɪdəns/ **noun** formal **1** [C] a building where someone lives: *the Queen's official residence* **2** [U] the fact of living somewhere: *He took up residence* (= started to live) *in St. Louis.* **3 in residence** living or working somewhere: *He was writer in residence with a professional theatre company.* → See also **hall of residence**

residence hall noun [C] US (also **dormitory**, UK **hall of residence**) a building where university or college students live

resident¹ /ˈrezɪdənt/ **noun** [C] **1** 🅱️ someone who lives in a particular place: *complaints from local residents* **2** US a doctor who is working in a hospital to get extra training in a particular area of medicine

resident² /ˈrezɪdənt/ **adj** living in a place: *She has been resident in Britain for most of her life.*

residential /ˌrezɪˈdenʃəl/ **adj 1** 🅱️ A residential area has only houses and not offices or factories. **2** UK A residential job or course is one where you live at the same place as you work or study.

residual /rɪˈzɪdjuəl/ **adj** remaining: *residual value*

residue /ˈrezɪdjuː/ **noun** [C] something that remains after most of a substance has gone or been removed

resign /rɪˈzaɪn/ **verb** [I, T] 🅱️ to officially tell your employer that you are leaving your job: *She resigned as headteacher.* ○ *Mr Aitken has resigned from the company.*

PHRASAL VERB **resign yourself to sth** to make yourself accept something that you do not like because you cannot easily change it: *He resigned himself to living alone.*

📋 **Word partners for resignation**

accept/call for sb's resignation • announce/hand in/tender your resignation • the resignation of sb • sb's resignation as [manager/chairman, etc] • a letter of resignation

---

resignation /ˌrezɪɡˈneɪʃən/ **noun 1** [C, U] the act of telling your employer that you are leaving your job: *a letter of resignation* ○ *I handed in my resignation yesterday.* **2** [U] the feeling that

you have to accept something that you do not like because you cannot easily change it

resilient /rɪˈzɪliənt/ **adj** strong enough to get better quickly after damage, illness, shock, etc: *Growth figures show that the economy is still fairly resilient.* • **resilience** /rɪˈzɪliəns/ **noun** [U]

resin /ˈrezɪn/ **noun** [C, U] **1** a thick, sticky substance that is produced by some trees **2** a substance that is used for making plastics

resist /rɪˈzɪst/ **verb** [I, T] **1** AVOID ▷ 🅱️ to stop yourself from doing something that you want to do: *I can't resist chocolate.* ○ *[+ doing sth] I just can't resist reading other people's mail.* **2** NOT ACCEPT ▷ to refuse to accept something and try to stop it from happening: *The President is resisting calls for him to resign.* **3** FIGHT ▷ to fight against someone or something that is attacking you: *British troops resisted the attack for two days.*

resistance /rɪˈzɪstəns/ **noun** [U, no plural] **1** DISAGREE ▷ If there is resistance to a change, idea, etc, people disagree with it and refuse to accept it: *resistance to political change* **2** FIGHT ▷ If someone puts up resistance, they fight against someone who is attacking them: *She didn't put up much resistance.* **3** ILLNESS ▷ the ability of your body to not be affected by illnesses: *Cold weather may lower the body's resistance to infection.*

resistant /rɪˈzɪstənt/ **adj 1** not wanting to accept something, especially changes or new ideas: *They're resistant to change.* **2** not harmed or affected by something: *a water-resistant cover* ○ *Bacteria can become resistant to antibiotics.*

resolute /ˈrezəluːt/ **adj** formal determined not to change what you do or believe because you think that you are right: *a resolute opponent of the war* • **resolutely adv**

resolution /ˌrezəˈluːʃən/ **noun 1** DECISION ▷ [C] an official decision that is made after a group or organization have voted: *Congress passed a resolution in support of the plan* (= voted to support it). **2** PROMISE ▷ [C] a promise to yourself to do something: *My New Year's resolution is to do more exercise.* **3** SOLUTION ▷ [U, no plural] formal the solution to a problem: *a successful resolution to the crisis* **4** DETERMINATION ▷ [U] formal the quality of being determined

resolve¹ /rɪˈzɒlv/ **verb 1** [T] to solve or end a problem or difficulty: *an attempt to resolve the dispute* **2** [I, T] formal to decide that you will do something and be determined to do it: *[+ to do sth] I have resolved to keep my bedroom tidy.*

resolve² /rɪˈzɒlv/ **noun** [U] formal determination to do something

resonant /ˈrezənənt/ **adj** A resonant sound is loud and clear: *a deep, resonant voice* • **resonance** /ˈrezənəns/ **noun** [U]

resonate /ˈrezəneɪt/ **verb** [I] to make a loud, clear sound

resort¹ /rɪˈzɔːt/ **noun 1** 🅱️ [C] a place where many people go for a holiday: *a ski resort* **2 a last resort** something that you do because everything else has failed: *Soldiers were given the authority to shoot, but only as a last resort.*

---

yes | k cat | ŋ ring | ʃ she | θ thin | ð this | ʒ decision | dʒ jar | tʃ chip | æ cat | e bed | ə ago | ɪ sit | i cosy | ɒ hot | ʌ run | ʊ put |

resort² /rɪ'zɔːt/ **verb**

PHRASAL VERB **resort to sth/doing sth** to do something that you do not want to do because you cannot find any other way of achieving something: *They should be able to control the riots without resorting to violence.*

resound /rɪ'zaʊnd/ **verb** [I] to make a loud sound, or to be filled with a loud sound: *The whole hall resounded with applause.*

resounding /rɪ'zaʊndɪŋ/ **adj** [always before noun] **1** very loud: *resounding applause* **2 a resounding success/victory/failure, etc** a very great success, victory, etc

resource /rɪ'zɔːs/, /'riːsɔːrs/ **noun** [C] ⑱ something that a country, person, or organization has that they can use: [usually plural] *natural resources* → See also **human resources**

resourceful /rɪ'zɔːsfəl/ **adj** good at finding ways to solve problems • **resourcefulness noun** [U]

respect¹ /rɪ'spekt/ **noun 1** POLITE ▷ [U] ⑪ polite behaviour towards someone, especially because they are older or more important than you: *You should show more respect for your parents.* **2** ADMIRATION ▷ [U] ⑪ admiration for someone because of their knowledge, skill, or achievements: *She's an excellent teacher and I have the greatest respect for her.* **3** SHOW IMPORTANCE ▷ [U] behaviour that shows you think something is important or needs to be dealt with carefully: *Electricity can be dangerous and should always be treated with respect.* **4 in this respect/many respects** ⑫ in a particular way, or in many ways: *The school has changed in many respects.* **5 with respect to sth; in respect of sth** formal ⑫ relating to a particular thing: *I am writing with respect to your letter of 24 June.* **6 pay your respects a** formal to visit someone or go to talk to them **b** (also **pay your last respects**) to go to someone's funeral → See also **self-respect**

⊘ Word partners for **respect**

command respect • **have/show** [great/no, etc] respect for sb • **treat** sb/sth **with** respect

respect² /rɪ'spekt/ **verb** [T] **1** ⑪ to admire someone because of their knowledge, achievements, etc: *I respect him for his honesty.* **2** ⑫ If you respect someone's rights, customs, wishes, etc you accept their importance and are careful not to do anything they would not want.

respectable /rɪ'spektəbl/ **adj 1** ⑫ behaving in a socially acceptable way or looking socially acceptable: *a respectable family ○ a respectable hotel* **2** large enough or good enough: *a respectable income* • **respectably adv** • **respectability** /rɪ,spektə'bɪləti/ **noun** [U]

respected /rɪ'spektɪd/ **adj** ⑫ admired by people because of your knowledge, achievements, etc: *a highly respected doctor*

respectful /rɪ'spektfəl/ **adj** showing respect for someone or something • **respectfully adv**

respective /rɪ'spektɪv/ **adj** [always before noun] relating to each of the people or things that you have just talked about: *members of staff and their respective partners*

respectively /rɪ'spektɪvli/ **adv** in the same order as the people or things you have just talked about: *Mr Ewing and Mr Campbell gave £2000 and £250 respectively.*

respiration /,respər'eɪʃən/ **noun** [U] the proces of breathing

respiratory /rɪ'spɪrətəri/ ⑤ /'respərətɔːri/ **ad** [always before noun] relating to the process c breathing: *respiratory illnesses*

respite /'respaɪt/ ⑤ /'respɪt/ **noun** [U, no plural] short period of rest from something difficult o unpleasant: *The weekend was a brief respite from the pressures of work.*

respond /rɪ'spɒnd/ **verb** [I] **1** ⑫ to say or d something as an answer or reaction to some thing that has been said or done: [+ by + doin sth] *The government has responded by sendin food and medical supplies to the region. ○ Hou quickly did the police respond to the call?* **2** t improve as the result of a particular medica treatment: *She's responding well to drug treat ment.*

respondent /rɪ'spɒndənt/ **noun** [C] someon who has answered a request for information [usually plural] *More than half the respondents wer opposed to the new tax.*

response /rɪ'spɒns/ **noun** [C, U] ⑫ an answer o reaction to something that has been said o done: *The President's comments provoked a angry response from students. ○ I'm writing i response to your letter of 14 February.*

⊘ Word partners for **response**

in response to sth • sb's response **to** sth • **draw/elicit/provoke** a response • sb's **immediate/initial/instinctive** response

responsibility /rɪ,spɒnsə'bɪləti/ **noun 1** ⑫ [C U] something that it is your job or duty to dea with: *The head of the department has variou additional responsibilities. ○* [+ to do sth] *It is you responsibility to make sure that your homework i done on time.* **2 take/accept/claim responsibil ity for sth** ⑫ to say that you have done something or caused something to happen especially something bad: *No one has ye claimed responsibility for yesterday's bomb attack*

⊘ Word partners for **responsibility**

abdicate/accept/assume/claim/take/shirk responsibility • **collective/heavy/total** responsibility • responsibility **for** sth

responsible /rɪ'spɒnsəbl/ **adj 1 be responsible for sb/sth/doing sth** ⑪ to be the person whose duty is to deal with someone or something: *I'n responsible for looking after the children in th evenings.* **2 be responsible for sth/doing sth** ⑫ to be the person who caused something t happen, especially something bad: *Who wa responsible for the accident?* **3** ⑫ showing goo judgment and able to be trusted: *a responsibl attitude* → Opposite **irresponsible 4** ⑫ A responsible job is important because you hav to make decisions that affect other people. **5 b responsible to sb** If you are responsible t someone at work, they are in a higher positio

R

than you and you have to tell them what you have done.

esponsibly /rɪˈspɒnsəbli/ **adv** in a way that shows you have good judgment and can be trusted: *to behave/act responsibly*

esponsive /rɪˈspɒnsɪv/ **adj** listening to someone or something and having a positive and quick reaction to them: *a wonderfully responsive audience* ∘ *They have not been very responsive to the needs of disabled customers.* • **responsiveness noun** [U]

est¹ /rest/ **noun 1 the rest** **ⓐ** the part of something that remains, or the others that remain: *I'm not sure I want to spend the rest of my life with him.* ∘ *She was slightly older than the rest of us.* **2** **ⓐ** [C, U] a period of time when you relax or sleep: *Why don't you have a rest?* ∘ *I must get some rest.* **3 come to rest** to stop moving → See also **put/set sb's mind¹ at rest**

est² /rest/ **verb 1** **ⓑ** [I] to relax or sleep because you are tired after doing an activity or because you are sick: *Pete's resting after his long drive.* **2 rest your eyes/feet/legs, etc** **ⓑ** to stop using your eyes/feet, etc for a while because they are tired **3 rest (sth) on/against, etc** If something rests somewhere, or if you rest it somewhere, it is supported by something else: *She rested her elbows on the table.* → See also **rest on your laurels**

> ⚠ Common learner error: **rest**, **stay**, or **remain**?
>
> **Rest** means to relax or sleep because you are tired or ill.
>
> *The doctor told him to rest.*
>
> **Stay** means to continue to be in the same place, job, or particular state.
>
> *It was raining, so we stayed at home.*
>
> ~~It was raining, so we rested at home.~~
>
> **Remain** means to continue to be in the same state, or to continue to exist when everything or everyone else has gone.
>
> *He remained unconscious for a week after the accident.*
>
> *After the earthquake, nothing remained of the village.*

PHRASAL VERB **rest on/upon sth** formal to depend on something: *The whole future of the team rests on his decision.*

estart /ˌriːˈstɑːt/ **verb** [T] **1** to start something again that had stopped: *They want to restart the talks.* **2** If you restart a computer, you turn it off and then on again.

estaurant /ˈrestərɒnt/ **noun** [C] **ⓐ** a place where you can buy and eat a meal: *an Italian/vegetarian restaurant* ∘ *We had lunch at/in a restaurant near the station.*

> 🗒 Word partners for **restaurant**
>
> go to a restaurant • manage/own/run a restaurant • a restaurant offers/serves/specializes in sth • at/in a restaurant

estaurateur /ˌrestɒrəˈtɜːʳ/ **noun** [C] someone who owns a restaurant

restful /ˈrestfəl/ **adj** making you calm and relaxed: *restful music*

restive /ˈrestɪv/ **adj** formal unable to be quiet and calm

restless /ˈrestləs/ **adj 1** unable to be still or relax because you are bored or nervous: *The audience was getting restless.* **2** not satisfied with what you are doing now and wanting something new: *After a while in the same relationship I start to get restless.* • **restlessly adv** • **restlessness noun** [U]

restore /rɪˈstɔːʳ/ **verb** [T] **1 MAKE EXIST** ▷ to make something good exist again: *Three wins in a row helped restore the team's confidence.* ∘ *Peace has now been restored in the region.* **2 REPAIR** ▷ **ⓑ** to repair something old: *to restore antiques* **3 RETURN** ▷ formal to give something back to the person it was stolen from or who lost it: *The painting was restored to its rightful owner.* • **restoration** /ˌrestəˈreɪʃən/ **noun** [C, U] *The building is now closed for restoration* (= repair work). ∘ *the restoration* (= return) *of the former government*

restrain /rɪˈstreɪn/ **verb** [T] **1** to stop someone doing something, sometimes by using force: *He became violent and had to be physically restrained.* ∘ [+ from + doing sth] *I had to restrain myself from shouting at him.* **2** to limit something: *to restrain arms sales*

restrained /rɪˈstreɪnd/ **adj** calm and not showing emotions: *I was expecting him to be furious but he was very restrained.* → Opposite **unrestrained**

restraint /rɪˈstreɪnt/ **noun 1** [U] control over your feelings **2** [C] a control on something: *wage restraints*

restrict /rɪˈstrɪkt/ **verb** [T] to limit something: *They've brought in new laws to restrict the sale of cigarettes.* ∘ *I restrict myself to one cup of coffee a day.*

restricted /rɪˈstrɪktɪd/ **adj** controlled or limited: *They do good food but the choice is fairly restricted.*

restriction /rɪˈstrɪkʃən/ **noun** [C, U] a rule or law that limits what people can do: *There are restrictions on how many goods you can bring into the country.* ∘ *parking restrictions*

restrictive /rɪˈstrɪktɪv/ **adj** limiting activities too much: *restrictive practices*

restroom /ˈrestruːm/ **noun** [C] US a room with toilets that is in a public place, for example in a restaurant → See Note at **toilet**

restructure /ˌriːˈstrʌktʃəʳ/ **verb** [I, T] to organize a system or organization in a new way • **restructuring noun** [U]

result¹ /rɪˈzʌlt/ **noun 1 HAPPEN** ▷ [C, U] **ⓑ** something that happens or exists because something else has happened: *Unemployment has risen as a direct result of new economic policies.* ∘ *Most accidents are the result of human error.* **2 COMPETITION** ▷ [C] **ⓑ** the score or number of votes at the end of a competition or election: *The election results will be known by Sunday.* **3 INFORMATION** ▷ [C] **ⓑ** information that you get from something such as an exam, a scientific

R

experiment, or a medical test: *She's waiting for the results of a blood test.*

> **Word partners for result**
>
> the result **of** sth • **as a** result **of** sth • **with** the result **that** • with catastrophic/disastrous, etc results • excellent/good/disappointing/disastrous results

result² /rɪˈzʌlt/ **verb** [I] to happen or exist because something else has happened: *There was a food shortage resulting from the lack of rainfall.*

PHRASAL VERB **result in** sth ⑫ to be the reason something happens: *The improvements in training resulted in increased wins.*

resultant /rɪˈzʌltənt/ **adj** formal happening as a result of something else

resume /rɪˈzjuːm/ **verb** [I, T] formal If an activity resumes, or if you resume it, it starts again: *The talks are due to resume today.* • **resumption** /rɪˈzʌmʃən/ **noun** [no plural]

résumé /ˈrezəmeɪ/ **noun** [C] US (mainly UK **CV**) a document that describes your qualifications and the jobs that you have done, which you send to an employer that you want to work for

resurface /ˌriːˈsɜːfɪs/ **verb** [I] to appear again after having been lost or forgotten: *The story resurfaced in the news again last week.*

resurgence /rɪˈsɜːdʒəns/ **noun** [no plural] a time when something starts to happen again or people become interested in something again: *There has been a resurgence of interest in the game.* • **resurgent** /rɪˈsɜːdʒənt/ **adj** happening again

resurrect /ˌrezərˈekt/ **verb** [T] to make something exist again that has not existed for a long time: *He is trying to resurrect his acting career.*

resurrection /ˌrezərˈekʃən/ **noun** [U] **1** the process of starting to exist again after not existing for a long period: *the resurrection of a fashion* **2** in the Christian religion, Jesus Christ's return to life after he was killed

resuscitate /rɪˈsʌsɪteɪt/ **verb** [T] to make someone breathe again when they have stopped breathing • **resuscitation** /rɪˌsʌsɪˈteɪʃən/ **noun** [U]

retail¹ /ˈriːteɪl/ **noun** [U] the activity of selling products to the public in shops and on the internet: *jobs in retail*

retail² /ˈriːteɪl/ **verb** retail **at/for £50/$100, etc** to be sold to the public for a particular price: *This computer retails at $2,000.*

retailer /ˈriːteɪlər/ **noun** [C] someone who sells products to the public

retailing /ˈriːteɪlɪŋ/ **noun** [U] the business of selling products to customers in shops

retain /rɪˈteɪn/ **verb** [T] to continue to keep something: *Will this beauty queen retain her crown?*

retaliate /rɪˈtælieɪt/ **verb** [I] to do something bad to someone because they have done something bad to you: *They have threatened to retaliate against any troops that attack.* • **retaliation** /rɪˌtæliˈeɪʃən/ **noun** [U] *They bombed the hotel in* retaliation **for** the arrests. • **retaliatory** /rɪˈtæliətəri/ **adj** retaliatory measures

retention /rɪˈtenʃən/ **noun** [U] continuing keep something

rethink /ˌriːˈθɪŋk/ **verb** [I, T] (**rethought**) change what you think about something what you plan to do: *We've had to rethink ou strategy.* • **rethink** /ˈriːθɪŋk/ **noun** [no plural] *Th whole issue needs a fundamental rethink.*

reticent /ˈretɪsənt/ **adj** saying little about wha you think or feel: *He was reticent about h private life.* • **reticence** /ˈretɪsəns/ **noun** [U]

retina /ˈretɪnə/ **noun** [C] a part at the back of th eye, which is affected by light and send messages to the brain

retire /rɪˈtaɪər/ **verb** [I] **1** ⑪ to leave your job an stop working, usually because you are old: *Sh retired from the company in 2010.* **2** formal to g to another place where you can be alone c more private: *After dinner, he retired to h bedroom.*

retired /rɪˈtaɪəd/ **adj** ⑫ having stopped workin often because you are old: *a retired farme teacher*

retiree /rɪˈtaɪriː/ **noun** [C] US someone who ha stopped working, usually because they are old

retirement /rɪˈtaɪəmənt/ **noun** [C, U] **1** ⑫ th time at which you leave your job and sto working, usually because you are old: *He taking early retirement.* **2** ⑫ the period c your life after you have stopped working: *W wish you a long and happy retirement.*

> **Word partners for retirement**
>
> take early retirement • **in** retirement • retirement **from** sth • retirement **age**

retiring /rɪˈtaɪərɪŋ/ **adj** shy and quiet

retort /rɪˈtɔːt/ **verb** [T] formal to answer someon quickly in an angry or funny way: *"That doesn concern you," she retorted sharply.* • **retort nou** [C] formal

retrace /rɪˈtreɪs/ **verb** retrace your steps to g back somewhere the same way that you came: *was lost so I retraced my steps.*

retract /rɪˈtrækt/ **verb** [I, T] formal to admit tha something you said before was not true: *Severa key witnesses have retracted their statement. claims/allegations.*

retrain /ˌriːˈtreɪn/ **verb** [T] to learn a new skill s you can do a different job: *Owen used to be a actor but now he's retraining as a teacher.*

retraining /ˌriːˈtreɪnɪŋ/ **noun** [U] the process c learning new skills so that you can do a differer job

retreat¹ /rɪˈtriːt/ **verb** [I] **1** When soldiers retrea they move away from the enemy, especially t avoid fighting: *The army was forced to retrea* **2** retreat **to/into, etc** to go away to a place c situation that is safer or quieter: *She retreate into the bathroom for some peace and quiet.*

retreat² /rɪˈtriːt/ **noun 1** MOVE ▷ [U, no plural] move away, especially to a place or situation tha is safer or quieter: *He saw the dog comin towards him and beat a hasty retreat* (= move quickly away). **2** MILITARY ▷ [C, U] a move bac by soldiers or an army, especially to avoid fighting: *a strategic retreat* **3 PLACE** ▷ [C] a quiet place where you can go to rest or be alone: *a mountain retreat*

retrial /ˌriːˈtraɪəl/ *noun* [C] a new trial for a crime that has already been judged in a law court: *The judge ordered a retrial.*

retribution /ˌretrɪˈbjuːʃən/ *noun* [U] formal punishment for something morally wrong that was done: *They're seeking **retribution for** the killings.*

retrieve /rɪˈtriːv/ *verb* [T] to get something after first finding it: *I've just **retrieved** the ball **from** the bottom of the pond.* ∘ *computer tools for **retrieving information*** • **retrieval** *noun* [U] the act of retrieving something

retriever /rɪˈtriːvər/ *noun* [C] a large dog with thick black or light brown hair

retro /ˈretrəʊ/ *adj* looking or sounding like something from the past: *His clothes had a retro look.*

retrosexual /ˌretrəʊˈseksjuəl/ *noun* [C] a man who is sexually attracted to women and is not interested in fashion or the way he looks → Compare **metrosexual**

retrospect /ˈretrəʊspekt/ *noun* **in retrospect** thinking now about something in the past: *In retrospect, I should probably have told her.*

retrospective¹ /ˌretrəʊˈspektɪv/ *noun* [C] a show of work done by an artist over many years

retrospective² /ˌretrəʊˈspektɪv/ *adj* If a law or decision is retrospective, it affects situations in the past as well as in the future. • **retrospectively** *adv*

return¹ /rɪˈtɜːn/ *verb* **1 GO BACK** ▷ [I] Ⓐ₂ to go or come back to a place where you were before: *She **returned to** America in 1954.* ∘ *I won't **return from** my holiday till May.* **2 GIVE BACK** ▷ [T] Ⓐ₂ to give, send, or put something back where it came from: *He immediately **returned** the records **to** the files.* **3 return to sth a** Ⓑ₂ to start doing an activity again or talking about something again: *I **returned to** work three months after Susie was born.* **b** to go back to a previous condition: *Life has begun to **return to** normal now that the war is over.* **4 HAPPEN AGAIN** ▷ [I] Ⓑ₂ If something returns, it happens again: *If the pains **return** phone the doctor.* **5 DO THE SAME** ▷ [T] Ⓑ₂ to react to something that someone does or says by doing or saying the same: *I must **return** Michael's **call** (= telephone him because he telephoned me earlier).* **6 return a verdict/sentence** to announce if someone is guilty or not guilty or what punishment the person will be given in a law court: *The jury **returned** a verdict of guilty.* **7 SPORTS** ▷ [T] to hit or throw a ball back to someone when playing a sport

return² /rɪˈtɜːn/ *noun* **1 GOING BACK** ▷ [no plural] Ⓑ₁ an occasion when someone goes or comes back to a place where they were before: *On his **return** to Sydney, he started up a business.* **2 GIVING BACK** ▷ [no plural] the act of giving, putting, or sending something back: *the **return** of the stolen goods* **3 ACTIVITY** ▷ [no plural] a time when someone starts an activity again: *This film marks his **return to** acting.* **4 HAPPENING AGAIN** ▷ [no plural] a time when something

starts to happen or be present again: *What we are seeing here is **a return to** traditional values.* **5 TICKET** ▷ [C] UK (US **round-trip ticket**) Ⓑ₁ a ticket that lets you travel to a place and back again, for example on a train **6 PROFIT** ▷ [C, U] the profit that you get from an investment: *This fund has shown **high returns** for the last five years.* **7 in return** Ⓑ₂ in exchange for something or as a reaction to something: *I'd like to give them something **in return for** everything they've done for us.* **8 SPORTS** ▷ [C] an occasion when a ball is thrown or hit back to another player in a sports game: *She hit an excellent **return**.* **9 COMPUTER** ▷ [U] Ⓑ₁ a key on a computer keyboard that is used to make the computer accept information or to start a new line in a document: *Type in the password and **press return**.* → See also **day return**

returnable /rɪˈtɜːnəbl/ *adj* If something is returnable, it can be taken or given back: *a **returnable deposit***

reunification /ˌriːjuːnɪfɪˈkeɪʃən/ *noun* [U] a process in which a country that was divided into smaller countries is joined together again as one country: *the reunification of Germany*

reunion /ˌriːˈjuːniən/ *noun* [C] an occasion when people who have not met each other for a long time meet again: *a **family/school reunion***

> ☑ Word partners for **reunion**
>
> **have/go to** a reunion • an **emotional** reunion • a reunion **of** sb • sb's reunion **with** sb • a **family/school** reunion

reunite /ˌriːjuːˈnaɪt/ *verb* [I, T] to meet again after being apart for a long time, or to bring people together who have been apart for a long time: [often passive] *Years later, he was **reunited with** his brother.*

reuse /ˌriːˈjuːz/ *verb* [T] to find a new use for something so that it does not have to be thrown away: *Businesses are finding new ways to reuse materials.* • **reusable** *adj*

rev /rev/ *verb* [I, T] (**revving, revved**) (also **rev up**) to increase the engine speed of a vehicle: *He revved the engine and drove off.*

Rev written abbreviation for Reverend (= title of Christian official): *Rev Jo Harding*

revamp /ˌriːˈvæmp/ *verb* [T] to change something in order to make it better: *They're revamping the restaurant.*

Revd written abbreviation for Reverend (= title of Christian official): *the Revd Laurie Clow*

reveal /rɪˈviːl/ *verb* [T] **1** Ⓑ₂ to give someone a piece of information that is surprising or that was previously secret: [+ that] *It was revealed in this morning's papers that the couple intend to marry.* **2** to allow something to be seen that was previously hidden: *His shirt came up at the back, revealing an expanse of white skin.*

revealing /rɪˈviːlɪŋ/ *adj* **1** showing someone's true character or the true facts about someone or something: *a revealing biography/remark* **2** If clothes are revealing, they show a lot of your body.

R

revel /ˈrevᵊl/ **verb** (mainly UK **revelling, revelled,** US **reveling, reveled**)

PHRASAL VERB **revel in sth** to enjoy a situation or activity very much: *He revelled in his role as team manager.*

revelation /ˌrevᵊlˈeɪʃᵊn/ **noun 1** [C] a piece of information that is discovered although it was intended to be kept secret: *He resigned following **revelations about** his private life.* **2 be a revelation** to be an extremely pleasant surprise: *Anna's boyfriend was a revelation.*

revenge /rɪˈvendʒ/ **noun** [U] 🔲 something that you do to punish someone who has done something bad to you: *He's made life very difficult for me but I'll **get/take** my **revenge**. ◦ He was shot **in revenge** for the murder.*

> 🗹 Word partners for **revenge**
>
> **get/plot/seek/take** revenge • **in revenge for** sth • revenge **against/on** sb • an **act of** revenge

revenue /ˈrevᵊnjuː/ **noun** [U] (also **revenues**) large amounts of money received by a government as tax, or by a company

reverberate /rɪˈvɜːbᵊreɪt/ **verb** [I] If a sound reverberates, it is heard for a long time as it is sent back from different surfaces: *The sound of the shots reverberated around the building.*

revere /rɪˈvɪəʳ/ **verb** [T] formal to respect and admire someone very much: *a revered religious leader*

reverence /ˈrevᵊrᵊns/ **noun** [U] formal a strong feeling of respect and admiration

Reverend /ˈrevᵊrᵊnd/ **adj** used as a title before the name of some Christian officials: *the Reverend Alan Pringle*

reverie /ˈrevᵊri/ **noun** [C] formal a pleasant state in which you are thinking of something else, not what is happening around you

reversal /rɪˈvɜːsᵊl/ **noun** [C] a change to the opposite of something: *In a reversal of traditional roles, Paul stayed at home to look after the baby and Clare went out to work.*

reverse¹ /rɪˈvɜːs/ **verb 1** [I, T] 🔲 to drive a vehicle backwards: *I hate reversing into parking spaces.* **2** [T] to change a situation or change the order of things so that it becomes the opposite: *It is unlikely that the judge will **reverse** his decision.*

reverse² /rɪˈvɜːs/ **noun 1 the reverse** the opposite of what has been suggested: *"So, is he happier?" "Quite the reverse – I've never seen him look so miserable."* **2** 🔲 [U] (also re₊verse ˈgear) the method of controlling a vehicle that makes it go backwards: *Put the car **into** reverse.* **3 in reverse** in the opposite order or way: *Do the same steps but this time in reverse.*

reverse³ /rɪˈvɜːs/ **adj** [always before noun] opposite to the usual way or to the way you have just described: *I'm going to read out the names of the winners in reverse order.*

reversible /rɪˈvɜːsəbl/ **adj 1** If something is reversible, it can be changed back to what it was before: *Most of the damage done to the cells is*

reversible. → Opposite **irreversible 2** Reversibl clothes can be worn so that the inside is th outside: *a reversible jacket*

revert /rɪˈvɜːt/ **verb**

PHRASAL VERB **revert to sth/doing sth** to go bac to how something was before: *For a while I at low-fat food but then I reverted to my old eatin habits.* • **reversion** /rɪˈvɜːʃᵊn/ **noun** [U, no plural]

review¹ /rɪˈvjuː/ **noun 1** [C, U] the process o considering something again in order to mak changes to it: *a **review of** teachers' pay ◦ Th policy is now **under review** (= being considered* **2** [C] 🔲 a report in a newspaper, magazine, o programme that gives an opinion about a ne book, film, etc: *a book review ◦ The film has ha **mixed reviews** (= some good, some bad).*

> 🗹 Word partners for **review**
>
> **carry out** a review • a review **of** sth • be **under** review

review² /rɪˈvjuː/ **verb 1** CONSIDER ▷ [T] t consider something again in order to decide changes should be made: *The courts will revie her case.* **2** REPORT ▷ [T] 🔲 to give your opinio in a report about a film, book, televisio programme, etc: *He reviews films for the Time* **3** STUDY ▷ [I, T] US (UK **revise**) to study a subjec before you take a test

reviewer /rɪˈvjuːəʳ/ **noun** [C] someone wh writes reviews of a book, film, etc

reviled /rɪˈvaɪld/ **adj** hated: *He is possibly th most reviled man in Britain.*

revise /rɪˈvaɪz/ **verb 1** [T] 🔲 to change some thing so that it is more accurate: *a revised editio of the book* **2** [I, T] UK (US **review**) 🔲 to study subject before you take a test

revision /rɪˈvɪʒᵊn/ **noun 1** [C, U] a change t something to make it more accurate: *a dow ward revision of prices* **2** [U] UK 🔲 study that yo do before taking a test

revitalize (also UK **-ise**) /ˌriːˈvaɪtᵊlaɪz/ **verb** [T] t make something more active or exciting *attempts to revitalize the city*

revival /rɪˈvaɪvᵊl/ **noun 1** [C, U] a situation i which something becomes popular again: *revival in folk music ◦ Yoga is **enjoying** revival.* **2** [C] a performance of a play, oper etc that has not been performed for a long tim

revive /rɪˈvaɪv/ **verb 1** EXIST AGAIN ▷ [T] to mak something from the past exist again: *to reviv memories ◦ A lot of traditional skills are currentl being revived.* **2** CONSCIOUS ▷ [I, T] to becom conscious again or make someone consciou again: *A police officer tried unsuccessfully t revive her.* **3** FEEL BETTER ▷ [I, T] to start to fee healthier and more active again, or to mak someone feel this way: *A cup of tea an something to eat might revive you.*

revoke /rɪˈvəʊk/ **verb** [T] formal to stop someon having official permission to do something, o to change an official decision: *His work perm was revoked after six months.*

revolt¹ /rɪˈvəʊlt/ **noun** [C, U] a situation in whic people try to change a government, often usin violence, or in which they refuse to accept someone's authority: *a slave/peasant revolt*

revolt² /rɪˈvəʊlt/ **verb 1** [I] to try to change a government, often using violence, or to refuse to accept someone's authority: *Many were killed when nationalists **revolted against** the new government.* **2 be revolted by sth** to think that something is extremely unpleasant

revolting /rɪˈvəʊltɪŋ/ **adj** extremely unpleasant

revolution /ˌrevəˈluːʃən/ **noun 1** POLITICS ▷ [C, U] 🅱2 a change in the way a country is governed, usually to a different political system and often using violence or war: *the French Revolution* **2** CHANGE ▷ [C] 🅱2 a very important change in the way people think or do things: *the techno-logical revolution* ∘ *This discovery caused a **revolution in** medicine.* **3** CIRCLE ▷ [C, U] one whole circular movement around a central point, for example one whole movement of a wheel

revolutionary¹ /ˌrevəˈluːʃənəri/ **adj 1** 🅱2 com-pletely different from what was done before: *The twentieth century has brought about **revolution-ary changes** in our lifestyles.* **2** 🅱2 relating to a political revolution: *a revolutionary movement*

revolutionary² /ˌrevəˈluːʃənəri/ **noun** [C] someone who tries to cause or take part in a political revolution

revolutionize (also UK **-ise**) /ˌrevəˈluːʃənaɪz/ **verb** [T] to change something in every way so that it is much better: *This will revolutionize the way we do business.*

revolve /rɪˈvɒlv/ **verb** [I] to move in a circle around a central point: *A fan was revolving slowly.* • **revolving adj** [always before noun] *a revolving door*

PHRASAL VERB **revolve around/round sth/sb** to have something or someone as the only interest or subject: *Her whole life revolves around her children.*

revolver /rɪˈvɒlvər/ **noun** [C] a small gun

revue /rɪˈvjuː/ **noun** [C] a show in a theatre with jokes, songs, and dancing

revulsion /rɪˈvʌlʃən/ **noun** [U] a strong feeling that something is very unpleasant

reward¹ /rɪˈwɔːd/ **noun 1** [C, U] 🅱1 something good that you get or experience because you have worked hard, behaved well, etc: *There'll be a **reward for** whoever finishes first.* **2** [C] 🅱1 money that the police give to someone who gives them information about a crime

> 🗹 Word partners for **reward**
>
> **get/receive** a reward • a **big/handsome/sub-stantial** reward • a **reward for** sb/sth • a **reward of** [$500/$300, etc]

reward² /rɪˈwɔːd/ **verb** [T] 🅱2 to give a reward to someone: *She was **rewarded for** her bravery.*

rewarding /rɪˈwɔːdɪŋ/ **adj** making you feel satisfied that you have done something well: *Teaching is hard work but it's very rewarding.*

rewind /ˌriːˈwaɪnd/ **verb** [I, T] (**rewound**) to make a sound or television recording go back to the beginning

rework /ˌriːˈwɜːk/ **verb** [T] to change a piece of music or writing in order to improve it or make it more suitable: *The old system needs reworking.*

rewrite /ˌriːˈraɪt/ **verb** [T] (**rewrote, rewritten**) 🅱2 to write something again in order to improve it: *I had to rewrite my essay.*

rhapsody /ˈræpsədi/ **noun** [C] a piece of music for instruments

rhetoric /ˈretərɪk/ **noun** [U] language that is intended to make people believe things, often language that is not sincere: *It was the usual political speech, full of **empty rhetoric**.* • **rhetorical** /rɪˈtɒrɪkəl/ **adj** • **rhetorically adv**

rhetorical **question** /rɪˌtɒrɪkəlˈkwestʃən/ **noun** [C] a question that is not intended to be a real question because you do not expect anyone to answer it

rheumatism /ˈruːmətɪzəm/ **noun** [U] a disease in which there is swelling and pain in the joints (= parts of the body where bones join)

rhino /ˈraɪnəʊ/ **noun** [C] short for rhinoceros

rhinoceros /raɪˈnɒsərəs/ **noun** [C] a large animal from Africa or Asia that has thick skin and one or two horns on its nose

rhubarb /ˈruːbɑːb/ **noun** [U] a plant that has long, red stems that can be cooked and eaten as a fruit

rhyme¹ /raɪm/ **verb** [I] If a word rhymes with another word, the end part of the words sound the same: *'Moon' rhymes with 'June'.*

rhyme² /raɪm/ **noun 1** POEM ▷ [C] a short poem that has words that rhyme at the end of each line **2** STYLE ▷ [U] a style of writing or speaking that uses words that rhyme: *The story was written entirely in rhyme.* **3** WORD ▷ [C] a word that rhymes with another word → See also **nursery rhyme**

rhythm /ˈrɪðəm/ **noun** [C, U] 🅱2 a regular, repeating pattern of sound: *You need a **sense of rhythm** to be a good dancer.* • **rhythmic** /ˈrɪðmɪk/ **adj** with rhythm • **rhythmically adv**

rib /rɪb/ **noun** [C] 🅱2 one of the curved bones in the chest

ribbon /ˈrɪbən/ **noun** [C] a long, narrow piece of cloth that is used for tying things or used for decoration

rib cage noun [C] the structure of ribs (= curved bones) in the chest

rice /raɪs/ **noun** [U] 🅰2 small grains from a plant that are cooked and eaten → See colour picture **Food** on page Centre 11

rice paddy noun [C] (also UK **paddy field**) a field in which rice is grown

rich /rɪtʃ/ **adj 1** MONEY ▷ 🅰2 having much more money than most people, or owning things that could be sold for a lot of money: *She's the third richest woman in Britain.* ∘ *These cars are only for the rich.* **2** CONTAINING A LOT ▷ 🅱2 containing a lot of something that is important or valuable: *rich soil* ∘ *Both foods are **rich in** Vitamin C.* **3** FOOD ▷ 🅱2 Rich food has a lot of butter, cream, or eggs in it: *a rich sauce* **4** STRONG ▷ A rich sound is low and strong, and a rich colour is bright and strong. • **richness noun** [U]

R

🔲 Other ways of saying **rich**

The adjectives **wealthy** and **well off** are common alternatives to 'rich':

*Oliver's parents are very **wealthy/well off**.*

If someone is very rich, in informal situations you can use the adjective **loaded** or the expression **be rolling in it**:

*They don't have any money worries – they're **loaded**.*

*If he can afford a yacht, he must **be rolling in it**.*

If someone is richer than they were previously, the adjective **better off** is often used:

*We're a lot **better off** now that Jane's working again.*

The adjectives **affluent** and **prosperous** are sometimes used to describe areas where people are rich:

*It's a very **affluent** neighbourhood.*

*In a **prosperous** country like this, no one should go hungry.*

riches /'rɪtʃɪz/ noun [plural] literary a lot of money or valuable objects → See also **go from rags to riches**

richly /'rɪtʃli/ adv **1 be richly decorated/furnished, etc** to have a lot of beautiful or expensive decoration, furniture, etc: *a richly decorated church* **2 be richly rewarded** to be paid a lot of money **3 richly deserve** to very much deserve something: *Later that year he received the award he so richly deserved.*

rickety /'rɪkəti/ adj likely to break soon: *a rickety wooden chair*

ricochet /'rɪkəʃeɪ/ verb [I] to hit a surface and then be sent back through the air: *The bullet ricocheted off the wall.*

rid¹ /rɪd/ adj **1 get rid of sth a** 🔵 to throw something away or give something to someone because you do not want it now: *We must get rid of some of those old books.* **b** 🔵 to end something unpleasant: *I can't seem to get rid of this headache.* **2 get rid of sb** to make someone leave: *She was useless at her job so we had to get rid of her.* **3 be rid of sb/sth** to be without someone or something that you do not like or want: *I'd do anything to be rid of him.*

rid² /rɪd/ verb (**ridding, rid**)

PHRASAL VERBS **rid sth of sth** to remove something unpleasant from somewhere: *to rid the world of nuclear weapons* • **rid yourself of sth** to remove something that you do not want: *to rid yourself of a reputation*

riddance /'rɪdəns/ noun **Good riddance!** used to express pleasure when you have got rid of something or someone that you do not want

ridden /'rɪdən/ past participle of ride

riddle /'rɪdl/ noun [C] **1** a strange and difficult question that has a clever and often funny answer **2** a situation or event that you cannot understand: *Scientists may have **solved** the **riddle** of Saturn's rings.*

riddled /'rɪdld/ adj **be riddled with sth** to contain a large number of something bad: *The wall was riddled with bullets.*

ride¹ /raɪd/ verb (**rode, ridden**) **1** [I, T] 🔵 to travel by sitting on a horse, bicycle, or motorcycle and controlling it: *I ride my bike to work.* ∘ *She taught me to ride (= to ride a horse).* → See Note at **drive¹ 2** [T] US to travel in a vehicle as a passenger: *I've told her not to ride the subway at night.*

PHRASAL VERBS **ride on sth** If something important rides on a situation, it will succeed or fail depending on the situation: *There was $600,000 riding on the outcome of the deal.* • **ride out sth** to continue to exist during a bad situation: *to ride out a recession*

ride² /raɪd/ noun [C] **1 VEHICLE** ▷ 🔵 a journey in a vehicle or train: *Can I **give** you a **ride** to the station?* **2 BICYCLE** ▷ 🔵 a journey riding a bicycle, motorcycle, or horse: *He's gone out for a ride on his bike.* **3 PLAYING** ▷ 🔵 a machine at a fair (= event outdoors) that moves people up and down, round in circles, etc as they sit in it

🔲 Word partners for **ride** noun

go for/hitch a ride • a ride **in/on** sth • **give** sb a ride

rider /'raɪdər/ noun [C] 🔵 someone who rides a horse, bicycle, or motorcycle → See colour picture **Sports 1** on page Centre 14

ridge /rɪdʒ/ noun [C] **1** a long, narrow piece of high land, especially along the top of a mountain: *a mountain ridge* **2** a narrow, raised line on a flat surface

ridicule¹ /'rɪdɪkjuːl/ verb [T] to laugh at someone in an unkind way: *I was **ridiculed for** saying they might win.*

ridicule² /'rɪdɪkjuːl/ noun [U] unkind behaviour in which you laugh at someone

ridiculous /rɪ'dɪkjələs/ adj 🔵 very silly: *I've never heard anything so ridiculous.* • **ridiculously** adv *ridiculously expensive*

riding /'raɪdɪŋ/ noun [U] the sport or activity of riding horses

rife /raɪf/ adj [never before noun] Something unpleasant that is rife is very common: *Rumours were rife that the band would split up.*

rifle¹ /'raɪfl/ noun [C] a long gun that you hold against your shoulder when you shoot

rifle² /'raɪfl/ verb [T] (also **rifle through**) to quickly search through things, often in order to steal something: *I caught him rifling through my drawers.*

rift /rɪft/ noun [C] **1** a serious disagreement: *the deepening **rift between** the workers and management* **2** a very large hole that separates parts of the Earth's surface

🔲 Word partners for **rift**

create/heal a rift • a **deep/growing/huge/serious** rift • a rift **with** sb • a rift **between** sb and sb • a rift **over** sth

rig¹ /rɪg/ verb [T] (**rigging, rigged**) to arrange an election, competition, etc so that the results are not fair or true: *He accused the government of rigging the elections.*

PHRASAL VERB **rig sth up** to quickly make a piece of equipment from any materials you can find

rig² /rɪg/ **noun** [C] a large structure for removing gas or oil from the ground or the sea: *an oil rig*

rigging /ˈrɪgɪŋ/ **noun** [U] a system of ropes and chains used to support a ship's masts (= poles)

right¹ /raɪt/ **adj 1 CORRECT** ▷ **A1** correct or true: *He only got half the answers right.* ◦ *You're right about Alison – she's incredible!* ◦ *"You came here in 1979, didn't you?" "That's right."* **2 DIRECTION** ▷ [always before noun] **A2** on or towards the side of your body that is to the east when you are facing north: *your right hand* ◦ *There's a tree on the right side of the house.* **3 SUITABLE** ▷ **B1** suitable or best in a particular situation: *I'm not sure she's the right person for the job.* ◦ *Are we going in the right direction?* **4 ACCEPTABLE** ▷ **B2** fair or morally acceptable: *It's not right to criticize him behind his back.* **5 put sth right** to solve a problem **6 COMPLETE** ▷ [always before noun] UK informal used for emphasizing when something is bad: *His house is a right mess.* → See also **all right¹**

> ⚠ Common learner error: **right** or **true**?
>
> **Right** is usually used to say something is correct or to agree with something someone has said.
>
> *He gave the right answer.*
> *"That's right, they live in central London."*
>
> **True** is usually used to say something is based on facts.
>
> *Is it true that she's leaving?*
> *Everything I've told you is true.*

right² /raɪt/ **adv 1 EXACTLY** ▷ **B1** exactly in a place or time: *He's right here with me.* ◦ *I fell asleep right in the middle of her speech.* **2 CORRECTLY** ▷ **B2** correctly: *He guessed right most of the time.* **3 DIRECTION** ▷ **A2** to the right side: *Turn right after the bridge.* **4 right away/now/after** ▷ **B1** immediately: *Do you want to start right away?* **5 ALL** ▷ all the way: *Did you read it right through to the end?* **6 IN SPEECH** ▷ UK **A2** used at the beginning of a sentence to get someone's attention or to show you have understood someone: *Right, whose turn is it to tidy up?* ◦ *Right, so Helen's coming tomorrow and Trevor on Thursday.* **7 Right** used in the UK as part of the title of some politicians and Christian officials: *Right Honourable/Reverend*

IDIOM **It serves her/him/you right!** informal something you say about a bad thing that has happened to a person and that they deserve: *So she left him, did she? Serves him right!*

• **rightness noun** [U] → See also **be right up sb's alley**, **be right up sb's street**

right³ /raɪt/ **noun 1 LAW** ▷ [C] **B2** something that the law allows you to do: *the right to free speech* ◦ [+ to do sth] *the right to vote* **2 DIRECTION** ▷ [U] **A2** the right side of your body, or the direction towards this side: *You'll find her in the second room on the right.* **3 BEHAVIOUR** ▷ [U] **B2**

morally correct behaviour: *I've tried to teach them the difference between right and wrong.* **4 have a/no right to do sth** to have, or not have, a good reason for something: *He has a right to be angry.* ◦ *She had no right to speak to me like that.* **5 the Right/right** political groups that support capitalism (= a system in which industries and companies are owned by people and not the government): *The right campaigned against the president.*

right⁴ /raɪt/ **verb** [T] **1** to put something back in a vertical position, or to return to a vertical position: [often reflexive] *The boat righted itself and I rowed us back to the shore.* **2 right a wrong** to do something good to make an unfair situation seem better: *How can we right the wrongs of the past?*

right ˌangle noun [C] a 90 degree angle of the type that is in a square

ˌright ˈclick verb [I] to press the button on the right of a computer mouse (= a small piece of equipment that you move with your hand to control what the computer does)

righteous /ˈraɪtʃəs/ **adj** morally right and for good moral reasons: *righteous anger/indignation* • **righteousness noun** [U] → See also **self-righteous**

rightful /ˈraɪtfəl/ **adj** [always before noun] legally or morally correct: *The wallet was returned to its rightful owner.*

right-hand /ˌraɪtˈhænd/ **adj** [always before noun] **1** **A2** on the right of something: *On the right-hand side you'll see a sign.* **2 sb's right-hand man/woman** the person that you most trust and depend on, especially at work

right-handed /ˌraɪtˈhændɪd/ **adj** Someone who is right-handed uses their right hand to do most things.

rightly /ˈraɪtli/ **adv** **B2** in a correct way: *He is rightly concerned about the situation.*

rights /raɪts/ **noun** [plural] freedom to do and say things without fear of punishment → See also **civil rights**, **human rights**

right-wing /ˌraɪtˈwɪŋ/ **adj** supporting the ideas of parties on the political right: *a right-wing newspaper* • **right-winger noun** [C]

rigid /ˈrɪdʒɪd/ **adj** **1** not able to change or be changed easily: *I found the rules a little too rigid.* **2** not able to bend or move easily: *a rigid structure* • **rigidly adv** • **rigidity** /rɪˈdʒɪdəti/ **noun** [U] being unable to bend or change easily

rigorous /ˈrɪgərəs/ **adj** careful to look at or consider every part of something to make sure it is correct or safe: *rigorous testing* ◦ *a rigorous medical examination* • **rigorously adv**

rigour UK (US **rigor**) /ˈrɪgər/ **noun** [U] If you do something with rigour, you look at or consider every part of something to make sure it is correct or safe: *His arguments lack intellectual rigour.*

rigours UK (US **rigors**) /ˈrɪgəz/ **noun the rigours of sth** the difficult conditions of a particular situation: *the rigours of a harsh winter*

rim /rɪm/ **noun** [C] the edge of something round: *the rim of a wheel*

yes | k cat | ŋ ring | ʃ she | θ thin | ð this | ʒ decision | dʒ jar | tʃ chip | æ cat | e bed | ə ago | ɪ sit | i cosy | ɒ hot | ʌ run | ʊ put |

rind /raɪnd/ **noun** [C, U] the thick skin of fruits such as oranges and lemons and other foods, for example cheese

ring¹ /rɪŋ/ **noun** [C] **1** JEWELLERY ▷ **A2** a round piece of jewellery that you wear on your finger: *a **wedding ring*** ∘ *a gold ring* → See picture at **jewellery 2** CIRCLE ▷ **B2** something that is the shape of a circle: *The children sat in a ring around the teacher.* **3** SOUND ▷ the sound a bell makes: *The ring of the doorbell woke him up.* **4 a crime/drug/spy, etc ring** a group of people who are involved in an illegal activity together **5 a boxing/circus ring** an area with seats around it where boxers (= people fighting) or people in a circus (= show) perform **6 give sb a ring** mainly UK **A2** to telephone someone: *If you want anything, just give me a ring.* → See also **key ring**

ring² /rɪŋ/ **verb** (**rang**, **rung**) **1** SOUND ▷ [I, T] **B1** If something rings, it makes the sound of a bell, and if you ring a bell, you cause it to make a sound: *The **phone's** ringing.* ∘ *I rang the doorbell.* **2** TELEPHONE ▷ [I, T] UK (UK/US **call**) **A2** to telephone someone: *Have you rung your mother?* ∘ *I've **rung for** a taxi.* **3** EARS ▷ [I] If your ears are ringing, you can hear a loud sound after the sound has stopped. → See also **ring a bell, ring true**

PHRASAL VERBS **ring (sb) back** UK (UK/US **call (sb) back**) **B1** to telephone someone a second time, or to telephone someone who rang you earlier: *I'm a bit busy – can I ring you back later?* • **ring off** UK (UK/US **hang up**) to end a telephone conversation and put down the part of the telephone that you speak into: *She'd rung off before I could say goodbye.*

ring³ /rɪŋ/ **verb** [T] to make a circle around something: *Dozens of armed police ringed the building.*

ringleader /ˈrɪŋˌliːdər/ **noun** [C] the leader of a group who are doing something harmful or illegal: *the ringleader of a gang of drug smugglers*

ring road **noun** [C] UK a road built to take traffic around the outside of a city

ringtone /ˈrɪŋtəʊn/ **noun** [C] the sound that a telephone makes, especially a mobile phone, when someone is calling it

rink /rɪŋk/ **noun** [C] a large, flat surface made of ice or wood where you can skate (= move wearing boots with wheels or a piece of metal): *a roller skating rink* → See also **ice rink**

rinse¹ /rɪns/ **verb** [T] to wash something in clean water in order to remove dirt or soap: *Rinse the beans with cold water.*

PHRASAL VERB **rinse sth out** to quickly wash the inside of something with clean water: *I'll just rinse these glasses out and leave them to dry.*

rinse² /rɪns/ **noun** [C] **1** a wash in clean water to remove dirt or soap from something: *Give it a quick rinse, then squeeze it dry.* **2** a liquid that is used for changing the colour of someone's hair: *a dark brown rinse*

riot¹ /ˈraɪət/ **noun** [C] angry, violent behaviour by a crowd of people: *a race riot* ∘ *Riots started in several cities.*

IDIOM **run riot** to behave in a noisy, violent, or wild way without being controlled: *They allow their kids to run riot.*

☑ Word partners for **riot**
quell/spark a riot • a riot breaks out

riot² /ˈraɪət/ **verb** [I] to take part in a riot: *People were rioting in the streets.* • **rioter** **noun** [C]

rioting /ˈraɪətɪŋ/ **noun** [U] angry, violent behaviour by a group of people: *There was **widespread** rioting.*

riotous /ˈraɪətəs/ **adj 1** wild and not controlled by anyone: *a riotous party* **2** formal violent and not controlled: *He was charged with riotous behaviour and jailed for six months.*

rip¹ /rɪp/ **verb** (**ripping, ripped**) **1** **B2** [I, T] to tear quickly and suddenly, or to tear something quickly and suddenly: *She ripped her dress getting off her bike.* ∘ *He **ripped open** the parcel.* **2 rip sth out/off/from, etc** to remove something by pulling it away quickly: *Hedges had been ripped out to make larger fields.* **3** [T] to copy information from a CD onto an MP3 player (= a piece of electronic equipment or a computer program for storing music)

PHRASAL VERBS **rip sb off** informal to cheat someone by making them pay too much money for something: *We were ripped off by the first taxi driver.* • **rip sth off** to remove a piece of clothing very quickly and carelessly: *I ripped off my clothes and jumped in the shower.* • **rip through sth** to move through a place or building, destroying it quickly: *The bomb ripped through the building, killing six people.* • **rip sth up** to tear something into small pieces: *He ripped up all her letters.*

rip² /rɪp/ **noun** [C] a hole in the shape of a line when cloth or paper has been torn

ripe /raɪp/ **adj 1** **B2** developed enough and ready to be eaten: *ripe bananas* **2 ripe for sth** developed enough to be ready for something: *The country is ripe for change.* ∘ *The time is ripe for* (= It is the right time for) *investing in new technology.*

ripen /ˈraɪpən/ **verb** [I, T] to become ripe, or to make something become ripe: *The peaches had ripened in the sun.*

rip-off /ˈrɪpɒf/ **noun** [C] informal something that costs far too much money: *The drinks here are a complete rip-off.*

ripple¹ /ˈrɪpl/ **verb** [I, T] to move in small waves, or to make something move in small waves: *A field of wheat rippled in the breeze.*

ripple² /ˈrɪpl/ **noun** [C] **1** a small wave or series of small waves on the surface of water: *She dived in, sending ripples across the pool.* **2** something that spreads through a place in a gentle way: *a ripple of applause/laughter*

rise¹ /raɪz/ **verb** (**rose**, **risen**) **1** INCREASE ▷ **B2** to increase in level: *rising temperatures* ∘ *Prices rose by 10 percent.* **2** GO UP ▷ **B1** to move up: *The balloon rose slowly into the air.* **3** STAND ▷ to stand, especially after sitting: *He rose from his seat.* **4 rise to/through, etc** to become important, successful, or rich: *He quickly rose to stardom.* ▷ to become stronger or louder: *The wind is rising.* **6 HIGH** ▷ to be high above something: *The bridge rose almost 600 feet above the water.* **7 APPEAR** ▷ **B1** When the sun or moon rises, it appears in the sky: *The sun rises in the East.* **8 rise to the occasion/challenge, etc** to deal with a difficult job or opportunity successfully

> **!** Common learner error: **rise** or **raise**?
>
> Be careful not to confuse these two verbs.
> **Rise** means 'to increase or move up'. This verb cannot be followed by an object.
> *The price of petrol is rising.*
> ~~The price of petrol is raising.~~
> **Raise** means 'to lift something to a higher position or to increase an amount or level'. This verb must always be followed by an object.
> *The government has raised the price of petrol.*
> ~~The government has rised the price of petrol.~~

PHRASAL VERBS **rise above sth** to succeed in not allowing something harmful or bad to affect or hurt you • **rise up** to try to defeat and change a government

> **◪** Word partners for **rise**
>
> a **big/dramatic/massive/sudden** rise • a rise **in** sth • be **on the** rise • the rise **and fall of** sb/sth • a **pay/price** rise

ise² /raɪz/ **noun 1** [C] **B2** an increase in the level of something: *a tax rise* ∘ *a **rise in** interest rates* **2 sb's rise to fame/power, etc** the period when someone becomes very famous or powerful **3 give rise to sth** to cause something: *The bacteria live in the human body but do not give rise to any symptoms.* **4** [C] UK (US **raise**) an increase in the amount of money that you earn: *a **pay** rise*

isk¹ /rɪsk/ **noun 1** [C, U] **B2** the possibility of something bad happening: *the **risk of** heart disease* ∘ *People in the Northeast face the **highest** risk of being burgled.* ∘ [+ (that)] *There is a slight risk that the blood could have become infected.* **2** [C] something bad that might happen: *There are more **health risks** when older women get pregnant.* **3 at risk** **B2** being in a situation where something bad is likely to happen: *Releasing these prisoners into the community **puts** the public **at risk**.* **4 at your own risk** If you do something at your own risk, you are completely responsible for anything bad that you might happen because of it. **5 run the risk of sth** to do something although something bad might happen because of it: *I think I'll run the risk of hurting her feelings, and tell her the truth.* **6 take a risk** **B2** to do something although something bad might happen because of it: *This time I'm not taking any risks – I'm going to get insured.*

isk² /rɪsk/ **verb** [T] **1** **B2** If you risk something bad, you do something although that bad thing might happen: [+ doing sth] *I'd like to help you,*

but I can't risk losing my job. **2** **B2** If you risk something important, you cause it to be in a dangerous situation where you might lose it: *He risked his life to save me.*

> **◪** Word partners for **risk**
>
> **carry/increase/pose/minimize/reduce/take** a risk • **run the risk** of sth • a **great/high/serious/slight/small** risk • **the risk of** sth • **at** risk

risky /'rɪski/ **adj** **B2** dangerous because something bad might happen: *Investing in shares is always a **risky business**.*

rite /raɪt/ **noun** [C] a traditional ceremony in a particular religion or culture: *initiation/funeral rites*

ritual /'rɪtʃuəl/ **noun** [C] an activity or a set of actions that are always done in the same way or at the same time, sometimes as part of a religion: *Coffee and the paper are part of my morning ritual.* • **ritualistic** /ˌrɪtjuəl'ɪstɪk/ **adj** done as a ritual

rival¹ /'raɪvəl/ **noun** [C] someone or something that is competing with another person or thing: *business/political rivals* • **rival adj** [always before noun] *a rival company/gang* • **rivalry noun** [C, U] behaviour typical of rivals: *There is intense **rivalry between** the two teams.*

rival² /'raɪvəl/ **verb** [T] (mainly UK **rivalling, rivalled**, US **rivaling, rivaled**) to be good enough to compete with someone or something else: *Australian wine can now rival the best from France.*

river /'rɪvər/ **noun** [C] **A1** a long, natural area of water that flows across the land and into a sea, lake, or another river: *the River Thames*

riverside /'rɪvəsaɪd/ **noun** [no plural] the area of land at the side of a river: *a riverside path*

rivet¹ /'rɪvɪt/ **verb be riveted** to give something all of your attention because it is so interesting or important: *Her eyes were **riveted on/to** his face.*

rivet² /'rɪvɪt/ **noun** [C] a metal pin used to fasten pieces of metal together

riveting /'rɪvɪtɪŋ/ **adj** extremely interesting or exciting: *I found the film absolutely riveting.*

roach /rəʊtʃ/ **noun** [C] (plural **roach, roaches**) US a cockroach (= large insect that sometimes breeds in houses)

road /rəʊd/ **noun 1** **A1** [C, U] a long, hard surface built for vehicles to drive on: *Be careful when you **cross** the road.* ∘ *The journey takes about three hours **by road** (= in a car, bus, etc).* ∘ *Follow the **main road** (= large road) till you come to a church.* **2 Road** (written abbreviation **Rd**) **A1** used in the name of a road as part of an address: *142 Park Road* **3 along/down/up the road** a distance away on the same road: *There's a supermarket just down the road.* **4 over the road** UK (UK/US **across the road**) on the other side of the road: *Who lives in that big house over the road?* **5 on the road** driving or travelling, usually over a long distance: *We'd been on the road for 48 hours.*

IDIOMS **down the road** If an event is a particular period of time down the road, it will not happen

R

until that period has passed: *Why worry about something that's 10 years down the road?* • **go down that road** to decide to do something in a particular way: *I don't think we want to go down that road.*

→ See also **ring road, slip road, trunk road**

roadblock /'rəʊdblɒk/ **noun** [C] something that is put across a road to stop people who are driving down it: *The police had set up a road-block and were checking identity papers.*

road map noun [C] a plan for achieving something: *the road map for peace in the Middle East*

road rage noun [U] anger and violence between drivers: *a road rage incident*

roadshow /'rəʊdʃəʊ/ **noun** [C] a radio or television programme broadcast from a public place

roadside /'rəʊdsaɪd/ **noun** [C] the area next to a road: [usually singular] *They found an injured cat lying by the roadside.*

roadway /'rəʊdweɪ/ **noun** [C] the part of the road that the traffic drives on

roadworks /'rəʊdwɜːks/ **noun** [plural] UK repairs being done to the road

roadworthy /'rəʊd,wɜːði/ **adj** If a car is road-worthy, it is in good enough condition to be safe to drive.

roam /rəʊm/ **verb** [I, T] to move around a place without any purpose: *Gangs of youths roam the streets at night*

roar¹ /rɔːr/ **verb 1** [I] to make a loud, deep sound: *We could hear a lion roaring from the other side of the zoo.* ○ *She roared with laughter.* **2 roar past/down, etc** If a vehicle roars somewhere, it moves fast making a loud noise: *A huge motorcycle roared past.* **3** [I, T] to say something in a very loud voice: *"Stop that!" he roared.*

roar² /rɔːr/ **noun** [C] a loud, deep sound: *a lion's roar* ○ *the roar of a jet engine*

roaring /'rɔːrɪŋ/ **adj** [always before noun] **1** A roaring fire or wind is very powerful. **2** informal used to emphasize a situation or state: *The party was a roaring success.*

roast¹ /rəʊst/ **verb** [I, T] **⚫** If you roast food, you cook it in an oven or over a fire, and if food roasts, it is cooked in an oven or over a fire: *Roast the lamb in a hot oven for 35 minutes.* • **roast adj** [always before noun] **⚫** *roast beef/pork* → See picture at **cook**

roast² /rəʊst/ **noun** [C] a piece of roasted meat

rob /rɒb/ **verb** [T] (**robbing, robbed**) **1 ⚫** to steal from someone or somewhere, often using violence: *to rob a bank* ○ *Two tourists were robbed at gunpoint in the city centre last night.* **2 rob sb of sth** to take something important away from someone: *The war had robbed them of their innocence.*

robber /'rɒbər/ **noun** [C] someone who steals: *a bank robber* ○ *a gang of armed robbers*

robbery /'rɒbəri/ **noun** [C] **⚫** the crime of stealing from someone or somewhere: *a bank robbery* ○ *an armed robbery* ○ *to commit a robbery*

robe /rəʊb/ **noun** [C] a long, loose piece of clothing, often something that is worn for ceremonies or special occasions

robin /'rɒbɪn/ **noun** [C] a small, brown bird with a red chest

robot /'rəʊbɒt/ **noun** [C] a machine controlled by a computer, which can move and do other things that people can do • **robotic** /rəʊ'bɒtɪk/ **adj** relating to or like a robot

robust /rəʊ'bʌst/ **adj** strong and healthy: *He looks robust enough.* ○ *a robust economy*

rock¹ /rɒk/ **noun 1 SUBSTANCE** ▷ [U] **⚫** the hard, natural substance that forms part of the Earth's surface: *a layer of volcanic rock* **2 LARGE PIECE** ▷ [C] **⚫** a large piece of rock or stone: *Huge waves were crashing against the rocks.* **3 MUSIC** ▷ [U] **⚫** loud, modern music with a strong beat, often played with electric guitars and drums: *hard/soft rock* ○ *rock music* ○ *rock band/singer*

IDIOM **on the rocks a** If a relationship is on the rocks, it has problems and is likely to end soon. **b** If a drink is on the rocks, it is served with ice in it.

rock² /rɒk/ **verb 1** [I, T] to move backwards and forwards or from side to side, or to make someone or something do this: *She rocked back and forth on her chair.* ○ *He gently rocked the baby to sleep.* **2** [T] to shock a large number of people: [often passive] *The country has been rocked by a series of drug scandals.* → See also **rock the boat**

rock bottom noun informal **hit/reach rock bottom** to reach the lowest level possible: *The president's popularity has hit rock bottom.*

rocket¹ /'rɒkɪt/ **noun** [C] **1 ⚫** a tube-shaped vehicle for travelling in space **2** a tube-shaped weapon that carries a bomb

rocket² /'rɒkɪt/ **verb** [I] **1** to quickly increase in value or amount: *House prices have rocketed this year.* **2** to make quick progress: *She rocketed to stardom after modelling for Vogue last year.*

rocking chair noun [C] (also **rocker**) a chair built on two pieces of curved wood so that you can move forward and backward when you sit in it

rock 'n' roll /,rɒkən'rəʊl/ **noun** [U] (also **rock and roll**) a type of dance music that was especially popular in the 1950s

IDIOM **be the new rock 'n' roll** to now be the most fashionable and popular activity

rock star noun [C] a famous rock musician

rocky /'rɒki/ **adj** with lots of rocks: *a rocky beach*

rod /rɒd/ **noun** [C] a thin, straight pole: *a fishing rod* ○ *The concrete is strengthened with steel rods*

rode /rəʊd/ past tense of ride

rodent /'rəʊdənt/ **noun** [C] an animal with long, sharp teeth, such as a mouse or rabbit

rodeo /'rəʊdiəʊ/ **noun** [C] a competition in

which people show their skill at riding wild horses and catching cows

oe /rəʊ/ **noun** [U] fish eggs

ogue /rəʊg/ **adj** [always before noun] not behaving in the way that is expected or wanted: *a rogue state* ○ *rogue cells*

ole /rəʊl/ **noun** [C] **1** ⑱ the job someone or something has in a particular situation: *This part of the brain **plays an** important **role** in learning.* **2** ⑪ a part in a play or film: *In his latest movie, he **plays the role of** a violent gangster.* → See also **title role**

> ☑ Word partners for **role**
>
> **play** a role ● an **active/central/key/leading/ major** role ● **in** a role ● sb's role **as** sth ● sb/ sth's role **in** (doing) sth

ole ˌmodel noun [C] someone you try to behave like because you admire them: *Jane is such a good role model for her younger sister.*

ole-play /ˈrəʊlˌpleɪ/ **noun** [C, U] pretending to be someone else, especially as part of learning a new skill

oll¹ /rəʊl/ **verb 1 roll (sth) across/around/over, etc** ⑫ to move somewhere by turning in a circular direction, or to make something move this way: *The ball rolled through the goalkeeper's legs.* ○ *She rolled over onto her side.* **2 roll down/ in/off, etc** ⑫ to move somewhere smoothly: *Tears rolled down her face.* **3** ⑱ [T] to turn something around itself to make the shape of a ball or tube: *to roll a cigarette* **4 roll your eyes** to move your eyes so that they are looking up, usually to show surprise or disapproval → See also **set/start the ball rolling**

IDIOM **be rolling in it** informal to be very rich

PHRASAL VERBS **roll in** to arrive in large numbers: *She only set up the business last year and already the money's rolling in.* ● **roll sth up** to fold something around itself to make the shape of a ball or tube, or to make a piece of clothing shorter: *to roll up your sleeves/trouser legs* ○ *to roll up a carpet* → Opposite **unroll** ● **roll up** informal to arrive somewhere, usually late: *By the time Jim rolled up, the party had almost finished.*

oll² /rəʊl/ **noun** [C] **1** ROUND OBJECT ▷ ⑫ something that has been turned around itself into a round shape like a tube: *a roll of film* ○ *a roll of toilet paper* **2** BREAD ▷ ⑪ a small loaf of bread for one person: *Would you like a roll and butter with your soup?* **3** LIST ▷ a list of names: *the electoral roll* **4** SOUND ▷ a long, deep sound: *a roll of thunder* ○ *a drum roll* **be on a roll** informal to be having a successful period: *We were on a roll, winning our fourth game in a row.* → See also **rock 'n' roll, toilet roll**

oller /ˈrəʊlər/ **noun** [C] a piece of equipment in the shape of a tube which is rolled around or over something: *She uses rollers to curl her hair.*

Rollerblades /ˈrəʊləbleɪdz/ **noun** [plural] (also **in-line skates**) trademark boots with a single line of wheels on the bottom, used for moving across the ground ● **rollerblading noun** [U] *Lots of*

*people **go rollerblading** in Central Park.* → See colour picture **Sports 1** on page Centre 14

roller coaster /ˌrəʊləˈkəʊstər/ **noun** [C] an exciting entertainment that is like a fast train that goes up and down very steep slopes

ˈroller ˌskate noun [C] a boot with wheels on the bottom, used for moving across the ground ● **roller skating noun** [U]

ˈrolling ˌpin noun [C] a kitchen tool shaped like a tube that you roll over pastry to make it thinner before cooking → See colour picture **The Kitchen** on page Centre 2

Roman¹ /ˈrəʊmən/ **noun** [C] someone who lived in ancient Rome or its empire

Roman² /ˈrəʊmən/ **adj** relating to ancient Rome or its empire: *Roman remains*

ˌRoman ˈCatholic adj related to the part of the Christian religion that has the Pope (= a very important priest) as its leader ● **Roman Catholic noun** [C] ● **Roman Catholicism noun** [U] the beliefs of the Roman Catholic religion

romance /rəʊˈmæns/ **noun 1** LOVE ▷ [C, U] ⑪ an exciting relationship of love between two people, often a short one: *They got married last September after a **whirlwind romance**.* **2** STORY ▷ [C] a story about love **3** EXCITEMENT ▷ [U] a feeling of excitement or exciting danger: *the romance of the sea*

> ☑ Word partners for **romance**
>
> **find/look for** romance ● a romance **blossoms** ● a **whirlwind** romance ● a **holiday** romance ● the romance **between** sb and sb ● sb's romance **with** sb

ˌRoman ˈnumeral noun [C] a letter that represents a number in the Roman system in which I is 1, II is 2, V is 5, etc: *My watch has Roman numerals.*

romantic¹ /rəʊˈmæntɪk/ **adj 1** LOVE ▷ ⑪ relating to exciting feelings of love: *a romantic dinner for two* **2** STORY ▷ ⑪ relating to a story about love: *romantic fiction* ○ *a romantic comedy* **3** IDEAS ▷ thinking that things are better than they really are, and that things are possible which are not: *a romantic view of the world* ● **romantically adv**

romantic² /rəʊˈmæntɪk/ **noun** [C] someone who thinks that things are better than they really are, and that things are possible which are not

romanticize (also UK **-ise**) /rəʊˈmæntɪsaɪz/ **verb** [T] to make something seem much better or exciting than it really is: *a romanticized image of married life*

romp /rɒmp/ **verb romp around/in/through, etc** to run around in a happy, energetic way: *The children were romping around in the garden.* ● **romp noun** [C]

roof /ruːf/ **noun 1** ⓐ [C] the surface that covers the top of a building or vehicle: *a flat/sloping roof* ○ *He climbed onto the roof.* **2 the roof of your**

roof

mouth the top part of the inside of your mouth

IDIOMS **a roof over your head** somewhere to live • **go through the roof** If the level of something, especially a price, goes through the roof, it increases very quickly. • **hit the roof** informal to become very angry and start shouting: *If I'm late again he'll hit the roof.*

roofing /'ruːfɪŋ/ noun [U] material used to make a roof

rooftop /'ruːftɒp/ noun [C] the top of a roof: *a view across the city rooftops*

rook /rʊk/ noun [C] a large, black bird that lives in Europe

rookie /'rʊki/ noun [C] mainly US someone who has only recently started doing a job or activity and so has no experience: *a rookie cop*

room¹ /ruːm/, /rʊm/ noun **1** [C] 🅐 a part of the inside of a building, which is separated from other parts by walls, floors, and ceilings: *a hotel room* **2** [U] 🅑 space for things to fit into: *Is there enough room for all of us in your car?* ∘ *Can everyone move up a bit to make room for these people?* ∘ [+ to do sth] *There's hardly enough room to move in here.* **3 room for sth** a possibility for something to happen: *His work isn't bad but there's still some room for improvement.* → See also **changing room, chat room, dining room, drawing room, dressing room, elbow room, emergency room, living room, locker room, men's room, operating room, sitting room, waiting room**

📋 Word partners for **room**

leave/make room • take up room • room for sb/sth

room² /ruːm/, /rʊm/ verb **room with sb** US to share a bedroom with someone, usually at college

roommate /'ruːmmeɪt/ noun [C] **1** 🅑 someone who you share a room with **2** US (UK **flatmate, housemate**) 🅑 someone who you share your home with

room service noun [U] in a hotel, a service in which someone serves you food and drink in your room

roomy /'ruːmi/ adj having a lot of space: *It looks small, but it's really quite roomy inside.*

roost /ruːst/ noun [C] a place where birds go to rest or sleep

IDIOM **rule the roost** to be the person who makes all the decisions in a group

rooster /'ruːstər/ noun [C] a male chicken

root¹ /ruːt/ noun [C] **1** 🅑 the part of a plant that grows under the ground and gets water and food from the soil **2** the part of a hair or tooth that is under the skin **3 the root of sth** the cause of something, usually something bad: *the root of all evil* → See also **grass roots**

root² /ruːt/ verb

PHRASAL VERBS **root about/around (sth)** to search for something, especially by looking through other things: *She was rooting around in her drawer for a pencil.* • **root for sb** informal to show

support for someone who is in a competition o who is doing something difficult: *Good luck We're all rooting for you.* • **be rooted in sth** to b based on something or caused by something Most prejudices are rooted in ignorance.* • **roo sth/sb out** to find and get rid of the thing o person that is causing a problem: *It is our aim t root out corruption.*

roots /ruːts/ noun [plural] 🅑 where someone o something originally comes from: *the roots o modern jazz*

rope¹ /rəʊp/ noun [C, U] 🅑 very thick strin made from twisted thread

IDIOMS **be on the ropes** mainly US to be doin badly and likely to fail: *His career is on the ropes* • **learn/know the ropes** to learn/know how t do a job or activity

→ See also **at the end¹ of your tether, jum rope, skipping rope**

rope² /rəʊp/ verb [T] to tie things together wit rope

PHRASAL VERB **rope sb in** informal to persuad someone to help you with something, especiall when they do not want to

rosary /'rəʊzəri/ noun [C] a string of bead (= small, round balls) that is used to coun prayers in the Catholic religion

rose¹ /rəʊz/ noun [C] 🅑 a flower with a pleasan smell and thorns (= sharp points on the stem) that grows on a bush

rose² /rəʊz/ past tense of rise

rosé /'rəʊzeɪ/ Ⓤ /rəʊˈzeɪ/ noun [U] pink wine

rosemary /'rəʊzməri/ noun [U] a herb tha grows as a bush with thin, pointed leaves

rosette /rəʊˈzet/ noun [C] **1** (also US **ribbon**) decoration made of coloured cloth, which i given as a prize **2** UK a decoration made o coloured cloth in the shape of a rose, worn t show political support for someone

roster /'rɒstər/ noun [C] **1** a plan that shows wh must do which jobs and when they must d them: *a staff roster* **2** a list of names of peopl who belong to a team or organization

📋 Word partners for **roster**

draw up/organize a roster • a roster of sth • on a roster

rostrum /'rɒstrəm/ noun [C] a raised surfac that someone stands on to make a speech o receive a prize

rosy /'rəʊzi/ adj **1** Rosy faces are a healthy pin colour: *rosy cheeks* **2** very positive and happy The future looks rosy.*

rot¹ /rɒt/ verb [I, T] (**rotting, rotted**) If vegetabl or animal substances rot, they decay, and i something rots them, it makes them decay Sugar rots your teeth.* ∘ *the smell of rotting fish*

rot² /rɒt/ noun [U] decay: *There was rot in th woodwork.*

IDIOMS **the rot sets in** UK If the rot sets in, situation starts to get worse. • **stop the rot** UK t

R

do something to prevent a situation from continuing to get worse

ota /'rəutə/ **noun** [C] UK (also UK/US **roster**) a plan that shows who must do which jobs and when they must do them

otary /'rəutəri/ **adj** [always before noun] moving in a circular direction

otate /rəu'teɪt/ **verb** [I, T] **1** to turn in a circular direction, or to make something turn in a circular direction: *The television rotates for viewing at any angle.* **2** to change from one person or thing to another in a regular order: *Farmers usually rotate their crops to improve the soil.* • **rotation** /rəu'teɪʃⁿn/ **noun** [C, U] *the rotation of the Earth* ∘ *crop rotation*

otten /'rɒtⁿn/ **adj 1** ⑫ Rotten vegetable or animal substances are decaying: *rotten eggs* **2** informal very bad: *rotten weather*

ottweiler /'rɒtwaɪlər/ **noun** [C] a type of large, powerful dog

ough¹ /rʌf/ **adj 1 NOT SMOOTH** ▷ ⑪ A rough surface is not smooth: *rough hands* ∘ *rough ground* **2 APPROXIMATE** ▷ ⑪ approximate: *a rough estimate* ∘ *Can you give me a rough idea of the cost?* **3 FORCEFUL** ▷ ⑫ If the sea or weather is rough, there is a lot of strong wind and sometimes rain: *The boat sank in rough seas off the Swedish coast.* **4 SICK** ▷ [never before noun] UK sick: *I feel a bit rough after last night.* **5 DIFFICULT** ▷ ⑫ difficult or unpleasant: *She's having a rough time at work.* **6 DANGEROUS** ▷ dangerous or violent: *a rough part of town* ∘ *Hockey can be quite a rough game.* **7 NOT PERFECT** ▷ quickly done and not perfect: *These are just rough sketches.*

IDIOM **rough and ready a** produced quickly without preparation **b** not very polite or well-educated

• **roughness noun** [U]

ough² /rʌf/ **noun**

IDIOM **take the rough with the smooth** UK to accept the unpleasant parts of a situation as well as the pleasant parts

ough³ /rʌf/ **adv live/sleep rough** UK to live and sleep outside because you have nowhere else to live

ough⁴ /rʌf/ **verb rough it** to live in a way that is simple and not comfortable

oughage /'rʌfɪdʒ/ **noun** [U] a substance in fruit and vegetables that helps you to get rid of waste from the body

oughen /'rʌfⁿn/ **verb** [I, T] to become rough or to make something become rough: *Years of housework had roughened her hands.*

oughly /'rʌfli/ **adv 1** ⑫ approximately: *There's been an increase of roughly 30% since last year.* **2** forcefully or violently: *He pushed us roughly out of the door.*

oulette /ru:'let/ **noun** [U] a game in which a small ball moves around a dish with numbers on it, and people try to win money by guessing where the ball will stop

ound¹ /raund/ **adj 1** ⑫ in the shape of a circle or ball: *a round table/window* ∘ *round eyes* ∘ *a*

round face → See picture at **flat 2 round figures/numbers** numbers given to the nearest 10, 100, 1000, etc and not as the exact amounts

round² /raund/ **adv, preposition** mainly UK (also UK/US **around**) **1 IN A CIRCLE** ▷ ⑫ on all sides of something: *We sat round the table.* ∘ *She had a scarf round her neck.* **2 DIRECTION** ▷ ⑪ to the opposite direction: *She looked round.* ∘ *Turn the car round and let's go home.* **3 TO A PLACE** ▷ ⑪ to or in different parts of a place: *He showed me round the flat.* **4 SEVERAL PLACES** ▷ ⑪ from one place or person to another: *Could you pass these forms round, please?* **5 VISIT** ▷ ⑫ to someone's home: *Wendy's coming round this afternoon.* **6 NEAR** ▷ near an area: *Do you live round here?* **7 round about** at approximately a time or approximately an amount: *We'll be there round about 10 o'clock.* **8 round and round** ⑫ moving in a circle without stopping: *We drove round and round trying to find the hotel.*

round³ /raund/ **noun** [C] **1 first/second/third/etc, round** ⑫ a part of a competition: *He was beaten in the first round.* **2 EVENTS** ▷ a group of events that is part of a series: *a round of interviews* ∘ *a new round of talks between the two countries* **3 VISITS** ▷ (also US **rounds**) regular visits to a group of people or houses to give them something or to see them: *a milk/newspaper round* **4 DRINKS** ▷ drinks that you buy for a group of people: *It's your turn to buy the next round.* **5 round of applause** If something gets a round of applause, people clap their hands to show their approval or enjoyment: *The crowd gave him a huge round of applause.* **6 BULLETS** ▷ a bullet or a set of bullets to be fired at one time from a gun **7 round of golf** a game of golf

round⁴ /raund/ **verb** [T] to go around something: *They rounded the corner at high speed.*

PHRASAL VERBS **round sth down** to reduce a number to the nearest whole or simple number • **round sth off** to end an activity in a pleasant way: *We rounded off the lesson with a quiz.* • **round sb/sth up** to find and bring together a group of people or animals: *The police are rounding up the usual suspects.* • **round sth up** to increase a number to the nearest whole or simple number

R

roundabout

roundabout *UK*, traffic circle *US*

roundabout

roundabout¹ /'raundə,baut/ **noun** [C] UK **1** (US

traffic circle ⓐ a circular place where roads meet and where cars drive around until they arrive at the road that they want to turn into: *to go round a roundabout* **2** (US **merry-go-round**) an entertainment that goes round and round while children sit on it

roundabout² /ˈraʊndəˌbaʊt/ **adj** [always before noun] A roundabout way of doing something or going somewhere is not the direct way.

rounded /ˈraʊndɪd/ **adj** smooth and curved: *a table with rounded corners*

rounders /ˈraʊndəz/ **noun** [U] a British game in which you try to hit a small ball and then run round all four sides of a large square

roundly /ˈraʊndli/ **adv** If you criticize someone or something roundly, you do it very strongly: *The action was **roundly condemned** by French and German leaders.*

round-the-clock /ˌraʊndðəˈklɒk/ **adj** all day and all night: *round-the-clock nursing care*

round 'trip noun [C] a journey from one place to another and back to where you started

round-trip 'ticket noun [C] US (UK **return**) a ticket that lets you travel to a place and back again, for example on a train

round-up /ˈraʊndʌp/ **noun** [C] **1** the act of finding and bringing together a group of people or animals: *a police round-up* **2** a short report of all the facts or events relating to a subject: *a news round-up*

rouse /raʊz/ **verb** [T] **1** to cause a feeling or emotion in someone: *This issue is rousing a lot of public interest.* **2** formal to wake someone up: *He was roused from a deep sleep.*

rousing /ˈraʊzɪŋ/ **adj** making people feel excited and proud or ready to take action: *a rousing speech*

rout /raʊt/ **verb** [T] to defeat someone completely • **rout** *noun* [C] *an election rout*

route /ruːt/ ⓤ /ruːt/, /raʊt/ **noun** [C] **1** ⓑ the roads or paths you follow to get from one place to another place: *an escape route* ○ *Crowds gathered all **along the route** to watch the race.* **2** a method of achieving something: *A university education is seen by many as the best route to a good job.* → See also **en route**

> 🗹 Word partners for **route**
>
> **follow/take** a route • **plan/work out** a route • **along/on** a route • a route **between/from/to**

router /ˈruːtər/ **noun** [C] a piece of electronic equipment that connects computer networks to each other

> 🗹 Word partners for **routine**
>
> **get into/have/settle into** a routine • sb's **daily/normal** routine • a routine **of doing** sth

routine¹ /ruːˈtiːn/ **noun 1** [C, U] ⓑ the things you regularly do, and how and when you do them: *a **daily routine*** ○ *He longed to escape the routine of an office job.* **2** [C] a regular series of

movements, jokes, etc used in a performance: *dance routine*

routine² /ruːˈtiːn/ **adj 1** done regularly and no unusual: *a routine procedure* ○ *routine check* **2** done regularly and very boring: *His job is ver routine.*

routinely /ruːˈtiːnli/ **adv** regularly or often

roving /ˈrəʊvɪŋ/ **adj** [always before noun] movin around from one place to another place: *roving reporter*

row¹ /rəʊ/ **noun 1** [C] ⓑ a straight line of peopl or things: *a row of chairs/houses* ○ *My students s at desks in rows for most of the time.* **2** [C] ⓑ line of seats: *to sit on the **back/front row*** ○ *Isn that Sophie sitting in the row behind us?* **3 in row** ⓒ one after another without a break: *He just won the tournament for the fifth year in a rou* → See also **death row**

row² /rəʊ/ **verb** [I, T] ⓒ to move a boat or mov someone in a boat through the water using oar (= poles with flat ends) • **rowing** *noun* [U]

row³ /raʊ/ **noun** UK **1 LOUD ARGUMENT** ▷ [C] ⓒ a loud, angry argument: *a blazing row* ○ *Th couple next door are always **having row** **2 DISAGREEMENT** ▷ [C] a disagreement abou a political or public situation: *A row has erupte over defence policy.* **3 NOISE** ▷ [no plural] ver loud noise: *The kids were **making** a terrible rou upstairs.*

> 🗹 Word partners for **row** (= argument)
>
> **have** a row • an **almighty/blazing/heated** row • a row **about/over** sth • a row **with** sb • a row **between** sb and sb

rowdy /ˈraʊdi/ **adj** loud and uncontrolled *rowdy behaviour* ○ *rowdy football fans*

row ˌhouse noun [C] US (UK **terraced house** one of a row of houses that are joined togethe

rowing ˌboat noun [C] UK (US **rowboat**, ⓤ /ˈrəʊbəʊt/) a small boat moved by oars (= pole with flat ends)

royal¹ /ˈrɔɪəl/ **adj 1** ⓑ relating to a queen o king and their family: *the British royal famil* ○ *a royal visit* **2 Royal** used in the UK as part c the title of a royal person: *His Royal Highness, th Duke of York*

royal² /ˈrɔɪəl/ **noun** [C] informal a member of royal family: *a book about the royals*

royalist /ˈrɔɪəlɪst/ **noun** [C] someone who sup ports the principle of having a King or Quee • **royalist adj**

royalties /ˈrɔɪəltiz/ **noun** [plural] money that i paid to a writer, actor, etc each time their work i sold or performed: *He could receive as much as $ million **in royalties** over the next six years.*

royalty /ˈrɔɪəlti/ **noun** [U] the members of th royal family

RSI /ˌɑːresˈaɪ/ **noun** [C] abbreviation for repetitiv strain injury: a painful medical condition tha can damage the hands, arms, and backs c people, especially people who use computers

RSVP /ˌɑːresviːˈpiː/ used at the end of a writte invitation to mean 'please answer': *RSVP b October 9th*

---

rub¹ /rʌb/ **verb (rubbing, rubbed) 1** [T] 🅱️ to press your hand or a cloth on a surface and move it backwards and forwards: *She rubbed her hands together to warm them.* ∘ *Rub the stain with a damp cloth.* **2 rub sth into/on, etc** 🅱️ to move a substance backwards and forwards over a surface so that it covers it and goes into it: *I rubbed some suntan oil on her back.* ∘ *Rub the butter into the flour.* **3** [I, T] to touch and move against something, often causing pain or damage: *My new boots are rubbing against my toes.* → See also **rub shoulders (shoulder¹) with sb**, **rub sb up the wrong way¹**

IDIOM **rub it in** informal to upset someone by talking to them about something that you know they want to forget

PHRASAL VERBS **rub off** If a quality or characteristic of a particular person rubs off, other people begin to have it because they have been with that person: *His enthusiasm is starting to **rub off** on the rest of us.* • **rub sth out** UK 🅱️ to remove writing from something by rubbing it with a piece of rubber or a cloth

rub² /rʌb/ **noun** [C] the action of rubbing something: [usually singular] *Give it a rub and it'll feel better.*

rubber /ˈrʌbər/ **noun 1** [U] 🅱️ a strong material that bends easily, originally produced from the juice of a tropical tree, and used to make tyres, boots, etc **2** [C] UK (US **eraser**) 🅰️ a small object that is used to remove pencil marks from paper → See colour picture **The Classroom** on page Centre 6

rubber ˈband noun [C] (also UK **elastic band**) a thin circle of rubber used to hold things together

rubber ˈboot noun [C, plural] US (UK **wellies**) a large shoe made of rubber that covers your foot and part of your leg

rubber-stamp /ˌrʌbəˈstæmp/ **verb** [T] to officially approve a decision or plan without thinking very much about it

rubbery /ˈrʌbəri/ **adj** feeling or bending like rubber: *a rubbery piece of meat*

rubbish¹ /ˈrʌbɪʃ/ **noun** [U] mainly UK **1 WASTE** ▷ 🅱️ things that you throw away because you do not want them: *Our rubbish gets collected on Thursdays.* ∘ *a rubbish dump/bin* **2 NONSENSE** ▷ something that is nonsense or wrong: *Ignore him, he's talking rubbish.* **3 BAD QUALITY** ▷ informal 🅱️ something that is of bad quality: *There's so much rubbish on TV.*

rubbish² /ˈrʌbɪʃ/ **verb** [T] to criticize someone or something: *I wish you wouldn't rubbish everything about the concert – I really enjoyed it!*

rubbish³ /ˈrʌbɪʃ/ **adj** informal disappointing or of very bad quality: *I got a rubbish mark for chemistry.*

rubble /ˈrʌbl/ **noun** [U] pieces of broken bricks from a building that has been destroyed: *a pile of rubble*

rubella /ruːˈbelə/ **noun** [U] (also **German measles**) a disease that causes red spots on your skin

rubric /ˈruːbrɪk/ **noun** [C] a set of instructions or an explanation, especially in an examination paper or book

ruby /ˈruːbi/ **noun** [C] a valuable red stone that is used in jewellery

rucksack /ˈrʌksæk/ **noun** [C] UK a bag that you carry on your back → See picture at **bag**

rudder /ˈrʌdər/ **noun** [C] a piece of equipment that changes the direction of a boat or aircraft

ruddy /ˈrʌdi/ **adj** A ruddy face is red: *ruddy cheeks*

rude /ruːd/ **adj 1** 🅱️ behaving in a way that is not polite and upsets people: *a rude remark* ∘ *He complained that a member of staff had been **rude to** him.* ∘ [+ to do sth] *It would be rude to leave without saying goodbye.* **2** Rude words or jokes relate to sex or going to the toilet. • **rudely adv** • **rudeness noun** [U] → See also **a rude awakening**

➕ **Other ways of saying rude**

If someone is slightly rude or behaves without respect in a way that is funny, you might describe them as **cheeky** (*UK*):
*You asked your teacher how old she was? That was a bit **cheeky!***

A more formal alternative to 'rude' is the word **impolite**:
*She asks direct questions without being in any way **impolite**.*

If someone is rude or does not show respect to a person who is older or has more authority than they do, they might be described as **impertinent** or **insolent**:
*It was clear that they found his questions **impertinent**.*

The adjective **abrasive** describes someone's manner when they are rude and unfriendly:
*I found him rather **abrasive**.*

A person who is rude and unpleasant is sometimes described as **uncouth**:
*She found him loud-mouthed and **uncouth**.*

Language which is rude, referring to the body in an unpleasant way can be described as **vulgar** or **crude**:
*He told a rather **vulgar** joke over dinner.*

---

rudiments /ˈruːdɪmənts/ **noun** [plural] formal the **rudiments of sth** the most basic parts or principles of something • **rudimentary** /ˌruːdɪˈmentəri/ **adj** formal very basic

rueful /ˈruːfəl/ **adj** showing slight sadness about something but not in a serious way: *a rueful smile* • **ruefully adv**

ruffle /ˈrʌfl/ **verb** [T] If someone ruffles your hair, they rub it gently: *He **ruffled** my hair and kissed me.*

rug /rʌg/ **noun** [C] **1 FLOOR** ▷ 🅱️ a soft piece of material used to cover the floor: *The dog was lying on the rug in front of the fire.*

rug

→ See colour picture **The Living Room** on page Centre 4 **2 COVER** ▷ UK a soft cover that keeps you warm or comfortable

rugby /'rʌgbi/ **noun** [U] ⓐ a sport played by two teams with an oval ball and H-shaped goals: *a rugby player* → See colour picture **Sports 2** on page Centre 15

rugged /'rʌgɪd/ **adj 1** If an area of land is rugged, it looks rough and has lots of rocks: *a rugged coastline* **2** If a man looks rugged, his face looks strong and attractive: *a rugged face*

ruin¹ /'ruːɪn/ **verb** [T] **1** ⓑ to spoil or destroy something: [often passive] *They were late and the dinner was ruined.* **2** to cause someone to lose all their money or their job: *If the newspapers get hold of this story, they'll ruin him.*

ruin² /'ruːɪn/ **noun 1 DESTRUCTION** ▷ [U] the destruction of something: *Fonthill Abbey fell into ruin 10 years after it was built.* **2 BROKEN BUILDING** ▷ [C] ⓑ the broken parts that are left from an old building or town: *Thousand of tourists wander around these ancient ruins every year.* **3 LOSING EVERYTHING** ▷ [U] a situation in which someone has lost everything such as all their money or their job: *The collapse of the bank has left many people in financial ruin.* **4 be/lie in ruins** to be in a very bad state: *The war left one million people dead and the country in ruins.*

rule¹ /ruːl/ **noun 1 INSTRUCTION** ▷ [C] ⓑ an official instruction about what you must or must not do: *to break (= not obey) the rules.* ○ *to obey/follow the rules* ○ *You can't smoke at school, it's against the rules (= not allowed).* **2 LEADER** ▷ [U] control of a country by a particular person or country: *military rule* ○ *There have been reports of immense human suffering under his rule.* **3 USUAL WAY** ▷ [no plural] ⓑ the usual way something is: *an exception to the rule* ○ *Workers in the North are, as a rule, paid less than those in the South.* **4 PRINCIPLE** ▷ [C] ⓑ a principle of a system, such as a language or science: *the rules of grammar*

IDIOMS **a rule of thumb** a way of calculating something, which is not exact but which will help you to be correct enough • **bend/stretch the rules** to allow someone to do something that is not usually allowed: *We don't usually let students take books home, but I'll bend the rules on this occasion.*

→ See also **ground rules**

> ☑ Word partners for **rule**
>
> **apply/break/enforce/establish** a rule • a rule **forbids/prohibits** sth • a **strict/unwritten** rule • a rule **against** sth

rule² /ruːl/ **verb** [I, T] **1** to make an official legal decision: [+ (that)] *The judge ruled that it was wrong for a 16-year-old girl to be held in an adult prison.* **2** ⓑ to be in control of somewhere, usually a country: [often passive] *They were ruled for many years by a dictator.* ○ *the ruling party* → See also **rule the roost**

PHRASAL VERB **rule sb/sth out** to decide that something or someone is not suitable for a

particular purpose, or to decide that something is impossible: *The police have not ruled him out as a suspect.*

ruler /'ruːlər/ **noun** [C] **1** the leader of a country **2** ⓐ a flat, straight stick that is used to measure things → See colour picture **The Classroom** on page Centre 6

ruling /'ruːlɪŋ/ **noun** [C] an official legal decision, usually made by a judge

rum /rʌm/ **noun** [C, U] a strong, alcoholic drink made from sugar

rumble /'rʌmbl/ **verb** [I] to make a deep, long sound: *The smell of cooking made his stomach rumble.* • **rumble noun** [no plural] *the distant rumble of thunder*

rumbling /'rʌmblɪŋ/ **noun** [C] a deep, long sound: *the rumbling of a train passing by*

rumblings /'rʌmblɪŋz/ **noun** [plural] signs that people are angry about something: *rumblings of discontent*

rummage /'rʌmɪdʒ/ **verb rummage around/in/through, etc** to search inside something and move things around: *I found him rummaging through my drawers.*

rummage ,sale noun [C] US (UK **jumble sale**) a sale of old items, especially clothes, usually to make money for an organization

rumour¹ UK (US **rumor**) /'ruːmər/ **noun** [C] ⓑ a fact that a lot of people are talking about although they do not know if it is true: *to spread rumours* ○ *to deny rumours* ○ [+ (that)] *I heard a rumour that you were leaving.*

> ☑ Word partners for **rumour**
>
> **fuel/spark/spread/start** rumours • **deny/dismiss/hear** rumours • a rumour **circulates/goes around** • a **persistent/strong/unconfirmed** rumour • a rumour **about/of** sth

rumour² UK (US **rumor**) /'ruːmər/ **verb be rumoured** If a fact is rumoured, people are talking about it although they do not know if it is true: [+ (that)] *It's rumoured that the company director is about to resign.* ○ [+ to do sth] *The company is rumoured to be in financial difficulty.*

rump /rʌmp/ **noun** [C] the area above an animal's back legs

rumpled /'rʌmpld/ **adj** Rumpled clothes or sheets are untidy because they have folds in them.

run¹ /rʌn/ **verb** (**running, ran, run**) **1 MOVE FAST** ▷ [I, T] ⓐ to move on your feet at a faster speed than walking: *He ran away when I tried to pick him up.* ○ [+ to do sth] *We had to run to catch up with him.* ○ *I run about three miles every morning.* **2 ORGANIZE** ▷ [T] ⓑ to organize or control something: *She ran her own restaurant for five years.* **3 run sb/sth to/down, etc** to take someone or something somewhere, usually by car: *Could you run me to the station this afternoon?* **4 WORKING** ▷ [I, T] If a piece of equipment is running, it is switched on and working, and if you run it, you switch it on and make it work: *The engine is running more smoothly now.* **5 USE COMPUTER** ▷ [T] ⓑ If you run a computer program, you use it on your computer: *Did you* run a virus check this morning? **6 TRAVELLING** ▷ [I] ❷ If trains or buses are running, they are available to travel on: *The buses only run until 11 p.m.* **7 LIQUID** ▷ [I] ❷ If liquid runs somewhere, it flows: *Tears ran down her face.* **8 PUBLISH** ▷ [T] to publish something in a newspaper or magazine: *All the papers are **running** this story on the front page.* **9 run a bath** UK to fill a bath with water so that it is ready to use **10 run sth along/over/through, etc sth** to move something along, over, or through something else: *She ran her fingers through her hair.* **11 run through/down/along, etc** If something long and narrow runs somewhere, it is in that position: *There are wires running across the floor.* **12 CONTINUE** ▷ [I] If a play, film, etc runs for a period of time, it continues that long. **13 run in sb's/the family** If a quality, ability, disease, etc runs in the family, many members of the family have it: *A love of animals runs in our family.* **14 COLOUR** ▷ [I] If a colour runs, it comes out of some material when it is washed. **15 be running at sth** to be at a particular level: *Inflation is now running at 5.8%.* → See also **cast/run your/an eye**¹ over sth, run the **gauntlet**, run **riot**¹, run out of **steam**¹, run **wild**¹

PHRASAL VERBS **run across sb** to meet someone you know when you are not expecting to: *I ran across Jim in town the other day.* • **run after sb/sth** to chase someone or something that is moving away from you • **run around** to be very busy doing a lot of different things: *I'm exhausted, I've been running around all morning.* • **run away** ❷ to secretly leave a place because you are unhappy there: *to **run away from home*** • **run sth by sb** to tell someone about something so that they can give their opinion about it: *Can I run something by you, Sam?* • **run sb/sth down** informal to criticize someone or something, often unfairly • **run for sth** to compete in an election: *He's running for mayor again this year.* • **run into sb** ❷ to meet someone you know when you are not expecting to: *I ran into Emma on my way home.* • **run into sth 1 HIT** ▷ ❷ to hit something while you are driving a vehicle: *He skidded and ran into a tree.* **2 REACH A LEVEL** ▷ If an amount runs into thousands, millions, etc, it reaches that level. **3 PROBLEMS** ▷ If you run into difficulties, you begin to experience them: *to run into trouble* • **run off** informal to leave somewhere unexpectedly: *He **ran off** with all my money.* • **run on sth** If a machine runs on a supply of power, it uses that power to work: *The scanner runs on mains electricity and batteries.* • **run out 1** ❷ to use all of something so that there is none left: *I've nearly **run out of** money.* **2** ❷ If a supply of something runs out, there is none left because it has all been used: *Come on, time is running out.* • **run sb/sth over** ❷ to hit someone or something with a vehicle and drive over them, injuring or killing them: *He was run over by a bus as he crossed the road.* • **run through sth** to repeat something in order to practise it or to make sure that it is correct: *I just need to run through my speech one more time.* • **run sth up** If you run up a debt, you do things which cause

you to owe a large amount of money. • **run up against sth** If you run up against problems or difficulties, you begin to experience them.

run² /rʌn/ **noun 1 MOVING** ▷ [C] ❸ the activity of running for a period of time: [usually singular] *to **go for a run*** **2 SCORING** ▷ [C] ❷ in cricket or baseball, a single point: *to score a run* **3 a dummy/practice/trial run** an occasion when you do something to practise it before the real time **4 a run of sth** several things of the same type that happen without something different happening during that period: *a run of 10 games without a win* ∘ *a **run of good/bad luck*** **5 PERFORMANCES** ▷ [C] a period of performances of a play, film, etc **6 be on the run** to be trying to avoid being caught, especially by the police **7 make a run for it** informal to suddenly run fast in order to escape from somewhere

IDIOM **in the long/short run** ❷ at a time that is far away or near in the future

runaway¹ /ˈrʌnəˌweɪ/ **adj** [always before noun] **1 a runaway success/victory/winner, etc** something good that happens very quickly or easily **2** A runaway vehicle is moving away from somewhere without anyone controlling it: *a runaway car/train*

runaway² /ˈrʌnəˌweɪ/ **noun** [C] someone who has secretly left a place because they are unhappy there: *teenage runaways*

rundown /ˈrʌndaʊn/ **noun** [no plural] a report of the main facts relating to a subject: *He gave us **a rundown on** what happened at the meeting.*

run-down /ˌrʌnˈdaʊn/ **adj** Run-down buildings or areas are in very bad condition: *a run-down housing estate*

rung¹ /rʌŋ/ **noun** [C] one of the horizontal parts across a ladder (= structure for climbing up)

IDIOM **the first/highest/next, etc rung of the ladder** the first, highest, next, etc position, especially in society or in a job: *She's on the bottom rung of the management ladder.*

rung² /rʌŋ/ past participle of ring²

run-in /ˈrʌnɪn/ **noun** [C] informal an argument: *to have a run-in with someone*

runner /ˈrʌnər/ **noun 1** ❷ [C] someone who runs, usually in competitions: *a long-distance runner* **2 drug/gun runner** someone who takes drugs or guns illegally from one place to another → See also **front-runner**

runner ˈbean UK (US ˈrunner ˌbean) **noun** [C] a long, flat, green bean

runner-up /ˌrʌnərˈʌp/ **noun** [C] (plural **runners-up**) someone who finishes in second position in a competition

running¹ /ˈrʌnɪŋ/ **noun** [U] **1** ❷ the sport of moving on your feet at a speed faster than walking: *I **go running** three times a week.* ∘ *running shoes* → See colour picture **Sports 1** on page Centre 14 **2** the activity of controlling or looking after something: *He has recently handed over the **day-to-day running** of the museum to his daughter.* ∘ *running costs*

running² /ˈrʌnɪŋ/ **adj 1** [always before noun]

R

continuing for a long time: *a **running battle*** ∘ *a **running joke*** **2 second/third, etc day/week, etc running** ⑫ If something happens for the second/third, etc day/week, etc running, it happens on that number of regular occasions without changing: *He's won the Championship for the fifth year running.* **3 running water** If a place has running water, it has a working water system.

runny /'rʌni/ *adj* **1** A runny substance is more liquid than usual: *runny egg* **2 runny nose** If you have a runny nose, your nose is producing liquid all the time.

run-of-the-mill /ˌrʌnəvðə'mɪl/ *adj* ordinary and not special or exciting in any way: *He gave a fairly run-of-the-mill speech.*

run-up /'rʌnʌp/ *noun* **the run-up to sth** UK the period of time before an event: *Sales increased by 15% in the run-up to Christmas.*

runway /'rʌnweɪ/ *noun* [C] a large road that aircraft use to land on or to start flying from

rupture /'rʌptʃər/ *verb* [I, T] If you rupture something, you break or tear it, and if something ruptures, it breaks or tears: *He fell and ruptured a ligament in his knee.* • **rupture** *noun* [C]

rural /'rʊərəl/ *adj* ⑫ relating to the countryside and not to towns: *a rural area*

ruse /ruːz/ *noun* [C] a way of deceiving someone so that they do something that you want them to do: [+ to do sth] *The story was just a ruse to get her out of the house.*

rush¹ /rʌʃ/ *verb* **1** [I, T] ⑫ to hurry or move quickly somewhere, or to make someone or something hurry or move quickly somewhere: *We **rushed out** into the street to see what all the noise was.* ∘ *The UN has **rushed** medical supplies **to** the war zone.* ∘ [+ to do sth] *We had to rush to catch the bus.* **2 rush to do sth** to do something quickly and enthusiastically: *His friends rushed to congratulate him after the ceremony.* **3** [T] to make someone do something more quickly than they want to do it: [+ into + doing sth] *I refuse to be rushed into making a decision.*

rush² /rʌʃ/ *noun* [no plural] **1 MOVEMENT** ▷ a sudden fast movement of something: *a rush of air* **2 ACTIVITY** ▷ a lot of things happening or a lot of people trying to do something: [+ to do sth] *There was a **mad rush** to get tickets for the concert.* **3 HURRY** ▷ ⑫ a situation in which you have to hurry or move somewhere quickly: *I'm sorry I can't talk now, I'm **in a rush**.*

☑ Word partners for **rush**

a frantic/headlong/last-minute/mad rush • a rush for sth

rushes /rʌʃɪz/ *noun* [plural] tall plants that grow near water

rush hour *noun* [C, U] ⑫ the time when a lot of people are travelling to or from work and so roads and trains are very busy: *the morning/evening rush hour*

rust /rʌst/ *noun* [U] a dark orange substance that you get on metal when it has been damaged by air and water • **rust** *verb* [I, T]

rustic /'rʌstɪk/ *adj* simple and old-fashioned in style, in a way that is typical of the countryside

rustle /'rʌsl/ *verb* [I, T] If things such as paper or leaves rustle, or if you rustle them, they move about and make a soft, dry sound: *Outside, the trees rustled in the wind.*

PHRASAL VERB **rustle sth up** to produce something very quickly: *I managed to rustle up a meal from the bits and pieces I found in his fridge.*

rusty /'rʌsti/ *adj* **1** ⑫ Rusty metal has rust (= an orange substance) on its surface: *rusty nails* **2** ⑬ If a skill you had is now rusty, it is not now good because you have forgotten it: *My French is a bit rusty.*

rut /rʌt/ *noun* **1 in a rut** in a bad situation where you do the same things all the time, or where it is impossible to make progress: *He seems to be **stuck in a rut** at the moment.* **2** [C] a deep narrow mark in the ground made by a wheel

ruthless /'ruːθləs/ *adj* not caring if you hurt or upset other people when you try to get what you want: *ruthless ambition* ∘ *a ruthless dictator* **ruthlessly** *adv* • **ruthlessness** *noun* [U]

rye /raɪ/ *noun* [U] a plant that has grains which are used to make things such as bread and whisky: *rye bread*

R

S

S, s /es/ the nineteenth letter of the alphabet

the Sabbath /'sæbəθ/ **noun** a day of the week that many religious groups use for prayer and rest

sabbatical /sə'bætɪkəl/ **noun** [C, U] a period when a university teacher does not do their usual work and instead travels or studies: *He was on sabbatical last year.*

sabotage /'sæbətɑːʒ/ **verb** [T] **1** to damage or destroy something in order to prevent an enemy from using it: *Rebels sabotaged the roads and bridges.* **2** to spoil someone's plans or efforts in order to prevent them from being successful: *She tried to sabotage my chances of getting the job.* • **sabotage noun** [U] *an act of sabotage*

sac /sæk/ **noun** [C] a part in an animal or plant that is like a small bag

saccharin /'sækərɪn/ **noun** [U] a sweet, chemical substance that is used in food instead of sugar

sachet /'sæʃeɪ/ ⓤ /sæ'ʃeɪ/ **noun** [C] a small bag containing a small amount of something: *sachets of sugar and coffee powder*

sack¹ /sæk/ **noun 1** [C] a large bag made of paper, plastic, or cloth and used to carry or store things **2 the sack** UK ⓑ When someone gets the sack or is given the sack, they are told to leave their job: *He got the sack from his last job.*

 sack

sack² /sæk/ **verb** [T] UK ⓑ to tell someone to leave their job, usually because they have done something wrong: *He was sacked for being late.*

sacrament /'sækrəmənt/ **noun** [C] an important religious ceremony in the Christian Church: *the sacrament of marriage*

sacred /'seɪkrɪd/ **adj 1** relating to a religion or considered to be holy: *sacred music* ◦ *a sacred object* **2** too important to be changed or destroyed: *I don't work at weekends – my private time is sacred.*

sacrifice¹ /'sækrɪfaɪs/ **noun** [C, U] **1** something valuable that you give up in order to achieve something, or the act of giving it up: *Sometimes you have to **make sacrifices** to succeed.* **2** something offered to a god in a religious ceremony, especially an animal that is killed, or the act of offering it → See also **self-sacrifice**

sacrifice² /'sækrɪfaɪs/ **verb** [T] **1** to give up something that is valuable to you in order to achieve something: *There are thousands of men ready to **sacrifice** their lives **for** their country.* **2** to

kill an animal and offer it to a god in a religious ceremony

sacrilege /'sækrɪlɪdʒ/ **noun** [U, no plural] an act of treating something that is holy or important without respect

sacrosanct /'sækrəʊsæŋkt/ **adj** formal too important to be changed or destroyed: *Human life is sacrosanct.*

sad /sæd/ **adj** (**sadder, saddest**) **1 NOT HAPPY** ▷ ⓐ unhappy or making you feel unhappy: *I was very sad when our cat died.* ◦ *a sad book/movie* ◦ *[+ that] It's a bit sad that you'll miss our wedding.* ◦ *[+ to do sth] I was sad to see him go.* **2 NOT SATISFACTORY** ▷ [always before noun] not pleasant or satisfactory: *The sad truth is that we've failed.* **3 NOT FASHIONABLE** ▷ UK informal boring or not fashionable: *You enjoy reading timetables? You sad man!* • **sadness noun** [U]

➕ Other ways of saying sad

Unhappy and **miserable** mean the same as 'sad':

> She'd had a very **unhappy** childhood.
> I just woke up feeling **miserable**.

If someone is **upset**, they are unhappy because something bad has happened:

> They'd had an argument and she was still **upset** about it.
> Mike got very **upset** when I told him the news.

If someone is **broken-hearted** or **heartbroken** they are very sad because someone they love has ended a relationship with them:

> She was **broken-hearted** when Richard left.

If someone is **devastated** or **distraught**, they are extremely upset:

> She was **devastated** when he died.
> The missing child's **distraught** parents made an emotional appeal for information on TV.

The adjective **depressed** is often used when someone is very unhappy for a long time:

> She became deeply **depressed** after her husband died.

---

sadden /'sædən/ **verb** [T] formal to make someone feel sad or disappointed: [often passive] *We were saddened by his death.*

saddle¹ /'sædl/ **noun** [C] **1** a leather seat that you put on a horse so that you can ride it → See colour picture **Sports 1** on page Centre 14 **2** a seat on a bicycle or motorcycle

saddle

saddle² /'sædl/ **verb** [I, T] (also **saddle up**) to put a saddle on a horse

PHRASAL VERB **saddle sb with sth** to give someone a job or problem that will cause them a lot of work or difficulty

saddo /'sædəʊ/ **noun** [C] UK informal someone, especially a man, who is boring and not fashionable and has no friends

sadistic /sə'dɪstɪk/ **adj** getting pleasure from being cruel or violent: *sadistic behaviour* ∘ *a sadistic murderer* • **sadist** /'seɪdɪst/ **noun** [C] someone who gets pleasure from being cruel or violent • **sadism** /'seɪdɪzᵃm/ **noun** [U]

sadly /'sædli/ **adv** **1 NOT HAPPY** ▷ **B2** in a sad way: *She shook her head sadly.* **2 NOT SATISFACTORY** ▷ **B2** in a way that is not satisfactory: *Enthusiasm was sadly lacking these past few months at work.* **3 SORRY** ▷ used to say that you are sorry something is true: *Sadly, the marriage did not last.*

sae, SAE /eseɪ'iː/ **noun** [C] UK abbreviation for stamped addressed envelope or self-addressed envelope: an envelope that you put a stamp and your own address on and send to someone so that they can send you something back

safari /sə'fɑːri/ **noun** [C, U] a journey, usually to Africa, to see or hunt wild animals: *She is on safari in Kenya.*

safe¹ /seɪf/ **adj** **1 NOT DANGEROUS** ▷ **A2** not dangerous or likely to cause harm: *a safe driver* ∘ *Air travel is generally quite safe.* ∘ *We live in a safe neighbourhood.* ∘ [+ to do sth] *Is it safe to drink the water here?* → Opposite **unsafe 2 NOT HARMED** ▷ **B1** not harmed or damaged: *She returned safe and sound* (= not harmed in any way). **3 NOT IN DANGER** ▷ **A1** not in danger or likely to be harmed: *During the daylight hours we're safe from attack.* **4 safe to say** If it is safe to say something, you are sure it is correct: *I think it's safe to say that he'll be the next president.* **5 a safe place; somewhere safe** a place where something will not be lost or stolen: *It's very valuable so put it somewhere safe.*

IDIOM **play (it) safe** informal to be careful and not take risks

• **safely adv** **B1** *Make sure you drive safely.* ∘ *I can safely say* (= I am certain) *I have never met anyone as rude as him.* → See also **a safe bet**

safe² /seɪf/ **noun** [C] a strong metal box or cupboard with locks where you keep money, jewellery, and other valuable things

safeguard¹ /'seɪfgɑːd/ **verb** [T] to protect something from harm: *a plan to safeguard public health*

PHRASAL VERB **safeguard against sth** to do things that you hope will stop something unpleasant from happening: *A good diet will safeguard against disease.*

safeguard² /'seɪfgɑːd/ **noun** [C] a law, rule, or system that protects people or things from being harmed or lost

safe haven **noun** [C] a place where someone is safe from danger

safe sex **noun** [U] sex using a condom (= a thin rubber covering that a man wears on his penis) to avoid catching a disease

safety /'seɪfti/ **noun** [U] **1 B2** the state of being safe: *food/road safety* ∘ *The hostages were led to safety* (= to a safe place). ∘ *a safety valve* **2** how

safe something is: *Safety at the factory has been improved.* → See Note at **security**

Word partners for safety

ensure/guarantee sb's safety • safety is paramount

safety belt **noun** [C] a piece of equipment that keeps you fastened to your seat when you are travelling in a vehicle: *Please fasten your safety belt for take-off.*

safety net **noun** [C] **1** a plan or system that will help you if you get into a difficult situation: *Legal aid provides a safety net for people who can't afford a lawyer.* **2** a net that will catch someone if they fall from a high place

safety pin **noun** [C] a pin with a round cover that fits over the sharp end

saffron /'sæfrən/ **noun** [U] a yellow powder that is used as a spice

sag /sæg/ **verb** [I] (**sagging, sagged**) **1** to sink or bend down: *Our mattress sags in the middle* **2** informal to become weaker or less successful: *a sagging economy*

saga /'sɑːgə/ **noun** [C] a long story about a lot of people or events

sagacious /sə'geɪʃəs/ **adj** literary having or showing understanding and the ability to make good decisions and judgments

sage /seɪdʒ/ **noun** **1** [U] a herb whose leaves are used to give flavour to food **2** [C] literary a wise person

Sagittarius /ˌsædʒɪ'teəriəs/ **noun** [C, U] the sign of the zodiac that relates to the period of 22 November – 22 December, or a person born during this period → See picture at **the zodiac**

said /sed/ past of say

sail¹ /seɪl/ **verb** **1 TRAVEL** ▷ [I] **B1** to travel in a boat or a ship: *We sailed to Malta.* **2 CONTROL BOAT** ▷ [I, T] **B1** to control a boat that has no engine and is pushed by the wind: *She sailed the small boat through the storm.* **3 START JOURNEY** ▷ [I] When a ship sails, it starts its journey, and if people sail from a particular place or at a particular time, they start their journey: *This ship sails weekly from Florida to the Bahamas.* **4 sail over/past/through, etc** to move quickly through the air: *The ball sailed past me.*

PHRASAL VERB **sail through (sth)** to succeed very easily, especially in a test or competition: *She sailed through her exams.*

sail² /seɪl/ **noun** **1** [C] a large piece of material that is fixed to a pole on a boat to catch the wind and make the boat move **2 set sail** to start a journey by boat or ship

sailboat /'seɪlbəʊt/ **noun** [C] US a small boat with sails

sailing /'seɪlɪŋ/ **noun** [U] **A2** a sport using boats with sails: UK *a sailing boat*

IDIOM **be plain sailing** to be very easy

sailor /'seɪlər/ **noun** [C] **B1** someone who sails ships or boats as their job or as a sport

saint /seɪnt/ **noun** [C] **1** a dead person who has been officially respected by the Christian church

S

for living their life in a holy way: *Catherine of Siena was made a saint in 1461.* **2** a very kind or helpful person → See also **patron saint**

saintly /'seɪntli/ *adj* very good and kind

sake /seɪk/ *noun* **1 for the sake of sth** ⓑ for this reason or purpose: *For the sake of convenience, they combined the two departments.* **2 for the sake of sb** ⓑ in order to help or please someone: *He begged her to stay for the sake of the children.* **3 for God's/goodness/heaven's, etc sake** something you say when you are angry about something: *For heaven's sake, stop moaning!*

salad /'sæləd/ *noun* [C, U] ⓐ a cold mixture of vegetables that have not been cooked, usually eaten with meat, cheese, etc: *I made a big salad for lunch.* → See colour picture **Food** on page Centre 11

salad

salami /sə'lɑːmi/ *noun* [C, U] a spicy sausage (= tube of meat and spices) that is usually eaten cold in slices

salaried /'sæləʳrid/ *adj* receiving a fixed amount of money from your employer, usually every month

salary /'sæləri/ *noun* [C, U] ⓑ a fixed amount of money that you receive from your employer, usually every month → See Note at **pay²**

> **Word partners for salary**
>
> **earn** a salary • a **good/high/top** salary • an **annual** salary • a salary **cut/increase/rise**

sale /seɪl/ *noun* **1 SELLING THINGS** ▷ [U, no plural] ⓑ the act of selling something, or the time when something is sold: *The sale of alcohol is now banned.* ○ *to make a sale* **2 (up) for sale** ⓐ available to buy: *For sale: ladies' bicycle – good condition.* ○ *The house next to mine is up for sale.* **3 on sale a** ⓐ UK available to buy in a shop: *Her new book is now on sale.* **b** available for a lower price than usual: *This album was on sale for half price.* **4 EVENT** ▷ [C] an event where things are sold: *a sale of used books* **5 CHEAP PRICE** ▷ [C] ⓐ a time when a shop sells goods at a lower price than usual: UK *I bought this dress in the sale.* → See also **car boot sale, jumble sale**

saleable /'seɪləbl/ *adj* Something that is saleable can be sold easily: *He's painted some very saleable landscapes.*

sales /seɪlz/ *noun* **1** [plural] the number of items sold: *Our sales have doubled this year.* **2** [U] the part of a company that deals with selling things: *I used to work in sales.* ○ *a sales department*

sales assistant *noun* [C] (also US **salesclerk**, US /'seɪlzklɜːrk/) someone whose job is selling things in a shop

salesman, saleswoman /'seɪlzmən/, /'seɪlzwʊmən/ *noun* [C] (plural **salesmen, saleswomen**) ⓑ someone whose job is selling things

salesperson /'seɪlzˌpɜːsən/ *noun* [C] (plural **salespeople**) ⓐ someone whose job is selling things

sales rep *noun* [C] (formal **sales representative**) someone who travels to different places trying to persuade people to buy their company's products or services

salient /'seɪliənt/ *adj* formal The salient facts about something or qualities of something are the most important things about them.

saline /'seɪlaɪn/ US /'seɪliːn/ *adj* formal containing salt: *saline solution*

saliva /sə'laɪvə/ *noun* [U] the liquid that is made in your mouth

sallow /'sæləʊ/ *adj* Sallow skin is slightly yellow and does not look healthy.

salmon /'sæmən/ *noun* [C, U] (plural **salmon**) ⓑ a large, silver fish, or the pink meat of this fish: *fresh/smoked salmon*

salmonella /ˌsælmə'nelə/ *noun* [U] a type of bacteria that can make you very sick, sometimes found in food that is not cooked enough

salon /'sælɒn/ *noun* [C] a shop where you can have your hair cut or have your appearance improved: *a hair salon* → See also **beauty salon**

saloon /sə'luːn/ *noun* [C] **1** UK (US **sedan**) a large car with a separate, closed area for bags **2** US old-fashioned a public bar

salsa /'sælsə/ *noun* [U] **1** a cold, spicy sauce **2** a type of dance and music from Latin America: *a salsa club*

salt¹ /sɔːlt/, /sɒlt/ *noun* [U] ⓐ a white substance used to add flavour to food: *salt and pepper*

> IDIOM **take sth with a pinch of salt** UK (US **take sth with a grain of salt**) to not completely believe something that someone tells you

salt² /sɔːlt/, /sɒlt/ *verb* [T] to add salt to food

salt cellar *noun* [C] UK (US **salt shaker**) a small container with holes in for shaking salt on food

saltwater /'sɔːltˌwɔːtəʳ/ *adj* [always before noun] living in or containing water that has salt in it: *a saltwater fish*

salty /'sɔːlti/ *adj* tasting of or containing salt: *Is the soup too salty?*

salute¹ /sə'luːt/ *noun* [C] a sign of respect to someone of a higher rank in a military organization, often made by raising the right hand to the side of the head: *to give a salute*

salute² /sə'luːt/ *verb* [I, T] to give a salute to someone of a higher rank in a military organization

salvage¹ /'sælvɪdʒ/ *verb* [T] **1** to save things from a place where they have been damaged or lost: *gold coins salvaged from a shipwreck* **2** to try to make a bad situation better: *an attempt to salvage her reputation*

salvage² /'sælvɪdʒ/ *noun* [U] the activity of saving things from being damaged, or the things that are saved: *a salvage company*

salvation /sæl'veɪʃən/ *noun* [U] **1** in the Christian religion, the way that God saves someone from the bad effects of evil **2** something or someone that saves you from harm or a very unpleasant situation: *Getting a dog was Dad's salvation after Mum died.*

salwar kameez (also **shalwar kameez**) /ˌsalwɑːkə'miːz/ *noun* [C] a type of suit, worn especially by women in India, with loose trousers and a long shirt → See colour picture **Clothes** on page Centre 8

same¹ /seɪm/ *adj, pronoun* **1 the same a** **(A1)** exactly alike: *He's the same age as me.* ○ *We work at the same speed.* ○ *Cars cost the same here as they do in Europe.* **b** **(A1)** not another different thing or situation: *They met at the same place every week.* ○ *You meet the same people at all these events.* **c** **(B2)** not changed: *She's the same lively person she's always been.* ○ *He looks exactly the same as he did ten years ago.* **2 all/just the same** despite what has just been said: *He doesn't earn much. All the same, he ought to pay for some of his own drinks.* **3 Same here.** informal something that you say when something another person has said is also true for you: *"I think she's awful." "Same here."* **4 the same old arguments/faces/story, etc** informal something or someone you have seen or heard many times before

IDIOM **same old same old** informal used to say that a situation or someone's behaviour remains the same, especially when it it boring or annoying: *Most people just keep on doing the same old same old every day.*

→ See also **be in the same boat**, **in the same vein**, **be on the same wavelength**

same² /seɪm/ *adv* **the same** **(B2)** in the same way: *We treat all our children the same.*

same-sex /ˌseɪmˈseks/ *adj* A same-sex relationship, marriage, etc. is a romantic relationship between two men or two women.

sample¹ /ˈsɑːmpl/ *noun* [C] **1 SHOW** ▷ **(B2)** a small amount of something that shows you what it is like: *a **free sample** of chocolate* ○ *She brought in some **samples of** her work.* **2 EXAMINE** ▷ a small amount of a substance that a doctor or scientist collects in order to examine it: *a **blood/urine sample*** **3 NUMBER** ▷ **(B2)** a small number of people from a larger group that is being tested: *a sample of 500 male drivers*

> [!NOTE] **Word partners for sample**
> **analyse/collect/take/test** a sample • a sample **of** sth

sample² /ˈsɑːmpl/ *verb* [T] **1** to taste a small amount of food or drink to decide if you like it: *We sampled eight different cheeses.* **2** to experience a place or an activity, often for the first time: *an opportunity to sample the local night life*

sanatorium (plural **sanatoriums**, **sanatoria**) (also US **sanitarium**) /ˌsænəˈtɔːriəm/ *noun* [C] a hospital where people go to rest and get well after a long illness

sanction¹ /ˈsæŋkʃ°n/ *noun* **1** [C] a punishment for not obeying a rule or a law: *economic/trade sanctions against a country* **2** [U] official approval or permission

> [!NOTE] **Word partners for sanction**
> **impose/lift** sanctions • **tough** sanctions • sanctions **against/on** sb • economic/trade sanctions

sanction² /ˈsæŋkʃ°n/ *verb* [T] to formally

approve of something: *He refused to sanction the publication of his private letters.*

sanctity /ˈsæŋktəti/ *noun* formal **the sanctity o life/marriage, etc** the quality of being important and deserving respect

sanctuary /ˈsæŋktʃuəri/ *noun* **1 QUIET** ▷ [C, U] quiet and peaceful place: *After a busy day, I like to escape to the sanctuary of my garden* **2 PROTECTION** ▷ [C, U] a place that provide protection: *to **seek sanctuary*** **3 ANIMALS** ▷ [C a place where animals are protected and canno be hunted: *a bird/wildlife sanctuary*

sand¹ /sænd/ *noun* [U] **(B1)** a substance that i found on beaches and in deserts, which is made from very small grains of rock: *a grain of sand*

sand² /sænd/ *verb* [T] to make wood smooth by rubbing it with sandpaper (= strong paper with rough surface)

sandal /ˈsænd°l/ *noun* [C] **(B1)** a light shoe with straps that you wear in warm weather → Se colour picture **Clothes** on page Centre 9

sandcastle /ˈsændˌkɑːsl/ *noun* [C] a model of castle made of wet sand, usually built by children on a beach

sand dune *noun* [C] a hill of sand in the deser or on the coast

sandpaper /ˈsændˌpeɪpəʳ/ *noun* [U] stron paper with a rough surface that is rubbed against wood to make it smooth

sands /sændz/ *noun* [plural] a large area of san

sandstone /ˈsændstəʊn/ *noun* [U] rock made o sand

sandwich¹ /ˈsænwɪdʒ/ *noun* [C] **(A1)** two slices of bread with meat, cheese, etc between them: *a cheese/tuna sandwich* → See **Food** on page Centre 11

sandwich

sandwich² /ˈsænwɪdʒ/ *verb*

PHRASAL VERB **be sandwiched between sth/sb** informal to be in a small space between two people or things: *Andorra is a small country sandwiched between Spain and France.*

sandy /ˈsændi/ *adj* **(B1)** covered with or containing sand: *a sandy beach*

sane /seɪn/ *adj* **1** not suffering from menta illness **2** [always before noun] showing goo judgment: *a sane attitude/decision* → Opposite **insane**

sang /sæŋ/ past tense of sing

sanguine /ˈsæŋgwɪn/ *adj* formal positive and ful of hope: *The director is sanguine about th company's prospects.*

sanitarium /ˌsænɪˈteəriəm/ *noun* [C] (plura **sanitariums**, **sanitaria**) another US spelling o sanatorium (= a hospital where people rest an get well after a long illness)

sanitary /ˈsænɪt°ri/ *adj* relating to preventin disease by removing dirt and waste: *sanitar conditions*

sanitary towel *noun* [C] UK (US **sanitary napkin**) a thick piece of soft paper that woman wears to absorb blood from her period (= monthly blood from the uterus)

anitation /ˌsænɪˈteɪʃᵊn/ **noun** [U] a system for protecting people's health by removing dirt and waste

anity /ˈsænəti/ **noun** [U] **1** the quality of behaving calmly and showing good judgment: *Jogging helps me **keep** my **sanity**.* **2** the state of having a healthy mind and not being mentally ill → Opposite **insanity**

ank /sæŋk/ past tense of sink

anta /ˈsæntə/ **noun** [no plural] (also **Santa Claus** /ˈsæntəklɔːz/) a kind, fat, old man in red clothes who people say brings presents to children at Christmas

ap¹ /sæp/ **verb** [T] (**sapping, sapped**) to gradually make something weak: *Ten years of war had **sapped** the country's **strength**.*

ap² /sæp/ **noun** [U] the liquid inside plants and trees

apling /ˈsæplɪŋ/ **noun** [C] a young tree

apphire /ˈsæfaɪəʳ/ **noun** [C] a bright blue, transparent stone

arcasm /ˈsɑːkæzᵊm/ **noun** [U] the use of remarks in a way that says the opposite of what you mean, in order to insult someone or show them that you are annoyed: *"Oh, I am sorry," she said, her voice heavy with sarcasm.*

arcastic /sɑːˈkæstɪk/ **adj** using sarcasm: *a sarcastic comment/remark ∘ Are you being sarcastic?* • **sarcastically adv**

ardine /sɑːˈdiːn/ **noun** [C] a small sea fish that you can eat

ari (also **saree**) /ˈsɑːri/ **noun** [C] a dress, worn especially by women from India and Pakistan, made from a very long piece of thin cloth

ARS /sɑːz/ **noun** [U] abbreviation for Severe Acute Respiratory Syndrome: a serious disease that makes it difficult to breathe

ASE /ˌeseɪesˈiː/ **noun** [C] US abbreviation for self-addressed stamped envelope: an envelope that you put a stamp and your own address on and send to someone so that they can send you something back

ash /sæʃ/ **noun** [C] a long, narrow piece of cloth that is worn around the waist or over the shoulder, often as part of a uniform

assy /ˈsæsi/ **adj** US informal **1** very energetic and confident: *a smart, sassy young woman* **2** slightly rude, but not offensive: *a sassy remark*

at /sæt/ past of sit

at written abbreviation for Saturday

atan /ˈseɪtᵊn/ **noun** [no plural] the Devil (= enemy of God)

atanic /səˈtænɪk/ **adj** relating to the Devil (= enemy of God) : *a satanic cult/ritual*

atchel /ˈsætʃᵊl/ **noun** [C] a large bag with a strap that goes over your shoulder, often used for carrying school books → See **The Classroom** on page Centre 6

atellite /ˈsætᵊlaɪt/ **noun** [C] **1** ⱞ a piece of equipment that is sent into space around the Earth to receive and send signals or to collect information: *a spy/weather satellite* **2** a natural

object that moves around a planet in space: *The moon is the Earth's satellite.*

satellite dish noun [C] a round piece of equipment that receives television and radio signals broadcast from satellites

satellite television noun [U] (also **satellite TV**) television programmes that are broadcast using a satellite

satin /ˈsætɪn/ **noun** [U] a smooth, shiny cloth

satire /ˈsætaɪəʳ/ **noun 1** [U] the use of jokes and humour to criticize people or ideas: *political satire* **2** [C] a story, film, etc that uses satire • **satirist** /ˈsætɪrɪst/ **noun** [C] someone who uses satire

satirical /səˈtɪrɪkᵊl/ **adj** using satire: *a satirical magazine/novel*

satisfaction /ˌsætɪsˈfækʃᵊn/ **noun** [U] **1** ⱞ the pleasant feeling you have when you get something that you wanted or do something that you wanted to do: *job satisfaction* ∘ *She smiled **with satisfaction**.* ∘ *[+ of + doing sth] I had the satisfaction of knowing that I'd done everything I could.* **2** to sb's satisfaction as well as someone wants: *He won't get paid until he completes the job to my satisfaction.* → Opposite **dissatisfaction**

🗒 Word partners for **satisfaction**

derive/get satisfaction from sth • sth gives sb satisfaction • deep/immense satisfaction • a sense of satisfaction • job satisfaction

---

satisfactory /ˌsætɪsˈfæktᵊri/ **adj** ⱞ good enough: *We hope very much to find a **satisfactory** solution to the problem.* → Opposite **unsatisfactory** • **satisfactorily adv**

satisfied /ˈsætɪsfaɪd/ **adj 1** ⱞ pleased because you have got what you wanted, or because something has happened in the way that you wanted: *Are you **satisfied with** the new arrangement?* → Opposite **dissatisfied 2** be satisfied that If you are satisfied that something is true, you believe it: *The judge was satisfied that she was telling the truth.* → See also **self-satisfied**

satisfy /ˈsætɪsfaɪ/ **verb 1** ⱞ [T] to please someone by giving them what they want or need: *They sell 31 flavours of ice cream – enough to satisfy everyone!* **2** satisfy conditions/needs/requirements, etc to have or provide something that is needed or wanted: *She satisfies all the requirements for the job.* **3** satisfy sb that to make someone believe that something is true: *I satisfied myself that I had locked the door.*

satisfying /ˈsætɪsfaɪɪŋ/ **adj** making you feel pleased by providing what you need or want: *a satisfying meal* ∘ *My work is very satisfying.*

SATNAV /ˈsætnæv/ **noun** [U] abbreviation for satellite navigation: a system of computers and satellites (= equipment that is sent into space around the Earth to receive and send signals), used in cars and other places to tell a user where they are or where something is

saturate /ˈsætʃᵊreɪt/ **verb** [T] **1** to make something completely wet: *Heavy rain had saturated the playing field.* **2** to put as much of a substance that dissolves into a solution as is possible • **saturation** /ˌsætʃᵊrˈeɪʃᵊn/ **noun** [U]

S

saturated 'fat noun [C, U] a fat found in meat, milk, and eggs, which is thought to be bad for your health

Saturday /'sætədeɪ/ **noun** [C, U] (written abbreviation **Sat**) Ⓐ① the day of the week after Friday and before Sunday

Saturn /'sætən/ **noun** [no plural] the planet that is sixth from the Sun, after Jupiter and before Uranus

sauce /sɔːs/ **noun** [C, U] Ⓐ② a hot or cold liquid that you put on food to add flavour: *pasta with tomato sauce* → See also **soy sauce**

saucepan /'sɔːspən/ **noun** [C] Ⓑ① a deep, metal pan, usually with a long handle and a lid, that is used to cook food in → See colour picture **The Kitchen** on page Centre 2

saucer /'sɔːsər/ **noun** [C] Ⓑ① a small plate that you put under a cup: *a cup and saucer*

saucy /'sɔːsi/ **adj** slightly rude, or referring to sex in a funny way: *a saucy postcard/joke*

sauna /'sɔːnə/ **noun** [C] **1** a room that is hot and filled with steam where people sit to relax or feel healthy: *a gym with a pool and a sauna* **2 have a sauna** to spend time inside a sauna

saunter /'sɔːntər/ **verb saunter into/over/ through, etc** to walk somewhere in a slow and relaxed way: *He sauntered through the door two hours late.*

sausage /'sɒsɪdʒ/ **noun** [C, U] Ⓐ② a mixture of meat and spices pressed into a long tube

sausage

sauté /'səʊteɪ/, /səʊ'teɪ/ **verb** [T] to fry food quickly in a small amount of hot oil

savage[1] /'sævɪdʒ/ **adj 1** extremely violent: *a savage attack* **2** severe: *savage criticism* • **savagely adv**

savage[2] /'sævɪdʒ/ **verb** [T] **1** to attack violently: [often passive] *A sheep had been savaged by a dog.* **2** to severely criticize someone or something: [often passive] *Her performance was savaged by the critics.*

savage[3] /'sævɪdʒ/ **noun** [C] old-fashioned an offensive word for a person from a country at an early stage of development

save[1] /seɪv/ **verb 1 MAKE SAFE** ▷ [T] Ⓑ① to stop someone or something from being killed or destroyed: *He was badly injured, but the doctors saved his life.* ∘ *She saved the children from drowning.* ∘ *He had to borrow money to save his business.* **2 MONEY** ▷ [I, T] (also **save up**) Ⓐ② to keep money so that you can buy something with it in the future: *We've saved almost $900 for our wedding.* ∘ *Michael's saving up for a new computer.* **3 KEEP** ▷ [T] Ⓐ② to keep something to use in the future: *I've saved some food for you.* **4 save money/space/time, etc** to reduce the amount of money/space/time, etc that you have to use **5 save sb (from) doing sth** Ⓑ① to help someone avoid having to do something: *We'll eat in a restaurant – it'll save you having to cook.* **6 save files/work, etc** Ⓐ② to store work or

information electronically on or from a compu ter **7 save a goal** to prevent a player from scoring a goal: *He saved two goals in the las minute of the game.* → See also **save the day lose/save face**[1]

PHRASAL VERB **save on sth** to avoid using some thing so that you do not have to pay for it: *Sh walks to work to save on bus fares.*

save[2] /seɪv/ **noun** [C] the act of preventing a goa from being scored in a sport: *The goalkeepe made a great save.*

saver /'seɪvər/ **noun** [C] someone who save money in a bank

saving /'seɪvɪŋ/ **noun** [C] UK (US **savings**) If yo make a saving, you pay less money than yo would usually have to: [usually singular] *a savin of 20 euros*

savings /'seɪvɪŋz/ **noun** [plural] Ⓑ② money tha you have saved, usually in a bank: *I spent all m savings on a new kitchen.* ∘ *a savings account*

savings and 'loan associ,ation noun [C] U a bank that is owned by the people who kee their money in it and that lets them borro money to buy a house

saviour UK (US **savior**) /'seɪvjər/ **noun 1** [C someone who saves someone or somethin from harm or difficulty **2 the Saviour** i Christianity, Jesus Christ

savour UK (US **savor**) /'seɪvər/ **verb** [T] to enjo food or a pleasant experience as much and a slowly as possible: *to savour a meal* ∘ *W savoured our moment of victory.*

savoury UK (US **savory**) /'seɪvəri/ **adj** Savour food is not sweet: *savoury biscuits*

savvy /'sævi/ **noun** [U] informal practical knowl edge and ability: *business/political savv* • **savvy adj** informal having knowledge an ability: *a savvy consumer*

saw[1] /sɔː/ **noun** [C] a tool with a sharp edge tha you use to cut wood or other hard materia → See picture at **tool** • **saw verb** [I, T] (**sawed sawn**, mainly US **sawed**) to use a saw: *They sawe the door in half.*

saw[2] /sɔː/ past tense of see

sawdust /'sɔːdʌst/ **noun** [U] very small pieces o wood and powder that are produced when yo cut wood with a saw

saxophone /'sæksəfəʊn/ **noun** [C] (informal **sax** a metal musical instrument that you play b blowing into it and pressing keys to produc different notes • **saxophonist** /sæk'sɒfənɪst/ U /'sæksəfəʊnɪst/ **noun** [C] someone who plays th saxophone

say[1] /seɪ/ **verb** [T] (**says, said**) **1 WORDS** ▷ Ⓐ① t speak words: *"I'd like to go home," she said.* ∘ *I couldn't hear what they were saying.* ∘ *How d you say this word?* **2 TELL** ▷ Ⓑ① to tell someon about a fact, thought, or opinion: [+ questio word] *Did she say where she was going?* [+ (that)] *The jury said that he was guilty* **3 INFORMATION** ▷ Ⓑ① to give information i writing, numbers, or signs: *My watch says on o'clock.* ∘ *What do the papers say about th election?* **4 say sth to yourself** to think some thing but not speak: *"I hope she likes me," he sai* to himself. **5 SHOW** ▷ to show what you think without using words: *His smile seemed to say that I was forgiven.* **6 (let's) say...** used to introduce a suggestion or possible example of something: *Say you were offered a better job in another city – would you take it?* **7 You can say that again!** informal used to show that you completely agree with something that someone has just said: *"That was a very bad movie!" "You can say that again!"*

IDIOM **it goes without saying** ⬚ If something goes without saying, it is generally accepted or understood: *It goes without saying that smoking is harmful to your health.*

→ See also **Say cheese!**, **easier said than done (easy²)**

> ❗ Common learner error: **say** or **tell**?
>
> **Say** can refer to any type of speech.
> *"Good night," she said.*
> *She said she was unhappy.*
> *Jim said to meet him here.*
>
> **Tell** is used to report that someone has given information or an order. The verb **tell** is always followed by the person that the information or order is given to.
> *Simon told me about his new job.*
>
> **Say** is never followed by the person that the information or order is given to.
> *He told us to stay here.*
> ~~He said us to stay here.~~

ay² /seɪ/ **noun** [U] **1** If you have a say in something, you are involved in making a decision about it: *We had some say in how our jobs would develop.* **2 have your say** to give your opinion about something: *We can't vote yet – Christina hasn't had her say.*

> ✏ Word partners for **say (noun)**
>
> be given/have [a/no/some, etc] say • the final say • say in/on sth

aying /ˈseɪɪŋ/ **noun** [C] a famous phrase that people use to give advice about life: *Have you heard the saying, "misery loves company"?*

b written abbreviation for 'somebody' or 'someone' • **sb's** written abbreviation for 'somebody's' or 'someone's'

cab /skæb/ **noun** [C] a layer of dried blood that forms to cover a cut in the skin

caffolding /ˈskæfˀldɪŋ/ **noun** [U] a temporary structure made of flat boards and metal poles used to work on a tall building

cald /skɔːld/ **verb** [T] to burn something or someone with very hot liquid or steam: *She scalded her mouth on the hot soup.*

cale¹ /skeɪl/ **noun 1 SIZE** ▷ [no plural] ⬚ the size or level of something: *We don't yet know the scale of the problem.* ○ *Nuclear weapons cause destruction on a massive scale* (= cause a lot of destruction). **2 large-/small-scale** A large-/small-scale event or activity is large/small in size: *a large-scale investigation* **3 MEASURING SYSTEM** ▷ [C] ⬚ the set of numbers, amounts, etc used to measure or compare the level of something:

How would you rate her work on a scale of 1-10? **4 EQUIPMENT** ▷ [C] US (UK **scales** [plural]) a piece of equipment for measuring weight: *a bathroom/kitchen scale* → See colour picture **The Kitchen** on page Centre 2 → See colour picture **The Bathroom** on page Centre 3 **5 COMPARISON** ▷ [C, U] ⬚ how the size of things on a map, model, etc relates to the same things in real life: *a map with a scale of one centimetre per ten kilometres* **6 MUSIC** ▷ [C] a series of musical notes that is always played in order and that rises gradually from the first note **7 SKIN** ▷ [C] one of the flat pieces of hard material that covers the skin of fish and snakes

> ✏ Word partners for **scale**
>
> on a [grand/large/massive/small, etc] scale • the scale of sth

scale² /skeɪl/ **verb** [T] to climb something that is high or steep: *to scale a wall*

PHRASAL VERB **scale sth back** mainly US (UK/US **scale sth down**) to make something smaller than it was or smaller than it was planned to be

scales /skeɪlz/ **noun** [plural, C] UK (US **scale**) ⬚ a piece of equipment for measuring weight: *bathroom/kitchen scales* → See colour picture **The Kitchen** on page Centre 2 → See colour picture **The Bathroom** on page Centre 3

scallion /ˈskæliən/ **noun** [C] US (UK **spring onion**) a small onion with a white part at the bottom and long, green leaves which is eaten in salads

scallop /ˈskæləp/ **noun** [C] a small sea creature that lives in a shell and is eaten as food

scalp /skælp/ **noun** [C] the skin on the top of your head under your hair

scalpel /ˈskælpˀl/ **noun** [C] a small, sharp knife that doctors use to cut through skin during an operation

scalper /ˈskælpəʳ/ **noun** [C] US (UK **tout**) someone who unofficially sells tickets outside theatres, sports grounds, etc

scaly /ˈskeɪli/ **adj** If your skin is scaly, it is rough and falls off in small, dry pieces.

scam /skæm/ **noun** [C] informal an illegal plan for making money

scamper /ˈskæmpəʳ/ **verb** **scamper away/down/off, etc** to run quickly and with small steps, like a child or a small animal

scampi /ˈskæmpi/ **noun** [U] prawns (= small sea creatures) that have been fried

scan¹ /skæn/ **verb** [T] (**scanning, scanned**) **1 EXAMINE** ▷ to examine something with a machine that can see inside an object or body: *Airports use X-ray machines to scan luggage for weapons.* **2 COMPUTER** ▷ to use a piece of equipment that copies words or pictures from paper into a computer: *to scan photos into a computer* **3 LOOK** ▷ to look around an area quickly to try to find a person or thing: *She scanned the crowd for a familiar face.* **4 READ** ▷ (also **scan through**) to quickly read a piece of writing to understand the main meaning or to find a particular piece of information: *I scanned the travel brochures looking for a cheap holiday.*

S

scan² /skæn/ **noun** [C] a medical examination in which an image of the inside of the body is made using a special machine: *a brain scan*

scandal /'skændᵊl/ **noun** [C, U] ⓑ something that shocks people because they think it is morally wrong: *a **sex** scandal*

> **✓ Word partners for scandal**
>
> a scandal **breaks/erupts** • be at the **centre of/involved in** a scandal • a scandal **surrounding** sth • a **sex** scandal

scandalous /'skændᵊləs/ **adj** shocking or morally wrong: *a scandalous waste of money*

Scandinavian /ˌskændɪ'neɪviən/ **adj** from or relating to the countries of Sweden, Denmark, Norway, and sometimes Finland and Iceland
• **Scandinavian noun** [C]

scanner /'skænər/ **noun** [C] **1** a piece of equipment that copies words or pictures from paper into a computer **2** a piece of medical equipment used to examine images of the inside of someone's body

scant /skænt/ **adj** [always before noun] very little and not enough: *His work has received only scant attention outside this country.*

scantily /'skæntɪli/ **adv scantily clad/dressed** not wearing many clothes and showing a lot of the body

scanty /'skænti/ **adj** very small in size or quantity: *scanty clothing*

scapegoat /'skeɪpgəʊt/ **noun** [C] someone who is blamed for a bad situation, although they have not caused it: *He was **made** a scapegoat for the disaster.*

scar /skɑːr/ **noun** [C] **1** ⓑ a permanent mark left on the body from a cut or other injury **2** damage done to a person's mind by a very unpleasant event or situation: *a **psychological** scar* • **scar verb** [T] **(scarring, scarred)** to cause a scar: [often passive] *He was **scarred for life** by the accident.*

scarce /skeəs/ **adj** rare or not available in large amounts: *scarce resources*

scarcely /'skeəsli/ **adv 1** only just: *They had scarcely finished eating when the doorbell rang.* **2 can scarcely do sth** If you say you can scarcely do something, you mean it would be wrong to do it: *He's only two – you can scarcely blame him for behaving badly.*

scarcity /'skeəsəti/ **noun** [C, U] a situation in which there is not enough of something: *a scarcity of food/affordable housing*

scare¹ /skeər/ **verb** [T] **1** to frighten a person or animal: *Sudden, loud noises scare me.* **2 scare the hell/life/living daylights, etc out of sb** *informal* to make someone feel very frightened → See also **scare/frighten sb out of their wits**

PHRASAL VERBS **scare sb/sth away/off** to make a person or an animal so frightened that they go away: *She scared off her attacker by screaming.* • **scare sb away/off** to make someone worried about doing something so that they decide not to do it: *The recent bomb attacks have scared away the tourists.*

scare² /skeər/ **noun** [C] **1** a sudden feeling of fear or worry: *The earthquake **gave** us a scare.* **2** situation that worries or frightens people: *food/health scare*

> **✓ Word partners for scare**
>
> **give** sb/**have**/**suffer** a scare • a **food/health** scare

scarecrow /'skeəkrəʊ/ **noun** [C] a model of a person that is put in a field to frighten birds and stop them from eating the plants

scared /skeəd/ **adj** ⓑ frightened or worried: *Robert's **scared of** heights.* ∘ *I was **scared to death** (= very frightened).* ∘ [+ (that)] *We were scared that we'd be killed.*

> **➕ Other ways of saying scared**
>
> The adjectives **afraid** and **frightened** are common alternatives to 'scared':
> *Don't be **frightened**. The dog won't hurt you.*
> *Gerry has always been **afraid** of heights.*
> If someone is extremely scared, then you can use the adjectives **petrified**, **terrified**, **panic-stricken**, or the informal phrase **scared to death**:
> *I'm **petrified/terrified** of spiders.*
> *She was **panic-stricken** when her little boy disappeared.*
> *He's **scared to death** of having the operation.*
> If someone is scared because they are worrying about something, then you can use adjectives like **afraid** or **worried**:
> *I'm **afraid/worried** that something will go wrong.*

scarf¹ /skɑːf/ **noun** [C] (plural **scarves** /skɑːvz/, **scarfs**) ⓐ a piece of cloth that you wear around your neck, head, or shoulders to keep warm or for decoration → See colour picture **Clothes** on page Centre 9

scarf² /skɑːf/ **verb** [T] *US informal* (also **scarf down**, UK **scoff**) to eat a lot of something quickly: *Who scarfed all the cookies?*

scarlet /'skɑːlət/ **noun** [U] a bright red colour
• **scarlet adj**

scary /'skeəri/ **adj** *informal* ⓑ frightening: *a scary place/woman*

scathing /'skeɪðɪŋ/ **adj** criticizing something very strongly: *He was scathing about the report.*

scatter /'skætər/ **verb 1** [T] to throw objects over an area so that they land apart from each other: *He scattered some flower seeds in the garden.* **2** [I] to suddenly move apart in different directions: *The crowd scattered at the sound of gunshots.*

scatter

scattered /'skætəd/ **adj** covering a wide area: *His toys were* *scattered all over the floor.* ◦ *There will be* ***scattered showers*** *(= separate areas of rain) today.*

cattering /ˈskætərɪŋ/ **noun** [no plural] a small number of separate things, especially in a large area: *a scattering of houses*

cavenge /ˈskævɪndʒ/ **verb** [I, T] to search for food or for useful things that have been thrown away • **scavenger noun** [C] a person or animal who scavenges

cenario /sɪˈnɑːriəʊ/ **noun 1** [C] a description of a situation, or of a situation that may develop in the future **2 worst-case scenario** the worst situation that you can imagine

cene /siːn/ **noun 1 PART OF FILM** ▷ [C] [B1] a short part of a film, play, or book in which the events happen in one place: *a* ***love scene*** ◦ *the final scene* **2 VIEW** ▷ [C] [B2] a view or picture of a place, event, or activity: *scenes of everyday life* **3 PLACE** ▷ [C] [B2] a place where an unpleasant event has happened: *the scene of the crime* **4 the club/gay/music, etc scene** [B2] all the things connected with a particular way of life or activity **5 ARGUMENT** ▷ [C] If someone makes a scene, they have a loud argument or show strong emotions in a public place: [usually singular] *She* ***made a scene*** *when I told her she couldn't come with us.*

IDIOMS **behind the scenes** If something happens behind the scenes, it happens secretly. • **set the scene for sth** to make an event or situation possible or likely to happen

cenery /ˈsiːnəri/ **noun** [U] **1** [B1] the attractive, natural things that you see in the countryside: *The Grand Canyon is famous for its spectacular scenery.* **2** the large pictures of buildings, countryside, etc used on a theatre stage

cenic /ˈsiːnɪk/ **adj** having views of the attractive, natural things in the countryside: *a* ***scenic route*** ◦ *an area of great* ***scenic beauty***

cent /sent/ **noun 1 SMELL** ▷ [C] [B2] a pleasant smell: *the sweet scent of orange blossoms* **2 LIQUID** ▷ [C, U] a pleasant-smelling liquid that people put on their skin **3 ANIMAL** ▷ [C, U] the smell of an animal or a person that is left somewhere

cented /ˈsentɪd/ **adj** having a pleasant smell: *a scented candle*

ceptic UK (US **skeptic**) /ˈskeptɪk/ **noun** [C] someone who doubts that a belief or an idea is true or useful

ceptical UK (US **skeptical**) /ˈskeptɪkəl/ **adj** doubting that something is true or useful: *Scientists remain* ***sceptical about*** *astrology.* ◦ *She was* ***sceptical of*** *the new arrangement.*

cepticism UK (US **skepticism**) /ˈskeptɪsɪzəm/ **noun** [U] doubt that something is true or useful: *There was some* ***scepticism about*** *her ability to do the job.*

chedule¹ /ˈʃedjuːl/ [US] /ˈskedʒuːl/ **noun 1** [C, U] [B2] a plan that gives events or activities and the times that they will happen or be done: *I have a very* ***busy schedule*** *today.* ◦ *Will the work be completed* ***on schedule*** *(= at the expected time)?* ◦ *The project was finished* ***ahead of schedule*** *(= earlier than planned).* **2** [C] mainly US a list of times when buses, trains, etc arrive and leave

schedule² /ˈʃedjuːl/ [US] /ˈskedʒuːl/ **verb** [T] [B2] to arrange that an event or an activity will happen at a particular time: [often passive] *Your appointment has been* ***scheduled for*** *next Tuesday.* ◦ *a scheduled flight*

scheme¹ /skiːm/ **noun** [C] **1** mainly UK [B2] an official plan or system: *an insurance/savings scheme* ◦ *a training scheme for teenagers* **2** a plan for making money, especially in a dishonest way: *a scheme to steal money from investors*

> Word partners for **scheme**
>
> **come up with/devise** a scheme • **implement/introduce/launch/unveil** a scheme • a scheme **for** doing sth

scheme² /skiːm/ **verb** [I] to make a secret plan in order to get an advantage, usually by deceiving people

schizophrenia /ˌskɪtsəʊˈfriːniə/ **noun** [U] a serious mental illness in which someone cannot understand what is real and what is imaginary

schizophrenic¹ /ˌskɪtsəʊˈfrenɪk/ **adj** relating to schizophrenia: *schizophrenic patients/symptoms*

schizophrenic² /ˌskɪtsəʊˈfrenɪk/ **noun** [C] someone who suffers from schizophrenia

schmooze /ʃmuːz/ **verb** [I, T] informal to talk to someone in a friendly, informal way so that they will like you or do something for you: *politicians* ***schmoozing with*** *journalists*

scholar /ˈskɒləʳ/ **noun** [C] someone who has studied a subject and knows a lot about it: *a legal scholar*

scholarly /ˈskɒləli/ **adj 1** A scholarly article or book is a formal piece of writing by a scholar about a particular subject. **2** If someone is scholarly, they study a lot and know a lot about what they study.

scholarship /ˈskɒləʃɪp/ **noun 1** [C] an amount of money given to a person by an organization to pay for their education, usually at a college or university **2** [U] study of a subject for a long time

scholastic /skəˈlæstɪk/ **adj** [always before noun] relating to school and education: *scholastic achievements*

school /skuːl/ **noun 1 PLACE** ▷ [C] [A1] a place where children go to be educated: *Which* ***school*** *do you* ***go*** *to?* ◦ *I ride my bike to school.* **2 TIME** ▷ [U] [A2] the time that you spend at school: *I like school.* ◦ *We're going shopping after school.* **3 PEOPLE** ▷ [no plural] all the students and teachers at a school: *The whole school took part in the project.* **4 a dance/language/riding, etc school** [A2] a place where you can study a particular subject **5 PART** ▷ [C] a part of a college or university: *the University of Cambridge Medical School* **6 UNIVERSITY** ▷ [C, U] US informal in the US, any college or university, or the time you spend there: *Which schools did you apply to?* **7 FISH** ▷ [C] a group of fish or other sea animals

IDIOM **school of thought** the ideas and beliefs shared by a group of people

S

→ See also **boarding school, elementary school, grade school, grammar school, high school, junior high school, junior school, middle school, night school, nursery school, prep school, preparatory school, primary school, public school, secondary school, state school**

> 🗏 Word partners for **school**
>
> go to school • at school • a school holiday • a school year • school children/kids

schoolboy /'sku:lbɔɪ/ **noun** [C] a boy who goes to school

schoolchild /'sku:ltʃaɪld/ **noun** [C] (plural **schoolchildren**) ⓐ a child who goes to school

schooldays /'sku:ldeɪz/ **noun** [plural] UK the period in your life when you go to school

schoolgirl /'sku:lgɜ:l/ **noun** [C] a girl who goes to school

schooling /'sku:lɪŋ/ **noun** [U] education at school

schoolteacher /'sku:l‚ti:tʃər/ **noun** [C] someone who teaches children in a school

science /saɪəns/ **noun 1** [U] ⓐ the study and knowledge of the structure and behaviour of natural things in an organized way **2** [C, U] ⓑ a particular type of science: *computer science* ∘ *Chemistry, physics, and biology are all sciences.* → See also **natural sciences, social science**

science 'fiction noun [U] ⓑ stories about life in the future or in other parts of the universe

scientific /‚saɪən'tɪfɪk/ **adj** ⓑ relating to science, or using the organized methods of science: *scientific experiments/research* • **scientifically adv** ⓑ *a scientifically proven fact*

scientist /'saɪəntɪst/ **noun** [C] ⓑ someone who studies science or works in science

sci-fi /'saɪ‚faɪ/ **noun** [U] informal short for science fiction

scintillating /'sɪntɪleɪtɪŋ/ **adj** very interesting or exciting: *a scintillating performance*

scissors /'sɪzəz/ **noun** [plural] ⓐ a tool for cutting paper, hair, cloth, etc that you hold in your hand and that has two blades that move against each other: *a pair of scissors*

scissors

scoff /skɒf/ **verb 1** [I] to laugh at someone or something, or criticize them in a way that shows you do not respect them: *The critics scoffed at his work.* **2** [I, T] UK informal (US **scarf**) to eat a lot of something quickly: *Who scoffed all the chocolates?*

scold /skəʊld/ **verb** [T] old-fashioned to speak angrily to someone because they have done something wrong

scone /skɒn/, /skəʊn/ **noun** [C] a small, round cake: *tea and buttered scones*

scoop¹ /sku:p/ **verb** [T] to remove something from a container using a spoon, your curved hands, etc: *She scooped the ice cream into the dishes.*

PHRASAL VERB **scoop sth/sb up** to lift something or someone with your hands

scoop² /sku:p/ **noun** [C] **1** a large, deep spoon for lifting and moving an amount of something, or the amount that can be held in it: *an ice cream scoop* ∘ *a scoop of ice cream* **2** a piece of news discovered and printed by one newspaper before it appears anywhere else

scoot /sku:t/ **verb** informal **scoot along/down/over, etc** to go somewhere quickly

scooter /'sku:tər/ **noun** [C] **1** ⓐ a small motorcycle **2** a child's vehicle that has two wheels fixed to the ends of a long board and a long handle

scope /skəʊp/ **noun 1** [no plural] how much a subject or situation relates to: *Do we know the full scope of the problem yet?* **2** [U] the opportunity to do something: *There is plenty of scope for improvement.*

> 🗏 Word partners for **scope**
>
> expand/extend/limit/widen the scope of sth • be beyond/outside/within the scope of sth

scorch /skɔ:tʃ/ **verb** [T] to damage something with fire or heat

scorched /skɔ:tʃt/ **adj** slightly burnt, or damaged by fire or heat: *scorched earth/fields*

scorching /'skɔ:tʃɪŋ/ **adj** very hot: *a scorching hot day*

score¹ /skɔ:r/ **noun 1** [C] ⓑ the number of points someone gets in a game or test: *a high/low score* ∘ *What's the score?* **2 scores of sth** a large number of people or things: *Scores of teenage girls were waiting to get his autograph.* **3** [C] printed piece of music **4 on that/this score** about the thing or subject which you have just discussed: *The company will pay your travel expenses, so don't worry on that score.*

> 🗏 Word partners for **score**
>
> keep score • even/level the score • the final/latest score • a score of sth • a high/low score

score² /skɔ:r/ **verb** [I, T] ⓑ to get points in a game or test: *He scored just before half-time to put Liverpool 2-1 ahead.*

scoreboard /'skɔ:bɔ:d/ **noun** [C] a large board that shows the score of a game

scorer /'skɔ:rər/ **noun** [C] a player who scores points in a game: *Who was top scorer in the 2014 World Cup?*

scorn /skɔ:n/ **noun** [U] formal the feeling that something is stupid and does not deserve your respect • **scorn verb** [T] formal to show scorn for someone or something: *You scorned all my suggestions.*

scornful /'skɔ:nfəl/ **adj** formal showing that you think something is stupid and does not deserve your respect: *I'm very **scornful of** any findings that lack proper scientific data.* • **scornfully** adv

corpio /ˈskɔːpiəʊ/ **noun** [C, U] the sign of the zodiac that relates to the period of 23 October – 21 November, or a person born during this period → See picture at **the zodiac**

corpion /ˈskɔːpiən/ **noun** [C] a small, insect-like creature with a curved, poisonous tail

cotch /skɒtʃ/ **noun** [C, U] (also ˌScotch ˈwhisky) a type of whisky

cotch ˈtape noun [U] US trademark (UK trademark **Sellotape**) clear, thin tape used for sticking things, especially paper, together → See colour picture **The Classroom** on page Centre 6

he Scots /skɒts/ **noun** [plural] the people of Scotland

cottish /ˈskɒtɪʃ/ **adj** relating to Scotland: *Scottish history*

cour /skaʊəʳ/ **verb** [T] **1** to search for something very carefully, often over a large area: *The police scoured the surrounding countryside for possible clues.* **2** to clean something by rubbing it with something rough

courge /skɜːdʒ/ **noun** formal **the scourge of sth** something that causes a lot of suffering or trouble: *Drug-related crime is the scourge of modern society.*

cout¹ /skaʊt/ **noun 1** [C] (also **Boy Scout**) a member of an organization for young people which teaches them practical skills and encourages them to be good members of society **2 the Scouts** an organization for young people which teaches them practical skills and encourages them to be good members of society **3** [C] someone whose job is to find good musicians, sports people, etc to join an organization: *a talent scout*

cout² /skaʊt/ **verb** [I] (also **scout around**) to try to find something by looking in different places: *I'm scouting around for somewhere to park.*

cowl /skaʊl/ **verb** [I] to look at someone angrily: *He scowled at me from behind his paper.* • **scowl noun** [C]

crabble /ˈskræbl/ **verb**

PHRASAL VERB **scrabble about/around** to use your fingers to quickly find something that you cannot see: *She scrabbled around in her bag, trying to find her keys.*

cramble /ˈskræmbl/ **verb 1 scramble down/out/up, etc** to move or climb quickly but with difficulty, often using your hands: *We scrambled up the hill.* **2** [I] to compete with other people for something which there is very little of: [+ to do sth] *New teachers scramble to get jobs in the best schools.* • **scramble noun** [no plural] *There was a mad scramble for places near the front.*

crambled ˈeggs noun [plural] eggs that are mixed together and then cooked

crap¹ /skræp/ **noun 1 SMALL PIECE** ▷ [C] a small piece or amount of something: *He wrote his phone number on a scrap of paper.* ◦ *I've read every scrap of information I can find on the subject.* **2 OLD** ▷ [U] old cars and machines that are not now needed but have parts which can be

used to make other things: *scrap metal* ◦ *The car was so badly damaged we could only sell it as scrap.* **3 FIGHT** ▷ [C] informal a fight or an argument, usually one that is not very serious: *He was always getting into scraps at school.*

scrap² /skræp/ **verb** [T] (**scrapping, scrapped**) **1** informal to not continue with a plan or idea: *That project has now been scrapped.* **2** to get rid of something which you do not now want

scrapbook /ˈskræpbʊk/ **noun** [C] a book with empty pages where you can stick newspaper articles, pictures, etc, that you have collected and want to keep

scrape¹ /skreɪp/ **verb** [T] **1** to damage the surface of something by rubbing it against something rough: *Jamie fell over and scraped his knee.* **2** to remove something from a surface using a sharp edge: *The next morning I had to scrape the ice off the car.* **3 scrape a win/draw/pass** UK to succeed in a test or competition but with difficulty: *France scraped a 3-2 win over Norway.*

PHRASAL VERBS **scrape by** to manage to live when you do not have enough money • **scrape through (sth)** to succeed in something but with a lot of difficulty: *I scraped through my exams (= just passed).* • **scrape sth together** to manage with a lot of difficulty to get enough of something, often money: *I finally scraped together enough money for a flight home.*

scrape² /skreɪp/ **noun** [C] **1** the slight damage caused when you rub a surface with something rough: *He suffered a few cuts and scrapes but nothing serious.* **2** informal a difficult or dangerous situation that you cause yourself: *She's always getting into scrapes.*

scrappy /ˈskræpi/ **adj 1** UK untidy or organized badly: *They won but it was a scrappy match.* **2** US determined to win or achieve something: *a scrappy competitor*

scratch¹ /skrætʃ/ **verb 1 RUB SKIN** ▷ [I, T] to rub your skin with your nails, often to stop it itching (= feeling unpleasant): *He scratched his head.* **2 HURT/DAMAGE** ▷ [T] to make a slight cut or long, thin mark with a sharp object: *The surface was all scratched.* ◦ *I scratched myself on the roses.* **3 RUB SURFACE** ▷ [I, T] to rub a hard surface with a sharp object, often making a noise: *I could hear the cat scratching at the door.*

scratch² /skrætʃ/ **noun 1** [C] a slight cut or a long, thin mark made with a sharp object: *I've got all these scratches on my arm from the cat.* **2** [no plural] If you give something a scratch, you rub your skin with your nails, often to stop it itching (= feeling unpleasant).: *Could you give my back a scratch?* **3 from scratch** If you do something from scratch, you do it from the beginning.

IDIOM **not be/come up to scratch** informal to not be good enough: *She told me my work wasn't up to scratch.*

scrawl /skrɔːl/ **verb** [T] to write something quickly so that it is untidy: *She scrawled a note, but I couldn't read it.* • **scrawl noun** [C, U]

scrawny /ˈskrɔːni/ **adj** too thin: *a scrawny neck*

scream

640

scream¹ /skri:m/ **verb** [I, T] 🔵 to make a loud, high noise with your voice, or to shout something in a loud, high voice because you are afraid, hurt, or angry: *She screamed for help.* ∘ *I could hear a woman screaming, "Get me out of here!"*

scream² /skri:m/ **noun 1** 🔵 [C] the sound of someone screaming: *We heard screams coming from their apartment.* ∘ *We heard a **blood curdling** scream.* **2 be a scream** informal to be very funny: *You'd love Amanda – she's a scream.*

> 🔲 Word partners for **scream**
>
> let out a scream • a blood-curdling/piercing/shrill scream • a scream of [horror/pain/shock, etc]

screech /skri:tʃ/ **verb 1** [I, T] to make an unpleasant, high, loud sound: *A car came screeching around the corner.* ∘ *She was screeching at him at the top of her voice.* **2 screech to a halt/stop** If a vehicle screeches to a halt, it suddenly stops, making an unpleasant, high sound. • **screech noun** [C] *We could hear the screech of brakes.*

screen

screen¹ /skri:n/ **noun 1** COMPUTER/TV ▷ [C] 🅰️ the part of a television or computer that shows images or writing: *I spend most of my day working in front of a **computer screen**.* **2 on screen** 🅰️ using a computer: *Do you work on screen?* **3** FILM SURFACE ▷ [C] 🅰️ a large, flat surface where a film or an image is shown **4** CINEMA ▷ [U, no plural] cinema films: *an actor of **stage and screen** (= theatre and films)* ∘ *She first **appeared on screen** in 1965.* **5** NET ▷ [C] a wire net that covers a window or door and is used to stop insects coming in **6** SEPARATE ▷ [C] a vertical structure that is used to separate one area from another

screen² /skri:n/ **verb** [T] **1** MEDICAL ▷ to find out if people have an illness by doing medical tests on them: *Babies are routinely **screened for** the condition.* **2** GET INFORMATION ▷ to find out information about someone in order to decide if they are suitable for a particular job: *Applicants are screened to ensure that none of them is a security risk.* **3** SHOW ▷ to show something on television or at a cinema: [often passive] *The first episode will be screened tonight.*

PHRASAL VERB **screen sth off** to separate one area from another using a vertical structure: *Part of the room is screened off and used as an office.*

screenplay /'skri:npleɪ/ **noun** [C] a story that is written for television or for a film

'screen ˌsaver noun [C] (also **screensaver**) a program to protect a computer screen that automatically shows a moving image if the computer is not used for a few minutes

screw¹ /skru:/ **noun** [C] a small, pointed piece of metal that you turn round and round to fasten things together, especially pieces of wood → See picture at **tool**

screw² /skru:/ **verb 1 screw sth down/to/onto, etc** to fasten something with a screw: *You need to screw the cabinet to the wall.* **2 screw sth on/down/together, etc** to fasten something by turning it round until it is tight, or to be fastened this way: *The lid is **screwed on** so tight I can't get it off.* → Opposite **unscrew 3 screw up your eyes/face** to move the muscles of your face so that your eyes become narrow: *He screwed up his eyes in the bright sunlight.*

PHRASAL VERBS **screw (sth) up** informal to make a mistake, or to spoil something: *I screwed up my exams last year.* • **screw sth up** to twist and crush a piece of paper with your hands: *She screwed the letter up and threw it in the bin.*

screwdriver /'skru:ˌdraɪvər/ **noun** [C] a tool for turning screws → See picture at **tool**

screwed-up /ˌskru:d'ʌp/ **adj** informal If someone is screwed-up, they are unhappy and anxious because they have had a lot of bad experience

scribble /'skrɪbl/ **verb** [I, T] to write or draw something quickly and carelessly: *She scribbled some **notes** in her book.* • **scribble noun** [C, U] something that has been scribbled

script /skrɪpt/ **noun 1** [C] 🅱️ the words in a film, play, etc: *He wrote a number of **film scripts**.* **2** [C, U] a set of letters used for writing a particular language: *Arabic/Roman script*

scripted /'skrɪptɪd/ **adj** A scripted speech or broadcast has been written before it is read or performed.

scripture /'skrɪptʃər/ **noun** [U] (also **the scriptures**) the holy books of a religion

scriptwriter /'skrɪptˌraɪtər/ **noun** [C] someone who writes the words for films or radio or television programmes

scroll¹ /skrəʊl/ **noun** [C] a long roll of paper with writing on it, used especially in the past

scroll² /skrəʊl/ **verb scroll up/down/through, etc** to move text or an image on a computer screen so that you can look at the part that you want

scrollbar /'skrəʊlbɑ:r/ **noun** [C] on a computer screen, a thin rectangle on the side or bottom that you use to move text or an image

scrooge /skru:dʒ/ **noun** [C] informal someone who spends very little money

scrounge /skraʊndʒ/ **verb** [I, T] informal to get something from someone else instead of paying for it yourself: *He's always **scrounging** money off you.*

S

α: arm | ɜ: her | i: see | ɔ: saw | u: too | aɪ my | aʊ how | eə hair | eɪ day | əʊ no | ɪə near | ɔɪ boy | ʊə pure | aɪə fire | aʊə sour

scrub¹ /skrʌb/ **verb** [I, T] (**scrubbing, scrubbed**) to clean something by rubbing it hard with a brush: *to scrub the floor*

scrub² /skrʌb/ **noun 1** [U] bushes and small trees that grow in a dry area **2** [no plural] If you give something a scrub, you clean it by rubbing it with a brush: *I gave my hands a scrub.*

scruff /skrʌf/ **noun**

IDIOM **by the scruff of the/your neck** by the back of the neck: *She picked the cat up by the scruff of its neck.*

scruffy /'skrʌfi/ **adj** dirty and untidy: *scruffy jeans* ◦ *I don't like to look scruffy.*

scruple /'skru:pl/ **noun** [C] a belief that something is wrong which stops you from doing that thing: [usually plural] *She **has no scruples** about accepting bribes.*

scrupulous /'skru:pjələs/ **adj 1** very careful and giving great attention to details: *He's very scrupulous about making sure that all the facts are checked.* **2** always honest and fair → Opposite **unscrupulous**

scrutinize (also UK **-ise**) /'skru:tɪnaɪz/ **verb** [T] to examine something very carefully: *The evidence was carefully scrutinized.*

scrutiny /'skru:tɪni/ **noun** [U] careful examination of something: *Every aspect of her life **came under** public **scrutiny**.*

> **Word partners for scrutiny**
>
> **be under/come under** scrutiny • **careful/ close/rigorous** scrutiny • **public** scrutiny

scuba diving /'sku:bə͵daɪvɪŋ/ **noun** [U] a sport in which you swim under water using special equipment for breathing

scuff /skʌf/ **verb** [T] to make a mark on your shoes by rubbing them against something rough

scuffle /'skʌfl/ **noun** [C] a short fight in which people push each other: *A **scuffle broke out** (= started) behind the courtroom.*

sculptor /'skʌlptər/ **noun** [C] someone who makes sculpture

sculpture /'skʌlptʃər/ **noun 1** [C, U] ⬤ a piece of art that is made from stone, wood, clay, etc: *a wooden sculpture* ◦ *modern sculpture* **2** [U] ⬤ the art of making objects from stone, wood, clay, etc: *She teaches sculpture at an art school.*

scum /skʌm/ **noun 1** [U, no plural] an unpleasant, thick substance on the surface of a liquid **2** [U] informal an offensive way of referring to a very bad person

scurry /'skʌri/ **verb scurry along/around/away, etc** to walk quickly or run because you are in a hurry

scuttle /'skʌtl/ **verb scuttle across/along/away, etc** to run quickly using short steps: *A beetle scuttled across the floor.*

scythe /saɪð/ **noun** [C] a tool with a long handle and a curved blade that is used to cut tall grass and crops

sea /si:/ **noun 1** ⬤ [C, U] a large area of salt water: *I'd like to live by **the sea**.* ◦ *It was our third day **at sea** (= travelling on the sea).* ◦ *It's cheaper*

to send parcels **by sea** (= on a ship). **2 Sea** ⬤ a particular area of salt water: *the North Sea* ◦ *the Black Sea* **3 a sea of sth** a large number of something: *He looked across the room and saw a sea of faces.*

seabed /'si:bed/ **noun** [no plural] the floor of the sea

seafood /'si:fu:d/ **noun** [U] animals from the sea that are eaten as food, especially animals that live in shells

seafront /'si:frʌnt/ **noun** [C] UK a part of a town that is next to the sea: [usually singular] *We walked **along the seafront**.*

seagull /'si:gʌl/ **noun** [C] a grey and white bird that lives near the sea

seagull

seahorse /'si:hɔ:s/ **noun** [C] a small fish that has a head and neck the same shape as a horse's

seal¹ /si:l/ **noun** [C] **1 ANIMAL** ▷ ⬤ an animal with smooth fur that eats fish and lives near the sea **2 ON A CONTAINER** ▷ a piece of paper or plastic on a container that you break in order to open it **3 OFFICIAL MARK** ▷ an official mark made of wax, paper, or metal that is put on important documents **4 STOP LIQUID/AIR** ▷ an object or substance that stops liquid or air from leaving or entering a container

seal² /si:l/ **verb** [T] **1** (also **seal up**) to close an entrance or container so that air or liquid cannot enter or leave it: *She quickly sealed up the bottle.* **2** to close a letter or parcel by sticking the edges together: *to seal an envelope*

PHRASAL VERB **seal sth off** to prevent people from entering an area or building, often because it is dangerous: *Police immediately sealed off the streets.*

sea level noun [U] the level of the sea's surface, used to measure the height of an area of land

sea lion noun [C] a large seal (= sea animal)

seam /si:m/ **noun** [C] **1** a line of sewing where two pieces of cloth have been joined together **2** a long, thin layer of coal under the ground

seaman /'si:mən/ **noun** [C] (plural **seamen**) a sailor

seance /'seɪɒns/ **noun** [C] a meeting at which people try to communicate with spirits of dead people

search¹ /sɜ:tʃ/ **verb 1 TRY TO FIND** ▷ [I, T] ⬤ to try to find someone or something: *I've searched my bedroom but I can't find my watch.* ◦ *Police are still **searching** the woods **for** the missing girl.* **2 POLICE** ▷ [T] ⬤ If the police search someone, they look in their clothes and bags to see if they are hiding anything illegal, such as drugs: *They were searched at the airport.* **3 FIND ANSWER** ▷ [I] ⬤ to try to find an answer to a problem: *Doctors are still **searching for** a cure.* **4 COMPUTER** ▷ [I, T] to look for information on a computer or on the Internet: *She **searched** the Internet **for** information about the area.*

S

Common learner error: search or search for?

If you **search** a place or person, you are looking for something in that place or on that person.

The police searched the man (= looked in his clothes) *for drugs.*

I searched the kitchen (= looked in the kitchen) *for my watch.*

If you **search for** something or someone, you are looking for that thing or that person.

I searched for my watch.

~~I searched my watch.~~

search² /sɜːtʃ/ **noun 1** [C] 🅑 an attempt to find someone or something: [usually singular] *Police are continuing their **search for** the missing girl.* ○ *They went off **in search of** (= to find) a bar.* **2** [no plural] 🅑 an attempt to find an answer to a problem: *the search for happiness*

Word partners for search noun

carry out/conduct/make/mount a search • abandon/call off a search • a desperate/ frantic/painstaking/thorough search • a search **for** sb/sth • **in search of** sb/sth • an Internet search

search box noun [C] a rectangular space on a computer screen where you type words, in order to look for them automatically in a document, on a website, etc.

search engine noun [C] a computer program which finds information on the Internet by looking for words that you have typed in → See Study Page **The Web and the Internet** on page Centre 36

searching /sɜːtʃɪŋ/ **adj** A searching question or look is intended to discover the truth about something.

search party noun [C] a group of people who look for someone who is lost

search warrant noun [C] an official document that allows the police to search a building

searing /sɪərɪŋ/ **adj** [always before noun] extreme and unpleasant: *searing pain/heat*

sea shell noun [C] the empty shell of some types of sea animals

the seashore /siːʃɔːr/ **noun** the area of land along the edge of the sea

seasick /siːsɪk/ **adj** feeling sick because of the way a boat is moving

the seaside /siːsaɪd/ **noun** 🅑 an area or town next to the sea: *We had a picnic **at the seaside**.* ○ *a seaside resort/community*

season¹ /siːzən/ **noun** [C] **1** 🅑 one of the four periods of the year; winter, spring, summer, or autumn **2** 🅑 a period of the year when a particular thing happens: [usually singular] *the holiday season* ○ *the rainy/dry season* ○ *the football season* **3 in season a** 🅑 If vegetables or fruit are in season, they are available and ready to eat. **b** If a female animal is in season, she is ready to mate. **4 out of season a** If vegetables or fruit are out of season, they are not usually

available at that time. **b** If you go somewhere out of season, you go during a period of the year when few people are there.

season² /siːzən/ **verb** [T] to add salt or spices to food that you are cooking

seasonal /siːzənəl/ **adj** 🅑 happening or existing only at a particular time of the year: *a seasonal worker* ○ *the seasonal migration of birds*

seasoned /siːzənd/ **adj** [always before noun] having a lot of experience of doing something: *a seasoned traveller*

seasoning /siːzənɪŋ/ **noun** [C, U] salt or spices that you add to food

season ticket UK (US **season 'ticket**) **noun** [C] a ticket that you can use many times without having to pay each time

seat¹ /siːt/ **noun** [C] **1 SIT** ▷ 🅐 something that you sit on: *Please, **have/take a seat** (= sit down).* ○ *I've booked three seats for the cinema tonight.* ○ *the **back/front seat** of a car* **2 PART** ▷ the flat part of a chair, bicycle, etc that you sit on **3 POLITICS** ▷ a position in a parliament or other group that makes official decisions: *a seat in parliament* ○ *a congressional seat*

Word partners for seat

have/take a seat • in/on a seat • the back/ driver's/front/passenger seat

seat² /siːt/ **verb 1 seat yourself in/on/next to,** etc to sit somewhere: *I seated myself next to the fire.* **2 be seated a** 🅑 to be sitting down: *The director was seated on his right.* **b** used to politely ask a group of people to sit down: *Would the people at the back please be seated.* **3 seat 4/12, 200, etc** If a building, room, or vehicle seats a particular number of people, that many people can sit in it.

seat belt noun [C] a strap that you fasten across your body when travelling in a vehicle: *to **fasten** your seat belt* → See colour picture **Car** on page Centre 7

seating /siːtɪŋ/ **noun** [U] the seats in a public place, or the way that they are arranged

seaweed /siːwiːd/ **noun** [U] a plant that you find on the beach and that grows in the sea

sec /sek/ **noun** [C] informal a very short time: *Just a sec – I'm nearly ready.*

secluded /sɪˈkluːdɪd/ **adj** If a place is secluded, it is quiet and not near people: *a secluded beach/ garden*

seclusion /sɪˈkluːʒən/ **noun** [U] If someone is in seclusion, they are alone, away from other people: *He lived **in seclusion** for the rest of his life.*

second¹ /sekənd/ **adj, pronoun 1** 🅐 referring to the person, thing, or event that comes immediately after the first: *You're second on the list.* ○ *This is my second piece of chocolate cake.* ○ *She didn't win but she did **come second** (= was the one after the winner) in one race.* **2** 🅐 2nd written as a word → See also **second best, second-hand, second language, second nature, the second person, second-rate, second thought, second wind**

second² /sekənd/ **noun** [C] **1 TIME** ▷ 🅐 one of

the 60 parts a minute is divided into **2 SHORT TIME** ▷ informal ⑤ a very short period of time: *I'll be back in just a second.* **3 PRODUCT** ▷ something that is sold cheaply because it is damaged or not in perfect condition: [usually plural] *Some of those towels are seconds.*

second³ /'sekənd/ verb [T] to formally support an idea at a meeting: [often passive] *The chairperson's proposal was seconded by Ms Jones.*

second⁴ /sɪ'kɒnd/ verb [T] UK to send someone to another job for a fixed period of time: [often passive] *He was seconded from the police to the Department of Transport.*

secondary /'sekəndəri/ adj **1** ⑤ relating to the education of students aged between 11 and 18: *secondary education* **2** less important than something else: *What matters is the size of the office. The location is of secondary importance.*

secondary school noun [C] mainly UK a school for students aged between 11 and 18

second best adj not the best but the next best: *the second best candidate* • **second best** noun [U]

second-class /,sekənd'klɑːs/ adj **1** TRAVEL ▷ relating to the less expensive way of travelling in a train that most people use: *a second-class carriage/ticket* **2** NOT IMPORTANT ▷ less important than other people: *Women are still treated as second-class citizens.* **3** UNIVERSITY ▷ A second-class university degree is a good degree but not the best possible. • **second class** adv *We always travel second class.*

second-guess /,sekənd'ges/ verb [T] to guess what someone will do in the future

second-hand /,sekənd'hænd/ adj, adv ⑤ If something is second-hand, someone else owned or used it before you: *second-hand books/clothes* • *She buys a lot of clothes second-hand.*

second language noun [C] a language that you speak that is not the first language you learned as a child

secondly /'sekəndli/ adv ⑤ used for introducing the second reason, idea, etc: *I want two things: firstly, more money, and secondly, better working hours.*

second nature noun [U] something that you can do easily because you have done it many times before: *After a few years, teaching became second nature to me.*

the second person noun ⑤ the form of a verb or pronoun that is used when referring to the person being spoken or written to. For example 'you' is a second person pronoun

second-rate /,sekənd'reɪt/ adj of bad quality: *a second-rate writer*

second thought noun **1 on second thoughts** UK used when you want to change a decision you have made: *I'll have tea, please – on second thoughts, make that coffee.* **2 without a second thought** If you do something without a second thought, you do it without first considering if you should do it or not: *She'll spend a hundred pounds on a dress without a second thought.* **3 have second thoughts** to change your opinion about something or start to doubt it:

[+ about + doing sth] *I've been having second thoughts about doing the course.*

second wind noun [no plural] a return of energy that makes it possible to continue an activity: *I was feeling tired, but I got my second wind after lunch.*

secrecy /'siːkrəsi/ noun [U] the quality of being secret: *Politicians criticized the secrecy surrounding the air attack.*

> **☑ Word partners for secrecy**
>
> be **shrouded in** secrecy • do sth **in** secrecy • **absolute/strict** secrecy • the secrecy **of/surrounding** sth

secret¹ /'siːkrət/ adj **1** ⑤ If something is secret, other people are not allowed to know about it: *a secret affair/meeting* ○ *I'll tell you but you must keep it secret.* **2 secret admirer/drinker, etc** someone who does something or feels something without telling other people about it • **secretly** adv ⑤ *He secretly taped their conversation.* → See also **top-secret**

secret² /'siːkrət/ noun [C] **1** ⑤ something that you tell no one about or only a few people: *I'm having a party for him but it's a secret.* ○ *Can you keep a secret?* **2 the secret** ⑥ the best way of achieving something: *So what's the secret of your success?* **3 in secret** ⑥ without telling other people: *For years they met in secret.*

> **☑ Word partners for secret**
>
> keep a secret • let sb in on/reveal/tell sb a secret • a big/closely-guarded/well-kept secret

secret agent noun [C] someone who tries to find out secret information, especially about another country

secretarial /,sekrə'teəriəl/ adj relating to the work of a secretary (= office worker who types letters, etc): *secretarial skills* ○ *secretarial work*

secretary /'sekrət⁰ri/ noun [C] **1** ⑫ someone who works in an office, typing letters, answering the telephone, and arranging meetings, etc **2** (also **Secretary**) an official who is in charge of a large department of the government: *the Secretary of State*

secrete /sɪ'kriːt/ verb [T] to produce a substance: *A mixture of substances are secreted by cells within the stomach.* • **secretion** /sɪ'kriːʃ⁰n/ noun [C, U]

secretive /'siːkrətɪv/ adj not willing to tell people what you know or what you are doing: *He's very secretive about his relationships.* • **secretively** adv

Secret Service noun [no plural] **1** in the UK, a department of the government that tries to find out secret information about foreign countries **2** in the US, a government organization that protects the president

sect /sekt/ noun [C] a group of people with a set of religious or political beliefs, often extreme beliefs

sectarian /sek'teəriən/ adj relating to the differences between religious groups: *sectarian violence*

section /'sekʃ°n/ **noun** [C] **1** ⓖ one of the parts that something is divided into: *a non-smoking section in a restaurant* ∘ *the business section of a newspaper* ∘ *the tail section of an aircraft* **2** a model or drawing of something that shows how it would look if it were cut from top to bottom and seen from the side → See also **cross-section**

sector /'sektə⁼/ **noun** [C] **1** one part of a country's economy: *the private/public sector* ∘ *the financial/manufacturing sector* **2** one of the parts that an area is divided into: *the British sector of the North Sea*

secular /'sekjələ⁼/ **adj** not religious or not controlled by a religious group: *secular education* ∘ *a secular state*

secure¹ /sɪ'kjʊə⁼/ **adj 1** NOT FAIL ▷ ⓑ not likely to fail or be lost: *a secure investment/job* **2** SAFE ▷ ⓑ safe from danger: *I don't feel that the house is secure.* **3** CONFIDENT ▷ ⓑ confident about yourself and the situation that you are in: *I need to feel secure in a relationship.* **4** FIXED ▷ firmly fastened and not likely to fall or break: *Check that all windows and doors are secure.* → Opposite **insecure**

secure² /sɪ'kjʊə⁼/ **verb** [T] **1** ACHIEVE ▷ to achieve something, after a lot of effort: *to secure the release of hostages* **2** FASTEN ▷ to fasten something firmly: *He secured the bike to the gate.* **3** MAKE SAFE ▷ to make something safe

securely /sɪ'kjʊəli/ **adv** If something is securely fastened, it will not become loose.

security /sɪ'kjʊərəti/ **noun** [U] **1** BEING SAFE ▷ ⓑ the things that are done to keep someone or something safe: *airport/national security* ∘ *a security alarm* **2** SAFE SITUATION ▷ a situation in which something is not likely to fail or be lost: *financial security* ∘ *job security* **3** CONFIDENCE ▷ confidence about yourself and the situation that you are in: *the security of a long-term relationship* → Opposite **insecurity (insecure) 4** BORROWING ▷ something valuable that you offer to give someone when you borrow money if you cannot pay the money back **5** INFORMATION ▷ the protection of information against being stolen or used wrongly or illegally: *IT security* → See also **social security**

⚠ Common learner error: **security** or **safety**?

Security means activities or people that protect you from harm, or that try to stop crime.

He works as a security guard.
airport security

Safety is when you are safe or how safe something is.

Remember to wear your safety belt in the car.
Children should have lessons in road safety.

🗒 Word partners for **security**

lax/tight security • security **arrangements/ checks** • a security **breach/guard/lapse/ operation/risk** • **national** security

---

sedan /sɪ'dæn/ **noun** [C] US (UK **saloon**) a larg⁼ car with a separate, closed area for bags

sedate¹ /sɪ'deɪt/ **adj** calm and slow: *walking at ⁼ sedate pace*

sedate² /sɪ'deɪt/ **verb** [T] to give a person o⁼ animal a drug to make them feel calm • **sedation** /sɪ'deɪʃ°n/ **noun** [U] *She had to b⁼ put under sedation.*

sedative /'sedətɪv/ **noun** [C] a drug used t⁼ sedate a person or an animal

sedentary /'sed°nt°ri/ **adj** spending a lot of tim⁼ sitting down or not being active: *a sedentar⁼ job/lifestyle*

sediment /'sedɪmənt/ **noun** [C, U] a soli⁼ substance that forms a layer at the bottom of ⁼ liquid

seduce /sɪ'dju:s/ **verb** [T] **1** to persuade someon⁼ to have sex with you, especially someone youn⁼ **2** to persuade someone to do something the⁼ would not normally do: *I wouldn't have bought ⁼ but I was seduced by the low prices.*

seductive /sɪ'dʌktɪv/ **adj 1** sexually attractive: ⁼ *seductive smile/voice* **2** making you want to hav⁼ or do something: *the seductive power of money*

see /si:/ **verb** (**seeing, saw, seen**) **1** EYES ▷ [I, ⁼ ⓐ to notice people and things with your eyes ⁼ *Have you seen Jo?* ∘ *Turn the light on so I can se⁼* → See Note at **look¹ 2** UNDERSTAND ▷ [I, T] ⓑ t⁼ understand something: *I see what you mean.* ∘ ⁼ *don't see why I should go.* **3** MEET ▷ [T] ⓐ t⁼ meet or visit someone: *I'm seeing Peter tonigh⁼* ∘ *You should see a doctor.* **4** WATCH ▷ [T] ⓐ t⁼ watch a film, television programme, etc: *Did yo⁼ see that programme last night⁼* **5** INFORMATION ▷ [T] ⓑ to find out informa⁼ tion: [+ question word] *I'll just see what time th⁼ train gets in.* **6** IMAGINE ▷ [T] ⓑ to imagine o⁼ think about something or someone in a part⁼ cular way: *I just can't see him as a fathe⁼* **7** BELIEVE ▷ [T] to believe that something wil⁼ happen: *I can't see us finishing on time⁼* **8** HAPPEN ▷ [T] to be the time or place wher⁼ something happens: *This decade has seen hug⁼ technological advances.* **9 see that** If you as⁼ someone to see that something happens, yo⁼ want them to make sure it happens: *Could yo⁼ see that everyone gets a copy of this letter?* **10 se⁼ sb home/to the station, etc** to go somewher⁼ with someone, especially to make sure they ar⁼ safe: *Let me see you home.* **11 I'll/we'll see** use⁼ to say that you will make a decision abou⁼ something later: *"Dad, can I have a guitar?⁼ "We'll see."* **12 see you** informal ⓐ used for sayin⁼ goodbye → See also **be glad/happy, etc to se⁼ the back² of sb/sth, see eye¹ to eye (with sb⁼ see red²**

PHRASAL VERBS **see about sth/doing sth** to dea⁼ with something, or arrange for something to b⁼ done: *You should see about getting your hair cut.* ⁼ **see sth in sb/sth** to believe that someone o⁼ something has a particular quality: *I can⁼ understand what you see in her (= why you lik⁼ her).* • **see sb off** ⓑ to go to the place tha⁼ someone is leaving from in order to sa⁼ goodbye to them: *My parents came to th⁼ airport to see me off.* • **see sb out** to tak⁼

S

someone to the door of a room or building when they are leaving: *Don't worry, I'll see myself out* (= *leave the room/building by myself*). • **see through sb/sth** ⓑ to understand that someone is trying to deceive you: *I saw through him at once.* • **see to sth** ⓑ to deal with something: *Don't worry, I'll see to everything while you're away.*

eed¹ /si:d/ **noun 1** ⓑ [C, U] a small round or oval object produced by a plant that a new plant can grow from: *Sow the seeds* (= *plant them*) *near the surface.* **2 (the) seeds of sth** the beginning of something: *the seeds of hope/change* → See also **sesame seed**

eed² /si:d/ **verb 1** [T] to plant seeds in the ground **2 be seeded first/second, etc** in tennis, to be the first/second, etc on a list of players expected to succeed in a competition

eedless /ˈsiːdləs/ **adj** without seeds: *seedless grapes*

eedling /ˈsiːdlɪŋ/ **noun** [C] a young plant that has been grown from a seed

eedy /ˈsiːdi/ **adj** informal looking dirty or in bad condition and likely to be involved in immoral activities: *a seedy bar/hotel*

eeing ˈeye dog noun [C] US (UK/US **guide dog**) a dog that is trained to help blind people

eek /siːk/ **verb** [T] (**sought**) **1** ⓑ to try to find or get something: *to seek advice/a solution* **2** to try to do something: [+ to do sth] *They are seeking to change the rules.* ◦ *to seek re-election* → See also **hide-and-seek**

eem /siːm/ **verb seem happy/a nice person, etc; seem like/as if, etc** ⓑ to appear to be a particular thing or to have a particular quality: *She seemed happy enough.* ◦ *It seemed like a good idea at the time.* ◦ *There doesn't seem to be any real solution.* ◦ [+ (that)] *It seems that the bars close early here.* ◦ **It seems to me** (= I think) *that she's in the wrong job.*

eemingly /ˈsiːmɪŋli/ **adv** appearing to be something without really being that thing: *a seemingly harmless comment*

een /siːn/ past participle of see

eep /siːp/ **verb seep from/into/through, etc** to flow very slowly through something: *Water was seeping through the walls.*

eesaw

eesaw /ˈsiːsɔː/ **noun** [C] (also US **teeter-totter**) a long board that children play on by sitting at each end and using their feet on the ground to push the board up and down

seethe /siːð/ **verb** [I] to be very angry, often without showing it: *I left him **seething with** anger.*

segment /ˈsegmənt/ **noun** [C] one of the parts that something can be divided into: *a segment of the population/market* ◦ *an orange segment*

segregate /ˈsegrɪgeɪt/ **verb** [T] to separate one group of people from another, especially one sex or race from another: *At school the girls were **segregated from** the boys.* • **segregation** /ˌsegrɪˈgeɪʃən/ **noun** [U] *racial segregation*

seismic /ˈsaɪzmɪk/ **adj** relating to or caused by an earthquake (= when the earth shakes): *seismic activity*

seize /siːz/ **verb** [T] **1 HOLD** ▷ ⓑ to take hold of something quickly and firmly: *She seized my arm and pulled me towards her.* **2 OPPORTUNITY** ▷ ⓑ to do something quickly when you have the opportunity: *You need to **seize** every **opportunity**.* **3 PLACE** ▷ to take control of a place suddenly by using military force: *Troops **seized** control in the early hours of the morning.* **4 DRUGS ETC** ▷ to take away something that is illegal, for example drugs: *Officials seized 2.7 tons of cocaine from the ship.*

PHRASAL VERBS **seize on/upon sth** to quickly use something that will give you an advantage: *Her story was seized upon by the press.* • **seize up** If part of your body or a machine seizes up, it stops moving or working in the normal way: *His right leg suddenly seized up during the race.*

seizure /ˈsiːʒər/ **noun 1 CONTROL** ▷ [U] the act of taking control of a country, government, etc: *a seizure of power* **2 DRUGS ETC** ▷ [C] the act of taking away something that is illegal, for example drugs, by someone in authority: *a seizure of heroin* **3 ILLNESS** ▷ [C] a sudden attack of an illness: *an epileptic seizure*

seldom /ˈseldəm/ **adv** ⓑ not often: *We seldom go out in the evenings.*

select¹ /sɪˈlekt/ **verb** [T] ⓑ to choose someone or something: *We've selected three candidates.*

select² /sɪˈlekt/ **adj** consisting of only a small group of people who have been specially chosen: *a select group*

selection /sɪˈlekʃən/ **noun 1** [U] ⓑ the act of choosing someone or something: *the selection process* **2** [C] ⓑ a group of people or things that has been chosen: *We have a **wide selection of** imported furniture.* → See also **natural selection**

✓ Word partners for selection

a **good/wide** selection • a selection **of** sth

---

selective /sɪˈlektɪv/ **adj 1** careful about what you choose: *He's very selective about the people he spends time with.* **2** involving only people or things that have been specially chosen: *selective breeding*

self /self/ **noun** [C, U] (plural **selves** /selvz/) your characteristics, including your personality, your abilities, etc: *his true self*

self-assured /ˌselfəˈʃʊəd/ **adj** confident about yourself

self-catering /ˌselfˈkeɪtərɪŋ/ **adj** UK describes a

S

holiday in which you have a kitchen so that you can cook meals for yourself: *We decided to stay in self-catering accommodation rather than in a hotel.*

self-centred UK (US **self-centered**) /ˌselfˈsentəd/ **adj** interested only in yourself

self-confident /ˌselfˈkɒnfɪd³nt/ **adj** ⑫ feeling sure about yourself and your abilities • **self-confidence** **noun** [U] ⑫ being self-confident

self-conscious /ˌselfˈkɒnʃəs/ **adj** too aware of what other people are thinking about you and your appearance • **self-consciously adv** • **self-consciousness noun** [U]

self-contained /ˌselfkənˈteɪnd/ **adj** UK If a flat is self-contained, it has its own kitchen, bathroom, and entrance.

self-control /ˌselfkənˈtrəʊl/ **noun** [U] the ability to control your emotions and actions although you are very angry, upset, etc

self-defence UK (US **self-defense**) /ˌselfdɪˈfens/ **noun** [U] ways of protecting yourself from someone who is attacking you, for example by fighting: *He claimed he had acted **in self-defence**.*

self-destructive /ˌselfdɪˈstrʌktɪv/ **adj** A self-destructive action harms the person who is doing it.

self-discipline /ˌselfˈdɪsɪplɪn/ **noun** [U] the ability to make yourself do things that you do not want to do

self-employed /ˌselfɪmˈplɔɪd/ **adj** working for yourself and not for a company or other organization • **self-employment** /ˌselfɪmˈplɔɪmənt/ **noun** [U]

self-esteem /ˌselfɪˈstiːm/ **noun** [U] confidence in yourself and a belief in your qualities and abilities: *She suffers from **low self-esteem**.*

> ☑ Word partners for **self-esteem**
>
> boost/build/damage/raise self-esteem • high/low self-esteem

self-evident /ˌselfˈevɪd³nt/ **adj** obviously true and not needing to be explained

self-explanatory /ˌselfɪkˈsplænət³ri/ **adj** easy to understand and not needing to be explained

self-help /ˌselfˈhelp/ **adj** A self-help book, activity, organization, etc is designed to help you deal with your problems on your own: *a self-help group for alcoholics*

self-indulgent /ˌselfɪnˈdʌldʒ³nt/ **adj** doing or having things that you like although they are not necessary or are bad for you • **self-indulgence** /ˌselfɪnˈdʌldʒ³ns/ **noun** [C, U]

self-inflicted /ˌselfɪnˈflɪktɪd/ **adj** If an injury or a problem is self-inflicted, you have caused it yourself.

self-interest /ˌselfˈɪntrəst/ **noun** [U] interest in what will help you, and not what will help other people

selfish /ˈselfɪʃ/ **adj** ⑪ caring only about yourself and not other people: *It's very selfish of him.* • **selfishly adv** • **selfishness noun** [U]

selfless /ˈselfləs/ **adj** caring about other people and not about yourself

self-made /ˌselfˈmeɪd/ **adj** rich because you have

earned a lot of money yourself: *a self-mad* millionaire

self-pity /ˌselfˈpɪti/ **noun** [U] sadness for yourself because you think you have suffered so much especially when this is not true

self-portrait /ˌselfˈpɔːtreɪt/ **noun** [C] a pictur that you draw or paint of yourself

self-reliant /ˌselfrɪˈlaɪənt/ **adj** able to do thing yourself without depending on other people

self-respect /ˌselfrɪˈspekt/ **noun** [U] the feelin of pride in yourself and your character • **self respecting adj**

self-righteous /ˌselfˈraɪtʃəs/ **adj** believing tha you are morally better than other people

self-sacrifice /ˌselfˈsækrɪfaɪs/ **noun** [U] the act o not having or doing something so that you ca help other people

self-satisfied /ˌselfˈsætɪsfaɪd/ **adj** too please with yourself and what you have achieved

self-service /ˌselfˈsɜːvɪs/ **adj** ⑪ A self-servic restaurant or shop is one in which you serv yourself and are not served by the people wh work there.

self-sufficient /ˌselfsəˈfɪʃ³nt/ **adj** having every thing that you need yourself and not needin help from others

sell /sel/ **verb** (**sold**) **1 FOR MONEY** ▷ [I, T] ⑫ t give something to someone who gives yo money for it: *He **sold** his guitar **for** $50.* ∘ * sold my bike **to** Claire.* ∘ [+ two objects] *I'm hopin she'll sell me her car.* **2 OFFER** ▷ [T] ⑫ to offe something for people to buy: *Excuse me, do yo sell newspapers?* **3 sell for/at sth** to be availabl for sale at a particular price: *The shirts are sellin for £30 each.* **4 A LOT** ▷ [I, T] to be bought i large numbers: *His last book sold eight millio copies.* **5 MAKE YOU WANT** ▷ [T] to mak someone want to buy something: *Scandal sel newspapers.* **6 IDEA/PLAN** ▷ [T] to persuad someone that an idea or plan is good: *I'r currently trying to sell the idea to my boss.*

PHRASAL VERBS **sell sth off** to sell all or part of business • **sell out** ⑫ If a shop sells out o something, it sells all of that thing: *They'd sol out of bread by the time I got there.* • **sell up** U to sell your house or company in order to g somewhere else or do something else: *They sol up and moved to the country.*

'sell-by ˌdate **noun** [C] UK the date printed on food or drink container after which it should nc be sold

seller /ˈselər/ **noun** [C] **1** ⑪ someone who sell something: *a flower seller* **2** a product that company sells: *Our **biggest sellers** are th calendars.*

Sellotape /ˈseləʊteɪp/ **noun** [U] UK trademark (U trademark **Scotch tape**) clear, thin material wit glue on it, used to stick things togethe especially paper → See colour picture **The Class room** on page Centre 6

sellout /ˈseləʊt/ **noun** [no plural] **1** a performanc or event where all of the tickets have been sol **2** informal an example of someone doing som thing that is against their beliefs in order to ge money or power

elves /selvz/ plural of **self**

emantic /sɪˈmæntɪk/ **adj** connected with the meaning of language

emblance /ˈsembləns/ **noun semblance of normality/order, etc** a small amount of a quality, but not as much as you would like: *Our lives have now returned to some semblance of normality.*

emen /ˈsiːmən/ **noun** [U] the liquid that is produced by the male sex organs, that contains sperm (= cells that join with female eggs to make new life)

emester /sɪˈmestər/ **noun** [C] one of the two time periods that a school or college year is divided into

emi- /semi-/ **prefix** half or partly: *a semicircle* ○ *semifrozen*

emicircle

emicircle /ˈsemiˌsɜːkl/ **noun** [C] half a circle

emicolon /ˌsemiˈkəʊlən/ ⓤ /ˈsemiˌkəʊlən/ **noun** [C] ⓑ a mark (;) used to separate parts of a sentence, or items in a list which already has commas → See Study Page **Punctuation** on page Centre 33

emi-detached /ˌsemidɪˈtætʃt/ **adj** UK A semi-detached house has one wall that is joined to another house.

emifinal /ˌsemiˈfaɪnəl/ **noun** [C] ⓑ one of the two games in a sports competition that are played to decide who will play in the final game

eminar /ˈseminɑːr/ **noun** [C] ⓑ a meeting of a group of people with a teacher or expert for training, discussion, or study of a subject

emitic /sɪˈmɪtɪk/ **adj** relating to the Jewish or Arab races, or their languages

he Senate /ˈsenɪt/ **noun** [group] a part of a government in some countries

enator /ˈsenətər/ **noun** [C] someone who has been elected to the Senate: *Senator Moynihan*

end /send/ **verb** [T] (**sent**) **1** ⓐ to arrange for something to go or be taken somewhere, especially by post: [+ two objects] *I sent him a letter last week.* ○ *Do you think we should send flowers?* **2** ⓑ to make someone go somewhere: *I sent him into the house to fetch some glasses.* **3 send sb to sleep** to make someone start sleeping → See also **drive/send sb round the bend²**

PHRASAL VERBS **send sth back** ⓑ to return something to the person who sent it to you,

especially because it is damaged or not suitable: *I had to send the shirt back because it didn't fit me.* • **send for sb** to send someone a message asking them to come to see you: *Do you think we should send for a doctor?* • **send (off/away) for sth** to write to an organization to ask them to send you something: *I've sent off for a catalogue.* • **send sth in** to send something to an organization: *Viewers were asked to send in photographs of their pets.* • **send sb in** to send soldiers, police, etc to a place in order to deal with a dangerous situation • **send sth off** ⓑ to send a letter, document, or parcel by post • **send sb off** UK to order a sports player to leave the playing area because they have done something wrong • **send sth out 1** to send something to a lot of different people: *to send out invitations* **2** to produce light, sound, etc • **send sb/sth up** UK to make someone or something seem stupid by copying them in a funny way

send-off /ˈsendɒf/ **noun** [C] an occasion when a group of people say goodbye to someone at the same time: *I got a good send-off at the station.*

senile /ˈsiːnaɪl/ **adj** confused and unable to remember things because of old age • **senility** /sɪˈnɪləti/ **noun** [U] the state of being senile

senior¹ /ˈsiːniər/ **adj 1 MORE IMPORTANT** ▷ ⓑ having a more important job or position than someone else: *a senior executive* ○ *We work in the same team but she's senior to me.* **2 OLDER** ▷ older: *senior students* **3 NAME** ▷ (written abbreviation **Sr**) mainly US used at the end of a man's name to show that he is the older of two men in the same family who have the same name: *Hello, may I speak to Ken Griffey, Senior, please?*

senior² /ˈsiːniər/ **noun 1 be 20/30, etc years sb's senior** to be 20, 30, etc years older than someone: *She married a man 20 years her senior.* **2** [C] US a student in their last year of study at an American college or high school (= school for students aged 15 to 18)

senior citizen **noun** [C] an old person

seniority /ˌsiːniˈɒrəti/ **noun** [U] the state of being older or of having a more important position in an organization

sensation /senˈseɪʃən/ **noun 1 PHYSICAL** ▷ [C, U] ⓑ a physical feeling, or the ability to physically feel things: *a burning sensation* ○ *Three months after the accident she still has no sensation in her right foot.* **2 FEELING** ▷ [C] ⓑ a strange feeling or idea that you cannot explain: *I had the strangest sensation that I had met him before.* **3 EXCITEMENT** ▷ [no plural] ⓑ a lot of excitement, surprise, or interest, or the person or event that causes these feelings: *Their affair caused a sensation.*

sensational /senˈseɪʃənəl/ **adj 1** done in a way that is intended to shock people: *sensational journalism* **2** very exciting or extremely good: *a sensational performance*

sensationalism /senˈseɪʃənəlɪzəm/ **noun** [U] a way of telling a story that is intended to shock people

sense¹ /sens/ **noun 1 GOOD JUDGMENT** ▷ [U] ⓑ good judgment, especially about practical

S

things: *He had the **good sense** to book a seat in advance.* **2 ABILITY** ▷ [no plural] 🔵 the ability to do something: *a **sense of direction*** ∘ *good business sense* **3 NATURAL ABILITY** ▷ [C] 🔵 one of the five natural abilities of sight, hearing, touch, smell, and taste: *I have a very poor sense of smell.* **4 a sense of humour** UK (US **a sense of humor**) 🔵 the ability to understand funny things and to be funny yourself **5 a sense of loyalty/responsibility/security, etc** the quality or feeling of being loyal, responsible, safe, etc: *He has absolutely no sense of loyalty.* **6 MEANING** ▷ [C] 🔵 the meaning of a word, phrase, or sentence **7 in a sense/in some senses** thinking about something in a particular way: *In a sense, he's right.* **8 make sense a** 🔵 to have a meaning or reason that you can understand: *He's written me this note but it doesn't make any sense.* **b** 🔵 to be a good thing to do: [+ to do sth] *It makes sense to buy now while prices are low.* **9 make sense of sth** to understand something that is difficult to understand: *I'm trying to make sense of this document.*

IDIOM **come to your senses** to start to understand that you have been behaving stupidly

→ See also **common sense**

☑ Word partners for **sense**
have the sense to do sth • **good** sense

sense² /sens/ **verb** [T] to understand what someone is thinking or feeling without being told about it: [+ (that)] *I sensed that you weren't happy about this.*

senseless /ˈsensləs/ **adj 1** happening or done without a good reason: ***senseless violence*** **2** not conscious: *He was beaten senseless.*

sensibility /ˌsensɪˈbɪləti/ **noun** [C, U] formal someone's feelings, or the ability to understand what other people feel

sensible /ˈsensɪbl/ **adj 1** 🔵 showing good judgment: *a **sensible** decision* ∘ [+ to do sth] *Wouldn't it be more sensible to leave before the traffic gets bad?* **2** having a practical purpose: *sensible shoes/clothes* • **sensibly** adv *to eat/behave sensibly*

⚠ Common learner error: **sensitive** or **sensible**?

Remember that **sensible** does not mean 'easily upset' or 'able to understand what people are feeling'. The word you need to express that is **sensitive**.
Don't criticize her too much. She's very sensitive.

sensitive /ˈsensɪtɪv/ **adj 1 KIND** ▷ 🔵 able to understand what people are feeling and deal with them in a way that does not upset them: *I want a man who's kind and sensitive.* **2 EASILY UPSET** ▷ 🔵 easily upset by the things people say or do: *He was always **sensitive to** criticism.* ∘ *She's very **sensitive about** her weight.* **3 SUBJECT** ▷ 🔵 A sensitive subject or situation needs to be dealt with carefully in order to avoid upsetting people: *Gender is a very sensitive subject.* **4 EASILY DAMAGED** ▷ 🔵 easily

damaged or hurt: *sensitive eyes/ski* **5 EQUIPMENT** ▷ 🔵 Sensitive equipment i able to measure very small changes. → Opposit **insensitive** • **sensitively** adv *I think she dea with the problem very sensitively.* • **sensitivit** /ˌsensɪˈtɪvəti/ **noun** [U] the quality of bein sensitive

sensor /ˈsensər/ **noun** [C] a piece of equipmen that can find heat, light, etc: *Sensors detec movement in the room.*

sensual /ˈsensjuəl/ **adj** relating to physica pleasure, often sexual pleasure: *a sensual exper ence* ∘ *a sensual mouth* • **sensuality** /ˌsensjuˈ ləti/ **noun** [U] the quality of being sensual

sensuous /ˈsensjuəs/ **adj** giving physical plea sure: *the sensuous feel of silk sheets*

sent /sent/ past of send

sentence¹ /ˈsentəns/ **noun 1** [C] 🔵 a group c words, usually containing a verb, that expresse a complete idea **2** [C, U] 🔵 a punishment that judge gives to someone who has committed crime: *a 30-year sentence*

☑ Word partners for **sentence**
impose/receive/serve a sentence • a **jail/ prison** sentence • a sentence **for** sth

sentence² /ˈsentəns/ **verb** [T] 🔵 to give punishment to someone who has committed crime: [often passive] *She was **sentenced to** s months in prison.*

sentiment /ˈsentɪmənt/ **noun 1** [C, U] a opinion that you have because of the way yo feel about something: *nationalist/religious senti ments* **2** [U] emotional feelings such as sym pathy, love, etc, especially when they are nc considered to be suitable for a situation: *I fin her writing full of sentiment.*

sentimental /ˌsentɪˈmentəl/ **adj 1** showing kin feelings such as sympathy, love, etc, especiall in a silly way: *a sentimental song* ∘ *The British ar very sentimental about animals.* **2** related t feelings and memories and not related to ho much money something costs: *It wasn't a expensive ring but it had great **sentimenta value**.* • **sentimentality** /ˌsentɪmenˈtæləti noun** [U]

sentry /ˈsentri/ **noun** [C] a soldier who stand outside a building in order to guard it

separable /ˈsepərəbl/ **adj** able to be separate → Opposite **inseparable**

separate¹ /ˈsepərət/ **adj 1 NOT JOINED** ▷ 🔵 nc joined or touching anything else: *a separat compartment* ∘ *I try to keep meat **separate fron** other food.* **2 NOT AFFECTING** ▷ 🔵 not affectin or related to each other: *I've asked him to turn h music down on three **separate occasions**.* ∘ *have my professional life and my private and try to **keep** them **separate**.* **3 DIFFERENT** ▷ 🔵 different: *Use a separate sheet of pape* • **separately** adv

separate² /ˈsepəreɪt/ **verb 1 DIVIDE** ▷ [I, T] 🔵 t divide into parts, or to make something divid into parts: *I **separated** the class **into** three group* **2 MOVE APART** ▷ [I, T] 🔵 to move apart, or t make people move apart: *I shall separate you tw* *if you don't stop talking.* **3 HUSBAND/WIFE** ▷ [I] ⓑ to start to live in a different place from your husband or wife because the relationship has ended: *My parents separated when I was four.* → See Note at **married**

separation /ˌsepᵊrˈeɪʃᵊn/ **noun 1** [C, U] ⓑ the act of separating or being separated: *the separation of church and state* ∘ *Their working in different countries meant long periods of separation.* **2** [C] a legal agreement when two people stay married but stop living together

September /sepˈtembəʳ/ **noun** [C, U] (written abbreviation **Sept**) ⓐ the ninth month of the year

septic /ˈseptɪk/ **adj** infected by poisonous bacteria

sequel /ˈsiːkwᵊl/ **noun** [C] a film, book, etc that continues the story from an earlier one

sequence /ˈsiːkwᵊns/ **noun 1** [C] a series of related events or things that have a particular order: *the sequence of events that led to his death* **2** [U] the order that events or things should happen or be arranged in: *I got my slides mixed up and they appeared out of sequence.*

> 🗹 Word partners for **sequence**
>
> **in** a sequence • a sequence **of** sth • be **out of** sequence • a **logical** sequence

sequin /ˈsiːkwɪn/ **noun** [C] a small, flat, shiny circle that is sewn onto clothes for decoration

serenade /ˌserəˈneɪd/ **noun** [C] a song, usually about love

serendipity /ˌserᵊnˈdɪpəti/ **noun** [U] literary good luck that makes you find something interesting or valuable by chance

serene /sɪˈriːn/ **adj** calm and quiet: *a serene face/smile* • **serenely adv**

sergeant /ˈsɑːdʒᵊnt/ **noun** [C] **1** an officer of low rank in the police **2** a soldier of middle rank in the army or air force

serial /ˈsɪəriəl/ **noun** [C] a story in a magazine or on television or radio that is told in separate parts over a period of time

serial killer **noun** [C] someone who has murdered several people over a period of time

serial number **noun** [C] one of a set of numbers that is put on an item that is made in large quantities, such as computers, televisions, paper money, etc., so that you can tell one item from another

series /ˈsɪəriːz/ **noun** [C] (plural **series**) **1** ⓑ several things or events of the same type that come one after the other: *a series of lectures* **2** ⓑ a group of television or radio programmes that have the same main characters or deal with the same subject: *a four-part drama series*

serious /ˈsɪəriəs/ **adj 1 BAD** ▷ ⓑ A serious problem or situation is bad and makes people worry: *a serious accident/illness* ∘ *This is a serious matter.* **2 NOT JOKING** ▷ ⓑ thinking or speaking sincerely about something and not joking: *I'm being serious now – this is a very real problem.* ∘ *Are you serious about changing your job?* **3 QUIET** ▷ ⓑ A serious person is quiet and does not laugh often: *a serious child* • **seriousness noun** [U]

seriously /ˈsɪəriəsli/ **adv 1** ⓑ in a serious way: *seriously injured* ∘ *Smoking can seriously damage your health.* **2** ⓑ used to show that what you are going to say is not a joke: *Seriously though, you mustn't say that.* **3 take sb/sth seriously** ⓑ to believe that someone or something is important and that you should pay attention to them: *The police have to take any terrorist threat seriously.*

sermon /ˈsɜːmən/ **noun** [C] a religious speech given by a priest in church: *to deliver/give a sermon*

serotonin /ˌserəˈtəʊnɪn/ **noun** [U] a chemical in your brain which controls your moods

serpent /ˈsɜːpᵊnt/ **noun** [C] literary a snake

serrated /sɪˈreɪtɪd/ **adj** A serrated edge, usually of a knife, has sharp triangular points along it.

serum /ˈsɪərəm/ **noun** [U] a clear liquid in blood that contains substances that stop infection

serrated

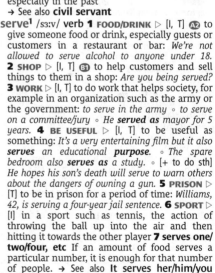

servant /ˈsɜːvᵊnt/ **noun** [C] ⓑ someone who works and lives in someone else's house doing their cooking and cleaning, especially in the past → See also **civil servant**

serve¹ /sɜːv/ **verb 1 FOOD/DRINK** ▷ [I, T] ⓐ to give someone food or drink, especially guests or customers in a restaurant or bar: *We're not allowed to serve alcohol to anyone under 18.* **2 SHOP** ▷ [I, T] ⓑ to help customers and sell things to them in a shop: *Are you being served?* **3 WORK** ▷ [I, T] to do work that helps society, for example in an organization such as the army or the government: *to serve in the army* ∘ *to serve on a committee/jury* ∘ *He served as mayor for 5 years.* **4 BE USEFUL** ▷ [I, T] to be useful as something: *It's a very entertaining film but it also serves an educational purpose.* ∘ *The spare bedroom also serves as a study.* ∘ [+ to do sth] *He hopes his son's death will serve to warn others about the dangers of owning a gun.* **5 PRISON** ▷ [T] to be in prison for a period of time: *Williams, 42, is serving a four-year jail sentence.* **6 SPORT** ▷ [I] in a sport such as tennis, the action of throwing the ball up into the air and then hitting it towards the other player **7 serves one/two/four, etc** If an amount of food serves a particular number, it is enough for that number of people. → See also **It serves her/him/you right²**!

serve² /sɜːv/ **noun** [C] in sports such as tennis, the act of throwing the ball up into the air and hitting it towards the other player to start play

server /ˈsɜːvəʳ/ **noun** [C] ⓑ a computer that is used only for storing and managing programs and information used by other computers: *an email/Internet server*

service¹ /ˈsɜːvɪs/ **noun 1 SHOP** ▷ [U] ⓑ help that

you get in a place such as a shop, restaurant, or hotel: *The food was nice, but the service wasn't very good.* **2** SYSTEM ▷ [C] 🔵 a system that supplies something that people need: *financial/ medical services* ○ *electricity/water services* ○ *They* **provide** *a free bus* **service** *from the station.* **3** WORK ▷ [U] the time you spend working for an organization: *He retired last week after 25 years' service.* **4** CEREMONY ▷ [C] a religious ceremony: *They* **held a** *memorial* **service** *for the victims of the bombing.* **5** CAR/ MACHINE ▷ [C] a check on a car or machine in which it is examined for faults and repaired **6** SPORT ▷ [C] the action of throwing a ball up into the air and hitting it towards the other player in sports such as tennis → See also **the Civil Service, community service, lip-service, the National Health Service, national service, Secret Service**

> ☑ Word partners for **service**
> offer/provide/use a service

service² /'sɜːvɪs/ *verb* [T] to examine and repair a car or machine

serviceable /'sɜːvɪsəbl/ *adj* able to be used, but not very good or attractive: *I have some old but serviceable chairs.*

'service ˌcharge *noun* [C] an amount of money that is added to what you pay in a restaurant for being helped and brought things: *a 10% service charge*

serviceman /'sɜːvɪsmən/ *noun* [C] (plural **servicemen**) a man who is in the army, navy, or airforce

'service proˌvider *noun* [C] a company that connects your computer to the Internet, and lets you use email and other services

the services /'sɜːvɪsɪz/ *noun* [plural] the military forces such as the army or navy

'service ˌstation *noun* [C] a place at the side of a road where you can buy fuel for cars, and food

servicewoman /'sɜːvɪswʊmən/ *noun* [C] (plural **servicewomen**) a woman who is in the army, navy, or airforce

serviette /ˌsɜːviˈet/ *noun* [C] UK (UK/US **napkin**) a piece of cloth or paper used when you eat, to keep your clothes clean and to clean your mouth and hands

servile /'sɜːvaɪl/ ⓤⓢ /'sɜːrvəl/ *adj* too willing to do things for other people

serving /'sɜːvɪŋ/ *noun* [C] an amount of food for one person to eat: *a large serving of rice*

sesame seed /'sesəmiˌsiːd/ *noun* [C] a small seed that is used to add a taste to food

session /'seʃən/ *noun* **1** [C] 🔵 a period during which you do one activity: *a weekly aerobics session* ○ *We're having a training session this afternoon.* **2** [C, U] a meeting of an official group of people such as in a court or in the government: *The court is now* **in session.**

set¹ /set/ *verb* (**setting, set**) **1** A TIME ▷ [T] 🔵 to arrange a time when something will happen: [often passive] *The next meeting is* **set for** *6 February.* **2** LEVEL ▷ [T] to decide the level of something: *The interest rate has been* **set at** *5%.*

3 MACHINE ▷ [T] 🔵 to press switches on a machine so that it will start when you want it to: *I've* **set** *the alarm* **for** *6.30.* ○ [+ to do sth] *You can set the oven to come on at any particular time.* **4 set an example/a record/a standard, etc** 🔵 to do something in a way that people will copy or try to improve on: *She's set a new world record with that jump.* **5 set fire to sth; set sth on fire** 🔵 to make something start burning **6 set sb free** 🔵 to allow someone to leave prison, or to allow a person or animal to escape **7 set sth alight** to make something start burning **8 set the table** to put plates, knives, forks, etc on the table before you have a meal **9** SUN ▷ [I] 🔵 When the sun sets, it moves down in the sky so that it cannot be seen: *The sun rises in the East and sets in the West.* **10** BECOME SOLID ▷ [I] If a liquid substance sets, it becomes solid. **11** SCHOOL WORK ▷ [T] UK 🔵 If you set work or an exam at a school or college, you ask the students to do it: [+ two objects] *Mr Harley forgot to set us any maths homework.* **12 set sth down/ on, etc** to put something somewhere: *She set the vase down on the table.* **13** BOOK/FILM/PLAY ▷ [T] 🔵 If a book, play, or movie is set in a place or period of time, the story happens there or at that time: [often passive] *It's a historical adventure set in India in the 1940s.* **14 set to work** to start working

PHRASAL VERBS **set about sth/doing sth** to start doing something, especially something that uses a lot of time or energy: *I got home and immediately set about cleaning the house.* • **be set against sth/doing sth** to not want to do or have something: *He is* **dead set against** *the move.* • **set sb/sth apart** If a quality sets someone or something apart, it makes them different from and usually better than others of the same type: *It's their intelligence which* **sets them apart from** *other rock bands.* • **set sth aside** to save something, usually time or money, for a special purpose • **set sb/sth back** to make something happen more slowly or later than it should: *The heavy traffic set us back about half an hour.* • **set sb back (sth)** informal to cost someone a large amount of money: *A car like that will probably set you back about £12,000.* • **set in** If something unpleasant sets in, it begins and seems likely to continue: *This rain looks as if it has set in for the rest of the day.* • **set off** 🔵 to start a journey: *What time are you setting off tomorrow morning?* • **set sth off** to make something begin or happen, especially a loud noise or a lot of activity: *He's always burning the toast and setting off the smoke alarm.* • **set sb/sth on/upon sb** to make a person or animal attack someone: *If you come any closer, I'll set the dog on you.* • **set out 1** to start doing something when you have already decided what you want to achieve: [+ to do sth] *I'd done what I set out to do.* **2** 🔵 to start a journey • **set sth out** 🔵 to give all the details of something, or to explain something clearly, especially in writing: *Your contract will set out the terms of your employment.* • **set sth up 1** 🔵 to start a company or organization: *A committee has been set up to investigate the problem.* **2** 🔵 to arrange for

S

something to happen: *I've set up a meeting with him for next week.* • **set sb up** to trick someone in order to make them do something, or in order to make them seem guilty of something that they have not done • **set (sth) up** to get all the necessary equipment ready for an activity: *I need one or two people to help me set up the display.*

set² /set/ noun [C] **1** GROUP ▷ ② a group of things that belong together: *a set of instructions/rules* ◦ *a set of keys/tools* **2** FILM/PLAY ▷ ② the place where a film or play is performed or recorded, and the pictures, furniture, etc that are used: *They first met on the set of 'Star Wars'.* **3** TENNIS ▷ ② one part of a tennis match: *Nadal is leading by four games to one in the third set.* **4** TV/RADIO ▷ ③ a television or radio: *a TV set* **5** MUSIC ▷ a group of songs or tunes that go together to make a musical performance **6** MATHS ▷ a group of numbers or things

set³ /set/ adj **1** fixed and never changing: *Most people work for a set number of hours each week.* ◦ *I have no set routine.* **2** be all set to be ready: [+ to do sth] *We were all set to go when the phone rang.* → See also **On your marks. Get set. Go!**

setback /'setbæk/ noun [C] a problem that makes something happen later or more slowly than it should: *The project has suffered a series of setbacks this year.*

> 🗹 Word partners for **setback**
>
> **suffer** a setback • a **major/serious** setback • a setback **for** sb • a setback **in/to** sth

set-piece /'set'piːs/ noun [C] a speech or set of actions that has been carefully planned and practised

settee /set'iː/ noun [C] UK (UK/US **sofa**) a large, comfortable seat for more than one person

setting /'setɪŋ/ noun [C] **1** ③ the place where something is or where something happens, often in a book, play, or film: *The house provided the setting for the TV series 'Pride and Prejudice'.* **2** a position on the controls of a piece of equipment: *Set the oven at the lowest setting.*

settle /'setl/ verb **1** ARGUMENT ▷ [T] ③ If you settle an argument, you solve the problem and stop arguing: *to settle a dispute* **2** LIVE ▷ [I] ③ to start living in a place where you are going to live for a long time: *He travelled around Europe for years before finally settling in Vienna.* **3** DECIDE ▷ [T] ③ to decide or arrange something: [often passive] *Right, that's settled. We're going to Spain.* **4** RELAX ▷ [I, T] to relax into a comfortable position: [often reflexive] *She settled herself into the chair opposite.* **5** PAY ▷ [T] If you settle a bill or a debt, you pay the money that you owe. **6** MOVE DOWN ▷ [I] to move down towards the ground or the bottom of something and then stay there: *Do you think the snow will settle?* → See also **the dust¹ settles**

PHRASAL VERBS **settle down 1** to start living in a place where you intend to stay for a long time, usually with a partner: *Do you think he'll ever settle down and have a family?* **2** ③ to start to

feel happy and confident with a new situation: *Has she settled down in her new job?* • **settle (sb) down** to become quiet and calm, or to make someone become quiet and calm: *Come on children, stop chatting and settle down please!* • **settle for sth** to accept something, especially something that is not exactly what you want: *He wants a full refund and he won't settle for anything less.* • **settle in** to begin to feel relaxed and happy in a new job: *Are you settling in OK?* • **settle on/upon sth** to agree on a decision: *We still haven't settled on a place to meet.* • **settle up** to pay someone the money that you owe them: *I need to settle up with you for the tickets.*

settled /'setld/ adj **1** be settled to feel happy and relaxed in a place or situation: *He seems quite settled now.* **2** regular and not often changing: *The weather's a lot more settled at this time of year.* → Opposite **unsettled**

settlement /'setlmənt/ noun [C] **1** an official agreement that finishes an argument: *a peace settlement* **2** a town or village that people built to live in after arriving from somewhere else: *a Jewish settlement*

> 🗹 Word partners for **settlement**
>
> **agree/negotiate/reach** a settlement • a settlement **between** sb and sb • a settlement **over** sth • a **peace** settlement

settler /'setlər/ noun [C] someone who moves to a new place where there were not many people before: *The first European settlers arrived in Virginia in 1607.*

set-top box /'settɒpˌbɒks/ noun [C] a piece of electronic equipment that allows you to watch digital broadcasts (= television sounds and pictures sent as signals in the form of numbers) on an ordinary television

set-up /'setʌp/ noun [C] informal **1** the way that something is arranged or organized: *It took me a while to get used to the set-up in my new job.* **2** a plan that is dishonest and is intended to trick someone

seven /'sevən/ ③ the number 7

seventeen /ˌsevən'tiːn/ ③ the number 17 • **seventeenth** 17th written as a word

seventh¹ /'sevənθ/ ② 7th written as a word

seventh² /'sevənθ/ noun [C] one of seven equal parts of something; ⅐

seventy /'sevənti/ **1** ② the number 70 **2** the seventies the years from 1970 to 1979 **3** be in your seventies to be aged between 70 and 79 • **seventieth** 70th written as a word

sever /'sevər/ verb [T] **1** to cut through something, especially a part of the body: *to sever an artery* ◦ [often passive] *Two of her fingers were severed in the accident.* **2** sever links/ties, etc with sb to end a relationship with someone

several /'sevərəl/ pronoun, determiner ② some, but not a lot: *Several people have complained about the scheme.* ◦ *Several of my friends studied in Manchester.*

severance /'sevərəns/ noun [U] a situation in

S

which an employer forces an employee to leave a job: *severance pay*

severe /sɪ'vɪəʳ/ **adj 1 BAD** ▷ 🅱️ extremely bad: *a severe headache* ∘ *severe weather conditions* **2 NOT KIND** ▷ not kind or gentle: *a severe punishment* **3 PERSON** ▷ 🅱️ A severe person looks unfriendly or very strict. • **severely adv** 🅱️ *to be severely injured* ∘ *She has been severely criticized for the speech.*

severity /sɪ'verəti/ **noun** [U] how severe something is

sew /səʊ/ **verb** [I, T] (**sewed, sewn, sewed**) 🅱️ to join things together with a needle and thread: *I need to sew a button on my shirt.*

PHRASAL VERB **sew sth up 1** to close or repair something by sewing the edges together **2 have sth sewn up** informal to be certain to win or succeed at something

sewage /'suːɪdʒ/ **noun** [U] waste water and waste from toilets: *a sewage treatment plant*

sewer /suəʳ/ **noun** [C] a large underground system of pipes that carries away sewage

sewing /'səʊɪŋ/ **noun** [U] **1** the activity of joining pieces of cloth together or repairing them with a needle and thread **2** the pieces of cloth that you are joining together or repairing with a needle and thread

'sewing ma,chine noun [C] a machine that joins pieces of cloth together with a needle and thread

sewn /səʊn/ past participle of sew

sex¹ /seks/ **noun 1** [U] 🅱️ sexual activity between people: *to have sex with someone* ∘ *sex education* **2** [U] 🅱️ the fact of being male or female: *Do you know what sex the baby is?* ∘ *sex discrimination* **3** the female/male/opposite, etc sex people who are female/male/the other sex from you, etc

sex² /seks/ **verb**

PHRASAL VERB **sex sth up** UK informal to make something seem more exciting than it really is: *It was said that the government had sexed up the report.*

sexism /'seksɪzᵊm/ **noun** [U] unfair treatment of someone because they are a woman or because they are a man • **sexist adj** *sexist attitudes/jokes*

'sex ,life noun [C] a person's sexual activities and relationships

sexual /'sekʃuəl/ **adj 1** 🅱️ relating to the activity of sex: *sexual experiences* ∘ *sexual organs* **2** relating to being male or female: *sexual discrimination* ∘ *sexual equality*

,sexual 'intercourse noun [U] formal the activity in which a man puts his penis into a woman's vagina

sexuality /,sekʃu'æləti/ **noun** [U] the way you feel about sexual activity and the type of sex you prefer

sexually /'sekʃuəli/ **adv** in a way that relates to the activity of sex: *sexually attractive* ∘ *a sexually transmitted disease*

sexy /'seksi/ **adj** attractive or exciting in a sexual way: *sexy underwear* ∘ *He's very sexy.*

SGML /esdʒiːem'el/ **noun** [U] abbreviation fc standard generalized markup language: system for organizing information on compu ters

sh (also **shh**) /ʃ/ **exclamation** used to tel someone to be quiet

shabby /'ʃæbi/ **adj 1** untidy and in bad condi tion: *shabby clothes/furniture* **2** Shabby beha viour or treatment is bad and unfair. • **shabbily adv** *shabbily dressed* ∘ *shabbily treated*

shack¹ /ʃæk/ **noun** [C] a small simple building that has been badly built

shack² /ʃæk/ **verb**

PHRASAL VERB **shack up with sb** very informal t start living in the same house as someone you are having a romantic relationship with

shackle /'ʃækl/ **verb** [T] **1** to fasten a prisoner' arms or legs together with chains **2 be shackled by sth** to be prevented from doing what yo want to do by something

shackles /'ʃæklz/ **noun** [plural] chains used t fasten together prisoners' arms or legs

shade¹ /ʃeɪd/ **noun 1 NO SUN** ▷ [U] 🅱️ an are where there is no light from the sun and so it i darker and not as hot: *I'd prefer to sit in th shade.* **2 COLOUR** ▷ [C] 🅱️ a colour, especiall when referring to how dark or light it is: *a pale dark shade of grey* ∘ *pastel shades* **3 COVER** ▷ [C a cover that stops too much light coming fron the sun or from an electric light: *a lampshade* **4 a shade** a small amount: *He's perhaps a shad taller.* **5 a shade of meaning/opinion, etc** slight difference in the meaning of something

shade

shade   shadow

shade² /ʃeɪd/ **verb** [T] to cover something i order to protect it from the sun: *He shaded hi eyes with his hand.*

shades /ʃeɪdz/ **noun** [plural] informal sunglasse (= dark glasses that protect your eyes from th sun)

shadow¹ /'ʃædəʊ/ **noun** [C, U] 🅱️ a dark are made by something that is stopping the light *The tree had cast* (= made) *a long shadow.* → Se picture at **shade**

IDIOMS **beyond/without a shadow of a doubt** I something is true beyond a shadow of a doubt, i is certainly true. • **cast a shadow over sth** t spoil a good situation with something unpleas ant: *The bombing has cast a shadow over the Queen's visit.*

☑ **Word partners for shadow**

sth **casts** a shadow • a shadow **crosses/falls across** sth • sth is **in** shadow • the shadow **of** sth

---

shadow² /ˈʃædəʊ/ **verb** [T] to follow someone secretly in order to see where they go and what they do: [often passive] *He was being shadowed by a private detective.*

shadowy /ˈʃædəʊi/ **adj 1** dark and full of shadows: *in a shadowy corner* **2** secret and mysterious: *the shadowy world of espionage*

shady /ˈʃeɪdi/ **adj 1** A shady place is protected from the sun and so it is fairly dark and cool: *We found a shady spot to sit in.* **2** informal dishonest and illegal: *shady deals*

shaft /ʃɑːft/ **noun** [C] **1** a long, vertical hole that people or things can move through, either inside a building or in the ground: *a mine shaft* ∘ *a ventilation shaft* **2** the handle of a tool or weapon **3** **a shaft of light** a beam of light

shake¹ /ʃeɪk/ **verb** (**shook, shaken**)

shake

1 MOVE ▷ [I, T] 🄐 to make quick, short movements from side to side or up and down, or to make something or someone do this: *He was shaking with nerves.* ∘ *Shake the bottle.* **2 shake hands** 🄑 to hold someone's hand and move it up and down when you meet them for the first time, or when you make an agreement with them: *The two leaders smiled and shook hands for the photographers.* ∘ *I shook hands with him.* **3 shake your head** 🄒 to move your head from side to side to mean 'no' **4 SHOCK** ▷ [T] to shock or upset someone: [often passive] *No one was injured in the crash, but the driver was badly shaken.* **5 VOICE** ▷ [I] If your voice shakes, you sound very nervous or frightened.

PHRASAL VERBS **shake sth off** to get rid of an illness or something that is causing you problems: *I hope I can shake off this cold before the weekend.* • **shake sb off** to succeed in escaping from someone who is following you • **shake sth out** to hold something that is made of cloth at one end and move it up and down in order to get rid of dirt • **shake sb up** If an unpleasant experience shakes someone up, it makes them feel shocked and upset: *The accident really shook him up.*

shake² /ʃeɪk/ **noun** [C] **1** the action of shaking something: *Give it a good shake before you open it.* **2** (also **milkshake**) a sweet drink made of milk and chocolate or fruit

shake-up /ˈʃeɪkʌp/ **noun** [C] If there is a shake-

up of a system or organization, big changes are made to it: *This is the biggest shake-up in the legal system for fifty years.*

shaky /ˈʃeɪki/ **adj 1 MOVING** ▷ making quick, short movements from side to side or up and down: *shaky hands* **2 NOT STRONG** ▷ not physically strong because you are nervous, old, or sick: *I felt a bit shaky when I stood up.* **3 LIKELY TO FAIL** ▷ not working well and likely to fail: *They managed to win the game, despite a very shaky start.*

shall strong /ʃæl/ weak /ʃəl/ **modal verb 1 shall I/ we...? a** 🄐 used to make an offer or suggestion: *Shall I cook dinner tonight?* ∘ *We'll ask him later, shall we?* **b** 🄐 used to ask someone what to do: *What restaurant shall we go to?* ∘ *Who shall I ask?* **2 I/we shall...** formal 🄑 used to say what you are going to do in the future: *I shall be talking to her tomorrow.* ∘ *I shan't forget to tell them.* → See Study Page **Modal verbs** on page Centre 22

❗ **Common learner error: shall and will**

Shall and **will** are both used to talk about what you are going to do in the future. **Shall** is usually used with 'I' or 'we' and is more formal than **will**.

---

shallot /ʃəˈlɒt/ **noun** [C] a vegetable like a small onion

shallow /ˈʃæləʊ/ **adj 1** 🄒 not deep: *shallow water* ∘ *a shallow dish* → See picture at **deep** **2** not showing any interest in serious ideas

the shallows /ˈʃæləʊz/ **noun** [plural] areas of shallow water

sham /ʃæm/ **noun** [no plural] something that is not what it seems to be and is intended to deceive people: *Newspapers have described their marriage as a sham.*

shambles /ˈʃæmblz/ **noun** **be a shambles** informal to be very badly organized: *The performance was a complete shambles.*

shame¹ /ʃeɪm/ **noun 1 a shame** 🄐 If you describe something as a shame, you mean you are disappointed that it has happened: [+ to do sth] *It's a real shame to waste all this food.* ∘ [+ (that)] *What a shame that they had to destroy such a beautiful building.* **2** [U] a feeling of being embarrassed and guilty about something bad that you have done: *to be filled with shame* **3 have no shame** to not feel embarrassed or guilty about doing bad or embarrassing things

IDIOM **put sb/sth to shame** to be much better than someone or something else: *Your cooking puts mine to shame.*

☑ **Word partners for shame**

bring shame **on** sb/sth • a **sense** of shame • the **shame** of (doing) sth

---

shame² /ʃeɪm/ **verb** [T] to make someone feel embarrassed and guilty about something: [+ into + doing sth] *His children are trying to shame him into giving up smoking.*

shameful /ˈʃeɪmfəl/ **adj** Something shameful is bad and should make you feel embarrassed and guilty: *shameful scenes* • **shamefully adv**

S

---

shameless /'ʃeɪmləs/ **adj** without feeling embarrassed or guilty although you should: *shameless behaviour/lies* • **shamelessly adv**

shampoo /ʃæm'puː/ **noun** [C, U] Ⓐ⓶ a liquid substance that you use to wash your hair: *a bottle of shampoo* • **shampoo verb** [T] (**shampooing, shampooed**)

shan't /ʃɑːnt/ mainly UK short for shall not: *I was invited to the party, but I shan't be going.*

shanty town /'ʃænti ˌtaʊn/ **noun** [C] an area on the edge of a town where poor people live in very simply built houses

shapes

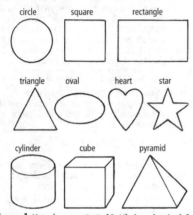

circle   square   rectangle

triangle   oval   heart   star

cylinder   cube   pyramid

shape¹ /ʃeɪp/ **noun 1** Ⓑ⓵ [C, U] the physical form of something made by the line around its outer edge: *a circular/rectangular shape* ◦ *You can recognize trees by the shape of their leaves.* **2 in good/bad/great, etc shape** Ⓑ⓶ in good/bad, etc health or condition: *She runs every day so she's in pretty good shape.* **3 out of shape** not healthy or physically strong **4 keep in shape** to stay healthy and physically strong **5 take shape** to start to develop and become more clear or certain: *The project is slowly beginning to take shape.*

IDIOM **all shapes and sizes** many different types of people or things: *We saw people there of all shapes and sizes.*

> ☑ Word partners for **shape**
> an **irregular/pleasing/strange/unusual** shape • **change** shape • **in** the shape **of** sth

shape² /ʃeɪp/ **verb** [T] **1** to influence the way that something develops: [often passive] *Their attitudes were shaped during the war.* **2** to make something become a particular shape: *Combine the meat and egg and shape the mixture into small balls.*

PHRASAL VERB **shape up** informal to develop or improve: *Things at work seem to be shaping up quite nicely.*

-shaped /ʃeɪpt/ **suffix** used after nouns to mean 'having a particular shape': *a heart-shaped cake* → See also **pear-shaped**

shapeless /'ʃeɪpləs/ **adj** not having a clear c well designed shape: *a shapeless dress*

shapely /'ʃeɪpli/ **adj** having an attractive shape *shapely legs*

share¹ /ʃeər/ **verb 1** [I, T] Ⓐ⓶ to have or us something at the same time as someone else *She **shares** a house **with** Paul.* **2** [I, T] Ⓐ⓶ to divid something between two or more people: *W shared a pizza and a bottle of wine.* ◦ *We **share** the cost of the wedding **between** us.* **3 share a interest/opinion, etc** Ⓑ⓵ to have the sam interest/opinion, etc as someone else: *The share a love of gardening.* **4 share you problems/thoughts/ideas, etc** to tell someon your problems/thoughts, etc

PHRASAL VERB **share sth out** to divide somethin into smaller amounts and give one amount t each person in a group: *Profits are **shared** ou equally **among** members of the group.*

share² /ʃeər/ **noun** [C] **1** one of the equal part that the value of a company is divided into whe it is owned by a group of people: *to **buy/sei** **shares*** ◦ *We own shares in a number c companies.* ◦ ***Share prices** have fallen for th third day running.* **2** Ⓑ⓶ a part of something tha has been divided: [usually singular] *When am going to get my share of the money?*

IDIOM **have your (fair) share of sth** to have a lc of something and enough of it, usually some thing bad: *We've had our fair share of rain alread this summer.*

> ☑ Word partners for **share** (noun)
> **buy/have/sell** shares • shares **in** sth • share **prices**

shareholder /'ʃeəˌhəʊldər/ **noun** [C] someon who owns shares in a company: *a shareholder. meeting*

shareware /'ʃeəweər/ **noun** [U] software tha you get from the Internet, that you can use for short time without paying for it

Sharia /ʃə'riːə/ **noun** [U] the holy law of Islam

shark /ʃɑːk/ **noun** [C]   **shark**
Ⓑ⓵ a large fish with
very sharp teeth

sharp¹ /ʃɑːp/ **adj**
1 ABLE TO CUT ▷ Ⓑ⓵
having a very thin or
pointed edge that can
cut things: *a sharp knife*
◦ *sharp claws/teeth* **2 a sharp rise/increase/drop, etc** Ⓑ⓶ a sudden an very large increase or reduction in somethin **3 a sharp contrast/difference/distinction, etc** very big and noticeable difference between tw things **4 QUICK** ▷ Ⓑ⓶ quick to notice an understand things: *a sharp mind* **5 a shar pain** a sudden, short, strong pain **6 SEVERE** ▷ severe and not gentle: *sharp criticism* ◦ *She ca be a bit sharp with people sometimes.* **7 a shar bend/turn, etc** a sudden large change in th direction you are travelling **8 SOUR** ▷ A shar taste is slightly sour. **9 CLEAR** ▷ A sharp image i very clear: *a photograph in sharp focus* **10**

S

sharp wit the ability to say things that are funny and clever **11 a sharp tongue** If you have a sharp tongue, you often upset people by saying unkind things to them. **12** FASHIONABLE ▷ If a piece of clothing or a style is sharp, it is fashionable and tidy: *young men in sharp suits* **13 C sharp/F sharp, etc** the musical note that is between the note C, F, etc and the note above it **14** TOO HIGH ▷ A sharp musical note sounds unpleasant because it is slightly higher than it should be. • **sharply** adv • **sharpness** noun [U]

harp² /ʃɑːp/ **adv 3 o'clock/8.30 p.m., etc sharp** at exactly 3 o'clock, 8.30 p.m., etc

harp³ /ʃɑːp/ **noun** [C] a musical note that is between a particular note and the note above it

harpen /ˈʃɑːpən/ **verb** [T] to make something sharper: *to sharpen a knife/pencil*

hatter /ˈʃætər/ **verb 1** [I, T] to break into very small pieces, or to make something break into very small pieces: *Someone threw a stone at the car, shattering the windscreen.* **2** [T] to destroy something good, such as your confidence, hopes, or belief in something: *The accident completely shattered her confidence.*

hattered /ˈʃætəd/ **adj 1** very upset **2** UK informal very tired

have¹ /ʃeɪv/ **verb** [I, T] ⬛ to cut hair off your face or body: *to shave your head/legs* ∘ *shaving cream/foam*

have

PHRASAL VERB **shave sth off** to cut a very thin piece off a surface

have² /ʃeɪv/ **noun** [C] When a man has a shave, he shaves the hair growing on his face.

IDIOM **a close shave** a situation in which something unpleasant or dangerous almost happens

haven /ˈʃeɪvən/ **adj** A shaven part of the body has had the hair cut off it: *a gang of youths with shaven heads*

haver /ˈʃeɪvər/ **noun** [C] a piece of electrical equipment used to cut hair off the head or body

havings /ˈʃeɪvɪŋz/ **noun** [plural] very thin pieces that have been cut off something: *wood shavings*

hawl /ʃɔːl/ **noun** [C] a piece of cloth that is worn by a woman around her shoulders or used to cover a baby

he strong /ʃiː/ weak /ʃi/ **pronoun** ⬛ used as the subject of the verb when referring to someone female who has already been talked about: *"When is Ruth coming?" "She'll be here soon."*

heaf /ʃiːf/ **noun** [C] (plural **sheaves** /ʃiːvz/) **1** several pieces of paper held together: *a sheaf of papers* **2** several pieces of wheat or corn (= plant for grain) tied together

hear /ʃɪər/ **verb** [T] (**sheared**, **sheared**, **shorn**) to cut the wool off a sheep

hears /ʃɪəz/ **noun** [plural] a cutting tool with two large blades, like a large pair of scissors: *a pair of garden shears*

sheath /ʃiːθ/ **noun** [C] a cover for the sharp blade of a knife

shed¹ /ʃed/ **noun** [C] ⬛ a small building used to store things such as tools: *a garden shed*

shed² /ʃed/ **verb** [T] (**shedding, shed**) **1 shed leaves/skin/hair, etc** to lose something because it falls off: *A lot of trees shed their leaves in the autumn.* **2** to get rid of something that you do not want or need: *A lot of companies are shedding jobs.* **3 shed tears** to cry **4 shed blood** to kill or injure someone → See also **cast/shed light on sth**

she'd /ʃiːd/ **1** short for she had: *By the time I got there, she'd fallen asleep.* **2** short for she would: *She knew that she'd be late.*

shedload /ˈʃedləʊd/ **noun** [C] informal a large amount: *They spent shedloads of money on that car.*

sheen /ʃiːn/ **noun** [no plural] a smooth shine on a surface

sheep /ʃiːp/ **noun** [C] (plural **sheep**) ⬛ a farm animal whose skin is covered with wool: *a flock of sheep*

sheepish /ˈʃiːpɪʃ/ **adj** slightly embarrassed, usually because you have done something stupid: *a sheepish grin/look* • **sheepishly** adv

sheer /ʃɪər/ **adj 1** EXTREME ▷ [always before noun] used to emphasize how strong a feeling or quality is: *a look of sheer delight/joy* ∘ *sheer determination/hard work* **2** LARGE ▷ [always before noun] used to emphasize the large size or amount of something: *The delays are due to the sheer volume of traffic.* **3** STEEP ▷ very steep: *a sheer cliff face* **4** CLOTH ▷ Sheer cloth is very thin and you can see through it: *sheer tights/nylons*

sheet

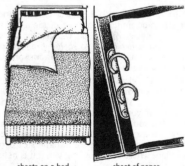

sheets on a bed   sheet of paper

sheet /ʃiːt/ **noun** [C] **1** ⬛ a large piece of cloth put on a bed to lie on or under: *a double fitted sheet* ∘ *to change the sheets* **2 a sheet of paper/glass/metal, etc** ⬛ a flat piece of paper/glass, etc: *a sheet of yellow paper* → See also **balance sheet**

sheeting /ˈʃiːtɪŋ/ **noun** [U] a large flat piece of material, usually used as a cover: *plastic sheeting*

Sheikh (also **Sheik**) /ʃeɪk/ **noun** [C] an Arab leader

shelf /ʃelf/ **noun** [C] (plural **shelves** /ʃelvz/) ⬛ a flat, horizontal board used to put things on,

S

often fixed to a wall or inside a cupboard: *a bookshelf* ○ *on the top/bottom shelf*

'shelf ˌlife noun [C] (plural **shelf lives**) A product's shelf life is the length of time it stays in good condition and can be used: [usually singular] *Fresh fruit has a very short shelf life.*

shell¹ /ʃel/ noun [C]
1 ⁶² the hard outer covering of some creatures and of eggs, nuts, or seeds: *a snail's shell* ○ *an egg shell* **2** a bomb fired from a large gun → See also **sea shell**

shell² /ʃel/ verb [T] to attack a place with bombs

PHRASAL VERB **shell out (sth)** informal to pay or give money for something, especially when you do not want to

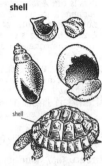

shell

shell

shell

she'll /ʃiːl/ short for she will: *She'll be away until Tuesday.*

shellfish /'ʃelfɪʃ/ noun [U] sea creatures that live in shells and are eaten as food

shelter¹ /'ʃeltə'/ noun **1** [C] ⁶² a place that protects you from bad weather or danger: *a bomb shelter* **2** [U] ⁶² protection from bad weather or danger: *We **took shelter** from the rain in a doorway.*

> **Word partners for shelter**
> find/provide/seek/take shelter • shelter from sth • under the shelter of sth

shelter² /'ʃeltə'/ verb **1 shelter from/in/under, etc sth** to go under a cover or inside a building to be protected from bad weather or danger: *They went under a tree to shelter from the rain.* **2** [T] to provide cover or protection for someone: *Many households are already sheltering refugees.*

sheltered /'ʃeltəd/ adj **1** covered or protected from bad weather or danger: *a sheltered spot by the wall* **2 a sheltered existence/life/upbringing, etc** If you have a sheltered life, you are protected too much and experience very little danger or excitement. **3 sheltered accommodation/housing** UK houses for old and sick people in a place where help can be given if it is needed

shelve /ʃelv/ verb [T] to decide not to continue with a plan: [often passive] *The project had to be shelved when they ran out of money.*

shelves /ʃelvz/ plural of shelf

shenanigans /ʃɪ'nænɪɡənz/ noun [plural] informal secret or dishonest behaviour: *political/sexual shenanigans*

shepherd¹ /'ʃepəd/ noun [C] someone whose job is to look after sheep

shepherd² /'ʃepəd/ verb [T] to go somewhere with someone in order to guide them or protect them: *Children were being shepherded to school by their parents.*

sheriff /'ʃerɪf/ noun [C] an elected law officer in the US

sherry /'ʃeri/ noun [C, U] a strong Spanish wine that is often drunk before a meal

she's /ʃiːz/ **1** short for she is: *She's a very good student.* **2** short for she has: *She's been working very hard.*

shh /ʃ/ exclamation used to tell someone to be quiet

Shia /'ʃiːə/ noun [C] a Shiite

shield¹ /ʃiːld/ noun [C] **1** a large, flat object that police officers and soldiers hold in front of their bodies to protect themselves **2** a person or thing used as protection: *The hostages are being used as human shields.*

shield² /ʃiːld/ verb [T] to protect someone or something from something dangerous or unpleasant: *to **shield** your **eyes** from the sun*

shift¹ /ʃɪft/ noun [C] **1 CHANGE** ▷ a change in something: *There has been a dramatic **shift** in public opinion on this matter.* **2 WORK** ▷ ⁶² a period of work in a place such as a factory or hospital: *afternoon/night shift* ○ *He works an eight-hour shift.* **3 COMPUTER** ▷ (also **shift key**) the key on a computer keyboard which allows you to create a capital letter (= a large letter of the alphabet used at the beginning of sentences and names)

> **Word partners for shift**
> a dramatic/fundamental/gradual/major shift • a shift (away) from/towards sth • a shift in sth

shift² /ʃɪft/ verb **1 CHANGE** ▷ [I, T] to change something: *We are trying to **shift** the emphasis from curing illness to preventing it.* **2 MOVE STH** ▷ [T] to move something to another place: *We need to shift all these boxes into the other room.* **3 MOVE YOURSELF** ▷ [I, T] to move into a different position: *He shifted uncomfortably in his seat.* **4 CHANGE SPEED** ▷ [T] (also **shift into**) US to change the position of the gears (= parts that control how fast the wheels turn) in a vehicle: *shift gears*

'shift ˌkey noun [C] (also **shift**) the key on a computer keyboard that allows you to create a capital letter (= a large letter of the alphabet used at the beginning of sentences and names)

shifty /'ʃɪfti/ adj informal Someone who looks shifty looks dishonest.

Shiite (also **Shi'ite**) /'ʃiːaɪt/ noun [C] a member of a large group within the Islamic religion • **Shiite** adj (also **Shi'ite**) describing the Shiites or the type of Islam

shilling /'ʃɪlɪŋ/ noun [C] a unit of money used in the past in the UK

shimmer /'ʃɪmə'/ verb [I] to shine gently and seem to be moving slightly: *The trees shimmered in the moonlight.*

shin /ʃɪn/ noun [C] the front part of a leg between the knee and the foot → See colour picture **The Body** on page Centre 13

shine¹ /ʃaɪn/ verb (shone, shined) **1 PRODUCE LIGHT** ▷ [I] ⁶¹ to produce bright light: *The sun was **shining** brightly through the window.*

S

2 POINT LIGHT ▷ [I, T] to point a light somewhere: *The car's headlights shone right into my eyes.* **3** REFLECT ▷ [I, T] If a surface shines, it reflects light, and if you shine it, you make it reflect light: *She polished her shoes until they shone.* **4** EYES/FACE ▷ [I] If your eyes or face shine, you look happy, healthy, or excited: *His eyes were shining with excitement.* **5** DO WELL ▷ [I] to do something very well, usually better than other people.

shine² /ʃaɪn/ noun [no plural] the quality of being bright from reflected light on the surface: *hair with body and shine*

IDIOMS **take a shine to sb** informal to like someone immediately: *I think he's taken a bit of a shine to you.* • **take the shine off sth** to spoil something pleasant

shingle /'ʃɪŋgl/ noun [U] UK a lot of very small pieces of stone on a beach

shiny /'ʃaɪni/ adj ⓑ A shiny surface is bright because it reflects light: *shiny hair*

ship¹ /ʃɪp/ noun [C] ⓐ a large boat that carries people or goods by sea: *a cargo ship*

ship² /ʃɪp/ verb [T] (**shipping**, **shipped**) to send something from one place to another: [often passive] *These vegetables have been shipped halfway around the world.*

shipment /'ʃɪpmənt/ noun **1** [C] an amount of goods sent from one place to another, especially by ship: *The first shipments of food arrived this month.* **2** [U] the movement of goods or industrial products from one place to another, especially by ship: *the shipment of nuclear waste*

shipping and 'handling noun [U] US postage and packing

shipwreck¹ /'ʃɪprek/ noun [C] an accident in which a ship is destroyed at sea

shipwreck² /'ʃɪprek/ verb be **shipwrecked** If someone is shipwrecked, the ship they are in is destroyed in an accident.

shipyard /'ʃɪpjɑːd/ noun [C] a place where ships are built or repaired

shirk /ʃɜːk/ verb [I, T] to avoid doing something because it is difficult or unpleasant: *to shirk your duties/responsibilities*

shirt /ʃɜːt/ noun [C] ⓐ a piece of clothing worn on the top part of the body, often made of thin material like cotton and fastened with buttons down the front → See colour picture **Clothes** on page Centre 9 → See also **polo shirt, T-shirt**

shish kebab /'ʃɪʃkəˌbæb/ noun [C] small pieces of meat or vegetables cooked on a long, thin stick

shit¹ /ʃɪt/ exclamation very informal a very impolite word used to show surprise, anger, disappointment, etc

shit² /ʃɪt/ noun [U] very informal a very impolite word for waste from the body of a person or animal that comes out of their bottom

shiver /'ʃɪvər/ verb [I] ⓑ to shake because you are cold or frightened: *She shivered with cold.* • **shiver** noun [C] *He felt a shiver run down his spine (= He felt afraid).*

shoal /ʃəʊl/ noun [C] a large group of fish swimming together

shock¹ /ʃɒk/ noun **1** SURPRISE ▷ [C, U] ⓑ a big, unpleasant surprise: *We got a nasty shock when he gave us the bill.* ◦ *Her death came as a terrible shock to him.* ◦ *They are still in shock (= feeling the effect of a shock) from the accident.* **2** ILLNESS ▷ [U] a medical condition when someone is extremely weak because of damage to their body: *He went into shock and nearly died.* **3** ELECTRICITY ▷ [C] (also **electric shock**) a sudden, painful feeling that you get when electricity flows through your body **4** MOVEMENT ▷ [C] a sudden movement caused by an explosion, accident, etc → See also **culture shock**

> ### ⊘ Word partners for **shock**
>
> **come as** a shock • **get/have** a shock • a **big/ nasty/real** shock • a shock **to sb** • **be in** shock

shock² /ʃɒk/ verb [I, T] ⓑ to surprise and upset someone: [often passive] *Many people were shocked by the violent scenes in the film.* • **shocked** adj ⓑ [+ to do sth] *We were shocked to find rat poison in our hotel room.*

shocking /'ʃɒkɪŋ/ adj **1** ⓑ very surprising and upsetting or immoral: *shocking news* ◦ *This report contains scenes that some people may find shocking.* **2** UK very bad: *My memory is shocking.* • **shockingly** adv

shoddy /'ʃɒdi/ adj very bad quality: *shoddy goods* ◦ *shoddy work/workmanship/treatment*

shoe /ʃuː/ noun [C] ⓐ a strong covering for the foot, often made of leather: *a pair of shoes* ◦ *to put your shoes on/take your shoes off*

IDIOM **be in sb's shoes** informal to be in the same situation as someone else, especially an unpleasant situation: *What would you do if you were in my shoes?*

shoelace /'ʃuːleɪs/ noun [C] a long, thin piece of material used to fasten shoes

shoestring /'ʃuːstrɪŋ/ noun

IDIOM **on a shoestring** If you do something on a shoestring, you do it using very little money.

shone /ʃɒn/ ⓤ /ʃəʊn/ past of shine

shoo /ʃuː/ verb (**shooing**, **shooed**) **shoo sb away/off/out, etc** to make a person or animal leave a place by chasing them or shouting 'shoo' at them • **shoo** exclamation

shook /ʃʊk/ past tense of shake

shoot¹ /ʃuːt/ verb (**shot**) **1** INJURE ▷ [T] ⓑ to injure or kill a person or animal by firing a bullet from a gun at them: [often passive] *He was robbed and then shot in the stomach.* ◦ *An innocent bystander was shot dead in the incident.* **2** FIRE BULLET ▷ [I, T] ⓑ to fire a bullet from a gun: *Don't shoot!* **3** SPORT ▷ [I] ⓑ to try to score points in sports such as football by hitting, kicking, or throwing the ball towards the goal **4** **shoot across/out/up, etc** to move somewhere very quickly: *She shot across the road without looking.* **5** FILM ▷ [T] to use a camera to record a film or take a photograph: [often passive] *Most of the film was shot in Italy.*

PHRASAL VERBS **shoot sb/sth down** to destroy an aircraft or make it fall to the ground by firing bullets or weapons at it • **shoot up** If a number or amount shoots up, it increases very quickly: *Prices have shot up by 25%.*

shoot² /ʃuːt/ noun [C] **1** a new branch or stem growing on a plant: *bamboo shoots* **2** an occasion when someone takes photographs or makes a film: *a **fashion shoot***

shooting /'ʃuːtɪŋ/ noun **1** [C] ②⃝ an occasion when someone is injured or killed by a bullet from a gun: *a fatal shooting* **2** [U] the sport of firing bullets from guns, sometimes to kill animals

shop¹ /ʃɒp/ noun [C] (mainly US **store**) ④⃝ a building or part of a building where you can buy things: *a book shop* ∘ *a shoe shop* ∘ *to go to the shops* ∘ *a shop window* → See also **charity shop**

> ⚠ Common learner error: **shop** or **store**?
>
> In **American English** the usual word for shop is **store**.
> *He went to the store to buy some cookies.*
> In **British English** the word **store** is only used to mean a very large shop where you can buy many different things.
> *Harrods is a famous department store.*

shop² /ʃɒp/ verb [I] (**shopping**, **shopped**) ⑥⃝ to buy things in shops: *I'm **shopping for** baby clothes.* ∘ *I usually **go shopping** on Saturday.*

PHRASAL VERB **shop around** to compare the price and quality of the same thing from different places before deciding which one to buy: *to shop around for a computer*

shop as,sistant noun [C] UK (US **sales clerk**) ④⃝ someone whose job is selling things in a shop

shop 'floor noun [no plural] the part of a factory where things are made and not the part where the managers' offices are

shopkeeper /'ʃɒpˌkiːpər/ noun [C] (also US **storekeeper**) ⑥⃝ someone who owns or manages a small shop

shoplifting /'ʃɒplɪftɪŋ/ noun [U] the crime of stealing things from a shop • **shoplifter** noun [C] • **shoplift** verb [I]

shopper /'ʃɒpər/ noun [C] someone who is buying things from shops

shopping /'ʃɒpɪŋ/ noun [U] **1** ④⃝ the activity of buying things from shops: *I love shopping.* ∘ *a shopping basket*/UK *trolley*/US *cart* **2** ④⃝ the things that you buy from a shop or shops: *Can you help me unpack the shopping?* ∘ *a shopping bag* → See also **window shopping**

> ✍ Word partners for **shopping**
>
> a shopping spree/trip • to go shopping

shopping basket noun [C] a place on a website where you collect things that you plan to buy from the website → See **basket**

shopping centre noun [C] UK (US **shopping**

center) a place where a lot of shops have been built close together

shopping mall noun [C] a large, covered shopping area

shore¹ /ʃɔːr/ noun [C, U] ⑥⃝ the area of land along the edge of the sea or a lake: *They had to abandon the boat and swim back to shore.*

shore² /ʃɔːr/ verb

PHRASAL VERB **shore sth up** to help or improve something that is likely to fail

shorn /ʃɔːn/ past participle of shear

short¹ /ʃɔːt/ adj **1** DISTANCE ▷ ④⃝ having a small distance from one end to the other: *short, brown hair* ∘ *short legs* ∘ *a short skirt* **2** TIME ▷ ④⃝ continuing for a small amount of time: *a short visit* ∘ *There's a short break for coffee between classes.* **3** BOOK ▷ ④⃝ A short book or other piece of writing has few pages or words: *a short article/story* **4** PERSON ▷ ④⃝ A short person is not as tall as most people: *She's short and slim with dark hair.* **5** NOT HAVING ENOUGH ▷ ⑥⃝ not having enough of something: *I'm a bit **short of** money at the moment.* ∘ *Would you like to play? We're a couple of people short.* ∘ *He seemed a bit **short of breath** (= having difficulty breathing).* **6** be short for sth ⑥⃝ to be a shorter way of saying the same thing: *'Mick' is short for 'Michael'.* **7** be short with sb to talk to someone quickly in an angry or rude way • **shortness** noun [U] → See also in the long/short run²

short² /ʃɔːt/ adv **1 short of doing sth** without doing something: *He did everything he could to get the money, short of robbing a bank.* **2 stop short of sth/doing sth** to almost do something but decide not to do it: *She stopped short of accusing him of lying.* **3 fall short of sth** to not reach a particular level, but only by a small amount: *Sales for the first half of this year fell just short of the target.* **4 cut sth short** to have to stop doing something before it is finished: *She had to cut her speech short when the fire alarm went off.*

short³ /ʃɔːt/ noun **1 in short** in a few words: *In short, we need more staff.* **2** [C] a short film **3** [C] UK a small amount of a strong alcoholic drink, like whisky

shortage /'ʃɔːtɪdʒ/ noun [C] ⑥⃝ a situation in which there is not enough of something: *a shortage of nurses* ∘ *food shortages*

> ✍ Word partners for **shortage**
>
> an acute/chronic/desperate/serious shortage • a shortage of sth

shortbread /'ʃɔːtbred/ noun [U] a hard, sweet biscuit

short-circuit /ˌʃɔːtˈsɜːkɪt/ noun [C] a fault in an electrical connection • **short-circuit** verb [I, T]

shortcoming /'ʃɔːtˌkʌmɪŋ/ noun [C] a fault [usually plural] *I like him despite his shortcomings.*

shortcut (also UK **short 'cut**) /'ʃɔːtkʌt/ noun [C] **1** a quicker and more direct way of getting somewhere or doing something: *I **took a shortcut** through the car park.* **2** In computing, a shortcut is a quick way to start or use a computer program: *a shortcut key*

ɑː arm | ɜː her | iː see | ɔː saw | uː too | aɪ my | aʊ how | eə hair | eɪ day | əʊ no | ɪə near | ɔɪ boy | ʊə pure | aɪə fire | aʊə sour

shorten /'ʃɔːtᵊn/ **verb** [I, T] to become shorter or to make something shorter: *Smoking shortens your life.*

shortfall /'ʃɔːtfɔːl/ **noun** [C] the difference between the amount that is needed and the smaller amount that is available: *a shortfall in government spending*

shorthand /'ʃɔːthænd/ **noun** [U] a fast way of writing using abbreviations and symbols

short-haul /'ʃɔːthɔːl/ **adj** travelling a short distance: *a **short-haul flight***

shortlist /'ʃɔːtlɪst/ **noun** [C] UK a list of people who are competing for a prize, job, etc, who have already been chosen from a larger list: *to be **on the shortlist*** • **shortlist verb** [T] UK *shortlisted candidates*

short-lived /ˌʃɔːt'lɪvd/ **adj** only lasting for a short time

shortly /'ʃɔːtli/ **adv 1** ⓑ² If something is going to happen shortly, it will happen soon: *Our plans for the next year will be announced shortly.* **2 shortly after/before sth** ⓑ¹ a short time after or before something: *He left here shortly after midnight.*

short-range /ˌʃɔːt'reɪndʒ/ **adj** intended to go a short distance: *a **short-range** missile*

shorts /ʃɔːts/ **noun** [plural] **1** ⓐ² a very short pair of trousers that stop above the knees: *T-shirt and shorts* ∘ *cycling shorts* **2** US men's underwear to wear under trousers → See also **boxers**

short-sighted /ˌʃɔːt'saɪtɪd/ **adj 1** not able to see far without wearing glasses **2** not thinking enough about how an action will affect the future: *a **short-sighted** policy*

short-term /ˌʃɔːt'tɜːm/ **adj** ⓑ² lasting a short time: ***short-term** memory*

short-wave /'ʃɔːtweɪv/ **noun** [U] a system used to broadcast radio signals around the world: *short-wave radio*

shot¹ /ʃɒt/ **noun** [C] **1 GUN** ▷ ⓑ² the action of firing a bullet from a gun: *Three **shots** were **fired**.* **2 SPORT** ▷ ⓑ² an attempt to score points in sports such as football by hitting or throwing the ball: *Good shot!* **3 PHOTOGRAPH** ▷ ⓑ² a photograph: *I got a good shot of them leaving the hotel together.* **4 give sth a shot; have/take a shot at sth** informal to try to do something, often for the first time: *I've never played football, but I'll give it a shot.* **5 MEDICINE** ▷ an amount of medicine put into the body with a special needle **6 DRINK** ▷ a small amount of a strong alcoholic drink: *a shot of whisky*

IDIOMS **like a shot** If someone does something like a shot, they do it quickly and enthusiastically. • **a shot in the dark** an attempt to guess something when you have no information or knowledge about it

→ See also **long shot**

shot² /ʃɒt/ past of shoot

shotgun /'ʃɒtgʌn/ **noun** [C] a long gun that fires small, metal balls

should strong /ʃʊd/ weak /ʃəd/ **modal verb 1 BEST** ▷ ⓑ¹ used to say or ask what is the correct or best thing to do: *He should have gone to the doctor.* ∘ *Should I apologize to her?* ∘ *You*

shouldn't be so angry with him. **2 EXPECT** ▷ ⓑ¹ used to say that you expect something to be true or that you expect something to happen: *She should be feeling better by now.* ∘ *The letter should arrive by Friday.* **3 POSSIBLE** ▷ formal used to refer to a possible event in the future: *Should you have any further queries, please do not hesitate to contact me.* **4 why should/ shouldn't...?** ⓑ² used to ask or give the reason for something, especially when you are surprised or angry about it: *He told me to forgive her, but why should I?* → See Study Page **Modal verbs** on page Centre 22

shoulder¹ /'ʃəʊldəʳ/ **noun** [C] **1** ⓑ¹ where your arm joins your body next to your neck: *He put his arm around my shoulder.* → See colour picture **The Body** on page Centre 13 **2** US (UK **hard shoulder**) the area on the edge of a main road, where a car can stop in an emergency

shoulder
shoulder
shoulder
shoulder blade

IDIOMS **rub shoulders with sb** to spend time with famous people • **a shoulder to cry on** someone who gives you sympathy when you are upset

→ See also **have a chip¹ on your shoulder**

shoulder² /'ʃəʊldəʳ/ **verb shoulder the blame/ burden/responsibility, etc** to accept that you are responsible for something difficult or bad

'shoulder ,bag noun [C] a bag with a long strap that you hang from your shoulder

'shoulder ,blade noun [C] a large, flat bone on each side of your back below your shoulder

shoulder-length /'ʃəʊldəleŋθ/ **adj** If your hair is shoulder-length, it goes down as far as your shoulders.

shouldn't /'ʃʊdᵊnt/ short for should not: *I shouldn't have said that.*

should've /'ʃʊdəv/ short for should have: *She should've finished by now.*

shout¹ /ʃaʊt/ **verb** [I, T] ⓐ² to say something very loudly: *"Look out!" she shouted.* ∘ *I was angry and I **shouted at** him.* ∘ *I **shouted out** her name but she didn't hear me.*

shout² /ʃaʊt/ **noun** [C] ⓑ¹ the sound made when you say something very loudly or make a very loud sound with your voice: *He was woken by a loud shout.*

> ✏ Word partners for **shout** (noun)
>
> **give a shout** • **a shout of** [anger, etc] • **an angry shout**

shouty /'ʃaʊti/ **adj** informal Someone who is shouty shouts a lot because they get angry very easily.

shove /ʃʌv/ **verb** [I, T] **1** to push someone or something in a rough way: *He wouldn't move, so I shoved him out of the way.* **2 shove sth into/in/**

S

under, etc to put something somewhere in a quick, careless way: *She shoved the suitcase under the bed.* • **shove** noun [C] *to give someone a shove* → See also **if/when push²** comes to shove

shovel /'ʃʌvəl/ noun [C] a tool with a long handle, used for digging or moving things such as soil or snow • **shovel** verb [I, T] (mainly UK **shovelling, shovelled,** US **shoveling, shoveled**)

show¹ /ʃəʊ/ verb (**showed, shown**) **1** PROVE ▷ [T] **B2** If numbers, results, facts, etc show something, they prove that it is true: [+ (that)] *Research shows that 40% of the programme's viewers are aged over 55.* ◦ *Sales figures showed a significant increase last month.* **2** LET SOMEONE SEE ▷ [T] **A1** to let someone look at something: [+ two objects] *Show me your photos.* ◦ *Show your passport to the officer.* **3 show sb what to do/how to do sth** **B1** to teach someone how to do something by explaining it or by doing it yourself while they watch: *She showed me how to use the new computer system.* ◦ *Have you shown him what to do?* **4** EXPRESS ▷ [T] **B2** to express a feeling so that other people are able to notice it: *He hasn't shown any interest so far.* ◦ *If she was upset, she certainly didn't show it.* **5** EASY TO SEE ▷ [I, T] to be easy to see, or to make something easy to see: *The sadness really shows on her face.* ◦ *Light-coloured carpets show the dirt.* **6 show sb into/around/round, etc** **B1** to take someone to or round a place: *She showed me round the factory.* **7** IMAGE ▷ [T] **B1** If a picture, film, map, etc shows something, that thing can be seen in the picture, movie, etc.: *A diagram shows the levels of rainfall in different parts of the country.* **8** FILM ▷ [I, T] If a cinema shows a film or a film is showing somewhere, you can go and see it there.

PHRASAL VERBS **show off** **B2** to try to make people admire your abilities or achievements in a way which other people find annoying: *He was the kind of kid who was always showing off to his classmates.* • **show sb/sth off** to show something or someone you are proud of to other people: *I couldn't wait to show off my new ring.* • **show up** informal **B1** to arrive somewhere: *I waited for nearly half an hour, but he didn't show up.* • **show sb up** to behave in a way that makes someone you are with feel embarrassed: *I didn't want my parents there, showing me up in front of all my friends.*

> ☑ Word partners for **show** noun
>
> host/present a show • a show is broadcast/screened • be on a show

show² /ʃəʊ/ noun **1** [C] **A2** a television or radio programme or a theatre performance: *He's got his own show on Channel 5.* **2** [C] **B2** an event at which a group of similar things are brought together for the public to see: *a fashion show* **3 a show of sth** an expression of a feeling which can be clearly seen by other people: *Crowds gathered in the central square in a show of support for the government.* **4 for show** for looking at only, and not for using: *The cakes are just for show – you can't eat them.* **5 on show** being shown to the

public: *Her designs are currently on show at the Museum of Modern Art.* → See also **chat show, game show, talk show**

show business noun [U] (informal **show biz**) the entertainment industry, including films, television, theatre, etc

showcase /'ʃəʊkeɪs/ noun [C] an event that is intended to show the best qualities of something: *The exhibition acts as a showcase for French design.*

showdown /'ʃəʊdaʊn/ noun [C] an argument or fight that is intended to end a period of disagreement: *Opponents of the changes are heading for a showdown with party leaders.*

> ☑ Word partners for **showdown**
>
> face/be heading for a showdown • a showdown **between** sb and sb • a showdown **with** sb

shower¹ /ʃaʊəʳ/ noun [C] **1** WASH ▷ **A1** If you have or take a shower, you wash your whole body while standing under a flow of water: *I go up, had a shower and got dressed.* **2** BATHROOM EQUIPMENT ▷ **A1** a piece of bathroom equipment that you stand under to wash your whole body: *He likes to sing in the shower.* → See colour picture **The Bathroom** on page Centre 3 **3** RAIN ▷ **B1** a short period of rain **4 a shower of sth** a lot of small things in the air, especially falling through the air: *a shower of glass*

shower² /ʃaʊəʳ/ verb [I] to wash standing under a shower

PHRASAL VERB **shower sb with sth** to give a lot of something to someone: *I was showered with gifts.*

showerhead /'ʃaʊəhed/ noun [C] the part of a shower that water flows out of

showing /'ʃəʊɪŋ/ noun **1** [C] a broadcast of a television programme at a particular time or of a film at a cinema: *There's a repeat showing of Wednesday's episode on Saturday morning.* **2 a good/poor/strong, etc showing** how successful someone is in a competition, election, etc: *She made a good showing in the world champion-ships.*

showman /'ʃəʊmən/ noun [C] (plural **showmen**) someone who is very good at entertaining people

shown /ʃəʊn/ past participle of show

show-off /'ʃəʊɒf/ noun [C] someone who tries to make other people admire their abilities or achievements in a way which is annoying

showroom /'ʃəʊruːm/ noun [C] a large room where you can look at large items for sale, such as cars or furniture

shrank /ʃræŋk/ past tense of shrink

shrapnel /'ʃræpnəl/ noun [U] small, sharp pieces of metal that fly through the air when a bomb explodes

shred¹ /ʃred/ noun [C] **1** a very small piece that has been torn from something: [usually plural] *She tore the letter to shreds.* **2 not a shred of sth** not the smallest amount of something: *There is not a shred of evidence to support his story.*

hred² /ʃred/ **verb** [T] (**shredding**, **shredded**) to tear or cut something into small, thin pieces: *shredded cabbage*

hrewd /ʃruːd/ **adj** good at judging situations and making decisions that give you an advantage: *a shrewd businessman* ○ *a shrewd investment* • **shrewdly adv**

hriek /ʃriːk/ **verb** [I, T] to make a sudden, loud, high noise because you are afraid, surprised, excited, etc: *to shriek with laughter* ○ *"It's about to explode!" she shrieked.* • **shriek noun** [C]

hrill /ʃrɪl/ **adj** A shrill sound is very high, loud, and often unpleasant: *a shrill voice*

hrimp /ʃrɪmp/ **noun** [C] a small, pink, sea animal that you can eat, with a curved body and a shell

hrine /ʃraɪn/ **noun** [C] a place where people go to pray because it is connected with a holy person or event

hrink¹ /ʃrɪŋk/ **verb** [I, T] (**shrank**, **shrunk**) ⓑ₂ to become smaller, or to make something smaller: *My shirt shrank in the wash.* ○ *Its forests have shrunk to almost half the size they were 10 years ago.*

PHRASAL VERB **shrink from sth/doing sth** to avoid doing something that is difficult or unpleasant: *We will not shrink from using force.*

hrink² /ʃrɪŋk/ **noun** [C] informal a doctor trained to help people with mental or emotional problems

hrivel /ʃrɪvəl/ **verb** [I] (mainly UK **shrivelling**, **shrivelled**, US **shriveling**, **shriveled**) If something shrivels, it becomes smaller, dryer, and covered in lines, often because it is old. • **shrivelled adj** *There were a few shrivelled apples at the bottom of the bowl.*

hroud¹ /ʃraʊd/ **noun** [C] a cloth used to cover the body of a dead person

hroud² /ʃraʊd/ **verb 1 be shrouded in darkness/fog/mist** to be hidden or covered by the dark/fog, etc: *The island was shrouded in sea mist.* **2 be shrouded in mystery/secrecy** to be difficult to find out about or to know the truth about: *Details of the president's trip remain shrouded in secrecy.*

hrub /ʃrʌb/ **noun** [C] a large plant, smaller than a tree, that has several main stems

hrubbery /ʃrʌbəri/ **noun 1** [C, U] an area of a garden with shrubs in it **2** [U] US shrubs considered as a group

hrug /ʃrʌg/ **verb** [I, T] (**shrugging**, **shrugged**) to move your shoulders up and down to show that you do not care about something or that you do not know something: *I told him we weren't happy with it but he just shrugged his shoulders.* • **shrug noun** [C]

PHRASAL VERB **shrug sth off** to not worry about something and treat it as not important: *The team manager shrugged off criticism.*

hrunk /ʃrʌŋk/ past participle of shrink

hrunken /ʃrʌŋkən/ **adj** having become smaller or having been made smaller: *a shrunken old man*

hudder /ʃʌdər/ **verb** [I] to shake, usually because you are thinking of something unpleasant: *I still shudder at the thought of the risks we took.* ○ *She shuddered with horror.* • **shudder noun** [C]

shuffle /ʃʌfl/ **verb 1 WALK** ▷ [I] to walk slowly without lifting your feet off the floor: *I heard him shuffling around downstairs.* **2 ARRANGE** ▷ [I, T] If you shuffle papers or cards, you mix them or arrange them in a different order. **3 MOVE** ▷ [I, T] to move your body or feet a little because you feel nervous or uncomfortable: *People started shuffling their feet and looking at their watches.*

shun /ʃʌn/ **verb** [T] (**shunning**, **shunned**) to avoid or ignore someone or something: *He was shunned by colleagues and family alike.* ○ *She has always shunned publicity.*

shunt /ʃʌnt/ **verb** [T] to move someone or something from one place to another, usually because they are not wanted: *As a teenager he was shunted between different children's homes.*

shut¹ /ʃʌt/ **verb** [I, T] (**shutting**, **shut**) **1** ⓐ₂ to close something, or to become closed: *Shut the door.* ○ *He lay back and shut his eyes.* ○ *The lid shut with a bang.* **2** UK (UK/US **close**) ⓐ₂ When a shop, restaurant, etc shuts, it stops serving customers and does not allow people to enter: *The museum shuts at 4 o'clock on a Friday.* ○ *Several schools were shut because of the bad weather.*

PHRASAL VERBS **shut sb/sth away** to put someone or something in a place from which they cannot leave or be taken away • **shut (sth) down** ⓑ₂ If a business or a large piece of equipment shuts down or someone shuts it down, it stops operating: *Many factories have been forced to shut down.* • **shut sb/sth in (sth)** to prevent someone or something from leaving a place by shutting a door or gate: *We normally shut the dog in the kitchen when we go out.* • **shut sth off** to stop a machine working, or to stop the supply of something: *Shut the engine off.* ○ *Oil supplies have been shut off.* • **shut sth/sb out** to stop someone or something from entering a place or from being included in something: *The curtains shut out most of the light from the street.* • **shut (sb) up** informal ⓑ₂ to stop talking or making a noise, or to make someone do this: *Just shut up and get on with your work!* • **shut sb/sth up** to keep a person or animal somewhere and prevent them from leaving: *You can't keep it shut up in a cage all day.*

shut² /ʃʌt/ **adj** [never before noun] **1** ⓑ₁ closed: *Her eyes were shut and I thought she was asleep.* **2** UK (UK/US **closed**) ⓑ₁ When a shop, restaurant, etc is shut, it has stopped serving customers and does not allow people to enter it.

shutdown /ʃʌtdaʊn/ **noun** [C] a time when a business or a large piece of equipment stops operating, usually for a temporary period

shutter /ʃʌtər/ **noun** [C] **1** a wooden or metal cover on the outside of a window **2** the part at the front of a camera that opens quickly to let in light when you take a photograph

shuttle¹ /ʃʌtl/ **noun** [C] **1** a bus, train, plane etc that travels regularly between two places,

S

usually a short distance: *the London-Glasgow shuttle* ◦ *There's a shuttle service between the airport and the city centre.* **2** (also ˈspace ˌshuttle) a spacecraft that can go into space and return to Earth more than once

shuttle² /ˈʃʌtl/ **verb** [I, T] to travel or take people regularly between the same two places: *He shuttles between Ireland and England.*

shuttlecock /ˈʃʌtlkɒk/ **noun** [C] mainly UK (US **birdie**) a small object with feathers that is used like a ball in badminton (= sport like tennis)

shy¹ /ʃaɪ/ **adj** (**shyer**, **shyest**) ⓑ① not confident, especially about meeting or talking to new people: *He was too shy to say anything to her.* • **shyly** adv *She smiled shyly.* • **shyness** noun [U]

shy² /ʃaɪ/ **verb** [I] If a horse shies, it moves backwards suddenly because it has been frightened by something.

PHRASAL VERB **shy away from sth** to avoid doing something, usually because you are not confident enough to do it: *He tends to shy away from public speaking.*

sibling /ˈsɪblɪŋ/ **noun** [C] formal a sister or brother

sic /sɪk/ **adv** (**sic**) used in writing after a word that you have copied to show that you know it has been spelt or used wrongly

sick¹ /sɪk/ **adj 1** ⓐ② ill: *He was off work sick for most of last week.* ◦ *They provide care for the sick.* **2 be sick** ⓑ① If you are sick, food and drink comes up from your stomach and out of your mouth: *The baby was sick all down his shirt.* **3 feel sick** ⓐ② to feel that the food or drink in your stomach might soon come up through your stomach: *I was so nervous I felt quite sick.* **4 be sick of sth** informal ⓑ② to be bored with or annoyed about something that has been happening for a long time: *I'm sick of people telling me how to run my life.* **5 It makes me sick.** informal something you say when you are jealous of someone: *She looks fantastic whatever she wears – it makes me sick.* **6** cruel and unpleasant: *He's got a sick mind.* ◦ *a sick joke*

> **❗ Common learner error: sick, ill, and be sick**
>
> In British English **ill** is the word that is usually used to mean 'not well'. In American English the word for this is **sick**.
>
> *He went home early because he felt ill/sick.*
>
> In British English to **be sick** is to bring food up from the stomach. Another way of saying this is the word **vomit**, which is used both in British and American English.

sick² /sɪk/ **noun** [U] UK informal food or liquid that has come up from someone's stomach and out of their mouth

sicken /ˈsɪkⁿn/ **verb** [T] to shock someone and make them very angry: *Sickened by the violence, she left.*

sickening /ˈsɪkⁿnɪŋ/ **adj** causing shock and anger: *a sickening act of violence*

sickle /ˈsɪkl/ **noun** [C] a tool with a round blade used to cut long grass or grain crops

ˈsick ˌleave **noun** [U] a period during which you are away from your work because you are sick

sickly /ˈsɪkli/ **adj 1** weak and often sick: *a sickly child* **2** unpleasant and making you feel slightly sick: *a sickly smell*

sickness /ˈsɪknəs/ **noun 1** ILL ▷ [U] ⓑ② the state of being sick: *She's had three weeks off for sickness this year.* **2** VOMIT ▷ [U] the act of vomiting, or the act of being about to vomit: *morning/travel sickness* **3** ILLNESS ▷ [C, U] a particular illness: *radiation sickness*

> **🗪 Word partners for side**
>
> on the [right/left] side • the side of sth

side¹ /saɪd/ **noun** [C] **1** PART OF SOMETHING ▷ ⓐ② one of the two parts that something would divide into if you drew a line down the middle: *In most countries people drive on the right side of the road.* ◦ *Which side of the bed do you sleep on?* **2** SURFACE ▷ ⓐ② a flat, outer surface of an object, especially one that is not its top, bottom, front, or back: *The ingredients are listed on the side of the box.* ◦ *The side of the car was badly scratched.* **3** EDGE ▷ ⓐ② one edge of something: *A square has four sides.* ◦ *There were chairs round the sides of the room.* **4** NEXT TO SOMETHING ▷ ⓑ① the area next to something: *trees growing by the side of the road* **5** PAPER/COIN ETC ▷ ⓐ② either of the two surfaces of a thin, flat object such as a piece of paper or a coin: *Write on both sides of the paper.* **6** ARGUMENT ▷ ⓑ② one of the people or groups who are arguing, fighting, or competing: *Whose side is he on?* ◦ *Whenever we argue he always takes Alice's side* (= gives support to Alice). **7** TEAM ▷ UK the players in a sports team: *He's been selected for the national side.* **8** PART OF A SITUATION ▷ ⓑ② part of a situation that can be considered or dealt with separately: *She looks after the financial side of things.* **9** CHARACTER ▷ ⓑ② a part of someone's character: *She has a very practical side.* **10** BODY ▷ the two areas of your body from under your arms to the tops of your legs: *Stand with your arms by your sides.* ◦ *She lay on her side.* **11** STORY ▷ Someone's side of a story is the way in which they explain how something happened: *I thought I'd better listen to Clare's side of the story.* ◦ *So far they'd only heard the story from the wife's side.* **12** TELEVISION/RADIO ▷ UK a number on a television that you can choose in order to receive a broadcast: *Which side is the film on?* **13 from side to side** ⓑ② If something moves from side to side, it moves from left to right and back again repeatedly: *swinging from side to side* **14 side by side** ⓑ② If two things or people are side by side, they are next to each other: *sitting side by side on the sofa* **15** RELATIVES ▷ the part of your family who are either your mother's relatives or your father's relatives: *They tend to be tall on my mother's side of the family.*

IDIOMS **err on the side of caution** to be very careful instead of taking a risk or making a mistake • **on the side** in addition to your main job: *She does a bit of bar work on the side.* • **pu** sth **to one side** to not use or deal with something now, but keep it for a later time

→ See also **the flip side**

de² /saɪd/ **verb**

PHRASAL VERB **side with sb** to support one person or group in an argument: *If ever there was any sort of argument, she'd always side with my father.*

ideboard /'saɪdbɔːd/ **noun** [C] a piece of furniture with a flat top and low cupboards and drawers, used for storing dishes and glasses, etc in the room you eat in

ideburns /'saɪdbɜːnz/ **noun** [plural] hair that grows on the sides of a man's face in front of the ear

ide dish noun [C] a small serving of food, especially vegetables, served in addition to the main course of a meal

ide effect /'saɪdɪfekt/ **noun** [C] **1** another effect that a drug has on your body in addition to the main effect for which the doctor has given you the drug: *Headaches are one side effect of this drug.* **2** an unexpected result of a situation

idekick /'saɪdkɪk/ **noun** [C] someone who helps, or is friends with, a more powerful and important person

ideline¹ /'saɪdlaɪn/ **noun** [C] a job or business in addition to your main job or business: *He works in a bank but teaches English as a sideline.*

ideline² /'saɪdlaɪn/ **verb** [T] to stop someone from being included in an activity that they usually do, especially in a sport: [often passive] *He's broken his ankle and could be sidelined for weeks.*

idelines /'saɪdlaɪnz/ **noun** [plural] the outside edge of the playing area of a sport such as football: *The coach was shouting instructions from the sidelines.*

IDIOM **on the sidelines** not really involved in something

idelong /'saɪdlɒŋ/ **adj** **a sidelong glance/look** a very short look at someone, moving your eyes to the side, and not looking at them directly

ide mirror noun [C] US (UK **wing mirror**) a small mirror on the side of a car or truck → See colour picture **Car** on page Centre 7

ide order noun [C] (also US **side**) a small serving of food sold at a restaurant, usually to be eaten with other food

ideshow /'saɪdʃəʊ/ **noun** [C] an event or activity that is considered less important than another event or activity

idestep /'saɪdstep/ **verb** [T] (**sidestepping, sidestepped**) to avoid talking about a subject, especially by starting to talk about something else: *She neatly sidestepped questions about her recent divorce.*

idetrack /'saɪdtræk/ **verb** [T] to make someone forget what they were doing or speaking about and start doing or speaking about something different: [often passive] *Sorry, I was talking about staffing and I got sidetracked.*

idewalk /'saɪdwɔːk/ **noun** [C] US (UK **pavement**) a path with a hard surface by the side of a road that people walk on

sideways /'saɪdweɪz/ **adv** in a direction to the left or right, not forwards or backwards: *He glanced sideways.*

siding /'saɪdɪŋ/ **noun** **1** [C] a short railway track, connected to a main track, where trains are kept when they are not being used **2** [U] US material that covers the outside walls of a building, usually in layers

sidle /'saɪdl/ **verb** **sidle along/over/up, etc** to walk towards someone, trying not to be noticed: *He sidled up to her and whispered something in her ear.*

SIDS /sɪdz/ **noun** [U] US (UK **cot death**) abbreviation for sudden infant death syndrome: the sudden death of a sleeping baby for no obvious reason

siege /siːdʒ/ **noun** [C, U] a period when an army or the police stand around a building or city to stop supplies from entering it, in order to force the people inside to stop fighting: *The city is under siege from rebel forces.*

siesta /si'estə/ **noun** [C] a short period of rest or sleep in the afternoon

sieve /sɪv/ **noun** [C] a piece of kitchen equipment with a wire or plastic net which separates large pieces of food from liquids or powders: *Pass the sauce through a sieve to remove any lumps.* → See colour picture **The Kitchen** on page Centre 2 • **sieve verb** [T]

sift /sɪft/ **verb** [T] **1** to put flour, sugar, etc through a sieve (= wire net shaped like a bowl) to break up large pieces: *Sift the flour into a large bowl.* **2** (also **sift through**) to carefully look at every part of something in order to find something: *to sift through evidence*

sigh /saɪ/ **verb** [I, T] ⬤ to breathe out slowly and noisily, often because you are annoyed or unhappy: *He sighed deeply and sat down.* • **sigh noun** [C] ⬤ *a sigh of relief*

sight¹ /saɪt/ **noun** **1** ABILITY ▷ [U] ⬤ the ability to use your eyes to see: *Doctors managed to save his sight.* **2** **the sight of sb/sth** ⬤ the fact of seeing someone or something: *The sight of so much blood had shocked him.* ∘ informal *I can't stand the sight of her* (= I hate her). → See Note at **view¹** **3** AREA SEEN ▷ [U] ⬤ the area that it is possible for you to see: *I looked for her but she was nowhere in sight.* ∘ *I was able to park within sight of the house.* ∘ *Security guards were waiting out of sight* (= where they could not be seen). **4** VIEW ▷ [C] something that you see, especially something interesting: *the sights and sounds of the market* **5** **at first sight** ⬤ the first time you see or hear about something or someone: *It may, at first sight, seem a surprising choice.* **6** **the sights** ⬤ the beautiful or interesting places in a city or country, that a lot of people visit: *He took me around New York and showed me the sights.*

IDIOMS **lose sight of sth** to forget about an important idea or fact because you are thinking too much about other, less important things: *We mustn't lose sight of the original aims of this project.* • **set your sights on sth** to decide to achieve something: *She's set her sights on becoming an actress.*

S

sight² /saɪt/ **verb** [T] to see something that is difficult to see or that you have been looking for: [often passive] *The ship was last sighted off the French coast at 8 o'clock yesterday evening.*

sighted /'saɪtɪd/ **adj** A sighted person is able to see.

-sighted /'saɪtɪd/ used after a word describing a person's ability to see: *long-/short-sighted* ∘ *partially-sighted*

sighting /'saɪtɪŋ/ **noun** [C] an occasion when you see something that is rare or unusual: *UFO sightings*

sightseeing /'saɪtsiːɪŋ/ **noun** [U] 🅐🅑 the activity of visiting places that are interesting because they are historical, famous, etc: *a sightseeing tour of London* • **sightseer** /'saɪtˌsiːər/ **noun** [C] a person who goes sightseeing

---
🗹 **Word partners for sightseeing**

do some/go sightseeing • a sightseeing **tour/ trip**

---

sign¹ /saɪn/ **noun** [C] **1 PROOF** ▷ 🅑🅐 something that shows that something is happening: *Flowers are the first sign of Spring.* ∘ [+ (that)] *It's a sign that things are improving.* ∘ *Staff are showing signs of strain.* **2 NOTICE** ▷ 🅐🅑 a symbol or message in a public place that gives information or instructions: *a road sign* ∘ *a 'no-smoking' sign* **3 SYMBOL** ▷ 🅑🅑 a symbol that has a particular meaning: *a dollar/pound sign* ∘ *the sign of the cross* **4 MOVEMENT** ▷ 🅑🅐 a movement you make to give someone information or tell them what to do → See also **star sign**

🗹 **Word partners for sign**

see/take sth **as a** sign • **show (no)** signs **of** sth • a **clear/sure** sign • a sign **of** sth

---

sign² /saɪn/ **verb** [I, T] 🅑🅐 to write your name on something to show that you wrote/painted, etc it or to show that you agree to it: *He signs his letters 'Prof. James D. Nelson'.* ∘ *to sign a contract/ treaty*

PHRASAL VERBS **sign for sth** UK If a player signs for a football team, he signs a formal agreement saying that he will play for that team. • **sign (sb) in** to write your name or someone else's name in a book when you arrive at a building such as an office or hotel • **sign on 1** to sign a document saying that you will work for someone: *She's signed on with a temp agency.* **2** UK to sign a form at a government office to say that you do not have a job and that you want to receive money from the government • **sign (sb) out** to write your name or someone else's name in a book when leaving a building such as an office or factory • **sign up** 🅑🅐 to arrange to do an organized activity: *I've signed up for evening classes at the local college.*

signal¹ /'sɪɡnəl/ **noun** [C] **1 ACTION** ▷ 🅑🅐 a movement, light, or sound that gives information, or tells people what to do: *Don't move until I give the signal.* **2 WAVE** ▷ 🅑🅐 a series of electrical waves that are sent to a radio, television, or mobile phone **3 PROOF** ▷ something that shows that something else exists or is

likely to happen: *The changing colour of t. leaves on the trees is a signal that it will soon ▪ autumn.* **4 TRAINS** ▷ a piece of equipment th tells trains to stop or to continue **5 VEHICLE PEOPLE** ▷ US a piece of equipment that show people or vehicles when to stop, go, or mo carefully: *a traffic signal*

signal² /'sɪɡnəl/ **verb** [I, T] (mainly UK **signallin signalled**, US **signaling, signaled**) **1** to make movement that gives information or tells peop what to do: *He signalled for them to be quiet.* [+ to do sth] *He signalled the driver to stop.* **2** ▪ show that you intend or are ready to ◆ something: [+ (that)] *The US signalled that the were ready to enter talks.*

signatory /'sɪɡnətəri/ **noun** [C] formal a perso or country that signs an official document

signature /'sɪɡnətʃər/ **noun** [C] 🅑🅐 your nam written in your own way which is difficult f someone else to copy

significance /sɪɡ'nɪfɪkəns/ **noun** [U] the impo tance or meaning of something: *I still dor understand the significance of his remark.*

🗹 **Word partners for significance**

play down/realize/understand the signifi- cance **of** sth • **have** significance **for** sb • **be of** [great/little/major/no] significance

---

significant /sɪɡ'nɪfɪkənt/ **adj** 🅑🅐 important ◆ noticeable: *These measures will save a significa. amount of money.* ∘ *It is significant that Falkn did not attend the meeting himself.* → Oppos **insignificant** • **significantly** adv

signify /'sɪɡnɪfaɪ/ **verb** [T] to be a sign ◆ something: *Red signifies danger.*

signing /'saɪnɪŋ/ **noun** [C] **1** UK a player who ha joined a sports team or a musician who ha joined a record company **2** the act of signir something: [usually singular] *the signing of th declaration*

sign language noun [C, U] a system ◆ communication using hand movements, use by people who are deaf (= cannot hear)

signpost /'saɪnpəʊst/ **noun** [C] 🅑🅐 a sign by th side of the road that gives information abou routes and distances

Sikh /siːk/ **noun** [C] someone who believes in a Indian religion based on belief in a single go and on the teachings of Guru Nanak • **Sikh adj** *Sikh temple* • **Sikhism noun** [U]

silence¹ /'saɪləns/ **noun 1 NO SOUND** ▷ [U] 🅑🅑 there is silence, there is no sound: *The three me ate in silence.* ∘ *No sound broke the silence ▪ the wintry landscape.* **2 NO TALKING** ▷ [U] situation in which someone says nothing abou a particular subject: *She ended her silenc yesterday and spoke to a TV reporter about th affair.* **3 PERIOD OF TIME** ▷ [C] 🅑🅑 a period ◆ time when there is no sound or no talking: *a awkward/embarrassed silence*

🗹 **Word partners for silence**

in silence • **deafening/stunned** silence • **break** the silence • **lapse into** silence • silence **falls/descends/ensues**

---

silence² /'saɪləns/ **verb** [T] **1** to stop something making a sound or stop someone from talking: *He silenced the alarm.* **2** to stop people from criticizing you by giving a good argument to support your opinion: *He seems to have silenced his critics.*

silencer /'saɪlənsər/ **noun** [C] **1** UK (US **muffler**) a part of a vehicle that reduces noise **2** a piece of equipment that you use on a gun to reduce the sound of it firing

silent /'saɪlənt/ **adj 1** NO SOUND ▷ ⑤ without any sound: *The building was dark and silent.* ° *At last the guns fell silent.* **2** NO TALKING ▷ ⑥ without talking: *He remains silent about his plans.* **3** LETTER ▷ If a letter in a word is silent, it is not pronounced: *The 'p' in 'receipt' is silent.* • **silently** **adv**

silhouette /ˌsɪlu'et/ **noun** [C, U] the shape of something when the light is behind it so that you cannot see any details: *He saw a woman in silhouette.* • **silhouetted** **adj** *the roofs silhouetted against the night sky*

silicon /'sɪlɪkən/ **noun** [U] a chemical element used in making electronic equipment such as computers, and materials such as glass and concrete: *a silicon chip*

silk /sɪlk/ **noun** [U] ⑤ a type of cloth that is light and smooth: *a silk dress/shirt*

silken /'sɪlkən/ **adj** literary soft and smooth, like silk: *her silken skin*

silky /'sɪlki/ **adj** soft and smooth, like silk: *a large, silky, grey cat*

silly /'sɪli/ **adj 1** ⑤ stupid: *silly games/hats* ° *I feel silly in this hat.* ° *It's a bit silly spending all that money on something we don't need.* **2** ⑤ small and not important: *She gets upset over such silly things.* • **silliness** **noun** [U]

silt /sɪlt/ **noun** [U] sand and clay that has been carried along by a river and is left on land

silver¹ /'sɪlvər/ **noun 1** METAL ▷ [U] ⑫ a valuable, shiny, grey-white metal used to make coins and jewellery: *silver and gold* ° *a solid silver ring* **2** OBJECTS ▷ [U] objects made of silver **3** PRIZE ▷ [C] a silver medal (= a small, round disc given to someone for finishing second in a race or competition)

silver² /'sɪlvər/ **adj 1** ⑫ made of silver: *a silver coin* ° *a silver necklace* **2** ⑫ being the colour of silver: *a silver sports car*

silver 'medal **noun** [C] a small, round disc given to someone for finishing second in a race or competition

silver 'surfer **noun** [C] a person aged over about 50 who uses the Internet

silverware /'sɪlvəweər/ **noun** [U] US (UK **cutlery**) knives, forks, spoons, etc that are used for eating

silver 'wedding anniversary **noun** [C] the date that is 25 years after the day that two people married

silvery /'sɪlvəri/ **adj** shiny and pale, like silver: *a silvery light*

sim card /'sɪm kɑːd/ **noun** [C] a plastic card in a mobile phone that contains information about you and makes you able to use the phone

similar /'sɪmɪlər/ **adj** ⑤ Something which is similar to something else has many things the same, although it is not exactly the same: *The two houses are remarkably similar.* ° *The style of cooking is similar to that of Northern India.* → Opposite **dissimilar**

similarity /ˌsɪmɪ'lærəti/ **noun** [C, U] ⑫ the state of being similar, or a way in which people or things are similar: *There are a number of similarities between the two systems.* ° *He bears a striking similarity to his grandfather.*

similarly /'sɪmɪləli/ **adv** in a similar way

simile /'sɪmɪli/ **noun** [C] a phrase that compares one thing to something else, using the words 'like' or 'as', for example 'as white as snow'

simmer /'sɪmər/ **verb** [I, T] to gently cook a liquid or something with liquid in it so that it is very hot, but does not boil

simple /'sɪmpl/ **adj 1** EASY ▷ ⑫ not difficult to do or to understand: [+ to do sth] *It's very simple to use.* ° *Just mix all the ingredients together – it's as simple as that.* **2** NOT COMPLICATED ▷ ⑥ not complicated or containing details that are not necessary: *a simple life* ° *a simple black dress* (= *dress without decoration*) **3** IMPORTANT ▷ ⑫ used to describe the one important fact, truth, etc: *We chose her for the simple reason that she's the best person for the job.*

simplicity /sɪm'plɪsəti/ **noun** [U] **1** the quality of not being complicated and having few details or little decoration: *I admire the simplicity of his designs.* **2** the quality of being easy to understand

simplify /'sɪmplɪfaɪ/ **verb** [T] to make something less complicated or easier to do or to understand: *We need to simplify the instructions.* • **simplification** /ˌsɪmplɪfɪ'keɪʃən/ **noun** [C, U]

simplistic /sɪm'plɪstɪk/ **adj** making something complicated seem simple by ignoring many of the details: *a simplistic explanation*

simply /'sɪmpli/ **adv 1** EMPHASIS ▷ ⑫ used to emphasize what you are saying: *We simply don't have the time.* **2** ONLY ▷ ⑫ only: *A lot of people miss out on this opportunity simply because they don't know about it.* **3** NOT COMPLICATED ▷ ⑫ in a way which is not complicated or difficult to understand: *simply prepared food*

simulate /'sɪmjəleɪt/ **verb** [T] to do or make something that behaves or looks like something real but which is not real: *The company uses a computer to simulate crash tests of its new cars.* • **simulation** /ˌsɪmjə'leɪʃən/ **noun** [C, U]

simulator /'sɪmjəleɪtər/ **noun** [C] a machine on which people can practise operating a vehicle or an aircraft without having to drive or fly: *a flight simulator*

simultaneous /ˌsɪmᵊl'teɪniəs/ **adj** If two or more things are simultaneous, they happen or exist at the same time: *simultaneous translation* • **simultaneously** **adv** ⑫ *It was broadcast simultaneously in Britain and France.*

sin¹ /sɪn/ **noun 1** [C, U] something that is against the rules of a religion: *the sin of pride* **2** [no plural] informal something that you should not do because it is morally wrong: *You've only got one life and it's a sin to waste it.*

S

⊠ Word partners for **sin**

commit a sin • the sin of [pride/greed, etc]

sin² /sɪn/ **verb** [I] (**sinning**, **sinned**) to do something that is against the rules of a religion • **sinner** noun [C] someone who does something against the rules of a religion

since¹ /sɪns/ **adv, preposition** ⓐ₂ from a time in the past until a later time or until now: *They've been waiting since March.* ∘ *The factory had been closed since the explosion.* ∘ *I've felt fine ever since.*

❗ Common learner error: **since** or **for**?

When you talk about the beginning of a period of time, use **since**.

I have lived here since 1997.

When you talk about the whole period of time, use **for**.

I have lived here for five years.

~~I have lived here since five years.~~

since² /sɪns/ **conjunction 1** ⓑ₁ from a time in the past until a later time or until now: *He's been much happier since he started his new job.* ∘ *I've known Tim since he was seven.* **2** ⓑ₁ because: *He drove quite slowly since we had plenty of time.*

sincere /sɪnˈsɪər/ **adj 1** honest and saying or showing what you really feel or believe: *He seems to be sincere.* → Opposite **insincere 2 sincere apologies/thanks, etc** formal used to add emphasis when you are expressing a feeling: *The family wishes to express their sincere thanks to all the staff at the hospital.* • **sincerity** /sɪnˈserəti/ noun [U] *No one doubted his sincerity.*

sincerely /sɪnˈsɪəli/ **adv 1** in a sincere way: *I sincerely hope that this never happens again.* **2 Yours sincerely** formal ⓑ₁ used at the end of formal letters when you know the name of the person you are writing to

sinful /ˈsɪnfəl/ **adj** against the rules of a religion or morally wrong: *sinful thoughts*

sing /sɪŋ/ **verb** [I, T] (**sang, sung**) ⓐ₁ to make musical sounds with your voice: *They all sang 'Happy Birthday' to him.* ∘ *She sings in the church choir.*

singer /ˈsɪŋər/ **noun** [C] ⓐ₂ someone who sings: *a jazz singer*

singing /ˈsɪŋɪŋ/ **noun** [U] ⓐ₂ the activity of singing

single¹ /ˈsɪŋɡl/ **adj 1 ONE** ▷ [always before noun] ⓑ₂ only one: *There was a single light in the corner of the room.* **2 every single** ⓑ₁ used to emphasize that you are talking about each one of a group or series: *I call him every single day.* **3 MARRIAGE** ▷ ⓐ₂ not married: *He's young and single.* → See Note at **married 4 PARENT** ▷ [always before noun] ⓑ₁ looking after your children alone without a partner or the children's other parent: *a single mother* ∘ *a single-parent family* **5 FOR ONE** ▷ [always before noun] ⓐ₂ for only one person: *a single bed*

single² /ˈsɪŋɡl/ **noun** [C] **1** a record or CD that includes only one main song **2** UK (US **one-way ticket**) ⓑ₁ a ticket for a journey that is from one place to another but not back again: *Could I have a single to London, please?*

single³ /ˈsɪŋɡl/ **verb**

PHRASAL VERB single sb/sth out to choose one person or thing from a group to criticize or praise them: *The report **singled** him **out** for special criticism.*

single-handedly /ˌsɪŋɡlˈhændɪdli/ **adv** (also **single-handed**) on your own, without anyone's help: *After his partner left, he kept the business going single-handedly.* • **single-handed** /ˌsɪŋɡlˈhændɪd/ **adj** [always before noun] *a single-handed round-the-world yacht race*

single-minded /ˌsɪŋɡlˈmaɪndɪd/ **adj** very determined to achieve something: *She had a single-minded determination to succeed in her career.*

single ˈparent noun [C] (also UK **lone parent**) someone who has a child or children but no husband, wife, or partner that lives with them

singles /ˈsɪŋɡlz/ **noun** [U] a game in sports such as tennis, in which one person plays against another: *He won the men's singles title two years running.*

singly /ˈsɪŋɡli/ **adv** separately or one at a time: *We don't sell them singly, only in packs of four or ten.*

singular¹ /ˈsɪŋɡjələr/ **adj 1** ⓐ₂ The singular form of a word is used to talk about one person or thing. For example 'woman' is the singular form of 'women'. **2** formal very special, or found only in one person or situation: *a landscape of singular beauty*

singular² /ˈsɪŋɡjələr/ **noun the singular** ⓐ₂ the singular form of a word

singularly /ˈsɪŋɡjələli/ **adv** formal very: *Fulbright was singularly uninterested in his comments.*

sinister /ˈsɪnɪstər/ **adj** making you feel that something bad or evil might happen: *a sinister figure dressed in black*

sink¹ /sɪŋk/ **verb** (**sank**, also US **sunk, sunk**) **1 WATER** ▷ [I, T] ⓑ₁ to go down or make something go down below the surface of water and not come back up: *The Titanic sank after hitting an iceberg.* → See picture at **float 2 SOFT SUBSTANCE** ▷ [I, T] ⓑ₁ to go down, or make something go down, into something soft: *My feet keep sinking into the sand.* **3 MOVE DOWN** ▷ [I] ⓑ₂ to move down slowly: *The sun sank below the horizon.*

PHRASAL VERBS sink in If an unpleasant or surprising fact sinks in, you gradually start to believe it and understand what effect it will have on you: *It still hasn't sunk in that I'll never see her again.* • **sink sth into sth** to spend a large amount of money in a business or other piece of work: *Millisat has already sunk $25 million into the Hong Kong project.* • **sink into sth** to slowly move into a sitting or lying position, in a relaxed or tired way: *I just want to go home and sink into a hot bath.*

sink² /sɪŋk/ **noun** [C] ⓐ₂ a bowl that is fixed to the wall in a kitchen or bathroom that you wash dishes or your hands, etc in → See colour picture

The Kitchen on page Centre 2 → See colour picture
The Bathroom on page Centre 3

·inus /'saɪnəs/ **noun** [C] one of the spaces inside the head that are connected to the back of the nose

·ip /sɪp/ **verb** [I, T] (**sipping, sipped**) to drink, taking only a small amount at a time: *She sipped her champagne.* • **sip noun** [C] *He took a sip of his coffee and then continued.*

·iphon¹ /'saɪfᵊn/ **noun** [C] a piece of equipment for moving liquid from one place to another

·iphon² /'saɪfᵊn/ **verb** [T] **1** to remove liquid from a container using a siphon **2** (also **siphon off**) to dishonestly take money from an organization or other supply over a period of time

·ir /sɜːʳ/ **noun 1** (also **Sir**) 🅐 You call a man 'sir' when you are speaking to him politely: *Excuse me, sir, is this seat taken?* **2** 🅑 You write 'Sir' at the beginning of a formal letter to a man when you do not know his name: *Dear Sir, I am writing to...* **3 Sir** a title used in the UK before the name of a man who has been officially respected or who has a high social rank: *Sir Cliff Richard*

·iren /'saɪərən/ **noun** [C] a piece of equipment that makes a loud sound as a warning: *a police siren*

> 🗷 **Word partners for siren**
>
> a siren **goes off/sounds** • a siren **blares/ wails** • a **police** siren

·ister /'sɪstəʳ/ **noun** [C] **1 RELATIVE** ▷ 🅐 a girl or woman who has the same parents as you: *an older/younger sister* ∘ *my big/little sister* **2 RELIGION** ▷ (also **Sister**) a nun (= woman who lives in a female religious group): *Sister Bridget* **3 NURSE** ▷ (also **Sister**) a female nurse in the UK who is responsible for a hospital ward (= an area of a hospital containing beds for sick people) **4 MEMBER** ▷ a woman who is a member of the same race, religious group, organization, etc

·ister-in-law /'sɪstᵊrɪnlɔː/ **noun** [C] (plural **sisters-in-law**) 🅑 the woman married to your brother, or the sister of your husband or wife

·isterly /'sɪstᵊli/ **adj** experienced by or for a sister: *sisterly love*

·it /sɪt/ **verb** (**sitting, sat**) **1 BODY POSITION** ▷ [I] 🅐 to be in a position with the weight of your body on your bottom and the top part of your body up, for example, on a chair: *Emma was sitting on a stool.* ∘ *The children sat at the table by the window.* ∘ *We sat by the river and had a picnic.* **2 MOVE BODY** ▷ [I] (also **sit down**) 🅑 to move your body into a sitting position after you have been standing: *She came over and sat beside him.* ∘ *She sat down on the grass.* → See colour picture **Phrasal Verbs** on page Centre 16 **3 sit sb down/at/in, etc** to make someone sit somewhere: *She sat me down and told me the bad news.* ∘ *I thought we'd sit the children at the end of the table.* **4 STAY** ▷ [I] to stay in one place for a long time and not be used: *He hardly ever drives the car. It just sits in the garage.* **5 MEETING** ▷ [I] If a court, parliament, etc sits, it has a meeting to do its work: *The board will be sitting next week.*

6 TEST/EXAM ▷ [T] UK to take a test or exam: *The changes will affect many students sitting their exams this summer.* → See also **sit on the fence¹**

PHRASAL VERBS **sit about/around** to spend time sitting down and doing very little: [+ doing sth] *He just sits around all day watching television.* • **sit back 1** to relax in a chair so that your back is against the back of the chair: *Just sit back and enjoy the show.* **2** to wait for something to happen without making any effort to do anything yourself: *You can't just sit back and expect someone else to deal with the problem.* • **sit in** to go to a meeting or class to watch: *I sat in on a couple of classes before choosing a course.* • **sit sth out 1** to not do an activity such as a game or dance because you are tired or have an injury: *I think I'll sit out the next dance.* **2** to wait for something unpleasant to finish before you do anything: *The government is prepared to sit out the strike rather than agree to union demands.* • **sit through sth** to stay until the end of a meeting, performance, etc that is very long or boring: *We had to sit through two hours of speeches.* • **sit up 1** to move your body to a sitting position after you have been lying down: *I sat up and opened my eyes.* **2** to stay awake and not go to bed although it is late: [+ doing sth] *We sat up talking all night.*

sitcom /'sɪtkɒm/ **noun** [C, U] a funny television programme that is about the same group of people every week in different situations

site¹ /saɪt/ **noun 1 HISTORY** ▷ [C] 🅑 the place where something important happened in the past: *a historic site* ∘ *the site of a battle* **2 AREA** ▷ [C] 🅑 an area that is used for something or where something happens: *a building site* **3 on site** inside a factory, office building, etc: *There are two restaurants on site.* ∘ *They provide on-site childcare facilities for employees.* **4 INTERNET** ▷ [C] 🅐 short for website (= an area on the Internet where information about a particular subject, organization, etc can be found)

site² /saɪt/ **verb** formal **site sth in/on, etc** to build something in a particular place: [often passive] *The company's head office is sited in Geneva.*

sitter /'sɪtəʳ/ **noun** [C] mainly US a babysitter (= someone who looks after children when their parents go out)

sitting /'sɪtɪŋ/ **noun** [C] **1** a meeting of a parliament, court, etc: *a late-night sitting of parliament* **2** one of the times when a meal is served to a large group of people who cannot all eat at the same time

·sitting room **noun** [C] UK 🅑 the room in a house where people sit to relax and, for example, watch television

situated /'sɪtjueɪtɪd/ **adj** formal **be situated in/ on/by, etc** 🅑 to be in a particular place: *a hotel situated by Lake Garda*

·situation /ˌsɪtju'eɪʃᵊn/ **noun** [C] **1** 🅑 the set of things that are happening and the conditions that exist at a particular time and place: *the economic/political situation* ∘ *He's in a difficult*

S

situation. **2** formal the position of a town, building, etc: *The park's situation was perfect.*

> ☑ **Word partners for situation**
>
> **bring about/rectify/improve** a situation • a situation **arises/deteriorates/worsens** • a **complicated/dangerous/difficult/stressful** situation • **in** a situation

six /sɪks/ ⓐ the number 6

sixteen /ˌsɪk'stiːn/ ⓐ the number 16 • **sixteenth** 16th written as a word

sixth¹ /sɪksθ/ ⓐ 6th written as a word

sixth² /sɪksθ/ **noun** [C] one of six equal parts of something; ⅙

sixth ˌform noun [C] in Britain, the part of a school for students between the ages of 16 and 18

sixty /'sɪksti/ **1** ⓐ the number 60 **2 the sixties** the years from 1960 to 1969 **3 be in your sixties** to be aged between 60 and 69 • **sixtieth** 60th written as a word

sizable /'saɪzəbl/ **adj** another spelling of sizeable

size¹ /saɪz/ **noun 1** [C, U] ⓐ how big or small something is: *It's an area about the size of Oxford.* ◦ *The size of some of those trees is incredible (= they are very large).* **2** [C] ⓐ one of the different measurements in which things, for example clothes, food containers, etc are made: *a size 10 skirt* ◦ *What size shoes do you take?* ◦ *I usually buy the 1.5 litre size.* → See also **all shapes and sizes**

> ☑ **Word partners for size**
>
> **take/wear** a size [10/39, etc] • **come in** [all/different/various, etc] sizes

size² /saɪz/ **verb**

PHRASAL VERB **size sb/sth up** to look at someone or think about something carefully before making a judgment: *I could see her trying to size me up.*

sizeable (also **sizable**) /'saɪzəbl/ **adj** quite large: *a sizeable crowd*

-sized /saɪzd/ **suffix** used at the end of a word to mean 'of a particular size': *a medium-sized pizza* ◦ *a good-sized bedroom*

sizzle /'sɪzl/ **verb** [I] to make the sound of food cooking in hot oil

skanky /'skæŋki/ **adj** informal very unpleasant or dirty

skate¹ /skeɪt/ **noun** [C] **1** (also **roller skate**) ⓐ a boot with wheels on the bottom, used for moving across the ground: *a pair of skates* **2** (also **ice skate**) ⓐ a boot with a metal part on the bottom, used for moving across ice → See colour picture **Sports 1** on page Centre 14

IDIOM **get/put your skates on** UK informal used to tell someone to hurry

skate² /skeɪt/ **verb** [I] ⓔ to move using skates • **skater noun** [C] • **skating noun** [U]

skateboard /'skeɪtbɔːd/ **noun** [C] ⓐ a board with wheels on the bottom, that you stand on and move forward by pushing one foot on the

ground → See colour picture **Sports 1** on pag Centre 14

skateboarding /'skeɪtbɔːdɪŋ/ **noun** [U] ⓐ th activity of moving using a skateboard → Se colour picture **Sports 1** on page Centre 14

skeletal /'skelɪtᵊl/ **adj** like a skeleton, or relatin to skeletons

skeleton /'skelɪtᵊn/ **noun 1** ⓑ [C] the structur made of all the bones in the body of a person c animal **2 a skeleton crew/staff/service** th smallest number of people that you need t keep an organization working

IDIOM **have a skeleton in the cupboard** UK (U **have a skeleton in the closet**) to have a embarrassing or unpleasant secret about some thing that happened in the past

skeptic /'skeptɪk/ **noun** [C] US spelling of sceptic

skeptical /'skeptɪkᵊl/ **adj** US spelling of sceptical

skepticism /'skeptɪsɪzᵊm/ **noun** [U] US spelling c scepticism

sketch¹ /sketʃ/ **noun** [C] **1 PICTURE** ▷ a pictur that you draw quickly and with few details: *H did a quick sketch of the cat.* **2 ACTING** ▷ a shor piece of acting about a funny situatio **3 DESCRIPTION** ▷ a short description of some thing without many details

sketch² /sketʃ/ **verb** [T] to draw a sketch: *sketched a map for him on a scrap of paper.*

PHRASAL VERB **sketch sth out** to give a shor description with few details, especially of an ide or plan: *I've sketched out some ideas for my ne book.*

sketchy /'sketʃi/ **adj** with few details: *Report about the accident are still sketchy.*

ski¹ /skiː/ **noun** [C] (plural **skis**) ⓔ one of a pair o long, thin pieces of wood or plastic that yo wear on the bottom of boots to move over sno → See colour picture **Sports 1** on page Centre 14

ski² /skiː/ **verb** [I] (**skiing, skied**) ⓔ to move ove snow wearing skis • **skier noun** [C] • **skiin noun** [U] ⓐ *I'd like to go skiing in Switzerland* → See also **water-skiing** → See colour pictur **Sports 1** on page Centre 14

skid /skɪd/ **verb** [I] (**skidding, skidded**) If vehicle skids, it slides along a surface and yo cannot control it: *The car skidded on ice and hit tree.* • **skid noun** [C]

skies /skaɪz/ **noun** [plural] the sky in a particula place or in a particular state: *beautiful, clear, blu skies*

skilful UK (US **skillful**) /'skɪlfᵊl/ **adj 1** ⓑ good a doing something: *a skilful artist* **2** done or mad very well: *skilful use of language* • **skilfully ad** UK

skill /skɪl/ **noun** [C, U] ⓔ the ability to do a activity or job well, especially because you hav practised it: *You need good communication skill to be a teacher.*

> ☑ **Word partners for skill**
>
> **acquire/develop/learn/master/require** a skill • **consummate/great** skill • a **basic/neces-sary/useful** skill • skill **at/in** sth

skilled /skɪld/ **adj 1** 🅱️2 having the abilities needed to do an activity or job well: *a highly skilled* (= very skilled) *photographer* ∘ *He has become skilled in dealing with the media.* **2** Skilled work needs someone who has had special training to do it. → Opposite **unskilled**

skillet /'skɪlɪt/ **noun** [C] mainly US a large, heavy pan with a long handle, used for frying food

skillful /'skɪlfʊl/ **adj** US spelling of skilful

skim /skɪm/ **verb** (**skimming, skimmed**) **1** MOVE OVER ▷ [I, T] to move quickly, and almost or just touch the surface of something: *Birds skimmed the surface of the pond.* **2** REMOVE ▷ [T] (also **skim off**) to remove something from the surface of a liquid: *Skim off any excess fat before serving.* **3** READ QUICKLY ▷ [T] (also **skim through**) to read or look at something quickly without looking at the details: *She began skimming through the reports on her desk.*

skimmed 'milk noun [U] mainly UK (US **'skim milk**) milk that has had the fat removed from it

skimp /skɪmp/ **verb**

PHRASAL VERB **skimp on sth** to not spend enough time or money on something, or not use enough of something: *We've got plenty of cheese so don't skimp on it.*

skimpy /'skɪmpi/ **adj** Skimpy clothes show a lot of your body: *a skimpy bikini/dress*

skin¹ /skɪn/ **noun** [C, U] **1** BODY ▷ 🅱️1 the outer layer of a person or animal's body: *dark/fair skin* **2** ANIMAL ▷ the outer layer of a dead animal used as leather, fur, etc: *a leopard skin rug* **3** FRUIT ▷ 🅱️2 the outer layer of a fruit or vegetable: *a banana/potato skin* **4** LIQUID ▷ a thin, solid layer that forms on the top of a liquid: *A skin had formed on the top of the milk.* **5** COMPUTERS ▷ the particular way that information is arranged and shown on a computer screen

IDIOMS **do sth by the skin of your teeth** informal to only just succeed in doing something: *They held on by the skin of their teeth to win 1-0.* • **have (a) thick skin** to not care if someone criticizes you

> 🔲 Word partners for **skin**
>
> dark/fair/olive skin • dry/oily/sensitive skin

skin² /skɪn/ **verb** [T] (**skinning, skinned**) **1** to remove the skin from something **2** (also UK **graze**) to injure your skin by rubbing it against something rough: *Mary fell and skinned her knees.*

skinhead /'skɪnhed/ **noun** [C] a man who has extremely short hair, especially one who behaves in a violent way

skinny /'skɪni/ **adj** Someone who is skinny is too thin.

skip¹ /skɪp/ **verb** (**skipping, skipped**) **1** MOVE FORWARD ▷ [I] to move forward, jumping quickly from one foot to the other: *She watched her daughter skipping down the street.* **2** JUMP ▷ [I] (US **skip 'rope**) to jump over a rope while you or two other people move it over and then under your body again and again: *I skip for*

ten minutes every day to keep fit. **3** NOT DO ▷ [T] 🅱️2 to not do something that you usually do or that you should do: *I think I'll skip lunch today – I'm not very hungry.* **4** AVOID ▷ [T] (also **skip over**) to avoid reading or talking about something by starting to read or talk about the next thing instead: *I usually skip the boring bits.*

skip² /skɪp/ **noun** [C] **1** UK (US trademark **Dumpster**) a very large, metal container for big pieces of rubbish **2** a movement of jumping quickly from one foot to the other

skipper /'skɪpər/ **noun** [C] informal the leader of a team, an aircraft, a ship, etc

skipping rope noun [C] UK (US **jump rope**) a rope that you move over your head and then jump over as you move it under your feet

skirmish /'skɜːmɪʃ/ **noun** [C] a small fight

skirt¹ /skɜːt/ **noun** [C] 🅰️1 a piece of women's clothing that hangs from the waist and has no legs → See colour picture **Clothes** on page Centre 8

skirt² /skɜːt/ **verb** [T] (also **skirt around**) **1** to avoid talking about something: *I deliberately skirted the question of money.* **2** to move around the edge of something: *We skirted around the edge of the field.*

skittle /'skɪtl/ **noun 1** [C] one of a set of bottle-shaped objects that you try to knock down with a ball as a game **2** **skittles** [U] a game in which you try to knock down bottle-shaped objects with a ball

skive /skaɪv/ **verb** [I, T] (also **skive off**) UK to not go to school or work when you should, or to leave school or work earlier than you should • **skiver** noun [C] UK informal someone who skives

skulk /skʌlk/ **verb skulk about/behind/in, etc** to hide somewhere or move around quietly in a way that makes people think you are going to do something bad: *I saw a man skulking behind the shed.*

skull /skʌl/ **noun** [C] the part of your head that is made of bone and which protects your brain

skull cap noun [C] a small round hat worn especially by some religious men

skunk /skʌŋk/ **noun** [C] a black and white animal that produces a very unpleasant smell in order to defend itself

> 🔲 Word partners for **sky**
>
> the sky darkens/lightens • in the sky • a clear/cloudy/overcast sky

sky /skaɪ/ **noun** [U, no plural] 🅰️2 the area above the Earth where you can see clouds, the sun, the moon, etc: *a beautiful, blue sky* ∘ *The sky suddenly went dark.* → See also **skies**

skydiving /'skaɪˌdaɪvɪŋ/ **noun** [U] the sport of jumping out of an aircraft with a parachute (= large piece of cloth that allows you to fall slowly to the ground)

skylight /'skaɪlaɪt/ **noun** [C] a window in the roof of a building

skyline /'skaɪlaɪn/ **noun** [C] the pattern that is made against the sky by tall buildings: *the New York skyline*

sky marshal noun [C] a person whose job is to

S

carry a gun and protect the passengers on an aircraft

skyline

skyscraper /'skaɪˌskreɪpər/ **noun** [C] a very tall building

slab /slæb/ **noun** [C] a thick, flat piece of something, especially stone: *a slab of concrete*

slack¹ /slæk/ **adj**
1 LOOSE ▷ loose or not tight: *Suddenly the rope became slack.* **2 BUSINESS** ▷ If business is slack, there are not many customers. **3 LAZY** ▷ not trying hard enough in your work: *slack management*

slack² /slæk/ **verb** [I] informal (also US **slack off**) to work less hard than usual: *I'm afraid I haven't been to the gym recently – I've been slacking.*

slacken /'slækən/ **verb** [I, T] **1** to become slower or less active, or to make something become slower or less active: *Economic growth is slackening.* **2** to become loose, or to make something become loose: *As you get older your muscles slacken.*

slacks /slæks/ **noun** [plural] mainly US trousers

slag /slæg/ **verb** (**slagging, slagged**)

PHRASAL VERB **slag sb/sth off** UK informal to criticize someone or something in an unpleasant way

slain /sleɪn/ past participle of slay

slalom /'slɑːləm/ **noun** [C] a race in which you go forwards by moving from side to side between poles

slam /slæm/ **verb** (**slamming, slammed**) **1** ⬛ [I, T] to close with great force, or to make something close with great force: *Kate heard the front door slam.* **2 slam sth down/onto/into, etc** ⬛ to put something somewhere with great force: *She slammed the phone down.* • **slam noun** [C] [usually singular] *the slam of a car door*

slander /'slɑːndər/ **noun** [C, U] the crime of saying bad things about someone that are not true • **slander verb** [T] • **slanderous** /'slɑːndərəs/ **adj** saying bad things about someone that are not true

slang /slæŋ/ **noun** [U] informal language, often language that is only used by people who belong to a particular group: *prison slang*

slant¹ /slɑːnt/ **verb** [I, T] to slope in a particular direction, or to make something slope in a particular direction: *Pale sunlight slanted through the curtain.*

slant² /slɑːnt/ **noun** [no plural] **1** a position that is sloping: *The road is on/at a slant.* **2** a way of writing about something that shows who or what you support: *a political slant* ○ *It's certainly a new slant on the subject.*

slap¹ /slæp/ **verb** [T] (**slapping, slapped**) ⬛ to hit

someone with the flat, inside part of your hand: *She slapped him across the face.*

PHRASAL VERB **slap sth on** to quickly put or spread something on a surface: *I'll just slap some make up on.*

slap² /slæp/ **noun** [C] a hit with the flat, inside part of your hand

IDIOM **a slap in the face** something someone does that insults or upsets you: *After all that hard work, losing my job was a real slap in the face.*

slapdash /'slæpdæʃ/ **adj** done quickly and without being careful: *Her work has been a bit slapdash recently.*

slapstick /'slæpstɪk/ **noun** [U] entertainment in which actors do funny things like falling down, hitting each other, etc to make people laugh

slap-up /'slæpˌʌp/ **adj slap-up meal/dinner, etc** UK informal a large and very good meal

slash¹ /slæʃ/ **verb** [T] **1** to cut something by making a quick, long cut with something very sharp: *His throat had been slashed.* **2** to reduce the amount of something by a lot: *to slash prices*

slash² /slæʃ/ **noun** [C] **1** a long, deep cut **2** ⬛ mark (/) used in writing to separate words or numbers, often to show a choice or connection

slate¹ /sleɪt/ **noun** [C, U] a dark grey rock that can easily be cut into thin pieces, or a small, flat piece of this used to cover a roof

slate² /sleɪt/ **verb 1** [T] UK to criticize someone or something severely: [often passive] *The film has been slated by critics.* **2 be slated** US to be expected to happen in the future, or to be expected to be or do something in the future: [+ to do sth] *Filming is slated to begin next spring.*

slaughter¹ /'slɔːtər/ **verb** [T] **1 ANIMAL** ▷ to kill an animal for meat **2 PEOPLE** ▷ to kill a lot of people in a very cruel way **3 DEFEAT** ▷ informal to defeat someone very easily

slaughter² /'slɔːtər/ **noun** [U] the killing of a lot of people or animals in a cruel way

slaughterhouse /'slɔːtəhaʊs/ **noun** [C] (plural **slaughterhouses** /'slɔːtəhaʊzɪz/) a place where animals are killed for meat

slave¹ /sleɪv/ **noun 1** ⬛ [C] someone who is owned by someone else and has to work for them: *He treats his mother like a slave.* **2 be a slave to sth** to be completely controlled or influenced by something: *You're a slave to fashion.*

slave² /sleɪv/ **verb** [I] (also **slave away**) to work very hard: *Giorgio was slaving away at his homework.*

slavery /'sleɪvəri/ **noun** [U] the system of owning slaves, or the condition of being a slave

slay /sleɪ/ **verb** [T] (**slew, slain**) literary to kill someone in a very violent way

sleaze /sliːz/ **noun** [U] political or business activities that are morally wrong

sleazy /'sliːzi/ **adj** unpleasant and morally wrong, often in a way that relates to sex: *He spent the night drinking in a sleazy bar.*

ledge¹ /sledʒ/ **noun** [C] UK (US **sled**, ⓤⓢ /sled/) a vehicle that is used for travelling on snow

ledge² /sledʒ/ **verb** [I] UK (US **sled** /sled/) to travel on snow using a sledge

leek /sliːk/ **adj 1** Sleek hair is smooth and very shiny. **2** A sleek car is attractive and looks expensive.

leep¹ /sliːp/ **verb** (**slept**) **1** ⓐ [I] to be in the state of rest when your eyes are closed, your body is not active, and your mind is unconscious: *Did you sleep well?* **2 sleep four/six, etc** If a place sleeps four, six, etc, it is big enough for that number of people to sleep in. → See also **not sleep a wink²**

IDIOM **sleep on it** to wait until the next day before making a decision about something important so that you can think about it carefully

PHRASAL VERBS **sleep in** to sleep longer in the morning than you usually do • **sleep sth off** to sleep until you feel better, especially after drinking too much alcohol • **sleep over** to sleep in someone else's home for a night: *After the party, I slept over at Tom's house.* • **sleep through sth** to continue to sleep although there is noise: *I don't know how you slept through the storm.* • **sleep with sb** informal to have sex with someone

leep² /sliːp/ **noun 1** ⓑ [U, no plural] the state you are in when you are sleeping, or a period of time when you are sleeping: *I haven't had a good night's sleep* (= a long sleep at night) *for weeks.* ∘ *You need to go home and get some sleep.* ∘ *It took me ages to get to sleep* (= to succeed in sleeping). ∘ *He slept peacefully in his sleep.* **2 go to sleep a** ⓑ to begin to sleep: *Babies often go to sleep after a feed.* **b** informal If part of your body goes to sleep, you cannot feel it: *I'd been sitting on my feet and they'd gone to sleep.* **3 put sth to sleep** to kill an animal that is very old or sick **4 could do sth in your sleep** to be able to do something very easily

IDIOM **lose sleep over sth** to worry about something

☑ Word partners for **sleep noun**

get [no/some, etc] sleep • get to/go to sleep • **have** a sleep • a good night's sleep • in your sleep

leeper /ˈsliːpər/ **noun 1** a **light/heavy sleeper** someone who wakes up easily/does not wake up easily **2** TRAIN ▷ [C] a train or a part of a train that has beds in it **3** SUPPORT ▷ [C] UK (US **railroad tie**) a piece of wood that is used to support a railway track (= the thing a train moves along on) **4** JEWELLERY ▷ [C] UK a small gold or silver ring worn in the ear

leeping ˌbag noun [C] a long bag made of thick material that you sleep inside

leeping ˌpill noun [C] a medicine that you take to help you sleep

leepless /ˈsliːpləs/ **adj sleepless night** a night when you are not able to sleep: *He'd spent a*

sleepless night worrying about his exam. • **sleeplessness noun** [U]

sleep-over /ˈsliːpəʊvər/ **noun** [C] (also **sleepover**) a party when a group of young people stay at a friend's house for the night

sleepwalk /ˈsliːpˌwɔːk/ **verb** [I] to get out of bed and walk around while you are sleeping • **sleepwalker noun** [C]

sleeping bag

sleepy /ˈsliːpi/ **adj 1** ⓑ feeling tired and wanting to go to sleep: *The heat had made me sleepy.* **2** quiet and with little activity: *a sleepy little town* • **sleepily adv** • **sleepiness noun** [U]

sleet /sliːt/ **noun** [U] a mixture of snow and rain • **sleet verb** [I] *It was sleeting when I looked outside.*

sleeve /sliːv/ **noun** [C] ⓑ the part of a jacket, shirt, etc that covers your arm: *He rolled up his sleeves to do the dishes.* → See picture at **jacket**

IDIOM **have sth up your sleeve** informal to have a secret plan: *They were worried he might have another nasty surprise up his sleeve.*

☑ Word partners for **sleeve**

long/short sleeves • roll up your sleeves

-sleeved /sliːvd/ **suffix short-sleeved/long-sleeved** having short/long sleeves: *a short-sleeved shirt*

sleeveless /ˈsliːvləs/ **adj** describes a piece of clothing with no sleeves: *a sleeveless dress*

sleigh /sleɪ/ **noun** [C] a large vehicle that is pulled by animals and used for travelling on snow

slender /ˈslendər/ **adj** thin in an attractive way: *a slender woman with long, red hair*

slept /slept/ past of sleep

sleuth /sluːθ/ **noun** [C] old-fashioned a police officer whose job is to discover who has committed a crime

slew /sluː/ past tense of slay

slice¹ /slaɪs/ **noun 1** ⓐ [C] a flat piece of food that has been cut from a larger piece: *a slice of bread/cake/meat* → See colour picture **Pieces and Quantities** on page Centre 1 **2 a slice of sth** a part of something that is being divided: *a large slice of the profits* → See also **fish slice**

slice² /slaɪs/ **verb 1** [T] (also **slice up**) ⓑ to cut food into thin, flat pieces: *Could you slice the tomatoes?* **2 slice into/off/through, etc** [I, T] to cut into or through something with a knife or something sharp: *I almost sliced my finger off.* → See also the **best/greatest thing since sliced bread**

slick /slɪk/ **adj 1** done with a lot of skill: *a slick presentation* **2** attractive but in a way that is not sincere or honest: *He was a bit slick – I didn't trust him.*

S

slide¹ /slaɪd/ **verb** (**slid**) **1 slide (sth) across/down/along, etc** B2 to move smoothly over a surface, or to make something move smoothly over a surface: *He slid the letter into his pocket.* **2 slide (sth) into/out of/through, etc** to move somewhere quietly, or to make something move quietly: *She slid out of the room, being careful not to wake Alan.*

slide² /slaɪd/ **noun 1 PHOTOGRAPH** ▷ [C] a small piece of film that you shine light through in order to see a photograph **2 GAME** ▷ [C] a large object that children climb and slide down as a game **3 GLASS** ▷ [C] a small piece of glass that you put something on when you want to look at it under a microscope (= equipment used to make things look bigger) **4 LESS/WORSE** ▷ [no plural] a reduction in the level or quality of something : *a price slide*

slight¹ /slaɪt/ **adj 1** B2 small and not important: *slight differences in colour* ∘ *We're having a slight problem with our computer system.* **2** Someone who is slight is thin.

slight² /slaɪt/ **noun** [C] an action or remark that insults someone

slighted /ˈslaɪtɪd/ **adj be/feel slighted** to feel insulted because someone has done or said something which shows that they think you are not important: *Annie felt slighted because she hadn't been invited to the meeting.*

slightest /ˈslaɪtɪst/ **adj 1 the slightest** [always before noun] the smallest: *The slightest movement will disturb these shy animals.* **2 not in the slightest** not at all: *"Do you mind if I open the window?" "Not in the slightest."*

slightly /ˈslaɪtli/ **adv** B2 a little: *I think I did slightly better in my exams this time.* ∘ *I find it slightly worrying.*

slim¹ /slɪm/ **adj** (**slimmer**, **slimmest**) **1** A1 Someone who is slim is thin in an attractive way. **2** small and not as much as you would like: *There's a **slim chance** he'll succeed.*

slim² /slɪm/ **verb** [I] (**slimming**, **slimmed**) UK to eat less in order to become thinner

PHRASAL VERBS **slim down** to become thinner • **slim sth down** to reduce the size of something: *It is not our intention to slim down the workforce.*

slime /slaɪm/ **noun** [U] a thick, sticky liquid that is unpleasant to touch

slimy /ˈslaɪmi/ **adj 1** covered in slime **2** informal too friendly in a way that is not sincere

sling¹ /slɪŋ/ **noun** [C] **1** a piece of cloth that you wear around your neck and put your arm into to support it when it is injured **2** a piece of cloth or a strap that you tie around your body to carry things in: *She had her baby in a sling.*

sling² /slɪŋ/ **verb** (**slung**) **1 sling sth over/around/on, etc** to put something in a position where it hangs loosely: *He slung his bag over his shoulder.* **2 sling sth into/onto/under, etc** to throw something somewhere in a careless way: *She slung her coat onto the bed.*

slingshot /ˈslɪŋʃɒt/ **noun** [C] US (UK **catapult**) a Y-shaped object with a piece of elastic across it, used by children to shoot small stones

slink /slɪŋk/ **verb** (**slunk**) **slink away/off/out, etc** to move somewhere quietly so that no one will notice you: *I caught him slinking out of the meeting.*

slip¹ /slɪp/ **verb** (**slipping**, **slipped**) **1 FALL** ▷ [I] B1 to slide by accident and fall or almost fall: *She slipped on the ice and broke her ankle.* **2 OUT OF POSITION** ▷ [I] B1 to slide out of the correct position: *The photo had slipped from the frame.* **3 slip away/through, etc** to go somewhere quietly or quickly: *I'll slip out of the room if I get bored.* **4 slip sth into/through, etc** to put something somewhere quickly or secretly: *She slipped the letter into an envelope and sealed it.* **5 GIVE SECRETLY** ▷ [+ two objects] informal to give something to someone secretly: *I slipped her a five euro note.* **6 GET LESS/WORSE** ▷ [I] to get less or worse in level or quality: *His school grades have slipped recently.* **7 let sth slip** to forget that something is a secret and tell someone about it
→ See also **slip your mind¹**

PHRASAL VERBS **slip into sth** to quickly put on a piece of clothing • **slip sth off** to quickly take off a piece of clothing: *Slip your shirt off and I'll listen to your heart.* • **slip sth on** to quickly put on a piece of clothing: *I'll just slip my shoes on.* **slip out** If a remark slips out, you say it without intending to: *I didn't mean to tell anyone you were getting married – it just slipped out.* • **slip out of sth** to quickly take off a piece of clothing • **slip up** to make a mistake

slip² /slɪp/ **noun** [C] **1 PAPER** ▷ a small piece of paper: *He wrote the number on a **slip of paper***. **2 FALL** ▷ the movement of sliding by accident and falling or almost falling **3 WOMEN'S CLOTHING** ▷ a piece of clothing that a woman wears under a dress or skirt **4 MISTAKE** ▷ small mistake

IDIOMS **give sb the slip** informal to escape from someone you do not want to be with • **a slip of the tongue** a mistake made by using the wrong word

slipper /ˈslɪpər/ **noun** [C] a soft, comfortable shoe that you wear in the house → See colour picture **Clothes** on page Centre 8

slippery /ˈslɪpəri/ **adj** smooth and wet and difficult to hold or walk on: *Be careful – the floor's slippery.*

IDIOM **a slippery slope** a bad situation that is likely to get worse

'slip ˌroad noun [C] UK (US **ramp**) a short road that is used to drive onto or off a motorway (= wide, fast road)

slit¹ /slɪt/ **noun** [C] a long, narrow cut or hole in something: *Make a slit in the pastry to allow the steam to escape.*

slit² /slɪt/ **verb** [T] (**slitting**, **slit**) to make a long, narrow cut in something: *She slit her **wrists**.*

slither /ˈslɪðər/ **verb** [I] to move smoothly by twisting and sliding

sliver /ˈslɪvər/ **noun** [C] a thin piece of something that has come off a larger piece: *slivers of glass*

slob /slɒb/ **noun** [C] informal a lazy or dirty person

slog¹ /slɒg/ **verb** (**slogging**, **slogged**) inform-

slog up/down/through, etc to move forward with difficulty: *We slogged up the hill in silence.*

PHRASAL VERB **slog away** informal to work very hard for a long time: *I've been slogging away at this for hours and I'm exhausted.*

slog² /slɒɡ/ noun [U, no plural] UK informal a period of hard work: *Studying for all the exams was a hard slog.*

slogan /ˈsləʊɡən/ noun [C] a short phrase that is easy to remember and is used to make people notice something: *an advertising slogan*

> ☑ Word partners for **slogan**
>
> sth bears/carries a slogan • a slogan of sth • an advertising slogan

slop /slɒp/ verb (**slopping, slopped**) **slop (sth) about/around/into, etc** If liquid slops about, it moves around or over the edge of its container, and if you slop it about, you make it move around or over the edge of its container: *Her hand shook, making her tea slop into the saucer.*

slope¹ /sləʊp/ noun [C] ⑫ a surface or piece of land that is high at one end and low at the other: *There's a steep slope to climb before we're at the top.* → See also **a slippery slope**

slope² /sləʊp/ verb [I] to be high at one end and low at the other: *The field slopes down to the river.*

sloppy /ˈslɒpi/ adj **1 CARELESS** ▷ not done carefully: *His work was sloppy and full of spelling mistakes.* **2 CLOTHES** ▷ Sloppy clothes are loose and untidy: *a girl wearing a sloppy sweater and torn jeans* **3 TOO WET** ▷ A sloppy substance has too much liquid in it. • **sloppily** adv • **sloppiness** noun [U]

slosh /slɒʃ/ verb **slosh against/over/around, etc** If liquid sloshes, it moves against or over the edge of its container: *Water sloshed over the edge of the pool as the swimmers dived in.*

sloshed /slɒʃt/ adj informal drunk

slot¹ /slɒt/ noun [C] **1** a long, narrow hole that you put something into, especially money **2** a period of time that you allow for something in a plan: *The programme is being moved to a later slot.*

slot² /slɒt/ verb [I, T] (**slotting, slotted**) to fit into a slot, or to make something fit into a slot

PHRASAL VERB **slot sb/sth in** to find time for someone or something in a period of time that has already been planned: *Dr O'Neil can slot you in around 9.30.*

sloth /sləʊθ/ noun **1** [C] an animal that moves very slowly and lives in Central and South America **2** [U] literary lazy behaviour

slot ma,chine noun [C] a machine that you put money into in order to try to win money

slouch¹ /slaʊtʃ/ verb [I] to stand, sit, or walk with your shoulders forward so that your body is not straight: *Stop slouching and stand up straight.*

slouch² /slaʊtʃ/ noun **1** [no plural] the position your body is in when you slouch **2 be no slouch** informal to work very hard and be good at something: *He's no*

slouch when it comes to cooking.

slouch

slovenly /ˈslʌvᵊnli/ adj lazy, untidy, and dirty: *slovenly habits* • **slovenliness** noun [U]

slow¹ /sləʊ/ adj **1 NOT FAST** ▷ Ⓐ moving, happening, or doing something without much speed: *I'm making slow progress with the painting.* ◦ *He's a very slow reader.* **2 be slow to do sth; be slow in doing sth** to take a long time to do something: *The government has been slow to react to the problem.* ◦ *The ambulance was very slow in coming.* **3 CLOCK** ▷ If a clock is slow, it shows a time that is earlier than the correct time. **4 BUSINESS** ▷ If business is slow, there are few customers. **5 NOT CLEVER** ▷ not quick at learning and understanding things **6 NOT EXCITING** ▷ not exciting: *I find his films very slow.*

slow² /sləʊ/ verb [I, T] to become slower or to make something become slower: *The car slowed to a halt* (= moved more and more slowly until it stopped).

PHRASAL VERBS **slow (sth) down** Ⓑ to become slower or to make something become slower: *Slow down, Claire, you're walking too fast!* • **slow down** Ⓑ If someone slows down, they become less active: *The doctor told me I should slow down and not work so hard.*

slowdown /ˈsləʊdaʊn/ noun [C] a period when business activity becomes slower: *an economic slowdown* ◦ *The figures show a slowdown in retail sales.*

slowly /ˈsləʊli/ adv Ⓐ at a slow speed: *Could you speak more slowly, please?*

slow 'motion noun [U] a way of showing pictures from a film or television programme at a slower speed than normal: *They showed a replay of the goal in slow motion.*

sludge /slʌdʒ/ noun [U] soft, wet soil, or a substance that looks like this

slug¹ /slʌɡ/ noun [C] **1** a small, soft creature with no legs that moves slowly and eats plants → See picture at **snail 2** a small amount of a drink, especially an alcoholic drink: *He took a slug of whisky from the bottle.*

slug² /slʌɡ/ verb [T] (**slugging, slugged**) informal to hit someone with your fist (= closed hand)

PHRASAL VERB **slug it out** informal to fight, argue, or compete with someone until one person wins: *Federer and Nadal slugged it out for a place in the final.*

sluggish /ˈslʌɡɪʃ/ adj moving or working more slowly than usual: *a sluggish economy* ◦ *I felt really sluggish after lunch.*

S

slum /slʌm/ **noun** [C] a poor and crowded area of a city where the buildings are in a very bad condition: *He grew up in the slums of Mexico City.* ∘ *slum areas*

slumber /'slʌmbər/ **noun** [C, U] literary sleep: *She lay down on the bed and fell into a deep slumber.* • **slumber verb** [I] literary

'**slumber** ˌparty **noun** [C] US a party when a group of children spend the night at one child's house

slump¹ /slʌmp/ **verb 1** [I] If a price, value, or amount slumps, it goes down suddenly: *Sales have slumped by 50%.* **2 slump back/down/over, etc** to fall or sit down suddenly because you feel tired or weak: *She slumped back in her chair, exhausted.*

slump² /slʌmp/ **noun** [C] **1** a sudden fall in prices or sales: *a slump in world oil prices* **2** a period when there is very little business activity and not many jobs: *It's been the worst economic slump for 25 years.*

> **Word partners for slump noun**
>
> a **dramatic/severe** slump • a slump **in** sth

slung /slʌŋ/ past of sling

slunk /slʌŋk/ past of slink

slur¹ /slɜːr/ **verb** [I, T] (**slurring, slurred**) to speak without separating your words clearly, often because you are tired or drunk: *He'd drunk too much and was slurring his words.*

slur² /slɜːr/ **noun** [C] a criticism that will make people have a bad opinion of someone or something: *a racial slur* ∘ *She regarded it as a slur on her character.*

> **Word partners for slur**
>
> **cast** slurs • a slur **against/on** sb/sth

slurp /slɜːp/ **verb** [I, T] informal to drink in a noisy way: *He slurped his tea.* • **slurp noun** [C] informal

slush /slʌʃ/ **noun** [U] snow that has started to melt

sly /slaɪ/ **adj** (**slyer, slyest**) **1** deceiving people in a clever way to get what you want **2 sly smile** a smile that shows you know something that other people do not: *"I know why Chris didn't come home yesterday," she said with a sly smile.* • **slyly adv**

smack¹ /smæk/ **verb 1** [T] to hit someone with the flat, inside part of your hand: *Do you think it's right to smack children when they're naughty?* **2 smack sth against/onto/down, etc** to hit something hard against something else: *Ray smacked the ball into the net.*

PHRASAL VERB **smack of sth** If something smacks of an unpleasant quality, it seems to have that quality: *a policy that smacks of racism*

smack² /smæk/ **noun** [C] a hit with the flat, inside part of your hand: *Stop shouting or I'll give you a smack!*

smack³ /smæk/ **adv** informal (also UK '**smack** ˌbang , also US ˌsmack 'dab) **1** exactly in a particular place: *She lives smack in the middle of Edinburgh.* **2** suddenly and with a lot of force: *He braked too late and ran smack into the car in front.*

small¹ /smɔːl/ **adj 1** LITTLE ▷ **A1** little in size or amount: *They live in a small apartment near Times Square.* ∘ *We teach the children in small groups.* **2** YOUNG ▷ **A1** A small child is very young: *a woman with three small children* **3** NOT IMPORTANT ▷ **A2** not important or serious: *a small mistake* **4 feel small** to feel stupid or unimportant: *Simon was always trying to make me feel small.*

> ⚠ Common learner error: **small** or **little**?
>
> **Small** refers to size and is the usual opposite of 'big' or 'large'.
>
> *Could I have a hamburger and a small Coke please?*
>
> *Our house is quite small.*
>
> **Little** refers to size but also expresses the speaker's feelings. For example, it can suggest that the speaker likes or dislikes something.
>
> *They live in a beautiful little village.*
>
> *Rats are horrible little animals.*
>
> The comparative and superlative forms of **little** are not usually used in British English. Use **smaller** or **smallest** instead.
>
> *My car is smaller than yours.*
>
> ~~My car is littler than yours.~~

> ➕ Other ways of saying **small**
>
> **Little** is a very common alternative to 'small', and can describe things or people:
>
> *I'll just have a little piece of cake.*
>
> *She's so little.*
>
> If someone is extremely small, you can say that they are **tiny** or **minute**, and if something is extremely small, you can say that it is **minute**, **tiny**, or, in more formal contexts, **microscopic** or **minuscule**:
>
> *Inside the pram was a tiny baby.*
>
> *The phone he pulled out of his pocket was minute.*
>
> *The cost of vaccination is minuscule compared to the cost of treatment.*
>
> The adjectives **dwarf** and **miniature** are sometimes used to describe things that are smaller than the normal size:
>
> *There were dwarf fir trees in pots on the patio.*
>
> *It's a miniature bath for the doll's house.*
>
> If a woman or girl is small in an attractive way, you can use the adjectives **dainty** or **petite**:
>
> *She had dainty feet.*
>
> *Like all his girlfriends, Emma was dark and petite.*
>
> You can use the informal adjective **poky** to describe a room or other area that is too small:
>
> *They live in a poky little flat in south London.*
>
> The adjective **slight** is sometimes used with abstract nouns to describe things that are small and not important:
>
> *There was a slight difference in colour.*

S

small² /smɔːl/ **adv** in a small size: *Emma knitted the sweater far too small.*

small ˌad noun [C] UK a small advertisement that you put in a newspaper if you want to buy or sell something

small ˈchange noun [U] coins that have little value

small ˌfry noun [U] informal people or activities that are not considered important: *Compared to companies that size we're just small fry.*

small ˈprint noun [U] the part of a written agreement that is printed smaller than the rest and that contains important information: *Make sure you read the small print before you sign.*

small-scale /ˌsmɔːlˈskeɪl/ **adj** A small-scale activity or organization is not big and involves few people.

small ˌtalk noun [U] polite conversation between people at social events: *He's not very good at **making small talk**.*

small-time /ˈsmɔːlˌtaɪm/ **adj** [always before noun] informal not important or successful: *a small-time criminal*

smart¹ /smɑːt/ **adj 1 INTELLIGENT** ▷ 🔵 intelligent: *Rachel's one of the smartest kids in the class.* **2 TIDY** ▷ 🔵 If you look smart or your clothes are smart, you look clean and tidy: *a smart, blue suit* ∘ *I need to look a bit smarter for my interview.* **3 FASHIONABLE** ▷ fashionable and expensive: *a smart, new restaurant* **4 MACHINE/WEAPON** ▷ A smart machine, weapon, etc uses advanced computer systems: *smart bombs* • **smartly adv**

smart² /smɑːt/ **verb** [I] **1** to feel upset because someone has said or done something unpleasant to you: *The team are still **smarting from** last week's defeat.* **2** If part of your body smarts, it hurts with a sharp, burning pain: *The smoke from the fire made her **eyes smart**.*

smart ˌcard noun [C] a small, plastic card that can be read by a computer and can be used to pay for things or to store personal information

smarten /ˈsmɑːtᵊn/ **verb**

PHRASAL VERB **smarten (sb/sth) up** to make a person or place look more clean and tidy: *plans to smarten up the city centre*

smartphone /ˈsmɑːtfəʊn/ **noun** [C] a mobile phone that has software like the software on a small computer, and that connects to the Internet

smash¹ /smæʃ/ **verb**   **smash**

1 [I, T] 🔵 to break into a lot of pieces with a loud noise, or to make something break into a lot of pieces with a loud noise: *Thieves smashed the shop window and stole $50,000 worth of computer equipment.* **2 smash (sth) against/ into/through, etc** to hit a hard object or surface with a lot of f orce, or to make

something do this: *The car skidded and smashed into a tree.* ∘ *He smashed the glass against the wall.* **3** [T] to destroy a political or criminal organization: *attempts to smash a drug smuggling ring*

PHRASAL VERB **smash sth up** to damage or destroy something: *They were arrested for smashing up a hotel bar.*

smash² /smæʃ/ **noun** [C] (also ˌsmash ˈhit) a very successful film, song, play, etc: *the smash hit movie 'Titanic'*

smashing /ˈsmæʃɪŋ/ **adj** UK old-fashioned extremely good or attractive: *We had a smashing time at Bob and Vera's party.*

smear¹ /smɪəʳ/ **verb** [T] **1** to spread a thick liquid or sticky substance over something: *His shirt was **smeared with** paint.* ∘ *He smeared sun cream **over** his face and neck.* **2** to say unpleasant and untrue things about someone in order to harm them, especially in politics

smear² /smɪəʳ/ **noun** [C] **1** a dirty mark: *There was a smear of oil on his cheek.* **2** an unpleasant and untrue story about someone that is meant to harm them, especially in politics: *a **smear campaign***

smell¹ /smel/ **verb (smelled,** also UK **smelt) 1 smell of/like; smell delicious/horrible, etc** 🔵 to have a particular quality that people notice by using their nose: *I've been cooking, so my hands smell of garlic.* ∘ *That soup smells delicious – what's in it?* **2 NOTICE** ▷ [T] 🔵 to notice something by using your nose: *I think I can smell something burning.* **3 UNPLEASANT** ▷ [I] 🔵 to have an unpleasant smell: *Your running shoes really smell!* **4 PUT YOUR NOSE NEAR** ▷ [T] 🔵 to put your nose near something and breathe in so that you can notice its smell: *Come and smell these flowers.* **5 ABILITY** ▷ [I] 🔵 to have the ability to notice smells: *Dogs can smell much better than humans.*

smell² /smel/ **noun 1 QUALITY** ▷ [C] 🔵 the quality that something has which you notice by using your nose: *The **smell of** roses filled the room.* ∘ *There was a delicious smell coming from the kitchen.* **2 UNPLEASANT** ▷ [C] an unpleasant smell: *I wish I could get rid of that smell in the bathroom.* **3 ABILITY** ▷ [U] 🔵 the ability to notice smells: *Smoking can affect your **sense of smell**.*

smelly /ˈsmeli/ **adj** having an unpleasant smell: *smelly feet*

smelt /smelt/ UK past of smell

smile¹ /smaɪl/ **verb** [I] 🔵 to make a happy or friendly expression in which the corners of your mouth curve up: *She **smiled at** me.*

> ❗ Common learner error: **smile at** someone/ something
>
> Be careful to choose the right preposition after the verb **smile**.
> *She **smiled at** the little girl.*
> ~~She smiled to the little girl.~~

smile² /smaɪl/ **noun** [C] 🔵 a happy or friendly expression in which the corners of your mouth curve up: *"I passed my driving test,"* she said with a smile.

smiley /'smaɪli/ **noun** [C] an image such as :-) which looks like a face when you look at it from the side, made using keyboard symbols and used in emails to express emotions → See Study Page **Emailing and texting** on page Centre 37

smirk /smɜːk/ **verb** [I] to smile in an annoying or unkind way: *What are you smirking at?* • **smirk noun** [C]

smitten /'smɪtᵊn/ **adj** [never before noun] loving someone or liking something very much: *He's absolutely **smitten with** this Carla woman.*

smog /smɒg/ **noun** [U] air pollution in a city that is a mixture of smoke, gases, and chemicals

smoke¹ /sməʊk/ **noun 1** [U] 🔵 the grey or black gas that is produced when something burns **2** [no plural] when someone has a smoke, they smoke a cigarette: *I'm just going outside for a smoke.*

smoke² /sməʊk/ **verb 1** CIGARETTE ▷ [I, T] 🔵 to breathe smoke into your mouth from a cigarette: *Do you mind if I smoke?* ∘ *She smokes thirty cigarettes a day.* **2** MEAT/FISH ▷ [T] to give meat or fish a special taste by hanging it over burning wood: *smoked ham/salmon* **3** PRODUCE SMOKE ▷ [I] to produce or send out smoke: *smoking chimneys* → See also **chain-smoke**

smoker /'sməʊkər/ **noun** [C] 🔵 someone who smokes cigarettes regularly: *He used to be a **heavy smoker** (= someone who smokes a lot).* → Opposite **non-smoker**

smoking /'sməʊkɪŋ/ **noun** [U] 🔵 the activity or habit of smoking cigarettes: *The new law will restrict smoking in public places.* → See also **passive smoking**

smoky /'sməʊki/ **adj 1** filled with smoke: *a smoky bar/room* **2** having the smell, taste, or appearance of smoke: *That ham has a delicious, smoky flavour.*

smolder /'sməʊldər/ **verb** [I] US spelling of smoulder

smooth¹ /smuːð/ **adj 1** SURFACE ▷ 🔵 having a regular surface that has no holes or lumps in it: *soft, smooth skin* ∘ *a smooth wooden table* **2** SUBSTANCE ▷ 🔵 A substance that is smooth has no lumps in it: *Mix the butter and sugar together until smooth.* **3** MOVEMENT ▷ happening without any sudden movements or changes: *The plane made a smooth landing.* **4** PROCESS ▷ happening without problems or difficulties: *Her job is to help students make a smooth transition from high school to college.* **5** PERSON ▷ too polite and confident in a way that people do not trust: *a smooth salesman* • **smoothness noun** [U]

smooth² /smuːð/ **verb** [T] (also **smooth down/**

out, etc) to move your hands across something in order to make it flat: *He straightened his tie and smoothed down his hair.*

PHRASAL VERB **smooth sth over** to make a disagreement or problem seem less serious especially by talking to the people involved in it: *Would you like me to smooth things over between you and Nick?*

smoothie /'smuːði/ **noun** [C, U] a thick, cold drink made mainly from fruit, sometimes with milk, cream, or ice cream (= cold, sweet food)

smoothly /'smuːðli/ **adv 1** **go smoothly** 🔵 to happen without any problems or difficulties: *Everything was going smoothly until Darren arrived.* **2** without any sudden movements or changes: *The car accelerated smoothly.*

smother /'smʌðər/ **verb** [T] **1** KILL ▷ to kill someone by covering their face with something so that they cannot breathe **2** LOVE ▷ to give someone too much love and attention so that they feel they have lost their freedom: *I try not to smother him.* **3** PREVENT ▷ to prevent something from happening: *I tried to smother my cough* **4** FIRE ▷ to make a fire stop burning by covering it with something

PHRASAL VERB **smother sth in/with sth** to cover something completely with a substance: *She took a slice of chocolate cake and smothered it in cream.*

smoulder UK (US **smolder**) /'sməʊldər/ **verb** [I] **1** to burn slowly, producing smoke but no flames: *a smouldering bonfire* **2** to have a strong feeling, especially anger, but not express it: *I could see he was **smouldering with** anger.*

SMS /esem'es/ **noun** [U] abbreviation for short message service: a system for sending written messages from one mobile phone to another • **SMS verb** [T, I]

smudge¹ /smʌdʒ/ **noun** [C] a dirty mark: *a smudge of ink*

smudge² /smʌdʒ/ **verb** [I, T] If ink, paint, etc smudges, or if it is smudged, it becomes dirty or not clear because someone has touched it: *Be careful you don't smudge the drawing.*

smug /smʌg/ **adj** too pleased with your skill or success in a way that annoys other people: *a smug smile* • **smugly adv** *"I've never lost a match yet,"* she said smugly.

smuggle /'smʌgl/ **verb** [T] to take something into or out of a place in an illegal or secret way: *He was arrested for smuggling cocaine into Britain.* • **smuggler noun** [C] *drug smugglers* • **smuggling noun** [U]

snack¹ /snæk/ **noun** [C] 🔵 a small amount of food that you eat between meals: *Do you want a quick snack before you go out?* ∘ *snack food*

snack² /snæk/ **verb** [I] informal to eat a snack: *I've been **snacking on** chocolate and biscuits all afternoon.*

'**snack ˌbar noun** [C] a place where you can buy a small meal such as a sandwich

snag¹ /snæg/ **noun** [C] informal a problem or difficulty: *I'd love to come – the only snag is I have to be home by 3 o'clock.*

> ☑ **Word partners for snag**
>
> hit a snag • the (only) snag is • a snag in/ with sth

snag² /snæg/ **verb** [T] (**snagging, snagged**) **1** If you snag something, it becomes stuck on a sharp object and tears: *I snagged my coat on the wire.* **2** US informal to get, catch, or win something: *She managed to snag a seat in the front row.*

snail /sneɪl/ **noun** [C] a small creature with a long, soft body and a round shell

IDIOM **at a snail's pace** very slowly: *There was so much traffic that we were travelling at a snail's pace.*

snail mail noun [U] humorous informal letters or messages that are not sent by email but by post

snake¹ /sneɪk/ **noun** [C] ⓐ a long, thin creature with no legs that slides along the ground

snake² /sneɪk/ **verb** **snake across/around/ through, etc** to follow a route that has a lot of bends: *The river snakes through some of the most spectacular countryside in France.*

snap¹ /snæp/ **verb** (**snapping, snapped**) **1** BREAK ▷ [I, T] If something long and thin snaps, it breaks making a short, loud sound, and if you snap it, you break it, making a short, loud sound: *The twigs snapped as we walked on them.* **2 snap (sth) open/shut/together, etc** to suddenly move to a particular position, making a short, loud noise, or to make something do this: *The suitcase snapped open and everything fell out.* **3** SPEAK ANGRILY ▷ [I, T] to say something suddenly in an angry way: *I was snapping at the children because I was tired.* **4** LOSE CONTROL ▷ [I] to suddenly be unable to control a strong feeling, especially anger: *She asked me to do the work again and I just snapped.* **5** PHOTOGRAPH ▷ [T] informal to take a photograph of someone or something: *Photographers snapped the Princess everywhere she went.* **6** ANIMAL ▷ [I] If an animal snaps, it tries to bite someone: *The dog was barking and snapping at my ankles.* → See also **snap your fingers (finger¹)**

PHRASAL VERBS **snap out of sth** informal to force yourself to stop feeling sad, angry, upset etc: *He's in a bad mood now but he'll soon snap out of it.* • **snap sth up** informal to buy or get something quickly because it is cheap or exactly what you want: *The dress was perfect, so I snapped it up.* • **snap sb up** informal to immediately accept someone's offer to join your company or team because you want them

very much: *She was snapped up by a large law firm.*

snap² /snæp/ **noun 1** SOUND ▷ [no plural] a sudden, short, loud sound like something breaking or closing: *I heard a snap as I sat on the pencil.* **2** PHOTOGRAPH ▷ [C] UK informal (also UK/ US **snapshot**) a photograph: *holiday snaps* **3** FASTENING ▷ [C] US (UK **popper**) a metal or plastic object made of two parts which fit together with a short, loud sound, used to fasten clothing **4** GAME ▷ [U] a card game in which you say "snap" when you see two cards that are the same **5 be a snap** US informal to be very easy: *The French test was a snap.*

snap³ /snæp/ **adj snap decision/judgment** A snap decision or judgment is made very quickly and without careful thought.

snappy /ˈsnæpi/ **adj 1** written or spoken in a short and interesting way: *a snappy title* **2** Snappy clothes are fashionable: *a snappy new suit*

IDIOM **make it snappy** informal used to tell someone to hurry

snapshot /ˈsnæpʃɒt/ **noun** [C] a photograph that you take quickly without thinking

snare¹ /sneəʳ/ **noun** [C] a piece of equipment used to catch animals

snare² /sneəʳ/ **verb** [T] **1** to catch an animal using a snare **2** to trick someone so that they cannot escape from a situation: *She's trying to snare a rich husband.*

snarl /snɑːl/ **verb 1** [I, T] to speak angrily: *"Go away!" he snarled.* ◦ *She snarled at me.* **2** [I] If an animal snarls, it shows its teeth and makes an angry sound. • **snarl noun** [C]

snatch¹ /snætʃ/ **verb** [T] **1** to take something or someone quickly and suddenly: *Bill snatched the telephone from my hand.* ◦ *The child was snatched from his bed.* **2** to do or get something quickly because you only have a short amount of time: *I managed to snatch some lunch.*

snatch² /snætʃ/ **noun** [C] a short part of a conversation, song, etc that you hear: *I keep hearing snatches of that song on the radio.*

sneak¹ /sniːk/ **verb** (**sneaked**, also US informal **snuck**) **1 sneak into/out/around, etc** to go somewhere quietly because you do not want anyone to hear you: *I sneaked into his bedroom while he was asleep.* **2 sneak sth into/out of/ through, etc** to take something somewhere without anyone seeing you: *We tried to sneak the dog into the hotel.* **3 sneak a look/glance at sb/sth** to look at someone or something quickly and secretly: *I sneaked a look at the answers.*

PHRASAL VERB **sneak up** to move close to someone without them seeing or hearing you: *Don't sneak up on me like that – you scared me!*

sneak² /sniːk/ **noun** [C] informal UK someone who you do not like because they tell people when someone else has done something bad

sneaker /ˈsniːkəʳ/ **noun** [C] US (UK **trainer**) a soft sports shoe → See colour picture **Clothes** on page Centre 9

S

sneaking /'sni:kɪŋ/ *adj* **1 have a sneaking feeling/suspicion** to think that something is true but not be sure: [+ (that)] *I have a sneaking feeling that the English test is going to be very difficult.* **2 have a sneaking admiration/fondness for sb** UK to like someone secretly, especially when you do not want to

sneaky /'sni:ki/ *adj* doing things in a secret and unfair way

sneer /snɪəʳ/ *verb* [I] to talk about, or look at someone or something in a way that shows you do not approve of them: *Carlos sneered at my attempts to put the tent up.* • **sneer** *noun* [C]

sneeze /sni:z/ *verb* [I] ⑫ If you sneeze, air suddenly comes out through your nose and mouth: *He had a cold and was sneezing a lot.* • **sneeze** *noun* [C]

snicker /'snɪkəʳ/ *verb* [I] US (mainly UK **snigger**) to laugh quietly in a rude way • **snicker** *noun* [C]

snide /snaɪd/ *adj* A snide remark criticizes someone in an unpleasant way.

sniff /snɪf/ *verb* **1** [I] to breathe air in through your nose in a way that makes a noise: *Sam had a cold and she kept sniffing.* **2** [I, T] to breathe air in through your nose in order to smell something: *She sniffed the flowers.* • **sniff** *noun* [C]

snigger /'snɪgəʳ/ *verb* [I] mainly UK (US **snicker**) to laugh quietly in a rude way: *The boys were sniggering at the teacher.* • **snigger** *noun* [C]

snip¹ /snɪp/ *verb* [I, T] (**snipping, snipped**) to cut something using scissors (= tool with two flat blades) with quick, small cuts: *She snipped the article out of the magazine.*

snip² /snɪp/ *noun* **1** [C] a small, quick cut with scissors (= tool with two flat blades) **2 be a snip** UK informal to be very cheap

snipe /snaɪp/ *verb* [I] **1** to criticize someone in an unpleasant way: *I hate the way politicians snipe at each other.* **2** to shoot people from a place that they cannot see: *Rebels were indiscriminately sniping at civilians.* • **sniping** *noun* [U]

sniper /'snaɪpəʳ/ *noun* [C] **1** someone who shoots at people from a place they cannot see **2** on a website, someone who makes an offer for an item just before the end of an auction (= a sale in which things are sold to the person who offers the most money)

snippet /'snɪpɪt/ *noun* [C] a small piece of information, news, conversation, etc: *I kept hearing snippets of conversation.*

snob /snɒb/ *noun* [C] someone who thinks they are better than other people because they are in a higher social position • **snobbery** /'snɒbᵊri/ *noun* [U] behaviour and opinions that are typical of a snob

snobbish /'snɒbɪʃ/ *adj* (also **snobby**) like a snob: *a snobbish attitude*

snog /snɒg/ *verb* [I, T] (**snogging, snogged**) UK informal If two people snog, they kiss each other for a long time. • **snog** *noun* [C] UK informal

snooker /'snu:kəʳ/ *noun* [U] a game in which two people use long sticks to hit coloured balls into holes at the edge of a table

snoop /snu:p/ *verb* [I] to look around a place secretly in order to find out information about someone: *I found her snooping around in my bedroom.* • **snoop** *noun* [no plural]

snooty /'snu:ti/ *adj* Someone who is snooty behaves in an unfriendly way because they think they are better than other people.

snooze /snu:z/ *verb* [I] informal to sleep for a short time, especially during the day: *Grandpa was snoozing in his chair.* • **snooze** *noun* [C] informal *Why don't you have a snooze?*

snore /snɔːʳ/ *verb* [I] ⑫ to breathe in a very noisy way while you are sleeping: *I couldn't sleep because my brother was snoring.* • **snore** *noun* [C]

snorkel¹ /'snɔːkᵊl/ *noun* [C] a tube that you use to help you breathe if you are swimming with your face under water

snorkel² /'snɔːkᵊl/ *verb* [I] (mainly UK **snorkelling, snorkelled**, US **snorkeling, snorkeled**) to swim using a snorkel

snort /snɔːt/ *verb* [I, T] to breathe out noisily through your nose, especially to show that you are annoyed or think something is funny: *"Stupid man!" he snorted.* ◦ *Rosie started snorting with laughter.* • **snort** *noun* [C]

snot /snɒt/ *noun* [U] informal the thick liquid that is produced in your nose

snout /snaʊt/ *noun* [C] the long nose of some animals, such as pigs

snow¹ /snəʊ/ *noun* [U] ⓐ soft white pieces of frozen water that fall from the sky when the weather is cold: *children playing in the snow*

> ☑ **Word partners for snow (noun)**
>
> snow **falls/melts** • a snow **flurry/shower** • **deep/heavy** snow • [walk/tramp, etc] **through** the snow

snow² /snəʊ/ *verb* **1 it snows** ⑫ If it snows, snow falls from the sky: *It snowed all day yesterday.* **2 be snowed in** to be unable to leave a place because there is too much snow: *We were snowed in for two days.*

IDIOM **be snowed under** to have too much work: *I'm snowed under with homework.*

snowball¹ /'snəʊbɔːl/ *noun* [C] a ball made from snow that children throw at each other

snowball² /'snəʊbɔːl/ *verb* [I] If a problem, idea or situation snowballs, it quickly grows bigger or more important: *The whole business idea snowballed from one phone call.*

snowboard /'snəʊbɔːd/ *noun* [C] ⑥ a large board that you stand on to move over snow → See colour picture **Sports 1** on page Centre 14

snowboarding /'snəʊbɔːdɪŋ/ *noun* [U] ⑫ a sport in which you stand on a large board and move over snow • **snowboarder** *noun* [C] → See colour picture **Sports 1** on page Centre 14

snowdrift /'snəʊdrɪft/ *noun* [C] a deep pile of snow that the wind has blown

snowdrop /'snəʊdrɒp/ *noun* [C] a small, white flower that you can see at the end of winter

snowfall /'snəʊfɔːl/ *noun* [C, U] the snow that falls at one time, or the amount of snow that falls: *a heavy snowfall (= a lot of snow)*

snowflake /'snəʊfleɪk/ *noun* [C] a small piece of snow that falls from the sky

S

snowman /'snəʊmæn/ **noun** [C] (plural **snowmen**) something that looks like a person and is made from snow: *The kids made a snowman in the garden.*

snowplough UK (US **snowplow**) /'snəʊplaʊ/ **noun** [C] a vehicle used for moving snow off roads and railways

snowstorm /'snəʊstɔːm/ **noun** [C] a storm when a lot of snow falls

snowy /'snəʊi/ **adj** snowing or covered with snow: *a cold, snowy day*

Snr UK (UK/US **Sr**) written abbreviation for senior (= the older of two men in a family with the same name): *Thomas Smith, Snr*

snub /snʌb/ **verb** [T] (**snubbing, snubbed**) to be rude to someone, especially by not speaking to them • **snub noun** [C]

snuck /snʌk/ US informal past of sneak

snuff¹ /snʌf/ **noun** [U] tobacco powder that people breathe in through their noses, especially in the past

snuff² /snʌf/ **verb**

PHRASAL VERB **snuff sth out 1** informal to suddenly end something: *England's chances were snuffed out by three brilliant goals from the Italians.* **2** to stop a candle flame from burning by covering it or pressing it with your fingers

snug /snʌg/ **adj 1** warm and comfortable: *a snug little house* **2** Snug clothes fit tightly: *a pair of snug shoes* • **snugly adv**

snuggle /'snʌgl/ **verb snuggle up/down/into, etc** to move into a warm, comfortable position: *I snuggled up to him on the sofa.*

so¹ /səʊ/ **adv 1 VERY** ▷ Ⓐ❷ used before an adjective or adverb to emphasize what you are saying, especially when there is a particular result: *I was so tired when I got home.* ∘ *[+ (that)] I was so upset that I couldn't speak.* **2 ANSWER** ▷ Ⓐ❷ used to give a short answer to a question to avoid repeating a phrase: *"Is Ben coming to the party?" "I hope so."* **3 so did we/so have I/so is mine, etc** Ⓑ❶ used to say that someone else also does something or that the same thing is true about someone or something else: *"We went to the cinema last night." "Oh, so did we."* **4 GET ATTENTION** ▷ used to get someone's attention when you are going to ask them a question or when you are going to start talking: *So, when are you two going to get married?* **5 SHOW SOMETHING** ▷ used with a movement of your hand to show someone how to do something or show them the size of something: *The box was so big.* ∘ *For this exercise, you have to put your hands like so.* **6 so it is/so they are, etc** used to agree with something that you had not noticed before: *"The cat's hiding under the chair." "So it is."* **7 or so** Ⓑ❶ used after a number or amount to show that it is not exact: *"How many people were at the party?" "Fifty or so, I guess."* **8 I told you so** used to say that you were right and that someone should have believed you **9 So (what)?** used to say that you do not think something is important, especially in a rude way: *"She might tell Emily." "So what?"* **10 and so on/forth** Ⓐ❷ used after a list of things to show that you could

have added other similar things: *She plays a lot of tennis and squash and so on.* **11 so as (not) to do sth** Ⓑ❷ used to give the reason for doing something: *He went in very quietly so as not to wake the baby.* **12 only so much/many** used to say that there are limits to something: *There's only so much help you can give someone.* **13 so much for...** informal used to say that something has not been useful or successful: *"The computer's crashed again." "So much for modern technology."*

so² /səʊ/ **conjunction 1** Ⓐ❷ used to say that something is the reason why something else happens: *I was tired so I went to bed.* ∘ *Greg had some money so he bought a bike.* **2 so (that)** Ⓑ❶ in order to make something happen or be possible: *He put his glasses on so that he could see the television better.* **3** Ⓐ❷ used at the beginning of a sentence to connect it with something that was said or happened previously: *So we're not going away this weekend after all?*

so³ /səʊ/ **adj be so** to be correct or true: *"Apparently, she's moving to Canada." "Is that so?"*

soak /səʊk/ **verb** [I, T] **1** Ⓑ❷ If you soak something, or let it soak, you put it in a liquid for a period of time: *He left the pan in the sink to soak.* ∘ *Soak the bread in the milk.* **2** If liquid soaks somewhere or soaks something, it makes something very wet: *The rain soaked my clothes.* ∘ *The ink soaked through the paper onto the table.*

PHRASAL VERB **soak sth up** Ⓑ❷ If a dry substance soaks up a liquid, the liquid goes into the substance: *Fry the potatoes until they soak up all the oil.*

soaked /səʊkt/ **adj** Ⓑ❷ completely wet: *My shirt was soaked.*

soaking /'səʊkɪŋ/ **adj** Ⓑ❷ completely wet: *You're soaking – why didn't you take an umbrella?* ∘ *The dog was soaking wet.*

so-and-so /'səʊəndsəʊ/ **noun** [C] **1** used to talk about someone or something without saying a particular name: *It was the usual village news – so-and-so got married to so-and-so, and so-and-so's having a baby.* **2** informal someone who you do not like: *He's a lazy so-and-so.*

soap /səʊp/ **noun 1** [U] Ⓐ❷ a substance that you use for washing: *a bar of soap* ∘ *soap powder* → See colour picture **The Bathroom** on page Centre 3 **2** [C] (also **soap opera**) Ⓑ❶ a television programme about the lives of a group of people that is broadcast several times every week

soap opera noun [C] (informal **soap**) Ⓑ❶ a series of television or radio programmes that continues over a long period and is about the lives of a group of characters

soapy /'səʊpi/ **adj** containing soap, or covered with soap: *soapy hands*

soar /sɔːr/ **verb** [I] **1** to increase to a high level very quickly: *House prices have soared.* **2** to move quickly and smoothly in the sky, or to move quickly up into the sky: *The birds were soaring high above.* • **soaring adj**

sob /sɒb/ **verb** [I] (**sobbing, sobbed**) Ⓑ❷ to cry in a noisy way • **sob noun** [C]

S

sober¹ /'səʊbər/ **adj 1 NOT DRUNK** ▷ Someone who is sober is not drunk. **2 SERIOUS** ▷ Someone who is sober is serious and thinks a lot: *He was in a sober mood.* **3 NOT BRIGHT** ▷ UK Clothes or colours that are sober are plain and not bright: *a sober, grey dress* • **soberly adv**

sober² /'səʊbər/ **verb**

PHRASAL VERB **sober (sb) up** to become less drunk or to make someone become less drunk: *You'd better sober up before you go home.*

sobering /'səʊbərɪŋ/ **adj** making you feel serious: *a **sobering thought***

so-called /ˌsəʊ'kɔːld/ **adj** [always before noun] **B2** used to show that you think a word that is used to describe someone or something is wrong: *My so-called friend has stolen my girlfriend.*

soccer /'sɒkər/ **noun** [U] (also UK **football**) a game in which two teams of eleven people kick a ball and try to score goals → See colour picture **Sports 2** on page Centre 15

sociable /'səʊʃəbl/ **adj B1** Someone who is sociable enjoys being with people and meeting new people.

social /'səʊʃəl/ **adj 1 B2** relating to society and the way people live: *social problems* ∘ *social and political changes* **2 B1** relating to the things you do with other people for enjoyment when you are not working: *I have a very good **social life**.* • **socially adv** → Compare **anti-social**

socialism /'səʊʃəlɪzəm/ **noun** [U] a political system in which the government owns important businesses and industries, and which allows the people to share the money and opportunities equally

socialist /'səʊʃəlɪst/ **noun** [C] someone who supports socialism • **socialist adj** *socialist principles*

socialize (also UK **-ise**) /'səʊʃəlaɪz/ **verb** [I] **B2** to spend time enjoying yourself with other people: *The cafe is a place where students can **socialize** with teachers.*

social 'media noun [U or plural] forms of electronic communication that allow people to share information using the Internet or mobile phones: *Blogs, podcasts and other forms of social media are creating new opportunities for businesses to reach the public.*

social 'networking noun [U] **B1** the activity of using a website to share information and communicate with people

social 'science noun [C, U] the study of society and the way people live

social se'curity noun [U] money that the government gives to people who are old, sick, or not working

social ,worker noun [C] someone whose job is to help people who have problems because they are poor, old, have difficulties with their family, etc • **social work noun** [U]

society /sə'saɪəti/ **noun 1** [C, U] **B1** a large group of people who live in the same country or area and have the same laws, traditions, etc: *The US is a multicultural society.* **2** [C] **B2** an organization for people who have the same interest or aim:

the London Zoological Society → See also **building society**

☑ **Word partners for society**

a **democratic/free/modern/multicultural/secular** society

---

socio- /ˌsəʊsiəʊ-/ **prefix** relating to society: *socio-economic*

sociology /ˌsəʊsi'ɒlədʒi/ **noun** [U] the study of society and the relationship between people in society • **sociologist** /ˌsəʊsi'ɒlədʒɪst/ **noun** [C] someone who studies sociology

sociopath /'səʊsiəʊpæθ/ **noun** [C] someone who is completely unable to behave in a way that is acceptable to society

sock /sɒk/ **noun** [C] (plural **socks**, also US **sox**) **A2** something that you wear on your foot inside your shoe: [usually plural] *a pair of black socks* → See colour picture **Clothes** on page Centre 9

socket /'sɒkɪt/ **noun** [C] **1** the place on a wall where you connect electrical equipment to the electricity supply **2** a hollow place where one thing fits inside another thing: *Your eyeball is in your eye socket.*

soda /'səʊdə/ **noun 1** [U] (also **'soda ,water**) water with bubbles in it that you mix with other drinks **2** [C, U] (also old-fashioned **'soda ,pop**) US sweet drink with bubbles: *a can of soda*

sodden /'sɒdən/ **adj** extremely wet: *Your shoes are sodden!*

sodium /'səʊdiəm/ **noun** [U] a chemical element that is found in salt and food: *a low-sodium diet*

sofa /'səʊfə/ **noun** [C] **A2** a large, comfortable seat for more than one person → See colour picture **The Living Room** on page Centre 4

sofa

soft /sɒft/ **adj 1 NOT HARD** ▷ **A2** not hard, and easy to press: *a soft cushion* ∘ *Cook the onion until it's soft* **2 SMOOTH** ▷ **A2** smooth and pleasant to touch: *soft hair/skin* **3 SOUND** ▷ **B1** A soft sound is very quiet: *He spoke in a soft voice* **4 COLOUR/LIGHT** ▷ **B1** A soft colour or light is not bright: *soft lilac paint* **5 PERSON** ▷ too kind and not angry enough when someone does something wrong: *The kids are naughty because she's too **soft on** them.* **6 DRUGS** ▷ Soft drugs are illegal drugs that some people think are not dangerous. • **softness noun** [U] → See also **have soft spot¹ for sb**

softball /'sɒftbɔːl/ **noun** [U] a game that is like baseball but played with a larger and softer ball

soft 'drink UK (US **'soft ,drink**) **noun** [C] **A2** cold, sweet drink that does not have alcohol in it

soften /'sɒfən/ **verb** [I, T] **1** to become softer or to make something become softer: *Heat the butter until it softens.* **2** to become more gentle or to make someone or something become more gentle: *Her voice softened.*

softly /'sɒftli/ **adv B1** in a quiet or gentle way: *"Are you OK?" she said softly.*

soft 'option noun [C] UK a choice that is easier

S

than other choices: *The cookery course is not a soft option.*

oft-spoken /ˌsɒftˈspəʊkən/ **adj** having a quiet, gentle voice: *a small, soft-spoken man*

oftware /ˈsɒftweəʳ/ **noun** [U] 🅰🅲 programs that you use to make a computer do different things: *educational software*

oggy /ˈsɒgi/ **adj** very wet and soft: *soggy ground*

oil¹ /sɔɪl/ **noun** [C, U] 🅱🅲 the top layer of earth that plants grow in: *clay/sandy soil*

oil² /sɔɪl/ **verb** [T] formal to make something dirty • **soiled adj** dirty: *soiled clothes*

olace /ˈsɒləs/ **noun** [U, no plural] formal comfort when you are feeling sad: *Music was a great solace to me.*

olar /ˈsəʊləʳ/ **adj** 🅱🅲 relating to, or involving, the sun: *solar panels*

olar ˈenergy noun [U] energy that uses the power of the sun

olar ˈpanel noun [C] a piece of equipment that changes light from the sun into electricity

olar ˈpower noun [U] electricity produced by using the energy from the sun

he ˈsolar ˌsystem noun the sun and planets that move around it

old /səʊld/ past of sell

oldier /ˈsəʊldʒəʳ/ **noun** [C] 🅱🅳 a member of an army

ole¹ /səʊl/ **adj** [always before noun] **1** only: *the sole survivor* **2** not shared with anyone else: *She has sole responsibility for the project.*

ole² /səʊl/ **noun 1 FOOT** ▷ [C] the bottom part of your foot that you walk on **2 SHOE** ▷ [C] the part of a shoe that is under your foot **3 FISH** ▷ [C, U] (plural **sole**) a small, flat fish that you can eat

olely /ˈsəʊlli/ **adv** only, and not involving anyone or anything else: *I bought it solely for that purpose.*

olemn /ˈsɒləm/ **adj 1** serious or sad: *solemn music* **2** A solemn promise, warning, etc is serious and sincere. • **solemnly adv** • **solemnity** /səˈlemnəti/ **noun** [U]

olicit /səˈlɪsɪt/ **verb 1** [T] formal to ask someone for money, information, or help: *to solicit donations for a charity* **2** [I] to offer sex for money, usually in a public place

oliciting /səˈlɪsɪtɪŋ/ **noun** [U] offering to have sex for money

olicitor /səˈlɪsɪtəʳ/ **noun** [C] in Britain, a lawyer who gives legal advice and help, and who works in the lower courts of law → See Note at **lawyer**

olid¹ /ˈsɒlɪd/ **adj 1 HARD/FIRM** ▷ 🅱🅲 hard and firm without holes or spaces, and not liquid or gas: *solid ground* ∘ *solid food* **2 STRONG** ▷ 🅱🅲 strong and not easily broken or damaged: *solid furniture* **3 solid gold/silver/wood, etc** gold/silver/wood, etc with nothing added: *a solid silver bracelet* **4 TIME** ▷ continuing for a period of time without stopping: *The noise continued for two solid hours/two hours solid.* **5 INFORMATION** ▷ [always before noun] Solid information, proof, etc is based on facts and you are certain that it is correct: *This provides solid evidence that he committed the crime.*

6 PERSON ▷ honest and able to be trusted • **solidity** /səˈlɪdəti/ **noun** [U] • **solidly adv**

solid² /ˈsɒlɪd/ **noun** [C] **1** a substance or object that is not a liquid or a gas **2** a shape that has length, width, and height, and is not flat

solidarity /ˌsɒlɪˈdærəti/ **noun** [U] agreement and support between people in a group who have similar aims or beliefs

solidify /səˈlɪdɪfaɪ/ **verb** [I] If a liquid solidifies, it becomes solid.

solids /ˈsɒlɪdz/ **noun** [plural] food that is not liquid: *Three weeks after the operation he still couldn't eat solids.*

solipsism /ˈsɒlɪpsɪzᵊm/ **noun** [U] the belief that in life you can only really know yourself and your own experiences

solitaire /ˌsɒlɪˈteəʳ/ 🆄🆂 /ˈsɒlɪteəʳ/ **noun** [U] US (UK **patience**) a card game for one person

solitary /ˈsɒlɪtᵊri/ **adj 1** A solitary person or thing is the only person or thing in a place: *a solitary figure/walker* **2** A solitary activity is done alone: *solitary walks*

ˌsolitary conˈfinement noun [U] a punishment in which a prisoner is kept in a room alone: *He was kept in solitary confinement for ten days.*

solitude /ˈsɒlɪtjuːd/ **noun** [U] being alone: *He went upstairs to read the letter in solitude.*

solo¹ /ˈsəʊləʊ/ **adj, adv** 🅱🅲 done alone by one person only: *a solo performance* ∘ *to perform solo*

solo² /ˈsəʊləʊ/ **noun** [C] 🅱🅲 a piece of music for one person or one instrument

soloist /ˈsəʊləʊɪst/ **noun** [C] a musician who performs a solo

solstice /ˈsɒlstɪs/ **noun** [C] the longest day or the longest night of the year: *the summer/winter solstice*

soluble /ˈsɒljəbl/ **adj** If a substance is soluble, it will dissolve in water: *soluble vitamins* ∘ *These tablets are soluble in water.*

solution /səˈluːʃᵊn/ **noun** [C] **1** 🅱🅳 the answer to a problem: *There's no easy solution to this problem.* **2** a liquid which a substance has been dissolved into

> ❗ Common learner error: **solution to** a problem
>
> Be careful to choose the correct preposition after **solution**.
>
> *This could be one solution to the problem.*
> ~~This could be one solution of the problem.~~

> 🗹 Word partners for **solution**
>
> find/offer/provide/seek a solution • a diplomatic/good/long-term/peaceful/simple/workable solution • a solution to sth

solve /sɒlv/ **verb** [T] 🅱🅳 to find the answer to something: *to solve a problem* ∘ *to solve a mystery/puzzle* ∘ *Police are still no nearer to solving the crime.*

solvent¹ /ˈsɒlvənt/ **noun** [C] a liquid that is used to dissolve other substances

S

solvent² /'sɒlvənt/ **adj** having enough money to pay your debts

sombre UK (US **somber**) /'sɒmbər/ **adj 1** sad and serious: *a sombre expression/mood* **2** dark and without bright colours: *a sombre colour*

some¹ strong /sʌm/ weak /səm/ **pronoun, quantifier 1 UNKNOWN AMOUNT** ▷ **A1** used to refer to an amount of something without saying exactly how much or how many: *You'll need a pair of scissors and some glue.* ∘ *I can't eat all this chocolate, would you like some?* ∘ *Could I have some more (= an extra amount of) paper, please?* **2 NOT ALL** ▷ **A1** used to refer to part of a larger amount or number of something and not all of it: *In some cases it's possible to fix the problem right away.* ∘ *Some of the children were frightened.* **3 UNKNOWN NAME** ▷ used to refer to someone or something when you do not know the name of it or exact details about it: *Some girl phoned for you, but she didn't leave a message.* **4 some time/distance, etc** **B2** a large amount of time, distance, etc: *I'm afraid it'll be some time before it's ready.*

> ⚠ Common learner error: **some** or **any**?
>
> Be careful not to confuse these two words. **Any** is used in questions and negative sentences.
>
> *Have you got any friends in America?*
> *I haven't got any money.*
>
> **Some** is used in positive sentences.
>
> *I've got some friends in America.*
>
> Sometimes **some** is used in questions, especially when the speaker thinks that the answer will be 'yes'.
>
> *Have you got some money I could borrow?*
>
> The same rules are true for 'something/anything' and 'someone/anyone'.
>
> *I didn't see anyone I knew.*
> *I saw someone I knew at the party.*

some² strong /sʌm/ weak /səm/ **adv** used before a number to show that it is not the exact amount: *He died some ten years ago.*

somebody /'sʌmbədi/ **pronoun** **A2** another word for someone

someday /'sʌmdeɪ/ **adv** at an unknown time in the future: *We plan to get married someday.*

somehow /'sʌmhaʊ/ **adv** **B1** in a way which you do not know or do not understand: *Don't worry, we'll fix it somehow.* ∘ **Somehow or other** (= *I do not know how) they managed to get in.*

someone /'sʌmwʌn/ **pronoun** (also **somebody**) **1** **A2** used to refer to a person when you do not know who they are or when it is not important who they are: *There's someone at the door.* ∘ *Will someone please answer the phone?* **2 someone else** **A2** a different person: *Sorry, I thought you were talking to someone else.*

someplace /'sʌmpleɪs/ **adv** US used to refer to a place when you do not know where it is or when it is not important where it is: *They live someplace in the South.* ∘ *If they don't like it here, they can go someplace else (= to a different place).*

somersault /'sʌməsɔːlt/ **noun** [C] a movement in which you roll your body forwards or backwards so that your feet go over your head and come back down to the ground again • **somersault verb** [I]

something /'sʌmθɪŋ/ **pronoun 1** **A1** used to refer to a thing when you do not know what it is or when it is not important what it is: *As soon as I walked in, I noticed that something was missing.* ∘ *We know about the problem and we're trying to do something about it.* ∘ *It's not something that will be easy to change.* ∘ *There's something else (= another thing) I wanted to tell you.* **2 or something (like that)** **A2** used to show that what you have just said is only an example or you are not certain about it: *Why don't you go to a movie or something?* **3 something like** similar to or approximately: *He paid something like $2000 for his car.* **4 be something** informal to be a thing which is important, special, or useful: *The President visiting our hotel – that would really be something.* **5 something of a sth** used to describe a person or thing in a way which is partly true but not completely or exactly: *It came as something of a surprise.* **6 be/have something to do with sth/sb** to be related to something or a cause of something but not in a way which you know about or understand exactly: *It might have something to do with the way it's made.*

sometime /'sʌmtaɪm/ **adv** used to refer to a time when you do not know exactly what it is or when it is not important what it is: *sometime before June* ∘ *You must come over and visit sometime.*

sometimes /'sʌmtaɪmz/ **adv** **A1** on some occasions but not always or often: *He does cook sometimes, but not very often.* ∘ *Sometimes I feel like no one understands me.*

somewhat /'sʌmwɒt/ **adv** formal slightly: *We were somewhat disappointed with the food.*

somewhere /'sʌmweər/ **adv 1** **A2** used to refer to a place when you do not know exactly where it is or when it is not important where it is: *They had difficulties finding somewhere to live.* ∘ *He comes from somewhere near London.* ∘ *Can you think of somewhere else (= a different place) we could go?* **2 somewhere around/between, etc** **B2** approximately: *He earns somewhere around £50,000 a year.*

IDIOM **get somewhere** to achieve something or to make progress: *Right, that's the printer working. Now we're getting somewhere!*

son /sʌn/ **noun** [C] **A1** your male child

sonar /'səʊnɑːr/ **noun** [U] a system, used especially on ships, which uses sound waves to find the position of things in the water

sonata /sə'nɑːtə/ **noun** [C] a piece of music written to be played on a piano or on another instrument and the piano together

song /sɒŋ/ **noun** [C] **A2** words that go with a short piece of music: *a folk/love song* ∘ *to sing a song*

> ☑ Word partners for **song**
>
> sing/write a song • a song about sth • a love song

ongwriter /ˈsɒŋˌraɪtəʳ/ **noun** [C] someone who writes songs

onic /ˈsɒnɪk/ **adj** relating to sound

on-in-law /ˈsʌnɪnlɔː/ **noun** [C] (plural **sons-in-law**) ⓑ your daughter's husband

onnet /ˈsɒnɪt/ **noun** [C] a poem with 14 lines, written in a particular pattern: *Shakespeare's sonnets*

oon /suːn/ **adv 1** ⓐ after a short period of time: *I've got to leave quite soon.* ○ *It's too soon to make a decision.* ○ *He joined the company soon after leaving college.* **2 as soon as** ⓑ at the same time or a very short time after: *As soon as I saw her, I knew there was something wrong.* ○ *They want it as soon as possible.* **3 sooner or later** ⓑ used to say that you do not know exactly when something will happen, but you are sure that it will happen: *Sooner or later they'll realize that it's not going to work.* **4 would sooner** would prefer: *I'd sooner spend a bit more money than take chances with safety.* **5 no sooner … than** used to show that something happens immediately after something else: *No sooner had we got home than the phone rang.*

oot /sʊt/ **noun** [U] a black powder produced when coal, wood, etc is burnt

oothe /suːð/ **verb** [T] **1** to make something feel less painful: *I had a long, hot bath to soothe my aching muscles.* **2** to make someone feel calm or less worried: *to soothe a crying baby* ● **soothing** **adj** making you feel calm or in less pain: *soothing music* ○ *a soothing effect/voice*

ophisticated /səˈfɪstɪkeɪtɪd/ **adj 1** ⓑ well-educated and having experience of the world or knowledge of culture **2** ⓑ A sophisticated machine or system is very advanced and works in a clever way: *a sophisticated computer system* ● **sophistication** /səˌfɪstɪˈkeɪʃᵊn/ **noun** [U]

ophomore /ˈsɒfəmɔːʳ/ **noun** [C] US a student studying in the second year of a course at a US university or high school (= school for students aged 15 to 18)

oprano /səˈprɑːnəʊ/ **noun** [C] a female singer who sings the highest notes

ordid /ˈsɔːdɪd/ **adj** unpleasant, dirty, or immoral: *a sordid affair*

ore¹ /sɔːʳ/ **adj 1** ⓑ painful, especially when touched: *a sore throat/knee* ○ *Her eyes were red and sore.* **2 sore point/spot/subject** a subject that causes disagreement or makes people angry when it is discussed: *Money is a bit of a sore point with him at the moment.* → See also **stick/stand out like a sore thumb**

ore² /sɔːʳ/ **noun** [C] an area of skin that is red and painful because of an infection

orely /ˈsɔːli/ **adv** formal very much: *to be sorely disappointed/tempted* ○ *He will be sorely missed by everyone.*

orority /səˈrɒrɪti/ **noun** [C] in the US, a social organization for female college students

orrow /ˈsɒrəʊ/ **noun** [C, U] formal the feeling of being very sad ● **sorrowful adj** formal

orry /ˈsɒri/ **adj 1 (I'm) sorry** ⓑ something that you say to be polite when you have done something wrong, or when you cannot agree with someone or accept something: *Sorry I'm late.* ○ *Oh, I'm sorry. I didn't see you there.* ○ *Tom, I'm so sorry about last night – it was all my fault.* ○ *I'm sorry, but I just don't think it's a good idea.* **2** ⓑ used to show sympathy or sadness for a person or situation: *I feel sorry for the children – it must be very hard for them.* ○ *I was sorry to hear about your brother's accident.* ○ [+ (that)] *I'm sorry that things didn't work out for you.* **3 Sorry?** mainly UK used as a polite way to say that you did not hear what someone has just said: *Sorry? What was that?* **4** used to say that you wish something in the past had not happened or had been different: [+ (that)] *I'm sorry that I ever met him.* **5 a sorry sight/state/tale** a bad condition or situation: *Her car was in a sorry state after the accident.*

sort¹ /sɔːt/ **noun 1** ⓐ [C] a type of something: *We both like the same sort of music.* ○ *What sort of shoes does she wear?* ○ *I'm going to have a salad of some sort.* **2 all sorts of sth** ⓐ many different types of something **3 sort of** informal ⓑ used to describe a situation approximately: *It's a sort of pale orange colour.* **4 (and) that sort of thing** informal ⓑ used to show that what you have just said is only an example from a larger group of things: *They sell souvenirs, postcards, that sort of thing.* **5 of sorts** informal used to describe something that is not a typical example: *He managed to make a curtain of sorts out of an old sheet.*

sort² /sɔːt/ **verb 1** ⓑ [T] to arrange things into different groups or types or into an order: *They sort the paper into white and coloured for recycling.* ○ *The names are sorted alphabetically.* **2 be sorted/get sth sorted** UK informal If something is sorted or you get something sorted, you successfully deal with it and find a solution or agreement: *Did you manage to get everything sorted?*

PHRASAL VERBS **sort sth out** ⓑ to successfully deal with something, such as a problem or difficult situation: *Have you sorted out your schedule yet?* ● **sort through sth** to look at a number of things to organize them or to find something: *I had the sad task of sorting through her papers after she died.*

so-so /ˈsəʊsəʊ/ **adj** informal not very good, but not bad: *"Are you feeling better today?" "So-so."*

soufflé /ˈsuːfleɪ/ ⓤ /suːˈfleɪ/ **noun** [C, U] a light food made by baking the white part of eggs: *chocolate/cheese soufflé*

sought /sɔːt/ past of seek

sought-after /ˈsɔːtˌɑːftəʳ/ **adj** wanted by lots of people, but difficult to get: *a house in a sought-after location*

soul /səʊl/ **noun 1** SPIRIT ▷ [C] ⓑ the part of a person that is not their body, which some people believe continues to exist after they die **2** MUSIC ▷ [U] (also **soul music**) ⓐ popular music that expresses deep feelings, originally performed by African-Americans **3** PERSON ▷ [C] informal ⓑ a person: *I didn't see a soul when I went out.* → See also **heart and soul**

S

soulful /ˈsəʊlfəl/ **adj** expressing deep feelings, often sadness: ***soulful eyes***

soulless /ˈsəʊlləs/ **adj** without any interesting or attractive characteristics: *a soulless housing estate*

soul-searching /ˈsəʊlˌsɜːtʃɪŋ/ **noun** [U] careful thought about something to decide if it is the right thing to do: *After much soul-searching, he decided to leave his job.*

sound¹ /saʊnd/ **noun 1** A2 [C, U] something that you hear or that can be heard: *I could **hear** the **sounds** of the city through the open window.* ◦ *She stood completely still, not **making a sound**.* ◦ *Can you turn the sound up (= make a radio, television, etc louder)?* **2 the sound of sth** informal how something seems to be, from what you have been told or heard: *I like the sound of the beef in red wine sauce.* ◦ *He's really enjoying college, **by the sound of it**.*

> **Word partners for sound**
> emit/make/produce a sound • hear/listen to a sound • the sound of sth

sound² /saʊnd/ **verb 1 sound good/interesting/strange, etc** A2 to seem good/interesting/strange, etc, from what you have heard or read: *Your job sounds really interesting.* **2 sound like/as if/as though** B1 to seem like something, from what you have heard or read: *That sounds like a really good idea.* **3 sound angry/happy/rude, etc** B2 to seem angry/happy/rude, etc when you speak: *You don't sound too sure about it.* **4** [I, T] to make a noise: *It looks and **sounds like** a real bird.* ◦ *If the alarm sounds, you must leave the building immediately.*

sound³ /saʊnd/ **adj** good or safe and able to be trusted: ***sound advice/judgment*** ◦ *The building is quite old, but still **structurally sound**.* → Opposite **unsound**

sound⁴ /saʊnd/ **adv sound asleep** in a deep sleep

soundbite /ˈsaʊndbaɪt/ **noun** [C] a short statement that is easy to remember, usually used by a politician to get attention on television, in newspapers, etc

ˈsound ˌcard noun [C] a small piece of electronic equipment inside a computer that makes it able to record and play sound

ˈsound efˌfects noun [plural] B1 sounds that are produced artificially and are intended to sound like real sounds in a play, movie, etc.

soundly /ˈsaʊndli/ **adv 1 sleep soundly** to sleep well **2 soundly beaten/defeated** beaten/defeated easily and by a large amount

soundtrack /ˈsaʊndtræk/ **noun** [C] B2 the music used in a film

soup /suːp/ **noun** [U] A1 a hot, liquid food, made from vegetables, meat, or fish: *chicken/tomato soup* → See colour picture **Food** on page Centre 11

sour¹ /saʊəʳ/ **adj 1** B1 having a sharp, sometimes unpleasant, taste or smell, like a lemon, and not sweet: *These plums are a bit sour.* **2** very unfriendly or unpleasant: *Their relationship suddenly **turned sour**.*

sour² /saʊəʳ/ **verb** [T] to make something unpleasant or unfriendly: *This affair has **soured relations** between the two countries.*

source /sɔːs/ **noun** [C] **1** B2 where something comes from: *a source of income/information* ◦ *Oranges are a good **source of** vitamin C.* **2** someone who gives information to the police, newspapers, etc

> **Word partners for source**
> a [good/important/major, etc] source of sth

ˌsour ˈcream noun [U] (also UK **soured cream**) cream that is made sour by adding special bacteria, used in cooking

south, South /saʊθ/ **noun** [U] **1** A2 the direction that is on your right when you face towards the rising sun **2 the south** A2 the part of an area that is further towards the south than the rest • **south adj** A2 *the south side of the house* • **south adv** A2 towards the south: *Birds fly south in winter.*

southbound /ˈsaʊθbaʊnd/ **adj** going or leading towards the south

southeast, Southeast /ˌsaʊθˈiːst/ **noun** [U] **1** B1 the direction between south and east **2 the southeast** B1 the southeast part of a country • **southeast, Southeast adj, adv**

southeastern, Southeastern /ˌsaʊθˈiːstən/ **adj** in or from the southeast

southerly /ˈsʌðəli/ **adj 1** towards or in the south: *We continued in a southerly direction.* **2** A southerly wind comes from the south.

southern, Southern /ˈsʌðən/ **adj** B1 in or from the south part of an area: *the southern half of the country*

southerner, Southerner /ˈsʌðənəʳ/ **noun** [C] someone from the south part of a country

southernmost /ˈsʌðənməʊst/ **adj** The southernmost part of an area is the part furthest to the south.

south-facing /ˈsaʊθˌfeɪsɪŋ/ **adj** [always before noun] positioned towards the south: *a south-facing garden/window*

the ˌSouth ˈPole noun a point on the Earth's surface that is furthest south

southward, southwards /ˈsaʊθwəd/, /ˈsaʊθwədz/ **adv** B1 towards the south • **southward adj** *a southward direction*

southwest, Southwest /ˌsaʊθˈwest/ **noun** [U] **1** B1 the direction between south and west **2 the southwest** B1 the southwest part of the country • **southwest, Southwest adj, adv**

southwestern, Southwestern /ˌsaʊθˈwestən/ **adj** in or from the southwest

souvenir /ˌsuːvənˈɪəʳ/ **noun** [C] B1 something that you buy or keep to remember a special event or holiday: *a **souvenir shop*** ◦ *I kept the ticket as a **souvenir of** my trip.*

sovereign, Sovereign /ˈsɒvərɪn/ **noun** [C] formal a king or queen

sovereign /ˈsɒvərɪn/ **adj** A sovereign country or state is completely independent. • **sovereignty** /ˈsɒvrənti/ **noun** [U] the power of a country to control its own government

S

ow[1] /səʊ/ **verb** [T] (**sowed**, **sown**, **sowed**) to put seeds into the ground: *to sow seeds/crops*

ow[2] /saʊ/ **noun** [C] a female pig

oya bean /ˈsɔɪəˌbiːn/ **noun** [C] UK (US **soybean**) a bean used to produce oil, and which is used in many foods

oy sauce /ˌsɔɪˈsɔːs/ **noun** [U] a dark brown sauce made from soya beans, used in Chinese and Japanese cooking

pa /spɑː/ **noun** [C] a place where people go to improve their health by exercising or by having baths in special water: *a **health spa*** ∘ *a spa town*

pace[1] /speɪs/ **noun 1** [C, U] **A2** an empty area that is available to be used: *a **parking space*** ∘ *We need more **open spaces** for children to play in.* ∘ *There wasn't enough **space** for everyone.* ∘ [+ to do sth] *We don't have the space to store it all.* **2** [U] **B1** the area outside the Earth: *They plan to send another satellite into space.* ∘ *space travel* **3** **in the space of six weeks/three hours, etc** during a period of six weeks/three hours, etc: *It all happened in the space of 10 minutes.* → See also **breathing space, outer space**

> 🗹 Word partners for **space**
>
> create/make space • fill a/occupy a/take up space • space for sb/sth • an open space

---

pace[2] /speɪs/ **verb** [T] to arrange things so that there is some distance or time between them: [often passive] *They will have to be spaced at least two metres apart.*

pace bar **noun** [C, usually singular] on a computer keyboard, the long key below the letter keys that you press in order to make a space between words

pacecraft /ˈspeɪskrɑːft/ **noun** [C] (plural **space-craft**) a vehicle that can travel outside the Earth and into space

paceman /ˈspeɪsˌmæn/ **noun** [C] (plural **space-men**) a man who travels into space

paceship /ˈspeɪsʃɪp/ **noun** [C] a vehicle that can travel outside the Earth and into space, especially one which is carrying people

pace shuttle **noun** [C] a vehicle in which people travel into space and back again

pacious /ˈspeɪʃəs/ **adj** large and with a lot of space: *a spacious apartment/office*

pade /speɪd/ **noun** [C]
1 a tool with a long handle and a flat, metal part at one end used for digging
2 **spades** playing cards with black leaf shapes on them: *the ace of spades*

spade

paghetti /spəˈɡeti/ **noun** [U] long, thin pieces of pasta

pam /spæm/ **noun** [U] emails that you do not want, usually advertisements • **spam verb** [T] • **spammer noun** [C] a person who sends spam

pan /spæn/ **noun** [C] **1** the period of time that something exists or happens: *a short **attention span*** ∘ *an average **life span** of seventy years*

2 the length of something from one end to the other: *a **wing span** of five metres* • **span verb** [T] (**spanning**, **spanned**) to exist or continue for a particular distance or length of time: *Her acting **career spanned** almost forty years.*

spaniel /ˈspænjəl/ **noun** [C] a dog with long hair and long ears

spank /spæŋk/ **verb** [T] to hit someone, usually a child, on their bottom

spanner /ˈspænər/ **noun** [C] UK (US **wrench**) a tool with a round end that is used to turn nuts and bolts (= metal objects used to fasten things together) → See picture at **tool**

spar /spɑːr/ **verb** [I] (**sparring**, **sparred**) to fight or argue with someone in a friendly way

spare[1] /speər/ **adj 1** **B1** If something is spare, it is available to use, because it is extra and not being used: *a spare bedroom* ∘ *spare cash* • ***spare parts*** **2** **spare time** **A2** time when you are not working: *I enjoy gardening **in my spare time**.*

spare[2] /speər/ **noun** [C] an extra thing that is not being used and which can be used instead of a part which is broken, lost, etc

spare[3] /speər/ **verb 1** [T] to give time or money to someone: *I have to go soon, but I can spare a few minutes.* ∘ [+ two objects] *Can you spare me some change?* **2** [+ two objects] to prevent someone from having to experience something unpleasant: [often passive] *I was spared the embarrassment of having to sing in front of everybody.* **3** **to spare** If you have time, money, etc to spare, you have more than you need: *I arrived at the station with more than an hour to spare.* **4** **spare no effort/expense, etc** to use a lot of effort/ expense, etc to do something: [+ to do sth] *We will spare no effort to find out who did this.* **5** **spare sb's life** to not kill someone → See also **spare a thought**[1] **for sb**

sparingly /ˈspeərɪŋli/ **adv** carefully using only a very small amount of something: *to eat/drink sparingly* • **sparing adj**

spark[1] /spɑːk/ **noun** [C] **1** FIRE ▷ a very small, bright piece of burning material: *The fire was caused by a spark from a cigarette.* **2** ELECTRICITY ▷ a small flash of light caused by electricity **3** START ▷ a small idea or event that causes something bigger to start: *a spark of hope/inspiration*

spark[2] /spɑːk/ **verb** [T] (also **spark off**) to cause an argument, fight, etc to start happening: *to **spark** a **debate/protest*** ∘ *to **spark criticism/ fears***

sparkle[1] /ˈspɑːkl/ **verb** [I] **1** to shine brightly because of reflected light: *water sparkling in the sun* ∘ *Her **eyes sparkled** with excitement.* **2** to do something in a special or exciting way: *The concert gave her an opportunity to sparkle.*

sparkle[2] /ˈspɑːkl/ **noun 1** [C, U] the light from something reflecting on a shiny surface **2** [U] the quality of being special or exciting: *The performance lacked a bit of sparkle.*

sparkling /ˈspɑːklɪŋ/ **adj 1** **B2** shining brightly because of reflected light **2** special or exciting: *a **sparkling performance*** ∘ *sparkling*

S

conversation **3 sparkling water/wine** ⓑ1 water/wine with bubbles in it

spark plug noun [C] a part in an engine that makes the fuel burn

sparrow /ˈspærəʊ/ noun [C] a small, brown bird that is common in towns and cities

sparse /spɑːs/ adj **1** existing only in small amounts over a large area: *sparse population/vegetation* **2** A room that is sparse contains little furniture and does not seem very comfortable. • **sparsely** adv *sparsely populated/furnished*

spartan /ˈspɑːtən/ adj very simple and not comfortable or luxurious: *The rooms were clean but spartan.*

spasm /ˈspæzəm/ noun [C, U] a sudden movement in your body caused when a muscle gets tight in a way that you cannot control: *a back/muscle spasm* ∘ *to go into spasm*

spasmodic /spæzˈmɒdɪk/ adj happening suddenly for short periods of time and not in a regular way

spat /spæt/ past of spit

spate /speɪt/ noun **a spate of accidents/crimes/thefts, etc** a large number of bad things that happen at about the same time

spatial /ˈspeɪʃəl/ adj relating to the position, area, and size of things • **spatially** adv

spatter /ˈspætər/ verb [T] to cover someone or something with small drops of liquid without intending to: [often passive] *His shirt was spattered with blood.*

spatula /ˈspætjələ/ noun [C] a tool with a wide flat blade, used in cooking for mixing, spreading, or lifting food → See colour picture **The Kitchen** on page Centre 2

spawn /spɔːn/ verb [T] to cause a lot of other things to be produced or to exist: *Her death spawned several films and books.*

speak /spiːk/ verb (**spoke, spoken**) **1** [I] ⓐ1 to say something using your voice: *to speak loudly/quietly* ∘ *There was complete silence – nobody spoke.* **2 speak to sb** (mainly US **speak with sb**) ⓐ1 to talk to someone: *Could I speak to Mr Davis, please?* ∘ *Have you spoken with your new neighbors yet?* **3 speak about/of sth** to talk about something: *He refused to speak about the matter in public.* **4 speak English/French/German, etc** ⓐ1 to be able to communicate in English/French/German, etc: *Do you speak English?* **5** [I] to make a speech to a large group of people: *She was invited to speak at a conference in Madrid.* **6 speak for/on behalf of sb** to express the feelings, opinions, etc of another person or of a group of people: *I've been chosen to speak on behalf of the whole class.* **7 generally/personally, etc speaking** ⓑ2 used to explain that you are talking about something in a general/personal, etc way: *Personally speaking, I don't like cats.* **8 so to speak** used to explain that the words you are using do not have their usual meaning → See also **speak/talk of the devil**, **speak your mind¹**

PHRASAL VERBS **speak out** to give your opinion about something in public, especially on a subject that you have strong feelings about: *He decided to speak out against the bombing.* • **speak up 1** ⓑ2 to say something in a louder voice so that people can hear you: *Could you speak up a bit? I can't hear you.* **2** to give your opinion about something, especially about a problem or to support someone else: *It's getting bad – it's time someone spoke up about it.*

⚠ Common learner error: **speak** or **talk**?

Remember that you **speak** a language. You do not 'talk' it.
She speaks French.
~~She talks French.~~

speaker /ˈspiːkər/ noun [C] **1** ⓐ2 the part of a radio, CD player, etc which the sound comes out of → See colour picture **The Living Room** on page Centre 4 **2 an English/French/German, etc speaker** ⓑ1 someone who can speak English, French, etc **3** ⓑ1 someone who makes a speech to a group of people: *a guest speaker*

spear /spɪər/ noun [C] a long weapon with a sharp point at one end used for hunting

spearhead /ˈspɪəhed/ verb [T] to lead an attack or series of actions: *to spearhead a campaign*

spearmint /ˈspɪəmɪnt/ noun [U] a type of mint (= a herb used as a flavour for sweets): *spearmint chewing gum*

➕ Other ways of saying **special**

If someone or something is special because they are better than usual, you can describe them as **exceptional** or **outstanding**:
*Their standard of acting was very high but there was one **exceptional/outstanding** performance.*

The adjective **extraordinary** is sometimes used to describe someone or something that is special in a surprising way:
*Her capacity to remember things is **extraordinary**.*
*She has an **extraordinary** talent.*

The adjectives **deluxe** and **superior** are sometimes used to describe things which you can buy which are special because they are particularly good quality:
*The shop assistant tried to sell us the **deluxe/superior** model.*

The adjectives **rare** and **unique** are sometimes used instead of special when it means 'unusual':
*This is a **rare/unique** opportunity to see inside the building.*

If something is special because it is of extremely good quality, you can describe it as **out of this world**:
*Their chocolate cake is just **out of this world**.*

special¹ /ˈspeʃəl/ adj **1** ⓐ2 better or more important than usual things: *a special friend* ∘ *I'm cooking **something special** for her birthday.* **2 special attention/care/treatment** ⓑ2 treatment that is better than usual **3 special offer** UK ⓑ1 a price that is lower than usual: *A*

S

bought them because they were **on special offer.**
4 ⬤ different from normal things, or used for a particular purpose: *You need to use a special kind of paint.*

special² /ˈspeʃ°l/ **noun** [C] **1** a television programme made for a particular reason or occasion and not part of a series: *The Christmas special had 24.3 million viewers.* **2** a dish in a restaurant that is not usually available: *Today's specials are written on the board.*

special edu'cation noun [U] (also **special ed**) US education for children who need to be taught in a different way because they have an illness or condition that makes it difficult for them to do the things that other people do

special ef'fects noun an unusual type of action in a film, or an entertainment on stage, created by using special equipment: *The Harry Potter film includes some very frightening special effects.*

specialist /ˈspeʃ°lɪst/ **noun** [C] ⬤ someone who has a lot of experience, knowledge, or skill in a particular subject: *a cancer/software specialist* ◦ *He's **a specialist in** childhood illnesses.*

> 🗹 Word partners for **specialist**
>
> a **leading** specialist • a specialist **in** sth • specialist **knowledge**

speciality /ˌspeʃiˈæləti/ **noun** [C] UK (US **specialty**, ⓤⓢ /ˈspeʃ°lti/) a product, skill, etc that a person or place is especially known for: *We tasted a local speciality made from goat's cheese.*

specialize (also UK **-ise**) /ˈspeʃ°laɪz/ **verb** [I] ⬤ to spend most of your time studying one particular subject or doing one type of business: *She works for a company **specializing in** business law.* • **specialization** /ˌspeʃ°laɪˈzeɪʃ°n/ **noun** [U]

specialized (also UK **-ised**) /ˈspeʃ°laɪzd/ **adj** relating to a particular subject or activity and not general: *specialized equipment/language*

specially /ˈspeʃ°li/ **adv** ⬤ for a particular purpose: *They searched the building with specially trained dogs.* ◦ *I made this **specially for** you.*

> ⓘ Common learner error: **specially** or **especially?**
>
> Sometimes these two words both mean 'for a particular purpose'.
>   *I cooked this meal specially/especially for you.*
> **Specially** is often used before an adjective made from a past participle, e.g. specially prepared, specially trained.
>   *He uses a specially adapted wheelchair.*
> **Especially** is used to give emphasis to a person or thing. This word is not usually used at the beginning of a sentence.
>   *I like all kinds of films, especially horror films.*

special 'needs adj describes something that is intended for people who have an illness or condition that makes it difficult for them to do the things that other people do: *a special needs school*

species /ˈspiːʃiːz/ **noun** [C] (plural **species**) ⬤ a group of plants or animals that share similar characteristics: *a rare species of bird* → See Note at **race¹**

specific /spəˈsɪfɪk/ **adj 1** ⬤ used to refer to a particular thing and not something general: *a **specific purpose/reason*** ◦ *Could we arrange a specific time to meet?* **2** exact or containing details: *Could you **be** more **specific about** the problem?*

specifically /spəˈsɪfɪk°li/ **adv 1** for a particular reason, purpose, etc: *They're designed **specifically for** children.* ◦ [+ to do sth] *She bought it specifically to wear at the wedding.* **2** exactly or in detail: *I specifically told them that she doesn't eat meat.*

specification /ˌspesɪfɪˈkeɪʃ°n/ **noun** [C] formal a detailed description of how something should be done, made, etc: *They are made exactly **to** the customer's **specifications.***

specifics /spəˈsɪfɪks/ **noun** [plural] exact details about something: *I can't comment on the specifics of the case.*

specify /ˈspesɪfaɪ/ **verb** [T] ⬤ to say or describe something in a detailed way: [+ question word] *They didn't specify what colour they wanted.*

specimen /ˈspesəmɪn/ **noun** [C] **1** an animal, plant, etc used as an example of its type, especially for scientific study: *This is one of the museum's finest specimens.* **2** a small amount of a substance, such as blood, that is used for a test

speck /spek/ **noun** [C] a very small spot or a very small amount of something: *a **speck of dirt/dust*** ◦ *I watched the car until it was just a tiny speck in the distance.*

speckled /ˈspekld/ **adj** covered in a pattern of very small spots: *a speckled egg*

specs /speks/ **noun** [plural] informal short for **spectacles**

spectacle /ˈspektəkl/ **noun** [C] **1** an event that is exciting or unusual to watch **2** **make a spectacle of yourself** to do something that makes you look stupid and that makes other people look at you: *He got drunk and made a real spectacle of himself.*

spectacles /ˈspektəklz/ **noun** [plural] old-fashioned glasses: *a pair of spectacles*

spectacular /spekˈtækjələʳ/ **adj** ⬤ extremely good, exciting, or surprising: *a **spectacular success*** ◦ *a **spectacular view*** ◦ *spectacular scenery* • **spectacularly adv** *a spectacularly beautiful country*

spectator /spekˈteɪtəʳ/ **noun** [C] ⬤ someone who watches an event, sport, etc: *They won 4-0 in front of over 40,000 cheering spectators.* • **spectate** /spekˈteɪt/ **verb** [I] to watch an event, sport, etc

spectre UK (US **specter**) /ˈspektəʳ/ **noun 1 the spectre of sth** the idea of something unpleasant that might happen in the future: *This attack **raises the spectre of** a return to racial violence.* **2** [C] literary a ghost (= dead person's spirit)

spectrum /ˈspektrəm/ **noun** [C] (plural **spectra**) **1** all the different ideas, opinions, possibilities, etc that exist: *He has support from **across the***

S

whole political **spectrum**. **2** the set of colours into which light can be separated

speculate /'spekjəleɪt/ **verb** [I, T] to guess possible answers to a question when you do not have enough information to be certain: *The police refused to **speculate about** the cause of the accident.* ○ [+ that] *The newspapers have speculated that they will get married next year.*

speculation /ˌspekjə'leɪʃən/ **noun** [U] guesses about something without having enough information to be certain: [+ that] *She has dismissed the claims as **pure speculation**.*

speculative /'spekjələtɪv/ **adj** based on a guess and not on information: *The article was dismissed as **highly/purely speculative**.* • **speculatively** adv

sped /sped/ past of speed

speech /spiːtʃ/ **noun 1** [U] 🔵 someone's ability to talk, or an example of someone talking: *His speech was very slow and difficult to understand.* ○ *These changes can be seen in both speech and writing.* **2** [C] 🔵 a formal talk that someone gives to a group of people: *I had to **make a speech** at my brother's wedding.* **3 free speech/freedom of speech** the right to say or write what you want → See also **figure of speech**, **reported speech**

> ❗ Common learner error: **make/give a speech**
>
> Be careful to choose the correct verb.
> *I have to make a speech.*
> ~~I have to do a speech.~~
> *He gave a speech at the conference.*
> ~~He said a speech at the conference.~~

> 🗒 Word partners for **speech**
>
> careful/continuous/human/normal speech • slur your speech

speechless /'spiːtʃləs/ **adj** unable to speak because you are so angry, shocked, surprised, etc: *I couldn't believe what he was telling me – I was speechless.*

speed¹ /spiːd/ **noun 1** [C, U] 🔵 how fast something moves or happens: *high/low speed* ○ *He was travelling **at a speed of** 90 mph.* **2** [U] 🔵 very fast movement: *He put on a sudden burst of speed.*

IDIOM **up to speed** having all the most recent information about a subject or activity: *The course should bring you up to speed with the latest techniques.*

> 🗒 Word partners for **speed**
>
> gain/gather/pick up speed • lower/reduce sb's/sth's speed • reach a speed of [100kph/70mph, etc] • at a speed of [100kph/70mph, etc]

speed² /spiːd/ **verb** (**sped**, **speeded**) **1 speed along/down/past,** etc to move somewhere or happen very fast: *The three men jumped into a car*

and sped away. **2 be speeding** to be driving faster than you are allowed to

PHRASAL VERB **speed (sth) up** to move or happen faster, or to make something move or happen faster: *Can you try to speed up a bit please?*

speedboat /'spiːdbəʊt/ **noun** [C] a small, fast boat with an engine

'speed ˌdating noun [U] a way to meet people for possible romantic relationships, in which you talk with lots of people for a short amount of time to see if you like them

'speed ˌdial noun [U] a feature on a telephone that makes it possible for you to call a number by pressing only one button • **speed dial verb** [I, T]

speeding /'spiːdɪŋ/ **noun** [U] driving faster than you are allowed to: *They were stopped by the police for speeding.*

'speed ˌlimit noun [C] the fastest speed that a vehicle is allowed to travel on a particular road: *to **break** the **speed limit***

speedometer /spiː'dɒmɪtər/ **noun** [C] a piece of equipment in a vehicle that shows how fast it is moving → See colour picture **Car** on page Centre 7

speedy /'spiːdi/ **adj** done quickly: *a **speedy recovery*** • **speedily** adv

spell¹ /spel/ **verb** (**spelled**, also UK **spelt**) **1** [T] 🔵 to write down or tell someone the letters that are used to make a word: *How do you spell that?* ○ *Her name's spelt S-I-A-N.* **2** [I] If you can spell you know how to write the words of a language correctly: *My grammar's all right, but I can't spell.* **3 spell disaster/trouble, etc** If something spells disaster, trouble, etc, you think it will cause something bad to happen in the future: *The new regulations could spell disaster for small businesses.*

PHRASAL VERB **spell sth out** to explain something in a very clear way with details: *They sent me a letter, **spelling out the details** of the agreement.*

spell² /spel/ **noun** [C] **1** a period of time: *a short spell in Australia* ○ *a spell of dry weather* **2** a magic instruction: *The witch **cast a spell** over him and he turned into a frog.*

spell-check (also **spellcheck**) /'speltʃek/ **verb** [T] to use a computer program to make certain that the words in a document have the correct letters in the correct order • **spell-check noun** [C] *to run a spell-check*

spelling /'spelɪŋ/ **noun 1** [C] 🔵 how a particular word is spelt: *There are two possible spellings of this word.* ○ **spelling mistakes 2** [U] 🔵 someone's ability to spell words: *My spelling is terrible.*

'spelling ˌbee noun [C] US a competition in which people, often students, try to spell difficult words

spelt /spelt/ UK past of spell

spend /spend/ **verb** [T] (**spent**) **1** 🔵 to use money to buy or pay for something: *The company has **spent** $1.9 million **on** improving its computer network.* ○ *She **spends** too much **money** on clothes.* ○ *How much did you spend?* **2** 🔵 to use time doing something or being somewhere: *He spent 18 months working on the project.* ○ *He'* *planning to* **spend** *some* **time** *at home with his family.* ◦ *How long did you spend in Edinburgh?*

Other ways of saying spend

The most common alternative is the verb **pay**:

When you booked the tickets, how much did you **pay**?

I **paid** *an extra £30 to get a double room.*

The verb **invest** is used when someone spends money on something because they hope to get a profit:

She's **invested** *all her savings in the business.*

If someone spends a lot of money on something, the phrasal verb **pay out** is sometimes used:

I've just **paid out** *£700 to get the car fixed.*

If someone spends a lot of money on something that they want but do not need, you can use the phrasal verb **splash out**:

We've just **splashed out** *£12,000 on a new kitchen.*

The phrasal verb **dip into** is sometimes used when someone spends part of a supply of money that they have been keeping:

We had to **dip into** *our savings to pay for the repairs.*

If someone spends money on something when they do not want to, the phrasal verbs **fork out** and **shell out** are often used:

We had to **shell out** *two thousand euros to get the roof fixed.*

I'm not going to **fork out** *another five hundred quid for their tickets.*

---

spending /ˈspendɪŋ/ **noun** [U] the money that is used for a particular purpose, especially by a government or organization: *government spending on health* ◦ *spending cuts*

spent¹ /spent/ **adj** already used, so not useful or effective any more: *spent bullets*

spent² /spent/ past of spend

sperm /spɜːm/ **noun** [C] (plural **sperm**) a small cell produced by a male animal that joins an egg from a female animal to create a baby

spew /spjuː/ **verb** [I, T] (also **spew out**) If something spews liquid or gas, or liquid or gas spews from something, it flows out in large amounts: *The factory spews out clouds of black smoke.*

SPF /ˌespiːˈef/ **noun** [C] abbreviation for sun protection factor: the letters and numbers on a bottle of sunscreen (= a substance which protects your skin in the sun) which shows how effective the sunscreen is

sphere /sfɪəʳ/ **noun** [C] **1** a subject or area of knowledge, work, etc: *the political sphere* **2** a round object shaped like a ball

---

Word partners for sphere

in a sphere • a sphere of **activity/influence/ life**

---

spice¹ /spaɪs/ **noun 1** [C, U] 🔵 a substance made from a plant, which is used to give a special taste to food: *herbs and spices* **2** [U] something that

makes something else more exciting: *A scandal or two* **adds** *a little* **spice** *to office life.*

spice² /spaɪs/ **verb** [T] to add spice to something: [often passive] *The apples were* **spiced with** *nutmeg and cinnamon.*

PHRASAL VERB **spice sth up** to make something more interesting or exciting: *You can always spice up a talk with a few pictures.*

spicy /ˈspaɪsi/ **adj** 🔵 containing strong flavours from spice: **spicy food** ◦ *a spicy sauce*

spider /ˈspaɪdəʳ/ **noun** [C] 🔵 a small creature with eight long legs which catches insects in a web (= structure like a net)

spidery /ˈspaɪdəri/ **adj** thin and often untidy, looking like a spider: *spidery handwriting*

spike /spaɪk/ **noun** [C] a long, thin piece of metal, wood, etc with a sharp point at one end • **spiky adj** covered with spikes or having that appearance: *spiky hair*

spill /spɪl/ **verb** [T] (**spilled**, also UK **spilt**) 🔵 to pour liquid somewhere without intending to: *Someone at the party spilled red wine on the carpet.* • **spill noun** [C] *an oil spill*

PHRASAL VERBS **spill out 1** to flow or fall out of a container: *The contents of the truck spilled out across the road.* **2** If people spill out of a place, large numbers of them move out of it: *The crowd spilled out onto the street.* • **spill over** If a bad situation spills over, it begins to have an unpleasant effect on another situation or group of people: *There are fears that the war could spill over into neighbouring countries.*

spin¹ /spɪn/ **verb** [I, T] (**spinning, spun**) **1** If something spins or you spin something, it turns around and around quickly: *The car spun across the road.* **2** to make thread by twisting together cotton, wool, etc

PHRASAL VERBS **spin (sb) around/round** If you spin around, or someone spins you around, your body turns quickly to face the opposite direction. • **spin sth out** to make something such as a story or an activity last as long as possible

spin² /spɪn/ **noun 1** TURN ▷ [C, U] the movement of something turning round very quickly: *The skater did a series of amazing spins and jumps.* **2** IDEA ▷ [no plural] a clever way of expressing an idea to make it seem better than it really is, especially in politics: *This report* **puts** *a different* **spin on** *the issue.* **3** CAR ▷ [no plural] informal a short journey by car

spinach /ˈspɪnɪtʃ/ **noun** [U] 🔵 a vegetable with large, dark green leaves and a strong taste

spinal /ˈspaɪnəl/ **adj** relating to the spine: *a spinal injury*

spin doctor noun [C] informal someone whose job is to make ideas, events, etc seem better than they really are, especially in politics

spine /spaɪn/ **noun** [C] **1** the long structure of bones down the centre of your back, which supports your body **2** the narrow part of a book cover where the pages are joined together and which you can see when it is on a shelf

spineless /ˈspaɪnləs/ **adj** A spineless person has a weak personality and is frightened easily.

spin-off /ˈspɪnɒf/ **noun** [C] a product that develops from another more important product

spinster /ˈspɪnstəʳ/ **noun** [C] old-fashioned a woman who has never married

spiral /ˈspaɪərəl/ **noun** [C] a shape made by a curve turning around and around a central point: *a spiral staircase*

 spiral

IDIOM **a downward spiral** a situation that is getting worse very quickly, and which is difficult to control

spire /spaɪəʳ/ **noun** [C] a tall, pointed tower on the top of a building such as a church

spirit¹ /ˈspɪrɪt/ **noun 1 FEELING** ▷ [no plural] ⑫ the way people think and feel about something: *a spirit of optimism* ∘ *Everyone soon got into the spirit of* (= started to enjoy) *the carnival – singing, dancing, and having fun.* **2 community/team, etc spirit** a feeling of enthusiasm about being part of a group **3 in good/high/low spirits** ⑫ feeling good/excited/unhappy **4 NOT BODY** ▷ [C] ⑫ the part of a person that is not their body, which some people believe continues to exist after they die **5 NOT ALIVE** ▷ [C] ⑫ something that people believe exists but does not have a physical body, such as a ghost: *evil spirits* **6 the spirit of the law/an agreement, etc** the intended meaning of the law/an agreement, etc and not just the written details **7 DRINK** ▷ [C] a strong alcoholic drink, such as whisky or vodka: [usually plural] *I don't often drink spirits.*

spirit² /ˈspɪrɪt/ **verb be spirited away/out/to, etc** to be moved somewhere secretly: *He was spirited away to a secret hideout in Mexico.*

spirited /ˈspɪrɪtɪd/ **adj** enthusiastic and determined, often in a difficult situation: *a spirited performance*

spiritual /ˈspɪrɪtʃuəl/ **adj** ⑫ relating to deep feelings and beliefs, especially religious beliefs: *a spiritual leader*

spiritualism /ˈspɪrɪtʃuᵊlɪzᵊm/ **noun** [U] the belief that living people can communicate with people who are dead • **spiritualist noun** [C] someone who is involved with spiritualism

spit¹ /spɪt/ **verb** [I, T] (**spitting, spat**, also US **spit**) **1** to force out the liquid in your mouth: *I don't like to see people spitting in public.* ∘ *He took a mouthful of coffee and then spat it out.* **2 Spit it out!** informal used to tell someone to say more quickly what it is they want to say: *Come on, spit it out!*

spit² /spɪt/ **noun 1** [U] informal the liquid that is made in your mouth **2** [C] a long, thin stick used for cooking meat over a fire

spite /spaɪt/ **noun 1 in spite of sth** ⑪ although something exists or happens: *He still smokes, in spite of all the health warnings.* **2** [U] a feeling of anger towards someone which makes you want to hurt or upset them: *He hid my new jacket out of spite.*

spiteful /ˈspaɪtfᵊl/ **adj** intentionally hurting or upsetting someone: *That was a very spiteful thing to do.* • **spitefully adv**

splash¹ /splæʃ/ **verb** [I, T] **1** ⑫ If a liquid splashes or you splash a liquid, drops of it hit or fall on something: *The paint splashed onto his new shirt.* ∘ *She splashed some cold water on her face.* **2 splash about/around/through, etc** ⑫ to move in water so that drops of it go in all directions: *The children splashed about in the puddles.* **3 be splashed across/all over sth** to be the main story in a newspaper, usually on the front page, which many people will see: *His picture was splashed across the front pages of all the newspapers the next morning.*

PHRASAL VERB **splash out (sth)** UK to spend a lot of money on something that you want but do not need: *He splashed out on the best champagne for the party.*

splash² /splæʃ/ **noun** [C] **1** a drop of liquid that has fallen on something, or the mark made by it: *There were several small splashes of paint on the carpet.* **2** ⑫ the sound of something falling into or moving in water: *They sat listening to the splash of raindrops on the lake.* **3 a splash of colour** a small area of colour that makes something look brighter: *The flowers added a splash of colour to the room.*

IDIOM **make a splash** informal to get a lot of public attention: *The film made quite a splash in the US.*

splatter /ˈsplætəʳ/ **verb** [I, T] If a liquid splatters or you splatter it, it falls onto a surface, often in many small drops: [often passive] *His clothes were splattered with blood.*

splendid /ˈsplendɪd/ **adj** very good or very beautiful, special, etc: *a splendid idea* ∘ *a splendid view* • **splendidly adv**

splendour UK (US **splendor**) /ˈsplendəʳ/ **noun** [C, U] the quality of being extremely beautiful or luxurious: *Tourists marvelled at the splendour of the medieval cathedral.*

splinter /ˈsplɪntəʳ/ **noun** [C] **1** a small, sharp piece of wood, glass, etc which has broken from a large piece: *I've got a splinter in my finger.* **2 a splinter group** a small group of people that forms after leaving a larger organization, such as a political party • **splinter verb** [I] to break into small, sharp pieces

split¹ /splɪt/ **verb** (**splitting, split**) **1 BREAK** ▷ [I, T] ⑫ If something splits or if you split it, it tears so that there is a long, thin hole in it: *He split his trousers when he bent over.* ∘ *Her shoes were splitting apart at the sides.* **2 DIVIDE** ▷ [I, T] (also **split up**) ⑫ to divide into smaller parts or groups, or to divide something into smaller parts or groups: *The children split up into three groups.* **3 SHARE** ▷ [T] to share something by dividing it into smaller parts: *The cost of the wedding will be split between the two families.* **4 DISAGREE** ▷ [I, T] If a group of people splits, or something splits them, they disagree and form smaller groups: [often passive] *The government*

S

was **split on** the issue of hunting. → See also **split hairs**

PHRASAL VERB **split up** ⓑ If two people split up, they end their relationship: She **split up with** her boyfriend.

plit² /split/ noun [C] **1** BREAK ▷ a long, thin hole in something where it has broken apart: There's a **split in** my trousers. **2** DISAGREEMENT ▷ the division of a group of people into smaller groups because they disagree about something: This issue is likely to cause a major **split in** the party. **3** RELATIONSHIP ▷ the end of a marriage or relationship: Very few of their friends were surprised when they announced their split last week.

┌─────────────────────────────────────┐
│ ⨯ Word partners for **split (noun)** │
│   │
│ cause/create a split • a split **develops** • a │
│ split **between** sb and sb • a split **in** sth • a │
│ split **on/over** sth │
└─────────────────────────────────────┘

plit³ /split/ adj **a split second** a very short period of time: It was all over in a split second. ° a **split second decision**

plitting 'headache noun [C] a very bad pain in your head: I've got a splitting headache.

plurge /splɜːdʒ/ verb [I, T] to spend a lot of money on something that you want but do not need: We could either save the money or splurge **on** a new car. • **splurge** noun [C]

┌─────────────────────────────────────┐
│ ✚ Other ways of saying **spoil**   │
│   │
│ **Ruin** is a very common alternative to 'spoil': │
│ I put too much salt in the sauce and **ruined** │
│ it. │
│ The verb **deface** is sometimes used when │
│ someone spoils the appearance of something │
│ by writing or drawing on it: │
│ Many of the library books had been **defaced**. │
│ The verb **disfigure** is sometimes used when │
│ a person's physical appearance has been │
│ spoilt: │
│ Her face was **disfigured** by the scar. │
│ If something spoils a friendship or other rela │
│ tionship, you can use the verbs **sour** or │
│ **poison**: │
│ The long dispute has **poisoned/soured** rela │
│ tions between the two countries. │
│ In informal situations you can use the │
│ phrasal verbs **mess up** and **screw up** to say │
│ that something has been spoilt: │
│ Laurie's illness has completely **messed up** all │
│ our holiday plans. │
│ That new software has really **screwed up** my │
│ computer. │
└─────────────────────────────────────┘

poil /spɔɪl/ verb (spoiled, spoilt) **1** MAKE BAD ▷ [T] ⓑ to stop something from being enjoyable or successful: The picnic was spoiled by the bad weather. **2** CHILD ▷ [T] If you spoil a child, you let them have anything they want or do anything they want, usually making them badly behaved. **3** TREAT WELL ▷ [T] to treat someone very well, buying them things or doing things for them: He's always sending flowers – he absolutely spoils

me! **4** FOOD ▷ [I] formal If food spoils, it starts to decay and you cannot eat it.

spoils /spɔɪlz/ noun [plural] formal things that are taken by the winners of a war: **the spoils of war**

spoilt /spɔɪlt/ adj UK (US **spoiled** /spɔɪld/) badly behaved because you are always given what you want or allowed to do what you want: He was behaving like a **spoilt child**.

spoke¹ /spəʊk/ noun [C] one of the thin pieces of metal that connects the middle of a wheel to the outside edge, for example, on a bicycle

spoke² /spəʊk/ past tense of speak

spoken /'spəʊkən/ past participle of speak

spokesman, spokeswoman /'spəʊksmən/, /'spəʊks,wʊmən/ noun [C] (plural **spokesmen**, **spokeswomen**) a man/woman who is chosen to speak officially for a group or organization: A spokesman for the company refused to comment on the reports.

spokesperson /'spəʊks,pɜːsən/ noun [C] (plural **spokespeople**) someone who is chosen to speak officially for a group or organization

sponge /spʌndʒ/ noun [C, U] **1** a soft substance full of small holes, which absorbs liquid very easily and is used for washing things **2** (also 'sponge cake) a soft, light cake

sponge

spongy /'spʌndʒi/ adj soft and full of small holes

sponsor¹ /'spɒnsər/ verb [T] ⓑ to give money to someone to support an activity, event, or organization, sometimes as a way to advertise your company or product: The event is sponsored by local companies. ° UK a sponsored walk (= a walk for charity) • **sponsorship** noun [U] an arrangement in which someone gives money to support something

sponsor² /'spɒnsər/ noun [C] ⓑ a person or organization that gives money to support an activity, event, etc

spontaneous /spɒn'teɪniəs/ adj happening naturally and suddenly and without being planned: a spontaneous reaction ° The crowd broke into spontaneous applause. • **spontaneity** /,spɒntə'neɪəti/ noun [U] the quality of being spontaneous • **spontaneously** adv

spoof /spuːf/ noun [C] a funny television programme, film, article, etc that copies the style of a real programme, film, article, etc: They did a **spoof of** the Oscars, giving awards for the worst films of the year.

spooky /'spuːki/ adj informal strange and frightening: There's something spooky about that place.

spoon /spuːn/ noun [C] ⓐ an object with a handle and a round, curved part at one end, used for eating and serving food: knives, forks, and spoons • **spoon** verb [T] to move or serve food using a spoon: Spoon the sauce over the fish.

spoonful /'spuːnfʊl/ noun [C] the amount of something that can be held on a spoon: Then add a spoonful of yoghurt.

S

sporadic /spəˈrædɪk/ **adj** not happening regularly or happening in different places: *sporadic violence* • **sporadically adv**

sport¹ /spɔːt/ **noun 1** [C] **ⓐ** a game or activity that people do to keep healthy or for enjoyment, often competing against each other: *winter sports* ∘ *team sports* → See colour picture **Sports 1 & 2** on page on pages Centre 14, 15 **2** [U] UK (US **sports**) **ⓐ** all types of physical activity that people do to keep healthy or for enjoyment → See also **blood sport**

⟦ **Z** Word partners for **sport**

do/play a sport • **spectator/team** sports ⟧

sport² /spɔːt/ **verb** [T] humorous to wear something, especially something that people notice: *He turned up sporting a bright red baseball cap and sunglasses.*

sporting /ˈspɔːtɪŋ/ **adj** relating to sports: *a sporting hero*

sports car noun [C] a car designed to go very fast, often with only two seats and an open roof

sports centre noun [C] UK (US **sports center**) **ⓐ** a building with places where you can play different sports

sportsman, sportswoman /ˈspɔːtsmən/, /ˈspɔːtsˌwʊmən/ **noun** [C] (plural **sportsmen**, **sportswomen**) a man/woman who is good at sports

sportsmanship /ˈspɔːtsmənʃɪp/ **noun** [U] behaviour in sport that is fair and shows respect for other players: *We hope to teach children good sportsmanship.*

sportswear /ˈspɔːtsweəʳ/ **noun** [U] clothes, shoes, etc for people to wear when they play sports: *a sportswear shop*

sporty /ˈspɔːti/ **adj 1** Sporty cars, clothes, etc are attractive, comfortable, and stylish. **2** Sporty people are good at sports.

spot¹ /spɒt/ **noun** [C] **1 ROUND MARK** ▷ **ⓑ** a small, round mark that is a different colour to the surface it is on: *a blue shirt with white spots* ∘ *I noticed a small spot of oil on my jacket.* **2 SKIN** ▷ UK (US **pimple**) an unpleasant, small, red mark on your skin: *He suffered badly with spots as a teenager.* **3 PLACE** ▷ **ⓑ** a place: *We found a good spot to sit and have our picnic.* **4 a spot of sth** UK old-fashioned a small amount of something: *a spot of lunch/shopping* **5 on the spot a** immediately: *I accepted the job on the spot.* **b** in the place where something happens: *The police were called and they were on the spot within three minutes.*

IDIOMS **have a soft spot for sb** to like someone a lot: *I've always had a soft spot for her.* • **put sb on the spot** to ask someone a question that is difficult or embarrassing to answer at that time

→ See also **beauty spot, blind spot**

spot² /spɒt/ **verb** [T] (**spotting, spotted**) **ⓑ** to see or notice something or someone: *They were spotted together in London last week.* ∘ *She soon spotted the mistake.*

spotless /ˈspɒtləs/ **adj** completely clean: *By the*

time I'd finished, the whole room was spotless • **spotlessly adv spotlessly clean**

spotlight /ˈspɒtlaɪt/ **noun 1** [C] a strong light that can be pointed in different directions **2 the spotlight** If someone is in the spotlight, they ge public attention by being on television, in the newspapers, etc.: *She's rarely out of the media spotlight these days.* • **spotlight verb** [T] (**spotlighted, spotlit**)

⟦ **Z** Word partners for **spotlight**

be under/come under the spotlight • the spotlight **falls on/is on** sb/sth • **put/turn** the spotlight **on** sb/sth • **in/out of** the spotlight • the **media/public** spotlight ⟧

spot on adj [never before noun] UK exactly correct: *Her imitation of Ann was spot on.*

spotty /ˈspɒti/ **adj 1 SKIN** ▷ UK having a lot of unpleasant, small, red marks on your skin: *a spotty young man with greasy hair* **2 PATTERN** ▷ with a pattern of round marks: *a spotty dress* **3 NOT GOOD/REGULAR** ▷ US (UK **patchy**) If an action, quality, supply, etc is spotty, it is not all good or regular: *Sales of tickets for the concer have been spotty.*

spouse /spaʊs/ **noun** [C] formal your husband o wife

spout¹ /spaʊt/ **noun** [C] an opening of a container, in the shape of a tube which liquid flows out through: *the spout of a teapot*

spout² /spaʊt/ **verb** [I, T] **1** If a liquid spouts or i something makes it spout, it flows out of something with force. **2** informal to talk a lo about something, often when other people are not interested: *He was spouting his usual rubbish about politics.*

sprain /spreɪn/ **verb** [T] to injure part of you body by twisting it, but not so badly that i breaks: *I slipped on the ice and sprained my ankle* • **sprain noun** [C]

sprang /spræŋ/ past tense of spring

sprawl /sprɔːl/ **verb** [I] **1** (also **sprawl out**) to si or lie in a relaxed, untidy position with you arms and legs stretched out: *He sprawled out o the sofa.* **2** to cover a large area, often in a way which is not tidy or not planned: *sprawlin suburbs* • **sprawl noun** [U] *urban sprawl*

spray¹ /spreɪ/ **noun 1** [C, U] **ⓑ** liquid in a container which is forced out in small drops *hair spray* ∘ *spray paint* **2** [U] many small drop of liquid blown through the air: *sea spray*

spray² /spreɪ/ **verb 1** [T] **ⓑ** to force liquid out o a container in many small drops: *The fields ar sprayed with pesticides.* ∘ *She sprayed a littl perfume on her wrists.* **2** [I, T] If small pieces o something spray somewhere or if somethin sprays them, they are sent through the air in a directions: *A brick shattered the window, spraying the room with pieces of broken glass.*

spread¹ /spred/ **verb** (**spread**) **1 spread st across/over/through, etc** **ⓑ** to arrange some thing so that it covers a large area: *He spread th cards out on the table.* **2 TIME** ▷ [T] (also **sprea out**) **ⓑ** to arrange for something to happen over a period of time and not at once: *Th* *payments* will be **spread** over two years. **3** INCREASE ▷ [I] ⓑ to increase, or move to cover a larger area or affect a larger number of people: *The virus is spread by rats.* **4** SURFACE ▷ [T] to move a soft substance across a surface so that it covers it: *hot buttered toast* **spread with** *strawberry jam* ∘ *He* **spread** *a thin layer of glue* **on** *the paper.* **5** INFORMATION ▷ [I, T] ⓑ If information spreads or if someone spreads it, it is communicated from one person to another: *News of his death spread quickly.*

PHRASAL VERB **spread out** ⓑ If people spread out, they move from being close together in a group to being in different places across a larger area: *They spread out to search the whole area.*

spread² /spred/ **noun 1** MOVEMENT ▷ [U] ⓑ the degree to which something moves to cover a larger area or affect a larger number of people, or the fact of doing this: *They are looking for ways to slow down* **the spread of** *the disease.* **2** FOOD ▷ [C, U] a soft food that you put on bread: *cheese spread* **3** NEWSPAPER ▷ [C] an article that covers one or more pages of a newspaper or magazine: *a double-page spread*

> 🗹 Word partners for **spread** noun
>
> the spread of sth • control/halt/limit/prevent the spread of sth

spreadsheet /'spredʃi:t/ **noun** [C] ⓑ a computer program that helps you to do business calculations and planning

spree /spri:/ **noun a shopping/spending, etc spree** a short period when someone does a lot of shopping/spending, etc

sprig /sprɪg/ **noun** [C] a small piece of a plant with leaves: *a sprig of parsley*

sprightly /'spraɪtli/ **adj** A sprightly person is able to move about easily and quickly although they are old.

spring¹ /sprɪŋ/ **noun 1** SEASON ▷ [C, U] ⓐ the season of the year between winter and summer, when the weather becomes warmer and plants start to grow again: *I'm starting a new course* **in the spring.** ∘ *spring flowers/weather* **2** METAL ▷ [C] a piece of metal that curves round and round and that returns to its original shape after being pushed or pulled: *bed springs* **3** WATER ▷ [C] a place where water comes out of the ground: *hot springs* **4** MOVEMENT ▷ [C, U] a sudden movement or jump somewhere

> 🗹 Word partners for **spring**
>
> in (the) spring • early/late spring • last/next spring

spring² /sprɪŋ/ **verb (sprang, also US sprung, sprung) 1 spring back/forward/out, etc** to jump or move somewhere suddenly: *The cat sprang onto the sofa.* ∘ *I tried to shut the door, but it kept springing open.* **2 spring to life** to suddenly become very active: *After about 8 o'clock, the city springs to life.* **3 spring to mind** If a word or idea springs to mind, you suddenly think of it: *He asked if I knew any good places to go, but nothing sprang to mind.*

PHRASAL VERBS **spring from sth** to come from or be the result of something: *Many of his problems spring from his strict religious upbringing.* • **spring sth on sb** to suddenly tell or ask someone something when they do not expect it: *I'm sorry to spring this on you, but could you give a talk at tomorrow's meeting?* • **spring up** to appear suddenly: *A lot of new hotels have sprung up along the coast recently.*

spring ˈclean noun [no plural] UK (UK/US **spring ˈcleaning**) If you give a place a spring clean, you clean it more carefully and using more effort than usual: *I gave the kitchen a spring clean at the weekend.* • **spring clean verb** [I, T] UK

spring ˈonion noun [C, U] UK (US **scallion**) a small onion with a white part at the bottom and long, green leaves, which is eaten in salads

sprinkle /'sprɪŋkl/ **verb** [T] to gently drop small pieces of something over a surface: *Sprinkle the cake with sugar before serving.* • **sprinkling noun** [no plural] a small amount of a powder or liquid that has been sprinkled on a surface: *a sprinkling of pepper/snow*

sprinkle

sprinkler /'sprɪŋklə^r/ **noun** [C] a piece of garden equipment that automatically spreads drops of water over grass and plants

sprint /sprɪnt/ **verb** [I] to run very fast for a short distance: *She sprinted along the road to the bus stop.* • **sprinter noun** [C] someone who runs short distances in competitions • **sprint noun** [C] *a 100m sprint*

sprout¹ /spraʊt/ **verb** [I, T] If a plant sprouts, or if it sprouts something, it begins to produce leaves, flowers, etc.: *The seeds I planted are just beginning to sprout.*

PHRASAL VERB **sprout up** If a large number of things sprout up, they suddenly appear or begin to exist: *New buildings are sprouting up all over the city.*

sprout² /spraʊt/ **noun** [C] **1** (also **brussel sprout**) a small, green vegetable that is round and made of leaves **2** a part of a plant that is just beginning to grow

spruce /spru:s/ **verb**

PHRASAL VERB **spruce sb/sth up** to make someone or something cleaner or more tidy: [often reflexive] *I'd like to spruce myself up a bit before we go out.*

sprung /sprʌŋ/ **1** past participle of spring **2** US past tense of spring

spun /spʌn/ past tense of spin

spur¹ /spɜː^r/ **verb** [T] (**spurring, spurred**) (also **spur on**) to encourage someone to do something or something to happen: *Spurred on by his fans, he won the next three games easily.*

spur² /spɜː^r/ **noun** [C] a sharp, pointed piece of

S

metal fixed to the boot of someone riding a horse

IDIOM **on the spur of the moment** If you do something on the spur of the moment, you do it suddenly, without planning it.

spurious /ˈspjʊəriəs/ adj formal false and not based on the truth

spurn /spɜːn/ verb [T] formal to not accept someone or something: *He spurned my offer/suggestion.* ○ *a spurned lover*

spurt[1] /spɜːt/ verb **1** [I, T] (also **spurt out**) If something spurts liquid or fire, or if liquid or fire spurts from somewhere, it flows out suddenly with force: *Blood was spurting out of his stomach.* **2 spurt ahead/into/past, etc** to increase your speed, effort, or activity: *She spurted ahead in the final lap.*

spurt[2] /spɜːt/ noun [C] **1** a sudden, short increase in speed, effort, or activity: *He works in short spurts.* **2** a sudden, powerful flow of liquid: *The water came out of the tap in spurts.*

sputter /ˈspʌtər/ verb [I] to make several quick, explosive sounds: *The car sputtered to a halt.*

spy[1] /spaɪ/ noun [C] ⑤ someone who secretly tries to discover information about a person, country, etc

spy[2] /spaɪ/ verb **1** [I] to secretly try to discover information about a person, country, etc **2** [T] literary to see someone or something, often from a distance: *I spied him on the dance floor.*

PHRASAL VERB **spy on sb** to secretly watch someone: *He spied on her through the keyhole.*

sq written abbreviation for square in measurements: *an area of 70 sq km (= square kilometres)*

squabble /ˈskwɒbl/ verb [I] to argue about something that is not important: *They're always squabbling over money.* ● **squabble** noun [C]

squad /skwɒd/ noun [C] **1 bomb/drug/fraud, etc squad** a group of police officers who have special skills to deal with particular problems **2 death/firing/hit, etc squad** a group of people who are trained to kill, usually with guns **3** a sports team: *the New Zealand rugby squad*

squadron /ˈskwɒdrən/ noun [C] a group of soldiers, ships, aircraft, etc in a military organization: *a squadron of fighter jets*

squalid /ˈskwɒlɪd/ adj **1** very dirty and unpleasant: *squalid conditions* **2** morally bad: *a squalid affair*

squall /skwɔːl/ noun [C] a sudden storm with strong winds

squalor /ˈskwɒlər/ noun [U] extremely dirty and unpleasant conditions: *They were found living in absolute squalor.*

squander /ˈskwɒndər/ verb [T] to waste time, money, etc: *He squandered all his money on alcohol and drugs.*

square[1] /skweər/ noun [C] **1 SHAPE** ▷ ⑫ a shape with four equal sides and four 90° angles → See picture at **shape 2 PLACE** ▷ ⑫ an open area with buildings around it, often in the centre of a town: *Trafalgar Square* **3 NUMBER** ▷ a number

that results from multiplying a number by itself: *The square of 3 is 9.*

IDIOM **back to square one** back to the beginning of a long process or piece of work: *None of the applicants were suitable, so we had to go back to square one and advertise the job again.*

→ See also **fair**[3] **and square**

square[2] /skweər/ adj **1** ⑫ having the shape of a square: *a square room* ○ *He has broad shoulders and a square jaw.* **2 square centimetre/metre/mile, etc** the area of a square with sides that are a centimetre/metre/mile, etc long: *3000 square feet of office space*

IDIOM **a square meal** a big, healthy meal: *You need three square meals a day.*

square[3] /skweər/ verb **2/3/4, etc squared** 2/3/4, etc multiplied by itself: *Four squared is sixteen.*

PHRASAL VERBS **square off** US to prepare to fight, compete, or argue with someone: *The two teams will square off in the finals next Saturday* ● **square up 1** UK to prepare to fight, compete, or argue with someone: *The players squared up to each other and started shouting.* **2** informal to pay someone the money that you owe them: *If you pay for it now, I'll square up with you later* ● **square with sth** to match or to agree with something: *Her story doesn't quite square with the evidence.*

square brackets noun [plural] a pair of marks [ ] used in text around information that is separate from the main part

squarely /ˈskweəli/ adv directly: *I looked him squarely in the eye.* ○ *The report put the blame squarely on the police.*

square root noun **the square root of 16/64/144, etc** the number you multiply by itself to get 16/64/144, etc: *The square root of 144 is 12.*

squash[1] /skwɒʃ/ noun **1 SPORT** ▷ [U] ⑤ a sport in which two people hit a small rubber ball against the four walls of a room: *a game of squash* ○ *a squash court/racket* **2 it's a squash** UK used to say that there are too many people or things in a small space: *We managed to get in but it was a squash.* **3 DRINK** ▷ [U] UK a sweet drink that tastes like fruit **4 VEGETABLE** ▷ [C, U] a fruit with hard skin, a soft inside, and large seeds that you cook and eat as a vegetable

squash[2] /skwɒʃ/ verb **1** [T] ⑫ to crush something into a flat shape: *I stepped on a spider and squashed it.* **2** [I, T] ⑫ to push someone or something into a small space: [often passive] *The kids were all squashed into the back seat.*

squat[1] /skwɒt/ verb [I] (**squatting, squatted**) **1** (also **squat down**) to bend your legs so that you are sitting with your bottom very close to the ground: *He squatted down beside me.* **2** to live in an empty building without the owner's permission

squat[2] /skwɒt/ adj short and wide: *a squat little man*

squat[3] /skwɒt/ noun [C] a building that people are living in without the owner's permission

quatter /ˈskwɒtəʳ/ **noun** [C] someone who lives in a building without the owner's permission

quawk /skwɔːk/ **verb** [I] If a bird squawks, it makes a loud, unpleasant noise. • **squawk noun** [C]

queak /skwiːk/ **verb** [I] to make a short, high sound: *His shoes squeaked loudly as he walked.* • **squeak noun** [C]

queaky /ˈskwiːki/ **adj 1** making short, high sounds: *a squeaky voice* **2 squeaky clean** very clean

queal /skwiːl/ **verb** [I] to make a loud, high sound, often because of fear or excitement: *She squealed with delight.* • **squeal noun** [C] *squeals of laughter*

queamish /ˈskwiːmɪʃ/ **adj** If you are squeamish about something such as blood, you find it very unpleasant and it makes you feel ill.

queeze¹ /skwiːz/ **verb 1** ⑫ [T] to press something firmly: *She squeezed his hand and said goodbye.* **2 squeeze into/through/past, etc** ⑫ to move somewhere where there is very little space: *She squeezed through a narrow gap in the wall.* **3 squeeze a lemon/orange, etc** to press a lemon/orange, etc to get juice from it: *freshly squeezed orange juice*

PHRASAL VERB **squeeze sth/sb in** to manage to do something or see someone when you are very busy: *The doctor will try to squeeze you in this afternoon.*

queeze² /skwiːz/ **noun 1** [C] the action of firmly pressing something: *He gave her hand a little squeeze.* **2 it's a squeeze** used to say that there are too many people or things in a small space: *We all got in, but it was a tight squeeze.* **3 a squeeze of lemon/orange, etc** a small amount of juice from a lemon/orange, etc

quid /skwɪd/ **noun** [C] (plural **squid**) a sea creature with a long body and ten long arms

quiggle /ˈskwɪgl/ **noun** [C] informal a short, curly line: *Her signature just looks like a squiggle.*

quint /skwɪnt/ **verb** [I] to look at something with your eyes partly closed: *She was squinting at her computer screen.*

quirm /skwɜːm/ **verb** [I] to twist your body because you are embarrassed, nervous, etc

quirrel /ˈskwɪrəl/ ⑤ /ˈskwɜːrəl/ **noun** [C] a small animal with a big, fur tail that climbs trees and eats nuts

squirrel

quirt /skwɜːt/ **verb 1** [I, T] If liquid squirts, it comes out suddenly and with force, and if you squirt liquid, you make it come out suddenly and with force: *Water squirted out all over the floor.* **2 squirt sb with sth** to hit someone with a liquid

r (also UK **Snr**) written abbreviation for senior (= the older of two men in a family with the same name): *Joseph Kennedy, Sr.*

t 1 written abbreviation for street (= a road in a town or city that has houses or other buildings): *42 Oxford St* **2** written abbreviation for saint (= a dead person who has been officially respected

by the Christian Church for living their life in a holy way): *St Patrick*

stab¹ /stæb/ **verb** [T] (**stabbing, stabbed**) ⑫ to push a knife into someone: *He was stabbed several times in the chest.*

stab² /stæb/ **noun** [C] **1** the act of pushing a knife into someone: *He had a deep stab wound in his neck.* **2 a stab of guilt/jealousy/regret, etc** a sudden, unpleasant emotion: *She felt a stab of guilt.* **3 have a stab at sth/doing sth** informal to try to do something, or to try an activity that you have not done before: *She had a stab at solving the problem.*

stabbing /ˈstæbɪŋ/ **noun** [C] an attack in which someone is stabbed: *Where were you on the night of the stabbing?* ∘ US *a stabbing death*

stabbing pain noun [C] a sudden, strong pain

stability /stəˈbɪləti/ **noun** [U] the quality of not being likely to change or move: *political/financial stability* → Opposite **instability**

stabilize (also UK **-ise**) /ˈsteɪbəlaɪz/ **verb** [I, T] If you stabilize something, or if something stabilizes, it stops changing or moving: *The economy has finally stabilized.* • **stabilization** /ˌsteɪbəlaɪˈzeɪʃ³n/ **noun** [U]

stable¹ /ˈsteɪbl/ **adj 1** SITUATION ▷ not likely to change or end suddenly: *a stable relationship* ∘ *The doctor said his condition was stable.* **2** OBJECT ▷ fixed or safe and not likely to move: *Be careful! That chair isn't very stable.* **3** PERSON ▷ mentally calm and not easily upset → Opposite **unstable**

stable² /ˈsteɪbl/ **noun** [C] a building where horses are kept

stack¹ /stæk/ **noun** [C] **1** a tidy pile of things: *a stack of books/CDs* **2 stacks of sth** informal a lot of something: *There are stacks of studies linking salt to high blood pressure.*

stack² /stæk/ **verb** [T] (also **stack up**) to arrange things in a tidy pile: *Can you help me stack these chairs?*

stadium /ˈsteɪdiəm/ **noun** [C] ⑫ a large, open area with seats around it, used for playing and watching sports: *a football/baseball stadium*

staff¹ /stɑːf/ **noun** [group] ⑫ the people who work for an organization: *The company has a staff of over 500 employees.* ∘ *Please talk to a member of staff.*

> ☑ Word partners for **staff**
>
> administrative/experienced/extra/full-time/senior staff • employ/lay off/train staff • join the staff • on the staff

staff² /stɑːf/ **verb** [T] to provide workers for an organization: [often passive] *The charity was staffed by volunteers.*

stag /stæg/ **noun** [C] a male deer

stage¹ /steɪdʒ/ **noun 1** [C] ⑫ a period of development, or a particular time in a process: *an early stage in his career* ∘ *Our project is in its final stages.* ∘ *I'm not prepared to comment at this stage.* **2** [C] ⑫ the raised area in a theatre where actors perform: *He's on stage for most of* *the play.* **3 the stage** performances in theatres: *He's written plays for television and the stage.*

IDIOM **set the stage for sth** to make something possible or likely to happen: *The meeting set the stage for future cooperation between the companies.*

> ☑ Word partners for **stage**
>
> **reach** a stage • **at** [one/some/this/that] stage • the **closing/early/final** stages • a stage **in/ of** sth

stage² /steɪdʒ/ **verb 1 stage a demonstration/ protest, etc** to organize and take part in a public meeting to complain about something **2 stage a concert/show, etc** to organize and produce a performance of music or a play, etc: *They staged a free concert in Central Park.*

stagger /'stægər/ **verb 1** [I] to walk as if you might fall: *He staggered drunkenly towards the door.* **2** [T] to arrange events so that they do not happen at the same time: *We stagger our lunch breaks at work.*

staggered /'stægəd/ **adj** [never before noun] very shocked or surprised: *I was staggered at the prices.*

staggering /'stægərɪŋ/ **adj** very shocking and surprising: *He earns a staggering amount of money.*

stagnant /'stægnənt/ **adj 1** Stagnant water or air does not flow and becomes dirty and smells unpleasant: *a stagnant pond* **2** A stagnant economy, society, or organization does not develop or grow.

stagnate /stæg'neɪt/ ⑤ /'stægneɪt/ **verb** [I] to stay the same and not grow or develop: *He expects the economy to stagnate and unemployment to rise.* • **stagnation** /stæg'neɪʃᵊn/ **noun** [U]

stag ˌnight noun [C] a night when a group of men go out just before one of them gets married → Compare **hen night**

staid /steɪd/ **adj** serious and old-fashioned: *a staid, middle-aged man*

stain¹ /steɪn/ **noun 1** [C] ⑫ a dirty mark on something that is difficult to remove: *a blood/ grass stain* ∘ *a stain on the carpet* **2** [C, U] a thin, clear paint that you put on wood to make it darker: *wood stain*

stain² /steɪn/ **verb 1** [I, T] to leave a dirty mark on something that is difficult to remove, or to become dirty in this way: *That wine I spilt has stained my shirt.* **2** [T] to paint a wooden surface with a thin paint in order to change its colour: *She stained the bookcase to match the desk.*

ˌstained ˈglass noun [U] coloured glass that is used to make pictures in windows: *a stained-glass window*

stainless steel /ˌsteɪnləs'stiːl/ **noun** [U] a type of steel (= strong metal) that is not damaged by water

stair /steər/ **noun** [C] one of the steps in a set of steps

staircase /'steəkeɪs/ **noun** [C] a set of stairs and the structure around them: *a spiral staircase*

stairs /steəz/ **noun** [plural] ⑫ a set of steps from

one level in a building to another: *to climb th stairs* ∘ *a flight* (= set) *of stairs*

> ☑ Word partners for **stairs**
>
> **climb/fall down/go down/go up** the stairs • the **bottom of/foot of** the stairs • the **head of/top of** the stairs • **on** the stairs • a **flight of** stairs

stairway /'steəweɪ/ **noun** [C] a set of stairs an the structure around them

stake¹ /steɪk/ **noun 1 be at stake** If something i at stake, it is in a situation where it might be los or damaged: *We have to act quickly – people lives are at stake.* **2** [C] a part of a business tha you own, or an amount of money that you hav invested in a business: *He has a 30 percent stak in the company.* **3** [C] a strong stick with pointed end that you push into the ground: *wooden stake*

stake² /steɪk/ **verb stake a/your claim** to sa that you want something and that you shoul have it

PHRASAL VERBS **stake sth on sth** to risk somethin on the result of a competition or situation: *H has staked his reputation on the film's success.* **stake sth out** to watch a place in order to catcl criminals or to see a famous person: *The polic are staking out the house where the terrorists ar hiding.*

stakes /steɪks/ **noun** [plural] money or othe advantages that you may get or lose in competition or situation: *People get very compe titive because the stakes are so high.*

stale /steɪl/ **adj 1** old and not fresh: *stale brea* ∘ *Cake goes stale quickly if it's not covered* **2** boring or bored, and not producing or feelin excitement or enthusiasm like before: *I'd bee too long in the same job and was getting stale.*

stalemate /'steɪlmeɪt/ **noun** [C, U] a situation i which neither side in an argument can win: *Th talks ended in a stalemate.*

stalk¹ /stɔːk/ **verb 1** [T] to follow a person o animal closely and secretly, often to try to catcl or attack them: *She claimed that the man ha been stalking her for a month.* **2 stalk out/off, et** to walk in an angry or proud way: *She stalked ou of the restaurant.*

stalk² /stɔːk/ **noun** [C] the main stem of a plan

stalker /'stɔːkər/ **noun** [C] someone who follow a person or animal closely and secretly, often t try to catch or attack them

stall¹ /stɔːl/ **noun** [C]   **stall**
1 mainly UK ⑪ a small shop with an open front or a table from which goods are sold: *a market stall* **2** US a small area in a room for washing or using the toilet: *a shower stall*

stall² /stɔːl/ **verb 1** ENGINE ▷ [I, T] If an engin stalls, or if you stall it, it stops working suddenly *The car stalled when I stopped at the traffic lights*

2 STOP ▷ [I] to stop making progress: *The peace talks have stalled over the issue of nuclear weapons.* **3 MORE TIME** ▷ [T] to intentionally make someone wait or make something happen later so that you have more time: *She wanted an answer immediately, but I managed to stall her.*

stallion /ˈstæljən/ **noun** [C] an adult male horse

the stalls /stɔːlz/ **noun** [plural] UK (US **orchestra**) the seats on the main floor near the front of a theatre or cinema: *a seat in the stalls*

stalwart /ˈstɔːlwət/ **noun** [C] someone who supports an organization, team, etc in a very loyal way • **stalwart** adj

stamina /ˈstæmɪnə/ **noun** [U] the physical or mental energy that allows you to do something for a long time: *Marathon runners need a lot of stamina.*

> ⏹ Word partners for **stamina**
>
> have stamina • build up/improve/increase stamina • mental/physical stamina • stamina for sth • a test of stamina

stammer /ˈstæmər/ **verb** [I] to pause a lot and repeat sounds because of a speech problem or because you are nervous: *He blushed and began to stammer.* • **stammer** noun [C] *He has a stammer.*

stamp¹ /stæmp/ **noun** [C] **1** (also **postage stamp**) Ⓐ a small, official piece of paper that you buy and stick onto a letter or parcel before you post it **2** a tool for putting a special ink mark on something, or the mark made by it: *a stamp in a passport* **3 stamp of approval** official, public approval: *The president has put his stamp of approval on the proposal.*

stamp² /stæmp/ **verb 1** [T] Ⓑ to make a mark on something with a tool that you put ink on and press down: *She stamped the date on the invoice.* **2** [I, T] to put your foot down on the ground hard and quickly, often to show anger: *"No!" she shouted, stamping her foot.* → See also **rubber-stamp**

PHRASAL VERB **stamp sth out** to get rid of something that is wrong or harmful: *a campaign to stamp out racism*

stampede /stæmˈpiːd/ **noun** [C] a sudden uncontrolled movement of a large group of animals or people, often in the same direction: *Gunfire caused a stampede in the marketplace.* • **stampede** verb [I]

stance /stæns/ **noun** [C] **1** an opinion or belief about something, especially if you say it in public: [usually singular] *What's their stance on nuclear energy?* ∘ *They are taking a very tough stance against drugs.* **2** formal the way that someone stands: [usually singular] *an awkward stance*

> ⏹ Word partners for **stance**
>
> take a stance • change your stance • a hard-line/tough stance • a stance against sb/sth • sb's stance on sth

stand¹ /stænd/ **verb** (**stood**) **1 ON FEET** ▷ [I] Ⓐ to be in a vertical position on your feet: *We'd been*

standing for hours. **2 RISE** ▷ [I] (also **stand up**) Ⓐ to rise to a vertical position from sitting or lying down: *I get dizzy if I stand up too quickly.* ∘ *Please stand when the bride arrives.* → See colour printer **Phrasal Verbs** on page Centre 16 **3 stand in line** US (UK **queue**) to wait for something as part of a line of people: *We stood in line all afternoon.* **4 stand (sth) in/against/by, etc sth** Ⓑ to be in or to put something in a particular place or position: *His walking stick stood by the door.* ∘ *You'll have to stand the sofa on its end to get it through the door.* **5 can't stand sb/sth** informal Ⓑ to hate someone or something: *I can't stand him.* ∘ [+ doing sth] *She can't stand doing housework.* **6 ACCEPT** ▷ [T] to be able to accept or deal with a difficult situation: *She couldn't stand the pressures of the job.* **7 stand at sth** to be at a particular level, amount, height, etc: *Inflation currently stands at 3 percent.* **8 where you stand on sth** what your opinion is about something: *We asked the senator where she stood on gun control.* **9 where you stand (with sb)** what someone thinks about you, how they expect you to behave, and how they are likely to behave: *She said she will never leave her husband, so now at least I know where I stand.* **10 OFFER** ▷ [I] If an offer still stands, it still exists: *You're welcome to visit any time – my invitation still stands.* **11 as it stands** as something is now, without changes in it: *The law as it stands is very unclear.* **12 stand trial** If someone stands trial, they appear in a law court where people decide if they are guilty of a crime: *to stand trial for murder* **13 stand to gain/lose sth** to be in a situation where you can get/lose money or an advantage: *He stands to gain a fortune if the company is sold.* **14 ELECTION** ▷ [I] UK (US **run**) to compete in an election for an official position: *to stand for office* → See also **stand your ground¹**, not have a **leg to stand on**, it **stands to reason¹**, stand on your own two feet (**foot¹**), stand sb in good **stead**

PHRASAL VERBS **stand about/around** to spend time standing somewhere and doing very little: *They stood around waiting for the store to open.* • **stand aside** to leave a job or position so that someone else can do it instead • **stand back** Ⓑ to move a short distance away from something or someone: *Stand back while I light the fire.* • **stand by 1** to be ready to do something or to help: *Doctors were standing by to treat the injured passengers.* **2** to do nothing to prevent something unpleasant from happening: *We can't stand by while millions of people starve.* • **stand by sb** Ⓑ to continue to support someone when they are in a difficult situation: *She stood by him throughout his troubled career.* • **stand by sth** If you stand by an agreement, decision, etc, you do not change it: *The government stood by its promise to improve education.* • **stand down** UK to leave a job or position so that someone else can do it instead: *He stood down as party leader.* • **stand for sth 1 LETTER** ▷ Ⓑ If a letter stands for a word, it is used to represent it: *UFO stands for 'unidentified flying object'.* **2 SUPPORT** ▷ Ⓑ If a group of people stand for a set of ideas, they support those ideas: *The party stands for low*

Ⓢ

yes | k cat | ŋ ring | ʃ she | θ thin | ð this | ʒ decision | dʒ jar | tʃ chip | æ cat | e bed | ə ago | ɪ sit | i cosy | ɒ hot | ʌ run | ʊ put |

taxes and individual freedom. **3 not stand for sth** B2 If you will not stand for something, you will not accept a situation or someone's behaviour: *He can't speak to me like that – I won't stand for it!* • **stand in** to do something that someone else was going to do because they cannot be there: *She stood in for me when I was sick.* • **stand out** **1** B2 to be very easy to see or notice: *The bright blue letters really stand out on the page.* **2** B2 to be better than other similar things or people: *His application stood out from all the rest.* → See also stick/stand out like a sore **thumb¹** • **stand up** If an idea or some information stands up, it is proved to be correct. • **stand sb up** B2 to fail to meet someone when you said you would: *He's stood me up twice now.* • **stand up for sth/sb** B2 to support an idea or a person who is being criticized: [often reflexive] *Never be afraid to stand up for yourself.*

stand² /stænd/ **noun** **1** SHOP ▷ [C] a small shop with an open front or a table from which goods are sold: *a hot dog stand* ○ *Visit our stand at the trade fair.* **2** SPORT ▷ [C] UK (US **stands**) a structure in a sports ground where people can stand or sit to watch an event **3** FURNITURE ▷ [C] a piece of furniture for holding things: *a music/hat stand* **4 the (witness) stand** (also **the dock**) the place in a law court where people sit or stand when they are being asked questions: *The judge asked her to take the stand* (= go into the witness stand). **5** OPINION ▷ [C] an opinion or belief about something, especially if you say it in public: [usually singular] *What's the President's stand on gun control?* **6 take a stand** to express your opinion about something publicly: *He refuses to take a stand on this issue.* **7 make a stand** to publicly defend something or stop something from happening

standard¹ /ˈstændəd/ **noun** [C] **1** B2 a level of quality, especially a level that is acceptable: *a high standard of service* ○ *low safety standards* ○ *His work was below standard* (= not acceptable). ○ *She sets very high standards for herself.* **2** a level of behaviour, especially a level that is acceptable: [usually plural] *high moral standards* → See also double **standard**

> ⊘ **Word partners for standard**
>
> **come up to** standard • **below/(not) up to** standard • **set** standards • **comply with/conform to/meet** standards • **exacting/high/low/rigorous** standards • standards **of sth**

standard² /ˈstændəd/ **adj** B2 usual and not special: *standard procedure/practice*

standardize (also UK **-ise**) /ˈstændədaɪz/ **verb** [T] to change things so that they are all the same: *I wish someone would standardize clothing sizes.* • **standardization** /ˌstændədaɪˈzeɪʃən/ **noun** [U] *the standardization of computer terms*

standard of ˈliving **noun** [C] (plural **standards of living**) B2 how much money and comfort someone has: *a high standard of living*

standby /ˈstændbaɪ/ **noun** [C] (plural **standbys**) **1** someone or something extra that is ready to be used if needed: *We kept our old TV set as a*

standby in case the new one broke. **2 be on standby** to be ready to do something or to be used if needed: *Police were on standby in case there was any trouble after the game.*

stand-in /ˈstændɪn/ **noun** [C] someone who does what another person was going to do because the other person cannot be there

standing¹ /ˈstændɪŋ/ **noun** [U] Your standing is the opinion that other people have of you: *Last week's speech has improved the Prime Minister's standing in the polls.*

standing² /ˈstændɪŋ/ **adj** [always before noun] **1** permanent and not only created when necessary: *a standing committee* ○ *He has a standing invitation to stay at our house.* **2 a standing joke** a situation that a group of people often make jokes about: *The poor quality of his work has become a standing joke in the office.* → See also long-**standing**

standing ˈorder **noun** [C] UK an instruction to a bank to pay someone a fixed amount of money at regular times from your account

standing oˈvation **noun** [C] If someone gets a standing ovation, people stand while clapping to show that they have enjoyed the performance or speech very much.

stand-off UK (US **standoff**) /ˈstændɒf/ **noun** [C] a situation in which an argument or fight stops for a period of time because no one can win or get an advantage

standpoint /ˈstændpɔɪnt/ **noun** [C] a particular way of thinking about a situation or problem: *to look at something from a political/religious standpoint*

standstill /ˈstændstɪl/ **noun** [no plural] a situation in which all movement or activity has stopped: *The traffic came to a standstill in the thick fog.*

stand-up /ˈstændʌp/ **adj** [always before noun] A stand-up comedian is someone who stands in front of a group of people and tells jokes as a performance: *stand-up comedy*

stank /stæŋk/ past tense of stink

staple¹ /ˈsteɪpl/ **adj** [always before noun] A staple food, product, etc is basic and very important: *a staple diet of rice and fish*

staple² /ˈsteɪpl/ **noun** [C] a small piece of wire that you put through pieces of paper to join them together • **staple verb** [T] to join pieces of paper together with staples

stapler /ˈsteɪplər/ **noun** [C] a piece of equipment used for putting staples through paper

star¹ /stɑːr/ **noun** [C] **1** SKY ▷ A2 a ball of burning gases that you see as a small point of light in the sky at night **2** FAMOUS PERSON ▷ A2 a famous singer, actor, sports person, etc: *a pop star* **3** BEST PERSON ▷ someone in a group of people who is the best at doing something: *Messi is one of our star players.* **4** SHAPE ▷ A2 a shape that has five or more points → See picture at **shape** **5 two-star/three-star, etc** used to show how good a restaurant or hotel is: *a five-star hotel* **6 sb's stars/the stars** UK informal something you read that tells you what will happen to you based on the position of the stars in the sky: *My*

tar

stars said it would be a good month for romance.* → See also **co-star, film star, rock star**

> **Word partners for star**
> become/make sb a star • a **big** star • a **pop** star

tar² /stɑːʳ/ **verb** [I, T] (**starring**, **starred**) [B1] If a film, play, etc stars someone, or if someone stars in a film, play, etc, they are the main person in it: *a film starring Cameron Diaz* ◦ *Colin Firth **starred in** 'The King's Speech'.* → See also **co-star**

tarboard /ˈstɑːbəd/ **noun** [U] the right side of a ship or aircraft

tarch /stɑːtʃ/ **noun 1** [C, U] a substance in foods such as rice, bread, and potatoes **2** [U] a substance used to make cloth stiff • **starchy adj** containing a lot of starch

tardom /ˈstɑːdəm/ **noun** [U] the quality of being very famous for acting, singing, etc

tare /steəʳ/ **verb** [I] [B2] to look at someone or something for a long time and not move your eyes: *Sean was **staring at** me.* • **stare noun** [C]

tark¹ /stɑːk/ **adj 1** unpleasantly clear and obvious: *His death is a **stark warning** to other people about the dangers of drugs.* **2 stark difference/contrast** a total difference: *Jerry is very lazy, in stark contrast to his sister who works very hard.* **3** with a very plain and simple appearance and not very attractive: *a stark, snowy landscape* • **starkly adv**

tark² /stɑːk/ **adv stark naked** wearing no clothes

tarry /ˈstɑːri/ **adj** A starry sky or night is one in which you can see a lot of stars.

tar ˌsign noun [C] UK (US **sign**) one of the twelve signs that are based on star positions when you are born, which some people believe shows what type of person you are: *"What star sign are you?" "I'm Capricorn."*

tart¹ /stɑːt/ **verb 1 BEGIN DOING** ▷ [I, T] [A1] to begin doing something: [+ doing sth] *He started smoking when he was eighteen.* ◦ [+ to do sth] *Maria started to laugh.* ◦ *We start work at nine o'clock.* **2 BEGIN HAPPENING** ▷ [I, T] [B1] to begin to happen or to make something begin to happen: *The programme starts at seven o'clock.* ◦ *Police believe the fire started in the kitchen.* **3 BUSINESS** ▷ [I, T] (also **start up**) [B2] If a business, organization, etc starts, it begins to exist, and if you start it, you make it begin to exist: *She started her own computer business.* ◦ *A lot of new restaurants have started up in the area.* **4 CAR** ▷ [I, T] (also **start up**) [B2] If a car or engine starts, it begins to work, and if you start it, you make it begin to work: *The car won't start.* ◦ *Start up the engine.* **5 to start with a** used to talk about what a situation was like at the beginning before it changed: *I was happy at school to start with, but later I hated it.* **b** used before saying the first thing in a list of things: *To start with, we need better computers. Then we need more training.* **6 MOVE SUDDENLY** ▷ [I] to move suddenly because you are frightened or surprised → See also **set/start the ball rolling**, **get/start off on the wrong foot¹**

PHRASAL VERBS **start (sth) off** [B1] to begin by doing something, or to make something begin by doing something: *She started off the meeting with the monthly sales report.* • **start on sth** to begin doing something: *Have you started on your homework yet?* • **start out** to begin your life or the part of your life when you work, in a particular way: *My dad started out as a sales assistant in a shop.* • **start over** US to begin something again: *If you make a mistake, you'll have to start over.*

start² /stɑːt/ **noun 1 BEGINNING** ▷ [C] [B1] the beginning of something: [usually singular] *Our teacher checks who is in class **at the start of** each day.* ◦ *Ivan has been involved in the project **from the start**.* ◦ *The meeting **got off to a bad start** (= began badly).* **2 make a start** to begin doing something: *I'll **make a start on** the washing-up.* **3 for a start** used when you are giving the first in a list of reasons or things: *I won't be going – I've got too much homework for a start.* **4 ADVANTAGE** ▷ [C] an advantage that you have over someone else when you begin something: [usually singular] *I'm grateful for the start I had in life.* **5 the start** the place where a race begins **6 SUDDEN MOVEMENT** ▷ [no plural] a sudden movement that you make because you are frightened or surprised: *Kate sat up **with a start**.* → See also **false start**

> **Word partners for start**
> at the start • from the start • the start of sth

starter /ˈstɑːtəʳ/ **noun 1** [C] mainly UK (US **appetizer**) something that you eat as the first part of a meal **2** [C] US in sports, a member of a team who is involved in a competition from the beginning: *At only 20, he's the team's youngest starter.* **3 for starters** informal used to say that something is the first in a list of things: *Try this exercise for starters.* → See also **non-starter**

starting-point /ˈstɑːtɪŋˌpɔɪnt/ **noun** [C] an idea, subject, etc that you use to begin a discussion or process

startle /ˈstɑːtl/ **verb** [T] to suddenly surprise or frighten someone: *The sound startled me.* • **startled adj** *a **startled expression***

startling /ˈstɑːtlɪŋ/ **adj** making you feel very surprised: *startling news*

S

start-up /ˈstɑːtʌp/ **adj** [always before noun] relating to starting a business: *start-up costs*

starve /stɑːv/ **verb** [I, T] to become sick or die because you do not have enough food, or to make someone sick or die because they do not have enough food: *Many people have **starved to death** in parts of Africa.* ● **starvation** /stɑːˈveɪʃən/ **noun** [U] *Children were dying of starvation.*

starved /stɑːvd/ **adj 1 be starved of sth** UK (US **be starved for sth**) to not have enough of something that you need very much: *a child starved of love* **2** mainly US informal very hungry

starving /ˈstɑːvɪŋ/ **adj 1** ⓑ dying because there is not enough food: *starving people* **2** informal ⓑ very hungry: *I'm absolutely starving.*

stash¹ /stæʃ/ **verb** [T] (also **stash away**) to keep a lot of something in a safe, secret place: *His money was stashed away in a cupboard.*

stash² /stæʃ/ **noun** [C] informal a lot of something that you keep in a safe, secret place: *He had a stash of whisky under the bed.*

state¹ /steɪt/ **noun 1 CONDITION** ▷ [C] ⓑ the condition that something or someone is in: *the state of the economy* ∘ *The building is in a terrible state.* **2 in/into a state** informal very upset or nervous: *Ben was in a real state before the exam.* **3 PART OF COUNTRY** ▷ [C] (also **State**) one of the parts that some countries such as the US are divided into: *Washington State* ∘ *Alaska is the largest state in the US.* **4 COUNTRY** ▷ [C] a country: *a union of European states* → See Note at **country¹ 5 the state** the government of a country: *financial help from the state* **6 state visit/occasion, etc** an important visit/occasion, etc involving the leader of a government **7 the States** the United States of America → See also **police state, welfare state**

state² /steɪt/ **verb** [T] ⓑ to officially say or write something: [+ (that)] *Two medical reports stated that he was mentally ill.*

stately /ˈsteɪtli/ **adj** formal and slow: *a stately procession through the streets*

stately ˈhome noun [C] a big, old house in the countryside that people pay to visit in Britain

statement /ˈsteɪtmənt/ **noun** [C] **1** ⓑ something that someone says or writes officially: *The prime minister is expected to **make a statement** later today.* **2** (also **bank statement**) a piece of paper that shows how much money you have put into your bank account and how much you have taken out

> 🗹 Word partners for **statement**
>
> issue/make/prepare/release a statement ● a false/joint/public/sworn statement ● a statement about/on sth

state of afˈfairs noun [no plural] a situation: *a sad state of affairs*

state of ˈmind noun [C] (plural **states of mind**) how you are feeling at a particular time: *to be in a positive state of mind*

state-of-the-art /ˌsteɪtəvðiˈɑːt/ **adj** using the newest ideas, designs, and materials: *a computer system that uses **state-of-the-art** technology*

ˈstate ˌschool noun [C] UK (US **public school**) a

school that is free to go to because the government provides the money for it

statesman /ˈsteɪtsmən/ **noun** [C] (plural **statesmen**) an important politician, especially one who people respect

static¹ /ˈstætɪk/ **adj** not moving or changing: *The number of students on the course has remained static.*

static² /ˈstætɪk/ **noun** [U] **1** (also ˌstatic elecˈtricity) electricity that you get when two surfaces rub together **2** noise on a radio or television that is caused by electricity in the air

station¹ /ˈsteɪʃən/ **noun** [C] **1 TRAINS** ▷ ⓐ a building where trains stop so that you can get on or off them: *Dad met me at the station.* **2 bus station** (also UK **coach station**) ⓐ a building where a bus starts or ends its journey **3 SERVICE** ▷ a building where a particular service is based: UK *a petrol station*/US *a gas station* **4 RADIO/TV** ▷ ⓑ a company that broadcasts television or radio programmes: *a classical music station* → See also **filling station, fire station, police station, polling station, power station, service station**

> ❗ Common learner error: **station** or **stop**?
>
> **Station** is used for trains.
> *the train/railway station*
> *the underground/tube station*
> **Stop** or **bus stop** is used for buses.
> *I stood at the bus stop for over half an hour.*
> *Get off at the third stop.*
> A **bus station** is a place where many buses start or end their journeys.

station² /ˈsteɪʃən/ **verb be stationed at/in, etc** If someone such as a soldier is stationed somewhere, they are sent there to work for a period of time: *He met some US soldiers stationed in Germany.*

stationary /ˈsteɪʃənəri/ **adj** not moving: *stationary cars*

stationer's /ˈsteɪʃənəz/ **noun** [C] UK a shop where you can buy pens, paper, and other things for writing

stationery /ˈsteɪʃənəri/ **noun** [U] things that you use for writing, such as pens and paper

ˈstation ˌwagon noun [C] US (UK **estate car**) a big car with a large space for bags behind the back seat

statistic /stəˈtɪstɪk/ **noun** [C] a fact in the form of a number that shows information about something: [usually plural] ***Statistics show** that skin cancer is becoming more common.* ● **statistical adj** relating to statistics: *statistical evidence* ● **statistically adv**

> 🗹 Word partners for **statistic**
>
> collect/gather statistics ● statistics confirm/indicate/reveal/show sth ● according to statistics ● statistics on sth

statistics /stəˈtɪstɪks/ **noun** [U] ⓑ the subject that involves collecting and studying numbers to show information about something

statue /ˈstætʃuː/ **noun** [C] ⓑ a model that looks

like a person or animal, usually made from stone or metal

stature /ˈstætʃəʳ/ noun [U] formal **1** the importance that someone has because of their work: *a scientist of international stature* **2** your height: *a man of small stature*

status /ˈsteɪtəs/ noun [U] **1** the position that you have in relation to other people because of your job or social position: *The pay and status of nurses has improved.* **2** the legal position of someone or something: *What's your marital status (= are you married or not)?*

the status quo /ˌsteɪtəsˈkwəʊ/ noun formal the situation that exists now, without any changes: *They only want to maintain the status quo.*

status symbol noun [C] something that someone owns that shows they have a high position in society

statute /ˈstætʃuːt/ noun [C] formal a law or rule

statutory /ˈstætjətʳri/ adj formal decided or controlled by law: *a statutory minimum wage*

staunch /stɔːnʃ/ adj [always before noun] very loyal in your support for someone or your belief in something: *a staunch supporter of the Communist party*

stave /steɪv/ verb

PHRASAL VERB **stave sth off** to stop something bad from happening now although it may happen later: *He had a bar of chocolate to stave off his hunger.*

stay¹ /steɪ/ verb **1** NOT LEAVE ▷ [I] 🅐1 to continue to be in a place, job, etc and not leave: *The weather was bad so we stayed at home.* ∘ *Do you want to stay in teaching?* **2** IN A STATE ▷ [T] 🅱1 to continue to be in a particular state: *The supermarket stays open late.* ∘ *I was tired and couldn't stay awake.* **3** VISIT ▷ [I] 🅐2 to spend a short period of time in a place: *We stayed in a hotel.* ∘ *We're going to stay with my grandmother.* **4** stay put informal to continue to be in the same place: *He told me to stay put while he fetched the car.* → See Note at **rest²**

PHRASAL VERBS **stay behind** 🅱1 to not leave a place when other people leave: *I stayed behind after class to speak to the teacher.* • **stay in** 🅱1 to stay in your home: *Let's stay in tonight and watch a DVD.* • **stay on** to continue to be in a place, job, or school after other people have left: *I stayed on an extra two years at school.* • **stay out** 🅱2 to not go home at night, or to go home late: *He stayed out all night.* • **stay out of sth** to not become involved in an argument or discussion: *It's better to stay out of their arguments.* • **stay up** 🅱2 to go to bed later than usual: [+ to do sth] *She stayed up to watch a film.*

stay² /steɪ/ noun [C] 🅱1 a period of time that you spend in a place: *Did you enjoy your stay in Tokyo?*

staycation /ˌsteɪˈkeɪʃᵊn/ noun [C] informal a holiday that someone spends in their own country or at home, rather than travelling somewhere else

stead /sted/ noun

IDIOM **stand sb in good stead** to be useful to someone in the future: *The course will stand you in good stead.*

steadfast /ˈstedfɑːst/ adj formal refusing to change your beliefs or what you are doing: *He is steadfast in his support for political change.*
• **steadfastly** adv

steady¹ /ˈstedi/ adj **1** GRADUAL ▷ 🅱2 happening at a gradual, regular rate: *steady economic growth* ∘ *He has had a steady flow/stream of visitors.* **2** STILL ▷ 🅱2 still and not shaking: *You need steady hands to be a dentist.* → Opposite **unsteady 3** NOT CHANGING ▷ not changing: *She drove at a steady speed.* **4** steady job/work a job that is likely to continue for a long time and pay you regular money • **steadily** adv
• **steadiness** noun [U]

steady² /ˈstedi/ verb **1** [T] to make something stop shaking or moving: *He managed to steady the plane.* **2** steady yourself to stop yourself from falling: *She grabbed hold of the rail to steady herself.*

steak /steɪk/ noun [C, U] 🅐2 a thick, flat piece of meat or fish: *steak and chips*

steal /stiːl/ verb (stole, stolen) **1** 🅐2 [I, T] to secretly take something that does not belong to you, without intending to return it: *Burglars broke into the house and stole a computer.* ∘ *stolen cars* **2** steal away/in/out, etc to move somewhere quietly and secretly

stealth /stelθ/ noun [U] secret, quiet behaviour
• **stealthy** adj behaving in a secret, quiet way
• **stealthily** adv

stealth tax noun [C] a tax that is collected in a way that is not very obvious, so people may not realize that they are paying it

steam¹ /stiːm/ noun [U] 🅱2 the gas that water produces when you heat it

steam

IDIOMS **let off steam** to get rid of your anger, excitement, etc by being noisy or using a lot of energy • **run out of steam** to not have enough energy to finish doing something

steam² /stiːm/ verb **1** [T] to cook something using steam: *steamed rice* **2** [I] to produce steam: *a steaming bowl of soup*

PHRASAL VERB **steam (sth) up** If glass steams up, or if you steam it up, it becomes covered in steam.

steamer /ˈstiːməʳ/ noun [C] **1** a pan used for cooking food using steam **2** a ship that uses steam power

steamy /ˈstiːmi/ adj **1** hot and full of steam: *a*

S

steamy kitchen **2** sexually exciting: *a steamy love story*

steel[1] /stiːl/ **noun** [U] ⓑ a very strong metal made from iron, used for making knives, machines, etc → See also **stainless steel**

steel[2] /stiːl/ **verb steel yourself** to prepare yourself to do something difficult or unpleasant: *He was steeling himself for an argument.*

steely /'stiːli/ **adj** [always before noun] very strong and determined: *a steely determination to succeed*

steep[1] /stiːp/ **adj 1 SLOPE** ▷ ⓑ A steep slope, hill, etc goes up or down very quickly: *The hill was too steep to cycle up.* **2 CHANGE** ▷ A steep increase or fall in something is very big and quick: *a steep rise in prices* **3 PRICE** ▷ informal very expensive: *Hotel prices are steep at $300 for a room.* • **steeply** adv *Food prices have risen steeply.* • **steepness** noun [U]

steep[2] /stiːp/ **verb be steeped in sth** to have a lot of something around or to be strongly influenced by something: *The town is steeped in history.*

steeple /'stiːpl/ **noun** [C] a church tower that has a point at the top

steer /stɪər/ **verb 1** [I, T] ⓑ to control the direction of a vehicle: *I tried to steer the boat away from the bank.* **2** [T] to influence the way a situation develops: *I managed to steer the conversation away from my exam results.* **3 steer sb into/out of/towards, etc** to guide someone somewhere, especially by putting your hand on their back: *He steered me towards the door.* → See also **steer clear**[3] of sb/sth

steering /'stɪərɪŋ/ **noun** [U] the parts of a vehicle that control its direction

'steering ˌwheel noun [C] ⓑ a wheel that you turn to control the direction of a vehicle → See colour picture **Car** on page Centre 7

stem[1] /stem/ **noun** [C] the long, thin part of a plant that the leaves and flowers grow on

stem[2] /stem/ **verb** [T] (**stemming**, **stemmed**) to stop something from continuing or increasing: *The new procedures are intended to stem the flow of drugs into the country.*

PHRASAL VERB **stem from sth** to develop as the result of something: *Her problems stem from childhood.*

'stem ˌcell noun [C] a cell, especially one taken from a person or animal in a very early stage of development, that can develop into any other type of cell

stench /stenʃ/ **noun** [C] a very unpleasant smell: *the stench of rotten fruit*

stencil /'stensəl/ **noun** [C] a piece of paper or plastic with patterns cut into it, that you use to paint patterns onto a surface • **stencil verb** [I, T] (mainly UK **stencilling**, **stencilled**, US **stenciling**, **stenciled**) to use a stencil to paint patterns onto a surface

step[1] /step/ **noun** [C] **1 MOVEMENT** ▷ ⓑ one of the movements you make with your feet when you walk: *She took a few steps forward and then started to speak.* **2 METHOD** ▷ ⓑ one of the

things that you do to achieve something: *Thi meeting is the first step towards a peace agree ment.* ○ *The company has taken steps to improv its customer service.* **3 STAIR** ▷ ⓑ one of the surfaces that you walk on when you go up o down stairs **4 in step (with sb/sth)** having the same ideas, opinions, etc as other people: *Thi time, Britain is in step with the rest of Europe* **5 out of step (with sb/sth)** having differen ideas, opinions, etc from other people: *Her view are out of step with government policy.*

IDIOMS **be one step ahead (of sb)** to have don something before someone else • **watch you step a** used to tell someone to be careful abou where they are walking **b** to be careful abou what you say and do

---

🗹 Word partners for **step noun**

take steps to do sth • a big/important/major step • the **first/next** step • a step **towards** sth • a step **in** (doing) sth

---

step[2] /step/ **verb** (**stepping, stepped**) **1 step back/forward/over, etc** ⓑ to move somewhere by lifting your foot and putting it down in a different place: *She stepped carefully over th dog.* **2 step on/in sth** ⓑ to put your foot on o in something: *I accidentally stepped on her foot*

PHRASAL VERBS **step down** to leave an importan job: *He stepped down as manager of the Italia team.* • **step in** to become involved in a difficul situation in order to help: [+ to do sth] *A Japanes bank stepped in to provide financial help.* • **ste sth up** to increase what you are doing to try t achieve something: *Police have stepped up thei efforts to find the man.*

stepbrother /'stepˌbrʌðər/ **noun** [C] not you parent's son but the son of the person you parent has married

step-by-step /ˌstepbaɪ'step/ **adj** [always befor noun] A step-by-step method, plan, etc, deal with one thing and then another thing in a fixe order: *a step-by-step guide to buying a house*

'step ˌchange noun [C] a very big change: *Ther is a step change taking place in communication technology.*

stepchild /'steptʃaɪld/ **noun** [C] (plural **stepchil dren**) the child of your husband or wife from a earlier marriage

stepdaughter /'stepˌdɔːtər/ **noun** [C] the daugh ter of your husband or wife from an earlie marriage

stepfather /'stepˌfɑːðər/ **noun** [C] ⓑ the ma who has married your mother but is not you father

stepmother /'stepˌmʌðər/ **noun** [C] ⓑ th woman who has married your father but is no your mother

stepping-stone /'stepɪŋstəʊn/ **noun** [C] **1** a event or experience that helps you achiev something else: *Education is a stepping-ston to a good job.* **2** one of several stones that yo walk on to cross a stream

stepsister /'stepˌsɪstər/ **noun** [C] not you

S

parent's daughter but the daughter of the person your parent has married

tepson /'stepsʌn/ **noun** [C] the son of your husband or wife from an earlier marriage

tereo /'steriəʊ/ **noun 1** [C] a piece of equipment for playing CDs, listening to the radio, etc that has two speakers (= parts where sound comes out) : *a car stereo* → See colour picture **The Living Room** on page Centre 4 **2** [U] a system for hearing music, speech, etc through two speakers (= parts where sound comes out): *The concert was broadcast in stereo.* ∘ *stereo sound*

tereotype¹ /'steriəʊtaɪp/ **noun** [C] a fixed idea that people have about what a particular type of person is like, especially an idea that is wrong: *racial stereotypes* • **stereotypical** /ˌsteriəʊ'tɪpɪkəl/ **adj** having the qualities that you expect a particular type of person to have: *a stereotypical student*

☑ **Word partners for stereotype**

challenge/fit a stereotype • a **negative** stereotype • a stereotype **of** sth • a **racial** stereotype

---

tereotype² /'steriəʊtaɪp/ **verb** [T] to have a fixed idea about what a particular type of person is like, especially an idea that is wrong: [often passive] *Young people are often **stereotyped as** being lazy.*

terile /'steraɪl/ **adj 1 CLEAN** ▷ completely clean and without any bacteria: *a sterile needle* **2 NO CHILDREN** ▷ unable to produce children **3 NO IDEAS** ▷ not having enough new ideas: *a sterile discussion* • **sterility** /stə'rɪləti/ **noun** [U]

terilize (also UK **-ise**) /'sterᵊlaɪz/ **verb** [T] **1** to make something clean and without bacteria: *a sterilized needle* **2** to perform a medical operation on someone to make them unable to have children • **sterilization** /ˌsterᵊlaɪ'zeɪʃᵊn/ **noun** [U]

terling /'stɜ:lɪŋ/ **noun** [U] British money

tern¹ /stɜ:n/ **adj** very serious and without any humour: *a **stern expression/face*** ∘ *stern criticism* • **sternly** adv

tern² /stɜ:n/ **noun** [C] the back part of a ship

teroid /'sterɔɪd/ **noun** [C] a drug for treating injuries, that some people use illegally in sport to make their muscles stronger

tethoscope /'steθəskəʊp/ **noun** [C] a piece of equipment that a doctor uses to listen to your heart and breathing

tew /stju:/ **noun** [C, U] a dish made of vegetables and meat cooked together slowly in liquid: *beef/lamb stew* • **stew verb** [T] to cook food slowly in liquid: *stewed fruit*

teward /'stju:əd/ **noun** [C] **1** a man who looks after people on an aircraft, boat, or train: *an air steward* **2** someone who helps to organize a race or big event

tewardess /'stju:ədes/ **noun** [C] a woman who looks after people on an aircraft, boat, or train: *an air stewardess*

th written abbreviation for something • **sth's** written abbreviation for something's

tick¹ /stɪk/ **verb** (**stuck**) **1** [I, T] 🔵 to become joined to something or to make something

---

become joined to something else, usually with a substance like glue: *Anne stuck a picture of her boyfriend on the wall.* ∘ *The stamp wouldn't **stick to** the envelope.* **2 stick sth in/on/under, etc** informal to put something somewhere: *Just stick your bag under the table.* **3 stick (sth) in/into/through, etc** 🔵 If something sharp sticks into something, it goes into it, and if you stick something sharp somewhere, you push it into something: *She stuck the needle into his arm.* **4** [I] to become fixed in one position and not be able to move: *This drawer has stuck – I can't open it.* **5 can't stick sb/sth** UK informal to not like someone or something: *I can't stick her.* → See also **stick to your guns** (**gun¹**), **poke/stick your nose¹ into sth**, **stick/put your oar in**

The boy stuck his tongue out.

PHRASAL VERBS **stick around** informal to stay somewhere for a period of time: *Stick around after the concert and you might meet the band.* • **stick at sth** to continue trying hard to do something difficult: *I know it's hard learning to drive but stick at it.* • **stick by sb** to continue to support someone when they are having problems • **stick out 1** 🔵 If part of something sticks out, it comes out further than the edge or surface: *His ears stick out a bit.* **2** to be very easy to notice: *She certainly sticks out in a crowd.* → See also **stick/stand out like a sore thumb¹** • **stick sth out** to make part of your body come forward from the rest of your body: *The little boy stuck his tongue out.* • **stick it out** informal to continue doing something that is boring, difficult, or unpleasant • **stick to sth** 🔵 to continue doing or using something and not change to anything else: *I'll stick to lemonade – I'm driving.* • **stick together** 🔵 If people stick together, they support and help each other. • **stick up** to point up above a surface and not lie flat: *I can't go out with my hair sticking up like this.* • **stick up for sb/sth** informal to support someone or something when they are being criticized • **stick with sb/sth** 🔵 to continue using someone or doing something and not change to anyone or anything else: *He's a good builder – I think we should stick with him.*

stick² /stɪk/ **noun** [C] **1** 🔵 a long, thin piece of wood, usually broken or fallen from a tree **2 walking/hockey, etc stick** 🔵 a long, thin piece of wood that you use when you are walking/playing hockey, etc **3** a long, thin piece of something: *a stick of candy/celery* → See also **carrot and stick**, **get (hold of) the wrong end¹ of the stick**

sticker /'stɪkər/ **noun** [C] a piece of paper or plastic with writing or a picture on it that you stick onto a surface: *a car sticker* → See also **bumper sticker**

sticky /'stɪki/ **adj 1** 🔵 made of or covered with a substance that can stick to other things: *sticky fingers* ∘ *sticky tape* **2** Sticky weather is unpleasantly hot. **3 a sticky moment/problem/**

S

---

situation, etc informal a moment/problem/situation, etc that is difficult or embarrasses you

stiff¹ /stɪf/ adj **1 HARD** ▷ 🄱🄲 hard and difficult to bend: *stiff material* **2 NOT MOVING** ▷ 🄱🄲 A door, drawer, etc that is stiff does not move as easily as it should. **3 HURTING** ▷ If a part of your body is stiff, it hurts and is difficult to move: *I've got a stiff neck.* **4 SEVERE** ▷ very severe or difficult: *stiff competition/opposition* ∘ *We need stiffer penalties for drink driving.* **5 FORMAL** ▷ behaving in a way that is formal and not relaxed **6 THICK** ▷ A stiff substance is thick and does not move around easily: *Whip the cream until it is stiff.* **7 stiff drink/whisky/vodka, etc** a strong alcoholic drink: *I need a stiff brandy.* **8 stiff wind/breeze** a wind that is quite strong • **stiffly** adv • **stiffness** noun [U]

stiff² /stɪf/ adv **bored/scared/worried, etc stiff** 🄱🄲 extremely bored, worried, etc: *The lecture was awful – I was bored stiff.*

stiffen /'stɪfᵊn/ verb [I, T] to become stiff or to make something become stiff **2** [I] to suddenly stop moving because you are frightened or angry: *She stiffened at the sound of the doorbell.*

stifle /'staɪfl/ verb [T] to stop something from happening or continuing: *to stifle a sneeze/yawn* ∘ *Large supermarkets stifle competition.*

stifling /'staɪflɪŋ/ adj extremely hot: *a stifling summer in Rome*

stigma /'stɪɡmə/ noun [C, U] If there is a stigma attached to something, people disapprove of it, especially when this is unfair: *There is still a stigma attached to being mentally ill.* • **stigmatize** (also UK **-ise**) verb [T] to treat someone or something unfairly by disapproving of them: [often passive] *Unmarried mothers are stigmatized by society.*

> 🄦 Word partners for **stigma**
>
> sth **carries** a stigma • the stigma **attached to/surrounding** sth • sth **loses** its stigma • a **social** stigma • the stigma **of (doing)** sth

stiletto /stɪ'letəʊ/ noun [C] a shoe with a very high, pointed heel (= part at the bottom and back of a shoe): *a pair of stilettos*

still¹ /stɪl/ adv **1 CONTINUING** ▷ 🄰🄲 used to say that something is continuing to happen now or that someone is continuing to do something now: *He's still here if you want to speak to him.* ∘ *Do you still play basketball?* **2 POSSIBLE** ▷ used to say that something continues to be possible: *We could still catch the train if we leave now.* **3 EMPHASIS** ▷ 🄱🄵 used to emphasize that you did not expect something to happen because something else makes it surprising: *He didn't do much work but still came top of the class.* ∘ *The weather was terrible. Still, we had a good holiday.* **4 better/harder/worse, etc still** 🄱🄲 better/harder/worse, etc than something else

still² /stɪl/ adj **1 stand/stay/sit, etc still** 🄱🄵 to stand, stay, sit, etc without moving: *Sit still so I can brush your hair.* **2** A still place is calm and quiet: *It was night and the whole village was still.* **3** UK 🄱🄵 A still drink does not have any bubbles in it. • **stillness** noun [U]

still³ /stɪl/ noun [C] a photograph from o[ne] moment in a film

stillborn /ˌstɪl'bɔːn/ ⓤⓢ /'stɪlˌbɔːn/ adj born dea[d]: *a stillborn baby*

stilt /stɪlt/ noun [C] **1** one of two long poles th[at] you can stand on and use to walk above th[e] ground: [usually plural] *a clown on stilts* **2** one [of] several poles that support a building above th[e] ground: [usually plural] *a house on stilts*

stilted /'stɪltɪd/ adj talking or writing in a form[al] way that does not sound natural: *a stilte[d] conversation*

stimulant /'stɪmjələnt/ noun [C] a drug tha[t] makes you feel more active and awake: *Coff[ee] contains caffeine which is a stimulant.*

stimulate /'stɪmjəleɪt/ verb [T] **1** 🄱🄲 to mak[e] something happen or develop more: *It stim[u]lates the production of red blood cells.* **2** 🄱🄲 [to] make someone feel interested and excite[d:] *Colourful pictures can stimulate a child.* • **stim[u]lation** /ˌstɪmjə'leɪʃᵊn/ noun [U]

stimulating /'stɪmjəleɪtɪŋ/ adj interesting an[d] making you think: *a stimulating discussion*

stimulus /'stɪmjələs/ noun [C, U] (plural **stimul[i]** /'stɪmjəlaɪ/) something that makes somethin[g] else happen, grow, or develop more: *The repo[rt] provided the stimulus for more studies.*

> 🄦 Word partners for **stimulus**
>
> **act as/provide** a stimulus • a stimulus **for/to** sth

sting¹ /stɪŋ/ verb (**stung**) **1 CAUSE PAIN** ▷ [T] [If] an insect, plant, etc stings you, it causes pain b[y] putting poison into your skin: *He was stung by [a] wasp.* **2 FEEL PAIN** ▷ [I, T] If your eyes, skin, e[tc] sting, or if something makes them sting, yo[u] feel a sudden, burning pain: *That shampoo real[ly] made my eyes sting.* **3 UPSET** ▷ [T] to upse[t] someone: [often passive] *She was clearly stung b[y] his criticism.*

sting² /stɪŋ/ noun **1 WOUND** ▷ [C] a painf[ul] wound that you get when an insect, plant, e[tc] puts poison into your skin: *a wasp/bee stin[g]* **2 PAIN** ▷ [no plural] a sudden, burning pain [in] your eyes, skin, etc **3 UPSET** ▷ [no plural] th[e] feeling of being upset by something: *the sting [of] defeat*

stingy /'stɪndʒi/ adj informal not generous: *He['s] too stingy to buy any drinks.*

stink¹ /stɪŋk/ verb [I] (**stank**, also US **stunk** stunk) **1** to smell very bad: *The kitchen stinks [of] fish.* **2** informal to be very bad and dishonest: [If] you ask me, the whole affair stinks.*

stink² /stɪŋk/ noun **1 make/cause/create, etc [a] stink** informal to complain about something [in a] forceful way **2** [no plural] a very bad smell

stint /stɪnt/ noun [C] a period of time spe[nt] doing something: *He had a two-year stint as [a] teacher in Spain.*

stipulate /'stɪpjəleɪt/ verb [T] formal to sa[y] exactly what must be done: [+ (that)] *The rule[s] stipulate that smoking is not allowed.* • **stipula[-] tion** /ˌstɪpjə'leɪʃᵊn/ noun [C]

stir¹ /stɜːʳ/ verb (**stirring, stirred**) **1 MIX** ▷ [T] 🄱[?] to mix food or liquid by moving a spoon roun[d]

S

and round in it: *Stir the **mixture** until it is smooth.* **2 MOVE** ▷ [I, T] to move slightly or make someone move slightly: *The baby stirred in its sleep.* **3 FEEL** ▷ [T] to make someone feel a strong emotion: *The case has **stirred** great **anger** among the public.*

PHRASAL VERB **stir sth up 1** to cause arguments or bad feelings between people, often intentionally: *I think she just likes to **stir up trouble.*** **2** If something stirs up memories, it makes you remember events in the past: *The photographs **stirred up** some painful **memories**.*

stir² /stɜːʳ/ noun **1 cause/create a stir** to make people excited or surprised: *Her new book has caused quite a stir.* **2** [no plural] the action of mixing food or liquid with a spoon: *Could you give the soup a stir?*

stir-fry /ˈstɜːˌfraɪ/ verb [T] to fry small pieces of vegetable, meat, etc very quickly while mixing them around • **stir-fry** noun [C]

stirring /ˈstɜːrɪŋ/ adj making people feel excitement or other strong emotions: *a **stirring** performance/speech*

stirrup /ˈstɪrəp/ noun [C] one of the two metal parts that support your feet when you are riding a horse

stitch¹ /stɪtʃ/ noun **1 THREAD** ▷ [C] a short line of thread that is sewn through a piece of material **2 WOUND** ▷ [C] one of the small pieces of thread that is used to sew together a cut: *She needed 50 stitches in her head.* **3 WOOL** ▷ [C] one of the small circles of wool that you make when you are knitting (= making something from wool) **4 PAIN** ▷ [no plural] a sudden pain that you get in the side of your body when you exercise too much: *to get a stitch* **5 in stitches** laughing a lot: *He had the whole audience in stitches.*

stitch² /stɪtʃ/ verb [I, T] to sew two things together or to repair something by sewing: *I need to get my shoes stitched.*

PHRASAL VERB **stitch sth up** to sew together the two parts of something that have come apart: *The nurse stitched up my finger.*

stock¹ /stɒk/ noun **1 SHOP** ▷ [U] all the goods that are available in a shop: *We're expecting some new stock in this afternoon.* **2 be in stock/out of stock** to be available/not available in a shop **3 SUPPLY** ▷ [C] a supply of something that is ready to be used: [usually plural] *stocks of food/weapons* **4 COMPANY** ▷ [C, U] the value of a company, or a share in its value: *to buy/sell stock* ◦ *falling/rising **stock prices*** **5 LIQUID** ▷ [U] a liquid made by boiling meat, bones, or vegetables and used to make soups, sauces, etc: *chicken/vegetable stock* **6 take stock (of sth)** to think carefully about a situation before making a decision → See also **laughing stock**

stock² /stɒk/ verb [T] to have something available for people to buy: *They stock a wide range of books and magazines.*

PHRASAL VERB **stock up** to buy a lot of something: *We'd better **stock up on** food for the holiday.*

stock³ /stɒk/ adj **stock answer/phrase, etc** an answer/phrase, etc that is always used and so is not really useful

stockbroker /ˈstɒkˌbrəʊkəʳ/ noun [C] someone whose job is to buy and sell stocks and shares in companies for other people

the ˈstock exˌchange noun (also **the ˈstock ˌmarket**) **1** the place where stocks and shares in companies are bought and sold **2** the value of stocks and shares being bought and sold

stocking /ˈstɒkɪŋ/ noun [C] a very thin piece of clothing that covers a woman's foot and leg: *a pair of stockings*

stockpile /ˈstɒkpaɪl/ verb [T] to collect a lot of something, usually so that it can be used in the future: *to stockpile food* • **stockpile** noun [C] *a stockpile of weapons*

stocky /ˈstɒki/ adj having a wide, strong, body: *a short, stocky man*

stoic /ˈstəʊɪk/ adj formal dealing with pain, problems, etc, but never complaining • **stoically** adv • **stoicism** /ˈstəʊɪsɪzᵊm/ noun [U] stoic behaviour

stole /stəʊl/ past tense of steal

stolen /ˈstəʊlᵊn/ past participle of steal

stolid /ˈstɒlɪd/ adj calm and not showing emotion or excitement

stomach¹ /ˈstʌmək/ noun [C] (plural **stomachs**) **1** ⓐ the organ inside your body where food goes after it has been eaten and where it starts to be digested **2** ⓐ the front part of your body just below your chest: *He punched me in the stomach.* → See colour picture **The Body** on page Centre 13 **3 have no stomach for sth** to not feel brave enough to do something unpleasant → See also **have butterflies (in your stomach) (butterfly)**

stomach² /ˈstʌmək/ verb informal **can't stomach sth** to be unable to deal with, watch, etc something unpleasant: *I can't stomach horror movies.*

ˈstomach ˌache noun [C, U] ⓐ pain in your stomach: *I've got terrible stomach ache.*

stomp /stɒmp/ verb [I] to put your foot down on the ground hard and quickly, or to walk with heavy steps, usually because you are angry: *He stomped off to his room.*

stone¹ /stəʊn/ noun **1 SUBSTANCE** ▷ [U] ⓑ a hard, natural substance that is found in the ground: *a stone wall* **2 ROCK** ▷ [C] ⓑ a small rock or piece of rock **3 JEWEL** ▷ [C] ⓑ a hard, valuable substance that is often used in jewellery: *precious stones* **4 WEIGHT** ▷ [C] (plural **stone**) UK a unit for measuring weight, equal to 6.35 kilograms or 14 pounds: *I gained two stone when I was pregnant.* → See Study Page **Measurements** on page Centre 31 **5 SEED** ▷ [C] the hard seed that is at the centre of some fruits: *a cherry stone* → See also **stepping-stone**

stone² /stəʊn/ verb [T] to kill or hurt someone by throwing stones (= small rocks) at them, usually as a punishment: [often passive] *Two men were **stoned to death** by the crowd.*

stoned /stəʊnd/ adj informal **1** relaxed or excited because of the effect of drugs **2** drunk

stonemason /ˈstəʊnˌmeɪsᵊn/ **noun** [C] someone who makes things from stone

stony /ˈstəʊni/ **adj 1** covered with or containing stones (= small rocks): *a stony path/road* **2** not friendly, usually because you are angry: *a stony silence*

stood /stʊd/ past of stand

stool /stuːl/ **noun** [C] **B2** a seat that does not have a back or arms: *a piano/bar stool*

stool

stoop¹ /stuːp/ **verb** [I] to bend the top half of your body forward and down: *He stooped to pick up the letter.*

PHRASAL VERB **stoop to sth/doing sth** to do something bad that will give you an advantage: *I can't believe he would stoop to blackmail.*

stoop² /stuːp/ **noun 1** [no plural] If someone has a stoop, the upper part of their body is bent forwards. **2** [C] US a raised area in front of the door of a house, with steps leading up to it

stop¹ /stɒp/ **verb** (**stopping, stopped**) **1 FINISH** ▷ [I, T] **A1** to finish doing something that you were doing: [+ doing sth] *Stop laughing – it's not funny.* ∘ *He started to say something and then stopped.* ∘ *I'm trying to work but I keep having to stop to answer the phone* (= stop so that I can answer the telephone). **2 FOR A SHORT TIME** ▷ [I] **A2** to stop a journey or an activity for a short time: *He stopped at a pub for lunch.* **3 NOT OPERATE** ▷ [I, T] **B1** to not continue to operate, or to make something not continue to operate: *My watch has stopped.* ∘ *Can you stop the tape for a minute?* **4 FINISH MOVING** ▷ [I, T] **B1** to not move any more, or make someone or something not move any more: *A car stopped outside the house.* ∘ *I stopped someone in the street to ask for directions.* **5 BUS/TRAIN** ▷ [I] **A2** If a bus, train, etc stops at a particular place, it pauses at that place so that people can get on and off: *Does this train stop at Cambridge?* **6 END** ▷ [T] **B1** to make something end: *We must find a way to stop the war.* **7 PREVENT** ▷ [T] **B1** to prevent something from happening or someone from doing something: [+ from + doing sth] *Health workers are trying to stop the disease from spreading.* **8 Stop it/that!** **A1** used to tell someone to finish doing something, usually something annoying: *Stop it! I can't concentrate if you keep making a noise.* **9 stop a cheque** UK (US **stop a check**) to prevent money from being paid from a cheque (= a piece of paper that you sign to pay for things) → See also **stop at nothing, stop the rot²**

PHRASAL VERBS **stop by (sth)** to visit a person or place for a short time: *If you're passing our house, why don't you stop by sometime?* • **stop off** to visit a place for a short time when you are going somewhere else: *We stopped off in Paris for a couple of days before heading south.*

! Common learner error: **stop doing** something or **stop to do** something?

Stop doing something means 'not continue with an activity'.
Suddenly, everyone stopped talking.
~~Suddenly, everyone stopped to talk.~~

Stop to do something means 'stop one activity so that you can do something else'.
We stopped to look at the map.

stop² /stɒp/ **noun** [C] **1** **A1** a place where a bus or train stops so that people can get on or off: *We need to get off at the next stop.* → See Note at **station¹ 2** put a stop to sth to end something unpleasant: *We must put a stop to the violence.* **3** a place where you stop on a journey, or the time that you spend there: *We had an overnight stop in Singapore.* **4 come to a stop** **B1** to stop moving: *The car came to a stop in front of an old cottage.*

IDIOM **pull out all the stops** to do everything you can to make something succeed

→ See also **bus stop, full stop**

stoplight /ˈstɒplaɪt/ **noun** [C] US a set of red, green, and yellow lights that is used to stop and start traffic

stopover /ˈstɒpˌəʊvəʳ/ **noun** [C] **B2** a short stop between parts of a journey, especially a plane journey

stoppage /ˈstɒpɪdʒ/ **noun** [C] an occasion when people stop working because they are angry about something their employers have done

ˈstop ˌsign noun [C] a sign on the road which tells drivers of vehicles to stop and not to continue until all other vehicles have gone past

stopwatch /ˈstɒpwɒtʃ/ **noun** [C] a watch that can measure exactly how long it takes to do something, and that is often used in sports activities

storage /ˈstɔːrɪdʒ/ **noun** [U] **B2** If things are in storage, they have been put in a safe place until they are needed: *We had to put our furniture into storage.*

store¹ /stɔːʳ/ **noun** [C] **1** mainly US **B1** a shop: *a book store* ∘ *She works at a men's clothing store.* → See Note at **shop¹ 2** a supply of something that you are keeping to use later: *a store of grain* **3 be in store (for sb)** If something is in store for you, it will happen to you in the future: *There's a surprise in store for you!*

IDIOM **set great store by sth** to believe that something is very important: *Martina sets great store by physical strength and fitness.*

→ See also **chain store, convenience store, department store, liquor store**

store² /stɔːʳ/ **verb** [T] **1** (also **store away**) **B2** to put something somewhere and not use it until you need it: *We have a lot of old clothes stored in the attic.* **2** **B2** to keep information on a computer: *All the data is stored on the server.*

storekeeper /ˈstɔːˌkiːpəʳ/ **noun** [C] US (UK **shopkeeper**) someone who owns or manages a small shop

toreroom /'stɔːrruːm/ **noun** [C] a room where goods are kept until they are needed

torey UK (US **story**) /'stɔːri/ **noun** [C] ⓑ a level of a building: *a three-storey house*

tork /stɔːk/ **noun** [C] a large, white bird with very long legs that walks around in water to find its food

torm¹ /stɔːm/ **noun** [C] **1** ⓐ very bad weather with a lot of rain, snow, wind, etc: *a snow/thunder storm* **2 a storm of controversy/protest, etc** a strong, negative reaction to something that has been said or done

---
🗒 Word partners for **storm**

an **approaching/gathering** storm • a **fierce/ severe/violent** storm • a storm **breaks** • a storm **abates/passes**
---

torm² /stɔːm/ **verb 1** [T] to attack a building, town, etc, using violence: *Armed police stormed the embassy and arrested hundreds of protesters.* **2 storm into/out of, etc** to enter or leave a place in a very noisy way because you are angry: *He stormed out of the meeting.*

torm surge noun [C] a lot of water that is pushed from the sea onto the land, usually caused by a hurricane (= a violent storm with very strong winds)

tormy /'stɔːmi/ **adj 1** If it is stormy, the weather is bad with a lot of wind and rain: *a stormy night* ∘ *stormy seas* **2** A stormy relationship or situation involves a lot of anger and arguments: *a stormy relationship* ∘ *a stormy meeting/ debate*

tory /'stɔːri/ **noun** [C] **1 DESCRIPTION** ▷ ⓐ a description of a series of real or imaginary events which is intended to entertain people: *a horror/detective story* ∘ *the story of the revolution* ∘ *Tell us a story, Grandpa.* ∘ *She reads stories to the children every night.* **2 REPORT** ▷ a report in a newspaper, magazine, or news programme: *Today's main story is the hurricane in Texas.* **3 EXPLANATION** ▷ an explanation of why something happened, which may not be true: *Did he tell you the same story about why he was late?* **4 BUILDING** ▷ US spelling of storey

---
🗒 Word partners for **story**

read/listen to a story • **tell sb** a story • a story **about/of** sth
---

tout¹ /staʊt/ **adj 1** quite fat: *a short, stout man* **2** If shoes or other objects are stout, they are strong and thick.

tout² /staʊt/ **noun** [C, U] a very dark beer

tove /stəʊv/ **noun** [C] **1** a piece of equipment that you cook on: *I've left some soup on the stove for you.* → See colour picture **The Kitchen** on page Centre 2 **2** a piece of equipment that burns coal, gas, wood, etc and is used for heating a room

tow /stəʊ/ **verb** [T] (also **stow away**) to put something in a particular place until it is needed: *Our camping equipment is stowed away in the loft.*

towaway /'stəʊəˌweɪ/ **noun** [C] someone who hides on a ship or aircraft so that they can travel without paying

straddle /'strædl/ **verb** [T] **1** to sit or stand with one leg on either side of something: *He straddled the chair.* **2** to be on both sides of a place: *Niagara Falls straddles the Canadian border.*

straggle /'strægl/ **verb** [I] **1** to move more slowly than other members of a group: *Some runners are straggling a long way behind.* **2** to grow or spread out in an untidy way: *I could see a line of straggling bushes.*

straggly /'strægli/ **adj** growing or spreading out in an untidy way: *a straggly beard*

straight¹ /streɪt/ **adj 1 NOT CURVED** ▷ ⓐ not curved or bent: *a straight road* ∘ *straight hair* **2 LEVEL** ▷ ⓑ in a position that is level or vertical: *That shelf's not straight.* **3 IN A SERIES** ▷ [always before noun] one after another: *They've won five straight games so far.* **4 HONEST** ▷ ⓑ honest: *a straight answer* **5 DRINK** ▷ An alcoholic drink that is straight is not mixed with water, ice, etc. **6 get sth straight** to make sure that you completely understand a situation: *Let me get this straight – am I paying for this?* **7 NOT HOMOSEXUAL** ▷ informal not homosexual → See also **keep a straight face**

straight² /streɪt/ **adv 1** ⓐ in a straight line: *It's straight ahead.* ∘ *He was looking straight at me.* **2** ⓑ immediately: *I went straight back to sleep.* **3 sit up/stand up straight** ⓑ to sit or stand with your body vertical **4 not think straight** If you cannot think straight, you are not thinking clearly about something: *I was so tired, I couldn't think straight.* **5 tell sb straight (out)** to tell someone the truth in a clear way: *I told him straight that he wasn't getting a pay increase.* **6 straight away** ⓑ immediately: *Go there straight away.*

straighten /'streɪtᵊn/ **verb** [I, T] to become straight or to make something straight

---
PHRASAL VERBS **straighten sth out** to successfully deal with a problem or a confusing situation: *We need to straighten a few things out.* • **straighten sth up** to make a place tidy: *Could you straighten up your room?* • **straighten up** to stand so that your back is straight
---

straightforward /ˌstreɪt'fɔːwəd/ **adj 1** ⓑ easy to do or understand: *The task looked fairly straightforward.* **2** saying clearly and honestly what you think: *She's very straightforward.*

strain¹ /streɪn/ **noun 1 FEELING** ▷ [C, U] ⓑ a feeling of being worried and nervous about something: *The strain of the last few months had exhausted her.* **2 put a strain on sb/sth** to cause problems for someone or to make a situation difficult: *Children put tremendous strains on a marriage.* **3 INJURY** ▷ [C, U] an injury to part of your body that is caused by using it too much: *back strain* **4 STRETCH** ▷ [U] ⓑ the fact of being pulled or stretched too tightly: *The rope broke under the strain.* **5 DISEASE/PLANT** ▷ [C] a type of disease or plant: *a new strain of virus*

🗒 Word partners for **strain**

feel the strain • be **under** strain • the strain **of doing sth**
---

strain² /streɪn/ **verb 1 TRY HARD** ▷ [I, T] to try

S

hard to do something, usually to see or hear something: [+ to do sth] *I had to strain to hear the music.* **2 INJURE** ▷ [T] ⏥ to injure part of your body by using it too much: *I think I've strained a muscle.* **3 CAUSE PROBLEMS** ▷ [T] to cause problems for a situation or relationship: *The incident has strained relations between the two countries.* **4 MONEY** ▷ [T] to cause too much of something to be used, especially money: *The war is straining the defence budget.* **5 SEPARATE** ▷ [T] to separate solids from a liquid by pouring the mixture into a container with small holes in it: *Strain the sauce to remove the seeds and skins.*

strained /streɪnd/ **adj 1** showing that someone is nervous or anxious: *We had a rather **strained conversation**.* **2** If a relationship is strained, problems are spoiling that relationship: *Relations are still **strained** between the two countries.* ○ *They have a rather **strained relationship**.*

strainer /'streɪnər/ **noun** [C] a kitchen tool with a lot of holes in it, used for separating pieces of food from liquid

strait /streɪt/ **noun** [C] a narrow area of sea that connects two large areas of sea: [usually plural] *the straits of Florida*

strait-jacket /'streɪtˌdʒækɪt/ **noun** [C] a jacket that prevents people from moving their arms, especially used in the past for mentally ill people

strand /strænd/ **noun** [C] **1** a thin piece of hair, thread, rope, etc: *She tucked a **strand of hair** behind her ear.* **2** one part of a story, situation, idea, etc: *There are a number of different strands to the plot.*

stranded /'strændɪd/ **adj** unable to leave a place: *We were stranded at the airport for ten hours.*

strange /streɪndʒ/ **adj 1** ⏥ If something is strange, it is surprising because it is unusual or unexpected: [+ (that)] *It's strange that she hasn't called.* ○ *It's midnight and he's still at work – that's strange.* ○ *What a strange-looking man.* **2** ⏥ A strange person or place is one that you are not familiar with: *I was stuck in a strange town with no money.* ● **strangely adv** ⏥ *She's been behaving very strangely (= in an unusual way) recently.*

> ➕ **Other ways of saying strange**
>
> Other ways of saying 'strange' are **odd, bizarre**, and **weird**:
>
> *I always thought there was something a bit **odd** about her.*
>
> *I had a really **bizarre/weird** dream last night.*
>
> If something is strange because it is not what you usually expect, you can use the adjectives **curious, funny**, or **peculiar**:
>
> *This lemonade tastes **funny**.*
>
> *The chicken had a **peculiar** smell.*
>
> *A **curious** thing happened to me yesterday.*
>
> If someone always behaves strangely, you might describe them as **eccentric**:
>
> *The whole family are **eccentric**.*

stranger /'streɪndʒər/ **noun** [C] **1** ⏥ someon• you have never met before: *I can't just walk up• a complete stranger and start speaking to ther* **2 be no stranger to sth** to have a lot • experience of something: *He's no stranger to ha• work himself.*

strangle /'stræŋgl/ **verb** [T] **1** to kill someone I pressing their throat with your hands, a rop• wire, etc: [often passive] *Police believe the victi• was strangled.* **2** to prevent something fro• developing: *High-level corruption is strangling t• economy.*

stranglehold /'stræŋglhəʊld/ **noun** [no plural] position of complete control that preven• something from developing: *Two major comp• nies have a **stranglehold on** the market.*

strap /stræp/ **noun** [C] a narrow piece of materi• used to fasten two things together or to car• something: *a watch strap* ○ *a bra strap* ○ *I want• bag with a shoulder strap.* ● **strap verb** [(strapping, strapped)** to fasten somethir• using a strap

strategic /strə'tiːdʒɪk/ **adj 1 PLAN** ▷ helping • achieve a plan, usually in business or politic• *strategic planning* **2 WAR** ▷ related to fightir• a war: *strategic weapons* **3 POSITION** ▷ something is in a strategic position, it is in • useful place for achieving something. ● **strat• gically adv**

strategy /'strætədʒi/ **noun 1** [C] ⏥ a plan th• you use to achieve something: *an econom• strategy* ○ *a long-term strategy* **2** [U] the act • planning how to achieve something: *a militar• strategy*

> ☑ Word partners for **strategy**
>
> **adopt/develop/have** a strategy ● a strategy **for doing sth** ● the strategy **of doing sth** ● an **economic** strategy ● a **long-term/short-term** strategy ● a **sales** strategy

straw /strɔː/ **noun 1** [U] the long, dried stems • plants such as wheat (= plant for grain), ofte• given to animals for sleeping on and eating: *straw hat* **2** [C] a thin plastic or paper tube th• you use for drinking through

IDIOM **the final/last straw** the last in a series • unpleasant events that finally makes you sto• accepting a bad situation: *Last week he cam• home drunk at five in the morning, and that w• the last straw.*

strawberry /'strɔːbəri/ **noun** [C] ⏥ a small, re• fruit with a green leaf at the top and sma• brown seeds on its surface

stray[1] /streɪ/ **verb** [I] **1** to move away from th• place where you should be, without intendin• to: *I suddenly realized that I had **strayed** far fro• the village.* **2** to start thinking or talking about• different subject from the one you should I giving attention to: *We seem to have **straye• from** the original **subject**.*

stray[2] /streɪ/ **adj** [always before noun] **1** A stra• animal is lost or has no home: *a **stray dog*** **2** • stray piece of something has become separate• from the main part: *a stray hair*

stray³ /streɪ/ **noun** [C] an animal that is lost or has no home

streak¹ /striːk/ **noun** [C] **1** a thin line or mark: *She has a streak of white hair.* **2** a quality in someone's character, especially a bad one: *Tom has a **mean/ruthless streak**.* **3 a winning/losing streak** a period of always winning/losing a game: *I'm **on a winning streak**.*

streak² /striːk/ **verb 1 streak across/down/ through, etc** to move quickly: *The plane streaked across the sky.* **2 be streaked with sth** to have thin lines of a different colour: *His dark hair was lightly streaked with grey.*

stream

stream   stream of water

stream¹ /striːm/ **noun** [C] **1** ⒶⒷ a small river **2 a stream of sth a** ⒷⒷ a line of people or vehicles moving in the same direction: *a constant stream of traffic* **b** a large number of similar things that happen or appear one after another: *He has produced a steady stream of books.* **c** ⒷⒷ a moving line of liquid, gas, smoke, etc: *A stream of smoke was coming from the chimney.*

stream² /striːm/ **verb 1 stream down/in/ through, etc** to move or flow continuously in one direction: *Tears were streaming down her face.* **2** [T] to listen to or watch something on a computer directly from the Internet

streamer /ˈstriːmər/ **noun** [C] a long, narrow piece of coloured paper that you use to decorate a room or place for a party

streamline /ˈstriːmlaɪn/ **verb** [T] **1** to make an organization or process simpler and more effective: *We need to streamline our production procedures.* **2** to give a vehicle a smooth shape so that it moves easily through air or water

street /striːt/ **noun** [C] ⒶⒷ a road in a town or city that has houses or other buildings: *We live on the same street.* ∘ *a street map*

IDIOMS **the man/person, etc in the street** a typical, ordinary person • **be right up sb's street** UK informal (US **be right up sb's alley**) to be exactly the type of thing that someone knows about or likes to do: *I've got a little job here which should be right up your street.* • **be streets ahead (of sb/sth)** UK to be much better or more advanced than someone or something else:

American film companies are streets ahead of their European rivals.

→ See also **high street, Wall Street**

streetcar /ˈstriːtkɑːr/ **noun** [C] US (also US **trolley**, mainly UK **tram**) an electric vehicle for carrying passengers, mostly in cities, which runs along metal tracks in the road

street light **noun** [C] (also **street lamp**) a light on a tall post next to a street → See picture at **light**

streetwise /ˈstriːtwaɪz/ **adj** (also US **street-smart**) Someone who is streetwise knows how to manage dangerous or difficult situations in big towns or cities.

strength /streŋθ/ **noun 1 STRONG** ▷ [U] ⒷⒷ the quality of being strong: *upper-body strength* ∘ *A good boxer needs skill as well as strength.* **2 INFLUENCE** ▷ [U] the power or influence that an organization, country, etc has: *economic strength* **3 BEING BRAVE** ▷ [U] the quality of being brave or determined in difficult situations: *I think she showed great **strength of character**.* **4 GOOD QUALITIES** ▷ [C] a good quality or ability that makes someone or something effective: *We all have our **strengths and weaknesses**.* ∘ *The great strength of this arrangement is its simplicity.* **5 STRONG FEELING** ▷ [U] how strong a feeling or opinion is: *There is great **strength of feeling** against tax increases.* **6 VALUE** ▷ [U] the value of a country's money: *The strength of the dollar has traders worried.* **7 at full strength** with the necessary number of people: *Our team is now at full strength.* **8 on the strength of sth** If you do something on the strength of facts or advice, you do it because of them: *On the strength of this year's sales figures, we've decided to expand the business.*

IDIOM **go from strength to strength** UK to continue to become more successful

→ See also a **tower¹ of strength**

> **☑ Word partners for strength**
> **full/great/superhuman** strength • **draw/have/ muster/regain/sap** strength

strengthen /ˈstreŋθən/ **verb** [I, T] ⒷⒷ to become stronger or make something become stronger: *exercises to strengthen the leg muscles*

strenuous /ˈstrenjuəs/ **adj** using or needing a lot of effort: *strenuous exercise*

> **☑ Word partners for stress**
> **be under** stress • **cope with/deal with/handle** stress • **alleviate/combat/reduce/relieve** stress • stress **levels**

stress¹ /stres/ **noun 1 WORRY** ▷ [C, U] ⒷⒷ feelings of worry caused by difficult situations such as problems at work: *work-related stress* ∘ *She's been **under** a lot of **stress** recently.* **2 IMPORTANCE** ▷ [U] special importance that you give to something: *At school, they **laid** great **stress** on academic achievement.* **3 PHYSICAL FORCE** ▷ [C, U] physical force on something: *Jogging **puts** a lot of **stress on** your knee joints.* **4 STRONG PART** ▷ [U] ⒷⒷ the emphasis you put

S

on one part of a word: *In the word 'blanket', the* **stress** *is* **on** *the first syllable.*

stress² /stres/ **verb 1** [T] 🄱🄲 to emphasize something in order to show that it is important: [+ (that)] *I stressed that this was our policy.* **2** [I] informal to be worried: *Stop stressing about tonight – it'll be fine.*

stressed /strest/ **adj** (also **stressed out**) 🄱🄱 worried and not able to relax: *Tanya's really stressed out about her exams.*

stressful /'stresfʊl/ **adj** 🄱🄱 making you stressed: *a stressful job*

stretch¹ /stretʃ/ **verb 1** [I, T] 🄱🄲 to become longer or wider, or to pull something so that it becomes longer or wider: *Don't pull my sweater – you'll stretch it.* **2** [I, T] 🄱🄲 to make your body or part of your body straighter and longer: *Stretch your arms above your head.* **3 stretch away/into, etc** to cover a large area: *The fields stretched away into the distance.* **4 stretch into/over, etc** to continue for a long period of time: *The discussions will probably stretch into next month.* → See also **stretch your legs, bend/stretch the rules (rule¹)**

PHRASAL VERB **stretch out** to lie with your legs and arms spread out in a relaxed way

stretch² /stretʃ/ **noun** [C] **1 LAND/WATER** ▷ an area of land or water: *a stretch of coastline* **2 TIME** ▷ a continuous period of time: *He often worked ten hours* **at a stretch.** **3 BODY** ▷ the action of stretching part of your body: *I always* **do** *a few* **stretches** *before I go jogging.*

IDIOM **not by any stretch of the imagination** used to say that something, often a description, is certainly not true: *She was never a great player, not by any stretch of the imagination.*

stretcher /'stretʃər/ **noun** [C] a flat structure covered with cloth which is used to carry someone who is sick or injured

stretcher

stricken /'strɪkᵊn/ **adj** suffering from the effects of something bad, such as illness, sadness, etc: *a child stricken by fear* → See also **panic-stricken, poverty-stricken**

strict /strɪkt/ **adj 1 PERSON** ▷ 🄱🄱 A strict person makes sure that children or people working for them behave well and does not allow them to break any rules: *a strict teacher* ∘ *My parents were very* **strict with** *us.* **2 RULE** ▷ 🄱🄲 If a rule, law, etc is strict, it must be obeyed: *She gave me* **strict** *instructions to be there by ten.* **3 BEHAVIOUR** ▷ [always before noun] 🄱🄲 always behaving in a particular way because of your beliefs: *a strict Muslim* **4 EXACT** ▷ exactly correct: *a strict translation of a text*

strictly /'strɪktli/ **adv 1** 🄱🄲 exactly or correctly: *That's not* **strictly** *true.* ∘ *Strictly speaking* (= *The rules say*), *we're not allowed to give you any advice.* **2** done or existing for a particular person or purpose: *Her visit is strictly business.*

3 strictly forbidden/prohibited 🄱🄲 used to emphasize that something is not allowed

stride¹ /straɪd/ **verb** (**strode**) **stride across, down/into, etc** to walk somewhere with long steps: *She strode across the stage.*

stride² /straɪd/ **noun** [C] a long step when walking or running

IDIOMS **get into your stride** UK (US **hit your stride**) to start to do something well and with confidence because you have been doing it for a period: *Once I get into my stride, I'm sure I'll work much faster.* ● **take sth in your stride** UK (US **take sth in stride**) to calmly deal with something that is unpleasant and not let it affect what you are doing: *There are often problems at work but she seems to take it all in her stride.*

strident /'straɪdᵊnt/ **adj 1** expressed in a strong way: *strident criticism* **2** loud and unpleasant: *a strident voice*

strife /straɪf/ **noun** [U] formal trouble or disagreement between people

strike¹ /straɪk/ **verb** (**struck**) **1 HIT** ▷ [T] 🄱🄱 to hit someone or something: *His car went out of control and struck a tree.* ∘ *I've never heard of anyone being* **struck by lightning.** **2 THINK** ▷ [T] 🄱🄲 If a thought or idea strikes you, you suddenly think of it: [+ (that)] *It struck me that I'd forgotten to order the champagne.* **3 strike sb as sth** If someone strikes you as having a particular quality, they seem to have that quality: *He didn't strike me as a passionate man.* **4 NOT WORK** ▷ [I] 🄱🄲 to stop working for a period of time because you want more money, etc: *Bus drivers are threatening to strike.* **5 EFFECT** ▷ [T] If something bad strikes something or someone, it affects them strongly and quickly: *The hurricane struck the coast at about eight in the morning.* **6 ATTACK** ▷ [I] to attack suddenly: *The marines will strike at dawn.* **7 CLOCK** ▷ [I, T] If a clock strikes, a bell rings to show what the time is. **8 strike gold, oil, etc** to find a supply of gold, oil, etc in the ground **9 strike a match** to light a match in order to produce fire **10 strike a balance** to give two things the same amount of attention: *It's important to* **strike a balance** *between spending and saving.* **11 strike a deal** If two people strike a deal, they promise to do something for each other that will give them both an advantage: *The book's author has struck a deal with a major film company.* → See also **strike a chord (with sb), be struck dumb**

PHRASAL VERBS **strike back** to attack someone who has attacked you ● **strike out 1** to start moving towards somewhere in a determined way: *She struck out for the opposite bank.* **2** US informal to fail at something: *I really struck out with her – she wouldn't even let me kiss her goodbye.* ● **strike sth out** to draw a line through something wrong that you have written ● **strike up sth** to start a conversation or relationship with someone: *I struck up a* **conversation** *with a guy who worked behind the bar.*

strike² /straɪk/ **noun 1** [C, U] 🄱🄱 a period of time when people are not working because they want more money, etc: *Teachers are planning to* **go on**

strike next month. **2** [C] a sudden military attack: *an air strike* → See also **hunger strike**

🔲 Word partners for **strike noun**

be on/go on strike • a strike **over** sth • strike **action**

triker /'straɪkər/ noun [C] **1** someone who is on strike **2** a football player whose job is to try to score goals

triking /'straɪkɪŋ/ adj **1** 🅑2 easily noticed: *There's a **striking resemblance** between them.* **2** very attractive: *She's very striking.*

tring¹ /strɪŋ/ noun **1** [C, U] 🅑2 very thin rope used for tying things: *a ball of string* **2** [C] 🅑2 a piece of wire that is part of a musical instrument: *guitar strings* **3** a **string of beads/pearls** a set of decorative things joined together on a thread, worn as jewellery **4** a **string of** sth a number of similar things: *a string of questions* ∘ *As a writer, she's enjoyed a string of successes.*

IDIOMS **no strings (attached)** If there are no strings attached to an offer or arrangement, there is nothing that is unpleasant that you have to accept: *I'll drive you home – no strings attached.* • **pull strings** to secretly use the influence that you have over important people to get something or to help someone

tring² /strɪŋ/ verb [T] (**strung**) to hang something somewhere with string: *They had strung flags across the entrance to welcome us home.*

PHRASAL VERBS **string sb along** to deceive someone for a long time about what you are intending to do • **be strung out** If a group of things or people are strung out somewhere, they are in a line with spaces between them: *There were chairs strung out across the room.*

tringent /'strɪndʒənt/ adj Stringent controls, rules, etc are very strict or extreme.

he strings /strɪŋz/ noun [plural] the people in a musical group who play instruments with strings on them such as the violin

trip¹ /strɪp/ verb (**stripping, stripped**) **1** [I, T] (also UK **strip off**) to remove all your clothes, or to remove all of someone else's clothes: *She was stripped and searched by the guards.* ∘ *He stripped off his clothes and ran into the sea.* **2** [T] (also **strip off**) to remove a covering from the surface of something: *to strip paint/wallpaper off the wall*

PHRASAL VERB **strip sb of sth** to take something important away from someone as a punishment: *He was stripped of his gold medal.*

trip² /strɪp/ noun [C] **1** PIECE ▷ a long, narrow piece of something: *a strip of paper/plastic* **2** AREA ▷ a long, narrow area of land or water **3** REMOVING CLOTHES ▷ entertainment in which someone takes off their clothes in a sexually exciting way: *a strip club/show* → See also **comic strip**

tripe /straɪp/ noun [C] 🅑1 a long, straight area of colour: *white with blue stripes* → See picture at **horizontal**

triped /straɪpt/ adj with a pattern of stripes: *a striped shirt*

stripey /'straɪpi/ adj another spelling of stripy

stripper /'strɪpər/ noun [C] someone who takes off their clothes in a sexually exciting way to entertain people

striptease /'strɪptiːz/ noun [C, U] entertainment in which someone takes off their clothes in a sexually exciting way

stripy (also **stripey**) /'straɪpi/ adj with a pattern of stripes: *stripy trousers*

strive /straɪv/ verb [I] (**strove, strived, striven, strived**) formal to try very hard to do or achieve something: *to **strive for** happiness/peace* ∘ *[+ to do sth] We are constantly striving to improve our service.*

strode /strəʊd/ past of stride

stroke¹ /strəʊk/ noun [C] **1** ILLNESS ▷ 🅑2 a sudden problem in your brain that changes the flow of blood and makes you unable to move part of your body: *to **have/suffer** a stroke* **2** MOVEMENT ▷ a movement that you make against something with your hand, a pen, brush, etc: *a brush stroke* **3** SWIMMING ▷ a style of swimming **4** SPORT ▷ the action of moving your arm and hitting the ball in sports such as tennis, golf, etc

IDIOM **a stroke of luck** something good that happens to you by chance: *He had exactly the part that I needed so that was a stroke of luck.*

stroke² /strəʊk/ verb [T] 🅑2 to gently move your hand over a surface: *to stroke a cat/dog* ∘ *He stroked her hair.*

stroll /strəʊl/ verb **stroll along/down/through, etc** to walk somewhere in a slow and relaxed way: *They strolled along the beach.* • **stroll** noun [C] *Shall we **go for a stroll** around the garden?*

stroller /'strəʊlər/ noun [C] US (UK **pushchair**) a chair on wheels that is used to move small children

strong /strɒŋ/ adj **1** PHYSICALLY POWERFUL ▷ 🅐2 A strong person or animal is physically powerful: *Are you strong enough to lift this table on your own?* **2** NOT BREAK ▷ 🅑1 A strong object does not break easily or can support heavy things: *a strong box/chair* **3** QUALITY ▷ 🅑2 of a good quality or level and likely to be successful: *a strong competitor/team* ∘ *a strong economy* **4** FEELING ▷ 🅑2 A strong feeling, belief, or opinion is felt in a very deep and serious way: *a strong sense of pride* **5** NOTICEABLE ▷ 🅑1 If a taste, smell, etc is strong, it is very noticeable: *There's a strong smell of burning.* **6** PERSONALITY ▷ 🅑2 If a person or their personality is strong, they are confident and able to deal with problems well. **7** ALCOHOL ▷ containing a lot of alcohol: *a strong drink* **8** RELATIONSHIP ▷ 🅑1 If a friendship, relationship, etc is strong, it is likely to last for a long time. **9** **strong chance/possibility, etc** something that is very likely to happen: *There's a strong possibility of rain this afternoon.* **10** **strong opposition/support, etc** a lot of opposition/support, etc **11** **strong language** words that some people might consider to be offensive **12** **sb's strong point** something that someone is very good at: *Cooking is not my strong point.*

13 be still going strong continuing to be successful after a long time

strongly /ˈstrɒŋli/ adv ⓑ very much or in a very serious way: *He is **strongly opposed** to violence of any sort.* ∘ *I **strongly believe** that we should take action.*

strong-willed /ˌstrɒŋˈwɪld/ adj very determined to do what you want to do

stroppy /ˈstrɒpi/ adj UK informal angry or arguing a lot: *a stroppy teenager*

strove /strəʊv/ past tense of strive

struck /strʌk/ past of strike

structural /ˈstrʌktʃərəl/ adj relating to the structure of something: ***structural damage*** ∘ *The last five years have seen big **structural changes** in the company.* • **structurally** adv

structure¹ /ˈstrʌktʃər/ noun **1** [C, U] ⓑ the way that parts of something are arranged or put together: *cell structure* ∘ *grammatical structure* **2** [C] a building or something that has been built

structure² /ˈstrʌktʃər/ verb [T] to arrange something in an organized way: *How is the course structured?*

struggle¹ /ˈstrʌɡl/ verb [I] **1** ⓑ to try very hard to do something difficult: [+ to do sth] *He's struggling to pay off his debts.* **2** ⓑ to fight someone when they are holding you: *She struggled but couldn't break free.*

PHRASAL VERB **struggle on** to continue doing something that is difficult

struggle² /ˈstrʌɡl/ noun [C] **1** ⓑ a situation in which you try very hard to do something difficult: *It was a real struggle to stay awake during the film.* **2** ⓑ a fight between people

> 🗹 Word partners for **struggle** noun
>
> a **constant/ongoing/uphill** struggle • a struggle **for** [justice/survival, etc]

strum /strʌm/ verb [I, T] (**strumming, strummed**) to move your fingers across the strings of a guitar

strung /strʌŋ/ past of string

strut /strʌt/ verb (**strutting, strutted**) **strut along/around/down, etc** to walk somewhere with big steps in a proud way → See also **strut your stuff**

stub¹ /stʌb/ noun [C] the short end piece of something such as a cigarette or pencil that is left after it has been used: *There were **cigarette stubs** all over the floor.*

stub² /stʌb/ verb (**stubbing, stubbed**) **stub your toe** to hit your toe against a hard surface by accident

PHRASAL VERB **stub sth out** to stop a cigarette from burning by pressing the burning end against a hard surface

stubble /ˈstʌbl/ noun [U] **1** very short, stiff hairs, usually on a man's face **2** the short bits of dried plant stems left in a field after it has been cut

stubborn /ˈstʌbən/ adj ⓑ determined not to change your ideas, plans, etc, although other people want you to • **stubbornly** adv • **stubbornness** noun [U]

stubby /ˈstʌbi/ adj short and thick: *stubby leg fingers*

stuck¹ /stʌk/ adj [never before noun] **1** ⓑ not ab to move anywhere: *My car **got stuck in** a ditc* ∘ *We were stuck at the airport for twelve hour* **2** not able to continue reading, answerin questions, etc because something is too difficul *I keep **getting stuck** on difficult words.* **3 be stuc with sb/sth** to have to deal with someone o something unpleasant because no one els wants to: *Whenever we eat out, I always g stuck with the bill.*

stuck² /stʌk/ past of stick

stud /stʌd/ noun [C] **1** JEWELLERY ▷ a smal metal piece of jewellery that is put through part of your body such as your ear or nose → Se picture at **jewellery 2** DECORATION ▷ a sma piece of metal that is fixed to the surface o something, usually for decoration **3** ANIMALS (also **'stud ˌfarm**) a place where horses are kep for breeding

student /ˈstjuːdənt/ noun [C] ⓐ someone who studying at a school or university: *a law studen* ∘ *a foreign student* → See also **mature studen**

studies /ˈstʌdiz/ noun [plural] the work that yo do while you are at a college or university: *I'n enjoying my studies a lot more this year.*

studio /ˈstjuːdiəʊ/ noun [C] **1** ART ▷ ⓑ a roon where an artist or photographer works **2** T RADIO ▷ ⓑ a room where television/radi programmes or musical recordings are mad **3** FILMS ▷ ⓑ a film company or a place wher films are made

studious /ˈstjuːdiəs/ adj spending a lot of tim studying • **studiously** adv

study¹ /ˈstʌdi/ verb **1** [I, T] ⓐ to learn about subject, usually at school or university: *I studie biology before going into medicine.* → See Note **learn 2** [T] ⓑ to look at something ver carefully: *He studied his face in the mirror.*

study² /ˈstʌdi/ noun **1** FINDING OU INFORMATION ▷ [C] ⓑ the activity of studyin a subject in detail in order to discover ne information: *For years, **studies** have **shown** th link between smoking and cancer.* **2** LEARNING [U] ⓑ the activity of learning about a subjec usually at school or university: *the study English literature* **3** ROOM ▷ [C] ⓑ a room in house where you can read, write, etc → See als **case study**

> 🗹 Word partners for **study** noun
>
> **carry out/conduct/undertake** a study • a study **examines/focuses on** sth • a study **concludes/finds/shows/suggests** sth • a study **into** sth

stuff¹ /stʌf/ noun [U] informal ⓑ used to refer t a substance or a group of things or ideas, e without saying exactly what they are: *There some sticky stuff on the carpet.* ∘ *They sell brea and cakes and stuff like that.* ∘ *Can I leave m stuff at your house?*

IDIOMS **know your stuff** informal to know a l about a subject, or to be very good at doin something: *She's an excellent teacher – she reall* *knows her stuff.* • **strut your stuff** humorous informal to dance

stuff² /stʌf/ **verb** [T] **1 stuff sth in/into/behind, etc** to push something into a small space, often quickly or in a careless way: *He stuffed the papers into his briefcase and left.* **2 FILL** ▷ to completely fill a container with something: *an envelope stuffed with money* **3 FOOD** ▷ to fill meat, vegetables, etc with a mixture of food before you cook them: *stuffed peppers* **4 DEAD ANIMAL** ▷ to fill the body of a dead animal with special material so that it looks as if it is still alive

stuffing /'stʌfɪŋ/ **noun** [U] **1** a mixture of food that is put into meat, vegetables, etc before they are cooked **2** material that is used to fill the inside of things such as soft chairs, beds, toys, etc

stuffy /'stʌfi/ **adj 1** If a room or a building is stuffy, it is hot and unpleasant and the air is not fresh. **2** old-fashioned, formal, and boring: *a stuffy club for wealthy old men*

stumble /'stʌmbl/ **verb** [I] **1** to step badly and almost fall over: *Mary stumbled on the loose rocks.* **2** to make a mistake, such as pausing or repeating a word, while speaking or performing: *He kept **stumbling over** the same word.*

PHRASAL VERB **stumble across/on/upon sth/sb** to discover something by chance, or to meet someone by chance: *I stumbled across these photographs while I was cleaning out my desk.*

stumbling block **noun** [C] a problem that makes it very difficult to do something: *Lack of money has been the main stumbling block.*

stump¹ /stʌmp/ **noun** [C] **1** the short part of something that is left after most of it has been removed: *a tree stump* **2** one of the three vertical wooden sticks that you throw a ball at in the game of cricket → See colour picture **Sports 2** on page Centre 15

stump² /stʌmp/ **verb 1 be stumped by sth** informal to not be able to answer a question or solve a problem because it is too difficult: *Scientists are completely stumped by this virus.* **2** [I] US to travel to different places to get political support

PHRASAL VERB **stump up (sth)** UK informal to provide money for something, especially when you do not want to

stun /stʌn/ **verb** [T] (**stunning, stunned**) **1** to shock or surprise someone very much: [often passive] *Friends and family were stunned by her sudden death.* **2** to make a person or animal unconscious, usually by hitting them on the head

stung /stʌŋ/ past of sting

stunk /stʌŋk/ **1** past participle of stink **2** US past tense of stink

stunning /'stʌnɪŋ/ **adj** ⓑ very beautiful: *stunning views over the city* ◦ *She's stunning.* • **stunningly** adv *a **stunningly beautiful** woman*

stunt¹ /stʌnt/ **noun** [C] **1** something dangerous that needs great skill, usually done by someone in a film: *He always **does** his own stunts.*

2 something that is done to get people's attention: *Their marriage was just a cheap publicity stunt.*

stunt² /stʌnt/ **verb** [T] to stop the normal growth or development of something: *They say that smoking **stunts** your **growth**.*

stupefied /'stjuːpɪfaɪd/ **adj** so shocked, tired, etc that you cannot think • **stupefying** adj making you stupefied • **stupefy** verb [T]

stupendous /stjuː'pendəs/ **adj** extremely good or large: *a stupendous performance* • **stupendously** adv *stupendously successful*

stupid /'stjuːpɪd/ **adj 1** ⓔ silly or not intelligent: *That was a really stupid thing to do.* ◦ *How could you be so stupid?* **2** [always before noun] informal used to show that you are annoyed about something which is causing a problem: *I can never get this stupid machine to work!* • **stupidity** /stjuː'pɪdəti/ **noun** [U] • **stupidly** adv

stupor /'stjuːpər/ **noun** [no plural] If someone is in a stupor, they are almost unconscious and cannot think clearly, especially because they have drunk too much alcohol: *He staggered into the room in a **drunken stupor**.*

sturdy /'stɜːdi/ **adj** very strong and solid: *sturdy walking boots*

stutter /'stʌtər/ **verb** [I, T] to repeat the first sound of a word several times when you talk, usually because you have a speech problem: *"C-c-can we g-go now?" she stuttered.* • **stutter** noun [no plural] *He has a really bad stutter.*

style¹ /staɪl/ **noun 1 WAY** ▷ [C, U] ⓔ a way of doing something that is typical of a particular person, group, place, or period: *a **style of** painting/writing* **2 DESIGN** ▷ [C, U] ⓔ a way of designing hair, clothes, furniture, etc: *She's had her hair cut in a really nice style.* **3 QUALITY** ▷ [U] the quality of being attractive and fashionable or behaving in a way which makes people admire you: *She's got style.* **4 do sth in style** to do something in a way that people admire, usually because it involves spending a lot of money: *If we ever get married, we'll do it in style.*

IDIOM **cramp sb's style** to prevent someone from enjoying themselves, especially by going somewhere with them

> **Ɔ Word partners for style**
>
> a **distinctive** style • **in** a style • a style **of** doing sth

style² /staɪl/ **verb** [T] to shape or design hair, clothes, furniture, etc in a particular way: *He spends hours in the bathroom styling his hair.*

-style /staɪl/ **suffix** used at the end of words to mean 'looking or behaving like something or someone': *antique-style furniture* ◦ *Japanese-style management* → See also **old-style**

stylish /'staɪlɪʃ/ **adj** ⓔ fashionable and attractive: *a stylish, black suit* • **stylishly** adv *stylishly dressed*

Styrofoam /'staɪrəfəʊm/ **noun** [U] trademark polystyrene (= light plastic material used to protect objects when they are packed)

suave /swɑːv/ **adj** If someone, especially a man,

S

is suave, they are polite and confident in a way that is attractive but may be false: *suave and sophisticated*

sub- /sʌb-/ **prefix 1** under or below: *substandard workmanship* **2** less important or a smaller part of a larger whole: *a subsection*

subconscious¹ /sʌb'kɒnʃəs/ **adj** Subconscious thoughts and feelings influence your behaviour without you being aware of them: *a subconscious fear* • **subconsciously adv**

subconscious² /sʌb'kɒnʃəs/ **noun** [no plural] the part of your mind that contains thoughts and feelings that you are not aware of but which influence your behaviour: *The memory was buried deep within my subconscious.*

subcontract /ˌsʌbkən'trækt/ **verb** [T] to pay someone else to do part of a job that you have agreed to do

subculture /'sʌbˌkʌltʃər/ **noun** [C] a group of people with beliefs, interests, etc that are different from the rest of society

subdivide /ˌsʌbdɪ'vaɪd/ **verb** [T] to divide something into smaller parts: [often passive] *Each chapter is subdivided into smaller sections.* • **subdivision** /ˌsʌbdɪ'vɪʒən/ **noun** [C, U]

subdue /səb'dju:/ **verb** [T] (**subduing, subdued**) to start to control someone or something, especially by using force

subdued /səb'dju:d/ **adj 1** quiet because you are feeling sad or worried: *She seemed a bit subdued.* **2** Subdued lights or colours are not bright: *subdued lighting*

subject¹ /'sʌbdʒɪkt/ **noun** [C] **1 WHAT** ▷ 🅑🅕 what someone is writing or talking about: *a series of programmes on the subject of homelessness* **2 STUDY** ▷ 🅐🅕 an area of knowledge studied in school or university: *Chemistry is my favourite subject.* **3 GRAMMAR** ▷ 🅑🅕 the person or thing that performs the action described by the verb. In the sentence 'Bob phoned me yesterday.', 'Bob' is the subject. **4 PERSON** ▷ someone who is from a particular country, especially one with a king or queen: *a British subject*

> **⚡ Word partners for subject**
>
> **bring up/broach/raise** a subject • **get onto** a subject • **change/drop/get off** a subject • **on** the subject (of sth)

subject² /'sʌbdʒɪkt/ **adj subject to sth a** often affected by something, especially something unpleasant: *Departure times are subject to alteration.* **b** only able to happen if something else happens: *The pay rise is subject to approval by management.*

subject³ /səb'dʒekt/ **verb**

PHRASAL VERB **subject sb/sth to sth** to make someone or something experience something unpleasant: *In prison, he was subjected to beatings and interrogations.*

subjective /səb'dʒektɪv/ **adj** influenced by someone's beliefs or feelings, instead of facts: *a subjective judgment* • **subjectively adv** • **subjectivity** /ˌsʌbdʒek'tɪvəti/ **noun** [U] being influenced by beliefs or feelings instead of facts

subject line /'sʌbdʒɪkt laɪn/ **noun** [C] the short line at the top of an email that tells you the subject of the message

subject matter /'sʌbdʒɪkt mætə/ **noun** [U] what is being talked or written about: *I'm not sure whether the subject matter is suitable for children.*

subjunctive /səb'dʒʌŋktɪv/ **noun** [no plural] the form of the verb that is used to express doubt, possibility, or wish. In the sentence 'I wish I were rich.', 'were' is in the subjunctive. • **subjunctive adj**

sublime /sə'blaɪm/ **adj** extremely good, beautiful, or enjoyable: *sublime scenery* • **sublimely adv**

submarine /ˌsʌbmər'i:n/ **noun** [C] a boat that travels under water

submerge /səb'mɜ:dʒ/ **verb** [I, T] to cause something to be under the surface of water, or to move below the surface of water: *The floods destroyed farmland and submerged whole villages.* • **submerged adj**

submission /səb'mɪʃən/ **noun 1** [U] the act of accepting that someone has complete control over you: *They tried to starve her into submission.* **2** [C, U] the act of sending a document, plan, etc to someone so that they can consider it, or the document, plan, etc that you send: *The deadline for submissions is 29 April.*

submissive /səb'mɪsɪv/ **adj** always doing what other people tell you to do: *a quiet, submissive wife*

submit /səb'mɪt/ **verb** (**submitting, submitted**) **1** [T] 🅑🅖 to send a document, plan, etc to someone so that they can consider it: *Applications must be submitted before 31 January.* **2** [I] to accept that someone has control over you and do what they tell you to do: *He was forced to submit to a full body search.*

subordinate¹ /sə'bɔ:dənət/ **adj** less important or lower in rank: *a subordinate position/role* ○ *An individual's needs are subordinate to those of the group.*

subordinate² /sə'bɔ:dənət/ **noun** [C] someone who has a less important position than someone else in an organization

subordinate³ /sə'bɔ:dɪneɪt/ **verb** [T] formal to put someone or something into a less important position • **subordination** /səˌbɔ:dɪ'neɪʃən/ **noun** [U]

subordinate clause /sə'bɔ:dɪneɪt klɔ:z/ **noun** [C] in grammar, a clause that cannot form a separate sentence but adds information to the main clause

subpoena /səb'pi:nə/ **noun** [C] a legal document ordering someone to go to court • **subpoena verb** [T] to give someone a subpoena

subscribe /səb'skraɪb/ **verb** [I] to pay money to an organization so that you regularly receive a service or product, such as a magazine or newspaper: *to subscribe to a magazine/an internet service* • **subscriber noun** [C]

PHRASAL VERB **subscribe to sth** formal to agree with an opinion, belief, etc: *I certainly don't subscribe to the view that women are morally superior to men.*

ubscription /səbˈskrɪpʃən/ noun [C] an amount of money that you pay regularly to receive a product or service or to be a member of an organization: *an annual subscription*

☑ Word partners for **subscription**

cancel/pay/take out a subscription • a subscription **to** sth • an **annual** subscription

---

ubsequent /ˈsʌbsɪkwənt/ adj [always before noun] happening after something else: *The mistakes were corrected in a subsequent edition of the book.* • **subsequently** adv

ubservient /səbˈsɜːviənt/ adj always doing what other people want you to do

ubside /səbˈsaɪd/ verb [I] **1** to become less strong or extreme: *The violence seems to be subsiding at last.* **2** If a building subsides, it sinks down to a lower level.

ubsidence /səbˈsaɪdəns/ noun [U] the effect of buildings subsiding or land sinking down to a lower level

ubsidiary /səbˈsɪdiəri/ noun [C] a company that is owned by another larger company

ubsidize (also UK -ise) /ˈsʌbsɪdaɪz/ verb [T] If a government or other organization subsidizes something, it pays part of the cost of it, so that prices are reduced: *We have a subsidized restaurant at work.*

ubsidy /ˈsʌbsɪdi/ noun [C] money given by a government or other organization to pay part of the cost of something: *housing subsidies for the poor*

ubsist /səbˈsɪst/ verb [I] to manage to live when you only have a very small amount of food or money • **subsistence** noun [U]

ubstance /ˈsʌbstəns/ noun **1** [C] ⓑ a solid, liquid, or gas: *a dangerous substance* ○ *illegal substances* (= *illegal drugs*) **2** [U] truth or importance: *There's no substance to the allegations.* **3** the substance of sth the most important part of what someone has said or written

---

☑ Word partners for **substance**

a **dangerous/hazardous/toxic** substance • a **powdery/sticky/waxy** substance

---

ubstandard /sʌbˈstændəd/ adj Something that is substandard is not as good as it should be: *substandard conditions/housing*

ubstantial /səbˈstænʃəl/ adj **1** ⓑ large in amount: *a substantial change/increase* ○ *a substantial amount of money/time* **2** large and strong: *a substantial building* → Opposite **insubstantial**

ubstantially /səbˈstænʃəli/ adv by a large amount: *House prices are substantially higher in the south.*

ubstantiate /səbˈstænʃieɪt/ verb [T] formal to provide facts that prove that something is true: *His claims have never been substantiated.*

ubstantive /ˈsʌbstəntɪv/ adj formal important or serious: *a substantive issue*

ubstitute¹ /ˈsʌbstɪtjuːt/ noun [C] ⓑ someone or something that is used instead of another

person or thing: *Margarine can be used as a substitute for butter.* ○ *a substitute teacher*

substitute² /ˈsʌbstɪtjuːt/ verb **1** ⓑ [T] to use someone or something instead of another person or thing: *You can substitute pasta for the rice, if you prefer.* **2** substitute for sb to do someone's job because they are not there: *I'm substituting for her while she's on holiday.* • **substitution** /ˌsʌbstɪˈtjuːʃən/ noun [C, U]

subsume /səbˈsjuːm/ verb [T] formal to include someone or something as part of a larger group: [often passive] *The company has been subsumed by a large US bank.*

subterfuge /ˈsʌbtəfjuːdʒ/ noun [C, U] formal a trick or a dishonest way of achieving something: *They obtained the information by subterfuge.*

subterranean /ˌsʌbtəˈreɪniən/ adj under the ground: *subterranean passages*

subtitles /ˈsʌbˌtaɪtlz/ noun [plural] words shown at the bottom of a cinema or television screen to explain what is being said: *It's a French film with English subtitles.*

subtle /ˈsʌtl/ adj **1** NOT OBVIOUS ▷ not obvious or easy to notice: *a subtle change/difference* ○ *a subtle hint* **2** NOT STRONG ▷ A subtle flavour, colour, etc is delicate and not strong or bright. **3** CLEVER ▷ clever in a way that does not attract attention: *a subtle way of solving the problem* • **subtly** adv

subtlety /ˈsʌtlti/ noun **1** [U] the quality of being subtle **2** [C] something that is subtle

subtract /səbˈtrækt/ verb [T] to take a number or amount away from another number or amount: *You need to subtract 25% from the final figure.* • **subtraction** /səbˈtrækʃən/ noun [C, U]

suburb /ˈsʌbɜːb/ noun [C] ⓑ an area where people live outside the centre of a city: *a suburb of New York* • **suburban** /səˈbɜːbən/ adj relating to a suburb: *a suburban area/home*

suburbia /səˈbɜːbiə/ noun [U] the suburbs of towns and cities generally

subversive /səbˈvɜːsɪv/ adj trying to destroy the authority of a government, religion, etc: *subversive literature* • **subversive** noun [C] someone who is subversive

subvert /sʌbˈvɜːt/ verb [T] formal to try to destroy the authority of a government, religion, etc: *a plot to subvert the government* • **subversion** /səbˈvɜːʃən/ noun [U] formal

subway /ˈsʌbweɪ/ noun [C] **1** UK (also UK/US **underpass**) ⓑ a passage under a road or railway for people to walk through **2** US (UK **underground**) a system of trains that travel underground: *We can take the subway to Grand Central Station.* → See Note at **metro¹**

sub-zero /ˈsʌbˌzɪərəʊ/ adj Sub-zero temperatures are temperatures below zero degrees.

succeed /səkˈsiːd/ verb **1** [I] ⓑ to achieve what you are trying to achieve: *She has the skill and determination to succeed.* ○ [+ in + doing sth] *He has finally succeeded in passing his exams.* **2** [T] to take an official job or position after someone else: *The Queen was succeeded by her eldest son when she died.*

Common learner error: succeed

Remember that **succeed** is often followed by the preposition **in + doing something**. It is not used with 'to do something'.

Two prisoners succeeded in escaping.

~~Two prisoners succeeded to escape.~~

success /sək'ses/ **noun 1** [U] 🔒 the achievement of what you want to achieve: *Her success is due to hard work and determination.* **2** [C] 🔒 something that has a good result or that is very popular: *His first film was a great success.*

❗ Common learner error: success

Be careful to choose the correct verb with this noun.

*The evening **was** a great success.*

*They tried for weeks but **had** little success.*

*They are determined to **make** a success of the scheme.*

~~She reached success as a writer.~~

✍ Word partners for success

achieve/have success • the key to/secret of success • success in (doing) sth • without success

successful /sək'sesf°l/ **adj 1** ACHIEVEMENT ▷ 🔒 achieving what you want to achieve: *If the operation is successful, she should be walking within a few months.* **2** WORK ▷ 🔒 having achieved a lot or made a lot of money through your work: *a successful businessman* **3** POPULAR ▷ 🔒 very popular: *a successful book/film* → Opposite **unsuccessful** • **successfully adv**

succession /sək'seʃ°n/ **noun 1** [no plural] a number of similar events or people that happen, exist, or come after each other: *to suffer a succession of injuries* ◦ *a succession of boyfriends* **2 in quick/rapid succession** If several things happen in quick/rapid succession, they happen very quickly after each other: *She had her first three children in quick succession.* **3** [U] an arrangement in which someone takes an official position or job after someone else

successive /sək'sesɪv/ **adj** happening after each other: *He has just won the World Championship for the third successive year.*

successor /sək'sesər/ **noun** [C] **1** someone who has a position or job after someone else: *He is her most likely successor.* **2** an organization, product, etc that follows and takes the place of an earlier one

✍ Word partners for successor

appoint/choose/find a successor • a natural/worthy successor • a successor to sb

succinct /sək'sɪŋkt/ **adj** said in a very clear way using only a few words: *a succinct explanation* • **succinctly adv**

succulent /'sʌkjələnt/ **adj** If food is succulent, it is good to eat because it has a lot of juice: *a succulent piece of meat*

succumb /sə'kʌm/ **verb** [I] formal **1** to not be able

to stop yourself doing something: *I succumbe to temptation and had some cheesecake.* **2** to di or suffer badly from an illness

such /sʌtʃ/ **pronoun, determiner 1** 🔒 used t refer to something or someone that you wer just talking about, or something or someone o that type: *It's difficult to know how to treat suc cases.* **2** 🔒 used to emphasize a quality o someone or something: *She's such a nice person* ◦ *It's such a shame that he's leaving.* **3 such as** 🅐 for example: *She can't eat dairy products, such a milk and cheese.* **4 as such** used after a word o phrase in negative statements to mean in th exact meaning of that word or phrase: *There ar no rules as such, just a few guidelines.* **5 such.. that** used to talk about the result of somethinɡ *The whole thing was such a worry that I began t lose sleep over it.* **6 there's no such thing person (as)...** 🔒 used to say that something o someone does not exist: *There's no such thing a ghosts.*

such-and-such /'sʌtʃ°nsʌtʃ/ **determiner** infor mal used instead of referring to a particular o exact thing: *If they tell you to arrive at such-and such a time, get there a couple of minutes before.*

suck /sʌk/ **verb 1** [I, T] to have something in you mouth and use your tongue, lips, etc to pull o it or to get liquid, air, etc out of it: *to suck sweet/lollipop* ◦ *to suck your thumb* **2 suck sth in under/up, etc** to pull something somewher using the force of moving air, water, etc: *He wa sucked under the boat and drowned.* **3 be sucke into sth** to become involved in something ba when you do not want to **4 he/it/this, etc sucks** US very informal If someone or something sucks they are bad or unpleasant.

PHRASAL VERB **suck up to sb** very informal to try t make someone who is in authority like you b doing and saying things that will please them

sucker /'sʌkər/ **noun** [C] **1** informal someone wh believes everything that you tell them and i easy to deceive **2** something that helps a animal or object stick to a surface

suction /'sʌkʃ°n/ **noun** [U] the force that pull something into a container or space by remov ing air

sudden /'sʌd°n/ **adj 1** 🔒 done or happeninɡ quickly and unexpectedly: *a sudden change increase* ◦ *His sudden death was a great shock t us all.* **2 all of a sudden** 🔒 unexpectedly: *All of sudden she got up and walked out.* • **suddennes noun** [U]

sudden infant death syndrome noun [U SIDS

suddenly /'sʌd°nli/ **adv** 🔒 quickly and unex pectedly: *I suddenly realized who she was.* ◦ *It a happened so suddenly that I can't remember muc about it.*

Sudoku (also **Su Doku**) /su:'dɒku:/ **noun** [C, U number game in which you have to write number between 1 and 9 in each small box of 9x9 square

suds /sʌdz/ **noun** [plural] small bubbles mad from soap and water

sue /su:/ **verb** [I, T] (**suing, sued**) to take legɑ action against someone and try to get money from them because they have harmed you: *He's threatening to sue the newspaper for slander.*

suede /sweɪd/ **noun** [U] leather that has a slightly rough surface

suffer /'sʌfər/ **verb 1** [I, T] ⓑ2 to experience pain or unpleasant emotions: *I can't bear to see animals suffering.* **2 suffer from sth** ⓑ1 to have an illness or other health problem: *She suffers from severe depression.* **3 suffer a broken leg/a heart attack, etc** ⓑ2 to experience an injury or other sudden health problem: *He suffered a serious neck injury in the accident.* **4 suffer damage/defeat/loss, etc** ⓑ2 to experience something bad such as damage/defeat/loss, etc **5** [I] to become worse in quality: *If you're tired all the time, your work tends to suffer.*

sufferer /'sʌfərər/ **noun** [C] someone who suffers from an illness or other health problem: *AIDS/cancer sufferers*

suffering /'sʌfərɪŋ/ **noun** [U] ⓑ2 experiences such as pain or unpleasant emotions: *human suffering*

☑ Word partners for **suffering**

create/endure/relieve suffering • human suffering • unnecessary/unspeakable suffering • the suffering of sb

suffice /sə'faɪs/ **verb** [I] formal to be enough: *You don't need to give a long speech – a few sentences will suffice.*

sufficient /sə'fɪʃ°nt/ **adj** ⓑ2 as much as is necessary: *She didn't have sufficient time to answer all the questions.* → Opposite **insufficient** • **sufficiently** adv *I was sufficiently close to hear what they were saying.* → See also **self-sufficient**

suffix /'sʌfɪks/ **noun** [C] ⓑ2 a group of letters that you add to the end of a word to make another word. In the word 'slowly', '-ly' is a suffix. → Compare **prefix** → See Study Page **Word formation** on page Centre 28

suffocate /'sʌfəkeɪt/ **verb** [I, T] to die because you cannot breathe or to kill someone by stopping them from breathing: *He suffocated her with a pillow.* • **suffocation** /ˌsʌfə'keɪʃ°n/ **noun** [U]

sugar /'ʃʊgər/ **noun 1** [U] ⓐ1 a very sweet substance used to give flavour to food and drinks: *coffee with milk and sugar* **2** [C] a spoon of sugar in a cup of tea or coffee: *He likes two sugars in his tea.*

suggest /sə'dʒest/ **verb** [T] **1 IDEA** ▷ ⓑ1 to express an idea or plan for someone to consider: [+ (that)] *I suggest that we park the car here and walk into town.* ∘ [+ doing sth] *He suggested having the meeting at his house.* **2 ADVICE** ▷ ⓑ1 to say that someone or something is suitable for something: *to suggest someone for a job* ∘ *Can you suggest a good hotel?* **3 SEEM TRUE** ▷ ⓑ2 to make something seem likely to be true: *All the evidence suggests that she did it.*

suggestion /sə'dʒestʃ°n/ **noun 1** ⓑ1 [C] an idea or plan that someone suggests: *to make a suggestion* ∘ *Have you got any suggestions for improvements?* **2 a suggestion of/that sth**

something that makes something seem likely to be true: *There's no suggestion of any connection between the two men.* **3 at sb's suggestion** following the advice that someone has given you: *We went to that restaurant at Paul's suggestion.*

☑ Word partners for **suggestion**

bristle at/deny/make/reject/welcome a suggestion • an alternative/constructive/helpful/ridiculous/sensible suggestion • at sb's suggestion

➕ Other ways of saying **suggestion**

A suggestion about what to do is sometimes described as a **thought** or **idea**:
  Rebecca has a few ideas about how we could improve things.
  I've had a thought about what we might do this summer.
If someone suggests a plan or action, especially in business, you can use nouns such as **proposal** or **proposition**:
  The proposal for a new sports hall has been rejected.
  He wrote to me with a very interesting business proposition.

suggestive /sə'dʒestɪv/ **adj 1** making you think about sex: *suggestive comments/remarks* **2 suggestive of sth** formal similar to something and making you think about it: *The shapes are suggestive of human forms.* • **suggestively** adv

suicidal /ˌsuːɪ'saɪd°l/ **adj 1** so unhappy that you want to kill yourself: *to feel suicidal* **2** likely to have an extremely bad result: *a suicidal decision*

suicide /'suːɪsaɪd/ **noun** [C, U] **1** the act of intentionally killing yourself: *He committed suicide after a long period of depression.* **2** [U] something you do that will have an extremely bad result for you: *political suicide*

suicide bomber **noun** [C] a person who has a bomb hidden on their body and who kills themselves in the attempt to kill others

suit¹ /suːt/ **noun** [C] **1** ⓐ2 a jacket and trousers or a jacket and skirt that are made from the same material: *She wore a dark blue suit.* → See colour picture **Clothes** on page Centre 8 **2** one of the four types of cards with different shapes on them in a set of playing cards

IDIOM **follow suit** to do the same as someone else has just done: *If other shops lower their prices, we will have to follow suit.*

→ See also **bathing suit, pant suit, trouser suit, wet suit**

suit² /suːt/ **verb** [T] **1** ⓑ2 to make someone look more attractive: *Green really suits you.* **2** ⓑ2 to be acceptable or right for someone: *It would suit me better if we left a bit earlier.* → See Note at **fit¹ 3 be suited to/for sth** to be right for someone or something: *These plants are better suited to a warm climate.* → See also **suit sb down to the ground¹**

suitable /'suːtəbl/ **adj** ⓑ1 acceptable or right for someone or something: *a suitable time to call*

S

◦ *This film is **suitable for** children.* → Opposite **unsuitable** • **suitably** adv ⑫ *suitably dressed*

> ➕ Other ways of saying **suitable**
>
> A common alternative to 'suitable' is the adjective **appropriate**:
> *Is this film **suitable** for young children?*
> *You should bring **appropriate** footwear.*
>
> If an action is suitable for a particular situation, you can use the adjectives **apt** or **fitting**:
> *'Unusual', yes, that's a very **apt** description.*
> *The promotion was a **fitting** reward for all his hard work.*
>
> The adjective **right** can also be used to show that someone or something is suitable for a particular situation:
> *I'm not sure that she's the **right** person for the job.*
> *Is this the **right** way to do it?*
>
> If someone or something is very suitable, you can use the adjective **perfect**:
> *It's a **perfect** day for a picnic.*
> *She'd be **perfect** for the job.*
>
> The expression **in keeping with** is sometimes used when something is suitable for a particular style or tradition:
> *The antique desk was very much **in keeping with** the rest of the furniture in the room.*

suitcase /ˈsuːtkeɪs/ **noun** [C] ⑫ a rectangular case with a handle that you use for carrying clothes when you are travelling: *to **pack** your suitcase* → See picture at **luggage**

suite /swiːt/ **noun** [C] **1** several pieces of furniture that go together: *a bedroom suite* **2** a set of hotel rooms that are used together → See also **en suite**

suitor /ˈsuːtər/ **noun** [C] old-fashioned a man who wants to marry a particular woman

sulfur /ˈsʌlfər/ **noun** [U] US spelling of sulphur

sulk /sʌlk/ **verb** [I] to look unhappy and not speak to anyone because you are angry about something: *He's upstairs sulking in his bedroom.* • **sulky** adj *a sulky teenager*

sullen /ˈsʌlən/ **adj** in an unpleasant mood and not smiling or speaking to anyone

sulphur UK (US **sulfur**) /ˈsʌlfər/ **noun** [U] a yellow chemical element that has an unpleasant smell

sultan /ˈsʌltən/ **noun** [C] a ruler in some Muslim countries

sultana /sʌlˈtɑːnə/ **noun** [C] UK a dried grape (= small round fruit) often used in cakes

sultry /ˈsʌltri/ **adj** **1** If a woman is sultry, she behaves in a sexually attractive way: *a sultry voice* **2** If the weather is sultry, it is hot and wet: *a sultry summer night*

sum¹ /sʌm/ **noun** [C] **1** MONEY ▷ ⑬ an amount of money: *a large/small sum of money* **2** MATHS ▷ a simple mathematical calculation such as adding two numbers together: *Kids these days can't **do** sums without a calculator.* **3** TOTAL ▷ the total amount that you get when you add two or more numbers together: *The sum of six and seven is thirteen.* → See also **lump sum**

sum² /sʌm/ **verb** (**summing, summed**)

PHRASAL VERBS **sum (sth/sb) up** ⑫ to describe briefly the important facts or characteristics of something or someone: *The purpose of a conclusion is to sum up the main points of an essay.* • **sum sth/sb up** to quickly decide what you think about something or someone: *I think she summed up the situation very quickly.*

summarize (also UK **-ise**) /ˈsʌməraɪz/ **verb** [I, T] ⑫ to describe briefly the main facts or ideas of something

summary¹ /ˈsʌməri/ **noun** [C] ⑫ a short description that gives the main facts or idea about something: *He gave a brief summary of what happened.*

> 🗓 Word partners for **summary** noun
>
> **give/produce/provide** a summary • a **brief/quick/short** summary • a summary **of** sth

summary² /ˈsʌməri/ **adj** [always before noun] formal decided or done quickly, without the usual discussions or legal arrangements: *summary arrest/execution*

summer /ˈsʌmər/ **noun** [C, U] ⓐ the season of the year between spring and autumn, when the weather is warmest: *We usually go away **in the summer**.* ◦ *a long, hot summer* • **summery** adj typical of or suitable for summer

> 🗓 Word partners for **summer**
>
> **in (the)** summer • **last/next** summer • **early/late** summer • the summer **months**

summer holiday noun [C] (US **summer vacation**) the time during the summer when you do not have to go to school

summer school noun [C] an educational course that happens during the summer when other courses have finished

summertime /ˈsʌmətaɪm/ **noun** [U] the period when it is summer: *In the summertime, we often eat outside.*

summit /ˈsʌmɪt/ **noun** [C] **1** an important meeting between the leaders of two or more governments: *a two-day summit* ◦ *a summit meeting* **2** the top of a mountain: *The climbers hope to **reach the summit** before nightfall.*

summon /ˈsʌmən/ **verb** [T] **1** formal to officially order someone to come to a place: *He was summoned to a meeting.* **2** summon (up) the courage/strength, etc to make a great effort to do something: [+ to do sth] *He tried to summon up the courage to speak to her.*

summons /ˈsʌmənz/ **noun** [C] an official order saying that you must go to a court of law

sun¹ /sʌn/ **noun** **1 the sun** ⓐ the large, bright star that shines in the sky during the day and provides light and heat for the Earth **2** ⓐ [U, no plural] the light and heat that comes from the sun: *I can't sit **in the sun** for too long.*

sun² /sʌn/ **verb** (**sunning, sunned**) **sun yourself** to sit or lie in the sun: *She was sitting on the deck sunning herself.*

Sun written abbreviation for Sunday

sunbathe /ˈsʌnbeɪð/ **verb** [I] ⑬ to sit or lie in

the sun so that your skin becomes brown • **sunbathing noun** [U]

unbed /'sʌnbed/ **noun** [C] (US **tanning bed**) a piece of equipment with a flat area like a bed and a strong light, which you lie on in order to make your skin go darker

unblock /'sʌnblɒk/ **noun** [C, U] sunscreen

unburn /'sʌnbɜːn/ **noun** [U] painful red skin caused by being in the sun too long • **sunburnt** (also **sunburned**) adj

undae /'sʌndeɪ/ **noun** [C] a sweet dish made of ice cream with fruit and nuts

unday /'sʌndeɪ/ **noun** [C, U] (written abbreviation **Sun**) ⓐ the day of the week after Saturday and before Monday

undry /'sʌndri/ **adj 1** [always before noun] of different types: *sundry items* **2** all and sundry old-fashioned (also US **various and sundry**) everyone: *I don't want all and sundry knowing about my problems.*

unflower /'sʌnflaʊəʳ/ **noun** [C] a tall, yellow flower with a large, black centre full of seeds

ung /sʌŋ/ past participle of sing

unglasses /'sʌnˌglɑːsɪz/ **noun** [plural] ⓐ dark glasses that you wear to protect your eyes from the sun → See colour picture **Clothes** on page Centre 9

unk /sʌŋk/ **1** past participle of sink **2** US past tense of sink

unken /'sʌŋkən/ **adj** [always before noun] **1** at a lower level than the surrounding area: *a sunken bath* **2** having fallen down to the bottom of the sea: *a sunken ship* **3** sunken eyes/cheeks eyes or cheeks that make you look sick because they go too far into your face

unlight /'sʌnlaɪt/ **noun** [U] ⓑ the light from the sun

unlit /'sʌnlɪt/ **adj** [always before noun] A sunlit place is bright because of light from the sun: *a sunlit room*

un ˌlotion noun [C, U] sunscreen

unni /'sʊni/ **noun** [C] a member of a large group within the Islamic religion • **Sunni adj** describing the Sunni or their type of Islam

unny /'sʌni/ **adj 1** ⓐ bright because of light from the sun: *a lovely sunny day* **2** behaving in a happy way: *a sunny smile/personality*

unrise /'sʌnraɪz/ **noun** [C, U] ⓑ the time when the sun appears in the morning and the sky becomes light

unroof /'sʌnruːf/ **noun** [C] part of a roof of a car that you open to allow air and light from the sun to come in

unscreen /'sʌnskriːn/ **noun** [C, U] a substance that protects your skin in the sun

unset /'sʌnset/ **noun** [C, U] ⓑ the time when the sun disappears in the evening and the sky becomes dark

unshine /'sʌnʃaɪn/ **noun** [U] ⓑ the light from the sun: *Let's sit over there in the sunshine.*

unstroke /'sʌnstrəʊk/ **noun** [U] an illness caused by spending too much time in the sun

untan /'sʌntæn/ **noun** [C] (also **tan**) If you have

a suntan, your skin is brown from being in the sun: *suntan oil* • **suntanned** (also **tanned**) adj

super /'suːpəʳ/ **adj, adv** informal old-fashioned very good: *We had a super time.*

super- /suːpəʳ-/ **prefix** extremely or more than usual: *a supermodel* ∘ *super-rich*

superb /suːˈpɜːb/ **adj** ⓑ excellent: *a superb performance/restaurant* • **superbly adv**

superbug /'suːpəbʌg/ **noun** [C] a type of bacteria (= very small living things that cause disease) that is very difficult to destroy

superficial /ˌsuːpəˈfɪʃəl/ **adj 1 NOT SERIOUS** ▷ If someone is superficial, they never think about things that are serious or important. **2 NOT COMPLETE** ▷ not complete and involving only the most obvious things: *superficial knowledge* ∘ *a superficial resemblance* **3 NOT DEEP** ▷ only on the surface of something: *superficial damage/injuries* • **superficially adv**

superfluous /suːˈpɜːfluəs/ **adj** not needed, or more than is needed: *superfluous details/information*

superhuman /ˌsuːpəˈhjuːmən/ **adj** superhuman effort/strength, etc more effort/strength, etc than a normal human being

superimpose /ˌsuːpərɪmˈpəʊz/ **verb** [T] to put an image, text, etc over something so that the thing under it can still be seen

superintendent /ˌsuːpərɪnˈtendənt/ **noun** [C] **1** in Britain, a police officer of high rank **2** in the US, an official responsible for a place, event, etc

superior¹ /suːˈpɪəriəʳ/ **adj 1** better than other things: *superior quality* ∘ *This car is far superior to the others.* **2** thinking that you are better than other people: *She has a very superior manner.*

superior² /suːˈpɪəriəʳ/ **noun** [C] someone in a higher position than you at work: *I will have to report this to my superiors.*

superiority /suːˌpɪəriˈɒrəti/ **noun** [U] **1** the quality of being better than other things: *the superiority of modern design* **2** the opinion that you are better than other people: *She has an air of superiority.*

superlative /suːˈpɜːlətɪv/ **noun** [C] ⓐ the form of an adjective or adverb that is used to show that someone or something has more of a particular quality than anyone or anything else. For example 'best' is the superlative of 'good' and 'slowest' is the superlative of 'slow'. → Compare **comparative** noun

supermarket /'suːpəˌmɑːkɪt/ **noun** [C] ⓐ a large shop that sells food, drink, products for the home, etc

supermodel /'suːpəˌmɒdəl/ **noun** [C] a very famous model (= someone whose job is to wear fashionable clothes for photographs)

the supernatural /ˌsuːpəˈnætʃərəl/ **noun** ⓑ things that cannot be explained by our knowledge of science or nature • **supernatural adj** ⓑ *supernatural forces/powers*

superpower /'suːpəˌpaʊəʳ/ **noun** [C] a country that has great military and political power in the world

supersede /ˌsuːpəˈsiːd/ **verb** [T] to take the place

S

of someone or something that went before: [often passive] *Records were superseded by CDs.*

supersize /ˈsuːpəsaɪz/ **adj** (also **supersized**) describes something that is much bigger than normal: *a supersize cheeseburger*

supersonic /ˌsuːpəˈsɒnɪk/ **adj** faster than the speed of sound: *supersonic aircraft*

superstar /ˈsuːpəstɑːʳ/ **noun** [C] a very famous singer, performer, etc

superstition /ˌsuːpəˈstɪʃᵊn/ **noun** [C, U] the belief that particular actions or objects are lucky or unlucky

superstitious /ˌsuːpəˈstɪʃəs/ **adj** believing that particular objects or events are lucky or unlucky: *Are you superstitious about the number 13?*

superstore /ˈsuːpəstɔːʳ/ **noun** [C] a very large shop that sells many different things, often outside a town

supervise /ˈsuːpəvaɪz/ **verb** [I, T] ⑫ to watch a person or activity and make certain that everything is done correctly, safely, etc: *Students must be supervised by a teacher at all times.* • **supervisor noun** [C] someone who supervises

supervision /ˌsuːpəˈvɪʒᵊn/ **noun** [U] the activity of supervising someone or something: *He needs constant supervision.*

> ☑ Word partners for **supervision**
>
> be **under** supervision • **close/constant** supervision • the **supervision of** sb/sth

supper /ˈsʌpəʳ/ **noun** [C, U] ⑫ a meal that you eat in the evening: *What are we having for supper?*

supplant /səˈplɑːnt/ **verb** [T] formal to take the place of someone or something

supple /ˈsʌpl/ **adj** able to bend or move easily: *a supple body*

supplement /ˈsʌplɪmənt/ **noun** [C] an extra amount or part added to something: *to take a vitamin supplement* ○ *a newspaper with a colour supplement* • supplement /ˈsʌplɪment/ **verb** [T] *She works part-time to supplement her pension.*

supplementary /ˌsʌplɪˈmentᵊri/ **adj** (also US **supplemental**) added to something: *supplementary materials*

supplier /səˈplaɪəʳ/ **noun** [C] ⑫ someone who provides things that people want or need, often over a long period of time

supplies /səˈplaɪz/ **noun** [plural] ⑫ the food, equipment, etc that is needed for a particular activity, holiday, etc

supply¹ /səˈplaɪ/ **verb** [T] ⑫ to provide things that people want or need, often over a long period of time: *to supply food/drugs to people* ○ *This lake supplies the whole town with water.*

supply² /səˈplaɪ/ **noun 1** [C] ⑫ an amount of something that is ready to be used: *a supply of water* ○ *food supplies* **2 in short supply** If something is in short supply, there is little of it available. **3** [C] the system of supplying something to people: *Someone has turned off the electricity supply.*

> ☑ Word partners for **supply noun**
>
> a supply of sth • a constant/endless/plentiful supply

support¹ /səˈpɔːt/ **verb** [T] **1 AGREE** ▷ ⑫ to agree with an idea, group, or person: *Do you support their views on nuclear weapon* **2 PROVE** ▷ to help to show that something true: *There's no evidence to support his story.* **3 HOLD** ▷ ⑫ to hold the weight of someone something: *Is this ladder strong enough to support me?* **4 PAY** ▷ ⑪ to look after someone by paying for their food, clothes, etc: *She has three children to support.* **5 SPORT** ▷ mainly UK ⑪ to like a particular sports team and want them to win: *Who do you support?*

support² /səˈpɔːt/ **noun 1 AGREEMENT** ▷ [U] agreement with an idea, group, or person: *there much public support for the death penalty* **2 in support of sb/sth** agreeing with someone or something: *The minister spoke in support military action.* **3 HELP** ▷ [U] ⑪ help encouragement: *emotional/financial support* **4 OBJECT** ▷ [C] an object that can hold the weight of something → See also **child support, income support, moral support**

> ☑ Word partners for **support noun**
>
> **enlist/express/give/lose/rally** support • **overwhelming/public/strong/tacit/widespread** support • support **for** sb/sth

supporter /səˈpɔːtəʳ/ **noun** [C] **1** ⑫ someone who supports a particular idea, group, person: *a strong supporter of the government* **2** mainly UK ⑪ someone who likes a particular sports team and wants them to win: *English football supporters*

> ☑ Word partners for **supporter**
>
> a **keen/loyal/staunch/strong** supporter • a supporter **of** sth

supportive /səˈpɔːtɪv/ **adj** giving help encouragement: *a very supportive friend*

suppose /səˈpəʊz/ **verb 1 be supposed to do sth a** ⑪ to be expected or intended to do something, especially when this does not happen: *These drugs are supposed to reduce the pain.* ○ *He was supposed to be here by nine.* **b** If you are supposed to do something, the rule say that you should do it: *You're supposed to pay by the end of the month.* ○ *You're not supposed* (= you should not) *smoke in here.* **2 be supposed to be sth** ⑫ to be considered by many people to be something: *The scenery is supposed to be fantastic.* **3** ⑪ [T] to think that something likely to be true: [+ (that)] *I suppose that you've already heard the news?* **4 suppose/supposing (that)** used to introduce an idea for someone to consider: *Suppose he phones tonight. What should I say?* **5 I suppose** ⑫ used to show that you are not certain or not completely happy about something: *It was quite interesting, I suppose.* **6 I suppose so** ⑪ used to show agreement to something when you do not really want to: *"Can I come with you?" "I suppose so."*

S

supposed /sə'pəʊzd/ **adj** [always before noun] used to show that you do not believe that someone or something really is what many people consider them to be: *a supposed genius* • **supposedly** /sə'pəʊzɪdli/ **adv** *The building is supposedly in good condition.*

supposition /ˌsʌpə'zɪʃən/ **noun** [C, U] formal the belief that something is true although there is no proof

suppress /sə'pres/ **verb** [T] **1 FEELINGS** ▷ to control feelings so that they do not show: *I could barely suppress my anger.* **2 INFORMATION** ▷ to prevent information from being known: *to suppress evidence/news* **3 FIGHT** ▷ to stop someone or something by using force: [often passive] *The rebellion was suppressed by government forces.* • **suppression** /sə'preʃən/ **noun** [U]

supremacy /suː'preməsi/ **noun** [U] a situation in which a country or group of people is more powerful, successful, etc than anyone else: *a battle/struggle for supremacy*

supreme /suː'priːm/ **adj 1** of the highest rank or greatest importance: *the supreme ruler* **2** very great: *supreme confidence/effort* • **supremely adv** very: *supremely confident*

the su,preme 'court noun the court of law that has the most authority in a state or country

surcharge /'sɜːtʃɑːdʒ/ **noun** [C] an extra amount of money that you have to pay for something: *There is a surcharge for single rooms.*

sure /ʃɔːr/ **adj 1** ⏦ [never before noun] certain: [+ (that)] *I'm sure that he won't mind.* ◦ [+ question word] *She's not sure what she's going to do next.* ◦ *I'm quite sure about the second answer.* → Opposite **unsure 2 make sure (that)** ⏦ to take action so that you are certain that something happens, is true, etc: *Make sure that you close all the windows before you leave.* **3 be sure of sth** ⏦ to be confident that something is true: *He'll win, I'm sure of it.* **4 for sure** ⏦ without any doubts: *I think he's from Korea but don't know for sure.* **5 be sure of yourself** ⏦ to be confident of your own abilities, qualities, etc: *She's always been very sure of herself.* **6 be sure to do sth a** If you are sure to do something, it is certain that you will do it: *He's sure to go back there again.* **b** used to tell someone what they must remember to do: *Be sure to tell her I called.* **7 a sure sign of/that sth** something that makes something seem certain to be true **8 a sure thing** something that is certain to happen: *Death is the one sure thing about life.* **9 sure** (also US **sure thing**) ⏦ used to show agreement: *"Can I borrow your pen please?" "Sure."* **10 sure enough** ⏦ as expected: *He said the book was on his desk, and sure enough, there it was.*

surely /'ʃɔːli/ **adv** ⏦ used to express surprise that something has happened or is going to happen: *You surely didn't tell him, did you?* ◦ *Surely you're not going to go out dressed like that?*

surf¹ /sɜːf/ **verb 1** ⏦ [I] to ride on a wave in the sea using a special board **2 surf the Internet/Net/Web** ⏦ to look at information on the Internet by moving from one page to another using electronic links (= connections) → See

Study Page **The Web and the Internet** on page Centre 36 • **surfer noun** [C] someone who surfs • **surfing noun** [U]

surf² /sɜːf/ **noun** [U] the top of the waves in the sea as it moves onto the coast

surface¹ /'sɜːfɪs/ **noun 1** [C] ⏦ the top or outside part of something: *the Earth's surface* ◦ *The sun was reflected on the surface of the water.* **2** [no plural] ⏦ what someone or something seems to be like when you do not know much about them: *On the surface he seemed very pleasant.* → See also **work surface**

> ✓ Word partners for **surface**
>
> a flat/hard/level/smooth/uneven surface • cover the surface • above/below/beneath/on the surface

surface² /'sɜːfɪs/ **verb 1 APPEAR** ▷ [I] to appear or become public, often after being hidden: *This problem first surfaced about two weeks ago.* ◦ *So when did these allegations surface?* **2 RISE** ▷ [I] to rise to the surface of water: *The submarine surfaced a few miles off the coast.* **3 COVER** ▷ [T] to cover a road with a hard substance

'surface ,mail noun [U] letters, parcels, etc that are sent by road, sea, or train and not by aircraft

surfboard /'sɜːfbɔːd/ **noun** [C] a long piece of wood or plastic that you use to ride on waves in the sea

surfeit /'sɜːfɪt/ **noun** [no plural] formal too much of something: *We've had a surfeit of applications from women for this job.*

surfing /'sɜːfɪŋ/ **noun** [U] **1** ⏦ the sport of riding on a wave on a special board **2** the activity of looking at a lot of different things on the Internet

surge¹ /sɜːdʒ/ **verb 1 surge forward/into/through, etc** to move somewhere with great strength: *The crowd surged against the barriers.* **2** [I] to increase very quickly: *Prices surged on the stock exchange.*

surge² /sɜːdʒ/ **noun** [C] **1** a large increase in something: *a surge in spending* **2** a sudden movement forward

surgeon /'sɜːdʒən/ **noun** [C] a doctor who does medical operations → See also **veterinary surgeon**

surgeon

surgery /'sɜːdʒəri/ **noun 1** [U] ⏦ the activity in which a doctor cuts people's bodies open and repairs or removes something: *to have surgery* ◦ *heart/knee surgery* **2** [C] UK ⏦ a place where doctors or other medical workers treat people → See also **plastic surgery**

surgical /'sɜːdʒɪkəl/ **adj** relating to medical operations: *surgical instruments/gloves* • **surgically adv**

surly /'sɜːli/ **adj** unfriendly and rude: *a surly teenager*

S

surmount /səˈmaʊnt/ **verb** [T] formal to deal successfully with a problem

surname /ˈsɜːneɪm/ **noun** [C] ⓐ the name that you and other members of your family all have: *His surname is Walker.*

surpass /səˈpɑːs/ **verb** [T] formal to be or do better than someone or something else: *The book's success* **surpassed** *everyone's* **expectations.**

surplus /ˈsɜːpləs/ **noun** [C, U] an amount of something that is more than you need: *Every year we produce a huge* **surplus of** *meat.* • **surplus adj** *surplus wheat*

surprise¹ /səˈpraɪz/ **noun 1** [C] ⓐ an event that you did not expect to happen: *I didn't know that my parents were coming – it was a lovely surprise.* ◦ *Her resignation* **came as a** *complete* **surprise** (= *was very surprising*). ◦ *a* **surprise party 2** [U] ⓑ the feeling that you get when something happens that you did not expect: *He agreed to everything, much* **to my surprise. 3 take/catch sb by surprise** to be unexpected and make someone feel surprise: *I wasn't expecting her to be so angry – it took me by surprise.*

🖉 Word partners for **surprise**

come as a surprise • a **big/nice/unpleasant** surprise • a surprise **to** sb • a surprise **party**

➕ Other ways of saying **surprise**

An unpleasant surprise is often described as a **shock**:
We got a nasty **shock** *when he gave us the bill.*
His death came as a terrible **shock.**
A **blow** is a surprising event that causes someone to feel very sad and disappointed:
Losing his job was a terrible **blow** *to him.*
Something which is so surprising that it is almost difficult to believe is sometimes described as a **miracle**:
It's a **miracle** *that she survived the accident.*
If I pass this exam it'll be a **miracle.**
The expression **a rude awakening** is sometimes used if someone has an unpleasant surprise when they discover the truth about a situation:
She'll be in for **a rude awakening** *when she has to pay her own bills.*
If you want to say informally that an event is a surprise to you, you can use the expression **be news to**:
Sarah is leaving? Well that's **news to** *me.*

---

surprise² /səˈpraɪz/ **verb** [T] **1** ⓑ to make someone feel surprise: *I didn't tell her I was coming home early – I thought I'd surprise her.* **2** to find or attack someone when they are not expecting it

surprised /səˈpraɪzd/ **adj** ⓐ feeling surprise because something has happened that you did not expect: [+ to do sth] *I'm surprised to see you here.* ◦ *She wasn't* **surprised at** *his decision.* ◦ [+ (that)] *I'm surprised that you've decided to leave.*

surprising /səˈpraɪzɪŋ/ **adj** ⓑ not expected and making someone feel surprised: *It's not surprising you're putting on weight, the amount you're eating!* • **surprisingly adv** ⓑ *surprisingly good*

surreal /səˈrɪəl/ **adj** (also **surrealistic** /səˌrɪəˈlɪstɪk/) strange and not real, like something in a dream: *His paintings have a surreal quality.*

surrender /səˈrendər/ **verb 1** [I] to stop fighting and admit that you have been beaten: *Rebel troops are refusing to surrender.* **2** [T] formal to give something to someone else because you have been forced or officially asked to give it to them: *He was released on the condition that he surrendered his passport.* • **surrender noun** [C, U]

surreptitious /ˌsʌrəpˈtɪʃəs/ **adj** done secretly so that other people do not see: **surreptitious glances** *at the clock* • **surreptitiously adv**

surrogate /ˈsʌrəgɪt/ **adj** [always before noun] used instead of someone or something else: *Twenty years older than her, he effectively became a surrogate father.* • **surrogate noun** [C] someone or something that is used instead of someone or something else: *He seemed to regard her as a* **surrogate for** *his dead mother.*

surrogate ˈmother noun [C] a woman who has a baby for a woman who is not able to have a baby herself

surround /səˈraʊnd/ **verb** [T] **1** ⓑ to be or go everywhere around something or someone: *The house is surrounded by a large garden.* ◦ *The police have surrounded the building.* ◦ *the surrounding countryside* **2 be surrounded by sb/sth** to have a lot of people or things near you: *She's surrounded by the people she loves.* **3** If a feeling or situation surrounds an event, it is closely connected with it: *Mystery still* **surrounds** *the exact circumstances of his death.*

surroundings /səˈraʊndɪŋz/ **noun** [plural] ⓑ the place where someone or something is and the things that are in it: *Have you got used to your new surroundings?*

surveillance /sɜːˈveɪləns/ **noun** [U] the activity of watching someone carefully, especially by the police or army, because they are expected to do something wrong: *The police have* **kept** *the man* **under** *strict* **surveillance.**

survey¹ /ˈsɜːveɪ/ **noun** [C] **1 QUESTIONS** ▷ ⓑ an examination of people's opinions or behaviour made by asking people questions: *Holidays in the UK are becoming more popular, according to a* **recent survey. 2 BUILDING** ▷ UK an examination of the structure of a building in order to find out if there is anything wrong with it: *The bank have refused a loan until we've had a survey done on the property.* **3 LAND** ▷ an examination of an area of land in which its measurements and details are recorded, especially in order to make a map

---

🖉 Word partners for **survey**

carry out/conduct/take part in a survey • a survey **finds/reveals/shows/suggests** sth • a survey **of** sth • **in** a survey • **according to** a survey • a **recent** survey

---

survey² /səˈveɪ/ **verb** [T] **1 EXAMINE** ▷ to look at or examine something carefully: *I got out of the car to survey the damage.* **2 QUESTION** ▷ to ask people questions in order to find out about their opinions or behaviour: *75% of midwives surveyed were in favour of home births.* **3 LAND** ▷ to measure and record the details of an area of land **4 BUILDING** ▷ UK to examine the structure of a building in order to find out if there is anything wrong with it

surveyor /sə'veɪər/ **noun** [C] **1** UK someone whose job is to examine the structure of buildings **2** someone whose job is to measure and record the details of an area of land

survival /sə'vaɪvəl/ **noun** [U] 🅱2 the fact of continuing to live or exist, especially after a difficult or dangerous situation: *Flood victims had to fight for survival.*

survive /sə'vaɪv/ **verb 1 NOT DIE** ▷ [I, T] 🅱2 to continue to live after almost dying because of an accident, illness, etc: *He was born with a heart problem and only survived ten days.* ○ *No one survived the plane crash.* **2 EXIST** ▷ [I, T] to continue to exist after being in a difficult or dangerous situation: *Only two buildings survived the earthquake.* **3 LIVE LONGER** ▷ [T] If you survive someone, you continue to live after they have died.

survivor /sə'vaɪvər/ **noun** [C] 🅱2 someone who continues to live after almost dying because of an accident, illness, etc: *Rescuers have given up hope of finding any more survivors.*

susceptible /sə'septəbl/ **adj** easily influenced or harmed by something: *Older people are more susceptible to the virus.* ○ *a susceptible young teenager* • **susceptibility** /sə,septə'bɪləti/ **noun** [U] the fact of being susceptible to something

sushi /'suːʃi/ **noun** [U] Japanese food made of cold rice and fish which has not been cooked: *a sushi bar*

suspect¹ /'sʌspekt/ **noun** [C] 🅱2 someone who may have committed a crime: *He's the prime suspect (= the most likely suspect) in the murder case.*

IDIOM **the usual suspects** the people you would expect to be present somewhere or doing a particular thing: *"Who was at the party?" "Oh, Adrian, John, Dave – the usual suspects."*

> ☑ Word partners for **suspect**
>
> the **chief/main/prime** suspect • a suspect **for/ in** sth

suspect² /'sʌspekt/ **adj** difficult to trust or believe: *His explanation was highly suspect.*

suspect³ /sə'spekt/ **verb** [T] **1 CRIME** ▷ 🅱2 to think that someone may have committed a crime or done something bad: *He was suspected of drug dealing.* ○ *suspected terrorists* **2 THINK LIKELY** ▷ 🅱2 to think that something is probably true, or is likely to happen: [+ (that)] *They suspected that he was lying.* **3 NOT TRUST** ▷ to not trust someone or something: *She suspected his motives for offering to help.*

suspend /sə'spend/ **verb** [T] **1** to stop something happening for a short time: *The semifinal was suspended because of bad weather.* **2 suspend sth**

from/between, etc to hang something from somewhere: [often passive] *A light bulb was suspended from the ceiling.* **3** 🅱1 to not allow someone to go to work or school for a period of time because they have done something wrong: [often passive] *She was suspended from school for fighting.*

suspenders /sə'spendəz/ **noun** [plural] **1** UK (US **garters**) pieces of elastic fixed to a belt that hold up a woman's stockings (= very thin pieces of clothing that cover a woman's foot and leg) **2** US (UK **braces**) two straps fixed to a pair of trousers that go over your shoulders and stop the trousers from falling down

suspense /sə'spens/ **noun** [U] the feeling of excitement that you have when you are waiting for something to happen: *What's your answer then? Don't keep me in suspense.*

suspension /sə'spenʃən/ **noun 1 STOP** ▷ [U] the act of stopping something happening for a period of time: *an immediate suspension of all imports and exports* **2 JOB/SCHOOL** ▷ [C, U] the punishment of not allowing someone to go to work or school for a period of time **3 VEHICLE** ▷ [C, U] equipment that is fixed to the wheels of a vehicle in order to make it move more smoothly

suspicion /sə'spɪʃən/ **noun 1** [C, U] 🅱2 a feeling or belief that someone has done something wrong: *They were arrested on suspicion of drug dealing.* ○ *Several members of staff are under suspicion of stealing money.* **2** [C] an idea that something may be true: [+ (that)] *I had a sneaking suspicion that the two events might be connected.*

> ☑ Word partners for **suspicion**
>
> **have** a suspicion • **confirm** sb's suspicion • a **deep/sneaking/strong** suspicion

suspicious /sə'spɪʃəs/ **adj 1** 🅱2 making you feel that something is wrong or that something bad or illegal is happening: *suspicious behaviour/ circumstances* ○ *I called airport security after noticing a suspicious package.* **2** 🅱2 not trusting someone: *Many of them remain suspicious of journalists.* • **suspiciously adv** 🅱2 *She's been acting very suspiciously lately.*

sustain /sə'steɪn/ **verb** [T] **1** to cause or allow something to continue for a period of time: *The team may not be able to sustain this level of performance.* **2** to support someone or something so that they can live or exist: *The money he received was hardly enough to sustain a wife and five children.* **3 sustain damage/injuries/losses** formal to be injured/damaged, etc.

sustainable /sə'steɪnəbl/ **adj 1** able to continue over a period of time: *sustainable development/ growth* **2** causing little or no damage to the environment, and therefore able to continue for a long time

sustained /sə'steɪnd/ **adj** continuing for a period of time without getting weaker: *a sustained attack* ○ *sustained pressure*

SUV /,esjuː'viː/ **noun** [C] abbreviation for sports utility vehicle: a large vehicle with an engine

S

that supplies power to all four wheels, so that the vehicle can travel easily over rough ground

svelte /svelt/ *adj* thin in an attractive way

swab /swɒb/ *noun* [C] a small piece of material used for cleaning an injury or for taking a small amount of a substance from someone's body so that it can be tested

swagger /ˈswægər/ *verb* [I] to walk in a way that shows that you are confident and think that you are important: *A group of young men swaggered around in leather jackets.* • **swagger** *noun* [no plural]

swallow¹ /ˈswɒləʊ/ *verb* **1** FOOD OR DRINK ▷ [T] ⑫ to move your throat in order to make food or drink go down: *The snake swallowed the bird whole.* **2** THROAT ▷ [I] to make a movement with your throat as if you are eating, sometimes because you are nervous: *Claire swallowed hard, opened the door and stepped inside.* **3** ACCEPT ▷ [T] to accept something unpleasant: *They found the final decision hard to swallow.* **4** BELIEVE ▷ [T] informal to believe something, usually something that is not true: *I told him we were journalists and he seemed to swallow it.* → See also **swallow your pride**

PHRASAL VERB **swallow sth up** to make something disappear: *Many small businesses are being swallowed up by large international companies.*

swallow² /ˈswɒləʊ/ *noun* [C] **1** a small bird with long, pointed wings and a tail with two points **2** the movement of swallowing

swam /swæm/ past tense of swim

swamp¹ /swɒmp/ *noun* [C, U] an area of very wet, soft land

swamp² /swɒmp/ *verb* [T] **1** to give someone more of something than they can deal with: [often passive] *The company was swamped with calls about its new service.* ○ *The market has been swamped by cheap imports.* **2** If an area is swamped, it becomes covered with water: *Heavy rain has swamped many villages in the region.*

swan /swɒn/ *noun* [C] ⑫ a large, white bird with a long neck that lives on lakes and rivers

swap /swɒp/ *verb* [I, T] (**swapping, swapped**) to give something to someone and get something from them in return: *Would you mind swapping places with me?* • **swap** *noun* [C] *We'll do a swap.*

swarm¹ /swɔːm/ *noun* [C] a large group of things, usually insects, moving together: *a swarm of bees*

swarm² /swɔːm/ *verb* [I] to move in a large group: *TV reporters swarmed outside the pop star's home.*

PHRASAL VERB **swarm with sb/sth** If a place is swarming with people, insects, etc, there are a lot of them moving around in it: *The house was swarming with police.*

swarthy /ˈswɔːði/ *adj* having dark skin

swat /swɒt/ *verb* [T] (**swatting, swatted**) to hit something, especially an insect, with a flat object: *He swatted a fly with his newspaper.*

sway /sweɪ/ *verb* **1** [I] to move slowly from one side to the other: *The trees swayed gently in the*

wind. **2** [T] to persuade someone to change their opinion or decision: *I think I was swayed by what James said.*

swear /sweər/ *verb* (**swore, sworn**) **1** BAD LANGUAGE ▷ [I] ⑫ to use language that people think is rude or offensive: *He was sent home because he swore at the teacher.* **2** PROMISE ▷ [I, T] ⑫ to make a serious promise: [+ to do sth] *I swear to tell the truth.* [+ (that)] *She swore that she was at home at the time of the accident.* **3** TRUE ▷ [T] used to say that you are sure something is true: [+ (that)] *I could have sworn that she said she lived in Canterbury* (= *I was sure she lived in Canterbury, but now have found that it is not true*).

PHRASAL VERBS **swear by sth** to believe strongly that something is useful or effective: *Have you tried using vinegar to clean windows? My Mum swears by it.* • **swear sb in** to make someone such as a president, judge, etc officially promise to be honest and responsible when they start their job: [often passive] *Mr Stein was sworn in as City Council president.*

swearing /ˈsweərɪŋ/ *noun* [U] the use of rude or offensive language: *He was always getting into trouble for swearing.*

'swear ˌword *noun* [C] a word which people think is rude or offensive

sweat /swet/ *verb* [I] ⑫ to produce liquid through your skin because you are hot or nervous: *I'd been running and I was sweating.* • **sweat** *noun* [U] ⑫ *The sweat was running down his face.*

PHRASAL VERBS **sweat it out** informal to wait nervously for an unpleasant situation to improve or end: *I don't get my exam results till the end of June so I'll just have to sweat it out till then.* • **sweat over sth** to work hard at something: *She's been sweating over the preparations for the party all weekend.*

sweater /ˈswetər/ *noun* [C] (also UK **jumper**) ⑫ a warm piece of clothing that covers the top of your body and is pulled on over your head → See colour picture **Clothes** on page Centre 8

sweats /swets/ *noun* [plural] US a sweatshirt and sweatpants (= loose, comfortable trousers), often worn for exercising → See colour picture **Clothes** on page Centre 9

sweatshirt /ˈswetʃɜːt/ *noun* [C] ⑪ a piece of clothing made of soft cotton which covers the top of your body and is pulled on over your head → See colour picture **Clothes** on page Centre

sweatshop /ˈswetʃɒp/ *noun* [C] a small factory where workers are paid very little and work many hours in very bad conditions

sweaty /ˈsweti/ *adj* covered in sweat: *He was hot and sweaty from working in the garden.*

swede /swiːd/ *noun* [C, U] UK a round, yellow vegetable that grows in the ground

sweep¹ /swiːp/ *verb* (**swept**) **1** [I, T] (also **sweep up**) ⑫ to clean the floor using a brush: *She's just swept the floor.* ○ *He swept up the pieces of broken glass* (= *removed them from the floor with a brush*). **2 be swept along/away, etc** ⑫ to be pushed or carried along, often by something strong that you cannot control: *Many trees were swept away in the flood.* **3** [I, T] to quickly affect a large area: *The disease is **sweeping the country**.* ◦ *Panic swept through the crowd.* **4 sweep along/into/ past, etc** to move quickly, especially in a way that shows you think you are important: *She swept past me in the corridor.*

weep² /swiːp/ noun [C] **1** a long movement: [usually singular] *With a sweep of his arm, he gestured towards the garden.* **2** something shaped in a long curve: *a long sweep of sandy beach* → See also **chimney sweep**

weeping /ˈswiːpɪŋ/ adj **1** [always before noun] affecting many things or people: *sweeping changes/reforms* **2 sweeping statement/gener- alization** something someone says that is very general and has not been carefully thought about

weepstake /ˈswiːpsteɪk/ noun [C] UK (US **sweepstakes**) a type of betting (= risking money on a competition) in which the winner receives all the money

weet¹ /swiːt/ adj **1** TASTE ▷ ⓐ with a taste like sugar: *It was covered in a very sweet chocolate sauce.* **2** ATTRACTIVE ▷ ⓐ attractive, often because of being small: *Look at that kitten – isn't she sweet?* **3** KIND ▷ ⓑ kind and friendly: *It was really sweet of you to come.* **4** SMELL/ SOUND ▷ A sweet smell or sound is pleasant. • **sweetness** noun [U]

weet² /swiːt/ noun [C] UK (US **candy**) ⓐ a small piece of sweet food, often made of sugar or chocolate: *You shouldn't eat so many sweets – they're bad for your teeth.*

weetcorn /ˈswiːtkɔːn/ noun [U] UK (US **corn**) the sweet, yellow seeds of maize (= a plant) which are eaten as a vegetable → See colour picture **Fruit and Vegetables** on page Centre 10

weeten /ˈswiːtᵊn/ verb [T] to make something sweeter, for example by adding more sugar: *She gave me a hot lemon drink, sweetened with honey.*

weetener /ˈswiːtᵊnər/ noun [C] **1** something that is used to make something taste sweeter: *an artificial sweetener* **2** something that is used to persuade someone to do something

weetheart /ˈswiːthɑːt/ noun [C] You call someone 'sweetheart' to show affection or to be friendly: *Come here, sweetheart.*

weetly /ˈswiːtli/ adv in an attractive or kind way: *She smiled sweetly.*

weet poˈtato (plural **sweet potatoes**) UK (US **sweet poˌtato**) noun [C, U] a long, orange vegetable like a potato but that tastes slightly sweet

well¹ /swel/ verb (**swelled, swollen, swelled**) **1** [I] (also **swell up**) to increase in size: *One side of his face had swollen up where he'd been stung.* **2** [I, T] to increase in amount because more things are added: *The population of the region was swollen by refugees from across the border.*

well² /swel/ noun **1** [C, U] the movement of waves in the sea, or the waves themselves: *ocean swells* **2** [C] an increase

swell³ /swel/ adj US old-fashioned good or pleasant: *Everyone's having a swell time.*

swelling /ˈswelɪŋ/ noun [C, U] a part of your body that has become bigger because of illness or injury: *The doctor gave me drugs to reduce the swelling in my ankle.*

sweltering /ˈsweltərɪŋ/ adj so hot that you feel uncomfortable: *It was a sweltering afternoon in August.*

swept /swept/ past of sweep

swerve /swɜːv/ verb [I] to change direction suddenly, especially when you are driving a vehicle: *He swerved to avoid a cyclist and hit another car.*

swift /swɪft/ adj happening or moving quickly: *a swift response* • **swiftly** adv

swig /swɪg/ verb [T] (**swigging, swigged**) informal to drink something, taking a lot of liquid into your mouth at a time • **swig** noun [C] *He took a swig of his beer and carried on with the story.*

swill¹ /swɪl/ verb [T] **1** (also **swill out**) to clean something by making liquid move around it: *The dentist handed me a glass of water to swill my mouth out.* **2** to quickly drink a large amount of something, especially alcohol

swill² /swɪl/ noun [U] waste food that is fed to pigs

swim¹ /swɪm/ verb (**swimming, swam, swum**) **1** THROUGH WATER ▷ [I, T] ⓐ to move through water by moving your body: *I learnt to swim when I was about 5 years old.* ◦ *I swim thirty lengths of the pool most mornings.* → See colour picture **Sports 1** on page Centre 14 **2** HEAD ▷ [I] If your head swims, you feel confused and are unable to see or think clearly. **3** SEEM TO MOVE ▷ [I] to seem to move about: *I got up suddenly and the room started swimming.* • **swimming** noun [U] ⓐ *I usually go swim- ming about twice a week.* • **swimmer** noun [C] ⓑ *I'm not a very strong swimmer.*

swim² /swɪm/ noun [C] ⓐ a time when you swim: *I went for a swim before breakfast.*

ˈswimming ˌcostume noun [C] UK (US **bathing suit**) ⓐ a piece of clothing that you wear to go swimming → See colour picture **Clothes** on page Centre 9

ˈswimming ˌpool noun [C] ⓐ an area of water that has been made for people to swim in

ˈswimming ˌtrunks noun [plural] a piece of clothing that boys and men wear when they swim → See colour picture **Clothes** on page Centre 9

swimsuit /ˈswɪmsuːt/ noun [C] a piece of clothing that girls and women wear to go swimming → See colour picture **Clothes** on page Centre 9

swindle /ˈswɪndl/ verb [T] to get money from someone by cheating or deceiving them: [often passive] *She was swindled out of thousands of dollars.* • **swindle** noun [C] *a multi-million-pound swindle* • **swindler** noun [C]

swine /swaɪn/ noun **1** [plural] formal pigs **2** [C] informal an unpleasant person

swing¹ /swɪŋ/ verb (**swung**) **1** BACKWARDS/ FORWARDS ▷ [I, T] ⓑ to move smoothly backwards and forwards, or to make something do this: *She really swings her arms when she walks.* **2 CURVE** ▷ [I, T] to move smoothly in a curve, or to make something do this: *The door swung shut.* ○ *Watch the ball as you swing the bat.* **3 CHANGE** ▷ [I] If someone's opinion or their feelings swing, they suddenly change: *Her moods swing with absolutely no warning.*

PHRASAL VERBS **swing around/round** to turn around quickly • **swing at sb** informal to try to hit someone

swing² /swɪŋ/ noun [C] **1 FOR CHILDREN** ▷ **B2** a chair hanging on two ropes that children sit on and swing backwards and forwards **2 HIT** ▷ an attempt to hit someone: *Isn't that the boy Mark took a swing at (= tried to hit)?* **3 CHANGE** ▷ a sudden change: *He suffered terrible mood swings.*

IDIOM **be in full swing** If an event is in full swing, everything has started and there is a lot of activity: *By ten o'clock, the party was in full swing.*

swipe¹ /swaɪp/ verb [T] **1** (also **swipe at**) to move your arm in order to try to hit someone or something **2** informal to steal something

swipe² /swaɪp/ noun [C] an attempt to hit someone

'swipe ,card noun [C] UK a small piece of plastic that contains electronic information, used to open doors, etc

swirl /swɜːl/ verb [I, T] to move around and around quickly, or to make something do this: *The mist swirled round the castle.* • **swirl** noun [C]

swish /swɪʃ/ verb [I, T] to move quickly through the air making a soft sound, or to make something do this • **swish** noun [C] *the swish of curtains closing*

switch¹ /swɪtʃ/ verb [I, T] **1** **B2** to change from one thing to another: *We're trying to encourage people to switch from cars to bicycles.* ○ *He's just switched jobs.* **2** to exchange something with someone else: *After a couple of months we switched roles.*

PHRASAL VERBS **switch (sth) off** **B1** to turn off a light, television, etc by using a switch: *Have you switched the computer off?* • **switch off** UK to stop giving your attention to someone or something: *I'm afraid I just switch off when she starts telling me about her problems.* • **switch (sth) on** **B1** to turn on a light, television, etc by using a switch • **switch over 1** UK to change from one television or radio station to another **2** to change from doing one thing to another: *We've decided to switch over to low fat milk.*

switch² /swɪtʃ/ noun [C] **1** **B1** a small object that you push up or down with your finger to turn something electrical on or off **2** a change: *There has been a switch in policy.*

☑ Word partners for **switch**

flick/press a switch • the on/off switch

---

switchboard /'swɪtʃbɔːd/ noun [C] a piece of equipment that is used to direct all the telephone calls made from and to a building

swivel /'swɪvəl/ verb [I, T] (mainly UK **swivelling,**

swivelled, US **swiveling, swiveled**) (also **swivel around**) to turn round, or to make something turn round

swollen¹ /'swəʊlən/ adj **B2** bigger than usual: *swollen wrist/ankle* ○ *swollen rivers*

swollen² /'swəʊlən/ past participle of swell

swoop /swuːp/ verb [I] **1** to suddenly move very quickly down through the air: *Huge birds swoop down from the sky.* **2** to suddenly attack: *The day before police had swooped on his home.* • **swoop** noun [C]

swop /swɒp/ verb [I, T] (**swopping, swopped**) another UK spelling of swap (= to give something to someone and get something from them in return)

sword /sɔːd/ noun [C] **B2** a weapon with a long, metal blade and a handle, used especially in the past

swordfish /'sɔːdfɪʃ/ noun [C, U] (plural **swordfish**) a large fish with a long, pointed part at the front of its head, that can be eaten as food

swore /swɔːr/ past tense of swear

sworn¹ /swɔːn/ adj **1 sworn statement/testimony, etc** something that you have officially said is true **2 sworn enemies** two people, or two groups of people who are completely against each other

sworn² /swɔːn/ past participle of swear

swot¹ /swɒt/ verb [I] (**swotting, swotted**) UK informal (US **cram**) to study a lot: *I'm swotting for tomorrow's exam.*

PHRASAL VERB **swot up (on sth)** to learn as much as you can about a subject, especially before an examination

swot² /swɒt/ noun [C] UK informal someone who studies too much

swum /swʌm/ past participle of swim

swung /swʌŋ/ past of swing

sycamore /'sɪkəmɔːr/ noun [C, U] a tree with leaves that are divided into five parts and with seeds that turn around as they fall

sycophantic /ˌsɪkəʊ'fæntɪk/ adj formal Someone who is sycophantic praises people in authority in a way that is not sincere, especially in order to get an advantage for themselves. • **sycophant** /'sɪkəfænt/ noun [C]

syllable /'sɪləbl/ noun [C] **B2** a word or part of a word that has one vowel sound: *'But' has one syllable and 'apple' has two syllables.*

syllabus /'sɪləbəs/ noun [C] (plural **syllabuses, syllabi**) a list of the subjects that are included in a course of study

symbol /'sɪmbəl/ noun [C] **1** **B2** a sign or object that is used to represent something: *A heart shape is the symbol of love.* **2** a number, letter, or sign that is used instead of the name of a chemical substance, another number, etc: *Another symbol for oxygen is O.* → See also **status symbol**

symbolic /sɪm'bɒlɪk/ adj representing something: *The blue, white, and red of the French flag are symbolic of liberty, equality, and fraternity.* • **symbolically** adv

symbolism /'sɪmbəlɪzəm/ noun [U] the use of

signs and objects in art, films, etc to represent ideas

ymbolize (also UK **-ise**) /'sɪmbªlaɪz/ **verb** [T] to represent something: *The lighting of the Olympic torch symbolizes peace and friendship among the nations of the world.*

ymmetrical /sɪ'metrɪkªl/ **adj** (also **symmetric**) having the same shape or size on both halves: *Faces are roughly symmetrical.*

ymmetry /'sɪmətri/ **noun** [U] the quality of being symmetrical

ympathetic /ˌsɪmpə'θetɪk/ **adj 1** ⑫ showing that you understand and care about someone's problems: *My boss is very sympathetic about my situation.* **2** agreeing with or supporting someone's ideas or actions: *He was sympathetic to their views.* → Opposite **unsympathetic** • **sympathetically adv**

> **⚠ Common learner error: sympathetic**
>
> Be careful not to use **sympathetic** when you simply want to say that someone is **nice**, **friendly**, or **kind**. Remember that if someone is **sympathetic**, they understand your problems.

ympathize (also UK **-ise**) /'sɪmpəθaɪz/ **verb** [I] **1** to understand and care about someone's problems: *It's a really bad situation – I do sympathize with her.* **2** to agree with or support someone's ideas or actions: *I sympathize with the general aims of the party.*

ympathizer (also UK **-iser**) /'sɪmpəθaɪzəʳ/ **noun** [C] someone who supports a particular political organization, or believes in a particular set of ideas: *a communist sympathizer*

ympathy /'sɪmpəθi/ **noun** [U] **1** ⑫ the feeling that you understand and care about someone's problems: *I have no sympathy for people who say they can't find work but are really just too lazy to look.* **2** agreement with or support for someone's ideas or actions: *Scott was in sympathy with this view.*

> **✍ Word partners for sympathy**
>
> have/express/feel [every/little/no, etc] sympathy **for** sb • look **for** sympathy • deep/great/heartfelt sympathy • words of sympathy

ymphony /'sɪmfəni/ **noun** [C] a long piece of music for an orchestra (= large group of different musicians)

ymptom /'sɪmptəm/ **noun** [C] **1** ⑫ a physical feeling or problem that shows that you have a particular illness: *The inability to sleep is often a symptom of some other illness.* **2** a problem that is caused by and shows a more serious problem: *The drinking was just a symptom of his general unhappiness.* • **symptomatic** /ˌsɪmptə'mætɪk/ **adj** relating to a symptom

ynagogue /'sɪnəgɒg/ **noun** [C] a building in which Jewish people pray

ync /sɪŋk/ **noun** informal **1 be in sync** to be happening at the same time **2 be out of sync** to not be happening at the same time

synchronize (also UK **-ise**) /'sɪŋkrənaɪz/ **verb** [T] **1** to make something happen at the same time as something else: *We had a problem synchronizing the music and the images.* **2 synchronize watches** to make two or more watches show exactly the same time • **synchronization** /ˌsɪŋkrənaɪ'zeɪʃªn/ **noun** [U]

syndicate /'sɪndɪkət/ **noun** [C] a group of people or companies who join together in order to achieve something: *a bank syndicate* ◦ *a crime syndicate*

syndrome /'sɪndrəʊm/ **noun** [C] a combination of physical problems that often go together in a particular illness

synergy /'sɪnədʒi/ **noun** [C, U] a situation in which two companies or groups work together and achieve more success than they would separately: *a synergy between the two software companies*

synonym /'sɪnənɪm/ **noun** [C] a word or phrase that means the same as another word or phrase

synonymous /sɪ'nɒnɪməs/ **adj 1** If one thing is synonymous with another, they are very closely connected with each other in people's minds: *It is a country where wealth is synonymous with corruption.* **2** If one word is synonymous with another, they have the same meaning.

synopsis /sɪ'nɒpsɪs/ **noun** [C] (plural **synopses**) a short description of a book, film, etc

syntax /'sɪntæks/ **noun** [U] the grammatical arrangement of words in a sentence

synthesis /'sɪnθəsɪs/ **noun** [C, U] (plural **syntheses** /'sɪnθəsiːz/) formal the mixing of several things to make another whole new thing

synthesize (also UK **-ise**) /'sɪnθəsaɪz/ **verb** [T] to mix several things in order to make something else

synthesizer (also UK **-iser**) /'sɪnθəsaɪzəʳ/ **noun** [C] an electronic musical instrument that can copy the sounds made by other musical instruments

synthetic /sɪn'θetɪk/ **adj** not made from natural substances: *synthetic rubber* • **synthetically adv**

syphilis /'sɪfɪlɪs/ **noun** [U] a serious disease caught during sex, that spreads slowly from the sex organs to all parts of the body

syringe /sɪ'rɪndʒ/ **noun** [C] a piece of medical equipment used to push liquid into or take liquid out of someone's body

syringe

syrup /'sɪrəp/ **noun** [U] a very sweet liquid made from sugar and water

system /'sɪstəm/ **noun** [C] **1 METHOD** ▷ ⑫ a way or method of doing things: *the American legal system* ◦ *the public transport system* **2 EQUIPMENT** ▷ ⑪ a set of connected pieces of equipment that operate together: *They've had an alarm system installed at their home.* **3 BODY** ▷ parts of the body that work together in order to make something happen: *the body's immune*

S

system **4 the system** the laws and rules of a society

IDIOM **get sth out of your system** to get rid of a strong feeling or a need to do something, especially by expressing that feeling or doing the thing you want to do: *It's not a bad idea to travel before getting a job – that way you get it out of your system.*

→ See also **immune system, nervous system, operating system, public address system, the solar system**

systematic /ˌsɪstəˈmætɪk/ **adj** done using fixed and organized plan: *the systematic collection and analysis of information* • **systematically adv**

T

T, t /tiː/ the twentieth letter of the alphabet

ta /tɑː/ **exclamation** UK informal thank you

tab /tæb/ **noun** [C] **1** PAPER/METAL ETC ▷ a small piece of paper, metal, etc that is fixed to something and that you use to open it or find out information about it: *Pull tab to open.* **2** AMOUNT OF MONEY ▷ an amount of money that you owe for something you have bought or for a service you have used: *Officials said the tab for the new bridge would be $8 million.* **3** INTERNET ▷ a small symbol on a website that gives you information about the different pages you can open on that website: *Move between pages by clicking on the tabs at the top of the screen.* **4** COMPUTING ▷ (also **tab stop**) a fixed position on a line of text that you are writing on a computer, etc that can be reached by pressing the tab key **5 pick up the tab** to pay for something, especially a meal in a restaurant

IDIOM **keep tabs on sb/sth** informal to watch someone or something carefully to check they do nothing wrong

tabby /ˈtæbi/ **noun** [C] a cat that has stripes in its fur

tab key noun [C] the key on a computer keyboard that allows you to move the cursor (= a symbol which shows you where you are working) forward a few spaces

table¹ /ˈteɪbl/ **noun** [C]

1 FURNITURE ▷ ⒶⒷ a piece of furniture with four legs, used for eating off, putting things on, etc: *the kitchen table* **2 lay the table** UK (UK/US **set the table**) ⒷⒶ to put plates, knives, forks, etc on the table to prepare for a meal **3** NUMBERS/WORDS ▷ ⒷⒶ a set of numbers or words written in rows that go across and down the page: *The table below shows the results of the experiment.* **4** COMPUTER ▷ a collection of a particular kind of information in a database

table

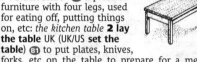

IDIOM **turn the tables on sb** to change a situation so that you have an advantage over someone who before had an advantage over you

→ See also **put/lay your cards on the table**, **coffee table**, **dressing table**

table² /ˈteɪbl/ **verb** [T] **1** UK to formally suggest that a particular subject is discussed **2** US to decide to discuss something later

tablecloth /ˈteɪblklɒθ/ **noun** [C] a piece of material that covers a table, especially during a meal

tablespoon /ˈteɪblspuːn/ **noun** [C] a large spoon used for measuring or serving food, or the amount this spoon can hold

tablet

tablet /ˈtæblət/ **noun** [C] **1** MEDICINE ▷ ⒷⒶ a small,

round object containing medicine that you swallow → See picture at **medicine 2** STONE ▷ a square piece of stone that has words cut into it **3** PAPER ▷ US (UK/US **pad**) sheets of paper that have been fastened together at one edge, used for writing or drawing **4** COMPUTER ▷ a small computer that you can use by touching the screen

> 🗒 Word partners for **tablet**
>
> take a tablet • a tablet for sth • sleeping tablets • headache tablets

table tennis noun [U] (also informal **Ping-Pong**) ⒶⒶ a game in which two or four people hit a small ball over a low net on a large table

tabloid /ˈtæblɔɪd/ **noun** [C] ⒷⒶ a small newspaper with a lot of pictures and short, simple news stories

taboo /təˈbuː/ **noun** [C, U] something that you should not say or do because people generally think it is morally wrong, unpleasant, or embarrassing: *Sex is a taboo in this country.* • **taboo adj** *Suicide is a taboo subject.*

tacit /ˈtæsɪt/ **adj** formal understood without being said: *a tacit agreement*

taciturn /ˈtæsɪtɜːn/ **adj** formal saying very little and not seeming friendly

tack¹ /tæk/ **noun 1 take/try a different tack** to try to deal with a problem in a different way: *I've tried being nice to her and it doesn't work so I might take a different tack.* **2** [C] a small, sharp nail with a flat top: *carpet tacks* **3** [C] US (UK **drawing pin**) a short pin with a flat, round top, used for fastening pieces of paper to the wall

tack² /tæk/ **verb** [T] **1** to fasten something to a wall with a tack **2** to sew something loosely

PHRASAL VERB **tack sth on** to add something that you had not planned to add

tackle¹ /ˈtækl/ **verb** [T] **1** DEAL WITH ▷ ⒷⒶ to try to deal with a problem: *new ways to **tackle** crime* **2** SPEAK TO ▷ UK to speak to someone about something bad that they have done: *I decided to tackle him about his absences.* **3** BALL ▷ ⒷⒶ to try to get the ball from someone in a game such as football

tackle² /ˈtækl/ **noun 1** [C] an attempt to get the ball from someone in a game such as football **2** [U] all the things you need for a particular activity: *fishing tackle*

tacky /ˈtæki/ **adj 1** informal cheap and of bad quality: *tacky holiday souvenirs* **2** slightly sticky

tact /tækt/ **noun** [U] the ability to talk to people about difficult subjects without upsetting them

tactful /ˈtæktfəl/ **adj** careful not to say or do anything that could upset someone • **tactfully adv**

tactic /ˈtæktɪk/ **noun** [C] a way of doing something that you plan in order to achieve what you want: [usually plural] *These bomb attacks represent a **change of tactics** by the terrorists.*

tactical /'tæktɪkəl/ **adj** relating to tactics, or done in order to achieve something: *tactical voting* ◦ *a tactical error* • **tactically** adv

tactless /'tæktləs/ **adj** not being careful about saying or doing something that could upset someone

tad /tæd/ **noun** informal **a tad** a little: *It was a tad expensive, I thought.*

tadpole /'tædpəʊl/ **noun** [C] a small, black animal that lives in water and will become a frog (= green jumping animal)

taffeta /'tæfɪtə/ **noun** [U] a stiff, shiny cloth used in women's formal dresses

TAFN internet abbreviation for that's all for now: used at the end of an email or message

tag[1] /tæg/ **noun** [C] a small piece of paper or plastic with information on it that is fixed to something: *a price tag*

tag[2] /tæg/ **verb** [T] (**tagging**, **tagged**) to put a tag on something

PHRASAL VERB **tag along** informal to go somewhere with someone, especially when they have not asked you to

t'ai chi /taɪ'tʃiː/ **noun** [U] a form of Chinese exercise that involves a series of slow movements

tail[1] /teɪl/ **noun** [C] **1** 🔵 the long, narrow part that sticks out at the back of an animal's body: *The dog's pleased to see you – he's **wagging** his tail.* **2** the back part of something long, such as a plane

tail

IDIOM **the tail end of sth** the last part of something: *the tail end of the eighties*

tail[2] /teɪl/ **verb** [T] to secretly follow someone, especially because you think they have done something wrong

PHRASAL VERB **tail off** to gradually become quieter, smaller, less frequent, etc: *His voice tailed off.*

tailback /'teɪlbæk/ **noun** [C] UK a line of cars that have stopped or are moving very slowly because of an accident or other problem on the road in front of them

tailcoat /'teɪl‚kəʊt/ **noun** [C] a formal coat that has a short front part and a long back part that is divided in two

tailgate /'teɪlgeɪt/ **verb** [I, T] to drive too closely to the car in front of you • **tailgating noun** [U]

tail ‚light noun [C] US (UK **rear light**) one of the two red lights on the back of a car → See **Car** on page Centre 7

tailor[1] /'teɪlər/ **noun** [C] someone whose job is to make or repair clothes, especially men's clothes

tailor[2] /'teɪlər/ **verb** [T] to make or change

something so that it is suitable: *The kitchen ca[n] then be **tailored** exactly **to** the customer's needs.*

tailor-made /‚teɪlə'meɪd/ **adj 1** perfect for [a] particular person or purpose: *It sounds as [if] you're **tailor-made for** the job.* **2** Tailor-mad[e] clothes are made by a tailor.

tailpipe /'teɪlpaɪp/ **noun** [C] US (mainly U[K] **exhaust pipe**) the pipe that waste gas from [a] vehicle's engine flows through → See colo[ur] picture **Car** on page Centre 7

tails /teɪlz/ **noun** [plural] **1** the side of a coin tha[t] does not have someone's head on it: *Let's toss [a] coin – **heads or tails**?* **2** a formal coat that has [a] short front part and a long back part that i[s] divided in two

taint /teɪnt/ **verb** [T] **1** to spoil people's opinio[n] of someone: [often passive] *a government tainte[d] by scandal* **2** to spoil something, especially foo[d] or blood, by adding a harmful substance

take /teɪk/ **verb** [T] (**took, taken**) **1** CARRY ▷ 🄰 to get and carry something with you when yo[u] go somewhere: *I always **take** my mobile phon[e] **with** me.* **2** GO ▷ 🄰 to go somewhere wit[h] someone, often paying for them or bein[g] responsible for them: *I **took** the kids **to** th[e] park.* → See Note at **bring 3** WITHOU[T] PERMISSION ▷ 🄱 to remove something without permission: *Someone's taken my coa[t].* **4** GET HOLD ▷ 🄱 to get hold of something an[d] move it: *He reached across and took the glass fro[m] her.* **5** ACCEPT ▷ 🄱 to accept something: *So, ar[e] you going to take the job? ◦ Do you take cred[it] cards?* **6** NEED ▷ 🄰 If something takes [a] particular amount of time, or a particula[r] quality, you need that amount of time or tha[t] quality in order to be able to do it: [+ to do st[h]] *It's taken me three days to get here. ◦ It takes a lo[t] of courage to stand up and talk in front of so man[y] people.* **7** MEDICINE ▷ 🄰 to swallow or us[e] medicine: *Take two tablets, three times a day[.]* **8** MEASURE ▷ to measure something: *Have yo[u] taken her temperature?* **9** CLOTHES ▷ 🄱 to wear [a] particular size of clothes: *I take a size 12 i[n] trousers.* **10** SPACE ▷ to have enough space for [a] particular number of people or things: *There'[s] six of us and the car only takes five.* **11** TRAVEL [▷] 🄰 to travel somewhere by using a bus, train, ca[r] etc, or by using a particular road: *Are you takin[g] the train to Edinburgh?* **12** take a break/rest, et[c] 🄱 to stop working for a period **13** tak[e] pleasure/pride/an interest, etc 🄱 to have [a] particular, good feeling about something tha[t] you do: *I take great pleasure in cooking. ◦ Thes[e] women take their jobs very seriously (= think thei[r] jobs are very important).* **14** take a look 🄱 t[o] look at something: *Take a look at these photo[s]* **15** UNDERSTAND ▷ to understand something i[n] a particular way: *Whatever I say she'll take it th[e] wrong way.* **16** I take it (that) used when yo[u] think that what you say is probably true: *I take i[t] you're not coming with us.* **17** can't take sth 🄱 t[o] not be able to deal with an unpleasant situatio[n:] *We argue all the time – I really can't take it an[y] more.* **18** take it from me accept that what I sa[y] is true, because I know or have experienced i[t:] *You could be doing a much less interesting jo[b]* *take it from me.* **19 take sth as it comes** to deal with something as it happens, without planning for it **20 BY FORCE** ▷ to get control of something by force: *By morning they had taken the city.*

> ❗ Common learner error: **take part in** or **take place**?
>
> If someone **takes part in** something, they join other people in doing it.
> *All the children took part in the competition.*
> If someone **takes place**, it happens.
> *The festival takes place every summer in the castle gardens.*

PHRASAL VERBS **take after sb** ⑫ to be similar to an older member of your family: *Peter's very tall – he takes after his father.* • **take sth apart** to separate something into its different parts: *He spent the whole afternoon taking his bike apart.* • **take sth away 1** ⑫ to remove something: *The waitress took our plates away.* ◦ *Supermarkets are taking business away from small local shops.* **2** ⑪ to subtract a number: *Take 3 away from 20.* • **take sb away** to make someone leave a place and go with you • **take sth back 1** ⑪ to return something to the place you borrowed or bought it from **2** to admit that your opinion was wrong: *You're right, he's nice – I take back everything I said about him.* • **take sth down 1** to write something: *Did you take down the telephone number?* **2** ⑫ to remove something that is on a wall or something that is temporary: *I've taken the pictures down.* • **take sth in 1 UNDERSTAND** ▷ to understand something: *It was an interesting lecture but there was just too much to take in.* **2 FILM/BUILDING ETC** ▷ to go to see a film, visit an interesting building, etc for enjoyment: *I thought we might get something to eat and then take in a movie.* **3 CLOTHES** ▷ to make a piece of clothing narrower • **take sb in 1** If the police take someone in, they take that person to the police station. **2** to let someone stay in your house: *You could earn some extra cash by taking in foreign students.* **3 be taken in** ⑫ to be deceived by someone • **take sth off 1** ⑫ to remove something: *If you're hot, take your jacket off.* → See colour picture **Phrasal Verbs** on page Centre 16 **2** ⑫ to spend time away from your work: *I'm taking Friday off to get some things done around the house.* • **take off 1 AIRCRAFT** ▷ ⑫ If an aircraft takes off, it begins to fly. **2 SUCCESSFUL** ▷ ⑫ to suddenly become successful: *Her career had just taken off.* **3 LEAVE** ▷ to suddenly leave without telling anyone where you are going: *He took off in the middle of the night.* • **take sth on** ⑫ to accept a responsibility: *I don't want to take on too much work.* • **take sb on 1** ⑫ to begin to employ someone: *We'll be taking on two new members of staff.* **2** to compete against someone: *I might take you on at tennis sometime.* • **take on sth** to begin to have a particular quality: *Her voice took on a tone of authority.* • **take sth out** ⑪ to remove something from somewhere: *He reached into his bag and took out a book.* • **take sb out** ⑪ to go somewhere with someone and pay for them: *Are you taking her out for her birthday?*

• **take sth out on sb** to unfairly treat someone badly because you are upset: *Don't take it out on me!* • **take (sth) over** ⑫ to get control of or responsibility for something: *They've recently been taken over by a larger company.* ◦ *Who'll be taking over from Cynthia when she retires?* • **take sb through sth** to explain something to someone • **take to sb/sth** to start to like someone or something: *For some reason, I just didn't take to him.* • **take to sth/doing sth** to start doing something: *Dad's taken to swimming every morning.* • **take sth up 1** ⑪ to start doing a particular job or activity: *I thought I might take up cycling.* **2** ⑫ to use an amount of time or space: *This desk takes up too much space.* • **take sb up on sth** to accept an offer: *Could I take you up on your offer of a ride home?* • **take sth up with sb** to discuss something with someone: *You'll have to take the matter up with your manager.*

takeaway /ˈteɪkəweɪ/ noun [C] UK (US **takeout**, ⑤ /ˈteɪkaʊt/) ⑪ a meal that you buy in a restaurant but eat at home, or a shop that sells this type of meal

take-off /ˈteɪkɒf/ noun **1** [C, U] the time when an aircraft leaves the ground and begins to fly **2** [C] a film, book, etc that copies someone else's style in a way that is funny

takeout /ˈteɪkaʊt/ noun [C, U] US (UK **takeaway**) a meal that you buy in a restaurant but eat at home

takeover /ˈteɪkˌəʊvər/ noun [C] a situation in which a company gets control of another company

takings /ˈteɪkɪŋz/ noun [plural] UK (US **receipts**) all the money that a business gets from selling things

talcum powder /ˈtælkəmˌpaʊdər/ noun [U] (also **talc**) white powder that you put on your skin after a bath

tale /teɪl/ noun [C] ⑫ a story, especially one that is not true or is difficult to believe: *My grandfather used to tell us tales of his time as a pilot during the war.* → See also **fairy tale**

talent /ˈtælənt/ noun [C, U] ⑪ a natural ability to do something: *She showed an early talent for drawing.* • **talented** adj ⑪ showing natural ability in a particular area: *a talented young musician*

> 🗹 Word partners for **talent**
>
> **have/show** a talent for sth • a **natural** talent
> • sb's **talent as** sth

talisman /ˈtælɪzmən/ noun [C] (plural **talismans**) an object that people think will make them lucky

talk¹ /tɔːk/ verb **1** [I] ⑪ to say things to someone: *We were just talking about Simon's new girlfriend.* ◦ *It was nice talking to you.* ◦ mainly US *It was nice talking with you.* → See Note at **speak** **2** [I] ⑫ to discuss something with someone, often to try to find a solution to a disagreement: *The two sides have agreed to talk.* **3 talk about sth/doing sth** to think about or make plans to do something in the future: *They're talking about* *building a new fire station just up the road.* **4 talk business/politics, etc** to discuss a particular subject: *I don't like to talk business over lunch.* **5 talking of sth** UK (US **speaking of sth**) used when you are going to start talking about something that is related to what has just been said: *Talking of holidays, did you hear about Lesley's skiing trip?* → See also **speak/talk of the devil**

PHRASAL VERBS **talk at sb** to talk to someone without letting them say anything or without listening to them • **talk back** If a child talks back to an adult, they answer them rudely. • **talk down to sb** to talk to someone in a way that shows you think they are not intelligent or not important • **talk sb into/out of (doing) sth** [B2] to persuade someone to do or not do something: *We managed to talk Lisa into doing the cooking.* • **talk sth over** [B2] to discuss something with someone, often to find out their opinion or to get advice before making a decision

> **Other ways of saying talk**
>
> The most common alternatives are **speak** and **say**:
>
> *Could you **speak** more quietly, please?*
> *I couldn't hear what they were **saying**.*
>
> The verb **chat** or the expression **have a chat** are often used if a person is talking with someone in a friendly, informal way:
>
> *We were just **chatting** about the party on Saturday.*
> *Give me a call and we'll **have a chat**.*
>
> If people talk for a long time about things that are not important, verbs such as **chatter**, **natter** (*UK, informal*), and the expression **have a natter** (*UK, informal*) are sometimes used:
>
> *She spent the morning **chattering** away to her friends.*
> *We **had a** long **natter** over coffee.*
>
> If someone talks about something too much in an annoying way, you can use the phrasal verb **go on** (*UK*):
>
> *He's always **going on** about how much he hates his work.*
>
> If someone talks quietly so that their voice is difficult to hear, often because they are complaining about something, then the verbs **mumble** and **mutter** are used:
>
> *She walked past me, **muttering** to herself.*
> *He **mumbled** something about it being a waste of time.*
>
> The verb **whisper** is used when someone talks extremely quietly so that other people cannot hear:
>
> *What are you two girls **whispering** about?*

talk² /tɔːk/ **noun 1 CONVERSATION** ▷ [C] [B1] a conversation between two people, often about a particular subject: *I **had a long talk with** Chris at the weekend about going to university.* **2 PEOPLE** ▷ [U] a situation in which people talk about what might happen or be true: *There's been some **talk of** possible job losses.* **3 TO A GROUP** ▷ [C] [B2] an occasion when someon speaks to a group of people about a particula subject: *Someone's coming to the school to **give** **talk about** road safety.*

IDIOM **be all talk (and no action)** If someone i all talk, they never do the brave or excitin things they often say they will do.

→ See also **small talk**

> **Word partners for talk noun**
>
> **have** a talk • a talk **with** sb • a talk **about** sth • a **long/serious** talk

talkative /ˈtɔːkətɪv/ **adj** A talkative person talk a lot.

talks /tɔːks/ **noun** [plural] formal meeting especially between political leaders, to discus a problem and to try to reach an agreemen *peace talks ◦ US officials are **holding talks wit** EU leaders over trade.*

> **Word partners for talks**
>
> **attend/have/hold/resume** talks • talks **break down/take place** • **lengthy/secret/urgent** talks • talks **about/on** sth

ˈtalk ˌshow noun [C] US (UK **chat show**) a informal television or radio programme wher people are asked questions about themselve and their lives

tall /tɔːl/ **adj 1** [A1] having a greater than averag height: *He's tall and thin. ◦ It's one of the talles buildings in the city.* **2** [A2] used to describe or as about the height of someone or something: *Ho tall is she? ◦ He's almost 2 metres tall.*

tally¹ /ˈtæli/ **noun** [C] the number of things yo have achieved, used, won, etc until now: *Thi adds to his **tally of** 12 race wins so far this year.*

tally² /ˈtæli/ **verb 1** [I] If two numbers or storie tally, they are the same. **2** [T] (also **tally up**) t find out the total number

the Talmud /ˈtælmʊd/ **noun** the ancient Jewis written laws and traditions

talon /ˈtælən/ **noun** [C] a sharp nail on the foo of a bird that it uses to catch animals

tambourine /ˌtæmbᵊrˈiːn/ **noun** [C] a musica instrument with a wooden ring and small meta discs loosely fixed to it which you play b shaking or hitting

tame¹ /teɪm/ **adj 1** If an animal is tame, it is no wild and not frightened of people. **2** too cor trolled and not exciting: *His TV show is very tam in comparison with his live performances.*

tame² /teɪm/ **verb** [T] to make a wild anima tame

tamper /ˈtæmpəʳ/ **verb**

PHRASAL VERB **tamper with sth** to touch or mak changes to something that you should no often in order to damage it

tampon /ˈtæmpɒn/ **noun** [C] a small roll c cotton that a woman puts in her vagina t absorb her monthly flow of blood

tan¹ /tæn/ **noun** [C] (also **suntan**) [B2] brown ski from being in the sun

tan² /tæn/ **verb** [I, T] (**tanning**, **tanned**) t

become brown from the sun, or to make a person or body part become brown: *I tan quite easily.*

tan³ /tæn/ *adj* **1** being a pale yellow-brown colour: *a tan jacket* **2** US (UK/US **tanned**) having darker skin because you have been in the sun

tandem /'tændəm/ *noun* **1 in tandem (with sb)** If someone does something in tandem with someone else, they do it together or at the same time. **2** [C] a bicycle for two people

tangent /'tændʒªnt/ *noun* [C] a straight line that touches but does not cross a curve

IDIOM **go off at/on a tangent** to suddenly start talking about a different subject

tangerine /ˌtændʒəˈriːn/ *noun* [C] a fruit like a small orange

tangible /'tændʒəbl/ *adj* Something that is tangible is real and can be seen, touched, or measured: *tangible benefits/evidence* → Opposite **intangible**

tangle¹ /'tæŋgl/ *noun* [C] several things that have become twisted together in an untidy way: *a tangle of hair/wires*

tangle² /'tæŋgl/ *verb* [I, T] to become twisted together, or to make things become twisted together → Opposite **disentangle, untangle**

tangled /'tæŋgld/ *adj* **1** (also **tangled up**) twisted together in an untidy way: *The wires are all tangled.* **2** confused and difficult to understand: *tangled finances* **3 be tangled up in/with sth** to be involved in something unpleasant or complicated that is difficult to escape from

tango /'tæŋgəʊ/ *noun* [C] a South American dance

tangy /'tæŋi/ *adj* having a strong, sharp but pleasant taste or smell: *a tangy lemon drink* • **tang** *noun* [no plural]

tank /tæŋk/ *noun* [C] **1** a large container for storing liquid or gas: UK *a petrol tank*/US *a gas tank* ◦ *a hot-water tank* **2** a large, strong military vehicle with a gun on it which moves on wheels inside large metal belts → See also **think tank**

tanker /'tæŋkər/ *noun* [C] a ship or truck used to carry large amounts of liquid or gas: *an oil tanker*

tank top *noun* [C] a piece of clothing that covers the upper part of the body but not the arms

tanned /tænd/ *adj* (also US **tan**) having darker skin than usual because you have been in the sun

tanning bed *noun* [C] US a sun bed

tannoy /'tænɔɪ/ *noun* [no plural] UK trademark (also UK/US **public address system**) a system of equipment used in public places that someone speaks into in order to make their voice loud enough to be heard

tantalizing (also UK **-ising**) /'tæntəlaɪzɪŋ/ *adj* Something that is tantalizing is very attractive and makes you want it, although often you cannot have it: *a tantalizing glimpse of blue sea*

tantamount /'tæntəmaʊnt/ *adj* **be tantamount to sth** to be almost as bad as something

else: *Resignation would be tantamount to admitting he was guilty.*

tantrum /'tæntrəm/ *noun* [C] a short period of very angry behaviour by a child, usually because they cannot have something: *Tom threw a tantrum in the middle of the supermarket.*

tap¹ /tæp/ *noun* [C]   **tap** *UK*, **faucet** *US*
1 WATER ▷ UK (US **faucet**) 🔊 the part at the end of a pipe that controls the flow of water: *the cold/hot tap* ◦ *to turn a tap on/off* ◦ *She rinsed the cup under the tap.*
2 KNOCK ▷ 🔊 a gentle knock or touch, or the noise made by knocking something gently: *I felt a tap on my shoulder.* ◦ *There was a tap at the door.*
3 TELEPHONE ▷ a small piece of equipment that can be fixed to someone's telephone in order to listen to their telephone calls **4 on tap** easily available: *They have all that sort of information on tap.*

🖊 Word partners for **tap**

turn on/turn off a tap • a tap is **dripping/running** • the **cold/hot** tap • **under** the tap • **tap** water

---

tap² /tæp/ *verb* (**tapping, tapped**) **1** KNOCK ▷ [I, T] 🔊 to knock or touch something gently: *I tapped on the window to try and get her attention.* **2** A SUPPLY ▷ [T] If you tap a supply of something, you use what is available: *There are immense natural resources here waiting to be tapped.* **3** TELEPHONE ▷ [T] to use a special piece of equipment to listen to someone's telephone calls: [often passive] *I think the phone's been tapped.*

PHRASAL VERB **tap into sth** to use part of a large supply of something for your own advantage

tap dancing *noun* [U] a type of dancing where the dancer wears special shoes with pieces of metal on the bottom which make a noise • **tap dance** *verb* [I] • **tap dancer** *noun* [C]

tape¹ /teɪp/ *noun* **1** RECORDING ▷ [C, U] a long, thin piece of plastic that is used to store sound, pictures, or information, or a plastic box containing it: *I've got the match on tape.* **2** STICKY ▷ [U] a thin piece of plastic that has glue on one side and is used for sticking things together: *adhesive/sticky tape* **3** MATERIAL ▷ [C, U] a long, thin piece of material used, for example, in sewing or to tie things together → See also **red tape, Scotch tape**

tape² /teɪp/ *verb* **1** [T] to record something onto tape **2 tape sth to/onto, etc** to stick something somewhere using tape

tape measure *noun* [C] a long, thin piece of cloth, metal, or plastic used to measure lengths

taper /'teɪpər/ **verb** [I, T] to become gradually narrower at one end • **tapered adj**

PHRASAL VERB **taper off** to become gradually smaller or less frequent: *Sales have gradually tapered off.*

tape re,corder noun [C] a machine used to record sound onto tape • **tape recording** noun [C] something which has been recorded on tape

tapestry /'tæpɪstri/ noun [C] a picture or pattern created by sewing different coloured threads onto heavy cloth

tap ,water noun [U] water that comes out of a tap (= part at the end of a pipe)

tar /tɑːr/ noun [U] **1** a thick, black substance that is sticky when hot and is used to cover roads **2** a black, sticky substance that is produced when tobacco burns • **tar** verb [T] (**tarring, tarred**) to cover something with tar

tarantula /tə'ræntjələ/ noun [C] a large, hairy spider that is often poisonous

target[1] /'tɑːgɪt/ noun [C] **1** ATTACK ▷ ⓐ something or someone that you attack, shoot at, try to hit, etc: *It's very difficult to* **hit** *a moving* **target**. ∘ *Foreign businesses in the region have become a* **target for** *terrorist attacks.* **2** ACHIEVE ▷ ⓐ something that you intend to achieve: *I'm hoping to save 3,000 euros by June – that's my* **target**. ∘ *If you want to lose weight, you have to* **set** *yourself (= decide) a* **target**. **3** BLAME ▷ the person or thing that people are criticizing or blaming for something: *Such extreme views have recently made him the target of criticism.* **4 be on target** to have made enough progress in order to achieve something that you intended to achieve: [+ to do sth] *We're on target to finish the project in June.* **5 target audience/market, etc** the group of people that a programme, product, etc is aimed at

> ☑ Word partners for **target**
>
> **attack/hit/miss/strike** a target • an **obvious/prime** target • a target **for** sth

target[2] /'tɑːgɪt/ **verb** [T] **1** to aim an attack at a particular person or place: *They mostly targeted military bases.* **2** to aim advertising, criticism, or a product at someone: [often passive] *The products are* **targeted at** *people in their late twenties.*

tariff /'tærɪf/ noun [C] **1** an amount of money that has to be paid for goods that are brought into a country: *import tariffs* **2** a list of prices

Tarmac /'tɑːmæk/ noun (also **tarmac**) trademark **1** [U] UK (US **asphalt**) a thick, black substance that is sticky when hot and is used to cover roads **2 the tarmac** the area at an airport where aircraft land and take off

tarnish /'tɑːnɪʃ/ verb **1** [T] to spoil the way in which people think of someone so that they do not respect them: *to tarnish someone's image/reputation* **2** [I, T] If a metal tarnishes or something tarnishes it, it becomes less bright and shiny.

tarpaulin /tɑː'pɔːlɪn/ noun [C, U] (also US **tarp**) a large piece of plastic or cloth that water cannot

go through which is used to cover and prote things

tart[1] /tɑːt/ noun [C]
1 an open pastry case with a sweet filling, often of fruit: *an apple tart* **2** UK very informal an offensive word for a woman who dresses or behaves in a way to attract a lot of attention from men

tart

tart[2] /tɑːt/ adj having a sour, bitter taste

tartan /'tɑːtən/ noun [C, U] cloth with a patte of different coloured squares and crossing line *a tartan kilt*

task /tɑːsk/ noun [C] ⓐ a piece of wor especially something unpleasant or difficu [+ of + doing sth] *I was given the task of sorti out all the stuff in the garage.*

taskbar /'tɑːskbɑːr/ noun [C] on a comput screen, a set of symbols that shows th programs you are using and allows you change them

task ,force noun [C] a group of people, often military group, who are brought together order to do a particular job

tassel /'tæsəl/ noun [C] a decoration, made of group of short threads tied together, which hung on curtains, furniture, etc

taste[1] /teɪst/ noun **1** FOOD ▷ [C, U] ⓑ the flavo of a particular food in your mouth: *a swee* **bitter taste** ∘ *It's got quite a* **strong tas** **2** ABILITY ▷ [U] ⓑ the ability to feel differe flavours in your mouth: *When you've got a co you often lose your* **sense of taste**. **3 a taste** small amount of food that you have in order try it: *Could I* **have** *just a* **taste** *of the sauc* **4** WHAT YOU LIKE ▷ [C, U] ⓑ the particul. things you like, such as styles of music, clothe decoration, etc: *I don't like his* **taste in** *mus* ∘ *It's okay, but it's not really* **to** *my* **taste**. **5** AR **STYLE ETC** ▷ [U] the ability to judge what attractive or suitable, especially in things relate to art, style, beauty, etc: *Everything in his house beautiful – he's got very* **good taste**. **6 be in goo taste** to be acceptable in a way that will n upset or anger people **7 be in bad/poor taste** be unacceptable in a way that will upset or ang people: *He told a joke about a plane crash which thought was in rather poor taste.* **8 a taste for st** when you like or enjoy something: *I've deve oped a bit of a taste for opera.* **9 taste of sth** ⓑ short experience of something new: *That was m first taste of Mexican culture.*

> ☑ Word partners for **taste**
>
> **disguise/improve/like/spoil** a taste • a **bitter/pleasant/strong/unpleasant/unusual** taste

taste[2] /teɪst/ verb **1 taste funny/nice/sweet, e** ⓑ If food tastes a particular way, it has th flavour: *This sauce tastes strange.* ∘ *It* **tastes** chocolate. **2 can taste sth** to be able experience a particular flavour in a food: *Yc can really taste the garlic in it.* **3** ⓑ [T] to put foo or drink in your mouth to find out what its flavour is like: *I always taste food while I'm cooking it.*

taste ˌbuds noun [plural] the cells on your tongue that allow you to taste different foods

tasteful /'teɪstf³l/ **adj** attractive and chosen for style and quality: *a tasteful beige suit* • **tastefully adv** *tastefully dressed/decorated*

tasteless /'teɪstləs/ **adj 1** UGLY ▷ ugly or without style **2** OFFENSIVE ▷ likely to upset or anger people: *a tasteless joke* **3** FOOD ▷ having no flavour: *The meat was dry and tasteless.*

tasty /'teɪsti/ **adj** ⑤ Food that is tasty has a good flavour and is nice to eat.

tattered /'tætəd/ **adj** old and badly torn: *tattered clothes*

tatters /'tætəz/ **noun in tatters** badly torn, damaged, or spoilt: *The yacht finally made it to the harbour, its sails in tatters.* ∘ *His reputation is in tatters.*

tattoo /tæt'uː/ **noun** [C] a design on someone's skin that is put on using ink and a needle • **tattoo verb** [T] **(tattooed)**

tattoo

tatty /'tæti/ **adj** UK informal untidy and in bad condition: *He turned up wearing a pair of tatty old jeans.*

taught /tɔːt/ past of teach

taunt /tɔːnt/ **verb** [T] to repeatedly say unkind things to someone in order to upset them or make them angry: *He was taunted by his classmates because of his size.* • **taunt noun** [C]

Taurus /'tɔːrəs/ **noun** [C, U] the sign of the zodiac that relates to the period of 21 April – 22 May, or a person born during this period → See picture at **the zodiac**

taut /tɔːt/ **adj** stretched very tight: *My skin feels taut.*

tavern /'tævən/ **noun** [C] mainly US a place where people go to drink alcohol

tawdry /'tɔːdri/ **adj 1** unpleasant and immoral **2** cheap and of bad quality

tawny /'tɔːni/ **adj** being a light yellow-brown colour

tax¹ /tæks/ **noun** [C, U] ⑤ money that you have to pay to the government from what you earn or when you buy things: *They're putting up the tax on cigarettes.* ∘ *Do you have to pay tax on that?* → See also **income tax**

☑ Word partners for **tax**

deduct/increase/pay tax • high/low taxes • a tax on sth • after/before tax

tax² /tæks/ **verb** [T] **1** to make someone pay a tax: *Goods such as clothes are taxed at 15%.* **2** to need a lot of effort: *It's only a short report – it shouldn't tax me too much.*

taxable /'tæksəbl/ **adj** If something is taxable, you have to pay tax on it: *taxable income*

taxation /tæk'seɪʃ³n/ **noun** [U] the system of making people pay taxes

tax-free /ˌtæks'friː/ **adj** If something is tax-free, you do not pay tax on it.

taxi /'tæksi/ **noun** [C] ⑥ a car with a driver who you pay to take you somewhere: *a taxi driver* ∘ *I'll take a taxi to the airport.*

☑ Word partners for **taxi**

call/get/hail/order/take a taxi • a taxi driver/fare/firm

taxing /'tæksɪŋ/ **adj** difficult and needing a lot of thought or effort to do or understand

taxi ˌrank noun [C] UK (US **taxi ˌstand**) a place where you can go to get a taxi

taxpayer /'tæksˌpeɪər/ **noun** [C] a person who pays tax

TB /ˌtiː'biː/ **noun** [U] abbreviation for tuberculosis (= a serious infectious disease of the lungs)

tbsp written abbreviation for tablespoonful: the amount that can be held by a large spoon used for measuring food

tea /tiː/ **noun** [C, U] **1** DRINK ▷ ⑥ a hot drink that you make by pouring water onto dried leaves, or the leaves that you use to make this drink: *herbal teas* ∘ *Would you like a cup of tea or coffee?* **2** AFTERNOON MEAL ▷ UK ⑤ a small afternoon meal of cakes, biscuits, etc and tea to drink: *They invited us for afternoon tea.* **3** EVENING MEAL ▷ UK a word used by some people for the meal that is eaten in the evening

teabag /'tiːbæg/ **noun** [C] a small paper bag with dried leaves inside, used for making tea

teach /tiːtʃ/ **verb** **(taught) 1** GIVE LESSONS ▷ [I, T] ⑥ to give lessons in a particular subject at a school, university, etc: *She taught at Harvard University for several years.* ∘ *He teaches history.* **2** SHOW HOW TO ▷ [T] ⑥ to show or explain to someone how to do something: [+ to do sth] *My dad taught me to drive.* ∘ *Can you teach me how to knit?* **3** GET KNOWLEDGE ▷ [T] ⑤ If a situation teaches you something, it gives you new knowledge or helps you to understand something: [+ to do sth] *The whole experience taught him to be more careful with money.* → See Note at **learn** → See also **teach sb a lesson**

teacher /'tiːtʃər/ **noun** [C] ⑥ someone whose job is to teach in a school, college, etc: *a history/science teacher* → See colour picture **The Classroom** on page Centre 6 → See Note at **lecturer**

teaching /'tiːtʃɪŋ/ **noun** [U] ⑤ the job of being a teacher: *He decided to go into teaching* (= become a teacher).

teachings /'tiːtʃɪŋz/ **noun** [plural] the ideas or beliefs of someone, such as a political or religious leader: *the teachings of Martin Luther King*

teacup /'tiːkʌp/ **noun** [C] a cup that you drink tea from

team¹ /tiːm/ **noun** [group] **1** ⑥ a group of people who play a sport or game together against another group of players: *a basketball/football team* **2** ⑤ a group of people who work together to do something: *a management team* ∘ *a team of advisers*

T

team² /tiːm/ **verb**

PHRASAL VERB **team up** to join someone and work together with them to do something: *I teamed up with Brendan for the doubles tournament.*

teammate /'tiːmmeɪt/ **noun** [C] a member of your team

teamwork /'tiːmwɜːk/ **noun** [U] a situation in which a group of people work well together

teapot /'tiːpɒt/ **noun** [C] a container used for making and serving tea, which has a lid, a handle, and a spout (= tube that liquid comes out of) → See colour picture **The Kitchen** on page Centre 2

teapot

tear¹ /teər/ **verb** (**tore**, **torn**) **1** [T] ⓪ to pull paper, cloth, etc into pieces, or to make a hole in it by accident: *The nail had* **torn a hole in** *my skirt.* **2** [I] ⓪ If paper, cloth, etc tears, it becomes damaged because it has been pulled. **3 tear sth out of/off/down, etc** to remove something by pulling something quickly and violently: *She tore his picture down from the wall.*

tear

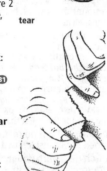

4 tear along/about/past, etc informal to move somewhere very quickly: *The kids were tearing around the house.* **5 be torn between sth and sth** to be unable to decide between two choices: *I'm torn between the apple pie and the chocolate mousse.* → See also **pull/tear your hair out**

PHRASAL VERBS **tear sth apart 1** to make a group of people argue or fight with each other: *The country was torn apart by 12 years of civil war.* **2** to destroy something: *The building was torn apart by the bomb blast.* • **tear sb apart** to make someone very unhappy • **tear sb away** to make someone stop doing something that they enjoy, in order to do something else: *I'll bring Ian, if I can* **tear** *him* **away from** *his computer games.* • **tear sth down** to intentionally destroy a building or structure: *They tore down the old hospital and built some offices.* • **tear sth off** to quickly remove your clothes: *He tore off his shirt and jumped into the stream.* • **tear sth up** ⓪ to tear paper into a lot of small pieces: *He tore up her photograph.*

tear² /teər/ **noun** [C] a hole in a piece of cloth, paper, etc where it has been torn

tear³ /tɪər/ **noun** [C] ⓪ a drop of water that comes from your eye when you cry: *Suddenly he* **burst into tears** (= started crying). ○ *I was in* **tears** (= crying) by the end of the film. • **tearful**

adj crying: *a tearful goodbye* • **tearfully ad**
→ See also **in floods of tears**

'tear ˌgas noun [U] a gas that makes people eyes hurt, used by the police or army to contr violent crowds

tease /tiːz/ **verb** [I, T] ⓬ to laugh at someone say unkind things to them, either because yc are joking or because you want to upset ther *They were* **teasing** *Dara* **about** *her new haircu* ○ *Don't get upset, I'm only teasing.*

teaspoon /'tiːspuːn/ **noun** [C] ⓬ a small spoc that is used for mixing drinks and measurir small amounts of food, or the amount th spoon can hold

teatime /'tiːtaɪm/ **noun** [C, U] UK the time in tł afternoon or evening when people have a me

'tea ˌtowel noun [C] UK (US **dishtowel**) a clo that is used for drying plates, dishes, etc

tech¹ /tek/ **adj** mainly US short for technical: *onlir tech support*

tech² /tek/ **noun** mainly US **1** [U] short f technology: *high/low tech* ○ *tech stocks* **2** [informal short for technician: *Bill was a lab tech NYU.*

techie /'teki/ **noun** [C] informal someone who h a strong interest in technology, usually comp ters

technical /'teknɪkəl/ **adj 1** SCIENCE/INDUSTRY ⓬ relating to the knowledge, machines, • methods used in science and industry: *We' having a few* **technical problem 2** SPECIALIZED ▷ relating to the knowledg and methods of a particular subject or job: *The are a few* **technical terms** *here that I dor understand.* **3** PRACTICAL SKILL ▷ ⓬ relating t practical skills and methods that are used in particular activity: *As a dancer she had gre technical skill.*

technicalities /ˌteknɪˈkælətiz/ **noun** [plural] tł exact details of a system or process: *tł technicalities of photography*

technicality /ˌteknɪˈkæləti/ **noun** [C] a sma detail of a law or rule

technically /'teknɪkəli/ **adv 1** relating to tł knowledge, machines, or methods used i science and industry: *technically advance weapons* **2** according to the exact details of rule, law, or fact: *Technically, you shouldn't I cats drink cow's milk.*

technician /tekˈnɪʃən/ **noun** [C] someone whos job involves practical work with scientific • electrical equipment: *a lab technician*

technique /tekˈniːk/ **noun** [C, U] ⓪ a particula or special way of doing something: [+ for + doir sth] *Scientists have developed a new technique f taking blood samples.*

techno /'teknəʊ/ **noun** [U] UK a type of electron dance music

techno- /teknəʊ-/ **prefix** relating to technolog *a technophile* (= *a person who loves technology*)

technology /tekˈnɒlədʒi/ **noun** [C, U] ⓪ know edge, equipment, and methods that are used i science and industry: *computer technolog* • **technological** /ˌteknəˈlɒdʒɪkəl/ **adj** ⓬ relatin to, or involving technology: *technologic* *developments* • **technologically** adv → See also **information technology**

🗹 Word partners for **technology**

advanced/cutting-edge/modern technology • develop/harness technology

---

eddy bear /'tedi,beə/ *noun* [C] (also UK **teddy**) a soft, toy bear

edious /'ti:diəs/ *adj* boring: *a tedious job* • **tediously** adv

ee /ti:/ *noun* [C] a small stick that is used for holding a golf ball

eem /ti:m/ *verb*

PHRASAL VERB **be teeming with sb/sth** to contain large numbers of people or animals

eeming /'ti:mɪŋ/ *adj* full of people: *the teeming city*

een¹ /ti:n/ *noun* [C] short for teenager

een² /ti:n/ *adj* [always before noun] informal relating to, or popular with, people who are between 13 and 19 years old: *a teen idol*

eenage /'ti:neɪdʒ/ *adj* [always before noun] 🅱1 aged between 13 and 19 or suitable for people of that age: *a teenage daughter* ○ *a teenage disco*

eenager /'ti:n,eɪdʒə/ *noun* [C] 🅐2 someone who is between 13 and 19 years old

eens /ti:nz/ *noun* [plural] the part of your life between the age of 13 and 19: *Her youngest daughter is still in her teens.*

ee shirt *noun* [C] another spelling of T-shirt (= a piece of cotton clothing for the top part of the body with short sleeves and no collar)

eeter /'ti:tə^r/ *verb* **1 be teetering on the brink/ edge of sth** to be in a situation where something bad might happen very soon: *The economy is teetering on the brink of collapse.* **2 teeter about/across/around, etc** to look as if you are going to fall: *She teetered around the room in six-inch heels.*

eeter-totter /,ti:tə'tɒtə^r/ *noun* [C] US (UK/US **seesaw**) a long board that children play on by sitting at each end and using their feet on the ground to push the board up and down

eeth /ti:θ/ *plural of* tooth

teeth

eethe /ti:ð/ *verb* **1 be teething** If a baby is teething, it is getting its first teeth. **2 teething problems/ troubles** problems that happen because something is new and has not been done before

eetotal /,ti:'təʊt^əl/ *adj* never drinking any alcohol • **teetotaller** mainly UK (US **teetotaler**) *noun* [C] someone who never drinks alcohol

TEFL /'tefl/ *noun* [U] abbreviation for Teaching English as a Foreign Language

el written abbreviation for telephone number: *Tel 0113 246369*

ele- /telɪ-/ *prefix* **1** TELEPHONE ▷ done using a telephone: *telesales* **2** TELEVISION ▷ connected with television: *telecast* (= *something that is* *broadcast on television*) **3** DISTANCE ▷ over a long distance: *telephoto lens* (= *a camera lens that makes distant objects look nearer*)

telecommunications /,telɪkə,mju:nɪ'keɪʃ^ənz/ *noun* [U, group] 🅱2 the process or business of sending information or messages by telephone, radio, etc

telecommuting /,telɪkə'mju:tɪŋ/ ⓤⓢ /'telɪkə,mju:tɪŋ/ *noun* [U] US (UK **teleworking**) working at home, while communicating with your office by computer and telephone • **telecommuter** *noun* [C] US

telecoms /'telɪkɒmz/ *noun* [U] short for telecommunications

teleconference /,telɪ'kɒnf^ərəns/ *noun* [C] a meeting between people in different places using computers, telephones, televisions, etc to allow them to talk to each other and see each other

telegram /'telɪgræm/ *noun* [C] a message that is sent by telegraph and printed on paper

telegraph /'telɪgrɑ:f/ *noun* [U] an old-fashioned system of sending messages using radio or electrical signals

telemarketing /'telɪ,mɑ:kɪtɪŋ/ *noun* [U] (also UK **telesales**) the selling of goods or services by telephone

telepathy /tə'lepəθi/ *noun* [U] the ability to know what someone is thinking or to communicate thoughts without speaking or writing • **telepathic** /,telɪ'pæθɪk/ *adj* having or involving telepathy

telephone¹ /'telɪfəʊn/ *noun* (also **phone**) **1** [U] 🅐2 a communication system that is used to talk to someone who is in another place: *a telephone call* ○ *I'm sorry, he's on the telephone* (= *using the telephone*) *at the moment.* **2** [C] 🅐2 a piece of equipment that is used to talk to someone who is in another place: *The telephone rang and she hurried to pick it up.* ○ *Could you answer the telephone?*

🗹 Word partners for **telephone**

answer/pick up/put down the telephone • the telephone rings • on the telephone • a telephone call

---

telephone² /'telɪfəʊn/ *verb* [I, T] (also **phone**) 🅐2 to communicate with someone by telephone

---

❗ Common learner error: **telephone** and **phone**

Telephone and **phone** mean the same thing, but we usually use **phone** for both the noun and the verb.

I'll phone you this evening.

Can I use your phone, please?

When the phone rings or when you want to make a phone call, you **pick** it **up**.

I picked up the phone and dialled his number.

When you finish a phone call, you **put** the phone **down** or you **hang up**.

Don't hang up – I can explain everything!

She thanked him and put the phone down.

~~She thanked him and hung up the phone.~~

T

telephone di,rectory noun [C] a book that contains the telephone numbers of people who live in a particular area

telephone ,number noun [C] (also **phone number**) the number of a particular telephone

telesales /'telɪseɪlz/ noun [U] UK (UK/US **tele-marketing**) the selling of goods or services by telephone

telescope /'telɪskəʊp/ noun [C] ⓑ a piece of equipment, in the shape of a tube, that makes things that are far away look bigger or nearer

telescope

Teletext /'telɪ,tekst/ noun [U] trademark a system that gives written information on many subjects, such as news, on a television screen

televise /'telɪvaɪz/ verb [T] to show something on television: *The concert will be televised live around the world.*

television /'telɪvɪʒ³n/ noun **1** EQUIPMENT ▷ [C] ⓐ a piece of equipment, with a screen on the front, used for watching programmes **2** PROGRAMMES ▷ [U] ⓐ the programmes that are shown on a television: *I mostly watch television in the evening.* ◦ *I saw it on television.* ◦ *a television programme* **3** SYSTEM ▷ [U] ⓑ the system or business of making and broadcasting programmes for television → See also **closed-circuit television, satellite television**

> ⚠ Common learner error: **watch television**
>
> Be careful to choose the correct verb with **television**.
> *My children watch too much television.*
> ~~My children look too much television.~~

> ✓ Word partners for **television**
>
> **watch** television • **see/watch** sth **on** television • **on** television • a television **channel/presenter/programme/series**

teleworking /'telɪ,wɜːkɪŋ/ noun [U] UK (US **telecommuting**) working at home, while communicating with your office by computer and telephone • **teleworker** noun [C] UK

tell /tel/ verb (**told**) **1** SAY ▷ [T] ⓐ to say something to someone, usually giving them information: *He told me about his new school.* ◦ [+ (that)] *Sally told me that the play didn't start until 9 o'clock.* ◦ [+ question word] *Can you tell me what time the next bus leaves?* → See Note at **say¹** **2** **tell sb to do sth** ⓐ to order someone to do something: *I told you to stay here.* **3** **can tell** ⓑ to know or recognize something from what you hear, see, etc: [+ (that)] *You could tell that he was tired.* ◦ [+ question word] *You can never tell whether Hajime's being serious or not.* ◦ *I can't tell the difference between them.* **4** UNDER-STAND FROM ▷ [T] ⓑ If something tells you something, it gives you information: *What does the survey tell us about the lives of teenagers?* **5** **(I'll) tell you what** used to suggest a plan: *Tell you what, let's go swimming and then get a pizza.* **6** EFFECT ▷ [I] to have a bad effect on someone:

The worry of the last few months was starting t **tell on** him. **7** **(I) told you so!** informal used whe someone has caused problems for themselve by doing something that you told them not t → See also **tell sb's fortune**

PHRASAL VERBS **tell sb/sth apart** to be able to se the difference between two things or people tha are very similar: *It's impossible to tell the twin apart.* • **tell sb off** ⓑ to tell someone that the have done something wrong and that you ai angry about it: [+ for + doing sth] *Darren got tol off for talking in class.* → See colour picture **Phrasa Verbs** on page Centre 16

teller /'telər/ noun [C] US someone who works i a bank and gives out or takes in money → Se also **fortune-teller**

telling /'telɪŋ/ adj showing the truth about situation, or showing what someone reall thinks: *a telling comment*

telltale /'telteɪl/ adj [always before noun] showin something that someone is trying to kee secret: *She was showing all the telltale signs c pregnancy.*

telly /'teli/ noun [C, U] UK informal short fo television

temp /temp/ noun [C] someone who works in a office for a short time while someone else i away, sick, etc • **temp** verb [I] to work as a tem in an office

temper¹ /'tempər/ noun **1** ⓑ [C, U] If someon has a temper, they become angry very easily *He's got a really bad temper.* **2** **be in a bad/fou etc temper** to be feeling angry: *I'd avoid her if were you – she's in a foul temper.* **3** **lose you temper (with sb)** ⓑ to suddenly become ver angry: *I lost my temper with the children th morning.* **4** **keep your temper** to succeed i staying calm and not becoming angry

temper² /'tempər/ verb [T] formal to make some thing less strong, extreme, etc: *I learnt to tempe my criticism.*

temperament /'temp³rəmənt/ noun [C, U] th part of your character that affects your moo and the way you behave: *I don't think he's got th right temperament to be a teacher.*

temperamental /,temp³rə'ment³l/ adj **1** becom ing angry or upset very often and suddenly **2** machine, vehicle, etc that is temperament does not always work correctly

temperate /'temp³rət/ adj formal havin weather that is not very hot and not very col *a temperate climate*

temperature /'temprətʃər/ noun **1** ⓐ [C, U how hot or cold something is: *The room's kept a temperature of around 20°C.* **2** **sb's tempera ture** ⓐ how hot or cold someone's body is: *Th doctor examined him and took his temperatur (= measured his temperature).* **3** **have a tempera ture** to be hotter than usual because you ar sick

> ✓ Word partners for **temperature**
>
> **average/extreme/high/low** temperatures • temperatures **drop/fall/rise/soar**

template /'templeɪt/ **noun** [C] **1** a metal, plastic, etc pattern that is used for making many copies of a shape **2** a system that helps you arrange information on a computer screen

temple /'templ/ **noun** [C] **1** 🔵 a building where people in some religions go to pray or worship: *a Buddhist temple* **2** the area on each side of your head in front of the top of your ear

tempo /'tempəʊ/ **noun** **1** [U, no plural] the speed at which an activity happens: *The tempo of the game increased in the second half.* **2** [C, U] formal the speed of a piece of music

temporary /'tempᵊrᵊri/ **adj** 🔵 existing or happening for only a short or limited time: *a temporary job* ∘ *temporary accommodation/ housing* • **temporarily adv**

> ➕ Other ways of saying **temporary**
>
> The phrase **for now** can be used to say that something should happen or be done now but can be changed later:
>
> > *Just put everything on the table **for now** – I'll sort it all out later.*
>
> The adjective **disposable** can be used to describe objects which are intended to be used temporarily and then thrown away:
>
> > *I bought a **disposable** camera at the airport.*
>
> If something is temporary and low quality, you can say that it is **makeshift**:
>
> > *We built a **makeshift** shelter under the trees.*
>
> The adjective **short-lived** can be used instead of 'temporary' when it means 'lasting for a short time':
>
> > *I had a few relationships at college, most of which were fairly **short-lived**.*
>
> The expression **acting manager/chairman**, etc is often used to describe someone who does a job temporarily while the person who usually does it is not there:
>
> > *He'll be the **acting** director until they appoint a permanent one.*

tempt /tempt/ **verb** [T] 🔵 to make someone want to have or do something, especially something that they do not need or something that is wrong: [+ to do sth] *She's trying to tempt me to go shopping with her.*

temptation /temp'teɪʃᵊn/ **noun** **1** [C, U] 🔵 a feeling that you want to do or have something, although you know you should not: [+ to do sth] *I resisted the temptation* to (= *I did not) have another piece of chocolate cake.* **2** [C] something that makes you want to do or have something although you know you should not: *He knew crime was wrong but the money was too great a temptation.*

> 🔲 Word partners for **temptation**
>
> **avoid/resist (the) temptation** • **give in to/ succumb to** temptation • **a strong** temptation • the temptation **of** doing sth

tempting /'temptɪŋ/ **adj** Something that is tempting makes you want to have or do it: *a tempting invitation/offer*

ten /ten/ 🔵 the number 10

tenacious /tɪ'neɪʃəs/ **adj** very determined to do something and not wanting to stop • **tenaciously adv** • **tenacity** /tɪ'næsəti/ **noun** [U]

tenancy /'tenənsi/ **noun** [C, U] the period of time when someone rents a room, house, etc

tenant /'tenənt/ **noun** [C] someone who pays rent to live in a room, house, etc

tend /tend/ **verb 1 tend to do sth** 🔵 to often do a particular thing or be likely to do a particular thing: *I tend to wear dark colours.* ∘ *July and August tend to be our busiest months.* **2** [T] (also **tend to**) to look after someone or something: *He spends most afternoons tending his vegetable garden.*

tendency /'tendənsi/ **noun** [C] something that someone often does, or something that often happens: [+ to do sth] *She has a tendency to talk for too long.* ∘ *There is a growing tendency for companies to employ people on short contracts.*

tender¹ /'tendər/ **adj 1 GENTLE** ▷ kind and gentle: *a tender kiss/look* **2 FOOD** ▷ Tender meat or vegetables are soft and easy to cut. **3 PAINFUL** ▷ If part of your body is tender, it is painful when you touch it. **4 at the tender age of 8/17/25, etc** literary at the young age of 8/ 17/25, etc • **tenderness noun** [U]

tender² /'tendər/ **verb** formal **1** [I] to make a formal offer to do a job or to provide a service **2** [T] formal to formally offer a suggestion, idea, money, etc: *He tendered his resignation* (= *offered to leave his job*).

tender³ /'tendər/ **noun** [C, U] a formal offer to do some work: *The work has been put out to tender* (= *people have been asked to make offers to do the work*).

tenderly /'tendəli/ **adv** in a kind and gentle way: *He looked at her tenderly.*

tendon /'tendən/ **noun** [C] a strong piece of tissue in your body that connects a muscle to a bone

tenement /'tenəmənt/ **noun** [C] a large building that is divided into apartments, usually in a poor area of a city

tenet /'tenɪt/ **noun** [C] a principle or belief of a theory or religion: *one of the basic tenets of Islam*

tenner /'tenər/ **noun** [C] UK informal a piece of paper money that has a value of £10

tennis /'tenɪs/ **noun** [U] 🔵 a sport in which two or four people hit a small ball to each other over a net → See colour picture **Sports 2** on page Centre 15 → See also **table tennis**

tenor /'tenər/ **noun** [C] a male singer with a high voice

tense¹ /tens/ **adj 1 FEELING** ▷ 🔵 nervous, worried, and not able to relax: *The students looked tense as they waited for their exam results.* **2 SITUATION** ▷ 🔵 A tense situation makes you feel nervous and worried: *There were some tense moments in the second half of the game.* **3 MUSCLE** ▷ A tense muscle feels tight and stiff.

tense² /tens/ **verb** [I, T] (also **tense up**) If your muscles tense, they become tight and stiff, and if you tense them, you make them do this.

tense³ /tens/ **noun** [C, U] 🔵 the form of a verb that shows the time at which an action happened. For example 'I sing' is in the present tense and 'I will sing' is in the future tense.

tension /'tenʃən/ **noun 1 NO TRUST** ▷ [C, U] ⓑ a feeling of fear or anger between two groups of people who do not trust each other: *ethnic/ racial tension* ◦ *There are growing tensions between the two countries.* **2 BEING NERVOUS** ▷ [U] ⓑ a feeling that you are nervous, worried, and not relaxed: *You could feel the tension in the room as we waited for her to arrive.* **3 TIGHT** ▷ [U] how tight or stiff a muscle, rope, etc, is, or the quality of being tight or stiff

> ☑ **Word partners for tension**
>
> create/defuse/ease tension • tension mounts
> • growing/increased/mounting tension •
> tension between sb and sb • ethnic/racial
> tensions

tent /tent/ **noun** [C] ⓑ a structure made of metal poles and cloth which is fixed to the ground with ropes and used as a cover or to sleep under: *It only took twenty minutes to put the tent up (= make it ready to use).*

tent

tentacle /'tentəkl/ **noun** [C] one of the long, arm-like parts of some sea creatures

tentative /'tentətɪv/ **adj 1** A tentative idea, plan, agreement, etc is not certain: *The two companies have announced a tentative deal.* **2** doing something in a way that shows you are not confident: *a child's tentative first steps* • **tentatively adv**

tenth¹ /tenθ/ 10th written as a word

tenth² /tenθ/ **noun** [C] one of ten equal parts of something; ¹⁄₁₀; 0.1

tenuous /'tenjuəs/ **adj** A tenuous connection, idea, or situation is weak and possibly does not exist: *The court is unlikely to accept such tenuous evidence.* • **tenuously adv**

tenure /'tenjər/ **noun** [U] **1 BUILDING/LAND** ▷ the legal right to live in a building or use a piece of land for a period **2 TIME** ▷ the period of time when someone has an important job: *his tenure as president* **3 PERMANENT** ▷ If you have tenure in your job, your job is permanent.

tepid /'tepɪd/ **adj** A tepid liquid is slightly warm.

term¹ /tɜːm/ **noun 1 WORD** ▷ [C] ⓑ a word or phrase that is used to refer to a particular thing, especially in a technical or scientific subject: *a legal/technical term* **2 TIME** ▷ [C] the fixed period of time when someone does an important job or is in a particular place: *a prison term* ◦ *The government has been elected for another four-year term.* **3 SCHOOL** ▷ [C] ⓐ one of the periods of time that the school or university year is divided into: *We've got a test at the end of term.* **4 in the long/short, etc term** ⓑ a long/ short, etc period of time from now → See also **half-term**

term² /tɜːm/ **verb** [T] formal to use a particular word or phrase to describe something: *Critics termed the movie a 'disaster'.*

terminal¹ /'tɜːmɪnəl/ **noun** [C] **1** ⓑ a building where you can get onto an aircraft, bus, or ship: *a terminal building* **2** a screen and keyboard which you can use a computer

terminal² /'tɜːmɪnəl/ **adj** A terminal illness will cause death: *terminal cancer* • **terminally adv** *terminally ill*

terminate /'tɜːmɪneɪt/ **verb** [I, T] formal If something terminates, it ends, and if you terminate something, you make it end: *His contract has been terminated.* • **termination** /ˌtɜːmɪ'neɪʃən/ **noun** [C, U]

terminology /ˌtɜːmɪ'nɒlədʒi/ **noun** [C, U] the special words and phrases that are used in a particular subject: *medical/scientific terminology*

terminus /'tɜːmɪnəs/ **noun** [C] the place where a train or bus finishes its journey

term paper noun [C] US the main report written by a student for a particular class or subject in the middle of each school term

terms /tɜːmz/ **noun** [plural] **1** ⓑ the rules of an agreement: *Under the terms of their contract employees must give 3 months notice if they want to leave.* **2 be on good/bad/friendly, etc terms** to have a good/bad, etc relationship with someone **3 not be on speaking terms** to not speak to someone because you have argued with them **4 in ... terms** (also **in terms of sth**) ⓑ used to explain which part of a problem or situation you are referring to: *In financial terms the project was not a success.* **5 in no uncertain terms** in a direct and often angry way: *I told him to go away in no uncertain terms.* **6 come to terms with sth** to accept a sad situation: *He still hasn't come to terms with his brother's death.* → See also a **contradiction** in terms

> ☑ **Word partners for terms**
>
> agree terms • break/meet the terms of sth •
> under the terms of sth

terrace /'terɪs/ **noun** [C] **1** ⓑ a flat area outside a house, restaurant, etc where you can sit **2** UK row of houses that are joined together

terraced house noun [C] UK (US **row house**) one of a row of houses that are joined together

the terraces /'terɪsɪz/ **noun** [plural] in the UK wide, concrete steps where people stand to watch a football game

terrain /tə'reɪn/ **noun** [C, U] a particular type of land: *rough terrain*

terrestrial /tə'restriəl/ **adj** formal relating to the Earth, not space

terrible /'terəbl/ **adj** ⓐ very bad, of low quality, or unpleasant: *a terrible accident* ◦ *The weather was terrible.*

terribly /'terəbli/ **adv 1** ⓑ very: *She seemed terribly upset.* **2** ⓑ very badly: *I slept terribly last night.*

terrier /'teriər/ **noun** [C] a type of small dog

terrific /tə'rɪfɪk/ **adj 1** ⓑ excellent: *a terrific opportunity* ◦ *I thought she looked terrific.* **2** [always before noun] very large, great, or serious: *a terrific increase in prices* ◦ *a terrific storm* • **terrifically adv**

terrified /'terəfaɪd/ **adj** ⓑ very frightened: *I'm*

terrified of flying. ○ [+ (that)] *Maggie was terrified that her parents would discover the truth.*

errify /ˈterəfaɪ/ **verb** [T] ⓑ to make someone feel very frightened: *The idea of parachuting out of an aircraft terrifies me.* • **terrifying adj** ⓑ *a terrifying experience*

erritorial /ˌterɪˈtɔːriəl/ **adj** relating to the land that is owned or controlled by a particular country: *a territorial dispute*

erritory /ˈterɪtˀri/ **noun 1 LAND** ▷ [C, U] ⓑ land that is owned or controlled by a particular country: *Spanish territory* **2 PERSON/ANIMAL** ▷ [C, U] ⓑ an area that an animal or person thinks belongs to them: *Cats like to protect their territory.* **3 AREA OF KNOWLEDGE** ▷ [U] an area of knowledge or experience: *With this project we'll be moving into unknown territory.*

error /ˈterər/ **noun** [U] ⓑ a feeling of being very frightened: *There was a look of terror on his face.* → See also **reign¹ of terror**

errorism /ˈterˀrɪzˀm/ **noun** [U] ⓑ the use of violence for political purposes, for example putting bombs in public places: *an act of terrorism*

errorist /ˈterərɪst/ **noun** [C] ⓑ someone who is involved in terrorism: *a terrorist attack*

errorize (also UK **-ise**) /ˈterəraɪz/ **verb** [T] to make someone feel very frightened by saying that you will hurt or kill them: *A gang of young men with knives have been terrorizing local people.*

erse /tɜːs/ **adj** said or written in a few words, often showing that you are annoyed • **tersely adv**

ertiary /ˈtɜːʃˀri/ **adj** UK formal Tertiary education is education at university or college level: *a tertiary institution*

ESOL /ˈtiːsɒl/ **noun** [U] abbreviation for Teaching English to Speakers of Other Languages

est¹ /test/ **noun** [C] **1 EXAM** ▷ ⓐ a set of questions to measure someone's knowledge or ability: *a driving test.* ○ *You have to take a test.* ○ *Only two students in the class failed the test.* ○ *Did you pass the biology test?* **2 MEDICAL** ▷ ⓑ a short medical examination of part of your body: *an eye test* ○ *a pregnancy test* **3 EXPERIMENT** ▷ something that you do to discover if something is safe, works correctly, etc: *a safety test* **4 SITUATION** ▷ ⓑ a situation that shows how good something is: *This will be a real test of his ability.*

☑ Word partners for **test**
do/sit/take a test • **fail/pass** a test • a test **on** sth

est² /test/ **verb** [T] **1 EXPERIMENT** ▷ ⓑ to do something in order to discover if something is safe, works correctly, etc: *None of our products are tested on animals.* **2 MEDICAL** ▷ to do a medical examination of part of someone's body: *I'm going to get my hearing tested.* **3 EXAM** ▷ ⓑ to give someone a set of questions, in order to measure their knowledge or ability: *You'll be tested on all the things we've studied this term.*

4 SITUATION ▷ ⓑ If a situation tests someone, it proves how good, strong, etc they are.

testament /ˈtestəmənt/ **noun a testament to sth** formal proof of something good: *It's a testament to Jane's popularity that so many people are celebrating with her today.* → See also **the New Testament, the Old Testament**

testicle /ˈtestɪkl/ **noun** [C] one of the two round, male sex organs that produce sperm

testify /ˈtestɪfaɪ/ **verb** [I] to say what you know or believe is true in a law court: [+ that] *Elliott testified that he had met the men in a bar.*

testimony /ˈtestɪməni/ **noun 1** [C, U] a formal statement about what someone knows or believes is true, especially in a law court: *the testimony of a witness* **2 testimony to sth** formal proof of something good: *The book's continued popularity is testimony to the power of clever marketing.*

test tube **noun** [C] a glass tube that is closed at one end and is used in scientific experiments

tetanus /ˈtetˀnəs/ **noun** [U] a serious disease that makes your muscles stiff and is caused by an infection that gets into the body through a cut

tether /ˈteðər/ **verb** [T] to tie an animal to something so that it cannot move away • **tether noun** [C] → See also **at the end of your tether**

text¹ /tekst/ **noun 1 WRITING** ▷ [C, U] ⓑ the written words in a book, magazine, etc, not the pictures: *a page of text* **2 BOOK/DOCUMENT** ▷ [C] ⓑ a book or piece of writing that you study as part of a course **3 MESSAGE** ▷ ⓐ [C] a written message sent from one mobile phone to another

text² /tekst/ **verb** [I, T] ⓐ to send a text message (= written message from a mobile phone)

textbook /ˈtekstbʊk/ **noun** [C] ⓐ a book about a particular subject, written for students: *a chemistry/French textbook* → See **The Classroom** on page Centre 6

textile /ˈtekstaɪl/ **noun** [C] any type of cloth that is made by weaving (= crossing threads under and over each other)

text message **noun** [C] ⓐ a written message sent from one mobile phone to another • **text messaging noun** [U]

☑ Word partners for **text message**
get/send a text message • a text message **saying** sth • a text message **from/to** sb

texture /ˈtekstʃər/ **noun** [C, U] the way that something feels when you touch it: *wood with a rough texture*

than strong /ðæn/ weak /ðˀn/ **preposition, conjunction** ⓐ used to compare two different things or amounts: *Susannah's car is bigger than mine.* ○ *Tom's a bit taller than Sam.* ○ *It cost less than I expected.*

thank /θæŋk/ **verb** [T] **1** ⓐ to tell someone that you are grateful for something they have done or given you: *I haven't thanked her for her present yet.* ○ [+ for + doing sth] *Yu Yin thanked the boys for helping her.* **2 thank God/goodness/Heavens, etc** ⓑ something that you say when

T

you are happy because something bad did not happen: *Thank goodness you're okay – I was really worried.*

thankful /'θæŋkfᵊl/ **adj** pleased or grateful about something: [+ (that)] *We were thankful that none of the children saw the accident.*

thankfully /'θæŋkfᵊli/ **adv** used at the beginning of a sentence to show that you are pleased or grateful about something: *Thankfully, nobody was hurt.*

thankless /'θæŋkləs/ **adj** A thankless job is difficult or unpleasant and no one thanks you for doing it: *Nursing can be a **thankless job**.*

thanks¹ /θæŋks/ **exclamation** informal **1** ⓐ used to tell someone that you are grateful because they have given you something or done something for you: *Can you pass me the book? Thanks very much.* ∘ ***Thanks for** all your help.* **2 thanks/ no, thanks** ⓐ used to accept or refuse someone's offer: *"Would you like a cup of coffee?" "No, thanks."*

thanks² /θæŋks/ **noun** [plural] **1** ⓑ words that show you are grateful for something someone has given to you or done for you: *He sent a message of thanks.* **2 thanks to sb/sth** ⓑ because of someone or something: *I passed my driving test, thanks to the extra help my Dad gave me.*

Thanksgiving /ˌθæŋks'gɪvɪŋ/ **noun** [C, U] a holiday in the autumn in the US and Canada, when families have a big meal together

'thank ˌyou exclamation 1 ⓐ used to tell someone that you are grateful because they have given you something or done something for you: ***Thank you** very much **for** the birthday card.* ∘ *"Here's the money I promised you." "Thank you."* **2 thank you/no, thank you** ⓐ used to accept or refuse someone's offer: *"Would you like something to eat?" "No, thank you."*

thank-you /'θæŋkju/ **noun** [C] something that you say or do to thank someone for doing something: [+ for + doing sth] *I bought Emma some chocolates as a thank-you for looking after the dog.* ∘ *a **thank-you present***

that¹ /ðæt/ **determiner** (plural **those**) **1** ⓐ used to refer to something or someone that has already been talked about or seen: *Did you know that woman in the post office?* ∘ *How much are those shoes?* **2** ⓐ used to refer to something or someone that is not near you: *He went through that door.* ∘ *Have you seen that man over there?* → See Note at **this¹**

that² /ðæt/ **pronoun** (plural **those**) **1** ⓐ used to refer to something that has already been talked about or seen: *That looks heavy.* ∘ *You can't possibly wear those!* **2** ⓐ used to refer to something that is not near you: *What's that in the corner?* **3 that's it a** ⓑ used to say that something is correct: *You need to push the two pieces together. That's it.* **b** ⓑ used to say that something has ended: *Well that's it then, we've finished.* **4 that's that** used to say that something has happened or a decision has been made and there is nothing more to say or do: *I won't agree to it and that's that.* **5 that is (to say)** used to correct something you have said or give more information about something: *Everybody*

was at the meeting, well everyone except Jeanne that is.

> ❗ Common learner error: **this/these** or **that/ those**?
>
> Use **this** or **these** to talk about people and things that are close to the speaker.
>   *This is my sister Sarah.*
>   *Do you like these earrings I'm wearing?*
> Use **that** or **those** to talk about people and things that are further away from the speaker.
>   *That girl over there is called Sarah.*
>   *I liked those earrings you wore last night.*

that³ strong /ðæt/ weak /ðət/ **conjunction 1** ⓐ used after some verbs, nouns, and adjectives to introduce a new part of a sentence: *He said tha he'd collect it later.* ∘ *Is it true that she's pregnant* **2** ⓑ used instead of 'who' or 'which' at th beginning of a relative clause: *Have you eaten a the cake that I made yesterday?*

that⁴ /ðæt/ **adv 1** ⓑ used when describing th size, amount, or state of something or someone *I've never seen a fish that big before.* **2 not (all that big/good/warm, etc** ⓑ not very big/good warm, etc: *It hasn't been all that cold this winte*

thatched /θætʃt/ **adj** A thatched building has roof that is made of straw (= dried grass-lik stems): *a **thatched cottage***

thaw /θɔː/ **verb 1** [I, T] (also **thaw out**) ▶ something that is frozen thaws, it become warmer and softer or changes to liquid, and ▶ you have something that is frozen, you make ▶ do this: *Allow the meat to thaw before cooking i* **2** [I] If a relationship between people thaws, ▶ becomes more friendly after being bad. ● **thaᵥ noun** [C]

the strong /ðiː/ weak /ðɪ/, /ðə/ **determine 1 ALREADY KNOWN** ▷ ⓐ used before nouns t refer to particular things or people that hav already been talked about or are already known *Can you pass the salt?* ∘ *I'll pick you up at th station.* ∘ *That's the new restaurant I told yo about.* **2 ONLY ONE** ▷ ⓐ used before noun when only one of something exists: *Have yo seen the Eiffel Tower?* ∘ *I'd love to travel round th world.* **3 SINGULAR NOUN** ▷ used before singular noun to refer to all the things c people described by that noun: *The tiger ha become extinct in many countries.* **4 ADJECTIVE** [used before some adjectives to make them int nouns: *a home for the elderly* ∘ *relatives of th deceased* **5 COMPARE** ▷ ⓑ used before each c two adjectives or adverbs to show how one thin changes depending on another: *The longer w live here, the more we like it.* **6 EACH** ▷ used wit units or measurements to mean each or ever *How many US dollars to the pound?* **7 BODY** ▷ ⓑ used when referring to a part of the body: *H held her tightly by the arm.* **8 TIME** ▷ ⓑ use before numbers that refer to dates or periods c time: *the sixties* ∘ *Thursday the 29th of Apr* **9 MUSIC** ▷ used with the names of musica instruments or dances to mean the type c instrument or dance in general: *Can you play the violin?*

theatre UK (US **theater**) /ˈθɪətər/ **noun 1** BUILD-ING WITH STAGE ▷ [C] **A2** a building with a stage where people go to watch plays: *the Arts Theatre* **2** BUILDING FOR FILMS ▷ [C] US a building where people go to watch films: *a movie theater* **3** WORK ▷ [U] the work of writing, acting in, and producing plays **4** MEDICAL ▷ [C, U] UK a room in a hospital where doctors do operations

> **Word partners for theatre**
>
> go to the theatre • at the theatre • musical theatre • street theatre • a theatre company/director

theatrical /θiˈætrɪkəl/ **adj 1** [always before noun] relating to the theatre: *theatrical make-up* **2** doing and saying things in a very obvious way that is intended to make people notice you

theft /θeft/ **noun** [C, U] **B2** the action or crime of stealing something: *car theft*

their /ðeər/ **determiner 1** **A1** belonging to or relating to a group of people, animals, or things that have already been talked about: *It was their problem, not mine.* **2** **B1** used to refer to what belongs to or relates to a person when you want to avoid saying 'his' or 'her' or when you do not know if the person is male or female: *Did this person give their name?*

theirs /ðeəz/ **pronoun** **A2** the things that belong or relate to a group of people, animals, or things that have already been talked about: *I think she's a relation of theirs.*

them strong /ðem/ weak /ðəm/ **pronoun 1** **A1** used after a verb or preposition to refer to a group of people, animals, or things that have already been talked about: *I'm looking for my keys – have you seen them?* **2** **B1** used after a verb or preposition to refer to a person when you want to avoid saying 'him' or 'her' or when you do not know if the person is male or female: *When each passenger arrives we ask them to fill in a form.*

theme /θiːm/ **noun 1** **B2** [C] the subject of a book, film, speech, etc: *The theme of loss runs through most of his novels.* **2 theme music/song/ tune** the music that is played at the beginning and end of a particular television or radio programme

> **Word partners for theme**
>
> a theme **runs through** sth • the **central/ main** theme • a **recurring** theme • the theme **of** sth • **on** the theme of sth

theme ˌpark **noun** [C] a park with entertainments, such as games, machines to ride on, restaurants, etc, that are all based on one idea

themselves /ðəmˈselvz/ **pronoun 1** **A2** the reflexive form of the pronoun 'they': *They're both 16 – they're old enough to look after themselves.* **2** **B2** used to emphasize the pronoun 'they' or the particular group of people you are referring to: *They've decided to run the club themselves.* **3 (all) by themselves** **A2** alone or without anyone else's help: *The kids*

arranged the party all by themselves. **4 (all) to themselves** for their use only: *They had the whole campsite to themselves.*

then[1] /ðen/ **adv 1** TIME ▷ **A1** at that time: *Call me tomorrow – I'll have time to speak then.* ○ *Tim and I were at school together, but I haven't seen him since then.* **2** NEXT ▷ **A1** next, or after something has happened: *She trained as a teacher and then became a lawyer.* ○ *Let me finish my drink, then we'll go.* **3** SO ▷ **A2** so or because of that: *Have a rest now, then you won't be tired this evening.* ○ *"My interview's at 9 o'clock." "You'll be catching an early train, then?"* **4** IN ADDITION ▷ **B2** used in order to add something to what you have just said: *I've got two essays to write and then my science project to finish.* **5 now then/right then/ okay then** used to introduce a question or a suggestion: *Right then, what do you want to drink?*

then[2] /ðen/ **adj** [always before noun] used to refer to something that was true in the past but that is not true now: *the then Prime Minister Margaret Thatcher*

thence /ðens/ **adv** formal from there: *The oil is shipped to Panama and thence to Texan refineries.*

theology /θiˈɒlədʒi/ **noun** [U] the study of religion and religious belief • **theological** /ˌθiːəˈlɒdʒɪkəl/ **adj** *theological college*

theoretical /ˌθɪəˈretɪkəl/ **adj 1** based on the ideas that relate to a subject, not the practical uses of that subject: *theoretical physics* **2** related to an explanation that has not been proved

theoretically /ˌθɪəˈretɪkəli/ **adv** in a way that obeys some rules but is not likely: *It is theoretically possible.*

theorist /ˈθɪərɪst/ **noun** [C] someone who develops ideas about the explanation for events: *a political theorist*

theorize (also UK **-ise**) /ˈθɪəraɪz/ **verb** [I, T] to develop a set of ideas about something: [+ that] *Investigators theorized that the crash was caused by engine failure.*

theory /ˈθɪəri/ **noun 1** [C] **B2** an idea or set of ideas that is intended to explain something: *Darwin's theory of evolution* **2** [U] the set of principles on which a subject is based: *economic theory* **3 in theory** **B2** If something is possible in theory, it should be possible but often it does not happen this way.

> **Word partners for theory**
>
> challenge/formulate/prove/test a theory • a popular/plausible/new theory • a theory about sth

therapeutic /ˌθerəˈpjuːtɪk/ **adj 1** helping to cure a disease or improve your health: *the therapeutic benefits of massage* **2** helping you to feel happier and more relaxed: *I find gardening very therapeutic.*

therapist /ˈθerəpɪst/ **noun** [C] someone whose job is to treat a particular type of mental or physical illness: *a speech therapist*

therapy /ˈθerəpi/ **noun** [C, U] **B2** the work of treating mental or physical illness without using an operation: *cancer therapy* ○ *She's now in*

therapy to help her deal with her alcohol problem.
→ See also **physical therapy**

there¹ strong /ðeə^r/ weak /ðə^r/ **pronoun there is/ are/was, etc** Ⓐ❶ used to show that something exists or happens: *There are three girls in my family.* ◦ *There's not much room in the back of the car.* ◦ *There have been a lot of accidents on this road.* ◦ *Is there any milk?*

there² /ðeə^r/ **adv 1 PLACE** ▷ Ⓐ❶ in or at a particular place: *We live in York because my wife works there.* ◦ *I went to the party but I didn't know anyone there.* ◦ *We'll never get there* (= *arrive*) *in time!* **2 DIRECTION** ▷ Ⓐ❶ used when you are pointing or looking at something in order to make someone look in the same direction: *Put them in that box there.* ◦ *Your bag's over there by the door.* **3 AVAILABLE** ▷ present or available: *They were all there – Mark, Jill, and the three kids.* ◦ *That money is there for you if you need it.* **4 POINT** ▷ Ⓑ❷ at a particular point in a process or activity: *Do you want to play another game or do you want to stop there?* ◦ *Keep on trying – you'll get there* (= *succeed*) *in the end.* **5 there and then** If you do something there and then, you do it immediately: *I showed James the ring I liked and he bought it there and then.* **6 There you are/go. a** Ⓐ❷ used when you are giving something to someone: *Do you want a tissue? There you are.* **b** used to emphasize that you were right: *There you go – I told you you'd win!*

thereabouts /ˈðeərəbaʊts/ **adv** mainly UK near the number, amount, or time that has just been given: *For this recipe you'll need 1kg of tomatoes, or thereabouts.*

thereafter /ˌðeəˈrɑːftə^r/ **adv** formal after a particular amount, time, or event: *Faxes cost $1.20 for the first page, and 60 cents for each page thereafter.*

thereby /ˌðeəˈbaɪ/ **adv** formal as a result of a particular action or event: *The new dam will improve the water supply and thereby reduce hunger and disease.*

therefore /ˈðeəfɔː^r/ **adv** Ⓑ❶ for that reason: *The region has suffered severe flooding and tourists are therefore advised not to travel there.*

therein /ˌðeəˈrɪn/ **adv** formal **1** in a particular document or place: *We recommend that you study the report and the proposals contained therein.* **2 therein lies sth** because of the reason that has just been given: *But the medicines are expensive, and therein lies the problem.*

thereof /ˌðeəˈrɒv/ **adv** formal relating to what has just been said: *It's gospel music, traditional country, jazz, and some strange combinations thereof.*

thermal /ˈθɜːm^əl/ **adj** [always before noun] **1** relating to heat: *thermal energy* **2** Thermal clothes are made to keep you warm: *thermal underwear*

thermo- /ˈθɜːməʊ-/ **prefix** relating to heat or temperature: *a thermostat* (= *a piece of equipment that controls temperature*) ◦ *a thermometer*

thermometer /θəˈmɒmɪtə^r/ **noun** [C] Ⓑ❷ a piece of equipment that measures the temperature of the air or of your body

Thermos /ˈθɜːmɒs/ **noun** [C] trademark a container that keeps hot liquids hot or cold liquids cold: UK *a Thermos flask*/US *a Thermos bottle* → See picture at **flask**

thermometer

thermostat /ˈθɜːməstæt/ **noun** [C] a piece of equipment that controls the temperature of something or of a place

thesaurus /θɪˈsɔːrəs/ **noun** [C] a book in which words with similar meanings are put together in groups

these /ðiːz/ **pronoun, determiner** Ⓐ❶ plural of this → See Note at **that²**, **this**

thesis /ˈθiːsɪs/ **noun** [C] (plural **theses** /ˈθiːsiːz/) **1** Ⓑ❷ a long piece of writing that you do as pa of an advanced university course: *a master's/Ph thesis* **2** formal a theory that is suggested and ca then be argued with or agreed with: *That is th central thesis of the book.*

they /ðeɪ/ **pronoun 1 GROUP** ▷ Ⓐ❶ used as th subject of the verb when referring to a group o people, animals, or things that have alread been talked about: *I saw Kate and Nigel yesterda – they came over for dinner.* ◦ *"Have you seen m car keys?" "They're on the kitchen table* **2 PERSON** ▷ Ⓑ❶ used to refer to a person whe you want to avoid saying 'he' or 'she' or whe you do not know if the person is male or femal *Someone I met at a party said they knew yo* **3 PEOPLE** ▷ Ⓑ❷ people in general: *They say th breaking a mirror brings you seven years' bad luc*

they'd /ðeɪd/ **1** short for they had: *They'd ju moved in when I saw them.* **2** short for they woul *They'd be to take us out to dinner.*

they'll /ðeɪl/ short for they will: *They'll be i Scotland next week.*

they're /ðeə^r/ short for they are: *They're both fro Washington.*

they've /ðeɪv/ short for they have: *They've g three children – two girls and a boy.*

thick¹ /θɪk/ **adj**

thick

1 DISTANCE ▷ Ⓑ❶ Something that is thick is larger than usual between its opposite sides: *a thick slice of meat* ◦ *a thick layer of snow* **2 10cm/2m, etc** thick Ⓑ❶ being 10cm/ 2m, etc thick: *a piece of wood 2cm thick* **3 LARGE AMOUNT** ▷ Ⓑ❶ growing very close together and in larg amounts: *thick, dark hair* **4 SMOKE** ▷ Ⓑ❷ Thic smoke, cloud, or fog is difficult to see throug *Thick, black smoke was pouring out of th chimney.* **5 LIQUID** ▷ A thick substance liquid has very little water in it and does ne

thick   thin

α: arm | ɜː her | iː see | ɔː saw | uː too | aɪ my | aʊ how | eə hair | eɪ day | əʊ no | ɪə near | ɔɪ boy | ʊə pure | aɪə fire | aʊə sou flow easily: *Stir the sauce over a low heat until thick.* **6 STUPID** ▷ UK informal not intelligent **7 be thick with sth** If something is thick with a particular substance, it is covered in or full of that substance: *The air was thick with petrol fumes.*

IDIOM **thick and fast** quickly and in large numbers: *Calls were coming in thick and fast by the end of the programme.*

→ See also **have (a) thick skin¹**

thick² /θɪk/ **noun be in the thick of sth** to be involved in a situation at the point where there is most activity: *He loves being in the thick of the action.*

IDIOM **through thick and thin** If you support or stay with someone through thick and thin, you always support or stay with them in easy and difficult situations: *We've been together through thick and thin.*

thicken /'θɪkən/ **verb** [I, T] to become thicker, or to make something thicker: *Boil the sauce until it thickens.*

thickly /'θɪkli/ **adv** in thick pieces, or in a thick layer: *toast* **thickly spread** *with butter*

thickness /'θɪknəs/ **noun** [C, U] the distance between the opposite sides of something

thick-skinned /ˌθɪk'skɪnd/ **adj** If someone is thick-skinned, they do not get upset when other people criticize them.

thief /θiːf/ **noun** [C] (plural **thieves** /θiːvz/) someone who steals things: *a car thief* ◦ *Thieves stole $500,000 worth of computer equipment.*

thigh /θaɪ/ **noun** [C] the top part of your leg above your knee → See colour picture **The Body** on page Centre 13

thimble /'θɪmbl/ **noun** [C] a small metal or plastic object that you use to protect your finger when you are sewing

thin¹ /θɪn/ **adj** (**thinner, thinnest**) **1 DISTANCE** ▷ Something that is thin is smaller than usual between its opposite sides: *a thin slice of ham* ◦ *The walls are very thin.* → See picture at **thick** **2 PERSON** ▷ A thin person or animal has very little fat on their body. **3 LIQUID** ▷ A thin substance or liquid has a lot of water in it and flows easily: *thin soup* **4 AMOUNT** ▷ having only a small number of people or a small amount of something: *His hair is going thin on top.* **5 AIR** ▷ Thin air does not have enough oxygen in it.

IDIOM **wear thin a** If your patience wears thin, you become less and less patient with someone who is annoying you. **b** If a joke or explanation wears thin, it becomes less effective because it has been used too much.

→ See also **disappear/vanish into thin air¹, be thin on the ground¹, through thick² and thin**

thin² /θɪn/ **verb** [T] (**thinning, thinned**) to make a substance less thick, often by adding a liquid to it

PHRASAL VERB **thin out** If a large number of people or things thin out, they become fewer in number.

thing /θɪŋ/ **noun 1 OBJECT** ▷ [C] used to refer to an object without saying its name: *How do I switch this thing off?* ◦ *I need to get a few things in town.* **2 PERSON** ▷ [C] used to refer to a person or animal when you are expressing your feelings towards them: *You look tired, you poor thing.* **3 IDEA** ▷ [C] used to refer to an idea, event, or activity: *I can't believe Nick would say such a thing!* ◦ *Meeting Nina was the best thing that's ever happened to me.* **4 for one thing** used to give a reason for something: *You can't give Amy that shirt – for one thing it's too small for her.* **5 the thing is** informal used to introduce a problem that relates to something that you have just said: *I'd love to go out tonight, but the thing is, I've got to finish my report.* **6 a thing** used instead of 'anything' in order to emphasize what you are saying: *I haven't got a thing to wear!* **7 have a thing about sth/sb** informal to like or dislike something or someone very much: *He's got a thing about blonde women.* **8 it's a good thing** informal If it is a good thing that something happened, it is lucky that it happened: [+ (that)] *It's a good thing that Jo was there to help you.* **9 first/last thing** informal at the beginning/end of the day: *I'll phone him first thing and tell him I can't come.* ◦ *She likes a glass of milk last thing at night.* **10 be sb's thing** informal If an activity or subject is someone's thing, they are very interested in it and like doing it: *Jogging's just not my thing – I prefer team sports.*

IDIOM **the best/greatest thing since sliced bread** humorous extremely good: *When I first got this computer I thought it was the best thing since sliced bread.*

things /θɪŋz/ **noun** [plural] **1** what is happening in your life: *Don't worry – things will get better soon.* **2** the objects that you own: *I'll just gather my things and then I'll be ready.* **3 be hearing/seeing things** to imagine that you can hear or see things that do not exist

thingy /'θɪŋi/ **noun** [C] UK informal used to refer to something or someone when you cannot remember their name: *We ate that beef thingy for lunch.*

think¹ /θɪŋk/ **verb** (**thought**) **1 OPINION** ▷ [I, T] to have an opinion about something or someone: *Do you think it's going to rain?* ◦ [+ (that)] *I don't think that Emma will get the job* (= I believe she will not get it). ◦ *What did you think of the film?* ◦ *What do you think about modern art?* **2 CONSIDER** ▷ [I] to consider an idea or a problem: *He thought for a few seconds before answering.* ◦ *You should think about where you want to live.* **3 EXPECT** ▷ [I, T] to believe that something is true, or to expect that something will happen, although you are not sure: *I think she's called Joanna.* ◦ *"Does this train stop at Oxford?" "Yes, I think so."* ◦ [+ (that)] *I never thought that I would see Steven again.* **4 think about/of doing sth** to consider doing something: *I'm thinking of moving to Sydney.* ◦ *We thought about getting married, but decided not to.* **5 think about/of sb/sth** to use your mind to imagine a situation: *I'm sorry I can't be at the wedding, but I'll be thinking of you.* **6 think of**

sth **G1** to use your imagination and intelligence to produce an idea, a solution to a problem, or an answer to a question: *When did you first think of the idea?* **7 think a lot of sb/sth** **A1** to admire someone, or to believe that something is good quality: *Simon thinks a lot of you, you know.* **8 not think much of sb/sth** **G1** to not like someone, or to believe that something is not good quality: *I don't think much of the food here.* **9 I think** used to introduce a suggestion or explanation in order to be polite: [+ (that)] *It's getting late – I think that we should go.* **10 Who would have thought...?** used to express how surprising something is: [+ (that)] *Who would have thought that buying a house could take so long!* → See also **think the world¹ of sb**

> **!** Common learner error: **think about** or **think of**?
>
> **Think about** someone/something means to have thoughts in your mind about a person or thing, or to consider them.
>
> *I was thinking about my mother.*
> *I thought about the question before answering.*
> ~~I thought the question before answering.~~
>
> **Think of/about** something/someone also means to have an opinion about something or someone.
>
> *What do you think of/about the colour?*
> ~~What do you think the colour?~~
>
> **Think of doing something** means to consider the possibility of doing something.
>
> *We are thinking of having a party.*
> ~~We are thinking to have a party.~~

IDIOM **think outside the box** to use new ideas instead of traditional ideas when you think about something

PHRASAL VERBS **think back** to remember something that happened in the past: *I thought back to the time when I was living in Toronto.* • **think sth out** to consider all the possible details of something: *The scheme was well thought out.* • **think sth over** **B2** to consider an idea or plan carefully before making a decision • **think sth through** **B2** to carefully consider the possible results of doing something • **think sth up** to produce a new idea or plan: *I don't want to go tonight and I'm trying to think up an excuse.*

think² /θɪŋk/ **noun** UK **have a think** to consider something carefully: *Have a think about it and then tell me what you've decided.*

thinker /'θɪŋkər/ **noun** [C] someone who considers important subjects or produces new ideas: *a political/religious thinker*

> **✓** Word partners for **thinking**
>
> the thinking **behind/on** sth • the **current** thinking

thinking /'θɪŋkɪŋ/ **noun** [U] **1** the use of your mind to consider something: *This problem requires careful thinking.* **2** someone's ideas or opinions: *The book discusses the impact of*

Christian thinking on western society. → See als **wishful thinking**

'think ,tank noun [C] a group of people wh advise the government or an organization abou particular subjects and who suggest new ideas

thinly /'θɪnli/ **adv 1** in thin pieces, or in a thi layer: *She sliced the bread thinly.* **2** with only small number of people or things: *thinl populated areas*

third¹ /θɜːd/ **A2** 3rd written as a word

third² /θɜːd/ **noun** [C] **1** **B2** one of three equa parts of something; ⅓ **2 a third** in the UK, on of the lowest exam results you can achieve at th end of a university course

third-generation /ˌθɜːdʒenəˈreɪʃᵊn/ **adj** [alway before noun] (also **3G** /ˌθriːˈdʒiː/) relating t technology that gives mobile phone and con puter users a fast internet connection as well a good video and other advanced features: *a 3 network* ∘ *third-generation wireless technology*

thirdly /'θɜːdli/ **adv** used in order to introduc the third thing in a list

,third 'party noun [C] someone who is not on of the two main people or groups that ar involved in a situation

the ,third 'person noun **B2** the form of a ver or pronoun that is used when referring to th person or thing being spoken about o described. For example 'she' and 'they' ar third person pronouns.

the ,Third 'World noun the countries i Africa, Asia, and South America, which do no have well-developed economies

thirst /θɜːst/ **noun 1** **B2** [U, no plural] the feelin that you want to drink something: *I had a lon cold drink to* **quench** *my* **thirst** (= stop me feelin thirsty). **2 a thirst for sth** a strong wish fo something: *a thirst for adventure*

thirsty /'θɜːsti/ **adj** **A2** wanting or needing drink: *I felt really hot and thirsty after my rur* • **thirstily adv**

thirteen /ˌθɜːˈtiːn/ **A1** the number 13 • **thi teenth** 13th written as a word

thirty /'θɜːti/ **1** **A2** the number 30 **2 the thirtie** the years from 1930 to 1939 **3 be in you thirties** to be between the ages of 30 and 3 • **thirtieth** 30th written as a word

this¹ /ðɪs/ **determiner** (plural **these**) **1** ALREAD TALKED ABOUT ▷ **A1** used to refer to somethin that you have already talked about: *Most peopl don't agree with this decision.* ∘ *How did you hea about this course?* **2** NEAR ▷ **A1** used to refer t something or someone that is near you or tha you are pointing to: *How much does this CD cos* ∘ *David gave me these earrings for my birthda* **3** TIME ▷ **A1** used to refer to the present wee month, year, etc or the one that comes next: *I' see you this evening.* ∘ *Kate and Nigel are gettin married this June.* **4** NOW TALKING ABOUT [informal used to refer to a particular person o thing that you are going to talk about: *We wer to this really great club last night.* → See Note a **that²** → See also **be out of this world¹**

this² /ðɪs/ **pronoun** (plural **these**) **1** ALREAD TALKED ABOUT ▷ **A2** used to refer to somethin that you have already talked about: *When did this happen?* ∘ *This is the best news I've heard all week!* **2 NEAR** ▷ Ⓐ❷ used to refer to something or someone that is near you or that you are pointing to: *Try some of this – it's delicious.* ∘ *Are these your keys?* ∘ *This is my girlfriend, Beth.* **3 SAY/ASK WHO** ▷ used to say or ask who someone is when speaking on the telephone, radio, etc: *"Hello, is this Julie Hawkins?" "Yes, who's this?"*

IDIOM **this and that** different things that are not very important: *"What are you doing today?" "Oh, just this and that."*

❗ Common learner error: **this/that** or **these/those**?

Remember **this** and **that** are used before a singular noun. **These** and **those** are used before a plural noun.
Look at this photo.
Look at these photos.
Can you pass me that book please?
Can you pass me those books please?

---

his³ /ðɪs/ **adv** used when describing the size, amount, or state of something or someone: *I need a piece of wood this big.* ∘ *I've never seen her this angry.*

histle /ˈθɪsl̩/ **noun** [C] a wild plant with purple flowers and sharp points

THNX informal written abbeviation for thank you: used in emails and text messages

hong /θɒŋ/ **noun** [C] **1** a piece of underwear or the bottom part of a bikini (= a piece of clothing with two parts that women wear for swimming) which does not cover the bottom **2** US a flip-flop

horn /θɔːn/ **noun** [C] a small, sharp point on the stem of a plant

horny /ˈθɔːni/ **adj 1** covered in thorns **2** A thorny problem, question, subject, etc is difficult to deal with.

horough /ˈθʌrə/ Ⓤ /ˈθɜːrəʊ/ **adj** ❷ careful and covering every detail: *The government has promised a thorough investigation of the matter.* • **thoroughness noun** [U]

horoughbred /ˈθʌrəbred/ **noun** [C] a horse especially bred for racing

horoughly /ˈθʌrəli/ **adv 1** ❷ very carefully: *Wash the spinach thoroughly before cooking.* **2** ❷ very, or very much: *We thoroughly enjoyed ourselves.*

hose /ðəʊz/ **pronoun, determiner** Ⓐ❶ plural of that → See Note at **that²**, **this²**

hough¹ /ðəʊ/ **conjunction 1** ❶ used to introduce a fact or opinion that makes the other part of the sentence seem surprising: *And though she's quite small, she's very strong.* ∘ *Nina didn't phone, **even though** she said she would.* **2** ❷ but: *They're coming next week, though I don't know when.* ∘ *The restaurant serves good, though extremely expensive, food.*

hough² /ðəʊ/ **adv** ❷ used to add a new fact or opinion that changes what you have just said: *Okay, I'll come to the party – I'm not staying late though.*

thought¹ /θɔːt/ **noun 1 IDEA** ▷ [C] ❺❶ an idea or opinion: *Do you have any **thoughts about/on** where you want to spend Christmas?* ∘ [+ of + doing sth] *The thought of seeing her again filled him with happiness.* ∘ informal *"Why don't we invite Ben?" "**That's a thought** (= That's a good idea)."* **2 THINKING** ▷ [U] ❷ the activity of thinking, or when you think about something carefully: *She sat staring at the picture, **deep in thought**.* ∘ *You'll need to **give** the matter **some thought**.* **3 CARE** ▷ [no plural] something you do that shows you care about someone: *Thanks for the card – it was a really kind thought.* **4 SET OF IDEAS** ▷ [U] a set of ideas about a particular subject: *The book examines his influence on recent political thought.*

IDIOM **spare a thought for sb** to think about someone who is in a bad situation: *Spare a thought for all the people who have lost their homes.*

→ See also **school** of thought, **second thought**

🔲 Word partners for **thought**

give sth some thought • have a thought • a secret/sobering/terrible thought

---

thought² /θɔːt/ past of think

thoughtful /ˈθɔːtfʰl/ **adj 1** quiet because you are thinking about something: *You look thoughtful.* **2** ❷ kind and always thinking about how you can help other people: *Thank you for the card – it was very **thoughtful of** you.* • **thoughtfully adv** *She gazed thoughtfully into the distance.* • **thoughtfulness noun** [U]

thoughtless /ˈθɔːtləs/ **adj** not considering how your actions and words might upset someone else: *I should have called her to say we'd be late – it was a bit thoughtless of me.* • **thoughtlessly adv**

thought-provoking /ˈθɔːtprəˌvəʊkɪŋ/ **adj** making you think a lot about a subject: *a thought-provoking book/film*

thousand /ˈθaʊzᵊnd/ **1** Ⓐ❷ the number 1000 **2 thousands** informal ❷ a lot: *She tried on **thousands of** dresses but didn't like any of them.*

thousandth¹ /ˈθaʊzᵊndθ/ 1000th written as a word

thousandth² /ˈθaʊzᵊndθ/ **noun** [C] one of a thousand equal parts of something; ⅟₁₀₀₀; .001: *a thousandth of a second*

thrash /θræʃ/ **verb 1 HIT** ▷ [T] to hit a person or animal several times as a punishment **2 MOVE** ▷ [I] to move from side to side in a violent way: *He was screaming in pain and **thrashing around** on the floor.* **3 DEFEAT** ▷ [T] informal to win against someone very easily

PHRASAL VERB **thrash sth out** to discuss a plan or problem in detail until you reach an agreement or find a solution

thrashing /ˈθræʃɪŋ/ **noun** [C] **1** informal a very easy win against someone **2** old-fashioned the act of hitting a person or animal several times as a punishment

thread¹ /θred/ **noun 1 MATERIAL** ▷ [C, U] a long, thin piece of cotton, wool, etc that is used

T

for sewing: *a needle and thread* **2 CONNECTION** ▷ [C] the connection between different events or different parts of a story or discussion: *By that point I'd lost the thread of the conversation.* **3 INTERNET** ▷ [C] a group of pieces of writing on the Internet in which people discuss one subject

thread² /θred/ *verb* [T] **1 thread a needle** to push thread through the hole in a needle **2 thread your way through/between, etc** to move carefully through a crowded place, changing direction in order to avoid people or things

threadbare /'θredbeər/ *adj* Threadbare material or clothes are very thin because they have been used too much: *a threadbare carpet*

threat /θret/ *noun* **1 HARM** ▷ [C] ⬤ If someone makes a threat, they say they will kill or hurt you, or cause problems for you if you do not do what they want: *a death threat* ∘ *I was scared he would carry out his threat* (= do what he said he would do). **2 DAMAGE** ▷ [C] ⬤ someone or something that is likely to cause harm or damage: [usually singular] *a threat to the environment* ∘ *Smoking poses* (= is) *a serious threat to your health.* **3 POSSIBILITY** ▷ [no plural] the possibility that something bad will happen: *the threat of invasion*

> ☑ Word partners for **threat**
>
> a threat to sb/sth • **pose** a threat • a **potential** threat • a **growing/serious** threat • a **security/terrorist** threat

threaten /'θretən/ *verb* **1 HARM** ▷ [T] ⬤ to tell someone that you will kill or hurt them, or cause problems for them if they do not do what you want: *He threatened the staff with a gun and demanded money.* ∘ [+ to do sth] *He threatened to report her to the police.* **2 DAMAGE** ▷ [T] to be likely to cause harm or damage to something or someone: *His knee problem is threatening his cycling career.* **3 HAPPEN** ▷ [I] If something bad threatens to happen, it is likely to happen: [+ to do sth] *The conflict threatened to spread to neighbouring countries.* • **threatening** *adj* **threatening behaviour** • **threateningly** *adv*

three /θriː/ ⬤ the number 3

three-dimensional /ˌθriːdɪˈmenʃənəl/ *adj* (also **3-D** /ˌθriːˈdiː/) having length, depth, and height: *three-dimensional computer graphics*

threshold /'θreʃhəʊld/ *noun* **1** [C] the level at which something starts to happen: *He had a low boredom threshold.* **2 on the threshold of sth** at the start of a new and important time or development: *We're on the threshold of a new era in European relations.* **3** [C] the floor of an entrance

threw /θruː/ past tense of throw

thrift /θrɪft/ *noun* [U] careful use of money so that you do not spend too much • **thrifty** *adj*

'thrift ˌshop *noun* [C] US (UK **charity shop**) a shop that sells goods given by the public, especially clothes, to make money for a particular charity

thrill¹ /θrɪl/ *noun* [C] a strong feeling of excitement and pleasure: *It was a big thrill*

meeting the stars of the show. ∘ [+ of + doing sth] *the thrill of winning a competition*

> ☑ Word partners for **thrill**
>
> **feel** a thrill • **get** a thrill **from/out** of doing sth • a **big/great** thrill • the thrill **of** (doing) sth • a thrill **seeker**

thrill² /θrɪl/ *verb* [T] to make someone feel excited and happy: *Woods thrilled the golf world with his performances.*

thrilled /θrɪld/ *adj* very excited and pleased: *Sh was thrilled with your present.*

thriller /'θrɪlər/ *noun* [C] ⬤ a book or film with an exciting story, often about crime

thrilling /'θrɪlɪŋ/ *adj* very exciting: *a thrilling game*

thrive /θraɪv/ *verb* [I] to grow very well, or t become very healthy or successful: *The busines is thriving.* ∘ *He seems to thrive on hard work* • **thriving** *adj a thriving economy*

throat /θrəʊt/ *noun* [C] **1** ⬤ the back part c your mouth and the passages inside your neck *a sore throat* **2** ⬤ the front of your neck: *H grabbed her round the throat.* → See colour pictur **The Body** on page Centre 13 **3 clear your throa** to cough once so that you can speak mor clearly

throb /θrɒb/ *verb* [I] (**throbbing, throbbed**) **1** I a part of your body throbs, you feel pain in it i a series of regular beats: *My head was throbbing* **2** to make a strong, regular sound or movemen *The whole house throbbed with the music* • **throb** *noun* [C] *the throb of the engine*

throes /θrəʊz/ *noun* **in the throes of sth** in difficult or unpleasant situation: *a country in th throes of war*

throne /θrəʊn/ *noun* **1** [C] the special chair tha a king or queen sits on **2 the throne** th position of being king or queen: *He came to th throne in 1936.*

throng¹ /θrɒŋ/ *noun* [C] literary a large group c people

throng² /θrɒŋ/ *verb* [I, T] to be or go somewher in very large numbers: *drunken people throngin the streets* ∘ *The street was thronged wit shoppers and tourists.*

throttle¹ /'θrɒtl/ *verb* [T] to press someone' throat tightly so they cannot breathe

throttle² /'θrɒtl/ *noun* [C] the part of a vehicl that controls how much fuel or power goes t the engine

through¹ /θruː/ *preposition* **1 ONE SIDE T ANOTHER** ▷ ⬤ from one end or side c something to the other: *The River Seine flow through Paris.* ∘ *The sun was shining through th window.* ∘ *She cut through the wire.* **2 START T END** ▷ ⬤ from the start to the end c something: *He worked through the night.* ∘ *Th phone rang halfway through the programme* **3 BECAUSE OF** ▷ ⬤ because of someone c something, or with someone's help: *I got the jo through my mum's friend.* ∘ *He became ill throug eating undercooked meat.* **4 UNTIL** ▷ US (UK/US to from a particular time until and includin

---

another time: *The store is open Monday through Friday.*

through² /θruː/ adv **1** 🅱️ from one end or side to another: *He opened the door and walked through.* **2 read/think/talk, etc sth through** to read/think/talk to someone, etc very carefully about something from the start to the end: *I've thought it through and decided not to take the job.* **3** connected to someone by telephone: *I tried to phone David but I couldn't get through.* ∘ *Can you put me through to the manager, please?*

through³ /θruː/ adj **1 be through with sth** informal to have finished using something or doing something: *Let me know when you're through with the iron.* **2 be through (with sb)** informal to not have a relationship with someone any more **3** [always before noun] A through train goes all the way from one place to another place without the passenger having to change trains.

throughout /θruːˈaʊt/ adv, preposition **1** in every part of a place: *The same laws apply throughout much of Europe.* ∘ *The house was painted pink throughout.* **2** 🅱️2️⃣ during the whole of a period of time: *He yawned throughout the performance.*

throw¹ /θrəʊ/ verb [T] (**threw**, **thrown**) **1 THROUGH THE AIR** ▷ 🅰️2️⃣ to make something move through the air by pushing it out of your hand: *Amy threw the ball to the dog.* ∘ *He threw the book at the wall.* ∘ [+ two objects] *Throw me a chocolate.* ∘ *How far can you throw?* **2 throw sth in/on, etc** to put something somewhere quickly and without thinking about it: *He threw his clothes on the floor and got into bed.* **3 throw sth around/down/on, etc** to suddenly and quickly move your body or a part of your body: *She threw her arms around the child.* ∘ *Gabriela threw herself onto the bed and started to cry.* **4 throw sb from/forward, etc** to make someone move somewhere suddenly or fall down: [often passive] *The bus suddenly stopped and we were thrown forward.* **5 CONFUSE** ▷ to make someone feel shocked or confused: *It threw me completely when he asked me to marry him.* **6 LIGHT** ▷ to make light or shadows (= dark shapes) appear on something: *The trees threw shadows across the road.* → See also **throw caution¹ to the wind**, **throw sb in at the deep end¹**, **throw down the gauntlet**, **throw in the towel**, **throw your weight around**

PHRASAL VERBS **throw sth away 1** 🅱️1️⃣ to get rid of something that you do not want any more: *He read the magazine and then threw it away.* → See colour picture **Phrasal Verbs** on page Centre 16 **2** to waste a skill or opportunity: *You've spent three years studying – don't throw it all away.* • **throw sth in** to add something extra when you sell something and not increase the price: *They're selling computers with a free printer thrown in.* • **throw sth out** 🅱️1️⃣ to get rid of something that you do not want any more: *I must throw some of my old clothes out.* • **throw sb out** 🅱️2️⃣ to force someone to leave: *He was thrown out of school for taking drugs.* • **throw (sth) up** informal 🅱️2️⃣ to vomit • **throw sth up** to produce new problems or ideas: *The meeting threw up some interesting ideas.*

throw² /θrəʊ/ noun [C] the act of throwing something: *a throw of the dice*

throwback /ˈθrəʊbæk/ noun [C] something that is like something of the same type in the past: *Her style of playing is **a throwback to** the early days of jazz.*

thru /θruː/ adj, adv, preposition mainly US informal another spelling of through, used in signs and advertisements

thrust¹ /θrʌst/ verb (**thrust**) **thrust sth behind/into/through, etc** to push something somewhere suddenly and with force: *She thrust a letter into my hand and told me to read it.*

PHRASAL VERB **thrust sth on/upon sb** to force someone to accept or deal with something: [often passive] *Fatherhood had been thrust on him.*

thrust² /θrʌst/ noun **1** [C, U] a strong push or the power used to push something forward **2 the thrust of sth** the main part or ideas of what someone says or does: *The main thrust of our work involves helping victims of crime.*

thruway /ˈθruːˌweɪ/ noun [C] (also **throughway**) US a wide road for fast-moving traffic, with a limited number of places where drivers can enter and leave it

thud /θʌd/ noun [C] the sound that is made when something heavy falls or hits something else: *There was a thud as he fell on the floor.* • **thud** verb [I] (**thudding, thudded**)

thug /θʌg/ noun [C] an unpleasant person who behaves violently

thumb¹ /θʌm/ noun [C] 🅱️1️⃣ the short, thick finger on the side of your hand that can touch the top of all your other fingers → See colour picture **The Body** on page Centre 13

IDIOMS **have a green thumb** US (UK **have green fingers**) to be good at gardening and making plants grow well • **be under sb's thumb** If you are under someone's thumb, they control you completely. • **stick/stand out like a sore thumb** to be very different from all the other people or things around: *I was the only one in uniform and I stuck out like a sore thumb.*

→ See also a **rule¹ of thumb**

thumb² /θʌm/ verb → See **thumb your nose¹ at sth/sb**

PHRASAL VERB **thumb through sth** to quickly turn the pages of a book or magazine

thumbtack /ˈθʌmtæk/ noun [C] US (UK **drawing pin**) a pin with a wide, flat top, used for fastening pieces of paper to a wall

thump /θʌmp/ verb **1 HIT** ▷ [T] UK to hit someone with your fist (= closed hand) **2 NOISE** ▷ [I, T] to hit something and make a noise: *She thumped the tambourine.* **3 HEART** ▷ [I] If your heart thumps, it beats very quickly because you are excited or frightened. • **thump** noun [C]

thunder¹ /ˈθʌndər/ noun [U] 🅱️1️⃣ the loud noise in the sky that you hear during a storm: *thunder and lightning*

thunder² /'θʌndər/ verb **1 it thunders** When it thunders during a storm, a loud noise comes from the sky. **2 thunder along/down/through, etc** to move in a way that makes a deep, loud, continuous sound: *Traffic thunders through the village all day.*

thunderous /'θʌndərəs/ adj extremely loud: *the **thunderous roar** of the aircraft's engine*

thunderstorm /'θʌndəstɔːm/ noun [C] ⓐ a storm that has thunder (= loud noise) and lightning (= sudden flashes of light in the sky)

Thursday /'θɜːzdeɪ/ noun [C, U] (written abbreviation **Thur, Thurs**) ⓐ the day of the week after Wednesday and before Friday

thus /ðʌs/ adv formal **1** ⓑ used after saying a fact to introduce what then happened as a result: *The guard fell asleep, thus allowing Bates to escape.* **2** in this way: *They limit the number of people allowed into the forest, thus preventing damage to the trails.*

thwart /θwɔːt/ verb [T] to prevent someone from doing what they had planned to do

thyme /taɪm/ noun [U] a herb used in cooking

thyroid /'θaɪrɔɪd/ noun [C] an organ in the neck that produces a substance that helps your body to grow and develop

TIA internet abbreviation for thanks in advance: used in an email when you have asked someone for something

tick¹ /tɪk/ noun [C] **1 CLOCK** ▷ the sound that some clocks or watches make every second **2 MARK** ▷ UK (US **check**) ⓑ a mark (✓) that shows something is correct or has been done **3 INSECT** ▷ a small insect that sucks the blood of animals **4 TIME** ▷ UK informal a short time: *Wait a tick!*

tick² /tɪk/ verb **1** [I] If a clock or watch ticks, it makes a sound every second. **2** [T] UK ⓑ to mark something with a tick

IDIOM **what makes sb tick** informal the reasons for someone's behaviour

PHRASAL VERBS **tick away/by** If seconds or minutes tick away or by, they pass: *With the final seconds ticking away, Milan scored a goal.* • **tick sth off** UK (US **check sth off**) to put a small mark next to something on a list to show that you have dealt with it • **tick sb off** informal **1** UK to tell someone that they have done something wrong and that you are angry about it: *I got ticked off for not going to the meeting.* **2** US to annoy someone • **tick over/along** UK If a business or system ticks over, it continues to work but makes little progress: *Carlton managed to **keep** the business **ticking over**.*

ticket /'tɪkɪt/ noun [C] **1** ⓐ a small piece of paper that shows you have paid to do something, for example travel on a bus, watch a film, etc: *a lottery ticket ○ plane tickets* **2** a piece of paper that orders you to pay money because you have put your car in an illegal place, drive too fast, etc: *a parking ticket* → See also **round trip ticket**, **season ticket**

'ticket ,office noun [C] a place where you can buy a ticket

tickets

tickle /'tɪkl/ verb **1 TOUCH LIGHTLY** ▷ [T] to touch someone lightly with your fingers, in order to make them laugh **2 PART OF THE BODY** ▷ [I, T] If a part of your body tickles, or something tickles it, it feels uncomfortable and you want to rub it: *My nose is tickling.* **3 AMUSE** ▷ [T] to make someone smile or laugh: *I was very tickled by his comments.* • **tickle** noun [C]

tidal /'taɪdəl/ adj relating to the regular rising and falling of the sea

'tidal ,wave noun [C] a very large wave that destroys things, often caused by an earthquake (= when the Earth shakes)

tidbit US (UK **titbit**) /'tɪdbɪt/ noun [C] a small piece of nice food, or an interesting piece of information

tide¹ /taɪd/ noun **1** [C] ⓑ the regular rise and fall in the level of the sea: *high/low tide* **2** [no plural] an increase in something that is developing: *the rising tide of drug-related deaths*

tide² /taɪd/ verb

PHRASAL VERB **tide sb over (sth)** to help someone through a difficult time, especially by giving them money

tidy¹ /'taɪdi/ adj **1** ⓐ having everything in the right place and arranged in a good order: *He room was clean and tidy.* **2** ⓐ liking to keep things in the correct place and arranged in a good order: *I'm afraid I'm not very tidy.* • Opposite **untidy** • **tidily** adv • **tidiness** noun [U]

tidy² /'taɪdi/ verb [I, T] (also **tidy up**) UK ⓐ to make a place tidy: *I'm tidying up before our guests arrive.*

PHRASAL VERB **tidy sth away** UK to put things back in drawers, cupboards, etc after you have used them

tie¹ /taɪ/ verb (**tying, tied**) **1 tie sth to/together/around, etc** ⓑ to fasten something with string, rope, etc: *The dog was tied to a tree.* **2** [T] ⓑ to make a knot in a piece of string, rope, etc: *She tied the scarf.* → Opposite **untie 3** [I] to have the same score as someone else at the end of a competition or game: *Sweden **tied with** France*

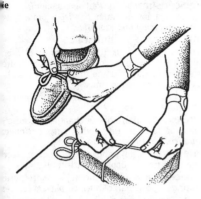

in the winter sports competition. → See also **tie the knot¹**

PHRASAL VERBS **tie sb down** to limit someone's freedom: *I don't want to be tied down by having children.* • **tie in** If one idea or statement ties in with another one, they have some of the same information in them: *His story **ties in with** what Gemma told me.* • **tie sb/sth up** ⑫ to tie a part of someone's body with a rope or something similar so they cannot move → Opposite **untie** • **tie sth up** to fasten something together using string, rope, etc • **be tied up** to be very busy and unable to speak to anyone, go anywhere, etc

tie² /taɪ/ noun [C] **1** CLOTHES ▷ ⓐ a long, thin piece of cloth that a man wears around his neck with a shirt → See colour picture **Clothes** on page Centre 9 **2** CONNECTION ▷ a relationship that connects you with a place, person, etc: [usually plural] *The two countries have **close ties with** each other.* **3** GAME/COMPETITION ▷ the result of a game or competition when two people or teams have the same score → See also **bow tie**

┌─────────────────────────────────────┐
│ ☑ Word partners for **tie**   │
│   │
│ create/forge ties • cut/sever (all) ties • have │
│ ties with sb/sth • close/strong ties • ties │
│ between sb and sb • ties to/with sb/sth │
└─────────────────────────────────────┘

tie-break /'taɪbreɪk/ noun [C] an extra part that is played when a game or competition ends in a tie, to decide who is the winner

tier /tɪəʳ/ noun [C] one of several rows or layers: *the upper tier of seats in a stadium*

tiger /'taɪgəʳ/ noun [C] ⑪ a large wild cat that has yellow fur with black lines on it

tight¹ /taɪt/ adj **1** FIRM ▷ ⑫ firm and difficult to move: *Make sure the knot is tight.* **2** CLOTHES ▷ ⑪ fitting your body very closely: *a tight skirt* **3** CONTROLLED ▷ ⑫ controlled and obeying all rules completely: *tight security* ∘ *They kept tight control of the school budget.* **4** STRAIGHT ▷ If cloth, wire, skin, etc is tight, it has been pulled so that it is straight or smooth. **5** NOT MUCH ▷ If money, time, or space is tight, there is only just enough of it: *We should get six people into the car but it will be tight.* • **tightly** adv • **tightness** noun [U] → See also **keep a tight rein on sb/sth**

tight² /taɪt/ adv ⑫ very firmly or closely: *He held her tight.*

tighten /'taɪtᵊn/ verb [I, T] ⑫ to become tighter or to make something become tighter: *His hand tightened around her arm.* → See also **tighten your belt¹**

PHRASAL VERBS **tighten sth up** to make something become firmer and less easy to move: *Tighten up the screws.* • **tighten (sth) up** to make a rule, system, or law more difficult to avoid: *I think they should **tighten up** the laws **on** gun ownership.*

tightrope /'taɪtrəʊp/ noun [C] a rope high above the ground that a performer walks along at a circus (= show)

tights /taɪts/ noun [plural] **1** ⑫ UK (US **pantyhose**) a piece of women's clothing made of very thin material that covers the legs and bottom: *a pair of black tights* → See colour picture **Clothes** on page Centre 9 **2** the same type of clothing made from thicker material and worn by dancers and people doing physical exercises for health: *Ballet students should wear a leotard and tights.*

tile /taɪl/ noun [C] one of the flat, square pieces that are used for covering roofs, floors, or walls • **tile** verb [T] *a tiled kitchen*

till¹ /tɪl/ preposition, conjunction ⑫ until: *The supermarket is open till midnight.* ∘ *I lived with my parents till I was twenty.*

till² /tɪl/ noun [C] **1** UK a machine that holds the money in a shop and shows how much you have to pay **2** US a drawer where money is kept in a store

tilt /tɪlt/ verb [I, T] to move into a position where one end or side is higher than the other, or to make something move into this position: *He tilted backwards on his chair.* • **tilt** noun [no plural]

timber /'tɪmbəʳ/ noun **1** WOOD ▷ [U] UK (US **lumber**) wood that is used for building **2** TREE ▷ [U] US trees that are grown to provide wood for building **3** PIECE OF WOOD ▷ [C] a large piece of wood: *The roof was supported by timbers.*

time¹ /taɪm/ noun **1** HOURS/YEARS ETC ▷ [U] ⑫ Time is what we measure in minutes, hours, days, etc.: *He wants to **spend** more **time** with his family.* ∘ *Time seems to **pass** so slowly when you're unhappy.* **2** PARTICULAR POINT ▷ [C, U] ⑪ a particular point in the day or night: *What time is it?* ∘ *What time do you leave for school in the mornings?* ∘ *Can you tell me the times of the trains to London, please?* → See Note at **hour 3 it's time (for/to do sth)** used to say that something should happen or be done now: *It's time to get up.* **4 in (good) time** ⑪ early or at the right time: *We arrived in time to catch the train.* **5 on time** ⑪ not early or late: *I got to school on time.* **6 can tell the time** to be able to know what time it is by looking at a clock or watch **7** PERIOD ▷ [no plural] ⑫ a period of minutes, hours, years, etc: *I lived in Switzerland for a **long time**.* ∘ *It **takes time** (= takes a long time) to make friends at a new school.* **8 have time** ⑪ to have enough time to do something: *Do you have time for a cup of coffee?* ∘ [+ to do sth] *I never have time to eat breakfast.* **9 in no time** very soon: *We'll be home* *in no time.* **10 OCCASION** ▷ [C] ② an occasion when something happens: *Give me a call the **next time** you're in Seattle.* ◦ *I can't remember the **last time** we went away.* ◦ *How many **times** have you been to Germany?* **11 at the same time** ③ If two things happen at the same time, they happen together: *We arrived at the same time.* **12 one/two/six, etc at a time** one/two/six, etc on one occasion: *He carried the chairs, three at a time.* **13 time after time** again and again on repeated occasions **14 all the time a** ② very often: *"She's been late twice this week." "It happens all the time."* **b** ② during the whole of a period of time: *He was ill all the time we were in Spain.* **15 three/eight/nine, etc times** ③ used to say how much bigger/better/worse, etc one thing is than another thing: *Ben earns three times more than me.* **16 in a day's/two months', etc time** ③ a day/two months, etc from now: *I have to go to the doctor again in a month's time.* **17 at times** sometimes: *At times, I wish I didn't have to go to school.* **18 for the time being** for now but not permanently: *I'm living with my parents for the time being.* **19 IN THE PAST** ▷ [C] ② a period of time in the past: *Did you enjoy your time in Japan?* **20 at one time** at a time in the past: *At one time, you could drive without taking a driving test.* **21 before sb's time** before someone was born **22 from time to time** ③ sometimes, but not often: *I still see my ex-boyfriend from time to time.* **23 RACE** ▷ [C] the amount of time that someone takes in a race: *a winning time of three minutes* **24 IN A PLACE** ▷ [U] the time in a particular place: *The plane arrives at 20.50, New York time.*

IDIOMS **be ahead of your time** to have new ideas a long time before other people think that way • **behind the times** not fashionable or modern: *Dad's a bit behind the times.* • **bide your time** to wait for an opportunity to do something: *She was biding her time until she could get her revenge.* • **give sb a hard time** to criticize someone and make them feel guilty about something they have done: *Ever since I missed the goal, the other players have been giving me a hard time.* • **have no time for sb/sth** to have no respect for someone or something: *I have no time for people who are racist.* • **kill time** to do something while you are waiting for something else: *I went shopping to kill some time before my job interview.* • **play for time** UK to try to make something happen more slowly because you want more time or because you do not want it to happen • **take your time** to do something without hurrying

→ See also **half-time**, **local time**, **in the nick² of time**, **night-time**, **prime time**, **a race¹ against time/the clock**

time² /taɪm/ **verb** [T] **1** to decide that something will happen at a particular time: *They timed the release of the new album so it came out just before Christmas.* ◦ *Her comment was **well timed**.* **2** ③ to measure how long it takes for something to happen or for someone to do something: *It's a good idea to time yourself while you do the exercises.* → See also **two-time**

time-consuming /'taɪmkənˌsjuːmɪŋ/ **a**◦ needing a lot of time: *The legal process w▪ time-consuming and expensive.*

time ˌframe → See **timescale**

time-honoured UK (US **time-honored**) /'taɪ▪ ˌɒnəd/ **adj** [always before noun] A time-honoure▪ tradition or way of doing things is one that h▪ been used for a long time.

time ˌlag **noun** [C] a period of time between tw▪ things happening

timeless /'taɪmləs/ **adj** not changing because ▪ time or fashion: *Her clothes have a **timele**▪ **quality**.* ◦ *a timeless classic*

timely /'taɪmli/ **adj** happening or done at exact▪ the right time → Opposite **untimely**

time-out /ˌtaɪm'aʊt/ **noun** [C] a short perio▪ during a sports game in which players can re▪

timer /'taɪmər/ **noun** [C] a piece of equipmen▪ that measures time

times /taɪmz/ **preposition** ③ used to say th▪ one number is multiplied by another numbe▪ *Two times three is six.*

timescale /'taɪmskeɪl/ **noun** [C] (also **tim▪ frame**) the amount of time that somethin▪ takes or during which something happens

timetable /'taɪmˌteɪbl/ **noun** [C] **1** (also ▪ **schedule**) ③ a list of times when buses, train▪ etc arrive and leave **2** ② a list of dates and time▪ that shows when things will happen → See colo▪ picture **The Classroom** on page Centre 6

> 🔲 Word partners for **timetable**
>
> **draw up/give/keep to/set** a timetable • a timetable **for** (doing) sth

time ˌzone **noun** [C] one of the areas of th▪ world that has a different time from all the oth▪ areas: *London and New York are five time zon▪ apart.*

timid /'tɪmɪd/ **adj** shy and easily frightene▪ *a timid little boy* • **timidly adv** • **timidit▪** /tɪ'mɪdəti/ **noun** [U]

timing /'taɪmɪŋ/ **noun** [U] **1** ② the time whe▪ something happens: *the timing of the announc▪ ment* **2** the ability to do something at exactly th▪ right time: *You need great timing to be a goo▪ football player.*

tin /tɪn/ **noun 1 METAL CONTAINER** ▷ [C] UK (U▪ US **can**) ③ a metal container in which food ▪ sold: *a tin of beans/soup* → See picture ▪ **container 2 CONTAINER WITH LID** ▷ [C] main▪ UK ② a metal container with a lid that you kee▪ food or other substances in: *a biscuit tin* ◦ ▪ *paint tin* **3 COOKING EQUIPMENT** ▷ [C] UK (U▪ **pan**) a flat pan that you cook food in: *a roastin▪ tin* **4 METAL** ▷ [U] a soft, silver metal that ▪ often combined with other metals or used ▪ cover them

tinfoil /'tɪnfɔɪl/ **noun** [U] metal made into ve▪ thin sheets like paper and used mainly f▪ covering food

tinge /tɪndʒ/ **noun** [C] a small amount of a s▪ feeling or colour: *"Goodbye," he said, with a tin▪ of sadness.* • **tinged adj** *Her dark hair is no▪ tinged with grey.*

tingle /'tɪŋgl/ **verb** [I] If a part of your body tingles, the skin feels slightly uncomfortable: *My hands are starting to tingle with the cold.* • **tingle** **noun** [C]

tinker /'tɪŋkə^r/ **verb** [I] to make small changes to something in order to improve or repair it: *Tim loves **tinkering with** car engines.*

tinkle /'tɪŋkl/ **verb** [I] to make a soft, high, ringing sound • **tinkle noun** [C]

tinned /tɪnd/ **adj** UK (UK/US **canned**) Tinned food is sold in metal containers.

tin opener noun [C] UK (UK/US **can opener**) a piece of kitchen equipment for opening metal food containers → See colour picture **The Kitchen** on page Centre 2

tinsel /'tɪnsəl/ **noun** [U] long, shiny, coloured string, used as a decoration at Christmas (= a Christian holiday)

tint¹ /tɪnt/ **noun** [C] a particular colour: *the yellow and red tints of autumn*

tint² /tɪnt/ **verb** [T] to add a small amount of a colour to something: *Do you think he tints his hair?*

tinted /'tɪntɪd/ **adj** Tinted glass has colour added to it: *tinted sunglasses*

tiny /'taɪni/ **adj** ⑤ extremely small: *a tiny baby* ◦ *a tiny little room*

tip¹ /tɪp/ **noun** [C] **1 END** ▷ the end of something long and narrow: *the tips of your fingers* **2 ADVICE** ▷ ⑥ a piece of useful advice: *gardening tips* ◦ *Emma was giving me some **tips on** how to grow tomatoes.* **3 MONEY** ▷ ⑥ an extra amount of money that you give to a driver, someone working in a restaurant, etc to thank them: *We **left** a **tip** because the waiter was so friendly.* **4 WASTE** ▷ UK (also UK/US **dump**) a place where people take things that they want to get rid of: *We took our old fridge to the tip.* **5 UNTIDY PLACE** ▷ UK informal (also UK/US **dump**) a place that is dirty and untidy: *His bedroom is an absolute tip.*

IDIOMS **be on the tip of your tongue** If a word is on the tip of your tongue, you want to say it but cannot remember it. • **be the tip of the iceberg** to be a small part of a very big problem

> ☑ Word partners for **tip**
>
> give/pass on/pick up tips • a handy/helpful/hot/useful tip • tips for/on sth

tip² /tɪp/ **verb** (**tipping, tipped**) **1** [I, T] to move so that one side is higher than the other side, or to make something move in this way: *The table tipped and all the drinks fell on the floor.* **2 tip sth into/onto/out of sth** to make the contents of a container fall out by holding the container in a position where this happens: *She tipped the contents of her purse onto the table.* **3** [I, T] to give an extra amount of money to a driver, someone working in a restaurant, etc to thank them **4 be tipped as/to do/for sth** UK If someone is tipped to achieve something, most people say it will happen: *Christie was tipped to win the race.*

PHRASAL VERBS **tip sb off** to warn someone secretly about something so that they can take

action or prevent it happening • **tip-off** /'tɪpɒf/ **noun** [C] a piece of information that you give someone secretly, so that they can take action or prevent something happening • **tip (sth) over** If something tips over, or if you tip it over, it falls onto its side.

tiptoe¹ /'tɪptəʊ/ **noun on tiptoe** standing on your toes with the rest of your feet off the ground

tiptoe² /'tɪptəʊ/ **verb tiptoe across/down/through, etc** to walk quietly on your toes

tire¹ /taɪə^r/ **noun** [C] US spelling of tyre → See colour picture **Car** on page Centre 7

tire² /taɪə^r/ **verb** [I, T] to become tired or to make someone become tired: *He tires easily.*

PHRASAL VERBS **tire of sth/doing sth** to become bored with something: *He never tires of playing games on his computer.* • **tire sb out** to make someone very tired

tired /taɪəd/ **adj 1** ⑤ feeling that you want to rest or sleep: *He was **tired out** (= very tired) by the end of the day.* ◦ *She never seems to **get tired**.* **2 tired of doing sth** ⑥ bored or annoyed by something that has happened too often: *I'm tired of listening to her problems.* • **tiredness noun** [U]

> ❗ Common learner error: **tired of** or **tired from**?
>
> If you are **tired of** something or **of doing** something, you are bored or annoyed by it.
> *I'm tired of hearing his awful jokes.*
> If you are **tired from** something, you want to rest because of it.
> *I'm tired from the long journey.*

> ➕ Other ways of saying **tired**
>
> If someone is extremely tired, you can say that they are **exhausted**, **worn-out**, or, in informal situations in the UK, **shattered**:
> *I'm too **exhausted** to take the dog for a walk tonight.*
> *By the time I got home, I was absolutely **shattered**.*
> You can use the adjectives **burnt out** and **drained** to describe someone who is tired because they have been working very hard:
> *He was completely **burnt out** after a full week of performances.*
> *I'd worked a twelve-hour day and was absolutely **drained**.*
> If someone is tired and wants to go to sleep, you can describe them as **drowsy** or **sleepy**:
> *The heat had made me **drowsy/sleepy**.*

tireless /'taɪələs/ **adj** working very hard at something and not stopping: *He was a **tireless campaigner/worker** for children's organizations.* ◦ *I want to thank James for his **tireless efforts** on behalf of the company.*

tiresome /'taɪəsəm/ **adj** formal making you feel annoyed or bored: *a tiresome little boy*

tiring /'taɪərɪŋ/ **adj** ⑥ making you feel tired: *a long and tiring day*

T

tissue /'tɪʃuː/ noun **1** ANIMAL/PLANT ▷ [C, U] the material that animals and plants are made of: *human brain tissue* **2** FOR YOUR NOSE ▷ [C] a soft piece of paper that you use for cleaning your nose **3** FOR WRAPPING ▷ [U] (also ˈtissue ˌpaper) soft, thin paper that you cover things with in order to protect them

tit /tɪt/ noun [C] very informal a woman's breast

IDIOM **tit for tat** informal doing something bad to someone because they have done something bad to you

titbit UK (US **tidbit**) /'tɪtbɪt/ noun [C] a small piece of nice food, or an interesting piece of information

title /'taɪtl/ noun [C] **1** BOOK/FILM ETC ▷ the name of a book, film, etc **2** SPORTS ▷ what you get if you win an important sports competition: *He won the 2010 world motor racing title.* **3** SOMEONE'S NAME ▷ a word such as 'Lord', 'Dr', etc that is used before someone's name

> ☑ Word partners for **title**
>
> defend/lose/retain/take/win the title • the world title

titled /'taɪtld/ adj having a title such as 'Lord', 'Lady', or 'Duke' that shows you have a high social position

title-holder /'taɪtlˌhəʊldər/ noun [C] someone who has won a sports competition: *the World Grand Prix title-holder*

ˈtitle ˌrole noun [C] the person in a play or film who has the same name as the play's or film's title

titter /'tɪtər/ verb [I] to laugh in a nervous way • **titter** noun [C]

T-junction /'tiːˌdʒʌŋkʃən/ noun [C] UK (US **T-intersection**) a place where two roads join and make the shape of the letter 'T'

to¹ /tə/ **1** used with a verb to make the infinitive: *I want to learn Spanish.* ○ *He forgot to feed the cat.* **2** used to give the reason for doing something: *I'm just going out to get some milk.*

to² strong /tuː/ weak /tʊ/, /tə/ preposition **1** DIRECTION ▷ in the direction of somewhere: *Dimitri is going to Germany next week.* ○ *I ran to the door.* **2** ANOTHER PERSON ▷ used to show who receives something or experiences an action: *Could you give these keys to Pete?* ○ *Anna was speaking to her mother on the phone.* ○ *I lent my bike to Tom.* **3** POSITION ▷ almost touching or facing something: *She stood with her back to the window.* **4** from … to … a used to give information about periods of time and distances: *The museum is open from Monday to Saturday.* ○ *The bus goes from London to Cambridge.* **b** including: *The book deals with everything from childhood to old age.* **5** BEFORE ▷ used to say 'before' the hour when you are saying what time it is: *It's five to three.* **6** COMPARE ▷ used to compare two things: *I prefer football to rugby.* **7** UNTIL ▷ until a particular time or state: *It's only two weeks to my birthday.* ○ *She nursed him back to health.* **8** SOMEONE'S OPINION ▷ used to say what

someone's opinion is: *Fifty euros is nothing to Paul* (= he would not think it was a lot of money). **9** to sb's disappointment/relief/surprise, etc used to say that someone feels disappointed, relieved/surprised, etc by something: *To Pierre's disappointment, Monique wasn't at the party.* **10** MEASUREMENT ▷ used to say how many parts make up a whole unit of measurement or money: *There are 100 pence to the British pound.* **11** BELONGING ▷ belonging to or connected with: *Can you give me the keys to the car?*

to³ /tuː/ adv UK If you push or pull a door to, you close it.

IDIOM **to and fro** backwards and forwards: *The sign was swinging to and fro in the wind.*

toad /təʊd/ noun [C] a small, brown animal with long back legs for swimming and jumping

toadstool /'təʊdstuːl/ noun [C] a poisonous fungus (= organism like a plant) with a short stem and round top

toast¹ /təʊst/ noun **1** [U] bread that has been heated to make it brown: *a slice of toast* **2** [C] a time when people lift their glasses and drink because they want someone to be successful, happy, etc: *At the wedding, there was a toast to the happy couple.*

toast² /təʊst/ verb [T] **1** to lift your glass and drink with other people because you want someone to be successful, happy, etc **2** to heat bread so that it becomes brown

toaster /'təʊstər/ noun [C] a machine that heats bread so that it becomes brown → See colour picture **The Kitchen** on page Centre 2

toasty /'təʊsti/ adj warm and comfortable: *It's nice and toasty near the fire.*

tobacco /tə'bækəʊ/ noun [U] dried leaves that are inside cigarettes

toboggan /tə'bɒgən/ noun [C] a board that you sit or lie on, used for going down a hill on a surface of snow

today /tə'deɪ/ noun [U], adv **1** this day, or on this day: *It's Johann's birthday today.* ○ *Today is Friday.* **2** the period of time that is happening now or in this period of time: *More young people smoke today than in the past.*

toddle /'tɒdl/ verb **toddle down/off/to, etc** informal to walk somewhere: *Sophie said goodbye and toddled off towards the station.*

toddler /'tɒdlər/ noun [C] a child who has just learned to walk

toe¹ /təʊ/ noun [C] **1** one of the five separate parts at the end of your foot: *your big toe* (= largest toe) ○ *your little toe* (= smallest toe) → See colour picture **The Body** on page Centre 13 **2** the part of a shoe or sock that covers your toes

IDIOM **keep sb on their toes** to make sure that someone gives all their attention to what they are doing and is ready for anything that might happen

toe² /təʊ/ verb → See also **toe the (party) line¹**

toenail /'təʊneɪl/ noun [C] one of the hard, flat parts on top of the end of your toes → See colour picture **The Body** on page Centre 13

ɑː arm | ɜː her | iː see | ɔː saw | uː too | aɪ my | aʊ how | eə hair | eɪ day | əʊ no | ɪə near | ɔɪ boy | ʊə pure | aɪə fire | aʊə sour

toffee /'tɒfi/ **noun** [C, U] a sticky sweet, made by boiling sugar and butter together

tofu /'təʊfuː/ **noun** [U] (also **bean curd**) a soft pale food made from the soya bean plant

together[1] /tə'geðər/ **adv 1** WITH SOMEONE ▷ **A1** with each other: *We went shopping together.* ◦ *They live together.* **2** CONNECTED ▷ **B2** used to say that two or more things are joined to each other, mixed with each other, etc: *She tied the two pieces of rope together.* **3** SAME PLACE ▷ **B2** in the same place or close to each other: *We all sat together.* **4** SAME TIME ▷ **B1** at the same time: *We'll deal with the next two items on the list together.* **5 together with sth** in addition to something: *She sent some flowers together with a card.* → See also **get your act**[2] **together**, **get-together**

together[2] /tə'geðər/ **adj** informal Someone who is together thinks clearly and organizes their life well.

togetherness /tə'geðənəs/ **noun** [U] a feeling of friendship

toil /tɔɪl/ **verb** [I] literary to do difficult work for a long time • **toil noun** [U] literary

toilet /'tɔɪlɪt/ **noun** [C] **1** **A1** a bowl that you sit on or stand near when you get rid of waste substances from your body → See colour picture **The Bathroom** on page Centre 3 **2** mainly UK (US **bathroom**) a room with a toilet in it

> ⚠ Common learner error: **toilet**
>
> **Toilet** is the most general word. In **British English** the informal word **loo** is often used. In **American English** the word **bathroom** is usually used to mean toilet, especially in the home. In public places toilets are usually called **the ladies** or **the gents** in Britain and the **men's room**, **ladies' room**, or **restroom** in America. The **lavatory** is slightly formal and **WC** is only used in **British English**. These two words are not used much today.

> ✍ Word partners for **toilet**
>
> **be on/go to/flush/need** the toilet • toilet **facilities** • a toilet **seat**

toilet paper noun [U] paper used for cleaning your body after you have used the toilet → See colour picture **The Bathroom** on page Centre 3

toiletries /'tɔɪlɪtriz/ **noun** [plural] things such as soap, toothpaste (= substance for cleaning teeth), etc that you use for making yourself clean

toilet roll noun [C] UK paper for cleaning your body after using the toilet that is folded around a tube → See colour picture **The Bathroom** on page Centre 3

token[1] /'təʊkən/ **noun** [C] **1** LOVE/THANKS ▷ something that you give to someone in order to show them love, to thank them, etc: *I gave Helen some chocolates as **a token of** thanks for all her help.* **2** INSTEAD OF MONEY ▷ a round piece of metal or plastic that you put in some machines instead of money: *You need a token to get out of the car park.* **3** PAPER ▷ UK (US **gift certificate**) a piece of paper that you give someone which

they can exchange for a book, CD, etc: *a book/record/gift token*

token[2] /'təʊkən/ **adj** [always before noun] **1** A token person is chosen so that an organization can pretend that they care about that type of person: *a token woman* **2** A token action is small or unimportant and may show your future intentions or may only pretend to: *He made a **token effort** to find a job.*

told /təʊld/ past of tell

tolerable /'tɒlərəbl/ **adj** acceptable but not excellent: *The food was just about tolerable but the service was terrible.* → Opposite **intolerable** • **tolerably adv**

tolerance /'tɒlərəns/ **noun** [U] the quality of allowing people to do or believe what they want although you do not agree with it: *religious/racial tolerance* → See also **zero tolerance**

> ✍ Word partners for **tolerance**
>
> **show** tolerance • tolerance **of/towards** sb/sth • sb's tolerance **level** • **racial/religious** tolerance

tolerant /'tɒlərənt/ **adj** allowing people to do what they want especially when you do not agree with it: *a tolerant attitude* ◦ *I think we're becoming more **tolerant of** children in public places.* → Opposite **intolerant**

tolerate /'tɒləreɪt/ **verb** [T] **1** **B2** to accept or allow something although you do not like it: *We will not tolerate racism of any sort.* **2** to be able to deal with something unpleasant and not be harmed by it: *These plants can tolerate very low temperatures.* • **toleration** /ˌtɒlər'eɪʃən/ **noun** [U]

toll[1] /təʊl/ **noun 1** [C] money that you pay to use a bridge, road, etc **2** [no plural] the number of people who are killed or injured

> IDIOM **take its toll** to have a bad effect on someone or something, especially over a long period of time: *The stress was starting to **take its toll** on him.*

→ See also **death toll**

toll[2] /təʊl/ **verb** [I] When a bell tolls, it rings slowly, especially because someone has died.

toll-free /ˌtəʊl'friː/ **adj** US (UK **freephone**) A toll-free number is a telephone number that you can connect to without paying.

tomato /tə'mɑːtəʊ/ ⓤ /tə'meɪtəʊ/ **noun** [C, U] (plural **tomatoes**) **A1** a soft, round, red fruit eaten in salad or as a vegetable → See colour picture **Fruit and Vegetables** on page Centre 10

tomb /tuːm/ **noun** [C] **B2** a place where a dead person is buried, usually with a monument (= stone structure)

tomboy /'tɒmbɔɪ/ **noun** [C] a young girl who behaves and dresses like a boy

tombstone /'tuːmstəʊn/ **noun** [C] a stone that shows the name of a dead person who is buried under it

tomcat /'tɒmkæt/ **noun** [C] a male cat

tomorrow /tə'mɒrəʊ/ **noun** [U], **adv 1** **A1** the day after today or on the day after today: *It's my birthday tomorrow.* ◦ *Tomorrow is Friday.* **2** the future, or in the future: *the children of tomorrow*

T

ton /tʌn/ **noun** [C] (plural **tons**, **ton**) **1** ⓑ2 a unit for measuring weight, equal to 1016 kilograms in the UK and 907 kilograms in the US → Compare **tonne 2 tons of sth** informal ⓑ a lot of something: *We've got tons of cheese left.* **3 weigh a ton** informal to be very heavy

tone¹ /təʊn/ **noun 1 SOUND QUALITY** ▷ [C, U] ⓑ2 the quality of a sound, especially of someone's voice: *I knew by her **tone of voice** that she was serious.* **2 FEELING/STYLE** ▷ [U, no plural] the general feeling or style that something has: *Then the director arrived and the whole tone of the meeting changed.* **3 TELEPHONE** ▷ [C] ⓑ an electronic sound made by a telephone: *a dialling tone/an engaged tone* **4 COLOUR** ▷ [C] one of the many types of a particular colour

tone² /təʊn/ **verb** [T] (also **tone up**) to make your muscles or skin firmer and stronger: *Try these exercises to tone up your stomach muscles.*

PHRASAL VERB **tone sth down** to make a piece of writing, a speech, etc less offensive or rude: *The show was toned down for television.*

tone-deaf /ˌtəʊnˈdef/ ⓤ /ˈtəʊndef/ **adj** unable to sing the correct musical notes or hear the difference between musical notes

tongs /tɒŋz/ **noun** [plural] a tool used for picking things up, that has two pieces joined together at one end

tongue /tʌŋ/ **noun 1 MOUTH** ▷ [C] ⓑ1 the soft thing inside your mouth that you move and use for tasting and speaking **2 FOOD** ▷ [C, U] the tongue of some animals that you can eat as meat **3 LANGUAGE** ▷ [C] formal a language: *Japanese is her **native tongue** (= the language she learnt to speak as a child).* → See also **mother tongue**, a **slip²** of the tongue, be on the **tip¹** of your tongue

tongue-in-cheek /ˌtʌŋɪnˈtʃiːk/ **adj, adv** said or done as a joke

tongue-tied /ˈtʌŋtaɪd/ **adj** unable to say anything because you are nervous

'tongue ˌtwister noun [C] a phrase or sentence that is difficult to say quickly because it has many similar sounds in it

tonic /ˈtɒnɪk/ **noun 1** [C, U] (also **'tonic ˌwater**) a drink with bubbles in it that has a slightly bitter taste and is often added to alcoholic drinks **2** [no plural] something that makes you feel better: *Spending time with Leo is always a tonic.*

tonight /təˈnaɪt/ **noun, adv** [U] ⓐ the night of this day, or during the night of this day: *What are you doing tonight?* ○ *I'm looking forward to tonight.*

tonne /tʌn/ **noun** [C] (plural **tonnes**, **tonne**) UK a metric ton (= unit for measuring weight, equal to 1000 kilograms) → Compare **ton**

tonsil /ˈtɒnsəl/ **noun** [C] one of the two small, soft parts at the back of your mouth

tonsillitis /ˌtɒnsəlˈaɪtɪs/ **noun** [U] an illness that makes your tonsils very painful

too /tuː/ **adv 1 too small/heavy/much, etc** ⓐ used before adjectives and adverbs to mean 'more than is allowed, necessary, possible, etc': *The film is also far too long.* ○ *There are too many cars on the roads these days.* ○ *[+ to do sth] I*

decided it was too early to get up and went back to sleep. **2** ⓐ also: *Do you know Jason too?* ○ *I'll probably go there next year too.* **3 not too** ⓐ used before adjectives and adverbs to mean 'not very': *"How was your exam?" "Not too bad, I suppose."* ○ *I didn't play too well today.*

took /tʊk/ past tense of take

tools

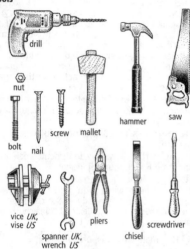

drill
nut
bolt
nail
screw
mallet
hammer
saw
vice *UK*, vise *US*
spanner *UK*, wrench *US*
pliers
chisel
screwdriver

tool /tuːl/ **noun** [C] **1** ⓑ2 a piece of equipment that you use with your hands in order to help you do something **2** something that helps you to do a particular activity: *Computers are an essential tool for modern scientists.* → See also **power tool**

toolbar /ˈtuːlbɑːʳ/ **noun** [C] on a computer screen, a row of icons (= small pictures that you choose in order to make the computer do something)

'tool ˌbox noun [C] a container in which you keep and carry small tools

toot /tuːt/ **verb** (also **honk**) **toot your horn** If a driver toots their horn, they make a short sound with the horn (= thing you press to make a warning noise). • **toot noun** [C]

tooth /tuːθ/ **noun** [C] (plural **teeth**) **1** ⓐ one of the hard, white objects in your mouth that you use for biting and crushing food: *You should **brush** your teeth twice a day.* **2** one of the row of metal or plastic points that stick out from a tool such as a comb (= thing used to make your hair tidy), or saw (= thing used to cut wood)

IDIOM **grit your teeth** to accept a difficult situation and deal with it in a determined way

→ See also a **kick²** in the teeth, do sth by the **skin¹** of your teeth, **wisdom tooth**

┌─────────────────────────────────────┐
│ ☑ Word partners for **tooth** │
│ │
│ brush/clean your teeth • your back/front │
│ teeth • **have** a tooth **removed/taken out** • a │
│ **set** of teeth │
└─────────────────────────────────────┘

toothache /'tu:θeɪk/ **noun** [U] ⓐ a pain in one of your teeth

toothbrush /'tu:θ- brʌʃ/ **noun** [C] ⓐ a small brush that you use to clean your teeth

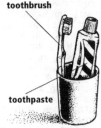

toothbrush

toothpaste

toothpaste /'tu:θpeɪst/ **noun** [U] ⓐ a substance that you use to clean your teeth → See colour picture **The Bathroom** on page Centre 3

toothpick /'tu:θpɪk/ **noun** [C] a small, thin stick that you use to remove pieces of food from between your teeth

top¹ /tɒp/ **noun 1 HIGHEST PART** ▷ [C] ⓐ the highest part of something: *They were waiting for him at the top of the stairs.* ○ *I want a cake with cherries on top.* **2 SURFACE** ▷ [C] the flat, upper surface of something: *the table top* **3 LID** ▷ [C] the lid or cover of a container, pen, etc: *Put the top back on the bottle.* **4 CLOTHING** ▷ [C] ⓑ a piece of women's clothing worn on the upper part of the body **5 TOY** ▷ [C] a toy that turns round and round when you move its handle up and down **6 the top** the most important position in a company, team, etc: *At forty he was already at the top of his profession.* **7 at the top of your voice** UK (US **at the top of your lungs**) shouting very loudly

IDIOMS **from top to bottom** completely: *I've searched the house from top to bottom and still can't find it.* • **get on top of sb** UK If a difficult situation gets on top of someone, it upsets them. • **off the top of your head** informal If you say a fact off the top of your head, you say it immediately, from memory: *"What date is their wedding?" "I couldn't tell you off the top of my head."* • **on top of sth a** ⓑ in addition to something else that is bad: *And then, on top of everything else, her car was stolen.* **b** able to deal with or in control of something: *I'm not at all sure that he's on top of the situation.* • **be on top of the world** informal to be very happy • **over the top** mainly UK informal too extreme and not suitable: *I thought her performance was way over the top.*

☐ Word partners for **top**

reach the top • **at** the top • **on** top • **the top of** sth

top² /tɒp/ **adj** [always before noun] **1** ⓑ the best, most important, or most successful: *He's one of the country's top athletes.* **2** ⓑ at the highest part of something: *I can't reach the top shelf.*

top³ /tɒp/ **verb** [T] (**topping, topped**) **1** to be better or more than something: *I don't think film makers will ever top 'Gone With The Wind'.* **2 be topped with sth** to be covered with something: *lemon tart topped with cream*

PHRASAL VERBS **top sth off** informal to finish something in an enjoyable or successful way • **top sth up** UK (US **top sth off**) **1** to add more

liquid to a container in order to make it full **2** to add more of something, especially money, to an existing amount to create the total you need: *Can I top up my mobile phone here?*

top 'hat UK (US **'top ˌhat**) **noun** [C] a tall, black or grey hat worn by men on some formal occasions

topic /'tɒpɪk/ **noun** [C] ⓑ a subject that you talk or write about

☐ Word partners for **topic**

cover/discuss/raise a topic • a **controversial/ hot** topic • the **(main) topic of** sth • a **topic of conversation/discussion**

topical /'tɒpɪkəl/ **adj** relating to things that are happening now

topless /'tɒpləs/ **adj** without clothes on the upper part of your body

topmost /'tɒpməʊst/ **adj** [always before noun] highest: *the topmost branches of a tree*

topography /tə'pɒgrəfi/ **noun** [U] the shape and other physical characteristics of a piece of land

topping /'tɒpɪŋ/ **noun** [C, U] food that is put on top of other food in order to give it more flavour, or to make it look attractive

topple /'tɒpl/ **verb 1** [I, T] to fall, or to make something or someone fall **2** [T] to make a leader lose their position of power

top-secret /ˌtɒp'siːkrət/ **adj** Top-secret information is very important and must not be told to anyone.

topsy-turvy /ˌtɒpsi'tɜːvi/ **adj** informal confused or badly organized

'top-up ˌcard noun [C] a card you can buy that gives you a special number so that you can use your mobile phone for longer

the Torah /'tɔːrə/ **noun** the holy books of the Jewish religion, especially the first five books of the Bible

torch¹ /tɔːtʃ/ **noun** [C] **1** UK (US **flashlight**) ⓑ a small electric light that you hold in your hand **2** a long stick with material that burns tied to the top of it

torch² /tɔːtʃ/ **verb** [T] informal to destroy something by burning it: *A number of houses were torched.*

tore /tɔːʳ/ past tense of tear

torment¹ /tɔː'ment/ **verb** [T] to make someone suffer or worry a lot: *All evening the question tormented her.* • **tormentor noun** [C]

torment² /'tɔːment/ **noun** [C, U] extreme unhappiness or pain

torn /tɔːn/ past participle of tear

tornado /tɔː'neɪdəʊ/ **noun** [C] (plural **tornados, tornadoes**) (also US **twister**) ⓑ an extremely strong and dangerous wind that blows in a circle and destroys buildings as it moves along

torpedo /tɔː'piːdəʊ/ **noun** [C] (plural **torpedoes**) a long, thin bomb that is fired from a ship and moves under water to destroy another ship

torrent /'tɒrənt/ **noun** [C] **1 a torrent of sth** a lot of something unpleasant: *a torrent of abuse* **2** a large amount of water that is moving very fast

T

torrential /təˈrenʃ³l/ **adj** Torrential rain is very heavy rain.

torso /ˈtɔːsəʊ/ **noun** [C] the main part of a human body without its arms, legs, or head

tortilla /tɔːˈtiːə/ **noun** [C] a type of thin round Mexican bread

tortoise /ˈtɔːtəs/ **noun** [C] an animal with a thick, hard shell that it can move its head and legs into for protection

tortoise

tortuous /ˈtɔːtʃuəs/ **adj** formal **1** very complicated or difficult: *Gaining permission to build was a long and tortuous process.* **2** A tortuous road has many turns in it: *a tortuous path/route*

torture¹ /ˈtɔːtʃər/ **verb** [T] to cause someone severe pain, often in order to make them tell you something • **torturer noun** [C]

torture² /ˈtɔːtʃər/ **noun** [C, U] **1** the act of torturing someone **2** a very unpleasant experience: *I had to sit there listening to her for two whole hours – it was torture!*

Tory /ˈtɔːri/ **noun** [C] someone who supports the Conservative Party in the UK: *a Tory voter*

toss¹ /tɒs/ **verb 1 toss sth away/into/on, etc** to throw something somewhere carelessly: *He read the letter quickly, then tossed it into the bin.* **2** [I, T] (also **toss up**) to throw a coin in the air and guess which side will land facing upwards as a way of deciding something

toss² /tɒs/ **noun 1 a toss of a coin** the action of throwing a coin in the air and guessing which side will land facing upwards, as a way of deciding something **2 a toss of your head/hair** the action of moving your head quickly backwards

tot /tɒt/ **noun** [C] informal **1** a small child **2** UK a small amount of strong alcohol

total¹ /ˈtəʊt³l/ **adj** [always before noun] **1** ❶ including everything: *The total cost of the work was $800.* **2** ❷ extreme or complete: *The whole evening was a total disaster.*

total² /ˈtəʊt³l/ **noun** [C] ❶ the amount you get when you add several smaller amounts together: *In total we made over 3,000 euros.*

🗒 **Word partners for total noun**

sth **brings/takes** the total **to** [500/4000, etc] • **reach** a total **of** [500/4000, etc] • the **final/overall/sum** total • [500/4000, etc] **in total**

---

total³ /ˈtəʊt³l/ **verb** [T] (mainly UK **totalling, totalled**, US **totaling, totaled**) to add up to a particular amount

totalitarian /təʊˌtælɪˈteəriən/ **adj** belonging to a political system in which the people in power have complete control and do not allow anyone to oppose them • **totalitarianism noun** [U]

totally /ˈtəʊt³li/ **adv** ❶ completely: *They look totally different.* ∘ *I totally disagree.*

tote bag /ˈtəʊtˌbæg/ **noun** [C] a large bag with handles and an open top

totter /ˈtɒtər/ **verb** [I] to walk in a way that looks as if you are going to fall: *She tottered around the dance floor.*

touch¹ /tʌtʃ/ **verb 1** HAND ▷ [T] ❶ to put your hand on something: *You can look at them but please don't touch them.* **2** GET CLOSE ▷ [I, T] ❷ If two things touch, they are so close to each other that there is no space between them: *These two wires must not touch.* **3** EMOTION ▷ [T] ❷ If something kind that someone says or does touches you, it makes you feel pleased or a little sad: [often passive] *I was deeply touched by her letter.* **4 not touch sth** to not eat or drink something **5 not touch sb/sth** to not harm someone or not damage something → See also **touch/cover all the bases (base¹), hit/touch a (raw) nerve**

PHRASAL VERBS **touch down** When a plane touches down, it lands. • **touch on sth** to briefly talk about something: *We only touched on the subject.* • **touch sth up** to improve something by making small changes

touch² /tʌtʃ/ **noun 1** HAND ▷ [no plural] ❷ the action of putting your hand on something: *I felt the touch of his hand on my face.* **2** ABILITY ▷ [U] ❷ the ability to feel things by putting your hand on them: *It was cold to the touch (= when touched it).* **3** DETAIL ▷ [C] a small detail that makes something better: *Having flowers on the tables was a nice touch.* **4 a touch** a little: *Add a little olive oil and a touch of vinegar.* **5 be/get/keep, etc in touch** ❶ to communicate or continue to communicate with someone by telephoning, or writing to them **6 lose touch** ❷ to stop communicating with someone usually because they do not live near you now **7 be out of touch** to know little about what has recently happened

touchdown /ˈtʌtʃdaʊn/ **noun 1** [C, U] the moment when an aircraft lands **2** [C] the act of carrying or throwing the ball over a line in order to score points in rugby or American football

touched /tʌtʃt/ **adj** pleased or a little sad because someone has done something kind: *She was touched that he had remembered her birthday.*

touching /ˈtʌtʃɪŋ/ **adj** making you feel sadness or sympathy: *a touching performance*

touch screen noun [C] a screen on a computer, phone, etc. that you touch in order to give it instructions, rather than using a keyboard

touchstone /ˈtʌtʃstəʊn/ **noun** [no plural] something that other things can be judged against

touchy /ˈtʌtʃi/ **adj 1** easily upset: *Why are you so touchy today?* **2 touchy subject/issue, etc** a subject that you have to talk about carefully because it is likely to upset someone

tough /tʌf/ **adj 1** DIFFICULT ▷ ❷ difficult: *He's had a tough time at work recently.* ∘ *We've had to make some tough decisions.* **2** SEVERE ▷ Tough rules are severe: *tough new laws on noise pollution* **3** STRONG THING ▷ ❷ not easily damaged, cut, etc: *Children's shoes have to be tough.* ∘ *This meat's very tough.* **4** STRONG PERSON ▷ ❷ physically strong and not afraid of violence: *a tough guy* **5** DETERMINED ▷ determined and not easily upset: *You have to be tough to survive in politics.* **6** UNFAIR ▷ unfair or unlucky: *It can be tough on kids when parents get divorced.*

oughen /ˈtʌfᵊn/ verb [I, T] (also **toughen up**) to become stronger, or to make something or someone stronger: *School tends to toughen kids up.*

oupee /ˈtuːpeɪ/, /tuːˈpeɪ/ noun [C] a piece of artificial (= not natural) hair worn by a man to cover part of his head where there is no hair

our¹ /tʊər/ noun [C, U] ⓐ a visit to and around a place, area, or country: *a tour of Europe* ∘ *We went on a guided tour of the cathedral.* ∘ *The band are on tour (= travelling and performing in different places).*

> ☑ Word partners for **tour**
>
> be on/go on a tour • a guided/sightseeing/ world tour • a tour of sth

our² /tʊər/ verb [I, T] ⓑ to travel around a place for pleasure: *to tour the States*

our guide noun [C] ⓐ someone whose job is to show visitors a place or area: *Our tour guide explained the church's history.*

ourism /ˈtʊərɪzᵊm/ noun [U] ⓑ the business of providing services for tourists, including organizing their travel, hotels, entertainment, etc

ourist /ˈtʊərɪst/ noun [C] ⓐ someone who visits a place for pleasure and does not live there

ournament /ˈtʊənəmənt/ noun [C] ⓑ a competition with a series of games between many teams or players, with one winner at the end: *a golf/tennis tournament*

> ☑ Word partners for **tournament**
>
> host/play in/pull out of/take part in/win a tournament • in a tournament • a major tournament • a round/stage of a tournament

ourniquet /ˈtʊənɪkeɪ/ ⓤ /ˈtɜːrnɪkɪt/ noun [C] a long piece of cloth that you tie tightly around an injured arm or leg to stop the blood coming out

ousled /ˈtaʊzld/ adj Tousled hair is untidy.

out¹ /taʊt/ verb **1** [T] to praise someone or something in order to make people think that they are important: [often passive] *He is being touted as the next big star.* **2** [I, T] UK to try to persuade people to buy something: *Drug dealers were seen touting for business outside schools.*

out² /taʊt/ noun [C] UK (US **scalper**) someone who unofficially sells tickets outside theatres, sporting events, etc

ow¹ /təʊ/ verb [T] to pull a car, boat, etc, using a rope or chain connected to another vehicle: *His car was towed away by the police.*

ow² /təʊ/ noun informal **in tow** If you have someone in tow, you have them with you: *Shopping can be very stressful with young children in tow.*

owards /təˈwɔːdz/ preposition mainly UK (mainly US **toward**) **1** DIRECTION ▷ ⓑ in the direction of someone or something: *She stood up and walked towards him.* **2** POSITION ▷ near to a time or place: *Your seats are towards the back of the theatre.* ∘ *He only became successful towards the*

end of his life. **3** FEELING ▷ ⓑ used when talking about feelings about something or someone: *His attitude towards work needs to improve.* **4** PURPOSE ▷ for the purpose of buying or achieving something: *We're asking people for a contribution towards the cost.* ∘ *This piece of work counts towards your final mark.*

towel /taʊəl/ noun [C] ⓐ a soft piece of cloth or paper that you use for drying yourself or for drying something: *a bath/beach towel* ∘ *a paper towel* → See colour picture **The Bathroom** on page Centre 3

IDIOM **throw in the towel** to stop trying to do something because you do not think you can succeed

→ See also **sanitary towel**, **tea towel**

towel rail noun [C] UK (US **towel rack**) a horizontal bar on the wall that you hang towels on → See picture at **rail**

tower¹ /taʊər/ noun [C] ⓑ a very tall, narrow building, or part of a building: *a church tower* ∘ *the Eiffel Tower*

IDIOM **a tower of strength** someone who helps you a lot during a difficult time

tower² /taʊər/ verb **tower over/above sb/sth** to be much taller or higher than someone or something else: *David towers over his mother.*

tower block noun [C] UK a very tall building divided into apartments or offices

towering /ˈtaʊərɪŋ/ adj [always before noun] very tall: *towering mountains/trees*

town /taʊn/ noun **1** [C] ⓐ a place where people live and work, usually larger than a village but smaller than a city: *It's a small town in the north of England.* **2** [U] ⓐ the central area of a town where the shops are: *I usually go into town on a Saturday.* ∘ *Shall I meet you in town?*

IDIOMS **go to town (on sth)** to spend a lot of money or time doing something in order to make it special: *They've really gone to town on the decorations.* • **out on the town** informal enjoying yourself in bars, restaurants, etc in the evening

→ See also **ghost town**, **shanty town**

> ☑ Word partners for **town**
>
> go into town • in town • a part of/side of town • the town centre

town hall noun [C] a large building where local government is based

township /ˈtaʊnʃɪp/ noun [C] in South Africa in the past, an area where only black people lived

toxic /ˈtɒksɪk/ adj ⓑ poisonous: *toxic chemicals/ fumes* ∘ *toxic waste (= poisonous waste materials produced by industry)* • **toxicity** /tɒkˈsɪsəti/ noun [U] formal how poisonous a substance is

toxin /ˈtɒksɪn/ noun [C] formal a poisonous substance

toy¹ /tɔɪ/ noun [C] ⓐ an object for children to play with: *a toy car/train* ∘ *He was happily playing with his toys.*

T

toy² /tɔɪ/ **verb**

PHRASAL VERB **toy with sth 1** to briefly think about doing something, but not really intend to do it: *I've toyed with the idea of going to work abroad.* **2** to move something around in your hands without any clear purpose: *He sat toying with his empty glass.*

trace¹ /treɪs/ **verb** [T] **1** FIND ▷ to find someone or something that was lost: *Police have so far failed to trace the missing woman.* **2** ORIGIN ▷ to find the origin of something: *She's **traced** her family **back** to the sixteenth century.* ∘ *They were able to **trace** the call (= find out the number of the telephone used).* **3** DEVELOPMENT ▷ to describe the way something has developed over time: *The book traces the development of women's art since the start of the century.* **4** COPY ▷ to copy a picture by putting transparent paper on top and following the outer line of the picture with a pen: *tracing paper*

trace² /treɪs/ **noun 1** [C, U] 🅱️2 proof that someone or something was in a place: *There was **no trace** of her anywhere.* ∘ *Ships have **disappeared without trace** (= completely).* **2** [C] a small amount of something: *They found traces of blood on his clothing.*

📗 **Word partners for trace**

find no/leave no trace(of sth) • disappear without/vanish without trace

---

track¹ /træk/ **noun 1** PATH ▷ [C] 🅱️1 a narrow path or road: *We followed a dirt track off the main road.* **2** RAILWAY ▷ [C] the long metal lines that a train travels along: *UK a railway track/US a railroad track* **3** RACE ▷ [C] 🅱️1 a path, often circular, used for races: *a race track* ∘ *track events* **4** SPORT ▷ [U] US 🅱️2 the sport of running in races around a wide circular path made for this sport **5** MUSIC ▷ [C] 🅱️2 one song or piece of music on a CD, record, etc **6 keep track** to continue to know what is happening to someone or something: *He changes jobs so often – I find it hard to keep track of what he's doing.* **7 lose track** 🅱️2 to not know what is happening to someone or something any more: *I've lost track of how much we've spent.* **8 on track** making progress and likely to succeed: *[+ to do sth] A fighter from Edinburgh is on track to become world heavyweight boxing champion.*

IDIOMS **a fast track (to sth)** a very quick way of achieving or dealing with something: *These intensive courses claim to offer a fast track to wealth and success.* • **off the beaten track** in a place where few people go

track² /træk/ **verb** [T] **1** to follow a person or animal by looking for proof that they have been somewhere, or by using electronic equipment: *The wolves are tracked by using radio collars.* **2** to record the progress or development of something over a period: *The project tracks the effects of population growth on the area.*

PHRASAL VERB **track sth/sb down** to find something or someone after looking for them in a lot

of different places: *The man was finally tracked down by French police.*

track and field **noun** [U] US (UK **athletics**) the sports that include running, jumping, and throwing → See colour picture **Sports 1** on page Centre 14

track record UK (US **track record**) **noun** [C] how well or badly you have done in the past: *This company has an impressive track record in completing projects on time.*

tracks /træks/ **noun** [plural] 🅱️2 the marks left on the ground by a person, animal, or vehicle: *We followed their tracks in the snow.*

tracksuit /ˈtræksuːt/ **noun** [C] UK 🅱️1 loose, comfortable clothes, usually trousers and a top, especially worn for exercising → See colour picture **Clothes** on page Centre 9

tract /trækt/ **noun** [C] **1** a system of connected tubes in someone's body which has a particular purpose: *the **digestive/respiratory tract*** **2** large area of land

tractor /ˈtræktər/ **noun** [C] a strong vehicle with large back wheels used on farms for pulling things

trade¹ /treɪd/ **noun 1** BUYING AND SELLING ▷ [U] 🅱️1 the buying and selling of large numbers of goods or services, especially between countries: *a **trade agreement/dispute*** ∘ *They rely heavily on **trade with** Europe.* ∘ *The laws ban the international **trade in** ivory.* **2** BUSINESS ▷ [C] particular area of business or industry: *the building/tourist trade* **3** JOB ▷ [C] 🅱️2 someone job, especially one which needs skill in using their hands: *He's a builder **by trade**.*

📗 **Word partners for trade noun**

trade **agreement/deal/policy** • trade **between** [two countries/regions] • trade **with** [a country] • trade **in** sth • a trade **dispute**

---

trade² /treɪd/ **verb 1** [I] 🅱️2 to buy and sell goods or services, especially between countries: *They will increase costs for companies **trading with** Asia.* **2** [T] mainly US to give something to someone and receive something else in exchange: *He **traded** his guitar **for** a leather jacket.* • **trading noun** [U]

PHRASAL VERB **trade sth in** to give something as part of your payment for something else: *He traded his old car in for a new model.*

trademark /ˈtreɪdmɑːk/ **noun** [C] the name of a particular company or product which cannot be used by anyone else

trade-off /ˈtreɪdɒf/ **noun** [C] a situation where you accept something bad in order to have something good: *There's always **a trade-off between** speed and quality.*

tradesman /ˈtreɪdzmən/ **noun** [C] (plural **tradesmen**) UK someone who works in trade or in a trade that needs skill in using their hands, usually in the building industry

trade union **noun** [C] UK (US **labor union**) an organization that represents people who do a particular job

---

tradition /trəˈdɪʃᵊn/ **noun** [C, U] 🅱2 a custom or way of behaving that has continued for a long time in a group of people or a society: *There is a* **strong tradition** *of dance in St Petersburg.* ∘ *We decided to* **break with tradition** (= *not behave as usual*) *this year and go away for Christmas.*

> 🗹 Word partners for **tradition**
>
> break with/follow/revive/uphold a tradition • an ancient/old/proud/rich/strong tradition

traditional /trəˈdɪʃᵊnᵊl/ **adj** 🅱1 following the customs or ways of behaving that have continued in a group of people or society for a long time: *traditional Hungarian dress* ∘ *traditional farming methods* • **traditionally adv**

traditionalist /trəˈdɪʃᵊnᵊlɪst/ **noun** [C] someone who believes in traditional ideas and ways of doing things

traffic /ˈtræfɪk/ **noun** [U] **1 CARS ETC** ▷ 🅰2 the cars, trucks, etc using a road: *Traffic is* **heavy** (= *there are a lot of cars, etc*) *in both directions.* ∘ *a* **traffic accident** ∘ *Sorry we're late – we got* **stuck in traffic**. **2 PLANES AND SHIPS** ▷ the planes or ships moving around an area: *air traffic control* **3 ILLEGAL** ▷ the illegal buying and selling of goods, such as drugs, weapons, etc: *the* **traffic in** *illegal drugs*

> 🗹 Word partners for **traffic**
>
> reduce/ease/divert/slow down traffic • bad/heavy traffic • be stuck in traffic • a traffic accident

traffic ˌ**circle noun** [C] US (UK **roundabout**) a circular place where roads meet and where cars drive around until they arrive at the road that they want to turn into → See picture at **roundabout**

traffic ˌ**jam noun** [C] 🅱1 a line of cars, trucks, etc that are moving slowly or not moving at all: *They got stuck in a traffic jam.*

trafficking /ˈtræfɪkɪŋ/ **noun** [U] the activity of illegally buying and selling goods, such as drugs or weapons: **arms/drug trafficking** • **trafficker noun** [C]

traffic ˌ**lights noun** [plural] (also **lights**) 🅰2 a set of red, green, and yellow lights that is used to stop and start traffic: [usually plural] *Turn left at the traffic lights.* → See picture at **light**

traffic ˌ**warden noun** [C] UK someone whose job is to make sure that people do not leave their cars in illegal places

tragedy /ˈtrædʒədi/ **noun 1** [C, U] 🅱2 an event or situation that is very sad, often involving death: *the tragedy of their daughter's death* **2** [C] a play with a sad end: *a Greek tragedy*

tragic /ˈtrædʒɪk/ **adj** 🅱2 very sad, often relating to death and suffering: *a* **tragic accident/death** • **tragically adv** *He was tragically killed in a flying accident at the age of 25.*

trail¹ /treɪl/ **noun** [C] **1** a line of marks that someone or something leaves behind as they move: *He left a trail of muddy footprints across the kitchen floor.* **2** 🅱2 a path through the countryside, often where people walk: *a* **nature trail**

trail² /treɪl/ **verb 1 FOLLOW** ▷ [T] to follow

someone, especially without them knowing, in order to watch or catch them: *He suspected he was being trailed by undercover police.* **2 HANG DOWN** ▷ [I, T] UK to hang down and touch the ground, or to make something do this: *Your coat's trailing in the mud.* **3 LOWER SCORE** ▷ [I, T] to have a lower score than someone else, especially in a sporting event: *City were trailing United 2-1 at half time.*

PHRASAL VERB **trail away/off** If someone's voice trails away or off, it gradually becomes quieter until it stops.

trailer /ˈtreɪlər/ **noun** [C] **1 CONTAINER** ▷ a container with wheels that can be pulled by a car or a truck **2 HOUSE** ▷ mainly US a house on wheels that can be pulled by a car **3 FILM** ▷ short parts of a film or television programme which are shown in order to advertise it

trailer ˌpark noun [C] US a place where trailers (= vehicles that people live in) can park

train¹ /treɪn/ **noun 1** 🅰1 [C] a long, thin vehicle that travels along metal tracks and carries people or goods: *a train journey* ∘ *We could go* **by train**. ∘ *You'll have to* **catch/get** *the next train.* **2 train of thought/events** a series of connected thoughts, ideas, or events that come or happen one after the other: *I was interrupted and lost my train of thought.*

train² /treɪn/ **verb 1 TEACH** ▷ [T] 🅱2 to teach someone how to do something, usually a skill that is needed for a job: *We are* **training** *all our staff* **in** *how to use the new computer system.* ∘ [+ to do sth] *The aid workers trained local people to give the injections.* **2 LEARN** ▷ [I] 🅱2 to learn the skills you need to do a job: *He* **trained as** *a lawyer in Vienna.* ∘ *I'm* **trained in** *basic first aid.* **3 SPORT** ▷ [I, T] 🅱1 to practise a sport or exercise, often in order to prepare for a sporting event, or to help someone to do this: *He's been training hard for the race for several weeks now.*

trainee /ˌtreɪˈniː/ **noun** [C] someone who is learning how to do something, especially a job: *a trainee accountant/teacher*

trainer /ˈtreɪnər/ **noun** [C] **1 PERSON** ▷ 🅱1 someone who trains people: *a fitness trainer* **2 ANIMALS** ▷ 🅱1 a person who trains animals: *a racehorse trainer* **3 SHOE** ▷ UK (US **sneaker**) 🅰2 a soft sports shoe: *a pair of trainers* → See colour picture **Clothes** on page Centre 9

training /ˈtreɪnɪŋ/ **noun** [U] **1** 🅱1 the process of learning the skills you need to do a particular job or activity: *a* **training course** ∘ *computer/management training* **2** 🅱1 preparation for a sport or competition: *weight training* ∘ *He's* **in training** *for the big match next month.*

> 🗹 Word partners for **training**
>
> have/receive/undergo training • give sb/provide training • training in/on sth • a training course/day/programme/session

ˈ**train** ˌ**station noun** (also UK **railway station**, also US **railroad station**) a place where trains stop so that you can get on or off: *We have to be at the train station by 11.*

T

---

yes | k cat | ŋ ring | ʃ she | θ thin | ð this | ʒ decision | dʒ jar | tʃ chip | æ cat | e bed | ə ago | ɪ sit | i cosy | ɒ hot | ʌ run | ʊ put |

trait /treɪt/ **noun** [C] a quality, good or bad, in someone's character: *a family trait*

traitor /ˈtreɪtəʳ/ **noun** [C] someone who is not loyal to their country or to a group that they are a member of

trajectory /trəˈdʒektəri/ **noun** [C] formal the curved line that something follows as it moves through the air

tram /træm/ **noun** [C] @ an electric vehicle for carrying passengers, mostly in cities, which moves along metal lines in the road

tramp[1] /træmp/ **noun** [C] someone who has no home, job, or money and who lives outside

tramp[2] /træmp/ **verb** [I, T] to walk a long way, or to walk with heavy steps because you are tired: *We spent all day tramping around the city looking for somewhere cheap to stay.*

trample /ˈtræmpl/ **verb** [T] (also **trample on**) to walk on something, usually damaging or hurting it: *She shouted at the boys for trampling on her flowers.* ∘ *Two people were **trampled to death** in the panic.*

trampoline /ˈtræmpəliːn/ **noun** [C] a piece of sports equipment that you jump up and down on, made of a metal structure with a piece of strong material fixed to it

trance /trɑːns/ **noun** [C] a condition in which you are not completely conscious of what is happening around you or able to control what you are doing: *He sat staring out of the window as if **in a trance**.*

tranquil /ˈtræŋkwɪl/ **adj** calm and quiet: *a tranquil garden* • **tranquility** (also **tranquillity**) /træŋˈkwɪləti/ **noun** [U] *I love the tranquility of the woods.*

tranquilizer (also UK **-iser**) /ˈtræŋkwɪˌlaɪzəʳ/ **noun** [C] a drug that is used to make people or animals sleep or to make them calm

trans- /træns-/, /trænz-/ **prefix 1** across: *transatlantic flights* **2** showing a change: *to transform* ∘ *to translate*

transaction /trænˈzækʃn/ **noun** [C] formal the buying or selling of something, or an exchange of money: *a business/financial transaction*

transatlantic /ˌtrænzətˈlæntɪk/ **adj** crossing the Atlantic: *a transatlantic flight/phone call*

transcend /trænˈsend/ **verb** [T] formal to be better or more important than something else: *Somehow her appeal transcends class barriers.*

transcribe /trænˈskraɪb/ **verb** [T] to make a written record of something you hear, such as speech or music: *I later transcribed the tapes of the interviews.* • **transcription** /trænˈskrɪpʃn/ **noun** [C, U] a written record of speech, music, etc, or the process of making it

transcript /ˈtrænskrɪpt/ **noun** [C] an exact written record of speech, music, etc

transfer /trænsˈfɜːʳ/ **verb** (**transferring**, **transferred**) **1** MOVE ▷ [T] @ to move someone or something from one place to another: *She was later **transferred to** a different hospital.* ∘ *I'll transfer some money **into** my other account.* **2** CHANGE JOB/TEAM ETC ▷ [I, T] @ to change to a different job, team, place of work, etc, or to make someone do this: *After a year he trans-*

ferred to University College, Dublin. **3** CHANGE OWNER ▷ [T] to change who owns or controls something: *We had all the documents transferred to my name.* • **transfer** /ˈtrænsfɜːʳ/ **noun** [C, U] @ *I'm hoping for a transfer to the Brussels office.*

transfixed /trænsˈfɪkst/ **adj** unable to move or stop looking at something because you are so interested, surprised, or frightened: *We all sat in silence, transfixed by what we saw on the screen.*

transform /trænsˈfɔːm/ **verb** [T] @ to change something completely, usually to improve it: *Within weeks they had **transformed** the area into a beautiful garden.* • **transformation** /ˌtrænsfəˈmeɪʃn/ **noun** [C, U] a complete change: *The company has **undergone** a dramatic transformation in the past five years.*

transformer /trænsˈfɔːməʳ/ **noun** [C] a piece of equipment that changes the strength of an electrical current

transfusion /trænsˈfjuːʒn/ **noun** [C] (also **blood transfusion**) a process in which blood is put into someone's body

transgress /trænzˈgres/ **verb** [I, T] formal to do something that is against a law or rule • **transgression** /trænzˈgreʃn/ **noun** [C]

transient[1] /ˈtrænziənt/ **adj** formal **1** lasting only for a short time: *transient pleasures* **2** staying in one place only for a short time

transient[2] /ˈtrænziənt/ **noun** [C] US someone who has no home and stays in a place for only a short time

transistor /trænˈzɪstəʳ/ **noun** [C] a small piece of electrical equipment used in radios, televisions etc

transit /ˈtrænzɪt/ **noun** [U] formal the movement of goods or people from one place to another: *Some things got damaged **in transit** (= while they were being moved).*

transition /trænˈzɪʃn/ **noun** [C, U] formal a change from one system or method to another, often a gradual one: *The country is in the process of **making the transition from** military rule **to** democracy.* • **transitional adj** ∘ *transitional period/phase* ∘ *a transitional government*

transitive /ˈtrænsətɪv/ **adj** @ A transitive verb always has an object. In the sentence 'I'll make a drink.', 'make' is a transitive verb. → See Study Page **Verb patterns** on page Centre 27 → Compare **intransitive**

transitory /ˈtrænsɪtəri/ **adj** formal lasting only for a short time: *the transitory nature of life*

translate /trænzˈleɪt/ **verb** [I, T] **1** @ to change written or spoken words from one language to another: *The book has now been **translated from** Spanish **into** more than ten languages.* **2** formal If an idea or plan translates into an action, it makes it happen: *So how does this theory **translate into** practical policy?*

translation /trænzˈleɪʃn/ **noun** [C, U] @ something that has been translated from one language to another, or the process of translating

translator /trænzˈleɪtəʳ/ **noun** [C] someone

whose job is to change written or spoken words from one language to another

translucent /trænz'lu:s³nt/ **adj** If something is translucent, light can pass through it and you can almost see through it: *translucent fabric*

transmission /trænz'mɪʃ³n/ **noun** **1 BROADCAST** ▷ [C, U] the process of broadcasting something by radio, television, etc, or something that is broadcast: *radio/satellite transmission* **2 SPREADING** ▷ [U] formal the process of passing something from one person or place to another: *There is still a risk of transmission of the virus through infected water.* **3 CAR** ▷ [U] the system in a car that moves power from its engine to its wheels: *automatic/manual transmission*

transmit /trænz'mɪt/ **verb** [T] (**transmitting**, **transmitted**) **1** to broadcast something, or to send out signals using radio, television, etc: [often passive] *The information is transmitted electronically to the central computer.* **2** formal to pass something from one person or place to another: *The **disease** is **transmitted** by mosquitoes.* • **transmitter** noun [C] *a radio/television transmitter*

transparency /træn'spær³nsi/ **noun** [C] a photograph or picture printed on plastic which you can see on a screen by shining a light through it

transparent /træn'spær³nt/ **adj** 🅱️ If a substance or material is transparent, you can see through it: *transparent plastic*

transpire /træn'spaɪər/ **verb** formal **1 It transpires that** If it transpires that something has happened, this fact becomes known: *It later transpired that he had known about the plan from the beginning.* **2** [I] to happen

transplant /'trænsplɑːnt/ **noun** [C] an operation in which a new organ is put into someone's body: *a heart/kidney transplant* • **transplant** /træn'splɑːnt/ **verb** [T] to remove an organ or other body part from one person and put it into someone else's body

> ☑ Word partners for **transplant**
>
> have/perform/undergo a transplant • a transplant **donor/operation/patient/surgeon**

transport[1] /'trænspɔːt/ **noun** [U] **1** 🅱️ a vehicle or system of vehicles, such as buses, trains, aircraft, etc for getting from one place to another: *He can't drive so he has to rely on **public transport**.* ∘ *the city's **transport system*** **2** 🅱️ the activity of moving people or goods from one place to another: *the transport of live animals*

> ☑ Word partners for **transport**
>
> provide/arrange/improve transport • free/ cheap transport • public transport • the transport **system**

transport[2] /træn'spɔːt/ **verb** [T] 🅱️ to move people or goods from one place to another

transportation /ˌtrænspɔː'teɪʃ³n/ **noun** [U] **1** US (UK **transport**) a vehicle or system of vehicles, such as buses, trains, etc for getting from one

place to another **2** the activity of moving people or goods from one place to another: *transportation costs*

transvestite /trænz'vestaɪt/ **noun** [C] someone, especially a man, who likes to wear the clothes of someone of the opposite sex

trap[1] /træp/ **noun** [C] **1** 🅱️ a piece of equipment for catching animals: *a mouse trap* **2** 🅱️ a dangerous or unpleasant situation that is difficult to escape from: [usually singular] *Such families **get caught in** the poverty **trap**.* → See also **booby trap**

trap[2] /træp/ **verb** [T] (**trapping**, **trapped**) **1 CANNOT ESCAPE** ▷ 🅱️ If someone or something is trapped, they cannot move or escape from a place or situation: *The car turned over, trapping the driver underneath.* **2 ANIMAL** ▷ to catch an animal using a trap **3 TRICK** ▷ to trick someone into doing or saying something that they do not want to

trap door noun [C] a small door that you cannot see in a floor or ceiling

trappings /'træpɪŋz/ **noun** [plural] things that you usually get when you are rich and successful, such as a big house and car: *the trappings of success/power*

trash[1] /træʃ/ **noun** [U] **1** US (UK **rubbish**) things that you throw away because you do not want them **2** informal something that is of bad quality: *It's better than the trash she usually reads.*

trash[2] /træʃ/ **verb** [T] informal to destroy something: *Vandals broke in and trashed the place.*

trash can noun [C] US a container for waste, often one that is kept outdoors → See colour picture **The Office** on page Centre 5

trashy /'træʃi/ **adj** informal of very bad quality: *a trashy novel/movie*

trauma /'trɔːmə/ **noun** [C, U] severe shock caused by an unpleasant experience, or the experience that causes this feeling: *the trauma of marriage breakdown*

traumatic /trɔː'mætɪk/ **adj** If an experience is traumatic, it makes you feel very shocked and upset: *His parents split up when he was eight, which he found very traumatic.*

traumatized (also UK **-ised**) /'trɔːmətaɪzd/ **adj** very shocked and upset for a long time: *The violence that he witnessed left him traumatized.*

travel[1] /'træv³l/ **verb** (mainly UK **travelling**, **travelled**, US **traveling**, **traveled**) **1** [I, T] 🅰️ to make a journey: *I spent a year travelling around Asia.* ∘ *He has to travel abroad a lot on business.* **2** [I] 🅱️ If light, sound, or news travels, it moves from one place to another: *News of the accident travelled fast.* → See Note at **move**[1]

travel[2] /'træv³l/ **noun** **1** 🅱️ [U] the activity of travelling: *air/rail travel* ∘ *travel expenses/ insurance* **2 sb's travels** someone's journey: *I meet all kinds of interesting people **on my travels**.*

travel agency noun [C] (also **travel agent's**) a company or shop that makes travel arrangements for people

travel agent noun [C] 🅱️ someone whose job is making travel arrangements for people

traveller /'træv³lər/ **noun** [C] **1** mainly UK (also US

> ❗ **Common learner error: travel, journey, or trip?**
>
> The noun **travel** is a general word that means the activity of travelling.
> *Air travel has become much cheaper.*
> Use **journey** to talk about when you travel from one place to another.
> *He fell asleep during the train journey.*
> *Did you have a good journey?*
> ~~Did you have a good travel?~~
> A **trip** is a journey in which you visit a place for a short time and come back again.
> *a business trip*
> *a three-day trip to Spain*

traveler) ⓐ someone who is travelling or who often travels: *We're doing a survey of business travellers.* **2** UK another word for gypsy (= a member of a race of people who travel from place to place, especially in Europe)

traveller's cheque UK (US **traveler's check**) noun [C] a special piece of paper that you buy at a bank and exchange for local money when you are in another country

traverse /trə'vɜːs/ verb [T] formal to move across something

travesty /'trævəsti/ noun [C] formal If something is a travesty, it is very badly done or unfair and does not represent how that thing should be: *She described the trial as **a travesty of justice**.*

trawl /trɔːl/ verb

PHRASAL VERB **trawl through sth** mainly UK to look through a lot of things in order to find something: *to trawl through data*

trawler /'trɔːlər/ noun [C] a large ship that is used for catching fish by pulling a large net through the sea behind it

tray /treɪ/ noun [C] ⓐ a flat object with higher edges, used for carrying food and drinks: *She came back carrying a tray of drinks.*

treacherous /'tretʃərəs/ adj **1** very dangerous, especially because of bad weather conditions: *Ice had made the roads treacherous.* **2** formal If someone is treacherous, they deceive people who trust them.

treachery /'tretʃəri/ noun [U] formal behaviour in which a person deceives someone who trusts them

treacle /'triːkl/ noun [U] UK (UK/US **molasses**) a sweet, thick, dark liquid used in sweet dishes

tread¹ /tred/ verb (**trod**, **trodden**) **1** [I, T] mainly UK to put your foot on something or to press something down with your foot: *I trod on a piece of broken glass.* ∘ *David trod in some paint.* ∘ *The kids were treading cake crumbs into the carpet.* **2 tread carefully/gently/lightly, etc** to be careful what you say so that you do not upset someone **3 tread water** to float vertically in the water by moving your arms and legs up and down

tread² /tred/ noun **1** [C, U] the pattern of lines on the surface of a tyre **2** [no plural] the sound of someone putting their feet down when walking

treadmill /'tredmɪl/ noun [C] **1** a machine with moving part that you walk or run on for exercis **2** a job that is boring because you have to repea the same thing again and again

treason /'triːzən/ noun [U] the crime of doin something that harms your country or govern ment, especially by helping its enemies

treasure¹ /'treʒər/ noun **1** [U] ⓐ a collection o gold, silver, jewellery, and valuable object especially in children's stories: *buried treasur* **2** [C] a very valuable object: [usually plural] *ar treasures*

treasure² /'treʒər/ verb [T] If you treasur something, it is very important to you an gives you a lot of pleasure: *I shall treasure thos memories of her.*

treasurer /'treʒərər/ noun [C] someone who i responsible for the money of an organization

treasury /'treʒəri/ noun [C] the governmen department that controls a country's mone supply and economy

treat¹ /triːt/ verb [T] **1 DEAL WITH** ▷ ⓑ to behav towards or deal with someone in a particula way: *He treats her really badly.* ∘ *She felt she' been unfairly treated by her employer.* ∘ *The treat her like one of their own children* **2 CONSIDER** ▷ ⓑ to consider something in a particular way: *He treated my suggestion as a joke.* **3 ILLNESS/INJURY** ▷ ⓑ to give medical car to someone for an illness or injury: *He's being treated for cancer at a hospital in California* **4 SPECIAL** ▷ ⓑ to do or buy something specia for someone: *I'm going to treat her to dinner a that nice Italian restaurant.* **5 PROTECT** ▷ to put substance on something in order to protect it The wood is then treated with a special chemica to protect it from the rain.

treat² /triːt/ noun [C] something special that yo buy or do for someone else: *a birthday trea* ∘ *As a special treat I'm taking him out for dinne* ∘ *Annie, put your money away, this is my trea (= I am paying).* → See also **Trick or treat!**

treatise /'triːtɪz/ noun [C] a formal piece o writing that examines a particular subject

treatment /'triːtmənt/ noun **1** [C, U] ⓑ some thing that you do to try to cure an illness o injury, especially something suggested or don by a doctor: *She's receiving treatment for a lun infection.* **2** [U] ⓑ the way you deal with o behave towards someone or something: *Ther have been complaints about the treatment o prisoners.*

> ✓ **Word partners for treatment**
>
> get/have/receive/undergo treatment • give/ provide treatment • respond to treatment • treatment for sth

treaty /'triːti/ noun [C] a written agreemen between two or more countries: *a peace treat* ∘ *an international treaty*

> ✓ **Word partners for treaty**
>
> draw up/ratify/sign a treaty • the terms of a treaty • under a treaty • a treaty between sb and sb • a treaty on sth • a peace treaty • an international treaty

reble /'trebl/ **verb** [I, T] to increase three times in size or amount, or to make something do this

tree

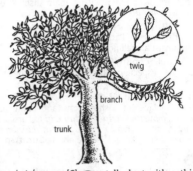

twig

branch

trunk

tree /triː/ **noun** [C] ⓐ a tall plant with a thick stem that has branches coming from it and leaves → See also **Christmas tree, family tree, palm tree**

trek /trek/ **noun** [C] a long, difficult journey that you make by walking: *They started out on the long trek across the mountains.* • **trek verb** [I] (**trekking, trekked**)

trellis /'trelɪs/ **noun** [C] a wooden structure fixed to a wall for plants to grow up

tremble /'trembl/ **verb** [I] ⓑ to shake slightly, especially because you are nervous, frightened, or cold: *My hands were trembling so much I could hardly hold the pen.*

tremendous /trɪ'mendəs/ **adj 1** ⓑ extremely good: *I think she's doing a tremendous job.* **2** ⓑ very large, great, strong, etc: *a tremendous amount of money* • **tremendously adv** ⓑ very much

tremor /'tremər/ **noun 1** a slight earthquake (= when the Earth shakes) **2** a slight shaking of part of your body that you cannot control

trench /trenʃ/ **noun** [C] a long, narrow hole dug into the ground

trenchant /'trenʃənt/ **adj** formal expressing strong criticism: *trenchant criticism/views*

trenchcoat /'trentʃkəʊt/ **noun** [C] a long coat that does not let water through, similar in style to a military coat

trend /trend/ **noun** [C] ⓑ a general development or change in a situation: *There's a trend towards more locally produced television programmes.* ○ *I'm not familiar with the latest trends in teaching methodology.*

trendy /'trendi/ **adj** informal fashionable at the moment

trepidation /ˌtrepɪ'deɪʃən/ **noun** [U] formal fear or worry about something you are going to do: *It was with trepidation that I accepted Klein's invitation.*

trespass /'trespəs/ **verb** [I] to go on someone's land without their permission • **trespasser noun** [C]

tri- /traɪ-/ **prefix** three: *a triangle* ○ *a tripod*

trial /traɪəl/ **noun** [C, U] **1** ⓑ a legal process to decide if someone is guilty of a crime: *The two*

men are now **on trial for** attempted murder. ○ *He will be taken to the US to **stand trial**.* **2** a test of something new to find out if it is safe, works correctly, etc: *The drug is currently undergoing **clinical trials**.* **3 trial and error** a way of learning the best way to do something by trying different methods: *There aren't any instructions with it – it's just a matter of trial and error.*

> ❷ Word partners for **trial**
>
> be on/stand trial (for sth) • be awaiting/be facing trial • a trial court/date/judge

trials /traɪəlz/ **noun** [plural] a sports competition to find out how good a player is

IDIOM **trials and tribulations** problems and suffering: *the trials and tribulations of growing up*

triangle /'traɪæŋgl/ **noun** [C] **1** ⓑ a flat shape with three sides → See picture at **shape 2** a small musical instrument made of a piece of metal with three sides which you hit with a metal bar • **triangular** /traɪ'æŋgjələr/ **adj** shaped like a triangle

tribe /traɪb/ **noun** [C] ⓑ a group of people who live together, usually in areas far away from cities, and who share the same culture and language and still have a traditional way of life: *Native American tribes* • **tribal adj** relating to a tribe: *a tribal dance*

tribulations /ˌtrɪbjə'leɪʃənz/ **noun** [plural] see **trials and tribulations**

tribunal /traɪ'bjuːnəl/ **noun** [C] an official court or group of people whose job is to deal with a particular problem or disagreement → See also **industrial tribunal**

tributary /'trɪbjətri/ **noun** [C] a river or stream that flows into a larger river

tribute /'trɪbjuːt/ **noun** [C, U] **1** something that you do or say to show that you respect and admire someone, especially in a formal situation: *The concert was organized as **a tribute to** the singer who died last year.* ○ *The President **paid tribute to** (= expressed his admiration for) the brave soldiers who had defended the country.* **2 be a tribute to sb/sth** to show how good someone or something is: *It's a tribute to Mark's hard work that the project is finished.*

tribute band noun [C] a group of musicians who play the music of a famous pop group and pretend to be that group: *a Rolling Stones tribute band*

trick¹ /trɪk/ **noun** [C] **1 DECEIVE** ▷ ⓑ something you do to deceive or cheat someone, or to make someone look stupid as a joke: *a **trick question*** ○ *I wasn't really ill – it was just a trick.* ○ *My little brother liked to **play tricks on** me* (= do things to deceive me as a joke). **2 METHOD** ▷ ⓑ an effective way of doing something: *What's the **trick to** pulling out this sofa bed?* **3 MAGIC** ▷ ⓑ something that is done to entertain people and that seems to be magic: *a card trick*

IDIOM **do the trick** If something does the trick, it solves a problem or has the result you want: *If*

T

I've got a headache, a couple of aspirins usually do the trick.

→ See also **hat trick**

> 🔲 Word partners for **trick**
>
> **play** a trick (on sb) • a cheap/cruel/dirty/sneaky trick • a trick **question**

trick² /trɪk/ **verb** [T] ⑫ to deceive someone: [+ into + doing sth] *They tricked him into signing the papers.*

trickery /ˈtrɪkˀri/ **noun** [U] the use of tricks to deceive or cheat people

trickle /ˈtrɪkl/ **verb 1 trickle down/from/out of, etc** If liquid trickles somewhere, it flows slowly and in a thin line: *She could feel the sweat trickling down her back.* **2 trickle in/into/out, etc** to go somewhere slowly in small numbers: *People began to trickle into the classroom.* • **trickle noun** [C] *a trickle of blood*

,**Trick or 'treat! 1** something that children say on Halloween (= a holiday on 31 October), when they dress to look frightening and visit people's houses to ask for sweets **2 go trick or treating** If children go trick or treating, they visit people's houses on Halloween to ask for sweets.

tricky /ˈtrɪki/ **adj** ⑫ difficult to deal with or do: *a tricky question/situation*

tricycle /ˈtraɪsɪkl/ **noun** [C] a bicycle with one wheel at the front and two at the back

trifle /ˈtraɪfl/ **noun 1 a trifle** formal slightly: *It does seem a trifle odd.* **2** [C, U] UK a cold, sweet dish that has layers of cake, fruit, custard (= sweet, yellow sauce), and cream **3** [C] formal something silly or unimportant

trigger¹ /ˈtrɪgər/ **verb** [T] (also **trigger off**) to make something begin to happen: *His arrest triggered mass protests.*

trigger² /ˈtrɪgər/ **noun** [C] **1** the part of a gun that you pull when you shoot **2** an event or situation that makes something else happen: *Stress can be a **trigger for** many illnesses.*

trillion /ˈtrɪljən/ the number 1,000,000,000,000

trilogy /ˈtrɪlədʒi/ **noun** [C] a series of three books, plays, etc with the same characters or subject

trim¹ /trɪm/ **verb** [T] (**trimming, trimmed**) **1** (also **trim off**) to cut a small amount from something to make it tidy or to remove parts that you do not need: *I've had my hair trimmed.* ○ *Trim the fat off the meat.* **2** to reduce something: *to trim costs* **3 be trimmed with sth** to be decorated with something around the edges: *a silk dress trimmed with lace*

trim² /trɪm/ **noun 1** [no plural] If something has a trim, it is cut so that it looks tidy: *The hedge needs a trim.* **2** [U, no plural] decoration that is added to something such as clothes or a car: *The car has a CD player, sunroof, and leather trim.*

trim³ /trɪm/ **adj** looking thin and healthy

trimester /trɪˈmestər/ ⑩ /traɪˈmestər/ **noun** [C] mainly US one of the periods of time that the year is divided into in some US schools and colleges

trimming /ˈtrɪmɪŋ/ **noun** [C, U] decoration on the edge of something such as a piece of clothing

trimmings /ˈtrɪmɪŋz/ **noun** [plural] extra dishe that are often eaten with a main dish: *a roas dinner with all the trimmings*

the Trinity /ˈtrɪnəti/ **noun** the existence of Go in three forms, Father, Son, and Holy Spirit, i the Christian religion

trio /ˈtriːəʊ/ **noun** [C] a group of three things o people, especially three musicians who pla together

trip¹ /trɪp/ **noun** [C] ⑫ a journey in which yo visit a place for a short time and come bac again: *a **business trip** to Paris* ○ *W might **take a trip to** Spain later in the summe* → See Note at **travel²** → See also **round trip**

> 🔲 Word partners for **trip**
>
> **go on/take** a trip • a day/two-day/weekend trip • **on** a trip • a trip **around/to** sth • a **business** trip

trip² /trɪp/ **verb** (**tripping, tripped**) **1** [I] ⑫ to fa or fall because you hit your foot o something when you are walking or runnin *Careful you don't **trip over** the cat!* ○ *He **trippe on** a stone and hurt his ankle.* **2** [T] to mak someone fall by putting your foot in front c their foot

PHRASAL VERB **trip (sb) up 1** UK to fall because yo hit your foot on something, or to make someon fall by putting your foot in front of their foo **2** to make a mistake, or to make someone mak a mistake: *I tripped up on the last question.*

triple¹ /ˈtrɪpl/ **adj** having three parts of the sam type, or happening three times: *a triple worl champion*

triple² /ˈtrɪpl/ **verb** [I, T] to increase three time in size or amount, or to make something do thi *Sales have tripled in the past five years.*

triplet /ˈtrɪplət/ **noun** [C] one of three childre who are born to the same mother at the sam time

tripod /ˈtraɪpɒd/ **noun** [C] a piece of equipmen with three legs, used for supporting a camera o a container in a science laboratory

trite /traɪt/ **adj** A trite remark, idea, etc does no seem sincere or true because it has been used s much before or is too simple.

triumph¹ /ˈtraɪəmf/ **noun 1** [C] an importan success, achievement, or victory: *Barcelona's 2-triumph over Manchester United* **2** [U] the feelin of happiness that you have when you wi something or succeed

triumph² /ˈtraɪəmf/ **verb** [I] to win or succeed *The Democrats once again triumphed in recen elections.*

triumphant /traɪˈʌmfənt/ **adj** feeling ver pleased because you have won something o succeeded: *the President's triumphant return t the White House* • **triumphantly adv**

trivia /ˈtrɪviə/ **noun** [U] small facts or details tha are not important

rivial /'trɪviəl/ **adj** ⓫ small and not important: *a trivial matter/offence*

rivialize (also UK **-ise**) /'trɪviəlaɪz/ **verb** [T] to make something seem less important or serious than it really is: *I don't mean to trivialize the problem.*

rod /trɒd/ past tense of tread

rodden /'trɒdᵊn/ past participle of tread

rolley

supermarket trolley *UK*, shopping cart *US*

luggage trolley *UK*, luggage cart *US*

rolley /'trɒli/ **noun** [C] **1** UK (US **cart**) ⓬ a metal structure on wheels that is used for carrying things: *a supermarket trolley* ∘ *a luggage trolley* **2** US (mainly UK **tram**, also US **streetcar**) an electric vehicle for carrying passengers, mostly in cities, which runs along metal tracks in the road

IDIOM **off your trolley** informal UK mad

rombone /trɒm'bəʊn/ **noun** [C] a metal musical instrument that you play by blowing into it and sliding a tube up and down

roop¹ /truːp/ **noun** [C] a group of people or animals

roop² /truːp/ **verb** informal **troop into/through/out of, etc** to walk somewhere in a large group: *We all trooped into the hall in silence.*

rooper /'truːpər/ **noun** [C] a police officer in the US state police force

roops /truːps/ **noun** [plural] soldiers: *UN troops have been sent to help in the rescue effort.*

rophy /'trəʊfi/ **noun** [C] ⓬ a prize, such as a silver cup, that you get for winning a race or competition

trophy

ropical /'trɒpɪkᵊl/ **adj** ⓬ from or in the hottest parts of the world: *a tropical climate*

he tropics /'trɒpɪks/ **noun** [plural] the hottest parts of the world, near to the Equator (= imaginary line around the Earth's middle)

rot¹ /trɒt/ **verb** (**trotting, trotted**) **1** [I] If a horse trots, it runs slowly with short steps. **2 trot down/up/along, etc** to walk with quick, short steps: *The little boy trotted along behind his father.*

PHRASAL VERB **trot sth out** informal to say something that has been said many times before and does not seem sincere: *They always trot out the same old statistics.*

trot² /trɒt/ **noun 1** [no plural] the speed that a horse moves when it trots **2 on the trot** If you do several things on the trot, you do them one after the other: *They won three games on the trot.*

trouble¹ /'trʌbl/ **noun 1 PROBLEMS** ▷ [C, U] ⓫ problems, difficulties, or worries: [+ doing sth] *We had trouble finding somewhere to park.* ∘ *She's been having a lot of trouble with her boss recently.* ∘ *I'd like to go to the party, but the trouble is my parents won't let me.* **2 the trouble with sb/sth** ⓬ used to say what is wrong with someone or something: *The trouble with a white floor is that it gets dirty so quickly.* **3 NOT WORKING** ▷ [U] a problem that you have with a machine or part of your body: *back trouble* ∘ *car trouble* **4 FIGHTING** ▷ [U] ⓬ a situation in which people are fighting or arguing: *The trouble started after a group of drunken football fans started to throw bottles.* **5 DIFFICULT SITUATION** ▷ [U] ⓬ a difficult or dangerous situation: *The company was in trouble and had huge debts.* **6 PUNISHMENT** ▷ [U] ⓫ a situation in which you have done something wrong and are likely to be punished: *Her children are always in trouble.* ∘ *They got into trouble with the police.* **7 EXTRA WORK** ▷ [U] ⓬ a situation in which you use extra time or energy to do something: [+ to do sth] *He took the trouble to write to each of them personally.*

> ⚠ Common learner error: **trouble** or **problem**?
>
> **Problem** means 'a situation that causes difficulties and that needs to be dealt with'. You can talk about **a problem** or **problems**.
> *Tell me what the problem is.*
> *There's a problem with the engine.*
> *He's having a few problems at work.*
> **Trouble** means 'problems, difficulties, or worries' and is used to talk about problems in a more general way. **Trouble** is almost always uncountable so do not use **a** before it.
> *We had some trouble while we were on holiday.*
> *He helped me when I was in trouble.*
> *I had trouble with the car last night.*
> ~~I had a trouble with the car last night.~~

> ▣ Word partners for **trouble**
>
> have trouble with sth • get into/run into trouble • the trouble is • without any trouble

trouble² /'trʌbl/ **verb** [T] **1** If something troubles you, you think about it a lot and it makes you worry: *The situation has been troubling me for a while.* **2** formal used to ask someone politely to help you: *I'm sorry to trouble you, but could you tell me how to get to the station?*

troubled /'trʌbᵊld/ **adj** worried or having a lot of problems: *You look troubled.*

troublemaker /'trʌbl,meɪkər/ **noun** [C] someone who intentionally causes problems

T

troublesome /'trʌblsəm/ **adj** causing a lot of problems, especially over a long period of time: *a troublesome knee injury*

trough /trɒf/ **noun** [C] **1** a long, narrow container that animals eat or drink from **2** formal a low point in a series of high and low points: *peaks and troughs*

troupe /tru:p/ **noun** [C] a group of singers, dancers, etc who perform together

trouser /'trauzər/ **verb** [T] informal to get a large amount of money, especially in an unfair or illegal way: *She did all the work, yet her husband trousered the profits.*

trousers /'trauzəz/ **noun** [plural] (also US **pants**) ⓐ a piece of clothing that covers the legs and has a separate part for each leg: *a pair of trousers* → See colour picture **Clothes** on page Centre 8, 9

'trouser ,suit noun [C] UK (US **pant suit**) a woman's jacket and trousers made of the same material

trout /traut/ **noun** [C, U] (plural **trout**) a type of river fish, or the meat from this fish

truant /'tru:ənt/ **noun** [C] a child who stays away from school without permission

IDIOM **play truant** UK to stay away from school without permission

• **truancy** /'tru:ənsi/ **noun** [U] the problem of children playing truant

truce /tru:s/ **noun** [C] an agreement between two enemies to stop fighting for a period of time

> ☑ Word partners for **truce**
>
> agree/call/offer a truce • a fragile/uneasy truce • a truce **between** sb and sb • a truce **with** sb

truck /trʌk/ **noun** [C] (also UK **lorry**) ⓑ a large road vehicle for carrying goods from place to place → See picture at **vehicle**

trucker /'trʌkər/ **noun** [C] mainly US someone whose job is driving trucks

trudge /trʌdʒ/ **verb trudge along/through/up, etc** to walk slowly with heavy steps, especially because you are tired: *We trudged back up the hill.*

true /tru:/ **adj 1** ⓐ based on facts and not imagined: *a true story* ○ [+ (that)] *Is it true that Martin and Sue are getting married?* → Opposite **untrue** → See Note at **right¹ 2** [always before noun] ⓑ real: *a true friend* ○ *true love* **3 come true** ⓑ If a dream or hope comes true, it really happens. **4 be true to sb/sth** to be loyal and sincere even in a difficult situation: *It's important to be true to your principles.*

IDIOM **ring true** to seem to be the truth: *Something about the story didn't ring true.*

truffle /'trʌfl/ **noun** [C] **1** a soft sweet that is made with chocolate **2** a fungus (= organism like a plant) that you can eat, which grows under the ground

truly /'tru:li/ **adv 1 NOT FALSE** ▷ used to emphasize that something is true in every way: *The project was truly a team effort.* **2 VERY** ▷ used to emphasize a description of somethin It's truly amazing to watch a baby being bor **3 SINCERE** ▷ used to emphasize that somethir is sincere or honest: *I truly believe that he innocent.*

trump /trʌmp/ **noun** [C] a card that has a high value than other cards in some card games

IDIOM **come/turn up trumps** UK to be successfu or provide something that is needed, especial when people do not expect you to: *He's real come up trumps with this latest book.*

'trump ,card noun [C] an advantage that w help you succeed, especially one that oth people do not know about

trumpet /'trʌmpɪt/ **noun** [C] ⓑ a metal musical instrument that you play by blowing into it and pressing buttons to make different notes • **trumpeter noun** [C]

trumpet

truncheon /'trʌnʃən/ **noun** [C] UK (US **night-stick**) a short stick that police officers carry to use as a weapon

truncheon

trundle /'trʌndl/ **verb trundle (sth) along/ down/up, etc** to move slowly on wheels, or to push something slow on wheels: *The bus trundled along the lane.*

trunk /trʌŋk/ **noun** [C] **1 TREE** ▷ ⓑ the thic stem of a tree that the branches grow from → S picture at **tree 2 CAR** ▷ US (UK **boot**) a close space at the back of a car for storing things → See colour picture **Car** on page Centre 7 **3 NOSE** the long nose of an elephant (= large, gr animal) **4 CONTAINER** ▷ a large box with a li that you store things in **5 BODY** ▷ the main pa of your body, not your head, legs, or arms

'trunk ,road noun [C] UK a main road across country or area

trunks /trʌŋks/ **noun** [plural] **1** (also **swimmin trunks**) a piece of clothing that boys and me wear when they swim **2** underwear worn by me → See colour picture **Clothes** on page Centre 9

trust¹ /trʌst/ **verb 1** ⓑ [T] to believe th someone is good and honest and will n harm you: *My sister warned me not to trust hir* → Opposite **distrust, mistrust 2 trust sb to d sth** to be sure that someone will do the rig thing or what they should do: *I trust them make the right decision.* **3 trust sb with sb/sth** allow someone to look after someone or som thing because you believe they will be careful: *wouldn't trust him with my car.* **4 Trust sb (to d sth)!** mainly UK informal used to say that it typical of someone to do something stupid: *Tru Chris to leave the tickets at home!* **5 I trust (tha** formal used to say that you hope something true: *I trust that you had an enjoyable stay.*

trust² /trʌst/ **noun 1** [U] ⓑ the belief that yo can trust someone or something: *a marriag*

based on love and trust ○ They **showed** a lot of **trust** in me right from the beginning. → Opposite **distrust, mistrust 2** [C, U] a legal arrangement that allows a person or organization to control someone else's money

☑ Word partners for **trust** noun

have/show trust in sb • earn/gain/win sb's trust • betray sb's trust • trust between [two people]

trustee /trʌsˈtiː/ noun [C] someone who has legal control over someone else's money or possessions

trusting /ˈtrʌstɪŋ/ adj always believing that other people are good or honest and will not harm or deceive you

trustworthy /ˈtrʌstˌwɜːði/ adj Someone who is trustworthy can be trusted.

truth /truːθ/ noun (plural **truths** /truːðz/) **1 the truth** ⓑ the real facts about a situation: Do you think he was **telling the truth**? ○ I don't think we'll ever know **the truth about** what really happened. **2** [U] ⓑ the quality of being true: There may be some truth in their claim. **3** [C] a fact or idea that people accept is true: moral/religious truths → Opposite **untruth**

☑ Word partners for **truth**

tell the truth • discover/find out/learn/uncover the truth • the truth comes out/emerges • the awful/honest/simple truth • the truth about sb/sth

truthful /ˈtruːθfᵊl/ adj honest and not containing or telling any lies: a truthful answer • **truthfully** adv • **truthfulness** noun [U]

try¹ /traɪ/ verb **1** ATTEMPT ▷ [I] ⓐ to attempt to do something: [+ to do sth] I tried to open the window but couldn't. ○ Try not to drop anything this time. **2** TEST ▷ [T] ⓑ to do, test, taste, etc something to discover if it works or if you like it: I tried that recipe you gave me last night. ○ [+ doing sth] Why don't you try using a different shampoo? **3** LAW ▷ [T] to examine facts in a court of law to decide if someone is guilty of a crime: [often passive] He was **tried for** attempted murder.

PHRASAL VERBS **try sth on** ⓐ to put on a piece of clothing to discover if it fits you or if you like it: Could I try this dress on, please? • **try sth out** ⓑ to use something to discover if it works or if you like it: We're going to try out that new restaurant tonight.

try² /traɪ/ noun **1** [C] ⓑ an attempt to do something: She suggested I should **have a try**. **2 give sth a try** to do something in order to find out if it works or if you like it **3** [C] a way of scoring points in rugby (= game played with an oval ball) by putting the ball on the ground behind the other team's goal line

trying /ˈtraɪɪŋ/ adj annoying and difficult: I've had a very **trying day/time**.

tsar (also **czar**) /zaːr/ noun [C] **1** a male Russian ruler before 1917 **2** a powerful official who makes decisions for the government about a particular activity

T-shirt (also **tee shirt**) /ˈtiːʃɜːt/ noun [C] ⓐ a piece of cotton clothing for the top part of the body with short sleeves and no collar → See colour picture **Clothes** on page Centre 8

tsp written abbreviation for teaspoonful: the amount that can be held by a small spoon used for measuring food

tub /tʌb/ noun [C] **1** LARGE CONTAINER ▷ a large, round container with a flat base and an open top: Outside was a stone patio with tubs of flowering plants. **2** FOOD CONTAINER ▷ a small, plastic container with a lid, used for storing food: a tub of ice cream/margarine → See picture at **container 3** BATH ▷ US (UK **bath**) a large container that you fill with water and sit in to wash → See colour picture **The Bathroom** on page Centre 3

tuba /ˈtjuːbə/ noun [C] a large, metal musical instrument that produces low notes, and is played by blowing into it

tube /tjuːb/ noun **1** [C] ⓑ a pipe made of glass, plastic, metal, etc, especially for liquids or gases to flow through **2** [C] ⓑ a long, thin container for a soft substance, that you press to get the substance out: a tube of toothpaste → See picture at **container 3 the Tube** ⓑ the system of railways under the ground in London: I got the Tube to Oxford Circus. → See also **test tube**

tuberculosis /tjuːˌbɜːkjəˈləʊsɪs/ noun [U] (abbreviation **TB**) a serious infectious disease of the lungs

tubing /ˈtjuːbɪŋ/ noun [U] a long piece of metal, plastic, etc in the shape of a tube: steel tubing

tubular /ˈtjuːbjələr/ adj in the shape of a tube

tuck /tʌk/ verb **1 tuck sth into/behind/under, etc** to push a loose piece of clothing or material somewhere to make it tidy: Tuck your shirt in. **2 tuck sth behind/under/in, etc** to put something in a small place so that it is safe and cannot move: I found an old letter tucked in the back of the book.

PHRASAL VERBS **tuck sth away** to put something in a safe place: Helen tucked the money away in her purse. • **be tucked away** to be in a place that is hidden, or in a place that few people go to: He lives in a cottage tucked away in the countryside. • **tuck in/tuck into sth** UK informal to start eating something, especially with enthusiasm: I was just about to tuck into a huge bowl of pasta. • **tuck sb in/up** to make someone, especially a child, comfortable in bed by putting the covers around them

Tuesday /ˈtjuːzdeɪ/ noun [C, U] (written abbreviation **Tue, Tues**) ⓐ the day of the week after Monday and before Wednesday

tuft /tʌft/ noun [C] a small group of hairs, grass, etc

tug¹ /tʌg/ verb [T] (**tugging, tugged**) to pull something suddenly and strongly: Tom **tugged** at his mother's arm.

tug² /tʌg/ noun [C] **1** a sudden, strong pull on something **2** (also **tugboat** /ˈtʌgbəʊt/) a boat used for pulling larger ships

tuition /tjuˈɪʃᵊn/ noun [U] **1** the teaching of one person or of a small group of people: French

T

tuition **2** mainly US money that you pay for being taught, especially at college or university

> ☑ Word partners for **tuition**
>
> get/be given/offer/receive tuition • expert tuition • individual/one-to-one/private tuition • tuition in sth

tulip /'tjuːlɪp/ *noun* [C] a brightly coloured spring flower in the shape of a cup

tumble /'tʌmbl/ *verb* [I] **1** to suddenly fall: *He tumbled down the stairs.* **2** If the price or value of something tumbles, it suddenly becomes lower: *Share prices tumbled by 20%.* • **tumble** *noun* [C]

tumble dryer *noun* [C] UK (UK/US **dryer**) a machine that dries clothes

tumbler /'tʌmblər/ *noun* [C] a glass that you drink out of, that has straight sides and no handle

tummy /'tʌmi/ *noun* [C] informal stomach

tumour UK (US **tumor**) /'tjuːmər/ *noun* [C] a group of cells in someone's body that are not growing normally

tumultuous /tjuː'mʌltjuəs/ *adj* full of noise and excitement: *tumultuous applause* ∘ *a tumultuous reception/welcome*

tuna /'tjuːnə/ *noun* [C, U] (plural **tuna**) 🔵 a large sea fish, or the meat from this fish

tune¹ /tjuːn/ *noun* **1** 🔵 [C] a series of musical notes that are pleasant to listen to: *He was humming a tune as he dried the dishes.* **2 in tune** singing or playing the right notes **3 out of tune** singing or playing the wrong notes: *The piano is out of tune.*

IDIOMS **change your tune** to suddenly change your opinion about something • **be in tune with sb** to be able to understand what someone wants or needs: *The government is not in tune with the voters.*

> ☑ Word partners for **tune**
>
> hum/play/sing/whistle a tune • a catchy tune

tune² /tjuːn/ *verb* [T] **1** to make slight changes to a musical instrument so that it plays the right notes **2** to make changes to a television or radio so that it receives programmes from a particular company: *Stay tuned for* (= continue watching or listening for) *more details.* ∘ *The radio is tuned to Radio 5.*

PHRASAL VERBS **tune in** to watch or listen to a particular television or radio programme: *Be sure to tune in to next week's show.* • **tune (sth) up** to make slight changes to a musical instrument before you play it so that it produces the right notes: *The orchestra were tuning up.*

tunic /'tjuːnɪk/ *noun* [C] a loose piece of clothing that covers the top part of your body

tunnel¹ /'tʌnəl/ *noun* [C] 🔵 a long passage under the ground or through a mountain: *The train went into the tunnel.* → See also **light**¹ at the end of the tunnel

tunnel² /'tʌnəl/ *verb* [I, T] (mainly UK **tunnelling**, **tunnelled**, US **tunneling**, **tunneled**) to dig a tunnel

tunnel

turban /'tɜːbən/ *noun* [C] a long piece of cloth that men from some religions fold around their heads

turbine /'tɜːbaɪn/ *noun* [C] a large machine that produces power by using gas, steam, etc to turn a wheel

turbulent /'tɜːbjələnt/ *adj* **1** A turbulent situation, time, etc is one in which there are a lot of sudden changes, arguments, or violence: *a turbulent relationship* **2** Turbulent air or water moves very strongly and suddenly. • **turbulence** /'tɜːbjələns/ *noun* [U]

turf¹ /tɜːf/ *noun* [U] short, thick grass and the soil it is growing in

turf² /tɜːf/ *verb*

PHRASAL VERB **turf sb out** UK informal to make someone leave

turkey /'tɜːki/ *noun* [C, U] 🔵 a bird that looks like a large chicken, or the meat of this bird

turmoil /'tɜːmɔɪl/ *noun* [U, no plural] a situation in which there is a lot of trouble, confusion, or noise: *The whole region is in turmoil.*

> ☑ Word partners for **turmoil**
>
> be in/be thrown into turmoil • a state of turmoil • emotional/political turmoil • the turmoil of (doing) sth

turn¹ /tɜːn/ *verb* **1** MOVE YOUR BODY ▷ [I] 🔵 to move your body so that you are facing a different direction: *Ricky turned and saw Sue standing in the doorway.* **2** CHANGE DIRECTION ▷ [I, T] 🔵 to change direction when you are moving, or to make a car do this: *Turn left at the traffic lights.* **3** CHANGE POSITION ▷ [T] to move something round so that it faces a different direction: *Ella turned the cup to hide the crack in it.* **4** GO ROUND ▷ [I, T] 🔵 to move around a central point in a circle, or to make something do this: *Turn the steering wheel as quickly as you can.* **5 turn blue/cold/sour, etc** 🔵 to become blue, cold, etc: *The sky turned black and it started to rain.* **6 turn 16/21, etc** to become a particular age: *He turned 18 last May.* **7 turn a page** 🔵 to move a page in a book or magazine in order to see the next one → See also **turn your back**² on sb/sth, turn/put the **clock**¹ back, turn a blind **eye**¹ (to sth), turn over a new **leaf**¹, turn your **nose**¹ up at sth, turn the tables (**table**¹) on sb, come/turn up **trumps**, turn sth **upside down**¹

PHRASAL VERBS **turn sb away** to not allow someone to enter a place: *By 10 o'clock the club was already full and they were turning people away.* • **turn (sb) back** 🔵 to return in the direction you have come from, or to make someone do this: *They had to turn back because of the bad weather.* • **turn sb/sth down** 🔵 to refuse an offer or request: *They did offer me the job, but I turned it down.* • **turn sth down** 🔵 to reduce the level of sound or heat that a machine produces: *Could you turn the radio down, please?* • **turn (sb/sth) into sb/sth** 🔵 to change and become someone or something different, or to make someone or something do this: *There are plans to turn his latest book into a film.* • **turn off (sth)** to leave the road you are driving along and drive on a different road • **turn sth off** 🔵 to move the switch on a machine, light, etc so that it stops working, or to stop the supply of water, electricity, etc: *How do you turn the computer off?* → See colour picture **Phrasal Verbs** on page Centre 16 • **turn sth on** 🔵 to move the switch on a machine, light, etc so that it starts working, or to start the supply of water, electricity, etc: *Ben turned the TV on.* → See colour picture **Phrasal Verbs** on page Centre 16 • **turn out 1** 🔵 to happen in a particular way, or to have a particular result: *The bomb warning turned out to be a false alarm.* ◦ [+ (that)] *I got talking to her and it turned out that we'd been to the same school.* **2** 🔵 If people turn out for an event, they go to be there or watch: *Over 800 people turned out for the protest.* • **turn sth out 1** to produce something: *The factory turns out more than 600 vehicles a month.* **2** to move the switch on a light so that it stops working • **turn (sth) over** UK to change to a different television station: *Are you watching this or can I turn over?* • **turn to sb** 🔵 to ask someone for help or advice: *Eventually she turned to her aunt for help.* • **turn to sth 1** to find a page in a book: *Turn to page 105.* **2** to start to do something bad, especially because you are unhappy: *She turned to drugs after the break-up of her marriage.* • **turn up 1** informal 🔵 to arrive: *Fred turned up late again.* **2** If something that you have been looking for turns up, you find it. • **turn sth up** 🔵 to increase the level of sound or heat that a machine produces: *I'm cold, could you turn the heating up please?*

turn² /tɜːn/ *noun* **1** TIME ▷ [C] 🔵 the time when you can or must do something, usually before or after someone else: [+ to do sth] *It's your turn to feed the rabbit – I did it yesterday.* ◦ *You'll have to be patient and wait your turn.* **2** **take turns** (also UK **take it in turns**) 🔵 If two or more people take turns, one person does something, then another person does something, etc.: [+ doing sth] *They all took turns carrying the suitcase.* ◦ [+ to do sth] *The children took it in turns to hold the baby.* **3** **in turn** one after another: *He spoke to the three boys in turn.* **4** CHANGE DIRECTION ▷ [C] 🔵 a change in the direction in which you are moving or facing: *a right/left turn* **5** BEND ▷ [C] a bend and corner in a road, river, etc: *Take the next turn on the right.* **6** **turn of events** the way in which a situation develops, especially a sudden or unexpected change **7** **take a turn for the better/worse** to become better or worse suddenly **8** **do sb a good turn** to do something to help someone **9** **the turn of the century** the start of a new century → See also **U-turn**

turnaround /'tɜːnəraʊnd/ *noun* [C] a change from a bad situation to a good one

turning /'tɜːnɪŋ/ *noun* [C] UK 🔵 a corner where

one road meets another: *Take the second turning on the left.*

turning point *noun* [C] a time when an important change begins to happen: *This event marked a turning point in the country's history.*

🔲 Word partners for **turning point**

mark/prove/reach a turning point • the turning point came • be at a turning point • the turning point in/of sth • the turning point for sb • a crucial/important/major/real turning point

---

turnip /'tɜːnɪp/ *noun* [C, U] a large, round, pale yellow vegetable that grows under the ground

turn-off /'tɜːnɒf/ *noun* **1** [C] a place where you can leave a main road to go onto another road **2** [no plural] informal something that you dislike or that makes you feel less interested, especially sexually: *Greasy hair is a real turn-off.*

turnout /'tɜːnaʊt/ *noun* [C] the number of people at an event, such as a meeting or election: [usually singular] *They blamed the low turnout on the bad weather.*

turnover /'tɜːnˌəʊvər/ *noun* **1** [no plural] how much money a business earns in a period of time **2** [U, no plural] the rate at which workers leave an organization and new workers join it: *a high turnover of staff*

turnpike /'tɜːnpaɪk/ *noun* [C] US a main road intended for fast travel, which you usually have to pay to use

turn signal *noun* [C] US (UK **indicator**) a light that flashes on a vehicle to show that the driver intends to turn right or left → See colour picture **Car** on page Centre 7

turnstile /'tɜːnstaɪl/ *noun* [C] a gate that only allows one person to go through it at a time

turpentine /'tɜːpəntaɪn/ *noun* [U] (also UK **turps** /tɜːps/) a clear liquid that has a strong smell and is used for removing paint

turquoise /'tɜːkwɔɪz/ *noun* [U] a blue-green colour • **turquoise** adj

turret /'tʌrɪt/ *noun* [C] a small tower that is part of a building

turtle /'tɜːtl/ *noun* [C] an animal with four legs and a hard shell that lives mainly in water

turtleneck /'tɜːtlnek/ *noun* [C] US (UK **polo neck**) a piece of clothing that covers the top part of the body and has a tube-like part covering the neck: *a turtleneck sweater* → See picture at **polo neck**

tusk /tʌsk/ *noun* [C] one of the two long, pointed teeth that come out of the mouth of some animals

tussle /'tʌsl/ *noun* [C] a fight or argument, especially between two people who want to have the same thing

tut /tʌt/ *exclamation* (also **tut-tut**) a sound you make when you do not approve of something

tutor /'tjuːtər/ *noun* [C] **1** 🔵 someone who teaches one person or a very small group of people: *a private tutor* **2** UK a university teacher who is responsible for a small group of students • **tutor** verb [T]

---

tutorial /tjuːˈtɔːriəl/ **noun** [C] **1** a class in which a small group of students talks about a subject with their tutor, especially at a British university **2** a set of instructions and exercises that teaches you how to use a computer program

tux /tʌks/ **noun** [C] US short for tuxedo

tuxedo /tʌkˈsiːdəʊ/ **noun** [C] **1** US a black or white suit that a man wears on a very formal occasion → See picture at **dinner jacket 2** (also UK **dinner jacket**) a black or white jacket that a man wears on a very formal occasion

TV (also **tv**) /ˌtiːˈviː/ **noun** [C, U] ⒶⒷ abbreviation for television: *What's on TV tonight?* ○ *We could stay in and watch TV.* → See colour picture **The Living Room** on page Centre 4

twang /twæŋ/ **noun** [C] the sound that is made by pulling a tight string or wire • **twang verb** [I, T]

tweak /twiːk/ **verb** [T] **1** to change something slightly to try to improve it **2** to pull or twist something quickly and suddenly: *Dad sat there tweaking his beard.* • **tweak noun** [C]

tweed /twiːd/ **noun** [U] a thick, rough cloth made of wool

Tweet¹ /twiːt/ **noun** [C] trademark a message put on Twitter™ to let people know what you are doing, thinking, feeling, etc.

Tweet² /twiːt/ **verb** [I or T] to communicate on Twitter™ using short messages: *Many famous people Tweet regularly.*

tweezers /ˈtwiːzəz/ **noun** [plural] a small tool with two narrow pieces of metal joined at one end, used for picking up or pulling out very small things

tweezers

twelfth¹ /twelfθ/ 12th written as a word

twelfth² /twelfθ/ **noun** [C] one of twelve equal parts of something; ¹⁄₁₂

twelve /twelv/ ⒶⒷ the number 12

twenty /ˈtwenti/ **1** ⒶⒷ the number 20 **2 the twenties** the years from 1920 to 1929 **3 be in your twenties** to be aged between 20 and 29 • **twentieth** 20th written as a word

twice /twaɪs/ **adv** ⒶⒷ two times: *I've been there twice.* ○ *I have to take the tablets twice a day.*

twiddle /ˈtwɪdl/ **verb** [I, T] to move your fingers around, or turn something around many times, especially because you are bored: *Karen just sat there twiddling with her hair.*

twig /twɪg/ **noun** [C] a small, thin branch on a tree → See picture at **tree**

twilight /ˈtwaɪlaɪt/ **noun** [U] the time just before it becomes completely dark in the evening

twin¹ /twɪn/ **noun** [C] ⒷⒶ one of two children who are born to the same mother at the same time → See also **identical twin**

> 🗌 **Word partners for twin**
>
> a **set** of twins • sb's twin **brother/sister** • **identical** twins

twin² /twɪn/ **adj** [always before noun] used to describe two similar things that are a pair: *twin towers*

twin³ /twɪn/ **verb** UK **be twinned with sth** If a town in one country is twinned with a town in another country, the two towns have a special relationship: *Leeds in England is twinned with Dortmund in Germany.*

twin bed **noun** [C] one of a pair of two beds which are each big enough for one person

twinge /twɪndʒ/ **noun** [C] **1** a sudden, slight emotion: *a twinge of guilt* **2** a sudden, slight pain

twinkle /ˈtwɪŋkl/ **verb** [I] **1** If light twinkles, it shines and seems to be quickly flashing on and off: *The lights of the town twinkled in the distance* **2** If someone's eyes twinkle, they look bright and happy. • **twinkle noun** [C]

twin room **noun** [C] a room in a hotel that has two beds, each for one person

twirl /twɜːl/ **verb** [I, T] to turn around and around quickly, or to make something do this • **twirl noun** [C]

twist¹ /twɪst/ **verb**

twist

1 TURN ▷ [T] to turn something using your hand: *She sat there nervously twisting the ring around on her finger.* **2 BEND** ▷ [T] to bend and turn something many times and change its shape: *The wheels of the bike had been twisted in the accident.* **3 TURN YOUR BODY** ▷ [I, T] to turn part of your body to face a different direction: *She twisted her head so she could see what was happening.* **4 CHANGE DIRECTION** ▷ [I] If a road, river, etc twists, it has a lot of bends in it: *The path twisted and turned up the side of the mountain.* **5 INJURE** ▷ [T] If you twist a part of your body, such as your knee, you injure it by turning it suddenly. **6 CHANGE MEANING** ▷ [T] to unfairly change the meaning of something that someone has said: *Journalists had twisted his remarks.* → See also **twist sb's arm¹**

twist² /twɪst/ **noun** [C] **1 UNEXPECTED CHANGE** ▷ a sudden change in a story or situation that you do not expect: *The story has an unusual twist at the end.* **2 MOVEMENT** ▷ the movement of twisting something **3 PART** ▷ a part of something that is twisted: *There's a twist in the wire* **4 SHAPE** ▷ a shape that is made by twisting something: *Finally, add a twist of lemon for decoration.* **5 RIVER/ROAD** ▷ a bend in a river road, etc

twisted /ˈtwɪstɪd/ **adj 1** ⒷⒶ Something that is twisted is bent a lot of times and does not have its usual shape. **2** strange and slightly unpleasant or cruel: *He'd become bitter and twisted.*

twister /ˈtwɪstər/ **noun** [C] US another word for tornado (= an extremely strong and dangerous wind that blows in a circle) → See also **tongue twister**

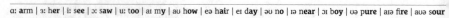

twit /twɪt/ **noun** [C] informal a silly person

twitch /twɪtʃ/ **verb** [I] If a part of your body twitches, it suddenly makes a slight movement in a way that you cannot control: *His face twitched nervously.* • **twitch noun** [C]

twitter /'twɪtə^r/ **verb** [I] If a bird twitters, it makes a series of short, high sounds.

Twitter /'twɪtə^r/ **noun** [U] trademark a social website on the Internet for communicating with people quickly

two /tuː/ **1** ⓐ the number 2 **2 in two** ⓑ into two pieces: *She broke the chocolate in two.*

IDIOM **put two and two together** to guess the truth from details that you notice about a situation: *She didn't tell me she was pregnant – I just put two and two together.*

→ See also the **lesser of two evils**, **be in two minds**, **stand on your own two feet (foot¹)**

two-time /ˌtuː'taɪm/ **verb** [T] informal If someone two-times their partner, they secretly have a romantic relationship with someone else.

two-way /'tuːˌweɪ/ **adj** moving, or allowing something to move or work in two directions: *a two-way street*

tycoon /taɪ'kuːn/ **noun** [C] someone who is very successful and powerful in business and has a lot of money: *a media tycoon* ∘ *a property/ shipping tycoon*

tying /'taɪɪŋ/ present participle of tie

Tylenol /'taɪlənɒl/ **noun** [C, U] trademark a common drug used to reduce pain and fever

type¹ /taɪp/ **noun** [C] **1** ⓐ a person or thing that is part of a group of people or things that have similar qualities, or a group of people or things that have similar qualities: *They sell over 20 different types of cheese.* ∘ *Illnesses of this type are very common in children.* **2** someone who has particular qualities or interests: *He's the outdoor type* (= enjoys being outside). **3 not be sb's type** informal to not be the type of person that someone thinks is attractive: *I like Bertrand but he's not really my type.* → See also **blood type**

☑ Word partners for **type**
of this type • **all** types **of sth** • **different/ various** types

type² /taɪp/ **verb** [I, T] ⓑ to write something using a keyboard • **typing noun** [U]

typewriter /'taɪpˌraɪtə^r/ **noun** [C] a machine with keys that you press to produce letters and numbers on paper • **typewritten** /'taɪpˌrɪtªn/ **adj** printed using a typewriter: *a typewritten letter*

typhoid /'taɪfɔɪd/ **noun** [U] a serious infectious disease that is caused by dirty water or food

typhoon /taɪ'fuːn/ **noun** [C] a violent storm with very strong winds

typical /'tɪpɪkªl/ **adj** ⓑ having all the qualities you expect a particular person, object, place, etc to have: *typical German food* ∘ *This style of painting is typical of Monet.*

typically /'tɪpɪkªli/ **adv 1** ⓑ used for saying that something is typical of a person, thing, place, etc: *Such behaviour is typically English.* **2** ⓑ used for saying what usually happens: *Schools in the area typically start at 8.30.*

typify /'tɪpɪfaɪ/ **verb** [T] to be a typical example or quality of something: *Emma's opinions typify the attitude of many young people.*

typist /'taɪpɪst/ **noun** [C] old-fashioned someone who types (= writes using a machine)

typo /'taɪpəʊ/ **noun** [C] informal a small mistake in a text, made when it was typed or printed

tyranny /'tɪrªni/ **noun** [U] a situation in which a leader or government has too much power and uses that power in a cruel and unfair way • **tyrannical** /tɪ'rænɪkªl/ **adj** using or involving tyranny

tyrant /'taɪªrªnt/ **noun** [C] someone who has total power and uses it in a cruel and unfair way

tyre UK (US **tire**) /taɪə^r/ **noun** [C] ⓑ a thick, round piece of rubber filled with air, that fits around a wheel: *It's got a **flat tyre** (= tyre with no air in it).* → See colour picture **Car** on page Centre 7

T

U

U, u /juː/ the twenty-first letter of the alphabet

uber- /'uːbər-/ **prefix** humorous used before nouns to mean 'extreme' or 'extremely good or successful': *uber-billionaire*

ubiquitous /juː'bɪkwɪtəs/ **adj** formal seeming to be in all places: *the ubiquitous security cameras*

udder /'ʌdər/ **noun** [C] the part of a female cow, goat, etc that hangs under its body and produces milk

UFO /ˌjuːef'əʊ/ **noun** [C] abbreviation for unidentified flying object: something strange that you see in the sky that could be from another part of the universe

ugh /ʌg/ **exclamation** used to show that you think something is very unpleasant: *Ugh! What a smell!*

ugly /'ʌgli/ **adj 1** ⑬ unpleasant to look at: *an ugly city* **2** An ugly situation is very unpleasant, usually because it involves violence: *There were **ugly scenes** outside the stadium.* • **ugliness noun** [U] → See also **rear/raise its ugly head**¹

uh US spoken (mainly UK **er**) /ə/ **exclamation** something that you say when you are thinking what to say next: *It's not too far – it's about, uh, five miles from here.*

UK /ˌjuː'keɪ/ **noun** abbreviation for United Kingdom

ulcer /'ʌlsər/ **noun** [C] a painful, infected area on your skin or inside your body: *a mouth/stomach ulcer*

ulterior /ʌl'tɪəriər/ **adj ulterior motive/purpose, etc** a secret purpose or reason for doing something

ultimate¹ /'ʌltɪmət/ **adj** [always before noun] **1** ⑫ better, worse, or greater than all similar things: *Climbing Mount Everest is the ultimate challenge.* ◦ *the ultimate insult* **2** final or most important: *the ultimate aim/solution*

ultimate² /'ʌltɪmət/ **noun the ultimate in sth** the best or greatest example of something: *It describes the hotel as 'the ultimate in luxury'.*

ultimately /'ʌltɪmətli/ **adv 1** finally, after a series of things have happened: *The disease ultimately killed him.* **2** used to emphasize the most important fact in a situation: *Ultimately, he'll have to decide.*

ultimatum /ˌʌltɪ'meɪtəm/ **noun** [C] a statement that you will do something that will affect someone badly if they do not do what you want: *The children were **given** an **ultimatum** – finish their work quietly or stay behind after class.*

🗒 **Word partners for ultimatum**

deliver/give sb/issue an ultimatum • an ultimatum demands sth • an ultimatum **from**/**to** sb

---

ultra- /ʌltrə-/ **prefix** extremely: *ultra-modern architecture* ◦ *ultra-careful*

ultrasonic /ˌʌltrə'sɒnɪk/ **adj** involving ultra sound

ultrasound /'ʌltrəsaʊnd/ **noun 1** [U] very high sound waves, especially those that are used in medical examinations to produce an image of something inside your body: *an **ultrasound scan*** **2** [C] a medical examination that produce an image of something that is inside the body especially a baby, using sound waves: *An ultrasound revealed a perfectly healthy baby.*

ultraviolet /ˌʌltrə'vaɪələt/ **adj** Ultraviolet ligh makes your skin become darker.

um /əm/ **exclamation** spoken something that you say while you are thinking about what to say next: *Well, um, I don't know, actually.*

umbilical cord /ʌm'bɪlɪklˌkɔːd/ **noun** [C] the tube that connects a baby to its mother before i is born

umbrella /ʌm'brelə/ **noun** [C] **1** ⑫ a thing that you hold above your head to keep yourself dry when it is raining **2 umbrella group/organization, etc** a large organization that is made of many smaller organizations

umbrella

umpire /'ʌmpaɪər/ **noun** [C] someone whose job is to watch a sports game and make sure that the player obey the rules: *a tennis/cricket umpire* • **umpire verb** [I, T]

umpteen /ʌm'tiːn/ **quantifier** informal very many: *I've been there **umpteen times** and I stil can't remember the way.* • **umpteenth** *I drank m umpteenth cup of coffee.*

un- /ʌn-/ **prefix** not or the opposite of: *unhapp* ◦ *unfair* ◦ *to unfasten*

the UN /juː'en/ **noun** abbreviation for the Unite Nations: an international organization that trie to solve world problems in a peaceful way

unable /ʌn'eɪbl/ **adj be unable to do sth** ⑬ t not be able to do something: *Some days he i. unable to get out of bed.*

unabridged /ˌʌnə'brɪdʒd/ **adj** An unabridge book, play, etc is in its original form and has no been made shorter.

unacceptable /ˌʌnək'septəbl/ **adj** ⑫ too bad t be allowed to continue: *The water contain. unacceptable levels of pollution.* ◦ *I find that sor of behaviour **completely unacceptable**.* • **unac ceptably adv**

🗒 **Word partners for unacceptable**

find sth unacceptable • completely/totally/wholly unacceptable • unacceptable **to** sb

---

unaccompanied /ˌʌnə'kʌmpənid/ **adj** no

having anyone with you when you go somewhere: *Unaccompanied children are not allowed in the museum.*

unaccountable /ˌʌnəˈkaʊntəbl/ **adj 1** impossible to explain: *For some **unaccountable reason**, I've got three copies of the same book.* **2** not having to give reasons for your actions or decisions • **unaccountably** adv

unadulterated /ˌʌnəˈdʌltᵊreɪtɪd/ **adj 1** complete: *I've never heard such unadulterated nonsense in all my life!* **2** pure and with nothing extra added: *People using drugs can never be sure that they're using unadulterated substances.*

unaffected /ˌʌnəˈfektɪd/ **adj** not changed by something: *Smaller colleges will be **unaffected by** the new regulations.*

unaided /ʌnˈeɪdɪd/ **adj, adv** without help: *He's now well enough to **walk unaided**.*

unanimous /juːˈnænɪməs/ **adj** agreed by everyone: *The jury was unanimous in finding him guilty.* • **unanimity** /ˌjuːnəˈnɪməti/ **noun** [U] a situation in which everyone agrees about something • **unanimously** adv *The members **unanimously agreed** to the proposal.*

unannounced /ˌʌnəˈnaʊnst/ **adj, adv** without telling anyone first: *an **unannounced visit***

unappealing /ˌʌnəˈpiːlɪŋ/ **adj** not attractive or enjoyable: *Five hours on a train with Mike is a fairly **unappealing prospect**.* ∘ *an **unappealing character***

unarmed /ʌnˈɑːmd/ **adj** not carrying a weapon

unashamedly /ˌʌnəˈʃeɪmɪdli/ **adv** in a way that shows you are not embarrassed or worried about what other people think of you: *They are unashamedly in love.*

unassuming /ˌʌnəˈsjuːmɪŋ/ **adj** not wanting to be noticed: *a shy, unassuming man*

unattached /ˌʌnəˈtætʃt/ **adj** not married or having a romantic relationship

unattended /ˌʌnəˈtendɪd/ **adj** not being watched or looked after: *Passengers should not **leave bags unattended**.*

unattractive /ˌʌnəˈtræktɪv/ **adj 1** not beautiful or nice to look at: *I felt old and unattractive.* **2** not interesting or useful: *an unattractive proposition*

unauthorized (also UK **-ised**) /ʌnˈɔːθᵊraɪzd/ **adj** done without official permission: *an unauthorized use of company money*

unavailable /ˌʌnəˈveɪləbl/ **adj 1** not able to talk to someone or meet them, especially because you are doing other things: *The manager was **unavailable for comment**.* **2** ⑫ impossible to buy or get: *The book is unavailable in Britain.*

unavoidable /ˌʌnəˈvɔɪdəbl/ **adj** impossible to avoid or prevent: *an unavoidable delay*

unaware /ˌʌnəˈweəʳ/ **adj** [never before noun] ⑫ not knowing about something: *He seems **totally unaware of** the problem.*

☑ Word partners for **unaware**

blissfully/completely/seemingly/totally unaware • unaware of sth

unawares /ˌʌnəˈweəz/ **adv catch/take sb unawares** If something catches or takes you

unawares, it happens when you do not expect it to: *The rain caught me unawares and I didn't have my umbrella.*

unbalanced /ʌnˈbælənst/ **adj 1** slightly mentally ill **2** false and not fair: *He gave an unbalanced view of the situation.*

unbearable /ʌnˈbeərəbl/ **adj** ⑫ too painful or unpleasant for you to continue to experience: *The heat was almost unbearable.* • **unbearably** adv

unbeatable /ʌnˈbiːtəbl/ **adj** much better than everyone or everything else: *We aim to sell the best products at unbeatable prices.*

unbeaten /ʌnˈbiːtᵊn/ **adj** in sports, having won every game: *Manchester United **remain unbeaten** this season.*

unbelievable /ˌʌnbɪˈliːvəbl/ **adj 1** ⑪ extremely bad or good and making you feel surprised: *It's unbelievable how lucky she's been.* **2** ⑫ not probable and difficult to believe • **unbelievably** adv

unborn /ʌnˈbɔːn/ **adj** not yet born: *the **unborn child***

unbreakable /ˌʌnˈbreɪkəbl/ **adj** impossible to break: *unbreakable glass/plastic*

unbridled /ʌnˈbraɪdld/ **adj** An unbridled feeling is one that you do not try to hide or control: *unbridled enthusiasm/passion*

unbroken /ʌnˈbrəʊkᵊn/ **adj** continuous and with no pauses: *unbroken sunshine*

unbutton /ʌnˈbʌtᵊn/ **verb** [T] to open the buttons on a piece of clothing: *He unbuttoned his jacket.*

uncalled for /ʌnˈkɔːldfɔːʳ/ **adj** If an action or remark is uncalled for, it is unfair or unkind: *That was uncalled for, Tess – apologize to your brother.*

uncanny /ʌnˈkæni/ **adj** strange and impossible to explain: *an **uncanny resemblance*** • **uncannily** adv

uncaring /ʌnˈkeərɪŋ/ **adj** without sympathy for people with problems: *victims of an uncaring society*

uncertain /ʌnˈsɜːtᵊn/ **adj 1** ⑫ not sure or not able to decide about something: *Bridie was **uncertain about** meeting him.* **2** ⑫ not known, or not completely certain: *The museum faces an **uncertain future**.* • **uncertainly** adv

uncertainty /ʌnˈsɜːtᵊnti/ **noun** [C, U] the state of being uncertain: *Life is full of uncertainties.*

☑ Word partners for **uncertainty**

face uncertainty • the uncertainty surrounding sth • uncertainty about/as to/over sth • continuing/great/growing uncertainty • the uncertainty of sth

unchanged /ʌnˈtʃeɪndʒd/ **adj** ⑫ staying the same: *The area has **remained** virtually **unchanged** in fifty years.*

uncharacteristic /ˌʌnkærəktəˈrɪstɪk/ **adj** not typical • **uncharacteristically** adv

unchecked /ʌnˈtʃekt/ **adj** If something bad continues unchecked, it is not stopped.

U

uncle /ˈʌŋkl/ **noun** [C] Ⓐ⒉ the brother of your mother or father, or the husband of your aunt

unclean /ʌnˈkliːn/ **adj** morally bad, as described by the rules of a religion

unclear /ʌnˈklɪəʳ/ **adj 1** Ⓑ⒉ not easy to understand: *The situation at the moment is unclear.* ○ [+ question word] *It's unclear what actually happened that night.* **2** Ⓑ⒉ If you are unclear about something, you do not understand it exactly: *I'm **unclear about** exactly who's doing what.*

uncomfortable /ʌnˈkʌmftəbl/ **adj 1** Ⓑ⒈ not feeling comfortable and pleasant, or not making you feel comfortable and pleasant: *These shoes are really uncomfortable.* **2** slightly embarrassed, or making you feel slightly embarrassed: *an uncomfortable silence* • **uncomfortably adv**

uncommon /ʌnˈkɒmən/ **adj** unusual: [+ for + to do sth] *It's not uncommon for people to become sick* (= *they often become sick*) *when they travel.* • **uncommonly adv**

uncompromising /ʌnˈkɒmprəmaɪzɪŋ/ **adj** determined not to change your ideas or decisions: *an **uncompromising attitude***

unconcerned /ˌʌnkənˈsɜːnd/ **adj** not worried by something: *The baby seemed **unconcerned by** all the noise.*

unconditional /ˌʌnkənˈdɪʃᵊnᵊl/ **adj** done or given without any limits and without asking for anything for yourself: *unconditional love* • **unconditionally adv**

unconfirmed /ˌʌnkənˈfɜːmd/ **adj** An unconfirmed report or story may not be true because there is no proof yet.

unconnected /ˌʌnkəˈnektɪd/ **adj** If two or more things are unconnected, there is no connection between them: *The stomach ailment was **unconnected with** his cancer.*

unconscious¹ /ʌnˈkɒnʃəs/ **adj 1** Ⓑ⒉ in a state as though you are sleeping, for example because you have been hit on the head: *She was **knocked unconscious**.* **2** An unconscious thought or feeling is one that you do not know you have: *an unconscious fear* • **unconsciousness noun** [U]

unconscious² /ʌnˈkɒnʃəs/ **noun** [no plural] the part of your mind that contains feelings and thoughts that you do not know about, and that influences the way you behave

unconsciously /ʌnˈkɒnʃəsli/ **adv** If you do something unconsciously, you do it without knowing that you are doing it.

unconstitutional /ʌnˌkɒnstɪˈtjuːʃᵊnᵊl/ **adj** not allowed by the rules of an organization or political system

uncontrollable /ˌʌnkənˈtrəʊləbl/ **adj** unable to be controlled: *uncontrollable anger* ○ *an uncontrollable desire to cry* • **uncontrollably adv**

unconventional /ˌʌnkənˈvenʃᵊnᵊl/ **adj** doing things in a way that is different from most people: *an unconventional lifestyle*

unconvincing /ˌʌnkənˈvɪntsɪŋ/ **adj** not seeming true or real: *an unconvincing explanation*

uncool /ʌnˈkuːl/ **adj** embarrassing and not stylish or fashionable

uncountable noun /ʌnˌkaʊntəbᵊlˈnaʊn/ **noun** [C] (also **uncount noun**) Ⓑ⒈ a noun that does not have a plural form and cannot be used with 'a' or 'one'. For example 'music' and 'furniture' are uncountable nouns. → See Study Page **Countable and uncountable nouns** on page Centre 20

uncouth /ʌnˈkuːθ/ **adj** behaving in a rude, unpleasant way

uncover /ʌnˈkʌvəʳ/ **verb** [T] **1** to discover something that had been secret or hidden: *The inspectors **uncovered evidence** of corruption.* **2** to remove a cover from something

---

☑ **Word partners for uncover**

uncover **evidence/a plot/a secret/the truth** • an **investigation** uncovers sth

---

undaunted /ʌnˈdɔːntɪd/ **adj** not frightened to do something that is difficult or dangerous: *Keiko spoke, **undaunted by** the crowd.*

undecided /ˌʌndɪˈsaɪdɪd/ **adj** If you are undecided about something, you have not made a decision yet: *I'm still undecided about whether to apply for the job.*

undefeated /ˌʌndɪˈfiːtɪd/ **adj** in sports, having won every game: *Both teams **remain undefeated** in the final weeks of the season.*

undeniable /ˌʌndɪˈnaɪəbl/ **adj** certainly true: *an undeniable fact* • **undeniably adv**

under- /ˈʌndəʳ-/ **prefix 1** not enough: *undercooked potatoes* **2** below: *underwear* ○ *an underpass*

under¹ /ˈʌndəʳ/ **preposition 1** **BELOW** ▷ Ⓐ below something: *She pushed her bag under the table.* ○ *The children were sitting under a tree.* **2** **BELOW THE SURFACE** ▷ Ⓐ⒈ below the surface of something: *He could only keep his head under the water for a few seconds.* **3** **LESS THAN** ▷ Ⓐ⒉ less than a number, amount, or age: *You can buy the whole system for just under $2000.* ○ *We don't serve alcohol to anyone under 18.* **4** **CONTROLLED BY** ▷ controlled or governed by a particular person, organization, etc: *a country under military rule* ○ *The restaurant is under new management.* **5** **RULE/LAW** ▷ according to a rule, law, etc: *Under the new law, all new buildings must be approved by the local government.* **6** **IN A PARTICULAR STATE** ▷ Ⓑ⒉ in a particular state or condition: *The President is under pressure to resign.* ○ *Students are allowed to miss school under certain circumstances.* **7** **IN PROGRESS** ▷ Ⓑ⒉ used to say that something is happening at the moment but is not finished: *a new 16-screen cinema is under construction* ○ *Several different plans are under discussion.* **8** **NAME** ▷ using a particular name, especially one that is not your usual name: *He also wrote several detective novels under the name Edgar Sandys.* **9** **PLACE IN LIST** ▷ used to say which part of a list, book, library, etc you should look in to find something: *Books about health problems are under 'Medicine'.*

under² /ˈʌndəʳ/ **adv 1** below the surface of something: *The child was swimming and suddenly started to go under.* **2** less than a particular number, amount, or age: *I want a computer that is £500 or under.*

U

under-age /ˌʌndər'eɪdʒ/ **adj** younger than the legal age when you are allowed to do something: *under-age drinking/sex*

underarm /'ʌndərɑːm/ **adj** [always before noun] of or for use in the armpit (= the area under the arm where the arm joins the body): *underarm deodorant*

undercover /ˌʌndə'kʌvəʳ/ **adj, adv** working secretly in order to get information for the police or government: *an **undercover police officer***

undercut /ˌʌndə'kʌt/ **verb** [T] (**undercutting, undercut**) to sell something at a lower price than someone else

the underdog /'ʌndədɒg/ **noun** the person or team that is expected to lose a race or competition

underestimate /ˌʌndəˈr'estɪmeɪt/ **verb** [T] **1** 🔵 to not understand how large, strong, or important something is: *Many people underestimate the cost of owning a car.* **2** to not understand how powerful or clever someone is: *I thought it would be an easy game but I had underestimated my opponent.* → Opposite **overestimate**

underfoot /ˌʌndə'fʊt/ **adv** under your feet as you walk: *Several people were **trampled underfoot** in the rush to escape.*

undergo /ˌʌndə'gəʊ/ **verb** (**undergoing, underwent, undergone**) to experience something, especially a change or medical treatment: *The country is currently **undergoing** major political **change**.* ∘ *He is **undergoing surgery** for a heart problem.*

undergraduate /ˌʌndə'grædʒuət/ **noun** [C] (*informal* **undergrad** /'ʌndəgræd/) a student who is studying for their first university degree (= qualification)

underground¹ /'ʌndəgraʊnd/ **adj, adv 1** 🔵 under the surface of the ground: *underground caves* ∘ *an animal that lives underground* **2** Underground political activities are secret and illegal: *an underground political organization*

underground² /'ʌndəgraʊnd/ **noun** [no plural] UK (US **subway**) 🔵 a system of trains that is built under a city: *the London Underground* → See Note at **metro¹**

> 🔲 Word partners for **underground** noun
> take the underground • on the underground
> • an underground **station/train**

undergrowth /'ʌndəgrəʊθ/ **noun** [U] short plants and bushes that grow around trees

underhand /ˌʌndə'hænd/ **adj** (also **underhanded**) secret and not honest: ***underhand business deals***

underline /ˌʌndə'laɪn/ **verb** [T] **1** 🔵 to draw a line under a word or sentence **2** 🔵 to emphasize the importance or truth of something: *The report **underlines the need** for more teachers in schools.*

underlying /ˌʌndə'laɪŋ/ **adj** [always before noun] An underlying reason or problem is the real reason or problem, although it is not obvious: *We need to look at the **underlying reasons** for ill health.*

undermine /ˌʌndə'maɪn/ **verb** [T] to make

someone less confident or make something weaker: *A series of scandals have **undermined** people's **confidence** in the government.*

underneath¹ /ˌʌndə'niːθ/ **adv, preposition** 🔵 under something: *Florian was wearing a jacket with a red shirt underneath.* ∘ *Deborah pushed her shoes underneath the bed.*

underneath² /ˌʌndə'niːθ/ **noun the underneath** the bottom part of something

underpaid /ˌʌndə'peɪd/ **adj** not earning enough for your work

underpants /'ʌndəpænts/ **noun** [plural] 🔵 a piece of underwear that covers the area between your waist and the top of your legs → See colour picture **Clothes** on page Centre 9 → See Note at **underwear**

underpass /'ʌndəpɑːs/ **noun** [C] a road or path that goes under another road

underprivileged /ˌʌndə'prɪvəlɪdʒd/ **adj** poor and having fewer opportunities than most people: *underprivileged families*

underrate /ˌʌndə'reɪt/ **verb** [T] to think that someone or something is not as good as they really are: *Don't underrate her. She's a great tennis player.* • **underrated adj** *I think he's really underrated as an actor.* → Opposite **overrated**

underscore /ˌʌndə'skɔːʳ/ **verb** [T] mainly US to emphasize the importance of something

undershirt /'ʌndəʃɜːt/ **noun** [C] US (UK **vest**) a piece of underwear that you wear under a shirt

the underside /'ʌndəsaɪd/ **noun** the bottom surface of something: *There was some damage to the underside of the car.*

understand /ˌʌndə'stænd/ **verb** [I, T] (**understood**) **1** KNOW MEANING ▷ 🔵 to know the meaning of something that someone says: *I don't understand half of what he says.* ∘ *She didn't understand so I explained it again.* **2** KNOW WHY/ HOW ▷ 🔵 to know why or how something happens or works: [+ question word] *We still don't fully understand how the brain works.* **3** KNOW FEELINGS ▷ 🔵 to know how someone feels or why they behave in a particular way: *I don't understand James sometimes.* ∘ [+ question word] *I understand why she's so angry.* **4 I/we understand (that)...** *formal* used to say that you believe something is true because someone has told you it is: *I understand that the school is due to close next year.* **5 make yourself understood** to say something to someone in a way that they understand: *I had a little difficulty making myself understood.*

understandable /ˌʌndə'stændəbl/ **adj** 🔵 An understandable feeling or action is one that you would expect in that particular situation: *It's understandable that he's angry.* • **understandably adv** *She's understandably upset.*

understanding¹ /ˌʌndə'stændɪŋ/ **noun 1** KNOWLEDGE ▷ [U, no plural] 🔵 knowledge about a subject, situation, etc or about how something works: *We now **have a better understanding of** this disease.* **2** AGREEMENT ▷ [C] an informal agreement between two people: [usually singular, + that] *We **have** an **understanding** that we don't discuss the subject in front of his mother.*

U

3 SYMPATHY ▷ [U] 🅱2 sympathy: *Thank you for your understanding.* **4 my/her/his, etc understanding** what you thought to be true: *It was my understanding that she was coming alone.* **5 ABILITY** ▷ [U] the ability to learn or think about something

📄 Word partners for **understanding**

develop/gain/have an understanding (of sth) • a **better/clear** understanding • an understanding **of** sth

understanding² /ˌʌndəˈstændɪŋ/ *adj* 🅱2 showing sympathy for someone's problems: *Fortunately, my girlfriend is very understanding.*

understated /ˌʌndəˈsteɪtɪd/ *adj* simple and attractive in style: *an understated black dress*

understatement /ˌʌndəˈsteɪtmənt/ *noun* [C, U] a statement in which you say that something is less extreme than it really is: *'Quite big', did you say? That's an understatement – he's enormous!*

understood /ˌʌndəˈstʊd/ past of understand

understudy /ˈʌndəˌstʌdi/ *noun* [C] an actor in the theatre who learns the words and actions of another character so that they can perform if the usual actor is sick

undertake /ˌʌndəˈteɪk/ *verb* (**undertook, undertaken**) formal **1** [T] to start work on something that will take a long time or be difficult: *Max has undertaken the task of restoring an old houseboat.* **2 undertake to do sth** to promise to do something

undertaker /ˈʌndəˌteɪkəʳ/ *noun* [C] someone whose job is to organize funerals and prepare dead bodies to be buried or burned

undertaking /ˈʌndəˌteɪkɪŋ/ *noun* [C] **1** a difficult or important piece of work, especially one that takes a long time: [usually singular] *Building your own house is a **major undertaking**.* **2** UK a legal or official promise to do something: [usually singular] *The newspaper has **given an undertaking** not to print the story.*

📄 Word partners for **undertaking**

give/sign an undertaking • a **written** undertaking • an undertaking **by/from** sb

undertone /ˈʌndətəʊn/ *noun* [C] a feeling or quality that exists but is not obvious: *an article with worrying political undertones*

undertook /ˌʌndəˈtʊk/ past tense of undertake

undervalued /ˌʌndəˈvæljuːd/ *adj* If someone or something is undervalued, they are more important or useful than people think they are.

underwater /ˌʌndəˈwɔːtəʳ/ *adj, adv* under the surface of water: *an underwater camera* ∘ *Seals can hear very well underwater.*

underwear /ˈʌndəweəʳ/ *noun* [U] 🅱1 the clothes that you wear next to your skin, under your other clothes

underweight /ˌʌndəˈweɪt/ *adj* too light

underwent /ˌʌndəˈwent/ past tense of undergo

underworld /ˈʌndəwɜːld/ *noun* [no plural] criminals and their activities: *the **criminal underworld*** ∘ *the London underworld*

undesirable /ˌʌndɪˈzaɪərəbl/ *adj* formal Some-

❗ Common learner error: types of underwear

Underpants are a piece of underwear that cover the bottom. In British English **underpants** are only worn by men or boys, but in American English they can also be worn by women and girls. The American English word **panties** is a piece of underwear for women or girls that covers the bottom. The British English word for **panties** is **knickers** or **pants**.

thing that is undesirable is not wanted because it is bad or unpleasant: *an undesirable influence*

undeveloped /ˌʌndɪˈveləpt/ *adj* Undeveloped land has no buildings on it and is not used for anything.

undid /ʌnˈdɪd/ past tense of undo

undisclosed /ˌʌndɪsˈkləʊzd/ *adj* If official information is undisclosed, it is secret: *The meeting is taking place at an undisclosed location.*

undisputed /ˌʌndɪˈspjuːtɪd/ *adj* If something is undisputed, everyone agrees about it: *an **undisputed fact*** ∘ *the **undisputed champion/master***

undisturbed /ˌʌndɪˈstɜːbd/ *adj* not interrupted or changed in any way: *undisturbed sleep*

undivided /ˌʌndɪˈvaɪdɪd/ *adj* **undivided attention/loyalty/support, etc** complete attention, support, etc: *There, now you can have my undivided attention.*

undo /ʌnˈduː/ *verb* [T] (**undoing, undid, undone**) **1** 🅱2 to open something that is tied or fastened: *I took off my hat and undid my coat.* **2** 🅱2 to get rid of the effects of something that has been done before: *Some of the **damage** caused by pollution cannot be **undone**.*

undoing /ʌnˈduːɪŋ/ *noun* **be sb's undoing** to be the thing that makes someone fail: *It was a policy that proved to be the President's undoing.*

undone /ʌnˈdʌn/ *adj* **1** not fastened or tied: *Her coat was undone.* **2** not done: *I don't think I've left anything undone.*

undoubted /ʌnˈdaʊtɪd/ *adj* [always before noun] used to emphasize that something is true: *The project was an **undoubted success**.* ∘ *her undoubted ability/talent*

undoubtedly /ʌnˈdaʊtɪdli/ *adv* 🅱2 used to emphasize that something is true: *Stress has undoubtedly contributed to her illness.*

undress /ʌnˈdres/ *verb* [I, T] 🅱1 to remove your clothes or someone else's clothes • **undressed** *adj* 🅱2 *I got undressed and went to bed.*

undue /ʌnˈdjuː/ *adj* [always before noun] formal more than is necessary: *I don't want to cause undue alarm.*

undulating /ˈʌndjəleɪtɪŋ/ *adj* formal having slight slopes or curves, or moving slightly up and down: *undulating roads*

unduly /ʌnˈdjuːli/ *adv* formal more than necessary: *She didn't seem **unduly concerned/worried**.*

unearth /ʌnˈɜːθ/ *verb* [T] **1** to find something in the ground: [often passive] *Thousands of dinosaur bones have been unearthed in China.* **2** to find something that has been secret or hidden: *Reporters **unearthed evidence** of criminal activity.*

unearthly /ʌnˈɜːθli/ **adj** strange and frightening: *an **unearthly light/beauty***

unease /ʌnˈiːz/ **noun** [U] a feeling of worry because you think something bad might happen

uneasy /ʌnˈiːzi/ **adj** 🅱2 worried because you think something bad might happen: *I feel a bit **uneasy about** her travelling alone.*

uneconomic /ˌʌnˌiːkəˈnɒmɪk/ **adj** (also **uneconomical**) **1** using too much money, fuel, time, etc: *Big cars can be uneconomic to run.* **2** not making enough profit: *plans to close uneconomic factories*

unemployed /ˌʌnɪmˈplɔɪd/ **adj** 🅱1 not having a job: *I've been unemployed for six months.* ◦ *The government is helping to create jobs for **the unemployed**.*

unemployment /ˌʌnɪmˈplɔɪmənt/ **noun** [U] **1** 🅱1 the number of people who are unemployed: *a **rise/fall** in unemployment* ◦ *The **unemployment rate** has increased to 20 percent.* **2** the state of not having a job

> 🔲 Word partners for **unemployment**
>
> unemployment **drops/falls/increases/rises** • **high/low/rising/soaring** unemployment • the unemployment **rate** • a **drop/fall/increase/rise** in unemployment

unending /ʌnˈendɪŋ/ **adj** seeming to continue forever: *an **unending series** of problems*

unequal /ʌnˈiːkwəl/ **adj 1** different in size, level, amount, etc **2** unfair: *the unequal distribution of wealth* • **unequally** adv

unequivocal /ˌʌnɪˈkwɪvəkəl/ **adj** formal clear and certain: *an unequivocal answer* • **unequivocally** adv

unethical /ʌnˈeθɪkəl/ **adj** morally bad: *unethical business methods*

uneven /ʌnˈiːvən/ **adj** not level or smooth: *an uneven floor* • **unevenly** adv

uneventful /ˌʌnɪˈventfəl/ **adj** without problems and without anything exciting happening: *The journey itself was fairly uneventful.*

unexpected /ˌʌnɪkˈspektɪd/ **adj** 🅱1 Something that is unexpected surprises you because you did not know it was going to happen: *His death was completely unexpected.* • **unexpectedly** adv

unfailing /ʌnˈfeɪlɪŋ/ **adj** An unfailing quality or ability is one that someone always has: *unfailing support/courtesy* • **unfailingly** adv

unfair /ʌnˈfeəʳ/ **adj 1** 🅱1 not treating people in an equal way: *an unfair system* ◦ *The test was unfair because some people had seen it before.* **2** 🅱2 not true and morally wrong: [+ to do sth] *It's unfair to blame Frank for everything.* • **unfairly** adv • **unfairness** noun [U]

unfaithful /ʌnˈfeɪθfəl/ **adj** having sex with someone who is not your wife, husband, or usual sexual partner: *She was **unfaithful to** me.*

unfamiliar /ˌʌnfəˈmɪljəʳ/ **adj 1** 🅱2 not known to you: *an unfamiliar face* ◦ *His name was unfamiliar to me.* **2** **be unfamiliar with sth** 🅱2 to not

have any knowledge or experience of something: *Many older people are **unfamiliar with** computers.*

unfashionable /ʌnˈfæʃənəbl/ **adj** not fashionable or popular at a particular time

unfasten /ʌnˈfɑːsən/ **verb** [T] to open something that is closed or fixed together: *to unfasten a seat belt*

unfavourable UK (US **unfavorable**)/ʌnˈfeɪvʳrəbl/ **adj 1** negative and showing that you do not like something: *unfavourable publicity* **2** not good and likely to cause problems: *unfavourable weather conditions* • **unfavourably** adv

unfeeling /ʌnˈfiːlɪŋ/ **adj** not having sympathy for other people

unfettered /ʌnˈfetəd/ **adj** formal not limited by rules: *The UN inspectors were given **unfettered access** to all nuclear sites.*

unfinished /ʌnˈfɪnɪʃt/ **adj** not completed: *an unfinished novel/portrait*

unfit /ʌnˈfɪt/ **adj 1** 🅱2 not suitable or good enough: *The food was judged **unfit for** human consumption.* **2** UK 🅱1 not healthy because you do too little exercise

unflattering /ʌnˈflætʳrɪŋ/ **adj** making someone look less attractive or seem worse than usual: *an unflattering photo/dress/colour*

unfold /ʌnˈfəʊld/ **verb 1** [I] If a situation or story unfolds, it develops or becomes known: *The nation watched on TV as the tragic events unfolded.* **2** [I, T] to become open and flat, or to make something become open and flat: *I unfolded the map.*

unforeseen /ˌʌnfɔːˈsiːn/ **adj** not expected: *The concert was cancelled due to **unforeseen circumstances**.*

unforgettable /ˌʌnfəˈgetəbl/ **adj** 🅱1 Something that is unforgettable is so good, interesting, etc that you remember it for a long time: *Seeing Niagara Falls was an **unforgettable experience**.*

unfortunate /ʌnˈfɔːtʃʳnət/ **adj 1** 🅱2 used to show that you wish something was not true or had not happened: *an unfortunate mistake* ◦ [+ (that)] *It was unfortunate that she lost her job just as her husband became ill.* **2** 🅱2 unlucky: *One unfortunate person failed to see the hole and fell straight into it.*

unfortunately /ʌnˈfɔːtʃʳnətli/ **adv** 🅰2 used to say that you wish something was not true or that something had not happened: *I'd love to come, but unfortunately I have to work.*

unfounded /ʌnˈfaʊndɪd/ **adj** not based on facts: *unfounded allegations/rumours*

unfriendly /ʌnˈfrendli/ **adj** 🅱1 not friendly

unfulfilled /ˌʌnfʊlˈfɪld/ **adj 1** An unfulfilled wish, hope, etc is one that has not happened or not been achieved: *an **unfulfilled ambition/dream*** ◦ *unfulfilled potential* **2** unhappy because you think you should be achieving more in your life

unfurnished /ʌnˈfɜːnɪʃt/ **adj** If a room, apartment, etc. is unfurnished, there is no furniture in it.

ungainly /ʌnˈgeɪnli/ **adj** moving in a way that is not attractive: *an ungainly walk*

U

ungrateful /ʌnˈɡreɪtfᵊl/ **adj** not thanking or showing that you are pleased with someone who has done something for you

unhappy /ʌnˈhæpi/ **adj 1** ⓐ sad: *an unhappy childhood* **2** ⓑ not satisfied: *Giorgio was unhappy with his test results.* ∘ *I'm unhappy about the situation.* • **unhappily** adv • **unhappiness** noun [U]

> ➕ Other ways of saying **unhappy**
>
> **Sad** and **miserable** mean the same as unhappy:
> *I felt so **sad** after he left.*
> *I just woke up feeling **miserable**.*
> If someone is **upset**, they are unhappy because something bad has happened:
> *They'd had an argument and she was still **upset** about it.*
> *Mike got very **upset** when I told him the news.*
> If someone is **broken-hearted** or **heartbroken** they are very sad because someone they love has ended a relationship with them:
> *She was **broken-hearted** when Richard left.*
> If someone is **devastated**, or **distraught**, they are extremely upset:
> *She was **devastated** when he died.*
> *The missing child's **distraught** parents made an emotional appeal for information on TV.*
> The adjective **depressed** is often used when someone is very unhappy for a long time:
> *She became deeply **depressed** after her husband died.*

unharmed /ʌnˈhɑːmd/ **adj** [never before noun] not harmed or damaged: *Both children **escaped unharmed** from the burning building.*

unhealthy /ʌnˈhelθi/ **adj 1 CAUSE ILLNESS** ▷ ⓑ likely to damage your health: *Eating too much is unhealthy.* **2 ILL** ▷ ⓑ not strong, and likely to become sick: *She looks pale and unhealthy.* **3 NOT NORMAL** ▷ not normal and slightly unpleasant: *an **unhealthy interest** in weapons*

unheard /ʌnˈhɜːd/ **adj** not listened to or considered: *Her cries **went unheard**.*

un'heard ,of adj [never before noun] never having happened before: *Thirty years ago the disease was unheard of.*

unhelpful /ʌnˈhelpfʊl/ **adj 1** not improving a situation: *an unhelpful remark* **2** ⓑ not wanting to help someone, in a way that seems unfriendly: *The taxi driver was rude and unhelpful.*

unhurt /ʌnˈhɜːt/ **adj** not harmed

unicorn /ˈjuːnɪkɔːn/ **noun** [C] an imaginary white horse with a horn growing from the front of its head

unidentified /ˌʌnaɪˈdentɪfaɪd/ **adj** not recognized: *The body of an unidentified woman was found in a field last night.*

unification /ˌjuːnɪfɪˈkeɪʃᵊn/ **noun** [U] a process in which two or more countries join together and become one country: *the unification of East and West Germany*

uniform¹ /ˈjuːnɪfɔːm/ **noun** [C, U] ⓐ a special set

of clothes that are worn by people who do a particular job or people who go to a particular school: *a **school uniform*** ∘ *a nurse's uniform* ∘ *Tom looks completely different **in uniform*** (= wearing a uniform). • **uniformed** adj *uniformed police officers*

uniform² /ˈjuːnɪfɔːm/ **adj** being the same size, shape, amount, etc: *a row of houses of uniform height* • **uniformity** /ˌjuːnɪˈfɔːməti/ **noun** [U] • **uniformly** adv

unify /ˈjuːnɪfaɪ/ **verb** [T] to join together two or more countries or groups to make a single one: *We need a leader who can unify the party.* • **unified** adj *Many people want a more unified Europe.*

unilateral /ˌjuːnɪˈlætᵊrᵊl/ **adj** A unilateral action or decision is done or made by one country, group, etc without waiting for others to agree: *unilateral nuclear disarmament* • **unilaterally** adv

unimaginable /ˌʌnɪˈmædʒɪnəbl/ **adj** Something that is unimaginable is difficult to imagine because it is so bad, good, big, etc: *unimaginable pain/wealth* • **unimaginably** adv

unimportant /ˌʌnɪmˈpɔːtᵊnt/ **adj** ⓑ not important

uninhabitable /ˌʌnɪnˈhæbɪtəbl/ **adj** too cold, dangerous, etc to live in

uninhabited /ˌʌnɪnˈhæbɪtɪd/ **adj** If a place is uninhabited, no one lives there: *an uninhabited island*

uninhibited /ˌʌnɪnˈhɪbɪtɪd/ **adj** feeling free to behave in any way that you want without worrying about other people's opinions

uninstall /ˌʌnɪnˈstɔːl/ **verb** [T] to remove a computer program from a computer

unintelligible /ˌʌnɪnˈtelɪdʒəbl/ **adj** impossible to understand

unintentional /ˌʌnɪnˈtentʃᵊnᵊl/ **adj** not planned or intended: *If I did offend her, it was entirely unintentional.*

uninterested /ʌnˈɪntrəstɪd/ **adj** ⓑ not interested: *He's completely **uninterested in** politics.*

uninterrupted /ʌnˌɪntᵊrˈʌptɪd/ **adj** continuous: *I want a radio station that offers uninterrupted music.*

union /ˈjuːnjən/ **noun 1** [C] (also UK **trade union**, also US **labor union**) ⓑ an organization that represents people who do a particular job: *teachers'/firefighters' union* **2** [U, no plural] ⓑ a situation in which two or more countries, groups, etc join together to make one country, group, etc: *a move towards full economic union of EU countries* → See also **the European Union**

> 🗹 Word partners for **union**
>
> join a union • a union member/official/leader/representative

Union 'Jack noun [C] (**Union flag**) the red, white and blue flag of the United Kingdom

unique /juːˈniːk/ **adj 1** ⓑ different from every one and everything else: *Everyone's fingerprints are unique.* **2** ⓑ unusual and special: *a unique opportunity* **3 be unique to sb/sth** to exist in only one place, or be connected with only one

U

person or thing: *It's a method of education that is unique to this school.* • **uniquely** adv • **uniqueness** noun [U]

> **!** Common learner error: **unique** or **only**?
>
> **Unique** describes something that is special or unusual because only one example of it exists. If something is not special or important, but only one of it exists, you should use **only**.
> *It is the only bus that goes to the airport.*
> ~~It is the unique bus that goes to the airport.~~

unisex /'juːnɪseks/ adj for both men and women: *unisex clothes* ∘ *a unisex hairdresser*

unison /'juːnɪsən/ noun **in unison** If people do something in unison, they all do it at the same time.

unit /'juːnɪt/ noun [C] **1 GROUP** ▷ a group of people who are responsible for a particular part of an organization: *an anti-terrorist unit* **2 MEASURE** ▷ a measure used to express an amount or quantity: *The kilogram is a unit of weight.* **3 SINGLE** ▷ ⓑ a single, complete thing that may be part of a larger thing: *a French course book with ten units* **4 FURNITURE** ▷ a piece of furniture that fits together with other pieces: *kitchen units* **5 MACHINE** ▷ a small machine, or part of a machine, that has a particular purpose: *a computer's central processing unit* **6 BUILDING** ▷ a single apartment, office, etc in a larger building

unite /juː'naɪt/ verb [I, T] to join together as a group, or to make people join together as a group: *We need a leader who can unite the party.*

united /juː'naɪtɪd/ adj **1** ⓑ If people are united, they all agree about something: *On the issue of education the party is united.* **2** ⓑ joined together: *a united Germany*

the U₁nited ¹Nations noun [group] an international organization that tries to solve world problems in a peaceful way

unity /'juːnəti/ noun [U] a situation in which everyone agrees with each other or wants to stay together: *national unity* ∘ *family unity*

> **✍** Word partners for **unity**
>
> achieve/maintain/restore unity • unity among/between sb • a show of unity

universal /ˌjuːnɪ'vɜːsəl/ adj ⓑ relating to everyone in the world, or to everyone in a particular group: *Kittens and puppies have an almost universal appeal.* • **universally** adv *It's a style of music that is universally popular.*

the universe /'juːnɪvɜːs/ noun ⓑ everything that exists, including stars, space, etc: *Many people believe that there is life elsewhere in the universe.*

university /ˌjuːnɪ'vɜːsəti/ noun [C, U] ⓐ a place where students study at a high level to get a degree (= type of qualification): *the University of Cambridge* ∘ *I applied to three universities.* ∘ *mainly UK Sarah studied chemistry* **at university.** ∘ *mainly UK I want to* **go to university** *when I finish school.*

> **✍** Word partners for **university**
>
> go to university • at university • a university course

unjust /ʌn'dʒʌst/ adj not fair: *unjust treatment/laws/sanctions* • **unjustly** adv

unjustified /ʌn'dʒʌstɪfaɪd/ adj done without a reason and not deserved: *unjustified criticism*

unkempt /ʌn'kempt/ adj untidy: *Her hair was long and unkempt.*

unkind /ʌn'kaɪnd/ adj ⓑ slightly cruel: *I didn't tell her the truth because I thought it would be unkind.* • **unkindly** adv • **unkindness** noun [U]

unknown¹ /ʌn'nəʊn/ adj **1** ⓑ not known: *The cause of his death is still unknown.* **2** not famous: *an unknown actor* → See also **an unknown quantity**

unknown² /ʌn'nəʊn/ noun **1 the unknown** things that you have not experienced and know nothing about: *It's normal to fear the unknown.* **2** [C] someone who is not famous: *The game was won by a complete unknown.*

unlawful /ʌn'lɔːfəl/ adj formal illegal: *unlawful possession of guns* • **unlawfully** adv

unleaded /ʌn'ledɪd/ adj Unleaded fuel does not contain lead (= a metal).

unleash /ʌn'liːʃ/ verb [T] to suddenly cause a strong reaction: *The newspaper report unleashed a storm of protest from readers.*

unless /ən'les/ conjunction ⓑ except if: *I won't call you unless there are any problems.*

unlike /ʌn'laɪk/ preposition **1** ⓑ different from someone or something: *Jackie's really clever, unlike her sister.* ∘ *The furniture was unlike anything she had ever seen.* **2** not typical of someone or something: *It's unlike her to be quiet – was there something wrong?*

unlikely /ʌn'laɪkli/ adj **1** ⓑ not expected to happen: *[+ (that)] It's unlikely that I'll be able to come to the party.* ∘ *[+ to do sth] He's unlikely to arrive before midday.* **2** probably not true: *an unlikely explanation*

unlimited /ʌn'lɪmɪtɪd/ adj ⓑ without any limits: *a service that offers unlimited Internet access*

unload /ʌn'ləʊd/ verb **1** [I, T] to remove things from a vehicle: *Can you help me unload the car?* **2** [I] If a ship, aircraft, etc unloads, goods are taken off it.

unlock /ʌn'lɒk/ verb [T] ⓑ to open something which is locked using a key

unlucky /ʌn'lʌki/ adj ⓑ having or causing bad luck: *[+ to do sth] The team played well and was unlucky to lose.* ∘ *Some people think it's unlucky to walk under ladders.* • **unluckily** adv

unmarked /ʌn'mɑːkt/ adj having no signs or words that show what something is: *an unmarked grave*

unmarried /ʌn'mærɪd/ adj not married

unmatched /ʌn'mætʃt/ adj better than anyone or anything else: *Horses have an athletic beauty unmatched by any other animal.*

unmistakable /ˌʌnmɪ'steɪkəbl/ adj Something that is unmistakable is very obvious and cannot

U

be confused with anything else: *an unmistakable look of disappointment* • **unmistakably** adv

unmoved /ʌnˈmuːvd/ adj not feeling any emotion: *It's impossible to remain unmoved by pictures of starving children.*

unnamed /ʌnˈneɪmd/ adj An unnamed person or thing is talked about but their name is not said: *The money was given by an unnamed businessman.*

unnatural /ʌnˈnætʃʳrᵊl/ adj 🔵 not normal or right: *an unnatural interest in death* • **unnaturally** adv *unnaturally thin*

unnecessary /ʌnˈnesəsᵊri/ adj **1** 🔵 not needed: *You don't want to make any unnecessary car journeys in this weather.* **2** unkind: *Why did she say that? That was unnecessary.* • **unnecessarily** /ʌnˈnesəsᵊrᵊli/ adv

unnerve /ʌnˈnɜːv/ verb [T] to make someone feel nervous or frightened

unnerving /ʌnˈnɜːvɪŋ/ adj making you feel nervous or frightened: *He kept looking at me which I found unnerving.*

unnoticed /ʌnˈnəʊtɪst/ adj without being seen or noticed: *We managed to slip away unnoticed.*

unobtrusive /ˌʌnəbˈtruːsɪv/ adj not attracting attention: *He was quiet and unobtrusive.* • **unobtrusively** adv

unoccupied /ʌnˈɒkjəpaɪd/ adj An unoccupied building, room, seat, etc has no one in it.

unofficial /ˌʌnəˈfɪʃᵊl/ adj not said or done by the government or someone in authority: *Unofficial reports suggest the death toll from the earthquake is around 600.* • **unofficially** adv

unorthodox /ʌnˈɔːθədɒks/ adj unusual and different from most people's opinions, methods, etc: *unorthodox ideas/views* ∘ *an unorthodox style of teaching*

unpack /ʌnˈpæk/ verb [I, T] 🔵 to take things out of a bag, box, etc: *Bella unpacked her suitcase.* ∘ *I haven't had time to unpack yet.*

unpaid /ʌnˈpeɪd/ adj **1** An unpaid debt, tax, etc has not been paid. **2** working without getting any money: *unpaid work*

unpalatable /ʌnˈpælətəbl/ adj formal shocking and difficult to accept: *an unpalatable fact*

unpack

unparalleled /ʌnˈpærᵊleld/ adj formal better, greater, worse, etc than anything else: *an act of unparalleled cruelty*

unplanned /ʌnˈplænd/ adj not planned or expected: *an unplanned pregnancy*

unpleasant /ʌnˈplezᵊnt/ adj **1** 🔵 not enjoyable or pleasant: *an unpleasant experience/smell* **2** rude and angry: *The waiter got quite unpleasant with us.* • **unpleasantly** adv

unplug /ʌnˈplʌg/ verb [T] to stop a piece of electrical equipment being connected to an electricity supply by pulling its plug (= object at the end of a cable) out of the wall

unpopular /ʌnˈpɒpjələʳ/ adj 🔵 disliked by most people: *an unpopular idea* ∘ *an unpopular teacher* • **unpopularity** /ʌnˌpɒpjəˈlærəti/ noun [U]

unprecedented /ʌnˈpresɪdᵊntɪd/ adj never having happened before: *The Internet has given people unprecedented access to information.*

unpredictable /ˌʌnprɪˈdɪktəbl/ adj 🔵 changing so much that you do not know what will happen next: *unpredictable weather conditions* • **unpredictability** /ˌʌnprɪˌdɪktəˈbɪləti/ noun [U]

unprofessional /ˌʌnprəˈfeʃᵊnᵊl/ adj behaving badly at work: *an unprofessional attitude*

unprovoked /ˌʌnprəˈvəʊkt/ adj An unprovoked attack is one in which the person who is attacked has done nothing to cause it.

unqualified /ʌnˈkwɒlɪfaɪd/ adj **1** without the qualifications or knowledge to do something [+ to do sth] *She was totally unqualified to look after children.* **2** [always before noun] formal total and not limited in any way: *an unqualified success*

unquestionably /ʌnˈkwestʃənəbli/ adv in a way that is obvious and causes no doubt: *She is unquestionably the best person for the job.*

unravel /ʌnˈrævᵊl/ verb [I, T] (mainly UK **unravelling, unravelled**, US **unraveling, unraveled**) **1** If you unravel a difficult situation or story, or if it unravels, it becomes clear and easier to understand: *No one has yet unravelled the mystery of his death.* **2** to stop being twisted together, or to move pieces of string, etc so that they are no twisted together

unreal /ʌnˈrɪəl/ adj Something that is unreal seems so strange that it is difficult to believe: *For a while I couldn't believe she was dead – it all seemed unreal.* • **unreality** /ʌnriˈæləti/ noun [U]

unrealistic /ˌʌnrɪəˈlɪstɪk/ adj 🔵 not thinking about what is likely to happen or what you can really do: *She has a totally unrealistic view of life* ∘ [+ to do sth] *It's unrealistic to expect their decision before Tuesday.*

unreasonable /ʌnˈriːzᵊnəbl/ adj 🔵 not fair: *unreasonable demands/behaviour* ∘ [+ to do sth] *It seems unreasonable to expect one person to do both jobs.* • **unreasonably** adv

unrelated /ˌʌnrɪˈleɪtɪd/ adj having no connection: *Police said his death was unrelated to the attack.*

unrelenting /ˌʌnrɪˈlentɪŋ/ adj formal never stopping or getting any less extreme: *unrelenting pressure* ∘ *The heat was unrelenting.*

unreliable /ˌʌnrɪˈlaɪəbl/ adj 🔵 not able to be trusted or depended on: *an unreliable witness.* ∘ *The trains were noisy, dirty, and unreliable.*

unremarkable /ˌʌnrɪˈmɑːkəbl/ adj ordinary and not interesting: *an unremarkable town*

unremitting /ˌʌnrɪˈmɪtɪŋ/ adj formal never stopping or getting any less extreme: *unremitting hostility/pressure* ∘ *unremitting efforts*

unrepentant /ˌʌnrɪˈpentənt/ adj not feeling sorry about something bad that you have done

unreservedly /ˌʌnrɪˈzɜːvɪdli/ adv completely: *The minister has apologized unreservedly.*

unresolved /ˌʌnrɪˈzɒlvd/ **adj** formal If a problem or question is unresolved, there is still no solution or answer: *The question of who owns the land remains unresolved.*

unrest /ʌnˈrest/ **noun** [U] a situation in which a lot of people are angry about something and are likely to become violent: *political/social unrest*

> ☑ Word partners for **unrest**
>
> cause unrest • continuing/growing unrest • unrest **among** sb • unrest **over** sth • **a wave of** unrest • **political/social** unrest

unrestrained /ˌʌnrɪˈstreɪnd/ **adj** not limited or controlled: *unrestrained anger*

unrivalled mainly UK (US **unrivaled**) /ʌnˈraɪvəld/ **adj** better than any other of the same type: *The museum has an **unrivalled collection** of modern American paintings.* ∘ *an **unrivalled reputation***

unroll /ʌnˈrəʊl/ **verb** [T] to open something that was rolled into a tube shape and make it flat: *He unrolled the carpet.*

unruly /ʌnˈruːli/ **adj** **1** behaving badly and difficult to control: *unruly children* **2** Unruly hair is difficult to keep tidy.

unsafe /ʌnˈseɪf/ **adj** **1** dangerous: *The building is unsafe.* ∘ [+ to do sth] *The water was dirty and unsafe to drink.* **2** If you feel unsafe, you feel that you are in danger: *Many women feel unsafe on the streets at night.*

unsatisfactory /ʌnˌsætɪsˈfæktəri/ **adj** ⑫ not good enough to be acceptable: *Many school buildings are in an unsatisfactory condition.*

unsavoury UK (US **unsavory**) /ʌnˈseɪvəri/ **adj** unpleasant and morally offensive: *an unsavoury reputation/incident/character*

unscathed /ʌnˈskeɪðd/ **adj** [never before noun] not harmed: *The driver of the car was killed but both passengers escaped unscathed.*

unscrew /ʌnˈskruː/ **verb** [T] **1** to remove something by twisting it: *I can't unscrew the lid.* **2** to remove something by taking the screws (= small, metal pieces) out of it

unscrupulous /ʌnˈskruːpjələs/ **adj** behaving in a way that is dishonest or unfair in order to get what you want: *an unscrupulous financial adviser*

unseat /ʌnˈsiːt/ **verb** [T] to remove someone from a powerful position: *Who would be most likely to unseat the President at the next election?*

unseen /ʌnˈsiːn/ **adj, adv** not seen or noticed: *an exhibition of previously unseen photographs*

unsettled /ʌnˈsetld/ **adj** **1** changing often: *The weather continues to be unsettled.* **2** anxious and not able to relax or feel happy in a situation: *Children tend to get unsettled if you keep changing their routine.*

unsettling /ʌnˈsetlɪŋ/ **adj** making you feel anxious: *an unsettling experience/feeling*

unsightly /ʌnˈsaɪtli/ **adj** unpleasant to look at: *unsightly piles of litter*

unskilled /ʌnˈskɪld/ **adj** **1** without special skills or qualifications: *an unskilled labourer/worker* **2** Unskilled work does not need people with special skills or qualifications.

unsociable /ʌnˈsəʊʃəbl/ **adj** not wanting to be with other people

unsolicited /ˌʌnsəˈlɪsɪtɪd/ **adj** not asked for and often not wanted: *unsolicited advice/offer*

unsolved /ʌnˈsɒlvd/ **adj** having no answer or solution: *an unsolved mystery/murder/crime*

unsound /ʌnˈsaʊnd/ **adj** **1** based on ideas, facts, and reasons that are wrong: *an unsound practice* **2** in a bad condition: *The bridge was structurally unsound.*

unspeakable /ʌnˈspiːkəbl/ **adj** extremely bad or shocking: *unspeakable crimes/suffering* • **unspeakably adv**

unspecified /ʌnˈspesɪfaɪd/ **adj** If something is unspecified, you are not told what it is: *The court awarded her an unspecified amount of money.*

unspoiled (also UK **unspoilt**) /ʌnˈspɔɪlt/ **adj** An unspoiled place is beautiful because it has not been changed or damaged by people: *an island with clean, unspoiled beaches*

unspoken /ʌnˈspəʊkən/ **adj** not said, but thought or felt: *unspoken doubts*

unstable /ʌnˈsteɪbl/ **adj** **1 CHANGE** ▷ likely to change or end suddenly: *an unstable situation* ∘ *an unstable economy* **2 PERSON** ▷ If someone is unstable, their moods and behaviour change suddenly, especially because they are mentally ill. **3 MOVE** ▷ not fixed or safe and likely to move: *That chair looks a bit unstable.*

unsteady /ʌnˈstedi/ **adj** moving slightly from side to side, as if you might fall: *The alcohol had made her unsteady on her feet.*

unstuck /ʌnˈstʌk/ **adj come unstuck a** If something comes unstuck, it stops being fixed to something: *One of the photos has come unstuck.* **b** UK informal to experience difficulties and fail: *The negotiations came unstuck at a crucial stage.*

unsubscribe /ˌʌnsəbˈskraɪb/ **verb** [I, T] to remove your name from an Internet mailing list (= a list of names and addresses that an organization sends information to)

unsuccessful /ˌʌnsəkˈsesfəl/ **adj** ⑫ not achieving what was wanted or intended: *an unsuccessful attempt/effort* • **unsuccessfully adv**

unsuitable /ʌnˈsuːtəbl/ **adj** ⑫ not acceptable or right for someone or something: *My parents considered the programme unsuitable for children.*

unsung /ʌnˈsʌŋ/ **adj** not famous or praised although you have done something very well: *He was the unsung hero of the match.*

unsure /ʌnˈʃʊər/ **adj** **1** ⑫ not certain or having doubts: *I'm a bit unsure about what to do.* **2 unsure of yourself** without confidence

unsuspecting /ˌʌnsəˈspektɪŋ/ **adj** [always before noun] not aware that something bad is happening: *In each case the unsuspecting victim had been invited into Cooper's home.*

unsustainable /ˌʌnsəˈsteɪnəbl/ **adj** **1** Something that is unsustainable cannot continue at the same rate **2** causing damage to the environment by using more of something than can be replaced naturally: *unsustainable fishing methods*

unsympathetic /ˌʌnsɪmpəˈθetɪk/ **adj** **1** showing that you do not understand or care about someone's problems: *I told him I'd got a cold*

U

but he was completely unsympathetic. **2** not agreeing with or supporting someone's ideas or actions

untangle /ʌnˈtæŋgl/ **verb** [T] **1** to separate pieces of string, hair, wire, etc that have become twisted together: *I'm trying to untangle these wires.* **2** to understand the different parts of a situation that has become confused or very complicated: *Historians have tried to untangle the complex issues behind the events.*

untapped /ʌnˈtæpt/ **adj** not yet used: *untapped potential*

untenable /ʌnˈtenəbl/ **adj** formal If an argument, action, or situation is untenable, it cannot be supported or defended from criticism: *an untenable position*

unthinkable /ʌnˈθɪŋkəbl/ **adj** If something is unthinkable, it is so strange that you cannot imagine it will ever happen: *Thirty years ago a no-smoking restaurant would have been unthinkable.*

untidy

untidy /ʌnˈtaɪdi/ **adj** ⓑ1 not tidy: *an untidy room* ◦ *She's really untidy at home.*

untie /ʌnˈtaɪ/ **verb** [T] **(untying, untied)** ⓑ2 to open a knot or something that has been tied with a knot: *I untied my shoelaces and kicked off my shoes.*

until /ənˈtɪl/ **preposition, conjunction** (also **till**) **1** ⓐ1 continuing to happen before a particular time or event and then stopping: *The show will be on until the end of the month.* ◦ *Whisk the egg whites until they look white and fluffy.* **2** ⓐ2 as far as: *Carry on until you reach the traffic lights and turn right.* **3** **not until** ⓑ1 not before a particular time or event: *It doesn't open until 7.* ◦ *We won't start until Jeanne arrives.*

untie

untimely /ʌnˈtaɪmli/ **adj** happening too soon: *her untimely death from cancer*

untold /ʌnˈtəʊld/ **adj** [always before noun] too much to be measured or counted: *untold riches* ◦ *untold damage*

untouched /ʌnˈtʌtʃt/ **adj** **1** not changed or damaged in any way: *Most of the island remains untouched by tourism.* **2** If food is untouched, it has not been eaten.

untoward /ˌʌntəˈwɔːd/ **adj** formal unexpected and causing problems: *If nothing untoward happens, we should be there by midday.*

untrained /ʌnˈtreɪnd/ **adj** **1** never having been taught the skills for a particular job: *untrained staff* **2** **the untrained eye** someone without the skill or knowledge to judge what they see: *To the untrained eye, most fake diamonds look real.*

untried /ʌnˈtraɪd/ **adj** not yet used or tested: *new and untried technology*

untrue /ʌnˈtruː/ **adj** false

untruth /ʌnˈtruːθ/ **noun** [C] formal a lie, or something that is not true

unused¹ /ʌnˈjuːzd/ **adj** not used now or not used before now: *an unused room*

unused² /ʌnˈjuːst/ **adj** **be unused to sth** to not have experience of something: *I was unused to city life.*

unusual /ʌnˈjuːʒuəl/ **adj** ⓐ2 different and not ordinary, often in a way that is interesting or exciting: *an unusual name* ◦ [+ to do sth] *It's fairly unusual to keep insects as pets.*

unusually /ʌnˈjuːʒuəli/ **adv** **1** **unusually big, strong/good, etc** ⓑ2 bigger/stronger/better, etc than is normal: *unusually warm weather* **2** **unusually for sb** in a way that is not usual for someone: *Unusually for me, I actually couldn't finish my meal.*

unveil /ʌnˈveɪl/ **verb** [T] **1** to tell the public about an idea or plan that was secret before: *The new policy is due to be unveiled later this month.* **2** to remove the cover from an object as part of an official ceremony

unwanted /ʌnˈwɒntɪd/ **adj** not wanted: *an unwanted gift*

unwarranted /ʌnˈwɒrəntɪd/ **adj** formal without a good reason: *unwarranted intrusion*

unwary /ʌnˈweəri/ **adj** not aware of possible dangers: *Unwary travellers* can easily get lost in these parts.

unwelcome /ʌnˈwelkəm/ **adj** not wanted: *unwelcome publicity* ◦ *an unwelcome visitor*

unwell /ʌnˈwel/ **adj** [never before noun] formal sick: *to feel/look unwell*

unwieldy /ʌnˈwiːldi/ **adj** An unwieldy object is difficult to carry because it is heavy, large, or a strange shape.

unwilling /ʌnˈwɪlɪŋ/ **adj** ⓑ2 not wanting to do something: [+ to do sth] *A lot of people are unwilling to accept change.* ● **unwillingly** adv ● **unwillingness** noun [U]

unwind /ʌnˈwaɪnd/ **verb** **(unwound)** **1** [I] informal to relax, especially after working: *Music helps me to unwind.* **2** [I, T] If you unwind something or if something unwinds, it stops being curled or twisted round something else and is made straight: *He unwound the bandage.*

unwise /ʌnˈwaɪz/ **adj** stupid and likely to cause problems: *an unwise decision* ● **unwisely** adv

unwittingly /ʌnˈwɪtɪŋli/ **adv** without intending to do something: *I apologized for the chaos I had unwittingly caused.*

unworkable /ʌnˈwɜːkəbl/ **adj** A plan that is unworkable is impossible: *The policy has been described as unworkable.*

unwrap /ʌnˈræp/ **verb** [T] (**unwrapping, unwrapped**) to remove the paper, cloth, etc that is covering something: *She carefully unwrapped the present.*

unwrap

unwritten /ʌnˈrɪtᵊn/ **adj** an **unwritten agreement/law/rule** an agreement/law, etc that is accepted and obeyed by most people but is not formally written

unzip /ʌnˈzɪp/ **verb** [T] (**unzipping, unzipped**)
1 to open something by using its zip (= two rows of metal or plastic points that fasten two sides together): *He unzipped his trousers.* **2** to make a file bigger again after it has been zipped (= made smaller so that you can send or store it) so that it can easily be used

up¹ /ʌp/ **adv, preposition 1 HIGHER PLACE** ▷ ⓐ₂ towards or in a higher place: *He ran up the stairs.* ∘ *Pick up your clothes and put them away.* ∘ *She looked up and smiled at me.* **2 VERTICAL** ▷ ⓐ₁ vertical or as straight as possible: *He stood up.* ∘ *She opened her eyes and sat up.* **3 INCREASE** ▷ ⓑ₂ to a greater degree, amount, volume, etc: *Inflation keeps pushing prices up.* ∘ *Can you turn up the heat? I'm freezing!* ∘ *Please speak up* (= speak louder), *I can't hear you.* **4 COMPLETELY** ▷ ⓑ₂ used to emphasize that someone completes an action or uses all of something: *I used up all my money.* ∘ *Eat up the rest of your dinner.* **5 up the road/street, etc** ⓐ₂ along or further along the street/road, etc: *My best friend lives up the street from me.* ∘ *He ran up the path and hugged her.* **6 go/walk, etc up to sb/ sth** ⓑ₁ to walk directly towards someone or something until you are next to them: *He walked straight up to me and introduced himself.* **7 DIRECTION** ▷ in or towards a particular direction, usually north: *We moved from London up to Scotland.* ∘ *Chris lives up north.* **8 up and down** ⓑ₂ If something or someone moves up and down, they move repeatedly in one direction and then in the opposite direction: *The children were constantly running up and down the stairs.* **9 up to 10/20, etc** ⓑ₁ any amount under 10/20, etc: *We can invite up to 65 people.* **10 up to** ⓑ₁ until a particular time: *You can call me up to midnight.* **11 up to sth** equal in quality or achievement: *His work wasn't up to his usual standard.* **12 up to sth/doing sth** able to do something: *It'll be a while before I feel up to walking again.* **13 be up to sth** informal ⓑ₁ to be doing or planning something, often something

secret and bad: *Joe, what are you up to?* **14 be up to sb** ⓑ₁ If an action or decision is up to someone, they are responsible for doing or making it: *I can't decide for you Jack, it's up to you.* ∘ [+ to do sth] *It's up to her to decide whether she wants to enter the competition.* **15 be up against sb/sth** If you are up against a situation or a person, they make it very difficult for you to achieve what you want to achieve: *We were up against some of the best players in the world.*

up² /ʌp/ **adj** [never before noun] **1 NOT IN BED** ▷ not in bed: *I was up all night with the baby.* ∘ *Is she up yet?* **2 be up and around/about** to be well enough after an illness to get out of bed and move around **3 FINISHED** ▷ If a period of time is up, it has ended: *My health club membership is up.* **4 INCREASE** ▷ If a level or amount is up, it has increased: *Profits are up by 26%.* **5 ROAD** ▷ UK If a road is up, it is being repaired. **6 OPERATING** ▷ If a computer system is up, it is operating. **7 SPORT** ▷ US In baseball and similar sports, if a player is up, they are taking a turn to play. **8 be up and running** If a system, organization, or machine is up and running, it is operating.

IDIOM **be up for sth** informal to want to do something: *We're going clubbing tonight if you're up for it.*

up³ /ʌp/ **verb** [T] (**upping, upped**) to increase something: *Dad's upped my allowance by fifty cents a week.*

up-and-coming /ˌʌpᵊŋˈkʌmɪŋ/ **adj** [always before noun] becoming popular and likely to achieve success: *He's a young, up-and-coming DJ.*

upbeat /ˈʌpbiːt/ **adj** informal positive and expecting a situation to be good or successful: *He remains upbeat about the future.*

upbringing /ˈʌpˌbrɪŋɪŋ/ **noun** [no plural] ⓑ₂ the way your parents treat you when you are growing up: *a middle-class/religious upbringing*

upcoming /ˈʌpˌkʌmɪŋ/ **adj** [always before noun] An upcoming event will happen soon: *the upcoming elections*

update¹ /ʌpˈdeɪt/ **verb** [T] **1** ⓑ₁ to add new information: *We've just updated our website.* ∘ *I'll update you on* (= tell you about) *any developments.* **2** ⓑ₂ to make something more modern: *They need to update their image.*

update² /ˈʌpdeɪt/ **noun** [C] **1** ⓑ₂ new information: *I'll need regular updates on your progress.* **2** ⓑ₂ a new form of something that existed at an earlier time: *It's an update of an old 60's movie.*

┌───┐
│ **✍ Word partners for update noun**   │
│   │
│ get/give/provide an update • an update on│
│ sth • an update from sb   │
└───┘

upfront¹ /ˌʌpˈfrʌnt/ **adj 1** paid or obtained before work starts: *an upfront payment/fee* **2** behaving in a way that makes your beliefs and intentions obvious to other people: *She's very upfront about her dislike of men.*

upfront² /ˌʌpˈfrʌnt/ **adv** If you pay someone upfront, you pay them before they work for you.

upgrade /ʌpˈɡreɪd/ **verb** [T] ⓑ₂ to improve

U

something so that it is of a higher quality or a newer model: *to upgrade a computer* • **upgrade** /ˈʌpɡreɪd/ **noun** [C]

upheaval /ʌpˈhiːvəl/ **noun** [C, U] a very big change that causes difficulty or confusion: *political/social upheaval*

uphill[1] /ʌpˈhɪl/ **adj an uphill battle/struggle/task** something that is difficult to do and needs a lot of effort: *I can lose weight but it's a real uphill struggle.*

uphill[2] /ʌpˈhɪl/ **adv** towards the top of a hill: *We'd walked half a mile uphill.*

uphold /ʌpˈhəʊld/ **verb** [T] (**upheld**) **1** to agree with a decision, especially a legal one, and say it was correct: *The court upheld the ruling.* **2** to support a decision, principle, or law: *Police officers are expected to uphold the law.*

upholstery /ʌpˈhəʊlstəri/ **noun** [U] the material that covers chairs and other types of seats

upkeep /ˈʌpkiːp/ **noun** [U] the process of keeping something in good condition, or of keeping a person or animal healthy

upland /ˈʌplənd/ **adj** [always before noun] existing on a hill or mountain: *upland areas*

uplands /ˈʌpləndz/ **noun** [plural] high areas of land: *the uplands of Nepal*

uplifting /ʌpˈlɪftɪŋ/ **adj** making you feel happy and full of good feelings: *an uplifting film*

upload /ʌpˈləʊd/ **verb** [T] 🔵 to copy computer programs or information electronically, usually from a small computer to a larger one or to the Internet: *I uploaded the file as soon as I had finished working on it.* → Compare **download** → See Study Page **The Web and the Internet** on page Centre 36

upmarket /ˌʌpˈmɑːkɪt/ **adj** mainly UK (US **upscale**) expensive and used by people who are rich and from a high social class: *an upmarket hotel/restaurant*

upon /əˈpɒn/ **preposition** formal 🔵

upper /ˈʌpər/ **adj** [always before noun] **1** 🔵 at a higher position: *an upper floor* ∘ *the upper lip* ∘ *the upper body* **2** of a higher social class **3 the upper limit** the highest amount or level, or the longest time that something is allowed → See also **get/gain the upper hand**

upper 'case noun [U] letters written as capitals

upper 'class noun [C] the highest social class of people: *members of the upper classes* • **upper-class adj** *an upper-class accent*

uppermost /ˈʌpəməʊst/ **adj 1** highest: *the building's uppermost floors* **2 be uppermost in sb's mind** to be the most important thing someone is thinking about: *The safety of her children was uppermost in her mind.*

upright[1] /ˈʌpraɪt/ **adv** 🔵 vertical and as straight as possible: *to sit/stand upright* → See also **bolt upright**

upright[2] /ˈʌpraɪt/ **adj 1** 🔵 straight up or vertical: *Please return your seat to an upright position and fasten your seat belt.* **2** honest and morally good: *an upright citizen*

uprising /ˈʌpˌraɪzɪŋ/ **noun** [C] a situation in which a large group of people try to make political changes or change the government by

fighting: [usually singular] *a general/popular uprising*

uproar /ˈʌprɔːr/ **noun** [U, no plural] a situation in which many people complain about something angrily: *The book caused an uproar in the United States.* ∘ *Local residents are UK in uproar/US in an uproar over plans for the new road.*

> ✏️ Word partners for **uproar**
>
> cause/provoke (an) uproar • be UK in/US in an uproar • uproar among sb • uproar at/over sth

uproot /ʌpˈruːt/ **verb** [T] **1** to pull a tree or plant out of the ground: *Hundreds of trees were uprooted in the storm.* **2** to make someone leave a place where they have been living for a long time: *The war has uprooted nearly half the country's population.*

ups and 'downs noun [plural] the mixture of good and bad things that happen to people: *Like most married couples, we've had our ups and downs.*

upscale /ˈʌpˌskeɪl/ **adj** US (mainly UK **upmarket**) expensive and used by people who are rich and from a high social class: *an upscale restaurant/neighborhood*

upset[1] /ʌpˈset/ **adj 1** 🅰️ unhappy or worried because something unpleasant has happened: *They'd had an argument and she was still upset about it.* ∘ *Mike got very upset when I told him the news.* **2 upset stomach/tummy** an illness in the stomach

upset[2] /ʌpˈset/ **verb** [T] (**upsetting**, **upset**) **1** 🔵 to make someone feel unhappy or worried: *The phone call had clearly upset her.* **2** to cause problems for something: *If I arrived later, would that upset your plans?* **3 upset sb's stomach** to make someone feel sick in the stomach

upset[3] /ˈʌpset/ **noun** [C] **1** a situation in which someone beats the player or team that was expected to win: *They caused a major upset by beating the top team 3-1.* **2 a stomach/tummy upset** UK an illness in the stomach **3** a difficulty or problem: *We had the usual upsets but overall the day went well.*

upsetting /ʌpˈsetɪŋ/ **adj** making you feel unhappy or worried: *I found the programme very upsetting.*

the upshot /ˈʌpʃɒt/ **noun** the final result of a discussion or series of events: *The upshot is that we've decided to move to Sydney.*

upside 'down[1] **adv** 🔵 turned so that the part that is usually at the top is now at the bottom: *One of the pictures had been hung upside down.* ∘ *Turn the jar upside down and shake it.*

IDIOM **turn sth upside down a** to make a place very untidy while looking for something **b** to change someone's life or a system completely: *Their lives were turned upside down when their son was arrested.*

upside 'down[2] **adj** 🔵 turned so that the part that is usually at the top is now at the bottom: *Why is this box upside down?*

upstage /ʌpˈsteɪdʒ/ **verb** [T] to do something

upside down

that takes people's attention away from someone or something and gives it to you instead: *You mustn't upstage the bride.*

upstairs /ʌpˈsteəz/ **adv** 🅐🄫 on or to a higher level of a building: *He ran upstairs to answer the phone.* • **upstairs adj** 🄑 *an upstairs bedroom*

upstart /ˈʌpstɑːt/ **noun** [C] someone who has just started a job but already thinks they are very important

upstate /ˌʌpˈsteɪt/ **adj** US in the northern part of a US state (= one of the parts into which the country is divided): *upstate New York* • **upstate adv** *She's taken a trip upstate with some friends.*

upstream /ʌpˈstriːm/ **adv** along a river in the opposite direction to the way that the water is moving

upsurge /ˈʌpsɜːdʒ/ **noun** [C] a sudden increase: *an upsurge in violent crime*

uptake /ˈʌpteɪk/ **noun** informal **be slow/quick on the uptake** to be slow/quick to understand something

uptight /ʌpˈtaɪt/ **adj** informal worried or nervous and not able to relax

up-to-date /ˌʌptəˈdeɪt/ **adj 1** 🄑 modern, and using the most recent technology or knowledge **2** 🄑 having the most recent information: *The Internet keeps us up-to-date.*

up-to-the-minute /ˌʌptəðəˈmɪnɪt/ **adj** most recent: *up-to-the-minute news*

uptown /ʌpˈtaʊn/ **adj, adv** US in or to the northern part of a city: *She lives uptown.*

upturn /ˈʌptɜːn/ **noun** [C] an improvement, especially in economic conditions or a business: *There's been a sharp upturn in sales.*

upturned /ʌpˈtɜːnd/ **adj** pointing up, or turned so the under side faces up: *an upturned boat*

upward /ˈʌpwəd/ **adj** [always before noun] moving towards a higher place or level: *an upward glance* ○ *an upward trend in sales*

upwards /ˈʌpwədz/ **adv** mainly UK (mainly US

upward) 1 towards a higher place or level: *House prices have started moving upwards again.* **2 upwards of sth** more than a particular amount: *Double rooms cost upwards of 70 euros a night.*

uranium /jʊəˈreɪniəm/ **noun** [U] a heavy, grey metal that is used in the production of nuclear power

Uranus /ˈjʊərⁿnəs/ **noun** [no plural] the planet that is seventh from the Sun, after Saturn and before Neptune

urban /ˈɜːbⁿn/ **adj** 🄑 belonging or relating to a town or city: *urban areas* ○ *urban development*

urbane /ɜːˈbeɪn/ **adj** confident, relaxed, and polite: *With his good looks and urbane manner, he was very popular.*

urbanize (also UK **urbanise**) /ˈɜːbⁿnaɪz/ **verb** [T] to build on land in the countryside so that the area becomes part of a town or city

urge¹ /ɜːdʒ/ **verb** [T] **1 urge sb to do sth** to try to persuade someone to do something: *His parents urged him to go to university.* **2** formal to strongly advise an action: *Financial experts are **urging caution**.*

PHRASAL VERB **urge sb on** to encourage someone to do or achieve something: *The crowd was cheering and urging her on.*

urge² /ɜːdʒ/ **noun** [C] a strong wish or need: [+ to do sth] *I resisted a powerful **urge** to slap him.*

> 🔲 Word partners for **urge noun**
>
> feel/have/resist/satisfy an urge • an irresistible/overwhelming/strong/sudden/uncontrollable urge

urgency /ˈɜːdʒⁿnsi/ **noun** [U] the state of being very important and needing you to take action immediately: *a **matter of** great **urgency***

> 🔲 Word partners for **urgency**
>
> a **matter of** urgency • a **sense of** urgency • the urgency **of** sth

urgent /ˈɜːdʒⁿnt/ **adj** 🄑 very important and needing you to take action immediately: *an urgent message* ○ *The refugees were **in urgent need of** food and water.* • **urgently adv** 🄑 *I need to **speak to** you **urgently**.*

urinate /ˈjʊərɪneɪt/ **verb** [I] to get rid of urine from your body

urine /ˈjʊərɪn/ **noun** [U] the liquid that comes out of your body when you go to the toilet

URL /juːɑːrˈel/ abbreviation for uniform resource locator: a website address → See Study Page **The Web and the Internet** on page Centre 36

urn /ɜːn/ **noun** [C] **1** a round container that is used for plants or to store someone's ashes (= the powder that is left after a dead body has been burned) **2** a metal container that is used to make a large amount of coffee or tea and to keep it hot

us strong /ʌs/ weak /əs/, /s/ **pronoun** 🄐 used after a verb or preposition to refer to the person who is speaking or writing and one or more other people: *She gave us all a present.* ○ *Would you like to have dinner with us next Saturday?*

U

USA /ˌjuːesˈeɪ/ **noun** abbreviation for United States of America

usage /ˈjuːsɪdʒ/ **noun 1** [C, U] the way that words are used: *a guide to English grammar and usage* **2** [U] the amount of something that is used, or the way that something is used: *restrictions on water usage*

USB /ˌjuːesˈbiː/ **noun** [C] abbreviation for Universal Serial Bus: a part of a computer that allows you to connect extra devices, such as printers and cameras

use¹ /juːz/ **verb** [T] **(used) 1** PURPOSE ▷ **A1** If you use something, you do something with it for a particular purpose: *Can I use your pen?* ∘ *She uses her car for work.* ∘ [+ to do sth] *Nick used the money to buy a new computer.* **2** MAKE LESS ▷ **B1** to take an amount from a supply of something: *A shower uses less water than a bath.* **3** PERSON ▷ to treat someone badly in order to get what you want: *He was just using me to make his girlfriend jealous.* **4** WORD ▷ to say or write a particular word or phrase: *'Autumn' is used in British English and 'fall' in American English.* **5** could use sth mainly US informal something that you say when you want or need something: *I could use some help with these packages, please.*

PHRASAL VERB **use sth up** **B2** to finish a supply of something: *Someone's used up all the milk.*

use² /juːs/ **noun 1** USING ▷ [U] **A2** the act of using something, or of being used: *an increase in the use of mobile phones* ∘ *Guests have free use of the hotel swimming pool.* ∘ *Turn the machine off when it's not in use* (= being used). **2** PURPOSE ▷ [C] **B1** a purpose for which something is used: *A food processor has a variety of uses in the kitchen.* ∘ *Can you find a use for this box?* **3** be (of) any/some use **B2** to be useful: *Is this book of any use to you?* **4** be (of) no use **B2** to not be useful: *His advice was no use at all.* **5** be no use; be no use doing sth **B2** used to say that trying to do something has no effect: *It was no use talking to him – he wouldn't listen.* **6** WORD ▷ [C] **B1** one of the meanings of a word, or the way that a particular word is used: *Can you list all the uses of the verb 'go'?* **7** the use of sth permission to use something, or the ability to use something: *Martin has offered me the use of his car.* **8** make use of sth to use something that is available: *We were encouraged to make use of all the facilities.*

used¹ /juːst/ **adj** used to sth/doing sth **B1** If you are used to something, you have done it or experienced it many times before: *He's used to working long hours.* ∘ *We've been living here for two years and we've* UK *got used to/*US *gotten used to the heat.* → Opposite **unused**

used² /juːzd/ **adj** Something that is used is not new and has been owned by someone else: *a used car* → Opposite **unused**

used to /ˈjuːsttuː/ **modal verb** used to do/be sth **B1** If something used to happen or a situation used to exist, it happened regularly or existed in the past but it does not happen or exist now: *I used to go out every night when I was a student.* ∘ *He used to be a lot fatter.*

useful /ˈjuːsfəl/ **adj 1** **A2** helping you to do or

! Common learner error: **used to** and **be used to**

Used to + verb is for talking about a situation or regular activity in the past.
  My dad used to smoke when he was younger.
  I used to live in Italy, but now I live in England.
When you make **used to + verb** into a question or negative using the verb **do**, the correct form is **use to**.
  My dad didn't use to smoke.
  Where did you use to live?
  ~~Where did you used to live?~~
The expression **be used to something/doing something** is for talking about something that you have done or experienced a lot before.
  I don't mind the heat. I'm used to hot weather.
  He's not used to working long hours.
  ~~He's not use to working long hours.~~

achieve something: *useful information* **2** come in useful UK to be useful and help someone do or achieve something, especially when there is nothing else to help them: *You should keep that paint – it might come in useful.* • **usefully adv**

+ Other ways of saying **useful**

If something is **useful** because it helps you do or achieve something, you can describe it as **helpful** or **valuable**:
  *They gave us some really **helpful** advice.*
  *He was able to provide the police with some **valuable** information.*
The adjective **invaluable** means 'extremely useful':
  *The Internet is an **invaluable** resource for teachers.*
An activity which requires a lot of effort but is useful, is sometimes described as **worthwhile**:
  *It's a difficult course but it's very **worthwhile**.*
Something which is useful because it is simple to use is often described as **handy**:
  *That's a **handy** little gadget.*
The expression **come in handy** is often used when you think something will be useful in the future:
  *Don't throw that away – it'll **come in handy** for the party.*
If speech or writing contains a lot of useful information, you can describe it as **informative** or **instructive**:
  *It's an interesting and highly **informative** book.*

useless /ˈjuːsləs/ **adj 1** **B1** If something is useless it does not work well or it has no effect: *This umbrella's useless – there's a big hole in it.* ∘ [+ doing sth] *It's useless arguing with her.* **2** UK informal having no skill in an activity: *Dave's useless at football.*

U

ser /ˈjuːzəʳ/ **noun** [C] **B1** someone who uses a product, machine, or service: *drug users* ∘ *a new service for Internet users*

ser ac,count noun [C] an agreement allowing you to use a particular computer system, website, etc.: *To log on to the site, please enter your user account password.*

ser-friendly /ˌjuːzəˈfrendli/ **adj** A machine or system that is user-friendly is easy to use or understand: *user-friendly software*

ser I'D noun [U] information that proves who a person using a computer system is

sername noun [C] (also **user name**) a name or other word that you sometimes need to use together with a password (= secret word) before you can use a computer or the internet

sher[1] /ˈʌʃəʳ/ **verb** usher sb into/to/across, etc to show someone where to go or sit: *She ushered me into her office.*

PHRASAL VERB **usher in sth** formal to be at the start of a period when important changes happen, or to cause important changes to start happening: *His presidency ushered in a new era of democracy.*

sher[2] /ˈʌʃəʳ/ **noun** [C] someone who shows people where to sit in a theatre or at a formal event

sual /ˈjuːʒuəl/ **adj 1** **B1** normal and happening most often: *I went to bed at my usual time.* ∘ *This winter has been much colder than usual.* → Opposite **unusual 2 as usual** **A2** in the way that happens most of the time: *As usual, Ben was the last to arrive.*

sually /ˈjuːʒəli/ **adv** **A2** in the way that most often happens: *I usually get home at about six o'clock.* ∘ *Usually I just have a sandwich.*

surp /juːˈzɜːp/ **verb** [T] formal to take someone's job or power when you should not

tensil /juːˈtensəl/ **noun** [C] a tool that you use for doing jobs in the house, especially cooking:

wooden cooking utensils → See colour picture **The Kitchen** on page Centre 2

uterus /ˈjuːtərəs/ **noun** [C] the organ inside a woman's body where a baby grows

utilitarian /ˌjuːtɪlɪˈteəriən/ **adj** designed to be useful and not beautiful: *utilitarian furniture*

utility /juːˈtɪləti/ **noun** [C] (also **public utility**) an organization that supplies the public with water, gas, or electricity

utilize formal (also UK **-ise**) /ˈjuːtɪlaɪz/ **verb** [T] to use something in an effective way: *The vitamins come in a form that is easily utilized by the body.*

utmost[1] /ˈʌtməʊst/ **adj** [always before noun] formal used to emphasize how important or serious something is: *a matter of the **utmost importance*** ∘ *The situation needs to be handled **with** the **utmost** care.*

utmost[2] /ˈʌtməʊst/ **noun do your utmost** to try as hard as you can to do something: [+ to do sth] *We did our utmost to finish the project on time.*

utopia /juːˈtəʊpiə/ **noun** [C, U] an imaginary place where everything is perfect

utopian /juːˈtəʊpiən/ **adj** A utopian idea or plan is based on the belief that things can be made perfect: *a **utopian vision** of society*

utter[1] /ˈʌtəʳ/ **adj** [always before noun] used to emphasize something: *She dismissed the article as utter nonsense.*

utter[2] /ˈʌtəʳ/ **verb** [T] formal to say something: *She left without **uttering a word**.*

utterance /ˈʌtərəns/ **noun** [C] formal something that you say

utterly /ˈʌtəli/ **adv** completely: *It's **utterly ridiculous**.*

U-turn /ˈjuːtɜːn/ **noun** [C] **1** a change of direction that you make when driving in order to travel in the opposite direction **2** a complete change from one opinion or plan to an opposite one: *the government's **U-turn on** economic policy*

U

V

V, v /viː/ the twenty-second letter of the alphabet

v UK (also UK/US **vs**) /viː/ **preposition** abbreviation for versus (= used to say that one team or person is competing against another): *Germany v France*

V written abbreviation for volt (= a unit for measuring an electric current): *a 9V battery*

vacancy /'veɪkᵊnsi/ **noun** [C] **1** a room that is not being used in a hotel: *Do you have any vacancies?* **2** a job that is available for someone to do: *Tell me if you hear of any vacancies for secretaries.*

vacant /'veɪkᵊnt/ **adj 1 EMPTY** ▷ ⑫ Somewhere that is vacant is available because it is not being used: *a vacant building* **2 JOB** ▷ ⑫ A vacant job is available for someone to do. **3 EXPRESSION** ▷ A vacant expression on someone's face shows they are not thinking about anything. • **vacantly** adv

vacate /vəˈkeɪt/ ⑤ /'veɪkeɪt/ **verb** [T] formal to leave a room, building, chair, etc so that someone else can use it

vacation¹ /vəˈkeɪʃᵊn/ ⑤ /veɪˈkeɪʃᵊn/ **noun** [C, U] **1** US (UK **holiday**) a period of time when you are not at home but are staying somewhere else for enjoyment: *We're **taking a vacation** in Florida.* ◦ *We met Bob and Wendi **on vacation**.* **2** mainly US a period of the year when schools or colleges are closed: *the summer vacation* ◦ *He's **on vacation** for three months.*

vacation² /vəˈkeɪʃᵊn/ ⑤ /veɪˈkeɪʃᵊn/ **verb** US (UK **holiday**) **vacation in/on/by**, etc to go on vacation: *Sam was vacationing in Guatemala.*

vaccinate /'væksɪneɪt/ **verb** [T] to give someone a vaccine to stop them from getting a disease: *Have you been **vaccinated against** polio?* • **vaccination** /ˌvæksɪˈneɪʃᵊn/ **noun** [C, U]

vaccine /'væksiːn/ **noun** [C, U] a substance that is given to people to stop them from getting a particular disease

vacuum¹ /'vækjuːm/ **noun 1** [C] a space that has no air or other gas in it **2** [no plural] a situation in which someone or something important is not now in your life and you are unhappy: *When her husband died, it left a big vacuum in her life.*

vacuum² /'vækjuːm/ **verb** [I, T] to clean somewhere using a vacuum cleaner

ˈvacuum ˌcleaner noun [C] (also UK **Hoover**) an electric machine that cleans floors by sucking up dirt

vagaries /'veɪɡəriz/ **noun** [plural] sudden changes that are not expected or known about before they happen: *the **vagaries of** the English weather*

vagina /vəˈdʒaɪnə/ **noun** [C] the part of a woman's body that connects her outer sex organs to the place where a baby grows

vagrant /'veɪɡrᵊnt/ **noun** [C] formal someone who has no job and no home and who lives outside

vague /veɪɡ/ **adj 1** not clear or certain: *I have a vague idea of where the hotel is.* ◦ *He was a bit vague about directions.* **2** showing that someone is not thinking clearly or does not understand: *a vague expression* • **vaguely** adv *I **vaguely remember** (= slightly remember) meeting her* • **vagueness** noun [U]

> ☑ Word partners for **vague**
>
> a vague **feeling/idea/impression/memory/ promise**

vain /veɪn/ **adj 1 in vain** without any success: *... tried in vain to start a conversation.* **2 vain attempt/effort/hope** an attempt/effort, etc that does not have the result you want **3** too interested in your own appearance and thinking you are very attractive • **vainly** adv

Valentine /'vælᵊntaɪn/ **noun** [C] (also **'Valentine ˌcard**) a card (= stiff, folded paper with a message inside) that you give someone on Valentine's Day

Valentine's Day /'vælᵊntaɪnzˌdeɪ/ **noun** [C, U] 14 February, a day when you give a Valentine to someone you have a romantic relationship with or want a romantic relationship with

valet /'væleɪ/ **noun** [C] **1** someone who parks your car when you arrive at a restaurant, hotel or airport **2** a male servant who looks after a man's clothes and helps him to dress

valiant /'væliᵊnt/ **adj** formal very brave: *a valiant effort* • **valiantly** adv

valid /'vælɪd/ **adj 1** ⑫ based on good reasons or facts that are true: *a **valid argument*** **2** ⑫ A valid ticket or document is legally acceptable: *The ticket is valid for three months.* → Opposite **invalid** • **validity** /vəˈlɪdəti/ **noun** [U]

validate /'vælɪdeɪt/ **verb** [T] formal to prove that something is true • **validation** /ˌvælɪˈdeɪʃᵊn/ **noun** [C, U]

valley /'væli/ **noun** [C] ⑥ an area of low land between hills or mountains

valley

valour UK literary (US **valor**) /'vælər/ **noun** [U] great bravery, especially during a war

valuable /'væljuəbl/ **adj 1** ⑥ Valuable objects could be sold for a lot of money: *valuable paintings and antiques* **2** ⑫ Valuable information, help, advice, etc is very helpful.

➕ Other ways of saying **valuable**

If something is valuable because it helps you do or achieve something, you can describe it as **helpful** or **useful**:
*They gave us some really **helpful** advice.*
*She made a really **useful** contribution to the project.*
Something which is valuable because it produces useful results may be described as **constructive** or **productive**:
*It was a very **constructive** discussion.*
*We had a very **productive** meeting and sorted out a lot of problems.*
An activity which is valuable but requires a lot of effort, is sometimes described as **worthwhile**:
*It's a difficult course but it's very **worthwhile**.*
If speech or writing contains a lot of valuable information, you can describe it as **informative** or **instructive**:
*It's an interesting and highly **informative** book.*

valuables /ˈvæljuəblz/ **noun** [plural] small things that you own which could be sold for a lot of money: *valuables such as jewellery and watches*

valuation /ˌvæljuˈeɪʃ°n/ **noun** [C, U] a judgment about how much money something could be sold for

value¹ /ˈvæljuː/ **noun 1** [C, U] 🔵 how much money something could be sold for: *The new road has affected the **value of** these houses.* ○ *Cars quickly **go down** in **value**.* **2** [U] 🔵 how useful or important something is: *a document of great historical value* **3 good value (for money)** 🔵 If something is good value, it is of good quality or there is a lot of it so you think the amount of money you spent on it was right: *The meal was very good value.* → See also **face value**

🔲 Word partners for **value**

the value of sth • of [any/great/real] value • values go up/increase • values decrease/go down • a drop/fall/increase/rise in value

value² /ˈvæljuː/ **verb** [T] (**valuing, valued**) **1** 🔵 If you value something or someone, they are very important to you: *I always **value** his opinion.* **2** to judge how much money something could be sold for: *The ring was **valued at** $1000.*

values /ˈvæljuːz/ **noun** [plural] 🔵 your beliefs about what is morally right and wrong and what is most important in life

valve /vælv/ **noun** [C] something that opens and closes to control the flow of liquid or gas

vampire /ˈvæmpaɪəʳ/ **noun** [C] in stories, a dead person who bites people's necks and drinks their blood

van /væn/ **noun** [C] 🔵 a vehicle that is used for carrying things but that is smaller than a truck → See picture at **vehicle**

vandal /ˈvændəl/ **noun** [C] someone who intentionally damages things in public places: *Vandals had smashed the shop window.*

vandalism /ˈvændəlɪzəm/ **noun** [U] the crime of intentionally damaging things in public places

vandalize (also UK **-ise**) /ˈvændəlaɪz/ **verb** [T] to intentionally damage things in public places

vanguard /ˈvæŋɡɑːd/ **noun in the vanguard of sth** involved in the most recent changes in technology and understanding: *Libraries are in the vanguard of the electronic revolution.*

vanilla /vəˈnɪlə/ **noun** [U] a substance that is used to give flavour to some sweet foods: *vanilla ice cream*

vanish /ˈvænɪʃ/ **verb** [I] 🔵 to disappear suddenly: *The sun vanished behind the trees.* ○ *The report mysteriously vanished from the files.* → See also **disappear/vanish into thin air¹**

vanity /ˈvænəti/ **noun** [U] behaviour which shows someone is too interested in their own appearance and thinks they are very attractive

vantage point /ˈvɑːntɪdʒˌpɔɪnt/ **noun** [C] **1** the way you think about a subject when you are in a particular situation: *From my vantage point, it is difficult to see how things can improve.* **2** a place from which you can see something very well

vapour UK (US **vapor**) /ˈveɪpəʳ/ **noun** [U] many small drops of liquid in the air, which look like a cloud

variable¹ /ˈveəriəbl/ **adj** changing often: *The sound quality on the recording is variable.* • **variability** /ˌveəriəˈbɪləti/ **noun** [U]

variable² /ˈveəriəbl/ **noun** [C] a number, amount, or situation that can change: *A patient's recovery time depends on so many variables, such as age, weight, and general health.*

variance /ˈveəriəns/ **noun** formal **at variance with sb/sth** If two things or people are at variance with each other, they do not agree or are very different: *The statement seems to be at variance with government policy.*

variant /ˈveəriənt/ **noun** [C] something that is a slightly different form from the usual one: *There are several **variants of** the virus.* ○ *spelling variants*

variation /ˌveəriˈeɪʃ°n/ **noun 1** [C, U] 🔵 a difference in amount or quality: *variations in price* **2** [C] something that is slightly different from the usual form: *It's a **variation on** the standard apple pie.*

varied /ˈveərid/ **adj** 🔵 consisting of many different types of things: *a long and varied career*

variety /vəˈraɪəti/ **noun 1 a variety of sth/sb** 🔵 many different types of things or people: *Ben has done a **variety of** jobs.* **2** [C] a different type of something: *a new **variety of** potato* **3** [U] 🔵 a lot of different activities, situations, people, etc: *I need more variety in my life.*

🔲 Word partners for **variety**

a bewildering/great/infinite/wide variety • offer/provide variety

various /ˈveəriəs/ **adj** 🔵 many different: *They have offices in various parts of the country.* ○ *I started learning Spanish for various reasons.*

variously /ˈveəriəsli/ **adv** in many different ways: *The event was variously described as "terrible", "shocking", and "unbelievable".*

V

varnish¹ /ˈvɑːnɪʃ/ noun [C, U] a clear liquid that you paint onto wood to protect it and make it shine → See also **nail polish**

varnish² /ˈvɑːnɪʃ/ verb [T] to put varnish on a surface

vary /ˈveəri/ verb **1** BE DIFFERENT ▷ [I] ② If things of the same type vary, they are different from each other: *Car prices vary greatly across Europe.* ○ *Roses vary widely in size and shape.* **2** CHANGE ▷ [I] ② to change: *Temperatures vary depending on the time of year.* **3** INTENTIONALLY CHANGE ▷ [T] ② to often change something that you do: *I try to vary what I eat.*

vase /vɑːz/ ⓤ /veɪs/ noun [C] ⓑ a container that you put flowers in

vase

vasectomy /vəˈsektəmi/ noun [C] a medical operation that is done to stop a man having children

vast /vɑːst/ adj ② extremely big: *a vast amount of money* ○ *vast forest areas*

vastly /ˈvɑːstli/ adv very much: *Life now is vastly different from 100 years ago.*

VAT /ˌviːeɪˈtiː/ noun [U] abbreviation for value added tax: a tax on goods and services in the UK

vault¹ /vɔːlt/ noun [C] **1** a special room in a bank where money, jewellery, and other valuable objects are kept **2** a room under a church where people are buried

vault² /vɔːlt/ verb [I, T] to jump over something by first putting your hands on it: *Rick vaulted the gate and ran off.* → See also **pole vault**

VCR /ˌviːsiːˈɑːr/ noun [C] mainly US (UK **video**) abbreviation for video cassette recorder: a machine that you use for recording television programmes and playing videos (= recorded films or programmes) → See colour picture **The Living Room** on page Centre 4

VDU /ˌviːdiːˈjuː/ noun [C] UK abbreviation for visual display unit: a machine with a screen that shows information from a computer

've /v/ short for have: *I've already eaten.*

veal /viːl/ noun [U] meat from a very young cow

veer /vɪər/ verb **veer across/off/towards, etc** to suddenly change direction: *The car veered off the road and hit a tree.*

veg /vedʒ/ noun [C, U] (plural **veg**) UK informal short for vegetables: *fruit and veg*

vegan /ˈviːgən/ noun [C] someone who does not eat meat, fish, eggs, milk, or cheese • **vegan** adj

vegetable /ˈvedʒtəbl/ noun [C] ⓐ a plant that you eat, for example potatoes, onions, beans, etc → See colour picture **Fruit and Vegetables** on page Centre 10

vegetarian¹ /ˌvedʒɪˈteəriən/ noun [C] ⓑ someone who does not eat meat or fish

vegetarian² /ˌvedʒɪˈteəriən/ adj ⓑ not eating, containing, or using meat or fish: *All her children are vegetarian.* ○ *a vegetarian restaurant/pizza*

vegetation /ˌvedʒɪˈteɪʃən/ noun [U] the plants and trees that grow in a particular area

veggie /ˈvedʒi/ noun [C] UK informal a vegetarian • **veggie** adj

vehement /ˈviːəmənt/ adj formal showing strong, often negative, feelings about something: *vehement criticism/opposition* • **vehemently** adv

vehicles

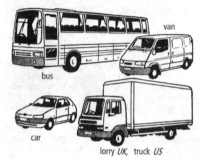

van
bus
car
lorry *UK*, truck *US*

vehicle /ˈviːɪkl/ noun **1** ⓑ [C] formal something such as a car or bus that takes people from one place to another, especially using roads **2** a **vehicle for sth/doing sth** something that you use as a way of telling people your ideas or opinions: *The paper was merely a vehicle for his political beliefs.*

veil /veɪl/ noun [C] a thin piece of material that covers a woman's face

IDIOM **draw a veil over sth** UK to not talk any more about a subject because it could cause trouble or embarrassment

veiled /veɪld/ adj said so that the true meaning or purpose is not clear: *veiled criticism*

vein /veɪn/ noun [C] **1** one of the tubes in your body that carries blood to your heart **2** one of the thin lines on a leaf

IDIOM **in the same vein** in the same style or speaking or writing

Velcro /ˈvelkrəʊ/ noun [U] trademark material that consists of two pieces of cloth that stick together, used to fasten clothes

velocity /vɪˈlɒsəti/ noun [C, U] the speed at which something moves

velvet /ˈvelvɪt/ noun [U] cloth that has a thick, soft surface on one side: *a black velvet jacket*

vendetta /venˈdetə/ noun [C] If someone has a vendetta against you, they try to do something bad to you over a period of time because they have been treated badly by you: *He had a vendetta against the company after he lost his job.*

vending machine /ˈvendɪŋməˌʃiːn/ noun [C] a machine that sells drinks, cigarettes, etc

vendor /ˈvendɔːr/ noun [C] **1** someone who sells something outside: *an ice cream vendor* **2** formal a company that sells goods or services

V

veneer /vəˈnɪər/ noun **1** [C, U] a thin layer of wood that covers a piece of furniture that is made of a cheaper material **2 a veneer of sth** formal a way of behaving that is not sincere and hides someone's real character or emotions: *a thin veneer of calm/respectability*

venerable /ˈvenərəbl/ adj old and very much respected: *a venerable institution/tradition*

Venetian blind /vənˌiːʃənˈblaɪnd/ noun [C] a covering for a window that is made from long, flat, horizontal pieces of metal or wood which you can move to let in light

vengeance /ˈvendʒəns/ noun **1** [U] the act of doing something bad to someone who has done something bad to you, or the feeling of wanting to do this: *an act of vengeance* **2 with a vengeance** If something happens with a vengeance, it happens a lot or in a very strong way: *The disease swept across the country with a vengeance.*

vengeful /ˈvendʒfəl/ adj formal wanting vengeance

venison /ˈvenɪsən/ noun [U] meat from a deer

venom /ˈvenəm/ noun [U] **1** poison that some snakes and insects produce **2** a feeling of extreme anger or hate: *Much of his venom was directed at his boss.* • **venomous** adj containing or involving venom

vent¹ /vent/ noun [C] a hole in a wall or machine that lets air in and allows smoke or smells to go out

vent² /vent/ verb **vent your anger/frustration, etc** to do or say something to show your anger or another strong, bad feeling

ventilate /ˈventɪleɪt/ verb [T] to let air come into and go out of a room or building • **ventilation** /ˌventɪˈleɪʃən/ noun [U] *a ventilation system*

venture¹ /ˈventʃər/ noun [C] a new activity that may not be successful: *a business venture* → See also **joint venture**

venture² /ˈventʃər/ verb formal **1 venture into/out/outside, etc** to leave a safe place and go somewhere that may involve risks: *If the snow stops I might venture out.* **2** [T] to be brave enough to say something that might be criticized: *I didn't dare venture an opinion.*

venue /ˈvenjuː/ noun [C] 🅱️ a place where a sports game, musical performance, or special event happens

Venus /ˈviːnəs/ noun [no plural] the planet that is second from the Sun, after Mercury and before the Earth

veranda (also **verandah**) /vəˈrændə/ noun [C] a room that is joined to the outside of a house and has a roof and floor but no outside wall

verb /vɜːb/ noun [C] 🅰️ a word that is used to say that someone does something or that something happens. For example the words 'arrive', 'make', 'be', and 'feel' are verbs. → See also **auxiliary verb, modal verb, phrasal verb**

verbal /ˈvɜːbəl/ adj **1** spoken and not written: *a verbal promise* **2** relating to words or the use of words: *verbal ability/skills* • **verbally** adv

verbatim /vɜːˈbeɪtɪm/ adj, adv using the exact words that were originally used

verdict /ˈvɜːdɪkt/ noun [C] **1** a decision in a court of law saying if someone is guilty or not: *a guilty verdict* ○ *The jury took nine hours to reach a verdict.* **2** someone's opinion about something after experiencing it, often for the first time: *You tried out that Italian restaurant? What was the verdict?*

> 🔲 Word partners for **verdict**
>
> **deliver/reach/return** a verdict • a **guilty/not guilty** verdict

verge¹ /vɜːdʒ/ noun [C] **1** UK the edge of a road or path that is usually covered in grass **2 be on the verge of sth/doing sth** to be going to happen or to do something very soon: *a company on the verge of financial disaster*

verge² /vɜːdʒ/ verb

PHRASAL VERB **verge on sth** to almost be a particular state or quality: *His constant questions verged on rudeness.*

verify /ˈverɪfaɪ/ verb [T] to prove that something is true, or do something to discover if it is true: *It was impossible to verify her statement.* • **verification** /ˌverɪfɪˈkeɪʃən/ noun [U]

veritable /ˈverɪtəbl/ adj [always before noun] formal used to emphasize how extreme something is: *Their house was a veritable palace (= was very large).*

vermin /ˈvɜːmɪn/ noun [plural] small animals that damage crops and can give people diseases

versatile /ˈvɜːsətaɪl/ ⓊⓈ /ˈvɜːrsətəl/ adj **1** having many different skills: *a versatile player/performer* **2** useful for doing a lot of different things: *a versatile tool* • **versatility** /ˌvɜːsəˈtɪləti/ noun [U]

verse /vɜːs/ noun **1** [C] 🅱️ one of the parts that a song or poem is divided into: *I only know the first verse.* **2** [U] words that are in the form of poetry: *The story was told in verse.*

version /ˈvɜːʃən/ noun [C] **1** 🅱️ one form of something that is slightly different to other forms of the same thing: *I saw the original version of the film.* **2** someone's description of what has happened: *Bates gave his version of events to the police.*

> 🔲 Word partners for **version**
>
> a **new/the latest** version • a version **of** sth • **in** a version

versus /ˈvɜːsəs/ preposition **1** used to say that one team or person is competing against another: *It's Arsenal versus Barcelona in the final.* **2** used to compare two things or ideas, especially when you have to choose between them: *private education versus state education*

vertical /ˈvɜːtɪkəl/ adj pointing straight up from a surface: *a vertical line* • **vertically** adv → See picture at **horizontal**

vertigo /ˈvɜːtɪɡəʊ/ noun [U] a medical condition in which you feel slightly sick because you are in a high place and feel as if you might fall

verve /vɜːv/ noun [U] formal energy and enthusiasm

very¹ /ˈveri/ adv **1** 🅰️ used to emphasize an adjective or adverb: *She was very pleased.*

V

○ *Marie speaks very slowly.* ○ *Thank you very much.* **2 not very good/tall/happy, etc** 🄐 not good/happy, etc: *The film wasn't very good.*

very² /'veri/ **adj** [always before noun] used to emphasize a noun: *This is the very house where we stayed.*

vessel /'ves³l/ **noun** [C] **1** formal a ship or large boat **2** old-fashioned a container for liquids → See also **blood vessel**

vest /vest/ **noun** [C] **1** UK (US **undershirt**) a piece of underwear that you wear under a shirt **2** US (UK **waistcoat**) a piece of clothing with buttons at the front and no sleeves, that you wear over a shirt → See colour picture **Clothes** on page Centre 9

vested interest /ˌvestɪd'ɪntrest/ **noun** [C] If you have a vested interest in something, you want it to happen because it will give you advantages.

vestige /'vestɪdʒ/ **noun** [C] a very small amount of something that still exists after most of it has gone: *There is still a vestige of hope that she might be found alive.*

vet¹ /vet/ **noun** [C] 🄑 someone whose job is to give medical care to animals that are sick or hurt

vet² /vet/ **verb** [T] (**vetting, vetted**) to look at details of someone's life, in order to make sure that they are suitable for a particular job: [often passive] *Applicants for the job are carefully vetted.*

veteran /'vet³r³n/ **noun** [C] **1** someone who has been in an army or navy during a war: *a veteran of World War Two* **2** someone who has done a job or activity for a long time: *a 20-year veteran of BBC news*

veterinarian /ˌvet³rɪ'neəriən/ **noun** [C] US a vet

veterinary /'vet³rɪn³ri/ **adj** formal relating to medical care given to animals that are sick or hurt

veterinary surgeon **noun** [C] UK formal a vet

veto¹ /'vi:təʊ/ **verb** [T] (**vetoing, vetoed**) If someone in authority vetoes something, they do not allow it to happen, although other people have agreed to it: *The plan was vetoed by the President.*

veto² /'vi:təʊ/ **noun** [C, U] (plural **vetoes**) a decision by someone in authority to not allow something to happen

vexed /vekst/ **adj vexed question/issue, etc** a situation that causes problems and is difficult to deal with: *the vexed issue of unemployment*

via /vaɪə/ **preposition 1** 🄑 going through or stopping at a place on the way to another place: *The train to Utrecht goes via Amsterdam.* **2** 🄑 using a particular machine, system, or person to send or receive something: *I receive all my work via e-mail.*

viable /'vaɪəbl/ **adj** effective and able to be successful: *a viable alternative to nuclear power* ○ *an economically viable plan* • **viability** /ˌvaɪə'bɪləti/ **noun** [U]

viaduct /'vaɪədʌkt/ **noun** [C] a long, high bridge across a valley

vibes /vaɪbz/ **noun** [plural] informal the way a person or place makes you feel: *I get bad/good vibes from her.*

vibrant /'vaɪbrənt/ **adj 1** full of excitement and energy: *a vibrant city* ○ *a vibrant, young performer* **2** A vibrant colour is very bright.

vibrate /vaɪ'breɪt/ ⓤ /'vaɪbreɪt/ **verb** [I, T] to shake with small, quick movements or to make something shake this way: *The music was so loud that the floor was vibrating.* • **vibration** /vaɪ'breɪʃ³n/ **noun** [C, U]

vicar /'vɪkər/ **noun** [C] a priest in some Christian churches

vicarage /'vɪk³rɪdʒ/ **noun** [C] the house where a vicar lives

vicarious /vɪ'keəriəs/ **adj** [always before noun] A vicarious feeling is one you get from seeing or hearing about another person's experiences: *It gives me vicarious pleasure to watch him eat.*

vice /vaɪs/ **noun 1 BAD HABIT** ▷ [C] something bad that someone often does: *Smoking is his only vice.* **2 CRIME** ▷ [U] crime that involves sex or drugs **3 TOOL** ▷ [C] UK (US **vise**) a tool used for holding something tightly while you cut it, make it smooth, etc → See picture at **tool**

vice president **noun** [C] **1** the person who is a rank lower than the president of a country **2** US someone who is responsible for part of a company: *She's vice president of sales and marketing.*

vice versa /ˌvaɪs'vɜːsə/ **adv** used for referring to the opposite of what you have just said: *Never use indoor lights outside and vice versa.*

vicinity /vɪ'sɪnəti/ **noun in the vicinity (of sth)** formal in the area near a place: *A number of buildings in the vicinity of the fire were damaged.*

vicious /'vɪʃəs/ **adj 1** violent and dangerous: *a vicious attack on a child* ○ *a vicious dog* **2** intended to upset someone: *a vicious rumour* • **viciously adv**

vicious circle **noun** [no plural] (also **vicious cycle**) a situation in which one problem causes another problem, which then makes the first problem worse

victim /'vɪktɪm/ **noun** [C] 🄑 someone who has suffered the effects of violence, illness, or bad luck: *victims of crime* ○ *hurricane/flood victims*

victimize (also UK **-ise**) /'vɪktɪmaɪz/ **verb** [T] to treat someone unfairly because you do not like or approve of them: *Ben feels he has been victimized by his teacher.*

victor /'vɪktər/ **noun** [C] formal the person who wins a fight or competition

Victorian /vɪk'tɔːriən/ **adj** from or relating to the period between 1837 and 1901 in Britain: *a Victorian house*

victorious /vɪk'tɔːriəs/ **adj** having won a fight or competition: *a victorious army*

victory /'vɪkt³ri/ **noun** [C, U] 🄑 a win in a fight or competition: *Phoenix managed a 135-114 victory over Denver.*

🗹 Word partners for **victory**

claim/secure victory • a comfortable/easy/impressive victory • a victory for/over sb

---

video¹ /'vɪdiəʊ/ **noun 1 RECORDING** ▷ [C] 🄑 an electronic recording of moving images, for example a film or TV programme, that can be watched on television, a computer, a camera, etc.: *Caroline and Yann showed us their wedding video last night.* **2** **TAPE** ▷[U] **A2** a film or television programme recorded on videotape: *a copy of 'Lord of the Rings'* **on video** **3** **SYSTEM** ▷ [U] a system used for electronically recording moving images: *The website uses video to enhance learning.* **4** [C] (also **VCR**, **video recorder**) a machine that you use for recording a television programme or watching a video → See colour picture **The Living Room** on page Centre 4

video² /'vɪdiəʊ/ verb [T] (**videoing**, **videoed**) **1** to film something using a video camera **2** to record a television program using a video recorder

video ˌblog noun [C] a blog (= record of thoughts that someone puts on the Internet) that contains a lot of video

video ˌcamera noun [C] a piece of equipment used to record moving pictures and sound

video ˌclip noun [C] **B1** a short video recording

videoconferencing (also **video conferencing**) /ˌvɪdiəʊ'kɒnfᵊrᵊnsɪŋ/ noun [U] a system that allows people in different places to see each other on screens and communicate with each other, so they do not have to travel to meetings: *videoconferencing equipment*

video ˌgame noun [C] **A2** a game in which you make pictures move on a screen

videophone /'vɪdiəʊfəʊn/ noun [C] a telephone with a small screen so that you can see the person you are talking to

video reˌcorder noun [C] a machine that records and plays videos

videotape /'vɪdiəʊteɪp/ noun [C, U] a thin strip of material inside a plastic box that is used for recording television programmes and films

vie /vaɪ/ verb [I] (**vying**, **vied**) to try hard to do something more successfully than someone else: *The children were vying for attention.* ∘ [+ to do sth] *Film crews were vying with each other to get the best pictures.*

view¹ /vjuː/ noun **1** **OPINION** ▷ [C] **B1** your opinion: *We have different* **views about/on** *education.* ∘ **In** *her* **view** *this is wrong.* **2** **THINGS YOU SEE** ▷ [C] **A2** the things that you can see from a place: *There was a lovely view of the lake from the bedroom window.* **3** **ABILITY TO SEE** ▷ [no plural] **B2** how well you can see something from a particular place: *We had a great view of the procession.* **4** **POSITION** ▷ [U] a position from which something can be seen: *The house was hidden from view behind a wall.* ∘ *He turned the corner and the harbour* **came into view.** **5** **in full view of sb** happening where someone can easily see: *All this happened in full view of the cameras.* **6** **in view of sth** formal **B2** because of something: *In view of recent events, we have decided to cancel the meeting.* **7** **with a view to doing sth** formal so that you can do something: *He's doing some improvements on the house with a view to selling it.* → See also **point of view**

view² /vjuː/ verb [T] formal **1** to have a particular opinion about someone or something: *In all three countries he is* **viewed as** *a terrorist.* **2** to

! Common learner error: **view** or **sight**?

View means the countryside, buildings, things, etc. that you can see from a place, or how well you can see something. A **view** is usually pleasant.
 We had a wonderful view from the aircraft.
 ~~We had a wonderful sight from the aircraft.~~
Sight means an occasion when you see something, or the ability to see.
 The sight of blood makes me feel sick.
 ~~The view of blood makes me feel sick.~~

☑ Word partners for **view**

express/have/hold a view • strong views • in sb's view • sb's views about/on sth • an exchange of views

watch something: *They were able to view the city from a helicopter.*

viewer /'vjuːəʳ/ noun [C] **B2** someone who watches a television programme

viewpoint /'vjuːpɔɪnt/ noun [C] a way of thinking about a situation: *From* *his* **viewpoint** *the action seemed entirely justified.*

vigil /'vɪdʒɪl/ noun [C, U] a period when people stay somewhere quietly in order to show that they support someone, disagree with something, etc: *an all-night vigil for peace*

vigilant /'vɪdʒɪlənt/ adj watching carefully and always ready to notice anything dangerous or illegal: *Police have asked people to be vigilant after yesterday's bomb attack.* • **vigilance** /'vɪdʒɪləns/ noun [U]

vigilante /ˌvɪdʒɪ'lænti/ noun [C] a member of a group of people who try to catch criminals and punish them without having any legal authority

vigor /'vɪɡəʳ/ noun [U] US spelling of vigour

vigorous /'vɪɡᵊrəs/ adj **1** showing or needing a lot of physical energy: **vigorous exercise** **2** showing strong, often negative, feelings about something: *a vigorous debate* ∘ *He was a* **vigorous opponent** *of the government.* • **vigorously** adv *Bates* **vigorously denies** (= strongly denies) *murdering his wife.*

vigour UK (US **vigor**) /'vɪɡəʳ/ noun [U] strength and energy: *She set about her work* **with** *great* **vigour.**

vile /vaɪl/ adj extremely unpleasant: *a vile attack* ∘ *The bathroom was vile.*

vilify /'vɪlɪfaɪ/ verb [T] formal to say bad things about someone so that other people will not like or approve of them

villa /'vɪlə/ noun [C] a large house, especially one used for holidays in a warm country

village /'vɪlɪdʒ/ noun [C] **A1** a place where people live in the countryside that includes buildings such as shops and a school but which is smaller than a town: *She lives in a small village outside Oxford.* ∘ *a village shop*

villager /'vɪlɪdʒəʳ/ noun [C] someone who lives in a village

villain /'vɪlən/ noun [C] a bad person in a film, book, etc

V

vindicate /ˈvɪndɪkeɪt/ **verb** [T] formal to prove that what someone said or did was right after people generally thought it was wrong • **vindication** /ˌvɪndɪˈkeɪʃən/ **noun** [C, U] formal

vindictive /vɪnˈdɪktɪv/ **adj** intending to harm or upset someone who has harmed or upset you

vine /vaɪn/ **noun** [C] a plant that grapes (= small, green or purple fruit used for making wine) grow on

vinegar /ˈvɪnɪɡər/ **noun** [U] 🅱2 a sour liquid that is used in cooking, often made from wine

vineyard /ˈvɪnjəd/ **noun** [C] an area of land where someone grows grapes (= small, green or purple fruit) for making wine

vintage¹ /ˈvɪntɪdʒ/ **adj 1 WINE** ▷ Vintage wine is wine of a good quality that was made in a particular year. **2 VERY GOOD** ▷ having all the best or most typical qualities of something, especially from the past: *a vintage Hollywood movie* **3 CAR** ▷ A vintage car was made between 1919 and 1930.

vintage² /ˈvɪntɪdʒ/ **noun** [C] the wine that was made in a particular year: *The 1993 vintage is one of the best.*

vinyl /ˈvaɪnəl/ **noun** [U] a type of very strong plastic

viola /viˈəʊlə/ **noun** [C] a wooden instrument, larger than a violin, that you hold against your neck and play by moving a special stick across strings

violate /ˈvaɪəleɪt/ **verb** [T] formal **1** to not obey a law, rule, or agreement: *Countries that violate international law will be dealt with severely.* **2** to not allow someone something that they should morally be allowed to have: *They were accused of violating human rights.* • **violation** /ˌvaɪəˈleɪʃən/ **noun** [C, U] *a violation of privacy*

violence /ˈvaɪələns/ **noun** [U] **1** 🅱2 behaviour intended to hurt or kill someone: *an act of violence* ∘ *A number of people were killed in the violence.* ∘ ***Violence against*** *women has increased in recent years.* **2** extreme force and energy, especially of something causing damage: *Such was the violence of the explosion that three buildings collapsed.*

> 🗌 Word partners for **violence**
>
> erupt into/renounce/use violence • escalating/extreme/gratuitous violence • violence against/towards sb

violent /ˈvaɪələnt/ **adj 1 ACTION** ▷ 🅱2 involving violence: *a victim of **violent crime*** ∘ *a violent protest* ∘ *I don't like violent films* (= films that show violence). **2 PERSON** ▷ 🅱2 likely to hurt or kill someone else: *a violent criminal* **3 DAMAGE** ▷ sudden and causing damage: *a violent explosion/storm* **4 EMOTIONS** ▷ showing very strong feelings, especially anger: *violent emotions* • **violently adv** → See also **non-violent**

violet /ˈvaɪələt/ **noun 1** [C] a small plant with a small, purple flower **2** [U] a pale purple colour

violin /ˌvaɪəˈlɪn/ **noun** [C] 🅰2 a wooden musical instrument that you hold against your neck and play by moving a bow (= special stick) across strings • **violinist** /ˌvaɪəˈlɪnɪst/ **noun** [C]

someone who plays a **violin**

VIP /ˌviːaɪˈpiː/ **noun** [C] abbreviation for very important person: someone who is famous or powerful and is treated in a special way: *The airport has a separate lounge for VIPs.*

viper /ˈvaɪpər/ **noun** [C] a small, poisonous snake

viral /ˈvaɪrəl/ **adj 1** caused by or relating to a virus (= infectious organism): *a viral infection* **2** spreading or becoming popular very quickly through communication from one person to another, especially on the Internet: *viral advertising*

virgin¹ /ˈvɜːdʒɪn/ **noun** [C] someone who has never had sex

virgin² /ˈvɜːdʒɪn/ **adj** Virgin land, forest, etc has not been used or damaged by people.

virginity /vəˈdʒɪnəti/ **noun** [U] the quality of never having had sex: *Emma **lost her virginity*** (= had sex for the first time) *at sixteen.*

Virgo /ˈvɜːɡəʊ/ **noun** [C, U] the sign of the zodiac that relates to the period of 23 August – 22 September, or a person born during this period → See picture at **the zodiac**

virile /ˈvɪraɪl/ ⑤ /ˈvɪrəl/ **adj** A virile man is strong and has sexual energy. • **virility** /vɪˈrɪləti/ **noun** [U]

virtual /ˈvɜːtʃuəl/ **adj** [always before noun] **1** almost a particular thing or quality: *They played the game in virtual silence.* **2** 🅱2 used to describe something that can be done or seen using computers or the Internet instead of going to a place, meeting people in person, etc.: *a virtual art gallery*

virtually /ˈvɜːtʃuəli/ **adv** 🅱2 almost: *They're virtually the same.* ∘ *I've virtually finished.*

virtual re'ality noun [U] 🅱2 computer images and sounds that make you feel an imagined situation is real

virtue /ˈvɜːtjuː/ **noun 1 ADVANTAGE** ▷ [C, U] an advantage or useful quality: *The great **virtue of** having a small car is that you can park it easily.* **2 GOOD QUALITY** ▷ [C] a good quality that someone has: *Patience is not among his virtues.* **3 MORAL BEHAVIOUR** ▷ [U] behaviour that is morally good **4 by virtue of sth** formal because of something: *She succeeded by virtue of hard work rather than talent.*

virtuoso /ˌvɜːtjuˈəʊsəʊ/ **noun** [C] someone who is extremely good at doing something, especially playing a musical instrument

virtuous /ˈvɜːtʃuəs/ **adj** behaving in a good and moral way • **virtuously adv**

virulent /ˈvɪrʊlənt/ **adj 1** A virulent disease or poison causes severe illness very quickly **2** formal criticizing or hating someone or something very much: *a virulent attack on the government*

virus /ˈvaɪrəs/ **noun** [C] **1** 🅱2 an infectious organism too small to be seen that causes disease, or an illness that it causes: *The doctor* says *I've got a virus.* **2** ⓑ a program that is secretly put onto a computer in order to destroy the information that is stored on it

> ☑ Word partners for **virus**
>
> carry/contract/have/transmit a virus • a deadly/rare virus

visa /'viːzə/ noun [C] ⓑ an official mark in your passport (= document which proves your nationality) that allows you to enter or leave a particular country: *She went to Miami **on** a tourist **visa**.*

vis-à-vis /ˌviːzə'viː/ preposition relating to something, or in comparison with something: *I have to speak to James vis-à-vis the conference arrangements.*

vise /vaɪs/ noun [C] US spelling of vice (= a tool used for holding something tightly while you cut it, make it smooth, etc) → See picture at **tool**

visibility /ˌvɪzə'bɪləti/ noun [U] how far or how well you can see because of weather conditions: *good/poor visibility* ∘ *It was foggy and visibility was down to 50 metres.*

visible /'vɪzəbl/ adj ⓑ able to be seen: *The fire was **visible from** five kilometres away.* → Opposite **invisible** • **visibly** adv *She was visibly upset.*

vision /'vɪʒən/ noun **1** IDEA ▷ [C] ⓑ an idea or image in your mind of what something could be like in the future: *a vision of a better society* **2** SEE ▷ [U] ⓑ the ability to see: *He has poor vision in his left eye.* **3** ABILITY TO PLAN ▷ [U] the ability to make plans for the future that are imaginative and wise: *As a leader, he lacked vision.* **4** RELIGION ▷ [C] someone or something that you see that no one else can see as part of a religious experience

visionary /'vɪʒənəri/ adj able to make plans for the future that are imaginative and wise: *a visionary leader* • **visionary** noun [C]

visit¹ /'vɪzɪt/ verb **1** SEE A PERSON ▷ [I, T] ⓐ to go to someone's home and spend time with them: *We have friends coming to visit this weekend.* **2** SEE A PLACE ▷ [I, T] ⓐ to go to a place and spend a short amount of time there: *Did you visit St Petersburg while you were in Russia?* **3** INTERNET ▷ [T] ⓐ to look at a website
PHRASAL VERB **visit with sb** US to spend time talking with someone who you know: *Mom was visiting with our neighbor.*

visit² /'vɪzɪt/ noun [C] ⓑ an occasion when you visit a place or a person: *the President's **visit to** Hong Kong* ∘ *Why don't you **pay** him **a visit** (= visit him)?*

> ☑ Word partners for **visit**
>
> a visit to sth • a visit from sb • on a visit • pay sb a visit • have a visit from sb • a brief/flying visit

visitor /'vɪzɪtər/ noun [C] ⓐ someone who visits a person or place: *The museum attracts large numbers of visitors.*

visor /'vaɪzər/ noun [C] **1** PART OF HAT ▷ the part of a helmet (= hard hat that protects your head) that you can pull down to cover your face

2 HAT ▷ (also 'sun ˌvisor) a hat that has a curved part above your eyes to protect them from the sun → See colour picture **Clothes** on page Centre 9 **3** CAR ▷ the parts in the front window of a car that you pull down to protect your eyes from the sun → See colour picture **Car** on page Centre 7

vista /'vɪstə/ noun [C] a view, especially a beautiful view that you look at from a high place

visual /'vɪʒuəl/ adj ⓑ relating to seeing: *The film has some powerful **visual effects**.* • **visually** adv *visually appealing*

visual 'aid noun [C] something that helps you understand or remember information, such as a picture or film

visualize (also UK **-ise**) /'vɪʒuəlaɪz/ verb [T] to create a picture in your mind of someone or something: *I was very surprised when I met Geoff – I'd visualized someone much older.* • **visualization** /ˌvɪʒuəlaɪ'zeɪʃən/ noun [U]

vital /'vaɪtəl/ adj **1** ⓑ necessary: *Tourism is vital to the country's economy.* ∘ [+ (that)] *It's vital that you send off this form today.* **2** formal full of energy

vitality /vaɪ'tæləti/ noun [U] energy and strength: *At 48, he still projects an image of youth and vitality.*

vitally /'vaɪtəli/ adv in a very important way: *Safety at work is **vitally important**.*

vitamin /'vɪtəmɪn/ ⓤ /'vaɪtəmɪn/ noun [C] ⓑ one of a group of natural substances in food that you need to be healthy: *Oranges are full of vitamin C.*

vitriolic /ˌvɪtri'ɒlɪk/ adj formal criticizing someone in a very severe and unpleasant way

viva /'vaɪvə/ noun [C] UK a spoken examination at university

vivacious /vɪ'veɪʃəs/ adj A vivacious person, especially a woman, is full of energy and enthusiasm.

vivid /'vɪvɪd/ adj **1** ⓑ Vivid descriptions or memories produce strong, clear images in your mind: *He gave a very **vivid description** of life in Caracas.* **2** ⓑ A vivid colour is very bright. • **vividly** adv ⓑ *I remember my first day at school very vividly.*

vivisection /ˌvɪvɪ'sekʃən/ noun [U] the use of living animals in scientific experiments, especially in order to discover the effects of new drugs

vixen /'vɪksən/ noun [C] a female fox (= wild dog with red-brown fur)

V-neck /'viːnek/ noun [C] a V-shaped opening for your neck on a piece of clothing, or a sweater, dress, etc with this opening: *a V-neck jumper* • **V-necked** /viː'nekt/ adj *a V-necked dress*

> ☑ Word partners for **vocabulary**
>
> a limited/wide vocabulary • be in sb's vocabulary • widen your vocabulary

vocabulary /vəʊ'kæbjələri/ noun **1** WORDS ▷ [C, U] ⓐ all the words you know in a particular language: *Reading helps to widen your vocabulary.* **2** LANGUAGE ▷ [no plural] all the words that exist in a language, or that are used when discussing a particular subject: *Computing has its*

V

---

own specialist vocabulary. **3 LIST** ▷ [no plural] a list of words and their meanings

vocal /ˈvəʊkəl/ **adj 1** expressing your opinions in a strong way: *She is a **vocal supporter** of women's rights.* **2** involving or relating to the voice, especially singing: *vocal music*

vocal cords (also **vocal chords**) **noun** [plural] folds of skin at the top of your throat that make sounds when air from your lungs moves over them

vocalist /ˈvəʊkəlɪst/ **noun** [C] the person who sings in a group of people who play popular music

vocals /ˈvəʊkəlz/ **noun** [plural] the part of a piece of music that is sung

vocation /vəʊˈkeɪʃən/ **noun** [C, U] a strong feeling that you are right for a particular type of work, or a job that gives you this feeling: *He knew that teaching was his true vocation.*

vocational /vəʊˈkeɪʃənəl/ **adj** Vocational education and skills prepare you for a particular type of work: *The college offers both vocational and academic courses.*

vociferous /vəˈsɪfərəs/ **adj** formal expressing your opinions in a loud and strong way: *She has become increasingly **vociferous in** her opposition to the scheme.*

vodka /ˈvɒdkə/ **noun** [C, U] a strong alcoholic drink that is popular in Russia and Poland

vogue /vəʊg/ **noun** [U, no plural] If there is a vogue for something, it is very fashionable: *This period saw a **vogue for** Japanese painting.* ○ *Flat shoes are **in vogue** (= fashionable) this spring.*

voice¹ /vɔɪs/ **noun 1 SOUNDS** ▷ [C] **B1** the sounds that you make when you speak or sing: *I could hear voices in the next room.* ○ *Jessie has a beautiful singing voice.* ○ *Could you please **keep your voices down** (= speak more quietly)?* ○ *He **raised his voice** (= spoke more loudly) so that everyone could hear.* **2 lose your voice** **B2** to become unable to speak, often because of an illness: *She had a bad cold and was losing her voice.* **3 OPINION** ▷ [C] someone's opinion about a particular subject: *The programme gives people the opportunity to make their voices heard.* **4 PERSON** ▷ [no plural] someone who expresses the opinions or wishes of a group of people: *It's important that students have a **voice on** the committee.* → See also **passive** noun

> ☑ **Word partners for voice**
>
> a deep/husky/low voice • lose your voice • lower/raise your voice • in a [bored/stern, etc.] voice • your tone of voice

voice² /vɔɪs/ **verb** [T] to say what you think about a particular subject: *He has voiced concern about the new proposals.*

voice-activated /ˌvɔɪsˈæktɪveɪtɪd/ **adj** A machine that is voice-activated can recognize and follow spoken instructions.

voice mail **noun** [U] (also **voicemail**) **1** an electronic telephone answering system **2** a phone message recorded by someone when you do not answer their call

void¹ /vɔɪd/ **adj 1** [never before noun] not legally or officially acceptable: *The contracts were declared void.* **2 be void of sth** formal to be without something: *His last statement was entirely void of meaning.*

void² /vɔɪd/ **noun** [no plural] **1** a situation in which someone or something important is not now in your life and you are unhappy: *Her husband's death **left a void** in her life.* **2** a large hole or empty space

vol written abbreviation for volume

volatile /ˈvɒlətaɪl/ ⓤⓢ /ˈvɑːlətəl/ **adj 1** A volatile person can suddenly become angry or violent. **2** A volatile situation might suddenly change: *a volatile political situation* • **volatility** /ˌvɒləˈtɪləti/ **noun** [U]

volcano /vɒlˈkeɪnəʊ/ **noun** [C] (plural **volcanoes**, **volcanos**) **B2** a mountain with a large hole at the top which sometimes explodes and produces hot, melted rock and smoke • **volcanic** /vɒlˈkænɪk/ **adj** relating to a volcano: *volcanic ash*

volcano

vole /vəʊl/ **noun** [C] a small animal like a mouse

volition /vəʊˈlɪʃən/ **noun** [U] formal the power to make your own decisions: *He left the firm **of his own volition** (= because he decided to).*

volley¹ /ˈvɒli/ **noun 1** [C] in sports, a kick or hit in which a player returns a ball before it touches the ground **2 a volley of shots/gunfire, etc** a lot of bullets shot at the same time: *A volley of bullets ripped through the floorboards.* **3 a volley of abuse/complaints, etc** a lot of insults, complaints, etc said at the same time

volley² /ˈvɒli/ **verb** [I, T] in sports, to return a ball by kicking or hitting it before it touches the ground

volleyball /ˈvɒlibɔːl/ **noun** [U] **A2** a game in which two teams use their hands to hit a ball over a net without allowing it to touch the ground → See colour picture **Sports 2** on page Centre 15

volleyball

volt /vɒlt/ **noun** [C] (written abbreviation **V**) a unit for measuring the force of an electric current

voltage /ˈvəʊltɪdʒ/ **noun** [C, U] the force of an electric current, measured in volts

volume /ˈvɒljuːm/ **noun 1 SOUND** ▷ [U] **B1** the level of sound produced by a television, radio, etc: *to turn the volume up/down* **2 AMOUNT** ▷ **B2** the number or amount of something especially when it is large: *the volume of work involved* **3 SPACE** ▷ [U] the amount of space inside an object: *Which of the bottles has the larger volume?* **4 BOOK** ▷ [C] a book, especially one of a set: *a new dictionary in two volumes*

voluminous /vəˈluːmɪnəs/ **adj** formal very large: *voluminous trousers*

voluntary /ˈvɒləntˀri/ **adj 1** Voluntary work is done without being paid and usually involves helping people: *She does voluntary work for the Red Cross.* ∘ *voluntary organizations* **2** done or given because you want to and not because you have been forced to: *voluntary contributions* → Opposite **involuntary** • **voluntarily** /ˌvɒlənˈteərˀli/ **adv** *She left voluntarily.*

volunteer¹ /ˌvɒlənˈtɪər/ **verb 1 OFFER** ▷ [I, T] to offer to do something without being asked or told to do it: [+ to do sth] *Rob volunteered to look after the kids.* **2 ARMY** ▷ [I] to join the army, navy, etc without being officially told to join: *In 1939 he volunteered for active service.* **3 INFORMATION** ▷ [T] to give information without being asked: *No one volunteered the truth.*

volunteer² /ˌvɒlənˈtɪər/ **noun** [C] **1** 🆎 someone who does work without being paid, especially work that involves helping people: *a Red Cross volunteer* **2** someone who does or gives something because they want to and not because they have been forced to: *Any volunteers to help me move these books?*

voluptuous /vəˈlʌptʃuəs/ **adj** A voluptuous woman has a sexually attractive body, often with large breasts.

vomit¹ /ˈvɒmɪt/ **verb** [I, T] If someone vomits, the food or liquid that was in their stomach comes up and out of their mouth: *She was vomiting blood.*

vomit² /ˈvɒmɪt/ **noun** [U] the food or liquid that comes from your mouth when you vomit

voodoo /ˈvuːduː/ **noun** [U] a religion involving magic and praying to spirits

voracious /vəˈreɪʃəs/ **adj** wanting to do something a lot, especially wanting to eat a lot of food: *She has a voracious appetite.* ∘ *a voracious reader of historical novels* • **voraciously adv** • **voracity** /vəˈræsəti/ **noun** [U]

vote¹ /vəʊt/ **verb** [I, T] 🆎 to show your choice or opinion in an election or meeting by writing a cross on an official piece of paper or putting your hand up: *Who did you vote for?* ∘ *The unions voted against strike action.* ∘ [+ to do sth] *Staff have voted to accept the pay offer.*

vote² /vəʊt/ **noun** [C] **1** 🆎 the act of showing your choice or opinion in an election or meeting by writing a cross on an official piece of paper or putting your hand up: *He lost the election by twenty votes.* **2** 🆎 a way of making a decision by asking a group of people to vote: *We called a meeting in order to take a vote on the proposal.* **3 the vote a** the total number of votes given or received in an election: *The Green party got 10% of the vote.* **b** the right to vote in elections: *In some countries women still don't have the vote.*

> ☑ Word partners for **vote**
>
> cast your vote • a vote against/for sb/sth • a vote on sth

voter /ˈvəʊtər/ **noun** [C] someone who votes or who is officially allowed to vote

vouch /vaʊtʃ/ **verb**

PHRASAL VERB **vouch for sb/sth** to say that you know from experience that something is true or good, or that someone has a good character

voucher /ˈvaʊtʃər/ **noun** [C] a piece of paper that can be used instead of money to pay for goods or services: *a discount voucher*

vow¹ /vaʊ/ **verb** [T] to make a serious promise or decision: [+ (that)] *She vowed that she would never leave the children again.* ∘ [+ to do sth] *I've vowed never to go there again.*

vow² /vaʊ/ **noun** [C] a serious promise or decision: *marriage vows* ∘ *I made a vow that I would write to him once a week.*

vowel /vaʊəl/ **noun** [C] 🆑 a speech sound that you make with your lips and teeth open, shown in English by the letters 'a', 'e', 'i', 'o' or 'u'

voyage /ˈvɔɪdʒ/ **noun** [C] 🆎 a long journey, especially by ship, or in space: *The ship sank on its maiden voyage* (= first journey).

vs (also UK **v**) **preposition** written abbreviation for versus (= used to say that one team or person is competing against another)

vulgar /ˈvʌlgər/ **adj 1** rude and likely to upset or anger people, especially by referring to sex and the body in an unpleasant way: *vulgar jokes/ language* **2** not showing good judgment about what is suitable or pleasant to look at: *a vulgar shade of yellow* • **vulgarity** /vʌlˈgærəti/ **noun** [U]

vulnerable /ˈvʌlnˀrəbl/ **adj** easy to hurt or attack physically or emotionally: *She was a vulnerable sixteen-year-old.* ∘ *The troops are in a vulnerable position.* ∘ *He's more vulnerable to infection because of his injuries.* • **vulnerability** /ˌvʌlnˀrəˈbɪləti/ **noun** [U]

vulture /ˈvʌltʃər/ **noun** [C] a large bird with no feathers on its head or neck that eats dead animals

vying /ˈvaɪɪŋ/ present participle of vie

V

W

W, w /ˈdʌblju:/ the twenty-third letter of the alphabet

W written abbreviation for watt (= a unit for measuring electrical power): *a 40W light bulb*

wacky /ˈwæki/ **adj** informal unusual in a funny or surprising way: *a wacky sense of humour*

wad /wɒd/ **noun** [C] **1** a thick pile of pieces of paper, especially paper money: *a wad of cash* **2** a piece of soft material in the shape of a ball: *a wad of cotton wool* UK/ *cotton* US

waddle /ˈwɒdl/ **verb** [I] A duck (= water bird) or fat person that waddles walks with short steps, moving from side to side.

wade /weɪd/ **verb wade across/through, etc** to walk through water: *He waded across the river.*

PHRASAL VERB **wade through sth** to read a lot of boring or difficult information

wafer /ˈweɪfər/ **noun** [C] a light, thin biscuit

waffle¹ /ˈwɒfl/ **noun 1** [U] informal speech or writing that says nothing important **2** [C] a square, flat cake with a pattern of holes in it, eaten especially in the US

waffle² /ˈwɒfl/ **verb** [I] (also **waffle on**) to talk or write a lot and say nothing important

waft /wɒft/ **verb waft from/through, etc** to gradually move through the air: *The smell of coffee wafted through the room.*

wag /wæg/ **verb** [I, T] (**wagging, wagged**) **1** If a dog wags its tail, it moves it from side to side. **2** If you wag your finger, you move it from side to side, often to tell someone not to do something.

wage¹ /weɪdʒ/ **noun** [no plural] (also **wages** [plural]) ⑥ the amount of money a person regularly receives for their job: *weekly wages* ∘ *the minimum wage* → See Note at **pay²**

> ✷ Word partners for **wage**
>
> earn a wage • a decent wage • a wage increase/rise • the minimum wage

wage² /weɪdʒ/ **verb wage a battle/campaign/ war, etc** to fight or organize a series of activities in order to achieve something: *They're currently waging a campaign to change the law.*

wager /ˈweɪdʒər/ **verb** [T] to risk money on the result of a game, race, competition, etc • **wager noun** [C]

wagon /ˈwægən/ **noun** [C] a large vehicle with four large wheels pulled by horses

wail /weɪl/ **verb 1** [I, T] to cry loudly because you are very unhappy: *"I've lost my mummy," she wailed.* **2** [I] If a siren (= loud noise to warn of danger) wails, it makes a noise: *Somewhere in the distance a police siren was wailing.* • **wail noun** [C]

waist /weɪst/ **noun** [C] **1** ⑥ the part around the middle of your body where you wear a belt: *She had a 26 inch waist.* → See colour picture **The Body**

on page Centre 13 **2** the part of a piece of clothing that fits round the waist

waist

waistband /ˈweɪstbænd/ **noun** [C] the strip of material at the top of a pair of trousers or a skirt that goes around the waist

waistcoat /ˈweɪstkəʊt/ **noun** [C] UK (US **vest**) a piece of clothing with buttons at the front and no sleeves, that you wear over a shirt → See **Clothes** on page Centre ⑤

waistline /ˈweɪstlaɪn/ **noun** [C] how big or small your waist is, or the part of a piece of clothing that goes around the waist

wait¹ /weɪt/ **verb** [I] **1** ⓐ to stay in a place until someone or something arrives or someone or something is ready for you: *I'm waiting for Clive.* ∘ *How long did you wait for a taxi?* ∘ [+ to do sth] *I'm still waiting to use the phone.* **2** to not do something until something else happens: *We'll wait till Jane gets here before we start eating.* **3 can't wait** informal ⓐ used to say how excited you are about something that you are going to do: [+ to do sth] *I can't wait to see him.* **4 keep sb waiting** ⓑ to be late so that someone has to wait for you: *I'm sorry to have kept you waiting.* **5 wait and see** to wait to discover what will happen: *We'll wait and see what she says.* → See also **be waiting in the wings**

> **!** Common learner error: **wait** or **expect**?
>
> When you **wait**, you stay somewhere until a person or thing arrives or is ready.
>
> *I waited twenty minutes for the bus.*
> *She's waiting for her exam results.*
>
> When you **expect** something, you think that it will happen.
>
> *I'm expecting the bus to arrive in about five minutes.*
> *She expected to do well in the exam.*
> ~~She waited to do well in the exam.~~

> **!** Common learner error: **wait**
>
> **Wait** must always be followed by **for** or **to do sth**. It cannot be followed by the thing you are waiting for.
>
> *I am waiting for my mother.*
> ~~I am waiting my mother.~~

PHRASAL VERBS **wait about/around** to stay in a place and do nothing while you wait for someone to arrive or something to happen • **wait in** UK to stay at home because you are expecting someone to visit or telephone you • **wait on sb** to bring a meal to someone, especially in a restaurant • **wait up** to not go to bed at night until someone has come home: *I'll be quite late, so don't **wait up for** me.*

wait² /weɪt/ noun [no plural] 🔵 a period when you stay in a place until someone or something arrives or someone or something is ready for you: *We **had** a **long wait** at the airport.*

> 🔲 Word partners for **wait**
>
> face/have a wait • an agonizing/anxious/long wait • the wait for sth • sth is (well) worth the wait

waiter /'weɪtər/ noun [C] 🅰️ a man who works in a restaurant, bringing food to customers

waiting list noun [C] a list of people who are waiting until it is their time to have or do something: *a hospital waiting list*

waiting room noun [C] a room in which people wait for something, for example to see a doctor or take a train

waitress /'weɪtrəs/ noun [C] 🅰️ a woman who works in a restaurant, bringing food to customers

waive /weɪv/ verb [T] **1** to allow someone not to obey the usual rule or not to pay the usual amount of money: *He agreed to waive his fee to help us.* **2** to decide not to have something that you are allowed by law to have: *She **waived** her **right** to have a lawyer representing her.*

wake¹ /weɪk/ verb [I, T] (**woke, woken**) (also **wake up**) 🅰️ to stop sleeping or to make someone stop sleeping: *I've only just woken up.* ◦ *Could you wake me up before you go?* ◦ *You woke me up making so much noise.* → See colour picture **Phrasal Verbs** on page Centre 16

PHRASAL VERB **wake up to sth** to start to understand something that is important: *We need to wake up to the fact that the Earth's resources are limited.*

wake² /weɪk/ noun **1 in the wake of sth** after something has happened, and often because it has happened: *Airport security was extra tight in the wake of last week's bomb attacks.* **2** [C] the waves behind a moving ship **3** [C] an occasion when people come together to remember someone who has recently died

wake-up call noun [C] **1** a telephone call to wake you in the morning, especially when you are staying in a hotel **2** something bad that happens and shows you that you need to take action to change a situation

walk¹ /wɔːk/ verb **1** 🅰️ [I, T] to move forward by putting one foot in front of the other and then repeating the action: *She walks to school.* ◦ *We walked twenty miles in all.* **2 walk sb home/to sth** to walk with someone in order to guide them or keep them safe: *He walked me to my house.* **3 walk the dog** to walk with a dog to give the dog exercise

IDIOM **walk all over sb** informal to treat someone badly

> 🔲 Common learner error: **walk** or **go on foot?**
>
> The expression **go on foot** means **walk**, usually when you are describing how you get somewhere.
>
> *How do you get to school? I **go on foot**/I walk.*

PHRASAL VERBS **walk into sth** to get a job easily • **walk off with sth** to win something easily: *She walked off with the top prize.* • **walk out** to leave a job, meeting, or performance because you are angry or do not approve of something: *He was so disgusted by the film he walked out.* • **walk out on sb** to suddenly leave your husband, wife, or partner and end your relationship with them: *He walked out on his wife and kids.*

walk² /wɔːk/ noun **1** [C] 🅰️ a journey that you make by walking, often for enjoyment: *We usually **go for a walk** on Sunday afternoons.* ◦ *He took the dog for a walk.* **2 a short/ten-minute, etc walk** a journey that takes a short time/ten minutes, etc when you walk: *The station is just a five-minute walk from the house.* **3** [C] a path or route where people can walk for enjoyment: *There are some lovely walks in the forest.*

IDIOM **walk of life** People from different walks of life have different jobs and different experiences in life.

> 🔲 Word partners for **walk**
>
> go for/take a walk • a brisk walk • a long/short walk

walker /'wɔːkər/ noun [C] someone who walks for exercise or enjoyment

walkie talkie /ˌwɔːki'tɔːki/ noun [C] a radio that you carry with you and that lets you talk to someone else with a similar radio

walking /'wɔːkɪŋ/ noun [U] 🅰️ the activity of going for a walk, especially for pleasure in the countryside: *I love walking on the beach.*

Walkman /'wɔːkmən/ noun [C] trademark a small piece of equipment with parts that you put in your ears which allows you to listen to music that no one else can hear

wall /wɔːl/ noun [C] **1** 🅰️ one of the vertical sides of a room or building: *There were several large paintings on the wall.* **2** 🅰️ a vertical structure made of brick or stone that divides areas that are owned by different people: *a garden wall*

IDIOM **drive sb up the wall** informal to make someone very angry: *She drives me up the wall.*

→ See also **fly²** on the wall, be banging your **head¹** against a brick wall

walled /wɔːld/ adj **walled garden/city** a garden/city with walls around it

wallet /'wɒlɪt/ noun [C] (also US **billfold**) 🅰️ a small, flat container for paper money and credit cards (= plastic cards used for paying with), usually used by a man

wallop /'wɒləp/ verb [T] informal to hit someone or something hard • **wallop** noun [no plural] informal

wallow /'wɒləʊ/ verb [I] **1** to allow yourself to

W

feel too much sadness in a way that stops people respecting you: *There's no use **wallowing** in self-pity.* **2** to lie or move around in soil or water, especially for pleasure

wallpaper /ˈwɔːlˌpeɪpər/ noun [C, U] **1** paper, usually with a pattern, that you decorate walls with **2** a design or image that you choose to appear on the screen of your computer • **wallpaper** verb [T]

Wall Street noun the financial area of New York where shares (= small, equal parts of the value of a company) are bought and sold: *The company's shares rose **on Wall Street** yesterday.*

wally /ˈwɒli/ noun [C] UK informal a silly person

walnut /ˈwɔːlnʌt/ noun **1** [C] a nut that is in two halves inside a brown shell, and whose surface has curves and folds in it **2** [U] the hard wood of the tree that produces walnuts, used to make furniture

walrus /ˈwɔːlrəs/ noun [C] a large sea animal that has two tusks (= long, pointed teeth that come out of the mouth)

waltz[1] /wɒls/ noun [C] a dance for two partners performed to music that has a rhythm of three beats, or the music for the dance

waltz[2] /wɒls/ verb [I] **1** to dance a waltz **2** **waltz in/off, etc** to walk somewhere quickly and confidently, often in a way that annoys other people: *You can't just waltz into my bedroom – it's private!*

wan /wɒn/ adj pale and looking sick or tired

wand /wɒnd/ noun [C] a thin stick that someone who performs magic tricks holds in their hand

wander /ˈwɒndər/ verb **1** [I, T] to walk slowly about a place without any purpose: *They wandered aimlessly around the town.* **2** [I] (also **wander off**) to walk away from the place where you should be: *He was here a moment ago – he must have wandered off.* **3** **sb's attention/mind/thoughts, etc wander** If someone's attention/mind, etc wanders, they start thinking about one subject when they should be thinking about a different subject: *I was bored and my thoughts started to wander.*

wane /weɪn/ verb [I] to become less powerful, important, or popular: *Interest in the product is starting to wane.*

wangle /ˈwæŋɡl/ verb [T] informal to succeed in getting something that a lot of people want, by being clever or tricking someone: *He managed to wangle an invitation to the party.*

> ⚠ Common learner error: **want** something/someone **to do** something
>
> Be careful to use the correct form after this expression. You cannot say 'that' after **want**.
> *I just want him to enjoy himself.*
> ~~I just want that he enjoy himself.~~
> *They don't want the school holidays to end.*
> ~~They don't want that the school holidays end.~~

want[1] /wɒnt/ verb [T] **1** to hope to have or do something, or to wish for something: *He wants a new car.* ○ *[+ to do sth] I don't want to talk about it.* ○ *You can't always do what you want.* ○ *We can*

go later if you want. ○ *I want him to explain why.* **2** to need something: *This soup wants more salt.* **3** **want to do sth** UK informal used to give advice to someone: *You want to go to bed earlier and then you won't be so tired.* **4** **be wanted** to be needed for a particular activity or in a particular place: *You're wanted on the phone.*

want[2] /wɒnt/ noun **want of sth** a situation in which there is not enough of something: *If we fail, it won't be **for want of** effort (= it is not because we have not tried).*

wanted /ˈwɒntɪd/ adj If someone is wanted, the police think they have committed a serious crime and are trying to find them: *He is **wanted for** murder.*

wanton /ˈwɒntən/ adj formal done in order to cause suffering or destruction but with no other reason: *wanton cruelty/violence*

wants /wɒnts/ noun [plural] the things you want or need

war /wɔːr/ noun **1** FIGHTING ▷ [C, U] fighting using soldiers and weapons, between two or more countries, or two or more groups inside a country: *They've been **at war** for the past five years.* ○ *He was only a child when the **war broke out** (= started).* ○ *If this country **goes to war** (= starts to fight in a war), thousands of people will die.* **2** COMPETING ▷ [C, U] a situation in which two or more groups are trying to be more successful than each other: *a **price war** between supermarkets* **3** TO STOP ▷ [no plural] an attempt to stop something bad or illegal: *the **war against** crime/drugs* → See also **civil war, prisoner of war, world war**

> 🗎 Word partners for **war**
>
> all-out/full-scale war • declare/go to war • wage war on sb • war breaks out • war against sb

war crime noun [C] a crime during a war that breaks the international rules of war • **war criminal** noun [C] someone guilty of a war crime

ward[1] /wɔːd/ noun [C] a room in a hospital where people receiving treatment stay, often for the same type of illness: *the maternity ward*

ward[2] /wɔːd/ verb

PHRASAL VERB **ward sth off** to prevent something unpleasant happening: *I take vitamin C to ward off colds.*

-ward, -wards /-wəd/, /-wədz/ suffix makes an adverb meaning 'towards a direction or place': *inward* ○ *forward* ○ *homeward*

warden /ˈwɔːdən/ noun [C] **1** US (UK **governor**) someone who is responsible for controlling a prison **2** someone who is responsible for looking after a particular place or the people in it → See also **traffic warden**

warder /ˈwɔːdər/ noun [C] UK a prison guard

wardrobe /ˈwɔːdrəʊb/ noun **1** [C] (also US **closet**) a large cupboard for keeping clothes in **2** [no plural] all the clothes that you own

warehouse /ˈweəhaʊs/ noun [C] (plural **warehouses** /ˈweəhaʊzɪz/) a large building for storing goods that are going to be sold

W

wares /weəz/ **noun** [plural] literary goods that are for sale, especially not in a shop: *People were selling their wares at the side of the road.*

warfare /'wɔːfeər/ **noun** [U] fighting in a war, especially using a particular type of weapon: *chemical/modern warfare*

warhead /'wɔːhed/ **noun** [C] the part of a missile (= weapon) that explodes when it reaches the place it is aimed at: *a nuclear warhead*

warlord /'wɔːlɔːd/ **noun** [C] a military leader who controls a particular area of a country

warm¹ /wɔːm/ **adj 1 TEMPERATURE** ▷ **A1** having a temperature between cool and hot: *It's nice and warm in here.* ○ *Are you warm enough?* ○ *Make sure you keep warm.* **2 CLOTHES** ▷ **A2** Warm clothes or covers keep your body warm: *a warm sweater* **3 FRIENDLY** ▷ **B1** friendly and showing affection: *a warm smile/welcome*

warm² /wɔːm/ **verb** [I, T] **B2** to become warm or to make something become warm: *She warmed her feet against his.* ○ *I'll warm the soup.*

PHRASAL VERBS **warm to sb/sth** to start to like a person or idea • **warm up** to do gentle exercises in order to prepare yourself for more energetic exercise: *They were warming up before the match.* • **warm-up** /'wɔːmʌp/ **noun** [C] • **warm (sb/sth) up** to become warmer or to make someone or something warmer: *The house soon warms up with the heating on.*

warmly /'wɔːmli/ **adv** **B2** in a friendly way

warmth /wɔːmθ/ **noun** [U] **1** **B2** the heat that is produced by something: *the warmth of the fire* **2** **B2** the quality of being friendly and showing affection: *There was no warmth in his eyes.*

warn /wɔːn/ **verb** [T] **1** **B1** to tell someone that something bad may happen in the future, so that they can prevent it: [+ that] *I warned you that it would be cold but you still wouldn't wear a coat.* ○ *I've been warning him for months.* **2** to advise someone not to do something that could cause danger or trouble: [+ to do sth] *I warned you not to tell her.*

warning /'wɔːnɪŋ/ **noun** [C, U] **B1** something that tells or shows you that something bad may happen: *All cigarette packets carry a warning.* ○ *The bombs fell completely without warning.*

> ☑ Word partners for **warning**
> deliver/give/heed/ignore/issue a warning • a blunt/final/stern warning • without warning

warp¹ /wɔːp/ **verb 1** [I, T] to become bent into the wrong shape or to make something do this: *The window frames had warped.* **2** [T] If something warps your mind, it makes you strange and cruel.

warp² /wɔːp/ **noun the warp** the threads that go from one end to the other in a piece of cloth, and which the other threads are twisted over and under

warpath /'wɔːpɑːθ/ **noun**

IDIOM **be on the warpath** informal to be trying to find someone in order to be angry with them

warped /wɔːpt/ **adj** strange and cruel: *You've got a warped mind!*

warplane /'wɔːˌpleɪn/ **noun** [C] an aircraft for carrying bombs

warrant¹ /'wɒrənt/ **noun** [C] an official document that allows someone to do something, for example that allows a police officer to search a building: *The police have a warrant for his arrest.* → See also **search warrant**

warrant² /'wɒrənt/ **verb** [T] to make something necessary: *None of her crimes is serious enough to warrant punishment.*

warranty /'wɒrənti/ **noun** [C, U] a written promise made by a company to change or repair one of its products if it has a fault: *a five-year warranty*

warren /'wɒrən/ **noun** [C] (also **'rabbit ˌwarren**) a group of connected underground holes where rabbits live

warring /'wɔːrɪŋ/ **adj warring factions/parties/ sides, etc** groups that are fighting against each other

warrior /'wɒriər/ **noun** [C] a person who has experience and skill in fighting in a war, especially in the past

warship /'wɔːʃɪp/ **noun** [C] a ship with weapons, used in war

wart /wɔːt/ **noun** [C] a small, hard lump that grows on the skin

wartime /'wɔːtaɪm/ **noun** [U] a period when a country is fighting a war

war-torn /'wɔːˌtɔːn/ **adj** damaged by war: *a war-torn country*

wary /'weəri/ **adj** If you are wary of someone or something, you do not trust them completely: *She's still wary of strangers.* • **warily adv** • **wariness noun** [U]

was /wɒz/ past simple I/he/she/it of be

wash¹ /wɒʃ/ **verb 1** [T] **A1** to make something clean using water, or water and soap: *Dad was washing the dishes.* **2** [I, T] **A1** to clean part of your body with water and soap: *Have you washed your hands?* ○ *I got washed and dressed.* **3 be washed away/out/up, etc** If something is washed away/out, etc, it is moved there by water: *A lot of the waste is washed out to sea.* **4 wash against/on, etc** If water washes somewhere, it flows there: *Waves washed against the base of the cliff.*

PHRASAL VERBS **wash sth away** If water washes something away, it removes that thing: *Floods washed away much of the soil.* • **wash sth down** to drink something with food or medicine to make it easier to swallow: *I had a plate of sandwiches, washed down with a glass of cool beer.* • **wash out** If a colour or dirty mark washes out, it disappears when you wash something: *Most hair dye washes out after a few weeks.* • **wash (sth) up** UK **A2** to wash the dishes, pans, and other things you have used for cooking and eating a meal → See colour picture **Phrasal Verbs** on page Centre 16 • **wash up** US to wash your hands, especially before a meal: *Go and wash up – your dinner's ready.*

W

wash² /wɒʃ/ **noun 1 a wash a** ⓐ2 UK If you have a wash, you wash a part of your body. **b** ⓐ2 mainly UK If you give something a wash, you wash it: *Could you give the car a wash?* **2** [C, U] clothes, sheets, etc that are being washed together: *Your jeans are in the wash.*

washable /ˈwɒʃəbl/ **adj** Something that is washable will not be damaged by being washed.

washbasin /ˈwɒʃˌbeɪsən/ **noun** [C] UK (also UK/US **sink**) a bowl in a bathroom that water can flow into, used for washing your face or hands

washcloth /ˈwɒʃklɒθ/ **noun** [C] US (UK **flannel**) a small cloth that you use to wash your face and body → See colour picture **The Bathroom** on page Centre 3

washed-out /ˌwɒʃtˈaʊt/ **adj** looking pale and tired

washer /ˈwɒʃər/ **noun** [C] **1** a thin, flat ring that is put between a nut and a bolt (= metal objects used to fasten things together) **2** a machine that washes clothes

washing /ˈwɒʃɪŋ/ **noun** [U] clothes, sheets, and similar things that are being washed or have been washed, or the activity of washing these: *I'm doing the washing this morning.* ∘ *He does his own washing and ironing.*

washing maˌchine noun [C] ⓐ2 a machine that washes clothes

washing ˌpowder noun [C] UK (US **laundry detergent**) a soap in the form of a powder that is used to wash clothes

washing-up /ˌwɒʃɪŋˈʌp/ **noun** [U] UK ⓐ2 the activity of washing the dishes, pans, and other things you have used for cooking and eating a meal: *He was doing the washing-up.*

washing-ˈup ˌliquid noun [C, U] UK (US **dish soap**) a thick liquid soap used to wash pans, plates, knives and forks, etc

washout /ˈwɒʃaʊt/ **noun** [no plural] informal an event that fails badly: *No one came to the fete – it was a complete washout.*

washroom /ˈwɒʃruːm/ **noun** [C] US a room where you can go to the toilet or wash your hands and face

wasn't /ˈwɒzənt/ short for was not: *I wasn't hungry this morning.*

wasp /wɒsp/ **noun** [C] ⓑ2 a flying insect with a thin, black and yellow body: *a wasp sting*

wasp

wastage /ˈweɪstɪdʒ/ **noun** [U] the fact of wasting something: *fuel wastage*

waste¹ /weɪst/ **noun 1** [U, no plural] ⓑ1 a bad use of something useful, such as time or money, when there is a limited amount of it: *Meetings are a waste of time.* ∘ *They throw away loads of food – it's such a waste.* ∘ *a waste of energy/resources* **2** [U] ⓑ2 things that are not wanted, especially what remains after you have used something: *household/nuclear waste* **3 go to waste** to not be used: *I hate to see good food go to waste.*

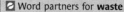

🗹 Word partners for **waste**

a waste **of** sth • a waste **of effort/money/ time** • household/nuclear/toxic waste • waste **disposal** • go to waste

waste² /weɪst/ **verb** [T] **1** ⓑ1 to use too much of something or use something badly when there is a limited amount of it: *I don't want to waste any more time so let's start.* ∘ *Why waste your money on things you don't need?* **2 be wasted on sb** to be clever or of high quality in a way that someone will not understand or enjoy: *Good coffee is wasted on Joe – he prefers instant.*

PHRASAL VERB **waste away** to become thinner and weaker

waste³ /weɪst/ **adj** [always before noun] ⓑ1 Waste material is not now needed and can be got rid of: *waste paper*

wasteful /ˈweɪstfəl/ **adj** using too much of something, or using something badly when there is a limited amount of it

wasteland /ˈweɪstlænd/ **noun** [C, U] an area of land that cannot be used in any way

ˈwastepaper ˌbasket noun [C] (also US **wastebasket**) a container that is used inside buildings for putting rubbish such as paper into

watch¹ /wɒtʃ/ **verb 1 LOOK AT** ▷ [I, T] ⓐ1 to look at something for a period of time: *I watched him as he arrived.* ∘ *The kids are watching TV.* ∘ *I want to watch the news (= programme on television)* → See Note at **look¹ 2 BE CAREFUL** ▷ [T] ⓑ2 to be careful about something: *She has to watch what she eats.* ∘ *Watch how you cross the road!* **3 GIVE ATTENTION TO** ▷ [T] to give attention to a situation that is changing: *We'll be watching the case with interest.* → See also **bird-watching, watch your step¹**

PHRASAL VERBS **watch out** ⓑ2 used to tell someone to be careful because they are in danger: *Watch out! There's a car coming!* ∘ *Drivers were told to watch out for black ice on the road.* • **watch over sb** to look after someone and protect them if it is necessary

watch² /wɒtʃ/ **noun 1** [C] ⓐ1 a small clock on a strap that you fasten round your wrist (= lower arm): *I don't wear a watch.* **2** [U, no plural] If you keep a watch on something or someone, you watch or give attention to them, especially to make sure nothing bad happens: *We're keeping a close watch on the situation.*

watch

🗹 Word partners for **watch noun**

wear a watch • glance at/look at your watch

watchdog /ˈwɒtʃdɒg/ **noun** [C] an organization whose job is to make sure that companies behave legally and provide good services

watchful /ˈwɒtʃfəl/ **adj** careful to notice things and ready to deal with problems: *They were playing outside under the watchful eye of a teacher.*

watchword /'wɒtʃwɜːd/ **noun** [no plural] a word or phrase that describes the main ideas or most important part of something: *As regards fashion, the watchword this season is simplicity.*

water¹ /'wɔːtər/ **noun** [U] **1 🅐** the clear liquid that falls from the sky as rain and that is in seas, lakes, and rivers: *hot/cold water* ∘ *a drink of water* **2** (also **waters**) 🅐 an area in the sea or in a river or lake: *coastal waters*

IDIOMS **be in deep water** to be in a difficult situation that is hard to deal with: *They tried to adopt a baby illegally and ended up in very deep water.* • **be (like) water off a duck's back** If criticisms, insults, etc are like water off a duck's back to you, they do not affect you at all: *She calls him lazy and useless, but it's like water off a duck's back.*

→ See also **drinking water, mineral water, tap water**

water² /'wɔːtər/ **verb 1 PLANTS** ▷ [T] 🅑 to pour water over plants **2 MOUTH** ▷ [I] If food makes your mouth water, it makes you want to eat it, sometimes making your mouth produce liquid: *The smells from the kitchen are making my mouth water.* **3 EYES** ▷ [I] If your eyes water, they produce liquid because something is hurting them: *The smoke was making my eyes water.*

PHRASAL VERB **water sth down 1** to add water to a drink, especially an alcoholic drink **2** to make a plan or idea less extreme, usually so that people will accept it

watercolour UK (US **watercolor**) /'wɔːtəˌkʌlər/ **noun** [C] a type of paint that is mixed with water, or a picture made with this paint

water cooler noun [C] a machine for providing cool drinking water, usually in an office or other public place

watercress /'wɔːtəkres/ **noun** [U] a small, strong-tasting plant that is eaten in salads

waterfall /'wɔːtəfɔːl/ **noun** [C] 🅒 a stream of water that flows from a high place, often to a pool below

water fountain noun [C] a device, usually in a public place, which supplies water for drinking

waterfront /'wɔːtəfrʌnt/ **noun** [C] a part of a town that is next to the sea, a lake, or a river: *waterfront restaurants*

waterhole /'wɔːtəhəʊl/ **noun** [C] a small pool of water in a dry area where animals go to drink

watering can noun [C] a container used for watering plants in the garden

waterlogged /'wɔːtəlɒgd/ **adj** Waterlogged land is too wet.

watermark /'wɔːtəmɑːk/ **noun** [C] a pattern or picture on paper, especially paper money, which you can only see when a strong light is behind it

watermelon /'wɔːtəˌmelən/ **noun** [C, U] a large, round, green fruit that is pink inside with a lot of black seeds

waterproof /'wɔːtəpruːf/ **adj** 🅑 Waterproof material or clothing does not let water through: *a waterproof sleeping bag*

waters /'wɔːtəz/ **noun** [plural] the part of a sea around the coast of a country that legally belongs to that country

watershed /'wɔːtəʃed/ **noun** [no plural] an important event after which a situation completely changes: *The discovery marked a watershed in the history of medicine.*

water-skiing /'wɔːtəskiːɪŋ/ **noun** [U] a sport in which someone is pulled behind a boat while standing on skis (= long, narrow pieces of wood or plastic fastened to the feet)

watertight /'wɔːtətaɪt/ **adj 1** Something that is watertight prevents any water from entering it. **2** A watertight reason or excuse is one that no one can prove is false: *a watertight alibi*

waterway /'wɔːtəweɪ/ **noun** [C] a river or canal (= river made by people, not nature) that people can use to travel along

watery /'wɔːtəri/ **adj 1** made with too much water: *watery soup* **2** Watery eyes are wet with tears.

watt /wɒt/ **noun** [C] (written abbreviation **W**) a unit for measuring electrical power: *a 60 watt light bulb*

wave

a wave   She's waving.

wave¹ /weɪv/ **verb 1** [I] 🅒 to raise your hand and move it from side to side in order to attract someone's attention or to say goodbye: *Wave goodbye to Grandma.* ∘ *She waved at him.* **2 wave sb in/on/through, etc** to show which way you want someone to go by moving your hand in that direction: *The police waved him on.* **3** [I, T] (also **wave about/around**) to move from side to side in the air or make something move this way: *The long grass waved in the breeze.* ∘ *He started waving his arms about wildly.*

PHRASAL VERBS **wave sth aside** to refuse to consider what someone says: *She waved aside all my objections.* • **wave sb off** to wave your hand to someone as they are leaving in order to say goodbye: *We went to the station to wave him off.*

wave² /weɪv/ **noun** [C] **1 WATER** ▷ 🅒 a line of higher water that moves across the surface of the sea or a lake: *I could hear the waves crashing against the rocks.* **2 GROUP** ▷ a group of people or things that arrive or happen together or in a short period of time: *There has been a wave of kidnappings in the region.* ∘ *Another wave of refugees is arriving at the border.* **3 a wave of hatred/enthusiasm/sadness, etc** an emotion

W

that you suddenly feel: *She felt a sudden wave of sadness.* **4 HAND** ▷ a movement of your hand from side to side in order to attract someone's attention or say goodbye: *She gave a little wave as the train left.* **5 ENERGY** ▷ 🅑🅑 a piece of sound, light, or other energy that travels up and down in a curved pattern: *a radio wave* → See also **new wave**, **tidal wave**

wavelength /ˈweɪvleŋθ/ *noun* [C] **1** the length of radio wave used by a radio company for broadcasting its programmes **2** the distance between one sound or light wave, etc and the next

IDIOM **be on the same wavelength** If two people are on the same wavelength, they have the same way of thinking and it is easy for them to understand each other.

waver /ˈweɪvəʳ/ *verb* [I] **1** to start to be uncertain about a belief or decision: *Her support for him never wavered.* ∘ *I'm wavering between the blue shirt and the red.* **2** to shake slightly or lose strength: *His voice wavered and I thought he was going to cry.*

wavy /ˈweɪvi/ *adj* with slight curves: *wavy hair*

wax¹ /wæks/ *noun* [U] a solid substance that becomes soft when warm and melts easily, often used to make candles

wax² /wæks/ *verb* [T] **1** to put wax on something, especially to make it shiny: *They cleaned and waxed my car.* **2** If you wax your legs, you remove the hair from them by using wax.

way¹ /weɪ/ *noun* **1 METHOD** ▷ [C] 🅐🅑 how you do something: [+ to do sth] *I must find a way to help him.* ∘ [+ of + doing sth] *We looked at various ways of solving the problem.* ∘ [+ (that)] *It was the way that she told me that I didn't like.* **2 ROUTE** ▷ [C] 🅐🅑 the route you take to get from one place to another: [usually singular] *Is there another way out of here?* ∘ *I must buy a paper on the way home.* ∘ *Can you find your way back to my house?* ∘ *I took the wrong road and lost my way* (= got lost). **3 make your way to/through/towards**, etc 🅑🅑 to move somewhere, often with difficulty: *We made our way through the shop to the main entrance.* **4 be on her/my/its**, etc **way** to be arriving soon: *Apparently she's on her way.* **5 in/out of the/sb's way** 🅑🅑 in/not in the area in front of someone that they need to pass or see through: *I couldn't see because Bill was in the way.* ∘ *Sorry, am I in your way?* ∘ *Could you move out of the way, please?* **6 a third of the way/most of the way**, etc used to say how much of something is completed: *A third of the way through the film she dies.* **7 get in the way of sth/sb** to prevent someone from doing or continuing with something: *Don't let your new friends get in the way of your studies.* **8 be under way** to be already happening: *Building work is already under way.* **9 give way (to sb/sth) a** to allow someone to get what they want, or to allow something to happen after trying to prevent it: *The boss finally gave way when they threatened to stop work.* **b** UK (US **yield**) to allow other vehicles to go past before you move onto a road **10 give way to sth** to change into something else: *Her excitement quickly gave way to horror.* **11 give**

way If something gives way, it falls because it is not strong enough to support the weight on top of it: *Suddenly the ground gave way under me.* **12 get sth out of the way** to finish something: *I'll go shopping when I've got this essay out of the way.* **13 DIRECTION** ▷ [C] 🅑🅑 a direction something faces or travels: *This bus is going the wrong way.* ∘ *Which way up does this picture go* (= which side should be at the top)? ∘ *UK He always wears his baseball cap the wrong way round* (= backwards). **14 SPACE/TIME** ▷ [no plural] 🅑🅑 an amount of space or time: *We're a long way from home.* ∘ *The exams are still a long way away/off.* **15 make way** to move away so that someone or something can pass **16 make way for sth** If you move or get rid of something to make way for something new, you do so in order to make a space for the new thing: *They knocked down the old houses to make way for a new hotel.* **17 in a way/in many ways** 🅑🅑 used to say that you think something is partly true: *In a way his behaviour is understandable.* **18 in no way** not at all: *This is in no way your fault.* **19 there's no way** informal 🅑🅑 If there is no way that something will happen, it is certainly not allowed or not possible: *There's no way that dog's coming in the house.* **20 No way!** informal 🅑🅑 certainly not: *"Would you invite him to a party?" "No way!"* **21 get/have your (own) way** to get what you want, although it might upset other people: *She always gets her own way in the end.* **22 in a big/small way** informal used to describe how much or little you do a particular thing: *They celebrate birthdays in a big way.* **23 a/sb's way of life** 🅑 the way someone lives: *Violence has become a way of life there.*

IDIOMS **by the way** 🅐🅑 used when you say something that does not relate to what is being discussed: *Oh, by the way, my name's Julie.* • **go out of your way to do sth** to try very hard to do something pleasant for someone: *He went out of his way to make us feel welcome.* • **rub sb up the wrong way** UK (US **rub sb the wrong way**) to annoy someone without intending to

→ See also **the Milky Way**

way² /weɪ/ *adv* informal used to emphasize how extreme something is: *The room was way too hot.* ∘ *He's in second place but he's way behind off.*

way 'out *noun* [C] **1** UK (UK/US **exit**) a door that takes you out of a building **2** a way of avoiding doing something unpleasant: *I'm supposed to be going to this meeting at 2.00 and I'm looking for a way out.*

wayside /ˈweɪsaɪd/ *noun*

IDIOM **fall by the wayside** to fail to complete something or be completed: *Many students fall by the wayside during their first year at college.*

wayward /ˈweɪwəd/ *adj* literary behaving badly in a way that causes trouble for other people

WC /ˌdʌbljuːˈsiː/ *noun* [C] UK abbreviation for water closet: a toilet, especially in a public place → See Note at **toilet**

we strong /wiː/ weak /wi/ *pronoun* **1** 🅐🅐 used a

the subject of the verb when the person speaking or writing is referring to themselves and one or more other people: *My wife and I both play golf and we love it.* **2** ⓑ people generally: *The world in which we live is very different.*

weak /wiːk/ **adj 1 BODY** ▷ ⓑ not physically strong: *He felt too weak to sit up.* ∘ *The children were* **weak with/from** *hunger.* **2 CHARACTER** ▷ ⓑ not powerful, or not having a strong character: *a weak government/leader* **3 LIKELY TO FAIL** ▷ likely to fail: *a weak economy* ∘ *a weak team* **4 LIKELY TO BREAK** ▷ ⓑ likely to break and not able to support heavy things: *a weak bridge* **5 TASTE** ▷ ⓑ A weak drink has little taste or contains little alcohol: *weak coffee/beer* **6 REASON** ▷ ⓑ A weak reason or excuse is one that you cannot believe because there is not enough proof to support it. **7 NOT GOOD** ▷ ⓑ not good at something: *She reads well but her spelling is weak.* **8 SLIGHT** ▷ ⓑ difficult to see or hear: *He spoke in a weak voice.* ∘ *a weak light* • **weakly adv**

weaken /ˈwiːkən/ **verb** [I, T] **1** to become less strong or powerful, or to make someone or something less strong or powerful: *A number of factors have weakened the economy.* **2** to become less certain or determined about a decision, or to make someone less determined: *I told him he wasn't having any more money but then I weakened.*

weakling /ˈwiːklɪŋ/ **noun** [C] someone who is physically weak

weakness /ˈwiːknəs/ **noun 1** [U] ⓑ the state of not being strong or powerful: *Asking for help is not a* **sign of weakness.** **2** [C] ⓑ a particular part or quality of something or someone that is not good: *What do you think are your weaknesses as a manager?* ∘ *There are a number of weaknesses in this proposal.* **3 have a weakness for sth/sb** to like a particular thing or person very much: *She has a real weakness for ice cream.*

wealth /welθ/ **noun 1** ⓑ [U] a large amount of money or valuable possessions that someone has: *He enjoyed his new wealth and status.* **2 a wealth of sth** a large amount of something good: *a wealth of experience/information*

wealthy /ˈwelθi/ **adj** ⓑ rich: *a wealthy businessman/nation* ∘ *Only the very* **wealthy** *can afford to live here.*

wean /wiːn/ **verb** [T] to start to give a baby food to eat instead of its mother's milk

PHRASAL VERB wean sb off sth to make someone gradually stop using something that is bad for them: *I'm trying to wean myself off fatty food generally.*

weapon /ˈwepən/ **noun** [C] ⓑ a gun, knife, or other object used to kill or hurt someone: *nuclear weapons* ∘ *Police have found the murder weapon.* • **weaponry noun** [U] weapons

☑ Word partners for **weapon**

biological/chemical/nuclear weapons •
deadly/lethal/offensive weapons • carry/
possess a weapon

wear¹ /weəʳ/ **verb** (**wore**, **worn**) **1 DRESS** ▷ [T] ⓐ

to have a piece of clothing, jewellery, etc on your body: *I wear jeans a lot of the time.* ∘ *She wears glasses.* ∘ *I don't usually wear make-up for work.* **2 FACE** ▷ [T] to show a particular emotion on your face: *He was wearing a smile/frown.* **3 HAIR** ▷ [T] to arrange or grow your hair in a particular way: *She usually wears her hair in a ponytail.* **4 SPOIL** ▷ [I, T] to become thin and damaged after being used a lot, or to make this happen: *The carpet is already starting to wear in places.* ∘ *He keeps* **wearing holes in** *his socks.* → See also **wear thin¹**

PHRASAL VERBS **wear (sth) away** to disappear after a lot of time or use, or to make something disappear in this way: *The words on the gravestone had worn away completely.* • **wear sb down** to make someone feel tired and less able to argue: *Their continual nagging just wears me down.* • **wear off** ⓑ If a feeling or the effect of something wears off, it gradually disappears: *The anaesthetic is starting to wear off.* • **wear on** If a period of time wears on, it passes, especially slowly: *As time wore on she became more and more unhappy.* • **wear sb out** ⓑ to make someone extremely tired: *All this walking is wearing me out.* • **wear (sth) out** ⓑ to use something so much that it is damaged and cannot be used any more, or to become damaged in this way: *He's already worn out two pairs of shoes this year.*

wear² /weəʳ/ **noun** [U] **1** (also **wear and tear**) damage that happens to something when it is used a lot: *The furniture is already showing signs of wear.* **2** how much you wear a piece of clothing: *These clothes are not for everyday wear.* **3 be the worse for wear** to be in a bad state or condition: *He looked a little the worse for wear this morning.*

-wear /weəʳ/ **suffix** used at the end of words that describe a particular type of clothes: *menswear/swimwear*

wearing /ˈweərɪŋ/ **adj** making you tired or annoyed

weary /ˈwɪəri/ **adj 1** tired: *You look weary, my love.* **2 weary of sth/sb** bored with something or someone: *She* **grew weary of** *the children and their games.* • **wearily adv** • **weariness noun** [U]

weasel /ˈwiːzəl/ **noun** [C] a small animal with a long body that kills and eats other small animals

weather¹ /ˈweðəʳ/ **noun** [U] ⓐ the temperature or conditions outside, for example if it is hot, cold, sunny, etc: *The flight was delayed because of* **bad weather.**

IDIOM **be/feel under the weather** to feel ill

☑ Word partners for **weather**

bad/cold/good/hot/stormy/warm/wet weather
• weather brightens up/improves/worsens

weather² /ˈweðəʳ/ **verb** [T] to deal with a difficult situation or difficult conditions: *to weather criticism/a recession*

weathered /ˈweðəd/ **adj** looking rough and old: *a weathered face*

W

weather forecast noun [C] ③ a description of what the weather will be like

weave /wiːv/ verb **1 weave in and out; weave through** (**weaved**) to go somewhere by moving around a lot of things: *to weave in and out of the traffic* ∘ *to weave through the crowd* **2** [I, T] (**wove**, **woven**) to make cloth on a machine by crossing threads under and over each other

web /web/ noun [C] **1** ③ a type of net made by a spider (= small creature with eight legs) to catch other insects: *a spider's web* **2 the Web** ④ (also **the World Wide Web**) part of the Internet that consists of all the connected websites (= pages of text and pictures) → See Study Page **The Web and the Internet** on page Centre 36

web ad,dress noun [C] (US **'web ,address**) an email or website address → See Study Page **The Web and the Internet** on page Centre 36

web ,browser noun [C] a computer program that allows you to look at pages on the Internet

webcam /ˈwebkæm/ noun [C] ③ a camera that records moving pictures and sound, and allows these to be shown on the Internet as they happen

webcast /ˈwebkɑːst/ noun [C] a broadcast made on the Internet

web de,veloper (also **Web developer**) noun [C] someone whose job is to create websites: *She works as a web developer for a financial services company.*

webinar /ˈwebɪnɑːʳ/ noun [C] (also **web-based seminar**) an occasion when a group of people go online at the same time to study or discuss something

web ,page noun [C] ④ a part of a website that can be read on a computer screen → See Study Page **The Web and the Internet** on page Centre 36

website /ˈwebsaɪt/ noun [C] ④ an area on the Internet where information about a particular subject, organization, etc can be found: *For more information, visit our website.* → See Study Page **The Web and the Internet** on page Centre 36

we'd /wiːd/ **1** short for we had: *By the time she arrived we'd eaten.* **2** short for we would: *We'd like two tickets for the three o'clock show, please.*

Wed (also **Weds**) written abbreviation for Wednesday

wedding /ˈwedɪŋ/ noun [C] ③ an official ceremony at which a man and woman get married: *We're going to a wedding on Saturday.* ∘ *a wedding dress/ring* → See also **golden wedding**

> ☑ Word partners for **wedding**
>
> go to/be invited to/plan a wedding • at a wedding • sb's wedding to sb • sb's wedding day • a wedding dress/guest/present/reception/ring

wedge¹ /wedʒ/ noun [C] a piece of something that is thin at one end and thicker at the other: *a big wedge of cheese*

wedge² /wedʒ/ verb [T] **1 wedge sth open/shut** to use a wedge or similar shaped object to keep a door or window firmly open or closed: *The*

room was hot so I wedged the door open. **2** to push something into a narrow space: *I wc wedged between Andy and Pete in the back of th car.*

Wednesday /ˈwenzdeɪ/ noun [C, U] (writte abbreviation **Wed, Weds**) ④ the day of the wee after Tuesday and before Thursday

wee¹ /wiː/ noun [no plural] mainly UK informal I someone has a wee, they urinate: *to have a we* ∘ *I need a wee.* • **wee** verb [I] (**weeing, weed**)

wee² /wiː/ adj small, usually used by Scottis speakers: *a wee girl*

weed¹ /wiːd/ noun [C] a wild plant that you d not want to grow in your garden: *Dandelions ar common weeds.*

weed² /wiːd/ verb [I, T] to remove wild plant from a garden where they are not wanted

PHRASAL VERB **weed sb/sth out** to get rid of peopl or things that you do not want from a group: *Th government plans to weed out bad teachers.*

weedy /ˈwiːdi/ adj UK informal thin and weak: *H looks too weedy to be an athlete.*

week /wiːk/ noun **1** ④ [C] a period of seven days: *last week/next week* ∘ *I've got three exam this week.* ∘ *We get paid every week.* **2 the wee** ④ the five days from Monday to Friday whe people usually go to work or school: *I don't g out much during the week.*

weekday /ˈwiːkdeɪ/ noun [C] ④ one of the fiv days from Monday to Friday, when peopl usually go to work or school: *This road is ver busy on weekdays.*

weekend /ˌwiːkˈend/ ⑤ /ˈwiːkend/ noun [C **1** ④ Saturday and Sunday, the two days in th week when many people do not work: *Are yo doing anything this weekend?* ∘ *I'm going hom for the weekend.* **2 at the weekend** UK (US **on th weekend**) on Saturday or Sunday: *He's going to football match at the weekend.*

weekly /ˈwiːkli/ adj, adv ④ happening once week or every week: *a weekly newspaper* ∘ *We'r paid weekly.*

weeknight /ˈwiːknaɪt/ noun [C] the evening o night of any day of the week except Saturda and Sunday

weep /wiːp/ verb [I, T] (**wept**) literary to cry usually because you are sad

weigh /weɪ/ verb **1** weigh 200g/75kg/10 stone etc ③ to have a weight of 200g/75kg/10 stone etc: *How much do you weigh?* **2** [T] ③ to measur how heavy someone or something is: *Can yo weigh that piece of cheese for me?* ∘ *She weigh herself every day.* **3** [T] (also UK **weigh up**) ④ t consider something carefully, especially in orde to make a decision: *The jury must weigh th evidence.* ∘ *He needs to weigh up the pros an cons of going to college.*

PHRASAL VERBS **weigh sth against sth** to judg which of two things is more important befor making a decision: *The advantages have to b weighed against the possible disadvantages.* • **b weighed down by/with sth 1** to be carrying o holding too much: *She was weighed down wit shopping bags.* **2** to be very worried abou

something: *be weighed down by problems/debts*
• **weigh on/upon sb/sth** If a problem or responsibility weighs on you, it makes you worried or unhappy: *Problems at work are weighing on me.*
• **weigh sth out** to measure an amount of something: *Weigh out 8 ounces of flour.*

weight /weɪt/ noun **1** AMOUNT ▷ [U] ③ how heavy someone or something is: *He's about* **average** *height and* **weight**. **2** lose weight If someone loses weight, they become lighter and thinner: *I need to* **lose** *a bit of* **weight**. **3** put on/ gain weight If someone puts on weight or gains weight, they become heavier and fatter. **4** HEAVINESS ▷ [U, no plural] ③ the quality of being heavy: *The shelf collapsed under the weight of the books.* **5** OBJECT ▷ [C] ③ something that is heavy: *You're not supposed to lift heavy weights after an operation.*

IDIOMS **carry weight** to be considered important and effective in influencing someone: *His opinions carry a lot of weight with the scientific community.* • **pull your weight** to work as hard as other people in a group: *The rest of the team complained that Sarah wasn't pulling her weight.*
• **throw your weight around** to behave as if you are more important or powerful than other people • **a weight off your mind** If something is a weight off your mind, a problem that has been worrying you stops or is dealt with: *Finally selling that house was a weight off my mind.*

→ See also **paper weight**

> ☑ Word partners for **weight**
>
> **gain/lose/put on** weight • **carry/lift/support** a weight • **average/excess/heavy/ideal/light** weight

weighted /ˈweɪtɪd/ adj be weighted in favour of/towards/against sth to give one group an advantage or disadvantage over other people: *The system is weighted in favour of families with young children.*

weights /weɪts/ noun [plural] heavy pieces of metal that you lift up and down to make your muscles stronger

weighty /ˈweɪti/ adj very serious and important: *The film deals with the* **weighty issues** *of religion and morality.*

weir /wɪər/ noun [C] UK a low wall built across a river to control the flow of water

weird /wɪəd/ adj ③ very strange: *I had a really weird dream last night.*

weirdo /ˈwɪədəʊ/ noun [C] informal a person who behaves strangely

welcome¹ /ˈwelkəm/ exclamation ③ used to greet someone who has just arrived somewhere: *Welcome home!* ∘ *Welcome to the UK.*

welcome² /ˈwelkəm/ verb [T] **1** ③ to greet someone who has arrived in a place: *Both families were there to welcome us.* **2** ③ to be pleased about something and want it to happen: *The decision was welcomed by everybody.* ∘ *I would welcome your advice.*

welcome³ /ˈwelkəm/ adj **1** ③ If something is welcome, people are pleased about it and want it

to happen: *a* **welcome change** ∘ *Your comments are very welcome.* → Opposite **unwelcome** **2** You're welcome. ③ used to be polite to someone who has thanked you: *"Thank you." "You're welcome."* **3** make sb (feel) welcome ③ to make a visitor feel happy and comfortable in a place by being kind and friendly to them: *They made me very welcome in their home.* **4** be welcome to do sth ③ used to tell someone that they can certainly do something, if they want to: *Anyone who is interested is welcome to come along.* **5** be welcome to sth used to tell someone that they can certainly have something, if they want it, because you do not

welcome⁴ /ˈwelkəm/ noun [no plural] ③ the way someone is greeted when they arrive somewhere: *He was* **given a warm** (= friendly) **welcome** *by his fans.*

IDIOM **outstay/overstay your welcome** to stay somewhere too long so that people want you to leave

> ☑ Word partners for **welcome** noun
>
> **get/be given** a [big/friendly/warm, etc] welcome

weld /weld/ verb [T] to join pieces of metal together by heating them until they almost melt and then pressing them together

welfare /ˈwelfeər/ noun [U] **1** ③ Someone's welfare is their health and happiness: *He is concerned about the welfare of young men in prison.* **2** US (UK **social security**) money paid by a government to people who are poor, sick, or who do not have jobs: *to be* **on welfare** (= getting welfare)

welfare ˈstate UK (US **ˈwelfare ˌstate**) noun [no plural] a system in which the government looks after and pays for people who are sick, old, or who cannot get a job

well¹ /wel/ adj [never before noun] (**better, best**) **1** ③ healthy: *to feel/look well* ∘ *I'm not very well.* ∘ *Are you feeling better now?* → Opposite **unwell** **2** all is well ③ everything is in a good or acceptable state: *I hope all is well with Jack.* **3** be all very well used to show that you do not agree with something or that you are annoyed about something: *It's all very well for her to say everything's fine, she doesn't have to live here.* **4** be (just) as well to say that something might be a good thing to do or happen: [+ (that)] *It was just as well that you left when you did.* → See also **be alive and kicking/well**

well² /wel/ adv (**better, best**) **1** ③ in a successful or satisfactory way: *I thought they played well.* ∘ *He's* **doing well** *at school/work.* **2** ③ in a complete way or as much as possible: *I know him quite well.* ∘ *Stir the mixture well.* → See Note at **good¹** **3** as well ③ also: *Are you going to invite Steve as well?* **4** as well as sth ③ in addition to something: *They have lived in the United States as well as Britain.* **5** may/might as well do sth ③ If you may/might as well do something, it will not spoil the situation if you do that thing: *If we're not waiting for Karen, we might as well go now.* **6** may/might/could well ③ used to say that

W

something is likely to be true: *He could well be at Michelle's house.* **7 well above/ahead/below, etc** ⑫ above/ahead/below, etc by a large amount: *It was well after seven o'clock when we got home.* **8 can't/couldn't very well do sth** used to say that something is not a suitable or practical thing to do: *I couldn't very well tell her while he was there.* **9 Well done!** ⑪ used to tell someone how pleased you are about their success: *"I passed my exams." "Well done!"*

well³ /wel/ *exclamation* **1** ⑪ used at the beginning of a sentence to pause slightly or to express doubt or disagreement: *"You'll go, won't you?" "Well, I'm not sure."* ○ *"You said the food was bad." "Well, I didn't exactly say that."* **2** (also **well, well**) used to express surprise: *Well, well, I never expected that to happen.* **3 oh well** ⑪ used to say that a situation cannot be changed although it might be disappointing: *Oh well, it doesn't matter, I can always buy another one.*

well⁴ /wel/ *noun* [C] a deep hole in the ground from which you can get water, oil, or gas

we'll /wiːl/ short for we shall or we will: *We'll be home on Friday.*

well-balanced /ˌwelˈbælənst/ *adj* **1 a well-balanced diet/meal** ⑫ food that includes all the different types of food that the body needs to be healthy **2** Well-balanced people are calm and have good judgment.

well-behaved /ˌwelbɪˈheɪvd/ *adj* behaving in a polite and quiet way: *a well-behaved child*

well-being /ˈwelˌbiːɪŋ/ *noun* [U] how healthy, happy, and comfortable someone is

well-built /ˌwelˈbɪlt/ *adj* ⑫ having a large, strong body

well-connected /ˌwelkəˈnektɪd/ *adj* having important or powerful friends

well-done /ˌwelˈdʌn/ *adj* Meat that is well-done has been cooked completely and is not pink inside.

well-dressed /ˌwelˈdrest/ *adj* ⑪ wearing attractive, good quality clothes

well-earned /ˌwelˈɜːnd/ *adj* **well-earned break/holiday/rest, etc** a rest that you deserve because you have been working hard

well-educated /ˌwelˈedʒʊkeɪtɪd/ *adj* having had a good education

well-established /ˌwelɪˈstæblɪʃt/ *adj* having existed for a long time: *a well-established tradition*

well-fed /ˌwelˈfed/ *adj* having eaten enough good food: *a well-fed cat*

well-heeled /ˌwelˈhiːld/ *adj* having a lot of money, expensive clothes, etc

wellies /ˈweliz/ *noun* [plural] UK informal (US **rubber boots**) large rubber boots that you wear outside when the ground is wet and dirty: *a pair of wellies*

well-informed /ˌwelɪnˈfɔːmd/ *adj* knowing a lot of useful information

wellingtons /ˈwelɪŋtənz/ *noun* [plural] UK wellies

well-intentioned /ˌwelɪnˈtenʃ³nd/ *adj* trying to be helpful and kind but not improving a situation

well-kept /ˌwelˈkept/ *adj* **1 a well-kept secre** something that has been carefully and success fully kept secret: *The recipe is a well-kept secre* **2** tidy and organized: *a well-kept kitchen*

well-known /ˌwelˈnəʊn/ *adj* ⑫ famous: *a wel known actor*

well-meaning /ˌwelˈmiːnɪŋ/ *adj* trying to b helpful and kind but not improving a situatior *well-meaning friends*

well-off /ˌwelˈɒf/ *adj* having a lot of money: *H parents are very well-off.*

well-organized (also UK **-ised**) /ˌwelˈɔːgᵊnaɪzd adj* ⑫ working in an effective and successfu way because of good organization

well-paid /ˌwelˈpeɪd/ *adj* ⑫ earning a lot o money

well-placed /ˌwelˈpleɪst/ *adj* in a very conven ent position or in a position that gives someon an advantage: [+ to do sth] *She's very well-place to find out what's going on.*

well-read /ˌwelˈred/ *adj* having read a lot o books on different subjects

well-to-do /ˌweltəˈduː/ *adj* old-fashioned having lot of money: *a well-to-do family*

well-wisher /ˈwelˌwɪʃəʳ/ *noun* [C] someone wh wants another person to be happy, successful, o healthy: *A crowd of well-wishers gathered outsid the hospital.*

Welsh /welʃ/ *noun* [U] **1** a language that i spoken in some parts of Wales **2 the Welsh** th people of Wales

went /went/ past tense of go

wept /wept/ past of weep

were /wɜːʳ/ past simple you/we/they of be

we're /wɪəʳ/ short for we are: *Hurry! We're late!*

weren't /wɜːnt/ short for were not: *They weren' there.*

west, West /west/ *noun* [U] **1** ⑫ the directio that you face to see the sun go down **2 the wes** ⑫ the part of an area that is further towards th west than the rest **3 the West** ⑫ the countrie of North America and western Europe • **wes** *adj* ⑫ *the west coast of Ireland* • **west** *adv* ⑪ towards the west: *They lived in a village fou miles west of Oxford.*

the West End *noun* a part of central Londo that has a lot of shops, theatres, restaurants, et

westerly /ˈwestᵊli/ *adj* **1** towards or in the west *Senegal is the most westerly country in Africa.* **2 /** westerly wind comes from the west: *westerl breezes*

western, Western /ˈwestən/ *adj* [always befor noun] **1** ⑪ in or from the west part of an area *western France* **2** ⑪ related to the countries o North America and western Europe: *a Wester diplomat*

western /ˈwestən/ *noun* [C] a film or story tha happens in the west of the US at the time whe Europeans started living there

westerner, Westerner /ˈwestᵊnəʳ/ *noun* [C someone who is from a country in Nort America or western Europe

westernized (also UK **-ised**) /ˈwestᵊnaɪzd/ *ad* having a culture like North America and wester

Europe: *Some Asian countries are becoming increasingly westernized.*

West ˈIndian adj belonging or relating to the West Indies: *a West Indian island* • **West Indian** noun [C] someone from the West Indies

the ˌWest ˈIndies noun [plural] a group of islands in the Caribbean Sea

westward, westwards /ˈwestwəd/, /ˈwest-wədz/ adv towards the west: *They were travelling westward.* • **westward** adj

wet¹ /wet/ adj (**wetter, wettest**) **1** WATER ▷ **A2** covered in water or another liquid: *a wet towel* ◦ *We got soaking wet in the rain.* ◦ UK *Look at you – you're wet through* (= very wet)! **2** RAIN ▷ **A2** raining: *a wet and windy day* **3** NOT DRY ▷ **B1** not dry yet: *wet paint* **4** PERSON ▷ UK informal Someone who is wet has a weak personality.

wet² /wet/ verb [T] (**wetting, wet, wetted**) **1 wet the bed/your pants/yourself, etc** to urinate in your bed or in your underwear without intending to **2** to make something wet

ˈwet ˌsuit noun [C] a piece of clothing covering the whole body that keeps you warm and dry when you are under water

we've /wiːv/ short for we have: *We've bought a house.*

whack /wæk/ verb [T] informal to hit someone or something in a quick, strong way: *She whacked him on the head with her book.* • **whack** noun [C] informal

whale /weɪl/ noun [C]   **whale**
B1 a very large animal
that looks like a large
fish, lives in the sea,
and breathes air
through a hole at the
top of its head

whaling /ˈweɪlɪŋ/
noun [U] the activity
of hunting whales

wharf /wɔːf/ noun [C] (plural **wharves** /wɔːvz/) an area next to the sea or a river where goods can be put on or taken off ships

what /wɒt/ pronoun, determiner **1** INFORMATION ▷ **A1** used to ask for information about something: *What's this?* ◦ *What time is it?* ◦ *What happened?* → See Note at **how¹ 2** THE THING ▷ **B1** used to refer to something without naming it: *I heard what he said.* ◦ *Do you know what I mean?* ◦ *What I like most about her is her honesty.* **3** NOT HEARD ▷ informal used when you have not heard what someone has said and you want them to repeat it. Some people think this use is not very polite: *"Do you want a drink Tom?" "What?"* **4** REPLY ▷ informal used to ask what someone wants when they call you: *"Hey Jenny?" "Yes, what?"* **5 what a/an ...** ▷ **B1** used to give your opinion, especially when you have strong feelings about something: *What a mess!* ◦ *What an awful day!* **6 what about...?** ▷ **A2** used to suggest something: *What about asking Martin to help?* **7 what ... for?** ▷ **B2** used to ask about the reason for something: *What are you doing that for?* ◦ *"We really need a bigger car." "What for?"* **8 what if...?** ▷ **B1** used to ask about something

that could happen in the future, especially something bad: *What if I don't pass my exams?* **9 what's up (with sb)** informal used to ask why someone is unhappy or angry: *What's up, Angie? You look troubled.* **10 what with** informal used to talk about the reasons for a particular situation, especially a bad or difficult situation: *I'm tired, what with travelling all day yesterday and sleeping badly.* **11 what's more** **B2** used to add something surprising or interesting to what you have just said

> **!** Common learner error: **what**
>
> When you have not heard what someone has said and you want them to repeat it, you can say **what?**, but this is not polite. It is better to say **sorry?** or **pardon?**.
>
> *"It's ten o'clock." "Sorry/Pardon?" "I said it's ten o'clock."*

whatever /wɒtˈevər/ adv, pronoun, determiner **1** ANYTHING ▷ **B1** anything or everything: *Do whatever you want.* ◦ *He eats whatever I put in front of him.* **2** NO DIFFERENCE ▷ **B2** used to say that what happens is not important because it does not change a situation: *Whatever happens I'll still love you.* ◦ *We'll support you, whatever you decide.* **3** QUESTION ▷ used to ask for information when you are surprised or angry about something: *Whatever do you mean?* **4** ANGRY ▷ informal something that you say when you are angry with someone who is asking you something: *'Isabel, will you just listen when I'm talking to you?' 'Whatever.'* **5 or whatever** **B2** or something similar: *The children are usually outside playing football or whatever.*

whatnot /ˈwɒtnɒt/ **and whatnot** informal and other things of a similar type: *They sell cards and wrapping paper and whatnot.*

whatsoever /ˌwɒtsəʊˈevər/ adv (also **whatever**) **no...whatsoever** none at all: *There's no evidence whatsoever that she was involved.*

wheat /wiːt/ noun [U] **B2** a plant whose grain is used for making flour, or the grain itself

wheel¹ /wiːl/ noun **1** **A2** [C] a circular object fixed under a vehicle so that it moves smoothly over the ground: *My bike needs a new front wheel.* **2 the wheel** **B2** a steering wheel (= circular object you turn to direct a vehicle): *You should drive with both hands on the wheel.* ◦ *He fell asleep at the wheel* (= while driving).

IDIOM **reinvent the wheel** to waste time trying to create something that has been done before

→ See also **Ferris wheel**

wheel² /wiːl/ verb **wheel sth around/into/to, etc** to push something that has wheels somewhere: *He wheeled his bicycle into the garden.*

PHRASAL VERB **wheel around/round** to quickly turn around: *She wheeled around to face him.*

wheelbarrow /ˈwiːlˌbærəʊ/ noun [C] a big, open container with a wheel at the front and handles that is used to move things, especially around in a garden

wheelchair /ˈwiːltʃeər/ noun [C] **B1** a chair with wheels used by someone who cannot walk

W

wheeze /wiːz/ **verb** [I] to make a noisy sound when breathing because of a problem in your lungs

when¹ /wen/ **adv** Ⓐ1 used to ask at what time something happened or will happen: *When's your birthday?* ∘ *When did he leave?* ∘ *When are you going away?*

when² /wen/ **conjunction 1** Ⓐ2 used to say at what time something happened or will happen: *I found it when I was cleaning out the cupboards.* ∘ *We'll go when you're ready.* **2** Ⓑ2 although: *Why are you doing this when I've asked you not to?*

whenever /wen'evər/ **conjunction** Ⓑ1 every time or at any time: *You can go whenever you want.* ∘ *I try to help them out whenever possible.*

where¹ /weər/ **adv** Ⓐ1 used to ask about the place or position of someone or something: *Where does she live?* ∘ *Where are my car keys?*

where² /weər/ **conjunction 1** Ⓐ2 at, in, or to a place or position: *He's not sure where they are.* ∘ *I know where to go.* **2** Ⓑ2 relating to a particular part of a process or situation: *We've now reached the point where we can make a decision.*

whereabouts¹ /ˌweərə'baʊts/ **adv** used to ask in what place or area someone or something is: *Whereabouts does he live?*

whereabouts² /'weərəbaʊts/ **noun sb's whereabouts** the place where someone or something is: *His whereabouts are unknown.*

whereas /weər'ræz/ **conjunction** Ⓑ2 compared with the fact that: *His parents were rich, whereas mine had to struggle.*

whereby /weə'baɪ/ **adv** formal by which: *They've introduced a system whereby people share cars.*

wherein /weə'rɪn/ **adv** formal in which

whereupon /'weərəpɒn/ **conjunction** formal after which: *We decided to have a picnic, whereupon it started to rain.*

wherever¹ /weə'revər/ **conjunction 1** Ⓑ1 in or to any place or every place: *You can sit wherever you like.* **2 wherever possible** Ⓑ2 every time it is possible: *We try to use natural fabrics wherever possible.*

wherever² /weə'revər/ **adv** used to ask in what situation or place something happened, especially when the person asking feels surprised: *Wherever did you get that idea?*

wherewithal /'weəwɪðɔːl/ **noun the wherewithal to do sth** the money, skills, or other things that are needed to do something

whether /'weðər/ **conjunction 1** Ⓑ1 used to talk about a choice between two or more possibilities: *Someone's got to tell her, whether it's you or me.* ∘ *I didn't know whether or not to go.* **2** Ⓑ1 if: *I wasn't sure whether you'd like it.*

whew /fjuː/ **exclamation** used when you are happy that something is not going to happen, or when you are tired or hot

which /wɪtʃ/ **pronoun, determiner 1 CHOICE** ▷ Ⓐ2 used to ask or talk about a choice between two or more things: *Which of these do you like best?* ∘ *Which way is it to the station?* ∘ *I just don't know which one to choose.* **2 REFERRING TO SOMETHING** ▷ Ⓐ2 used at the beginning of a relative clause to show what thing is being

referred to: *These are principles which we a* believe in. **3 EXTRA INFORMATION** ▷ Ⓑ1 used t give more information about something: *Th book, which includes a map, gives you all th information you need about Venice.* **4 GIVIN OPINION** ▷ Ⓑ2 used when you give an opinio about what you have just said: *He took us bot out for lunch, which I thought was very kind c him.*

> **❗ Common learner error: which or who?**
>
> Use **which** to refer to a thing.
> *The restaurant which is next to the pub is good.*
> ~~The restaurant who is next to the pub is good.~~
> Use **who** to refer to a person.
> *The boy who is wearing the red coat is called Paul.*
> ~~The boy which is wearing the red coat is called Paul.~~
> Sometimes it is possible to use 'that' or no word instead of **which** or **who**.
> *He's the man (that) I saw in the bar.*
> *This is the shirt (that) I bought yesterday.*

whichever /wɪ'tʃevər/ **pronoun, determine 1** Ⓑ2 used to say that what happens is no important because it does not change a situa tion: *Whichever option we choose there'll b disadvantages.* ∘ *It's a sad situation whicheve way you look at it.* **2** Ⓑ2 any of a group of simila things: *Choose whichever bedroom you want.*

whiff /wɪf/ **noun** [no plural] a smell that you onl smell for a short time: *I just caught a whiff o garlic from the kitchen.*

while¹ /waɪl/ **conjunction** (also UK **whilst** /waɪlst/ **1 DURING** ▷ Ⓐ2 during the time that: *I read magazine while I was waiting.* ∘ *I can't talk t anyone while I'm driving.* ∘ *While you're away, might decorate the bathroom.* **2 ALTHOUGH** ▷ Ⓑ although: *And while I like my job, I wouldn't want t do it forever.* **3 COMPARING** ▷ Ⓑ1 used to compar two different facts or situations: *Tom is ver confident while Katy is shy and quiet.*

while² /waɪl/ **noun a while** Ⓑ1 a period of time *a long/short while* ∘ *I'm going out for a while*

> **🔁 Word partners for while noun**
>
> take/wait a while • after/for/in a while • quite a while • a short while • a while ago

while³ /'waɪl/ **verb**
PHRASAL VERB **while sth away** to spend time in relaxed way because you are waiting for some thing or because you have nothing to do: *W played a few games to while away the time.*

whim /wɪm/ **noun** [C] a sudden wish to d something without having a reason: *We booke the holiday on a whim.*

whimper /'wɪmpər/ **verb** [I] to make quie crying sounds because of fear or pain: *The do was whimpering with pain.*

whimsical /'wɪmzɪkəl/ **adj** unusual in a way tha is slightly funny: *a whimsical tale*

whine /waɪn/ verb [I] **1** to complain in an annoying way: *She's always whining about something.* **2** to make a long, high, sad sound: *The dog whined and scratched at the door.* • **whine** noun [C]

whinge /wɪndʒ/ verb [I] (**whingeing, whinging**) UK informal to complain in an annoying way: *Oh, stop whingeing!* • **whinge** noun [C] UK *He was just having a whinge.*

whip¹ /wɪp/ noun [C] a long piece of leather fixed to a handle and used to hit an animal or person

whip² /wɪp/ verb (**whipping, whipped**) **1** [T] to hit a person or animal with a whip **2** [T] to make a food such as cream more solid by mixing it hard with a kitchen tool **3 whip (sth) away/off/out, etc** informal to move or make something move in a fast, sudden way: *She opened the bag and whipped out her camera.*

PHRASAL VERB **whip up sth 1** to try to make people have strong feelings about something: *to whip up enthusiasm/hatred* **2** to prepare food very quickly: *I could whip up a plate of spaghetti if you like.*

whir /wɜːʳ/ noun, verb (**whirring, whirred**) US spelling of whirr

whirl¹ /wɜːl/ verb [I, T] to move or make something move quickly round and round

whirl² /wɜːl/ noun [no plural] **1** a situation in which a lot of exciting or confusing things happen at the same time: *a whirl of activity* **2** a sudden turning movement **3 give sth a whirl** informal to try to do something, often for the first time: *I've never danced salsa before but I'll give it a whirl.*

whirlpool /'wɜːlpuːl/ noun [C] an area of water that moves round and round very quickly

whirlwind¹ /'wɜːlwɪnd/ adj a whirlwind **romance/visit/tour, etc** a relationship/visit, etc that only lasts a short time

whirlwind² /'wɜːlwɪnd/ noun **1 a whirlwind of sth** a lot of sudden activity, emotion, etc: *a whirlwind of activity* **2** [C] a strong wind that moves round and round very quickly

whirr (also US **whir**) /wɜːʳ/ noun [no plural] a low, continuous sound: *the whirr of machinery* • **whirr** (also US **whir**) verb [I]

whisk¹ /wɪsk/ verb [T] **1 whisk sb away/off/into, etc** informal to take someone somewhere quickly: *They whisked him off to the police station.* **2** to mix food such as eggs, cream, etc very quickly using a fork or whisk: *Whisk the mixture until smooth.*

whisk² /wɪsk/ noun [C] a kitchen tool made of wire that is used to mix eggs, cream, etc, or to make such food thicker → See colour picture **The Kitchen** on page Centre 2

whisker /'wɪskəʳ/ noun [C] one of the long, stiff hairs that grows around the mouths of animals such as cats

whiskers /'wɪskəz/ noun [plural] old-fashioned hairs growing on a man's face

whiskey /'wɪski/ noun [C, U] whisky in Ireland or the United States

whisky /'wɪski/ noun [C, U] ⑫ a strong, alcoholic drink made from grain

whisper /'wɪspəʳ/ verb **whisper**
[I, T] ⑫ to speak extremely quietly so that other people cannot hear: *She whispered something to the girl sitting next to her.*
• **whisper** noun [C]

whistle¹ /'wɪsl/ verb
1 [I, T] ⑫ to make a sound by breathing air out through a small hole made with your lips or through a whistle: *Someone whistled at her as she walked past.* **2** [I] to produce a sound when air passes through a narrow space: *He could hear the wind whistling through the trees.*

whistle² /'wɪsl/ noun [C] **1** ⑫ a small, simple instrument that makes a high sound when you blow through it: *The referee blew the whistle to end the game.* **2** the sound made by someone or something whistling

white¹ /waɪt/ adj **1 COLOUR** ▷ ⓐ being the colour of snow or milk: *a white T-shirt* ∘ *white walls* → See colour picture **Colours** on page Centre 12 **2 PERSON** ▷ ⑬ Someone who is white has skin that is pale in colour: *He's described as a white man in his early thirties.* **3 OF WHITE PEOPLE** ▷ relating to white people: *the white community* **4 FACE** ▷ having a pale face because you are sick or you are feeling shocked: *He was white with shock.* **5 COFFEE** ▷ UK White coffee has milk or cream added to it: *Two coffees please, one black and one white.* **6 WINE** ▷ ⓐ White wine is a pale yellow colour. • **whiteness** noun [U] → See also **black and white**

white² /waɪt/ noun **1 COLOUR** ▷ [C, U] ⓐ the colour of snow or milk → See colour picture **Colours** on page Centre 12 **2 PERSON** ▷ [C] a white person: *For a long time, whites controlled the economy here.* **3 EGG** ▷ [C] the part of an egg that is white when it is cooked: *Mix the egg whites with the sugar.* → See also **in black and white**

whiteboard /'waɪtbɔːd/ noun [C] **1** (also **interactive whiteboard**) a piece of electronic equipment in the shape of a flat, white board which is connected to a computer and which you can write on using a special pen that also controls the computer **2** a large board with a white surface that teachers write on → See colour picture **The Classroom** on page Centre 6

white-collar /ˌwaɪt'kɒləʳ/ adj relating to work in an office or in a job that needs special knowledge and education: *white-collar jobs/workers*

the White House noun **1** the US president and government **2** the building that is the official home and offices of the US president • **White House** adj *a White House spokesman*

white lie noun [C] a lie that is not important and is usually said to avoid upsetting someone

white meat noun [U] a meat that is pale in colour, such as chicken

whiten /'waɪtⁿn/ verb [I, T] to become white or to make something become white

W

White Paper noun [C] a government report in the UK giving information or suggestions on a subject: *a White Paper on employment*

whitewash /ˈwaɪtwɒʃ/ **noun** [no plural] an attempt to hide the truth about a serious mistake, crime, etc from the public: *The newspaper accused the government of a whitewash.* ● **whitewash verb** [T]

whizz (also **whiz**) /wɪz/ **verb whizz by/past/ through, etc** informal to move somewhere very quickly: *She whizzed down the street in her new sports car.*

whizzkid (also **whizkid**) /ˈwɪzˌkɪd/ **noun** [C] a young person who is very successful or good at doing something: *a computer whizzkid*

who /huː/ **pronoun 1 NAME** ▷ Ⓐ used to ask about someone's name or which person or group someone is talking about: *Who told you?* ◦ *Who's that?* **2 WHICH PERSON** ▷ Ⓐ used at the beginning of a relative clause to show which person or group of people you are talking about: *That's the man who I saw in the bank.* **3 ADD INFORMATION** ▷ Ⓑ used to give more information about someone: *My brother, who's only just seventeen, has already passed his driving test.* → See Note at **which**

who'd /huːd/ **1** short for who had: *I was reading about a man who'd sailed around the world.* **2** short for who would: *Who'd have thought we'd still be friends?*

whoever /huːˈevər/ **pronoun 1 WHICH PERSON** ▷ Ⓑ the person who: *Whoever broke the window will have to pay for it.* ◦ *Could I speak to whoever is in charge please?* **2 ANY PERSON** ▷ Ⓑ used to say that it is not important which person or group does something: *Can whoever leaves last lock up, please?* **3 SURPRISE** ▷ used to ask who a person is when expressing surprise: *Whoever could that be phoning at this time?* ◦ *Whoever would believe such a ridiculous story?*

whole¹ /həʊl/ **adj 1** [always before noun] Ⓐ complete, including every part: *She spent the whole afternoon studying.* ◦ *The whole family went to the show.* **2** [never before noun] as a single object and not in pieces: *The chick swallowed the worm whole.* → See also **a whole new ball game**, **the whole world¹**

whole² /həʊl/ **noun 1 the whole of sth** Ⓑ all of something: *His behaviour affects the whole of the class.* **2 as a whole** Ⓑ when considered as a group and not in parts: *The population as a whole is getting healthier.* **3 on the whole** Ⓑ generally: *We've had a few problems, but on the whole we're very happy.*

wholefood /ˈhəʊlfuːd/ **noun** [U] UK food that is as natural as possible, without artificial things added to it: *a wholefood shop*

wholehearted /ˌhəʊlˈhɑːtɪd/ **adj wholehearted agreement/approval/support, etc** complete agreement/approval/support, etc without any doubts ● **wholeheartedly adv** *I agree wholeheartedly.*

wholemeal /ˈhəʊlmiːl/ **adj** UK (also UK/US **whole wheat**) made using whole grains, or made from flour that contains whole grains: *wholemeal bread/flour*

wholesale /ˈhəʊlseɪl/ **adj 1** relating to product that are sold in large amounts, usually at cheaper price: *wholesale prices* **2** [always befor noun] complete or affecting a lot of thing people, places, etc: *wholesale changes* ● **whole sale adv**

wholesaler /ˈhəʊlˌseɪlər/ **noun** [C] a compan that sells products in large amounts to shop which then sell them to customers

wholesome /ˈhəʊlsəm/ **adj 1** Wholesome food good for your health. **2** morally good: *whole some family entertainment*

whole wheat adj (also UK **wholemeal**) mad using whole grains, or made from flour tha contains whole grains: *whole wheat bread/flou*

who'll /huːl/ short for who will: *Who'll be at you party?*

wholly /ˈhəʊlli/ **adv** completely: *His behaviour i wholly unacceptable.*

whom /huːm/ **pronoun** formal Ⓑ used instea of 'who' as the object of a verb or preposition: *met a man with whom I used to work.*

> **⚠ Common learner error: whom or who?**
>
> **Whom** is very formal and most people use **who** instead.
> *Whom did you see at the party?*
> *Who did you see at the party?*
> **Whom** should be used after a preposition but most people avoid this by putting the preposition at the end of the sentence and using **who**.
> *With whom did you go to the party?*
> *Who did you go to the party with?*

---

whoop /wuːp/ **noun** [C] a loud, excited shout: *H gave a loud whoop of delight.*

whooping cough /ˈhuːpɪŋˌkɒf/ **noun** [U] serious children's disease in which a cough i followed by a 'whoop' noise

whoops /wʊps/ **exclamation** used when yo make a mistake or have a small accident

whopping /ˈwɒpɪŋ/ **adj** [always before nour informal extremely large: *a whopping 50 percer increase*

whore /hɔːr/ **noun** [C] an offensive word fo someone whose job is having sex with people

who're /ˈhuːər/ short for who are: *Who're th people we're going to see?*

who's /huːz/ **1** short for who is: *Who's your ne friend?* **2** short for who has: *Who's been using m computer?*

whose /huːz/ **pronoun, determiner 1** Ⓑ use to ask who something belongs to or wh someone or something is connected with *Whose gloves are these?* ◦ *Whose car shall w use?* **2** Ⓑ used to say that something c someone is connected with or belongs to person: *She has a brother whose name I can remember.*

who've /huːv/ short for who have: *I know peopl who've bought their homes on the Internet.*

why /waɪ/ **adv 1** Ⓐ used to ask or talk about th reasons for something: *Why didn't you call me* ◦ *I wonder why he didn't come.* ◦ *So that's th* *reason why* he asked her! **2 Why don't you?/ Why not do sth?** Ⓐ2 used to make a suggestion: *Why don't you come with us?* ∘ *Why not give it a try?* **3 why not?** informal Ⓑ1 used to agree with something that someone has suggested: *"Let's have an ice cream." "Yes, why not?"*

wicked /'wɪkɪd/ adj **1 BAD** ▷ extremely bad and morally wrong: *a wicked man* **2 AMUSING** ▷ funny or enjoyable in a way that is slightly bad or unkind: *a wicked sense of humour* **3 GOOD** ▷ very informal extremely good: *They sell some wicked clothes.*

wicker /'wɪkər/ adj made from thin branches crossed over and under each other: *a wicker basket*

wicket /'wɪkɪt/ noun [C] in cricket, an arrangement of three long, vertical poles with two short poles across the top

wide¹ /waɪd/ adj **1 LONG DISTANCE** ▷ Ⓐ2 measuring a long distance or longer than usual from one side to the other: *a wide river/ road* ∘ *I have very wide feet.* → See picture at **narrow 2 5 miles/3 inches/6 metres, etc wide** Ⓑ1 having a distance of 5 miles/3 inches/6 metres, etc from one side to the other: *The swimming pool is five metres wide.* **3 a wide range/selection/variety, etc** Ⓑ1 a lot of different types of thing: *The library is a good source of a wide range of information.* **4 EYES** ▷ If your eyes are wide, they are completely open: *Her eyes were wide with fear.* **5 BALL** ▷ If a ball, shot, etc is wide, it does not go near enough to where it was intended to go. → See also **be wide of the mark¹**

wide² /waɪd/ adv **1 wide apart/open** Ⓑ2 as far apart/open as possible: *The window was wide open.* **2 wide awake** completely awake

wide-eyed /ˌwaɪd'aɪd/ adj with your eyes completely open because of surprise, fear, happiness, etc: *The children looked on, wide-eyed with wonder.*

widely /'waɪdli/ adv **1** Ⓑ2 including a lot of different places, people, subjects, etc: *widely known* ∘ *He has travelled widely in Europe.* **2 differ/vary widely** Ⓑ2 to be very different: *Prices vary widely from shop to shop.*

widen /'waɪdən/ verb [I, T] **1** Ⓑ2 to become wider or make something become wider: *The road is being widened to two lanes.* **2** Ⓑ2 to increase or make something increase in number or degree: *to widen choice*

wide-ranging /ˌwaɪd'reɪndʒɪŋ/ adj including a lot of subjects: *a wide-ranging discussion/ interview*

widescreen /'waɪdskriːn/ adj describes a very wide cinema or television screen which shows very clear pictures: *widescreen TV*

widespread /'waɪdspred/ adj affecting or including a lot of places, people, etc: *a wide-spread problem* ∘ *widespread support*

widow /'wɪdəʊ/ noun [C] **1** Ⓑ2 a woman whose husband has died **2** in printing, the last line of a paragraph, separated from the rest which is on the page before

widowed /'wɪdəʊd/ adj If someone is widowed, their husband or wife has died.

widower /'wɪdəʊər/ noun [C] a man whose wife has died

width /wɪtθ/ noun **1** [C, U] Ⓑ2 the distance from one side of something to the other side: *a width of 2 metres* ∘ *height, length, and width* → See picture at **length 2** [C] the distance across the shorter side of a swimming pool when you swim across it

❷ Word partners for **width**
the width **of** sth • [1 metre/5 feet, etc] **in** width • the **full** width **of** sth

wield /wiːld/ verb [T] **1** to hold a weapon or tool and look as if you are going to use it: *They were confronted by a man wielding a knife.* **2 wield influence/power, etc** to have a lot of influence or power over other people

wiener /'wiːnər/ noun [C] US a long thin sausage (= tube of meat and spices) that is usually eaten in bread

wife /waɪf/ noun [C] (plural **wives** /waɪvz/) Ⓐ1 the woman that a man is married to: *I've never met William's wife.*

wi-fi /'waɪfaɪ/ noun [U] a system used for connecting computers and other electronic equipment to the Internet without using wires

wig /wɪɡ/ noun [C] a covering of real or artificial hair that you wear on your head: *She was wearing a blonde wig.*

wiggle /'wɪɡl/ verb [I, T] to make small movements from side to side or to make something else move from side to side: *He was wiggling his hips to the music.* • **wiggle** noun [no plural]

wild¹ /waɪld/ adj **1 ANIMAL** ▷ Ⓐ2 A wild animal or plant lives or grows in its natural environment and not where people live: *a wild dog* ∘ *wild flowers* **2 LAND** ▷ Ⓑ2 Wild land is in a completely natural state: *a wild garden* **3 ENERGETIC** ▷ Ⓑ2 very energetic and not controlled: *a wild party* ∘ *wild dancing* **4 WEATHER** ▷ with a lot of wind, rain, etc: *a wild and stormy night* **5 a wild accusation/ guess/rumour, etc** something that you say which is not based on facts and is probably wrong **6 be wild about sth** informal to be very enthusiastic about something: *He's wild about jazz.*

IDIOM **run wild** If someone, especially a child, runs wild, they behave as they want to and no one controls them: *Their nine-year-old son is left to run wild.*

• **wildness** noun [U] → See also **beyond your wildest dreams (dream¹)**

wild² /waɪld/ noun **1 in the wild** in a natural environment: *Animals are better off in the wild than in a zoo.* **2 the wilds** an area that is far from where people usually live: *the wilds of Alaska*

wild boar noun [C] a wild pig

wildcard /'waɪldkɑːd/ noun [C] a sign that is used to represent any letters, numbers, or symbols: *a wildcard search*

wild card noun [C] someone or something that you know nothing about: *a wild-card candidate in the election*

wilderness /'wɪldənəs/ **noun** [C] a place that is in a completely natural state without houses, industry, roads, etc: [usually singular] *a beautiful mountain wilderness*

wildlife /'waɪldlaɪf/ **noun** [U] 🅐 animals, birds, and plants living in their natural environment: *a wildlife park*

wildly /'waɪldli/ **adv 1** 🅑 in a very energetic way and without control: *They cheered wildly.* **2** extremely: *It hasn't been wildly successful.*

wiles /waɪlz/ **noun** [plural] tricks or clever ways of making people do what you want: *I'll use my **womanly wiles**.*

wilful UK (US **willful**) /'wɪlfⁿl/ **adj** doing what you want to do, although you are not allowed to or other people tell you not to: *wilful disobedience* • **wilfully adv**

will¹ strong /wɪl/ weak /wəl/, /əl/ **modal verb 1 FUTURE** ▷ 🅐 used to talk about what is going to happen in the future, especially things that you are certain about: *Claire will be five next month.* ∘ *I'll see him on Saturday.* ∘ *She'll have a great time.* → See Note at **shall 2 ABLE/WILLING** ▷ 🅐 used to talk about what someone or something is willing or able to do: *Ask Susie if she'll take them.* ∘ *I've asked her but she won't come.* ∘ *The car won't start.* **3 ASK** ▷ 🅐 used to ask someone to do something or to politely offer something to someone: *Will you give me her address?* ∘ *Will you have a drink with us, Phil?* **4 IF** ▷ 🅐 used in conditional sentences that start with 'if' and use the present tense: *If he's late again I'll be very angry.* **5 HAPPENING OFTEN** ▷ used to talk about something that often happens, especially something annoying: *Accidents will happen.* ∘ *He will keep talking when I'm trying to concentrate.* **6 it/that will be** mainly UK used to talk about what is probably true: *That will be Helen at the front door.* ∘ *That will be his mother with him.* → See Study Page **Modal verbs** on page Centre 22

will² /wɪl/ **noun 1 MENTAL POWER** ▷ [C, U] 🅑 the mental power to control your thoughts and actions or to succeed in doing something difficult: *She has a very strong will.* ∘ [+ to do sth] *He lacks the will to win.* **2 WANT** ▷ [no plural] what someone wants: *She was forced to marry him **against** her **will**.* **3 DOCUMENT** ▷ [C] a legal document that gives instructions about what should happen to your money and possessions after you die: *She left me some money **in** her **will**.* → See also **free will, ill will**

> 🅩 Word partners for **will**
>
> make/write a will • in sb's will • leave sb sth in your will

willful /'wɪlfⁿl/ **adj** US spelling of wilful

willing /'wɪlɪŋ/ **adj 1 be willing to do sth** 🅑 to be happy to do something, if you need to: *He's willing to pay a lot of money for that house.* **2** wanting to do something: *He is a very willing assistant.* → Opposite **unwilling** • **willingly adv** 🅑 *He would willingly risk his life for her.* • **willingness noun** [U]

willow /'wɪləʊ/ **noun** [C] a tree with long, thin leaves that grows near water

willowy /'wɪləʊi/ **adj** tall and attractively thin: *willowy blonde*

willpower /'wɪlpaʊər/ **noun** [U] the ability t make yourself do difficult things or to sto yourself from doing enjoyable things that ar bad for you: *It takes great willpower to los weight.*

wilt /wɪlt/ **verb** [I] If a plant wilts, it starts to ben because it is dying or needs water.

wily /'waɪli/ **adj** good at getting what you wan especially by deceiving people

wimp /wɪmp/ **noun** [C] informal someone who i not brave and tries to avoid dangerous o difficult situations: *I'm too much of a wimp t go rock climbing.* • **wimpy adj** informal

win¹ /wɪn/ **verb** (**winning**, **wo 1 COMPETITION** ▷ [I, T] 🅐 to get the mos points in a competition or game, or the mos votes in an election: *Barcelona won the game 6-* ∘ *Who do you think will win the election* **2 ARGUMENT** ▷ [I, T] 🅑 to be successful in war, fight, or argument: *Protesters have won the battle to stop the road being built.* **3 PRIZE** ▷ [T] 🅐 to get a prize in a game or competition: *He wo $500.* ∘ *She won a gold medal at the Olympic.* **4 win approval/respect/support, etc** to ge approval/respect/support, etc because of you skill and hard work: *Her plans have won th support of many local people.* **5 sb can't wi** informal used to say that nothing someone doe in a situation will succeed or please peopl *Whatever I do seems to annoy her – I just can win.*

> ❗ Common learner error: **win** or **beat**?
>
> You **win** a game or competition.
> *Who do you think will win the football game?*
> You **beat** someone, or a team you are playing against.
> *We beat both teams.*
> ~~We won both teams.~~

PHRASAL VERB **win sb over** to persuade someon to support you or agree with you

win² /wɪn/ **noun** [C] an occasion when someon wins a game or competition: *The Jets have onl had three wins this season.*

> 🅩 Word partners for **win** noun
>
> a **comfortable/convincing/emphatic** win • a win **against/over** sb • a win **for** sb

wince /wɪns/ **verb** [I] to suddenly look as if yo are suffering because you feel pain or becaus you see or think about something unpleasant: *makes me wince just to think about eye operation.*

winch /wɪnʃ/ **noun** [C] a machine with a thic chain, used for lifting heavy things • **winch ver** [T] to lift someone or something with a winc *The injured climber was **winched to safety** by helicopter.*

wind¹ /wɪnd/ **noun 1** [C, U] 🅐 a natural, fas movement of air: *The weather forecast said ther* *would be **strong winds** and rain.* **2** [U] UK (US **gas**) gas or air in your stomach that makes you feel uncomfortable and sometimes makes noises **3 get wind of sth** to discover something that is intended to be a secret: *Dad got wind of our plans for a party.* **4 get your wind (back)** to breathe easily again, for example after you have been running → See also **throw caution¹ to the wind, second wind**

> **Word partners for wind**
>
> the wind **blows** • a **gust** of wind • a **biting/ light/strong** wind • **high** winds • **in the** wind

wind² /wɪnd/ *verb* [T] to make someone have difficulty breathing, often by hitting them in the stomach

wind³ /waɪnd/ *verb* (**wound**) **1 wind sth around/round, etc sth** ⓑ to turn or twist something long and thin around something else several times: *She wound the rope around the tree.* → Opposite **unwind 2 wind (up) a clock/ toy/watch, etc** to make a clock/toy/watch, etc work by turning a small handle or button several times: *Did you remember to wind the alarm clock?* **3 wind along/down/through, etc** ⓑ If a river, road, etc winds somewhere, it bends a lot and is not straight: *The path winds along the edge of the bay.*

PHRASAL VERBS **wind (sth) down** to gradually end, or to make something gradually end: *to wind down a business* • **wind down** (also **unwind**) to gradually relax after doing something that has made you tired or worried • **wind up** to finally be somewhere or do something, especially without having planned it: *If he carries on like this, he'll wind up in prison.* ∘ [+ doing sth] *I wound up having to start the course from the beginning again.* • **wind (sth) up** to end, or to make something end: *It's time to wind up the game now.* • **wind sb up** UK informal **1** to tell someone something that is not true, as a joke: *Have I really won or are you winding me up?* **2** to annoy someone: *He keeps complaining and it really winds me up.*

windfall /ˈwɪndfɔːl/ *noun* [C] an amount of money that you get that you did not expect: *Investors each received a windfall of £1000.*

wind ˌfarm *noun* [C] an area of land or sea where there is a group of wind turbines (= machines with long parts at the top that are turned by the wind) that are used for producing electricity

winding /ˈwaɪndɪŋ/ *adj* **a winding path/road/ street, etc** ⓑ a path/road, etc that bends a lot and is not straight

wind ˌinstrument *noun* [C] a musical instrument that you play by blowing into it: *A flute is a wind instrument.*

windmill /ˈwɪndmɪl/ *noun* [C] a building with long parts at the top that turn in the wind, used for producing power or crushing grain

window /ˈwɪndəʊ/ *noun* [C] **1** ⓐ a space in the wall of a building or vehicle that has glass in it, used for letting light and air inside and for

looking through: *Open the **window** if you're too hot.* ∘ *I could see the children's faces **at** the **window**.* ∘ *a window **frame/ledge*** → See colour picture **The Living Room** on page Centre 4 **2** ⓑ a separate area on a computer screen showing information and which you can move around: *to minimize/maximize a window* → See also **French windows**

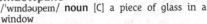
windmill

windowpane /ˈwɪndəʊpeɪn/ *noun* [C] a piece of glass in a window

Windows *noun* [U] trademark a software system produced by Microsoft with many commonly used software products: *Click here to download Windows™ updates.*

window ˌshopping *noun* [U] the activity of looking at things in shops but not buying anything

windowsill /ˈwɪndəʊsɪl/ *noun* [C] a shelf at the bottom of a window → See colour picture **The Living Room** on page Centre 4

windpipe /ˈwɪndpaɪp/ *noun* [C] the tube that carries air from your throat to your lungs

wind ˌpower *noun* [U] electricity produced using wind turbines (= machines with long parts at the top that are turned by the wind)

windscreen /ˈwɪndskriːn/ *noun* [C] UK (US **windshield**, ⓤ /ˈwɪndʃiːld/) ⓑ the window at the front end of a car, bus, etc → See colour picture **Car** on page Centre 7

windscreen ˌwiper *noun* [C] UK (US **windshield ˌwiper**) one of two long, metal and rubber parts that move against a windscreen to remove rain → See colour picture **Car** on page Centre 7

windsurfing /ˈwɪndsɜːfɪŋ/ *noun* [U] ⓑ a sport in which you sail across water by standing on a board and holding onto a large sail • **windsurfer** *noun* [C]

windswept /ˈwɪndswept/ *adj* **1** A windswept place often has strong winds: *a remote, windswept hill* **2** looking untidy because you have been in the wind: *windswept hair*

wind ˌturbine *noun* [C] a machine with long parts at the top that are turned by the wind, used to make electricity

windy /ˈwɪndi/ *adj* ⓐ with a lot of wind: *a windy day* ∘ *Outside it was cold and windy.*

wine /waɪn/ *noun* [C, U] ⓐ an alcoholic drink that is made from the juice of grapes (= small, green or purple fruit), or sometimes other fruit: *a **glass of wine*** ∘ *red/white wine*

> **Word partners for wine**
>
> a **bottle of/glass of** wine • **dry/red/sparkling/ sweet/white** wine

W

wing

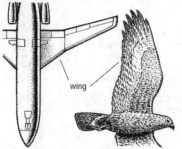

wing

wing /wɪŋ/ **noun** [C] **1 CREATURE** ▷ ⓐ one of the two parts that a bird or insect uses to fly **2 AIRCRAFT** ▷ ⓑ one of the two long, flat parts at the sides of an aircraft that make it stay in the sky **3 CAR** ▷ UK (US **fender**) one of the parts at each corner of a car above the wheels **4 BUILDING** ▷ a part of a large building that is joined to the side of the main part: *Their offices are in the West wing.* **5 POLITICS** ▷ a group of people in an organization or political party who have the same beliefs: *the nationalist wing of the party*

IDIOM **take sb under your wing** to help and protect someone who is younger than you or who has less experience than you

winged /wɪŋd/ **adj** with wings: *a winged insect*

wing mirror noun [C] UK (US **side mirror**) a small mirror on the side of a car or truck → See colour picture **Car** on page Centre 7

the wings /wɪŋz/ **noun** [plural] the area behind the sides of a stage where actors wait just before they perform

IDIOM **be waiting in the wings** to be ready to do something or be used at any time

wink

wink¹ /wɪŋk/ **verb** [I] to quickly close and then open one eye, in order to be friendly or to show that something is a joke: *She smiled and winked at me.*

wink² /wɪŋk/ **noun** [C] the action of winking at someone: *He gave me a friendly wink.*

IDIOM **not sleep a wink** to not have any sleep: *I was so excited last night – I didn't sleep a wink.*

winner /ˈwɪnər/ **noun** [C] ⓐ someone who wins a game, competition, or election: *the winners of the World Cup*

winnings /ˈwɪnɪŋz/ **noun** [plural] money that you win in a competition

winter /ˈwɪntər/ **noun** [C, U] ⓐ the coldest season of the year, between autumn and spring: *We went skiing last winter.* ∘ *a mild winter* • **wintry** /ˈwɪntri/ **adj** cold and typical of winter: *wintry showers* (= *snow mixed with rain*) → See also **the dead³ of night/winter**

🗹 Word partners for **winter**

in (the) winter • a **cold/severe** winter • a **mild** winter • **last/next** winter • the winter **months**

---

win-win /ˈwɪnwɪn/ **adj** A win-win situation is one in which something good happens to everyone.

wipe¹ /waɪp/ **verb** [T] **1** ⓑ to clean or dry something by moving a cloth across it: *I had a job wiping tables in a cafe.* ∘ *She wiped her hands on the towel.* **2 wipe sth from/away/off, etc** ⓒ to remove dirt, water, a mark, etc from something with a cloth or your hand: *He wiped a tear from his eye.* **3** if someone or something wipes a computer's, phone's, etc. memory, it removes all the data from the memory: *The virus wiped the memory of my computer.*

PHRASAL VERBS **wipe sth out** to destroy something completely: *The earthquake wiped out many villages.* • **wipe sth up** to remove a substance, usually liquid, with a cloth: *Have you got something I could wipe this mess up with?*

wipe² /waɪp/ **noun** [C] **1** the act of cleaning or drying something with a cloth: *I'll give the table a wipe.* **2** a thin cloth or piece of paper used for cleaning: *baby wipes*

wiper /ˈwaɪpər/ **noun** [C] (also **windscreen wiper**) a long, metal and rubber part that removes rain from the front window of a vehicle

wire¹ /waɪər/ **noun 1** [C, U] ⓑ thin, metal thread used to fasten things or to make fences, cages etc **2** [C] ⓑ a long, thin piece of metal thread, usually covered in plastic, that carries electricity: *electrical wires* → See also **barbed wire**

wire² /waɪər/ **verb** [T] **1 ELECTRICITY** ▷ (also **wire up**) to connect wires so that a piece of electrical equipment will work: *Do you know how to wire a burglar alarm?* **2 JOIN** ▷ to join two things together using wire **3 SEND** ▷ US to send a message or money using an electrical communication system

wireless /ˈwaɪələs/ **adj** without a cable: *a wireless keyboard*

wireless internet noun [U] a way of being able to connect to the internet or other computer network without using any kind of cable: *Most Europeans can now access high-speed wireless internet from their homes.*

wiring /ˈwaɪərɪŋ/ **noun** [U] the system of wires

W

that carry electricity around a building: *The fire was caused by* **faulty wiring.**

wiry /ˈwaɪəri/ adj **1** Someone who is wiry is strong but quite thin. **2** Wiry hair is thick and stiff, like wire: *a wiry beard*

wisdom /ˈwɪzdəm/ noun **1** ⓑ② [U] the ability to use your knowledge and experience to make good decisions and judgments **2** **the wisdom of sth/doing sth** If you doubt the wisdom of something, you think it is probably not a good plan: *Many people have questioned the wisdom of spending so much money on weapons.*

wisdom ˌtooth noun [C] (plural **wisdom teeth**) one of the four teeth at the back of your mouth that are the last to grow

wise¹ /waɪz/ adj **1** ⓑ① A wise decision or action shows good judgment and is the right thing to do: *I think we've made a wise choice.* ◦ [+ to do sth] *It's always wise to see a doctor if you're worried about your health.* → Opposite **unwise** **2** ⓑ① A wise person is able to use their knowledge and experience to make good decisions and give good advice. **3** **be none the wiser** informal to still not understand something after someone has tried to explain it to you • **wisely** adv

wise² /waɪz/ verb

PHRASAL VERB **wise up** informal to start to understand the truth about a situation: *Employers are starting to* **wise up to** *the fact that people want flexible working hours.*

-wise /-waɪz/ suffix changes a noun into an adverb meaning 'relating to this subject': *Weather-wise, the holiday was great.* ◦ *How are we doing time-wise?*

wish¹ /wɪʃ/ verb **1** **wish (that)** ⓑ① to want a situation that is different from the one that exists: *I wish that I didn't have to go to work.* ◦ *I* **wish** *he* **would** *leave.* ◦ *I* **wish** *I* **had** *been there.* **2** **wish to do sth** formal to want to do something: *I wish to speak to the manager.* **3** **wish sb luck/success, etc** ⓑ① to say that you hope someone will be lucky/successful, etc: *I wished him luck for his test.* **4** **I/you wish!** informal used to say that you would like something to be true although you know it is not true: *"Have your exams finished yet?" "I wish!"*

wish² /wɪʃ/ noun [C] **1** ⓑ② what you want to do or what you want to happen: *The hospital always tries to* **respect** *the* **wishes** *of its patients.* ◦ *I* **have no wish** *to travel the world.* **2** something that you say secretly to yourself about what you want to have or happen: *She closed her eyes and* **made a wish.** **3** **best wishes** ⓐ② something you say or write at the end of a letter, to show that you hope someone is happy and has good luck: *Please give her my best wishes when you see her.*

> ⚡ Word partners for **wish** noun
>
> ignore/respect sb's wishes • get your wish • have no wish to do sth • according to/against sb's wishes

wishful thinking /ˌwɪʃfəlˈθɪŋkɪŋ/ noun [U] the act of wanting something to happen or be true when it is impossible

wisp /wɪsp/ noun [C] **1** **a wisp of cloud/smoke/steam** a small, thin line of cloud/smoke/steam **2** **a wisp of hair/grass, etc** a thin piece of hair/grass, etc • **wispy** adj in the form of wisps: *wispy hair* ◦ *a wispy cloud*

wistful /ˈwɪstfəl/ adj slightly sad because you are thinking about something you cannot have: *a wistful look/smile* • **wistfully** adv

wit /wɪt/ noun [U] the ability to say things that are funny and clever: *a woman of great intelligence and wit*

witch /wɪtʃ/ noun [C] in stories, a woman who has magical powers that she uses to do bad or strange things

witch

witchcraft /ˈwɪtʃkrɑːft/ noun [U] the use of magic to make bad or strange things happen

witch-hunt /ˈwɪtʃhʌnt/ noun [C] an attempt by a group of people to blame someone and punish them for something, in a way that is unfair

with /wɪð/ preposition **1** TOGETHER ▷ ⓐ① used to say that people or things are in a place together or are doing something together: *Emma lives with her boyfriend.* ◦ *Hang your coat with the others.* **2** HAVING ▷ ⓐ① having or including something: *a house with a swimming pool* ◦ *a woman with brown eyes* **3** USING ▷ ⓐ② using something: *She hit him over the head with a tennis racket.* **4** HOW ▷ ⓑ① used to describe the way someone does something: *He plays with great enthusiasm.* ◦ *She shut the drawer with a bang.* **5** WHAT ▷ ⓑ① used to say what fills, covers, etc something: *a bucket filled with water* ◦ *shoes covered with mud* **6** CAUSE ▷ ⓑ② because of something: *She was trembling with fear.* **7** RELATING TO ▷ ⓑ② relating to something or someone: *There's something wrong with the car.* ◦ *The doctors are very pleased with his progress.* **8** POSITION ▷ used to describe the position of someone's body: *She sat with her legs crossed.* **9** **be with me/you** informal to understand what someone is saying: *Sorry, I'm not with you – can you say that again?*

withdraw /wɪðˈdrɔː/ verb (**withdrew, withdrawn**) **1** MONEY ▷ [T] to take money out of a bank account: *She withdrew $50.* **2** REMOVE ▷ [T] to remove something, especially because of an official decision: *This product has been* **withdrawn from** *sale.* ◦ *He has threatened to withdraw his support.* **3** MILITARY ▷ [I, T] If a military force withdraws, or if someone withdraws it, it leaves the place where it is fighting: *The President has ordered troops to be* **withdrawn from** *the area.* **4** COMPETITION ▷ [I] to decide that you will not now be in a race, competition, etc: *He was forced to* **withdraw from** *the race because of injury.* **5** SOMETHING SAID ▷ [T] formal to say that you want people to ignore something you said before because it was not true: *He admitted taking the money, but later* **withdrew** *his* **confession.**

W

withdrawal /wɪðˈdrɔːʳəl/ noun **1** MONEY ▷ [C] the act of taking money out of a bank account: *This account allows you to make withdrawals whenever you want to.* **2** STOP ▷ [C, U] the act of stopping doing something, for example helping someone or giving money: [usually singular] *the withdrawal of financial support* **3** MILITARY ▷ [C, U] the movement of a military force out of an area: [usually singular] *the withdrawal of troops* **4** DRUGS ▷ [U] the unpleasant feelings that someone gets when they stop taking a drug that they have taken for a long time: *withdrawal symptoms* **5** ALONE ▷ [U] behaviour which shows someone prefers to be alone and does not want to talk to other people: *Withdrawal can be a symptom of depression.*

withdrawn /wɪðˈdrɔːn/ adj [never before noun] quiet and not talking to other people

wither /ˈwɪðəʳ/ verb [I] (also **wither away**) If a plant withers, it becomes dry and starts to die.

withering /ˈwɪðərɪŋ/ adj **withering attack/ contempt/look** criticism or an expression that shows that someone strongly disapproves of someone or something: *He published a withering attack on the government's policies.*

withhold /wɪðˈhəʊld/ verb [T] (**withheld**) to not give someone the information, money, etc that they want: *The company has decided to withhold payment until the job has been finished.*

within¹ /wɪˈðɪn/ preposition **1** TIME ▷ 🅱1 before a particular period of time has finished: *The ambulance arrived within 10 minutes.* ∘ *Consume within two days of purchase.* **2** DISTANCE ▷ 🅱1 less than a particular distance from something: *She was born within 20 miles of New York.* ∘ *The hotel is within easy reach of (= near) the airport.* **3** INSIDE ▷ inside an area, group, or system: *a dispute within the department* ∘ *There's a pharmacy within the hospital building.* **4** LIMIT ▷ 🅱2 not outside the limits of something: *The project was completed well within budget.* **5** **within the law/the rules/your rights, etc** allowed according to the law/the rules/your rights, etc: *You're perfectly within your rights to complain.*

within² /wɪˈðɪn/ adv inside something: *The organization needs to change from within.*

without /wɪˈðaʊt/ preposition **1** 🅰2 not having, using, or doing something: *I did the test without any problems.* ∘ *I can't see without my glasses.* ∘ *He went to school without eating any breakfast.* **2** 🅰2 not with someone: *You can start the meeting without me.* **3** **go/do without (sth)** to not have something important: *They went without sleep for three days.*

withstand /wɪðˈstænd/ verb [T] (**withstood**) to not be damaged or broken by something: *The bridge is designed to withstand earthquakes.*

witness¹ /ˈwɪtnəs/ noun [C] **1** COURT ▷ someone in a court of law who says what they have seen and what they know about a crime: *The witness was called to the stand.* **2** SEE ▷ 🅱2 someone who sees an accident or crime: *Police are appealing for witnesses to the shooting.* **3** DOCUMENT ▷ someone who signs their name on an official document to say that they were present when someone else signed in

📌 Word partners for **witness**

appeal for a witness • a witness to sth • a character/key witness • a witness account/ testimony

witness² /ˈwɪtnəs/ verb [T] **1** 🅱2 to see something happen, especially an accident or crime: *Did anyone witness the attack?* **2** to sign your name on an official document to say that you were present when someone else signed it

'witness ˌbox noun [C] UK (UK/US **'witness ˌstand**) the place in a court of law where a witness stands or sits when they are answering questions

wits /wɪts/ noun [plural] **1** intelligence and the ability to think quickly **2** **keep/have your wits about you** to be ready to think quickly in a situation and react to things that you are not expecting: *You have to keep your wits about you when you're cycling.*

IDIOMS **be at your wits' end** to be very worried about something and not know what you should do next • **scare/frighten sb out of their wits** to make someone very frightened

witty /ˈwɪti/ adj 🅱2 using words in a funny and clever way: *a witty comment* ∘ *He was witty and charming.*

wives /waɪvz/ plural of wife

wizard /ˈwɪzəd/ noun [C] **1** MAGIC ▷ in stories, a man who has magical powers **2** SKILL ▷ informal someone who is very good at something or knows a lot about something: *a computer wizard* **3** COMPUTER ▷ a computer program that gives the user a series of questions or instructions to help them use a particular system

WMD /ˌdʌbəljuːemˈdiː/ noun [plural] abbreviation for weapons of mass destruction: weapons, such as nuclear bombs, which cause a lot of damage and death when used

wobble /ˈwɒbl/ verb [I, T] If something wobbles or you make something wobble, it moves from side to side, often because it is not on a flat surface: *The ladder started to wobble.* ∘ *Stop wobbling the table.* • **wobbly** adj likely to wobble: *a wobbly chair*

woe /wəʊ/ noun [U] literary sadness: *full of woe*

woeful /ˈwəʊfəl/ adj very bad and showing no skill: *a woeful attempt/performance* • **woefully** adv

woes /wəʊz/ noun [plural] formal **your woes** your problems and worries

wok /wɒk/ noun [C] a large, bowl-shaped pan that is used for frying Chinese food

woke /wəʊk/ past tense of wake

woken /ˈwəʊkən/ past participle of wake

wolf¹ /wʊlf/ noun [C] (plural **wolves** /wʊlvz/) 🅱2 a wild animal like a large dog

wolf² /wʊlf/ verb [T] (also **wolf down**) to eat something very quickly: *I gave her a plate of pasta and she wolfed it down.*

woman /ˈwʊmən/ noun [C] (plural **women** /ˈwɪmɪn/) 🅰1 an adult female person: *a 30-year-old woman* ∘ *There were two women at the bus*

W

stop. • **womanhood** noun [U] the state of being a woman

womanly /'wʊmənli/ **adj** having the qualities and appearance that people think a woman should have: *womanly charms*

womb /wuːm/ **noun** [C] the organ inside a woman's body where a baby grows

women /'wɪmɪn/ plural of woman

women's room noun [C] (also **ladies' room**) US a room in a public place where there are women's toilets

won /wʌn/ past of win

wonder¹ /'wʌndəʳ/ **verb 1** ⓑ [I, T] to want to know something or to try to understand the reason for something: [+ question word] *I wonder what he's making for dinner.* ○ *I wonder why she left so suddenly.* **2 I/we wonder if/whether …** ⓑ used to politely ask someone for something or to suggest something: *I wonder if you could help me?* ○ *We were wondering if you'd like to come over for a meal sometime.*

wonder² /'wʌndəʳ/ **noun 1** [U] surprise and admiration: *The boys gazed in wonder at the shiny, red Ferrari.* **2** [C] something that makes you feel surprise or admiration: [usually plural] *the wonders of modern medicine* **3 no wonder** ⓑ used to say that you are not surprised about something: *No wonder she failed the test if she didn't do any work.* **4 it's a wonder (that)** used to say that you are surprised about something: *It's a wonder he's still alive.*

wonderful /'wʌndəfəl/ **adj** ⓐ very good: *a wonderful idea* ○ *We had a wonderful time in Spain.* • **wonderfully adv**

won't /wəʊnt/ short for will not: *I won't be home before midnight.*

woo /wuː/ **verb** [T] (**wooing, wooed**) to try to persuade someone to support you or to use your business: *a political party trying to woo young voters*

wood /wʊd/ **noun 1** [C, U] ⓐ the hard material that trees are made of: *a piece of wood* **2** [C] (also **woods** [plural]) ⓐ a large area of trees growing near each other: *We went for a walk in the woods.*

wooded /'wʊdɪd/ **adj** covered with trees: *a wooded area*

wooden /'wʊdən/ **adj** ⓐ made of wood: *a wooden chair*

woodland /'wʊdlənd/ **noun** [C, U] an area of land with a lot of trees

woodwind /'wʊdwɪnd/ **noun** [U] the group of musical instruments that you play by blowing into them: *woodwind instruments*

woodwork /'wʊdwɜːk/ **noun** [U] **1** the parts of a building that are made from wood **2** the activity of making things from wood

woof /wʊf/ **noun** [C] the sound made by a dog

wool /wʊl/ **noun** [U] **1** the soft, thick hair on a sheep **2** ⓐ thick thread or material that is made from the hair of a sheep: *a wool suit* ○ *a ball of wool* • See also **cotton wool**

woollen UK (US **woolen**) /'wʊlən/ **adj** made of wool: *woollen gloves*

woolly UK (US **wooly**) /'wʊli/ **adj** made of wool,

or made of something that looks like wool: *a green woolly hat*

word¹ /wɜːd/ **noun 1** ⓐ [C] a group of letters or sounds that mean something, or a single letter or sound that means something: *'Hund' is the German word for 'dog'.* ○ *He has difficulty spelling long words.* **2 not believe/understand/hear, etc a word** ⓑ to not believe/understand/hear, etc anything: *I don't believe a word he says.* **3 a word of warning/advice/thanks, etc** something that you say to warn someone/give them advice/ thank them, etc: *Just a word of warning – he doesn't like people being late.* **4 have a word with sb** ⓑ to talk to someone for a short time: *I'll have a word with Ted and see if he wants to come.* **5 put in a good word for sb** to praise someone, often to someone who might be able to employ them **6 give sb your word** to promise someone something: *He gave me his word that he wouldn't tell anyone.* **7 take sb's word for it** ⓑ to believe what someone says without any proof **8 in other words** ⓑ used to explain what something means in a different way: *He said he's too busy, in other words, he isn't interested.* **9 in sb's words** used when you repeat what someone said: *In the manager's words, the game was 'a total disaster'.* **10 word for word** using the exact words that were originally used: *She repeated word for word what he had told her.*

IDIOMS **have the last word** to say the last thing in a discussion or argument or make the final decision about something • **not breathe a word** to not tell people a secret: *Don't breathe a word about this to anyone.* • **not get a word in edgeways** mainly UK (US **not get a word in edgewise**) to be unable to say anything because someone else is talking so much

→ See also **a play² on words**, **swear word**

word² /wɜːd/ **verb** [T] to choose the words you use when you are saying or writing something: *How should I word this letter?*

wording /'wɜːdɪŋ/ **noun** [U] the words that are used when someone says or writes something

Word partners for wording

change the wording • the exact wording • the wording of sth • a form of wording

word processor noun [C] a computer or computer program that you use for writing letters, reports, etc • **word processing noun** [U]

wore /wɔːʳ/ past tense of wear

work¹ /wɜːk/ **verb 1** JOB ▷ [I, T] ⓐ to do a job, especially the job you do to earn money: *Helen works for a computer company.* ○ *He works as a waiter in an Italian restaurant.* ○ *My dad works very long hours* (= he works a lot of hours). **2** MACHINE ▷ [I] ⓐ If a machine or piece of equipment works, it is not broken: *Does this radio work?* ○ *The washing machine isn't working.* **3** SUCCEED ▷ [I] ⓑ If something works, it is effective and successful: *Her plan to get rid of me didn't work.* **4 can work sth; know how to work sth** to know how to use a machine or piece of equipment: *Do you know how to work the dishwasher?* **5** EFFORT ▷ [I, T] to do something that needs a lot of time or effort, or to make someone do this: [+ to do sth] *He's been working to improve his speed.* ◦ *Our teacher works us very hard.* **6 work your way around/through/up, etc sth** to achieve something gradually: *I have a pile of homework to work my way through.*

PHRASAL VERBS **work against sb** to make it more difficult for someone to achieve something: *Age can work against you when you are looking for a job.* • **work at sth** to try hard to achieve something: [+ doing sth] *You need to work at improving your writing.* • **work on sth** to spend time repairing or improving something: *Tim loves working on old cars.* • **work sth out 1** ⓔ to calculate an amount: *I'm trying to work out the total cost.* **2** to understand something or decide something after thinking very carefully: [+ question word] *I haven't worked out what to do yet.* • **work out 1** ⓔ If a problem or difficult situation works out, it gradually becomes better: *Don't worry – everything will work out in the end.* **2** ⓑ to do exercises to make your body stronger → See colour picture **Phrasal Verbs** on page Centre 16 **3 work out badly/well, etc** to happen or develop in a particular way: *Changing schools worked out really well for me.* **4 work out at sth** to be the result when you calculate something: *If we share the costs, it works out at $10 per person.* • **work sb out** UK to understand the reasons for someone's behaviour: *I can't work him out at all.* • **work up to sth** to gradually prepare yourself for something difficult

> ❗ Common learner error: work, job, or occupation?
>
> **Work** is something you do to earn money. Remember that this noun is uncountable.
> *She enjoys her work in the hospital.*
> *He's looking for work.*
> ~~He's looking for a work.~~
>
> **Job** is used to talk about the particular work activity that you do.
> *He's looking for a job in computer programming.*
> *Teaching must be an interesting job.*
> ~~Teaching must be an interesting work.~~
>
> **Occupation** is a formal word that means the job that you do. It is often used on forms.
> See also: **career** and **profession**.

work² /wɜːk/ noun **1** EFFORT ▷ [U] ⓑ the use of physical or mental effort to do something: *Decorating that room was* **hard work.** **2** PLACE ▷ [U] ⓐ the place where you go to do your job: *He had an accident* **at work.** **3** JOB ▷ [U] ⓐ something you do as a job to earn money: *Has she got any work yet?* ◦ *Many young people are* **out of work** (= *they do not have a job*). **4** ACTIVITY ▷ [U] ⓐ the activities that you have to do at school, for your job, etc: *Have you got a lot of work to do?* ◦ *The teacher said she was pleased with my work.* **5 get/set to work (on sth)** to start doing something **6** ART/MUSIC ETC ▷ [C, U] ⓑ a painting, book, piece of music, etc: *The exhibition includes works by Picasso and Klee.* ◦ *the* **complete works** *of Shakespeare*

IDIOMS **do sb's dirty work** to do something unpleasant or difficult for someone else because they do not want to do it themselves • **have your work cut out** to have something very difficult to do: *It's a demanding job – she's going to have her work cut out for her.*

→ See also **donkey work, work of art**

> ☑ Word partners for **work**
> do/find/finish/have work • clerical/dirty/ hard/part-time/pioneering work • at work

workable /ˈwɜːkəbl/ **adj** A workable plan or system can be used or done easily and i effective. → Opposite **unworkable**

workaholic /ˌwɜːkəˈhɒlɪk/ **noun** [C] informa someone who works too much and does no have time to do anything else

workbook /ˈwɜːkbʊk/ **noun** [C] a book with questions and exercises in it that you use when you are learning something

worked 'up **adj** very nervous, angry, or excite

worker /ˈwɜːkəʳ/ **noun 1** ⓐ [C] someone who works for a company or organization but does not have a powerful position: *an office worker* **2** a **quick/slow/good, etc worker** ⓑ someone who works quickly/slowly/well, etc → See also **socia worker**

workforce /ˈwɜːkfɔːs/ **noun** [group] **1** all the people who work for a company or organization **2** all the people in a country who are able to do a job: *10% of the workforce are unemployed.*

working /ˈwɜːkɪŋ/ **adj** [always before noun] **1** ⓑ relating to your job: *good working conditions* **2** a **working man/woman, etc** someone who has a job: *a working mother* **3** a **working knowledge of sth** ⓑ knowledge about something that i good enough to be useful: *She has a working knowledge of German and Russian.* → See also **hard-working**

working 'class **noun** [C] the social class o people who have little money and who usually do physical work • **working-class** /ˌwɜːkɪŋˈklɑːs, **adj** *a working-class family*

workings /ˈwɜːkɪŋz/ **noun the workings of sth** how something works: *the workings of the mind*

workload /ˈwɜːkləʊd/ **noun** [C] the amount o work that you have to do: *Nurses have a very* **heavy workload** (= *they work hard*).

workman /ˈwɜːkmən/ **noun** [C] (plura **workmen**) someone who does a physical jot such as building

workmanship /ˈwɜːkmənʃɪp/ **noun** [U] the skil that is used in making something

work of 'art **noun** [C] (plural **works of art**) **1** a very beautiful and important painting, drawing etc: *They stole several valuable works of art.* **2 be a work of art** to be something that is beautifu or needed a lot of skill to create: *Have you seer the wedding cake? It's a work of art.*

workout /ˈwɜːkaʊt/ **noun** [C] ⓑ a series o exercises to make your body strong and healthy *a daily workout at the gym*

workplace /ˈwɜːkpleɪs/ noun [C] the place where you work: *We are trying to get rid of bullying in the workplace.*

worksheet /ˈwɜːkʃiːt/ noun [C] a piece of paper with questions and exercises for students

workshop /ˈwɜːkʃɒp/ noun [C] **1** an event at which a group of people meet to learn more about something by discussing it and doing practical exercises: *a workshop on crime prevention* **2** a place where people use tools and machines to make or repair things

workspace /ˈwɜːkspeɪs/ noun [C] **1** the office, desk, etc. where someone works **2** the area on a computer screen where you work, and the way that this is arranged: *Once you have created your workspace, you can then save it for future use.*

workstation /ˈwɜːkˌsteɪʃᵊn/ noun [C] a computer and the area around it where you work in an office

work ˌsurface noun [C] (also **worktop** /ˈwɜːk-tɒp/) a flat surface for preparing food in a kitchen → See colour picture **The Kitchen** on page Centre 2

world¹ /wɜːld/ noun **1 the world** Ⓐ the Earth and all the people, places, and things on it: *Everest is the highest mountain in the world.* ∘ *She's travelled all over the world.* **2** Ⓑ [C] the people and things that are involved in a particular activity or subject: [usually singular] *the entertainment world* ∘ *the world of politics* **3 the developing/industrialized/Western, etc world** a particular area of the Earth **4 the plant/ animal, etc world** plants/animals, etc as a group **5 your world** Ⓐ your life and experiences: *His whole world fell apart when she left.*

IDIOMS **do sb a/the world of good** informal to make someone feel much happier or healthier: *That swim has done me a world of good.* • **be out of this world** informal to be of extremely good quality: *Their chocolate cake is just out of this world!* • **think the world of sb** to like and admire someone very much • **the whole world** informal everyone: *The whole world knew she was getting married before I did.*

→ See also **have the best³ of both worlds**, **not be the end¹ of the world**, **the Old World**, **the outside world**, **the Third World**, **be on top¹ of the world**

🖉 Word partners for **world**
travel the world • **in** the world • **across/all over** the world

world² /wɜːld/ adj [always before noun] relating to the whole world: *world peace* ∘ *the world championships*

world-class /ˌwɜːldˈklɑːs/ adj one of the best in the world: *a world-class swimmer*

world-famous /ˌwɜːldˈfeɪməs/ adj known by people everywhere in the world: *The Eiffel Tower is a world-famous landmark.*

worldly /ˈwɜːldli/ adj **1 sb's worldly goods/ possessions** everything that someone owns: *She lost all her worldly possessions in a fire.* **2** having had a lot of experience of life: *a worldly woman*

world ˈwar noun [C] a war in which several large or important countries fight

worldwide /ˌwɜːldˈwaɪd/ adj, adv Ⓑ in all parts of the world: *10 million copies have been sold worldwide.*

the ˌWorld Wide ˈWeb noun all the websites (= pages of text and pictures) on the Internet → See Study Page **The Web and the Internet** on page Centre 36

worm¹ /wɜːm/ noun [C] **1** Ⓑ a small creature with a long, thin, soft body and no legs → See also **a can² of worms 2** a computer program that can send copies of itself to other computers and is designed to prevent the computers from working normally

worm² /wɜːm/ verb **worm your way into sth** to gradually get into a situation by making people like you and trust you, especially by deceiving them: *He wormed his way into the family.*

worn¹ /wɔːn/ adj
Worn clothing or objects have been used a lot and show damage: *a worn leather chair*

worn² /wɔːn/ past participle of **wear**

worn

worn-out /ˌwɔːnˈaʊt/ adj **1** extremely tired: *I was absolutely worn-out after all that dancing.* **2** Something that is worn-out is so old or has been used so much that it is damaged too much to repair: *a worn-out carpet*

worried /ˈwʌrid/ adj Ⓐ anxious because you are thinking about problems or unpleasant things that might happen: *She's really worried about her son.* ∘ [+ (that)] *I'm worried that she'll tell Maria.*

worry¹ /ˈwʌri/ verb **1** [I] Ⓐ to think about problems or unpleasant things that might happen in a way that makes you feel anxious: *Don't worry – she'll be all right.* ∘ *She's always worrying about something.* ∘ [+ (that)] *I worry that he might run away.* **2** [T] Ⓑ to make someone feel anxious because of problems or unpleasant things that might happen: *It worries me that he hasn't phoned yet.*

❗ Common learner error: **worry about** something or someone
Be careful to use the correct preposition after this verb.
They were worried about the weather.
~~They were worried for the weather.~~

🖉 Word partners for **worry** noun
allay/ease/express a worry • a **constant/lin-gering/nagging/real** worry • a worry **about/ over** sth

worry² /ˈwʌri/ noun **1** [C] Ⓑ a problem that makes you feel anxious: *health worries* **2** [U] Ⓑ

W

the feeling of being anxious about something: *She's been sick with worry.*

worrying /'wʌriɪŋ/ **adj** **B2** making you feel anxious: *a worrying situation* • **worryingly adv** *She's worryingly thin.*

worse¹ /wɜːs/ **adj 1** **A2** comparative of **bad**: more unpleasant or difficult than something else that is also bad: *The exam was worse than I expected.* ◦ *We'll have to stop the game if the rain gets any worse.* **2** **B1** more sick: *The drugs aren't working, he just seems to be getting worse.* **3 be none the worse for sth** to not be harmed or damaged by something: *He seemed none the worse for the experience.* **4 worse luck** UK informal used to show that you are annoyed or unhappy about something: *I've got to work on Saturday, worse luck!*

worse² /wɜːs/ **noun** [U] **1** something that is more unpleasant or difficult: *It was a nasty accident, although I've seen worse.* **2 for the worse** If a situation changes for the worse, it becomes worse.

worse³ /wɜːs/ **adv** **B1** comparative of **badly**: less well: *He was treated much worse than I was.*

worsen /'wɜːsⁿn/ **verb** [I, T] to become worse or to make something become worse: *His condition suddenly worsened last week.*

worse off adj [never before noun] poorer or in a more difficult situation: *If Rick loses his job we'll be even worse off.*

worship /'wɜːʃɪp/ **verb** (**worshipping, worshipped**, also US **worshiping, worshiped**) **1** [I, T] to show respect for a god by saying prayers or performing religious ceremonies **2** [T] to love and respect someone very much: *She worshipped her mother.* • **worship noun** [U] *a place of worship* (= *a religious building*) • **worshipper noun** [C]

worst¹ /wɜːst/ **adj** **A2** superlative of **bad**: the most unpleasant or difficult: *What's the worst job you've ever had?*

worst² /wɜːst/ **noun 1 the worst** **B1** the most unpleasant or difficult thing, person, or situation: *I've made some mistakes in the past, but this is definitely the worst.* **2 at worst** used to say what the most unpleasant or difficult situation could possibly be: *At worst, we might lose our money.* **3 if the worst comes to the worst** UK (US **if worse/worst comes to worst**) if a situation develops in the most unpleasant or difficult way

worst³ /wɜːst/ **adv** **B2** superlative of **badly**: the most badly: *the worst affected area*

worth¹ /wɜːθ/ **adj 1 be worth sth** **B1** to have a particular value, especially in money: *Our house is worth about 600,000 euros.* **2 be worth doing/seeing/trying, etc** **B1** to be useful or enjoyable to do/see/try, etc: *It's not as good as his last book but it's definitely worth reading.* **3 be worth it** **B1** to be useful or enjoyable despite needing a lot of effort: *It was a long climb up the mountain but the view was worth it.* ◦ *Don't bother complaining – it's really not worth it.* **4 be worth your while** If it is worth your while doing something, it is useful or enjoyable despite needing a lot of

effort: *It isn't worth my while going all that wa[y] just for one day.*

> **ℹ** **Common learner error: be worth doing something**
>
> When **worth** is followed by a verb, the verb is always in the **-ing** form.
> *Do you think it's worth asking Patrick first?*
> ~~*Do you think it's worth to ask Patrick first?*~~

worth² /wɜːθ/ **noun 1 £20/$100, etc worth of st[h]** the amount of something that you can buy fo[r] £20/$100, etc: *I've put £2 worth of stamps on th[e] letter.* **2 a month's/year's, etc worth of sth** th[e] amount of something that can be done or use[d] in a month/year, etc: *an hour's worth of fre[e] phone calls* **3** [U] how important or usefu[l] someone or something is: *She's finally prove[d] her worth.*

worthless /'wɜːθləs/ **adj 1** not important o[r] useful: *He made me feel stupid and worthless[.]* **2** having no value in money: *The painting's [a] fake – it's completely worthless.*

worthwhile /ˌwɜːθ'waɪl/ **adj** **B2** useful an[d] enjoyable, despite needing a lot of effort: *It's [a] difficult course but it's very worthwhile.*

worthy /'wɜːði/ **adj 1** deserving respect, admira[-] tion, or support: *a worthy cause* ◦ *a worth[y] champion* **2 be worthy of attention/respect, et[c]** to deserve attention/respect, etc

would strong /wʊd/ weak /wəd/ **modal ver[b]** **1** **IF** ▷ **B1** used to say what might happen i[f] something else happens: *What would you do i[f] you lost your job?* **2 SAID/THOUGHT** ▷ **B1** used a[s] the past form of 'will' to talk about wha[t] someone has said or thought: *Sue promise[d] that she would help.* ◦ *They thought that sh[e] would never recover.* **3 WILLING** ▷ **B1** used as th[e] past form of 'will' to talk about what someon[e] was willing to do or what something was able t[o] do: *I asked her to talk to him, but she wouldn't[.]* ◦ *The car wouldn't start this morning.* **4 woul[d] like/love sth** **A1** used to say politely that yo[u] want something: *I'd* (= *I would*) *like a cup o[f] coffee, please.* **5 would you** **A1** used to politel[y] ask someone something: *Would you like a drink[.]* ◦ *Would you come with me, please?* **6 IMAGINE** ▷ **B1** used to talk about a situation that you ca[n] imagine happening: *It would be lovely to go t[o] New York.* **7 I would imagine/think, etc** used t[o] give an opinion in a polite way: *I would imagin[e] she'll discuss it with her husband first.* **8 OFTEN** ▷ **B2** used to talk about things that happene[d] often in the past: *He would always turn and wav[e] at the end of the street.* **9 She/he/you would** mainly UK used to show that you are no[t] surprised by someone's annoying behaviou[r] *Margot spent $500 on a dress for the occasion bu[t] she would, wouldn't she?* → See Study Page **Moda[l] verbs** on page Centre 22

wouldn't /'wʊdⁿnt/ short for would not: *Sh[e] wouldn't let us watch TV.*

wound¹ /wuːnd/ **verb** [T] **1** **B2** to injur[e] someone, especially with a knife or gun: *[often] passive] He was badly wounded in the attack[*

W

◦ *wounded soldiers* **2** to upset someone: [often passive] *She was deeply wounded by his rejection.*

wound² /wuːnd/ **noun** [C] ⓑ an injury, especially one that is made by a knife or bullet

> **☑ Word partners for wound noun**
>
> inflict/sustain a wound • a wound heals (up) • bullet/gunshot/stab wounds • a wound on/to [sb's arm/back, etc] • an open wound

wound³ /waʊnd/ past of wind³

wound 'up adj very nervous, worried, or angry: *He gets very wound up before an important game.*

wove /wəʊv/ past tense of weave

woven /ˈwəʊvᵊn/ past participle of weave

wow /waʊ/ **exclamation** informal ⓐ something that you say to show surprise, excitement, admiration, etc: *Wow! Look at that car!*

wrangle¹ /ˈræŋgl/ **noun** [C] a long and complicated argument: *a legal wrangle*

> **☑ Word partners for wrangle**
>
> be involved in/get into a wrangle • a bitter/legal wrangle • a wrangle over sth • a wrangle between sb and sb • a wrangle with sb

wrangle² /ˈræŋgl/ **verb** [I] to argue with someone for a long time: *They're still wrangling over money.*

wrap /ræp/ **verb** [T] (**wrapping, wrapped**) **1** ⓑ (also **wrap up**) to cover something or someone with paper, cloth, etc: *to wrap a present* ◦ *They wrapped him in a blanket.* → Opposite **unwrap** **2 wrap sth around sb/sth** ⓑ to fold paper, cloth, etc around something to cover it: *He wrapped a towel around his waist.* **3 wrap your arms/fingers, etc around sb/sth** to put your arms/fingers, etc around someone or something: *She wrapped her arms around my neck.*

PHRASAL VERBS **wrap sth up 1** ⓑ to fold paper, cloth, etc around something to cover it: *Have you wrapped up Jenny's present?* **2** to finish an activity successfully: *We hope to have this deal wrapped up by Monday.* • **wrap up** to dress in warm clothes: *Wrap up well – it's cold outside.* • **be wrapped up in sth** to give so much of your attention to something that you do not have time for other things or people: *She's so wrapped up in her work that she hardly sees her kids.*

wrapper /ˈræpər/ **noun** [C] a piece of paper or plastic that covers something that you buy, especially food: UK *sweet wrappers*/US *candy wrappers*

wrapping /ˈræpɪŋ/ **noun** [C, U] paper or plastic that is used to cover and protect something

wrapping paper noun [U] decorated paper that is used to cover presents

wrath /rɒθ/ ⓤ /ræθ/ **noun** [U] literary extreme anger

wreak /riːk/ **verb** (**wrought, wreaked**) **wreak havoc** to cause a lot of damage or harm: *Floods have wreaked havoc in central Europe.*

wreath /riːθ/ **noun** [C] (plural **wreaths** /riːðz/) a large ring of leaves and flowers used as a decoration or to show respect for someone who has died

wreck¹ /rek/ **verb** [T] to destroy something completely: *The explosion wrecked several cars and damaged nearby buildings.*

wreck² /rek/ **noun** [C] **1 VEHICLE** ▷ a car, ship, or aircraft that has been very badly damaged **2 PERSON** ▷ informal someone who is in a bad physical or mental condition: [usually singular] *I was a complete wreck by the end of my exams.* **3 ACCIDENT** ▷ mainly US a bad accident involving a car or train: *a car/train wreck*

wreckage /ˈrekɪdʒ/ **noun** [U] the parts that remain of a car, ship, or aircraft that has been destroyed: *Two survivors were **pulled from the wreckage**.*

> **☑ Word partners for wreckage**
>
> be cut (free) from/pulled from/recovered from the wreckage • be trapped in the wreckage • a piece of wreckage • the tangled wreckage of sth

wren /ren/ **noun** [C] a very small, brown bird

wrench¹ /renʃ/ **verb** [T] **1 wrench sth from/off, etc sb/sth** to pull something violently away from a fixed position: *The phone had been wrenched off the wall.* **2** to injure part of your body by turning it suddenly: *I wrenched my right shoulder playing tennis.*

wrench² /renʃ/ **noun 1** [no plural] a situation in which you are very sad because you have to leave someone or something: *She found leaving home a real wrench.* **2** [C] US (UK **spanner**) a tool with a round end that is used to turn nuts and bolts (= metal objects used to fasten things together) → See picture at **tool**

wrestle /ˈresl/ **verb** [I] to fight with someone by holding them and trying to push them to the ground

PHRASAL VERB **wrestle with sth** to try very hard to deal with a difficult problem or decision: *He's still wrestling with his conscience.*

wrestling /ˈreslɪŋ/ **noun** [U] a sport in which two people fight and try to push each other to the ground • **wrestler noun** [C]

wretched /ˈretʃɪd/ **adj 1 UNHAPPY** ▷ very unhappy or sick: *I'd been feeling wretched all day so I went to bed early.* **2 BAD** ▷ very bad or of poor quality: *The refugees were living in **wretched conditions**.* **3 ANNOYED** ▷ [always before noun] used to show that something or someone makes you angry: *This wretched phone won't work!*

wriggle /ˈrɪgl/ **verb** [I, T] **1** to twist your body or move part of your body with short, quick movements: *She wriggled her toes in the warm sand.* **2 wriggle out of sth/doing sth** to avoid doing something that you have agreed to do: *Are you trying to wriggle out of going to the meeting?*

wring /rɪŋ/ **verb** [T] (**wrung**) (also **wring out**) to twist a cloth or piece of clothing with your hands to remove water from it: *He wrung out his socks* and hung them up to dry. → See also **wring your hands**

wrinkle /'rɪŋkl/ noun [C]
1 a small line on your face that you get when you grow old **2** a small fold in a piece of cloth • **wrinkle** verb [I, T] *a wrinkled face*

wrinkles

wrist /rɪst/ noun [C] ⓑ the part of your body between your hand and your arm

wristband /'rɪstbænd/ noun [C] **1** a piece of material that goes around the wrist (= the part of your body between your hand and your arm), for example to hold a watch **2** a piece of material in a particular colour that goes around the wrist and shows that the person wearing it supports a certain charity

wristwatch /'rɪstwɒtʃ/ noun [C] a watch that you wear on your wrist (= the part of your body between your hand and your arm)

writ /rɪt/ noun [C] a legal document that orders someone to do something

write /raɪt/ verb (wrote, written) **1 WORDS** ▷ [I, T] ⓐ to produce words, letters, or numbers on a surface using a pen or pencil: *Write your name at the top of the page.* ∘ *She can't read or write.* **2 BOOK** ▷ [I, T] ⓑ to create a book, story, article, etc or a piece of music: *He's writing a book on Russian literature.* ∘ *She writes for Time magazine.* **3 LETTER** ▷ [I, T] ⓐ to send someone a letter: [+ two objects] *I wrote her a letter last week.* ∘ *Has Bill written to you recently?* **4 DOCUMENT** ▷ [T] (also **write out**) to put all the information that is needed on a document: *He wrote out a cheque for £250.* **5 COMPUTER** ▷ [T] to create a computer program

---

❗ Common learner error: write

Remember to use the correct grammar after **write**.

write to someone
Rachel wrote to me last week.

write someone **a letter**
Rachel wrote me a letter last week.

write someone (American English)
Rachel wrote me last week.

PHRASAL VERBS **write back** to reply to someone's letter • **write sth down** ⓑ to write something on a piece of paper so that you do not forget it: *Did you write Jo's phone number down?* • **write in** to write a letter to a newspaper, television company, etc: *Lots of people have written in to complain about the show.* • **write off** to write a letter to an organization asking them to send you something: *I've written off for an information pack.* • **write sth off 1** to accept that an amount of money has been lost or will never be paid to you: *to write off debts* **2** UK to damage a vehicle so badly that it cannot be repaired • **write sb/sth off** to decide that someone or something is not useful or important: *They had written him off before they even met him.* • **write**

sth up ⓑ to write something in a complet... form, usually using notes that you made earlie... *Have you written up that report yet?*

write-off /'raɪtɒf/ noun [C] UK a vehicle that ... damaged so badly in an accident that it canne... be repaired: *I wasn't hurt, but the car was ... complete write-off.*

writer /'raɪtər/ noun [C] ⓑ someone whose jo... is writing books, stories, articles, etc

write-up /'raɪtʌp/ noun [C] an article in ... newspaper or magazine in which someon... gives their opinion about a performance... product, etc: *The film got a very good write-u... in yesterday's paper.*

writhe /raɪð/ verb [I] to twist your body in ... violent way, often because you are in pain: *Sh... lay on her bed, writhing in agony.*

writing /'raɪtɪŋ/ noun [U] **1 SKILL** ▷ ⓐ the ski... or activity of producing words on a surface... *Teachers focus on reading and writing in the firs... year.* **2 WORDS** ▷ ⓐ words that have bee... written or printed: *The writing was too small t... read.* **3 STYLE** ▷ ⓑ the way that someone write... *You've got very neat writing.* **4 BOOKS** ▷ ⓑ th... books, stories, articles, etc written by a particu... lar person or group of people: *She's studyin... women's writing of the 1930s.* **5 JOB** ▷ ⓑ th... activity or job of creating books, stories, o... articles **6 in writing** ⓑ An agreement that is i... writing is official because it has been written... and not only spoken: *Please confirm you... reservation in writing.*

written¹ /'rɪtən/ adj [always before noun] ⓑ... presented as a document on paper: *a writte... statement/warning*

written² /'rɪtən/ past participle of write

wrong¹ /rɒŋ/ adj **1 NOT CORRECT** ▷ ⓐ no... correct: *the wrong answer* ∘ *We're going th... wrong way.* **2 be wrong** ⓐ to think or sa... something that is not correct: *You were wron... about the party – it's today, not tomorrow.* **3 ge... sth wrong** ⓑ to produce an answer or resul... that is not correct: *I got most of the answer... wrong.* **4 PROBLEM** ▷ [never before noun] ⓑ... something is wrong, there is a problem: *There ... something wrong with my computer.* ∘ *What'... wrong?* **5 NOT MORAL** ▷ [never before noun] ⓑ... morally bad: [+ to do sth] *It's wrong to tell lie... **6 NOT SUITABLE** ▷ not suitable: *I think she ... wrong for this job.* → See also get (hold of) th... wrong end¹ of the stick, get/start off on th... wrong foot¹, not put a foot¹ wrong, rub s... up the wrong way¹

wrong² /rɒŋ/ adv **1** ⓐ in a way that is no... correct: *He always says my name wrong.* **2 g... wrong** ⓑ to develop problems: *Something ... gone wrong with my computer.* **3 Don't get m... wrong.** informal used when you do not wan... someone to think that you do not like someon... or something: *Don't get me wrong, I like her, bu... she can be very annoying.*

wrong³ /rɒŋ/ noun **1** [C, U] something that i... not morally right: *She's old enough to know th... difference between right and wrong.* **2 be in th...

α: arm | ɜ: her | i: see | ɔ: saw | u: too | aɪ my | aʊ how | eə hair | eɪ day | əʊ no | ɪə near | ɔɪ boy | ʊə pure | aɪə fire | aʊə sour

wrong to be responsible for a mistake or something bad that has happened

wrong⁴ /rɒŋ/ **verb** [T] formal to treat someone unfairly: *a wronged man*

wrongdoing /'rɒŋˌduːɪŋ/ **noun** [C, U] formal an activity that is illegal or not honest

wrongful /'rɒŋfᵊl/ **adj wrongful arrest/conviction/imprisonment, etc** a situation in which someone is accused of something or punished for something unfairly or illegally • **wrongfully adv** *wrongfully arrested*

wrongly /'rɒŋli/ **adv 1** 🅑 in a way that is not correct: *The letter was wrongly addressed.* **2 wrongly accused/convicted/imprisoned, etc** accused or punished unfairly or illegally: *She was wrongly convicted of drug smuggling.*

wrote /rəʊt/ past tense of write

wrought /rɔːt/ past of wreak

wrought iron noun [U] iron that can be bent into shapes and used to make gates, furniture, etc

wrung /rʌŋ/ past of wring

wry /raɪ/ **adj** A wry expression or remark shows your humour despite being in a difficult or disappointing situation: *a **wry smile*** • **wryly adv**

www /ˌdʌbljuːˌdʌbljuːˈdʌbljuː/ **noun** abbreviation for World Wide Web (= part of the Internet that consists of all the connected websites) → See Study Page **The Web and the Internet** on page Centre 36

X

X, x /eks/ **1 LETTER** ▷ the twenty-fourth letter of the alphabet **2 WRONG** ▷ used to show that an answer is wrong **3 KISS** ▷ used to represent a kiss at the end of a letter **4 UNKNOWN** ▷ used to represent an unknown person or thing

xenophobia /ˌzenəʊˈfəʊbiə/ **noun** [U] extreme dislike or fear of people from other countries • **xenophobic** /ˌzenəʊˈfəʊbɪk/ **adj**

XL /ˌeksˈel/ abbreviation for extra large: the largest size of clothes

Xmas /ˈkrɪstməs/ **noun** [U] informal used as a short way of writing 'Christmas' (= a Christian holiday), mainly on signs or cards: *Happy Xmas!*

XML /ˌeksemˈel/ **noun** abbreviation for extensible markup language: a system of organizing information on computers

X-ray /ˈeksreɪ/ **noun** [C] **1** 🅱️ a photograph that shows the inside of your body: *They took an X-ray of his leg.* **2** a wave of energy that can pass through solid materials • **X-ray verb** [T] to take a photograph that shows the inside of something

xylophone /ˈzaɪləfəʊn/ **noun** [C] a musical instrument consisting of a row of flat, metal bars that you hit with sticks

Y

y /waɪ/ the twenty-fifth letter of the alphabet

a /jə/ **pronoun** informal you: *See ya later.*

acht /jɒt/ **noun** [C]
B2 a large boat with sails, used for pleasure or in races: *a luxury yacht*

yacht

am /jæm/ **noun** [C] an orange vegetable with yellow flesh that tastes slightly sweet

ank /jæŋk/ **verb** [T] informal to pull something with a strong, sudden movement: *She yanked the drawer open.* ∘ *He yanked at the rope.*

ank /jæŋk/ **noun** [C] informal someone from the US, sometimes considered an offensive word

ap /jæp/ **verb** [I] (**yapping, yapped**) If a small dog yaps, it makes lots of short, high sounds.

ard /jɑːd/ **noun** [C] **1** UNIT ▷ (written abbreviation **yd**) **B1** a unit for measuring length, equal to 0.9144 metres or 3 feet: *There's a bus stop a few hundred yards up the road.* → See Study Page **Measurements** on page Centre 31 **2** HOUSE ▷ US (UK **garden**) an area of land in front of or behind a house **3** AREA ▷ a small area of ground next to a building, often with a fence or wall around it: *a school yard*

ardstick /'jɑːdstɪk/ **noun** [C] something that you use to judge how good or successful something else is: *If popularity is the yardstick of success, he's done very well.*

arn /jɑːn/ **noun 1** [U] thread used for making cloth **2** [C] informal a long story that is probably not true

awn /jɔːn/ **verb** [I] **B2** to take a deep breath with your mouth wide open, because you are tired or bored: *She yawned and looked at her watch.* • **yawn noun** [C]

yawn

awning /'jɔːnɪŋ/ **adj** **a yawning gap** a very big gap (= space or difference)

d written abbreviation for yard (= a unit for measuring length)

eah /jeə/ **exclamation** informal spoken **A2** yes: *Yeah, I agree.*

ear /jɪəʳ/ **noun** [C] **1** **A1** a period of 12 months, or 365 or 366 days, especially from 1 January to 31 December: *last year/next year* ∘ *He joined the company a year ago.* **2** **the academic/ financial, etc year** **A2** the period of a year that is used by universities/businesses, etc to organize their activities **3** **be two/twelve/37, etc years old** **A1** to be a particular age: *Her son is six years old.* **4** **a two-/twelve-/37-, etc year-old** someone who is a particular age **5** UK a group of students who start college or a course together:

He was in my year at school. **6 years** **B1** a long time: *I haven't seen Linda for years.* → See also for **donkey's years, leap year, new year**

> ☑ Word partners for **year**
>
> each/every/last/next year • the past year • [2/5, etc] years ago

> ❗ Common learner error: describing age
>
> If you describe someone's age by saying 'Tom is eight years old', you always write the age as three separate words.
> *My son is eight years old.*
> You can use also use eight-year-old, etc. as an adjective. When you do this, the words are written together using hyphens.
> *I've got a twelve-year-old son.*
> You can also do the same with days, weeks, and months.
> *I've got a ten-week-old rabbit.*
> *The baby is three months old.*
> *a three-month-old baby*

yearbook /'jɪəbʊk/ **noun** [C] a book produced every year by a school or organization, containing information about its activities, members, etc

yearly /'jɪəli/ **adj, adv** happening once a year or every year: *a yearly fee* ∘ *Interest is paid yearly.*

yearn /jɜːn/ **verb yearn for sth; yearn to do sth** to want something very much with a feeling of sadness: *They yearned for peace.* ∘ *She yearned to get away.* • **yearning noun** [C, U]

yeast /jiːst/ **noun** [U] a substance used to make bread rise and to make beer and wine

yell /jel/ **verb** [I, T] **B2** to shout something very loudly: *The policeman yelled at them to stop.* • **yell noun** [C]

yellow /'jeləʊ/ **adj** **A1** being the same colour as a lemon or the sun: *a bright yellow tablecloth* • **yellow noun** [C, U] **A2** the colour yellow → See colour picture **Colours** on page Centre 12

yellow '**card noun** [C] in football, a small card shown to a player as a warning that the player has not obeyed a rule → Compare **red card**

the ,**Yellow** '**Pages** UK trademark (US **the** '**Yellow** ,**Pages**) **noun** [plural] a big, yellow book containing telephone numbers of shops and businesses

yelp /jelp/ **verb** [I] If a dog yelps, it gives a sudden cry because of pain or shock.

yep /jep/ **exclamation** informal spoken yes

yes¹ /jes/ **exclamation 1** AGREE ▷ **A1** used to agree with something, or to give a positive answer to something: *"Can I borrow your pencil?" "Yes, of course."* ∘ *"Are you feeling better?" "Yes, thanks."* ∘ *"Coffee?" " Yes, please."* **2** ANSWER ▷ **A1** used as an answer when someone calls you: *"Jack!" "Yes?"* **3** DISAGREE ▷ **A2** used to disagree with a negative announcement: *"He's not here yet." "Yes he is, I've just seen him."*

yes² /jes/ **noun** [C] a positive reaction or agreement with something: *Was that a yes or a no?*

yesterday /'jestədeɪ/ **noun** [U], **adv** 🅐 the day before today: *I went to see the doctor yesterday.* ∘ *yesterday morning/afternoon*

yet¹ /jet/ **adv** **1** 🅐 before now or before that time: *Have you read his book yet?* ∘ *"Has he called?" "No, not yet."* **2** 🅐 now or as early as this time: *I don't want to go home yet.* **3 the best/ worst, etc yet** 🅑 the best/worst, etc until now: *That was my worst exam yet.* **4 be/have yet to do sth** to not have done something that was expected before this time: *They have yet to make a decision.* **5 yet again/another/more, etc** 🅑 used to show that you are surprised or annoyed that something is being repeated or increased: *He's given us yet more work to do.* **6 could/may/might, etc yet** used to say there is still a possibility that something will happen: *He may win yet.*

yet² /jet/ **conjunction** 🅑 used to add something that seems surprising because of what you have just said: *simple yet effective*

yew /juː/ **noun** [C, U] a tree with dark, needle-shaped leaves, or the wood of this tree

yield¹ /jiːld/ **verb** **1** [T] to produce or provide something: *to **yield a profit*** ∘ *The investigation **yielded** some unexpected **results**.* **2 yield to demands/pressure, etc** to be forced to do something **3** [I] US (UK **give way**) to stop in order to allow other vehicles to go past before you drive onto a bigger road

> 🔲 Word partners for **yield**
>
> yield **clues/information/a profit/a result**

yield² /jiːld/ **noun** [C] the amount of something that is produced

yo /jəʊ/ **exclamation** mainly US informal used as a greeting

yob /jɒb/ **noun** [C] UK informal a rude or violent young man

yoga /'jəʊɡə/ **noun** [U] 🅑 a set of exercises for the mind and body, based on the Hindu religion: *She does yoga three times a week.*

yoghurt (also **yogurt**) /'jɒɡət/ 🆄🆂 /'jəʊɡərt/ **noun** [C, U] 🅐 a thick, liquid food with a slightly sour taste which is made from milk: *a low-fat strawberry yoghurt* → See colour picture **Food** on page Centre 11

yolk /jəʊk/ **noun** [C] the round, yellow part in the middle of an egg

Yom Kippur /ˌjɒmkɪ'pʊər/ **noun** [U] a Jewish holy day in September or October

yonder /'jɒndər/ **adv, determiner** literary in that place or direction

you strong /juː/ weak /ju/, /jə/ **pronoun 1** 🅐 used to refer to the person or people you are talking to: *I love you.* ∘ *You said I could go with you.* **2** 🅐 people generally: *You learn to accept these things as you get older.*

you'd /juːd/ **1** short for you had: *You'd better g home now.* **2** short for you would: *I expect you' like some lunch.*

you'll /juːl/ short for you will: *I hope you'll com again.*

young¹ /jʌŋ/ **adj** 🅐 having lived or existed fo only a short time and not old: *young childrer people* ∘ *We were very young when we met.*

young² /jʌŋ/ **noun** [plural] **1 the young** 🅑 young people generally: *It's the sort of music tha appeals mainly to the young.* **2 sth's young** a animal's babies

youngster /'jʌŋstər/ **noun** [C] a young persor especially an older child: *He talked to th youngsters about the dangers of drugs.*

your strong /jɔːr/ weak /jər/ **determiner 1** 🅐 belonging or relating to the person or peopl you are talking to: *Can I borrow your pen?* ∘ *It not your fault.* **2** 🅑 belonging or relating t people in general: *You never stop loving you children.*

you're /jɔːr/ short for you are: *You're my bes friend.*

yours /jɔːz/ **pronoun 1** 🅐 the things that belon or relate to the person or people you are talkin to: *Is this pen yours?* ∘ *Our tent's smaller tha yours.* **2 Yours faithfully/sincerely, etc** 🅑 use just before your name at the end of a polite c formal letter **3 yours truly** humorous I or me

yourself /jɔː'self/ **pronoun** (plural **yourselves 1** 🅐 the reflexive form of the pronoun 'you' *Don't cut yourself with that sharp knife.* **2** 🅑 use to emphasize the pronoun 'you' when talkin about the actions of the person you are speak ing to: *Did you make the dress yourself?* **3 (all) b yourself/yourselves** 🅐 alone or without anyon else's help: *I'm amazed you managed to mou those boxes all by yourself.* **4 (all) to yourself** fo your use only: *So you've got the whole house t yourself this weekend?*

youth /juːθ/ **noun 1** YOUNG MAN ▷ [C] a youn man: *gangs of youths* **2** YOUNG PEOPLE ▷ [grou 🅑 young people generally: *the youth of toda* ∘ *a youth club* **3 sb's youth** 🅑 the period c time when someone is young: *I was very shy i my youth.* **4** QUALITY ▷ [U] the quality of bein young

> 🔲 Word partners for **youth**
>
> **recapture/relive** your youth • **in** sb's youth

youth club noun [C] UK a place where olde children can go to play sports and do othe social activities

youthful /'juːθfəl/ **adj** typical of a young persor *youthful energy/good looks*

youth hostel noun [C] a cheap, simple hote especially for young people who are travellin around

you've /juːv/ short for you have: *If you've finishe your work, you can go.*

yo-yo /'jəʊjəʊ/ **noun** [C] a small, round toy tha you make go up and down on a string that yo hang from your finger

Y

uck /jʌk/ **exclamation** informal used to say that something looks or tastes very unpleasant

um /jʌm/ **exclamation** (also ˌyum ˈyum) used to say that something tastes very good

yummy /ˈjʌmi/ **adj** informal If food or drink is yummy, it tastes very good.

yuppie /ˈjʌpi/ **noun** [C] a young person who earns a lot of money and likes expensive things

Z

Z, z /zed/ the twenty-sixth and last letter of the alphabet

zany /ˈzeɪni/ **adj** funny in a strange way: *zany humour*

zap /zæp/ **verb** [T] (**zapping, zapped**) informal to attack or destroy something in a fast and powerful way

zeal /ziːl/ **noun** [U] extreme enthusiasm: *religious zeal*

zealous /ˈzeləs/ **adj** extremely enthusiastic
• **zealously adv**

zebra /ˈzebrə/ ⓤⓢ /ˈziːbrə/ **noun** [C] ⓑ② an animal like a horse with black and white lines

zebra ˈcrossing **noun** [C] UK a part of the road painted with black and white lines where people can cross over safely

Zen /zen/ **noun** [U] a religion that developed from Buddhism

zenith /ˈzenɪθ/ ⓤⓢ /ˈziːnɪθ/ **noun** [no plural] literary the highest or most successful point of something: *The city reached its zenith in the 1980s.*

zero /ˈzɪərəʊ/ ⓐ② the number 0

> ☑ Word partners for **zero**
>
> sth drops to/falls to zero • above/below zero

ˌzero ˈtolerance **noun** [U] a way of dealing with bad behaviour in which you do not accept any bad behaviour at all, often by using laws to prevent it: *zero tolerance of crime*

zest /zest/ **noun** [U] **1** excitement and enthusiasm: *a zest for life* **2** the outer skin of a lemon or orange used to give flavour to food

zigzag /ˈzɪgzæg/ **noun** [C] a line that changes direction from left to right and back again at sharp angles • **zigzag verb** [I] (**zigzagging, zigzagged**) to make a movement or pattern like a zigzag

zillion /ˈzɪljən/ **quantifier** informal a very large number: *a zillion times*

zinc /zɪŋk/ **noun** [U] a blue-white metal that is used to make or cover other metals

zip¹ /zɪp/ **noun** [C] UK (US **zipper**) ⓑ② a thing for fastening clothes, bags, etc consisting of two rows of very small parts that connect together: *Your zip's undone.*

zip² /zɪp/ **verb** (**zipping, zipped**) **1** [T] (also **zip up**) to fasten something with a zip: *He zipped up his jacket.* **2** [T] (also **zip up**) to reduce the size of a computer file (= collection of information) so that it uses less space and can be sent or stored more easily **3** **zip along/around/past, etc** informal to move somewhere very quickly

ˈzip ˌcode **noun** [C] a set of numbers that go after someone's address in the US → Compare **postcode**

ˈzip ˌdrive **noun** [C] a device used for copying large documents onto special disks → See also **Memory Stick**

ˈzip ˌfile **noun** [C] a computer file (= collection of information) that has been made smaller so that it uses less space

zipper /ˈzɪpər/ **noun** [C] US a zip¹

zodiac

Capricorn Aquarius Pisces

Aries Taurus Gemini

Cancer Leo Virgo

Libra Scorpio Sagittarius

the **zodiac** /ˈzəʊdiæk/ **noun** the twelve signs representing groups of stars that are thought by some people to influence your life and personality: *What **sign of the zodiac** are you?*

zombie /ˈzɒmbi/ **noun** [C] **1** a dead body that walks around because of magic **2** like a zombie informal in a very tired, slow way: *The day after the party I was walking around like a zombie.*

zone /zəʊn/ **noun** [C] ⓑ① an area where a particular thing happens: *a war zone* ○ *a nuclear-free zone* → See also **buffer zone**

zoo /zuː/ **noun** [C] ⓐ① a place where wild animals are kept and people come to look at them

zoological /ˌzəʊəˈlɒdʒɪkəl/ **adj** relating to the scientific study of animals

zoology /zuˈɒlədʒi/ ⓤⓢ /zəʊˈɒlədʒi/ **noun** [U] the scientific study of animals and how they behave
• **zoologist noun** [C] someone who studies zoology

zoom /zuːm/ **verb** informal **zoom along/down/past, etc** to travel somewhere very fast, especially with a loud noise

PHRASAL VERB **zoom in** to make something appear much closer and larger when using a camera or computer: *The TV cameras zoomed in on her face.*

ˈzoom ˌlens **noun** [C] a lens (= part of a camera) that can make something appear much closer and larger

zucchini /zʊˈkiːni/ **noun** [C, U] (plural **zucchini**, **zucchinis**) US (UK **courgette**) a long, green vegetable which is white inside

Appendices

Common first names

These lists give you the most common names for males and females in English-speaking countries, along with their pronunciation. The names in brackets are short, informal forms of the names.

Male names

Adam /ˈædəm/
Alan /ˈælən/
Alexander /ˌælɪgˈzɑːndər/
  (Alex) /ˈælɪks/
Andrew /ˈændruː/
  (Andy) /ˈændi/
Anthony
  UK /ˈæntəni/
  US /ˈænθəni/
  (Tony) /ˈtəʊni/
Benjamin /ˈbendʒəmɪn/
  (Ben) /ben/
Charles /tʃɑːlz/
  (Charlie) /ˈtʃɑːli/
Christopher /ˈkrɪstəfər/
  (Chris) /krɪs/
Daniel /ˈdænjəl/
  (Dan) /dæn/
Darren /ˈdærən/
David /ˈdeɪvɪd/
  (Dave) /deɪv/
Edward /ˈedwəd/
  (Ed) /ed/
  (Ted) /ted/

Geoffrey /ˈdʒefri/
  (Geoff) /dʒef/
George /dʒɔːdʒ/
Harry /ˈhæri/
Jack /dʒæk/
James /dʒeɪmz/
  (Jim) /dʒɪm/
John /dʒɒn/
Jonathan /ˈdʒɒnəθən/
Joseph /ˈdʒəʊzɪf/
  (Joe) /dʒəʊ/
Joshua /ˈdʒɒʃjuə/
  (Josh) /dʒɒʃ/
Ian /ˈiːən/
Kevin /ˈkevɪn/
Liam /ˈliːəm/
Mark /mɑːk/
Martin /ˈmɑːtɪn/
Matthew /ˈmæθjuː/
  (Matt) /mæt/
Michael /ˈmaɪkəl/
  (Mike) /maɪk/
  (Mick) /mɪk/
Nicholas /ˈnɪkələs/

  (Nick) /nɪk/
Patrick /ˈpætrɪk/
Paul /pɔːl/
Peter /ˈpiːtə/
  (Pete) /piːt/
Philip /ˈfɪlɪp/
  (Phil) /fɪl/
Richard /ˈrɪtʃəd/
  (Ricky) /ˈrɪki/
  (Dick) /dɪk/
Robert /ˈrɒbət/
  (Bob) /bɒb/
  (Rob) /rɒb/
Samuel /ˈsæmjuəl/
  (Sam) /sæm/
Simon /ˈsaɪmən/
Thomas /ˈtɒməs/
  (Tom) /tɒm/
Timothy /ˈtɪməθi/
  (Tim) /tɪm/
William /ˈwɪljəm/
  (Billy) /ˈbɪli/
  (Will) /wɪl/

Female names

Alice /ˈælɪs/
Alison /ˈælɪsən/
Amanda /əˈmændə/
  (Mandy) /ˈmændi/
Amy /ˈeɪmi/
Ann/Anne /æn/
Bridget /ˈbrɪdʒɪt/
Carol /ˈkærəl/
Caroline /ˈkærəlaɪn/
Catherine/Kathryn
  /ˈkæθrɪn/
  (Kate) /keɪt/
  (Katie) /ˈkeɪti/
  (Cath) /kæθ/
Charlotte /ˈʃɑːlət/
Chloe /ˈkləʊi/
Christine /ˈkrɪstiːn/
  (Chris) /krɪs/

Clare/Claire /kleər/
Deborah /ˈdebrə/
  (Debbie) /ˈdebi/
Diane /daɪˈæn/
Elizabeth /ɪˈlɪzəbəθ/
  (Beth) /beθ/
  (Liz) /lɪz/
Emily /ˈemɪli/
Emma /ˈemə/
Hannah /ˈhænə/
Helen /ˈhelən/
Jane /dʒeɪn/
Jennifer /ˈdʒenɪfə/
  (Jenny) /ˈdʒeni/
Joanne /dʒəʊˈæn/
  (Jo) /dʒəʊ/
Julie /ˈdʒuːli/
Karen /ˈkærən/

Laura /ˈlɔːrə/
Linda /ˈlɪndə/
Lucy /ˈluːsi/
Margaret /ˈmɑːgərət/
  (Maggie) /ˈmægi/
Mary /ˈmeəri/
Rachel /ˈreɪtʃəl/
Rebecca /rɪˈbekə/
  (Becky) /ˈbeki/
Ruth /ruːθ/
Sarah /ˈseərə/
Sharon /ˈʃærən/
Sophie /ˈsəʊfi/
Susan /ˈsuːzən/
  (Sue) /suː/
Tracy /ˈtreɪsi/
Valerie /ˈvæləri/

Geographical names

This list shows the spellings and pronunciations of countries, regions, and continents.

Each name is followed by its related adjective. Most of the time you can use the adjective to talk about a person who comes from each place. However, in some cases you must use a special word, which is listed in the column labelled 'Adjective/Person' (for example, **Finland, Finnish, Finn**).

To talk about more than one person from a particular place, add '**s**', except for:

■ words ending in '**ese**' or '**s**', which remain the same (**Chinese, Swiss**)

■ words ending in '**man**' or '**woman**', which change to '**men**' and '**women**' (one **Irishman**, two **Irishmen**).

This list is for reference only. Inclusion does not imply or suggest status as a sovereign nation.

Name	Adjective/Person
Afghanistan /æfˈgænɪstæn/	Afghan /ˈæfgæn/
Africa /ˈæfrɪkə/	African /ˈæfrɪkən/
Albania /ælˈbeɪniə/	Albanian /ælˈbeɪniən/
Algeria /ælˈdʒɪəriə/	Algerian /ælˈdʒɪəriən/
Central America /ˌsentrəl əˈmerɪkə/	Central American /ˌsentrəl əˈmerɪkən/
North America /ˌnɔːθ əˈmerɪkə/	North American /ˌnɔːθ əˈmerɪkən/
South America /ˌsaʊθ əˈmerɪkə/	South American /ˌsaʊθ əˈmerɪkən/
Andorra /ænˈdɔːrə/	Andorran /ænˈdɔːrən/
Angola /æŋˈgəʊlə/	Angolan /æŋˈgəʊlən/
Antarctica /ænˈtɑːktɪkə/	Antarctic /ænˈtɑːktɪk/
Antigua and Barbuda /ænˌtiːgə ənd bɑːˈbjuːdə/	Antiguan /ænˈtiːgən/, Barbudan /bɑːˈbjuːdən/
The Arctic /ˈɑːktɪk/	Arctic /ˈɑːktɪk/
Argentina /ˌɑːdʒənˈtiːnə/	Argentine /ˈɑːdʒəntaɪn/, Argentinian /ˌɑːdʒənˈtɪniən/
Armenia /ɑːˈmiːniə/	Armenian /ɑːˈmiːniən/
Asia /ˈeɪʒə/	Asian /ˈeɪʒən/
Australasia /ɒstrəˈleɪʒə/	Australasian /ɒstrəˈleɪʒən/
Australia /ɒsˈtreɪliə/	Australian /ɒsˈtreɪliən/
Austria /ˈɒstriə/	Austrian /ˈɒstriən/
Azerbaijan /ˌæzəbaɪˈdʒɑːn/	Azerbaijani /ˌæzəbaɪˈdʒɑːni/; Person: Azeri /əˈzeəri/
The Bahamas /bəˈhɑːməz/	Bahamian /bəˈheɪmiən/
Bahrain /bɑːˈreɪn/	Bahraini /bɑːˈreɪni/
Bangladesh /ˌbæŋɡləˈdeʃ/	Bangladeshi /ˌbæŋɡləˈdeʃi/
Barbados /bɑːˈbeɪdɒs/	Barbadian /bɑːˈbeɪdiən/
Belarus /ˌbeləˈruːs/	Belorussian /ˌbeləˈrʌʃən/
Belgium /ˈbeldʒəm/	Belgian /ˈbeldʒən/
Belize /bəˈliːz/	Belizean /bəˈliːziən/
Benin /beˈniːn/	Beninese /ˌbenɪˈniːz/
Bhutan /buːˈtɑːn/	Bhutanese /ˌbuːtəˈniːz/
Bolivia /bəˈlɪviə/	Bolivian /bəˈlɪviən/
Bosnia-Herzegovina /ˌbɒzniəˌhɜːtsəˈɡɒvɪnə/	Bosnian /ˈbɒzniən/
Botswana /bɒtˈswɑːnə/	Botswanan /bɒtˈswɑːnən/; Person: Motswana /mɒtˈswɑːnə/
Brazil /brəˈzɪl/	Brazilian /brəˈzɪliən/
Britain /ˈbrɪtən/	British /ˈbrɪtɪʃ/; Person: Briton /ˈbrɪtən/

Brunei /bruːˈnaɪ/ — Bruneian /bruːˈnaɪən/
Bulgaria /bʌlˈɡeəriə/ — Bulgarian /bʌlˈɡeəriən/
Burkina Faso /bɜːˌkiːnə ˈfæseʊ/ — Burkinabe /bɜːˈkiːnəˌbeɪ/
Burma /ˈbɜːmə/ — Burmese /bɜːˈmiːz/
Burundi /bʊˈrʊndi/ — Burundian /bʊˈrʊndiən/
Cambodia /ˌkæmˈbəʊdiə/ — Cambodian /ˌkæmˈbəʊdiən/
Cameroon /ˌkæməˈruːn/ — Cameroonian /ˌkæməˈruːniən/
Canada /ˈkænədə/ — Canadian /kəˈneɪdiən/
Cape Verde /ˌkeɪp ˈvɜːd/ — Cape Verdean /ˌkeɪp ˈvɜːdiən/
The Caribbean /ˌkærɪˈbiːən/ — Caribbean /ˌkærɪˈbiːən/
The Central African Republic /ˌsentrəl ˌæfrɪkən rɪˈpʌblɪk/ — Central African /ˌsentrəl ˈæfrɪkən/
Chad /tʃæd/ — Chadian /ˈtʃædiən/
Chile /ˈtʃɪli/ — Chilean /ˈtʃɪliən/
China /ˈtʃaɪnə/ — Chinese /tʃaɪˈniːz/
Colombia /kəˈlɒmbiə/ — Colombian /kəˈlɒmbiən/
Comoros /ˈkɒmərəʊz/ — Comoran /kəˈmɔːrən/
The Democratic Republic of Congo /ˌdeməˌkrætɪk rɪˌpʌblɪk əv ˈkɒŋɡəʊ/ — Congolese /ˌkɒŋɡəˈliːz/
The Republic of Congo /rɪˌpʌblɪk əv ˈkɒŋɡəʊ/ — Congolese /ˌkɒŋɡəˈliːz/
Costa Rica /ˌkɒstə ˈriːkə/ — Costa Rican /ˌkɒstə ˈriːkən/
Côte d'Ivoire /ˌkəʊt diːˈvwɑːˈ/ — Ivorian /aɪˈvɔːriən/
Croatia /krəʊˈeɪʃə/ — Croatian /krəʊˈeɪʃ°n/;
    Person: Croat /ˈkrəʊæt/
Cuba /ˈkjuːbə/ — Cuban /ˈkjuːbən/
Cyprus /ˈsaɪprəs/ — Cypriot /ˈsɪpriət/
The Czech Republic /ˌtʃek rɪˈpʌblɪk/ — Czech /tʃek/
Denmark /ˈdenmɑːk/ — Danish /ˈdeɪnɪʃ/;
    Person: Dane /deɪn/
Djibouti /dʒɪˈbuːti/ — Djiboutian /dʒɪˈbuːtiən/
Dominica /dəˈmɪnɪkə/ — Dominican /dəˈmɪnɪkən/
The Dominican Republic /dəˌmɪnɪkən rɪˈpʌblɪk/ — Dominican /dəˈmɪnɪkən/
East Timor /ˌiːst ˈtiːmɔːˈ/ — East Timorese /ˌiːst ˌtiːmɔːˈriːz/
Ecuador /ˈekwədɔːˈ/ — Ecuadorian /ˌekwəˈdɔːriən/
Egypt /ˈiːdʒɪpt/ — Egyptian /ɪˈdʒɪpʃ°n/
El Salvador /ˌel ˈsælvədɔːˈ/ — Salvadoran /ˌsælvəˈdɔːrən/
England /ˈɪŋɡlənd/ — English /ˈɪŋɡlɪʃ/;
    Person: Englishman /ˈɪŋɡlɪʃmən/
Equatorial Guinea /ˌekwətɔːriəl ˈɡɪni/ — Equatorial Guinean /ˌekwətɔːriəl ˈɡɪniən/
Eritrea /ˌerɪˈtreɪə/ — Eritrean /ˌerɪˈtreɪən/
Estonia /esˈtəʊniə/ — Estonian /esˈtəʊniən/
Ethiopia /ˌiːθiˈəʊpiə/ — Ethiopian /ˌiːθiˈəʊpiən/
Europe /ˈjʊərəp/ — European /ˌjʊərəˈpiːən/
Fiji /ˈfiːdʒiː/ — Fijian /fiˈdʒiːən/
Finland /ˈfɪnlənd/ — Finnish /ˈfɪnɪʃ/; Person: Finn /fɪn/
France /frɑːns/ — French /frentʃ/;
    Person: Frenchman /ˈfrentʃmən/
Gabon /ɡæbˈɒn/ — Gabonese /ˌɡæbəˈniːz/
Gambia /ˈɡæmbiə/ — Gambian /ˈɡæmbiən/
Georgia /ˈdʒɔːdʒə/ — Georgian /ˈdʒɔːdʒən/
Germany /ˈdʒɜːməni/ — German /ˈdʒɜːmən/
Ghana /ˈɡɑːnə/ — Ghanaian /ɡɑːˈneɪən/

Great Britain /ˌɡreɪt ˈbrɪtᵊn/
Greece /ɡriːs/
Greenland /ˈɡriːnlənd/

Grenada /ɡrəˈneɪdə/
Guatemala /ˌɡwɑːtəˈmɑːlə/
Guinea /ˈɡɪni/
Guinea-Bissau /ˌɡɪnɪbɪˈsaʊ/
Guyana /ɡaɪˈænə/
Haiti /ˈheɪti/
Honduras /hɒnˈdjʊərəs/
Hungary /ˈhʌŋɡᵊri/
Iceland /ˈaɪslənd/

India /ˈɪndiə/
Indonesia /ˌɪndəˈniːʒə/
Iran /ɪˈrɑːn/
Iraq /ɪˈrɑːk/
Ireland /ˈaɪələnd/

Israel /ˈɪzreɪl/
Italy /ˈɪtᵊli/
Jamaica /dʒəˈmeɪkə/
Japan /dʒəˈpæn/
Jordan /ˈdʒɔːdᵊn/
Kazakhstan /ˌkæzækˈstɑːn/
Kenya /ˈkenjə/
Kiribati /ˌkɪrəˈbæs/
North Korea /ˌnɔːθ kəˈriːə/
South Korea /ˌsaʊθ kəˈriːə/
Kuwait /kuːˈweɪt/
Kyrgyzstan /ˌkɜːɡɪˈstɑːn/
Laos /laʊs/
Latvia /ˈlætviə/
Lebanon /ˈlebənən/
Lesotho /ləˈsuːtuː/

Liberia /laɪˈbɪəriə/
Libya /ˈlɪbiə/
Liechtenstein /ˈlɪktᵊnstaɪn/

Lithuania /ˌlɪθjuˈeɪniə/
Luxembourg /ˈlʌksᵊmbɜːɡ/

The Former Yugoslav Republic of
  Macedonia /ˌfɔːmə ˌjuːɡəslɑːv
  rɪˌpʌblɪk əv ˌmæsəˈdəʊniə/
Madagascar /ˌmædəˈɡæskəʳ/
Malawi /məˈlɑːwi/
Malaysia /məˈleɪziə/
The Maldives /ˈmɔːldiːvz/
Mali /ˈmɑːli/
Malta /ˈmɔːltə/
The Marshall Islands /ˈmɑːʃᵊl ˌaɪləndz/
Mauritania /ˌmɒrɪˈteɪniə/

British /ˈbrɪtɪʃ/; Person: Briton /ˈbrɪtᵊn/
Greek /ɡriːk/
Greenland /ˈɡriːnlənd/;
  Person: Greenlander /ˈɡriːnləndəʳ/
Grenadian /ɡrəˈneɪdiən/
Guatemalan /ˌɡwɑːtəˈmɑːlən/
Guinean /ˈɡɪniən/
Guinea-Bissauan /ˌɡɪnɪbɪˈsaʊən/
Guyanese /ˌɡaɪəˈniːz/
Haitian /ˈheɪʃᵊn/
Honduran /hɒnˈdjʊərən/
Hungarian /hʌŋˈɡeəriən/
Icelandic /aɪsˈlændɪk/;
  Person: Icelander /ˈaɪsləndəʳ/
Indian /ˈɪndiən/
Indonesian /ˌɪndəˈniːʒᵊn/
Iranian /ɪˈreɪniən/
Iraqi /ɪˈrɑːki/
Irish /ˈaɪrɪʃ/;
  Person: Irishman /ˈaɪrɪʃmən/
Israeli /ɪzˈreɪli/
Italian /ɪˈtæliən/
Jamaican /dʒəˈmeɪkən/
Japanese /ˌdʒæpᵊnˈiːz/
Jordanian /dʒɔːˈdeɪniən/
Kazakh /ˈkæzæk/
Kenyan /ˈkenjən/
Kiribati /ˌkɪrəˈbæs/
North Korean /ˌnɔːθ kəˈriːən/
South Korean /ˌsaʊθ kəˈriːən/
Kuwaiti /kuːˈweɪti/
Kyrgyz /ˈkɜːɡɪz/
Laotian /ˈlaʊʃᵊn/
Latvian /ˈlætviən/
Lebanese /ˌlebəˈniːz/
Basotho /bəˈsuːtuː/;
  Person: Mosotho /məˈsuːtuː/
Liberian /laɪˈbɪəriən/
Libyan /ˈlɪbiən/
Liechtenstein /ˈlɪktᵊnstaɪn/;
  Person: Liechtensteiner
  /ˈlɪktᵊnstaɪnəʳ/
Lithuanian /ˌlɪθjuˈeɪniən/
Luxembourg /ˈlʌksᵊmbɜːɡ/;
  Person: Luxembourger /ˈlʌksᵊmbɜːɡəʳ/
Macedonian /ˌmæsəˈdəʊniən/

Malagasy /ˌmæləˈɡæsi/
Malawian /məˈlɑːwiən/
Malaysian /məˈleɪziən/
Maldivian /mɔːlˈdɪviən/
Malian /ˈmɑːliən/
Maltese /mɔːlˈtiːz/
Marshallese /ˌmɑːʃᵊlˈiːz/
Mauritanian /ˌmɒrɪˈteɪniən/

Mauritius /məˈrɪʃəs/
Mexico /ˈmeksɪkəʊ/
Micronesia /ˌmaɪkrəˈniːziə/
Moldova /mɒlˈdəʊvə/
Monaco /ˈmɒnəkəʊ/
Mongolia /mɒŋˈgəʊliə/
Montenegro /ˌmɒntɪˈniːgrəʊ/
Morocco /məˈrɒkəʊ/
Mozambique /ˌməʊzæmˈbiːk/
Myanmar /ˈmjænmɑːʳ/
Namibia /nəˈmɪbiə/
Nauru /nɑːˈuːruː/
Nepal /nəˈpɔːl/
The Netherlands /ˈneðələndz/

New Zealand /ˌnjuː ˈziːlənd/

Nicaragua /ˌnɪkəˈrægʊə/
Niger /niːˈʒeəʳ/
Nigeria /naɪˈdʒɪəriə/
Northern Ireland /ˌnɔːðˑn ˈaɪələnd/

Norway /ˈnɔːweɪ/
Oman /əʊˈmɑːn/
Pakistan /ˌpɑːkɪˈstɑːn/
Palau /pəˈlaʊ/
Palestine /ˈpæləstaɪn/
Panama /ˈpænəmɑː/
Papua New Guinea /ˌpæpuə njuː ˈgɪni/

Paraguay /ˈpærəgwaɪ/
Peru /pəˈruː/
The Philippines /ˈfɪlɪpiːnz/

Poland /ˈpəʊlənd/
Portugal /ˈpɔːtʃəgəl/
Qatar /ˈkʌtɑːʳ/
Romania /rʊˈmeɪniə/
Russia /ˈrʌʃə/
Rwanda /ruˈændə/
St Kitts and Nevis /sˑnt kɪts ˑnd ˈniːvɪs /
St Lucia /sˑnt ˈluːʃə/
St Vincent and the Grenadines
/sˑnt ˌvɪnsˑnt ˑnd ðə ˌgrenəˈdiːnz/
Samoa /səˈməʊə/
San Marino /ˌsæn məˈriːnəʊ/
São Tomé and Príncipe
/ˌsaʊ təˌmeɪ ˑnd ˈprɪnsɪpeɪ/
Saudi Arabia /ˌsaʊdi əˈreɪbiə/
Scandinavia /ˌskændɪˈneɪviə/
Scotland /ˈskɒtlənd/

Senegal /ˌsenɪˈgɔːl/

Mauritian /məˈrɪʃˑn/
Mexican /ˈmeksɪkˑn/
Micronesian /ˌmaɪkrəˈniːziən/
Moldovan /mɒlˈdəʊvən/
Monégasque /mɒneɪˈgæsk/
Mongolian /mɒŋˈgəʊliən/
Montenegrin /ˌmɒntɪˈniːgrən/
Moroccan /məˈrɒkən/
Mozambican /ˌməʊzæmˈbiːkən/
Burmese /bɜːˈmiːz/
Namibian /nəˈmɪbiən/
Nauruan /nɑːuːˈruːən/
Nepalese /ˌnepˑlˈiːz/
Dutch /dʌtʃ/;
  Person: Dutchman /ˈdʌtʃmən/
New Zealand /ˌnjuː ˈziːlənd/;
  Person: New Zealander /ˌnjuː ˈziːləndəʳ/
Nicaraguan /ˌnɪkəˈrægʊən/
Nigerien /niːˈʒeəriən/
Nigerian /naɪˈdʒɪəriən/
Northern Irish /ˌnɔːðˑn ˈaɪrɪʃ/;
  Person: Northern Irishman
  /ˌnɔːðˑn ˈaɪrɪʃmən/
Norwegian /nɔːˈwiːdʒˑn/
Omani /əʊˈmɑːni/
Pakistani /ˌpɑːkɪˈstɑːni/
Palauan /pəˈlaʊən/
Palestinian /ˌpæləˈstɪniən/
Panamanian /ˌpænəˈmeɪniən/
Papua New Guinean
  /ˌpæpuə njuː ˈgɪniən/
Paraguayan /ˌpærəˈgwaɪən/
Peruvian /pəˈruːviən/
Philippine /ˈfɪlɪpiːn/;
  Person: Filipino /ˌfɪlɪˈpiːnəʊ/,
  Filipina /ˌfɪlɪˈpiːnə/
Polish /ˈpəʊlɪʃ/; Person: Pole /pəʊl/
Portuguese /ˌpɔːtʃəˈgiːz/
Qatari /kʌˈtɑːri/
Romanian /rʊˈmeɪniən/
Russian /ˈrʌʃˑn/
Rwandan /ruˈændən/
Kittsian /ˈkɪtsiən/, Nevisian /niːˈvɪsiən/
St Lucian /sˑnt ˈluːʃˑn/
Vincentian /vɪnˈsɪntiən/

Samoan /səˈməʊən/
Sanmarinese /ˌsænmærɪˈniːz/
São Tomean /ˌsaʊ təˈmeɪən/

Saudi /ˈsaʊdi/
Scandinavian /ˌskændɪˈneɪviən/
Scottish /ˈskɒtɪʃ/; Person: Scot /skɒt/,
Scotsman /ˈskɒtsmən/
Senegalese /ˌsenɪgəˈliːz/

Serbia /'sɜːbiə/
The Seychelles /seɪ'ʃelz/

Serbian /'sɜːbiən/; Person: Serb /sɜːb/
Seychelles /seɪ'ʃelz/;
   Person: Seychellois /ˌseɪʃel'wɑː/

Sierra Leone /siˌerə li'əʊn/
Singapore /ˌsɪŋə'pɔːʳ/
Slovakia /slə'vækiə/
Slovenia /slə'viːniə/

Sierra Leonean /siˌerə li'əʊniən/
Singaporean /ˌsɪŋə'pɔːriən/
Slovak /'sləʊvæk/
Slovenian /slə'viːniən/;
   Person: Slovene /'sləʊviːn/

The Solomon Islands /'sɒləmən ˌaɪləndz/
Somalia /sə'mɑːliə/
South Africa /ˌsaʊθ 'æfrɪkə/
Spain /speɪn/
Sri Lanka /ˌsri: 'læŋkə/
Sudan /su:'dɑːn/
Suriname /ˌsʊərɪ'næm/
Swaziland /'swɑːzilænd/
Sweden /'swiːdᵊn/
Switzerland /'swɪtsələnd/
Syria /'sɪriə/
Taiwan /ˌtaɪ'wɑːn/
Tajikistan /tɑːˌdʒiːkɪ'stɑːn/
Tanzania /ˌtænzə'niːə/
Thailand /'taɪlænd/
Tibet /tɪ'bet/
Togo /'təʊgəʊ/
Tonga /'tɒŋə/
Trinidad and Tobago
   /ˌtrɪnɪdæd ᵊnd tə'beɪgəʊ/
Tunisia /tju:'nɪziə/
Turkey /'tɜːki/
Turkmenistan /tɜːkˌmenɪ'stɑːn/
Tuvalu /tu:'vɑːlu:/
Uganda /ju:'gændə/
Ukraine /ju:'kreɪn/
The United Arab Emirates
   /ju:ˌnaɪtɪd ˌærəb 'emɪrəts/
The United Kingdom (UK)
   /ju:ˌnaɪtɪd 'kɪŋdəm/
The United States of America (USA)
   /ju:ˌnaɪtɪd ˌsteɪts əv ə'merɪkə/
Uruguay /'jʊərəgwaɪ/
Uzbekistan /ʊzˌbekɪ'stɑːn/
Vanuatu /ˌvænu'ɑːtu:/
Vatican City /ˌvætɪkən 'sɪti/
Venezuela /ˌvenɪ'zweɪlə/
Vietnam /ˌvjet'næm/
Wales /weɪlz/

Somali /sə'mɑːli/
South African /ˌsaʊθ 'æfrɪkən/
Spanish /'spænɪʃ/; Person: Spaniard /'spænjəd/
Sri Lankan /ˌsri: 'læŋkən/
Sudanese /ˌsuːdᵊn'iːz/
Surinamese /ˌsʊərɪnæm'iːz/
Swazi /'swɑːzi/
Swedish /'swiːdɪʃ/; Person: Swede /swiːd/
Swiss /swɪs/
Syrian /'sɪriən/
Taiwanese /ˌtaɪwə'niːz/
Tajik /tɑː'dʒiːk/
Tanzanian /ˌtænzə'niːən/
Thai /taɪ/
Tibetan /tɪ'betᵊn/
Togolese /ˌtəʊgə'liːz/
Tongan /'tɒŋᵊn/
Trinidadian /ˌtrɪnɪ'dædiən/

Tunisian /tju:'nɪziən/
Turkish /'tɜːkɪʃ/; Person: Turk /tɜːk/
Turkmen /'tɜːkmen/
Tuvaluan /ˌtu:vɑː'lu:ən/
Ugandan /ju:'gændən/
Ukrainian /ju:'kreɪniən/
Emirati /emɪ'rɑːti/

British /'brɪtɪʃ/; Person: Briton /'brɪtᵊn/

American /ə'merɪkən/

Uruguayan /ˌjʊərə'gwaɪən/
Uzbek /'ʊzbek/
Vanuatuan /ˌvænuɑː'tu:ən/
Vatican /'vætɪkən/
Venezuelan /ˌvenɪ'zweɪlən/
Vietnamese /ˌvjetnə'miːz/
Welsh /welʃ/;
   Person: Welshman /'welʃmən/

Western Sahara /ˌwestən sə'hɑːrə/
Yemen /'jemən/
Zambia /'zæmbiə/
Zimbabwe /zɪm'bɑːbweɪ/

Sahrawian /sɑː'rɑːwiən/
Yemeni /'jeməni/
Zambian /'zæmbiən/
Zimbabwean /zɪm'bɑːbwiən/

Regular verb tenses

The simple tenses

Present Simple

used for action in the present, for things that are always true or that happen regularly, and for opinions and beliefs

| I/we/you/they | arrive (**do not** arrive) |
| he/she/it | arrives (**does not** arrive) |

Past Simple

used for completed actions and events in the past

| I/we/you/they | arrive**d** (**did not** arrive) |
| he/she/it | arrive**d** (**did not** arrive) |

Future Simple

used for actions and events in the future

| I/we/you/they | **will** arrive (**will not** arrive) |
| he/she/it | **will** arrive (**will not** arrive) |

Present Perfect

used to show that an event happened or an action was completed at some time before the present

| I/we/you/they | **have** arrived (**have not** arrived) |
| he/she/it | **has** arrived (**has not** arrived) |

Past Perfect

used to show that an event happened or an action was completed before a particular time in the past

| I/we/you/they | **had** arrived (**had not** arrived) |
| he/she/it | **had** arrived (**had not** arrived) |

Future Perfect

used to show that something will be completed before a particular time in the future

| I/we/you/they | **will have** arrived (**will not have** arrived) |
| he/she/it | **will have** arrived (**will not have** arrived) |

The continuous/progressive tenses

Present Continuous/Progressive

used for actions or events that are happening or developing now, for future plans, or to show that an event is repeated

I	**am** arriving (**am not** arriving)
we/you/they	**are** arriving (**are not** arriving)
he/she/it	**is** arriving (**is not** arriving)

Past Continuous/Progressive

used for actions or events in the past that were not yet finished or that were interrupted

I	**was** arriving (**was not** arriving)
we/you/they	**were** arriving (**were not** arriving)
he/she/it	**was** arriving (**was not** arriving)

Future Continuous/Progressive

used for actions or events in the future that will continue into the future

I/we/you/they	**will be** arriving (**will not be** arriving)
he/she/it	**will be** arriving (**will not be** arriving)

Present Perfect Continuous/Progressive

used for actions or events that started in the past but are still happening now, or for past actions which only recently finished and their effects are seen now

I/we/you/they	**have been** arriving (**have not been** arriving)
he/she/it	**has been** arriving (**has not been** arriving)

Past Perfect Continuous/Progressive

used for actions or events that happened for a period of time but were completed before a particular time in the past

I/we/you/they	**had been** arriving (**had not been** arriving)
he/she/it	**had been** arriving (**had not been** arriving)

Future Perfect Continuous/Progressive

used for actions or events that will already be happening at a particular time in the future

I/we/you/they	**will have been** arriving (**will not have been** arriving)
he/she/it	**will have been** arriving (**will not have been** arriving)

Irregular verbs

This list gives the infinitive form of the verb, its past tense, and then the past participle.

If two forms are given, look the verb up in the dictionary to see whether they have a different meaning.

Infinitive	Past Tense	Past Participle	Infinitive	Past Tense	Past Participle
arise	arose	arisen	dream	dreamed,	dreamed,
awake	awoke	awoken		dreamt	dreamt
be	was/were	been	drink	drank	drunk
bear	bore	borne	drive	drove	driven
beat	beat	beaten,	dwell	dwelt, dwelled	dwelt, dwelled
		also US beat	eat	ate	eaten
become	became	become	feed	fed	fed
befall	befell	befallen	fall	fell	fallen
begin	began	begun	feel	felt	felt
bend	bent	bent	fight	fought	fought
bet	bet, betted	bet, betted	find	found	found
bid	bid, bade	bid, bidden	flee	fled	fled
bind	bound	bound	fling	flung	flung
bite	bit	bitten	fly	flew	flown
bleed	bled	bled	forbid	forbade	forbidden
blow	blew	blown	forecast	forecast,	forecast,
break	broke	broken		forecasted	forecasted
breed	bred	bred	foresee	foresaw	foreseen
bring	brought	brought	forget	forgot	forgotten
broadcast	broadcast,	broadcast,	forgive	forgave	forgiven
	also US	*also US*	forgo	forwent	forgone
	broadcasted	broadcasted	forsake	forsook	forsaken
build	built	built	freeze	froze	frozen
burn	burnt, burned	burnt, burned	get	got	got, *also US* gotten
burst	burst	burst	give	gave	given
bust	bust, *US* busted	bust, *US* busted	go	went	gone
buy	bought	bought	grind	ground	ground
cast	cast	cast	grow	grew	grown
catch	caught	caught	hang	hung, hanged	hung, hanged
choose	chose	chosen	have	had	had
cling	clung	clung	hear	heard	heard
come	came	come	hide	hid	hidden
cost	cost	cost	hit	hit	hit
creep	crept	crept	hold	held	held
cut	cut	cut	hurt	hurt	hurt
deal	dealt	dealt	input	inputted, input	inputted, input
dig	dug	dug	keep	kept	kept
dive	dived,	dived	kneel	knelt, kneeled	knelt, kneeled
	also US dove		know	knew	known
draw	drew	drawn	lay	laid	laid

Infinitive	Past Tense	Past Participle	Infinitive	Past Tense	Past Participle
lead	led	led	rid	rid	rid
lean	leaned, also UK leant	leaned, also UK leant	ride	rode	ridden
			ring	rang	rung
leap	leapt, leaped	leapt, leaped	rise	rose	risen
learn	learned, also UK learnt	learned, also UK learnt	run	ran	run
			saw	sawed	sawn, also US sawed
leave	left	left			
lend	lent	lent	say	said	said
let	let	let	see	saw	seen
lie	lay	lain	seek	sought	sought
light	lit, lighted	lit, lighted	sell	sold	sold
lose	lost	lost	send	sent	sent
make	made	made	set	set	set
mean	meant	meant	sew	sewed	sewn, sewed
meet	met	met	shake	shook	shaken
mislay	mislaid	mislain	shed	shed	shed
mislead	misled	misled	shine	shone	shone
misread	misread	misread	shoot	shot	shot
misspell	misspelled, also UK misspelt	misspelled, also UK misspelt	show	showed	shown, showed
			shrink	shrank	shrunk
mistake	mistook	mistaken	shut	shut	shut
misunderstand	misunderstood	misunderstood	sing	sang	sung
mow	mowed	mown, mowed	sink	sank	sunk
outdo	outdid	outdone	sit	sat	sat
outgrow	outgrew	outgrown	slay	slew	slain
overcome	overcame	overcome	sleep	slept	slept
overdo	overdid	overdone	slide	slid	slid
overhang	overhung	overhung	slit	slit	slit
overhear	overheard	overheard	smell	smelled, also UK smelt	smelled, also UK smelt
override	overrid	overridden			
overrun	overrun	overrun	sow	sowed	sown, sowed
oversee	oversaw	overseen	speak	spoke	spoken
oversleep	overslept	overslept	speed	sped, speeded	sped, speeded
overtake	overtook	overtaken	spell	spelled, also UK spelt	spelled, also UK spelt
overthrow	overthrew	overthrown			
pay	paid	paid	spend	spent	spent
plead	pleaded, also US pled	pleaded, also US pled	spill	spilled, also UK spilt	spilled, also UK spilt
			spin	spun	spun
prove	proved, proven	proved, proven	spit	spat, also US spit	spat, also US spit
put	put	put			
quit	quit	quit	split	split	split
read	read	read	spoil	spoiled, spoilt	spoiled, spoilt
rebuild	rebuilt	rebuilt	spread	spread	spread
repay	repaid	repaid	spring	sprang	sprung
rethink	rethought	rethought	stand	stood	stood
rewind	rewound	rewound	steal	stole	stolen
rewrite	rewrote	rewritten			

Infinitive	Past Tense	Past Participle	Infinitive	Past Tense	Past Participle
stick	stuck	stuck	undercut	undercut	undercut
sting	stung	stung	undergo	underwent	undergone
stink	stank, also US stunk	stunk	understand	understood	understood
			undertake	undertook	undertaken
stride	strode	strode	undo	undid	undone
strike	struck	struck	unwind	unwound	unwound
string	strung	strung	uphold	upheld	upheld
strive	strove	striven	upset	upset	upset
swear	swore	sworn	wake	woke	woken
sweep	swept	swept	wear	wore	worn
swell	swelled	swollen, swelled	weave	wove, weaved	woven, weaved
swim	swam	swum	weep	wept	wept
swing	swung	swung	wet	wet, wetted	wet, wetted
take	took	taken	win	won	won
teach	taught	taught	wind	wound	wound
tear	tore	torn	withdraw	withdrew	withdrawn
tell	told	told	withstand	withstood	withstood
think	thought	thought	withhold	withheld	withheld
thrust	thrust	thrust	wring	wrung	wrung
throw	threw	thrown	write	wrote	written
tread	trod	trodden			

Word beginnings and endings

You can change the meaning of many English words simply by adding a group of letters to the beginning or the ending of a word.

Prefixes

A group of letters added to the beginning of a word is called a **prefix**. Here is a list of the most common prefixes and examples of how they are used.

Anglo- relating to the UK or England *an Anglophile* (= someone who loves England)

anti- 1 opposed to or against *anti-racist laws* 2 preventing or destroying *an anti-aircraft missile*

astro- relating to stars or outer space *astronomer • astrophysics*

audio- relating to hearing or sound *audiotape*

auto- 1 operating without being controlled by humans *autopilot* (= a computer that directs an aircraft) 2 self *an autobiography* (= a book that someone writes about their own life)

bi- two *bilingual* (= speaking two languages) • *bimonthly* (= happening twice in a month or once every two months)

bio- relating to living things or human life *biodiversity • bioethics*

centi-, cent- hundred *a centimetre • a century*

co- with or together *a co-author • coexist*

contra- against or opposite *contradict* (= say the opposite) • *contraception* (= something that is used to prevent pregnancy)

counter- opposing or as a reaction to *a counter-attack* (= an attack on someone who has attacked you)

cross- 1 across *cross-border* 2 including different groups or subjects *a cross-party committee* (= one formed from many political parties) • *cross-cultural*

cyber- relating to electronic communications, especially the Internet *cyberspace*

de- to take something away *deforestation* (= when the trees in an area are cut down)

demi- half, partly *demitasse* (= a small coffee cup) • *demigod* (= a creature that is part god and part human)

dis- not or the opposite of *dishonest • disbelief • disagree*

e- electronic, usually relating to the Internet *email • e-commerce*

eco- relating to the environment *eco-friendly tourism* (= tourism which does not damage the environment)

equi- equal, equally *equidistant* (= the same distance from two or more places)

Euro- relating to Europe *Europop* (= modern, young people's music from Europe)

ex- from before *an ex-boyfriend • an ex-boss*

extra- outside of or in addition to *extracurricular activities* (= activities that are in addition to the usual school work)

geo- of the earth *geothermal* (= of or connected with the heat inside the earth)

hydro- relating to water *hydroponic* (= a method of growing plants in water)

hyper- having a lot of or too much of a quality *hyperactive • hypersensitive* (= more than normally sensitive)

ill- in a way which is bad or not suitable *ill-prepared • an ill-judged remark*

in-, il-, im-, ir- not *incorrect • illegal • impossible • irregular*

inter- between or among *international • an interdepartmental meeting*

intra- within *an intranet*

kilo- a thousand *a kilometre • a kilogram*

macro- on a large scale *macroeconomics* (= the study of financial systems at a national level)

mega- 1 informal extremely *megarich* (= extremely rich) 2 one million *40 megabytes*

micro- very small *a microchip • microscopic* (= extremely small)

mid- in the middle of *mid-July • a man in his mid-forties • mid-afternoon/-morning*

milli- a thousandth *a millisecond*

mini- small *a miniskirt* (= very short skirt) • *a minibus*

mis- not or badly *mistrust • misbehave*

mono- one or single *monolingual • a monologue*

multi- many *a multi-millionaire • a multi-storey car park*

nano- 1 one billionth *nanometre* 2 extremely small *nanotechnology*

neo- new *neo-fascists*

non- not or the opposite of *non-alcoholic drinks • non-smokers*

out- more than or better than *outgrow • outnumber • outdo someone* (= to show that you are better than someone)

over- too much *overeat • overpopulated*

poly- many *polygamy* (= having more than one husband or wife at the same time) • *a polygon* (= shape with many sides)

post- after or later than *postwar • a postgraduate*

pre- before or earlier than *pre-tax profits • pre-school*

pro- supporting *pro-democracy demonstrations*

pseudo- false *a pseudonym* (= false name used especially by a writer) • *pseudo-academic*

quasi- partly *quasi-religious ideas*

re- again *remarry* • *a reusable container*

semi- half or partly *a semicircle* • *semi-frozen*

socio- relating to society *socio-economic*

sub- 1 under or below *subzero temperatures* **2** less important or a smaller part of a larger whole *a subsection*

super- extremely or more than usual *a supermodel* • *super-rich*

techno- relating to technology *technophile* (= a person who loves technology)

tele- 1 done using a telephone *telesales* **2** connected with television *telecast* (= something that is broadcast on television) **3** over a long distance *telephoto lens* (= a camera lens that makes distant objects look nearer)

thermo- relating to heat or temperature *a thermostat* (= piece of equipment that controls temperature) • *a thermometer*

trans- 1 across *transatlantic flights* **2** showing a change *transform* • *translate*

tri- three *a triangle* • *a tripod*

ultra- extremely *ultra-modern architecture* • *ultra-careful*

uber- *humorous* used before nouns to mean 'extreme' or 'extremely good or successful' *uber-billionare*

un- not or the opposite of *unhappy* • *unfair* • *unfasten*

under- 1 not enough *undercooked potatoes* • *underprivileged children* **2** below *underwear* • *an underpass*

Suffixes

A **suffix** is a group of letters at the end of a word which changes the word's meaning and often its part of speech. Here is a list of the most common suffixes and examples of how they are used.

-able, -ible changes a verb into an adjective meaning 'able to be' *avoid → avoidable* • *admire → admirable* • *like → likeable*

-age changes a verb into a noun meaning 'the action described by the verb or the result of that action' *marry → marriage* • *break → breakage* • *spill → spillage*

-aholic unable to stop doing or taking something *chocaholic* (= someone who cannot stop eating chocolate)

-al 1 changes a noun into an adjective meaning 'relating to' *culture → cultural* • *nation → national* • *nature → natural* **2** changes a verb into a noun meaning 'the action described by the verb' *approve → approval* • *remove → removal*

-an, -ian 1 makes a noun meaning 'a person who does something' *historian* • *politician* **2** makes an adjective meaning 'belonging somewhere' *American*

-ance, -ence, -ancy, -ency makes a noun meaning 'an action, state, or quality' *performance* • *independence* • *preference*

-athon an event or activity that lasts a long time, usually to raise money for charity *a walkathon* (= a long walk)

-ation, -ion changes a verb into a noun meaning 'the process of the action described by the verb, or the result of that action' *educate → education* • *explain → explanation* • *connect → connection*

-ed makes an adjective meaning, 'having this thing or quality' *bearded* • *coloured* • *surprised*

-ee changes a verb into a noun meaning 'someone that something is done to' *employ → employee* • *interview → interviewee* • *train → trainee*

-en changes an adjective into a verb meaning 'to become or make something become' *thick → thicken* • *fat → fatten* • *soft → soften*

-ence, -ency See -ance

-er, -or changes a verb into a noun meaning 'the person or thing that does the activity' *dance → dancer* • *employ → employer* • *act → actor* • *cook → cooker* (= a machine for cooking) • *time → timer*

-ese of a place, the language spoken there *Lebanese* • *Chinese*

-esque in the style of *Kafka-esque* (= in the style of writer Franz Kafka)

-est makes superlative adjectives and adverbs *bravest* • *latest*

-ful changes a noun into an adjective meaning, 'having a particular quality' *beauty → beautiful* • *power → powerful* • *use → useful*

-hood makes a noun meaning 'the state of being something and the time when someone is something' *childhood* • *motherhood*

-ian See -an

-ible See -able

-ical changes a noun ending in **-y** or **-ics** into an adjective meaning 'relating to' *history → historical* • *politics → political*

-ify to produce a state or quality *simplify*

-in an activity in which many people take part *a sit-in*

-ing makes an adjective meaning 'making someone feel something' *interest → interesting • surprise → surprising • shock → shocking*

-ion See -ation

-ise See -ize

-ish makes an adjective meaning **1** slightly *a greyish colour • a smallish* (= quite small) *house* **2** typical of or similar to *a childish remark* **3** approximately *fiftyish* (= about fifty)

-ist 1 makes a noun meaning 'a person who does a particular activity' *artist • novelist • scientist* **2** makes a noun and an adjective meaning 'someone with a particular set of beliefs' *communist • feminist*

-ive changes a verb into an adjective meaning 'having a particular quality or effect' *attract → attractive • create → creative • explode → explosive*

-ize, -ise changes an adjective into a verb meaning 'to make something become' *modern → modernize • commercial → commercialize*

-less changes a noun into an adjective meaning 'without' *homeless people • a meaningless statement • a hopeless situation*

-let small, not very important *piglet*

-like changes a noun into an adjective meaning 'typical of or similar to' *childlike trust • a cabbage-like vegetable*

-ly 1 changes an adjective into an adverb describing the way that something is done *She spoke slowly. • Drive safely.* **2** makes an adjective and an adverb meaning 'happening every day, night, week, etc' *a daily newspaper • We hold the meeting weekly.* **3** changes a noun into an adjective meaning 'like that person or thing' *mother → motherly • coward → cowardly*

-ment changes a verb into a noun meaning 'the action or process described by a verb, or its result' *develop → development • disappoint → disappointment*

-ness changes an adjective into a noun meaning 'the quality or condition described by the adjective' *sweet → sweetness • happy → happiness • dark → darkness • ill → illness*

-ology makes a noun meaning 'the study of something' *psychology* (= the study of the mind) • *sociology* (= the study of society)

-or See -er

-ous changes a noun into an adjective meaning 'having that quality' *danger → dangerous • ambition → ambitious*

-phile makes a noun meaning 'enjoying or liking something' *a Francophile* (= someone who loves France) • *a bibliophile* (= someone who loves books)

-phobe someone who hates something *commitment-phobe* (= a person who hates commitment)

-ship makes a noun showing involvement between people *friendship • a relationship • partnership*

-ster a person who is associated with something *gangster*

-ward, -wards makes an adverb meaning 'towards a direction or place' *inward • forward • homeward*

-wise changes a noun into an adverb meaning 'relating to this subject' *Weather-wise, the holiday was great. • How are we doing time-wise?*

-y changes a noun into an adjective meaning 'having a lot of something (often something bad)' *noise → noisy • dirt → dirty • smell → smelly*

Word building

It is useful to know how to build up word families using the prefixes and suffixes listed on pages 845–847, and for some exams you need to know these word families. In the list below, words in heavy type are words which are very common and important to learn. The other words on each line are words in the same family, often formed with prefixes and suffixes, or sometimes just a different part of speech (e.g. anger, which is a noun and a verb). All the words in this list have entries in the dictionary except for some beginning with 'un-', 'im-', 'in-' or 'ir-', or ending with '-ly' or '-ily', where the meaning is always regular. Sometimes words in a word family can have meanings which are quite different from others in the group, so you should always check in the dictionary if you are not sure of the meaning.

Nouns	Adjectives	Verbs	Adverbs
ability, disability, inability	**able**, unable, disabled	enable, disable	ably
acceptance	**acceptable**, unacceptable, accepted	**accept**	acceptably, unacceptably
accident	accidental		accidentally
accuracy, inaccuracy	**accurate**, inaccurate		accurately, inaccurately
accusation, the accused, accuser	accusing	**accuse**	accusingly
achievement, achiever	achievable	**achieve**	
act, **action**, inaction, interaction, reaction, transaction	acting	**act**	
activity, inactivity	**active**, inactive, interactive, proactive	activate	actively
addition	additional	**add**	additionally
admiration, admirer	admirable	**admire**	admirably
advantage, disadvantage	advantageous, disadvantaged		advantageously
advertisement, advertiser, **advertising**		advertise	
advice, adviser	advisable, inadvisable, advisory	**advise**	
agreement, disagreement	agreeable	**agree**, disagree	agreeably
aim	aimless	**aim**	aimlessly
amazement	amazed, **amazing**	amaze	amazingly
anger	angry	anger	angrily
announcement, announcer	unannounced	**announce**	unannounced
appearance, disappearance, reappearance		**appear**, disappear, reappear	
applicant, application	applicable, applied	**apply**	
appreciation	appreciable, appreciative	**appreciate**	appreciatively
approval, disapproval	approving, disapproving	**approve**, disapprove	approvingly
approximation	approximate	approximate	**approximately**

Nouns	Adjectives	Verbs	Adverbs
argument	arguable, argumentative	**argue**	arguably
arrangement		**arrange**, rearrange	
art, artist, artistry	artistic		artistically
shame	**ashamed**, unashamed, shameful, shameless	shame	shamefully, shamelessly
attachment	attached, unattached, detachable, detached	**attach**, detach	
attack, counter-attack, attacker		**attack**, counter-attack	
attention	attentive, inattentive	attend	attentively
attraction, attractiveness	**attractive**, unattractive	attract	attractively
authority, authorization	authoritarian, authoritative, unauthorized	authorize	
availability	**available**, unavailable		
avoidance	avoidable, unavoidable	**avoid**	
awareness	**aware**, unaware		unawares
base, the basics, basis	baseless, **basic**	base	basically
bearer	bearable, unbearable	**bear**	
beat, beating	unbeatable, unbeaten	**beat**	
beautician, **beauty**	beautiful		beautifully
beginner, **beginning**	begin		
behaviour/US **behavior**, misbehaviour/US misbehavior	behavioural/US behavioral	**behave**, misbehave	
belief, disbelief	believable, unbelievable	**believe**, disbelieve	unbelievably
block, blockage	blocked, unblocked	**block**, unblock	
blood, bleeding	bloodless, bloody	bleed	
the boil, boiler	boiling	**boil**	
bore, boredom	**bored, boring**	bore	boringly
break, outbreak, breakage	unbreakable, **broken**, unbroken	**break**	
breath, breather, breathing	breathless	**breathe**	breathlessly
brother, brotherhood	brotherly		
build, builder, **building**		build, rebuild	
burn, burner	burning, burnt	**burn**	
burial	buried	**bury**	
calculation, calculator	incalculable, calculated, calculating	**calculate**	
calm, calmness	**calm**	calm	calmly
capability	**capable**, incapable		capably

Nouns	Adjectives	Verbs	Adverbs
care, carer	careful, careless, caring, uncaring	**care**	carefully, carelessly
celebration, celebrity	celebrated, celebratory	**celebrate**	
centre/US **center**, centralization, decentralization	**central**, centralized	centre/US center, centralize, decentralize	centrally
certainty, uncertainty	**certain**, uncertain		certainly, uncertainly
challenge, challenger	challenging	challenge	
change	changeable, interchangeable, unchanged, changing	**change**	
character, characteristic, characterization	characteristic, uncharacteristic	characterize	characteristically
chemical, chemist, chemistry	chemical		chemically
circle, semicircle, circulation	circular	circle, circulate	
cleaner, cleaning, cleanliness	**clean**, unclean	**clean**	clean, cleanly
clarity, clearance, clearing	**clear**, unclear	**clear**	clear, **clearly**
close, closure	closed, closing	**close**	
closeness	**close**		close, closely
clothes, clothing	clothed, unclothed	clothe	
collection, collector	collected, collective	**collect**	collectively
colour/US **color**, colouring/US coloring	coloured/US colored, discoloured/US discolored, colourful/US colorful, colourless/US colorless	colour/US color	colourfully/US colorfully
combination	combined	**combine**	
comfort, discomfort	**comfortable**, uncomfortable, comforting	comfort	comfortably
commitment	noncommittal, committed	**commit**	
communication, communicator	communicative, uncommunicative	**communicate**	
comparison	comparable, incomparable, comparative	**compare**	comparatively
competition, competitor	competitive, uncompetitive	**compete**	competitively
completion, incompleteness	**complete**, incomplete	**complete**	**completely**, incompletely
complication	**complicated**, uncomplicated	complicate	

Nouns	Adjectives	Verbs	Adverbs
computer, computing, computerization		computerize	
concentration	concentrated	**concentrate**	
concern	**concerned**, unconcerned	**concern**	
conclusion	concluding, conclusive, inconclusive	conclude	conclusively
condition, precondition, conditioner, conditioning	conditional, unconditional	condition	conditionally, unconditionally
confidence	confident, confidential	confide	confidently, confidentially
confirmation	confirmed, unconfirmed	**confirm**	
confusion	confused, confusing	**confuse**	confusingly
connection	connected, disconnected, unconnected	**connect**, disconnect	
subconscious, consciousness, unconscious, unconsciousness	unconscious, **conscious**, subconscious,		consciously, unconsciously
consequence	consequent, inconsequential		consequently
consideration	considerable, considerate, inconsiderate, considered	**consider**, reconsider	considerably, considerately
continent	continental, intercontinental		
continuation, continuity	continual, continued, **continuous**	**continue**, discontinue	continually, continuously
contribution, contributor	contributory	**contribute**	
control, controller	controlling, uncontrollable	**control**	uncontrollably
convenience, inconvenience	**convenient**, inconvenient	inconvenience	conveniently
	convinced, convincing, unconvincing	**convince**	convincingly
cook, cooker, cookery, **cooking**	cooked, uncooked	**cook**	
cool, coolness	**cool**	cool	coolly
correction, correctness	**correct**, incorrect, corrective	**correct**	correctly, incorrectly
count, recount	countable, uncountable, countless	**count**, recount	
cover, coverage, covering	undercover, uncovered	**cover**, uncover	undercover
creation, creativity, creator	creative, uncreative	**create**, recreate	creatively
crime, **criminal**, criminologist	criminal, incriminating	incriminate	criminally

Nouns	Adjectives	Verbs	Adverbs
critic, **criticism**	critical, uncritical	**criticize**	critically
crowd, overcrowding	**crowded**, overcrowded	crowd	
cruelty	**cruel**		cruelly
cry, outcry	crying	cry	
culture, subculture	cultural, cultured		culturally
cure	cured, incurable	**cure**	
custom, customer, customs	customary	accustom	customarily
cut, cutting	cutting	**cut**, undercut	
damage, damages	damaging	**damage**	
danger	endangered, **dangerous**	endanger	dangerously
dare, daring	daring	**dare**	daringly
dark, darkness	**dark**, darkened, darkening	darken	darkly
date	dated, outdated	date, predate	
day, midday	daily		daily
dead, **death**	dead, deadly, deathly	deaden	deadly, deathly
deal, dealer, dealings	**deal**		
deceit, deceiver, deception	deceitful, deceptive	**deceive**	deceptively
decision, indecision	decided, undecided, decisive, indecisive	**decide**	decidedly, decisively, indecisively
decoration, decorator	decorative	**decorate**	decoratively
deep, **depth**	deep, deepening	deepen	deeply
defeat, defeatism, defeatist	undefeated, defeatist	**defeat**	
defence/US **defense**, defendant, defender	defenceless/US defenseless, indefensible, defensive	**defend**	defensively
definition	**definite**, indefinite	define	**definitely**, indefinitely
demand, demands	demanding, undemanding	**demand**	
democracy, democrat	democratic, undemocratic		democratically
demonstration, demonstrator	demonstrable, demonstrative	**demonstrate**	demonstrably
denial	undeniable	**deny**	undeniably
dependant, dependence, independence, dependency	dependable, dependent, independent	**depend**	dependably, independently
description	describable, indescribable, nondescript, descriptive	**describe**	descriptively

Nouns	Adjectives	Verbs	Adverbs
desire	desirable, undesirable, desired, undesired	desire	
destroyer, destruction	indestructible, destructive	**destroy**	destructively
determination, determiner	**determined**, predetermined, indeterminate	determine	determinedly
developer, **development**, redevelopment	developed, undeveloped, developing	**develop**, redevelop	
difference, indifference, differentiation	**different**, indifferent	differ, differentiate	differently
directness, **direction**, directions, **director**	**direct**, indirect	**direct**, redirect	directly, indirectly
disagreement	disagreeable	**disagree**	disagreeably
disappointment	**disappointed**, disappointing	disappoint	disappointingly
disaster	disastrous		disastrously
disciplinarian, **discipline**	disciplinary, disciplined, undisciplined	discipline	
discoverer, **discovery**		**discover**	
distance	distant	distance	distantly
disturbance	disturbed, undisturbed, disturbing	**disturb**	disturbingly
divide, division, subdivision	divided, undivided, divisible, divisive	**divide**, subdivide	
divorce, divorcee	divorced	divorce	
do, doing	done, overdone, undone	**do**, outdo, overdo, redo, undo	
doubt, doubter	undoubted, doubtful, doubtless	**doubt**	undoubtedly, doubtfully
dream, dreamer	dream, dreamless, dreamy	**dream**	dreamily
dress, dresser, dressing	dressed, undressed, dressy	**dress**, redress, undress	
drink, drinker, drinking, drunk, drunkenness	**drunk**, drunken	**drink**	drunkenly
drive, **driver**, driving	driving	**drive**	
due, dues	**due**, undue		due, duly, unduly
earner, earnings		**earn**	
earth	earthy, earthly, unearthly	unearth	
ease, unease, easiness	**easy**, uneasy	ease	**easily**, uneasily, easy
east, easterner	east, easterly, eastern		east, eastward(s)
economics, economist, **economy**	**economic**, economical, uneconomic(al)	economize	economically

Nouns	Adjectives	Verbs	Adverbs
education	educated, uneducated, educational	educate	educationally
effect, effectiveness, ineffectiveness	**effective**, ineffective, ineffectual	effect	effectively, ineffectively
effort	effortless		effortlessly
election, re-election, elector, electorate	unelected, electoral	elect, re-elect	
electrician, **electricity**	electric, **electrical**	electrify	electrically
electronics	**electronic**		electronically
embarrassment	**embarrassed, embarrassing**	embarrass	embarrassingly
emotion	emotional, emotive		emotionally
emphasis	emphatic	**emphasize**	emphatically
employee, **employer, employment**, unemployment	unemployed	**employ**	
encouragement, discouragement	encouraged, encouraging, discouraging	**encourage**, discourage	encouragingly
end, ending	unending, endless	**end**	endlessly
energy	energetic	energize	energetically
enjoyment	enjoyable	**enjoy**	enjoyably
enormity	**enormous**		enormously
entrance, entrant, **entry**		**enter**	
entertainer, **entertainment**	entertaining	entertain	entertainingly
enthusiasm, enthusiast	**enthusiastic**, unenthusiastic	enthuse	enthusiastically, unenthusiastically
environment, environmentalist	environmental		environmentally
equality, inequality	**equal**, unequal	equalize	**equally**, unequally
escape, escapism	escaped, inescapable	**escape**	inescapably
essence, essentials	**essential**		essentially
estimate, estimation	estimated	**estimate**, overestimate, underestimate	
event, non-event	eventful, uneventful, eventual		eventfully, eventually
exam, examination, cross-examination, examiner		examine, cross-examine	
excellence	**excellent**	excel	excellently
excitement	excitable, **excited, exciting**, unexciting	excite	excitedly, excitingly
excuse	excusable, inexcusable	**excuse**	inexcusably

Nouns	Adjectives	Verbs	Adverbs
existence	non-existent, existing, pre-existing	**exist**, coexist	
expectancy, expectation	expectant, unexpected	**expect**	expectantly, unexpectedly
expenditure, **expense**, expenses	**expensive**, inexpensive	expend	expensively, inexpensively
experience, inexperience	**experienced**, inexperienced	experience	
experiment	experimental	experiment	experimentally
expert, expertise	expert, inexpert		expertly
explanation	unexplained, explanatory, explicable, inexplicable	**explain**	inexplicably
explosion, explosive	exploding, explosive	**explode**	explosively
exploration, explorer	exploratory	**explore**	
expression	expressive	**express**	expressively
extreme, extremism, extremist, extremity	**extreme**, extremist		**extremely**
fact	factual		factually
fail, failure	unfailing	**fail**	unfailingly
fairness	**fair**, unfair		**fairly**, unfairly
faith, faithfulness	faithful, unfaithful		faithfully
familiarity, **family**	familiar, unfamiliar	familiarize	familiarly
fame	famed, **famous**, infamous		famously, infamously
fashion	fashionable, unfashionable	fashion	fashionably, unfashionably
fat	**fat**, fattening, fatty	fatten	
fastener		**fasten**, unfasten	
fault	faultless, faulty	fault	faultlessly
fear	fearful, fearless, fearsome	fear	fearfully, fearlessly
feel, **feeling**, feelings	unfeeling	**feel**	
fiction, nonfiction	fictional		
fill, refill, filling	filling	**fill**, refill	
final, semifinal, finalist	**final**	finalize	**finally**
finish	finished, unfinished	**finish**	
firmness, infirmity	**firm**, infirm		firmly
fish, fishing	fishy	fish	fishily
fit, fittings	fitted, fitting	**fit**	fittingly
fix, fixation, fixture	fixed, transfixed, unfixed	**fix**	
flat	flat	flatten	flat, flatly

Nouns	Adjectives	Verbs	Adverbs
flower	flowered, flowery, flowering	flower	
fold, folder	folded, folding	**fold**, unfold	
follower, following	following	**follow**	
force	forceful, forcible	**force**	forcefully, forcibly
forest, deforestation, forestry	forested		
forgetfulness	forgetful, unforgettable	**forget**	forgetfully
forgiveness	forgiving, unforgiving	**forgive**	
form, formation, transformation, reformer, transformer	reformed	**form**, reform, transform	
formality	**formal**, informal	formalize	formally, informally
fortune	fortunate, unfortunate		**fortunately**, unfortunately
freebie, **freedom**	free	free	free, freely
freeze, freezer, freezing	freezing, frozen	**freeze**	
frequency, infrequency	**frequent**, infrequent	frequent	**frequently**, infrequently
freshness, refreshments	**fresh**, refreshing	freshen, refresh	freshly, refreshingly
friend, friendliness	friendly, unfriendly	befriend	
fright	**frightened**, **frightening**, frightful	**frighten**	frighteningly, frightfully
fruit, fruition	fruitful, fruitless, fruity		fruitfully, fruitlessly
fund, refund, funding	funded	fund, refund	
furnishings, **furniture**	furnished, unfurnished	furnish	
garden, gardener, gardening		garden	
generalization	**general**	generalize	**generally**
generosity	**generous**		generously
gentleness	**gentle**		gently
gladness	**glad**	gladden	gladly
glass, glasses	glassy		
good, goodies, goodness, goods	**good**		
government, governor	governmental, governing	govern	governmentally
gratitude, ingratitude	**grateful**, ungrateful		gratefully
greatness	**great**		greatly
green, greenery, greens	**green**		

Nouns	Adjectives	Verbs	Adverbs
ground, underground, grounding, grounds	groundless, underground	ground	underground
grower, **growth**, undergrowth	growing, grown, overgrown	**grow**, outgrow	
guilt, guiltiness	**guilty**		guiltily
habit	habitual		habitually
hair, hairiness	hairless, hairy		
hand, handful	underhand, handy	**hand**	
handle, handler, handling		**handle**	
hanger	hanging	**hang**, overhang	
happiness, unhappiness	**happy**, unhappy		happily, unhappily
hardship	**hard**	harden	**hard**, hardly
harm	unharmed, harmful, harmless	**harm**	harmlessly
head, heading	overhead, heady	head, behead	overhead
health	healthy, unhealthy		healthily, unhealthily
hearing	unheard, unheard of	**hear**, overhear	
heart	heartened, heartening, heartless, hearty		heartily, heartlessly
heat, heater, heating	heated, unheated	heat, overheat	heatedly
height, heights	heightened	heighten	
help, helper, helpfulness, helping	helpful, unhelpful, helpless	**help**	helpfully, helplessly
Highness	**high**		high, highly
historian, **history**	historic, prehistoric, historical		historically
hold, holder, holding		**hold**	
home	homeless, homely	home	**home**
honesty, dishonesty	**honest**, dishonest		honestly, dishonestly
hope, hopefulness, hopelessness	hopeful, hopeless	**hope**	**hopefully**, hopelessly
human, humanism, humanity, inhumanity	**human**, inhuman, superhuman, inhumane		humanly, humanely
hunger	**hungry**		hungrily
hurry	hurried, unhurried	**hurry**	hurriedly
hurt	unhurt, hurtful	**hurt**	hurtfully
ice, icicle, icing	icy	ice	icily
identification, identity	identifiable, unidentified	**identify**	

858

Nouns	Adjectives	Verbs	Adverbs
imagination	imaginable, unimaginable, imaginary, imaginative	**imagine**	unimaginably, imaginatively
importance	important, unimportant		importantly
impression	impressionable, impressive	impress	impressively
improvement	improved	**improve**	
increase	increased	**increase**	increasingly
credibility, incredulity	**incredible**, credible, incredulous		incredibly, incredulously
independence, independent	**independent**		independently
industrialist, **industry**, industrialization	**industrial**, industrialized, industrious		industrially, industriously
infection, disinfectant	infectious	infect, disinfect	infectiously
inflation	inflatable, inflated, inflationary	inflate, deflate	
informant, **information**, informer	informative, uninformative, informed, uninformed	inform, misinform	
injury	injured, uninjured	**injure**	
innocence	**innocent**		innocently
insistence	insistent	**insist**	insistently
instance, instant	**instant**, instantaneous		instantly, instantaneously
instruction, instructor	instructive	instruct	instructively
intelligence	intelligent, unintelligent, intelligible, unintelligible		intelligently
intent, **intention**	intended, unintended, intentional, unintentional	**intend**	intentionally, unintentionally
interest	interested, disinterested, uninterested, **interesting**	interest	interestingly
interruption	uninterrupted	**interrupt**	
interview, interviewee		interview	
introduction	introductory	**introduce**	
invention, inventiveness, inventor	inventive	**invent**, reinvent	inventively
invitation, invite	uninvited, inviting	**invite**	invitingly
involvement	involved, uninvolved	**involve**	
item	itemized	itemize	
joke, joker		joke	jokingly
journal, journalism, **journalist**	journalistic		
judge, **judg(e)ment**	judgmental	**judge**	

Nouns	Adjectives	Verbs	Adverbs
juice, juices	juicy		
keenness	**keen**		keenly
keep, keeper, keeping	kept	**keep**	
kill, overkill, killer, killing		**kill**	
kindness, unkindness	**kind**, unkind		kindly, unkindly
knowledge	knowing, knowledgeable, known, unknown	**know**	knowingly, unknowingly, knowledgeably
enlargement	**large**	enlarge	largely
laugh, **laughter**	laughable	**laugh**	laughably
law, **lawyer**, outlaw	lawful, unlawful	outlaw	lawfully, unlawfully
laziness	**lazy**		lazily
lead, **leader**, leadership	lead, leading	**lead**	
learner, learning	learned, unlearned	**learn**	
legality, illegality, legalization	**legal**, illegal	legalize	legally, illegally
length	lengthening, lengthy	lengthen	lengthily
liar, **lie**	lying	lie	
life	lifeless, lifelike, lifelong		lifelessly
light, lighter, lighting, lightness	**light**	light, lighten	lightly
dislike, liking	likeable	**like**, dislike	
likelihood	**likely**, unlikely		likely
limit, limitation, limitations	limited, unlimited	**limit**	
literature, literacy	literary, literate, illiterate		
liveliness, living	**live**, lively, living	**live**, outlive, relive	live
local, location, relocation	**local**	dislocate, relocate	locally
loser, **loss**	lost	**lose**	
	loud		aloud, loud/loudly
love, lover	lovable, unlovable, loveless, lovely, loving	**love**	lovingly
low	**low**, lower, lowly	lower	low
luck	lucky, unlucky		luckily, unluckily
machine, machinery, mechanic, mechanics, mechanism	mechanical, mechanized		mechanically
magic, magician	magic, magical		magically

Nouns	Adjectives	Verbs	Adverbs
make, remake, maker, making	unmade	**make**, remake	
man, manhood, mankind	manly, manned, unmanned	man	
management, manager	manageable, unmanageable, managerial	**manage**	
mark, marker, markings	marked, unmarked	**mark**	markedly
market, marketing	marketable	market	
marriage	married, unmarried	**marry**, remarry	
match	matching, unmatched	**match**	
material, materialism, materialist, materials	material, immaterial, materialistic	materialize	
meaning	meaningful, meaningless	**mean**	meaningfully
measure, **measurement**	measurable, immeasurable	**measure**	immeasurably
medical, medication, **medicine**	**medical**, medicated, medicinal		medically
memorial, **memory**	memorable	memorize	memorably
mentality	**mental**		mentally
method, methodology	methodical, methodological		methodically
militancy, militant, the military, militia	**military**, militant		militantly, militarily
mind, minder, reminder	mindless	**mind**, remind	mindlessly
minimum	minimal, **minimum**	minimize	minimally
miss	**missing**	**miss**	
mistake	mistaken, unmistakable	mistake	unmistakably, mistakenly
mix, mixer, **mixture**	mixed	**mix**	
modernity, modernization	**modern**	modernize	
moment	momentary, momentous		momentarily
mood, moodiness	moody		moodily
moral, morals, morality, immorality	**moral**, amoral, immoral		morally
mother, motherhood	motherly		
move, **movement**, removal, remover	movable, unmoved, moving	**move**, remove	movingly
murder, murderer	murderous	**murder**	murderously
music, musical, musician	musical, unmusical		musically
name	named, unnamed, nameless	**name**, rename	namely

Nouns	Adjectives	Verbs	Adverbs
nation, national, multinational, nationalism, nationalist, nationality, nationalization	**national**, international, multinational, nationalistic	nationalize	nationally, internationally
nature, naturalist, naturalization, naturalness, the supernatural	**natural**, supernatural, unnatural, naturalistic	naturalize	naturally, unnaturally
necessity	**necessary**, unnecessary	necessitate	necessarily, unnecessarily
need, needs	needless, needy	**need**	needlessly
nerve, nerves, nervousness	**nervous**		nervously
news, renewal	**new**, renewable, renewed	renew	newly
night, midnight			overnight, nightly
noise	noisy		noisily
normality/US normalcy, abnormality	**normal**, abnormal		**normally**, abnormally
north, northerner	north, northerly, northern		north, northward(s)
notice	noticeable, unnoticed	**notice**	noticeably
number, numeral	innumerable, numerical, numerous	number, outnumber	
nurse, nursery, nursing		nurse	
obedience, disobedience	obedient, disobedient	**obey**, disobey	obediently, disobediently
occasion	occasional		occasionally
offence/US **offense**, offender, offensive	offensive, inoffensive	**offend**	offensively
office, officer, official	**official**, unofficial		officially, unofficially
the open, opener, opening, openness	**open**, opening	**open**	openly
operation, cooperation, operative, cooperative, operator	operational, operative, cooperative	**operate**, cooperate	operationally
opposition, opposite	opposed, opposing, **opposite**	**oppose**	opposite
option	optional	opt	optionally
order, disorder	disordered, orderly, disorderly	**order**	
organization, disorganization, reorganization, organizer	organizational, organized, disorganized	**organize**, disorganize, reorganize	

Nouns	Adjectives	Verbs	Adverbs
origin, original, originality, originator	**original**, unoriginal	originate	**originally**
owner, ownership		**own**, disown	
pack, package, packaging, packet, packing	packed	**pack**, unpack, package	
pain	pained, **painful**, painless	pain	painfully, painlessly
paint, painter, **painting**		**paint**	
part, counterpart, parting, partition	partial, parting	part, partition	part, partially, **partly**
pass, overpass, underpass, passage, passing	passing	**pass**	
patience, impatience, **patient**	**patient**, impatient		patiently, impatiently
pay, **payment**, repayment	unpaid, underpaid	**pay**, repay	
peace	peaceful		peacefully
perfection, imperfection, perfectionist	**perfect**, imperfect	perfect	**perfectly**
performance, performer		**perform**	
permission, permit	permissible, impermissible, permissive	permit	
person, **personality**	personal, impersonal, personalized	personalize, personify	personally
persuasion	persuasive	**persuade**, dissuade	persuasively
photo, **photograph**, photographer, photography	photogenic, photographic	photograph	
picture	pictorial, picturesque	picture	
place, placement, displacement, replacement	misplaced	place, displace, replace	
plan, planner, planning	unplanned	**plan**	
plant, transplant, plantation		plant, transplant	
play, interplay, replay, **player**, playfulness	playful	**play**, outplay, replay	playfully
pleasantry, **pleasure**, displeasure	**pleasant**, unpleasant, **pleased**, displeased, pleasing, pleasurable	please, displease	pleasantly, unpleasantly
poem, poet, **poetry**	poetic		
point, pointer	pointed, pointless	**point**	pointlessly
politeness	**polite**, impolite		politely, impolitely
politician, **politics**	political, politicized	politicize	politically

Nouns	Adjectives	Verbs	Adverbs
popularity, unpopularity, popularization	**popular**, unpopular	popularize	popularly
population	populated, unpopulated, populous	populate	
possibility, impossibility, the impossible	**possible**, impossible		**possibly**, impossibly
post, postage	postal	**post**	
power, superpower	**powerful**, overpowering, powerless	power, empower, overpower	powerfully
practical, practicalities, practicality	practicable, **practical**, impractical		practically
practice, practitioner	practised/US practiced, practising/US practicing	**practise/US practice**	
precision	**precise**, imprecise		precisely
preference	preferable, preferential	**prefer**	preferably
preparation, preparations	prepared, unprepared, preparatory	**prepare**	
presence, **present**, presentation, presenter	**present**, presentable	present, represent	presently
press, **pressure**	pressed, pressing, pressurized	**press**, pressure/ pressurize	
prevention	preventable, preventive/ preventative	**prevent**	
price	overpriced, priceless, pricey/pricy	price	
print, printer, printing	printed	**print**	
prison, prisoner, imprisonment		imprison	
privacy, private, privatization	**private**	privatize	privately
probability	probable, improbable		**probably,** improbably
process, processing, procession, processor	processed	process	
produce, producer, **product, production,** reproduction, productivity	productive, counterproductive, reproductive, unproductive	**produce**, reproduce	
profession, professional, professionalism	**professional,** unprofessional		professionally
profit, profitability	profitable, unprofitable	profit	profitably
progress, progression	progressive	progress	progressively
proof	proven, unproven	prove, disprove	
protection, protector	protected, unprotected, protective	**protect**	protectively

Nouns	Adjectives	Verbs	Adverbs
provider, provision, provisions	provisional	**provide**	provisionally
public, publication, publicist, publicity	**public**	publicize	publicly
publisher, publishing	published, unpublished	**publish**	
punishment	punishable, punishing	**punish**	
purification, purist, purity, impurity	**pure**, impure	purify	purely
purpose	purposeful		purposefully, purposely
push, pusher	pushed, pushy	**push**	
qualification, disqualification, qualifier	qualified, unqualified	qualify, disqualify	
quarter, quarters	quarterly	quarter	quarterly
question, questioning	questionable, unquestionable	question	unquestionably
quiet, disquiet	**quiet**	quieten/quiet	quietly
race, racism, racist	racial, multiracial, racist		racially
rarity	**rare**		rarely
rate, rating	overrated, underrated	rate, underrate	
reaction, reactor	reactionary	**react**, overreact	
read, reader, readership, **reading**	readable, unreadable	**read**	
readiness	**ready**		readily
realism, realist, reality, unreality, realization	**real**, unreal, realistic, unrealistic	**realize**	real, **really**, realistically
reason, reasoning	reasonable, unreasonable	reason	reasonably, unreasonably
receipt, receipts, receiver, reception	receptive	**receive**	
recognition	recognizable, unrecognizable	**recognize**	recognizably
record, recorder, recording	recorded, unrecorded	**record**	
referee, reference, referral		**refer**, referee	
reflection	reflective	**reflect**	
regret	regrettable, regretful	**regret**	regrettably, regretfully
regular, regularity, irregularity	**regular**, irregular		**regularly**, irregularly
relation, relations, **relationship**, **relative**	**related**, unrelated, relative	relate	relatively
relaxation	**relaxed**, relaxing	**relax**	

Nouns	Adjectives	Verbs	Adverbs
reliability, reliance	**reliable**, unreliable, reliant	**rely**	reliably
religion	religious, irreligious		religiously
the remainder, remains	remaining	**remain**	
remark	remarkable, unremarkable	remark	remarkably
repair, disrepair	irreparable	**repair**	irreparably
repeat, repetition	repeated, repetitive/ repetitious	**repeat**	repeatedly, repetitively
report, reporter	unreported	**report**	reportedly
representation, representative	representative unrepresentative	**represent**	
reputation, disrepute	reputable, disreputable, reputed		reputedly
respect, disrespect, respectability	respectable, respected, respectful, disrespectful, respective	**respect**	respectably, disrespectfully, respectfully, respectively
respondent, **response**, responsiveness	responsive, unresponsive	**respond**	
responsibility, irresponsibility	**responsible**, irresponsible		responsibly, irresponsibly
rest, unrest, restlessness	restless	**rest**	restlessly
retiree, retirement	retired, retiring	**retire**	
reward	rewarding, unrewarding	reward	
riches, richness, enrichment	**rich**	enrich	richly
ride, rider, riding	overriding	**ride**, override	
right, rightness, rights, righteousness	right, righteous, rightful	right	**right**, rightly, rightfully
roll, roller		**roll**, unroll	
romance, romantic	**romantic**, unromantic, romanticized	romance, romanticize	romantically
rough, roughage, roughness	**rough**	rough, roughen	rough, **roughly**
round, rounders, roundness	**round**, rounded	round	**round**, roundly
royal, royalist, royalty	**royal**, royalist		royally
rudeness	**rude**		rudely
rule, ruler, ruling	ruling, unruly	rule, overrule	
run, rerun, runner, running	running, runny	**run**, outrun, overrun	
sadness	**sad**	sadden	sadly
safe, **safety**	safe, unsafe		safely

Nouns	Adjectives	Verbs	Adverbs
satisfaction, dissatisfaction	**satisfactory,** unsatisfactory, **satisfied,** dissatisfied, unsatisfied, satisfying	satisfy	satisfactorily, unsatisfactorily
save, saver, saving, savings, saviour/US savior		**save**	
	scared, scary	scare	
school, pre-school, schooling	pre-school		
science, scientist	scientific, unscientific		scientifically
score, scorer		**score,** outscore, underscore	
search, research, researcher	searching	**search,** research	
seat, seating	seated	seat, unseat	
secrecy, secret	**secret,** secretive		secretly, secretively
sense, nonsense, sensibility, sensitivity, insensitivity	**sensible,** senseless, sensitive, insensitive	sense	sensibly, sensitively, insensitively
separation	separable, inseparable, **separate**	**separate**	inseparably, separately
seriousness	**serious**		**seriously**
servant, serve, server, **service,** disservice, the services, serving	serviceable, servile	**serve,** service	
sex, sexism, sexuality	sexist, **sexual,** bisexual, sexy		sexually
shadow	shadowy	shadow, overshadow	
shake	shaky	**shake**	shakily
shape	shapeless, shapely	shape	
(pencil) sharpener, sharpness	**sharp**	sharpen	sharp, sharply
shine	shiny	**shine,** outshine	
shock	shocked, shocking	**shock**	shockingly
shop, shopper, **shopping**		shop	
short, shortage, shortness, shorts	**short**	shorten	short, shortly
shyness	**shy**	shy	shyly
sick, sickness	**sick,** sickening, sickly	sicken	sickeningly
sight, insight, oversight, sighting	sighted, unsightly	sight	
sign, signal, signatory, signature, signing	signed, unsigned	**sign,** signal	

Nouns	Adjectives	Verbs	Adverbs
significance, insignificance	**significant**, insignificant	signify	significantly, insignificantly
silence, silencer	**silent**	silence	silently
similarity	**similar**, dissimilar		similarly
simplicity, simplification	**simple**, simplistic	simplify	simply
singer, singing	unsung	**sing**	
single, singles	**single**, singular	single	singly
skill	skilful/*US* skillful, skilled, unskilled		skilfully/*US* skillfully
sleep, sleeper, sleepiness, sleeplessness	asleep, sleepless, sleepy	**sleep**	sleepily
slight	**slight**, slighted, slightest		**slightly**
slip, slipper	slippery	**slip**	
smoke, smoker, non-smoker, smoking	smoked, smoking, non-smoking, smoky	**smoke**	
smoothness	**smooth**	smooth	smoothly
society, sociologist, sociology	sociable, unsociable, **social**, anti-social, unsocial	socialize	socially
softness	**soft**	soften	softly
solid, solidarity, solidity, solids	**solid**	solidify	solidly
solution, solvent	soluble, insoluble, unsolved, solvent	**solve**	
south, southerner	south, southerly, southern		south, southward(s)
speaker, **speech**	unspeakable, speechless, outspoken, unspoken	**speak**	unspeakably
special, specialist, speciality/*US* specialty, specialization	**special**, specialized	specialize	**specially**
speed, speeding	speedy	speed	speedily
spelling		**spell**, misspell	
spoils	spoilt/spoiled, unspoiled/unspoilt	**spoil**	
sport	sporting, sporty	sport	
spot	spotted, spotless, spotty	spot	spotlessly
stand, standing	standing, outstanding	**stand**	outstandingly
standard, standardization	standard, substandard	standardize	
start, starter, non-starter		**start**, restart	
statement, understatement	understated	state, overstate	
steam, steamer	steamy	steam	

Nouns	Adjectives	Verbs	Adverbs
steepness	**steep**		steeply
sticker	sticky, stuck, unstuck	**stick**	
stiffness	**stiff**	stiffen	stiff, stiffly
stone	stoned, stony	stone	
stop, stoppage	non-stop	**stop**	non-stop
storm	stormy	storm	
	straight	straighten	**straight**
stranger	**strange**		strangely
strength	strong	strengthen	strongly
stress	stressed, stressful	stress	
strike, striker	striking	**strike**	
structure, restructuring	structural	structure, restructure	structurally
student, study	studious	**study**	studiously
stupidity	**stupid**		stupidly
style	stylish	style	stylishly
substance	substantial, insubstantial, substantive	substantiate	substantially
success, succession, successor	**successful**, unsuccessful, successive	**succeed**	successfully, unsuccessfully
suddenness	**sudden**		**suddenly**
sufferer, suffering	insufferable	**suffer**	insufferably
suggestion	suggestive	**suggest**	suggestively
summer, midsummer	summery		
supplier, supplies, **supply**		**supply**	
support, supporter	supportive	**support**	
supposition	supposed	**suppose**, presuppose	supposedly
surface	surface, resurface		
surprise	surprised, surprising	surprise	surprisingly
surroundings	surrounding	**surround**	
survival, survivor		**survive**	
suspect, suspicion	suspect, suspected, unsuspecting, suspicious	**suspect**	suspiciously
swearing	sworn	**swear**	
sweet, sweetener, sweetness	**sweet**	sweeten	sweetly
swim, swimmer, swimming		**swim**	
symbol, symbolism	symbolic	symbolize	symbolically
sympathy, sympathizer	**sympathetic**, unsympathetic	sympathize	sympathetically
system	systematic		systematically

Nouns	Adjectives	Verbs	Adverbs
takings, undertaking		**take**, overtake, undertake	
talk, talks	talkative	**talk**	
taste, distaste	tasteful, distasteful, tasteless, tasty	**taste**	tastefully, distastefully
tax, taxation	taxable, taxing	tax	
teacher, teaching, teachings		**teach**	
tear	tearful		tearfully
technicalities, technicality, technician, technique	**technical**		technically
technology	technological		technologically
thanks	thankful, thankless	**thank**	thankfully
theorist, **theory**	theoretical	theorize	theoretically
thick, thickness	**thick**	thicken	thickly
thinness	**thin**	thin	thinly
think, rethink, thinker, thinking	unthinkable	**think**, rethink	
thirst	**thirsty**		thirstily
thought, thoughtfulness	thoughtful, thoughtless		thoughtfully, thoughtlessly
threat	threatening	**threaten**	threateningly
tightness	**tight**	tighten	tight, tightly
time, overtime, timer, timing	timeless, timely, untimely	time	
tiredness	**tired**, tireless, tiresome, tiring	tire	tirelessly
title, subtitles	titled	entitle	
top, topping	**top**, topless, topmost	top	
touch	touched, untouched, touching, touchy	**touch**	touchingly
tough		toughen	toughly
trade, trader, trading		trade	
tradition, traditionalist	**traditional**		traditionally
trainee, trainer, **training**, retraining	untrained	**train**	
transport, transportation		transport	
treat, **treatment**, mistreatment	untreated	**treat**, mistreat	
trick, trickery	tricky	trick	
trouble	troubled, troublesome	trouble	
trust, distrust, mistrust, trustee	trusting, trustworthy	**trust**, distrust, mistrust	

Nouns	Adjectives	Verbs	Adverbs
truth, untruth, truthfulness	**true**, untrue, truthful		truly, truthfully
try	trying, untried	**try**	
turn, upturn, turning	upturned	**turn**, overturn	
twist, twister	twisted	**twist**	
type	typical	typify	typically
understanding, misunderstanding	understandable, understanding, misunderstood	**understand**, misunderstand	understandably
upset	**upset**, upsetting	upset	
urgency	**urgent**		urgently
usage, **use**, disuse, misuse, usefulness, user	reusable, **used**, disused, unused, **useful**, **useless**	**use**, misuse, reuse	usefully
valuables, **value**, values	**valuable**, invaluable, undervalued	value, devalue	
variable, variance, variant, **variety**	variable, varied, **various**	vary	invariably, variously
view, overview, preview, review, viewer		view, preview, review	
violence	violent, non-violent	violate	violently
visit, **visitor**		**visit**, revisit	
vote, voter		**vote**	
want, wants	wanted, unwanted	**want**	
war, warfare, warrior	postwar, warring		
warmth	**warm**	warm	warmly
wash, washer, washing	washable, unwashed	**wash**	
wastage, **waste**	waste, wasteful	**waste**	wastefully
watch	watchful	**watch**	
water, waters	underwater, waterproof, watery	water	underwater
way, subway			midway
weakling, weakness	**weak**	weaken	weakly
wear, underwear	wearing, worn	**wear**	
week, midweek	weekly, midweek		weekly, midweek
weight, weights	overweight, underweight, weighted, weighty	**weigh**, outweigh	
welcome	welcome, unwelcome	**welcome**	
west, western, westerner	westerly, western		west, westward(s)
white, whiteness	**white**	whiten	
whole	whole, wholesome, unwholesome		

Nouns	Adjectives	Verbs	Adverbs
width	**wide**	widen	**wide, widely**
wild, wildness	**wild**		wildly
willingness, unwillingness	**willing**, unwilling		willingly, unwillingly
win, **winner**, winnings		**win**	
winter, midwinter	wintry		
wire, wireless, wiring	wiry	wire	
woman, womanhood	womanly		
wonder	**wonderful**	wonder	wonderfully
wood	wooded, wooden		
wool	woollen/*US* woolen, woolly/*US* wooly		
word, wording		word	
work, workaholic, worker, workings	workable, unworkable, overworked, working	**work**, rework	
world, underworld	world, worldly, unworldly, worldwide		worldwide
worry	**worried**, unworried, worrying	**worry**	worryingly
worth	worth, worthless, worthwhile, worthy, unworthy		
riter, **writing**	written, unwritten	**write**, rewrite	
rong	**wrong**, wrongful	wrong	**wrong**, wrongly, wrongfully
ar	yearly		yearly
ng, youngster, youth	**young**, youthful		

Pronunciation symbols

iː	see	aɪ	my	f	fat
i	baby	ɔɪ	boy	v	van
ɪ	sit	aʊ	how	θ	thin
e	bed	ɪə	near	ð	this
æ	cat	eə	hair	s	sun
ɑː	father	ʊə	pure	z	zoo
ɒ	hot	aɪə	fire	ʃ	she
ɔː	saw	aʊə	sour	ʒ	decision
uː	too			h	hat
u	influence	p	pen	m	map
ʊ	put	b	bee	n	name
ʌ	run	t	ten	ŋ	ring
ɜː	bird	d	do	l	light
ə	ago	k	cat	r	red
		g	go	j	yes
eɪ	day	tʃ	chip	w	wet
əʊ	no	dʒ	jar		

ᵊ as in **sudden** /sʌdᵊn/, can be pronounced or not. Say /sʌdᵊn/ or /sʌdn/

ʳ as in **teacher** /ˈtiːtʃəʳ/, is pronounced in UK English when followed by a vowel sound and not when followed by a consonant sound. In US English it is always pronounced.

ˈ shows a primary stress (the part of the word that is said most strongly), as in **above** /əˈbʌv/.

ˌ shows a secondary stress (the part of the word that is said strongly, but less strongly than ˈ, for example the first part of **information** /ˌɪnfəˈmeɪʃən/)